With the aid of the alphabetical thumb index at the edge of the page you can quickly locate the letter you need to find in the German-English and English-German dictionary. Once you have localized the letter you need on the thumb index, simply flip to the correspondingly marked part of the dictionary.

If you are left-handed, you can use the thumb index at the end of this book.

Mit Hilfe der alphabetischen Daumenleiste am rechten Seitenrand, kann man die gesuchte Stelle im Alphabet des deutsch-englischen und des englisch-deutschen Wörterbuches schnell finden. Wurde die gewünschte Stelle im Alphabet auf der Leiste ausgewählt, schlägt man das Wörterbuch an der entsprechend markierten Stelle auf und befindet sich dann in der richtigen Buchstabenstrecke.

Falls Sie Linkshänder(in) sind, können Sie die Buchstabenleiste in der hinteren Umschlagklappe benutzen.

D1132293

A
B
C
D
E
F
G
H
I
J
K
L
M
N
O
P
Q
R
S
T
U
V
W
X
Y
Z

Benutzerhinweise

Blaue Stichwörter.	**maßvoll** I. *adj* moderate ...
Markierung der Phrasal Verb Einträge.	
Kennzeichnung gleich geschriebener Wörter mit unterschiedlicher Bedeutung (Homographen).	**Plastik**[1] ... *nt kein pl* plastic **Plastik**[2] ... *f* (*Kunstwerk*) sculpture
Angabe der Aussprache in internationaler Lautschrift. Die Trennungspunkte geben die Sprechsilben wider. Diese Trennung entspricht nicht immer der orthographischen Silbentrennung.	**übersehbar** [y:bɐ·ˈzeː·baːɐ̯] ... **übersehen*** [y:bɐ·ˈzeː·ən] ... **übersetzen***[1] [y:bɐ·ˈzɛt·tsn̩] ...
Bei Stichwörtern ohne Phonetik wird die Betonung direkt im Stichwort angegeben.	**verschneit** *adj* ... **verschnörkelt** *adj* ...
Unregelmäßige Pluralformen, Verb- und Steigerungsformen werden in spitzen Klammern angegeben.	**verschleißen** <verschliss, verschlissen> *vt, vi sein* to wear out
Kennzeichnung der Trennbarkeit von Verben.	**ab|bringen** *vt irreg* ...
Die alte Schreibung wird durch das hochgestellte Zeichen ᴬᴸᵀ kenntlich gemacht, die neue durch ᴿᴿ.	**Stängel**ᴿᴿ <-s, -> [ˈʃtɛŋl̩] *m* ... **Stengel**ᴬᴸᵀ <-s, -> [ˈʃtɛŋl̩] *m s.* **Stängel**
Mit römischen Ziffern wird ein Eintrag unter grammatischen Gesichtspunkten gegliedert. Die arabischen Ziffern bezeichnen die unterschiedlichen Bedeutungen des Stichworts.	**langsam** [ˈlaŋ·zaːm] I. *adj* ❶ (*nicht schnell*) slow ❷ (*allmählich*) gradual II. *adv* ❶ (*nicht schnell*) slowly ❷ (*fam: allmählich*) gradually
Die Tilde ersetzt in Wendungen das Stichwort. Das Zeichen ▶ leitet den Block der festen Wendungen ein. Die Unterstreichung dient der besseren Orientierung.	**Bach** <-[e]s, Bäche> [bax] *m* brook ▶WENDUNGEN: **den ~ runtergehen** (*fam*) to go down the drain
Das Symbol ◯ bei Phrasal Verb Einträgen und die Angabe *sep* in Übersetzungen geben an, dass die Reihenfolge von Objekt und Ergänzung vertauscht werden kann.	**beladen*** *irreg vt* to load [up *sep*]
Wegweiser zur treffenden Übersetzung:	
• Sachgebietsangaben (geben den Wissensbereich an)	**unfruchtbar** [ˈʊn·frʊxt·baːɐ̯] *adj* MED infertile; (*agr a.*) barren
• Bedeutungserklärungen, Kontextpartner oder Synonyme	**echt** [ˈɛçt] I. *adj* ❶ (*nicht künstlich, wirklich*) real; *Haarfarbe* natural; ...
• Regionale Bedeutungen	**berichten*** I. ... ❷ SCHWEIZ **falsch/recht berichtet** wrong/right; ...
• Stil-, Alters- und rhetorische Angaben	**Bücherwurm** *m* (*hum*) bookworm

N'S Foreign Language Guides
-English Pocket Dictionary
1wörterbuch Deutsch-Englisch

lition for the United States and Canada published in 2015 by Barron's Educational

on for the United States and Canada published in 2008 by Barron's Educational

Management: Ursula Martini
tors: Anette Dralle, Caroline Reul

ing: Dörr + Schiller GmbH, Stuttgart

ries should be addressed to:
Educational Series, Inc.
eless Boulevard
ge, New York 11788
arronseduc.com

8-1-4380-0608-6
f Congress Control No.: 2014938589

n China
5 4

How to use the dictionary

coach [koʊtʃ] I. *n* ① SPORT …	Blue headwords.
bring <brought, brought> [brɪŋ] … ◆ **bring about** *vt* verursachen …	English phrasal verbs come directly after the base verb and are marked with a diamond (◆).
incense[1] … Weihrauch *m* **incense**[2] [ɪnˈsens] *vt* empören	Homographs marked with superscript numbers.
flexibility [ˌflek·səˈbɪl·ɪ·t̬i] … **flexible** [ˈflek·sə·bəl] … **flextime** [ˈfleks·taɪm] …	Phonetic transcriptions. Centered dots are used for syllable division. Please note that this does not always correspond with the orthographic division into syllables.
'time bomb *n* … **'time-consuming** *adj* …	Where no phonetic code is given, the main spoken emphasis of the headword is indicated by a stress mark.
'daughter-in-law <*pl* daughters-> … **begin** <-nn-, began, begun> …	Angle brackets are used to show irregular plural forms and, forms of irregular verbs and adjectives.
	Indication of separability of verbs.
	Old spellings are marked with a superscript ALT symbol. New spellings are marked with a superscript RR symbol.
balance [ˈbæl·ənts] I. *n* ① Gleichge-wicht *nt a. fig* ② FIN Kontostand *m* II. *vt* balancieren; (*achieve equilibri-um*) ein Gleichgewicht herstellen	Roman numerals are used for the parts of speech of a word, and Arabic numerals for sense divisions.
ballistic [bəˈlɪs·t̬ɪk] *adj* ballistisch ▶PHRASES: **to go** ~ (*fam*) ausflippen *fam*	The swung dash substitutes the entry word in phrases. The ▶ sign introduces a block of set expressions, idioms and proverbs. Key words are underlined as a guide.
◆ **win back** *vt* ① SPORT **to ~ back** ◯ **the trophy** den Pokal zurückholen ② *customers* zurückgewinnen	The symbol ◯ in phrasal verb entries and the label *sep* in translations show that the sequence of object and complement can be reversed.
	Guides to the correct translation:
horn [hɔrn] *n* ① ZOOL Horn *nt* ② MUS Horn *nt* ③ AUTO Hupe *f*	• Subject labels (which indicate areas of specialization)
wild … ① (*undomesticated*) wild ② (*un-cultivated*) *landscape* rau, wild; …	• Definitions, context partners or synonyms
dinner [ˈdɪn·ər] *n* … DIAL (*warm lunch*) Mittagessen *nt;* …	• Regional labels
jump [dʒʌmp] I. *n* (*a. fig*) Sprung …	• Usage Labels (which indicate restriction to a particular level or style of usage)

BARRON

FOREIGN LANGUAGE G

GERMAI
ENGLIS
Pocket Diction

~~~

Taschenwörterbu
DEUTSCH–ENGLIS

Second Edition

BARR●
Germa
Tasch●

Second
Series, I
First edi
Series, ●

© Copy
Series, ●

Editor●
Contri

Types●

All righ
form o●

All inq
Barron
250 W
Haupp
www.

ISBN:
Library

Printe
9 8 7 ●

Inhalt

Contents

Lautschriftzeichen für Deutsch
German phonetic symbols

Vokale
Vowels

[a]	matt		[oː]	Boot, drohen
[ɐ]	bitter		[o̜]	loyal
[ɐ̯]	Uhr		[ɔ]	Post
[ã]	Arangement		[õ]	Fondue
[ãː]	Gourmand		[õː]	Fonds
[e]	Etage		[ø]	Ökonomie
[eː]	Beet, Mehl		[øː]	Öl
[ɛ]	Nest, Wäsche		[œ]	Götter
[ɛː]	wählen		[œː]	Server
[ɛ̃]	Cousin		[u]	zunächst
[ɛ̃ː]	Teint		[uː]	Hut
[ə]	halte		[u̯]	aktuell
[ɪ]	Bitte		[ʊ]	Mutter
[i]	Vitamin		[y]	Aerodynamik
[iː]	Bier		[yː]	Typ
[i̯]	Studie		[ỹ]	Etui
[j]	ja		[ʏ]	füllen
[o]	Oase			

Diphthonge
Diphthongs

[ai]	heiß
[au]	Haus
[ɔy]	Mäuse

Konsonanten
Consonants

[b]	Ball		[ŋ]	Ring, blinken
[ç]	ich		[p]	Papst
[d]	dicht		[pf]	Pfeffer
[dʒ]	Budget, Job		[r]	Rad
[f]	Fett, viel		[s]	Rast, besser, heiß
[g]	Geld		[ʃ]	Schaum, sprechen, Chef
[h]	Hut		[t]	Test
[k]	Kohl, Computer		[ts]	Zaun
[kv]	Quadrat		[tʃ]	Matsch, Tschüs
[l]	Last		[v]	wann
[l̩]	Nebel		[x]	Schlauch
[m]	Meister		[ks]	Fix, Axt, Lachs
[n]	nett		[z]	Hase, sauer
[n̩]	sprechen		[ʒ]	Genie

Zeichen
Signs

ʔ	glottal stop
'	primary stress
ˌ	secondary stress
:	length symbol
·	syllable division

English phonetic symbols
Lautschriftzeichen für Englisch

Vowels
Vokale

[a]	farm, not	[ɪ]	sit, wish, near
[æ]	cat, man, sad	[ɔ]	caught, all, law, sauce, floor
[e]	best, get, hair, dare	[u]	moose, lose, you
[ə]	Africa, better, actor, potato, anonymous, virus	[ʊ]	book, put, sure, tour
[ɜ]	bird, berth, curb	[ʌ]	bust, multi
[i]	read, meet, belief, hobby	[ã]	genre

Diphthongs
Diphthonge

[aɪ]	ride, my, buy	[oʊ]	rope, piano, road, toe, show, plateau
[aʊ]	house, now	[ju]	accuse, beauty
[eɪ]	rate, lame		
[ɔɪ]	boy, noise		

Consonants
Konsonanten

[b]	big, blind		[ŋ]	long, sing, prank
[d]	dad, had		[p]	paper, happy
[ð]	father, bathe		[r]	right, dry, current, player, part
[dʒ]	edge, juice, object		[s]	soft, yes, cent, capacity
[f]	fast, wolf		[ʃ]	shift, station, fish
[g]	beg, gold		[t]	take, fat
[h]	hello		[t̬]	butter, interstate
[j]	yellow		[θ]	think, bath
[ʒ]	pleasure		[tʃ]	chip, patch
[k]	cat, king, milk		[v]	vitamin, live
[l]	little, ill, oil		[w]	wish, why, wore
[m]	man, am		[z]	zebra, jazz, gaze
[n]	nice, manner			

Signs
Zeichen

'	primary stress
ˌ	secondary stress
[·]	syllable division

Aa

A, a <-, -> [aː] *nt* ① (*Buchstabe*) A, a; ~ **wie Anton** A as in Alpha ② MUS A, a; **A-Dur/a-Moll** A major/A minor ▶WEN-DUNGEN: **das ~ und [das] O** the be all and end all; **von ~ bis Z** from beginning to end

Aal <-[e]s, -e> [aːl] *m* eel

aalen ['aːlən] *vr* (*fam*) ■**sich** *akk* **auf dem Sofa** ~ to stretch out on the sofa; ■**sich** *akk* **in der Sonne** ~ to bask in the sun

aalglatt ['aːl·lˈglat] *adj* slippery

Aas <-es, -e> [aːs] *nt* (*Tierleiche*) carrion

Aasgeier *m* vulture *a. pej*

ab [ap] I. *adv* ① (*weg, entfernt*) off; **mein Knopf ist** ~ I've lost a button; **erst muss die alte Farbe** ~ first you have to remove the old paint ② **links/ rechts** ~ off to the left/right ③ **weit ~ liegen** to be far away ▶WENDUNGEN: ~ **und zu** now and then II. *präp* +*dat* from; **Kinder** ~ **14 Jahren** children age 14 and older; ~ **heute** starting today; ~ **Köln** from Cologne

ab|ändern *vt* to amend; *Programm* to change

abartig *adj* abnormal

Abbau <-s> *m kein pl* ① *von Boden-schätzen* mining ② (*Verringerung*) **der** ~ **von Arbeitsplätzen** job cuts *pl;* **der** ~ **von Vorurteilen** the breaking down of prejudices

ab|bauen I. *vt* ① *Bodenschätze* to mine ② *Schrank* to dismantle ③ (*verringern*) to reduce II. *vi* ■**jd baut ab** sb is wilting; (*geistig*) sb is deteriorating

ab|bekommen* *vt irreg s.* **abkriegen**

ab|bestellen* *vt Zeitung, Reservierung* to cancel; **den Klempner** ~ to tell the plumber he doesn't need to come anymore

ab|bezahlen* *vt* to pay off *sep*

ab|biegen *irreg vi sein* [**nach**] **links/**

rechts ~ to turn left/right; *Straße* to curve

Abbiegespur *f* turning lane

ab|bilden *vt* **auf dem Foto war ... abgebildet** the photo showed ...

ab|blasen *vt irreg* (*fam*) to call off *sep*

Abblendlicht *nt* AUTO low beam headlights

ab|blitzen *vi sein* (*fam*) ■**bei jdm** ~ **to** not get anywhere with sb; **jdn** ~ **lassen** to turn down *sep* sb

ab|brechen *irreg* I. *vt haben* ① (*lösen*) to break off *sep* ② (*beenden*) to stop; **eine Beziehung** ~ to break up; **einen Streik** ~ to call off *sep* strike; **das Studium** ~ to drop out of college; **den Urlaub** ~ to cut short *sep* one's vacation II. *vi sein* ① (*sich lösen*) to break off ② (*aufhören*) to stop; *Beziehung* to end

ab|bringen *vt irreg* ■**jdn von etw** *dat* ~ to get sb to give up sth; (*abraten*) to change sb's mind about sth; ■**jdn davon** ~, **etw zu tun** to prevent sb from doing sth

Abbruch *m* ① *eines Gebäudes* demolition ② *einer Beziehung* break-up

abbruchreif *adj* ① *Gebäude* dilapidated ② SCHWEIZ (*schrottreif*) ready for the junk yard *pred*

ab|buchen *vt Bank* to debit; **etw [vom Konto]** ~ to deduct sth [from a/one's bank account]

Abc-Schütze, -Schützin [aːbeːˈtseː-] *m, f* child attending school for the first time

ab|danken *vi* to resign; *König* to abdicate

ab|decken *vt* to cover

ab|dichten *vt* to seal

ab|drehen *vt* to turn off *sep*

Abdruck *m* ① <-drücke> (*Spur*) print ② <-drucke> (*Veröffentlichung*) printing

A **ab|drucken** *vt* to print

abend^{ALT} *adv s.* **Abend**

Abend <-s, -e> ['a:bnt] *m* evening;
am ~ in the evening; **gestern/morgen ~** yesterday/tomorrow evening;
heute ~ tonight; **~ für ~** night after
night; **den ganzen ~ über** the whole
evening; **gegen ~** toward evening;
jdm guten ~ wünschen to wish sb a
good evening; **zu ~ essen** to eat dinner

Abendbrot *nt* DIAL *s.* **Abendessen**

Abendessen *nt* dinner

abend|füllend *adj* evening, all-night *attr*, lasting
all evening *pred*

Abendkasse *f* evening box office

Abendkleid *nt* evening dress

Abendkurs *m* evening class

Abendland *nt kein pl* (*geh*) West, Occident

Abendmahl *nt* [Holy] Communion; **das
Letzte ~** the Last Supper

Abendrot <-s> ['a:bnt·ro:t] *nt kein pl*
[red] sunset; **im ~** in the evening glow

abends ['a:bnts] *adv* in the evening

Abenteuer <-s, -> ['a:bn·tɔye] *nt* ❶ adventure ❷ (*Liebesabenteuer*) fling; **auf
[ein] ~ aus sein** to be looking for a one-night stand

abenteuerlich ['a:bn·tɔye·lɪç] *adj*
Geschichte fantastic; *Vorhaben* risky

Abenteurer, Abenteu(r)erin <-s, ->
['a:bn·tɔy·re, 'a:bn·tɔy·(r)ə·rɪn] *m, f*
adventurer

aber ['a:be] *konj* but; **~ dennoch ...** but
in spite of this ...; **oder ~** or else

Aber <-s, -> ['a:be] *nt* but *fam*; **kein ~!**
no buts [about it]!

Aberglaube *m* superstition

abergläubisch ['a:be·glɔy·bɪʃ] *adj*
superstitious

abermals ['a:be·ma:ls] *adv* once again

abfahrbereit *adj, adv* ready to depart
pred

ab|fahren *irreg* **I.** *vi sein* to depart ▶WENDUNGEN: **auf jdn/etw ~** (*fam*) to be
crazy about sb/sth; **jdn ~ lassen** (*fam*)
to turn down sb **II.** *vt* ❶ *sein o
haben Strecke* to [drive along and]

check ❷ *haben Reifen* to wear down
sep

Abfahrt *f* ❶ (*Wegfahren*) departure
❷ (*Autobahnabfahrt*) exit ❸ (*beim Skifahren, Rodeln*) run; (*Abfahrtsstrecke*)
slope

Abfahrtszeit *f* departure time

Abfall *m* garbage

Abfallbeseitigung *f* garbage [*or* trash]
removal, waste disposal

Abfalleimer *m* garbage can

abfällig **I.** *adj* **~e Bemerkung** derogatory remark **II.** *adv* disparagingly; **sich
akk ~ über jdn/etw äußern** to make
derogatory remarks about sb/sth

Abfallverwertung *f* recycling

ab|finden *irreg* **I.** *vt* (*entschädigen*) to
compensate **II.** *vr* (*fam*) ■**sich
akk mit etw** *dat* **~** to put up with sth

Abfindung <-, -en> *f* compensation;
(*bei Entlassung*) severance pay

ab|flauen *vi sein Wind, Sturm* to abate;
Nachfrage to decrease; *Lärm* to drop;
Interesse to wane

ab|fliegen *vi irreg sein* to take off

Abflug *m* departure, takeoff

Abfluss^{RR} *m* (*Rohr*) drain pipe

Abfuhr <-, -en> *f* snub; **jdm eine ~
erteilen** to snub sb

ab|führen **I.** *vt* ❶ ■**jdn ~** *Polizei* to lead
sb away ❷ *Geld* to pay **II.** *vi* MED to loosen the bowels

Abführmittel *nt* laxative

ab|füllen *vt* ❶ *Flüssigkeit* to fill (**in** +*akk*
into); (*in Flaschen*) to bottle ❷ (*sl:
betrunken machen*) to get drunk

Abgangszeugnis *nt* diploma

Abgas *nt* exhaust

abgasarm *adj* low-emission

ab|geben *irreg* **I.** *vt* ❶ (*geben*) ■**jdm
etw ~** to give sb sth [*or* sth to sb]; **jdm
die Hälfte** [**von etw** *dat*] **~** to go
halves [on sth] with sb; **jdm nichts ~**
to not share with sb ❷ *Diplomarbeit
etc.* to hand in *sep* sth ❸ (*hinterlassen*) ■**etw** [**bei jdm**] **~** to leave sth
[with sb]; **das Gepäck ~** to check in
one's luggage; **den Mantel an der
Garderobe ~** to check one's coat

④ *Erklärung, Urteil* to make; **seine Stimme ~** to cast one's vote **⑤** (*darstellen*) to be; **die perfekte Hausfrau ~** to be the perfect wife II. *vr* ■ **sich** *akk* **mit jdm ~** to associate with sb

abgebrannt *adj* (*fam*) broke

abgebrüht *adj* (*fam*) unscrupulous

abgedroschen *adj* (*pej fam*) hackneyed

ab|gehen *irreg vi sein* **①** (*sich lösen*) to come off **②** **von der Schule ~** to drop out of school **③** (*abzweigen*) to branch off

abgekartet *adj* (*fam*) ▶WENDUNGEN: **ein ~es <u>Spiel</u> treiben** to play a double game

abgelegen *adj* remote

abgeneigt *adj* ■ **nicht ~ sein, etw zu tun** to not be averse to doing sth

Abgeordnete(r) [ˈap·gə·ʔɔrd·nə·tɐ, -tə] *f(m) dekl wie adj* representative

Abgeordnetenhaus *nt* ≈ House of Representatives

abgerissen *pp von* **abreißen**

Abgesandte(r) *f(m) dekl wie adj* envoy

abgeschieden *adj* isolated

abgesehen I. *adj* **es auf jdn ~ haben** (*schikanieren wollen*) to have it in for sb; **es auf etw** *akk* **~ haben** to have one's eye on sth; **du hast es nur darauf ~, mich zu ärgern** you're just out to annoy me II. *adv* ■ **~ von jdm/ etw** except for sb/sth; ■ **~ davon, dass ...** apart from the fact that ...

abgespannt *adj, adv* tired out

abgestanden *adj Bier, Wasser* stale

ab|gewöhnen I. *vt* ■ **jdm etw ~** to get sb to stop doing sth II. *vr* ■ **sich** *dat* **etw ~** to give up sth

abgöttisch *adv* **jdn ~ lieben** to idolize sb

Abgrund *m* abyss; **am Rande des ~s stehen** to be on the brink of disaster

abgrundtief [ˈapgrʊnt·ˈtiːf] *adj Hass* profound

ab|gucken *vt* ■ **etw [von jdm] ~** to copy sth [from sb]

ab|hacken *vt* to chop down *sep; Finger* to chop off *sep*

ab|haken *vt* **①** (*in einer Liste*) to check

off *sep* **②** (*vergessen*) to forget; **die Sache ist abgehakt** the affair is over and done with

ab|halten *vt irreg* **①** (*hindern*) ■ **jdn von etw** *dat* **~** to keep sb from sth **②** (*fernhalten*) *Hitze* to protect from; *Insekten* to repel **③** (*veranstalten*) to hold; *Demonstration* to stage

abhanden|kommen^{RR} [apˈhandn̩-] *vi irreg sein* to get lost

Abhang <-[e]s, Abhänge> *m* slope

ab|hängen *vi irreg* **①** (*bedingt sein*) to depend (**von** +*dat* on); **das hängt davon ab** that [all] depends **②** (*angewiesen sein*) to be dependent (**von** +*dat* on) **③** (*sl: nichts tun*) to hang out

abhängig *adj* **①** (*bedingt*) ■ **von etw** *dat* **~ sein** to depend on sth **②** (*angewiesen*) ■ **von jdm ~ sein** to be dependent on sb **③** (*süchtig*) addicted; ■ **[von etw** *dat*] **~ sein** to be addicted [to sth]

ab|härten *vt, vi* to harden (**gegen** +*akk* to)

ab|hauen <haute ab, abgehauen> *vi sein* (*fam*) to skip out of town; **hau ab!** get lost!

ab|heben *irreg* I. *vi* **①** *Flugzeug* to take off **②** (*am Telefon*) to answer [the phone] II. *vt Geld* to withdraw

ab|hetzen *vr* ■ **sich** *akk* **~** to stress oneself out

Abhilfe *f kein pl* remedy

ab|holen *vt* to pick up *sep*

Abholzung <-, -en> *f* deforestation

Abi <-s, -s> [ˈabi] *nt pl selten* (*fam*), **Abitur** <-s, -e> [abiˈtuːɐ̯] *nt pl selten* Abitur (*written and oral final examination usually taken at the end of the 13th year of school*)

Abiturient(in) <-en, -en> [abiˈtuˈriɛnt] *m(f)* Abitur student (*student who is taking or has passed the Abitur*)

ab|kapseln *vr* ■ **sich** *akk* **~** to cut oneself off

ab|kaufen *vt* (*a. fig*) ■ **jdm etw ~** to buy sth off sb; **das kaufe ich dir nicht ab!** (*fig*) I don't buy that!

ab|kochen *vt* to boil

A

ablkommen *vi irreg sein* von der Straße to veer off; vom Weg to stray from; **von einer Meinung ~** to change one's mind; **vom Thema ~** to digress from the topic

Abkommen <-s, -> *nt* agreement; **ein ~ abschließen** to sign a treaty

ablkratzen I. *vt haben* to scratch off *sep* **II.** *vi sein* (*sl*) to kick the bucket

ablkriegen *vt* (*fam*) ❶ *Anteil* to get one's share; **die Hälfte von etw** *dat* ~ to receive half of sth ❷ (*beschädigt werden*) to get damaged; (*verletzt werden*) to be injured

ablkühlen I. *vi sein* to cool [down]; *Begeisterung* to wane **II.** *vr haben* ■**sich** ~ *Person* to cool off; *Wetter* to get cooler

ablkürzen *vt* ❶ *Wort* to abbreviate ❷ *Weg, Gespräch* to cut short *sep*

Abkürzung *f* ❶ *eines Wortes* abbreviation ❷ (*Weg*) shortcut; **eine ~ nehmen** to take a shortcut

ablladen *vt irreg* ❶ *Müll* to dump ❷ *Ladung, Waren* to unload ❸ (*fam: absetzen*) ■**jdn** ~ to drop off *sep* sb ❹ (*abreagieren*) **seinen Ärger bei jdm ~** to take out one's anger on sb ❺ (*abwälzen*) ■**etw auf jdn ~** to shift sth onto sb

abllassen *irreg vt Wasser, Öl* to drain; *Dampf* ~ (*a. fig*) to let off steam

Ablauf <-es, -läufe> *m* ❶ (*Verlauf*) course; von Verbrechen, Unfall sequence of events ❷ **nach/vor ~ der Frist** after/before a deadline

abllaufen *irreg* **I.** *vi sein* ❶ (*verlaufen*) to proceed ❷ (*abfließen*) to run; **das Badewasser ~ lassen** to drain the bathtub ❸ (*ungültig werden*) to expire **II.** *vt haben Schuhe* to wear down *sep*

abllegen I. *vt* ❶ (*an einen Ort*) to put ❷ **einen Eid ~** to take an oath; **ein Geständnis ~** to make a confession; **eine Prüfung ~** to pass an exam **II.** *vi* NAUT to set sail

abllehnen I. *vt* ❶ (*zurückweisen*) to turn down *sep*; *Person, Antrag* to reject ❷ (*sich weigern*) ■**[es] ~, etw zu tun**

to refuse to do sth ❸ (*missbilligen*) to disapprove of **II.** *vi* (*nein sagen*) to refuse

Ablehnung <-, -en> *f* ❶ (*Zurückweisung*) rejection ❷ (*Missbilligung*) disapproval; **auf ~ stoßen** to meet with disapproval

abllenken I. *vt* ❶ to distract; ■**sich** *akk* **von etw** *dat* ~ **lassen** to be distracted by sth; **Gartenarbeit lenkt ihn ab** working in the garden helps him to relax **II.** *vi* to distract; **vom Thema ~** to change the subject

Ablenkung *f* distraction; **zur ~** in order to relax

abllesen *irreg vt Messgeräte, Strom* to read

ablliefern *vt Paket* to deliver (**bei** +*dat* to); *Manuskript* to hand in *sep*

abllösen I. *vt* ❶ (*abmachen*) to remove; *Pflaster* to peel off *sep* ❷ **einen Kollegen ~** to take over for a colleague; **die Wache ~** to change the guard ❸ (*fig: ersetzen*) to replace **II.** *vr* ■**sich** *akk* ~ ❶ (*abgehen*) to peel off ❷ (*abwechseln*) to take turns (**bei** +*dat* at); **sich** *akk* **bei der Arbeit ~** to work in shifts

ablmachen *vt* ❶ (*entfernen*) to take off *sep* ❷ (*vereinbaren*) ■**etw [mit jdm] ~** to arrange sth [with sb]

Abmachung <-, -en> *f* agreement; **sich** *akk* **[nicht] an eine ~ halten** to [not] keep an agreement

ablmelden I. *vt* ❶ **jdn von einer Schule ~** to withdraw sb from a school ❷ **ein Auto ~** to cancel one's car registration; **das Telefon ~** to have one's phone disconnected **II.** *vr* ■**sich** *akk* ~ (*bei Umzug*) to notify the authorities of a change of address

ablmessen *vt irreg* to measure

ablnabeln *vr* ■**sich** *akk* [**von jdm/ etw**] ~ to become independent [of sb/ sth]

Abnahme <-, -n> ['ap·na:·mə] *f* reduction [in]; *der Kräfte* weakening

ablnehmen *irreg* **I.** *vi* ❶ (*an Gewicht*) to lose weight ❷ (*sich verringern*) to decrease; *Nachfrage* to drop ❸ (*am Tele-*

fon) to answer [the phone] **II.** *vt* ❶(*wegnehmen*) ■ **jdm etw ~** to take sth [away *sep*] from sb ❷(*herunternehmen*) to take down *sep;* **den Hut ~** to take off *sep* one's hat ❸**den Telefonhörer ~** to pick up *sep* the phone ❹(*übernehmen*) ■ **jdm etw ~** to take over *sep* sth for sb; **deine Arbeit kann ich dir nicht ~** I can't do your work for you

Abneigung *f* dislike (**gegen** +*akk* of)

ab|nutzen, ab|nützen SÜDD, ÖSTERR **I.** *vt* to wear out *sep;* ■ **abgenutzt** worn **II.** *vr* ■ **sich** *akk* **~** to wear

abonnieren* [abɔ·'niː·rən] *vt* to subscribe to

Abordnung *f* delegation

ab|plagen *vr* ■ **sich** *akk* [**mit etw** *dat*] **~** to struggle [with sth]

ab|prallen *vi sein* to rebound (**von** +*dat* off [of]); ■ **an jdm ~** to bounce off sb

ab|putzen *vt* to clean; **putz dir die Schuhe ab!** wipe your shoes!

ab|raten *vi irreg* ■ **jdm von etw** *dat* **~** to advise sb against sth

ab|räumen *vt* **den Tisch ~** to clear the table

ab|reagieren* ['ap·rea·giː·rən] **I.** *vt* *Wut, Frust* to work off *sep* **II.** *vr* ■ **sich** *akk* **~** to calm down

ab|rechnen *vi* (*zur Rechenschaft ziehen*) ■ **mit jdm ~** to call sb to account

Abrechnung *f* **die ~ machen** to add up the bill

ab|regen *vr* (*fam*) ■ **sich** *akk* **~** to calm down; **reg dich ab!** calm down!, relax!

Abreise *f kein pl* departure

ab|reisen *vi sein* to depart

ab|reißen *irreg* **I.** *vt haben* to tear (**von** +*dat* off); *Gebäude* to tear down *sep* **II.** *vi sein* ❶(*sich lösen*) to tear off ❷(*aufhören*) to break off; **den Kontakt nicht ~ lassen** to not lose contact

ab|riegeln *vt Fenster, Tür* to bolt; *Gebiet, Straße* to cordon off *sep*

ab|rufen *vt irreg* **Daten ~** to retrieve data

ab|runden *vt* ❶*Betrag, Zahl* to round

(**auf** +*akk* to) ❷**ein Essen ~** to round off a meal

ab|rüsten *vi* MIL to disarm

Abrüstung *f kein pl* MIL disarmament

ABS <-> [aːbeː'ʔɛs] *nt Abk von* **Antiblockiersystem** ABS

ab|sacken *vi sein* (*fam*) *Blutdruck, Boden* to sink; *Flugzeug, Leistung* to drop (**auf** +*akk* to); **sie ist in ihren Leistungen sehr abgesackt** her performance has deteriorated considerably

Absage <-, -n> *f* rejection

ab|sagen I. *vt Termin, Verabredung* to cancel **II.** *vi* ■ **jdm ~** to decline sb's invitation; **ich muss leider ~** I'm afraid I have to cancel *fam;* **hast du ihr schon abgesagt?** have you already told her you're not going?

ab|sägen *vt Ast* to saw off *sep; Baum* to cut down *sep*

Absatz *m* ❶(*am Schuh*) heel ❷(*Abschnitt*) paragraph ❸(*Verkauf*) sales *pl;* **~ finden** to find a market

ab|schaffen *vt* to abolish; **die Todesstrafe ~** to abolish the death penalty

ab|schalten I. *vt* (*abstellen*) to turn off *sep* **II.** *vi* (*fam: entspannen*) to relax

ab|schätzen *vt* ❶(*einschätzen*) to assess; **ich kann ihre Reaktion schlecht ~** I can't even guess what her reaction will be ❷(*ungefähr schätzen*) to estimate

ab|schauen *vt* SÜDD, ÖSTERR, SCHWEIZ *s.* **abgucken**

Abschaum *m kein pl* (*pej*) scum

abscheulich [ap·'ʃɔy·lɪç] **I.** *adj* revolting; *Verbrechen* horrifying **II.** *adv* **~ wehtun** to hurt like hell *fam;* **~ kalt/warm** awfully cold/hot

ab|schieben *irreg vt* (*ausweisen*) to deport

Abschied <-[e]s, -e> ['ap·ʃiːt] *m* farewell; **der ~ fiel ihr nicht leicht** she found it difficult to say goodbye; **sie gab ihm zum ~ einen Kuss** she gave him a goodbye kiss; **von jdm ~ nehmen** to say goodbye to sb

ab|schlachten *vt* to slaughter

ab|schlagen *irreg vt* ❶(*abtrennen*) to

A

knock (**von** +*dat* off); *Ast* to knock down; **jdm den Kopf** ~ to chop off *sep* sb's head ❷ ■ **jdm etw** ~ to refuse sb sth; **er kann keinem etwas** ~ he can't refuse anybody anything

Abschlag(s)zahlung *f* partial payment

ab|schleppen *vt* ❶ *Fahrzeug, Schiff* to tow [away *sep*] ❷ (*fam*) *Person* to pick up *sep*; **jede Woche schleppt er eine andere ab** he comes home with a different girl every week

Abschleppseil *nt* tow rope

Abschleppwagen *m* tow truck

ab|schließen *irreg* I. *vt* ❶ *Tür* to lock ❷ (*beenden*) to finish; *Diskussion* to end ❸ (*vereinbaren*) *Geschäft* to close; *Versicherung* to take out *sep*; *Vertrag* to sign; *Wette* to place II. *vi* (*zuschließen*) to lock up

abschließend *adj* ~**e Bemerkungen** closing remarks

Abschluss^RR *m* ❶ *kein pl* (*Ende*) conclusion; **zum** ~ **kommen** to draw to a conclusion; **kurz vor dem** ~ **stehen** to be nearly over ❷ *SCH, UNIV* degree; **welchen** ~ **haben Sie?** what degree do you have? ❸ (*das Vereinbaren*) settlement; *einer Versicherung* taking out; *eines Vertrags* signing

Abschlussprüfung^RR *f SCH* final [exam]

Abschlusszeugnis^RR *nt SCH* diploma

ab|schminken *vr* ❶ (*Make-up entfernen*) ■ **sich** *akk* ~ to take off one's make-up ❷ (*fig fam: aufgeben*) ■ **sich** *dat* **etw** ~ to give up *sep* sth; **das können Sie sich** ~! you can forget about that!

ab|schnallen *vr* ■ **sich** *akk* ~ to unfasten one's seat belt

ab|schneiden *irreg* I. *vt* to cut [off *sep*]; **jdm den Weg** ~ to intercept sb; **jdm das Wort** ~ to cut sb short II. *vi* (*fam*) **bei etw** *dat* **gut/schlecht** ~ to do well/poorly on sth

Abschnitt *m* ❶ (*im Text*) passage ❷ (*Zeitabschnitt*) period; **ein neuer** ~ **der Geschichte** a new era in history; **ein neuer** ~ **in seinem Leben** a new

chapter of his life ❸ (*Unterteilung*) part; *einer Autobahn* section

ab|schrauben *vt* to unscrew

ab|schrecken I. *vt* KOCHK to shock II. *vi* to deter

abschreckend I. *adj* deterrent; **ein** ~**es Beispiel** a warning II. *adv* ~ **wirken** to act as a deterrent

ab|schreiben *irreg vt* ❶ *Text* to copy ❷ (*fam: verloren geben*) to write off *sep*

Abschürfung <-, -en> *f MED* scrape

abschüssig ['ap·ʃʏ·sɪç] *adj* steep

ab|schütteln *vt* to shake off *sep*

ab|schweifen *vi sein Gedanken* to deviate; **bitte schweifen Sie nicht ab!** please stick to the point!; **vom Thema** ~ to digress [from a topic]

absehbar ['ap·ze:·ba:ɐ̯] *adj* foreseeable; **das Ende ist nicht** ~ the end is not in sight; **in** ~**er Zeit** in the foreseeable future

abseits ['ap·zaits] *präp* +*gen* **ein wenig** ~ **der Straße** not far from the road

abseits|stehen^RR *vi irreg* to stand on the sidelines

Absender(in) <-s, -> *m(f)* sender

ab|setzen I. *vt* ❶ *Hut, Brille* to take off *sep* ❷ (*hinstellen*) to put down *sep* ❸ (*aussteigen lassen*) ■ **jdn** ~ to drop off *sep* sb ❹ **etw von der Steuer** ~ to deduct sth from one's taxes ❺ *Medikament* to stop taking II. *vr* ■ **sich** *akk* ~ ❶ *Dreck, Staub* to settle ❷ (*fam: verschwinden*) to clear out; **sich** *akk* **ins Ausland** ~ to leave the country

Absicht <-, -en> *f* intention; ~ **sein** to be intentional; **das war nicht meine** ~! I didn't mean to do it!; **mit/ohne** ~ intentionally/unintentionally; **die** ~ **haben, etw zu tun** to intend to do sth

absichtlich ['ap·zɪçt·lɪç] *adv* on purpose

absolut [ap·zo·'lu:t] I. *adj* absolute; ~**e Ruhe** complete calm II. *adv* (*fam*) absolutely; ~ **nicht/nichts** absolutely not/nothing

ab|sondern I. *vt* (*ausscheiden*) to secrete II. *vr* ■ **sich** *akk* ~ to keep oneself apart

A

ab|speichern *vt* COMPUT to store; (*Daten sichern*) to save

abspenstig ['ap-ʃpɛnstɪç] *adj* **jdm etw ~ machen** to take away *sep* sth from sb

ab|sperren I. *vt* ❶ (*versperren*) to cordon off *sep* ❷ (*abstellen*) *Strom, Wasser* to cut off *sep* ❸ SÜDD (*zuschließen*) to lock II. *vi* SÜDD (*zuschließen*) to lock up

ab|spielen I. *vr* ■ **sich** *akk* ~ to happen; **was hat sich hier abgespielt?** what happened here? II. *vt* ❶ *Musik* to play ❷ *Ball* to pass

Absprache *f* agreement; **eine ~ treffen** to come to an agreement

ab|sprechen *irreg* I. *vt* (*vereinbaren*) to agree on II. *vr* ■ **sich** *akk* **mit jdm** (**wegen** +*gen* **on**) to come to an agreement with sb

Absprung *m* (*fam: Ausstieg*) getting out; **den ~ schaffen** to make a getaway; **den ~ verpassen** to miss the boat

ab|spülen I. *vt* to wash off *sep;* **das Geschirr ~** to do the dishes II. *vi* to do the dishes

Abstand *m* ❶ (*räumlich*) distance; **ein ~ von 20 Metern** a distance of 65 feet; **in einigem ~** at some distance; **~ halten** to maintain a distance; **fahr nicht so dicht auf, halt ~!** don't tailgate! ❷ (*zeitlich*) interval; **in kurzen/regelmäßigen Abständen** at short/regular intervals ❸ (*emotional*) aloofness

ab|stauben *vt Möbel* to dust

Abstecher <-s, -> *m* (*Ausflug*) trip

ab|stehen *vi irreg* to stick out; **er hat ~de Ohren** his ears stick out

ab|steigen *vi irreg sein* ❶ (*heruntersteigen*) to dismount; **von einer Leiter ~** to get down off a ladder ❷ (*fam*) **in einem Hotel ~** to stay in a hotel ❸ **beruflich/gesellschaftlich ~** to slide down the job/social ladder

ab|stellen *vt* ❶ *Gerät* to turn off *sep* ❷ *Wasser, Strom* to cut off *sep;* **den Haupthahn ~** to turn off the main shut-off valve ❸ (*absetzen*) to put down *sep* ❹ *Fahrzeug* to park

Abstellgleis *nt* siding

ab|stempeln *vt* ❶ *Brief* to stamp ❷ (*fig*) ■ [**als etw** *akk*] **abgestempelt** branded [as sth]

ab|sterben *vi irreg sein Blätter, Zellen* to die; *Finger, Zehen* to go numb

Abstieg <-[e]s, -e> *m* descent; **der berufliche/gesellschaftliche ~** descent down the job/social ladder

ab|stimmen I. *vi* to vote; [**über etw** *akk*] **~ lassen** to [have a] vote [on sth] II. *vt* (*in Einklang bringen*) ■ **Dinge aufeinander ~** to coordinate things [with each other]; *Farben, Kleidung* to match

Abstimmung *f* POL vote (**über** +*akk* **on**)

abstinent [ap-sti-'nɛnt] *adj* abstinent; ■ **~ sein** to be a teetotaler

ab|stoßen *irreg vt* ❶ MED to reject ❷ (*anwidern*) to repel

abstoßend *adj Aussehen* repulsive; *Geruch* disgusting

ab|stottern *vt* (*fam*) to pay in installments

abstrakt [ap-'strakt] *adj* abstract

ab|streiten *vt irreg* to deny; **er stritt ab, sie zu kennen** he denied knowing her

ab|stumpfen *vi sein* to blunt (**gegen** +*akk* to)

Absturz *m* fall; *von Computer, Flugzeug* crash

ab|stürzen *vi sein* ❶ (*in die Tiefe*) to fall; *Computer, Flugzeug* to crash ❷ (*sich betrinken*) to get hammered *sl*

ab|suchen *vt* to search (**nach** +*dat* for)

absurd [ap-'zʊrt] *adj* absurd

Abszess^{RR} <-es, -e>, **Abszeß**^{ALT} <-sses, -sse> [aps-'tsɛs] *m* MED abscess

Abt, Äbtissin <-[e]s, Äbte> [apt, ɛp-'tɪsɪn] *m, f* abbot *masc,* abbess *fem*

ab|tanzen *vi* (*sl*) to boogie *fam*

ab|tasten *vt* to search (**nach** +*dat* for); **jdn nach Waffen ~** to frisk sb for weapons

ab|tauen I. *vi sein Eis* to thaw II. *vt haben Kühlschrank* to defrost

Abtei <-, -en> *f* abbey

Abteil *nt* compartment

ab|teilen *vt* to partition off *sep*

A **Abteilung** *f* department; *eines Krankenhauses* ward

Abteilungsleiter(in) *m(f)* department manager

ab|treiben *irreg vt, vi* MED to have an abortion

Abtreibung <-, -en> *f* MED abortion

ab|trennen *vt* ❶ (*ablösen*) to detach ❷ (*abteilen*) to divide off *sep* ❸ *Körperteil* to cut off *sep*

ab|treten *irreg vt* ❶ (*übertragen*) *Rechte* to transfer; *Land* to cede ❷ (*fam: überlassen*) ▪ **jdm etw ~** to give sth to sb; **er hat ihr seinen Platz abgetreten** he gave up his seat to her ❸ **seine Schuhe ~** to wipe off *sep* one's shoes

ab|trocknen *vt* to dry; **das Geschirr ~** to dry the dishes

abturnend ['ap·tœː̯ɐ̯·nənt] *adj* (*sl*) repulsive

ab|wägen *vt irreg* to weigh; **die Vor- und Nachteile ~** to weigh the advantages and disadvantages

ab|wälzen *vt* ▪ **etw [auf jdn] ~** to unload sth [on|to sb]; *Kosten* to pass on *sep*; *Verantwortung* to shift

ab|warten I. *vi* to wait II. *vt* ▪ **etw ~** to wait for sth; **das bleibt abzuwarten** that remains to be seen

abwärts ['ap·vɛrts] *adv* down, downward[s]; (*bergab*) downhill; **den Fluss ~** downstream

Abwasch[1] <-[e]s> *m kein pl* (*Geschirr*) dirty dishes *pl*; **den ~ machen** to do the dishes

Abwasch[2] <-, -en> *f* ÖSTERR (*Spülbecken*) sink

ab|waschen *irreg* I. *vt Schmutz* to wash off *sep*; **das Geschirr ~** to do the dishes II. *vi* to do the dishes

Abwasser <-wässer> *nt* waste water; *von Industrieanlagen* effluent

Abwasserkanal *m* sewer

ab|wechseln [-vɛk·sl̩n] *vr* ▪ **sich** *akk* **~** (*bei Tätigkeit*) to take turns

abwechselnd [-vɛk·sl̩nt] *adv* alternately

Abwechslung <-, -en> [-vɛks·lʊŋ] *f* change; **die ~ lieben** to like variety; **zur ~** for a change

abwegig ['ap·veː·gɪç] *adj* absurd; *Idee* far-fetched; *Verdacht* unfounded

ab|wehren *vt Angriff* to fend off *sep*; *Ball* to clear

Abwehrkräfte *pl* the body's defenses

ab|weisen *vt irreg* ❶ (*wegschicken*) to turn away *sep*; **sich** *akk* [**von jdm**] **nicht ~ lassen** to not take no for an answer [from sb] ❷ (*ablehnen*) to turn down *sep*; *Antrag, Bitte* to deny

abweisend *adj* cold

ab|wenden *vr reg o irreg* ▪ **sich** *akk* **~** to turn away

ab|werben *vt irreg* to entice away *sep*

ab|werten *vt* ❶ *Währung* to devalue (**um** +*akk* by) ❷ (*Bedeutung mindern*) to debase

abwesend ['ap·veː·zn̩t] *adj* absent

Abwesenheit <-, -en> *f pl selten* absence

ab|wickeln *vt Auftrag* to process; *Geschäft* to carry out

ab|wimmeln *vt* (*fam*) ▪ **jdn ~** to get rid of sb; ▪ **etw ~** to get out of [doing] sth

ab|wischen *vt* to wipe; **sich** *dat* **die Tränen ~** to dry one's tears; **sich** *dat* **den Schweiß von der Stirn ~** to wipe the sweat from one's brow

ab|würgen *vt* (*fam*) ❶ *Motor* to stall ❷ (*unterbrechen*) ▪ **jdn ~** to cut sb short

ab|zahlen *vt* (*in Raten*) to pay in installments

ab|zeichnen I. *vt* ❶ (*abmalen*) to copy ❷ (*signieren*) to initial II. *vr* (*erkennbar werden*) ▪ **sich** *akk* **~** to become apparent

ab|ziehen *irreg* I. *vi sein* ❶ *Truppen* to withdraw ❷ *Rauch* to clear ❸ (*fam: weggehen*) to go away; **zieh ab!** beat it! *sl* II. *vt haben* ❶ (*einbehalten*) to deduct ❷ MATH to subtract ❸ *Truppen* to withdraw ❹ *Bett* to strip ❺ *Schlüssel* to take out *sep* ❻ SCHWEIZ (*ausziehen*) to take off *sep*

Abzocke <-> *f kein pl* (*pej fam*) price gouging

ab|zocken *vt* (*fam*) ■ **jdn ~** to swindle sb

Abzug *m* ➊ ÖKON deduction ➋ *von Truppen* withdrawal

abzüglich ['ap·tsy:k·lɪç] *präp* +*gen* minus sth

Abzugshaube *f* exhaust hood

ab|zweigen I. *vi sein* to branch off; **nach links/rechts ~** to turn off to the left/right II. *vt* (*fam*) **Geld ~** to put aside *sep* money

Abzweigung <-, -en> *f* turnoff

Ach [ax] *nt* ►WENDUNGEN: **mit ~ und Krach** (*fam*) by the skin of one's teeth

Achse <-, -n> ['ak·sə] *f* ➊ AUTO axle ➋ (*Linie*) axis ►WENDUNGEN: **auf ~ sein** (*fam*) to be on the move

Achsel <-, -n> ['ak·sl] *f* ANAT armpit; **mit den ~n zucken** to shrug one's shoulders

Achselhöhle *f* armpit

acht[1] [axt] *adj* eight; **das kostet ~ Euro** that costs eight euros; **die Linie ~ fährt zum Bahnhof** the No. 8 [bus/ streetcar] goes to the train station; **es steht ~ zu drei** it's eight to three; **[Jahre alt] sein/werden** to be/turn eight [years old]; **mit ~ [Jahren]** at the age of eight; **~ Uhr sein** to be eight o'clock; **gegen ~ [Uhr]** [at] about eight [o'clock]; **um ~** at eight [o'clock]; **... [Minuten] nach/vor ~ ...** [minutes] after/to eight [o'clock]; **alle ~ Tage** every eight days; **heute/Freitag in ~ Tagen** a week from today/Friday; **heute/ Freitag vor ~ Tagen** a week ago today/Friday

acht[2] [axt] *adv* **wir waren zu ~** there were eight of us

Acht[1] <-, -en> [axt] *f* eight; **auf dem Eis eine ~ laufen** to skate a figure eight on the ice; **die Kreuzacht** the eight of clubs

Acht[RR2] [axt] *f* **~ geben** to be careful; **sie gab genau Acht, was der Professor sagte** she paid careful attention to what the professor said; **auf jdn/etw ~ geben** to look after sb/sth; **etw außer ~ lassen** to not take sth into account;

sich *akk* [**vor jdm/etw**] **in ~ nehmen** to be wary [of sb/sth]

achte(r, s) ['ax·tə, -te, -təs] *adj* ➊ (*an achter Stelle*) eighth; **an ~r Stelle** [in] eighth [place]; **die ~ Klasse** eighth grade ➋ (*Datum*) eighth; **am ~n August** on August eighth

Achte(r) ['ax·tə, -te] *f(m) dekl wie adj* ➊ (*Person*) ■ **der/die/das ~** the eighth; **du bist jetzt der ~, der fragt** you're the eighth person to ask; **als ~ an der Reihe sein** to be the eighth [in line]; **~[r] sein/werden** to be/finish [in] eighth [place]; **als ~r durchs Ziel gehen** to finish eighth, to cross the line in eighth place; **jeder ~** every eighth person, one in eight [people] ➋ (*bei Datumsangabe*) ■ **der ~** [*o geschrieben* **der 8.**] the eighth *spoken,* the 8th *written;* **heute ist der ~** it's the eighth today; ■ **am ~n** on the eighth ➌ (*Namenszusatz*) **Karl der ~** [*o geschrieben* **Karl VIII.**] Karl the Eighth *spoken* [*or written* Karl VIII]

achtel ['ax·tl] *adj* eighth

Achtel <-s, -> ['ax·tl] *nt* eighth

achten ['ax·tn̩] I. *vt* to respect II. *vi* ■ **auf jdn/etw ~** to pay attention to sb/sth; ■ **darauf ~, etw zu tun** to make sure to do sth; **achtet darauf, dass ihr nichts umwerft!** be careful not to knock anything over!

achtens ['ax·tn̩s] *adv* eighthly

Achterbahn *f* roller coaster

achtfach, 8fach ['axt·fax] *adj, adv* eightfold; **die ~e Menge** eight times the amount

achtjährig, 8-jährig[RR] ['axt·jɛː·rɪç] *adj* ➊ (*Alter*) eight-year-old *attr,* eight years old *pred;* **das ~e Jubiläum einer S.** *gen* the eighth anniversary of sth ➋ (*Zeitspanne*) eight-year *attr;* **eine ~e Amtszeit** an eight-year term of office

achtlos I. *adj* careless II. *adv* without noticing

achtmal, 8-mal[RR] *adv* eight times

achttägig, 8-tägig[RR] ['axt·tɛː·gɪç] *adj* eight-day *attr,* lasting eight days *pred*

A

Achtung <-> ['ax·tʊŋ] *f kein pl* respect (**vor** +*dat* for); ~! attention!

achtzehn ['axt·seːn] *adj* eighteen; **ab ~ frei|gegeben| sein** *Film* ≈ NC-17; **■ ~ Uhr** 6 p.m.; MIL 1800 hrs *written*, eighteen hundred hours *spoken*; *s. a.* **acht** [1]

achtzehnte(r, s) *adj* eighteenth; (*Datum*) 18th; *s. a.* **achte(r, s) 1, 2**

achtzig ['axt·sɪç] *adj* ❶ (*Zahl*) eighty; **die Linie ~ fährt zum Bahnhof** the No. 80 |bus/streetcar| goes to the train station; **~ [Jahre alt] sein** to be eighty |years old|; **mit ~ [Jahren]** at the age of eighty ❷ (*fam: Stundenkilometer*) eighty |kilometers an hour|; **[mit] ~ fahren** to do eighty |kilometers an hour| ▶WENDUNGEN: **jdn auf ~ bringen** (*fam*) to make sb's blood boil

achtzigste(r, s) ['axt·sɪç·stə, -tə, -təs] *adj* eightieth; *s. a.* **achte(r, s) 1**

Acker <-s, Äcker> ['akɐ] *m* field

Ackerbau *m kein pl* |arable| farming

Ackerland *nt kein pl* arable |farm|land

Adapter <-s, -> [a'dap·tɐ] *m* adapter

addieren* [a'diː·rən] *vt* to add up *sep*

Adel <-s> ['aːdl] *m kein pl* aristocracy

Ader <-, -n> ['aːdɐ] *f* ❶ (*Vene*) vein; (*Schlagader*) artery ❷ (*Begabung*) eine **künstlerische ~ haben** to have an artistic bent

Adjektiv <-s, -e> ['at·jɛk·tiːf] *nt* adjective

Adler <-s, -> ['aːd·lɐ] *m* eagle

adlig ['aːd·lɪç] *adj* aristocratic; **■ ~ sein** to have a title

Adlige(r) ['aːd·lɪ·gə, -gə] *f(m) dekl wie adj* aristocrat

adoptieren* [ad·ɔp·'tiː·rən] *vt* to adopt

Adoption <-, -en> [adɔp·'tsi̯oːn] *f* adoption; **ein Kind zur ~ freigeben** to put a child up for adoption

Adoptiveltern [ad·ɔp·'tiːf-] *pl* adoptive parents

Adoptivkind *nt* adopted child

Adrenalin <-s> [ad·re·na·'liːn] *nt kein pl* adrenalin

Adressat(in) <-en, -en> [adrɛ·'saːt] *m(f)* addressee

Adressbuch^RR *nt* address book

Adresse <-, -n> [a'drɛ·sə] *f* address

adressieren* [adrɛ·'siːr·ən] *vt* to address (**an** +*akk* to)

Adria <-> ['aːdria] *f* Adriatic |Sea|

Advent <-s, -e> [at·'vɛnt] *m* Advent |season|; **■im ~** during |the| Advent |season|; **erster ~** first Sunday of/in Advent

Adverb <-s, -ien> [at·'vɛrp] *nt* adverb

Advokat(in) <-en, -en> [at·vo·'kaːt] *m(f)* ÖSTERR, SCHWEIZ (*Rechtsanwalt*) lawyer

Advokatur <-, -en> [at·vo·ka·'tuːɐ̯] *f* SCHWEIZ (*Anwaltskanzlei*) lawyer's office

Affe <-n, -n> ['afə] *m* ❶ (*Tier*) ape, monkey ❷ (*fam: blöder Kerl*) dope; **ein eingebildeter ~** a conceited jackass

Affekt <-[e]s, -e> [a'fɛkt] *m* affect; **im ~ handeln** to act in the heat of the moment

affektiert [afɛk·'tiːɐ̯t] *adj* affected

Affenhitze ['afn·hɪtsə] *f* (*fam*) scorching heat

Afghane, Afghanin <-n, -n> [af·'gaː·nə, -nɪn] *m, f* Afghan; *s. a.* **Deutsche(r)**

Afrika <-s> ['aːfri·ka] *nt* Africa

Afrikaner(in) <-s, -> [afri·'kaː·nɐ] *m(f)* African

afrikanisch [afri·'kaː·nɪʃ] *adj* African

Afroamerikaner(in) ['aːfro-] *m(f)* African-American

afroamerikanisch *adj* African-American

After <-s, -> ['af·tɐ] *m* ANAT anus

Agent(in) <-en, -en> [a'gɛnt] *m(f)* ❶ (*Spion*) spy ❷ (*Vertreter*) agent

Agentur <-, -en> [agɛn·'tuːɐ̯] *f* agency

Ägypten <-s> ['ɛ'gʏp·tn] *nt* Egypt; *s. a.* **Deutschland**

Ägypter(in) <-s, -> ['ɛ'gʏp·tɐ] *m(f)* Egyptian; *s. a.* **Deutsche(r)**

ägyptisch ['ɛ'gʏp·tɪʃ] *adj* Egyptian; *s. a.* **deutsch**

ähneln ['ɛ:nln] *vt* to resemble, to look like; **du ähnelst meiner Frau** you remind me of my wife

ahnen ['aːnən] *vt* to suspect; **das kann/**

konnte ich doch nicht ~! how can/could I know that?

ähnlich ['ɛːnˌlɪç] **I.** *adj* similar **II.** *adv* similarly; ∎**jdm ~ sehen** to look like sb

Ähnlichkeit <-, -en> *f* resemblance; ∎**mit jdm/etw ~ haben** to resemble sb/sth

Ahnung <-, -en> *f* ❶ (*Vermutung*) suspicion; **es ist eher so eine ~** it's more of a hunch *fam* ❷ (*Idee*) **hast du eine ~!** (*iron fam*) that's what you think!; **keine ~ haben** to have no idea; **keine ~!** (*fam*) [I have] no idea!

ahnungslos *adj* unsuspecting

Ahorn <-s, -e> ['aːhɔrn] *m* maple [tree]

Aids <-> [eːts] *nt Akr von* **acquired immune deficiency syndrome** AIDS

Airbag <-s, -s> ['ɛːɐˌbɛk] *m* airbag

Airbus ['ɛːɐˌbʊs] *m* airbus

Akademie <-, -n> [akaˈdeˈmiː] *f* academy

Akademiker(in) <-s, -> [akaˈdeːmiˈkɐ] *m(f)* university graduate

akklimatisieren* [akliˈmaˈtiˈziːˈrən] *vr* ∎**sich *akk* ~** ❶ (*klimatisch*) to become acclimated ❷ (*sich einleben*) to get used to sth

Akkordarbeit *f* piecework

Akkordeon <-s, -s> [aˈkɔrˈdeˈɔn] *nt* accordion

Akku <-s, -s> ['aku] *m* (*fam*) *kurz für* **Akkumulator** rechargeable battery

Akkusativ <-s, -e> ['akuˈzaˈtiːf] *m* accusative [case]

Akne <-, -n> ['aknə] *f* acne

Akrobat(in) <-en, -en> [akroˈbaːt] *m(f)* acrobat

akrobatisch *adj* acrobatic

Akt¹ <-[e]s, -e> [akt] *m* ❶ (*Gemälde*) nude [painting] ❷ (*Handlung*) act; **ein ~ der Rache** an act of revenge ❸ THEAT act

Akt² <-[e]s, -en> [akt] *m* ÖSTERR (*Akte*) file

Akte <-, -n> ['aktə] *f* file; **die ~ Borgfeld** the Borgfeld file ▶WENDUNGEN: **etw zu den ~n legen** to lay sth to rest

Aktenordner *m* file

Aktentasche *f* briefcase

Aktenzeichen *nt* file reference [number]

Aktie <-, -n> ['akˈtsiə] *f* BÖRSE stock; **die ~n stehen gut/schlecht** the stock is doing well/badly; (*fig*) things are/aren't looking good

Aktiengesellschaft *f* joint stock company

Aktienkurs *m* stock price

Aktion <-, -en> [akˈtsioːn] *f* action; **in ~ sein** to be [constantly] in action; **in ~ treten** to come into action

Aktionär(in) <-s, -e> [akˈtsioˈnɛːɐ] *m(f)* FIN stockholder

aktiv [akˈtiːf] *adj* active

Aktiv <-s, -e> ['akˈtiːf] *nt pl selten* LING active [voice]

aktivieren* [akˈtiˈviːˈrən] *vt* to activate

Aktivität <-, -en> [akˈtiˈviˈtɛːt] *f* activity

aktualisieren* *vt* to update

aktuell [akˈtʊɛl] *adj* current

Akupunktur <-, -en> [akuˈpʊŋkˈtuːɐ̯] *f* acupuncture

Akustik <-> [aˈkʊsˈtɪk] *f kein pl* acoustics + *pl vb*

akustisch [aˈkʊsˈtɪʃ] *adv* acoustically; **ich habe dich rein ~ nicht verstanden** I just didn't hear what you said

akut [aˈkuːt] *adj* acute

Akzent <-[e]s, -e> [akˈtsɛnt] *m* ❶ (*Aussprache*) accent ❷ LING (*Zeichen*) accent ❸ (*Betonung*) stress ❹ (*Schwerpunkt*) emphasis; **den ~ auf etw *akk* legen** to emphasize sth

akzeptieren* [akˈtsɛpˈtiːˈrən] *vt* to accept

Alarm <-[e]s, -e> [aˈlarm] *m* alarm; ∎**~ schlagen** to sound the alarm

Alarmanlage *f* alarm [system]

alarmieren* [alarˈmiːˈrən] *vt* **die Polizei ~** to call the police

Albaner(in) <-s, -> [alˈbaːˈnə] *m(f)* Albanian; *s. a.* **Deutsche(r)**

Albanien <-s> [alˈbaːniən] *nt* Albania; *s. a.* **Deutschland**

albanisch [alˈbaːnɪʃ] *adj* Albanian; *s. a.* **deutsch**

A **albern** ['al·bɐn] **I.** *adj* childish **II.** *vi* to fool around

Albtraum^RR *m* nightmare

Album <-s, Alben> ['al·bʊm] *nt* album

Alge <-, -n> ['al·gə] *f* alga

Alibi <-s, -s> ['aːli·bi] *nt* alibi

Alimente [ali·'mɛn·tə] *pl* alimony

Alkohol <-s, -e> ['al·ko·hoːl] *m* alcohol

Alkoholeinfluss^RR *m* influence of alcohol

alkoholfrei *adj* nonalcoholic

alkoholhaltig *adj* alcoholic

Alkoholiker(in) <-s, -> [al·ko·'hoː·li·kɐ] *m(f)* alcoholic; **~ sein** to be an alcoholic

Alkoholismus <-> [al·ko·ho·'lɪs·mʊs] *m kein pl* alcoholism

all <-s> [al] *pron indef* all; **ihr Geld** all her money

All <-s> [al] *nt kein pl* space

alle ['alə] *adj pred* (*fam*) ❶ (*aufgebraucht*) ▪ **~ sein** to be all gone; **etw ~ machen** to finish sth off *sep* ❷ (*erschöpft*) ▪ **~ sein** to be finished

alle(r, s) ['alə, -lə, -ləs] *pron indef* ❶ (*mit Singular*) all; [**ich wünsche dir**] **~s Gute** [I wish you] all the best ❷ (*mit Plural*) all; **~e Anwesenden** all those present ❸ *substantivisch* (*jeder*) ▪ **~** everyone; **und damit sind ~ gemeint** and that means everyone; **ihr seid ~ beide Schlitzohren!** you're both a couple of sly little weasels!; **wir haben ~ kein Geld mehr** none of us have any money left; ▪ **~ die**[**jenigen**]**, die ...** everyone, who ...; **~ auf einmal** all at once ❹ *substantivisch* (*alle Dinge*) ▪ **~s** everything; **das ist ~s** that's everything; **ist das schon ~s?** is that it? ❺ *substantivisch* (*insgesamt*) ▪ **~s** all [that]; **das ist doch ~s Unsinn** that's all nonsense ❻ (*bei Zeit- und Maßangaben*) every; **~ fünf Minuten/Meter** every five minutes/meters ▶WENDUNGEN: **~s in ~m** all in all; [**wohl**] **nicht mehr ~ haben** (*fam*) to have a screw loose; **vor ~m** above all

Allee <-, -n> [a'leː] *f* avenue

allein [a'lain] **I.** *adj pred* alone; (*einsam*) lonely; (*ohne Hilfe*) on one's own; **sind Sie ~ oder in Begleitung?** are you by yourself or with someone?; **jdn ~ lassen** to leave sb alone **II.** *adv* ❶ (*bereits*) just; **~ der Schaden war schon schlimm genug** the damage alone was bad enough; **~ der Gedanke daran** the mere thought of it ❷ (*ausschließlich*) exclusively; **das ist ~ deine Entscheidung** it's your decision [and yours alone] ❸ (*ohne Hilfe*) by oneself; **er kann sich schon ~ anziehen** he can already get himself dressed; **~ erziehend sein** to be a single parent; **von ~** by itself/oneself; **ich wäre auch von ~ darauf gekommen** I would have thought of it [by] myself

Alleinerziehende(r) *f(m) dekl wie adj* single parent

alleinstehend *adj* single

allemal ['alə·'maːl] *adv* was er kann, **kann ich ~** whatever he can do, I can do too ▶WENDUNGEN: **ein für ~** once and for all

allenfalls ['alən·'fals] *adv* at [the] most

allerbeste(r, s) ['alɐ·'bɛstə, -tə, -təs] *adj* very best; **ich wünsche dir das A~** I wish you all the best

allerdings ['alɐ·'dɪŋs] *adv* ❶ (*aber*) although; **ich rufe dich an, ~ erst morgen** I'll call you, though not until tomorrow ❷ (*in der Tat*) definitely; **~!** indeed!, you bet! *fam*; **hast du mit ihm gesprochen? ~ ~!** did you speak to him? — I certainly did!

allererste(r, s) ['alɐ·'?ɛːɐstə, -tə, -təs] *adj* the [very] first; **~ als A~r** the first; ▪ **als A~s** first of all

Allergie <-, -n> [alɛr·'giː] *f* allergy (**gegen** +*akk* to); **~ auslösend** allergenic

allergisch [a'lɛr·gɪʃ] **I.** *adj* allergic (**gegen** +*akk* to) **II.** *adv* **~ auf etw** *akk* **reagieren** MED to have an allergic reaction to sth; (*fig*) to get steamed up about sth

Allerheiligen <-> ['alɐ·'hai·lɪ·gn̩] *nt* All Saints' Day

allerlei ['alɐ·'lai] *adj* ❶ *substantivisch* a

lot; **ich muss noch ~ erledigen** I still have a lot to do ❷ *attr* all sorts of

allerletzte(r, s) ['alɐ·'lɛts·tə, -tɐ, -təs] *adj* [very] last ▶WENDUNGEN: **das A~ sein** (*fam*) to be beyond the pale *fam*; **er ist das A~!** he's the worst!

allermeiste(r, s) ['alɐ·'mais·tə, -tɐ, -təs] *adj* most; ■**am ~n** most of all; **die ~n Leute** the vast majority of the people

allerneueste(r, s) [...] *adj* latest; **auf dem ~n Stand** state-of-the-art; ■**das A~** the latest

Allerseelen <-> ['alɐ·'zeː·lən] *nt* All Souls' Day

allerwenigste(r, s) *adj* ❶(*zählbar*) fewest; **in den ~n Fällen** in only very few cases ❷(*unzählbar*) least; **das ~ Geld** the least money; ■**am ~n** the least

allesamt ['alə·'zamt] *adv* all [of them/ you/us]

allgemein ['al·ɡə·'main] **I.** *adj* general; **von ~em Interesse sein** to be of general interest; **zur ~en Überraschung** to everyone's surprise ▶WENDUNGEN: **im A~en** (*normalerweise*) generally speaking; (*insgesamt*) on the whole **II.** *adv* generally; **~ bekannt sein** to be common knowledge; **~ gültig** general; **~ verständlich** intelligible to everybody

Allgemeinbildung *f kein pl* general education

Allgemeinheit <-> ['al·ɡə·'main·hait] *f kein pl* general public

allgemeinverständlich *adj s.* **allgemein II**

Allheilmittel *nt* cure-all

Allianz <-, -en> [a'liː·ants] *f* alliance

Alliierte(r) [ali·'iːɐ·tə -tɐ] *f(m) dekl wie adj* ally; ■**die ~n** the Allies

alljährlich ['al·'jɛːɐ·lɪç] *adj attr* annual

allmählich [al·'mɛː·lɪç] **I.** *adj attr* gradual **II.** *adv* gradually; **~ geht er mir auf die Nerven** he's beginning to get on my nerves; **wir sollten jetzt ~ gehen** it's time we left

Allradantrieb *m* four-wheel drive

Alltag ['al·taːk] *m kein pl* everyday life

alltäglich ['al·tɛːk·lɪç] *adj* ❶ *attr* (*tagtäglich*) daily, everyday ❷(*gang und gäbe*) usual ❸(*gewöhnlich*) ordinary

allzu ['al·tsuː] *adv* **~ oft** only too often; **nicht ~ oft** not [all] too often; **~ sehr/ viel** too much

Allzweckhalle *f* multipurpose hall

Allzweckreiniger *m* general-purpose cleaner

Alm <-, -en> [alm] *f* mountain pasture

Alpen ['al·pn] *pl* ■**die ~** the Alps

Alphabet <-[e]s, -e> [al·fa·'beːt] *nt* alphabet

alphabetisch [al·fa·'beː·tɪʃ] *adj* alphabetical

Alptraum ['alp·traum] *m* nightmare

als [als] *konj* ❶(*zeitlich*) when, as; **ich kam, ~ er ging** I came as he was leaving; **gleich, ~ ...** as soon as ...; **damals, ~ ...** back in the days when ...; **gerade ~ ...** just when ... ❷ *nach Komparativ* than; **Joe ist größer ~ Tom** Joe is taller than Tom ❸(*wie*) as; **alles andere ~ ...** everything but ...; **anders ~ jd sein** to be different from sb; **niemand anders ~ ...** (*a. hum, iron*) none other than ... ❹ ■**...,~ habe/könne/sei/ würde ...** as if; ..., **als habe er es schon geahnt**, as if he had already known; **es sieht aus, ~ würde es bald schneien** it looks like snow ❺(*in der Eigenschaft*) as; **schon ~ Kind hatte er immer Albträume** even as a child, he had nightmares; **sich** *akk* **~ wahr/ falsch erweisen** to prove to be true/ false

also ['alzo] *adv* so

alt <älter, älteste> [alt] *adj* old; (*von früher*) ancient; **wie ~ ist er? – er ist 8 Jahre ~** how old is he? — he's 8 [years old]; ■**älter sein/werden** to be/get older; **ältere Mitbürger** senior citizens; **A~ und Jung** young and old alike ▶WENDUNGEN: **~ aussehen** (*fam*) to look like a complete fool

Altar <-s, Altäre> [al·'taːɐ̯] *m* altar

altbacken *adj* ❶ *Backwaren* stale ❷(*altmodisch*) old-fashioned

A

Altbau <-bauten> *m* old building
altbewährt ['alt·bə·'vɛːɐ̯t] *adj* tried-and-true
Alter <-s, -> ['altɐ] *nt* ❶ (*Lebensalter*) age; **in jds** *dat* ~ **at sb's age**; **in jds** ~ **sein** to be the same age as sb; **er ist in meinem** ~ he's my age; **mittleren** ~**s** middle-aged ❷ (*Bejahrtheit*) old age; **im** ~ **in old age** ▶WENDUNGEN: ~ **schützt vor** Torheit **nicht** (*prov*) there's no fool like an old fool *prov*
altern ['al·tɐn] *vi sein Mensch* to age
alternativ [al·tɐr·na·'tiːf] *adv* ~ **leben** to live an alternative lifestyle
Alternative <-, -n> [al·tɐr·na·'tiː·və] *f* alternative
Altersgruppe *f* age group
Altersheim *nt* retirement home
Altersrente *f* social security
Altersschwäche *f kein pl* infirmity
Altersversorgung *f* pension; (*betrieblich*) retirement plan
Altglascontainer *m* glass recycling container
altklug ['alt·'kluːk] *adj* precocious
ältlich ['ɛlt·lɪç] *adj* oldish
altmodisch ['alt·moːdɪʃ] **I.** *adj* old-fashioned **II.** *adv* ~ **gekleidet** dressed in old-fashioned clothes; ~ **eingerichtet** furnished in an old-fashioned style
Altöl *nt* used oil
Altpapier *nt* waste paper
Altstadt *f* old town center
Altweibersommer [alt·'vaibɐ·zɔ·mɐ] *m* Indian summer
Alu ['aːlu] *nt kurz für* **Aluminium**
Alufolie *f* aluminum foil
Aluminium <-s> [alu·'miː·nɪ·ʊm] *nt kein pl* aluminum
am [am] ❶ = **an dem** *s.* **an** ❷ + *superl* **ich fände es** ~ **besten, wenn** ... I think it would be best if ...; **es wäre mir** ~ **liebsten, wenn** ... I would prefer it if ...; ~ **schnellsten/schönsten sein** to be [the] fastest/most beautiful
Amateur(in) <-s, -e> [ama·'tøːɐ̯] *m(f)* amateur
Ambulanz <-, -en> [am·bu·'lants] *f*

❶ (*im Krankenhaus*) outpatient department ❷ (*Unfallwagen*) ambulance
Ameise <-, -n> ['aː·mai·zə] *f* ant
Ameisenbär *m* anteater
Ameisenhaufen *m* anthill
Amen <-s, -> ['aːmɛn] *nt* Amen
Amerika <-s> [a'meː·ri·ka] *nt* ❶ (*Kontinent*) America ❷ (*USA*) the USA, the United States, the States *fam*
Amerikaner(in) <-s, -> [ame·ri·'kaː·nɐ] *m(f)* American; *s. a.* **Deutsche(r)**
amerikanisch [ameri·'kaː·nɪʃ] *adj* American
Amok ['aːmɔk] *m* ~ **laufen** to run amok
amortisieren* [amɔr·ti·zi··rən] *vr* ■ **sich** *akk* ~ to pay for itself
Ampel <-, -n> ['am·pl] *f* traffic light; **die** ~ **ist auf Rot gesprungen** the light turned red; **du hast eine rote** ~ **überfahren** you just ran a red light
Amphibie <-, -n> [am·'fiː·bjə] *f* amphibian
amputieren* [am·pu·'tiː·rən] *vt, vi* to amputate
Amsel <-, -n> ['amzl] *f* blackbird
Amt <-[e]s, Ämter> [amt] *nt* ❶ (*Behörde*) office; **aufs** ~ **gehen** (*fam*) to go to the authorities ❷ (*öffentliche Stellung*) post; **ein** ~ **antreten** to take up one's post; **ein** ~ **innehaben** to hold an office; **im** ~ **sein** to be in office
amtlich *adj* official
Amtsgericht *nt* ≈ district court
Amtsrichter(in) *m(f)* ≈ district court judge
Amtszeit *f* term of office
Amulett <-[e]s, -e> [amu·'lɛt] *nt* amulet
amüsant [amy·'zant] *adj* amusing
amüsieren* [amy·'ziː·rən] **I.** *vr* ■ **sich** *akk* ~ to enjoy oneself; **amüsiert euch gut!** have a good time!; ■ **sich** *akk* **mit jdm** ~ to have a good time with sb; ■ **sich** *akk* **über jdn/etw** ~ to laugh at sb/sth **II.** *vt* ■ **jdn** ~ to amuse sb
an [an] **I.** *präp* ❶ + *dat* (*räumlich*) ■ **etw hängt** ~ **der Wand** sth is hanging on the wall; **am Telefon sein** to be on the phone; **am Tisch sitzen** to sit at the ta-

ble; **Tür ~ Tür wohnen** to be next-door neighbors; **~ Krücken gehen** to walk on crutches ② +*akk* (*räumlich*) **etw ~ die Tafel schreiben** to write sth on the board; **~s Telefon gehen** to answer the telephone; **sich** *akk* **~ den Tisch setzen** to sit down at the table; **jdn ~ die Hand nehmen** to take sb by the hand ③ +*dat* (*zeitlich*) **am Freitag** on Friday; **am Morgen** in the morning; **~ jenem Morgen** that morning; **~ Weihnachten** at Christmas; (*25. Dezember*) on Christmas Day ④ +*dat* (*Eigenschaft*) **das Angenehme ~ etw** *dat* the pleasant thing about sth, **was ist ~ ihm** so besonders? what's so special about him? ⑤ +*dat* (*mittels*) **jdn ~ der Stimme erkennen** to recognize sb by his/her voice ▶WENDUNGEN: **~ [und für] sich** actually II. *adj pred* (*angeschaltet*) ▪**~ sein** to be on III. *adv* (*ungefähr*) ▪**~ die ...** approximately ...

analog [ana·ˈloːk] *adj* TECH analog

Analphabet(in) <-en, -en> [ˈanʔalfaˌbeːt] *m(f)* illiterate

Analyse <-, -n> [anaˈlyːzə] *f* analysis

analysieren* [analyˈziːrən] *vt* to analyze

Ananas <-, -> [ˈananas] *f* pineapple

anatomisch [anaˈtoːmɪʃ] *adj* anatomic

an|bahnen *vr* ▪**sich** *akk* **~** to be in the making; **zwischen ihnen bahnt sich etwas an** there's sth going on there

Anbau¹ *m kein pl* AGR cultivation

Anbau² <-bauten> *m* (*Nebengebäude*) annex

an|bauen *vt* ① *Gemüse* to grow ② ▪**etw [an etw** *akk*] **~** to build an extension [to sth]

an|beten *vt* to adore; REL to worship

an|biedern [ˈanˌbiːdɐn] *vr* (*pej*) ▪**sich** *akk* **bei jdm ~** to curry favor with sb

an|bieten *irreg* I. *vt* ▪**[jdm] etw ~** to offer [sb] sth II. *vr* ① (*zur Verfügung stellen*) ▪**sich** *akk* **~** to offer one's services; ▪**sich** *akk* **~, etw zu tun** to offer to do sth ② (*naheliegen*) ▪**etw bietet sich an** sth is just the right thing

an|binden *vt irreg* to tie (**an** +*akk* to)

an|blicken *vt* to look at

an|brennen *irreg vi sein* to burn; ▪**etw ~ lassen** to let sth burn; **es riecht hier so angebrannt** something smells burned in here ▶WENDUNGEN: **nichts ~ lassen** (*fam*) to not hesitate

Anbruch *m kein pl* **bei ~ des Tages** at the break of day; **bei ~ der Dunkelheit** at dusk

andächtig [ˈanˌdɛçtɪç] *adv* ① REL devoutly ② (*ehrfürchtig*) reverently; (*inbrünstig*) raptly

an|dauern *vi* to continue; *Gespräche* to go on

andauernd I. *adj* continuous II. *adv* continuously

Andenken <-s, -> *nt* ① (*Souvenir*) souvenir ② (*Erinnerungsstück*) keepsake ③ *kein pl* (*Erinnerung*) memory; **zum ~ an jdn** in memory of sb

andere(r, s) [ˈanˌdəʁə, -ʁe, -ʁəs] *pron indef* ① (*abweichend*) different, other; **das ist eine ~ Frage** that's another question; **das ~ Geschlecht** the opposite sex; **ein ~s Mal** another time ② (*weitere*) other; **haben Sie noch ~ Fragen?** do you have any more questions? ③ *substantivisch* **es gibt noch ~, die warten!** there are others waiting!; ▪**ein ~r/eine ~** someone else; **alle ~n** all [the] others; **wir ~n** the rest of us; **das T-Shirt ist schmutzig – hast du noch ein ~s** this T-shirt is dirty — do you have another one?; **das ist etwas ganz ~s!** that's something entirely different; **es bleibt uns nichts ~s übrig** there's nothing else we can do; **unter ~m ... ...** among other things

ändern [ˈɛndɐn] *vt, vr* ▪**[sich** *akk*] **~** to change; **ich kann es nicht ~** I can't do anything about it; **daran kann man nichts ~** there's nothing you can do about it; **es hat sich nichts geändert** nothing's changed; **seine Meinung ~** to change one's mind

anders [ˈandɐs] *adv* differently; ▪**~ als ...** different from [*or* than] ...; **es ging**

A

A

leider nicht ~ I'm afraid I couldn't do anything about it; ~ **kann ich es mir nicht erklären** I can't think of another explanation; ~ **als sonst** different than usual; ~ **denkend** dissenting; **jemand/niemand** ~ somebody/nobody else; **es sich** *dat* ~ **überlegen** to change one's mind ▶WENDUNGEN: **nicht** ~ **können** (*fam*) to be unable to help it; **jdm wird ganz** ~ sb feels dizzy

anderswo ['an·dɐs·vo:] *adv* somewhere else

anderthalb ['an·dɐt·'halp] *adj* one and a half; ~ **Stunden** an hour and a half

Änderung <-, -en> *f* change

anderweitig ['an·dɐ·vai·tɪç] I. *adj attr* other II. *adv* ~ **beschäftigt sein** to be otherwise busy; **etw** ~ **verwenden** to use sth in a different way

an|deuten *vt* to imply

Andeutung *f* hint; **eine versteckte** ~ an insinuation; **eine** ~ **machen** to imply

Andrang *m kein pl* rush

an|eignen *vr* ■ **sich** *dat* **etw** ~ ❶ (*an sich nehmen*) to take sth ❷ (*lernen*) to learn sth

aneinander [an·ʔai·'nan·dɐ] *adv* to one another; **etw** ~ **finden** to see sth in each other; ~ **vorbeireden** to be working at cross-purposes

aneinander|geraten* *vi irreg sein* to have a fight

aneinander|reihen *vt* to string together *sep*

an|ekeln *vt* ■ **jdn** ~ to make sb sick; ■ **von etw** *dat* **angeekelt sein** to be disgusted by sth

Anemone <-, -n> [ane·'mo:·nə] *f* BOT anemone

an|erkennen* ['an·ʔɛɐ·kɛ·nən] *vt irreg* ❶ (*akzeptieren*) *Forderung* to accept; *Kind* to acknowledge; *Meinung* to respect ❷ (*würdigen*) to appreciate

an|fahren *irreg* I. *vi sein* to drive off; *Zug* to pull in II. *vt haben* ❶ (*mit Fahrzeug*) to hit ❷ (*schelten*) ■ **jdn** ~ to snap at sb ❸ TRANSP to stop at; **einen Hafen** ~ to pull in at a port

Anfall *m* ❶ MED attack; **epileptischer** ~ epileptic seizure ❷ (*Wutanfall*) fit [of rage]; **einen** ~ **kriegen** to throw a fit ❸ (*Anwandlung*) ■ **in einem** ~ **von etw** *dat* in a fit of sth

an|fallen *irreg vt* to attack

anfällig *adj* to be prone (**für** +*akk* to)

Anfang <-[e]s, -fänge> *m* ❶ (*Beginn*) beginning, start; **der Täter war ca.** ~ **40** the perpetrator was in his early 40s; **am** ~ (*zu Beginn*) in the beginning; (*anfänglich*) to begin with; **den** ~ **machen** to start; **einen neuen** ~ **machen** to make a fresh start; ~ **September/der Woche** at the beginning of September/the week; **von** ~ **an** from the [very] start; **von** ~ **bis Ende** from start to finish ❷ (*Ursprung*) origin[s] *usu pl* ▶WENDUNGEN: **der** ~ **vom Ende** the beginning of the end; **aller** ~ **ist schwer** (*prov*) the first step is always the hardest

an|fangen *irreg* I. *vi* to start II. *vt* ❶ (*beginnen*) to start ❷ (*machen*) **etw anders** ~ to do sth differently ❸ (*zu tun wissen*) **jd kann mit etw** *dat***/jdm nichts** ~ sth/sb is [of] no use to sb; **was soll ich damit** ~**?** what am I supposed to do with that?; **mit jdm ist nichts anzufangen** nothing can be done with sb; **nichts mit sich** *dat* **anzufangen wissen** to not know what to do with oneself

Anfänger(in) <-s, -> *m(f)* beginner; (*im Straßenverkehr*) student driver; ~ **sein** to be a novice

anfänglich *adj attr* initial *attr*

anfangs *adv* at first

Anfangsbuchstabe *m* first letter

Anfangsstadium *nt* initial stage[s] *usu pl*

an|fassen I. *vt* to touch II. *vi* **mit** ~ to lend a hand

an|fechten *vt irreg* JUR to contest

an|fertigen *vt* to make

an|flehen *vt* to beg (**um** +*akk* for)

Anflug *m* LUFT approach ▶WENDUNGEN: **ein** ~ **von Eifersucht** a fit of jealousy

an|fordern *vt* to request; *Katalog* to order

Anforderung *f* ❶ *kein pl* (*das Anfordern*) request; *von Katalog* ordering ❷ *meist pl* (*Anspruch*) demands; **~en [an jdn] stellen** to place demands [on sb]; **du stellst zu hohe ~en** you're too demanding

Anfrage *f* inquiry; ■**auf ~** [up]on request

an|fragen *vi* to ask

an|freunden ['an·frɔyn·dn̩] *vr* ■**sich** *akk* **~** to become friends; ■**sich** *akk* **mit jdm ~** to make friends with sb; ■**sich** *akk* **mit etw** *dat* **~** to get to like sth

an|führen *vt* ❶ *Gruppe* to lead ❷ (*zitieren*) to quote; **ein Beispiel/einen Grund ~** to give an example/a reason ❸ (*benennen*) to name

Anführer(in) *m(f)* leader

Anführungsstrich *m*, **Anführungszeichen** *nt meist pl* quotation mark[s]

Angabe <-, -n> *f* ❶ *meist pl* (*Information*) details *pl*; **genauere ~n** further details; **~n zur Person** personal details; **~n machen** to give details ❷ *kein pl* (*Prahlerei*) boasting

an|geben *irreg* I. *vt* ❶ (*nennen*) to give; **seinen Namen ~** to give one's name; **jdn als Zeugen ~** to cite sb as a witness ❷ (*behaupten*) to claim ❸ (*anzeigen*) to indicate ❹ (*bestimmen*) to set; *Takt* to give; **das Tempo ~** to set the pace II. *vi* (*prahlen*) to brag (**mit** +*dat* about)

Angeber(in) <-s, -> *m(f)* poser

angeblich ['an·ge:p·lɪç] I. *adj attr* alleged II. *adv* allegedly; **er hat ~ nichts gewusst** he didn't know anything about it

angeboren *adj* innate; *MED* congenital

Angebot *nt* offer; **im ~** on sale; **~ und Nachfrage** supply and demand

angebracht *adj* ❶ (*sinnvoll*) sensible ❷ (*angemessen*) suitable

angegossen *adj* ►WENDUNGEN: **wie ~ sitzen** (*fam*) to fit like a glove

angeheitert ['an·gə·hai·tɐt] *adj* (*fam*) tipsy

an|gehen *irreg* I. *vi sein* ❶ *Licht, Radio* to come on ❷ (*bekämpfen*) ■**gegen jdn/etw ~** to fight sb/sth II. *vt haben* (*betreffen*) to concern; **was geht mich das an?** what's that got to do with me?; **das geht dich nichts an!** (*fam*) that's none of your business!; **was mich angeht, ...** as far as I am concerned, ...

an|gehören* *vi* to belong to

Angehörige(r) *f(m) dekl wie adj* ❶ (*Verwandte(r)*) relative; **die nächsten ~n** the next of kin ❷ (*Mitglied*) member

Angeklagte(r) *f(m) dekl wie adj* accused

Angel <-, -n> ['aŋl] *f* fishing pole

Angelegenheit <-, -en> *f* matter; **sich** *akk* **um seine eigenen ~en kümmern** to mind one's own business

angeln ['aŋln] I. *vi* to fish (**nach** +*dat* for) II. *vt* to catch; **sich** *dat* **einen Mann ~** (*fam*) to catch oneself a man

Angelrute *f* fishing rod

angemessen I. *adj* appropriate; **~es Verhalten** appropriate behavior II. *adv* appropriately; **~ bezahlt** appropriately paid

angenehm *adj* pleasant; *Nachricht* good; *Wetter* agreeable ►WENDUNGEN: **das A~e mit dem Nützlichen verbinden** to mix business with pleasure

angesehen I. *adj* respected; *Firma* of good standing II. *pp von* **ansehen**

angesichts *präp* +*gen* in the face of

Angestellte(r) *f(m) dekl wie adj* employee

angestrengt *pp von* **anstrengen**

angetan I. *adj* ■**von jdm/etw ~ sein** to be taken with sb/sth; ■**es jdm ~ haben** to appeal to sb II. *pp von* **antun**

angetrunken *adj* tipsy

angewandt I. *adj attr* applied II. *pp von* **anwenden**

angewiesen I. *adj* dependent (**auf** +*akk* [up]on) II. *pp von* **anweisen**

an|gewöhnen* *vt* ■**sich** *dat* **etw ~** to get into the habit of [doing] sth

Angewohnheit *f* habit

Angler(in) <-s, -> ['aŋ·lɐ] *m(f)* angler

angreifbar *adj* contestable

an|greifen *irreg vt, vi* to attack

A **angrenzend** *adj attr* bordering; **die ~ en Bauplätze** the adjoining building sites

Angriff *m* attack ▶WENDUNGEN: **etw in ~ nehmen** to tackle sth

angriffslustig *adj* aggressive

angst [aŋst] *adj* ■**jdm ist/wird ~ [und bange]** sb is/becomes afraid

Angst <-, Ängste> [aŋst] *f* fear (**vor** +*dat* of); **~ bekommen** to get scared; **~ [vor etw** *dat***] haben** to be afraid [of sth]; **~ um etw** *akk* **haben** to be worried about sth; **jdm ~ machen** to frighten sb

ängstigen [ˈɛŋs·tɪ·gn̩] I. *vt* to frighten II. *vr* ■**sich** *akk* **~** to be afraid

ängstlich [ˈɛŋst·lɪç] *adj* timid

Angstmacherei <-> [ˈaŋst·ma·xə·rai] *f kein pl* scaremongering

Anhalter(in) <-s, -> [ˈan·hal·te] *m(f)* hitchhiker; **per ~ fahren** to hitchhike

Anhang <-[e]s, -hänge> *m* ➊ (*Nachtrag*) appendix ➋ *kein pl* (*Angehörige*) [close] family, dependants ➌ COMPUT attachment

an|hängen *vt* ➊ (*fam: anlasten*) ■**jdm etw ~** to blame sth on sb ➋ COMPUT to attach

Anhänger <-s, -> *m* ➊ AUTO trailer ➋ (*Schmuck*) pendant ➌ (*für Gepäck*) label

Anhänger(in) <-s, -> *m(f)* fan

anhänglich [ˈan·hɛŋ·lɪç] *adj* devoted; **die Kinder sind sehr anhänglich** the children won't leave their mother's side

an|heben *irreg vt* ➊ (*hochheben*) to lift [up *sep*] ➋ (*fig*) *Löhne, Preise* to increase

Anhieb *m* **auf ~** right away; **das kann ich nicht auf ~ sagen** I can't say off the top of my head

an|himmeln *vt* (*fam*) to idolize

an|hören I. *vt* ■**[sich** *dat***] etw ~** to listen to sth; ■**jdm etw ~** to hear sth in sb['s voice]; **dass er Däne ist, hört man ihm nicht an** you can't tell from his accent that he's Danish II. *vr* ■**sich** *akk* **~** to sound

Animateur(in) <-s, -e> [anima·ˈtøːɐ̯] *m(f)* host *masc*, hostess *fem*

animieren* [ani·ˈmiː·rən] *vt* to encourage

Anis <-[es], -e> [aˈniːs] *m* ➊ (*Pflanze*) anise ➋ (*Gewürz*) aniseed

Ankauf *m* buy

Anker <-s, -> [ˈaŋ·kɐ] *m* anchor; **vor ~ gehen** to drop anchor [somewhere]; **den ~ lichten** to weigh anchor; **vor ~ liegen** to lie at anchor

an|ketten *vt* to chain up (**an** +*akk* to)

Anklage <-, -n> *f* ➊ (*Beschuldigung*) accusation ➋ *kein pl* JUR charge; **gegen jdn ~ [wegen etw** *gen***] erheben** to charge sb [with sth]; **unter ~ stehen** to be charged

an|klagen *vt* ➊ JUR to charge ➋ (*beschuldigen*) to accuse

Anklang *m* ▶WENDUNGEN: **~ finden** to meet with approval

an|klicken *vt* COMPUT to click on

an|klopfen *vi* to knock

an|knüpfen *vi* ■**an etw** *akk* **~** to resume sth

an|kommen *irreg* I. *vi sein* to arrive; **seid ihr gut angekommen?** did you arrive safely?; ■**[bei jdm] ~** *Sache* to go over well [with sb]; *Person* to make an impression [on sb]; ■**gegen jdn/etw ~** to get the better of sb/sth II. *vi impers sein* ➊ (*wichtig sein*) ■**es kommt darauf an, dass ...** what matters is that ... ➋ (*abhängen von*) ■**auf jdn/ etw ~** to be dependent on sb/sth; **das kommt darauf an** it depends

an|kündigen *vt* to announce

Ankündigung *f* announcement

Ankunft <-, -künfte> [ˈan·kʊnft] *f* arrival

an|kurbeln *vt* ÖKON to boost

an|lächeln *vt* to smile at

AnlassRR <-es, -lässe>, **Anlaß**ALT

an|haben *vt irreg* ➊ *Kleidung* to have on ➋ (*schaden*) **jdm nichts ~ können** to be unable to harm sb

an|halten *irreg* I. *vi* ➊ (*stoppen*) to stop ➋ (*fortdauern*) to continue II. *vt* (*stoppen*) to bring to a stop

anhaltend *adj Hitze* continuing; *Lärm* incessant; *Schmerz* persistent

<-sses, -lässe> ['an·las] *m* ❶ (*Gelegenheit*) occasion; **dem ~ entsprechend** to fit the occasion ❷ (*Grund*) reason; **es besteht kein ~ zu etw** *dat/*, **etw zu tun** there are no grounds for sth/to do sth; **[jdm] ~ zu etw geben** to give [sb] grounds for sth; **keinen ~ haben, etw zu tun** to have no grounds to do sth; **etw zum ~ nehmen, etw zu tun** to use sth as an opportunity to do sth

anlassen *irreg vt* ❶ AUTO to start [up *sep*] ❷ (*fam*) *Kleidung* to keep on *sep* ❸ **das Licht ~** to leave on *sep* the light

Anlasser <-s, -> *m* AUTO starter [motor]

anlässlich^RR, **anläßlich**^ALT ['an·lɛs·lɪç] *präp +gen* on the occasion of

Anlauf <-[e]s, -läufe> *m* SPORT - **nehmen** to take a running start

anlaufen *irreg vi sein* ❶ *Metall* to tarnish ❷ **vor Wut rot ~** to turn purple with rage

Anlaufschwierigkeiten *pl meist pl* initial difficulties

Anlaufstelle *f* refuge

anlegen I. *vt* ❶ *Liste* to draw up; *Garten, Park* to lay out; *Vorräte* to stock up ❷ ÖKON *Geld* to invest II. *vi Schiff* to berth III. *vr* ■ **sich** *akk* **mit jdm ~** to pick a fight with sb

anlehnen I. *vt* to lean [against]; *Tür* to leave ajar II. *vr* ■ **sich** *akk* **~ an** to lean against

anleiern *vt* (*fam*) to get going

anleiten *vt* to instruct

Anleitung *f* instructions *pl;* **unter jds** *dat* **~** under sb's guidance

Anliegen <-s, -> *nt* request

anlocken *vt* to attract; *Tier* to lure

anlügen *vt irreg* to lie to

anmachen *vt* ❶ *Licht, Gerät* to turn on *sep; Zigarette* to light ❷ *Salat* to dress ❸ (*sl: aufreizen*) to turn on *sep* ❹ (*sl: aufreißen wollen*) to pick up *sep* ❺ (*sl: rüde ansprechen*) ■ **jdn ~** to have a go at sb

anmailen ['an·mer·lən] *vt* (*fam*) to e-mail

anmaßend ['an·ma:·sṇt] *adj* arrogant

anmelden I. *vt* ❶ **ein Kind in der Schule ~** to enroll a child at a school; **jdn zu einem Kurs ~** to enroll sb in a course ❷ **ein Auto ~** to register a car; **ein Fernsehgerät/Radio ~** to get a TV/radio reception license; **das Telefon ~** to get phone service II. *vr* ■ **sich** *akk* ~ ❶ (*zu einem Besuch*) to give notice of a visit (**bei** +*dat* to) ❷ (*zu einem Kurs*) to sign up ❸ (*bei einem Umzug*) to register one's change of address with the authorities

Anmeldung <-, -en> *f* ❶ (*Ankündigung*) [advance] notice [of a visit]; **ohne ~** without an appointment ❷ SCH enrollment ❸ (*Registrierung*) registration ❹ (*Anmelderaum*) reception

anmerken *vt* ■ **jdm etw ~** to notice sth in sb; **er ließ sich nichts ~** he didn't let it show

Anmerkung <-, -en> *f* ❶ (*Fußnote*) footnote ❷ (*Kommentar*) comment

anmutig *adj* graceful

annähen *vt* **einen Knopf ~** to sew a button on

Annäherungsversuche *pl* advances; **~e machen** to make advances

Annahme <-, -n> ['an·na:·mə] *f* **von einer ~ ausgehen** to proceed on the assumption; **in der ~, dass ...** on the assumption that ...

annehmbar *adj* acceptable

annehmen *irreg* I. *vt* ❶ (*übernehmen*) to accept; *Auftrag, Job, Patienten, Schüler* to take on *sep; Kind* to adopt ❷ (*voraussetzen*) to assume; ■ **angenommen, das stimmt ...** assuming that's right ... II. *vr* ❶ (*sich kümmern*) ■ **sich** *akk* **jds** *gen* **~** to look after sb ❷ (*erledigen*) ■ **sich** *akk* **einer S.** *gen* **~** to take care of sth

Annehmlichkeiten <-, -en> *pl* conveniences

Anno, anno ['ano] *adv* ÖSTERR in the year ▶WENDUNGEN: **von ~ dazumal** (*fam*) from long ago

Annonce <-, -n> [a'nõ:·sə] *f* advertisement

A anonym [ano·'nyːm] *adj* anonymous;
~ **bleiben** to remain anonymous

Anorak <-s, -s> ['ano·rak] *m* anorak

an|ordnen *vt* ❶ (*bestimmen*) to order
❷ (*ordnen*) to arrange (**nach** +*dat* according to)

an|packen I. *vt* to tackle; **packen wir's
an!** let's get started! II. *vi* **mit** ~ to lend
a hand

an|passen I. *vt* to adjust II. *vr* ■ **sich**
akk **jdm/etw** ~ to fit in with sb/
sth; (*gesellschaftlich*) to conform to
sth

anpassungsfähig *adj* adaptable

Anpassungsfähigkeit *f* adaptability

an|pflanzen *vt* to grow

Anprobe *f* fitting

an|probieren* *vt* to try on *sep*

an|pumpen *vt* (*fam*) ■ **jdn** ~ to pump sb
for cash *sl;* **jdn um 100 Euro** ~ to hit
sb up for 100 euros *sl*

an|rechnen *vt* (*gutschreiben*) **die 200
Euro werden auf die Gesamtsumme
angerechnet** the 200 euros will be
deducted from the total ▶WENDUNGEN:
**dass er ihr geholfen hat, rechne ich
ihm hoch an** I think very highly of him
for having helped her

an|regen *vt* ❶ (*ermuntern*) ■ **jdn** [**zu
etw** *dat*] ~ to encourage sb [to do sth]
❷ (*vorschlagen*) to suggest ❸ (*stimulieren*) to stimulate; **den Appetit** ~ to
whet the appetite

anregend *adj* stimulating; (*sexuell*) sexually arousing

Anregung *f* **auf jds** ~ at sb's suggestion

Anreise *f* trip [here/there]

Anreiz *m* incentive

an|rempeln *vt* to bump into

Anrichte <-, -n> *f* sideboard

an|richten *vt* *Speisen* to prepare; *Schaden, Unheil* to cause; **was hast du da
wieder angerichtet!** what have you
done now!; **Unfug** ~ to be up to no
good

anrüchig ['an·rʏ·çɪç] *adj* indecent

Anruf *m* [phone] call

Anrufbeantworter <-s, -> *m* answering machine

an|rufen *irreg vt, vi* to phone; ■ **angerufen werden** to get a [phone] call

Ansage *f* announcement

an|sagen I. *vt* to announce II. *vr* ■ **sich**
akk ~ to announce a visit

Ansager(in) <-s, -> ['an·za·ɡɐ] *m(f)*
RADIO announcer

ansässig ['an·zɛ·sɪç] *adj* resident; **in
einer Stadt** ~ **sein** to reside in a city

an|schaffen I. *vt* to buy; ■ **sich** *dat*
etw ~ to buy oneself sth II. *vi* (*sl*) ~
[**gehen**] to hook *pej fam*

Anschaffung <-, -en> *f* purchase; **eine**
~ **machen** to make a purchase

an|schalten *vt* to switch on

an|schauen *vt, vr s.* **ansehen**

anschaulich I. *adj* illustrative; **ein** ~**es
Beispiel** a good example II. *adv* vividly

Anschein *m* appearance; **allem** ~ **nach**
to all appearances; **den** ~ **erwecken,
als** [**ob**] … to give the impression
that …; **den** ~ **haben, als** [**ob**] … to
seem that …

anscheinend *adv* apparently

Anschlag *m* attempted assassination;
einen ~ **auf jdn/etw verüben** to
make an attack on sb/sth; **einen** ~ **auf
jdn vorhaben** (*hum fam*) to have a request for sb

an|schließen *irreg* I. *vt* TECH to connect (**an** +*akk* to) II. *vr* ❶ (*sich zugesellen*) ■ **sich** *akk* **jdm** ~ to join sb
❷ (*beipflichten*) ■ **sich** *akk* **jdm/
etw** ~ to fall in with sb/sth; **dem
schließe ich mich an** I think I'd go
along with that

Anschluss^RR *m* ❶ TELEK connection; **der**
~ **ist gestört** there's a disturbance in
the line ❷ **im** ~ **an etw** *akk* after sth
❸ *kein pl* (*Kontakt*) contact; ~ **finden**
to make friends; ~ **suchen** to try to
make friends ❹ BAHN, LUFT (*Verbindung*)
connection; **den** ~ **verpassen** to miss
one's connecting train/flight

an|schmiegen *vr* ■ **sich** *akk* [**an jdn/
etw**] ~ to cuddle up [to sb/sth]; *Katze,
Hund* to nestle [up to sb/into sth]

anschmiegsam *adj* ❶ (*anlehnungsbedürftig*) affectionate ❷ (*weich*) soft

anschnallen *vr* ■**sich** *akk* ~ to fasten one's seat belt

anschnauzen *vt* (*fam*) to yell at

anschneiden *vt irreg Brot, Fleisch* to cut; *Thema* to touch on

anschreiben *irreg* I. *vt* ■**jdn** ~ to write to sb II. *vi* (*fam*) ■~ **lassen** to buy on credit

anschreien *vt irreg* to shout at

Anschrift *f* address

anschwemmen *vt* to wash up *sep*

ansehen *irreg vt* ❶ (*ins Gesicht sehen*) to look at; **jdn böse** ~ to give sb an angry look ❷ (*betrachten*) *Film* to watch; *Theaterstück, Fußballspiel* to see; **etw genauer** ~ to take a closer look at sth; **hübsch anzusehen sein** to be pretty to look at ❸ (*ablesen können*) **jdm sein Alter nicht** ~ sb doesn't look his/her age; **ihre Erleichterung war ihr deutlich anzusehen** her relief was obvious ❹ (*hinnehmen*) ■**etw mit** ~ to stand by and watch sth; **das kann ich nicht länger mit** ~ I can't stand it anymore

Ansehen <-s> *nt kein pl* reputation

ansehnlich *adj* considerable; **eine** ~**e Leistung** an impressive performance

ansetzen I. *vt* ❶ ■**jdn auf jdn/etw** ~ *Detektiv* to put sb on sb/sth ❷ **Fett** ~ to put on weight II. *vi* to start; **zum Überholen** ~ to begin to pass

Ansicht <-, -en> *f* opinion; **ich bin ganz Ihrer** ~ I agree with you completely; **in etw** *dat* **geteilter** ~ **sein** to have a different view of sth; **der** ~ **sein, dass ...** to be of the opinion that ...; **meiner** ~ **nach** in my opinion

Ansichtskarte *f* [picture] postcard

Anspannung *f* strain

anspielen *vi* to allude (**auf** +*akk* to); **worauf willst du** ~? what are you driving at?

Anspielung <-, -en> *f* allusion (**auf** +*akk* to)

anspornen *vt* to spur on; *Spieler* to cheer on

Ansprache *f* speech; **eine** ~ **halten** to make a speech

ansprechen *irreg* I. *vt* ❶ (*anreden*) ■**jdn** ~ to speak to sb; **jdn** [**mit Peter/mit seinem Namen**] ~ to address sb [as Peter/by his name] ❷ (*erwähnen*) ■**etw** ~ to mention sth ❸ (*gefallen*) ■**jdn** ~ to appeal to sb II. *vi* MED, TECH to respond (**auf** +*akk* to)

ansprechend *adj* appealing

Ansprechpartner(in) *m(f)* contact [person]

anspringen *irreg vi sein Motor* to start

Anspruch *m* ❶ (*Recht*) claim (**auf** +*akk* to); ~ **auf etw** *akk* **erheben** to make a claim for sth; ~ **auf etw** *akk* **haben** to be entitled to sth ❷ (*Anforderung*) demand; **den Ansprüchen** [**voll**] **gerecht werden** to [fully] meet the requirements; **Ansprüche stellen** to be very demanding ▶WENDUNGEN: **etw in** ~ **nehmen** to claim sth; **jds Hilfe in** ~ **nehmen** to accept help from sb

anspruchslos *adj* undemanding; *Film, Lektüre* trivial; **ein** ~**er Mensch** a modest person

anspruchsvoll *adj* demanding; *Lesestoff, Film* a. highbrow; *Geschmack* discriminating

Anstalt <-, -en> ['anʃtalt] *f* (*fam: für psychisch Kranke*) asylum

Anstand *m kein pl* decency; **keinen** ~ **haben** to have no sense of decency

anständig I. *adj* decent II. *adv* ❶ (*gesittet*) decently; **sich** *akk* ~ **benehmen** to behave oneself ❷ (*fam: gut*) properly; ~ **essen/ausschlafen** to get a decent meal/a good night's sleep

anstarren *vt* to stare at

anstatt [anˈʃtat] I. *präp* +*gen* instead of II. *konj* ■~ **etw zu tun** instead of doing sth

anstecken I. *vt* ❶ *Gebäude* to set on fire; *Zigarette* to light [up] ❷ (*infizieren*) to infect; **ich möchte dich nicht** ~ I don't want to give you my cold II. *vr* ■**sich** *akk* [**bei jdm**] ~ to catch sth [from sb]; **sich** *akk* **leicht/schnell** ~ to get sick easily

ansteckend *adj* contagious; ~**e Krankheit** contagious disease

A

an|stehen *vi irreg haben o* SÜDD *sein* ❶ *(Schlange stehen)* ■ **nach etw** *dat* ~ to line up for sth ❷ *(zu erledigen sein)* ■ **etw steht an** sth must be dealt with; **steht bei dir heute etwas an?** are you planning on doing anything today?

an|steigen *vi irreg sein* ❶ *(sich erhöhen)* to go up (**auf** +*akk* to, **um** +*akk* by) ❷ *(steiler werden)* to ascend; **steil** ~ to ascend steeply

anstelle [an·'ʃtɛ·lə] *präp* +*gen* instead of

an|stellen I. *vt* ❶ *(einschalten)* to turn on *sep* ❷ *(beschäftigen)* to employ ❸ *(durchführen)* **Nachforschungen** [**über etw** *akk*] ~ to conduct inquiries [into sth]; **Vermutungen [über etw** *akk*] ~ to make assumptions [about sth] ❹ *(fam: bewerkstelligen)* to manage; **etw geschickt** ~ to pull sth off ❺ *(fam: anrichten)* **Blödsinn** ~ to be up to no good; **was hast du da wieder angestellt?** what have you done now? *fam* II. *vr* ■ **sich** *akk* ~ ❶ *(Schlange stehen)* to line up; **sich** *akk* **hinten** ~ to get in the back of a line ❷ *(fam: sich verhalten)* to act; **sich** *akk* **dumm** ~ to play the fool ❸ *(wehleidig sein)* to make a fuss; **stell dich nicht [so] an!** don't make such a fuss!

an|stiften *vt* ■ **jdn [dazu]** ~, **etw zu tun** to incite sb to do sth; **jdn zu einem Verbrechen** ~ to incite sb to commit a crime

Anstoß *m* ❶ *(Ansporn)* impetus (**zu** +*dat* for); **den ~ zu etw** *dat* **bekommen** to be encouraged to do sth; **jdm den ~ geben, etw zu tun** to encourage sb to do sth ❷ *(Ärgernis)* ~ **erregen** to be annoying; **an etw** *dat* ~ **nehmen** to take offense at sth ❸ SPORT start of the game; *(Billard)* break; *([am.] Fußball)* kickoff; *(Eishockey)* face-off ❹ SCHWEIZ *(Angrenzung)* border

an|stoßen *irreg* I. *vi* ❶ *sein* **mit dem Kopf an etw** *akk o dat* ~ to bump one's head on sth ❷ *haben* **auf jdn/etw** ~ to drink to sb/sth; **lasst uns ~!** let's drink to it/that! II. *vt haben* ❶ *(leicht stoßen)* to bump ❷ *(in Gang setzen)* to set in

motion III. *vr haben* **sich** *dat* **den Kopf** ~ to bang one's head

anstößig *adj* offensive

an|streichen *vt irreg* ❶ *(mit Farbe)* to paint; **etw neu/frisch** ~ to give sth a new/fresh coat of paint ❷ *(markieren)* to mark; **etw rot** ~ to mark sth [in] red

Anstreicher(in) <-s, -> *m(f)* [house] painter

an|strengen I. *vr* ■ **sich** *akk* ~ to try hard; **sich** *akk* **mehr** ~ to make a greater effort II. *vt* ■ **jdn** ~ to tire sb out

anstrengend *adj* strenuous; *(geistig)* taxing; *(körperlich)* exhausting; **das ist ~ für die Augen** it's a strain on the eyes

Anstrengung <-, -en> *f* effort; **mit letzter** ~ with one last effort

Ansturm *m* rush

Antarktis <-> [ant·'ʔark·tɪs] *f* Antarctic

antarktisch [ant·'ʔark·tɪʃ] *adj* Antarctic *attr*

an|tasten *vt* ❶ **jds Ehre/Würde** ~ to offend sb's honor/dignity; **jds Rechte** ~ to encroach [up]on sb's rights ❷ **Ersparnisse/Vorräte** ~ to dip into savings/supplies

Anteil ['an·tail] *m* share (**an** +*dat* of); **der ~ an Asbest** the proportion of asbestos ▶ WENDUNGEN: ~ **an etw** *dat* **nehmen** to show an interest in sth

anteilig *adj* proportionate

Anteilnahme <-> ['an·tail·na:·mə] *f kein pl* sympathy

Antenne <-, -n> [an·'tɛ·nə] *f* antenna

antiautoritär [an·ti·ʔau·to·ri·'tɛːɐ̯] *adj* anti[-]authoritarian

Antibabypille [an·ti·'be:·bi·pɪ·lə] *f* *(fam)* ■ **die** ~ the [contraceptive] pill

Antibiotikum <-s, -biotika> [an·ti·'bi̯oː·ti·kʊm] *nt* antibiotic

Antiblockiersystem [an·ti·blɔ·'kiːɐ̯·] *nt* antilock [braking] system, ABS

antik [an·'tiːk] *adj* Möbel antique

Antike <-> [an·'tiː·kə] *f kein pl* antiquity; **die Kunst der** ~ the art of the ancient world

Antikörper *m* MED antibody

Antilope <-, -n> [an·ti·'loː·pə] *f* antelope

Antiquariat <-[e]s, -e> [anˌtiˌkvaˈriˌaːt] *nt* secondhand bookstore

Antiquität <-, -en> [anˌtiˌkviˈtɛːt] *f* antique

Antrag <-[e]s, -träge> [ˈanˌtraːk] *m* ❶(*Beantragung*) application (**auf** +*akk* for); **einen ~ stellen** to put in an application ❷(*Heiratsantrag*) [marriage] proposal; **jdm einen ~ machen** to propose to sb

Antragsformular *nt* application form

an|treffen *vt irreg* ◼**jdn ~** to catch sb; ◼**etw ~** to come across sth

an|treiben *irreg vt* ❶(*vorwärtstreiben*) to drive [on *sep*] ❷(*drängen*) ◼**jdn ~, etw zu tun** to urge sb to do sth; (*aufdringlicher*) to push sb to do sth ❸TECH to drive

Antrieb *m* AUTO, LUFT drive ▶WENDUNGEN: **aus eigenem ~** on one's own initiative

Antritt *m kein pl* **nach ~ seines Amtes** after assuming office; **nach ~ der Erbschaft** after coming into the inheritance

an|tun *vt irreg* ◼**jdm etwas/nichts ~** to do something/not to do anything to sb; **tu mir das nicht an!** (*hum fam*) spare me, please! ▶WENDUNGEN: **sich** *dat* **etwas ~** to kill oneself

Antwort <-, -en> [ˈantˌvɔrt] *f* answer (**auf** +*akk* to); **jdm [eine] ~ geben** to give sb an answer; **als ~ auf etw** *akk* in response to sth

antworten [ˈantˌvɔrˌtn̩] *vi* ◼**jdm/auf etw** *akk*] ~ to answer [sb/sth]; **mit Ja/ Nein ~** to answer yes/no; **schriftlich ~** to answer in writing

an|vertrauen* [ˈanˌfɛɐ̯ˌtrauˌən] I. *vt* ◼**jdm etw ~** (*übergeben*) to entrust sb with sth; (*erzählen*) to confide sth to sb II. *vr* ◼**sich** *akk* **jdm ~** to confide in sb

Anwalt, Anwältin <-[e]s, -wälte> [ˈanˌvalt, ˈanˌvɛlˌtɪn] *m, f* lawyer; **sich** *dat* **einen ~ nehmen** to hire a lawyer

an|weisen *vt irreg* ◼**jdn ~, etw zu tun** to order sb to do sth

Anweisung <-, -en> *f* order

anwendbar *adj* applicable (**auf** +*akk* to); **in der Praxis ~** practicable

an|wenden *vt reg o irreg* to use (**bei** +*dat* on)

Anwender(in) <-s, -> *m(f)* COMPUT user

anwenderfreundlich *adj* COMPUT user-friendly

Anwendung *f* ❶(*Gebrauch*) use ❷MED administration

anwesend *adj* present *pred* (**bei** +*dat* at)

Anwesenheit <-> *f kein pl* presence; *von Studenten* attendance; **in jds ~** in sb's presence

an|widern [ˈanˌviːˌdən] *vt* to disgust

Anzahl *f kein pl* number

Anzahlung *f* down payment

an|zapfen *vt* to tap

Anzeige <-, -n> *f* ❶(*Strafanzeige*) charge (**wegen** +*gen* of) ❷(*Inserat*) ad[vertisement]

an|zeigen *vt* ❶◼**jdn** [**wegen einer S.** *gen*] ~ to report sb [for sth] ❷*Gerät, Uhr* to show; (*digital*) to display

an|ziehen *irreg* I. *vt* ❶*Kleidung* to put on *sep* ❷(*festziehen*) *Schraube* to tighten; *Handbremse* to put on ❸*Arm, Bein* to draw up ❹(*anlocken*) to attract; **sich** *akk* **von jdm/etw angezogen fühlen** to be attracted to sb/sth ❺SCHWEIZ **das Bett frisch ~** to change the bed II. *vr* ◼**sich** *akk* ~ to get dressed; **sich** *akk* **warm ~** to dress warm[ly]; **sich** *akk* **schick ~** to dress up

anziehend *adj* attractive

Anziehungskraft *f* ❶PHYS **~ der Erde** [force of] gravitation ❷*kein pl* (*fig*) **auf jdn eine ~ ausüben** to appeal to sb

Anzug *m* ❶(*Kleidung*) suit ❷SCHWEIZ (*Bezug*) duvet cover

anzüglich [ˈanˌtsyːkˌlɪç] *adj Bemerkung* insinuating; **~ werden** to get personal

an|zünden *vt Feuer, Zigarette* to light; *Haus* to set on fire

apart [aˈpart] *adj* striking

Apartment <-s, -s> [aˈpartˌmənt] *nt* apartment

apathisch [aˈpaːtɪʃ] *adj* apathetic

Apfel <-s, Äpfel> [ˈapˌfl̩] *m* apple ▶WENDUNGEN: **in den sauren ~ beißen** (*fam*) to bite the bullet; **der ~ fällt**

A nicht weit vom <u>Stamm</u> (*prov*) like father, like son

Apfelbaum *m* apple tree

Àpfelsaft *m* apple juice

Apfelsine <-, -n> [apˈfl̩ˈziːnə] *f* orange

Àpfelwein *m* hard cider

Apostel <-s, -> [aˈpɔsˑtl̩] *m* apostle

Apostroph <-s, -e> [apoˈstroːf] *m* apostrophe

Apotheke <-, -n> [apoˈteːkə] *f* pharmacy

Apotheker(in) <-s, -> [apoˈteːkɐ] *m(f)* pharmacist

Apparat <-[e]s, -e> [apaˈraːt] *m* ❶ TECH apparatus *form*; (*kleineres Gerät*) gadget ❷ (*Telefon*) telephone; **am ~ bleiben** to hold on; **am ~!** speaking!

appellieren* [apɛˈliːrən] *vi* **an jds Vernunft ~** to appeal to sb's common sense

Appetit <-[e]s> [apeˈtiːt] *m kein pl* appetite; **guten ~!** enjoy your meal!; **~ auf etw haben** to feel like [having] sth; **[jdm] ~ machen** to whet sb's appetite; **jdm den ~ verderben** to spoil sb's appetite

appetitlich *adj* appetizing

Appetitlosigkeit <-> *f kein pl* lack of appetite

applaudieren* [aplauˈdiːrən] *vi* to applaud

Applaus <-es, -e> [aˈplaus] *m pl selten* applause

Aprikose <-, -n> [apriˈkoːzə] *f* apricot

April <-s, -e> [aˈprɪl] *m pl selten* April; *s. a.* **Februar** ▶ WENDUNGEN: **~! ~!** April fool!; **jdn in den ~ schicken** to make an April fool of sb

Aprilscherz *m* April fools' joke

apropos [aproˈpoː] *adv* by the way; **~ Männer, …** speaking of men, …

Aquarell <-s, -e> [akvaˈrɛl] *nt* watercolor [painting]

Äquator <-s> [ɛˈkvaːˑtoːɐ] *m kein pl* equator

Araber(in) <-s, -> [ˈaraˑbɐ] *m(f)* Arab

arabisch [aˈraːˑbɪʃ] *adj* ❶ GEOG Arabian; **A~ es Meer** Arabian Sea ❷ LING Arabic; **auf ~** in Arabic

Arbeit <-, -en> [ˈarˌbait] *f* ❶ (*Tätigkeit*) work; **gute/schlechte ~ leisten** to do a good/bad job; **sich** *akk* **an die ~ machen** to get down to work ❷ (*Arbeitsplatz*) job ❸ SCH test; **eine ~ schreiben** to take a test; **eine schriftliche ~** a [term] paper ❹ *kein pl* (*Mühe*) effort; **sich** *dat* **~ machen** to take the trouble ▶ WENDUNGEN: **erst die ~, dann das <u>Vergnügen</u>** (*prov*) business before pleasure *prov*

arbeiten [ˈarˌbaiˑtn̩] *vi* to work; *Körperorgan* to function; ■ **an etw** *dat* **~** to be working on sth; **~ gehen** to have a job

Arbeiter(in) <-s, -> *m(f)* (*Industrie*) [blue-collar] worker; (*Landwirtschaft*) laborer

Arbeitgeber(in) <-s, -> *m(f)* employer

Àrbeitnehmer(in) <-s, -> *m(f)* employee

Àrbeitsamt *nt* unemployment office

Àrbeitsbedingungen *pl* working conditions *pl*

Àrbeitsbeschaffungsmaßnahme *f* job creation plan

Àrbeitserlaubnis *f* work permit

Àrbeitsessen *nt* business lunch/dinner

Àrbeitsgericht *nt a court that handles labor disputes*

arbeitsintensiv *adj* labor-intensive

Àrbeitskleidung *f* work clothes *pl*

Àrbeitskraft *f* ❶ *kein pl* (*Leistungskraft*) work capacity ❷ (*Mitarbeiter*) worker

arbeitslos *adj* unemployed

Àrbeitslose(r) *f(m) dekl wie adj* unemployed person; ■ **die ~n** the unemployed

Àrbeitslosengeld *nt* unemployment benefit

Àrbeitslosenhilfe *f* unemployment aid

Àrbeitslosigkeit <-> *f kein pl* unemployment *no indef art, + sing vb*

Àrbeitsmarkt *m* job market

Àrbeitsniederlegung *f* walkout

Àrbeitsplatz *m* ❶ (*Arbeitsstätte*) work-

place; **am ~** at work ②(*Stelle*) job;
freier ~ vacancy

Ạrbeitsspeicher *m* COMPUT main
memory

Ạrbeitstag *m* work day

ạrbeitsunfähig *adj* unable to work; **jdn
~ schreiben** to put sb on sick leave

Ạrbeitsunfall *m* work-related accident

Ạrbeitsvertrag *m* employment contract

Ạrbeitszeit *f* working hours *pl*; **glei
tende ~** flexitime

Ạrbeitszeugnis *nt* reference

Ạrbeitszimmer *nt* study

Archäologe, Archäologin <-n, -n>
[ar·ços·loː·ɡə, arços·loː·ɡɪn] *m, f* ar-
chaeologist

Archäologie <-> [arços·lo·ˈɡiː] *f kein
pl* archaeology

Architẹkt(in) <-en, -en> [ar·çi·ˈtɛkt]
m(f) architect

Architektur <-, -en> [ar·çi·tɛk·ˈtuːɐ̯] *f*
architecture

Archịv <-s, -e> [ar·ˈçiːf] *nt* archives *pl*

Arena <-, Arenen> [aˈreː·na] *f* ①(*Manege*) [circus] ring ② SPORT [sports] arena
③(*für Stierkampf*) [bull]ring

arg <ärger, ärgste> [ark] *bes* SÜDD **I.** *adj*
bad; *Enttäuschung* big **II.** *adv* badly; **tut
es ~ weh?** does it hurt badly?

Argentịnien <-s> [ar·ɡɛn·ˈtiː·ni̯·ən] *nt*
Argentina; *s. a.* **Deutschland**

Argentịnier(in) <-s, -> [ar·ɡɛn·ˈtiː·ni̯ɐ]
m(f) Argentinian; *s. a.* **Deutsche(r)**

argentịnisch [ar·ɡɛn·ˈtiː·nɪʃ] *adj* Argentinian; *s. a.* **deutsch**

Ạ̈rger <-s> [ˈɛrɡɐ] *m kein pl* trouble;
~ bekommen to get into trouble;
~ haben to have problems; **[jdm] ~
machen** to cause [sb] trouble

ärgerlich *adj* ①(*verärgert*) annoyed
②(*unangenehm*) annoying

ärgern [ˈɛr·ɡɐn] **I.** *vt* ①(*ungehalten
machen*) to annoy ②(*reizen*) to tease
(**wegen** +*gen* about) **II.** *vr* **sich** *akk* **~**
to be annoyed; **ich ärgere mich, dass
ich nicht hingegangen bin** I'm upset
with myself for not going

arglos *adj* innocent

Argumẹnt <-[e]s, -e> [arɡu·ˈmɛnt] *nt*

argument; **das ist kein ~** (*unsinnig*)
that's a poor argument; (*keine Entschuldigung*) that's no excuse

argumentieren* *vi* to argue; **mit etw
dat ~** to use sth as an argument

argwöhnisch [ˈark·vøː·nɪʃ] *adj* suspicious

Aristokrạt(in) <-en, -en> [arɪs·to·
ˈkraːt] *m(f)* aristocrat

aristokrạtisch *adj* aristocratic

Ạrktis <-> [ˈark·tɪs] *f* Arctic

ạrktisch [ˈark·tɪʃ] *adj* arctic

arm <ärmer, ärmste> [arm] *adj* poor;
~ dran sein to have a hard time

Ạrm <-[e]s, -e> [arm] *m* arm; **jdn im ~
halten** to hold sb in one's arms ►WEN-
DUNGEN: **jdm [mit etw *dat*] unter die
~e greifen** to help sb out [with sth];
jdn auf den ~ nehmen to pull sb's leg

Armaturenbrett *nt* AUTO dashboard

Ạrmband <-bänder> *nt* ①(*an Uhr*)
[watch] strap ②(*Schmuck*) bracelet

Ạrmbanduhr *f* [wrist]watch

Armee <-, -n> [arˈmeː] *f* army

Ạ̈rmel <-s, -> [ˈɛr·ml] *m* sleeve

Ạ̈rmelkanal *m* **der ~** the [English]
Channel

Ạrmlehne *f* armrest

ärmlich [ˈɛrm·lɪç] **I.** *adj* poor; (*Kleidung*)
shabby; **aus ~en Verhältnissen** from
humble backgrounds **II.** *adv* poorly;
~ gekleidet sein to be shabbily dressed

ạrmselig *adj* ①*Kleidung* shabby
②(*dürftig*) miserable

Ạrmut <-> [ˈar·muːt] *f kein pl* poverty

Arọma <-s, Aromen> [aˈroː·ma] *nt*
①(*Geruch*) aroma; (*Geschmack*) taste
②(*Aromastoff*) flavor[ing]

aromạtisch [aro·ˈmaː·tɪʃ] *adj* aromatic;
~ schmecken to have a distinctive
taste

Arrẹst <-[e]s, -e> [aˈrɛst] *m* JUR detention

arrogạnt [aro·ˈɡant] *adj* arrogant

Arrogạnz <-> [aro·ˈɡants] *f kein pl* arrogance

Ạrsch <-[e]s, Ärsche> [arʃ] *m* (*derb*)
①(*Hintern*) ass ②(*pej: blöder Kerl*)
asshole ►WENDUNGEN: **am ~ der Welt**

A

(sl) out in the boonies; **jdm in den ~ kriechen** (sl) to kiss sb's ass sl; **jdn [mal] am ~ lecken können** (sl) sb can shove it; **im ~ sein** (sl) to be screwed

Arschkriecher(in) <-s, -> m(f) (pej derb) ass kisser

Arschloch nt (derb) asshole

Arsen <-s> [ar·'ze:n] nt kein pl CHEM arsenic

Art <-, -en> [a:ɐt] f ❶ (Sorte) kind ❷ (Methode) way; **auf diese ~ und Weise** [in] this way; **das ist doch keine ~!** that's no way to behave! ❸ (Wesen) nature ❹ BIOL species ▶WENDUNGEN: **nach ~ des Hauses** à la maison

Artenschutz m protection of species

Arterie <-, -n> [ar·'te:·riə] f artery

artig ['a:ɐ·tɪç] adj well-behaved

Artikel <-s, -> [ar·'ti:·kl] m ❶ (in der Zeitung) article ❷ (Ware) item ❸ LING article

Artischocke <-, -n> [ar·ti·'ʃɔ·kə] f artichoke

Artist(in) <-en, -en> [ar·'tɪst] m(f) performer

Arznei <-, -en> [a:ɐts·'nai] f medicine

Arzneimittel nt drug

Arzt, Ärztin <-es, Ärzte> [a:ɐtst, 'ɛ:ɐts·tɪn] m, f doctor; **~ für Allgemeinmedizin** family physician, GP

Arzthelfer(in) m(f) doctor's assistant

ärztlich ['ɛ:ɐtst·lɪç] I. adj medically; II. adv medically; **sich** akk **~ behandeln lassen** to get medical advice

AsALT <-ses, -se> [as] nt s. **Ass**

Asche <-, -n> ['aʃə] f ash

Aschenbecher m ashtray

Aschermittwoch [aʃe·'mɪt·vɔx] m REL Ash Wednesday

Asiat(in) <-en, -en> m(f) Asian

asiatisch [a'zɪa·tɪʃ] adj Asiatic; Kultur, Sprache Asian

Asien <-s> ['a:zɪən] nt Asia

asozial ['azo·tsɪa:l] adj antisocial

Asphalt <-[e]s, -e> [as·'falt] m asphalt

asphaltieren* [as·fal·'ti:·ran] vt to tar

AssRR <-es, -e> nt ace ▶WENDUNGEN:

[noch] **ein ~ im Ärmel haben** to have an ace up one's sleeve

Assistent(in) <-en, -en> [asɪs·'tɛnt] m(f) assistant

Assistenzarzt, -ärztin m, f [hospital] intern

assistieren* [asɪs·'ti:·ran] vi to assist (**bei** + dat with)

Ast <-[e]s, Äste> [ast] m branch ▶WENDUNGEN: **auf dem absteigenden ~ sein** (fam) sb/sth is going downhill

Aster <-, -n> ['as·te] f aster

ästhetisch [ɛs·'te:·tɪʃ] adj aesthetic

Asthma <-s> ['ast·ma] nt kein pl asthma

asthmatisch [ast·'ma:·tɪʃ] adj asthmatic

Astrologe, Astrologin <-n, -n> [as·tro·'lo:·gə, -gɪn] m, f astrologer

Astrologie <-> [as·tro·lo·'gi:] f kein pl astrology

astrologisch [as·tro·'lo:·gɪʃ] adj astrological

Astronom(in) <-en, -en> [as·tro·'no:m] m(f) astronomer

Astronomie <-> [as·tro·no·'mi:] f kein pl astronomy

Asyl <-s, -e> [a'zy:l] nt asylum; **um ~ bitten** to apply for [political] asylum; **jdm ~ gewähren** to grant sb [political] asylum

Asylbewerber(in) m(f) asylum seeker

Atelier <-s, -s> [atə·'lɪe:] nt KUNST studio

Atem <-s> ['a:təm] m kein pl breath; **den ~ anhalten** to hold one's breath; **~ holen** to take a breath; **wieder zu ~ kommen** to catch one's breath; **außer ~** out of breath ▶WENDUNGEN: **den längeren ~ haben** to have the upper hand; **jdn in ~ halten** to keep sb on their toes; **jdm den ~ verschlagen** to take sb's breath away

atemberaubend adj breathtaking

Atemgerät nt respirator; (von Taucher) breathing apparatus

atemlos adv breathlessly

Atemnot f kein pl shortness of breath

Atemwege pl respiratory tracts pl

Atemzug m breath

Atheist(in) <-en, -en> [ate·'ɪst] *m(f)* atheist

Äthiopien <-s> [ɛˈti̯oː·pi̯·ən] *nt* Ethiopia; *s. a.* **Deutschland**

Äthiopier(in) <-s, -> [ɛˈti̯oː·pi̯·e] *m(f)* Ethiopian; *s. a.* **Deutsche(r)**

äthiopisch [ɛˈti̯oː·prʃ] *adj* Ethiopian; *s. a.* **deutsch**

Athlet(in) <-en, -en> [at·'leːt] *m(f)* athlete

athletisch [at·'leː·trʃ] *adj* athletic

Atlantik <-s> [at·'lan·tɪk] *m* Atlantic

Atlas <-, Atlanten> [ˈat·las] *m* atlas

atmen [ˈaːt·mən] *vt, vi* to breathe

Atmosphäre <-, -n> [at·mo·'sfɛː·rə] *f* atmosphere

Atmung <-> *f kein pl* breathing

Atom <-s, -e> [a'toːm] *nt* atom

Atomausstieg *m* denuclearization, nuclear [power] phase-out

Atombombe *f* nuclear bomb

Atomenergie *f* nuclear energy

Atomindustrie *f* nuclear industry

Atomkraft *f kein pl* nuclear power

Atomkraftwerk *nt* nuclear power plant

Attentat <-[e]s, -e> [ˈatn·taːt] *nt* attempt on sb's life; **ein ~ auf jdn verüben** to make an attempt on sb's life

Attentäter(in) [ˈatn·tɛː·te] *m(f)* assassin

Attest <-[e]s, -e> [a'tɛst] *nt* certificate; **jdm ein ~ ausstellen** to certify sth

Attrappe <-, -n> [a'trapə] *f* dummy

ätzend *adj* ① *Substanz* corrosive ② *Geruch* pungent ③ (*sl: sehr übel*) lousy

Aubergine <-, -n> [obɛr·'ʒiː·nə] *f* eggplant

auch [aux] *adv* ① (*ebenfalls*) too, also, as well; **ich ~** me too; **~ nicht** not … either, … [n]either; **ich ~ nicht** me [n]either; **ich gehe nicht mit! — ich ~ nicht!** I'm not going [along]! — neither am I!; **wenn du nicht hingehst, gehe ich ~ nicht** if you don't go, I won't either ② (*sogar*) even; **~ wenn** even if ③ (*einräumend*) **wie dem ~ sei** whatever

Audienz <-, -en> [au·'diː·ɛnts] *f* audience

auf [auf] I. *präp* ① +*dat* on; **~ dem Stuhl** on the chair ② +*akk* on, onto; **sie fiel ~ den Rücken** she fell on[to] her back ③ +*akk* (*zu*) to; **~ die Post/das Fest** to the post office/party ④ +*akk* (*bei Zeitangaben*) on; **etw ~ morgen verlegen** to postpone sth until tomorrow II. *adv* (*fam*) ① (*geöffnet*) **~ sein** to be open ② (*nicht mehr im Bett*) **~ sein** to be up ▶ WENDUNGEN: **~ und ab** up and down; **~ und davon** up and away

auf|**atmen** *vi* [**erleichtert**] **~** to heave a sigh of relief

auf|**bauen** *vt* ① (*zusammenbauen*) to assemble ② (*errichten*) *Zelt* to put up *sep*; *Haus, Stadt* to build; **ein Haus neu ~** to rebuild a house ③ (*aufmuntern*) **jdn [wieder] ~** to cheer up *sep* sb ④ (*schaffen*) *Partei, Existenz* to build

auf|**bekommen*** *vt irreg* (*fam*) ① (*öffnen*) to get open *sep* ② *Hausaufgaben* to get as homework

auf|**bereiten*** *vt Trinkwasser* to purify

auf|**bessern** *vt* to improve; *Gehalt* to increase

auf|**bewahren*** *vt* ① (*aufheben*) to keep ② (*lagern*) to store

Aufbewahrung <-> *f kein pl* [safe]keeping

auf|**blasen** *irreg vt Luftballon* to blow up *sep*

auf|**bleiben** *vi irreg sein* ① (*nicht zu Bett gehen*) to stay up ② (*geöffnet bleiben*) to stay open

auf|**blühen** *vi sein* ① *Blume* to bloom ② (*aufleben*) to blossom out

auf|**brauchen** *vt* to use up *sep*

auf|**brausen** *vi sein* to flare up

auf|**brechen** *irreg* I. *vt haben* to break open *sep*; **ein Auto ~** to break into a car II. *vi sein* ① (*aufplatzen*) to break up; *Wunde* to open ② (*sich auf den Weg machen*) to start off; **ich glaube, wir müssen ~** I think we have to go

auf|**bringen** *vt irreg Geld* to raise; *Geduld, Kraft, Mut* to summon [up *sep*]

Aufbruch *m kein pl* departure

auf|**decken** *vt Skandal, Verbrechen* to reveal

A

auf|donnern vr (fam) ■**sich** akk ~ to doll oneself up

auf|drängen I. vt ■**jdm etw** ~ to force sth on sb II. vr ■**sich** akk **jdm** ~ to impose oneself on sb

auf|drehen I. vt ❶(öffnen) to turn on sep; Flasche, Ventil to open; Schraubverschluss to unscrew ❷(fam: lauter stellen) to turn up sep II. vi (fam) ■**aufgedreht sein** to be full of go

aufdringlich adj Benehmen obtrusive; Geruch pungent; Person insistent

auf|drücken vt ❶ Tür to push open sep ❷(fam: aufzwingen) ■**jdm etw** ~ to impose sth on sb

aufeinander [auf·ʔai·ˈnan·dɐ] adv ❶(räumlich) on top of each other ❷(zeitlich) after each other; **dicht ~ folgen** to come hard and fast a. hum; **~ folgend** successive ❸(gegeneinander) **~ losgehen** to hit away at each other ❹(wechselseitig) **~ angewiesen sein** to be dependent [up]on each other; **~ zugehen** to approach each other

aufeinander|folgen vi sein s. **aufeinander 2**

aufeinanderfolgend adj s. **aufeinander 2**

aufeinander|stoßen vi irreg sein to clash

Aufenthalt <-[e]s, -e> [ˈauf·ʔɛnt·halt] m stay; BAHN stop[over]; **wie lange haben wir in Köln ~?** how long are we stopping in Cologne?

Aufenthaltsort m whereabouts + sing/pl vb

Aufenthaltsraum m day room; (in Firma) employee lounge

Auferstehung <-, -en> f REL resurrection; **Christi ~** the Resurrection [of Christ]

auf|essen irreg vt, vi to eat up sep

Auffahrunfall m collision; (mehrere Fahrzeuge) pile-up

auffallend I. adj striking II. adv **~ schön** strikingly beautiful

auffällig adj conspicuous; ■**an jdm ~ sein** to be noticeable about sb; ■**etwas A~es** something conspicuous

Auffanglager nt reception camp

auf|fassen vt to interpret; **etw falsch ~** to misinterpret sth

Auffassung f opinion; **ich bin der ~, dass ...** I think [that] ...; **nach jds ~** in sb's opinion

auf|finden vt irreg to find

auf|fliegen vi irreg sein ❶ Tür to fly open ❷(fam: bekannt werden) to leak out; Betrug, Machenschaften to be exposed; ■**jdn/etw ~ lassen** to blow the whistle on sb/sth

auf|fordern vt ■**jdn ~, etw zu tun** to ask sb to do sth; **jdn zum Tanz ~** to ask sb to dance

auf|frischen I. vt haben Beziehung to renew; Erinnerung to refresh; Kenntnisse to polish up sep; Make-up to touch up; **sein Englisch ~** to brush up on one's English II. vi sein o haben Wind to freshen

Auffrischungskurs m refresher course

auf|führen I. vt ❶ Theaterstück to perform ❷(auflisten) to list; Beispiele, Zeugen to cite II. vr ■**sich** akk ~ to behave; **sich** akk ~, **als ob ...** to act as if ...

Aufführung f THEAT performance

auf|füllen vt to fill up sep

Aufgabe <-, -n> f ❶(Pflicht) job, task ❷meist pl (Übung) exercise; (Hausaufgabe) homework; **eine schwierige ~ lösen** to solve a difficult problem

auf|gabeln vt (fam) to pick up sep

Aufgabenbereich nt area of responsibility

auf|geben irreg I. vt ❶ Brief, Päckchen to mail ❷ Gepäck to register; LUFT to check in ❸ Anzeige to place ❹**eine Gewohnheit** to break [with] a habit; **das Rauchen ~** to quit smoking ❺(verloren geben) ■**jdn ~** to give up on sb II. vi to give up; MIL to surrender

aufgeblasen I. adj (pej) self-important II. pp von **aufblasen**

aufgebracht I. adj outraged (**über** +akk with); II. pp von **aufbringen**

aufgedunsen adj bloated; Gesicht puffy

auf|gehen vi irreg sein ❶(sich öffnen)

A

to open; *Vorhang* to rise; *Knoten, Reißverschluss etc.* to come undone ❷ *Sonne, Mond* to rise ❸ *Teig* to rise ❹ *(Erfüllung finden)* ■ **in etw** *dat* ~ to be wrapped up in sth

aufgelegt I. *adj* **gut/schlecht ~ sein** to be in a good/bad mood; ■ **dazu ~ sein, etw zu tun** to feel like doing sth II. *pp von* **auflegen**

aufgeregt I. *adj* excited II. *pp von* **aufregen**

aufgeschmissen *adj (fam)* ■ **~ sein** to be in a jam

aufgeweckt I. *adj* bright II. *pp von* **aufwecken**

auf|greifen *vt irreg* **einen Punkt ~** to take up a point; **ein Gespräch ~** to continue a conversation

aufgrund, auf Grund [auf·'grʊnt] *präp* +*gen* because of

auf|haben *irreg (fam)* I. *vt Hut, Mütze* to wear II. *vi Geschäft, Museum* to be open

auf|halten *irreg* I. *vt* ❶ **jdn ~** to hold up sb *sep;* **den Verkehr ~** to tie up traffic ❷ **die Hand ~** to hold out *sep* one's hand; **jdm die Tür ~** to hold open *sep* the door for sb II. *vr* ❶ *(verweilen)* ■ **sich** *akk* ~ to stay somewhere ❷ *(sich befassen)* ■ **sich** *akk* **mit jdm/etw ~** to spend time [dealing] with sb/sth

auf|hängen I. *vt Bild, Mantel* to hang up *sep; Mensch* to hang II. *vr* ■ **sich** *akk* ~ to hang oneself

auf|heben *irreg vt* ❶ *(vom Boden)* to pick up *sep* ❷ *(behalten)* to keep ❸ *Gesetz* to abolish; *Urteil* to reverse; *Verbot* to lift

auf|heitern I. *vt* to cheer up *sep* II. *vr impers* ■ **sich** *akk* ~ *Himmel* to brighten up

auf|hetzen *vt (pej)* to incite

auf|holen I. *vt* to make up *sep* II. *vi* to catch up; *Läufer, Rennfahrer* to make up ground

auf|horchen *vi* to prick up one's ears

auf|hören *vi* to stop

auf|klappen *vt Buch* to open [up *sep*];

Messer to unclasp; *Verdeck* to fold back *sep*

auf|klären I. *vt* to inform *(über +akk* about); *(sexuell)* to explain the facts of life; *Irrtum, Missverständnis* to resolve; *Verbrechen* to clear up *sep* II. *vr* ■ **sich** *akk* ~ ❶ *Geheimnis, Irrtum* to resolve itself ❷ *(sonniger werden)* to brighten [up]

Aufkleber *m* sticker

auf|kommen *vi irreg sein* ❶ *(finanziell)* ■ **für etw** *akk* ~ to pay for sth; ■ **für jdn ~** to pay for sb's upkeep ❷ *Nebel, Regen* to set in; *Wind* to pick up

auf|laden *irreg vt* ❶ **etw auf den Wagen ~** to load on[to] a vehicle ❷ ■ **jdm etw ~** to burden sb with sth ❸ *Batterie* to charge

Auflage <-, -n> *f* ❶ *eines Buchs* edition ❷ *(Auflagenhöhe) eines Buchs* number of copies; *einer Zeitung* circulation ❸ *(Bedingung)* condition; **die ~ haben, etw zu tun** to be obliged to do sth

auf|lassen *vt irreg (fam)* ❶ *Fenster, Tür* to leave open *sep* ❷ *Hut* to leave on *sep*

auf|lauern *vi* ■ **jdm ~** to lie in wait for sb

Auflauf *m* KOCHK casserole

auf|laufen *vi irreg sein (fam)* ■ **jdn ~ lassen** to show sb up

auf|leben *vi sein* to liven up

auf|legen *vt* ❶ **ein Buch neu ~** to reprint a book ❷ **eine CD ~** to put on *sep* a CD ❸ **den Hörer ~** to hang up

auf|lehnen *vr* ■ **sich** *akk* ~ to revolt

auf|leuchten *vi sein o haben* to light up

auf|lockern I. *vt* **die Erde ~** to break up *sep* the earth ❶ SPORT **die Muskeln ~** to loosen up one's muscles ❷ **das Gespräch ~** to liven up the conversation

auf|lösen I. *vt* ❶ *(in Flüssigkeit)* to dissolve ❷ *(aufklären)* to clear up *sep* ❸ *Konto, Geschäft* to close; *Haushalt* to break up *sep; Parlament* to dissolve; *Partei, Verein* to disband II. *vr* ■ **sich** *akk* ~ ❶ *(in Flüssigkeit)* to dissolve

A

❷(*sich klären*) to resolve itself **❸** *Bewölkung* to break up; *Nebel a.* to lift

Auflösung f **❶** *eines Geschäfts, Kontos* closing; *eines Haushalts* breaking up; *des Parlaments* dissolution; *einer Partei, eines Vereins* disbanding **❷** *eines Rätsels* solution **❸** (*Bildqualität*) resolution

auf|machen I. *vt Tür* to open; *Knopf* to undo **II.** *vi* **❶** (*Tür öffnen*) to open the door **❷** *Geschäft* to open up **III.** *vr* ■ **sich** *akk* ~ to set out (**nach** +*akk* for)

aufmerksam *adj* attentive; **das ist sehr** ~ [**von Ihnen**]! that's most kind [of you]; **jdn auf etw** *akk* ~ **machen** to draw sb's attention to sth; **auf etw** *akk* ~ **werden** to take notice of sth

auf|muntern *vt* to cheer up *sep*

aufmüpfig *adj* (*fam*) rebellious

Aufnahme <-, -n> f **❶** *von Musik, Videos* recording **❷** *von Tätigkeit* start **❸** (*in Verein*) admission

Aufnahmeprüfung f entrance examination

auf|nehmen *vt irreg* **❶** *Foto* to take; *Film, Video* to record **❷** ■ **jdn** [**bei sich** *dat*] ~ to take in *sep* sb **❸** (*verstehen*) ■ **etw** ~ to grasp sth; **wie hat sie es aufgenommen?** how did she take it? **❹** (*auflisten*) to include **❺** *Tätigkeit* to take up *sep*; **Kontakt mit jdm** ~ to contact sb

auf|opfern *vr* ■ **sich** *akk* ~ to sacrifice oneself

auf|passen *vi* to pay attention; **pass auf!** (*sei aufmerksam*) [be] careful!; (*Vorsicht*) watch out!; **genau** ~ to pay close attention; **auf die Kinder** ~ to watch the children

auf|peppen ['auf·pɛpn̩] *vt* (*sl*) to jazz up *sep*

Aufprall <-[e]s, -e> *m* impact

auf|prallen *vi sein* ■ **auf etw** *akk* ~ to hit sth; *Mensch, Fahrzeug a.* to run into sth

Aufpreis *m* surcharge; **gegen** ~ for an additional charge

auf|pumpen *vt* to pump up *sep*

Aufputschmittel *nt* stimulant

auf|raffen *vr* ■ **sich** *akk* **zu etw** *dat* ~ to bring oneself to do sth

auf|räumen I. *vt Zimmer* to clean [up *sep*]; *Schrank* to clear out; *Schreibtisch* to clear [off *sep*]; *Spielsachen* to put away *sep* **II.** *vi* to clean up; ■ **mit etw** *dat* ~ to do away with sth

aufrecht ['auf·rɛçt] *adj, adv* upright

aufrecht|erhalten* ['auf·rɛçt·?ɐg·hal·tn̩] *vt irreg* to maintain; *Freundschaft* to keep up *sep*; **seine Behauptung** ~ to stick to one's claim

auf|regen I. *vt* to excite; (*nervös machen*) to make nervous **II.** *vr* ■ **sich** *akk* ~ to get worked up (**über** +*akk* about); **reg dich nicht so auf!** don't get [yourself] so worked up!

Aufregung f excitement; **nur keine** ~! don't get flustered; **in heller** ~ in utter confusion; **jdn in** ~ **versetzen** to make sb lose their composure *fam*

auf|reißen *irreg vt haben* **❶** (*öffnen*) *Augen, Mund* to open wide *sep*; *Fenster, Tür* to fling open *sep*; *Geschenk, Tüte* to tear open *sep* **❷ eine Frau/ einen Mann** ~ (*sl*) to pick up *sep* a woman/man

aufrichtig *adj* honest; *Gefühl* sincere; *Liebe* true

Aufrichtigkeit <-> f *kein pl* sincerity

auf|rufen *irreg* **I.** *vt* **❶** *Schüler, Zeuge* to call [out *sep*] **❷** COMPUT *Datei* to call up *sep*; *Daten* to retrieve **II.** *vi* ■ **zu etw** *dat* ~ to call for sth

Aufruhr <-[e]s, -e> ['auf·ʁuːɐ̯] *m* **❶** *kein pl* (*Unruhe*) turmoil; (*in der Stadt/im Volk*) unrest **❷** (*Aufstand*) revolt

aufrührerisch *adj* rebellious

auf|runden *vt* to round up *sep* (**auf** +*akk* to)

auf|sagen *vt* to recite

auf|sammeln *vt* to pick up *sep*

aufsässig ['auf·zɛ·sɪç] *adj* rebellious

Aufsatz *m* LING essay

auf|schichten *vt* to stack

auf|schieben *vt irreg Termin* to postpone ▶WENDUNGEN: **aufgeschoben ist**

A

nicht aufgehoben (*prov*) there'll be another opportunity

auf|schlagen *irreg* I. *vi* ① *sein* **mit dem Kopf** [**auf etw** *akk o dat*] ~ to hit one's head [on sth] ② *haben* (*sich verteuern*) to go up (**um** +*akk* by) II. *vt haben* ① *Buch* to open; **Seite 35** ~ to turn to page 35 ② *Nuss* to break open *sep* ③ *Zelt* to put up *sep* ④ (*verteuern*) to raise (**um** +*akk* by)

auf|schließen *irreg* I. *vt Tür* to unlock II. *vi* ■**jdm** ~ to unlock the door [for sb]

aufschlussreich^RR *adj* informative; (*enthüllend*) revealing

auf|schnappen *vt* (*fam*) to pick up *sep*

Aufschnitt *m kein pl* ① (*Wurst*) cold cuts *npl* ② (*Käse*) assorted sliced cheese[s *pl*]

auf|schrauben *vt* to unscrew; *Flasche* to take the cap off

auf|schrecken I. *vt* <schreckte auf, aufgeschreckt> *haben* to startle II. *vi* <schreckte auf, aufgeschreckt> *sein* to start [up]

auf|schreiben *vt irreg* to write down *sep*; ■**sich** *dat* **etw** ~ to make a note of sth

Aufschub *m* delay; **jdm** ~ **gewähren** to grant sb an extension

auf|schwatzen *vt* DIAL (*fam*) ■**jdm etw** ~ to palm sth off *sep* sth on sb; ■**sich** *dat* **etw** ~ **lassen** to get talked into buying sth

Aufschwung *m* ① (*Auftrieb*) impetus; **jdm neuen** ~ **geben** to give sb a boost ② (*Aufwärtstrend*) upswing

Aufsehen <-s> *nt kein pl* sensation; **ohne** [**großes**] ~ without any [real] fuss; **etw erregt** [**großes**] ~ sth causes a [great] sensation; ~ **erregend** sensational

auf|setzen I. *vt* ① *Hut, Brille* to put on *sep* ② *Essen, Wasser* to put on *sep* ③ (*zur Schau tragen*) to put on *sep* II. *vr* ■**sich** *akk* ~ to sit up

Aufsichtsrat *m* supervisory board

auf|spielen *vr* (*fam*) ■**sich** *akk* ~ to show off

auf|spüren *vt* to track down *sep*

auf|stacheln *vt* ■**jdn** [**zu etw** *dat*] ~ to incite sb [to do sth]; ■**jdn gegen jdn** ~ to turn sb against sb

Aufstand *m* rebellion

auf|stehen *vi irreg* ① *sein Person* to stand up; (*aus dem Bett*) to get up ② *haben Fenster, Tür* to be open

auf|stellen I. *vt* ① (*aufbauen*) to put up *sep*; *Maschine* to install; *Denkmal* to erect; *Falle* to set ② *Rekord* to set ③ *Kandidat* to nominate ④ *Wache* to post ⑤ SCHWEIZ (*aufmuntern*) to perk up *sep* II. *vr* ■**sich** *akk* ~ to stand; **sich** *akk* **hintereinander** ~ to line up; **sich** *akk* **im Kreis** ~ to form a circle

Aufstieg <-[e]s, -e> ['auf·ʃtiːk] *m* climb (**auf** +*akk* up); **sozialer** ~ social advancement; **den** ~ **ins Management schaffen** to work one's way up into management

auf|stocken *vt* to increase (**um** +*akk* by); **ein Team** ~ to add players to a team

auf|tanken *vt, vi* to fill up *sep*; *Flugzeug* to refuel

auf|tauchen *vi sein* ① *Taucher* to come up ② *verlorener Gegenstand* to be found ③ (*plötzlich da sein*) to suddenly appear

auf|tauen I. *vi sein* ① *Eis* to thaw ② (*fig*) to open up II. *vt haben* to thaw [out *sep*]

auf|teilen *vt* ① (*aufgliedern*) to divide [up *sep*] (**in** +*akk* into) ② (*verteilen*) to share *sep* (**unter** +*dat* among)

Auftrag <-[e]s, Aufträge> ['auf·traːk] *m* order; **jdm den** ~ **geben, etw zu tun** to instruct sb to do sth; „~ **erledigt!**" "mission accomplished!"

auf|tragen *irreg vt* ① *Creme, Farbe* to apply (**auf** +*akk* to) ② ■**jdm etw** ~ to instruct sb to do sth

Auftraggeber(in) <-s, -> *m(f)* client

auf|treiben *vt irreg* (*fam*) to get [a] hold of

auf|treten *irreg* I. *vi sein* ① *Problem, Schwierigkeiten* to occur ② THEAT to appear [on the stage] ③ **selbstbewusst** ~

A

to exhibit self-confidence II. *vt haben* **Tür** to kick open *sep*

Auftreten <-s> *nt kein pl* behavior

Auftritt *m* MUS, THEAT appearance

auf|tun *irreg vr* ■ **sich** *akk* ~ *Möglichkeit* to open [up]

auf|wachen *vi sein* to wake [up]

auf|wachsen [-ks-] *vi irreg sein* to grow up

Aufwand <-[e]s> ['auf·vant] *m kein pl* expenditure; **der ~ war umsonst** it was a waste of energy/money/time; **[großen] ~ treiben** to be [very] extravagant

Aufwandsentschädigung *f* expense allowance

auf|wärmen I. *vt Essen* to heat up *sep* II. *vr* ■ **sich** *akk* ~ to warm oneself [up]

aufwärts ['auf·vɛrts] *adv* up, upward[s]; (*bergauf*) uphill; **den Fluss ~** upstream

auf|wecken *vt, vi* to wake [up *sep*]

auf|weisen *vt irreg* to show; **zahlreiche Fehler ~** to be full of mistakes

auf|wenden *vt irreg o reg vt* to use; *Zeit, Mühe* to expend; *Geld* to spend; **viel Energie ~, etw zu tun** to put a lot of energy into doing sth

auf|werfen *irreg vt Frage* to raise

auf|werten *vt* ❶ *Währung* to revalue ❷ (*fig*) to increase the value of

Aufwertung <-, -en> *f* ❶ *einer Währung* revaluation ❷ (*fig*) enhancement

auf|wischen *vt, vi* to wipe [up *sep*]

auf|wühlen *vt* ■ **jdn** [**innerlich**] ~ to stir up *sep* sb

auf|zählen *vt* to list

Aufzeichnung *f* ❶ (*Aufnahme*) recording; (*auf Band a.*) taping; (*auf Videoband a.*) videotaping ❷ *meist pl* (*Notizen*) notes

auf|ziehen *irreg* I. *vt haben* ❶ *Schublade* to open; *Reißverschluss* to unzip; *Vorhänge* to draw back *sep* ❷ *Kind* to raise ❸ (*fam: verspotten*) to tease (**mit** +*dat* about) II. *vi sein Wolken* to gather

Aufzucht *f* raising

Aufzug *m* elevator; [**mit dem**] ~ **fahren** to take the elevator

Augapfel ['auk·ʔapfl̩] *m* eyeball

Auge <-s, -n> ['au·gə] *nt* eye; **gute/ schlechte ~n haben** to have good/ poor eyesight *sing* ▶WENDUNGEN: **mit einem** blauen ~ **davonkommen** (*fam*) to get off lightly; **ins ~ gehen** (*fam*) to backfire; **jdn nicht aus den ~n lassen** to not let sb out of one's sight; **ins ~ springen** to catch sb's eye; **etw aus den ~n verlieren** to lose track of sth; **sich** *akk* **aus den ~n verlieren** to lose touch with; **die ~n vor etw** *dat* **verschließen** to close one's eyes to sth; **unter vier ~n** in private; **ein ~ auf jdn/etw werfen** to have one's eye on sb/sth; **ein ~/beide ~n zudrücken** (*fam*) to turn a blind eye to; **kein ~ zutun** (*fam*) to not sleep a wink; **~n zu und durch** (*fam*) take a deep breath and do it

Augenarzt, -ärztin *m, f* optometrist

Augenblick ['au·gn̩·blɪk] *m* moment; **im ersten ~** for a moment; **im letzten ~** at the [very] last moment; **~ mal!** just a minute!

augenblicklich ['au·gn̩·blɪk·lɪç] *adv* ❶ (*sofort*) immediately; (*herausfordernd*) at once ❷ (*zurzeit*) at present

Augenbraue *f* eyebrow; **die ~n hochziehen** to raise one's eyebrows

Augenlid *nt* eyelid

Augentropfen *pl* eye drops *npl*

Augenzeuge, -zeugin *m, f* eyewitness (**bei** +*dat* to)

August <-[e]s, -e> [au·'gʊst] *m* August; *s. a.* **Februar**

Auktion <-, -en> *f* auction

Aula <-, Aulen> ['au·la] *f* [assembly] hall

aus [aus] I. *präp* +*dat* ❶ (*von innen nach außen*) out of; **~ dem Fenster/ der Tür** out of the window/door; **das Öl tropfte ~ dem Fass** the oil was dripping from the barrel ❷ (*Herkunft*) from; **~ Stuttgart kommen** to be from Stuttgart; **~ dem 17. Jahrhundert stammen** to be [from the] 17th century; **Zigaretten ~ dem Automaten** cigarettes from a vending machine ❸ (*Ursache*) **~ Angst/Dummheit/ Verzweiflung** out of fear/stupidity/

desperation; **~ einer Laune heraus** on a whim; **~ Unachtsamkeit** due to carelessness ④ (*Material*) **~ Glas/Holz** [made] of glass/wood II. *adv* (*fam*) ① (*gelöscht*) out ② (*ausgeschaltet*) off ③ (*zu Ende*) **■ ~ sein** to have finished; *Krieg* to have ended; *Schule* to be out; **mit etw** *dat* **ist es ~** sth is over; **es ist ~** [**zwischen jdm**] (*fam*) it's over [between sb] ▶WENDUNGEN: **auf jdn/etw ~ sein** to be after sb/sth; **~ und vorbei sein** to be over and done with

aus|atmen *vt, vi* to exhale

aus|bauen *vt* ① *Gebäude* to extend (**zu** +*dat* into); (*innen*) to remodel ② (*herausmontieren*) to remove (**aus** +*dat* from)

aus|bessern *vt* to repair

aus|beuten *vt* to exploit

Ausbeutung <-, -en> *f* exploitation

aus|bezahlen* *vt Betrag* to pay out *sep*; *Person* to pay off *sep*

aus|bilden *vt* to train; (*akademisch*) to educate; **jdn zum Arzt ~** to train sb to be a doctor

Ausbilder(in) <-s, -> *m(f)*, **Ausbildner(in)** <-s, -> *m(f)* ÖSTERR, SCHWEIZ trainer; MIL instructor

Ausbildung <-, -en> *f* training; (*akademisch*) education; **in der ~ sein** to be in training

Ausbildungsplatz *m* internship

aus|blenden *vt* (*fam*) *Problem* to forget

aus|brechen *irreg vi sein* ① (*aus dem Gefängnis*) to escape ② *Vulkan* to erupt ③ *Feuer, Seuche, Panik* to break out ④ **in Gelächter/Tränen ~** to burst into laughter/tears

aus|breiten I. *vt* ① *Decke, Landkarte* to spread [out *sep*] ② *Arme, Flügel* to spread [out *sep*] II. *vr* **■ sich** *akk* **~** to spread (**auf** +*akk* to)

Ausbruch *m* ① (*aus dem Gefängnis*) escape (**aus** +*dat* from) ② (*Beginn*) outbreak ③ *eines Vulkans* eruption

aus|bürsten *vt* to brush [out *sep*]

Ausdauer *f kein pl* endurance

aus|dehnen I. *vr* **■ sich** *akk* **~** ① (*größer werden*) to expand ② (*sich ausbreiten*) to spread (**auf** +*akk* to) II. *vt* ① *Zeitraum* to extend ② (*erweitern, vergrößern*) *Aktivitäten, Streik* to expand (**auf** +*akk* to)

aus|denken *vr irreg* **■ sich** *dat* **etw ~** to think up *sep* sth; **sich** *akk* **eine Überraschung ~** to plan a surprise

Ausdruck[1] <-drücke> *m* expression; **etw zum ~ bringen** to express sth; **als ~ der Dankbarkeit** as an expression of one's gratitude

Ausdruck[2] <-drucke> *m* [computer] printout; **einen ~** [**von etw** *dat*] **machen** to run off *sep* a copy [of sth]

aus|drucken *vt* to print [out *sep*]

aus|drücken I. *vt* ① (*zeigen*) to show; **Gefühle ~** to express feelings ② (*formulieren*) to put into words; **anders ausgedrückt** in other words; **einfach ausgedrückt** put simply ③ *Zigarette* to snuff out *sep* II. *vr* **■ sich** *akk* **~** to express oneself; **sich** *akk* **falsch ~** to use the wrong word

ausdrücklich ['aus·drʏk·lɪç] *adj attr* explicit

ausdruckslos *adj* inexpressive; *Blick* vacant; *Gesicht* expressionless

ausdrucksvoll *adj* expressive

Ausdrucksweise *f* way one expresses oneself

auseinander [aus·ʔai·'nan·dɐ] *adv* apart

auseinander|biegen *vt* to bend apart *sep*

auseinander|fallen *vi irreg sein* to fall apart

auseinander|falten *vt* to unfold

auseinander|gehen *vi irreg sein* ① *Menschen* to part ② *Beziehung* to break up; *Ehe a.* to fall apart ③ *Meinungen* to differ ④ (*fam: dick werden*) to [start to] fill out *a. hum*

auseinander|setzen I. *vt* **jdm etw ~** to explain sth to sb II. *vt* **■ sich** *akk* **mit etw** *dat* **~** to tackle sth

Auseinandersetzung <-, -en> [aus·ʔai·'nan·dɐ·zɛtsʊŋ] *f* argument

Ausfahrt *f* exit; (*mit Tor*) gateway

aus|fallen *vi irreg sein Veranstaltung* to

A

be canceled; ■etw ~ **lassen** to cancel sth

ausfällig *adj* abusive; ■~ **werden** to become abusive

ausfindig *adj* ■jdn/etw ~ **machen** to locate sb/sth

aus|flippen *vi sein* (*fam*) ❶ (*aus Wut*) to freak out ❷ (*aus Freude*) to jump for joy

Ausflucht <-, Ausflüchte> *f* excuse; **Ausflüchte machen** to make excuses

Ausflug *m* outing; SCH field trip

aus|fragen *vt* to question

aus|fressen *vt irreg* (*fam*) ■etwas/ nichts ausgefressen haben to have done something/nothing wrong

Ausfuhr <-> *f kein pl* export[ation]

Ausfuhrbestimmungen *pl* export regulations *pl*

aus|führen *vt* ❶ *Auftrag* to carry out *sep*; *Befehl* to execute ❷ jdn zum Essen ~ to take sb out *sep* for dinner ❸ (*exportieren*) to export (in +*akk* to)

ausführlich ['aus·fy:ɐ̯·lɪç] I. *adj* detailed II. *adv* in detail; **sehr ~** in great detail

aus|füllen *vt* ❶ *Formular* to fill in *sep* ❷ jdn [*ganz*] ~ to satisfy sb [completely] ❸ seine Zeit mit etw *dat* ~ to fill one's time with sth

Ausgabe *f* ❶ MEDIA, LIT edition ❷ *pl* (*Kosten*) expenses

Ausgang *m* exit

aus|geben *irreg* I. *vt* ❶ *Geld* to spend (**für** +*akk* on) ❷ (*austeilen*) to distribute (**an** +*akk* to) ❸ (*fam: spendieren*) ■jdm etw ~ to treat sb to sth; **eine Runde** ~ to buy a round; [jdm] **einen** ~ (*fam*) to buy sb a drink II. *vr* ■sich *akk* als jd/etw ~ to pass oneself off as sb/ sth

ausgebucht *adj* booked up

ausgedehnt I. *adj* extensive II. *pp von* **ausdehnen**

ausgefallen I. *adj* unusual II. *pp von* **ausfallen**

ausgeglichen I. *adj* Mensch easy-going II. *pp von* **ausgleichen**

aus|gehen *vi irreg sein* ❶ (*zum Essen etc.*) to go out ❷ *Feuer, Licht* to go out

❸ *Haare* to fall out ❹ ■von etw *dat* ~ to take sth as a basis; ■davon ~, **dass ...** to assume that ...; **davon kann man nicht** ~ you can't go by that ❺ (*enden*) to end; ■gut/schlecht ~ *Buch, Film* to have a happy/sad ending

ausgelassen I. *adj* wild II. *adv* **es wurde ~ gefeiert** there was a lively party going on III. *pp von* **auslassen**

ausgemacht I. *adj attr* ~er Unsinn utter nonsense II. *pp von* **ausmachen**

ausgenommen I. *konj* except; **wir kommen, ~ es regnet** we'll come, but only if it doesn't rain II. *pp von* **ausnehmen**

ausgepowert [-pauɐt] *adj* (*fam*) beat

ausgeprägt *adj* distinctive; *Interesse* pronounced

ausgerechnet ['aus·gə·rɛç·nət] I. *adv* ~ **er** he of all people; ■~ **jetzt** now of all times; ■~ **gestern/heute** yesterday/today of all days II. *pp von* **ausrechnen**

ausgeschlossen I. *adj pred* **es ist nicht ~, dass ...** it is still possible that ...; ■[völlig] ~! [that's] [completely] out of the question II. *pp von* **ausschließen**

ausgeschnitten *adj* **tief ~** *Kleid, Bluse* low-cut

ausgesprochen I. *adv* really II. *pp von* **aussprechen**

ausgestorben I. *adj* ❶ *Tier-, Pflanzenart* extinct ❷ *Straßen* deserted II. *pp von* **aussterben**

ausgesucht *pp von* **aussuchen**

ausgewogen *adj* balanced

ausgezeichnet ['aus·gə·tsaiç·nət] I. *adj* excellent II. *adv* extremely well III. *pp von* **auszeichnen**

ausgiebig ['aus·gi:·bɪç] I. *adj* extensive; *Mahlzeit* substantial II. *adv* extensively; ~ **schlafen** to have a good [long] sleep

aus|gleichen *irreg* I. *vt* Konto to balance; *Mangel* to compensate for; *Unterschied* to even out II. *vr* ■sich *akk* ~ to balance out

aus|graben *vt irreg* ❶ (*aus der Erde*) to dig up *sep*; *Altertümer* to excavate

A

❷ (*hervorholen*) to dig out *sep*; **alte Geschichten ~** to bring up *sep* old stories

Ausgrabungen *pl* excavations *pl*

Ausguss^{RR} *m* (*Spüle*) sink

aus|**halten** *irreg vt* ❶ (*ertragen*) to bear; **hältst du es noch eine Stunde aus?** can you hold out [for] another hour?; **es ist nicht [länger] auszuhalten** it's [getting to be] unbearable; **es lässt sich hier ~** it's not a bad place; **den Druck ~** to [with]stand the pressure; **die Kälte ~** to endure the cold; **eine hohe Temperatur ~** to withstand a high temperature; **viel ~** to take a lot ❷ (*finanziell*) to support

aus|**händigen** ['aus·hɛn·dɪ·gn] *vt* to hand over *sep*

Aushang *m* notice

aus|**harren** *vi* to wait [patiently]

aus|**helfen** *vi irreg* to help out *sep*

Aushilfe *f* temporary worker; **[bei jdm] als ~ arbeiten** to temp [for sb] *fam*

aus|**horchen** *vt* (*fam*) to sound out *sep*

aus|**kennen** *vr irreg* ❶ ■**sich** *akk* **irgendwo ~** to know one's way around somewhere ❷ ■**sich** *akk* **[in etw** *dat*] **~** to know a lot [about sth]

Ausklang *m kein pl* **zum ~ des Abends** to conclude the evening

aus|**klopfen** *vt Teppich* to beat

aus|**kommen** *vi irreg sein* ❶ ■**mit etw** *dat* **~** to get by on sth; ■**ohne jdn/etw ~** to manage without sb/sth ❷ ■**mit jdm [gut] ~** to get along [well] with sb ❸ ÖSTERR (*entkommen*) to escape

Auskommen <-s> *nt kein pl* **sein ~ haben** to get by

aus|**kosten** *vt* **das Leben ~** to enjoy life to the fullest; **den Moment/seine Rache ~** to savor the moment/one's revenge

Auskunft <-, Auskünfte> ['aus·kʊnft] *f* ❶ (*Information*) information; **nähere ~** more information ❷ (*Schalter*) information counter ❸ TELEK ■**die ~** the operator

aus|**lachen** *vt* to laugh at

aus|**laden** *irreg vt* ❶ (*entladen*) to unload ❷ (*Einladung widerrufen*) ■**jdn ~** to tell sb not to come

Ausland ['aus·lant] *nt kein pl* ■**[das] ~** foreign countries *pl*; ■**aus dem ~** from abroad; ■**im/ins ~** abroad

Ausländer(in) <-s, -> ['aus·lɛn·dɐ] *m(f)* foreigner; JUR alien

Ausländerbeauftragte(r) *f(m) dekl wie adj* Commissioner for Foreigners' Affairs

ausländerfeindlich *adj* racist

ausländisch ['aus·lɛn·dɪʃ] *adj attr* foreign

Auslandseinsatz *m* MIL foreign [military] deployment

Auslandsgespräch *nt* TELEK international call

Auslandskorrespondent(in) *m(f)* foreign correspondent

aus|**lassen** *irreg* **I.** *vt* ❶ (*weglassen*) to omit; (*überspringen*) to skip ❷ (*fam: ausgeschaltet*) to keep turned off ❸ ■**etw an jdm ~** *Wut* to vent sth on sb **II.** *vr* ■**sich** *akk* **über jdn/etw ~** to go on about sb/sth *pej* **III.** *vi* ÖSTERR to let go

aus|**laufen** *irreg vi sein* ❶ *Schiff* to [set] sail (**nach +***dat* for) ❷ *Vertrag* to expire ❸ (*undicht sein*) to leak

aus|**leeren** *vt Gefäß* to empty [out *sep*]; *Inhalt* to pour away *sep*

aus|**legen** *vt* to interpret; **etw falsch ~** to misinterpret sth

aus|**leihen** *irreg vt* ■**jdm etw** *akk* **~** to lend sb sth; ■**[sich** *dat*] **etw** *akk* **von jdm ~** to borrow sth from sb

Auslese <-> *f kein pl* selection; **die natürliche ~** natural selection

aus|**liefern** *vt* ❶ *Waren* to deliver ❷ (*fig*) ■**jdm/etw ausgeliefert sein** to be at the mercy of sb/sth

Auslieferung *f* ❶ *von Waren* delivery ❷ JUR extradition

aus|**löschen** *vt* to extinguish

aus|**losen** *vi* to draw lots

Auslöser <-s, -> *m* ❶ FOTO [shutter] release ❷ (*Anlass*) trigger

Auslosung <-, -en> *f* draw

A

aus|machen vt ❶ *Feuer* to extinguish ❷ *Gerät, Licht* to turn off *sep* ❸ (*vereinbaren*) to agree [up]on ❹ (*bewirken*) ■**kaum etwas ~** to hardly make any difference; ■**nichts ~** to not make any difference; ■**viel ~** to make a big difference ❺ (*stören*) ■**es macht jdm nichts/viel aus, etw zu tun** sb doesn't mind/really does mind doing sth; **macht es Ihnen etwas aus, wenn …?** do you mind if …?

aus|malen vr ■**sich** *dat* **etw ~** to imagine sth

Ausmaß nt ❶ (*Größe*) size; **das ~ von etw** *dat* **haben** to cover the area of sth ❷ (*fig: Tragweite*) extent

aus|messen vt *irreg* to measure [out]

aus|misten vt ❶ *Stall* to muck out ❷ (*fam*) *Zimmer* to clean up *sep; alte Sachen* to throw out *sep*

Ausnahme <-, -n> ['aʊs·naː·mə] f exception ▶WENDUNGEN: **~n bestätigen die** <u>Regel</u> (*prov*) the exception proves the rule *prov*

Ausnahmezustand m POL state of emergency; **den ~ verhängen** to declare a state of emergency (**über** +*akk* in)

ausnahmslos adv without exception

ausnahmsweise adv for a change

aus|nehmen *irreg* vt ❶ *Tiere* to gut; *Geflügel* to draw ❷ (*ausschließen*) to exempt; **ich nicht ausgenommen** myself not excepted ❸ (*fam: Geld abnehmen*) ■**jdn ~** to fleece sb *fam*; (*beim Glücksspiel*) to clean out *sep* sb *fam*

ausnehmend adv exceptionally; **das gefällt mir ~ gut** I really like it a lot

aus|nutzen I. vt ❶ ■**jdn ~** to exploit sb ❷ ■**etw ~** to make the most of sth; **jds Leichtgläubigkeit ~** to take advantage of sb's gullibility

aus|packen I. vt to unpack; *Geschenk* to unwrap II. vi (*fam: gestehen*) to talk

aus|plaudern vt to let out *sep*

aus|plündern vt *Menschen* to plunder; *Laden* to loot

aus|posaunen* vt (*fam*) to broadcast

aus|pressen vt **eine Orange/ Zitrone ~** to squeeze an orange/a lemon; **den Saft ~** to squeeze out *sep* the juice

aus|probieren* I. vt to try [out *sep*] II. vi ■**~, ob/wie …** to see whether/how …

Auspuff <-[e]s, -e> m exhaust system

Auspuffrohr nt exhaust pipe

aus|quetschen vt ■**jdn ~** to pump sb [for information]; *Polizei* to grill sb

aus|radieren* vt (*mit Radiergummi*) to erase

aus|rangieren* [-raŋ·ʒiː·rən] vt to throw out *sep*

aus|rauben vt to rob

aus|räumen vt ❶ *Möbel* to move out *sep; Zimmer* to clear out *sep* ❷ *Missverständnis, Zweifel* to dispel

aus|rechnen vt to calculate

Ausrede f excuse

aus|reichen vi to be sufficient

aus|reisen vi *sein* to leave the country

Ausreisevisum [-viː-] nt exit visa

aus|reißen *irreg* I. vt *haben* to pull out *sep; Haare* to tear out *sep* II. vi *sein* (*fam*) to run away

Ausreißer(in) <-s, -> m(f) (*fam*) runaway

aus|renken vt to dislocate

aus|richten vt ❶ (*übermitteln*) ■**jdm etw ~** to tell sb sth; **kann ich etwas ~?** can I give him/her a message?; **richten Sie ihr einen Gruß [von mir] aus** give her my regards ❷ (*erreichen*) ■**bei jdm etwas/nichts ~** to achieve something/nothing with sb ❸ ÖSTERR (*schlechtmachen*) to badmouth ❹ SCHWEIZ (*zahlen*) ■**jdm etw ~** to pay sb sth

aus|rotten vt *Ungeziefer* to destroy; *Unkraut* to wipe out *sep; Volk* to exterminate

aus|rufen vt *irreg* to call out *sep; Streik* to call; *Krieg* to declare; ■**jdn ~** to put out a call for sb

Ausrufungszeichen nt, **Ausrufzeichen** nt ÖSTERR, SCHWEIZ exclamation point

aus|ruhen *vi, vr* ■ |*sich akk*| ~ to rest; ■ **ausgeruht** |**sein**| |to be| well rested

Ausrüstung <-, -en> *f* equipment

aus|rutschen *vi sein* to slip; **sie ist ausgerutscht** she slipped; **mir ist die Hand ausgerutscht** I lost my temper and slapped him/her

Ausrutscher <-s, -> *m* (*fam*) slip-up

Aussage *f* statement; (*Zeugenaussage*) evidence; **eine ~ machen** to make a statement

aus|sagen *vt* ■ **etw** |**über jdn/etw**| ~ to say sth |about sb/sth|

aus|schalten *vt* Gerät, Licht to turn off *sep*

Ausschau *f* ■ ~ **halten** to keep an eye out (**nach** +*dat* for)

aus|scheiden *irreg* I. *vi sein* ❶ aus Amt, Beruf to retire; aus Verein to leave ❷ SPORT to drop out ❸ (*nicht in Betracht kommen*) to be ruled out II. *vt haben* (*absondern*) to excrete

aus|schlafen *irreg vi, vr* ■ |*sich akk*| ~ to sleep in

Ausschlag *m* MED rash ▶WENDUNGEN: |**bei etw** *dat*| **den ~ geben** to be the decisive factor |for/in sth|

aus|schlagen *irreg vt* ❶ Angebot to turn down *sep*; (*höflicher*) to decline; ■ **jdm etw** ~ to refuse sb sth; **eine Erbschaft** ~ to disclaim an estate ❷ **jdm einen Zahn** ~ to knock out *sep* one of sb's teeth

ausschlaggebend *adj* decisive; **von ~er Bedeutung sein** to be of primary importance

aus|schließen *irreg* I. *vt* ❶ (*entfernen*) to exclude; (*als Strafe a.*) to bar; Mitglied to expel; (*vorübergehend*) to suspend ❷ (*für unmöglich halten*) to rule out *sep* II. *vr* ■ **sich** *akk* ~ to lock oneself out

ausschließlich ['aus·ʃliːs·lɪç] I. *adv* exclusively; **darüber habe ~ ich zu bestimmen** I'm the one to decide on this matter II. *präp* excluding; (*geschrieben a.*) excl.

Ausschluss^RR *m* exclusion; von Mitglied expulsion; (*vorübergehend*) sus-

pension; **unter ~ der Öffentlichkeit stattfinden** to be closed to the public

aus|schneiden *vt irreg* to cut out *sep*

Ausschnitt *m* ❶ (*an Kleidung*) neckline; **ein tiefer ~** a low neckline ❷ (*Teil*) part

aus|schöpfen *vt* Möglichkeiten, Reserven to exhaust

Ausschreitungen *pl* riots *pl*

Ausschuss^RR *m* committee

aus|schütten *vt* Gefäß to empty; Inhalt to pour out

ausschweifend *adj* Leben hedonistic; Fantasie wild

aus|sehen *vi irreg* to look; ■ ~ **wie ...** to look like ...; **es sieht gut/schlecht aus** things are looking good/not looking too good; **nach Schnee/Regen ~** to look like it's going to snow/rain; **wie sieht's aus?** how're things?

Aussehen <-s> *nt kein pl* appearance; ■ **dem ~ nach** judging by appearances

außen ['ausn̩] *adv* on the outside; **links/rechts ~** on the outside left/right; ■ **von ~** from the outside ▶WENDUNGEN: **jdn/etw ~ vor lassen** to leave sb/sth out; **~ vor sein** to be left out

Außenbezirk *m* outer district

Außenhandel *m* foreign trade

Außenminister(in) *m(f)* Secretary of State

Außenministerium *nt* State Department

Außenpolitik ['ausn̩·po·li·tiːk] *f* foreign policy

außenpolitisch ['ausn̩·po·li·tɪʃ] *adj* foreign policy *attr*; **~er Sprecher** foreign policy spokesman

Außenseiter(in) <-s, -> *m(f)* outsider

Außenspiegel *m* AUTO |out|side mirror

außer ['ause] I. *präp* +*dat* ❶ (*abgesehen von*) apart from ❷ (*zusätzlich zu*) in addition to ❸ ~ **Betrieb/Sicht/Gefahr sein** to be out of order/sight/danger ▶WENDUNGEN: |**über jdn/etw**| ~ **sich** *dat* **sein** to be beside oneself |about sb/sth| II. *konj* ■ ~ **wenn** except when

außerdem ['ause·deːm] *adv* besides

äußere(r, s) ['ɔy·sə·rə, -rə, -rəs] *adj* outer; ~ **Einflüsse/Verletzung** external influences/injury

Äußere(s) ['ɔy·sə·rə, -rəs] *nt dekl wie adj* outward appearance

außerehelich *adj* extramarital; *Kind* illegitimate

außergewöhnlich ['au·se·gə·'vøːn·lɪç] I. *adj* unusual; *Leistung* extraordinary; *Mensch* remarkable II. *adv* extremely

außerhalb ['au·se·halp] I. *adv* outside; **von ~** from out of town II. *präp +gen* outside

äußerlich ['ɔy·se·lɪç] *adj* external

äußern ['ɔy·sen] I. *vr* ■**sich** *akk* **über jdn/etw** to make comments about sb/sth II. *vt* to say; *Kritik* to voice; *Wunsch* to express

außerordentlich ['au·se·'ʔɔr·dnt·lɪç] *adj* extraordinary

außerplanmäßig ['au·se·plaːn·mɛː·sɪç] *adj* unscheduled; *Ausgaben, Kosten* nonbudgetary

äußerst ['ɔy·sest] *adv* extremely

außerstande [au·se·'ʃtan·də] *adj* ■**~, etw zu tun** unable to do sth

äußerste(r, s) *adj* ❶ (*entfernteste*) outermost; **am ~n Ende der Welt** at the farthest point of the globe; **der ~ Norden/Süden** the extreme north/south ❷ (*höchste*) utmost; **von ~r Wichtigkeit** of supreme importance; **der ~ Preis** the ultimate price

äußerstenfalls ['ɔy·sestn̩·'fals] *adv* at the most

Äußerung <-, -en> *f* comment

aus|setzen I. *vt* ❶ *Kind, Haustier* to abandon ❷ **eine Belohnung ~** to offer a reward ❸ (*preisgeben*) ■**jdn/etw etw** *dat* **~** to expose sb/sth to sth ❹ (*bemängeln*) **an etw** *dat* **etwas auszusetzen haben** to find fault with sth; **was hast du an ihr auszusetzen?** what don't you like about her?; **daran ist nichts auszusetzen** there's nothing wrong with that; *Motor* to fail II. *vi* (*versagen*) to stop; *Motor* to fail

Aussicht *f* ❶ (*Blick*) view; **ein Zimmer mit ~ aufs Meer** a room overlooking the sea ❷ (*Chance*) prospect; ■**die ~**

auf etw *akk* the chance of sth; **etw in ~ haben** to have good prospects of sth; **jdm etw in ~ stellen** to promise sb sth

aussichtslos *adj* hopeless

Aussichtsturm *m* lookout tower

aus|söhnen ['aus·zøː·nən] *vr* ■**sich** *akk* **~** to make [it] up; ■**sich** *akk* **mit jdm/etw ~** to reconcile with sb/to become reconciled with sth

aus|spannen I. *vi* to relax II. *vt* **jdm die Freundin/den Freund ~** (*fam*) to steal sb's girlfriend/boyfriend

aus|sperren I. *vt* ■**jdn ~** to lock sb out II. *vr* ■**sich** *akk* **~** to lock oneself out

aus|spielen *vt* ■**jdn gegen jdn ~** to play sb off against sb

aus|spionieren* *vt* to spy out

Aussprache *f* ❶ LING pronunciation ❷ (*Unterredung*) talk

aus|sprechen *irreg* I. *vt* ❶ LING to pronounce ❷ (*äußern*) to express; *Warnung* to issue; **ein Lob ~** to give a word of praise II. *vr* ■**sich** *akk* **~** ❶ (*sein Herz ausschütten*) to talk things over ❷ ■**sich** *akk* **für/gegen jdn/etw ~** to voice one's support for/opposition against sb/sth III. *vi* to finish [speaking]

Ausstand *m* ❶ (*Streik*) **im ~ sein** to be on strike; **in den ~ treten** to go on strike ❷ ÖSTERR, SCHWEIZ, SÜDD (*Ausscheiden aus Stelle o Schule*) going away; **seinen ~ geben** to hold a going-away party

aus|statten ['aus·ʃtatn̩] *vt* to equip; *Wohnung* to furnish

aus|stehen *irreg* I. *vt* **jdn/etw nicht ~ können** to not be able to stand sb/sth II. *vi* to be due; **die Antwort steht seit 5 Wochen aus** the reply has been due for 5 weeks

aus|steigen *vi irreg sein* (*aus Bus, Flugzeug, Zug*) to get off; (*aus dem Auto*) to get out of; **du kannst mich dort ~ lassen** you can drop me off over there

aus|stellen *vt* ❶ (*auf Messe, in Museum*) to exhibit ❷ **jdm] eine Rechnung ~** to issue [sb] an invoice; **sie ließ sich die Bescheinigung ~** she had the certificate made out in her name

Ausstellung f KUNST exhibition

aus|sterben vi irreg sein Pflanze, Tier to become extinct

Aussteuer <-, -n> f dowry

Ausstieg <-[e]s, -e> m ❶ (Öffnung) exit ❷ (fig) ■ **der ~ aus etw** dat abandoning sth; **der ~ aus der Kernenergie** abandoning [of] nuclear energy

aus|stoßen vt irreg ❶ Gase to emit ❷ Seufzer to utter; Schrei to give [out]; Laute to make ❸ ■ **jdn aus etw ~** to expel sb from sth

Ausstrahlung f ❶ (Charisma) **eine besondere ~ haben** to have a special charisma ❷ RADIO, TV broadcast[ing]

aus|strecken I. vt Hände, Beine to stretch out II. vr ■ **sich** akk **[auf dem Sofa] ~** to stretch oneself out [on the sofa]

aus|suchen vt to choose; ■ **[sich** dat**] etw ~** to choose sth; ■ **[sich** dat**] jdn ~** to pick sb

Austausch m exchange

austauschbar adj interchangeable; defekte Teile, Mensch replaceable

aus|tauschen I. vt ❶ (ersetzen) to replace (**gegen** +akk with) ❷ (miteinander wechseln) to exchange II. vr ■ **sich** akk **über etw/etw ~** to exchange stories about sb/sth

aus|teilen vt to distribute

Auster <-, -n> ['aus·tɐ] f oyster

Austernpilz m oyster mushroom

aus|toben vr ■ **sich** akk ~ to romp around

aus|tragen vt irreg ❶ Post, Zeitung to deliver ❷ Baby to carry to [full] term ❸ **einen Streit mit jdm ~** to have it out with sb ❹ SPORT Wettkampf to hold

aus|treiben irreg vt ❶ ■ **jdm etw ~** to knock sth out of sb ❷ Teufel to exorcise

aus|treten irreg I. vi sein Öl to leak; Gas to escape II. vt haben ❶ Feuer, Zigarette to stamp out ❷ Schuhe to wear out

aus|tricksen vt (fam) to trick

aus|üben vt ❶ Beruf to practice; Amt to hold; Aufgabe, Funktion to perform

❷ Macht, Recht to exercise; Druck, Einfluss to exert; Wirkung to have

aus|ufern ['aus·ʔuːfɐn] vi sein to escalate (**zu** +dat into)

Ausverkauf m clearance sale

ausverkauft adj sold out

Auswahl f ❶ (Warenangebot) selection (**an** +dat of) ❷ kein pl (das Aussuchen) **eine ~ treffen** to make one's choice (**unter** +dat from) ❸ SPORT all-star team

aus|wählen vt, vi to choose (**unter** +dat from)

Auswanderer, -wanderin m, f emigrant

aus|wandern vi sein to emigrate

auswärtig ['aus·vɛr·tɪç] adj attr POL **Auswärtiges ~** State Department

aus|wechseln [-ks-] vt to replace (**gegen** +akk with); Spieler to substitute (**gegen** +akk for)

Ausweg m way out; **der letzte ~** the last resort

ausweglos adj hopeless

aus|weichen vi irreg sein ❶ (vermeiden) ■ **etw** dat ~ to get out of the way [of sth] ❷ (als Alternative) ■ **auf etw** akk ~ to fall back on sth

Ausweis <-es, -e> ['aus·vais] m ID, identity card

aus|weisen irreg I. vt (abschieben) to deport II. vr ■ **sich** akk ~ to identify oneself; **können Sie sich ~?** do you have any [means of] identification?

Ausweispapiere pl identification [or ID] papers pl

Ausweisung f ADMIN deportation

aus|weiten I. vt to expand II. vr ■ **sich** akk ~ to extend; ■ **sich** akk **zu etw** dat ~ to escalate [into sth]

auswendig adv by heart; **etw ~ können** to know sth by heart

aus|wirken vr ■ **sich** akk ~ to have an effect

Auswirkung f effect

aus|wischen vt to wipe [clean] ►WENDUNGEN: **jdm eins ~** (fam) to put one over on sb

aus|zahlen I. vt ❶ Lohn, Betrag to pay

A

out ❷ *Kompagnon, Miterben* to buy out *sep* II. *vr* ■ **sich** *akk* [**für jdn**] ~ to pay [off] [for sb]

aus|zählen *vt* to count

aus|zeichnen I. *vt* ❶ *Ware* to price ❷ (*ehren*) to honor; **jdn mit einem Preis** ~ to give sb an award ❸ (*hervorheben*) **jdn** ~ to distinguish sb [from all others] II. *vr* ■ **sich** *akk* ~ to stand out

Auszeichnung *f* (*Medaille*) medal; (*Orden*) decoration; (*Preis*) award

aus|ziehen *irreg* I. *vt haben* ❶ *Kleidung* to take off *sep* ❷ *Zahn* to pull out *sep* II. *vr haben* ■ **sich** *akk* **ausziehen** to get undressed III. *vi sein* [**aus einem Haus**] ~ to move out [of a house]

Auszubildende(r) *f(m) dekl wie adj* trainee

Auszug *m* ❶ (*aus Wohnung*) move ❷ (*Ausschnitt*) excerpt ❸ (*Kontoauszug*) statement ❹ PHARM extract

authentisch [auˈtɛn·tɪʃ] *adj* authentic

Auto <-s, -s> [ˈauto] *nt* car; ~ **fahren** to drive; **mit dem ~ fahren** to take the car

Autoatlas *m* road atlas

Autobahn *f* highway, freeway; (*in Deutschland a.*) autobahn

Autobahndreieck *nt* highway junction

Autobahnkreuz *nt* highway intersection

Autobahnraststätte *f* service area

Autobiografieᴿᴿ, **Autobiographie** [au·to·bio·gra·ˈfiː] *f* autobiography

Autobus [ˈau·to·bʊs] *m*, **Autocar** [ˈau·to·kaːɐ̯] *m* SCHWEIZ bus

Autofahrer(in) *m(f)* [car] driver

autogen [au·to·ˈgeːn] *adj* ~**es Training** relaxation through self-hypnosis

Autogramm <-s, -e> [au·to·ˈgram] *nt* autograph

Autokennzeichen *nt* license plate; (*Länderkennzeichen*) international license plate code

Automat <-en, -en> [au·to·ˈmaːt] *m* (*Geldautomat*) ATM; (*Musikautomat*) jukebox; (*Spielautomat*) slot machine; (*Verkaufsautomat*) vending machine

Automatik <-, -en> [au·to·ˈmaː·tɪk] *f* AUTO automatic transmission

automatisch [au·to·ˈmaː·tɪʃ] *adj* automatic

automatisieren* [au·to·ma·ti·ˈziː·rən] *vt* to automate

autonom [au·to·ˈnoːm] *adj* POL autonomous

Autonomie <-, -n> [au·to·no·ˈmiː] *f* POL autonomy

Autopsie <-, -n> [au·tɔ·ˈpsiː] *f* MED autopsy

Autor, Autorin <-s, Autoren> [ˈauˑtɐ, auˈtoː·rɪn] *m, f* author

Autoradio *nt* car radio

Autoreifen *m* car tire

Autorennen *nt* motor race

autorisieren* [au·to·ri·ˈziː·rən] *vt* to authorize; **ich habe ihn dazu autorisiert** I gave him authorization for it

autoritär [au·to·ri·ˈtɛːɐ̯] *adj* authoritarian

Autorität <-, -en> [au·to·ri·ˈtɛːt] *f* authority

Autovermietung <-, -en> *f* car rental company

Axt <-, Äxte> [akst] *f* ax

Azoren [aˈtsoː·rən] *pl* ■ **die** ~ the Azores *npl*

Azubi [aˈtsuː·bi] *m* <-s, -s>, *f* <-, -s> *kurz für* **Auszubildende(r)**

Bb

B

B, b <-, -> [beː] *nt* ❶ (*Buchstabe*) B, b;
~ **wie Berta** B as in Bravo ❷ MUS
(*Note*) B flat

Baby <-s, -s> [ˈbeː·bi] *nt* baby

Babyklappe [ˈbeː·bi-] *f* hatch or container in which unwanted babies can be left anonymously

Babypause [ˈbeː·bi-] *f* parental leave

Babysitter(in) <-s, -> [ˈbeː·bi·zi·tɐ]
m(f) babysitter

Bach <-[e]s, Bäche> [bax] *m* brook
▶WENDUNGEN: **den ~ runtergehen**
(*fam*) to go down the drain

Backblech *nt* baking sheet

Backbord <-[e]s> [ˈbak·bɔrt] *nt kein pl*
NAUT port [side]

Backe <-, -n> [ˈba·kə] *f* cheek

backen <backt, backte, gebacken>
[ˈba·kn̩] *vt, vi* (*im Ofen*) to bake; (*in Fett*) to fry

Backenknochen *m* cheekbone

Backenzahn *m* molar

Bäcker(in) <-s, -> [ˈbɛ·kɐ] *m(f)* baker;
beim ~ at the baker's [shop]

Bäckerei <-, -en> [bɛ·kə·ˈrai] *f* bakery

Backfisch [ˈbak·fɪʃ] *m* batter-fried fish

Backform *f* baking pan

Backofen *m* oven

Backpulver *nt* baking powder

Bad <-[e]s, Bäder> [baːt] *nt* ❶ bath;
jdm/sich *dat* **ein ~ einlassen** to run
sb/oneself a bath ❷ (*Badezimmer*)
bathroom ❸ (*Schwimmbad*) swimming
pool ❹ (*Heilbad*) spa; (*Seebad*) seaside
resort

Badeanzug *m* swimsuit

Badehose *f* swim[ming] trunks *npl*

Badekappe *f* swim[ming] cap

Bademantel *m* bathrobe

Bademeister(in) *m(f)* lifeguard

baden [ˈbaː·dn̩] **I.** *vi* ❶ (*in Wanne*) to
take a bath ❷ (*schwimmen*) to swim;
~ **gehen** to go for a swim **II.** *vt* to bathe
III. *vr* ■**sich** *akk* ~ to take a bath

Badeort *m* ocean resort; (*Kurort*) spa resort

Badetuch *nt* bath towel

Badewanne *f* bathtub

Badezimmer *nt* bathroom

baff [baf] *adj* (*fam*) ■~ **sein** to be flabbergasted

Bagatelle <-, -n> [ba·ga·ˈtɛ·lə] *f* trifle

Bagger <-s, -> [ˈbagɐ] *m* BAU excavator

Bahamas [ba·ˈhaː·mas] *pl* ■**die ~** the
Bahamas *pl*

Bahn <-, -en> [baːn] *f* ❶ (*Eisenbahn*)
train; (*Straßenbahn*) streetcar; **mit der**
~ **fahren** to take the train/streetcar
❷ SPORT track; (*beim Schwimmen*) lane
▶WENDUNGEN: **freie ~ haben** to have
the go-ahead; **auf die schiefe ~ kommen** to get off the straight and narrow;
jdn aus der ~ werfen to get sb off
course

bahnen *vt* **sich** *dat* **einen Weg durch
etw** *akk* ~ to fight one's way through
sth

Bahnfahrt *f* train trip

Bahnhof *m* train station ▶WENDUNGEN:
nur [noch] ~ verstehen (*fam*) to not
have the foggiest [idea]

Bahnpolizei *f* railroad police

Bahnsteig <-[e]s, -e> *m* [train] platform

Bahnübergang *m* grade crossing

Bahnverbindung *f* [train] connection

Bahre <-, -n> [ˈbaː·rə] *f* stretcher

Bakterie <-, -n> [bak·ˈteː·ri̯ə] *f meist pl*
bacterium

Balance <-, -n> [ba·ˈlãː·sə] *f* balance

balancieren* [ba·lã·ˈsiː·rən] *vt, vi* to
balance

bald [balt] *adv* soon; **bis ~!** see you later!; **nicht so ~** not as soon; **wird's ~?**
move it!

Baldrian <-s, -e> *m* BOT valerian

Balearen [ba·le·ˈaː·rən] *pl* ■**die ~** the
Balearic Islands *pl*

B

Balkan <-s> ['bal·ka:n] m ❶ (Halbinsel, Länder) ■ der ~ the Balkans pl; auf dem ~ on the Balkans ❷ (Gebirge) Balkan Mountains pl

Balken <-s, -> ['bal·kn] m (a. sport) beam ►WENDUNGEN: **lügen, dass sich die ~ biegen** (fam) to lie through one's teeth

Balkon <-s, -s -s> [bal·'kɔŋ] m ❶ ARCHIT balcony ❷ THEAT dress circle

Ball¹ <-[e]s, Bälle> [bal] m ball ►WENDUNGEN: **am ~ bleiben/sein** to stay/be on the ball

Ball² <-[e]s, Bälle> [bal] m (Fest) ball

Ballast <-[e]s, -e> ['ba·last] m pl selten ❶ NAUT, LUFT ballast ❷ (fig) burden

Ballaststoffe pl fiber

ballen ['ba·lən] I. vt Faust to clench II. vr ■ **sich** akk to crowd [together]; Wolken to gather

Ballett <-[e]s, -e> [ba·'lɛt] nt ballet

Ballon <-s, -s> [ba·'lɔŋ] m balloon

Ballungsgebiet nt metropolitan area

Balsam <-s, -e> ['bal·za:m] m (a. fig) balm

Baltikum <-s> ['bal·ti·kʊm] nt ■ **das ~** the Baltic States

baltisch ['bal·tɪʃ] adj Baltic; s. a. **deutsch**

Bambus <-ses, -se> ['bam·bʊs] m bamboo

Bambussprossen pl bamboo shoots pl

banal [ba·'na:l] adj banal; Angelegenheit trivial

Banane <-, -n> [ba·'na:·nə] f banana

band [bant] imp von **binden**

Band¹ <-[e]s, Bänder> [bant] nt ❶ (aus Stoff) ribbon ❷ (Tonband) [recording] tape; **etw auf ~ aufnehmen** to tape[-record] sth ❸ meist pl ANAT ligament ►WENDUNGEN: **am laufenden ~** nonstop

Band² <-[e]s, Bände> [bant] m (Buch) volume ►WENDUNGEN: **Bände sprechen** to speak volumes

Band³ <-, -s> [bɛnt] f MUS band

Bandage <-, -n> [ban·'da:·ʒə] f bandage

bandagieren* [ban·da·'ʒi:·rən] vt to bandage

Bandbreite f ❶ (Spektrum) range ❷ INET, RADIO bandwidth

Bande <-, -n> ['ban·də] f gang

BänderrissRR ['bɛn·dɐ-] m torn ligament

bändigen ['bɛn·dɪ·gn] vt to tame

Bandit(in) <-en, -en> [ban·'di:t] m(f) bandit

Bandmaß nt tape measure

Bandscheibe f ANAT [intervertebral] disc; **es an den ~n haben** to have a slipped disc

Bandwurm m tapeworm

Bank¹ <-, Bänke> [baŋk] f bench ►WENDUNGEN: **[alle] durch die ~** every single one [of them]; **etw auf die lange ~ schieben** to put sth off

Bank² <-, -en> [baŋk] f FIN bank; **ein Konto bei einer ~ haben** to have a bank account

Bankangestellte(r) f(m) bank employee

Bankett <-[e]s, -e> [baŋ·'kɛt] nt banquet

Bankier <-s, -s> [baŋ·'kje:] m banker

Bankkonto nt bank account

Bankleitzahl f [bank] routing number

bankrott [baŋk·'rɔt] adj bankrupt; **jdn ~ machen** to bankrupt sb

Bankrott <-[e]s, -e> [baŋk·'rɔt] m bankruptcy

bankrott|gehenRR vi irreg sein to go bankrupt

Bankverbindung f bank account

Banner <-s, -> ['ba·nɐ] nt banner

bar [ba:ɐ̯] adj FIN cash; **[in] ~ bezahlen** to pay [in] cash

Bar <-, -s> [ba:ɐ̯] f bar

Bär <-en, -en> [bɛ:ɐ̯] m bear; **wie ein ~ schlafen** to sleep like a log ►WENDUNGEN: **jdm einen ~en aufbinden** to put sb on

Baracke <-, -n> [ba·'ra·kə] f shack

Bardame f barmaid

barfuß ['ba:ɐ̯·fu:s] adj pred barefoot[ed]

Bargeld nt cash

bargeldlos I. adj cashless II. adv without using cash

Barkauf m cash purchase

barmherzig [barm·ˈhɛr·tsɪç] *adj* compassionate; ■~ **sein** to show compassion

Barmherzigkeit <-> *f kein pl* mercy

Barmixer(in) <-s, -> *m(f)* bartender

Barock <-[s]> [ba·ˈrɔk] *nt o m kein pl* baroque

Barometer <-s, -> [baro·ˈmeː·tɐ] *nt* barometer

Barren <-s, -> [ˈba·rən] *m* ① SPORT parallel bars *pl* ② (*Goldbarren*) bar

Barriere <-, -n> [ba·ˈri̯eː·rə] *f* (*a. fig*) barrier

Barrikade <-, -n> [ba·ri·ˈkaː·də] *f* barricade

barsch [barʃ] *adj* curt

Barsch <-[e]s, -e> [barʃ] *m* perch

Bart <-[e]s, Bärte> [baːɐt] *m* ① beard; **sich** *dat* **einen ~ wachsen lassen** to grow a beard ② ZOOL whiskers

Barzahlung *f* cash payment

Basar <-s, -e> [ba·ˈzaːɐ] *m* bazaar

Base <-, -n> [ˈbaː·zə] *f* ① (*veraltet: Cousine*) cousin ② SCHWEIZ *s.* **Tante** aunt

basieren* [ba·ˈziː·rən] *vi* to be based

Basilikum <-s> [ba·ˈziː·li·kʊm] *nt kein pl* basil

Basis <-, Basen> [ˈbaː·zɪs] *f* ① (*Grundlage*) basis ② POL ■**die ~** the grass roots ③ MIL base

Baskenland *nt* ■**das ~** the Basque region

Baskenmütze *f* beret

BassRR <-es, Bässe>, **Baß**ALT <-sses, Bässe> [bas] *m* bass

basteln [ˈbas·tl̩n] I. *vi* ① (*als Hobby*) to do arts and crafts ② ■**an etw** *dat* **~** to work on sth II. *vt* to make

Batterie <-, -n> [ba·tə·ˈriː] *f* ELEK, MIL battery

batteriebetrieben *adj* battery-powered

Bau <-[e]s, -ten> [bau] *m* ① *kein pl* **im ~ sein** to be under construction ② (*Gebäude*) building ③ **auf dem ~ arbeiten** to work on a building site

Bauarbeiten *pl* construction [work] *sing*; **wegen ~ gesperrt** closed for repairs

Bauarbeiter(in) *m(f)* construction worker

Bauch <-[e]s, Bäuche> [baux] *m* belly; **sich** *dat* **den ~ vollschlagen** (*fam*) to stuff oneself ▶WENDUNGEN: **aus dem ~** from the heart; **aus dem hohlen ~** [heraus] off the top of one's head

Bauchfellentzündung *f* peritonitis

Bauchgefühl *nt kein pl* gut feeling

bauchig [ˈbaux·ɪç] *adj* bulbous

Bauchnabel *m* navel

Bauchschmerzen *pl* stomachache

Bauchspeicheldrüse *f* ANAT pancreas

Bauchtanz *m* belly dance

bauen [ˈbau·ən] I. *vt* to build II. *vi* ① (*Haus*) to build ② (*vertrauen*) ■**auf jdn/etw ~** to rely on sb/sth

Bauer, Bäuerin <-n, -n> [ˈbau·ɐ, ˈbɔyə·rɪn] *m*, *f* ① (*Landwirt*) farmer ② (*pej: ungehobelter Mensch*) yokel ③ (*Schachfigur*) pawn

Bauernhaus *nt* farmhouse

Bauernhof *m* farm

baufällig *adj* dilapidated

Baufirma *f* construction company

Baugelände *nt* construction site

Baugerüst *nt* scaffolding

Baugrube *f* [building] excavation

Bauholz *nt* lumber

Bauingenieur(in) *m(f)* civil engineer

Baujahr *nt* ① *von Gebäude* year of construction ② (*Produktionsjahr*) year of manufacture

Baukasten *m* construction set

Baum <-[e]s, Bäume> [baum] *m* tree ▶WENDUNGEN: **jd könnte Bäume ausreißen** sb is full of energy

Baumarkt *m* building supplies store

baumeln [ˈbau·ml̩n] *vi* to dangle (**an** + *dat* from)

Baumgrenze *f* tree line

Baumschule *f* tree nursery

Baumstamm *m* tree trunk

Baumsterben *nt* dying[-off] of trees

Baumwolle *f* cotton

Bauplan *m* building plans *pl*

Bauplatz *m* [construction] site

Bauschutt *m* construction waste

bausparen *vi nur infin* to have an account with a mortgage lender

B **Bausparkasse** *f* mortgage lender

Bausparvertrag *m* savings account for home construction

Baustelle *f* construction site

Bauunternehmer(in) *m(f)* builder

Bauwerk *nt* building; (*Brücke etc.*) construction

Bayer(in) <-n, -n> ['bai·ɐ] *m(f)* Bavarian; *s. a.* **Deutsche(r)**

bayerisch ['baiə·rɪʃ] *adj* Bavarian; *s. a.* **deutsch**

Bayern <-s> ['bai·ɐn] *nt* Bavaria; *s. a.* **Deutschland**

beabsichtigen* [bə·'ʔap·zɪç·tɪ·gn̩] *vt* to intend; **das hatte ich nicht beabsichtigt!** I didn't mean to do that!

beachten* [bə·'ʔax·tn̩] *vt* ① (*befolgen*) to observe; *Anweisung, Rat* to follow; **die Vorfahrt ~** to yield [the right of way] ② (*Aufmerksamkeit schenken*) ■**jdn/etw ~** to pay attention to sb/sth; **bitte ~ Sie, dass ...** please note that ...

beachtlich *adj* considerable; *Erfolg, Leistung* notable; *Verbesserung* marked

Beachtung *f* ① (*Befolgung*) observance; **~ der Vorschriften** compliance with the regulations ② (*Aufmerksamkeit*) **~ finden** to receive attention; **keine ~ finden** to be ignored; **jdm/etw ~ schenken** to pay attention to sb/sth

Beamte(r) [bə·'ʔam·tə, bə·'ʔam·te] *m dekl wie adj*, **Beamtin** <-, -nen> [bə·'ʔam·tɪn] *f* civil servant

beängstigend *adj* alarming

beanspruchen* [bə·'ʔan·ʃprʊ·xn̩] *vt* ① (*fordern*) to claim ② (*brauchen*) to require; *Platz, Zeit* to take up ③ (*Anforderungen stellen*) ■**jdn ~** to make demands on sb; **ich will Sie nicht länger ~** I don't want to take up any more of your time; ■**etw ~** to demand sth; **jds Zeit ~** to make demands on sb's time; **jds Geduld ~** to try sb's patience

beanstanden* [bə·'ʔan·ʃtan·dn̩] *vt* to complain about; **das ist beanstandet worden** there have been complaints about that

beantragen* *vt* to apply for; POL to propose

beantworten* *vt* to answer; ■**etw mit etw** *dat* **~** to respond to sth with sth

bearbeiten* *vt* ① (*behandeln*) to work on; **Holz ~** to work wood ② (*auf jdn einwirken*) ■**jdn ~** to work on sb; **wir haben ihn so lange bearbeitet, bis er zugesagt hat** we pressed him until he agreed

beatmen* *vt* to give artificial respiration to

beaufsichtigen* [bə·'ʔauf·zɪç·tɪ·gn̩] *vt* to supervise; *Kinder* to look after; (*bei Prüfung*) to proctor

beauftragen* *vt Architekt, Künstler* to commission; *Firma* to hire; ■**jdn mit etw** *dat* **~** to give sb the job of doing sth; ■**jdn ~, etw zu tun** to ask sb to do sth

Beauftragte(r) *f(m) dekl wie adj* representative

bebauen* *vt* ① *Grundstück* to build on; **dicht bebaut sein** to be heavily built-up ② *Acker, Feld* to cultivate

beben ['be:·bn̩] *vi* to tremble; **vor Zorn ~** to shake with anger

Becher <-s, -> ['bɛ·çɐ] *m* glass; (*aus Plastik*) cup; (*für Tee/Kaffee*) mug

Becken <-s, -> ['bɛ·kn̩] *nt* ① (*Bassin*) basin; (*Spülbecken*) sink; (*von Toilette*) bowl; (*Schwimmbecken*) pool ② ANAT pelvis ③ MUS cymbals *pl*

bedacht [bə·'daxt] **I.** *pp von* **bedenken** **II.** *adj* ① (*überlegt*) cautious ② ■**auf etw** *akk* **~ sein** to be concerned about sth

bedächtig [bə·'dɛç·tɪç] **I.** *adj* ① (*ohne Hast*) deliberate ② (*besonnen*) thoughtful **II.** *adv* ① (*ohne Hast*) deliberately; **~ sprechen** to speak in measured tones ② (*besonnen*) carefully

bedanken* *vr* ■**sich** *akk* **~** to express one's thanks; ■**sich** *akk* **bei jdm ~** to thank sb; **ich bedanke mich!** thank you!

Bedarf <-[e]s> [bə·'darf] *m kein pl* need (**an** +*dat* for); **der tägliche ~ an Vitaminen** the daily requirement of vitamins; **Dinge des täglichen ~s** everyday necessities; **bei ~** if required; **[je] nach ~** as required

bedauerlich adj regrettable; **sehr ~!** how unfortunate!; **■~ sein, dass …** to be unfortunate that …

bedauerlicherweise adv unfortunately

bedauern* vt ❶ **■etw ~** to regret sth ❷ **■jdn ~** to feel sorry for sb

Bedauern <-s> nt kein pl regret

bedauernswert adj Mensch pitiful; **ein ~er Zwischenfall** an unfortunate incident

bedeckt adj pred (bewölkt) overcast ▸WENDUNGEN: **sich** akk **~ halten** to keep a low profile

bedenken* irreg vt to consider; **[jdm] etw zu ~ geben** to ask [sb] to consider sth; **[jdm] zu ~ geben, dass …** to ask [sb] to keep in mind that …

Bedenken <-s, -> nt meist pl doubt; **~ haben** to have doubts; **moralische ~** moral scruples; **jdm kommen ~** sb has second thoughts; **ohne ~** without hesitation

bedenkenlos adv without hesitation

bedenklich adj ❶ (fragwürdig) questionable ❷ (Besorgnis erregend) disturbing; Gesundheitszustand serious; **jdn ~ stimmen** to give sb cause for concern

bedeuten* vt to mean; **das hat nichts zu ~** that doesn't mean a thing; **[jdm] etw ~** to mean something [to sb]

bedeutend adj ❶ (wichtig) important; Politiker leading; **eine ~e Rolle spielen** to play a significant role ❷ (beachtlich) considerable

bedeutsam adj ❶ (wichtig) important ❷ (vielsagend) meaningful

Bedeutung <-, -en> f ❶ (Sinn) meaning; **in wörtlicher/übertragener ~** in the literal/figurative sense ❷ (Wichtigkeit) importance; **[für jdn/etw] von ~ sein** to be of importance [to sb/sth]; **nichts von ~** nothing important

bedeutungslos adj insignificant

bedienen* I. vt ❶ Kunde, Gast to serve ❷ Maschine to operate ▸WENDUNGEN:

bedient sein (fam) to have had enough II. vi to serve; **wird hier nicht bedient?** isn't anyone working here? III. vr **■sich** akk [**mit etw** akk] **~** to help oneself [to sth]; **~ Sie sich!** help yourself!

Bedienung <-, -en> f ❶ (Kellner) waiter masc, waitress fem ❷ kein pl (Handhabung) operation ❸ kein pl (Service) service; **~ inbegriffen** service included

Bedienungsanleitung f [operating] instructions pl

bedingt adv **~ gültig** of limited validity

Bedingung <-, -en> f ❶ (Voraussetzung) condition; **unter der ~, dass …** on the condition that … ❷ pl (Umstände) conditions

bedingungslos adj unconditional; Gehorsam, Treue unquestioning

bedrohen* vt to threaten

bedrohlich adj threatening

bedrücken* vt to depress; **was bedrückt dich?** what's troubling you?

bedrückt adj depressed; **~es Schweigen** oppressive silence

Beduine, Beduinin <-n, -n> [bedu·'i:nə, bedu·'i:nɪn] m, f Bed[o]uin

Bedürfnis <-ses, -se> [bə·'dʏrf·nɪs] nt need; **die ~se des täglichen Lebens** everyday needs; **das ~ haben, etw zu tun** to feel the need to do sth

beeilen* vr **■sich** akk **~** to hurry [up]; **■sich** akk **~, etw zu tun** to hurry to do sth

beeindrucken* [bə·'ʔain·drʊ·kn̩] vt to impress; **sich** akk [**von etw** dat] **nicht ~ lassen** to not be impressed [by sth]

beeinflussen* [bə·'ʔain·flʊ·sn̩] vt to influence

beeinträchtigen* [bə·'ʔain·trɛç·tɪ·gn̩] vt to impair

beenden* vt to end

beerdigen* [bə·'ʔe:ɐ̯·dɪ·gn̩] vt to bury

Beerdigung <-, -en> f funeral

Beere <-, -n> ['be:rə] f berry

Beet <-[e]s, -e> [be:t] nt (Blumen) flower bed; (Gemüse) vegetable patch

befahren* adj Straße used; **kaum/ stark ~ sein** to be little/heavily used;

B

B

eine viel ~e Kreuzung a busy intersection

befangen [bəˈfaŋən] *adj* JUR biased; **jdn als ~ ablehnen** to disqualify sb on grounds of bias

befassen* *vr* **■sich** *akk* **mit etw** *dat* ~ to concern oneself with sth; **sich** *akk* **mit einem Problem ~** to tackle a problem; **■sich** *akk* **mit jdm ~** to spend time with sb

Befehl <-[e]s, -e> [bəˈfeːl] *m* order; **jdm den ~ geben, etw zu tun** to order sb to do sth

befehlen <befiehlt, befahl, befohlen> [bəˈfeːlən] *vt* to order; **von dir lasse ich mir nichts ~!** I won't take orders from you!

befestigen* *vt* to fasten (**an** +*dat* to)

befinden* *irreg* **I.** *vr* **■sich** *akk* **irgendwo ~** to be somewhere; **unter den Geiseln ~ sich zwei Deutsche** the hostages include two Germans **II.** *vi* **■über etw** *akk* ~ to decide [on] sth

befolgen* *vt Rat* to follow; *Befehl, Vorschrift* to obey

befördern* *vt* **①** (*transportieren*) to transport **②** (*beruflich*) to promote

Beförderung *f* **①** (*Transport*) transportation **②** (*beruflich*) promotion

befragen* *vt* to question

befreien* **I.** *vt* **①** *Gefangene* to free **②** *Volk, Land* to liberate **③** (*freistellen*) to excuse; *vom Wehrdienst* to exempt **④** (*von Schmerzen, Sorgen*) to free **II.** *vr* **■sich** *akk* **von etw** *dat* ~ to rid oneself of sth

Befreiung <-, -en> *f pl selten* **①** *von Gefangenen* release **②** *eines Volkes, Landes* liberation **③** (*Freistellung*) exemption

befreunden* [bəˈfrɔyn·dn̩] *vr* **■sich** *akk* **mit jdm ~** to make friends with sb; **mit jdm befreundet sein** to be friends with sb

befriedigen* [bəˈfriː·dɪ·gn̩] **I.** *vt* to satisfy; *Ansprüche, Wünsche* to fulfill; **leicht/schwer zu ~ sein** to be easily/not easily satisfied **II.** *vr* **■sich** *akk* [**selbst**] ~ to masturbate

befriedigend *adj* satisfactory; **■~ sein** to be satisfying

befristen* *vt* to limit (**auf** +*akk* to)

befugt [bəˈfuːkt] *adj* authorized

Befund <-[e]s, -e> *m* MED result[s *pl*]; **ohne ~** negative

befürchten* *vt* to fear; **■~, dass ...** to be afraid that ...

befürworten* [bəˈfyːɐ̯·vɔr·tn̩] *vt* to be in favor of

Befürworter(in) <-s, -> *m(f)* supporter

begabt [bəˈgaːpt] *adj* gifted, talented; **■für etw** *akk* ~ **sein** to have a gift for sth; **künstlerisch sehr ~ sein** to be very artistic

Begabung <-, -en> *f* gift, talent

begeben* *vr irreg* **sich** *akk* **in ärztliche Behandlung ~** to undergo medical treatment; **sich** *akk* **in Gefahr ~** to expose oneself to danger

begegnen* [bəˈgeːg·nən] **I.** *vi sein* **■jdm ~** to meet sb **II.** *vr sein* **■sich** *dat* ~ to meet

Begegnung <-, -en> *f* encounter

begehren* [bəˈgeː·ɐn] *vt* to desire

begehrenswert *adj* desirable

begehrt *adj Frau, Mann* desirable; *Preis* [much-]coveted; **ein ~er Junggeselle** an eligible bachelor

begeistern* **I.** *vt* to fill with enthusiasm **II.** *vr* **■sich** *akk* **für jdn/etw ~** to be enthusiastic about sb/sth

begeistert *adj* enthusiastic (**von** +*dat* about)

Begeisterung <-> *f kein pl* enthusiasm

Begierde <-, -n> [bəˈgiːɐ̯·də] *f* desire (**nach** +*dat* for)

begierig *adj* **①** (*gespannt*) eager (**auf** +*akk* for) **②** (*verlangend*) longing

Beginn <-[e]s> [bəˈgɪn] *m kein pl* beginning, start; **zu ~** at the beginning

beginnen <begann, begonnen> [bəˈgɪ·nən] *vt, vi* to begin

beglaubigen* [bəˈglau·bɪ·gn̩] *vt* to authenticate; **eine beglaubigte Kopie** a certified copy

begleichen* *vt irreg Schulden* to pay; *Rechnung* to settle

begleiten* *vt* (*a. fig*) to accompany; **jdn zur Tür ~** to show sb to the door

Begleiter(in) <-s, -> *m(f)* companion

Begleitung <-, -en> *f* company; **kommst du allein oder in ~?** are you coming by yourself or with someone?; **in** [jds *gen*] **~** accompanied by sb; **ohne ~** unaccompanied ❷ (*Begleiter(in)*]) companion ❸ MUS accompaniment; **ohne ~ spielen** to play unaccompanied

beglückwünschen* *vt* to congratulate (**zu** + *dat* on)

begnadigen* [bə·'gna:·dɪ·gn̩] *vt* to pardon

begnügen* *vr* **sich** *akk* **mit etw** *dat* **~** to be satisfied with sth

begraben* *vt irreg* ❶ (*beerdigen*) to bury ❷ (*aufgeben*) *Hoffnung, Plan* to abandon; **einen Streit ~** to bury the hatchet

Begräbnis <-ses, -se> [bə·'grɛp·nɪs] *nt* burial

begreifen* *irreg* I. *vt* to comprehend; **■~, dass ...** to realize that ...; **kaum zu ~ sein** to be incomprehensible II. *vi* **langsam/schnell ~** to be slow/quick on the uptake

begreiflich *adj* understandable; **jdm etw ~ machen** to make sth clear to sb

begrenzen* *vt* to limit; **die Geschwindigkeit auf ... km/h ~** to impose a speed limit of ... kmph

Begriff <-[e]s, -e> *m* ❶ (*Ausdruck*) term; **ein ~ aus der Philosophie** a philosophical term ❷ (*Vorstellung*) idea; **jdm ein/kein ~ sein** to mean sth/nothing to sb; **für jds ~e** in sb's opinion ▶WENDUNGEN: **im ~ sein, etw zu tun** to be about to do sth; **schnell/schwer von ~ sein** (*fam*) to be quick/slow on the uptake

begriffsstutzig *adj* slow on the uptake

begründen* *vt* to give reasons for; *Ablehnung, Forderung* to justify; *Behauptung, Verdacht* to substantiate

begründet *adj* well-founded; **in etw** *dat* **~ liegen** to be the result of sth

Begründung <-, -en> *f* reason

begrüßen* *vt* to greet; **es ist zu ~, dass ...** it is a good thing that ...

Begrüßung <-, -en> *f* greeting; **offizielle ~** official welcome

begünstigen [bə·'gyn·stɪ·gn̩] *vt Export, Wachstum* to encourage; **von etw** *dat* **begünstigt werden** to be helped by sth

behagen [bə·'ha:·gn̩] *vi* **■etw behagt jdm** sb likes sth

behaglich [bə·'ha:k·lɪç] *adj* ❶ (*gemütlich*) cozy; **es sich** *dat* **~ machen** to make oneself comfortable ❷ **ein ~es Schnurren** a contented purring

behalten* *vt irreg* ❶ (*nicht wegwerfen*) to keep ❷ (*nicht verraten*) **etw für sich** *akk* **~** to keep sth to oneself ❸ **die Nerven ~** to keep one's composure ❹ (*sich merken*) to remember; **etw im Kopf ~** to keep sth in one's head

Behälter <-s, -> *m* container

behandeln* *vt* to treat; **jdn gut/schlecht ~** to treat sb well/badly

Behandlung <-, -en> *f* treatment

beharren* *vi* to insist; **auf seiner Meinung ~** to stick to one's opinion

beharrlich *adv* persistently; **~ schweigen** to persist in remaining silent

behaupten* [bə·'haʊp·tn̩] I. *vt* to claim; **■von jdm ~, dass ...** to say of sb that ...; **■es wird behauptet, dass ...** it is said that ...; **seinen Vorsprung gegen jdn ~** SPORT to maintain one's lead over sb II. *vr* **■sich** *akk* **~** to assert oneself; **sich** *akk* **gegen die Konkurrenz ~ können** to hold one's own against the competition

Behauptung <-, -en> *f* assertion; **eine ~ aufstellen** to make an assertion

beheben* *vt irreg Fehler, Mangel* to rectify; *Missstände* to remedy; *Schaden, Störung* to repair

Behelf <-[e]s, -e> [bə·'hɛlf] *m* [temporary] replacement

beherbergen* *vt* to accommodate

beherrschen* I. *vt* ❶ *Land* to rule ❷ (*im Griff haben*) to control; **ein Fahrzeug ~** to have control over a vehicle ❸ **ein Instrument ~** to play an in-

B

strument well; **eine Sprache ~** to have good command of a language; **alle Tricks ~** to know all the tricks II. *vr* ∎ **sich** *akk* **~** to control oneself

behilflich [bə-'hɪlf·lɪç] *adj* ∎ **jdm ~ sein** to help sb

behindern* *vt* to hinder

behindert *adj* **geistig/körperlich ~** mentally/physically disabled

Behinderte(r) *f(m) dekl wie adj* disabled person; ∎ **die B~n** the disabled

Behinderung <-, -en> *f* ❶ TRANSP **es muss mit ~en gerechnet werden** delays should be expected ❷ MED **geistige/körperliche ~** mental/physical disability

Behörde <-, -n> [bə-'høːɐ̯·də] *f* department; ∎ **die ~n** the authorities

bei [bai] *präp* +*dat* ❶ (*in der Nähe*) near; **eine Stadt ~ Köln** a town near Cologne ❷ ∎ **~ jdm [zu Hause]** at sb's place; **~ uns zu Hause** at our place; **ich war ~ meinen Eltern** I was at my parents' [house]; **er ist ~ der Bahn** he works for the railroad; **~ wem nimmst du Klavierstunden?** who's your piano teacher?; **~m Bäcker/Friseur** at the bakery/hairdresser's ❸ **etw ~ sich** *dat* **haben** to have sth on one; **ich habe gerade kein Geld ~ mir** I don't have any money on me at the moment ❹ (*zeitlich*) **~ Tag/Nacht** by day/night; **~m Lesen kann ich nicht Radio hören** I cannot read and listen to the radio at the same time; **störe mich bitte nicht ~ der Arbeit!** please stop disturbing me while I'm working!; **~ dem Zugunglück starben viele Menschen** many people died in the train crash ❺ (*Begleitumstände*) **wir können das ja ~ einer Flasche Wein besprechen** let's talk about it over a bottle of wine; **~ deinen Fähigkeiten** with your talents; **~ 45° unter null** at 45° below zero [Celsius]; **~ dieser Hitze/Kälte** in such heat/cold; **~ Nebel/Regen** when it is foggy/raining; **~ Wind und Wetter** come rain or shine ❻ (*ungefähr*) around; **der Preis**

liegt ~ 1.000 Euro the price is around 1,000 euros

bei|behalten* *vt irreg* to maintain; *Tradition, Brauch* to uphold; *Meinung* to stick to

bei|bringen *vt irreg* ∎ **jdm etw ~** to teach sb sth ►WENDUNGEN: **jdm etw schonend ~** to break sth gently to sb

Beichte <-, -n> ['baiç·tə] *f* confession; **die ~ ablegen** to make one's confession; **jdm die ~ abnehmen** to hear sb's confession

beichten ['baiç·tn̩] I. *vt* ∎ [**jdm**] **etw ~** to confess sth [to sb] II. *vi* **~ gehen** to go to confession

beide ['bai·də] *pron* both; **meine ~n Töchter** my two daughters; **alle ~** both of them; **~ Mal[e]** both times; **keiner von ~n** neither of them; ∎ **ihr ~** the two of you; **ihr habt ~ Recht** both of you are right; ∎ **wir ~** the two of us; ∎ **die ~n** both [of them]; **die ersten/ letzten ~n** the first/last two; **einer von ~n** one of the two; ∎ **~s** both; **~s ist möglich** both are possible

beiderlei ['bai·dɐ·'lai] *adj attr* both

beieinander [bai·ʔai·'nan·dɐ] *adv* together ►WENDUNGEN: **gut/schlecht sein** (*fam: körperlich*) to be in good/bad shape; (*geistig*) to be with it/not all there

Beifahrer(in) *m(f)* front-seat passenger

Beifahrersitz *m* [front] passenger seat

Beifall <-[e]s> *m kein pl* applause; **[jds** *akk*] **~ finden** to meet with [sb's] approval; **~ klatschen** to applaud

bei|fügen *vt* ❶ (*mitsenden*) to enclose ❷ (*hinzufügen*) to add

beige [beːʃ, 'beː·ʒə] *adj* beige

bei|geben *vt irreg* ►WENDUNGEN: **klein ~** to give in

Beihilfe *f* financial aid

Beil <-[e]s, -e> [bail] *nt* [short-handled] ax

Beilage *f* ❶ (*Speise*) side dish ❷ (*Beiheft*) supplement

beiläufig *adv* **etw ~ erwähnen** to mention sth in passing

bei|legen *vt* ❶ **einem Brief einen**

Rückumschlag ~ to enclose a return envelope in a letter ② **einen Streit** ~ to settle a dispute

Beileid *nt* condolence[s *pl*]; **[mein] herzliches** ~ [you have] my heartfelt sympathy; **jdm [zu etw** *dat*] **sein** ~ **aussprechen** to offer sb one's condolences [on sth]

bei|**liegend** *adj* enclosed; ~ **finden Sie ...** please find enclosed ...

Bein <-[e]s, -e> [bain] *nt* leg; **jdm auf die** ~ **e helfen** to help sb back on his/her feet; **jdm ein** ~ **stellen** to trip sb; **die** ~ **e übereinanderschlagen** to cross one's legs; **unsicher auf den** ~ **en sein** to be unsteady on one's feet ►WENDUNGEN: **sich** *dat* **die** ~ **e in den Bauch stehen** to be standing around for ages; **wieder auf die** ~ **e kommen** (*gesundheitlich*) to be up on one's feet again; (*finanziell*) to regain one's financial standing; **mit dem linken** ~ **zuerst aufgestanden sein** to have gotten up on the wrong side of the bed; **auf den** ~ **en sein** (*auf sein*) to be up and about; **etw auf die** ~ **e stellen** to get sth going

beinahe ['bai·na:ə] *adv* almost

Beinbruch *m* leg fracture ►WENDUNGEN: **das ist kein** ~! (*fam*) it's not as bad as all that!

beinhalten* [bə·'ʔɪn·hal·tn̩] *vt* to contain

Beipackzettel *m* instruction sheet

beirren* *vt* ■ **sich** *akk* [**nicht**] ~ **lassen** to [not] let oneself be put off

Beisammensein *nt* get-together

beiseite [bai·'zai·tə] *adv* to one side

beiseite|**gehen**^RR *vi irreg sein* to step aside

beiseite|**legen**^RR *vi irreg* ■ **etw** ~ (*weglegen*) to put sth to one side; *Geld* to put aside *sep* sth

bei|**setzen** *vt* (*geh*) to inter; *Urne* to install

Beisetzung <-, -en> *f* (*geh*) interment; *einer Urne* installing [in its resting place]

Beispiel <-[e]s, -e> ['bai·ʃpi:l] *nt* example; **anschauliches** ~ illustration; **praktisches** ~ demonstration; **zum** ~

for example; **wie zum** ~ such as ►WENDUNGEN: **mit gutem** ~ **vorangehen** to set a good example

beispielsweise *adv* for example

beißen <biss, gebissen> ['bai·sn̩] **I.** *vt* to bite ►WENDUNGEN: **etw/nichts zu** ~ **haben** (*fam*) to have something/nothing to eat **II.** *vi* ① (*mit den Zähnen*) ■ **auf/in etw** *akk* ~ to bite into sth ② (*brennen*) to sting; *Säure* to burn; **in den Augen** ~ to make one's eyes sting ►WENDUNGEN: **an etw** *dat* **zu** ~ **haben** to have sth to chew on **III.** *vr* ① ■ **sich** *akk* **o** *dat* **auf die Zunge** ~ to bite one's tongue ② ■ **sich** *akk* [**mit etw** *dat*] ~ *Farben* to clash [with sth]

beißend *adj* ~ **er Geruch** pungent smell; ~ **e Kälte** bitter cold; ~ **e Kritik** sharp criticism; ~ **er Witz** caustic humor

bei|**stehen** *vi irreg* ■ **jdm** ~ to stand by sb

Beitrag <-[e]s, -träge> ['bai·tra:k] *m* ① (*für Verein*) fee; (*für Versicherung*) premium ② (*Artikel*) article ③ (*Mitwirkung*) contribution; **einen** ~ **zu etw** *dat* **leisten** to make a contribution to sth ④ SCHWEIZ (*Subvention*) subsidy

beitragspflichtig *adj* liable to pay contributions

Beitragssatz *m* membership rate

bei|**treten** *vi irreg sein* to join [as a member]; **der EU** ~ to join the EU

Beitritt *m* entry (**zu** +*dat* into); **der** ~ **zur EU** the accession to the EU

Beiwagen *m* sidecar

beizeiten [bai·'tsai·tn̩] *adv* in good time

beizen ['bai·tsn̩] *vt* ① **etw** [**braun/schwarz**] ~ to stain sth [brown/black] ② KOCHK to marinade

bejahen* [bə·'ja:·ən] *vt* ① *Frage* to say yes to ② (*gutheißen*) to approve [of]

bekämpfen* **I.** *vt* to fight; *Schädlinge* ~ to control pests **II.** *vr* ■ **sich** *akk* [**gegenseitig**] ~ to fight one another

bekannt [bə·'kant] *adj* ① (*allgemein gekannt*) well-known; **etw ist allgemein** ~ sth is common knowledge; **etw** ~ **geben** to announce sth; *Presse* to

B

publish sth; **etw ~ machen** to make sth known to the public ❷ *(berühmt)* **jdn ~ machen** to make sb famous; **~ werden** to become famous; **für etw** *akk* **~ sein** to be well-known for sth ❸ *(nicht fremd)* familiar; **ist dir dieser Name ~?** are you familiar with this name?; **mit jdm ~ sein** to be acquainted with sb

Be̱kannte(r) *f(m) dekl wie adj* acquaintance; **ein guter ~r** a friend

bekanntlgeben *vt irreg s.* **bekannt 1**

bekanntlich *adv* as is [generally] known

bekanntlmachen *vt s.* **bekannt 1, 2**

Bekanntschaft <-, -en> *f* ❶ *pl selten* *(das Bekanntsein)* acquaintance; **eine nette ~ machen** to meet a nice person; **mit etw** *dat* **~ machen** *(iron)* to get to know sth ❷ *(Bekannte[r])* acquaintance; *(Bekanntenkreis)* acquaintances *pl*

bekehren* *vt* to convert

bekennen* *irreg* I. *vt* to confess II. *vr* ❶ *(eintreten für)* ■ **sich** *akk* **zu jdm/etw ~** to declare one's support for sb/sth; **sich** *akk* **zu einem Glauben ~** to profess a faith ❷ *(zugeben)* **sich** *akk* **zu einem Irrtum/einer Tat ~** to admit [to] a mistake/doing sth

bekifft [bə·ˈkɪft] *adj (fam)* stoned

beklagen* I. *vt* to lament; **bei dem Unglück waren 23 Tote zu ~** the accident claimed 23 lives II. *vr* ■ **sich** *akk* [**bei jdm**] **~** to complain [to sb]

beklagenswert *adj* lamentable; *Irrtum, Versehen* unfortunate

bekleckern* *(fam)* I. *vt* to stain II. *vr* **sich** *akk* **mit Soße ~** to spill sauce all over oneself

Bekleidung *f* clothing

beklommen [bə·ˈklɔ·mən] *adj* anxious

bekloppt [bə·ˈklɔpt] *adj (fam) s.* **bescheuert**

bekömmlich [bə·ˈkœm·lɪç] *adj* [easily] digestible

bekümmert *adj* worried

beladen* *irreg vt* to load [up *sep*]

Belag <-[e]s, Beläge> [bə·ˈlaːk] *m* ❶ *(Schicht)* coating ❷ *(für Pizza, Brot)* topping; *(für Sandwich)* filling ❸ *(auf Zähnen)* film; *(auf Zunge)* fur

belagern* *vt* to besiege

belangen* *vt* JUR to prosecute (**wegen** +*gen* for)

belanglos *adj* irrelevant

belassen* *vt irreg* ❶ **es bei etw** *dat* **~** to leave it at sth; **~ wir es dabei!** let's leave it at that ❷ **etw an seinem Platz ~** to leave sth in its place

belasten* *vt* ❶ *(mit Gewicht)* to load ❷ *(seelisch)* to burden; **jdn mit Problemen ~** to burden sb with problems; **jdn [schwer] ~** to weigh [heavily] on one's mind; ■ **~d** crippling ❸ *(körperlich)* to strain; **jdn/etw zu sehr ~** to overstrain sb/sth; **etw belastet das Herz** sth puts a strain on the heart ❹ JUR to incriminate; **~des Material** incriminating evidence ❺ **die Umwelt ~** to pollute the environment ❻ FIN **ein Konto [mit 100 Euro] ~** to debit [100 euros from] an account; **etw mit einer Hypothek ~** to mortgage sth

belästigen* [bə·ˈlɛs·tɪ·ɡn] *vt* to pester; **jdn sexuell ~** to harass sb sexually

Belästigung <-, -en> *f* annoyance; **sexuelle ~** sexual harassment

Belastung <-, -en> *f* ❶ *(Gewicht)* load ❷ *(seelisch)* burden ❸ *(körperlich)* strain (**für** +*akk* on) ❹ ÖKOL pollution

belaufen* *vr irreg* ■ **sich** *akk* **auf etw** *akk* **~** to amount to sth

beleben* I. *vt Konjunktur* to stimulate; *Party, Unterhaltung* to liven up II. *vr* ■ **sich** *akk* **~** to liven up; *Konjunktur* to be stimulated

belebend *adj* refreshing

Beleg <-[e]s, -e> [bə·ˈleːk] *m* ❶ ÖKON receipt ❷ *(Beweis)* proof

belegen* *vt* ❶ **ein Brot mit etw** *dat* **~** to put sth on a slice of bread; **belegte Brote** [open-faced] sandwiches ❷ **eine Behauptung ~** to substantiate a claim; **ein Zitat ~** to give a reference for a quotation ❸ **einen Kurs ~** to enroll for a class ❹ *(besetzen)* to occupy; ■ **belegt sein** to be occupied; **ist der Stuhl hier schon belegt?** is this chair free?

⑤ SPORT **den vierten Platz ~** to take fourth place

Belegschaft <-, -en> f staff; (*Arbeiter*) workforce

belegt adj *Stimme* hoarse

belehren* vt **sich** akk **von jdm ~ lassen** to listen to sb

beleibt [bə·'laipt] adj corpulent

beleidigen* [bə·'lai·dɪ·ɡn̩] vt to insult

Beleidigung <-, -en> f insult

belesen [bə·'le:·zn̩] adj well-read

beleuchten* vt ① (*durch Licht*) to light [up *sep*] ② (*fig: betrachten*) to throw light on

Beleuchtung <-, -en> f ① pl selten lighting; **die ~ der Straßen** street lighting ② AUTO lights pl

Belgien <-s> ['bɛl·ɡiən] nt Belgium; *s. a.* **Deutschland**

Belgier(in) <-s, -> ['bɛl·ɡiɐ] m(f) Belgian; *s. a.* **Deutsche(r)**

belgisch ['bɛl·ɡɪʃ] adj Belgian; *s. a.* **deutsch**

Belichtung f FOTO exposure

Belieben nt [ganz] **nach ~** just as you/they etc. like

beliebig [bə·'li:·bɪç] I. adj any; **eine ~ e Zahl** any number at all; **jeder B~e** anyone at all II. adv ~ **lange/viele** as long/many as you like; **etw ~ verändern** to change sth at will

beliebt [bə·'li:pt] adj popular (**bei** + dat with); **sich** akk [**bei jdm**] **~ machen** to make oneself popular [with sb]

Beliebtheit <-> f kein pl popularity

beliefern* vt to supply

bellen ['bɛ·lən] vi to bark

belohnen* vt to reward

Belohnung <-, -en> f reward; **eine ~ aussetzen** to offer a reward

Belüftung f ventilation no indef art

belügen* irreg I. vt **jdn ~** to lie to sb II. vr **sich** akk selbst **~** to deceive oneself

bemängeln* [bə·'mɛ·ŋl̩n] vt to find fault with

bemerkbar adj noticeable; **sich** akk [**bei jdm**] **~ machen** to attract [sb's] attention; **ich werde mich schon ~**

machen, wenn ich Sie benötige I'll let you know when I need you

bemerken* vt ① (*wahrnehmen*) to notice ② (*äußern*) to say

bemerkenswert adj remarkable

Bemerkung <-, -en> f remark; **eine ~ über etw** akk **machen** to remark on sth; **eine ~ fallen lassen** to drop a remark

bemitleiden* [bə·'mɪt·lai·dn̩] I. vt to pity II. vr **sich** akk [**selbst**] **~** to feel sorry for oneself

bemitleidenswert adj pitiful

bemühen* vr **sich** akk **~** to try hard; **sich** akk **vergebens ~** to try in vain; **sich** akk **um eine Stelle ~** to try hard to get a job

Bemühung <-, -en> f effort; **danke für Ihre ~en** thank you for your trouble

bemuttern* [bə·'mʊ·tɐn] vt to mother

benachbart [bə·'nax·baːɐ̯t] adj neighboring attr; **das ~e Haus** the house next door

benachrichtigen* [bə·'naːx·rɪç·tɪɡn̩] vt to inform; (*amtlich*) to notify

Benachrichtigung <-, -en> f notification

benachteiligen* [bə·'naːx·tai·lɪ·ɡn̩] vt to put at a disadvantage; (*wegen Rasse, Geschlecht, Glaube*) to discriminate against

Benachteiligung <-, -en> f **die ~ einer Person** discrimination against sb

benehmen* vr irreg **sich** akk **~** to behave [oneself]; **benimm dich!** behave yourself!; **sich** akk **gut/schlecht ~** to behave well/badly

Benehmen <-s> nt kein pl manners pl

beneiden* vt **jdn [um etw] ~** to envy sb [sth]

beneidenswert adj enviable

benennen* vt irreg to name (**nach** + dat after); **Gegenstände ~** to denote objects

Bengel <-s, -[s]> ['bɛ·ŋl̩] m rascal

benommen [bə·'nɔ·mən] adj dazed; **jdn ~ machen** to throw sb

benötigen* vt to need

benutzen* vt, **benützen*** vt DIAL,

B

ÖSTERR ❶ (gebrauchen) to use; **den Aufzug ~** to take the elevator ❷ (ausnutzen) ■**jdn ~** to take advantage of sb; **sich akk benutzt fühlen** to feel [that one has been] used

Benutzer(in) <-s, -> m(f), **Benützer(in)** <-s, -> m(f) DIAL, ÖSTERR COMPUT user

Benutzerhandbuch nt user manual

Benutzername m COMPUT user name

Benutzeroberfläche f COMPUT user interface

Benutzung f, **Benützung** f DIAL, ÖSTERR use; **jdm etw zur ~ überlassen** to put sth at sb's disposal

Benzin <-s, -e> [bɛn·'tsi:n] nt gas[oline]

Benzintank m gas tank

Benzinverbrauch m gas consumption

beobachten* [bə·'ʔo:b·ax·tn̩] vt ❶ (betrachten) to observe; ■**jdn [bei etw dat] ~** to watch sb [doing sth]; **gut beobachtet!** good observation! ❷ (überwachen) ■**beobachtet werden** to be kept under surveillance; ■**jdn ~ lassen** to put sb under surveillance ❸ (bemerken) ■**etw an jdm ~** to notice sth in sb

Beobachter(in) <-s, -> m(f) observer

Beobachtung <-, -en> f ❶ (das Betrachten) observation ❷ (Überwachung) surveillance ❸ meist pl (Feststellung) observations pl

bequem [bə·'kve:m] adj ❶ (angenehm) comfortable; **es sich** dat **~ machen** to make oneself comfortable; **ein ~es Leben haben** to have an easy life ❷ (pej: träge) idle

Bequemlichkeit <-, -en> f ❶ (Behaglichkeit) comfort ❷ (Trägheit) idleness; **aus [reiner] ~** out of [sheer] laziness

beraten* irreg I. vt to advise; **jdn finanziell ~** to give sb financial advice; ■**sich** akk **[von jdm] ~ lassen** to ask sb's advice II. vi ■**über etw** akk **~** to discuss sth III. vr ■**sich** akk **[über etw** akk**] ~** to discuss sth; POL to debate sth

Berater(in) <-s, -> m(f) advisor

Beratung <-, -en> f ❶ kein pl (das Beraten) advice ❷ (Besprechung) dis-

cussion; POL debate ❸ (beratendes Gespräch) consultation

berauschend adj intoxicating

berechenbar [bə·'rɛ·çn̩·ba:g] adj ❶ MATH calculable ❷ (voraussehbar) predictable

berechnen* vt ❶ MATH to calculate ❷ (in Rechnung stellen) to charge

berechnend adj (pej) scheming

Berechnung f ❶ MATH calculation; **nach meiner ~** according to my calculations ❷ (pej: Eigennutz) scheming; **aus ~** in cold deliberation

berechtigt [bə·'rɛç·tɪçt] adj Anspruch, Frage, Hoffnung legitimate; **ein ~er Vorwurf** a just accusation; ■**[dazu] ~, etw zu tun** to be entitled to do sth

Bereich <-[e]s, -e> m area

bereichern* [bə·'rai·çɐn] vr ■**sich** akk **[an etw** dat**] ~** to grow rich [on sth]

bereisen* vt ■**etw ~** to travel around sth; **die Welt ~** to travel the world

bereit [bə·'rait] adj meist pred ❶ (fertig) ready; (vorbereitet) prepared ❷ (willens) ■**zu etw** dat **~ sein** to be prepared to do sth; **sich** akk **~ erklären, etw zu tun** to agree to do sth

bereiten* vt to cause; Freude, Überraschung to give; **jdm Kopfschmerzen ~** to give sb a headache

bereits [bə·'raits] adv already; **~ damals** even then

Bereitschaft <-, -en> [bə·'rait·ʃaft] f kein pl ❶ willingness; **seine ~ zu etw** dat **erklären** to express one's willingness to do sth ❷ kein pl (Bereitschaftsdienst) emergency service; **~ haben** Apotheke to provide emergency services; Arzt, Feuerwehr to be on call; (im Krankenhaus) to be on duty; Polizei, Soldaten to be on stand-by

Bereitschaftsdienst m emergency service

bereit|stellen vt ■**etw [für jdn/etw] ~** to provide [sb/sth with] sth

bereitwillig I. adj Auskunft given willingly; Helfer willing; Verkäufer obliging; **~e Hilfe** eager hands II. adv readily

B

bereuen* *vt* to regret; **das wirst du noch** ~! you'll be sorry [for that]!

Berg <-[e]s, -e> [bɛrk] *m* ① GEOG mountain; (*kleiner*) hill; **am** ~ **liegen** to lie at the foot of the hill ② (*große Menge*) ■ ~-**e von etw** *dat* piles of sth; ~**e von Papier** mountains of paper ▶WENDUNGEN: **über** alle ~**e sein** to be miles away; **mit etw** *dat* **hinterm** ~ halten to keep quiet about sth; **über den** ~ sein to be out of the woods; **die Patientin ist noch nicht über den** ~ the [female] patient is still in critical condition

bergab [bɛrk·ˈʔap] *adv* (*a. fig*) downhill; **mit seinem Geschäft geht es** ~ his business is going downhill

Bergarbeiter(in) *m(f)* miner

bergauf [bɛrk·ˈʔauf] *adv* uphill; **es geht wieder** ~ (*fig*) things are looking up

Bergbahn *f* mountain railroad

Bergbau *m kein pl* mining

bergen <birgt, barg, geborgen> [ˈbɛrgn] *vt* to rescue; (*aus* +*dat* from); *Giftstoffe, Tote* to recover; *Schiff* to salvage

Bergführer(in) *m(f)* mountain guide

Berggipfel *m* mountain top

Bergkette *f* mountain range

Bergrutsch *m* landslide

Bergsteigen <-s> *nt kein pl* mountain climbing

Bergsteiger(in) <-s, -> *m(f)* mountain climber

Bergung <-, -en> *f* rescuing; *eines Schiffs* salvaging; *von Toten* recovering

Bergwacht <-, -en> *f* mountain rescue service

Bergwand *f* mountain face

Bergwerk *nt* mine

Bericht <-[e]s, -e> [bə·ˈrɪçt] *m* report

berichten* I. *vt* ① (*mitteilen*) to tell ② SCHWEIZ **falsch/recht berichtet** wrong/right; **bin ich falsch/recht berichtet, wenn ich annehme ...?** am I wrong/right in assuming ...? II. *vi* ① ■ **über etw** *akk* ~ to report on sth; **wie unser Korrespondent berichtet** according to our correspondent; **wie soeben berichtet wird, ...** we are just

receiving reports that ... ② (*Bericht erstatten*) ■ **jdm** ~ to tell sb ③ SCHWEIZ (*erzählen*) to talk

Berichterstattung <-, -en> *f* reporting (**über** +*akk* on)

berichtigen* [bə·ˈrɪç·tɪ·gn] *vt* to correct

Berlin <-s> [bɛr·ˈliːn] *nt* Berlin

Berliner[1] <-s, -> [bɛr·ˈliː·nɐ] *m* (*Gebäck*) ≈ jelly donut

Berliner[2] [bɛr·ˈliː·nɐ] *adj attr* Berlin

Bernstein [ˈbɛrn·ʃtain] *m kein pl* amber

berüchtigt [bə·ˈrʏç·tɪçt] *adj* notorious (**für** +*akk* for)

berücksichtigen* [bə·ˈrʏk·zɪç·tɪ·gn] *vt* to take into consideration; ■ ~, **dass ...** to bear in mind that ...

Beruf <-[e]s, -e> [bə·ˈruːf] *m* occupation; (*Stellung*) job; **sie ist Ärztin von** ~ she's a doctor; **was sind Sie von** ~? what do you do [for a living]?; **ein akademischer** ~ an academic profession; **ein handwerklicher** ~ a trade

berufen[1] *adj* ■ **zu etw** *dat* ~ **sein** to have a vocation for sth; **sich** *akk* ~ **fühlen, etw zu tun** to feel a calling to do sth

berufen*[2] *irreg* I. *vt* ■ **jdn zu etw** *dat* ~ to appoint sb to sth II. *vr* ■ **sich** *akk* **auf jdn/etw** ~ to refer to sb/sth III. *vi* JUR ÖSTERR (*Berufung einlegen*) to [file an] appeal

beruflich I. *adj* professional; ~**e Aussichten** career prospects; ~**e Laufbahn** career II. *adv* as far as work is concerned; **was macht sie** ~? what does she do [for a living]?; **sich** *akk* ~ **weiterbilden** to attend professional seminars/workshops; ~ **unterwegs sein** to be away on business; ~ **verhindert sein** to be detained by work

Berufsakademie *f* university which combines three years of college-level academics with on-the-job training

Berufsausbildung *f* [professional] training; (*zum Handwerker*) apprenticeship

Berufsberater(in) *m(f)* career advisor

Berufsberatung *f* ① (*Beratungsstelle*)

B

career advisory service ② (*das Beraten*) career advice

berufserfahren *adj* [professionally] experienced

Berufskrankheit *f* occupational disease

Berufsleben *nt* professional life

Berufspendler(in) *m(f)* commuter

Berufsschule *f* vocational school

berufstätig *adj* working; **■ ~ sein** to be employed; **sie ist nicht mehr ~** she's no longer working

Berufsverkehr *m* rush-hour traffic

Berufung <-, -en> *f* ① JUR appeal; **in die ~ gehen** to file an appeal ② (*in ein Amt*) appointment ③ (*innerer Auftrag*) vocation (**zu** +*dat* for) ④ (*das Sichbeziehen*) **unter ~ auf jdn/etw** with reference to sb/sth

beruhen* *vi* **■ auf etw** *dat* **~** to be based on sth ▶WENDUNGEN: **etw auf sich** *akk* **~ lassen** to drop sth

beruhigen* [bə·'ruː·ɪ·gn] I. *vt* to calm down; *Sept; Nerven* to soothe; *Schmerzen* to ease; **dieses Getränk wird deinen Magen ~** this drink will settle your stomach; **jds Gewissen ~** to ease sb's conscience; **den Verkehr ~** to introduce traffic-calming measures II. *vr* **■ sich** *akk* **~** to calm down; *politische Lage* to stabilize; *Meer* to grow calm; *Unwetter* to die down

Beruhigungsmittel *nt* sedative

berühmt [bə·'ryːmt] *adj* famous

Berühmtheit <-, -en> *f* ① *kein pl* (*Ruf*) fame; **~ erlangen** to rise to fame ② (*Mensch*) celebrity

berühren* *vt* ① (*anfassen*) to touch ② (*seelisch*) **■ etw berührt jdn** sth moves sb; **das berührt mich überhaupt nicht!** I couldn't care less!

besänftigen* [bə·'zɛnf·tɪ·gn] I. *vt* to soothe II. *vr* **■ sich** *akk* **~** to calm down; *Sturm, Unwetter* to die down

Besatzung <-, -en> [bə·'za·tsʊŋ] *f* ① (*Mannschaft*) crew ② MIL occupation

besaufen* *vr irreg* (*fam*) **■ sich** *akk* **~** to get sloshed

beschädigen* *vt* to damage

Beschädigung <-, -en> *f* damage

beschaffen*¹ I. *vt* **■ [jdm] etw ~** to get sth [for sb] II. *vr* **■ sich** *dat* **etw ~** to get sth; **du musst dir Arbeit ~** you've got to find yourself a job

beschaffen² *adj* **■ so ~ sein, dass …** to be made in such a way that …

beschäftigen* [bə·'ʃɛf·tɪ·gn] I. *vt* ① *Firma etc.* to employ ② **■ jdn** [**mit etw** *dat*] to keep sb busy [with sth] ③ (*gedanklich*) **■ jdn ~** to be on sb's mind; **mit einer Frage/einem Problem beschäftigt sein** to be preoccupied with a question/problem II. *vr* **■ sich** *akk* [**mit etw** *dat*] **~** to occupy oneself [with sth]; **hast du genug, womit du dich ~ kannst?** do you have enough to do?; **■ sich** *akk* **mit jdm ~** to pay attention to sb; **du musst dich mehr mit den Kindern ~** you should spend more time with the children

beschäftigt [bə·'ʃɛf·tɪçt] *adj* ① (*angestellt*) employed; **wo bist du ~?** where do you work? ② (*befasst*) busy

Beschäftigte(r) *f(m) dekl wie adj* employee

Beschäftigung <-, -en> *f* ① (*Anstellung*) employment, job ② (*Tätigkeit*) occupation ③ *mit Literatur, Musik* study (**mit** +*dat* of)

beschämt *adj* **■ über etw** *akk* **~ sein** to be ashamed of sth

beschatten* *vt* to shadow

beschaulich *adj* peaceful; **ein ~es Leben führen** to lead a contemplative life

Bescheid <-[e]s, -e> [bə·'ʃait] *m* information; ADMIN answer; **~ erhalten** to be informed; **jdm ~ geben** to inform sb; **jdm ~ sagen, dass …** to let sb know that …; **ich habe noch keinen ~** I still haven't heard anything; [**über etw** *akk*] **~ wissen** to know [about sth] ▶WENDUNGEN: **jdm ordentlich ~ sagen** to give sb a piece of one's mind

bescheiden [bə·'ʃai·dn] *adj* modest; **ein ~es Leben führen** to lead a humble life

bescheinigen* [bə·'ʃai·nɪ·gn] *vt* **■ jdm etw ~** to certify sth for sb *form*; **■ [jdm]**

~, dass ... to confirm [to sb] in writing that ...; ■**sich** *dat* **etw ~ lassen** to have sth certified

Bescheinigung <-, -en> *f* certification

bescheißen* *irreg* (*derb*) **I.** *vt* ■**jdn ~** to rip off *sep* sb *sl* **II.** *vi* ■[**bei etw** *dat*] **~** to cheat [at sth]

beschenken* *vt* ■**jdn ~** to give sb a present; **reich beschenkt werden** to be showered with presents; ■**sich** *akk* [**gegenseitig**] **~** to give each other presents

Bescherung <-, -en> *f* giving of Christmas presents ▶WENDUNGEN: [**das ist ja**] **eine schöne ~!** (*iron*) what a fine mess!

bescheuert (*fam*) **I.** *adj* ❶ (*blöd*) screwy; **dieser ~e Kerl** that stupid idiot; **der ist etwas ~** he's got a screw loose *fam* ❷ (*unangenehm*) stupid; **so was B~es!** how stupid! **II.** *adv* stupidly; **du siehst total ~ aus** you look totally ridiculous; **sich** *akk* **~ anstellen** to act like an idiot

beschimpfen* *vt* to insult; ■**sich** *akk* [**gegenseitig**] **~** to insult each other

beschissen (*vulg*) **I.** *adj* lousy **II.** *adv* in a lousy fashion; **es geht ihr wirklich ~** she's miserable; **~ aussehen/behandelt werden** to look /be treated like shit *vulg*

beschlagen* *irreg* *vi* *sein* Spiegel, Scheibe to fog up

beschlagnahmen* [bə·ˈʃlaːk·naː·mən] *vt* to confiscate

beschleunigen* [bə·ˈʃlɔy·nɪ·gn̩] **I.** *vt* to accelerate; Tempo to increase; Schritte to quicken; Vorgang to speed up **II.** *vi* Fahrzeug to accelerate

Beschleunigung <-, -en> *f* acceleration

beschließen* *irreg* **I.** *vt* ❶ (*entscheiden*) to decide; **ein Gesetz ~** to pass a motion ❷ (*beenden*) to conclude **II.** *vi* ■**über etw** *akk* **~** to decide on sth

Beschluss^{RR} <-es, Beschlüsse> *m* decision

beschmutzen* **I.** *vt* ❶ to dirty up

❷ (*fig*) to tarnish **II.** *vr* ■**sich** *akk* **~** to get oneself dirty

Beschneidung <-, -en> *f* MED, REL circumcision

beschönigen* [bə·ˈʃøː·nɪ·gn̩] *vt* to gloss over

beschränken* **I.** *vt* to limit (**auf** +*akk* to); **jdn in seinen Rechten ~** to limit sb's rights **II.** *vr* ■**sich** *akk* [**auf etw** *akk*] **~** to restrict oneself [to sth]; **sich** *akk* **auf das Wesentliche ~** to keep to the essential points

beschränkt *adj* restricted; Sicht low; Intelligenz limited; Sichtweise narrow-minded; **finanziell/räumlich/zeitlich ~ sein** to have a limited amount of cash/space/time; **Gesellschaft mit ~er Haftung** corporation

Beschränkung <-, -en> *f* restriction

beschreiben* *vt* *irreg* (*darstellen*) to describe

Beschreibung <-, -en> *f* description; (*Gebrauchsanweisung*) instructions *pl*

beschriften [bə·ˈʃrɪf·tn̩] *vt* **einen Umschlag ~** to address an envelope

beschuldigen* [bə·ˈʃʊl·dɪ·gn̩] *vt* ■**jdn** [**einer S.** *gen*] **~** to accuse sb [of sth]

Beschuldigung <-, -en> *f* accusation

beschützen* *vt* to protect (**vor** +*dat* from)

Beschützer(in) <-s, -> *m(f)* protector

Beschwerde <-, -n> [bə·ˈʃveː·ɐ·də] *f* complaint; **Grund zur ~ haben** to have grounds for complaint; **~n mit etw** *dat* **haben** to have problems with sth; **mein Magen macht mir ~n** my stomach is giving me trouble

beschweren* [bə·ˈʃveː·rən] **I.** *vr* ■**sich** *akk* **~** to complain **II.** *vt* to weight [down]

beschwerlich *adj* difficult; **das Laufen ist für ihn sehr ~** walking is hard for him

beschwichtigen* [bə·ˈʃvɪç·tɪ·gn̩] *vt* to soothe

beschwingt **I.** *adj* lively; Mensch *a.* vivacious **II.** *adv* **sich** *akk* **~ fühlen** to feel elated

beschwipst [bə·ˈʃvɪpst] *adj* (*fam*) tipsy

B

beschwören* vt irreg ■ etw ~ to swear [to] sth; ~ **kann ich das nicht** I wouldn't like to swear to it

beseitigen* [bə·ˈzai·tɪ·gn̩] vt ① (*entfernen*) to dispose of; *Missverständnis, Zweifel* to clear up; *Hindernis* to clear away; *Fehler* to eliminate; *Ungerechtigkeiten* to abolish ② (*euph: umbringen*) to eliminate

Besen <-s, -> [ˈbeː·zn̩] m ① (*Kehrbesen*) broom; (*kleiner*) brush; *einer Hexe* broomstick ② (*pej fam: kratzbürstige Frau*) old bag ③ SÜDD (*fam*) Swabian vineyard's wine bar, indicated by a broom hanging outside the door ▶ WENDUNGEN: **ich fresse einen ~, wenn ...** (*fam*) I'll eat my hat if ...

besessen [bə·ˈzɛ·sn̩] adj obsessed (**von** +*dat* with); **wie ~** like crazy

besetzen* vt *Land, Stühle, Plätze* to occupy; **die Leitung ist besetzt** the line is busy; **ein Haus ~** to squat in a house; **einen Posten ~** to fill a post

Besetztzeichen nt busy signal

besichtigen* [bə·ˈzɪç·tɪ·gn̩] vt to visit; *Betrieb* to take a tour of; *Haus, Wohnung* to view

Besichtigung <-, -en> f visiting; *von Haus, Wohnung etc.* viewing; **eine ~ der Sehenswürdigkeiten** a sightseeing tour; **die ~ einer Stadt** a tour of a town

Besinnung <-> f kein pl consciousness; **die ~ verlieren** to faint; [**wieder**] **zur ~ kommen** to come around

besinnungslos adj ① unconscious; ■ **~ werden** to pass out ② (*fig*) *Wut* blind; **~ vor Angst** blind with fear

Besitz <-es> [bə·ˈzɪts] m kein pl ① (*Eigentum*) property; (*Vermögen*) possessions pl ② (*das Besitzen*) possession; **in den ~ einer S.** gen **gelangen** to come into possession of sth; **in privatem**/**staatlichem ~** privately-/state-owned

besitzen* vt irreg ① *Eigentum* to own ② (*haben*) to have [got]; **die Frechheit ~, etw zu tun** to have the nerve to do sth; **jds Vertrauen ~** to have sb's confidence

Besitzer(in) <-s, -> m(f) owner; *eines Geschäfts etc.* proprietor; **den ~ wechseln** to change hands

besitzergreifend adj possessive

besoffen [bə·ˈzɔfn̩] adj (*fam*) sloshed; **total ~** hammered sl

besondere(r, s) [bə·ˈzɔn·də·rə, -ərɐ, -ərəs] adj exceptional; **ein ~s Interesse an etw** dat **haben** to be especially interested in sth; **von ~r Bedeutung** of great significance; **~n Wert auf etw** akk **legen** to attach great importance to sth

besonders [bə·ˈzɔn·dɐs] adv ① (*außergewöhnlich*) particularly; [**nicht**] **~ klug**/**fröhlich** [not] especially bright/happy; **~ viel** a great deal ② (*vor allem*) in particular, above all ③ (*fam*) **nicht ~ sein** to be nothing out of the ordinary; **jd fühlt sich** akk **nicht ~** sb does not feel too good

besonnen [bə·ˈzɔ·nən] adj sensible; **~ bleiben** to stay calm

besorgen* vt ① (*kaufen*) to buy ② (*beschaffen*) to get; **sich** dat **einen Job ~** to find oneself a job ▶ WENDUNGEN: **es jdm ~** (*fam: verprügeln*) to beat up sep sb; (*derb: sexuell befriedigen*) to do sb

besorgt [bə·ˈzɔrkt] adj worried (**wegen** +*gen* about); ■ **um jdn**/**etw ~ sein** to be concerned about sb/sth; **ein ~es Gesicht machen** to look troubled

besprechen* irreg vt ① (*erörtern*) to discuss; **wie besprochen** as agreed ② *Buch, Film* to review ③ *Kassette* to make a recording on

Besprechung <-, -en> f ① (*Konferenz*) meeting ② (*Unterredung*) discussion

besser [ˈbɛ·sɐ] I. adj komp von **gut** better; *Qualität* superior; **etwas**/**nichts B~es** something/nothing better ▶ WENDUNGEN: **jdn eines B~en belehren** to enlighten sb; **ich lasse mich gerne eines B~en belehren** I'm willing to admit [it when] I'm wrong II. adv ① **es geht jdm ~** sb feels better ② (*fam: lieber*) better; **dem solltest du ~ aus dem Wege gehen!** it would be better if you avoided him! ▸WENDUNGEN: **es ~ haben** to be better off

bessern ['bɛ·sen] *vr* ■ **sich** *akk* ~ to improve; *Person* to better oneself

Besserung <-> *f kein pl* improvement; **gute ~!** get well soon!; **auf dem Weg der ~ sein** to be on one's way to recovery

Besserwisser(in) <-s, -> *m(f)* (*pej*) know-it-all

Bestand <-[e]s, Bestände> *m* ❶ *kein pl* (*Fortdauer*) survival; **~ haben** to be long-lasting ❷ (*Vorrat*) supply (**an** +*dat* of)

beständig *adj* ❶ (*gleich bleibend*) consistent; *Wetter* steady ❷ (*widerstandsfähig*) resistant (**gegen** +*akk* to)

Bestandteil *m* part; SCI component; **notwendiger ~** essential part; **etw in seine ~e zerlegen** to dismantle

bestärken* *vt* ■ **jdn** [**in etw** *dat*] ~ to encourage sb['s sth]; **jdn in einem Verdacht ~** to reinforce sb's suspicion

bestätigen* [bə·'ʃtɛː·tɪ·gn] I. *vt* to confirm; **die Richtigkeit einer S.** *gen* ~ to verify sth II. *vr* ■ **sich** *akk* ~ to prove to be true

Bestätigung <-, -en> *f* confirmation; (*Schriftstück*) certification

bestatten* [bə·'ʃta·tn] *vt* (*geh*) to bury

Bestattung <-, -en> *f* (*geh*) funeral

Bestattungsinstitut *nt* (*geh*) funeral home

beste(r, s) ['bɛs·tɐ, 'bɛs·tɐ, 'bɛs·təs] *adj superl von* **gut** *attr* best; **„mit den ~n Wünschen"** "best wishes"; **in ~r Laune** in the best of spirits; ■ **am ~n ...** it would be best if ...; **es wäre am ~n, wenn Sie jetzt gingen** you had better leave now

bestechen* *irreg* I. *vt* *Beamte* to bribe II. *vi* to be impressive; ■ **durch etw** *akk* ~ to impress with sth

bestechlich [bə·'ʃtɛç·lɪç] *adj* corrupt

Bestechung <-, -en> *f* bribery

Besteck <-[e]s, -e> [bə·'ʃtɛk] *nt* KOCHK cutlery *n sing*

bestehen* *irreg* I. *vt* *Prüfung* to pass; ■ **etw nicht ~** to fail sth; **die Prüfer**

ließen ihn nicht ~ the inspectors failed him II. *vi* ❶ (*existieren*) to be; + *Zeitangabe* to exist; **es ~ gute Aussichten, dass ...** the prospects are good that ...; **es besteht die Gefahr, dass ...** there is a danger of ...; **das Problem/der Unterschied besteht darin, dass ...** the problem/difference is that ...; **es besteht kein Zweifel** there is no doubt; **~ bleiben** to last; *Versprechen* to remain; **etw ~ lassen** to retain sth ❷ (*sich zusammensetzen*) to consist (**aus** +*dat* of); *Material* to be made (**aus** +*dat* [out] of) ❸ (*beharren*) ■ **auf etw** *dat* ~ to insist on sth; **auf einer Meinung ~** to stick to an opinion; ■ **darauf ~, dass ...** to insist that ...; **wenn Sie darauf ~!** if you insist!

besteigen* *vt irreg* *Berg* to climb [[up] onto]; *Bus* to get on; *Flugzeug* to board; *Pferd* to mount; *Podest* to get up onto; *Schiff* to go on board; *Taxi* to get into; *Thron* to ascend

bestellen* *vt* ❶ *Ware* to order (**bei** +*dat* from) ❷ *Tisch* to reserve ❸ (*Handwerker*) to ask to come; *Taxi* to call ❹ (*ausrichten*) to tell; **können Sie ihr etwas ~?** may I leave a message for her?; **[jdm] Grüße ~** to send [sb] one's regards ▸WENDUNGEN: **wie bestellt und nicht abgeholt** (*hum fam*) standing around looking like a lost sheep; **mit etw** *dat* **ist es schlecht bestellt** things look bad for sth

Bestellnummer *f* order number

Bestellung <-, -en> *f* order

bestenfalls ['bɛs·tn̩·'fals] *adv* at best

bestens ['bɛs·tn̩s] *adv* very well

bestialisch [bɛs·'tɪaː·lɪʃ] I. *adj* atrocious; *Gestank* revolting; *Schmerz* excruciating; **~ stinken** to stink to high heaven II. *adv* (*fam*) dreadfully

Bestie <-, -n> ['bɛs·tɪə] *f* ❶ (*Tier*) beast ❷ (*Mensch*) brute

bestimmen* I. *vt* ❶ (*festsetzen*) ■ **etw ~** to decide on sth; *Ort, Preis, Zeit* to fix ❷ (*vorsehen*) **für jdn/etw bestimmt sein** to be for sb/sth; **füreinander bestimmt** meant for each oth-

B

er II. *vi* ■ über jdn/etw ~ to control sb/sth

bestimmt [bə·ˈʃtɪmt] I. *adj* ❶ (*speziell*) particular; **ganz ~e Vorstellungen** very particular ideas ❷ (*festgelegt*) *Tag, Termin* set ❸ LING **ein ~er Artikel** a definite article ❹ (*entschieden*) *Auftreten* firm II. *adv* ❶ (*sicher*) definitely; **ganz ~** [sooner or later]; **Sie sind ~ derjenige, der …** you must be the person who …; **das ist ~ für dich** *Anruf, Besuch* it must be for you; **etw ganz ~ wissen** to be positive about sth; **~ nicht** certainly not ❷ (*entschieden*) determinedly

Bestimmung <-, -en> *f* ❶ (*Vorschrift*) regulation ❷ (*Schicksal*) destiny

bestmöglich [ˈbɛst·ˈmøːk·lɪç] *adj* best possible

bestrafen* *vt* to punish; **etw wird mit Gefängnis bestraft** sth is punishable by imprisonment

Bestrafung <-, -en> *f* punishment; **zur ~** as a punishment

Bestrahlung <-, -en> *f* MED radiotherapy

bestrebt *adj* ■ ~ **sein, etw zu tun** to be eager to do sth

bestreiken* *vt* to go on strike against; **dieser Betrieb wird bestreikt** there is a strike in progress at this company

bestreiten* *vt irreg* ❶ (*leugnen*) to deny; *Behauptung* to reject; **es lässt sich nicht ~, dass …** it cannot be denied that … ❷ (*finanzieren*) *Kosten* to cover; **seinen Unterhalt ~** to earn a living

bestürmen* *vt* to bombard

bestürzt I. *adj* upset; **zutiefst ~** deeply dismayed II. *adv* in a dismayed manner

Besuch <-[e]s, -e> [bə·ˈzuːx] *m* ❶ (*das Besuchen*) visit (**bei/in** +*dat* to); **jdm einen ~ abstatten** to pay sb a visit; (*kurz*) to drop in on sb; **[bei jdm] auf ~ sein** to be visiting [sb]; **ich bin hier nur zu ~** I'm just visiting ❷ (*Besucher*) visitor[s]; (*eingeladen*) guest[s]

besuchen* *vt* ❶ *Menschen, Museum etc.* to visit; *Konzert* to attend; **besuch mich bald mal wieder!** come again soon! ❷ (*teilnehmen*) **einen Kurs ~** to take a class; **die Schule ~** to go to school

Besucher(in) <-s, -> *m(f)* visitor, guest; *Kino* moviegoer; *Theater* theatergoer; *Sportveranstaltung* spectator; **ein regelmäßiger ~** a frequenter

Besuchszeit *f* visiting hours *pl*

betätigen* I. *vt Schalter* to press; *Hebel* to operate II. *vr* ■ **sich** *akk* ~ to busy oneself; **sich** *akk* **politisch ~** to be politically active; **sich** *akk* **sportlich ~** to exercise

betäuben* [bə·ˈtɔy·bn̩] *vt* ❶ (*narkotisieren*) to anesthetize; **die Entführer betäubten ihr Opfer** the kidnappers drugged their victim ❷ (*fig*) *Schmerz* to kill; **seinen Kummer mit Alkohol ~** to drown one's sorrows in alcohol

Betäubungsmittel *nt* anesthetic

beteiligen* [bə·ˈtai·lɪ·gn̩] I. *vt* to give a share (**an** +*dat* of/in) II. *vr* ■ **sich** *akk* [**an etw** *dat*] ~ to participate [in sth]; (*an einem Unternehmen*) to have a stake in

beteiligt [bə·ˈtai·lɪçt] *adj* ■ **an etw** *dat* ~ **sein** (*mit dabei*) to be involved in sth ❷ FIN, ÖKON to hold a stake in sth

beten [ˈbeː·tn̩] I. *vi* to pray II. *vt* to recite

beteuern* [bə·ˈtɔy·ɐn] *vt* ■ **jdm ~, dass …** to protest to sb that …; **seine Unschuld ~** to protest one's innocence

Beton <-s, *selten* -s> [be·ˈtɔŋ, be·ˈtõː] *m* concrete

betonen* *vt* ❶ (*hervorheben*) to stress; **die Figur** to accentuate ❷ LING *Wort* to stress

betonieren* [be·to·ˈniː·rən] *vt* to concrete

betont I. *adj* emphatic; **~e Höflichkeit** studied politeness II. *adv* markedly

Betonung <-, -en> *f* LING stress

Betracht [bə·ˈtraxt] *m* **in ~ kommen** to be considered; **etw außer ~ lassen** to disregard sth; **jdn/etw in ~ ziehen** to consider sb/sth

betrachten* *vt* ❶ (*anschauen*) to look at; **bei näherem B~** [up]on closer examination ❷ (*halten für*) to regard (**als +*akk*** as)

beträchtlich [bə'trɛçt·lɪç] *adj* considerable; *Schaden* extensive

Betrag <-[e]s, Beträge> [bə'traːk] *m* amount

betragen* *irreg* **I.** *vi* to be; **die Rechnung beträgt 10 Euro** the bill comes to 10 euros **II.** *vr* ■ **sich** *akk* ~ to behave

Betragen <-s> *nt kein pl* behavior; SCH conduct

betreffen* *vt irreg* ❶ (*angehen*) ■ **jdn** ~ to concern sb; ■ **etw** ~ to affect sth; **was das betrifft, ...** as far as that is concerned ❷ (*bestürzen*) ■ **jdn ...** ~ to affect sb ...

betreffend *adj attr* ❶ (*erwähnt*) in question *pred*; **die ~e Person** the person in question ❷ (*in Bezug auf*) concerning

betreten*¹ *vt irreg* Haus, Zimmer to enter

betreten² *adj* embarrassed

betreuen* [bə'trɔʏ·ən] *vt* Kind to look after

Betrieb <-[e]s, -e> [bə'triːp] *m* ❶ (*Firma*) company ❷ *kein pl* (*Betriebsamkeit*) activity; **heute war nur wenig/herrschte großer** ~ it was very quiet/busy today ❸ (*Tätigkeit*) operation; **etw in** ~ **nehmen** to put sth into operation; **außer** ~ out of order; **in** ~ in operation

Betriebsanleitung *f* [operating] instructions *pl*

Betriebsarzt, -ärztin *m, f* company doctor

Betriebsausflug *m* staff outing

Betriebsferien *pl* vacation close-down

Betriebsklima *nt* work atmosphere

Betriebskosten *pl* operating costs; *einer Maschine* running costs

Betriebsleitung *f* management

Betriebsrat *m* employee representative committee

Betriebssystem *nt* COMPUT operating system

Betriebsunfall *m* ≈ occupational accident (*accident at or on the way to or from work*)

Betriebswirtschaft *f* business management

betrinken* *vr irreg* ■ **sich** *akk* [**mit etw** *dat*] ~ to get drunk [on sth]

betroffen I. *pp von* **betreffen II.** *adj* shocked; **~es Schweigen** stunned silence **III.** *adv* **jdn** ~ **anschauen** to look at sb with dismay; ~ **schweigen** to be too upset to say anything

betrübt *adj* sad

Betrug <-[e]s, SCHWEIZ Betrüge> [bə'truːk] *m* fraud

betrügen* *irreg* **I.** *vt* ❶ (*vorsätzlich täuschen*) to cheat (**um +*akk*** out of); **ich fühle mich betrogen!** I feel betrayed! ❷ (*durch Seitensprung*) ■ **jdn** [**mit jdm**] ~ to be unfaithful to sb [with sb] **II.** *vr* **sich** *akk* **selbst** ~ to deceive oneself

Betrüger(in) <-s, -> [bə'tryː·gɐ] *m(f)* con man

betrunken [bə'trʊn·kn̩] *adj* drunken *attr*, drunk *pred*

Bett <-[e]s, -en> [bɛt] *nt* bed; **jdn ins** ~ **bringen** to put sb to bed; **ins** ~ **gehen** to go to bed; **jdn aus dem** ~ **holen** to get sb out of bed; **das** ~ **hüten müssen** to be confined to [one's] bed

Bettbezug *m* duvet cover

Bettdecke *f* blanket; (*Steppdecke*) duvet

betteln ['bɛ·tl̩n] *vi* to beg (**um +*akk*** for)

bettlägerig *adj* bedridden

Bettlaken *nt s.* **Betttuch**

Bettler(in) <-s, -> ['bɛt·lɐ] *m(f)* beggar

BetttuchRR, **Bettuch**ALT ['bɛt·tuːx] *nt* sheet

Bettwäsche *f* bed linens *pl*

Bettzeug *nt* bedding

betüddeln [bə'tʏ·dl̩n] *vt* (*fam*) to coddle

beugen ['bɔʏ·gn̩] **I.** *vt* ❶ (*neigen*) to bend; *Kopf* to bow ❷ LING (*konjugieren*) to conjugate; (*deklinieren*) to decline **II.** *vr* ❶ (*sich neigen*) **sich** *akk* **nach vorn/hinten** ~ to bend forward/backward; **sich** *akk* **aus dem Fenster** ~ to lean out [of] the window ❷ (*sich unterwerfen*) ■ **sich** *akk* [**jdm/etw**] ~ to

B

submit [to sb/sth]; **ich werde mich der Mehrheit ~** I will bow to the majority

Beule <-, -n> ['bɔy·lə] *f* ❶ (*Delle*) dent ❷ (*Schwellung*) bump

beunruhigen* [bə·'ʔʊn·ruː·ɪ·gn̩] *vt* to worry

beurkunden* [bə·'ʔuːɐ̯·kʊn·dn̩] *vt* to certify

beurlauben* [bə·'ʔuːɐ̯·lau·bn̩] *vt* ❶ (*Urlaub geben*) to give time off; **können Sie mich für eine Woche ~?** can you give me a week off? ❷ (*suspendieren*) to suspend; **Sie sind bis auf weiteres beurlaubt** you are suspended until further notice

beurteilen* *vt* ❶ (*einschätzen*) to judge ❷ (*abschätzen*) to assess

Beurteilung <-, -en> *f* assessment

Beute <-> ['bɔy·tə] *f kein pl* ❶ (*Jagdbeute*) prey ❷ (*erbeutete Dinge*) loot; **[fette] ~ machen** to make a [big] haul

Beutel <-s, -> ['bɔy·tl̩] *m* ❶ (*Tasche*) bag ❷ ZOOL pouch

Bevölkerung <-, -en> *f* population

bevölkerungsreich *adj* populous

bevollmächtigen* *vt* to authorize

bevor [bə·'foːɐ̯] *konj* before; **■ nicht ~** not until

bevormunden* [bə·'foːɐ̯·mʊn·dn̩] *vt* to treat like a child

bevor|stehen *vi irreg* ❶ (*zu erwarten haben*) **■ jdm ~** to await sb; **der schwierigste Teil steht dir erst noch bevor!** the most difficult part is yet to come! ❷ (*bald kommen*) **■ etw steht bevor** sth is approaching

bevorzugen* [bə·'foːɐ̯·tsuː·gn̩] *vt* to prefer; **keines unserer Kinder wird bevorzugt** none of our children receive preferential treatment; **hier wird niemand bevorzugt!** there's no favoritism around here!

bewachen* *vt* to guard

bewahren* *vt* ❶ (*schützen*) to save; **vor etw** *dat* **bewahrt bleiben** to be spared sth ❷ (*behalten*) **■ [sich** *dat*] **etw ~** to keep sth

bewähren* *vr* **■ sich** *akk* **~** ❶ *Gerät,*

Methode, Medikament to prove itself ❷ *Mensch* to prove oneself; **sich** *akk* **als Freund ~** to prove to be a friend

bewahrheiten* [bə·'vaːɐ̯·hai·tn̩] *vr* **■ sich** *akk* **~** to come true

bewährt *adj* proven

Bewährung <-, -en> *f* JUR probation; **eine Strafe zur ~ aussetzen** to suspend a sentence

Bewährungshelfer(in) *m(f)* JUR probation officer

bewältigen* [bə·'vɛl·tɪ·gn̩] *vt* ❶ (*meistern*) to cope with, to handle; *Schwierigkeiten* to overcome ❷ (*überwinden*) to get over; *Vergangenheit* to come to terms with

bewandert [bə·'van·dɐt] *adj* well-versed

bewässern* *vt Feld* to irrigate; *Garten* to water

bewegen*¹ [bə·'veː·gn̩] I. *vt* ❶ *Gegenstand, Körperteil* to move ❷ (*innerlich aufwühlen*) **■ etw bewegt jdn** sth moves sb ❸ (*bewirken*) to achieve; **etwas/nichts/viel/wenig ~** to achieve something/nothing/a lot/little II. *vr* **■ sich** *akk* **~** ❶ (*sich regen*) to move ❷ (*sich körperlich betätigen*) to [get some] exercise ❸ (*schwanken*) to range; **der Preis bewegt sich um die 3.000 Euro** the price is around 3,000 euros

bewegen*² <bewog, bewogen> [bə·'veː·gn̩] *vt* (*veranlassen*) **■ jdn dazu ~, etw zu tun** to move sb to do sth

Beweggrund *m* motive

beweglich [bə·'veːk·lɪç] *adj* movable; *Glieder* supple

bewegt *adj* ❶ (*innerlich gerührt*) moved; **mit ~er Stimme** in an emotional voice ❷ *Leben, Vergangenheit* eventful

Bewegung <-, -en> *f* movement; **jdn in ~ halten** to keep sb moving; **jd/ein Tier braucht ~** sb/an animal needs exercise

bewegungslos *adj* motionless

Beweis <-es, -e> [bə·'vais] *m* proof (**für** +*akk* of)

beweisen* *irreg vt* to prove

Beweismaterial *nt* JUR [body of] evidence

Bewerber(in) <-s, -> *m(f)* applicant

Bewerbung <-, -en> *f* application

Bewerbungsgespräch *nt* [job] interview

Bewerbungsschreiben *nt* application [letter]

bewerkstelligen* [bə·'vɛrk·ʃtɛ·lɪ·gn̩] *vt* to manage

bewerten* *vt* to assess; ■**jdn/etw nach etw** *dat* ~ to judge sb/sth according to sth; **etw zu hoch/niedrig** ~ to overvalue/undervalue sth

Bewertung *f* assessment

bewilligen* [bə·'vɪ·lɪ·gn̩] *vt* to approve; FIN to grant; *Stipendium* to award

bewirken* *vt* ① (*verursachen*) to cause ② (*erreichen*) **etwas** ~ to achieve something

bewirten* *vt* to entertain

bewohnbar *adj* habitable

bewohnen* *vt* ① *Gegend, Insel* to inhabit ② *Haus* to live in

Bewohner(in) <-s, -> *m(f)* ① (*Einwohner*) inhabitant ② *eines Hauses, Zimmers* occupant

bewölken* *vr* ■**sich** *akk* ~ to cloud over

bewölkt *adj* cloudy; **leicht** ~ partly cloudy

Bewunderer, Bewunderin <-s, -> [bə·'vʊnd·rɐ, bə·'vʊn·də·rɪn] *m, f* admirer

bewundern* *vt* to admire (**wegen** +*gen* for)

bewundernswert *adj* admirable

Bewunderung <-, -en> *f pl selten* admiration

bewusst^RR, **bewußt**^ALT [bə·'vʊst] I. *adj* ① (*vorsätzlich*) ~**es Nichtbefolgen von Anordnungen** willful disobedience of orders ② (*überlegt*) considered; **eine** ~**e Entscheidung** a deliberate decision; ~**e Lebensführung** socially and environmentally aware lifestyle ③ **jdm etw** ~ **machen** to make sb realize sth; **sich** *dat* **etw** ~ **machen** to

realize sth; ■**sich** *dat* **etw** *gen* ~ **sein** to be aware of sth; ■**jdm** ~ **sein** to be clear to sb II. *adv* ① (*vorsätzlich*) deliberately ② (*überlegt*) ~ **leben** to practice social and environmental awareness

bewusstlos^RR, **bewußtlos**^ALT [bə·'vʊst·lo:s] *adj* unconscious; ~ **werden** to faint

Bewusstsein^RR, **Bewußtsein**^ALT <-s> *nt kein pl* consciousness; **bei** [**vollem**] ~ **sein** to be [fully] conscious; **etw aus dem** ~ **verdrängen** to banish sth from one's mind; **jdm etw ins** ~ **rufen** to remind sb of sth

bezahlen* I. *vt* ① to pay; *Rechnung* to settle; *Getränke, Speisen* to pay for II. *vi* to pay; ~**, bitte!** [the] check, please!

Bezahlung *f* (*Lohn*) pay; **gegen** ~ for a fee

bezaubern* *vt, vi* to enchant

bezeichnen* I. *vt* ■**jdn/etw als jdn/ etw** ~ to call sb/sth sb/sth II. *vr* ■**sich** *akk* **als etw** *akk* ~ to call oneself sth

bezeichnend *adj* typical (**für** +*akk* of)

Bezeichnung *f* term

beziehen* *irreg* I. *vt* ① (*überziehen*) to cover; **das Bett neu** ~ to change the sheets ② *Haus, Wohnung* to move into ③ *Gehalt* to receive ④ *Standpunkt* to adopt; **zu etw** *dat* **Stellung** ~ to take a stand on sth ⑤ (*kaufen*) to obtain ⑥ (*in Beziehung setzen*) to apply (**auf** +*akk* to); **warum bezieht er immer alles gleich auf sich?** why does he always take everything personally? ⑦ SCHWEIZ (*einziehen*) to collect II. *vr* ① ■**sich** *akk* ~ *Himmel* to cloud over ② (*betreffen, sich berufen*) ■**sich** *akk* **auf jdn/ etw** ~ to refer to sb/sth

Beziehung <-, -en> [bə·'tsi:·ʊŋ] *f* ① (*Verhältnis*) relationship (**zu** +*dat* with); (*sexuell*) [romantic] relationship; **menschliche** ~**en** human relations ② (*Verbindung*) connection; **etw zu etw** *dat* **in** ~ **setzen** to connect sth to [*or* with] sth ③ *meist pl* (*fördernde Bekanntschaften*) ~**en haben** to have connections; **seine** ~**en spielen lassen** to pull [some] strings ④ (*Hinsicht*)

B

B

in jeder ~ in every respect; **in mancher** ~ in many respects

beziehungsweise *konj* or rather

Bezirk <-[e]s, -e> [bə·'tsɪrk] *m* district

bezug^ALT [bə·'tsu:k] *s.* **Bezug 2**

Bezug <-[e]s, Bezüge> [bə·'tsu:k] *m* ❶ *(für Kissen)* pillowcase; *(für Bett)* duvet cover ❷ *(Relation)* ■ **in ~ auf etw** *akk* with regard to sth; ~ **auf etw** *akk* **nehmen** to refer to sth; **etw zu etw** *dat* **in ~ setzen** to connect sth to [*or* with] sth

bezüglich [bə·'tsy:k·lɪç] *präp* +*gen* regarding

Bezugsperson *f* [personal] role model

bezwecken* [bə·'tsvɛ·kn̩] *vt* to aim to achieve; **was willst du damit ~?** what do you hope to achieve by doing that?

bezweifeln* *vt* to doubt

BH <-[s], -[s]> [be:·'ha:] *m* Abk von **Büstenhalter** bra

Bibel <-, -n> ['bi:·bl̩] *f* Bible

Biber <-s, -> ['bi:·be] *m* beaver

Bibliografie^RR, **Bibliographie** <-, -n> [bib·lio·gra·'fi] *f* bibliography

Bibliothek <-, -en> [bib·lio·'te:k] *f* library

Bibliothekar(in) <-s, -e> [bib·lio·te·'ka:ɐ̯] *m(f)* librarian

bieder ['bi:·dɐ] *adj (pej: spießig)* narrow-minded; *Geschmack* conservative

biegen <bog, gebogen> ['bi:·gn̩] *vt, vr* ■ **[sich** *akk***]** ~ to bend

biegsam ['bi:k·za:m] *adj Material* flexible

Biegung <-, -en> *f* ❶ *(Kurve)* bend; **eine ~ machen** to turn ❷ LING ÖSTERR *(Flexion)* inflection

Biene <-, -n> ['bi:·nə] *f* bee

Bienenhonig *m* [bee] honey

Bienenkönigin *f* queen bee

Bienenwabe *f* honeycomb

Bier <-[e]s, -e> [bi:ɐ̯] *nt* beer; ~ **vom Fass** draft beer ▶WENDUNGEN: **das ist dein ~** *(fam)* that's your business; **das ist nicht mein ~** *(fam)* that has nothing to do with me

Bierdose *f* beer can

Biest <-[e]s, -er> [bi:st] *nt* beast

bieten <bot, geboten> ['bi:·tn̩] **I.** *vt* ❶ *(anbieten)* to offer ❷ *(geben)* to give; *Gewähr, Sicherheit, Schutz* to provide ❸ *(zumuten)* **sich** *dat* **etw nicht ~ lassen** to not stand for sth **II.** *vr* ■ **sich** *akk* **|jdm|** ~ *Möglichkeit, Gelegenheit* to present itself [to sb]

Bikini <-s, -s> [bi·'ki:·ni] *m* bikini

Bilanz <-, -en> [bi·'lants] *f* ÖKON balance sheet ▶WENDUNGEN: ~ **ziehen** to take stock

Bild <-[e]s, -er> [bɪlt] *nt* picture ▶WENDUNGEN: **ein ~ für die Götter** *(fam)* a sight for sore eyes; **sich** *dat* **von jdm/etw ein ~ machen** to form an opinion about sb/sth; **im ~e sein** to be in the picture

bilden ['bɪl·dn̩] **I.** *vt* ❶ *(formen)* to form ❷ *Ausschuss* to set up *sep* ❸ *(darstellen)* to make up; *Gefahr, Problem* to constitute ❹ *(mit Bildung versehen)* to educate **II.** *vr* ❶ *(entstehen)* ■ **sich** *akk* ~ to develop; CHEM to form; BOT to grow ❷ *(sich Bildung verschaffen)* ■ **sich** *akk* ~ to educate oneself ❸ *(sich formen)* ■ **sich** *dat* **eine Meinung ~** to form an opinion III. *vi* ■ **etw bildet** sth broadens the mind

Bilderbuch *nt* picture book

Bilderrahmen *m* picture frame

Bildhauer(in) <-s, -> ['bɪlt·hauɐ̯] *m(f)* sculptor

bildhübsch ['bɪlt·'hypʃ] *adj* as pretty as a picture

bildlich *adv* figuratively; ~ **gesprochen** metaphorically speaking; **sich** *dat* **etw ~ vorstellen** to picture sth

Bildschirm *m* TV, COMPUT screen

Bildschirmschoner *m* screen saver

bildschön ['bɪlt·'ʃø:n] *adj s.* **bildhübsch**

Bildtelefon *nt* videophone

Bildung <-> *f kein pl* education; **keine ~ haben** to be uneducated

Bildungslücke *f* gap in one's education

Billard <-s, -e> ['bɪl·jart] *nt* billiards + *sing vb*, pool

Billardkugel ['bɪl·jart-] *f* billiard ball

Billardstock *m* billiard cue

Billett <-[e]s, -s> [bɪl·'jɛ(t)] *nt*

1 SCHWEIZ (*Fahrkarte*) ticket **2** SCHWEIZ (*Eintrittskarte*) admission ticket **3** ÖSTERR (*Glückwunschkarte*) greeting card
Billiarde <-, -n> [bɪˈl̩i̯arˌdə] *f* a thousand trillion
billig [ˈbɪlɪç] I. *adj* cheap II. *adv* cheaply; ~ **abzugeben** going cheap ►WENDUNGEN: ~ **davonkommen** (*fam*) to get off lightly
billigen [ˈbɪlɪgn̩] *vt* to approve of
Billigflieger *m* (*fam*) budget airline, no-frills airline
Billiglinie *f* low-cost airline
Billion <-, -en> [bɪˈl̩i̯oːn] *f* trillion
binär [biˈnɛːɐ̯] *adj* binary
Binde <-, -n> [ˈbɪndə] *f* **1** MED bandage; (*Schlinge*) sling **2** (*Monatsbinde*) sanitary napkin
Bindegewebe *nt* ANAT connective tissue
Bindehaut *f* ANAT conjunctiva
Bindehautentzündung *f* conjunctivitis
binden <band, gebunden> [ˈbɪndn̩] I. *vt* **1** (*befestigen*) to tie [up *sep*] (**an** +*akk* to) **2** (*zusammenbinden*) *Schnürsenkel* to tie; *Krawatte* to knot; *Blumenstrauß, Buch, Kranz* to bind ►WENDUNGEN: **mir sind die Hände gebunden** my hands are tied II. *vr* **1** (*sich verpflichten*) ■**sich** *akk* **an jdn/etw** ~ to commit oneself to sb/sth **2** (*feste Partnerschaft eingehen*) **ich will mich momentan nicht** ~ I don't want to tie myself down right now
bindend *adj* binding
Bindestrich *m* hyphen
Bindfaden *m* string
Bindung <-, -en> *f* **1** (*Verbundenheit*) bond (**an** +*dat* to) **2** (*Verpflichtung*) commitment; **eine vertragliche ~ eingehen** to enter into a binding contract **3** (*am Ski*) binding
Binnengewässer *nt* inland water *no indef art*
Binnenhafen *m* inland port
Binnenmarkt *m* domestic market; **der [Europäische] ~** the Single [European] Market
Bioabfall *m* ÖKOL organic waste [matter]
BiografieRR <-, -n> [bioˈɡraˈfiː] *f*

1 (*Buch*) biography **2** (*Lebenslauf*) life [history]
biografischRR [bioˈɡraːfɪʃ] *adj* biographical
Biographie <-, -n> [bioˈɡraˈfiː] *f s.* **Biografie**
biographisch [bioˈɡraːfɪʃ] *adj s.* **biografisch**
Bioladen *m* health food store
Biolandbau *m kein pl* organic farming
Biologe, Biologin <-n, -n> [bioˈloːɡə, -ɡɪn] *m, f* biologist
Biologie <-> [bioˈloˈɡiː] *f kein pl* biology
biologisch I. *adj* biological; (*natürlich*) natural II. *adv* biologically; ~ **abbaubar** biodegradable
Biosprit *m* biofuel, ethanol gas blend
Biotonne *f* bin for compostable waste
Biowaffe *f* biological weapon
Birke <-, -n> [ˈbɪrˌka] *f* birch [tree]
Birma <-s> [ˈbɪrˌma] *nt* Burma; *s. a.* **Deutschland**
Birnbaum *m* pear [tree]
Birne <-, -n> [ˈbɪrˌnə] *f* **1** (*Frucht*) pear **2** ELEK [light] bulb **3** (*fam: Kopf*) noggin *fam*
bis [bɪs] I. *präp* +*akk* **1** *zeitlich* until; (*nicht später als*) by; ~ **jetzt** up to now; ~ **bald/morgen!** see you soon/tomorrow! **2** *räumlich* as far as; ~ **dort/dorthin** [up] to there; ~ **hierher** up to this point **3** (*erreichend*) up to; **ich zähle ~ drei** I'll count [up] to three; **die Tagestemperaturen steigen ~ [zu] 30°C** daytime temperatures will reach 30°C; **Kinder ~ sechs Jahre** children up to the age of six **4** (*mit Ausnahme von*) ■~ **auf** [*o* SCHWEIZ ~ **an**] except [for] II. *konj* **1** (*ungefähre Angabe*) to; **400 ~ 500 Gramm Schinken** 400 to 500 grams of ham **2** *zeitlich* ~ **es dunkel wird, möchte ich zu Hause sein** I want to be home by the time it gets dark; **ich warte noch, ~ es dunkel wird** I'll wait until it gets dark
Bischof, Bischöfin <-s, Bischöfe> [ˈbɪʃɔf, ˈbɪʃœˌfɪn] *m, f* bishop
bisexuell [bizɛˈksu̯ɛl] *adj* bisexual

B

bisher [bɪsˈheːɐ̯] *adv* until now

Biskaya <-> [bɪsˈkaːja] *f* ■ **die ~** [the Bay of] Biscay

Biskuit <-[e]s, -s> [bɪsˈkviːt] *nt o m* sponge cake

bislang [bɪsˈlaŋ] *adv s.* **bisher**

Bison <-s, -e> [ˈbiːzɔn] *m* bison

biss^RR, **biß**^ALT [bɪs] *imp von* **beißen**

Biss^RR <-es, -e>, **Biß**^ALT <-sses, -sse> [bɪs] *m* bite ▶WENDUNGEN: **~ haben** to have drive

bisschen^RR, **bißchen**^ALT [ˈbɪsçən] *pron indef* ❶ + *Substantiv* ■ **ein ~ ...** a little ...; ■ **kein ~ ...** not one [little] bit of ...; ■ **das ~ ...** the little bit of ... ❷ + *adj/adv/vb* ■ **ein ~ ...** a bit ...; **das war ein ~ dumm von ihr!** that was a little stupid of her!; ■ **kein ~ ...** not the slightest bit ...

Bissen <-s, -> [ˈbɪsn̩] *m* morsel; **kann ich einen ~ von deinem Brötchen haben?** can I have a bite of your roll?; **er brachte keinen ~ herunter** he couldn't eat a thing

bissig [ˈbɪsɪç] *adj* ❶ **ein ~er Hund** a dog that bites ❷ (*sarkastisch*) sarcastic; *Kritik* scathing

Bistum <-s, Bistümer> [ˈbɪstuːm] *nt* bishopric

Bit <-[s], -[s]> [bɪt] *nt* COMPUT bit

bitte [ˈbɪtə] *interj* ❶ (*auffordernd*) please; **~ nicht!** please don't!; **ja, ~?** (*am Telefon*) hello?; **tun Sie [doch] ~ ...** won't you please ... ❷ (*Dank erwidernd*) **~ schön!** here you are!; **danke für die Auskunft! – ~[, gern geschehen]** thanks for the information — you're [very] welcome!; **danke, dass du mir geholfen hast! – ~[, gern geschehen]**! thanks for helping me — not at all!; **danke schön! – ~ schön, war mir ein Vergnügen!** thank you! — don't mention it, my pleasure!; **Entschuldigung! – ~!** Excuse me! — go right ahead!

Bitte <-, -n> [ˈbɪtə] *f* request (**um** +*akk* for)

bitten <bat, gebeten> [ˈbɪtn̩] *vt, vi* to ask (**um** +*akk* for); **könnte ich dich um einen Gefallen ~?** could I ask you a favor? ▶WENDUNGEN: **wenn ich ~ darf!** if you wouldn't mind!

bitter [ˈbɪtɐ] I. *adj* bitter; *Schokolade* dark; *Reue* deep II. *adv* (*sehr*) bitterly

bitterböse [ˈbɪtɐˈbøːzə] *adj* furious

bizarr [biˈtsar] *adj* bizarre

blähen [ˈblɛːən] I. *vr* ■ **sich** *akk* **~** to billow; MED to dilate II. *vi* MED to cause flatulence

Blähung <-, -en> *f meist pl* **~en haben** to have flatulence

Blamage <-, -n> [blaˈmaːʒə] *f* disgrace

blamieren* [blaˈmiːrən] I. *vt* to disgrace II. *vr* ■ **sich** *akk* **~** to make a fool of oneself

blank [blaŋk] I. *adj* ❶ (*glänzend, sauber*) shining ❷ *Unsinn* utter ❸ (*fam: pleite*) ■ **~ sein** to be broke II. *adv* **~ gewetzt** shiny; **~ poliert** brightly polished

Blase <-, -n> [ˈblaːzə] *f* ❶ ANAT bladder ❷ MED blister; **sich** *dat* **~n laufen** to get blisters on one's feet

blasen <bläst, blies, geblasen> [ˈblaːzn̩] *vt, vi* to blow

Blasenentzündung *f* bladder infection

Blasinstrument *nt* wind instrument

Blaskapelle *f* brass band

blass^RR, **blaß**^ALT [blas] *adj* ❶ (*bleich, hell*) pale; **~ um die Nase sein** to be green about the gills *hum* ❷ (*schwach*) vague; *Erinnerung* dim

Blatt <-[e]s, Blätter> [blat] *nt* ❶ BOT leaf ❷ (*Papierseite*) sheet ❸ (*Zeitung*) paper ▶WENDUNGEN: **kein ~ vor den Mund nehmen** to not mince one's words; **das ~ hat sich gewendet** things have changed

blättern [ˈblɛtɐn] *vi* **in einem Buch ~** to flip through a book

Blätterteig *m* puff pastry

Blattgold *nt* gold leaf

Blattlaus *f* aphid

blau [blau] *adj* ❶ (*Farbe*) blue ❷ **ein ~er Fleck** a bruise; **ein ~es Auge** a black eye ❸ *meist pred* (*fam: betrunken*) plastered *sl*

blauäugig adj ❶ (blaue Augen habend) blue-eyed ❷ (naiv) naïve

Blauhelm m blue beret

bläulich adj bluish

Blaulicht nt flashing blue light

blau|machen vi (fam) to call in sick; SCH to play hooky

Blausäure f hydrocyanic acid

Blazer <-s, -> ['ble:ze] m blazer

Blech <-[e]s, -e> [blɛç] nt ❶ kein pl (Material) sheet metal ❷ (Backblech) [baking] tray

Blechdose f tin

blechen ['blɛçn̩] vt, vi (fam) to fork out

Blechschaden m AUTO damage to the bodywork

Blei <-[e]s> [blai] nt kein pl lead

Bleibe <-, -n> ['blai·bə] f place to stay

bleiben <blieb, geblieben> ['blai·bn̩] vi sein ❶ (verweilen) to stay; **wo bleibst du so lange?** what's taking you so long [to get here]?; **wo sie nur so lange bleibt?** where the heck is she? ❷ (weiterhin sein) to remain; **unbeachtet ~** to go unnoticed; **wach ~** to stay awake; **das bleibt unter uns** that's [just] between you and me ❸ (übrig bleiben) **eine Möglichkeit bleibt uns noch** we still have one possibility left; **es blieb mir keine andere Wahl** I was left with no other choice

bleibend adj lasting

bleich [blaiç] adj pale

bleifrei adj lead-free

Bleistift m pencil

blenden ['blɛn·dn̩] vi to be dazzling

blendend I. adj brilliant; **~er Laune sein** to be in a fantastic mood II. adv wonderfully; **sich** akk **~ amüsieren** to have a great time

Blick <-[e]s, -e> [blɪk] m ❶ (das Blicken) look; **er warf einen ~ aus dem Fenster** he glanced out the window; **auf einen ~** at a glance; **auf den ersten ~** at first sight; **auf den zweiten ~** upon closer inspection; **jds ~ ausweichen** to avoid sb's gaze; **einen ~ auf jdn/etw werfen** to glance at sb/sth ❷ (Augenausdruck) look in one's eye

❸ (Aussicht) view; **ein Zimmer mit ~ auf den Strand** a room overlooking the beach

blicken ['blɪ·kn̩] vi ❶ (schauen) to look (auf +akk at) ❷ sich akk **~ lassen** to put in an appearance; **sie hat sich hier nicht wieder ~ lassen** she hasn't shown up here again

Blickkontakt m visual contact; **~ haben** to have eye contact

blind [blɪnt] adj blind; ▪**~ werden** to go blind; **~ vor Hass/Eifersucht sein** to be blinded by hatred/jealousy

Blinddarm m appendix

Blinddarmentzündung f appendicitis

Blinde(r) f(m) dekl wie adj blind person

Blindenhund m guide dog

Blindenschrift f Braille no art

blinken ['blɪŋ·kn̩] vi ❶ (funkeln) to gleam ❷ Fahrzeug to flash; (zum Abbiegen) to put one's turn signal on; **mit der Lichthupe ~** to flash one's [head]lights

Blinker <-s, -> ['blɪŋ·ke] m AUTO turn signal

Blitz <-es, -e> [blɪts] m lightning; FOTO flash; **vom ~ getroffen werden** to be struck by lightning ▶WENDUNGEN: **wie vom ~ getroffen** thunderstruck; **wie ein ~ einschlagen** to come as a bombshell; **wie der ~** (fam) like lightning

Blitzableiter <-s, -> m lightning rod

blitzblank adj squeaky clean

blitzen ['blɪ·tsn̩] I. vi impers ▪**es blitzt** there is [a flash of] lightning II. vt TRANSP ▪**geblitzt werden** to be photographed by a traffic camera

Blitzlicht nt FOTO flash[light]

Blitzschlag m lightning strike

Block <-[e]s, Blöcke> [blɔk] m block; **ein ~ Briefpapier** a stationery pad

Blockflöte f recorder

blockieren* [blɔ·ˈkiː·rən] I. vt to block; Stromzufuhr to interrupt; Verkehr to stop II. vi Bremse, Räder to lock

blöd [bløːt] I. adj (fam) silly; (stärker) stupid; Situation awkward; **ein ~es Gefühl** a funny feeling; **zu ~!** how annoying! II. adv (fam) idiotically; **frag**

B

B

doch nicht so ~! don't ask such stupid questions!; **sich** *akk* **~ anstellen** to act stupid

blödeln ['bløː·dl̩n] *vi* (*fam*) to tell silly jokes

Blödsinn *m kein pl* nonsense; **machen Sie keinen ~!** don't mess around!

blödsinnig ['bløːt·zɪnɪç] *adj* idiotic

blöken ['bløː·kn̩] *vi* to bleat

blond [blɔnt] *adj* blond[e]

Blondine <-, -n> [blɔn·ˈdiː·nə] *f* blonde

bloß [bloːs] **I.** *adj* **mit ~em Auge** with the naked eye; **mit ~em Oberkörper** stripped to the waist **II.** *adv* (*nur*) only **III.** *part* (*verstärkend*) **lass mich ~ in Ruhe!** just leave me alone!; **was er ~ hat?** what's his problem?

bloß|stellen *vt* (*blamieren*) to show up *sep*

bluffen ['blʊfn̩] *vi* to bluff

blühen ['blyː·ən] *vi* ❶ *Pflanze* to bloom ❷ (*fig: florieren*) to flourish ❸ (*fam: bevorstehen*) ■**jdm ~** to be in store for sb; **dann blüht dir aber was!** then you'll be in for it!

blühend *adj* ▶WENDUNGEN: **eine ~e Fantasie haben** to have a fertile imagination

Blume <-, -n> ['bluː·mə] *f* flower; (*Topfblume*) potted plant ▶WENDUNGEN: **jdm etw durch die ~ sagen** to say sth in a roundabout way to sb

Blumenbeet *nt* flower bed

Blumenkohl *m kein pl* cauliflower

Blumenstrauß <-sträuße> *m* bouquet of flowers

Blumentopf *m* flowerpot

Blumenvase *f* flower vase

blumig *adj* flowery

Bluse <-, -n> ['bluː·zə] *f* blouse

Blut <-[e]s> [bluːt] *nt kein pl* blood; **jdm ~ abnehmen** to take a blood sample from sb ▶WENDUNGEN: **~ geleckt haben** to have developed a liking for sth; **jdm im ~ liegen** to be in sb's blood; **[nur] ruhig ~!** [just] calm down!; **~ und Wasser schwitzen** to sweat blood [and tears]

Blutbad *nt* bloodbath

Blutbank <-banken> *f* blood bank

Blutdruck *m kein pl* blood pressure

Blüte <-, -n> ['blyː·tə] *f* ❶ *von Blume* bloom; *von Baum* blossom; **in voller ~ stehen** (*a. fig*) to be in full bloom; *Baum, Strauch* to be in full blossom ❷ (*fam: falsche Banknote*) fake [bill]

Blutegel *m* leech

bluten ['bluː·tn̩] *vi* to bleed

Blütenblatt *nt* petal

Blütenstaub *m* pollen

Bluter(in) <-s, -> ['bluː·tɐ] *m(f)* MED hemophiliac

BlutergussRR <-es, -ergüsse>, **Bluterguß**ÄLT <-sses, -ergüsse> *m* bruise

Blütezeit *f* ❶ BOT blossoming ❷ (*fig*) heyday

Blutgefäß *nt* blood vessel

Blutgerinnsel *nt* blood clot

Blutgruppe *f* blood group

Bluthund *m* bloodhound

blutig ['bluː·tɪç] *adj* ❶ bloody; (*blutbefleckt*) bloodstained ❷ KOCHK rare; **sehr ~** very rare

blutjung ['bluːt·ˈjʊŋ] *adj* very young

Blutorange *f* blood orange

Blutplasma *nt* blood plasma

Blutprobe *f* ❶ (*Untersuchung*) blood test ❷ (*Entnahme*) blood sample

blutrot *adj* blood-red

blutrünstig ['bluːt·rʏns·tɪç] *adj* bloodthirsty

Blutsauger *m* (*a. fig*) bloodsucker

Blutspender(in) *m(f)* blood donor

blutsverwandt *adj* related by blood *pred*

Blutsverwandte(r) *f(m)* blood relation

Blutung <-, -en> *f* ❶ (*das Bluten*) bleeding; **innere ~en** internal bleeding ❷ [*monatliche*] MED menstruation

blutunterlaufen *adj* *Augen* bloodshot

Blutvergießen <-s> *nt kein pl* bloodshed

Blutvergiftung *f* blood poisoning *no indef art*

Blutverlust *m* blood loss

Blutwäsche *f* MED hemodialysis

Blutwurst *f* blood sausage

Bö <-, -en> [bøː] *f* gust [of wind]

B

Bock <-[e]s, Böcke> [bɔk] m ❶ ZOOL buck; (*Schafsbock*) ram; (*Ziegenbock*) billy goat ❷ (*pej*) **ein alter ~** an old goat; **ein sturer ~** a stubborn bastard ▶WENDUNGEN: **~ [auf etw** *akk*] **haben** (*sl*) to feel like [doing sth]

bockig ['bɔ·kɪç] *adj* (*fam*) stubborn

Bockwurst *f* bockwurst (*type of sausage*)

Boden <-s, Böden> ['bo:·dn] m ❶ (*Erdreich*) soil; **magerer ~** barren soil ❷ (*Erdboden*) ground; (*Fußboden*) floor ❸ *kein pl* (*Territorium*) territory; **auf amerikanischem ~** on American soil ❹ (*Dachboden*) attic ❺ (*Grund*) bottom; *eines Gefäßes a.* base ▶WENDUNGEN: **am ~ zerstört sein** (*fam*) to be devastated; **etw [mit jdm] zu ~ reden** SCHWEIZ to chew over sth *sep* [with sb]

Bodenbelag *m* floor covering

Bodenfrost *m* light frost

bodenlos *adj* outrageous; **das ist eine ~e Frechheit!** that's absolutely outrageous!

Bodennebel *m* ground fog

Bodenpersonal *nt* LUFT ground crew

Bodenschätze *pl* mineral resources *pl*

Bodensee ['bo:·dn·ze:] *m* ■**der ~** Lake Constance

Body <-s, -s> ['bɔdi] *m* bodysuit

Bodybuilding <-s> [-bɪl·dɪŋ] *nt kein pl* bodybuilding

Bogen <-s, -> ['bo:·gn] m ❶ (*Kurve*) curve; **einen ~ machen** to curve [around] ❷ (*Blatt Papier*) sheet [of paper] ❸ (*Schusswaffe*) bow; **Pfeil und ~** bow and arrow[s *pl*] ❹ ARCHIT arch ▶WENDUNGEN: **in hohem ~ hinausfliegen** (*fam*) to be thrown out; **den ~ heraushaben** (*fam*) to have got the hang of it; **einen [großen] ~ um jdn/ etw machen** (*fam*) to steer clear of sb/ sth

bogenförmig *adj* arched

böhmisch ['bø:·mɪʃ] *adj* Bohemian

Bohne <-, -n> ['bo:·nə] *f* bean; **dicke/ grüne/rote/weiße ~n** broad/green/ kidney/navy beans

Bohnenkaffee *m kein pl* real coffee

Bohnenstange *f* (*a. hum*) beanpole *a. hum*

bohnern ['bo:·nɐn] *vt* to polish

Bohnerwachs [-vaks] *nt* floor polish

bohren ['bo:·rən] I. *vt* ❶ *Loch* to bore; (*mit Bohrmaschine*) to drill ❷ (*hineinstoßen*) to sink; **sie bohrte ihm das Messer in den Bauch** she plunged the knife into his stomach II. *vi* ❶ (*mit dem Bohrer*) to drill ❷ **in der Nase ~** to pick one's nose ❸ (*fam: drängen*) ■**so lange ~, bis ...** to keep on asking until ...

Bohrer <-s, -> *m* drill

Bohrinsel *f* drilling rig

Bohrturm *m* derrick

böig ['bø:·ɪç] *adj Wetter* windy

Boiler <-s, -> ['bɔy·lɐ] *m* hot-water tank

Boje <-, -n> ['bo:·jə] *f* buoy

Bolivianer(in) <-s, -> [boli·'vi̯a:·nɐ] *m(f)* Bolivian; *s. a.* **Deutsche(r)**

Bolivien <-s> [bo·'li:·vi̯·ən] *nt* Bolivia; *s. a.* **Deutschland**

bombardieren* [bɔm·bar·'di:·rən] *vt* ❶ MIL to bomb ❷ (*fig fam*) to bombard

Bombe <-, -n> ['bɔm·bə] *f* bomb; **wie eine ~ einschlagen** to come as a bombshell

Bombenerfolg *m* (*fam*) smash hit

Bombengeschäft *nt* (*fam*) booming business

Bombenstimmung *f kein pl* (*fam*) ■**in ~ sein** to be in a great mood; **auf der Party herrschte eine ~** that was one happening party *sl*

bombig ['bɔm·bɪç] *adj* (*fam*) fantastic

Bon <-s, -s> [bɔŋ, bõ:] m ❶ (*Kassenzettel*) receipt ❷ (*Gutschein*) coupon

Bonbon <-s, -s> [bɔŋ·'bɔŋ] *m* o ÖSTERR *nt* piece of candy

Bonus <-, -> ['bo:·nʊs] *m* FIN bonus

boomen ['bu:·mən] *vi* ÖKON to [be on the] boom

Boot <-[e]s, -e> [bo:t] *nt* boat; (*Segelboot*) yacht; **~ fahren** to go boating

Bootsfahrt *f* boat trip

Bootshaus *nt* boathouse

Bootsverleih *m* boat rental

Bord[1] [bɔrt] *m* **an ~** aboard; **an ~ gehen**

B

to board; **über ~ gehen** to go overboard; **Mann über ~!** man overboard!; **von ~ gehen** *Lotse* to leave the plane/ship; *Passagier a.* to disembark

Bord² <-[e]s, -e> [bɔrt] *nt* shelf

Bordell <-s, -e> [bɔr·'dɛl] *nt* brothel

Bordkarte *f* boarding pass

Bordpersonal *nt kein pl* crew

Bordstein *m* curb

borgen ['bɔr·gn] *vt* ① (*sich leihen*) to borrow ② (*verleihen*) to lend

Borke <-, -n> ['bɔr·kə] *f* BOT bark

Borkenkäfer *m* bark beetle

borniert [bɔr·'niːɐ̯t] *adj* (*pej*) bigoted

Börse <-, -n> ['bœr·zə] *f* FIN stock market; (*Gebäude*) stock exchange; **an die ~ gehen** to go public; **an der ~ [gehandelt]** [traded] on the exchange

Börsenmakler(in) *m(f)* stockbroker

Borste <-, -n> ['bɔrs·tə] *f* bristle

bösartig *adj* ① (*tückisch*) malicious; *Tier* vicious ② MED malignant

Böschung <-, -en> ['bœ·ʃʊŋ] *f* embankment

böse ['bøː·zə] **I.** *adj* ① (*schlecht*) bad; **~ Absicht** malice; **das war keine ~ Absicht!** no harm intended!; **nichts B~s ahnen** to not suspect anything is wrong; **ein ~s Ende nehmen** to end in disaster; **~ Folgen haben** to have dire consequences; **eine ~ Überraschung erleben** to have an unpleasant surprise; **ein ~r Zufall** a terrible coincidence ② (*verärgert*) angry; **ein ~s Gesicht machen** to scowl ③ (*fam: unartig*) naughty **II.** *adv* ① (*schlecht*) badly; **~ ausgehen** to end in disaster; **~ [für jdn] aussehen** to look bad [for sb] ② (*böswillig*) **das habe ich nicht ~ gemeint** I meant no harm; **~ lächeln** to give an evil smile ③ (*fam: sehr*) **sich** *akk* **~ irren** to make a serious mistake

Bösewicht <-[e]s, -er> ['bøː·zə·vɪçt] *m* ① (*hum: fam*) little rascal ② (*veraltend: Schurke*) villain

boshaft ['boːs·haft] **I.** *adj* malicious **II.** *adv* **~ grinsen** to give an evil grin

Bosheit <-, -en> *f* malice; (*Bemerkung*) nasty remark

Boss[RR] <-es, -e>, **Boß**[ALT] <-sses, -sse> [bɔs] *m* boss

böswillig *adj* malevolent; JUR willful

botanisch [bo·'taː·nɪʃ] *adj* botanical

Bote, Botin <-n, -nn> ['boː·tə, 'boː·tɪn] *m, f* courier; (*mit Nachricht*) messenger

Botschaft <-, -en> ['boːt·ʃaft] *f* ① (*Nachricht*) message; **hast du schon die freudige ~ gehört?** have you heard the good news yet? ② POL embassy

Botschafter(in) <-s, -> *m(f)* POL ambassador

Bottich <-[e]s, -e> ['bɔ·tɪç] *m* tub; (*für Wäsche*) washtub

Bouillon <-, -s> [bʊl·'jɔŋ] *f* [beef] bouillon

Boulevardpresse *f* (*fam*) yellow press

Boutique <-, -n> [bu·'tiːk] *f* boutique

Bowle <-, -n> ['boː·lə] *f* KOCHK punch

Bowling <-s, -s> ['boː·lɪŋ] *nt* [tenpin] bowling

Box <-, -en> [bɔks] *f* ① (*Behälter*) box ② (*fam: Lautsprecher*) loudspeaker

boxen ['bɔ·ksn] **I.** *vi* to box; ■ **gegen jdn ~** to fight sb **II.** *vt* to punch

Boxen <-s> ['bɔ·ksn] *nt kein pl* boxing *no art*

Boxer(in) <-s, -> ['bɔ·ksɐ] *m(f)* boxer

Boxhandschuh *m* boxing glove

Boxkampf *m* boxing match

boykottieren* [bɔɪ·kɔ·'tiː·rən] *vt* to boycott

brach [braːx] *imp von* **brechen**

Branche <-, -n> ['brã·ʃə] *f* ÖKON line of business

Branchenverzeichnis *nt* ≈ Yellow Pages

Brand <-[e]s, Brände> [brant] *m* fire; **in ~ geraten** to catch fire; **etw in ~ stecken** to set sth on fire

brandeilig *adj* (*fam*) extremely urgent

Brandherd *m* source of the fire

Brandmal <-s, -e> *nt* brand

brandmarken *vt* to brand

brandneu ['brant·'nɔy] *adj* (*fam*) brand-new

Brandschaden *m* fire damage

Brandschutz *m kein pl* fire protection

Brandstifter(in) <-s, -> *m(f)* arsonist

Brandstiftung *f* arson

Brandung <-, -en> *f* surf

Brandwunde *f* burn

Branntwein ['brant·vain] *m* spirits *pl*

Brasilianer(in) <-s, -> [bra·zi·'lịa·ne] *m(f)* Brazilian; *s. a.* **Deutsche(r)**

brasilianisch [bra·zi·'lịa·nɪʃ] *adj* Brazilian; *s. a.* **deutsch**

Brasilien <-s> [bra·'zi:·lị·ən] *nt* Brazil; *s. a.* **Deutschland**

braten <brät, briet, gebraten> ['bra:·tn] *vt, vi (in der Pfanne)* to fry; *(am Spieß)* to roast

Braten <-s, -> ['bra:·tn] *m* roast [meat]; **kalter ~** cold meat ▶WENDUNGEN: **ein fetter ~** *(fam)* a good catch; **den ~ riechen** *(fam)* to smell a rat *fam*

Brathähnchen *nt,* **Brathendl** <-s, -[n]> *nt* ÖSTERR, SÜDD grilled chicken

Bratkartoffeln *pl* fried potatoes *pl*

Bratpfanne *f* frying pan

Bratsche <-, -n> ['bra:·tʃə] *f* MUS viola

Bratwurst *f* bratwurst, [fried] sausage; *(vor dem Braten)* [frying] sausage

Brauch <-[e]s, Bräuche> [braux] *m* custom; **[bei jdm so] ~ sein** to be customary [with sb]

brauchbar *adj* useful; **nicht ~ sein** to be of no use

brauchen ['brau·xn] I. *vt* ❶ *(benötigen)* to need; **wozu brauchst du das?** what do you need that for?; **ich brauche bis zum Bahnhof eine Stunde** it takes me an hour to get to the train station ❷DIAL *(fam: gebrauchen)* to use; **kannst du die Sachen ~?** can you find a use for these things? II. *modal vb (müssen)* to need; **etw nicht [zu] tun ~** to not need to do sth; **du hättest doch nur etwas [zu] sagen ~** you should have just said something III. *vt impers* SCHWEIZ, SÜDD **es braucht etw** sth is needed

brauen ['brau·ən] *vt Bier* to brew

Brauerei <-, -en> [brau·ə·'rai] *f* brewery

braun [braun] *adj* ❶brown; *Haut* [sun]tanned ❷POL *(pej hist)* **die B~ en** *pl* the Brown Shirts *pl*

bräunen ['brɔy·nən] I. *vt Haut* to tan II. *vr* **sich** *akk* **~** *(sich sonnen)* to get a tan; *(braun werden)* to turn brown

Braunkohle *f* lignite

Brausetablette *f* effervescent tablet

Braut <-, Bräute> [braut] *f* bride

Bräutigam <-s, -e> ['brɔy·tɪ·gam] *m* [bride]groom

Brautjungfer *f* bridesmaid

Brautkleid *nt* wedding dress

brav [bra:f] *adj Kind* good; **sei schön ~!** be a good boy/girl!

brechen <bricht, brach, gebrochen> ['brɛ·çn] I. *vt haben* to break; **sein Schweigen ~** to break one's silence II. *vi* ❶ *sein (auseinander)* to break [apart] ❷ *haben* **mit jdm ~** to break with sb ❸ *(sich erbrechen)* to throw up

Brechreiz *m kein pl* nausea

Brei <-[e]s, -e> [brai] *m* KOCHK porridge ▶WENDUNGEN: **um den [heißen] herumreden** to beat around the bush *fam*

breit [brait] I. *adj* wide; *Schultern* broad; **etw ~er machen** to widen sth II. *adv* **~ gebaut** strongly built; **sich** *akk* **~ hinsetzen** to plump down

Breite <-, -n> ['brai·tə] *f* width; **von 4 cm** ~ 4 cm in width; **die ~ des Angebots** the wide range of offers

Breitengrad *m* [degree of] latitude

breitmachen *vr (fam)* **sich** *akk* **~** to spread oneself [out]

breitschlagen *vt irreg (fam)* to talk sb into sth

Bremse¹ <-, -n> ['brɛm·zə] *f (Bremsvorrichtung)* brake

Bremse² <-, -n> ['brɛm·zə] *f (Stechfliege)* horsefly

bremsen ['brɛm·zn] I. *vi Fahrzeug* to brake II. *vt* ❶ *Fahrzeug* to brake ❷ *(aufhalten)* to slow down *sep;* **sie ist nicht zu ~** there's no holding her back

Bremsflüssigkeit *f* brake fluid

Bremsklotz *m* brake pad

Bremslicht *nt* brake light

Bremsspur *f* skid mark

Bremsweg *m* braking distance
brennbar *adj* combustible

B

brennen <brannte, gebrannt> ['brɛ·nən]
I. *vi* ❶ *Feuer* to burn; *Gegenstand* to be
on fire; **es brennt!** fire! fire!; **in der
Fabrik brennt es** there's a fire in the
factory; **lichterloh ~** to be ablaze
❷ *Licht* to be burning; **das Licht ~ lassen** to leave the light on ❸ **auf der
Haut ~** to burn the skin ▶WENDUNGEN:
darauf ~, etw zu tun to be dying to do
sth II. *vt* ❶ *Schnaps* to distill ❷ *CD* to
burn

brennend I. *adj* burning; *Frage* urgent;
Wunsch fervent II. *adv* ▶WENDUNGEN:
etw interessiert jdn ~ sb is dying to
know sth

Brenner <-s, -> ['brɛ·nɐ] *m* TECH burner
Brennerei <-, -en> [brɛ·nə·'rai] *f* distill-
ery
Brennessel^ALT ['brɛn·nɛ·sl] *f s.* Brenn-
nessel
Brennholz *nt* firewood
Brennnessel^RR ['brɛn·nɛ·sl] *f* stinging
nettle
Brennspiritus *m* methylated spirit
Brennstoff *m* fuel
brenzlig ['brɛnts·lɪç] *adj* (*fam*) dicey;
die Situation wird mir zu ~ things are
getting too hot for me
Bretagne <-> [bre·'tan·jə] *f* ■ **die ~**
Brittany
Brett <-[e]s, -er> [brɛt] *nt* board;
(*Planke*) plank; (*Regalbrett*) shelf;
schwarzes ~ bulletin board ▶WENDUN-
GEN: **ein ~ vorm Kopf haben** (*fam*) to
be slow on the uptake
Bretterzaun *m* wooden fence
Brettspiel *nt* board game
Brezel <-, -n> ['bre:·tsl] *f* pretzel
Brief <-[e]s, -e> [bri:f] *m* letter
Briefbeschwerer <-s, -> *m* paper-
weight
Briefbogen *m* [sheet of] writing paper
Brieffreund(in) *m(f)* pen pal
Briefkasten *m* mailbox
Briefmarke *f* [postage] stamp
Brieföffner *m* letter opener
Briefpapier *nt* stationery

Brieftasche *f* wallet
Briefträger(in) *m(f)* mailman *masc*,
mailwoman *fem*
Briefumschlag *m* envelope
Briefwahl *f* absentee ballot
Brikett <-s, -s> [bri·'kɛt] *nt* briquette
brillant [brɪl·'jant] *adj* brilliant
Brillant <-en, -en> [brɪl·'jant] *m* brilliant
Brille <-, -n> ['brɪ·lə] *f* ❶ (*Sehhilfe*)
[eye]glasses *npl*; ■ **eine ~** a pair of glasses; **eine ~ tragen** to wear glasses
❷ (*Toilettenbrille*) [toilet] seat
Brillenetui *nt* eyeglass case
Brillengestell *nt* [eyeglass] frames
Brillenglas *nt* lens
bringen <brachte, gebracht> ['brɪ·ŋən]
vt ❶ (*hinbringen*) ■ **jdm etw ~** to bring
[sb] sth ❷ (*wegbringen*) ■ **jdn/etw
irgendwohin ~** to take sb/sth somewhere; **jdn nach Hause ~** to take sb
home; **den Müll nach draußen ~** to
take out the garbage; **die Kinder ins
Bett ~** to put the children to bed ❸ (*versetzen*) **jdn in Bedrängnis ~** to get sb
in[to] trouble; **jdn ins Gefängnis ~** to
put sb in prison; **jdn ins Grab ~** to be
the death of sb; **jdn in Schwierigkeiten ~** to put sb into a difficult position
❹ (*rauben*) ■ **jdn um etw** *akk* **~** to rob
sb of sth; **jdn um den Verstand ~** to
drive sb crazy ❺ (*einbringen*) **das
bringt nicht viel** that won't bring in
much money [for us] ❻ (*bewegen*)
■ **jdn dazu ~, etw zu tun** to get sb to
do sth ❼ + *substantiviertem Verb*
(*bewerkstelligen*) **jdn zum Laufen/
Singen/Sprechen ~** to make sb run/
sing/talk; **jdn zum Schweigen ~** to silence sb ❽ (*fam: tun*) **das kannst du
doch nicht ~!** you can't [go and] do
that! ❾ (*fam: gut sein*) **sie bringt's**
she's got what it takes; **das bringt er
nicht** he's not up to it; **das bringt
nichts** it's pointless; **das bringt's nicht**
that's useless ▶WENDUNGEN: **etw hinter
sich** *akk* **~** to get sth over [and done]
with; **etw bringt etw mit sich** sth
involves sth; **es nicht über sich** *akk* **~,**

etw zu tun to not be able to bring oneself to do sth

brisant [bri·'zant] *adj* explosive

Brise <-, -n> ['bri:·zə] *f* breeze

Brite, Britin <-n, -n> ['brɪ·tə, 'brɪ·tɪn] *m, f* Briton, Brit *fam; s. a.* **Deutsche(r)**

britisch ['brɪ·tɪʃ] *adj* British, Brit *attr fam; s. a.* **deutsch**

bröckeln ['brœ·k|n] *vi* to crumble

Brocken <-s, -> ['brɔ·kn̩] *m* ❶ *(Stück)* chunk ❷ *pl* LING **ein paar ~ Russisch** a smattering of Russian ▶WENDUNGEN: **ein harter ~ sein** *(fam)* to be a tough nut

Brokkoli <-s, -s> ['brɔ·ko·li] *m* broccoli

Brombeere ['brɔm·be:·rə] *f* blackberry; *(Strauch)* blackberry bush

Bronchie <-, -n> ['brɔn·çiə] *f meist pl* bronchial tube

Bronchitis <-, Bronchitiden> [brɔn·'çi:·tɪs] *f* bronchitis *no art*

Bronze <-, -n> ['brõ:·sə] *f* bronze

Bronzemedaille [-me·dal·jə] *f* bronze medal

Brosche <-, -n> ['brɔ·ʃə] *f* brooch

Broschüre <-, -n> [brɔ·'ʃy:·rə] *f* brochure

Brot <-[e]s, -e> [bro:t] *nt* bread; *(Laib)* loaf [of bread]; **ein ~ mit Käse** a slice of bread with cheese; **belegtes ~** [open-faced] sandwich

Brötchen <-s, -> ['brø:t·çən] *nt* [bread] roll ▶WENDUNGEN: **sich** *dat* **seine ~ verdienen** *(fam)* to earn one's living

Broteinheit *f* MED carbohydrate unit

Brotkasten *m* bread box

Brotrinde *f* [bread] crust

Browser <-s, -> ['brau·zɐ] *m* INET browser

Bruch <-[e]s, Brüche> [brʊx] *m* ❶ *eines Vertrags* infringement; *von Vertrauen* breach ❷ *(in Beziehung, Freundschaft)* rift; **in die Brüche gehen** to go to pieces ❸ *(Knochenbruch)* fracture; **ein komplizierter ~** a compound fracture ❹ MED **sich** *dat* **einen ~ heben** to give oneself a hernia

bruchfest *adj* unbreakable

brüchig ['brʏ·çɪç] *adj Leder, Stimme* cracked

Bruchteil *m* **im ~ einer Sekunde** in a split second **B**

Brücke <-, -n> ['brʏ·kə] *f* ❶ ARCHIT bridge ❷ *(Teppich)* rug

Brückenpfeiler *m* [bridge] pier

Bruder <-s, Brüder> ['bru:·dɐ] *m* brother; ■**die Brüder Schmitz/Grimm** die Schmitz brothers/the Brothers Grimm

brüderlich *adv* **~ teilen** to share and share alike

Bruderschaft <-, -en> *f* REL fraternity

Brühe <-, -n> ['bry:·ə] *f* KOCHK broth

Brühwürfel *m* bouillon cube

brüllen ['brʏ·lən] *vt* ■**jdm etw ins Ohr ~** to shout sth in sb's ear

brummen ['brʊ·mən] I. *vi Bass* to rumble; *Motor* to drone II. *vt* to mumble

Brummschädel *m* *(fam)* headache; *(durch Alkohol a.)* hangover

brünett [brʏ·'nɛt] *adj* brunet[te]

Brunnen <-s, -> ['brʊ·nən] *m* ❶ *(Wasserbrunnen)* well ❷ *(Springbrunnen)* fountain

brünstig ['brʏns·tɪç] *adj männliches Tier* rutting; *weibliches Tier* in heat *pred*

brüsk [brʏsk] *adj* brusque

brüskieren* [brʏs·'ki:·rən] *vt* to snub

Brüssel <-s> ['brʏ·sl̩] *nt* Brussels

Brust <-, Brüste> [brʊst] *f* ❶ breast; *(Brustkasten)* chest; **einem Kind die ~ geben** to breastfeed a baby; **es auf der ~ haben** to have chest trouble ▶WENDUNGEN: **schwach auf der ~ sein** *(hum fam: schwächlich)* to have weak lungs; *(finanziell)* to be a bit short on cash

Brustbein *nt* ANAT breastbone

Brustbeutel *m* [neck] travel pouch

Brustfellentzündung *f* MED pleurisy

Brustkorb *m* ANAT chest

Brustkrebs *m* breast cancer

Brustschwimmen *nt* breaststroke

Brustwarze *f* nipple

brutal [bru·'ta:l] *adj* brutal

Brutalität <-, -en> [bru·ta·li·'tɛːt] *f kein pl* brutality

B

Br<u>u</u>tkasten m MED incubator

br<u>u</u>tto ['bru·to] adv gross; **3.800 Euro ~ verdienen** to have a gross income of 3,800 euros

Bruttoeinkommen nt gross income

Bub <-en, -en> [bu:p] m SÜDD, ÖSTERR, SCHWEIZ boy

Buch <-[e]s, Bücher> [bu:x] nt book

B<u>u</u>chdrucker(in) m(f) [letterpress] printer

Buche <-, -n> ['bu:·xə] f beech

B<u>u</u>checker <-, -n> f BOT beechnut

Bücherei <-, -en> [by:·çə·'rai] f [lending] library

B<u>ü</u>cherregal nt bookshelf

B<u>ü</u>cherschrank m bookcase

B<u>ü</u>cherwurm m (hum) bookworm

B<u>u</u>chführung f bookkeeping

B<u>u</u>chhalter(in) m(f) bookkeeper

B<u>u</u>chhandel m book trade; **im ~ erhältlich** available in bookstores

B<u>u</u>chhändler(in) m(f) bookseller

B<u>u</u>chhandlung f bookstore

B<u>ü</u>chsenöffner m can opener

Buchstabe <-n[s], -n> ['bu:x·ʃta·bə] m letter

buchstabieren* [bu:x·ʃta·'bi:·rən] vt to spell

Bucht <-, -en> [buxt] f bay

B<u>u</u>chung <-, -en> f ❶ (Reservierung) booking, reservation ❷ FIN book entry

B<u>u</u>chweizen m buckwheat

b<u>ü</u>cken ['by·kn̩] vr ■**sich** akk [**nach etw** dat] ~ to bend down [to pick sth up]

buddeln ['bu·dl̩n] (fam) I. vi to dig [up] II. vt to dig [out sep]

Buddhismus <-> [bu·'dɪs·mʊs] m kein pl Buddhism

Buddhist(in) <-en, -en> [bu·'dɪst] m(f) Buddhist

Bude <-, -n> ['bu:·də] f (fam: Wohnung) pad; **sturmfreie ~ haben** (fam) to have the place [all] to oneself

Budget <-s, -s> [by·'dʒe:] nt budget

Büfett <-[e]s, -s> [by·'fɛt] nt, **Buffet** <-s, -s> [by·'fe:] nt bes ÖSTERR, SCHWEIZ ❶ (Essen) buffet ❷ (Anrichte) side-

board ❸ SCHWEIZ (Bahnhofsgaststätte) train station restaurant

Büffel <-s, -> ['bʏ·fl̩] m buffalo

B<u>ü</u>gelbrett nt ironing board

B<u>ü</u>geleisen <-s, -> nt iron

B<u>ü</u>gelfalte f crease

b<u>ü</u>gelfrei adj wrinkle-free

b<u>ü</u>geln ['by:·gl̩n] vt, vi to iron

Bühne <-, -n> ['by:·nə] f stage; **auf der ~ stehen** to be on [the] stage; **hinter der ~** behind the scenes ▶WENDUNGEN: **etw über die ~ bringen** (fam) to get sth over with; **über die ~ gehen** (fam) to take place

B<u>ü</u>hnenbild nt scenery

B<u>ü</u>hnenbildner(in) <-s, -> m(f) scene painter

B<u>ü</u>hnenstück nt [stage] play

Buhruf m [cry of] boo

Bulgare, Bulgarin <-n, -n> [bʊl·'ga:·rə, -rɪn] m, f Bulgarian; s. a. **Deutsche(r)**

Bulgarien <-s> [bʊl·'ga:·rj·ən] nt Bulgaria; s. a. **Deutschland**

bulgarisch [bʊl·'ga:·rɪʃ] adj Bulgarian; s. a. **deutsch**

Bullauge ['bʊl-] nt porthole

Bulldogge f bulldog

Bulldozer <-s, -> ['bʊl·do:·zɐ] m bulldozer

Bulle <-n, -n> ['bʊ·lə] m ❶ ZOOL bull ❷ (sl: Polizist) cop fam

Bullenhitze f kein pl (fam) stifling heat

Bumerang <-s, -s> ['bu:·mə·raŋ] m boomerang

Bummel <-s, -> ['bʊ·ml̩] m stroll

bummeln ['bʊ·ml̩n] vi ❶ sein (spazieren gehen) to stroll; **~ gehen** to go for a stroll ❷ haben (fam: trödeln) to dilly-dally

Bummelzug m (fam) local [passenger] train

bumsen ['bʊm·zn̩] vt, vi (derb) to screw

Bund[1] <-[e]s, Bünde> [bʊnt] m ❶ (Vereinigung) association ❷ (fam: Bundeswehr) ■**der ~** the [German] army; **beim ~ sein** to be serving in the military

Bund² <-[e]s, -e> [bʊnt] nt bunch; **ein ~ Petersilie** a bunch of parsley

Bündel <-s, -> ['bʏn·dl] nt bundle

Bundesbank f kein pl **die [Deutsche] ~** [German] Federal [Reserve] Bank

Bundesbürger(in) m(f) German citizen

Bundesgebiet nt BRD, ÖSTERR federal territory

Bundesgerichtshof m BRD [German] Federal Supreme Court

Bundeshauptstadt f federal capital

Bundesinnenminister(in) m(f) [German] Secretary of the Interior

Bundeskanzler(in) m(f) BRD German Chancellor; ÖSTERR Austrian Chancellor; SCHWEIZ Head of the Federal Chancellery

Bundesland nt federal state; **die alten/ neuen Bundesländer** the federal states of the former West/East Germany

Bundesliga f kein pl the highest level sports league, often divided into two subleagues, the 1st and 2nd Bundesliga

Bundespost f kein pl [German] Federal Post Office

Bundespräsident(in) m(f) BRD, ÖSTERR President of the Federal Republic of Germany/Austria; SCHWEIZ President of the Confederation

Bundesrat m ❶ BRD, ÖSTERR Bundesrat, ≈ Senate ❷ SCHWEIZ [Swiss] Federal Council (*executive body*)

Bundesregierung f federal government

Bundesrepublik f federal republic; **die ~ Deutschland** the Federal Republic of Germany

Bundesstaat m ❶ (*Staatenbund*) confederation ❷ (*Gliedstaat*) federal state; **im ~ Kalifornien** in the state of California

Bundesstraße f BRD, ÖSTERR highway

Bundestag m kein pl BRD Bundestag, ≈ House of Representatives

Bundestagswahl f Bundestag election

Bundesverfassungsgericht nt kein pl BRD [German] Federal Constitutional Court (*supreme legal body that settles issues relating to the basic constitution*)

Bundesversammlung f POL ❶ BRD Federal Assembly, ≈ U.S. Congress ❷ SCHWEIZ Parliament

Bundeswehr f [Federal] Armed Forces

Bündnis <-ses, -se> ['bʏnt·nɪs] nt alliance

Bunker <-s, -> ['bʊŋ·kɐ] m MIL bunker

bunt [bʊnt] adj colorful

Buntstift m colored pencil

Buntwäsche f colored laundry

Burg <-, -en> [bʊrk] f castle

bürgen vi ❶ **für jdn ~** to vouch for sb ❷ (*fig*) **für etw** akk **~** to be a guarantee of sth

Bürger(in) <-s, -> ['bʏr·gɐ] m(f) citizen

Bürgerinitiative f citizens' group

Bürgerkrieg m civil war

bürgerlich ['bʏr·gɐ·lɪç] adj ❶ attr (*den Staatsbürger betreffend*) civil; **~e Pflicht** civic duty ❷ (*dem Bürgerstand angehörend*) bourgeois pej

Bürgermeister(in) ['bʏr·gɐ·mais·tɐ] m(f) mayor

Bürgerrechtsbewegung f civil rights movement

Bürgersteig <-[e]s, -e> m sidewalk

Bürgerversammlung f public meeting

Burgund <-[s]> [bʊr·'gʊnt] nt Burgundy

Büro <-s, -s> [by·'ro:] nt office

Büroangestellte(r) f(m) office worker

Büroarbeit f office work

Büroklammer f paper clip

Bürokratie <-, -n> [by·ro·kra·'ti:] f bureaucracy

Bürste <-, -n> ['bʏrs·tə] f brush

bürsten ['bʏrs·tn] vt to brush

Bus <-ses, -se> [bʊs] m bus; (*Reisebus*) tour bus

Busbahnhof m bus station

Busch <-[e]s, Büsche> [bʊʃ] m shrub ▶WENDUNGEN: **mit etw** dat **hinter dem ~ halten** (*fam*) to keep sth to oneself; **da ist etw im ~** (*fam*) sth is up; **bei jdm auf den ~ klopfen** (*fam*) to sound sb out

Büschel <-s, -> ['bʏ·ʃl] nt tuft

Busen <-s, -> ['bu:·zn] m bust

Busfahrer(in) *m(f)* bus driver
Bushaltestelle *f* bus stop
Buslinie *f* bus route
Bussard <-s, -e> ['bʊ·sart] *m* buzzard
büßen ['by:·sn̩] I. *vt* to pay for; **das wirst du mir ~!** I'll make you pay for that! II. *vi* **dafür wird er mir ~!** I'll make him suffer for that!
Bußgeld *nt* fine (*for traffic or tax offenses*)
Büste <-, -n> ['bʏs·tə] *f* bust
Büstenhalter *m* bra[ssiere]

Butangas *nt* butane gas
Butter <-> ['bʊ·tɐ] *f kein pl* butter
▶WENDUNGEN: **weich wie ~** as soft as can be
Butterblume *f* buttercup
Butterbrot *nt* slice of buttered bread
Butterbrotpapier *nt* wax paper
Buttermilch *f* buttermilk
Butterschmalz *nt* clarified butter
butterweich ['bʊ·tɐ·vaiç] *adj* really soft
Byte <-s, -s> [bait] *nt* byte

Cc

C, c <-, -> [tse:] *nt* ❶ C, c; **~ wie Cäsar** C as in Charlie ❷ MUS C, c; **das hohe ~** high C
C *Abk von* **Celsius** C
ca. *Abk von* **circa** approx., ca
Café <-s, -s> [ka·'fe:] *nt* café
Cafeteria <-, -s> [ka·fe·tə·'ri:a] *f* cafeteria
Camping <-s> ['kɛm·pɪŋ] *nt kein pl* camping
Campingplatz *m* campsite
CD <-, -s> [tse:·'de:] *f Abk von* **Compactdisc** CD
CD-ROM <-, -s> [tse:·de:·'rɔm] *f* CD-ROM
CD-Spieler *m* CD player
Cellist(in) <-en, -en> [tʃɛ·'lɪst] *m(f)* cellist
Cello <-s, -s> ['tʃɛ·lo] *nt* cello
Celsius ['tsɛl·zi·ʊs] *kein art* Celsius
Cembalo <-s, -s> ['tʃɛm·ba·lo] *nt* harpsichord
Cent <-(s), -(s)> ['sɛnt] *m* cent
Champagner <-s, -> [ʃam·'pan·jɐ] *m* champagne
Champignon <-s, -s> ['ʃam·pɪn·jɔn] *m* mushroom
Chance <-, -n> ['ʃã·sə] *f* chance; **die ~n** *pl* **stehen gut** there's a good chance; **die ~n** *pl* **stehen schlecht** there's little chance
Chancengleichheit *f kein pl* equal opportunity
Chaos <-> ['ka:·ɔs] *nt kein pl* chaos
Chaot(in) <-en, -en> [ka·'o:t] *m(f)* chaotic person
chaotisch [ka·'o:tɪʃ] *adj* chaotic
Charakter <-s, -e> [ka·'rak·tɐ, *pl* -'te:·rə] *m einer Person* character; *einer Sache* nature *no indef art*
Charaktereigenschaft *f* characteristic
charakterfest *adj* with strength of character *pred*
charakterisieren* [ka·rak·te·ri·'zi:·rən] *vt* to characterize
charakteristisch [ka·rak·te·'rɪs·tɪʃ] *adj* characteristic (**für** +*akk* of)
Charakterzug *m* characteristic
charmant [ʃar·'mant] I. *adj* charming II. *adv* charmingly
Charme <-s> ['ʃarm] *m kein pl* charm
Chauffeur(in) <-s, -e> [ʃɔ·'fø:ɐ] *m(f)* chauffeur
Chauvinist(in) <-en, -en> [ʃo·vi·'nɪst] *m(f)* chauvinist
chauvinistisch [ʃo·vi·'nɪs·tɪʃ] I. *adj* chauvinistic II. *adv* chauvinistically

checken ['tʃɛ·kn̩] vt ① (*überprüfen*) to check ② (*sl: begreifen*) to get

Chef(in) <-s, -s> [ʃɛf] m(f) head; (*einer Firma*) manager

Chefarzt, -ärztin m, f head doctor

Chefkoch, -köchin m, f head cook

Chefredakteur(in) m(f) editor in chief

Chemie <-> [çe·'mi:] f kein pl chemistry

Chemiefaser f man-made fiber

Chemiker(in) <-s, -> ['çe·mi·kɐ] m(f) chemist

chemisch ['çe:·mɪʃ] adj chemical

Chemotherapie f chemotherapy

Chiffre <-, -n> ['ʃɪf·rə] f ① (*Kennziffer*) box number ② (*Zeichen*) cipher

Chile <-s> ['tʃi·le] nt Chile; s. a. **Deutschland**

Chilene, Chilenin <-n, -n> [tʃi·'le:·nə] m, f Chilean; s. a. **Deutsche(r)**

China <-s> ['çi:·na] nt China; s. a. **Deutschland**

Chinese, Chinesin <-n, -n> [çi·'ne:·zə, çi·'ne:·zɪn] m, f Chinese [person]; s. a. **Deutsche(r)**

chinesisch [çi·'ne:·zɪʃ] adj Chinese ▶WENDUNGEN: ~ **für jdn sein** (*fam*) to be all Greek to sb; s. a. **deutsch**

Chip <-s, -s> [tʃɪp] m ① COMPUT [micro]chip ② meist pl KOCHK chip usu pl

Chirurg(in) <-en, -en> [çi·'rʊrk] m(f) surgeon

Chirurgie <-, -n> [çi·rʊr·'gi:] f kein pl surgery

chirurgisch [çi·'rʊr·gɪʃ] adj surgical

Chlor <-s> [klo:ɐ̯] nt kein pl chlorine

Chloroform <-s> [klo·ro·'fɔrm] nt kein pl chloroform

Chlorophyll <-s> [klo·ro·'fyl] nt kein pl chlorophyll

Cholera <-> ['ko:·le·ra] f kein pl cholera

cholerisch [ko·'le:·rɪʃ] adj choleric

Cholesterin <-s> [kol·ɛs·te·'ri:n] nt kein pl cholesterol

Cholesterinspiegel m cholesterol level

Chor <-[e]s, Chöre> [ko:ɐ̯] m chorus; REL choir

Choral <-s, Choräle> [ko·'ra:l] m choral[e]

Choreograf(in)RR <-en, -en> [ko·reo·'gra:f] m(f) choreographer

ChoreografieRR <-, -n> [ko·reo·gra·'fi:] f choreography

Christ(in) <-en, -en> ['krɪst] m(f) Christian

Christbaum m DIAL Christmas tree

Christentum <-s> nt kein pl Christianity

Christkind nt ① (*Jesus*) Christ child ② (*weihnachtliche Gestalt*) Santa Claus; **ans ~ glauben** to believe in Santa Claus

christlich adj Christian

Christmette f Christmas mass

Christus <Christi, dat -, akk -> ['krɪs·tʊs] m Christ; **nach/vor ~** A.D./B.C.; **Christi Himmelfahrt** Ascension

Chrom <-s> ['kro:m] nt kein pl chrome

Chromosom <-s, -en> [kro·mo·'zo:m] nt chromosome

Chronik <-, -en> ['kro:·nɪk] f chronicle

chronisch ['kro:·nɪʃ] adj chronic; ■etw ist bei jdm ~ sb has [a] chronic [case of] sth

chronologisch [kro·no·'lo:·gɪʃ] adj chronological

circa ['tsɪr·ka] adv s. **zirka**

Clip <-s, -s> ['klɪp] m ① (*Klemme*) clip ② (*Ohrschmuck*) clip-on [earring] ③ (*Videoclip*) video

Clique <-, -n> ['klɪ·kə] f circle of friends

Clown(in) <-s, -s> [klaun] m(f) clown ▶WENDUNGEN: **sich** akk **zum ~ machen** to make a fool of oneself

CO₂-Fußabdruck [tse·'ʔo:·'tsvai-] m carbon footprint

Code <-s, -s> m s. **Kode**

Computer <-s, -> [kɔm·'pju:·tɐ] m computer; [etw] **auf ~ umstellen** to computerize [sth]

computergesteuert I. adj computer-controlled II. adv under computer control

Computerspiel nt computer game

D

Container <-s, -> [kɔn·'te:·nɐ] *m* container

Cookie <-s, -s> ['kʊ·kɪ] *nt* INET cookie

Cord <-s> ['kɔrt] *m kein pl* corduroy

Couch <-, -s> [kautʃ] *f o* SCHWEIZ *m* couch

Couchgarnitur *f* couch set

Couchtisch *m* coffee table

couragiert [ku·ra·'ʒi:ɐt] *adj* bold

Cousin, Cousine <-s, -s> [ku·'zɛ̃:, ku·'zi·nə] *m, f* cousin

Crack[1] <-s, -> ['krɛk] *m* (*ausgezeichneter Spieler*) ace

Crack[2] <-s> ['krɛk] *nt kein pl* (*Rauschgift*) crack

Creme <-, -s> ['kre:m, 'krɛ:m] *f* ❶ (*Salbe*) cream ❷ (*Sahnespeise*) mousse

cremefarben *adj* cream-colored

cremig *adj* creamy

Curry <-s, -s> ['kœri] *m o nt* curry

Dd

D, d <-, -> [de:] *nt* ❶ (*Buchstabe*) D, d; ~ **wie Dora** D as in Delta ❷ MUS D, d

da ['da:] **I.** *adv* ❶ (*dort*) there; (*hier*) here; ~ **sein** to be there/here; ~ **bist du ja!** there you are!; ~ **drüben/vorne** over there; ~ **hinten** back there; ~ **draußen/drinnen** out/in there; **der/die/das ...** ~ this ... [over] here [*or* that ... [over] there] ❷ (*dann*) then; **von** ~ **an herrschte endlich Ruhe** after that it was finally quiet ❸ (*in diesem Fall*) in this case; ~ **bin ich ganz deiner Meinung** I completely agree with you **II.** *konj* (*weil*) since, as

dabei [da·'bai] *adv* ❶ (*örtlich*) with [it/them]; **die Rechnung war nicht** ~ the bill was not enclosed; **direkt/nahe** ~ right next to/near it ❷ (*zeitlich*) at the same time; (*währenddessen*) while doing it ❸ (*anwesend, beteiligt*) there; ~ **sein** to be there; **bist du** ~? are you with us? ❹ (*damit verbunden*) through it/them; **was hast du dir denn** ~ **gedacht?** what [on earth] were you thinking?; **ich habe mir nichts** ~ **gedacht** I didn't mean anything by it; **da ist** [doch] **nichts** ~ there's nothing to it; **das Dumme/Schöne** ~ **ist, ...** the stupid/good thing about it is ...

dableiben *vi irreg sein* to stay there

Dach <-[e]s, Dächer> ['dax] *nt* (*Gebäudeteil, a. vom Auto*) roof ▶WENDUNGEN: **[von jdm] eins aufs** ~ **kriegen** (*fam*) to be given a talking-to [by sb]; **jdm aufs** ~ **steigen** (*fam*) to jump down sb's throat

Dachboden *m* attic

Dachdecker(in) <-s, -> *m(f)* roofer

Dachfenster *nt* skylight

Dachgepäckträger *m* roof rack

Dachrinne *f* gutter

Dachs <-es, -e> ['daks] *m* badger

Dachstuhl *m* roof truss

Dachziegel *m* [roofing] tile

Dackel <-s, -> ['da·kl] *m* dachshund

dadurch [da·'dʊrç] *adv* ❶ *örtlich* through [it/them] ❷ ■~, **dass ...** because ... ❸ (*auf diese Weise*) this is how

dafür [da·'fy:ɐ] *adv* ❶ (*für das*) for it/this/that; **warum ist er böse? er hat doch keinen Grund** ~ why's he angry? he has no reason to be; **es ist ein Beweis** ~, **dass ...** it's proof that ...; ~ **bin ich ja da** that's what I'm here for ❷ (*als Gegenleistung*) in return ❸ (*andererseits*) **in Mathematik ist er schlecht,** ~ **kann er gut Fußball spielen** he's bad at math, but he makes up for it with soccer; **er ist zwar nicht**

kräftig, ~ aber intelligent he may not be strong, but [at least] he's smart ❹ *(im Hinblick darauf)* ■**~, dass ...** seeing [that] ... ❺ ■**~ sein** *(zustimmen)* to be for it/that

dagegen [daˈgeːɡn̩] **I.** *adv* ❶ *(räumlich)* against it ❷ *(als Einwand, Ablehnung)* against it/that; **~ müsst ihr was tun** you have to do something about it; **etwas/nichts ~ haben** to mind/not mind sth; **ich habe nichts ~ [einzuwenden]** that's fine by me ❸ *(als Gegenmaßnahme)* **das hilft gut ~** this will help; **~ lässt sich nichts machen** you can't do anything about it ❹ *(vergleichen damit)* compared with it/that/them ❺ ■**~ sein** *(nicht zustimmen)* to be against it **II.** *konj (jedoch)* whereas

daheim [daˈhaim] *adv* SÜDD, ÖSTERR, SCHWEIZ at home

daher [daˈheːɐ̯] *adv* ❶ *(von da)* from there ❷ *(aus dieser Quelle)* **~ hat er das** that's where he got it [from]; **~ weißt du es also** so that's how you know [that] ❸ *(aus diesem Grund)* [and] that's why; **das kommt ~, dass ...** that is because ...

dahin [daˈhɪn] *adv* ❶ *(an diesen Ort)* there; **kommst du mit ~?** are you coming along?; **ist es noch weit bis ~?** is there still a ways to go? *fam* ❷ *(zeitlich)* ■**bis ~** until then ❸ *(in dem Sinne)* ■**äußerte sich ~ gehend, dass ...** he said something to the effect that ...

dahin|schmelzen *vi irreg sein (hum)* to melt, to get [all] gooey *fam*

dahinten [daˈhɪntn̩] *adv* back there

dahinter [daˈhɪntɐ] *adv* behind it/that/behind etc.

Dahlie <-, -n> [ˈdaːli̯ə] *f* dahlia

damalig [ˈdaːmaːlɪç] *adj attr* at that time *pred*

Dame <-, -n> [ˈdaːmə] *f* ❶ lady; **meine ~n und Herren!** ladies and gentlemen! ❷ *(Damespiel)* checkers + *sing vb* ❸ *(bei Schach, Karten)* queen

Damebrett [ˈdaːməbrɛt] *nt* checkerboard

Damenbinde *f* sanitary napkin

Damenfahrrad *nt* women's bicycle

Damespiel *nt* [game of] checkers + *sing vb*

damit [daˈmɪt] **I.** *adv* ❶ with it/that; **was soll ich ~?** what am I supposed to do with this/that?; **weißt du, was sie ~ meint?** do you know what she means by that?; **ist Ihre Frage ~ beantwortet?** has that answered your question?; **ich habe nichts ~ zu tun** I have nothing to do with this; **hör auf ~!** knock it off!; **sind Sie ~ einverstanden?** do you agree [to/with it/that]? **II.** *konj* so that

dämlich [ˈdɛːmlɪç] *(fam)* **I.** *adj* stupid **II.** *adv* **sich** *akk* **~ anstellen** to be awkward

Damm <-[e]s, Dämme> [ˈdam] *m* *(Staudamm)* dam; *(Deich)* dike ►WENDUNGEN: **wieder auf dem ~ sein** to be on one's feet again

dämmern [ˈdɛmɐn] **I.** *vi* ❶ *Tag, Morgen* to dawn; *Abend* to approach ❷ *(fig)* ■**jdm ~** to [gradually] dawn on sb **II.** *vi impers* ■**es dämmert** *(morgens)* dawn is breaking; *(abends)* night is falling

Dämmerung <-, -en> *f* twilight; *(abends)* dusk; *(morgens)* dawn

Dämon <-s, Dämonen> [ˈdɛːmɔn] *m* demon

Dampf <-[e]s, Dämpfe> [ˈdampf] *m* steam; *s. a.* **ablassen**

Dampfbügeleisen *nt* steam iron

dampfen [ˈdampfn̩] *vi* to steam

dämpfen [ˈdɛmpfn̩] *vt* ❶ *Gemüse* to steam ❷ *Stimme* to lower ❸ *Stoß, Begeisterung* to dampen

Dampfer <-s, -> [ˈdampfɐ] *m* steamship ►WENDUNGEN: **auf dem falschen ~ sein** to be barking up the wrong tree

Dampfmaschine *f* steam engine

Dampfwalze *f* steamroller

danach [daˈnaːx] *adv* ❶ *zeitlich* after it/that; *(nachher a.)* afterwards; **ein paar Minuten ~** a few minutes later ❷ *örtlich* behind [her/him/it/them etc.] ❸ *(laut dem)* according to that ❹ *(nach dieser Sache)* **~ greifen** to [make a] grab for it; **sich** *akk* ~ **sehnen** to long for it/that; ■**jdm ist ~/nicht ~** sb feels/doesn't feel like it

Däne, Dänin <-n, -n> ['dɛːnə, 'dɛːnɪn] *m, f* Dane; *s. a.* **Deutsche(r)**

daneben [daˈneːbn̩] *adv* ❶ *(räumlich)* next to her/him/it/that etc.; **links/rechts** ~ *(bei Gegenständen)* to the left/right of it/them; *(bei Menschen)* to her/his left/right ❷ *(verglichen damit)* compared with her/him/it/that etc. ❸ *(außerdem)* in addition [to that] ▶WENDUNGEN: ~ **sein** *(unangemessen)* to be inappropriate

daneben|gehen *vi irreg sein* ❶ *(Ziel verfehlen)* miss; *Pfeil, Schuss a.* to miss its/their mark ❷ *(scheitern)* to go wrong

Dänemark <-s> ['dɛːnəˌmark] *nt* Denmark; *s. a.* **Deutschland**

dänisch ['dɛːnɪʃ] *adj* Danish; *s. a.* **deutsch**

dank ['daŋk] *präp +gen* (*a. iron*) thanks to

Dank <-[e]s> ['daŋk] *m kein pl* gratitude; **vielen ~!** thank you very much!, thanks a lot; *fam;* **das ist der [ganze] ~ dafür!** that is/was all the thanks one gets/got!

dankbar ['daŋkˌbaːɐ̯] *adj* grateful; ■**jdm ~ sein** to be grateful to sb

Dankbarkeit <-> *f kein pl* gratitude

danke *interj* thank you, thanks *fam*

danken ['daŋkn̩] **I.** *vi* ■**jdm ~** to thank sb, to express one's thanks to sb; **nichts zu ~** you're welcome **II.** *vt* ■**jdm etw ~** to repay sb for sth; **wie kann ich Ihnen das jemals ~?** how can I ever thank you?

dann ['dan] *adv* ❶ *(danach)* then; **noch eine Woche, ~ ist Weihnachten** one more week until Christmas ❷ *(zu dem Zeitpunkt)* ■**immer ~, wenn ...** whenever ... ❸ *(unter diesen Umständen)* then; ■**wenn ..., ~ ...** if ..., [then] ...; ■**selbst ~** even then ❹ *(außerdem)* ■**und ~ auch noch ...** on top of that ... ▶WENDUNGEN: ~ **und wann** now and then

daran [daˈran] *adv* ❶ *(räumlich)* **halt deine Hand ~!** put your hand [up] against it; **etw ~ befestigen** to fasten sth to it; ~ **riechen** to smell it; ~ **vorbei** past it ❷ *(zeitlich)* **im Anschluss** ~ following that/this ❸ *(an dieser Sache)* **es ändert sich nichts ~** it won't change; **denk ~!** don't forget!; **das Gute ~ ist, dass ...** the good thing about it is that ...; **kein Interesse** ~ no interest in it/that; ~ **arbeiten** to work on it/that; **sich** *akk* ~ **beteiligen** to take part in it/that; **sich** *akk* ~ **erinnern** to remember it/that

daran|gehen *vi irreg sein* to get started

daran|machen *vr* ■**sich** *akk* ~ to get started

daran|setzen [daˈranˌzɛt·sn̩] *vt* **alles ~, etw zu tun** to make every effort to do sth

darauf [daˈrauf] *adv* ❶ *(räumlich)* on it/that/them etc. ❷ *(zeitlich)* after that; **bald** ~ shortly afterwards; **am Abend** ~ the next evening; **im Jahr [in] ~** the following year ❸ *(auf das)* **wir müssen** ~ **Rücksicht nehmen** we must take that into consideration; ~ **antworten** to reply to it/that; **etw** ~ **sagen** to say sth to it/this/that; **ein Recht** ~ a right to it/that; **sich** *akk* ~ **verlassen** to rely on it/that; **sich** *akk* ~ **vorbereiten** to prepare for it/that

daraufhin [daˌraufˈhɪn] *adv* ❶ *(nachher)* after that ❷ *(infolgedessen)* as a result [of this/that]

daraus [daˈraus] *adv* ❶ *(aus Gefäß, Raum)* out of it/that/them; **etw ~ entfernen** to remove sth from it ❷ *(aus diesem Material)* out of it/that/them ❸ *(aus dieser Tatsache)* ~ **folgt, dass ...** the result of which is that ...

Darbietung <-, -en> ['daːɐ̯biːˌtʊŋ] *f* performance

darin [daˈrɪn] *adv* ❶ *(in dem/der)* in there; *(in vorher Erwähntem)* in it/them; **was steht ~ [geschrieben]?** what does it say? ❷ *(in dem Punkt)* in that respect; ~ **übereinstimmen, dass** *akk* to agree that ...

dar|legen ['daːɐ̯·leː·gn̩] *vt* to explain

Darm <-[e]s, Därme> ['darm] *m* intestine

Darmgrippe *f* stomach flu

dar|stellen ['daːɐ̯·ʃtɛ·lən] *vt* ❶ (*wiedergeben*) to portray ❷ (*beschreiben*) to describe; **etw knapp ~** to give a brief description of sth ❸ (*bedeuten*) to represent

Darstellung <-, -en> *f* ❶ (*bildlich*) portrayal ❷ THEAT performance ❸ (*das Schildern*) representation

darüber [da·ˈryː·bɐ] *adv* ❶ (*räumlich*) over it/that/them; (*direkt auf etwas*) on top [of it/that]; (*oberhalb von etwas*) above [it/that/them]; (*über etwas hinweg*) over [it/that/them]; (*hinsichtlich einer Sache*) about it/that/them; **~ spricht er nicht gern** he doesn't like to talk about it/that ❸ (*dabei und deswegen*) in the process ❹ (*über dieser Grenze*) above [that]; **Kinder im Alter von 12 Jahren und ~** children 12 [years] and older/over; **10 Stunden oder ~** 10 hours and/or longer ▶WENDUNGEN: **~ hinaus** what is more; **~ hinweg sein** to have gotten over it

darum [da·ˈrʊm] *adv* ❶ (*deshalb*) that's why ❷ (*um das*) **~ bitten** to ask for it/that; **es geht nicht ~, wer zuerst kommt** it's not a question of who comes first; **~ geht es ja gerade!** that's just it!, that's exactly what I'm/we're talking about! ❸ (*räumlich*) ■~ [**herum**] around it

darunter [da·ˈrʊn·tɐ] *adv* ❶ (*räumlich*) under it/that; (*unterhalb von etw*) below [it/that]; **~ hervorgucken** to look out [from underneath] ❷ (*unter dieser Sache*) **was verstehst du ~?** what do you understand it/that to mean?; **~ kann ich mir nichts vorstellen** it doesn't mean anything to me ❸ (*dazwischen*) among[st] them ❹ (*unter dieser Grenze*) lower; **Kinder im Alter von 12 Jahren und ~** children 12 [years] and younger/under

das¹ <gen: des, dat: dem, akk: das, pl: die> ['das] *art def, sing nt* the; **~ Kind/**

Tier/Schiff the child/animal/ship; *s. a.* **der¹, die¹**

das² <gen: dessen, dat: dem, akk: das, pl: die> ['das] *pron dem* that; **~ Kind/Haus [da]** that child/house [there]; **was ist denn ~?** what on earth is that/this?; *s. a.* **der², die³**

das³ <gen: dessen, dat: dem, akk: das, pl: die> ['das] *pron rel, sing nt* that; (*Person a.*) who, whom *form*; (*Gegenstand, Tier a.*) which; **ich sah ein Auto, ~ um die Ecke fuhr** I saw a car driving around the corner; **ein Mädchen, ~ gut singen kann** a girl who can sing well; *s. a.* **der³, die⁵**

da|seinᴬᴸᵀ ['daː·zain] *vi irreg sein s.* **da I 1**

Dasein <-s> ['daː·zain] *nt kein pl* ❶ (*Existenz*) existence ❷ (*Anwesenheit*) presence

dasjenige <gen: desjenigen, dat: demjenigen, akk: dasjenige, pl: diejenigen> ['das·je·nɪ·ɡə] *pron dem* ❶ *substantivisch* ■~, **was ...** that which ... ❷ *adjektivisch* **~ Kind, das ...** the child that ...; *s. a.* **diejenige, derjenige**

dassᴿᴿ, **daß**ᴬᴸᵀ ['das] *konj* that; **ich habe gehört, ~ du Vater geworden bist** I heard [that] you became a father; **die Tatsache, ~ ...** the fact that ...

dasselbe <gen: desselben, dat: demselben, akk: dasselbe, pl: dieselben> *pron dem* **~ Kleid** the same dress; *s. a.* **derselbe, dieselbe**

Datei <-, -en> [da·ˈtai] *f* [data] file

Daten ['daː·tn̩] *pl* ❶ (*Angaben*) data ❷ *pl von* **Datum**

Datenabruf *m* data retrieval

Datenaufbereitung *f* data processing

Datenbank <-banken> *f* database

Datenhandschuh *m* data glove

Datenschutz *m* data [privacy] protection

Datensicherung *f* [data] backup

Datenträger *m* data medium

Datenverarbeitung *f* data processing

datieren* [da·ˈtiː·rən] *vt, vi* to date

Dativ <-s, -e> ['daː·tiːf] *m* dative [case]

Dattel <-, -n> ['da·tl̩] *f* date

D

Datum <-s, Daten> ['da:·tʊm] *nt* date; **welches ~ haben wir heute?** what's today's date?

Dauer <-> ['dau·ɐ] *f kein pl* duration; *eines Aufenthalts* length ▶WENDUNGEN: **von kurzer ~ sein** to be short-lived; **auf die ~** in the long run; **diesen Lärm kann auf die ~ keiner ertragen** nobody can stand this noise for any length of time

dauerhaft I. *adj Beziehung, Schaden* permanent; *Frieden, Wirkung* durable, lasting II. *adv* permanently

dauern ['dau·ɐn] *vi* ❶ (*anhalten*) to last; **der Film dauert 3 Stunden** the film is 3 hours long ❷ *impers* (*Zeit erfordern*) to take; **es wird nicht lange ~** it won't take long; **vier Stunden? das dauert mir zu lange** four hours? that's too long for me

dauernd ['dau·ɐnt] I. *adj* constant II. *adv* constantly; **etw ~ tun** to keep [on] doing sth

Dauerwelle *f* perm

Dauerzustand *m* permanent state of affairs

Daumen <-s, -> ['dau·mən] *m* thumb; **am ~ lutschen** to suck one's thumb ▶WENDUNGEN: **jdm die ~ drücken** to keep one's fingers crossed [for sb]

Daune <-, -n> ['dau·nə] *f* down

Daunendecke *f* duvet

davon [da·'fɔn] *adv* ❶ (*räumlich*) **links/rechts ~** to the left/right of it/that/them; **etw ~ lösen** to loosen sth from it/that ❷ (*von dieser Sache*) **was hältst du ~?** what do you think of it/that/them?; **~ weiß ich nichts** I don't know anything about it; **das Gegenteil ~** the opposite of it/that; **die Hälfte ~** half of it/that/them; **~ essen/trinken** to eat/drink some of it/that; **etwas/nichts ~ haben** to have some/not have any of it

davon|fliegen *vi irreg sein* to fly away; *Vögel a.* to fly off

davon|kommen *vi irreg sein* **mit dem Leben ~** to escape with one's life; **mit einem Schock ~** to come away with no more than a shock

davon|laufen *vi irreg sein* ■**jdm ~** ❶ (*weglaufen*) to run away from sb ❷ (*jdn abhängen*) to run ahead of sb ❸ (*überraschend verlassen*) to run out on sb

davon|machen *vr* ■**sich** *akk* **~** to slip away

davon|tragen *vt irreg* ❶ (*wegtragen*) to take away *sep* ❷ (*geh*) *Preis* to carry off *sep*; *Ruhm* to achieve; *Sieg* to score ❸ (*erleiden*) *Knochenbruch, Verletzung* to suffer

davor [da·'fo:ɐ] *adv* ❶ (*räumlich*) in front [of it/that/them]; **~ musst du links abbiegen** you have to turn left before [you get to] it ❷ (*zeitlich*) before [it/that/them/etc.] ❸ *mit Verben* **er hat Angst ~** he's afraid of it/that; **er hatte mich ~ gewarnt** he warned me about it/that

dazu [da·'tsu:, 'da:·tsu:] *adv* ❶ (*zu dem gehörend*) with it ❷ (*außerdem*) at the same time ❸ (*zu diesem Ergebnis*) **wie konnte es nur ~ kommen?** how could that happen?; **~ reicht das Geld nicht** we/I don't have enough money for that ❹ **im Gegensatz ~** in contrast to that; **im Vergleich ~** compared to that ❺ (*zu dieser Sache*) **ich würde dir ~ raten** I would advise you to do that; **ich bin noch nicht ~ gekommen** I haven't gotten around to it/that yet; **es gehört viel Mut ~** that takes a lot of courage ❻ (*dafür*) **ich bin ~ nicht bereit** I'm not prepared to do that; **~ ist es da** that's what it's there for ❼ (*darüber*) **er hat sich noch nicht ~ geäußert** he hasn't commented on it/that yet; **was meinst du ~?** what do you think about it/that?

dazu|gehören* *vi* ❶ (*zu der Sache gehören*) to belong [to it/etc.] ❷ (*nicht wegzudenken sein*) be a part of it

dazu|tun *vt irreg* to add

Dazutun *nt* **ohne jds ~** without sb's intervention

dazwischen [da·'tsvɪ·ʃn] *adv* ❶ (*zwi-*

schen zwei Dingen) [in] between; (*darunter*) among[st] them ❷ (*zeitlich*) in between

dazwischen|kommen *vi irreg sein* **wenn nichts dazwischenkommt!** if everything goes according to plan!; **leider ist [mir] etwas dazwischengekommen** I'm afraid something has come up

dealen ['diː·lən] *vi* (*sl*) [**mit Drogen** *dat*] ~ to deal [drugs]

Dealer(in) <-s, -> ['diː·lɐ] *m(f)* (*sl*) drug dealer

Debatte <-, -n> [de·'ba·tə] *f* debate; (*schwächer*) discussion; **zur ~ stehen** to be under discussion; **das steht hier nicht zur ~** that's beside the point

debattieren* [de·ba·'tiː·ʀən] *vt* to debate; (*schwächer*) to discuss

Deck <-[e]s, -s> [dɛk] *nt* deck

Decke <-, -n> ['dɛ·kə] *f* ❶ (*Zimmerdecke*) ceiling ❷ (*Tischdecke*) tablecloth ❸ (*Wolldecke*) blanket; (*Bettdecke*) covers *pl* ▶WENDUNGEN: **jdm fällt die ~ auf den Kopf** sb feels really cooped up; **an die ~ gehen** to go through the roof

Deckel <-s, -> ['dɛ·kl̩] *m* ❶ (*Verschluss*) lid; *von Glas, Schachtel a.* top ❷ (*Buchdeckel*) cover ▶WENDUNGEN: **jdm eins auf den ~ geben** to slap sb upside the head

decken ['dɛ·kn̩] I. *vt* ❶ *Tisch* to set ❷ *Dach* to shingle ❸ (*etw verheimlichen*) ▪**jdn ~** to cover up for sb; ▪**etw ~** to cover up *sep* sth ❹ *Nachfrage* to meet; *Kosten* to cover II. *vi* **diese Farbe deckt besser** this paint covers better III. *vr* ▪**sich** *akk* ~ *Aussagen* to correspond

Deckenbeleuchtung *f* ceiling lights *pl*

Deckname *m* code name

Deckung <-, -en> *f* ❶ (*Schutz*) cover ❷ ÖKON **die ~ der Kosten** to cover the costs; **die ~ der Nachfrage** to meet the demand

defekt [de·'fɛkt] *adj* faulty

Defekt <-[e]s, -e> [de·'fɛkt] *m* defect

Defensive [de·fɛn·'ziː·və] *f* **in die ~ gehen** to go on the defensive

definieren* [de·fi·'niː·ʀən] *vt* to define

Definition <-, -en> [de·fi·ni·'tsi̯oːn] *f* definition

definitiv [de·fi·ni·'tiːf] I. *adj* (*genau*) definite; (*endgültig a.*) definitive II. *adv* (*genau*) definitely; (*endgültig a.*) definitively

Defizit <-s, -e> ['deː·fi·tsɪt] *nt* deficit

dehnbar *adj* ❶ *Material* elastic ❷ *Begriff* flexible

dehnen ['deː·nən] *vt, vr* ▪**[sich** *akk*] ~ to stretch

Deich <-[e]s, -e> ['daiç] *m* dike

dein ['dain] *pron poss, adjektivisch* your; **herzliche Grüße, ~e Anita/~ Paul** best wishes, love Anita/Paul

deine(r, s) ['dai·nə] *pron poss, substantivisch* yours; **diese Tasche ist ~** this bag is yours

deinerseits ['dai·nɐ·'zaits] *adv* (*von dir aus*) on your part; (*auf deiner Seite*) for your part

deinetwegen ['dai·nət·ve··gn̩] *adv* ❶ (*wegen dir*) because of you ❷ (*dir zuliebe*) for your sake

Dekan(in) <-s, -e> [de·'kaːn] *m(f)* UNIV dean; REL deacon

deklinieren* [de·kli·'niː·ʀən] *vt* to decline

Dekor <-s, -s> [de·'koːɐ̯] *m o nt* pattern

Dekorateur(in) <-s, -e> [de·ko·ʀa·'tøːɐ̯] *m(f)* (*Schaufensterdekorateur*) window dresser

Dekoration <-, -en> [de·ko·ʀa·'tsi̯oːn] *f* decoration

dekorativ [de·ko·ʀa·'tiːf] *adj* decorative

dekorieren* [de·ko·'ʀiː·ʀən] *vt* to decorate

Delegierte(r) *f(m)* *dekl wie adj* delegate

DelfinRR <-s, -e> [dɛl·'fiːn] *m s.* **Delphin**

delikat [de·li·'kaːt] *adj* ❶ (*wohlschmeckend*) delicious ❷ (*heikel*) sensitive

Delikatesse <-, -n> [de·li·ka·'tɛ·sə] *f* delicacy

Delikt <-[e]s, -e> [de·'lɪkt] *nt* JUR ❶ (*Verstoß*) offense ❷ (*Straftat*) crime

D

Delirium <-s, -rien> [deˈliːrɪˌʊm] *nt* delirium

Delle <-, -n> [ˈdɛlə] *f* dent

Delphin <-s, -e> [dɛlˈfiːn] *m* dolphin

dem [deːm] **I.** *art def dat sing von* **der¹**, **das¹:** **er gab ~ Kind das Geld** he gave the money to the child; **ich werde es ~ Klaus sagen** (*fam*) I'll tell Klaus **II.** *pron dem dat sing von* **der²**, **das²:** **das Fahrrad gehört ~ Mann/Kind** [**da**] the bike belongs to that man/child [[over] there] **III.** *pron rel sing von* **der³:** **der Freund, mit ~ ich mich gut verstehe** the [male] friend that I get along so well with; **der Hund, ~ er zu fressen gibt** the dog that he is feeding

dementsprechend [ˈdeːmˌʔɛntˈʃprɛçnt] **I.** *adj* appropriate **II.** *adv* according-ly; **sich** *akk* **~ äußern** to utter words to that effect; **~ bezahlt werden** to be paid commensurately *form*

demnach [ˈdeːmˌnaːx] *adv* therefore

demnächst [deːmˈnɛːçst] *adv* soon

Demokrat(in) <-en, -en> [deˈmo-ˈkraːt] *m(f)* democrat

Demokratie <-, -n> [demokraˈtiː] *f* democracy

demokratisch [demoˈkraːtɪʃ] **I.** *adj* democratic **II.** *adv* democratically

demolieren* [demoˈliːrən] *vt Auto* to wreck; *Gebäude* to demolish

Demonstrant(in) <-en, -en> [demɔnˈstrant] *m(f)* demonstrator

Demonstration <-, -en> [demɔnstraˈtsi̯oːn] *f* demonstration (**für** +*akk* in support of, **gegen** +*akk* against)

demonstrativ [demɔnstraˈtiːf] **I.** *adj* demonstrative **II.** *adv* demonstratively

Demonstrativpronomen *nt* demon-strative pronoun

demonstrieren* [demɔnˈstriːrən] *vt, vi* to demonstrate (**für** +*akk* in support of, **gegen** +*akk* against)

Demut <-> [ˈdeːˌmuːt] *f kein pl* humil-ity (**gegenüber** +*dat* before)

demütig [ˈdeːˌmyːtɪç] **I.** *adj* humble **II.** *adv* humbly

demütigen [ˈdeːˌmyːtɪɡn] *vt* to hu-miliate

Demütigung <-, -en> *f* humiliation

den [deːn] **I.** *art def* ① *akk sing von* **der¹:** **er kennt ~ Mann** he knows the man; **grüße bitte ~ Klaus von mir** (*fam*) please give Klaus my regards ② *dat pl von* **die²:** **sie hilft ~ Armen** she helps the poor **II.** *pron dem akk sing von* **der²:** **~ Mann da** [**drüben**] that man [over] there **III.** *pron rel akk sing von* **der³:** **der Mann, ~ ich gesehen habe** the man [that] I saw; **der Hund, ~ er füttert** the dog [that] he is feeding

denkbar **I.** *adj* imaginable **II.** *adv* **das ~ beste/schlechteste Wetter** the best/worst possible weather

Denkblockade *f* PSYCH mental block

denken <dachte, gedacht> [ˈdɛŋkn] *vt, vi* ① (*überlegen*) to think (**an** +*akk* of); **langsam/schnell ~** to think slowly/quickly ② (*meinen*) to think; **ich denke nicht** I don't think so; **wer hätte das** [**von ihr**] **gedacht!** who'd have expected that/it [from her]? ③ (*ur-teilen*) to think (**über** +*akk* about); **wie ~ Sie darüber?** what's your view [on it/that]?; **ich denke genauso darüber** that's exactly what I think ④ (*sich erin-nern*) **solange ich ~ kann** [for] as long as I can remember; **die wird noch an mich ~!** she won't forget me in a hurry! ⑤ ■ **für jdn/etw gedacht sein** to be meant for sb/sth ⑥ (*beabsichtigen*) **ich habe mir nichts Böses dabei gedacht**[, **als** ...] I meant no harm [when ...] ▶WENDUNGEN: **jdm zu ~ geben** to give sb food for thought; **das gab mir zu ~** that made me think

Denkmal <-s, Denkmäler> [ˈdɛŋk-maːl] *nt* memorial

Denkmalschutz *m* **unter ~ stehen** to be designated as a historical landmark

denkwürdig *adj* memorable

denn [dɛn] *konj* ① (*weil*) because; **~ sonst** otherwise ② ■ **es sei** [**dass**] ... unless ... ③ **schöner ~ je** more beautiful than ever

dennoch [ˈdɛnɔx] *adv* still

denunzieren* [denʊnˈtsiːrən] *vt* to denounce

D

Deo <-s, -s> ['de:o] *nt* (*fam*) deodorant

Deoroller *m* roll-on [deodorant]

Deponie <-, -n> [de·po·'ni:] *f* disposal site

deponieren* [de·po·'ni:·rən] *vt* to deposit

deportieren* [de·pɔr·'ti:·rən] *vt* to deport

Depot <-s, -s> [de·'po:] *nt* ①(*Lager*) depot ②(*für Straßenbahnen, Omnibusse*) [streetcar/bus] depot ③ SCHWEIZ (*Flaschenpfand*) deposit

Depp <-en, -e[n]> ['dɛp] *m* ÖSTERR, SCHWEIZ, SÜDD (*fam*) idiot

Depression <-, -en> [de·prɛ·'si̯o:n] *f* PSYCH, ÖKON depression

depressiv [de·prɛ·'si:f] I. *adj* depressive; (*deprimiert*) depressed II. *adv* ~ **veranlagt** prone to depression

deprimieren* [de·pri·'mi:·rən] *vt* to be depressing

der[1] <*gen:* des, *dat:* dem, *akk:* den, *pl:* die> ['de:ɐ] *art def, sing m* the; ~ **Nachbar/Hengst/Käse** the neighbor/stallion/cheese; ~ **Papa hat's mir erzählt** (*fam*) dad told me; ~ **Andreas lässt dich grüßen** (*fam*) Andreas says hi; *s. a.* **das**[1], **die**[1]

der[2] <*gen:* dessen, *dat:* dem, *akk:* den, *pl:* die> ['de:ɐ] *pron dem, sing m* that; ~ **Mann/Hengst/Stuhl** [da] that man/stallion/chair [over] there]; ~ **mit den roten Haaren** the guy/man/one with the red hair; **wo ist dein Bruder?** – ~ **kommt gleich** where's your brother? – he'll be here soon; *s. a.* **das**[2], **die**[3]

der[3] <*gen:* dessen, *dat:* dem, *akk:* den, *pl:* die> ['de:ɐ] *pron rel, sing m* that; (*Person a.*) who; (*Gegenstand, Tier a.*) which; **der Mann,** ~ **es eilig hatte** the man who was in a hurry; **ein Film,** ~ **gut ankommt** a highly-acclaimed film; **ein Zahn,** ~ **wackelt** a tooth that is loose; *s. a.* **das**[3], **die**[5]

der[4] ['de:ɐ] I. *art def* ① *gen sing von* **die**: **die Augen** ~ **Katze** the eyes of the cat, the cat's eyes ② *dat sing von* **die**[1]: **er half** ~ **Frau** he helped the

woman; **an** ~ **Decke hängen** to hang from the ceiling; **ich werde es** ~ **Anne sagen** (*fam*) I'll tell Anne ③ *gen pl von* **die**[2]: **die Wünsche** ~ **Männer/Frauen/Kinder** the men's/women's/children's wishes; **das Ende** ~ **Ferien** the end of vacation II. *pron dem dat sing von* **die**[3]: **das Fahrrad gehört** ~ **Frau** [da] the bike belongs to that woman [over there] III. *pron rel dat sing von* **die**[5]: **die Freundin, mit** ~ **ich mich gut verstehe** my [girl]friend that I get along so well with; **die Katze,** ~ **er zu fressen gibt** the cat [that] he is feeding; **die Hitze, unter** ~ **sie leiden** the heat [that] they're suffering from

derart ['de:ɐ·'ʔa·ɐt] *adv s.* **dermaßen**

derartig ['de:ɐ·'ʔa·ɐ·tɪç] *adj, adv* such

derb ['dɛrp] I. *adj* ①(*grob*) coarse; *Manieren* rough; *Ausdrucksweise, Witz* crude ②(*fest*) *Material, Schuhe* strong II. *adv* **jdn** ~ **anfassen** to handle sb roughly; **sich** *akk* ~ **ausdrücken** to be crude

dergleichen [de·ɐ·'glai̯·çn̩] *pron dem* that sort of thing; **nichts** ~ nothing like it; **ich will nichts** ~ **hören!** I'm not interested in hearing any of that!

derjenige <*gen:* desjenigen, *dat:* demjenigen, *akk:* denjenigen, *pl:* diejenigen> ['de:ɐ·je:·nɪ·gə] *pron dem, sing m* ① *substantivisch* ■~, **der ...** *auf eine Person bezogen* the person who ..., whoever ...; *auf eine Sache bezogen* the one that ... ② *adjektivisch* that; ~ **Mann, der ...** the man who ...; *s. a.* **dasjenige, diejenige**

dermaßen ['de:ɐ·ma:sn̩] *adv* such; **jdn** ~ **unter Druck setzen, dass ...** to put sb under so much pressure that ...

derselbe <*gen:* desselben, *dat:* demselben, *akk:* denselben, *pl:* dieselben> [de:ɐ·'zɛlbə] *pron dem* the same; ~ **Pulli** the same sweater; *s. a.* **dasselbe, dieselbe**

derzeitig ['de:ɐ·tsai̯·tɪç] *adj attr* present

des ['dɛs] *art def gen sing von* **der**[1], **das**[1]: **das Aussehen** ~ **Kindes/Mannes** the child's/man's appearance; **ein**

D

Zeichen ~ Unbehagens a sign of un-easiness

desertieren* [de·zɛr·'tiː·rən] *vi sein* to desert

deshalb ['dɛs·'halp] *adv* because of it; ~ **frage ich ja** that's why I'm asking; **also** ~! [so] that's why!

Design <-s, -s> [di·'zaɪn] *nt* design

Designermode *f* designer fashion

Desinfektion <-, -en> [dɛs·ʔɪn·fɛk·'tsi̯oːn] *f* disinfection

Desinfektionsmittel *nt* disinfectant; (*für Wunden a.*) antiseptic

desinfizieren* [dɛs·ʔɪn·fi·'tsiː·rən] *vt* to disinfect

despotisch [dɛs·'poː·tɪʃ] I. *adj* despotic II. *adv* despotically

dessen ['dɛ·sn̩] I. *pron dem gen sing von* der², das²; **ein Freund und ~ Schwester** a [male] friend and his sister; **ein Buch und ~ Inhalt** a book and its contents II. *pron rel gen von* der³, das³ whose; (*von Sachen a.*) of which; **ein Junge, ~ Name ich nicht weiß** a boy whose name I do not know; **ein Buch, ~ Seiten verkleckst sind** a book that has stained pages

Dessert <-s, -s> [dɛ·'seːɐ̯, dɛ·'sɛːɐ̯] *nt* dessert

destillieren* [dɛs·tɪ·'liː·rən] *vt* to distill

desto ['dɛsto] *konj* **je einfacher ~ besser** the simpler the better; ~ **eher** the earlier; ~ **schlimmer** so much the worse

destruktiv [dɛs·trʊk·'tiːf] *adj* destructive

Detail <-s, -s> [de·'taɪ, de·'taːj] *nt* detail

detailliert [de·ta·'jiːɐ̯t] I. *adj* detailed II. *adv* in detail

Detektiv(in) <-s, -e> [de·tɛk·'tiːf] *m(f)* (*Privatdetektiv*) private investigator

deuten ['dɔy·tn̩] I. *vt* to interpret II. *vi* to point (**auf** +*akk* at)

deutlich ['dɔyt·lɪç] I. *adj* clear; *Umrisse* distinct; **das war ~!** that was very clear! II. *adv* clearly; **sich** *akk* ~ **ausdrücken** to make oneself clear

Deutlichkeit <-> *f kein pl* clarity; [**jdm**]

etw in aller ~ sagen to make sth perfectly clear [to sb]

deutsch ['dɔytʃ] *adj* German; **typisch ~ sein** to be typically German; ~**er Abstammung sein** to be of German origin; **die ~e Schweiz** German-speaking Switzerland; **die ~e Sprache** the German language; **die ~e Staatsbürgerschaft besitzen** to be a German citizen; **das ~e Volk** the German people; **die ~e Wiedervereinigung** the reunification of Germany

Deutsch ['dɔytʃ] *nt dekl wie adj* LING German; **können Sie ~?** do you speak/understand German?; **er spricht akzentfrei** ~ he speaks German without an accent; **sie spricht fließend** ~ she speaks fluent German; ~ **lernen** to learn German; ~ **sprechen** to speak German; ~ **verstehen** to understand German; **kein ~ verstehen** to not understand [any] German; ■ **auf ~** in German; **etw auf ~ sagen** to say sth in German; ~ **unterrichten** to teach German ►WENDUNGEN: **auf gut ~ [gesagt]** (*fam*) in plain English

Deutsche(r) *f(m) dekl wie adj* German; **er hat eine ~ geheiratet** he married a German [woman]; ■ **die ~n** the Germans; ~ **sein** to be German

Deutschland <-s> ['dɔytʃ·lant] *nt* Germany; **aus ~ kommen** to come from Germany; **in ~ leben** to live in Germany

deutschsprachig ['dɔytʃ·ʃpraː·xɪç] *adj* ❶ *Person* German-speaking *attr* ❷ *Literatur etc.* German[-language] *attr*

Devise <-, -n> [de·'viː·zə] *f* motto

Dezember <-s, -> [de·'tsɛm·bɐ] *m* December; *s. a.* **Februar**

dezent [de·'tsɛnt] I. *adj* discreet; *Farbe* subdued II. *adv* discreetly

dezentralisieren* [de·tsɛn·tra·li·'ziː·rən] *vt* to decentralize

dezimieren* [de·tsi·'miː·rən] *vt* (*geh*) to decimate

Dia <-s, -s> ['diː·a] *nt* slide

Diabetes <-> [dia·'beː·tɛs] *m kein pl* diabetes

D

Diabetiker(in) <-s, -> [dia·'be:·ti·kɐ] *m(f)* diabetic

Diagnose <-, -n> [dia·'gno:·zə] *f* diagnosis

diagnostizieren* [dia·gnɔs·ti·'tsi:·rən] *vt* to diagnose

diagonal [dia·go·'na:l] *adj* diagonal

Diagonale <-, -n> [dia·go·'na:·lə] *f* diagonal [line]

Diagramm <-s, -e> [dia·'gram] *nt* diagram

Diakon(in) <-s, -e[n]> [dia·'ko:n] *m(f)* deacon

Dialekt <-[e]s, -e> [dia·'lɛkt] *m* dialect

Dialog <-[e]s, -e> [dia·'lo:k] *m* dialogue

Diamant <-en, -en> [dia·'mant] *f* diamond

Diät <-, -en> [di·'ɛːt] *f* diet; ~ **halten** to keep to a diet; **auf** ~ **sein** to be on a diet; **jdn auf** ~ **setzen** to put sb on a diet

dich ['dɪç] **I.** *pron pers akk von* **du** you **II.** *pron refl* yourself; **du solltest** ~ **da raushalten** you should keep out of that/this; **wie fühlst du** ~? how do you feel?

dicht ['dɪçt] **I.** *adj* ❶ dense; *Haar* thick; *Verkehr* heavy ❷ (*wasserdicht*) **die Fenster sind wieder** ~ [now] the windows are sealed again ►WENDUNGEN: **nicht ganz** ~ **sein** (*pej fam*) to be out of one's mind *pej fam* **II.** *adv* ❶ (*nah*) closely; ~ **vor jdm** just in front of sb; ~ **beieinander** close together; ~ **gedrängt** squeezed together ❷ (*stark*) ~ **bevölkert** densely populated

Dichter(in) <-s, -> ['dɪç·tɐ] *m(f)* poet

dicht|halten ['dɪçt·haltn] *vi irreg* (*sl*) to keep one's mouth shut

Dichtung <-, -en> ['dɪç·tʊŋ] *f* ❶ *kein pl* LING poetry ❷ TECH seal[ing]

dick ['dɪk] **I.** *adj* ❶ (*von großem Umfang*) *Buch, Kleidung, Stamm* thick; *Bauch* fat; *Backen* chubby; **etwa fünf Meter** ~ about fifteen feet thick ❷ (*geschwollen*) swollen; *Beule* big ❸ (*dickflüssig*) thick ❹ (*fam*) *Freunde* close

II. *adv* ❶ (*warm*) **sich** *akk* ~ **anziehen** to dress warmly ❷ (*fig*) **mit jdm** ~ **befreundet sein** to be good friends with sb ►WENDUNGEN: ~ **auftragen** to lay it on thick *sl*; **jdn/etw** ~**[e] haben** (*fam*) to be sick of sb/sth

Dickdarm *m* large intestine

dickflüssig *adj* thick, viscous

Dickicht <-[e]s, -e> ['dɪ·kɪçt] *nt* thicket

dickköpfig *adj* stubborn, obstinate

die¹ <*gen:* der, *dat:* der, *akk:* die, *pl:* die> ['di:] *art def, sing fem* the; ~ **Tochter/ Stute/Theorie** the daughter/mare/theory; ~ **Mama hat's mir erzählt** (*fam*) mom told me; **ich bin** ~ **Susi** (*fam*) I'm Susi; *s. a.* **das¹, der¹**

die² <*gen:* der, *dat:* den, *akk:* die> ['di:] *art def, pl* ~ **Männer/Mütter/Pferde** the men/mothers/horses; *s. a.* **das¹, der¹**

die³ <*gen:* deren, *dat:* der, *akk:* die, *pl:* die> ['di:] *pron dem, sing fem* that; ~ **Frau/Stute/Tasche [da]** that woman/mare/bag [[over] there]; ~ **mit den roten Haaren** the girl/woman/one with the red hair; **wo ist deine Schwester?** – ~ **kommt gleich** where's your sister? — she'll be here soon; *s. a.* **das², der²**

die⁴ <*gen:* deren/derer, *dat:* denen, *akk:* die, *pl* ~ **Männer/Frauen/Stühle [da]** the men/women/chairs [over there]; ~ **mit den roten Haaren** the girls/women/ones with the red hair; ~ **waren es!** it was them!; **welche Bücher?** ~ **da?** *oder* ~ **hier?** which books? those [over there]? or these [over here]?; *s. a.* **das², der², die³**

die⁵ <*gen:* deren, *dat:* der, *akk:* die> ['di:] *pron rel, sing fem* that; (*Person a.*) who; (*Gegenstand, Tier a.*) which; **die Frau,** ~ **da drüben läuft** the woman walking along over there; **die Katze,** ~ **nicht fressen mag** the cat that doesn't want to eat; **eine Geschichte,** ~ **Millionen gelesen haben** a story [that has been] read by millions; *s. a.* **das³, der³**

die[6] <gen: **de**ren, dat: **de**nen, akk: **die**> ['diː] pron rel, pl that; (Person a.) who; (Gegenstand, Tier a.) which; **ich sah zwei Autos, ~ um die Ecke fuhren** I saw two cars driving around the corner; **die Abgeordneten, ~ dagegenstimmten** the members of Congress who voted against it; s. a. **das**[3], **der**[3], **die**[5]

Dieb(in) <-[e]s, -e> ['diːp] m(f) thief

Diebstahl <-[e]s, -stähle> ['diːp·ʃtaːl] m theft

Diebstahlsicherung f antitheft device

diejenige <gen: **der**jenigen, dat: **der**jenigen, akk: **die**jenige, pl: **die**jenigen> ['diː·jeː·nɪ·gə] pron dem ① substantivisch ■~, **die ... auf eine Person bezogen** the person who ...; **auf eine Sache bezogen** the one that ...; ■~, **die ... auf Personen bezogen** the people who ...; **auf Gegenstände bezogen** the ones that ... ② adjektivisch that; ~ **Frau, die ...** the woman who ...; s. a. **dasjenige, derjenige**

Diele <-, -n> ['diː·lə] f ① (Vorraum) hall ② (Bodenbrett) floorboard

dienen ['diː·nən] vi ① (nützlich sein) ■etw dat ~ to be [important] for sth; **einem guten Zweck ~** to be for a good cause ② (behilflich sein) **womit kann ich Ihnen ~?** how can I help you?; **jdm ist mit etw** dat **nicht/kaum gedient** sth is of no/little use to sb ③ (verwendet werden) ■[jdm] **als etw** ~ to serve [sb] as sth

Diener[1] <-s, -> ['diː·nɐ] m (Verbeugung) bow

Diener(in)[2] <-s, -> ['diː·nɐ] m(f) servant

Dienst <-[e]s, -e> ['diːnst] m ① kein pl (berufliche Tätigkeit) work; ~ **haben** to be on duty; **im ~** at work; **während/nach dem ~** during/outside working hours ② kein pl (Amt) **diplomatischer/öffentlicher ~** diplomatic/civil service ③ kein pl (Bereitschaftsdienst) ~ **haben** to be on call; **der ~ habende Arzt** the doctor on duty ④ (Service) service; ~ **am Kunden** customer service

▶WENDUNGEN: **jdm einen guten/ schlechten ~ erweisen** to do sb a service/disservice

Dienstag ['diːns·taːk] m Tuesday; **wir haben heute ~** today's Tuesday; **treffen wir uns ~?** would you like to get together on Tuesday?; **am ~** on Tuesday; **[am] ~ früh** early Tuesday [morning]; **an ~en** on Tuesdays; **an einem ~** one Tuesday; **am ~, den 4. März** on Tuesday, March 4th; **diesen ~** this Tuesday; **jeden ~** every Tuesday; **[am] nächsten ~** next Tuesday; **ab nächstem ~** from next Tuesday on; ~ **in acht Tagen** a week from Tuesday; **vor acht Tagen ~** a week ago Tuesday; **letzten ~** last Tuesday; **seit letztem ~** since last Tuesday; **den ganzen ~ über** all day Tuesday; **eines ~s** one Tuesday; **in der Nacht [von Montag] auf ~** [on] Monday night, in the early hours of Tuesday morning

dienstags ['diːns·taːks] adv [on] Tuesdays; ~ **abends/nachmittags/vormittags** [on] Tuesday evenings/afternoons/mornings

Dienstleistung f meist pl services npl

dienstlich I. adj official II. adv ~ **unterwegs sein** to be away on business

Dienstreise f business trip

Dienststelle f office

Dienststunden pl office hours npl

Dienstzeit f ① ADMIN tenure ② (Arbeitszeit) working hours pl

diesbezüglich ['diːs·bə·tsyːk·lɪç] I. adj relating to this II. adv with respect to this

diese(r, s) ['diː·zə] pron dem ① adjektivisch this sing, these pl ② substantivisch this one sing, these pl; ~ **und jenes** this and that

Diesel[1] <-s> ['diː·zl] nt kein pl diesel

Diesel[2] <-s, -> ['diː·zl] m (fam) ① (Wagen mit Dieselmotor) diesel ② s. **Dieselmotor**

dieselbe <gen: **der**selben, dat: **der**selben, akk: **die**selbe, pl: **die**selben> pron dem ~ **Frau** the same woman; ~**n**

Männer the same men; *s. a.* **dasselbe, derselbe**

Dieselmotor *m* diesel engine

diesig ['diː·zɪç] *adj* misty

diesjährig ['diːs·jɛːrɪç] *adj attr* this year's

diesmal ['diːs·maːl] *adv* this time

diesseits ['diːs·zaits] *präp +gen* this side of

Dietrich <-s, -e> ['diːt·rɪç] *m* picklock

differenzieren* [dɪfə·rɛn·'tsiː·rən] *vi* to discriminate

digital [di·gi·'taːl] *adj* digital

Diktator, Diktatorin <-s, -toren> [dɪk·'taː·toːɐ̯, dɪk·ta·'toː·rɪn] *m, f* dictator

Diktatur <-, -en> [dɪk·ta·'tuːɐ̯] *f* dictatorship

diktieren* [dɪk·'tiː·rən] *vt* to dictate

Diktiergerät *nt* Dictaphone®

Dill <-s, -e> ['dɪl] *m* dill

Dimension <-, -en> [di·mɛn·'zi̯oːn] *f* dimension

Ding <-[e]s, -e> ['dɪŋ] *nt* ❶ (*Gegenstand*) thing ❷ (*fam: Mädchen*) ein **junges** ~ a young thing ❸ (*Angelegenheit*) matters *pl;* **so wie die ~e liegen** as things stand [at the moment] ▸WENDUNGEN: **das ist** [ja] **ein ~!** (*fam*) wow!, get a load of that! *sl;* **krumme ~er drehen** (*fam*) to pull a fast one *sl;* **das ist nicht so ganz mein ~** that's not really my thing; **über den ~en stehen** to be above it all

Dingsbums <-> ['dɪŋs·bʊms] *nt kein pl* (*fam: Sache*) thingamajig

Dinosaurier <-s, -> [di·no·'zau·ri̯·ɐ] *m* dinosaur

Diphtherie <-, -n> [dɪf·te·'riː] *f* diphtheria

Diplom <-s, -e> [di·'ploːm] *nt* (*Hochschulabschluss*) degree; (*Zeugnis, Urkunde*) diploma

Diplomat(in) <-en, -en> [di·plo·'maːt] *m(f)* diplomat

diplomatisch [di·plo·'maː·tɪʃ] I. *adj* diplomatic II. *adv* diplomatically

Diplomingenieur(in) [-ɪn·ʒe·ni̯øːɐ̯] *m(f)* sb with a Master of Science in engineering

dir ['diːɐ̯] *pron* ❶ *pers dat von* **du** you; **ich hoffe, es geht ~ wieder besser** I hope you're feeling better; **Freunde von ~** friends of yours ❷ *refl dat von* **sich** yourself, you; **was wünscht du ~ zum Geburtstag?** what would you like for your birthday?; **du solltest ~ die Haare waschen** you should wash your hair

direkt [di·'rɛkt] I. *adj* direct; *Übertragung* live II. *adv* ❶ (*fam: geradezu*) almost; **das war ja ~ lustig** that was actually funny for a change ❷ (*unverblümt*) directly; **etw ~ zugeben** to admit sth outright ❸ (*mit Ortsangabe*) direct[ly]; **~ am Bahnhof** right by the train station ❹ (*unverzüglich*) immediately

Direktor, Direktorin <-s, -toren> [di·'rɛk·toːɐ̯, di·rɛk·'toː·rɪn] *m, f eines Unternehmens* manager; *einer öffentlichen Einrichtung* director; *einer Schule* principal

Direktübertragung *f* live broadcast

Dirigent(in) <-en, -en> [di·ri·'gɛnt] *m(f)* conductor

dirigieren* [di·ri·'giː·rən] *vt, vi* MUS to conduct

Diskette <-, -n> [dɪs·'kɛ·tə] *f* disk

Diskettenlaufwerk *nt* disk drive

Diskothek <-, -en> [dɪs·ko·'teːk] *f* discotheque

diskret [dɪs·'kreːt] I. *adj* ❶ (*vertraulich*) confidential ❷ (*unauffällig*) discreet II. *adv* **etw ~ behandeln** to treat sth confidentially; **sich** *akk* **~ verhalten** to behave discreetly

diskriminieren* [dɪs·kri·mi·'niː·rən] *vt* ■**jdn ~** to discriminate against sb

Diskriminierung <-, -en> *f* discrimination

Diskussion <-, -en> [dɪs·kʊ·'si̯oːn] *f* discussion

diskutieren* [dɪs·ku·'tiː·rən] *vt, vi* to discuss

disqualifizieren* [dɪs·kva·li·fi·'tsiː·rən] *vt* to disqualify (**wegen** *+gen* for)

Dissident(in) <-en, -en> [dɪ·si·'dɛnt] *m(f)* dissident

Distanz <-, -en> [dɪs·'tants] *f* distance

distanzieren* [dɪs·tan·'tsiː·rən] *vr* ■**sich** *akk* ~ to distance oneself (**von** +*dat* from)

Distel <-, -n> ['dɪs·tl̩] *f* thistle

Disziplin <-, -en> [dɪs·tsi·'pliːn] *f* discipline

diszipliniert [dɪs·tsi·pli·'niːɐ̯t] I. *adj* disciplined II. *adv* in a disciplined way

divers [di·'vɛrs] *adj attr* diverse

Dividende <-, -n> [di·vi·'dɛn·də] *f* dividend

dividieren* [di·vi·'diː·rən] *vt* to divide (**durch** +*akk* by)

DNS <-> [deː·ʔɛn·'ɛs] *f Abk von* **Desoxyribonukleinsäure** DNA

doch [dɔx] I. *konj* (*aber*) but II. *adv* ❶ (*dennoch*) even so; **zum Glück ist aber ~ nichts passiert** fortunately, nothing happened ❷ (*einräumend*) **du hattest ~ Recht** you were right after all ❸ (*Widerspruch ausdrückend*) **du gehst jetzt ins Bett – nein! – ~!** you need to go to bed now — no! — oh yes you do! ❹ (*ja*) yes; **hat es dir nicht gefallen? – ~[, ~]!** didn't you enjoy it? — yes, I did!

Docht <-[e]s, -e> ['dɔxt] *m* wick

Dock <-s, -s> ['dɔk] *nt* dock

Dogge <-, -n> ['dɔgə] *f* mastiff

Doktor, Doktorin <-s, -toren> ['dɔk·toːɐ̯, dɔk·'toː·rɪn] *m, f* doctor; **er ist ~ der Physik** he's got a PhD in physics

Doku <-, -s> ['do·ku] *f kurz für* **Dokumentarfilm, -bericht** documentary

Dokument <-[e]s, -e> [do·ku·'mɛnt] *nt* document

Dokumentarfilm *m* documentary [film]

dokumentieren* [do·ku·mɛn·'tiː·rən] *vt* to document

Dolch <-[e]s, -e> ['dɔlç] *m* dagger

Dollar <-[s], -s> ['dɔ·lar] *m* dollar

dolmetschen ['dɔl·mɛt·ʃn̩] *vt, vi* to interpret

Dolmetscher(in) <-s, -> ['dɔl·mɛt·ʃe] *m(f)* interpreter

Dom <-[e]s, -e> ['doːm] *m* (*Kirche*) cathedral

Domäne <-, -n> [do·'mɛː·nə] *f* domain

dominieren* [do·mi·'niː·rən] *vt, vi* to dominate

Dominikanische Republik *f* Dominican Republic

Domino <-s, -s> ['doː·mi·no] *nt* dominoes + *sing vb*

Dompteur(in) <-s, -e> [dɔmp·'tøːɐ̯] *m(f)*, **Dompteuse** <-, -n> [dɔmp·'tøːzə] *f* animal trainer

Domstadt *f kein pl* Cathedral City (*nickname for the city of Cologne*)

Donau <-> ['doː·nau] *f* ■**die ~** the Danube

Donner <-s, -> ['dɔ·ne] *m pl selten* thunder

donnern ['dɔ·nen] I. *vi impers* **haben hörst du, wie es donnert?** can you hear the thunder?; **es hat geblitzt und gedonnert** there was thunder and lightning II. *vi sein* (*krachen*) to crash (**gegen/in** +*akk* into) III. *vt* **haben** (*irgendwohin werfen*) to fling

Donnerstag ['dɔ·nes·taːk] *m* Thursday; *s. a.* **Dienstag**

Donnerwetter ['dɔ·ne·vɛ·te] *nt* (*fam: Schelte*) a tongue-lashing; **zum ~!** [god]damn it!

doof <doofer, doofste> ['doːf] *adj* (*fam*) stupid

Doppel <-s, -> ['dɔpl̩] *nt* ❶ (*Duplikat*) duplicate ❷ SPORT doubles; **gemischtes ~** mixed doubles

Doppelbett *nt* double bed

Doppeldecker <-s, -> *m* ❶ (*Flugzeug*) biplane ❷ (*Bus*) double-decker [bus]

doppeldeutig ['dɔpl̩·dɔy·tɪç] *adj* ambiguous

Doppelgänger(in) <-s, -> [-gɛŋe] *m(f)* look-alike

Doppelhaus *nt* duplex

Doppelleben *nt* double life

Doppelpunkt *m* colon

doppelt ['dɔplt] I. *adj* ❶ (*zweifach*) double; *Staatsangehörigkeit* dual; **die ~e Menge** double the amount ❷ (*verdoppelt*) doubled; **mit ~em Einsatz arbeiten** to redouble one's efforts II. *adv* ❶ (*zweimal*) twice; **~ so groß/klein** twice as big/small; **~ so viel/**

viele twice as much/many ② (*umso mehr*) doubly; **~ vorsichtig sein** to be doubly careful ▶WENDUNGEN: **~ sehen** to see double

Doppelzentner m ≈ 2.2 [short] hundredweights (*220 pounds*)

Doppelzimmer *nt* double [room]

Dorf <-[e]s, Dörfer> ['dɔrf] *nt* village

Dorn <-[e]s, -en> ['dɔrn] m thorn ▶WENDUNGEN: **jdm ein ~ im Auge sein** to be a thorn in sb's side

Dornröschen <-> [-'rø:s·çən] *nt kein pl* Sleeping Beauty

Dörrobst *nt* dried fruit

dort ['dɔrt] *adv* there; **~ drüben** over there

dorther ['dɔrt·'heːɐ̯] *adv* from [over] there

dorthin ['dɔrt·'hɪn] *adv* [over] there

dortig ['dɔr·tɪç] *adj attr* local

Dose <-, -n> ['doː·zə] f can

dösen ['døː·zn̩] *vi* to doze

Dosenbier *nt* canned beer

Dosenmilch f condensed milk

Dosenöffner m can opener

Dosenpfand *nt kein pl* deposit

dosieren* [do·'ziː·rən] *vt* to measure out *sep*

Dosis <-, Dosen> ['doː·zɪs] f dose

Dotter <-s, -> ['dɔ·te] m o *nt* yolk

Double <-s, -s> ['duː·bl̩] *nt* double

downloaden ['daʊn·loʊ·dn̩] *vt* INET to download

Dozent(in) <-en, -en> [do·'tsɛnt] $m(f)$ lecturer

Drache <-n, -n> ['dra·xə] m dragon

Drachen <-s, -> ['dra·xn̩] m ① (*Spielzeug*) kite; **einen ~ steigen lassen** to fly a kite ② (*Fluggerät*) hang glider ③ (*fam: zänkisches Weib*) witch

Draht <-[e]s, Drähte> ['draːt] m wire ▶WENDUNGEN: **zu jdm einen guten ~ haben** to be on good terms with sb

Drahtbürste f wire brush

Drahtgitter *nt* wire grating

drahtig *adj* wiry

Drahtseil *nt* wire cable

drall ['dral] *adj* well-rounded; *Mädchen* shapely

Drama <-s, -men> ['dra·ma] *nt* drama

dramatisch [dra·'maː·tɪʃ] *adj* dramatic

dramatisieren* [dra·ma·ti·'ziː·rən] *vt* ① LIT to dramatize ② (*fig: übertreiben*) to express in a dramatic way, to be dramatic about

dran ['dran] *adv* (*fam*) ① (*fertig*) [zu] früh/spät ~ sein to be [too] early/late ② (*an der Reihe*) **jetzt bist du ~!** now it's your turn!; **wer ist als Nächster ~?** who's next? ③ (*zutreffen*) **an dem Gerücht ist etwas/nichts** ~ there is something/nothing to the rumor ▶WENDUNGEN: **besser ~ sein als ...** to be better off than ...; **schlecht ~ sein** (*gesundheitlich*) to be in bad shape; (*schlechte Möglichkeiten haben*) to be having a hard time [of it]

drang ['draŋ] *imp von* dringen

Drang <-[e]s, Dränge> ['draŋ] m longing; **ein starker ~** a strong desire

drängeln ['drɛŋ·əln] I. *vi* to push II. *vt* ■**jdn ~** to pester sb

drängen ['drɛŋ·ən] I. *vi* ① ■**irgendwohin ~** to force one's way somewhere ② (*fordern*) ■**auf etw** *akk* ~ to insist [up]on sth; **warum drängst du so zur Eile?** why are you in such a hurry? ③ (*pressieren*) **die Zeit drängt** time is running out; **es drängt nicht** there's no hurry II. *vt* ① (*schiebend drücken*) to push ② (*antreiben*) ■**jdn ~, etw zu tun** to pressure sb into doing sth; ■**jdn** [**zu etw** *dat*] ~ to force sb [to do sth] III. *vr* ■**sich** *akk* ~ to crowd; **sich** *akk* **nach vorne ~** to push forward; **sich** *akk* **durch die Menge ~** to force one's way through the crowd

drangsalieren* [draŋ·za·'liː·rən] *vt* to plague

drastisch ['dras·tɪʃ] *adj* drastic

drauf ['draʊf] *adv* (*fam*) ① (*darauf*) on it/them ② **gut/schlecht ~ sein** (*fam*) to be in a good/bad mood ▶WENDUNGEN: **~ und dran sein, etw zu tun** to be on the verge of doing sth

Draufgänger(in) <-s, -> ['draʊf·gɛŋɐ] $m(f)$ go-getter *fam*

draufgehen ['draʊf·geː·ən] *vi irreg*

D

D

sein (*fam*) ❶ (*sterben*) to kick the bucket ❷ (*verbraucht werden*) to be spent ❸ (*kaputtgehen*) to break

drauf|haben *vt irreg* (*fam: Kenntnisse haben*) ■ **nichts/viel ~** to know nothing/a lot; **Mathe hat er drauf** he's brilliant at math

drauf|zahlen *vi* (*fam*) **500 Euro ~** to pay an extra 500 euros; **~ müssen** to lose money

draußen ['drau·sn] *adv* outside; **nach ~** outside

Dreck <-[e]s> ['drɛk] *m kein pl* ❶ (*Schmutz, Erde*) dirt ❷ (*Schlamm*) mud ❸ (*Müll*) trash ■ **jdn wie den** letzten **~ behandeln** to treat sb like dirt

dreckig I. *adj* dirty II. *adv* ▶WENDUNGEN: **jdm** geht **es ~** sb feels terrible; (*finanziell*) sb is not doing [too] well

Dreckspatz *m* filthy kid

Dreh <-s, -s> ['dre:] *m* ▶WENDUNGEN: **den ~** raushaben to get the hang of it

drehbar *adj, adv* revolving

Drehbuch *nt* screenplay

Drehbuchautor(in) *m(f)* screenplay writer

drehen ['dre:·ən] I. *vt* ❶ (*herumdrehen*) to turn ❷ *Zigarette* to roll ❸ FILM to shoot ❹ **das Radio lauter/leiser ~** to turn the radio up/down ▶WENDUNGEN: **wie man es auch dreht und** wendet no matter how you look at it II. *vi* ❶ FILM to shoot ■ **an etw** *dat* **~** to turn sth ❸ *Wind* to change III. *vr* ❶ (*rotieren*) ■ **sich** *akk* **~** to turn ❷ (*wenden*) **zur Seite, auf den Bauch** to turn ❸ (*betreffen*) ■ **sich** *akk* **um jdn/etw ~** to be about sb/sth; **das Gespräch dreht sich um Sport** the conversation revolves around sports ▶WENDUNGEN: **jdm dreht sich** alles **im Kopf** sb's head is spinning

Drehorgel *f* barrel organ

Drehtür *f* revolving door

Drehzahl *f* [number of] revolutions *pl; eines Motors* revolutions *pl* per minute

drei ['drai] *adj* three

Drei <-, -en> ['drai] *f* ❶ (*Zahl*) three ❷ (*Zeugnisnote*) C

Dreieck <-s, -e> ['drai·?ɛk] *nt* triangle

dreieckig, 3-eckigRR ['drai·?ɛ·kɪç] *adj* triangular

dreifach, 3fach ['drai·fax] I. *adj* threefold; **die ~e Arbeit** triple the work II. *adv* threefold, three times over

dreihundert ['drai·ˈhʊn·dɐt] *adj* three hundred

dreijährig, 3-jährigRR *adj* ❶ (*Alter*) three-year-old *attr;* three years old *pred; s. a.* **achtjährig 1** ❷ (*Zeitspanne*) three-year *attr; s. a.* **achtjährig 2**

Dreirad *nt* tricycle

dreißig ['drai·sɪç] *adj* thirty; *s. a.* **achtzig 1, 2**

dreißigjährig, 30-jährigRR ['drai·sɪç·jɛ:·rɪç] *adj attr* ❶ (*Alter*) thirty-year-old *attr,* thirty years old *pred* ❷ (*Zeitspanne*) thirty-year *attr*

dreißigste(r, s) *adj* ❶ (*an dreißigster Stelle*) thirtieth; *s. a.* **achte(r, s) 1** ❷ (*Datum*) thirtieth, 30th; *s. a.* **achte(r, s) 2**

dreist ['draist] *adj* brazen

dreistellig, 3-stelligRR *adj* three-figure *attr*

dreiteilig, 3-teiligRR *adj* three-part; *Besteck* three-piece

dreizehn ['drai·tse:n] *adj* thirteen; **~ Uhr** 1 p.m.; *s. a.* **acht**[1] ▶WENDUNGEN: **jetzt** schlägt's **aber ~** enough is enough

dreizehnte(r, s) *adj* ❶ (*an dreizehnter Stelle*) thirteenth; *s. a.* **achte(r, s) 1** ❷ (*Datum*) thirteenth, 13th; *s. a.* **achte(r, s) 2**

dreschen <drischt, drosch, gedroschen> ['drɛ·ʃn] *vt* ❶ AGR to thresh ❷ (*fam: prügeln*) to beat

dressieren* [drɛ·ˈsiː·rən] *vt* to train [an animal]

Dressman <-s, -men> ['drɛs·mən] *m* male model

Dressur <-, -en> [drɛ·ˈsuːɐ̯] *f* training [of animals]

drin ['drɪn] *adv* (*fam*) ❶ (*darin*) in it ❷ (*drinnen*) inside ▶WENDUNGEN: **bei**

D

jdm ist <u>alles</u> ~ anything is possible with sb; **für jdn ist noch <u>alles</u>** ~ anything is still possible for sb

dringen <drang, gedrungen> ['drɪŋ·ən] vi ① sein (stoßen) ■**durch/in** etw akk ~ to penetrate sth ② sein (vordringen) **an die Öffentlichkeit** ~ to leak to the public ③ haben (fordern) ■**auf** etw akk ~ to insist [up]on sth

dringend ['drɪŋ·ənt] I. adj urgent, pressing; **eine ~e Bitte** an urgent request II. adv urgently; **ich muss dich ~ sehen** I really need to see you

drinnen ['drɪ·nən] adv inside

dritt ['drɪt] adv **wir waren zu ~** there were three of us

dritte(r, s) ['drɪ·tə] adj ① (an dritter Stelle) third; s. a. **achte(r, s) 1** ② (Datum) third, 3rd; s. a. **achte(r, s) 2**

drittel ['drɪ·tl] adj third

drittens ['drɪ·tns] adv thirdly, in the third place

Droge <-, -n> ['dro:·gə] f drug

drogenabhängig adj addicted to drugs pred

Drogerie <-, -n> [dro·gə·'ri:] f drugstore

Drogist(in) <-en, -en> [dro·'gɪst] m(f) pharmacist

Drohbrief m threatening letter

drohen ['dro:·ən] vi to threaten

drohend I. adj ① (einschüchternd) threatening ② (bevorstehend) impending II. adv threateningly

dröhnen ['drø:·nən] vi ① (dumpf klingen) Donner to rumble; Lautsprecher, Musik, Stimme to boom ② **jdm dröhnt der Kopf** sb's head is ringing; **jdm ~ die Ohren** sb's ears are ringing

Drohung <-, -en> ['dro:·ʊŋ] f threat

drollig ['drɔ·lɪç] adj ① (belustigend) amusing ② (niedlich) cute

Dromedar <-s, -e> [dro·me·'da:ɐ̯] nt dromedary

Drossel <-, -n> ['drɔ·sl] f thrush

drosseln ['drɔ·sln] vt Heizung to turn down sep; Produktion to cut; Tempo to reduce

drüben ['dry:·bn] adv over there

drüber ['dry:·bɐ] adv (fam) s. **darüber**

Druck[1] <-[e]s, Drücke> ['drʊk] m pressure; **unter ~ stehen** to be under pressure; **jdn unter ~ setzen** to put pressure on sb

Druck[2] <-[e]s, -e> ['drʊk] m TYPO printing

Druckbuchstabe m **in ~n** in print

Drückeberger <-s, -> m (pej) shirker

drucken ['drʊ·kn] vt, vi to print

drücken ['dry·kn] I. vi ① (pressen) to push; **auf einen Knopf ~** to push a button ② Kleidung to pinch; **die Schuhe ~** the shoes are pinching my feet II. vt ① (pressen) to press; **einen Knopf ~** to press a button; ■**etw aus etw** dat ~ to squeeze sth from sth ② (Kleidung) ■**jdn ~** to be too tight for sb ③ (umarmen) ■**jdn ~** to hug sb ④ (herabsetzen) **den Preis ~** to force down the price III. vr ■**sich** akk [**vor etw** dat/**um etw** akk] ~ to dodge [sth]

drückend adj Hitze, Stimmung oppressive; Sorgen serious

Drucker <-s, -> m COMPUT printer

Drucker(in) <-s, -> m(f) printer

Drücker m ▸WENDUNGEN: **auf den letzten ~** at the last minute

Druckerei <-, -en> [drʊ·kə·'rai] f printer's, print shop

Druckfehler m typographical error

Druckknopf m snap

Druckluft f kein pl compressed air

Druckmittel nt **jdn/etw als ~ benutzen** to use sb/sth as a means of exerting pressure

druckreif adj ready for publication pred

Drucksache f printed matter

Druckschrift f **in ~ schreiben** to write in print

drum ['drʊm] adv (fam) s. **darum** ▸WENDUNGEN: **das D~ und <u>Dran</u>** the whole works, the whole shebang fam

drunter ['drʊn·tɐ] adv (fam) s. **darunter** ▸WENDUNGEN: **alles geht ~ und <u>drüber</u>** it's all chaos

Drüse <-, -n> ['dry:·zə] f gland

Dschungel <-s, -> ['dʒʊŋ·əl] m jungle

du <gen: de<u>i</u>ner, dat: dir, akk: dich>

D

['du:] *pron pers* you; **bist ~ das, Peter?** is that you, Peter?

Du <-[s], -[s]> ['du:] *nt* you, "du" *(familiar form of address)*; **jdm das ~ anbieten** to suggest that sb use the familiar form of address

Dübel <-s, -> ['dy:·bl] *m* drywall anchor

dubios [du·'bi·o:s] *adj* dubious

ducken ['dʊ·kn] *vr* ~ **sich** *akk* ~ to duck one's head

Duckmäuser(in) <-s, -> ['dʊk·mɔy·ze] *m(f)* *(pej)* yes man

Dudelsack ['du:·dl·zak] *m* bagpipes *pl*

Duell <-s, -e> [du·'ɛl] *nt* duel

Duft <-[e]s, Düfte> ['dʊft] *m* [pleasant] smell; *von Blume, eines Parfüms* scent; *von Essen, Kaffee* aroma

duften ['dʊf·tn] *vi* to smell (**nach** +*dat* of)

duftend *adj attr* fragrant

dulden ['dʊl·dn] *vt* to tolerate

dumm <dümmer, dümmste> ['dʊm] I. *adj* ❶ *(geistig beschränkt)* stupid ❷ *(unklug)* foolish; **kein ~er Vorschlag!** not a bad idea! ❸ *(albern)* silly; ▪ **etw wird jdm zu ~** sb has had enough of sth ❹ *(ärgerlich) Geschichte, Sache* unpleasant; **so etwas D~es!** how stupid! II. *adv* stupidly; **frag nicht so ~** don't ask such stupid questions ▸WENDUNGEN: ~ **dastehen** to look stupid; **jdn für ~ verkaufen** to take sb for a ride

dummerweise *adv* ❶ *(leider)* unfortunately ❷ *(unklugerweise)* stupidly

Dummheit <-, -en> *f* ❶ *kein pl (geringe Intelligenz)* stupidity ❷ *(unkluge Handlung)* foolish action

Dummkopf *m (pej)* idiot

dumpf ['dʊmpf] *adj* ❶ *(hohl klingend)* dull; *Geräusch, Ton* muffled ❷ *(unbestimmt)* vague; *Gefühl* sneaking; *Schmerz* dull ❸ *(feucht-muffig)* musty; *Atmosphäre, Luft* oppressive

Düne <-, -n> ['dy:·nə] *f* dune

Düngemittel *nt* fertilizer

düngen ['dʏŋən] *vt* to fertilize

Dünger <-s, -> *m* fertilizer

dunkel ['dʊŋ·kl] I. *adj* ❶ *(nicht hell)* dark; *Ton* deep ❷ *(unklar) Erinnerung* vague; **ein dunkles Kapitel** a dark chapter ❸ *(pej: zwielichtig) Gestalt* shady ▸WENDUNGEN: **im D~n tappen** to be groping around in the dark II. *adv* **sich** *akk* ~ **an etw** *akk* **erinnern** to remember sth vaguely

dunkelhäutig *adj* dark-skinned

Dunkelheit <-> *f kein pl* darkness

Dunkelziffer *f* number of unreported cases

dünn ['dʏn] I. *adj (nicht dick); Kleidung* light; *Strümpfe* fine II. *adv* thinly; ~ **besiedelt** sparsely populated; ~ **gesät** thinly scattered

Dünndarm *m* small intestine

Dunst <-[e]s, Dünste> ['dʊnst] *m* ❶ *(leichter Nebel)* haze; *(durch Abgase)* smog *npl* ❷ *(Dampf)* steam

dünsten ['dʏns·tn] *vt* KOCHK to steam

dunstig ['dʊns·tɪç] *adj* METEO hazy

durch ['dʊrç] I. *präp* ❶ *(räumlich)* through; ~ **den Fluss waten** to wade across the river; **mitten** ~ **etw** *akk* through the middle of sth ❷ *(vermittels)* by [means of]; ~ **[einen] Zufall** by chance ❸ *(zeitlich)* throughout; **die ganze Nacht** ~ all night long ❹ MATH divided by II. *adj pred* ❶ *(durchgetrennt)* through ❷ *(vorbei)* **es ist schon 12 Uhr** ~ it's already past 12 [o'clock]; **der Zug ist vor zwei Minuten** ~ the train left two minutes ago ❸ *(gar, reif)* Steak well-done; *Käse* ripe ❹ *(fertig)* ▪ **mit jdm/etw** ~ **sein** to be through with sb/sth

durcharbeiten ['dʊrç·ʔar·bai·tn] I. *vt* to go through II. *vi* to keep working [until the end]

durchatmen ['dʊrç·ʔa:t·mən] *vi* to breathe deeply

durchaus ['dʊrç·ʔaus] *adv* ~ **kein schlechtes Angebot** not a bad offer [at all]; **ich bin** ~ **deiner Meinung, aber ...** I completely agree with you, but ...; ~ **möglich sein** to be quite possible; ~ **nicht schlecht sein** to be by no means bad

durchblicken ['dʊrç·blɪ·kn] *vi*

① ■ *(durch etw akk)* ~ to look through [sth] **②** *(den Überblick haben)* to know what's going on **③** etw ~ lassen to hint at sth

durch|braten ['dʊrç·braː·tn̩] *irreg vt* **■** etw ~ to cook sth until it is well-done

durch|brechen¹ ['dʊrç·brɛ·çn̩] *irreg* I. *vt* haben to break in two II. *vi* sein *(zer-brechen)* to break in two

durchbrechen*² [dʊrç·'brɛ·çn̩] *vt irreg* Absperrung, Blockade to break through

durch|brennen ['dʊrç·brɛ·nən] *irreg vi* sein **①** ELEK to burn out; Sicherung to blow **②** *(weglaufen)* **■** jdm ~ to run away [from sb]

durch|bringen ['dʊrç·brɪŋən] *vt irreg* **①** *(finanziell)* to support **②** einen Kranken to pull through

Durchbruch ['dʊrç·brʊx] *m* **①** break-through **②** *(Öffnung)* opening

durch|drehen ['dʊrç·dreː·ən] *vi (fam)* to crack up

durch|dringen¹ ['dʊrç·drɪŋən] *irreg vi* sein **■** zu jdm ~ to make one's way up to sb

durchdringen*² [dʊrç·'drɪŋən] *irreg vt* to penetrate

durcheinander [dʊrç·ʔai·'nan·dɐ] *adj pred (in Unordnung)* in a mess; *(ver-wirrt)* confused

Durcheinander <-s> [dʊrç·ʔai·'nan·dɐ] *nt kein pl* **①** *(Unordnung)* mess **②** *(Wirrwarr)* confusion

durcheinander|bringen *vt irreg* **■** etw ~ *(in Unordnung bringen)* to mess up sep sth; *(verwechseln)* to mix up sep sth; **■** jdn ~ to confuse sb

durcheinander|reden *vi* to all talk at once

Durchfahrt ['dʊrç·faːɐt] *f (das Durch-fahren)* ~ verboten do not enter; auf der ~ sein to be passing through

Durchfall ['dʊrç·fal] *m* diarrhea

durch|fallen ['dʊrç·fa·lən] *vi irreg sein* **①** *(räumlich)* **■** *(durch etw akk)* ~ to fall through [sth] **②** *(fig: nicht bestehen)* bei einer Prüfung ~ to fail an exam

durch|fragen ['dʊrç·fraː·ɡn̩] *vr* **■** sich akk ~ to find one's way by asking

durchführbar *adj* feasible

Durchgang ['dʊrç·ɡaŋ] *m (Passage)* path[way]

Durchgangsverkehr *m* through traffic

durch|geben ['dʊrç·ɡeː·bn̩] *vt irreg* Lottozahlen to read; eine Meldung ~ to make an announcement

durch|gehen ['dʊrç·ɡeː·ən] *irreg vi* sein **①** *(hindurchgehen)* to go through **②** *(fam: weglaufen)* to run off **③** *(ange-nommen werden)* to go through; Antrag, Gesetz to pass **④** Pferd to bolt **⑤** *(gehalten werden)* **■** für etw akk ~ to pass for sth ▶ WENDUNGEN: jdm etw ~ lassen to let sb get away with sth

durchgehend ['dʊrç·ɡeː·ənt] I. *adj* **①** *(nicht unterbrochen)* continuous **②** BAHN direct II. *adv* „wir haben von 9 - 18 Uhr ~ geöffnet" "we're open from 9 a.m. - 6 p.m." *(not closed for lunch)*

durch|greifen ['dʊrç·ɡrai·fn̩] *vi irreg (wirksam vorgehen)* to take drastic action; hart ~ to crack down hard

durchgreifend I. *adj* Änderung, Maß-nahme drastic II. *adv* drastically

durch|halten ['dʊrç·hal·tn̩] *irreg* I. *vt* **①** Belastung to withstand **②** *(beibehal-ten)* to keep up sep II. *vi* to hold out

Durchhänger <-s, -> *m* einen [tota-len] ~ haben *(fam)* to be on a [real] downer

durch|kämmen¹ ['dʊrç·kɛ·mən] *vt* Haar to comb through sep

durchkämmen*² [dʊrç·'kɛ·mən] *vt* to comb *(nach +dat* for)

durch|kommen ['dʊrç·kɔ·mən] *vi irreg* sein **①** *(durchfahren)* **■** durch etw akk] ~ to come through [sth] **②** Sonne to come through **③** Charakterzug to become noticeable **④** *(Erfolg haben)* **■** mit etw dat ~ to get away with sth **⑤** *(durch eine Öffnung)* to get through sep **⑥** *(überleben)* to pull through

durchkreuzen* [dʊrç·'krɔy·tsn̩] *vt (ver-eiteln)* Plan to foil

durchlässig ['dʊrç·lɛ·sɪç] *adj* porous *(für +akk* to)

D

durch|lesen ['dʊrç·leː·zn] *vt irreg* to read through *sep*

durch|machen ['dʊrç·ma·xn] I. *vt Phase* to go through; *Krankheit* to suffer II. *vi* (*fam*) ① (*feiern*) **die ganze Nacht ~** to stay up all night ② (*durcharbeiten*) to keep working [until the end]

Durchmesser <-s, -> ['dʊrç·me·sɐ] *m* diameter

durch|mogeln *vr* (*fam*) ■ **sich** *akk* **~** to fake one's way through

durch|nehmen ['dʊrç·neː·mən] *vt irreg* SCH to do

durchqueren* [dʊrç·'kveː·rən] *vt* to cross

Durchsage <-, -n> ['dʊrç·zaː·gə] *f* announcement

durch|sagen ['dʊrç·zaː·gn] *vt* to announce

durchschauen*¹ [dʊrç·'ʃaʊ·ən] *vt* (*jds Absichten erkennen*) ■ **jdn ~** to see through sb

durch|schauen² ['dʊrç·ʃaʊ·ən] *vt s.* **durchsehen**

durch|schlagen ['dʊrç·ʃlaː·gn] *irreg* I. *vt haben* to split [in two] II. *vr haben* ■ **sich** *akk* **~** ① (*seine Existenz behaupten*) to struggle along ② (*ans Ziel gelangen*) to make one's way through

durchschlagend ['dʊrç·ʃlaː·gnt] *adj* ① (*überwältigend*) sweeping; *Erfolg* huge; **eine ~e Wirkung haben** to be extremely effective ② (*überzeugend*) convincing; *Beweis* conclusive

durch|schneiden ['dʊrç·ʃnaɪ·dn] *vt irreg* to cut through

Durchschnitt ['dʊrç·ʃnɪt] *m* average; **im ~** on average; **über/unter dem ~ liegen** to be above/below average

durchschnittlich ['dʊrç·ʃnɪt·lɪç] I. *adj* ① (*Mittelwert betreffend*) average *attr* ② (*mittelmäßig*) ordinary II. *adv* ① (*im Schnitt*) on average ② (*mäßig*) moderately; **~ intelligent** of average intelligence

Durchschnittsgeschwindigkeit *f* average speed

durch|sehen ['dʊrç·zeː·ən] *irreg* I. *vt*

■ **etw ~** to go over sth II. *vi* ■ **durch etw** *akk* **~** to look through sth

durch|setzen ['dʊrç·zɛ·tsn] I. *vt Maßnahmen* to impose; *Reformen* to carry out; *Ziel* to achieve; ■ **etw bei jdm ~** to get sb to agree to sth; **seinen Willen [gegen jdn] ~** to get one's own way [with sb] II. *vr* ① (*sich Geltung verschaffen*) ■ **sich** *akk* **~** to assert oneself; ■ **sich** *akk* **mit etw** *dat* **~** to be successful with sth ② (*Gültigkeit erreichen*) ■ **sich** *akk* **~** to gain acceptance; *Trend* to catch on

Durchsicht ['dʊrç·zɪçt] *f* inspection; **zur ~** for inspection

durchsichtig ['dʊrç·zɪç·tɪç] *adj* transparent *a. fig*; *Bluse, Kleid* see-through

durch|stehen ['dʊrç·ʃteː·ən] *vt irreg* to get through; *Qualen* to endure; *Schwierigkeiten* to cope

durch|streichen ['dʊrç·ʃtraɪ·çn] *vt irreg Fehler, Wort* to cross out *sep*

durchsuchen* [dʊrç·'zuː·xn] *vt* to search (**nach** +*dat* for)

Durchsuchung <-, -en> [dʊrç·'zuː·xʊn] *f* search

durchtrieben [dʊrç·'triː·bn] *adj* crafty

durchwachsen [dʊrç·'vak·sn] *adj* ① *Speck* marbled ② *pred* (*mittelmäßig*) so-so

durchweg ['dʊrç·vɛk] *adv* without exception

durch|wühlen¹ ['dʊrç·vyː·lən] *vr* ■ **sich** *akk* [**durch etw** *akk*] **~** to plow through [sth]

durchwühlen*² [dʊrç·'vyː·lən] *vt* (*durchstöbern*) to comb (**nach** +*dat* for)

durch|ziehen ['dʊrç·tsiː·ən] *irreg* I. *vt haben* ① (*durch eine Öffnung*) to pull through ② (*fam: vollenden*) to see through II. *vi sein* to come through III. *vr haben* ■ **sich** *akk* **durch etw** *akk* **~** to occur throughout sth

dürfen ['dʏr·fn] I. *modal vb* <darf, durfte, dürfen> ① (*Erlaubnis haben*) ■ **etw [nicht] tun ~** to [not] be allowed to do sth ② *verneint* **wir ~ den Zug nicht verpassen** we can't miss the train; **du darfst ihm das nicht übel nehmen** you shouldn't hold that against him ❸ *im Konjunktiv (sollen)* ■ **das/es dürfte ...** that/it should ...; **es dürfte wohl das Beste sein, wenn ...** it would probably be best if ... II. *vi* <darf, durfte, gedurft> **darf ich nach draußen?** may I go outside?; **sie hat nicht gedurft** she wasn't allowed to III. *vt* <darf, durfte, gedurft> ■ **etw ~** to be allowed to do sth; **darfst du das?** are you allowed to [do that]?

dürftig ['dʏrf·tɪç] I. *adj* ❶ *(karg)* paltry; *Unterkunft* poor ❷ *(schwach)* poor; *Ausrede* feeble; *Kenntnisse* little ❸ *(spärlich) Informationen* sparse II. *adv* scantily

dürr ['dʏr] *adj* ❶ *(trocken)* dry; *Laub* withered ❷ *(mager)* [painfully] thin

Dürre <-, -n> ['dʏ·rə] *f* drought

Durst <-[e]s> ['dʊrst] *m kein pl* thirst; **~ haben** to be thirsty

durstig ['dʊrs·tɪç] *adj* thirsty

durstlöschend *adj* thirst-quenching

Durststrecke *f* lean period

Dusche <-, -n> ['duː·ʃə] *f* shower; **unter die ~ gehen** to take a shower

duschen ['duː·ʃn] I. *vi* to take a shower II. *vr* ■ **sich** *akk* **~** to take a shower III. *vt* ■ **jdn ~** to give sb a shower

Duschgel *nt* body wash

Duschkabine *f* shower stall

Düse <-, -n> ['dyː·zə] *f* ❶ TECH nozzle ❷ LUFT jet

düsen ['dyː·zn] *vi sein (fam: fahren)* to race; *(schnell gehen)* to dash

Düsenantrieb *m* jet propulsion

Düsenflugzeug *nt* jet plane

dusselig ['dʊ·sə·lɪç] I. *adj* daft II. *adv* ❶ *(dämlich)* **sich** *akk* **~ anstellen** to act stupidly ❷ *(enorm viel)* **sich** *akk* **~ arbeiten** to work oneself silly

düster ['dyː·stɐ] *adj Himmel, Wetter* gloomy; **eine ~e Ahnung** a dark foreboding; **~e Gedanken** black thoughts; **eine ~e Miene** a gloomy face

Dutzend <-s, -e> ['dʊ·tsnt] *nt* dozen

dutzendweise ['dʊ·tsnt·vai·zə] *adv* by the dozen

dynamisch [dy·'naː·mɪʃ] I. *adj* dynamic II. *adv* dynamically

Dynamit <-s> [dy·na·'miːt] *nt kein pl* dynamite

Dynastie <-, -n> [dyn·as·'tiː] *f* dynasty

D

Ee

E, e <-, -> [e:] *nt* ❶ (*Buchstabe*) E, e;
~ **wie Emil** E as in Echo ❷ MUS E, e
Ebbe <-, -n> ['ɛbə] *f* low tide; (*Wasser-stand*) low water; ~ **und Flut** the tides *pl*
eben¹ ['e:bn̩] I. *adj* ❶ (*flach*) flat ❷ (*glatt*) level II. *adv* evenly
eben² ['e:bn̩] I. *adv* ❶ *zeitlich* ❷ (*nun einmal*) just; **das ist ~ so** that's [just] the way it is ❸ (*gerade noch*) just [about] ❹ (*kurz*) **mal ~** for a minute II. *part* ❶ (*genau das*) precisely ❷ (*Abschwächung von Verneinung*) **das ist nicht ~ billig** that's/it's not exactly cheap
Ebenbild *nt* image
ebenbürtig ['e:bn̩·byr·tɪç] *adj* equal (**an** +*dat* in); **einander** [nicht] **~ sein** to be [un]evenly matched
Ebene <-, -n> ['e:bə·nə] *f* ❶ (*Tiefebene*) plain; (*Hochebene*) plateau ❷ MATH, PHYS plane ❸ (*fig*) **auf wissenschaftlicher** ~ at the scientific level
ebenfalls ['e:bn̩·fals] *adv* as well; **danke, ~!** thanks, [and the] same to you
ebenso ['e:bn̩·zo:] *adv* ❶ (*genauso*) just as; **er schwimmt ~ gern wie ich** he likes to swim just as much as I do; ~ **gut/oft/lang(e)** just as well/often/long; ~ **sehr/viel** just as much; ~ **wenig** just as little ❷ (*auch*) as well
Eber <-s, -> ['e:bɐ] *m* boar
ebnen ['e:b·nən] *vt* to level [off] ►WENDUNGEN: **jdm/etw den Weg ~** to pave the way for sb/sth
EC¹ <-s, -s> [e:'tse:] *m Abk von* **Eurocity** Eurocity train
EC² <-s, -s> [e:'tse:] *m* FIN *Abk von* **Electronic Cash** electronic cash (*a debit card system*)
Echo <-s, -s> ['ɛço] *nt* ❶ (*Effekt*) echo ❷ (*Reaktion*) response (**auf** +*akk* to)
Echse <-, -n> ['ɛk·sə] *f* lizard

echt ['ɛçt] I. *adj* ❶ (*nicht künstlich, wirklich*) real; *Haarfarbe* natural; *Silber, Gold* pure ❷ (*aufrichtig*) *Freundschaft, Schmerz* sincere II. *adv* ❶ (*typisch*) typically ❷ (*fam: wirklich*) really
EC-Karte [e:'tse:-] *f* debit card
Eckball *m* SPORT corner [kick]
Ecke <-, -n> ['ɛkə] *f* ❶ (*spitze Kante*) corner; (*Tischkante*) edge ❷ (*Straßen-, Zimmerecke*) corner ❸ (*fam: Gegend*) area ❹ SPORT corner [kick]
eckig ['ɛk·ɪç] *adj* ❶ (*nicht rund*) square; *Gesicht* angular ❷ (*ungelenk*) *Bewegungen* jerky
Eckzahn *m* canine [tooth]
Ecuador <-s> [ekua·'do:ɐ̯] *nt* Ecuador; *s. a.* **Deutschland**
Ecuadorianer(in) <-s, -> [ekua·do·'ri̯a·nɐ] *m(f)* Ecuadorian; *s. a.* **Deutsche(r)**
edel ['e:dl̩] I. *adj* ❶ (*großherzig*) generous ❷ (*hochwertig*) fine ❸ (*aristokratisch*) noble II. *adv* nobly
Edelgas *nt* inert gas
Edelmetall *nt* precious metal
edelmütig ['e:dl̩·my:·tɪç] *adj* magnanimous
Edelstahl *m* stainless steel
Edelstein *m* precious stone
Edelweiß <-[es], -e> ['e:dl̩·vais] *nt* BOT edelweiss
editieren* [edi·'ti:·rən] *vt* COMPUT to edit
EDV <-> [e:·de:·'fau] *f* COMPUT *Abk von* **elektronische Datenverarbeitung** EDP
Efeu <-s> ['e:fɔy] *m kein pl* ivy
Effekt <-[e]s, -e> [ɛ'fɛkt] *m* effect
effektiv [ɛfɛk·'ti:f] I. *adj* ❶ (*wirksam*) effective ❷ *attr* (*tatsächlich*) actual *attr* II. *adv* ❶ (*wirksam*) effectively ❷ (*tatsächlich*) actually
EG <-> [e:'ge:] *f kein pl* (*hist*) *Abk*

von **Europäische Gemeinschaft** EC, European Community

egal [e'ga:l] *adj* ■jdm ~ **sein** to be all the same to sb; **das ist mir** ~ I don't care; (*unhöflicher*) I couldn't care less; ~, **was/wie/wo/warum ...** no matter what/how/where/why ...

Egoist(in) <-en, -en> [ego·'ɪst] *m(f)* ego[t]ist

egoistisch [ego·'ɪs·tɪʃ] *adj* ego[t]istical

ehe ['e:ə] *konj* before; ~ **das Wetter nicht besser wird ...** until the weather changes for the better ...

Ehe <-, -n> ['e:ə] *f* marriage

Ehebruch *m* adultery; ~ **begehen** to commit adultery

Ehefrau *f fem form von* **Ehemann** wife

Ehegatte *m* (*geh*) ❶ *s.* **Ehemann** ❷ *pl* (*Ehepartner*) ■**die ~n** [married] partners *pl*

Eheleute *pl* married couple + *sing/pl vb*

ehelich ['e:ə·lɪç] *adj* marital; *Kind* legitimate

ehemalig ['e:ə·ma:·lɪç] *adj attr* former

Ehemann <-männer> *m* husband

Ehepaar *nt* [married] couple + *sing/pl vb*

eher ['e:ɐ] *adv* ❶ (*früher*) sooner ❷ (*wahrscheinlicher*) more likely ❸ (*mehr*) more ❹ (*lieber*) rather

Ehering *m* wedding ring

Eheschließung *f* (*geh*) wedding

ehrbar ['e:ɐ·ba:ɐ] *adj* respectable

Ehre <-, -n> ['e:ɐə] *f* honor; **jdm eine ~ sein** to be an honor for sb; **jdm wird die ~ zuteil, etw zu tun** sb is given the honor of doing sth ►WENDUNGEN: **habe die ~!** ÖSTERR, SÜDD (*ich grüße Sie!*) [I'm] pleased to meet you

ehren ['e:r·ən] *vt* to honor

ehrenamtlich I. *adj* ~**e Tätigkeiten** volunteer work II. *adv* on a voluntary basis

Ehrenbürger(in) *m(f)* honorary citizen

Ehrengast *m* guest of honor

Ehrenkodex *m* code of honor

Ehrenplatz *m* place of honor

Ehrensache *f* matter of honor

ehrenvoll *adj* honorable

ehrenwert *adj s.* **ehrbar**

Ehrenwort <-worte> *nt* word of honor

Ehrfurcht *f kein pl* respect; (*fromme Scheu*) reverence; **vor jdm/etw ~ haben** to have [great] respect for sb/sth

ehrfürchtig ['e:ɐ·fʏrç·tɪç] I. *adj* reverent II. *adv* reverentially

Ehrgefühl *nt kein pl* sense of honor

Ehrgeiz ['e:ɐ·gaits] *m kein pl* ambition

ehrgeizig ['e:ɐ·gai·tsɪç] *adj* ambitious

ehrlich ['e:ɐ·lɪç] I. *adj* honest; ~**e Zuneigung** genuine affection II. *adv* (*legal*) ~ **verdientes Geld** honestly earned money ►WENDUNGEN: ~ **gesagt ...** to be [quite] honest ...

Ehrlichkeit *f kein pl* honesty

Ehrwürden <*bei Voranstellung* -[s] *o bei Nachstellung* -> ['e:ɐ·vʏr·dn] *m kein pl, kein art* REL Reverend

ehrwürdig ['e:ɐ·vʏr·dɪç] *adj* venerable

Ei <-[e]s, -er> ['ai] *nt* egg; (*Eizelle*) ovum; **ein hart/weich gekochtes ~** a hard-boiled/soft-boiled egg

Eiche <-, -n> ['ai·çə] *f* (*a. Holz*) oak

Eichel <-, -n> ['ai·çl̩] ❶ BOT acorn ❷ ANAT glans

eichen ['ai·çn̩] *vt Instrument, Messgerät* to calibrate

Eichhörnchen ['aiç·hœrn·çən] *nt* squirrel

Eid <-[e]s, -e> ['ait] *m* oath; **einen ~ ablegen** to swear an oath

Eidechse ['ai·dɛk·sə] *f* lizard

Eidgenossenschaft *f* **Schweizerische ~** the Swiss Confederation

Eierbecher *m* egg cup

Eierkuchen *m* pancake

Eierschale *f* eggshell

Eierstock *m* ANAT ovary

Eifer <-s> ['ai·fɐ] *m kein pl* enthusiasm ►WENDUNGEN: **im ~ des Gefechts** (*fam*) in the heat of the moment

Eifersucht ['ai·fe·zʊxt] *f kein pl* jealousy

eifersüchtig ['ai·fe·zʏç·tɪç] *adj* jealous

eifrig ['ai·frɪç] I. *adj* eager; *Leser, Sammler* avid II. *adv* eagerly; ~ **lernen** to study hard

Eigelb <-s, -e *o bei Zahlenangaben* -> *nt* egg yolk

E

eigen ['ai·gn̩] *adj* ❶ (*jdm gehörig*) own; **seine ~e Meinung/Wohnung haben** to have one's own opinion/apartment ❷ (*separat*) **mit ~em Eingang** with a separate entrance ❸ (*typisch*) **mit dem ihr ~en Optimismus ...** with her characteristic optimism ... ❹ (*eigenartig*) peculiar

Eigenart ['ai·gn̩·ʔaːɐ̯t] *f* characteristic

eigenartig ['ai·gn̩·ʔaːɐ̯·tɪç] *adj* strange

Eigenbedarf *m* **zum ~** for one's [own] personal use

eigenhändig ['aign·hɛn·dɪç] I. *adj* personal; *Brief* handwritten; *Testament* holographic II. *adv* personally

Eigenheim *nt* home of one's own

eigenmächtig ['aign·mɛç·tɪç] *adj* highhanded

Eigenname *m* LING proper noun

Eigennutz <-es> *m kein pl* self-interest

eigennützig ['aign·nʏ·tsɪç] *adj* selfish

Eigenschaft <-, -en> ['ai·gn̩·ʃaft] *f* ❶ (*Charakteristik*) quality; **gute/schlechte ~en** good/bad qualities ❷ (*Funktion*) capacity

Eigenschaftswort <-wörter> *nt* LING adjective

eigensinnig ['ai·gn̩·zɪ·nɪç] *adj* stubborn

eigentlich ['ai·gn̩t·lɪç] I. *adj* ❶ (*wirklich*) real; *Wesen* true ❷ (*ursprünglich*) original II. *adv* actually; **da hast du ~ Recht** you may be right there III. *part* (*überhaupt*) **was ist ~ mit dir los?** what [on earth] is wrong with you?; **wie alt bist du ~?** how old are you anyway?

Eigentor *nt* own goal

Eigentum <-s, *selten* -e> ['ai·gn̩·tuːm] *nt* property

Eigentümer(in) <-s, -> ['ai·gn̩·tyː·mɐ] *m(f)* owner

eigentümlich ['ai·gn̩·tyː·m·lɪç] I. *adj* ❶ (*merkwürdig*) strange ❷ (*typisch*) **jdm/etw ~** characteristic of sb/sth II. *adv* strangely

Eigentumswohnung *f* condominium

eigenwillig ['ai·gn̩·vɪ·lɪç] *adj* ❶ (*eigensinnig*) stubborn ❷ (*unkonventionell*) unconventional

eignen ['aig·nən] *vr* ■**sich** *akk* **für etw** *akk* **~** to be suited to sth

Eilbrief *m* express letter

Eile <-> ['ai·lə] *f kein pl* haste; **etw hat ~** sth is urgent; **in ~ sein** to be in a hurry

Eileiter <-s, -> *m* ANAT fallopian tube

eilen ['ai·lən] I. *vi* ■**etw eilt** sth is urgent II. *vi impers* ■**es eilt** it's urgent

eilig ['ai·lɪç] I. *adj* ❶ (*schnell*) hurried ❷ (*dringend*) urgent; **es ~ haben** to be in a hurry II. *adv* quickly

Eilzug *m* BAHN *a type of express train*

Eimer <-s, -> ['ai·mɐ] *m* bucket

ein¹ ['ain] *adv* (*eingeschaltet*) on; **E~/Aus** on/off

ein² ['ain], **eine** ['ai·nə], **ein** ['ain] I. *adj* one; **mir fehlt noch ~ Cent** I need one more cent ► WENDUNGEN: **~ für alle Mal** once and for all II. *art indef* ❶ (*einzeln*) a/an; **was für ~ Lärm!** what a noise! ❷ (*jeder*) a/an

einander [ai·'nan·dɐ] *pron* each other

ein|arbeiten I. *vr* ■**sich** *akk* **[in etw** *akk*] **~** to get used to [sth] II. *vt* ❶ (*praktisch vertraut machen*) ■**jdn [in etw** *akk*] **~** to train sb [for sth] ❷ ÖSTERR (*nachholen*) *Zeitverlust* to make up [for] sth

Einarbeitungszeit *f* training period

ein|äschern ['ain·ʔɛʃɐn] *vt Leiche* to cremate

ein|atmen *vt, vi* to breathe in *sep*

Einbahnstraße *f* one-way street

ein|balsamieren* *vt Leiche* to embalm

Einband <-bände> ['ain·bant] *m* [book] cover

einbändig ['ain·bɛn·dɪç] *adj Buch* one-volume *attr*

Einbau <-bauten> *m kein pl* installation

ein|bauen *vt* ❶ (*installieren*) ■**etw [in etw** *akk*] **~** to build sth in[to] sth; *Batterie, Motor* to install sth in[to] sth ❷ (*fam: einfügen*) to incorporate [into sth]

Einbauküche *f* fitted kitchen

Einbauschrank *m* built-in cupboard; (*im Schlafzimmer*) built-in closet

ein|berufen* vt irreg ❶ Versammlung to convene ❷ MIL to draft

Einberufung f ❶ einer Versammlung convention ❷ MIL draft card

ein|betten vt to embed

ein|beziehen* vt irreg to include

ein|biegen vi irreg sein to turn (in +akk into)

ein|bilden vr ❶ (glauben) ■ sich dat etw ~ to imagine sth; ■ sich dat ~, dass ... to think that ...; was bildest du dir eigentlich ein? (fam) what has gotten into your head? ❷ (stolz sein) ■ sich dat etw auf etw akk ~ to be proud of sth

Einbildung f kein pl ❶ (Fantasie) imagination ❷ (Arroganz) conceitedness

Einbildungskraft f kein pl [powers of] imagination

ein|blenden vt to insert; Geräusche, Musik to dub in

Einblick m insight; ~ in etw akk haben to have insight into sth

ein|brechen irreg vi ❶ sein o haben (Einbruch verüben) to break in ❷ sein Dämmerung, Nacht to fall ❸ sein (einstürzen) to cave in

Einbrecher(in) <-s, -> m(f) burglar

ein|bringen irreg I. vt ❶ Ernte to bring in ❷ (finanziell) to bring; Zinsen ~ to earn interest ❸ seine Erfahrung ~ to bring one's experience to sth II. vr ■ sich akk ~ to contribute

Einbruch <-[e]s, -brüche> ['ain-brʊx] m ❶ JUR break-in ❷ einer Mauer etc. collapse ❸ (plötzlicher Beginn) onset; bei ~ der Dunkelheit at nightfall

ein|bürgern ['ain-bʏr-gɐn] I. vt ADMIN ■ jdn ~ to naturalize sb II. vr ■ sich akk ~ Gewohnheiten etc. to become the habit (bei +dat with)

ein|checken [-tʃɛkn] I. vi to check in II. vt to check in sep

ein|cremen ['ain-kreː-mən] vt ■ sich dat etw ~ to put cream on sth

ein|decken vr ■ sich akk [mit etw dat] ~ to stock up [on sth]

eindeutig ['ain-dɔy-tɪç] I. adj ❶ (unmissverständlich) unambiguous ❷ (unzweifelhaft) clear II. adv ❶ (unmissverständlich) unambiguously ❷ (klar) clearly

ein|dicken ['ain-dɪkn] I. vt haben KOCHK to thicken II. vi sein to thicken

ein|dringen vi irreg sein ■ in etw akk ~ to force one's way into sth; MIL to penetrate [into] sth

Eindringling <-s, -e> ['ain-drɪŋ-lɪŋ] m intruder

Eindruck <-[e]s, -drücke> ['ain-drʊk] m (Vorstellung) impression; den ~ erwecken/haben, dass ... to give/have the impression that ...

eindrucksvoll adj impressive

eine(r, s) ['ai-nə] pron indef ❶ (jemand) someone, somebody; ~ s von den Kindern one of the children ❷ (fam: man) one; und das soll noch ~ r glauben? and I'm expected to swallow that? ❸ (ein Punkt) ■ ~ s one thing

eineiig ['ain-ʔai-ɪç] adj BIOL identical

eineinhalb ['ain-ʔain-'halp] adj one and a half

ein|engen ['ain-ɛŋ-ən] vt to restrict

einer ['ai-nɐ] pron s. eine(r, s)

einerlei ['ai-nɐ-'lai] adj pred (egal) das ist mir ganz ~ it's all the same to me

einerseits ['ai-nɐ-zaits] adv ~ ... andererseits ... on the one hand ..., on the other hand ...

einfach ['ain-fax] I. adj ❶ (leicht) easy ❷ (gewöhnlich) simple ❸ eine ~ e Fahrkarte a one-way ticket II. adv ❶ (leicht) easily; ~ zu verstehen easy to understand III. part simply, just; das geht ~ nicht! we/you just can't do that!

ein|fädeln ['ain-fɛː-dln] I. vt ❶ Faden to thread ❷ (fam: anbahnen) to engineer fig II. vr AUTO ■ sich akk ~ to merge

ein|fahren irreg I. vi sein ■ in etw akk ~ to pull in to sth; auf einem Gleis ~ to arrive on a platform II. vt haben ❶ Antenne, Objektiv to retract ❷ Gewinne to make ❸ Heu, Korn to harvest

Einfahrt <-, -en> f ❶ kein pl (das Einfahren) entry; eines Zuges arrival

E

E

➋ (*Zufahrt*) entrance; (*Auffahrt*) driveway

Einfall ['ain-fal] *m* ➊ (*Idee*) idea ➋ MIL invasion (**in** +*akk* of)

ein|fallen *vi irreg sein* ➊ (*in den Sinn kommen*) ■etw fällt jdm ein sth occurs to sb ➋ (*in Erinnerung kommen*) ■etw fällt jdm ein sb remembers sth ➌ (*einstürzen*) to collapse ➍ MIL **in ein Land** ~ to invade a country ➎ (*Wangen*) to become hollow

einfallslos *adj* unimaginative

einfältig ['ain-fɛl-tɪç] *adj* naive

Einfaltspinsel *m* (*pej fam*) simpleton

Einfamilienhaus *nt* single-family house

ein|fangen *irreg* I. *vt* ■jdn/ein Tier [wieder] ~ to [re]capture sb/an animal II. *vr* (*fam*) ■sich *dat* etw ~ to catch sth

einfarbig *adj* in one color

ein|fassen *vt* Edelstein, Diamant to set

ein|finden *vr irreg* ■sich *akk* [irgendwo] ~ to arrive [somewhere]

ein|flößen *vt* ➊ (*langsam eingeben*) ■jdm etw ~ to give sb sth ➋ (*erwecken*) jdm Angst/Vertrauen ~ to instill fear/confidence in sb

Einflugschneise *f* approach [path]

EinflussRR, **Einfluß**ALT <-flusses, -flüsse> ['ain-flus] *m* influence; **auf jdn/etw ~ haben** to have an influence on sb/sth

einflussreichRR *adj* influential

einförmig ['ain-fœr-mɪç] I. *adj* monotonous; *Landschaft* uniform II. *adv* monotonously

ein|frieren *irreg vt* ➊ (*konservieren*) to [deep-]freeze ➋ (*suspendieren*) to suspend; *Projekt* to shelve ➌ ÖKON to freeze

ein|fügen I. *vt* ■etw [in etw *akk*] ~ to fit sth in[to sth] II. *vr* ■sich *akk* [in etw *akk*] ~ ➊ (*sich anpassen*) to adapt [oneself] [to sth] ➋ (*hineinpassen*) to fit in [with sth]

Einfühlungsvermögen *nt* empathy

Einfuhr <-, -en> ['ain-fuːɐ̯] *f* importation

Einfuhrbestimmungen *pl* import regulations *pl*

ein|führen *vt* ➊ (*importieren*) to import ➋ (*bekannt machen*) to introduce; *Artikel, Firma* to establish ➌ (*vertraut machen*) ■jdn ~ to introduce sb (**in** +*akk* to) ➍ (*hineinschieben*) to insert (**in** +*akk* into)

Einführung *f* introduction

Einführungspreis *m* introductory price

Einfuhrzoll *m* import duty

Eingabe <-, -en> *f* ➊ (*Petition*) petition (**bei** +*dat* to) ➋ *kein pl von Daten, Informationen* entry

Eingabetaste *f* COMPUT enter key

Eingang <-[e]s, -gänge> ['ain-gaŋ] *m* ➊ (*Zugang*) entrance; „**kein ~!**" "no entry" ➋ *kein pl* (*Erhalt*) receipt

ein|geben *irreg vt* ➊ COMPUT **Daten** ~ to input data (**in** +*akk* into) ➋ ■jdm etw ~ *Medizin* to administer sth to sb

eingebildet *adj* ➊ (*pej: hochmütig*) conceited ➋ (*imaginär*) imaginary

Eingeborene(r) *f(m)* native

Eingebung <-, -en> *f* (*Inspiration*) inspiration

eingefallen *adj* hollow; *Gesicht* gaunt

ein|gehen *irreg* I. *vi sein* ➊ (*sich beschäftigen mit*) ■auf etw *akk* ~ to deal with sth; ■auf jdn ~ to pay attention to sb ➋ (*zustimmen*) ■auf etw *akk* ~ to agree to sth; (*sich einlassen*) to accept sth ➌ **in die Geschichte** ~ to go down in history ➍ ([*ab*]*sterben*) to die (**an** +*dat* of); *Laden* to go bust *fam* II. *vt sein* **ein Risiko** ~ to take a risk; **ich gehe jede Wette ein, dass ...** I'll bet you anything that ...

eingehend ['ain-geː-ənt] I. *adj* detailed; *Prüfung* extensive II. *adv* in detail

Eingemachte(s) *nt dekl wie adj* KOCHK preserved fruit

eingeschnappt *adj* (*fam*) miffed

eingeschrieben *adj* registered

Eingeständnis ['ain-gə-ʃtɛnt-nɪs] *nt* admission

ein|gestehen* *irreg* I. *vt* to admit II. *vr* ■sich *dat* ~, dass ... to admit to oneself that ...

eingestellt *adj* ➊ (*gesinnt*) fortschrittlich/ökologisch ~ progressively/environmentally minded; ■**jd ist gegen jdn** ~ sb is set against sb ❷ (*vorbereitet*) ■**auf etw** *akk* ~ **sein** to be prepared for sth

eingetragen *adj* Mitglied, Verein, Warenzeichen registered

Eingeweide <-s, -> ['ain·gə·vai·də] *nt meist pl* entrails *npl*

ein|**gewöhnen*** *vr* ■**sich** *akk* ~ to acclimatize

ein|**gießen** *vt irreg s.* einschenken

eingleisig ['ain·glai·zɪç] *adj* single-track

ein|**gliedern** I. *vt* ❶ (*integrieren*) ■**jdn** ~ to integrate sb (**in** +*akk* into) ❷ ADMIN, POL (*einbeziehen*) ■**etw** ~ to incorporate sth (**in** +*akk* into) II. *vr* ■**sich** *akk* ~ to integrate oneself (**in** +*akk* into)

ein|**greifen** *vi irreg* to intervene

Eingriff *m* <-, -en> ❶ (*Einschreiten*) intervention ❷ MED operation

Einhalt ['ain·halt] *m kein pl* jdm/etw ~ **gebieten** to put a stop to sb/sth

ein|**halten** *irreg vt* **eine Diät** ~ to stick to a diet; **einen Vertrag** ~ to honor [the terms of] a contract; **die Spielregeln/ Vorschriften** ~ to obey the rules

ein|**handeln** *vr* (*fam*) **sich** *dat* **eine Krankheit** ~ to catch a disease

einheimisch ['ain·hai·mɪʃ] *adj* ❶ (*ortsansässig*) local ❷ BOT, ZOOL indigenous

Einheit <-, -en> ['ain·hait] *f* unity; **Tag der deutschen** ~ Day of German Unity

einheitlich ['ain·hait·lɪç] I. *adj* ❶ (*gleich*) uniform ❷ (*in sich geschlossen*) integrated; *Front* united II. *adv* ~ **gekleidet** dressed the same

ein|**heizen** *vi* (*gründlich heizen*) to turn the heat on

ein|**holen** *vt* ❶ (*einziehen*) to pull in *sep; Fahne, Segel* to lower ❷ *Genehmigung* to ask for ❸ (*erreichen, nachholen*) ■**jdn/etw** ~ to catch up with sb/sth

einig ['ai·nɪç] *adj pred* (*einer Meinung*) ■**sich** *dat* [über etw *akk*] ~ **sein** to agree [on sth]

einige(r, s) ['ai·nɪ·gə] *pron indef* ❶ *sing, adjektivisch* (*etwas*) some;

nach ~**r Zeit** after some time ❷ *sing, substantivisch* (*viel*) ■~**s** quite a lot ❸ *pl, adjektivisch* (*mehrere*) several; **vor** ~**n Tagen** a few days ago ❹ *pl, substantivisch* (*mehrere*) some; ~ **von euch** some of you; ~ **wenige** a few

einigen ['ai·nɪgn] *vr* ■**sich** *akk* ~ to agree (**auf** +*akk* on)

einigermaßen ['ai·nɪ·gɐ·'maː·sn] *adv* ❶ (*ziemlich*) fairly ❷ (*leidlich*) all right

Einigkeit <-> ['ai·nɪç·kait] *f kein pl* ❶ (*Eintracht*) unity ❷ (*Übereinstimmung*) agreement

Einigung <-, -en> *f* ❶ POL unification ❷ (*Übereinstimmung*) agreement (**über** +*akk* on)

ein|**impfen** *vt* ■**jdm etw** ~ to drum sth into sb

einjährig, 1-jährig^RR ['ain·jɛː·rɪç] *adj* ❶ (*Alter*) one-year-old *attr*; one year old *pred; s. a.* **achtjährig 1** ❷ BOT annual ❸ (*Zeitspanne*) one-year *attr*, [of] one year *pred; s. a.* **achtjährig 2**

ein|**kalkulieren*** *vt* ■**etw** [mit] ~ to take sth into account

ein|**kassieren*** *vt* ❶ (*kassieren*) to collect ❷ (*fam: wegnehmen*) to confiscate

Einkauf *m* ❶ (*das Einkaufen*) shopping; **beim** ~ **von Lebensmitteln ...** when buying food ... ❷ (*gekaufte Ware*) purchase

ein|**kaufen** I. *vt* to buy II. *vi* ~ **gehen** to go shopping III. *vr* (*einen Anteil erwerben*) ■**sich** *akk* **in etw** *akk* ~ to buy [one's way] into sth

Einkaufsbummel *m* shopping trip

Einkaufspassage [-pa·sa:·ʒə] *f* galleria

Einkaufswagen *m* shopping cart

Einkaufszentrum *nt* shopping mall

ein|**kehren** *vi sein* (*veraltend*) to stop off (**in** +*dat* at)

ein|**klammern** *vt* LING to put in parentheses

Einklang *m* harmony

ein|**klemmen** *vt* ❶ (*quetschen*) to trap ❷ (*festdrücken*) to clamp

ein|**kochen** KOCHK I. *vt haben* to preserve II. *vi sein* to thicken

Einkommen <-s, -> *nt* income

E

E

ein|laden *irreg vt* ① (*zu Hochzeit, Party*) to invite (**zu** +*dat* to) ② (*Gegenstände*) to load (**in** +*akk* in[to])

Einladung *f* invitation

Einlage <-, -n> *f* ① FIN (*Bankguthaben*) deposit ② (*für Schuhe*) insole

ein|lagern *vt* to store

EinlassRR, **Einlaß**ALT <-lasses, -lässe> ['ain·las] *m* admission

ein|lassen *irreg* **I.** *vt* ① (*hereinlassen*) ■**jdn ~** to let sb in ② (*einlaufen lassen*) **jdm ein Bad ~** to run sb a bath **III.** *vr* ① (*auf etwas eingehen*) ■**sich** *akk* **auf etw** *akk* **~** to get involved in sth; *auf Abenteuer* to embark on sth; *auf Kompromiss* to accept sth ② (*bes pej: Kontakt aufnehmen*) ■**sich** *akk* **mit jdm ~** to get involved with sb

ein|laufen *irreg* **I.** *vi sein* ① *Kleidung* to shrink ② (*Badewasser*) to run ③ SPORT **als Erster ~** to come in first **II.** *vt haben* **Schuhe ~** to wear shoes in

ein|laufen *vr* ■**sich** *akk* **~** to settle in

ein|legen *vt* ① AUTO **den zweiten Gang ~** to shift into second [gear] ② KOCHK ■**etw [in etw** *dat o akk*] **~** to pickle sth [in sth] ③ **eine Pause ~** to take a break

ein|leiten *vt* ① (*in die Wege leiten*) to introduce; **Schritte [gegen jdn] ~** to take steps [against sb] ② MED to induce ③ ÖKON **Abwässer in einen Fluss ~** to discharge effluent into a river

einleitend **I.** *adj* introductory **II.** *adv* as an introduction

Einleitung *f* (*a. Vorwort*) introduction; *eines Verfahrens* institution; *einer Untersuchung* opening

ein|lenken *vi* (*nachgeben*) to give in

ein|leuchten *vi* to make sense

einleuchtend **I.** *adj* evident; *Argument* convincing; *Erklärung* plausible **II.** *adv* clearly

ein|liefern *vt* **jdn ins Krankenhaus ~** to admit sb to the hospital; **jdn ins Gefängnis ~** to send sb to prison

ein|loggen ['ain·lɔ·gn] *vr* ■**sich** *akk* **~** to log in

ein|lösen *vt* ① *Scheck* to cash ② *Pfand*

to redeem (**bei** +*dat* at) ③ *Versprechen* to honor

ein|machen *vt* to preserve; (*in Essig*) to pickle sth

Einmachglas *nt* [preserving] jar

einmal[1], **1-mal**RR ['ain·ma:l] *adv* once; **~ am Tag/in der Woche** once a day/ week; **es war ~** once upon a time; **irgendwann ~** sometime ▶WENDUNGEN: **auf ~** (*plötzlich*) all of a sudden; (*an einem Stück*) all at once; **~ ist keinmal** (*prov*) just once doesn't count

einmal[2] ['ain·ma:l] *part* ① (*eben*) **so liegen die Dinge nun ~** that's [just] the way things are ② (*einschränkend*) **nicht ~** not even

Einmaleins <-> ['ain·ma:l·ʔains] *nt kein pl* ■**das ~** multiplication tables *pl*

einmalig ['ain·ma:·lɪç] *adj* ① (*nicht nochmals*) *Chance, Gelegenheit* unique; *Zahlung* one-off ② (*fam: ausgezeichnet*) outstanding

Einmischung *f* interference

einmotorig *adj* single-engine

einmütig ['ain·my:·tɪç] *adj* unanimous

Einnahme <-, -n> ['ain·na:·mə] *f* ① FIN earnings *npl*; *bei einem Geschäft* receipts *npl* ② *kein pl von Arzneimitteln, Mahlzeiten* taking

ein|nehmen *vt irreg* ① *Geld* to take; *Steuern* to collect ② (*zu sich nehmen*) to take; *Mahlzeit* to have ③ *Platz* to take ④ *Raum* to take up ⑤ *Standpunkt* to hold ⑥ (*erobern*) to take ▶**jdn für sich** *akk* **~** to win favor with sb

einnehmend ['ain·ne:·mənt] *adj* engaging

ein|nicken *vi sein* (*fam*) to doze off

ein|nisten *vr* ■**sich** *akk* **~** ① (*sich niederlassen*) to ensconce oneself (**bei** +*dat* with) ② *Ungeziefer* to nest

Einöde ['ain·ʔø:də] *f* wasteland

ein|ordnen **I.** *vt* ① (*einsortieren*) ■**etw ~** to organize sth ② (*klassifizieren*) ■**jdn/etw ~** to classify sb/sth **II.** *vr* TRANSP ■**sich** *akk* **links/rechts ~** to merge [to the] left/right

ein|packen *vt* ① (*verpacken*) to wrap;

(*zum Verschicken*) to pack ② (*fam: ein-mummeln*) ▪**jdn** ~ to wrap sb up

ein|parken *vt, vi* to park; (*am Straßen-rand*) to parallel park

ein|planen *vt* to plan; ▪**etw** [**mit**] ~ to take sth into consideration

ein|prägen I. *vr* ① ▪**sich** *dat* **etw** ~ to make a mental note of sth ② ▪**sich** *akk* **jdm** ~ *Bilder, Eindrücke, Worte* to be imprinted on sb's memory II. *vt* ▪**jdm etw** ~ to drum sth into sb's head

einprägsam ['ain·prɛːk·zaːm] *adj* easy to remember *pred; Melodie* catchy

ein|rahmen *vt* to frame

ein|räumen *vt* ① (*hineintun*) to place ② (*gewähren*) ▪**jdm etw** ~ *Frist, Kre-dit* to give sb sth

ein|rechnen *vt* to include

ein|reden I. *vt* ▪**jdm etw** ~ to talk sb into thinking sth II. *vi* (*bedrängen*) ▪**auf jdn** ~ to pester sb *fam* III. *vr* ▪**sich** *dat* **etw** ~ to talk oneself into thinking sth

ein|reichen *vt* to submit

ein|reihen I. *vt* ▪**jdn/etw unter etw** *akk* ~ to classify sb/sth under sth II. *vr* ▪**sich** *akk* **in etw** *akk* ~ to join sth

Einreise *f* entry [into a country]

Einreisegenehmigung *f* entry permit

ein|reisen *vi sein* to enter

ein|renken ['ain·rɛŋ·kn̩] I. *vt* ① MED ▪[**jdm**] **etw** ~ to pop sth back in [place] [for sb] ② (*fam: bereinigen*) ▪**etw** [**wie-der**] ~ to straighten out *sep* sth [again] II. *vr* (*fam: ins Lot kommen*) ▪**sich** *akk* **wieder** ~ to sort itself out

ein|richten I. *vt* ① (*möblieren*) to fur-nish; *Praxis* to equip ② (*gründen*) to set up *sep* ③ *Konto* to open ④ (*arrangie-ren*) ▪**es** ..., **dass** ... arrange it so that ... ⑤ (*vorbereitet sein*) ▪**auf etw** *akk* **eingerichtet sein** to be prepared for sth II. *vr* ① (*mit Möbeln*) **ich richte mich völlig neu ein** I'm completely refurnishing my home ② (*sich einstel-len*) ▪**sich** *akk* **auf etw** *akk* ~ to be prepared for sth

Einrichtung <-, -en> *f* ① (*Möbel*) fur-nishings *npl*; (*Ausstattung*) decorations

npl ② (*das Möblieren*) furnishing; (*das Ausstatten*) decorating ③ (*das Installie-ren*) installation ④ FIN *eines Kontos* opening ⑤ (*Institution*) organization

eins ['ains] I. *adj* one; *s. a.* **acht**[1] ▶WEN-DUNGEN: ~ **A** (*fam*) first-class II. *adj pred* ▪~ **mit jdm/sich/etw sein** to be [at] one with sb/oneself/sth

einsam ['ain·zaːm] *adj* ① (*verlassen*) lonesome; *Leben* solitary ② (*abgele-gen*) isolated ③ (*menschenleer*) desert-ed ▶WENDUNGEN: **das war ~e Spitze!** it was absolutely fantastic!

ein|sammeln *vt* to collect

Einsatz <-es, Einsätze> *m* ① *beim Spiel* bet ② (*Verwendung*) use; *von Truppen* deployment ③ **im ~ sein** to be on duty ④ (*eingesetzte Leistung*) effort; **unter ~ ihres Lebens** by putting her own life at risk

einsatzbereit *adj* ready for use *pred; Menschen* ready for action; MIL ready for combat *pred*

ein|schalten I. *vt* ① *Gerät, Licht* to switch on *sep* ② (*hinzuziehen*) ▪**jdn** ~ to call in *sep* II. *vr* ▪**sich** *akk* [**in etw** *akk*] ~ ① RADIO, TV to tune in[to sth] ② (*sich einmischen*) to intervene [in sth]

Einschaltquote *f* [audience] ratings *npl*

ein|schärfen I. *vt* ▪**jdm etw** ~ to im-press on sb the importance of sth II. *vr* ▪**sich** *dat* **etw** ~ to remember sth

ein|schätzen *vt* to assess; **Sie haben ihn richtig eingeschätzt** your opinion of him was right

ein|schenken *vt* ▪**jdm etw** ~ to pour sb sth

ein|schiffen *vr* ▪**sich** *akk* ~ to embark

ein|schlafen *vi irreg sein* to fall asleep

ein|schläfern ['ain·ʃlɛː·fɐn] *vt* (*a. euph*) to put to sleep

einschläfernd ['ain·ʃlɛː·fɐnt] *adj* MED **ein ~es Mittel** a sleep-inducing drug

ein|schlagen *irreg* I. *vt haben* ① (*mit Gewalt*) **eine Tür** ~ to break down *sep* a door; **jdm die Zähne** ~ to knock sb's teeth out ② (*wählen*) *Laufbahn, Weg* to choose II. *vi* ① *sein o haben* ▪[**in etw**

E

akk] ~ *Blitz* to strike [sth] ② *sein Granaten* to fall ③ *haben* (*einprügeln*) ■ **auf jdn** ~ to hit sb ④ *haben* (*Anklang finden*) to catch on

ein|schließen *vt irreg* ① (*in einen Raum*) ■ **jdn** ~ to lock up *sep* sb ② (*wegschließen*) ■ **etw** ~ to lock away *sep* sth ③ (*einbeziehen*) ■ **jdn** ~ to include sb ④ (*einkesseln*) ■ **jdn/etw** ~ to surround sb/sth

einschließlich ['ain·ʃliːs·lɪç] **I.** *präp* ■ ~ **einer S.** *gen* including sth **II.** *adv* inclusive

ein|schmeicheln *vr* ■ **sich** *akk* [**bei jdm**] ~ to ingratiate oneself [with sb]

ein|schnappen *vi sein* ① *Tür* to click shut ② (*fam: beleidigt sein*) to get in a huff

einschneidend ['ain·ʃnai·dn̩t] *adj* **eine** ~ **Veränderung** a drastic change

Einschnitt *m* ① MED incision ② (*geschichtlich*) turning point

ein|schränken ['ain·ʃrɛŋ·kn̩] **I.** *vt* ① (*reduzieren*) to cut [back on] ② (*beschränken*) to curb **II.** *vr* ■ **sich** *akk* ~ to cut back (**in** +*dat* on)

Einschränkung <-, -en> *f* **ohne** ~**en** (*in vollem Umfang*) without restrictions; (*ohne Vorbehalt*) without reservations

ein|schreiben *irreg vr* SCH, UNI ■ **sich** *akk* ~ to register

Einschreiben *nt* registered letter

ein|schreiten *vi irreg sein* to take action

ein|schüchtern ['ain·ʃʏç·tɐn] *vt* ■ **jdn** ~ to intimidate sb

ein|schweißen *vt Bücher, Nahrungsmittel* to seal

ein|sehen *vt irreg* ■ ~, **dass** ... to see that ...

einseitig ['ain·zai·tɪç] **I.** *adj* ① MED *Lähmung* one-sided ② (*unausgewogen*) *Ernährung* unbalanced ③ (*voreingenommen*) *Sicht* bias[s]ed **II.** *adv* ① MED **gelähmt** on one side ② (*unausgewogen*) **sich** *akk* ~ **ernähren** to have an unbalanced diet ③ (*parteiisch*) from a one-sided point of view

ein|senden *vt irreg* to send (**an** +*akk* to)

Einsendeschluss^RR *m* deadline [for entries]

einsetzbar *adj* applicable

ein|setzen **I.** *vt* ① (*einfügen*) to insert ② *Kommission* to set up ③ (*zum Einsatz bringen*) to use; SPORT to put in *sep* **II.** *vi* (*beginnen*) to start **III.** *vr* ■ **sich** *akk* ~ to make an effort; ■ **sich** *akk* **für jdn/etw** ~ to support sb/sth

Einsicht *f* ① (*Vernunft*) sense; (*Erkenntnis*) insight; **jdn zur** ~ **bringen** to make sb see reason ② (*in Akten, Unterlagen*) ~ **in etw** *akk* **nehmen** to inspect sth

einsichtig ['ain·zɪç·tɪç] *adj* ① (*verständlich*) *Argument* understandable ② (*vernünftig*) *Person* reasonable

einsilbig ['ain·zɪl·bɪç] *adj* (*a. ling*) monosyllabic

ein|spannen *vt* ① (*in einen Schraubstock*) to clamp ② *Tiere* to harness ③ ■ **jdn** [**für etw** *akk*] ~ to call sb in [for sth]; ■ **sehr eingespannt sein** to be very busy

ein|sperren *vt* to lock up *sep*

ein|spielen **I.** *vr* ① ■ **sich** *akk* ~ *Methode, Regelung* to get going; ■ **sich** *akk* **aufeinander** ~ to get used to each other ② SPORT ■ **sich** *akk* ~ to warm up **II.** *vt* FILM to bring in *sep*

ein|springen *vi irreg sein* (*fam*) ① (*vertreten*) ■ **für jdn** ~ to cover [for sb] ② (*aushelfen*) ■ **mit etw** *dat* ~ to help out [with sth]

Einspruch *m* (*a. jur*) objection

einspurig ['ain·ʃpuː·rɪç] **I.** *adj* ① TRANSP one-lane ② (*pej*) ~**es Denken** one-track mind **II.** *adv* TRANSP **die Straße ist nur** ~ **befahrbar** only one lane of the road is open [to traffic]

einst ['ainst] *adv* ① (*früher*) once ② (*in der Zukunft*) one day

Einstand *m* ① (*Arbeitsanfang*) start of a new job ② TENNIS deuce

ein|stecken *vt* ① *Geld, Schlüssel* to put in one's pocket ② *Brief* to mail ③ (*fam: hinnehmen*) ■ **etw** ~ to put up with sth ④ ELEK to plug in *sep*

ein|stehen *vi irreg sein* ① (*sich verbür-*

gen) ■**für** jdn/etw ~ to vouch for sb/ sth ②(*aufkommen*) ■**für etw** akk ~ to take responsibility for sth

ein|steigen vi irreg sein ■ |**in etw** akk] ~ ①(*besteigen*) Auto to get in [sth]; Bus, Flugzeug to get on [sth] ②(*fam: hineinklettern*) to climb in[to sth] ③ÖKON to buy into sth ④(*sich engagieren*) to get involved [in sth]

ein|stellen I. vt ①(*anstellen*) to employ ②(*beenden*) to stop; Suche to call off; Projekt to shelve ③MIL to stop; **das Feuer** ~ to cease fire ④JUR to abandon ⑤FOTO, TECH to adjust ⑥TV, RADIO to tune ⑦SPORT **den Rekord** ~ to tie the record II. vr ①(*auftreten*) ■**sich** akk ~ Bedenken to begin; MED Fieber, Symptome to develop ②(*sich anpassen*) ■**sich** akk **auf jdn/etw** ~ to adapt to sb/sth ③(*sich vorbereiten*) ■**sich** akk **auf etw** akk ~ to prepare oneself for sth

Einstellung f ①(*Gesinnung*) attitude ②(*Anstellung*) employment ③(*Beendigung*) stopping ④FOTO adjustment ⑤FILM take ⑥TV, RADIO tuning

Einsturz m collapse; einer Decke a. cave-in; einer Mauer falling-down

ein|stürzen vi sein ①(*zusammenbrechen*) to collapse; Decke a. to cave in ②(*fig*) ■**auf jdn** ~ to overwhelm sb

einstweilig ['ainst·'vai·lɪç] adj attr JUR ~ **e Verfügung** temporary restraining order

eintägig, 1-tägigRR adj one-day attr, lasting one day pred

Eintagsfliege f ZOOL mayfly ►WENDUNGEN: **eine ~ sein** to be here today gone tomorrow

ein|tauchen I. vt haben to dip sth II. vi sein ■|**in etw** akk] ~ to dive in[to sth]

ein|teilen vt ①(*unterteilen*) ■**etw in etw** akk ~ to divide sth up into sth ②■|**sich** dat] **etw** ~ Geld, Vorräte, Zeit to be careful with sth ③(*zu Tätigkeit*) ■**jdn zu etw** dat ~ to assign sb to sth

Einteilung f ①von Vorräten, Zeit management ②(*Verpflichtung*) ■**jds ~ zu etw** dat sb's assignment to sth

eintönig ['ain·tø:·nɪç] I. adj monotonous II. adv monotonously; ~ **klingen** to sound monotonous

Eintopf m stew

einträchtig ['ain·trɛç·tɪç] adj harmonious

Eintrag <-[e]s, Einträge> ['ain·tra:k] m ①(*Vermerk*) note ②(*im Nachschlagewerk*) entry ③ADMIN record

ein|tragen vt irreg ①(*einschreiben*) ■**jdn** ~ to record sb's name ②(*amtlich registrieren*) to register ③(*einzeichnen*) ■**etw** ~ to note sth [down]

ein|treffen vi irreg sein ①(*ankommen*) to arrive ②(*in Erfüllung gehen*) to come true; Ereignis, Katastrophe to happen

ein|treiben vt irreg ■**etw** [**von jdm**] ~ to collect sth [from sb]

ein|treten irreg I. vi ①sein (*betreten*) to enter ②sein (*beitreten*) in Partei, Verein to join ③sein (*sich ereignen*) to occur; **sollte der Fall ~, dass ...** if it should happen that ... ④sein (*sich einsetzen*) ■**für jdn/etw** ~ to stand up for sb/sth ⑤haben (*wiederholt treten*) ■**auf jdn/ein Tier** ~ to kick sb/an animal [repeatedly] II. vt haben **eine Tür** ~ to kick in sep a door

Eintritt m ①(*Beitritt*) ■**jds ~ in etw** akk sb's joining sth ②(*Eintrittsgeld*) admission ③(*das Betreten*) ~ **verboten** do not enter

Eintrittskarte f [admission] ticket

ein|üben vt to practice; Rolle, Stück to rehearse

ein|verleiben* ['ain·fɛɐ·lai·bn̩] vr ■**sich** dat **etw** ~ ①ÖKON to incorporate sth ②(*hum fam: verzehren*) to put sth away

Einvernehmen <-s> nt kein pl agreement

einverstanden ['ain·fɛɐ·ʃtan·dn̩] adj pred ■ ~ **sein** to agree

Einverständnis ['ain·fɛɐ·ʃtɛnt·nɪs] nt **sein ~ geben** to give one's consent; **in beiderseitigem ~** by mutual agreement

E

Einwand <-[e]s, Einwände> ['ain·vant] *m* objection (**gegen** +*akk* to)

Einwanderer, -wand[r]erin *m, f* immigrant

ein|wandern *vi sein* to immigrate

Einwanderung *f* immigration (**nach** to, **in** into); **kontrollierte ~** selective [*or* controlled] immigration

einwandfrei ['ain·vant·frai] *adj* ❶ (*tadellos*) flawless; *Obst* perfect; *Qualität* excellent; *Benehmen* impeccable ❷ (*unzweifelhaft*) irrefutable

Einwegflasche *f* nonreturnable bottle

ein|weichen *vt* to soak sth

ein|weihen *vt* ❶ (*offiziell eröffnen*) ■etw ~ to open sth [officially] ❷ (*informieren*) ■jdn ~ to initiate sb (**in** +*akk* into)

ein|weisen *vt irreg* ❶ (*unterweisen*) ■jdn ~ to brief sb (**in** +*akk* about) ❷ MED to refer

ein|wenden *vt irreg* ■etw [gegen etw *akk*] ~ to object [to sth]

ein|werfen *irreg* ❶ *Brief* to mail ❷ *Fenster* to break ❸ SPORT to throw in *sep* ❹ *Bemerkung* to throw in *sep*

ein|wickeln *vt* ❶ (*in etwas wickeln*) to wrap [up *sep*] ❷ (*fam: überlisten*) ■jdn ~ to take sb in

ein|willigen ['ain·vɪ·lɪ·gn] *vi* to consent (**in** +*akk* to)

ein|wirken *vi* ■auf jdn/etw ~ to have an effect on sb/sth

Einwohner(in) <-s, -> ['ain·vo:·nɐ] *m(f)* inhabitant

Einwohnermeldeamt *nt* ≈ Town Clerk['s Office]

Einwurf *m* ❶ *von Münzen* insertion; *von Brief* mailing ❷ (*beim Fußball*) throw-in ❸ (*Zwischenbemerkung*) interjection

Einzahl ['ain·tsa:l] *f* LING singular

ein|zahlen *vt* to pay [in]

Einzahlung *f* FIN deposit

Einzelfahrschein *m* one-way ticket

Einzelgänger(in) <-s, -> *m(f)* (*Mensch, Tier*) loner

Einzelhaft *f* solitary confinement

Einzelhandel *m* retail trade

Einzelhändler(in) *m(f)* retailer

Einzelheit <-, -en> *f* detail

Einzelkind *nt* only child

einzeln ['ain·tsln] I. *adj* ❶ (*für sich allein*) individual ❷ (*Detail*) ■im E~en in detail ❸ (*individuell*) individual; **jede(r, s) E~e** each [and every] individual ❹ (*alleinstehend*) single ❺ *pl* (*einige wenige*) a few; **~e Schauer** METEO scattered showers II. *adv* separately

Einzelteil *nt* separate part

Einzelzimmer *nt* single room

ein|ziehen *irreg* I. *vt haben* ❶ *Beiträge, Gelder* to collect ❷ (*beschlagnahmen*) to take away *sep* ❸ MIL **jdn [zum Militär]** ~ to draft sb [into the army] ❹ (*zurückziehen*) to draw in *sep*; *Antenne, Periskop* to retract; **den Kopf ~** to duck one's head ❺ BAU **eine Wand ~** to put in *sep* II. *vi sein* ❶ (*in eine Wohnung*) ■bei jdm ~ to move in with sb ❷ SPORT, MIL (*einmarschieren*) ■in etw *akk* ~ to march into sth ❸ (*Flüssigkeit*) to soak

einzig ['ain·tsɪç] I. *adj* ❶ *attr* only ❷ (*alleinige*) ■der/die E~e the only one; ■das E~e the only thing II. *adv* only

einzigartig ['ain·tsɪç·ʔa:ɐ̯·tɪç] I. *adj* unique II. *adv* astoundingly

Eis <-es> ['ais] *nt kein pl* ice; (*Eiscreme*) ice cream

Eisbahn *f* SPORT skating rink

Eisbär *m* polar bear

Eisbecher *m* ❶ (*Behälter*) [ice-cream] carton ❷ (*Eiscreme*) sundae

Eisberg *m* GEOG iceberg

Eisbrecher *m* NAUT icebreaker

Eiscreme [-kre:m] *f* ice cream

Eisdiele *f* ice cream parlor

Eisen <-s, -> ['aizn] *nt kein pl* iron

Eisenbahn ['ai·zn·ba:n] *f* train

Eisenbahner(in) <-s, -> *m(f)* (*fam*) railroad employee

Eisenbahnwagen *m* (*Personenwagen*) passenger car; (*Güterwaggon*) freight car

eisern ['ai·zɐn] I. *adj* iron II. *adv* resolutely

eisgekühlt *adj* ice-cold
Eisglätte *f* black ice
Eishockey *nt* ice hockey
eisig ['ai·zɪç] I. *adj* ❶ (*bitterkalt*) icy ❷ (*abweisend*) icy; *Schweigen* frosty ❸ (*jäh*) chilling; **ein ~er Schreck durchfuhr sie** a cold shiver ran through her [body] II. *adv* coolly
eiskalt ['ais·'kalt] I. *adj* ❶ ice-cold ❷ (*fig*) cold-blooded II. *adv* (*fig*) coolly
Eiskunstlauf *m* figure skating
eis‖laufen *vi irreg sein* to ice-skate
Eisprung *m* ovulation
Eiswürfel *m* ice cube
Eiszapfen *m* icicle
Eiszeit *f* Ice Age
eitel ['ai·tl] *adj* vain
Eitelkeit <-, -en> ['ai·tl̩·kait] *f* vanity
Eiter <-s> ['ai·tɐ] *m kein pl* pus
eitern ['ai·tɐn] *vi* to fester
Eiweiß ['ai·vais] *nt* ❶ CHEM protein ❷ KOCHK egg white
Eizelle *f* ovum
Ekel[1] <-s> ['e:kl̩] *m kein pl* disgust; **~ erregend** revolting
Ekel[2] <-s, -> ['e:kl̩] *nt* (*fam*) disgusting person
ekelhaft *adj* disgusting
ekeln ['e:kl̩n] I. *vt* ■**jdn ~** to disgust sb II. *vt impers* **es ekelt mich vor diesem Geruch** this smell is disgusting III. *vr* ■**sich** *akk* **vor etw** *dat* **~** to find sth disgusting
eklig <-er, -ste> ['e:k·lɪç] *adj s.* **ekelhaft**
Ekstase <-, -n> [ɛk·'sta:·zə] *f* ecstasy
Ekzem <-s, -e> [ɛk·'tse:m] *nt* eczema
elastisch [e'las·tɪʃ] *adj* ❶ *Binde, Stoff* stretchy ❷ *Gelenk, Muskel, Mensch* supple; *Gang* springy
Elch <-[e]s, -e> ['ɛlç] *m* elk
Elefant <-en, -en> [ele·'fant] *m* elephant
elegant [ele·'gant] *adj* elegant
Elektriker(in) <-s, -> [e'lɛk·tri·kɐ] *m(f)* electrician
elektrisch [e'lɛk·trɪʃ] *adj* electric; **~e Geräte** electrical appliances

elektrisieren* [elɛk·tri·'zi:·rən] *vt* to electrify
Elektrizität <-> [elɛk·tri·tsi·'tɛːt] *f kein pl* electricity
Elektrizitätswerk *nt* [electric] power plant
Elektrofahrrad [e'lɛk·tro·fa:ɐ̯·ra:t] *nt* electric bicycle, e-bike
Elektroherd [e'lɛk·tro·he:ɐ̯t] *m* electric stove
Elektromotor [e'lɛk·tro·mo:·to:ɐ̯] *m* electric motor
Elektron <-s, -tronen> [elɛk·'tro:n] *nt* electron
Elektronenmikroskop *nt* electron microscope
Elektronik <-, -en> [elɛk·'tro:·nɪk] *f kein pl* electronics + *sing vb*
elektronisch [elɛk·'tro:·nɪʃ] I. *adj* electronic II. *adv* electronically
Elektrorasierer *m* electric razor
Elektrotechnik [elɛk·tro·'tɛç·nɪk] *f* electrical engineering
Element <-[e]s, -e> [ele·'mɛnt] *nt* element
elend ['e:lɛnt] *adj* ❶ (*beklagenswert*) miserable ❷ (*krank*) wretched ❸ (*erbärmlich*) dreadful ❹ (*gemein*) miserable
Elend <-[e]s> ['e:lɛnt] *nt kein pl* misery
Elendsviertel *nt* slum
elf ['ɛlf] *adj* eleven; *s. a.* **acht**[1]
Elf <-, -en> ['ɛlf] *f* ❶ (*Zahl*) eleven ❷ FBALL team, eleven
Elfe <-, -n> ['ɛl·fə] *f* elf
Elfenbein ['ɛl·fn̩·bain] *nt* ivory
Elfenbeinküste *f* Ivory Coast
Elfmeter [ɛlf·'me:·tɐ] *m* penalty kick; **einen ~ schießen** to take a penalty kick
elfte(r, s) ['ɛlf·tə] *adj* ❶ (*Zahl*) eleventh; *s. a.* **achte(r, s)** 1 ❷ (*Datum*) eleventh, 11th; *s. a.* **achte(r, s)** 2
elitär [eli·'tɛːɐ̯] *adj* elitist
Elite <-, -n> [e'li:·tə] *f* elite
Elixier <-s, -e> [eli·'ksi:ɐ̯] *nt* elixir
Ellipse <-, -n> [ɛ'lɪp·sə] *f* MATH ellipse; LING ellipsis

E

El Salvador <-s> [ɛl zal·va·'do:ɐ̯] *nt* El Salvador; *s. a.* **Deutschland**

Elsass^RR, **Elsaß**^ALT <-> ['ɛl·zas] *nt* ■ **das** ~ Alsace

Elsässer(in) <-s, -> ['ɛlzɛ·sɐ] *m(f)* inhabitant of Alsace

elsässisch ['ɛl·zɛ·sɪʃ] *adj* ❶ GEOG Alsatian ❷ LING Alsatian

Elster <-, -n> ['ɛl·stɐ] *f* magpie

Eltern ['ɛl·tɐn] *pl* parents *pl*

E-Mail <-, -s> ['i:me:l] *f* e-mail

Emanzipation <-, -en> [eman·tsi·pa·'tsi̯o:n] *f* emancipation

emanzipieren* [eman·tsi·'pi:·rən] *vr* ■ **sich** *akk* ~ to emancipate oneself

Embargo <-s, -s> [ɛm·'bar·go] *nt* embargo

Embryo <-s, -s> ['ɛm·bryo] *m o* ÖSTERR *nt* embryo

Emigrant(in) <-en, -en> [emi·'grant] *m(f)* emigrant

emigrieren* [emi·'gri:·rən] *vi sein* to emigrate

Emission <-, -en> [emɪ·'si̯o:n] *f* emission

Emotion <-, -en> [emo·'tsi̯o:n] *f* emotion

emotional [emo·tsi̯o·'na:l] *adj* emotional

empfahl [ɛm·'pfa:l] *imp von* **empfehlen**

empfand [ɛm·'pfant] *imp von* **empfinden**

Empfang <-[e]s, Empfänge> [ɛm·'pfaŋ] *m* ❶ *kein pl* (*das Entgegennehmen*) receipt ❷ (*Begrüßung*) reception ❸ *kein pl* TV, RADIO reception ❹ (*Hotelrezeption*) reception [desk]

empfangen <empfing, empfangen> [ɛm·'pfaŋən] *vt* ❶ RADIO, TV to receive ❷ (*begrüßen*) ■ **jdn mit etw** *dat* ~ to receive sb with sth

Empfänger(in) <-s, -> [ɛm·'pfɛŋɐ] *m(f)* ❶ (*Adressat*) addressee ❷ FIN payee

Empfänger <-s, -> [ɛm·'pfɛŋɐ] *m* RADIO, TV receiver

empfänglich [ɛm·'pfɛŋ·lɪç] *adj* ■ **für etw** *akk* ~ **sein** ❶ (*zugänglich*) to be receptive to sth ❷ (*beeinflussbar, anfällig*) to be susceptible to sth

Empfängnis <-, -se> [ɛm·'pfɛŋ·nɪs] *f pl selten* conception

Empfängnisverhütung *f* contraception

Empfangsbestätigung *f* [confirmation of] receipt

Empfangsdame *f* receptionist

empfehlen <empfahl, empfohlen> [ɛm·'pfe:·lən] I. *vt* ■ **jdm etw** ~ to recommend sth [to sb] II. *vr impers* ■ **es empfiehlt sich, etw zu tun** it is advisable to do sth

empfehlenswert *adj* ❶ (*wert, empfohlen zu werden*) recommendable ❷ (*ratsam*) ■ **es ist ~, etw zu tun** it is advisable to do sth

Empfehlung <-, -en> *f* recommendation; **auf ~ von jdm** on the recommendation of sb; **mit den besten ~en** with best regards

empfinden <empfand, empfunden> [ɛm·'pfɪn·dn̩] *vt* to feel

empfindlich [ɛm·'pfɪnt·lɪç] I. *adj* sensitive (**gegen** +*akk* to); *Gesundheit* delicate; ~ **gegen Kälte** sensitive to cold II. *adv* **auf etw** *akk* ~ **reagieren** to be very sensitive to sth

empfindsam [ɛm·'pfɪnt·za:m] *adj, adj* sensitive; (*einfühlsam*) empathetic

empfing [ɛm·'pfɪŋ] *imp von* **empfangen**

empfunden [ɛm·'pfʊn·dn̩] *pp von* **empfinden**

empor|arbeiten *vr* ■ **sich** *akk* ~ to work one's way up

Empore <-, -n> [ɛm·'po:·rə] *f* gallery

empören* [ɛm·'pø:·rən] I. *vt* ■ **jdn** ~ to fill sb with indignation II. *vr* ■ **sich** *akk* ~ to be outraged

empörend *adj* outrageous

empört I. *adj* scandalized (**über** +*akk* by) II. *adv* indignantly

emsig ['ɛm·zɪç] I. *adj* busy II. *adv* industriously; **überall wird ~ gebaut** they are busy building everywhere

Ende <-s, -n> ['ɛn·də] *nt* ❶ (*Schluss*) end; ~ **August/des Monats/~ 2007**

the end of August/the month/2007; **~ 20 sein** to be in one's late 20s; **damit muss es jetzt ein ~ haben** this must stop now; **etw** *dat* **ein ~ machen** to put an end to sth; **das nimmt gar kein ~** there's no end to it; **am ~** (*fam*) finally; **etw zu ~ bringen** to complete sth; **zu ~ sein** to be finished ② FILM, LIT ending ③ (*räumliches Ende*) end ►WEN-DUNGEN: **~ gut, alles gut** (*prov*) all's well that ends well

Endeffekt [ˈɛntˌʔɛfɛkt] *m* **im ~ in the** end

enden [ˈɛnˌdn̩] *vi* ① *haben* to end ② *ha-ben* LING ■**auf etw** *akk* **~ to end with** sth ③ *sein* (*fam: irgendwo landen*) to end up

Endergebnis *nt* final result

endgültig I. *adj* final; *Antwort* definitive II. *adv* finally

Endhaltestelle *f* terminal stop

Endlager *nt* ÖKOL permanent disposal site

endlich [ˈɛntˌlɪç] I. *adv* ① (*nunmehr*) at last; **lass mich ~ in Ruhe!** just leave me alone already! ② (*schließlich*) final-ly; **na ~!** (*fam*) at last! II. *adj* ASTRON, MATH finite

endlos I. *adj* endless II. *adv* intermi-nably

Endspurt *m* final spurt

Endstation *f* terminus, end of the line, final stop

Endung <-, -en> *f* ending

Endverbraucher(in) *m(f)* end-user

Energie <-, -n> [enɛrˈgiː] *f* energy

Energiebedarf *m* energy requirement[s]

Energiegewinnung *f kein pl* energy generation

Energieverbrauch *m* energy consump-tion

Energieverschwendung *f kein pl* waste of energy

Energieversorgung *f* energy supply

energisch [eˈnɛrˌgɪʃ] I. *adj* ① (*Tatkraft ausdrückend*) energetic ② (*entschlos-sen*) firm II. *adv* vigorously

eng [ˈɛŋ] I. *adj* ① (*schmal*) narrow ② (*knapp sitzend*) tight ③ (*beengt*)

cramped ④ (*wenig Zwischenraum habend*) close together *pred* ⑤ (*intim*) close ⑥ (*eingeschränkt*) limited; **im ~eren Sinn** in the stricter sense II. *adv* ① (*knapp*) **ein ~ anliegendes Kleid** a close-fitting dress ② (*dicht*) densely; **~ nebeneinanderstehen** to stand close to each other ③ (*intim*) closely; **~ befreundet sein** to be close friends ④ (*akribisch*) **etw zu ~ sehen** to take too narrow a view of sth

Engagement <-s, -s> [ãgaˈʒaˈmãː] *nt* ① (*Eintreten*) commitment (**für** +*akk* to) ② THEAT engagement

engagieren* [ãgaˈʒiːˈrən] I. *vt* ■**jdn ~** to engage sb II. *vr* ■**sich** *akk* [**für jdn/ etw**] **~** to be committed [to sb/sth]

engagiert [ãgaˈʒiːˈət] *adj* **politisch/ sozial ~** politically/socially committed

Enge <-, -n> [ˈɛŋə] *f* ① (*schmale Beschaffenheit*) narrowness ② *kein pl* (*Beschränktheit*) confinement

Engel <-s, -> [ˈɛŋl] *m* angel

England <-s, -> [ˈɛŋˌlant] *nt* ① (*Teil Großbritanniens*) England ② (*falsch für Großbritannien*) Great Britain; *s. a.* **Deutschland**

Engländer(in) <-s, -> [ˈɛŋˌlɛnˌde] *m(f)* Englishman *masc*, Englishwoman *fem*; ■**die ~** the English

englisch [ˈɛŋˌlɪʃ] *adj* English; *s. a.* **deutsch**

Englisch [ˈɛŋˌlɪʃ] *nt dekl wie adj* English; *s. a.* **Deutsch**

Engpass[RR] *m* ① GEOG [narrow] pass ② (*Fahrbahnverengung*) bottleneck ③ (*Verknappung*) bottleneck

engstirnig [ˈɛŋˌʃtɪrˌnɪç] *adj* nar-row-minded

Enkel(in) <-s, -> [ˈɛŋˌkl] *m(f)* grand-child

enorm [eˈnɔrm] I. *adj* enormous; *Summe* vast II. *adv* (*fam*) tremendous-ly; **~ viel/viele** an enormous amount/ number

Ensemble <-s, -s> [ãˈsãːˌbl] *nt* ensem-ble

ent|behren* [ɛntˈbeːˌrən] *vt* ■**jdn/**

E

etw ~ können to be able to do without sb/sth

Entbindung f delivery

entblößen* [ɛntˈbløː·sn̩] vt ■**sich** akk ~ to take one's clothes off

entdecken* vt ① (zum ersten Mal finden) to discover ② (ausfindig machen) to find; Fehler to spot

Entdecker(in) <-s, -> [ɛntˈdɛ·kɐ] m(f) discoverer

Entdeckung f discovery

Entdeckungsreise f voyage of discovery

Ente <-, -n> [ˈɛn·tə] f ① ORN duck ② (fam: Zeitungsente) canard ▶WENDUNGEN: **lahme ~** (fam) slowpoke

enteignen* vt ■**jdn** ~ to dispossess sb

enterben* vt ■**jdn** ~ to disinherit sb

entfachen* [ɛntˈfa·χn̩] vt ① Feuer to kindle; Brand to start ② (entfesseln) to provoke; Leidenschaft to arouse

entfalten* I. vt Fähigkeiten, Kräfte to develop II. vr ① (sich öffnen) ■**sich** akk [zu etw dat] ~ Blüte, Fallschirm to open [into sth] ② (sich voll entwickeln) ■**sich** akk ~ to fully develop

Entfaltung <-, -en> f (Entwicklung) development

entfernen* [ɛntˈfɛr·nən] I. vt ① (beseitigen) to remove (aus/von +dat from) ② MED **jdm den Blinddarm** ~ to take out sep sb's appendix ③ (weit abbringen) ■**jdn von etw** dat ~ to take sb away from sth II. vr ① (weggehen) ■**sich** akk ~ to go away (von/aus +dat from); **sich** akk **vom Weg** ~ to go off the path ② (nicht bei etwas bleiben) ■**sich** akk **von etw** dat ~ to depart from sth

entfernt I. adj ① Verwandte distant ② (gering) Ähnlichkeit slight; Ahnung vague ③ (weit weg) remote ④ **weit davon ~ sein, etw zu tun** to not have the slightest intention of doing sth II. adv vaguely

Entfernung <-, -en> f ① (Distanz) distance ② ADMIN (Ausschluss) removal

entfremden* [ɛntˈfrɛm·dn̩] I. vt to estrange; **etw seinem Zweck** ~ to use

sth for a different purpose; (falscher Zweck) to use sth for the wrong purpose II. vr ■**sich** akk **jdm** ~ to become estranged from sb

entführen* vt Person to abduct; Fahrzeug, Flugzeug to hijack

Entführer(in) m(f) kidnapper; eines Fahrzeugs/Flugzeugs hijacker

Entführung f kidnapping; eines Fahrzeugs/Flugzeugs hijacking

entgegen [ɛntˈgeː·gn̩] I. adv toward II. präp against

entgegengehen vi irreg sein ■**jdm** ~ to go to meet sb

entgegengesetzt [ɛntˈgeː·gn̩·gə·zɛtst] I. adj ① (gegenüberliegend) opposite ② (einander widersprechend) opposing; Auffassungen conflicting II. adv ~ **denken/handeln** to think/do the exact opposite

entgegenhalten vt irreg ① **jdm die Hand** ~ to hold out one's hand to sb ② (fig: gegenüberstellen) ■~, **dass** .... to counter that ...

entgegenkommen [ɛntˈgeː·gn̩·kɔ·mən] vi irreg sein ① (in jds Richtung kommen) ■**jdm** ~ to come [over] to meet sb ② (Zugeständnisse machen) **jdm/etw** ~ to accommodate sb/sth ③ (entsprechen) **jds Plänen** ~ to fit in sb's plans

Entgegenkommen <-s, -> [ɛntˈgeː·gn̩·kɔ·mən] nt kein pl cooperation

entgegenkommend adj obliging

entgegentreten vi irreg sein ① (in den Weg treten) ■**jdm** ~ to walk up to sb ② (sich zur Wehr setzen) ■**etw** dat ~ to counter sth

entgegnen* [ɛntˈgeːg·nən] vt to reply

entgehen* vi irreg sein ① (entkommen) ■**jdm/etw** ~ to escape sb/sth ② (nicht bemerkt werden) ■**etw entgeht jdm** sth escapes sb['s notice] ③ (versäumen) ■**sich** dat **etw** ~ **lassen** to miss sth

Entgelt <-[e]s, -e> [ɛntˈgɛlt] nt ① (Bezahlung) payment; (Entschädigung) compensation ② (Gebühr) **gegen ~** for a fee

entgleisen* [ɛnt·ˈɡlaɪzn̩] *vi sein* ❶ *Zug* to derail ❷ *(fig: ausfallend werden)* to make a gaffe

entgleiten* *vi irreg sein* ❶ *(aus den Händen)* ■ etw entgleitet jdm sb loses his/her grip on sth ❷ *(verloren gehen)* ■ jdm ~ to slip away from sb

enthalten* *irreg* **I.** *vt* ❶ *(in sich haben)* to contain ❷ *(einschließen)* Frühstück im Preis ~ breakfast included **II.** *vr* ■ sich *akk* ~ POL to abstain

enthaltsam [ɛnt·ˈhalt·za:m] *adj* abstinent

entheben* *vt irreg (geh)* jdn eines Amtes ~ to relieve sb of a position

Enthüllung <-, -en> *f* ❶ *(Aufdeckung)* disclosure; *von Lüge, Skandal* exposure ❷ *(das Enthüllen) von Denkmal, Gesicht* unveiling

enthusiastisch *adj* enthusiastic

entkoffeiniert [ɛnt·kɔ·fei·ˈni:ɐ̯t] *adj* decaffeinated

entkommen* *vi irreg sein* to escape

Entkommen <-s> *nt kein pl* escape

entkräften* [ɛnt·ˈkrɛf·tn̩] *vt* ❶ *(kraftlos machen)* ■ jdn ~ *(durch Anstrengung)* to weaken sb; *(durch Krankheit)* to debilitate sb *form* ❷ *(widerlegen)* ■ etw ~ to refute sth

entladen* *irreg* **I.** *vt* ❶ *Ladung* to unload ❷ ELEK to drain **II.** *vr* ■ sich *akk* ~ ❶ *(zum Ausbruch kommen)* Gewitter, Sturm to break ❷ ELEK *Akku, Batterie* to run down ❸ *(fig: plötzlich ausbrechen)* Begeisterung, Zorn etc. to be vented

entlang [ɛnt·ˈlaŋ] **I.** *präp (längs)* along; den Fluss ~ along the river **II.** *adv* ■ an etw *dat* ~ along sth

entlarven* [ɛnt·ˈlar·fn̩] *vt* Dieb, Spion to expose

entlassen* *vt irreg* ❶ *(kündigen)* ■ jdn ~ to dismiss sb ❷ MED, MIL to discharge sb ❸ *(entbinden)* ■ jdn aus etw *dat* ~ to release sb from sth

entlasten* *vt* ❶ JUR ■ jdn [von etw *dat*] ~ to clear sb [of sth] ❷ *(von Belastung befreien)* ■ jdn ~ to relieve sb

Entlastung <-, -en> *f* ❶ JUR exoneration ❷ *(das Entlasten)* relief

entlaufen*¹ *vi irreg sein* to run away

entlaufen² *adj (entflohen)* escaped; *(weggelaufen)* on the run *pred*

entledigen* [ɛnt·ˈle:·dɪ·ɡn̩] *vr* ■ sich *akk* einer S. *gen* ~ ❶ *(ablegen)* to put down *sep* sth; *Kleidungsstück* to remove sth ❷ *(loswerden)* to get rid of sth

entlegen [ɛnt·ˈle:·ɡn̩] *adj* remote

entmachten* [ɛnt·ˈmax·tn̩] *vt* to disempower

entmutigen* [ɛnt·ˈmu:·tɪ·ɡn̩] *vt* to discourage

entnehmen* *vt irreg* ❶ *(herausnehmen)* ■ [etw *dat*] etw ~ to take sth [from sth] ❷ MED ■ jdm etw ~ to take sth from sb ❸ *(fig: aus etwas schließen)* ■ aus etw ~, dass ... to gather from sth that ...

entpuppen* [ɛnt·ˈpʊ·pn̩] *vr (fig: sich enthüllen)* ■ sich *akk* [als ...] ~ to turn out to be ...

entreißen* *vt irreg* ❶ *(wegreißen)* ■ jdm etw ~ to snatch sth [away] from sb ❷ *(retten)* ■ jdn etw *dat* ~ to rescue sb from sth

entrümpeln* *vt* to clear out *sep*

entrüsten* **I.** *vt (empören)* ■ jdn ~ to make sb indignant; *(stärker)* to outrage sb **II.** *vr (sich empören)* ■ sich *akk* über jdn/etw ~ to be indignant about sb/sth; *(stärker)* to be outraged by sb/sth

entrüstet **I.** *adj* indignant *(über +akk* about/at) **II.** *adv* indignantly

Entschädigung *f* compensation

entschärfen* *vt (a. fig)* to defuse

entscheiden* *irreg* **I.** *vt* to decide; *(gerichtlich)* to rule **II.** *vi* to decide *(über +akk* on); ■ für/gegen jdn/etw ~ to decide in favor/against sb/sth; *(gerichtlich)* to rule in favor/against sb/sth **III.** *vr* ■ sich *akk* [dazu] ~, etw zu tun to decide [to do sth]

entscheidend [ɛnt·ˈʃai·dn̩t] *adj* decisive; ■ für jdn/etw ~ sein to be crucial for sb/sth

Entscheidung *f* ❶ *(Beschluss)* decision; eine ~ treffen to make a decision ❷ JUR ruling

entschieden [ɛntˈʃiːdn̩] I. *pp von* **entscheiden** II. *adj* ❶ (*entschlossen*) resolute ❷ (*eindeutig*) definite III. *adv* ❶ (*entschlossen*) **etw ~ ablehnen** to categorically reject sth ❷ (*eindeutig*) **diesmal bist du ~ zu weit gegangen** this time you've definitely gone too far

entschließen* *vr irreg* ■ **sich** *akk* [**zu etw** *dat*] ~ to decide [on sth]

entschlossen [ɛntˈʃlɔsn̩] I. *pp von* **entschließen** II. *adj* determined III. *adv* resolutely

Entschluss^RR, **Entschluß**^ALT <-schlusses, -schlüsse> [ɛntˈʃlʊs] *m* decision

entschuldbar [ɛntˈʃʊltˌbaːɐ̯] *adj* excusable

entschuldigen* [ɛntˈʃʊlˌdɪˌɡn̩] I. *vi* (*als Höflichkeitsformel*) ~ **Sie** excuse me II. *vr* ■ **sich** *akk* ~ ❶ (*um Verzeihung bitten*) to apologize ❷ (*eine Abwesenheit begründen*) to ask to be excused III. *vt* ❶ (*als verzeihlich begründen*) ■ **etw mit etw** *dat* ~ to use sth as an excuse for sth ❷ (*eine Abwesenheit begründen*) ■ **jdn bei jdm** ~ to ask sb to excuse sb ❸ (*als verständlich erscheinen lassen*) ■ **etw** ~ to excuse sth

Entschuldigung <-, -en> *f* ❶ (*Bitte um Verzeihung*) apology ❷ (*Begründung, Rechtfertigung*) **als ~ für etw** *akk* as an excuse for sth ❸ (*als Höflichkeitsformel*) ~! sorry! ❹ SCH note

entsetzen* I. *vt* (*in Grauen versetzen*) ■ **jdn** ~ to horrify sb II. *vr* (*die Fassung verlieren*) ■ **sich** *akk* ~ to be horrified (**über** +*akk* at/about)

Entsetzen <-s> *nt kein pl* horror; **mit** ~ horrified; **voller** ~ filled with horror

entsetzlich [ɛntˈzɛtsˌlɪç] I. *adj* ❶ (*schrecklich*) horrible ❷ (*fam: sehr stark*) terrible II. *adv* terribly

entsetzt I. *adj* horrified II. *adv* (*großes Entsetzen zeigend*) **sie schrie ~ auf** she let out a horrified scream

entspannen* I. *vr* ■ **sich** *akk* ~ to relax; (*pol a.*) to ease II. *vt* ❶ (*lockern*) ■ **etw** ~ to relax sth ❷ ÖKON, POL **die Situation** ~ to ease the situation

Entspannung *f* ❶ (*innerliche Ruhe*) relaxation ❷ POL easing of tension

entsprechen* *vi irreg* ■ **etw** *dat* ~ ❶ (*übereinstimmen mit*) to correspond to sth ❷ (*genügen*) **den Anforderungen** ~ to fulfill the requirements

entsprechend [ɛntˈʃprɛˌçnt] I. *adj* (*angemessen*) appropriate II. *präp* in accordance with

entstehen* *vi irreg sein* ■ [**aus etw** *dat*/**durch etw** *akk*] ~ ❶ (*zu existieren beginnen*) to come into being [from sth] ❷ (*verursacht werden*) to arise [from sth] ❸ CHEM (*sich bilden*) to be produced [from/through sth]

Entstehung <-, -en> *f* creation; **des Lebens** origin; **eines Gebäudes** construction

entstellen* *vt* ❶ (*verunstalten*) to disfigure; **jds Gesicht** ~ to disfigure sb's face; **der Schmerz entstellte ihre Züge** her features were contorted with pain ❷ (*verzerren*) **etw entstellt wiedergeben** to distort sth

enttäuschen* I. *vt* ❶ (*Erwartungen nicht erfüllen*) ■ **jdn** ~ to disappoint sb ❷ (*nicht entsprechen*) **jds Hoffnungen** ~ to dash sb's hopes II. *vi* (*enttäuschend sein*) to be disappointing

enttäuscht I. *adj* disappointed (**über** +*akk* about, **von** +*dat* by) II. *adv* disappointedly

Enttäuschung *f* disappointment

Entwarnung *f* all clear

entwässern* *vt* ❶ AGR, BAU to drain ❷ MED to dehydrate

entweder [ɛntˈveːˌdɐ] *konj* ~ ... **oder** ... either...or

entwerfen* *vt irreg* ❶ (*designen*) to design ❷ (*im Entwurf erstellen*) to draft

entwickeln* I. *vt* to develop II. *vr* ■ **sich** *akk* [**zu etw** *dat*] ~ to develop [into sth]; **na, wie entwickelt sich euer Projekt?** well, how is your project coming along?

Entwicklung <-, -en> *f* ❶ (*das Entwickeln, Foto*) development ❷ (*das*

Vorankommen) progression ❸ ÖKON, POL trend

Entwicklungshelfer(in) *m(f)* development aid worker

Entwicklungshilfe *f* development aid

Entwicklungsland *nt* developing country

Entwurf *m* ❶ (*Skizze*) sketch ❷ (*Design*) design ❸ (*Konzept*) draft

ent|ziehen* *irreg* I. *vt* ▪jdm etw ~ to withdraw sth from sb II. *vr* ▪ **sich** *akk* **jdm/etw** ~ to evade sth ❷ ▪ **sich** *akk* **etw** *dat* ~: **das entzieht sich meiner Kenntnis** that's beyond my knowledge

Entziehungskur *f* treatment for an addiction

ent|ziffern* [ɛnt-ˈtsɪ-fən] *vt* to decipher

ent|zücken* *vt* ▪jdn ~ to delight sb

Entzücken <-s> *nt kein pl* delight; [**über etw** *akk*] **in** ~ **geraten** to be ecstatic [about sth]

entzückend [ɛnt-ˈtsʏ-kn̩t] *adj* delightful

Entzug <-[e]s> *m kein pl* ❶ ADMIN revocation ❷ MED withdrawal; **auf** ~ **sein** (*sl*) to go [through] cold turkey *sl*

Entzugserscheinungen *pl* withdrawal symptoms

ent|zünden* *vr* ▪ **sich** *akk* ~ ❶ MED to become infected ❷ (*in Brand geraten*) to catch fire

entzündet *adj* MED infected

Entzündung *f* MED *eines Gelenks* inflammation

entzwei [ɛnt-ˈtsvai] *adj pred* in two [pieces]; (*zersprungen*) broken

entzwei|gehen *vi irreg sein* to break [in two]

Enzian <-s, -e> [ˈɛn-tsi̯ -aːn] *m* ❶ BOT gentian ❷ (*Schnaps*) spirit distilled from the roots of gentian

Enzyklopädie <-, -n> [ɛn-tsy-klo-pɛ-ˈdiː] *f* encyclopedia

Enzym <-s, -e> [ɛn-ˈtsyːm] *nt* enzyme

Epidemie <-, -n> [epi-de-ˈmiː] *f* epidemic

Epilepsie <-, -n> [epi-lɛ-ˈpsiː] *f* epilepsy

Epileptiker(in) <-s, -> [epiˈlɛp-ti-kɐ] *m(f)* epileptic

Epoche <-, -n> [eˈpɔ-xə] *f* epoch

Epos <-, Epen> [ˈeːpɔs] *nt* epic

er <*gen* seiner, *dat* ihm, *akk* ihn> [ˈeːɐ̯] *pron pers* he; **sie ist ein Jahr jünger als** ~ she is a year younger than him

Erachten <-s> [ɛɐ̯-ˈʔax-tn̩] *nt kein pl* **meines** ~ **s** in my opinion

Erbanlagen *pl* hereditary factors

er|barmen* [ɛɐ̯-ˈbar-mən] *vr* ▪ **sich** *akk* **jds/einer S.** ~ to take pity on sb/sth

Erbarmen <-s> [ɛɐ̯-ˈbar-mən] *nt kein pl* pity; ▪~ **mit jdm** [**haben**] [to have] pity for sb; **ohne** ~ merciless[ly]

erbärmlich [ɛɐ̯-ˈbɛrm-lɪç] I. *adj* (*pej*) ❶ (*fam: gemein*) miserable ❷ (*jämmerlich*) *Aussehen*, *Zustand* wretched II. *adv* (*pej*) ❶ (*gemein*) **sich** *akk* ~ **verhalten** to behave abominably ❷ (*fam: furchtbar*) ~ **kalt** terribly cold

erbarmungslos [ɛɐ̯-ˈbar-mʊŋs-loːs] *adj* merciless

er|bauen* I. *vt* ❶ (*errichten*) to build ❷ (*fam: begeistert sein*) ▪ **von etw** *dat* **erbaut sein** to be enthusiastic [about sth] II. *vr* (*sich innerlich erfreuen*) ▪ **sich** *akk* **an etw** *dat* ~ to be uplifted by sth

Erbauer(in) <-s, -> *m(f)* architect

Erbe <-s> [ˈɛr-bə] *nt kein pl* ❶ (*Erbschaft*) inheritance ❷ (*fig: Hinterlassenschaft*) legacy

Erbe, Erbin <-n, -n> [ˈɛr-bə] *m, f* heir *masc*, heiress *fem*

erben [ˈɛr-bn̩] I. *vt* to inherit II. *vi* (*Erbe sein*) to receive an inheritance

er|beuten* [ɛɐ̯-ˈbɔy-tn̩] *vt Diebesgut* to carry off *sep*; *Kriegsbeute* to capture

Erbfaktor *m* hereditary factor

Erbfolge *f* [line of] succession

Erbgut *nt kein pl* genetic makeup

Erbin <-, -nen> [ˈɛr-bɪn] *f fem form von* **Erbe** heiress

erbittert *adj* bitter

Erbkrankheit *f* hereditary disease

er|blassen* [ɛɐ̯-ˈbla-sn̩] *vi sein* to turn pale (**vor** +*dat* with)

erblich [ˈɛrp-lɪç] I. *adj* hereditary II. *adv* by inheritance

er|blinden* [ɛɐ̯-ˈblɪn-dn̩] *vi sein*

❸ E

■ **[durch etw** *akk*] ~ to go blind [as a result of sth]

er|brechen* *irreg* I. *vt Mageninhalt, Essen* to bring up *sep* II. *vr* ■ **sich** *akk* ~ to throw up *fam*

er|bringen* *vt irreg* ❶ FIN *Erlös* to raise ❷ JUR **den Beweis** ~ to produce evidence

Erbschaft <-, -en> ['ɛrp·ʃaft] *f* inheritance

Erbse <-, -n> ['ɛrp·sə] *f* pea

Erdachse ['eːɐ̯d·aksə] *f* earth's axis

Erdanziehung *f kein pl* earth's gravitational pull

Erdapfel *m* SÜDD, ÖSTERR (*Kartoffel*) potato

Erdatmosphäre *f* Earth's atmosphere

Erdbeben *nt* earthquake

Erdbeere ['eːɐ̯t·beː·rə] *f* strawberry

Erdboden *m* ground

Erde <-, -n> ['eːɐ̯·də] *f* ❶ *kein pl* (*Welt*) earth; **auf der ganzen** ~ in the whole world ❷ (*Erdreich*) earth ❸ (*Boden*) ground; **zu ebener** ~ at street level

erdenklich *adj attr* conceivable

Erdgas *nt* natural gas

ErdgeschossRR *nt* first floor

Erdkugel *f* globe

Erdkunde *f* geography

ErdnussRR *f* peanut

Erdoberfläche *f* Earth's surface

Erdöl *nt* oil

er|dreisten* [ɛg·'drai·stn̩] *vr* ■ **sich** *akk* ~ to take liberties; ■ **sich** *akk* ~, **etw zu tun** to have the audacity to do sth

er|drosseln* *vt* to strangle

er|drücken* *vt* ❶ (*Eigenständigkeit nehmen*) ■ **jdn** [**mit etw** *dat*] ~ to stifle sb [with sth] ❷ (*sehr stark belasten*) ■ **jdn** ~ to overwhelm sb

Erdrutsch *m* (*a. fig*) landslide

Erdstoß *m* seismic shock

Erdteil *m* continent

er|dulden* *vt Kränkungen, Leid* to endure

Erdumdrehung *f* Earth's rotation

Erdumlaufbahn *f* [Earth] orbit

er|eifern* *vr* ■ **sich** *akk* [**über etw** *akk*] ~ to get worked up [about sth]

er|eignen* [ɛg·'?aig·nən] *vr* ■ **sich** *akk* ~ to occur

Ereignis <-ses, -se> [ɛg·'?aig·nɪs] *nt* event

ereignisreich *adj* eventful

er|fahren¹ [ɛg·'faː·rən] *irreg* I. *vt* ❶ (*zu hören bekommen*) to hear ❷ (*erleben*) to experience II. *vi* (*Kenntnis erhalten*) ■ **von etw** *dat*/**über etw** *akk* ~ to learn of sth

erfahren² [ɛg·'faː·rən] *adj* (*versiert*) experienced

Erfahrung <-, -en> *f* ❶ (*prägendes Erlebnis*) experience; **nach meiner** ~ in my experience ❷ *kein pl* (*Übung*) experience; **jahrelange** ~ years of experience ❸ (*Kenntnis*) **etw in** ~ **bringen** to find out *sep* sth

erfahrungsgemäß *adv* in sb's experience; ~ **ist** ... experience shows ...

er|fassen* *vt* ❶ (*mitreißen*) *Auto, Strömung* to catch ❷ (*befallen*) *jdn* ~ *Furcht, Traurigkeit* to seize sb ❸ (*begreifen*) to understand ❹ ADMIN (*registrieren*) to record ❺ (*eingeben*) *Daten, Text* to enter

er|finden* [ɛg·'fɪn·dn̩] *vt irreg* to invent

Erfinder(in) [ɛg·'fɪn·dɐ] *m(f)* inventor

erfinderisch [ɛg·'fɪn·də·rɪʃ] *adj* inventive

Erfindung <-, -en> *f* invention

Erfolg <-[e]s, -e> [ɛg·'fɔlk] *m* success; ~ **versprechend** promising; **viel** ~! good luck!; **mit dem** ~, **dass** ... with the result that ...

er|folgen* *vi sein* to occur

erfolglos [ɛg·'fɔlk·loːs] *adj* ❶ (*ohne Erfolg*) unsuccessful ❷ (*vergeblich*) futile

erfolgreich *adj* successful

Erfolgsdruck *m kein pl* performance pressure

Erfolgserlebnis *nt* sense of achievement

erforderlich [ɛg·'fɔr·də·lɪç] *adj* necessary

er|fordern* *vt* to require

er|forschen* vt ❶ (*durchstreifen und erkunden*) to explore ❷ (*prüfen*) to investigate; *Gewissen* to examine

er|freuen* I. vt to please II. vr ❶ (*Freude haben*) ■ **sich** akk **an etw** dat ~ to take pleasure in sth ❷ (*genießen*) ■ **sich** akk **einer S.** gen ~ to enjoy sth

erfreulich [ɛɐ̯ˈfrɔy·lɪç] I. adj *Anblick* pleasant; *Nachricht* welcome II. adv happily

erfreulicherweise adv happily

er|frieren* vi irreg sein ❶ (*durch Frost eingehen*) to be killed by frost ❷ *Gliedmaßen* to get frostbitten ❸ (*an Kälte sterben*) to freeze to death

er|frischen* [ɛɐ̯ˈfrɪ·ʃən] I. vt ■ **jdn** ~ to refresh sb II. vi to be refreshing III. vr ■ **sich** akk ~ to refresh oneself

erfrischend adj refreshing

Erfrischung <-, -en> f refreshment

Erfrischungsgetränk nt refreshment

er|füllen* I. vt ❶ *Pflicht, Versprechen, Wunsch* to fulfill ❷ (*durchdringen*) to fill; **von Angst/Ekel erfüllt sein** to be filled with fear/disgust II. vr (*sich bewahrheiten*) ■ **sich** akk ~ to come true

er|gänzen* [ɛɐ̯ˈgɛn·tsn̩] vt ❶ (*auffüllen*) *Vorräte* to replenish ❷ (*erweitern*) *Sammlung* to complete ❸ **sie** ~ **sich** they complement each other

Ergänzung <-, -en> f ❶ (*das Auffüllen*) *von Vorräten* replenishment ❷ (*Erweiterung*) *einer Sammlung* completion; **zur** ~ **einer S.** gen for the completion of sth ❸ (*Zusatz*) addition

er|gattern* [ɛɐ̯ˈga·tən] vt (*fam*) to get [a] hold of

er|geben*[1] irreg I. vt ❶ MATH ■ **etw** ~ to amount to sth ❷ (*als Resultat haben*) ■ ~, **dass ...** to reveal that ... II. vr ❶ (*kapitulieren*) ■ **sich** akk [jdm] ~ to surrender [to sb] ❷ (*sich fügen*) **sich** akk **in sein Schicksal** ~ to resign oneself to one's fate ❸ (*sich hingeben*) **sich** akk **dem Glücksspiel** ~ to take to gambling ❹ (*daraus folgen*) ■ **sich** akk **aus etw** dat ~ to result from sth

er|geben[2] adj ❶ (*demütig*) humble ❷ (*treu*) devoted

Ergebnis <-ses, -se> [ɛɐ̯ˈgeːp·nɪs] nt result; SPORT score

ergebnislos adj without result

er|gehen* irreg I. vi sein ❶ JUR *Beschluss, Urteil* to be enacted ❷ (*geduldig hinnehmen*) **etw über sich** akk ~ **lassen** to endure sth II. vi impers sein (*widerfahren*) **und wie ist es dir im Urlaub so ergangen?** how did you fare on your holidays?; **es ergeht jdm schlecht** it's not going well for sb

ergiebig [ɛɐ̯ˈgiː·bɪç] adj ❶ (*sparsam im Verbrauch*) economical ❷ (*nützlich*) productive

er|greifen* vt irreg ❶ (*fassen*) to seize ❷ *Maßnahmen* to take ❸ JUR *Täter* to apprehend ❹ (*gefühlsmäßig bewegen*) ■ **jdn** ~ to seize sb; (*Angst*) to grip sb

ergreifend adj moving

ergriffen [ɛɐ̯ˈgrɪ·fn̩] adj moved

Erhalt <-[e]s> m kein pl ❶ (*das Bekommen*) receipt; **den** ~ **einer S.** gen **bestätigen** to confirm receipt of sth ❷ (*das Aufrechterhalten*) maintenance

er|halten* irreg I. vt ❶ (*bekommen*) to receive; *Befehl* to be given; **einen Eindruck** [von jdm/etw] ~ to get an impression [of sb/sth] ❷ (*bewahren*) to maintain ❸ BAU to preserve II. vr ❶ (*sich halten*) **sich** akk **gesund** ~ to keep [oneself] healthy ❷ (*bewahrt bleiben*) ■ **sich** akk ~ to remain preserved

erhältlich [ɛɐ̯ˈhɛlt·lɪç] adj obtainable

er|härten* I. vt ■ **etw** ~ *Vermutung, Verdacht* to support sth II. vr ■ **sich** akk ~ to be reinforced

er|heben* irreg I. vt ❶ (*hochheben*) to raise ❷ ADMIN, POL *Gebühr, Steuern* to levy ❸ *Daten, Informationen* to gather ❹ (*zum Ausdruck bringen*) *Protest* to voice; *Einspruch* to raise II. vr ■ **sich** akk ~ ❶ (*aufstehen*) to stand up (**von** + dat from) ❷ (*sich auflehnen*) to revolt ❸ (*aufragen*) to rise up (**über** + dat above) ❹ (*entstehen, aufkommen*) to start; *Wind* to pick up; *Sturm* to blow up

erheblich [ɛɐ̯ˈheːp·lɪç] I. adj ❶ (*be-*

E

trächtlich) considerable; *Nachteil, Vorteil a.* great; *Störung, Verspätung a.* major; *Verletzung* serious ②(*relevant*) relevant II. *adv* considerably

er|**heitern*** [ɛɐ̯ˈhai̯tɐn] *vt* to amuse

er|**hellen*** [ɛɐ̯ˈhɛlən] I. *vt* ①(*hell machen*) to light up *sep* ②(*klären*) to throw light on II. *vr* ■**sich** *akk* ~ to clear

er|**hitzen*** [ɛɐ̯ˈhɪtsn̩] I. *vt* to heat II. *vr* (*sich erregen*) ■**sich** *akk* ~ to get excited (**an** +*dat* about)

er|**hoffen*** *vt* ■[**sich** *dat*] **etw** ~ to hope for sth

er|**höhen*** [ɛɐ̯ˈhøː·ən] I. *vt* ①(*anheben*) *Löhne, Preise* to raise (**um** +*akk* by) ②(*verstärken*) *Produktion* to increase (**auf** +*akk* to, **um** +*akk* by) II. *vr* ■**sich** *akk* ~ to increase (**auf** +*akk* to, **um** +*akk* by)

er|**holen*** *vr* ■**sich** *akk* ~ ①(*von einer Krankheit*) to recover (**von** +*dat* from) ②(*von der Arbeit*) to take a break (**von** +*dat* from) ③BÖRSE to rally

er**holsam** [ɛɐ̯ˈhoːl·zaːm] *adj* relaxing

Er**holung** <-> *f kein pl* relaxation

er|**innern*** [ɛɐ̯ˈʔɪn·ɐn] I. *vt* ■**jdn an jdn/etw~** to remind sb of sb/sth; ■**jdn daran ~, etw zu tun** to remind sb to do sth II. *vr* (*sich entsinnen*) ■**sich** *akk* **an jdn/etw ~** to remember sb/sth III. *vi* ①(*in Erinnerung bringen*) ■**an jdn/etw ~** to be reminiscent of sb/sth *form* ②(*ins Gedächtnis rufen*) ■**daran ~, dass ...** to point out that ...

Er**innerung** <-, -en> *f* memory (**an** +*akk* of)

er|**kälten*** [ɛɐ̯ˈkɛl·tn̩] *vr* ■**sich** *akk* ~ to catch a cold

Er**kältung** <-, -en> *f* cold; **eine ~ bekommen** to catch a cold

er|**kämpfen*** *vt* ■**etw** ~ to fight to get sth

er**kennbar** *adj* ①(*auf Foto*) recognizable ②■**an etw** *dat* ~ **sein, dass ...** to be perceptible from sth that ...

er|**kennen*** *irreg* I. *vt* ①(*identifizieren*) to recognize (**an** +*dat* by) ②(*einsehen*)

einen Irrtum ~ to realize one's mistake II. *vi* ■~**, dass ...** to realize that ...

er**kenntlich** [ɛɐ̯ˈkɛnt·lɪç] *adj* grateful; **sich** *akk* ~ **zeigen** to show one's appreciation

Er**kenntnis** <-, -se> [ɛɐ̯ˈkɛnt·nɪs] *f* (*Einsicht*) insight; **zu der ~ kommen, dass ...** to realize that ...

Erker <-s, -> [ˈɛr·kɐ] *m* oriel

er|**klären*** I. *vt* ①(*erläutern*) ■**jdm etw ~** to explain sth [to sb]; **wie ~ Sie sich, dass ...** how do you explain that ... ②(*bekannt geben*) to announce ③(*offiziell bezeichnen*) ■**jdn für etw ~** *akk* to pronounce sb sth II. *vr* **sich** *akk* **bereit ~, etwas zu tun** to volunteer to do sth

er**klärt** *adj attr* declared

Er**klärung** *f* ①(*Erläuterung*) explanation ②(*Mitteilung*) statement

Er**krankung** <-, -en> *f* illness

er|**kunden*** [ɛɐ̯ˈkʊn·dn̩] *vt* ①(*auskundschaften*) to scout out *sep* ②(*in Erfahrung bringen*) to discover

er|**kundigen*** [ɛɐ̯ˈkʊn·dɪ·ɡn̩] *vr* ■**sich** *akk* [**nach jdm/etw**] ~ to ask [about sb/sth]

er|**langen*** [ɛɐ̯ˈlaŋən] *vt* to obtain

er|**lassen*** *vt irreg* ①JUR (*verfügen*) to issue ②(*von etw befreien*) ■**jdm etw ~** to remit sb's sth

er|**lauben*** [ɛɐ̯ˈlau̯·bn̩] I. *vt* ①(*gestatten*) ■**jdm etw ~** to allow sb to do sth ②(*zulassen*) **ich komme, soweit es meine Zeit erlaubt** if time permits, I'll come ▸WENDUNGEN: ~ **Sie mal!** what do you think you're doing? II. *vr* ①(*sich gönnen*) ■**sich** *dat* **etw ~** to allow oneself sth ②(*sich herausnehmen*) ■**sich** *dat* ~**, etw zu tun** to take the liberty of doing sth

Er**laubnis** <-, *selten* -se> *f* permission; (*schriftlich*) permit

er|**läutern*** *vt* ■[**jdm**] **etw** ~ to explain sth [to sb]

Er**läuterung** <-, -en> *f* explanation

Erle <-, -n> [ˈɛr·lə] *f* alder

er|**leben*** *vt* ①(*im Leben mitmachen*) ■**etw** ~ to live to see sth ②(*erfah-*

ren) to experience ③ (*durchmachen*) ■ etw ~ to go through sth ④ (*mit ansehen*) ■ es ~, dass/wie ... to see that/how ...; **so wütend habe ich ihn noch nie erlebt** I've never seen him so furious

Erlebnis <-ses, -se> [ɛɐˈleːpnɪs] *nt* experience

er|ledigen* [ɛɐˈleːdɪɡn̩] I. *vt* ① (*ausführen*) ■ etw ~ to take care of sth ② (*fam: erschöpfen*) ■ jdn ~ to wear out *sep* sb ③ (*sl: umbringen*) ■ jdn ~ to bump off *sep* sb II. *vr* ■ etw erledigt sich [von selbst] sth sorts itself out [on its own]

er|legen* *vt* ① (*töten*) ■ ein Tier ~ to shoot an animal ② ÖSTERR (*bezahlen*) to pay

er|leichtern* [ɛɐˈlaiçtɐn] *vt* ① (*einfacher machen*) ■ etw ~ to make sth easier ② (*innerlich beruhigen*) ■ jdn ~ to be a relief to sb ③ (*fam: beklauen*) ■ jdn um etw *akk* ~ to relieve sb of sth

er|leiden* *vt irreg* to suffer

erlesen *adj* exquisite

er|liegen* *vi irreg sein* ■ etw *dat* ~ ▶WENDUNGEN: **zum E~ kommen** to come to a standstill

Erlös <-es, -e> [ɛɐˈløːs] *m* proceeds *npl*

er|mächtigen* [ɛɐˈmɛçtɪɡn̩] *vt* to authorize

er|mahnen* *vt* ① (*warnend mahnen*) ■ jdn ~ to warn sb ② (*anhalten*) ■ jdn zu etw *dat* ~ to admonish sb to do sth

Ermäßigung <-, -en> *f* reduction

Ermessen <-s> *nt kein pl* **nach jds ~** in sb's discretion

er|mitteln* I. *vt* ① (*herausfinden*) to find out *sep*; **den Täter ~** to establish the culprit's identity ② (*errechnen*) to determine; *Gewinner* to decide [on] II. *vi* (*eine Untersuchung durchführen*) ■ [gegen jdn] ~ to investigate [sb]

Ermittlung <-, -en> *f* ① *kein pl* (*das Ausfindigmachen*) determining ② (*Untersuchung*) investigation

er|möglichen* [ɛɐˈmøːklɪçn̩] *vt* ■ jdm etw ~ to enable sb to do sth

er|morden* *vt* to murder

er|müden* [ɛɐˈmyːdn̩] I. *vt haben* ■ jdn ~ to tire [out *sep*] sb II. *vi sein* ① (*müde werden*) to become tired ② TECH to wear

ermüdend *adj* tiring

Ermüdung <-, selten -en> *f* ① (*das Ermüden*) tiredness ② TECH wear

er|mutigen* [ɛɐˈmuːtɪɡn̩] *vt* ■ jdn [zu etw *dat*] ~ to encourage sb [to do sth]

er|nähren* I. *vt* (*mit Nahrung versorgen*) to feed II. *vr* ■ sich *akk* von etw *dat* ~ ① (*essen*) to live on sth ② (*sich finanzieren*) to support oneself by doing sth

Ernährung <-> *f kein pl* ① (*das Ernähren*) feeding ② (*Nahrung*) diet ③ (*finanziell*) support

Ernährungsberater, -beraterin *m, f* nutritionist

er|nennen* *vt irreg* to appoint (**zu** +*dat* as)

Ernennung *f* appointment (**zu** +*dat* as)

erneuerbar *adj* renewable

er|neuern* [ɛɐˈnɔyɐn] *vt* ① (*auswechseln*) *Fenster, Reifen* to replace; *Öl* to change ② (*wiederbeleben*) *Freundschaft* to renew

er|niedrigen* [ɛɐˈniːdrɪɡn̩] *vt* ■ jdn/sich ~ to demean sb/oneself

ernst [ɛrnst] *adj* ① (*gravierend*) serious ② (*aufrichtig*) genuine; **es ~ meinen [mit jdm/etw]** to be serious [about sb/sth]; **jdn/etw ~ nehmen** to take sb/sth seriously ③ *Anlass* solemn

Ernstfall *m* emergency

ernsthaft I. *adj* ① (*gravierend*) serious ② (*aufrichtig*) sincere II. *adv* seriously

ernten [ˈɛrntn̩] *vt* ① *Gemüse, Obst* to harvest ② (*erzielen*) *Anerkennung* to gain; *Applaus* to win; *Lob, Spott* to earn

er|nüchtern* [ɛɐˈnʏçtɐn] *vt* ■ jdn ~ ① (*wieder nüchtern machen*) to sober up *sep* sb ② (*in die Realität zurückholen*) to bring sb back to reality

Ernüchterung <-, -en> *f* disillusionment

er|obern* [ɛɐˈʔoːbɐn] *vt* ① (*mit Waffengewalt*) *Gebiet, Land, Stadt* to con-

E

quer ② *Markt* to capture ③ (*für sich einnehmen*) *Mensch* to win sb's heart

Eroberung <-, -en> f ① (*das Erobern*) conquest ② (*fam: eroberte Person*) conquest *hum*

Eröffnung f ① *eines Geschäfts, Museums etc.* opening ② (*Mitteilung*) revelation

er|örtern* [ɛɐˈœrtən] *vt* to discuss [in detail]

Erörterung <-, -en> f discussion

Erotik <-> [eˈroːtɪk] f *kein pl* eroticism

erotisch [eˈroːtɪʃ] *adj* erotic

Erpel <-s, -> [ˈɛrpl̩] m drake

erpicht [ɛɐˈpɪçt] *adj* ■ auf etw *akk* ~ sein to be after sth

er|pressen* *vt* ■ jdn ~ to blackmail sb

Erpresser(in) <-s, -> m(f) blackmailer

Erpressung <-, -en> f blackmail

er|proben* *vt* to test

erprobt *adj* ein ~es Mittel a reliable remedy

er|raten* *vt irreg* to guess

er|rechnen* *vt* to calculate

er|regen* *vt* ① (*aufregen*) ■ jdn ~ to excite sb; (*sexuell a.*) to arouse sb ② (*hervorrufen*) ■ etw ~ *Aufmerksamkeit* to attract; *Aufsehen* to cause

Erreger <-s, -> m pathogen

erreichbar *adj* ■ [für jdn] ~ sein to be able to be reached [by sb]

er|reichen* *vt* to reach

er|richten* *vt* ① (*aufstellen*) to erect *form* ② (*gründen*) to found sth

er|röten* *vi sein* to blush

Errungenschaft <-, -en> [ɛɐˈrʊŋənʃaft] f achievement

Ersatz <-es> [ɛɐˈzats] m *kein pl* ① (*ersetzender Mensch*) substitute; (*ersetzender Gegenstand*) replacement ② (*Entschädigung*) compensation

Ersatzbank f SPORT bench

Ersatzdienst m nonmilitary service for conscientious objectors

Ersatzmann <-männer *o* -leute> m substitute

Ersatzreifen m spare tire

Ersatzteil nt spare part

er|schaffen* *vt irreg* to create

er|scheinen* *vi irreg sein* ① (*auftreten*) to appear ② (*sichtbar werden*) to be able to be seen ③ (*veröffentlicht werden*) *Buch, CD etc.* to come out ④ (*scheinen*) to seem; **das erscheint mir recht weit hergeholt** that seems pretty far-fetched to me

Erscheinen <-s> nt *kein pl* ① (*das Auftreten*) appearance ② (*die Veröffentlichung*) publication

Erscheinung <-, -en> f ① (*Phänomen*) phenomenon ② (*Persönlichkeit*) ■ eine bestimmte ~ a certain figure ③ (*Vision*) vision ▶WENDUNGEN: in ~ treten to appear

er|schießen* *irreg vt* ■ jdn ~ to shoot sb dead

er|schlagen*¹ *vt* ■ jdn ~ *irreg* ① (*totschlagen*) to beat sb to death ② (*durch Darauffallen töten*) *Gegenstand* to fall down and kill sb; *Blitz* to strike sb dead ③ (*fig: überwältigen*) to overwhelm sb

erschlagen² *adj* (*fam*) wie ~ sein to be pooped *sl*

er|schließen* *irreg* I. *vt* *Land* to develop II. *vr* ■ sich *dat* jdm ~ to reveal oneself to sb

er|schöpfen* *vt* ① (*ermüden*) ■ jdn ~ to exhaust sb ② (*aufbrauchen*) ■ etw ~ to exhaust sth

erschöpfend I. *adj* ① (*zur Erschöpfung führend*) exhausting ② (*ausführlich*) exhaustive II. *adv* exhaustively

Erschöpfung <-, selten -en> f exhaustion

er|schrak *imp von* **erschrecken** II

er|schrecken I. *vt* <erschreckte, erschreckt> *haben* ■ jdn ~ ① (*in Schrecken versetzen*) to give sb a scare ② (*bestürzen*) to shock sb II. *vi* <erschrickt, erschreckte *o* erschrak, erschreckt *o* erschrocken> *sein* to be scared (**vor** +*dat* by) III. *vr* <erschrickt, erschreckte, erschreckt *o* erschrocken> *haben* (*fam*) ■ sich *akk* [**über etw** *akk*] ~ to be shocked [by sth]

erschrocken I. *pp von* **erschrecken** II, III II. *adj* alarmed *pred* III. *adv* with a start er|schüttern* [ɛɐ̯·ˈʃʏ·tɐn] vt ①(zum Beben bringen) Boden, Gebäude to shake ②(in Frage stellen) Ansehen to damage; Glaubwürdigkeit to undermine; Vertrauen to shake ③(tief bewegen) ■jdn ~ to shake sb

er|schweren* [ɛɐ̯·ˈʃveː·rən] vt to make more difficult

erschwinglich [ɛɐ̯·ˈʃvɪŋ·lɪç] adj affordable

er|sehen* vt irreg to see (aus +dat from)

er|setzen* vt ①(austauschen) ■etw [durch etw akk] ~ to replace sth [with sth] ②(vertreten) ■jdn/etw ~ to replace sb/sth ③(erstatten) ■jdm etw ~ to reimburse sb for sth

ersichtlich adj apparent; ■aus etw ~ sein, dass ... to be apparent from sth that ...

er|sparen* vt ①(von Ärger verschonen) ■jdm etw ~ to spare sb sth ②(durch Sparen erwerben) ■[sich dat] etw ~ to save up [to buy] sth

Ersparnis <-, -se> [ɛɐ̯·ˈʃpaɐ̯·nɪs] f savings npl

erst ['eːɐ̯st] I. adv ①(zuerst) [at] first ②(nicht früher als) only; wecken Sie mich bitte ~ um 8 Uhr! please don't wake me up until 8 o'clock! II. part (verstärkend) an deiner Stelle würde ich ~ gar nicht anfangen zu ... if I were in your shoes I wouldn't even start to ... ▶WENDUNGEN: ~ recht all the more

er|statten* [ɛɐ̯·ˈʃta·tn̩] vt ①(ersetzen) ■[jdm] etw ~ to reimburse [sb] for sth ②Anzeige ~ to report a crime

Erstattung <-, -en> f von Auslagen, Unkosten reimbursement

Erstaufführung f première

Erstaunen nt amazement; jdn in ~ versetzen to amaze sb

erstaunlich [ɛɐ̯·ˈʃtaʊn·lɪç] adj amazing

erstaunlicherweise adv amazingly

erstaunt I. adj amazed II. adv in amazement

erste(r, s) ['eːɐ̯s·tə] adj ①(an erster Stelle) first; das E~, was ... the first thing that ...; s. a. achte(r, s) 1 ②(Da-

tum) first, 1st; s. a. achte(r, s) 2 ③(führend) leading ▶WENDUNGEN: fürs E~ to begin with

Erste-Hilfe-Kasten [eːɐ̯s·tə·ˈhɪl·fə·kas·tn̩] m first-aid kit

er|sticken* I. vt haben ①(durch Erstickung töten) to suffocate ②Brand to extinguish II. vi sein ①(durch Erstickung sterben) ■an etw dat ~ to choke to death on sth ②(erlöschen) Feuer to go out ③(übermäßig viel haben) ■in etw dat ~ to drown in sth

erstklassig ['eːɐ̯st·klasɪç] adj first-class

erstmalig ['eːɐ̯st·maː·lɪç] I. adj first II. adv s. erstmals

erstmals ['eːɐ̯st·maːls] adv for the first time

er|strecken* I. vr ①(sich ausdehnen) ■sich akk [über etw akk] ~ to extend [over sth] ②(betreffen) ■sich akk auf etw akk ~ to include sth II. vt SCHWEIZ (verlängern) to extend

er|tappen* vt, vr ■jdn/sich [bei etw dat] ~ to catch sb/oneself [doing sth]

Ertrag <-[e]s, Erträge> [ɛɐ̯·ˈtraːk] m ①(Ernte) yield; ~ bringen to bring yields ②meist pl (Einnahmen) revenue

er|tragen* vt irreg to bear

erträglich [ɛɐ̯·ˈtrɛːk·lɪç] adj bearable

er|trinken* vi irreg sein to drown

er|übrigen* [ɛɐ̯·ˈʔyː·brɪ·gn̩] I. vr ■sich akk ~ to be superfluous II. vt (aufbringen) etw ~ können Geld, Zeit to spare sth

er|wachen* vi sein to wake up

erwachsen [ɛɐ̯·ˈvak·sn̩] adj adult

Erwachsene(r) f(m) adult

Erwachsenenbildung [ɛɐ̯·ˈvak·se·nən-] f adult education

er|wägen* vt irreg to consider

er|wähnen* vt to mention

er|wärmen* I. vt to warm [up] II. vr ①(warm werden) ■sich akk ~ to warm up ②(sich begeistern) ■sich akk für jdn/etw ~ to work up enthusiasm for sb/sth

Erwärmung <-, -en> f warming [up]; globale ~ global warming

er|warten* I. vt to expect II. vr (sich

E

versprechen) ■**sich** *dat* **etw von jdm/etw ~** to expect sth from sb/sth

Erwartung <-, -en> f ❶ *kein pl (Ungeduld)* anticipation ❷ *pl (Hoffnung)* expectations *pl;* **den ~en entsprechen** to fulfill expectations

erwartungsvoll I. *adj* expectant, full of expectation *pred* **II.** *adv* expectantly

er|wecken* *vt* ❶ *(nachweisen)* to arouse; **den Eindruck ~, ...** to give the impression ...

er|weisen* *irreg* **I.** *vt* ❶ *(nachweisen)* to prove ❷ *(zeigen)* ■**etw wird ~, dass/ob ...** sth will show that/whether ... ❸ **jdm einen Dienst/Gefallen ~** to do somebody a service/favor **II.** *vr* ❶ *(sich herausstellen)* ■**sich akk als etw ~** to prove to be sth ❷ *(sich zeigen)* **sie sollte sich dankbar [ihm gegenüber] ~** she should be grateful [to him]

er|weitern* **I.** *vt* ❶ *Straße, Kleidung* to widen **(um** +*akk* by) ❷ *(vergrößern)* to expand **(um** +*akk* by) ❸ *(umfangreicher machen)* to increase **(um** +*akk* by) **II.** *vr* ❶ *(sich verbreitern)* ■**sich akk ~** to widen **(um** +*akk* by) ❷ MED, ANAT ■**sich** *akk* **~** to dilate

Erwerb <-[e]s> [ɛɐ̯ˈvɛrp] *m kein pl* purchase

er|werben* *vt irreg* ❶ *(kaufen)* to purchase ❷ *(gewinnen)* Vertrauen to win

erwerbsfähig *adj* fit for gainful employment *pred*

erwerbslos *adj* unemployed

erwerbsunfähig *adj* unfit for gainful employment

er|widern* [ɛɐ̯ˈviːdən] *vt* ❶ *(antworten)* to reply ❷ *(zurückgeben)* Gefühle, Liebe to return

erwiesenermaßen [ɛɐ̯viːzəˈneˈmaːsn̩] *adv* as has been proved

er|wischen* [ɛɐ̯ˈvɪʃn̩] *vt (fam)* ❶ *(ertappen)* ■**jdn [bei etw** *dat*] **~** to catch sb [doing sth] ❷ *(ergreifen, erreichen)* ■**jdn/etw ~** to catch sb/sth

Erz <-es, -e> [ˈeːɐ̯ts] *nt* ore

er|zählen* **I.** *vt* ❶ *(anschaulich berichten)* to explain ❷ *(sagen)* to tell **II.** *vi* to tell a story/stories

Erzähler(in) <-s, -> [ɛɐ̯ˈtsɛːlɐ] *m(f)* storyteller; *(Schriftsteller(in))* author; *(Romanperson)* narrator

Erzählung f ❶ *(Geschichte)* story ❷ *kein pl (das Erzählen)* telling

Erzbischof, -bischöfin [ˈeːɐ̯ts-bɪʃɔf, -bɪ-ʃœ-fɪn] *m, f* archbishop

Erzengel [ˈɛrts-ʔɛŋl̩] *m* archangel

er|zeugen* *vt* ❶ ÖKON *(produzieren)* to produce ❷ ELEK, SCI to generate ❸ *(hervorrufen)* to create

Erzeuger(in) <-s, -> *m(f)* ❶ *(Produzent)* producer ❷ *(hum fam: Vater)* father

Erzeugnis <-ses, -se> [ɛɐ̯ˈtsɔyk-nɪs] *nt* product

Erzfeind(in) *m(f)* archenemy

erziehbar *adj* educable; **schwer ~ sein** to have behavioral problems

er|ziehen* *vt irreg* ❶ *(aufziehen)* **gut/schlecht erzogen sein** to be well/badly brought-up ❷ *(anleiten)* ■**jdn zu etw** *dat* **~** to teach sb to be sth

Erziehung f *kein pl* ❶ *(das Erziehen)* education ❷ *(anerzogene Manieren)* manners *npl*

Erziehungsurlaub *m* maternity/paternity leave *(for up to 3 years)*

er|zielen* *vt* ❶ *(erreichen)* to achieve; *Einigung* to reach ❷ SPORT to score

er|zwingen* *vt irreg* ■**etw [von jdm] ~** to force sth [out of sb]; **ein Geständnis [von jdm] ~** to make sb confess

es <*gen seiner, dat* ihm, *akk* es> [ˈɛs] *pron pers, unbestimmt* ❶ *auf Dinge bezogen (das, diese)* it; **wer ist da? – ich bin ~** who's there? — it's me ❷ *auf vorangehenden Satzinhalt bezogen* it; **kommt er auch? – ich hoffe ~** is he coming too? — I hope so ❸ *rein formales Subjekt* it; **hier stinkt ~** something smells bad in here; **~ gefällt mir** I like it ❹ *rein formales Objekt* **er hat ~ gut** he's got it made ❺ *Subjekt bei unpersönl. Ausdrücken* **~ klopft** there's a knock at the door; **~ regnet** it's raining ❻ *Einleitewort mit folgendem Subjekt* **~ waren Tausende** there were thousands

Esche <-, -n> ['ɛʃə] f ash

Esel(in) <-s, -> ['e:zl] m(f) ① (Tier) donkey ② nur m (fam: Dummkopf) idiot

Eselsbrücke f (fam) mnemonic [device]

Eselsohr nt dog-ear

eskalieren* [ɛs·ka·'li:·rən] vt, vi to escalate (**zu** + dat into)

Eskimo, -frau <-s, -s> ['ɛs·ki·mo] m, f Eskimo

Espe <-, -n> ['ɛs·pə] f aspen

Espenlaub nt ►WENDUNGEN: **zittern wie ~** to be shaking like a leaf

essbar^RR, **eßbar**^ALT adj edible

essen <isst, aß, gegessen> ['ɛsn] I. vt to eat; **~ Sie gern Äpfel?** do you like apples?; **etw zum Nachtisch ~** to have sth for dessert II. vi to eat; **griechisch/italienisch ~** to eat Greek/Italian food

Essen <-s, -> ['ɛsn] nt ① (Mahlzeit) meal ② (Nahrung) food

Essen(s)marke f meal voucher

Essig <-s, -e> ['ɛsɪç] m vinegar

Essiggurke f pickle

Essigsäure f acetic acid

Esskastanie^RR f sweet chestnut

Esslöffel^RR m ① (Essbesteck) soup spoon ② (Maßeinheit beim Kochen) tablespoon

Esszimmer^RR nt dining room

Este, Estin <-n, -n> ['e:stə, 'e:s·tɪn] m, f Estonian; s. a. **Deutsche(r)**

Estland <-s> ['e:st·lant] nt Estonia; s. a. **Deutschland**

estnisch ['e:st·nɪʃ] adj Estonian; s. a. **deutsch**

Estragon <-s> ['ɛs·tra·gɔn] m kein pl tarragon

etabliert adj (geh) established

Etage <-, -n> [e'ta:·ʒə] f floor; **auf der 5. ~** on the 6th floor

Etagenwohnung [e'ta:·ʒən-] f apartment (occupying a whole floor)

Etappe <-, -n> [e'tapə] f ① (Abschnitt) stage ② (Teilstrecke) leg ③ MIL communications zone

Etat <-s, -s> [e'ta:] m budget

etepetete [e:tə·pe·'te:·tə] adj pred (fam) finicky

Ethik <-> ['e:tɪk] f kein pl ① (Wissen-

schaft) ethics + sing vb ② (moralische Haltung) ethics npl

ethisch ['e:tɪʃ] adj ethical

Etikett <-[e]s, -e> [eti·'kɛt] nt ① (Preisschild) price tag ② (Aufnäher) label

etliche(r, s) ['ɛt·lɪ·çə] pron indef ① adjektivisch, sing o pl quite a lot of ② substantivisch, plural quite a few ③ substantivisch, sing ■ ~s quite a lot

Etui <-s, -s> [ɛt·'vi:, e'tÿi:] nt case; (verziert a.) etui

etwa ['ɛt·va] I. adv ① (ungefähr; annähernd) about; **in ~** more or less ② (zum Beispiel) **wie ~ mein Bruder** like my brother for instance II. part ① (womöglich) **soll das ~ heißen, dass …?** is that supposed to mean [that] …?; **willst du ~ schon gehen?** you don't want to go already, do you? ② (Verstärkung der Verneinung) **ist das ~ nicht wahr?** do you mean to say it's not true?

etwaig [ɛt·'va:·ɪç] adj attr any

etwas ['ɛt·vas] pron indef ① substantivisch (eine unbestimmte Sache) something; (bei Fragen) anything ② adjektivisch (nicht näher bestimmt) something; (bei Fragen) anything; **~ anderes** something else; **[noch] ~ Kaffee** some [more] coffee ③ adverbial (ein wenig) a little

Etwas <-> ['ɛt·vas] nt kein pl ►WENDUNGEN: **das gewisse ~** that certain something

EU [e:·'u:] f Abk von **Europäische Union** EU, European Union

euch ['ɔyç] I. pron pers akk o dat von **ihr** you[-all], you guys sl; **ein Freund/eine Freundin von ~** a friend of yours II. pron refl **beeilt ~!** hurry up!; **macht ~ fertig!** get [fam yourselves] ready!

euere(r, s) ['ɔyə·rə] pron poss, substantivisch s. **eure(r, s)**

Eukalyptus <-, -lypten> [ɔy·ka·'lʏp·tʊs] m ① (Baum) eucalyptus [tree] ② (Öl) eucalyptus [oil]

EU-Kommission f EU Commission

EU-Land nt EU country

Eule <-, -n> ['ɔy·lə] f owl

EU-Mitgliedsland nt EU member state

Eunuch <-en, -en> [ɔyˈnuːx] *m* eunuch

Euphorie <-, -n> [ɔyfoˈriː] *f* euphoria

euphorisch [ɔyˈfoːrɪʃ] *adj* euphoric

eure(r, s) [ˈɔyrə] *pron poss (geh)* ■ der/die/das] E~ yours; **tut ihr das E~** you do your part

euretwegen [ˈɔyrətˈveːgn] *adv (wegen euch)* because of you; *(euch zuliebe)* for your sake[s]

euretwillen [ˈɔyrətˈvɪlən] *adv* for your sake[s]

Euro [ˈɔyro] *m (Währungseinheit)* euro; **hundert ~ spenden** to donate a hundred euros

Eurocity [ˈɔyroˌsɪti] *m* Eurocity train *(connecting major European cities)*

Eurokrise *f* eurozone *[or euro]* crisis

Europa <-s> [ɔyˈroːpa] *nt* Europe

Europäer(in) <-s, -> [ɔyroˈpɛːɐ] *m(f)* European

europäisch [ɔyroˈpɛːɪʃ] *adj* European; **E~e Einheitswährung** single European currency, euro; **E~e Gemeinschaft** *[o* **EG]** European Community, EC; **E~er Gerichtshof** European Court of Justice; **E~es Parlament** European Parliament; **E~er Rat** European Council; **die ~en Staaten** the European countries

Europameister(in) *m(f) (als Einzelner)* European champion; *(als Team, Land)* European champions *pl*

Europameisterschaft *f* European championship

Europaparlament *nt* the European Parliament

Europapokal *m* European cup tournament

Europarat *m kein pl* Council of Europe

Europawahlen *pl* European elections *pl*

Euro-Rettungsschirm, **Eurorettungsschirm** *m kein pl* FIN *(organization)* European Financial Stability Facility, EFSF; *(fund)* euro bailout fund

Eurozone <-> *f kein pl* Eurozone

Euter <-s, -> [ˈɔytɐ] *nt o m* udder

evakuieren* [evakuˈiːrən] *vt* to evacuate

evangelisch [evaŋˈgeːlɪʃ] *adj* Protestant

Evangelium <-s, -lien> [evaŋˈgeːliʊm] *nt* Gospel; *(fig)* gospel

eventuell [evɛnˈtuˌɛl] I. *adj attr* possible; **bei ~en Rückfragen wenden Sie sich bitte an ...** if you have any questions, please contact ... II. *adv* possibly

Evolution <-, -en> [evoluˈtsi̯oːn] *f* evolution

EWG <-> [eːveːˈgeː] *f kein pl (hist) Abk von* **Europäische Wirtschaftsgemeinschaft** EEC, [European] Economic Community

EWI <-[s]> *nt kein pl Abk von* **Europäisches Währungsinstitut** HIST EMI, European Monetary Institute

ewig [ˈeːvɪç] I. *adj* ❶ *(immer während)* eternal ❷ *(pej fam: ständig)* ~es **Gejammer** never-ending moaning and groaning II. *adv* ❶ *(dauernd)* eternally; *(seit jeher)* always ❷ *(fam: ständig)* always ❸ *(fam: lange Zeitspanne)* for ages

Ewigkeit <-, -en> [ˈeːvɪçkait] *f* eternity; **eine [halbe] ~ dauern** *(hum fam)* to last forever

EWS <-> [eːveːˈɛs] *nt kein pl* HIST *Abk von* **Europäisches Währungssystem** EMS, European Monetary System

EWWU <-> [eːveːveːˈuː] *f Abk von* **Europäische Wirtschafts- und Währungsunion** EEMU, European Economic and Monetary Union

exakt [ɛˈksakt] I. *adj* exact II. *adv* exactly; ~ **arbeiten** to be accurate in one's work

Examen <-s, -> [ɛˈksaːmən] *nt* **mündliches/schriftliches ~** oral/written exam; **das ~ bestehen** to pass one's final [exam]; **durch das ~ fallen** to fail one's final [exam]

Exemplar <-s, -e> [ɛksɛmˈplaːɐ] *nt* specimen; *(Ausgabe) von Buch, Heft* copy; *einer Zeitung* issue

Exil <-s, -e> [ɛˈksiːl] *nt* exile

Existenz <-, -en> [ɛksɪsˈtɛnts] *f* ❶ *kein pl (das Vorhandensein)* existence ❷(*Lebensgrundlage, Auskommen*) livelihood ❸(*Dasein, Leben*) life

Existenzgründer(in) *m(f)* founder of a new business

Existenzgrundlage *f* basis of one's livelihood

Existenzminimum *nt* subsistence level

Existenzrecht *nt kein pl* right to existence

existieren* [ɛksɪsˈtiːrən] *vi* ❶(*vorhanden sein*) to exist ❷(*sein Auskommen haben*) ■ |**von etw** *dat*| ~ to live [on sth]

exklusiv [ɛksˈkluˈziːf] *adj* exclusive

Exkrement <-[e]s, -e> [ɛksˈkreˈmɛnt] *nt meist pl* (*geh*) excrement

Exkursion <-, -en> [ɛksˈkʊrˈzjoːn] *f* UNIV study trip; SCH field trip

exotisch [ɛˈksoːtɪʃ] *adj* ❶(*aus fernem Land*) exotic ❷(*fam: ausgefallen*) unusual

Expedition <-, -en> [ɛksˈpeˈdiˈtsjoːn] *f* expedition

Experiment <-[e]s, -e> [ɛksˈpeˈriˈmɛnt] *nt* experiment

experimentieren* [ɛksˈpeˈriˈmɛnˈtiːrən] *vi* to experiment

Experte, Expertin <-n, -n> [ɛksˈpɛrtə] *m, f* expert

explodieren* [ɛksˈploˈdiːrən] *vi sein* (*a. fig*) to explode *a. fig*

Explosion <-, -en> [ɛksˈploˈzjoːn] *f* (*a. fig*) explosion *a. fig*; **etw zur ~ bringen** to detonate sth

Explosionsgefahr *f* danger of explosion

explosiv [ɛksˈploˈziːf] *adj* explosive

Export <-[e]s, -e> [ɛksˈpɔrt] *m kein pl* export

Exportartikel *m* exported article; *pl* exports

Exporteur(in) <-s, -e> [ɛkspɔrˈtøːɐ̯] *m(f)* exporter

exportieren* [ɛksˈpɔrˈtiːrən] *vt* to export

Express[RR], **Expreß**[ALT] <Expresses> [ɛksˈprɛs] *m kein pl* ❶(*Eilzug*) express [train] ❷(*schnell*) **etw per ~ senden** to send sth express

Expressionismus <-> [ɛksˈprɛsˈjoˈnɪsˈmʊs] *m kein pl* expressionism

extern [ɛksˈtɛrn] *adj* external

extra [ˈɛksˈtra] *adv* ❶(*besonders*) extra ❷(*zusätzlich*) extra ❸(*eigens*) just ❹(*fam: absichtlich*) on purpose ❺(*gesondert*) separately; KOCHK on the side

Extrablatt *nt* special supplement

Extrakt <-[e]s, -e> [ɛksˈtrakt] *m o nt* extract

extravagant [ɛksˈtraˈvaˈgant] *adj* extravagant

extravertiert [ɛksˈtraˈvɛrˈtiːɐ̯t] *adj* extroverted

extrem [ɛksˈtreːm] **I.** *adj* extreme **II.** *adv* (*sehr*) extremely; **~ links/rechts** POL ultra-left/right

Extremist(in) <-en, -en> [ɛksˈtreˈmɪst] *m(f)* extremist

Extremitäten [ɛksˈtreˈmiˈtɛːtn̩] *pl* extremities *npl*

exzellent [ɛksˈtsɛˈlɛnt] (*geh*) **I.** *adj* excellent **II.** *adv* excellently; **sich** *akk* ~ **fühlen** to feel great; **~ schmecken** to taste delicious

exzentrisch [ɛksˈtsɛnˈtrɪʃ] *adj* eccentric

Exzess[RR], **Exzeß**[ALT] <Exzesses, Exzesse> [ɛksˈtsɛs] *m meist pl* excess; **etw bis zum ~ treiben** to take sth to extremes

exzessiv [ɛksˈtsɛˈsiːf] *adj* excessive

EZB <-> [eːˈtsɛtˈbeː] *f kein pl* FIN *Abk von* **Europäische Zentralbank** ECB, European Central Bank

E

Ff

F, f <-, -> [ɛf] *nt* F, f; **~ wie Friedrich** F as in Foxtrot

Fabrik <-, -en> [faˈbriːk] *f* factory

Fabrikarbeiter(in) *m(f)* factory worker

Fabrikgelände *nt* factory site

fabrikneu *adj* brand-new

Fach <-[e]s, Fächer> [fax] *nt* ① (*im Schrank*) shelf ② (*Sachgebiet*) subject; **vom ~ sein** to be a specialist

Facharbeiter(in) *m(f)* skilled worker

Facharzt, -ärztin *m, f* specialist

Fachausdruck *m* technical term; **juristischer ~** legal term

Fächer <-s, -> [ˈfɛ·çɐ] *m* fan

Fachgebiet *nt* field of expertise

Fachhändler(in) *m(f)* retail dealer

Fachhochschule *f* ≈ University of Applied Sciences

Fachkenntnisse *pl* specialized knowledge *sing*

fachlich *adv* **sich** *akk* **~ qualifizieren** to gain expertise in one's field

Fachliteratur *f* technical literature

Fachmann, -frau <-leute> *m, f* expert

Fachsprache *f* [technical] jargon

Fachwerkhaus *nt* half-timbered house

Fachwissen *nt* specialized knowledge

Fachwort *nt* technical term

Fachwörterbuch *nt* technical dictionary; **ein medizinisches ~** a dictionary of medical terms

Fachzeitschrift *f* technical journal

Fackel <-, -n> [ˈfa·kl] *f* torch

Faden <-s, Fäden> [ˈfaː·dn̩] *m* thread; **die Fäden ziehen** MED to remove sb's stitches ►WENDUNGEN: **der rote ~** the central theme; **den ~ verlieren** to lose one's train of thought

fähig [ˈfɛ·ɪç] *adj* able, competent; **zu etw** *dat* **[nicht] ~ sein** to be [in]capable of sth

Fähigkeit <-, -en> *f* ability

fahnden [ˈfaːn·dn̩] *vi* to search (**nach** +*dat* for)

Fahndung <-, -en> *f* search; **eine ~ nach jdm einleiten** to put out an APB for sb

Fahne <-, -n> [ˈfaː·nə] *f* flag; (*Alkoholgeruch*) smell of alcohol *no indef art*

Fahrausweis *m* ① (*Fahrkarte*) ticket ② SCHWEIZ (*Führerschein*) driver's license

Fahrbahn *f* road; **von der ~ abkommen** to leave the road

Fähre <-, -n> [ˈfɛː·rə] *f* ferry

fahren <fährt, fuhr, gefahren> [ˈfaː·rən] I. *vi sein* to go; (*als Fahrer*) to drive; (*losfahren*) to leave; **die Bahn fährt alle 20 Minuten** the train runs every 20 minutes; **mit dem Auto/ Bus/Zug ~** to take the car/bus/train; **in Urlaub ~** to go on vacation; **gegen etw** *akk* **~** to drive into sth; **was ist denn in dich ge~?** (*fig*) what's gotten into you?; **gut/schlecht ~** (*fig*) to do/ not do well II. *vt* ① *haben* (*lenken*) to drive ② *sein* **Fahrrad/Motorrad ~** to ride a bicycle/motorcycle; **Schlittschuh ~** to ice-skate; **90 [km/h] ~** to be doing 90 kmph ③ *haben* (*befördern*) to take; **ich fahr dich nach Hause** I'll take you home III. *vr haben* **der Wagen fährt sich gut** the car handles well

Fahrer(in) <-s, -> [ˈfaː·rɐ] *m(f)* driver; (*auf Motorrad*) biker *fam*

Fahrerflucht *f* hit-and-run

Fahrgast *m* passenger

Fahrgemeinschaft *f* carpool; **eine ~ bilden** to carpool

Fahrkarte *f* ticket (**nach** +*dat* to)

Fahrkartenautomat *m* ticket machine

Fahrkartenschalter *m* ticket office

fahrlässig [ˈfaːɐ̯·lɛ·sɪç] I. *adj* negligent; **grob ~** reckless II. *adv* negligently; **~ handeln** to act with negligence

Fahrlässigkeit <-, -en> *f* negligence; **grobe ~** recklessness

Fahrlehrer(in) *m(f)* driving instructor

Fahrplan m schedule

Fahrpreis m fare

Fahrprüfung f driving test

Fahrrad ['faːɐ̯·raːt] nt bicycle, bike fam; **~ fahren** to ride a bicycle

Fahrradweg m bicycle path

Fahrschein m ticket

Fahrschule f driving school

Fahrschüler(in) m(f) student driver

Fahrspur f [traffic] lane

Fahrstuhl m elevator

Fahrt <-, -en> [faːɐ̯t] f trip; **gute ~!** [have a] safe trip!; **eine einfache ~** a one-way [ticket]; **eine ~ ins Blaue** a Sunday drive ▶WENDUNGEN: **in ~ kommen/sein** (fam: in Wut) to get/be all riled up fam; (in Schwung) to get going

Fährte <-, -n> ['fɛɐ̯·tə] f trail; **auf der falschen/richtigen ~ sein** (fig) to be on the wrong/right track

fahrtüchtig adj Fahrzeug roadworthy; Mensch fit to drive pred

Fahrzeug <-s, -e> nt vehicle

Fahrzeughalter(in) m(f) vehicle owner

Faktor <-s, -toren> ['fak·toːɐ̯] m factor

Fakultät <-, -en> [fa·kʊl·'tɛt] f department

Falke <-n, -n> ['fal·kə] m falcon

Fall <-[e]s, Fälle> [fal] m ❶ kein pl (Sturz) fall; (fig: Untergang) downfall ❷ (Umstand) case, circumstance; **auf alle Fälle** in any case; **auf keinen ~** under no circumstances; **für alle Fälle** just in case; **im besten/schlimmsten ~[e]** at best/worst; **in diesem ~** in this case; **klarer ~!** you bet!; **von ~ zu ~** from case to case ❸ JUR, MED case ▶WENDUNGEN: **[nicht] jds ~ sein** (fam) to [not] be sb's cup of tea

Falle <-, -n> ['fa·lə] f trap; **in der ~ sitzen** to be trapped; **~n stellen** to set traps

fallen <fällt, fiel, gefallen> ['fa·lən] vi sein ❶ (nach unten) to fall; Person, Preise to fall; Gegenstand, Klappe, Temperatur, Vorhang to drop; Fieber, Wasserstand to go down; ■ **über etw** akk **~** to trip over sth ❷ (fig) **eine Bemerkung ~ lassen** to drop a remark; **jdn/**

etw ~ lassen to abandon sb/sth ❸ (fam: nicht bestehen) ■ **durch etw** akk **~** to fail sth ❹ (im Krieg) to be killed ❺ (stattfinden) **der 1. Mai fällt auf einen Montag** May 1st falls on a Monday

fällen ['fɛ·lən] vt **einen Baum ~** to fell a tree; **eine Entscheidung ~** to come to a decision; **ein Urteil ~** JUR to pass judgment

fällig ['fɛ·lɪç] adj due usu pred

falls [fals] konj if

Fallschirm m parachute

Fallschirmspringer(in) m(f) parachutist

falsch [falʃ] I. adj ❶ (verkehrt) wrong; **~e Anschuldigung** false accusation; **einen ~en Namen angeben** to give a false name; **~e Scham** false shame; **~e Vorstellung** wrong idea ❷ (hinterhältig) two-faced II. adv wrongly; **etw ~ aussprechen** to mispronounce sth; **jdn ~ informieren** to misinform sb; **~ singen** to sing out of tune

fälschen ['fɛl·ʃn] vt to forge; **Geld ~** to counterfeit money; **gefälschter Scheck** forged check

Falschgeld nt kein pl counterfeit money

falschliegen vi irreg ■ [mit etw dat] **~** to be wrong [in sth]

falschspielen vi to cheat

Fälschung <-, -en> f forgery

fälschungssicher adj counterfeit-proof

Faltblatt nt leaflet

Falte <-, -n> ['fal·tə] f ❶ (in Kleidung) crease; **~n bekommen** to get wrinkled ❷ (in Stoff) fold; **~n werfen** to fall in folds ❸ (in Haut) wrinkle; **die Stirn in ~n legen** to furrow one's brow

falten ['fal·tn] vt to fold

Falter <-s, -> ['fal·tɐ] m (Tagfalter) butterfly; (Nachtfalter) moth

faltig ['fal·tɪç] adj wrinkled

familiär [fa·mi·'liːɛɐ̯] adj family attr; **aus ~en Gründen** for family reasons; **in ~er Atmosphäre** in an informal atmosphere

Familie <-, -n> [fa·'miː·liə] f family;

„~ **Lang**" "The Lang Family"; **das liegt in der** ~ it runs in the family; **eine vierköpfige** ~ a family of four; ~ **haben** to have a family

Familienname m last name, surname

Familienstand m marital status

Fan <-s, -s> [fɛn] m fan

Fanatiker(in) <-s, -> [faˈnaːtiˌkɐ] m(f) fanatic; **politischer** ~ extremist

fanatisch [faˈnaːtɪʃ] adj fanatical

fand [fant] imp von finden

Fang <-[e]s, Fänge> [faŋ] m catch; **einen guten** ~ **machen** (a. fig) to make a good catch

fangen <fängt, fing, gefangen> [ˈfaŋən] I. vt, vi to catch; **F~ spielen** to play catch II. vr ■ **sich** akk ~ to steady oneself

Fangfrage f trick question

Fantasie <-, -n> [fantaˈziː] f kein pl imagination

fantasieren* [fantaˈziːrən] vi to fantasize (**von** +dat about)

fantasievoll adj [highly] imaginative

fantastisch adj fantastic; **das klingt** ~ that sounds incredible

Farbe <-, -n> [ˈfarbə] f color; (Anstreichmittel) paint; (Färbemittel) dye; **sanfte ~n** soft hues ▶WENDUNGEN: ~ **bekennen** to come clean

färben [ˈfɛrbn̩] I. vt to dye II. vr ■ **sich** akk ~ to change color; **die Blätter ~ sich gelb** the leaves are turning yellow

farbenblind adj color blind

Farbfilm m color film

farbig [ˈfarbɪç] adj ❶ (bunt) colored ❷ (anschaulich) colorful ❸ attr (Hautfarbe) of color; **die ~e Bevölkerung** people of color

Farbige(r) f(m) dekl wie adj person of color; (Schwarzamerikaner) African-American

Farbkopierer m color copier

farblos [ˈfarpˌloːs] adj colorless; (langweilig) dull

Farbskala f color scale

Farbstift m colored pencil

Farbstoff m (in Nahrungsmitteln) artificial coloring

Farbton m shade

Farn <-[e]s, -e> [farn] m, **Farnkraut** nt fern

Fasan <-s, -e[n]> [faˈzaːn] m pheasant

Fasching <-s, -e> [ˈfaʃɪŋ] m SÜDD, ÖSTERR carnival

Faschismus <-> [faˈʃɪsˌmʊs] m kein pl fascism

Faschist(in) <-en, -en> [faˈʃɪst] m(f) fascist

Faser <-, -n> [ˈfaːzɐ] f fiber

faserig [ˈfaːzəˌrɪç] adj fibrous

Fass[RR] <-es, Fässer>, **Faß**[ALT] <-sses, Fässer> [fas] nt barrel; **Bier vom** ~ draft beer ▶WENDUNGEN: **das** ~ **zum Überlaufen bringen** to be the final straw

fassen [ˈfasn̩] I. vt ❶ (ergreifen) to grasp; **jdn am Arm** ~ to grab sb's arm; **jdn bei der Hand** ~ to take sb by the hand; **den Täter** ~ to apprehend the culprit ❷ (fig) **einen Entschluss/Vorsatz** ~ to make a decision/resolution; **keinen klaren Gedanken** ~ **können** to not be able to think clearly ❸ (begreifen) to comprehend; **er konnte sein Glück kaum** ~ he could hardly believe his luck ❹ (enthalten) to contain II. vi to grip; **fass!** Hund sic [him/her]! III. vr ■ **sich** akk ~ to pull oneself together

Fassung <-, -en> f ❶ (Rahmen) mounting ❷ (Brillengestell) frame ❸ (für Lampen) socket ❹ (Bearbeitung) version, draft ❺ kein pl (Selbstbeherrschung) composure; **die** ~ **bewahren** to maintain one's composure; **jdn aus der** ~ **bringen** to rattle sb; **die** ~ **verlieren** to lose one's self-control

fassungslos I. adj stunned II. adv in bewilderment; ~ **zusehen, wie ...** to watch in disbelief as ...

Fassungsvermögen nt capacity

fast [fast] adv almost; ~ **nie** hardly ever

fasten [ˈfastn̩] vi to fast

Fastenzeit f REL Lent

Fast Food[RR], **Fastfood**[RR], **Fast food**[ALT] <-> [ˈfaːstˌfuːt] nt kein pl fast food

Fastnacht ['fast·naxt] f kein pl DIAL carnival

faszinieren* [fas·tsi·'niː·rən] vt, vi to fascinate

faszinierend adj fascinating

fatal [fa·'taːl] adj fatal; ~e **Folgen** fatal repercussions; ~e **Lage** awkward position

fauchen ['fau·xn̩] vi ❶ Tier to hiss ❷ (wütend zischen) to spit

faul [faul] adj ❶ lazy ❷ (verfault) rotten ▶WENDUNGEN: **an etw** dat **ist etw ~** something's fishy about sth

faulen ['fau·lən] vi sein o haben to rot

faulenzen ['fau·lɛn·tsn̩] vi to laze around

Faulenzer(in) <-s, -> ['fau·lɛn·tsɐ] m(f) (pej) slacker pej

Faulheit <-> f kein pl laziness

faulig ['fau·lɪç] adj rotten; Geruch foul

Fäulnis <-> ['fɔy·lnɪs] f kein pl decay, rot

Faulpelz m (pej fam) lazybones pej

Faultier nt ZOOL sloth

Fauna <-, Faunen> ['fau·na] f fauna

Faust <-, Fäuste> [faust] f fist ▶WENDUNGEN: **auf eigene ~** on one's own initiative

Fausthandschuh m mitten

Faustregel f rule of thumb

Fax <-, -e> [faks] nt fax

faxen ['faksn̩] vt, vi to fax

Faxen ['faksn̩] pl ▶WENDUNGEN: **lass die ~!** stop clowning around!

Fazit <-s, -s> ['faː·tsɪt] nt result

FCKW <-s, -s> [ɛf·tseː·kaː·'veː] m Abk von **Fluorchlorkohlenwasserstoff** CFC

Februar <-[s], selten -e> ['feː·bru·aːɐ̯] m February; **Anfang/Ende ~** at the beginning/end of February; **Mitte ~** in the middle of February, mid-February; **im ~** in February; **diesen/jeden ~** this/every February; **bis in den ~ [hinein]** well into February; **den ganzen ~ über** throughout February; **am 14. ~** on February 14th; **am Freitag, dem** [o **den**] **14. Februar** on Friday, February [the] 14th; **Hamburg, den**

14. ~ 2005 Hamburg, February 14, 2005; **auf den 14. ~ fallen/legen** to fall on/to schedule for February 14th

fechten <fechtet, focht, gefochten> ['fɛç·tn̩] vi to fence

Fechten <-s> ['fɛç·tn̩] nt kein pl fencing

Feder <-, -n> ['feː·dɐ] f ❶ von Vögeln feather; (Schreibfeder) quill ❷ (aus Metall) spring ❸ (Bett) **raus aus den ~n!** (fam) rise and shine!; **noch in den ~n liegen** (fam) to still be in bed

Federball m kein pl badminton

Federbett nt duvet

Federgewicht nt kein pl SPORT featherweight

federn ['feː·dɐn] vi to be springy

Federung <-, -en> f springing; (von Auto) suspension

Fee <-, -n> [feː] f fairy

Fegefeuer ['feː·gə-] nt purgatory

fegen ['feː·gn̩] vt, vi ❶ (kehren) to sweep ❷ SCHWEIZ (feucht wischen) to wipe

Fehlbetrag m ÖKON deficit

fehlen ['feː·lən] I. vi ❶ (nicht da sein) ■etw fehlt sth is missing; ■jdm fehlt etw sb is missing sth; unentschuldigt ~ to be absent without an excuse ❷ (vermissen) ■jd fehlt jdm sb misses sb ❸ (an etw leiden) **fehlt Ihnen etwas?** is there something wrong [with you]? II. vi impers ❶ **es fehlt etw** sth is missing; ■jdm fehlt es an etw dat sb is lacking sth; **jdm fehlt es an nichts** sb wants for nothing

Fehler <-s, -> ['feː·lɐ] m mistake; (Mangel) defect; **einen ~ machen** to make a mistake; **jds ~ sein** to be sb's fault

Fehlermeldung f COMPUT error message

Fehlgeburt f miscarriage

Fehlgriff m mistake

Fehlkonstruktion f **eine totale ~ sein** to be poorly constructed

fehl|schlagen vi irreg sein to fail

Fehlstart m SPORT false start

Feier <-, -n> ['faiɐ] f celebration; **zur ~ des Tages** in honor of the occasion

Feierabend ['faiɐ·ʔaː·bn̩t] m end of work; **~!** that's it for today!; **schö-**

F

nen ~! have a nice evening!; **hoffentlich ist bald** ~! I hope it's time to go home soon!; ~ **machen** to finish work for the day

feierlich ['fai·ɐ·lɪç] I. *adj* Akt ceremonial; **ein** ~**er Anlass** a formal occasion II. *adv* etw ~ **begehen** to celebrate sth

Feierlichkeiten *pl* celebrations

feiern *vt, vi* to celebrate; **eine Party** ~ to have a party

Feiertag ['fai·ɐ·ta:k] *m* holiday

Feige <-, -n> ['fai·gə] *f* fig

Feigheit <-> *f kein pl* cowardice

Feigling <-s, -e> ['faik·lɪŋ] *m* (pej) coward

Feile <-, -n> ['fai·lə] *f* file

feilen ['fai·lən] *vt, vi* ■**an etw** *dat* ~ to file sth; (fig) to polish sth

feilschen ['fail·ʃn] *vi* (pej) to haggle (**um** + *akk*)

fein [fain] I. *adj* ❶ (nicht grob) fine; (zart) delicate ❷ (vornehm) distinguished; **jd ist sich** *dat* **für etw** *akk* **zu** ~ sth is beneath sb; **sich** ~ **machen** to get dressed up ❸ (sehr gut) exquisite; **vom** F~**sten** of the highest quality ❹ (fam: anständig) decent; (iron) fine ❺ (fam: erfreulich) ■~, **dass** ... it's great that ... ►WENDUNGEN: ~ **raus sein** to be in a nice position II. *adv* ~ **gemahlen** fine-ground; ~ **säuberlich** accurate

Feind(in) <-[e]s, -e> [faint] *m(f)* enemy; **sich** *dat* **jdn zum** ~ **machen** to make an enemy of sb; ■**ein** ~ **einer S.** *gen* an opponent of sth

feindlich *adj* hostile; MIL enemy *attr*

Feindschaft <-, -en> *f kein pl* animosity

feindselig ['faint·ze:·lɪç] *adj* hostile

Feindseligkeit <-> *f kein pl* hostility

feinfühlig ['fain·fy:·lɪç] *adj* sensitive

Feingefühl *nt kein pl* sensitivity

feinkörnig *adj* fine-grained; Foto fine-grain

Feinkostgeschäft *nt* gourmet shop

Feinmechanik *f* precision engineering

Feinschmecker(in) <-s, -> *m(f)* gourmet

Feld <-[e]s, -er> [fɛlt] *nt* field; (auf Spielbrett) square; (Bereich) area; **ein weites** ~ **sein** to be a broad subject ►WENDUNGEN: **das** ~ **räumen** to clear the way; **jdm das** ~ **überlassen** to leave the field open to sb

Feldsalat *m* mâche

Feldwebel(in) <-s, -> ['fɛlt·ve:·bl] *m(f)* sergeant major

Feldweg *m* field path

Feldzug *m* campaign

Felge <-, -n> ['fɛl·gə] *f* rim

Fell <-[e]s, -e> [fɛl] *nt* fur ►WENDUNGEN: **ein dickes** ~ **haben** to be thick-skinned

Felsblock <-blöcke> *m* boulder

Felsen <-s, -> ['fɛl·zn] *m* cliff

felsenfest ['fɛl·zn·fɛst] *adv* ~ **von etw** *dat* **überzeugt sein** to be firmly convinced of sth

felsig ['fɛl·zɪç] *adj* rocky

Felswand *f* rock face

feminin [fe·mi·'ni:n] *adj* feminine

Feminismus <-> [fe·mi·'nɪs·mʊs] *m kein pl* feminism

Feminist(in) <-en, -en> [fe·mi·'nɪst] *m(f)* feminist

feministisch *adj* feminist

Fenchel <-s> ['fɛn·çl] *m kein pl* BOT fennel

Fenster <-s, -> ['fɛn·stɐ] *nt* window

Fensterbank <-bänke> *f* windowsill

Fensterladen *m* shutter

Fensterplatz *m* window seat

Fensterputzer(in) <-s, -> *m(f)* window cleaner

Fensterrahmen *m* window frame

Fensterscheibe *f* window pane

Ferien ['fe:·rɪ·ən] *pl* vacation; **in die** ~ **fahren** to go on vacation; **die großen** ~ summer vacation; ~ **haben** to be on vacation

Ferienhaus *nt* vacation home

Ferienkurs *m* summer school

Ferienlager *nt* vacation camp

Ferienwohnung *f* vacation apartment

Ferienzeit *f* vacation

Ferkel <-s, -> ['fɛr·kl] *nt* ❶ ZOOL piglet

② (*pej fam: unsauberer Mensch*) pig; (*obszöner Mensch*) filthy pig

fern [fɛrn] **I.** *adj* distant **II.** *präp + dat* far [away] from

Fernbedienung *f* remote control

fern|bleiben *vi irreg sein* (*geh*) to stay away

ferner ['fɛr·nɐ] **I.** *adj komp von* **fern: in der ~en Zukunft** in the distant future **II.** *konj* furthermore

Fernfahrer(in) *m(f)* long-distance truck driver

Ferngespräch *nt* long-distance call

ferngesteuert *adj* remote-controlled

Fernglas *nt* [pair of] binoculars

fern|halten *vr irreg* ■ **sich** *akk* **von jdm/etw** to keep away from sb/sth

Fernkurs *m* correspondence course

Fernlicht *nt* AUTO high beams

Fernost ['fɛrn·'ʔɔst] *kein art* **aus/in/ nach ~** from/in/to the Far East

Fernrohr *nt* telescope

Fernsehansager(in) *m(f)* television announcer

Fernsehantenne *f* television antenna

Fernsehen <-s> ['fɛrn·ze:ən] *nt kein art* television; **im ~ kommen** to be on television

fern|sehen ['fɛrn·ze:ən] *vi irreg* to watch television

Fernseher <-s, -> *m* television [set]

Fernsehsender *m* television station

Fernsehsendung *f* television program

Fernsehübertragung *f* television broadcast

Fernsehzeitschrift *f* TV guide

Fernsicht *f* view; **bei guter ~** with good visibility

Fernsteuerung *f* remote control

Fernstudium *nt* correspondence course

Fernverkehr *m* long-distance traffic

Fernweh <-[e]s> *nt kein pl* (*geh*) wanderlust

Ferse <-, -n> ['fɛr·zə] *f* heel ▶WENDUNGEN: **jdm** [**dicht**] **auf den ~n sein** to be [hot] on sb's tail

fertig ['fɛr·tɪç] **I.** *adj* **①** (*abgeschlossen*) finished; **etw ~ haben** to have finished sth; **mit etw** *dat* **~ sein** to be finished

with sth; **mit etw** *dat* **~ werden** to finish sth **②** (*bereit*) ready **③** (*fam: erschöpft*) exhausted **④** (*im Griff haben*) **mit jdm/etw ~ werden** to cope with sb/sth **II.** *adv* **①** (*zu Ende*) **etw ~ bekommen** to complete sth; **etw ~ machen** [*o* **stellen**] to finish sth **②** (*bereit*) **sich** *akk* **~ machen** to get ready [for sth] ▶WENDUNGEN: **auf die Plätze, ~, los!** on your marks, get set, go!

Fertiggericht *nt* instant meal

Fertighaus *nt* prefabricated house

fertig|machen I. *vt, vr s.* **fertig II 1, II 2 II.** *vt* (*fam*) **①** (*zermürben*) ■**etw macht jdn fertig** sth wears out *sep* sb **②** **jdn ~** (*schikanieren*) to wear sb down *sep*; (*sl: zusammenschlagen*) to beat sb up *sep*

fertig|stellen *vt s.* **fertig II 1**

fesch [fɛʃ] *adj* SÜDD, ÖSTERR (*fam: flott*) chic

Fessel <-, -n> ['fɛsl] *f* **①** *meist pl* (*Kette*) shackles *npl* **②** ANAT (*von Mensch*) ankle; (*von Huftier*) pastern

fesseln ['fɛsl̩n] *vt* ■**jdn ~** to tie sb up; (*faszinieren*) to captivate sb

fesselnd *adj* captivating

fest [fɛst] **I.** *adj* firm; (*erstarrt*) solidified; **~e Freundschaft** lasting friendship; **~er Händedruck** firm handshake; **~e Schuhe** sturdy shoes; **~er Termin** fixed date; **~e Zusage** firm promise **II.** *adv* **①** (*kräftig*) firmly; **jdn ~ an sich** *akk* **drücken** to give someone a big hug **②** (*nicht locker*) tightly; **~ anziehen** to screw in tightly; **jdm etw ~ versprechen** to make sb a firm promise **③** (*dauernd*) permanently; **~ angestellt sein** to have a permanent job

Fest <-[e]s, -e> [fɛst] *nt* celebration; **ein ~ geben** to throw a party; **frohes ~!** Merry Christmas/Happy Easter, etc. ▶WENDUNGEN: **man soll die ~e feiern, wie sie fallen** (*prov*) one should make hay while the sun shines *prov*

festangestellt *adj s.* **fest II 3**

Festessen *nt* banquet

fest|fahren *vr irreg* ■**sich** *akk* ~ to get stuck

fest|halten *irreg* I. *vt* to grab (**an** +*dat* by); (*gefangen halten*) to detain II. *vi* ■**an etw** *dat* ~ to adhere to sth III. *vr* ■**sich** *akk* ~ to hold on (**an** +*dat* to)

Festiger <-s, -> *m* setting lotion

Festland ['fɛst·lant] *nt kein pl* mainland

fest|legen I. *vt* to determine; ■~, **dass ...** to stipulate that ...; ■**jdn [auf etw** *akk*] ~ to oblige sb [to do sth] II. *vr* ■**sich** *akk* ~ to commit [oneself] (**auf** +*akk* to)

festlich *adv* festively; ~ **gekleidet sein** to be dressed up

Festlichkeit <-, -en> *f* festivity

fest|liegen *vi irreg* to be determined; **die Termine liegen jetzt fest** the schedules have now been set

fest|nageln *vt* ❶ (*mit Nägeln*) to nail (**an** +*akk* to) ❷ (*fam: festlegen*) ■**jdn** ~ to nail sb down (**auf** +*akk* to)

Festnahme <-, -n> ['fɛst·na:·mə] *f* arrest

fest|nehmen *vt irreg* to take into custody; **Sie sind festgenommen** you're under arrest

Festnetz *nt* TELEK landline; **jdn vom** [*o* **aus dem**] ~ **anrufen** to call sb on the landline

Festplatte *f* COMPUT hard disk

Festplattenlaufwerk *nt* COMPUT hard disk drive

fest|schnallen *vr* ■**sich** *akk* ~ to fasten one's seat belt

fest|schrauben *vt* to screw tight *sep*

fest|sitzen *vi irreg* to be stuck

fest|stehen *vi irreg* to be certain; ■**es steht fest, dass ...** it is certain that ...; **steht das Datum schon fest?** has the date been set yet?

fest|stellen *vt* (*bemerken*) to detect; **zu meinem Erstaunen muss ich ~, dass ...** I am astounded to see that ...

Feststellung *f* remark; (*Beobachtung*) observation; **zu der ~ kommen, dass ...** to come to the conclusion that ...; **die ~ machen, dass ...** to see that ...

Festung <-, -en> ['fɛs·tʊŋ] *f* fortress

fett [fɛt] *adj* fat; (*fetthaltig*) fatty; ~ **gedruckt** in bold [type] *pred*

Fett <-[e]s, -e> [fɛt] *nt* fat; (*zum Schmieren*) grease; ~ **ansetzen** *Mensch* to gain weight; *Tier* to put on fat; **pflanzliches/tierisches** ~ vegetable/animal fat

fettarm *adj* low-fat

Fettfleck, Fettflecken *m* grease mark

fettgedruckt *adj attr s.* **fett**

fettig ['fɛ·tɪç] *adj* greasy

Fettnäpfchen *nt* ►WENDUNGEN: **ins ~ treten** to put one's foot in one's mouth

Fetzen <-s, -> ['fɛtsn̩] *m* ❶ (*Stück*) scrap; **etw in ~ reißen** to tear sth to pieces ❷ *einer Unterhaltung* fragments *pl* ❸ (*sl: billiges Kleid*) rag ►WENDUNGEN: **... dass die ~ fliegen** (*fam*) ... like crazy

feucht [fɔɪçt] *adj* damp; ~**e Hände/ Stirn** clammy hands/forehead; ~**es Klima** humid climate; ~**e Luft** humid air

Feuchtigkeit <-> ['fɔɪç·tɪç·kaɪt] *f kein pl* dampness; *von Luft* humidity; (*Wassergehalt*) moisture

Feuchtigkeitscreme [-kre:m] *f* moisturizing cream

Feuer <-s, -> ['fɔy·ɐ] *nt* ❶ (*Flamme, Brand*) fire; **am** ~ by the fire; ~ **fangen** to catch [on] fire; ~ **machen** to make a fire; **das olympische** ~ the Olympic flame ❷ (*für Zigarette*) **jdm** ~ **geben** to give sb a light; ~ **haben** to have a light ❸ (*Kochstelle*) **etw vom** ~ **nehmen** to take sth off the heat ❹ MIL (*Beschuss*) fire; ~ **frei!** open fire!; **das** ~ **eröffnen/ einstellen** to open/cease fire ►WENDUNGEN: ~ **und Flamme [für etw] sein** (*fam*) to be enthusiastic [about sth]; **mit dem** ~ **spielen** to play with fire

Feueralarm *m* fire alarm

Feuerbestattung *f* cremation

feuerfest *adj* fireproof; ~**es Geschirr** ovenproof dishes

Feuerleiter *f* fire escape

Feuerlöscher *m* fire extinguisher

Feuermelder <-s, -> *m* fire alarm

feuern I. *vi* to fire II. *vt* (*fam*) to fire *fam;* ■**gefeuert werden** to get the ax

feuersicher ['fɔy·ɐ·zɪ·çɐ] *adj* fireproof

Feuerwehr <-, -en> *f* fire department

Feuerwehrauto *nt* fire engine

Feuerwehrmann, -frau <-leute> *m, f* firefighter, fireman *masc,* firewoman *fem*

Feuerwerk *nt* fireworks *npl*

Feuerwerkskörper *m* firework

Feuerzeug *nt* lighter

Feuilleton <-s, -s> [fœ·jə·'tõː] *nt* culture section

Fichte <-, -n> [fɪç·tə] *f* spruce

ficken ['fɪ·kn̩] *vt, vi* (*vulg*) to fuck *vulg*

Fidschiinseln *pl* Fiji Islands *pl*

Fieber <-s, -> ['fiː·bɐ] *nt* fever; **~ haben** to have a temperature

fieberhaft *adj* feverish

Fieberthermometer *nt* [clinical] thermometer

fiebrig ['fiː·brɪç] *adj* feverish

fiel ['fiːl] *imp von* **fallen**

fies [fiːs] *adj* (*fam*) mean

Figur <-, -en> [fi·'guːɐ̯] *f* figure; FILM, LIT character

Filet <-s, -s> [fi·'leː] *nt* fillet

Filetsteak [fi·'leː·steːk] *nt* fillet steak

Filiale <-, -n> [fi·'lɪ̯aː·lə] *f* branch

Filialleiter(in) *m(f)* branch manager

Film <-[e]s, -e> [fɪlm] *m* film; (*Spielfilm a.*) movie; **beim ~ arbeiten** to work in the movie industry

filmen ['fɪl·mən] *vt, vi* to film

Filmkamera *f* movie camera

Filmregisseur(in) *m(f)* movie director

Filmvorschau *f* [movie] preview

Filter <-s, -> ['fɪl·tɐ] *nt o m* filter

Filterkaffee *m* filter coffee

filtern ['fɪl·tɐn] *vt* to filter

Filterpapier *nt* filter paper

Filterzigarette *f* filter cigarette

Filz <-es, -e> [fɪlts] *m* felt

Filzstift *m* felt-tip pen

Finale <-s, -s> [fi·'naː·lə] *nt* final

Finanzamt *nt* ■**das ~** the Department of the Treasury

Finanzen [fi·'nan·tsn̩] *pl* finances *npl;*

jds **~ übersteigen** to be beyond sb's means

finanziell [fi·nan·'tsi̯ɛl] *adj* financial

finanzieren* [fi·nan·'tsiː·rən] *vt* to finance; **etw** [**nicht**] **~ können** to [not] be able to afford sth

Finanzierung <-, -en> *f* financing

Finanzminister(in) *m(f)* Secretary of the Treasury

Finanzministerium *nt* Department of the Treasury, Treasury [Department]

F

finden <fand, gefunden> ['fɪn·dn̩] I. *vt* ❶ to find; **Unterstützung ~** to receive support; **einen Vorwand** [**für etw** *akk*] **~** to find an excuse [for sth]; **Zustimmung** [**bei jdm**] **~** to meet with approval [from sb] ❷ (*meinen*) to think; **ich finde, die Ferien sind zu kurz** I think the vacation is too short; **jdn blöd/nett ~** to think [that] sb is stupid/nice; **es kalt/warm ~** to find it cold/warm ▶WENDUNGEN: **etwas an jdm/ etw ~** to see sth in sb/sth; **nichts an jdm/etw ~** to not think much of sb/sth II. *vi* ❶ (*den Weg finden*) ■**zu jdm/ etw ~** to find one's way to sb/sth; **zu sich** *dat* **selbst ~** to find oneself ❷ (*meinen*) to think; **~ Sie?** [do] you think so?

Finderlohn *m* reward [for the finder]

fing ['fɪŋ] *imp von* **fangen**

Finger <-s, -> ['fɪŋ·ɐ] *m* finger; **~ weg!** hands off!; **der kleine ~** the little finger ▶WENDUNGEN: **etw in die ~ bekommen** (*fam*) to get one's hands on sth; **keinen ~ krumm machen** (*fam*) to not lift a finger; **die ~ von jdm/etw lassen** (*fam*) to keep away from sb/sth; **sich** *dat* **etw aus den ~n saugen** (*fam*) to conjure up *sep* sth; **sich** *dat* **nicht die ~ schmutzig machen** to not get one's hands dirty; **überall seine ~ im Spiel haben** (*fam*) to have a finger in every pie

Fingerabdruck *m* fingerprint

Fingerhut *m* thimble

Fingernagel *m* fingernail; **an den Fingernägeln kauen** to bite one's nails

Fink <-en, -en> [fɪŋk] *m* finch

F

Finne, **Finnin** <-n, -n> ['fɪnə, 'fɪnɪn] *m*, *f* Finn, Finnish man/woman/boy/girl; ∎ ~ **sein** to be Finnish

finnisch ['fɪnɪʃ] *adj* Finnish

Finnland <-s> ['fɪn·lant] *nt* Finland

finster ['fɪns·tɐ] *adj* dark; (*fig*) grim

Firma <-, Firmen> ['fɪr·ma] *f* company

Firmenwagen *m* company car

Firmung <-, -en> *f* confirmation

First <-[e]s, -e> [fɪrst] *m* roof ridge

Fisch <-[e]s, -e> [fɪʃ] *m* ❶ (*Tier*) fish ❷ *kein pl* ASTROL Pisces ▸WENDUNGEN: **weder ~ noch Fleisch sein** to be neither fish nor fowl; **ein großer/kleiner ~** a big fish/small fry

fischen ['fɪʃn] *vi* to fish; ∎ **das F~** fishing

Fischer(in) <-s, -> ['fɪ·ʃɐ] *m(f)* fisher, fisherman *masc*, fisherwoman *fem*

Fischfang *m kein pl* fishing

Fischhändler(in) *m(f)* fishmonger

Fischotter *m* otter

Fischstäbchen *nt* fish stick

Fischzucht *f* fish farming

Fisole <-, -n> [fi·'zoː·lə] *f* ÖSTERR green bean

fit [fɪt] *adj pred* fit; **sich** *akk* ~ **halten** to keep fit

FitnessRR, **Fitneß**ALT <-> ['fɪ·tnɛs] *f kein pl* fitness

FitnesscenterRR <-sɛn·tɐ> *nt* gym

FitnessgerätRR ['fɪt·nɛs-] *nt* fitness equipment

fix [fɪks] *adj* quick ▸WENDUNGEN: ~ **und fertig sein** (*erschöpft*) to be exhausted; (*am Ende*) to be at the end of one's rope; **jdn** ~ **und fertig machen** (*fam*) to wear out sb *sep*

fixieren* [fɪk·'siː·rən] *vt* to stare at

FKK-Strand *m* nude beach

flach [flax] **I.** *adj* flat; (*nicht hoch*) low; (*nicht steil*) gentle **II.** *adv* ~ **abfallen** to slope down gently; ~ **atmen** to take shallow breaths

Flachbildschirm *m* flat screen

Flachdach *nt* flat roof

Fläche <-, -n> ['flɛ·çə] *f* expanse; (*mit Maßangaben*) area

Flachland *nt* lowland

flackern ['flakɐn] *vi* to flicker

Fladenbrot *nt* KOCHK ≈ [thick] pita bread

Flagge <-, -n> ['fla·gə] *f* flag

Flame, **Flamin** *o* **Flämin** <-n, -n> ['flaː·mə, flaː·mɪn, flɛː·mɪn] *m*, *f* Flemish man/woman/boy/girl

Flamingo <-s, -s> [fla·'mɪŋ·go] *m* flamingo

flämisch ['flɛː·mɪʃ] *adj* Flemish

Flamme <-, -n> ['fla·mə] *f* flame; **in ~ aufgehen** to go up in flames; **etw auf großer/kleiner ~ kochen** to cook sth on high/low heat

Flandern <-s> ['flan·dɐn] *nt* Flanders + *sing vb*

Flanke <-, -n> ['flaŋ·kə] *f* ❶ ANAT flank ❷ (*im Fußball*) cross

Flasche <-, -n> ['fla·ʃə] *f* ❶ bottle; **einem Kind die ~ geben** to bottle-feed a child ❷ (*fig*) loser

Flaschenbier *nt* bottled beer

Flaschenöffner *m* bottle opener

flattern ['fla·tɐn] *vi* to flutter

flau [flau] *adj* **ein ~es Gefühl im Magen** a queasy feeling

Flaum <-[e]s> [flaum] *m kein pl* down

flauschig *adj* fleecy

Flaute <-, -n> ['flau·tə] *f* (*Windstille*) calm; ÖKON lull

Flechte <-, -n> ['flɛç·tə] *f* BOT, MED lichen

flechten <flocht, geflochten> ['flɛç·tn] *vt Haare* to braid; *Korb, Kranz* to weave

Fleck <-[e]s, -e> [flɛk] *m* ❶ (*Schmutzfleck*) stain; ~**en machen** to stain ❷ (*dunkle Stelle*) mark; **ein blauer ~** a bruise ❸ (*Stelle*) spot; **sich** *akk* **nicht vom ~ rühren** to not move [an inch]

fleckig ['flɛ·kɪç] *adj* stained; ~**e Haut** blotchy skin

Fledermaus ['fleː·dɐ·maus] *f* bat

Flegel <-s, -> ['fleː·gl] *m* (*pej*) lout

flehen ['fleː·ən] *vi* (*geh*) to beg (**um** +*akk* for)

Fleisch <-[e]s> ['flaiʃ] *nt kein pl* ❶ (*Nahrungsmittel*) meat; ~ **fressend** carnivorous ❷ (*Gewebe*) flesh ▸WENDUNGEN: **jdm in ~ und Blut übergehen** to become sb's second nature; **sich**

dat o akk **ins eigene ~ schneiden** to cut off one's nose to spite one's face

Fleischbrühe *f* bouillon

Fleischer(in) <-s, -> ['flai·ʃɐ] *m(f)* butcher

Fleischklößchen *nt* [small] meatball

Fleischwolf *m* meat grinder

Fleischwurst *f* ≈ pork sausage (*similar to bologna*)

fleißig ['flai·sɪç] *adj* industrious

flexibel [flɛˈkˌsiː·bl̩] *adj* flexible; (*elastisch*) pliable

Flexibilität <-> [flɛk·si·bi·liˈtɛːt] *f* flexibility

flicken ['flɪ·kn̩] *vt* to mend; **einen Fahrradschlauch ~** to patch [up *sep*] a bicycle tube

Flicken <-s, -> ['flɪ·kn̩] *m* patch

Flickzeug *nt kein pl* ❶(*für Fahrräder*) [flat] repair kit ❷(*Nähzeug*) sewing kit

Flieder <-s, -> ['fliː·dɐ] *m* lilac

Fliege <-, -n> ['fliː·gə] *f* ❶(*Insekt*) fly ❷MODE bow tie

fliegen <flog, geflogen> ['fliː·gn̩] *vi sein* to fly

Fliegengewicht *nt kein pl* flyweight

Fliegenklatsche *f* fly swatter

Fliegenpilz *m* fly agaric

Flieger <-s, -> *m* (*fam*) plane

fliehen <floh, geflohen> ['fliː·ən] *vi sein* to flee; **aus dem Gefängnis ~** to escape from prison

Fliese <-, -n> [fliː·zə] *f* tile

Fliesenleger(in) <-s, -> *m(f)* tiler

Fließband <-bänder> *nt* assembly line; **am ~ arbeiten** to work on the production line

fließen <floss, geflossen> ['fliː·sn̩] *vi sein* to flow

fließend *adv* **~ Französisch sprechen** to speak French fluently; **~ warmes und kaltes Wasser** running hot and cold water

flimmern ['flɪ·mɐn] *vi* to flicker

flink [flɪŋk] *adj* quick

Flinte <-, -n> ['flɪn·tə] *f* shotgun ►WENDUNGEN: **die ~ ins Korn werfen** (*fam*) to throw in the towel

flippern ['flɪ·pɐn] *vi* to play pinball

flippig *adj* (*fam*) hip

flirten ['flœɐ·tn̩] *vi* to flirt

Flitterwochen *pl* honeymoon *n sing*

flitzen ['flɪ·tsn̩] *vi sein* to dash

flocht ['flɔxt] *imp von* **flechten**

Flocke <-, -n> ['flɔ·kə] *f* flake

flog ['floːk] *imp von* **fliegen**

Floh <-[e]s, Flöhe> [floː] *m* flea

Flohmarkt *m* flea market

Floskel <-, -n> ['flɔs·kl̩] *f* set phrase

Floß <-es, Flöße> [floːs] *nt* raft

flossᴿᴿ, **floß**ᴬᴸᵀ ['flɔs] *imp von* **fließen**

Flosse <-, -n> ['flɔ·sə] *f* ❶(*Fischflosse*) fin ❷(*Schwimmflosse*) flipper

Flöte <-, -n> ['fløː·tə] *f* ❶MUS pipe; (*Querflöte*) flute; (*Blockflöte*) recorder ❷(*Kelchglas*) flute [glass]

Flötist(in) <-en, -en> [fløˈtɪst] *m(f)* flutist

flott [flɔt] I.*adj* ❶(*zügig*) quick; **aber ein bisschen ~!** (*fam*) make it snappy!; **ein ~es Tempo** [a] high speed ❷(*schick*) smart II.*adv* ❶(*zügig*) fast ❷(*schick*) smartly

Flotte <-, -n> ['flɔ·tə] *f* fleet

flott|machen *vt* **etw [wieder] ~** to get sth back in working order; **ein Auto ~** to get a car back on the road

Fluch <-[e]s, Flüche> [fluːx] *m* curse

fluchen ['fluː·xn̩] *vi* to curse (**auf/über** +*akk* at)

Flucht <-, -en> [flʊxt] *f* escape; **auf der ~ sein** to be on the run; **die ~ ergreifen** (*geh*) to take flight

fluchtartig *adv* hastily

flüchten ['flʏç·tn̩] I.*vi sein* to flee; (*entkommen*) to escape II.*vr haben* ■**sich** *akk* **irgendwohin ~** to seek refuge somewhere; ■**sich** *akk* **in etw** *akk* ~ (*fig*) to take refuge in sth; **sich** *akk* **in Ausreden ~** to resort to excuses

flüchtig ['flʏç·tɪç] I.*adj* ❶(*geflüchtet*) fugitive *attr*; ■~ **sein** to be a fugitive ❷(*kurz*) brief ❸(*oberflächlich*) cursory; **eine ~e Bekanntschaft** a passing acquaintance II.*adv* ❶(*kurz*) briefly ❷(*oberflächlich*) cursorily; **jdn ~ kennen** to have met sb briefly

Flüchtigkeitsfehler *m* careless mistake

F

Flüchtling <-s, -> ['flʏçt·lɪŋ] *m* refugee

Flug <-[e]s, Flüge> [fluːk] *m* flight
►WENDUNGEN: **wie im** ~|e] in a flash

Flugbegleiter(in) *m(f)* flight attendant, steward *masc,* stewardess *fem*

Flugblatt *nt* flyer

Flügel <-s, -> ['flyː·gl̩] *m* wing; MUS grand piano

Flügeltür *f* double door

Fluggast *m* passenger

Fluggeschwindigkeit *f* (*von Flugzeug*) flying speed; (*von Rakete, Geschoss*) velocity; (*von Vögeln*) speed of flight

Fluggesellschaft *f* airline

Flughafen *m* airport

Flughöhe *f* altitude

Fluglotse, -lotsin *m, f* air traffic controller

Flugplatz *m* airfield

Flugverkehr *m* air traffic

Flugzeit *f* flight time

Flugzeug <-[e]s, -e> *nt* [air]plane; **mit dem** ~ by [air]plane

Flugzeugbesatzung *f* flight crew

Flugzeughalle *f* hangar

Flugzeugträger *m* aircraft carrier

flunkern ['flʊŋ·kɐn] *vi* (*fam*) to fib

Fluor <-s> ['fluː·oːɐ̯] *nt kein pl* fluorine

Flur <-[e]s, -e> [fluːɐ̯] *m* hall[way]

Fluss^RR <-es, Flüsse>, **Fluß**^ALT <-sses, Flüsse> [flʊs] *m* river; **am** ~ next to the river

flussab^RR [flʊs·ˈʔap], **flussabwärts**^RR [flʊs·ˈʔap·vɛrts] *adv* downriver

flussaufwärts^RR [flʊs·ˈʔauf·vɛrts] *adv* upriver

Flussbett^RR *nt* riverbed

flüssig ['flʏ·sɪç] I. *adj* liquid II. *adv* ~ **lesen** to read effortlessly; ~ **sprechen** to speak fluently

Flüssigkeit <-, -en> *f* liquid

Flusskrebs^RR *m* crayfish

Flusspferd^RR *nt* hippopotamus

Flussufer^RR *nt* river bank

flüstern ['flʏs·tɐn] *vt, vi* to whisper

Flut <-, -en> [fluːt] *f* ❶ GEOL high tide; **bei** ~ at high tide; **die** ~ **geht zurück** the tide is going out; **es ist** ~ the tide's in; **die** ~ **kommt** the tide is coming in ❷ (*große Menge*) ■**eine** ~ **von etw** *dat* a flood of sth

fluten ['fluː·tn̩] *vt, vi* to flood

Fluthilfe *f* flood relief

Flutlicht *nt kein pl* floodlight

Flutwelle *f* tidal wave

focht ['fɔxt] *imp von* **fechten**

Fohlen <-s, -> ['foː·lən] *nt* foal

Föhn^RR <-[e]s, -e> [føːn] *m* ❶ (*Wind*) foehn [wind] ❷ (*Haartrockner*) hair dryer

föhnen^RR *vt* to blow-dry

Folge <-, -n> ['fɔl·gə] *f* ❶ (*Auswirkung*) consequence; **etw zur** ~ **haben** to result in sth; **als** ~ **von etw** *dat* as a consequence of sth ❷ (*Abfolge*) series; *von Bildern, Tönen a.* sequence; **in rascher** ~ in quick succession ❸ *einer TV-Serie* episode

folgen ['fɔl·gn̩] *vi sein* ■**jdm** ~ to follow sb; ■**auf etw** *akk* ~ to come after sth; ■**aus etw** *dat* ~ to follow from sth; ■**es folgt, dass ...** it follows that ...; **wie folgt** as follows; **jdm/etw** ~ **können** to be able to follow sb/sth; **einem Vorschlag** ~ to act on a suggestion

folgend ['fɔl·gnt] *adj* following; ■**F**~**es** the following; ■**im F**~**en** in the following

folgendermaßen ['fɔl·gn̩·dɐ·ˈmaː·sn̩] *adv* as follows

folgenschwer *adj* serious; **eine** ~**e Entscheidung** a momentous decision

folgerichtig *adj* logical

folgern ['fɔl·gɐn] *vt* to conclude (**aus** +*dat* from)

folglich ['fɔlk·lɪç] *adv* therefore

folgsam ['fɔlk·zaːm] *adj* obedient

Folie <-, -n> ['foː·liə] *f* ❶ (*Plastikfolie*) [plastic] film; KOCHK plastic wrap; (*Metallfolie*) foil ❷ (*Projektorfolie*) slide

Folter <-, -n> ['fɔl·te] *f* torture ►WENDUNGEN: **jdn auf die** ~ **spannen** to keep sb on tenterhooks

foltern ['fɔl·ten] *vt* to torture

Folterung <-, -en> *f* torture

Fonds <-, -> [fõː] *m* FIN fund

fönen^ALT ['føː·nən] *vt s.* **föhnen**

Fontäne <-, -n> [fɔnˈtɛː·nə] f fountain

Förderband <-bänder> nt conveyor belt

förderlich adj useful

fordern ['fœr·dɐn] vt ① (verlangen) to demand ② (erfordern) to require ③ (Leistung abverlangen) ■jdn ~ to make demands on sb

fördern ['fœr·dɐn] vt ① (unterstützen) to support; ■jdn ~ Sponsor to sponsor; **die Verdauung ~** to aid digestion ② (steigern) to promote; **den Umsatz ~** to boost sales ③ (abbauen) to mine for; **Erdöl** to drill for

Forderung <-, -en> f demand; ÖKON debt claim; **jds ~en erfüllen** to meet sb's demands; **~en [an jdn] stellen** to make demands [on sb]

Forelle <-, -n> [foˈrɛ·lə] f trout

Form <-, -en> [fɔrm] f ① (äußere Gestalt) shape; **~ annehmen** to take shape; **in ~ bleiben** to stay in shape; **nicht in ~ sein** to be out of shape; **seine ~ verlieren** to lose shape ② (Art und Weise) form; **in ~ von etw** dat in the form of sth; **in mündlicher/ schriftlicher ~** verbally/in writing; **die ~ wahren** to remain polite ③ (Gussform) mold

formal [fɔrˈmaːl] adj formal

Formalität <-, -en> [fɔr·ma·li·ˈtɛt] f formality

Format <-[e]s, -e> [fɔrˈmaːt] nt format ▶WENDUNGEN: **[kein] ~ haben** to have [no] class

formatieren* [fɔr·ma·ˈtiː·rən] vt to format

Formatierung f formatting

formbar adj malleable

Formel <-, -n> ['fɔrml̩] f ① CHEM, MATH formula ② in Brief, Eid wording

formell [fɔrˈmɛl] adj official

förmlich ['fœrm·lɪç] I. adj Bitte, Entschuldigung formal II. adv ① (unpersönlich) formally ② (geradezu) really

Förmlichkeit <-, -en> f kein pl formality

formlos adj ~**er Antrag** informal application

Formular <-s, -e> [fɔr·mu·ˈlaːɐ̯] nt form

formulieren* [fɔr·mu·ˈliː·rən] vt to formulate; **... wenn ich es mal so ~ darf** ... if I might put it that way

forsch [fɔrʃ] adj bold

forschen ['fɔr·ʃn̩] vi to research; ■**nach jdm/etw ~** to search for sb/sth

Forscher(in) <-s, -> m(f) researcher; (Forschungsreisender) explorer

Forschung <-, -en> f research; **~ und Lehre** research and teaching

Forst <-[e]s, -e[n]> [fɔrst] m [commercial] forest

Forstamt nt Forest Service

Förster(in) <-s, -> ['fœr·stɐ] m(f) forester

Forstwirtschaft f kein pl forestry

fort [fɔrt] adv ① (weg) away; **nur ~ von hier!** let's get out of here ② (weiter) **und so ~** and so on; **in einem ~** constantly

fort|bewegen* vt, vr ■[sich akk] ~ to move

Fortbewegung f kein pl movement

Fortbewegungsmittel nt means of locomotion

fort|bilden vr ■sich akk ~ to further one's training

Fortbildung f kein pl supplementary training

fort|bringen ['fɔrt·brɪŋən] vt irreg to take away sep

fort|dauern vi to continue

fort|fahren vi sein ① (wegfahren) to drive [away/off] ② (weitermachen) to continue

fort|führen vt ① (wegführen) to lead away ② (fortsetzen) to continue

fort|gehen vi sein to go away

fortgeschritten adj advanced; **im ~en Alter** at an advanced age

fortgesetzt adj constant

fort|jagen vt to chase away

fort|laufen vi irreg sein to run away; **uns ist unsere Katze fortgelaufen** our cat has disappeared

fortlaufend adj consecutive

fort|pflanzen vr ■sich akk ~ to reproduce

F

F

Fortpflanzung f kein pl reproduction

fort|schaffen vt to get rid of

fort|schicken vt to send away

Fortschritt ['fɔrt·ʃrɪt] m progress; [gute] ~ e machen to make progress

fortschrittlich adj progressive

fort|setzen vt, vi to continue

Fortsetzung <-, -en> ['fɔrt·zɛ·tsʊŋ] f eines Buches, Films sequel; einer TV-Serie, eines Hörspiels episode; „~ folgt" "to be continued"

fortwährend ['fɔrt·vɛː·rənt] adj attr constant

Fossil <-s, -ien> [fɔ·'siːl] nt fossil

Foto <-s, -s> ['foː·to] nt photo, picture; ein ~ |von jdm/etw| machen to take a photo |of sb/sth|

Fotoapparat m camera

Fotograf(in) <-en, -en> [fo·to·'graːf] m(f) photographer

Fotografie <-, -n> [fo·to·gra·'fiː] f photography

fotografieren* [fo·to·gra·'fiː·rən] I. vt ■ jdn/etw ~ to take a picture II. vi to take pictures

Fotokopie [fo·to·ko·'piː] f photocopy

fotokopieren* [fo·to·ko·'piː·rən] vt to photocopy

Fötus <-[ses], Föten> ['føː·tʊs] m fetus

foulen ['fau·lən] vt, vi to foul

Fracht <-, -en> ['fraxt] f freight

Frachter <-s, -> ['frax·tɐ] m freighter

Frachtgut nt cargo

Frachtschiff nt cargo boat; (groß) cargo ship

Frack <-[e]s, Fräcke> [frak] m tails npl; ■im ~ in tails; einen ~ tragen to wear tails

Frage <-, -n> ['fraː·gə] f question; ~ en aufwerfen to raise questions; eine ~ zu etw dat haben to have a question about sth; keine ~ no problem; in ~ kommen to be worthy of consideration; nicht in ~ kommen to be out of the question; ohne ~ without |a| doubt; jdm eine ~ stellen to ask sb a question; eine strittige ~ a controversial issue; ungelöste ~ en unresolved issues

Fragebogen m questionnaire

fragen ['fraː·gŋ] I. vi to ask; man wird ja wohl noch ~ dürfen I was only asking; ■nach jdm ~ to ask for sb; nach der Uhrzeit/dem Weg ~ to ask for the time/for directions; nach jds Gesundheit ~ to inquire about sb's health; ohne zu ~ without asking questions II. vr ■sich akk ~, ob/wann/wie ... to wonder whether/when/how ...; ■es fragt sich, ob ... it is doubtful whether ... III. vt ■|jdn| etw ~ to ask |sb| sth

Fragesatz m LING interrogative clause

Fragezeichen nt question mark

fraglich ['fraː·k·lɪç] adj ❶ (fragwürdig) suspect; eine ~ e Angelegenheit a suspicious matter ❷ (unsicher) doubtful; ■es ist ~, ob ... it's doubtful whether ... ❸ attr (betreffend) in question pred; zur ~ en Zeit at the time in question

fragwürdig ['fraːk·vʏr·dɪç] adj dubious

Fraktion <-, -en> [frak·'tsi̯oːn] f faction

Fraktionsvorsitzende(r) f(m) dekl wie adj chairman of a political party

frankieren* [fraŋ·'kiː·rən] vt to put postage on

Frankreich <-s> ['fraŋk·raiç] nt France; s. a. **Deutschland**

Franse <-, -n> ['fran·zə] f fringe

Franzose <-n, -n> [fran·'tsoː·zə] m adjustable wrench

Franzose, Französin <-n, -n> [fran·'tsoː·zə, fran·'tsøː·zɪn] m, f Frenchman masc, Frenchwoman fem; ~ sein to be French; ■die ~ n the French; s. a. **Deutsche(r)**

französisch [fran·'tsøː·zɪʃ] adj French; ~ es Bett double bed; s. a. **deutsch**

Französisch [fran·'tsøː·zɪʃ] nt dekl wie adj French; auf ~ in French; s. a. **Deutsch**

Fraß <-es, selten -e> [fraːs] m (pej fam: schlechtes Essen) slop

fraß ['fraːs] imp von **fressen**

Fratze <-, -n> ['fra·tsə] f grotesque face; (Grimasse) grimace

Frau <-, -en> [frau] f woman; (Ehefrau) wife; (Anrede) Mrs., Ms.; ~ Doktor Doctor; gnädige ~ (geh) my dear lady

Frauen**arzt**, **-ärztin** *m, f* gynecologist

Frauen**bewegung** *f kein pl* women's rights movement

Frauen**haus** *nt* women's shelter

Fräulein <-s, -> ['frɔy·laɪn] *nt* (*hum veraltend*) young [unmarried] woman; (*Anrede*) Miss

frech [frɛç] *adj* ❶ (*dreist*) brazen; ~ **sein** to be rude; *Kind* to backtalk ❷ (*kess*) daring; ~**e Frisur** sassy hairstyle

Frechdachs *m* (*fam*) little rascal

Frechheit <-, -en> *f* ❶ *kein pl* (*Dreistigkeit*) impudence; **die ~ haben, etw zu tun** to have the nerve to do sth ❷ (*Äußerung*) rude remark; (*Handlung*) insolent behavior

frei [fraɪ] **I.** *adj* ❶ (*nicht gefangen, unabhängig*) free; ~**e Meinungsäußerung** freedom of speech; ~**er Mitarbeiter/ ~e Mitarbeiterin** freelance[r]; **aus ~en Stücken** of one's own free will ❷ (*freie Zeit*) **er hat heute ~** he's off today; ~ **haben/nehmen** to have/take time off; **eine Woche ~ haben** to have a week off ❸ (*verfügbar*) available; ■ **sich** *akk* **[für jdn/etw] ~ machen** to make oneself available [for sb/sth] ❹ (*nicht besetzt*) free; *Stuhl, Zimmer* vacant; **ist dieser Platz ~?** is this seat taken?; ~**e Stelle** vacancy; **eine Zeile ~ lassen** to skip a line ❺ (*kostenlos*) free; „**Eintritt ~**" "admission free"; „**Lieferung ~ Haus**" "free [home] delivery" ❻ (*ohne etw*) ■ ~ **von etw** *dat* **sein** to be free of sth; ~**e Rede** impromptu speech ❼ (*unbekleidet*) bare; **sich** *akk* ~ **machen** to get undressed ❽ (*ungefähr*) ~ **nach ...** roughly quoting... **II.** *adv* freely; **er läuft immer noch ~ herum!** he's still on the loose!; ~ **atmen** to breathe easy; **sich** *akk* ~ **bewegen können** to be able to move [around] freely; ~ **erfunden** to be completely made up; ~ **laufend** *Tiere* free-range; ~ **lebend** living in the wild; ~ **sprechen** to speak off the cuff

Freibad *nt* outdoor swimming pool

freiberuflich *adj* freelance

Freibetrag *m* allowance

Freie(r) *f(m) dekl wie adj* freeman

freigeben *vt irreg* (*Urlaub geben*) to give time off

freihalten *vt irreg Ausfahrt* to keep clear; **einen Platz für jdn** ~ to save a seat for sb

Freihandelszone *f* free trade zone

freihändig ['fraɪ·hɛn·dɪç] *adv* ~ **zeichnen** to draw freehand; ~ **Rad fahren** to ride a bike with no hands

Freiheit <-, -en> ['fraɪ·haɪt] *f* ❶ *kein pl* (*das Nichtgefangensein*) freedom; **in ~ sein** to have escaped ❷ (*[Vor]recht*) liberty; **sich** *dat* **die ~ nehmen, etw zu tun** to take the liberty of doing sth; **dichterische ~** poetic license

Freiheitsstrafe *f* prison sentence

Freikarte *f* free ticket

Freikörperkultur *f kein pl* nudism

freilassen *vt irreg* to free

freilegen *vt* to uncover

Freilichtbühne *f* open-air theater

freimachen **I.** *vt* (*frankieren*) to stamp **II.** *vi* (*fam: nicht arbeiten*) to take time off

Freimaurer ['fraɪ·mau·rɐ] *m* Freemason

freimütig ['fraɪ·my:·tɪç] *adj* frank

freischaffend *adj attr* freelance

freisprechen *vt irreg* JUR to acquit

Freispruch *m* acquittal; **auf ~ plädieren** to plead for an acquittal

Freistaat *m* free state

freistehen *vi irreg* ■ **jdm steht es frei, etw zu tun** sb is free to do sth

Freistoß *m* free kick

Freitag <-[e]s, -e> ['fraɪ·taːk] *m* Friday; *s. a.* **Dienstag**

freiwillig ['fraɪ·vɪ·lɪç] *adv* voluntarily; **sich** *akk* ~ **versichern** to take out a voluntary insurance policy

Freiwillige(r) ['fraɪ·vɪ·lɪ·gə, 'fraɪ·vɪ·lɪ·gɐ] *f(m) dekl wie adj* volunteer

Freizeichen *nt* dial tone

Freizeit *f* free time

Freizeitkleidung *f* leisurewear

Freizeitpark *m* amusement park

freizügig *adj* ~**es Kleid** revealing dress

fremd [frɛmt] *adj* **ich bin hier ~** I'm not from around here; ~**es Eigentum**

F

F

somebody else's property; **~e Länder/ Sitten** foreign countries/customs

Fremde(r) [ˈfrɛm·də, -ee] *f(m) dekl wie adj* stranger; (*Ausländer*) foreigner

Fremdenführer(in) *m(f)* [tour] guide

Fremdenlegion *f kein pl* [French] Foreign Legion

Fremdenverkehr *m* tourism

Fremdkörper *m* MED foreign body

Fremdsprache *f* foreign language

fremdsprachlich *adj* foreign-language *attr*

Fremdwort *nt* borrowed word

Frequenz [fre·ˈkvɛnts] *f* frequency

Fresko <-s, Fresken> [ˈfrɛs·ko] *nt* fresco

Fressalien [frɛ·ˈsaː·li·ən] *pl* (*fam*) grub

Fresse <-, -n> [ˈfrɛsə] *f* (*derb*) (*Mund*) trap; (*Gesicht*) mug ▶WENDUNGEN: **die ~ halten** to shut up, to shut one's face; **jdm die ~ polieren** to smash sb's face in

fressen <fraß, gefressen> [ˈfrɛ·sn̩] I. *vi* ❶ (*von Tieren*) to eat ❷ (*pej derb: von Menschen*) to gobble ❸ (*fig: langsam zerstören*) to eat away (**an** +*dat* at) II. *vt* ❶ *Tiere* to eat; (*sich ernähren*) to feed on; **etw leer ~** to lick sth clean ❷ (*fig: verbrauchen*) **Energie ~** to gobble up *sep* energy ▶WENDUNGEN: **jdn zum F~ gernhaben** (*fam*) sb is good enough to eat

Frettchen <-s, -> [ˈfrɛt·çən] *nt* ferret

Freude <-, -n> [ˈfrɔy·də] *f* joy, delight; **was für eine ~, dich wiederzusehen!** what a pleasure to see you again!; **~ an etw** *dat* **haben** to get pleasure from sth; **jdm eine ~ machen** to make sb happy; **etw macht jdm ~** sb enjoys sth; **zu unserer großen ~** to our great delight

Freudengeschrei *nt* cries of joy

freudestrahlend *adv* joyfully

freudig [ˈfrɔy·dɪç] I. *adj* joyful; **~es Ereignis** happy event; **~e Nachricht/ Überraschung** joyful news/surprise II. *adv* with joy; **~ überrascht** pleasantly surprised

freudlos [ˈfrɔyt·loːs] *adj* cheerless

freuen [ˈfrɔy·ən] I. *vr* ■**sich** *akk* **~** to be happy (**über** +*akk* about); ■**sich** *akk* **auf etw** *akk* **~** to look forward to sth; ■**sich** *akk* **für jdn ~** to be happy for sb; ■**sich** *akk* **mit jdm ~** to share sb's happiness II. *vt impers* ■**es freut mich, dass ...** I'm pleased that ...

Freund(in) <-[e]s, -e> [ˈfrɔynt, ˈfrɔyn·dɪn] *m(f)* friend; (*Anhänger*) lover; (*intimer Bekannter*) boyfriend; (*intime Bekannte*) girlfriend; **jdn zum ~ haben** to be going [out] with sb

freundlich [ˈfrɔynt·lɪç] I. *adj* friendly; *Person a.* kind; *Farben* cheerful; **das ist sehr ~ von Ihnen** that's very kind of you; **bitte recht ~!** smile please!; **eine ~e Einstellung** a friendly attitude II. *adv* in a friendly way, kindly

Freundlichkeit <-, -en> *f kein pl* friendliness, kindness

Freundschaft <-, -en> *f kein pl* friendship; **~ schließen** to make friends

freundschaftlich I. *adj* **~e Gefühle** feelings of friendship II. *adv* **jdm ~ auf die Schulter klopfen** to give sb a friendly slap on the back; **jdm ~ gesinnt sein** to be well-disposed toward sb

Frieden <-s, -> [ˈfriː·dn̩] *m* peace; **ich traue dem ~ nicht** there's something fishy going on; **im ~** in peacetime; **der häusliche ~** domestic harmony; **jdn in ~ lassen** to leave sb in peace; **~ schließen** to make peace; **~ stiften** to bring about peace

Friedensbewegung *f* peace movement

Friedenseinsatz *m* MIL peacekeeping troops *pl*

Friedensrichter(in) *m(f)* justice of the peace

Friedensverhandlungen *pl* peace negotiations

Friedensvertrag *m* peace treaty

friedfertig *adj* peaceable

Friedhof *m* graveyard; (*in Städten*) cemetery

friedlich [ˈfriːt·lɪç] *adj* peaceful; *Tier* placid

frieren <fror, gefroren> [ˈfriː·rən] I. *vi*

❶ *haben* (*sich kalt fühlen*) ■**jd friert** sb is freezing **❷** *sein* (*gefrieren*) to freeze **II.** *vi impers* haben ■**es friert** it's freezing

Frikadelle <-, -n> [fri·ka·'dɛ·lə] *f* hamburger

frisch [frɪʃ] **I.** *adj* fresh; *Farbe* wet; *Wind a.* cool; **sich** *akk* ~ **machen** to freshen up; ~ **und munter sein** (*fam*) to be [as] fresh as a daisy **II.** *adv* freshly; **die Betten ~ beziehen** to change the sheets; ~ **gebacken** freshly baked; ~ **gestrichen** newly painted

Frischhaltefolie *f* plastic wrap

Frischkäse *m* cream cheese

Friseur <-s, -e> [fri·'zø:ɐ̯] *m* hairdresser's; (*Herrensalon*) barbershop; **zum ~ gehen** to go to the hairdresser's/barbershop

Friseur(in) <-s, -e> [fri·'zø:ɐ̯] *m(f)*, **Friseuse** <-, -n> [fri·'zø:·zə] *f* hairdresser; (*Herrenfriseur*) barber

frisieren* [fri·'zi:·rən] *vt* ■**jdn ~** to do sb's hair

Frisiersalon *m* hair stylist['s]; (*für Damen*) hairdresser's; (*für Herren*) barbershop

Frisör <-s, -e> [fri·'zø:ɐ̯] *m*, **Frisöse** <-, -n> [fri·'zø:·zə] *f s.* **Friseur(in)**

Frist <-, -en> [frɪst] *f* period; (*Aufschub*) respite; (*bei Zahlung*) extension; **festgesetzte ~** fixed time; **gesetzliche ~** statutory period; **innerhalb einer ~ von zwei Wochen** within two week deadline

fristlos *adv* without notice; **jdn ~ entlassen** to fire sb on the spot

Frisur <-, -en> [fri·'zu:ɐ̯] *f* hairstyle

frittieren*ᴿᴿ, **fritieren*ᴬᴸᵀ** [frɪ·'ti:·rən] *vt* to [deep-]fry

froh [fro:] *adj* happy; ■~ **sein** to be pleased (*über* +*akk* with/about); ~**e Feiertage!** have a nice holiday!; ~**es Ostern/Weihnachten!** Happy Easter/Merry Christmas!; **eine ~e Botschaft** good news; **die F~e Botschaft** ʀᴇʟ the Gospel; ~ **gelaunt** cheerful

fröhlich ['frø:·lɪç] *adj* cheerful

Fröhlichkeit <-> *f kein pl* cheerfulness

fromm <frömmer, frömmste> [frɔm] *adj* devout

Front <-, -en> [frɔnt] *f* face, front; **in vorderster ~ stehen** to be on the front lines ▶ᴡᴇɴᴅᴜɴɢᴇɴ: **klare ~en schaffen** to clarify one's position

frontal [frɔn·'ta:l] **I.** *adj attr* frontal; ~ **er Zusammenstoß** head-on collision **II.** *adv* frontally; ~ **zusammenstoßen** to collide head-on

Frontscheibe *f* ᴀᴜᴛᴏ windshield

fror ['fro:ɐ̯] *imp von* **frieren**

Frosch <-[e]s, Frösche> [frɔʃ] *m* frog ▶ᴡᴇɴᴅᴜɴɢᴇɴ: **einen ~ im Hals haben** (*fam*) to have a frog in one's throat

Froschschenkel *m* frog's leg

Frost <-[e]s, Fröste> [frɔst] *m* frost; ~ **abbekommen** to get frostbitten

frösteln ['frœs·tln] *vi* to shiver

frostig ['frɔs·tɪç] *adj* frosty

Frostschutzmittel *nt* antifreeze

Frottee <-s, -s> [frɔ·'te:] *nt o m* terrycloth

frotzeln ['frɔ·tsln] *vi* (*fam*) to tease

Frucht <-, Früchte> [frʊxt] *f* fruit; **kandierte Früchte** candied fruit; **Früchte tragen** to bear fruit

fruchtbar ['frʊxt·ba:ɐ̯] *adj* fertile

Fruchtbarkeit <-> *f kein pl* fertility

fruchten ['frʊx·tn] *vi* ■**nichts/wenig ~** to be of no/little use

Fruchtfleisch *nt* [fruit] pulp

fruchtlos *adj* (*fig*) fruitless

Fruchtsaft *m* fruit juice

Fruchtwasser *nt* ᴍᴇᴅ amniotic fluid

Fruchtzucker *m* fructose

früh [fry:] **I.** *adj* early; ~ **am Morgen** early in the morning; **der ~e Goethe** the young Goethe; **ein ~ er Picasso** an early Picasso **II.** *adv* early; **Montag ~** Monday morning; ~ **genug** early enough; **von ~ bis spät** from morning until night

Frühaufsteher(in) <-s, -> *m(f)* early riser

Frühe <-> ['fry:·ə] *f kein pl* **in aller ~** at the crack of dawn; **in der ~** early in the morning

früher ['fry:·ɐ̯] **I.** *adj* **❶** (*vergangen*) earlier; **in ~en Zeiten** in the past ② (*ehemalig*) former; *Adresse* previous; **~e Freundin** ex[-girlfriend] II. *adv* ① (*eher*) earlier; **~ geht's nicht** it can't be done any earlier; **~ oder später** sooner or later ② (*ehemals*) **ich habe ihn ~ [mal] gekannt** I used to know him; **~ war das alles anders** things were different in the [good] old days; **von ~** from the past

Früherkennung *f* early diagnosis

frühestens *adv* at the earliest

Frühgeburt *f* premature birth; (*Baby*) premature baby

Frühjahr ['fryːˌjaːɐ̯] *nt* spring

Frühjahrsmüdigkeit *f* springtime lethargy

Frühling <-s, -e> ['fryːlɪŋ] *m* spring[time]; **es wird ~** spring is coming

Frühlingsrolle *f* spring roll

frühmorgens [fryːˈmɔrɡn̩s] *adv* early in the morning

Frühpensionierung *f* early retirement

frühreif *adj* precocious

Frühschicht *f* morning shift; **~ haben** to be on the morning shift

Frühstück <-s, -e> ['fryːˌʃtʏk] *nt* breakfast; **zum ~** for breakfast; **zweites ~** midmorning snack

frühstücken ['fryːˌʃtʏkŋ̍] *vt, vi* ▪ **[etw] ~** to have [sth for] breakfast

frühzeitig ['fryːˌtsaɪtɪç] *adj, adv* early; **möglichst ~** as soon as possible

Frust <-[e]s> [frʊst] *m kein pl* (*fam*) frustration; **einen ~ haben** to be frustrated

Frustration <-, -en> [frʊstraˈtsi̯oːn] *f* frustration

frustrieren* [frʊsˈtriːrən] *vt* (*fam*) ▪ **jdn frustriert etw** sth is frustrating sb

Fuchs, Füchsin <-es, Füchse> [fʊks, ˈfʏkˌsɪn] *m, f* fox; (*weiblich*) vixen

Fuchsbau *m* [fox's] den

Fuchsschwanz *m* ① ZOOL [fox's] tail ② (*Säge*) [straight back] hand saw

fuchsteufelswild [fʊksˈtɔɪˌfl̩sˈvɪlt] *adj* (*fam*) mad as hell

Fuchtel <-, -n> ['fʊxtl̩] *f* (*fam*) **unter**

jds ~ stehen to be [well] under sb's control

Fuge <-, -n> ['fuːɡə] *f* joint; **aus den ~n geraten** (*fig*) to be turned upside down

fügen ['fyːɡn̩] *vr* ▪ **sich** *akk* **~** to toe the line; ▪ **sich** *akk* **in etw** *akk* **~** to submit to sth; ▪ **sich** *akk* **jdm ~** to bow to sb; **sich** *akk* **den Anordnungen ~** to obey instructions

Fügung <-, -en> *f* stroke of fate; **eine ~ des Schicksals** an act of fate; **eine glückliche ~** a stroke of luck; **eine göttliche ~** divine providence

fühlbar *adj* noticeable

fühlen ['fyːlən] I. *vt, vi* to feel II. *vr* **wie ~ Sie sich?** how do you feel?; **sich** *akk* **besser ~** to feel better

fuhr ['fuːɐ̯] *imp von* **fahren**

Fuhre <-, -n> ['fuːrə] *f* [cart]load

führen ['fyːrən] I. *vt* ① (*leiten*) **ein Geschäft ~** to run a business; **eine Armee ~** to command an army; ▪ **jdn ~** ② ▪ **etw mit sich** *dat* **~** to carry sth ③ (*geleiten*) **was führt Sie zu mir?** what brings you to me?; **jdn auf Abwege ~** to lead sb astray; **jdn durch ein Museum ~** to show sb around a museum ④ ÖKON to stock II. *vi* ① SPORT **mit drei Punkten ~** to lead by three points ② (*verlaufen*) *Weg* to lead; *Kabel* to run ③ (*als Ergebnis haben*) ▪ **zu etw** *dat* **~** to lead to sth

führend *adj* leading *attr*

Führer <-s, -> ['fyːrɐ] *m* (*Buch*) guide[book]

Führer(in) <-s, -> ['fyːrɐ] *m(f)* leader; (*Fremdenführer*) [tour] guide; ▪ **der ~** HIST (*Hitler*) the Führer

Führerschein *m* driver's license; **den ~ machen** (*Unterricht nehmen*) to learn to drive; (*Prüfung machen*) to take one's driving test

Führerscheinentzug *m* driver's license revocation

Fuhrpark *m* fleet [of vehicles]

Führung <-, -en> *f* ① (*Besichtigung*) guided tour ② *kein pl* MIL command ③ *kein pl* (*Vorsprung*) **in ~ liegen/**

gehen to be in/take the lead ◉ *kein pl* (*Betragen*) **bei guter ~** for good conduct

Führungskraft *f* executive [officer]

Führungszeugnis *nt* **polizeiliches ~** [criminal] background check

Fuhrunternehmen [fuːɐ̯-] *nt* trucking company

Fülle <-> ['fʏ·lə] *f kein pl* ▶WENDUNGEN: **in Hülle und ~** in abundance

füllen ['fʏ·lən] **I.** *vt* to fill; *Gans, Ente, etc.* to stuff; ■ **etw in etw** *akk* **~** to put sth into sth; **etw in Flaschen ~** to bottle sth **II.** *vr* ■ **sich** *akk* **~** to fill [up]

Füller <-s, -> ['fʏ·lɐ] *m* fountain pen; (*mit Patrone*) cartridge pen

Füllung <-, -en> *f* stuffing

fummeln ['fʊ·mln] *vi* (*fam*) ◉ (*hantieren*) to fumble [around] ◉ (*sexuell*) to pet

fundamental [fʊn·da·mɛn·'taːl] *adj* fundamental

Fundbüro *nt* lost-and-found [office]

Fundsachen *pl* lost and found items

fünf [fʏnf] *adj* five; *s. a.* **acht**[1]

Fünf <-, -en> [fʏnf] *f* ◉ (*Zahl*) five; *s. a.* **Acht**[1] ◉ (*Note*) "unsatisfactory", ≈ "F"

fünffach, 5fach ['fʏnf·fax] *adj* fivefold; **die ~e Menge** five times the amount

fünfhundert ['fʏnf·'hʊn·dɐt] *adj* five hundred

fünfmal, 5-mal[RR] *adv* five times; *s. a.* **achtmal**

fünftausend ['fʏnf·'tau·znt] *adj* five thousand

fünfte(r, s) ['fʏnf·tɐ, 'fʏnf·tə, 'fʏnf·təs] *adj* (*Zahl*) fifth; (*Datum*) 5th; *s. a.* **achte(r, s) 1, 2**

fünftel ['fʏnf·tl] *adj* fifth

fünftens ['fʏnf·tns] *adv* in [the] fifth place

fünfzehn ['fʏnf·tseːn] *adj* fifteen; **~ Uhr** 3 p.m.; *s. a.* **acht**[1]

fünfzehnte(r, s) *adj* (*Zahl*) fifteenth; (*Datum*) 15th; *s. a.* **achte(r, s) 1, 2**

fünfzig ['fʏnf·tsɪç] *adj* fifty; *s. a.* **achtzig 1, 2**

fünfzigste(r, s) *adj* fiftieth; *s. a.* **achte(r, s) 1**

Funk <-s> [fʊŋk] *m kein pl* radio

Funke <-ns, -n> ['fʊŋ·kə], **Funken** <-s, -> ['fʊŋ·kn] *m* spark; **~n sprühen** to emit sparks; **ein ~ [von] Anstand** (*fig*) a shred of decency; **ein ~ Hoffnung** (*fig*) a gleam of hope; **der zündende ~** (*fig*) the vital spark

funkeln ['fʊŋ·kln] *vi* to sparkle; *Edelsteine, Gold* to glitter

funken ['fʊŋ·kn] **I.** *vt* to radio; **SOS ~** to send out *sep* an SOS **II.** *vi impers* (*fam: sich verlieben*) **zwischen den beiden hat's gefunkt** those two have really clicked

Funkgerät *nt* radiotelephone unit; (*Sprechfunkgerät*) walkie-talkie

Funkstille *f* ▶WENDUNGEN: **bei jdm herrscht ~** sb is [completely] incommunicado

Funktion <-, -en> [fʊŋk·'tsi̯oːn] *f* function; **in ihrer ~ als etw** in her capacity as sth

Funktionär(in) <-s, -e> [fʊŋk·tsi̯o·'nɛɐ̯] *m(f)* official; **ein hoher ~** a high-ranking official

funktionell [fʊŋk·tsi̯o·'nɛl] *adj* MED **eine ~e Störung** a dysfunction

funktionieren* [fʊŋk·tsi̯o·'niː·rən] *vi* to work; *Maschine a.* to operate; *Organisation* to run smoothly

Funkverbindung *f* radio contact

Funkverkehr *m* radio communication *no art*

für [fyːɐ̯] *präp + akk* for; ■ **~ jdn/etw** for sb/sth; **er hat es ~ 45 Dollar bekommen** he got it for 45 dollars; **sind Sie ~ diesen Kandidaten?** do you support this candidate?; **~ ihr Alter ist sie noch rüstig** she's in great shape for someone her age; **~ diese Jahreszeit ist es ziemlich kalt** it's pretty cold for this time of year; **was Sie da sagen, hat manches ~ sich** there's something to what you're saying; **ich halte sie ~ intelligent** I think she is intelligent; **~ ganz** SCHWEIZ (*für immer*) for good, forever; **~ sich** *akk* **bleiben** to remain by oneself; **was ~ ein ...** what ...; **~ ein Blödsinn!** what nonsense!; **was**

~ ein Pilz ist das? what kind of mushroom is that?

Für <-> [fyːɐ] *nt* **das ~ und Wider** the pros and cons

Furche <-, -n> ['fʊrçə] *f* furrow

Furcht <-> ['fʊrçt] *f kein pl* fear; **~ [vor jdm/etw] haben** to fear sb/sth; **~ erregend** terrifying

furchtbar *adj* terrible

fürchten ['fʏrçtn] **I.** *vt* to fear; ■**zum F~** frightful; ■**~, dass ...** to be afraid that ... **II.** *vr* **sich** *akk* **~** to be afraid **(vor** +*dat* of); **sich** *akk* **im Dunkeln ~** to be afraid of the dark

fürchterlich *adj s.* **furchtbar**

furchterregend *adj s.* **Furcht**

furchtlos *adj* fearless

füreinander [fyːɐ'ʔai̯·nan·dɐ] *adv* for each other; **~ einspringen** to help each other out

Furie <-, -n> ['fuː·riə] *f* fury

Furnier <-s, -e> [fʊr·'niːɐ] *nt* veneer

furnieren* [fʊr·'niː·rən] *vt* to veneer

Fürsorge ['fyːɐ·zɔr·gə] *f kein pl* ① (*Betreuung*) care ② (*fam: Sozialhilfe*) **von der ~ leben** to live on welfare

fürsorglich ['fyːɐ·zɔrk·lɪç] *adj* considerate

Fürst(in) <-en, -en> [fʏrst] *m(f)* prince *masc*, princess *fem*

Fürstentum *nt* principality; **das ~ Monaco** the principality of Monaco

fürstlich ['fʏrst·lɪç] *adv* **~ speisen** to eat like a king

Furz <-[e]s, Fürze> [fʊrts] *m* (*derb*) fart

furzen ['fʊr·tsn̩] *vi* (*derb*) to fart

Fusion <-, -en> [fu·'zi̯oːn] *f* ÖKON merger

Fuß <-es, Füße> [fuːs] *m* foot; **bei ~!** heel!; **gut/schlecht zu ~ sein** to be steady/not so steady on one's feet; **etw ist zu ~ zu erreichen** sth is within walking distance; **zu ~ gehen** to walk ▸WENDUNGEN: **auf eigenen Füßen stehen** to stand on one's own two feet; **auf großem ~[e] leben** to live the high life; **kalte Füße bekommen** to get cold feet; **jdm zu Füßen liegen** to lie at sb's

feet; **keinen ~ vor die Tür setzen** to not set foot outside; **sich** *dat* **die Füße vertreten** to stretch one's legs; **auf wackligen Füßen stehen** to rest on shaky ground

Fußball ['fuːs·bal] *m* soccer; (*Ball*) soccer ball

Fußballer(in) <-s, -> ['fuːs·ba·lɐ] *m(f)* (*fam*) soccer player

Fußballmannschaft *f* soccer team

Fußballplatz *m* soccer field

Fußballspiel *nt* soccer game

Fußballspieler(in) *m(f)* soccer player

Fußballstadion *nt* soccer stadium

Fußbank <-bänke> *f* footrest

Fußboden *m* floor

fusselig ['fʊ·sə·lɪç] *adj* fluffy, lint-covered *attr*, full of lint *pred*

Fußgänger(in) <-s, -> *m(f)* pedestrian

Fußgängerüberweg *m*, **Fußgängerstreifen** *m* SCHWEIZ pedestrian crossing

Fußgängerzone *f* pedestrian zone

Fußgelenk *nt* ankle

Fußnagel *m* toenail

Fußnote *f* LIT footnote

Fußpilz *m kein pl* athlete's foot

Fußstapfen <-s, -> *m* ▸WENDUNGEN: **in jds ~ treten** to follow in sb's footsteps

Fußtritt *m* kick

Fußweg *m* footpath; **es sind nur 15 Minuten ~** it's only a 15 minute walk

Futter¹ <-s, -> ['fʊ·tɐ] *nt* (*Tiernahrung*) [animal] feed

Futter² <-s> ['fʊ·tɐ] *nt kein pl* (*Innenstoff*) lining

Futteral <-s, -e> [fʊ·tə·'raːl] *nt* case

füttern¹ ['fʏ·tɐn] *vt* (*mit Nahrung*) to feed

füttern² ['fʏ·tɐn] *vt* (*mit Stofffutter*) to line

futtern ['fʊ·tɐn] **I.** *vi* (*hum fam*) to stuff oneself **II.** *vt* (*hum fam*) ■**etw ~** to scarf sth down *sep sl*

Fütterung <-, -en> *f* feeding

Futur <-s, -e> [fu·'tuːɐ] *nt* LING future [tense]

futuristisch [fu·tu·'rɪs·tɪʃ] *adj* futurist[ic]

Gg

G, g <-, -> [ge:] nt ① (Buchstabe) G, g; **~ wie Gustav** G as in Golf ② MUS G, g

g Abk von **Gramm** g

gab ['ga:p] imp von **geben**

Gabe <-, -n> ['ga:·bə] f ① (geh: Geschenk) gift; **eine milde ~** alms pl ② (Begabung) gift ③ SCHWEIZ (Preis, Gewinn) prize

Gabel <-, -n> ['ga:·bl] f ① (Essensgabel) fork ② (Heu-, Mistgabel) pitchfork ③ (Radgabel) fork ④ TELEK cradle

gabeln ['ga:·bln] vr ■ **sich** akk **~** Straße, Ast to fork

Gabelstapler <-s, -> ['-ʃta:p·lɐ] m forklift

Gabelung <-, -en> ['ga:·bə·lʊŋ] f fork

gackern ['ga·kɐn] vi ① Huhn to cluck ② (fig fam) to cackle

Gage <-, -n> ['ga:·ʒə] f THEAT fee

gähnen ['gɛː·nən] vi to yawn

galant [ga·lant] adj (veraltend) chivalrous

Galeere <-, -n> [ga·le:·rə] f galley

Galerie <-, -n> [ga·lə·riː] f ① ARCHIT gallery ② (Gemäldegalerie) art gallery; (Kunsthandlung) art dealership ③ ÖSTERR, SCHWEIZ (Tunnel mit fensterartigen Öffnungen) gallery

Galgen <-, -> ['gal·gn] m gallows + sing vb

Galgenfrist f (fam) stay of execution

Galle <-, -n> ['ga·lə] f ① (Gallenblase) gall bladder ② (Gallenflüssigkeit) bile

Galopp <-s, -s> [ga·lɔp] m gallop

galoppieren* [ga·lɔ·piː·rən] vi sein o haben to gallop

galt ['galt] imp von **gelten**

Gämse^RR <-, -n> ['gɛm·zə] f chamois

Gang^1 <-[e]s, Gänge> ['gaŋ] m ① kein pl (Gangart) gait ② (Weg) walk; (Besorgung) errand ③ (Ablauf) course; **alles geht wieder seinen gewohnten ~** everything is back to normal ④ (in einer Speisenfolge) course ⑤ AUTO gear; (Fahrrad a.) speed ⑥ (eingefriedeter Weg) passageway; (Korridor) corridor; (im Theater, Flugzeug, Laden) aisle ▶WENDUNGEN: **etw in ~ bringen** to get sth going; (a. fig) **in ~ kommen** Mensch to get going; Geschäft to get off the ground

Gang^2 <-, -s> [gɛŋ] f (Bande) gang

Gangart f walk; (bei Pferden) pace

gängig ['gɛŋɪç] adj ① (üblich) Praxis common ② (gut verkäuflich) Buch, Modell popular

Gangschaltung f gearshift

Ganove <-n, -n> [ga·noː·və] m (pej fam) crook

Gans <-, Gänse> ['gans] f goose

Gänseblümchen nt daisy

Gänsefüßchen pl (fam) quotation marks pl

Gänsehaut f kein pl goose bumps pl

Gänsemarsch m kein pl **im ~** in single file

ganz ['gants] I. adj ① (vollständig) all; **den ~en Tag** all [or the whole] day; **die ~e Wahrheit** the whole truth ② (unbestimmtes Zahlwort) **eine ~e Menge** quite a lot ③ (fam: unbeschädigt) intact; **etw wieder ~ machen** to fix sth ④ (fam: nicht mehr als) **~ 10 Minuten** no more than 10 minutes II. adv ① (sehr, wirklich) really; **das war ~ lieb von dir** that was really kind of you; **~ besonders** particularly ② (ziemlich) quite ③ (vollkommen) completely; **~ und gar** completely; **~ und gar nicht** not at all; **~ hinten/vorne** all the way in [the] back/up front

Ganze(s) nt ① (alles zusammen) whole; **im ~n** on the whole ② (die ganze Angelegenheit) the whole business

ganzheitlich adj **~e Behandlung/Medizin** holistic treatment/medicine

gänzlich ['gɛnts·lɪç] adv completely

Ganztagsschule f all-day school

gar[1] ['ga:ɐ̯] *adj* KOCHK done

gar[2] ['ga:ɐ̯] *adv* ❶ (*überhaupt*) at all, whatsoever; ~ **keine[r]** no one at all; **hattest du denn ~ keine Angst?** weren't you even the least bit scared?; ~ **nichts** nothing at all [*or* whatsoever] ❷ ÖSTERR, SCHWEIZ, SÜDD (*sehr*) really

Garage <-, -n> [ga·'ra:·ʒə] *f* garage

Garantie <-, -n> [ga·ran·'ti:] *f* guarantee

garantieren* [ga·ran·'ti:·rən] *vt, vi* to guarantee

Garde <-, -n> ['gar·də] *f* guard

Garderobe <-, -n> [gar·də·'ro:·bə] *f* ❶ (*Kleiderablage*) coat rack; (*Aufbewahrungsraum*) cloakroom ❷ *kein pl* (*Kleidung*) wardrobe ❸ THEAT (*Ankleideraum*) dressing room

Gardine <-, -n> [gar·'di:·nə] *f* curtain

gären ['gɛ:·rən] *vi sein o haben* ❶ (*sich in Gärung befinden*) to ferment ❷ (*fig*) to seethe

Garn <-[e]s, -e> ['garn] *nt* thread

Garnele <-, -n> [gar·'ne:·lə] *f* prawn

garnieren* [gar·'ni:·rən] *vt* KOCHK to garnish

Garnitur <-, -en> [gar·ni·'tu:ɐ̯] *f* set

Garten <-s, Gärten> ['gar·tn̩] *m* garden

Gartenarbeit *f* gardening

Gartenbau *m kein pl* horticulture

Gartenlokal *nt* open-air restaurant

Gärtner(in) <-s, -> ['gɛrt·nɐ] *m(f)* gardener

Gärtnerei <-, -en> [gɛrt·nə·'rai] *f* nursery

Gas <-es, -e> ['ga:s] *nt* gas; ~ **geben** to accelerate; (*fig*) to speed up on it

Gasflasche *f* gas canister

gasförmig *adj* gaseous

Gasheizung *f* gas heating [system]

Gasherd *m* gas stove

Gaskocher *m* camping stove

Gasleitung *f* gas pipe

Gasmaske *f* gas mask

Gaspedal *nt* gas [pedal]

Gasse <-, -n> ['ga·sə] *f* ❶ (*schmale Straße*) alley[way] ❷ ÖSTERR (*Straße*) street

Gast <-es, Gäste> ['gast] *m* guest; ~ **in einem Land sein** to be visiting country

Gastarbeiter(in) *m(f)* guest worker

Gästebuch *nt* guest book

Gästezimmer *nt* guestroom

gastfreundlich *adj* hospitable

Gastfreundschaft *f* hospitality

Gastgeber(in) <-s, -> *m(f)* host *masc*, hostess *fem*

Gasthaus, Gasthof *m* inn

Gastritis <-, Gastritiden> [gas·'tri:·tɪs] *f* gastritis

Gastronomie <-,-n> [gas·tro·no·'mi:] *f* ❶ (*Gaststättengewerbe*) catering trade ❷ (*Kochkunst*) gastronomy

gastronomisch *adj* gastronomic

Gastspiel *nt* THEAT guest performance

Gaststätte *f* restaurant

Gastwirt(in) *m(f)* restaurant manager; *einer Kneipe* barkeeper

Gastwirtschaft *f* s. **Gaststätte**

Gaszähler *m* gas meter

Gatte, Gattin <-n, -nen> ['ga·tə, 'ga·tɪn] *m, f* (*geh*) spouse

Gatter <-s, -> ['ga·tɐ] *nt* fence

Gattung <-, -en> ['ga·tʊŋ] *f* ❶ BIOL genus ❷ KUNST, LIT genre

GAU <-s, -s> ['gau] *m Akr von* **größter anzunehmender Unfall** MCA

Gaudi <-> ['gau·di] *f o nt kein pl* ÖSTERR, SÜDD (*fam: Spaß*) fun

Gaul <-[e]s, Gäule> ['gaul] *m* nag

Gaumen <-s, -> ['gau·mən] *m* palate

Gauner(in) <-s, -> ['gau·nɐ] *m(f)* ❶ (*Betrüger*) crook ❷ (*Schelm*) rogue

Gaunerei <-, -en> [gau·nə·'rai] *f* cheating

Gazelle <-, -n> [ga·'tsɛ·lə] *f* gazelle

Gebäck <-[e]s, -e> [gə·'bɛk] *nt* ❶ *pl selten* (*Plätzchen*) cookies *pl* ❷ (*Teilchen*) pastries *pl*

gebacken *pp von* **backen**

geballt I. *adj* ❶ (*konzentriert*) concentrated ❷ (*zur Faust gemacht*) ~**e Fäuste** clenched fists II. *adv* in clusters

gebar [gə·'ba:ɐ̯] *imp von* **gebären**

gebären* [gə·'bɛ:ɐ̯·dn̩] *vr haben* ■ **sich ~** *akk* ~ to behave

gebären <gebiert, gebar, geboren>

[gə-ˈbɛː-rən] I. vt ① (zur Welt bringen) ■geboren werden to be born ② (eine natürliche Begabung haben) ■zu etw dat geboren sein to be born to sth II. vi (ein Kind zur Welt bringen) to give birth

Gebärmutter f womb

Gebäude <-s, -> [gə-ˈbɔy-də] nt building

Gebein <-[e]s, -e> [gə-ˈbain] nt ■-e pl bones pl; eines Heiligen relics pl

geben <gibt, gab, gegeben> [ˈgeː-bn̩] I. vt ① (reichen) ■jdm etw akk ~ to give sb sth [or sth to sb]; (beim Kartenspiel) to deal sb sth; jdm etw zu tun ~ to give sb sth to do ② (schenken) to give [as a present] ③ (mitteilen) jdm seine Telefonnummer ~ to give sb one's telephone number ④ (verkaufen) ~ Sie mir bitte fünf Brötchen I'd like five rolls please ⑤ (spenden) Schutz/ Schatten ~ to give protection/shade ⑥ TELEK ■jdm jdn ~ to put sb through to sb; ~ Sie mir bitte Frau Kuhn can I please speak to Mrs. Kuhn? ⑦ Pressekonferenz to hold ⑧ (zukommen lassen) jdm einen Namen ~ to name sb ⑨ (veranstalten) ein Fest ~ to give a party ⑩ KOCHK to add ⑪ (ergeben) 7 mal 7 gibt 49 7 times 7 equals 49; keinen Sinn ~ to make no sense ⑫ (äußern) ■etw von sich dat ~ to utter sth II. vi ① KARTEN to deal ② SPORT (Aufschlag haben) to serve; du gibst! it's your serve III. vt impers ① (gereicht werden) was gibt es zum Frühstück? what's for breakfast?; freitags gibt es bei uns immer Fisch we always have fish on Fridays ② (eintreten) heute gibt es noch Regen it's going to rain [later] today ③ (existieren, passieren) das gibt's doch nicht! (fam) I can't believe it!; was gibt's? (fam) what's up? IV. vr ① (nachlassen) ■etw gibt sich sth is letting up; (sich erledigen) sth sorts itself out ② (sich benehmen, aufführen) sie gab sich sehr überrascht she acted very surprised

Gebet <-[e]s, -e> [gə-ˈbeːt] nt prayer

gebeten [gə-ˈbeː-tn̩] pp von bitten

Gebiet <-[e]s, -e> [gə-ˈbiːt] nt ① (Fläche) area; (Region a.) region; (Staatsgebiet) territory ② (Fach) field

gebieten* [gə-ˈbiː-tn̩] irreg vt (geh) etw dat Einhalt ~ to put an end to sth; es ist Vorsicht geboten care must be taken

Gebilde <-s, -> [gə-ˈbɪl-də] nt ① (Ding) thing ② (Form) shape; (Struktur) structure

gebildet adj educated

Gebirge <-s, -> [gə-ˈbɪr-gə] nt mountain range

gebirgig [gə-ˈbɪr-gɪç] adj mountainous

Gebiss^RR <-es, -e>, Gebiß^ALT <-sses, -sse> [gə-ˈbɪs] nt ① (Zähne) [set of] teeth ② (Zahnprothese) dentures npl

gebissen [gə-ˈbɪ-sn̩] pp von beißen

geblasen pp von blasen

geblieben [gə-ˈbliː-bn̩] pp von bleiben

geboren [gə-ˈboː-rən] I. pp von gebären II. adj der ~e Koch sein to be a born cook

geborgen [gə-ˈbɔr-gn̩] I. pp von bergen II. adj safe

Gebot <-[e]s, -e> [gə-ˈboːt] nt ① (Gesetz) law; (Verordnung) decree ② REL die zehn ~e the Ten Commandments ③ ÖKON bid

geboten [gə-ˈboː-tn̩] pp von bieten, gebieten

gebracht [gə-ˈbraxt] pp von bringen

gebraten pp von braten

Gebrauch <-[e]s, Gebräuche> [gə-ˈbraux] m ① kein pl (Verwendung) use; (Anwendung) application ② meist pl Sitten und Gebräuche manners and customs

gebrauchen* vt (verwenden) to use

gebräuchlich [gə-ˈbrɔyç-lɪç] adj ① (allgemein üblich) customary; (in Gebrauch) in use ② (herkömmlich) conventional

Gebrauchsanweisung f operating instructions pl, directions pl

gebraucht adj secondhand

Gebrauchtwagen m used car

gebrechlich [gə-ˈbrɛç-lɪç] adj frail

G

gebrochen [gəˈbrɔ·xn̩] I. *pp von* **brechen** II. *adj (völlig entmutigt)* broken III. *adv* imperfectly; **sie sprach nur ~ Deutsch** she only spoke broken German

Gebrüder [gəˈbryː·dɐ] *pl (veraltet)* brothers

Gebühr <-, -en> [gəˈbyːɐ̯] *f* charge; *(Beitrag, Honorar)* fee

gebührend I. *adj (angemessen)* appropriate II. *adv* appropriately

gebührenfrei *adj, adv* free [of charge]

gebührenpflichtig *adj, adv* subject to a charge

gebunden [gəˈbʊn·dn̩] I. *pp von* **binden** II. *adj* ~es Buch hardcover; **vertraglich ~ sein** to be bound by contract

Geburt <-, -en> [gəˈbuːɐ̯t] *f* birth

gebürtig [gəˈbʏr·tɪç] *adj* by birth; **er ist ~er Brasilianer** he is a native Brazilian

Geburtsdatum *nt* date of birth

Geburtsjahr *nt* year of birth

Geburtsort *m* place of birth

Geburtstag *m* birthday; *(Geburtsdatum)* date of birth; **„herzlichen Glückwunsch zum ~"** "Happy Birthday [to you]"

Geburtsurkunde *f* birth certificate

Gebüsch <-[e]s, -e> [gəˈbʏʃ] *nt* bushes *pl; (Unterholz)* undergrowth

gedacht [gəˈdaxt] *pp von* **denken, gedenken**

Gedächtnis <-ses, -se> [gəˈdɛçt·nɪs] *nt* memory

Gedanke <-ns, -n> [gəˈdaŋ·kə] *m* ① *(das Gedachte, Überlegung)* thought; **jdn auf andere ~n bringen** to take sb's mind off [of] sth; **sich** *dat* **über etw** *akk* **~n machen** to be worried about sth ② *(Einfall)* idea

gedankenlos *adj* thoughtless

Gedankenstrich *m* dash

Gedeck <-[e]s, -e> [gəˈdɛk] *nt* place setting

gedenken *vi irreg (geh)* ① *(ehrend zurückdenken)* ■ jds/einer S. ~ to remember sb/sth ② *(beabsichtigen)* ■~, etw zu tun to intend to do sth

Gedenken <-s> [gəˈdɛŋ·kn̩] *nt kein pl* memory

Gedenkfeier *f* commemoration

Gedenkminute *f* moment of silence

Gedenktag *m* day of remembrance

Gedicht <-[e]s, -e> [gəˈdɪçt] *nt* poem

gediegen [gəˈdiː·gn̩] *adj* ① *(solide gearbeitet)* high quality ② *(gründlich)* ~e Kenntnisse haben to have sound knowledge

Gedränge <-s> [gəˈdrɛŋə] *nt kein pl* ① *(drängende Menschenmenge)* crowd ② *(das Drängen)* jostling

gedroschen [gəˈdrɔ·ʃn̩] *pp von* **dreschen**

gedrungen [gəˈdrʊŋən] I. *pp von* **dringen** II. *adj Körperbau* stocky

Geduld <-> [gəˈdʊlt] *f kein pl* patience

gedulden* *vr* ■ sich *akk* ~ to be patient

geduldig [gəˈdʊl·dɪç] *adj* patient

gedurft [gəˈdʊrft] *pp von* **dürfen**

geehrt *adj* honored; **sehr ~e Damen, sehr ~e Herren!** ladies and gentlemen!; *(Anrede in Briefen)* **sehr ~e Damen und Herren!** Dear Sir or Madam

geeignet [gəˈʔaig·nət] *adj* suitable

Gefahr <-, -en> [gəˈfaːɐ̯] *f* danger; **jdn in ~ bringen** to endanger sb; **auf eigene ~** at one's own risk

gefährden* *vt* ■ sich/jdn/etw ~ to endanger oneself/sb/sth; **den Erfolg einer S.** *gen* ~ to jeopardize the success of sth

gefahren *pp von* **fahren**

gefährlich [gəˈfɛːɐ̯·lɪç] *adj* dangerous; *(risikoreich)* risky

gefahrlos [gəˈfaːɐ̯·loːs] *adj* safe

gefallen <gefiel, gefallen> I. *vi* ■ etw **gefällt jdm** sth pleases sb, sb likes sth II. *vr (fam)* ■ sich *dat* etw ~ lassen to put up with sth

Gefallen <-s, -> *m* favor; **jdn um einen ~ bitten** to ask sb for a favor; **jdm einen ~ tun** to do sb a favor

Gefallene(r) *f(m)* soldier killed in action

gefällig [gəˈfɛ·lɪç] *adj* ① *(hilfsbereit)* helpful ② *(ansprechend)* pleasant ③ *(a.*

iron form: gewünscht) **Kaffee ~?** would you care for [some] coffee? *form*

Gefälligkeit <-, -en> *f* ❶ (*Gefallen*) favor ❷ *kein pl* (*Hilfsbereitschaft*) helpfulness

gefangen [gəˈfaŋən] **I.** *pp von* **fangen II.** *adj* ❶ (*in Gefangenschaft*) **jdn ~ halten** to hold sb captive; **jdn ~ nehmen** MIL to take sb prisoner; (*verhaften*) to arrest sb ❷ (*beeindruckt*) **jdn ~ halten** to captivate sb

Gefangene(r) *f(m)* captive; (*im Gefängnis*) prisoner; (*im Krieg*) prisoner of war

gefangen|halten^ALT *vt irreg s.* **gefangen II 2**

Gefangennahme <-, -n> *f* ❶ MIL capture ❷ (*Verhaftung*) arrest

Gefangenschaft <-, *selten* -en> *f* captivity

Gefängnis <-ses, -se> [gəˈfɛŋˌnɪs] *nt* ❶ (*Haftanstalt*) prison, jail; **ins ~ kommen** to be sent to prison ❷ *kein pl* (*Haftstrafe*) imprisonment

Gefängnisstrafe *f* prison sentence

Gefäß <-es, -e> [gəˈfɛːs] *nt* ❶ (*Behälter*) container ❷ MED (*Ader*) vessel

gefasst^RR, **gefaßt**^ALT **I.** *adj* ❶ (*beherrscht*) composed ❷ (*eingestellt*) ■ **auf etw** *akk* **~ sein** to be prepared for sth **II.** *adv* calmly

Gefecht <-[e]s, -e> [gəˈfɛçt] *nt* (*a. fig*) battle

Gefieder <-s, -> [gəˈfiːdɐ] *nt* plumage

geflochten [gəˈflɔxtn̩] *pp von* **flechten**

geflogen [gəˈfloːɡn̩] *pp von* **fliegen**

geflohen [gəˈfloːən] *pp von* **fliehen**

geflossen [gəˈflɔsn̩] *pp von* **fließen**

Geflügel <-s> [gəˈflyːɡl̩] *nt kein pl* poultry

geflügelt [gəˈflyːɡlt] *adj* winged

gefochten [gəˈfɔxtn̩] *pp von* **fechten**

Gefolge <-s, -> [gəˈfɔlɡə] *nt* retinue

gefräßig [gəˈfrɛːsɪç] *adj* ❶ (*fressgierig*) voracious ❷ (*pej: unersättlich*) greedy

gefressen [gəˈfrɛsn̩] *pp von* **fressen**

ge|frieren* *vi irreg sein* to freeze

Gefrierfach *nt* freezer [compartment]

Gefrierpunkt *m* freezing point

gefroren [gəˈfroːrən] *pp von* **frieren, gefrieren**

gefügig [gəˈfyːɡɪç] *adj* compliant

Gefühl <-[e]s, -e> [gəˈfyːl] *nt* feeling; **ein ~ für etw** *akk* [**haben**] [to have] a feeling for sth

gefühllos I. *adj* ❶ *Bein, Fuß* numb ❷ (*herzlos*) insensitive **II.** *adv* insensitively

Gefühlsausbruch *m* emotional outburst

gefühlsbetont *adj* emotional

gefühlsmäßig *adv* instinctively

gefühlvoll I. *adj* sensitive **II.** *adv* with feeling

gefunden [gəˈfʊndn̩] *pp von* **finden**

gegangen [gəˈɡaŋən] *pp von* **gehen**

gegebenenfalls [gəˈɡeːbəˌnənˈfals] *adv* if necessary

gegen [ˈɡeːɡn̩] **I.** *präp* +*akk* ❶ (*wider*) against; (*jur, sport a.*) versus; ■ **~ jdn/ etw sein** to be against sb/sth; **etwas ~ eine Erkältung** sth for a cold ❷ (*für*) for; **~ Kaution/Quittung** with a deposit/receipt ❸ (*verglichen mit*) compared with ❹ (*ungefähr*) **~ Abend/Morgen** toward evening/morning **II.** *adv* **er kommt ~ drei Uhr an** he's arriving around three o'clock

Gegenangriff *m* counterattack

Gegenargument *nt* counterargument

Gegend <-, -en> [ˈɡeːɡnt] *f* ❶ (*Gebiet*) region; **durch die ~ fahren/laufen** to drive/walk around ❷ (*Wohngegend*) neighborhood ❸ (*Nähe*) area

Gegendarstellung *f* MEDIA reply

gegeneinander [ɡeːɡn̩ʔaɪˈnandɐ] *adv* against each other

gegeneinander|prallen *vi sein* to collide

Gegengift *nt* antidote

Gegenleistung *f* **eine/keine ~ erwarten** to expect something/nothing in return

Gegensatz *m* ❶ (*Gegenteil*) opposite; ■ **im ~ zu jdm/etw** unlike sb/sth ❷ *pl* differences; **unüberbrückbare Gegensätze** irreconcilable differences

gegensätzlich ['ge:·gn̩·zɛts·lɪç] I. *adj* conflicting; *Menschen, Temperamente* different II. *adv* differently

Gegenseite *f* other side

gegenseitig ['ge:·gn̩·zai·tɪç] *adj* mutual

Gegenseitigkeit <-> *f kein pl* **auf ~ beruhen** to be mutual

Gegenspieler(in) *m(f)* opponent

Gegenstand <-[e]s, Gegenstände> *m* ① *(Ding)* object ② *(Thema)* subject

Gegenteil ['ge:·gn̩·tail] *nt* opposite

gegenteilig ['ge:·gn̩·tai·lɪç] I. *adj* opposite II. *adv* to the contrary

gegenüber [ge:·gn̩·'?y:·bɐ] I. *präp* +*dat* ■**jdm/etw ~** ① *(örtlich)* opposite sb/sth ② *(in Bezug auf)* toward sb/sth ③ *(im Vergleich zu)* in comparison with sb/sth II. *adv* opposite

gegenüberliegend *adj attr* opposite

gegenüberIstehen *irreg* I. *vi* ① *(örtlich)* ■**jdm ~** to stand opposite sb ② *(eingestellt sein)* ■**jdm/etw [...] ~** to have a [...] attitude toward sb/sth II. *vr* ■**sich** *dat* **~** to face each other

gegenüberIstellen *vt* ① *(konfrontieren)* ■**jdm jdn ~** to confront sb with sb ② *(vergleichen)* ■**etw** *dat* **etw ~** to compare sth with sth

Gegenüberstellung *f* JUR police lineup

Gegenverkehr *m* oncoming traffic

Gegenwart <-> ['ge:·gn̩·vart] *f kein pl* ① *(jetziger Augenblick)* present ② *(heutiges Zeitalter)* present [day]; **die Literatur/Musik der ~** contemporary literature/music ③ LING present [tense] ④ *(Anwesenheit)* presence

gegenwärtig ['ge:·gn̩·vɛr·tɪç] I. *adj attr (derzeitig)* present II. *adv* currently

Gegenwind *m* headwind

gegessen [gə·'gɛ·sn̩] *pp von* **essen**

geglichen [gə·'glɪ·çn̩] *pp von* **gleichen**

geglitten [gə·'glɪ·tn̩] *pp von* **gleiten**

Gegner(in) <-s, -> ['ge:g·nɐ] *m(f)* ① *(Feind)* enemy ② *(Gegenspieler, Sport)* opponent

gegnerisch *adj attr* opposing

gegolten [gə·'gɔl·tn̩] *pp von* **gelten**

gegoren [gə·'go:·rən] *pp von* **gären**

gegossen [gə·'gɔ·sn̩] *pp von* **gießen**

gegraben *pp von* **graben**

gegriffen [gə·'grɪ·fn̩] *pp von* **greifen**

Gehalt[1] <-[e]s, Gehälter> [gə·'halt] *nt* o ÖSTERR *m* salary

Gehalt[2] <-[e]s, -e> [gə·'halt] *m (Anteil)* content **(an** +*dat* of)

Gehaltserhöhung *f* pay raise

gehaltvoll *adj (nahrhaft)* nutritious

gehangen [gə·'haŋən] *pp von* **hängen**

gehässig [gə·'hɛ·sɪç] *adj* spiteful

gehauen *pp von* **hauen**

Gehäuse <-s, -> [gə·'hɔy·zə] *nt* casing; *einer Kamera a.* body

gehbehindert *adj* **leicht/stark ~ sein** to have a slight/severe mobility handicap

Gehege <-s, -> [gə·'he:·gə] *nt* enclosure

geheim [gə·'haim] I. *adj* secret II. *adv* secretly; **etw [vor jdm] ~ halten** to keep sth secret [from sb]

Geheimagent(in) *m(f)* secret agent

Geheimdienst *m* secret service

geheimIhaltenALT *vt irreg s.* **geheim** II

Geheimnis <-ses, -se> [gə·'haim·nɪs] *nt* secret

geheimnisvoll *adj* mysterious

Geheimnummer *f* ① TELEK unlisted number ② *(Geheimzahl)* PIN

GeheimtippRR *m* inside tip

Geheimzahl *f* FIN PIN

geheißen *pp von* **heißen**

gehen <ging, gegangen> ['ge:·ən] I. *vi* sein ① *(sich fortbewegen)* to go; *(zu Fuß)* to walk ② *(besuchen)* ■**zu jdm ~** to go [and] visit sb; **in die Kirche/Schule/ins Theater ~** to go to church/school/the theater ③ *(weggehen)* to go; *(abfahren a.)* to leave; **ich muss jetzt ~** I have to go; **wann geht der Zug nach Hamburg?** when does the train to Hamburg leave? ④ *(führen)* to go; **die Brücke geht über den Fluss** the bridge crosses the river; **wohin geht dieser Weg?** where does this path lead [to]? ⑤ *(funktionieren)* to work; **meine Uhr geht nicht mehr** my watch [has] stopped ⑥ *(gelingen)*

versuch's einfach, es geht ganz leicht just try it — it's really easy; **kannst du mir bitte erklären, wie das Spiel geht?** can you please explain how the game goes? ➐ ÖKON **das Geschäft geht vor Weihnachten immer gut** business is always good before Christmas ➑ (*hineinpassen*) **es ~ über 450 Besucher in das neue Theater** the new theater holds over 450 people; **wie viele Leute ~ in deinen Wagen?** how many people [can] fit in your car? ➒ (*dauern*) **der Film geht drei Stunden** the movie lasts three hours ➓ (*reichen*) **der Rock geht ihr bis zum Knie** the skirt goes down to her knee; **in die Tausende ~** to run into the thousands ⑪ KOCHK *Teig* to rise ⑫ (*möglich sein*) **haben Sie am nächsten Mittwoch Zeit? – nein, das geht [bei mir] nicht** are you free next Wednesday? — no, that's no good [for me]; **ich muss mal telefonieren – geht das?** I have to make a phone call — would that be alright? ⑬ (*beeinträchtigen*) **zu viel Alkohol geht auf die Leber** too much alcohol is bad for your liver; **das geht [mir] ganz schön an die Nerven** that really wears on my nerves ⑭ (*gerichtet sein*) ■ **an jdn ~** to be addressed to sb ⑮ (*fam: liiert sein*) ■ **mit jdm ~** to be going out with sb ⑯ (*überschreiten*) **zu weit ~** to go too far ⑰ (*fam: akzeptabel sein*) **er geht gerade noch, aber seine Frau ist furchtbar** he's not that bad, but his wife is awful; **wie ist das Hotel? – es geht [so]** how's the hotel? — it's ok ►WENDUNGEN: **es geht nichts über jdn/etw** *akk* there's nothing like sb/sth II. *vi impers sein* ➊ + *adv* (*sich befinden*) **wie geht es Ihnen? – danke, mir geht es gut!** how are you? — fine, thank you!; **nachher ging es ihr wieder besser** afterwards she felt better again ➋ + *adv* (*verlaufen*) **wie war denn die Prüfung? – ach, es ging ganz gut** how was the exam? — oh, it went quite well ➌ (*sich handeln um*)

worum geht es in diesem Film? what is this movie about? ➍ (*wichtig sein*) **worum geht es dir eigentlich?** what are you trying to say?; **es geht mir ums Prinzip** it's a matter of principle ➎ (*ergehen*) **mir ist es ähnlich/ genauso gegangen** it was the same/ just the same with me; **lass es dir gut ~!** take care of yourself! ➏ (*sich machen lassen*) **ich werde arbeiten, solange es geht** I will continue working as long as possible; **geht es, oder soll ich dir tragen helfen?** can you manage, or should I help you carry it/ them? ➐ (*nach jds Kopf gehen*) **wenn es nach mir ginge** if it were up to me III. *vr haben* ➊ *impers* **in diesen Schuhen geht es sich bequem** these shoes are very comfortable for walking ➋ (*sich nicht beherrschen*) **sich** *akk* **~ lassen** to lose one's self-control; (*nachlässig sein*) to let oneself go

gehen|lassen* *vr irreg s.* **gehen III 2**
geheuer [gəˈhɔy·ɐ] *adj* **[jdm] nicht [ganz] ~ sein** to seem [a bit] suspicious [to sb]
Gehilfe, Gehilfin <-n, -n> [gəˈhɪl·fə, gəˈhɪl·fɪn] *m, f* assistant
Gehirn <-[e]s, -e> [gəˈhɪrn] *nt* brain
Gehirnerschütterung *f* concussion
Gehirnschlag *m* stroke
geholfen [gəˈhɔl·fn̩] *pp von* **helfen**
Gehör <-[e]s, *selten* -e> [gəˈhøːɐ̯] *nt* hearing; **sich** *dat* **~ verschaffen** to make oneself heard
gehorchen* *vi* ■ **jdm/etw ~** to obey sb/sth
ge|hören* I. *vi* ➊ (*jds Eigentum sein*) ■ **jdm ~** to belong to sb; **ihm ~ mehrere Häuser** he owns several houses ➋ (*jdm zugewandt sein*) ■ **jdm/etw ~** to belong to sb/sth; **ihre ganze Liebe gehört ihrem Sohn** she gives all her love to her son ➌ (*den richtigen Platz haben*) **die Kinder ~ ins Bett** the children belong in bed ➍ (*angebracht sein*) **nicht zum Thema ~** to be beside the point ➎ (*Mitglied sein*) ■ **zu jdm/ etw ~** to belong to sb/sth; **zur Fami-**

   G

lie ~ to be one of the family ⑥ (*Teil sein von*) ■ **zu etw** *dat* ~ to be [a] part of sth ⑦ (*Voraussetzung, nötig sein*) to require; **es gehört viel Mut dazu, ...** it takes a lot of courage to ... II. *vr* ■ **sich** *akk* ~ to be fitting; **wie es sich gehört** as it should be; **sich** *akk* [**einfach**] **nicht** ~ to be [simply] not good manners

gehörig [gə·ˈhøː·rɪç] I. *adj* ❶ *attr* (*fam: beträchtlich*) good *attr* ❷ (*geh: gehörend*) belonging (**zu** +*dat* to) II. *adv* (*fam*) **jdn** ~ **ausschimpfen** to really tell sb off

Gehörlose(r) *f/m* deaf person

gehorsam [gə·ˈhoːɐ̯·zaːm] *adj* obedient

Gehorsam <-s> [gə·ˈhoːɐ̯·zaːm] *m kein pl* obedience

Gehweg *m* ❶ *s.* **Bürgersteig** ❷ (*Fußweg*) walk

Geier <-s, -> [ˈgai·ɐ] *m* vulture

Geige <-, -n> [ˈgai·gə] *f* violin, fiddle *fam*

geil [ˈgail] I. *adj* ❶ (*lüstern*) lecherous; ■ ~ **auf jdn sein** to have the hots for sb ❷ (*sl: toll*) cool II. *adv* ❶ (*lüstern*) lecherously ❷ (*sl: toll*) cool

Geisel <-, -n> [ˈgai·zl̩] *f* hostage

Geiselnehmer(in) <-s, -> [ˈgai·zl̩] *m(f)* kidnapper, abductor

Geist <-[e]s, -er> [ˈgaist] *m* ❶ *kein pl* (*Vernunft*) mind ❷ *kein pl* (*Esprit*) spirit ❸ *kein pl* (*Wesen, Sinn, Gesinnung*) spirit ❹ (*körperloses Wesen*) ghost; **böse/gute ~er** evil/good spirits; **der Heilige ~** the Holy Ghost ▶WENDUNGEN: **den ~ aufgeben** (*fam*) to give up the ghost; **von allen guten ~ern verlassen sein** (*fam*) to have taken leave of one's senses

geistesabwesend *adj* absent-minded

geistesgegenwärtig I. *adj* quick-witted II. *adv* with great presence of mind

geistesgestört *adj* mentally disturbed

Geisteskrankheit *f* mental illness

Geisteswissenschaften *pl* humanities

geistig [ˈgais·tɪç] *adj* ~**es Eigentum** JUR intellectual property

Geistliche(r) *f/m* clergyman *masc*, clergywoman *fem*

geistlos *adj* ❶ (*dumm*) witless ❷ (*einfallslos*) inane

geistreich *adj* ❶ *Mensch* witty ❷ (*iron: dumm*) bright *iron*

geizen [ˈgai·tsn̩] *vi* ■ **mit etw** *dat* ~ ❶ (*knauserig sein*) to be stingy with sth ❷ (*zurückhaltend sein*) to be sparing with sth

Geizhals *m* cheapskate

geizig [ˈgai·tsɪç] *adj* stingy

Gejammer <-s> [gə·ˈja·mɐ] *nt kein pl* (*pej fam*) whining

gekannt [gə·ˈkant] *pp von* **kennen**

geklungen [gə·ˈklʊŋən] *pp von* **klingen**

gekniffen [gə·ˈknɪ·fn̩] *pp von* **kneifen**

gekommen *pp von* **kommen**

Gekritzel <-s> [gə·ˈkrɪtsl̩] *nt kein pl* (*pej*) scrawl

gekrochen [gə·ˈkrɔ·xn̩] *pp von* **kriechen**

Gel <-s, -e> [ˈgeːl] *nt* gel

Gelächter <-s, selten -> [gə·ˈlɛç·tɐ] *nt* laughter

geladen I. *pp von* **laden** II. *adj* (*fam*) *pred* (*wütend*) furious

gelähmt *adj* paralyzed

Gelände <-s, -> [gə·ˈlɛn·də] *nt* ❶ (*Land*) terrain ❷ (*bestimmtes Stück Land*) site

Geländer <-s, -> [gə·ˈlɛn·dɐ] *nt* handrail; (*Treppengeländer*) banister

Geländewagen *m* all-terrain vehicle, ATV

gelang [gə·ˈlaŋ] *imp von* **gelingen**

gelangen* *vi sein* ❶ (*hinkommen*) **ans Ziel** ~ to reach one's destination ❷ (*erwerben*) ■ **zu etw** *dat* ~ to achieve sth; *Ruhm, Reichtum* to gain

gelassen [gə·ˈla·sn̩] I. *pp von* **lassen** II. *adj* calm

Gelassenheit <-> *f kein pl* calmness

gelaufen *pp von* **laufen**

geläufig [gə·ˈlɔy·fɪç] *adj* familiar

gelaunt [gə·ˈlaunt] *adj pred* **gut/schlecht** ~ **sein** to be in a good/bad mood

gelb [ˈgɛlp] *adj* yellow

Gelb <-s, -> [ˈgɛlp] *nt* yellow

Geld <-[e]s, -er> ['gɛlt] *nt kein pl (Zahlungsmittel)* money ▸WENDUNGEN: **jdm das ~ aus der Tasche ziehen** to squeeze money out of sb

Geldanlage *f* [financial] investment

Geldautomat *m* automated teller machine, ATM

Geldbeutel *m* SÜDD, **Geldbörse** *f* ÖSTERR *(sonst geh: Portmonee)* wallet

Geldschein *m* bill

Geldstrafe *f* fine

Geldwechsel *m* foreign exchange

Gelee <-s, -s> [ʒeˈleː, ʒəˈleː] *m o nt* jelly

gelegen [gəˈleː.gn̩] I. *pp von* **liegen** II. *adj (passend)* convenient; **jdm ~ kommen** to come at the right time for sb

Gelegenheit <-, -en> [gəˈleː.gn̩.haɪt] *f* ❶ *(günstiger Moment)* opportunity ❷ *(Anlass)* occasion

Gelegenheitsarbeiter(in) *m(f)* casual laborer

gelegentlich [gəˈleː.gn̩t.lɪç] I. *adj attr* occasional II. *adv* ❶ *(manchmal)* occasionally ❷ *(bei Gelegenheit)* **wenn Sie ~ in der Nachbarschaft sind ...** if you happen to be in the neighborhood ...

gelehrt *adj* learned

Geleitschutz *m* escort; **jdm/etw ~ geben** to escort sb/sth

Gelenk <-[e]s, -e> [gəˈlɛŋk] *nt* ANAT, TECH joint

Gelenkentzündung *f* arthritis

gelenkig [gəˈlɛŋ.kɪç] *adj* supple

gelesen *pp von* **lesen**

Geliebte(r) *f/m* lover

geliehen [gəˈliː.ən] *pp von* **leihen**

gelingen [gəˈlɪŋ.ən] *(gelang, gelungen)* [gəˈlɪŋən] *vi sein* ■**jdm gelingt es, etw zu tun** sb manages to do sth; ■**jdm gelingt es nicht, etw zu tun** sb fails to do sth

gelitten [gəˈlɪ.tn̩] *pp von* **leiden**

gelogen [gəˈloː.gn̩] *pp von* **lügen**

gelten <gilt, galt, gegolten> ['gɛl.tn̩] I. *vi* ❶ *(gültig sein)* ■**für jdn** ~ *Regelung* to be valid [for sb]; *Bestimmungen* to apply [to sb]; *Gesetz* to be in force ❷ *(bestimmt sein für)* ■**jdm/etw ~** to be meant for sb/sth; *Buhrufe* to be aimed at sb/sth; *Frage* to be directed at sb ❸ *(gehalten werden)* ■**als etw ~** to be regarded as sth ▸WENDUNGEN: **etw ~ lassen** to accept sth II. *vi impers* ■**es gilt, etw zu tun** it is necessary to do sth; **das gilt nicht!** that's not allowed!

geltend *adj attr* ❶ *(gültig)* current ❷ *(vorherrschend)* *Meinung* prevailing ❸ **Ansprüche/Forderungen ~ machen** to make claims/demands

Geltung <-> *f kein pl (Gültigkeit)* validity ▸WENDUNGEN: **etw zur ~ bringen** to show off *sep* sth to its advantage

Gelübde <-s, -> [gəˈlʏp.də] *nt (geh)* vow

gelungen [gəˈlʊŋən] I. *pp von* **gelingen** II. *adj attr* successful

Gemälde <-s, -> [gəˈmɛːl.də] *nt* painting

gemäß [gəˈmɛːs] I. *präp +dat* in accordance with; **~ § 198** according to § 198 II. *adj* ■**jdm/etw ~** appropriate for sb/sth

gemäßigt *adj* ❶ METEO temperate ❷ *(moderat)* moderate

gemein [gəˈmaɪn] I. *adj* ❶ *(niederträchtig)* mean; *(böse)* nasty ❷ *attr, kein komp/superl* BOT, ZOOL common ❸ *pred (gemeinsam)* **etw mit jdm/etw ~ haben** to have sth in common with sb/sth II. *adv (fam)* horribly

Gemeinde <-, -n> [gəˈmaɪn.də] *f* ❶ ADMIN *(politische Einheit)* municipality ❷ REL *(Pfarrgemeinde)* parish; *(Gläubige a.)* parishioners *pl*

Gemeindehaus *nt* REL parish house

Gemeinderat[1] *m (Organ der Gemeinde)* town council

Gemeinderat, -rätin[2] *m, f (Gemeinderatsmitglied)* councilman *masc*, councilwoman *fem*

Gemeindeverwaltung *f* town council

gemeingefährlich *adj* constituting a public danger *pred*

Gemeinheit <-, -en> *f* ❶ *kein pl (Niedertracht)* meanness ❷ *(niederträch-*

G

tige Bemerkung, Handlung) **so eine ~!** that was a mean thing to say/do!

gemeinnützig [gə·'main·nʏ·tsɪç] *adj* charitable

gemeinsam [gə·'main·za:m] I. *adj* ❶ *(mehreren gehörend)* common; *Konto* joint; *Freund* mutual; **etw ~ haben** to have sth in common ❷ *(von mehreren unternommen)* joint *attr* II. *adv* jointly

Gemeinschaft <-, -en> *f* ❶ POL community; ■ **die Europäische ~** the European Community ❷ *kein pl (gegenseitige Verbundenheit)* sense of community

Gemeinschaftspraxis *f* joint practice

Gemenge <-s, -> [gə·'mɛŋə] *nt* ❶ *(Mischung)* mixture *(aus +dat of)* ❷ *(Gewühl)* crowd ❸ *(Durcheinander)* jumble

Gemetzel <-s, -> [gə·'mɛ·tsl̩] *nt* bloodbath

gemieden [gə·'mi:·dn̩] *pp von* **meiden**

Gemisch <-[e]s, -e> [gə·'mɪʃ] *nt* mixture *(aus +dat of)*

gemischt *adj* mixed

gemocht [gə·'mɔxt] *pp von* **mögen**

gemolken [gə·'mɔl·kn̩] *pp von* **melken**

GemseALT <-, -n> *f s.* **Gämse**

Gemüse <-s, *selten* -> [gə·'my:·zə] *nt* vegetables *pl;* ■ **ein ~** a vegetable

Gemüsehändler(in) *m(f)* produce market

gemusstRR, **gemußt**ALT [gə·'mʊst] *pp von* **müssen**

gemustert *adj* patterned

gemütlich I. *adj* ❶ *(bequem)* cozy; **es sich/jdm ~ machen** to make oneself/ sb comfortable ❷ *(gesellig)* pleasant; *(ungezwungen)* informal II. *adv* ❶ *(gemächlich)* leisurely ❷ *(behaglich)* comfortably

Gemütlichkeit <-> *f kein pl* ❶ *(Behaglichkeit)* coziness ❷ *(Ungezwungenheit)* informality

Gemütsmensch *m (fam)* good-natured person

Gemütsruhe *f* **in aller ~** *(fam)* at one's own pace

Gemütszustand *m* mood

Gen <-s, -e> ['ge:n] *nt* gene

genannt [gə·'nant] *pp von* **nennen**

genau [gə·'nau] I. *adj* ❶ *(exakt)* exact; **man weiß noch nichts G~es** nobody knows any details yet ❷ *(gewissenhaft)* meticulous II. *adv* exactly; **~ in der Mitte** right in the middle; **~ genommen** strictly speaking

genaugenommen *adv s.* **genau** II

Genauigkeit <-> [gə·'nau·ɪç·kait] *f kein pl* exactness; *von Daten* accuracy

genauso [gə·'nau·zo:] *adv* just the same; **~ gut/viel/wenig** just as well/ much/little

Gendefekt *m* BIOL, MED genetic defect

genehmigen* [gə·'ne:·mɪ·gn̩] I. *vt* ■ **jdm] etw ~** to grant [sb] permission to do sth II. *vr* ■ **sich** *dat* **etw ~** to indulge in sth

Genehmigung <-, -en> *f* ❶ *(das Genehmigen)* approval ❷ *(Berechtigungsschein)* permit

geneigt *adj* ■ **~ sein, etw zu tun** to be inclined to do sth

General(in) <-[e]s, -e> [ge·nə·'ra:l] *m(f)* general

Generaldirektor(in) *m(f)* general manager

Generalprobe *f* ❶ THEAT dress rehearsal ❷ MUS final rehearsal

Generalstreik *m* general strike

Generaluntersuchung *f* complete checkup

Generation <-, -en> [ge·nə·ra·'tsi̯o:n] *f* generation

Generator <-s, -toren> [ge·nə·'ra:·to:ɐ̯] *m* generator

generell [ge·nə·'rɛl] I. *adj* general II. *adv* generally

genervt [gə·'nɛrft] *adj* annoyed; *(stärker)* at the end of one's rope

Genesung <-, *selten* -en> [gə·'ne:·zʊŋ] *f (geh)* convalescence

Genetik <-> [ge·'ne:·tɪk] *f kein pl* genetics + *sing vb*

genetisch [ge·'ne:·tɪʃ] *adj* genetic

Genforschung *f* genetic research

genial [ge·'ni̯a:l] *adj* ❶ *(überra-*

gend) brilliant; (*erfinderisch*) ingenious ② *Idee* inspired

Genick <-[e]s, -e> [gəˈnɪk] *nt* neck ▶WENDUNGEN: **jdm das ~ brechen** to finish [off *sep*] sb

Genie <-s, -s> [ʒeˈniː] *nt* genius

genieren* [ʒeˈniː·rən] *vr* ■ **sich** *akk* ~ to be embarrassed

ge|nießen <genoss, genossen> [gəˈniː·sn] *vt* ① (*auskosten*) to enjoy ② (*essen*) to eat

Genießer(in) <-s, -> *m(f)* gourmet

Genitiv <-s, -e> [ˈgeː·ni·tiːf] *m* genitive [case]

genommen [gəˈnɔ·mən] *pp von* **nehmen**

genormt *adj* standardized

genossRR, **genoß**ALT [gəˈnɔs] *imp von* **genießen**

Genosse, Genossin <-n, -n> [gəˈnɔ·sə, gəˈnɔ·sɪn] *m, f* comrade

genossen [gəˈnɔ·sn] *pp von* **genießen**

Genossenschaft <-, -en> [gəˈnɔ·sn̩·ʃaft] *f* cooperative

Gentechnik *f* genetic engineering

genug [gəˈnuːk] *adv* enough

Genüge [gəˈnyː·gə] *f kein pl* **zur ~** [quite] enough; (*oft genug*) often enough

ge|nügen* [gəˈnyː·gn̩] *vi* ① (*ausreichen*) ■ **jdm** ~ to be enough [for sb] ② (*gerecht werden*) ■ **etw** *dat* ~ to fulfill sth

genügsam [gəˈnyːk·za:m] *adj* (*bescheiden*) modest

Genugtuung <-, *selten* -en> [gəˈnuːk·tu:·ʊŋ] *f* satisfaction

Genus <-, Genera> [ˈgɛ·nʊs] *nt* gender

GenussRR <-es, Genüsse>, **Genuß**ALT <-sses, Genüsse> [gəˈnʊs] *m* ① (*Köstlichkeit*) [culinary] delight ② *kein pl* (*das Zusichnehmen*) consumption ③ (*das Genießen*) enjoyment; **in den ~ einer S.** *gen* **kommen** to [come to] enjoy sth; (*aus etw Nutzen ziehen a.*) to benefit from sth

genüsslichRR, **genüßlich**ALT I. *adj* pleasurable II. *adv* with [great] pleasure

GenussmittelRR *nt* luxury foods, alcohol and tobacco

Geograf(in)RR <-en, -en> *m(f)* s. **Geograph**

GeografieRR <-> *f kein pl* s. **Geographie**

geografischRR *adj* s. **geographisch**

Geograph(in) <-en, -en> [geoˈgraːf] *m(f)* geographer

Geographie <-> [geo·graˈfiː] *f kein pl* geography

geographisch [geoˈgraː·fɪʃ] *adj* geographic[al]

geologisch [geoˈloː·gɪʃ] *adj* geological

Geometrie <-> [geo·meˈtriː] *f kein pl* geometry

geometrisch [geoˈmeː·trɪʃ] *adj* geometric

Gepäck <-[e]s> [gəˈpɛk] *nt kein pl* luggage, baggage

Gepäckabfertigung *f* luggage [or baggage] check-in

Gepäckausgabe *f* luggage [or baggage] claim

Gepäckstück *nt* piece of luggage [or baggage]

Gepäckträger *m* (*am Fahrrad*) rear rack

Gepäckträger(in) *m(f)* porter

Gepäckwagen *m* luggage cart

gepfeffert *adj* (*fam*) s. **gesalzen**

gepfiffen [gəˈpfɪ·fn̩] *pp von* **pfeifen**

gepflegt *adj* ① (*nicht vernachlässigt*) well looked after; *Aussehen* well-groomed; *Garten* well-tended; *Park* well-kept ② (*fam: kultiviert*) civilized; *Ausdrucksweise* sophisticated

gepriesen [gəˈpriː·zn̩] *pp von* **preisen**

gequollen [gəˈkvɔ·lən] *pp von* **quellen**

gerade [gəˈraː·də] I. *adj* ① (*nicht krumm*) straight; (*aufrecht*) upright; **~ sitzen/stehen** to sit/stand up straight ② MATH even II. *adv* (*fam*) ① (*im Augenblick, soeben*) just; **haben Sie ~ einen Moment Zeit?** do you have a minute?; **da du ~ da bist, ...** while you're here, ...; **ich wollte mich ~ ins Bad begeben, da ...** I was just about to take a bath when ...; **da wir ~**

G

von Geld sprechen, ... speaking of money, ... ➋ (*knapp*) just; **sie hat die Prüfung ~ so bestanden** she [just] barely passed the exam ➌ (*genau*) just; **~ heute habe ich an dich gedacht** I was just thinking of you today III. *part* (*ausgerechnet*) **warum ~ er/ich?** why him/me of all people?; **warum ~ jetzt?** why now of all times?; **~ deswegen** that's exactly why ►WENDUNGEN: **das hat ~ noch gefehlt!** (*iron*) that's all I need!; **~, weil ...** especially because ...

Gerade <-n, -n> [gə·ˈraː·də] *f* MATH straight line

geradeaus [gə·raː·də·ˈʔaus] *adv* straight ahead

gerade|biegen *vt irreg* (*fam: in Ordnung bringen*) to straighten out *sep*

geradeheraus [gə·raː·də·hɛ·ˈraus] I. *adj pred* straightforward II. *adv* frankly

gerade|stehen^ALT1 *vi irreg* (*aufrecht stehen*) s. **gerade II 1**

gerade|stehen[2] *vi irreg* (*einstehen*) ■**für jdn/etw ~** to answer for sb/sth

geradezu [gə·raː·də·ˈtsuː] *adv* really

geradlinig *adj, adv* straight

Geranie <-, -n> [ge·ˈraː·ni̯ə] *f* geranium

gerann [gə·ˈran] *imp von* **gerinnen**

gerannt [gə·ˈrant] *pp von* **rennen**

Gerät <-[e]s, -e> [gə·ˈrɛːt] *nt* ➊ (*Vorrichtung*) device, gadget ➋ ELEK, TECH appliance; (*Fernseher, Radio*) set ➌ (*Werkzeug*) tool ➍ SPORT (*Turngerät*) apparatus ➎ *kein pl* (*Ausrüstung*) equipment; *eines Handwerkers* tools *pl*

ge|raten[1] <gerät, geriet, geraten> *vi sein* ➊ (*unbeabsichtigt kommen*) ■**in etw** *akk* **~** to get into sth; **in Schwierigkeiten/eine Schlägerei ~** to get into difficulties/a fight; **in Armut ~** to end up in poverty; **in Brand ~** to catch fire; **in eine Falle ~** to fall into a trap; **in Gefangenschaft ~** to be taken prisoner; **ins Schleudern ~** to go into a skid; **in einen Stau ~** to get stuck in a traffic jam; **ins Schwärmen/Träumen ~** to fall into a rapture/dream; **in**

einen Sturm ~ to get caught in a storm; **in Vergessenheit ~** to fall into oblivion ➋ (*erfüllt werden von*) **in Panik ~** to start to panic; **in Verlegenheit/Wut ~** to get embarrassed/angry ➌ **zu groß/klein ~** to turn out too big/short ➍ (*gelingen*) to turn out; **das Soufflé ist mir nicht ~** my soufflé turned didn't turn out well ➎ (*fam: kennen lernen*) ■**an jdn ~** to come across sb ➏ (*arten*) ■**nach jdm ~** to take after sb

ge|raten[2] *pp von* **raten**

Geratewohl [gə·raː·tə·ˈvoːl] *nt* ►WENDUNGEN: **aufs ~** (*fam: auf gut Glück*) on the off chance; (*willkürlich*) randomly

geräumig [gə·ˈrɔy·mɪç] *adj* spacious

Geräusch <-[e]s, -e> [gə·ˈrɔyʃ] *nt* sound; (*unerwartet, unangenehm a.*) noise

geräuschempfindlich *adj* sensitive to noise *pred*

geräuschlos *adj* silent

geräuschvoll *adj* loud

gerben [ˈɡɛr·bn̩] *vt* to tan

gerecht [gə·ˈrɛçt] I. *adj* just; ■**etw** *dat* **~ werden** to fulfill sth; **Erwartungen ~ werden** to meet expectations II. *adv* justly

Gerechtigkeit <-> [gə·ˈrɛç·tɪç·kait] *f kein pl* justice

Gerede <-s> [gə·ˈreː·də] *nt kein pl* gossip; (*Geschwätz*) talk; **kümmere dich nicht um das ~ der Leute** don't worry about what [other] people are saying

gereizt I. *adj* (*verärgert*) irritated; (*nervös*) edgy II. *adv* irritably

Gericht[1] <-[e]s, -e> [gə·ˈrɪçt] *nt* (*Speise*) dish

Gericht[2] <-[e]s, -e> [gə·ˈrɪçt] *nt* ➊ JUR court [of justice]; (*Gebäude*) law courts *pl* ➋ (*die Richter*) court ►WENDUNGEN: **mit jdm ins ~ gehen** to sharply criticize sb

gerichtlich I. *adj attr* judicial II. *adv* legally; **~ gegen jdn vorgehen** to take sb to court

Gerichtshof *m* court of law

Gerichtssaal *m* courtroom

Gerichtsverfahren *nt* legal proceedings *pl*; **ein ~ gegen jdn einleiten** to take legal action against sb

Gerichtsverhandlung *f* trial; (*zivil*) hearing

Gerichtsvollzieher(in) <-s, -> *m(f)* U.S Marshal

geriet [gəˈriːt] *imp von* **geraten**[1]

gering [gəˈrɪŋ] *adj* ① (*niedrig*) low; *Anzahl, Menge* small; **das stört mich nicht im G~sten** it doesn't bother me in the slightest; **von ~em Wert** of little value ② (*unerheblich*) slight; *Bedeutung* minor; *Chance* slim

geringfügig [gəˈrɪŋfyːgɪç] I. *adj* insignificant; *Betrag, Einkommen* small; *Unterschied, Vergehen, Verletzung* minor II. *adv* slightly

geringschätzig [gəˈrɪŋʃɛtsɪç] *adj s.* **abfällig**

ge|rinnen <gerann, geronnen> *vi sein* to coagulate; *Blut a.* to clot; *Milch a.* to curdle

Gerippe <-s, -> [gəˈrɪpə] *nt* skeleton

gerissen [gəˈrɪsn̩] I. *pp von* **reißen** II. *adj* (*fam*) crafty; *Plan* cunning

geritten [gəˈrɪtn̩] *pp von* **reiten**

Germane, Germanin <-n, -n> [gɛrˈmaːnə, gɛrˈmaːnɪn] *m, f* Teuton

germanisch [gɛrˈmaːnɪʃ] *adj* ① HIST Teutonic ② LING Germanic

Germanistik <-> [gɛrmaˈnɪstɪk] *f kein pl* German [studies *npl*]

gern(e) <lieber, am liebsten> [ˈgɛrn(ə)] *adv* ① (*freudig*) with pleasure; **ich mag ihn sehr ~** I like him a lot; **etw ~ tun** to like doing/to do sth; **seine Arbeit ~ machen** to enjoy one's work; **ich hätte ~ gewusst, ...** I would like to know ... ② (*ohne weiteres*) **das kannst du ~ haben** you're welcome to [have] it; **das glaube ich ~!** I [really] believe it! ►WENDUNGEN: **~ geschehen!** don't mention it!

gerochen [gəˈrɔxn̩] *pp von* **riechen**

Geröll <-[e]s, -e> [gəˈrœl] *nt* scree *spec*, talus; (*größer*) boulders *pl*

Gerste <-, -n> [ˈgɛrstə] *f* barley

Geruch <-[e]s, Gerüche> [gəˈrʊx] *m*

smell; *einer Blume, eines Parfüms* scent; (*Gestank*) stench

geruchlos *adj* odorless

Geruch(s)sinn *m kein pl* sense of smell

Gerücht <-[e]s, -e> [gəˈrʏçt] *nt* rumor; **ein ~ in die Welt setzen** to start a rumor

gerufen *pp von* **rufen**

Gerümpel <-s> [gəˈrʏmpl̩] *nt kein pl* junk

Gerundium <-s, -ien> [geˈrʊndiʊm] *nt* gerund *spec*

gerungen [gəˈrʊŋən] *pp von* **ringen**

Gerüst <-[e]s, -e> [gəˈrʏst] *nt* ① BAU scaffold[ing] ② (*Grundplan*) framework

gesalzen [gəˈzaltsn̩] *adj* (*fam*) *Preis, Strafe* steep

gesamt [gəˈzamt] *adj attr* whole, entire; *Kosten* total

Gesamtbetrag *m* total [amount]

Gesamteindruck *m* overall impression

Gesamtkosten *pl* total cost[s *pl*]

Gesamtschule *f* ≈ integrated school

gesandt [gəˈzant] *pp von* **senden**[2]

Gesandte(r) [gəˈzantə] *f/m* envoy

Gesang <-[e]s, Gesänge> [gəˈzaŋ] *m* ① *kein pl* (*das Singen*) singing ② (*Lied*) song; **ein Gregorianischer ~** a Gregorian chant

Gesangbuch *nt* hymn book

Gesangverein *m* glee club

Gesäß <-es, -e> [gəˈzɛːs] *nt* rear end *fam*

geschaffen *pp von* **schaffen**[2]

Geschäft <-[e]s, -e> [gəˈʃɛft] *nt* ① (*Laden*) store, shop ② (*Gewerbe, Handel*) business; **mit jdm ins ~ kommen** (*einmalig*) to make a deal with sb; (*dauerhaft*) to do business with sb; **wie gehen die ~e?** how's business? ③ (*Geschäftsabschluss*) deal; **ein gutes ~ machen** to get a good deal ►WENDUNGEN: **kleines/großes ~** (*fam*) number one/number two

geschäftig [gəˈʃɛftɪç] *adj* busy

geschäftlich [gəˈʃɛftlɪç] I. *adj* business *attr* II. *adv* on business; **~ verreist** away on business

Geschäftsbrief *m* business letter

G

Geschäftsfrau f fem form von **Geschäftsmann** businesswoman fem

Geschäftsführer(in) m(f) ① ADMIN manager ② (in einem Verein) secretary

Geschäftsmann m businessman

Geschäftsreise f business trip

Geschäftsschluss^{RR} m (Ladenschluss) closing time

Geschäftsstelle f (Büro) office; einer Bank, Firma branch

geschäftstüchtig adj business-minded

Geschäftszeit f business hours pl

geschah [gə·ˈʃaː] imp von **geschehen**

ge|schehen <geschah, geschehen> [gə·ˈʃeː·ən] vi sein ① (stattfinden) to happen; **es muss etwas ~** something has to be done ② (widerfahren) ■**jdm geschieht etw** sth happens to sb; **das geschieht dir recht!** [it] serves you right!; **nicht wissen, wie einem geschieht** to not know whether one is coming or going ③ (hin und weg sein) **als sie ihn sah, war es um sie ~** she was lost the moment she set eyes on him

Geschehen <-s, -> [gə·ˈʃeː·ən] nt events pl

gescheit [gə·ˈʃaɪt] adj clever

Geschenk <-[e]s, -e> [gə·ˈʃɛŋk] nt present

Geschenkpapier nt wrapping paper

Geschichte <-, -n> [gə·ˈʃɪçtə] f ① kein pl (Historie) history; **Alte/Neue ~** ancient/modern history ② (Erzählung) story ③ (fam: Angelegenheit, Sache) business; **die ganze ~** everything; **das sind ja schöne ~n!** (iron) that's a fine state of affairs!

geschichtlich [gə·ˈʃɪçt·lɪç] adj historical

Geschichtsbuch nt history book

Geschick[1] <-[e]s> [gə·ˈʃɪk] nt kein pl (Fertigkeit) skill

Geschick[2] <-[e]s, -e> [gə·ˈʃɪk] nt (Schicksal) fate

Geschicklichkeit <-> f kein pl skill

geschickt I. adj skillful; Verhalten diplomatic II. adv skillfully

geschieden [gə·ˈʃiː·dn̩] I. pp von **scheiden** II. adj divorced

geschienen [gə·ˈʃiː·nən] pp von **scheinen**

Geschirr <-[e]s, -e> [gə·ˈʃɪr] nt ① kein pl (Haushaltsgefäße) dishes pl ② (Service) [tea/dinner] service ③ (Riemenzeug) harness

Geschirrspülmaschine f dishwasher

Geschirrspülmittel nt dish soap

Geschirrtuch nt dishcloth

geschissen [gə·ˈʃɪ·sn̩] pp von **scheißen**

geschlafen pp von **schlafen**

geschlagen pp von **schlagen**

Geschlecht <-[e]s, -er> [gə·ˈʃlɛçt] nt ① kein pl BIOL gender; **das andere ~** the opposite sex; **männlichen/weiblichen ~s** male/female ② (Sippe) family ③ LING gender

Geschlechtskrankheit f sexually transmitted disease

Geschlechtsteil nt genitals npl

Geschlechtsverkehr m sexual intercourse

geschlichen [gə·ˈʃlɪ·çn̩] pp von **schleichen**

geschliffen [gə·ˈʃlɪ·fn̩] I. pp von **schleifen**[2] II. adj polished

geschlossen [gə·ˈʃlɔ·sn̩] I. pp von **schließen** II. adj ① (gemeinsam) united; Ablehnung unanimous ② (nicht geöffnet) closed III. adv (einheitlich) unanimously

geschlungen [gə·ˈʃlʊŋən] pp von **schlingen**

Geschmack <-[e]s, Geschmäcke> [gə·ˈʃmak] m ① kein pl (Aroma) taste ② kein pl (Geschmackssinn) sense of taste ③ (ästhetisches Empfinden) taste; **einen guten/keinen guten ~ haben** to have good/bad taste; **auf den ~ kommen** to acquire a taste for sth ▶WENDUNGEN: **über ~ lässt sich [nicht] streiten** (prov) there's no accounting for taste

geschmacklos adj ① KOCHK bland ② (taktlos) tasteless

Geschmacklosigkeit <-, -en> f ① (Taktlosigkeit) tastelessness; (taktlose Bemerkung) tasteless remark ② KOCHK tastelessness geschmackvoll *adj* tasteful

geschmeidig [gə·ˈʃmai·dɪç] **I.** *adj*
① (*weich*) sleek; *Haar, Fell* silky; *Haut*
soft; *Leder* supple; *Masse, Teig* smooth
② (*biegsam*) supple **II.** *adv* (*biegsam*)
supplely

geschmissen [gə·ˈʃmɪ·sn̩] *pp von*
schmeißen

geschmolzen [gə·ˈʃmɔl·tsn̩] *pp von*
schmelzen

geschnitten [gə·ˈʃnɪ·tn̩] *pp von* **schneiden**

geschoben [gə·ˈʃoː·bn̩] *pp von* **schieben**

gescholten [gə·ˈʃɔl·tn̩] *pp von* **schelten**

geschoren [gə·ˈʃoː·rən] *pp von* **scheren**¹

Geschoss^RR <-es, -e>, Geschoß^ALT
<-sses, -sse> [gə·ˈʃɔs] *nt* ① MIL projec-
tile ② (*Wurfgeschoss*) missile ③ (*Stockwerk*) floor, story

geschossen [gə·ˈʃɔ·sn̩] *pp von* **schießen**

geschraubt *adj* (*pej*) affected

Geschrei <-s> [gə·ˈʃrai] *nt kein pl*
① (*Schreien*) shouting; (*schrill*) shriek-
ing ② (*fam: Lamentieren*) fuss

geschrieben [gə·ˈʃriː·bn̩] *pp von*
schreiben

geschrie(e)n [gə·ˈʃriː·(ə)n] *pp von*
schreien

geschritten [gə·ˈʃrɪ·tn̩] *pp von* **schreiten**

geschunden [gə·ˈʃʊn·dn̩] *pp von*
schinden

Geschwätz <-es> [gə·ˈʃvɛts] *nt kein pl*
(*pej fam*) ① (*dummes Gerede*) hot air
pej fam ② (*Klatsch*) gossip

geschwätzig [gə·ˈʃvɛ·tsɪç] *adj* (*pej*)
talkative

geschweige [gə·ˈʃvai·gə] *konj* ■~
[denn] never mind, let alone

geschwiegen [gə·ˈʃviː·gn̩] *pp von*
schweigen

geschwind [gə·ˈʃvɪnt] *adv* DIAL quickly

Geschwindigkeit <-, -en> [gə·ˈʃvɪn·
dɪç·kait] *f* speed

Geschwindigkeitsbegrenzung *f* speed
limit

Geschwister [gə·ˈʃvɪs·tɐ] *pl* siblings *pl*

geschwollen [gə·ˈʃvɔ·lən] **I.** *pp von*
schwellen **II.** *adj* (*pej*) pompous
III. *adv* in a pompous way

geschwommen [gə·ˈʃvɔ·mən] *pp von*
schwimmen

Geschworene(r) *f(m)* juror; **die ~n** the
jury

Geschwulst <-, Geschwülste> [gə·
ˈʃvʊlst] *f* tumor

geschwunden [gə·ˈʃvʊn·dn̩] *pp von*
schwinden

Geschwür <-s, -e> [gə·ˈʃvyː·ɐ] *nt* ulcer **G**

gesehen *pp von* **sehen**

ge|sellen* [gə·ˈzɛ·lən] *vr* ① (*sich
anschließen*) ■**sich** *akk* **zu jdm ~** to
join sb ② (*hinzukommen*) ■**sich** *akk*
zu etw *dat* ~ to add to sth

gesellig [gə·ˈzɛ·lɪç] **I.** *adj* sociable;
Abend convivial; **ein ~es Beisammensein** a friendly get-together **II.** *adv*
~ zusammensitzen to sit together and
chat

Geselligkeit <-, -en> *f* gregariousness

Gesellschaft <-, -en> [gə·ˈzɛl·ʃaft] *f*
① POL, SOZIOL society ② ÖKON corporation
③ (*Fest*) party ④ (*Kreis von Menschen*)
group of people; **in schlechte ~ geraten** to get in with the wrong crowd;
jdm ~ leisten to join sb ⑤ (*Umgang*)
company

Gesellschafter(in) <-s, -> *m(f)* (*Teilha-
ber*) shareholder

gesellschaftlich *adj* social

gesellschaftsfähig *adj* socially acceptable

gesessen [gə·ˈzɛ·sn̩] *pp von* **sitzen**

Gesetz <-es, -e> [gə·ˈzɛts] *nt* law

Gesetzbuch *nt* statute book; **Bürgerli-
ches ~** Civil Code

Gesetzentwurf *m* draft legislation

Gesetzgeber <-s, -> *m* legislature

Gesetzgebung <-, -en> *f* legislation

gesetzlich [gə·ˈzɛts·lɪç] *adj* legal

Gesetzmäßigkeit <-, -en> *f* ① (*Ge-
setzlichkeit*) legality ② (*Rechtmäßig-
keit*) legitimacy ③ (*Regelmäßigkeit*)
regularity

gesetzt **I.** *adj* dignified **II.** *konj* ■~, ...

(*angenommen, ...*) assuming that ...; (*vorausgesetzt, dass ...*) providing that ...

gesichert I. *pp von* **sichern** II. *adj* secure[d]; *Erkenntnisse* solid; **~es Einkommen** fixed income; **~e Existenz** secure livelihood

Gesicht <-[e]s, -er> [gə·ˈzɪçt] *nt* face; **jdm etw am ~ ablesen** to see sth from sb's expression; **ein böses/trauriges ~ machen** to look angry/sad ▶WENDUNGEN: **jdm wie aus dem ~ geschnitten** to be the spitting image of sb; **sein <u>wahres</u> ~ zeigen** to show one's true colors

Gesichtsfarbe *f* complexion

Gesichtspunkt *m* point of view

Gesindel <-s> [gə·ˈzɪn·dl̩] *nt kein pl* (*pej*) riffraff

gesinnt [gə·ˈzɪnt] *adj meist pred* minded; **jdm gut/übel ~ sein** to be well-disposed/ill-disposed toward sb

Gesinnungswandel *m* change in attitude

gesittet [gə·ˈzɪ·tət] I. *adj* well-brought up II. *adv* **sich** *akk* **~ benehmen** to be well-behaved

gesoffen [gə·ˈzɔ·fn̩] *pp von* **saufen**

gesogen [gə·ˈzo·ɡn̩] *pp von* **saugen**

gespalten [gə·ˈʃpal·tn̩] *pp von* **spalten**

gespannt *adj* ❶ (*sehr erwartungsvoll*) expectant; **~ sein, ob/was ...** to be anxious to see whether/what ... ❷ (*konfliktträchtig*) tense

Gespenst <-[e]s, -er> [gə·ˈʃpɛnst] *nt* ghost

gespenstisch [gə·ˈʃpɛns·tɪʃ] *adj* eerie

gesponnen [gə·ˈʃpɔ·nən] *pp von* **spinnen**

Gespött <-[e]s> [gə·ˈʃpœt] *nt kein pl* mockery; **sich/jdn zum ~ [der Leute] machen** to make a laughing stock of oneself/sb

Gespräch <-[e]s, -e> [gə·ˈʃprɛːç] *nt* ❶ (*Unterredung*) conversation; **mit jdm ins ~ kommen** to get into a conversation with sb ❷ (*Anruf*) [tele]phone call

gesprächig [gə·ˈʃprɛː·çɪç] *adj* talkative

gesprochen [gə·ˈʃprɔ·xn̩] *pp von* **sprechen**

gesprossen [gə·ˈʃprɔ·sn̩] *pp von* **sprießen**

gesprungen [gə·ˈʃprʊ·ŋən] *pp von* **springen**

Gespür <-s> [gə·ˈʃpyːɐ̯] *nt kein pl* instinct; **ein gutes ~ für Farben** a good feel for colors

Gestalt <-, -en> [gə·ˈʃtalt] *f* ❶ (*Mensch*) figure; **eine verdächtige ~** a suspicious character ❷ (*Wuchs*) build ❸ (*Person, Persönlichkeit*) character; **in ~ jds** in the form of sb ▶WENDUNGEN: **~ annehmen** to take shape

gestalten* [gə·ˈʃtal·tn̩] I. *vt* to design; *Garten* to lay out; *Schaufenster* to dress; **etw anders/neu ~** to redesign sth II. *vr* ■ **sich** *akk* **irgendwie ~** to turn out to be somehow

Gestaltung <-, -en> *f* ❶ (*das Einrichten*) design; *eines Gartens* laying out; *eines Schaufensters* window dressing ❷ (*das Organisieren*) organization ❸ ARCHIT building

gestand *imp von* **gestehen**

geständig [gə·ˈʃten·dɪç] *adj* ■ **~ sein** to have confessed

Geständnis <-ses, -se> [gə·ˈʃtɛnt·nɪs] *nt* admission; *eines Verbrechens* confession

Gestank <-[e]s> [gə·ˈʃtaŋk] *m kein pl* stench

gestatten* [gə·ˈʃta·tn̩] I. *vt s.* **erlauben I 1,2** II. *vi* **wenn Sie ~, das war mein Platz!** if you don't mind, that was my seat! III. *vr s.* **erlauben II**

Geste <-, -n> [ˈɡɛːs·tə] *f* gesture

gestehen <gestand, gestanden> *vt, vi* to confess

Gestein <-[e]s, -e> [gə·ˈʃtain] *nt* rock

Gestell <-[e]s, -e> [gə·ˈʃtɛl] *nt* ❶ (*Bretterregal*) shelves *pl* ❷ (*Brillengestell*) frame

gestern [ˈɡɛs·tɐn] *adv* (*der Tag vor heute*) yesterday; **~ vor einer Woche** a week ago yesterday ▶WENDUNGEN: **nicht <u>von</u> ~ sein** (*fam*) to not be born yesterday

gestiegen [gə·ˈʃtiː·gn̩] *pp von* **steigen**

gestochen [gə·ˈʃtɔ·xn̩] I. *pp von* **stechen** II. *adv* ~ **scharf** crystal clear

gestohlen [gə·ˈʃtoː·lən] *pp von* **stehlen**

gestorben [gə·ˈʃtɔr·bn̩] *pp von* **sterben**

gestoßen [gə·ˈʃtoː·sn̩] *pp von* **stoßen**

Gestotter <-s> [gə·ˈʃtɔ·tɐ] *nt kein pl* stammering

gestreift *adj* striped

gestrichen [gə·ˈʃtrɪ·çn̩] I. *pp von* **streichen** II. *adj* level III. *adv* ~ **voll** full to the brim

gestrig [ˈɡɛst·rɪç] *adj attr* yesterday's *attr,* [of] yesterday *pred*

gestritten [gə·ˈʃtrɪ·tn̩] *pp von* **streiten**

Gestrüpp <-[e]s, -e> [gə·ˈʃtrʏp] *nt* undergrowth

gestunken [gə·ˈʃtʊŋ·kn̩] *pp von* **stinken**

gesucht *adj* (*gefragt*) in demand *pred,* much sought-after

gesund <gesünder, gesündeste> [gə·ˈzʊnt] *adj* healthy; **Rauchen ist nicht ~** smoking is bad for you; **geistig und körperlich ~** of sound mind and body; **~ und munter** in good shape

Gesundheit <-> *f kein pl* health; **~!** gesundheit!, bless you!

gesundheitlich I. *adj* health; **aus ~en Gründen** for health reasons II. *adv* (*hinsichtlich der Gesundheit*) with regard to health; **wie geht es Ihnen ~?** how are you doing, healthwise?

Gesundheitsamt *nt* local public health department

gesungen [gə·ˈzʊŋən] *pp von* **singen**

gesunken [gə·ˈzʊŋ·kn̩] *pp von* **sinken**

getan [gə·ˈtaːn] *pp von* **tun**

getragen [gə·ˈtraː·gn̩] *pp von* **tragen**

Getränk <-[e]s, -e> [gə·ˈtrɛŋk] *nt* drink

Getränkeautomat *m* drink dispenser

ge|trauen* *vr* (*wagen*) ■**sich** *akk* **~, etw zu tun** to dare to do sth

Getreide <-s, -> [gə·ˈtrai·də] *nt* cereal; (*geerntet*) grain

getrennt *adj* separate

getreten *pp von* **treten**

Getriebe <-s, -> [gə·ˈtriː·bə] *nt* TECH transmission

getrieben [gə·ˈtriː·bn̩] *pp von* **treiben**

getroffen [gə·ˈtrɔ·fn̩] *pp von* **treffen**

getrogen [gə·ˈtroː·gn̩] *pp von* **trügen**

getrost [gə·ˈtroːst] *adv* (*ohne weiteres*) safely

getrunken [gə·ˈtrʊŋ·kn̩] *pp von* **trinken**

Getto <-s, -s> [ˈɡɛ·to] *nt* ghetto

Getue <-s> [gə·ˈtuː·ə] *nt kein pl* (*pej*) fuss

geübt *adj* experienced; *Auge, Griff, Ohr* trained

gewachsen I. *pp von* **wachsen¹** II. *adj* (*ebenbürtig*) equal; **sie ist der Aufgabe ~** she is certainly up to the task; **einem Gegner ~ sein** to be a match for an opponent

Gewächshaus *nt* greenhouse

gewagt *adj* ❶ (*kühn*) audacious; (*gefährlich*) risky ❷ (*freizügig*) risqué

Gewähr <-> [gə·ˈvɛːɐ̯] *f kein pl* guarantee; **ohne ~** subject to change

ge|währen* [gə·ˈvɛː·rən] *vt* ❶ (*einräumen*) ■**[jdm] etw ~** to grant [sb] sth; **jdm einen Rabatt ~** to give sb a discount; **jdn ~ lassen** to give sb free rein ❷ (*zuteilwerden lassen*) *Trost* to afford

gewährleisten* [gə·ˈvɛːɐ̯·lais·tn̩] *vt* to guarantee

Gewalt <-, -en> [gə·ˈvalt] *f* ❶ (*Machtbefugnis, Macht*) power; ■**in jds ~ sein** to be in sb's hands; **höhere ~** JUR act of God; **ein Gebiet/Land in seine ~ bringen** to bring a region/country under one's control; **~ über jdn haben** to exercise [complete] control over sb; **sich** *akk* **in der ~ haben** to have oneself under control ❷ *kein pl* (*gewaltsames Vorgehen*) force; (*Gewalttätigkeit*) violence; **nackte ~** brute force; **sich** *dat* **~ antun** to force oneself ❸ *kein pl* (*Heftigkeit*) force

Gewaltherrschaft *f kein pl* tyranny

gewaltig [gə·ˈval·tɪç] I. *adj* ❶ (*heftig*) enormous; *Orkan* violent ❷ (*riesig, wuchtig*) huge; *Bauwerke* monumental; *Last* heavy ❸ (*fam: sehr groß*) tremendous II. *adv* (*fam: sehr*) considerably;

sich *akk* ~ **irren** to be very much mistaken

gewaltlos I. *adj* nonviolent II. *adv* without violence

Gewaltlosigkeit <-> *f kein pl* nonviolence

gewaltsam [gə·'valt·za:m] I. *adj* violent II. *adv* by force

gewalttätig *adj* violent

Gewalttätigkeit *f* violence

gewandt [gə·'vant] I. *pp von* **wenden** II. *adj* skillful; *Auftreten* confident; *Bewegung* deft; *Redner* good

gewann [gə·'van] *imp von* **gewinnen**

gewaschen *pp von* **waschen**

Gewässer <-s, -> [gə·'vɛ·sɐ] *nt* body of water

Gewebe <-s, -> [gə·'ve:·bə] *nt* ① (*Stoff*) fabric ② ANAT, BIOL tissue

Gewehr <-[e]s, -e> [gə·'ve:ɐ] *nt* rifle; (*Schrotflinte*) shotgun

Geweih <-[e]s, -e> [gə·'vai] *nt* antlers *pl*

Gewerbe <-s, -> [gə·'vɛr·bə] *nt* ① (*Betrieb*) [commercial] business ② (*Handwerk, Handel*) trade

Gewerbesteuer *f* business tax

gewerblich [gə·'vɛrp·lɪç] I. *adj* (*handwerklich*) trade; (*kaufmännisch*) commercial; (*industriell*) industrial II. *adv* **Räume** ~ **nutzen** to use rooms for commercial purposes

Gewerkschaft <-, -en> [gə·'vɛrk·ʃaft] *f* [trade] union

Gewerkschaft(l)er(in) <-s, -> [gə·'vɛrk·ʃaft(l)ɐ] *m(f)* trade unionist

Gewerkschaftsmitglied *nt* [trade] union member

gewichen [gə·'vɪ·çn̩] *pp von* **weichen**

Gewicht <-[e]s, -e> [gə·'vɪçt] *nt* ① *kein pl* (*Schwere eines Körpers*) weight + *sing vb*; **ein geringes/großes ~ haben** to be very light/heavy ② *kein pl* (*fig: Wichtigkeit*) weight; **ins ~ fallen** to count; **auf etw** *akk* [**großes**] ~ **legen** to attach importance to sth ③ (*Metallstück zum Beschweren*) weight

gewichtig [gə·'vɪç·tɪç] *adj* significant

Gewichtszunahme *f* weight gain

gewieft [gə·'vi:ft] (*fam*) I. *adj* crafty II. *adv* with cunning

gewiesen [gə·'vi:·zn̩] *pp von* **weisen**

Gewimmel <-s> [gə·'vɪ·ml̩] *nt kein pl* (*von Insekten*) swarm; (*von Menschen*) throng

Gewinde <-s, -> [gə·'vɪn·də] *nt* TECH thread

Gewinn <-[e]s, -e> [gə·'vɪn] *m* ① ÖKON profit; ~ **bringen** to make a profit ② (*Preis*) prize; (*beim Lotto, Wetten*) winnings *npl* ③ *kein pl* ([*innere*] *Bereicherung*) gain

Gewinnbeteiligung *f* profit sharing

gewinnen <gewann, gewonnen> [gə·'vɪ·nən] I. *vt* ① (*als Gewinn erhalten*) to win ② (*überzeugen*) ■**jdn** ~ to win sb over; **jdn als Freund** ~ to win sb as a friend; **jdn als Kunden** ~ to gain sb as a customer ③ (*erzeugen*) to obtain; *Kohle, Metall* to extract (**aus** +*dat* from) ④ *Einfluss, Selbstsicherheit* to gain II. *vi* ① (*Gewinner sein*) to win (**bei/in** +*dat* at) ② (*profitieren*) to profit (**bei** +*dat* from)

gewinnend *adj* charming

Gewinner(in) <-s, -> *m(f)* winner; (*mil a.*) victor

Gewinnung <-> *f kein pl* extraction

gewissRR, **gewiß**ALT [gə·'vɪs] I. *adj* ① *attr* (*nicht näher bezeichnet*) certain; **eine ~e Frau Schmidt** a [certain] Ms. Schmidt ② (*sicher*) ■**sich** *dat* **etw** *gen* ~ **sein** to be certain of sth II. *adv* (*geh*) certainly; **aber ~**! sure!

Gewissen <-s> [gə·'vɪ·sn̩] *nt kein pl* conscience; **jdn/etw auf dem ~ haben** to have sb/sth on one's conscience; **jdm ins ~ reden** to appeal to sb's conscience

gewissenhaft *adj* conscientious

gewissenlos I. *adj* unscrupulous II. *adv* without scruple[s] *pl*

Gewissensbisse *pl* ~ **haben** to have a bad conscience

Gewissenskonflikt *m* moral conflict

gewissermaßen *adv* so to speak

GewissheitRR, **Gewißheit**ALT <-, -en> *f selten pl* certainty; ~ **haben** to be certain; **sich** *dat* ~ [**über etw** *akk*] **verschaffen** to find out for certain [about sth]

Gewitter <-s, -> [gə·ˈvɪ·tɐ] *nt* thunderstorm

ge|wittern* *vi impers* ■**es gewittert** it's thundering

gewittrig [gə·ˈvɪt·rɪç] *adj* thundery; ~**e Schwüle** oppressive heat

gewoben [gə·ˈvoː·bn̩] *pp von* **weben**

gewogen [gə·ˈvoː·gn̩] I. *pp von* **wiegen** II. *adj* ■**jdm/etw** ~ **sein** to be well-disposed toward[s] sb/sth

ge|wöhnen* [gə·ˈvøː·nən] I. *vt* ■**jdn an etw** *akk* ~ to accustom sb to sth II. *vr* ■**sich** *akk* **an jdn/etw** ~ to get used to sb/sth; ■**sich** *akk* **daran** ~, **etw zu tun** to get used to doing sth

Gewohnheit <-, -en> *f* habit

Gewohnheitsmensch *m* creature of habit

Gewohnheitsrecht *nt* (*als Rechtssystem*) common law *no art*

gewöhnlich [gə·ˈvøː·n·lɪç] I. *adj* ❶ *attr* (*üblich*) usual ❷ (*normal*) normal ❸ (*pej: ordinär*) common II. *adv* (*üblicherweise*) usually; **für** ~ normally; **wie** ~ as usual

gewohnt [gə·ˈvoːnt] *adj* usual; *Umgebung* familiar; ■**etw** ~ **sein** to be used to sth; ■**es** ~ **sein, etw zu tun** to be used to doing sth

Gewölbe <-s, -> [gə·ˈvœl·bə] *nt* vault

gewölbt *adj Dach, Decke* vaulted; *Stirn* domed; *Rücken* rounded

gewonnen [gə·ˈvɔ·nən] *pp von* **gewinnen**

geworben [gə·ˈvɔr·bn̩] *pp von* **werben**

geworden [gə·ˈvɔr·dn̩] *pp von* **werden**

geworfen [gə·ˈvɔr·fn̩] *pp von* **werfen**

Gewühl <-[e]s> [gə·ˈvyːl] *nt kein pl* ❶ (*Gedränge*) throng ❷ (*pej: andauerndes Kramen*) rummaging around

gewunken [gə·ˈvʊŋ·kn̩] DIAL *pp von* **winken**

Gewürz <-es, -e> [gə·ˈvʏrts] *nt* spice

Gewürzgurke *f* gherkin

gewusst^RR, **gewußt**^ALT [gə·ˈvʊst] *pp von* **wissen**

gezackt *adj* jagged; *Hahnenkamm* toothed; *Blatt* serrated

Gezeiten [gə·ˈtsai·tn̩] *pl* tide[s *pl*]

Gezeter <-s> [gə·ˈtseː·tɐ] *nt kein pl* (*pej fam*) racket

gezielt I. *adj* well-directed; *Fragen* specific II. *adv* specifically; ~ **fragen** to ask questions with sth mind

geziert *adj* (*pej*) affected

gezogen [gə·ˈtsoː·gn̩] *pp von* **ziehen**

Gezwitscher <-s> [gə·ˈtsvi·tʃə] *nt kein pl* chirping

gezwungen [gə·ˈtsvʊŋən] I. *pp von* **zwingen** II. *adj* (*gekünstelt*) forced; *Benehmen* stiff III. *adv* (*gekünstelt*) stiffly; ~ **lachen** to give a forced laugh

gezwungenermaßen *adv* of necessity

Ghetto <-s, -s> *nt s.* **Getto**

Gicht <-> [ˈgɪçt] *f kein pl* gout

Giebel <-s, -> [ˈgiː·bl̩] *m* gable [end]

Gier <-> [ˈgiːɐ] *f kein pl* greed (**nach** +*dat* for); (*nach etw Ungewöhnlichem*) craving (**nach** +*dat* for)

gierig [ˈgiː·rɪç] I. *adj* greedy II. *adv* greedily; **etw** ~ **trinken** to gulp down *sep* sth

gießen <goss, gegossen> [ˈgiː·sn̩] I. *vt* ❶ (*bewässern*) to water ❷ (*schütten*) to pour (**auf** +*akk* on, **über** +*akk* over) ❸ TECH to cast II. *vi impers* (*stark regnen*) **es gießt in Strömen** it's pouring

Gießkanne *f* watering can

Gift <-[e]s, -e> [ˈgɪft] *nt* poison; (*Schlangengift*) venom ▶WENDUNGEN: ~ **und** G̲a̲l̲l̲e̲ **spucken** (*fam*) to vent one's spleen; **darauf kannst du ~ ne̲h̲-m̲e̲n̲** (*fam*) you can bet your life on that

Giftgas *nt* poison gas

giftig [ˈgɪf·tɪç] I. *adj* ❶ (*Gift enthaltend*) poisonous ❷ (*boshaft*) venomous ❸ (*grell*) garish II. *adv* (*pej*) ~ **antworten** to give a nasty reply

Giftmüll *m* toxic waste

Giftschlange *f* poisonous snake

Giftstoff *m* toxic substance

Gigant(in) <-en, -en> [gi·ˈgant] *m(f)* giant; (*fig a.*) colossus

gigantisch [gi·ˈgan·tɪʃ] *adj* gigantic

ging [ˈgɪŋ] *imp von* **gehen**

G

Ginster <-s, -> ['gɪnstɐ] *m* broom

Gipfel <-s, -> ['gɪpfl̩] *m* ❶ (*Bergspitze*) peak; (*höchster Punkt*) summit; DIAL (*Wipfel*) treetop ❷ (*fig: Zenit*) peak; (*Höhepunkt*) height ❸ POL summit

Gipfeltreffen *nt* summit [meeting]

Gips <-es, -e> ['gɪps] *m* ❶ (*Baumaterial*) plaster; (*in Mineralform*) gypsum; (*zum Modellieren*) plaster of Paris ❷ (*Kurzform für Gipsverband*) [plaster] cast; **den Fuß in ~ haben** to have one's foot in a cast

Gipsbein *nt* (*fam*) leg in a cast

gipsen ['gɪpsn̩] *vt* ❶ *Wand* to plaster ❷ MED *Bruch* to put in a cast

Gipsverband *m* plaster cast

Giraffe <-, -n> [gi·'ra·fə] *f* giraffe

Girlande <-, -n> [gɪr·'lan·də] *f* garland (**aus** +*dat* of)

Girokonto ['ʒi·ro·] *nt* ≈ checking account

Gischt <-[e]s, -e (m) o -, -en (f)> ['gɪʃt] *m o f pl selten* [sea] spray

Gitarre <-, -n> [gi·'ta·rə] *f* guitar

Gitarrist(in) <-en, -en> [gi·ta·'rɪst] *m(f)* guitarist

Gitter <-s, -> ['gɪtɐ] *nt* (*Absperrung*) fencing; (*vor Türen, Fenstern: engmaschig*) screen; (*grobmaschig*) grate; (*parallel laufende Stäbe*) bars *pl*; (*für Gewächse*) trellis ▶WENDUNGEN: **jdn hinter ~ bringen** (*fam*) to put sb behind bars

Gitterfenster *nt* barred window

glamourös [gla·mu·'rø:s] *adj* glamorous

Glanz <-es> ['glants] *m kein pl* ❶ (*das Glänzen*) shine; *von Augen* sparkle; *von Lack* gloss; *von Perlen, Seide* sheen ❷ (*herrliche Pracht*) splendor

glänzen ['glɛn·tsn̩] *vi* ❶ (*widerscheinen*) to shine; *polierte Oberfläche* to gleam; *Augen* to sparkle; *Haut, Stoff* to be shiny; *Wasseroberfläche* to glisten; *Sterne* to twinkle ❷ (*fig: sich hervortun*) to shine

glänzend ['glɛn·tsn̩t] I. *adj* ❶ (*widerscheinend*) shining; *Oberfläche* gleaming; *Augen* sparkling; *Haar* shiny;

Papier glossy ❷ (*hervorragend*) brilliant II. *adv* (*sehr*) splendidly; **sich** *akk* **~ amüsieren** to have a great time

Glanzleistung *f* brilliant achievement

glanzvoll *adj* brilliant

Glas <-es, Gläser> ['gla:s] *nt* ❶ (*Werkstoff*) glass *no indef art, + sing vb*; „**Vorsicht ~!**" "glass — handle with care" ❷ (*Trinkgefäß*) glass

Glascontainer [-kɔn·te:·nɐ] *m* recycling container for glass

Glaserei [gla:·zə·'rai] *f* glazier's workshop

Glasfaserkabel *nt* fiber optic cable

glasig ['gla:·zɪç] *adj* KOCHK *Zwiebeln* transparent

glasklar I. *adj* ❶ (*durchsichtig*) transparent ❷ (*fig: klar und deutlich*) crystal clear II. *adv* (*klar und deutlich*) in no uncertain terms

Glasscheibe *f* ❶ (*dünne Glasplatte*) sheet of glass ❷ (*Fensterscheibe*) pane of glass

Glasscherbe *f* glass shard

Glasur [gla·'zu:ɐ] *f* ❶ (*Keramikglasur*) glaze ❷ KOCHK icing

glatt <-er *o fam* glätter, -este *o fam* glätteste> ['glat] I. *adj* ❶ *Fläche, Haut* smooth; *Gesicht* unlined; *Haar* straight; **~ rasiert** clean-shaven; **etw ~ streichen** to smooth out *sep* sth ❷ *Straße* slippery ❸ (*problemlos*) smooth ❹ *attr* (*fam: eindeutig*) outright; *Lüge* downright II. *adv* (*fam: rundweg*) plainly; (*ohne Umschweife*) straight up; *leugnen* flatly

Glatteis [gla·'zu:ɐ] *nt* [thin sheet of] ice; „**Vorsicht ~!**" "danger — black ice" ▶WENDUNGEN: **sich** *akk* **auf ~ begeben** to skate on thin ice

glätten ['glɛ·tn̩] I. *vt* (*glatt streichen*) to smooth out *sep* II. *vr* ■**sich** *akk* **~** ❶ *Meer, Wellen* to subside ❷ (*fig*) *Wut, Erregung* to die down

glattweg ['glat·vɛk] *adv* (*fam*) just like that; **etw ~ ablehnen** to turn sth down flat out; **etw ~ abstreiten** to flatly deny sth

Glatze <-, -n> ['glatsə] *f* bald head;

eine ~ bekommen/haben to go/be bald

Glatzkopf m (fam) ❶ (Kopf) bald head ❷ (Mann) baldy

Glaube <-ns> ['glau·bə] m kein pl ❶ (Überzeugung) belief (an +akk in); (gefühlsmäßige Gewissheit) faith (an +akk in); in gutem ~n in good faith; den festen ~n haben, dass ... to firmly believe that ...; jdm/etw [keinen] ~n schenken to [not] believe sb/sth; den ~n an jdn/etw verlieren to lose faith in sb/sth ❷ REL [religious] faith

glauben ['glau·bn̩] I. vt ❶ (für wahr halten) to believe; kaum zu ~ incredible ❷ (wähnen) sich akk unbeobachtet ~ to think [that] nobody is watching II. vi ❶ (vertrauen) ■jdm ~ to believe sb; jdm aufs Wort ~ to take sb's word for it; ■an jdn/etw ~ to believe in sb/sth ❷ (für wirklich halten) ■an etw akk ~ to believe in sth ▶WENDUNGEN: dran müssen (sl: sterben müssen) to kick the bucket; (weggeworfen werden müssen) to get tossed out; (etw tun müssen) to be stuck with it

Glaubensbekenntnis nt (Religionszugehörigkeit) profession [of faith]

gläubig ['glɔy·bɪç] adj (religiös) religious

Gläubige(r) ['glɔy·bɪ·gə] f(m) believer

Gläubiger(in) <-s, -> ['glɔy·bɪ·gɐ] m(f) ÖKON creditor

glaubwürdig adj credible

Glaubwürdigkeit <-> f kein pl credibility

gleich ['glaiç] I. adj ❶ (übereinstimmend) same; 2 mal 2 [ist] ~ 4 2 times 2 is 4; ~ alt the same age; ~ groß equal in size; ~ schwer equally heavy; ~ gesinnt like-minded ❷ (unverändert) es ist immer das [ewig] G~e it's always the same [old thing]; ~ bleibend gut consistently good ❸ (gleichgültig) ■jdm ~ sein to be all the same to sb; ■ganz ~ wer/was [...] no matter who/what [...] II. adv ❶ (sofort, bald) right away; bis ~! see you soon!; (sofort) see you in a minute!; ich

komme ~! I'll be right there!; ~ darauf soon afterward; (sofort) right away; ~ morgen [first thing] tomorrow; ~ nach dem Frühstück right after breakfast ❷ (unmittelbar daneben/danach) immediately; ■~ als ... as soon as ...; ~ daneben right beside it ❸ (zugleich) at once III. part ❶ in Aussagesätzen (emph) just as well ❷ in Fragesätzen (noch) again; wie war doch ~ Ihr Name? what was your name again?

gleichalt(e)rig ['glaiç·ʔalt(ə)·rɪç] adj [of] the same age pred

gleichberechtigt adj ■~ sein to have equal rights

Gleichberechtigung f kein pl equal rights + sing/pl vb

gleichbleibend adj, adv s. gleich I 2

gleichen <glich, geglichen> ['glai·çn̩] vt ■jdm/etw ~ to be [just] like sb/sth; ■sich dat ~ to be alike

gleichfalls adv likewise; danke ~! thanks, [and the] same to you! a. iron

gleichförmig adj uniform

gleichgeschlechtlich adj (homosexuell) homosexual; ~e Ehe same-sex [or gay] marriage

gleichgesinnt adj s. gleich I 1

Gleichgewicht nt kein pl balance; im ~ sein to be balanced; aus dem ~ kommen to lose one's balance

gleichgültig I. adj ❶ (uninteressiert) indifferent (gegenüber +dat to[ward]) ❷ (teilnahmslos) apathetic (gegenüber +dat toward) ❸ (unwichtig) immaterial; etw ist jdm vollkommen ~ sb couldn't care less about sth II. adv ❶ (uninteressiert) with indifference ❷ (teilnahmslos) with apathy

Gleichgültigkeit ['glaiç·gyl·tɪç·kait] f kein pl indifference

Gleichheitszeichen nt equal[s] sign

gleichmäßig I. adj even; Bewegungen regular; Puls, Tempo steady II. adv ❶ (in gleicher Stärke/Menge) equally; ~ atmen to breathe regularly; ~ schlagen Herz, Puls to beat steadily ❷ (ohne Veränderungen) consistently

G

Gleichnis <-ses, -se> ['glaiç·nɪs] *nt* allegory; (*aus der Bibel*) parable

gleich|setzen *vt* to equate (**mit** +*dat* with)

Gleichstand *m kein pl* tie

Gleichstrom *m* ELEK direct current

Gleichung <-, -en> ['glai·çʊŋ] *f* equation

gleichwertig *adj* equal; ■**~ sein** to be equally matched

gleichzeitig **I.** *adj* simultaneous **II.** *adv* ① (*zur gleichen Zeit*) simultaneously ② (*ebenso, zugleich*) at the same time

Gleis <-es, -e> ['glais] *nt* track; (*einzelne Schiene*) rail; (*Bahnsteig*) platform; **~ 2** track 2

gleiten <glitt, geglitten> ['glai·tn̩] *vi* ① *sein* (*schweben*) to glide; *Wolke* to sail ② *sein* (*streichen, huschen*) ■**über etw** *akk* **~** *Augen* to wander over sth; *Blick* to pass over sth; *Finger* to explore sth; *Hand* to slide over sth ③ *sein* (*rutschen*) to slide; **ins Wasser ~** to slip into the water

Gleitmittel *nt* lubricant

Gleitzeit *f* (*fam*) flextime

Gletscher <-s, -> ['glɛ·tʃɐ] *m* glacier

Gletscherspalte *f* crevasse

glich ['glɪç] *imp von* **gleichen**

Glied <-[e]s, -er> ['gliːt] *nt* ① (*Körperteil*) limb ② (*Penis*) [male] member *form* ③ (*Kettenglied*) link *a. fig* ④ (*Teil*) part

gliedern ['gliː·dɐn] **I.** *vt Aufsatz, Buch* to [sub]divide (**in** +*akk* into) **II.** *vr* ■**sich akk in etw** *akk* **~** to be [sub]divided into sth

Gliederschmerz *pl* rheumatic pains

Gliedmaßen *pl* limbs

GlimmstängelRR, **Glimmstengel**ALT *m* (*hum fam*) smoke

glimpflich ['glɪmpf·lɪç] **I.** *adj* ① (*ohne schlimmere Folgen*) without serious consequences *pred* ② (*mild*) *Strafe* mild **II.** *adv* ① (*ohne schlimmere Folgen*) **~ abgehen** to pass [by] without serious consequences; ② (*davonkommen*) to get off lightly ② (*mild*) **mit jdm ~ umgehen** to treat sb leniently

glitschig ['glɪt·ʃɪç] *adj* (*fam*) slippery

glitt ['glɪt] *imp von* **gleiten**

glitz(e)rig ['glɪ·ts(ə)·rɪç] *adj* sparkly

glitzern ['glɪ·tsɐn] *vi* to glitter; *Stern* to twinkle

global [glo·'baːl] **I.** *adj* ① (*weltweit*) global ② (*umfassend*) general **II.** *adv* ① (*weltweit*) globally ② (*ungefähr*) generally

Globalisierung <-> *f* globalization

Globus <-, Globen> ['gloː·bʊs] *m* globe

Glocke <-, -n> ['glɔ·kə] *f* ① (*Läutewerk*) bell ② (*glockenförmiger Deckel*) [glass] cover ▶WENDUNGEN: **etw an die große ~ hängen** (*fam*) to shout sth from the rooftops

Glockenblume *f* bellflower

Glockenspiel *nt* ① (*in Kirch- oder Stadttürmen*) carillon ② (*Musikinstrument*) glockenspiel

Glockenturm *m* belfry

Glossar <-s, -e> [glɔ·'saːɐ̯] *nt* glossary

glotzen ['glɔ·tsn̩] *vi* (*pej fam*) to gape (**auf** +*akk* at)

Glück <-[e]s> ['glʏk] *nt kein pl* ① (*günstige Fügung*) luck, fortune; **ein ~, dass …** it is/was lucky that …; **viel ~ [bei etw** *dat*]! good luck [with sth]!; **~/kein ~ haben** to be lucky/unlucky; **zum ~** luckily ② (*Freude*) happiness ▶WENDUNGEN: **etw auf gut ~ tun** to do sth on the off chance; **~ im Unglück haben** it could have been much worse [for sb]; **mehr ~ als Verstand haben** to have more luck than brains

glücken ['glʏ·kn̩] *vi sein* (*gelingen*) to be successful; ■**jdm glückt etw** sb succeeds in sth

gluckern ['glʊ·kɐn] *vi* to gurgle

glücklich ['glʏk·lɪç] **I.** *adj* ① (*vom Glück begünstigt*) lucky ② (*vorteilhaft, erfreulich*) happy; *Umstand* fortunate ③ (*froh*) happy (**mit** +*dat* with, **über** +*akk* about) **II.** *adv* ① (*vorteilhaft, erfreulich*) happily ② (*froh und zufrieden*) **~ [mit jdm] verheiratet sein** to be happily married [to sb]

glücklicherweise *adv* luckily

Glücksbringer <-s, -> *m* lucky charm

Glücksfall *m* stroke of luck

Glückspilz *m* (*fam*) lucky devil

Glückssache *f* ■etw ist [**reine**] ~ sth's a matter of [sheer] luck

Glücksspiel *nt* game of chance

Glückstreffer *m* stroke of luck; (*beim Schießen*) lucky shot

Glückwunsch *m* congratulations *npl* (**zu** +*dat* on)

Glückwunschkarte *f* greeting card

Glühbirne *f* light bulb

glühen ['gly:·ən] *vi* to glow; **vor Scham** ~ to burn with shame

glühend I. *adj* ❶ (*rot vor Hitze*) glowing; *Metall* [red-]hot ❷ (*brennend, sehr heiß*) burning; *Hitze* blazing II. *adv* ~ **heiß** burning hot

Glühwein *m* [hot] mulled wine

Glühwürmchen <-s, -> *nt* glowworm; (*fliegend*) firefly

Glut <-, -en> ['glu:t] *f* embers *npl*

glutrot *adj* fiery red

GmbH <-, -s> [ge:·ʔɛm·be:·ha:] *f Abk von* **Gesellschaft mit beschränkter Haftung** ≈ Inc.

Gnade <-, -n> ['gna:·də] *f* mercy; ~ **vor Recht ergehen lassen** to temper justice with mercy

Gnadenfrist *f* [temporary] reprieve

gnadenlos *adj* merciless

gnädig ['gnɛ:·dɪç] I. *adj* ❶ (*herablassend*) gracious *a. iron* ❷ (*Nachsicht zeigend*) merciful ❸ (*veraltend: verehrt*) ~**e Frau** madam; ~**es Fräulein** madam; (*jünger*) miss; ~**er Herr** (*veraltet*) sir II. *adv* ❶ (*herablassend*) graciously ❷ (*milde*) leniently

Gnom <-en, -en> ['gno:m] *m* (*pej*) gnome

Gold <-[e]s> ['gɔlt] *nt kein pl* gold

▶WENDUNGEN: **es ist nicht alles** ~, **was glänzt** (*prov*) all that glitters is not gold

Goldbarren *m* gold ingot

golden ['gɔl·dn̩] I. *adj attr* gold[en *liter*] II. *adv* like gold

Goldfisch *m* goldfish

goldgelb *adj* golden yellow; KOCHK golden brown

Goldgrube *f* (*fig*) goldmine

Goldhamster *m* [golden] hamster

goldig ['gɔl·dɪç] *adj* ❶ (*fam: allerliebst*) cute ❷ *pred* DIAL (*fam: rührend nett*) sweet *a. iron* ❸ DIAL (*iron fam*) **du bist aber** ~! very funny!

Goldmedaille [-me·dal·jə] *f* gold [medal]

goldrichtig *adj* (*fam*) ❶ (*völlig richtig*) absolutely right ❷ *pred* (*in Ordnung*) all right

Goldschmied(in) *m(f)* goldsmith

Goldstück *nt* ❶ (*veraltet*) piece of gold ❷ (*Kosewort*) treasure *fam*

Golf¹ <-[e]s, -e> ['gɔlf] *m* GEOL gulf

Golf² <-s> ['gɔlf] *nt kein pl* SPORT golf

Golfplatz *m* golf course + *sing/pl vb*

Golfspieler(in) *m(f)* golfer

Golfstaat *m* ■**die** ~**en** the Gulf States

Golfstrom *m* GEOL ■**der** ~ the Gulf Stream

Gondel <-, -n> ['gɔn·dl̩] *f* ❶ (*Boot in Venedig*) gondola ❷ (*Seilbahngondel*) cable car ❸ (*Ballongondel*) basket

gönnen ['gœ·nən] I. *vt* ❶ (*gern zugestehen*) ■**jdm etw** ~ to not begrudge sb sth; **ich gönne ihm diesen Erfolg von ganzem Herzen!** I'm absolutely delighted that he succeeded! ❷ (*iron*) ■**es jdm** ~, **dass** ... to be pleased [to see] that sb ... *iron* II. *vr* ■**sich** *dat* **etw** ~ to allow oneself sth; **sich** *akk* **ein Glas Wein** ~ to treat oneself to a glass of wine

gor ['go:ɐ̯] *imp von* **gären**

Göre <-, -n> ['gø:·rə] *f* (*fam*) brat

Gorilla <-s, -s> [go·'rɪ·la] *m* gorilla

gossᴿᴿ, **goß**ᴬᴸᵀ ['gɔs] *imp von* **gießen**

Gotik <-> ['go:·tɪk] *f kein pl* Gothic period

gotisch ['go:·tɪʃ] *adj* Gothic

Gott, Göttin <-es, Götter> ['gɔt] *m, f* ❶ (*ein Gott*) god *masc*, goddess *fem* ❷ *kein pl* (*das höchste Wesen*) God; ~ **sei Dank!** (*a. fig fam*) thank God!

▶WENDUNGEN: **ach** ~ (*resignierend*) oh God!; (*tröstend*) oh dear; **ach du lieber** ~! good heavens!; ~ **bewahre!** God forbid!; **wie** ~ **in Frankreich leben** to live in the lap of luxury;

grüß ~! *bes* SÜDD, ÖSTERR hello!**; um ~es willen!** (*emph: o je!*) [oh] my God!; (*bitte*) for God's sake!; **~ weiß was/wann ...** (*fam*) God [only] knows what/when ...; **über ~ und die Welt reden** to talk about everything under the sun

Gottesdienst *m* [church] service

Gotteslästerung *f* blasphemy

Göttin <-, -nen> ['gœtɪn] *f fem form von* **Gott** goddess

göttlich ['gœtlɪç] *adj* divine

gottlos *adj* godless

gottverlassen *adj* (*emph fam*) godforsaken *pej*

Grab <-[e]s, Gräber> ['gra:p] *nt* grave
▶WENDUNGEN: **sich** *dat* **sein eigenes ~ schaufeln** to dig one's own grave; **schweigen können wie ein ~** to be [as] silent as the grave; **jd würde sich** *akk* **im ~[e] umdrehen, wenn ...** (*fam*) sb would turn in their grave if ...

graben <grub, gegraben> ['gra:bn̩] **I.** *vi* to dig (**nach** +*dat* for) **II.** *vt Loch to* dig

Graben <-s, Gräben> ['gra:bn̩] *m* ① (*Vertiefung in der Erde*) ditch ② MIL trench ③ (*Festungsgraben*) moat

Grabmal *nt* ① (*Grabstätte*) mausoleum ② (*Gedenkstätte*) memorial

Grabstein *m* gravestone

Grad <-[e]s, -e> ['gra:t] *m* ① SCI, MATH degree; **2 ~ unter/über null** 2 degrees below/above [zero] ② (*Maß, Stufe*) level; **in hohem ~[e]** to a great extent
▶WENDUNGEN: **um [ein]hundertachtzig ~** (*fam*) complete[ly]

Graf, Gräfin <-en, -en> ['gra:f] *m, f* count *masc,* countess *fem*

Grafik ['gra:fɪk] *f* ① *kein pl* (*grafische Technik*) graphic arts *pl* ② (*grafische Darstellung*) graphic ③ (*Schaubild*) diagram

Grafiker(in) <-s, -> ['gra:fi·kɐ] *m(f)* graphic artist

Grafikkarte *f* COMPUT graphics card

Gräfin <-, -nen> ['grɛ:fɪn] *f fem form von* **Graf** countess *fem*

Grafit^RR <-s, -e> [gra·ˈfi:t] *m s.* **Graphit**

Grafschaft <-, -en> *f* HIST count's land

Gramm <-s, -e *o bei Zahlenangaben* -> ['gram] *nt* gram

Grammatik <-, -en> [gra·ˈma·tɪk] *f* grammar

grammatisch [gra·ˈma·tɪʃ] *adj* grammatical

Granat <-[e]s, -e *o* ÖSTERR -en> [gra·ˈna:t] *m* garnet

Granate <-, -n> [gra·ˈna:·tə] *f* shell

grandios [gran·ˈdi·oːs] *adj* magnificent

Granit <-s, -e> [gra·ˈni:t] *m* granite

Grapefruit <-, -s> ['gre:p·fru:t] *f* grapefruit

Graphik <-, -en> *f s.* **Grafik**

Graphit <-s, -e> [gra·ˈfi:t] *m* graphite

Gras <-es, Gräser> ['gra:s] *nt* BOT grass
▶WENDUNGEN: **ins ~ beißen** (*sl*) to bite the dust; **das ~ wachsen hören** to have a sixth sense; **über etw** *akk* **wächst ~** (*fam*) [the] dust settles on sth

grasen ['gra:·zn̩] *vi* to graze

Grashalm *m* blade of grass

Grashüpfer <-s, -> *m* (*fam*) grasshopper

grässlich^RR, **gräßlich**^ALT ['grɛs·lɪç] **I.** *adj* horrible; **was für ein ~es Wetter!** what lousy weather! **II.** *adv* (*fam*) terribly

Grat <-[e]s, -e> ['gra:t] *m* ① (*oberste Kante*) ridge ② ARCHIT hip

Gräte <-, -n> ['grɛ:·tə] *f* [fish]bone

gratis ['gra:·tɪs] *adv* free [of charge]

Gratisprobe *f* free sample

gratulieren* [gra·tu·ˈli··rən] *vi* ■**[jdm] ~** to congratulate [sb] (**zu** +*dat* on); **[ich] gratuliere!** [my] congratulations!; **jdm zum Geburtstag ~** to wish sb a happy birthday

grau ['grau] *adj* ① (*Farbe*) gray; **~ meliert** (*leicht ergraut*) graying; MODE flecked with gray *pred* ② (*trostlos*) drab; **der ~e Alltag** the dullness of everyday life

Graubrot *nt* DIAL (*Mischbrot*) bread made from rye and wheat flour

Gräueltat^RR *f* atrocity

grauen ['grau·ən] *vi impers* ■ **es graut jdm vor jdm/etw** sb is terrified of sb/sth

Grauen <-s> ['grau·ən] *nt kein pl* horror; ~ **erregend** terrible

grauenerregend *adj s.* **Grauen**

grauenhaft *adj* ❶ (*furchtbar*) terrible ❷ (*fam: schlimm*) dreadful

grauhaarig *adj* gray-haired

gräulich ['grɔʏ·lɪç] *adj* grayish

Graupelschauer *m* sleet shower

grausam ['grau·za:m] *adj* ❶ (*brutal*) cruel ❷ (*furchtbar*) terrible

Grausamkeit <-, -en> *f* ❶ *kein pl* (*Brutalität*) cruelty ❷ (*grausame Tat*) act of cruelty

Gravierung <-, -en> *f* engraving

Gravitation <-> [gra·vi·ta·tsi̯o:n] *f kein pl* gravitation[al pull]

greifbar *adj* ❶ *pred* (*verfügbar*) **etw** ~ **haben** to have sth handy ❷ (*konkret*) tangible

greifen <griff, gegriffen> ['grai·fn̩] **I.** *vt* ■ [**sich** *dat*] **etw** ~ to take hold of sth **II.** *vi* ❶ (*fassen*) to reach (**in** +*akk* into, **nach** +*dat* for); **zu Drogen/zur Zigarette** ~ to turn to drugs/reach for a cigarette ❷ TECH ■ **etw greift** *Reifen, Zahnrad* sth grips ❸ (*wirksam werden*) *Methoden* to take effect ▶WENDUNGEN: **um sich** *akk* ~ (*sich ausbreiten*) to spread

Greis(in) <-es, -e> ['grais] *m(f)* very old man/woman

grell ['grɛl] **I.** *adj* ❶ (*hell*) *Licht, Sonne* glaring ❷ (*schrill*) *Stimme, Schrei* piercing ❸ (*auffallend*) *Muster* loud **II.** *adv* ❶ (*sehr hell*) dazzlingly ❷ (*schrill*) ~ **klingen** to sound shrill

Gremium <-s, -ien> ['gre:·mi̯ʊm] *nt* committee

Grenze <-, -n> ['grɛn·tsə] *f* ❶ (*Landesgrenze*) border; **an der** ~ on the border; **über die** ~ **fahren** to cross the border ❷ (*Trennlinie*) boundary ❸ (*äußerstes Maß*) limit; **alles hat seine ~n** there is a limit to everything; **seine ~n kennen** to know one's limitations; **sich** *akk* **in ~n halten** to be limited

grenzen ['grɛn·tsn̩] *vi* to border (**an** +*akk* on)

grenzenlos I. *adj* ❶ (*unbegrenzt*) endless ❷ (*maßlos*) extreme; *Vertrauen* blind **II.** *adv* extremely

Grenzfall *m* borderline case

Grenzgebiet *nt* POL border area

Grenzlinie *f* SPORT line [marking the boundary of a playing surface]

Grenzübergang *m* border crossing point

Grenzwert *m* limiting value

Grieche, Griechin <-n, -n> ['gri:·çə] *m, f* Greek; *s. a.* **Deutsche(r)**

Griechenland <-s> ['gri:·çn̩·lant] *nt* Greece; *s. a.* **Deutschland**

griechisch ['gri:·çɪʃ] *adj* Greek; *s. a.* **deutsch**

Grieß <-es, -e> ['gri:s] *m* semolina

Grießbrei *m* semolina

griff ['grɪf] *imp von* **greifen**

Griff <-[e]s, -e> ['grɪf] *m* ❶ (*Zugriff*) grip ❷ (*Handgriff*) movement; **mit einem** ~ in a flash ❸ SPORT hold ❹ (*Öffnungsmechanismus*) *einer Tür, eines Revolvers* handle; *eines Messers* hilt ▶WENDUNGEN: **etw in den** ~ **bekommen** (*fam*) to get the hang of sth; **jdn/ etw im** ~ **haben** to have sb/sth under control

griffbereit *adj* **etw** ~ **haben** to have sth handy

Grill <-s, -s> ['grɪl] *m* ❶ (*Gerät*) grill ❷ (*Grillrost*) barbecue; **vom** ~ grilled

Grille <-, -n> ['grɪ·lə] *f* cricket

grillen ['grɪ·lən] **I.** *vi* to have a barbecue **II.** *vt* to grill

Grimasse <-, -n> [gri·ˈma·sə] *f* grimace; ~ **schneiden** to make faces

grimmig ['grɪ·mɪç] *adj* grim

grinsen ['grɪn·zn̩] *vi* to grin; **frech** ~ to smirk; **höhnisch** ~ to sneer

Grinsen <-s> ['grɪn·zn̩] *nt kein pl* grin; **freches** ~ smirk; **höhnisches** ~ sneer

Grippe <-, -n> ['grɪ·pə] *f* influenza, flu *fam*

grob <gröber, gröbste> ['gro:p] **I.** *adj* ❶ (*nicht fein*) coarse ❷ (*ungefähr*) rough ❸ (*unhöflich*) rude ❹ (*unsanft,*

G

unsensibel) rough ▶WENDUNGEN: **aus dem Gröbsten heraus** <u>sein</u> the worst is over II. *adv* ❶ (*nicht fein*) coarsely; ~ **gemahlen** coarsely ground ❷ (*in etwa*) roughly; ~ **geschätzt** at a rough estimate ❸ (*unhöflich*) rudely ❹ (*unsanft, unsensibel*) roughly ❺ (*schlimm*) **sich** *akk* ~ **täuschen** to be badly mistaken

Groll <-[e]s> ['ɡrɔl] *m kein pl* resentment; [**einen**] ~ **gegen jdn hegen** to harbor a grudge against sb

grollen ['ɡrɔ·lən] *vi* ■**jdm** ~ to be resentful [of sb]

Grönland ['ɡrøːn·lant] *nt* Greenland; *s. a.* **Deutschland**

groß <größer, größte> ['ɡroːs] I. *adj* ❶ (*flächenmäßig*) large, big ❷ (*lang*) long ❸ (*hoch*) *Gebäude* high ❹ (*hoch gewachsen*) tall; **du bist** ~ **geworden** you've grown; **er ist 1,78 m** ~ he is 1.78 m [*or* 5 feet 10 inches] [tall] ❺ (*das Maß oder Ausmaß betreffend*) **in** ~**en Größen** in large sizes; **mit** ~**er Geschwindigkeit** at high speed; **die** ~**e Masse** the majority of [the] people ❻ (*fig: bedeutend, beträchtlich*) great; *Durchbruch, Reinfall* major; *Misserfolg* abject; *Nachfrage* big; *Schrecken* nasty; *Schwierigkeiten* serious; *Unternehmen* leading; ~ **e Angst haben** to be terribly afraid ❼ (*fig: in Eigennamen*) **Friedrich der G~e** Frederick the Great ▶WENDUNGEN: **im G~en und** <u>Ganzen</u> [**gesehen**] on the whole II. *adv* ❶ (*fam: besonders*) **was soll man da schon** ~ **sagen?** there's really not much to say; **ich habe mich nie** ~ **für Politik interessiert** I've never been particularly interested in politics ❷ MODE **etw größer machen** to let out *sep* sth ❸ (*von weitem Ausmaß*) ~ **angelegt** large-scale

großartig ['ɡroːs·ʔaːɐ̯·tɪç] I. *adj* ❶ (*prächtig*) magnificent ❷ (*hervorragend*) brilliant ❸ (*wundervoll*) wonderful II. *adv* magnificently

Großaufnahme *f* close-up

Großbetrieb *m* large business; AGR large farm

Großbritannien <-s> [ɡroːs·briˈtanjən] *nt* Great Britain; *s. a.* **Deutschland**

Großbuchstabe *m* capital [letter]

Größe <-, -n> ['ɡrøː·sə] *f* ❶ (*räumliche Ausdehnung, Mode*) size ❷ (*Höhe, Länge*) height ❸ MATH, PHYS quantity ❹ *kein pl* (*Erheblichkeit*) magnitude; *eines Problems* seriousness; *eines Erfolgs* extent ❺ *kein pl* (*Bedeutsamkeit*) significance

Großeinkauf *m* bulk purchase

Großeltern *pl* grandparents *pl*

großenteils *adv* largely

Größenwahn(sinn) *m* megalomania

Großfahndung *f* large-scale search

Großfamilie *f* extended family

Großhandel *m* wholesale trade; **etw im** ~ **kaufen** to buy sth wholesale

Großhändler(in) *m(f)* wholesaler

großherzig *adj* magnanimous

Großhirn *nt* cerebrum

Großkind *nt* SCHWEIZ (*Enkelkind*) grandchild

großkotzig *adj* (*pej sl*) swanky

Großmaul *nt* (*pej fam*) big mouth

Großmutter *f* grandmother, grandma *fam*, granny *fam*

Großraum *m* **im** ~ **Berlin** in Greater Berlin

Großraumbüro *nt* open-plan office

großspurig *adj* (*pej*) boastful

Großstadt ['ɡroːs·ʃtat] *f* [big] city

großstädtisch ['ɡroːs·ʃtɛː·tɪʃ] *adj* big-city *attr*

Großteil *m* ❶ (*ein großer Teil*) ■**ein** ~ a large part ❷ (*der überwiegende Teil*) ■**der** ~ the majority; **zum** ~ for the most part

größtenteils *adv* for the most part

Großvater *m* grandfather, grandpa *fam*

groß|ziehen ['ɡroːs·tsiː·ən] *vt irreg Kind* to raise; *Tier* to rear

großzügig *adj* ❶ (*generös*) generous ❷ (*nachsichtig*) lenient ❸ (*in großem Stil*) grand

Großzügigkeit <-> *f kein pl* ❶ (*Generosität*) generosity ❷ (*Toleranz*) leniency ❸ (*Weiträumigkeit*) spaciousness

grotesk [groˈtɛsk] *adj* grotesque

Grotte <-, -n> [ˈgrɔtə] *f* grotto

grub [ˈgruːp] *imp von* **graben**

Grube <-, -n> [ˈgruːbə] *f* ❶ (*größeres Erdloch*) [large] hole ❷ (*Bergwerk*) pit
▶WENDUNGEN: **wer andern eine ~ gräbt, fällt selbst hinein** (*prov*) you can easily fall into your own trap

grübeln [ˈgryːbl̩n] *vi* to brood (**über** +*akk* over)

Gruft <-, Grüfte> [ˈgrʊft] *f* (*Grabgewölbe*) vault; (*Kirche*) crypt

grün [ˈgryːn] *adj* (*Farbe, Politik*) green
▶WENDUNGEN: **sich** *akk* **~ und blau ärgern** to be furious; **jdn ~ und blau schlagen** (*fam*) to beat sb black and blue

Grün <-s, -> [ˈgryːn] *nt* (*Farbe*) green
▶WENDUNGEN: **das ist dasselbe in ~** (*fam*) it's one and the same [thing]

Grünanlage *f* green space

Grund <-[e]s, Gründe> [ˈgrʊnt] *m*
❶ (*Ursache, Veranlassung*) reason (**zu** +*dat* for); **keinen/nicht den geringsten ~** no/not the slightest reason; **jdm ~ [zu etw** *dat*] **geben** to give sb reason [to do sth] ❷ (*Motiv*) grounds *pl*; **~ zu der Annahme haben, dass ...** to have reason to believe that ...; **aus finanziellen/gesundheitlichen Gründen** for financial/health reasons; **aus gutem ~** with good reason; **aus unerfindlichen Gründen** for some obscure reason; **aus diesem/welchem ~[e]** for this/what reason ❸ *kein pl* (*Erdboden*) ground ❹ DIAL (*Land, Acker*) land; **~ und Boden** land ❺ *eines Gewässers* bottom ▶WENDUNGEN: **auf ~ einer S.** *gen* on the basis of sth; **jdn in ~ und Boden reden** to shoot sb's arguments to pieces; **im ~e jds Herzens** in one's heart of hearts; **im ~e [genommen]** basically; **von ~ auf** completely; (*von Anfang an*) from scratch

Grundausbildung *f* basic training

Grundbesitz *m* real estate

Grundbesitzer(in) *m(f)* landowner

Grundbuch *nt* real property register

gründen [ˈgrʏndn̩] **I.** *vt* to found; *Firma*

to set up; *Partei* to form **II.** *vr* ■ **sich** *akk* **auf etw** *akk* ~ to be based on sth

Gründer(in) <-s, -> *m(f)* founder

Grundfläche *f* area

Grundgebühr *f* basic charge

Grundgesetz *nt* basic [*or* fundamental] law

grundieren* [grʊnˈdiːrən] *vt* to prime

Grundlage *f* basis

grundlegend *adj* fundamental

gründlich [ˈgrʏntlɪç] **I.** *adj* thorough **II.** *adv* ❶ (*fam: total*) completely ❷ (*gewissenhaft*) thoroughly

Gründlichkeit <-> *f kein pl* thoroughness

grundlos I. *adj* (*unbegründet*) unfounded **II.** *adv* groundlessly

Grundnahrungsmittel *nt* basic food[stuff]

Gründonnerstag [gryːnˈdɔnɐstaːk] *m* Maundy Thursday

Grundrecht *nt* basic right

Grundriss^RR *m* ❶ BAU floor plan ❷ (*Abriss*) outline

Grundsatz [ˈgrʊntzats] *m* principle

grundsätzlich [ˈgrʊntzɛtslɪç] **I.** *adj* ❶ (*grundlegend*) fundamental; *Bedenken, Zweifel* serious ❷ (*prinzipiell*) in principle *pred* **II.** *adv* ❶ (*völlig*) completely ❷ (*prinzipiell*) in principle ❸ (*kategorisch*) absolutely

Grundschule *f* elementary school

Grundstein *m* foundation stone; **den ~ zu etw** *dat* **legen** to lay the foundation for sth

Grundstück *nt* [piece of] property

Grundstücksmakler(in) *m(f)* real estate agent

Gründung <-, -en> *f* ❶ (*das Gründen*) foundation; *eines Betriebs* establishment ❷ BAU foundation

grundverschieden [ˈgrʊntfɛɐ̯ˈʃiːdn̩] *adj* completely different

Grundwasser *nt* ground water

Grundwasserspiegel *m* groundwater level

Grundwortschatz *m* basic vocabulary

Grüne(r) [ˈgryːnə] *f(m)* POL [member of

G

the] Green [Party]; **die ~n** the Green Party

Grüner Punkt *indicates that cartons and other packages can be recycled according to a special recycling system*

Grünfläche *f* green space

Grünkohl *m* (curly) kale

grünlich ['gry:n·lɪç] *adj* greenish

Grünschnabel *m* (*fam*) greenhorn

Grünspan ['gry:n·ʃpa:n] *m kein pl* verdigris

Grünstreifen *m* median [strip]; (*am Straßenrand*) grassy shoulder

grunzen ['grʊn·tsn̩] *vt, vi* to grunt

Grünzeug *nt* (*fam*) ❶ (*Kräuter*) herbs *pl* ❷ (*Salat*) green salad ❸ (*Gemüse*) greens *pl*

Gruppe <-, -n> ['grʊ·pə] *f* group

Gruppenarbeit *f kein pl* teamwork

gruppenweise *adv* in groups

gruppieren* [grʊˈpiː·rən] I. *vt* to group II. *vr* **sich** *akk* ~ to be grouped

Gruppierung <-, -en> *f* ❶ (*Gruppe*) group ❷ (*Aufstellung*) grouping

Gruselgeschichte *f* horror story

Gruß <-es, Grüße> ['gruːs] *m* ❶ (*Begrüßung*) greeting; MIL salute; **einen [schönen] ~ an Ihre Frau** [please] give my regards to your wife, say hi to your wife for me *fam* ❷ (*am Briefschluss*) regards; **mit freundlichen Grüßen** sincerely; **herzliche Grüße** best wishes

grüßen ['gryː·sn̩] I. *vt* ❶ (*begrüßen*) to greet; **grüß dich!** DIAL hello [there]! ❷ (*Grüße übermitteln*) **jdn von jdm ~** to send sb sb's regards; **jdn ~ lassen** to say hello to sb II. *vi* to say hello III. *vr* **sich** *akk* ~ to say hello to one another

gucken ['gʊ·kn̩] *vi* ❶ (*sehen*) to look; (*heimlich*) to peek; **was guckst du so dumm!** wipe that silly look off your face! ❷ (*ragen*) **aus etw** *dat* ~ to stick out of sth

Guckloch *nt* peephole

Guerillakrieg [geˈrɪl·ja-] *m* guerrilla war[fare]

Gulasch <-[e]s, -e> ['gʊ·laʃ] *nt o m* goulash

gültig ['gʏl·tɪç] *adj* ❶ (*Geltung besitzend*) valid; **der Sommerfahrplan ist ab dem 1. April ~** the summer schedule takes effect April 1st ❷ (*allgemein anerkannt*) universal

Gummi <-s, -s> ['gʊmi] *nt o m* ❶ (*Material*) rubber ❷ (*fam: Radiergummi*) eraser ❸ (*fam: Gummiband*) rubber band ❹ (*Gummizug*) elastic ❺ (*fam: Kondom*) rubber *sl*

Gummiband *nt* rubber band

Gummibaum *m* ❶ (*Kautschukbaum*) rubber tree ❷ (*Zimmerpflanze*) rubber plant

Gummihandschuh *m* rubber glove

Gummizelle *f* padded cell

Gunst <-> ['gʊnst] *f kein pl* ❶ (*Wohlwollen*) goodwill; **in jds ~ stehen** to be in sb's favor ❷ (*Vergünstigung*) **zu jds ~en** in sb's favor

günstig ['gʏns·tɪç] *adj* ❶ (*zeitlich gut gelegen*) convenient ❷ (*begünstigend*) favorable ❸ (*preisgünstig*) reasonable

Gurgel <-, -n> ['gʊr·gl̩] *f* throat

gurgeln ['gʊr·gln̩] *vi* ❶ (*den Rachen spülen*) to gargle ❷ (*von ablaufender Flüssigkeit*) to gurgle

Gurke <-, -n> ['gʊr·kə] *f* cucumber; (*Essiggurke*) pickle

gurren ['gʊ·rən] *vi* Tauben to coo; (*fam*) Mensch to purr

Gurt <-[e]s, -e> ['gʊrt] *m* ❶ (*Riemen*) strap ❷ (*Sicherheitsgurt*) seat belt ❸ (*breiter Gürtel*) belt

Gürtel <-s, -> ['gʏr·tl̩] *m* belt

Gürtelschnalle *f* belt buckle

Gurtpflicht *f* seatbelt law

GussRR <-es, Güsse>, **Guß**ALT <-sses, Güsse> ['gʊs] *m* ❶ (*fam: Regenguss*) downpour ❷ (*Zuckerguss*) icing

GusseisenRR *nt* cast iron

GussformRR *f* mold

gut <besser, beste> ['guːt] I. *adj* ❶ (*nicht schlecht*) good (**in** +*dat* at, **gegen** +*akk* for); **jdm geht es ~/nicht ~** sb is fine/not well ❷ *attr* (*lieb*) good; *Freund, Freundin* close ❸ (*in Wünschen*) good; **~en Appetit!** enjoy your meal!; **~e Besserung!** get well soon!; **~e Fahrt!** have a nice trip!; **ein ~es neues Jahr!** Happy New Year! ▶WENDUNGEN: **~!** (*in Ordnung!*) OK!; **also ~!** well, all right then!; **~ beieinander sein** to be a bit chubby; **~ drauf sein** (*fam*) to be in a good mood; **das kann nicht ~ gehen!** this won't be good!; **lass mal ~ sein!** (*fam*) let's drop the subject!; **schon ~!** (*fam*) all right!; **~ so!** that's great! [*or* perfect!]; **und das ist auch ~ so** and it's/that's a good thing, too; **sei so ~ und ...** would you be kind enough to ...; **wer weiß, wozu es ~ ist** perhaps it's for the best; **etw wird wieder ~ werden** sth will be all right; **wozu ist das ~?** (*fam*) what's the use of that?; **[wie] ~, dass ...** it's a good thing that ... II. *adv* ❶ (*nicht schlecht*) well; **du sprichst aber ~ Englisch!** your English is really good!; **~ aussehend** *attr* good-looking; **~ bezahlt** *attr* well-paid; **~ gehend** *attr* flourishing; **~ gelaunt** in a good mood; **~ gemeint** *attr* well-meant; **~ verdienend** *attr* high-income *attr* ❷ (*geschickt*) well ❸ (*reichlich*) **es dauert noch ~ eine Stunde, bis Sie an der Reihe sind** it'll be a good hour before it's your turn ❹ (*einfach, recht*) **ich kann ihn jetzt nicht ~ im Stich lassen** I can't just leave him like that [now] ❺ (*leicht, mühelos*) **hast du die Prüfung ~ hinter dich gebracht?** did you make it through the exam all right?; **~ leserlich** very legible ❻ (*angenehm*) **hm, wonach riecht das denn so ~ in der Küche?** hmm, what's that great smell coming from the kitchen?; **schmeckt es dir auch ~?** do you like it, too? ▶WENDUNGEN: **~ und gern** easily; **so ~ es geht** as best one can; **[das hast du] ~ gemacht!** good job!; **es ~ haben** to be lucky; **das kann ~ sein** that's quite possible; **mach's ~!** (*fam*) bye!; **pass ~ auf!** be [very] careful!; **sich** *akk* **~ mit jdm stellen** to get in good with sb

Gut <-[e]s, Güter> ['guːt] *nt* ❶ (*Landgut*) estate ❷ (*Ware*) commodity

Gutachten <-s, -> ['guːt·ʔax·tn̩] *nt* [expert's] report

Gutachter(in) <-s, -> *m(f)* expert

gutartig *adj* ❶ MED benign ❷ (*nicht widerspenstig*) good-natured

gutbürgerlich ['guːt·bʏr·gə·lɪç] *adj* middle-class; KOCHK homemade; **~e Küche** home-style cooking

Gute(s) *nt* ❶ (*Positives*) [etwas] **~s** [something] good; **man hört viel ~s über ihn** you hear a lot of good things about him; **alles ~!** all the best!; **das ~ daran** the good thing about it; [auch] **sein ~s haben** to have its good points [too]; **ein ~s hat die Sache** there is one good thing about it; **jdm schwant nichts ~s** sb has a bad feeling about sth; **~s tun** to do good; **was kann ich dir denn ~s tun?** how can I spoil you?; **nichts ~s versprechen** to not sound very promising; **sich** *akk* **zum ~n wenden** to take a turn for the better ❷ (*friedlich*) **im ~n** amicably; **lass dir's im ~n gesagt sein, dass ich das nicht dulde** take a bit of friendly advice — I won't put up with it/that!; **sich** *akk* **im ~n trennen** to part on friendly terms ❸ (*gute Charakterzüge*) **das ~ im Menschen** the good in man ▶WENDUNGEN: **alles hat sein ~s** (*prov*) every cloud has a silver lining *prov*; **Gut und Böse** good and evil; **im ~n wie im Bösen** (*mit Güte wie mit Strenge*) every way possible; (*in guten und schlechten Zeiten*) through good [times] and bad; **des ~n zu viel sein** to be too much [of a good thing]; **das ist wirklich des ~n zu viel!** that's really overdoing it/things!

Güte <-> ['gyː·tə] *f kein pl* ❶ (*milde Einstellung*) kindness; **die ~ haben, zu ...** to be so kind as to ... ❷ (*Qualität*) [good] quality ▶WENDUNGEN: **erster ~** (*fam*) of the first order; **ach du liebe ~!** (*fam*) oh my goodness! *fam*; **in ~** amicably

Güterbahnhof *m* freight depot

Gütergemeinschaft *f* JUR community

property; **in ~ leben** to have community property

Gütertrennung f JUR separation of property; **in ~ leben** to have separate property

Güterzug m freight train

Gütezeichen nt mark of quality

gutgläubig adj gullible

gut|haben vt irreg ■ **etw bei jdm ~** to be owed sth by sb

Guthaben <-s, -> nt credit balance

gut|heißen vt irreg to approve of

gütig ['gy:·tɪç] adj kind; **würden Sie so ~ sein, zu …** (geh) would you be so kind as to …; **[danke,] zu ~!** (iron) [thank you,] you're too kind!

gutmütig ['gu:t·my:·tɪç] adj good-natured

Gutsbesitzer(in) m(f) landowner

Gutschein m coupon

gut|schreiben vt irreg ■ **jdm etw** akk ~ to credit sb with sth

Gutschrift f ÖKON voucher

Gutshof m estate, manor

gutwillig adj (entgegenkommend) obliging

Gymnasiast(in) <-en, -en> [gym·na·'zi̯·ast] m(f) ≈ high-school student

Gymnasium <-s, -ien> [gym·'na:·zi̯·ʊm] nt ≈ high school

Gymnastik <-> [gym·'nas·tɪk] f kein pl gymnastics + sing vb

Gynäkologe, Gynäkologin <-n, -n> [gy·nɛ·ko·'lo:·gə] m, f gynecologist

Hh

H, h <-, -> [ha:] nt ① (Buchstabe) H, h; **~ wie Heinrich** H as in Hotel ② MUS B, b

h Abk von hora[e] hr. ① gesprochen: Uhr (Stunde der Uhrzeit) **22 ~** 2200 hrs.; **Abfahrt des Zuges: 9 h 17** train departure: 9:17 a.m. ② gesprochen: Stunde (Stunde) h

ha [ha:] Abk von **Hektar** ha

Haar <-[e]s, -e> [ha:ɐ̯] nt ① (einzelnes Haar) hair ② sing o pl (gesamtes Kopfhaar) hair; **graue ~e bekommen** to go gray; **sich** dat **die ~e schneiden lassen** to have one's hair cut ▶WENDUNGEN: **jdm stehen die ~e zu** Berge (fam) sb's hair is standing on end; **sich** dat **in die ~e geraten** to argue; **etw ist an den ~en herbeigezogen** sth is farfetched; **um ein ~** within a hair's breadth

Haarausfall m hair loss

Haarbürste f hairbrush

haaren ['ha:·rən] vi to molt

Haarfarbe f color of one's hair

haarig ['ha:·rɪç] adj ① (behaart) hairy ② (fig: heikel) hairy; **Angelegenheit** tricky

Haarnadel f hairpin

haarscharf adv (ganz knapp) by a hair's breadth

Haarschnitt m haircut

Haarspalterei <-, -en> [ha:ɐ̯·ʃpal·te·'rai̯] f (pej) splitting hairs

Haarspange f barrette

haarsträubend ['ha:ɐ̯·ʃtrɔy·bn̩t] adj hair-raising

Haartrockner m hair dryer

Hab [ha:p] nt **~ und Gut** belongings npl

haben <hatte, gehabt> ['ha:·bn̩] I. vt ① (besitzen, aufweisen) to have ② (erhalten) to have; **ich hätte gern ein Bier** I'd like a beer, please ③ in Maßangaben **ein Meter hat 100 Zentimeter** there are 100 centimeters in a meter ④ (von etw erfüllt sein) **Angst/Durst/Hunger/Sorgen ~** to be afraid/thirsty/hungry/worried; **gute/ schlechte Laune ~** to be in a good/ bad mood ⑤ (*herrschen*) **wir ~ heute den 13.** it's the 13th today ⑥ + *adj* **es bei jdm gut ~** to have got it made with sb ⑦ (*tun müssen*) ■**etw zu tun ~** to have sth to do; **ich habe noch zu arbeiten** I still have work to do ⑧ DIAL (*geben*) ■**es hat ...** there is/are ... ⑨ + *prep* **etw an sich** *dat* **~** to be sth about one; **jetzt weiß ich, was ich an ihr habe** now I know how lucky I am to have her; **das hast du jetzt davon!** now look where it's gotten you!; **nichts davon ~** to not gain a thing from it; ■**jdn vor sich** *dat* **haben** to deal with sb; **wissen Sie überhaupt, wen Sie vor sich haben?** do you have any idea who you are dealing with? ▶WENDUNGEN: **noch/nicht mehr zu ~ sein** (*fam*) to still/no longer be available; **da haben wir's!** (*fam*) there you are!; **was hat es damit auf sich?** what's all this about?; **wie gehabt** as usual II. *aux vb* ■**etw getan ~** to have done sth; **also, ich hätte das nicht gemacht** well, I wouldn't have done that

Haben <-s-> ['haːbn̩] *nt kein pl* credit; **mit etw** *dat* **im ~ sein** to be in the black by sth

Habenichts <-[es], -e> ['haːbənɪçts] *m* (*fam*) have-not *usu pl*

habgierig ['haːpˌgiːrɪç] *adj* (*pej*) greedy

Habicht <-s, -e> ['haːbɪçt] *m* hawk

Habseligkeiten ['haːpˌzeːlɪçkaitn̩] *pl* [meager] belongings *npl*

Hackbraten *m* meat loaf

Hacke <-, -n> ['hakə] *f* ① (*Gartengerät*) hoe ② ÖSTERR (*Axt*) ax ③ DIAL (*Ferse*) heel

hacken[1] ['hakn̩] I. *vt* ① *Gemüse, Nüsse* to chop [up *sep*] ② *Boden* to hoe ③ (*in Stücke zerteilen*) to hack (**in** +*akk* into) II. *vi* ① (*mit dem Schnabel*) to peck ② (*mit der Hacke*) to hoe

hacken[2] ['hɛkn̩] *vi* COMPUT (*sl*) ■**das H~** hacking

Hacker(in) <-s, -> ['hɛkə] *m(f)* (*sl*: *Computerpirat*) hacker

Hackfleisch *nt* ground meat

hadern ['haːdən] *vi* to argue (**mit** +*dat* with); **mit seinem Schicksal ~** to rail against one's fate

Hafen <-s, Häfen> ['haːfn̩] *m* harbor, port

Hafenarbeiter(in) *m(f)* docker

Hafenstadt *f* port [city]

Hafer <-s, -> ['haːfɐ] *m* oats *pl*

Haferflocken *pl* oatmeal

Haft <-> [haft] *f kein pl* ① (*Haftstrafe*) imprisonment ② (*Haftzeit*) prison sentence; **in ~ sein** to be in custody

haftbar ['haftˌbaːɐ̯] *adj* ■**für etw** *akk* **~ sein** to be liable for sth; **jdn für etw** *akk* **~ machen** to hold sb responsible for sth

Haftbefehl *m* [arrest] warrant

haften[1] ['haftn̩] *vi* ① ÖKON to be liable (**für** +*akk* for, **mit** +*dat* with) ② (*die Haftung übernehmen*) to be responsible (**für** +*akk* for)

haften[2] ['haftn̩] *vi* (*festkleben*) to adhere (**an/auf** +*dat* to)

Häftling <-s, -e> ['hɛftlɪŋ] *m* prisoner

Haftnotiz *f* sticky note, Post-it®

Haftpflicht *f* ① (*Schadenersatzpflicht*) liability ② (*fam*) *s.* **Haftpflichtversicherung**

Haftpflichtversicherung *f* personal liability insurance; AUTO third-party insurance

Haftung[1] <-, -en> ['haftʊŋ] *f* JUR liability

Haftung[2] <-> ['haftʊŋ] *f kein pl* AUTO road handling

Hagebutte <-, -n> ['haːgəˌbuːtə] *f* rose hip

Hagel <-s> ['haːgl̩] *m kein pl* METEO hail

Hagelkorn <-körner> *nt* hailstone

hageln ['haːgl̩n] I. *vi impers* to hail II. *vt impers* (*fam*) ■**es hagelt etw** there is a hail of sth

hager ['haːgɐ] *adj* gaunt

Hahn[1] <-[e]s, Hähne> [haːn] *m* rooster

Hahn[2] <-[e]s, Hähne> [haːn] *m* ① (*Wasserhahn*) faucet ② (*an Schusswaffen*) hammer

H

Hai <-[e]s, -e> ['hai] *m*, **Haifisch** ['hai·fɪʃ] *m* shark

Hain <-[e]s, -e> [hain] *m* (*geh, poet*) grove

Haiti <-s> [ha·'i:ti] *nt* Haiti; *s. a.* **Deutschland**

häkeln ['hɛ·kln] *vt, vi* to crochet

Häkelnadel *f* crochet hook

Haken <-s, -> ['ha:·kn] *m* ❶ (*gebogene Halterung*) hook ❷ (*beim Boxen*) hook ❸ (*hakenförmiges Zeichen*) check [mark] ❹ (*fam: hindernde Schwierigkeit*) **einen ~ haben** (*fam*) to have a catch

Hakennase *f* hooked nose

halb [halp] **I.** *adj* ❶ (*die Hälfte von*) half ❷ (*halbe Stunde der Uhrzeit*) **es ist genau ~ sieben** it is exactly six[-]thirty ❸ *kein art* (*ein Großteil*) **~ Deutschland verfolgt die Fußballweltmeisterschaft** half of Germany is following the World Cup ▶WENDUNGEN: **nichts H~es und nichts Ganzes** neither this nor that **II.** *adv* ❶ *vor vb* (*zur Hälfte*) half; *etw nur* **~ machen** to only half do sth; **~ so ... sein** to be half as ...; **~ ..., ~ ... half ..., half ...** ❷ *vor adj, adv* (*halbwegs*) half; **~ nackt/voll** half-naked/half-full ▶WENDUNGEN: **[mit jdm] ~e-~e machen** to go halves with sb; **das ist ~ so schlimm** it's not as bad as all that

Halbbruder *m* half brother

halber ['hal·bɐ] *präp +gen nachgestellt* ■ **der ... ~** for the sake of ...

halbfertig *adj attr* half-finished

Halbgott, -göttin *m, f* demigod *masc*, demigoddess *fem*

halbieren* [hal·'bi:·rən] *vt* ❶ (*teilen*) to divide in half ❷ (*um die Hälfte vermindern*) to halve

Halbinsel ['halp·ʔɪn·zl] *f* peninsula

Halbjahr *nt* half year

halbjährig ['halp·jɛː·rɪç] *adj attr* ❶ (*ein halbes Jahr dauernd*) six-month *attr* ❷ (*ein halbes Jahr alt*) six-month-old *attr*

halbjährlich ['halp·jɛ:ɐ·lɪç] **I.** *adj* half-yearly **II.** *adv* every six months, twice a year

Halbkreis *m* semicircle

Halbkugel *f* hemisphere

Halbmond *m* ❶ ASTRON half moon ❷ (*Figur*) crescent

Halbpension *f* breakfast and dinner

Halbschuh *m* low shoe

Halbschwester *f* half sister

halbtags *adv* on a part-time basis; **~ arbeiten** to work half-time

halbwegs ['halp·'ve:ks] *adv* ❶ (*einigermaßen*) partly ❷ (*nahezu*) almost ❸ (*veraltend: auf halbem Wege*) halfway

Halbwert(s)zeit *f* PHYS half-life

Halbwüchsige(r) *f(m) dekl wie adj* adolescent

Halbzeit *f* halftime

Halde <-, -n> ['hal·də] *f* ❶ (*Müllhalde*) landfill ❷ BERGB slag heap ❸ (*unverkaufte Ware*) stockpile

half ['half] *imp von* **helfen**

Hälfte <-, -n> ['hɛlf·tə] *f* half; **um die ~** by half

Halle <-, -n> ['halə] *f* ❶ (*großer Raum*) hall ❷ (*Werkhalle*) workshop ❸ (*Sporthalle*) gymnasium; **in der ~** indoors

hallen ['ha·lən] *vi* to echo

Hallenbad *nt* indoor swimming pool

Halligalli <-s> [ha·li·ga·li] *nt kein pl* (*meist pej fam*) hubbub

hallo [ha·'lo:] *interj* hello

Hallo <-s, -s> [ha·'lo:] *nt* hello

Halm <-[e]s, -e> [halm] *m* ❶ (*Stängel*) stalk ❷ (*Trinkhalm*) straw

Hals <-es, Hälse> [hals] *m* ❶ ANAT neck; **den ~ recken** to crane one's neck ❷ (*Kehle*) throat ❸ (*Flaschenhals*) neck ▶WENDUNGEN: **~ über Kopf** in a hurry; **aus vollem ~[e]** at the top of one's voice

Halsabschneider(in) *m(f)* (*pej fam*) shark

Halsband *nt* ❶ (*für Haustiere*) collar ❷ (*Samtband*) choker

halsbrecherisch ['hals·brɛ·çə·rɪʃ] *adj* breakneck *attr*

Halsentzündung *f* sore throat

Halskette *f* necklace

Halsschlagader *f* carotid [artery]

Halsschmerzen *pl* sore throat

Halstuch *nt* neckerchief

halt[1] [halt] *interj* halt!

halt[2] [halt] *adv* DIAL *s.* **eben**[2] I 2

Halt <-[e]s, -e> [halt] *m* ❶ (*Stütze*)
hold; ~ **geben** to support; **den ~ ver-**
lieren to lose one's grip ❷ (*inneres*
Gleichgewicht)   stability   ❸ (*Stopp*)
stop; ~ **machen** to stop

haltbar ['halt·baːɐ̯] *adj* ❶ (*nicht leicht*
verderblich) nonperishable; ■~ **sein** to
keep; ~ **machen** to preserve ❷ (*wider-*
standsfähig) durable

Haltbarkeit <-> *f kein pl* ❶ (*Lagerfä-*
higkeit) shelf life ❷ (*Widerstandsfähig-*
keit) durability

Haltbarkeitsdatum *nt* sell-by date

halten <hielt, gehalten> ['hal·tn̩] I. *vt*
❶ (*festhalten, stützen*) to hold ❷ (*auf-*
halten) to stop ❸ (*zurückhalten*) to
keep (*in Position bringen*) to put; **er**
hielt die Hand in die Höhe he put his
hand up ❺ (*besitzen*) to keep ❻ (*weiter*
innehaben) to hold on to ❼ (*in einem*
Zustand erhalten) to keep ❽ (*abhalten*)
Rede, Vortrag) to give ❾ (*erfüllen*) **der**
Film hält nicht, was der Titel ver-
spricht the film doesn't live up to its title ►WENDUNGEN: **das** <u>kannst</u> **du ~, wie**
du willst that's completely up to you;
viel/nichts <u>davon</u> **~**, **etw zu tun** to
consider/not consider it important to
do sth; **jdn/etw** <u>für</u> **jdn/etw ~** to take
sb/sth for sb/sth; **etw** <u>von</u> **jdm/etw ~**
to think sth of sb/sth **II.** *vi* ❶ (*festhal-*
ten) to hold ❷ (*haltbar sein*) to keep
❸ (*anhalten*) to stop ►WENDUNGEN: **an**
sich *akk* ~ to control oneself; **zu jdm ~**
to stand by sb **III.** *vr* ❶ (*sich festhalten*)
■**sich an etw** *dat* ~ to hold on to
sth *akk* METEO (*konstant bleiben*) ■**sich**
akk ~ to last ❸ (*eine Richtung beibehal-*
ten) ■**sich** *akk* **irgendwohin/nach**
... ~ to keep to somewhere/heading
toward ... ❹ (*sich richten nach*) ■**sich**
akk **an etw** *akk* ~ to stick to sth ❺ (*eine*
bestimmte Haltung haben) ■**sich** *akk*
irgendwie ~ to carry oneself in a certain manner ►WENDUNGEN: **sich** *akk* <u>gut</u>

gehalten haben (*fam*) to have worn
well

Haltestelle *f* stop

Halteverbot *nt kein pl* no stopping [any
time]; **eingeschränktes ~** ≈ loading/
unloading zone

haltlos *adj* ❶ (*labil*) weak; *Mensch* unsteady ❷ (*unbegründet*) unfounded

Haltung[1] <-, -en> ['hal·tʊŋ] *f* ❶ (*Kör-*
perhaltung) posture; (*typische Stel-*
lung) stance ❷ (*Einstellung*) attitude
❸ *kein pl* (*Verhalten*) manner ►WEN-
DUNGEN: ~ <u>bewahren</u> to keep one's
composure

Haltung[2] <-> ['hal·tʊŋ] *f kein pl von*
Tieren keeping

Halunke <-n, -n> [ha·'lʊŋ·kə] *m*
❶ (*pej: Gauner*) scoundrel ❷ (*hum:*
Schlingel) rascal

hämisch ['hɛː·mɪʃ] *adj* malicious

Hammel <-s, -> ['ha·ml̩] *m* ❶ (*Tier*)
wether ❷ *kein pl* (*Fleisch*) mutton

Hammelfleisch *nt* mutton

Hammer <-s, Hämmer> ['ha·mɐ] *m*
❶ (*Werkzeug*) hammer ❷ SPORT (*Wurf-*
gerät) hammer ❸ (*fam: schwerer Feh-*
ler) major mistake ❹ (*fam: Unver-*
schämtheit) outrageous thing

hämmern ['hɛ·mɐn] *vt, vi* ❶ (*mit dem*
Hammer arbeiten) to hammer ❷ (*wie*
Hammerschläge ertönen) to make a
hammering noise ❸ (*fam: auf dem Kla-*
vier spielen) to hammer away on the
piano ❹ (*rasch pulsieren*) to pound

Hämorrhoide <-, -n> [hɛ·mɔ·'riː·də] *f*
meist pl hemorrhoids *pl*

Hampelmann <-männer> ['ham·pl̩·
man] *m* ❶ (*Spielzeug*) jumping jack
❷ (*pej fam: labiler Mensch*) puppet

Hamster <-s, -> ['ham·stɐ] *m* hamster

hamstern ['ham·stɐn] *vt, vi* to hoard

Hand <-, Hände> [hant] *f* ❶ ANAT hand;
Hände hoch! hands up!; **jdm etw in**
die ~ drücken to slip sth into sb's
hand; **jdm die ~ geben** to shake sb's
hand; **etw in die ~ nehmen** to pick up
sep sth; **Hände weg!** [get your] hands
off! ❷ *kein pl* SPORT (*Handspiel*) handball ❸ (*Besitz*) hands; **der Besitz**

H

H

gelangte in fremde Hände the property passed into foreign hands ▶WENDUNGEN: **an ~ einer S.** gen with the aid of sth; [**bar**] **auf die ~** (fam) cash in hand; **mit der bloßen ~** with one's bare hand[s]; **aus erster/zweiter ~** first-hand/secondhand; **in festen Händen sein** (fam) to be spoken for; **~ und Fuß haben** to be well thought-out; **etw gegen jdn in der ~ haben** to have sth on sb; **~ in ~** hand in hand; [**klar**] **auf der ~ liegen** (fam) to be [perfectly] obvious; **jds rechte ~ sein** to be sb's right-hand man; **die Hände in den Schoß legen** to sit back and do nothing; [**bei etw** dat] **die Hände im Spiel haben** to have a hand in sth; **eine starke ~** a firm hand; **alle Hände voll zu tun haben** to have one's hands full; **von ~** by hand; **zu Händen von jdm** attn: sb, for sb's attention; **zur ~ sein** to be on hand

Handarbeit f ❶ (Gegenstand) handicraft; **~ sein** to be handmade ❷ (Nähen, Stricken etc.) needlework; (Gegenstand) needlework

Handball m o fam nt SPORT handball

Handbewegung f gesture

Handbremse f hand brake

Handbuch nt manual

Händchen <-s, -> ['hɛnt·çən] nt dim von **Hand** small hand ▶WENDUNGEN: **für etw** akk **ein ~ haben** (fam) to have a knack for sth; **~ halten** (fam) to hold hands

Händedruck m kein pl handshake

Handel <-s> ['han·dl̩] m kein pl ❶ (Wirtschaftszweig der Händler) commerce ❷ (Warenverkehr) trade; **im ~ sein** to be on the market ❸ (fam: Abmachung, Geschäft) deal ❹ (das Handeln) dealing (**mit** +dat in)

handeln ['han·dl̩n] I. vi ❶ (kaufen und verkaufen) to trade (**mit** +dat in); **mit Drogen ~** to deal drugs ❷ (feilschen) to haggle (**um** +akk about/over) ❸ (agieren) to act ❹ (befassen) ■**von etw** dat **~** to be about [or deal with] sth II. vr impers ■**sich** akk **um jdn/etw ~**

to concern [or be about] sb/sth III. vt (angeboten und verkauft werden) ■[**für etw** akk] **gehandelt werden** to be traded [at/for sth]

Handelsbank f merchant bank

Handelsbeziehungen pl trade relations

Handelskammer f chamber of commerce

Handelsregister nt register of business names

Handelsschule f business school

Handelsvertreter(in) m(f) commercial agent

Handelsware f commodity

Handfeger <-s, -> m hand brush

Handfeuerwaffe f handgun

Handfläche f palm of one's hand

handgearbeitet adj handmade

Handgelenk nt wrist ▶WENDUNGEN: **etw aus dem ~ schütteln** (fam) to do sth effortlessly

Handgemenge nt scuffle

Handgepäck nt carry-on luggage

handgeschrieben adj handwritten

handgreiflich ['hant·graif·lɪç] adj violent (**gegen** +akk toward)

Handgriff m ❶ (Aktion) movement; **mit einem ~** with a flick of the wrist ❷ (Griff) handle

handhaben ['hant·ha:·bn̩] vt ❶ (bedienen) to handle; Maschine a. to operate ❷ (anwenden) to apply ❸ (verfahren) to manage

Handkoffer m small suitcase

HandkussRR m kiss on the hand

Handlanger(in) <-s, -> ['hant·laŋe] m(f) ❶ (Helfer) laborer ❷ (pej: Erfüllungsgehilfe) stooge

Händler(in) <-s, -> ['hɛnd·lɐ] m(f) dealer; **fliegender ~** hawker

handlich ['hant·lɪç] adj ❶ (bequem zu handhaben) easy to handle ❷ (leicht lenkbar) maneuverable

Handlung <-, -en> ['hand·lʊŋ] f ❶ (Tat) act ❷ (im Buch, Film etc.) plot

Handlungsweise f conduct

Handrücken m back of the hand

Handschelle f meist pl handcuffs pl

Handschrift ['hant·ʃrɪft] f ❶ (*Schrift*) handwriting ❷ (*Text*) manuscript

handschriftlich I. *adj* handwritten II. *adv* (*von Hand*) by hand

Handschuh *m* glove

Handschuhfach *nt* glove compartment

Handtasche *f* purse

Handtuch <-tücher> *nt* towel

Handumdrehen ['hant·ʔʊm·dre:·ən] *nt* ▸WENDUNGEN: **im** ~ in a jiffy

Handvoll <-, -> *f* handful

Handwerk *nt* trade ▸WENDUNGEN: **jdm das** ~ **legen** to put an end to sb's game; **sein** ~ **verstehen** to know one's job

Handwerker(in) <-s, -> *m(f)* tradesman

Handy <-s, -s> ['hɛn·di] *nt* TELEK cell[ular] [tele]phone

Handzettel *m* leaflet

Hanf <-[e]s> [hanf] *m kein pl* hemp

Hang <-[e]s, Hänge> [haŋ] *m* ❶ (*Abhang*) slope ❷ *kein pl* (*Neigung*) tendency; **sie hat einen** ~ **zu Übertreibungen** she tends to exaggerate; **den** ~ **haben, etw zu tun** to be inclined to do sth

Hängebrücke *f* suspension bridge

Hängematte *f* hammock

hängen ['hɛŋ·ən] I. *vi* <hing, gehangen> ❶ (*angebracht sein*) *Gegenstand, Verbrecher* to hang (**an** +*dat* on, **über** +*dat* over, **von** +*dat* from) ❷ (*sich neigen*) to lean ❸ (*befestigt sein*) ■**an etw** *dat* ~ *Anhänger, Wohnwagen* to be attached to sth ❹ (*fam: angeschlossen sein*) ■**an etw** *dat* ~ *Patient* to be connected to sth ❺ (*fam: emotional*) ■**an jdm/etw** ~ to be attached to sb/sth ❻ (*festhängen*) [**mit etw** *dat*] **an etw** *dat* ~ **bleiben** to get [sth] caught on sth ❼ (*fam: sich aufhalten*) **er hängt den ganzen Tag vorm Fernseher** he spends all day in front of the television ❽ (*fam: zu erledigen sein*) **etw bleibt an jdm** ~ sth is up to sb ❾ (*fam: in der Erinnerung bleiben*) ■**[bei jdm]** ~ **bleiben** to stick [in sb's mind] ❿ (*nach unten*) **etw** ~ **lassen** to dangle sth II. *vt* <hängte *o* DIAL hing, gehängt *o* DIAL

gehangen> ❶ (*anbringen*) to hang (**an/auf** +*akk* on) ❷ (*henken*) to hang ❸ (*anschließen*) to attach (**an** +*akk* to) ❹ (*im Stich lassen*) ■**jdn** ~ **lassen** to let sb down III. *vr* <hängte *o* DIAL hing, gehängt *o* DIAL gehangen> ❶ (*sich festhalten*) ■**sich** *akk* **an jdn/etw** ~ to hang on to sb/sth ❷ (*sich gehen lassen*) ■**sich** *akk* ~ **lassen** to let oneself go

Hanse <-> ['hanzə] *f kein pl* HIST Hanseatic League

hänseln ['hɛn·zl̩n] *vt* to tease (**wegen** +*gen* about)

Hantel <-, -n> ['han·tl̩] *f* SPORT dumbbell

hantieren* [han·'ti:·rən] *vi* ❶ (*sich beschäftigen*) to be busy (**mit** +*dat* with) ❷ (*herumwerkeln*) to work (**an** +*dat* on)

hapern ['ha:·pɐn] *vi impers* (*fam*) ❶ (*fehlen*) ■**an etw** *dat* ~ to be lacking sth ❷ (*schlecht bestellt sein*) ■**es hapert** [**bei jdm**] **mit etw** *dat* sb has a problem with sth

Happen <-s, -> ['hapn̩] *m* (*fam: kleine Mahlzeit*) snack

happig ['ha·pɪç] *adj* (*fam: hoch*) *Preis* steep

Harfe <-, -n> ['har·fə] *f* harp

harmlos I. *adj* ❶ (*ungefährlich*) harmless ❷ (*arglos*) innocent II. *adv* ❶ (*ungefährlich*) harmlessly ❷ (*arglos*) innocently

Harmonie <-, -n> [har·mo·'ni:] *f* harmony

harmonieren* [har·mo·'ni:·rən] *vi* ❶ (*zusammenklingen*) to harmonize ❷ (*zueinander passen*) to go with ❸ (*gut zusammenpassen*) to get along well [with each other]

Harmonika <-, -s> [har·'mo:·ni·ka] *f* accordion

harmonisch [har·'mo:·nɪʃ] *adj* harmonious

Harn <-[e]s, -e> [harn] *m* urine

Harnblase *f* bladder

Harpune <-, -n> [har·'pu:·nə] *f* harpoon

hart <härter, härteste> [hart] I. *adj*

H

H

① (nicht weich) hard; (straff) firm
② (heftig) Aufprall, Ruck, Winter severe ③ Akzent harsh ④ Schnaps strong; Drogen hard; Pornografie hardcore ⑤ (brutal) Film, Konflikt violent ⑥ (abgehärtet) Kerl tough ⑦ (streng, unerbittlich) Gesetze, Regime, Worte harsh; Mensch hard; Strafe severe; ■ ~ mit jdm sein to be hard on sb ⑧ (schwer zu ertragen) cruel; Zeiten hard; Realität, Wahrheit harsh; der Tod ihres Mannes war für sie ein ~ er Schlag the death of her husband was a cruel blow for her ⑨ (mühevoll) tough; Arbeit hard ▶WENDUNGEN: [in etw dat] ~ bleiben to remain firm [about sth]; ~ im Nehmen sein to be resilient II. adv ① (nicht weich) hard; ~ gefroren frozen hard pred; ~ gekocht hard-boiled ② (rau) harshly; die Sprache klingt ziemlich ~ the language sounds quite harsh ③ (mühevoll) hard; ~ arbeiten to work hard ▶WENDUNGEN: jdn ~ treffen to hit sb hard

Härte <-, -n> ['hɛr·tə] f ① (Härtegrad) hardness ② kein pl (Wucht) force ③ kein pl (Robustheit) robustness ④ kein pl (Stabilität) stability ⑤ kein pl (Strenge) severity; (Unerbittlichkeit) relentlessness ⑥ (schwere Erträglichkeit) cruelty

Härtefall m hardship case
Härtetest m endurance test
hartherzig adj hard-hearted
hartnäckig I. adj ① (beharrlich) persistent ② (langwierig) stubborn II. adv (beharrlich) persistently
Hartz IV [haːʁts·'fiːɐ̯] Hartz IV (German labor market reform of 2005 that regulates and brings together unemployment and social security benefits)
Harz <-es, -e> [haːʁts] nt resin
harzig ['haːʁ·ʦɪç] adj resinous
Haschisch <-[s]> ['ha·ʃɪʃ] nt o m kein pl hashish
Hase <-n, -n> ['haː·zə] m ① (wild lebendes Nagetier) hare ② (Kaninchen) rabbit

HaselnussRR ['haː·zl̩·nʊs] f ① (Nuss) hazelnut ② (Hasel) hazel
HassRR <-es>, **Haß**ALT <-sses> [has] m kein pl hatred; ■ aus ~ out of hatred; einen ~ auf jdn haben to hate sb
hassen ['ha·sn̩] vt to hate; ■ es ~, etw zu tun to hate doing sth
hasserfülltRR adj, adv full of hate
hässlichRR, **häßlich**ALT ['hɛs·lɪç] I. adj ① (unschön) ugly ② (gemein) nasty ③ (unerfreulich) unpleasant II. adv (gemein) nastily
HässlichkeitRR, **Häßlichkeit**ALT <-, -en> f ugliness
hasten ['has·tn̩] vi sein (geh) to hurry
hastig ['has·tɪç] I. adj hurried; nicht so ~! not so fast! II. adv hastily
hätscheln ['hɛː·tʃl̩n] vt ① (liebkosen) to cuddle ② (gut behandeln) to pamper ③ (gerne pflegen) to cherish
hatte ['ha·tə] imp von haben
Haube <-, -n> ['hau·bə] f ① (weibliche Kopfbedeckung) bonnet ② (Trockenhaube) hair dryer ③ (Motorhaube) hood ④ ÖSTERR, SÜDD (Mütze) cap
Hauch <-[e]s, -e> [haux] m ① (Atemhauch) breath ② (Luftzug) breath of air ③ (leichter Duft) whiff ④ (Flair) aura
hauchdünn ['haux·dʏn] adj ① (äußerst dünn) wafer-thin; Stoff airy ② (äußerst knapp) Mehrheit narrow
hauchen ['hau·xn̩] vt (flüstern) to whisper
Haue <-, -n> ['hauə] f ① SÜDD, SCHWEIZ, ÖSTERR (Hacke) hoe ② kein pl (fam: Prügel) thrashing
hauen <haute, gehauen o DIAL gehaut> ['hau·ən] I. vt ① (fam: schlagen) to hit ② (fam: verprügeln) to hit; ■ sie ~ sich they're beating each other up ③ (meißeln) to carve II. vr (fam: sich setzen, legen) ■ sich akk auf/in etw akk ~ to throw oneself onto/into sth
Haufen <-s, -> ['hau·fn̩] m ① (Anhäufung) heap, pile ② (fam: große Menge) ton; du erzählst da einen ~ Quatsch! what a bunch of nonsense! ③ (Schar) crowd ④ (Gruppe, Gemeinschaft)

bunch ▶WENDUNGEN: **auf einem ~** (fam) in one place; **jdn über den ~ fahren/rennen** (fam) to run over sep sb; **etw über den ~ werfen** (fam) to mess up sep sth

haufenweise adv ❶(in Haufen) in piles ❷(fam) in great quantities; **etw ~ haben** to have tons of sth

häufig ['hɔy·fɪç] I. adj frequent II. adv frequently

Häufigkeit <-, -en> f frequency

Haupt <-[e]s, Häupter> [haupt] nt (geh) head; **gesenkten/erhobenen ~es** with one's head bowed/raised

Hauptbahnhof m main [train] station

hauptberuflich I. adj full-time II. adv on a full-time basis

Hauptdarsteller(in) m(f) leading actor

Haupteingang m main entrance

Hauptfach nt SCH major

Hauptgericht nt main course

Hauptgeschäftszeit f peak shopping hours pl, main business hours pl

Hauptgewinn m first prize

Häuptling <-s, -e> ['hɔypt·lɪŋ] m chief

Hauptperson f LIT main character

Hauptquartier nt headquarters npl

Hauptrolle f leading role ▶WENDUNGEN: [bei etw dat] **die ~ spielen** to play a leading part [in sth]

Hauptsache ['haupt·za·xə] f main thing; **~, du bist glücklich!** the main thing is that you're happy!

hauptsächlich ['haupt·zɛç·lɪç] I. adj main II. adv mainly

Hauptsaison [-zɛ·zɔŋ] f peak season

Hauptsatz m LING main clause

Hauptschlagader f aorta

Hauptschule f ≈ junior high school (a school for grades 5 to 10 in Germany or grades 5 to 8 in Austria)

Hauptstadt f capital [city]

Hauptverkehrsstraße f main road

Hauptverkehrszeit f rush hour

Hauptwort nt noun

Haus <-es, Häuser> [haus] nt ❶(Gebäude) house; **jdn nach ~ bringen** to take sb home; **außer ~ essen** to eat out; **sich** akk **wie zu ~e fühlen** to feel at home; **frei ~ liefern** to deliver free of charge; **nach ~e** [o ÖSTERR, SCHWEIZ a. nachhause] home; **zu ~e** [o ÖSTERR, SCHWEIZ a. zuhause] at home; **bei jdm zu ~e** [o ÖSTERR, SCHWEIZ a. zuhause] at sb's house ❷(Familie) household; **er ist ein alter Freund des ~es** he's an old friend of the family; **aus gutem ~e** from a good family ❸(Unternehmen) company; ■**im ~e sein** to be in; **das erste ~ am Platze** the best company in the area ❹POL (Kammer) House ▶WENDUNGEN: **~ halten** to be economical; **von ~e aus** originally

Hausangestellte(r) f(m) domestic servant

Hausarbeit f ❶(Arbeit im Haushalt) housework ❷SCH (Schulaufgaben) homework; (wissenschaftliche Arbeit) assignment

Hausarrest m ❶(elterliche Strafe) **~ haben** to be grounded ❷JUR house arrest

Hausarzt, -ärztin m, f family physician

Hausaufgaben pl SCH homework sing

Hausbesitzer(in) m(f) homeowner; (Vermieter) landlord

Hausbewohner(in) m(f) tenant

Häuschen <-s, -> ['hɔys·çən] nt ❶dim von **Haus** small house ❷SCHWEIZ (Kästchen auf kariertem Papier) square

Hauseingang m entrance [to a house]

hausen ['hau·zn] vi ❶(pej fam: erbärmlich wohnen) to live [in poor conditions] ❷(wüten) to wreak havoc

Hausflur m entrance hall

Hausfrau f ❶(nicht berufstätige Frau) housewife ❷ÖSTERR, SÜDD (Zimmerwirtin) landlady

Hausfriedensbruch m trespassing

Hausgebrauch m **für den ~** for domestic use; (für durchschnittliche Ansprüche) for average requirements

Haushalt <-[e]s, -e> m ❶(Hausgemeinschaft) household ❷(Haushaltsführung) housekeeping; [jdm] **den ~ führen** to keep house [for sb] ❸MED, BIOL balance ❹ÖKON budget

haus|halten *vi irreg* to be economical (**mit** +*dat* with)

Haushaltsgeld *nt* money for household expenses

Hausherr(in) <-en, -en> *m(f)* head of the household; (*Gastgeber*) host

haushoch ['haus·hoːx] I. *adj* ① (*euph: sehr hoch*) huge; *Flammen, Wellen* gigantic ② SPORT (*eindeutig*) clear; *Niederlage* crushing; *Sieg* overwhelming; *Favorit* obvious II. *adv* (*eindeutig*) clearly

hausieren* [hau·'ziː·rən] *vi* to hawk; **H~ verboten!** no soliciting!

Hausierer(in) <-s, -> *m(f)* solicitor

Hauslehrer(in) *m(f)* private tutor

häuslich ['hɔys·lɪç] I. *adj* ① (*die Hausgemeinschaft betreffend*) domestic ② (*das Zuhause liebend*) home-loving II. *adv* **sich** *akk* ~ **einrichten** to make oneself at home; **sich** *akk* ~ **niederlassen** to settle down

Hausmädchen *nt* maid

Hausmann ['haus·man] *m* house husband

Hausmannskost *f kein pl* KOCHK home cooking

Hausmeister(in) *m(f)* janitor

Hausmittel *nt* household remedy

Hausordnung *f* house rules *pl*

Hausrat *m kein pl* household contents *pl*

Hausratversicherung *f* home owner's insurance

Hausschlüssel *m* house key

Hausschuh *m* slipper

Haustier *nt* pet

Haustür *f* front door

Haut <-, Häute> [haut] *f* skin; **nass bis auf die** ~ soaked to the skin [*or* bone] ▶WENDUNGEN: **aus der** ~ **fahren** (*fam*) to hit the roof; **auf der faulen** ~ **liegen** (*fam*) to take it easy; **mit** ~ **und Haar|en** (*fam*) completely; **mit heiler** ~ **davonkommen** (*fam*) to escape unscathed; **jd möchte nicht in jds ~stecken** sb would not like to be in sb's shoes; **sich** *akk* **nicht wohl in seiner ~ fühlen** (*fam*) to not feel too good

Hautabschürfung *f* graze

Hautausschlag *m* [skin] rash

Hautcreme *f* skin cream

häuten ['hɔy·tn̩] I. *vt* to skin II. *vr* **sich** *akk* ~ *Schlange* to shed one's skin

hauteng *adj, adv* skin-tight

Hebamme <-, -n> ['heːp·ʔamə] *f* midwife

Hebebühne *f* hydraulic lift

Hebel <-s, -> ['heː·bl̩] *m* lever ▶WENDUNGEN: **am längeren ~ sitzen** (*fam*) to hold the upper hand

heben <hob, gehoben> ['heː·bn̩] I. *vt* ① (*nach oben bewegen*) to raise ② (*verbessern*) *Stimmung, Niveau* to improve ③ SÜDD (*halten*) to hold II. *vr* **sich** *akk* ~ *Vorhang* to rise III. *vi* ① (*Lasten hochhieven*) to lift loads; **er musste den ganzen Tag schwer ~** he had to do a lot of heavy lifting all day ② SÜDD (*haltbar sein*) *Lebensmittel* to keep

Hebräer(in) <-s, -> [he·'brɛː·ɐ] *m(f)* Hebrew

hebräisch [he·'brɛː·ɪʃ] *adj* Hebrew

Hecht <-[e]s, -e> [hɛçt] *m* pike ▶WENDUNGEN: **ein toller ~** (*fam*) an incredible guy

Heck <-[e]s, -e> [hɛk] *nt* ① AUTO rear, back ② NAUT stern ③ LUFT tail

Hecke <-, -n> ['hɛ·kə] *f* hedge

Heckenschütze, -schützin *m, f* sniper

Heckklappe *f* AUTO tailgate

Heckscheibe *f* AUTO rear window

Heer <-[e]s, -e> [heːɐ] *nt* ① (*Armee*) armed forces *npl* ② (*fig: große Anzahl*) **ein ~ von ...** an army of ...

Hefe <-, -n> ['heː·fə] *f* yeast

Hefeteig *m* yeast dough

Heft <-[e]s, -e> [hɛft] *nt* ① (*Schreibheft*) notebook ② (*Zeitschrift*) magazine; (*Ausgabe*) issue

heften ['hɛf·tn̩] *vt* ① (*befestigen*) to stick (**an** +*akk* to) ② (*mit Heftklammer*) to staple (**an** +*akk* to) ③ (*nähen*) *Naht, Saum* to baste

Hefter <-s, -> *m* ① (*Mappe*) [loose-leaf] folder ② (*Heftmaschine*) stapler

heftig ['hɛf·tɪç] I. *adj* ① (*stark*) *Aufprall, Schlag* violent; *Kämpfe* fierce; *Kopf-*

schmerzen splitting; *Regen, Schneefall* heavy ❷ (*intensiv*) *Leidenschaft, Sehnsucht* intense ❸ (*scharf*) *Kritik* fierce; *Reaktion* vehement **II.** *adv* **etw ~ dementieren** to vehemently deny sth

He̱ftklammer *f* staple

He̱ftpflaster *nt* Band-Aid®

He̱ftzwecke *f* thumbtack

Heide <-, -n> ['hai·də] *f* ❶ (*Heideland*) heath, moor ❷ *s.* **Heidekraut**

Heide, Heidin <-n, -n> ['hai·də, 'hai·dɪn] *m, f* REL heathen, pagan

He̱idekraut *nt* BOT heather

He̱idelbeere ['hai·dl·beː·rə] *f* blueberry

He̱idenangst *f* mortal fear; ■**eine ~ vor etw** *dat* **haben** to be scared stiff of sth

He̱idenspaß *m* (*fam*) great fun

he̱ikel ['hai·kl] *adj* delicate; *Frage, Situation a.* tricky

heil [hail] *adj, adv* ❶ (*unverletzt*) uninjured ❷ (*unbeschädigt*) intact

he̱ilbar *adj* curable

He̱ilbutt <-s, -e> ['hail·but] *m* halibut

he̱ilen ['hai·lən] **I.** *vi sein* (*gesund werden*) to heal [up] **II.** *vt* ❶ (*gesund machen*) to cure (**von** +*dat* of) ❷ (*kurieren*) ■**von jdm/etw geheilt sein** to have gotten over sb/sth

he̱ilfroh ['hail·'froː] *adj pred* (*fam*) really glad

he̱ilig ['hai·lɪç] *adj* ❶ (*geweiht*) holy; **die ~e Kommunion** Holy Communion ❷ (*bei Namen von Heiligen*) Saint; **die H~e Jungfrau** the Blessed Virgin

He̱iligabend [hai·lɪç·'ʔaː·bn̩t] *m* Christmas Eve

He̱ilige(r) ['hai·lɪ·gə, -gə] *f(m) dekl wie adj* saint

he̱ilig|sprechen *vt irreg* to canonize

He̱ilkraft *f* healing power

He̱ilkraut *nt meist pl* medicinal herb

He̱ilkunde *f kein pl* medicine

he̱illos ['hail·loːs] **I.** *adj* terrible **II.** *adv* hopelessly

He̱ilpflanze *f* medicinal plant

He̱ilpraktiker(in) *m(f)* nonmedical practitioner

He̱ilquelle *f* medicinal spring

he̱ilsam ['hail·zaːm] *adj* salutary

Heilung <-, -en> ['hai·luŋ] *f* ❶ (*Genesungsprozess*) recovery ❷ (*Krankenbehandlung*) curing ❸ (*Abheilen einer Wunde*) healing

heim [haim] *adv* DIAL home

Heim <-[e]s, -e> [haim] *nt* ❶ (*Zuhause*) home ❷ (*Seniorenheim, Jugendanstalt*) home ❸ (*Stätte eines Clubs*) club[house] ❹ (*Erholungsheim*) convalescent home

Heimat <-, -en> ['hai·maːt] *f* hometown; (*Heimatland*) homeland; BOT, ZOOL natural habitat

he̱imatlich *adj* native; *Brauchtum, Lieder* local

he̱imatlos *adj* homeless; POL stateless

He̱imatstadt *f* hometown

He̱imfahrt *f* trip [*or* ride] home

he̱imisch ['hai·mɪʃ] *adj* ❶ (*einheimisch*) native; **sich** *akk* **~ fühlen** to feel at home ❷ (*bewandert*) ■**in etw** *dat* **~ sein** to be at home with sth

He̱imkehr <-> *f kein pl* return home

he̱im|kehren ['haim·keː·rən] *vi sein* to return home (**aus/von** +*dat* from)

he̱imlich ['haim·lɪç] *adj* ❶ (*geheim*) secret ❷ (*verstohlen*) furtive

He̱imlichtuerei <-, -en> [haim·lɪç·tuː·ə·'rai] *f* (*pej*) secretiveness

He̱imreise *f* trip home

he̱imtückisch ['haim·ty·kɪʃ] *adj* ❶ (*tückisch*) malicious ❷ (*gefährlich*) insidious

He̱imweg *m* way home; **sich** *akk* **auf den ~ machen** to head home

He̱imweh <-[e]s> *nt kein pl* homesickness; *kein pl, kein art;* ~ **haben** to be homesick (**nach** +*dat* for)

he̱im|zahlen *vt* ■**jdm etw ~** to pay sb back for sth

Heirat <-, -en> ['hai·raːt] *f* marriage

he̱iraten ['hai·raː·tn̩] **I.** *vt* to marry **II.** *vi* to get married; **sie hat reich geheiratet** she married into money

Heiratsantrag *m* [marriage] proposal; **jdm einen ~ machen** to propose to sb

heiser ['hai·zɐ] **I.** *adj Stimme* hoarse; (*rauchig*) husky **II.** *adv* hoarsely

Heiserkeit <-, *selten* -en> *f* hoarseness
heiß [hais] **I.** *adj* ❶ (*sehr warm*) hot; ∎ jdm ist/wird es ~ sb is/is getting hot; **etw ~ machen** to heat up *sep* sth ❷ *Debatte* heated; *Kampf* fierce ❸ *Liebe* burning; *Wunsch* fervent ❹ (*fam: aufreizend*) hot; *Kleid* sexy ❺ (*fam: gestohlen*) hot ❻ (*brisant*) **ein ~es Thema** an explosive issue ❼ (*aufregend*) *Musik, Party* hot ❽ *attr* (*fam: aussichtsreich*) hot; **die Polizei ist auf einer ~en Fährte** the police are on a hot trail ❾ (*sl: großartig*) fantastic; **echt ~** really cool ❿ (*fam: brünstig*) in heat **II.** *adv* ❶ (*sehr warm*) hot; ~ **laufen** (*Maschinenteil*) to overheat ❷ (*innig*) ardently; ~ **ersehnt** greatly longed for; ~ **geliebt** dearly beloved ❸ (*erbittert*) fiercely; ~ **umstritten** hotly disputed

heißblütig ['hais·bly:·tɪç] *adj* ❶ (*impulsiv*) hot-tempered ❷ (*leidenschaftlich*) passionate

heißen <hieß, geheißen> ['hai·sn] **I.** *vi* ❶ (*den Namen haben*) to be called; **wie ~ Sie?** what's your name? ❷ (*bedeuten*) to mean; **"ja" heißt auf Japanisch "hai"** "hai" is Japanese for "yes"; **was heißt eigentlich "Liebe" auf Russisch?** how do you say "love" in Russian?; **was soll das [denn] ~?** what's that supposed to mean?; **das heißt, ...** that is to say ...; (*vorausgesetzt*) that is, ...; (*sich verbessernd*) or should I say, ... ❸ (*lauten*) **das Sprichwort heißt anders** that's not how the proverb goes **II.** *vi impers* ❶ (*zu lesen sein*) **Auge um Auge, wie es im Alten Testament heißt** an eye for an eye, as it says in the Old Testament ❷ (*als Gerücht kursieren*) ∎ **es heißt, dass ...** there is a rumor [going around] that ...

Heißhunger *m* craving; **mit ~** ravenously

Heißluft *f kein pl* hot air

heiter ['hai·tɐ] *adj* ❶ (*fröhlich*) cheerful ❷ (*fröhlich stimmend*) amusing ❸ METEO *Wetter* bright

Heizanlage *f* heater
Heizdecke *f* electric blanket
heizen ['hai·tsn] **I.** *vi* ❶ (*die Heizung betreiben*) **mit Gas/Öl ~** to heat with natural gas/oil ❷ (*Wärme abgeben*) to give off heat **II.** *vt* ❶ (*beheizen*) to heat ❷ (*anheizen*) to stoke
Heizkessel *m* boiler
Heizkissen *nt* heating pad
Heizkörper *m* radiator
Heizlüfter *m* fan heater
Heizöl *nt* fuel oil
Heizung <-, -en> *f* ❶ (*Zentralheizung*) heating ❷ (*Heizkörper*) radiator
Heizungskeller *m* boiler room
Hektar <-s, -e *o bei Maßangaben* -> [hɛkt·'a:ɐ̯] *nt o m* hectare
Hektik <-> ['hɛk·tɪk] *f kein pl* hectic pace; **nur keine ~!** take it easy!
hektisch ['hɛk·tɪʃ] **I.** *adj* hectic **II.** *adv* frantically
Held(in) <-en, -en> [hɛlt] *m(f)* hero *masc*, heroine *fem*
heldenhaft *adj* heroic
Heldentat *f* heroic deed
helfen <half, geholfen> ['hɛl·fn] *vi* ❶ (*unterstützen*) to help (**bei** +*dat* with); **warte mal, ich helfe dir** wait, I'll help you ❷ (*dienen, nützen*) ∎ **jdm ist mit etw** *dat* **geholfen/nicht geholfen** sth is of help/no help to sb; **Knoblauch soll gegen Arteriosklerose ~** garlic is supposed to help prevent arteriosclerosis ▶WENDUNGEN: **ich kann mir nicht ~, [aber]** ... I'm sorry, but ...; **man muss sich** *dat* **nur zu ~ wissen** you just have to be resourceful
Helfer(in) <-s, -> ['hɛl·fɐ] *m(f)* ❶ (*unterstützende Person*) helper; (*Komplize*) accomplice ❷ (*fam: nützliches Gerät*) aid
hell [hɛl] **I.** *adj* ❶ (*nicht dunkel*) light; **es wird ~** it's getting light [out] ❷ (*kräftig leuchtend*) bright ❸ (*gering gefärbt*) light-colored; *Haar, Haut* fair ❹ *Stimme, Ton* clear ❺ (*fam: aufgeweckt*) bright; **du bist ein ~es Köpfchen** you've got brains ❻ *attr* (*rein, pur*) *Freude* sheer,

H

pure **II.** *adv* ❶ (*licht*) brightly ❷ (*hoch*) high and clear

hellhörig ['hɛl·høː·rɪç] *adj* badly sound-proofed ▸WENDUNGEN: ~ **werden** to prick up one's ears

Helligkeit <-, -en> *f* ❶ *kein pl* (*Licht-fülle*) lightness; (*helles Licht*) [bright] light ❷ (*Lichtstärke*) brightness ❸ ASTRON (*Leuchtkraft*) luminosity

Hellseher(in) ['hɛl·zeːɐ] *m(f)* clairvoyant

hellwach ['hɛl·'vax] *adj* wide-awake

Helm <-[e]s, -e> ['hɛlm] *m* helmet

Hemd <-[e]s, -en> [hɛmt] *nt* shirt; (*Unterhemd*) undershirt

hemmen [hɛ·mən] *vt* ❶ (*ein Hemmnis sein*) to hinder ❷ (*bremsen*) to stop ❸ PSYCH to inhibit

Hemmschwelle *f* PSYCH inhibition level

Hemmung <-, -en> *f* ❶ *kein pl* (*das Hemmen*) obstruction ❷ (*Bedenken, Skrupel*) ~**en haben** to feel inhibited; **nur keine ~en!** don't hold back! ❸ *pl* PSYCH inhibitions *pl*

hemmungslos I. *adj* ❶ (*zügellos*) unrestrained ❷ (*skrupellos*) unscrupulous **II.** *adv* ❶ (*zügellos*) without restraint ❷ (*skrupellos*) unscrupulously

Hengst <-[e]s, -e> [hɛŋst] *m* (*männliches Pferd*) stallion; (*männlicher Esel, männliches Kamel*) male

Henkel <-s, -> ['hɛŋ·kl] *m* handle

Henne <-, -n> ['hɛ·na] *f* hen

Hepatitis <-, Hepatitiden> [he·pa·'tiː·tɪs] *f* MED hepatitis

her [heːɐ] *adv* ❶ (*raus*) here, to me; ~ **damit!** (*fam*) give it here! ❷ (*herum*) ■**um jdn** ~ all around sb ❸ (*von einem Punkt aus*) ■**von etw** *dat* ~ räumlich from sth; **von weit** ~ from a long way away; ■**von ...** ~ zeitlich from ...; **ich kenne ihn von meiner Studienzeit** ~ I know him from my college days; **lang** ~ **sein, dass ...** to have been a long time since ... ❹ (*verfolgen*) ■**hinter etw** *dat* ~ **sein** to be after sth

herab|lassen *irreg* **I.** *vt* (*geh: herunter-lassen*) to let down *sep* **II.** *vr* ■**sich** *akk* [**zu etw** *dat*] ~ to lower oneself [to [do]

sth]; ■**sich** *akk* [**dazu**] ~, **etw zu tun** to condescend to doing sth

herablassend *adj* condescending

herab|sehen *vi irreg* to look down (**auf** +*akk* [**up**]**on**)

herab|setzen *vt* ❶ (*reduzieren*) Geschwindigkeit, Preise to reduce ❷ (*schlechtmachen*) to belittle

heran [hɛ·'ran] *adv* near, close up (**an** +*akk* to)

heran|kommen *vi irreg sein* ❶ (*herbei-kommen*) to approach; (*bis an etwas kommen*) to get to ❷ (*herangelangen können*) to reach ❸ (*sich beschaffen können*) to get [a] hold of ❹ (*in persön-lichen Kontakt kommen*) ■**an jdn** ~ to get a hold of sb ❺ (*gleichwertig sein*) to be up to the standard of

heran|machen *vr* (*fam*) ■**sich** *akk* an jdn ~ to approach sb

heran|wachsen [-'vak·sn] *vi irreg sein* (*geh*) to grow up (**zu** +*dat* into)

heran|wagen *vr* ■**sich** *akk* **an etw** *akk* ~ ❶ (*heranzukommen wagen*) to dare to go near sth ❷ (*sich zu beschäftigen wagen*) to dare to attempt sth

heran|ziehen *irreg* **I.** *vt* ❶ (*näher holen*) to pull (**an** +*akk* to/toward) ❷ (*einset-zen*) ■**jdn** [**zu etw** *dat*] ~ to use sb [for [or as] sth]

herauf [hɛ·'rauf] **I.** *adv* **von da unten bis oben** ~ from down there all the way up here **II.** *präp* +*akk* up; **sie ging die Treppe** ~ she went up the stairs

herauf|beschwören* *vt irreg* ❶ (*wach-rufen*) to evoke ❷ (*herbeiführen*) to cause

herauf|kommen *vi irreg sein* to come up (**zu** +*dat* to)

herauf|ziehen *irreg* **I.** *vt haben* to pull up *sep* **II.** *vi sein* Gewitter to approach

heraus [hɛ·'raus] *adv* ❶ (*nach draußen*) out; ■**aus etw** *dat* ~ out of sth ❷ (*ent-fernt sein*) ■~ **sein** to have been taken out [*or* removed] ❸ MEDIA (*veröffentlicht sein*) ■~ **sein** to be out ❹ (*hinter sich haben*) ■**aus etw** *dat* ~ **sein** to leave behind *sep* sth; **aus dem Alter bin ich** ~ that's all behind me ❺ (*gesagt*

H

worden sein) ■~ **sein** to have been said

heraus|bekommen* *vt irreg* ❶ (*entfernen*) to get out (**aus** +*dat* of) ❷ (*herausfinden*) to find out *sep* ❸ (*ausgezahlt bekommen*) to get back

heraus|bringen *vt irreg* ❶ (*nach draußen bringen*) to bring sth out[side] ❷ (*auf den Markt bringen*) to launch ❸ (*der Öffentlichkeit vorstellen*) to publish ❹ (*sagen*) to utter

heraus|finden *irreg* I. *vt* ❶ (*dahinterkommen*) to find out ❷ (*herauslesen*) to find (**aus** +*dat* from amongst) II. *vi* (*den Weg finden*) to find one's way out (**aus** +*dat* of)

Herausforderer, **-forderin** <-s, -> *m, f* challenger

heraus|fordern I. *vt* ❶ (*auffordern*) to challenge (**zu** +*dat* to) ❷ (*provozieren*) to provoke ❸ (*heraufbeschwören*) to invite; *Gefahr* to court; **das Schicksal** ~ to tempt fate II. *vi* ■**etw fordert zu etw** *dat* **heraus** sth invites sth

herausfordernd *adj* provocative

Herausforderung *f* challenge

heraus|geben *irreg* I. *vt* ❶ (*veröffentlichen*) to publish ❷ *Geld* to return II. *vi* to give change; **falsch** ~ to give [back] the wrong change

Herausgeber(in) <-s, -> *m(f)* MEDIA (*Verleger*) publisher; (*editierender Lektor*) editor

heraus|gehen *vi irreg sein* ❶ (*herauskommen*) to go out (**aus/von** +*dat* of) ❷ (*entfernt werden können*) to come out (**aus** +*dat* of) ❸ (*lebhaft werden*) ■**aus sich** *dat* ~ to come out of one's shell

heraus|greifen *vt irreg* to pick up *sep* (**aus** +*dat* from)

heraus|halten *irreg* I. *vt* ❶ (*nach draußen halten*) to hold out (**aus** +*dat* of) ❷ (*nicht verwickeln*) to keep out (**aus** +*dat* of) II. *vr* ■**sich** *akk* [**aus etw** *dat*] ~ to keep out [of sth]

heraus|kommen [hɛraus·kɔ·mən] *vi irreg sein* ❶ (*nach draußen kommen*) to come out (**aus** +*dat* of) ❷ (*etw ver-*

lassen können) ■**aus etw** *dat* ~ to get out of sth ❸ (*aufhören können*) ■**aus etw** *dat* **kaum/nicht** ~ to hardly/not be able to stop doing sth ❹ (*fam: überwinden können*) **aus Schwierigkeiten** ~ to get over one's difficulties ❺ (*auf den Markt kommen*) to be launched; (*erscheinen*) to come out ❻ (*bekannt gegeben werden*) to be published; *Gesetz, Verordnung* to be enacted ❼ (*bekannt werden*) ■**es kam heraus, dass …** it came out that … ❽ (*zur Sprache bringen*) ■**mit etw** *dat* ~ to come out with sth ❾ (*als Resultat haben*) ■**bei etw** *dat* ~ to come of sth; **und was soll dabei** ~? and what good will that do?; **auf dasselbe** ~ to amount to the same thing ▸ WENDUNGEN: **groß** ~ (*fam*) to be a great success

heraus|nehmen *irreg* I. *vt* ❶ (*entnehmen*) to take out (**aus** +*dat* of); *Zahn* to pull ❷ (*aus einer Umgebung entfernen*) ■**jdn aus etw** *dat* ~ to take sb away from sth II. *vr* ❶ (*pej: frech für sich reklamieren*) ■**sich** *dat* **etw** ~ to take liberties; **sich** *dat* **zu viel** ~ to go too far ❷ (*sich erlauben*) ■**sich** *dat* ~, **etw zu tun** to have the nerve to do sth

heraus|ragen *vi s.* hervorragen

heraus|reißen *vt irreg* ❶ (*aus etw reißen*) to tear out (**aus** +*dat* of); *Baum, Wurzel* to pull out ❷ (*ablenken*) **jdn aus seiner Arbeit** ~ to interrupt sb in their work ❸ (*fam: wettmachen*) to save

heraus|rutschen *vi sein* ❶ (*aus etw rutschen*) to slip out [of sth] ❷ (*fam: ungewollt entschlüpfen*) ■**etw rutscht jdm heraus** sb lets sth slip out

heraus|stellen I. *vt* ❶ (*nach draußen stellen*) to put outside ❷ (*hervorheben*) to emphasize II. *vr* ❶ (*ans Licht kommen*) ■**sich** *akk* ~ to come to light ❷ (*sich erweisen*) ■**sich** *akk* **als …** ~ to be shown to be …; **es stellte sich heraus, dass …** it turned out that …

herb [hɛrp] I. *adj* ❶ (*bitter-würzig*) sharp, astringent; *Duft, Parfüm* tangy; *Wein* dry ❷ (*schmerzlich*) bitter;

Erkenntnis sobering ③ *(etwas streng)* severe; *Schönheit* austere ④ *(scharf) Kritik* harsh II. *adv* ~ **duften** to smell tangy; ~ **schmecken** to taste sharp

herbei|eilen *vi sein* to rush over

herbei|führen [hɛɐ̯ˈbaɪ·fyː·rən]   *vt* *(bewirken)* to bring about *sep*

Herberge <-, -n> [ˈhɛr·bɛr·gə] *f* hostel

Herbst <-[e]s, -e> [hɛrpst] *m pl selten* fall

herbstlich [ˈhɛrpst·lɪç] *adj* fall *attr*, autumnal

Herd <-[e]s, -e> [heːɐ̯t] *m* ① *(Küchenherd)* stove ② *(Krankheitsherd)* focus ③ GEOL *(Zentrum)* epicenter

Herde <-, -n> [ˈheːɐ̯·də] *f* herd; *(Schafherde)* flock

herein [hɛˈraɪn] *adv* in [here]; ~**!** come in!

herein|brechen [hɛˈraɪn·brɛ·çn̩] *vi irreg sein* ■ **über jdn/etw** ~ *Katastrophe, Unglück* to befall [sb/sth]

herein|fallen *vi irreg sein* ① *(nach innen fallen)* to fall (**in** +*akk* in[to]) ② *(fam: betrogen werden)* to be taken in (**auf** +*akk* by)

herein|kommen *vi irreg sein* to come in; **wie bist du hier hereingekommen?** how did you get in here?

herein|lassen *vt irreg* to let in

herein|legen *vt* ① *(fam: betrügen)* to cheat (**mit** +*dat* with) ② *(nach drinnen legen)* to put in

herein|platzen *vi sein* *(fam)* ■ **[bei jdm]** ~ to burst in [on sb]; ■ **bei etw** *dat* ~ to burst into sth

Herfahrt *f* trip [over] here; **auf der** ~ on the way here

her|fallen *vi irreg sein* ① *(überfallen)* ■ **über jdn** ~ to attack sb; *(kritisieren)* to tear sb to pieces; *(mit Fragen)* to besiege sb (**mit** +*dat* with) ② *(sich stürzen)* ■ **über jdn/etw** ~ to fall upon sth

Hergang <-[e]s> *m kein pl* course of events

her|geben *irreg* I. *vt* ① *(weggeben)* to give away *sep* ② *(aushändigen)* to hand over *sep* [to] ③ *(fam: erbringen)* to say; **der Artikel gibt eine Fülle an Infor-**

mation her the article contains a lot of information ④ *(leihen)* **seinen guten Namen für etw** *akk* ~ to lend one's name to sth II. *vr* ■ **sich** *akk* **für etw** *akk* ~ to have something to do with sth

her|gehen *irreg* I. *vi sein* ① *(entlanggehen)* ■ **neben/vor jdm** ~ to walk beside/in front of sb ② *(sich erdreisten)* ~ **und ...** to just go [ahead] and ... ③ SÜDD, ÖSTERR *(herkommen)* to come [[over] here] II. *vi impers sein* *(fam: zugehen)* **bei der Diskussion ging es heiß her** it was a heated discussion

Hering <-s, -e> [ˈheː·rɪŋ] *m* ① *(Fisch)* herring ② *(Zeltpflock)* [tent] peg

her|kommen *vi irreg sein* ① *(herbeikommen)* to come [over] here ② *(herstammen)* to come from

Herkunft <-, selten Herkünfte> [ˈheːɐ̯·kʊnft] *f* ① *(Abstammung)* origins *pl*, descent ② *(Ursprung)* origin

Herkunftsland *nt* country of origin

her|machen I. *vr* *(fam)* ① *(beschäftigen)* ■ **sich** *akk* **über etw** *akk* ~ to dive into sth ② *(Besitz ergreifen)* ■ **sich** *akk* **über etw** *akk* ~ to pounce on sth ③ *(herfallen)* ■ **sich** *akk* **über jdn** ~ to attack sb II. *vt* *(fam)* **das macht doch nicht viel her!** that's not very impressive!

Hermelin <-s, -e> [hɛr·məˈliːn] *nt* ZOOL *(braun)* stoat; *(weiß)* ermine

hermetisch [hɛrˈmeː·tɪʃ] *adj* hermetic

Heroin <-s> [heˑroˈiːn] *nt kein pl* heroin

Herpes <-> [ˈhɛr·pɛs] *m kein pl* herpes

Herr(in) <-n, -en> [hɛr] *m(f)* ① *nur m (männliche Anrede)* Mr.; **die ~en Schmidt und Schrader** Mr. Schmidt and Mr. Schrader; **sehr geehrter ~ ...** Dear Mr. ...; **sehr geehrte ~en!** Dear Sirs! ② *nur m (geh: Mann)* gentleman ③ *(Herrscher)* ruler *(über* +*akk* of); ~ **der Lage sein** to be master of the situation; **sein eigener** ~ **sein** to be one's own boss ④ REL *(Gott)* Lord ▸ WENDUNGEN: **aus aller ~en Länder** from all over the world

Herrenbekleidung *f* menswear

H

H

Herren(fahr)rad nt men's bicycle
Herrenhaus nt manor house
herrenlos adj abandoned; Hund, Katze stray
Herrentoilette f men's restroom
Herrgott ['hɛr·gɔt] m SÜDD, ÖSTERR (fam) ■ der ~ the Lord
Herrin <-, -nen> f fem form von **Herr** mistress
herrisch ['hɛ·rɪʃ] I. adj overbearing; Ton commanding II. adv imperiously
herrlich I. adj ❶ (prächtig) marvelous; Aussicht magnificent; Sonnenschein glorious; Urlaub delightful; **das Wetter ist ~ heute!** the weather is great today! ❷ (köstlich) delicious II. adv (prächtig) **sich** akk **~ amüsieren** to have a wonderful time
Herrschaft <-, -en> ['hɛr·ʃaft] f ❶ kein pl (Macht, Kontrolle) reign ❷ pl (Damen und Herren) ■ **die ~en** ladies and gentlemen; **darf ich den ~en sonst noch etwas bringen?** would any of you ladies or gentlemen care for anything else?
herrschaftlich adj grand
herrschen ['hɛrʃn] I. vi ❶ to rule (über +akk over); Meinung to prevail; Ruhe, Stille to reign; Hunger, Krankheit, Not to be rampant II. vi impers ■ **es herrscht ...** there is ...
herrschend adj ruling; Meinung prevailing; Mode current
Herrscher(in) <-s, -> m(f) ruler (über +akk of)
Herrscherhaus nt [ruling] dynasty
herrschsüchtig adj domineering
herrühren vi ■ **von etw** dat ~ to come from sth
herstellen vt ❶ (erzeugen) to produce ❷ (gesundheitlich) **jdn wieder ~** to restore sb back to health ❸ (irgendwohin stellen) to put [over] here
Hersteller(in) <-s, -> m(f) producer
Herstellung f kein pl production
herüber [hɛ·'ryː·bɐ] adv over here
herum [hɛ·'rʊm] adv ❶ (um etw im Kreis) ■ **um etw** akk ~ around sth ❷ (überall in jds Nähe) ■ **um jdn ~**

[all] around sb ❸ (gegen) ■ **um ... ~** around ...
herumärgern vr (fam) ■ **sich** akk **mit jdm/etw** ~ to keep getting worked up about sb/sth
herumdrehen I. vt ❶ (um die Achse drehen) to turn ❷ (wenden) to turn over II. vr ■ **sich** akk ~ to turn around
herumführen I. vt ■ **jdn** ~ to show sb around II. vi ■ **um etw** akk ~ to go around sth
herumgehen vi irreg sein ❶ (einen Kreis gehen) to walk around (in a circular pattern) ❷ (ziellos umhergehen) to wander around ❸ (herumgereicht werden) to be passed around ❹ (weitererzählt werden) to go around ❺ (vorübergehen) to pass
herumkommandieren* I. vt (fam) to boss around II. vi (fam) to give orders
herumkommen vi irreg sein (fam) ❶ (herumfahren können) to get around ❷ (vermeiden können) to get out of ❸ (reisen) to get around; **viel ~** to do a lot of traveling
herumlaufen vi irreg sein ❶ (um etwas laufen) to run around ❷ (fam: umherlaufen) to go around; [noch] **frei ~** to be [still] at large
herumliegen vi irreg (fam) to lie around; ■ **etw ~ lassen** to leave sth lying around
herumlungern vi (fam) to hang around; JUR to loiter
herumschlagen irreg vr (fam) ■ **sich** akk **mit jdm/etw** ~ to struggle with sb/sth
herumschnüffeln vi (pej fam: spionieren) to snoop around (in +dat in)
herumstehen vi irreg sein ❶ (fam: irgendwo in der Gegend stehen) to stand around ❷ (gruppiert sein) ■ **um jdn/etw** ~ to stand around sb/sth
herumtreiben vr irreg ■ **sich** akk **irgendwo** ~ to hang around somewhere
herumziehen irreg vi sein ■ **mit jdm** ~ to move around with sb
herunter [hɛ·'rʊn·tɐ] I. adv down;

~ **vom Sofa!** [get] off the sofa!; ~ **mit der Mütze!** take off that hat! **II.** *präp nachgestellt* **den Berg ~ geht es leichter als hinauf** it's easier to go down the hill than up it

her·unter|fallen *vi irreg sein* to fall off; **mir ist der Hammer heruntergefallen** I dropped the hammer

her·unter|gehen *vi irreg sein* ❶ *(nach unten gehen)* to go down ❷ *(fig: sinken)* **Preise** to drop ❸ *(Flughöhe verringern)* to descend ❹ *(reduzieren)* to reduce; **mit der Geschwindigkeit ~** to slow down

her·unter·gekommen *adj (pej)* ❶ *(abgewohnt)* rundown, dilapidated ❷ *(verwahrlost)* down-and-out

her·unter|handeln *vt (fam)* to talk down *sep*

her·unter|kippen *vt (fam)* **Schnaps, Bier** to chug [down *sep*]

her·unter|klappen *vt* to put down *sep;* **Kragen** to turn down; **Deckel** to close

her·unter|kommen *vi irreg sein* to come down

her·unter|laden *vt* COMPUT to download

her·unter|machen *vt (fam)* ❶ *(schlechtmachen)* to tear to pieces ❷ *(zurechtweisen)* to tell off

her·unter|wirtschaften *vt (pej fam)* to ruin

her·vor|heben *vt irreg* to emphasize, to stress

her·vor|holen *vt* to take out *sep* **(aus** +*dat* from)

her·vor|ragen [hɛɡ·ˈfoːɐ̯·raː·gn̩] *vi* ❶ *(vorstehen)* to jut out **(aus** +*dat* from) ❷ *(fig: sich auszeichnen)* to stand out

her·vor·ragend *adj* excellent, outstanding

her·vor|rufen *vt irreg* to evoke; **Bestürzung, Entsetzen** to cause

her·vor|treten *vi irreg sein* ❶ *(heraustreten)* to step out **(hinter** +*dat* from behind) ❷ *Wangenknochen, Kinn* to protrude ❸ *(erkennbar werden)* to become evident

her·vor|tun *vr irreg (fam)* ■ **sich** *akk* ~ to distinguish oneself **(mit** +*dat* with)

Herz <-ens, -en> [hɛrts] *nt* ❶ ANAT heart ❷ *(Gemüt, Gefühl)* heart; **mit ganzem ~en** wholeheartedly; **von ganzem ~en** sincerely; **im Grunde seines ~ens** in his heart of hearts; **leichten ~ens** lightheartedly; **schweren ~ens** with a heavy heart; **jds ~ erweichen** to soften up *sep* sb ❸ *(Zentrum)* heart ❹ *(Schatz, Liebling)* dear, love ❺ KARTEN hearts *pl* ▶WENDUNGEN: **jdm das ~ brechen** to break sb's heart; **etw nicht übers ~ bringen** to not have the heart to do sth; **etw auf dem ~en haben** to have sth on one's mind; **jds ~ hängt an etw** *dat* sb is attached to sth; **jds ~ höherschlagen lassen** to make sb's heart beat faster; **jdm etw ans ~ legen** to entrust sb with sth; **jdm liegt etw am ~en** sb is concerned about sth; **jdn in sein ~ schließen** to take sb into one's heart; **ein ~ und eine Seele sein** to be the best of friends; **seinem ~en einen Stoß geben** to pluck up the courage; **jd wächst jdm ans ~** sb is growing fond of sb

Herz·anfall *m* heart attack

her·zens·gut [ˈhɛr·tsn̩s·ˈguːt] *adj* good-hearted

herz·er·grei·fend *adj* heart-rending

Herz·fehler *m* heart defect

herz·haft I. *adj* ❶ *(würzig-kräftig)* savory; **Essen, Eintopf** hearty ❷ *(kräftig)* substantial **II.** *adv* ❶ *(würzig-kräftig)* **~ schmecken** to be tasty ❷ *(kräftig)* heartily; **~ gähnen** to yawn loudly

her·ziehen *irreg* **I.** *vt* ■ **etw hinter/neben sich** *dat* ~ to pull sth [along] behind/beside oneself **II.** *vi (fam: sich auslassen)* ■ **über jdn/etw ~** to tear sb/sth to pieces

herzig [ˈhɛr·tsɪç] *adj* cute

Herz·infarkt *m* heart attack

Herz·klopfen *nt kein pl* pounding of the heart, palpitations *pl*

herz·krank *adj* ■ **~ sein** to have a heart condition

herz·lich I. *adj* ❶ *(warmherzig)* warm,

friendly, cordial; *Lachen* hearty ❷ (*in Grußformeln*) kind **II.** *adv* ❶ (*aufrichtig*) warmly; **sich** *akk* **bei jdm ~ bedanken** to thank sb very much; **jdn ~ gratulieren** to congratulate sb warmly ❷ (*recht*) really; **~ wenig** precious little

Herzlichkeit <-> *f kein pl* warmth

herzlos *adj* heartless

Herzog(in) <-s, Herzöge> ['hɛr·tso:k] *m(f)* duke *masc*, duchess *fem*

Herzogtum <-s, -tümer> *nt* duchy, dukedom

Herzschlag *m* MED ❶ (*Kontraktion des Herzmuskels*) heartbeat ❷ (*Herzstillstand*) heart failure

Herzschrittmacher *m* MED pacemaker

Herzstillstand *m* MED cardiac arrest

herzzerreißend *adj* heart-rending

heterosexuell [he·te·ro·zɛ·ˈksu̯·ɛl] *adj* heterosexual

hetzen ['hɛtsn̩] **I.** *vi* ❶ *haben* (*sich abhetzen*) to rush around ❷ *sein* (*eilen*) to rush ❸ *haben* (*pej: Hass schüren*) to stir up hatred (**gegen** +*akk* against) **II.** *vt haben* ❶ (*jagen*) to hunt ❷ (*losgehen lassen*) ■**jdn/einen Hund auf jdn ~** to set sb/a dog on sb ❸ (*fam: antreiben*) to rush ❹ (*vertreiben*) to chase (**von** +*dat* off)

Hetzkampagne *f* (*pej*) smear campaign

Heu <-[e]s> [hɔy] *nt kein pl* hay ▶WEN-DUNGEN: **Geld wie ~ haben** to have heaps of money

Heuchelei <-, -en> [hɔy·çaˑˈlai] *f* (*pej*) ❶ (*Heucheln*) hypocrisy ❷ (*heuchlerische Äußerung*) hypocritical remark

heucheln ['hɔy·çl̩n] **I.** *vi* to be hypocritical **II.** *vt* to feign

Heuchler(in) <-s, -> ['hɔy·çlɐ] *m(f)* (*pej*) hypocrite

heuchlerisch *adj* (*pej*) hypocritical

heuer ['hɔy·ɐ] *adv* SÜDD, ÖSTERR, SCHWEIZ (*in diesem Jahr*) this year

heulen ['hɔy·lən] *vi* ❶ (*fam: weinen*) to cry; **es ist zum H~** (*fam*) it's enough to make you cry ❷ *Sturm, Wolf* to howl; *Motor* to wail; *Flugzeug, Motorrad* to roar

Heuschnupfen *m* hay fever

Heuschrecke <-, -n> *f* grasshopper; (*Wanderheuschrecke*) locust

heute ['hɔy·tə] *adv* ❶ (*an diesem Tag*) today; **~ Abend** this evening; **~ Nacht** tonight; **~ früh** [early] this morning; **ab ~** as of today; **~ in/vor acht Tagen** a week from today/ago today ❷ (*der Gegenwart*) today; **von ~ auf morgen** all of a sudden, overnight ❸ (*heutzutage*) nowadays

heutig ['hɔy·tɪç] *adj attr* ❶ (*heute stattfindend*) today's ❷ (*von heute*) Nachrichten, Zeitung today's; **der ~e Anlass** this occasion ❸ (*gegenwärtig*) **die ~e Zeit** nowadays; **der ~e Stand der Technik** today's technology

heutzutage ['hɔyt·tsu·taˑˈgə] *adv* nowadays, these days

Hexe <-, -n> ['hɛ·ksə] *f* ❶ (*böses Fabelwesen*) witch ❷ (*pej fam: zeternde Frau*) shrew; **eine alte ~** an old hag

hexen ['hɛ·ksn̩] *vi* to cast spells, to do magic; **ich kann doch nicht ~** (*fig*) I can't work miracles

Hexenschuss^RR *m kein pl* (*fam*) lumbago

Hexerei <-, -en> [hɛ·ksəˑˈrai] *f* sorcery

hieb ['hi:p] *imp von* hauen

Hieb <-[e]s, -e> [hi:p] *m* ❶ (*Schlag*) blow ❷ *pl* (*Prügel*) beating *sing*, thrashing *sing*

hieb- und stichfest *adj* irrefutable; *Alibi* iron]

hielt ['hi:lt] *imp von* halten

hier [hi:ɐ] *adv* ❶ here; **er müsste doch schon längst wieder ~ sein!** he should have been back a long time ago!; **~ ist/spricht Dr. Günther** [this is] Dr. Günther [speaking]; **~ draußen/drinnen** out/in here; **~ entlang** this way; **~ oben/unten** up/down here; **~ vorn/hinten** here at the front/at the back; **von ~ aus** from here; **von ~ sein** to be from here ❷ (*in diesem Moment*) at this point ▶WENDUNGEN: **~ und da** (*stellenweise*) here and there; (*gelegentlich*) now and then

Hierarchie <-, -n> [hie·rar·'çi:] *f* hierarchy

hierauf ['hi:r·'auf] *adv* ① (*obendrauf*) here, on this ② (*daraufhin*) as a result of this/that

hieraus ['hi:r·'aus] *adv* ① (*aus diesem Gegenstand*) from [*or* out of] here ② (*aus diesem Material*) out of this ③ (*aus dem Genannten*) from this

hierbei ['hi:ɐ·'bai] *adv* ① (*währenddessen*) while doing this ② (*dabei*) here; ~ **sind gewisse Punkte zu beachten** you need to pay attention to certain things here

hierdurch ['hi:ɐ·'dʊrç] *adv* ① (*hier hindurch*) through here ② (*dadurch*) in this way

hierfür ['hi:ɐ·'fy:ɐ] *adv* for this

hierher ['hi:ɐ·'he:ɐ] *adv* here; **bis** ~ up to here; **bis** ~ **und nicht weiter** this far and no farther

hierin ['hi:r·'ɪn] *adv* ① (*in diesem Raum*) in here ② (*was das angeht*) in this

hiermit ['hi:ɐ·'mɪt] *adv* with this; ~ **erkläre ich, dass ...** I hereby declare that ...; ~ **wird bescheinigt, dass ...** this is to certify that ...; ~ **ist die Angelegenheit erledigt** that is the end of the matter

hierüber ['hi:r·'y:bɐ] *adv* ① (*über diese Stelle*) over here ② (*über diese Angelegenheit*) about this

hiervon ['hi:ɐ·'fɔn] *adv* ① (*von diesem Gegenstand*) of this/these ② (*über dieses Thema*) about this

hierzu ['hi:ɐ·'tsu:] *adv* ① (*dazu*) with it ② (*zu dieser Kategorie*) ~ **gehört ...** this includes ... ③ (*zu diesem Punkt*) to this; **sich** *akk* ~ **äußern** to say something about this

hierzulande, **hier zu Lande** ['hi:ɐ·tsu·'lan·də] *adv* [here] in these parts, around here *fam*

hieß ['hi:s] *imp von* **heißen**

Hi-Fi-Anlage ['hai·fi·] *f* stereo system, hi-fi

Hilfe <-, -n> ['hɪl·fə] *f* ① *kein pl* (*Beistand, Unterstützung*) help, assistance; **jdn um** ~ **bitten** to ask sb for help; **jdm**

zu ~ **kommen** to come to sb's assistance; **um** ~ **rufen** to call for help; [**zu**] ~**!** help!; **ohne fremde** ~ without outside help; **erste** ~ first aid ② (*Zuschuss*) **finanzielle** ~ financial aid; (*für Notleidende*) relief; **wirtschaftliche** ~ economic aid ③ (*Hilfsmittel*) aid ④ (*Haushaltshilfe*) help

Hilferuf *m* cry for help

hilflos ['hɪlf·lo:s] **I.** *adj* ① (*auf Hilfe angewiesen*) helpless ② (*ratlos*) at a loss *pred* **II.** *adv* ① (*schutzlos*) helplessly; **jdm/etw** ~ **ausgeliefert sein** to be at the mercy of sb/sth ② (*ratlos*) at a loss

hilfreich *adj* helpful; (*nützlich a.*) useful

Hilfsaktion *f* aid program

hilfsbedürftig *adj* ① (*auf Hilfe angewiesen*) in need of help *pred* ② FIN (*bedürftig*) needy

hilfsbereit *adj* helpful

Hilfsmittel *nt* ① MED [health] aid [product] ② *pl* (*Geldmittel*) [financial] aid

Himbeere ['hɪm·be:·rə] *f* raspberry

Himmel <-s, *poet* -> ['hɪ·ml] *m* ① (*Firmament*) sky; **unter freiem** ~ outdoors ② (*Himmelreich*) heaven; **in den** ~ **kommen** to go to heaven ③ (*Baldachin*) canopy ④ AUTO [interior] roof ▸WENDUNGEN: **aus heiterem** ~ out of the blue; **um** ~**s willen** (*fam*) for heaven's sake

himmelblau ['hɪ·ml·blau] *adj* sky-blue

Himmelfahrt *f* ① (*Feiertag*) [**Christi**] ~ Ascension Day ② (*Auffahrt*) ascension into heaven

Himmelskörper *m* celestial body

Himmelsrichtung *f* direction; **die vier** ~**en** the four points of the compass

himmelweit ['hɪ·ml·vait] **I.** *adj* (*fam*) enormous; *Unterschied* considerable **II.** *adv* **sich** *akk* ~ **unterscheiden** to be completely different

himmlisch ['hɪm·lɪʃ] **I.** *adj attr* divine **II.** *adv* divinely, wonderfully

hin [hɪn] *adv* ① *räumlich* (*dahin*) there; ~ **und her laufen** to run back and forth; **der Balkon liegt zur Straße** ~ the balcony faces the street; ~ **und**

H

zurück there and back ❷ *zeitlich* (*sich hinziehend*) **über die Jahre ~** over the years ❸ (*fig*) **auf jds Bitte/Vorschlag ~** at sb's request/suggestion; **auf jds Rat ~** on sb's advice; **auf die Gefahr ~, dass ich mich wiederhole** at the risk of repeating myself ▶ WENDUNGEN: **nach langem H~ und Her** after careful consideration; **~ und wieder** from time to time

hin|arbeiten *vi* ■ **auf etw** *akk* **~** to work [one's way] toward sth

hinauf [hɪˈnauf] *adv* up; **den Fluss ~** upstream; **bis ~ zu etw** *dat* up to sth

hinauf|fahren *irreg vi sein* to go up

hinauf|gehen *vi irreg sein* ❶ (*nach oben gehen*) to go up (**auf** +*akk* to) ❷ (*steigen*) *Preise* to go up ❸ (*hochgehen*) **mit dem Preis ~** to raise the price

hinauf|steigen *vi irreg sein* to climb up (**auf** +*akk* onto)

hinaus [hɪˈnaus] **I.** *interj* (*nach draußen*) get out [of here]! **II.** *adv* ❶ (*von hier nach draußen*) out; **hier/dort ~ bitte!** this/that way out, please!; ■ **aus etw** *dat* **~** out of sth; **nach hinten/vorne ~ liegen** to be [situated] at the back/front [of a house] ❷ (*fig*) ■ **über etw** *akk* **~ sein** to be past sth; **über etw** *akk* **~ reichen** to include sth ❸ (*zeitlich*) **auf Jahre ~** for years to come; ■ **über etw** *akk* **~** more than sth

hinaus|gehen [hɪˈnaus·ge:·ən] *irreg* **I.** *vi sein* ❶ (*nach draußen gehen*) to go out (**aus** +*dat* of) ❷ (*gerichtet sein*) to go out to the street ■ **auf etw** *akk* **~** to look out onto sth; **nach Osten ~** to face east ❸ (*überschreiten*) ■ [**weit**] **über etw** *akk* **~** to go [far] beyond sth **II.** *vi impers sein* **es geht dort hinaus!** that's the way out!

hinaus|laufen *vi irreg sein* ❶ (*nach draußen laufen*) to run out ❷ (*gleichbedeutend mit etw sein*) ■ **auf etw** *akk* **~** to be the same as sth; **auf was soll das ~?** what's that supposed to mean?; **auf dasselbe ~** to come to the same thing

hinaus|lehnen *vr* ■ **sich** *akk* **~** to lean out

hinaus|schieben *vt irreg* ❶ (*nach draußen schieben*) to push out ❷ (*auf später verschieben*) to put off

hinaus|werfen *vt irreg* ❶ (*nach draußen werfen*) to throw out (**aus** +*dat* of) ❷ (*fam: entlassen*) to fire

hinaus|wollen *vi irreg* ❶ (*nach draußen wollen*) **auf den Hof/in den Garten ~** to want to go out into the courtyard/garden ❷ (*etw anstreben*) ■ **auf etw** *akk* **~** to get at sth; **worauf wollen Sie hinaus?** what are you getting at?

hinaus|zögern **I.** *vt* to put off *sep*, to delay **II.** *vr* ■ **sich** *akk* **~** to be delayed

hin|biegen *vt irreg* (*fam*) ❶ (*bereinigen*) to sort out *sep*; *Problem a.* to iron out ❷ (*pej: drehen*) ■ **es so ~, dass ...** to manage it so that ...

Hinblick *m* **im ~ auf etw** *akk* (*angesichts*) in view of sth; (*in Bezug auf*) with regard to sth

hinderlich [ˈhɪn·dɐ·lɪç] *adj* ❶ (*behindernd*) ■ **~ sein** to be a hindrance ❷ (*ein Hindernis darstellend*) ■ **jdm/für etw** *akk* **~ sein** to be an obstacle for sb/sth

hindern [ˈhɪn·dɐn] *vt* ❶ (*abhalten*) ■ **jdn daran ~, etw zu tun** to prevent sb from doing sth ❷ (*hemmen*) ■ **jdn bei etw** *akk* **~** to hamper sb in [doing] sth

Hindernis <-ses, -se> [ˈhɪn·dɐ·nɪs] *nt* obstacle; **jdm ~se in den Weg legen** to put obstacles in sb's way; (*bei Leichtathletik*) hurdle

hin|deuten *vi* ■ **auf etw** *akk* **~** to suggest sth

Hindu <-[s], -[s]> [ˈhɪn·du] *m* Hindu

hindurch [hɪnˈdʊrç] *adv* ❶ *räumlich* through ❷ *zeitlich* through, throughout; **die ganze Zeit ~** all the time

hinein [hɪˈnain] *adv* in; **~ mit dir!** (*fam*) in with you!, get in there!

hinein|gehen *vi irreg sein* ❶ (*betreten*) to go in[to], to enter ❷ (*fam*) *s.* **hineinpassen**

hinein|passen vi ■ **in etw** akk ~ to fit in [to] sth

hinein|reden vi ■ **jdm in seine Angelegenheiten** ~ to meddle in sb's affairs

hinein|stecken vt ❶ (in etw stecken) to put in [to]; **Nadel** to stick in [to] ❷ (investieren) to put in [to]

hinein|versetzen* vr ■ **sich** akk **in jdn** ~ to put oneself in sb's place; ■ **sich** akk **in etw** akk ~ to acquaint oneself with sth

hin|fahren irreg I. vi sein ■ **irgendwo** ~ to go somewhere II. vt haben ■ **jdn** ~ to take sb; **jdn zum Flughafen** ~ to drive sb to the airport

Hinfahrt f drive, trip; **auf der** ~ on the way there

hin|fallen vi irreg sein to fall [down]

hinfällig adj ❶ (gebrechlich) frail ❷ (ungültig) invalid

Hinflug m flight

hin|führen I. vt (irgendwohin geleiten) ■ **jdn** [**irgendwo**] ~ to take sb [somewhere] II. vi (in Richtung auf etw verlaufen) to lead [to]

hing ['hɪŋ] imp von **hängen**

Hingabe f kein pl (rückhaltlose Widmung) dedication; (zu einem Mensch) devotion; **sie spielt die Flöte mit** ~ she plays the flute with passion

hin|geben irreg vr ■ **sich** akk **etw** dat ~ to abandon oneself to sth

hingebungsvoll I. adj dedicated; **Blick, Pflege** devoted II. adv with dedication

hingegen [hɪn'ge:·gn̩] konj but, however

hin|gehen vi irreg sein ❶ (dorthin gehen) to go ❷ (geh: vergehen) to pass

hin|halten vt irreg ❶ (entgegenhalten) ■ **jdm etw** ~ to hold sth out to sb ❷ (aufhalten) to keep waiting

hin|hauen irreg I. vi (fam) ❶ (klappen) to work ❷ (ausreichen) to be enough ❸ (zuschlagen) to take a swing II. vr (sl) ■ **sich** akk ~ ❶ (schlafen) to turn in ❷ (sich hinflegeln) to plunk [oneself] down III. vt (fam: schlampig erledigen) to rush through; **Schriftstück** to dash off

hinken ['hɪŋ·kn̩] vi ❶ haben (das Bein nachziehen) to limp ❷ haben (nicht ganz zutreffen) **der Vergleich hinkt** that's not a good comparison

hin|knien vi, vr vi: sein to kneel down

hin|legen I. vt ❶ (niederlegen) to put down ❷ (flach lagern) to lay down ❸ (ins Bett bringen) to put to bed ❹ (fam: bezahlen) **Geldbetrag** to fork out II. vr ■ **sich** akk ~ ❶ (schlafen gehen) to go sleep ❷ (fam: hinfallen) to fall [over]

hin|nehmen vt irreg to accept; **eine Niederlage/einen Verlust** ~ [müssen] to [have to] suffer a defeat/a loss

hinreichend adj sufficient; **Gehalt, Einkommen** adequate

Hinreise f trip [somewhere]; (mit dem Auto) drive

hin|reißen vt irreg ❶ (begeistern) to enchant ❷ (spontan verleiten) **sich** akk **zu etw** dat ~ **lassen** to allow oneself to be provoked into doing sth

hinreißend adj enchanting, captivating; **Schönheit** striking

hin|richten vt to execute

Hinrichtung f execution

hin|schmeißen vt irreg (fam) s. **hinwerfen**

hin|setzen I. vr ■ **sich** akk ~ to sit down II. vt to put down

Hinsicht f kein pl **in gewisser** ~ in certain respects

hinsichtlich präp +gen with regard to

hin|stellen I. vt ❶ (an einen Platz) to put ❷ (fam: bauen) to put up ❸ **Fahrzeug** to park ❹ (charakterisieren) ■ **jdn als ...** ~ to make sb out to be ... II. vr ■ **sich** akk ~ to stand up straight; ■ **sich** akk **vor jdn** ~ to plant oneself in front of sb

hinten ['hɪn·tn̩] adv at the back; ~ **im Buch** at the back of the book; **sich** akk ~ **anstellen** to get in line [at the back]; **das wird weiter** ~ **erklärt** that's explained further toward the end

hinter ['hɪn·tɐ] I. präp +dat ❶ (dahinter) behind; ~ **dem Baum** behind the tree ❷ (jenseits von etw) behind; ~ **der Grenze** on the other side of the border

H

❸ (*fig: herausfinden*) ~ **etw kommen** to find out about sth ❹ (*unterstützen*) **sich** *akk* ~ **jdn stellen** to back sb up **II.** *präp* +*akk* ❶ (*örtlich*) behind ❷ *zeitlich* after; **etw** ~ **sich** *akk* **bringen** to get sth over with **III.** *part* (*fam*) *s.* **dahinter**

Hinterachse [-ak·sə] *f* rear axle

Hinterbein *nt* hind leg

hintere(r, s) ['hɪn·tə·rə, -rə, -rəs] *adj* ■ **der/die/das ~ ...** the rear ...

hintereinander [hɪn·tɐ·ʔain·'an·dɐ] *adv* ❶ *räumlich* one behind the other ❷ *zeitlich* one after the other; **mehrere Tage** ~ several days in a row

Hintergedanke *m* ulterior motive

hintergehen* [hɪn·tɐ·'ge:·ən] *vt irreg* (*betrügen*) to deceive; (*sexuell*) to two-time; (*um Profit zu machen*) to double-cross

Hintergrund *m* background; ■ **die Hintergründe einer S.** *gen* the [true] facts about sth

Hinterhalt *m* (*pej*) ambush

hinterhältig ['hɪn·tɐ·hɛl·tɪç] **I.** *adj* (*pej*) underhanded **II.** *adv* (*pej*) in an underhanded manner

hinterher [hɪn·tɐ·'he:ɐ] *adv* ❶ *räumlich* behind; ■ **jdm** ~ **sein** to be after sb ❷ *zeitlich* after that, afterwards

hinterher|laufen [hɪn·tɐ·'he:ɐ·lau·fn̩] *vi irreg sein* to run after

Hinterhof *m* courtyard; (*Garten*) backyard

Hinterland *nt kein pl* hinterland

hinterlassen* [hɪn·tɐ·'la·sn̩] *vt irreg* to leave; **bei jdm einen Eindruck** ~ to leave an impression on sb

hinterlegen* [hɪn·tɐ·'le:·gn̩] *vt* ■ **etw** [**bei jdm**] ~ to leave sth [with sb]; *Sicherheitsleistung, Betrag* to supply [sth with] sth

hinterlistig *adj* shifty

Hintermann <-**männer**> *m* ❶ (*räumlich*) the person behind ❷ *meist pl* (*Drahtzieher*) ringleader, brains [behind the operation]

hintern ['hɪn·tɐn] = **hinter den** *s.* **hinter**

Hintern <-s, -> ['hɪn·tɐn] *m* (*fam: Gesäß*) butt

Hinterrad *nt* rear wheel

Hinterradantrieb *m* rear-wheel drive

hinterrücks ['hɪn·tɐ·rʏks] *adv* ❶ (*von hinten*) from behind ❷ (*im Verborgenen*) behind sb's back

hinterste(r, s) ['hɪn·tes·tɐ, -stə, -stəs] *adj superl von* **hintere(r, s)** last; (*entlegenste*) farthest

Hintertür *f*, **Hintertürl** <-s, -[n]> *nt* ÖSTERR ❶ (*hintere Eingangstür*) back entrance; (*zu einem privaten Haus*) back door ❷ (*fam: Ausweg*) back door, loophole

hinterziehen* [hɪn·tɐ·'tsi:·ən] *vt irreg* **Steuern** ~ to evade tax[es]

hinüber [hɪ·'ny:·bɐ] *adv* ❶ (*nach drüben*) across, over ❷ (*fam: verdorben*) bad ❸ (*fam: kaputt, erschöpft*) ■ **etw/jd ist** ~ sth has had it

hinunter [hɪ·'nʊn·tɐ] *adv* down

hinunter|gehen [hɪ·'nʊn·tɐ·ge:·ən] *vi irreg sein* ❶ (*nach unten gehen*) to go down ❷ (*die Flughöhe verringern*) to descend (**auf** +*akk* to)

hinunter|schlucken *vt* ❶ (*schlucken*) to swallow [down *sep*] ❷ (*fam: sich verkneifen*) to suppress; **eine Antwort** ~ to stifle a reply

hinunter|spülen *vt* ❶ (*wegspülen*) to flush down *sep* ❷ (*mit einem Getränk*) to wash down *sep*

hinunter|werfen *vt irreg* to throw down

hinweg [hɪn·'vɛk] *adv* **über jdn/etw** ~ **sein** to have gotten over sb/sth

Hinweg ['hɪn·ve:k] *m* way there

hinweg|gehen [hɪn·'vɛk·ge:·ən] *vi irreg sein* ■ **über etw** *akk* ~ to disregard sth

hinweg|kommen *vi irreg sein* ■ **über etw** *akk* ~ to get over sth

hinweg|sehen *vi irreg* ■ **über jdn/etw** ~ ❶ (*darüber sehen*) to see over sb['s head]/sth ❷ (*nicht wichtig nehmen*) to overlook sb/sth

hinweg|setzen *vr* ■ **sich** *akk* **über etw** *akk* ~ to disregard sth

Hinweis <-es, -e> ['hɪnˌvais] *m* ① (*Rat*) advice, tip ② (*Anhaltspunkt*) clue

hin|weisen *irreg* I. *vt* ■**jdn darauf ~, dass ...** to point out [to sb] that ... II. *vi* ■**auf jdn/etw ~** to point to sb/sth

hin|werfen *irreg vt* ① (*zuwerfen*) ■**jdm etw ~** to throw sth to sb ② (*auf den Boden werfen*) to throw down *sep* ③ (*fam: aufgeben*) to give up *sep* ④ *Bemerkung* to drop ⑤ (*flüchtig zu Papier bringen*) to dash off

hin|ziehen *irreg* I. *vt haben* ① (*zu sich ziehen*) ■**jdm/etw zu sich dat ~** to pull sb/sth toward oneself ② (*anziehen*) ■**es zieht jdn zu jdm/etw hin** *dat* sb is attracted to sb/sth ③ (*hinauszögern*) to delay II. *vi sein* (*an einen Ort*) to move III. *vr* ■**sich** *akk* ~ ① (*zeitlich*) to drag on ② (*räumlich*) to extend along

hinzu [hɪnˈtsuː] *adv* in addition, besides

hinzu|kommen [hɪnˈtsuːˌkɔmən] *vi irreg sein* ① (*eintreffen*) to arrive; **die anderen Gäste kommen dann später hinzu** the other guests will come along later ② (*sich noch ereignen*) ■**es kommt [noch] hinzu, dass ...** there is also the fact that ... ③ (*zu einem Kauf*) **kommt sonst noch etwas hinzu?** can I get you anything else?

hinzu|ziehen *vt irreg* to consult

Hirn <-[e]s, -e> [hɪrn] *nt* ① (*Gehirn*) brain ② (*Hirnmasse*) brains *pl*

Hirngespinst *nt* fantasy

Hirnhautentzündung *f* MED meningitis

hirnrissig *adj* (*pej fam*) harebrained

Hirntod *m* MED brain death

hirnverbrannt *adj* (*fam*) s. **hirnrissig**

Hirsch <-es, -e> [hɪrʃ] *m* ① (*Rothirsch*) deer ② (*Hirschfleisch*) venison

Hirschgeweih *nt* antlers *pl*

Hirschkuh *f* hind

Hirse <-, -n> ['hɪrzə] *f* millet

Hirt(in) <-en, -en> ['hɪrt] *m(f)* herdsman *masc*; (*Schafhirt*) shepherd *masc*, shepherdess *fem*

historisch [hɪsˈtoːrɪʃ] *adj s.* **geschichtlich**

Hitze <-, *fachspr* -n> ['hɪtsə] *f* heat;

bei mittlerer ~ backen to bake at medium heat

hitzebeständig *adj* heat-resistant

Hitzewelle *f* heat wave

hitzig ['hɪtsɪç] I. *adj* ① (*leicht aufbrausend*) *Mensch* hotheaded, quick-tempered; *Reaktion* heated; *Temperament* fiery ② (*leidenschaftlich*) passionate; *Debatte* heated II. *adv* passionately

Hitzkopf *m* (*fam*) hothead

Hitzschlag *m* heatstroke; (*von der Sonne a.*) sunstroke

HIV <-[s]> [haːˈʔiːˈfau] *nt Abk von* **human immunodeficiency virus** HIV

HIV-infiziert [haːˈʔiːˈfau-] *adj* HIV-positive

HIV-positiv [haːˈʔiːˈfau-ˈpoːˈziːˈtiːf] *adj* HIV-positive

H-Milch ['haː] *f* UHT milk

hob ['hoːp] *imp von* **heben**

Hobby <-s, -s> ['hɔbi] *nt* hobby

Hobel <-s, -> ['hoːbl̩] *m* ① (*Werkzeug*) plane ② (*Küchengerät*) slicer

hobeln ['hoːbl̩n] *vt, vi* ① (*mit dem Hobel glätten*) to plane ② (*mit dem Hobel schneiden*) to slice

hoch [hoːx] I. *adj* <*attr* hohe(r, s), höher, *attr* höchste(r, s)> ① *Berg* high; *Gebäude a.* tall; *Baum* tall ② (*beträchtlich, groß*) large; *Kosten* high; *Druck, Geschwindigkeit, Lebensstandard* high; *Verlust* severe; *Sachschaden* extensive ③ (*bedeutend*) great, high; *Position* senior ▶WENDUNGEN: **etw ist jdm zu hoch** sth is above sb's head II. *adv* <höher, am höchsten> ① (*nach oben*) **etw ~ halten** to hold up *sep* sth ② (*in einiger Höhe*) **~ gelegen** high-lying *attr*; **~ oben** high up ③ (*sehr*) highly; **~ konzentriert arbeiten** to be completely focused on one's work; **jdm etw ~ anrechnen** to give sb a lot of credit for sth; **jdn/etw ~ schätzen** to appreciate sb/sth very much ④ (*eine hohe Summe umfassend*) highly; **~ gewinnen** to win big *fam*; **~ verschuldet** deep in debt *pred* ⑤ MATH (*Bezeichnung der Potenz*) **2 - 4** 2 to the power of 4 ▶WENDUNGEN: **etw**

~ und heilig versprechen to promise sth faithfully; **wenn es ~ kommt** (*fam*) at the most

Hoch <-s, -s> [hoːx] *nt* METEO high

Hochachtung *f* deep respect

hochachtungsvoll *adv* (*geh*) your obedient servant *dated form*

hochaktuell *adj* ❶ (*äußerst aktuell*) [most] up-to-date ❷ MODE highly fashionable, all the rage *pred*

hoch|arbeiten *vr* ■ **sich** *akk* ~ to work one's way up

Hochbahn *f* elevated railroad

Hochbau *m kein pl* structural engineering

hochbetagt *adj* (*geh*) aged

Hochbetrieb *m* intense activity; **~ haben** to be very busy

Hochburg *f* stronghold

hochdeutsch [ˈhoːxˌdɔytʃ] *adj* Standard German

Hochdruck *m kein pl* high pressure

Hochebene *f* plateau

hocherfreut *adj* overjoyed

Hochgebirge *nt* high mountains *pl*

Hochgefühl *nt* elation

hoch|gehen *vi irreg sein* ❶ (*hinaufgehen*) to go up ❷ (*fam: detonieren*) to go off *sep* ❸ (*fam: wütend werden*) to blow one's top ❹ (*fam*) *Preise* to go up ❺ (*fam: enttarnt werden*) to get caught

Hochgenuss^RR *m* real delight

Hochgeschwindigkeitszug *m* high-speed train

Hochglanz *m* FOTO high gloss

Hochglanzmagazin *nt* glossy magazine

hochgradig *adj* extreme

hoch|halten *vt irreg* ❶ (*in die Höhe halten*) to hold up *sep* ❷ (*fig: ehren*) to uphold

Hochhaus *nt* high-rise building

hoch|heben *vt irreg* ❶ *Last* to lift up *sep* ❷ *Arm, Hand, Kind* to put up *sep*

hochkant [ˈhoːxˌkant] *adv* **etw ~ stellen** to stand sth on end

Hochkonjunktur *f* [economic] boom

hoch|laden *vt irreg* INET to upload

Hochland *nt* highland *usu pl*

Hochleistung *f* first-rate performance

hochmodern I. *adj* ultramodern II. *adv* in the latest fashion[s]

hochmütig [ˈhoːxˌmyːtɪç] *adj* (*pej*) arrogant

hochnäsig [ˈhoːxˌnɛːzɪç] *adj* (*pej fam*) conceited

Hochofen *m* blast furnace

Hochrechnung *f* projection

Hochsaison *f* ❶ (*Zeit stärksten Betriebes*) busy season ❷ (*Hauptsaison*) high season

Hochschule [ˈhoːxˌʃuːlə] *f* ❶ (*Universität*) university ❷ (*Fachhochschule*) college

Hochschullehrer(in) *m(f)* college/university professor

hochschwanger *adj* in an advanced stage of pregnancy *pred*

Hochseefischerei *f* deep-sea fishing

Hochsommer *m* midsummer, height of summer

Hochspannung *f* ❶ ELEK high voltage ❷ *kein pl* (*Belastung*) enormous tension

Hochsprung *m* high jump

höchst [høːçst] *adv* most, extremely

Hochstapler(in) <-s, -> [ˈhoːxˌʃtaːplə] *m(f)* (*pej*) con man

höchste(r, s) *attr* I. *adj superl von* **hoch** ❶ (*räumlich*) *Baum* tallest; *Berg* highest ❷ (*bedeutendste*) highest; *Profit* largest; **aufs H~** extremely, most; **von ~r Bedeutung sein** to be of the utmost importance II. *adv* ❶ (*räumlich*) the highest ❷ (*in größtem Ausmaß*) the most, most of all ❸ (*die größte Summe umfassend*) the most

höchstens [ˈhøːçstns] *adv* ❶ (*bestenfalls*) at [the] most, at best ❷ (*nicht mehr als*) not more than

Höchstgeschwindigkeit *f* ❶ (*mögliche Geschwindigkeit*) maximum speed ❷ (*zulässige Geschwindigkeit*) speed limit

Höchstmaß *nt* maximum amount

höchstpersönlich *adv* in person, personally

höchstwahrscheinlich [ˈhøːçstˌvaːɐ̯ˈʃainˌlɪç] *adv* most likely

H

Hochtour f ① SPORT (*Hochgebirgstour*) high-altitude mountain climbing trip ② *pl* TECH (*größte Leistungsfähigkeit*) **auf ~en laufen** to operate at full speed; (*fig*) to be in full swing

hochtrabend *adj* (*pej*) pompous

Hochverrat *m* high treason

Hochwasser *nt* ① (*Flut*) high tide ② (*überhoher Wasserstand*) high [level of] water ③ (*Überschwemmung*) flood

hochwertig ['hoːxˌveːɐ̯tɪç] *adj* ① (*von hoher Qualität*) [of *pred*] high quality ② (*von hohem Nährwert*) highly nutritious

Hochzeit¹ <-, -en> ['hɔxˌtsait] f (*Heirat*) wedding

Hochzeit² <-, -en> ['hoːxˌtsait] f (*geh: Blütezeit*) golden age

Hochzeitsfeier f wedding reception

Hochzeitsreise f honeymoon

Hochzeitstag *m* ① (*Tag der Hochzeit*) wedding day ② (*Jahrestag*) wedding anniversary

hoch|ziehen *irreg vt* ① (*nach oben*) to pull up *sep* ② (*fam: rasch bauen*) to build [rapidly]

Hocke <-, -n> ['hɔˌkə] f ① (*Körperhaltung*) crouching position; **in die ~ gehen** to squat [down] ② (*Turnübung*) squat vault

hocken ['hɔˌkn̩] *vi* ① *haben* (*kauern*) to crouch, to squat ② *haben* (*fam: sitzen*) to sit ③ *sein* SPORT to squat-vault (**über** +*akk* over)

Hocker <-s, -> *m* stool

Höcker <-s, -> ['hœˌkɐ] *m* (*eines Kamels*) hump

Hoden <-s, -> ['hoːˌdn̩] *m* testicle

Hodensack *m* ANAT, MED scrotum

Hof <-[e]s, Höfe> [hoːf] *m* ① (*Innenhof*) courtyard; (*Schulhof*) schoolyard, playground ② (*Bauernhof*) farm ③ HIST (*Fürstensitz, Hofstaat*) court

hoffen ['hɔfn̩] I. *vi* to hope (**auf** +*akk* for) II. *vt* **das will ich ~** I hope so

hoffentlich ['hɔˌfn̩tlɪç] *adv* hopefully; **~ nicht** I hope not

Hoffnung <-, -en> ['hɔfˌnʊŋ] f hope (**auf** +*akk* for/of); **jds letzte ~ sein** to

be sb's last hope; **sich** *dat* **~en machen** to have hope

hoffnungslos I. *adj* hopeless II. *adv* ① (*ohne Hoffnung*) without hope ② (*völlig*) hopelessly; **sich** *akk* **~ in jdn verlieben** to fall head over heels in love with sb

Hoffnungsschimmer *m* glimmer of hope

höflich ['høːfˌlɪç] *adj* polite

hohe(r, s) ['hoːˌə, 'hoːˌɐ, 'hoːˌəs] *adj s.* **hoch**

Höhe <-, -n> ['høːˌhə] f ① (*Ausdehnung nach oben*) height; **aus der ~** from above; **auf halber ~** halfway up; **in einer ~ von** at a height of ② (*Gipfel*) summit, top ③ (*Ausmaß*) amount, level; **ein Betrag in ~ von ...** an amount totaling ...; **die ~ des Schadens** the extent of the damage; **in die ~ gehen** *Preise* to rise ▶WENDUNGEN: **das ist doch die ~!** (*fam*) enough is enough [already]!

Hoheit <-, -en> ['hoːˌhait] f ① (*Mitglied einer fürstlichen Familie*) member of the royal family; **Ihre Königliche ~** Your Royal Highness ② *kein pl* (*oberste Staatsgewalt*) sovereignty

Hoheitsgebiet *nt* sovereign territory

Hoheitsgewässer *pl* territorial waters *npl*

Höhenmesser *m* LUFT altimeter

Höhenunterschied *m* difference in altitude

Höhepunkt *m* ① (*bedeutendster Teil*) high point; *einer Veranstaltung* highlight ② (*Gipfel*) height, peak; **die Krise hatte ihren ~ erreicht** the crisis had reached its climax ③ (*Orgasmus*) climax

höher ['høːˌɐ] I. *adj komp von* **hoch** ① (*räumlich*) higher, taller ② (*bedeutender, größer*) Druck, Forderungen, Verlust greater; Gewinn, Preis, Temperatur higher; Strafe more severe II. *adv komp von* **hoch** ① (*weiter nach oben*) higher, taller ② (*mit gesteigertem Wert*) higher; **sich** *akk* **~ versichern** to increase one's insurance

H

hohl [ho:l] *adj, adv* ① (*leer*) hollow; **mit der ~en Hand** with cupped hands; **~e Wangen** sunken cheeks ② (*fig, pej: nichts sagend*) empty

Höhle <-, -n> ['hø:·lə] *f* ① (*Felshöhle*) cave ② (*Tierbehausung*) cave, den ③ (*Höhlung*) hollow

Hohlraum *m* cavity, hollow space

Hohlspiegel *m* concave mirror

Hohn <-[e]s> [ho:n] *m kein pl* scorn, mockery

höhnisch ['hø:·nɪʃ] *adj* sneering

holen ['ho:·lən] I. *vt* ① (*hervorholen*) to get (**aus** +*dat* out of, **von** +*dat* from) ② (*herholen*) **Sie können den Patienten jetzt ~** you can send for the patient now; **■jdn ~ lassen** to go get sb; **Hilfe ~** to get help II. *vr* (*fam*) **■sich** *dat* **etw ~** ① (*sich nehmen*) to get oneself sth (**aus** +*dat* out of, **von** +*dat* from) ② (*sich zuziehen*) to catch sth (**an** +*dat* from, **bei** +*dat* in); **bei dem kalten Wetter holst du dir eine Erkältung** you'll catch a cold in this chilly weather ③ (*sich einhandeln*) *Abfuhr, Rüge* to get

Holland <-s> ['hɔ·lant] *nt* ① (*fam: Niederlande*) the Netherlands *npl*, Holland; *s. a.* **Deutschland** ② (*Provinz der Niederlande*) Holland

Holländer <-s> ['hɔ·lɛn·dɐ] *m kein pl* (*Käse*) Dutch cheese

Holländer(in) <-s, -> ['hɔ·lɛn·dɐ] *m(f)* (*fam*) Dutchman *masc*, Dutchwoman *fem*; **■die ~** the Dutch + *pl vb*

holländisch ['hɔ·lɛn·dɪʃ] *adj* (*fam*) Dutch; *s. a.* **deutsch**

Hölle <-, -n> ['hœ·lə] *f* (*pl selten*) hell ▶WENDUNGEN: **jdm die ~ heißmachen** (*fam*) to give sb hell; **die ~ ist los** (*fam*) all hell has broken loose

Höllenlärm ['hœ·lən·lɛrm] *m* racket

höllisch ['hœ·lɪʃ] *adj* ① *attr* infernal ② (*fam: fürchterlich*) terrible *pred*; **ein ~er Lärm** an awful noise

holp(e)rig ['hɔl·p(ə)·rɪç] *adj* ① *Straße* bumpy, uneven ② *Sprache, Stil* clumsy

Holunder <-s, -> [ho·ˈlʊn·dɐ] *m* elder

Holz <-es, Hölzer> [hɔlts] *nt* ① *kein pl*

(*Material*) wood; **~ fällen** to cut down *sep* trees; **tropische Hölzer** tropical wood; **aus ~** wood[en]; **massives ~** solid wood ② *pl* (*Bauhölzer*) timber ③ SPORT (*beim Golf*) wood

hölzern ['hœl·tsɐn] *adj* wooden

Holzfäller(in) <-s, -> *m(f)* lumberjack

Holzhammer *m* mallet

Holzhammermethode *f* (*fam*) sledgehammer approach

Holzklotz *m* wooden block

Holzkohle *f* charcoal

Holzschuh *m* clog, wooden shoe

Holzwurm *m* woodworm

Homo-Ehe *f* (*fam*) gay marriage

homogenisieren* [ho·mo·ge·ni·ˈziː·rən] *vt* to homogenize

homöopathisch [ho·møo·ˈpaː·tɪʃ] *adj* homeopathic

homosexuell [ho·mo·zɛ·ˈksu̯·ɛl] *adj* homosexual

Homosexuelle(r) *f(m) dekl wie adj* homosexual

Honig <-s, -e> ['ho:·nɪç] *m* honey; **türkischer ~** halva[h] ▶WENDUNGEN: **jdm ~ ums Maul schmieren** (*fam*) to butter up *sep* sb

Honigbiene *f* honeybee

Honigmelone *f* honeydew melon

Honorar <-s, -e> [ho·no·ˈraːɐ̯] *nt* fee; *eines Autors* royalties *npl*; **gegen ~** for a fee

honorieren* [ho·no·ˈriː·rən] *vt* ① (*würdigen*) to appreciate ② (*bezahlen*) to pay

Hopfen <-s, -> ['hɔp·fn̩] *m* hops *pl* ▶WENDUNGEN: **bei jdm ist ~ und Malz verloren** (*fam*) sb is a hopeless case

hoppla ['hɔp·la] *interj* ① (*o je!*) [wh]oops! ② (*Moment!*) hang on!; **~, wer kommt denn da?** hello, who's that [coming over this way]?

hopsen ['hɔp·sn̩] *vi sein* (*fam*) to skip; (*auf einem Bein*) to hop

hörbar *adj* audible

Hörbuch *nt* audio book

horchen ['hɔr·çn̩] *vi* to listen in (**an** +*dat* on); (*heimlich a.*) to eavesdrop

Horde <-, -n> ['hɔr·də] f (wilde Schar) horde

hören ['høː··rən] **I.** vt **❶** (mit dem Gehör vernehmen) to hear; **..., wie ich höre** I hear ...; **wie man hört, ...** word has it ...; **nie gehört!** never heard of him/her/it!; **das will ich nicht gehört haben** I'll ignore that comment; **sich** akk **gern reden ~** to like the sound of one's own voice **❷** (anhören) to listen ▶WENDUNGEN: **etwas [von jdm] zu ~ bekommen** to get chewed out [by sb]; **ich kann das nicht mehr ~!** enough [of that] already!; **etw/nichts von sich** dat **~ lassen** to keep/not keep in touch **II.** vi **❶** (zuhören) to listen; **hör mal!/~ Sie mal!** listen! **❷** (vernehmen) ■**~, was/wie ...** to hear what/how ...; **gut/schlecht ~** to have good/poor hearing **❸** (erfahren) ■**~, dass ...** to hear [that] ...; ■**von jdm/etw ~** to hear of [or about] sb/sth **❹** (gehorchen) to listen (**auf** +akk to); **auf dich hört er!** he listens to you! ▶WENDUNGEN: **lass von dir/lassen Sie von sich ~!** keep in touch!; **na hör/~ Sie mal!** (euph) [now] look here!; **man höre und staune!** would you believe it!?

Hörensagen ['høː·rən·za:·gŋ] nt **vom ~** from hearsay

Hörer <-s, -> m (Telefonhörer) receiver; **den ~ auflegen** to hang up [on sb]

Hörer(in) <-s, -> m(f) listener

Hörfunk m radio

Hörgerät nt hearing aid

hörig ['høː·rɪç] adj (sexuell abhängig) sexually dependent

Horizont <-[e]s, -e> [ho·ri·'tsɔnt] m horizon; **am ~** on the horizon; **über jds ~ gehen** to be beyond sb

horizontal [ho·ri·tsɔn·'ta:l] adj horizontal

Horizontale [ho·ri·tsɔn·'ta:·lə] f dekl wie adj horizontal [line]

Hormon <-s, -e> [hɔr·'moːn] nt hormone

Hörmuschel f TELEK earpiece

Horn <-[e]s, Hörner> [hɔrn] nt horn; **das ~ von Afrika** the Horn of Africa

Hörnchen <-s, -> ['hœrn·çən] nt **❶** dim von **Horn** small horn **❷** (Gebäck) crescent roll; (aus Plunderteig) croissant

Hornhaut f **❶** (des Auges) cornea **❷** (der Haut) callus

Hornisse <-, -n> [hɔr·'nɪ·sə] f hornet

Hornochs(e) m (fam) stupid idiot

Horoskop <-s, -e> [ho·ro·'sko:p] nt horoscope

Hörsaal m lecture hall

Hörspiel nt **❶** kein pl (Gattung) radio drama **❷** (Stück) radio play

Horst <-[e]s, -e> [hɔrst] m **❶** (Nest) nest, aerie **❷** MIL (Fliegerhorst) military airbase

Hörsturz m sudden hearing loss

horten ['hɔr·tŋ] vt to hoard

Hörweite f hearing range, earshot; **in/außer ~** within/out of earshot

Hose <-, -n> ['hoː·zə] f pants npl, trousers npl; **kurze ~[n]** shorts npl ▶WENDUNGEN: **in die ~ gehen** to be a failure; **jdm ist das Herz in die ~ gerutscht** (fam) sb's heart was in their mouth; **[sich** dat**] in die ~[n] machen** to wet oneself; **tote ~** (sl) boring as hell; **jd hat die ~n [gestrichen] voll** (sl) sb is scared shitless

Hosenanzug m pantsuit

Hosenschlitz m fly; **dein ~ ist offen!** your fly is down!

Hosentasche f pants pocket

Hosenträger pl suspenders npl

Hospital <-s, -e> [hɔs·pi·'ta:l] nt DIAL hospital

Hostie <-, -n> ['hɔs·tiə] f REL host

Hotel <-s, -s> [ho·'tɛl] nt hotel

Hotelfachschule f school of hotel management

Hotelier <-s, -s> [ho·tə·'liːeː] m hotelier

Hotellerie <-> [ho·tɛ·lə·'ri:] f kein pl hospitality

HTML <-, -> [ha:·te:·?ɛm·'?ɛl] nt o f kein pl COMPUT Abk von **hypertext markup language** HTML

Hubraum m cubic capacity

hübsch [hʏpʃ] adj **❶** (Aussehen) pretty; **na, ihr zwei H~en?** (fam) well, my two lovelies?; **sich** *akk* **~ machen** to get all dressed up ➋ (*fam: beträchtlich*) real, pretty; **ein ~es Sümmchen** a pretty penny ➌ (*fam: sehr angenehm*) nice and ...; **das wirst du ~ bleiben lassen** you'll do no such thing

Hubschrauber <-s, -> *m* helicopter

huckepack ['hʊ·kə·pak] *adv* piggyback; **jdn ~ nehmen** to give sb a piggyback ride

Huf <-[e]s, -e> [huːf] *m* hoof

Hufeisen *nt* horseshoe

Hüfte <-, -n> ['hʏf·tə] *f* ➊ (*Körperpartie*) hip ➋ *kein pl* KOCHK (*Fleischstück*) inside round; (*vom Rind*) top sirloin

Hüftgelenk *nt* hip joint

Hügel <-s, -> ['hyː·ɡl] *m* hill; (*Erdhaufen*) mound

hüg(e)lig ['hyː·ɡ(ə)·lɪç] *adj* hilly; **eine ~e Landschaft** rolling countryside

Huhn <-[e]s, Hühner> [huːn] *nt* ➊ (*Haushuhn*) hen, chicken; **frei laufende Hühner** free-range chickens ➋ (*Hühnerfleisch*) chicken ➌ (*Person*) **dummes ~!** stupid idiot!; **ein verrücktes ~** a nutcase ▶WENDUNGEN: **da lachen ja die Hühner** (*fam*) you must be joking

Hühnchen <-s, -> ['hyːn·çən] *nt dim von* Huhn spring chicken ▶WENDUNGEN: **mit jdm ein ~ zu rupfen haben** (*fam*) to have a bone to pick with sb

Hühnerauge *nt* corn

Hühnerei *nt* chicken egg

Hühnerstall *m* hencoop

Hühnerstange *f* chicken roost

Hülle <-, -n> ['hʏ·lə] *f* cover ▶WENDUNGEN: **in ~ und Fülle** (*geh*) in abundance

hüllenlos *adj* naked, in one's birthday suit *hum*

Hülse <-, -n> ['hʏl·zə] *f* ➊ BOT (*Schote*) pod ➋ (*röhrenförmige Hülle*) capsule

Hülsenfrucht ['hʏl·zn̩] *f meist pl* legume

human [hu·'maːn] *adj* ➊ (*menschenwürdig*) humane; *Strafe* lenient ➋ *Chef, Lehrer* considerate (**gegen**

über +*dat* toward) ➌ (*Menschen betreffend*) human

humanitär [hu·ma·ni·'tɛːɐ̯] *adj* humanitarian

Hummel <-, -n> ['hʊ·ml̩] *f* bumblebee ▶WENDUNGEN: **~n im Hintern haben** (*fam*) to have ants in one's pants

Hummer <-s, -> ['hʊ·mɐ] *m* lobster

Humor <-s, -e> [hu·'moːɐ̯] *m* (*pl selten*) ➊ (*Laune*) good humor, cheerfulness ➋ (*Witz, Wesensart*) [sense of] humor; **etw mit ~ nehmen** to take sth good-humoredly; **[einen Sinn für] ~ haben** to have a sense of humor

humorlos *adj* humorless

humorvoll *adj* humorous

Humpeln ['hʊm·pl̩n] *vi sein o haben* to limp

Humus ['huː·mʊs] *m kein pl* humus

Hund <-[e]s, -e> [hʊnt] *m* ➊ (*Tier*) dog; (*Jagdhund*) hound; „**Vorsicht, bissiger ~!**" "beware of dog!" ➋ (*Mensch*) swine; **ein armer ~ sein** (*fam*) to be a poor soul; **[du] gemeiner ~** [you] dirty dog ▶WENDUNGEN: **da liegt der ~ begraben** (*fam*) that's the crux of the matter; **~e, die bellen, beißen nicht** (*prov*) sb's bark is worse than their bite; **bekannt sein wie ein bunter ~** (*fam*) to be known far and wide; **das ist ja ein dicker ~** (*sl*) that is absolutely outrageous

hundeelend ['hʊn·də·'ʔeːlɛnt] *adj* (*fam*) **jd fühlt sich** *akk* **~** sb feels awful

Hundehütte *f* doghouse

Hundeleine *f* dog leash

hundemüde ['hʊn·də·'myː·də] *adj pred* (*fam*) dog-tired

hundert ['hʊn·dɐt] *adj* ➊ (*Zahl*) [a [*or* one]] hundred ➋ (*fam: sehr viele*) a hundred, hundreds ➌ *pl, auch großgeschrieben* (*viele hundert*) hundreds *pl*; *s. a.* **Hundert**[1]

Hundert[1] <-s, -e> ['hʊn·dɐt] *nt* ➊ (*Einheit von 100*) hundred; **mehrere ~** several hundred ➋ *pl, auch kleingeschrieben* (*viele hundert*) hundreds *pl*; **einige/viele ~e ...** a few/several hundred ...; **~e von ...** hundreds of ...; **in**

die ~e gehen (*fam*) *Kosten, Schaden* to run into the hundreds; **~e und aber ~e** hundreds upon hundreds

Hundert[2] <-, -en> ['hʊn·dɛt] *f* [one [*or* a]] hundred

hundertprozentig ['hʊn·dɛt·pro·tsɛn·tɪç] **I.** *adj* ❶ (*100 % umfassend*) one hundred percent; (*Alkohol*) pure ❷ (*fam: typisch*) through and through; **er ist ein ~er Bayer** he's a Bavarian through and through **II.** *adv* (*fam*) absolutely, completely; **das weiß ich ~** I know that for certain; **sich** *dat* **~ sicher sein** to be absolutely sure

Hundertstel <-s, -> ['hʊn·dɛts·tl̩] *nt o* schweiz *m* hundredth

Hündin ['hʏn·dɪn] *f* bitch

Hüne <-n, -n> ['hyː·nə] *m* giant

hünenhaft *adj* gigantic

Hunger <-s> ['hʊŋɐ] *m kein pl* ❶ (*Hungergefühl*) hunger; **~ bekommen/ haben** to get/be hungry; **~ auf etw** *akk* **haben** to feel like [eating] sth; **~ leiden** to starve; **~ wie ein Bär haben** to be [as] hungry as a bear ❷ (*Hungersnot*) famine ❸ (*großes Verlangen*) ■**jds ~ nach etw** *dat* sb's thirst for sth ►WENDUNGEN: **~ ist der beste Koch** (*prov*) hunger is the best sauce *prov*

Hungerhilfe *f kein pl* famine relief

Hungerlohn *m* (*pej*) pittance; **für einen ~ arbeiten** to work for peanuts

hungern *vi* ❶ (*Hunger leiden*) to starve; (*fam: fasten*) to fast ❷ (*fig: verlangen*) to hunger (**nach** +*dat* for)

Hungersnot *f* famine

Hungerstreik *m* hunger strike; **in den ~ treten** to go on a hunger strike

hungrig ['hʊŋ·rɪç] *adj* hungry; **etw macht ~** sth works up an appetite

Hupe <-, -n> ['huː·pə] *f* horn; **auf die ~ drücken** to honk the horn

hupen ['huː·pn̩] *vi* to honk [the horn]

hüpfen ['hʏp·fn̩] *vi sein* to hop; *Lamm, Zicklein* to frolic; *Ball* to bounce; **vor Freude ~** to jump for joy

Hürde <-, -n> ['hʏr·də] *f* SPORT hurdle; **110 Meter ~n laufen** to run the

110-meter hurdles ►WENDUNGEN: **eine ~ nehmen** to overcome an obstacle

Hürdenlauf *m* hurdling, hurdles *npl*

Hure <-, -n> ['huː·rə] *f* whore

huschen ['hʊ·ʃn̩] *vi sein* to dart, to flit; *Maus* to scurry; *Licht* to flash; **ein Lächeln huschte über ihr Gesicht** a smile flitted across her face

husten ['huː·s·tn̩] **I.** *vi* to cough **II.** *vt* (*auswerfen*) **Blut/Schleim ~** to cough up blood/mucus

Husten <-s> ['huː·s·tn̩] *m kein pl* cough

Hustenbonbon *m o nt* cough drop

Hustenreiz *m* tickly throat

Hustensaft *m* cough syrup

Hut[1] <-[e]s, Hüte> [huːt] *m* ❶ (*Kopfbedeckung*) hat; **den ~ abnehmen/aufsetzen** to take off/put on one's hat ❷ BOT (*von Pilzen*) cap ►WENDUNGEN: **~ ab [vor jdm]!** (*fam*) hats off to sb!; **etw unter einen ~ bringen** to reconcile sth; (*Termine*) to fit in *sep* sth; **mit etw** *dat* **nichts am ~ haben** (*fam*) to not really have anything in common with sth; **vor jdm/etw den ~ ziehen** to take one's hat off to sb/sth

Hut[2] <-> [huːt] *f* **auf der ~ [vor etw** *dat*] **sein** to be on one's guard [against sth]

hüten ['hyː·tn̩] **I.** *vt Schafe* to tend **II.** *vr* (*sich in Acht nehmen*) ■**sich vor etw** *dat* **~** to be on one's guard against sth; ■**sich** *akk* **~, etw zu tun** to take care not to do sth

Hütte <-, -n> ['hʏ·tə] *f* ❶ (*kleines Haus*) hut; (*ärmlich*) shack ❷ (*Berghütte*) [mountain] hut; (*Holzhütte*) cabin

Hüttenkäse *m* cottage cheese

Hyäne <-, -n> ['hʏɛː·nə] *f* hyena

Hyazinthe <-, -n> [hʏa·ˈtsɪn·tə] *f* hyacinth

Hydrant <-en, -en> [hy·ˈdrant] *m* hydrant

hydraulisch [hy·ˈdrau·lɪʃ] *adj* hydraulic

Hydrokultur *f* hydroponics + *sing vb* spec

Hygiene <-> [hy·ˈɡiɛː·nə] *f kein pl* hygiene

hygienisch [hy·'gie:·nɪʃ] *adj* hygienic
Hymne <-, -n> ['hʏm·nə] *f* hymn
Hyperaktivität [hype·ak·ti·vi·'tɛt] *f* hyperactivity
Hypnose <-, -n> [hʏp·'no:·zə] *f* hypnosis; **jdn in ~ versetzen** to hypnotize sb
hypnotisieren* *vt* to hypnotize
Hypothek <-, -en> [hy·po·'te:k] *f* mortgage

Hypothese <-, -n> [hy·po·'te:zə] *f* hypothesis; **eine ~ aufstellen/widerlegen** to advance/refute a hypothesis
hypothetisch [hy·po·'te:·tɪʃ] *adj* hypothetical
Hysterie <-, -n> [hʏs·te·'ri:] *f* hysteria
hysterisch [hʏs·'te:·rɪʃ] *adj* hysterical

I i

I, i <-, -> [i:] *nt* I, i; **~ wie Ida** I as in India
i [i:] *interj* (*fam*) (*Ausdruck von Ablehnung, Ekel*) ugh; **~, wie ekelig** yuck, how disgusting ▶WENDUNGEN: **~ wo!** DIAL no way! *fam*
IC <-s, -s> [i:·'tse:] *m Abk von* **Intercity**
ICE <-s, -s> [i:·tse:·'?e:] *m Abk von* **Intercity Express** *a high-speed train*
ich <*gen* meiner, *dat* mir, *akk* mich> ['ɪç] *pron pers* I, me; **~ bin/war es** it's/it was me; **~ nicht!** not me!; **~ selbst** I myself
Ich <-[s], -s> ['ɪç] *nt* ❶ (*das Selbst*) self ❷ PSYCH (*Ego*) ego; **jds anderes ~** sb's alter ego; **jds besseres ~** sb's better self
ideal [ide·'a:l] *adj* ideal
Ideal <-s, -e> [ide·'a:l] *nt* ideal
Idee <-, -n> [i'de:] *f* ❶ (*Einfall, Vorstellung*) idea; **eine fixe ~** an obsession; **keine ~ haben** to have no idea; **jdn auf eine ~ bringen** to give sb an idea; **jdn auf andere ~n bringen** to take sb's mind off of sth/it; **auf eine ~ kommen** to get an idea ❷ (*fam: ein wenig*) **keine ~ besser sein** to be not one bit better; **eine ~ ...** a little bit ...
identifizieren* [idɛn·ti·fi·'tsi:·rən] **I.** *vt* to identify **II.** *vr* ■**sich** *akk* **mit jdm/etw ~** to identify with sb/sth
identisch [i'dɛn·tɪʃ] *adj* identical (**mit** +*dat* to)

Ideologie <-, -n> [ideo·lo·'gi:] *f* ideology
idiomatisch [idio·'ma:·tɪʃ] *adj* idiomatic
Idiot(in) <-en, -en> [i'di̯·o:t] *m(f)* (*pej fam*) idiot
idiotisch [i'di̯o:·tɪʃ] *adj* (*fam*) idiotic
Idol <-s, -e> [i'do:l] *nt* idol
idyllisch [i'dʏ·lɪʃ] *adj* idyllic
Igel <-s, -> ['i:gl] *m* hedgehog
igitt(igitt) [i'gɪt·(igɪt)] *interj* ugh, yuck
Ignoranz <-> [ɪg·no·'rants] *f kein pl* (*pej geh*) ignorance
ignorieren* [ɪg·no·'ri:·rən] *vt* to ignore
ihm [i:m] *pron pers dat von* **er, es** ❶ (*dem Genannten*) him; **es geht ~ nicht gut** he's not feeling very well; *nach Präpositionen:* **ich war gestern bei ~** I was at his place yesterday; **das ist ein Freund von ~** that's a friend of his ❷ *bei Tieren und Dingen* (*dem genannten Tier oder Ding*) it; (*bei Haustieren*) him
ihn ['i:n] *pron pers akk von* **er** ❶ (*den Genannten*) him ❷ *bei Tieren und Dingen* (*das genannte Tier oder Ding*) it; (*bei Haustieren*) him
ihnen ['i:·nən] *pron pers dat pl von* **sie** them; *nach Präpositionen* them; **ich war die ganze Zeit bei ~** I was at their place the whole time

Ihnen ['iːnən] *pron pers dat sing o pl von* **Sie** you; *nach Präpositionen* you [all]

ihr[1] *<gen* euer, *dat* euch, *akk* euch*>* ['iːɐ̯] *pron pers 2. pers pl nomin von* **sie** you [all]

ihr[2] ['iːɐ̯] *pron pers dat sing von* **sie** (*der Genannten*) her

ihr[3] ['iːɐ̯] *pron poss, adjektivisch* ❶ *sing* her ❷ *pl* their

ihre(r, s) *pron poss, substantivisch* ❶ *sing* (*dieser weiblichen Person*) her; **das ist nicht seine Aufgabe, sondern ~** he's not responsible for doing that, she is; ■**der/die/das ~** hers ❷ *pl* theirs

Ihre(r, s)[1] *pron poss, substantivisch, auf „Sie" bezüglich* ❶ *sing* your; ■**der/die/das ~** yours ❷ *pl* your; ■**der/die/das ~** yours ❸ *sing und pl* (*Angehörige*) ■**die ~n** your loved ones ❹ *sing und pl* (*Eigentum*) ■**das ~** yours; **Sie haben alle das ~ getan** you have all done your part

Ihre(r, s)[2] *pron poss, substantivisch, auf „sie" sing bezüglich* ❶ (*Angehörige*) ■**der/[die] ~[n]** her loved one[s] ❷ (*Eigentum*) ■**das ~** hers

Ihre(r, s)[3] *pron poss, substantivisch, auf „sie" pl bezüglich* ❶ (*Angehörige*) ■**der/[die] ~[n]** their loved ones ❷ (*Eigentum*) ■**das ~** their things

ihrer *pron pers gen von* **sie** ❶ *sing* (*geh*) her ❷ *pl* them

Ihrer *pron pers* (*geh*) *gen von* **Sie** ❶ *sing* [of] you ❷ *pl* you

ihresgleichen ['iːrəsˈɡlaɪ̯çn̩] *pron* ❶ *sing* people *npl* like her; (*pej: Leute wie sie*) her [own] kind ❷ *pl* people like them; (*pej: Leute wie sie*) their [own] kind

Ihresgleichen ['iːrəsˈɡlaɪ̯çn̩] *pron* ❶ *sing* people like you ❷ *pl* (*pej: Leute wie Sie*) your [own] kind; **ich kenne [Sie und] ~** I know your kind!

illegal ['ɪleˌɡaːl] *adj* illegal

Illusion <-, -en> [ɪluˈzi̯oːn] *f* illusion; **sich** *akk* **der ~ hingeben, [dass]** to be under the illusion [that]; **sich** *dat* **keine ~en machen** to not have any illusions

illusorisch [ɪluˈzoːrɪʃ] *adj* ❶ (*trügerisch*) illusory ❷ (*zwecklos*) futile

Illustration <-, -en> [ɪlʊstraˈtsi̯oːn] *f* illustration

illustrieren* [ɪlʊsˈtriːrən] *vt* to illustrate

Illustrierte <-n, -n> *f* magazine

Iltis <-ses, -se> ['ɪltɪs] *m* polecat

im ['ɪm] = **in dem** ❶ (*örtlich*) in the; **~ Bett/Haus** in bed/the house; **~ Januar** in January ❷ (*zeitlich*) while; **~ Bau sein** to be under construction; **~ Begriff sein, etw zu tun** to be about to do sth; **etw ist ~ Kommen** sth is coming

Image <-[s], -s> ['ɪmɪtʃ] *nt* image

Imbiss[RR] <-es, -e> ['ɪmˌbɪs], **Imbiß**[ALT] <-sses, -sse> *m* ❶ (*kleine Mahlzeit*) snack ❷ (*fam*) s. **Imbissstube**

Imbissstube[RR] *f* snack bar

imitieren* [imiˈtiːrən] *vt* to imitate sth; (*im Kabarett*) to impersonate

Imker(in) <-s, -> ['ɪmkɐ] *m(f)* beekeeper

immatrikulieren* [ɪmatrikuˈliːrən] *vr* ■**sich** *akk* **~** to matriculate

immer ['ɪmɐ] I. *adv* ❶ (*ständig, jedes Mal*) always, all the time; **für ~** forever; **~ und ewig** for ever and ever; **~ wenn** every time; **wie ~** as usual; **~ mit der Ruhe** take it easy; **etw ~ wieder tun** to keep on doing sth ❷ (*zunehmend*) increasingly; **~ häufiger** more and more frequently; **~ mehr** more and more ❸ (*fam: jeweils*) each; **~ am vierten Tag** every fourth day II. *part* [*nur*] **her damit!** (*fam*) hand it/them over!; **~ mal** (*fam*) now and again; **~ noch** still; **~ noch nicht** still not; **wann/was/wer/wie/wo [auch] ~** whenever/whatever/whoever/however/wherever

immerhin ['ɪmɐˈhɪn] *adv* ❶ (*wenigstens*) at least ❷ (*schließlich*) after all ❸ (*allerdings, trotz allem*) all the same

Immigrant(in) <-en, -en> [ɪmiˈɡrant] *m(f)* immigrant

Immobilie <-, -n> [ɪmoˈbiːli̯ə] *f meist pl* real estate; ■**~n** property

Immobilienmakler(in) *m(f)* real estate agent

immun [ɪˈmuːn] *adj* (*a. fig*) immune (**gegen** +*akk* to)

Immunsystem *nt* immune system

Imperativ <-s, -e> [ˈɪm·pe·ra·tiːf] *m* LING imperative [form] *spec*

Imperfekt <-s, -e> [ˈɪm·pɛr·fɛkt] *nt* imperfect [tense] *spec*

Imperialismus <-, selten -lismen> [ɪm·pe·riˈa·lɪs·mʊs] *m* imperialism

impfen [ˈɪm·pfn̩] *vt* to vaccinate (**gegen** +*akk* against)

Impfpass^RR *m* vaccination card

Impfstoff *m* vaccine

Impfung <-, -en> *f* vaccination

implantieren [ɪm·planˈtiː·rən] *vt* ▪ **jdm** etw ~ to implant sth [into sb]

imponieren* [ɪm·poˈniː·rən] *vi* to impress

imponierend *adj* impressive

Import <-[e]s, -e> [ɪmˈpɔrt] *m* import

importieren* [ɪm·pɔrˈtiː·rən] *vt* to import

imprägnieren* [ɪm·prɛgˈniː·rən] *vt* (*wasserabweisend machen*) to waterproof

Impressionismus <-> [ɪm·prɛ·si̯o·ˈnɪs·mʊs] *m* Impressionism

impressionistisch *adj* Impressionist

improvisieren* [ɪm·pro·viˈziː·rən] *vt, vi* to improvise

impulsiv [ɪm·pʊlˈziːf] *adj* impulsive

imstande, im Stande [ɪmˈʃtan·də] *adj pred* ▪ **in etw** zu etw ~ **sein** to be capable of doing sth; ~ **sein, etw zu tun** to be able to do sth; **zu allem** ~ **sein** to be capable of anything; **zu nichts mehr** ~ **sein** to be exhausted

in^1 [ˈɪn] *präp* ❶ +*dat* (*darin befindlich*) in; **bist du schon mal** ~ **New York gewesen?** have you ever been to New York?; **ich arbeite seit einem Jahr** ~ **dieser Firma** I've been working for this company for a year ❷ +*akk* (*hin zu einem Ziel*) into; ~ **die Kirche/Schule gehen** to go to church/school ❸ +*dat* (*innerhalb von*) in; ~ **diesem Augenblick** at the moment; ~ **diesem Jahr/**

Monat/Sommer this year/month/summer; ~ **einem Jahr bin ich 18** in a year I'll be 18 ❹ +*akk* (*bis zu einer Zeit*) until ❺ +*dat* (*Verweis auf ein Objekt*) in; **er ist Fachmann** ~ **seinem Beruf** he is an expert in his field; **sich** *akk* ~ **jdm täuschen** to be wrong about sb ❻ +*dat* (*auf eine Art und Weise*) in; ~ **Wirklichkeit** in reality

in^2 [ˈɪn] *adj* (*fam*) in *fam*; ▪ ~ **sein** to be in

inbegriffen [ˈɪn·bə·ɡrɪ·fn̩] *adj pred* inclusive; ▪ **in etw** *dat* ~ **sein** to be included in sth

indem [ɪnˈdeːm] *konj* (*dadurch, dass*) by

Inder(in) <-s, -> [ˈɪn·dɐ] *m(f)* Indian; *s. a.* **Deutsche(r)**

indessen [ɪnˈdɛ·sn̩] **I.** *adv* ❶ (*inzwischen*) in the meantime ❷ (*dagegen*) however **II.** *konj* (*geh*) while

Indianer(in) <-s, -> [ɪnˈdi̯aː·nɐ] *m(f)* Indian *esp pej*, Native American

Indien <-s> [ˈɪn·di̯ən] *nt* India; *s. a.* **Deutschland**

Indikativ <-s, -e> [ˈɪn·di·ka·tiːf] *m* indicative [mood] *spec*

indirekt [ˈɪn·di·rɛkt] *adj* indirect

indisch [ˈɪn·dɪʃ] *adj* Indian; *s. a.* **deutsch**

individuell [ɪn·di·vi·ˈdu̯·ɛl] *adj* individual

Individuum <-s, -duen> [ɪn·diˈviː·du̯·ʊm] *nt* individual

Indiz <-es, -ien> [ɪnˈdiːts] *nt* ❶ JUR piece of circumstantial evidence ❷ (*Anzeichen*) ▪ **ein** ~ **für etw** *akk* **sein** to be a sign of sth

Indonesien <-s> [ɪn·doˈneː·zi̯ən] *nt* Indonesia; *s. a.* **Deutschland**

indonesisch [ɪn·doˈneː·zɪʃ] *adj* Indonesian; *s. a.* **deutsch**

Industrie <-, -n> [ɪn·dʊsˈtriː] *f* industry *no art*

Industriegebiet *nt* industrial area

Industrie- und Handelskammer *f* Chamber of Commerce

Industriezweig *m* branch of industry

ineinander [ɪn·ʔaiˈnan·dɐ] *adv* in each

other; **~ verliebt sein** to be in love with each other; **~ übergehen** to merge

ineinander|greifen *vi irreg* to mesh

Infektion <-, -en> [ɪn·fɛk·ˈtsi̯oːn] *f* ① (*Ansteckung*) infection ② (*fam: Entzündung*) inflammation

Infinitiv <-s, -e> [ˈɪn·fi·niˈtiːf] *m* infinitive *spec*

infizieren* [ɪn·fiˈtsiː·rən] I. *vt* to infect II. *vr* ■**sich** *akk* [an etw *dat*/bei jdm] ~ to be infected [by sth/sb]

Inflation <-, -en> [ɪn·flaˈtsi̯oːn] *f* ① ÖKON inflation ② (*übermäßig häufiges Auftreten*) proliferation

infolge [ɪn·ˈfɔl·ɡə] I. *präp +gen* owing to II. *adv* ■**~ von etw** *dat* as a result of sth

infolgedessen [ɪn·fɔl·ɡə·ˈdɛ·sn̩] *adv* consequently

Informatik <-> [ɪn·fɔrˈmaː·tɪk] *f kein pl* computer science

Informatiker(in) <-s, -> [ɪn·fɔrˈmaː·ti·ke] *m(f)* computer specialist

Information <-, -en> [ɪn·fɔr·maˈtsi̯oːn] *f* ① (*Mitteilung, Hinweis*) [a piece of] information ② (*das Informieren*) informing; **zu Ihrer ~** for your information ③ (*Informationsstand*) information desk

informativ [ɪn·fɔr·maˈtiːf] I. *adj* informative II. *adv* in an informative manner *pred*

informieren* [ɪn·fɔrˈmiː·rən] I. *vt* to inform (**über** *+akk* about); **jd ist gut informiert** sb is well-informed II. *vr* ■**sich** *akk* [über etw *akk*] ~ to find out [about sth]

Ingenieur(in) <-s, -e> [ɪn·ʒeˈni̯øːɐ̯] *m(f)* engineer

Ingwer <-s> [ˈɪŋ·ve] *m kein pl* ginger

Inhaber(in) <-s, -> [ˈɪn·haː·bɐ] *m(f)* ① (*Besitzer*) owner ② (*Halter*) holder; *von Scheck* bearer

Inhalt <-[e]s, -e> [ˈɪn·halt] *m* ① (*enthaltene Gegenstände*) contents *pl* ② (*Sinngehalt*) content ③ (*wesentliche Bedeutung*) meaning ④ MATH (*Flächeninhalt*) area; (*Volumen*) volume

Inhaltsangabe *f* summary; *von Buch, Film, Theaterstück* synopsis

Inhaltsverzeichnis *nt* table of contents *npl*

Initiative <-, -n> [in·itsi̯a·ˈtiː·və] *f* ① (*erster Anstoß*) initiative; **aus eigener ~** on one's own initiative; [**in etw** *dat*] **die ~ ergreifen** to take the initiative [in sth] ② *kein pl* (*Unternehmungsgeist*) drive ③ (*Bürgerinitiative*) pressure group ④ SCHWEIZ (*Volksbegehren*) demand for a referendum

Injektion <-, -en> [ɪn·jɛk·ˈtsi̯oːn] *f* injection

inklusive [ɪn·kluˈziː·və] I. *präp +gen* including II. *adv* **vom 25. bis zum 28. ~** from 25th to 28th inclusive

Inkrafttreten <-s> *nt kein pl* coming into effect

Inlandflug *m* domestic flight

innen [ˈɪnən] *adv* ① (*im Inneren*) on the inside; **~ und außen** [on the] inside and outside; **nach ~** inside; **die Tür geht nach ~ auf** the door opens inwards; **von ~** from the inside ② (*auf der Innenseite*) on the inside ③ *bes* ÖSTERR (*drinnen*) inside

Innendienst *m* office work

Innenminister(in) *m(f)* Secretary of the Interior, Interior Secretary

Innenministerium *nt* Department of the Interior

Innenpolitik *f* domestic policy

Innenraum *m* interior

Innenspiegel *m* AUTO rearview mirror

Innenstadt *f* downtown

innere(r, s) [ˈɪna·rə] *adj* ① *Tasche* inside ② (*a. med, anat*) inner, internal

Innere(s) [ˈɪna·rə] *nt* ① (*innerer Teil*) inside ② PSYCH **tief in seinem ~n war ihm klar, dass ...** deep down, he knew that ...

Innereien [ɪna·ˈrai̯·ən] *pl* KOCHK innards *npl*

innerhalb [ˈɪne·halp] I. *präp +gen* ① (*räumlich*) inside ② (*zeitlich*) within II. *adv* **~ von etw** *dat* within sth

innerlich [ˈɪne·lɪç] I. *adj* ① MED internal ② PSYCH inner II. *adv* ① (*im Inneren des*

Körpers) internally ❷PSYCH inwardly; **~ war er sehr aufgewühlt** he was in inner turmoil

Innerste(s) ['ɪnɛs·tə(s)] *nt* core being; **tief in ihrem ~n wusste sie ...** deep down, she knew ...

innig ['ɪnɪç] **I.** *adj* ❶(*tief empfunden*) deep; *Dank* heartfelt ❷ *Beziehung* intimate **II.** *adv* deeply

Innovation <-, -en> [ɪno·va·'tsi̯o:n] *f* innovation

innovativ [ɪno·va·'ti:f] *adj* innovative

Innung <-, -en> ['ɪn·ʊŋ] *f* guild

inoffiziell *adj* unofficial

in puncto [ɪn 'pʊŋk·to] *adv* (*fam*) concerning

ins ['ɪns] = **in das** *s.* **in**

Insasse, Insassin <-n, -n> ['ɪn·za·sə] *m, f* *eines Gefängnisses, Lagers* inmate

insbesondere [ɪns·bə·'zɔn·də·rə] *adv* especially

Insekt <-[e]s, -en> [ɪn·'zɛkt] *nt* insect

Insektenstich *m* insect sting

Insel <-, -n> ['ɪn·zl̩] *f* island

Inserat <-[e]s, -e> [ɪnze·'ra:t] *nt* advertisement

inserieren* [ɪn·ze·'ri:·rən] *vt, vi* to advertise

insgeheim [ɪns·gə·'haim] *adv* secretly

insgesamt [ɪns·gə·'zamt] *adv* ❶ (*alles zusammen*) altogether ❷ (*im Großen und Ganzen*) on the whole

insofern [ɪn·zo·'fɛrn, ɪn·'zo:·fɛrn] **I.** *adv* in this respect; **~ ..., als** in that **II.** *konj* ÖSTERR (*vorausgesetzt, dass*) if; **~ als** insofar as

insoweit [ɪn·'zo·vait] *adv, konj s.* **insofern**

Inspektion <-, -en> [ɪn·spɛk·'tsi̯o:n] *f* ❶ (*technische Wartung*) service ❷ (*Überprüfung*) inspection

Inspektor, Inspektorin <-s, -en> [ɪn·'spɛk·to:ɐ̯] *m, f* ❶ADMIN executive officer; (*Kriminalpolizei*) inspector ❷ (*Prüfer*) supervisor

Installateur(in) <-s, -e> [ɪn·sta·la·'tø:ɐ̯] *m(f)* ❶ (*Elektroinstallateur*) electrician ❷ (*Klempner*) plumber

installieren* [ɪn·sta·'li:·rən] *vt* ❶TECH (*einbauen*) ■**jdm** etw ~ to install sth [for sb] ❷COMPUT (*einprogrammieren*) ■**jdm** etw [auf etw *akk*] ~ to install sth [for sb] [on sth]

instand, in Stand [ɪn·'ʃtant] *adj* in working order; **etw ~ halten** to keep sth in good condition; **etw ~ setzen** to repair sth

inständig ['ɪn·ʃtɛn·dɪç] **I.** *adj* Bitte etc. urgent **II.** *adv* urgently; **~ um etw** *akk* **bitten** to beg for sth

Instanz <-, -en> [ɪn·'stants] *f* ❶ADMIN authority ❷ (*Stufe eines Gerichtsverfahrens*) **in erster/zweiter/oberster ~** trial court/appellate court/supreme court

Instinkt <-[e]s, -e> [ɪn·'stiŋkt] *m* instinct

instinktiv [ɪn·stɪŋk·'ti:f] *adj* instinctive

Institut <-[e]s, -e> [ɪn·sti·'tu:t] *nt* institute

Institution <-, -en> [ɪn·sti·tu·'tsi̯o:n] *f* institution

Instrument <-[e]s, -e> [ɪn·stru·'mɛnt] *nt* ❶MUS instrument; (*Gerät für wissenschaftliche Zwecke*) instrument ❷ (*a. fig geh: Werkzeug*) tool

Insulin <-s> [ɪn·zu·'li:n] *nt kein pl* insulin

inszenieren* [ɪns·tse·'ni:·rən] *vt* ❶ (*dramaturgisch gestalten*) to stage ❷ (*pej*) to stage-manage

Inszenierung <-, -en> *f* ❶FILM, MUS, THEAT production ❷ (*pej: Bewerkstelligung*) engineering

intakt [ɪn·'takt] *adj* ❶ (*unversehrt*) intact ❷ (*voll funktionsfähig*) in working order

Integration <-, -en> [ɪn·te·gra·'tsi̯o:n] *f* integration

integrieren* [ɪn·te·'gri:·rən] **I.** *vt* (*eingliedern*) to integrate (**in** +*akk* into) **II.** *vr* (*sich einfügen*) ■**sich** *akk* [**in etw** *akk*] ~ to become integrated [into sth]

Intellekt <-[e]s> [ɪn·tɛ·'lɛkt] *m kein pl* intellect

intellektuell [ɪn·tɛ·lɛk·'tu̯·ɛl] *adj* intellectual

Intellektuelle(r) *f(m)* intellectual

intelligent [ɪn·tɛ·li·ˈgɛnt] *adj* intelligent, smart

Intelligenz <-, -en> [ɪn·tɛ·li·ˈgɛnts] *f kein pl* intelligence

Intensität <-, *selten* -en> [ɪn·tɛn·zi·ˈtɛːt] *f* intensity

intensiv [ɪn·tɛn·ˈziːf] **I.** *adj* ➊ *(gründlich)* intensive ➋ *(eindringlich, durchdringend)* Duft, Schmerz intense **II.** *adv* ➊ *(gründlich)* intensively; **~ bemüht sein, etw zu tun** to make intense efforts to do sth ➋ *(eindringlich, durchdringend)* strongly

intensivieren* [ɪn·tɛn·zi·ˈviː·rən] *vt* to intensify

Intensivkurs *m* intensive course

Intensivstation *f* intensive care unit

interaktiv [ɪn·tɛ·ʔak·ˈtiːf] *adj* interactive

Intercity <-s, -s> [ɪn·tɛ·ˈsɪ·ti] *m* intercity [train]

interessant [ɪn·tə·rɛ·ˈsant] **I.** *adj* ➊ *(Interesse erweckend)* interesting; **sich** *akk* **[bei jdm] ~ machen** to attract [sb's] attention ➋ Angebot, Gehalt attractive **II.** *adv* interestingly; **der Vorschlag hört sich ~ an** the proposal sounds interesting

Interesse <-s, -n> [ɪn·tə·ˈrɛ·sə] *nt* ➊ *kein pl (Aufmerksamkeit)* interest; **~ [an jdm/etw] haben** to be interested [in sb/sth]; **hätten Sie ~ daran, für uns tätig zu werden?** would you be interested in working for us? ➋ *pl (Neigungen)* interests *pl;* **aus ~** out of interest ➌ *pl (Belange)* interests *pl* ➍ *(Nutzen)* interest; **für jdn von ~ sein** to be of interest [to sb]; **in jds ~ liegen** to be in sb's interest

Interessengemeinschaft *f* community of interests

Interessent(in) <-en, -en> [ɪn·tə·rɛ·ˈsɛnt] *m(f)* ➊ *(an einer Teilnahme Interessierter)* interested party ➋ *(an einem Kauf Interessierter)* potential buyer

interessieren* [ɪn·tə·rɛ·ˈsiː·rən] **I.** *vt* to interest **II.** *vr* ■ **sich** *akk* **für jdn/etw ~** to be interested in sb/sth

Internat <-[e]s, -e> [ɪn·tɛ·ˈnaːt] *nt* boarding school

international [ɪn·tɛ·na·tsi̯o·ˈnaːl] *adj* international

Internet <-s> [ˈɪntɛ·nɛt] *nt kein pl* Internet; **im ~ surfen** to surf the Internet

Internetportal *nt* INET web [*or* Internet] portal

Internist(in) <-en, -en> [ɪn·tɛ·ˈnɪst] *m(f)* internist

interpretieren* [ɪn·tɛ·pre·ˈtiː·rən] *vt* to interpret

Interpunktion <-> [ɪn·tɛ·pʊŋk·ˈtsi̯oːn] *f kein pl* punctuation

Interview <-s, -s> [ˈɪn·tɛ·vjuː] *nt* interview

interviewen* [ɪn·tɛ·ˈvjuː·ən] *vt* ➊ *(durch ein Interview befragen)* ■ **jdn [zu etw** *dat***] ~** to interview sb [about sth]; ■ **sich** *akk* **[von jdm] ~ lassen** to give [sb] an interview ➋ *(hum fam: befragen)* ■ **jdn ~ [ob/wann/wo etc.]** to consult sb about [whether/when/where, etc.]

intim [ɪn·ˈtiːm] *adj* ➊ *(innig, persönlich)* intimate; Bekannter, Freund close ➋ *(sexuell liiert)* ■ **mit jdm ~ sein/werden** to be/become intimate with sb

Intimität <-, -en> [ɪn·ti·mi·ˈtɛːt] *f* intimacy

Intimsphäre *f* private life

intolerant [ˈɪn·to·le·rant] *adj* intolerant

intransitiv [ˈɪn·tran·zi·tiːf] *adj* intransitive

Intrige <-, -n> [ɪn·ˈtriː·gə] *f* conspiracy

introvertiert [ɪn·tro·vɛr·ˈtiːɐ̯t] *adj* introverted

invalide [ɪn·va·ˈliː·də] *adj* invalid

Invalide, Invalidin <-n, -n> [ɪn·va·ˈliː·də] *m, f* invalid

Invasion <-, -en> [ɪn·va·ˈzi̯oːn] *f* invasion

Inventar <-s, -e> [ɪn·vɛn·ˈtaːɐ̯] *nt* inventory

Inventur <-, -en> [ɪn·vɛn·ˈtuːɐ̯] *f* inventory; **~ machen** to take inventory

investieren* [ɪn·vɛs·ˈtiː·rən] *vt* to invest

Investition <-, -en> [ɪnˈvɛsˌtiˈtsi̯oːn] f investment

inwiefern [ɪnˈviˈfɛrn] adv in what way

Inzucht [ˈɪnˈtsʊxt] f inbreeding

inzwischen [ɪnˈtsvɪʃn] adv in the meantime

Irak <-s> [iˈraːk] m ▪ **[der]** ~ Iraq; s. a. **Deutschland**

Iraker(in) <-s, -> [iˈraːˈkɐ] m(f) Iraqi; s. a. **Deutsche(r)**

Iran <-s> [iˈraːn] m ▪ **der** ~ Iran; s. a. **Deutschland**

Iraner(in) <-s, -> [iˈraːˈnɐ] m(f) Iranian; s. a. **Deutsche(r)**

Ire, Irin <-n, -n> [ˈiːrə] m, f Irishman masc, Irishwoman fem; ▪ **die** ~**n** the Irish; **[ein]** ~ **sein** to be Irish; s. a. **Deutsche(r)**

irgend [ˈɪrˈɡnt] adv at all; **wenn** ~ **möglich** if at all possible; „**wer war am Apparat?**“ – „**ach, wieder** ~ **so ein Spinner!**“ "who was that on the phone?" — "oh, some lunatic again"

irgendein [ˈɪrˈɡntˈʔain], **irgendeine(r, s)** [ˈɪrˈɡntˈʔainə], **irgendeins** [ˈɪrˈɡntˈʔains] pron indef ❶ adjektivisch some; **haben Sie noch irgendeinen Wunsch?** would you like anything else?; **ich will nicht irgendein Buch, sondern diesen Roman** I don't just want any old book, I want this novel ❷ substantivisch any [old] one; **ich werde doch nicht irgendeinen einstellen** I'm not going to hire just anybody

irgendetwas[RR] [ˈɪrˈɡntˈʔɛtˈvas] pron indef something; (bei Fragen) anything; ~ **anderes** something else; **nicht [einfach]** ~ not just anything

irgendjemand[RR] [ˈɪrˈɡntˈʔjeːˈmant] pron indef pron someone, somebody; (fragend, verneinend) anyone, anybody; ~ **anderer** sb else; **nicht [einfach]** ~ not just anybody

irgendwann [ˈɪrˈɡntˈvan] adv some time or other

irgendwas [ˈɪrˈɡntˈvas] pron indef (fam) s. **irgendetwas**

irgendwie [ˈɪrˈɡntˈviː] adv somehow [or

other]; **Sie kommen mir** ~ **bekannt vor** you seem familiar somehow

irgendwo [ˈɪrˈɡntˈvoː] adv somewhere [or other]

irisch [ˈiːrɪʃ] adj Irish; s. a. **deutsch**

Irland [ˈɪrˈlant] nt Ireland, Eire; s. a. **Deutschland**

Ironie <-, selten -n> [iroˈniː] f irony

ironisch [iˈroːˈnɪʃ] I. adj ironic II. adv ironically; ~ **lächeln** to give an ironic smile

irrational [ˈɪraˈtsi̯oˈnaːl] adj irrational

Irre <-> [ˈɪrə] f **jdn in die** ~ **führen** to mislead sb

irre|führen vt to mislead; ▪ **sich** akk **von jdm/etw** ~ **lassen** to be misled by sb/sth

irreführend adj misleading

irren [ˈɪrən] I. vi to be wrong ▶WENDUNGEN: **I**~ **ist menschlich** (prov) to err is human II. vr ▪ **sich** akk ~ to be wrong (**in** +dat about); **da irrst du dich** you're wrong there; **wenn ich mich nicht irre, ...** if I am not mistaken ...

Irrenhaus nt (veraltet o pej) insane asylum; **wie im** ~ (fam) like [in] a loony bin

irritieren* [ɪriˈtiːˈrən] vt ❶ (verwirren) to confuse ❷ (stören) to annoy

Irrsinn [ˈɪrˈzɪn] m kein pl ❶ (veraltet: psychische Krankheit) insanity ❷ (fam: Unsinn) [sheer] madness

irrsinnig [ˈɪrˈzɪˈnɪç] I. adj ❶ (veraltet: psychisch krank) insane ❷ (fam: völlig wirr, absurd) crazy ❸ (fam: stark, intensiv) tremendous; **Hitze, Kälte, Verkehr** incredible; **Kopfschmerzen** terrible II. adv (fam: äußerst) terribly

Irrtum <-[e]s, Irrtümer> [ˈɪrˈtuːm] m ❶ (irrige Annahme) error; **[schwer] im** ~ **sein** to be [badly] mistaken ❷ (fehlerhafte Handlung) mistake

irrtümlich [ˈɪrˈtyːmˈlɪç] adj attr mistaken

Ischias <-> [ˈɪʃi̯as] m o nt kein pl sciatica

Islam <-s> [ɪsˈlaːm, ˈɪsˈlam] m kein pl Islam; ▪ **der** ~ Islam

islamisch [ɪsˈlaːˈmɪʃ] adj Islamic

Island ['i:sˑlant] *nt* Iceland; *s. a.* **Deutschland**

Isländer(in) <-s, -> ['i:sˑlɛnˑdə] *m(f)* Icelander; **~ sein** to be an Icelander; *s. a.* **Deutsche(r)**

isländisch ['i:sˑlɛnˑdɪʃ] *adj* Icelandic; *s. a.* **deutsch**

Isolation <-, -en> [iz·ola·'tsi̯o:n] *f* ① TECH insulation ② (*das Isolieren*) *von Patienten, Häftlingen, etc.* isolation ③ (*Abgeschlossenheit*) isolation (**von** +*dat* from)

isolieren* [izoˑ'li:·rən] **I.** *vt* ① TECH to insulate (**gegen** +*akk* against) ② JUR, MED to isolate (**von** +*dat* from) **II.** *vr* (*sich absondern*) ■ **sich** *akk* [**von jdm/ etw**] **~** to isolate oneself [from sb/sth]

Israel <-s> ['ɪsˑra·e:l] *nt* Israel; *s. a.* **Deutschland**

Israeli [ɪsˑra·'e:li] *m* <-[s], -[s]>, *f* <-, -[s]> Israeli; *s. a.* **Deutsche(r)**

israelisch [ɪsˑra·'e:lɪʃ] *adj* Israeli; *s. a.* **deutsch**

Italien <-s> [iˑ'ta:ˑli̯·ən] *nt* Italy; *s. a.* **Deutschland**

Italiener(in) <-s, -> [itaˑ'li̯e:·nɐ] *m(f)* Italian; **~ sein** to be [an] Italian; *s. a.* **Deutsche(r)**

italienisch [itaˑ'li̯e:·nɪʃ] *adj* Italian; *s. a.* **deutsch**

IWF <-> [iːˑveːˑ'ʔɛf] *m kein pl Abk von* **Internationaler Währungsfonds** IMF

J

J j

J, j <-, -> [jɔt] *nt* J, j; **~ wie Julius** J as in Juliet

ja ['ja:] *part* ① (*bestätigend: so ist es*) yes; **~, bitte?** yes, [how] may I help you?; **das sag ich ~!** (*fam*) that's exactly what I'm talking about!; **aber ~!** [yes,] of course! ② (*fragend: so? tatsächlich?*) really?; **ach ~?** [oh] really? ③ (*warnend: bloß*) make sure; **sei ~ vorsichtig mit dem Messer!** be sure to be careful with the knife! ④ (*abschwächend, einschränkend: schließlich*) after all; **ich kann es ~ mal versuchen** I can certainly give it a try ⑤ (*revidierend, steigernd: und zwar*) in fact ⑥ (*anerkennend, triumphierend: doch*) **siehst du, ich habe es ~ immer gesagt!** see — what did I tell you?; **es musste ~ mal so kommen!** it was bound to happen!; **wo steckt nur der verfluchte Schlüssel? ach, da ist er ~!** where's the damn key? oh, there it is! ⑦ (*bekräftigend: allerdings*) **das ist ~ kaum zu glauben!** that is really hard to believe!; **ich verstehe das ~, aber trotzdem finde ich's nicht gut** I do understand what you're saying, but I still don't think it's okay; **das ist ~ die Höhe!** that is [absolutely] outrageous!; **es ist ~ immer dasselbe** some things will never change ⑧ (*na*) well ⑨ (*als Satzabschluss: nicht wahr?*) isn't it?; **es bleibt doch bei unserer Abmachung, ~?** we're sticking to what we agreed to, right? ⑩ (*ratlos: nur*) **ich weiß ~ nicht, wie ich es ihm beibringen soll** I have no idea how [I'm going to] teach him that ⑪ (*beschwichtigend*) **ich komm ~ schon!** okay! okay! I'm coming! ▶WENDUNGEN: **~ und amen zu etw sagen** (*fam*) to give sth one's blessing; **wenn ~** if so

Ja <-s, -[s]> ['ja:] *nt* yes

Jacke <-, -n> ['ja·kə] *f* ① (*Stoffjacke*) jacket ② (*Strickjacke*) cardigan

Jackett <-s, -s> [ʒa·'kɛt] *nt* jacket

Jagd <-, -en> ['ja:kt] *f* ① (*das Jagen*) hunting; **auf der ~ sein** to be [out]

hunting ② (*Verfolgung*) hunt (**auf** +*akk* for) ③ (*wildes Streben*) pursuit (**nach** +*dat* of)

Jagdhund *m* hound

Jagdrevier *nt* preserve

Jagdschein *m* hunting license

jagen ['ja:·ɡn̩] I. *vt* ① (*auf der Jagd verfolgen*) to hunt ② (*hetzen*) to pursue ③ (*fam: antreiben, vertreiben*) ■**jdn aus etw** *dat* ~ to drive sb out of sth ▶WENDUNGEN: **jdn mit etw** *dat* ~ **können** (*fam*) to not be able to stand sth II. *vi* to hunt

Jäger(in) <-s, -> ['jɛ:·ɡɐ] *m(f)* hunter

Jaguar <-s, -e> ['ja:·ɡu̯·aːɐ̯] *m* jaguar

jäh ['jɛ:] *adj* ① (*abrupt, unvorhergesehen*) abrupt; *Bewegung* sudden ② (*steil*) steep

Jahr <-[e]s, -e> ['jaːɐ̯] *nt* ① (*Zeitraum von 12 Monaten*) year; **die 20er-/ 30er~e** the twenties/thirties + *sing/ pl vb*; **anderthalb ~e** a year and a half; **ein dreiviertel ~** nine months; **das ganze ~ über** throughout the whole year, all year long; **das neue ~** the New Year; **~ für ~** year after year; **zweimal im ~** twice a year; **letztes/ nächstes ~** last/next year; **in diesem/im nächsten ~** this/next year; **vor einem ~** a year ago; **alle ~e wieder** every year; **Buch des ~es** book of the year ② (*Lebensjahre*) **er ist 10 ~e alt** he's 10 years old ▶WENDUNGEN: **in den besten ~en [sein]** [to be] in one's prime; **in die ~e kommen** (*euph fam*) to be getting on in years

jahrelang ['jaː·rə·laŋ] I. *adj attr* lasting for years; **die Früchte ~er Forschungen** the fruits of years of research II. *adv* for years

Jahrestag *m* anniversary

Jahreswechsel *m* turn of the year; **zum ~** at the turn of the year

Jahreszahl *f* year

Jahreszeit *f* season

Jahrgang *m* ① (*Personen eines Geburtsjahrs*) people born in the same year; (*Gesamtheit der Schüler eines*

Schuljahres) class of [a year] ② (*Erntejahr von Wein*) vintage

Jahrhundert <-s, -e> [jaːɐ̯·'hʊn·dɐt] *nt* century

Jahrhundertwende *f* turn of the century

jährlich ['jɛ:ɐ̯·lɪç] *adj* annual

Jahrmarkt *m* fair

Jahrtausend <-s, -e> [jaːɐ̯·'tau̯·zn̩t] *nt* millennium

Jahrzehnt <-[e]s, -e> [jaːɐ̯·'tseːnt] *nt* decade

jähzornig *adj* irascible

Jalousie <-, -n> [ʒa·lu·'ziː] *f* venetian blind

jämmerlich ['jɛ·mɐ·lɪç] *adj attr* ① (*beklagenswert*) wretched ② (*kummervoll*) sorrowful ③ (*fam*) *Ausrede* pathetic ④ (*pej fam: verächtlich*) miserable

jammern ['jam·ɐn] *vi* ① (*a. pej: lamentieren*) to whine (**über** +*akk* about, **wegen** +*dat* about); **lass das J~** stop [your] moaning ② (*wimmernd verlangen*) to beg (**nach** +*dat* for)

Jänner <-s, -> ['jɛ·nɐ] *m* ÖSTERR January

Januar <-[s], selten -e> ['ja·nu·aːɐ̯] *m* January; *s. a.* **Februar**

Japan <-s> ['ja:·pan] *nt* Japan; *s. a.* **Deutschland**

Japaner(in) <-s, -> [ja·'pa:·nɐ] *m(f)* Japanese; ■**die ~** the Japanese; *s. a.* **Deutsche(r)**

japanisch [ja·'pa:·nɪʃ] *adj* Japanese; *s. a.* **deutsch**

Jasmin <-s, -e> [jas·'miːn] *m* jasmine

jäten ['jɛ:·tn̩] I. *vt* ① (*aushacken*) to hoe ② (*von Unkraut befreien*) to weed II. *vi* to weed

jauchzen ['jau̯·xtsn̩] *vi* (*geh*) to shout with joy

jaulen ['jau̯·lən] *vi* to howl

Jawort *nt* **jdm das ~ geben** to agree to marry sb; (*bei Trauung*) to say "I do"

Jazz <-> ['dʒɛs, 'jats] *m kein pl* jazz

je ['je:] I. *adv* ① (*jemals*) ever ② (*jeweils*) each II. *präp* +*akk* (*pro*) per III. *konj* ~ **öfter du übst, desto besser kannst du dann spielen** the more you practice, the better you will be able to play; **~ nachdem!** it [all] depends!; **~ nachdem, ob/wann/wie ...** depending on whether/when/how ...

Jeans <-, -> ['dʒiːnz] *f meist pl* jeans *npl*

jede(r, s) ['jeːdə] *pron indef* ❶ *attr* (*alle einzelnen*) each, every; **~ s Mal** every time; **~ Woche** each week ❷ *attr* (*jegliche*) **ohne ~ Anstrengung** without any effort ❸ *attr* (*beliebige*) **zu ~ r Zeit** at any time ❹ *substantivisch* everyone; (*stärker*) each and every one; **das weiß doch ein ~ r!** everybody knows that!; DIAL (*jeweils der/die einzelne*) each [one]; **~ e[r, s]** zweite/dritte ... one in two/three ...

jedenfalls ['jeː·dn̩·'fals] *adv* ❶ (*immerhin*) in any case ❷ (*auf jeden Fall*) anyhow, anyway

jederzeit ['jeː·dɐ·'tsait] *adv* ❶ (*zu jeder beliebigen Zeit*) at any time ❷ (*jeden Augenblick*) at any moment

jedesmalᴬᴸᵀ *adv s.* **Mal**¹ 1

jedoch [je·'dɔx] *konj, adv* however

jemals ['jeː·maːls] *adv* ever

jemand ['jeː·mant] *pron indef* somebody; (*bei Fragen, Negation etc.*) anyone

jene(r, s) ['jeː·nə] *pron dem* (*geh*) that *sing*, those *pl*

jenseits ['jeːn·zaits] **I.** *präp +gen* (*auf der anderen Seite*) on the other side **II.** *adv* (*über ... hinaus*) ■ **~ von etw** *dat* beyond sth

Jenseits <-> ['jeːn·zaits] *nt kein pl* hereafter

Jesuit <-en, -en> [je·zu·'iːt] *m* Jesuit

Jesus <*gen o dat* Jesu, *akk* Jesum> ['jeː·zʊs] *m* Jesus; **~ Christus** Jesus Christ

jetzig ['jɛt·sɪç] *adj attr* current

jetzt ['jɛtst] *adv* ❶ (*zurzeit*) now; **bis ~** so far; **~ gleich** right now; **~ oder nie!** [it's] now or never!; **~ schon?** already? ❷ (*verstärkend: nun*) now; **habe ich ~ den Brief eingeworfen oder nicht?** did I just mail the letter or not?; **wer ist das ~ schon wieder?** now who is it? ❸ (*heute*) now[adays]

jeweils ['jeː·vails] *adv* ❶ (*jedes Mal*) each time; **die Miete ist ~ monatlich**

im Voraus fällig the rent is due each month in advance ❷ (*immer zusammengenommen*) each; **~ drei Pfadfinder mussten sich einen Teller Eintopf teilen** there was only one plate of stew for every three scouts ❸ (*zur entsprechenden Zeit*) at the time

jobben ['dʒɔ·bn̩] *vi* (*fam*) to work odd jobs

Jockey <-s, -s> ['dʒɔ·ke, 'dʒɔ·ki] *m* jockey

jodeln ['joː·dln̩] *vi* to yodel

Joga <-[s]> ['joː·ga] *m o nt kein pl* yoga

joggen ['dʒɔ·gn̩] *vi* ❶ *haben* (*eine Strecke laufen*) to jog ❷ *sein* ■ **irgendwohin ~** to jog somewhere

Jogger(in) <-s, -> ['dʒɔ·ge] *m(f)* jogger

Jogginganzug ['dʒɔ·gɪŋ-] *m* tracksuit

Joghurt, Jogurtᴿᴿ <-[s], -[s]> ['joː·gʊrt] *m o nt* yog[h]urt

Johannisbeere [jo·'ha·nɪs-] *f* currant; **rote/schwarze ~** red/black currant

johlen ['joː·lən] *vi* to yell

Jo-Jo <-s, -s> [jo'joː] *nt* yo-yo

jonglieren* [ʒɔŋ·'liː·rən] *vi* to juggle

Jordanien <-s> [jɔr·'daː·ni̯·ən] *nt* Jordan; *s. a.* **Deutschland**

Jordanier(in) <-s, -> [jɔr·'daː·ni̯·ɐ] *m(f)* Jordanian; *s. a.* **Deutsche(r)**

jordanisch [jɔr·'daː·nɪʃ] *adj* Jordanian; *s. a.* **deutsch**

Journal <-s, -e> [ʒʊr·'naːl] *nt* journal

Journalist(in) <-en, -en> [ʒʊr·na·'lɪst] *m(f)* journalist

jubeln ['juː·bln̩] *vi* ■ **[über etw** *akk*] **~** to celebrate [sth]

Jubiläum <-s, Jubiläen> [ju·bi·'lɛː·ʊm] *nt* anniversary

jucken ['jʊ·kn̩] **I.** *vi* (*Juckreiz erzeugen*) to itch **II.** *vi impers* to itch **III.** *vt impers* ❶ (*zum Kratzen reizen*) **mich juckt's am Rücken** my back's itching ❷ (*fam: reizen*) ■ **jdn juckt es, etw zu tun** sb's itching to do sth **IV.** *vt* ❶ (*kratzen*) **das Unterhemd juckt mich** my undershirt is itchy ❷ *meist verneint* (*fam: kümmern*) **das juckt mich doch nicht** I couldn't care less **V.** *vr* (*fam: sich krat-*

zen) ■sich *akk* [**an etw** *dat*] ~ to scratch [one's sth]

Juckreiz *m* itch[ing]

Jude, Jüdin <-n, -n> ['juː·də] *m, f* Jew *masc*, Jewess *fem*; ~ **sein** to be Jewish

Judentum <-s> *nt kein pl* Jewry, Jews *pl*

Jüdin <-, -nen> ['jyː·dɪn] *f fem form von* **Jude**

jüdisch ['jyː·dɪʃ] *adj* Jewish

Judo <-s> ['juː·do] *nt kein pl* judo

Jugend <-> ['juː·gnt] *f kein pl* ❶ (*Jugendzeit*) youth; **frühe/früheste** ~ early/earliest youth; **in jds** ~ in sb's youth; **in meiner** ~ ... when I was young, ... ❷ (*Jungsein*) youthfulness ❸ (*junge Menschen*) **die heutige** ~ young people today

Jugendherberge *f* youth hostel

jugendlich ['juː·gnt·lɪç] *adj* ❶ (*jung*) young ❷ (*jung wirkend*) youthful

Jugendliche(r) *f(m)* young person

Jugoslawien <-s> [ju·go·'slaː·vi·ən] *nt* (*hist*) Yugoslavia; *s. a.* **Deutschland**

jugoslawisch [ju·go·'slaː·vɪʃ] *adj* (*hist*) Yugoslav[ian]; *s. a.* **deutsch**

Juli <-[s], -s> ['juː·li] *m* July; *s. a.* **Februar**

jung <jünger, jüngste> ['jʊŋ] **I.** *adj* young; ■**jünger** [**als jd**] **sein** to be younger [than sb]; ■**der/die Jüngere/der/die Jüngste** the younger/the youngest; **das hält** ~! it keeps you young! **II.** *adv* (*in jungen Jahren*) young; ~ **heiraten** to marry

Junge <-n, -n> ['jʊŋə] *m* boy ▶WENDUNGEN: **alter** ~ (*fam*) old buddy, dude *sl*; **mein** ~ (*fam*) my boy, son; ~**, ~!** (*fam*) boy, oh boy!

Junge(s) ['jʊŋə(s)] *nt* ORN, ZOOL young

jünger ['jʏŋɐ] *adj komp von* **jung** younger

Jünger(in) <-s, -> ['jʏŋɐ] *m(f)* disciple

Jungfrau ['jʊŋ·frau] *f* ❶ (*Frau*) virgin; **die** ~ **Maria** the Virgin Mary; **die** ~ **von Orléans** Joan of Arc ❷ ASTROL Virgo

jungfräulich ['jʊŋ·frɔy·lɪç] *adj* (*a. fig*) virgin

Junggeselle, -gesellin ['jʊŋ·gə·zɛ·lə] *m, f* bachelor

Jüngling <-s, -e> ['jʏŋ·lɪŋ] *m* (*geh*) young man

jüngste(r, s) *adj* ❶ *superl von* **jung** youngest; [*auch*] **nicht mehr der/die Jüngste sein** (*hum*) to be no spring chicken anymore [either] ❷ (*nicht lange zurückliegend*) [most] recent ❸ (*neueste*) latest

Juni <-[s], -s> ['juː·ni] *m* June; *s. a.* **Februar**

Junior, Juniorin <-s, -en> ['juː·ni̯oːɐ̯] *m, f* ❶ (*Juniorchef*) boss' [*or* owner's] son *masc*/daughter *fem* ❷ (*fam: Sohn*) junior ❸ *pl* (*junge Sportler zwischen 18 und 23*) [*members of the*] junior team

Jura[1] ['juː·ra] *kein art* SCH law

Jura[2] <-s> ['juː·ra] *m* GEOL Jurassic [period/system]

Jura[3] <-s> ['juː·ra] *m kein pl* GEOG ❶ (*Gebirge in der Ostschweiz*) Jura Mountains *pl* ❷ (*Schweizer Kanton*) Jura

Jurist(in) <-en, -en> [ju·'rɪst] *m(f)* jurist

Jury <-, -s> [ʒy·'riː] *f* jury

Justiz <-> [jʊs·'tiːts] *f kein pl* JUR ❶ (*Gerichtsbarkeit*) justice ❷ (*Justizbehörden*) legal authorities *pl*

Justizbeamte(r) *m,* **Justizbeamtin** *f* judicial officer

Justizminister, -ministerin *m, f* Attorney General

Justizministerium *nt* Department of Justice

Juwel[1] <-s, -en> [ju·'veːl] *m o nt* ❶ (*Schmuckstein*) gem[stone], jewel ❷ *pl* (*Schmuck*) jewelry

Juwel[2] <-s, -e> [ju·'veːl] *nt gem*; **das** ~ **der Sammlung** the jewel of the collection; **ein** ~ **von einer Köchin sein** to be a great cook

Jux <-es, *selten* -e> ['jʊks] *m* (*fam: Scherz*) joke; **aus** ~ as a joke; **aus** [**lauter**] ~ **und Tollerei** (*fam*) out of sheer fun

Kk

K, k <-, -> [ka:] *nt* K, k; **~ wie Kaufmann** K as in Kilo
Kabarett <-s, -e> [ka·ba·'rɛt] *nt* cabaret
Kabel <-s, -> ['ka:·bl̩] *nt* ❶ ELEK wire; (*größer*) cable ❷ TELEK, TV cable
Kabelfernsehen *nt* cable TV
Kabeljau <-s, -e> ['ka:·bl̩·jau] *m* cod
Kabine <-, -n> [ka·'bi:·nə] *f* ❶ (*Umkleidekabine*) changing room ❷ NAUT cabin
Kabinett <-s, -e> [ka·bi·'nɛt] *nt* POL cabinet
Kachel <-, -n> ['ka·xl̩] *f* tile
Kachelofen ['ka·xl̩·ʔo:·fn̩] *m* tiled masonry heater
Kadaver <-s, -> [ka·'da:·vɐ] *m* carcass
Kader <-s, -> ['ka:·dɐ] *m* ❶ MIL cadre ❷ SPORT squad
Käfer <-s, -> ['kɛ·fɐ] *m* ❶ ZOOL beetle ❷ (*fam: Volkswagen*) [VW] bug [*or* beetle]
Kaff <-s, -s> ['kaf] *nt* (*pej fam*) hole
Kaffee <-s, -s> ['ka·fe] *m* coffee
Kaffeehaus *nt* ÖSTERR coffee house
Kaffeekanne *f* coffeepot
Kaffeemaschine *f* coffeemaker
Kaffeepad <-s, -s> [-pɛd] *nt* K-cup®, coffee pod
Kaffeepause *f* coffee break
Käfig <-s, -e> ['kɛ:·fɪç] *m* cage
kahl [ka:l] **I.** *adj* ❶ (*ohne Kopfhaar*) bald ❷ *Baum, Wand* bare; *Landschaft* barren **II.** *adv* **etw ~ fressen** to strip sth bare; **jdn ~ scheren** to shave sb's head; **~ geschoren** shaved
Kahlkopf *m* bald head
kahlköpfig ['ka:l·kœp·fɪç] *adj* bald-headed
Kahn <-[e]s, Kähne> [ka:n] *m* (*flaches Boot*) small boat; (*Schleppkahn*) barge
Kai <-s, -e> [kai] *m* quay
Kaiser(in) <-s, -> ['kai·zɐ] *m(f)* emperor *masc*, empress *fem*
kaiserlich ['kai·zɐ·lɪç] *adj* imperial
Kaiserschmarr(e)n *m* KOCHK ÖSTERR, SÜDD *a warm dessert of sliced crepes and raisins, topped with powdered sugar, often served with apple sauce or plum jam*
Kaiserschnitt *m* Caesarean [section]
Kajüte <-, -n> [ka·'jy:·tə] *f* cabin
Kakao <-s, -s> [ka·'kau] *m* cocoa; (*heiß*) hot chocolate; (*Pulver*) cocoa [powder]
Kakerlake <-, -n> ['ka:·kɐ·la·kə] *f* cockroach
Kaktus <-, Kakteen> ['kak·tʊs] *m* cactus
Kalb <-[e]s, Kälber> [kalp] *nt* calf
kalben ['kal·bn̩] *vi* to calve
Kalbfleisch *nt* veal
Kalbsschnitzel *nt* veal cutlet
Kalender <-s, -> [ka·'lɛn·dɐ] *m* calendar
Kalenderjahr *nt* calendar year
Kalifornien <-s> [ka·li·'fɔr·ni̯·ən] *nt* California
Kalium <-s> ['ka:·li̯·ʊm] *nt kein pl* potassium
Kalk <-[e]s, -e> [kalk] *m* ❶ (*Kalziumkarbonat*) lime ❷ BAU whitewash ❸ (*Kalzium*) calcium
kalkhaltig *adj* chalky; *Wasser* hard
Kalkulation <-, -en> [kal·ku·la·'tsi̯o:n] *f* calculation
kalkulierbar *adj* calculable
kalkulieren* [kal·ku·'li:·rən] *vt, vi* to calculate (**mit** + *dat* with)
Kalorie <-, -n> [ka·lo·'ri:] *f* calorie
kalorienarm **I.** *adj* low-calorie **II.** *adv* **~ essen** to eat diet food
kalt <kälter, kälteste> [kalt] **I.** *adj* cold; **mir ist ~** I'm cold **II.** *adv* ❶ (*mit kaltem Wasser*) **~ duschen** to take a cold shower ❷ (*ohne Aufwärmen*) **etw ~ essen** to eat sth cold ❸ (*an einen kühlen Ort*) **etw ~ stellen** to chill sth ▸WENDUNGEN: **jdn überläuft es ~** cold shivers run down sb's back
kaltblütig ['kalt·bly:·tɪç] **I.** *adj* cold-blooded **II.** *adv* in cold blood

K

Kälte <-> ['kɛl·tə] f kein pl cold; **vor ~** with cold

kälteempfindlich adj sensitive to cold pred

Kälteschutzmittel nt antifreeze

kaltlassen vi irreg ■ etw lässt jdn kalt sth leaves sb cold

Kaltluft f cold air

kaltschnäuzig (fam) I. adj callous II. adv callously

Kalzium <-s> ['kal·tsi̯·ʊm] nt kein pl calcium

Kamel <-[e]s, -e> [ka·'me:l] nt camel

Kamera <-, -s> ['ka·mə·ra] f camera

Kamerad(in) <-en, -en> [ka·mə·'ra:t] m(f) comrade

kameradschaftlich I. adj friendly II. adv on a friendly basis

Kamerun <-s> ['ka·mə·ru:n] nt Cameroon; s. a. **Deutschland**

Kamille <-, -n> [ka·'mɪ·lə] f camomile

Kamin <-s, -e> [ka·'mi:n] m o DIAL nt ① (offene Feuerstelle) fireplace ② (Schornstein) chimney

Kaminfeger(in) <-s, -> m(f) DIAL (Schornsteinfeger) chimney sweep

Kamm <-[e]s, Kämme> [kam] m ① (Frisierkamm) comb ② eines Vogels comb ③ (Bergrücken) ridge

kämmen ['kɛ·mən] vt to comb

Kammer <-, -n> ['ka·mɐ] f ① (kleiner Raum) small room ② POL, JUR chamber ③ (Berufsvertretung) professional association

Kampagne <-, -n> [kam·'pan·jə] f campaign

Kampf <-[e]s, Kämpfe> [kampf] m ① (a. fig: Auseinandersetzung) fight (**gegen** +akk against) ② (innerlich) struggle ③ (das Ringen) struggle (**um** +akk for) ④ MIL battle ⑤ SPORT fight (**um** +akk for) ►WENDUNGEN: **jdm/etw den ~ ansagen** to declare war on sb/sth

kämpfen ['kɛmp·fn̩] I. vi ① to fight ② (ringen) ■ **mit sich** dat/etw dat ~ to struggle with oneself/sth II. vr ■ **sich** akk **durch etw** akk ~ to struggle through sth

kämpferisch I. adj ① SPORT attacking

② (Kampfgeist aufweisend) aggressive ③ MIL fighting II. adv aggressively

Kampfhund m fighting dog

Kampfsport m kein pl martial arts pl

kampieren* [kam·'pi:·rən] vi to camp [out]

Kanada <-s> ['ka·na·da] nt Canada; s. a. **Deutschland**

Kanadier(in) <-s, -> [ka·'na:·di̯ɐ] m(f) Canadian; s. a. **Deutsche(r)**

kanadisch [ka·'na:·dɪʃ] adj Canadian; s. a. **deutsch**

Kanal <-s, Kanäle> [ka·'na:l] m ① NAUT, TRANSP canal ② (Abwasserkanal) sewer ③ kein pl (Ärmelkanal) ■ **der ~** the [English] Channel ④ RADIO, TV channel

Kanalinseln pl ■ **die ~** the Channel Islands pl

Kanalisation <-, -en> [ka·na·li·za·'tsi̯o:n] f sewage system

Kanaltunnel m ■ **der ~** the Channel Tunnel

Kandidat(in) <-en, -en> [kan·di·'da:t] m(f) candidate

kandidieren* [kan·di·'di:·rən] vi POL ■ **[für etw** akk**] ~** to run [for sth]

kandiert adj candied

Kandiszucker ['kan·dɪs-] m kein pl rock candy

KänguruRR, **Känguruh**ALT <-s, -s> ['kɛŋ·gu·ru] nt kangaroo

Kaninchen <-s, -> [ka·'ni:n·çən] nt rabbit

Kanister <-s, -> [ka·'nɪs·tɐ] m canister

Kanne <-, -n> ['ka·nə] f (Wasserkanne) pitcher; (Kaffee-, Teekanne) pot; (Gießkanne) watering can

Kannibale <-n, -n> [ka·ni·'ba:·lə] m cannibal

Kanone <-, -n> [ka·'no:·nə] f ① (Geschütz) cannon ② (sl: Pistole) pistol ►WENDUNGEN: **unter aller ~ sein** (fam) to be lousy

Kante <-, -n> ['kan·tə] f (Rand) edge ►WENDUNGEN: **etw auf die hohe ~ legen** (fam) to put sth away [for a rainy day]

kantig ['kan·tɪç] adj angular

Kantine <-, -n> [kan·'ti:·nə] f cafeteria

Kanton <-s, -e> [kan·'tɔːn] m canton

Kanu <-s, -s> ['kaː·nu] nt canoe

Kanzlei <-, -en> [kants·'lai] f office

Kanzler(in) <-s, -> ['kants·lɐ] m(f) chancellor

Kanzleramt nt POL ❶ (Büro) chancellor's office ❷ kein pl (Amt) chancellorship

Kap <-s, -s> [kap] nt cape; **~ der Guten Hoffnung** Cape of Good Hope

Kapazität <-, -en> [ka·pa·tsi·'tɛt] f capacity

Kapelle¹ <-, -n> [ka·'pɛ·lə] f REL chapel

Kapelle² <-, -n> [ka·'pɛ·lə] f MUS orchestra

Kaper <-, -n> ['kaː·pɐ] f caper

kapieren* [ka·'piː·rən] vt (fam) to get; ■ ~, **dass/wie ...** to understand that/ how ...

Kapital <-s, -e> [ka·pi·'taːl] nt FIN, ÖKON capital ▶ WENDUNGEN: **~ aus etw** dat **schlagen** to cash in on sth

Kapitalismus <-> [ka·pi·ta·'lɪs·mʊs] m kein pl capitalism

Kapitalist(in) <-en, -en> [ka·pi·ta·'lɪst] m(f) capitalist

kapitalistisch adj capitalist[ic]

Kapitalverbrechen nt capital offense

Kapitän(in) <-s, -e> [ka·pi·'tɛːn] m(f) captain

Kapitel <-s, -> [ka·'pɪ·tl̩] nt chapter

Kapitulation <-, -en> [ka·pi·tu·la·'tsi̯oːn] f capitulation

kapitulieren* [ka·pi·tu·'liː·rən] vi to capitulate; ■ **vor etw** dat **~** to give up in the face of sth

Kaplan <-s, Kapläne> [ka·'plaːn] m chaplain

Kappe <-, -n> ['ka·pə] f ❶ (Mütze) cap, hat ❷ (Verschluss) top

kappen ['ka·pn̩] vt ❶ (durchtrennen) to cut ❷ (fam: beschneiden) Zuschüsse to cut back [on]

Kapsel <-, -n> ['kap·sl̩] f PHARM, RAUM capsule

kaputt [ka·'pʊt] adj (fam) ❶ (zerbrochen) broken ❷ (beschädigt) damaged ❸ (erschöpft) shattered ❹ (ruiniert) ruined

kaputt|gehen vi irreg sein (fam) ❶ (zerstört werden) to break; Gerät to break down ❷ (beschädigt werden) to become damaged ❸ (ruiniert werden) ■ [an etw dat] **~** to be ruined [because of sth]; (Ehe, Partnerschaft) to break up [because of sth]

kaputt|lachen vr (fam) ■ **sich** akk **~** to die laughing

kaputt|machen (fam) **I.** vt ❶ (zerstören) to break ❷ (ruinieren) to ruin ❸ (erschöpfen) ■ **jdn ~** to wear sb out **II.** vr ■ **sich** akk **~** to wear oneself out

Kapuze <-, -n> [ka·'puː·tsə] f hood

Karaffe <-, -n> [ka·'ra·fə] f carafe

Karambolage <-, -n> [ka·ram·bo·'laː·ʒə] f pile-up

Karamelᴬᴸᵀ, **Karamell**ᴿᴿ <-s> [ka·ra·'mɛl] m kein pl caramel

Karate <-[s]> [ka·'ra:·tə] nt kein pl karate

Kardamom <-s> [kar·da·'moːm] m o nt kein pl cardamom

Kardinal <-s, Kardinäle> [kar·di·'naːl] m REL, ORN cardinal

Kardinalzahl f cardinal number

Karfiol <-s> [kar·'fi̯oːl] m kein pl SÜDD, ÖSTERR (Blumenkohl) cauliflower

Karfreitag [ka:ɐ̯·'frai·ta:k] m Good Friday

karg [kark] **I.** adj ❶ (unfruchtbar) barren ❷ (dürftig) sparse; Einkommen, Mahl meager **II.** adv sparsely; **die Portionen sind ~ bemessen** they're stingy with the portions

kärglich ['kɛrk·lɪç] adj ❶ (ärmlich) shabby ❷ (sehr dürftig) meager; **ein ~er Lohn** a pittance

Karibik <-> [ka·'riː·bɪk] f ■ **die ~** the Caribbean

kariert [ka·'riːrt] adj ❶ Stoff plaid ❷ Papier squared

Karies <-> ['ka·ri̯·ɛːs] f kein pl tooth decay

Karikatur <-, -en> [ka·ri·ka·'tuːɐ̯] f (a. pej) caricature

karikieren* [ka·ri·'kiː·rən] vt to caricature

Karneval <-s, -e> ['kar·nə·val] *m* carnival

Kärnten <-s> ['kɛrn·tn̩] *nt* Carinthia

Karo <-s, -s> ['kaː·ro] *nt* ❶ (*Raute*) rhombus ❷ *kein pl* KARTEN diamonds *pl*

Karosse <-, -n> [ka·'rɔ·sə] *f* (*Prunkkutsche*) state carriage

Karosserie <-, -n> [ka·rɔ·sə·'riː] *f* bodywork

Karotte <-, -n> [ka·'rɔ·tə] *f* carrot

Karpfen <-s, -> ['kar·pfn̩] *m* carp

Karren <-s, -> ['ka·rən] *m* ❶ (*fam: Auto*) old clunker ❷ (*Schubkarre*) wheelbarrow ❸ (*offener Pferdewagen*) cart ▶WENDUNGEN: **den ~ [für jdn] aus dem** <u>Dreck</u> **ziehen** to get [sb] out of a mess

Karriere <-, -n> [ka·'rie̯ː·rə] *f* career

Karrierefrau *f* career woman

Karte <-, -n> ['kar·tə] *f* ❶ (*Ansichtskarte*) [post]card ❷ (*Eintritts-, Fahrkarte*) ticket ❸ (*Visitenkarte*) [business] card ❹ FBALL **die gelbe/rote ~** the yellow/red card ❺ (*Auto-, Landkarte*) map ❻ (*Speisekarte*) menu ❼ (*Spielkarte*) card

Kartei <-, -en> [kar·'tai̯] *f* card index

Karteikarte *f* index card

Kartenspiel *nt* ❶ (*Spiel*) game of cards ❷ (*Satz Karten*) pack of cards

Kartentelefon *nt* a public telephone that accepts phone cards

Kartenvorverkauf *m* advance ticket sales

Kartoffel <-, -n> [kar·'tɔ·fl̩] *f* potato

Kartoffelbrei *m* mashed potatoes *pl*

Kartoffelchips *pl* [potato] chips *pl*

Kartoffelpuffer <-s, -> *m* potato pancake, latke

Kartoffelsalat *m* potato salad

Karton <-s, -s> [kar·'tɔŋ] *m* ❶ (*Schachtel*) cardboard box ❷ (*Pappe*) cardboard

Karussell <-s, -s> [ka·rʊ·'sɛl] *nt* merry-go-round

Karzinom <-s, -e> [kar·tsi·'noːm] *nt* carcinoma

kaschieren * [ka·'ʃiː·rən] *vt* to conceal

Kaschmir[1] <-s> ['kaʃ·miːɐ̯] *nt* GEOG Kashmir

Kaschmir[2] <-s, -e> ['kaʃ·miːɐ̯] *m* (*Wolle*) cashmere

Käse <-s, -> ['kɛː·zə] *m* ❶ (*Lebensmittel*) cheese; **weißer ~** DIAL quark (*low-fat curd cheese*) ❷ (*pej fam: Quatsch*) nonsense

Käsekuchen *m* cheesecake

käsig ['kɛː·sɪç] *adj* (*fam*) *Aussehen* pasty

Kasse <-, -n> ['ka·sə] *f* ❶ (*Zahlstelle*) [cash] register; (*im Supermarkt*) checkout counter ❷ (*Kartenverkauf*) ticket office ❸ (*Registrierkasse*) cash register ▶WENDUNGEN: **gut/schlecht bei ~ sein** (*fam*) to be well-off/not well-off; **jdn zur ~ bitten** to ask sb to pay

Kassenautomat *m* pay station

Kassenbon *m* [sales] receipt

Kassenpatient(in) *m(f)* ≈ HMO patient

Kassenzettel *m s.* Kassenbon

Kassette <-, -n> [ka·'sɛ·tə] *f* ❶ (*Videokassette*) videotape; (*Musikkassette*) [cassette] tape ❷ (*Kästchen*) case ❸ (*Schutzkarton*) box

Kassettenrekorder *m* cassette recorder

kassieren * [ka·'siː·rən] **I.** *vt Miete* to collect; *Abfindung, Zinsen* to pick up **II.** *vi* to settle the bill; **darf ich schon [bei Ihnen] ~?** would you mind paying the check now?

Kassierer(in) <-s, -> [ka·'siː·rɐ] *m(f)* cashier

Kastanie <-, -n> [kas·'taː·niə] *f* (*Rosskastanie*) [horse] chestnut; (*Esskastanie*) chestnut

Kasten <-s, Kästen> ['kas·tn̩] *m* ❶ (*kantiger Behälter*) box ❷ (*offene Kiste*) crate ❸ ÖSTERR, SCHWEIZ (*Schrank*) cupboard

kastrieren * [kas·'triː·rən] *vt* to castrate

Kasus <-, -> ['kaː·zʊs] *m* LING case

Katalog <-[e]s, -e> [ka·ta·'loːk] *m* catalog

Katalysator <-s, -toren> [ka·ta·ly·'zaː·toːɐ̯] *m* ❶ AUTO catalytic converter; **geregelter ~** regulated catalytic converter ❷ CHEM catalyst

K

Katarr[RR], **Katarrh** <-s, -e> [ka·ˈtar] *m* catarrh

katastrophal [ka·tas·tro·ˈfaːl] **I.** *adj* catastrophic **II.** *adv* catastrophically

Katastrophe <-, -n> [ka·ta·ˈstroː·fə] *f* catastrophe

Katastrophenhilfe *f kein pl* disaster aid

Kategorie <-, -n> [ka·te·go·ˈriː] *f* category

kategorisch [ka·te·ˈgoː·rɪʃ] **I.** *adj* categorical **II.** *adv* categorically

Kater[1] <-s, -> [ˈkaː·tɐ] *m* tomcat

Kater[2] <-s, -> [ˈkaː·tɐ] *m* (*fam*) hangover

Kathedrale <-, -n> [ka·te·ˈdraː·lə] *f* cathedral

Katholik(in) <-en, -en> [ka·to·ˈliːk] *m(f)* [Roman] Catholic

katholisch [ka·ˈtoː·lɪʃ] *adj* Roman Catholic

katzbuckeln [ˈkats·bʊ·kl̩n] *vi* (*pej fam*) to grovel

Katze <-, -n> [ˈka·tsə] *f* cat ▶WENDUNGEN: **die ~ aus dem Sack lassen** (*fam*) to let the cat out of the bag; **die ~ im Sack kaufen** (*fam*) to buy a pig in a poke

Katzenjammer *m* (*fam*) the blues + *sing vb*

Katzensprung *m* (*fam*) [nur] **einen ~ entfernt sein** to be [only] a stone's throw away

Katzenwäsche *f* (*hum fam*) ≈ quick shower

Kauderwelsch <-[s]> [ˈkau·dɐ·vɛlʃ] *nt kein pl* (*pej: Sprachgemisch*) gibberish

kauen [ˈkau·ən] *vt, vi* to chew (**an** +*dat* on)

kauern [ˈkau·ɐn] **I.** *vi* to be huddled [up] **II.** *vr* ▪**sich** *akk* **hinter etw** *akk* **~** to crouch behind sth; **sich** *akk* **in eine Ecke ~** to cower in a corner

Kauf <-[e]s, Käufe> [kauf] *m* buying; **etw zum ~ anbieten** to offer sth for sale ▶WENDUNGEN: **etw in ~ nehmen** to accept sth

kaufen [ˈkau·fn̩] *vt* ① (*einkaufen*) to buy ② (*fam: bestechen*) ▪**jdn ~** to buy sb [off *sep*]

Käufer(in) <-s, -> [ˈkɔy·fɐ] *m(f)* buyer

Kauffrau *f* businesswoman

Kaufhaus *nt* department store

Kaufkraft *f* ① (*Geldwert*) purchasing power ② (*Finanzkraft*) spending power

käuflich *adj* ① (*zu kaufen*) for sale *pred* ② (*bestechlich*) bribable

Kaufmann <-leute> [ˈkauf·man] *m* businessman

kaufmännisch *adj* commercial

Kaufpreis *m* purchase price

Kaufvertrag *m* bill of sale

Kaugummi *m* chewing gum

kaum [kaum] *adv* hardly

Kaution <-, -en> [kau·ˈtsi̯oːn] *f* ① JUR bail ② (*Mietkaution*) deposit

Kauz <-es, Käuze> [kauts] *m* ① (*Eulenvogel*) [tawny] owl ② (*Sonderling*) oddball *fam*

Kavalier <-s, -e> [ka·va·ˈliːɐ] *m* gentleman **K**

Kavaliersdelikt *nt* petty offense

Kaviar <-s, -e> [ˈkaː·vi̯·ar] *m* caviar[e]

keck [kɛk] **I.** *adj* cheeky **II.** *adv* cheekily

Kegel <-s, -> [ˈkeː·gl̩] *m* ① (*Spielfigur*) pin ② MATH, GEOG cone

Kegelbahn *f* (*Anlage*) bowling alley

kegeln [ˈkeː·gl̩n] *vi* to go bowling

Kehle <-, -n> [ˈkeː·lə] *f* throat

Kehlkopf *m* larynx

kehren[1] [ˈkeː·rən] *vt* ▶WENDUNGEN: **jdm/ etw den Rücken ~** to turn one's back on sb/sth

kehren[2] [ˈkeː·rən] *vt, vi* DIAL (*fegen*) to sweep

Kehrschaufel *f* dustpan

Kehrseite *f* (*Schattenseite*) downside

kehrt|machen *vi* to turn [around and go] back

Kehrwoche *f* SÜDD *a week in which it is a resident's turn to clean the common areas in and around an apartment building*

keifen [ˈkai·fn̩] *vi* (*pej*) to nag

Keil <-[e]s, -e> [kail] *m* TECH wedge

Keilerei <-, -en> [kai·lə·ˈrai] *f* (*fam*) scuffle

Keilriemen *m* AUTO fan belt

Keim <-[e]s, -e> [kaim] *m* ① BOT shoot

❷ (befruchtete Eizelle) embryo ❸ (Erreger) germ ▶WENDUNGEN: **etw im ~ ersticken** to nip sth in the bud

keimen ['kai·mən] vi ❶ BOT to germinate ❷ (fig) to stir

keimfrei adj sterile; **etw ~ machen** to sterilize sth

Keimling <-s, -e> m BOT shoot

kein [kain] I. pron indef, attr ❶ (verneint Substantiv) no, not any; **ich habe ~ Geld/~e Freunde** I don't have any money/friends, I have no money/friends; **ich habe jetzt wirklich ~ Zeit** I don't really have any time now; **er sagte ~ Wort** he didn't say a word ❷ (verneint Adjektiv) not; **das ist ~ dummer Gedanke** that's not a bad idea; **das ist ~ großer Unterschied** that's not much of a difference ❸ (vor Zahlwörtern) less than, not; **er wartete ~e 3 Minuten** he waited less than 3 minutes; **die Reparatur dauert ~e 5 Minuten** it won't even take 5 minutes to repair it II. pron indef, substantivisch ❶ (von Menschen) nobody, no one; **~e(r) von uns** none of us; **ich habe ~en gesehen** I didn't see anyone; **~e(r) von beiden** neither [of them] ❷ (von Gegenständen) none, any; **ist Saft da? – nein, ich habe ~en gekauft** is there any juice? — no, I didn't buy any; **~s von beiden** neither [of them]; **~ von beiden gefällt mir** I don't like either of them ❸ (nachgestellt) **Lust habe ich schon, aber Zeit habe ich ~e** I'd like to, it's just that I don't have time; **ich gehe zu der Verabredung, aber Lust hab ich ~e** I'm going to keep the appointment, but I don't feel like going

keinerlei ['kai·nɐ·'lai] adj attr no ... at all

keinesfalls ['kai·nəs·'fals] adv under no circumstances

keineswegs ['kai·nəs·'ve:ks] adv by no means

Keks <-es, -e> [ke:ks] m cookie ▶WENDUNGEN: **jdm auf den ~ gehen** (fam) to get on someone's nerves

Keller <-s, -> ['kɛ·lɐ] m cellar

Kellergeschoss^RR nt basement

Kellner(in) <-s, -> ['kɛl·nɐ] m(f) waiter masc, waitress fem

Kelte, Keltin <-n, -n> ['kɛl·tə, 'kɛl·tɪn] m, f Celt

keltern ['kɛl·tɐn] vt to press

Keltin <-, -nen> f fem form von **Kelte**

Kenia <-s> ['ke:·nja] nt Kenya; s. a. **Deutschland**

kennen <kannte, gekannt> ['kɛ·nən] vt ❶ (jdm bekannt sein) ■jdn/etw ~ to know sb/sth; **du kennst dich doch!** you know what you're like; **kennst du mich noch?** do you remember me?; **so kenne ich dich gar nicht** I've never seen you like this; **jdn ~ lernen** to get to know sb; **sich** akk **~ lernen** (erstmals begegnen) to meet ❷ (jdm vertraut sein) ■etw ~ to be familiar with sth; **kennst du das Buch/diesen Film?** have you read this book/seen this movie?; **das ~ wir [schon]** (iron) we've heard all that before ▶WENDUNGEN: **jdn noch ~ lernen** (fam) to still have sb to deal with

Kenner(in) <-s, -> ['kɛ·nɐ] m(f) expert

Kenntnis <-, -se> ['kɛnt·nɪs] f ❶ kein pl (Vertrautheit) knowledge; **etw zur ~ nehmen** to make [a] note of sth; **zur ~ nehmen, dass ...** to note that ...; **jdn von etw** dat **in ~ setzen** (geh) to inform sb of sth ❷ pl (Wissen) knowledge

Kennwort <-wörter> nt ❶ (Codewort) code word ❷ (Losungswort) password

Kennzeichen nt ❶ (Autokennzeichen) license plate ❷ (Merkmal) mark

kennzeichnen ['kɛn·tsai·ç·nən] vt ❶ (markieren) to mark ❷ (charakterisieren) to characterize

kentern ['kɛn·tɐn] vi sein to capsize

Keramik <-, -en> [ke·'ra:·mɪk] f ❶ kein pl (Töpferwaren) pottery no indef art ❷ (einzelner Gegenstand) piece of pottery

Kerbe <-, -n> ['kɛr·bə] f notch ▶WENDUNGEN: **in die gleiche ~ hauen** (fam) to take the same line

Kerl <-s, -e> [kɛrl] m (fam) guy

Kern <-[e]s, -e> [kɛrn] *m* ❶ *von Kernobst* pip; *von Steinobst* pit ❷ (*Atom-, Zellkern*) nucleus ❸ (*wichtigster Teil*) core ▶WENDUNGEN: **in ihr steckt ein guter ~** she's good at heart; **einen wahren ~ haben** to contain a core of truth

kerngesund *adj* fit as a fiddle *pred*

kernig ['kɛr·nɪç] *adj* ❶ (*voller Obstkerne*) pithy ❷ (*urwüchsig*) earthy

Kernkraft *f* nuclear power

Kernkraftwerk *nt* nuclear power plant

Kernseife *f* tallow soap

Kernstück *nt* crucial part

Kerosin <-s, -e> [ke·ro·'zi:n] *nt* kerosene

Kerze <-, -n> ['kɛr·tsə] *f* ❶ (*Wachskerze*) candle ❷ AUTO spark plug

kerzengerade I. *adj* erect II. *adv* [as] straight as an arrow

Kerzenlicht *nt kein pl* candlelight

Kerzenständer *m* candlestick

kessRR, **keß**ALT [kɛs] I. *adj* ❶ (*frech und pfiffig*) cheeky ❷ (*flott*) jaunty II. *adv* cheekily

Kessel <-s, -> ['kɛ·səl] *m* ❶ (*Wasserkessel*) kettle ❷ (*großer Kochtopf*) pot

Ketchup, KetschupRR <-[s], -s> ['kɛt·ʃap] *m o nt* ketchup

Kette <-, -n> ['kɛ·tə] *f* ❶ chain; (*zum Schmuck*) necklace ❷ (*Serie*) line; **eine ~ von Ereignissen** a chain of events; **eine ~ von Unglücksfällen** a series of accidents

Kettenraucher(in) *m(f)* chain smoker

Kettenreaktion *f* chain reaction

Ketzer(in) <-s, -> ['kɛ·tsɐ] *m(f)* heretic

ketzerisch *adj* heretical

keuchen ['kɔy·çn̩] *vi* to pant

Keuchhusten *m* whooping cough *no art*

Keule <-, -n> ['kɔy·lə] *f* ❶ (*Waffe*) club ❷ KOCHK leg

keusch [kɔyʃ] I. *adj* chaste II. *adv* **~ leben** to lead a chaste life

Kichererbse ['kɪçɐ·ʔɛrp·sə] *f* chickpea

kichern ['kɪ·çɐn] *vi* to giggle

kidnappen ['kɪt·nɛ·pn̩] *vt* to kidnap

Kiefer[1] <-, -n> ['ki:·fɐ] *f* BOT pine

Kiefer[2] <-s, -> ['ki:·fɐ] *m* ANAT jaw [bone]

Kieferorthopäde, -orthopädin <-n, -n> *m, f* orthodontist

Kieme <-, -n> ['ki:·mə] *f* gill

Kies <-es, -e> [ki:s] *m* gravel

Kieselstein *m* pebble

Kilo <-s, -[s]> ['ki:·lo] *nt* kilo

Kilobyte ['ki:·lo·bait] *nt* kilobyte

Kilogramm *nt* kilogram

Kilometer [ki·lo·'me:·tɐ] *m* kilometer

Kilometerzähler *m* mileage counter

Kind <-[e]s, -er> [kɪnt] *nt* child; **ein ~ [von jdm] bekommen** to be expecting a baby [from sb]; **von ~ auf** from an early age; **ein großes ~ sein** to be a big baby ▶WENDUNGEN: **mit ~ und Kegel** (*hum fam*) with the whole family; **wir werden das ~ schon schaukeln** (*fam*) we'll manage to sort it out; **kein ~ von Traurigkeit sein** (*hum*) to be sb who enjoys life

Kinderarzt, -ärztin *m, f* pediatrician

Kindergarten *m* kindergarten

Kindergärtner(in) *m(f)* kindergarten teacher

Kindergeld *nt a monthly government subsidy paid to parents or guardians for each child under 18*

Kinderhort *f* day-nursery

Kinderkrankheit *f* ❶ (*Krankheit*) childhood disease ❷ *meist pl* (*Anfangsproblem*) teething troubles *pl*

Kinderlähmung *f* polio

kinderleicht ['kɪn·dɐ·laiçt] (*fam*) I. *adj* very easy; ■ **~ sein** to be child's play II. *adv* very easily

kinderlieb ['kɪn·dɐ·li:p] *adj* fond of children *pred*

kinderlos *adj* childless

Kindermädchen *f* nanny

kinderreich *adj* with many children *pred*; **eine ~e Familie** a large family

Kindersitz *m* (*im Auto*) child safety seat; (*am Fahrrad*) child carrier [seat]

Kinderspiel *nt* children's game ▶WENDUNGEN: **[für jdn] ein ~ sein** to be child's play [for sb]

Kinderspielplatz *m* playground

K

Kịnderteller m child's portion

Kịnderwagen m baby carriage

Kịndheit <-> f kein pl childhood; **von ~ an** from childhood

kịndisch ['kɪn·dɪʃ] I. adj childish II. adv childishly

kịndlich ['kɪnt·lɪç] adj childlike

Kịnn <-[e]s, -e> [kɪn] nt chin

Kịnnhaken m hook to the chin

Kịno <-s, -s> ['ki:·no] nt [movie] theater; **im ~ kommen** to be playing at the movies

Kiọsk <-[e]s, -e> ['ki:·ɔsk] m kiosk

Kịpfe(r)l <-s, -[n]> nt ÖSTERR (Hörn·chen) croissant

Kịppe <-, -n> ['kɪ·pə] f (fam) ❶ (Deponie) dump ❷ (Zigarettenstummel) cigarette butt; (Zigarette) cigarette ►WENDUNGEN: **es steht auf der ~, ob ...** it's touch and go whether ...

kịppen ['kɪ·pn̩] I. vt haben ❶ (schütten) to tip ❷ (schräg stellen) to tilt ❸ (fam: scheitern lassen) Gesetzesvorlage to vote down sep; Urteil to overturn ►WENDUNGEN: **[gerne] einen/ein paar ~** (fam) to like a drink [or two] II. vi sein ❶ (umfallen) to topple over ❷ (fallen) **von etw** dat **~** to fall off [of] sth ❸ (scheitern) System to collapse

Kịrche <-, -n> ['kɪr·çə] f ❶ (Gebäude, Gottesdienst) church ❷ (Glaubensgemeinschaft, Institution) Church

Kịrchenchor m church choir

Kịrchenfest nt religious festival

Kịrchengemeinde f ❶ (Bezirk) parish ❷ (Angehörige) church members pl

Kịrchenlied nt hymn

Kịrchensteuer f taxes taken out of one's paycheck which are allotted to the state church one belongs to

kịrchlich ['kɪrç·lɪç] I. adj church attr, ecclesiastical; **ein ~er Feiertag** a religious holiday II. adv ~ **bestattet werden** to have a church funeral; **sich** akk ~ **trauen lassen** to get married in church

Kịrchturm m [church] steeple

Kịrschbaum ['kɪrʃ·baum] m cherry tree

Kịrsche <-, -n> ['kɪr·ʃə] f cherry

Kịssen <-s, -> ['kɪ·sn̩] nt (Kopfkissen) pillow; (Zierkissen) cushion

Kịssenbezug m (für Kopfkissen) pillowcase; (für Zierkissen) cushion cover

Kịste <-, -n> ['kɪs·tə] f ❶ (Behälter) box, crate ❷ (fam: Auto) [old] clunker ❸ (fam: Fernseher) tube ❹ (fam: Bett) sack; **ab in die ~!** hit the sack!

Kịtsch <-es> [kɪtʃ] m kein pl kitsch

kịtschig ['kɪt·ʃɪç] adj kitschy

Kịttchen <-s, -> ['kɪt·çən] nt (fam) slammer sl

Kịttel <-s, -> ['kɪ·tl̩] m smock; eines Arztes/Laboranten lab coat

kịtten ['kɪ·tn̩] vt ❶ (verspachteln) to putty ❷ (fig: in Ordnung bringen) to patch up sep

kịtzelig ['kɪ·tsə·lɪç] adj ticklish

kịtzeln ['kɪ·tsl̩n] I. vt ■**jdn irgendwo ~** to tickle sb somewhere II. vi to tickle III. vt impers ❶ (jucken) **es kitzelt mich** it tickles ❷ (fig: reizen) **es kitzelt mich sehr, da mitzumachen** I'm really itching to join in

Kiwi <-, -s> ['ki:·vi] f kiwi [fruit]

klạffen ['kla·fn̩] vi to yawn; Schnitt, Wunde to gape

klạ̈ffen ['klɛ·fn̩] vi (pej fam) to yap

Klạge <-, -n> ['kla:·ɡə] f ❶ (geh: Wehklage) lament[ation] ❷ (Beschwerde) complaint (**über** +akk about) ❸ JUR [legal] action; **eine ~ abweisen** to dismiss a suit; **eine ~ auf Schadenersatz** a claim for compensation

klạgen ['kla:·ɡn̩] I. vi ❶ (jammern) to moan (**über** +akk about) ❷ (sich beklagen) to complain (**über** +akk about); **ich kann nicht ~** I can't complain; **ohne zu ~** without complaining ❸ JUR to take legal action (**gegen** +akk against); **auf Schadenersatz ~** to sue for damages II. vt ■**jdm sein Leid ~** to tell sb one's troubles ❷ ÖSTERR (verklagen) ■**jdn ~** to take legal action against sb

Klạ̈ger(in) <-s, -> m(f) JUR plaintiff

klạmm [klam] adj ❶ Finger numb ❷ Kleidung, Wäsche dank ❸ (sl: knapp *bei Kasse)* ■~ **sein** to be [a little] strapped for cash *fam*

Klammer <-, -n> ['kla·mɐ] *f* ① *(Wäscheklammer)* clothespin; *(Heftklammer)* staple; *(Haarklammer)* [hair] clip; MED clip ② *(Zahnklammer)* braces *pl* ③ *(grafisches Zeichen: rund)* parentheses; *(eckig)* square bracket; *(spitz)* angle bracket; **in ~n** *(rund)* in parentheses; *(eckig o spitz)* in brackets

Klammeraffe *m* ① ZOOL spider monkey ② INET "at" symbol

klammheimlich ['klam·'haim·lɪç] *(fam)* I. *adj* clandestine II. *adv* clandestinely; **sich** *akk* ~ **fortstehlen** to slip away [unseen]

klang [klaŋ] *imp von* **klingen**

Klang <-[e]s, Klänge> [klaŋ] *m* sound

klangvoll *adj* sonorous; *Melodie* tuneful; *Stimme* melodious

Klappe <-, -n> ['kla·pə] *f* ① *(Deckel)* flap ② *(sl: Mund)* trap; **halt die ~!** shut up!; **eine große ~ haben** to have a big mouth

klappen ['kla·pn] I. *vt* to fold II. *vi (fam: funktionieren)* to work out; **alles hat geklappt** everything went as planned

Klapperkiste *f (fam: Auto)* rattletrap

klappern ['kla·pɐn] *vi* to rattle

Klapperschlange *f* rattlesnake

Klappfahrrad *nt* folding bicycle

Klappmesser *nt* switchblade

klapprig ['klap·rɪç] *adj* rickety

Klappstuhl *m* folding chair

Klaps <-es, -e> [klaps] *m (fam)* smack

Klapsmühle *f (sl)* funny farm *pej*

klar [klaːɐ] I. *adj* clear; *Antwort* straight; *Frage* direct; *Ergebnis* clear-cut; **alles ~?** *(fam)* is everything okay?; **na ~!** *(fam)* of course!; ■**jdm** ~ **sein** to be clear to sb; ■**sich** *dat* **über etw** *akk* ~ **werden** to get sth clear in one's mind II. *adv* clearly; **etw** ~ **erkennen** to see sth clearly; ~ **und deutlich** clearly and unambiguously; ~ **denkend** clear-thinking; **jdm etw** ~ **zu verstehen geben** to make sth clear to sb; ~ **im Vorteil sein** to be at a clear advantage

Kläranlage *f* sewage plant

klären ['klɛː·rən] I. *vt* ① *(aufklären)* to clear up *sep; Frage* to settle; *Problem* to resolve ② *Abwässer* to treat II. *vr (sich aufklären)* ■**sich** *akk* ~ to be cleared up

klargehen *vi irreg sein (fam)* to go okay

klarkommen *vi irreg sein (fam)* ① *(bewältigen)* ■**[mit etw** *dat]* ~ to manage [sth] ② *(zurechtkommen)* ■**mit jdm** ~ to cope with sb

klarmachen *vt* ■**jdm etw** ~ to make sth clear to sb; ■**sich** *dat* **etw** ~ to realize sth

Klartext *m* ▶WENDUNGEN: **mit jdm** ~ **reden** *(fam)* to be frank with sb

klasse ['kla·sə] *(fam)* I. *adj* fantastic, great II. *adv* fantastically, very well

Klasse <-, -n> ['kla·sə] *f* ① *(Schulklasse)* class, grade; **eine ~ wiederholen/überspringen** to repeat/skip a grade ② *einer Gesellschaft* class ③ *(Güteklasse)* class; **wir fahren immer erster** ~ we always travel first class

K

Klassenkamerad(in) *m(f)* classmate

Klassenlehrer(in) *m(f)* teacher

Klassenzimmer *nt* classroom

klassifizieren* [kla·si·fi·'tsiː·rən] *vt* to classify **(als** +*akk* as)

Klassik <-> ['kla·sɪk] *f kein pl (Musik)* classical music

klassisch ['kla·sɪʃ] *adj* KUNST, LIT, MUS classical

Klatsch <-[e]s> [klatʃ] *m kein pl (pej fam)* ~ **[und Tratsch]** gossip

klatschen ['klat·ʃn] I. *vi* ① *(mit den Händen)* to clap; **in die Hände** ~ to clap one's hands ② *(applaudieren)* to applaud ③ *(fam: tratschen)* to gossip **(über** +*akk* about) II. *vt* ① *(applaudieren)* **jdm Beifall** ~ to applaud sb ② *(fam: werfen)* ■**etw irgendwohin** ~ to chuck sth somewhere

klatschnass^RR *adj (fam)* soaking wet; ■~ **sein/werden** to be/get soaked

Klatschspalte *f (pej fam)* gossip column

Klaue <-, -n> ['klauə] *f* claw

klauen ['klau·ən] *(fam)* I. *vt* ■**[jdm]**

etw ~ to steal sth [from sb] **II.** *vi* to steal [things]

Klausel <-, -n> ['klau·zl̩] *f eines Ver-trags* clause

Klavier <-s, -e> [kla·'vi:ɐ̯] *nt* piano

Klavierspieler(in) *m(f)* pianist

kleben ['kle:·bn̩] **I.** *vi* ❶ (*klebrig sein*) to be sticky ❷ (*haften*) to stick (**an** +*dat* to); [an jdm/etw] ~ **bleiben** to stick [to sb/sth] ❸ (*fig: festhalten*) to cling (**an** +*dat* to) **II.** *vt* ❶ (*reparieren*) to glue ❷ (*befestigen*) to stick (**an** +*akk* to) ▸WENDUNGEN: **jdm eine** ~ (*fam*) to clock sb

klebrig ['kle:·brɪç] *adj* sticky

Klebstoff *m* adhesive

Klebstreifen *m* [adhesive] tape

kleckern ['klɛ·kɐn] (*fam*) **I.** *vt* ■ etw irgendwohin ~ to spill sth somewhere **II.** *vi* (*beim Essen*) to make a mess; ■ mit etw *dat* ~ to spill sth ▸WENDUNGEN: nicht ~, sondern klotzen! think big!

Klecks <-es, -e> ['klɛks] *m* ❶ (*Fleck*) stain ❷ (*kleine Menge*) blob

klecksen ['klɛk·sn̩] *vi* ❶ *haben* (*Kleckse verursachen*) ■ mit etw *dat* ~ to make a mess [with sth] ❷ *sein* (*tropfen*) ■ etw kleckst irgendwohin sth is spilling on[to] sth

Klee <-s> [kle:] *m kein pl* clover

Kleeblatt *nt* cloverleaf; **vierblättriges** ~ four-leaf clover

Kleid <-[e]s, -er> [klait] *nt* ❶ (*Damenkleid*) dress ❷ *pl* (*Bekleidungsstücke*) clothes *npl*

kleiden ['klai·dn̩] *vt, vr* ■ [sich *akk*] ~ to dress

Kleiderbügel *m* coat hanger

Kleiderbürste *f* clothes brush

Kleiderhaken *m* coat hook

Kleiderschrank *m* clothes closet

Kleidung <-, -en> *f pl selten* clothing

Kleidungsstück *nt* garment

klein [klain] **I.** *adj* small, little **II.** *adv* ~ **gedruckt** *attr* in small print *pred*; **etw** ~ **hacken** to chop up *sep* sth ▸WENDUNGEN: ~ **anfangen** to start [off]

small; ~ **beigeben** to give in [quietly]; **von** ~ **auf** from childhood

Kleinasien [klain·'ʔa:zi̯·ən] *nt* Asia Minor

Kleingeld *nt* [small] change

Kleinholz *nt kein pl* chopped wood ▸WENDUNGEN: aus jdm/etw ~ machen (*fam*) to make mincemeat [out] of sb/sth

Kleinigkeit <-, -en> ['klai·nɪç·kait] *f* ❶ (*Bagatelle*) small matter; **muss ich mich um jede** ~ **kümmern?** do I have to do every little thing myself?; **wegen jeder** ~ for the slightest reason, at every opportunity ❷ (*ein wenig*) **eine** ~ **zu hoch/low** a little too high/low ❸ (*Sache*) little something; **ich habe dir eine** ~ **mitgebracht** I brought you a little something; **eine** ~ **essen** to have a bite to eat ▸WENDUNGEN: [jdn] eine ~ kosten (*iron*) to cost [sb] a pretty penny

kleinkariert **I.** *adj* ❶ (*mit kleinen Karos*) finely checkered ❷ (*fam: engstirnig*) narrow-minded **II.** *adv* in a narrow-minded way

Kleinkind *nt* toddler

Kleinkram *m* (*fam*) ❶ (*Zeug*) odds and ends ❷ (*Trivialitäten*) trivialities *pl*

klein|kriegen *vt* (*fam*) ❶ (*kaputtmachen*) to smash ❷ (*gefügig machen*) ■ jdn ~ to bring sb into line

kleinlaut **I.** *adj* sheepish; (*gefügig*) subdued **II.** *adv* sheepishly

kleinlich ['klain·lɪç] *adj* (*pej*) ❶ (*knauserig*) mean ❷ (*engstirnig*) petty

Kleinstadt *f* small town

kleinstädtisch *adj* small-town *attr*

Kleinwagen *m* subcompact car

Klemme <-, -n> ['klɛ·mə] *f* (*fam: schwierige Lage*) jam

klemmen ['klɛ·mən] **I.** *vt* to stick **II.** *vr* **sich** *dat* **den Finger in der Tür** ~ to get one's finger caught in the door ▸WENDUNGEN: **sich** *akk* **hinter etw** ~ to get on sth; **ich werde mich mal hinter die Sache** ~ I'll get on it **III.** *vi* ❶ (*blockieren*) to jam ❷ (*angeheftet sein*) to be stuck

Klempner(in) <-s, -> ['klɛmp·nɐ] *m(f)* plumber

Klerus <-> ['kle:·rʊs] *m kein pl* clergy

Klette <-, -n> ['klɛ·tə] *f* ❶ (*Pflanze*) burdock ❷ (*pej fam: anhänglicher Mensch*) nuisance; **an jdm wie eine ~ hängen** (*fam*) to stick to sb like glue

klettern ['klɛ·tɐn] *vi sein* to climb; **auf einen Baum ~** to climb a tree

KlettverschlussRR *m* Velcro® fastener

Klima <-s, Klimata> ['kli:·ma] *nt* climate

Klimaanlage *f* air-conditioning

Klimakatastrophe *f kein pl* climate[-related] disaster

klimatisiert *adj* air-conditioned

Klimaveränderung *f* climate change

klimpern ['klɪm·pɐn] *vi Münzen* to jingle; *Schlüssel* to jangle; ■**auf einer Gitarre ~** to pluck away on a guitar *fam*

Klinge <-, -n> ['klɪŋə] *f* blade

Klingel <-, -n> ['klɪŋl̩] *f* bell

klingeln ['klɪŋl̩n] *vi* to ring; **an der Tür ~** to ring the doorbell ▶WENDUNGEN: **hat es jetzt endlich geklingelt?** do you get it, finally?

klingen <klang, geklungen> ['klɪŋən] *vi* ❶ (*erklingen*) *Glas* to clink; *Glocke* to ring ❷ (*sich anhören*) to sound; **das klingt gut/interessant** that sounds good/interesting

Klinik <-, -en> ['kli:·nɪk] *f* clinic

Klinke <-, -n> ['klɪŋ·kə] *f* [door] handle

Klippe <-, -n> ['klɪ·pə] *f* cliff; (*im Meer*) [coastal] rock

klirren ['klɪ·rən] *vi* ❶ *Gläser* to tinkle; *Fensterscheiben* to rattle ❷ *Lautsprecher, Mikrophon* to crackle

Klo <-s, -s> [klo:] *nt* (*fam*) john

Kloake <-, -n> [klo·'aː·kə] *f* (*a. fig*) cesspool

klobig ['klo:·bɪç] *adj* bulky; *Hände* massive

klonen ['klo:·nən] *vt* to clone

klönen ['klø:·nən] *vi* (*fam*) to chat

klopfen ['klɔp·fn̩] I. *vi* to knock (**auf** +*akk* on, **gegen** +*akk* against); ■**jdm auf etw** *akk* **~** (*mit der flachen Hand*) to pat sb on sth; (*mit dem Finger*) to tap sb on sth II. *vt Teppich, Fleisch* to beat

kloppen ['klɔ·pn̩] *vr* DIAL (*fam*) ■**sich** *akk* [**mit jdm**] **~** to fight [with sb]

Klops <-es, -e> [klɔps] *m* (*Fleischkloß*) meatball

Klosett <-s, -e> [klo·'zɛt] *nt* (*veraltend*) privy *old*

Kloß <-es, Klöße> [klo:s] *m* dumpling ▶WENDUNGEN: **einen ~ im Hals haben** (*fam*) to have a lump in one's throat

Kloster <-s, Klöster> ['klo:s·tɐ] *nt* (*Mönchskloster*) monastery; (*Nonnenkloster*) convent

Klotz <-es, Klötze> [klɔts] *m* block [of wood]; (*hässliches Gebäude*) monstrosity ▶WENDUNGEN: **[jdm] ein ~ am Bein sein** (*fam*) to be a heavy burden for sb

Klub <-s, -s> [klʊp] *m* club

Kluft[1] <-, Klüfte> [klʊft] *f* GEOG [deep] fissure

Kluft[2] <-, -en> [klʊft] *f* DIAL (*hum*) uniform

klug <klüger, klügste> [klu:k] I. *adj* smart, clever; (*vernünftig*) wise; *Entscheidung* prudent; *Rat* sound; **es wäre klüger, ...** it would be more sensible ...; **da soll einer draus ~ werden** I can't make heads or tails of it; **genauso ~ wie zuvor sein** to be none the wiser II. *adv* (*a. iron*) cleverly

klumpen ['klʊm·pn̩] *vi* to get lumpy; *Salz* to cake

Klumpen <-s, -> ['klʊm·pn̩] *m* lump; **~ bilden** to get lumpy

Klüngel <-s, -> ['klʏŋl̩] *m* (*pej fam*) clique

knabbern ['kna·bɐn] I. *vi* ❶ (*essen*) to nibble (**an** +*dat* on) ❷ (*emotional verarbeiten*) to chew (**an** +*dat* on) II. *vt* to nibble; **etwas zum K~** something to nibble on

Knabe <-n, -n> ['kna:·bə] *m* (*veraltend geh*) boy; **na, alter ~!** (*fam*) hey, dude! *sl*

Knäckebrot *nt* crispbread

knacken [kna·kn̩] I. *vt* to crack II. *vi* to crack; *Diele* to creak; *Zweige* to snap

K

Knạcker <-s, -> *m* DIAL (*fam*) guy; **ein alter ~** an old geezer

Knạcki <-s, -s> ['kna·ki] *m* (*sl*) ex-con

Knạckpunkt *m* (*fam*) crucial point

Knạcks <-es, -e> [knaks] *m* ❶ (*Laut*) crack ❷ (*Schaden*) problem; **einen ~ haben** *Ehe* to be in trouble; *Freundschaft* to be suffering; *Mensch* to have a screw loose

Knạll <-[e]s, -e> [knal] *m* bang; *vom Korken* pop; *einer Tür* bang ▸WENDUNGEN: **~ auf Fall** (*fam*) all of a sudden; **einen ~ haben** (*fam*) to be off one's rocker

knạllen ['knalən] I. *vi* ❶ haben (*ertönen*) to bang; *Auspuff* to backfire; *Feuerwerkskörper* to [go] bang; *Korken* to [go] pop; *Schuss* to ring out ❷ sein (*fam: stoßen*) to bang (**auf** +*akk* on, **gegen** +*akk* against) II. *vi impers* haben ▪ **es knallt** there's a bang; **..., sonst knallt's!** (*fam: oder es gibt eine Ohrfeige!*) ... or I'll slap you!; (*oder ich schieße!*) ... or I'll shoot! III. *vt* (*werfen*) to slam ▸WENDUNGEN: **jdm eine ~** (*fam*) to whack sb

knạllhart ['knal·'hart] (*fam*) I. *adj* ❶ (*rücksichtslos*) really tough, [as] tough as nails *pred* ❷ *Schuss* fierce; *Schlag* crushing II. *adv* brutally; **~ verhandeln** to drive a hard bargain

knạllrot ['knal·'ro:t] *adj* bright red

knạpp [knap] I. *adj* ❶ (*gering*) meager; *Geld* tight; ▪ **[mit etw** *dat*] **~ sein** to be short [on sth] ❷ (*eng*) tight[-fitting] ❸ (*noch genügend*) just enough; *Mehrheit, Sieg* narrow; *Ergebnis* close ❹ (*nicht ganz*) almost; **in einer ~en Stunde** in just under an hour ❺ *Antwort, Worte* succinct II. *adv* ❶ (*mäßig*) sparingly; **seine Zeit ist ~ bemessen** he only has a limited amount of time ❷ (*nicht ganz*) almost; **eine Stunde** just under an hour ❸ (*haarscharf*) narrowly

Knạrre <-, -n> ['kna·rə] *f* (*sl*) gun

knạrren ['kna·rən] *vi* to creak

Knạst <-[e]s, Knäste> [knast] *m* (*sl*) prison; ▪ **im ~** in the slammer; **im ~ sitzen** to do time

knạttern ['kna·tən] *vi* to clatter; *Motorrad* to roar

Knäuel <-s, -> ['knɔ·yəl] *m o nt* ball

Knauf <-[e]s, Knäufe> [knauf] *m* knob

knauserig ['knau·zə·rɪç] *adj* (*pej fam*) stingy

knausern ['knau·zən] *vi* (*pej fam*) to be stingy (**mit** +*dat* with)

knautschen ['knau·tʃn] *vi* to crease

Knebel <-s, -> ['kne:·bl] *m* gag

knebeln ['kne:·bln] *vt* (*a. fig*) to gag

kneifen <kniff, gekniffen> ['knai·fn] I. *vt* to pinch; ▪ **jdn in etw** *akk* **~** to pinch sb's sth II. *vi* ❶ (*zwicken*) to pinch ❷ (*fam: zurückscheuen*) ▪ **vor etw** *dat*] **~** to chicken out [of sth]; ▪ **vor jdm ~** to shy away from sb

Kneipe <-, -n> ['knai·pə] *f* (*fam*) bar

Knete <-> ['kne:·tə] *f kein pl* ❶ (*sl: Geld*) bread ❷ (*fam*) Play-Doh®

kneten ['kne:·tn] *vt* ❶ (*durchwalken*) to knead ❷ (*formen*) to model

knicken ['knɪ·kn] *vt* to fold; **„nicht ~!"** "[please] do not bend!"

knickerig ['knɪ·kə·rɪç] *adj* (*fam: knauserig*) penny-pinching, stingy

Knie <-s, -> [kni:, *pl* 'kni:ə] *nt* knee ▸WENDUNGEN: **etw übers ~ brechen** (*fam*) to rush into sth; **weiche ~ bekommen** (*fam*) to go weak at the knees

Kniebeuge *f* kneebend

Kniegelenk *nt* knee joint

Kniekehle *f* back of the knee

knien [kni:n] I. *vi* to kneel II. *vr* ▪ **sich** *akk* **~** ❶ (*auf die Knie gehen*) to kneel [down] (**auf** +*akk* on) ❷ (*fam: sich intensiv beschäftigen*) ▪ **sich** *akk* **in etw** *akk* **~** to get down to sth

Kniescheibe *f* kneecap

Kniestrumpf *m* knee sock

kniff [knɪf] *imp von* **kneifen**

Kniff <-[e]s, -e> [knɪf] *m* ❶ (*Kunstgriff*) trick ❷ (*Falte*) fold; (*unabsichtlich a.*) crease

knifflig ['knɪf·lɪç] *adj* (*fam*) tricky

Knilch <-s, -e> [knɪlç] *m* (*pej sl: Scheiß-kerl*) bastard *vulg*; (*Niete*) loser *fam*

knipsen ['knɪp·sn̩] I. *vt* ❶ (*fam: fotografieren*) ∎ **jdn/etw ~** to take a picture of sb/sth ❷ (*lochen*) to punch II. *vi* (*fam*) to take pictures; (*wild drauflos*) to snap away

knirschen ['knɪr·ʃn̩] *vi* to crunch; *Getriebe* to grind

knistern ['knɪs·tɐn] *vi Feuer* to crackle; *Papier* to rustle; ∎ **mit etw** *dat* ~ to rustle sth

knittern ['knɪ·tɐn] *vt, vi* to crease

knobeln ['kno:·bl̩n] *vi* (*würfeln*) to play dice

Knoblauch <-[e]s> *m kein pl* garlic

Knoblauchzehe *f* clove of garlic

Knöchel <-s, -> ['knœ·çl̩] *m* ❶ (*Fußknöchel*) ankle ❷ (*Fingerknöchel*) knuckle

Knochen <-s, -> ['knɔ·xn̩] *m* bone ▸WENDUNGEN: **bis auf die ~ abgemagert sein** to be all skin and bone[s]

Knochenarbeit *f* (*fam*) backbreaking work

Knochenbruch *m* fracture

Knochengerüst *nt* skeleton

Knochenmark *nt* bone marrow

knochig ['knɔ·xɪç] *adj* bony

Knödel <-s, -> ['knø:·dl̩] *m* SÜDD, ÖSTERR dumpling

Knolle <-, -n> ['knɔ·lə] *f* ❶ BOT nodule; *der Kartoffel* tuber ❷ (*fam: dicke Nase*) bulbous nose

Knopf <-[e]s, Knöpfe> [knɔpf] *m* button

Knopfloch *nt* buttonhole

Knorpel <-s, -> ['knɔr·pl̩] *m* ANAT cartilage; KOCHK gristle

knorpelig ['knɔr·pə·lɪç] *adj* ANAT cartilaginous *spec*; KOCHK gristly

Knospe <-, -n> ['knɔs·pə] *f* bud

knoten ['kno:·tn̩] *vt* to knot

Knoten <-s, -> ['kno:·tn̩] *m* ❶ (*Verschlingung*) knot ❷ MED lump ❸ (*Haarknoten*) bun

Knotenpunkt *m* AUTO, BAHN junction

knotig ['kno:·tɪç] *adj* ❶ *Finger* knotty; *Haar* full of knots *pred* ❷ MED nodular

Knüller <-s, -> ['knʊ·lɐ] *m* (*fam: Nachricht*) scoop

knüpfen ['knʏp·fn̩] I. *vt* ❶ (*verknoten*) to tie; *Netz* to mesh; *Teppich* to knot ❷ (*gedanklich*) **eine Bedingung an etw** *akk* ~ to attach a condition to sth; **Hoffnungen an etw** *akk* ~ to pin hopes on sth II. *vr* ∎ **sich** *akk* **an etw** *akk* ~ to be linked with sth

Knüppel <-s, -> ['knʏ·pl̩] *m* cudgel, club; (*Polizeiknüppel*) nightstick

knurren ['knʊ·rən] *vt, vi* to growl; (*wütend*) to snarl

knusprig ['knʊs·prɪç] *adj Brot, Braten* crisp[y]; *Brot a.* crusty; *Gebäck, Nüsse* crunchy

knutschen ['knu:·tʃn̩] (*fam*) I. *vt* to kiss II. *vi* to smooch (**mit** + *dat* with)

Knutschfleck *m* (*fam*) love bite

Koalition <-, -en> [ko·ʔali·ˈtsi̯o:n] *f* coalition   **K**

Koch, Köchin <-s, Köche> [kɔx, 'kœ·çɪn] *m, f* cook

Kochbuch *nt* cookbook

kochen ['kɔ·xn̩] I. *vi* ❶ (*Speisen zubereiten*) to cook ❷ (*brodeln*) to boil; **etw zum K~ bringen** to bring sth to a boil; **~d heiß** boiling hot ❸ (*in Aufruhr sein*) to seethe; **vor Wut ~** to seethe with rage II. *vt* ❶ (*zubereiten*) to cook; **Kaffee/Suppe ~** to make coffee/soup ❷ *Wäsche* to wash hot

Köchin <-, -nen> ['kœ·çɪn] *f fem form von* **Koch**

Kochlöffel *m* wooden spoon

Kochnische *f* kitchenette

Kochplatte *f* ❶ (*Herdplatte*) hotplate ❷ (*transportabler Kocher*) small [electric] stove

Kochrezept *nt* recipe

Kochtopf *m* [cooking] pot; (*mit Stiel*) saucepan

Kochwäsche *f* laundry that can be washed in boiling-hot water

Kode <-s, -s> ['ko:t] *m* code

Köder <-s, -> ['kø:·dɐ] *m* bait

ködern ['kø:·dɐn] *vt* to lure; **sich** *akk* **von jdm/etw ~ lassen** to be tempted by sb/sth

Koffein <-s> [kɔ·fe·'iːn] *nt kein pl* caffeine

koffeinfrei *adj* decaffeinated

Koffer <-s, -> ['kɔ·fɐ] *m* suitcase

Kofferraum *m* trunk

Kognak <-s, -s> ['kɔn·jak] *m* brandy

Kohl <-[e]s, -e> [koːl] *m* cabbage

Kohle <-, -n> ['koː·lə] *f* ❶ (*Brennstoff*) coal ❷ (*sl: Geld*) dough *no indef art* ►WENDUNGEN: **wie auf [glühenden] ~n sitzen** to be on tenterhooks

Kohlendioxid *nt kein pl* carbon dioxide

Kohlenhydrat <-[e]s, -e> *nt* carbohydrate

Kohlensäure *f* carbonic acid; **mit/ohne ~** carbonated/noncarbonated

kohlrabenschwarz ['koːl·ˈraː·bn̩·ˈʃvarts] *adj* jet-black

Kohlrabi <-[s], -[s]> [koːl·ˈraː·bi] *m* kohlrabi

Koje <-, -n> ['koː·jə] *f* NAUT bunk

Kojote <-n, -n> [ko·ˈjoː·tə] *m* coyote

Kokain <-s> [ko·ka·ˈiːn] *nt kein pl* cocaine

kokett [ko·ˈkɛt] I. *adj* flirtatious II. *adv* flirtatiously

kokettieren* [ko·kɛ·ˈtiː·rən] *vi* (*flirten*) to flirt

KokosnussRR *f* coconut

Koks[1] <-es, -e> [koːks] *m* (*Brennstoff*) coke

Koks[2] <-es> [koːks] *m o nt kein pl* (*sl: Kokain*) coke *fam*

Kolben <-s, -> ['kɔl·bn̩] *m* ❶ AUTO piston ❷ (*Gewehrkolben*) butt ❸ CHEM retort ❹ (*Maiskolben*) cob

Kolik <-, -en> ['koː·lɪk] *f* colic

Kollaps <-es, -e> ['kɔ·laps] *m* collapse

Kollege, Kollegin <-n, -n> [kɔ·ˈleː·gə] *m, f* colleague

kollegial [kɔ·le·ˈgi̯aːl] I. *adj* considerate and friendly (*towards one's colleagues*) II. *adv* in a considerate and friendly way

kollidieren* [kɔ·li·ˈdiː·rən] *vi* ❶ *sein* (*zusammenstoßen*) to collide ❷ *sein o haben* (*unvereinbar sein*) to clash

Kollision <-, -en> [kɔ·li·ˈzi̯oːn] *f* collision

Köln <-s> [kœln] *nt* Cologne

Kölnisch Wasser ['kœl·nɪʃ·va·sɐ] *nt* [eau de] cologne

Kolonie <-, -n> [ko·lo·ˈniː] *f* colony

kolonisieren* [ko·lo·ni·ˈziː·rən] *vt* to colonize

Kolonne <-, -n> [ko·ˈlɔ·nə] *f* AUTO line [of traffic]; (*von Polizei*) convoy

KolossRR <-es, -e>, **Koloß**ALT <-sses, -sse> [ko·ˈlɔs] *m* ❶ (*fam: riesiger Mensch*) colossus ❷ (*gewaltiges Gebilde*) colossal thing

kolossal [ko·lɔ·ˈsaːl] I. *adj* colossal; **eine ~e Dummheit begehen** to do sth incredibly stupid II. *adv* tremendously; **sich** *akk* **~ verschätzen** to make a huge miscalculation

Kolumbien <-s> [ko·ˈlʊm·bi̯·ən] *nt* Colombia; *s. a.* **Deutschland**

Kolumne <-, -n> [ko·ˈlʊm·nə] *f* column

Kolumnist(in) <-en, -en> [ko·lʊm·ˈnɪst] *m(f)* columnist

Koma <-s, -s> ['koː·ma] *nt* coma

Kombi <-s, -s> ['kɔm·bi] *m* (*fam*) station wagon

Kombination <-, -en> [kɔm·bi·na·ˈtsi̯oːn] *f* ❶ (*Verbindung*) combination ❷ MODE outfit

kombinieren* [kɔm·bi·ˈniː·rən] I. *vt* to combine II. *vi* to deduce; **gut ~ können** to be good at deducing; **falsch/richtig ~** to come to the wrong/right conclusion

Komet <-en, -en> [ko·ˈmeːt] *m* comet

Komfort <-s> [kɔm·ˈfoːɐ̯] *m kein pl* comfort

komfortabel [kɔm·fɔr·ˈtaː·bl̩] *adj* ❶ (*großzügig ausgestattet*) luxurious ❷ (*bequem*) comfortable

Komiker(in) <-s, -> ['koː·mi·kɐ] *m(f)* comedian

komisch ['koː·mɪʃ] I. *adj* ❶ (*zum Lachen reizend*) funny ❷ (*sonderbar*) strange; **etw kommt jdm ~ vor** (*eigenartig*) sth seems funny/strange to sb; (*suspekt*) sth seems fishy to sb; **sich** *akk* **~ fühlen** to feel funny II. *adv* (*eigenartig*) strangely

Komitee <-s, -s> [ko·mi·ˈteː] *nt* committee

Komma <-s, -s> ['kɔma] nt ❶ (Satzzeichen) comma ❷ MATH [decimal] point

Kommando <-s, -s> [kɔ'man·do] nt command; **auf ~** on command; **das ~ haben** to be in command

kommen <kam, gekommen> ['kɔmən]
I. vi sein ❶ (eintreffen, hinkommen) to come; **ich komme schon!** I'm coming!; **der Zug kommt aus Paris** the train is coming from Paris; **da kommt Anne/der Bus** there's Anne/the bus; **ist Post für mich gekommen?** was there any mail for me?; **wann soll das Baby ~?** when's the baby due?; **das Schlimmste kommt noch** the worst is yet to come; **als Erster/Letzter ~** to be the first/last to arrive; **mit dem Auto/Fahrrad ~** to come by car/bike; **zu Fuß ~** to come on foot ❷ (besuchen) ■ **zu jdm ~** to visit sb, to come and see sb ❸ (gelangen) ■ **irgendwohin ~** to get somewhere; **wie komme ich von hier zum Bahnhof?** how do I get to the train station from here?; **zu Fuß kommt man am schnellsten dahin** the quickest way [to get] there is to walk; **ans Ziel ~** to reach the finish line; **zu der Erkenntnis ~, dass ...** to realize that ...; **zu Geld ~** to come into money; **zu Kräften ~** to gain strength; **zu sich** dat **~** to regain consciousness ❹ (gehen, fahren) to come; **kommst du mit uns ins Kino?** are you coming to the movies with us?; **durch einen Ort/Tunnel ~** to pass through a place/tunnel ❺ (stammen) ■ **irgendwoher ~** to come from somewhere; **woher kommst du?** where are you from?; **ich komme aus Germersheim** I'm from Germersheim ❻ (an der Reihe sein) **jd kommt an die Reihe** it's sb's turn; **ich komme zuerst an die Reihe** I'm first; **wer kommt [jetzt]?** whose turn is it [now]? ❼ (Aufenthalt beginnen) **ins Gefängnis/Krankenhaus ~** to go to prison/to be admitted to a hospital; **in die Schule/Lehre ~** to start school/an apprenticeship ❽ **den Arzt/ein Taxi ~**

lassen to send for the doctor/a taxi ❾ (herannahen) to approach; (eintreten, geschehen) to come about; **das kam doch anders als erwartet** it/that turned out differently than expected; **es kam eins zum anderen** one thing led to another; **und so kam es, dass ...** and that's how it came about that ...; **wie kommt es, dass ...?** how come ...?; **es musste ja so ~** it/that was bound to happen; **es hätte viel schlimmer ~ können** it could have been much worse; **was auch immer ~ mag** whatever happens; **so weit ~, dass ...** to get to the point where ... ❿ (erfassen) ■ **über jdn ~** Gefühl to come over sb; **jdm ~ die Tränen** sb is starting to cry; **jdm ~ Zweifel, ob ...** sb doubts whether ... ⓫ (geraten) **wir kamen plötzlich ins Schleudern** we suddenly started to skid; **in Gefahr/Not ~** to get into danger/difficulty; **in Verlegenheit ~** to get embarrassed ⓬ (Grund haben) **das kommt davon, dass ...** that's because ...; **das kommt davon, wenn ...** that's what happens when ... ⓭ (sich erinnern) ■ **auf etw** akk **~** to remember sth ⓮ (Idee haben) ■ **auf etw** akk **~: wie kommst du darauf?** what makes you think that? ⓯ ■ **hinter etw** akk **~** Pläne to find out sep sth; **hinter ein Geheimnis ~** to uncover a secret ⓰ RADIO, TV (gesendet werden) to be on ⓱ (Zeit finden) ■ **zu etw** dat **~** to get around to doing sth ⓲ (ansprechen) **auf etw** akk **zu sprechen ~** to get around to [talking about] sth ⓳ (sl: Orgasmus haben) to come II. vt sein (fam) **die Reparatur kam mich sehr teuer** the repairs cost a lot [of money]

kommend adj coming, next; **in den ~en Jahren** in the years to come

Kommentar <-s, -e> [kɔ·mɛn·'taːɐ̯] m ❶ (Stellungnahme) statement; **kein ~!** no comment! ❷ (Meinung) opinion; **einen ~** [zu etw dat] **abgeben** to comment [on] sth ❸ (kommentierendes Werk) commentary

K

kommentieren* [kɔ·mɛn·ˈtiː·rən] *vt* to comment on

Kommissar(in) <-s, -e> [kɔ·mɪ·ˈsaːɐ̯] *m(f)* (*bei der Polizei*) inspector

Kommission <-, -en> [kɔ·mɪ·ˈsi̯oːn] *f* ❶ (*Gremium, Ausschuss*) committee ❷ (*EU-Kommission*) Commission ❸ (*Auftrag*) commission; **etw in ~ geben** to commission sb to sell sth

Kommode <-, -n> [kɔ·ˈmoː·də] *f* bureau, dresser

kommunal [kɔ·mu·ˈnaːl] *adj* municipal

Kommunalpolitik *f* local politics *pl*

Kommunalwahl *f* local [government] elections *pl*

Kommune <-, -n> [kɔ·ˈmuː·nə] *f* ❶ (*Gemeinde*) local authority ❷ (*Wohngemeinschaft*) commune

K Kommunikation <-, -en> [kɔ·mu·ni·ka·ˈtsi̯oːn] *f* communication

Kommunion <-, -en> [kɔ·mu·ˈni̯oːn] *f* REL Holy Communion; (*Erstkommunion*) First Communion

Kommunismus <-> [kɔ·mu·ˈnɪs·mʊs] *m kein pl* communism

Kommunist(in) <-en, -en> [kɔ·mu·ˈnɪst] *m(f)* communist

kommunistisch [kɔ·mu·ˈnɪs·tɪʃ] *adj* communist

Komödie <-, -n> [ko·ˈmøː·di̯ə] *f* ❶ (*Bühnenstück*) comedy ❷ (*pej: Verstellung*) play-acting

kompakt [kɔm·ˈpakt] *adj* compact

Komparativ <-s, -e> [ˈkɔm·pa·ra·tiːf] *m* comparative

KompassRR <-es, -e>, **Kompaß**ALT <-sses, -sse> [ˈkɔm·pas] *m* compass

kompatibel [kɔm·pa·ˈtiː·bl̩] *adj* compatible

kompensieren* [kɔm·pɛn·ˈziː·rən] *vt* to compensate

kompetent [kɔm·pe·ˈtɛnt] **I.** *adj* ❶ (*sachverständig*) competent ❷ (*zuständig*) responsible **II.** *adv* competently

komplett [kɔm·ˈplɛt] **I.** *adj* complete **II.** *adv* completely

komplex [kɔm·ˈplɛks] **I.** *adj* complex

II. *adv* complexly, in a complicated manner *pred*

Komplex <-es, -e> [kɔm·ˈplɛks] *m* complex

Komplikation <-, -en> [kɔm·pli·ka·ˈtsi̯oːn] *f* complication

Kompliment <-[e]s, -e> [kɔm·pli·ˈmɛnt] *nt* compliment; **jdm ein ~ machen** to pay sb a compliment

Komplize, Komplizin <-n, -n> [kɔm·ˈpliː·tsə] *m, f* accomplice

kompliziert **I.** *adj* complicated **II.** *adv* in a complicated manner *pred*

Komplizin <-, -nen> *f fem form von* **Komplize**

Komplott <-[e]s, -e> [kɔm·ˈplɔt] *nt* plot

komponieren* [kɔm·po·ˈniː·rən] *vt, vi* to compose

Komponist(in) <-en, -en> [kɔm·po·ˈnɪst] *m(f)* composer

Kompost <-[e]s, -e> [kɔm·ˈpɔst] *m* compost

kompostieren* [kɔm·pɔs·ˈtiː·rən] *vt* to compost

Kompott <-[e]s, -e> [kɔm·ˈpɔt] *nt* compote

komprimieren* [kɔm·pri·ˈmiː·rən] *vt* to compress

KompromissRR <-es, -e>, **Kompromiß**ALT <-sses, -sse> [kɔm·pro·ˈmɪs] *m* compromise; **fauler ~** false compromise

kompromisslosRR *adj* uncompromising

kondensieren* [kɔn·dɛn·ˈziː·rən] *vt, vi sein o haben* to condense

Kondensmilch *f* condensed milk

Konditor(in) <-s, -toren> [kɔn·ˈdiː·toːɐ̯, kɔn·di·ˈtoː·rɪn] *m(f)* pastry chef, confectioner

Konditorei <-, -en> [kɔn·di·to·ˈrai] *f* pastry shop

Kondom <-s, -e> [kɔn·ˈdoːm] *m o nt* condom

Kondor <-s, -e> [ˈkɔn·doːɐ̯] *m* condor

Konfekt <-[e]s, -e> [kɔn·ˈfɛkt] *nt* confections *pl*

Konfektionsgröße *f* size

Konferenz <-, -en> [kɔn·fe·ˈrɛnts] *f* conference

Konfession <-, -en> [kɔn·fɛ·ˈsi̯oːn] *f* denomination

konfessionslos *adj* not belonging to any denomination

Konfirmation <-, -en> [kɔn·fɪr·ma·ˈtsi̯oːn] *f* confirmation

konfiszieren* [kɔn·fɪs·ˈtsiː·rən] *vt* to confiscate

Konfitüre <-, -n> [kɔn·fi·ˈtyː·rə] *f* jam, preserves *pl*

Konflikt <-s, -e> [kɔn·ˈflɪkt] *m* conflict

Konfrontation <-, -en> [kɔn·frɔn·ta·ˈtsi̯oːn] *f* confrontation

konfrontieren* [kɔn·frɔn·ˈtiː·rən] *vt* to confront

konfus [kɔn·ˈfuːs] I. *adj* confused II. *adv* confusedly

Kongress^{RR} <-es, -e>, **Kongreß**^{ALT} <-sses, -sse> [kɔn·ˈgrɛs] *m* ① (*Fachtagung*) congress ② (*Parlament der USA*) ■ **der** ~ Congress

König <-s, -e> [ˈkøː·nɪç] *m* king

Königin <-, -nen> [ˈkøː·nɪ·gɪn] *f fem form von* **König** queen

königlich [ˈkøː·nɪk·lɪç] *adj* ① (*dem König gehörend*) royal ② (*großzügig*) handsome

Königreich [ˈkøː·nɪk·raiç] *nt* kingdom

Konjugation <-, -en> [kɔn·ju·ga·ˈtsi̯oːn] *f* conjugation

konjugieren* [kɔn·ju·ˈgiː·rən] *vt* to conjugate

Konjunktur <-, -en> [kɔn·jʊnk·ˈtuːɐ] *f* state of the economy; **steigende/ rückläufige** ~ [economic] boom/ slump

konkret [kɔn·ˈkreːt] I. *adj* concrete II. *adv* specifically; **das kann ich Ihnen noch nicht ~ sagen** I can't tell you for sure yet

konkretisieren* [kɔn·kre·ti·ˈziː·rən] *vt* to clearly define

Konkurrent(in) <-en, -nen> [kɔn·kʊ·ˈrɛnt] *m(f)* competitor

Konkurrenz <-, -en> [kɔn·kʊ·ˈrɛnts] *f* ① (*Konkurrent*) competitor; **keine ~ [für jdn] sein** to be no competition [for sb] ② *kein pl* (*Wettbewerb*) competition; **mit jdm in ~ stehen** to be in

competition with sb; **außer ~** unofficially

konkurrieren* [kɔn·kʊ·ˈriː·rən] *vi* to compete

Konkurs <-es, -e> [kɔn·ˈkʊrs] *m* bankruptcy; ~ **machen** (*fam*) to go bankrupt; ~ **anmelden** to declare oneself bankrupt

können [ˈkœ·nən] I. *vt* <kann, konnte, gekonnt> ① (*beherrschen*) ■ **etw** ~ to know sth; **eine Sprache** ~ to speak a language ② (*verantwortlich sein*) **etwas/nichts für etw** *akk* ~ to be able to/to not be able to do anything about sth ►WENDUNGEN: **du kannst mich mal** [*euph sl*] kiss my ass! *vulg*, fuck off! *vulg* II. *vi* <kann, konnte, gekonnt> to be able to; **nicht mehr** ~ (*erschöpft sein*) to not be able to go on; (*überfordert sein*) to have had enough; (*satt sein*) to be full; **noch** ~ (*weitermachen können*) to be able to continue; (*weiteressen können*) to be able to eat more; **wie konntest du nur!** how could you?! III. *modal vb* <kann, konnte, können> ① (*fähig sein*) ■ **etw tun** ~ to be able to do sth ② (*dürfen*) **kann ich das Foto sehen?** can I see the picture? ③ (*möglicherweise sein*) **solche Dinge** ~ **eben manchmal passieren** these things [can] happen sometimes; [**ja,**] **kann sein** [yes,] that's possible; **könnte es nicht sein, dass ...?** could it be that ...?

Können <-s> [ˈkœ·nən] *nt kein pl* ability

konsequent [kɔn·ze·ˈkvɛnt] I. *adj* consistent; ■ ~ **sein** to be consistent (**bei/ in** +*dat* in) II. *adv* consistently

Konsequenz <-, -en> [kɔn·ze·ˈkvɛnts] *f* ① (*Folge*) consequence; ~ **en [für jdn] haben** to have consequences [for sb]; **die ~ en tragen** to take the consequences ② *kein pl* (*Unbeirrbarkeit*) consistency

konservativ [kɔn·zɛr·va·ˈtiːf] I. *adj* conservative II. *adv* ~ **eingestellt sein** to have a conservative attitude

K

Konserve <-, -n> [kɔnˈzɛr·və] f preserved food

Konservendose f can

konservieren* [kɔn·zɛr·ˈviː·rən] vt to preserve

Konservierungsmittel nt preservative

Konsonant <-en, -en> [kɔn·zo·ˈnant] m consonant

konstant [kɔnˈstant] I. adj constant II. adv constantly

Konstante <-[n], -n> [kɔnˈstan·tə] f constant

Konstitution <-, -en> [kɔn·sti·tu·ˈtsi̯oːn] f constitution

konstitutionell [kɔn·sti·tu·tsi̯o·ˈnɛl] adj constitutional; **~e Monarchie** constitutional monarchy

konstruieren* [kɔn·stru·ˈiː·rən] vt ❶ (aufbauen) to construct ❷ (entwerfen) to design

Konstruktion <-, -en> [kɔn·strʊk·ˈtsi̯oːn] f ❶ (Bauweise) construction ❷ (Entwurf) design

konstruktiv [kɔn·strʊk·ˈtiːf] I. adj constructive II. adv constructively

Konsul(in) <-s, -n> [ˈkɔn·zʊl] m(f) consul

Konsulat <-[e]s, -e> [kɔn·zu·ˈlaːt] nt consulate

konsultieren* [kɔn·zʊl·ˈtiː·rən] vt to consult (**wegen** +gen about)

Konsum <-s> [kɔnˈzuːm] m kein pl consumption

Konsument(in) <-en, -en> [kɔn·zu·ˈmɛnt] m(f) consumer

Konsumgesellschaft f consumer society

Konsumgüter pl consumer goods

konsumieren* [kɔn·zu·ˈmiː·rən] vt to consume

Kontakt <-[e]s, -e> [kɔnˈtakt] m (a. elek) contact; **mit jdm ~ aufnehmen** to get in touch with sb; [**mit jdm**] **in ~ bleiben** to keep in touch [with sb]; **keinen ~ mehr** [**zu jdm**] **haben** to have lost touch [with sb]; **mit jdm in ~ kommen** to come into contact with sb

kontaktfreudig adj sociable

Kontaktlinse f contact lens

kontern [ˈkɔn·ten] vt, vi to counter

Kontext <-[e]s, -e> [ˈkɔn·tɛkst] m context

Kontinent <-[e]s, -e> [ˈkɔn·ti·nɛnt] m continent

Kontingent <-[e]s, -e> [kɔn·tɪŋ·ˈgɛnt] nt ❶ MIL contingent ❷ (Teil einer Menge) quota

kontinuierlich [kɔn·ti·nu·ˈiːɐ̯·lɪç] I. adj continuous II. adv continuously

Kontinuität <-> [kɔn·ti·nui·ˈtɛt] f kein pl (geh) continuity

Konto <-s, Konten> [ˈkɔn·to] nt account ▶WENDUNGEN: **auf jds ~ gehen** (fam: verantworten) to be sb's fault; (bezahlen) to be on sb

Kontoauszug m bank statement

Kontoinhaber(in) m(f) account holder

Kontonummer f account number

Kontostand m account balance

Kontrahent(in) <-en, -en> [kɔn·tra·ˈhɛnt] m(f) (geh) adversary

konträr [kɔnˈtrɛːɐ̯] adj (geh) contrary

Kontrast <-[e]s, -e> [kɔnˈtrast] m contrast

Kontrastprogramm nt alternative program

kontrastreich adj rich in contrast

Kontrolle <-, -n> [kɔnˈtrɔ·lə] f ❶ (Überprüfung) check ❷ (Überwachung) monitoring ❸ (Herrschaft) control (**über** +akk of); **etw unter ~ bringen** to bring sth under control; **jdn/ etw unter ~ haben** to have sb/sth under control; **die ~ über sich** akk/etw akk **verlieren** to lose control of sth/ oneself

kontrollierbar adj ❶ (beherrschbar) controllable ❷ (überprüfbar) verifiable

kontrollieren* [kɔn·trɔ·ˈliː·rən] vt ❶ (überprüfen) to check (**auf** +akk for) ❷ (überwachen) to monitor ❸ (beherrschen) to control

KontrolllampeRR f indicator light

Kontrollturm m control tower

Kontroverse <-, -n> [kɔn·tro·ˈvɛr·zə] f conflict

Kontur <-, -en> [kɔnˈtuːɐ̯] f meist pl contour

K

Konvention <-, -en> [kɔn·vɛn·ˈtsi̯oːn] f convention

Konventionalstrafe f fixed penalty

konventionell [kɔn·vɛn·tsi̯oˈnɛl] I. adj conventional II. adv conventionally

Konversation <-, -en> [kɔn·vɛr·za·ˈtsi̯oːn] f conversation

konvertieren* [kɔn·vɛr·ˈtiː·rən] vi sein o haben to convert (**zu** +dat to)

Konvoi <-s, -s> [ˈkɔn·vɔy] m convoy

Konzentrat <-[e]s, -e> [kɔn·tsɛn·ˈtraːt] nt concentrate

Konzentration <-, -en> [kɔn·tsɛn·tra·ˈtsi̯oːn] f concentration (**auf** +akk on)

Konzentrationsfähigkeit f kein pl ability to concentrate

Konzentrationslager nt concentration camp

konzentrieren* [kɔn·tsɛn·ˈtriː·rən] vt, vr ■[sich akk] ~ to concentrate (**auf** +akk on)

Konzept <-[e]s, -e> [kɔn·ˈtsɛpt] nt ❶ (Entwurf) draft ❷ (Plan) plan, concept; **jdn aus dem ~ bringen** to throw sb for a loop fam; **aus dem ~ geraten** to lose one's train of thought; **jdm nicht ins ~ passen** to not fit in with sb's plans

Konzern <-s, -e> [kɔn·ˈtsɛrn] m group

Konzert <-[e]s, -e> [kɔn·ˈtsɛrt] nt concert

Konzertflügel m concert grand

konzipieren* [kɔn·tsi·ˈpiː·rən] vt to plan

Kooperation <-, -en> [ko·ʔope·ra·ˈtsi̯oːn] f cooperation

Koordination <-, -en> [ko·ʔɔr·di·na·ˈtsi̯oːn] f coordination

koordinieren* [ko·ʔɔr·di·ˈniː·rən] vt to coordinate

Kopf <-[e]s, Köpfe> [kɔpf] m ❶ (Haupt) head; **von ~ bis Fuß** from head to toe; **einen roten ~ bekommen** to go red [in the face] ❷ (oberer Teil) head; (Briefkopf) letterhead; **~ oder Zahl?** (bei Münzen) heads or tails? ❸ (Gedanken) head; **sich dat etw durch den ~ gehen lassen** to mull sth over; **nichts als Sport im ~ haben** to think of nothing but sports;

sich dat [**über etw** akk] **den ~ zerbrechen** (fam) to rack one's brain [over sth]; **nicht ganz richtig im ~ sein** (fam) to be not quite right in the head ❹ (Wille) mind; **seinen eigenen ~ haben** (fam) to have a mind of one's own; **seinen ~ durchsetzen** to get one's way ❺ (Person) head; ■**der ~ einer S.** gen the person behind sth; **pro ~** per person ▶WENDUNGEN: **nicht auf den ~ gefallen sein** (fam) to not have been born yesterday; **etw auf den ~ hauen** (fam) to spend all of sth; **~ hoch!** [keep your] chin up!; [**bei etw** dat] **~ und Kragen riskieren** (fam) to risk life and limb [doing sth]; **etw auf den ~ stellen** (gründlich durchsuchen) to turn sth upside down; (ins Gegenteil verkehren) to turn sth on its head; **jdn vor den ~ stoßen** to offend sb; **mit dem ~ durch die Wand [rennen] wollen** (fam) to be determined to get one's way

Kopfball m header

Kopfbedeckung f headgear

Köpfchen [ˈkœpf·çən] nt ▶WENDUNGEN: **~ haben** (fam) to have brains

köpfen [ˈkœp·fn̩] vt (fam: enthaupten) to behead

Kopfende nt head

Kopfhaut f scalp

Kopfhörer m headphones pl

Kopfkissen nt pillow

kopflos I. adj (verwirrt) confused II. adv in a bewildered manner

Kopfrechnen nt mental arithmetic

Kopfsalat m lettuce

Kopfschmerz m meist pl headache

Kopfstand m headstand

Kopfsteinpflaster nt cobblestones pl

Kopfstütze f headrest

Kopftuch nt headscarf

kopfüber [kɔpf·ˈʔyː·bɐ] adv head first

Kopfweh nt DIAL s. **Kopfschmerz**

Kopie <-, -n> [ko·ˈpiː] f copy

kopieren* [ko·ˈpiː·rən] vt to copy

Kopierer <-s, -> m [photo]copier

Koppel <-, -n> [ˈkɔ·pl̩] f pasture

Koralle <-, -n> [ko·ˈra·lə] f coral

K

Koran <-s> [ko·'ra:n] *m kein pl* Koran

Korb <-[e]s, Körbe> [kɔrp] *m* ❶ (*a. sport*) basket ❷ *kein pl* (*Weidengeflecht*) wicker ❸ (*fam: Abfuhr*) rejection; [**von jdm**] **einen ~ bekommen** to be rejected [by sb]; (*bei einer Verabredung*) to get stood up [by sb]; **jdm einen ~ geben** to turn sb down; (*bei einer Verabredung*) to stand sb up

Korbball *m* netball (*a game that resembles basketball without the backboards*)

Kord <-[e]s, -e> [kɔrt] *m s.* **Cord**

Korea <-s> [ko·'re:a] *nt* Korea; *s. a.* **Deutschland**

Koreaner(in) [ko·re·'a:·nɐ] *m(f)* Korean; *s. a.* **Deutsche(r)**

Koriander <-s, -> [ko·'rian·dɐ] *m* coriander

Korinthe <-, -n> [ko·'rın·tə] *f* current

Kork <-[e]s, -e> [kɔrk] *m* cork

Korken <-s, -> ['kɔr·kn̩] *m* cork

Korkenzieher <-s, -> *m* corkscrew

Korn[1] <-[e]s, Körner> [kɔrn] *nt* ❶ (*Samenkorn*) grain ❷ (*Getreide*) corn, grain

Korn[2] <-[e]s, -> [kɔrn] *m* (*Kornbranntwein*) schnapps

Körper <-s, -> ['kœr·pɐ] *m* body; **am ganzen ~** all over

Körperbau *m kein pl* physique

Körperbehinderte(r) *f(m)* physically disabled person

Körpergewicht *nt* weight

Körpergröße *f* size

körperlich I. *adj* physical II. *adv* physically; **~ arbeiten** to do physical labor

Körperpflege *f* personal hygiene

Körpersprache *f* body language

Körperteil *m* part of the body, body part

Körperverletzung *f* bodily harm; **fahrlässige ~** bodily injury caused by negligence; **schwere ~** aggravated assault

korpulent [kɔr·pu·'lɛnt] *adj* (*geh*) corpulent

korrekt [ko·'rɛkt] I. *adj* correct II. *adv* correctly

Korrektur <-, -en> [ko·rɛk·'tu:ɐ] *f* correction; *von Schularbeiten* grading; [**etw**] **~ lesen** to proofread [sth]

Korrespondent(in) <-en, -en> [ko·rɛs·pɔn·'dɛnt] *m(f)* correspondent

Korrespondenz <-, -en> [ko·rɛs·pɔn·'dɛnts] *f* correspondence

korrespondieren* *vi* ❶ (*in Briefwechsel stehen*) to correspond (**mit** +*dat* with) ❷ (*geh: entsprechen*) ■ **mit etw** *dat* ~ to correspond to sth

Korridor <-s, -e> ['kɔ·ri·do:ɐ] *m* corridor

korrigieren* [ko·ri·'gi:·rən] *vt* to correct; *Klassenarbeit, Aufsatz* to grade; *Manuskript* to proofread

korrupt [ko·'rʊpt] *adj* corrupt

Korruption <-, -en> [ko·rʊp·'tsio:n] *f* corruption

Korse, Korsin <-n, -n> ['kɔr·zə] *m, f* Corsican; *s. a.* **Deutsche(r)**

Korsin <-, -nen> *f fem form von* **Korse**

koscher ['ko:·ʃe] I. *adj* kosher ▶ WENDUNGEN: **nicht [ganz] ~ sein** to not be [entirely] on the level II. *adv* according to kosher requirements

Kosename *m* pet name

Kosewort *nt* term of endearment

Kosmetik <-> [kɔs·'me:·tɪk] *f kein pl* cosmetics *pl*

Kosmetiker(in) <-s, -> [kɔs·'me:·ti·kɐ] *m(f)* beautician

kosmetisch [kɔs·'me:·tɪʃ] I. *adj* cosmetic II. *adv* cosmetically

kosmisch ['kɔs·mɪʃ] *adj* cosmic

Kosmopolit(in) <-en, -en> [kɔs·mo·po·'li:t] *m(f)* (*geh*) cosmopolitan

Kosmos <-> ['kɔs·mɔs] *m kein pl* cosmos

Kost <-> [kɔst] *f kein pl* food; [**freie**] **~ und Logis** [free] room and board

kostbar ['kɔst·ba:ɐ] *adj* valuable, precious; **jdm ~ sein** to mean a lot to sb

Kostbarkeit <-, -en> *f* ❶ (*Gegenstand*) precious object ❷ *kein pl* (*Erlesenheit*) preciousness

kosten[1] ['kɔs·tn̩] *vt* ❶ (*als Preis haben*) to cost ❷ (*erfordern*) to take [up]

kosten[2] ['kɔs·tn̩] *vt, vi* (*probieren*) to taste

Kosten ['kɔs·tn̩] *pl* costs *pl*, expenses *pl*; **auf ~ von jdm/etw** *dat* at the expense of sb/sth ▸WENDUNGEN: **auf seine ~ kommen** to get one's money's worth

kostendeckend I. *adj* cost-effective II. *adv* cost-effectively

kostenlos *adj, adv* free [of charge]

Kostenvoranschlag *m* quotation; **sich** *dat* **einen ~ machen lassen** to get an estimate

köstlich ['kœst·lɪç] I. *adj* ❶ (*herrlich*) delicious ❷ (*fam: amüsant*) priceless II. *adv* (*herrlich*) deliciously; **sich** *akk* **~ amüsieren** to have a wonderful time

Kostprobe *f* (*Vorgeschmack*) sample

kostspielig *adj* expensive

Kostüm <-s, -e> [kɔs·'ty:m] *nt* ❶ MODE suit ❷ HIST, THEAT costume

Kot <-[e]s> [ko:t] *m kein pl* excrement

Kotelett <-s, -s> [kɔt·'lɛt] *nt* chop

Köter <-s, -> ['kø:·tɐ] *m* (*pej*) mutt

Kotflügel *m* wing

Kotzbrocken *m* (*pej sl*) slimeball

Kotze <-> ['kɔ·tsə] *f kein pl* (*fam*) puke *sl*

kotzen ['kɔ·tsn̩] *vi* (*fam*) to puke; **das ist zum K~** that makes me want to puke *sl*

Krabbe <-, -n> ['kra·bə] *f* ❶ ZOOL (*Taschenkrebs*) crab ❷ KOCHK (*Garnele*) prawn

krabbeln ['kra·bl̩n] *vi sein* to crawl

Krach <-[e]s, Kräche> [krax] *m* ❶ *kein pl* (*Lärm*) noise ❷ (*fam: Streit*) quarrel; **sie haben ~** they're not on speaking terms; **mit jdm ~ kriegen** to get into trouble with sb

krachen ['kra·xn̩] *vi* ❶ *haben* (*laut hallen*) to crash; *Ast* to creak; *Schuss* to ring out ❷ *sein* (*fam: prallen*) to crash

krächzen ['krɛç·tsn̩] *vt, vi* ❶ ORN to caw ❷ (*fam: heiser sprechen*) to croak

Kraft <-, Kräfte> [kraft] *f* ❶ ([*körperliche*] *Stärke*) strength; **mit frischer ~** with renewed energy; **mit letzter ~** with one's last ounce of strength; **mit vereinten Kräften** with combined efforts; **aus eigener ~** by oneself; **die treibende ~** the driving force; **wieder zu Kräften kommen** to regain one's strength; **über jds Kräfte gehen** to be more than sb can cope with ❷ (*Gel-*

tung) power; **in ~ sein** to be in effect; **in ~ treten** to take effect; **außer ~ sein** to be no longer in effect; **etw außer ~ setzen** to cancel sth ❸ PHYS (*Energie*) power ❹ *meist pl* (*Einfluss ausübende Gruppe*) force

Kraftakt *m* act of strength

Kraftfahrer(in) *m(f)* driver

Kraftfahrzeug *nt* motor vehicle

Kraftfahrzeugbrief *m* title

Kraftfahrzeugsteuer *f* motor vehicle tax

Kraftfahrzeugversicherung *f* auto insurance

kräftig ['krɛf·tɪç] I. *adj* ❶ (*stark*) strong; *Händedruck* firm; *Haarwuchs* healthy; *Stimme* powerful; *Farbe* rich ❷ KOCHK hearty II. *adv* ❶ (*angestrengt*) vigorously ❷ METEO (*stark*) heavily

kraftlos I. *adj* weak II. *adv* feebly

Kraftprobe *f* test of strength

Kraftrad *nt* motorcycle

Kraftstoff *m* fuel

kraftvoll I. *adj* strong; *Stimme* powerful II. *adv* forcefully; **~ zubeißen** to take a hearty bite

Kraftwagen *m* motor vehicle

Kraftwerk *nt* power plant

Kragen <-s, -> ['kra:·gən] *m* collar ▸WENDUNGEN: **jdm geht es an den ~** (*derb*) sb is in for it; **etw kostet jdn den ~** (*derb*) sth is sb's downfall; **jdm platzt der ~** (*fam*) sb is blowing his/her top

Kragenweite *f* collar size ▸WENDUNGEN: **genau/nicht jds ~ sein** (*fam*) to be just/not sb's cup of tea

Krähe <-, -n> ['krɛː·ə] *f* crow

Krake <-n, -n> ['kra:·kə] *m* octopus

krakeelen* [kra·'ke:·lən] *vi* (*pej fam*) to make a racket

Kralle <-, -n> ['kra·lə] *f* ORN, ZOOL claw ▸WENDUNGEN: **jdn in seine ~ bekommen** to get one's claws into sb

krallen ['kra·lən] I. *vr* ■ **sich** *akk* **an jdn/etw** to cling onto sb/sth II. *vt* ■ **etw in etw** *akk* ~ to dig sth into sth

Kram <-[e]s> [kra:m] *m kein pl* (*fam*) ❶ (*Krempel*) junk ❷ (*Angelegenheit*)

affairs *pl;* **den ganzen ~ hinschmeißen** to pack it all in; **jdm in den ~ passen** to suit sb fine; **jdm nicht in den ~ passen** to be a real nuisance to sb

Krampf <-[e]s, Krämpfe> [krampf] *m* cramp

krampfhaft I. *adj* ❶ *(angestrengt)* desperate ❷ MED convulsive II. *adv* desperately

Kran <-[e]s, Kräne> [kra:n] *m* TECH crane

krank <kränker, kränkste> [kraŋk] *adj* sick, ill ►WENDUNGEN: **du bist wohl ~!** *(iron)* are you out of your mind?; **jdn [mit etw** *dat***] ~ machen** to get on sb's nerves [with sth]

Kranke(r) *f(m) dekl wie adj* sick person

kränkeln ['krɛŋ·kl̩n] *vi* to be in poor health

kränken ['krɛŋ·kn̩] *vt* ■**jdn ~** to hurt sb's feelings; ■**gekränkt sein** to feel hurt; ■**es kränkt jdn, dass ...** it hurts sb['s feelings], that ...; ■**~-d** hurtful

Krankengeld *nt* sick pay

Krankengymnastik *f* physical therapy

Krankenhaus *nt* hospital, clinic; **ins ~ kommen/müssen** to go/have to go to the hospital; **im ~ liegen** to be in a hospital

Krankenkasse *f* health insurance company

Krankenpflege *f* nursing

Krankenpfleger(in) *m(f)* male nurse

Krankenschwester *f* nurse

Krankenversicherung *f* health insurance

Krankenwagen *m* ambulance

krank|feiern *vi (fam)* to call in sick

krankhaft I. *adj* morbid II. *adv* morbidly

Krankheit <-, -en> *f* disease

Krankheitserreger *m* pathogen

kränklich ['krɛŋk·lɪç] *adj* sickly

krank|melden[RR] *vr* ■**sich** *akk* **~** to call in sick

Krankmeldung *f* notification of illness

krank|schreiben[RR] *vt* ■**jdn ~** to excuse sb from [going to] work because he/she is sick

Kränkung <-, -en> *f* insult

Kranz <-es, Kränze> [krants] *m* ❶ *(Ring aus Pflanzen)* wreath ❷ DIAL *(Hefekranz)* Danish ring

krass[RR], **kraß**[ALT] [kras] I. *adj Beispiel* glaring; *Bemerkung* crass; *Unterschied* extreme II. *adv (sl)* crassly

Krätze <-> ['krɛ·tsə] *f kein pl* scabies

kratzen ['kra·tsn̩] I. *vt* ❶ *(mit den Nägeln ritzen)* to scratch; ■**etw von etw** *dat* **~** to scratch sth off [of] sth ❷ *(fam: kümmern)* **das kratzt mich nicht** I couldn't care less about that II. *vi* to scratch

Kratzer <-s, -> ['kra·tse] *m* scratch

kraulen[1] ['krau·lən] *vi sein o haben (schwimmen)* to do [or swim] the crawl

kraulen[2] ['krau·lən] *vt (streicheln)* to fondle; **einen Hund zwischen den Ohren ~** to scratch a dog between its ears

kraus [kraus] *adj Haare* frizzy; *Stirn* wrinkled

Kraut <-[e]s, Kräuter> [kraut] *nt* ❶ BOT herb ❷ *kein pl* DIAL *(Kohl)* cabbage; *(Sauerkraut)* sauerkraut ►WENDUNGEN: **wie ~ und Rüben durcheinanderliegen** *(fam)* to lie around all over the place

Kräutertee *m* herbal tea

Krawall <-s, -e> [kra·'val] *m* ❶ *(Tumult)* riot ❷ *kein pl (fam: Aufruhr, Lärm)* racket

Krawatte <-, -n> [kra·'va·tə] *f* tie

kreativ [krea·'ti:f] I. *adj* creative II. *adv* creatively

Kreativität <-> [krea·ti·vi·'tɛt] *f kein pl* creativity

Krebs <-es, -e> [kre:ps] *m* ❶ ZOOL crayfish ❷ *kein pl* KOCHK *(Krebsfleisch)* crab ❸ MED cancer ❹ *kein pl* ASTROL Cancer

Krebserreger *m* carcinogen

Krebsfrüherkennung *f kein pl* early cancer diagnosis

Krebsgeschwür *nt* cancerous ulcer

Krebsvorsorgeuntersuchung *f* cancer checkup

Kredit <-[e]s, -e> [kre·'di:t] *m* credit; *(Darlehen)* loan

Kreditkarte *f* credit card

Kreide <-, -n> ['krai·də] *f* chalk

kreidebleich *adj* as white as a sheet

Kreidezeichnung *f* chalk drawing

kreieren* [kre·'i:·rən] *vt* to create

Kreis <-es, -e> [krais] *m* ❶ (*a. math*) circle; **die Hochzeit fand im engsten ~ statt** only close friends and family were invited to the wedding ❷ ADMIN district

kreischen ['krai·ʃn] *vi* ❶ ORN to squawk ❷ (*hysterisch schreien*) to shriek ❸ *Bremsen, Reifen* to screech

Kreisel <-s, -> ['krai·zl] *m* ❶ (*Spielzeug*) top ❷ TRANSP (*fam*) traffic circle

kreisen ['krai·zn] *vi sein o haben* ❶ ASTRON, RAUM ■ **um etw** *akk* ~ to orbit sth ❷ LUFT, ORN to circle (**über** +*dat* above) ❸ (*in einem Kreislauf sein*) to circulate (**in** +*dat* through) ❹ (*fig*) ■ **um jdn/ etw** ~ to revolve around sb/sth

kreisförmig I. *adj* circular II. *adv* in a circle

Kreislauf *m* ❶ MED circulation ❷ (*Zirkulation*) cycle

Kreislaufstörungen *pl* circulatory disorder

Kreisstadt *f* county seat

Kreisverkehr *m* traffic circle

Krematorium <-s, -rien> [kre·ma·'to:·ri·ʊm] *nt* crematorium

Krempe <-, -n> ['krɛm·pə] *f* brim

Krempel <-s> ['krɛm·pl] *m kein pl* (*pej fam*) ❶ (*ungeordnete Sachen*) stuff ❷ (*Ramsch*) junk ▶WENDUNGEN: **den ganzen ~ hinwerfen** to throw in the towel *fam*

krepieren* [kre·'pi:·rən] *vi sein* (*sl: zugrunde gehen*) to croak

Kresse <-, -n> ['krɛ·sə] *f* cress

kreuz [krɔyts] ▶WENDUNGEN: ~ **und quer** all over the place

Kreuz <-es, -e> [krɔyts] *nt* ❶ (*Zeichen X*) cross; **über** ~ crosswise ❷ REL cross; (*Kruzifix*) crucifix; **jdn ans ~ schlagen** to crucify sb ❸ (*fam: Teil des Rückens*) **es im ~ haben** (*fam*) to have back trouble ❹ (*Autobahnkreuz*) intersection ❺ *kein pl* KARTEN clubs *pl* ▶WENDUNGEN: **jdn aufs ~ legen** (*fam*) to fool sb; **drei**

~**e machen** (*fam*) to be so relieved; **das Rote** ~ the Red Cross

Kreuzer <-s, -> ['krɔy·tsɐ] *m* NAUT cruiser

Kreuzfahrt *f* cruise

Kreuzfeuer *nt* crossfire ▶WENDUNGEN: **ins** ~ [**der Kritik**] **geraten** to come under fire

kreuzigen ['krɔy·tsi·gn] *vt* to crucify

Kreuzigung <-, -en> *f* crucifixion

Kreuzotter *f* adder

Kreuzspinne *f* cross [*or* garden] spider

Kreuzung <-, -en> *f* ❶ (*Straßenkreuzung*) crossroad *usu pl* ❷ *kein pl* BIOL (*das Kreuzen*) crossbreeding ❸ ZOOL, BIOL (*Bastard*) mongrel

Kreuzworträtsel *nt* crossword [puzzle]

Kreuzzug *m* crusade

kribbeln ['kri·bln] *vi* (*prickeln*) **das kribbelt so schön auf der Haut** it's so nice and tingly on the skin

Kricket <-s, -s> ['kri·kət] *nt* SPORT cricket

kriechen <kroch, gekrochen> ['kri:·çn] *vi* ❶ *sein* (*auf dem Bauch*) to crawl ❷ *sein Zeit* to creep by; *Verkehr* to creep ❸ *sein o haben* (*pej: unterwürfig sein*) to grovel (**vor** +*dat* before)

Krieg <-[e]s, -e> [kri:k] *m* war

kriegen ['kri:·gn] *vt* (*fam*) ❶ (*bekommen*) to get; **den Schrank in den Aufzug** ~ to get the cupboard into the elevator; **ich kriege noch 20 Euro von dir** you still owe me 20 euros; **hast du die Arbeit auch bezahlt gekriegt?** did you get paid for the work?; **ein Kind** ~ to have a baby; **eine Krankheit** ~ to get a disease ❷ (*erwischen*) to catch; **den Zug** ~ to catch the train ❸ (*es schaffen*) ■ **jdn dazu** ~, **etw zu tun** to get sb to do sth; **ich kriege das schon geregelt** I'll take care of it ▶WENDUNGEN: **es mit jdm zu tun** ~ to be in trouble with sb

Krieger(in) <-s, -> ['kri:·gɐ] *m(f)* warrior

kriegerisch I. *adj* ❶ (*kämpferisch*) warlike ❷ (*militärisch*) military II. *adv* belligerently

K

Kriegsausbruch m outbreak of war

Kriegsbeil nt tomahawk ▶WENDUNGEN: **das ~ begraben** to bury the hatchet

Kriegsberichterstatter(in) m(f) war correspondent

Kriegsbeschädigte(r) f(m) dekl wie adj sb wounded in action, disabled vet[eran]

Kriegsdienstverweigerer <-s, -> m conscientious objector

Kriegsgefangene(r) f(m) prisoner of war

Kriegsgefangenschaft f captivity; **in ~ geraten** to become a prisoner of war

Kriegsgericht nt court martial

Kriegsschiff nt warship

Kriegsverbrecher(in) m(f) war criminal

Krimi <-s, -s> ['kriː·mi] m (fam) ❶ (Buch) detective novel ❷ (Film) [crime] thriller

Kriminalbeamte(r) m, **-beamtin** f detective

Kriminalität <-> [kri·mi·na·liˈtɛt] f kein pl criminality

Kriminalpolizei f criminal investigation department

Kriminalroman m detective novel

kriminell [kri·miˈnɛl] adj criminal

Kriminelle(r) [kri·miˈnɛ·lə, -lə] f(m) dekl wie adj criminal

Krimskrams <-es> ['krims·krams] m kein pl (fam) junk

Kringel <-s, -> ['krɪŋl] m ❶ KOCHK ring-shaped cookie ❷ (Schnörkel) squiggle

Kripo <-, -s> ['kriː·po] f (fam) kurz für **Kriminalpolizei**

Krippe <-, -n> ['krɪ·pə] f ❶ manger ❷ s. **Kinderhort**

Krise <-, -n> ['kriː·zə] f crisis

kriseln ['kriː·zln] vi impers (fam) **es kriselt** a crisis is looming

krisenfest adj crisis-proof

Krisenherd m trouble spot

Kristall <-s, -e> [krɪsˈtal] m crystal

Kriterium <-s, -rien> [kri·ˈteː·ri·ʊm] nt criterion

Kritik <-, -en> [kri·ˈtiːk] f ❶ kein pl (Beurteilung) criticism; **an jdm/etw ~ üben** to criticize sb/sth ❷ MEDIA (Rezension) review; **gute/schlechte ~en bekommen** to receive good/bad reviews ▶WENDUNGEN: **unter aller ~ sein** (pej) to be beneath contempt

Kritiker(in) <-s, -> ['kriː·ti·kɐ] m(f) critic

kritiklos I. adj uncritical II. adv uncritically

kritisch ['kriː·tɪʃ] I. adj critical II. adv critically

kritisieren* [kri·ti·ˈziː·rən] vt to criticize

Kritzelei <-, -en> [krɪ·tsə·ˈlai] f (pej fam: Gekritzel) scribble

kritzeln ['krɪ·tsln] vt, vi to scribble

Krokette <-, -n> [kro·ˈkɛ·tə] f croquette

Krokodil <-s, -e> [kro·ko·ˈdiːl] nt crocodile

Krokodilstränen pl (fam) crocodile tears pl

Krone <-, -n> ['kroː·nə] f ❶ (Kopfschmuck, Zahnkrone) crown ❷ (Baumkrone) top ❸ (Währungseinheit: in Skandinavien) krone; (in der Tschechei) crown ▶WENDUNGEN: **einen in der ~ haben** (fam) to have had one too many; **die ~ sein** (fam) to beat everything

krönen ['krøː·nən] vt to crown

Kronprinz, -prinzessin m, f crown prince masc, crown princess fem

Krönung <-, -en> f ❶ (Höhepunkt) high point ❷ (das Krönen) coronation

Kropf <-[e]s, Kröpfe> [krɔpf] m ORN crop

Kröte <-, -n> ['krøː·tə] f ❶ ZOOL toad ❷ pl (sl: Geld) pennies pl ❸ (pej: Kind) brat

Krücke <-, -n> ['krʏ·kə] f crutch; **an ~n gehen** to walk on crutches

Krug <-[e]s, Krüge> [kruːk] m (Gefäß) jug; (Trinkgefäß) tankard

Krümel <-s, -> ['kryː·ml] m crumb

krümelig ['kryː·mə·lɪç] adj crumbly

krumm [krʊm] I. adj ❶ (verbogen) crooked; **~ und schief** askew ❷ (gebogen) Nase hooked; Rücken hunched; Beine bowed ❸ (pej fam: unehrlich) crooked; **ein ~es Ding drehen** to pull a fast one sl; **es auf die ~e Tour versu-**

chen to try to pull some monkey business with sth *s/*II. *adv* ~ **gehen** to walk with a stoop ►WENDUNGEN: **sich** *akk* ~ **und schief lachen** (*fam*) to bust a gut laughing

krümmen ['krʏ·mən] I. *vt* to bend II. *vr* ■ **sich** *akk* ~ *Fluss* to wind; *Straße* to bend; **sich** *akk* ~ **vor Schmerzen/ Lachen** ~ to double up in pain/with laughter

krummlnehmen *vt irreg* (*fam*) ■ **[jdm] etw** ~ to take offense at sth [sb said or did]

Kruste <-, -n> ['krʊs·tə] *f* crust; *eines Bratens* cracklings *pl*; *einer Wunde* scab

Kruzifix <-es, -e> ['kru·tsi·fɪks] *nt* crucifix

Krypta <-, Krypten> ['krʏp·ta] *f* crypt

Kuba <-s> ['ku:·ba] *nt* Cuba; *s. a.* **Deutschland**

Kubaner(in) <-s, -> [ku·'ba:·nɐ] *m(f)* Cuban; *s. a.* **Deutsche(r)**

Kübel <-s, -> ['ky:·bl̩] *m* ❶ (*großer Eimer*) bucket ❷ (*Pflanzkübel*) container

Kubikmeter [ku·'bi:k-] *m o nt* cubic meter

Küche <-, -n> ['kʏ·çə] *f* kitchen

Kuchen <-s, -> ['ku:·xn̩] *m* cake

Küchenchef(in) *m(f)* chef

Kuchenform *f* cake pan

Küchenherd *m* stove

Küchenschabe *f* cockroach

Kuckuck <-s, -e> ['kʊ·kʊk] *m* ORN cuckoo ►WENDUNGEN: **[das] weiß der ~!** (*fam*) God only knows!; **zum ~ [noch mal]!** (*fam*) [god]damn it!

Kuddelmuddel <-s> *m o nt kein pl* (*fam*) ❶ muddle; (*Unordnung*) mess ❷ (*Verwirrung*) confusion

Kugel <-, -n> ['ku:·gl̩] *f* ❶ MATH sphere ❷ SPORT ball; (*Kegelkugel*) bowling ball ❸ (*Geschoss*) bullet ►WENDUNGEN: **eine ruhige ~ schieben** (*fam*) to have it pretty easy

kugelförmig *adj* spherical

kugeln ['ku:·gl̩n] *vi sein* to roll ►WENDUNGEN: **zum K~ sein** (*fam*) to be hilarious

kugelrund ['ku:·gl̩·'rʊnt] *adj* ❶ (*kugelförmig*) round as a ball *pred* ❷ (*fam: dick*) tubby

Kugelschreiber *m* ballpoint pen

kugelsicher *adj* bulletproof

Kuh <-, Kühe> [ku:] *f* ❶ ZOOL cow ❷ (*pej fam: Frau*) bitch; **blöde ~** stupid chick

Kuhhandel *m* (*pej fam*) horse trade

kühl [ky:l] I. *adj* ❶ (*recht kalt*) cool ❷ (*reserviert*) cool II. *adv* ❶ (*recht kalt*) **etw ~ lagern** to store sth in a cool place ❷ (*reserviert*) coolly

Kühlbox *f* cooler

kühlen ['ky:·lən] I. *vt* to chill II. *vi* to cool

Kühler <-s, -> ['ky:·lɐ] *m* AUTO radiator

Kühlerhaube *f* hood

Kühlraum *m* cold [*or* refrigerated] storage room

Kühlschrank *m* refrigerator, fridge *fam*

Kühltruhe *f* freezer [chest]

Kühlwasser *nt kein pl* coolant

kühn [ky:n] *adj* ❶ (*wagemutig*) brave ❷ (*gewagt*) *Behauptung etc.* bold

Kuhstall *m* cowshed

Küken <-s, -> ['ky:·kn̩] *nt* chick

kulant [ku·'lant] *adj* obliging

Kuli <-s, -s> ['ku:·li] *m* (*fam*) pen

kulinarisch [ku·li·'na:·rɪʃ] *adj* culinary

Kulisse <-, -n> [ku·'lɪ·sə] *f* THEAT scenery ►WENDUNGEN: **hinter die ~n blicken** to look behind the scenes

kullern ['kʊ·lɐn] *vi sein* (*fam*) to roll

Kult <-[e]s, -e> [kʊlt] *m* cult

Kultfigur *f* cult figure

kultivieren* [kʊl·ti·'vi:·rən] *vt* to cultivate

kultiviert [kʊl·ti·'vi:·ɐt] I. *adj* (*gepflegt*) *Mensch* cultured; *Benehmen* refined II. *adv* (*gepflegt*) in a refined manner

Kultstätte *f* place of ritual worship

Kultur <-, -en> [kʊl·'tu:ɐ] *f* culture

Kulturbanause *m* (*pej fam*) philistine

Kulturbeutel *m* toiletries bag

kulturell [kʊl·tu·'rɛl] I. *adj* cultural II. *adv* culturally

Kümmel <-s, -> ['kʏ·ml̩] *m* caraway

Kummer <-s> ['kʊ·mɐ] *m kein pl* grief

K

kümmerlich ['kʏ·mɐ·lɪç] I. *adj* ❶ (*pej: armselig*) miserable; *Mahlzeit* measly ❷ (*miserabel*) pitiful II. *adv* (*notdürftig*) in a miserable way

kümmern ['kʏ·mɐn] I. *vt* ■ **etw/jd kümmert jdn** sth/sb concerns sb; **was kümmert mich das?** what concern is that of mine? II. *vr* ■ **sich** *akk* **um jdn ~** to look after sb; ■ **sich** *akk* **um etw ~** to take care of sth; ■ **sich** *akk* **darum ~, dass ...** to see to it that ...; **kümmere dich um deine eigenen Angelegenheiten** mind your own business

Kumpan(in) <-s, -e> [kʊm·'pa:n] *m(f)* (*pej fam*) pal

Kumpel <-s, -> *m* ❶ (*Bergmann*) miner ❷ (*fam: Kamerad*) buddy

Kunde, Kundin <-n,-n> ['kʊn·də, 'kʊn·dɪn] *m, f* customer

Kundendienst *m* customer service

Kundenkarte *f* customer card

Kundennummer *f* customer account number

Kundgebung <-, -en> *f* rally

kündigen ['kʏn·dɪ·gn̩] I. *vi* ❶ (*Arbeitsverhältnis beenden*) ■ **jdm ~** to give sb notice, to lay off *sep* sb; **jdm fristlos ~** to lay off *sep* sb without notice ❷ (*Mietverhältnis beenden*) **dem Mieter/Vermieter ~** to give a tenant/landlord notice II. *vt* (*Arbeitsverhältnis beenden*) ■ **jdn ~** to give sb notice, to lay off *sep* sb; **jdn fristlos ~** to lay off *sep* sb without notice

Kündigung <-, -en> *f* ❶ (*durch den Arbeitnehmer*) handing in one's notice; (*durch den Arbeitgeber*) dismissal, layoff; **fristlose ~** dismissal without notice ❷ *eines Abonnements, Kredits* cancellation; *eines Vertrags* termination

Kündigungsfrist *f* period of notice

Kundin <-, -nen> *f fem form von* **Kunde**

Kundschaft <-, -en> ['kʊnt·ʃaft] *f* customers *pl*; (*bei Dienstleistungen*) clientele

künftig ['kʏnf·tɪç] I. *adj* future II. *adv* in the future

Kunst <-, Künste> [kʊnst] *f* art ►WENDUNGEN: **keine ~ sein** (*fam*) to be easy

Kunstausstellung *f* art exhibt[ion]

Kunstfaser *f* synthetic fiber

kunstfertig I. *adj* skillful II. *adv* skillfully

Kunstgegenstand *m* objet d'art, piece of art

Kunstgriff *m* trick

Kunstleder *nt* imitation leather

Künstler(in) <-s, -> ['kʏnst·lɐ] *m(f)* [visual] artist

künstlerisch ['kʏnst·lə·rɪʃ] I. *adj* artistic II. *adv* artistically

Künstlername *m* pseudonym; *eines Schauspielers* stage name

künstlich ['kʏnst·lɪç] I. *adj* artificial II. *adv* artificially

Kunstsammlung *f* art collection

Kunstseide *f* imitation silk

Kunststoff *m* synthetic material

Kunststück *nt* ❶ (*artistische Leistung*) trick ❷ (*schwierige Leistung*) feat; **das ist doch kein ~!** (*fam*) there's nothing to it!

Kunstwerk *nt* work of art

kunterbunt ['kʊn·tɐ·bʊnt] I. *adj* ❶ (*vielfältig*) varied ❷ (*sehr bunt*) colorful ❸ (*wahllos gemischt*) motley; **ein ~es Durcheinander** a jumble II. *adv* (*ungeordnet*) ~ **durcheinander** completely jumbled up

Kupfer <-s, -> ['kʊ·pfɐ] *nt* copper

Kuppe <-, -n> ['kʊ·pə] *f* ❶ (*Bergkuppe*) [rounded] hilltop ❷ (*Fingerkuppe*) tip

Kuppel <-, -n> ['kʊ·pl̩] *f* dome

kuppeln ['kʊ·pl̩n] I. *vi* AUTO to work the clutch II. *vt* to couple (**an** +*akk* to)

Kupplung <-, -en> ['kʊp·lʊŋ] *f* ❶ AUTO clutch ❷ (*Anhängevorrichtung*) coupling

Kur <-, -en> [ku:ɐ] *f* treatment [at a health resort]

Kurbel <-, -n> ['kʊr·bl̩] *f* crank

Kurbelwelle *f* crankshaft

Kürbis <-ses, -se> ['kʏr·bɪs] *m* pumpkin

Kurhaus *nt* main facility at a spa

Kurier <-s, -e> [ku·'ri:ɐ] *m* courier

Kurierdienst *m* courier [service]

kurieren* [ku·ˈriː·rən] *vt* to cure (**von** +*dat* of)

kurios [ku·ˈri̯oːs] (*geh*) **I.** *adj* curious **II.** *adv* curiously

Kuriosität <-, -en> [ku·ri̯o·zi·ˈtɛt] *f* (*geh*) ❶ *kein pl* (*kuriose Art*) oddity ❷ (*kurioser Gegenstand*) curiosity

Kurort *m* spa, health resort

Kurs <-es, -e> [kʊrs] *m* ❶ (*Richtung*) course ❷ (*Lehrgang*) course ❸ (*Wechselkurs*) exchange rate

kursieren* [kʊr·ˈziː·rən] *vi Falschgeld* to be in circulation; *Gerücht* to circulate

kursiv [kʊr·ˈziːf] **I.** *adj* italic **II.** *adv* in italics

Kursivschrift *f* italics

Kurve <-, -n> [ˈkʊr·və] *f* ❶ MATH, TRANSP curve; **aus der ~ fliegen** (*fam*) to wipe out on a curve ❷ *pl* (*fam: Körperrundung*) curves *pl* ▶WENDUNGEN: **die ~ kratzen** (*fam*) to scram *sl*, to beat it *sl*

kurvig [ˈkʊr·vɪç] *adj* curvy

kurz <kürzer, kürzeste> [kʊrts] **I.** *adj* ❶ (*räumlich*) short ❷ (*zeitlich*) brief, short ❸ (*knapp*) brief ▶WENDUNGEN: **den Kürzeren ziehen** (*fam*) to draw the short straw **II.** *adv* ❶ (*räumlich*) short; **jdm**| **etw kürzer machen** MODE to shorten sth [for sb] ❷ (*zeitlich*) for a short time; **etw ~ braten** to flash-fry sth; **~ gesagt** in a word; **jdn ~ sprechen** to have a quick word with sb; **~ bevor** just before; **~ nachdem** shortly after; **vor ~em** just a little while ago; **bis vor ~em** up until recently ▶WENDUNGEN: **~ entschlossen** without a moment's hesitation; **~ und gut** in a word; **|bei etw *dat*| zu ~ kommen** to lose out [on sth]; **über ~ oder lang** sooner or later; **~ und schmerzlos** (*fam*) quick[ly] and painless[ly]

Kurzarbeit *f kein pl* reduced working hours

kurz|arbeiten *vi* to work reduced hours

kurzärm(e)lig *adj* short-sleeved

kürzen [ˈkʏr·tsn̩] *vt* ❶ (*Länge/Umfang verringern*) to shorten (**um** +*akk* by) ❷ (*verringern*) to cut, to reduce

kurzerhand [ˈkʊr·tse·ˈhant] *adv* there and then

Kurzfassung *f* abridged version

Kurzfilm *m* short film

Kurzform *f* shortened form

kurzfristig [ˈkʊrts·frɪs·tɪç] **I.** *adj* ❶ (*innerhalb kurzer Zeit*) on short notice ❷ (*für kurze Zeit*) short-term **II.** *adv* ❶ (*innerhalb kurzer Zeit*) within a short [period of] time ❷ (*für kurze Zeit*) briefly

Kurzgeschichte *f* short story

kurzlebig [ˈkʊrts·leː·bɪç] *adj* short-lived

kürzlich [ˈkʏrts·lɪç] *adv* not long ago

Kurznachrichten *pl* news in brief + *sing vb*

Kurzschluss[RR] *m* ELEK short circuit

Kurzschlussreaktion[RR] *f* knee-jerk reaction

kurzsichtig I. *adj* (*a. fig*) shortsighted **II.** *adv* (*beschränkt*) in a shortsighted manner

Kurzstreckenflug *m* short-haul flight

Kürzung <-, -en> *f* ❶ *Text* abridgement ❷ FIN cut

Kurzwaren *pl* dry goods *npl*

kurzweilig [ˈkʊrts·vai·lɪç] *adj* entertaining

Kurzwelle *f* short wave

Kurzzeitgedächtnis *m* short-term memory

kuscheln [ˈkʊ·ʃln̩] **I.** *vr* ■ **sich** *akk* **an jdn ~** to cuddle up to sb; ■ **sich** *akk* **in etw** *akk* **~** to snuggle up in sth **II.** *vi* to cuddle (**mit** +*dat* with)

Kuschelrock <-s, -> *m kein pl* MUS soft rock

kuschen [ˈkʊ·ʃn̩] *vi* ■ **|vor jdm|** **~** to obey [sb]

Kusine <-, -n> [ku·ˈziː·nə] *f fem form von* **Cousin** cousin

Kuss[RR] <-es, Küsse>, **Kuß**[ALT] <-sses, Küsse> [kʊs] *m* kiss

küssen [ˈkʏ·sn̩] *vt, vi* to kiss

Küste <-, -n> [ˈkʏs·tə] *f* coast

Küstengewässer *pl* coastal waters *pl*

Küstenschifffahrt[RR] *f kein pl* coastal shipping

Kutsche <-, -n> [ˈkʊt·ʃə] *f* carriage

Kutte <-, -n> [ˈkʊ·tə] *f* habit

K

Kuttel <-, -n> ['kʊ·tl̩] *f meist pl* tripe *sing*

Kutter <-s, -> ['kʊ·tɐ] *m* cutter

Kuvert <-s, -s> [ku·'veːɐ̯] *nt* envelope

Kuwait <-s> ['kuː·vait] *nt* Kuwait; *s. a.* **Deutschland**

Kuwaiter(in) *m(f)* Kuwaiti; *s. a.* **Deutsche(r)**

KZ <-s, -s> [kaː·'tsɛt] *nt Abk von* **Konzentrationslager**

L

L, l <-, -> [ɛl] *nt* L, l; **~ wie Ludwig** L as in Lima

l [ɛl] *Abk von* **Liter** l

labil [la·'biːl] *adj* ❶ MED *Gesundheit, Kreislauf etc.* poor ❷ *(geh: instabil)* unstable

Labor <-s, -s> [la·'boːɐ̯] *nt* laboratory, lab *fam*

Laborant(in) <-en, -en> [la·bo·'rant] *m(f)* laboratory technician

Labyrinth <-[e]s, -e> [la·by·'rɪnt] *nt* maze

Lache <-, -n> ['la·xə] *f (zusammengelaufene Flüssigkeit)* puddle

lächeln ['lɛ·çl̩n] *vi* to smile

Lächeln <-s> ['lɛ·çl̩n] *nt kein pl* smile

lachen ['la·xn̩] *vi* to laugh **(über** +*akk* at) ▶WENDUNGEN: **gut ~ haben** to be all right for sb to laugh

Lachen <-s> ['la·xn̩] *nt kein pl* ❶ *(Gelächter)* laughter ❷ *(Lache)* laugh

lächerlich ['lɛ·çe·lɪç] **I.** *adj* ❶ *(albern)* ridiculous; **sich/jdn ~ machen** to make a fool of oneself/sb ❷ *(geringfügig)* trivial **II.** *adv (sehr)* ridiculously

lachhaft *adj* laughable

Lachs <-es, -e> [laks] *m* salmon

Lack <-[e]s, -e> [lak] *m* ❶ *(Lackierung)* paint [job] ❷ *(Lackfarbe)* glossy paint; *(transparent)* varnish

lackieren* [la·'kiː·rən] *vt a. Fingernägel* to paint; *Holz* to varnish

Lackleder <-s> *nt* patent leather

laden¹ <lädt, lud, geladen> ['laː·dn̩] **I.** *vt* ❶ *(packen)* to load **(auf** +*akk* on[to], **in** +*akk* in[to]), to unload **(aus** +*dat* from/out of) ❷ COMPUT to load ❸ *(sich aufbürden)* ■ **etw auf sich** *akk* ~ to saddle oneself with sth ❹ *(mit Munition versehen)* to load **(mit** +*dat* with) ❺ ELEK to charge **II.** *vi* ▶WENDUNGEN: **geladen sein** *(fam)* to be hopping mad

laden² <lädt, lud, geladen> ['laː·dn̩] *vt* JUR to summon

Laden¹ <-s, Läden> ['laː·dn̩] *m (Geschäft)* store, shop

Laden² <-s, Läden> ['laː·dn̩] *m* shutter

Ladendieb(in) *m(f)* shoplifter

Ladenhüter *m (pej)* slow seller

Ladenpreis *m* retail price

Ladenschluss^RR *m kein pl* closing time

Laderampe *f* loading ramp

Laderaum *m* LUFT, NAUT cargo space

lädieren* [lɛ·'diː·rən] *vt* to damage

Ladung¹ <-, -en> *f* ❶ *(Fracht)* load; *von Flugzeug, Schiff* cargo ❷ *(fam: größere Menge)* load ❸ *(Munition, Sprengstoff)* charge

Ladung² <-, -en> *f* JUR summons + *sing vb*

Lage <-, -n> ['laː·gə] *f* ❶ *(geographisch)* location ❷ *(Liegeposition)* position ❸ *(Situation)* situation; **zu etw** *dat* **in der ~ sein** to be in a position to do sth; **sich** *akk* **in jds ~ versetzen** to put oneself in sb's position ❹ *(Schicht)* layer

Lager <-s, -> ['laː·gɐ] *nt* ❶ *(Warenlager)* warehouse; **etw auf ~ haben** to have sth in stock ❷ (*vorübergehende Unterkunft*) camp ❸ (*ideologische Gruppierung*) camp ❹ TECH bearing

Lagerfeuer *nt* campfire

lagern ['laː·gən] I. *vt* (*aufbewahren*) to store II. *vi* ❶ (*aufbewahrt werden*) **dunkel/kühl ~** to be stored in the dark/a cold place ❷ (*liegen*) to lie (**auf** +*dat* on) ❸ (*sich niederlassen*) to camp

Lagerraum *m* ❶ (*Raum*) storeroom ❷ (*Fläche*) storage space

Lagerung <-, -en> *f* storage, warehousing

lahm [laːm] *adj* ❶ (*gelähmt*) Arm, Bein lame ❷ (*fam: steif*) stiff ❸ (*fam: ohne Schwung arbeitend*) sluggish ❹ (*fam: schwach*) lame; *Erklärung* feeble

lähmen ['lɛː·mən] *vt* to paralyze

lahm|legen *vt* Verkehr to bring to a standstill

Lähmung <-, -en> *f* paralysis

Laib <-[e]s, -e> [laip] *m bes* SÜDD loaf; (*Käse*) block

Laich <-[e]s, -e> [laiç] *m* spawn

laichen ['lai·çn̩] *vi* to spawn

Laie, Laiin <-n, -n> ['laiə, 'lai·ɪn] *m, f* layman, layperson

Lake <-, -n> ['laː·kə] *f* brine

Laken <-s, -> ['laː·kn̩] *nt* sheet

Lakritze <-, -n> [la·'krɪt·sə] *f* licorice

lallen ['la·lən] *vt, vi* to slur

Lama <-s, -s> ['laː·ma] *nt* ZOOL llama

Lamelle <-, -n> [la·'mɛ·lə] *f* ❶ (*dünne Platte*) slat ❷ (*Segment*) rib ❸ BOT lamella

Lametta <-s> [la·'mɛ·ta] *nt kein pl* tinsel

Lamm <-[e]s, Lämmer> [lam] *nt* (*a. Fleisch*) lamb

Lammfell *nt* lambskin

Lampe <-, -n> ['lam·pə] *f* lamp

Lampenfieber *nt* stage fright

Lampenschirm *m* lampshade

Land <-[e]s, Länder> [lant] *nt* ❶ (*Staat*) country; **andere Länder, andere Sitten** every country has its own customs ❷ (*Bundesland*) [federal] state ❸ NAUT land; **~ in Sicht!** land ahoy!; **an ~ gehen** to go ashore; **jdn/**

etw an ~ ziehen to pull sb/sth ashore ❹ *kein pl* (*Gelände*) land ❺ *kein pl* (*ländliche Gegend*) country; **auf dem ~[e]** in the country

Landarbeiter(in) *m(f)* farm hand

Landebahn *f* runway

landeinwärts *adv* inland

landen ['lan·dn̩] I. *vi sein* ❶ (*niedergehen*) Flugzeug, Raumschiff, Vogel to land (**auf** +*dat* on) ❷ (*fam: hingelangen o enden*) to end up ❸ (*fam: Eindruck machen*) **mit deinen Schmeicheleien kannst du bei mir nicht ~** your flattery won't get you very far with me II. *vt haben* LUFT, RAUM, MIL to land

Ländereien [lɛn·də·'rai·ən] *pl* estates *pl*

Landesgrenze *f* ❶ (*Staatsgrenze*) border ❷ (*Grenze eines Bundeslandes*) state border [*or* line]

Landesinnere(s) *nt* interior

Landesregierung *f* state government

Landesverrat *m* treason

Landfriedensbruch *m* disturbing the peace

Landgericht *nt* district court

Landhaus *nt* country manor

Landkarte *f* map

Landkreis *m* administrative district

landläufig *adj* generally accepted; *Ansicht* popular

Landleben *nt* country life

ländlich ['lɛnt·lɪç] *adj* rural; *Idylle* pastoral

Landschaft <-, -en> ['lant·ʃaft] *f* landscape

landschaftlich *adv* ~ **schön** scenic

Landsmann, -männin <-leute> *m, f* compatriot

Landstraße *f* country road

Landstreicher(in) <-s, -> *m(f)* tramp

Landtag *m* state parliament

Landung <-, -en> *f* (*a. mil*) landing

Landungsbrücke *f* pier

Landvermessung *f* [land] surveying

Landwirt(in) *m(f)* farmer

Landwirtschaft *f* ❶ *kein pl* (*Tätigkeit*) agriculture ❷ (*landwirtschaftlicher Betrieb*) farm

landwirtschaftlich I. adj agricultural; Betrieb farm **II.** adv agriculturally

lang <länger, längste> [laŋ] **I.** adj ① (räumlich ausgedehnt) long ② (zeitlich ausgedehnt) long; **noch/schon ~** for a long time ③ (fam: groß gewachsen) tall **II.** adv ① (eine lange Dauer) long; **die Verhandlungen ziehen sich schon ~e hin** the negotiations have been dragging on for a long time; **wo bist du denn so ~e geblieben?** where have you been all this time? ② (für die Dauer von etwas) **sie hielt einen Moment ~ inne** she paused for a moment ③ (der Länge nach) **~ gestreckt** long; **~ gezogen** prolonged

langatmig adj (pej) long-winded

lange ['laŋə] adv s. **lang II 1**

Länge <-, -n> ['lɛŋə] f ① (räumlich) length; **der ~ nach** lengthwise; **Pfähle von drei Metern ~** ten-foot-long poles ② (zeitlich) length, duration; **in voller ~** in its entirety; **sich** akk **in die ~ ziehen** to drag on ③ (fam: Größe) height ④ SPORT length ⑤ (Abstand vom Nullmeridian) longitude

langen ['laŋən] **I.** vi (fam) ① (ausreichen) ▪ **[jdm] ~** to be enough [for sb] ② (fassen, reichen) to reach; **lange bloß nicht mit der Hand an die Herdplatte** make sure you don't touch the hot plate with your hand ③ impers (fam) **jetzt langt's aber!** I've just about had enough! **II.** vt (fam) (reichen) ▪ **jdm etw ~** to hand sb sth ▶WENDUNG: **jdm eine ~** (fam) to smack sb in the mouth

Längengrad m degree of longitude

längerfristig I. adj fairly long-term **II.** adv on a fairly long-term basis

Langeweile <-> ['laŋə·vai·lə] f kein pl boredom

langfristig I. adj long-term **II.** adv on a long-term basis

langjährig adj of many years' standing; Freundschaft long-standing

Langlauf m kein pl cross-country skiing

langlebig adj ① (lange lebend) long-

lived ② (lange Zeit zu gebrauchen) long-lasting ③ (hartnäckig) persistent

länglich ['lɛŋ·lɪç] adj longish

längs [lɛŋs] **I.** präp +gen ▪ **~ einer S.** gen along sth **II.** adv (der Länge nach) lengthwise; **~ gestreift** with vertical stripes

langsam ['laŋ·za:m] **I.** adj ① (nicht schnell) slow ② (allmählich) gradual **II.** adv ① (nicht schnell) slowly ② (fam: allmählich) gradually

Langsamkeit <-> f kein pl slowness

Langschläfer(in) m(f) late riser

längst [lɛŋst] adv ① (lange) long since, for a long time ② (bei weitem) **~ nicht** by no means

längste(r, s) adj, adv superl von **lang**

längstens ['lɛŋ·stns] adv ① (höchstens) at the most ② (spätestens) at the latest

Langstreckenflug m long-haul flight

Languste <-, -n> [laŋ·ˈɡʊs·tə] f crayfish

langweilen ['laŋ·vai·lən] **I.** vt to bore **II.** vi (pej) to be boring **III.** vr ▪ **sich** akk ~ to be bored

langweilig ['laŋ·vai·lɪç] **I.** adj boring **II.** adv boringly

Langwelle f long wave

langwierig ['laŋ·vi:·rɪç] adj long-drawn-out

Langzeitarbeitslose(r) f(m) dekl wie adj long-term unemployed person

Langzeitarbeitslosigkeit f long-term unemployment

Langzeitgedächtnis nt long-term memory

Lanze <-, -n> ['lan·tsə] f lance

Lappalie <-, -n> [la·ˈpa:·liə] f trifle

Lappen <-s, -> ['lapn] m rag ▶WENDUNG: **jdm durch die ~ gehen** (fam) to slip through sb's fingers

läppisch ['lɛpɪʃ] **I.** adj ① (fam: lächerlich) Betrag ridiculous ② (pej: albern) silly **II.** adv (pej) in a silly manner

Laptop <-s, -s> ['lɛp·tɔp] m laptop

Lärche <-, -n> ['lɛr·çə] f BOT larch

Lärm <-[e]s> [lɛrm] m kein pl noise

Lärmbelästigung f noise pollution

lärmempfindlich adj sensitive to noise

lärmen ['lɛr·mən] vi to be noisy

Lärmpegel *m* noise level
Lärmschutz *m* noise protection
Larve <-, -n> ['lar·fə] *f* larva, grub
lasch [laʃ] I. *adj* (*fam*) ❶ (*schlaff*) feeble; *Händedruck* limp ❷ (*nachsichtig*) lax II. *adv* (*fam: schlaff*) limply
Lasche <-, -n> ['la·ʃə] *f* flap; (*Kleidung*) loop
Laser <-s, -> ['le:·zɐ] *m* laser
Laserdrucker *m* laser printer
lassen <lässt, ließ, gelassen> ['la·sn̩]
I. *vt* ❶ (*unterlassen*) to stop; **wenn du keine Lust dazu hast, dann lass es doch** if you don't feel like it, [then] don't do it; **er kann es nicht ~** he can't help [*or* stop] it ❷ (*zurücklassen*) ■**jdn/etw irgendwo ~** to leave sb/sth somewhere ❸ (*überlassen, behalten lassen*) ■**jdm etw ~** to let sb have sth; **ich lasse dir das Auto** you can have the car ❹ (*gehen lassen*) to let; **lass den Hund nicht nach draußen** don't let the dog out ❺ (*in einem Zustand lassen*) **jdn ohne Aufsicht ~** to leave sb unsupervised ❻ (*fam: loslassen*) ■**jdn/etw ~** to let sb/sth go ❼ (*in Ruhe lassen*) ■**jdn ~** to leave sb alone ❽ (*gewähren lassen*) **ich möchte so gerne mit, lässt du mich?** I really want to go along — will you let me? ❾ (*hineinlassen*) **frische Luft ins Zimmer ~** to let some fresh air into the room ❿ (*hinauslassen*) **sie haben mir die Luft aus den Reifen gelassen!** they let the air out of my tires! ⓫ (*zugestehen*) **eines muss man ihm ~, er versteht sein Handwerk** you have to give him one thing: he knows his job ▶WENDUNGEN: **einen ~** (*fam*) to let one rip II. *aux vb* <lässt, ließ, lassen> *modal* (*veranlassen*) ■**jdn etw tun ~** to have sb do sth; **jdn kommen ~** to send for sb; **~ Sie Herrn Braun hereinkommen** send Mr. Braun in; **der Chef hat es nicht gerne, wenn man ihn warten lässt** the boss doesn't like to be kept waiting; ■**etw machen ~** to have sth done; **ich lasse mir die Haare schneiden** I'm going to get a haircut ❷ (*zulas-*

sen) ■**jdn etw tun ~** to let sb do sth; **lass sie gehen!** let her go!; **er lässt sich nicht so leicht betrügen** it won't be that easy to trick him; **das lasse ich nicht mit mir machen** I won't stand for it!; **viel mit sich machen ~** to put up with a lot ❸ (*belassen*) **das Wasser sollte man eine Minute kochen ~** the water should be allowed to boil for one minute ❹ (*Möglichkeit ausdrückend*) **das lässt sich machen!** that can be done! ❺ *als imper* **lass uns jetzt lieber gehen** let's go now III. *vi* <lässt, ließ, gelassen> (*ablassen*) **sie kann einfach nicht von ihm ~** she simply can't part from him; **vom Alkohol ~** to give up alcohol; **lass nur!** that's all right!

lässig ['lɛsɪç] I. *adj* (*ungezwungen*) casual II. *adv* ❶ (*ungezwungen*) casually ❷ (*fam: mit Leichtigkeit*) no problem
Last <-, -en> [last] *f* ❶ (*zu tragender Gegenstand*) load ❷ (*schweres Gewicht*) weight ❸ (*Bürde*) burden ❹ *pl* (*finanzielle Belastung*) burden; **zu jds ~en gehen** to be charged to sb ▶WENDUNGEN: **jdm zur ~ fallen** to become a burden on sb
lasten ['las·tn̩] *vi* ❶ (*als Last liegen auf*) to rest (**auf** +*dat* on) ❷ (*eine Bürde sein*) ■**auf jdm ~** *Verantwortung* to rest with sb ❸ (*stark belasten*) ■**auf etw** *dat* ~ to weigh heavily on sth
Laster[1] <-s, -> ['las·tɐ] *m* (*fam: Lastwagen*) truck
Laster[2] <-s, -> ['las·tɐ] *nt* (*schlechte Gewohnheit*) vice
lästern ['lɛs·tɐn] *vi* to make disparaging remarks (**über** +*akk* about)
lästig ['lɛs·tɪç] *adj* ❶ (*unangenehm*) *Husten, Kopfschmerzen etc.* irritating ❷ (*störend, nervend*) annoying; *Person a.* tiresome
Lastwagen *m* truck
Lastzug *m* tractor-trailer
Lasur <-, -en> [la·'zuːɐ] *f* (*clear*) varnish
Latein <-s> [la·'tain] *nt* Latin ▶WENDUNGEN: **mit seinem ~ am Ende sein** to be at one's wits' end

L

Lateinamerika nt Latin America
Lateinamerikaner(in) <-s, -> m(f) Latin American; *s. a.* **Deutsche(r)**
lateinamerikanisch adj Latin American; *s. a.* **deutsch**
lateinisch adj Latin
Laterne <-, -n> [la·'tɛr·nə] f lantern; (Straßenlaterne) street lamp
Laternenpfahl m lamppost
Latex <-, Latizes> ['la:·tɛks] m latex
latschen ['la:t·ʃn] vi sein (fam) ① (schlurfen) to trudge ② (lässig gehen) to wander
Latschen <-s, -> ['la:t·ʃn] m (fam) ① (Hausschuh) slipper ② (pej: ausgetretener Schuh) worn-out shoe ▶WENDUNGEN: **aus den ~ kippen** (fam) to keel over; (sehr überrascht sein) to be bowled over
Latschenkiefer f mountain pine
Latte <-, -n> ['la·tə] f ① (kantiges Brett) slat ② SPORT bar ③ (Torlatte) crossbar ▶WENDUNGEN: **eine ganze ~ von etw** dat (fam) a slew of sth
Lattenzaun m picket fence
Latz <-es, Lätze o ÖSTERR -e> [lats] m bib
Latzhose f overalls npl
lau [lau] adj ① (mild) mild ② (lauwarm) lukewarm; (mäßig) moderate ③ (halbherzig) half-hearted
Laub <-[e]s> [laup] nt kein pl foliage
Laubbaum m deciduous tree
Laube <-, -n> ['lau·bə] f arbor
Laubfrosch m tree frog
Laubsäge f jigsaw
Laubwald m deciduous forest
Lauch <-[e]s, -e> [laux] m leek
Lauer <-> ['laue] f **auf der ~ liegen** to lie in wait
lauern ['lau·en] vi ① (in einem Versteck warten) to lie in wait (auf +akk for) ② (fam) **die anderen lauerten nur darauf, dass sie einen Fehler machte** the others were just waiting for her to make a mistake
Lauf <-[e]s, Läufe> [lauf] m ① kein pl (das Laufen) run ② SPORT (Durchgang) round; (Rennen) heat ③ kein pl eines

Flusses course; *eines Sterns* path ④ (Verlauf, Entwicklung) course; **das ist der ~ der Dinge** that's the way things go; **seinen ~ nehmen** to take its course ⑤ (Gewehrlauf) barrel ▶WENDUNGEN: **etw** dat **freien ~ lassen** to give sth free rein
Laufbahn f career
laufen <läuft, lief, gelaufen> ['lau·fn] I. vi sein ① (rennen, Sport) to run ② (fam: gehen) to go ③ (zu Fuß gehen) to walk ④ (fließen) to run; **jdm eiskalt über den Rücken ~** (fig) a chill runs down sb's spine ⑤ (funktionieren) to work; *Getriebe, Maschine, Motor* to run; (eingeschaltet sein) to be on ⑥ FILM, THEAT (gezeigt werden) **was läuft [im Kino]?** what's playing [at the movies]? ⑦ (gültig sein) *Vertrag* to run ⑧ (seinen Gang gehen) to go; **wie läuft es?** how's it going? ⑨ (geführt werden) **auf jds Namen ~** to be issued in sb's name ▶WENDUNGEN: **die Sache ist gelaufen** it's too late now II. vt haben o sein ① SPORT to run; **einen Rekord ~** to set a record ② (zurücklegen) to run ③ (fahren) **Rollschuh/ Schlittschuh/Ski ~** to roller-skate/ice-skate/ski III. vr impers haben **mit diesen Schuhen wird es sich besser ~** it will be easier to walk in these shoes
laufend I. adj attr ① (geh: derzeitig) current ② (ständig) constant ▶WENDUNGEN: **jdn [über etw** akk] **auf dem L~en halten** to keep sb up-to-date [on sth] II. adv (fam) constantly
Läufer[1] <-s, -> ['lɔy·fe] m ① (Schachfigur) bishop ② (Teppich) runner
Läufer(in)[2] <-s, -; -nen> ['lɔy·fe] m(f) runner
läufig ['lɔy·fɪç] adj in heat
Laufkundschaft f kein pl window-shoppers
Laufmasche f run
Laufschritt m **im ~** at a quick pace; MIL double time
Laufstall m playpen
Laufsteg m catwalk
Laufwerk nt einer Maschine drive

mechanism; *einer Uhr* clockwork; *eines Computers* disk drive

Lauge <-, -n> ['lau·gə] *f* ❶ *(Seifenlauge)* soapy water, suds ❷ *(wässrige Lösung einer Base)* lye; *(von Salz)* salt solution

Laune <-, -n> ['lau·nə] *f* ❶ *(Stimmung)* mood; **schlechte ~ haben** to be in a bad mood; **seine ~n an jdm auslassen** to take it out on sb *fig fam* ❷ *(abwegige Idee)* whim

Laus <-, Läuse> [laus] *f* ❶ *(Blut saugendes Insekt)* louse ❷ *(Blattlaus)* aphid

lauschen ['lau·ʃn] *vi (heimlich zuhören)* to eavesdrop

lauschig ['lau·ʃɪç] *adj (veraltend: gemütlich)* snug

lausen ['lau·zn] *vt* to delouse

lausig ['lau·zɪç] *(pej)* **I.** *adj* ❶ *(fam: entsetzlich) Arbeit, Zeiten etc.* awful, lousy ❷ *(fam: geringfügig)* measly **II.** *adv* ❶ *(entsetzlich)* terribly ❷ *(geringfügig)* **~ bezahlt** paid badly

laut[1] [laut] **I.** *adj* ❶ *(weithin hörbar)* loud; **etw ~er stellen** to turn up *sep* sth; **musst du immer gleich ~ werden?** do you always have to get so upset right away? ❷ *(voller Lärm)* noisy **II.** *adv (weithin hörbar)* loudly; **kannst du ~er sprechen?** can you speak up?; **~ denken** to think out loud

laut[2] [laut] *präp +gen o dat* **~ Zeitungsberichten ...** according to newspaper reports ...

Laut <-[e]s, -e> [laut] *m* noise; **keinen ~ von sich geben** to not make a sound

lauten ['lau·tn] *vi* ❶ *(zum Inhalt haben)* to read; **wie lautet die Frage?** what is the question?; **wie lautet der letzte Absatz?** how does the final paragraph go?; **die Anklage lautete auf Erpressung** the charge is blackmail ❷ *(ausgestellt sein)* **die Papiere ~ auf seinen Namen** the papers are in his name

läuten ['lɔy·tn] **I.** *vi Klingel, Telefon* to ring; *Glocke a.* to chime; *(feierlich)* to toll **II.** *vi impers* **es hat geläutet** there was a ring at the door

lauter ['lau·tɐ] *adj* just; **das sind ~**

Lügen that's nothing but lies; **vor ~ Arbeit** because of all the work I have

lauthals ['laut·hals] *adv* at the top of one's lungs *pred*

lautlos ['laut·lo:s] **I.** *adj* noiseless, silent **II.** *adv* noiselessly, silently

Lautschrift *f* phonetic alphabet

Lautsprecherbox *f* speaker

lautstark **I.** *adj* loud; *Protest* strong **II.** *adv* loudly, strongly

Lautstärke *f* volume

lauwarm ['lau·varm] *adj* lukewarm

Lava <-, Laven> [ˈlaː·vn] *f* lava

Lavendel <-s, -> [la·ˈvɛn·dl] *m* lavender

Lawine <-, -n> [la·ˈviː·nə] *f (a. fig)* avalanche

lax [laks] *adj* lax

Lazarett <-[e]s, -e> [la·tsa·ˈrɛt] *nt* military hospital

leben ['leː·bn] *vi* to live; **Gott sei Dank, er lebt** [noch] thank God, he's [still] alive; **vegetarisch ~** to be [a] vegetarian; **getrennt ~** to live apart; **vom Schreiben ~** to make a living as a writer ▶WENDUNGEN: **leb[e] wohl!** farewell!

Leben <-s, -> ['leː·bn] *nt* life; **am ~ sein** to be alive; **[bei etw *dat*] ums ~ kommen** to die [doing sth]; **sich *dat* das ~ nehmen** *(euph)* to take one's life; **das tägliche ~** everyday life; **so ist das ~ [eben]** that's life ▶WENDUNGEN: **nie im ~** *(fam)* never; **etw ins ~ rufen** to establish sth; **[bei etw *dat*] sein ~ aufs Spiel setzen** to risk one's life [doing sth]; **es geht um ~ und Tod** it's a matter of life and death

lebend **I.** *adj* living **II.** *adv* alive

lebendig [le·ˈbɛn·dɪç] *adj* ❶ *(lebend)* living; **■ ~ sein** to be alive ❷ *(anschaulich, lebhaft)* vivid; *Kind* lively

Lebendigkeit <-> *f kein pl* vividness

Lebensabend *m (geh)* twilight years *pl*

Lebensabschnitt *m* chapter in one's life

Lebensbedingungen *pl* living conditions

Lebensdauer *f* ❶ *(Dauer des Lebens)* life span ❷ *(Dauer der Funktionsfähigkeit)* [working] life

Lebenserfahrung *f* life experience

Lebenserwartung f life expectancy

Lebensfreude f kein pl love of life

lebensfroh adj full of life pred

Lebensgefahr f mortal danger; **jd ist in/außer ~** sb's life is in/no longer in danger

lebensgefährlich I. adj extremely dangerous; (Krankheiten) life-threatening **II.** adv ① (mit Lebensgefahr verbunden) ~ **verletzt** seriously injured ② (fam: sehr gefährlich) dangerously

Lebensgefährte, -gefährtin m, f (geh) partner

Lebenshaltungskosten pl cost of living

Lebenslage f situation [in life]

lebenslänglich ['leː·bns·lɛŋ·lɪç] **I.** adj JUR life attr, for life pred; **„~" bekommen** (fam) to get life [in prison] **II.** adv all one's life

Lebenslauf m résumé

Lebensmittel nt meist pl food

Lebensmittelgeschäft nt grocery store

Lebensmittelvergiftung f food poisoning

Lebenspartnerschaft f domestic partnership; **eingetragene ~** civil union

Lebensqualität f kein pl quality of life

Lebensraum m (Biotop) habitat

Lebensretter(in) m(f) lifesaver

Lebensstandard m kein pl standard of living

Lebensunterhalt m kein pl living; **das deckt noch nicht einmal meinen ~** that doesn't even cover my basic needs

Lebensversicherung f life insurance

Lebensweise f lifestyle

Lebensweisheit f ① (weise Lebenserfahrung) worldly wisdom ② (Wahlspruch) maxim

lebenswert adj worth living pred

lebenswichtig adj vital, essential

Lebenszeichen nt (a. fig) sign of life

Lebenszeit f lifetime; **auf ~** for life

Leber <-, -n> ['leː·bɐ] f liver

Leberfleck m liver spot; (Muttermal) mole

Leberpastete f liver pâté

Lebertran m cod-liver oil

Leberwurst f liver sausage

Lebewesen nt living thing; **menschliches ~** human being

Lebewohl <-[e]s, -s o geh -e> [leː·bə·'voːl] nt (geh) farewell

lebhaft ['leːp·haft] **I.** adj ① (temperamentvoll) lively ② (angeregt) lively; Beifall thunderous ③ (belebt) lively; Verkehr brisk ④ (anschaulich) Darstellung vivid **II.** adv ① (anschaulich) vividly ② (sehr stark) intensely

Lebkuchen ['leːp·kuː·xn̩] m gingerbread

leblos ['leːp·loːs] adj lifeless

Lebzeiten pl **zu jds ~** (Zeit) in sb's day; (Leben) in sb's lifetime

lechzen ['lɛç·tsn̩] vi (geh) to long (nach +dat for)

Leck <-[e]s, -s> [lɛk] nt leak

lecken ['lɛ·kn̩] vi (schlecken) to lick

lecker ['lɛ·kɐ] **I.** adj delicious **II.** adv deliciously

Leckerbissen m delicacy

Leder <-s, -> ['leː·dɐ] nt leather; **zäh wie ~** (fam) tough as nails

Lederjacke f leather jacket

Lederwaren pl leather goods

ledig ['leː·dɪç] adj single

lediglich ['leː·dɪk·lɪç] adv (geh) merely

leer [leːɐ̯] **I.** adj empty; Blatt Papier blank; Blick vacant; Versprechungen, Worte empty **II.** adv **wie ~ gefegt sein** to be deserted ▶WENDUNGEN: **[bei etw dat] ~ ausgehen** to go away empty-handed

Leere <-> ['leː·rə] f kein pl emptiness

leeren ['leː·rən] vt, vr ▪[sich akk] ~ to empty; **sie leerte ihre Tasse nur halb** she only drank half of her cup

Leergut nt kein pl empties pl fam

Leerlauf m ① (Gangeinstellung) neutral [gear] ② (unproduktive Phase) unproductiveness

Leertaste f space bar

Leerung <-, -en> f emptying; von Post collection

legal [leˈɡaːl] **I.** adj legal **II.** adv legally

legalisieren* [leˈɡaˈliˈziː·rən] vt to legalize

Legalität <-> [le·ga·li·'tɛːt] f kein pl legality

Legastheniker(in) <-s, -> [le·gas·'teː·ni·kɐ] m(f) dyslexic

legen ['leː·gn] I. vt ■ jdn/etw irgendwohin ~ to put sb/sth somewhere; **seinen Arm um jdn** ~ to put one's arm around sb; ~ **Sie ihn auf den Rücken** lay him on his back ② **die Stirn in Falten** ~ to frown ③ Teppich, Kabel, Eier to lay II. vr ■ sich akk ~ ① (hinlegen) to lie down; **sich** akk **ins ` Bett/in die Sonne/auf den Rücken** ~ to go to bed/lie down in the sun/lie on one's back ② (nachlassen) Aufregung, Empörung, Sturm, Begeisterung to subside; Nebel to lift

legendär [le·gɛn·'dɛːɐ̯] adj legendary

Legende <-, -n> [le·'gɛn·də] f ① (fromme Sage) legend ② (Lügenmärchen) myth

leger [le·'ʒeːɐ̯] I. adj ① (bequem) loose-fitting ② (ungezwungen) casual II. adv casually

Legierung <-, -en> f alloy

Legion <-, -en> [le·'gi̯oːn] f legion

Legionär <-s, -e> [le·gi̯o·'nɛːɐ̯] m legionary

Legislative <-n, -n> [le·gɪs·la·'tiː·və] f legislative power

Legislaturperiode [le·gɪs·la·'tuːɐ̯-] f legislative period

Lehm <-[e]s, -e> [leːm] m clay

lehmig ['leː·mɪç] adj (aus Lehm bestehend) clay; (voller Lehm) clayey; Weg muddy

Lehne <-, -n> ['leː·nə] f (Armlehne) armrest; (Rückenlehne) back

lehnen ['leː·nən] I. vt (anlehnen) to lean (an/gegen +akk against) II. vi (schräg angelehnt sein) to lean (an +dat against) III. vr (sich beugen) ■ sich akk an jdn/etw ~ to lean on sb/sth; ■ sich akk über etw akk ~ to lean over sth

Lehnstuhl m armchair

Lehramt ['leːɐ̯-] nt (geh) ■ das ~ the position of teacher; (Studiengang) teacher training [program]

Lehrbeauftragte(r) f(m) visiting [or adjunct] lecturer

Lehrberuf m teaching profession

Lehre <-, -n> ['leː·rə] f ① ([handwerkliche] Ausbildung) apprenticeship ② (Erfahrung, aus der man lernt) lesson; **jdm eine ~ erteilen** to teach sb a lesson ③ (ideologisches System) doctrine ④ (Theorie) theory

lehren ['leː·rən] vt (unterrichten) to teach; **die Erfahrung hat uns gelehrt, dass ...** experience has taught us that ...

Lehrer(in) <-s, -> ['leː·rɐ] m(f) teacher

Lehrfach nt subject

Lehrgang <-gänge> m course; **auf einem ~ sein** to be at a seminar

Lehrkörper m teaching staff + sing/pl vb

Lehrling <-s, -e> ['leːɐ̯·lɪŋ] m (veraltend) s. **Auszubildende(r)**

Lehrmittel nt (fachspr) teaching aid

Lehrplan m syllabus

lehrreich adj instructive

Lehrsatz m theorem

Lehrstelle f apprenticeship

Lehrstuhl m chair, professorship

Leib <-[e]s, -er> [laip] m (Körper) body; **etw** akk **am eigenen ~ erfahren** to experience sth firsthand; **bei lebendigem ~** alive ▸ WENDUNGEN: **mit ~ und Seele** wholeheartedly

Leibgericht nt favorite meal

leiblich ['laip·lɪç] adj ① (körperlich) physical ② (blutsverwandt) natural; ~ **e Verwandte** blood relations

Leibwächter(in) m(f) bodyguard

Leiche <-, -n> ['lai·çə] f corpse, body ▸ WENDUNGEN: **über ~ n gehen** (pej fam) to stop at nothing

leichenblass RR adj deathly pale

Leichenhalle f mortuary

Leichenschauhaus nt morgue

Leichenverbrennung f cremation

Leichnam <-s, -e> ['laiç·naːm] m (geh) corpse, body

leicht [laiçt] I. adj ① (geringes Gewicht habend) light ② (dünn) light ③ (einfach) easy; **nichts ~ er als das!** no problem!; ~ **e Lektüre** light reading ④ METEO (*schwach*) *Regen* light; *Donner* distant ⑤(*sacht*) light; *Akzent* slight; *Schlag* gentle ⑥ *Eingriff*, *Verbrennung* minor ⑦(*nicht belastend*) *Mahlzeit* light; *Zigarette* mild ⑧(*unbeschwert*) ■**jdm ist ~ er** sb is relieved ⑨(*nicht massiv*) lightweight II. *adv* ❶~ **bekleidet** dressed in light clothing ❷(*einfach*) easily; **etw geht [ganz] ~** sth is [quite] easy; **es jdm ~ machen** to make it easy for sb ❸METEO (*schwach*) lightly ❹(*nur wenig, etwas*) lightly; **~ verärgert sein** to be slightly annoyed ❺(*schnell*) easily; **das sagst du so ~!** that's easy for you to say!; **~ zerbrechlich** fragile ❻(*problemlos*) easily

Leichtathlet(in) *m(f)* track and field athlete

Leichtathletik *f* track and field + *sing vb, no art*

leichtfertig I. *adj* thoughtless II. *adv* thoughtlessly

Leichtgewicht *nt* ❶ *kein pl* (*Gewichtsklasse*) lightweight category ❷(*fig: Sportler*) lightweight *a. fig*

leichtgläubig *adj* gullible

Leichtigkeit <-> *f* ❶ *kein pl* (*Einfachheit*) simplicity; **mit ~** effortlessly ❷(*Leichtheit*) lightness

Leichtmetall *nt* light metal

leicht|nehmen *vt irreg* ■**etw ~** to take sth lightly

Leichtsinn ['laiçt·zɪn] *m kein pl* carelessness

leichtsinnig ['laiçt·zɪnɪç] I. *adj* careless II. *adv* carelessly

leid [lait] *adj pred* (*überdrüssig*) **ich bin es ~, das immer tun zu müssen** I'm sick of having to do this all the time

Leid <-[e]s> [lait] *nt kein pl* sorrow; **jdm sein ~ klagen** to tell sb one's troubles

leiden <litt, gelitten> ['lai·dn̩] I. *vi* to suffer; *Möbelstück, Stoff* to get damaged; ■**an etw** *dat* **~** to suffer from sth; ■**unter jdm ~** to suffer because of sb; ■**unter etw** *dat* **~** to suffer from sth II. *vt* ►WENDUNGEN: **jdn/etw ~ können**

to like sb/sth; **ich kann das nicht ~** I can't stand that

Leiden <-s, -> ['lai·dn̩] *nt* ❶(*chronische Krankheit*) ailment ❷ *pl* (*leidvolle Erlebnisse*) suffering

Leidenschaft <-, -en> ['lai·dn̩·ʃaft] *f* passion

leidenschaftlich I. *adj* passionate II. *adv* passionately; ■**etw ~ gern tun** to love doing sth; **ich esse ~ gern Himbeereis** I [absolutely] love raspberry ice cream

leidenschaftslos I. *adj* dispassionate II. *adv* dispassionately

leider ['lai·dɐ] *adv* unfortunately; **ich habe das ~ vergessen** I'm sorry, I forgot about that; **das ist ~ so** that's just the way it is

leidig ['lai·dɪç] *adj attr* (*pej*) tedious; **immer alles ~ e Geld!** it always comes down to money!

Leidtragende(r) *f(m)* ■**der/die ~** the one to suffer

leid|tunRR *vi irreg* **es tut mir leid** I'm sorry; **es tut mir [so] leid, dass …** I'm [so] sorry that …; **er tut mir leid** I feel sorry for him

leidvoll *adj* (*geh*) sorrowful *liter*

Leidwesen *nt kein pl* ■**zu jds ~** much to sb's regret

Leier <-, -n> ['laiɐ] *f* MUS lyre

Leierkasten *m* (*fam*) *s.* **Drehorgel**

leihen <lieh, geliehen> ['lai·ən] *vt* ❶(*ausleihen*) to lend ❷(*borgen*) ■**sich** *dat* **etw** *akk* **[von jdm] ~** to borrow sth [from sb]

Leihgabe *f* loan

Leihhaus *nt* pawn shop

Leihmutter *f* surrogate mother

leihweise *adv* on loan

Leim <-[e]s, -e> [laim] *m* glue

leimen ['lai·mən] *vt* ❶(*kleben*) to glue together ❷(*fam: hereinlegen*) ■**jdn ~** to take sb for a ride

Leine <-, -n> ['lai·nə] *f* ❶(*dünnes Seil*) rope ❷(*Wäscheleine*) [clothes]line ❸(*Hundeleine*) leash

Leinen <-s, -> ['lai·nən] *nt* linen

Leinsamen m linseed

Leintuch <-tücher> nt DIAL (Laken) sheet

Leinwand f ① (Projektionswand) screen ② kein pl (Gewebe aus Flachsfasern) canvas

leise ['lai·zə] I. adj ① (nicht laut) quiet; etw ~ stellen to turn down sep sth ② (gering) slight; Ahnung, Verdacht vague; es fiel ~r Regen it was drizzling II. adv ① (nicht laut) quietly ② (kaum merklich) slightly

Leiste <-, -n> ['lais·tə] f ① (schmale Latte) strip ② ANAT groin

leisten ['lais·tn̩] I. vt ① (erbringen) ganze Arbeit ~ to do a good job; viel ~ to get a lot done ② TECH, PHYS to generate ③ Funktionsverb Hilfe ~ to help; eine Anzahlung ~ to make a down payment; gute Dienste ~ to serve sb well II. vr ① (sich gönnen) ■ sich dat etw ~ to treat oneself to sth ② (sich herausnehmen) da hast du dir ja was geleistet! you've really outdone yourself!; er hat sich eine Dummheit geleistet he behaved stupidly; (tragen können) tolles Kleid – sie kann es sich ~, bei der Figur! great dress — she can certainly get away with it with a figure like that! ③ (finanziell in der Lage sein) sich dat etw ~ können to be able to afford sth; es sich dat ~ können, etw zu tun to be able to afford to do sth

Leistenbruch m hernia

Leistung <-, -en> f ① kein pl (das Leisten) performance ② (geleistetes Ergebnis) accomplishment; eine hervorragende/sportliche ~ an outstanding piece of work/athletic achievement; schulische ~en performance at school; ihre ~en lassen zu wünschen übrig her work leaves a lot to be desired ③ TECH, PHYS power; einer Fabrik output ④ FIN (Entrichtung) payment

Leistungsdruck m kein pl pressure to perform

leistungsfähig adj ① (zu hoher Arbeitsleistung fähig) efficient ② (zu hoher Produktionsleistung fähig) productive ③ (zur Abgabe großer Energie fähig) powerful ④ FIN competitive

Leistungsgesellschaft f meritocracy

Leitartikel m editorial [article]

Leitbild nt [role] model

leiten ['lai·tn̩] I. vt ① (verantwortlich sein) Firma to run; eine Abteilung/ Schule ~ to be head of a department/ school ② (den Vorsitz führen) to lead; Sitzung, Debatte to chair ③ TECH (transportieren) to conduct; Erdöl to pipe ④ TRANSP Zug to divert ⑤ (führen) to lead, to guide; ■ sich akk durch etw akk ~ lassen to [let oneself] be guided by sth; ■ sich akk von etw dat ~ lassen to [let oneself] be governed by sth II. vi PHYS to conduct; gut/schlecht ~ to be a good/bad conductor

leitend I. adj ① (führend) leading ② (in hoher Position) managerial; ~er Angestellter executive; ~er Redakteur editor in chief ③ PHYS conductive II. adv ~ tätig sein to hold a managerial position

Leiter¹ <-, -n> ['lai·tɐ] f (Sprossenleiter) ladder; (Stehleiter) stepladder

Leiter² <-s, -> ['lai·tɐ] m PHYS conductor

Leiter(in) <-s, -> ['lai·tɐ] m(f) head; einer Firma, eines Geschäfts manager; einer Schule principal; ~ einer Diskussion person chairing a discussion

Leitfaden m MEDIA compendium

Leitgedanke m central idea

Leitmotiv nt central theme; (in der Musik, Literatur) leitmotiv

Leitplanke f guardrail

Leitung <-, -en> f ① kein pl (Führung) management ② (leitendes Gremium) management ③ (Rohr) pipe ④ (Kabel) cable ⑤ TELEK line; die ~ ist gestört it's a bad connection ►WENDUNGEN: eine lange ~ haben (hum fam) to be slow on the uptake

Leitungsrohr nt pipe

Leitungswasser nt tap water

Leitzins m prime rate

Lektion <-, -en> [lɛkˈtsjoːn] f SCH (Kapitel) chapter; (Stunde) lesson

L

►WENDUNGEN: **jdm eine ~ erteilen** to teach sb a lesson

Lektor(in) <-s, -toren> ['lɛk·to:ɐ̯, lɛk·'to:·rɪn] *m(f)* ❶ (*in einem Verlag*) editor ❷ (*an der Universität*) lecturer who teaches in his/her native language at a university in a foreign country

Lektüre <-, -n> [lɛk·'ty:·rə] *f* ❶ (*das Lesen*) reading ❷ (*Lesestoff*) reading material

Lende <-, -n> ['lɛn·də] *f* ANAT, KOCHK loin

Lendenschurz *m* loincloth

Lendenstück *nt* KOCHK tenderloin

lenken ['lɛŋ·kn̩] **I.** *vt* to direct; *Fahrzeug, Unterhaltung* to steer; (*politisch*) to control; **jds Aufmerksamkeit auf etw** *akk* **~** to draw sb's attention to sth **II.** *vi* to drive

Lenker <-s, -> *m* handlebar *usu pl*

Lenkrad *nt* steering wheel

Leopard <-en, -en> [leo·'part] *m* leopard

Lepra <-> ['le:·pra] *f kein pl* leprosy

Lerche <-, -n> ['lɛr·çə] *f* ORN lark

lernbehindert *adj* with learning difficulties *pred*; ■**~ sein** to have learning difficulties

lernen ['lɛr·nən] **I.** *vt* ❶ (*sich als Kenntnis aneignen*) to learn ❷ (*fam: eine Ausbildung machen*) ■**etw ~** to train to be sth ►WENDUNGEN: **gelernt ist [eben] gelernt** once learned, never forgotten; **etw will gelernt sein** sth takes [a lot of] practice **II.** *vi* ❶ (*für die Schule*) to study, to [do school]work ❷ (*beim Lernen unterstützen*) ■**mit jdm ~** to tutor sb ❸ (*eine Ausbildung machen*) to apprentice (**bei** + *dat* with); **er hat bei verschiedenen Firmen gelernt** he has apprenticed with several companies; **sie lernt noch** she is still an apprentice

lesbar ['le:s·ba:ɐ̯] *adj Handschrift* legible

Lesbe <-, -n> ['lɛs·bə] *f* lesbian

lesbisch ['lɛs·bɪʃ] *adj* lesbian

Lesebuch *nt* reader

Leselampe *f* reading lamp

lesen <liest, las, gelesen> ['le:·zn̩] **I.** *vt* to read **II.** *vi* ❶ (*als Lektüre*) to read ❷ (*Hochschulwesen*) to lecture (**über** + *akk* on/about) **III.** *vr* **etw liest sich leicht** sth is easy to read

lesenswert *adj* worth reading *pred*

Leser(in) <-s, -> ['le:·zɐ] *m(f)* reader

Leseratte *f* (*hum fam*) bookworm

Leserbrief *m* letter to the editor

leserlich *adj* legible; **gut ~ sein** to be easy to read

Lesesaal *m* reading room

Lesestoff *m* reading material

Lesezeichen *nt* bookmark

Lesung <-, -en> *f* reading

Lette, Lettin <-n, -nn> ['lɛ·tə] *m*, *f* Latvian; *s. a.* **Deutsche(r)**

lettisch ['lɛ·tɪʃ] *adj* Latvian; *s. a.* **deutsch**

Lettland ['lɛt·lant] *nt* Latvia; *s. a.* **Deutschland**

letzte(r, s) *adj* ❶ (*am Ende einer Reihenfolge*) last; *Angebot, Versuch* final; *Zug* last; **sie saß in der ~n Reihe** she sat in the back row; **sie ging als ~ Läuferin durchs Ziel** she was the last runner to cross the finish line; **das ~ Brot** the last of the bread; **L~(r) werden** to finish last; **der L~ des Monats** the last [day] of the month; **das ist das L~, was ...** this is the last thing that ...; **in ~r Minute** at the last minute; **es ist das ~ Mal, dass ...** this is the last time that ...; **zum ~n Mal** the last time ❷ (*vorig*) **beim ~n Mal** last time; **im ~n Jahr** last year ❸ (*neueste*) *Nachricht, Mode* latest ❹ (*fam: schlechteste*) **das ist doch der ~ Kerl!** what a total loser!

letztendlich ['lɛtst·ʔɛnt·lɪç] *adv s.* **letztlich**

letztens ['lɛts·tn̩s] *adv* recently; **erst ~** just the other day

letztlich ['lɛtst·lɪç] *adv* in the end

Leuchtboje *f* light buoy

Leuchtdiode *f* light-emitting diode

Leuchte <-, -n> ['lɔɪç·tə] *f* (*Stehlampe*) floor lamp ►WENDUNGEN: **nicht gerade**

eine ~ **sein** (*fam*) to not be all that bright

leuchten ['lɔyçtn̩] *vi* ❶ (*Licht ausstrahlen*) to shine; *Abendsonne* to glow; **leuchte mit der Lampe mal hier in die Ecke** shine the light over here in the corner [please] ❷ (*Licht reflektieren*) to glow; **die Kinder hatten vor Freude ~de Augen** the children's eyes were sparkling with joy

leuchtend *adj* ❶ (*strahlend*) bright; *Farben* glowing, bright ❷ **ein ~es Beispiel** a shining example

Leuchter <-s, -> *m* candlestick; (*mehrarmig*) candelabra

Leuchtfeuer *nt* beacon; (*auf der Landebahn*) runway lights

Leuchtrakete *f* [rocket] flare

Leuchtreklame *f* neon sign

Leuchtschrift *f* neon lettering *pl*

Leuchtturm *m* lighthouse

leugnen ['lɔygnən] **I.** *vt* to deny; **es ist nicht zu ~, dass ...** there is no denying the fact that ... **II.** *vi* to deny it

Leukämie <-, -n> [lɔykε'mi:] *f* leukemia

Leute ['lɔytə] *pl* ❶ (*Menschen*) people *npl*; **alle/keine/kaum ~** everybody/nobody/hardly anybody; **unter ~ gehen** to get out and about ❷ (*fam: Kameraden, Verwandte*) folks *npl* ❸ MIL, NAUT (*Mitarbeiter*) men *pl* ▸WENDUNGEN: **etw unter die ~ bringen** (*fam*) to make sth known

Leviten [le·'vi:·tən] *pl* ▸WENDUNGEN: **jdm die ~ lesen** (*fam*) to read sb the riot act

Lexikon <-s, Lexika> ['lεk·si·kɔn] *nt* encyclopedia

Libanese, Libanesin <-n, -n> [li·ba·'ne:·zə] *m, f* Lebanese; *s. a.* **Deutsche(r)**

libanesisch [li·ba·'ne:·zɪʃ] *adj* Lebanese; *s. a.* **deutsch**

Libanon <-[s]> ['li:·ba·nɔn] *m* ▪**der ~** Lebanon; *s. a.* **Deutschland**

Libelle <-, -n> [li·'bε·lə] *f* dragonfly

liberal [li·be·'ra:l] *adj* liberal

liberalisieren* [li·be·ra·li·'zi:·rən] *vt* to liberalize

Liberia <-s> [li·'be:·ri̯a] *nt* Liberia; *s. a.* **Deutschland**

Libero <-s, -s> ['li:·be·ro] *m* FBALL sweeper

Libyen <-s> ['li:·bỳ·ən] *nt* Libya; *s. a.* **Deutschland**

Libyer(in) <-s, -> ['li:·bỳ·ɐ] *m(f)* Libyan; *s. a.* **Deutsche(r)**

libysch ['li:·bɣʃ] *adj* Libyan; *s. a.* **deutsch**

Licht <-[e]s, -er> [lɪçt] *nt* ❶ *kein pl* (*Helligkeit*) light ❷ ELEK light; **das ~ brennt** the light is on; **das ~ ausschalten** to turn out the light[s]; **etw gegen das ~ halten** to hold sth up to the light ▸WENDUNGEN: **etw erscheint in einem anderen ~** sth appears in a different light; **etw ans ~ bringen** to bring sth to light; **jdn hinters ~ führen** to hoodwink sb; **mir geht ein ~ auf** (*fam*) now I see, it has suddenly dawned on me; **kein großes ~ sein** (*fam*) to be no great genius; **grünes ~ [für etw akk] geben** to give [sth] the go-ahead; **das ~ der Welt erblicken** (*geh*) to [first] see the light of day

Lichtbild *nt* (*veraltend geh: Passbild*) passport photograph

Lichtblick *m* ray of hope

lichtdurchlässig *adj* translucent

lichtempfindlich *adj* sensitive to light *pred*; FOTO photosensitive

lichten ['lɪç·tn̩] **I.** *vt* HORT to thin out *sep* **II.** *vr* ▪**sich** *akk* ~ ❶ (*dünner werden*) to [grow] thin ❷ (*spärlicher werden*) to go down ❸ (*klarer werden*) to be cleared up

lichterloh ['lɪç·tɐ·'lo:] *adv* ~ **brennen** to be ablaze

Lichtgeschwindigkeit *f kein pl* **mit ~** at the speed of light

Lichthupe *f* **die ~ betätigen** to flash one's high beams

Lichtjahr *nt* light year

Lichtmaschine *f* generator

Lichtquelle *f* light source

Lichtschacht *m* light well

Lichtschalter *m* light switch
Lichtschutzfaktor *m* [sun] protection factor
Lichtstrahl *m* light beam
lichtundurchlässig *adj* opaque
Lichtung <-, -en> *f* clearing
Lichtverhältnisse *pl* lighting conditions *pl*
Lid <-[e]s, -er> [liːt] *nt* [eye]lid
Lidschatten *m* eye shadow
Lidstrich *m* eyeliner
lieb [liːp] *adj* ❶ (*liebenswürdig*) kind, nice; **seien Sie/sei so ~ und ...** would you be so kind as to ... ❷ (*artig*) good; **sei ein ~es Mädchen!** be a good girl! ❸ (*niedlich*) cute ❹ (*geschätzt*) dear; **L~er Karl, L~e Amelie,** (*als Anrede in Briefen*) Dear Karl and Amelie,; [**mein**] **L~es** [my] love; [**ach**] **du ~e Güte** (*fam*) good heavens!; **jdn ~ haben** to love sb; **man muss ihn einfach ~ haben** it's impossible not to like him ❺ (*angenehm*) welcome; **das wäre mir weniger ~** I'd rather you didn't [do it]
liebäugeln [ˈliːp·ʔɔy·gln] *vi* ■ **mit etw** *dat* ~ to have one's eye on sth; ■ **damit ~, etw** *akk* **zu tun** to toy with the idea of doing sth
Liebe <-, -n> [ˈliː·bə] *f* ❶ *kein pl* (*Gefühl starker Zuneigung*) love; **aus ~ zu jdm** out of love for sb; **aus ~ zu etw** *dat* for the love of sth; **aus ~ heiraten** to marry for love ❷ (*Mensch*) love; **die ~ meines Lebens** the love of my life ▶WENDUNGEN: **~ auf den ersten Blick** love at first sight; **~ macht blind** (*prov*) love is blind
lieben [ˈliː·bn] I. *vt* ❶ (*Liebe entgegenbringen*) to love; ■ **sich** *akk* ~ to love each other ❷ (*gerne mögen*) to love ❸ (*euph: Geschlechtsverkehr miteinander haben*) ■ **jdn ~** to make love to sb; ■ **sich** *akk* ~ to make love II. *vi* to be in love
liebenswert *adj* lovable
liebenswürdig *adj* kind
Liebenswürdigkeit <-, -en> *f* kind-

ness; **würden Sie die ~ haben, ...?** (*geh*) would you be so kind as to ...?
lieber [ˈliː·bɐ] I. *adj komp von* **lieb**: **mir wäre es ~, wenn ...** I would prefer it if ...; **was ist Ihnen ~, das Theater oder das Kino?** would you prefer to go to the theater or the movies? II. *adv* ❶ *komp von* **gern(e)** rather; **etw ~ mögen** to prefer sth; **ich würde ~ in der Karibik als an der Ostsee Urlaub machen** I would rather take a vacation in the Caribbean than on the Baltic ❷ (*besser*) better; **darüber schweige ich ~** I think it's better to remain silent; **wir sollten ~ gehen** we [really] should get going; **das hätten Sie ~ nicht gesagt** you shouldn't have said that; **das möchte ich dir ~ nicht sagen** I'd rather not tell you that
Liebesbrief *m* love letter
Liebeserklärung *f* declaration of love; **jdm eine ~ machen** to declare one's love to sb
Liebeskummer *m* lovesickness; **~ haben** to be lovesick
Liebeslied *nt* love song
Liebespaar *nt* lovers *pl*
liebevoll I. *adj* loving; *Kuss* affectionate II. *adv* ❶ (*zärtlich*) affectionately ❷ (*mit besonderer Sorgfalt*) lovingly
Liebhaber(in) <-s, -> [ˈliːp·haˌbɐ] *m(f)* ❶ (*Partner*) lover ❷ (*Freund* (*der Künste*)) enthusiast
Liebhaberei <-, -en> [liːp·haːbəˈrai] *f* hobby
liebkosen* [liːp·ˈkoːzn] *vt* (*geh*) to caress
lieblich [ˈliːp·lɪç] I. *adj* ❶ (*angenehm süß*) sweet; *Wein* medium sweet ❷ (*erhebend*) lovely; *Töne* melodious II. *adv* **~ duften/schmecken** to smell/taste sweet
Liebling <-s, -e> [ˈliːp·lɪŋ] *m* ❶ (*Geliebte(r)*) darling ❷ (*Favorit*) favorite
lieblos [ˈliːp·loːs] I. *adj* ❶ (*herzlos*) unloving ❷ (*Nachlässigkeit zeigend*) unfeeling II. *adv* (*nachlässig*) carelessly
Lieblosigkeit <-, -en> *f* ❶ *kein pl*

(*Herzlosigkeit*) lack of feeling ❷ (*herzlose Handlung*) unkind act

liebste(r, s) ['li:psˑtə, -tə, -təs] *adj superl von* **lieb** dearest; **das mag ich am ~n** I like that the best; **ich mag Vollmilchschokolade am ~n** milk chocolate is my favorite; **am ~n möchte ich schlafen** I'd really just like to sleep; **am ~n hätte ich ja abgelehnt** I would have rather said no

Liebste(r) ['li:psˑtə, -tə] *f(m)* sweetheart

Lied <-[e]s, -er> [li:t] *nt* song ▸WENDUNGEN: **es ist immer das alte ~** (*fam*) it's always the same old story; **ein ~ von etw** *dat* **singen können** to be able to tell sb a thing or two about sth

Liederbuch *nt* songbook

Liedermacher(in) *m(f)* singer-songwriter

Lieferant(in) <-en, -en> [li·fə·ˈrant] *m(f)* ❶ (*Firma*) supplier ❷ (*Auslieferer*) deliveryman *masc*, deliverywoman *fem*

lieferbar *adj* ❶ (*erhältlich*) available, in stock ❷ (*zustellbar*) **Ihre Bestellung ist leider erst später ~** unfortunately, we won't be able to ship your order until a later date

Lieferbedingungen *pl* terms of delivery

liefern ['li:·fɐn] **I.** *vt* ❶ (*ausliefern*) ■**jdm**] **etw** *akk* ~ to deliver sth [to sb] ❷ (*Beweis*) to provide ❸ (*erzeugen*) to yield ❹ SPORT **ein spannendes Spiel ~** to put on an exciting game **II.** *vi* to deliver

Lieferschein *m* packing slip

Lieferung <-, -en> *f* ❶ (*das Liefern*) delivery; **bei ~** on delivery ❷ (*gelieferte Ware*) consignment

Lieferwagen *m* delivery van; (*offen*) pickup truck

Liege <-, -n> ['li:·gə] *f* ❶ (*Bett ohne Fuß-/Kopfteil*) day bed ❷ s. **Liegestuhl**

liegen <lag, gelegen> ['li:·gn̩] *vi haben o* SÜDD *sein* ❶ (*sich in horizontaler Lage befinden*) to lie; **ich liege noch im Bett** I'm still [lying] in bed; **deine Brille müsste eigentlich auf dem Schreibtisch ~** your glasses must be on the

desk; **in diesem Liegestuhl liegt man am bequemsten** this is the most comfortable lounge chair [to lie in]; **~ bleiben** (*nicht aufstehen*) to stay in bed; (*nicht mehr aufstehen*) to remain lying down; **etw ~ lassen** to leave sth [where it is] ❷ (*sich abgesetzt haben*) **hier liegt oft bis Mitte April noch Schnee** there will often be snow on the ground until mid-April here; **über allen Möbeln lag eine dicke Staubschicht** a thick layer of dust covered all the furniture ❸ (*lagern*) **Hände weg, das Buch bleibt** [da] **~!** hands off — that book's not going anywhere!; **~ bleiben** (*nicht verkauft werden*) to remain unsold ❹ (*vergessen werden*) **irgendwo ~ bleiben** to be left behind somewhere ❺ (*geografisch gelegen sein*) to lie; **Cannes liegt in Frankreich** Cannes is in France ❻ (*eine bestimmte Lage haben*) to be situated; **ihr Haus liegt an einem See** they have a house on a lake; **diese Wohnung liegt zur Straße** this apartment faces [out onto] the street ❼ (*begraben sein*) **irgendwo ~** to be buried somewhere ❽ (*vertäut sein*) NAUT to be moored ❾ AUTO **~ bleiben** to break down ❿ SPORT **~** to be; **wie ~ unsere Schwimmer im Wettbewerb?** how are our swimmers doing in the competition? ⓫ (*angesiedelt sein*) **der Preis dürfte bei 4.500 Euro ~** the price is probably around 4,500 euros ⓬ (*verursacht sein*) **das liegt nur an dir** it's all your fault; **woran mag es nur ~, dass ...** why is it that ... ⓭ (*wichtig sein*) **du weißt doch, wie sehr mir daran liegt** you know how important it is to me; **mir ist viel daran gelegen** this means a lot to me ⓮ *meist verneint* (*zusagen*) **Sport liegt mir nicht** I don't like sports; **körperliche Arbeit liegt ihr nicht** she's not really cut out for physical work ⓯ (*lasten*) ■**auf jdm ~ Schuld** to weigh down on sb ⓰ (*abhängig sein*) **das liegt ganz bei Ihnen** it's entirely up to you ⓱ (*nicht ausgeführt werden*) **~ bleiben** *Arbeit* to be left undone

▶WENDUNGEN: **an mir soll** es nicht ~**!** don't let me stop you!

Liegesitz *m* recliner

Liegestuhl *m* chaise longue; (*Stuhl*) deck chair

Liegewagen *m* couchette car

Lift <-[e]s, -e> [lɪft] *m* elevator

Liga <-, Ligen> ['liː·ga] *f* league

Likör <-s, -e> [li·'køːɐ̯] *m* liqueur

lila ['liː·la] *adj* purple

Lilie <-, -n> ['liː·liə] *f* lily

Liliputaner(in) <-s, -> [li·li·pu·'taː·nɐ] *m(f)* dwarf

Limonade <-, -n> [li·mo·'naː·də] *f* lemon-lime soda

Limousine <-, -n> [li·mu·'ziː·nə] *f* sedan; (*größerer Luxuswagen*) limousine

Linde <-, -n> ['lɪn·də] *f* BOT linden [tree]

lindern ['lɪn·dɐn] *vt* to alleviate; *Husten, Sonnenbrand* to soothe

Linderung <-> *f kein pl* relief

Lineal <-s, -e> [li·ne·'aːl] *nt* ruler

Linie <-, -n> ['liː·niə] *f a.* TRANSP line; **nehmen Sie am besten die ~ 19** it's best if you take the [number] 19 ▶WENDUNGEN: **die schlanke ~** (*fam*) one's figure

Linienbus *m* regular [service] bus

Linienflug *m* scheduled flight

Linienrichter *m* (*beim Fußball*) linesman; (*beim Tennis*) line judge

liniert *adj* lined

link [lɪŋk] *adj* (*fam*) shady

Link <-s, -s> [lɪŋk] *nt* COMPUT link

Linke <-n, -n> ['lɪŋ·kə] *f* ❶ (*linke Hand*) left hand ❷ (*im Boxen*) left ❸ POL ■**die ~** the left

linke(r, s) *adj attr* ❶ left; *Fahrbahn, Spur* left-hand ❷ POL left-wing

linken ['lɪŋ·kn̩] *vt* (*sl*) to take for a ride *fam*

linkisch ['lɪŋ·kɪʃ] *adj* clumsy

links [lɪŋks] I. *adv* ❶ (*auf der linken Seite*) on the left; ■**~ neben/von ...** to the left of ...; **~ oben/unten** in the top [*or* upper]/bottom [*or* lower] left-hand corner; **nach ~** [to the] left; **von ~** from the left ❷ TRANSP **~ abbiegen** to turn [to the] left; **sich** *akk* **~ einordnen** to go

into the left lane; **sich** *akk* **~ halten** to keep [to the] left ❸ MODE **~ stricken** to purl ❹ *etw auf* **~ waschen** to wash sth inside out ❺ POL left-wing ❻ MIL **~ um!** left face! ▶WENDUNGEN: **jdn ~ liegen lassen** (*fam*) to ignore sb; **mit ~** (*fam*) easily II. *präp +gen* ■**~ einer S.** to the left of sth

Linksaußen <-, -> [lɪŋks·'ʔau̯·sn̩] *m* ❶ SPORT left winger ❷ POL (*fam*) extreme left-winger

Linkshänder(in) <-s, -> ['lɪŋks·hɛn·dɐ] *m(f)* left-hander

Linkskurve *f* left-hand curve

linksradikal *adj* radical left-wing *attr*

Linoleum <-s> [li·'noː·le·ʊm] *nt kein pl* linoleum

Linse <-, -n> ['lɪn·zə] *f* ❶ *meist pl* BOT, KOCHK lentil ❷ ANAT, PHYS lens

Lippe <-, -n> ['lɪpə] *f* ANAT lip ▶WENDUNGEN: **etw nicht über die ~n bringen** to not be able to bring oneself to say sth

Lippenstift *m* lipstick

Liquidität <-> [li·kvi·di·'tɛːt] *f kein pl* ÖKON [financial] solvency

lispeln ['lɪs·pl̩n] *vi* to lisp

List <-, -en> [lɪst] *f* trick ▶WENDUNGEN: **mit ~ und Tücke** (*fam*) with cunning and trickery

Liste <-, -n> ['lɪs·tə] *f* list ▶WENDUNGEN: **auf der schwarzen ~ stehen** to be blacklisted

listig ['lɪs·tɪç] *adj* cunning

Litauen <-s> ['liː·tau̯·ən] *nt* Lithuania; *s. a.* **Deutschland**

Litauer(in) <-s, -> ['liː·tau̯·ɐ] *m(f)* Lithuanian; *s. a.* **Deutsche(r)**

litauisch ['liː·tau̯·ɪʃ, lɪ·tau̯·ɪʃ] *adj* Lithuanian; *s. a.* **deutsch**

Liter <-s, -> ['liː·tɐ] *m o nt* liter

literarisch [lɪ·tə·'raː·rɪʃ] *adj* literary

Literatur <-, -en> [lɪ·tə·ra·'tuːɐ̯] *f* literature

Literaturangabe *f* bibliographical reference

Literaturpreis *m* literary prize

Literaturwissenschaft *f* literary studies *pl*

Litfaßsäule ['lɪt·fas·zɔy·lə] f advertising column

live [laif] adj pred live

Livesendung^RR f live broadcast

Lizenz <-, -en> [li·'tsɛnts] f license

Lizenziat^RR <-[e]s, -e> [li·tsɛn·'tsi̯a:t] m SCHWEIZ (akademischer Grad) licentiate

Lkw-Maut [ɛl·ka·'ve:-] f truck toll

Lob <-[e]s, selten -e> [lo:p] nt praise

Lobby <-, -s> ['lɔbi] f lobby

loben ['lo:bn̩] vt, vi to praise

lobenswert adj commendable

löblich ['lø:p·lɪç] adj s. lobenswert

Loch <-[e]s, Löcher> [lɔx] nt ① (offene Stelle) hole; **ein ~ in den Bauch** fragen (fam) to flood sb with questions; **auf dem letzten ~ pfeifen** (fam: finanziell am Ende sein) to be broke; (völlig erschöpft sein) to be on one's last legs; **saufen wie ein ~** (fam) to drink like a fish

Locher <-s, -> ['lɔ·xɐ] m hole punch[er]

Locke <-, -n> ['lɔ·kə] f curl; **~n haben** to have curly hair

locken^1 ['lɔ·kn̩] vt, vr ■ **sich** akk ~ to curl

locken^2 ['lɔ·kn̩] vt ① (anlocken) to lure; **mich lockt es jedes Jahr in die Karibik** every year I feel the lure of the Caribbean ② (verlocken) to tempt; **Ihr Vorschlag könnte mich schon ~** I'm [very] tempted by your offer

Lockenstab m curling iron

Lockenwickler <-s, -> m roller

locker ['lɔ·kɐ] I. adj ① (nicht stramm) loose ② (nicht fest) loose, loosely-packed attr, loosely packed pred ③ KOCHK light ④ (nicht gespannt) slack; **Muskeln** relaxed ⑤ **ein ~es Mundwerk haben** (fig fam) to have a big mouth ⑥ (leger, unverkrampft) relaxed, laid-back attr fam, laid back pred fam ⑦ (oberflächlich) casual II. adv ① (nicht stramm) loosely; **~ sitzen** Kleidungsstück to be loose ② (sl:

ohne Schwierigkeiten) **das mache ich ganz ~** I can do it no problem fam

lockerlassen vi irreg (fam) **nicht ~** don't give up

lockermachen vt (fam) to shell out

lockern ['lɔ·kɐn] I. vt ① (locker machen) to loosen ② (entspannen) **Muskeln** to loosen up sep ③ (weniger streng gestalten) **Regeln** to relax II. vr ■ **sich** akk ~ ① (locker werden) Backstein, Schraube, Zahn to work loose; **Bremsen** to come loose; **Bewölkung, Nebel** to lift ② SPORT (die Muskulatur entspannen) to loosen up ③ (sich entkrampfen) **die Verkrampfung lockerte sich zusehends** the tension eased visibly

lockig ['lɔ·kɪç] adj Haar curly

Lockvogel m (a. pej) decoy

lodern ['lo:·dɐn] vi Feuer to blaze

Löffel <-s, -> ['lœ·fl̩] m ① (als Besteck) spoon ② (Maßeinheit) a spoonful [of] ▶ WENDUNGEN: **den ~ abgeben** (sl) to kick the bucket; **sich** dat **etw hinter die ~ schreiben** to get sth into one's head

Loge <-, -n> ['lo:·ʒə] f ① FILM, THEAT box ② (Pförtnerloge) lodge ③ (Geheimgesellschaft von Freimaurern) lodge

Logik <-> ['lo:·gɪk] f kein pl logic

logisch ['lo:·gɪʃ] adj ① (in sich stimmig) logical ② (fam: selbstverständlich) [na,] ~! of course!

Logo <-s, -s> ['lo:·go] nt logo

Logopäde, Logopädin <-n, -n> [lo·go·'pɛ:·də] m, f speech therapist

Lohn <-[e]s, Löhne> [lo:n] m ① (Arbeitsentgelt) wage[s pl], pay ② kein pl (Belohnung) reward

Lohnabrechnung f payroll [accounting]

lohnen ['lo:·nən] I. vr ① (sich bezahlt machen) ■ **sich** akk [für jdn] ~ to be worthwhile [for sb]; **unsere Mühe hat sich gelohnt** our efforts were worth it ② (es wert sein) ■ **sich** akk ~, **etw zu tun** to be worth doing sth II. vt ① (rechtfertigen) **das lohnt den Aufwand kaum** it is hardly worth the effort ② (belohnen) **sie hat mir meine**

L

Hilfe mit Undank gelohnt she repaid my help with ingratitude

lohnend adj ① (einträglich) lucrative ② (nutzbringend) worthwhile

Lohnerhöhung f pay raise

Lohnfortzahlung f continued payment of wages

Lohnsteuer f income tax

Lohnsteuerjahresausgleich m ≈ tax return

Lohnsteuerkarte f ≈ W-2 [form]

lokal [loˈkaːl] adj local

Lokal <-s, -e> [loˈkaːl] nt bar, pub; (Restaurant) restaurant

lokalisieren* [lokaliˈziːrən] vt ① (örtlich bestimmen) to locate ② (eingrenzen) to localize (auf +akk in)

Lokomotive <-, -n> [lokomoˈtiːvə] f locomotive

Lokomotivführer(in) m(f) engineer

Lorbeer <-s, -en> [ˈlɔrbeːɐ] m ① (Baum) laurel [tree] ② (Gewürz) bay leaf ►WENDUNGEN: **sich** akk **auf seinen ~ en ausruhen** (fam) to rest on one's laurels

los [loːs] I. adj pred ① (von etwas getrennt) **~ sein** to have come off ② (fam: losgeworden) **jdn/etw ~ sein** to be rid of sb/sth; **er ist sein ganzes Geld ~** he's lost all his money ►WENDUNGEN: **mit jdm ist etwas ~** (fam) sth's up with sb; **dort ist nichts ~** (fam) nothing is going on there; **da ist immer viel ~** (fam) that's where the action always is; **mit jdm ist nichts ~** (fam: jd ist langweilig) sb is really boring; **was ist ~?** (fam) what's up?; **was ist denn hier/da ~?** (fam) what's going on here/there? II. adv ① (fortgegangen) **Ihre Frau ist schon vor fünf Minuten ~** your wife left five minutes ago ② (gelöst) **etw ist ~** sth is loose; **noch ein paar Umdrehungen, dann ist die Schraube ~!** just a couple more turns and the screw is out! ►WENDUNGEN: **~!** (mach!) come on!

Los <-es, -e> [loːs] nt ① (Lotterielos) [lottery] ticket; (Kirmeslos) [raffle] ticket ② (für Zufallsentscheidung) lot

③ kein pl (geh: Schicksal) fate ►WENDUNGEN: **jd hat mit jdm/etw das große ~ gezogen** sb has hit the jackpot with sb/sth

los|binden vt irreg to untie (**von** +dat from)

los|brechen irreg I. vt haben to break off II. vi sein ① (abbrechen) to break off ② (plötzlich beginnen) to break out

löschen [ˈlœʃn̩] I. vt ① (auslöschen) Feuer, Flammen to extinguish; Licht to turn off ② (tilgen) to delete ③ Musikkassette, Videokassette to erase II. vi to extinguish a fire

Löschfahrzeug nt fire engine

Löschpapier nt blotting paper

lose [ˈloːzə] adj loose

Lösegeld [ˈløːzə-] nt ransom

losen [ˈloːzn̩] vi to draw lots (**um** +akk for)

lösen [ˈløːzn̩] I. vt ① (ablösen) to remove (**von** +dat from) ② (aufbinden) to untie; Fesseln, Knoten to undo ③ Bremse to release ④ Schraube, Verband to loosen ⑤ (klären) to solve; Konflikt, Schwierigkeit to resolve ⑥ (aufheben, annullieren) to break off; Verbindung to sever; Vertrag to cancel ⑦ (zergehen lassen) to dissolve II. vr **sich** akk **~** ① (sich ablösen) to come off (**von** +dat of) ② (sich freimachen, trennen) to free oneself (**von** +dat of) ③ (sich aufklären) to be solved ④ (sich auflösen) to dissolve (**in** +akk in) ⑤ (sich lockern) to loosen; **langsam löste sich die Spannung** (fig) the tension [slowly] faded away

los|fahren vi irreg sein to drive off, to leave

los|gehen irreg I. vi sein ① (weggehen) to leave [on foot] ② (auf ein Ziel zu) **auf etw** akk **~** to set off for/toward sth; **wir gingen früh los** we set off early ③ (fam: beginnen) to start; **das Konzert geht erst in einer Stunde los** the concert doesn't start for another hour ④ (angreifen) **mit etw** dat **auf jdn ~** to lay into sb [with sth] ⑤ Schusswaffen to go off II. vi impers sein (fam:

beginnen) to start; **jetzt geht's los** (*fam*) here we go

los|kommen *vi irreg sein* (*fam*) ❶ (*wegkommen*) to get away ❷ (*sich befreien*) ■**von jdm ~** to free oneself of sb; **von einer Sucht ~** to overcome an addiction

los|lassen *vt irreg* ❶ (*nicht mehr festhalten*) to let go ❷ (*beschäftigt halten*) **der Gedanke lässt mich nicht mehr los** I can't get the thought out of my mind

löslich ['lø:sˌlɪç] *adj* soluble

Lösung <-, -en> ['lø:zʊŋ] *f* ❶ CHEM solution ❷ (*Aufhebung*) cancellation; *einer Beziehung/Verlobung* breaking off ❸ (*das Sichlösen*) breaking away (**von** +*dat* from)

Lösungsmittel *nt* solvent

los|werden *vt irreg sein* ❶ (*sich entledigen*) to get rid of ❷ (*aussprechen*) to tell ❸ (*fam: ausgeben*) to shell out ❹ (*fam: verkaufen*) to sell [off], to move

Lot <-[e]s, -e> [lo:t] *nt* ▶WENDUNGEN: **im ~ sein** (*fig*) to be all right

löten ['lø:tn̩] *vt* to solder (**an** +*akk* to)

Lothringen <-s> ['lo:trɪŋən] *nt* Lorraine

Lotion <-, -en> [loˈtsi̯o:n] *f* lotion

Lötkolben ['lø:tˌ-] *m* soldering iron

Lotse, Lotsin <-n, -n> ['lo:tsə] *m, f* pilot

lotsen ['lo:tsn̩] *vt* ❶ (*als Lotse dirigieren*) to pilot ❷ (*fam: führen*) ■**jdn irgendwohin ~** to take sb somewhere

Lotterielos *nt* lottery ticket

Lotto <-s, -s> ['lɔto] *nt* (*Zahlenlotto*) lottery; **~ spielen** to play the lottery

Löwe ['lø:və] *m* ❶ (*Raubtierart*) lion ❷ ASTROL Leo

Löwenzahn *m kein pl* dandelion

loyal [lo̯aˈja:l] *adj* loyal

Loyalität <-, *selten* -en> [lo̯aˌjaˌliˈtɛ:t] *f* loyalty (**gegenüber** +*dat* to)

Luchs <-es, -e> [lʊks] *m* lynx

Lücke <-, -n> ['lʏkə] *f* ❶ (*Zwischenraum*) gap ❷ (*Unvollständigkeit*) gap; (*Gesetzeslücke*) loophole

lückenhaft *adj* ❶ (*leere Stellen aufwei-*

send) full of gaps ❷ (*unvollständig*) fragmentary; *Wissen, Sammlung* incomplete; *Bericht, Erinnerung* sketchy

lückenlos *adj* (*vollständig*) complete; *Alibi* solid; *Kenntnisse* thorough

Luft <-, *liter* Lüfte> [lʊft] *f* ❶ *kein pl* (*Atemluft*) air; **die ~ anhalten** to hold one's breath; **an die** [**frische**] **~ gehen** to get some fresh air; [**tief**] **~ holen** to take a deep breath; **nach ~ schnappen** to gasp for breath ❷ *pl geh* (*Raum über dem Erdboden*) **in die ~ gehen** (*a. fig fam*) to explode; **etw ist aus der ~ gegriffen** (*fig*) sth is completely made up ❸ *kein pl* (*Platz, Spielraum*) space ▶WENDUNGEN: **sich in ~ auflösen** to vanish into thin air; **da ist dicke ~** (*fam*) the mood is tense; **die ~ ist rein** (*fam*) the coast is clear

Luftabwehr *f* air defense

Luftangriff *m* air raid

Luftballon *m* balloon

Luftblase *f* bubble

luftdicht *adj* airtight

Luftdruck *m kein pl* air pressure

lüften ['lʏftn̩] **I.** *vt* ❶ (*mit Frischluft versorgen*) to air ❷ (*preisgeben*) to reveal; *Geheimnis* to disclose **II.** *vi* (*Luft hereinlassen*) to let some air in

Luftfahrt *f kein pl* (*geh*) aviation

Luftfeuchtigkeit *f* humidity

Luftfracht *f* ❶ (*Frachtgut*) air freight ❷ (*Frachtgebühr*) air freight charge

Luftgewehr *nt* air gun

luftig ['lʊftɪç] *adj* (*gut belüftet*) well ventilated ❷ (*dünn und luftdurchlässig*) airy; *Kleid* light

Luftkissenboot *nt* air-cushion vehicle

Luftkurort *m* health resort area with particularly good air

luftleer *adj pred* vacuous

Luftlinie *f* as the crow flies

Luftmatratze *f* inflatable mattress

Luftpost *f* airmail (**per** +*dat* by)

Luftpumpe *f* pump; (*für Fahrrad*) bicycle pump

Luftraum *m* airspace

Luftröhre *f* windpipe

Luftschlange *f* [paper] streamer

Luftschutzbunker *m* air raid bunker

Lüftung <-, -en> *f* ① (*das Lüften*) ventilation ② (*Ventilationsanlage*) ventilation system

Luftverschmutzung *f* air pollution

Luftwaffe *f* air force + *sing vb*

Luftzufuhr *f kein pl* air supply

Luftzug *m* breeze; (*durch das Fenster*) draft

Lüge <-, -n> ['ly:·gə] *f* lie ►WENDUNGEN: **~n haben kurze Beine** (*prov*) the truth will come out

lügen <log, gelogen> ['ly:·gn] *vi* to lie; **das ist gelogen!** that's a lie! ►WENDUNGEN: **~ wie gedruckt** (*fam*) to lie one's head off

Lügner(in) <-s, -> ['ly:g·nɐ] *m(f)* (*pej*) liar

Luke <-, -n> ['lu:·kə] *f* ① *bes* NAUT (*verschließbarer Einstieg*) hatch ② (*Dachluke*) skylight; (*Kellerluke*) trapdoor

lukrativ [lu·kra·'ti:f] *adj* (*geh*) lucrative

Lumpen <-s, -> ['lʊm·pn] *m* ① *pl* (*pej: zerschlissene Kleidung, Stofffetzen*) rags *pl* ② DIAL (*Putzlappen*) rag

Lunge <-, -n> ['lʊŋə] *f* lung

Lungenentzündung *f* pneumonia

Lupe <-, -n> ['lu:·pə] *f* magnifying glass ►WENDUNGEN: **jdn/etw unter die ~** **nehmen** (*fam*) to examine sb/sth with a fine-tooth[ed] comb

Lust <-> [lʊst] *f kein pl* desire; **~/keine ~ zu etw** *dat* **haben** to feel like/not feel like doing sth

lüstern ['lʏs·tɐn] *adj* lustful

lustig ['lʊs·tɪç] *adj* cheerful; *Abend* fun; **sich** *akk* **über jdn/etw ~ machen** to make fun of sb/sth

lustlos *adj* listless

Lustschloss^{RR} *nt* summer residence

Lustspiel *nt* comedy

lutschen ['lʊ·tʃn] *vt, vi* to suck

Lutscher <-s, -> *m* lollipop

Luxemburg <-s> ['lʊ·ksm·bʊrk] *nt* Luxembourg; *s. a.* **Deutschland**

Luxemburger(in) <-s, -> ['lʊ·ksm·bʊr·gə] *m(f)* Luxembourger; *s. a.* **Deutsche(r)**

luxemburgisch ['lʊ·ksm·bʊr·gɪʃ] *adj* Luxembourgian; *s. a.* **deutsch**

luxuriös [lʊ·ksu·'riø:s] *adj* luxurious

Luxus <-> ['lʊ·ksʊs] *m kein pl* luxury

Luxusartikel *m* luxury item

Luxushotel *nt* luxury hotel

Lymphknoten *m* lymph node

lynchen ['lʏn·çn] *vt* (*a. hum*) to lynch

Lyrik <-> ['ly:·rɪk] *f kein pl* lyric [poetry]

Mm

M, m <-, -> [ɛm] *nt* M, m; **~ wie Martha** M as in Mike

m *m kurz für* **Meter** m

Machart *f* style

machen ['ma·xn̩] I. *vt* ❶ *(tun, unternehmen)* to do; **eine Reise/einen Spaziergang ~** to go on a trip/for a walk ❷ *(erzeugen, verursachen)* to make; *Fotos* to take; **jdm Angst ~** to frighten sb; **sich** *dat* **Sorgen ~** to worry; **jdm Hoffnung/Mut ~** to give sb hope/ courage ❸ *(zubereiten)* Tee, Kaffee to make ❹ *(absolvieren)* to do; **einen Kurs ~** to take a course; **eine Ausbildung ~** to train to be sth ❺ *(kosten)* **das macht zehn Euro** that's ten euros [please]; **was macht das zusammen?** what does that come to? ❻ *(ausmachen)* |**das**| **macht** |**doch**| **nichts!** never mind!; **macht das was?** does it matter? ▸WENDUNGEN: **mach's gut** *(fam)* take care [*or* it easy] II. *vi* ❶ *(werden lassen)* **Liebe macht blind** love is blind ❷ *(aussehen lassen)* **Querstreifen ~ dick** horizontal stripes make you look fat III. *vr* ❶ *(viel leisten)* **die neue Sekretärin macht sich gut** the new secretary is doing a good job ❷ *(passen)* **das Bild macht sich gut an der Wand** the picture looks good on the wall ❸ *(sich begeben)* **sich** *akk* **an die Arbeit ~** to get down to work ❹ *(gewinnen)* **sich** *dat* **Feinde ~** to make enemies ❺ + *adj (werden lassen)* **sich** *akk* **verständlich ~** to make oneself understood ❻ *(gelegen sein)* **sich** *dat* **etwas/viel/wenig aus jdm/etw ~** to care/care a lot/not care much for sb/ sth

Macher(in) <-s, -> *m(f) (fam)* doer

Macho <-s, -s> ['ma·tʃo] *m (fam)* macho

Macht <-, Mächte> ['maxt] *f* power; **an die ~ kommen** to come [in]to power

Machthaber(in) <-s, -> [-haː·bɐ] *m(f)* ruler

mächtig I. *adj* ❶ *(einflussreich)* powerful ❷ *(gewaltig)* mighty II. *adv (fam: sehr)* extremely

Machtkampf *m* power struggle

machtlos *adj* powerless

Machtprobe *f* test of strength

Macke <-, -n> ['ma·kə] *f (fam)* ❶ *(Schadstelle)* defect ❷ *(fam: Tick, Eigenart)* quirk

Mädchen <-s, -> ['mɛːt·çən] *nt* girl ▸WENDUNGEN: **~ für alles** *(fam)* jack-of-all-trades

mädchenhaft *adj* girlish

Mädchenname *m* ❶ *(Vorname)* girl's name ❷ *(Geburtsname einer Ehefrau)* maiden name

Made <-, -n> ['maː·də] *f* maggot ▸WENDUNGEN: **wie die ~**|**n**| **im Speck leben** *(fam)* to live the life of Riley

madig ['maː·dɪç] *adj* worm-eaten

madig|machen^{RR} *vt* to belittle; ■**jdm etw ~** *(fam)* to spoil sth for sb

Magazin <-s, -e> [ma·ga·ˈtsiːn] *nt* magazine

Magen <-s, Mägen> ['maː·gn̩] *m* stomach; **auf nüchternen ~** on an empty stomach ▸WENDUNGEN: **jdm dreht sich der ~ um** sb's stomach is turning; **etw schlägt jdm auf den ~** *(fam)* sth gets to sb

Magenbitter <-s, -> *m* bitters *npl*

Magengeschwür *nt* stomach ulcer

Magensäure *f* stomach acid

Magenschmerzen *pl* stomachache

Magenverstimmung *f* upset stomach

mager ['maː·gɐ] *adj* ❶ *(dünn)* thin ❷ *(fettarm)* low-fat; *Fleisch* lean ❸ *(dürftig)* feeble; *Ernte* poor

Magermilch *f* skim milk

Magersucht *f kein pl* anorexia

Magie <-> [ma·ˈgiː] *f kein pl* magic

Magier(in) <-s, -> ['maːɡiɐ] *m(f)* magician

magisch ['maːɡɪʃ] *adj* magic

Magister Artium *m the most commonly awarded degree in the humanities and social sciences at German universities*

Magnesium <-s> [ma'gneːzjʊm] *nt kein pl* magnesium

Magnet <-[e]s, -e[n]> [ma'gneːt] *m* magnet

Magnetfeld *nt* magnetic field

magnetisch [ma'gneːtɪʃ] *adj* magnetic

Mahagoni <-s> [maha'goːni] *nt kein pl* mahogany

Mähdrescher <-s, -> *m* combine harvester

mähen ['mɛːən] *vt Gras* to mow; *Feld* to harvest

Mahl <-[e]s, -e> ['maːl] *nt pl selten* (*geh*) meal

mahlen <mahlte, gemahlen> ['maːlən] *vt* to grind

Mahlzeit ['maːltsait] *f* meal; **~!** *DIAL* (*fam*) ≈ [good] afternoon! (*greeting used during the lunch break in parts of Germany and Austria*)

Mähne <-, -n> ['mɛːnə] *f* mane

mahnen ['maːnən] *vt* ① (*nachdrücklich erinnern*) to warn ② (*an eine Rechnung erinnern*) to remind

Mahnung <-, -en> *f* ① (*mahnende Äußerung*) warning ② (*Mahnbrief*) reminder

Mai <-[e]s, -e> ['mai] *m* May; *s. a.* **Februar**

Maiglöckchen *nt* lily of the valley

Mailand <-s> ['mailant] *nt* Milan

Mailbox <-, -en> ['meːlbɔks] *f* INET mailbox

Mais <-es, -e> ['mais] *m* ① (*Anbaupflanze*) corn ② (*Maisfrucht*) sweet corn

Maiskolben *m* corncob

majestätisch [majɛs'tɛːtɪʃ] *adj* majestic

Majonäse <-, -n> [majo'nɛːzə] *f* mayonnaise

Majoran <-s, -e> ['maːjoran] *m* marjoram

makaber [ma'kaːbɐ] *adj* macabre

Makel <-s, -> ['maːkl] *m* flaw

makellos *adj* ① (*untadelig*) *Ruf* untarnished ② (*fehlerlos*) perfect

mäkeln ['mɛːkln] *vi* to whine [about sth]

Make-up <-s, -s> [meːk'ʔap] *nt* make-up

Makkaroni [maka'roːni] *pl* macaroni

Makler(in) <-s, -> ['maːklɐ] *m(f)* broker; (*Immobilienmakler*) realtor

Makrele <-, -n> [ma'kreːlə] *f* mackerel

mal[1] ['maːl] *adv* ① MATH times; **drei ~ drei ergibt neun** three times three is nine ② (*eben so*) **gerade ~** (*fam*) only

mal[2] [maːl] *adv* (*fam*) *kurz für* **einmal**

Mal[1] <-[e]s, -e *o nach Zahlwörtern:* -> [maːl] *nt* (*Zeitpunkt*) time; **einige/ etliche ~e** sometimes/very often; **ein/ kein einziges ~** once/not once; **jedes ~** every time; **zum ersten/letzten ~** for the first/last time; **bis zum nächsten ~!** see you [around]!; **das x-te ~** (*fam*) the millionth time; **das eine oder andere ~** [every] now and again ▸WENDUNGEN: **ein für alle ~** once and for all; **mit einem ~[e]** all of a sudden

Mal[2] <-[e]s, -e> ['maːl] *nt* mark; (*Muttermal*) birthmark

Malaria <-> [ma'laːrɪa] *f kein pl* malaria

Malaysia <-s> [ma'laizɪa] *nt* Malaysia; *s. a.* **Deutschland**

malen ['maːlən] *vt, vi* ① (*ein Bild herstellen*) to paint ② DIAL (*anstreichen*) to paint

Maler(in) <-s, -> ['maːlɐ] *m(f)* painter

Malerei <-, -en> [maːlə'rai] *f* ① *kein pl* (*Malkunst*) painting ② *meist pl* (*Gemälde*) picture, painting

malerisch *adj* picturesque

Malheur <-s, -s> [ma'løːɐ] *nt* mishap

Malta <-s> ['malta] *nt* Malta; *s. a.* **Deutschland**

Malteser(in) <-s, -> [mal'teːzɐ] *m(f)* Maltese; *s. a.* **Deutsche(r)**

M

maltesisch [mal·'te:·zɪʃ] *adj* Maltese; *s. a.* **deutsch**

Malz <-es> ['malts] *nt kein pl* malt

Mama <-, -s> ['ma·ma] *f*, **Mami** <-, -s> ['ma·mi] *f (fam)* mommy

man <*dat* einem, *akk* einen> ['man] *pron indef* ➊ *(irgendjemand)* one *form,* you; **das hat ~ mir gesagt** that's what I was told ➋ *(die Leute)* people; **so etwas tut ~ nicht** that's not the way things work [around here] ➌ *(ich)* **~ versteht sein eigenes Wort nicht** I can't hear myself think

Management <-s, -s> ['mɛn·ɪtʃ·mənt] *nt* management + *sing/pl vb*

Manager(in) <-s, -> ['mɛ·ni·dʒɐ] *m(f)* manager

manche(r, s) *pron indef* ➊ + *pl (einige)* some ➋ + *sing* **~r Mann/~ Frau** many a man/woman

mancherlei ['man·çɐ·'lai] *pron indef, adjektivisch* various

manchmal ['manç·ma:l] *adv* ➊ *(gelegentlich)* sometimes ➋ SCHWEIZ *(oft)* often

Mandarine <-, -n> [man·da·'ri:·nə] *f* mandarin

Mandel <-, -n> ['man·dl] *f* ➊ *(Frucht)* almond ➋ *meist pl* ANAT tonsils *pl*

Mandelentzündung *f* tonsillitis

Manege <-, -n> [ma·'ne:·ʒə] *f* ring

Mangel¹ <-s, Mängel> ['ma·ŋl] *m* ➊ *(Fehler)* flaw ➋ *kein pl (Knappheit)* lack **(an** +*dat* of); **ein ~ an Vitamin C** vitamin C deficiency

Mangel² ['ma·ŋl] *f* ►WENDUNGEN: **jdn in die ~ nehmen** *(fam)* to grill sb

Mangelerscheinung *f* deficiency symptom

mangelhaft *adj* ➊ *(unzureichend)* inadequate ➋ *(Mängel aufweisend)* faulty ➌ *(Schulnote)* ≈ E

mangeln ['ma·ŋln] *vi* ■**es mangelt an etw** *dat* there is a shortage of sth

Mango <-, -gonen> ['maŋ·go] *f* mango

Manie <-, -n> [ma·'ni:] *f (geh)* obsession

Manifest <-[e]s, -e> [ma·ni·'fɛst] *nt* manifesto

Maniküre <-> [ma·ni·'ky:·rə] *f kein pl* manicure

Manipulation <-, -en> [ma·ni·pu·la·'tsi̯o:n] *f* manipulation

manipulieren* [ma·ni·pu·'li:·rən] *vt* to manipulate

Mann <-[e]s, Männer> ['man] *m* ➊ *(männlicher Mensch)* man; ■**Männer** men; *(im Gegensatz zu den Frauen a.)* males ➋ *(Ehemann)* husband ►WENDUNGEN: **der ~ auf der Straße** the man in the street, John Doe; **jd ist ein gemachter ~** sb has got it made

Mannequin <-s, -s> ['ma·nə·kɛ̃] *nt* model

männlich ['mɛn·lɪç] *adj* ➊ male; *Aussehen, Duft, Züge* masculine ➋ LING masculine

Mannschaft <-, -en> *f* ➊ SPORT team ➋ *(Schiffs- o Flugzeugbesatzung)* crew ➌ *(Gruppe von Mitarbeitern)* staff + *sing/pl vb*

Manöver <-s, -> [ma·'nø:·ve] *nt* ➊ MIL maneuver ➋ *(pej: Winkelzug)* trick

Mantel <-s, Mäntel> ['man·tl] *m* coat

manuell [ma·'nṵ·ɛl] I. *adj* manual II. *adv* manually

Mappe <-, -n> ['ma·pə] *f* ➊ *(Schnellhefter)* folder ➋ *(Aktenmappe)* briefcase

Maracuja <-, -s> [ma·ra·'ku:·ja] *f* passion fruit

Marathon <-s, -s> ['ma:·ra·tɔn] *m (a. fig)* marathon

Märchen <-s, -> ['mɛːɐ·çən] *nt* fairy tale

Marder <-s, -> ['mar·dɐ] *m* marten

Margarine <-, -n> [mar·ga·'ri:·nə] *f* margarine

Marienkäfer *m* ladybug

Marille <-, -n> [ma·'rɪ·lə] *f* ÖSTERR apricot

Marine <-, -n> [ma·'ri:·nə] *f* NAUT, MIL navy; ■**bei der ~** in the navy

Marionette <-, -n> [ma·ri̯o·'nɛ·tə] *f* puppet *a. fig*

Mark¹ <-, - o hum Märker> ['mark] *f (hist)* mark; **Deutsche ~** German mark

Mark² <-[e]s> ['mark] *nt kein pl* mar-

M

row ▸WENDUNGEN: **etw geht jdm durch ~ und <u>Bein</u>** sth sets sb's teeth on edge

markant [marˈkant] adj ❶ (ausgeprägt) bold ❷ (auffallend) striking

Marke <-, -n> [ˈmarkə] f ❶ (fam: Briefmarke) stamp; **eine ~ zu 55 Cent** a 55-cent stamp ❷ (Warensorte) brand; **das ist ~ Eigenbau** (hum) I made it myself

Markenartikel m brand-name product

Markenzeichen nt trademark a. fig

markieren* [marˈkiːrən] vt ❶ (kennzeichnen) to mark ❷ (fam: vortäuschen) to play

Markierung <-, -en> f marking

Markise <-, -n> [marˈkiːzə] f awning

Markt <-[e]s, Märkte> [ˈmarkt] m ❶ (Wochenmarkt) market ❷ (Marktplatz) marketplace ❸ ÖKON, FIN market; **etw auf den ~ bringen** to put sth on the market

Marktführer m market leader

Marktlücke f niche in the market

Marktplatz m marketplace

Marmelade <-, -n> [marməˈlaːdə] f jam; (aus Zitrusfrüchten) marmalade

Marmor <-s, -e> [ˈmarmoːɐ̯] m marble

Marokkaner(in) <-s, -> [maˈrɔˈkaːnɐ] m(f) Moroccan; s. a. **Deutsche(r)**

marokkanisch [maˈrɔˈkaːnɪʃ] adj Moroccan; s. a. **deutsch**

Marokko <-s> [maˈrɔˈko] nt Morocco; s. a. **Deutschland**

Marone <-, -n> [maˈroːnə] f [edible] chestnut

Mars <-> [ˈmars] m ∎ **der ~** Mars

Marsch <-[e]s, Märsche> [ˈmarʃ] m (a. mus) march

marschieren* [marˈʃiːrən] vi sein ❶ MIL to march ❷ (zu Fuß gehen) to walk quickly

Märtyrer(in) <-s, -> [ˈmɛrˈtyːrɐ, ˈmɛrtyˈrəˈrɪn] m(f) (a. fig) martyr

Marxismus <-> [marˈksɪsˈmʊs] m kein pl Marxism

Marxist(in) <-en, -en> [marˈksɪst] m(f) Marxist

März <-[es], -e> [ˈmɛrts] m March; s. a. **Februar**

Marzipan <-s, -e> [marˈtsiˈpaːn] nt o m marzipan

Masche <-, -n> [ˈmaʃə] f ❶ (Strickmasche) stitch ❷ (fam: Trick) trick

Maschendraht m wire mesh

Maschine <-, -n> [maˈʃiːnə] f ❶ (Automat) machine ❷ (Motorrad) bike ❸ (Schreibmaschine) typewriter; **~ schreiben** to type

maschinell [maʃiˈnɛl] I. adj machine attr II. adv by machine

Maschinenbau m kein pl ❶ (das Bau) machine construction ❷ (Fachgebiet) mechanical engineering

Masern [ˈmaːzɐn] pl measles

Maske <-, -n> [ˈmaskə] f (a. fig) mask

maskieren* [masˈkiːrən] I. vt to disguise II. vr ∎ **sich** akk ❶ (sich verkleiden) to dress up ❷ (sich vermummen) to put on a mask

Masochist(in) <-en, -en> [mazɔˈxɪst] m(f) masochist

masochistisch adj masochistic

maß [ˈmaːs] imp von **messen**

Maß¹ <-es, -e> [ˈmaːs] nt ❶ (Maßeinheit) measure ❷ pl (gemessene Größe) measurements; (Raum) dimensions; **bei jdm ~ nehmen** to measure sb ❸ (Ausmaß) extent ▸WENDUNGEN: **in ~en** in moderation; **das ~ ist voll** enough is enough

Maß² <-, -> [ˈmaːs] f SÜDD liter [mug] of beer

Massage <-, -n> [maˈsaːʒə] f massage

Massaker <-s, -> [maˈsaːkɐ] nt massacre

massakrieren* [masaˈkriːrən] vt to massacre

Masse <-, -n> [ˈmasə] f ❶ (breiiges Material) mass ❷ (Menschenmasse) crowd ❸ (große Anzahl) mass; **eine [ganze] ~** a lot [of] ❹ PHYS mass

Massenandrang m crush [of people]

Massenarbeitslosigkeit f mass unemployment no art

massenhaft I. adj on a huge scale II. adv (fam) in droves

Massenmedien pl mass media + sing/ pl vb

Massentierhaltung f factory farming

Massentourismus m kein pl mass tourism

Masseur(in) <-s, -e> [ma·ˈsøːɐ̯] m(f) masseur masc, masseuse fem

Masseuse <-, -n> [ma·ˈsøː·zə] f ❶ (veraltend) fem form von **Masseur** ❷ (euph: Prostituierte) masseuse

maßgeblich [ˈmaːs·geːp·lɪç] **I.** adj ❶ (ausschlaggebend) decisive ❷ (bedeutend) significant **II.** adv decisively; **an etw** dat ~ **beteiligt sein** to play a leading role in sth

massieren* [ma·ˈsiː·rən] vt to massage

massig [ˈma·sɪç] adj massive

mäßig [ˈmɛː·sɪç] **I.** adj ❶ (maßvoll, gering) moderate ❷ (mittelmäßig) mediocre, indifferent **II.** adv ❶ (in Maßen) with moderation ❷ (nicht besonders) indifferently

mäßigen [ˈmɛː·sɪ·gn̩] **I.** vt to curb **II.** vr ■ **sich** akk ~ to restrain oneself

massiv [ma·ˈsiːf] adj ❶ (solide) solid attr ❷ (wuchtig) solid, massive ❸ (drastisch, heftig) serious; Kritik heavy

Massiv <-s, -e> [ma·ˈsiːf] nt massif

maßlos I. adj extreme; ■~ **sein** to be immoderate **II.** adv ❶ (äußerst) extremely ❷ (unerhört) hugely

Maßlosigkeit <-> f kein pl lack of moderation

Maßnahme <-, -n> [ˈmaːs·naː·mə] f measure

Maßstab [ˈmaːs·ʃtaːp] m ❶ (Größenverhältnis) scale; **im** ~ **1:250.000** on a scale of 1:250,000 ❷ (Kriterium) criterion

maßstab(s)gerecht adj true to scale

maßvoll I. adj moderate **II.** adv moderately

Mast¹ <-[e]s, -en> [ˈmast] m ❶ NAUT mast ❷ (Stange) pole

Mast² <-, -en> [ˈmast] f pl selten (das Mästen) fattening

mästen [ˈmɛs·tn̩] vt to fatten

masturbieren* [mas·tʊr·ˈbiː·rən] vi to masturbate

Material <-s, -ien> [ma·te·ˈri̯aːl] nt material

Materialismus <-> [ma·te·ri̯a·ˈlɪs·mʊs] m kein pl materialism

Materialist(in) <-en, -en> [ma·te·ri̯a·ˈlɪst] m(f) materialist

materialistisch [ma·te·ri̯a·ˈlɪs·tɪʃ] adj materialist[ic]

Materie <-, -n> [ma·ˈteː·ri̯ə] f ❶ kein pl PHYS, CHEM matter ❷ (Thema) subject

materiell [ma·te·ˈri̯ɛl] adj ❶ (stofflich) material ❷ (finanziell) financial

Mathematik <-> [ma·te·ma·ˈtiːk] f kein pl mathematics + sing vb, math fam

mathematisch [ma·te·ˈmaː·tɪʃ] adj mathematical

Matratze <-, -n> [ma·ˈtra·tsə] f mattress

Matrose <-n, -n> [ma·ˈtroː·zə] m sailor

Matsch <-[e]s> [ˈmatʃ] m kein pl ❶ (schlammige Erde) mud; (Schneematsch) slush ❷ (breiige Masse) mush

matschig [ˈmat·ʃɪç] adj (fam) ❶ Erde muddy; Schnee slushy ❷ (breiig) mushy

matt [ˈmat] **I.** adj ❶ (erschöpft, schwach) weak; Händedruck limp; Lächeln, Stimme faint; Licht dim ❷ (glanzlos) mat[te]; Augen dull; Farben pale **II.** adv ❶ (schwach) dimly ❷ (ohne Nachdruck) feebly

Matte¹ <-, -n> [ˈma·tə] f (Fußmatte etc.) mat

Matte² <-, -n> [ˈma·tə] f SCHWEIZ, ÖSTERR (Bergwiese) alpine meadow

Mauer <-, -n> [ˈmau·ɐ] f (a. fig) wall

mauern [ˈmau·ɐn] vt to build

Maul <-[e]s, Mäuler> [ˈmaul] nt ❶ (bei Tieren) mouth; Raubtier jaws pl ❷ (derb: Mund) trap ►WENDUNGEN: **halt's** ~! (vulg) shut up!; **jdm das** ~ **stopfen** (vulg) to shut sb up

Maulesel [ˈmaul·ˈʔeː·zl̩] m mule

Maulkorb m muzzle

Maultaschen pl KOCHK SÜDD large pasta squares filled with meat, cheese, spinach, etc.

Maultier [ˈmaul·tiːɐ̯] nt s. **Maulesel**

M

Maulwurf <-[e]s, -würfe> ['maul·vʊrf] *m* (*a. fig*) mole

Maurer(in) <-s, -> ['mau·rɐ] *m(f)* bricklayer

Maus <-, Mäuse> ['maus] *f* ❶ (*a. comput*) mouse ❷ *pl* (*sl: Geld*) dough *sing*

Mausefalle *f* mousetrap

Maut <-, -en> ['maut] *f* toll [charge]

maximal [ma·ksi·'ma:l] I. *adj* maximum *attr;* (*höchste a.*) highest *attr* II. *adv* at maximum; **das ~ zulässige Gesamtgewicht** the maximum weight; **~ 25.000 Euro** 25,000 euros at most

Maximum <-s, Maxima> ['ma·ksi·mʊm] *nt* maximum (**an** +*dat* of)

Mayonnaise <-, -n> [ma·jɔ·'nɛː·zə] *f s.* **Majonäse**

Mazedonien <-s> [ma·tse·'do:·ni·ən] *nt* Macedonia; *s. a.* **Deutschland**

Mechanik <-, -en> [me·'ça:·nɪk] *f* mechanics + *sing vb*

Mechaniker(in) <-s, -> [me·'ça:·ni·kɐ] *m(f)* mechanic

mechanisch [me·'ça:·nɪʃ] *adj* (*a. fig*) mechanical

Mechanismus <-, -nismen> [me·ça·'nɪs·mʊs] *m* mechanism

meckern ['mɛ·kɐn] *vi* ❶ (*der Ziege*) to bleat ❷ (*fig fam*) to complain, to bellyache *fam* (**über** +*akk* about)

Medaille <-, -n> [me·'dal·jə] *f* medal

Medien ['me:·di·ən] *pl* ■ **die ~** the media + *sing/pl vb;* **die digitalen ~** digital media

Medikament <-[e]s, -e> [me·di·ka·'mɛnt] *nt* medicine

Medikamentenmissbrauch[RR] *m* drug abuse

medikamentös [me·di·ka·mɛn·'tøːs] *adj* medicinal

Meditation <-, -en> [me·di·ta·'tsi̯o:n] *f* meditation (**über** +*akk* about/on)

mediterran [me·di·tɛ·'ra:n] *adj* Mediterranean

meditieren* [me·di·'ti:·rən] *vi* to meditate

Medizin <-, -en> [me·di·'tsi:n] *f*

❶ *kein pl* (*Heilkunde*) medicine ❷ (*fam: Medikament*) medicine

Mediziner(in) <-s, -> [me·di·'tsi:·nɐ] *m(f)* doctor

medizinisch [me·di·'tsi:·nɪʃ] I. *adj* ❶ (*ärztlich*) medical ❷ (*heilend*) medicinal II. *adv* medically; **jdn ~ behandeln** to give sb medical treatment

Medizinmann <-männer> [-man] *m* (*indianisch*) medicine man; (*afrikanisch*) witch doctor

Meer <-[e]s, -e> ['me:ɐ] *nt* sea; (*Weltmeer*) ocean; **am ~** by the water; **ans ~ fahren** to go to the ocean; **das Schwarze/Tote ~** the Black/Dead Sea

Meerenge *f* strait

Meeresalge *f* seaweed + *sing vb*

Meeresfrüchte *pl* seafood + *sing vb*

Meeresspiegel *m* sea level

Meerrettich *m* horseradish

Meerschweinchen *nt* guinea pig

Meerwasser *nt* sea water

Megabyte ['me:·ga·bait] *nt* COMPUT megabyte

Mehl <-[e]s, -e> ['me:l] *nt* flour

mehlig ['me:·lɪç] *adj Kartoffeln* floury

mehr ['me:ɐ] I. *pron indef komp von* **viel** more; **immer ~** more and more; **~ oder weniger** more or less II. *adv* more; **nicht ~** no longer; **es war keiner ~ da** there was nobody left; **ich kann nicht ~** I can't take it any longer; **nie ~** never again; **niemand ~** nobody else

mehrdeutig *adj* ambiguous

mehrdimensional *adj* multidimensional

mehrere ['me:·rə·rə] *pron indef* ❶ *adjektivisch* (*einige*) several *attr;* (*verschiedene*) various ❷ *substantivisch* (*einige*) several; **~ davon** several [of them]

Mehrfamilienhaus [-liən-] *nt* multi-family house

mehrfarbig *adj* multicolored

Mehrheit <-, -en> *f* majority

mehrjährig *adj attr* several years of *attr,* of several years *pred*

Mehrkosten *pl* additional costs *pl*

mehrmals ['me:ɐ̯·ma:ls] *adv* repeatedly

mehrsprachig *adj* multilingual

mehrstündig *adj* lasting several hours *pred*

mehrtägig *adj* lasting several days *pred*

Mehrwegflasche *f* deposit [*or* returnable] bottle

Mehrwegverpackung *f* reusable packaging

Mehrwertsteuer *f* ≈ sales tax

mehrwöchig *adj* lasting several weeks *pred*

Mehrzahl *f kein pl* ❶ (*Mehrheit*) majority ❷ LING plural [form]

meiden <mied, gemieden> ['maɪ·dn̩] *vt* to avoid

Meile <-, -n> ['maɪ·lə] *f* mile

Meilenstein *m* (*a. fig*) milestone

meilenweit ['maɪ·lən·vaɪt] *adv* for miles

mein ['maɪn] *pron poss, adjektivisch* my

meine(r, s) ['maɪ·nə] *pron poss, substantivisch* mine

Meineid ['maɪn·ʔaɪt] *m* JUR perjury; **einen ~ leisten** to commit perjury

meinen ['maɪ·nən] *vt, vi* ❶ (*denken, annehmen*) to think; **und was ~ Sie dazu?** and what do you think about that?; **~ Sie?** [do] you think so? ❷ (*sagen wollen*) **was ~ Sie [damit]?** what do you mean [by that]? ❸ (*ansprechen*) **damit bist du gemeint** that means you ❹ (*beabsichtigen*) to mean, to intend; **ich meine es ernst** I'm serious [about it]; **es gut ~** to mean well; **es gut mit jdm ~** to do one's best for sb; **so war das nicht gemeint** I didn't mean it like that

meinetwegen ['maɪ·nət·'veː·gn̩] *adv* ❶ (*wegen mir*) because of me ❷ (*mir zuliebe*) for my sake ❸ (*von mir aus*) as far as I'm concerned; **darf ich? – ~!** may I? — sure! [*or* go right ahead!]

Meinung <-, -en> ['maɪ·nʊŋ] *f* opinion; (*Anschauung a.*) view; **jdm die ~ sagen** to give sb a piece of one's mind

Meinungsforschung *f kein pl* opinion polling

Meinungsumfrage *f* opinion poll

Meinungsverschiedenheit *f* ❶ (*unter-schiedliche Ansichten*) difference of opinion ❷ (*Auseinandersetzung*) argument

Meise <-, -n> ['maɪ·zə] *f* ORN tit ►WENDUNGEN: **eine ~ haben** (*fam*) to have a screw loose

meist ['maɪst] *adv s.* **meistens**

meiste(r, s) *pron indef superl von* **viel** ❶ *adjektivisch* most; **das ~ Geld** the most money; (*als Anteil*) most of the money; **die ~ Zeit** most of the time; (*meistens*) most of the time ❷ *substantivisch* ■**die ~n** most people; **die ~n von uns** most of us; ■**das ~** most of it; (*als Anteil*) the most; ■**das ~ von dem, was ...** most of what ...; ■**am ~n** [the] most

meistens ['maɪs·tn̩s] *adv* mostly, more often than not; (*zum größten Teil*) for the most part

Meister(in) <-s, -> ['maɪs·tɐ] *m(f)* ❶ (*Handwerksmeister*) master [craftsman]; **seinen ~ machen** to take one's master craftsman's exam ❷ SPORT champion ►WENDUNGEN: **es ist noch kein ~ vom Himmel gefallen** (*prov*) practice makes perfect

meisterhaft **I.** *adj* masterly; (*geschickt*) masterful **II.** *adv* in a masterly manner; (*geschickt*) masterfully

meistern ['maɪs·tɐn] *vt* to master

Meisterschaft <-, -en> *f* ❶ (*Wettkampf*) championship; (*Veranstaltung*) championships *pl* ❷ *kein pl* (*Können*) mastery

Melancholie <-, -n> [me·laŋ·ko·'liː] *f* melancholy

melancholisch [me·laŋ·'koː·lɪʃ] *adj* melancholy

Meldeamt *nt* (*fam*) ≈ city/town clerk['s office]

melden ['mɛl·dn̩] **I.** *vt* ❶ (*anzeigen*) to report ❷ RADIO, TV to report; **für morgen ist Schneefall gemeldet** snow is in the forecast for tomorrow ►WENDUNGEN: **nichts zu ~ haben** (*fam*) to have no say **II.** *vr* ❶ (*sich zur Verfügung stellen*) **sich** *akk* **zu etw** *dat* **freiwillig ~** to volunteer for sth ❷ **sich** *akk* **[am**

M

Telefon] ~ to answer the telephone; **es meldet sich keiner** there's no answer ❸ (*in Kontakt bleiben*) ■**sich** *akk* [**bei jdm**] ~ to get in touch [with sb]

Meldepflicht *f kein pl* obligation to report sth; **polizeiliche** ~ *legal obligation in Germany to register one's residence with the local authorities*

meldepflichtig *adj* ~**e Krankheit** disease doctors are required to report

Meldung <-, -en> *f* ❶ (*Nachricht*) piece of news ❷ (*offizielle Mitteilung*) report

meliert [me·'li:ɐt] *adj* ❶ (*Haar*) graying ❷ (*Gewebe*) flecked, mottled

Melisse <-, -n> [me·'lɪ·sə] *f* [lemon] balm

melken <melkte, gemolken *o* gemelkt> ['mɛl·kn̩] *vt* ❶ *Kuh* to milk ❷ (*fam*) *Person* to fleece

Melodie <-, -n> [me·lo·'di:] *f* melody, tune

melodisch [me·'lo:·dɪʃ] I. *adj* melodic II. *adv* melodically

Melone <-, -n> [me·'lo:·nə] *f* ❶ (*Frucht*) melon ❷ (*fam: Hut*) bowler [hat], derby

Memoiren [me·'mo̯a:·rən] *pl* memoirs

Menge <-, -n> ['mɛ·ŋə] *f* ❶ (*bestimmte Anzahl*) amount, quantity ❷ (*große Anzahl*) **eine** ~ **Geld** a lot of money; **eine** ~ **zu sehen** a lot to see; **jede** ~ **Arbeit** a ton of work ❸ (*Menschenmenge*) crowd ▶WENDUNGEN: **in rauen** ~**n** (*fam*) in vast quantities

Mensa <-, Mensen> ['mɛn·za] *f* university cafeteria

Mensch <-en, -en> ['mɛnʃ] *m* ❶ (*menschliches Lebewesen*) man; ■**die** ~**en** man *sing, no art*, human beings *pl*; **auch nur ein** ~ **sein** to be only human ❷ (*Person, Persönlichkeit*) person; ■~**en** people; **kein** ~ no one ▶WENDUNGEN: **wie der erste** ~ (*fam*) very clumsily

Menschenaffe *m* [anthropoid] ape

Menschenfresser(in) <-s, -> *m(f)* cannibal

Menschenhandel *m kein pl* human trafficking

Menschenkenner(in) <-s, -> *m(f)* judge of character

Menschenkenntnis *f kein pl* ability to judge character

Menschenleben *nt* ❶ (*Todesopfer*) life ❷ (*Lebenszeit*) lifetime

menschenleer *adj* ❶ (*unbesiedelt*) uninhabited ❷ (*unbelebt*) deserted

Menschenrecht *nt meist pl* human right *usu pl*

Menschenrechtsverletzung *f* human rights violation

Menschenseele ['mɛn·ʃn̩·'ze:·lə] *f* human soul; **keine** ~ not a [living] soul

menschenunwürdig I. *adj* inhumane; (*Behausung*) unfit for human habitation II. *adv* in an inhumane way, inhumanely

Menschenverstand *m* **gesunder** ~ common sense

Menschenwürde *f kein pl* human dignity

Menschheit <-> *f kein pl* ■**die** ~ mankind, humanity

menschlich ['mɛnʃ·lɪç] *adj* ❶ (*des Menschen*) human ❷ (*human*) humane; *Vorgesetzter* sympathetic

Menschlichkeit <-> *f kein pl* humanity

Menstruation <-, -en> [mɛns·trua·'tsi̯o:n] *f* menstruation

Mentalität <-, -en> [mɛn·ta·li·'tɛːt] *f* mentality

Menü <-s, -s> [me·'ny:] *nt* (*a. comput*) menu

merken ['mɛr·kn̩] I. *vt, vi* ❶ (*spüren*) to feel; **es war kaum zu** ~ it was barely noticeable ❷ (*wahrnehmen*) to notice; **ich habe nichts davon gemerkt** I didn't notice a thing ❸ (*behalten*) **leicht zu** ~ **sein** to be easy to remember II. *vr* (*im Gedächtnis behalten*) ■**sich** *dat* **etw** ~ to remember sth

Merkmal <-s, -e> ['mɛrk·ma:l] *nt* feature

merkwürdig I. *adj* strange II. *adv* strangely

messbar[RR], **meßbar**[ALT] *adj* measurable

Messe[1] <-, -n> ['mɛ·sə] *f* (*Gottesdienst*) mass

Messe[2] <-, -n> ['mɛ·sə] *f* (*Ausstellung*) trade show, convention

Messehalle *f* exhibit hall

messen <misst, maß, gemessen> ['mɛ·sn̩] I. *vt* ❶ (*Ausmaß oder Größe ermitteln*) to measure; *Blutdruck, Temperatur* to take ❷ (*beurteilen nach*) to judge (**an** +*dat* by) II. *vr* (*geh*) **sich** *akk* **mit jdm ~ können** to be able to compete with sb

Messer <-s, -> ['mɛ·sə] *nt* knife ▶WENDUNGEN: **bis aufs ~** (*fam*) to the bitter end; **jdn ans ~ liefern** (*fam*) to betray sb

Messerspitze *f* tip of a knife; **eine ~ Muskat** a pinch of nutmeg

Messias <-> [mɛ·'si·as] *m* REL Messiah

Messing <-s> ['mɛ·sɪŋ] *nt kein pl* brass

Messinstrument[RR] *nt* measuring instrument

Metall <-s, -e> [me·'tal] *nt* metal

Metallarbeiter(in) *m(f)* metalworker

metallisch [me·'ta·lɪʃ] I. *adj* ❶ (*aus Metall*) metal ❷ (*metallartig*) metallic II. *adv* like metal

Metapher <-, -n> [me·'ta·fɐ] *f* metaphor

Metastase <-, -n> [me·ta·'sta:·zə] *f* MED metastasis

Meteorologe, Meteorologin <-n, -n> [me·te·o·ro·'lo:·gə, me·te·o·ro·'lo:·gɪn] *m, f* meteorologist

Meter <-s, -> ['me:·tɐ] *m o nt* meter

Methode <-, -n> [me·'to:·də] *f* method

Metropole <-, -n> [me·tro·'po:·lə] *f* metropolis

Metzger(in) <-s, -> ['mɛts·gɐ] *m(f)* butcher

Metzgerei <-, -en> [mɛts·gə·'rai] *f* butcher shop

Meute <-, -n> ['mɔy·tə] *f* ❶ (*pej: Gruppe*) mob ❷ (*Jägersprache*) pack [of hounds]

Meuterei <-, -en> [mɔy·tə·'rai] *f* mutiny

Meuterer <-s, -> *m* mutineer

meutern ['mɔy·tɐn] *vi* ❶ (*sich auflehnen*) to mutiny ❷ (*fam: meckern*) to grumble, complain

Mexikaner(in) <-s, -> [mɛ·ksi·'ka:·nɐ] *m(f)* Mexican; *s. a.* **Deutsche(r)**

mexikanisch [mɛ·ksi·'ka:·nɪʃ] *adj* Mexican; *s. a.* **deutsch**

Mexiko <-s> ['mɛ·ksi·ko] *nt* Mexico; *s. a.* **Deutschland**

miauen* [mi·'au·ən] *vi* to meow

mich ['mɪç] I. *pron pers akk von* **ich** me II. *pron refl* myself; **ich fühle ~ nicht so gut** I don't feel very well

Mief <-s> ['mi:f] *m kein pl* (*fam*) stench

Miene <-, -n> ['mi:·nə] *f* expression ▶WENDUNGEN: **ohne eine ~ zu verziehen** without turning a hair

mies ['mi:s] *adj* (*fam*) lousy, rotten

mies|machen *vt* (*fam*) *s.* **madigmachen**

Miesmuschel ['mi:s·mʊ·ʃl] *f* [blue] mussel

Mietauto *nt* rental car

Miete <-, -n> ['mi:·tə] *f* rent; **zur ~ wohnen** to rent

mieten ['mi:·tn̩] *vt Boot, Wagen* to rent; *Haus, Wohnung, Büro a.* to lease

Mieter(in) <-s, -> *m(f)* tenant

Mietshaus *nt* apartment building

Mietvertrag *m* rental agreement

Mietwagen *m* rental car

Mietwohnung *f* rented apartment

Migräne <-, -n> [mi·'grɛː·nə] *f* migraine

Mikrochip [-tʃɪp] *m* microchip

Mikrofon <-s, -e> [mi·kro·'fo:n] *nt* microphone

Mikroskop <-s, -e> [mi·kro·'sko:p] *nt* microscope

Mikrowelle ['mi:·kro·vɛ·lə] *f* microwave

Milbe <-, -n> ['mɪl·bə] *f* mite

Milch <-> ['mɪlç] *f kein pl* milk

Milchflasche *f* milk bottle; (*für Babys*) baby's bottle

Milchkaffee *m* [caffe] latte

Milchprodukt *nt* milk product

Milchpulver *nt* powdered milk

M

Milchreis m ① (Gericht) rice pudding ② (Reis) arborio rice

Milchstraße f ■die ~ the Milky Way

Milchzahn m milk tooth

mild ['mɪlt] adj, adv mild

mildern ['mɪl·dɐn] vt to alleviate; ~de Umstände mitigating circumstances

Milieu <-s, -s> [mi·'lĭøː] nt environment

Militär <-s> [mi·li·'tɛːɐ̯] nt kein pl armed forces pl, military

Militärdiktatur f military dictatorship

militärisch [mi·li·'tɛː·rɪʃ] adj military

Miliz <-, -en> [mi·'liːts] f ① (Bürgerwehr) militia ② (in sozialistischen Staaten: Polizei) police

Milliardär(in) <-s, -e> [mɪ·lĭar·'dɛːɐ̯] m(f) billionaire

Milliarde <-, -n> [mɪ·'lĭar·də] f billion

Millimeter <-s, -> ['mɪ·li·meː·tɐ] m o nt millimeter

Million <-, -en> [mɪ·'lĭoːn] f million

Millionär(in) <-s, -e> [mɪ·lĭo·'nɛːɐ̯] m(f) millionaire masc, millionairess fem

Millionenstadt f city with a million inhabitants or more

Milz <-, -en> ['mɪlts] f spleen

Mimik <-> ['miː·mɪk] f kein pl (gestures and) facial expression(s)

Minderheit <-, -en> f minority

minderjährig ['mɪn·dɐ·jɛː·rɪç] adj underage

Minderjährige(r) f(m) dekl wie adj minor

mindern ['mɪn·dɐn] vt to reduce (um +akk by)

minderwertig adj inferior

Minderwertigkeit <-> f kein pl inferiority

Minderwertigkeitsgefühl nt feeling of inferiority

Minderwertigkeitskomplex m inferiority complex

Minderzahl f kein pl minority

Mindestalter nt minimum age

mindeste(r, s) adj attr slightest; das wäre das M~ gewesen that's the least he/she/you etc. could have done

mindestens ['mɪn·dəs·tns] adv at least

Mine <-, -n> ['miː·nə] f ① eines Bleistifts lead; eines Filz-, Kugelschreibers refill ② (Sprengkörper) mine ③ (Bergwerk) mine

Mineral <-s, -e> [mi·ne·'raːl] nt mineral

Mineralöl nt mineral oil

Mineralölsteuer f tax on oil

Mineralwasser nt mineral water

minimal [mi·ni·'maːl] adj minimal

Minimum <-s, Minima> ['miː·ni·mʊm] nt minimum (an +dat of)

Minirock m miniskirt

Minister(in) <-s, -> [mi·'nɪs·tɐ] m(f) POL Secretary

Ministerium <-s, -rien> [mi·nɪs·'teː·rĭʊm] nt POL department

Ministerpräsident(in) m(f) (eines Landes) prime minister; (eines Bundeslandes) minister-president (leader of a German state)

minus ['miː·nʊs] präp, konj, adv minus; ~ 15°C minus 15°C

Minus <-, -> ['miː·nʊs] nt ① (Minuszeichen) minus ② ÖKON (Fehlbetrag) deficit; ~ machen to lose money; [mit etw dat] im ~ sein to be in the red [with sth]

Minuszeichen nt minus sign

Minute <-, -n> [mi·'nuː·tə] f minute; in letzter ~ at the last minute; auf die ~ on the dot

Minutenzeiger m minute hand

Minze <-, -n> ['mɪn·tsə] f mint

mir ['miːɐ̯] pron ① pers dat von ich me; eine alte Bekannte von ~ an old acquaintance of mine; komm mit zu ~ come back to my place ② refl dat von sich one's; ich wasche ~ die Haare morgen I'll wash my hair tomorrow ▶WENDUNGEN: ~ <u>nichts</u>, dir nichts (fam) just like that

Mirabelle <-, -n> [mi·ra·'bɛlə] f Mirabelle [plum]

Mischbrot nt bread made from rye and wheat flour

Mischehe f mixed marriage

mischen ['mɪ·ʃn̩] I. vt to mix; KARTEN to shuffle II. vr ■sich akk ~ ① (sich ver-

M

mengen) to mix (**mit** +*dat* with) ❷ (*sich mengen*) to mingle (**unter** +*akk* with) ❸ (*sich einmischen*) to interfere (**in** +*akk* in)

Mischling <-s, -e> ['mɪʃ·lɪŋ] *m* ❶ (*Mensch*) person of mixed parentage ❷ ZOOL half-breed; (*Hund*) mongrel

Mischung <-, -en> *f* mixture; (*Kaffee, Tee, Tabak*) blend

miserabel [mi·zə·'ra:·bl] I. *adj* miserable II. *adv* ~ **schlafen** to sleep really badly

Misere <-, -n> [mi·'ze:·rə] *f* (*geh*) misery

missachten*RR, **mißachten***ALT [mɪs·'ʔax·tn̩] *vt* ❶ (*ignorieren*) to disregard ❷ (*gering schätzen*) ■ **jdn** ~ to be disdainful of sb; ■ **etw** ~ to disdain sth

MissachtungRR, **Mißachtung**ALT ['mɪs·ʔax·tʊŋ] *f* ❶ (*Ignorierung*) disregard ❷ (*Geringschätzung*) disdain

missbilligen*RR, **mißbilligen***ALT [mɪs·'bɪ·lɪ·gn̩] *vt* to disapprove of

MissbilligungRR, **Mißbilligung**ALT <-, -en> [mɪs·'bɪ·lɪ·gʊŋ] *f pl selten* disapproval

MissbrauchRR, **Mißbrauch**ALT ['mɪs·braux] *m* abuse

missbrauchen*RR, **mißbrauchen***ALT [mɪs·'brau·çn̩] *vt* to abuse

missen ['mɪs·n̩] *vt* **jdn**/**etw nicht** ~ **wollen** (*geh*) not to want to do without sb/sth; **mein Telefon möchte ich nicht** ~ I wouldn't want to have to do without my [tele]phone

MisserfolgRR, **Mißerfolg**ALT *m* failure

missfallen*RR, **mißfallen***ALT [mɪs·'fa·lən] *vi irreg* ■ **jdm missfällt etw** [**an jdm**] sb dislikes sth [about sb]

MissgeburtRR, **Mißgeburt**ALT ['mɪs·gə·bu:ɐt] *f* (*pej*) monster

MissgeschickRR, **Mißgeschick**ALT <-[e]s, -e> ['mɪs·gə·ʃɪk] *nt* mishap

missglücken*RR, **mißglücken***ALT [mɪs·'glʏ·kn̩] *vi sein* to fail

missgönnen*RR, **mißgönnen***ALT [mɪs·'gœ·nən] *vt* **jdm seinen Erfolg** ~ to resent sb's success

MissgunstRR, **Mißgunst**ALT ['mɪs·gʊnst] *f* envy

missgünstigRR, **mißgünstig**ALT I. *adj* envious II. *adv* enviously

misshandeln*RR, **mißhandeln***ALT [mɪs·'han·dl̩n] *vt* to mistreat

MisshandlungRR, **Mißhandlung**ALT [mɪs·'hand·lʊŋ] *f* mistreatment

Mission <-, -en> [mɪ·'sjo:n] *f* mission

Missionar(in) <-s, -e> [mɪ·sjo·'na:ɐ̯] *m(f)* missionary

misslingenRR, **mißlingen**ALT <misslang, misslungen> [mɪs·'lɪŋən] *vi sein* to fail

MisslingenRR, **Mißlingen**ALT <-s> [mɪs·'lɪŋən] *nt kein pl* failure

MissmutRR, **Mißmut**ALT ['mɪs·mu:t] *m* moroseness

missmutigRR, **mißmutig**ALT *adj* morose, sullen

missraten*RR, **mißraten***ALT [mɪs·'ra:·tn̩] *vi irreg sein* to go wrong; **ein** ~ **es Kind** a child who has turned out badly

MissstandRR, **Mißstand**ALT *m* sorry state of affairs; **soziale Missstände** social evils

misstrauen*RR, **mißtrauen***ALT [mɪs·'trau·ən] *vi* to mistrust

misstrauischRR, **mißtrauisch**ALT ['mɪs·trau·ɪʃ] I. *adj* mistrustful; (*argwöhnisch*) suspicious II. *adv* mistrustfully; (*argwöhnisch*) suspiciously

missverständlichRR, **mißverständlich**ALT I. *adj* unclear; ■ ~ **sein** to be easily misunderstood II. *adv* unclearly

MissverständnisRR, **Mißverständnis**ALT <-ses, -se> ['mɪs·fɛɐ̯·ʃtɛnt·nɪs] *nt* misunderstanding

missverstehen*RR, **mißverstehen***ALT ['mɪs·fɛɐ̯·ʃte:·ən] *vt irreg* to misunderstand

Mist <-es> [mɪst] *m kein pl* ❶ (*Stalldünger*) dung; ~! shit! *vulg* ❷ (*fam: Quatsch*) nonsense ❸ (*fam: Schund*) junk ►WENDUNGEN: ~ **bauen** (*fam*) to screw up; **so ein** ~! (*fam*) damn [it]!

Mistel <-, -n> ['mɪs·tl̩] *f* mistletoe

Misthaufen *m* dunghill

M

Mịststück *nt* (*fam*) bastard *masc vulg*, bitch *vulg*

mit ['mɪt] I. *präp +dat* ❶ with; ■ ~ **jdm** [**zusammen**] [together] with sb ❷ (*per*) by; ~ **der Bahn/dem Fahrrad/der Post** by train/bicycle/mail ❸ ~ **18** [**Jahren**] at [the age of] 18 II. *adv* too, as well; ~ **dabei sein** to be there [too]

Mịtarbeit *f kein pl* ❶ (*Arbeitsbeteiligung*) collaboration ❷ scH participation

mịt|arbeiten ['mɪt·ʔar·baɪ·tn̩] *vi* ❶ (*als Mitarbeiter*) to collaborate (**bei** *+dat* on) ❷ scH to participate (**in** *+dat* in)

Mịtarbeiter(in) *m(f)* employee; **freier** ~ freelancer

mịt|bekommen* *vt irreg* ❶ (*mitgegeben bekommen*) ■ **etw** [**von jdm**] ~ to be given sth [by sb] ❷ (*wahrnehmen*) ■ **etw** ~ to be aware of sth ❸ (*verstehen*) **hast du etwas davon** ~? did you catch any of that? ❹ (*fam: vererbt bekommen*) ■ **etw von jdm** ~ to get sth from sb

mịt|benutzen* *vt*, **mịt|benützen*** *vt* sÜDD to share

mịt|bestimmen* I. *vi* to have a say (**bei** *+dat* in) II. *vt* to have an influence on

Mịtbestimmung *f kein pl* participation

Mịtbewohner(in) *m(f)* housemate; (*in einem Zimmer*) roommate

mịt|bringen ['mɪt·ʔbrɪŋən] *vt irreg* ❶ to bring; **hast du denn niemanden mitgebracht?** didn't you bring anyone along? ❷ *Voraussetzungen* to meet

Mịtbürger(in) *m(f)* fellow citizen

mịt|denken *vi irreg* ■ **bei etw** *dat* ~ to follow sth

miteinander [mɪt·ʔaɪ·ˈnan·dɐ] *adv* ❶ (*jeder mit dem anderen*) with each other; ~ **reden** to talk to each other ❷ (*zusammen*) together; **alle** ~ all together

mịt|erleben* *vt* *Ereignisse* to live through; *eine Zeit* to witness; *im Fernsehen* to follow

Mịtesser <-s, -> *m* blackhead

mịt|fahren *vi irreg sein* ❶ (*begleiten*) **bei jdm** [**im Auto**] ~ to go [or ride along] with sb [in his/her car] ❷ (*Mit-*

fahrgelegenheit haben) **darf ich** [**bei Ihnen**] ~? can you give me a lift [or ride]?

Mịtfahrer(in) *m(f)* fellow passenger

mịt|fühlen *vi* ■ **mit jdm** ~ to sympathize with sb; **ich kann** ~, **wie dir zu Mute sein muss** I can imagine how you must feel

mịtfühlend *adj* sympathetic

mịt|geben *vt irreg* ■ **jdm etw** ~ to give sb sth to take with him/her

Mịtgefühl *nt kein pl* sympathy

mịt|gehen *vi irreg sein* ❶ (*begleiten*) ■ **mit jdm** ~ to come [or go] [along] with sb ❷ (*stehlen*) **etw** ~ **lassen** to walk off with sth

mịtgenommen I. *adj* (*fam*) worn-out II. *pp von* **mitnehmen**

Mịtglied ['mɪt·gli:t] *nt* member

mịt|halten *vi irreg* (*fam*) to keep up (**bei** *+dat* with)

mịt|helfen *vi irreg* to help (**bei** *+dat* with)

Mịthilfe ['mɪt·hɪl·fə] *f kein pl* assistance

mịt|hören *vt*, *vi* to listen in; **ein Gespräch** ~ to listen in on a conversation; (*zufällig*) to overhear a conversation

mịt|kommen *vi irreg sein* ❶ (*begleiten*) to come along ❷ (*Schritt halten können*) to keep up ❸ (*fam: verstehen*) **da komme ich nicht mit** that's [or it's] beyond me

mịt|kriegen *vt* (*fam*) *s.* **mitbekommen**

Mịtleid ['mɪt·laɪt] *nt kein pl* sympathy (**mit** *+dat* for), pity; **ein** ~ **erregender Anblick** a sorry sight

Mịtleidenschaft *f* **jdn in** ~ **ziehen** to affect sb

mịtleidig ['mɪt·laɪ·dɪç] I. *adj* ❶ (*mitfühlend*) sympathetic ❷ (*verächtlich*) pitying II. *adv* ❶ (*voller Mitgefühl*) sympathetically ❷ (*verächtlich*) pityingly

mịt|machen I. *vi* ❶ (*teilnehmen*) to take part (**bei** *+dat* in) ❷ (*fam: gut funktionieren*) **wenn das Wetter mitmacht** if the weather cooperates; **solange meine Beine** ~ as long as my legs hold out II. *vt* (*fam*) ❶ (*hineh-*

men) to go along with ❷(*erleiden*) **viel ~** to go through a lot

Mitmensch *m* fellow man

mit|nehmen *vt irreg* ❶(*mit sich nehmen*) to take [along] ❷(*transportieren*) to take [along]; **könnten Sie mich ~?** (*im Auto*) could you give me a lift? [*or* ride] ❸(*erschöpfen*) to take it out of sb

mit|reden *vi* ❶(*mitbestimmen*) to have a say (**bei** +*dat* in) ❷(*beim Gespräch*) **da kann ich nicht ~** I wouldn't know anything about that

Mitreisende(r) *f(m)* fellow passenger

mit|reißen *vt irreg* ❶(*mit sich reißen*) to sweep away ❷(*begeistern*) to get going

mit|schicken *vt* (*im Brief*) to enclose, to include

mit|schreiben *irreg* I. *vt* to write [*or* take] down II. *vi* to take notes

mitschuldig *adj* ■**an etw** *dat* **~ sein** to be partly to blame for sth

Mitschüler(in) *m(f)* classmate

mit|singen *irreg vi* to sing along

mit|spielen *vi* ❶ SPORT to play ❷ FILM, THEAT to act (**bei/in** +*dat* in) ❸(*bei Kinderspielen*) to play ❹(*fam: mitmachen*) to go [along] with it; **das Wetter spielte nicht mit** the weather didn't cooperate ❺(*wichtig sein*) to play a [big] part (**bei** +*dat* in) ❻**jdm übel ~** to play a nasty trick on sb

Mitspracherecht *nt kein pl* right to have a say; **ein ~ bei etw** *dat* **haben** to have a say in sth

Mittag <-[e]s, -e> ['mɪ·taːk] *m* ❶(*zwölf Uhr*) noon, midday; (*Essenszeit*) lunchtime; **gegen ~** around noon; [**etw**] **zu ~ essen** to have [sth for] lunch ❷(*fam: Mittagspause*) **~ machen** to take one's lunch break

Mittagessen *nt* lunch

mittags ['mɪ·taːks] *adv* in the middle of the day, at lunchtime

Mittagspause *f* lunch break

Mittagsschlaf *m* [afternoon] nap; **einen ~ machen** to take a nap

Mittagszeit *f kein pl* lunchtime; ■**in der ~** at lunchtime

Mitte <-, -n> ['mɪ·tə] *f* ❶(*räumlich*) middle; **in der ~ zwischen ...** halfway between ... ❷(*Mittelpunkt*) center ❸(*zur Hälfte*) **~ Januar** mid-January; **~ des Jahres** in the middle of the year; **sie ist ~ dreißig** she's in her mid-thirties ▸WENDUNGEN: **die goldene ~** a happy medium

mit|teilen ['mɪt·tai·lən] I. *vt* to tell II. *vr* ■**sich** *akk* [**jdm**] **~** to communicate [with sb]

Mitteilung *f* notification

Mittel <-s, -> ['mɪ·tl̩] *nt* ❶(*Hilfsmittel*) means *sing*; **es gibt ein ~, das herauszufinden** there is a way to find that out ❷(*Heilmittel*) remedy (**gegen** +*akk* for) ❸ *pl* (*Geldmittel*) funds ❹(*Mittelwert*) average; **im ~** on average ▸WENDUNGEN: **ein ~ zum Zweck** a means to an end

Mittelalter ['mɪ·tl̩·ʔal·tə] *nt kein pl* ■**das ~** the Middle Ages *npl*

mittelalterlich ['mɪ·tl̩·ʔal·tə·lɪç] *adj* medieval

Mittelamerika ['mɪ·tl̩·ʔaˈmeː·ri·ka] *nt* Central America

Mitteleuropa ['mɪ·tl̩·ʔɔyˈroː·pa] *nt* Central Europe

mitteleuropäisch ['mɪ·tl̩·ʔɔy·roˈpɛː·ɪʃ] *adj* Central European

Mittelfinger *m* middle finger

mittellos *adj* destitute

mittelmäßig I. *adj* average; (*pej*) mediocre II. *adv* **er spielte nur ~** his performance was just mediocre

Mittelmäßigkeit <-> *f kein pl* mediocrity

Mittelmeer ['mɪ·tl̩·meːɐ] *nt* ■**das ~** the Mediterranean [Sea]

Mittelpunkt *m* center

mittels ['mɪ·tl̩s] *präp* +*gen* (*geh*) by means of

Mittelstand *m* ❶ SOZIOL middle class ❷(*Unternehmen*) medium-sized business

mittelständisch *adj* medium-sized

Mittelweg *m* middle course ▸WENDUNGEN: **der goldene ~** a happy medium

M

mitten ['mɪ·tn̩] adv ■~ **auf/in** dat in the middle of; ~ **unter Menschen** in the midst of people

Mitternacht ['mɪ·tɐ·naxt] f kein pl midnight no art

mittlere(r, s) ['mɪt·lə·rə] adj attr ❶ (in der Mitte zwischen zweien) middle; **mein ~r Bruder** my second oldest/ youngest [or middle] brother ❷ (durchschnittlich) average attr or pred ❸ (mittelgroß) medium-sized

mittlerweile ['mɪt·lɐ·'vai·lə] adv (unterdessen) in the meantime; (seit dem) since then; (bis zu diesem Zeitpunkt) by now

Mittwoch <-s, -e> ['mɪt·vɔx] m Wednesday; s. a. **Dienstag**

mittwochs ['mɪt·vɔxs] adv [on] Wednesdays; s. a. **dienstags**

mitverantwortlich adj jointly responsible pred

mitwirken vi (beteiligt sein) to collaborate (**bei/an** +dat on)

mitwollen ['mɪt·vɔ·lən] vi to want to go [or come], too

mitzählen I. vi to count II. vt to include

mixen ['mɪk·sn̩] vt to mix

Mixer <-s, -> ['mɪk·sɐ] m blender

Mobbing <-s> ['mɔ·bɪŋ] nt kein pl bullying in the workplace

Möbel <-s, -> ['mø:·bl̩] nt ❶ sing piece of furniture ❷ pl furniture

mobil [mo·'bi:l] adj ❶ (beweglich) mobile ❷ (fam: munter) lively

Mobilfunk m mobile communications pl

Mobilfunkanbieter m wireless carrier, cell phone provider

Mobilität <-> [mo·bi·li·'tɛːt] f kein pl mobility

Mobiltelefon nt cell phone

möblieren* [mø·'bli:·rən] vt to furnish

Mode <-, -n> ['mo:·də] f fashion, style; **aus der/in ~ kommen** to go out of/ come into fashion

Modell <-s, -e> [mo·'dɛl] nt model

Modem <-s, -s> ['mo:·dɛm] nt o m TELEK modem

Modenschau f fashion show

Moderator, Moderatorin <-s, -toren> [mo·de·'ra:·toɐ̯, mo·de·ra·'to:·rɪn] m, f RADIO, TV host, presenter

modern¹ ['mo:·dɐn] vi sein o haben to decay, to get moldy

modern² [mo·'dɛrn] adj ❶ (zeitgemäß) modern; ~**ste Technik** state-of-the-art technology ❷ (modisch) fashionable

modernisieren* [mo·dɛr·ni·'zi:·rən] vt to modernize

Modeschmuck m costume jewelry

Modeschöpfer(in) m(f) fashion designer

modisch ['mo:·dɪʃ] I. adj fashionable II. adv fashionably

Modus <-, Modi> ['mɔ·dʊs] m COMPUT mode

Mofa <-s, -s> ['mo:·fa] nt moped

mogeln ['mo:·gln̩] vi (fam) to cheat (**bei** +dat at/on)

mögen ['mø:·gn̩] I. modal vb <mag, mochte, mögen> ❶ (wollen) **etw tun ~** to want to do sth; **ich möchte gerne kommen** I'd like to come ❷ (Vermutung) **sie mag Recht haben** she may be right; **das mag schon stimmen** that might [well] be true; **was mag das wohl bedeuten?** what's that supposed to mean? II. vt <mag, mochte, gemocht> ❶ (gernhaben) to like; (lieben) to love ❷ (Gefallen finden) ~ **Sie Fisch?** do you like fish?; **ich mag lieber Bier** I prefer beer; **am liebsten mag ich Eintopf** stew is my favorite [meal] ❸ (haben wollen) to want; **möchtest du ein Bier?** would you like a beer?; **ich möchte ein Stück Kuchen** I'd like a piece of cake

möglich ['mø:k·lɪç] adj possible; **alle ~en ...** all kinds [or sorts] of ...; **es für ~ halten, dass ...** to consider it possible that ...; **sein M~stes tun** to do everything in one's power; **schon ~** (fam) maybe

möglicherweise adv possibly

Möglichkeit <-, -en> f ❶ (Gelegenheit) opportunity ❷ (Möglichsein) possibility; **nach ~** if possible

möglichst *adv* ~ **bald** as soon as possible

Mohn <-[e]s, -e> ['mo:n] *m* poppy; (*Mohnsamen*) poppy seed

Möhre <-, -n> ['mø:·rə] *f* carrot

Mokka <-s, -s> ['mɔ·ka] *m* mocha

Molke <-> ['mɔl·kə] *f kein pl* whey

Molkerei <-, -en> [mɔl·kə·'rai] *f* dairy

mollig ['mɔ·lɪç] *adj* (*fam*) ❶ (*rundlich*) plump ❷ (*behaglich*) cozy ❸ (*angenehm warm*) snug

Moment <-[e]s, -e> [mo·'mɛnt] *m* moment; ■ **im** ~ at the moment; **im ersten** ~ at first; **im falschen/letzten** ~ at the wrong/last moment; **einen [kleinen]** ~! just a minute!

momentan [mo·mɛn·'ta:n] I. *adj* ❶ (*derzeitig*) present *attr,* current *attr* ❷ (*vorübergehend*) momentary II. *adv* ❶ (*derzeit*) at present ❷ (*vorübergehend*) momentarily

Monarch(in) <-en, -en> [mo·'narç, mo·'nar·çɪn] *m(f)* monarch

Monarchie <-, -n> [mo·nar·'çi:] *f* monarchy

Monat <-[e]s, -e> ['mo:·nat] *m* month; **im vierten** ~ **sein** to be four months pregnant

monatlich ['mo:·nat·lɪç] *adj, adv* monthly

Monatsbinde *f* sanitary napkin

Monatsblutung *f s.* **Menstruation**

Mönch <-[e]s, -e> ['mœnç] *m* monk

Mond <-[e]s, -e> ['mo:nt] *m* moon; **der** ~ **nimmt ab/zu** the moon is waning/waxing ▶WENDUNGEN: **hinter dem** ~ **leben** to be out of touch [with the world]

Mondfinsternis *f* eclipse of the moon

Mondschein *m* moonlight

Mongole, Mongolin <-n, -n> [mɔŋ·'go:·lə] *m, f* Mongol, Mongolian; *s. a.* **Deutsche(r)**

Mongolei <-> [mɔŋ·go·'lai] *f* ■ **die** ~ Mongolia; *s. a.* **Deutschland**

mongolisch [mɔŋ·'go:·lɪʃ] *adj* Mongolian; *s. a.* **deutsch**

Monitor <-s, -toren> ['mo:·ni·to:ɐ] *m* monitor

Monolog <-[e]s, -e> [mo·no·'lo:k] *m* monolog[ue]

Monopol <-s, -e> [mo·no·'po:l] *nt* monopoly (**auf** +*akk* on)

monoton [mo·no·'to:n] I. *adj* monotonous II. *adv* monotonously

Monotonie <-, -n> [mo·no·to·'ni:] *f* monotony

Monster <-s, -> ['mɔns·tɐ] *nt* monster

Monsun <-s, -e> [mɔn·'zu:n] *m* monsoon

Montag <-s, -e> ['mo:n·ta:k] *m* Monday; *s. a.* **Dienstag**

Montage <-, -n> [mɔn·'ta:·ʒə] *f* ❶ (*Zusammenbau*) assembly ❷ (*fam*) **auf** ~ **sein** to be away on a job

Monteur(in) <-s, -e> [mɔn·'tø:ɐ] *m(f)* mechanic, fitter

montieren* [mɔn·'ti:·rən] *vt* ❶ (*zusammenbauen*) to assemble ❷ (*installieren*) to install (**an/auf** +*akk* on)

Monument <-[e]s, -e> [mo·nu·'mɛnt] *nt* monument

Moor <-[e]s, -e> ['mo:ɐ] *nt* swamp

Moos <-es, -e> ['mo:s] *nt* ❶ (*Pflanze*) moss ❷ *kein pl* (*fam: Geld*) dough

Moped <-s, -s> ['mo:·pɛt] *nt* moped

Mops <-es, Möpse> ['mɔps] *m* ❶ (*Hund*) pug [dog] ❷ (*fam: dicke Person*) pudge ❸ *pl* (*fam: Brüste*) boobs *pl sl,* tits *pl vulg*

Moral <-> [mo·'ra:l] *f kein pl* ❶ (*ethische Grundsätze*) morals *pl* ❷ (*einer Geschichte*) moral

moralisch [mo·'ra:·lɪʃ] I. *adj* moral II. *adv* morally

Moralpredigt *f* homily

Mord <-[e]s, -e> ['mɔrt] *m* murder ▶WENDUNGEN: **dann gibt es** ~ **und Totschlag** there'll be hell to pay

Mordanschlag *m* attempt on sb's life; (*pol a.*) assassination attempt

Morddrohung *f* death threat

morden ['mɔr·dn̩] *vi* to murder, to kill

Mörder(in) <-s, -> ['mœr·dɐ] *m(f)* murderer, killer

Mordfall *m* murder case

Mordkommission *f* homicide [division]

Mordsglück *nt* (*fam*) incredibly good

M

luck; **ein ~ haben** to be incredibly lucky

Mordskrach m (fam) ① kein pl (Lärm) terrible racket, a real commotion ② (Streit) big argument

morgen ['mɔr·ɡn̩] adv tomorrow; **~ Früh/Mittag** tomorrow morning/at lunchtime; **bis ~!** see you tomorrow!

Morgen <-s, -> ['mɔr·ɡn̩] m morning; **am ~** in the morning; **eines ~s** one morning; **den ganzen ~ [über]** all morning [long]; **guten ~!** good morning!; **zu ~ essen** SCHWEIZ (frühstücken) to have breakfast

morgendlich ['mɔr·ɡn̩t·lɪç] adj ① (morgens üblich) morning attr ② (morgens stattfindend) in the morning pred

Morgenessen nt SCHWEIZ (Frühstück) breakfast

Morgengrauen <-s, -> nt daybreak

Morgenmuffel <-s, -> m (fam) **ein [großer] ~ sein** to always be [very] grumpy in the morning

morgens ['mɔr·ɡn̩s] adv in the morning

morgig ['mɔr·ɡɪç] adj attr tomorrow's; **der ~e Termin** tomorrow's appointment

Morphium <-s> ['mɔr·fi̯·ʊm] nt kein pl morphine

morsch ['mɔrʃ] adj rotten

Mosaik <-s, -e[n]> [mo·za·'i:k] nt mosaic

Moschee <-, -n> [mo·'ʃe:] f mosque

Mosel <-> ['mo:·zl̩] f ■ **die ~** the Moselle

Moskito <-s, -s> [mɔs·'ki:·to] m mosquito

Moslem, Moslemin <-s, -s> ['mɔs·lɛm, mɔs·'le:·mɪn] m, f Muslim

moslemisch [mɔs·'le:·mɪʃ] adj attr Muslim

Most <-[e]s> ['mɔst] m kein pl ① (Fruchtsaft) fruit juice ② SÜDD, SCHWEIZ, ÖSTERR (Obstwein) hard cider

Motiv <-s, -e> [mo·'ti:f] nt motive

Motivation <-, -en> [mo·ti·va·'tsi̯o:n] f motivation

motivieren* [mo·ti·'vi:·rən] vt to motivate

Motor <-s, Motoren> ['mo:·to:ɐ̯] m (Verbrennungsmotor) engine; (Elektromotor) motor

Motorboot nt motor boat

Motorhaube f hood

Motorrad [mo·'to:·rat] nt motorcycle, motorbike fam

Motorradfahrer(in) m(f) motorcyclist

Motorroller m [motor] scooter

Motorschaden m engine damage

Motte <-, -n> ['mɔ·tə] f moth

Motto <-s, -s> ['mɔ·to] nt motto

motzen ['mɔ·tsn̩] vi (fam) to complain (**über** +akk about)

Möwe <-, -n> ['mø:·və] f [sea]gull

Mücke <-, -n> ['mʏ·kə] f mosquito
▶WENDUNGEN: **aus einer ~ einen Elefanten machen** to make a mountain out of a molehill

Mückenstich m mosquito bite

Mucks ['mʊks] m (fam) **keinen ~ sagen** to not say a word; **ohne einen ~** without a murmur

mucksmäuschenstill ['mʊks·mɔys·çən·'ʃtɪl] adj (fam) completely quiet; **~ sein** to not make a sound

müde ['my:·də] adj ① (schlafbedürftig) tired ② (überdrüssig) ■ **einer S.** gen ~ **sein/werden** to be/grow tired of sth; ■ **nicht ~ werden, etw zu tun** to never tire of doing sth

Müdigkeit <-> ['my:·dɪç·kait] f kein pl tiredness

Muffel <-s, -> ['mʊ·fl̩] m (fam) grouch

muffig ['mʊ·fɪç] I. adj ① (dumpf) musty ② (schlecht gelaunt) grumpy II. adv ① (dumpf) musty ② (lustlos) listlessly

Mühe <-, -n> ['my:·ə] f trouble; **der ~ wert sein** to be worth the trouble; **sich** dat [große] ~ **geben[, etw zu tun]** to take [great] pains [to do sth]; **sich** dat **keine ~ geben[, etw zu tun]** to make no effort [to do sth]; **~ haben, etw zu tun** to have trouble doing sth; **[jdn] ~ kosten** to be hard work [for sb]; **machen Sie sich keine ~!** [please] don't go to any trouble! ▶WENDUNGEN: **mit ~ und Not** [just] barely

mühelos I. *adj* effortless II. *adv* effortlessly

Mühle <-, -n> ['myːlə] *f* mill

mühsam ['myːzaːm] I. *adj* arduous II. *adv* laboriously

Mulde <-, -n> ['mʊldə] *f* (*Bodenvertiefung*) hollow

Müll <-[e]s> ['mʏl] *m kein pl* garbage

Müllabfuhr <-, -en> *f* garbage [*or* trash] collection

Müllbeseitigung *f kein pl* garbage [*or* trash] collection

Mullbinde *f* MED gauze bandage

Mülldeponie *f* garbage [*or* trash] dump

Mülleimer *m s.* **Mülltonne**

Mülltonne *f* garbage [*or* trash] can

mulmig ['mʊlmɪç] *adj* (*fam: unbehaglich*) uneasy; **jdm ist ~ zumute** sb has butterflies in their stomach

multikulturell *adj* multicultural

multiplizieren* [mʊltipliˈtsiːrən] *vt* to multiply (**mit** +*dat* by)

Mumie <-, -n> ['muːmiə] *f* mummy

Mumm <-s> ['mʊm] *m kein pl* guts *npl*

Mumps <-> ['mʊmps] *m kein pl* MED [the] mumps + *sing/pl vb*

Mund <-[e]s, Münder> ['mʊnt] *m* mouth ▶WENDUNGEN: **halt den ~!** shut up!; **den ~ [zu] voll nehmen** to talk [too] big

münden ['mʏndn̩] *vi sein o haben Fluss* to flow (**in** +*akk* into); *Weg* to lead (**in** +*akk* into)

Mundgeruch *m* bad breath *no indef art*, halitosis *no indef art*

Mundharmonika *f* harmonica

mündig ['mʏndɪç] *adj* ■**~ sein/werden** to be/come of age

mündlich ['mʏntlɪç] I. *adj* oral II. *adv* orally

Mundpropaganda *f* word of mouth

Mündung <-, -en> ['mʏndʊn] *f* ❶ *eines Flusses* mouth ❷ *einer Schusswaffe* muzzle

Mundwasser *nt* mouthwash

Mundwerk *nt* **ein loses ~ haben** to be foul-mouthed

Mund-zu-Mund-Beatmung *f* mouth-to-mouth resuscitation

Munition <-, -en> [muˈniˈtsi̯oːn] *f* ammunition

Münster <-s, -> ['mʏnstə] *nt* cathedral

munter ['mʊntə] *adj* ❶ (*aufgeweckt*) bright ❷ (*heiter*) lively ❸ (*wach*) awake

Münzautomat *m* vending machine

Münze <-, -n> ['mʏntsa] *f* coin ▶WENDUNGEN: **etw für bare ~ nehmen** to take sth at face value

murmeln ['mʊrml̩n] I. *vi* to murmur II. *vt* to mutter

Murmeltier ['mʊrml̩tiːɐ̯] *nt* marmot, woodchuck ▶WENDUNGEN: **wie ein ~ schlafen** to sleep like a log

mürrisch ['mʏrɪʃ] I. *adj* grumpy II. *adv* grumpily

Muschel <-, -n> ['mʊʃl] *f* ❶ (*a. kochk*) mussel ❷ (*Muschelschale*) [sea] shell

Museum <-s, Museen> [muˈzeːʊm] *nt* museum

Musik <-, -en> [muˈziːk] *f* music

musikalisch [muziˈkaːlɪʃ] I. *adj* musical II. *adv* musically

Musikant(in) <-en, -en> [muziˈkant] *m(f)* musician

Musiker(in) <-s, -> ['muːzikɐ] *m(f)* musician

Musikinstrument *nt* [musical] instrument

Musikkapelle *f* band

musizieren* [muziˈtsiːrən] *vi* to play a musical instrument

Muskel <-s, -n> ['mʊskl] *m* muscle

Muskelkater *m kein pl* sore muscles *pl*

Muskelprotz <-es, -e> *m* (*fam*) muscleman

Muskelzerrung *f* pulled muscle

Muskulatur <-, -en> [mʊskulaˈtuːɐ̯] *f* musculature

muskulös [mʊskuˈløːs] I. *adj* muscular II. *adv* **~ gebaut sein** to have a muscular build

Müsli <-[s], -s> ['myːsli] *nt* muesli

muss^RR, **muß**^ALT ['mʊs] *3. pers sing pres von* **müssen**

Muße <-> ['muːsə] *f kein pl* leisure

müssen ['mʏsn] I. *modal vb* <muss, musste, müssen> ❶ (*gezwungen sein*) ■**etw tun ~** to have to do sth

M

❷(notwendig sein) ■ etw [nicht] tun ~ to [not] need to do sth; **warum muss es heute regnen?** why does it have to rain today?; **muss das [denn] sein?** is that really necessary? ❸(eigentlich sollen) ought to; ■ jd müsste etw tun sb should do sth; **ich hätte es ahnen ~!** I should have known! ❹(Vermutung) **es müsste jetzt acht Uhr sein** it must be eight o'clock [now]; **es müsste bald ein Gewitter geben** there's supposed to be a thunderstorm soon; **das muss wohl stimmen** that must be true II. vi <muss, musste, gemusst> ❶(gehen müssen) to have to go; **ich muss zur Post** I have to go to the post office ❷(gebracht werden müssen) ■ irgendwohin ~ to have to get somewhere; **dieser Brief muss heute noch zur Post** this letter has to be mailed today ❸(euph fam) [mal] ~ to have to go [to the bathroom]

müßig ['my:·sɪç] adj (geh: zwecklos) futile, pointless

Muster <-s, -> ['mʊs·tɐ] nt ❶(Warenmuster) sample ❷ MODE pattern

Musterknabe m (iron) paragon of virtue

mustern ['mʊs·tɐn] vt (eingehend betrachten) to scrutinize

Mut <-[e]s> ['mu:t] m kein pl courage

mutig ['mu:·tɪç] I. adj brave II. adv bravely

mutlos adj discouraged

Mutlosigkeit <-> f kein pl discouragement

Mutter[1] <-, Mütter> ['mʊ·tɐ] f mother; **~ werden** to be having a baby

Mutter[2] <-, -n> ['mʊ·tɐ] f TECH nut

Mutterleib m womb

mütterlich ['mʏ·tɐ·lɪç] adj ❶(von der Mutter) maternal ❷(umsorgend) motherly; **ein ~er Typ sein** to be the maternal type

Mutterliebe f motherly love

Muttermal nt birthmark; (kleiner) mole

Muttermilch f breast milk

Muttersöhnchen <-s, -> nt (pej fam) mama's boy fam

Muttersprache f native language

Muttersprachler(in) <-s, -> [-ʃpra:·xlɐ] m(f) native speaker

Muttertag m Mother's Day

Mutti <-, -s> ['mʊ·ti] f (fam) mommy

Mütze <-, -n> ['mʏ·tsə] f cap, hat

MwSt. f Abk von **Mehrwertsteuer** VAT, ≈ sales tax

mysteriös [mʏs·tə·'rjø:s] adj mysterious

Mythos <-, Mythen> ['my:·tɔs] m myth

Nn

N, n <-, -> [ɛn] *nt* N, n; **~ wie Nordpol** N as in November

Nabel <-s, -> ['naːbl̩] *m* navel

Nabelschnur *f* (*a. fig*) umbilical cord

nach [naːx] *präp* +*dat* ❶ (*räumlich: bis hin zu*) to; **der Weg führt ~ ...** this is the way to ... ❷ (*räumlich: hinter*) behind; **du stehst ~ mir auf der Liste** you're after me on the list ❸ (*zeitlich: im Anschluss an*) after ❹ (*gemäß*) according to; **~ allem, was ich gehört habe** from what I've heard ❺ (*in Anlehnung an*) after ▶WENDUNGEN: **~ und ~** little by little; **~ wie vor** still

nach|ahmen *vt* ❶ (*imitieren*) to imitate ❷ (*kopieren*) to copy

Nachahmung <-, -en> *f* ❶ *kein pl* (*Imitation*) imitation ❷ (*Kopie*) copy

Nachbar(in) <-n, -n> ['naxˌbaːɐ̯] *m(f)* neighbor; (*nebenan sitzend*) sb sitting next to one

Nachbarhaus *nt* house next door

Nachbarschaft <-, -en> *f* ❶ (*nähere Umgebung*) neighborhood ❷ (*die Nachbarn*) neighbors

Nachbildung *f* reproduction; (*exakt*) copy

nachdem [naːxˈdeːm] *konj* ❶ *zeitlich* after ❷ (*da*) since

nach|denken *vi irreg* to contemplate (**über** +*akk* about); **laut ~** to think out loud

nachdenklich ['naːxˌdɛŋkˌlɪç] *adj* pensive; **jdn ~ machen** to make sb think

Nachdruck[1] *m kein pl* emphasis; **~ auf etw** *akk* **legen** to stress sth; **etw mit ~ sagen** to say sth emphatically

Nachdruck[2] <-[e]s, -e> *m* VERLAG ❶ (*nachgedrucktes Werk*) reprint ❷ *kein pl* (*das Nachdrucken*) reprinting

nachdrücklich ['naːxˌdrʏkˌlɪç] **I.** *adj* insistent; *Warnung* firm **II.** *adv* firmly

nach|eifern *vi* (*geh*) to emulate

nacheinander [naːxˈʔaiˈnanˈdɐ] *adv* one after another

nach|empfinden* *vt irreg* ■**etw ~ können** to empathize with sth

nach|erzählen* *vt* to retell

nach|fahren *vi irreg sein* ❶ (*hinterherfahren*) to follow ❷ (*später fahren*) to come [along] later

Nachfolger(in) <-s, -> *m(f)* successor

Nachforschung *f* inquiry; (*polizeilich*) investigation

Nachfrage *f* ÖKON demand (**nach** +*dat* for)

nach|fragen *vi* to inquire

nach|fühlen *vt s.* **nachempfinden**

nach|füllen *vt Behältnis* to refill; **Zucker ~** to fill back up with sugar

Nachfüllpack <-s, -s> *m* refill [pack]

nach|geben *irreg vi* ❶ (*einlenken*) to give in ❷ (*nicht standhalten*) *Boden, Knie* to give way

nach|gehen *vi irreg sein* ❶ (*hinterhergehen*) to follow ❷ *Uhr* to be slow ❸ (*fig: verfolgen*) **einem Problem ~** to look into a problem ❹ (*form: ausüben*) to practice; *Interessen* to pursue

nachgiebig ['naːxˌgiːˌbɪç] *adj* accommodating; **jdm gegenüber zu ~ sein** to be too soft [on sb]

nach|gucken *vt, vi s.* **nachsehen I 1, 2, II**

nachhaltig ['naːxˌhalˌtɪç] **I.** *adj* ❶ (*dauerhaft*) lasting ❷ ÖKOL sustainable **II.** *adv* **jdn ~ beeindrucken** to leave a lasting impression on sb

Nachhaltigkeit <-> *f kein pl* ÖKOL sustainability

nach|helfen *vi irreg* ❶ (*zusätzlich beeinflussen*) to help along *sep* ❷ (*auf die Sprünge helfen*) ■**jdm ~** to give sb a helping hand

nachher ['naːxˈeːɐ̯] *adv* ❶ (*danach*) afterwards ❷ (*irgendwann später*) later; **bis ~!** see you later! ❸ (*fam: womöglich*) possibly

Nachhilfe *f* private tutoring

Nachhilfestunde *f* private lesson

nach|holen *vt* ❶ (*aufholen*) to make up for ❷ (*zu sich holen*) **seine Familie ~** to have one's family join one

nach|jagen *vi sein* ❶ (*zu erreichen trachten*) to pursue ❷ (*eilends hinterherlaufen*) to chase after

nach|kaufen *vt* to buy later

Nachkomme <-n, -n> ['na:x·kɔ·mə] *m* descendant

nach|kommen *vi irreg sein* ❶ (*folgen*) to come [along] later; **■jdn ~ lassen** to have sb join one later; **sein Gepäck ~ lassen** to have one's luggage sent on ❷ (*Schritt halten*) to keep up ❸ (*erfüllen*) *Anordnung, Pflicht* to carry out *sep*; *Forderung* to meet ❹ SCHWEIZ (*verstehen*) to follow

Nachkriegszeit *f* postwar period

Nachlass^RR <-es, -e> *m* ❶ (*hinterlassene Werke*) unpublished works *npl* ❷ (*hinterlassener Besitz*) estate ❸ (*Rabatt*) discount (**auf** +*akk* on)

nach|lassen *irreg* I. *vi* to diminish; *Druck, Schmerz* to ease off; *Gehör, Sehkraft* to deteriorate; *Nachfrage* to fall; *Sturm* to die down II. *vt* [*jdm*] **10 % vom Preis ~** to give [sb] a 10% discount

nachlässig ['na:x·lɛ·sɪç] I. *adj* careless; *Arbeit a.* slipshod *pej* II. *adv* carelessly

Nachlässigkeit <-, -en> *f* ❶ *kein pl* (*Art*) carelessness ❷ (*Handlung*) negligence

nach|laufen *vi irreg sein* (*a. fig*) to run after

nach|lösen *vt* **eine [Fahr]karte ~** to buy a ticket (*after boarding a train, bus etc.*)

nach|machen *vt* ❶ (*imitieren*) to imitate ❷ (*nachahmen*) **■jdm etw ~** to copy sth from sb ❸ (*fam: nachträglich anfertigen*) to make up *sep*

nach|messen *irreg vt* to measure again

Nachmieter(in) *m(f)* new tenant *no indef art*

Nachmittag ['na:x·mɪ·ta:k] *m* after-

noon; **am [frühen] ~** in the [early] afternoon; **im Laufe des ~s** during [the course of] the afternoon

nachmittags *adv* in the afternoon

Nachnahme <-, -n> ['na:x·na:·mə] *f* cash [*or* collect] on delivery; **etw per ~ schicken** to send sth COD

Nachname *m* surname, last name

nach|prüfen *vt, vi* to verify

Nachrede *f* **üble ~** slander, defamation [of character] *form*

nach|reichen *vt* to hand [*or* turn] in later

Nachricht <-, -en> ['na:x·rɪçt] *f* ❶ MEDIA news *no indef art,* + *sing vb;* **■eine ~** a news item; **■die ~en** the news + *sing vb* ❷ (*Mitteilung*) message; **■eine gute ~** [a piece of] good news; **jdm ~ geben** to let sb know

Nachrichtenagentur *f* news agency

Nachrichtendienst *m* ❶ (*Geheimdienst*) intelligence service ❷ *s.* **Nachrichtenagentur**

Nachrichtensprecher(in) *m(f)* newscaster

nach|rüsten I. *vt* to update; *Computer* to upgrade II. *vi* MIL to deploy new arms

nach|sagen *vt* ❶ (*von jdm behaupten*) **jdm Schlechtes ~** to say bad things about sb; **es wird ihr nachgesagt, dass ...** she is accused of ..., supposedly she ... ❷ (*nachsprechen*) **■[jdm] etw ~** to repeat sth [after sb]

Nachsaison [-zɛ·zõ:, -zɛ·zɔŋ] *f* off-season

nach|schauen *vt, vi s.* **nachsehen** I 1, 2, II

nach|schicken *vt* ❶ (*nachsenden*) to forward ❷ (*hinterher schicken*) **■jdn jdn ~** to send sb after sb

nach|schlagen *irreg* I. *vt* to look up *sep* (**in** +*dat* in) II. *vi* ❶ *haben* **in einem Wörterbuch ~** to consult a dictionary ❷ *sein* (*geh: ähneln*) **■jdm ~** to take after sb

nach|sehen *irreg* I. *vt* ❶ (*nachschlagen*) to look up *sep* (**in** +*dat* in) ❷ (*überprüfen*) *Auto, Schularbeiten* to check ❸ (*verzeihen*) **■jdm etw ~** to forgive sb for sth II. *vi* ❶ (*mit Blicken* *folgen*) ■jdm/etw ~ to follow sb/sth with one's eyes ❷ (*hingehen und prüfen*) to have a look ❸ (*nachschlagen*) to look it up

Nachsehen *nt* ▸WENDUNGEN: [bei etw *dat*] das ~ haben to come off worse [in sth]; (*leer ausgehen*) to be left empty-handed [in sth]; (*keine Chance haben*) to not get anywhere [with sth]

nach|senden *vt irreg* to forward

nachsichtig I. *adj* lenient; (*verzeihend*) merciful II. *adv* leniently

Nachspeise *f* dessert

Nachspiel *nt* (*unangenehme Folgen*) consequences *pl*

nach|sprechen *irreg vt* ■[jdm] etw ~ to repeat sth [after sb]

nächste(r, s) ['nɛːçs·tə] *adj superl von* **nahe** ❶ *räumlich* (*zuerst folgend*) next; **im ~n Haus** next door; (*nächstgelegen*) nearest ❷ *Angehörige* close ❸ *temporal* (*darauf folgend*) next; **bis zum ~n Mal!** until next time!; **am ~n Tag** the next day; **in den ~n Tagen** in the next few days; **als N~s** next

nach|stellen I. *vt* ❶ LING ■[etw *dat*] **nachgestellt werden** to be put after [sth] ❷ TECH (*neu einstellen*) to adjust; (*wieder einstellen*) to readjust; (*korrigieren*) to correct; *Uhr* to turn back *sep* ❸ (*nachspielen*) to reconstruct II. *vi* ■jdm ~ ❶ (*geh: verfolgen*) to follow sb ❷ (*umwerben*) to pester sb

Nächstenliebe *f* compassion

nächstliegend *adj attr* most plausible

Nacht <-, Nächte> ['naxt] *f* night; ■~ **sein/werden** to be/get dark; **bis weit in die ~** far into the night; **bei ~** at night; **in der ~** at night; **über ~** overnight; **über ~ bleiben** to stay the night; **diese/letzte ~** tonight/last night ▸WENDUNGEN: **bei ~ und Nebel** (*fam*) in the dead of night; **die ~ zum Tage machen** to stay up all night; **zu ~ essen** SÜDD, ÖSTERR to have dinner

Nachteil <-[e]s, -e> ['naːx·tail] *m* disadvantage; **sich** *akk* **zu seinem ~ verändern** to change for the worse

nachteilig ['naːx·tai·lɪç] I. *adj* disadvan-

tageous (**für** +*akk* for) II. *adv* unfavorably

nächtelang ['nɛç·tə·laŋ] *adv* for nights on end

Nachtessen *nt* SÜDD, ÖSTERR, SCHWEIZ (*Abendessen*) dinner, supper

Nachthemd *nt* nightgown

Nachtigall <-, -en> ['nax·tɪgal] *f* nightingale

Nachtisch *m s.* **Nachspeise**

Nachtleben *nt* nightlife

Nachtlokal *nt* nightclub

Nachtrag <-[e]s, -träge> ['naːx·traːk] *m* ❶ (*im Brief*) postscript ❷ *pl* (*Ergänzungen*) supplement

nach|tragen *vt irreg* ❶ (*hinterhertragen*) to carry after ❷ (*nachträglich ergänzen*) to add ❸ (*nicht verzeihen können*) ■jdm etw ~ to hold sth against sb; ■jdm ~, dass ... to hold it against sb that ...

nachtragend ['naːx·traː·gnt] *adj* unforgiving

nachträglich ['naːx·trɛːk·lɪç] I. *adj* later; (*verspätet*) belated II. *adv* later, belatedly

nach|trauern *vi* ■jdm/etw ~ to shed a tear for sb/sth

nachts ['naxts] *adv* at night; **montags ~** [on] Monday nights

Nachtschicht *f* night shift

Nachtschwester *f* night nurse

Nachttisch *m* bedside table

Nachtwache *f* night duty

Nachtwächter(in) *m(f)* night watchman

Nachuntersuchung *f* follow-up examination

nachvollziehbar *adj* comprehensible; **es ist für mich nicht ganz ~, wie ...** I don't quite understand how ...

nach|vollziehen* *vt irreg* to understand

nach|weinen *vi* ■jdm/etw ~ to shed a tear for sb/sth

Nachweis <-es, -e> ['naːx·vais] *m* proof

nachweisbar I. *adj* provable; *Giftstoffe* detectable; *Fehler* demonstrable II. *adv* provably

nach|weisen *vt irreg* ❶ (*beweisen*) to

N

establish proof of; **man kann mir nichts ~** nothing can be proved against me ❷ (*finden*) to detect (**in** +*dat* in)
nach|werfen *vt irreg* ❶ (*hinterherwerfen*) ■**jdm etw ~** to throw sth at sb ❷ (*fam: überlassen*) ■**jdm etw ~** to [practically] give sth away to sb
Nachwirkung *f* aftereffect; (*fig*) consequence
Nachwuchs *m kein pl* ❶ (*fam: Kinder*) offspring ❷ (*junge Fachkräfte*) young professionals *pl*
nach|zahlen *vt* ❶ (*nachträglich*) to pay at a later date ❷ (*zusätzlich*) to pay extra
Nachzahlung *f* ❶ (*nachträglich*) back payment ❷ (*zusätzlich*) additional payment
nach|ziehen *irreg vt* ❶ *Schraube* to tighten [up *sep*] ❷ *Bein* to drag ❸ *Linie* to go over; **sich** *dat* **die Augenbrauen ~** to pencil in *sep* one's eyebrows
Nachzügler(in) <-s, -> ['naːxˌtsyːklɐ] *m(f)* late arrival
N **Nacken** <-s, -> ['nakŋ] *m* neck ▶WENDUNGEN: **jdm im ~ sitzen** to breathe down sb's neck
nackt ['nakt] **I.** *adj* ❶ (*unbekleidet*) naked, nude; *Haut, Arme* bare ❷ (*kahl*) *Wand* bare ❸ (*unverblümt*) naked; *Tatsachen* bare; *Wahrheit* plain **II.** *adv* naked, in the nude
Nadel <-, -n> ['naːdl] *f* ❶ (*Nähnadel, Tannennadel*) needle ❷ (*Zeiger*) needle ▶WENDUNGEN: **an der ~ hängen** (*sl*) to be hooked on heroin
Nadelbaum *m* conifer
Nagel <-s, Nägel> ['naːgl] *m* (*Metallstift, Fingernagel*) nail ▶WENDUNGEN: **jdm brennt es unter den Nägeln, etw zu tun** (*fam*) sb is dying to do sth; **etw an den ~ hängen** (*fam*) to give up *sep* sth; **sich** *dat* **etw unter den ~ reißen** (*sl*) to steal [*or* make off with] sth
Nagelfeile *f* nail file
Nagellack *m* nail polish
Nagellackentferner *m* nail polish remover

nageln ['naːgln] *vt* to nail (**an** +*akk* to)
nagelneu ['naːglˈnɔy] *adj* (*fam*) brand-new
nagen ['naːgn] **I.** *vt, vi* to gnaw (**an** +*dat* at/on) **II.** *vi* (*quälen*) ■**an jdm ~** to nag [at] sb
nagend ['naːgnt] *adj* nagging; *Hunger* gnawing
Nagetier *nt* rodent
nah ['naː] *adj, adv s.* **nahe** ▶WENDUNGEN: **von ~ und fern** from near and far
nahe <näher, nächste> ['naːə] **I.** *adj* ❶ *räumlich* nearby, close [by] *pred*; **von ~m** from close up ❷ *zeitlich* near, approaching ❸ (*eng*) close; ■**jdm ~ sein** to be close to sb **II.** *adv* ❶ *räumlich* nearby, close [by]; ■**~ an/bei etw** *dat* close to sth ❷ *zeitlich* close ❸ (*fast*) **sie war ~ am Aufgeben** she almost gave up ❹ (*eng*) closely; **~ mit jdm verwandt sein** to be a close relative of sb ▶WENDUNGEN: **jdm zu ~ treten** to offend sb **III.** *präp* +*dat* near to
Nähe <-> ['nɛːə] *f kein pl* (*geringe Entfernung*) proximity; **aus der ~** from close up; **in der ~** near
nahebei ['naːəˈbai] *adv* nearby
nahe|kommen *vr irreg sein* ■**sich** *dat* ~ to become close
nahe|legen *vt* ■**jdm ~, etw zu tun** to advise sb to do sth
naheliegend *adj* **~ sein** to seem to suggest itself; **aus ~en Gründen** for obvious reasons
nahen ['naːən] *vi sein* (*geh*) to approach
nähen ['nɛːən] *vt* to sew; MED to stitch
näher ['nɛːɐ] **I.** *adj komp von* **nahe** ❶ (*in geringerer Entfernung*) nearer, closer ❷ (*kürzer bevorstehend*) closer, sooner *pred*; *Zukunft* near ❸ (*detaillierter*) further *attr*; **die ~en Umstände** the precise circumstances ❹ (*enger*) closer; *Verwandte* immediate **II.** *adv komp von* **nahe** ❶ (*in geringerem Abstand*) closer, nearer; **kommen Sie ~!** come closer! ❷ (*eingehender*) in more detail; **etw ~ ansehen** to have a closer look at sth; **sich** *akk* **~ mit etw**

dat **befassen** to go into sth in greater detail ③ (*enger*) closer; **jdn/etw ~ kennen** to know sb/sth well; **jdn/etw ~ kennen lernen** to get to know sb/sth better

nähern ['nɛːɐn] *vr* ❶ (*näher herankommen*) ■**sich** *akk* [**jdm/etw**] **~** to get closer [to sb/sth] ❷ (*einen Zeitpunkt erreichen*) ■**sich** *akk* **etw** *dat* **~** to get close to sth; **unser Urlaub nähert sich seinem Ende** our vacation is drawing to a close

nahe|stehen *vr irreg* ■**sich** *dat* **~** to be close

nahezu ['naːʔɐ·ʦuː] *adv* almost, virtually

Nähgarn *nt* cotton

Nähmaschine *f* sewing machine

Nähnadel *f* [sewing] needle

nahrhaft *adj* nutritious

Nährstoff *m* nutrient

Nahrung <-> ['naːrʊŋ] *f kein pl* food; **flüssige/feste ~** liquids/solids *pl*

Nahrungsmittel *nt* food

Nährwert *m* nutritional value

Naht <-, **Nähte**> ['naːt] *f* ❶ (*bei Kleidung*) seam ❷ MED suture *spec* ❸ TECH weld

Nahverkehr *m* local traffic; **der öffentliche ~** local public transportation

Nahverkehrszug *m* local train

naiv [na·'iːf] *adj* naive

Naivität <-> [na·ivi·'tɛːt] *f kein pl* naivety

Name <-ns, -n> ['naːmə] *m* name; **in jds ~s** on behalf of sb; **jdn nur dem ~n nach kennen** to only know sb by name

namenlos *adj* nameless; *Helfer, Spender* anonymous

namens ['naːməns] *adv* by the name of

Namenstag *m* Saint's day

nämlich ['nɛːm·lɪç] *adv* namely

Napf <-[e]s, **Näpfe**> ['napf] *m* bowl

Narbe <-, -n> ['narbə] *f* scar

Narkose <-, -n> [nar·'koː·zə] *f* anesthesia

Narr, Närrin <-en, -en> ['nar, 'nɛ·rɪn] *m, f* fool; **jdn zum ~en halten** to make a fool of sb; **sich** *akk* **zum ~en machen** to make a fool of oneself

närrisch ['nɛ·rɪʃ] *adj* (*verrückt*) crazy; (*unvernünftig*) foolish; ■**ganz** **~ auf jdn/etw sein** (*fam*) to be crazy about sb/sth

Narzisse <-, -n> [nar·'ʦɪ·sə] *f* narcissus

naschen ['na·ʃn̩] I. *vi* to snack, to nosh *fam;* **etwas zum N~** something sweet [to snack on] II. *vt* (*essen*) ■**etw ~** to snack on sth

Naschkatze *f* (*fam*) person with a sweet tooth

Nase <-, -n> ['naː·zə] *f* nose; **sich** *dat* **die ~ putzen** to blow one's nose ▶WENDUNGEN: **jdm etw auf die ~ binden** (*fam*) to tell sb sth; **sich** *dat* **an seine eigene ~ fassen** (*fam*) to blame oneself; **auf die ~ fliegen** (*fam*) to fall flat on one's face; **sich** *dat* **eine goldene ~ verdienen** to earn a fortune; **die ~ vorn haben** to be one step ahead; **jdn an der ~ herumführen** (*fam*) to lead sb on; **jdm auf der ~ herumtanzen** (*fam*) to walk all over sb; **pro ~** (*hum fam*) per person; **die ~ von jdm/etw voll haben** (*fam*) to be fed up with sb/sth; **jdm etw aus der ~ ziehen** (*fam*) to get sth out of sb

Nasenbluten <-s> *nt kein pl* nosebleed

Nasenspitze *f* tip of the nose ▶WENDUNGEN: **jdm etw an der ~ ansehen** to be able to tell sth from sb's face

Naseweis <-es, -e> ['naː·zə·vais] *m* (*Besserwisser*) know-it-all *fam,* wise guy *fam*

Nashorn *nt* rhino[ceros]

nass^{RR}, **naß**^{ALT} <nasser *o* nässer, nasseste *o* nässeste> ['nas] *adj* wet; **~ geschwitzt** soaked with sweat *pred*

Nässe <-> ['nɛ·sə] *f kein pl* wetness; **vor ~ triefen** to be soaking wet

nasskalt^{RR} *adj* cold and damp

Nation <-, -en> [na·'ʦjoːn] *f* nation; **die Vereinten ~en** the United Nations

national [na·ʦjo·'naːl] I. *adj* ❶ national ❷ (*patriotisch*) nationalist II. *adv* nationalistic

Nationalhymne *f* national hymn

N

Nationalist(in) <-en, -en> [na·tsi̯o·na·'lɪst] *m(f)* nationalist

nationalistisch *adj, adv* nationalist[ic]

Nationalität <-, -en> [na·tsi̯o·na·li·'tɛːt] *f* nationality

Nationalmannschaft *f* national team

Nationalrat *m kein pl* ① ÖSTERR National Assembly ② SCHWEIZ National Council

Nationalsozialismus [na·tsi̯o·'na·l·zo·tsi̯a·lɪs·mʊs] *m* National Socialism

Natter <-, -n> ['na·tɐ] *f* adder

Natur <-, -en> [na·'tuːɐ̯] *f* ① *kein pl* BIOL nature ② *kein pl* (*Landschaft*) countryside; **in freier ~** in the wild ③ (*Wesensart*) nature; **von ~ aus** by nature

Naturereignis *nt* natural phenomenon

Naturfreund(in) *m(f)* nature lover

naturgetreu *adj, adv* true to life

Naturkatastrophe *f* natural disaster

Naturkostladen *m* health food store

natürlich [na·'tyːɐ̯·lɪç] **I.** *adj* natural **II.** *adv* naturally, of course

Natürlichkeit <-> *f kein pl* naturalness

Naturprodukt *nt* natural product

Naturschutz *m* [nature] conservation; **unter ~ stehen** to be protected

Naturschutzgebiet *nt* nature reserve

Naturvolk *nt* primitive people

Naturwissenschaften *pl* natural sciences *pl*

Naturwissenschaftler(in) *m(f)* natural scientist

naturwissenschaftlich *adj* natural-scientific

Navi <-s, -s> ['na·vi, 'na·vi] *nt* (*fam*) *Abk von* **Navigationsgerät** GPS

Navigationsgerät *nt*, **Navigationssystem** *nt* navigation system; (*tragbares Gerät*) GPS

Nazi <-s, -s> ['na·tsi] *m* Nazi

Nebel <-s, -> ['neː·bl̩] *m* ① fog; **bei ~** in foggy conditions ② ASTRON nebula

Nebelscheinwerfer *m* fog light

neben ['neː·bn̩] *präp* ① +*akk, dat* beside, next to ② +*dat* (*außer*) apart from ③ +*dat* (*verglichen mit*) compared to

nebenan [ne·bn̩·'ʔan] *adv* next door

nebenbei [ne·bn̩·'bai̯] *adv* ① (*neben der Arbeit*) on the side ② (*beiläufig*) incidentally; **~ [bemerkt]** by the way

Nebenbeschäftigung *f* side job, sideline

Nebenbuhler(in) <-s, -> *m(f)* rival

nebeneinander [ne·bn̩·ʔai̯·'nan·dɐ] *adv* ① (*Seite an Seite*) side by side ② (*gleichzeitig*) simultaneously, at the same time

NebenflussRR *m* tributary

Nebengebäude *nt* (*benachbartes Gebäude*) neighboring building

nebenher [ne·bn̩·'heːɐ̯] *adv* in addition

Nebenkosten *pl* additional costs *pl*

Nebenmann <-es, -männer> *m* neighbor; **mein ~** the person next to me

Nebenrolle *f* FILM, THEAT supporting role

Nebensache *f* trivial matter; **~ sein** to be irrelevant

nebensächlich *adj* irrelevant

Nebensaison *f* off-season

Nebenverdienst *m* additional income

Nebenwirkung *f* side effect

Nebenzimmer *nt* next room [over]

neblig ['neː·blɪç] *adj* foggy

necken ['nɛ·kn̩] *vt* to tease

Neffe <-n, -n> ['nɛ·fə] *m* nephew

negativ ['neː·ga·tiːf] **I.** *adj* negative **II.** *adv* negatively

Negativ <-s, -e> ['neː·ga·tiːf] *nt* negative

nehmen <nimmt, nahm, genommen> ['neː·mən] *vt* to take; **nimm dir noch Kuchen** help yourself to more cake; **jdn ~, wie er ist** to take sb as he is; **den Bus/die Bahn/ein Taxi ~** to take the bus/the train/a taxi; ■**jdm etw ~** to take sth [away] from sb; **jdm die Sicht ~** to block sb's view ▶WENDUNGEN: **es sich** *dat* **nicht ~ lassen, etw zu tun** to insist on doing sth

Neid <-[e]s> ['nai̯t] *m kein pl* jealousy, envy (**auf** +*akk* of)

neidisch ['nai̯·dɪʃ] *adj* jealous, envious (**auf** +*akk* of)

neigen ['nai̯·gn̩] **I.** *vr* ■**sich** *akk* **~** ① (*sich beugen*) ■**sich** *akk* **zu jdm ~** to lean over to sb; **sich** *akk* **nach vorne ~** to lean forward ② (*schräg* *abfallen*) to slope ❸ (*sich biegen*) Äste to bow down II. *vt* (*beugen*) to bend III. *vi* ❶ (*anfällig sein für*) ■ **zu etw** *dat* ~ (*Krankheiten*) to be prone to sth ❷ (*tendieren*) ■ **zu etw** *dat* ~ to tend to [do] sth

Neigung <-, -en> *f* ❶ (*Vorliebe*) inclination ❷ (*Tendenz*) tendency ❸ (*Gefälle*) slope

nein ['nain] *adv* no

Nein <-s> ['nain] *nt kein pl* no

Neinstimme *f* no, "no" vote

Nektar <-s, -e> ['nɛk·tar] *m* nectar

Nektarine <-, -n> [nɛk·ta·'riː·nə] *f* nectarine

Nelke <-, -n> ['nɛl·kə] *f* ❶ BOT carnation ❷ KOCHK clove

nennen <nannte, genannt> ['nɛ·nən] *vt* ❶ (*anreden, benennen*) to call; **wie nennt man das?** what do you call that? ❷ (*sagen*) *Namen* to name; *Grund* to give; **können Sie mir einen guten Anwalt** ~ ? can you give me the name of a good lawyer?

Neofaschismus <-> ['ne·o·fa·ʃɪs·mʊs] *m kein pl* neofascism

Neon <-s> ['ne·ɔn] *nt kein pl* neon

Neonazi <-s, -s> ['ne·o·na·tsi] *m kurz für* **Neonazist** neo-Nazi

Neonlicht *nt* neon light

Nerv <-s, -en> ['nɛrf] *m* nerve ►WENDUNGEN: **die** ~**en behalten/verlieren** to keep calm/lose one's cool; **jdm auf die** ~**en gehen** (*fam*) to get on sb's nerves; **du hast vielleicht** ~**en!** (*fam*) you've got some nerve!

nerven ['nɛr·fn̩] *vt* (*fam*) ■ **jdn [mit etw** *dat*] ~ to bug sb [with sth]

nervenaufreibend *adj* nerve-racking

Nervenbündel *nt* (*fam*) bundle of nerves

Nervensäge *f* (*fam*) pain in the neck

Nervensystem *nt* nervous system

Nervenzusammenbruch *m* nervous breakdown

nervös [nɛr·'vøːs] *adj* nervous

Nervosität <-> [nɛr·vo·zi·'tɛːt] *f kein pl* nervousness

Nerz <-es, -e> ['nɛrts] *m* mink

Nessel <-, -n> ['nɛ·sl̩] *f* BOT nettle ►WENDUNGEN: **sich** *akk* **in die** ~**n setzen** (*fam*) to put one's foot in one's mouth

Nest <-[e]s, -er> ['nɛst] *nt* ❶ ORN nest ❷ (*fam: Kaff*) hole ►WENDUNGEN: **sich** *akk* **ins gemachte** ~ **setzen** (*fam*) to have got it made

Netiquette <-, -n> [nɛ·ti·'kɛ·tə] *f* netiquette

nett ['nɛt] *adj* nice; **sei so** ~ **und ...** would you mind ...

netto ['nɛ·to] *adv* net

Nettoeinkommen *nt* net income

Nettogewicht *nt* net weight

Netz <-es, -e> ['nɛts] *nt* ❶ (*a. sport*) net ❷ (*Einkaufsnetz*) string bag ❸ (*Gepäcknetz*) baggage net ❹ (*Spinnennetz*) web ❺ ELEK, TELEK network; (*Strom*) power grid ❻ *kein pl* COMPUT network; ■ **das** ~ the Net ❼ TRANSP system, network

Netzhaut *f* retina

Netzstecker *m* power plug

Netzwerk *nt a.* COMPUT network; **soziales** ~ social network

neu ['nɔy] I. *adj* ❶ (*nicht alt*) new; **die** ~**este Mode** the latest fashion; **ein** ~**eres System** a more up-to-date system; **was gibt's N**~**es?** (*fam*) what's new?; **was gibt's N**~**es?** what's new?; ■ **der/die N**~**e** the newcomer; ■ **das N**~**e [an etw** *dat*] the new thing [about sth]; ■ **das N**~**este** the latest [thing] ❷ (*abermalig*) new; **einen** ~ **en Anfang machen** to make a fresh start ►WENDUNGEN: **auf ein N**~**es!** here's to a fresh start!; **seit** ~**[e]stem** [since] recently; **von** ~ **em** all over again II. *adv* ❶ (*von vorn*) ~ **bearbeitet** MEDIA revised; ~ **anfangen** to start all over again; ~ **gestalten** to redesign ❷ (*zusätzlich*) anew; **33 Mitarbeiter** ~ **einstellen** to hire 33 new employees ❸ (*erneut*) again ❹ (*seit kurzem da*) newly; ~ **eröffnet** newly opened; (*erneut eröffnet*) reopened ►WENDUNGEN: **wie** ~ **geboren** like a new man/woman

N

Neuankömmling <-s, -e> *m* newcomer

neuartig [ˈnɔy·ʔaːɐ̯·tɪç] *adj* new, new type of

Neuauflage *f* ❶ (*unveränderter Nachdruck*) reprint ❷ (*veränderte Neuausgabe*) new edition

Neubau <-bauten> [ˈnɔy·bau] *m* ❶ *kein pl* (*neue Errichtung*) [new] building ❷ (*neu erbautes Gebäude*) new building

Neubaugebiet *nt* development area; (*schon bebaut*) new development

Neubauwohnung *f* newly built apartment

neuerdings [ˈnɔy·ɐ·dɪŋs] *adv* recently

Neuerscheinung *f* new publication

Neuerung <-, -en> [ˈnɔy·ə·rʊŋ] *f* reform

Neufundland <-s> [nɔy·ˈfʊnt·lant] *nt* Newfoundland

Neugeborene(s) *nt* newborn

Neugier(de) <-> [ˈnɔy·giːɐ̯(·də)] *f kein pl* curiosity

neugierig I. *adj* curious; **~ sein, ob ...** to be curious [to know] whether ...; **sei nicht so ~!** don't be so nosy! **II.** *adv* curiously, full of curiosity

Neuigkeit <-, -en> [ˈnɔy·ɪç·kait] *f* news

Neujahr *nt kein pl* New Year; **prost ~!** here's to the New Year!

neulich [ˈnɔy·lɪç] *adv* the other day

Neuling <-s, -e> [ˈnɔy·lɪŋ] *m* beginner

neumodisch *adj* (*pej*) newfangled

Neumond *m kein pl* new moon

neun [ˈnɔyn] *adj* nine; *s. a.* **acht**[1]

neunte(r, s) [ˈnɔyn·tə(ɐ, s)] *adj* ❶ (*an neunter Stelle*) ninth; *s. a.* **achte(r, s)** 1 ❷ (*Datum*) ninth, 9th; *s. a.* **achte(r, s)** 2

neuntel [ˈnɔn·t̩l] *nt* ninth

neunzehn [ˈnɔyn·tseːn] *adj* nineteen; *s. a.* **acht**[1]

neunzehnte(r, s) *adj* ❶ (*an neunzehnter Stelle*) nineteenth; *s. a.* **achte(r, s)** 1 ❷ (*Datum*) nineteenth, 19th; *s. a.* **achte(r, s)** 2

neunzig [ˈnɔyn·tsɪç] *adj* ninety; *s. a.* **achtzig** 1, 2

neunzigste(r, s) [ˈnɔyn·tsɪç·stə] *adj* ninetieth; *s. a.* **achte(r, s)** 1

Neurologe, Neurologin <-n, -n> [nɔy·ro·ˈloː·gə] *m, f* neurologist

Neurose <-, -n> [nɔy·ˈroː·zə] *f* neurosis

Neurotiker(in) <-s, -> [nɔy·ˈroː·ti·kɐ] *m(f)* neurotic

neurotisch [nɔy·ˈroː·tɪʃ] *adj* neurotic

Neuschnee *m* fresh snow

Neuseeland <-s> [nɔy·ˈzeː·lant] *nt* New Zealand; *s. a.* **Deutschland**

Neuseeländer(in) <-s, -> [nɔy·ˈzeː·lɛn·də] *m(f)* New Zealander; *s. a.* **Deutsche(r)**

neuseeländisch [nɔy·ˈzeː·lɛn·dɪʃ] *adj* New Zealand *attr,* from New Zealand *pred*

neutral [nɔy·ˈtraːl] *adj, adv* neutral

Neutralität <-> [nɔy·tra·li·ˈtɛːt] *f kein pl* neutrality

neuwertig *adj* as new

nicht [nɪçt] *adv* not; **ich weiß ~** I don't know; **ich bin es ~ gewesen** it wasn't me; **~ öffentlich** not open to the public *pred*; **~ [ein]mal** not even; **~ mehr** not any more, no longer; **~ mehr als ...** no more than ...; **bitte ~!** please don't!

Nichtbeachtung *f* noncompliance

Nichte <-, -n> [ˈnɪç·tə] *f* niece

Nichterscheinen <-s> *nt kein pl* failure to appear

nichtig [ˈnɪç·tɪç] *adj* ❶ (*ungültig*) invalid ❷ (*geh: belanglos*) trivial

Nichtigkeit <-, -en> *f* ❶ *kein pl* (*Ungültigkeit*) invalidity ❷ *meist pl* (*geh*) triviality

Nichtraucher(in) *m(f)* nonsmoker

nichts [ˈnɪçts] *pron indef* ❶ (*nicht etwas*) not anything, nothing; **es ist ~** it's nothing; **~ als ...** (*nur*) nothing but ...; **~ mehr** nothing more [or else]; **~ wie raus!** let's get out of here!; **~ ahnend** unsuspecting; **~ sagend** meaningless; **damit will ich ~ zu tun haben** I don't want anything to do with it ❷ *vor substantiviertem adj* nothing; **~ anderes [als ...]** nothing other [than ...]; **hoffentlich ist es ~ Ernstes**

I hope it's nothing serious ►WENDUNGEN: **~ da!** (*fam*) no chance!; **für** ~ for nothing; **für ~ und wieder ~** (*fam*) [all] for nothing

Nichts <-, -e> ['nıçts] *nt* ① *kein pl* (*leerer Raum*) void ② (*unbedeutender Mensch*) nonentity ►WENDUNGEN: **aus dem ~ auftauchen** to show up from out of nowhere; **vor dem ~ stehen** to be left with nothing

Nichtschwimmer(in) *m(f)* non-swimmer

nichtsdestoweniger [nıçts·dɛs·to·'ve:·nı·ge] *adv* nevertheless

Nichtsnutz <-es, -e> ['nıçts·nʊts] *m* (*pej*) good-for-nothing

Nickel <-s> ['nı·kl] *nt kein pl* nickel

nicken ['nı·kn] *vi* to nod

Nickerchen <-s, -> ['nı·kɐ·çən] *nt* (*fam*) nap; **ein ~ machen** to take a nap

nie [ni:] *adv* never; **~ mehr** never again; **das hätte ich ~ im Leben gedacht** I never would have thought that ►WENDUNGEN: **~ und nimmer** never ever

Niedergang <-[e]s> *m kein pl* decline

niedergeschlagen [-gə·ʃla:·gn] *adj* downcast

Niederlage *f* defeat

Niederlande ['ni:·dɐ·lan·də] *pl* ■ **die ~** the Netherlands; *s. a.* **Deutschland**

Niederländer(in) <-s, -> ['ni:·dɐ·lɛn·də] *m(f)* Dutchman *masc*, Dutchwoman *fem*; *s. a.* **Deutsche(r)**

niederländisch ['ni:·dɐ·lɛn·dıʃ] *adj* Dutch; *s. a.* **deutsch**

nieder|lassen *vr irreg* ■ **sich** *akk* ~ ① (*ansiedeln*) to settle down ② (*beruflich etablieren*) to establish oneself; **niedergelassener Arzt** *licensed doctor with his/her own practice* ③ (*geh: hinsetzen*) to sit down (**auf** +*akk* on); *Vogel* to settle (**auf** +*akk* on)

Niederlassung <-, -en> *f* (*Zweigstelle*) branch

nieder|legen *vt* ① (*hinlegen*) to put down *sep* ② (*aufgeben*) to give up; *Amt, Mandat* to resign; *Arbeit* to stop

Niederschlag *m* (*Regen*) rainfall; (*Schnee*) snowfall; (*Hagel*) hail

nieder|schlagen *irreg* I. *vt* ① (*zu Boden schlagen*) to floor ② (*unterdrücken*) to crush; *Streik* to break up; *Unruhen* to suppress II. *vr* ■ **sich** *akk* ~ ① (*kondensieren*) to condense (**an** +*dat* on) ② (*zum Ausdruck kommen*) to find expression (**in** +*dat* in)

niederschmetternd ['ni:·dɐ·ʃmɛ·tɐnt] *adj* deeply distressing; *Nachricht* devastating

Niedertracht <-> *f kein pl* ① (*Gesinnung*) malice ② (*Tat*) despicable act

niederträchtig *adj* contemptible; *Einstellung, Lüge, Person a.* despicable

niedlich ['ni:t·lıç] I. *adj* cute, sweet II. *adv* sweetly

niedrig ['ni:·drıç] I. *adj* ① (*nicht hoch*) low ② (*gering*) low; *Betrag* small II. *adv* low

niemals ['ni:·ma:ls] *adv* never

niemand ['ni:·mant] *pron indef* nobody, no one; (*bei Fragen und Verneinung*) anyone, anybody

Niemandsland ['ni:·mants·lant] *nt kein pl* no man's land

Niere <-, -n> ['ni:·rə] *f* kidney ►WENDUNGEN: **jdm an die ~n gehen** (*fam*) to get to sb

N

Nierenstein *m* kidney stone

Nierenversagen *nt kein pl* kidney failure

nieseln ['ni:·zln] *vi impers* ■ **es nieselt** it's drizzling

Nieselregen ['ni:·zl-] *m* drizzle

niesen ['ni:·zn] *vi* to sneeze

Niete¹ <-, -n> ['ni:·tə] *f* ① (*Nichttreffer*) blank ② (*fam: Versager*) loser

Niete² <-, -n> ['ni:·tə] *f* TECH rivet

niet- und nagelfest ['ni:·t?ʊnt·'na:·gl·fɛst] *adj* ►WENDUNGEN: **alles, was nicht ~ ist** (*fam*) everything that's not nailed down

Nikolaus <-, -e> ['nı·ko·laus] *m* ① (*verkleidete Gestalt*) St. Nicholas (*figure who brings children presents on December 6*) ② *kein pl* (*6. Dezember*) St. Nicholas' Day

Nikotin <-s> [ni·ko·'ti:n] *nt kein pl* nicotine

nikotinfrei adj nicotine-free
Nilpferd nt hippo[potamus]
nippen ['nɪ·pn̩] vi to sip (**an** +dat on)
Nippes ['nɪ·pəs, 'nɪps, 'nɪp] pl knick-
knacks pl
nirgends ['nɪr·gn̩ts], **nirgendwo** ['nɪr·
gn̩t·'voː] adv nowhere; **ich konnte ihn
~ finden** I couldn't find him anywhere
Nische <-, -n> ['niː·ʃə] f niche
nisten ['nɪs·tn̩] vi to nest
Nitrat <-[e]s, -e> [ni·'traːt] nt nitrate
Niveau <-s, -s> [ni·'voː] nt ① (Anspruch) caliber; **~ haben** to have class;
kein ~ haben to be lowbrow; **das ist
unter meinem ~** this is beneath me fig
② (Höhe einer Fläche) level
niveaulos [ni·'voː-] adj primitive
niveauvoll adj intellectually stimulating
Nixe <-, -n> ['nɪk·sə] f mermaid
nobel ['noː·bl̩] I. adj ① (edel) noble
② (luxuriös) luxurious ③ (großzügig)
generous II. adv ① (edel) honorably
② (großzügig) generously
Nobelpreis [no·'bɛl·prais] m Nobel
Prize
noch ['nɔx] I. adv ① (bis jetzt) still; **ein
~ ungelöstes Problem** an as yet unsolved problem; ■**~ immer** [nicht]
still [not]; ■**~ nicht** not yet; ■**~
nichts** nothing yet; ② (irgendwann)
some time; **er kommt schon ~** he will eventually
come ③ (nicht später als) by the end
of; **~ gestern habe ich davon nichts
gewusst** even yesterday I didn't know
a thing about it; **~ heute** today ④ (bevor etw anderes geschieht) **bleib ~
ein wenig** stay a little longer ⑤ (womöglich) **wir kommen ~ zu spät**
we're going to end up being late
⑥ (zusätzlich) in addition; **möchtest
du ~ etwas essen?** would you like
something else to eat?; **möchten Sie
~ eine Tasse Kaffee?** would you like
another cup of coffee?; ■**~ eine(r, s)**
another ⑦ (vor etw mehr als) even
[more] II. konj ■**weder ... ~ ...** neither ... nor ...
nochmals ['nɔx·maːls] adv again

N

Nomade, Nomadin <-n, -n> [no·'maː·
də] m, f nomad
Nominativ <-[e]s, -e> ['noː·mi·na·
tiːf] m nominative
nominieren* [no·mi·'niː·rən] vt to
nominate
Nonne <-, -n> ['nɔ·nə] f nun
Nordamerika ['nɔrt·ʔa'meː·ri·ka] nt
North America
Norden <-s> ['nɔr·dn̩] m kein pl, kein
indef art ① (Himmelsrichtung) north;
aus/im/nach ~ from/in/to the north;
in Richtung ~ to[ward] the north
② (nördliche Gegend) north; **er wohnt
im ~ der Stadt** he lives in the northern
part of town
Nordeuropa ['nɔrt·ʔɔy·'roː·pa] nt
Northern Europe
Nordhalbkugel f Northern Hemisphere
Nordirland ['nɔrt·'ʔɪr·lant] nt Northern
Ireland
nördlich ['nœrt·lɪç] I. adj ① (Himmelsrichtung) northern ② (im Norden liegend) northern; **weiter ~ liegen** to lie
farther [to the] north ③ (von/nach Norden) northerly; **in ~e Richtung** northward II. adv ■**~ von ...** north of ...
III. präp +gen **~ der Stadt** [to the]
north of the town
Nordosten [nɔrt·'ʔɔs·tn̩] m kein indef
art northeast; s. a. **Norden**
nordöstlich [nɔrt·'ʔœst·lɪç] I. adj
① (Himmelsrichtung) northeastern
② (im Nordosten liegend) northeastern
③ (von/nach Nordosten) northeast-
ward II. adv ■**~ von ...** northeast of ...
III. präp +gen northeast of; s. a. **nördlich**
Nordpol ['nɔrt·poːl] m kein pl ■**der ~**
the North Pole
Nordsee ['nɔrt·zeː] f ■**die ~** the North
Sea; **an der ~** on the North Sea coast
Nordwesten [nɔrt·'vɛs·tn̩] m kein indef
art northwest; s. a. **Norden**
nordwestlich [nɔrt·'vɛst·lɪç] I. adj
① (Himmelsrichtung) northwestern
② (im Nordwesten liegend) northwestern ③ (von/nach Nordwesten) north-
westward II. adv ■**~ von ...** northwest

of ... III. *präp* +*gen* northwest of; *s. a.*
nördlich

Nordwind *m* north wind

Nörgelei <-, -en> *f* ❶(*Äußerung*)
moaning [and groaning] ❷ *kein pl* (*das
Nörgeln*) nagging

nörgeln ['nœr·gln] *vi* to moan (**über**
+*akk* about)

Norm <-, -en> ['nɔrm] *f* ❶(*festgelegte Größe*) standard ❷(*verbindliche
Regel*) norm ❸(*Durchschnitt*) ∎**die ~**
the norm

normal [nɔr·'maːl] I. *adj* ❶(*üblich*) normal ❷ *meist verneint* (*fam: zurechnungsfähig*) right in the head; **du bist
wohl nicht ~!** you are out of your
mind! II. *adv* normally

Normalbenzin *nt* regular [unleaded]
[gas]

Normalverbraucher(in) *m(f)* average
consumer; **Otto ~** (*fam*) the man in the
street

normen ['nɔr·mən] *vt* to standardize

Norwegen <-s> ['nɔr·ve:·gn] *nt* Nor-
way; *s. a.* **Deutschland**

Norweger(in) <-s, -> ['nɔr·ve:·gɐ] *m(f)*
Norwegian; *s. a.* **Deutsche(r)**

norwegisch ['nɔr·ve:·gɪʃ] *adj* Norwegian; *s. a.* **deutsch**

Nostalgie <-> [nɔs·tal·'giː] *f kein pl*
(*geh*) nostalgia

nostalgisch [nɔs·'tal·gɪʃ] *adj* (*geh*) nostalgic

Not <-, Nöte> ['noːt] *f* ❶ *kein pl*
(*Armut*) poverty ❷(*Bedrängnis*) distress; **in ~ geraten** to be in dire straits;
jdm seine ~ klagen to pour out one's
troubles to sb ▶WENDUNGEN: **~ macht
erfinderisch** (*prov*) necessity is the
mother of invention; **mit knapper ~**
just; **zur ~** if need[s] be

Notar(in) <-s, -e> [no·'taːɐ̯] *m(f)* notary
[public]

Notariat <-[e]s, -e> [no·ta·'rɪaːt] *nt*
(*Kanzlei*) notary's office

Notarzt, -ärztin *m, f* ❶(*bei Unfällen*)
emergency doctor ❷(*Arzt im Notdienst*) on-call physician

Notaufnahme *f* ❶(*eines Kranken*)

emergency admission ❷(*Krankenhaus-
station*) emergency room

Notausgang *m* emergency exit

Notbremse *f* emergency brake

Notdienst *m* **~ haben** to be on duty

Note <-, -n> ['noː·tə] *f* ❶MUS note; **~n
lesen** to read music ❷SCH, UNIV grade
❸(*Banknote*) [bank]note

Notebook <-s, -s> ['noʊt·bʊk] *nt* COM-
PUT notebook

Notfall *m* emergency

notfalls ['noːt·fals] *adv* if need be

notgedrungen *adv* willy-nilly

notieren* [no·'tiː·rən] *vt* to write down

nötig ['nøː·tɪç] *adj* necessary; ∎**alles
N~e** everything necessary; ∎**das
N~ste** the essentials; **etw [bitter] ~
haben** to be in [urgent] need of sth; **das
haben wir nicht ~!** we don't have to
put up with that!

Nötigung <-, -en> *f* (*Zwang*) coercion

Notiz <-, -en> [no·'tiːts] *f* ❶(*Vermerk*)
note ❷(*Zeitungsmeldung*) short report
▶WENDUNGEN: **[keine]** | **[von jdm/etw]
nehmen** to take [no] notice [of sb/sth]

Notizblock <-blöcke> *m* notepad

Notlage *f* desperate situation

Notlandung *f* emergency landing

Notlösung *f* stopgap [solution]

notorisch [no·'toː·rɪʃ] I. *adj* (*geh*) notorious II. *adv* (*geh*) notoriously

Notruf *m* ❶(*Anruf*) emergency call
❷(*Notrufnummer*) emergency number

Notstand *m* ❶(*Notlage*) desperate
situation ❷JUR [state of] emergency

Notstandsgebiet *nt* disaster area

Notunterkunft *f* emergency accommodations *pl*

Notwehr <-> *f kein pl* self-defense

notwendig ['noːt·vɛn·dɪç] I. *adj* necessary II. *adv* necessarily

Notwendigkeit <-, -en> [noːt·'vɛn·dɪç·
kaɪt] *f* necessity

Nougat <-s, -s> ['nuː·gat] *m o nt s.*
Nugat

November <-s, -> [no·'vɛm·bɐ] *m* November; *s. a.* **Februar**

Nu ['nuː] *m* **im ~** in a flash

nüchtern ['nʏç·tɐn] *adj* ❶(*mit leerem*

N

Magen) with an empty stomach ②(*nicht betrunken*) sober ③(*realitätsbewusst*) down-to-earth ④ *Tatsachen* plain; *Einrichtung* austere

Nudel <-, -n> ['nuː·dl̩] *f meist pl* pasta + *sing vb, no indef art*; (*Suppennudel*) noodle *usu pl*

Nugat <-s, -s> *m o nt* nougat

nuklear [nu·kle·'aːɐ̯] **I.** *adj attr* nuclear **II.** *adv* with nuclear weapons *pred*

null ['nʊl] *adj* zero ▶WENDUNGEN: **gleich ~ sein** to be [practically] zero, to be extremely unrealistic; **in ~ Komma nichts** (*fam*) in a flash; **~ und nichtig sein** to be null and void

Null <-, -en> ['nʊl] *f* ①(*Zahl*) zero ②(*fam: Versager*) nothing

Nulldiät *f* starvation diet

Nullpunkt *m kein pl* freezing point ▶WENDUNGEN: **auf den ~ sinken** to reach rock bottom

numerieren*ALT [nu·mə·'riː·rən] *vt s.* **nummerieren**

Numerus <-, Numeri> ['nuː·me·rʊs] *m* number; **~ clausus** enrollment limits

N **Nummer** <-, -n> ['nʊ·mɐ] *f* ①(*Zahl, Telefonnummer*) number ②MEDIA (*Ausgabe*) issue ③(*Größe*) size ④(*sl: Koitus*) fuck *vulg*; **eine ~ [mit jdm] schieben** (*sl*) to get it on [with sb] *sl* ▶WENDUNGEN: **auf ~ Sicher gehen** (*fam*) to play it safe

nummerieren*RR *vt* to number

Nummernschild *nt* license plate

nun ['nuːn] *adv* ①(*jetzt*) now ②(*eben*) **es ist ~ [ein]mal so** that's [just] the way it is

nur ['nuːɐ̯] *adv* ①(*lediglich*) only; **sie**

fährt gut, ~ zu schnell she drives well, but too fast ②(*bloß*) just; **wie konnte ich das ~ vergessen!** how on earth could I forget that! ③(*ruhig*) just; **~ zu!** go [right] ahead!

nuscheln ['nʊ·ʃl̩n] *vt, vi* (*fam*) to mumble

NussRR, **Nuß**ALT <-, Nüsse> ['nʊs] *f* nut ▶WENDUNGEN: **dumme ~** (*fam*) moron, idiot

NussbaumRR *m* nut tree

Nutte <-, -n> ['nʊ·tə] *f* (*sl*) whore

nutz ['nʊts] *adj pred* SÜDD, ÖSTERR *s.* **nütze**

nütze ['nʏ·tsə] *adj pred* ■**zu etw** *dat* **~ sein** to be useful for sth; ■**zu nichts ~ sein** to be good for nothing

nutzen ['nʊ·tsn̩], **nützen** ['nʏ·tsn̩] **I.** *vi* (*von Nutzen sein*) to be of use; ■**[jdm] nichts ~** to not do [sb] any good **II.** *vt* ①(*in Gebrauch nehmen*) to use ②(*ausnutzen*) to exploit; **eine Gelegenheit ~** to take advantage of an opportunity

Nutzen <-s> ['nʊ·tsn̩] *m kein pl* benefit; **welchen ~ versprichst du dir davon?** what do you hope to gain from it?; **[jdm] ~ bringen** to be advantageous [to sb]; **[jdm] von ~ sein** to be of use [to sb]

nützlich ['nʏts·lɪç] *adj* ①(*nutzbringend*) useful ②(*hilfreich*) helpful

nutzlos I. *adj* useless **II.** *adv* in vain *pred*

Nutzlosigkeit <-> *f kein pl* uselessness

Nutzpflanze *f* [economically] useful plant

Nutzung <-, -en> *f* use

Oo

O, o <-, -> [oː] *nt* O, o; **~ wie Otto** O as in Oscar

Oase <-, -n> [oˈaːzə] *f* oasis

ob [ɔp] *konj* whether; **~ er morgen kommt?** I wonder if he's coming tomorrow?

Obdach <-[e]s> [ˈɔp·dax] *nt kein pl* (*geh*) shelter

obdachlos *adj* homeless

Obdachlose(r) *f(m)* homeless person

Obdachlosenheim *nt* homeless shelter

O-Beine *pl* bow legs *pl*

oben [ˈoːbn̩] *adv* ① (*in der Höhe*) top; **ich möchte die Flasche ~ links** I'd like the bottle [that's] on the top left; ■ **~ auf etw** *dat o akk* on top of sth; **dort/ hier ~** up there/here; **ganz ~** at the very top; **hoch ~** high; **bis ~ [hin]** up to the top; **nach ~** up; **nach ~ zu** further up; **von ~** (*vom oberen Teil*) from above ② (*im oberen Stockwerk*) upstairs; **nach ~** upstairs; **von ~** from upstairs ③ (*fam: auf höherer Ebene*) **der Befehl kommt von ~** the order comes from the top ④ (*vorher*) above; **der/ die/das ~** the above-mentioned ▶WENDUNGEN: **dieser Job steht mir bis [hier] ~** (*fam*) I'm fed up with this job *sl;* **~ ohne** (*fam*) topless; **von ~ bis unten** from top to bottom; **ich weiß nicht mehr, wo ~ und unten ist** (*fam*) I don't know whether I'm coming or going *sl*

obendrein [ˈoːbn̩·ˈdraɪn] *adv* on top

Ober <-s, -> [ˈoːbɐ] *m* waiter

Oberarm *m* upper arm

Oberarzt, -ärztin *m*, *f* assistant medical director

Oberbefehlshaber(in) *m(f)* commander in chief

Oberbegriff *m* generic term

Oberbürgermeister(in) [ˈoːbɐ·bʏr·gə· maistɐ] *m(f)* mayor

obere(r, s) [ˈoːbə·rə, -rɛ, -rəs] *adj attr* ① (*oben befindlich*) top ② (*rangmäßig höher*) higher ③ (*vorhergehend*) previous ④ (*höher gelegen*) upper

Oberfläche [ˈoːbɐ·flɛ·çə] *f* surface

oberflächlich [ˈoːbɐ·flɛç·lɪç] I. *adj* superficial II. *adv* superficially; (*flüchtig*) in a slapdash manner *pred*

Oberflächlichkeit <-> *f kein pl* superficiality

Obergeschoss[RR] *nt* top floor

oberhalb [ˈoːbɐ·halp] I. *präp* +*gen* above II. *adv* above

Oberhaupt *nt* head

oberirdisch I. *adj* aboveground; *Leitung* overhead II. *adv* aboveground

Oberkörper *m* torso

Oberlippe *f* upper lip

Oberschenkel *m* thigh

Oberschicht *f* (*der Gesellschaft*) upper class

Oberseite *f* top

oberste(r, s) [ˈoːbɐ·stə, -stɛ, -stəs] *adj* ① (*räumlich*) top ② (*rangmäßig*) highest

Oberstufe *f* ≈ sixth grade

obgleich [ɔpˈglaiç] *konj* although

Objekt <-[e]s, -e> [ɔpˈjɛkt] *nt* ① (*Gegenstand, a. Grammatik*) object ② (*Immobilie*) [piece of] property ③ (*Kunstgegenstand*) objet d'art, work of art

objektiv [ɔpjɛkˈtiːf] I. *adj* objective II. *adv* objectively

Objektiv <-s, -e> [ɔpjɛkˈtiːf] *nt* lens

Objektivität <-> [ɔpjɛk·tivi·ˈtɛːt] *f kein pl* objectivity

obligatorisch [obliga·ˈtoː·rɪʃ] *adj* (*geh*) mandatory

Obst <-[e]s> [ˈoːpst] *nt kein pl* fruit

Obstbaum *m* fruit tree

Obstkuchen *m* fruit tart

Obstsalat *m* fruit salad

obszön [ɔpsˈtsøːn] *adj* obscene

Obszönität <-, -en> [ɔps·tsø·ni·ˈtɛːt] *f* obscenity

O

obwohl [ɔp·'voːl] *konj* although

Ochse <-n, -n> ['ɔksə] *m* ox

Ọchsenschwanzsuppe *f* oxtail soup

öde ['øːdə] *adj* ① (*verlassen*) desolate ② (*fade*) *Landschaft* dull ③ (*langweilig*) tedious, dull

oder ['oːdɐ] *konj* ① (*eines oder anderes*) or; ~ **aber** or else; ~ **auch** or [even]; ~ **auch nicht** or [maybe] not ② (*stimmt's?*) **der Film hat dir auch gut gefallen, ~?** you liked the movie too, didn't you?; **er schuldet dir noch Geld, ~?** he still owes you money, doesn't he?

Ofen <-s, Öfen> ['oːfn̩] *m* ① (*Heizofen*) heater; (*Kohle-, Kachel-, Ölofen*) stove ② (*Backofen*) oven ③ DIAL (*Herd*) stove ▶WENDUNGEN: **jetzt ist der ~ aus** (*fam*) that does it

Ofenheizung *f* stove heating

offen ['ɔfn̩] I. *adj* open; *Punkt* moot; *Problem, Rechnung* unsettled; *Frage* unanswered; **bei ~em Fenster** with the window open; ~ **er Wein** wine by the glass/carafe; ~ **haben** *Laden, Geschäft* to be open II. *adv* openly; ~ **gestanden** to be [perfectly] honest

offenbar [ɔfn̩·'baːɐ̯] I. *adj* obvious II. *adv* obviously

Ọffenheit <-> *f kein pl* openness; **in aller** ~ quite frankly

offenherzig *adj* ① (*freimütig*) open ② (*hum fam: tief ausgeschnitten*) revealing

offensichtlich ['ɔfn̩·zɪçt·lɪç] I. *adj* obvious; *Irrtum, Lüge* blatant II. *adv* obviously

öffentlich ['œfn̩·tlɪç] I. *adj* public II. *adv* publicly

Öffentlichkeit <-> *f kein pl* ■ **die** ~ the [general] public + *sing/pl vb;* **in aller** ~ in public; **etw an die** ~ **bringen** to make sth public

offiziell [ɔfi·'tsi̯ɛl] I. *adj* ① (*amtlich*) official ② (*förmlich*) *Empfang, Feier* formal II. *adv* officially

Offizier(in) <-s, -e> [ɔfi·'tsiːɐ̯] *m(f)* officer

Offlinebetrieb[RR], **Off-line-Be-**

trieb[ALT] ['ɔf·lain-] *m kein pl* offline operation

öffnen ['œf·nən] I. *vt* to open II. *vi* ■ **[jdm]** ~ to open the door [for sb] III. *vr* ① (*aufgehen*) ■ **sich** *akk* ~ *Tür* to open; *Blüte, Fallschirm* to open up ② (*sich zuwenden*) ■ **sich** *akk* **[jdm/etw]** ~ to open up [to sb/sth]

Öffnung <-, -en> *f* ① (*offene Stelle*) opening ② *kein pl* (*das Öffnen*) opening

Öffnungszeiten *pl* hours of business *pl*

oft <öfter, am öftesten> ['ɔft] *adv* often

öfter(s) ['œf·tɐ(s)] *adv* [every] once in a while; **ist dir das schon ~ passiert?** has that happened to you often?

ọftmals *adv s.* oft

ohne ['oːnə] I. *präp* + *akk* ① (*nicht versehen mit*) without; ~ **Geld** without any money; ~ **Schutz** unprotected ② (*nicht eingerechnet*) excluding; ~ **mich!** count me out! II. *konj* ■ ~ **etw zu tun** without doing sth; ■ ~, **dass etw geschieht** without sth happening; ■ ~, **dass jd etw tut** without sb doing sth

Ohnmacht <-, -en> ['oːn·maxt] *f* ① (*Bewusstseinszustand*) faint; **in** ~ **fallen** to faint ② (*geh: Machtlosigkeit*) powerlessness

ohnmächtig ['oːn·mɛç·tɪç] I. *adj* ① (*bewusstlos*) unconscious; ~ **werden** to faint ② (*geh: machtlos*) powerless ③ *attr Wut* helpless II. *adv* helplessly

Ohr <-[e]s, -en> ['oːɐ̯] *nt* ear ▶WENDUNGEN: **es faustdick hinter den ~en haben** to be a sly one; **ganz ~ sein** (*hum fam*) to be all ears; **jdm eins hinter die ~en geben** (*fam*) to whack sb on the back of the head; **viel um die ~en haben** (*fam*) to have a lot on one's plate; **jdn übers ~ hauen** (*fam*) to pull a fast one on sb; **jdm [mit etw *dat*] in den ~en liegen** to nag sb [about sth]; **die ~en spitzen** (*fam*) to prick up one's ears; **bis über beide ~en verliebt sein** to be head over heels in love

ohrenbetäubend I. *adj* deafening II. *adv* deafeningly

Ọhrfeige <-, -n> *f* slap in the face

ohrfeigen *vt* ■ **jdn ~** to give sb a slap in the face

Ohrläppchen <-s, -> *nt* earlobe

Ohrring *m* earring

Ökologie <-> [øko·lo·'gi:] *f kein pl* ecology

ökologisch [øko·'lo:·gɪʃ] I. *adj* ecological II. *adv* ecologically

ökonomisch [øko·'no:·mɪʃ] I. *adj* ❶ (*die Wirtschaft betreffend*) economic ❷ (*sparsam*) economical II. *adv* economically

Ökosteuer *f* environmental tax (*tax on products or processes which damage the environment*)

Ökosystem *nt* ecosystem

Oktober <-s, -> [ɔk·'to:·bɐ] *m* October; *s. a.* **Februar**

Öl <-[e]s, -e> ['ø:l] *nt* (*fette Flüssigkeit, a. Erdöl*) oil; (*Heizöl*) fuel oil; (*Schmieröl*) lubricating oil ►WENDUNGEN: **~ ins Feuer gießen** to add fuel to the fire

Oldtimer <-s, -> ['o:lt·taimɐ] *m* (*Auto*) vintage car; (*Flugzeug*) vintage airplane

ölen ['ø:lən] *vt* to oil

Ölfarbe *f* oil-based paint; KUNST oil [paint]

Ölgemälde *nt* oil painting

Ölheizung *f* oil heater

ölig ['ø:lɪç] *adj* oily; (*fettig*) greasy

Olive <-, -n> [o·'li:·və] *f* olive

Olivenöl *nt* olive oil

olivgrün *adj* olive-green, olive *attr*

Ölleitung *f* oil pipe; (*Pipeline*) oil pipeline

Ölpest *f* oil pollution

Ölquelle *f* oil well

Ölsardine *f* sardine [in oil] ►WENDUNGEN: **wie die ~n** (*fam*) like sardines

Ölstand *m kein pl* oil level

Ölstandsmesser *m* oil pressure gauge

Öltanker *m* oil tanker

Ölwechsel *m* oil change

Olympiade <-, -n> [olʏm·'pi̯a:·də] *f* Olympic Games *pl*

olympisch [o·'lʏm·pɪʃ] *adj* Olympic *attr*

Oma <-, -s> ['o:ma] *f* (*fam*) granny *fam*, grandma *fam*

Omelett <-[e]s, -e> *nt,* **Omelette** <-, -n> [ɔm(ə)·'lɛt] *f* omelet

Omnibus ['ɔmni·bʊs] *m* bus

Omnibushaltestelle *f* bus stop

Onkel <-s, -> ['ɔŋ·kl] *m* uncle

Onlinebanking <-[s]> ['ɔn·lain·bɛŋ·kɪŋ] *nt kein pl* online banking

Onlinebetrieb ['ɔn·lain-] *m kein pl* online operation

Onlinedienst ['ɔn·lain-] *m* online service

Onlinehandel ['ɔn·lain-] *m* INET ■ **der ~** e-commerce

Onlineportal ['ɔn·lain-] *nt* INET web portal; ■ **im ~** on the web portal

Opa <-s, -s> ['o:pa] *m* (*fam*) grandpa

Oper <-, -n> ['o:pe] *f* opera

Operation <-, -en> [opə·ra·'tsi̯o:n] *f* operation

Operationssaal *m* operating room

operieren* [opə·'ri:·rən] *vt* ■ **jdn/ etw ~** to operate on sb/sth; **jdn am Bein ~** to operate on sb's leg; ■ **sich** *dat* **etw ~ lassen** to have sth operated on; ■ **sich** *akk* **~ lassen** to have an operation

Opernsänger(in) *m(f)* opera singer

Opfer <-s, -> ['ɔ·pfe] *nt* ❶ (*verzichtende Hingabe*) sacrifice; **~ bringen** to make sacrifices ❷ (*geschädigte Person*) victim; *von Unfall, Krieg* casualty; **jdm/ etw zum ~ fallen** to fall victim to sb/sth

opfern ['ɔ·pfen] *vt* to sacrifice

Opiat <-[e]s, -e> [o·'pi̯a:t] *nt* opiate

Opium <-s> ['o:·pi̯ʊm] *nt kein pl* opium

Opportunismus <-> [ɔpɔr·tu·'nɪs·mʊs] *m kein pl* (*geh*) opportunism

Opportunist(in) <-en, -en> [ɔp·ɔr·tu·'nɪst] *m(f)* opportunist

opportunistisch *adj* opportunistic

Opposition <-, -en> [ɔpo·zi·'tsi̯o:n] *f* POL ■ **die ~** opposition

Oppositionsführer(in) *m(f)* opposition leader

Optiker(in) <-s, -> ['ɔp·ti·kɐ] *m(f)* optometrist

optimal [ɔp·ti·'ma:l] I. *adj* optimal II. *adv* in the best possible way

optimieren* [ɔp·ti·'miː·rən] *vt* to optimize

Optimismus <-> [ɔp·ti·'mɪs·mʊs] *m kein pl* optimism

Optimist(in) <-en, -en> [ɔp·ti·'mɪst] *m(f)* optimist

optimistisch I. *adj* optimistic **II.** *adv* optimistically

optisch ['ɔp·tɪʃ] *adj* Eindruck, Täuschung optical

orange [o·'rãː·ʒə] *adj* orange

Orange <-, -n> [o·'rãː·ʒə] *f* orange

Orangensaft *m* orange juice

Orangenschale *f* orange peel

Orang-Utan <-s, -s> ['oː·raŋ·'ʔuːtan] *m* orangutan

Orchester <-s, -> [ɔr·'kɛs·tɐ] *nt* orchestra

Orchidee <-, -n> [ɔrçi·'deː·(ə)] *f* orchid

Orden <-s, -> ['ɔr·dn̩] *m* ❶ (Ehrenzeichen) decoration, medal; **jdm einen ~ [für etw** *akk***] verleihen** to decorate sb [for sth] ❷ (Gemeinschaft) [holy] order

ordentlich ['ɔr·dn̩·tlɪç] **I.** *adj* ❶ (aufgeräumt) neat ❷ (ordnungsliebend) Person orderly, neat ❸ (anständig) Leute respectable; Benehmen proper ❹ (fam: tüchtig) proper; Portion decent **II.** *adv* ❶ (säuberlich) neatly ❷ (anständig) **sich** *akk* **~ benehmen** to [really] behave oneself ❸ (fam: tüchtig) properly; **~ essen** to eat well

Ordinalzahl [ɔr·di·'naːl·] *f* ordinal [number]

ordinär [ɔr·di·'nɛːɐ̯] **I.** *adj* ❶ (vulgär) vulgar ❷ (alltäglich) ordinary **II.** *adv* crudely

ordnen ['ɔrd·nən] *vt* to arrange; **neu ~** to rearrange

Ordner <-s, -> *m* file; (Hefter) binder

Ordnung <-> ['ɔrd·nʊŋ] *f kein pl* order; **die öffentliche ~** public order; **~ schaffen** to straighten things up ▶WENDUNGEN: **etw in ~ bringen** (aufräumen) to clean sth up; (klären) to sort sth out; (reparieren) to fix sth; **es [ganz] in ~ finden, dass ...** to find it [perfectly] all right that ...; **geht in ~!** (fam) that's OK; **etw ist mit jdm/etw nicht in ~** there's something wrong with sb/sth; **wieder in ~ kommen** to turn out all right; **in ~ sein** (fam) to be OK; **nicht in ~ sein** (nicht funktionieren) to not be working right; (sich nicht gehören, nicht richtig sein) to not be OK

Ordnungsamt *nt* municipal authority responsible for registration, licensing, and regulating public events

ordnungsgemäß I. *adj* according to the rules *pred* **II.** *adv* in accordance with the regulations

Ordnungsstrafe *f* fine

ordnungswidrig I. *adj* improper **II.** *adv* improperly

Ordnungswidrigkeit *f* infringement [of the rules/law]

Organ <-s, -e> [ɔr·'gaːn] *nt* ❶ ANAT organ ❷ (fam: Stimme) voice ❸ (form: offizielle Zeitschrift/Einrichtung) organ

Organhandel *m* organ trafficking

Organisation <-, -en> [ɔr·ga·ni·za·'tsi̯oːn] *f* organization

Organisationstalent *nt* ❶ kein pl (Eigenschaft) organizational ability ❷ (Mensch) skilled organizer

organisatorisch [ɔr·ga·ni·za·'toː·rɪʃ] **I.** *adj* organizational **II.** *adv* organizationally

organisch [ɔr·'gaː·nɪʃ] **I.** *adj* organic **II.** *adv* organically

organisieren* [ɔr·ga·ni·'ziː·rən] **I.** *vt, vi* to organize; **er kann ausgezeichnet ~** he's an excellent organizer **II.** *vt* (fam: beschaffen) to get hold of; **wer organisiert einen CD-Spieler für die Party?** who is going to arrange for a CD player for the party? **III.** *vr* **sich** *akk* **~** to get organized

Organismus <-, -nismen> [ɔr·ga·'nɪs·mʊs] *m* organism

Organspende *f* organ donation

Organspender(in) *m(f)* organ donor

Organtransplantation *f*, **Organverpflanzung** *f* organ transplant

Orgasmus <-, Orgasmen> [ɔr·'gas·mʊs] *m* orgasm

Orgel <-, -n> ['ɔr·gl̩] *f* organ

Orgie <-, -n> ['ɔr·gi̯ə] *f* orgy

Orient <-s> ['oːriɛnt, oˈriɛnt] *m kein pl* ■ **der ~** the Orient; **der Vordere ~** the Middle East

Orientale, Orientalin <-n, -n> [oˈriɛnˈtaːlə] *m, f* Oriental

orientalisch [oˈriɛnˈtaːlɪʃ] *adj* oriental

orientieren* [oˈriɛnˈtiːrən] **I.** *vr* ■ **sich** *akk* **~** ❶ (*sich zurechtfinden*) to use as a point of reference; **sich** *akk* **an den Sternen ~** to get one's bearings by looking at the stars ❷ (*sich ausrichten*) **sich** *akk* **an etw** *dat* **~** *Bericht* to be based on; *Person* to adapt oneself to; **ich bin eher links orientiert** I tend more to the left **II.** *vt* to inform (**über** +*akk* about)

Orientierung <-, -en> [oˈriɛnˈtiːrʊŋ] *f* orientation; **die ~ verlieren** to lose one's sense of direction

Orientierungssinn *m kein pl* sense of direction

original [oˈriˈɡiˈnaːl] **I.** *adj* ❶ (*echt*) genuine ❷ (*ursprünglich*) original **II.** *adv* in the original (condition)

Original <-s, -e> [oˈriˈɡiˈnaːl] *nt* ❶ (*Urversion*) original ❷ (*Mensch*) character

originell [oˈriˈɡiˈnɛl] *adj* original

Orkan <-[e]s, -e> [ɔrˈkaːn] *m* hurricane

orkanartig *adj* hurricane-force *attr*

Ornament <-[e]s, -e> [ɔrnaˈmɛnt] *nt* ornament

Ort¹ <-[e]s, -e> [ɔrt] *m* place ▶WENDUNGEN: **an ~ und Stelle** on the spot

Ort² [ɔrt] *nt* (*fam*) ▶WENDUNGEN: **vor ~** on site

OrthografieRR, **Orthographie** <-, -n> [ɔrtoɡraˈfiː] *f* orthography, spelling

orthografischRR, **orthographisch** [ɔrtoˈɡraːfɪʃ] **I.** *adj* orthographic[al] *spec* **II.** *adv* orthographically *spec*

Orthopäde, Orthopädin <-n, -n> [ɔrtoˈpɛːdə] *m, f* orthopedist

orthopädisch [ɔrtoˈpɛːdɪʃ] *adj* orthopedic

örtlich ['œrtlɪç] **I.** *adj* ❶ (*lokal*) local ❷ METEO localized **II.** *adv* locally; **jdn ~ betäuben** to give sb a local anesthetic

Ortsangabe *f* (*Standortangabe*) [name of] location; (*in Anschrift*) [name of the] city/town

Ortsausgang *m* village/town exit

Ortschaft <-, -en> *f* village/[small] town; **eine geschlossene ~** a built-up area

Ortseingang *m* village/town entrance

ortsfremd *adj* ■ **~ sein** to be a stranger

Ortsgespräch *nt* local call

Ortsname *m* place name

Ortsschild *nt* sign for a town

Ortstarif *m* local [call] rate

Ortsteil *m* part of a town

Ortszeit *f* local time

Öse <-, -n> ['øːzə] *f* eye[let]

Ossi <-, -s> ['ɔsi] *m o f* (*fam*) East German

Ostasien *nt* East[ern] Asia

ostdeutsch ['ɔstˈdɔytʃ] *adj* East German

Ostdeutschland ['ɔstˈdɔytʃlant] *nt* East Germany

Osten <-s> ['ɔstn̩] *m kein pl, no indef art* ❶ (*Himmelsrichtung*) east; **der Ferne/Nahe ~** the Far/Middle East; *s. a.* **Norden 1** ❷ (*östliche Gegend*) east; *s. a.* **Norden 2**

Osterei *nt* Easter egg

Osterglocke *f* BOT daffodil

Osterhase *m* Easter bunny

Ostermontag ['oːsteˈmoːnˈtaːk] *m* Easter Monday

Ostern <-, -> ['oːstən] *nt* Easter; **frohe ~!** Happy Easter!

Österreich <-s> ['øːstəraiç] *nt* Austria; *s. a.* **Deutschland**

Österreicher(in) <-s, -> ['øːstəraiçe] *m(f)* Austrian; *s. a.* **Deutsche(r)**

österreichisch ['øːstəraiçɪʃ] *adj* Austrian; *s. a.* **deutsch**

Ostersonntag ['oːsteˈzɔnˈtaːk] *m* Easter Sunday

Osteuropa ['ɔstʔɔyˈroːpa] *nt* Eastern Europe

Ostfriese, -friesin <-n, -n> ['ɔstˈfriːzə] *m, f* East Frisian

ostfriesisch ['ɔstˈfriːzɪʃ] *adj* East Frisian

O

Ostfriesland [ɔstˈfriːsˌlant] *nt* East Friesland

östlich [ˈœstlɪç] I. *adj* ① (*Himmelsrichtung*) eastern; *s. a.* **nördlich I 1** ② (*im Osten liegend*) eastern; *s. a.* **nördlich I 2** ③ (*von/nach Osten*) eastward; *Richtung, Wind* easterly; *s. a.* **nördlich I 3** II. *adv* ■ ~ **von ...** east of ... III. *präp* +*gen* [to the] east of

Ostsee [ˈɔstzeː] *f* ■ **die ~** the Baltic [Sea]

Oststaaten *pl* (*in den USA*) Eastern states *pl*

Ost-West-Beziehungen [ˈɔstˈvɛst-] *pl* East-West relations *pl*

Otter¹ <-, -n> [ˈɔtɐ] *f* (*Schlangenart*) adder

Otter² <-s, -> [ˈɔtɐ] *m* (*Fischotter*) otter

oval [oˈvaːl] *adj* oval

Oxidation <-, -en> [ɔksiˈdaˈtsi̯oːn] *f* oxidation

oxidieren* [ɔksiˈdiːrən] *vt, vi sein o haben* to oxidize

Ozean <-s, -e> [ˈoːtseaːn] *m* ocean

Ozon <-s> [oˈtsoːn] *nt o m kein pl* ozone

Ozonloch *nt* ozone hole

Ozonschicht *f kein pl* ozone layer

Pp

P, p <-, -> [peː] *nt* P, p; ~ **wie Paula** P as in Papa

paar [paːɐ] *adj* ■ **ein ~ ...** a few ...; **ein ~ Mal** a couple of times; **alle ~ Tage** every few days

Paar <-s, -e> [paːɐ] *nt* ① (*Menschen*) couple ② (*Dinge*) pair; **ein ~ Würstchen** a couple [of] sausages

paaren [paːrən] *vr* ■ **sich** *akk* ~ ① (*kopulieren*) to mate ② (*sich verbinden*) to be coupled

paarweise *adv* in pairs

Pacht <-, -en> [paxt] *f* lease

pachten [ˈpaxtn̩] *vt* to lease

Pächter(in) <-s, -> [ˈpɛçtɐ] *m(f)* tenant

Pack¹ <-[e]s, -e> [pak] *m* (*Stapel*) stack; (*zusammengeschnürt*) pack

Pack² <-s> [pak] *nt kein pl* (*pej: Pöbel*) riffraff + *pl vb*

Päckchen <-s, -> [ˈpɛkçən] *nt* ① (*Postsendung*) small package ② (*Packung*) pack, packet ③ (*kleiner Packen*) small bundle

packen [ˈpakn̩] *vt* ① (*ergreifen*) to grab [hold of] (**bei, an** +*dat* by) ② (*vollpacken, verstauen*) to pack (**in** +*akk* in[to]); **ein Paket ~** to box up *sep* a package ③ (*überkommen*) to seize; **von Ekel gepackt** utterly disgusted ④ (*sl: bewältigen*) to manage; *Prüfung* to pass

Packen <-s, -> [ˈpakn̩] *m* stack; (*unordentlich a.*) pile; (*zusammengeschnürt*) bundle

packend *adj* absorbing; *Buch, Film* thrilling

Packung <-, -en> *f* pack[age]; **eine ~ Pralinen** a box of chocolates

Pad <-s, -s> [pɛt] *nt* ① COMPUT [mouse] pad ② (*Wattebausch*) cotton ball ③ (*Kaffeepad*) [coffee] pod

Pädagoge, Pädagogin <-n, -n> [pɛdaˈɡoːɡə] *m, f* ① (*Lehrer*) teacher ② (*Erziehungswissenschaftler*) education[al] theorist

Pädagogik <-> [pɛdaˈɡoːɡɪk] *f kein pl* pedagogy *spec*

pädagogisch [pɛdaˈɡoːɡɪʃ] I. *adj* educational *attr*; ~**e Fähigkeiten** teaching ability II. *adv* educationally

Paddel <-s, -> [ˈpadl̩] *nt* paddle

Paddelboot *nt* canoe

paddeln ['pa·d̩ln] *vi sein o haben* to paddle

Page <-n, -n> ['pa:·ʒə] *m* page

Paket <-[e]s, -e> [pa·ˈke:t] *nt* ❶ (*Postsendung*) package, parcel ❷ (*umhüllter Packen*) package ❸ (*Packung*) pack, packet ❹ (*Gesamtheit*) package ❺ (*Stapel*) stack

Pakistan <-s> ['pa:·kɪ·sta:n] *nt* Pakistan; *s. a.* **Deutschland**

Pakt <-[e]s, -e> [pakt] *m* pact

Palast <-[e]s, Paläste> [pa·ˈlast] *m* palace

Palästina <-s> [pa·lɛsˈti:·na] *nt* Palestine; *s. a.* **Deutschland**

Palästinenser(in) <-s, -> [pa·lɛs·tiˈnɛn·ze] *m(f)* Palestinian; *s. a.* **Deutsche(r)**

palästinensisch [pa·lɛs·tiˈnɛn·zɪʃ] *adj* Palestinian; *s. a.* **deutsch**

Palme <-, -n> ['pal·mə] *f* palm [tree] ▶WENDUNGEN: **jdn auf die ~ bringen** (*fam*) to drive sb up the wall

Palmsonntag [palmˈzɔn·ta:k] *m* Palm Sunday

Pampelmuse <-, -n> [pam·pl̩ˈmu:·zə] *f* grapefruit

Panama <-s> ['pa·na·ma] *nt* Panama; *s. a.* **Deutschland**

Panamaer(in) <-s, -> ['pa·na·ma·ɐ] *m(f)* Panamanian; *s. a.* **Deutsche(r)**

panieren* [pa·ˈni:·rən] *vt* to bread

Paniermehl *nt* breadcrumbs *pl*

Panik <-, -en> ['pa:·nɪk] *f* panic; **in ~ geraten** to panic

panisch ['pa:·nɪʃ] I. *adj attr* panic-stricken II. *adv* in panic

Panne <-, -n> ['pa·nə] *f* ❶ AUTO, TECH breakdown ❷ (*Missgeschick*) mishap

Pannendienst <-es, -e> *m* tow[ing] service

Panorama <-s, Panoramen> [pa·no·ˈra:·ma] *nt* panorama

panschen ['pan·ʃn] *vt* to water down *sep* (*an alcoholic drink*)

Panter[RR], **Panther** <-s, -> ['pan·tɐ] *m* panther

Pantoffel <-s, -n> [pan·ˈtɔ·fl̩] *m* [backless] slipper

Pantoffelheld *m* (*fam*) henpecked husband

Panzer <-s, -> ['pan·tsɐ] *m* ❶ MIL tank ❷ (*Schutzhülle*) shell; *eines Krokodils* bony plate; *eines Nashorns, Sauriers* armor

panzern ['pan·tsɐn] *vt* to armor-plate

Papa <-s, -s> ['pa·pa] *m* (*fam*) dad, daddy *esp childspeak*

Papagei <-s, -en> [pa·pa·ˈgai] *m* parrot

Papi <-s, -s> ['pa·pi] *m* (*fam*) *s.* **Papa**

Papier <-s, -e> [pa·ˈpi:ɐ] *nt* ❶ *kein pl* (*Material*) paper ❷ (*Schriftstück*) paper, document ❸ (*Ausweise*) ■ **~e** [identification] papers *pl*

Papierkorb *m* waste paper basket

Papierstau *m* paper jam

Papiertaschentuch *nt* tissue

Pappbecher *m* paper cup

Pappe <-, -n> ['pa·pə] *f* cardboard

Pappel <-, -n> ['pa·pl̩] *f* poplar

pappig ['pa·pɪç] *adj* (*fam*) ❶ (*klebrig*) sticky ❷ (*breiig*) mushy

Pappkarton *m* ❶ (*Pappschachtel*) cardboard box ❷ (*Pappe*) cardboard

Pappteller *m* paper plate

Paprika <-s, -[s]> ['pa·pri·ka] *m* ❶ (*Strauch, Schote*) pepper ❷ *kein pl* (*Gewürz*) paprika

Papst <-[e]s, Päpste> [pa:pst] *m* ■ **der ~** the Pope

päpstlich ['pɛːpst·lɪç] *adj* papal *a. pej*

Parabolantenne [pa·ra·ˈbo:l-] *f* satellite dish

Paradebeispiel *nt* perfect example

Paradeiser <-s, -> [pa·ra·ˈdai·zɐ] *m* ÖSTERR (*Tomate*) tomato

Paradies <-es, -e> [pa·ra·ˈdi:s] *nt* paradise *no def art* ▶WENDUNGEN: **das ~ auf Erden** heaven on earth

paradox [pa·ra·ˈdɔks] (*geh*) I. *adj* paradoxical II. *adv* paradoxically

Paragraf[RR], **Paragraph** <-en, -en> [pa·ra·ˈgra:f] *m* paragraph

parallel [pa·ra·ˈle:l] *adj, adv* parallel

Parallele <-, -n> [pa·ra·ˈle:·la] *f* (*a. fig*) parallel; **eine ~ [zu etw** *dat*] **ziehen** to draw a parallel [to [*or* with] sth]

paramilitärisch ['pa:·ra·mi·li·tɛ·rɪʃ] *adj* paramilitary

Parasit <-en, -en> [pa·ra·'zi:t] *m* parasite

Parfüm <-s, -e> [par·'fy:m] *nt* perfume

Parfümerie <-, -n> [par·fy·mə·'ri:] *f* perfumery

parfümieren* [par·fy·'mi:·rən] *vr* ■**sich** *akk* ~ to put on *sep* perfume

Pariser¹ [pa·'ri:·zɐ] *adj attr* ❶ (*in Paris befindlich*) in Paris ❷ (*aus Paris stammend*) Parisian

Pariser² <-s, -> [pa·'ri:·zɐ] *m* (*sl: Kondom*) condom

Park <-s, -s> [park] *m* park

parken ['par·kn] *vt, vi* to park

Parkett <-s, -e> [par·'kɛt] *nt* ❶ (*Holzfußboden*) parquet [flooring] ❷ (*Tanzfläche*) dance floor

Parkgebühr *f* parking fee

Parkhaus *nt* parking garage

Parklücke *f* parking space

Parkplatz *m* ❶ (*Parkbereich*) parking lot ❷ (*Parklücke*) parking space

Parkscheibe *f* parking disk (*for parking spaces with time limits to show what time the car was parked*)

Parksünder(in) *m(f)* parking offender

Parkuhr *f* parking meter

Parkverbot *nt* ❶ (*Verbot zu parken*) parking ban ❷ (*Parkverbotszone*) no-parking zone

Parkwächter(in) *m(f)* parking lot attendant

Parlament <-[e]s, -e> [par·la·'mɛnt] *nt* parliament; ■**das Europäische ~** the European Parliament

Parmesan(käse) <-s> [par·me·'za:n-] *m kein pl* Parmesan [cheese]

Partei <-, -en> [par·'tai] *f* ❶ POL, JUR party ❷ (*Mietpartei*) tenant ►WENDUNGEN: **für/gegen jdn ~ ergreifen** to side with/against sb

Parteigenosse, -genossin <-n, -n> *m, f* party member

parteiisch [par·'tai·ɪʃ] **I.** *adj* biased **II.** *adv* in a biased way

parteilos *adj* independent

Parteimitglied *nt* party member

Parteipolitik *f* party politics + *sing vb*

Parteiprogramm *nt* party platform

Parteitag *m* ❶ (*Parteikonferenz*) party conference ❷ (*Beschlussorgan*) party executive

Parteivorsitzende(r) *f(m)* party chairperson, party chairman *masc* [*or fem* -woman]

parterre [par·'tɛr] *adv* on the ground floor

Partie <-, -n> [par·'ti:] *f* ❶ (*Körperbereich*) area ❷ SPORT game; **eine ~ Schach** a game of chess ►WENDUNGEN: **eine gute ~ machen** to marry well; **mit von der ~ sein** to be in on it

Partikelfilter *m* AUTO particulate filter

Partizip <-s, -ien> [par·ti·'tsi:p] *nt* participle

Partner(in) <-s, -> ['part·nɐ] *m(f)* partner

Partnerschaft <-, -en> *f* partnership; **in einer ~ leben** to live with somebody

Partnerstadt *f* sister city

Party <-, -s> ['pa:ɐ·ti] *f* party

Partyservice ['pa:ɐ·ti·zø:ɐ·vɪs] *m* catering service

PassRR, **Paß**ALT <Passes, Pässe> [pas] *m* ❶ (*Dokument*) passport ❷ GEOG pass

Passage <-, -n> [pa·'sa:·ʒə] *f* ❶ LIT, NAUT passage ❷ (*Ladenstraße*) [shopping] galleria

Passagier(in) <-s, -e> [pa·sa·'ʒi:ɐ] *m(f)* passenger ►WENDUNGEN: **ein blinder ~** a stowaway

Passagierliste *f* passenger list

Passant(in) <-en, -en> [pa·'sant] *m(f)* passer-by

PassbildRR *nt* passport photo[graph]

passen ['pa·sn] *vi* ❶ (*von der Größe/Form her*) to fit ❷ (*harmonieren*) ■**zu jdm** ~ to suit sb; ■**zu etw** *dat* ~ to go well with sth; **sie passt einfach nicht in unser Team** she simply doesn't fit in with our team ❸ (*gelegen sein*) ■**jdm** ~ to suit sb; **der Termin passt mir zeitlich gar nicht** that day/time isn't convenient for me

P

at all; **würde Ihnen der Dienstag besser ~?** would Tuesday be better for you?; **passt es Ihnen, wenn wir ...** is it okay with you if we ... ❹ (*gefallen*) ■**jdm passt etw nicht** [an **jdm**] sb does not like sth [about sb] ❺ (*fam*) ■**[bei etw** *dat*] ~ **müssen** (*überfragt sein*) to have to pass [on sth]

passend *adj* ❶ *Größe, Form* fitting ❷ *Farbe, Stil* matching ❸ (*genehm*) convenient ❹ (*richtig*) suitable; (*angemessen*) appropriate; *Bemerkung* fitting; **die ~en Worte finden** to find the right words ❺ (*fam*) **es ~ haben** *Geldbetrag* to have exact change

Passfoto^RR *nt s.* **Passbild**

passieren* [pa·'si:·rən] **I.** *vi sein* to happen; **ist was passiert?** has something happened?; **wie konnte das nur ~?** how could that happen?; **... sonst passiert was!** (*fam*) ... or else!; **so etwas passiert eben** shit happens *fam vulg* **II.** *vt haben* ❶ (*vorbeigehen, -fahren*) to pass ❷ (*überqueren*) to cross

passioniert [pa·sio̯·'ni:ɐ̯t] *adj* (*geh*) passionate

Passionsfrucht *f* passion fruit

passiv ['pa·si:f] **I.** *adj* passive **II.** *adv* passively

Passiv <-s, -e> ['pa·si:f] *nt* passive

Passivrauchen *nt* passive smoking

Passkontrolle^RR *f* ❶ (*das Kontrollieren*) passport check ❷ (*Kontrollstelle*) passport checkpoint

Passstraße^RR *f* pass

Passwort^RR <-es, -wörter> *nt* password

Paste <-, -n> ['pas·tə] *f* paste

Pastellfarbe *f* pastel color

Pastete <-, -n> [pas·'te:·tə] *f* pâté

Pastor, Pastorin <-s, -toren> ['pas·to:ɐ̯, pas·'to:·rɪn] *m, f* DIAL *s.* **Pfarrer**

Pate, Patin <-n, -n> ['pa:·tə, 'pa:·tɪn] *m, f* godfather *masc*, godmother *fem*

Patenkind *nt* godchild

Patenonkel *m* godfather

Patent <-[e]s, -e> [pa·'tɛnt] *nt* ❶ (*amt-*

licher Schutz) patent ❷ SCHWEIZ (*staatliche Erlaubnis*) permit

Patentamt *nt* Patent Office

Patentante *f* godmother

patentieren* [pa·tɛn·'ti:·rən] *vt* ■**[jdm] etw ~** to patent sth [for sb]

Patient(in) <-en, -en> [pa·'tsi̯ɛnt] *m(f)* patient; **stationärer ~** inpatient

patriarchalisch [pa·tri·ar·'ça:·lɪʃ] *adj* patriarchal

Patriot(in) <-en, -en> [pa·tri·'o:t] *m(f)* patriot

patriotisch [pa·tri·'o:tɪʃ] **I.** *adj* patriotic **II.** *adv* patriotically

Patriotismus <-> [pa·trio·'tɪs·mʊs] *m kein pl* patriotism

Patrone <-, -n> [pa·'tro:·nə] *f* cartridge

Patsche ['pat·ʃə] *f* ▶WENDUNGEN: **jdm aus der ~ helfen** (*fam*) to get sb out of a jam; **in der ~ sitzen** (*fam*) to be in a jam

patschnass^RR ['patʃ·'nas] *adj* (*fam*) soaking wet

Patzer <-s, -> *m* ❶ (*fam: Fehler*) slip-up ❷ ÖSTERR (*Klecks*) blob

patzig ['pa·tsɪç] *adj* (*fam*) snotty

Pauke <-, -n> ['pau̯·kə] *f* MUS kettledrum ▶WENDUNGEN: **auf die ~ hauen** (*fam: angeben*) to toot one's [own] horn; (*ausgelassen feiern*) to paint the town red

pauken ['pau̯·kn̩] *vt, vi* (*fam*) to cram; **Mathe/Vokabeln ~** to cram for a math/vocabulary test

Pauker(in) <-s, -> ['pau̯·kɐ] *m(f)* (*fam*) teacher

pauschal [pau̯·'ʃa:l] **I.** *adj* ❶ (*undifferenziert*) sweeping ❷ FIN flat-rate *attr*, all-inclusive **II.** *adv* ❶ (*allgemein*) **etw ~ beurteilen** to make a wholesale judgment on sth ❷ FIN at a flat rate

Pauschalbetrag *m* lump sum

Pauschale <-, -n> [pau̯·'ʃa:·lə] *f* flat rate

Pauschalpreis *m* all-inclusive price

Pause <-, -n> ['pau̯·zə] *f* ❶ (*Unterbrechung*) break; SCH, POL recess; **[eine] ~ machen** to take a break ❷ (*Sprechpause*) pause

P

pausenlos *adj, adv s.* **ständig**
Pazifik <-s> [pa·'tsi:·fɪk] *m* ■**der ~** the Pacific
Pazifist(in) <-en, -en> [pa·tsi·'fɪst] *m(f)* pacifist
pazifistisch *adj* pacifist
PC <-s, -s> [pe:·'tse:] *m Abk von* **Personal Computer** PC
Pech <-[e]s> [pɛç] *nt kein pl* bad luck; **[bei etw** *dat*] **~ haben** to be unlucky [in/with sth]; **~ gehabt!** *(fam)* tough luck [*or fam vulg* shit]!
Pechvogel *m (fam)* walking disaster *hum*
Pedal <-s, -e> [pe·'da:l] *nt* pedal
Pedant(in) <-en, -en> [pe·'dant] *m(f)* pedant
pedantisch [pe·'dan·tɪʃ] I. *adj* pedantic II. *adv* pedantically
Pegelstand ['pe:·gl-] *m* water level
peinlich ['pain·lɪç] *adj* ❶ *(unangenehm)* embarrassing; *Frage, Lage, Situation* awkward; **es war ihr sehr ~** she was really embarrassed [about it] ❷ *(äußerst)* painstaking; *Genauigkeit* meticulous; *Sauberkeit* scrupulous
Peitsche <-, -n> ['pai·tʃə] *f* whip
peitschen ['pai·tʃn] I. *vt haben* to whip II. *vi sein Regen* to lash **(gegen** +*akk* against)
Pelikan <-s, -e> ['pe:·li·ka:n] *m* pelican
Pelle <-, -n> ['pɛ·lə] *f (fam: Haut)* skin ▶WENDUNGEN: **jdm auf die ~ rücken** *(fam: sich dicht herandrängen)* to crowd sb; *(jdn bedrängen)* to badger sb
pellen ['pɛ·lən] *vt (fam)* to peel
Pellkartoffeln *pl* potatoes boiled in their skin
Pelz <-es, -e> [pɛlts] *m* fur
Pelzmantel *m* fur coat
Pendel <-s, -> ['pɛn·dl] *nt* pendulum
pendeln ['pɛn·dln] *vi* ❶ *haben (schwingen)* ■**hin und her** **~** to swing [to and fro] ❷ *sein* TRANSP to commute
Pendelverkehr *m* ❶ *(Nahverkehrsdienst)* shuttle service ❷ *(Berufsverkehr)* commuter traffic
Pendler(in) <-s, -> ['pɛnd·lɐ] *m(f)* commuter

penetrant [pe·ne·'trant] I. *adj* ❶ *(durchdringend)* penetrating; *Geruch* pungent ❷ *(aufdringlich)* overbearing II. *adv* penetratingly
penibel [pe·'ni:·bl] *adj (geh) Ordnung* meticulous; *Mensch* fastidious **(in** +*dat* about)
Penis <-, -se> ['pe:·nɪs] *m* penis
Penizillin <-s, -e> [pe·ni·tsɪ·'li:n] *nt* penicillin
pennen ['pɛ·nən] *vi (fam)* to sleep
Penner(in) <-s, -> *m(f) (pej fam: Stadtstreicher)* bum
Pension <-, -en> [pã·'zjo:n, pɛn·'zjo:n] *f* ❶ TOURIST guesthouse ❷ *(Ruhegehalt)* pension; **in ~ gehen/sein** to retire/be retired
pensionieren* [pã·zjo·'ni:·rən] *vt* ■**pensioniert werden** to be retired off; ■**sich** *akk* **~ lassen** to retire
Pensum <-s, Pensa> ['pɛn·zʊm] *nt (geh)* work quota
Peperoni [pe·pe·'ro:·ni] *pl* ❶ *(scharfe Paprikas)* chili peppers *pl* ❷ SCHWEIZ *(Gemüsepaprikas)* bell peppers *pl*
peppig ['pɛ·pɪç] *adj (fam)* peppy
per [pɛr] *präp* ❶ *(durch)* by; **~ Post** by mail ❷ **mit jdm ~ du/Sie sein** to address sb with "du"/"Sie"
perfekt [pɛr·'fɛkt] I. *adj* perfect II. *adv* perfectly
Perfekt <-s, -e> ['pɛr·fɛkt] *nt* perfect [tense]
Perfektion <-> [pɛr·fɛk·'tsjo:n] *f kein pl* perfection
Pergamentpapier *nt* wax paper
Periode <-, -n> [pe·'rjo:·də] *f (a. biol)* period
Perle <-, -n> ['pɛr·lə] *f* ❶ *(Schmuckperle)* pearl ❷ *(Kügelchen, Tropfen)* bead
Perlenkette *f* pearl necklace
permanent [pɛr·ma·'nɛnt] *(geh)* I. *adj* permanent II. *adv* permanently
perplex [pɛr·'plɛks] *adj* dumbfounded
Perserteppich *m* Persian rug
Person <-, -en> [pɛr·'zo:n] *f (a. ling)* person

Personal <-s> [pɛr·zo·'na:l] *nt kein pl* staff

Personalausweis *m* identity card, ID

Personalien [pɛr·zo·'na:·li̯·ən] *pl* particulars *npl*

Personalpronomen *nt* personal pronoun

Personenkraftwagen *m* automobile

Personenverkehr *m* passenger transportation

persönlich [pɛr·'zø:n·lɪç] **I.** *adj* personal; **~ werden** to get personal **II.** *adv* personally; **~ erscheinen** to appear in person

Persönlichkeit <-, -en> *f* ❶ *kein pl* (*Eigenart*) personality ❷ (*markanter Mensch*) character ❸ (*Prominenter*) celebrity

Perspektive <-, -n> [pɛrs·pɛk·'ti:·və] *f* ❶ (*Blickwinkel*) perspective ❷ (*geh: Zukunftsaussicht*) prospect *usu pl*

perspektivlos *adj* without prospects

Perücke <-, -n> [pe·'rʏ·kə] *f* wig

pervers [pɛr·'vɛrs] *adj* ❶ (*widernatürlich*) perverted ❷ (*fam: abartig*) perverse

Perversion <-, -en> [pɛr·vɛr·'zi̯o:n] *f* perversion

Pessimismus <-> [pɛ·si·'mɪs·mus] *m kein pl* pessimism

Pessimist(in) <-en, -en> [pɛ·si·'mɪst] *m(f)* pessimist

pessimistisch [pɛ·si·'mɪs·tɪʃ] **I.** *adj* pessimistic **II.** *adv* pessimistically

Pest <-> [pɛst] *f kein pl* ■ **die ~** the plague ▶WENDUNGEN: **jdn wie die ~ hassen** (*fam*) to hate sb's guts; **wie die ~ stinken** (*fam*) to stink to high heaven

Petersilie <-, -n> [pe·tɐ·'zi:·li̯·ə] *f* parsley

Petroleum <-s> [pe·'tro:·le·ʊm] *nt kein pl* kerosene

petto ['pɛto] *adv* ▶WENDUNGEN: **etw in ~ haben** (*fam*) to have sth up one's sleeve

petzen ['pɛ·tsn̩] **I.** *vt* (*pej fam*) ■ **jdm** **etw ~** to tell [sb] about sth **II.** *vi* (*pej fam*) to tell

Pfad <-[e]s, -e> [pfa:t] *m* path

Pfadfinder(in) <-s, -> *m(f)* Boy Scout; (*Mädchen*) Girl Scout

Pfahl <-[e]s, Pfähle> [pfa:l] *m* post, stake

Pfand <-[e]s, Pfänder> [pfant] *nt* deposit

pfänden ['pfɛn·dn̩] *vt* ❶ (*beschlagnahmen*) to impound ❷ (*Pfandsiegel anbringen*) ■ **jdn ~** to seize some of sb's possessions

Pfandflasche *f* deposit bottle

Pfanne <-, -n> ['pfa·nə] *f* ❶ (*Bratpfanne*) [frying] pan ❷ SCHWEIZ (*Topf*) pot ▶WENDUNGEN: **jdn in die ~ hauen** (*sl*) to play a mean trick on sb

Pfannkuchen *m* pancake; (*dünner*) crepe

Pfarramt *nt* vicarage

Pfarrei <-, -en> [pfa·'rai̯] *f* ❶ (*Gemeinde*) parish ❷ *s.* **Pfarramt**

Pfarrer(in) <-s, -> ['pfa·rɐ] *m(f)* (*katholisch*) priest; (*evangelisch*) minister

Pfau <-[e]s, -en> [pfau̯] *m* peacock

Pfeffer <-s, -> ['pfɛ·fɐ] *m* pepper ▶WENDUNGEN: **hingehen, wo der ~ wächst** (*fam*) to go to hell

Pfefferminze *f kein pl* peppermint

Pfefferminztee *m* peppermint tea

Pfeffermühle *f* pepper mill

pfeffern ['pfɛ·fɐn] *vt* KOCHK to season with pepper

Pfeife <-, -n> ['pfai̯·fə] *f* ❶ (*Musikinstrument, Orgelpfeife*) pipe ❷ (*Trillerpfeife*) whistle ❸ (*Tabakpfeife*) pipe ❹ (*fam: Nichtskönner*) twit ▶WENDUNGEN: **nach jds ~ tanzen** to dance to sb's tune

pfeifen <pfiff, gepfiffen> ['pfai̯fn̩] **I.** *vt, vi* to whistle **II.** *vi* ■ **auf etw** *akk* **~** (*fam*) to not give a damn about sth

Pfeifton *m* whistle

Pfeil <-s, -e> [pfai̯l] *m* (*a. Richtungspfeil*) arrow

Pfeiler <-s, -> ['pfai̯·lɐ] *m* pillar

Pfennig <-s, -e *o meist nach Zahlenangaben* -> ['pfɛ·nɪç] *m* (*hist*) pfennig; **keinen ~ [Geld] haben** to be penniless ▶WENDUNGEN: **jeden ~ umdrehen** (*fam*) to think twice about every penny

P

one spends; **keinen ~ <u>wert</u> sein** (*fam*) to be worthless

Pferd <-[e]s, -e> [pfeːɐ̯t] *nt* ① (*Tier*) horse ② (*Schachfigur*) knight ▶WENDUNGEN: **die ~e <u>scheu</u> machen** (*fam*) to put people off; **ich glaub' mich <u>tritt</u> ein ~!** (*fam*) well I'll be damned!

Pferderennen *nt* horse race

Pferdeschwanz *m* ① (*vom Pferd*) horse's tail ② (*Frisur*) ponytail

Pferdestall *m* stable

pfiff [pfɪf] *imp von* **pfeifen**

Pfiff <-s, -e> [pfɪf] *m* (*fam: Reiz*) pizzazz

Pfifferling <-[e]s, -e> ['pfɪ·fɐ·lɪŋ] *m* chanterelle ▶WENDUNGEN: **keinen ~ wert sein** (*fam*) to be worthless

pfiffig ['pfɪ·fɪç] I. *adj* smart II. *adv* smartly

Pfingsten <-, -> ['pfɪŋs·tn̩] *nt meist ohne art* Whitsuntide

Pfingstsonntag *m* Pentecost, Whitsunday

Pfirsich <-s, -e> ['pfɪr·zɪç] *m* peach

Pflanze <-, -n> ['pflan·tsə] *f* plant

pflanzen ['pflan·tsn̩] *vt* to plant

Pflanzenschutzmittel *nt* pesticide

pflanzlich *adj attr* ① (*vegetarisch*) vegetarian ② (*aus Pflanzen gewonnen*) plant-based

Pflaster <-s, -> ['pflas·tɐ] *nt* ① MED band-aid ② BAU pavement ▶WENDUNGEN: **ein <u>gefährliches</u> ~** (*fam*) a dangerous place

Pflasterstein *m* paving stone

Pflaume <-, -n> ['pflau·mə] *f* ① (*Frucht*) plum ② (*fam*) *s.* **Pfeife**

Pflege <-> ['pfleː·ɡə] *f kein pl* ① *eines Kranken* [nursing] care ② *des Körpers* grooming ③ *von Pflanzen, des Gartens* care

pflegebedürftig *adj* in need of care *pred*

Pflegeeltern *pl* foster parents *pl*

Pflegefall *m* sb who needs long-term care

Pflegeheim *nt* nursing home

Pflegekind *nt* foster child

pflegeleicht *adj* ① *Waschprogramm* permanent press; *Textilien* easy-care *attr* ② *Mensch, Tier* easy-going *attr*, easy going *pred*

pflegen ['pfleː·ɡn̩] I. *vt* ① *Kranke* to care for, to look after ② *Körper* to treat ③ *Pflanzen, Garten* to tend ④ (*gewöhnlich tun*) ■**etw zu tun ~** to usually do sth II. *vr* ■**sich** *akk* **~** to take care of one's appearance

Pfleger(in) <-s, -> *m(f)* [male] nurse *masc*, nurse *fem*

Pflegesatz *m* [daily] hospital charges *pl*

Pflicht <-, -en> [pflɪçt] *f* duty

pflichtbewusst[RR] *adj* conscientious

Pflichtgefühl *nt kein pl* sense of duty

Pflichtverteidiger(in) *m(f)* court-appointed defense lawyer

pflücken ['pflʏ·kn̩] *vt* to pick

Pflug <-es, Pflüge> [pfluːk] *m* plow

pflügen *vt, vi* to plow

Pforte <-, -n> ['pfɔr·tə] *f* gate

Pförtner(in) <-s, -> ['pfœrt·nɐ] *m(f)* doorman

Pfosten <-s, -> ['pfɔs·tn̩] *m* (*a. sport*) post

Pfote <-, -n> ['pfoː·tə] *f* ① (*von Tieren*) paw ② (*fam: Hand*) paw

Pfund <-[e]s, -e *o nach Zahlenangaben* -> [pfʊnt] *nt* ① (*500 Gramm*) ≈ pound ② (*Währungseinheit*) pound; **in ~** in pounds

pfuschen ['pfʊ·ʃn̩] *vi* ① (*schlampen*) to be sloppy ② DIAL (*mogeln*) to cheat (**bei** +*dat* at/in/on)

Pfuscherei <-, -en> [pfʊ·ʃə·'rai] *f* bungling

Pfütze <-, -n> ['pfʏ·tsə] *f* puddle

Phänomen <-s, -e> [fɛ·no·'meːn] *nt* phenomenon

phänomenal [fɛ·no·me·'naːl] *adj* phenomenal

Phantasie <-, -n> [fan·ta·'ziː] *f s.* **Fantasie**

phantasieren* [fan·ta·'ziː·rən] *s.* **fantasieren**

phantasievoll *adj s.* **fantasievoll**

phantastisch [fan·'tas·tɪʃ] *adj, adv s.* **fantastisch**

Phantom <-s, -e> [fan·'to:m] *nt* phantom

Phantombild *nt* composite sketch

Pharmazie <-> [far·ma·'tsi:] *f kein pl* pharmacy

Philippinen [fi·lɪ·'pi:·nən] *pl* ▪ **die ~** the Philippines *pl*

Philippiner(in) <-s, -> [fi·lɪ·'pi:·nɐ] *m(f)* Filipino; *s. a.* **Deutsche(r)**

philippinisch [fi·lɪ·'pi:·nɪʃ] *adj* Filipino; *s. a.* **deutsch**

Philologe, Philologin <-n, -n> [fi·lo·'lo:·gə] *m, f* philologist

Philosoph <-en, -en> [fi·lo·'zo:f] *m(f)* philosopher

Philosophie <-, -n> [fi·lo·zo·'fi:] *f* philosophy

philosophieren* [fi·lo·zo·'fi:·rən] *vi* (*geh*) to philosophize (**über** +*akk* about)

philosophisch [fi·lo·'zo:·fɪʃ] *adj* philosophical

Phobie <-, -n> [fo·'bi:] *f* phobia

Phosphat <-[e]s, -e> [fɔs·'fa:t] *nt* phosphate

Phosphor <-s> ['fɔs·fo:ɐ] *m kein pl* phosphorus

Phrase <-, -n> ['fra:·zə] *f* (*pej*) empty phrase

Physik <-> [fy·'zi:k] *f kein pl* physics + *sing vb*, no art

physikalisch [fy·zi·'ka:·lɪʃ] *adj* physical

Physiker(in) <-s, -> ['fy:·zi·kɐ] *m(f)* physicist

Physiotherapeut(in) <-en, -en> [fy·zi̯o·te·ra·'pɔy̯t] *m(f)* physical therapist

Physiotherapie [fy·zi̯o·te·ra·'pi:] *f kein pl* physical therapy

physisch ['fy:·zɪʃ] *adj* physical

Pianist(in) <-en, -en> [pi̯a·'nɪst] *m(f)* pianist

Piano <-s, -s> ['pi̯a:·no] *nt* piano

Pickel <-s, -> ['pɪ·kl̩] *m* ❶ (*Hautunreinheit*) pimple, zit *fam* ❷ (*Spitzhacke*) pickax; (*Eispickel*) ice pick

pickelig ['pɪ·kə·lɪç] *adj* pimply

picken ['pɪ·kn̩] *vi* ORN to peck (**nach** +*dat* at)

Picknick <-s, -s> ['pɪk·nɪk] *nt* picnic

piepen ['pi:·pn̩] *vi* to peep; to squeak; *Gerät* to beep

Pier <-s, -s> [pi:ɐ] *m* pier

pietätlos [pi̯e·'tɛ:t·lo:s] *adj* (*geh*) irreverent

pikant [pi·'kant] I. *adj* ❶ KOCHK spicy ❷ (*frivol*) racy II. *adv* piquantly

pikiert [pi·'ki:ɐt] (*geh*) I. *adj* peeved II. *adv* peevishly

piksen ['pɪk·sn̩] I. *vt* (*fam*) to prick (**mit** +*dat* with) II. *vi* (*fam*) to prickle

Pilger(in) <-s, -> ['pɪl·gɐ] *m(f)* pilgrim

pilgern ['pɪl·gɐn] *vi sein* ❶ (*wallfahren*) to make a pilgrimage (**nach** to) ❷ (*fam: gehen, marschieren*) to wend one's way

Pille <-, -n> ['pɪ·lə] *f* pill; ▪ **die ~** (*Antibabypille*) the pill; **die ~ danach** the morning-after pill

Pilot(in) <-en, -en> [pi·'lo:t] *m(f)* pilot

Pils <-, -> [pɪls] *nt* pilsner

Pilz <-es, -e> [pɪlts] *m* ❶ BOT fungus; (*Speisepilz*) mushroom ❷ MED fungal skin infection ▶WENDUNGEN: **wie ~e aus dem Boden schießen** to shoot up

Pilzerkrankung *f* fungal disease

Pinguin <-s, -e> ['pɪŋ·gu̯i:n] *m* penguin

pinkeln ['pɪŋ·kl̩n] *vi* (*fam*) to pee

Pinnwand *f* bulletin board

Pinsel <-s, -> ['pɪn·zl̩] *m* brush

Pinte <-, -n> ['pɪn·tə] *f* (*fam*) bar, pub

Pinzette <-, -n> [pɪn·'tsɛ·tə] *f* tweezers *npl*

Pionier(in) <-s, -e> [pi̯o·'ni:ɐ] *m(f)* (*geh: Wegbereiter*) pioneer

Pirat(in) <-en, -en> [pi·'ra:t] *m(f)* pirate

pissen ['pɪ·sn̩] *vi* ❶ (*derb: urinieren*) to piss ❷ *impers* (*sl: stark regnen*) **es pisst** it's pouring

Pistazie <-, -n> [pɪs·'ta:·tsi̯ə] *f* pistachio

Piste <-, -n> ['pɪs·tə] *f* ❶ (*Skipiste*) ski slope [*or* run] ❷ (*Rollbahn*) runway

Pistole <-, -n> [pɪs·'to:·lə] *f* pistol ▶WENDUNGEN: **jdm die ~ auf die Brust setzen** (*fam*) to hold a gun to sb's head

Plackerei <-, -en> [pla·kə·'rai̯] *f* (*fam*) grind

P

plädieren* [plɛ·ˈdiː·rən] *vi* ① JUR ■**auf etw** *akk* ~ to plead sth; **auf schuldig** ~ to plead guilty ② (*fig geh*) ■**für etw** *akk* ~ to plead for sth

Plädoyer <-s, -s> [plɛ·dɔa·ˈjeː] *nt* JUR summation

Plage <-, -n> [ˈplaː·ɡə] *f* nuisance

plagen [ˈplaː·ɡn̩] **I.** *vt* ① *mit Fragen, Bitten* to pester ② (*quälen*) to bother; **Zweifel plagten ihn** he was plagued with doubt **II.** *vr* ■**sich** *akk* [mit etw *dat*] ~ ① (*sich abrackern*) to slave away [over sth] ② (*sich herumplagen*) to be bothered [by sth]

Plakat <-[e]s, -e> [pla·ˈkaːt] *nt* poster

Plakette <-, -n> [pla·ˈkɛ·tə] *f* ① (*Anstecker*) badge; (*Aufkleber, TÜV-Plakette*) sticker

Plan <-[e]s, Pläne> [plaːn] *m* ① (*Vorhaben*) plan; **nach** ~ **laufen** to go according to plan; **jds Pläne durchkreuzen** to thwart sb's plans ② GEOG, TRANSP map ③ (*zeichnerische Darstellung*) plan

Plane <-, -n> [ˈplaː·nə] *f* tarp *fam*

planen [ˈplaː·nən] *vt* to plan

Planet <-en, -en> [pla·ˈneːt] *m* planet

Planetarium <-s, -tarien> [pla·ne·ˈtaː·ri·ʊm] *nt* planetarium

Planierraupe *f* bulldozer

Planke <-, -n> [ˈplaŋ·kə] *f* plank

planlos *adj* ① (*ziellos*) aimless ② (*ohne System*) unsystematic

planmäßig **I.** *adj* ① TRANSP scheduled ② (*systematisch*) systematic **II.** *adv* ① TRANSP as scheduled, according to schedule ② (*systematisch*) systematically

Planschbecken *nt* kiddie pool

planschen [ˈplan·ʃn̩] *vi* to splash around

Plantage <-, -n> [plan·ˈtaː·ʒə] *f* plantation

Planung <-, -en> [ˈplaː·nʊŋ] *f* planning

Plappermaul *nt* (*bes pej fam*) blabbermouth

plappern [ˈpla·pɐn] (*fam*) **I.** *vi* to chatter **II.** *vt* **Unsinn** ~ to babble nonsense

Plastik¹ <-s> [ˈplas·tɪk] *nt kein pl* plastic

Plastik² <-, -en> [ˈplas·tɪk] *f* (*Kunstwerk*) sculpture

Plastikbecher *m* plastic cup

Plastikfolie *f* plastic wrap

Plastiktüte *f* plastic bag

Platin <-s> [ˈplaː·ti:n] *nt kein pl* platinum

platonisch [pla·ˈtoː·nɪʃ] *adj* (*geh*) platonic

plätschern [ˈplɛ·tʃɐn] *vi Brunnen* to splash; *Bach* to babble; *Regen* to patter

platt [plat] **I.** *adj* ① (*flach*) flat ② (*geistlos*) dull ③ (*fam: verblüfft*) ■~ **sein** to be flabbergasted **II.** *adv* flat; ~ **drücken** to flatten

Platt <-[s]> [plat] *nt kein pl*, **Plattdeutsch** [ˈplat·dɔytʃ] *nt* Low German

Platte <-, -n> [ˈpla·tə] *f* ① (*Steinplatte*) slab ② (*Metalltafel*) sheet ③ (*Schallplatte*) record ④ (*Servierteller, Gericht*) platter ⑤ (*Kochplatte*) burner

Plattenspieler *m* record player

Plattform *f* (*a. comput*) platform

Platz <-es, Plätze> [plats] *m* ① (*Ort, Stelle*) place ② (*öffentlicher Platz*) square ③ (*Sitzplatz*) seat; ~ **nehmen** (*geh*) to take a seat ④ (*freier Raum*) room ⑤ (*Sportplatz*) playing field ⑥ (*Rang*) place; **er liegt jetzt auf** ~ **drei** he's now in third place ►WENDUNGEN: **fehl am** ~[e] **sein** to be out of place

Platzangst *f* ① (*fam*) claustrophobia ② (*Agoraphobie*) agoraphobia

Plätzchen <-s, -> [ˈplɛts·çən] *nt* ① *dim von* **Platz** spot ② (*fam: scheitern*) cookie

platzen [ˈpla·tsn̩] *vi sein* ① (*zerplatzen*) to burst; **vor Ärger/Neugier** ~ (*fig*) to be bursting with anger/curiosity ② (*aufplatzen*) to split ③ (*fam: scheitern*) to fall through; **das Fest ist geplatzt** the party is off

platzieren*ᴿᴿ [pla·ˈtsi:·rən] *vt* to place

Platzkarte *f* seat reservation

Platzregen *m* cloudburst

Platzwunde *f* laceration

plaudern [ˈplau·dɐn] *vi* ① (*sich gemütlich unterhalten*) to [have a] chat ② (*fam: ausplaudern*) to gossip

plausibel [plau·'zi:·bl] *adj* plausible

Playboy <-s, -s> ['ple:·bɔy] *m* playboy

Plazenta <-, -s> [pla·'tsɛn·ta] *f* placenta

plazieren* ^{ALT} [pla·'tsi:·rən] *vt s.* **platzieren**

pleite ['plai·tə] *adj (fam)* broke

Pleite <-, -n> ['plai·tə] *f (fam)* ❶ *(Bankrott)* bankruptcy; ~ **machen** to go bust ❷ *(Reinfall)* flop

pleite|gehen^{RR} *vi irreg sein* to go bankrupt

Plombe <-, -n> ['plɔm·bə] *f* ❶ MED *(im Zahn)* filling ❷ *(Bleisiegel)* lead seal

plombieren* [plɔm·'bi:·rən] *vt* ❶ MED *Zahn* to fill ❷ *(amtlich versiegeln)* to seal

plötzlich ['plœts·lɪç] I. *adj* sudden II. *adv* suddenly, all of a sudden; **das kommt alles etwas/so ~** it's all happening rather/so suddenly

plump [plʊmp] I. *adj* ❶ *(massig)* plump ❷ *(schwerfällig)* ungainly ❸ *(dummdreist)* obvious; *Lüge* blatant II. *adv* ❶ *(schwerfällig)* clumsily ❷ *(dummdreist)* crassly

Plunder <-s> ['plʊn·dɐ] *m kein pl* junk

plündern ['plʏn·dɐn] I. *vt* ❶ *(ausrauben)* to plunder ❷ *(fam: leeren)* to raid II. *vi* to plunder

Plural <-s, -e> ['plu:·ra:l] *m* plural

plus [plʊs] *konj, präp, adv* plus; **6 ~ 4 ist 10** 6 plus 4 is 10; **wir haben fünf Grad ~** it's five degrees above zero

Plus <-, -> [plʊs] *nt* ❶ *(Pluszeichen)* plus ❷ ÖKON surplus; **~ machen** to make a profit; [**mit etw** *dat*] **im ~ sein** to be in the black [with sth]

Plüsch <-[e]s, -e> [plʏʃ] *m* plush

Plüschtier *nt* stuffed animal

Plusquamperfekt <-s, -e> ['plʊs·kvam·pɛr·fɛkt] *nt* past perfect, pluperfect

Po <-s, -s> [po:] *m (fam)* butt

pochen ['pɔ·xn] *vi* ❶ *(anklopfen)* to knock (**gegen/auf** +*akk* against/on) ❷ *Herz, Blut* to pound ❸ *(bestehen)* to insist (**auf** +*akk* on)

Pocken *pl* smallpox *no art*

Podest <-[e]s, -e> [po·'dɛst] *nt o m* podium, rostrum

Poesie <-> [poe·'zi:] *f kein pl* poetry

Poet(in) <-en, -en> [po·'e:t] *m(f)* poet

poetisch [po·'e:·tɪʃ] *adj* poetic[al]

Pointe <-, -> ['pɔɛ̃·tə] *f einer Erzählung* point; *eines Witzes* punch line

Pokal <-s, -e> [po·'ka:l] *m* ❶ *(Trinkbecher)* goblet ❷ SPORT trophy, cup

Poker <-s> ['po:·kɐ] *nt kein pl* poker

pokern ['po:·kɐn] *vi* ❶ KARTEN to play poker; ■**um etw ~** to gamble for sth ❷ *(viel riskieren)* to stake a lot

Pol <-s, -e> [po:l] *m* ELEK, GEOG, PHYS pole ▶WENDUNGEN: **der ruhende ~** the calming influence

Polarkreis *m* polar circle; **nördlicher/ südlicher ~** Arctic/Antarctic circle

Polarstern *m* Polaris

Pole, Polin <-n, -n> ['po:·lə] *m, f* Pole; *s. a.* **Deutsche(r)**

polemisch [po·'le:·mɪʃ] *adj (geh)* polemical

Polen <-s> ['po:·lən] *nt* Poland; *s. a.* **Deutschland**

polieren* [po·'li:·rən] *vt* to polish

Politesse <-, -n> [po·li·'tɛsə] *f* meter maid

Politik <-, -en> [po·li·'ti:k] *f* ❶ *kein pl* politics + *sing vb, no art* ❷ *(Strategie)* policy

Politiker(in) <-s, -> [po·'li:·ti·kɐ] *m(f)* politician

politisch [po·'li:·tɪʃ] I. *adj* ❶ POL political ❷ *(klug)* politic II. *adv* ❶ POL politically ❷ *(klug)* judiciously

Politologe, Politologin <-n, -n> [po·li·to·'lo:·gə] *m, f* political scientist

Polizei <-, -en> [po·li·'tsai] *f pl selten* ❶ *(Institution)* ■**die ~** the police + *sing/pl vb*; **bei der ~ sein** to be a police officer ❷ *kein pl (Dienstgebäude)* police station

Polizeibeamte(r) *m dekl wie adj*, **-beamtin** *f* police officer

polizeilich I. *adj attr* police *attr* II. *adv* by the police; **~ gemeldet sein** to be registered with the police

P

Polizeipräsident(in) m(f) chief of police

Polizeipräsidium nt police headquarters + sing/pl vb

Polizeirevier nt ① (Dienststelle) police station ② (Bezirk) [police] precinct

Polizeischutz m police protection

Polizeistreife f police patrol

Polizist(in) <-en, -en> [po·li·tsɪst] m(f) police officer, policeman masc, policewoman fem

Pollen <-s, -> ['pɔ·lən] m pollen

Pollenflug m kein pl pollen dispersal

polnisch ['pɔl·nɪʃ] adj Polish; s. a. **deutsch**

Polster <-s, -> ['pɔls·tɐ] nt o ÖSTERR m ① von Möbeln upholstery ② (an Kleidung) pad ③ (Rücklage) cushion; **ein finanzielles ~** financial reserves pl ④ ÖSTERR (Kissen) cushion

Polterabend ['pɔl·tɐ-] m party at the house of the bride's parents on the eve of a wedding, at which dishes are smashed to bring good luck

poltern ['pɔl·tɐn] vi ① haben (rumpeln) to bang ② sein (krachend fallen) **der Schrank polterte die Treppe hinunter** the cupboard went crashing down the stairs ③ sein (lärmend gehen) to stomp

P

Polyester <-s, -> [po·ly·'ʔɛs·tɐ] m polyester

Polygamie <-> [po·ly·ga·'mi:] f kein pl polygamy

Pomade <-, -n> [po·'ma:·də] f pomade

Pommes ['pɔ·məs] pl (fam), **Pommes frites** [pɔm·'frɪt] pl [French] fries pl

pompös [pɔm·'pø:s] I. adj grandiose II. adv grandiosely

Pony¹ <-s, -s> ['pɔ·ni] nt (Pferd) pony

Pony² <-s, -s> ['pɔ·ni] m bangs npl

Popo <-s, -s> [po·'po:] m (fam) butt

populär [po·pu·'lɛːɐ] adj popular

Popularität <-> [po·pu·la·ri·'tɛːt] f kein pl popularity

Pore <-, -n> ['po:·rə] f pore

Porno <-s, -s> ['pɔr·no] m (fam) porn

PornografieRR, **Pornographie** <-> [pɔr·no·gra·'fi:] f kein pl pornography

porös [po·'rø:s] adj porous

Portal <-s, -e> [pɔr·'ta:l] nt portal

Portemonnaie <-s, -s> [pɔrt·mɔ·'ne:] nt s. **Portmonee**

Portier <-s, -s> [pɔr·'tje:] m doorman

Portion <-, -en> [pɔr·'tsi̯o:n] f ① (beim Essen) portion ② (fam: Anteil) amount ▶WENDUNGEN: **eine halbe ~** (fam) a half-pint

PortmoneeRR <-s, -s> [pɔrt·mɔ·'ne:] nt wallet, change purse

Porto <-s, -s> ['pɔr·to] nt postage

Porträt <-s, -s> [pɔr·'trɛː] nt portrait

Portugal <-s> ['pɔr·tu·gal] nt Portugal; s. a. **Deutschland**

Portugiese, Portugiesin <-n, -n> [pɔr·tu·'gi:·zə] m, f Portuguese; s. a. **Deutsche(r)**

portugiesisch [pɔr·tu·'gi:·zɪʃ] adj Portuguese; s. a. **deutsch**

Portugiesisch [pɔr·tu·'gi:·zɪʃ] nt dekl wie adj Portuguese; s. a. **Deutsch 1**

Portwein ['pɔrt·vain] m port [wine]

Porzellan <-s, -e> [pɔr·tsɛ·'la:n] nt ① (Material) porcelain ② kein pl (Geschirr) china

Posaune <-, -n> [po·'zau·nə] f trombone

Pose <-, -n> ['po:·zə] f pose

Position <-, -en> [po·zi·'tsi̯o:n] f position

positiv ['po:·zi·ti:f] I. adj positive; ■~ [für jdn] sein to be good news [for sb] II. adv positively; **etw ~ beeinflussen** to have a positive influence on sth; **sich akk ~ verändern** to change for the better

Post <-> [pɔst] f kein pl ① (Institution) Post Office; **etw mit der/per ~ schicken** to send sth in the mail, to mail sth ② (Dienststelle) post office; **auf die/zur ~ gehen** to go to the post office ③ (Briefsendungen) mail; **elektronische ~** electronic mail

Postamt nt post office

Postbeamte(r) m dekl wie adj, **-beamtin** f post office clerk

Postbote, -botin m, f mail carrier, postman masc, mailman masc

Posten <-s, -> ['pɔs·tn̩] m ❶ (*zugewiesene Position*) post ❷ (*Anstellung*) position ❸ ÖKON (*Position*) item

posten ['poʊs·tn̩] *vt* INET to post

Postfach *nt* ❶ (*Schließfach*) post office [*or* PO] box ❷ (*offenes Fach*) pigeonhole

Postgiroamt [-ʒiː·ro-] *nt bank operated by the post office*

Postgirokonto [-ʒiː·ro-] *nt* postal checking account

Postkarte *f* postcard

Postleitzahl *f* Zip Code

Postscheck *m* postal check

Poststempel *m* (*Abdruck*) postmark

Potenz <-, -en> [po·'tɛnts] *f* (*sexuell*) potency

Pott <-[e]s, Pötte> [pɔt] *m* (*fam: Topf*) pot

Pracht <-> [praxt] *f kein pl* splendor
▶WENDUNGEN: **eine wahre ~ sein** (*fam*) to be [really] great

prächtig ['prɛç·tɪç] *adj* ❶ (*prunkvoll*) magnificent ❷ (*großartig*) splendid

Prädikat <-[e]s, -e> [prɛ·di·'kaːt] *nt* ❶ LING predicate ❷ (*Auszeichnung*) rating

Präfix <-es, -e> [prɛ·'fɪks, 'prɛː·fɪks] *nt* prefix

Prag <-s> [praːk] *nt* Prague

prägen ['prɛː·gn̩] *vt* ❶ *Münzen* to mint ❷ *Wort* to coin ❸ (*fig: formen*) ■**jdn ~** to leave its/their mark on sb

pragmatisch [praɡ·'maː·tɪʃ] **I.** *adj* pragmatic **II.** *adv* pragmatically

prähistorisch [prɛ·hɪs·'toː·rɪʃ] *adj* prehistoric

prahlen ['praː·lən] *vi* to boast, to brag *pej fam* (**mit** +*dat* about)

Prahler(in) <-s, -> *m(f)* bragger

prahlerisch *adj* boastful

Praktik <-, -en> ['prak·tɪk] *f meist pl* practice

Praktikant(in) <-en, -en> [prak·ti·'kant] *m(f)* intern

praktisch ['prak·tɪʃ] **I.** *adj* practical; *Beispiel* concrete **II.** *adv* ❶ (*so gut wie*) practically ❷ (*in der Praxis*) in practice

praktizieren* [prak·ti·'tsiː·rən] *vt, vi* to practice; **~ der Arzt** practicing doctor

Praline <-, -n> [pra·'liː·nə] *f* praline, [piece of] chocolate

prall [pral] *adj* ❶ (*sehr voll*) *Brüste* well-rounded; *Schenkel, Waden* sturdy; *Euter* swollen ❷ *Sonne* blazing ❸ **eine ~ gefüllte Brieftasche** a bulging wallet

prallen ['pra·lən] *vi sein* to crash (**gegen** +*akk* into); *Ball* to bounce

Prämie <-, -n> ['prɛː·mi̯ə] *f* ❶ (*zusätzliche Vergütung*) bonus ❷ (*Versicherungsbeitrag*) [insurance] premium ❸ (*staatliche Prämie*) [government] premium

Pranke <-, -n> ['praŋ·kə] *f* paw; (*hum a.*) mitt *sl*

Präposition <-, -en> [prɛ·po·zi·'tsi̯oːn] *f* preposition

Prärie <-, -n> [prɛ·'riː] *f* prairie

Präsens <-, Präsentia> ['prɛː·zɛns] *nt* present tense

Präsentation <-, -en> [prɛ·zɛn·ta·'tsi̯oːn] *f* presentation

präsentieren* [prɛ·zɛn·'tiː·rən] *vt* ■**jdm etw** *akk* **~** to present sb with sth

Präservativ <-s, -e> [prɛ·zɛr·va·'tiːf] *nt* condom

Präsident(in) <-en, -en> [prɛ·zi·'dɛnt] *m(f)* president

Präsidium <-s, Präsidien> [prɛ·'ziː·di̯um] *nt* ❶ (*Vorstand, Vorsitz*) chairmanship ❷ (*Führungsgruppe*) committee ❸ (*Polizeipräsidium*) [police] headquarters + *sing/pl vb*

prasseln ['pra·sl̩n] *vi* ❶ *sein Regen* to drum; (*stärker*) to beat ❷ *haben Feuer* to crackle

Praxis <-, Praxen> ['prak·sɪs] *f* ❶ (*Arztpraxis*) doctor's office; (*Anwaltspraxis*) law practice ❷ *kein pl* (*Erfahrung*) [practical] experience ❸ *kein pl* (*Anwendung*) practice *no art;* **etw in die ~ umsetzen** to put sth into practice

präzise [prɛ·'tsiː·zə] *adj* (*geh*) precise; *Beschreibung* exact

predigen ['preː·dɪ·gn̩] *vt, vi* to preach; ■**jdm etw** *akk* **~** (*fam*) to lecture sb on/about sth

P

Prediger(in) <-s, -> *m(f)* preacher

Predigt <-, -en> ['pre:·dɪçt] *f* (*a. fam*) sermon

Preis <-es, -e> [praɪs] *m* ❶ (*Kaufpreis*) price (**für** +*akk* of); **zum halben ~** at [*or* for] half-price ❷ (*Gewinn*) prize; **der erste ~** [the] first prize ▶WENDUNGEN: **um jeden ~** at all costs

Preisanstieg *m* price increase

Preisausschreiben *nt* competition, contest

Preiselbeere ['praɪ·zl̩·be:·rə] *f* (mountain *spec*) cranberry

Preisempfehlung *f* recommended price

preisen <pries, gepriesen> ['praɪ·zn̩] *vt* (*geh*) to praise

Preisermäßigung *f* price reduction

Preisfrage *f* ❶ (*Quizfrage*) contest question ❷ (*vom Preis abhängende Entscheidung*) question of price

preisgeben ['praɪs·ge:·bn̩] *vt irreg* (*geh*) ❶ *Geheimnis* to divulge; ■**jdm etw** *akk* **~** to betray sth to sb ❷ **jdn der Lächerlichkeit ~** to expose sb to ridicule

preisgekrönt *adj* award-winning *attr*

preisgünstig *adj* inexpensive; *Angebot* very reasonable; **etw ~ bekommen** to get a good deal on sth

Preis-Leistungs-Verhältnis *nt kein pl* cost-effectiveness, cost-benefit ratio

PreisnachlassRR *m* discount

Preisrätsel *nt* puzzle competition

Preisschild *nt* price tag

Preissenkung *f* reduction in prices

Preissteigerung *f* price increase

preiswert *adj s.* **preisgünstig**

Prellung <-, -en> *f* contusion *spec* (**an** +*dat* to)

Premiere <-, -n> [prə·'mi̯e:·rə] *f* première

Premierminister(in) *m(f)* prime minister

Presse <-, -n> ['prɛ·sə] *f* ❶ (*Gerät*) press; (*Fruchtpresse*) juice extractor ❷ *kein pl* ■**die ~** (*Zeitungen und Zeitschriften*) press

Presseagentur *f* press agency

Pressefreiheit *f kein pl* freedom of the press

Pressekonferenz *f* press conference

Pressemeldung *f* press report

pressen ['prɛ·sn̩] *vt* to press; *Saft* to squeeze (**aus** +*dat* out of)

Pressesprecher(in) *m(f)* spokesman

Prestige <-s> [prɛs·'ti:·ʒə] *nt kein pl* (*geh*) prestige

preußisch ['prɔy·sɪʃ] *adj* Prussian

prickeln ['prɪ·kl̩n] *vi* ❶ (*kribbeln*) to tingle; **ein P~ in den Beinen** pins and needles in one's legs ❷ (*erregen, reizen*) to thrill

prickelnd *adj Gefühl* tingling; *Humor* piquant; *Champagner* sparkling

Priester(in) <-s, -> ['pri:s·tɐ] *m(f)* priest *masc*, priestess *fem*

prima ['pri:·ma] *adj* (*fam*) great; **es läuft alles ~** everything is really going well

primitiv [pri·mi·'ti:f] *adj* primitive; **ein ~er Kerl** a big ape

Prinz <-en, -en> [prɪnts] *m* prince

Prinzessin <-, -nen> [prɪn·'tsɛ·sɪn] *f* princess

Prinzip <-s, -ien> [prɪn·'tsi:p] *nt* principle; **aus/im ~** on/in principle

prinzipiell [prɪn·tsi·'pi̯·ɛl] I. *adj* fundamental II. *adv* (*aus Prinzip*) on principle; (*im Prinzip*) in principle

Priorität <-, -en> [prio·ri·'tɛːt] *f* (*geh*) priority (**vor** +*dat* over)

Prise <-, -n> ['pri:·zə] *f* pinch

privat [pri·'va:t] I. *adj* private II. *adv* privately; **sich** *akk* **~ versichern** to take out private insurance

Privatdetektiv(in) *m(f)* private investigator

Privatgrundstück *nt* private property *npl*

Privatleben *nt kein pl* private life

Privatpatient(in) *m(f)* private patient

Privatschule *f* private school

Privatsekretär(in) *m(f)* private secretary

Privatsphäre *f kein pl* privacy

Privileg <-[e]s, -ien> [pri·vi·'le:k] *nt* (*geh*) privilege

pro [proː] *präp* per; **~ Kopf** a head; **~ Person** per person; **~ Stück** each

Pro <-> [proː] *nt kein pl* **[das] ~ und [das] Kontra** (*geh*) the pros and cons *pl*

Probe <-, -n> ['proːbə] *f* ❶ (*Warenprobe, Testmenge*) sample ❷ MUS, THEAT rehearsal ❸ (*Prüfung*) test ▶ WENDUNGEN: **auf ~** on probation; **jds Geduld auf eine harte ~ stellen** to try sb's patience; **jdn auf die ~ stellen** to put sb to the test; **zur ~** on a trial basis

Probealarm *m* fire drill

Probefahrt *f* test drive

proben ['proːbn̩] *vt, vi* to rehearse

Probezeit *f* probationary period

probieren* [proˈbiːrən] *vt, vi* to try; ■ **von etw** *dat* ~ to try some of sth; ■ **~, ob …** to try and see whether …

Problem <-s, -e> [proˈbleːm] *nt* problem

problematisch [probleˈmaːtɪʃ] *adj* problematic[al]; *Kind* difficult

problemlos I. *adj* problem-free, unproblematic *attr* II. *adv* without any problems

Produkt <-[e]s, -e> [proˈdʊkt] *nt* product

Produktion <-, -en> [prodʊkˈtsi̯oːn] *f* production

produktiv [prodʊkˈtiːf] *adj* (*geh*) productive

Produzent(in) <-en, -en> [produˈtsɛnt] *m(f)* producer

produzieren* [produˈtsiːrən] *vt* to produce

professionell [profɛsi̯oˈnɛl] *adj* professional

Professor, Professorin <-s, -soren> [proˈfɛsoːɐ̯, profɛˈsoːrɪn] *m, f* ❶ (*Universitätsprofessor*) professor ❷ ÖSTERR (*Gymnasiallehrer*) ≈ high-school teacher

Profi <-s, -s> ['proːfi] *m* (*fam*) pro

Profil <-s, -e> [proˈfiːl] *nt* ❶ *eines Reifens, einer Schuhsohle* tread ❷ (*Seitenansicht*) profile

Profit <-[e]s, -e> [proˈfiːt, proˈfɪt] *m* profit

profitabel [profiˈtaːbl̩] *adj* profitable; (*stärker*) lucrative

profitieren* [profiˈtiːrən] *vi* to profit (**von, bei** +*dat* from/with)

pro forma [proː ˈfɔrma] *adv* pro forma, as a formality

Prognose <-, -n> [proˈgnoːzə] *f* prognosis; (*Wetter*) forecast

Programm <-s, -e> [proˈgram] *nt* ❶ (*geplanter Ablauf*) program; (*Tagesordnung*) agenda; (*Zeitplan*) schedule; **ein volles ~ haben** to have a full day/week etc. ahead [of oneself]; **was steht für heute auf dem ~?** what's the agenda/program/schedule for today? ❷ RADIO, TV (*Sender*) channel ❸ (*Programmheft*) program ❹ COMPUT [computer] program

Programmfehler *m* COMPUT program error, bug

programmieren* [progra·ˈmiːrən] *vt* COMPUT to program

Programmierer(in) <-s, -> *m(f)* programmer

progressiv [progrɛˈsiːf] *adj* (*geh*) progressive

Projekt <-[e]s, -e> [proˈjɛkt] *nt* project

Projektleiter(in) <-s, -> *m(f)* project manager

Projektor <-s, -toren> [proˈjɛktoːɐ̯] *m* projector

projizieren* [proji·ˈtsiːrən] *vt* (*a. fig*) to project (**auf** +*akk* on[to])

Pro-Kopf-Einkommen [proːˈkɔpf-] *nt* per capita income

Prolet <-en, -en> [proˈleːt] *m* (*pej*) redneck *pej sl*

Proll <-s, -s> ['prɔl] *m* (*pej sl*) s. **Prolet**

Prolog <-[e]s, -e> [proˈloːk] *m* prolog[ue]

Promenade <-, -n> [promə·ˈnaːdə] *f* promenade

Promille <-[s], -> [proˈmɪlə] *nt* ❶ (*Tausendstel*) per mil[l] ❷ *pl* (*fam: Alkoholpegel*) [blood] alcohol level; **0,5 ~** blood alcohol level of 0.05 [percent]

Promillegrenze *f* legal [alcohol] limit

prominent [pro·mi·'nɛnt] *adj* prominent

Prominenz <-> [pro·mi·'nɛnts] *f kein pl* (*die Prominenten*) prominent figures *pl*

prompt [prɔmpt] **I.** *adj* prompt **II.** *adv* ❶ (*sofort*) promptly ❷ (*meist iron*) **er ist ~ auf den Trick hereingefallen** naturally, he fell for the trick

Pronomen <-s, -> [pro·'no:·mən] *nt* pronoun

Propaganda <-> [pro·pa·'gan·da] *f kein pl* ❶ POL (*a. pej*) propaganda ❷ (*Werbung*) publicity

Propangas *nt kein pl* propane [gas]

Propeller <-s, -> [pro·'pɛ·lə] *m* propeller

Prophet(in) <-en, -en> [pro·'fe:t] *m(f)* prophet *masc*, prophetess *fem*

prophezeien* [pro·fe·'tsai·ən] *vt* to prophesy, to predict

Prophezeiung <-, -en> *f* prophecy

prophylaktisch [pro·fy·'lak·tɪʃ] *adj* prophylactic

Proportion <-, -en> [pro·pɔr·'tsi̯o:n] *f* (*geh*) proportion

proportional [pro·pɔr·tsi̯o·'na:l] *adj* (*geh*) proportional (**zu** +*dat* to)

Prosa <-> ['pro:·za] *f kein pl* prose

Prospekt <-[e]s, -e> [prɔs·'pɛkt] *m* (*Werbebroschüre*) brochure; (*Werbezettel*) flier

prost [pro:st] *interj* cheers

Prostata <-, Prostatae> ['prɔs·ta·ta] *f* ANAT prostate gland

Prostituierte(r) [prɔs·ti·tu·'i:ɐ̯·tə, -tə] *f(m)* prostitute

Prostitution <-> [prɔs·ti·tu·'tsi̯o:n] *f kein pl* prostitution

Protein <-s, -e> [pro·te·'i:n] *nt* protein

Protest <-[e]s, -e> [pro·'tɛst] *m* protest

Protestant(in) <-en, -en> [pro·tɛs·'tant] *m(f)* Protestant

protestieren* [pro·tɛs·'ti:·rən] *vi* to protest

Prothese <-, -n> [pro·'te:·zə] *f* prosthesis *spec*

Protokoll <-s, -e> [pro·to·'kɔl] *nt* ❶ (*Niederschrift*) record[s *pl*]; (*einer Sitzung*) minutes *npl*; **etw zu ~ geben** (*bei der Polizei*) to make a statement ❷ DIAL (*Strafmandat*) ticket ❸ *kein pl* (*Zeremoniell*) **gegen das ~ verstoßen** to break with protocol

protzen ['prɔ·tsn̩] *vi* (*fam*) ■[**mit etw** *dat*] ~ to flaunt [sth]

protzig ['prɔ·tsɪç] *adj* (*fam*) showy; *Auto* fancy

Proviant <-s, -e> [pro·'vi̯ant] *m pl selten* provisions; MIL supplies

Provinz <-, -en> [pro·'vɪnts] *f* ❶ (*Verwaltungsgebiet*) province ❷ *kein pl* (*rückständige Gegend*) provinces *pl a. pej;* **in der ~ leben** to live [out] in the sticks *fam*

provinziell [pro·vɪn·'tsi̯ɛl] *adj* provincial *a. pej*

Provision <-, -en> [pro·vi·'zi̯o:n] *f* commission

provisorisch [pro·vi·'zo:·rɪʃ] **I.** *adj* provisional; *Unterkunft* temporary **II.** *adv* temporarily

Provokation <-, -en> [pro·vo·ka·'tsi̯o:n] *f* provocation

provozieren* [pro·vo·'tsi:·rən] *vt* to provoke; *Streit* to cause; ■**jdn zu etw** *dat* ~ to provoke sb into [doing] sth

Prozent <-[e]s, -e> [pro·'tsɛnt] *nt* ❶ (*Hundertstel*) percent ❷ (*Alkoholgehalt*) alcohol content ❸ *pl* (*Rabatt*) discount

Prozentsatz *m* percentage

Prozess^RR <-es, -e>, **Prozeß**^ALT <-sses, -sse> [pro·'tsɛs] *m* ❶ (*Gerichtsverfahren*) [court] case; (*Strafverfahren*) trial; **einen ~ [gegen jdn] führen** to take legal action [against sb] ❷ (*geh: Vorgang*) process ►WENDUNGEN: **[mit jdm/etw]** <u>kurzen</u> **~ machen** (*fam*) to make short work of sb/sth

prozessieren* [pro·tsɛ·'si:·rən] *vi* ■[**gegen jdn**] ~ to take [sb] to court

Prozession <-, -en> [pro·tsɛ·'si̯o:n] *f* procession

Prozesskosten^RR *pl* court costs

Prozessor <-s, -soren> [pro·tsɛ·so:ɐ̯, -'so:·rən] *m* COMPUT processor

prüde ['pry:·də] *adj* (*pej*) prudish

prüfen ['pry:·fn̩] vt ❶ (*überprüfen, untersuchen*) to check (**auf** +*akk* for); *Material* to test ❷ (*Kenntnisse abfragen*) to examine

Prüfung <-, -en> f ❶ (*Examen*) exam[ination]; (*für den Führerschein*) test; **mündliche ~ [in etw** *dat*] oral exam[ination] [in sth] ❷ (*Überprüfung*) checking; *von Material* test ❸ (*geh: Heimsuchung*) trial

Prüfungsangst f pre-exam jitters

Prügel ['pry:·gl̩] pl thrashing; **jdm eine Tracht ~ verabreichen** to give sb a [good] beating

Prügelei <-, -en> [pry:·gə·'lai] f (*fam*) [fist] fight

Prügelknabe m (*fam*) whipping boy

prügeln ['pry:·gl̩n] I. vt, vi to hit II. vr ■ **sich** *akk* ~ to fight

Prügelstrafe f ■ **die ~** corporal punishment

Prunk <-s> [prʊŋk] m kein pl magnificence

prusten ['pru:·stn̩] vi (*fam*) to snort; (*beim Trinken*) to splutter

Pseudonym <-s, -e> [psɔy·do·'ny:m] nt pseudonym

Psyche <-, -n> ['psy:·çə] f psyche

Psychiater(in) <-s, -> [psy·çi̯a:·te] m(f) psychiatrist

Psychiatrie <-, -n> [psyçi̯a·'tri:] f ❶ kein pl (*Fachgebiet*) psychiatry no art ❷ (*fam: Abteilung*) psychiatric ward

psychiatrisch [psy·çi̯a:·trɪʃ] adj psychiatric

psychisch ['psy:·çɪʃ] adj psychological, mental

Psychoanalytiker(in) [psy·ço·ʔana·'ly:·ti·ke] m(f) psychoanalyst

Psychologe, Psychologin <-n -n> [psy·ço·'lo:·gə] m, f psychologist

psychologisch [psy·ço·'lo:·gɪʃ] adj psychological

Psychopath(in) <-en, -en> [psy·ço·'pa:t] m(f) psychopath

Psychose <-, -n> [psy·'ço:·zə] f psychosis

psychosomatisch [psy·ço·zo·'ma:·tɪʃ] adj psychosomatic

Psychotherapeut(in) [psy·ço·te·ra·'pɔyt] m(f) psychotherapist

Pubertät <-> [pu·bɛr·'tɛ:t] f kein pl puberty no art

Publikum <-s> ['pu:·bli·kʊm] nt kein pl audience; (*im Theater a.*) house; (*beim Sport*) crowd

publizieren* [pu·bli·'tsi:·rən] vt to publish

Pudding <-s, -s> ['pʊ·dɪŋ] m KOCHK pudding

Pudel <-s, -> ['pu:·dl̩] m poodle

pudelwohl ['pu:·dl̩·'vo:l] adj (*fam*) **sich** *akk* ~ **fühlen** to feel like a million bucks

Puder <-s, -> ['pu:·de] m o fam nt powder

pudern ['pu:·den] vt to powder

Puderzucker m powdered [or confectioner's] sugar

Puff¹ <-[e]s, Püffe> [pʊf] m (*fam: Stoß*) thump; (*in die Seite*) prod

Puff² <-[e]s, -s> [pʊf] m (*fam*) brothel, whorehouse

Puffer <-s, -> ['pʊ·fe] m ❶ BAHN bumper ❷ (*Kartoffelpuffer*) potato pancake, ≈ latke

Pullover <-s, -> [pʊ·'lo:·ve] m sweater

Puls <-es, -e> [pʊls] m pulse

Pult <-[e]s, -e> [pʊlt] nt ❶ (*Rednerpult*) lectern ❷ (*Schaltpult*) control panel

Pulver <-s, -> ['pʊl·ve] nt powder

Pulverkaffee m instant coffee

Pulverschnee m powder[y] snow

Puma <-s, -s> ['pu:·ma] m puma, mountain lion, cougar

pummelig ['pʊ·mə·lɪç] adj (*fam*) chubby

Pump [pʊmp] m ▶WENDUNGEN: **auf ~** (*fam*) on credit

Pumpe <-, -n> ['pʊm·pə] f ❶ (*Gerät*) pump ❷ (*fam: Herz*) heart

pumpen ['pʊm·pn̩] vt ❶ (*mittels einer Pumpe*) to pump ❷ (*fam: leihen*) ■ **jdm etw** *akk* ~ to lend sb sth; ■ **sich** *dat* **etw** *akk* [**bei/von jdm**] ~ to borrow sth [from sb]

Punker(in) <-s, -> ['paŋ·ke] m(f) punk [rocker]

Punkt <-[e]s, -e> [pʊŋkt] m ❶ (*runder Fleck*) spot; (*in der Mathematik*) point ❷ (*Stelle*) spot; (*genauer*) point; **bis zu einem gewissen ~** up to a certain point ❸ (*Satzzeichen*) period; (*auf i, Auslassungszeichen*) dot ❹ (*Bewertungseinheit*) point ❺ (*Detailpunkt*) point; (*auf der Tagesordnung*) item ❻ **um ~ acht [Uhr]** at exactly eight [o'clock] ▶WENDUNGEN: **ein dunkler ~** [**in jds Vergangenheit**] a dark chapter [in sb's past]; **ohne ~ und Komma reden** (*fam*) to rattle on and on; **nun mach aber mal einen ~!** (*fam*) come off it!; **der springende ~** the crucial point

pünktlich ['pʏŋkt·lɪç] I. *adj* punctual II. *adv* punctually

Pünktlichkeit <-> f *kein pl* punctuality

Punktzahl f SPORT score

Punsch <-es, -e> [pʊnʃ] m [hot] punch

Pupille <-, -n> [pu·'pɪ·lə] f pupil

Puppe <-, -n> ['pʊ·pə] f (*Spielzeug*) doll ▶WENDUNGEN: **bis in die ~n** until the wee hours of the morning; **bis in die ~n schlafen** (*fam*) to sleep until all hours

Puppentheater nt puppet theater

P **pur** [puːɐ̯] *adj* ❶ (*rein, unverdünnt*) pure; **etw ~ trinken** to drink sth straight ❷ (*fam: blank, bloß*) sheer, pure; *Wahnsinn* absolute

Püree <-s, -s> [py·'reː] nt ❶ (*passiertes Gemüse/Obst*) purée ❷ (*Kartoffelbrei*) mashed potatoes pl

Purzelbaum ['pʊr·tsl̩-] m (*fam*) somersault

purzeln ['pʊr·tsl̩n] vi sein a. *Preise* to tumble

Puste <-> ['puːs·tə] f *kein pl* (*fam*) breath; **aus der ~ kommen** to get out of breath

Pustel <-, -n> ['pʊs·tl̩] f pimple

pusten ['puːs·tn̩] vt, vi (*fam*) to blow

Puter <-s, -> ['puː·tɐ] m tom, gobbler

puterrot ['puː·tɐ·'roːt] *adj* scarlet

Putsch <-[e]s, -e> [pʊtʃ] m coup [d'état]

Putschist(in) <-en, -en> [pʊt·'ʃɪst] m(f) rebel

putzen ['pʊ·tsn̩] I. vt to clean; *Gemüse* to prepare; *Spinat* to wash; **putz dir den Dreck von den Schuhen!** wipe the mud off your shoes!; **sich** *dat* **die Nase ~** to blow one's nose; **sich** *dat* **die Zähne ~** to brush one's teeth II. vi **~ gehen** to work as a housekeeper

Putzfrau f maid, cleaning lady

putzig ['pʊ·tsɪç] *adj* (*fam: niedlich*) sweet; *Tier* cute

Putzlappen m rag

Putzmittel nt detergent

Puzzle <-s, -s> ['pʊ·zl̩, 'pa·zl̩] nt jigsaw [puzzle]

Pyjama <-s, -s> [py·'dʒa:·ma] m pajamas npl

Pyramide <-, -n> [py·ra·'mi:·də] f pyramid

Pyrenäen [py·re·'nɛː·ən] pl ■**die ~** the Pyrenees npl

Pythonschlange f python

Q q

Q, q <-, -> [kuː] *nt* Q, q; **~ wie Quelle** Q as in Quebec

q [kuː] SCHWEIZ, ÖSTERR *Abk von* **Zentner** 100 kg

Quadrat <-[e]s, -e> [kvaˈdraːt] *nt* square

quadratisch *adj* square

Quadratmeter *m* square meter

quaken [ˈkvaːkn̩] *vi Frosch* to croak; *Ente* to quack

Qual <-, -en> [ˈkvaːl] *f* ❶ (*Quälerei*) struggle ❷ *meist pl* (*Pein*) agony ▶ WENDUNGEN: **die ~ der Wahl haben** (*hum*) to be spoiled for choice

quälen [ˈkvɛːlən] **I.** *vt* ❶ (*misshandeln*) *Mensch, Tier* to be cruel to ❷ (*peinigen*) *Gedanken, Gefühle* to torment *fig; Schmerzen* to trouble **II.** *vr* ❶ (*leiden*) ■ **sich** *akk* **~** to suffer ❷ (*sich herumquälen*) ■ **sich** *akk* **mit etw** *dat* **~** (*mit Gedanken, Gefühlen*) to torment oneself with sth; (*mit Hausaufgaben, Arbeit*) to struggle [hard] with sth ❸ (*sich mühsam bewegen*) ■ **sich** *akk* **~** to struggle

Quälerei <-, -en> [kvɛːləˈrai] *f* (*körperlich, seelisch*) torture

Qualifikation <-, -en> [kvaˈliˈfiˈkaˈtsi̯oːn] *f* ❶ (*beruflich*) qualifications *pl* ❷ SPORT qualifier

qualifizieren* [kvaˈliˈfiˈtsiːrən] **I.** *vr* ■ **sich** *akk* [**für etw** *akk*] **~** to qualify [for sth] **II.** *vt* ■ **jdn für etw** *akk* **~** to qualify sb for sth

Qualität <-, -en> [kvaˈliˈtɛːt] *f* ❶ (*Güte, Beschaffenheit*) quality ❷ *pl* (*gute Eigenschaften*) qualities *pl*

qualitativ [ˈkvaˈliˈtaˈtiːf] **I.** *adj* qualitative **II.** *adv* qualitatively

Qualle <-, -n> [ˈkvalə] *f* jellyfish

Qualm <-[e]s> [ˈkvalm] *m kein pl* [thick] smoke

qualmen [ˈkvalˈmən] **I.** *vi* (*a. fam: rauchen*) to smoke **II.** *vt* (*fam*) to puff away at

qualvoll **I.** *adj* agonizing **II.** *adv* **~ sterben** to die in agony

QuäntchenRR <-s, -> [ˈkvɛnt-] **ein ~ Glück** a little bit of luck; **ein ~ Hoffnung** a glimmer of hope

Quantität <-, -en> [kvanˈtiˈtɛːt] *f* quantity

quantitativ [ˈkvanˈtiˈtaˈtiːf] *adj* quantitative

Quarantäne <-, -n> [kaˈranˈtɛːnə] *f* quarantine; **unter ~ stehen/stellen** to be in/place under quarantine

Quark <-s> [ˈkvark] *m kein pl* ❶ KOCH quark, ≈ fromage frais ❷ (*fam: Quatsch*) nonsense

Quartal <-s, -e> [kvarˈtaːl] *nt* quarter

Quartier <-s, -e> [kvarˈtiːɐ̯] *nt* accommodation

Quarz <-es, -e> [ˈkvaːɐ̯ts] *m* quartz

quasi [ˈkvaːˈzi] *adv* almost, more or less *fam*

quasseln [ˈkvaˈsl̩n] *vi* (*fam*) to babble

Quasselstrippe <-, -n> *f* (*fam*) ❶ (*hum: Telefon*) **an der ~ hängen** to be on the phone ❷ (*pej: Person*) windbag

Quatsch <-es> [ˈkvatʃ] *m kein pl* (*fam*) nonsense; **~ machen** to mess [*or fam* screw] around

quatschen [ˈkvaˈtʃn̩] (*fam*) **I.** *vt* **dummes Zeug ~** to talk nonsense **II.** *vi* (*fam*) ❶ (*viel und dumm reden*) to babble ❷ (*sich unterhalten*) to chat ❸ (*etw ausplaudern*) to blab

Quatschkopf *m* (*pej fam*) babbling idiot

Quecksilber [ˈkvɛkˈzɪlˈbɐ] *nt* mercury

Quelle <-, -n> [ˈkvɛlə] *f* source

quellen <quillt, quoll, gequollen> [ˈkvɛlən] *vi sein* ❶ (*herausfließen*) ■ **aus etw** *dat*) **~** to pour out [of sth] ❷ (*aufquellen*) to swell [up]

Quellwasser *nt* spring water

Q

quengeln ['kvɛ·ŋln] *vi* (*fam*) ❶ (*weinerlich sein*) to whine ❷ (*nörgeln*) to moan

QuentchenALT <-s, -> ['kvɛnt·çən] *nt s.* **Quäntchen**

quer ['kveːɐ̯] *adv* ❶ (*der Breite nach*) diagonally; ~ **gestreift** horizontally striped ❷ ~ **durch/über etw** *akk* straight through/across sth

Quere ['kveː·rə] *f* ▶WENDUNGEN: **jdm in die ~ kommen** to get in sb's way

querfeldein [kveːɐ̯·fɛlt·'ʔain] *adv* through the countryside

Querflöte *f* flute

Querkopf *m* (*fam*) *person with a different agenda from everyone else's*

Querschnitt *m* cross section

Querstraße *f* crossroad

Querulant(in) <-en, -en> [kve·ru·'lant] *m(f)* querulous person

quetschen ['kvɛt·ʃn] I. *vt* **jdn gegen die Mauer ~** to crush sb against the wall; **Kleider in einen Koffer ~** to stuff clothes into a suitcase II. *vr* ❶ (*verletzen*) **sich** *dat* **den Fuß ~** to crush one's foot ❷ (*sich zwängen*) **sich** *akk* **in die U-Bahn ~** to squeeze into the subway train

Quetschung <-, -en> *f* MED bruise

quietschen ['kviːt·ʃn] *vi* Tür; Bett to squeak; **mit ~den Bremsen/Reifen** with screeching brakes/tires; **unter lautem Q~ kam das Fahrzeug zum Stehen** the vehicle came to a halt with a loud screech

quietschfidel ['kviːt·ʃfi·'deːl], **quietschvergnügt** ['kviːt·ʃfɛɐ̯·'gnyːkt] *adj* (*fam*) chipper *pred*

quitt ['kvɪt] *adj* ▪|**mit jdm**] ~ **sein** (*abgerechnet haben*) to be even [with sb] *fam*; (*sich getrennt haben*) to be finished [with sb]

Quitte <-, -n> ['kvɪ·tə] *f* quince

quittieren* [kvɪ·'tiː·rən] *vt* ÖKON ▪**etw** ~ to acknowledge [the] receipt of sth; ▪**jdm etw** ~ to give sb a receipt for sth; **sich** *dat* **etw** ~ **lassen** to obtain a receipt for sth

Quittung <-, -en> ['kvɪ·tʊŋ] *f* ❶ ÖKON receipt; **jdm eine ~ [für etw** *akk*] **ausstellen** to give sb a receipt [for sth] ❷ (*Folgen*) **das ist die ~ für deine Faulheit** that's what you get for being so lazy

Quiz <-, -> [kvɪs] *nt* quiz

Quote <-, -n> ['kvoː·tə] *f* ❶ (*Anteil*) proportion ❷ (*Rate*) rate, quota; TV ratings *npl*

Q

Rr

R, r <-, -> [ɛr] *nt* R, r; **~ wie Richard** R as in Romeo; **das ~ rollen** to roll one's r's

Rabatt <-[e]s, -e> [ra·'bat] *m* discount (**auf** +*akk* on)

Rabe <-n, -n> ['ra:·bə] *m* raven

rabenschwarz ['ra:·bn̩·'ʃvarts] *adj* jet-black

rabiat [ra·'bi̯a:t] I. *adj* ❶(*gewalttätig*) aggressive ❷(*rigoros*) ruthless II. *adv* ruthlessly

Rache <-> ['ra·xə] *f kein pl* revenge

Racheakt *m* act of revenge

Rachen <-s, -> ['ra·xn̩] *m* ❶(*von Mensch*) throat ❷(*von Tier*) jaws *pl*

rächen ['rɛ·çn̩] I. *vt* ■etw ~ to take revenge for sth; ■jdn ~ to avenge sb II. *vr* ■**sich** *akk* ~ to take [one's] revenge (**an** +*dat* on, **für** +*akk* for)

Rachitis <-> [ra·'xi:·tɪs] *f kein pl* rickets

rachsüchtig *adj* vindictive

Rad <-[e]s, Räder> [ra:t] *nt* ❶(*Fahrrad*) bicycle, bike *fam*; **~ fahren** to ride a bicycle, to bike *fam* ❷*eines Fahrzeugs* wheel ▶WENDUNGEN: **ein ~ ab haben** (*sl*) to have a screw loose *hum fam*

Radar <-s> [ra·'da:ɐ̯] *m o nt kein pl* radar

Radarkontrolle *f* radar speed enforcement

Radau <-s> [ra·'dau] *m kein pl* (*fam*) racket

radeln ['ra:·dln̩] *vi sein* (*fam*) to bike

Radfahrer(in) *m(f)* bicyclist

Radieschen <-s, -> [ra·'di:s·çən] *nt* radish

radikal [ra·di·'ka:l] I. *adj* ❶POL radical ❷(*völlig*) *Beseitigung, Bruch* complete ❸(*tief greifend*) *Veränderung* drastic II. *adv* ❶POL radically ❷(*völlig*) *brechen, entfernen* completely ❸(*tief greifend*) drastically

Radio <-s, -s> ['ra:·di̯o] *nt o* SCHWEIZ, SÜDD *m* radio; **im ~** on the radio

radioaktiv [ra·di̯o·ʔak·'ti:f] I. *adj* radioactive II. *adv* **~ verseucht** contaminated by radioactivity

Radioaktivität <-> [ra·di̯o·ʔak·ti·vi·'tɛ:t] *f kein pl* radioactivity

Radiowecker *m* alarm clock radio

Radius <-, Radien> ['ra:·di̯·ʊs] *m* radius

Radkappe *f* AUTO hub cap

Radrennen *nt* bike race

Radsport *m* cycling

Radtour [-tu:ɐ̯] *f* bike ride

raffen ['ra·fn̩] *vt* ❶(*eilig greifen*) to grab ❷(*in Falten legen*) to gather

raffgierig *adj* greedy

Raffinerie <-, -n> [ra·fi·nə·'ri:] *f* refinery

Raffinesse <-, -n> [ra·fi·'nɛ·sə] *f* ❶*kein pl* (*Durchtriebenheit*) cunning ❷(*Feinheit*) refinement

raffiniert I. *adj* ❶*Öl, Zucker* refined ❷(*gerissen*) *Person, Plan* cunning ❸(*ausgefallen*) *Kleidung* stylish II. *adv* ❶(*durchtrieben*) cunningly ❷(*ausgefallen*) stylishly

ragen ['ra:·gn̩] *vi* ❶(*in die Höhe*) to rise up (**aus** +*dat* out of); *Gebirge* to tower up ❷(*aus etwas heraus*) to stick out

Ragout <-s, -s> [ra·'gu:] *nt* ragout

Rahm <-[e]s> [ra:m] *m kein pl bes* SÜDD, SCHWEIZ (*Sahne*) cream

rahmen ['ra:·mən] *vt* to frame; *Dia* to mount

Rahmen <-s, -> ['ra:·mən] *m* ❶(*Einfassung*) frame ❷(*Gestell*) *eines Fahrrads* frame; *eines Autos* chassis ❸(*begrenzter Umfang/Bereich*) framework; **sich** *akk* **im ~ halten** to stay within reasonable limits; [**mit etw** *dat*] **aus dem ~ fallen** to stand out [because of sth]

Rahmsoße *f* cream[y] sauce

R

Rakete <-, -n> [ra·'keː·tə] f rocket; MIL missile

Rallye <-, -s> ['ra·li, 'rɛ·li] f rally

rammen ['ra·mən] vt to ram (**in** +akk into)

Rampe <-, -n> ['ram·pə] f ramp; (*Laderampe*) loading ramp

Rampenlicht nt THEAT spotlight, footlight ►WENDUNGEN: **im ~ |der Öffentlichkeit| stehen** to be in the limelight

ramponieren* [ram·po·'niː·rən] vt (fam) to ruin

Ramsch <-[e]s> [ramʃ] m kein pl (fam) junk

Rand <-es, Ränder> [rant] m ❶ (*obere Begrenzung*) eines Glases, einer Tasse brim; einer Wanne rim; ❷ (*äußere Begrenzung*) edge; eines Huts brim; ❸ eines Blatts Papier margin; ❹ (*Schatten, Spur*) mark; **Ränder um die Augen haben** to have rings [or bags] around one's eyes ►WENDUNGEN: **am ~e** in passing; **außer ~ und Band geraten** (fam) to be beside oneself; **mit jdm/etw zu ~e kommen** to get along with sb/cope with sth

rang [raŋ] imp von **ringen**

Rang <-[e]s, Ränge> [raŋ] m ❶ (*gesellschaftliche Position*) [social] standing; ❷ kein pl (*Stellenwert*) status; ❸ MIL rank ►WENDUNGEN: **alles, was ~ und Namen hat** everybody who is anybody

Rangelei <-, -en> [raŋə·'lai] f (fam) scuffle

rangeln ['ra·ŋln] vi (fam) to scuffle

rangieren* [rã·'ʒiː·rən] vi to rank, to be ranked

Rangliste f rankings, ranking list

Rangordnung f hierarchy

ranken ['raŋ·kn̩] vr ■ **sich** akk **um etw** akk ~ Pflanze to wind itself around sth; ■ **sich** akk **um jdn/etw** ~ Legende, Sage to have grown up around sb/developed around sth

Ranzen <-s, -> ['ran·tsn̩] m ❶ SCH ≈ backpack ❷ (fam: Bauch) gut

ranzig ['ran·tsɪç] adj rancid

rappelvoll adj (fam) jam-packed

Raps <-es, -e> [raps] m rape[seed]

rar [raːɐ̯] adj rare; **■ ~ sein/werden** to be/become hard to find

Rarität <-, -en> [ra·ri·'tɛːt] f rarity

rasant [ra·'zant] I. adj fast, rapid; Tempo breakneck II. adv rapidly

rasch [raʃ] I. adj quick II. adv quickly

rascheln ['ra·ʃln̩] vi to rustle

rasen ['raː·zn̩] vi ❶ sein (*schnell fahren*) to speed; **■ gegen/in etw** akk ~ to crash into sth ❷ sein Zeit to fly [by] ❸ haben **sie raste |vor Wut|** she was beside herself [with rage]

Rasen <-s, -> ['raː·zn̩] m lawn

rasend I. adj ❶ (*schnell*) breakneck ❷ (*wütend*) furious; **~ vor Wut sein** to be infuriated ❸ (*furchtbar*) terrible; Durst burning; Schmerz excruciating; Wut blind ❹ Beifall thunderous II. adv (fam) very; **ich würde das ~ gern tun** I'd love to do it

Rasenmäher <-s, -> m lawnmower

Raser(in) <-s, -> ['raː·zɐ] m(f) (fam) speeder

Rasierapparat m ❶ (*Elektrorasierer*) [electric] shaver ❷ (*Nassrasierer*) [safety] razor

rasieren* [ra·'ziː·rən] vt, vr **■ |sich** akk| ~ to shave; **sich** akk **trocken/ nass** ~ to dry-shave/wet-shave; **sich** dat **die Beine** ~ to shave one's legs

Rasierklinge f razor blade

Rasierschaum m shaving cream

Rasierwasser nt aftershave

Raspel <-, -n> ['ras·pl̩] f KOCHK grater

raspeln ['ras·pl̩n] vt KOCHK to grate

Rasse <-, -n> ['ra·sə] f (*bei Menschen*) race; (*bei Tieren*) breed

rasseln ['ra·sl̩n] vi ❶ haben to rattle; **■ mit etw** dat ~ to rattle sth ❷ sein (fam) **durch eine Prüfung** ~ to fail [or flunk] an exam

Rassendiskriminierung f racial discrimination

rassig ['ra·sɪç] adj spirited

Rassismus <-> [ra·'sɪs·mʊs] m kein pl racism

Rassist(in) <-en, -en> [ra·'sɪst] m(f) racist

rassistisch adj racist

Rast <-, -en> [rast] *f* break

rasten ['ras·tn̩] *vi* to take a break

rastlos *adj* ❶ (*unermüdlich*) tireless ❷ (*unruhig*) restless

Rastplatz *m* rest area [*or* stop]

Rat¹ <-[e]s> [ra:t] *m kein pl* advice; **jdm den ~ geben, etw zu tun** to advise sb to do sth; **sich** *dat* **keinen ~ [mehr] wissen** to be at one's wit's end; **jdn/etw zu ~e ziehen** to consult sb/ sth

Rat² <-[e]s, Räte> [ra:t, *pl* 'rɛ:·tə] *m* POL council; ■**der Europäische ~** the European Council

Rate <-, -n> ['ra:·tə] *f* installment

raten <rät, riet, geraten> ['ra:·tn̩] I. *vi* ❶ (*Ratschläge geben*) ■**jdm] zu etw** *dat* ~ to advise [sb to do] sth ❷ (*schätzen*) to guess II. *vt* ❶ (*als Ratschlag geben*) ■**jdm etw** ~ to advise sb to do sth ❷ (*erraten*) to guess

Ratenkauf *m* installment plan

Ratenzahlung *f* ❶ *kein pl* (*Zahlung in Raten*) payment in installments ❷ (*einzelne Zahlung*) installment payment

Rathaus *nt* city [*or* town] hall

Ration <-, -en> [ra·'tsi̯oːn] *f* ration

rational [ra·tsi̯o·'naːl] I. *adj* rational II. *adv* rationally

rationell [ra·tsi̯o·'nɛl] I. *adj* efficient II. *adv* efficiently

rationieren* [ra·tsi̯o·'niː·rən] *vt* to ration

ratlos I. *adj* helpless; **ich bin völlig ~** I'm completely at a loss II. *adv* helplessly

ratsam ['raːt·zaːm] *adj* advisable

Ratschlag <-s, Ratschläge> ['raːt·ʃlaːk] *m* advice

Rätsel <-s, -> ['rɛ:·tsl̩] *nt* ❶ (*Geheimnis*) mystery; **es ist [jdm] ein ~, warum/wie ...** it is a mystery [to sb] why/how ... ❷ (*Denkaufgabe*) riddle

rätselhaft *adj* mysterious

Ratte <-, -n> ['ra·tə] *f* (*a. fig*) rat

rattern ['ra·tɐn] *vi* ❶ *haben* (*klappern*) to rattle ❷ *sein* (*sich fortbewegen*) to rattle along

rauᴿᴿ [rau] *adj* ❶ (*spröde*) *Hände,*

Haut rough; *Lippen* chapped ❷ (*heiser*) *Stimme* hoarse; (*verführerisch*) husky ❸ (*unwirtlich*) *Klima, Wetter* harsh; *Gegend* inhospitable ❹ (*ungehobelt*) harsh; *Benehmen, Sitten* uncouth

Raub <-[e]s, -e> [raup] *m pl selten* ❶ (*das Rauben*) robbery ❷ (*das Geraubte*) loot

rauben ['rau·bn̩] I. *vt* (*stehlen*) to rob; **das hat mir viel Zeit geraubt** this has cost me a lot of time II. *vi* to rob

Räuber(in) <-s, -> ['rɔy·bɐ] *m(f)* robber

Raubkatze *f* big [predatory] cat

Raubkopie *f* pirate[d] copy

Raubmord *m* murder robbery

Raubtier *nt* predator

Raubüberfall *m* robbery; (*auf Geldtransport etc. a.*) holdup

Raubvogel *m* bird of prey

Rauch <-[e]s> [raux] *m kein pl* smoke ▶WENDUNGEN: **sich in ~ auflösen** to go up in smoke

rauchen ['rau·xn̩] *vt, vi* to smoke

Raucher(in) <-s, -> *m(f)* smoker

Raucherabteil *nt* BAHN smoking compartment [*or* car]

Räucherlachs *m* smoked salmon

räuchern ['rɔy·çɐn] *vt, vi* to smoke

rauchig ['rau·xɪç] *adj* smoky

Rauchverbot *nt* ban on smoking; **hier ist** [*o* **herrscht**] **~ there's** no smoking here, smoking isn't allowed here

Rauchwolke *f* cloud of smoke

raufen ['rau·fn̩] *vi, vr* ■**[sich** *akk*] ~ to fight (**um** +*akk* over)

rauhᴬᴸᵀ [rau] *adj s.* **rau**

Raum <-[e]s, Räume> [raum] *m* ❶ (*Zimmer*) room ❷ *kein pl* (*Platz*) room *no art,* space *no art* ❸ GEOG (*Gebiet*) region, area; **im ~ Hamburg** in the Hamburg area ▶WENDUNGEN: **im ~ stehen** to be unresolved; **etw in den ~ stellen** to raise sth

räumen ['rɔy·mən] *vt* ❶ (*entfernen*) to remove (**aus/von** +*dat* from) ❷ (*einsortieren*) to put away *sep* (**in** +*akk* in/ into) ❸ *Wohnung* to vacate; *Straße* to clear ❹ (*evakuieren*) to evacuate

Raumfähre *f* space shuttle

R

Raumfahrt f kein pl space travel no art; (einzelner Raumflug) space flight

Räumfahrzeug nt bulldozer; (für Schnee) snowplow

räumlich ['rɔʏm·lɪç] I. adj ❶ (den Raum betreffend) spatial ❷ (dreidimensional) three-dimensional II. adv ❶ (platzmäßig) spatially ❷ (dreidimensional) three-dimensionally

Raumpfleger(in) m(f) cleaner

Raumschiff nt spaceship

Raumstation f space station

Räumungsverkauf m clearance sale

Raupe <-, -n> ['rau·pə] f ❶ ZOOL caterpillar ❷ (Planierraupe) bulldozer

Rausch <-[e]s, Räusche> [rauʃ] m ❶ (Trunkenheit) intoxication; **einen ~ haben** to be drunk; **seinen ~ ausschlafen** to sleep it off ❷ (Ekstase) ecstasy

rauschen ['rau·ʃn] vi ❶ haben (anhaltendes Geräusch erzeugen) Wasser, Verkehr to roar; (sanft) to murmur; Baum, Blätter to rustle; Lautsprecher to hiss; Rock, Vorhang to swish ❷ sein (sich geräuschvoll bewegen) Wasser to rush; Vogelschwarm to swoosh ❸ sein (fam: zügig gehen) to sweep (aus +dat out of, in +akk into)

Rauschgift nt drug

Rauschgifthändler(in) m(f) drug dealer; (international) drug trafficker

rauschgiftsüchtig adj addicted to drugs pred

Rauschgiftsüchtige(r) f/m drug addict

raus|fliegen vi irreg sein (fam) ❶ (hinausgeworfen werden) **aus der Schule ~** to be kicked out of school; **aus einem Betrieb ~** to be given the boot ❷ (weggeworfen werden) to get thrown out

räuspern ['rɔʏs·pen] vr ■**sich** akk **~** to clear one's throat

raus|schmeißen vt irreg (fam) to throw out

Rausschmeißer <-s, -> m (fam) bouncer

Razzia <-, Razzien> ['ra·tsi̯a] f raid

Reagenzglas nt test tube

reagieren* [rea·ˈgiː·rən] vi (a. chem) to react (**auf** +akk to, **mit** +dat with)

Reaktion <-, -en> [reak·ˈtsi̯oːn] f reaction (**auf** +dat to)

Reaktor <-s, -toren> [re·ˈak·to·ɐ̯] m reactor

real [re·ˈaːl] adj real

realisierbar adj realizable; **schwer ~e Pläne** plans that are hard to accomplish

realisieren* [rea·li·ˈziː·rən] vt to realize

realistisch [rea·ˈlɪs·tɪʃ] I. adj realistic II. adv realistically

Realität <-, -en> [rea·li·ˈtɛːt] f ❶ (Wirklichkeit) reality ❷ pl (Gegebenheiten) facts ❸ pl ÖSTERR (Immobilien) real estate

realitätsfern adj unrealistic; Person out of touch with reality

realitätsnah adj realistic; Person in touch with reality

Realschule f ≈ junior high school (a school for grades 5–10 that prepares students either for the Gymnasium or for an apprenticeship in a trade or industry)

Rebe <-, -n> ['reː·bə] f [grape]vine

Rebell(in) <-en, -en> [re·ˈbɛl] m(f) rebel

rebellieren* [re·bɛ·ˈliː·rən] vi to rebel (**gegen** +akk against)

Rebellion <-, -en> [re·bɛ·ˈli̯oːn] f rebellion; (von Studenten) revolt

rebellisch [re·ˈbɛ·lɪʃ] adj rebellious

Rechenaufgabe f math problem

Rechenfehler m calculation mistake

Rechenschaft <-> f kein pl account; **jdm [über etw** akk] **~ schulden** to be accountable to sb [for sth]; **jdn [für etw** akk] **zur ~ ziehen** to call sb to account [for sth]

Recherche <-, -n> [re·ˈʃɛr·ʃə] meist pl f research

recherchieren* [re·ʃɛr·ˈʃiː·rən] vt, vi to investigate, to research

rechnen ['rɛç·nən] I. vt ❶ (mathematisch lösen) to calculate ❷ (veranschlagen) to estimate; **wir müssen mindestens zehn Stunden ~** we have to count on at least ten hours ❸ (berück-

sichtigen) to take into account ④ (*einstufen, gehören*) to count (**zu** +*dat* among); **ich rechne sie zu meinen besten Freundinnen** I consider her one of my best [girl]friends II. *vi* ① (*Rechenaufgaben lösen*) to do math; **ich konnte noch nie gut ~** I was never [any] good at math ② (*sich verlassen*) ■**auf jdn/etw ~** to count on sb/sth ③ (*einkalkulieren*) ■**mit etw** *dat* **~** to count on sth; **wann ~ Sie mit einer Antwort?** when do you expect an answer?; **mit allem/dem Schlimmsten ~** to be prepared for anything/the worst ④ (*fam: Haus halten*) to economize; **wir müssen mit jedem Cent ~** we have to watch every penny III. *vr* (*Gewinn einbringen*) ■**etw rechnet sich** [**nicht**] *akk* sth is [not] profitable

Rechnung <-, -en> *f* ① (*schriftliche Abrechnung*) bill; (*im Restaurant a.*) check; **das geht auf meine ~** I'll pay [for it], [you can] put that on my tab; [**jdm**] **etw in ~ stellen** to charge [sb] for sth ② (*Berechnung*) calculation; **die ~ stimmt nicht** the numbers don't add up ▶WENDUNGEN: **er hatte die ~ ohne den Wirt gemacht** there was one thing he failed to take into consideration

recht [rɛçt] I. *adj* ① (*passend*) right ② (*richtig*) right; **ganz ~!** that's right [all right]! ③ (*angenehm*) ■**jdm ist etw ~** sth is all right with sb; **dieser Kompromiss ist mir durchaus nicht ~** I'm not at all happy with this compromise ④ SCHWEIZ, SÜDD (*anständig*) decent; (*angemessen*) appropriate ▶WENDUNGEN: **jdm ~ geschehen** to serve sb right; **nach dem R~en sehen** to make sure that everything's okay II. *adv* ① (*richtig*) correctly; **höre ich ~?** am I hearing things?; **versteh mich bitte ~** please don't misunderstand me ② (*genau*) really; **nicht ~ wissen** to not really know ③ (*ziemlich*) rather; (*gehörig*) properly ④ (*fam: gelegen*) **jdm gerade ~ kommen** to come just in time for sb; (*iron*) to be all sb needs [right now]; **man kann es nicht allen**

~ machen you can't please everyone ▶WENDUNGEN: **jetzt erst ~** now more than ever

Recht <-[e]s, -e> [rɛçt] *nt* ① *kein pl* (*Rechtsordnung*) law ② (*Anspruch*) right; **jds gutes ~ sein** to be sb's [legal] right; **jdm ~ geben** to agree with sb; **~ haben** to be [in the] right; **ein ~ auf jdn/etw haben** to have a right to sb/sth ③ (*Befugnis*) right; **mit welchem ~?** by what right?; **mit ~** rightly; **und das mit ~!** and rightly so!

Rechte <-n, -n> ['rɛç·tə] *f* ① (*rechte Hand*) right [hand] ② POL right

Rechteck <-[e]s, -e> *nt* rectangle

rechteckig *adj* rectangular

rechtfertigen I. *vt* to justify (**gegenüber** +*dat* to) II. *vr* ■**sich** *akk* **~** to justify oneself

Rechtfertigung *f* justification

rechthaberisch *adj* (*pej*) dogmatic

rechtlich I. *adj* legal II. *adv* legally

rechtlos *adj* without rights *pred*

rechtmäßig *adj* ① (*legitim*) lawful ② (*legal*) legal

rechts [rɛçts] I. *adv* ① (*auf der rechten Seite*) on the right; **dein Schlüsselbund liegt ~ neben dir** your keys are just to your right; **~ oben/unten** on the top/bottom right; **nach/von ~ to/from the right** ② TRANSP (*nach rechts*) [to the] right; **halte dich ganz ~** keep [to the] right; **~ abbiegen/ranfahren** to turn off/pull over to the right ③ POL right; **~ eingestellt sein** to lean to the right ▶WENDUNGEN: **nicht mehr wissen, wo ~ und links ist** (*fam*) to not know whether one is coming or going II. *präp* +*gen* to [*or* on] the right of

Rechtsabteilung *f* legal department

Rechtsanwalt, -anwältin *m, f* lawyer, attorney; (*vor Gericht*) lawyer

Rechtschreibfehler *m* spelling mistake

Rechtschreibreform *f* German spelling reform which went into effect on August 1, 2006

Rechtschreibung *f* spelling

Rechtsextremismus *m kein pl* right-wing extremism

R

Rechtsextremist(in) *m(f)* right-wing extremist

rechtskräftig I. *adj* legally valid; *Urteil* final **II.** *adv* with the force of law; **jdn ~ verurteilen** to pass final sentence on sb

Rechtskurve *f* right-hand curve

Rechtslage *f* legal position

Rechtsprechung <-, -en> *f pl selten* dispensation of justice

rechtsradikal I. *adj* ultra-right-wing **II.** *adv* with ultra right-wing tendencies

Rechtsschutzversicherung *f* insurance that covers legal expenses

Rechtsstaat *m* state founded on the rule of law

rechtsstaatlich *adj* under the rule of law *pred*

Rechtsstreit *m* lawsuit

rechtswidrig *adj* unlawful

rechtzeitig I. *adj* punctual **II.** *adv* on time; **Sie hätten mich ~ informieren müssen** you should have given me enough [advance] notice

recken ['rɛ·kn̩] *vt, vr* ■**|sich|** *akk* ~ to stretch

Recycling <-s> [ri·'sai·klɪŋ] *nt kein pl* recycling

Redakteur(in) <-s, -e> [re·dak·'tø:ɐ] *m(f)* editor

Redaktion <-, -en> [re·dak·'tsi̯o:n] *f* ① (*Büro*) editorial department ② (*Redaktionsmitglieder*) editorial staff ③ *kein pl* (*das Redigieren*) editing

Rede <-, -n> ['re:·də] *f* ① (*Ansprache*) speech ② (*das Reden, Gespräch*) talk; **wovon ist die ~?** what's it [all] about?; **es war gerade von dir die ~** we/they were just talking about you; **die ~ kam auf jdn/etw** the conversation turned to sb/sth ▶WENDUNGEN: **jdm ~ und Antwort stehen** to justify oneself to sb; **davon kann keine ~ sein** that's out of the question; **jdn zur ~ stellen** to take sb to task; **nicht der ~ wert sein** to be not worth mentioning

redegewandt *adj* eloquent

reden ['re:·dn̩] **I.** *vi* ① (*sprechen*) to talk (**mit** +*dat* to/with, **über** +*akk* about) ② (*eine Rede halten*) to speak

(**über** +*akk* about/on) ③ (*diskutieren*) **darüber lässt sich ~** that's not out of the question; **mit sich** *dat* [**über etw** *akk*] **~ lassen** to be willing to discuss [sth] ▶WENDUNGEN: **du hast gut ~** that's easy for you to say **II.** *vt* ① (*sagen*) to say ② (*klatschen*) ■**etw** [**über jdn/etw**] **~** to say sth [about sb/sth]; **es wird über uns geredet** they're talking about us

Redewendung *f* idiom

redlich ['re:t·lɪç] **I.** *adj* honest **II.** *adv* honestly

Redner(in) <-s, -> ['re:d·nɐ] *m(f)* speaker

redselig ['re:t·ze:·lɪç] *adj* talkative

reduzieren* [re·du·'tsi:·rən] *vt* to reduce

Reederei <-, -en> [re:·də·'rai] *f* shipping company

reell [re·'ɛl] *adj* ① (*tatsächlich*) real ② (*anständig*) straight; *Angebot, Preis* fair; *Geschäft* sound

Referat <-[e]s, -e> [re·fe·'ra:t] *nt* [seminar] paper; SCH project; **ein ~** [**über jdn/etw**] **halten** to give a presentation [on sb/sth]

Referenz <-, -en> [re·fe·'rɛnts] *f meist pl* (*Beurteilung*) **gute ~en aufzuweisen haben** to have good references

reflektieren* [re·flɛk·'ti:·rən] **I.** *vt* to reflect **II.** *vi* (*zurückstrahlen*) to reflect ② (*nachdenken*) to reflect (**über** +*akk* on/upon)

Reflex <-es, -e> [re·'flɛks] *m* ① (*Nervenreflex*) reflex ② (*Lichtreflex*) reflection

Reflexion <-, -en> [re·flɛ·'ksi̯o:n] *f* reflection

Reform <-, -en> [re·'fɔrm] *f* reform

reformbedürftig *adj* in need of reform *pred*

Reformhaus *nt* health food store

reformieren* [re·fɔr·'mi:·rən] *vt* to reform

Reformkost *f* health food

Refrain <-s, -s> [re·'frɛ:, rə-] *m* refrain

Regal <-s, -e> [re·'ga:l] *nt* shelf, shelving, rack

Regatta <-, Regatten> [reˈɡaˌta] f regatta

rege [ˈreːɡə] **I.** adj (lebhaft) lively; Anteilnahme, Beteiligung active **II.** adv actively

Regel <-, -n> [ˈreːɡl̩] f ❶ (Grundsatz) rule; **sich** dat **etw zur ~ machen** to make a habit of sth; **in der ~** as a rule ❷ (Menstruation) period ▶WENDUNGEN: **nach allen ~n der Kunst** with all the tricks of the trade

regelmäßig I. adj regular **II.** adv ❶ (immer wieder) regularly ❷ (ständig) always; **sie kommt ~ zu spät** she is always late

Regelmäßigkeit <-> f kein pl regularity

regeln [ˈreːɡl̩n] **I.** vt ❶ (in Ordnung bringen) to settle; Problem to resolve ❷ (regulieren) to regulate **II.** vr ■ **sich** akk **(von selbst) ~** to sort itself out

regelrecht [ˈreːɡl̩ˌrɛçt] **I.** adj real; Frechheit downright **II.** adv really; **~ betrunken sein** to be hammered sl

Regelung <-, -en> [ˈreːɡəˌlʊŋ] f ❶ (festgelegte Vereinbarung) arrangement; (Bestimmung) ruling ❷ kein pl (das Regulieren) regulation

regelwidrig I. adj against the rules pred **II.** adv against the rules

regen [ˈreːɡn̩] vr ■ **sich** akk **~** ❶ (sich bewegen) to move ❷ (geh) Zweifel, Gewissen, Hoffnung to stir

Regen <-s, -> [ˈreːɡn̩] m rain; **saurer ~** acid rain; **bei strömendem ~** [the] pouring rain ▶WENDUNGEN: **vom ~ in die Traufe kommen** (prov) to jump out of the frying pan into the fire; **jdn im ~ stehen lassen** (fam) to leave sb in the lurch

Regenbogen m rainbow

Regenmantel m raincoat

Regenschauer m rain shower

Regenschirm m umbrella

Regent(in) <-en, -en> [reˈɡɛnt] m(f) ruler; (Vertreter des Herrschers) regent

Regenwald m rainforest

Regenwurm m earthworm

Regie <-, -n> [reˈʒiː] f FILM, THEAT direction; RADIO production; **[bei etw** dat**] die ~ haben** to direct [sth] ▶WENDUNGEN: **in eigener ~** on one's own

regieren* [reˈɡiːrən] vt, vi to rule (**über** +akk over); Monarch a. to reign

Regierung <-, -en> [reˈɡiːrʊŋ] f POL ❶ (Kabinett) government ❷ (Herrschaftsgewalt) rule; **die ~ antreten** to take power [or office]; **an der ~ sein** to be in power

Regierungschef(in) m(f) head of a government

Regierungserklärung f government statement

Regierungspartei f ruling party

Regierungssprecher(in) m(f) government spokesperson

Regime <-s, -s> [reˈʒiːm] nt (pej) regime

Region <-, -en> [reˈɡi̯oːn] f region

regional [reɡi̯oˈnaːl] **I.** adj regional **II.** adv regionally

Regisseur(in) <-s, -e> [reʒɪˈsøːɐ̯] m(f) FILM, THEAT director; RADIO producer

registrieren* [reɡɪsˈtriːrən] vt to register

Regler <-s, -> [ˈreːɡlɐ] m ELEK regulator; AUTO governor

reglos [ˈreːkloːs] adj s. regungslos

regnen [ˈreːɡnən] vi impers to rain; ■ **es regnet** it's raining

regnerisch adj rainy

regulär [reɡuˈlɛːɐ̯] adj ❶ (vorgeschrieben) regular ❷ (normal) normal

regulieren* [reɡuˈliːrən] **I.** vt (einstellen) to regulate **II.** vr ■ **sich** akk **[von selbst] ~** to regulate itself

Regung <-, -en> f ❶ (Bewegung) movement ❷ (Empfindung) feeling; **menschliche ~** human emotion

regungslos adj motionless; Miene impassive

Reh <-[e]s, -e> [reː] nt roe deer

Rehabilitationszentrum nt rehab[ilitation center]

rehabilitieren* [rehabiliˈtiːrən] vt to rehabilitate

Reibe <-, -n> [ˈraɪbə] f grater

Reibekuchen m KOCHK DIAL (*Kartoffel-puffer*) potato pancake, ≈ latke

reiben <rieb, gerieben> ['rai·bn̩] I. *vt* **1** (*zerkleinern*) to grate **2** (*reibend verteilen*) ■ **etw auf/in etw** *akk* ~ to rub sth onto/into sth **3** (*reibend entfernen*) ■ **etw aus/von etw** *dat* ~ to rub sth out of/off sth II. *vr* **sich** *dat* **die Augen/Hände** ~ to rub one's eyes/hands

Reibereien [rai·bə·'rai·ən] *pl* (*fam*) friction

Reibung <-, -en> *f kein pl* PHYS friction

reibungslos I. *adj* smooth II. *adv* smoothly

reich [raiç] I. *adj* **1** (*sehr wohlhabend*) rich, wealthy **2** (*in Fülle habend*) rich (**an** +*dat* in); ~ **an Erfahrung sein** to have a wealth of experience **3** (*ergiebig*) rich; *Ernte* abundant; *Ölquelle* productive; *Mahlzeit* lavish; *Erbschaft* substantial **4** (*vielfältig*) wide; *Möglichkeiten, Leben* rich; *Auswahl, Wahl* large; *Bestände* copious II. *adv* **1** (*reichlich*) richly; **jdn** ~ **beschenken** to shower sb with presents **2** (*mit viel Gelderwerb verbunden*) ~ **heiraten/erben** to marry into/inherit money **3** (*reichhaltig*) richly

Reich <-[e]s, -e> [raiç] *nt* **1** (*Imperium*) empire; **das** ~ **Gottes** the Kingdom of God; **das Dritte** ~ HIST the Third Reich; **das Römische** ~ HIST the Roman Empire **2** (*fig: Bereich*) realm

reichen ['rai·çn̩] I. *vi* **1** (*ausreichen*) to be enough; **die Vorräte** ~ **noch Monate** there are enough supplies to last for months **2** (*überdrüssig sein*) ■ **etw reicht jdm** sth is enough for sb; **mir reicht's!** I've had enough [of this]!; **jetzt reicht's** [**mir**] [**aber**]! enough is enough! **3** (*sich erstrecken*) ■ **bis zu etw** *dat* ~ to reach to sth II. *vt* (*geh*) **1** (*geben*) ■ **jdm etw** ~ to give [or pass] sb sth **2** (*zur Begrüßung*) ■ **jdm die Hand** ~ to hold out one's hand to sb; **sich** *dat* **die Hand** ~ to shake hands

reichhaltig ['raiç·hal·tɪç] *adj* **1** (*vielfältig*) wide; *Programm* varied **2** *Biblio-*

thek, Sammlung well-stocked **3** (*üppig*) rich

reichlich ['raiç·lɪç] I. *adj* large; *Belohnung* ample; *Trinkgeld* generous; ~ **Geld/Zeit haben** to have plenty of money/time II. *adv* (*ziemlich*) rather

Reichstag m seat of the federal government in Germany

Reichtum <-[e]s, Reichtümer> ['raiç·tu:m] *m* **1** *kein pl* (*große Wohlhabenheit*) wealth; **zu** ~ **kommen** to get rich **2** *pl* (*materieller Besitz*) riches *npl* **3** *kein pl* (*Reichhaltigkeit*) wealth (**an** +*dat* of)

Reichweite *f* range

reif [raif] *adj* **1** AGR, HORT ripe **2** (*ausgereift*) *a. Persönlichkeit* mature; **im** ~**en Alter von ...** at the ripe old age of ... **3** (*fam*) ■ ~ **für etw** *akk* **sein** to be ready for sth

Reif <-[e]s> [raif] *m kein pl* METEO hoarfrost

Reife <-> ['rai·fə] *f kein pl* (*charakterlich*) maturity

reifen ['rai·fn̩] *vi sein* **1** AGR, HORT to ripen **2** (*sich entwickeln*) to mature (**zu** +*dat* into)

Reifen <-s, -> ['rai·fn̩] *m* tire

Reifendruck *m* tire pressure

Reifenpanne *f* flat [tire]

reiflich ['raif·lɪç] I. *adj* thorough; **nach** ~**er Überlegung** after [very] careful consideration II. *adv* thoroughly, carefully

Reihe <-, -n> ['raiə] *f* **1** (*fortlaufende Folge*) row; **außer der** ~ out of [the usual] order; **der** ~ **nach** in order **2** (*das Drankommen*) ■ **jd ist an der** ~ it's sb's turn; **ich war jetzt an der** ~! I was next!; **jeder kommt an die** ~ everyone will get a turn **3** (*Menge*) **eine** [**ganze**] ~ **von** a [whole] lot of; **eine ganze** ~ **von Beschwerden** a slew of complaints **4** (*Linie von Menschen*) line; **sich** *akk* **in** ~**n aufstellen** to form lines ▶WENDUNGEN: **etw auf die** ~ **kriegen** (*fam: kapieren*) to get sth into one's head; (*in Ordnung bringen*)

R

to get sth together; **aus der ~ tanzen** to step out of line

Reihenfolge f order

Reihenhaus nt townhouse

reihenweise adv ➊ (*in großer Zahl*) by the dozen ➋ (*nach Reihen*) in rows

reihum [raiˈʔʊm] adv in turn; **etw ~ gehen lassen** to pass sth around

Reim <-[e]s, -e> [raim] m ➊ (*Endreim*) rhyme ➋ pl (*Verse*) verse[s]

reimen [ˈrai·mən] I. vt, vr ■ **sich** akk **~** to rhyme (**auf** +akk with, **mit** +dat with) II. vt ■ **etw ~** to rhyme sth III. vi to make up rhymes

rein[1] [rain] adv (*fam*) s. **herein, hinein**

rein[2] [rain] I. adj ➊ (*unvermischt*) pure; *Wahrheit* plain ➋ (*fam: absolut*) *Zufall, Glück* pure; *Blödsinn* sheer; *Unsinn* utter; **das Kinderzimmer ist der ~ste Schweinestall!** the children's room is an absolute pigsty! ➌ (*sauber*) clean; *Kleidung* fresh ➍ (*makellos*) clear ▶WENDUNGEN: **etw [für jdn] ins R~e bringen** to clear up sth sep [for sb]; **mit sich** dat [**selbst**]/**etw ins R~e kommen** to come to terms with oneself/sth; **etw ins R~e schreiben** to make a fair copy of sth II. adv ➊ (*ausschließlich*) purely; **eine ~ persönliche Meinung** a purely personal opinion ➋ (*fam: absolut*) absolutely; **~ zufällig** purely by chance

Reinfall [ˈrain·fal] m (*fam*) disaster

rein|**fallen** vi irreg sein (*fam*) ➊ (*eine schwere Enttäuschung erleben*) to be taken in (**mit** +dat by) ➋ (*hineinfallen*) to fall in

Reingewinn m net profit

Reinheitsgebot nt **Deutsches ~** *German beer purity regulation*

reinigen [ˈrai·nɪ·gn̩] vt to clean

Reinigung <-, -en> f ➊ kein pl (*das Reinigen*) cleaning ➋ (*Reinigungsbetrieb*) cleaner's; **die chemische ~** the dry cleaner's

reinlich adj clean

reinrassig adj thoroughbred

Reis <-es, -e> [rais] m AGR, BOT rice

Reise <-, -n> [ˈrai·zə] f trip, journey;

gute **~!** have a nice trip!; **eine ~ machen** to take a trip

Reiseandenken nt souvenir

Reisebüro nt travel agency

Reiseführer m travel [*or* tour] guide

Reisegepäck nt luggage

Reisegruppe f tour group

Reiseleiter(in) m(f) guide

reisen [ˈrai·zn̩] vi sein to travel (**nach** to)

Reisende(r) f(m) dekl wie adj traveler

Reisepass[RR] m passport

Reisescheck m traveler's check

Reisetasche f travel bag

Reiseveranstalter(in) m(f) tour operator

Reiseversicherung f travel insurance

Reiseziel nt destination

reißen <riss, gerissen> [ˈrai·sn̩] I. vi ➊ sein (*zerreißen*) *Seil, Faden* to break; *Papier, Stoff* to tear ➋ haben (*zerren*) to pull II. vt haben ➊ **etw in Stücke ~** to tear sth to pieces ➋ (*abreißen*) ■ **etw von etw** dat **~** *Ast, Bauteil* to break sth off [*of*] sth; *Papier, Stoff* to tear sth off [*of*] sth ➌ (*wegreißen*) **jdm etw aus der Hand ~** to snatch [*or* grab] sth from sb's hands ➍ (*sich bemächtigen*) ■ **etw an sich** akk **~** to seize sth III. vr haben (*fam*) ■ **sich** akk **um jdn/etw ~** to scramble to get/see sb's/sth; **um diese Arbeit reiße ich mich nicht** I'm not in any hurry to do this work

Reißverschluss[RR] m zipper

Reißzwecke <-, -n> f thumbtack

reiten <ritt, geritten> [ˈrai·tn̩] I. vi sein to ride [a horse/pony]; **im Galopp/Trab ~** to gallop/trot II. vt haben to ride

Reiter(in) <-s, -> [ˈrai·tɐ] m(f) [horseback] rider

Reiz <-es, -e> [raits] m ➊ (*Verlockung*) appeal, attraction; [**für jdn**] **den ~ verlieren** to lose its appeal [for sb] ➋ (*Stimulus*) stimulus

reizbar adj irritable

reizen [ˈrai·tsn̩] vt ➊ (*verlocken*) ■ **jdn ~** to appeal to sb; ■ **es reizt jdn, etw zu tun** sb is tempted to do sth ➋ MED to irritate ➌ (*provozieren*) to provoke (**zu** +dat into)

R

reizend I. *adj* delightful, charming; **das ist ja ~!** (*iron*) that's charming! *iron* **II.** *adv* charmingly

reizlos *adj* dull

Reizthema *nt* emotional topic

Reizüberflutung *f* overstimulation

Reizung <-, -en> *f* irritation

reizvoll *adj* attractive

Reklamation <-, -en> [re·kla·ma·'tsjo:n] *f* complaint

Reklame <-, -n> [re·'kla:·mə] *f* ❶ (*Werbeprospekt*) flyer ❷ (*Werbung*) commercials *pl*

reklamieren* [re·kla·'mi:·rən] *vt* (*bemängeln*) to complain about

rekonstruieren* [re·kɔn·stru·'i:·rən] *vt* to reconstruct

Rekord <-s, -e> [re·'kɔrt] *m* record

Rekordzeit *f* record time

Relation <-, -en> [re·la·'tsjo:n] *f* proportion; **in ~ zu etw** *dat* **stehen** to be proportional to sth; **in keiner ~ zu etw** *dat* **stehen** to bear no relation to sth

relativ [re·la·'ti:f] **I.** *adj* relative **II.** *adv* relatively

Religion <-, -en> [re·li·'gjo:n] *f* religion

Religionsfreiheit *f* freedom of religion

religiös [re·li·'gjø:s] **I.** *adj* religious **II.** *adv* in a religious manner

Rendezvous <-, -> [rã·de·'vu:] *nt* rendezvous *a. hum*

Rennbahn *f* racetrack

R

rennen <rannte, gerannt> ['rɛ·nən] *vi* **sein** ❶ (*laufen*) to run ❷ (*stoßen*) **■gegen etw** *akk* **~** to bump into sth

Rennen <-s, -> ['rɛ·nən] *nt* race

Renner <-s, -> ['rɛ·nɐ] *m* (*fam*) big seller

Rennfahrer(in) *m(f)* ❶ (*Autorennen*) racecar driver ❷ (*Radrennen*) bicycle racer

Rennsport *m* ❶ (*Motorrennen*) motor racing ❷ (*Radrennsport*) bicycle racing ❸ (*Pferderennsport*) horse racing

Rennwagen *m* racecar

renovieren* [re·no·'vi:·rən] *vt* to renovate

Renovierung <-, -en> *f* renovation

rentabel [rɛn·'ta:·bl̩] **I.** *adj* profitable **II.** *adv* profitably

Rente <-, -n> ['rɛn·tə] *f* ❶ (*Ruhestand*) **in ~ gehen/sein** (*fam*) to retire/be retired ❷ (*Altersruhegeld*) pension; (*staatlich*) social security

Rentenalter *nt* retirement age

Rentenversicherung *f* Social Security

Rentier ['rɛn·ti:ɐ̯] *nt* reindeer

rentieren* [rɛn·'ti:·rən] *vr* **■sich** *akk* **~** to be worthwhile

Rentner(in) <-s, -> *m(f)* retiree

Reparatur <-, -en> [re·pa·ra·'tu:ɐ̯] *f* repair

reparieren* [re·pa·'ri:·rən] *vt* to repair

Repertoire <-s, -s> [re·pɛr·'tqa:ɐ̯] *nt* repertoire

Reportage <-, -n> [re·pɔr·'ta:·ʒə] *f* documentary

Reporter(in) <-s, -> [re·'pɔr·tɐ] *m(f)* reporter

Repräsentant(in) <-en, -en> [re·prɛ·zɛn·'tant] *m(f)* representative

repräsentativ [re·prɛ·zɛn·ta·'ti:f] **I.** *adj* ❶ (*aussagekräftig*) *Ergebnis, Querschnitt* representative ❷ (*vorzeigbar*) *Aufmachung, Auftreten* prestigious **II.** *adv* imposingly

repräsentieren* [re·prɛ·zɛn·'ti:·rən] **I.** *vt* to represent **II.** *vi* to perform official and social functions

Reptil <-s, -ien> [rɛp·'ti:l] *nt* reptile

Republik <-, -en> [re·pu·'bli:k] *f* republic

Republikaner(in) <-s, -> [re·pu·bli·'ka:·nɐ] *m(f)* ❶ (*in den USA*) Republican ❷ (*in Deutschland*) member of the German Republican Party (*an ultra right-wing party*)

Reservat <-[e]s, -e> [re·zɛr·'va:t] *nt* reservation

Reserve <-, -n> [re·'zɛr·və] *f* (*a. fig*) reserve; **jdn aus der ~ locken** to bring sb out of his/her shell

Reservekanister *m* gas can

Reservrad *nt* spare tire

Reservespieler(in) *m(f)* substitute

reservieren* [re·zɛr·'vi:·rən] *vt* to reserve

Residenz <-, -en> [re·zi·'dɛnts] f residence

resolut [re·zo·'lu:t] I. adj resolute II. adv resolutely

Respekt <-s> [re·'spɛkt, rɛ-] m kein pl respect (**vor** +dat for); **sich** dat [**bei jdm**] **~ verschaffen** to earn [sb's] respect

respektieren* [re·spɛk·'ti:·rən, rɛ-] vt to respect

respektlos I. adj disrespectful II. adv disrespectfully

respektvoll I. adj respectful II. adv respectfully

Rest <-[e]s, -e o SCHWEIZ a. -en> [rɛst] m rest; **von Essen** leftovers npl; **der ~ ist für Sie!** (beim Bezahlen) keep the change! ►WENDUNGEN: **jdm den ~ geben** (fam) to be the final straw for sb

Restaurant <-s, -s> [rɛ·sto·'rã:] nt restaurant

restaurieren* [rɛ·stau·'ri:·rən, rɛ-] vt to restore

restlich adj remaining

Restmüll m trash (garbage that cannot be recycled or composted)

Resultat <-[e]s, -e> [re·zʊl·'ta:t] nt result

resultieren* [re·zʊl·'ti:·rən] vi (geh) to result (**aus** +dat from, **in** +dat in)

Retourbillett ['rə·tu:ɐ̯·bɪl·jɛt] nt SCHWEIZ (Rückfahrkarte) round-trip ticket

Retourgeld nt SCHWEIZ (Wechselgeld) change

retten ['rɛtn̩] I. vt to save (**vor** +dat from) ►WENDUNGEN: **bist du noch zu ~?** (fam) are you out of your mind? II. vr ■ **sich** akk **~** to save oneself (**vor** +dat from); **rette sich, wer kann!** run for your lives!; **sich** akk **vor etw** dat **nicht mehr ~ können** to not have a chance against sth

Retter(in) <-s, -> [m(f) rescuer

Rettich <-s, -e> ['rɛ·tɪç] m radish

Rettung <-, -en> f rescue; **für jdn gibt es keine ~ mehr** there is no saving sb ►WENDUNGEN: **jds letzte ~ sein** to be sb's last hope

Rettungsboot nt lifeboat

Rettungsring m ❶ NAUT life preserver ❷ (hum fam: Fettpolster) spare tire

Rettungswagen m ambulance

Reue <-> ['rɔyə] f kein pl remorse

reumütig ['rɔy·my:·tɪç] I. adj remorseful; Sünder repentant II. adv remorsefully

Revanche <-, -n> [re·'vã:ʃə, re·'vaŋʃə] f ❶ (Revanchespiel) rematch ❷ (Rache) revenge

revanchieren* [re·vã·'ʃi:·rən] vr (sich erkenntlich zeigen) **sich** akk **bei jdm für eine Einladung ~** to return sb's invitation

Revier <-s, -e> [re·'vi:ɐ̯] nt ❶ (Polizeidienststelle) police station ❷ (Jagdrevier) preserve ❸ (Zuständigkeitsbereich) area of responsibility

Revision <-, -en> [re·vi·'zi̯o:n] f ❶ FIN, ÖKON audit ❷ JUR appeal ❸ TYPO final proofreading

Revolte <-, -n> [re·'vɔl·tə] f revolt

Revolution <-, -en> [re·vo·lu·'tsi̯o:n] f revolution

revolutionär [re·vo·lu·tsi̯o·'nɛːɐ̯] adj revolutionary

Revolutionär(in) <-s, -e> [re·vo·lu·tsi̯o·'nɛːɐ̯] m(f) POL revolutionary

Revolver <-s, -> [re·'vɔl·və] m revolver

Revue <-, -n> [re·'vy:, rə·'vy:] f THEAT revue

Rezension <-, -en> [re·tsɛn·'zi̯o:n] f **R** review

Rezept <-[e]s, -e> [re·'tsɛpt] nt ❶ KOCHK recipe ❷ MED prescription

Rezeption <-, -en> [re·tsɛp·'tsi̯o:n] f reception

rezeptpflichtig adj requiring a prescription; ■ **~ sein** to be available only with a prescription

Rhabarber <-s, -> [ra·'bar·bə] m rhubarb

Rhein <-s> [rain] m Rhine

rhetorisch [re·'to:·rɪʃ] I. adj rhetorical II. adv rhetorically

Rheuma <-s> ['rɔy·ma] nt kein pl (fam) rheumatism

rheumatisch [rɔyˈmaːtɪʃ] *adj* rheumatic

Rheumatismus <-> [rɔy·ma·ˈtɪs·mʊs] *m kein pl* rheumatism

Rhinozeros <-[ses], -se> [riˈnoː·tse·rɔs] *nt* rhinoceros

rhythmisch [ˈrʏt·mɪʃ] *adj* rhythmic[al]

Rhythmus <-, Rhythmen> [ˈrʏt·mʊs] *m* rhythm

richten [ˈrɪç·tn̩] I. *vr* ❶ (*bestimmt sein*) ■ **sich** *akk* **an jdn** ~ to be directed at sb ❷ (*sich orientieren*) ■ **sich** *akk* **nach jdm/etw** ~ to comply with sb/sth; **wir richten uns ganz nach Ihnen** [we'll do] whatever is best for you II. *vt* ❶ (*lenken*) to direct (**auf** +*akk* toward/at); **eine Schusswaffe auf jdn** ~ to point a gun at sb ❷ (*adressieren*) to address (**an** +*akk*) ❸ DIAL (*reparieren*) to fix III. *vi* (*geh*) to pass judgment (**über** +*akk* on)

Richter(in) <-s, -> [ˈrɪç·tɐ] *m(f)* judge

Richtgeschwindigkeit *f* recommended speed limit

richtig [ˈrɪç·tɪç] I. *adj* ❶ (*korrekt*) right; *Lösung* correct ❷ (*angebracht*) right; **es war ~, dass du gegangen bist** you were right to leave ❸ (*am richtigen Ort*) ■ **irgendwo/bei jdm** ~ **sein** to be in the right place/at the right address ❹ (*echt*) real; **ein ~er Winter mit viel Schnee** a real winter with lots of snow ❺ (*fam: regelrecht*) **du bist ein ~er Idiot!** you're a real idiot! ❻ (*passend*) right (**für** +*dat* for) ❼ (*fam: in Ordnung*) all right II. *adv* ❶ (*korrekt*) correctly; **Sie haben irgendwie nicht ~ gerechnet** you've miscalculated somehow; **ich höre doch wohl nicht ~?** you must be joking [*or* kidding]!; **eine ~ gehende Uhr** an accurate watch; **sehr ~!** that's correct! ❷ (*fam: regelrecht*) really; **das schmeckt ~ gut** this tastes really good

richtig|liegen *vi irreg* (*fam*) ■ |**mit etw** *dat*] ~ to be right [about sth]; ■ **bei jdm** ~ to have come to the right person

richtig|stellen *vt* ■ **etw** ~ to correct sth

Richtlinie *f meist pl* guideline *usu pl*

Richtung <-, -en> [ˈrɪç·tʊŋ] *f* direction

richtungweisend *adj* pointing the way [ahead]

Richtwert *m* guideline

riechen <roch, gerochen> [ˈriː·çn̩] I. *vi* ❶ (*duften*) to smell (**nach** +*dat* of); (*stinken a.*) to stink *pej* ❷ (*schnuppern*) ■ **an jdm/etw** ~ to smell sb/sth II. *vt* to smell; **riechst du nichts?** don't you smell anything? ▶WENDUNGEN: **jdn nicht ~ können** to not be able to stand sb; **das konnte ich nicht ~!** how was I supposed to know that!

Riegel <-s, -> [ˈriː·gl̩] *m* ❶ (*Verschluss*) bolt; **vergiss nicht, den ~ vorzulegen** don't forget to bolt the door ❷ (*Schokoriegel*) bar ▶WENDUNGEN: **etw** *dat* **einen ~ vorschieben** to put a stop to sth

Riemen <-s, -> [ˈriː·mən] *m* (*schmaler Streifen*) strap ▶WENDUNGEN: **sich** *akk* **am ~ reißen** to pull oneself together

Riese, Riesin <-n, -n> [ˈriː·zə, ˈriː·zɪn] *m, f* giant

rieseln [ˈriː·tzl̩n] *vi sein* ❶ (*rinnen*) to trickle (**auf** +*akk* onto) ❷ (*bröckeln*) ■ **von etw** *dat* ~ to flake off [of] sth

riesengroß [ˈriː·zn̩·ˈgroːs] *adj* (*fam*) colossal, enormous; **eine ~e Dummheit** something really stupid; **eine ~e Enttäuschung/Überraschung** a huge disappointment/surprise

Riesenrad *nt* Ferris wheel

riesig [ˈriː·zɪç] I. *adj* ❶ (*ungeheuer groß*) gigantic ❷ (*gewaltig*) enormous; *Anstrengung, Enttäuschung* huge ❸ *pred* (*fam: gelungen*) great; **die Party war einfach ~** the party was really great II. *adv* (*fam*) enormously; **das war ~ nett von Ihnen** that was terribly nice of you

Riff <-[e]s, -e> [rɪf] *nt* reef

Rille <-, -n> [ˈrɪ·lə] *f* groove

Rind <-[e]s, -er> [rɪnt] *nt* ❶ (*Kuh*) cow ❷ *kein pl* (*Rindfleisch*) beef

Rinde <-, -n> [ˈrɪn·də] *f* ❶ *eines Baums* bark ❷ *von Brot* crust; *von Käse* rind

Rinderbraten *m* roast beef

Rinderfilet *nt* fillet of beef

Rinderwahnsinn *m kein pl* mad cow disease *fam*

Rindfleisch *nt* beef

Rindvieh <-viecher> *nt* ① *kein pl* (*Rinder*) cattle *no art*, + *pl vb* ② (*sl: Dummkopf*) ass

Ring <-[e]s, -e> [rɪŋ] *m* ① (*Fingerring, Öse*) ring ② (*Ringstraße*) beltway ③ (*Boxring*) ring

ringen <rang, gerungen> ['rɪ·ŋən] *vi* ① (*im Ringkampf kämpfen*) to wrestle ② (*kämpfen*) ■ **mit sich** *dat* ~ to wrestle with oneself ③ (*schnappen*) **nach Atem** ~ to gasp for breath ④ (*sich bemühen*) ■ **um etw** *akk* ~ to struggle for sth

Ringen <-s> ['rɪ·ŋən] *nt kein pl* wrestling

Ringer(in) <-s, -> *m(f)* wrestler

Ringfinger *m* ring finger

Ringkampf *m* wrestling match

ringsum ['rɪŋs·'ʔʊm] *adv* [all] around

Rinne <-, -n> ['rɪ·nə] *f* ① (*Furche*) furrow ② (*Dachrinne, Regenrinne*) gutter

rinnen <rann, geronnen> ['rɪ·nən] *vi sein* ① (*fließen*) to run ② (*sickern*) *Tränen* to trickle

Rinnstein *m* ① (*Gosse*) gutter ② (*Bordstein*) curb

Rippchen <-s, -> ['rɪp·çən] *nt* smoked pork ribs *pl*, spare rib *usu pl*

Rippe <-, -n> ['rɪ·pə] *f* ANAT, KOCHK rib

Rippenfellentzündung *f* pleurisy

Risiko <-s, -s *o* ÖSTERR Risken> ['riː·zi·ko] *nt* risk

Risikogruppe *f* [high-]risk group

riskant [rɪs·'kant] *adj* risky

riskieren* [rɪs·'kiː·rən] *vt* to risk; **ich riskiere es!** I'll chance it!; ■ **[es]** ~, **etw zu tun** to risk doing sth; **seinen Job** ~ to put one's job at risk; **sein Leben** ~ to risk one's life

riss^{RR}, **riß**^{ALT} [rɪs] *imp von* **reißen**

Riss^{RR} <-es, -e>, **Riß**^{ALT} <Risses, Risse> [rɪs] *m* (*in Kleidung, Muskel, Wand*) tear

rissig ['rɪ·sɪç] *adj Leder, Wand* cracked; *Hände, Lippen* chapped

ritt [rɪt] *imp von* **reiten**

Ritt <-[e]s, -e> [rɪt] *m* ride

Ritter <-s, -> ['rɪ·tɐ] *m* knight

Ritual <-s, -e> [ri·'tu̯·aːl] *nt* ritual

Ritze <-, -n> ['rɪ·tsə] *f* crack

ritzen ['rɪ·tsn̩] I. *vt* to carve II. *vr* ■ **sich** *akk* ~ to cut oneself

Rivale, Rivalin <-n, -n> [ri·'vaː·lə, ri·'vaː·lɪn] *m, f* rival

rivalisieren* [ri·va·li·'ziː·rən] *vi* (*geh*) ■ **mit jdm** ~ to compete with sb

Rivalität <-, -en> [ri·va·li·'tɛːt] *f* (*geh*) rivalry

Roaminggebühr ['roʊ·mɪŋ-] *f meist pl* TELEC roaming charge

Robbe <-, -n> ['rɔ·bə] *f* seal

Robe <-, -n> ['roː·bə] *f* ① (*langes Abendkleid*) evening gown ② (*Talar*) robe[s *pl*]

Roboter <-s, -> ['rɔ·bɔ·tɐ] *m* robot

robust [ro·'bʊst] *adj* robust

röcheln ['rœ·çl̩n] *vi* to breath rattles; *Sterbender* to give the death rattle *liter*

Rock <-[e]s, Röcke> [rɔk] *m* ① (*Damenrock*) skirt ② DIAL (*Jackett*) jacket ③ SCHWEIZ (*Kleid*) dress

Rodelbahn *f* toboggan run

rodeln ['roː·dl̩n] *vi sein o haben* to sled, to toboggan

Rogen <-s, -> ['roː·gn̩] *m* roe

Roggen <-s> ['rɔ·gn̩] *m kein pl* rye

Roggenbrot *nt* rye bread

roh [roː] I. *adj* ① (*nicht zubereitet*) raw ② (*unbearbeitet*) crude; *Holzklotz* rough ③ (*grob*) rough; **mit -er Gewalt** by brute force, with brute strength II. *adv* (*grob*) roughly

Rohbau <-bauten> *m* shell

Rohkost *f* raw vegetables *npl*

Rohling <-s, -e> ['roː·lɪŋ] *m* (*brutaler Kerl*) brute

Rohöl *nt* crude oil

Rohr <-[e]s, -e> [roːɐ̯] *nt* ① (*Röhre*) pipe; (*kleinerer Durchmesser, flexibel*) tube ② SÜDD, ÖSTERR (*Backofen*) oven

Rohrbruch *m* burst pipe

Röhre <-, -n> ['rø·rə] *f* ① (*Hohlkörper*) tube ② (*Leuchtstoffröhre*) neon tube ③ (*Backofen*) oven

Rohrleitung *f* pipe

R

Rohrzucker m cane sugar

Rohstoff m raw material

RolladenALT <-s, Rolläden> m s. **Roll-laden**

Rollbahn f LUFT runway

Rolle <-, -n> ['rɔ·lə] f ① (*Gerolltes*) roll; **eine ~ Draht/Toilettenpapier** a roll of wire/toilet paper ② (*Garnrolle*) reel ③ (*Laufrad*) roller; (*Möbelrolle*) caster ④ (*Turnübung*) roll ⑤ FILM, THEAT role, part; **eine ~ spielen** to play a part ⑥ (*Beteiligung, Part*) role, part; **das spielt doch keine ~**! that doesn't matter! ⑦ SOZIOL role ▶WENDUNGEN: **aus der ~ fallen** to behave badly

rollen ['rɔ·lən] I. vi *sein* to roll ▶WENDUNGEN: **etw ins R~ bringen** to set sth in motion II. vt ① (*zusammenrollen*) to roll [up *sep*] ② (*rollend fortbewegen*) to roll III. vr ■**sich** *akk* ~ to curl up

Rollenspiel nt role play

Roller <-s, -> ['rɔ·le] m ① (*Kinderfahrzeug*) scooter ② (*Motorroller*) [motor] scooter ③ ÖSTERR (*Rollo*) [roller] blind [*or* shade]

Rolli <-s, -s> ['rɔ·lli] m MODE (*fam*) turtleneck

Rollkragen m turtleneck

RollladenRR <-s, Rollläden> m storm shutters *npl*

Rollschuh m roller skate; **~ laufen** to roller-skate

Rollstuhl m wheelchair

Rollstuhlfahrer(in) m(f) wheelchair user

rollstuhlgerecht adj wheelchair-accessible

Rolltreppe f escalator

Rom <-s> [roːm] nt kein pl Rome

Roman <-s, -e> [roˈmaːn] m novel

romanisch [roˈmaːnɪʃ] adj ① LING, GEOG Romance ② HIST Romanesque *spec* ③ SCHWEIZ (*rätoromanisch*) Rhaeto-Romanic

Romanistik <-> [ro·maˈnɪs·tɪk] f kein pl Romance studies

Romanschriftsteller(in) m(f) novelist

Romantik <-> [roˈman·tɪk] f kein pl ① (*Epoche*) ■**die ~** the Romantic period ② (*gefühlsbetonte Stimmung*) romanticism; **[einen] Sinn für ~ haben** to be a romantic

romantisch [roˈman·tɪʃ] I. adj ① (*zur Romantik gehörend*) Romantic ② (*gefühlvoll*) romantic ③ (*malerisch*) picturesque II. adv picturesquely

Römer(in) <-s, -> m(f) Roman

römisch ['røː·mɪʃ] adj Roman

röntgen ['rœnt·gn̩] vt to X-ray; ■**sich** *akk* ~ **lassen** to be X-rayed

Röntgenstrahlen pl X-rays pl

rosa ['roː·za] adj pink

Rose <-, -n> ['roː·zə] f ① (*Strauch*) rose bush ② (*Blüte*) rose

Rosenkohl m [Brussels] sprouts

Rosenmontag m the Monday before Shrove Tuesday, the climax of the German carnival celebration

rosig ['roː·zɪç] adj rosy

Rosine <-, -n> [roˈziː·nə] f raisin

Rosmarin <-s> ['roːs·ma·riːn] m kein pl rosemary

RosskastanieRR [-ka·staː·niə] f [horse] chestnut

Rost[1] <-[e]s> [rɔst] m kein pl (*auf Eisen, Stahl*) rust

Rost[2] <-[e]s, -e> [rɔst] m ① (*Gitter*) grating ② (*Grillrost*) grill ③ (*Bettrost*) base

rosten ['rɔs·tn̩] vi sein o haben to rust

rösten ['rœs·tn̩] vt to roast; *Brot* to toast

rostfrei adj stainless

Rösti ['røː·s·ti] pl SCHWEIZ ≈ hash browns pl

rostig ['rɔs·tɪç] adj rusty

rot <-er o röter, -este o röteste> [roːt] adj red; ■**~ werden** to turn red; (*aus Scham a.*) to blush

rotblond adj Frau strawberry blond[e]; *Mann* sandy-haired

rotbraun adj reddish brown

Röteln ['røː·tl̩n] pl rubella *spec*

röten ['røː·tn̩] vr ■**sich** *akk* ~ to turn red; *Wangen a.* to blush

rothaarig adj red-haired; ■**~ sein** to have red hair

rotieren* [roˈtiː·rən] vi ① (*sich dre-*

hen) to rotate ②*(fam: hektisch agieren)* to run around like crazy

Rotkohl *m,* **Rotkraut** *nt* ÖSTERR, SÜDD red cabbage

rötlich ['rø:t·lɪç] *adj* reddish

Rotlichtviertel *nt* red-light district

Rotstift *m* red pencil/pen

Rotwein *m* red wine

Roulade <-, -n> [ru·'la:·də] *f* KOCHK roulade *spec*

Route <-, -n> ['ru:·tə] *f* route

Routine <-> [ru·'ti:·nə] *f kein pl* routine

routiniert [ru·ti·'ni:ɐt] *adj* experienced

Rowdy <-s, -s> ['rau·di] *m* hooligan

rubbeln ['rʊ·b|n] *vt, vi* to rub hard

Rübe <-, -n> ['ry:·bə] *f* KOCHK, BOT turnip; **Gelbe ~** SÜDD, SCHWEIZ carrot; **Rote ~** beet

Rubrik <-, -en> [ru·'bri:k] *f* ①*(Kategorie)* category ②*(Spalte)* column

Ruck <-[e]s, -e> [rʊk] *m* jolt ▶WENDUNGEN: **sich** *dat* **einen ~ geben** to pull oneself together

ruckartig I. *adj* jerky, jolting *attr* II. *adv* with a jerk

rücken ['rʏ·kn̩] I. *vi sein* to move; **zur Seite ~** to move aside; *(auf einer Bank a.)* to scoot over *fam* II. *vt haben* to move

Rücken <-s, -> ['rʏ·kn̩] *m* ①ANAT back; **jdm den ~ zudrehen** to turn one's back on sb; **auf dem ~** on one's back; **hinter jds ~** *(a. fig)* behind sb's back ②KOCHK saddle ③*(Buchrücken)* spine ▶WENDUNGEN: **jdm läuft es [eis]kalt über den ~** cold shivers run down sb's spine; **jdm in den ~ fallen** to stab sb in the back; **jdm den ~ stärken** to give sb moral support

Rückenmark *nt* spinal cord

Rückenschmerzen *pl* back pain, backache

Rückenschwimmen *nt* backstroke

Rückenwind *m* tail wind

Rückerstattung *f* refund; *von Verlusten* reimbursement *form*

Rückfahrkarte *f* return ticket

Rückfahrt *f* return trip

Rückfall *m* ①MED relapse *form* ②JUR second offense

rückfällig *adj* ①JUR *Täter* recidivist *attr* ②*Alkoholiker, Raucher, Patient* relapsed; **~ werden** to suffer a relapse

Rückflug *m* return flight

Rückfrage *f* question (**zu** +*dat* regarding)

Rückgabe *f* return

Rückgang *m* drop, fall

rückgängig *adj* **etw ~ machen** to cancel sth

Rückgrat <-[e]s, -e> *nt* ①*(Wirbelsäule)* spine ②*kein pl (fig: Stehvermögen)* backbone

Rückhalt *m* support

Rückkehr <-> *f kein pl* return

Rücklage *f (Ersparnisse)* savings *npl*

rückläufig ['rʏk·lɔy·fɪç] *adj* declining, falling

Rücklicht *nt* tail light; *eines Fahrrads a.* rear light

Rückreise *f* return trip

Rucksack ['rʊk·zak] *m* backpack

Rückschlag *m* ①*(Verschlechterung)* setback; **einen ~ erleiden** to suffer a setback ②*(von Schusswaffe)* recoil

Rückschritt *m* step backwards

Rückseite *f* ①*von Blatt, Buch, Münze* reverse [side] ②*von Gebäude, Gerät* back, rear

Rücksicht <-, -en> ['rʏk·zɪçt] *f* consideration; **~ [auf jdn] nehmen** to show consideration [for sb]; **~ auf etw** *akk* **nehmen** to take sth into consideration

rücksichtslos I. *adj* inconsiderate (**gegenüber** +*dat* toward) II. *adv* inconsiderately

Rücksichtslosigkeit <-> *f kein pl* thoughtlessness

rücksichtsvoll I. *adj* considerate (**zu** +*dat* toward) II. *adv* considerately

Rücksitz *m* rear seat

Rückspiegel *m* rearview mirror

Rückspiel *nt* rematch

Rückstand *m* ①*(Verzug)* arrears *npl;* **mit der Miete in ~ sein** to be behind on the rent ②*pl (fällige Zahlungen)*

R

outstanding payments *pl* ❸ *von Chemikalien* residue *form*

rückständig ['rʏk·ʃtɛn·dɪç] *adj* ❶ (*überfällig*) overdue ❷ (*zurückgeblieben*) backward

Rückstrahler <-s, -> *m* reflector

Rücktritt *m* ❶ (*Amtsniederlegung*) resignation ❷ *von einem Vertrag* withdrawal (*von* +*dat* from)

Rückwand *f* ❶ (*rückwärtige Mauer*) back wall ❷ (*rückwärtige Platte*) back [panel]

rückwärts ['rʏk·vɛrts] *adv* ❶ (*rücklings*) backwards; ~ **einparken** to back into a parking space ❷ (*nach hinten*) backward; **Salto** ~ backward somersault

Rückwärtsgang *m* reverse [gear]

Rückweg *m* way back; **sich** *akk* **auf den** ~ **machen** to head back

rückwirkend **I.** *adj* retroactive **II.** *adv* retroactively

Rückzahlung *f* repayment

Rückzieher <-s, -> *m* **einen** ~ **machen** (*fam: eine Zusage zurückziehen*) to back out [of a commitment]; (*nachgeben*) to back down

Rückzug *m* MIL retreat; **den** ~ **antreten** to retreat

Rüde <-n, -n> ['ryː·də] *m* [male] dog

Rudel <-s, -> ['ruː·dl] *nt* herd; *von Wölfen* pack; *von Menschen* swarm

Ruder <-s, -> ['ruː·dɐ] *nt* ❶ (*langes Paddel*) oar ❷ (*Steuerruder*) helm; *eines kleineren Bootes a.* rudder

Ruderboot *nt* rowboat

Ruderer, Ruderin <-s, -> *m*, *f* rower

rudern ['ruː·dɐn] *vi* sein o haben to row

Ruf <-[e]s, -e> [ruːf] *m* ❶ (*Ausruf*) shout; (*an jdn gerichtet*) call ❷ *kein pl* (*Ansehen*) reputation

rufen <rief, gerufen> ['ruː·fn] **I.** *vi* ❶ (*schreien*) to cry out ❷ (*a. fig: nach jdm/etw verlangen*) ~ **nach jdm** to call [for sb]; **die Pflicht ruft** duty calls **II.** *vt* ❶ (*ausrufen*) to shout ❷ (*herbestellen*) to call; ■**jdn zu sich** *dat* ~ to summon sb; ■**jdn** ~ **lassen** to send for sb

Rufmord *m* slander, character assassination

Rufname *m* name that sb is called

Rufnummer *f* [tele]phone number

Ruhe <-> ['ruː·ə] *f kein pl* ❶ (*Stille*) quiet, silence; ~! [be] quiet!, shhh! ❷ (*Frieden*) peace; **jdn** |**mit etw** *dat*| **in** ~ **lassen** to leave sb alone [about sth] ❸ (*Erholung*) rest; **sich** *dat* **keine** ~ **gönnen** to not allow oneself any rest; **jdm keine** ~ **lassen** to not give sb a moment's rest ❹ (*Gelassenheit*) calm[ness]; [**die**] ~ **bewahren** to keep calm; **jdn aus der** ~ **bringen** to throw sb [for a loop]; **sich** *akk* |**von jdm/etw**| **nicht aus der** ~ **bringen lassen** to not let oneself get rattled [by sb/sth]; **in** |**aller**| ~ [**really**] calmly; **immer mit der** ~! (*fam*) take it easy!, easy does it! ▶WENDUNGEN: **keine** ~ **geben, bis ...** to not rest until ...; **sich** *akk* **zur** ~ **setzen** to retire; **die** ~ **weghaben** (*fam*) to be unflappable

Ruhelosigkeit <-> *f kein pl* restlessness

ruhen ['ruː·ən] *vi* ❶ (*ausruhen*) to rest ❷ (*eingestellt sein*) to be suspended

Ruhestand *m kein pl* retirement; **in den** ~ **gehen** to retire; **im** ~ retired

Ruheständler(in) <-s, -> ['ruː·əʃtɛnt·lɐ] *m(f)* retiree

Ruhestörung *f* disturbance of the peace

Ruhetag *m* (*arbeitsfreier Tag*) day off; (*Feiertag*) day of rest

ruhig ['ruː·ɪç] **I.** *adj* ❶ (*still*) quiet; **sei** ~! (*fam*) [be] quiet!, shhh! ❷ (*geruhsam*) *Abend* quiet ❸ (*unbewegt*) *Meer* calm; *Blick, Hand* steady ❹ (*gelassen*) *Person, Stimme* calm; *Gewissen* clear **II.** *adv* (*gelassen*) calmly **III.** *part* (*fam*) **geh** ~, **ich komme schon alleine zurecht** it's okay if you leave; I can manage on my own; **du kannst** ~ **hierbleiben** you're welcome to stay here

Ruhm <-es> [ruːm] *m kein pl* fame

rühmen ['ryː·mən] **I.** *vt* to praise **II.** *vr* ■**sich** *akk* **einer S.** *gen* ~ to brag about sth

rühmlich adj praiseworthy

Rührei ['ry:ɐ̯ʔai] nt scrambled eggs pl

rühren ['ry:rən] I. vt ❶ (umrühren) to stir ❷ (innerlich) Herz to touch; ■jdn ~ to move sb II. vr (sich bewegen) ■sich akk ~ to move

rührend I. adj touching, moving II. adv touchingly

rührselig adj tear-jerking fam; ein ~er Film/ein ~es Buch a tearjerker fam

Rührung <-> f kein pl emotion

Ruin <-s> [ru·'iːn] m kein pl ruin

Ruine <-, -n> [ru·'iːnə] f ruin[s pl]

ruinieren* [rui·'niːrən] vt to ruin

rülpsen ['rʏlpsn̩] vi to burp

Rum <-s, -s> [rʊm] m rum

Rumäne, Rumänin <-n, -n> [ru·'mɛː-nə, ru·'mɛːnɪn] m, f Romanian; s. a. **Deutsche(r)**

Rumänien <-s> [ru·'mɛːni̯ən] nt Romania; s. a. **Deutschland**

rum|kriegen vt (sl) ❶ (zu etw bewegen) ■jdn [zu etw dat] ~ to talk sb into [doing] sth ❷ (verbringen) **den Tag irgendwie ~** to get through the day somehow

Rummel <-s> ['rʊ·ml̩] m kein pl ❶ (fam: Aufhebens) [hustle and] bustle ❷ (Betriebsamkeit) commotion ❸ DIAL s. **Rummelplatz**

Rummelplatz m fairground

Rumpf <-[e]s, Rümpfe> [rʊmpf] m ❶ (Torso) torso ❷ eines Flugzeugs fuselage; eines Schiffes hull

Rumpsteak ['rʊmp·ʃteːk] nt rump steak

rund [rʊnt] I. adj ❶ (kreisförmig) round ❷ (rundlich) plump; Hüften well-rounded; Wangen chubby ❸ (fam) **eine ~e Summe** a round sum; **~ fünf Jahre** a good five years ❹ **Geschmack** full II. adv ❶ ■~ **um ...** around ... ❷ (etwa) around; **~ 100 Euro** approximately 100 euros

Runde <-, -n> ['rʊn·də] f ❶ (Gesellschaft) company ❷ (Rundgang) rounds pl; eines Polizisten beat; eines Briefträgers route ❸ SPORT lap; (im Boxen) round ❹ (Bestellung) round [of drinks]; **eine ~ spendieren** to buy a [or the next] round ▶WENDUN-GEN: [**mit etw** dat] **über die ~n kommen** to make ends meet [with sth]

Rundfahrt f [sightseeing] tour

Rundflug m sightseeing flight

Rundfunk m ❶ (geh) radio; **im ~** on the radio ❷ (Sendeanstalt) broadcasting

Rundgang m walk; (zur Besichtigung) tour

rundlich ['rʊnt·lɪç] adj plump; Hüften well-rounded; Wangen chubby

Rundreise f tour (durch +akk of)

Rundung <-, -en> f ❶ (Wölbung) curve ❷ pl (fam) curves

Runzel <-, -n> ['rʊn·tsl̩] f wrinkle

runzelig ['rʊn·tsə·lɪç] adj wrinkled

runzeln ['rʊn·tsl̩n] vt to crease; Stirn to wrinkle

Rüpel <-s, -> ['ry:·pl̩] m lout

rupfen ['rʊp·fn̩] vt ❶ (Huhn) to pluck ❷ (zupfen) to pull up sep (aus +dat out of)

ruppig ['rʊ·pɪç] I. adj gruff; Antwort abrupt II. adv gruffly

Rüsche <-, -n> ['ry:·ʃə] f frill

Ruß <-es> [ruːs] m kein pl soot; (beim Dieselmotor) particulate

Russe, Russin <-n, -n> ['rʊ·sə] m, f Russian; s. a. **Deutsche(r)**

Rüssel <-s, -> ['rʏ·sl̩] m snout; eines Elefanten a. trunk

rußig ['ruː·sɪç] adj blackened [with soot pred]; (verschmutzt a.) sooty

russisch ['rʊ·sɪʃ] adj Russian; s. a. **deutsch**

RusslandRR, **Rußland**ALT <-s> ['rʊs-lant] nt Russia; s. a. **Deutschland**

rüsten ['rʏs·tn̩] vi to arm

rüstig ['rʏs·tɪç] adj sprightly

rustikal [rʊs·ti·'kaːl] I. adj rustic II. adv in a rustic style

Rüstung <-, -en> ['rʏs·tʊŋ] f ❶ kein pl (das Rüsten) [re]armament ❷ (Ritterrüstung) armor

Rüstungsindustrie f weapons industry

Rute <-, -n> ['ruː·tə] f ❶ (Gerte) switch ❷ (Angelrute) [fishing] rod

Rutsch <-es, -e> [rʊtʃ] m landslide

R

►WENDUNGEN: **in einem ~** (*fam*) in one go; **guten ~!** (*fam*) Happy New Year! **rutschen** ['rʊt·ʃn̩] *vi sein* ❶ (*ausrutschen*) to slip; *Auto* to skid ❷ (*fam: rücken*) to move; **auf dem Stuhl hin und her ~** to fidget in one's chair; **rutsch mal!** scoot over! ❸ (*gleiten*) to slide; *Kleidung* to slip [down]

rutschfest *adj* nonslip
rutschig ['rʊt·ʃɪç] *adj* slippery
rütteln ['rʏ·tl̩n] I. *vt* to shake II. *vi* ■**an etw** *dat* **~** to shake sth; **daran ist nicht zu ~** (*kein Zweifel*) there's no doubt about it

Ss

S, s <-, -> [ɛs] *nt* S, s; **~ wie Siegfried** S as in Sierra
s. *Abk von* **siehe**
Saal <-[e]s, Säle> [za:l] *m* hall
Saat <-, -en> [za:t] *f* ❶ *kein pl* (*das Säen*) sowing ❷ (*Saatgut*) seed[s *pl*]
Sabbat <-s, -e> ['za·bat] *m* the Sabbath
Säbel <-s, -> ['zɛː·bl̩] *m* saber
Sabotage <-, -n> [za·bo·'taː·ʒə] *f* sabotage
Sachbearbeiter(in) *m(f)* (*in einer Behörde*) official in charge
Sachbeschädigung *f* vandalism
Sachbuch *nt* nonfiction book
Sache <-, -n> ['za·xə] *f* ❶ (*Ding*) thing ❷ (*Angelegenheit*) matter; **eine gute ~** a good cause; **das ist meine ~** that's my business ❸ (*Aufgabe*) **mit jdm gemeinsame ~ machen** to collude with sb; **sie macht keine halben ~n** she finishes what she starts; **er macht seine ~ gut** he's doing well ❹ (*Sachlage*) **sich** *dat* **seiner ~ sicher sein** to be confident about what one's doing; **zur ~ kommen** to get to the point; **bei der ~ sein** to concentrate, to pay attention; **nichts zur ~ tun** to be irrelevant
Sachgebiet *nt* field
sachkundig *adj* [well-]informed
sachlich ['zax·lɪç] I. *adj* ❶ (*objektiv*) objective ❷ (*inhaltlich*) *Fehler* factual ❸ (*schmucklos*) *Stil* functional II. *adv*

❶ (*objektiv*) objectively ❷ (*inhaltlich*) factually
Sachschaden *m* property damage
Sachsen <-s> ['zak·sn̩] *nt* Saxony
sächsisch ['zɛk·sɪʃ] *adj* Saxon, of Saxony *pred*
sachte ['zax·tə] *adv* gently
Sachverständige(r) *f(m) dekl wie adj* expert
Sachwert *m* real value
Sack <-[e]s, Säcke> [zak] *m* ❶ (*großer Beutel*) sack, bag ❷ SÜDD, ÖSTERR, SCHWEIZ (*Hosentasche*) [pants] pocket ►WENDUNGEN: **jdm auf den ~ gehen** (*derb*) to get on sb's nerves
Sackgasse *f* (*a. fig*) dead end *a. fig*
Sadismus <-> [za·'dɪs·mʊs] *m kein pl* sadism
Sadist(in) <-en, -en> [za·'dɪst] *m(f)* sadist
sadistisch I. *adj* sadistic II. *adv* sadistically
säen ['zɛː·ən] *vt, vi* to sow
Safari <-, -s> [za·'faː·ri] *f* safari
Safran <-s, -e> ['zaf·ra:n] *m* saffron
Saft <-[e]s, Säfte> [zaft] *m* ❶ (*Fruchtsaft*) [fruit] juice ❷ (*Pflanzensaft*) sap ❸ (*fam: Strom*) juice
saftig ['zaf·tɪç] *adj* ❶ *Früchte* juicy ❷ (*fig*) *Rechnung* steep
Sage <-, -n> ['zaː·gə] *f* legend
Säge <-, -n> ['zɛː·gə] *f* ❶ (*Werkzeug*) saw ❷ ÖSTERR (*Sägewerk*) sawmill

sagen ['zaː·gn̩] I. *vt* ① (*äußern*) to say; **warum haben Sie das nicht gleich gesagt?** why didn't you say so before?; **was ich noch ~ wollte, ...** [oh, and] one more thing ... ② (*mitteilen*) to tell; **wem ~ Sie das!** you don't need to tell me [that]!; **das ist nicht gesagt** that is by no means certain; **nichts zu ~ haben** to have nothing to say ③ (*meinen*) **was ~ Sie dazu?** what do you think?; **das kann man wohl ~!** you can say that again! ④ (*bedeuten*) **jdm etwas ~** to mean something to sb; **das hat nichts zu ~** it doesn't mean a thing II. *vi* ■ **sag/~ Sie, ...** tell me, ...; **unter uns gesagt** between you and me; **sag bloß!** you don't say!

sägen ['zɛː·gn̩] *vt, vi* to saw

Sahara <-> [za·ˈhaː·ra] *f kein pl* ■ **die ~** the Sahara

Sahne <-> ['zaː·nə] *f kein pl* cream; (*Schlagsahne*) whipping cream

Sahnetorte *f* layer cake (*filled with whipped cream*)

Saison <-, -s *o* SÜDD, ÖSTERR -en> [zɛ·ˈzõː] *f* season; **außerhalb der ~** in the off-season

Saisonarbeiter(in) *m(f)* seasonal worker

Saite <-, -n> ['zai·tə] *f* MUS string ►WENDUNGEN: **andere ~n aufziehen** to get tough

Saiteninstrument *nt* string[ed] instrument

Sakko <-s, -s> ['zako] *m o nt* sports coat

Sakrament <-[e]s, -e> [za·kra·ˈmɛnt] *nt* sacrament

Salamander <-s, -> [za·la·ˈman·dɐ] *m* salamander

Salami <-, -s> [za·ˈlaː·mi] *f* salami

Salat <-[e]s, -e> [za·ˈlaːt] *m* ① (*Pflanze*) lettuce ② (*Gericht*) salad

Salatgurke *f* cucumber

Salatsoße *f* salad dressing

Salbe <-, -n> ['zal·bə] *f* ointment

Salbei <-s> ['zal·bai] *m kein pl* sage

Saldo <-s, -s> ['zal·do] *m* FIN balance

Salmonellenvergiftung *f* salmonella poisoning

salopp [za·ˈlɔp] I. *adj* ① (*leger*) casual ② (*ungezwungen*) *Ausdrucksweise* slangy II. *adv* ① (*leger*) casually ② (*ungezwungen*) **sich** *akk* ~ **ausdrücken** to use slang[y] expressions

Salto <-s, -s> ['zal·to] *m* somersault; **einen ~ machen** to somersault

Salz <-es, -e> [zalts] *nt* salt

salzen <salzte, gesalzen> ['zal·tsn̩] I. *vt* to salt II. *vi* to add salt

salzig ['zal·tsɪç] *adj* salty

Salzkartoffeln *pl* boiled potatoes

Salzsäure *f kein pl* hydrochloric acid

Salzstreuer <-s, -> *m* salt shaker

Salzwasser *nt kein pl* salt water

Samen <-s, -> ['zaː·mən] *m* ① (*Pflanzensamen*) seed ② *kein pl* (*Sperma*) sperm

sammeln ['za·mln̩] I. *vt* ① (*aufsammeln, zusammentragen*) to gather; *Belege* to keep ② *Briefmarken, Münzen, Unterschriften* to collect II. *vr* ■ **sich** *akk* ~ (*sich konzentrieren*) to collect oneself III. *vi* **für einen guten Zweck ~** to collect for a good cause

Sammler(in) <-s, -> *m(f)* collector

Sammlung <-, -en> *f* collection

Samstag <-[e]s, -e> ['zams·taːk] *m* Saturday; *s. a.* **Dienstag**

samstags *adv* [on] Saturdays

Samt <-[e]s, -e> [zamt] *m* velvet

sämtlich ['zɛmt·lɪç] *adj* all

Sanatorium <-, -rien> [za·na·ˈtoː·ri̯ʊm] *nt* sanatorium

Sand <-[e]s, -e> [zant] *m* sand ►WENDUNGEN: **das gibt es wie ~ am Meer** there are tons of them; **im ~e verlaufen** to peter out

Sandale <-, -n> [zan·ˈdaː·lə] *f* sandal

Sandbank <-bänke> *f* sandbank

sandig ['zan·dɪç] *adj* sandy, full of sand *pred*

Sandkasten *m* sandbox

Sandstein *m* sandstone

Sandstrand *m* sandy beach

sanft [zanft] I. *adj* ① *Berührung, Stimme* gentle ② *Farben, Musik* soft II. *adv* gently

sanftmütig *adj* gentle

Sänger(in) <-s, -> ['zɛŋɐ] *m(f)* singer
sanieren* [za·'niː·rən] *vt* ❶ *Gebäude* to refurbish ❷ *Unternehmen* to rehabilitate
Sanierung <-, -en> *f* ❶ *eines Gebäudes* renovation ❷ *eines Unternehmens* rehabilitation
sanitär [zani·'tɛːɐ] *adj attr* sanitary; **~e Anlagen** sanitation
Sanitäter(in) <-s, -> [zani·'tɛː·tɐ] *m(f)* paramedic
Sanktion <-, -en> [zaŋk·'tsi̯oːn] *f* sanction
sanktionieren* [zaŋk·tsi̯o·'niː·rən] *vt* to sanction
Saphir <-s, -e> [za·'fiːɐ] *m* sapphire
Sardelle <-, -n> [zar·'dɛlə] *f* anchovy
Sardine <-, -n> [zar·'diː·nə] *f* sardine
Sarg <-[e]s, Särge> [zark] *m* coffin, casket
Satan <-s, -e> ['zaː·tan] *m kein pl* Satan
satanisch [za·'taː·nɪʃ] I. *adj attr* satanic, diabolical II. *adv* diabolically
Satellit <-en, -en> [za·tɛ·'liːt] *m* satellite
Satin <-s, -s> [za·'tɛ̃ː] *m* satin
Satire <-, -n> [za·'tiː·rə] *f kein pl* satire (**auf** +*akk* about/on)
satt [zat] *adj* ❶ *(gesättigt)* full *pred fam;* **ich bin ~** I'm full; **Nudeln machen ~** pasta is filling; **sich** [**an etw** *dat*] **~ essen** to eat one's fill [of sth] ❷ *(kräftig) Farben* rich, deep ❸ *(fam: überdrüssig)* **etw ~ sein** to be fed up with sth
Sattel <-s, Sättel> ['za·tl̩] *m* saddle
satt|haben[RR] *vi irreg* ■**etw ~** to be fed up with sth
sättigen ['zɛ·tɪ·ɡn̩] *vi* to be filling
sättigend *adj* filling
Saturn <-s> [za·'tʊrn] *m kein pl* Saturn
Satz¹ <-es, Sätze> [zats] *m* ❶ LING sentence ❷ *(Set)* set; **ein ~ Weingläser** a set of wine glasses ❸ SPORT set
Satz² <-es, Sätze> [zats] *m* leap, jump; **einen ~ machen** to leap
Satz³ <-es> [zats] *m kein pl* dregs *npl;* *(Kaffeesatz)* grounds *npl*

Satzung <-, -en> ['za·tsʊŋ] *f* constitution, statutes *npl*
Satzzeichen *nt* LING punctuation mark
Sau <-, Säue> [zau] *f* ❶ *(weibliches Schwein)* sow ❷ *(sl: schmutziger Mensch)* filthy pig ►WENDUNGEN: **jdn zur ~ machen** to chew sb out; **die ~ rauslassen** to let it all hang out; **das ist unter aller ~** it's enough to make you puke
sauber ['zau·bɐ] I. *adj* ❶ *(rein)* clean ❷ *(stubenrein)* ■**~ sein** *Tier* to be housebroken; *Kind* to be potty trained ❸ *(sorgfältig)* neat ❹ *(anständig)* honest II. *adv (sorgfältig)* neatly
Sauberkeit <-> *f kein pl* cleanliness
säuberlich ['zɔy·bɐ·lɪç] I. *adj* neat II. *adv* neatly
säubern ['zɔy·bɐn] *vt* ❶ *(reinigen)* to clean ❷ *(euph: befreien)* to purge (**von** +*dat* of)
Sauce <-, -n> ['zoː·sə] *f s.* **Soße**
sauer ['zau·ɐ] *adj* ❶ *(nicht süß)* sour; *(sauer eingelegt)* pickled ❷ *(Säure enthaltend)* acid[ic] ❸ *(übel gelaunt)* mad (**auf** +*akk* at), pissed off *pred* (**auf** +*akk* at/with)
Sauerampfer <-, -n> *m* sorrel
Sauerbraten *m* sauerbraten *(beef roast marinated in vinegar and herbs)*
Sauerei <-, -en> [zauə·'rai̯] *f (fam)* ❶ *(schmutziger Zustand)* mess ❷ *(unmögliches Benehmen)* [downright] disgrace
Sauerkirsche *f* sour cherry
Sauerkraut *nt* DIAL sauerkraut
Sauerstoff ['zauɐ·ʃtɔf] *m kein pl* oxygen
Sauerstoffmangel *m kein pl* lack of oxygen
Sauerteig *m* sourdough
saufen <säuft, soff, gesoffen> ['zau·fn̩] I. *vt (fam)* to drink; *(schneller)* to knock back *sep* II. *vi* to drink
Säufer(in) <-s, -> ['zɔy·fɐ] *m(f) (fam)* drunk[ard], boozer
Sauferei <-, -en> [zau·fə·'rai̯] *f (fam)* ❶ *(Besäufnis)* drinking party ❷ *(übermäßiges Trinken)* boozing *fam*

saugen <sog o saugte, gesogen o gesaugt> ['zau·gn̩] vt, vi to suck (**an** +dat on)

säugen ['zɔy·gn̩] vt ■ **sein Junges** ~ to suckle its young

Säugetier nt mammal

Säugling <-s, -e> ['zɔyk·lɪŋ] m baby

Säule <-, -n> ['zɔy·lə] f ➊ ARCHIT column ➋ (a. fig: Stütze) pillar

Saum <-[e]s, Säume> [zaum] m hem

Sauna <-, -s> ['zau·na] f sauna

Säure <-, -n> ['zɔy·rə] f ➊ CHEM acid ➋ (saure Beschaffenheit) acidity, sourness

Saurier <-s, -> ['zau·ri̯ɐ] m dinosaur

sausen ['zau·zn̩] vi sein (sich schnell bewegen) to dash [off]; (schnell fahren) to roar ▶WENDUNGEN: **etw** ~ **lassen** to forget sth; **lass deine Verabredung doch** ~ forget about your date

Saustall m (fam) pigsty

Sauwetter nt (fam) lousy weather no indef art

Savanne <-, -n> [za·'va·nə] f savanna[h]

Saxofon[RR], **Saxophon** <-[e]s, -e> [zak·so·'fo:n] nt saxophone

SB [ɛs·'be:] Abk von **Selbstbedienung** self-service

S-Bahn [ɛs-] f rapid transit train

Schabe <-, -n> ['ʃa·bə] f [cock]roach

schaben ['ʃa·bn̩] vt to scrape

schäbig ['ʃɛ:·bɪç] adj ➊ (unansehnlich) shabby ➋ (gemein) mean ➌ (dürftig) paltry

Schablone <-, -n> [ʃa·'blo:·nə] f stencil

Schach <-s> [ʃax] nt kein pl ➊ (Spiel) chess; **eine Partie** ~ a game of chess ➋ (Stellung) check; ~ **und matt!** checkmate!

Schachbrett nt chessboard

Schachfigur f chess piece

schachmatt [ʃax·'mat] adj checkmate

Schacht <-[e]s, Schächte> [ʃaxt] m ➊ BERGB shaft ➋ eines Brunnens well

Schachtel <-, -n> ['ʃaxtl̩] f box; **eine** ~ **Zigaretten** a pack of cigarettes

Schachzug m move

schade ['ʃa·də] adj pred ➊ (bedauerlich) **wie** ~! that's too bad, what a

shame; **ich finde es** ~, **dass ...** it's too bad that ...; **es ist** ~ **um ihn** it's a shame about him ➋ (zu gut) ■**für etw** akk **zu** ~ **sein** to be too good for sth

Schädel <-s, -> ['ʃɛ:·dl̩] m skull ▶WENDUNGEN: **jdm brummt der** ~ (fam) sb's head is throbbing; **einen dicken** ~ **haben** (fam) to have a hangover

schaden ['ʃa·dn̩] vi ■**jdm** ~ to [do] harm [to] sb; ■**etw** dat ~ to damage sth

Schaden <-s, Schäden> ['ʃa:·dn̩] m damage (**durch** +akk caused by)

Schadenfreude f schadenfreude

schadenfroh I. adj malicious, gloating; ■~ **sein** to delight in others' misfortunes **II.** adv ~ **grinsen** to grin maliciously

schädigen ['ʃɛ:·dɪgn̩] vt to harm (**durch** +akk with)

schädlich ['ʃɛ:t·lɪç] adj harmful

Schädling <-s, -e> ['ʃɛ:t·lɪŋ] m pest

Schädlingsbekämpfungsmittel nt pesticide

Schadstoff m harmful substance; (in der Umwelt) pollutant

schadstoffarm adj Motor low-emission

Schadstoffbelastung f pollution

Schaf <-[e]s, -e> [ʃa:f] nt sheep

Schafbock m ram

Schäfer(in) <-s, -> ['ʃɛ:·fɐ] m(f) shepherd masc, shepherdess fem

Schäferhund m German shepherd

Schaffell nt sheepskin

schaffen¹ <schaffte, geschafft> ['ʃafn̩] vt ➊ (bewältigen) to manage; **Examen** ~ to pass; **es ist geschafft** it's done; ■**es** ~, **etw zu tun** to manage to do sth; **Ordnung** ~ to tidy things up ➋ (gelangen) **wir müssen es bis zur Grenze** ~ we have to get to the border

schaffen² <schuf, geschaffen> ['ʃafn̩] vt (herstellen) to create; **dafür bist du wie ge~** that's right up your alley fam

schaffen³ <schaffte, geschafft> ['ʃafn̩] vi ➊ SÜDD, ÖSTERR, SCHWEIZ (arbeiten) to work ➋ bes SÜDD, ÖSTERR, SCHWEIZ (tun) **nichts mit jdm/etw zu** ~ **haben** to have nothing to do with sb/sth ▶WEN-

S

DUNGEN: **jdm zu ~ machen** to give sb a hard time, to cause sb trouble

Schaffner(in) <-s, -> ['ʃaf·nɐ] *m(f)* conductor

Schafherde *f* flock of sheep

Schafott <-[e]s, -e> [ʃa·'fɔt] *nt* scaffold

Schafskäse *m* sheep's milk cheese; (*Feta*) feta

Schakal <-s, -e> [ʃa·'kaːl] *m* jackal

Schal <-s, -s> [ʃaːl] *m* scarf

Schale¹ <-, -n> ['ʃa·lə] *f* ❶ (*Nussschale*) shell ❷ (*Fruchtschale*) skin; (*abgeschält*) peel ▸WENDUNGEN: **eine raue ~ haben** to be a rough diamond

Schale² <-, -n> ['ʃa·lə] *f* bowl

schälen ['ʃɛː·lən] *vt, vr* ■**sich** *akk* ~ to peel

Schall <-s, -e> [ʃal] *m* sound

Schalldämpfer <-s, -> *m einer Schusswaffe* silencer; *eines Auspuffs* muffler

schalldicht *adj* soundproof

schallen ['ʃalən] *vi* to resound

Schallgeschwindigkeit *f kein pl* PHYS speed of sound

Schallplatte *f* record

Schallwelle *f* sound wave

schalten ['ʃaltn̩] I. *vi* ❶ AUTO to change gears, to shift ❷ (*fam: begreifen*) to get it ❸ (*sich einstellen*) **auf Rot ~** to switch to red II. *vt* (*einstellen*) to switch, to turn (**auf** +*akk* to)

Schalter <-s, -> ['ʃaltɐ] *m* ❶ ELEK switch ❷ ADMIN, BAHN counter

Schaltjahr *nt* leap year

Schaltknüppel *m* gearshift

Schaltung <-, -en> *f* ❶ AUTO gearshift ❷ ELEK circuit

Scham <-> [ʃaːm] *f kein pl* ❶ (*Beschämung*) shame ❷ (*Verlegenheit*) embarrassment

Schambein *nt* pubic bone

schämen ['ʃɛː·mən] *vr* ■**sich** *akk* ~ to be ashamed (**wegen** +*dat* of); ■**sich** *akk* **vor jdm** to be embarrassed in front of sb; **schäm dich!** shame on you!

Schamhaar *nt* pubic hair

schamhaft *adj* shy, bashful

Schamlippen *pl* labia *pl*

schamlos *adj* shameless, rude

Schande <-> ['ʃan·də] *f kein pl* disgrace, shame

schänden ['ʃɛn·dn̩] *vt Denkmal, Grab* to desecrate

Schanze <-, -n> ['ʃan·tsə] *f* ski jump

Schar <-, -en> [ʃaːɐ] *f von Vögeln* flock; *von Menschen* crowd

scharen ['ʃaː·rən] I. *vt Dinge/Menschen* **um sich** ~ to gather things/people around oneself II. *vr* ■**sich** *akk* **um jdn/etw** ~ to gather around sb/sth

scharenweise *adv* in hordes

scharf <schärfer, schärfste> [ʃarf] I. *adj* ❶ (*gut geschliffen*) sharp ❷ (*spitz zulaufend*) sharp; **eine ~e Kurve** a hairpin turn ❸ KOCHK spicy; (*hochprozentig*) strong ❹ (*ätzend*) Reinigungsmittel aggressive ❺ (*schonungslos, heftig*) harsh, severe, tough; *Kontrolle* rigorous; *Konkurrenz* fierce ❻ *Bombe* live ❼ (*konzentriert, präzise*) careful; *Beobachtung* astute ❽ *Foto, Umrisse* sharp; *Augen* keen ❾ (*fam: aufreizend*) spicy; ■**auf jdn ~ sein** to have the hots for sb; ■**auf etw** *akk* **~ sein** to be really interested in sth ❿ (*fam: toll*) fantastic, great II. *adv* ❶ (*intensiv gewürzt*) **etw ~ würzen** to highly season sth; **ich esse gerne ~** I like [eating] spicy food ❷ (*heftig*) sharply; *kritisieren* harshly; *verurteilen* strongly ❸ (*präzise*) **~ beobachten** to observe carefully ❹ (*abrupt*) abruptly; **~ bremsen** to slam on the brakes; **~ links/rechts abbiegen** to take a sharp left/right

Schärfe <-, -n> ['ʃɛr·fə] *f* ❶ *von Messer, Degen* sharpness ❷ (*Heftigkeit*) severity; *von Kritik* sharpness; *von Worten* harshness; *der Augen* keenness ❸ *von Foto, Bild* sharpness; *einer Brille* strength

schärfen ['ʃɛr·fn̩] *vt* to sharpen

scharfmachen *vt* (*fam: sexuell reizen*) ■**jdn** ~ to turn sb on

Scharfschütze, -schützin *m, f* marksman *masc*, markswoman *fem*

Scharfsinn *m kein pl* astuteness

scharfsinnig I. *adj* astute, perceptive II. *adv* astutely, perceptively

Scharlach <-s> ['ʃar·lax] *m kein pl* MED scarlet fever

Scharlatan <-s, -e> ['ʃar·la·tan] *m* (*Betrüger*) fraud

Scharnier <-s, -e> [ʃar·'niːɐ] *nt* hinge

Schaschlik <-s, -s> ['ʃaʃ·lɪk] *nt* shish kebab

Schatten <-s, -> ['ʃa·tn̩] *m* ① (*schattige Stelle*) shade; **30°C im ~** 30°C in the shade ② (*schemenhafte Gestalt, Umriss*) shadow; **einen ~** [**auf etw** *akk*] **werfen** to cast a shadow [over sth] ▶WENDUNGEN: **in jds ~ stehen** to be overshadowed by sb; **jdn/etw in den ~ stellen** to outshine sb/sth

Schattenseite *f* dark side

schattig ['ʃatɪç] *adj* shady

Schatz <-es, Schätze> [ʃats] *m* ① (*kostbare Dinge*) treasure ② (*fam: Liebling*) sweetheart

schätzen ['ʃɛtsn̩] I. *vt* ① (*einschätzen*) to guess; **meistens werde ich jünger geschätzt** people usually think I'm younger than I am; **grob geschätzt** roughly ② (*wertmäßig einschätzen*) to assess (**auf** +*akk* at) ③ (*würdigen*) to value (**als** +*akk* as); ▪ **jdn ~** to hold sb in high esteem; ▪ **etw ~** to appreciate sth II. *vi* to guess

Schätzung <-, -en> *f* ① *kein pl* (*wertmäßiges Einschätzen*) valuation ② (*Anschlag*) estimate

schätzungsweise *adv* approximately

Schau <-, -en> [ʃau] *f* show; **etw zur ~ stellen** to display sth

Schaubild *nt* diagram

Schauder <-s, -> ['ʃau·dɐ] *m* shudder

schauderhaft *adj s.* **schauerlich**

schaudern ['ʃau·dɐn] I. *vt impers* **es schaudert mich bei dem Gedanken** the thought alone makes me shudder II. *vi* (*erschauern*) to shudder; **vor Kälte** to shiver

schauen ['ʃau·ən] *vi* SÜDD, ÖSTERR, SCHWEIZ ① (*blicken*) to look (**auf** +*akk* at) ② (*darauf achten*) ▪ **auf etw** *akk* ~ to pay attention to sth ③ (*sich kümmern*) ▪ **nach jdm/etw** ~ to look after sb/sth ④ (*suchen*) ▪ [**nach etw** *dat*] ~

to look [for sth] ▶WENDUNGEN: **da schaust du aber!** (*fam*) how about that!

Schauer <-s, -> ['ʃau·ɐ] *m* ① (*Regenschauer*) shower ② *s.* **Schauder**

schauerlich *adj* (*grässlich*) ghastly, horrific; (*furchtbar*) awful

Schaufel <-, -n> ['ʃau·fl̩] *f* shovel; (*für Mehl o. Ä.*) scoop; (*für Kehricht*) dustpan

schaufeln ['ʃau·fl̩n] *vt, vi* to shovel, to dig

Schaufenster *nt* store window

Schaufensterpuppe *f* mannequin

Schaukel <-, -n> ['ʃau·kl̩] *f* swing

schaukeln ['ʃau·kl̩n] I. *vi* to swing; (*auf und ab wippen*) to rock II. *vt* to swing; *Baby* to rock

Schaukelpferd *nt* rocking horse

Schaukelstuhl *m* rocking chair

Schaum <-s, Schäume> [ʃaum] *m* foam; (*auf einer Flüssigkeit*) froth; (*Seifenschaum*) lather

Schaumbad *nt* bubble bath

schäumen ['ʃɔy·mən] *vi* to foam; *Flüssigkeit* to froth; *Seife* to lather

Schaumgummi *m* foam rubber

schaumig ['ʃau·mɪç] *adj* frothy

Schaumwein *m* sparkling wine

Schauplatz *m* scene

schaurig ['ʃau·rɪç] *adj* ① (*unheimlich*) eerie ② (*gruselig*) macabre, scary

Schauspiel ['ʃau·ʃpiːl] *nt* ① THEAT play, drama *no indef art* ② (*Anblick*) spectacle

Schauspieler(in) ['ʃau·ʃpiː·lɐ] *m(f)* actor *masc*, actress *fem*

Schauspielhaus *nt* theater, playhouse

Schauspielschule *f* drama school

Scheck <-s, -s> [ʃɛk] *m* check (**über** +*akk* for)

Scheckkarte *f* debit card

Scheibe <-, -n> ['ʃai·bə] *f* ① (*dünnes Glasstück*) [piece of] glass; (*Fensterscheibe*) window [pane] ② KOCHK slice ③ (*kreisförmiger Gegenstand*) disk

Scheibenwischer <-s, -> *m* windshield wiper

Scheich <-s, -e> [ʃaiç] *m* sheikh

S

Scheide <-, -n> ['ʃai·də] f ❶ (*Schwert-/ Dolchscheide*) scabbard ❷ (*Vagina*) vagina

scheiden <schied, geschieden> ['ʃai·dn̩] I. *vt haben* to divorce; **die Ehe wurde 2002 geschieden** the marriage was dissolved in 2002; ▪ **sich** *akk* ~ **lassen** to get divorced (**von** +*dat* from) II. *vi sein* **aus einem Amt** ~ to retire from a position

Scheidung <-, -en> f divorce; **die** ~ **einreichen** to start divorce proceedings

Schein <-[e]s, -e> [ʃain] m ❶ *kein pl* (*Lichtschein*) light ❷ *kein pl* (*Anschein*) appearance; **den** ~ **wahren** to keep up appearances ❸ (*Banknote*) bill, banknote ❹ (*fam: Bescheinigung*) certificate ❺ UNIV certificate (*after successfully completing a seminar*)

scheinbar *adj* apparent, seeming

scheinen <schien, geschienen> ['ʃai·nən] *vi* ❶ (*leuchten*) to shine ❷ (*den Anschein haben*) to appear, to seem

Scheinfirma f bogus company

scheinheilig ['ʃain·hai·lɪç] I. *adj* hypocritical; ~ **tun** to play the innocent II. *adv* hypocritically

Scheinwerfer m ❶ (*Strahler*) spotlight ❷ AUTO headlight

Scheinwerferlicht *nt* spotlight ▶WEN-DUNGEN: **im** ~ **stehen** to be in the public eye

Scheiß <-> [ʃais] m *kein pl* (*vulg: Quatsch*) crap; **he, was soll der** ~**!** hey, what [the hell] are you doing?; **lass doch den** ~ quit screwing around!; **mach keinen** ~**!** don't fuck around!; *vulg;* **so ein** ~**!** shit! *vulg*

Scheiße <-> ['ʃai·sə] f *kein pl* ❶ (*vulg: Darminhalt*) shit ❷ (*vulg: Mist*) ~**!** shit! *vulg* ▶WENDUNGEN: **in der** ~ **sitzen** (*vulg*) to be in deep shit *vulg*

scheißen <schiss, geschissen> ['ʃai·sn̩] *vi* ❶ (*derb*) to shit ❷ (*vulg: verzichten können*) to shit (**auf** +*akk* about)

Scheitel <-s, -> ['ʃai·tl̩] m part

scheitern ['ʃai·tɐn] *vi sein* to fail (**an** +*dat* because of)

Schellfisch m haddock

schelmisch *adj* mischievous

schelten <schilt, schalt, gescholten> ['ʃɛl·tn̩] *vt* to scold

Schema <-s, -ta> ['ʃe·ma] *nt* ❶ (*Muster*) pattern ❷ (*Diagramm*) diagram

schematisch [ʃe·'ma:·tɪʃ] I. *adj* schematic II. *adv* schematically; **etw** ~ **darstellen** to show sth with a chart

Schemel <-s, -> ['ʃe:·ml̩] m stool

Schenkel <-s, -> ['ʃɛŋ·kl̩] m thigh

schenken ['ʃɛŋ·kn̩] I. *vt* to give; ▪ **jdm etw** ~ to give sb sth [as a present]; **jdm Aufmerksamkeit** ~ to pay attention to sb; **jdm Vertrauen** ~ to trust sb II. *vi* to give presents III. *vr* (*sich sparen*) ▪ **sich** *dat* **etw** ~ to spare oneself sth

Scherbe <-, -n> ['ʃɛr·bə] f [sharp] piece; **von Glas** piece of glass

Schere <-, -n> ['ʃe:·rə] f (*Werkzeug*) scissors *npl*

scheren[1] <schor, geschoren> ['ʃe:·rən] *vt* **Fell** to shear; **Bart** to crop; **Hecke** to prune

scheren[2] ['ʃe:·rən] *vr* (*fam: sich kümmern*) ▪ **sich** *akk* **um etw** *akk* ~ to care about sth

Scherz <-es, -e> [ʃɛrts] m joke

scherzen ['ʃɛr·tsn̩] *vi* (*geh*) to crack a joke/jokes; **mit ihm ist nicht zu** ~ you shouldn't joke around with him

scherzhaft I. *adj* jocular II. *adv* jokingly

scheu [ʃɔy] *adj* shy

Scheu <-> [ʃɔy] f *kein pl* shyness

scheuchen ['ʃɔy·çn̩] *vt* (*treiben*) to shoo; **Tiere** to drive

scheuen ['ʃɔy·ən] I. *vt* **Auseinandersetzungen** ~ to avoid conflict II. *vi* **Pferd** to shy (**vor** +*dat* at)

scheuern ['ʃɔy·ɐn] I. *vt* to scour ▶WEN-DUNGEN: **jdm eine** ~ (*fam*) to hit somebody II. *vi* to rub, to chafe

Scheune <-, -n> ['ʃɔy·nə] f barn

scheußlich ['ʃɔys·lɪç] I. *adj* ❶ (*ekelhaft*) disgusting, revolting ❷ (*fam: schlimm*) awful II. *adv* ❶ (*widerlich*) in a disgusting manner ❷ (*fam: schlimm*) terribly

Schicht <-, -en> [ʃɪçt] f ❶ (*Lage*) layer; **Farbe** coat ❷ (*Gesellschaftsschicht*)

class ❸ (*Arbeitsschicht*) shift; ~ **arbeiten** to do shift work

Schichtarbeiter(in) *m(f)* shift worker

schichten ['ʃɪç·tn̩] *vt* to stack [up *sep*], to layer (**auf** +*akk* on/on top of)

Schichtwechsel [-vɛksl] *m* shift change

schick [ʃɪk] **I.** *adj* chic **II.** *adv* fashionably

schicken ['ʃɪkn̩] **I.** *vt* to send; **etw mit der Post ~** to send sth by mail **II.** *vi* ■ **nach jdm ~** to send for sb **III.** *vr* ■ **etw schickt sich** *akk* **nicht [für jdn]** sth is not suitable [for sb]

Schicksal [-s, -e] ['ʃɪk·za:l] *nt* fate

Schicksalsschlag *m* stroke of fate

Schiebedach *nt* sunroof

schieben <schob, geschoben> ['ʃi·bn̩] *vt* ❶ (*vorwärtsbewegen*) to push ❷ (*stecken*) to put, to stick; **die Pizza in den Ofen ~** to stick the pizza in the oven ❸ (*zuweisen*) ■ **etw auf jdn/ etw ~** to blame sb/sth for sth; **die Schuld auf jdn ~** to lay the blame on sb ❹ (*abweisen*) ■ **etw von sich** *dat* **~** to reject sth

Schiebetür *f* sliding door

Schiebung <-> *f kein pl* ❶ (*Begünstigung*) string-pulling ❷ SPORT fix

Schiedsgericht *nt* arbitration court

Schiedsrichter(in) *m(f)* SPORT referee; (*bei Tennis, Baseball*) umpire

schief [ʃi:f] **I.** *adj* crooked, not straight *pred* **II.** *adv* askew; **das Bild hängt ~** that picture isn't hanging straight ▶WEN-DUNGEN: **jdn ~ ansehen** to look at sb suspiciously

schief|gehen *vi irreg sein* (*fam*) to go wrong

schief|liegen *vi irreg* (*fam*) to miss the mark

schielen ['ʃi:·lən] *vi* ❶ MED to squint, to be cross-eyed ❷ (*haben wollen*) ■ **nach etw** *dat* **~** to steal a glance at sth

Schienbein ['ʃi:n·baɪn] *nt* shin, tibia

Schiene <-, -n> ['ʃi:·nə] *f* ❶ (*Führungsschiene*) rail *usu pl* ❷ MED splint

Schießbude *f* shooting gallery

schießen <schoss, geschossen> ['ʃi:·sn̩] *vt, vi* ❶ *haben* (*feuern*) to shoot (**auf** +*akk* at) ❷ *haben* FBALL to shoot;

ein Tor ~ to score [a goal] ❸ *sein* (*schnell bewegen*) **das Auto kam um die Ecke geschossen** the car came flying around the corner; **jdm durch den Kopf ~** to flash through sb's mind

Schießerei <-, -en> [ʃi:·sə·'raɪ] *f* shooting

Schießpulver *nt* gunpowder

Schiff <-[e]s, -e> [ʃɪf] *nt* ship

SchiffahrtALT *f s.* **Schifffahrt**

Schiffbau *m kein pl* shipbuilding

Schiffbruch *m* shipwreck; **~ erleiden** to be shipwrecked

SchifffahrtRR ['ʃɪf·fa:ɐ̯t] *f* shipping

Schikane <-, -n> [ʃi·'ka:·nə] *f* harassment *no indef art*

schikanieren* [ʃi·ka·'ni:·rən] *vt* to harass

Schild¹ <-[e]s, -er> [ʃɪlt] *nt* (*Hinweisschild*) sign

Schild² <-[e]s, -e> [ʃɪlt] *m* shield ▶WEN-DUNGEN: **etw im ~e führen** to be up to sth

Schilddrüse *f* thyroid [gland]

schildern ['ʃɪl·dɐn] *vt* to describe

Schilderung <-, -en> *f* description; *von Ereignissen a.* account

Schildkröte ['ʃɪlt·krø:·tə] *f* tortoise; (*Seeschildkröte*) turtle

Schilf <-[e]s, -e> [ʃɪlf] *nt* reeds *pl*

schillernd *adj* shimmering; *Persönlichkeit* flamboyant

Schimmel¹ <-s> ['ʃɪml] *m kein pl* mold

Schimmel² <-s, -> ['ʃɪml] *m* (*Tier*) white horse

schimmelig ['ʃɪmə·lɪç] *adj* moldy; *Leder, Buch* mildewed

schimmeln ['ʃɪmln̩] *vi sein o haben* to get moldy

Schimmer <-s> ['ʃɪmɐ] *m kein pl* shimmer; **ein ~ von Hoffnung** a glimmer of hope ▶WENDUNGEN: **keinen blassen ~ [von etw** *dat***] haben** (*fam*) to not have the faintest idea [about sth]

schimmern ['ʃɪmɐn] *vi* to shimmer

Schimpanse <-n, -n> [ʃɪm·'pan·zə] *m* chimpanzee

schimpfen ['ʃɪm·pfn̩] *vi* ❶ (*sich ärgerlich äußern*) to grumble (**über/auf**

S

+*akk* about) ❷(*fluchen*) to swear ❸(*zurechtweisen*) ■**mit jdm** ~ to scold sb, to tell sb off

Schimpfwort *nt* swear word

schinden <schindet, geschunden> ['ʃɪn·dn̩] *vr* ■**sich** *akk* ~ to slave [away]

Schinken <-s, -> ['ʃɪŋ·kn̩] *m* ham

Schirm <-[e]s, -e> ['ʃɪrm] *m* (*Regenschirm*) umbrella; (*Sonnenschirm*) sunshade; (*tragbar*) parasol

schiss^RR, **schiß**^ALT ['ʃɪs] *imp von* **scheißen**

Schiss^RR <-es>, **Schiß**^ALT <-sses> ['ʃɪs] *m kein pl* ~ [**vor jdm/etw**] **haben** (*sl*) to be scared shitless [of sb/sth]

schizophren [ʃi·tso·ˈfreːn] *adj* schizophrenic

Schizophrenie <-, *selten* -n> [ʃi·tso·fre·ˈniː] *f* schizophrenia

Schlacht <-, -en> [ʃlaxt] *f* battle

schlachten ['ʃlax·tn̩] *vt*, *vi* to slaughter

Schlachter(in) <-s, -> *m(f)* DIAL *s.* **Fleischer**

Schlachtfeld *nt* battlefield

Schlachtfest *nt* KOCHK slaughter festival (*celebration and feast following the slaughtering of a farm animal*)

Schlachthof *m* slaughterhouse

Schlaf <-[e]s> [ʃlaːf] *m kein pl* sleep; **einen festen/leichten** ~ **haben** to be a deep [*or* sound]/light sleeper; **jdn den** ~ **rauben** to keep sb awake ►WENDUNGEN: **nicht im** ~ **an etw** *akk* **denken** to not dream of [doing] sth; **etw im** ~ **können** (*fam*) to be able to do sth in one's sleep

Schlafanzug *m* pajamas *npl*

Schläfe <-, -n> ['ʃlɛː·fə] *f* temple

schlafen <schlief, geschlafen> ['ʃlaː·fn̩] *vi* to sleep; **er schläft noch** he is still asleep; ~ **gehen** to go to bed

schlaff [ʃlaf] I. *adj* ❶(*locker fallend*) slack ❷(*nicht straff*) sagging; **Händedruck** limp II. *adv* ❶(*locker fallend*) slackly ❷(*kraftlos*) feebly

Schlafgelegenheit *f* place to sleep

Schlaflosigkeit <-> *f kein pl* insomnia

Schlafmittel *nt* sleeping pill

schläfrig ['ʃlɛː·f·rɪç] *adj* sleepy, drowsy

Schlafsaal *m* dormitory

Schlafsack *m* sleeping bag

Schlaftablette *f* sleeping pill

Schlafwagen *m* sleeper

Schlafwandler(in) <-s, -> *m(f)* sleepwalker

Schlafzimmer *nt* bedroom

Schlag <-[e]s, Schläge> [ʃlaːk] *m* ❶(*Hieb*) blow, wallop *fam*; (*mit der Faust*) punch; (*mit der Hand*) slap; SPORT stroke, hit; (*Baseball*) hit; **Schläge bekommen** to get beaten up ❷(*rhythmisches Geräusch*) **die Schläge des Herzens** the heartbeats ❸(*Schicksalsschlag*) blow ❹ÖSTERR (*Schlagsahne*) whipped cream ❺(*Stromstoß*) shock; **einen** ~ **kriegen** to get an electric shock ❻(*Schlaganfall*) stroke; **einen** ~ **bekommen** to suffer a stroke ❼MODE **eine Hose mit** ~ flared pants ►WENDUNGEN: ~ **auf** ~ in rapid succession; **jdn trifft der** ~ (*fam*) sb is flabbergasted [*or* shocked]; **etw auf einen** ~ **tun** to get things done all at once

Schlagader *f* artery

Schlaganfall *m* stroke

schlagen <schlug, geschlagen> ['ʃlaː·gn̩] I. *vt haben* ❶(*hauen*) to hit; (*mit der Faust*) to punch; (*mit der Hand*) to slap; **einen Nagel in die Wand** ~ to hammer a nail into the wall ❷(*prügeln*) to beat; **jdn bewusstlos** ~ to beat sb senseless ❸(*besiegen*) to defeat; SPORT to beat (**in** +*dat* at) ❹ *Sahne* to whip; **Eier in die Pfanne** ~ to crack eggs into the [frying] pan ❺(*legen*) **ein Bein über das andere** ~ to cross one's legs; **die Decke zur Seite** ~ to throw the blanket aside II. *vi* ❶ *haben* (*hauen*) to hit; ■[**mit etw** *dat*] **um sich** *akk* ~ to lash out [with sth] ❷ *sein* (*auftreffen*) to strike (**gegen** +*akk* against) ❸ *haben* (*pochen*) to beat ❹ *haben* (*läuten*) *Uhr* to strike ❺ *sein* (*fam*: *jdm ähneln*) ■**nach jdm** ~ to take after sb III. *vr haben* ■**sich** *akk* ~ to fight (**umm** +*akk* over)

Schlager <-s, -> ['ʃlaː·gɐ] *m* MUS

① (*Lied*) pop song ② (*Erfolg*) [big] hit, great success

Schläger <-s, -> [ˈʃlɛːɡə] *m* SPORT (*beim Tennis*) racket; (*beim Tischtennis*) paddle; (*beim Golf*) golf club

Schlägerei <-, -en> [ʃlɛːɡəˈrai] *f* fight

schlagfertig I. *adj* quick-witted **II.** *adv* quick-wittedly

Schlaginstrument *nt* percussion instrument

Schlagloch *nt* pothole

Schlagsahne *f* (*flüssig*) whipping cream; (*geschlagen*) whipped cream

Schlagzeile *f* headline

Schlagzeug <-[e]s, -e> *nt* drums *pl*; (*im Orchester*) percussion

Schlagzeuger(in) <-s, -> *m(f)* drummer; (*im Orchester*) percussionist

Schlamassel <-s, -> [ʃlaˈmasl̩] *m o nt* mess

Schlamm <-[e]s, -e> [ʃlam] *m* mud; (*breiige Rückstände*) sludge

schlammig [ˈʃlamɪç] *adj* muddy

Schlammlawine *f* GEOG mudslide

Schlampe <-, -n> [ˈʃlampə] *f* slut

schlampig [ˈʃlampɪç] **I.** *adj* ① (*nachlässig*) sloppy; (*liederlich*) slovenly ② (*ungepflegt*) unkempt **II.** *adv* ① (*nachlässig*) sloppily ② (*ungepflegt*) in an unkempt way

Schlange <-, -n> [ˈʃlaŋə] *f* ① ZOOL snake ② (*lange Reihe*) line; **~ stehen** to stand in line

schlängeln [ˈʃlɛŋ·l̩n] *vr* ■ **sich** *akk* **~** (*sich winden*) to crawl; *Fluss, Straße* to meander

schlank [ˈʃlaŋk] *adj* thin, slim; *Handgelenk* slender; **du bist ~ geworden** you have lost weight

Schlankheitskur *f* diet

schlapp [ʃlap] *adj* ① *pred* (*erschöpft*) worn out ② (*ohne Antrieb*) feeble, listless

schlau [ʃlau] *adj* ① (*gescheit*) clever; **ich werde nicht ~ aus der Bedienungsanleitung** I can't make heads or tails of the operating instructions ② (*gerissen*) crafty, wily; *Plan* ingenious

Schlauch <-[e]s, Schläuche> [ʃlaux] *m*

① (*biegsame Leitung*) tube; (*für Wasser*) hose ② (*Reifenschlauch*) [inner] tube

Schlauchboot *nt* rubber boat

schlauchen [ˈʃlauxn̩] *vt, vi* to wear sb out; **das schlaucht ganz schön!** that really takes it out of you!

Schlaufe <-, -n> [ˈʃlaufə] *f* loop; (*aus Leder*) strap

schlecht [ʃlɛçt] **I.** *adj* ① (*nicht gut*) bad; *Augen* weak; *Gehalt, Leistung, Qualität* poor; *Zeiten* hard ② (*moralisch verkommen*) bad, wicked, evil; **ein ~es Gewissen haben** to have a bad conscience ③ (*übel*) **mir ist ~** I feel sick ④ (*verdorben*) bad; **das Fleisch ist ~ geworden** the meat has spoiled ▶ WENDUNGEN: **es sieht ~ aus** things don't look good **II.** *adv* ① (*nicht gut*) badly, poorly; **so ~ habe ich selten gegessen** I've rarely had such bad food; **die Geschäfte gehen ~** business is bad; **~ gelaunt** in a bad mood *pred*; (*dauernd*) bad-tempered ② MED **jdm geht es ~** sb doesn't feel good; **~ hören** to be hard of hearing; **~ sehen** to have poor eyesight

schlecht|machen *vt* ■ **jdn ~** to badmouth sb

schleichen <schlich, geschlichen> [ˈʃlai·çn̩] **I.** *vi sein* ① (*leise gehen*) to creep, to sneak ② (*langsam gehen/fahren*) to crawl along **II.** *vr haben* ■ **sich** *akk* **in das Zimmer ~** to sneak into the room; **sich** *akk* **aus dem Haus ~** to steal away softly

Schleier <-s, -> [ˈʃlaiɐ] *m* veil

schleierhaft *adj* ■ **~ sein** to be a mystery

Schleife <-, -n> [ˈʃlaifə] *f* ① MODE bow ② *Straße* loop

schleifen¹ [ˈʃlaifn̩] **I.** *vt haben* (*ziehen*) to drag **II.** *vi* ① *haben* (*reiben*) to rub (**an** +*dat* against) ② *sein o haben* (*gleiten*) to slide; *Schleppe* to trail

schleifen² <schliff, geschliffen> [ˈʃlaifn̩] *vt* ① (*schärfen*) to sharpen ② (*in Form polieren*) to polish; (*mit Sandpapier*) to sand; *Edelsteine* to cut

S

Schleifmaschine f sander
Schleim <-[e]s, -e> [ʃlaim] m ❶ MED mucus; (in Bronchien) phlegm ❷ (klebrige Masse) slime
Schleimhaut f mucous membrane
schleimig ['ʃlai·mɪç] I. adj ❶ MED mucous ❷ (glitschig) slimy ❸ (pej: unterwürfig) slimy, obsequious II. adv (pej) in a slimy way, obsequiously
schlemmen ['ʃlɛ·mən] vi to have a feast
schlendern ['ʃlɛn·dən] vi sein to stroll along
schlenkern ['ʃlɛŋ·ken] vi to dangle
Schleppe <-, -n> ['ʃlɛ·pə] f MODE train
schleppen ['ʃlɛ·pn̩] I. vt ❶ (tragen) to carry, to lug fam ❷ (zerren) to drag ❸ (abschleppen) to tow II. vr ■ sich akk ~ to drag oneself; Verhandlungen to drag on
schleppend I. adj ❶ (zögerlich) slow ❷ (schwerfällig) shuffling II. adv ❶ (zögerlich) slowly; ~ in Gang kommen to be slow in getting started ❷ (schwerfällig) ~ gehen to shuffle along
Schleppkahn m barge
Schlepplift m ski tow
schleudern ['ʃlɔy·den] I. vt haben ❶ (werfen) to hurl ❷ Wäsche to spin II. vi sein to skid; **ins S~ geraten** to go into a skid; (fig) to be losing control of a situation
schleunigst adv right away, at once
Schleuse <-, -n> ['ʃlɔy·zə] f lock; (Tor) sluice [gate]
schlicht [ʃlɪçt] I. adj ❶ (einfach) simple, plain ❷ (wenig gebildet) simple, unsophisticated ❸ attr (bloß) plain II. part (ganz einfach) simply
schließen <schloss, geschlossen> ['ʃliː·sn̩] I. vi ❶ (zugehen, zumachen) to close ❷ (schlussfolgern) to conclude; **etw lässt auf etw** akk ~ sth indicates sth II. vt ❶ (zumachen) to close; Lücke to fill ❷ (eingehen) Frieden, einen Pakt to make; **Freundschaft** ~ to become friends; **einen Kompromiss** ~ to reach a compromise ❸ (schlussfolgern) to conclude (aus +dat from) ❹ (umfas-

sen) jdn in die Arme ~ to take sb in one's arms
Schließfach nt (Gepäckschließfach) locker; (Bankschließfach) safe-deposit box; (Postfach) post office box
schließlich ['ʃliːs·lɪç] adv ❶ (endlich) at last, finally ❷ (immerhin) after all
schlimm [ʃlɪm] I. adj ❶ (übel) bad, terrible; ■**etwas S~es/S~eres** sth terrible/worse; **das ist nicht so** ~ that's not so bad ❷ (ernst) serious ❸ (moralisch schlecht) bad; Verbrechen serious ▶WENDUNGEN: **das ist halb so** ~ it's not as bad as all that; **ist nicht** ~! no problem!, don't worry [about it]! II. adv ❶ (gravierend) seriously ❷ (äußerst schlecht) dreadfully; **es hätte** ~**er kommen können** it could have been worse; ~ **dran sein** (fam) to be hard up; **umso** ~**er** so much the worse
schlimmstenfalls ['ʃlɪm·stn̩·'fals] adv if worst comes to worst
Schlinge <-, -n> ['ʃlɪŋə] f (Schlaufe) loop; (um jdn aufzuhängen) noose
schlingen¹ <schlang, geschlungen> ['ʃlɪŋən] I. vt to wind (um +akk around); **die Arme um jdn** ~ to wrap one's arms around sb II. vr ■**sich** akk **um etw** akk ~ to wind itself around sth
schlingen² <schlang, geschlungen> ['ʃlɪŋən] vi (fam) to gobble one's food
Schlingpflanze f creeper
Schlips <-es, -e> [ʃlɪps] m tie
Schlitten <-s, -> ['ʃlɪ·tn̩] m ❶ (Rodel) sledge, sled; (Rodelschlitten) toboggan; (mit Pferden) sleigh ❷ (sl: Auto) wheels pl
Schlittschuh ['ʃlɪt·ʃuː] m [ice] skate; ~ **laufen** to [ice-]skate
Schlittschuhbahn f ice rink
Schlittschuhläufer(in) m(f) [ice] skater
Schlitz <-es, -e> [ʃlɪts] m ❶ (Einsteckschlitz) slot ❷ (schmale Öffnung) slit
Schlitzohr nt rogue
schlossᴿᴿ, **schloß**ᴬᴸᵀ [ʃlɔs] imp von **schließen**
Schlossᴿᴿ <-es, Schlösser>, **Schloß**ᴬᴸᵀ <-sses, Schlösser> [ʃlɔs] nt ❶ (Palast) castle, palace ❷ (Türschloss)

S

lock; **ins ~ fallen** to snap shut ③ (*Verschluss*) catch ▶WENDUNGEN: **jdn hinter ~ und <u>Riegel</u> bringen** to put sb behind bars

Schlosser(in) <-s, -> [ˈʃlɔsɐ] *m(f)* locksmith

Schlosserei <-, -en> [ʃlɔsəˈrai] *f* locksmith's store

Schlucht <-, -en> [ʃlʊxt] *f* gorge

schluchzen [ˈʃlʊxtsn̩] *vi* to sob

Schluck <-[e]s, -e> [ʃlʊk] *m* mouthful; (*größer*) gulp; (*kleiner*) sip

Schluckauf <-s> [ˈʃlʊkˌʔauf] *m kein pl* hiccup

schlucken [ˈʃlʊkn̩] *vt, vi* (*a. fig*) to swallow; *Auto* to guzzle

Schluckimpfung *f* oral vaccination

schlummern [ˈʃlʊˌmɐn] *vi* to slumber

Schlund <-[e]s, Schlünde> [ʃlʊnt] *m* throat

schlüpfen [ˈʃlʏpfn̩] *vi sein* ① ORN, ZOOL to hatch (**aus** +*dat* out [of]) ② (*rasch kleiden*) to slip (**aus** +*dat* out of, **in** +*akk* into)

Schlüpfer <-s, -> [ˈʃlʏpfɐ] *m* panties *npl*

schlürfen [ˈʃlʏrfn̩] *vt, vi* to slurp

SchlussRR <-es, Schlüsse, Schluß**ALT** <Schlusses, Schlüsse> [ʃlʊs] *m* ① *kein pl* (*räumlich, zeitlich*) end; **~ für heute!** that's enough for today!; **~ damit!** stop it!; **~ [jetzt]!** [that's] enough [already]!; **zum ~ kommen** to finish; [**mit etw** *dat*] **~ machen** (*fam*) to stop [sth]; [**mit jdm**] **~ machen** to break up [with sb]; **zum ~** at the end; (*schließlich*) in the end ② (*Folgerung*) conclusion

Schlüssel <-s, -> [ˈʃlʏsl] *m* key

Schlüsselbein *nt* clavicle

Schlüsselloch *nt* keyhole

SchlussfolgerungRR, **Schlußfolgerung**ALT <-, -en> *f* conclusion

SchlussverkaufRR *m* sale

schmächtig [ˈʃmɛçtɪç] *adj* slight

schmackhaft *adj* tasty ▶WENDUNGEN: **jdm etw ~ <u>machen</u>** to make sth tempting for sb

schmal <-er *o* schmäler, -ste *o*

schmälste> [ʃmaːl] *adj* narrow; *Mensch* slim

Schmalz <-es, -e> [ʃmalts] *nt* KOCHK drippings *npl*; (*vom Schwein*) lard

schmalzig [ˈʃmaltsɪç] *adj* (*pej fam*) schmaltzy, corny

Schmarotzer <-s, -> *m* parasite

Schmarren [ˈʃmaˌrən] *m* SÜDD, ÖSTERR ① KOCHK *a warm dessert of sliced crepes and raisins, topped with powdered sugar, often served with apple sauce or plum jam* ② (*fam: Quatsch*) nonsense

schmatzen [ˈʃmatsn̩] *vi* to eat/drink noisily

schmecken [ˈʃmɛkn̩] **I.** *vi* ① (*Geschmack haben*) to taste (**nach** +*dat* of) ② (*munden*) **hat es geschmeckt?** did you enjoy it?; **das schmeckt aber gut** this tastes wonderful; **lass es dir ~!** enjoy your meal! ③ SÜDD, ÖSTERR, SCHWEIZ (*riechen*) smell **II.** *vt* to taste

Schmeichelei <-, -en> [ʃmaiçəˈlai] *f* flattery

schmeichelhaft *adj* flattering

schmeicheln [ˈʃmaiçln̩] *vi* to flatter; ▪**es schmeichelte ihm, dass ...** he was flattered that ...

schmeißen <schmiss, geschmissen> [ˈʃmaisn̩] **I.** *vt, vi* (*fam*) ① (*werfen*) to throw; (*mit Kraft*) to hurl, to fling ② (*sl: spendieren*) *Party* to throw ③ (*sl: managen*) to run ④ (*fam: abbrechen*) to quit **II.** *vr* (*sich fallen lassen*) ▪**sich** *akk* **~** to throw oneself (**auf** +*akk* onto, **vor** +*akk* in front of)

Schmeißfliege *f* blowfly

schmelzen <schmolz, geschmolzen> [ˈʃmɛltsn̩] **I.** *vi sein* to melt **II.** *vt haben* to melt; *Metall* to smelt

Schmelzkäse *m* KOCHK ① (*in Scheiben*) processed cheese ② (*streichfähig*) cheese spread

Schmelzpunkt *m* melting point

Schmerz <-es, -en> [ʃmɛrts] *m* pain; **~en haben** to be in pain

schmerzempfindlich *adj* sensitive to pain *pred*

S

schmerzen ['ʃmɛr·tsn̩] *vi* to hurt; ■**~d** painful, aching

Schmerzensgeld *nt* compensation

schmerzhaft *adj* painful

schmerzlich I. *adj* painful, distressing II. *adv* painfully

schmerzlos *adj* painless ▶WENDUNGEN: **kurz und ~** short and sweet

Schmerzmittel *nt* painkiller; MED analgesic

schmerzstillend *adj* painkilling; ■**~ sein** to be a painkiller

Schmerztablette *f* painkiller

Schmetterling <-s, -e> ['ʃmɛ·tɐ·lɪŋ] *m* butterfly

schmettern ['ʃmɛ·tɐn] *vt* ❶ (*schleudern*) to fling ❷ SPORT to smash ❸ MUS to blare out; *Lied* to bawl out

Schmied(in) <-[e]s, -e> [ʃmiːt] *m(f)* smith

schmiedeeisern *adj* wrought-iron

schmieden ['ʃmiː·dn̩] *vt* ❶ (*glühend hämmern*) to forge ❷ (*ausdecken*) *Plan* to make

schmiegen ['ʃmiː·gn̩] *vr* to snuggle (**an** +*akk* up to); ■**sich** *akk* **[an jdn]** ~ to cuddle up close [to sb]

schmieren ['ʃmiː·rən] I. *vt* ❶ (*streichen*) to spread; *Creme etc.* to rub, to smear ❷ (*fetten*) to lubricate, to grease ❸ (*fam: bestechen*) **jdn ~** to grease sb's palm ▶WENDUNGEN: **jdm eine ~** (*fam*) to whack sb; **wie geschmiert** (*fam*) like clockwork II. *vi* (*pej: unsauber schreiben*) to scribble; *Kuli* ~ to smudge

Schmiergeld *nt* (*fam*) bribe, kickback

schmierig ['ʃmiː·rɪç] *adj* ❶ (*nass und klebrig*) greasy ❷ (*pej: schleimig*) slimy

Schmieröl *nt* lubricating oil

Schmierseife *f* soft soap

Schmierzettel *m* piece of scratch paper

Schminke <-, -n> ['ʃmɪŋ·kə] *f* makeup

schminken ['ʃmɪŋ·kn̩] I. *vt* to put makeup on II. *vr* ■**sich** *akk* ~ to put on makeup

Schmirgelpapier ['ʃmɪrɡl̩-] *nt* sandpaper

schmollen ['ʃmɔ·lən] *vi* to sulk

Schmorbraten ['ʃmoːɐ̯-] *m* pot roast

schmoren ['ʃmoː·rən] *vt, vi* ❶ KOCHK to braise ❷ (*fam: schwitzen*) to swelter ▶WENDUNGEN: **jdn ~ lassen** (*fam*) to let sb stew

Schmuck <-[e]s> [ʃmʊk] *m kein pl* ❶ (*Schmuckstücke*) jewelry ❷ (*Verzierung*) decoration, ornamentation

schmücken ['ʃmʏ·kn̩] I. *vt* (*dekorieren*) to decorate, to embellish II. *vr* ■**sich** *akk* ~ to wear jewelry

schmuddelig ['ʃmʊdə·lɪç] *adj* grubby

Schmuggel <-s> ['ʃmʊɡl̩] *m kein pl* smuggling

schmuggeln ['ʃmʊɡl̩n] *vt* to smuggle

Schmuggelware *f* smuggled goods *pl*, contraband

Schmuggler(in) <-s, -> ['ʃmʊɡ·lɐ] *m(f)* smuggler

schmunzeln ['ʃmʊn·tsl̩n] *vi* to grin quietly to oneself (**über** +*akk* about)

Schmunzeln <-s> ['ʃmʊn·tsl̩n] *nt kein pl* grin

schmusen ['ʃmuː·zn̩] *vi* (*fam*) to cuddle, to neck

Schmutz <-es> [ʃmʊts] *m kein pl* dirt ▶WENDUNGEN: **jdn/etw in den ~ ziehen** to ruin sb's name/sth's reputation

schmutzig ['ʃmʊ·tsɪç] *adj* ❶ (*dreckig*) dirty; **sich** *akk* **[bei etw** *dat*] ~ **machen** to get dirty [doing sth] ❷ (*obszön*) smutty, lewd; *Witz* dirty ❸ (*pej: unlauter*) dubious, crooked; *Geld* dirty; *Geschäfte* shady

Schnabel <-s, Schnäbel> ['ʃna·bl̩] *m* ❶ (*Vogelschnabel*) beak ❷ (*lange Tülle*) spout ❸ (*fam: Mund*) trap; **halt den ~!** shut up!

Schnake <-, -n> ['ʃna·kə] *f* ❶ (*Weberknecht*) daddy longlegs *fam* ❷ DIAL (*Stechmücke*) mosquito

Schnalle <-, -n> ['ʃna·lə] *f* buckle

Schnäppchen <-s, -> ['ʃnɛp·çən] *nt* bargain

Schnäppchenmarkt *m* ÖKON (*fam*) bargain basement

schnappen ['ʃna·pn̩] I. *vi* to grab (**nach** +*dat* for), to snatch (**nach** +*dat* at); (*mit den Zähnen*) to snap (**nach** +*dat* at) **II.** *vt* (*fam*) ❶ (*ergreifen*) ■[**sich** *dat*] **etw ~** to grab sth; **etwas frische Luft ~** to get a breath of fresh air ❷ (*festnehmen*) to catch

SchnappschussRR *m* snapshot

Schnaps <-es, Schnäpse> [ʃnaps] *m* schnapps

schnarchen [ˈʃnar·çn̩] *vi* to snore

schnattern [ˈʃna·tɐn] *vi* ❶ ORN to cackle ❷ (*fam: schwatzen*) to chatter

schnauben <schnaubte, geschnaubt> [ˈʃnau·bn̩] *vi* to snort

schnaufen [ˈʃnau·fn̩] *vi* ❶ (*angestrengt atmen*) to puff, to pant ❷ *bes* SÜDD (*atmen*) to breathe

Schnauzbart *m* walrus mustache

Schnauze <-, -n> [ˈʃnau·tsə] *f* ❶ ZOOL snout ❷ (*sl: Mund*) trap; **eine große ~ haben** to have a big mouth; **die ~ halten** to shut up ▶WENDUNGEN: [**mit etw** *dat*] **auf die ~ fallen** (*sl*) to fall flat on one's face [with sth]; **die ~** [**von etw** *dat*] **voll haben** (*sl*) to be fed up [with sth]

schnäuzenRR [ˈʃnɔy·tsn̩] *vr* ■**sich** *akk* **~** to blow one's nose

Schnecke <-, -n> [ˈʃnɛ·kə] *f* ❶ ZOOL snail; (*Nacktschnecke*) slug ❷ (*Gebäck*) ≈ cinnamon roll with raisins ▶WENDUNGEN: **jdn zur ~ machen** to chew sb out

Schneckenhaus *nt* snail shell

Schneckentempo *nt* **im ~** at a snail's pace

Schnee <-s> [ʃneː] *m kein pl* snow ▶WENDUNGEN: **~ von gestern** [ancient] history

Schneeball *m* snowball

Schneebesen *m* whisk

Schneefall *m* snowfall

Schneeflocke *f* snowflake

Schneeglöckchen <-s, -> *nt* snowdrop

Schneegrenze *f* snow line

Schneekette *f meist pl* snow chain[s *pl*]

Schneemann *m* snowman

Schneematsch *m* slush

Schneepflug *m* snowplow

Schneeregen *m* sleet

Schneeschaufel *f* snow shovel

Schneesturm *m* snowstorm

Schneewittchen <-s> [ʃneː·ˈvɪt·çən] *nt* Snow White

schneiden <schnitt, geschnitten> [ˈʃnai·dn̩] **I.** *vt* ❶ (*zerteilen*) to cut ❷ (*kürzen*) to cut, to trim; **Baum** to prune ❸ (*knapp einscheren*) **Auto** to cut ❹ FILM to edit ❺ (*meiden*) to snub **II.** *vr* **sich** *akk* **in den Finger ~** to cut one's finger

schneidend *adj* ❶ (*durchdringend*) biting ❷ (*scharf*) sharp

Schneider(in) <-s, -> [ˈʃnai·dɐ] *m(f)* tailor ▶WENDUNGEN: **aus dem ~ sein** to be in the clear

Schneidezahn *m* incisor

schneien [ˈʃnai·ən] *vi impers* to snow

Schneise <-, -n> [ˈʃnai·zə] *f* aisle

schnell [ʃnɛl] **I.** *adj* ❶ (*mit hoher Geschwindigkeit*) fast ❷ (*zügig*) prompt, rapid ❸ *attr* (*baldig*) swift, speedy **II.** *adv* ❶ (*mit hoher Geschwindigkeit*) fast ❷ (*zügig*) quickly; **es geht ganz ~** it won't take long; **~ machen** to hurry up

Schnellhefter *m* loose-leaf binder

Schnelligkeit <-, *selten* -en> *f* speed

SchnellimbissRR *m* fast-food stand

Schnellkochtopf *m* pressure cooker

Schnellkurs *m* crash course

schnellstens *adv* as soon as possible

Schnellstraße *f* expressway

Schnellzug *m* fast train

schneuzenALT [ˈʃnɔy·tsn̩] *vr s.* **schnäuzen**

schniefen [ˈʃniː·fn̩] *vi* to sniffle

schnippisch [ˈʃnɪ·pɪʃ] *adj* snippy, snotty

Schnipsel <-s, -> [ˈʃnɪp·sl̩] *m o nt* shred

schnitt [ʃnɪt] *imp von* **schneiden**

Schnitt <-[e]s, -e> [ʃnɪt] *m* cut ▶WENDUNGEN: **im ~** on average

Schnitte <-, -n> [ˈʃnɪ·tə] *f* ❶ KOCHK slice ❷ DIAL (*belegtes Brot*) [open-faced] sandwich

Schnittlauch [ˈʃnɪt·laux] *m kein pl* chives *npl*

Schnittpunkt *m* point of intersection

Schnittstelle *f* COMPUT interface

Schnittwunde *f* cut

S

Schnitzel¹ <-s, -> ['ʃnɪ·ts̩l] *nt* KOCHK veal cutlet; **Wiener ~** Wiener schnitzel

Schnitzel² <-s, -> ['ʃnɪ·ts̩l] *nt o m* shred

schnitzen ['ʃnɪ·tsn̩] *vt, vi* to carve

Schnorchel <-s, -> ['ʃnɔr·çl̩] *m* snorkel

schnorren ['ʃnɔ·rən] *vt, vi* to sponge [*or* mooch]

Schnorrer(in) <-s, -> *m(f)* moocher, scrounger

schnüffeln ['ʃnʏ·fl̩n] *vi* ① (*schnuppern*) to sniff ② (*fam: spionieren*) to nose around

Schnuller <-s, -> ['ʃnʊ·lɐ] *m* pacifier, Binky® *fam*

Schnulze <-, -n> ['ʃnʊl·tsə] *f* corny love song

schnupfen ['ʃnʊpfn̩] I. *vi* to sniff II. *vt Tabak, Kokain* to snort

Schnupfen <-s, -> ['ʃnʊp·fn̩] *m* cold; [einen] **~ haben** to have a cold

schnuppern ['ʃnʊ·pɐn] *vt, vi* to sniff (**an** +*dat* at)

Schnur <-, Schnüre> ['ʃnuːɐ̯] *f* cord

schnüren ['ʃnyː·rən] *vt* to tie up *sep* (**zu** +*dat* into); *Schuhe* to tie

schnurlos *adj* cordless

Schnurrbart ['ʃnʊr·baːɐ̯t] *m* mustache

schnurren ['ʃnʊ·rən] *vi* ① (*Katze*) to purr ② (*surren*) to whir

Schnürsenkel *m* shoelace

Schnürstiefel *m* lace-up boot

Schock <-[e]s, -s> [ʃɔk] *m* shock; **unter ~ stehen** to be in [a state of] shock

schockieren* [ʃɔ·ki·rən] *vt* to shock; ■**schockiert sein** to be shocked (**über** +*akk* about)

Schöffe, Schöffin <-n, -n> ['ʃœfə, 'ʃœ·fɪn] *m, f* juror

Schokolade <-, -n> [ʃo·ko·ˈlaː·də] *f* (*Kakaomasse*) chocolate; (*Kakaogetränk*) hot chocolate

Scholle <-, -n> ['ʃɔ·lə] *f* ① ZOOL plaice ② (*flacher Erdklumpen*) clod [of earth] ③ (*Eisbrocken*) [ice] floe

schon [ʃoːn] I. *adv* ① (*bereits*) already, yet; **sind wir ~ da?** are we there yet?; **du willst ~ gehen?** you want to leave already?; **~ damals** even at that time; **~ lange** for a long time; **~ mal** ever; ~ **oft** several times [already] ② (*allein*) ~ **aus dem Grund** for that reason alone; ~ **die Tatsache, dass ...** the fact alone that ... ③ (*irgendwann*) in the end, one day; **es wird ~ noch klappen** it will [all] work out in the end ④ (*denn*) **was macht das ~?** what does it matter? ⑤ (*irgendwie*) all right; **danke, es geht ~** thanks, I can manage ⑥ (*ja*) **ich sehe ~, ...** I can see, ...; ~ **immer** always; ~ **längst** for ages, ages ago; ~ **wieder** [once] again; **und wenn ~!** so what? II. *part* ① (*auffordernd*) **geh ~!** go on!; **gib ~ her!** come on, give it here!; **mach ~!** hurry up!; [**nun**] **sag ~!** come on, tell me! ② (*nur*) **wenn ich das ~ höre!** I'm sick of hearing that!

schön [ʃøːn] I. *adj* ① (*hübsch*) beautiful; (*ansprechend*) nice ② (*angenehm*) good, great, nice; *Tag* beautiful; **ich wünsche euch ~e Ferien** have a nice vacation; [**das ist ja alles**] ~ **und gut, aber ...** that's all very well, but ...; **na ~** all right then ③ (*iron: unschön*) great; **das sind ja ~e Aussichten!** the future sure looks bright!; **das wird ja immer ~er!** things are getting worse and worse!; **das S~ste kommt erst noch** the best is yet to come ④ (*beträchtlich*) great, good II. *adv* ① (*ansprechend*) well; ~ **singen** to sing well ② (*fam: genau*) thoroughly ③ (*fam: besonders*) ~ **groß** nice and big ④ (*iron: ziemlich*) really; **das hat ganz schön wehgetan!** that really hurt!

schonen ['ʃoː·nən] I. *vt* ① (*pfleglich behandeln*) to take care of ② (*nicht überbeanspruchen*) to go easy on; **das schont die Gelenke** it's easy on the joints ③ (*verschonen*) to spare II. *vr* ■**sich** *akk* ~ to take it easy

schonend I. *adj* ① (*nicht strapazierend*) gentle; (*pfleglich*) careful ② (*rücksichtsvoll*) considerate II. *adv* ① (*pfleglich*) carefully, with care ② (*rücksichtsvoll*) **jdm etw ~ beibringen** to break sth to sb gently

Schönheit <-, -en> *f* beauty

Schönheitsfehler m ❶(*kosmetisch*) blemish ❷(*kleiner Makel*) flaw

Schonung <-> f *kein pl* ❶(*das pflegliche Behandeln*) care ❷(*Schutz*) protection ❸(*Rücksichtnahme*) consideration

schonungslos I. *adj* blunt, merciless; *Kritik* savage; *Offenheit* unabashed II. *adv* bluntly, mercilessly

schöpfen¹ ['ʃœp·fn] *vt* ❶(*mit einem Behältnis entnehmen*) to scoop; *Suppe* to ladle ❷ *Kraft* to summon [up]

schöpfen² ['ʃœp·fn] *vt* (*erschaffen*) to create; (*Ausdruck, Wort*) to coin

Schöpfer(in) <-s, -> m(f) creator; ■ **der ~** (*Gott*) the Creator

schöpferisch ['ʃœp·fə·rɪʃ] I. *adj* creative II. *adv* creatively

Schöpfung <-, -en> f creation; ■ **die ~** REL the Creation

Schöpfungsgeschichte f *kein pl* ■ **die ~** the story of the Creation

Schorf <-[e]s, -e> [ʃɔrf] m scab

Schornstein ['ʃɔrn·ʃtain] m chimney

Schornsteinfeger(in) <-s, -> m(f) chimney sweep

schossRR, **schoß**ALT [ʃɔs] *imp von* **schießen**

Schoß <-es, Schöße> [ʃɔs] m ❶ANAT lap ❷(*Mutterleib*) womb ▸WENDUNGEN: **etw fällt jdm in den ~** sth falls into sb's lap

Schoßhund m lapdog

Schote <-, -n> ['ʃo·tə] f pod

Schotte, Schottin <-n, -n> ['ʃɔ·tə, 'ʃɔ·tɪn] m, f Scot, Scotsman *masc*, Scotswoman *fem*; *s. a.* **Deutsche(r)**

Schottenrock m ❶(*Rock mit Schottenmuster*) plaid skirt ❷(*Kilt*) kilt

schottisch ['ʃɔ·tɪʃ] *adj* Scottish; *s. a.* **deutsch**

Schottland ['ʃɔt·lant] nt Scotland; *s. a.* **Deutschland**

schraffieren* [ʃra·fi:·rən] *vt* to hatch

schräg [ʃrɛːk] I. *adj* sloping; (*Linien*) diagonal II. *adv s.* **schief II**

Schrägstrich m slash

Schramme <-, -n> ['ʃra·mə] f ❶(*Schürfwunde*) scrape ❷(*Kratzer*) scratch

Schrank <-[e]s, Schränke> [ʃraŋk] m (*Geschirrschrank*) cupboard; (*Kleiderschrank*) closet

Schranke <-, -n> ['ʃraŋ·kə] f ❶BAHN barrier, gate ❷(*Grenze*) limit; **jdn in seine ~n weisen** to put sb in his/her place

schrankenlos *adj* unlimited, boundless

Schraube <-, -n> ['ʃrau·bə] f ❶TECH screw ❷NAUT propeller ❸SPORT twist ▸WENDUNGEN: **bei jdm ist eine ~ locker** (*fam*) sb has a screw loose

schrauben ['ʃrau·bn] *vt* to screw (**an** +*akk* into, **auf** +*akk* onto)

Schraubenschlüssel m wrench

Schraubenzieher <-s, -> m screwdriver

SchraubverschlussRR m screw top

Schrebergarten ['ʃre:·bɐ-] m *small garden plot on a piece of land managed by a gardening club*

Schreck <-s> [ʃrɛk] m *kein pl* fright; **einen ~ bekommen** to get a fright; **jdm einen ~ einjagen** to give sb a scare

Schrecken <-s, -> ['ʃrɛ·kn] m ❶ *kein pl s.* **Schreck** ❷ *pl* (*Gräuel*) horrors *pl*

Schreckgespenst nt bogey

schreckhaft *adj* jumpy

schrecklich ['ʃrɛk·lɪç] I. *adj* terrible, awful II. *adv* terribly, awfully

Schrei <-[e]s, -e> [ʃrai] m scream, cry ▸WENDUNGEN: **der letzte ~** (*fam*) the latest craze

Schreibblock <s, -blöcke> m writing pad

schreiben <schrieb, geschrieben> ['ʃrai·bn] I. *vt* to write; **etw falsch/richtig ~** to spell sth wrong/right II. *vi* to write; ■**jdm ~** to write to sb III. *vr* **wie schreibt sich das Wort?** how do you spell that word?

Schreiben <-s, -> ['ʃrai·bn] nt letter

Schreibkraft f typist

Schreibmaschine f typewriter

Schreibtisch m desk

Schreibung <-, -en> f spelling

schreien <schrie, geschrie[e]n> ['ʃrai·ən] I. *vi* ❶(*brüllen*) to yell ❷ORN, ZOOL

S

to cry ❸ (*laut rufen*) to shout (**nach** +*dat* for) II. *vt* to shout [out]

Schreihals *m* (*fam*) screamer

Schrein <-[e]s, -e> [ʃraɪn] *m* (*geh*) shrine

Schreiner(in) <-s, -> [ˈʃraɪ·nɐ] *m(f)* carpenter

Schreinerei <-, -en> [ʃraɪ·nəˈraɪ] *f* (*Tischlerei*) carpenter's workshop

schreiten <schritt, geschritten> [ˈʃraɪ·tn̩] *vi sein* ❶ (*gehen*) to stride ❷ (*etw in Angriff nehmen*) to proceed (**zu** +*dat* with)

Schrift <-, -en> [ʃrɪft] *f* ❶ (*Handschrift*) [hand]writing ❷ (*Schriftsystem*) script ❸ TYPO (*Druckschrift*) type; COMPUT font ❹ (*Abhandlung*) paper; **die Heilige ~** the [Holy] Scriptures *pl*

schriftlich [ˈʃrɪft·lɪç] I. *adj* written II. *adv* in writing

Schriftsprache *f* standard language

Schriftsteller(in) <-s, -> [ˈʃrɪft·ʃtɛ·lɐ] *m(f)* author, writer

schrill [ʃrɪl] I. *adj* ❶ (*durchdringend hell*) shrill ❷ (*nicht moderat*) brash; (*Farbe*) garish II. *adv* shrilly

schritt [ʃrɪt] *imp von* **schreiten**

Schritt <-[e]s, -e> [ʃrɪt] *m* ❶ (*Tritt*) step; [**mit jdm/etw**] **~ halten** to keep up [with sb/sth]; **~ für ~** step by step ❷ *kein pl* (*Gang*) walk, gait ❸ (*Maßnahme*) measure, step; **~e** [**gegen jdn/ etw**] **unternehmen** to take steps [against sb/sth] ❹ MODE crotch

Schritttempo^ALT *nt s.* **Schritttempo**

Schrittgeschwindigkeit *f* walking speed

Schrittmacher <-s, -> *m* pacemaker

Schritttempo^RR *nt* walking speed

schrittweise I. *adj* gradual II. *adv* gradually

schroff [ʃrɔf] I. *adj* ❶ (*barsch*) curt, brusque ❷ (*steil*) steep II. *adv* ❶ (*barsch*) curtly, brusquely ❷ (*steil*) steeply

Schrot <-[e]s, -e> [ʃroːt] *m o nt* ❶ *kein pl* AGR coarsely ground whole wheat ❷ (*aus Blei*) shot

Schrotflinte *f* shotgun

Schrott <-[e]s> [ʃrɔt] *m kein pl* ❶ (*Metallmüll*) scrap metal ❷ (*fam: wertloses Zeug*) junk; **ein Auto zu ~ fahren** (*fam*) to total a car

Schrotthändler(in) *m(f)* scrap dealer

Schrottplatz *m* junkyard

schrubben [ˈʃrʊbn̩] *vt, vi* to scrub

Schrubber <-s, -> [ˈʃrʊ·bɐ] *m* scrubbing brush

schrumpfen [ˈʃrʊmp·fn̩] *vi sein* to shrink; *Frucht* to shrivel; *Muskeln* to atrophy

Schubkarre *f* wheelbarrow

Schublade <-, -n> [ˈʃuːp·laː·də] *f* drawer

Schubs <-es, -e> [ʃʊps] *m* (*fam*) shove

schubsen [ˈʃʊp·sn̩] *vt* (*fam*) to shove

schüchtern [ˈʃʏç·tɐn] *adj* shy; *Versuch* half-hearted

Schüchternheit <-> *f kein pl* shyness

Schuft <-[e]s, -e> [ʃʊft] *m* villain

schuften [ˈʃʊf·tn̩] *vi* (*fam*) to slave away

Schufterei <-, -en> [ʃʊf·tə·ˈraɪ] *f* (*fam*) drudgery

Schuh <-[e]s, -e> [ʃuː] *m* shoe ►WENDUNGEN: **jdm etw in die ~e schieben** (*fam*) to put the blame for sth on sb

Schuhgeschäft *nt* shoe store

Schuhgröße *f* shoe size

Schuhmacher(in) <-s, -> [ˈʃuː·ma·xɐ] *m(f)* shoemaker, cobbler

Schuhsohle *f* sole [of a/one's shoe]

Schularbeiten *pl* ❶ *s.* **Hausaufgaben** ❷ ÖSTERR (*Klassenarbeit*) [written] test

Schulbildung *f kein pl* school education

Schulbuch *nt* schoolbook, textbook

Schulbus *m* school bus

schuld [ʃʊlt] *adj* ■ **~ sein** to be to blame (**an** +*dat* for)

Schuld <-> [ʃʊlt] *f kein pl* ❶ (*Verschulden*) fault, blame; **jdm** [**die**] **~ geben** to blame sb; **es ist jds ~, dass ...** it is sb's fault that ...; **die ~ auf sich nehmen** to take the blame ❷ (*verschuldete Missetat*) guilt; REL sin; **er ist sich keiner ~ bewusst** he's not aware of having done anything wrong ❸ *meist pl* FIN debt; **~en machen** to go into debt

schuldbewusst^{RR} I. *adj* guilty II. *adv* guiltily

schulden ['ʃʊl·dn̩] *vt* to owe

schuldenfrei *adj* free of debt

Schuldgefühl *nt* guilty feelings *pl*

schuldig ['ʃʊl·dɪç] *adj* ❶ JUR guilty; **sich** *akk* ~ **bekennen** to plead guilty; **jdn** ~ **sprechen** to find sb guilty ❷ ■**jdm etw** ~ **sein** *Geld, einen Gefallen etc.* to owe sb sth

Schuldige(r) *f(m) dekl wie adj* guilty party

schuldlos I. *adj* blameless II. *adv* blamelessly

Schuldner(in) <-s, -> ['ʃʊld·nɐ] *m(f)* debtor

Schule <-, -n> ['ʃuː·lə] *f* school; **in die** ~ **gehen** to go to school; **in die** ~ **kommen** to start school; **in der** ~ at school

schulen ['ʃuː·lən] *vt* to train

Schüler(in) <-s, -> ['ʃyː·lɐ] *m(f)* student; (*sch a.*) schoolchild

Schüleraustausch *m* high school exchange program

Schülerausweis *m* student ID [card]

Schulfach *nt* [school] subject

Schulferien *pl* summer vacation

schulfrei *adj* ~ **haben** to not have school

Schulgeld *nt* tuition

Schulheft *nt* notebook

Schulhof *m* school playground

Schuljahr *nt* SCH ❶ (*Zeitraum*) school year ❷ (*Klasse*) grade

Schulklasse *f* [school] class

Schulleiter(in) *m(f)* principal

Schulmedizin *f* classical medicine

Schulpflicht *f kein pl* mandatory school attendance

schulpflichtig *adj* of school age; ~ **sein** to be required to attend school

Schulschwänzer(in) ['ʃuː·l·ʃvɛn·tsɐ] *m(f)* SCH (*fam*) truant

Schulsprecher(in) *m(f)* student body president

Schulter <-, -n> ['ʃʊl·tɐ] *f* shoulder; **mit den** ~**n zucken** to shrug one's shoulders ►WENDUNGEN: **jdm die kalte** ~ **zeigen** to give sb the cold shoulder; **jd**

nimmt etw auf die leichte ~ sb takes sth very lightly, sb doesn't take sth very seriously

Schulterblatt *nt* shoulder blade

schulterlang *adj* shoulder-length

Schulung <-, -en> *f* training

Schulunterricht *m kein pl* [in-]class instruction

Schulverweis *m* SCH referral; (*befristet*) suspension

Schulweg *m* way to/from school

Schulzeit *f kein pl* school days *pl*

Schulzeugnis *nt* report card

schummeln ['ʃʊ·mln̩] *vi* (*fam*) to cheat

schummrig ['ʃʊm·rɪç] *adj* dim

Schund <-[e]s> [ʃʊnt] *m kein pl* (*pej*) trash

Schuppe <-, -n> ['ʃʊpə] *f* ❶ ZOOL scale ❷ *pl* MED dandruff

schuppen ['ʃʊ·pn̩] I. *vt* KOCHK to remove the scales II. *vr* ■**sich** *akk* ~ *Haut* to flake

Schuppen <-s, -> ['ʃʊ·pn̩] *m* ❶ (*Verschlag*) shed ❷ (*fam: Lokal*) joint

Schuppenflechte *f* MED psoriasis

schuppig ['ʃʊ·pɪç] *adj Haut* flaky; ~**e Haare haben** to have dandruff

Schürfwunde *f* scrape

Schurke <-n, -n> ['ʃʊr·kə] *m* (*veraltend*) scoundrel

Schurwolle *f* wool; „**reine** ~ " "pure new wool"

Schürze <-, -n> ['ʃyr·tsə] *f* apron

Schuss^{RR} <-es, Schüsse>, **Schuß**^{ALT} <-sses, Schüsse> [ʃʊs] *m* ❶ (*mit einer Waffe*) shot ❷ FBALL shot ❸ (*sl: Drogeninjektion*) shot; **sich** *dat* **einen** ~ **setzen** to shoot up ❹ (*Spritzer*) splash; **ein** ~ **Rum** a splash of rum; **mit** ~ with a shot (*of alcohol*) ►WENDUNGEN: **in** ~ in top shape; **weit vom** ~ **sein** (*fam*) to be miles away

Schüssel <-, -n> ['ʃy·sl̩] *f* bowl, dish

schusssicher^{RR} *adj* bulletproof

Schussverletzung^{RR} *f* bullet wound

Schusswaffe^{RR} *f* firearm

Schusswechsel^{RR} *m* exchange of fire

Schuster(in) <-s, -> ['ʃuː·s·tɐ] *m(f) s.* **Schuhmacher**

S

Schutt <-[e]s> [ʃʊt] *m kein pl* rubble *no indef art* ▶WENDUNGEN: **in ~ und Asche liegen** to be in ruins

Schüttelfrost *m* chills and fever

schütteln [ˈʃʏ·tl̩n] *vt* to shake

schütten [ˈʃʏ·tn̩] I. *vt* to pour II. *vi* ■**es schüttet** *impers* (*fam*) it's pouring

Schutz <-es, -e> [ʃʊts] *m kein pl* (*Sicherheit*) protection (**vor** +*dat* from); ~ **suchen** to seek refuge; **im ~[e] der Dunkelheit** under cover of darkness; **zu Ihrem ~** for your own protection; **jdn [vor etw** *dat*] **in ~ nehmen** to protect sb [from sth]

Schutzanzug *m* protective clothing

Schutzbrille *f* protective goggles *npl*

Schütze, Schützin <-n, -n> [ˈʃʏtsə, ˈʃʏt·sɪn] *m, f* ❶ SPORT marksman *masc,* markswoman *fem; (beim Fußball, Eishockey)* scorer ❷ (*Jagdwesen*) hunter ❸ MIL private, rifleman ❹ *kein pl* ASTROL Sagittarius

schützen [ˈʃʏtsn̩] I. *vt* to protect (**vor** +*dat* against/from) II. *vi* to give protection (**vor** +*dat* from)

schützend *adj* protective

Schutzengel *m* REL guardian angel

Schutzgebühr *f* nominal fee

Schutzhelm *m* protective helmet, hard hat

Schutzimpfung *f* vaccination

Schützling <-s, -e> [ˈʃʏts·lɪŋ] *m* protégé

schutzlos I. *adj* defenseless II. *adv* **jdm ~ ausgeliefert sein** to be at sb's mercy

Schutzmaske *f* protective mask

Schutzmaßnahme *f* precaution, precautionary measure

Schutzpatron(in) <-s, -e> *m(f)* REL patron saint

Schutzumschlag *m* dust jacket [*or* cover]

Schutzvorrichtung *f* safety device

Schutzweste *f* bulletproof vest

schwach <schwächer, schwächste> [ʃvax] I. *adj* ❶ (*nicht stark*) weak ❷ (*wenig leistend*) weak; *Schüler* poor; *Batterie* low ❸ (*gering*) weak; *Anzeichen* slight; *Beteiligung* poor; *Interesse,* *Trost* little ❹ (*leicht*) *Atmung* faint; *Bewegung* slight; *Druck, Wind, Strömung* light; ■**schwächer werden** to become fainter ▶WENDUNGEN: [**bei jdm/ etw**] **~ werden** (*fam*) to be unable to refuse [sb/sth] II. *adv* ❶ (*leicht*) faintly ❷ (*dürftig*) poorly

Schwäche <-, -n> [ˈʃvɛ·çə] *f* ❶ *kein pl* (*geringe Stärke*) weakness ❷ *kein pl* (*Unwohlsein*) [feeling of] faintness ❸ (*Vorliebe*) weakness

schwächen [ˈʃvɛ·çn̩] I. *vt* to weaken; ■**geschwächt** weakened II. *vi* to have a weakening effect

Schwachkopf *m* (*fam*) idiot, bonehead

schwächlich [ˈʃvɛç·lɪç] *adj* weakly, feeble

Schwächling <-s, -e> [ˈʃvɛç·lɪŋ] *m* weakling

Schwachsinn *m kein pl* (*fam: Quatsch*) nonsense

schwachsinnig *adj* (*fam: blödsinnig*) idiotic, ridiculous

Schwachstelle *f* weak spot

Schwager, Schwägerin <-s, Schwäger> [ˈʃvaː·ɡə, ˈʃvɛː·ɡə·rɪn] *m, f* brother-in-law *masc,* sister-in-law *fem*

Schwalbe <-, -n> [ˈʃval·bə] *f* ORN swallow

Schwall <-[e]s, -e> [ʃval] *m* torrent

schwamm [ʃvam] *imp von* **schwimmen**

Schwamm <-[e]s, Schwämme> [ʃvam] *m* ❶ (*zur Reinigung*) sponge ❷ SÜDD, ÖSTERR, SCHWEIZ (*essbarer Pilz*) mushroom ▶WENDUNGEN: **~ drüber!** let's forget it!

schwammig [ˈʃvamɪç] I. *adj* ❶ (*weich und porös*) spongy ❷ (*aufgedunsen*) puffy, bloated ❸ (*vage*) vague, woolly II. *adv* vaguely

Schwan <-[e]s, Schwäne> [ʃvaːn] *m* swan

schwanger [ˈʃvaŋe] *adj* pregnant (**von** +*dat* by)

Schwangere *f dekl wie adj* pregnant woman

Schwangerschaft <-, -en> *f* pregnancy

Schwangerschaftsabbruch m abortion

schwanken ['ʃvaŋ·kn̩] vi ❶ haben (schwingen) to sway ❷ sein (wanken) to stagger ❸ haben (nicht stabil sein) to fluctuate ❹ haben (unentschlossen sein) to be undecided; **zwischen zwei Dingen ~** to be torn between two things

Schwankung <-, -en> f fluctuation

Schwanz <-es, Schwänze> [ʃvants] m ❶ ZOOL tail ❷ ORN train, tail ❸ (sl: Penis) dick, cock ▶WENDUNGEN: **den ~ einziehen** (fam) to back down

schwänzen ['ʃvɛn·tsn̩] vt, vi SCH (fam) to play hooky

Schwarm[1] <-[e]s, Schwärme> [ʃvarm] m swarm; von Fischen school

Schwarm[2] <-[e]s> [ʃvarm] m (fam: verehrter Mensch) heartthrob

schwärmen[1] ['ʃvɛr·mən] vi sein to swarm

schwärmen[2] ['ʃvɛr·mən] vi ❶ haben (begeistert reden) to gush fam (von +dat about) ❷ (sich begeistern) ■**für jdn ~** to be crazy about sb; ■**für etw** akk ~ to have a passion for sth

Schwärmerei <-, -en> [ʃvɛr·mə·'rai] f ❶ (Wunschtraum) [pipe] dream ❷ (Passion) passion

Schwarte <-, -n> ['ʃvar·tə] f KOCHK rind

schwarz <schwärzer, schwärzeste> [ʃvarts] **I.** adj ❶ (Farbe) black ❷ attr (fam: illegal) illicit; Geld untaxed ▶WENDUNGEN: **~ auf weiß** in black and white **II.** adv ❶ (mit schwarzer Farbe) black ❷ (fam: auf illegale Weise) illicitly

Schwarz <-[es]> [ʃvarts] nt kein pl black

Schwarzarbeit f kein pl work that pays cash

schwarz|arbeiten vi to work under the table [or for cash]

Schwarzarbeiter(in) m(f) worker who gets paid under the table [or in cash]

Schwarzbrot nt DIAL ❶ (Roggenbrot) sourdough rye bread ❷ (festes Vollkornbrot) ≈ pumpernickel

Schwarze(r) f(m) dekl wie adj (Mensch) black

schwarz|fahren vi irreg sein to ride [public transportation] without paying the fare

Schwarzhandel m kein pl black market (**mit** +dat for)

Schwarzmarkt m black market

schwarz|sehen vi irreg ■**für jdn/ etw** ~ to be pessimistic [about sb/sth]

schwatzen ['ʃvatsn̩] vi, schwätzen ['ʃvɛtsn̩] vi SÜDD, ÖSTERR ❶ (sich unterhalten) to chat ❷ (etw ausplaudern) to blab fam ❸ (im Unterricht reden) to talk during class

Schwebe <-> ['ʃve:bə] f kein pl **in der ~ sein** to be in the balance; **etw in der ~ lassen** to leave sth undecided

Schwebebahn f (an Schienen) suspension railway ❷ s. **Seilbahn**

schweben ['ʃve:bn̩] vi haben to float; Vogel to hover; **in Lebensgefahr ~** to be in danger of one's life; (Patient) to be in critical condition

Schwede, Schwedin <-n, -nn> ['ʃve:·də, 'ʃve:·dɪn] m, f Swede; s. a. **Deutsche(r)**

Schweden <-s> ['ʃve:·dn̩] nt Sweden; s. a. **Deutschland**

schwedisch ['ʃve:·dɪʃ] adj Swedish; s. a. **deutsch**

Schwefel <-s> ['ʃve:·fl̩] m kein pl sulfur

Schwefeldioxid nt sulfur dioxide

schwefelhaltig adj sulfurous

schweifen ['ʃvai·fn̩] vi sein to roam, to wander; **seine Blicke ~ lassen** to let one's gaze wander

Schweigegeld nt hush money

Schweigeminute f minute of silence

schweigen <schwieg, geschwiegen> ['ʃvai·gn̩] vi to remain silent ▶WENDUNGEN: **ganz zu ~ von [etw]** dat let alone [sth]

Schweigen <-s> ['ʃvai·gn̩] nt kein pl silence; **jdn zum ~ bringen** to silence sb

Schweigepflicht f obligation to [maintain] confidentiality; **der ~ unterliegen** to be bound to maintain confidentiality

schweigsam ['ʃvaik·za:m] adj taciturn

S

Schwein <-s, -e> [ʃvain] *nt* ① ZOOL pig ② *kein pl* (*Schweinefleisch*) pork ③ (*pej fam: gemeiner Kerl*) bastard ④ (*fam: unsauberer Mensch*) pig ⑤ (*fam: obszöner Mensch*) lewd person, pervert ⑥ (*fam: bedauernswerter Mensch*) |**ein**| **armes** ~ [an] unlucky bastard ▸WENDUNGEN: [**großes**] ~ **haben** (*fam*) to be [really] lucky; **kein** ~ (*fam*) nobody

Schweinebraten *m* roast pork

Schweinefleisch *nt* pork

Schweinegrippe *f* MED swine flu, swine influenza

Schweinerei <-, -en> [ʃvai·nə·ˈrai] *f* (*fam*) ① (*Unordnung*) mess ② (*Gemeinheit*) dirty trick; ~! bullshit! *vulg sl* ③ (*Skandal*) scandal

Schweinestall *m* [pig]sty, [pig]pen

Schweiß <-es> [ʃvais] *m kein pl* sweat; **jdm bricht der ~ aus** sb breaks out in a sweat

schweißen [ʃvai·sn] *vt, vi* to weld

Schweißfuß *m meist pl* sweaty foot

schweißgebadet *adj* bathed in sweat *pred*

Schweiz <-> [ʃvaits] *f* Switzerland; **die französische/italienische ~** French-speaking/Italian-speaking Switzerland; *s. a.* **Deutschland**

Schweizer *adj attr* Swiss

Schweizer(in) <-s, -> [ʃvai·tsɐ] *m(f)* Swiss; *s. a.* **Deutsche(r)**

Schweizerdeutsch <-[s]> [ʃvai·tsɐ·dɔytʃ] *nt dekl wie adj* LING Swiss German; *s. a.* **Deutsch**

schwelgen [ʃvɛl·ɡn] *vi* to indulge oneself (**in** +*dat* in); **in Erinnerungen ~** to wallow in memories

Schwelle <-, -n> [ʃvɛ·lə] *f* ① (*Türschwelle*) threshold ② (*Bahnschwelle*) [railroad] tie

schwellen <schwoll, geschwollen> [ʃvɛ·lən] *vi sein* MED to swell [up]

Schwellung <-, -en> *f* swelling

Schwemme <-, -n> [ʃvɛ·mə] *f* (*Überangebot*) glut

schwemmen [ʃvɛ·mən] *vt* **etw an Land ~** to wash sth ashore

schwenken [ʃvɛŋ·kn̩] I. *vt* ① *Fahne, Stab* to wave ② KOCHK to toss II. *vi* TV, FILM *Kamera* to pan

schwer <schwerer, schwerste> [ʃveːɐ̯] I. *adj* ① (*nicht leicht*) heavy; ■ **30 kg ~ sein** to weigh 30 kilos ② (*beträchtlich*) serious; *Verlust* bitter; ~**e Mängel aufweisen** to be badly defective; ~**e Verwüstung[en] anrichten** to cause utter devastation ③ (*hart*) hard; *Schicksal* cruel; *Strafe* harsh ④ (*körperlich belastend*) serious, grave; *Operation* difficult ⑤ (*schwierig*) hard, difficult; *Lektüre* heavy ⑥ *attr* (*heftig*) *Sturm, Gewitter, Kämpfe* heavy II. *adv* ① (*hart*) hard; ~ **arbeiten** to work hard; **jdm ~ zu schaffen machen** to give sb a hard time ② (*mit schweren Lasten*) heavily; ~ **bepackt sein** to be heavily laden ③ (*fam: sehr*) deeply; ~ **betrunken** plastered *sl* ④ (*mit Mühe*) with [great] difficulty; **ein ~ erziehbares Kind** a problem child; ~ **verdaulich** indigestible ⑤ (*ernstlich*) seriously; **sich** *akk* ~ **erkälten** to catch a bad cold; ~ **verunglückt sein** to have had a bad accident; ~ **wiegend** serious ⑥ (*schwierig*) difficult, not easy; ~ **verständlich** (*kaum nachvollziehbar*) barely comprehensible; (*kaum zu verstehen*) hard to understand *pred*; **jdm das Leben ~ machen** to make life difficult for sb

Schwerarbeit *f kein pl* heavy labor

Schwerbehinderte(r) *f(m) dekl wie adj* severely disabled person

schwerelos *adj* weightless

schwer|fallen *vi irreg sein* ■ **etw fällt jdm schwer** sth is difficult for sb [to do]

schwerfällig <-er, -ste> I. *adj* (*plump*) clumsy II. *adv* (*plump*) clumsily

Schwergewicht *nt* ① (*Gewichtsklasse*) heavyweight ② (*Schwerpunkt*) emphasis

schwerhörig *adj* hard of hearing *pred*

Schwerkraft *f kein pl* gravity

Schwermetall *nt* heavy metal

Schwermut <-> *f kein pl* melancholy

schwermütig <-er, -ste> [ʃveːɐ̯·myː·tɪç] *adj* melancholy

schwer|nehmen *vt irreg* ▪ **etw ~** to take sth to heart

Schwerpunkt *m* ① (*Hauptgewicht*) main emphasis; **~e setzen** to set priorities ② PHYS center of gravity

Schwert <-[e]s, -er> [ʃveːɐ̯t] *nt* sword

Schwertfisch *m* swordfish

Schwertlilie *f* iris

Schwerverbrecher(in) *m(f)* dangerous criminal, felon

Schwerverletzte(r) *f(m) dekl wie adj* critically injured person

Schwester <-, -n> [ʃvɛste] *f* ① (*weibliches Geschwisterteil*) sister ② (*Krankenschwester*) nurse ③ (*Nonne*) nun

Schwiegereltern [ʃviːɡe-] *pl* parents-in-law *pl*, in-laws *pl fam*

Schwiegermutter *f* mother-in-law

Schwiegersohn *m* son-in-law

Schwiegertochter *f* daughter-in-law

Schwiegervater *m* father-in-law

Schwiele <-, -n> [ʃviːlə] *f* callus

schwierig [ʃviːrɪç] I. *adj* ① (*nicht einfach*) difficult, hard ② (*verwickelt*) complicated; *Situation* tricky II. *adv* with difficulty

Schwierigkeit <-, -en> *f* ① *kein pl* (*Problematik*) difficulty; *einer Lage, eines Problems* complexity; *einer Situation* trickiness ② *pl* (*Probleme*) problems *pl*; **jdn in ~en bringen** to get sb into trouble; **in ~en geraten** to get into trouble

Schwimmbad *nt* swimming pool

Schwimmbecken *nt* [swimming] pool

schwimmen <schwamm, geschwommen> [ʃvɪmən] *vt, vi sein o haben* to swim; **~ gehen** to go swimming

Schwimmer(in) <-s, -> [ʃvɪmɐ] *m(f)* swimmer

Schwimmflosse *f* flipper

Schwimmweste *f* life jacket

Schwindel <-s> [ʃvɪndl̩] *m kein pl* ① (*Betrug*) swindle, fraud ② MED dizziness, vertigo; **~ erregend** (*fig*) astronomical

Schwindelanfall *m* MED dizzy spell

schwindelfrei *adj* ▪ **~ sein** to not suffer from vertigo

schwindelig [ʃvɪndəlɪç] *adj pred* dizzy, giddy

schwindeln [ʃvɪndln̩] I. *vi* to lie II. *vi impers* ▪ **mir schwindelt [es]** I feel dizzy

schwinden <schwand, geschwunden> [ʃvɪndn̩] *vi sein* (*geh*) *Interesse* to be waning; *Wirkung* to be wearing off; *Zuversicht* to be failing

Schwindler(in) <-s, -> [ʃvɪndlɐ] *m(f)* ① (*Betrüger*) swindler ② (*Lügner*) liar

schwingen <schwang, geschwungen> [ʃvɪŋən] I. *vt haben* to swing; *Axt* to brandish; *Fahne* to wave II. *vi sein o haben* (*pendeln*) to swing III. *vr haben* ▪ **sich** *akk* **auf/in etw** *akk* **~** to jump onto/into sth; **sich** *akk* **aufs Fahrrad ~** to hop on one's bike

Schwingung <-, -en> *f* oscillation

Schwips <-es, -e> [ʃvɪps] *m* (*fam*) **einen ~ haben** to be tipsy

schwirren [ʃvɪrən] *vi sein Mücken* to buzz; *Vogel* to whir

schwitzen [ʃvɪtsn̩] *vi* to sweat; **nass geschwitzt** drenched with sweat

schwören <schwor, geschworen> [ʃvøːrən] I. *vi* to swear (**auf** +*akk* by) II. *vt* to promise

schwul [ʃvuːl] *adj* (*fam*) gay

schwül [ʃvyːl] *adj* humid, muggy

Schwule(r) *m dekl wie adj* (*fam*) gay

Schwüle <-> [ʃvyːlə] *f kein pl* humidity, mugginess

schwülstig [ʃvʏlstɪç] I. *adj* (*pej*) overly ornate, florid; *Stil* bombastic II. *adv* (*pej*) bombastically

Schwung <-[e]s, Schwünge> [ʃvʊŋ] *m* swing ▶WENDUNGEN: **in ~ kommen** to get going; **[richtig] in ~ sein** to be in full swing

schwungvoll I. *adj* ① (*weit ausholend*) sweeping ② (*mitreißend*) lively; *Rede* passionate II. *adv* lively

Schwur <-[e]s, Schwüre> [ʃvuːɐ̯] *m* ① (*Versprechen*) vow ② (*Eid*) oath

Schwurgericht *nt* jury court

sechs [zɛks] *adj* six; *s. a.* **acht¹**

Sechs <-, -en> [zɛks] *f* ① (*Zahl*) six

②SCH (schlechteste Zensur) ≈ F
③SCHWEIZ (beste Zensur) ≈ A

Sechseck nt hexagon

sechshundert ['zɛks·'hʊn·dɐt] adj six hundred

sechstausend ['zɛks·'tau·znt] adj six thousand

sechste(r, s) ['zɛks·tə, -tɐ, -təs] adj ①(an sechster Stelle) sixth; s. a. **achte(r, s) 1** ②(Datum) sixth, 6th; s. a. **achte(r, s) 2**

sechstel ['zɛks·tl̩] adj sixth

Sechstel <-s, -> ['zɛks·tl̩] nt sixth

sechstens ['zɛks·tn̩s] adv sixthly, in sixth place

sechzehn ['zɛç·tseːn] adj sixteen; s. a. **acht¹**

sechzehnte(r, s) adj ①(an sechzehnter Stelle) sixteenth; s. a. **achte(r, s) 1** ②(Datum) sixteenth, 16th; s. a. **achte(r, s) 2**

sechzig ['zɛç·tsɪç] adj sixty; s. a. **achtzig 1, 2**

sechzigste(r, s) adj sixtieth; s. a. **achte(r, s) 1**

Secondhandladen m secondhand store

See¹ <-s, -n> [zeː] m lake

See² <-, -n> [zeː] f ①(Meer) sea; **an der ~** by the sea; **auf ~** at sea; **auf hoher ~** on the high seas; **in ~ stechen** to put to sea ②(Seegang) heavy sea

Seefahrer m seafarer

Seefahrt f kein pl sea travel, seafaring no art

Seefisch m saltwater fish

Seehund m seal

Seekarte f nautical chart

seekrank adj seasick

Seelachs m coalfish

Seele <-, -n> ['zeː·lə] f soul; **mit Leib und ~** wholeheartedly; **das tut mir in der ~ weh** it breaks my heart ▶WENDUNGEN: **ein Herz und eine ~ sein** to be inseparable

seelenruhig ['zeː·lən·'ruː·ɪç] adv calmly

Seeleute pl von **Seemann**

seelisch ['zeː·lɪʃ] I. adj psychological, emotional; **~es Gleichgewicht** mental

balance II. adv **~ bedingt sein** to have psychological causes

Seelöwe, -löwin <-n, -n> m, f sea lion

Seelsorge f kein pl spiritual guidance

Seelsorger(in) <-s, -> ['zeː·l·zɔr·gə] m(f) pastor

Seemacht f naval power

Seemann <-leute> ['zeː·man] m sailor, seaman

Seemeile f nautical mile

Seenot f kein pl distress [at sea]

Seepferd(chen) nt sea horse

Seeräuber(in) m(f) pirate

Seereise f voyage; (Kreuzfahrt) cruise

Seerose f water lily

Seestern m starfish

Seetang m seaweed

seetüchtig adj seaworthy

Seeufer nt lakefront, lakeshore

Seeweg m sea route; **auf dem ~** by sea

Seezunge f sole

Segel <-s, -> ['zeː·gl̩] nt sail

Segelboot nt sailboat

Segelflugzeug nt glider

segeln ['zeː·gl̩n] vi sein to sail

Segeln <-s> ['zeː·gl̩n] nt kein pl sailing

Segelschiff nt sailing ship

Segen <-s, -> ['zeː·gn̩] m kein pl blessing; **ein wahrer ~ sein** to be a real godsend

Segler(in) <-s, -> ['zeː·glɐ] m(f) yachtsman masc, yachtswoman fem

Segment <-[e]s, -e> [zɛg·'mɛnt] nt segment

segnen ['zeːg·nən] vt to bless

sehen <sah, gesehen> ['zeː·ən] I. vt ①(erblicken, bemerken) to see; **ich kann kein Blut ~** I can't stand the sight of blood; **das muss man gehaben!** you have to see it to believe it!; **das sehe ich gar nicht gern!** I don't like that at all!; **das wollen wir [doch] erst mal ~!** [well,] we'll see about that!; **gut/schlecht zu ~ sein** to be easily/poorly visible; **etw kommen ~** to see sth coming; **sich** akk **~ lassen können** to be something to be proud of; **so ge~** from that point of view ②(ansehen, zusehen) to watch

③ (*treffen*) ▪**jdn ~** to meet sb **④** (*einschätzen*) **ich sehe das so: ...** the way I see it, ... II. *vi* **①** (*Sehvermögen haben*) to see; **gut/schlecht ~** to have good/bad eyesight **②** (*ansehen*) to look; **lass mal ~** let me see **③** (*blicken*) to look; **aus dem Fenster ~** to look out [of] the window **④** (*bemerken*) **~ Sie!/siehste!** (*fam*) [you] see? **⑤** (*sich kümmern um*) ▪**nach jdm/ etw ~** to check on sb/sth; **ich werde ~, was ich für Sie tun kann** I'll see what I can do for you **⑥** (*abwarten*) to wait and see III. *vr* **sich** *akk* **gezwungen ~, etw zu tun** to feel compelled to do sth

sehenswert *adj* worth seeing

Sehenswürdigkeit <-, -en> *f* sight

Sehfehler *m* visual defect

Sehkraft *f kein pl* [eye]sight

Sehne <-, -n> ['zeːnə] *f* ANAT tendon, sinew

sehnen ['zeːnən] *vr* ▪**sich** *akk* **nach jdm/etw ~** to long for sb/sth

Sehnerv *m* optic nerve

sehnig ['zeːnɪç] *adj* sinewy

Sehnsucht <-, -süchte> ['zeːnˌzʊxt] *f* longing (**nach** +*dat* for)

sehnsüchtig ['zeːnˌzʏç·tɪç] *adj attr* longing, yearning; *Blick* wistful; *Verlangen, Wunsch* ardent

sehr <[noch] mehr, am meisten> ['zeːɐ̯] *adv* **①** *vor vb* (*in hohem Maße*) very much, a lot; **danke ~!** thanks a lot; **bitte ~, bedienen Sie sich!** go ahead and help yourself!; **das will ich doch ~ hoffen** I very much hope so **②** *vor adj, adv* (*besonders*) very; **jdm ~ dankbar sein** to be very grateful to sb

Sehschärfe *f* visual acuity

Sehstörung *f* visual defect

Sehtest *m* eye test

seicht [zaiçt] *adj* shallow

Seide <-, -n> ['zai·də] *f* silk

seiden ['zai·dn] *adj attr* silk

Seidenraupe *f* silkworm

seidig ['zai·dɪç] *adj* silky

Seife <-, -n> ['zai·fə] *f* soap

Seifenoper *f* TV soap opera

Seil <-[e]s, -e> [zail] *nt* rope; (*Drahtseil*) cable

Seilbahn *f* (*Standseilbahn*) funicular; (*Drahtseilbahn*) gondola

seil|springen *vi irreg, nur infin und pp sein* to skip rope

Seiltänzer(in) *m(f)* tightrope acrobat

sein¹ <bin, bist, ist, sind, seid, war, gewesen> [zain] I. *vi sein* **①** (*existieren, sich befinden*) to be, to exist; **ich bin wieder da** I'm back [again]; **ist da jemand?** is anybody there? **②** (*Eigenschaft haben*) to be; **böse/klug ~** to be angry/clever; **er war so freundlich und hat das überprüft** he was kind enough to check it out; **sei so lieb und ...** I would be grateful if ... **③** (*gehören*) **das Buch ist meins** the book is mine **④** MATH to be, to equal **⑤** (*sich ereignen*) to be, to take place; **was ist mit dir?** what is the matter with you?; **was ist [denn schon wieder]?** what is it [now]?; **war was?** (*fam*) did anything happen?; **das wär's dann** that's it; **das darf doch nicht wahr ~!** that can't be true!; **muss das ~?** do you [really] have to?; **was ~ muss, muss ~** what will be will be; **etw ~ lassen** (*fam*) to stop [doing sth] **⑥** (*hergestellt sein*) ▪**aus etw** *dat* **~** to be [made of] sth **⑦** (*sich fühlen*) **mir ist heiß/kalt** I'm hot/cold; **mir ist übel** I feel sick II. *vi impers* **①** (*bei Zeitangaben*) **es ist jetzt 9 Uhr** it is now 9 o'clock; **es ist Januar/Nacht** it is January/night[time] **②** (*der Fall sein*) **mir ist es zu kalt** I'm too cold; **es sei denn, dass ...** unless ...; **wie wäre es mit ...?** how about ...?; **es war einmal ...** once upon a time ...; **wie dem auch sei** be that as it may, in any case III. *aux vb* **①** *zur Bildung des Perfekts* **jd ist gefahren/gegangen** sb drove/left **②** *zur Bildung des Zustandspassivs* **jd ist gebissen/verurteilt worden** sb has been bitten/convicted

sein² [zain] *pron poss, adjektivisch* **①** (*einem Mann gehörend*) his; (*zu einem Gegenstand gehörend*) its; (*einem Mädchen gehörend*) her; (*zu*

einer Stadt, einem Land gehörend) its
② *auf „man" bezüglich* one's; *auf
„jeder" bezüglich* his, their *fam;* **jeder
bekam ~ eigenes Zimmer** everyone
got his/her own room
Sein <-s> [zain] *nt kein pl* existence
seine(r, s) ['zai·nɐ, -nɐ, -nəs] *pron poss,
substantivisch* (*geh*) ■**das S~** his
[own]; **jedem das S~** to each his own;
■**die S~n** his family
seinerseits ['sai·nɐ·'saits] *adv* (*von ihm
aus*) on his part, as far as he is concerned
seinetwegen ['zai·nət·'ve:·gn] *adv* because of him
seinetwillen ['zai·nət·'vɪ·lən] *adv* **um ~**
for his sake
seit [zait] **I.** *präp* +*dat* ① (*Anfangs-
punkt*) since; **~ wann?** since when?;
~ Juni since June; **~ neuestem** recently ② (*Zeitspanne*) for; **~ drei Wochen**
for three weeks; **~ einiger Zeit** for a
while **II.** *konj* (*seitdem*) since
seitdem [zait·'de:m] **I.** *adv* since then
II. *konj* since
Seite <-, -n> ['zai·tə] *f* ① (*Fläche
eines Körpers*) side; **die vordere/
hintere/untere/obere** ② the front/
back/bottom/top ② (*rechts oder links
der Mitte*) **zur ~ gehen** to step aside;
jdn zur ~ nehmen to take sb aside
③ (*Papierblatt*) page; **gelbe ~n** Yellow
Pages ④ (*Beistand*) **jdm zur ~ stehen**
to stand by sb ⑤ (*Aspekt*) **alles hat
[seine] zwei ~n** there are two sides
to everything; **auf der einen ~...,
auf der anderen [~] ...** on the one
hand, ..., on the other [hand], ...;
**sich auf seiner besten ~ zei-
gen** to be on one's best behavior; **jds
starke ~ sein** (*fam*) to be sb's forte
⑥ (*Partei, Gruppe*) side; **auf jds ~
stehen** to be on sb's side; **die ~n
wechseln** to change sides ▶WENDUN-
GEN: **etw auf die ~ legen** to put sth
aside
Seitenangabe *f* page reference
Seitenausgang *m* side exit
Seiteneingang *m* side entrance

seitens ['zai·tns] *präp* +*gen* on the
part of
Seitensprung *m* (*fam*) affair
Seitenstechen *nt kein pl* stitch [in one's
side]
Seitenstreifen *m* hard shoulder
Seitenwind *m* crosswind
Seitenzahl *f* ① (*Anzahl der Seiten*)
number of pages ② (*Ziffer*) page number
seither [zait·'he:ɐ] *adv* since then
seitlich ['zait·lɪç] **I.** *adj* side *attr* **II.** *adv*
sideways **III.** *präp* +*gen* **~ der Straße**
at the side of the road
seitwärts ['zait·vɛrts] *adv* sideways
Sekretär(in) <-s, -e> [zek·re·'tɛ:ɐ] *m(f)*
secretary
Sekretariat <-[e]s, -e> [zek·re·ta·
'ri̯a:t] *nt* administrative office
Sekt <-[e]s, -e> [zɛkt] *m* sparkling wine
Sekte <-, -n> ['zɛk·tə] *f* sect
sekundär [ze·kʊn·'dɛ:ɐ] *adj* secondary
Sekunde <-, -n> [ze·'kʊn·də] *f* second;
auf die ~ genau to the second
Sekundenzeiger *m* second hand
selbst [zɛlpst] **I.** *pron dem* ① (*persönlich*) myself/yourself/himself etc.
② (*ohne Hilfe, alleine*) by oneself; **etw
~ machen** to do sth by oneself; **von ~**
automatically; **das versteht sich von ~**
it goes without saying ▶WENDUNGEN: **er
ist die Ruhe ~** he is calmness itself
II. *adv* ① (*eigen*) self; **~ ernannt**
self-appointed; **~ gemacht** homemade;
~ gestrickt hand-knit ② (*sogar*) even;
~ wenn even if
Selbstachtung *f* self-respect
selbständig ['zɛlp·ʃtɛn·dɪç] *adj* s.
selbstständig
Selbständigkeit <-> *f kein pl* s. **Selbstständigkeit**
Selbstauslöser *m* self-timer
Selbstbedienungsladen *m* ≈ supermarket
Selbstbefriedigung *f* masturbation
Selbstbeherrschung *f* self-control
Selbstbestimmungsrecht *nt kein pl*
right to self-determination
selbstbewusst^RR *adj* self-confident

SelbstbewusstseinRR *nt* self-confidence

Selbsterhaltungstrieb *m* survival instinct

selbstgefällig *adj* self-satisfied

Selbstgespräch *nt* monologue; **Selbstgespräche führen** to talk to oneself

Selbsthilfegruppe *f* self-help group

selbstklebend *adj* self-adhesive

Selbstkostenpreis *m* cost; **zum ~** at cost

Selbstkritik *f kein pl* self-criticism; **~ üben** to criticize oneself

selbstlos *adj* selfless, unselfish

Selbstmitleid *nt* self-pity

Selbstmord *m* suicide; **~ begehen** to commit suicide

Selbstmörder(in) *m(f)* suicidal person

Selbstmordversuch *m* suicide attempt

Selbstschutz *m* self-protection

selbstsicher *adj* self-confident

selbstständigRR ['zɛlpst·ʃtɛn·dɪç] *adj* ① (*eigenständig*) independent ② (*beruflich unabhängig*) self-employed; **sich** *akk* **~ machen** to start up *sep* one's own business

SelbstständigkeitRR <-> *f kein pl* ① (*Eigenständigkeit*) independence ② (*selbstständige Stellung*) self-employment

Selbsttäuschung *f* self-delusion

Selbstüberschätzung *f* overestimation of one's abilities

Selbstüberwindung *f* self-discipline

selbstverständlich I. *adj* natural; **das ist doch ~** don't mention it; **etw für ~ halten** to take sth for granted II. *adv* naturally, of course; [**aber**] **~!** [but] of course!

Selbstverständlichkeit <-, -en> *f* naturalness; **eine ~ sein** to be the least that could be done

Selbstverteidigung *f* self-defense

Selbstvertrauen *nt* self-confidence

Selbstverwaltung *f* self-government

Selbstverwirklichung *f* self-realization

Selbstzweck *m kein pl* end in itself

Selen <-s> [ze'le:n] *nt* selenium

selig ['ze:·lɪç] *adj* (*überglücklich*) over-

joyed ▶WENDUNGEN: **wer's glaubt, wird ~** (*iron fam*) that's a likely story

Sellerie <-s, -[s]> ['zɛ·ləri] *m* ① (*Knollensellerie*) celeriac ② (*Stangensellerie*) celery

selten ['zɛl·tn̩] I. *adj* rare II. *adv* rarely

Seltenheit <-, -en> *f* ① *kein pl* (*seltenes Vorkommen*) rare occurrence ② (*seltene Sache*) rarity

seltsam ['zɛlt·za:m] *adj* strange, weird, peculiar

Semester <-s, -> [ze'mɛs·tɐ] *nt* semester, term

Semikolon <-s, -s> [ze·mi·'ko:·lɔn] *nt* semicolon

Seminar <-s, -e *o* ÖSTERR -ien> [ze·mi·'na:ɐ̯] *nt* ① (*Lehrveranstaltung*) seminar ② (*Universitätsinstitut*) department

Semit(in) <-en, -en> [ze·'mi:t] *m(f)* Semite

semitisch [ze·'mi:·tɪʃ] *adj* Semitic

Semmel <-, -n> [zɛml] *f* DIAL roll ▶WENDUNGEN: **weggehen wie warme ~n** (*fam*) to go like hot cakes

Senat <-[e]s, -e> [ze·'na:t] *m* senate

Senator, Senatorin <-s, -toren> [ze·'na:·to:ɐ̯, ze·na·'to:·rɪn] *m, f* senator

Sendegebiet *nt* broadcast area

senden¹ ['zɛn·dn̩] I. *vt* to broadcast; *Botschaft* to transmit II. *vi* to be on the air

senden² <sandte *o* sendete, gesandt *o* gesendet> ['zɛn·dn̩] *vt* to send; *Truppen* to dispatch

Sender <-s, -> ['zɛn·dɐ] *m* ① (*Sendeanstalt*) TV channel; RADIO station ② (*Sendegerät*) transmitter

SendeschlussRR *m* end of a broadcast

Sendezeit *f* airtime; **zur besten ~** at prime time

Sendung¹ <-, -en> *f* TV, RADIO program; **auf ~ gehen/sein** to go/be on the air

Sendung² <-, -en> *f* (*Paketsendung*) package; (*Warensendung*) shipment

Senf <-[e]s, -e> [zɛnf] *m* mustard ▶WENDUNGEN: **seinen ~ dazugeben** *dat* (*fam*) to have one's say

senil [ze·'ni:l] *adj* senile

Senior <-s, Senioren> ['ze:·n̩jo:ɐ̯] *m meist pl* (*älterer Mensch*) senior citizen

S

Seniorenheim nt nursing [or retirement] home

senken ['zɛŋ·kn̩] I. vt ❶ (niedriger machen) to lower; Fieber to reduce ❷ (abwärtsbewegen) **den Kopf ~** to bow one's head II. vr ■**sich** akk ~ to sink, to drop

senkrecht ['zɛŋk·rɛçt] adj vertical

Senkung <-, -en> f ❶ kein pl der Preise reduction; der Löhne cut; der Steuern decrease ❷ (das Senken) drop, subsidence; der Stimme lowering

Sensation <-, -en> [zɛn·za·'tsi̯oːn] f sensation

sensationell [zɛn·za·tsi̯o·'nɛl] adj sensational

sensibel [zɛn·'ziː·bl̩] adj sensitive

Sensibilität <-, -en> [zɛn·zi·bi·li·'tɛːt] f sensitivity

Sensor <-s, -soren> ['zɛn·zoːɐ̯] m sensor

sentimental [zɛn·ti·mɛn·'taːl] adj sentimental

Sentimentalität <-, -en> [zɛn·ti·mɛn·ta·li·'tɛːt] f sentimentality

separat [ze·pa·'raːt] adj separate

Separatist(in) <-en, -en> [ze·pa·ra·'tɪst] m(f) separatist

September <-[s], -> [zɛp·'tɛm·bɐ] m September; s. a. **Februar**

Serbien <-s> ['zɛr·bi̯ən] nt Serbia; s. a. **Deutschland**

Serenade <-, -n> [ze·re·'naː·də] f serenade

Serie ['zeː·ri̯ə] f (a. media, tv) series + sing vb

serienmäßig adj ❶ (in Serienfertigung) mass-produced ❷ (bereits eingebaut sein) standard

Seriennummer f serial number

Serientäter(in) m(f) repeat offender

seriös [ze·'ri̯øːs] I. adj ❶ Mensch respectable; Angebot serious; Unternehmen reputable II. adv respectably

Serpentine <-, -n> [zɛr·pɛn·'tiː·nə] f winding road

Service¹ <-, -s> ['zœr·vɪs] m kein pl (Bedienung) service

Service² <-[s], -> [zɛr·'viːs] nt (Set) dinner/coffee service

servieren* [zɛr·'viː·rən] vt to serve

Serviette <-, -n> [zɛr·'vi̯ɛ·tə] f napkin

Servolenkung f power[-assisted] steering

servus ['zɛr·vʊs] interj ÖSTERR, SÜDD (hallo) hi; (tschüs) [good]bye

Sessel <-s, -> ['zɛ·sl̩] m armchair

Sessellift m chair lift

setzen ['zɛ·tsn̩] I. vt haben ❶ (platzieren) to put, to place ❷ (festlegen) to set; **eine Frist/ein Ziel ~** to set a deadline/a goal ❸ (bringen) **etw in Betrieb ~** to set sth in motion; **jdn auf Diät ~** to put sb on a diet ❹ (pflanzen) to plant ❺ (wetten) **Geld auf jdn/ etw ~** to bet money on sb/sth ❻ TYPO to set II. vr haben ■**sich** akk ~ ❶ (sich niederlassen) to sit [down]; **bitte ~ Sie sich doch!** please sit down!; ■**sich** akk **zu jdm ~** to sit next to sb; **wollen Sie sich nicht zu uns ~?** won't you join us?; **sich** akk **ins Auto ~** to get in the car ❷ (sich senken) Kaffeesatz to settle III. vi ❶ haben (wetten) ■**auf jdn/ etw ~** to bet on sb/sth ❷ sein o haben ■**über etw ~** (springen) to jump over sth; (überschiffen) to cross sth

Seuche <-, -n> ['zɔy·çə] f epidemic

Seuchenbekämpfung f epidemic control

seufzen ['zɔyf·tsn̩] vi to sigh

Seufzer <-s, -> m sigh

Sex <-[es]> [zɛks] m kein pl sex

siamesisch [zi̯a·'meː·zɪʃ] adj Siamese

Sibirien <-s> [zi·'biː·ri̯ən] nt Siberia

sich [zɪç] pron refl ❶ akk oneself; ■**er/ sie/es ... ~** he/she/it ... himself/herself/itself; ■**Sie ...** ~ you ... yourself/yourselves; ■**sie ...** ~ they ... themselves; **man fragt ~, was das soll** one wonders what it's all about; ~ **freuen/wundern** to be pleased/surprised; ~ **schämen** to be ashamed of oneself ❷ dat one's; ~ **etw einbilden** to imagine sth; ~ **etw kaufen** to buy sth for oneself; **die Katze leckte ~ die Pfote** the cat licked its paw

❸ pl (einander) each other, one another; ~ **lieben** to love each other **❹** unpersönlich **das Auto fährt ~ prima** the car drives really well **❺** ~ prep **er denkt immer nur an ~** he only ever thinks of himself; **wieder zu ~ kommen** to regain consciousness; **etw von ~ aus tun** to do sth of one's own accord

Sichel <-, -n> ['zɪ·çl̩] f **❶** (Werkzeug) sickle **❷** (Gebilde, von Mond) crescent

sicher ['zɪ·çɐ] I. adj **❶** (gewiss) certain, sure; Zusage definite; **sind Sie ~?** are you sure?; **es ist nicht ~, dass er kommt** it is not certain that he will come; ■ sich dat etw gen ~ **sein** to be sure of sth **❷** (ungefährdet) safe (vor +dat from); Anlage, Arbeitsplatz secure; ~ **ist ~** you can't be too careful **❸** (zuverlässig) reliable; Methode foolproof **❹** (geübt) competent **❺** (selbstsicher) self-assured II. adv **❶** (gewiss) surely; [aber] ~! (fam) sure!; **ich weiß das ganz ~** I know that for sure **❷** (ungefährdet) **sich** akk ~ **fühlen** to feel safe

Sicherheit <-, -en> f **❶** kein pl (gesicherter Zustand) safety; **etw in ~ bringen** to get sth to a safe place; **in ~ sein** to be safe **❷** kein pl (Gewissheit) certainty; **mit ~** for certain **❸** kein pl (Gewandtheit) competence **❹** (Kaution) surety

Sicherheitsabstand m safe distance

Sicherheitsgurt m seat [or safety] belt

sicherheitshalber adv to be on the safe side

Sicherheitsnadel f safety pin

Sicherheitsrat m kein pl POL Security Council

sicherlich adv surely

sichern ['zɪ·çɐn] vt **❶** (schützen) to safeguard (gegen +akk against) **❷** Schusswaffe to put a safety on **❸** (absichern) to protect; Bergsteiger, Tatort, Tür to secure; ■ **gesichert sein** to be protected **❹** COMPUT to save

sicher|stellen vt **❶** (in Gewahrsam nehmen) to confiscate **❷** (gewährleisten)

to guarantee; ■ ~, **dass ...** to ensure that ...

Sicherung <-, -en> f **❶** (das Sichern) securing, safeguarding **❷** ELEK fuse **❸** (Schutzvorrichtung) safety [catch] **❹** COMPUT backup

Sicherungskopie f COMPUT backup copy

Sicht <-, selten -en> [zɪçt] f **❶** (Aussicht) view; **du nimmst mir die ~** you're blocking my view; **die ~ beträgt heute nur 20 Meter** visibility is down to about 20 meters today; **in ~ sein** to be in sight; **Land in ~!** land ahoy!; **etw ist in ~** (fig) sth is on the horizon; **auf kurze/lange ~** (fig) in the short/long term **❷** (Meinung) [point of] view; **aus jds ~** from sb's point of view

sichtbar adj visible

sichten ['zɪ·çtn̩] vt **❶** (ausmachen) to sight **❷** (durchsehen) **die Akten ~** to look through the files

sichtlich adv ~ **beeindruckt sein** to be visibly impressed

Sichtverhältnisse pl visibility

Sichtweite f visibility; **außer/in ~ sein** to be out of/in sight

sickern ['zɪ·kɐn] vi sein to seep (aus +dat from, durch +akk through)

sie [ziː] pron pers, 3. pers **❶** <gen ihrer, dat ihr, akk sie> sing she; ~ **ist es!** it's her!; (weibliche Sache bezeichnend) it; (Tier bezeichnend) it; (bei weiblichen Haustieren) she **❷** <gen ihrer, dat ihnen, akk sie> pl they

Sie[1] <gen Ihrer, dat Ihnen, akk Sie> [ziː] pron pers, 2. pers sing o pl (förmliche Anrede) you

Sie[2] <-s> [ziː] nt kein pl **jdn mit ~ anreden** to address sb using the "Sie" form

Sieb <-[e]s, -e> [ziːp] nt (Küchensieb) sieve; (größer) colander; (Kaffeesieb, Teesieb) strainer

sieben[1] ['ziː·bn̩] adj seven; s. a. **acht**[1]

sieben[2] ['ziː·bn̩] vt to sieve

siebenhundert ['ziː·bn̩·'hʊn·dɐt] adj seven hundred

siebte(r, s) ['ziːp·tə, -tə, -təs] adj **❶** (an siebter Stelle) seventh; s. a. **achte(r, s)**

S

1 ⊚ (*Datum*) seventh, 7th; *s. a.* **achte(r, s) 2**

Siebtel <-s, -> ['zi:p·t̩l] *nt* seventh

siebzehn ['zi:p·tse:n] *adj* seventeen; *s. a.* **acht**[1]

siebzehnte(r, s) *adj* ⊙ (*an siebzehnter Stelle*) seventeenth; *s. a.* **achte(r, s) 1** ⊚ (*Datum*) seventeenth, 17th; *s. a.* **achte(r, s) 2**

siebzig ['zi:p·tsɪç] *adj* seventy; *s. a.* **achtzig 1, 2**

siebzigste(r, s) *adj* seventieth; *s. a.* **achte(r, s) 1**

siedeln ['zi:·d̩ln] *vi* to settle

sieden <siedete, gesiedet> ['zi:·d̩n] *vi* to boil

Siedepunkt *m* boiling point

Siedler(in) <-s, -> ['zi:d·lɐ] *m(f)* settler

Siedlung <-, -en> ['zi:d·lʊŋ] *f* ① (*Wohnhausgruppe*) housing development ② (*Ansiedlung*) settlement

Sieg <-[e]s, -e> [zi:k] *m* victory (**über** +*akk* over)

Siegel <-s, -> ['zi:·g̩l] *nt* seal; (*privates a.*) signet

siegen ['zi:·g̩n] *vt, vi* to win

Sieger(in) <-s, -> *m(f)* ① MIL victor ② SPORT winner

Siegerehrung *f* SPORT victory ceremony

Siegerurkunde *f* SPORT winner's certificate

siegessicher *adj* certain of victory *pred*

siegreich I. *adj* ① MIL victorious ② SPORT winning *attr*, successful II. *adv* in triumph

sieh(e) ['zi:·(ə)] *imp sing von* **sehen**

Signal <-s, -e> [zɪ·'gna:l] *nt* signal

signalisieren* [zɪ·gna·li·'zi:·rən] *vt* to signal

Signatur <-, -en> [zɪ·gna·'tu:ɐ] *f* signature

signieren* [zɪ·'gni:·rən] *vt* to sign; (*bei einer Autogrammstunde*) to autograph; ■ **signiert** signed, autographed

Silbe <-, -n> ['zɪl·bə] *f* syllable

Silbentrennung *f* hyphenation

Silber <-s> ['zɪl·bɐ] *nt kein pl* silver

Silberhochzeit *f* silver wedding anniversary

Silbermedaille *f* silver medal

silbern ['zɪl·bɐn] *adj* ① (*aus Silber bestehend*) silver ② (*Farbe*) silver[y]

Silhouette <-, -n> [zi·'lʊɛtə] *f* silhouette

Silizium <-s> [zi·'li:·tsi̯·ʊm] *nt kein pl* silicon

Silvester <-s, -> [zɪl·'vɛs·tɐ] *m o nt* New Year's Eve

simpel ['zɪm·p̩l] I. *adj* simple II. *adv* simply

Sims <-es, -e> [zɪms] *m o nt* (*Fenstersims*) windowsill; (*Kaminsims*) mantelpiece

simsen ['zɪm·zən] *vt, vi* TELEK (*fam*) to text, to send a text message

Simulant(in) <-en, -en> [zi·mu·'lant] *m(f)* malingerer

simulieren* [zi·mu·'li:·rən] I. *vi* to malinger II. *vt* SCI to [computer-]simulate

simultan [zi·mʊl·'ta:n] I. *adj* simultaneous II. *adv* simultaneously; ~ **dolmetschen** to simultaneously interpret

Sinfonie <-, -n> [zɪn·fo·'ni:] *f* symphony

singen <sang, gesungen> ['zɪŋ·ən] *vt, vi* to sing

Singular <-s, -e> ['zɪŋ·gu·la·ɐ̯] *m* LING singular

Singvogel *m* songbird

sinken <sank, gesunken> ['zɪŋ·kn] *vi sein* ① (*versinken*) to sink; *Schiff* to go down ② (*abnehmen*) to go down; *Fieber, Preis* to fall; *Hoffnung* to sink ▶ WENDUNGEN: **den Mut ~ lassen** to lose courage

Sinn <-[e]s, -e> [zɪn] *m* ① *meist pl* (*Organ der Wahrnehmung*) sense; **bist du noch bei ~ en?** have you taken leave of your senses?; **von ~ en sein** to be out of one's mind ② *kein pl* (*Bedeutung*) meaning; **im wahrsten ~ e des Wortes** in the truest sense of the word; **im übertragenen ~ e** in the figurative sense; **in diesem ~ e** in that respect ③ (*Zweck*) point; **der ~ des Lebens** the meaning of life; **es hat keinen ~[, etw zu tun]** there's no point [in doing sth] ④ *kein pl* (*Verständnis*) ~ **für**

etw *akk* **haben** to appreciate sth ⑤ (*Intention, Gedanke*) inclination; **in jds** *dat* ~ **handeln** to act according to sb's wishes; **was hast du mit ihm im ~?** what do you have in mind with him?

sinnbildlich I. *adj* symbolic **II.** *adv* symbolically

Sinnesorgan *nt* sense organ

Sinnestäuschung *f* hallucination

sinngemäß *adv* **etw ~ wiedergeben** to give the gist of sth

sinnlich I. *adj* ① (*sexuell*) carnal *form* ② (*sexuell verlangend*) sensual; (*stärker*) voluptuous ③ (*gern genießend*) sensuous, sensual ④ (*die Sinne ansprechend*) sensory, sensorial **II.** *adv* (*mit den Sinnen*) sensuously

Sinnlichkeit <-> *f kein pl* sensuality

sinnlos *adj* ① (*unsinnig*) senseless; *Bemühungen* futile; *Geschwätz* meaningless; **das ist doch ~!** that's pointless! ② (*pej: maßlos*) frenzied; *Hass, Wut* blind

Sinnlosigkeit <-, -en> *f* futility

sinnvoll I. *adj* ① (*zweckmäßig*) practical, appropriate (*Erfüllung bietend*) meaningful ③ (*eine Bedeutung habend*) meaningful, coherent **II.** *adv* sensibly

Sintflut ['zɪnt·fluːt] *f* ■ **die ~** the Flood ▶WENDUNGEN: **nach mir die ~** (*fam*) I don't care what happens after I leave

Sippe <-, -n> ['zɪ·pə] *f* ① SOZIOL [extended] family ② (*hum fam: Verwandtschaft*) family, clan *fam*

Sirene <-, -n> [zi·'reː·nə] *f* siren

Sirup <-s, -e> ['ziː·rʊp] *m* syrup

Sitte <-, -n> ['zɪtə] *f* custom ▶WENDUNGEN: **andere Länder, andere ~n** other countries, other customs

Sittlichkeitsverbrechen *nt* sex crime

Situation <-, -en> [zi·tu̯a·'t͡si̯oːn] *f* situation; (*persönlich a.*) position

Sitz <-es, -e> [zɪts] *m* ① (*Sitzgelegenheit*) seat ② (*Amtssitz*) seat; *von Verwaltung* headquarters + *sing/pl vb*; *von Unternehmen* head office

sitzen <saß, gesessen> ['zɪtsn̩] *vi* **haben** *o* SÜDD, ÖSTERR, SCHWEIZ **sein**

① (*sich gesetzt haben*) to sit; **im S~** while seated, sitting down; **bitte bleiben Sie ~!** please don't get up! ② (*beschäftigt sein*) **an einem Aufsatz ~** to be laboring over an essay ③ (*fam: inhaftiert sein*) to do time ④ MODE *Hosen, Rock* to fit ⑤ SCH ~ **bleiben** (*fam*) to repeat a grade ⑥ (*nicht absetzen können*) **auf etw** *dat* ~ **bleiben** to be left with sth ▶WENDUNGEN: **sie hat einen ~** (*fam*) she's had one too many; **jdn ~ lassen** (*fam: im Stich lassen*) to leave sb in the lurch; (*versetzen*) to stand sb up; (*nicht heiraten*) to jilt sb; **das lasse ich nicht auf mir ~!** I won't stand for this/that!

Sitzgelegenheit *f* seats *pl*, seating [accommodation]

Sitzplatz *m* seat

Sitzung <-, -en> *f* meeting; (*im Parlament*) [parliamentary] session

Sitzungssaal *m* conference hall

Sizilien <-s> [zi·'t͡siː·li̯ən] *nt* Sicily; *s. a.* **Deutschland**

Skala <-, Skalen> ['skaː·la] *f* ① (*Maßeinteilung*) scale ② (*Palette*) range

Skandal <-s, -e> [skan·'daːl] *m* scandal

skandalös [skan·da·'løːs] **I.** *adj* scandalous, outrageous **II.** *adv* outrageously, shockingly

Skandinavien <-s> [skan·di·'naː·vi̯ən] *nt* Scandinavia

skandinavisch [skan·di·'naː·vɪʃ] *adj* Scandinavian

Skateboard <-s, -s> ['skeːt·bɔːɐ̯t] *nt* skateboard; ~ **fahren** to skateboard

Skelett <-[e]s, -e> [ske·'lɛt] *nt* skeleton

Skepsis <-> ['skɛp·sɪs] *f kein pl* skepticism

skeptisch ['skɛp·tɪʃ] **I.** *adj* skeptical **II.** *adv* skeptically

Ski <-s, -> [ʃiː, 'ʃiːɐ̯] *m* ski; ~ **laufen** to ski

Skianzug *m* ski suit

Skifahrer(in) *m(f)* skier

Skilift *m* ski lift

Skinhead <-s, -s> ['skɪn·hɛt] *m* skinhead

Skipiste *f* ski run

Skispringen *nt kein pl* ski jumping

Skizze <-, -n> ['skɪ·tsə] f sketch

skizzieren* [skɪ·'tsiː·rən] vt ❶ (umreißen) Plan to outline ❷ KUNST (als Skizze darstellen) to sketch

Sklave, Sklavin <-n, -n> ['skla·və, 'skla·vɪn] m, f slave

Sklavenhandel m kein pl slave trade

Sklaverei <-, -en> [skla·və·'rai] f slavery no art

Skorpion <-s, -e> [skɔr·'pi̯oːn] m ❶ ZOOL scorpion ❷ ASTROL Scorpio

Skrupel <-s, -> ['skruː·pl̩] m meist pl scruple, qualms pl

skrupellos (pej) I. adj unscrupulous II. adv without scruple

Skrupellosigkeit <-> f kein pl unscrupulousness

Skulptur <-, -en> [skʊlp·'tuːɐ̯] f sculpture

Slalom <-s, -s> ['sla·lɔm] m slalom

Slawe, Slawin <-n, -n> ['sla·və, 'sla·vɪn] m, f Slav; s. a. **Deutsche(r)**

slawisch ['sla·vɪʃ] adj Slav[on]ic; s. a. **deutsch**

Slip <-s, -s> [slɪp] m panties pl

Slipeinlage f panty liner

Slowakei <-> [slo·va·'kai] f ▪ **die ~** Slovakia; s. a. **Deutschland**

Slowenien <-s> [slo·'veː·ni̯ən] nt Slovenia; s. a. **Deutschland**

Slum <-s, -s> [slam] m slum

Smaragd <-[e]s, -e> [sma·'rakt] m emerald

Smog <-[s], -s> [smɔk] m smog

Smogalarm m smog alert

Smoking <-s, -s> ['smoː·kɪŋ] m tuxedo, dinner jacket

SMS <-, -> [ɛs·ʔɛm·'ɛs] f MEDIA, TELEK Abk von **Short Message Service** text [message], IM; **jdm eine ~ schicken** to text sb

so [zoː] I. adv ❶ + adj/adv (derart) so; **es ist ~, wie du sagst** it is [just] as you say; **das ist ~ weit richtig, aber ...** generally speaking that is right, but ...; **~ viel [wie]** as much [as]; **~ weit sein** (fam) to be ready; **~ wenig wie möglich** as little as possible ❷ + vb (derart) **sie hat sich ~ darauf gefreut** she was really looking forward to it; **ich habe mich ~ über ihn geärgert!** I was so angry with him ❸ (auf diese Weise) like this/that, this/that way, thus form; **~ musst du es machen** this is how you have to do it; **~ ist das nun mal** (fam) that's the way things are; **~ ist es** that's [just] the way it is; **~, als ob ...** as if ...; **~ oder ~** either way, in the end; **und ~ weiter [und ~ fort]** et cetera[, et cetera]; **~ genannt** so-called ❹ (solch) **~ ein Buch haben wir nicht** we don't have a book like that; **~ etwas** such a thing; **~ etwas sagt man nicht** you shouldn't say such things ❺ (fam: etwa) **wir treffen uns ~ gegen 7 Uhr** we'll meet at around 7 o'clock ❻ (fam) **und/oder ~** or so; **ich gehe um 5 oder ~** I'm going around 5 or so ❼ (fam: umsonst) for nothing; **das können Sie ~ haben** you can have it [for free] II. konj ❶ (konsekutiv) ▪ **~ dass** so that ❷ (obwohl) **~ leid es mir auch tut** as sorry as I am III. interj ❶ (also) so, right; **~, jetzt gehen wir einkaufen** so, now let's go shopping ❷ (ätsch) so there! ❸ (ach) **~, ~!** (fam) is that a fact! iron

sobald [zo·'balt] konj as soon as

Socke <-, -n> ['zɔ·kə] f sock ▶WENDUNGEN: **sich** akk **auf die ~n machen** (fam) to get a move on

Sockel <-s, -> ['zɔ·kl̩] m ❶ von Statue plinth, pedestal ❷ (von Gebäude) plinth, base course

Sodbrennen [zoːt-] nt heartburn

soeben [zo·'ʔeː·bn̩] adv (geh) just

Sofa <-s, -s> ['zoː·fa] nt sofa

sofern [zo·'fɛrn] konj if, provided that

sofort [zo·'fɔrt] adv immediately

sofortig [zo·'fɔr·tɪç] adj immediate; **mit ~er Wirkung** with immediate effect

Softie <-s, -s> ['zɔf·ti] m (fam) softie

Software <-, -s> ['sɔft·veːɐ̯] f software

sogar [zo·'gaːɐ̯] adv even

Sohle <-, -n> ['zoː·lə] f sole

Sohn <-[e]s, Söhne> [zoːn] m son

Sojabohne f soybean

solange [zo·'laŋə] konj as long as

Solarenergie f solar energy

Solarium <-s, -rien> [zo·'la:·ri̯·ʊm] nt solarium

solch [zɔlç] adj such

solche(r, s) adj ① attr such; ~ **Frauen** women like that; **ich machte mir ~ Sorgen** I was really worried; **sie hatte ~ Angst ...** she was so afraid ... ② substantivisch (solche Menschen) people like that; **es gibt ~ und ~ Kunden** there are customers and then there are customers; **als ~(r, s)** as such, in itself; **der Mensch als ~r** man as such

Sold <-[e]s> [zɔlt] m kein pl MIL pay

Soldat(in) <-en, -en> [zɔl·'da:t] m(f) soldier

Söldner(in) <-s, -> ['zœld·nɐ] m(f) mercenary

solidarisieren* [zo·li·da·ri·'zi:·rən] vr ■ **sich** akk ~ to show [one's] solidarity

Solidarität <-> [zo·li·da·ri·'tɛ:t] f kein pl solidarity

Solidaritätszuschlag m POL solidarity tax (a tax to help finance the cost of the German reunification)

solide [zo·'li:·də] I. adj ① (haltbar, fest) solid; Kleidung durable ② (fundiert) Kenntnisse sound, thorough ③ (untadelig) Leben respectable ④ (seriös) Unternehmen well-established attr; sound II. adv (haltbar, fest) solidly

Solist(in) <-en, -en> [zo·'lɪst] m(f) MUS soloist

Soll <-[s], -[s]> [zɔl] nt ① (Sollseite) debit side; **~ und Haben** debit and credit ② (Produktionsnorm) target; **sein ~ erfüllen** to reach one's target

sollen ['zɔ·lən] I. aux vb <sollte, sollen> ① (etw zu tun haben) **du sollst herkommen, habe ich gesagt!** I said [you should] come here!; **man hat mir gesagt, ich soll Sie fragen** I was told to ask you; **was ~ wir machen?** what should we do? ② (falls) **sollte das passieren, ...** should that happen ... ③ (eigentlich müssen) **du sollst dich schämen!** you should be ashamed [of yourself]; **das solltest du unbedingt sehen** you have to see this; **so soll es sein** that's how it ought to be ④ (angeblich sein, tun) to be supposed to; **sie soll sehr reich sein** she is said to be very rich; **was soll das heißen?** what's that supposed to mean? ⑤ (dürfen) **du hättest das nicht tun ~** you should not have done that ⑥ in der Vergangenheit **es sollte ganz anders kommen** things were supposed to turn out quite differently II. vi <sollte, gesollt> ① (eine Anweisung befolgen) **soll er reinkommen? – ja, er soll** should he come in? — yes, he should ② (müssen) **du sollst sofort nach Hause** you should go home right away ③ (bedeuten) **was soll der Blödsinn?** (fam) what's all this nonsense about?; **was soll das?** (fam) what's that supposed to mean?; **was soll's?** (fam) who cares?

Solo <-s, Soli> ['zo:·lo] nt MUS solo

somit [zo·'mɪt] adv therefore, hence form

Sommer <-s, -> ['zɔ·mɐ] m summer

sommerlich I. adj summer attr; **~es Wetter** summer weather II. adv like in summer; **sich** akk **~ kleiden** to wear summer clothing

Sommersprosse f meist pl freckle

Sonate <-, -n> [zo·'na:·tə] f sonata

Sonde <-, -n> ['zɔn·də] f ① MED (Schlauchsonde) tube; (Operationssonde) probe ② (Raumsonde) probe

Sonderangebot nt special offer; **etw im ~ haben** to have sth on sale

sonderbar ['zɔn·dɐ·ba:ɐ] I. adj peculiar, strange, odd II. adv strangely

Sonderfall m special case

Sonderling <-s, -e> ['zɔn·dɐ·lɪŋ] m oddball

Sondermüll m hazardous waste

sondern ['zɔn·dɐn] konj but; **nicht sie war es, ~ er** it wasn't her, it was him

Sonderpreis m special [reduced] [or sale] price

Sonderregelung f special provision

Sonderschule f school for special education

Sonderstellung f special position

S

Sonderzug m special [or chartered] train

Sonett <-[e]s, -e> [zo·'nɛt] nt sonnet

Sonnabend ['zɔn·ʔa:bn̩t] m DIAL (*Samstag*) Saturday

sonnabends adv DIAL (*samstags*) [on] Saturdays

Sonne <-, -n> ['zɔnə] f kein pl sun; **die ~ geht auf/unter** the sun rises/sets

sonnen ['zɔ·nən] vr ① (*sonnenbaden*) ■ **sich** akk ~ to sunbathe ② (*genießen*) ■ **sich** akk **in etw** dat ~ to bask in sth

Sonnenaufgang m sunrise, sunup

Sonnenbad nt sunbathing; **ein ~ nehmen** to sunbathe

Sonnenblume f sunflower

Sonnenbrand m sunburn no art

Sonnenbrille f sunglasses npl, shades npl sl

Sonnenenergie f solar energy

Sonnenfinsternis f solar eclipse

Sonnenlicht nt kein pl sunlight

Sonnenmilch f suntan lotion

Sonnenschein m sunshine

Sonnenschirm m sunshade; (*tragbar*) parasol

Sonnenstich m sunstroke no art

Sonnenstrahl m sunbeam

Sonnensystem nt solar system

Sonnenuntergang m sunset, sundown

sonnig ['zɔ·nɪç] adj sunny

Sonntag ['zɔn·ta:k] m Sunday; s. a. **Dienstag**

sonntäglich adj [regular] Sunday attr

sonntags adv [on] Sundays

sonst [zɔnst] adv ① (*andernfalls*) or [else], otherwise ② (*gewöhnlich*) usually; **du hast doch ~ keine Bedenken** you don't usually have any doubts; **kälter als ~** colder than usual ③ (*außerdem*) ~ **noch Fragen?** any more questions?; **gibt es ~ noch etwas?** is there anything else?; ■ ~ **keine(r, s)** nothing/nobody else; ~ **nichts** nothing else; ~ **was** whatever

sonstig ['zɔns·tɪç] adj attr (*weitere[s]*) other; „**Sonstiges**" "miscellaneous"

Sopran <-s, -e> [zo·'pra:n] m kein pl soprano

Sorge <-, -n> ['zɔr·gə] f worry; **keine ~!** (*fam*) don't [you] worry; ■ **sich** akk **um etw** akk ~ **machen** to worry about sth; ~**n haben** to have problems

sorgen ['zɔr·gn̩] I. vi ① (*sich kümmern*) ■ **für jdn** ~ to provide for [or look after] sb ② (*besorgen*) **ich sorge dafür, dass ...** I'll see to it that ...; **dafür ist gesorgt** that's taken care of ③ (*bewirken*) **für Aufsehen** ~ to cause a sensation II. vr ■ **sich** akk **um jdn/etw** ~ to be worried about sb/sth

Sorgerecht nt kein pl custody

Sorgfalt <-> ['zɔrk·falt] f kein pl care

sorgfältig I. adj careful II. adv carefully

sorglos ['zɔrk·lo:s] I. adj ① (*achtlos*) careless ② (*sorgenfrei*) carefree II. adv ① (*achtlos*) carelessly ② (*sorgenfrei*) free of care

Sorte <-, -n> ['zɔr·tə] f ① (*Art*) kind, variety ② (*Marke*) brand

sortieren* [zɔr·'ti:·rən] vt to sort

Sortiment <-[e]s, -e> [zɔr·ti·'mɛnt] nt range [of products]

Soße <-, -n> ['zo:·sə] f sauce; (*Bratensoße*) gravy

Souterrain <-s, -s> ['zu:·tɛ·rɛ̃] nt basement

Souvenir <-s, -s> [zu·və·'ni:ɐ̯] nt souvenir

souverän [zu·və·'rɛːn] I. adj ① (*unabhängig*) sovereign attr ② (*überlegen*) superior II. adv with superior ease

Souveränität <-> [zu·və·rɛ·ni·'tɛːt] f kein pl sovereignty; (*Überlegenheit*) supremacy

soviel [zo·'fi:l] konj as far as; ~ **ich weiß ...** as far as I know ...; ~ **ich auch trinke ...** no matter how much I drink ...

soweit [zo·'vait] konj as far as

sowie [zo·'vi:] konj ① (*sobald*) as soon as, the moment [that] ② (*und auch*) as well as

sowieso [zo·vi·'zo:] adv anyway, anyhow

sowohl [zo·'vo:l] konj ■ ~ **... als auch ...** both ... and ..., ... as well as ...

sozial [zo·'tsi̯a:l] **I.** *adj* **①** *(gesellschaftlich)* social **②** *(für Hilfsbedürftige gedacht)* welfare *attr* **③** *(gesellschaftlich verantwortlich)* public-spirited **II.** *adv* ~ **schwache Familien** low-income families; ~ **denken** to be socially minded

Sozialabgaben *pl* social security contributions

Sozialamt *nt* Department of Social Services

Sozialarbeiter(in) *m(f)* social worker

Sozialdemokrat(in) *m(f)* social democrat

sozialdemokratisch *adj* social democratic

Sozialhilfe *f kein pl* welfare

Sozialismus <-> [zo·tsi̯a·'lɪs·mʊs] *m kein pl* socialism

Sozialist(in) <-en, -en> [zo·tsi̯a·'lɪst] *m(f)* socialist

sozialistisch [zo·tsi̯a·'lɪstɪʃ] *adj* **①** *(Sozialismus betreffend)* socialist **②** ÖSTERR *(sozialdemokratisch)* social democratic

Sozialleistungen *pl* social security benefits

Sozialstaat *m* welfare state

Sozialwohnung *f* [housing] project

Soziologe, Soziologin <-n, -n> [zo·tsi̯o·'lo:·gə, -'lo:·gɪn] *m, f* sociologist

Soziologie <-> [zo·tsi̯o·lo·'gi:] *f kein pl* sociology

sozusagen [zo:·tsu·'za:·gn̩] *adv* as it were, so to speak

Spachtel <-s, -> ['ʃpaxtl̩] *m* putty knife

Spagettiᴿᴿ, **Spaghetti** [ʃpa·'gɛ·ti] *f* spaghetti + *sing vb*

spähen ['ʃpɛ:·ən] *vi* **①** *(suchend blicken)* to peek *(durch +akk through)* **②** *(Ausschau halten)* to look out *(nach +dat for)*

Spalt <-[e]s, -e> [ʃpalt] *m* gap; *(Riss)* crack; *(Felsspalt)* crevice; **die Tür einen ~ öffnen/offen lassen** to open the door slightly/leave the door ajar

Spalte <-, -n> ['ʃpal·tə] *f* **①** *(Öffnung)* fissure; *(Felsspalte a.)* crevice **②** TYPO, MEDIA column

spalten ['ʃpal·tn̩] **I.** *vt* <pp gespalten o

gespaltet> **①** *(zerteilen)* to split; *Holz a.* to chop **②** *(trennen)* to divide **II.** *vr* <pp gespalten> ■ **sich** *akk* ~ **①** *(der Länge nach reißen)* to split **②** *(sich teilen)* to divide

Spamfilter ['spɛm-] *m* INET spam filter

Span <-[e]s, Späne> [ʃpaːn] *m* *(Holzspan)* [wood] chip; *(Bohrspan)* swarf, turnings *pl*

Spanferkel ['ʃpaːn·fɛr·kl̩] *nt* suckling pig

Spange <-, -n> ['ʃpaŋə] *f* **①** *(Haarspange)* barrette **②** *(Zahnspange)* braces *pl*, retainer

Spanien <-s> ['ʃpaː·ni̯ən] *nt* Spain; *s. a.* **Deutschland**

Spanier(in) <-s, -> ['ʃpaː·ni̯e] *m(f)* Spaniard; ■ **die** ~ the Spanish; *s. a.* **Deutsche(r)**

spanisch ['ʃpaː·nɪʃ] *adj* Spanish; *s. a.* **deutsch**

spann [ʃpan] *imp von* **spinnen**

Spannbetttuchᴿᴿ *nt* fitted sheet

Spanne <-, -n> ['ʃpanə] *f* **①** *(Gewinnspanne)* [profit] margin **②** *(Zeitspanne)* span

spannen ['ʃpa·nən] **I.** *vt* **①** *(straffen)* to tighten **②** *(aufspannen)* Wäscheleine to put up *sep*; *Seil* to stretch *(**zwischen** +akk between)* **③** *(anspannen)* Tier to harness *(**vor** +akk to)* **II.** *vr* ■ **sich** *akk* ~ *Seil* to become taut **III.** *vi* *(zu eng sitzen)* Hose to be [too] tight

spannend *adj* exciting; *(stärker)* thrilling

Spannung <-, -en> *f* **①** *kein pl (gespannte Erwartung)* suspense; **etw mit ~ erwarten** to anxiously await sth **②** *meist pl (Anspannung)* tension **③** ELEK voltage; **unter ~ stehen** to be live

Sparbuch *nt* bankbook

Sparbüchse *f* piggy bank

sparen ['ʃpaː·rən] **I.** *vt* **①** *(einsparen)* to save **②** *(ersparen)* ■ **sich/jdm etw** ~ to spare oneself/sb sth; **den Weg hätten wir uns ~ können** we could have saved ourselves that trip; **deine Ratschläge kannst du dir ~**

[you can] keep your advice to yourself II. vi ❶ FIN (*Geld zurücklegen*) to save; ■**für etw** *akk* ~ to save [up] for sth ❷ (*sparsam sein*) to economize (**an** + *dat* on)

Sparer(in) <-s, -> *m(f)* saver

Spargel <-s, -> ['ʃpar·gl̩] *m* asparagus

Sparkasse *f* bank (*supported publicly by a commune or district*)

spärlich ['ʃpɛːɐ̯·lɪç] I. *adj Haarwuchs, Vegetation* sparse; *Ausbeute, Reste* meager II. *adv* sparsely; ~ **bekleidet** scantily dressed; ~ **besucht** poorly attended

Sparmaßnahme *f* cost-cutting measure

Sparpreis *m* budget [*or* economy] price

sparsam ['ʃpaːɐ̯·zaːm] I. *adj* thrifty; (*ökonomisch im Verbrauch*) economical II. *adv* thriftily; (*ökonomisch beim Verbrauch*) sparingly

Sparsamkeit <-> *f kein pl* thriftiness

Sparschwein *nt* piggy bank

Sparte <-, -n> ['ʃpar·tə] *f* ❶ (*Branche*) line of business ❷ (*Spezialbereich*) area, branch ❸ (*Rubrik*) section, column

Spaß <-es, Späße> [ʃpaːs] *m* ❶ *kein pl* (*Vergnügen*) fun; **es macht mir ~, das zu tun** I enjoy doing that; **viel ~!** have fun! ❷ (*Scherz*) joke; **da hört der ~ auf** that's going a bit too far; ~ **sein** (*fam*) there's no harm in a joke; **keinen ~ verstehen** to not have a sense of humor; ~ **beiseite** joking apart; [**nur**] ~ **machen** to be [just] kidding ▶WENDUNGEN: **ein teurer ~ sein** to be an expensive business

spaßen ['ʃpaː·sn̩] *vi* to joke; **mit etw** *dat* **ist nicht zu ~** sth is no joking matter

spaßig ['ʃpaː·sɪç] *adj* funny

Spaßverderber(in) <-s, -> *m(f)* spoilsport

Spaßvogel *m* joker

spät [ʃpɛːt] I. *adj* late; **am ~en Abend** late in the evening II. *adv* late; **du kommst zu ~** you're too late; **wie ~ ist es?** what time is it?; **wie ~ kommst du heute nach Hause?** what time are you

coming home today?; ~ **dran sein** to be [running] late

Spaten <-s, -> ['ʃpaː·tn̩] *m* spade

später ['ʃpɛː·tɐ] I. *adj* later II. *adv* later [on]; **bis ~!** see you later!; **nicht ~ als** not later than; ~ [**ein**]**mal** some other time

spätestens ['ʃpɛː·təs·tn̩s] *adv* at the [very] latest

Spätschicht *f* late shift

Spätvorstellung *f* late show[ing]

Spatz <-en, -en> [ʃpats] *m* ORN sparrow

spazieren* [ʃpa·ˈtsiː·rən] *vi sein* to walk; ~ **fahren/gehen** to go for a drive/walk

Spazierfahrt *f* drive; **eine ~ machen** to go for a drive

Spaziergang <-gänge> *m* walk, stroll; **einen ~ machen** to go for a walk

Spaziergänger(in) <-s, -> *m(f)* stroller

Specht <-[e]s, -e> [ʃpɛçt] *m* woodpecker

Speck <-[e]s, -e> [ʃpɛk] *m* bacon

Spediteur(in) <-s, -e> [ʃpe·diˈtøːɐ̯] *m(f)* freight forwarder, shipper

Spedition <-, -en> [ʃpe·diˈtsi̯oːn] *f* (*Transportunternehmen*) trucking company; (*Umzugsunternehmen*) moving company

Speerwerfen *nt kein pl* SPORT the javelin

Speiche <-, -n> ['ʃpai̯·çə] *f* spoke

Speichel <-s> ['ʃpai̯·çl̩] *m kein pl* saliva

Speicher <-s, -> ['ʃpai̯·çɐ] *m* ❶ (*Dachboden*) attic, loft; **auf dem** ~ in the attic ❷ (*Lagerhaus*) storehouse ❸ COMPUT memory

Speicherkarte *f* COMPUT memory [*or* flash] card

speichern ['ʃpai̯·çɐn] *vt, vi* COMPUT to save; *Nummern im Handy* to store

Speicherplatz *m* COMPUT memory space; (*auf Festplatte*) disk space

Speicherung <-, -en> *f* COMPUT storage

Speise <-, -n> ['ʃpai̯·zə] *f meist pl* meal

Speisekarte *f* menu

speisen ['ʃpai̯·zn̩] *vi* to dine, to eat

Speiseöl *nt* cooking oil

Speiseröhre *f* esophagus, gullet

Speisewagen *m* dining car

spektakulär [ʃpɛk·ta·ku·ˈlɛːɐ̯] *adj* spectacular

Spekulant(in) <-en, -en> [ʃpe·ku·ˈlant] *m(f)* speculator

spekulieren* [ʃpe·ku·ˈliː·rən] *vi* to speculate (**mit** +*dat* in, **auf** +*akk* on)

spendabel [ʃpɛn·ˈdaː·bl̩] *adj* generous

Spende <-, -n> [ˈʃpɛn·də] *f* donation

spenden [ˈʃpɛn·dn̩] *vt*, *vi* to donate; *Blut* to give

Spender <-s, -> [ˈʃpɛn·dɐ] *m* (*Dosierer*) dispenser

Spender(in) <-s, -> [ˈʃpɛn·dɐ] *m(f)* ❶ (*jd, der spendet*) don[at]or ❷ MED donor

spendieren* [ʃpɛn·ˈdiː·rən] *vt* (*fam*) ■ **jdm] etw ~** to buy [sb] sth; **das Essen spendiere ich** [the] dinner's on me

Sperling <-s, -e> [ˈʃpɛr·lɪŋ] *m* sparrow

Sperma <-s, Spermen> [ˈʃpɛr·ma, ˈʃpɛr·ma] *nt* sperm

Sperre <-, -n> [ˈʃpɛ·rə] *f* ❶ (*Sperrvorrichtung*) barrier ❷ (*Spielverbot*) ban

sperren [ˈʃpɛ·rən] I. *vt* ❶ SÜDD, ÖSTERR (*schließen*) to close off (**für** +*akk* to) ❷ (*blockieren*) to block; *Konto* to freeze; *Scheck* to stop payment on ❸ (*einschließen*) to lock [up] ❹ (*ein Spielverbot verhängen*) to ban II. *vr* ■ **sich** *akk* ~ to back away (**gegen** +*akk* from)

Sperrmüll *m* bulky trash

Sperrstunde *f* closing time

Spesen [ˈʃpe·zn̩] *pl* expenses *npl*

Spezialgebiet *nt* special field

spezialisieren* [ʃpe·tsi̯a·li·ˈziː·rən] *vr* ■ **sich** *akk* ~ to specialize (**auf** +*akk* in)

Spezialisierung <-, -en> *f* specialization

Spezialist(in) <-en, -en> [ʃpe·tsi̯a·ˈlɪst] *m(f)* specialist

Spezialität <-, -en> [ʃpe·tsi̯a·li·ˈtɛːt] *f* specialty

speziell [ʃpe·ˈtsi̯ɛl] I. *adj* special II. *adv* |e]specially

spezifisch [ʃpe·ˈtsiː·fɪʃ] I. *adj* specific II. *adv* typically

Sphäre <-, -n> [ˈsfɛː·rə] *f* sphere

spicken [ˈʃpɪ·kn̩] *vt* ❶ KOCHK (*durchsetzen*) to lard ❷ (*fam: abschreiben*) to copy

Spiegel <-s, -> [ˈʃpiː·gl̩] *m* mirror

Spiegelbild *nt* mirror image

Spiegelei *nt* egg sunny side up

Spiegelei *nt* egg sunny side up

spiegeln [ˈʃpiː·gln̩] I. *vi* to reflect II. *vr* ■ **sich** *akk* **in etw** *dat* ~ to be reflected in sth

Spiegelreflexkamera *f* reflex camera

Spiel <-[e]s, -e> [ʃpiːl] *nt* game; (*im Tennis, Volleyball*) match ▸WENDUNGEN: **ein abgekartetes ~** (*fam*) a fix; **jdn/etw aus dem ~ lassen** to keep sb/sth out of it; **leichtes ~ haben** to have an easy job of it; **[bei etw] im ~ sein** to be involved [in sth]; **etw aufs ~ setzen** to put sth on the line; **auf dem ~ stehen** to be at stake; **jdm das ~ verderben** (*fam*) to ruin sb's plans

Spielautomat *m* gambling machine

Spielbank *f* casino

spielen [ˈʃpiː·lən] I. *vt* to play ▸WENDUNGEN: **was wird hier gespielt?** what's going on here? II. *vi* ❶ to play; (*beim Glücksspiel*) to gamble ❷ (*als Szenario haben*) **in Italien/im Mittelalter ~** to be set in Italy/in the Middle Ages

spielend *adv* easily

Spieler(in) <-s, -> [ˈʃpiː·lɐ] *m(f)* ❶ (*Mitspieler*) player ❷ (*Glücksspieler*) gambler

spielerisch I. *adj* playful II. *adv* playfully

Spielfeld [ˈʃpiːl·fɛlt] *nt* [playing] field

Spielfilm *m* feature film

Spielkamerad(in) *m(f)* playmate

Spielkarte *f* playing card

Spielkasino *nt* casino

Spielplatz *m* playground

Spielraum *m* leeway

Spielregel *f meist pl* rules *pl*

Spielsachen *pl* toys *pl*

Spielverderber(in) <-s, -> *m(f)* spoilsport

Spielzeit *f* ❶ THEAT season ❷ SPORT playing time

Spielzeug *nt* toy

Spieß <-es, -e> [ʃpiːs] *m* ❶ (*Bratspieß*)

spit; (*kleiner*) skewer ② (*Stoßwaffe*) spike ▶WENDUNGEN: **wie am ~ brüllen** to scream at the top of one's lungs; **den ~ umdrehen** to turn the tables

Spießbürger(in) *m(f)* s. Spießer

spießen ['ʃpiːsn̩] *vt* ▪**etw auf etw** *akk* ~ to skewer sth on sth

Spießer(in) <-s, -> ['ʃpiːsɐ] *m(f)* (*fam*) narrow-minded person

spießig ['ʃpiːsɪç] *adj* (*fam*) narrow-minded

Spießigkeit <-> *f kein pl* (*pej fam*) narrow-mindedness

Spinat <-[e]s> [ʃpiˈnaːt] *m kein pl* spinach

Spinne <-, -n> ['ʃpɪnə] *f* spider

spinnen <spann, gesponnen> ['ʃpɪnən] **I.** *vt* ① *Wolle* to spin ② *Geschichte* to invent **II.** *vi* (*fam: nicht bei Trost sein*) to be crazy [*or sl* nuts]; **sag mal, spinnt der?** is he out of his mind?

Spinner(in) <-s, -> ['ʃpɪnɐ] *m(f)* (*fam*) nutcase

Spinnerei <-, -en> [ʃpɪnəˈraɪ] *f* ① (*Betrieb*) spinning mill ② *kein pl* (*fam: Blödsinn*) nonsense

Spion(in) <-s, -e> [ʃpiˈoːn] *m(f)* spy

Spionage <-> [ʃpioˈnaːʒə] *f kein pl* espionage

spionieren* [ʃpioˈniːrən] *vi* to spy

Spirale <-, -n> [ʃpiˈraːlə] *f* ① (*gewundene Linie*) spiral ② MED IUD

Spirituosen [ʃpiriˈtu̯oːzn̩, sp-] *pl* spirits *pl*

S **Spital** <-s, Spitäler> [ʃpiˈtaːl] *nt* ÖSTERR, SCHWEIZ hospital

spitz [ʃpɪts] *adj* ① (*mit einer Spitze*) pointed; *Bleistift, Messer* sharp ② (*spitz zulaufend*) tapered; *Nase, Kinn* pointy ③ *Bemerkung* sharp **II.** *adv* ① (*V-förmig*) tapered ② (*spitzzüngig*) sharply

Spitze <-, -n> ['ʃpɪtsə] *f* ① (*spitzes Ende*) point ② (*vorderster Teil*) front ③ (*erster Platz, höchste Stelle eines Bergs*) top ④ (*Höchstwert*) peak ⑤ *pl* (*führende Leute*) *der Gesellschaft* the top; *eines Unternehmen* the heads ⑥ MODE lace ▶WENDUNGEN: **~ sein** (*fam*)

to be great; **etw auf die ~ treiben** to take sth to extremes

Spitzel <-s, -> ['ʃpɪtsl̩] *m* informer

spitzen ['ʃpɪtsn̩] *vt* to sharpen

Spitzenleistung *f* outstanding [*or* first-rate] performance

spitzfindig *adj* hairsplitting

Spitzname *m* nickname

Splitter <-s, -> ['ʃplɪtɐ] *m* splinter

Sponsion *f academic ceremony in Austria at which Master's degrees are awarded*

Sponsor, Sponsorin <-s, -soren> ['ʃpɔnzɐ, ʃpɔnˈzoːrɪn] *m, f* sponsor

spontan [ʃpɔnˈtaːn, sp-] *adj* spontaneous

sporadisch [spoˈraːdɪʃ, sp-] *adj* sporadic

Sport <-[e]s, *selten* -e> [ʃpɔrt] *m* ① SPORT sport[*s pl*]; **~ treiben** to play sports ② SCH PE, gym

Sportart *f* discipline, kind of sport

Sportlehrer(in) *m(f)* PE [*or* gym] teacher

Sportler(in) <-s, -> ['ʃpɔrtlɐ] *m(f)* athlete

sportlich ['ʃpɔrtlɪç] **I.** *adj* ① (*den Sport betreffend*) sporting ② (*trainiert*) *Figur* athletic; *Mensch* sporty ③ MODE casual **II.** *adv* ① SPORT (*in einer Sportart*) in sports ② (*flott*) casually

Sportplatz *m* [playing [*or* sports]] field

Sportveranstaltung *f* sports event

Sportverein *m* sports club

Sportwagen *m* AUTO sports car

Spott <-[e]s> [ʃpɔt] *m kein pl* mockery

spotten ['ʃpɔtn̩] *vi* to mock; ▪**über jdn/etw** ~ to make fun [of sb/sth]

spöttisch ['ʃpœtɪʃ] *adj* mocking

sprachbegabt *adj* linguistically talented; ▪**~ sein** to be good at languages

Sprache <-, -n> ['ʃpraːxə] *f* ① (*Kommunikationssystem*) language ② *kein pl* (*Sprechweise*) way of speaking ③ *kein pl* (*das Sprechen*) speech; **etw zur ~ bringen** to bring up *sep* sth; **zur ~ kommen** to come up ▶WENDUNGEN: **mit der ~ herausrücken** (*fam*) to come out with it; **jdm die ~ verschlagen** to leave sb speechless; **heraus mit der ~!** (*fam*) out with it!

Sprachfehler *m* speech impediment

Sprachkenntnisse *pl* language skills *pl*

Sprachkurs *m* language class [*or* course]

sprachlos *adj* speechless

Sprachwissenschaft *f* linguistics + *sing vb*

Spray <-s, -s> [ʃpreː, spreː] *m o nt* spray

sprechen <spricht, sprach, gesprochen> ['ʃprɛçn̩] **I.** *vi* ❶ (*reden*) to speak, to talk; **sprich nicht so laut** don't talk so loud; **sprich nicht in diesem Ton mit mir!** don't speak to me like that!; **wovon ~ Sie eigentlich?** what are you talking about?; **sein Benehmen spricht für sich [selbst]** his behavior speaks for itself; **mit sich selbst ~** to talk to oneself; **„hallo, wer spricht denn da?"** "hello, who's speaking?" ❷ (*empfehlen*) ■**für jdn/ etw ~** to speak well for sb/sth; ■**gegen jdn/etw ~** to not be in sb's/sth's favor **II.** *vt* ❶ (*können*) to speak; **~ Sie Chinesisch?** can you speak Chinese? ❷ (*sich unterreden*) ■**jdn ~** to speak to sb ▶WENDUNGEN: **nicht gut auf jdn zu ~ sein** to be on bad terms with sb; **wir ~ uns noch!** you haven't heard the last of this!; **für jdn/niemanden zu ~ sein** to be available for sb/to not be available for anyone

Sprecher(in) <-s, -> *m(f)* ❶ (*Wortführer*) spokesperson ❷ (*Beauftragter*) speaker ❸ RADIO, TV announcer; (*Nachrichtensprecher*) newscaster, anchorperson

Sprechstunde *f* office hours *pl*

Sprechstundenhilfe *f* receptionist

Sprechzimmer *nt* consultation room

spreizen ['ʃpraɪtsn̩] *vt* to spread

sprengen¹ ['ʃprɛŋən] **I.** *vt* ❶ (*zur Explosion bringen*) to blow up *sep* ❷ (*bersten lassen*) to burst ❸ (*gewaltsam auflösen*) to break up *sep* **II.** *vi* to blast

sprengen² ['ʃprɛŋən] *vt Rasen* to water

Sprengkörper *m* explosive device

Sprengkraft *f kein pl* explosive force

Sprengstoff *m* explosive

Sprengstoffanschlag *m* bomb attack

Sprichwort <-wörter> ['ʃprɪç·vɔrt] *nt* proverb

sprießen <spross *o* sprießte, gesprossen> ['ʃpriː·sn̩] *vi sein* BOT to sprout; *Haare* to grow

Springbrunnen *m* fountain

springen¹ <sprang, gesprungen> ['ʃprɪŋən] *vi sein* to shatter; (*einen Sprung bekommen*) to crack

springen² <sprang, gesprungen> ['ʃprɪŋən] *vi sein* to jump; (*in Sprüngen*) to leap; **er sprang hin und her** he jumped around ▶WENDUNGEN: **etw ~ lassen** (*fam*) to fork out sth

Springflut *f* spring tide

Spritze <-, -n> ['ʃprɪ·tsə] *f* ❶ (*Injektionsspritze*) syringe, needle ❷ (*Injektion*) injection, shot

spritzen ['ʃprɪ·tsn̩] **I.** *vi* ❶ (*in Tropfen*) to spray; *Fett* to spit; *Farbe* to splash ❷ *sein* (*im Strahl*) to spurt **II.** *vt haben* ❶ (*im Strahl verteilen*) to squirt ❷ (*bewässern*) to sprinkle ❸ (*injizieren*) to inject ❹ (*mit Bekämpfungsmittel besprühen*) to spray (**gegen** +*akk* against)

Spritzer <-s, -> *m* splash

spritzig ['ʃprɪ·tsɪç] *adj* ❶ (*prickelnd*) tangy ❷ (*flott*) sparkling

spröde ['ʃprøː·də] *adj* ❶ (*unelastisch*) brittle ❷ (*rau*) rough; *Haar* brittle; *Lippen* chapped ❸ (*abweisend*) aloof

sprossRR, **sproß**ALT ['ʃprɔs] *imp von* **sprießen**

SprossRR <-es, -e>, **Sproß**ALT <-sses, -sse> ['ʃprɔs] *m* BOT shoot

Sprosse <-, -n> ['ʃprɔ·sə] *f* rung, step

Spruch <-[e]s, Sprüche> ['ʃprʊx] *m* ❶ (*Ausspruch*) saying; (*Parole*) slogan ❷ (*Richterspruch*) verdict ▶WENDUNGEN: **Sprüche klopfen** (*fam*) to talk big

Sprudel <-s, -> ['ʃpruː·dl̩] *m* ❶ (*Mineralwasser*) sparkling mineral water ❷ DIAL (*Erfrischungsgetränk*) soft drink

sprudeln ['ʃpruː·dl̩n] *vi* ❶ *haben* (*aufschäumen*) to bubble, to foam ❷ *sein* (*heraussprudeln*) to bubble out

S

Sprühdose f aerosol [or spray] can

sprühen ['ʃpryːən] I. vt to spray II. vi **vor Begeisterung ~** to bubble with excitement

Sprung <-[e]s, Sprünge> [ʃprʊŋ] m ① (Riss) crack ② (Satz) leap, jump ▶WENDUNGEN: [mit etw dat] **keine gro-ßen Sprünge machen können** (fam) to not be able to live it up [with sth]; **jdm auf die Sprünge helfen** to give sb a helping hand; **auf dem ~ sein** to be in a hurry; **auf einen ~ [bei jdm] vorbei-kommen** (fam) to pop in [to see sb]

Sprungbrett nt ① (ins Wasser) diving board ② (Turngerät) springboard

Sprungschanze f ski jump

Spucke <-, -n> ['ʃpʊkə] f kein pl (fam) ▶WENDUNGEN: **jdm bleibt die ~ weg** sb is flabbergasted

spucken ['ʃpʊkn̩] I. vi to spit II. vt to spit out sep

spuken ['ʃpuːkn̩] vi impers to haunt; **hier spukt es** this place is haunted

Spüle <-, -n> ['ʃpyːlə] f [kitchen] sink

spülen ['ʃpyːlən] I. vi ① Geschirr to do the dishes ② Toilette to flush II. vt ① (abspülen) **das Geschirr ~** to do the dishes ② s. **schwemmen**

Spülmaschine f dishwasher

Spülmittel nt dish soap

Spülung <-, -en> f ① (Wasserspülung) flush ② (Haarspülung) conditioner

Spur <-, -en> [ʃpuːɐ̯] f ① (Anzeichen) trace; **~en hinterlassen** to leave traces; Schicksal a. to leave its mark; Verbrecher a. to leave clues; **jdm auf der ~ sein** to be on sb's trail; **auf die falschen/richtigen ~ sein** to be on the wrong/right track; **eine heiße ~** a firm lead; **jdm auf die ~ kommen** to be onto sb ② (Fußspuren) track[s pl], trail ③ (kleine Menge) trace; von Knob-lauch, etc. touch ④ (Fahrstreifen) lane

spüren ['ʃpyːrən] I. vt to feel; **etw zu ~ bekommen** to feel the brunt of sth II. vi ■~, dass ... to sense that ...; ■jdn ~ lassen, dass ... to leave sb with no doubt that ...

Spürhund m tracker dog

spurlos I. adj without a trace pred II. adv without [leaving] a trace; **die Scheidung ging nicht ~ an ihm vorü-ber** the divorce left its mark on him

Spurt <-s, -s> [ʃpʊrt] m spurt

spurten ['ʃpʊrtn̩] vi sein to spurt

Squash <-> [skvɔʃ] nt squash

Staat <-[e]s, -en> [ʃtaːt] m ① (Land) country ② (staatliche Institutionen) state ③ pl (USA) ■die ~en the States

Staatenbund <-bünde> m confedera-tion [of states]

staatlich I. adj ① (staatseigen) state-owned; (staatlich geführt) state-run; **~e Einrichtungen** government facilities ② (den Staat betreffend) state attr, na-tional ③ (aus dem Staatshaushalt stam-mend) government attr, state attr II. adv **~ anerkannt** state-approved; SCH, UNIV state-accredited; **~ gefördert** government-sponsored

Staatsakt m state ceremony

Staatsangehörige(r) f(m) dekl wie adj citizen

Staatsangehörigkeit f nationality

Staatsanwalt, -anwältin m, f district attorney

Staatsbeamte(r), -beamtin m, f civil servant

Staatsbesuch m state visit

Staatsbürger(in) m(f) citizen

Staatsdienst m civil service

Staatseigentum nt state [or govern-ment] property

Staatsexamen nt state exam[ination]; (zur Übernahme in den Staatsdienst) civil service exam[ination]

Staatsform f form of government

Staatsgebiet nt national territory

Staatshaushalt m national budget

Staatskosten pl public expenses pl

Staatsminister(in) <-s, -> m(f) secre-tary of state

Staatsoberhaupt nt head of state

Staatspräsident(in) m(f) president [of a republic]

Staatsstreich m coup [d'état]

Stab <-[e]s, Stäbe> [ʃtaːp] m ① (runde Holzlatte) rod; (Gitterstab) bar ② (Stab-

hochsprungstab) pole; (*Staffelstab*) baton ❸ (*beigeordnete Gruppe*) staff; *von Experten* panel

Stabhochsprung *m* pole vault

stabil [ʃtaˈbiːl, st-] *adj* ❶ (*strapazierfähig*) sturdy ❷ (*beständig*) *Preise, Währung, Zustand* stable ❸ (*nicht labil*) steady; *Gesundheit* sound

stabilisieren [ʃta·bi·liˈziː·rən] *vt, vr* ■|*sich akk*| ~ to stabilize

Stabilität <-> [ʃta·bi·liˈtɛːt, st-] *f kein pl* stability, solidity

Stachel <-s, -n> [ˈʃta·xl̩] *m* ❶ (*von Rose*) thorn; (*von Kakteen*) spine ❷ (*Giftstachel*) sting

Stachelbeere *f* gooseberry

Stacheldraht *m* barbed wire

stachelig [ˈʃta·xə·lɪç] *adj* prickly; *Rosen* thorny; *Kakteen* spiny

Stachelschwein *nt* porcupine

Stadion <-s, Stadien> [ˈʃta·di·ɔn] *nt* stadium, bowl

Stadium <-s, Stadien> [ˈʃta·di·ʊm] *nt* stage; **im letzten ~** MED at a terminal stage

Stadt <-, Städte> [ʃtat] *f* ❶ (*Ort*) town; (*Großstadt*) city ❷ (*Stadtverwaltung*) city/town council

Stadtbibliothek *f* city/town library

Städtepartnerschaft *f* sister city arrangement

Städter(in) <-s, -> [ˈʃtɛː·tɐ] *m(f)* city/town dweller

Stadtgebiet *nt* municipal area

städtisch [ˈʃtɛː·tɪʃ] *adj* ❶ (*kommunal*) municipal, city/town *attr* ❷ (*urban*) urban

Stadtmauer *f* city/town wall

Stadtmitte *f* downtown

Stadtplan *m* |street| map |of a city/ town|

Stadtrand *m* edge of town, outskirts *npl* of the city

Stadtrat *m* city/town council

Stadtrundfahrt *f* sightseeing tour of a city/town

Stadtteil *m* district, part of town

Stadtverwaltung *f* city/town council

Stadtviertel *nt* district

Stadtwerke *pl* public utilities *pl*

Stadtzentrum *nt* city/town center

Staffel <-, -n> [ˈʃta·fl̩] *f* ❶ SPORT relay team ❷ MIL (*Luftwaffeneinheit*) squadron ❸ TV season

Staffelei <-, -en> [ʃta·fəˈlai] *f* easel

Staffellauf *m* SPORT relay |race|

Stagnation <-, -en> [ʃta·gnaˈtsi̯oːn, st-] *f* stagnation

stagnieren* [ʃtaˈgniː·rən, st-] *vi* to stagnate

stahl [ʃtaːl] *imp von* **stehlen**

Stahl <-[e]s, -e> [ʃtaːl] *m* steel

Stahlbeton *m* reinforced concrete

Stahlhelm *m* steel helmet

Stahlindustrie *f kein pl* steel industry

Stall <-[e]s, Ställe> [ʃtal] *m* (*Hühnerstall*) coop; (*Kaninchenstall*) hutch; (*Kuhstall*) cowshed, |cow| barn; (*Pferdestall*) stable; (*Schweinestall*) |pig|sty, |pig|pen

Stamm <-[e]s, Stämme> [ʃtam] *m* ❶ (*Baumstamm*) |tree| trunk ❷ LING stem ❸ (*Volksstamm*) tribe

Stammbaum *m* family tree

stammeln [ˈʃta·ml̩n] *vt, vi* to stammer

stammen [ˈʃta·mən] *vi* to be (**aus** +*dat* from)

Stammgast *m* regular |guest|

Stammkunde, -kundin *m, f* regular |customer|

Stammlokal *nt* usual |or favorite| café/ restaurant/bar

Stammplatz *m* usual |or favorite| seat

Stammtisch *m* ❶ (*Tisch für Stammgäste*) table reserved for the regulars ❷ (*regelmäßiges Zusammentreffen*) |group of| regulars

stampfen [ˈʃtam·pfn̩] **I.** *vi* ❶ *haben* (*aufstampfen*) **mit dem Fuß auf den Boden ~** to stomp one's foot ❷ *sein s.* **stapfen II.** *vt haben* KOCHK *Gemüse, Kartoffeln* to mash

stand [ʃtant] *imp von* **stehen**

Stand <-[e]s, Stände> [ʃtant] *m* ❶ (*Verkaufsstand*) stand ❷ (*Anzeige*) reading; **laut ~ des Barometers** according to the barometer |reading| ❸ *kein pl* (*Zustand*) state; **der ~ der**

S

Dinge the [present] state of affairs; **sich** *akk* **auf dem neuesten ~ befinden** to be up-to-date ④ (*Spielstand*) score

Standard <-s, -s> [ˈʃtanˌdart, ˈstˑ] *m* standard

standardisieren* [ʃtanˑdarˑdiˑˈziˑrən, stˑ] *vt* to standardize

Stand-by-Betrieb [stɛndˈbaɪ-] *m*, **Stand-by-Modus** *m* TECH standby; **im ~** on standby

Ständer <-s, -> [ˈʃtɛnˑdɐ] *m* ① (*Gestell*) stand ② (*sl: erigierter Penis*) hard-on

Standesamt *nt* justice of the peace['s office]

standesamtlich *adv* **sich** *akk* **~ trauen lassen** to be married by the Justice of the Peace

Standesbeamte(r), -beamtin *m, f* Justice of the Peace

standhaft I. *adj* steadfast II. *adv* steadfastly

standhalten [ˈʃtantˑhalˑtn̩] *vi irreg* ■ **etw** *dat* **~** to hold out against sth

ständig [ˈʃtɛnˑdɪç] I. *adj* constant II. *adv* constantly

Standlicht *nt kein pl* parking lights *pl*

Standort <-[e]s, -e> *m* location

Standpunkt *m* [point of] view, standpoint; **den ~ vertreten, dass ...** to take the view that ...

Standspur *f* TRANSP shoulder

Standuhr *f* grandfather clock

Stange <-, -n> [ˈʃtaŋə] *f* ① (*Stab*) pole; (*kürzer*) rod ② (*Metallstange*) bar ③ **eine ~ Zigaretten** a carton of cigarettes ▸WENDUNGEN: **bei der ~ bleiben** (*fam*) to keep at it; **eine [schöne] ~ Geld kosten** (*fam*) to cost a pretty penny; **von der ~** (*fam*) off the rack

Stängel^{RR} <-s, -> [ˈʃtɛŋl̩] *m* stalk, stem

stänkern [ˈʃtɛŋˑkɐn] *vi* to stir things up

stanzen [ˈʃtanˑtsn̩] *vt* **Löcher in etw** *akk* **~** to punch holes in sth

Stapel <-s, -> [ˈʃtaːˑpl̩] *m* stack

Stapellauf *m* NAUT launch[ing]

stapeln [ˈʃtaːˑpl̩n] I. *vt* to stack [up *sep*] II. *vr* ■ **sich** *akk* **~** to pile up

stapfen [ˈʃtapˑfn̩] *vi sein* to tramp (**durch** +*akk* through)

Star¹ <-[e]s, -e> [ʃtaːɐ̯] *m* ① (*Vogel*) starling ② MED [**grauer**] **~** cataract; **grüner ~** glaucoma

Star² <-s, -s> [ʃtaːɐ̯, stˑ] *m* (*berühmte Person*) star

stark <stärker, stärkste> [ʃtark] I. *adj* ① (*kräftig*) strong ② (*mächtig*) powerful, strong ③ (*dick*) thick ④ *Hitze, Kälte* severe; *Regen* heavy; *Strömung* strong; *Sturm* violent ⑤ *Erkältung* bad; *Fieber* high ⑥ *Schlag* hard; *Druck* high ⑦ *Gefühle, Schmerzen* intense; *Bedenken* considerable; *Liebe* deep ⑧ (*leistungsfähig*) powerful ⑨ *Medikamente, Schnaps* strong II. *adv* ① (*heftig*) a lot; **~ regnen** to rain heavily ② (*erheblich*) **~ beschädigt** badly damaged; **~ bluten** to bleed profusely; **~ erkältet sein** to have a bad cold; **~ gewürzt** very spicy ③ (*in höherem Maße*) greatly, a lot; **~ vertreten** strongly represented

Stärke <-, -n> [ˈʃtɛrˑkə] *f* ① (*Kraft*) strength ② (*Macht, von Motor*) power ③ (*Dicke*) thickness ④ (*zahlenmäßiges Ausmaß*) size; *einer Armee* strength ⑤ (*Fähigkeit*) **jds ~ sein** to be sb's strong point ⑥ CHEM starch

stärken [ˈʃtɛrˑkn̩] I. *vt* to strengthen II. *vi* ■ **~d** fortifying III. *vr* ■ **sich** *akk* **~** to fortify oneself

starkmachen^{RR} *vr* (*fam*) ■ **sich** *akk* **für jdn/etw ~** to stand up for sb/sth

Starkstrom *m* high voltage

Stärkung <-, -en> *f kein pl* strengthening

starr [ʃtar] *adj* ① (*steif*) rigid ② (*erstarrt*) stiff; **~ vor Angst** paralyzed with fear; **~ vor Kälte** numb with cold; **~er Blick** [fixed] stare ③ (*rigide*) inflexible; *Haltung* unbending

starren [ˈʃtaˑrən] *vi* to stare

starrsinnig *adj* stubborn

Start <-s, -s> [ʃtart, start] *m* ① LUFT takeoff; RAUM liftoff, launch ② SPORT start ③ (*Beginn*) start; *eines Projekts* launch[ing]

Startbahn *f* LUFT runway

startbereit *adj* ① LUFT ready for takeoff *pred* ② SPORT ready to go *pred*

starten ['ʃtar·tn̩, 'st·] I. *vi sein* ① LUFT to take off; RAUM to lift off ② SPORT to start ③ (*beginnen*) to start; *Projekt* to be launched II. *vt haben* ① *Auto* to start ② *Computer* to initialize, to boot [up *sep*]; *Programm* to run ③ (*beginnen lassen*) to launch, to start

Starterlaubnis *f* takeoff clearance

Startkapital *nt* seed money

StartschussRR *m* starting signal

Statik <-> ['ʃta·tɪk, 'st·] *f* PHYS statics + *sing vb*

Station <-, -en> [ʃta·'tsi̯oːn] *f* ① (*Haltestelle*) stop ② (*Aufenthalt*) stopover; ~ **machen** to make a stop ③ (*Klinikabteilung*) ward ④ METEO, SCI, RADIO station

stationär [ʃta·tsi̯o·'nɛːɐ] I. *adj* MED inpatient *attr*; **ein ~er Aufenthalt** a stay in a hospital II. *adv* MED in the hospital

stationieren* [ʃta·tsi̯o·'niː·rən] *vt* **Truppen** ~ to station troops

Stationsschwester *f* senior nurse

Statist(in) <-en, -en> [ʃta·'tɪst] *m(f)* extra

Statistik <-, -en> [ʃta·'tɪs·tɪk] *f* statistics + *sing vb*

statistisch [ʃta·'tɪs·tɪʃ] I. *adj* statistical II. *adv* statistically

Stativ <-s, -e> [ʃta·'tiːf] *nt* tripod

statt [ʃtat] I. *präp* +*gen* instead of II. *konj* (*anstatt*) instead of

Stätte <-, -n> ['ʃtɛ·tə] *f* place

statt|finden ['ʃtat·fɪn·dn̩] *vi irreg* to take place; *Veranstaltung a.* to be held

stattlich ['ʃtat·lɪç] *adj* ① (*imposant*) imposing ② (*beträchtlich*) considerable

Statue <-, -n> ['ʃta·tu̯ə, 'st·] *f* statue

Status <-, -> ['ʃta·tʊs, 'st·] *m* status, position

Statussymbol *nt* status symbol

Stau <-[e]s, -e> [ʃtau] *m* ① (*Verkehrsstau*) traffic jam ② (*von Wasser etc.*) build-up

Staub <-[e]s, -e> [ʃtaup] *m kein pl* dust; ~ **saugen** to vacuum; ~ **wischen** to dust ▶WENDUNGEN: **sich** *akk* **aus dem** ~**[e] machen** to bolt

staubig ['ʃtau·bɪç] *adj* dusty

staubsaugen <*pp* staubgesaugt>,

Staub saugen <*pp* Staub gesaugt> *vt, vi* to vacuum

Staubsauger *m* vacuum [cleaner]

Staubtuch *nt* dust cloth

Staudamm *m* dam

Staude <-, -n> ['ʃtau·də] *f* HORT perennial [plant]

stauen ['ʃtau·ən] I. *vt* to dam [up *sep*] II. *vr* ■**sich** *akk* ~ ① (*sich anstauen*) to collect; (*von Wasser a.*) to rise ② (*Schlange bilden*) *Autos* to pile up

staunen ['ʃtau·nən] *vi* to be astonished (**über** +*akk* at)

Stausee *m* reservoir

stechen <sticht, stach, gestochen> ['ʃtɛ·çn̩] I. *vi* ① (*piksen*) to prick ② (*von Insekten*) to sting; *Mücken* to bite ③ (*mit spitzem Gegenstand eindringen*) to stab ④ KARTEN to take the trick II. *vt* to stab; *Insekt* to sting; *Mücken* to bite III. *vr* ■**sich** *akk* ~ to prick oneself

stechend *adj* ① (*scharf*) sharp ② (*durchdringend*) *Schmerzen* stabbing ③ (*beißend*) *Geruch* acrid

Stechmücke *f* mosquito

Stechuhr *f* time clock

Steckbrief *m* "wanted" poster

Steckdose *f* [wall] socket, electrical outlet

stecken ['ʃtɛ·kn̩] I. *vi* <steckte *o geh* stak, gesteckt> ① (*festsitzen*) ■**in etw** *dat* ~ to be stuck in sth; ~ **bleiben** to get stuck ② (*eingesteckt sein*) ■**hinter/in/zwischen etw** *dat* ~ to be behind/in/among sth; **den Schlüssel ~ lassen** to leave the key in the lock ③ (*verborgen sein*) **wo hast du denn gesteckt?** (*fam*) where have you been [hiding]?; **wo steckt er denn bloß wieder?** (*fam*) where did he disappear to again? ④ (*verwickelt sein*) **in einer Krise** ~ to be in the middle of a crisis; **in Schwierigkeiten** ~ to be in trouble ⑤ (*stocken*) ~ **bleiben** *in einer Rede* to falter; *im Verkehr* to get stuck II. *vt* <steckte, gesteckt> ① (*schieben*) ■**etw hinter/in/unter etw** *akk* ~ to put sth behind/in[to]/under sth ② (*fam:*

S

befördern) **jdn ins Gefängnis ~** to stick sb in prison ❸ (*fam: investieren*) **Geld in eine Firma ~** to put money into a company; **viel Zeit in etw** *akk* **~** to devote a lot of time to sth

Stecker <-s, -> *m* ELEK plug

Stecknadel *f* pin

Steckrübe *f* rutabaga

Steg <-[e]s, -e> [ʃteːk] *m* ❶ (*schmale Holzbrücke*) footbridge ❷ (*Bootssteg*) dock, pier

stehen <stand, gestanden> [ˈʃteː·ən] I. *vi* ❶ *haben o* SÜDD, ÖSTERR, SCHWEIZ *sein* ❶ (*in aufrechter Stellung sein*) to stand ❷ (*hingestellt sein*) to be; **wo steht das Auto?** where did you park the car?; **etw ~ lassen** to leave sth; (*nicht verrücken*) to leave sth where it is; (*vergessen*) to leave sth behind; **jdn einfach ~ lassen** to walk out on sb; **das Essen ~ lassen** to leave the food untouched; **alles ~ und liegen lassen** to drop everything ❸ (*gedruckt sein*) **wo steht das?** where does it say that?; **das steht auf Seite sechs** that's on page six; **was steht in seinem Brief?** what does his letter say? ❹ (*nicht mehr in Betrieb sein*) to have stopped; (*von Maschine a.*) to be at a standstill; **zum S~ kommen** to come to a stop ❺ (*anhalten*) **~ bleiben** to stop ❻ (*von etw betroffen sein*) **unter Drogen ~** to be under the influence of drugs; **unter Schock ~** to be in a state of shock ❼ (*passen zu*) **jdm [gut] ~** to suit sb [well]; **das steht dir nicht** it doesn't suit you ❽ (*einen bestimmten Spielstand haben*) **wie steht das Spiel?** what's the score? ❾ (*fam: fest sein*) Abmachung, Termin to be finally settled ❿ (*unterstützen*) ■**hinter jdm/etw ~** to support sb/sth; ■**zu jdm/etw ~** to stand by sb/sth ⓫ (*eingestellt sein*) **wie ~ Sie dazu?** what is your opinion on this? ⓬ (*anzeigen*) ■**auf etw** *dat* **~** to indicate sth; **die Ampel steht auf Rot** the traffic light is red ⓭ (*fam: gut finden*) ■**auf jdn ~** to be crazy about sb; **stehst du auf Techno?** are you into techno?

▶WENDUNGEN: **jdm steht etw bis hier** (*fam*) sb is sick and tired of sth II. *vi impers* (*gesundheitlich*) **es steht gut/schlecht um jdn** sb is in good/bad shape

Stehlampe *f* floor lamp

stehlen <stahl, gestohlen> [ˈʃteː·lən] I. *vt*, *vi* to steal; ■**das S~** stealing ▶WENDUNGEN: **jdm die Zeit ~** to take up sb's time; **das kann mir gestohlen bleiben!** (*fam*) to hell with it! II. *vr* to sneak; ■**sich** *akk* **von etw** *dat* **~** to sneak away from sth

steif [ʃtaif] I. *adj* ❶ (*starr*) stiff; Begrüßung formal ❷ (*erigiert*) erect ▶WENDUNGEN: **etw ~ und fest behaupten** to stubbornly maintain sth II. *adv* stiffly

Steigbügel [ˈʃtaik-] *m* stirrup

steigen <stieg, gestiegen> [ˈʃtai·gn̩] I. *vi sein* ❶ (*klettern*) ■**auf etw** *akk* **~** (*auf einen Berg*) to climb [up] sth; (*aufs Fahrrad, Pferd*) to get on[to] sth ❷ (*einsteigen*) ■**in etw** *akk* **~** to get in[to] sth; **in einen Zug ~** to get on a train ❸ (*aussteigen*) ■**aus etw** *dat* **~** to get out of sth; **aus einem Bus ~** to get off a bus ❹ (*absteigen*) ■**von etw** *dat* **~** to get off [of] sth ❺ (*sich aufwärts bewegen*) to rise [up]; **der Sekt ist mir zu Kopf gestiegen** the sparkling wine has gone to my head ❻ Achtung to rise; Flut to swell; Preis, Wert to increase; Temperatur to climb ❼ (*sich intensivieren*) to increase; Spannung, Ungeduld, a. to mount II. *vt sein* ■**Treppen ~** to climb [up] stairs

steigend *adj* ❶ (*sich erhöhend*) Preise, Löhne rising ❷ (*sich intensivierend*) Spannung, Ungeduld mounting

steigern [ˈʃtai·gɐn] I. *vt* ❶ (*erhöhen*) to increase (**auf** +*akk* to, **um** +*akk* by) ❷ (*verbessern*) to improve II. *vr* ■**sich** *akk* **~** to increase ❶ (*sich intensivieren*) Spannung a. to mount ❷ (*seine Leistung verbessern*) to improve

Steigerung <-, -en> *f* ❶ (*Erhöhung*) increase, rise ❷ (*Verbesserung*) improvement

Steigung <-, -en> *f* ❶ (*ansteigende*

Strecke) ascent ❷(*Anstieg*) slope; **eine ~ von 10 %** a 10% gradient

steil [ʃtail] I. *adj* ❶(*stark abfallend/ ansteigend*) steep ❷(*sehr rasch*) rapid II. *adv* steeply

Steilhang *m* steep slope

Steilküste *f* bluff

Stein <-[e]s, -e> [ʃtain] *m* ❶(*Gesteinsstück*) stone, rock ❷(*Obstkern*) stone ▶WENDUNGEN: **bei jdm einen ~ im <u>Brett</u> haben** (*fam*) to be in good with sb; **mir fällt ein ~ vom <u>Herzen</u>!** that's [taken] a load off [of] my mind!; **den ~ ins <u>Rollen</u> bringen** (*fam*) to start the ball rolling; **jdm ~e in den <u>Weg</u> legen** to put obstacles in sb's way

Steinbock *m* ❶ZOOL ibex ❷ASTROL Capricorn

Steinbruch *m* quarry

steinig [ʃtai·nɪç] *adj* stony

steinigen [ʃtai·nɪ·gn] *vt* to stone

Steinpilz *m* porcino

steinreich [ʃtain·'raiç] *adj* filthy rich

Steinschlag *m* falling rocks *pl*

Steinzeit *f kein pl* **die ~** the Stone Age

Steißbein *nt* ANAT coccyx

Stelle <-, -n> [ʃtɛ·lə] *f* ❶(*Platz*) place; (*genauer*) spot; **an dieser ~** in this place, here; (*fig*) at this point; **an anderer ~** elsewhere; **an erster/zweiter ~** in the first/second place; ■**an ~ von etw** *dat* instead of sth ❷(*umrissener Bereich*) spot; (*in einem Buch*) passage; **fettige/rostige ~** grease/rust spot ❸MATH digit; **eine Zahl mit sieben ~n** a seven-digit number ❹(*Posten*) place; **an jds ~ treten** to take sb's place; **an deiner ~ würde ich ...** if I were you, I would ... ❺(*Arbeitsplatz*) job; **eine freie ~** a vacancy ▶WENDUNGEN: **zur ~ <u>sein</u>** to be on hand; **auf der ~ <u>treten</u>** to make any progress; **<u>auf</u> der ~** at once; **er war auf der ~ tot** he died instantly

stellen [ʃtɛ·lən] I. *vt* ❶(*hin-, abstellen*) to put; **das Auto in die Garage ~** to put the car in the garage; **den Wein kalt ~** to chill the wine ❷(*aufrecht hinstellen*) to stand [up *sep*] ❸(*einstellen*)

die Heizung höher/kleiner ~ to turn up/down *sep* the heat; **den Fernseher lauter/leiser ~** to turn the television up/down; **den Wecker auf 7 Uhr ~** to set the alarm for 7 o'clock ❹(*vorgeben*) *Aufgabe* to set; *Bedingungen* to stipulate; **[jdm] eine Frage ~** to ask [sb] a question ❺(*richten*) **einen Antrag ~** to put forward a motion; **Forderungen ~** to make demands ▶WENDUNGEN: **auf sich** *akk* <u>selbst</u> **gestellt sein** to have to fend for oneself II. *vr* ❶(*sich hinstellen*) ■**sich** *akk* ~ to take up position ❷(*entgegentreten*) ■**sich** *akk* **jdm/etw ~** to face sb/sth ❸(*sich melden*) **sich** *akk* **der Polizei ~** to turn oneself in to the police ❹(*etw vorgeben*) **sich** *akk* **ahnungslos ~** to play innocent; **sich** *akk* **tot ~** to pretend to be dead

Stellenangebot *nt* job offer; **„~e"** "job market", "help wanted"

Stellenbeschreibung *f* job description

Stellengesuch *nt* "employment wanted" advertisement

Stellenvermittlung *f* ❶(*das Vermitteln*) job placement ❷(*Einrichtung*) employment agency

Stellplatz *m* parking space

Stellung <-, -en> *f* ❶(*Arbeitsplatz*) job ❷(*Rang, Körperhaltung, Position*) position ❸(*Standpunkt*) ~ **zu etw** *dat* **beziehen** to take a stand on sth; **~ zu etw** *dat* **nehmen** to express an opinion about/on sth

Stellungnahme <-, -n> *f* statement

stellvertretend I. *adj attr* (*vorübergehend*) acting *attr*; (*an zweiter Stelle stehend*) deputy *attr* II. *adv* ■**~ für jdn** on sb's behalf

Stellvertreter(in) *m(f)* deputy, substitute

Stemmeisen *nt* chisel

stemmen [ʃtɛ·mən] I. *vt* (*hochdrücken*) to lift II. *vr* ■**sich** *akk* **gegen etw** *akk* ~ to brace oneself against sth

Stempel <-s, -> [ʃtɛm·pl̩] *m* stamp

stempeln [ʃtɛm·pl̩n] *vt, vi* to stamp

Stengelᴬᴸᵀ <-s, -> [ʃtɛŋl̩] *m* s. **Stängel**

S

Stenografie <-, -n> [ʃte·no·gra·'fi:] *f* shorthand, stenography

Stenographie <-, -n> [ʃte·no·gra·'fi:] *f s.* **Stenografie**

Stenotypist(in) <-en, -en> [ʃte·no·ty·'pɪst] *m(f)* stenographer

Steppdecke *f* comforter

Steppe <-, -n> [ˈʃtɛ·pə] *f* steppe

Sterbehilfe *f kein pl* euthanasia

sterben <starb, gestorben> [ˈʃtɛr·bn̩] *vi sein* to die (**an** +*dat* of); **ich sterbe vor Durst** (*fig*) I'm dying of thirst ►WENDUNGEN: **für jdn ist jd/etw gestorben** sb is finished with sb/sth; **er ist für mich gestorben** I'm finished with him

Sterberate *f* death rate

Sterbeurkunde *f* death certificate

sterblich [ˈʃtɛrp·lɪç] *adj* (*geh*) mortal

Sterblichkeit <-> *f kein pl* mortality

Stereo <-> [ˈʃtɛ:·reo, -st-] *nt kein pl* stereo

Stereoanlage *f* stereo [system]

stereotyp [ʃte·reo·'ty:p, st-] I. *adj* stereotype *attr*; stereotypical II. *adv* stereotypically

Stereotyp <-s, -e> [ʃte·reo·'ty:p, st-] *nt* stereotype

steril [ʃte·'ri:l, st-] *adj* sterile

Sterilisation <-, -en> [ʃte·ri·li·za·'tsi̯o:n, st-] *f* sterilization

sterilisieren* [ʃte·ri·li·'zi:·rən] *vt* to sterilize; ■ **sich** *akk* ~ **lassen** to get sterilized

Stern <-[e]s, -e> [ʃtɛrn] *m star* ►WENDUNGEN: **in den ~en stehen** to be written in the stars

Sternbild *nt* constellation

Sternschnuppe <-, -n> *f* shooting star

Sternwarte *f* observatory

Stethoskop <-s, -e> [ʃte·to·'sko:p] *nt* stethoscope

stetig [ˈʃte:·tɪç] I. *adj* steady II. *adv* steadily

stets [ʃte:ts] *adv* at all times

Steuer¹ <-s, -> [ˈʃtɔy·ɐ] *nt* ❶ AUTO [steering] wheel ❷ NAUT helm

Steuer² <-, -n> [ˈʃtɔy·ɐ] *f* ÖKON tax; **etw von der ~ absetzen** to deduct sth from one's taxes

steuerbegünstigt *adj* tax-deductible

Steuerbelastung *meist sing f* tax burden

Steuerberater(in) *m(f)* tax consultant

Steuerbescheid *m* tax assessment

Steuerbord [ˈʃtɔy·ɐ·bɔrt] *nt kein pl* starboard

Steuererhöhung *f* tax increase

Steuererklärung *f* tax return

Steuerermäßigung *f* FIN tax reduction

steuerfrei I. *adj* tax-exempt *attr*; exempt from tax *pred* II. *adv* without paying tax

Steuergelder *pl* taxes *pl*, tax revenue[s *pl*]

Steuerhinterziehung *f* tax evasion

Steuerklasse *f* tax category

Steuermann <-männer> [ˈʃtɔy·ɐ·man] *m* NAUT helmsman

steuern [ˈʃtɔy·ɐn] I. *vt* ❶ (*lenken*) to steer ❷ LUFT to fly ❸ (*regulieren*) to control II. *vi* AUTO to drive

steuerpflichtig *adj* ❶ (*zu versteuern*) taxable ❷ (*zur Steuerzahlung verpflichtet*) obligated to pay tax *pred*

Steuerrad *nt* wheel, helm

Steuerruder *nt* rudder

Steuersatz *m* tax rate

Steuersenkung *f* tax cut

Steuerzahler(in) *m(f)* taxpayer

Steward <-s, -s> [ˈstju:·ɐt, ˈʃt(j)u:·ɐt] *m* steward

Stewardessᴿᴿ <-, -en>, **Stewardeß**ᴬᴸᵀ <-, -ssen> [stju:ɐ·'dɛs] *f* stewardess

Stich <-[e]s, -e> [ʃtɪç] *m* ❶ (*Messerstich*) stab; (*Stichwunde*) stab wound ❷ (*Insektenstich*) sting; (*Mückenstich*) bite ❸ (*stechender Schmerz*) stabbing pain ❹ (*Nadelstich*) stitch ❺ KUNST engraving ►WENDUNGEN: **jdn im ~ lassen** to leave sb in the lurch

sticheln [ˈʃtɪ·çl̩n] *vi* to make nasty remarks

stichhaltig I. *adj* Alibi solid; Argumentation sound; Beweis conclusive; ■ [**nicht**] ~ **sein** to [not] hold water II. *adv* (*schlüssig*) conclusively

Stichprobe *f* spot check

Stichtag *m* deadline

Stichwort ['ʃtɪç·vɔrt] *nt* **①** LING (*Haupteintrag*) headword **②** THEAT cue **③** *meist pl* (*Wort als Gedächtnisstütze*) **sich** *dat* **~e machen** to take notes

Stichwunde *f* knife wound

sticken ['ʃtɪ·kn̩] *vt, vi* to embroider

stickig ['ʃtɪ·kɪç] *adj* stuffy; *Luft* stale

Stickstoff ['ʃtɪk·ʃtɔf] *m kein pl* nitrogen

Stiefbruder ['ʃtiːf·] *m* stepbrother

Stiefel <-s, -> ['ʃtiː·fl̩] *m* boot

Stiefeltern *pl* stepparents *pl*

Stiefkind *nt* stepchild

Stiefmutter *f* stepmother

Stiefmütterchen *nt* BOT pansy

Stiefschwester *f* stepsister

Stiefsohn *m* stepson

Stieftochter *f* stepdaughter

Stiefvater *m* stepfather

Stiel <-[e]s, -e> ['ʃtiːl] *m* **①** (*Handgriff*) handle; (*Besenstiel*) broomstick **②** (*Blumenstiel*) stem, stalk

Stier <-[e]s, -e> ['ʃtiːɐ̯] *m* **①** (*Bulle*) bull **②** ASTROL Taurus

stieren ['ʃtiː·rən] *vi* to stare

Stierkampf *m* bullfight

Stift <-[e]s, -e> ['ʃtɪft] *m* **①** (*Stahlstift*) [steel] pin [*or* tack] **②** (*zum Schreiben*) pen, pencil

stiften ['ʃtɪf·tn̩] *vt* **①** (*spenden*) to donate **②** (*verursachen*) to cause; *Unruhe* **~** to create unrest

Stiftung <-, -en> *f* **①** (*Organisation*) foundation **②** (*Schenkung*) donation

Stigmatisierung [ʃtɪg·ma·ti·ˈziː·rʊŋ] *f* (*geh*) stigmatization

Stil <-[e]s, -e> ['ʃtiːl, st-] *m* (*Ausdrucksform*) style ►WENDUNGEN: **im großen ~** on a grand scale

still [ʃtɪl] *adj* **①** (*ruhig*) quiet, peaceful; **sei ~!** be quiet!; **in einer ~en Stunde** in a quiet moment **②** (*geräuschlos*) silent; *Vorwurf* silent **③** (*unbewegt*) still; **etw ~ halten** to keep sth still ►WENDUNGEN: **im S~en hoffen** to secretly hope

Stille <-> ['ʃtɪ·lə] *f kein pl* **①** (*Ruhe*) quiet; (*ohne Geräusch*) silence; **in aller ~** quietly **②** (*Abgeschiedenheit*) peace

StillebenALT *nt s.* **Stillleben**

stilllegenALT <stillgelegt> *vt s.* **stilllegen**

stillen ['ʃtɪ·lən] *vt* **①** (*säugen*) to breastfeed **②** (*befriedigen*) to satisfy; **den Durst ~** to quench sb's thirst **③** (*aufhören lassen*) to stop; *Blutverlust* to stanch

stillhalten *vi irreg* to keep still, to not move

StilllebenRR ['ʃtɪl·leː·bn̩] *nt* still life

stilllegenRR <stillgelegt> *vt* to close [down *sep*]

stillsitzen *vi irreg sein o haben* to sit still

Stillstand *m kein pl* standstill; **zum ~ kommen** (*zum Erliegen*) to come to a standstill; (*aufhören*) to stop

stillstehen *vi irreg sein o haben* **①** (*außer Betrieb sein*) to stand idle; *Verhandlungen, Verkehr* to be at a standstill **②** (*a. fig: sich nicht bewegen*) to stand still

Stilmöbel *nt meist pl* period furniture

Stimmband *nt meist pl* vocal cord

stimmberechtigt *adj* entitled to vote *pred*

Stimmbruch *m* **er war mit 12 im ~** his voice broke when he was 12

Stimme <-, -n> ['ʃtɪ·mə] *f* **①** (*Art des Sprechens*) voice **②** POL vote; **sich** *akk* **der ~ enthalten** to abstain **③** (*Meinungsäußerung*) voice

stimmen[1] ['ʃtɪ·mən] *vi* **①** (*zutreffen*) to be right; **es stimmt, dass ...** it is true that ...; **stimmt!** right! **②** (*korrekt sein*) to be correct; **da stimmt was nicht** there's something wrong here; **stimmt so** keep the change

stimmen[2] ['ʃtɪ·mən] *vt* MUS to tune

Stimmengleichheit *f* tie

Stimmenmehrheit *f* majority of votes

Stimmenthaltung *f* abstention

Stimmgabel *f* tuning fork

Stimmrecht *nt* right to vote

Stimmung <-, -en> *f* **①** (*Gemütslage*) mood; **~ sein** to be in the mood (**zu** +*dat* for); **in ~ kommen** to get in the [right] mood **②** (*Atmosphäre*) atmosphere

S

Stimmzettel *m* ballot

stimulieren* [ʃti·mu·ˈliː·rən] *vt* to stimulate

stinken <stank, gestunken> [ˈʃtɪŋ·kn̩] *vi* ① (*unangenehm riechen*) to stink (**nach** +*dat* of) ② (*verdächtig sein*) **die Sache stinkt** the whole business stinks ③ (*fam: zuwider sein*) ■**jdm stinkt etw** sb is sick and tired of sth

Stinktier *nt* skunk

Stipendium <-s, -dien> [ʃti·ˈpɛn·di·ʊm] *nt* scholarship

Stirn <-, -en> [ʃtɪrn] *f* forehead; **die ~ runzeln** to frown ▶WENDUNGEN: **jdm die ~ bieten** to stand up to sb

Stirnband <-bänder> *nt* headband

Stirnhöhle *f* sinus

stöbern [ˈʃtøː·bən] *vi* to rummage (**in** +*dat* in)

Stock¹ <-[e]s, Stöcke> [ʃtɔk] *m* ① (*Holzstange*) stick ② (*Topfpflanze*) plant

Stock² <-[e]s, -> [ʃtɔk] *m* floor, story; **der 1. ~** the second floor

stockbesoffen [ˈʃtɔk·bə·ˈzɔ·fn̩] *adj* (*fam*) plastered *fam*

stockdunkel [ˈʃtɔk·ˈdʊŋ·kl̩] *adj* pitch-dark

Stöckelschuh *m* high-heeled shoe

stocken [ˈʃtɔ·kn̩] *vi* ① (*innehalten*) to falter ② (*zeitweilig stillstehen*) to come to a halt

stockend *adj* ① *Unterhaltung* flagging ② *Verkehr* stop-and-go

Stockwerk *nt s.* **Stock²**

Stoff <-[e]s, -e> [ʃtɔf] *m* ① (*Textil*) material, fabric ② (*Material*) material ③ CHEM substance ④ (*thematisches Material*) material ⑤ (*Lehrstoff*) subject material ⑥ *kein pl* (*sl: Rauschgift*) dope

Stofftier *nt* stuffed animal

Stoffwechsel [-vɛksl̩] *m* metabolism

stöhnen [ˈʃtøː·nən] *vi* to moan; (*vor Schmerz*) to groan

Stollen <-s, -> [ˈʃtɔ·lən] *m* ① BERGB tunnel ② KOCHK stollen (*a sweet Christmas bread-like cake made with dried fruit, often filled with marzipan*)

stolpern [ˈʃtɔl·pɐn] *vi sein* to trip, to stumble

stolz [ʃtɔlts] **I.** *adj* proud **II.** *adv* proudly

Stolz <-es> [ʃtɔlts] *m kein pl* pride; **jds ganzer ~ sein** to be sb's pride and joy

Stop^ALT <-s, -s> [ʃtɔp] *m s.* **Stopp**

stopfen [ˈʃtɔp·fn̩] **I.** *vt* ① (*hineinzwängen*) to stuff; *Loch* to fill ② (*mit Nadel und Faden*) to darn **II.** *vi* (*die Verdauung hemmen*) to cause constipation

Stopp^RR <-s, -s> [ʃtɔp] *m* stop

Stoppelbart *m* stubbly beard

stoppen [ˈʃtɔ·pn̩] *vt, vi* ① (*anhalten*) to stop ② (*Zeit nehmen*) to time

Stoppschild <-schilder> *nt* stop sign

Stoppuhr *f* stopwatch

Stöpsel <-s, -> [ˈʃtœp·sl̩] *m* stopper; (*für Badewanne*) plug

Storch <-[e]s, Störche> [ʃtɔrç] *m* stork

stören [ˈʃtøː·rən] **I.** *vt* ① (*unterbrechen*) to disturb; **jdn bei der Arbeit ~** to disturb sb while he/she is working; **entschuldigen Sie, wenn ich Sie störe** I'm sorry to bother you ② (*beeinträchtigen*) **jds Pläne ~** to interfere with sb's plans ③ (*unangenehm berühren*) **stört es sie, wenn ich ...?** do you mind if I ...?; **das stört mich nicht** that doesn't bother me; **das stört mich!** that's getting on my nerves [*or* annoying [me]]! **II.** *vi* ① (*bei etw unterbrechen*) to disturb; **ich will nicht ~, aber ...** I'm sorry to bother you, but ... ② (*lästig sein*) to be irritating **III.** *vr* **er stört sich aber auch an allem** he lets absolutely everything bother him

stornieren* [ʃtɔr·ˈniː·rən] *vt* to cancel

Stornierung <-, -en> *f* ① HANDEL *eines Auftrags* cancellation ② FIN *einer Buchung* reversal, cancellation of an entry

störrisch [ˈʃtœ·rɪʃ] **I.** *adj* obstinate, stubborn **II.** *adv* obstinately, stubbornly

Störung <-, -en> *f* ① (*Unterbrechung*) interruption, disruption, disturbance ② (*Störsignale*) interference ③ (*technischer Defekt*) fault; (*Fehlfunktion*) malfunction

Stoß <-es, Stöße> [ʃtoːs] *m* ① (*Schubs*)

push; (*mit dem Ellbogen*) dig; (*mit der Faust*) punch; (*mit dem Fuß*) kick ② (*Erschütterung*) bump ③ (*Stapel*) pile, stack ►WENDUNGEN: **sich** *dat* **einen ~ geben** to pull oneself together

Stoßdämpfer *m* shock absorber

stoßen <stößt, stieß, gestoßen> ['ʃtoː- sn̩] I. *vt* (*schubsen*) to push, to shove (**aus** +*dat* out of, **von** +*dat* off) II. *vr* ■**sich** *akk* [**an** etw *dat*] ~ to hurt oneself [on sth]; **sich** *dat* **den Kopf** ~ to bang one's head III. *vi* ① *sein* (*aufschlagen*) ■**an/gegen** etw *akk* ~ to bump against/into sth; **mit dem Kopf an etw** *akk* ~ to bang one's head on sth ② *sein* (*grenzen*) ■**an** etw *akk* ~ to border on sth ③ *sein* (*treffen*) ■**zu jdm** ~ to join sb ④ *sein* (*finden*) ■**auf etw** *akk* ~ to find sth; **auf Erdöl** ~ to strike oil ⑤ *sein* (*konfrontiert werden*) **auf Ablehnung/Zustimmung** ~ to meet with disapproval/approval ⑥ SCHWEIZ (*schieben*) to push, to shove

Stoßstange *f* bumper

Stoßzeit *f* ① (*Hauptverkehrszeit*) rush hour ② (*Hauptgeschäftszeit*) peak business hour[s *pl*], busy time of day

stottern ['ʃtɔtɐn] *vi* ① (*stockend sprechen*) to stutter ② *Motor* to splutter

Strafanstalt *f* penal institution

Strafanzeige *f* [criminal] charge

Strafarbeit *f* extra work (*assigned as punishment*)

Strafbank *f* SPORT penalty box

strafbar *adj* punishable [by law]; **sich** *akk* ~ **machen** to make oneself liable to prosecution

Strafe <-, -n> ['ʃtraː·fə] *f* ① (*Bestrafung*) punishment; JUR penalty; **zur** ~ as a punishment ② (*Geldstrafe*) fine; (*Haftstrafe*) sentence; **seine** ~ **absitzen** to serve [out] one's sentence

strafen ['ʃtraː·fn̩] *vt* to punish; **jdn mit Verachtung** ~ to treat sb with contempt

StraferlassRR *m* remission of a sentence

straff [ʃtraf] I. *adj* ① (*fest gespannt*) taut, tight ② (*nicht schlaff*) firm II. *adv* tightly

straffällig *adj* JUR punishable, criminal *attr*; ■~ **werden** to become a criminal

straffen ['ʃtra·fn̩] *vt* ① (*straff anziehen*) to tighten ② (*kürzen*) *Artikel, Text* to shorten; (*präziser machen*) to tighten up *sep*

straffrei *adj* unpunished; ~ **bleiben** to go unpunished

Straffreiheit *f kein pl* immunity from criminal prosecution

Strafgefangene(r) *f(m) dekl wie adj* prisoner

Strafgesetzbuch *nt* penal code

sträflich ['ʃtrɛː·flɪç] *adj* criminal *attr*

Sträfling <-s, -e> ['ʃtrɛː·flɪŋ] *m* prisoner

Strafmaß *nt* sentence

strafmildernd *adj* mitigating

StrafprozessRR *m* trial

Strafpunkt *m* SPORT penalty point

Strafraum *m* FBALL penalty area [*or* box]

Strafrecht *nt* criminal law

Strafstoß *m* SPORT penalty [kick]

Straftat *f* [criminal] offense

Strafverteidiger(in) *m(f)* defense attorney

Strafvollzug *m* penal system

Strafzettel *m* ticket

Strahl <-[e]s, -en> [ʃtraːl] *m* ① (*Lichtstrahl*) ray [of light]; (*Sonnenstrahl*) sunbeam; (*konzentriertes Licht*) beam ② (*Wasserstrahl*) jet

strahlen ['ʃtraː·lən] *vi* ① (*leuchten*) to shine ② (*Radioaktivität abgeben*) to be radioactive ③ (*ein freudiges Gesicht machen*) to beam (**vor** +*dat* with) ④ (*glänzen*) to shine

Strahlenbelastung *f* radiation, radioactive contamination

Strahlentherapie *f* radiotherapy

strahlenverseucht *adj* contaminated with radioactivity *pred*

Strahlung <-, -en> *f* PHYS radiation; **radioaktive** ~ radioactivity

Strähne <-, -n> ['ʃtrɛː·nə] *f* strand

stramm [ʃtram] I. *adj* ① (*straff*) tight; **etw** ~ **ziehen** to tighten sth ② (*kräftig*) strong, brawny, strapping *hum fam* ③ (*drall*) taut; *Beine* sturdy ④ *Marsch* brisk II. *adv* ① (*eng anliegend*) tightly

S

② (*fam: intensiv*) intensively; ~ **marschieren** to march briskly

strammlstehen *vi irreg* to stand at attention

strampeln ['ʃtram·pl̩n] *vi* **①** (*heftig treten*) to kick around **②** (*fam: sich abmühen*) to struggle

Strand <-[e]s, Strände> [ʃtrant] *m* beach

stranden ['ʃtran·dn̩] *vi sein* (*auf Grund laufen*) to run aground ▶WENDUNGEN: **irgendwo gestrandet sein** to be stranded somewhere

Strandkorb *m* beach chair

strangulieren* [ʃtraŋ·gu·'liː·rən] *vt* to strangle

Strapaze <-, -n> [ʃtra·'paː·tsə] *f* stress, strain

strapazieren* [ʃtra·pa·'tsiː·rən] I. *vt* **①** (*stark beanspruchen*) to wear; (*abnutzen*) to wear out *sep* **②** (*überbeanspruchen*) jds Geduld ~ to tax sb's patience; jds Nerven ~ to get on sb's nerves II. *vr* ■sich *akk* [bei etw *dat*] ~ to overdo it [when doing sth], to wear oneself out

strapazierfähig *adj* durable

strapaziös [ʃtra·pa·'tsi̯øːs] *adj* strenuous

Straps <-es, -e> [ʃtraps] *m meist pl* garter

Straße <-, -n> ['ʃtraː·sə] *f* (*Verkehrsweg*) road; (*bewohnte Straße*) street; (*enge Straße auf dem Land*) lane ▶WENDUNGEN: **auf die ~ gehen** to demonstrate; **jdn auf die ~ setzen** to throw sb out; **auf der ~ sitzen** to be [out] on the streets; **auf offener ~** in broad daylight

Straßenbahn *f* streetcar

Straßenbahnhaltestelle *f* streetcar stop

Straßenbahnlinie *f* streetcar line

Straßenbau *m kein pl* road construction *no art*

Straßenbelag *m* road surface

Straßengraben *m* [roadside] ditch

Straßenkarte *f* road map

Straßenschild *nt* street sign

Straßensperre *f* roadblock

Straßenverkehr *m* [road] traffic

Strategie <-, -en> [ʃtra·te·'giː] *f* strategy

strategisch [ʃtra·'teː·gɪʃ] I. *adj* strategic II. *adv* strategically

sträuben ['ʃtrɔy·bn̩] *vr* **①** (*sich widersetzen*) ■sich *akk* [gegen etw *akk*] ~ to resist [sth] **②** (*sich aufrichten*) Fell, Haar to stand on end

Strauch <-[e]s, Sträucher> [ʃtraux] *m* shrub, bush

Strauß¹ <-es, Sträuße> [ʃtraus] *m* bunch [of flowers], bouquet

Strauß² <-es, -e> [ʃtraus] *m* ZOOL ostrich

streben ['ʃtreː·bn̩] *vi* (*sich bemühen*) to strive (**nach** +*dat* for)

Streber(in) <-s, -> ['ʃtreː·bɐ] *m(f)* (*pej fam*) dweeb *sl*

strebsam ['ʃtreːp·zaːm] *adj* industrious

Strecke <-, -n> ['ʃtrɛ·kə] *f* **①** (*Wegstrecke*) distance; **auf halber ~** halfway; **über weite ~n** for long stretches **②** BAHN stretch; **auf freier ~** between stations ▶WENDUNGEN: **auf der ~ bleiben** *dat* (*fam*) to fall by the wayside; **jdn zur ~ bringen** to hunt sb down

strecken ['ʃtrɛ·kn̩] I. *vt* to stretch; *Drogen etc.* to dilute II. *vr* ■sich *akk* ~ to stretch

streckenweise *adv* in parts

Streich <-[e]s, -e> [ʃtraiç] *m* prank; **jdm einen ~ spielen** to play a trick on sb

streicheln ['ʃtrai·çl̩n] *vt* to caress; *Katze, Hund* to pet

streichen <strich, gestrichen> ['ʃtrai·çn̩] I. *vt* haben **①** (*anmalen*) to paint **②** (*schmieren*) to spread **③** (*ausstreichen*) to delete **④** (*zurückziehen*) Auftrag, Projekt to cancel; *Zuschüsse* to withdraw II. *vi* **①** haben (*darüberfahren*) ■über etw *akk* ~ to stroke sth **②** sein (*streifen*) to prowl

Streichholz *nt* match

Streichinstrument *nt* string[ed] instrument

Streichwurst *f* spreadable sausage

streifen ['ʃtrai·fn̩] *vt* ❶ (*flüchtig berühren*) to touch; **ein Thema nur ~** to just touch on a subject ❷ (*überziehen*) ■**etw auf/über etw** *akk* **~** to slip sth on/over sth ❸ (*abstreifen*) ■**etw von etw** *dat* **~** to slip sth off [of] sth

Streifen <-s, -> ['ʃtrai·fn̩] *m* ❶ (*schmaler Abschnitt*) stripe ❷ (*schmales Stück*) strip

Streifenwagen *m* patrol car

Streik <-[e]s, -s> [ʃtraik] *m* strike; **in den ~ treten** to go on strike

Streikbrecher(in) *m(f)* strikebreaker, scab *pej fam*

streiken ['ʃtrai·kn̩] *vi* ❶ (*nicht arbeiten*) to be on strike, to strike ❷ (*hum fam: nicht funktionieren*) to call it quits ❸ (*fam: sich weigern*) to go on strike

Streikposten *m* picket; **~ aufstellen** to set up a picket line

Streikrecht *nt kein pl* right to strike

Streit <-[e]s, -e> [ʃtrait] *m* argument, dispute, fight; **[mit jdm] ~ [wegen etw** *dat*] **bekommen** to get into an argument [with sb] [about sth]; **~ haben/ suchen** to have/be looking for an argument; **im ~** during an argument

streiten <stritt, gestritten> ['ʃtrai·tn̩] *vi, vr* to argue, to fight (**über** +*akk* about); ■**sich** *akk* **um etw** *akk* **~** to argue [*or* fight] over sth

Streiterei <-, -en> [ʃtrai·tə·'rai] *f* (*fam*) arguing

Streitfall *m* dispute, conflict; **im ~** in case of dispute

streitig ['ʃtrai·tɪç] *adj* disputed; JUR contentious

Streitkräfte *pl* [armed] forces *pl*

streitlustig *adj* argumentative

streitsüchtig *adj* quarrelsome, contentious

streng [ʃtrɛŋ] I. *adj* strict; *Winter* severe; *Geruch* pungent II. *adv* strictly; **was riecht hier so ~?** what's that strong smell?

Strenge <-> ['ʃtrɛŋə] *f kein pl* ❶ (*Unnachsichtigkeit*) strictness ❷ (*Härte*) severity ❸ *von Geschmack* sharpness; *von Geruch* pungency

StressRR <-es, -e>, **Streß**ALT <-sses, -sse> [ʃtrɛs, ʃt-] *m* stress; **~ haben** to experience stress; **im ~ sein** to be under stress; **ich bin voll im ~** I am completely stressed out

stressen ['ʃtrɛ·sn̩] *vt* to put under stress

stressig ['ʃtrɛ·sɪç] *adj* stressful

streuen ['ʃtrɔy·ən] I. *vt* ❶ (*hinstreuen*) to scatter, to spread ❷ (*verbreiten*) to spread II. *vi* (*Streumittel anwenden*) to put down sand; *Salz* to salt [the roads]

streunen *vi sein o haben* to roam around; **~de Hunde** stray dogs

Streuselkuchen *m* streusel [cake]

strich [ʃtrɪç] *imp von* **streichen**

Strich <-[e]s, -e> [ʃtrɪç] *m* ❶ (*gezogene Linie*) line ❷ (*fam: Prostitution*) **auf den ~ gehen** to become a streetwalker ▶WENDUNGEN: **nach ~ und Faden** (*fam*) good and proper; **jd/etw macht jdm einen ~ durch die Rechnung** sb/sth messes up sb's plans; **jdm gegen den ~ gehen** (*fam*) to go against the grain; **einen ~ unter etw** *akk* **ziehen** to put an end to sth; **unterm ~** (*fam*) at the end of the day

stricheln ['ʃtrɪ·çl̩n] *vt* to sketch in *sep*; ■**gestrichelte Linie** dotted line; *auf Straße* broken line

Stricher <-s, -> *m* (*sl*) young male prostitute

Strichpunkt *m* semicolon

Strick <-[e]s, -e> [ʃtrɪk] *m* rope ▶WENDUNGEN: **wenn alle ~e reißen** (*fam*) if all else fails

stricken ['ʃtrɪ·kn̩] *vt, vi* to knit

Strickgarn *nt* knitting yarn

Strickjacke *f* cardigan

Strickwaren *pl* knitwear

striegeln ['ʃtri·gl̩n] *vt* to groom

strikt [ʃtrɪkt, ʃt-] I. *adj* strict; *Weigerung* point-blank II. *adv* strictly

Striplokal ['ʃtrɪp·lo·lo·ka:l] *nt* (*fam*) strip joint

strittig ['ʃtrɪ·tɪç] *adj* contentious; *Fall* controversial; *Grenze* disputed; ■**~ sein** to be in dispute; **der ~e Punkt** the point at issue

Stroh <-[e]s> [ʃtro:] *nt kein pl* straw

strohblond adj Mensch with sandy blonde hair; Haare sandy [blonde]

Strohhalm m straw

Strohhut m straw hat

Strohmann m front man

Strom <-[e]s, Ströme> [ʃtroːm, pl ˈʃtrøːmə] m ❶ ELEK electricity; **elektrischer ~** electric current; **grüner ~** green power ❷ (großer Fluss) [large] river ❸ (Schwarm) von Besuchern etc. stream ▶WENDUNGEN: **in Strömen gießen** to pour [down] [rain]; **mit dem/gegen den ~ schwimmen** to swim with/against the current; **unter ~ stehen** (elektrisch geladen sein) to be live; (überaus aktiv sein) to be a live wire fig

stromabwärts [ʃtroːmˈʔapˌvɛrts] adv downstream

stromaufwärts [ʃtroːmˈʔaufˌvɛrts] adv upstream

Stromausfall m power outage

strömen [ˈʃtrøːmən] vi sein to stream (**aus** + dat out of)

Stromerzeugung f electricity generation

Stromkabel nt power line

Stromkreis m [electric[al]] circuit

Stromnetz nt power grid

Stromstärke f current [strength]

Stromstoß m electric shock

Stromtankstelle f electric vehicle [or EV] charging station

Strömung <-, -en> f ❶ (fließendes Wasser) current ❷ (Tendenz) trend

S Stromverbrauch m power consumption

Stromversorgung f power supply

Stromzähler m electric meter

Strophe <-, -n> [ˈʃtroːfə] f verse

Strudel <-s, -> [ˈʃtruːdl̩] m ❶ (Wasserwirbel) whirlpool; (kleiner) eddy ❷ (Gebäck) strudel

Struktur <-, -en> [ʃtrʊkˈtuːɐ̯] f ❶ (Aufbau) structure ❷ (von Stoff etc.) texture

strukturell [ʃtrʊktuˈrɛl] adj structural

strukturschwach adj economically underdeveloped

Strumpf <-[e]s, Strümpfe> [ʃtrʊmpf] m ❶ (Kniestrumpf) knee-

high; (Socke) sock ❷ (Damenstrumpf) stocking

Strumpfhalter <-s, -> m garter

Strumpfhose f pantyhose, stockings; (fester) tights npl

struppig [ˈʃtrʊ·pɪç] adj Haare tousled; Fell shaggy

Stube <-, -n> [ˈʃtuː·bə] f DIAL (Wohnzimmer) living room

Stubenarrest m ~ **haben** (fam) to be confined to one's room

stubenrein adj housebroken

Stuck <-[e]s> [ʃtʊk] m kein pl stucco, cornices pl

Stück <-[e]s, -e o nach Zahlenangaben -> [ʃtʏk] nt ❶ (einzelnes Teil) piece; **ein ~ Kuchen** a piece of cake; **etw in ~e reißen** to tear sth to pieces; **~ für ~** bit by bit; **am ~** in one piece; **geschnitten oder am ~?** sliced or unsliced?; **5 Euro das ~** 5 euros each ❷ (besonderer Gegenstand) piece, item ❸ (Abschnitt) part; **ich begleite dich noch ein ~** I'll go part of the way with you; **ein ~ Land** a plot of land ❹ THEAT play ❺ MUS piece ▶WENDUNGEN: **jds bestes ~** (hum fam) sb's pride and joy; **aus freien ~en** of one's own free will; **große ~e auf jdn halten** (fam) to think highly of sb

Stückpreis m unit price

Student(in) <-en, -en> [ʃtuˈdɛnt] m(f) student

Studentenausweis m [college] student ID [card]

Studie <-, -n> [ˈʃtuː·di̯ə] f study

Studienfach nt subject

Studiengebühren pl tuition

Studienrat, -rätin m, f ≈ school board member

Studienreise f study trip

studieren* [ʃtuˈdiː·rən] vt, vi to study; **sie studiert noch** she is still a student; **ich will ~** I want to go to college

Studio <-s, -s> [ˈʃtuː·di̯o] nt studio

Studium <-, Studien> [ˈʃtuː·di̯·ʊm] nt ❶ (an Universität) studies pl; **ein ~ aufnehmen** to begin one's studies ❷ (eingehende Beschäftigung) study

Stufe <-, -n> ['ʃtu:·fə] *f* ❶ (*Treppenabschnitt*) step ❷ (*Niveau*) level ❸ (*Abschnitt*) stage, phase

stufenlos I. *adj* continuously variable II. *adv* smoothly

Stufenschnitt *m* (*Frisur*) layered cut

Stuhl <-[e]s, Stühle> [ʃtu:l] *m* chair

Stuhlbein *nt* chair leg

Stuhllehne *f* chair back

stumm [ʃtʊm] I. *adj* ❶ (*nicht sprechen können*) dumb ❷ (*schweigend*) silent; ■ ~ **werden** to go silent ❸ LING silent II. *adv* silently

Stummel <-s, -> ['ʃtʊ·məl] *m* Glied stump; *von Bleistift, Kerze* stub

Stummfilm *m* silent movie

Stümper(in) <-s, -> ['ʃtʏm·pɐ] *m(f)* (*pej*) incompetent

stumpf [ʃtʊmpf] *adj* ❶ (*nicht scharf*) blunt ❷ (*glanzlos*) dull ❸ (*abgestumpft*) apathetic

stumpfsinnig *adj* ❶ (*geistig träge*) apathetic ❷ (*stupide*) mindless, tedious

Stunde <-, -n> ['ʃtʊn·də] *f* ❶ (*60 Minuten*) hour; **nur noch eine knappe** ~ just under an hour to go; **zu später** ~ at a late hour; **in einer stillen** ~ in a quiet moment, fifteen minutes; **eine halbe** ~ half an hour; **anderthalb** ~**n** an hour and a half; **volle** ~ on the hour; **der Zug fährt jede volle** ~ the train departs every hour on the hour; **alle [halbe** ~ every [half [an]] hour ❷ *kein pl* (*festgesetzter Zeitpunkt*) time, hour *form;* **zur gewohnten** ~ at the usual time ❸ (*Unterrichtsstunde*) lesson, period ❹ *meist pl* (*Zeitraum von kurzer Dauer*) times *pl;* **sich** *akk* **nur an die angenehmen** ~**n erinnern** to only remember the good times ▶WENDUNGEN: **jds große** ~ sb's big moment; **jds letzte** ~ **hat geschlagen** sb's hour has come; **die** ~ **der Wahrheit** the moment of truth

stunden ['ʃtʊn·dn̩] *vt* ■ jdm etw ~ to give sb time to pay [for] sth

Stundenkilometer *pl* kilometers *pl* per hour

stundenlang I. *adj* lasting several hours *pred* II. *adv* for hours

Stundenlohn *m* hourly wage

Stundenplan *m* timetable, schedule

stundenweise I. *adv* for an hour or two [at a time] II. *adj* for a few hours *pred*

stündlich ['ʃtʏnt·lɪç] I. *adj* hourly II. *adv* hourly, every hour

Stupsnase *f* snub nose

stur [ʃtu:ɐ̯] I. *adj* stubborn, obstinate II. *adv* obstinately; **sich** *akk* ~ **stellen** (*fam*) to dig one's heels in

Sturheit <-> *f kein pl* stubbornness, obstinacy

Sturm <-[e]s, Stürme> [ʃtʊrm] *m* ❶ (*starker Wind*) storm ❷ FBALL forward line ❸ (*heftiger Andrang*) rush (**auf** +*akk* for) ▶WENDUNGEN: **gegen etw** *akk* ~ **laufen** to be up in arms against sth; ~ **läuten** to keep ringing the doorbell

stürmen ['ʃtʏr·mən] I. *vi impers haben* ■ **es stürmt** it's really windy out II. *vi* ❶ *haben* SPORT to attack ❷ *sein* (*rennen*) to storm III. *vt haben* to storm

Stürmer(in) <-s, -> ['ʃtʏr·mɐ] *m(f)* forward; FBALL striker

Sturmflut *f* storm tide

stürmisch ['ʃtʏr·mɪʃ] I. *adj* ❶ METEO blustery; (*mit Regen*) stormy; *See* rough ❷ (*vehement*) tumultuous; *Mensch* impetuous; *Beziehung* passionate; **nicht so** ~! take it easy! II. *adv* tumultuously

Sturmwarnung *f* storm warning

Sturz <-es, Stürze> [ʃtʊrts] *m* ❶ (*Fall*) fall ❷ (*drastisches Absinken*) **ein** ~ **der Temperaturen um 15° C** a drop in temperature of 15° C ❸ *eines Diktators, einer Regierung* overthrow

stürzen ['ʃtʏr·tsn̩] I. *vi sein* ❶ (*fallen*) to fall (**von** +*dat* off) ❷ (*rennen*) to rush; **ins Zimmer** ~ to burst into the room II. *vt haben* ❶ (*werfen*) **sich/jdn aus dem Fenster** ~ to throw oneself/sb out the window ❷ POL (*absetzen*) to bring down; *Minister* to force to resign; *Diktator* to overthrow; *Regierung* to topple ❸ KOCHK (*aus der Form kippen*) to turn upside down III. *vr* ❶ (*sich werfen*) ■ **sich** *akk* **auf jdn** ~ to pounce on

S

sb; **die Gäste stürzten sich aufs kalte Büfett** the guests stormed the cold buffet ❷ (*sich mit etw belasten*) ■ **sich** *akk* **in etw** *akk* ~ to plunge into sth; **sich** *akk* **in große Unkosten** ~ to go to great expense

Sturzflug *m* LUFT nosedive; ORN steep dive

Sturzhelm *m* crash helmet

Stute <-, -n> ['ʃtuː·tə] *f* mare

Stütze <-, -n> ['ʃtʏ·tsə] *f* ❶ (*Stützpfeiler*) support [pillar] ❷ (*Halt*) support, prop ❸ (*Unterstützung*) support ❹ (*fam: finanzielle Hilfe vom Staat*) welfare

stutzen¹ ['ʃtʊ·tsn̩] *vi* to hesitate, to stop short

stutzen² ['ʃtʊ·tsn̩] *vt* ❶ HORT to prune ❷ ZOOL to clip; **gestutzte Flügel** clipped wings ❸ (*kürzen*) to trim

stützen ['ʃtʏ·tsn̩] I. *vt* ❶ (*Halt geben*) to support ❷ (*aufstützen*) ■ **etw auf etw** *akk* ~ to rest sth on sth ❸ (*gründen*) ■ **etw auf etw** *akk* ~ to base sth on sth ❹ (*untermauern*) to back up *sep; Theorie* to support II. *vr* ❶ (*sich aufstützen*) ■ **sich** *akk* **auf jdn/etw** ~ to lean on sb/sth ❷ (*basieren*) ■ **sich** *akk* **auf etw** *akk* ~ to be based on sth

stutzig ['ʃtʊ·tsɪç] *adj* **jdn** ~ **machen** to make sb suspicious; ~ **werden** to begin to wonder

Stützpunkt *m* MIL base

Subjekt <-[e]s, -e> [zʊp·'jɛkt] *nt* subject

subjektiv ['zʊp·jɛk·tiːf] I. *adj* subjective II. *adv* subjectively

Substantiv <-s, -e> ['zʊp·stan·tiːf] *nt* noun

Substanz <-, -en> [zʊp·'stants] *f* substance

subtrahieren* [zʊp·tra·'hiː·rən] *vt, vi* to subtract (**von** +*dat* from)

Subtraktion <-, -en> [zʊp·trak·'tsi̯oːn] *f* subtraction

Subunternehmer(in) <-s, -> ['zʊp·ʔʊn·tɐ·neː·mɐ] *m(f)* subcontractor

Subvention <-, -en> [zʊp·vɛn·'tsi̯oːn] *f* subsidy

subventionieren* [zʊp·vɛn·tsi̯o·'niː·rən] *vt* to subsidize

Suche <-, -n> ['zuː·xə] *f* search (**nach** +*dat* for); **sich** *akk* **auf die** ~ [**nach jdm/etw] machen** to go in search [of sb/sth]; **auf der** ~ [**nach jdm/etw] sein** to be looking [for sb/sth]

suchen ['zuː·xn̩] I. *vt* ❶ (*zu finden versuchen*) to look for; (*intensiver*) to search for; **du hast hier nichts zu** ~**!** you've got no business being here! ❷ (*erstreben*) *Arbeit, Asyl, Schutz* to seek II. *vi* to search, to look (**nach** +*dat* for)

Suchfunktion *f* COMPUT search function

Suchlauf *m* search process

Suchmaschine *f* search engine

Sucht <-, Süchte> [zʊxt] *f* ❶ (*Abhängigkeit*) addiction; ~ **erzeugend** addictive ❷ (*Verlangen*) obsession; ■ **jds** ~ **nach etw** *dat* sb's craving for sth

Suchtgefahr *f* danger of addiction

süchtig ['zʏç·tɪç] *adj* ❶ (*abhängig*) addicted *pred;* ~ **machen** to be addictive ❷ (*begierig*) ■ ~ **sein** to be hooked (**nach** +*dat* on)

Süchtige(r) *f(m) dekl wie adj* addict

Suchtkranke(r) <-n, -n> *f (m) dekl adj* addict

Südafrika ['zyːt·ʔaːf·ri·ka] *nt* South Africa; *s. a.* **Deutschland**

südafrikanisch ['zyːt·ʔafri·'kaː·nɪʃ] *adj* South African; *s. a.* **deutsch**

Südamerika ['zyːt·ʔa'meː·ri·ka] *nt* South America; *s. a.* **Deutschland**

südamerikanisch *adj* South American; *s. a.* **deutsch**

süddeutsch ['zyːt·dɔʏtʃ] *adj* Southern German; *s. a.* **deutsch**

Süddeutschland ['zyːt·dɔʏtʃ·lant] *nt* Southern Germany; *s. a.* **Deutschland**

Süden <-s> ['zyː·dn̩] *m kein pl, kein indef art* ❶ (*Himmelsrichtung*) south; *s. a.* **Norden 1** ❷ (*südliche Gegend*) south; *s. a.* **Norden 2**

Südfrucht *f* tropical fruit

Südhalbkugel *f* Southern Hemisphere

südlich ['zyːt·lɪç] I. *adj* ❶ (*Himmelsrichtung*) southern; *s. a.* **nördlich I 1** ❷ (*im Süden liegend*) southern; *s. a.* **nördlich**

I 2 ❸ (*von/nach Süden*) southward, southerly; *s. a.* **nördlich I 3** II. *adv* ■ ~ **von** ... south of ... III. *präp* +gen ~ **der Stadt** [to the] south of the city/ town

Südosten [zy:t·'ʔɔs·tn̩] *m kein pl, kein indef art* southeast

südöstlich [zy:t·'ʔœst·lɪç] I. *adj* ❶ (*im Südosten gelegen*) southeastern ❷ (*von/nach Südosten*) southeastward, southeasterly II. *adv* southeast III. *präp* +gen [to the] southeast of sth

Südpol ['zy:t·po:l] *m* ■ **der** ~ the South Pole

Südsee ['zy:t·ze:] *f kein pl* ■ **die** ~ the South Seas *pl*, the South Pacific

Südstaaten ['zy:t·ʃta:·tn̩] *pl* (*in den USA*) ■ **die** ~ the South

Südwesten [zy:t·'vɛs·tn̩] *m kein pl, kein indef art* southwest

südwestlich [zy:t·'vɛst·lɪç] I. *adj* ❶ (*im Südwesten liegend*) southwestern ❷ (*von/nach Südwesten*) southwestward II. *adv* [to the] southwest III. *präp* +gen [to the] southwest of sth

suggerieren* [zʊ·ge·'ri:·rən] *vt* to suggest

sühnen ['zy:·nən] *vt* ■ **etw** ~ to atone for sth

Sultan, Sultanin <-s, -e> ['zʊl·ta:n, 'zʊl·ta·nɪn] *m, f* sultan *masc*, sultana *fem*

Summe <-, -n> ['zʊ·mə] *f* ❶ (*Additionsergebnis*) sum, total ❷ (*Betrag*) sum, amount

summen ['zʊ·mən] *vt, vi* to hum; *Biene* to buzz

summieren* [zʊ·'mi:·rən] I. *vt* to add up *sep* II. *vr* ■ **sich** *akk* **auf etw** *akk* ~ to amount [*or* add up] to sth

Sumpf <-[e]s, Sümpfe> [zʊmpf] *m* marsh, swamp; (*Moor*) bog

Sumpffieber *nt* malaria

Sumpfgebiet *nt* marsh[land], swamp[land]

sumpfig ['zʊm·pfɪç] *adj* marshy, swampy

Sünde <-, -n> ['zʏn·də] *f* sin

Sündenbock *m* scapegoat

Sünder(in) <-s, -> *m(f)* sinner

sündig ['zʏn·dɪç] *adj* ❶ REL sinful ❷ (*lasterhaft*) dissolute

super ['zu:·pɐ] I. *adj* super II. *adv* very well

Super <-s> ['zu:·pɐ] *nt kein pl* AUTO super, premium

Superlativ <-[e]s, -e> ['zu:·pɐ·la·ti:f] *m* superlative

Supermacht *f* superpower

Supermarkt ['zu:·pɐ·markt] *m* supermarket

superreich ['zu:·pɐ·] *adj* (*pej*) superrich

Suppe <-, -n> ['zʊ·pə] *f* soup; **klare** ~ consommé, broth ▸WENDUNGEN: **die** ~ **auslöffeln müssen** (*fam*) to have to face the music

Suppenhuhn *nt* boiling chicken

Suppenschüssel *f* soup tureen

Suppenteller *m* soup plate [*or* bowl]

Surfbrett ['zœf·] *nt* ❶ (*zum Windsurfen*) windsurfer ❷ (*zum Wellensurfen*) surfboard

Surfen <-s> ['zø:·ɐ·fn̩] *nt kein pl* surfing

surfen ['zœr·fn̩] *vi* to surf; **im Internet** ~ to surf the Internet

Surfer(in) <-s, -> *m(f)* surfer

surren ['zʊ·rən] *vi Insekt* to buzz; *Motor* to hum

suspekt *adj* (*geh*) suspicious; ■ **jdm** ~ **sein** to look suspicious to sb

suspendieren* [zʊs·pɛn·'di:·rən] *vt* to suspend (**von** +*dat* from)

süß [zy:s] I. *adj* sweet II. *adv* sweetly

süßen ['zy:·sn̩] *vt* to sweeten

Süßigkeit <-, -en> ['zy:·sɪç·kait] *f meist pl* sweets *pl*, candy

süßlich *adj* sickly sweet

süßsauer ['zy:s·'zau·ɐ] *adj* sweet-and-sour

Süßspeise *f* dessert

Süßstoff *m* sweetener

Süßwasser *nt* fresh water

Symbol <-s, -e> [zʏm·'bo:l] *nt* symbol

symbolisch [zʏm·'bo:·lɪʃ] I. *adj* symbolic II. *adv* symbolically

symbolisieren* [zʏm·bo·li·'zi:·rən] *vt* to symbolize

S

symmetrisch [zʏˈmeː·trɪʃ] I. *adj* symmetrical II. *adv* symmetrically

Sympathie <-, -en> [zʏm·paˈtiː] *f* sympathy

Sympathisant(in) <-en, -en> [zʏm·patiˈzant] *m(f)* sympathizer

sympathisch [zʏmˈpaː·tɪʃ] *adj* nice, likeable; **sie war mir gleich ~** I liked her right away

Symphonie <-, -en> [zʏm·foˈniː] *f* symphony

Symptom <-s, -e> [zʏmpˈtoːm] *nt* symptom (**für** +*akk* of)

Synagoge <-, -n> [zy·naˈgoː·gə] *f* synagogue

synchronisieren* [zʏn·kro·niˈziː·rən] *vt* ① FILM, TV to dub ② (*zeitlich abstimmen*) to synchronize

synonym [zy·noˈnyːm] *adj* synonym

Synonym <-s, -e> [zy·noˈnyːm] *nt* synonym

Syntax <-, -en> [ˈzʏn·taks] *f* syntax

Synthese <-, -n> [zʏnˈteː·zə] *f* synthesis

synthetisch [zʏnˈteː·tɪʃ] I. *adj* synthetic II. *adv* synthetically

Syphilis <-> [ˈzy·fi·lɪs] *f kein pl* syphilis

System <-s, -e> [zʏsˈteːm] *nt* system; **mit ~** systematically

systematisch [zʏs·te·ˈma:·tɪʃ] I. *adj* systematic II. *adv* systematically

Systemfehler *m* system error

Szene <-, -n> [ˈstseː·nə] *f* ① THEAT, FILM scene ② (*Krach*) scene; **eine ~ machen** to make a scene ③ *kein pl* (*Milieu*) scene

Szeneladen *m* (*fam: Kneipe*) trendy bar; (*Disco oder Club*) trendy club

Szenenwechsel *m* change of scene

Tt

T, t <-, -> [teː] *nt* T, t; **~ wie Theodor** T as in Tango

t *Abk von* **Tonne**

Tabak <-s, -e> [ˈta:·bak, ˈta·bak] *m* tobacco

Tabaksteuer *f* tobacco tax

Tabakwaren *pl* tobacco products *pl*

Tabelle <-, -n> [ta·ˈbɛ·lə] *f* table; SPORT [league] standings

Tabellenführer(in) *m(f)* SPORT league leader

Tablett <-[e]s, -s> [ta·ˈblɛt] *nt* tray

Tablette <-, -n> [ta·ˈblɛ·tə] *f* pill

tabu [ta·ˈbuː] *adj* taboo

Tachometer *m o nt* speedometer

Tadel <-s, -> [ˈta:·dl] *m* reprimand

tadellos I. *adj* (*einwandfrei*) perfect II. *adv* perfectly

tadeln *vt* to reprimand, to reproach

Tafel <-, -n> [ˈta:·fl] *f* ① (*Platte*) board, plaque; SCH [black]board ② **eine ~ Schokolade** a bar of chocolate ③ (*geh: festlicher Esstisch*) table

Tafelwasser *nt* table water

Tafelwein *m* table wine

Tag <-[e]s, -e> [ta:k] *m* ① (*Abschnitt von 24 Stunden*) day; **ein freier ~** a day off; **den ganzen ~ [lang]** all day; **guten ~!** hello!, good afternoon/morning!; **~ für ~** every day, day after day; **von einem ~ auf den anderen** overnight; **eines [schönen] ~es** one [fine] day ② (*Datum*) day; **~ der offenen Tür** open house; **der ~ X** D-Day; **bis zum heutigen ~** up to the present day ③ (*Tageslicht*) light; **am ~** during the day ④ *pl* (*fam: Menstruation*) period ▶WENDUNGEN: **es ist noch nicht aller ~e Abend** it's not over yet; **man soll den ~ nicht vor dem Abend loben**

(*prov*) don't count your chickens before they're hatched; **etw <u>kommt</u> an den ~** sth comes to light; **in den ~ hinein <u>leben</u>** to live from day to day; **über/ unter ~e** above/below ground
Tagebau *m kein pl* strip mining
Tagebuch *nt* diary
tagelang I. *adj* lasting for days; **nach ~em Warten** after days of waiting II. *adv* for days
Tagelöhner(in) <-s, -> ['ta:·gə·løː·nɐ] *m(f)* (*veraltend*) day laborer
tagen *vi* to meet; **der Kongress tagt** Congress is in session
Tagesablauf *m* daily routine
Tagesanbruch *m* daybreak
Tagesgeschäft *nt* BÖRSE day order
Tageskarte *f* ① (*Speisekarte*) menu of the day ② (*Eintrittskarte*) [one-]day pass
Tageslicht *nt kein pl* daylight (**bei** by/ in)
Tagesmutter *f* nanny
Tagesordnung *f* agenda; **etw auf die ~ setzen** to put sth on the agenda; **auf der ~ stehen** to be on the agenda ►WENDUNGEN: [**wieder**] **zur ~ überge- hen** to carry on [with business] as usual
Tageszeit *f* time [of day]
Tageszeitung *f* daily [[news]paper]
täglich ['tɛːk·lɪç] *adj, adv* daily
tagsüber ['taːks·ʔyː·bɐ] *adv* during the day
Tagung <-, -en> *f* ① (*Fachtagung*) con- ference ② (*Sitzung*) meeting
Taifun <-s, -e> [tai·ˈfuːn] *m* typhoon
Taille <-, -n> ['tal·jə] *f* waist
Takt <-[e]s, -e> ['takt] *m* ① MUS bar ② *kein pl* (*Rhythmus*) rhythm; **den ~ angeben** to beat time; **im ~ sein** in time to sth ③ *kein pl* (*Taktgefühl*) tact
Taktgefühl *nt* ① (*Feingefühl*) sense of tact ② MUS sense of rhythm
taktieren* [tak·ˈtiː·rən] *vi* to use tactics
Taktik <-, -en> ['tak·tɪk] *f* tactics *pl*
taktisch ['tak·tɪʃ] I. *adj* tactic[al] II. *adv* tactically
taktlos *adj* tactless
Taktlosigkeit <-, -en> *f* tactlessness; **so eine ~!** what a tactless thing to do!

Taktstock *m* baton
taktvoll *adj* tactful
Tal <-[e]s, Täler> [taːl] *nt* valley
Talar <-s, -e> [ta·ˈlaːɐ̯] *m* JUR robe; REL cassock; SCH gown
Talent <-[e]s, -e> [ta·ˈlɛnt] *nt* talent
talentiert [tal·ɛn·ˈtiːɐ̯t] I. *adj* talented II. *adv* in a talented way
Talisman <-s, -e> ['taː·lɪs·man] *m* lucky charm
Talkshow^RR <-, -s> ['tɔː·kʃoː] *f* talk show
Tampon <-s, -s> ['tam·pɔn] *m* tampon
Tang <-[e]s, -e> ['taŋ] *m* seaweed
Tangente <-, -n> [taŋ·ˈgɛn·tə] *f* MATH tangent
Tango <-s, -s> ['taŋ·go] *m* tango
Tank <-s, -s> [taŋk] *m* tank
tanken ['taŋ·kn̩] I. *vi* (*Auto*) to get gas; (*Flugzeug*) to refuel II. *vt* ① (*als Tank- füllung*) **Benzin ~** to fill up a car with gas ② (*fam: in sich aufnehmen*) **frische Luft/Sonne ~** to get some fresh air/sun ►WENDUNGEN: [**ganz schön**] **getankt haben** (*fam*) to have drunk a fair share
Tanker <-s, -> ['taŋ·kɐ] *m* tanker
Tankstelle *f* gas station
Tankwart(in) *m(f)* gas station attendant
Tanne <-, -n> ['ta·nə] *f* fir
Tannenbaum *m* ① (*Weihnachtsbaum*) Christmas tree ② *s.* **Tanne**
Tannenzapfen *m* pinecone
Tante <-, -n> ['tan·tə] *f* aunt
Tanz <-es, Tänze> ['tants] *m* dance
tanzen ['tan·tsn̩] *vt, vi* to dance
Tänzer(in) <-s, -> ['tɛn·tsɐ] *m(f)* dancer
Tanzfläche *f* dance floor
Tanzmusik *f* dance music
Tanzschule *f* dance school
Tapete <-, -n> [ta·ˈpeː·tə] *f* wallpaper
tapezieren* [ta·pe·ˈtsiː·rən] *vt* to wall- paper
tapfer ['tap·fɐ] *adj* brave
Tapferkeit <-> *f kein pl* courage
tappen ['ta·pn̩] *vi sein* **schlaftrunken tappte er zum Telefon** he shuffled drowsily to the phone
Tarantel <-, -n> [ta·ˈran·tl̩] *f* tarantula

T

Tarif <-[e]s, -e> [taˈriːf] m ❶ (*Gehaltsvereinbarung*) pay scale ❷ (*Gebühr*) charge

Tarifgruppe f wage group

tariflich I. adj negotiated II. adv by negotiation

Tariflohn m standard wage

Tarifverhandlungen pl collective bargaining negotiations pl

Tarifvertrag m collective bargaining agreement

tarnen [ˈtarnən] vt ❶ MIL to camouflage (**gegen** +akk against) ❷ (*Identität wechseln*) ■ **sich** akk ~ to disguise oneself

Tarnung <-, -en> f ❶ kein pl (*das Tarnen*) camouflage ❷ (*tarnende Identität*) cover

Tasche <-, -n> [ˈtaʃə] f bag; (*in Kleidung*) pocket ▶WENDUNGEN: **jdm auf der ~ liegen** (*fam*) to live off [of] sb['s money]; **jdn in die ~ stecken** (*fam*) to be head and shoulders above sb

Taschenbuch nt paperback

Taschendieb(in) m(f) pickpocket

Taschengeld nt allowance, spending money

Taschenlampe f [pocket] flashlight

Taschenmesser nt pocketknife

Taschenrechner m pocket calculator

Taschentuch nt handkerchief

Taschenuhr f pocket watch

Taskleiste [ˈtaːsk-] f COMPUT task bar

Tasse <-, -n> [ˈtasə] f cup; **eine ~ Tee** a cup of tea ▶WENDUNGEN: **nicht alle ~n im Schrank haben** (*fam*) to have a screw loose

Tastatur <-, -en> [tasta·ˈtuːɐ] f keyboard

Taste <-, -n> [ˈtastə] f key; (*am Telefon*) button

tasten [ˈtastn̩] vt, vi to feel (**nach** +dat for)

Tastsinn m kein pl sense of touch

tat [taːt] imp von **tun**

Tat <-, -en> [taːt] f ❶ (*Handlung*) act; **eine gute ~** a good deed; **etw in die ~ umsetzen** to put sth into effect ❷ (*Straftat*) crime; **jdn auf frischer ~ ertappen** to catch sb redhanded fig ▶WENDUNGEN: **in der ~** indeed

Tatbestand m ❶ (*Sachlage*) facts [of the matter] ❷ JUR elements of an offense

tatenlos adj idle; **~ zusehen** to stand back and do nothing

Täter(in) <-s, -> [ˈtɛːtɐ] m(f) perpetrator

tätig [ˈtɛːtɪç] adj ❶ (*beschäftigt*) employed; ■ **[irgendwo]** ~ **sein** to work [somewhere] ❷ (*aktiv*) active; ■ **[in etw dat]** ~ **werden** (geh) to act [on sth]

Tätigkeit <-, -en> f occupation

Tatkraft f kein pl drive

tatkräftig adj active

Tatort m scene of the crime

tätowieren* [tɛ·to·ˈviː·rən] vt to tattoo

Tätowierung <-, -en> f ❶ tattoo ❷ kein pl (*das Tätowieren*) tattooing

Tatsache [ˈtaːt·za·xə] f fact; **~ ist [aber], dass …** the fact of the matter is [however] that … ▶WENDUNGEN: **den ~n ins Auge sehen** to face the facts

tatsächlich [taːtˈzɛç·lɪç] I. adj attr actual attr, real II. adv ❶ (*in Wirklichkeit*) actually ❷ (*in der Tat*) really

tätscheln [ˈtɛːt·ʃl̩n] vt to pat

Tatze <-, -n> [ˈta·tsə] f (a. pej) paw

Tau¹ <-[e]s> [ˈtau] m kein pl (*Wasser*) dew

Tau² <-[e]s, -e> [ˈtau] nt (*Seil*) rope

taub [ˈtaup] adj ❶ (*gehörlos*) deaf ❷ (*gefühllos*) numb ❸ Nuss empty

Taube <-, -n> [ˈtau·bə] f pigeon

Taubheit <-> f kein pl ❶ (*Gehörlosigkeit*) deafness ❷ (*Gefühllosigkeit*) numbness

taubstumm adj deaf and dumb

Taubstumme(r) f(m) deaf-mute

tauchen [tau·xn̩] I. vi haben o sein to dive (**nach** +dat for) II. vt haben ❶ (*eintauchen*) to dip ❷ (*untertauchen*) to duck

Tauchen <-s> [ˈtau·xn̩] nt kein pl diving

Taucher(in) <-s, -> [ˈtau·xɐ] m(f) (a. orn) diver

Taucheranzug m diving suit

Tauchsieder <-s, -> *m* immersion heater

tauen ['tau·ən] *vi* ❶ *haben* ■**es taut** it's thawing [*or* starting to thaw] ❷ *sein* (*schmelzen*) to melt

Taufbecken *nt* baptismal font

Taufe <-, -n> ['tau·fə] *f* REL baptism

taufen ['tau·fn] *vt* ❶ (*die Taufe vollziehen*) to baptize ❷ (*in der Taufe benennen*) to christen ❸ (*fam: benennen*) to christen

Taufpate, -patin *m, f* godfather *masc*, godmother *fem*

taugen ['taugn] *vi* ❶ (*wert sein*) ■**etwas/viel/nichts ~** to be useful/very useful/useless ❷ (*geeignet sein*) to be suitable (**als/zu/für** for)

tauglich ['tauk·lɪç] *adj* ❶ (*geeignet*) suitable ❷ MIL fit [for military service]

taumeln ['tau·mln] *vi sein* to stagger

Tausch <-[e]s> [tauʃ] *m kein pl* swap, trade; **im ~ gegen** [*etw akk*] in exchange for [*sth*]

tauschen ['tau·ʃn] **I.** *vt* ❶ (*einwechseln*) to swap [*or* trade] (**mit** +*dat* with, **gegen** +*akk* for) ❷ (*austauschen*) to exchange **II.** *vi* to swap [*or* trade] ▶WEN-DUNGEN: **mit niemandem ~ wollen** to not wish to trade places with anyone

täuschen ['tɔy·ʃn] **I.** *vt* (*irreführen*) to deceive; **wenn mich nicht alles täuscht ....** if I'm not completely mistaken ...; **sich** *akk* [**von jdm/etw**] **nicht ~ lassen** to not be fooled [by sb/sth] **II.** *vr* (*sich irren*) ■**sich** *akk* **~** to be mistaken [*or* wrong] (**in** +*dat* about) **III.** *vi* to be deceptive

täuschend I. *adj* (*trügerisch*) deceptive; *Ähnlichkeit* striking **II.** *adv* (*trügerisch*) deceptively; **sie sieht ihrer Mutter ~ ähnlich** she bears a striking resemblance to her mother

Täuschung <-, -en> ['tɔy·ʃʊŋ] *f* ❶ (*Betrug*) deception ❷ (*Irrtum*) error; **optische ~** optical illusion

tausend ['tau·znt] *adj* ❶ (*Zahl*) a [*or* one] thousand ❷ (*fam: sehr viele*) thousands of ...

Tausend[1] <-s, -e o -> ['tau·znt] *nt*

❶ (*Einheit von 1000*) a [*or* one] thousand ❷ *pl, auch kleingeschrieben* (*viele tausend*) thousands *pl* (**von** +*dat* of); *s. a.* **Hundert**[1] 2

Tausend[2] <-, -en> ['tauznt] *f* thousand

Tausendfüßler <-s, -> ['tau·znt·fyːsˈlɐ] *m* centipede

Tausendstel ['tau·znt·stl] *nt o* SCHWEIZ *m* thousandth

Tauwetter *nt* thaw

Taxi <-s, -s> ['tak·si] *nt* taxi, cab

Taxifahrer(in) *m(f)* taxi [*or* cab] river

Taxistand *m* taxi [*or* cab] stand

Team <-s, -s> [tiːm] *nt* team

Teamarbeit ['tiːm-] *f* teamwork

Technik <-, -en> ['teç·nɪk] *f* ❶ *kein pl* (*Technologie*) technology ❷ *kein pl* (*technische Ausstattung*) technical equipment ❸ (*Methode*) technique ❹ ÖSTERR (*technische Hochschule*) college of technology

Techniker(in) <-s, -> ['teç·ni·kɐ] *m(f)* technician

technisch ['teç·nɪʃ] **I.** *adj* technical **II.** *adv* technically

Technologie <-, -n> [tɛç·no·lo·'giː] *f* technology

Tee <-s, -s> [teː] *m* tea; (*Kräutertee*) herbal tea; **eine Tasse ~** a cup of tea; **grüner/schwarzer ~** green/black tea ▶WENDUNGEN: **abwarten und ~ trinken** (*fam*) to wait and see

Teebeutel *m* tea bag

Teefilter *m* tea strainer

Teekanne *f* teapot

Teelöffel *m* ❶ (*Löffel*) teaspoon ❷ (*Menge*) teaspoon[ful]

Teer <-[e]s, -e> [teːɐ] *m* tar

Teeservice *nt* tea set

Teich <-[e]s, -e> [taiç] *m* pond

Teig <-[e]s, -e> [taik] *m* (*Hefe-, Rühr-, Nudelteig*) dough; (*Mürbe-, Blätterteig*) pastry; (*flüssig*) batter

Teigwaren *pl* pasta + *sing vb*

Teil[1] <-[e]s, -e> [tail] *m* ❶ (*Bruchteil*) part; **zum ~** partly; (*gelegentlich*) on occasion; **zum größten ~** for the most part ❷ (*Anteil*) share; **zu gleichen ~en** equally ❸ (*Bereich*) *einer Strecke*

stretch; *eines Gebäudes, einer Zeitung, eines Buches* section ▶WENDUNGEN: **sich** *dat* **seinen ~ denken** to draw one's own conclusions

Teil[2] <-[e]s, -e> [tail] *nt* component

teilbar *adj* MATH divisible (**durch** +*akk* by)

Teilchen <-s, -> *nt* ❶ (*Partikel*) particle ❷ KOCHK DIAL pastries *pl*

teilen ['tailən] I. *vt* ❶ (*aufteilen*) to share ❷ MATH (*dividieren*) to divide (**durch** +*akk* by) II. *vr* ❶ (*sich aufteilen, trennen*) ■**sich** *akk* ~ *akk* to split up ❷ (*gemeinsam benutzen, essen etc.*) ■**sich** *dat* **etw** [**mit jdm**] ~ to share sth [with sb] III. *vi* (*abgeben*) to share

Teilhaber(in) <-s, -> *m(f)* partner

Teilnahme <-, -en> ['tail·naː·mə] *f* participation (**an** +*dat* in)

teilnahmslos *adj* apathetic

teil|nehmen *vi irreg* ❶ (*anwesend sein*) ■[**an etw** *dat*] ~ to attend [sth] ❷ (*sich beteiligen*) to take part (**an** +*dat* in)

Teilnehmer(in) <-s, -> *m(f)* ❶ (*Anwesender*) person present ❷ (*Beteiligter*) participant (**an** +*dat* in) ❸ (*Telefoninhaber*) subscriber

teils ['tails] *adv* partly; ~, ~ yes and no

Teilung <-, -en> *f* division

teilweise ['tail·vai·zə] I. *adv* partly II. *adj attr* partial

Teilzeitarbeit *f* part-time work

Teint <-s, -s> ['tɛ̃ː] *m* complexion

Telebanking ['teː·lə·bɛn·kɪŋ] *nt* home banking

Telefon <-s, -e> [teː·le·foːn] *nt* [tele]phone

Telefonat <-[e]s, -e> [te·le·fo·ˈnaːt] *nt* telephone call, phone *fam*

Telefonauskunft *f* directory assistance

Telefonbuch *nt* [tele]phone book

Telefongespräch *nt* [tele]phone call

telefonieren* [te·le·fo·ˈniː·rən] *vi* to be on the phone; ■**mit jdm** ~ to talk on the phone with sb

telefonisch I. *adj* [tele]phone II. *adv* by [tele]phone

Telefonkarte *f* calling card

Telefonleitung *f* [tele]phone line

Telefonnummer *f* [tele]phone number

Telefonrechnung *f* [tele]phone bill

Telefonzelle *f* phone booth

telegrafieren* [te·le·gra·ˈfiː·rən] *vt, vi* to telegraph

Telegramm <-s, -e> [te·le·ˈgram] *nt* telegram

Telekommunikation *f* telecommunication

Teleobjektiv *nt* telephoto lens

Telepathie <-> [te·le·pa·ˈtiː] *f kein pl* telepathy

Teleskop <-s, -e> [te·le·ˈskoːp] *nt* telescope

Teller <-s, -> ['tɛ·lɐ] *m* ❶ (*Geschirrteil*) plate; **flacher/tiefer ~** dinner/soup plate ❷ (*Menge*) plate[ful]

Tempel <-s, -> ['tɛm·pl̩] *m* temple

Temperament <-[e]s, -e> [tɛm·pə·ra·ˈmɛnt] *nt* ❶ (*Wesensart*) temperament ❷ *kein pl* (*Lebhaftigkeit*) vivacity; ~ **haben** to be very lively

temperamentvoll I. *adj* lively, vivacious II. *adv* vivaciously

Temperatur <-, -en> [tɛm·pə·ra·ˈtuːɐ̯] *f* temperature; **seine ~ messen** to take one's temperature; [**erhöhte**] ~ **haben** to have a temperature

Tempo <-s, -s> ['tɛm·po] *nt* speed; **mit hohem ~** at high speed

Tempolimit *nt* speed limit

Tendenz <-, -en> [tɛn·ˈdɛnts] *f* ❶ (*Trend*) trend ❷ (*Neigung*) tendency (**zu** +*dat* to)

tendieren* [tɛn·ˈdiː·rən] *vi* to tend (**zu** +*dat* toward); ■**dazu ~, etw zu tun** to tend to do sth

Tennis <-> ['tɛ·nɪs] *nt kein pl* tennis

Tennisplatz *m* ❶ (*Spielfeld*) tennis court ❷ (*Anlage*) outdoor tennis complex

Tennisschläger *m* tennis racket

Tennisspiel *nt* ❶ (*Sportart*) tennis ❷ (*Einzelspiel*) game of tennis

Tenor <-s, Tenöre> [te·ˈnoːɐ̯] *m* MUS tenor

Teppich <-s, -e> ['tɛ·pɪç] *m* carpet; (*klein*) rug

Teppichboden *m* wall-to-wall carpeting

Termin <-s, -e> [tɛrˈmiːn] *m* ❶ (*verabredeter Zeitpunkt*) appointment; **einen ~ vereinbaren/verpassen** to set up/ miss an appointment; **sich** *dat* **einen ~ [für etw** *akk***] geben lassen** to make an appointment [for sth] ❷ (*Stichtag*) deadline

Terminal <-s-, -s> [ˈtøːɐ̯miˌnl] *nt* COMPUT, LUFT, TRANSP terminal

Terminkalender *m* [appointment] calendar

Termite <-, -n> [tɛrˈmiːtə] *f* termite

Terpentin <-s, -e> [tɛrpɛnˈtiːn] *nt o* ÖSTERR *m* turpentine; (*Terpentinöl a.*) oil of turpentine

Terrain <-s, -s> [tɛˈrɛ̃ː] *nt* ❶ (*Gelände*) terrain ❷ (*a. fig: [Bau]grundstück*) site

Terrasse <-, -n> [tɛˈrasə] *f* terrace

Territorium <-s, -rien> [tɛriˈtoːriˌʊm] *nt* territory

Terror <-s> [ˈtɛroːɐ̯] *m kein pl* ❶ (*terroristische Aktivitäten*) terrorism ❷ (*Furcht und Schrecken*) terror ❸ (*fam: Stunk*) huge fuss

Terroranschlag *m* terror[ist] attack

terrorisieren* [tɛroriˈziːrən] *vt* ❶ (*fam: schikanieren*) to intimidate ❷ (*in Angst und Schrecken versetzen*) to terrorize

Terrorismus <-> [tɛroˈrɪsˌmʊs] *m kein pl* terrorism

Terrorist(in) <-en, -en> [tɛroˈrɪst] *m(f)* terrorist

terroristisch *adj* terrorist *attr*

Terzett <-[e]s, -e> [tɛrˈtsɛt] *nt* MUS trio

Test <-[e]s, -s> [tɛst] *m* test

Testament <-[e]s, -e> [tɛstaˈmɛnt] *nt* ❶ JUR will ❷ REL **Altes/Neues ~** Old/ New Testament

testamentarisch [tɛstaˌmɛnˈtaːrɪʃ] I. *adj* testamentary II. *adv* in the will

Testamentseröffnung *f* reading of the will

testen [ˈtɛsˌtn̩] *vt* to test (**auf** *+akk* for)

teuer [ˈtɔyˌ•ɐ̯] I. *adj* ❶ (*viel kostend*) expensive II. *adv* (*geschätzt*) dearly; **das hast du aber zu ~ eingekauft** you

paid too much for that ▸WENDUNGEN: **etw** *akk* **~ bezahlen müssen** to pay a high price for sth; **jdn ~ zu stehen kommen** to cost sb dearly

Teuerungsrate *f* rate of price increase

Teufel <-s, -> [ˈtɔyfl̩] *m* ❶ *kein pl* (*Satan*) ■**der ~** the Devil ❷ (*teuflischer Mensch*) devil ▸WENDUNGEN: **geh zum ~!** (*fam*) go to hell!; **soll jdn [doch] der ~ holen** (*fam*) to hell with sb; **in ~s Küche kommen** (*fam*) to get into a hell of a mess; **irgendwo ist der ~ los** (*fam*) all hell is breaking loose somewhere; **den ~ an die Wand malen** to imagine the worst; **weiß der ~** (*fam*) who the hell knows

Teufelskreis *m* vicious circle

teuflisch [ˈtɔyfˌlɪʃ] I. *adj* diabolical II. *adv* ❶ (*diabolisch*) diabolically ❷ (*fam: höllisch*) like hell

Text <-[e]s, -e> [tɛkst] *m* text; *eines Lieds* lyrics; *einer Rede* script

Texter(in) <-s, -> *m(f)* songwriter; (*in der Werbung*) copywriter

Textilien [tɛksˈtiːlijˌən] *pl* textiles *pl*

Textilindustrie *f* textile industry

Textstelle *f* passage

Textverarbeitungsprogramm *nt* word processing program

Theater <-s, -> [teˈaːtɐ] *nt* ❶ (*Gebäude*) theater ❷ *kein pl* (*Schauspielkunst*) theater; **~ spielen** to act ❸ *kein pl* (*fam: Umstände*) fuss; **[ein] ~ machen** to make a fuss

Theateraufführung *f* theater performance

Theaterbesucher(in) *m(f)* theatergoer

Theaterstück *nt* play

Theke <-, -n> [ˈteːkə] *f* counter; (*in einem Lokal*) bar

Thema <-s, Themen> [ˈteːma] *nt* ❶ (*Gesprächsthema*) topic; **jdn vom ~ abbringen** to get [*or* throw] sb off the subject; **beim ~ bleiben** to stick to the subject; **ein ~ ist [für jdn] erledigt** a matter is closed [as far as sb is concerned] ❷ (*schriftliches Thema*) subject ❸ MUS theme ▸WENDUNGEN: **ein/kein ~ sein** to be/not be an issue

T

Thematik <-> [teˑmaˑˈtɪk] *f kein pl* topic

Theologe, Theologin <-n, -n> [teoˈloːgə] *m, f* theologian

Theologie <-, -n> [teoˑloˑˈgiː] *f* theology

theoretisch [teoˈreːtɪʃ] **I.** *adj* theoretical **II.** *adv* theoretically

Theorie <-, -n> [teoˈriː] *f* theory

Therapeut(in) <-en, -en> [teˑraˑˈpɔyt] *m(f)* therapist

Therapie <-, -n> [teˑraˑˈpiː] *f* therapy

therapieren [teˑraˑˈpiːˑrən] *vt* to treat

Thermalquelle [tɛrˈmaːl-] *f* thermal spring

Thermometer <-s, -> [tɛrˑmoˑˈmeːˑtə] *nt* thermometer

Thermometerstand *m* temperature

Thermostat <-[e]s, -e[n]> [tɛrˑmoˑˈstaːt] *m* thermostat

These <-, -n> [ˈteːˑzə] *f (geh)* thesis

Thrombose <-, -n> [trɔmˈboːˑzə] *f* thrombosis

Thron <-[e]s, -e> [ˈtroːn] *m* throne

Thronfolge *f* line of succession

Thronfolger(in) <-s, -> *m(f)* heir to the throne

Thunfisch [ˈtuːnˑfɪʃ] *m* tuna [fish]

Thüringen <-s> [ˈtyːˑrɪŋən] *nt* Thuringia

Thüringer(in) <-s, -> [ˈtyːˑrɪŋə] *m(f)* Thuringian

thüringisch [ˈtyːˑrɪŋɪʃ] *adj* Thuringian

Thymian <-s, -e> [ˈtyːˑmiˑaːn] *m* thyme

ticken [ˈtɪkn] *vi* to tick ▶WENDUNGEN: **nicht richtig ~** *(sl)* to be off one's rocker *sl*

tief [ˈtiːf] **I.** *adj* ① deep; **ein Meter ~** a meter deep ② *(niedrig)* Temperaturen, Tisch low; Ausschnitt low ③ Stimme deep ④ *(intensiv)* Bedauern, Schlaf, Schmerz deep ⑤ **im ~sten Winter** in the middle of winter **II.** *adv* ① *(in die Tiefe)* deep; **er stürzte 300 Meter ~** he fell 300 meters [down] ② *(niedrig)* low; **~ liegend** low-lying; **~ stehend** *(fig)* low-level ③ *(weit eindringend)* deep; **~ greifend** far-reaching

④ *(dumpf tönend)* low; **zu ~ singen** to sing flat ⑤ *(intensiv)* deeply; **etw ~ bedauern** to deeply regret sth; **~ schlafen** to sleep soundly

Tief <-[e]s, -s> [ˈtiːf] *nt* ① METEO low ② *(depressive Phase)* low [point]

Tiefe <-, -n> [ˈtiːˑfə] *f* depth

Tiefebene *f* lowland plain

Tiefenschärfe *f kein pl* depth of field

Tiefgang *m* NAUT draft ▶WENDUNGEN: **~ haben** to be profound

tiefgreifend *adj s.* **tief II 3**

Tiefkühlkost *f* frozen food

Tiefkühltruhe *f* freezer chest

Tiefland [ˈtiːfˑlant] *nt* lowlands *pl*

Tiefpunkt *m* low point

tiefsinnig *adj* profound

Tier <-[e]s, -e> [ˈtiːɐ] *nt* animal

Tierart *f* animal species + *sing vb*

Tierarzt, -ärztin *m, f* veterinarian, vet *fam*

tierisch [ˈtiːˑrɪʃ] **I.** *adj* ① Fett, Produkt animal *attr* ② *(fam: gewaltig)* **einen ~en Durst/Hunger haben** to be dying of thirst/hunger *fig* **II.** *adv (fam: heftig)* like hell; **~ schuften/schwitzen** to work/sweat like hell; **~ wehtun** to hurt like crazy

Tierkreiszeichen *nt* zodiac sign

tierlieb *adj* animal-loving *attr*; ■**~ sein** to be an animal lover

Tierquälerei [tiːɐˑkvɛːˑləˑˈrai] *f* cruelty to animals

Tierschutz *m* protection of animals

Tierschützer(in) *m(f)* animal welfare activist

Tierversuch *m* animal testing

Tiger <-s, -> [tiːˑgə] *m* tiger

tilgen [ˈtɪlgn] *vt* FIN Schulden to pay off

Tilgung <-, -en> *f* FIN von Schulden repayment

Tinte <-, -n> [ˈtɪnˑtə] *f* ink ▶WENDUNGEN: **in der ~ sitzen** *(fam)* to be in a scrape

Tintenfisch *m* squid

Tintenstrahldrucker *m* ink-jet printer

Tipp^RR, **Tip**^ALT <-s, -s> [ˈtɪp] *m* tip; **guter ~** good bet

tippen¹ [tɪpn] **I.** *vi* ① *(Lotto spielen)* to play the lottery ② *(fam: raten)* to guess;

darauf ~, dass ... to bet that ... **II.** *vt* **eine Zahl ~** to play a number

tippen² [tɪpn] **I.** *vi* ❶ (*fam: Schreibmaschine schreiben*) to type ❷ (*kurz anstoßen*) to tap (**an/auf** +*akk* on, **gegen** +*akk* against) **II.** *vt* (*fam*) to type

Tippfehler *m* typo

Tirol <-s> [ti·ˈroːl] *nt* Tyrol

Tiroler(in) <-s, -> [ti·ˈroː·lɐ] *m(f)* Tyrolean

Tisch <-[e]s, -e> [tɪʃ] *m* table ▶WENDUNGEN: **unter den ~ fallen** (*fam*) to fall by the wayside; **reinen ~ machen** to sort things out; **vom ~ sein** to be [all] cleared up; **sich** *akk* **[mit jdm] an einen ~ setzen** to come to the table [with sb]; **jdn über den ~ ziehen** (*fam*) to pull a fast one on sb

Tischdecke *f* tablecloth

Tischler(in) <-s -> [ˈtɪʃ·lɐ] *m(f)* carpenter

Tischlerei <-, -en> [tɪʃ·lə·ˈrai] *f* carpenter's workshop

Tischtennis *nt* table tennis, ping-pong

Tischtennisplatte *f* table-tennis [or ping-pong] table

Tischtennisschläger *m* table-tennis [or ping-pong] paddle

Titel <-s, -> [ˈtiː·tl] *m* ❶ (*Überschrift*) heading ❷ (*Namenszusatz*) [academic] title ❸ (*Adelstitel*) title ❹ MEDIA, SPORT title

Titelbild *nt* cover [picture]

Titelblatt *nt* einer Zeitung front page; einer Zeitschrift cover

Titelverteidiger(in) *m(f)* title holder

Toast <-[e]s, -e> [toːst] *m* ❶ kein pl (*Toastbrot*) toast ❷ (*Scheibe Toastbrot*) **ein ~** a slice of toast

Toaster <-s, -> [ˈtoːs·tɐ] *m* toaster

toben [ˈtoː·bn] *vi* ❶ haben (*wüten*) to be raging (**vor** +*dat* with) ❷ haben (*ausgelassen spielen*) to romp [around] ❸ sein (*fam: sich ausgelassen fortbewegen*) **irgendwohin ~** to romp somewhere

Tobsuchtsanfall *m* (*fam*) fit of rage

Tochter <-, Töchter> [ˈtɔx·tɐ] *f* ❶ (*weibliches Kind*) daughter ❷ *s.* **Tochtergesellschaft**

Tochtergesellschaft *f* subsidiary [company]

Tod <-[e]s, -e> [toːt] *m* death ▶WENDUNGEN: **jdn/etw auf den ~ nicht ausstehen können** (*fam*) to be unable to stand sb/sth; **sich** *dat* **den ~ holen** (*fam*) to catch one's death [of cold]; **sich** *akk* **zu ~e langweilen** (*fam*) to be bored to death

todernst [ˈtoːt·ˈʔɛrnst] **I.** *adj* deadly serious **II.** *adv* in a deadly serious manner

Todesangst *f* ❶ (*fam: große Angst*) mortal fear; **Todesängste ausstehen** (*fam*) to be scared to death ❷ (*Angst vor dem Sterben*) fear of death

Todesanzeige *f* obituary

Todesfall *m* death

Todesopfer *nt* casualty

Todesstrafe *f* death penalty; **auf etw** *akk* **steht die ~** sth is punishable by death

Todestag *m* anniversary of sb's death

Todesursache *f* cause of death

Todesurteil *nt* death sentence

todkrank [ˈtoːt·ˈkraŋk] *adj* terminally ill

tödlich [ˈtøːt·lɪç] **I.** *adj* deadly **II.** *adv* ❶ **~ verunglücken** to be killed in an accident ❷ (*fam: entsetzlich*) **sich** *akk* **~ langweilen** to be bored to death

Todsünde *f* deadly sin

Toilette <-, -n> [toa·ˈlɛ·tə] *f* restroom, bathroom *fam;* **ich muss mal auf die ~** I need to go to the restroom; **öffentliche ~** public restroom

Toilettenpapier *nt* toilet paper

tolerant [to·le·ˈrant] *adj* tolerant (**gegenüber** +*dat* toward)

Toleranz <-, en> [to·le·ˈrants] *f kein pl* tolerance (**gegenüber** +*dat* toward)

tolerieren* [to·le·ˈriː·rən] *vt* to tolerate

toll [tɔl] **I.** *adj* (*fam: sehr gut*) great **II.** *adv* (*fam: sehr gut*) very well

Tollpatschᴿᴿ <-es, -e> [ˈtɔl·patʃ] *m* (*fam*) clumsy fool

Tollwut *f* rabies

Tollpatschᴬᴸᵀ <-es, -e> *m s.* **Tollpatsch**

Tölpel <-s, -> [ˈtœl·pl] *m* (*fam*) fool

Tomate <-, -n> [to·'ma:·tə] f tomato ▶WENDUNGEN: **~n auf den Augen haben** (fam) to be blind; **du treulose ~!** (fam) you're a fine friend! iron

TomatenketchupRR, **Tomatenketchup** nt [tomato] ketchup [or catsup]

Tomatenmark nt tomato paste

Tombola <-, -s> ['tɔm·bo·la] f raffle

Tomographie, TomografieRR <-, -n> [to·mo·gra·'fi:] f tomography

Ton[1] <-[e]s, -e> ['to:n] m (Material) clay

Ton[2] <-[e]s, Töne> ['to:n] m ❶ (Laut) sound ❷ (Tonfall) tone; **ich verbitte mir diesen ~!** I will not be spoken to like that!; **einen anderen ~ anschlagen** to change one's tune ❸ (Farbton) tone ▶WENDUNGEN: **den ~ angeben** to set the tone; **große Töne spucken** (fam) to brag about sth fam; **keinen ~ herausbringen** to not be able to utter a word; **der ~ macht die Musik** (prov) it's not what you say, but the way you say it

Tonart f MUS key

Tonband nt tape; **etw** akk **auf ~ aufnehmen** to tape sth

tönen ['tø:·nən] vt to tint; Haare to color

Tonfall m tone of voice

Tonfilm m sound film

Tonhöhe f pitch

Tonleiter f scale

tonlos adj Stimme flat

Tonne <-, -n> ['tɔ·nə] f ❶ (Behälter) barrel ❷ (Mülltonne) garbage can; **grüne ~** recycling container for paper ❸ (Gewichtseinheit) ton ❹ (fam: fetter Mensch) fatso sl

Tonstörung f sound interference

Tontechniker(in) m(f) sound technician

Tonträger m sound carrier

Tönung <-, -en> f ❶ (das Tönen) tinting ❷ (Produkt für Haare) hair color ❸ (Farbton) shade

Topf <-[e]s, Töpfe> ['tɔpf] m ❶ (Kochtopf) pot, sauce pan ❷ (Nachttopf) bedpan ❸ (für Kleinkinder) potty fam ▶WENDUNGEN: **alles in einen ~ werfen** to lump everything together

Töpferei <-, -en> [tœp·fə·'rai] f pottery

Töpferscheibe f potter's wheel

Töpferwaren pl pottery

Topflappen m pot holder

Topfpflanze f potted plant

Tor <-[e]s, -e> ['to:ɐ̯] nt ❶ (breite Tür) gate; Garage door ❷ (Torbau) gateway ❸ SPORT goal; **ein ~ schießen** to score a goal; **im ~ stehen** to be the goalkeeper [or goalie]

Torbogen m archway

Torf <-[e]s, -e> ['tɔrf] m peat

töricht ['tø·rɪçt] I. adj (geh) foolish II. adv (geh) foolishly

torkeln ['tɔr·kl̩n] vi sein ❶ (taumeln) to reel ❷ (irgendwohin taumeln) to stagger

Torlinie f goal line

Tornado <-s, -s> [tɔr·'na:·do] m tornado, twister

Torpedo <-s, -s> [tɔr·'pe:·do] m torpedo

TorschlusspanikRR f (fam) **~ haben** to be afraid of missing the boat

Torschütze, -schützin m, f scorer

Torte <-, -n> ['tɔr·tə] f torte, cake; (Obstkuchen) tart

Torwart(in) m(f) goalkeeper, goalie

tot ['to:t] adj dead; **sich** akk **~ stellen** to play dead; **~ umfallen** to drop dead

total [to·'ta:l] adj total

totalitär [to·ta·li·'tɛ:ɐ̯] I. adj totalitarian II. adv in a totalitarian manner

Totalschaden m write-off

Tote(r) ['to:·tə] f(m) dead person; (Todesopfer) fatality

töten ['tø:·tn̩] vt to kill

Totenschein m death certificate

tot|fahren vt irreg (fam) to run over [and kill]

Totgeburt f stillbirth

tot|schießen vt irreg (fam) to shoot dead

Totschlag m kein pl manslaughter

tot|schlagen vt irreg (fam) to beat to death

Tötung <-, *selten* -en> *f* killing; **fahrlässige ~** [involuntary] manslaughter

Toupet <-s, -s> [tu·'peː] *nt* toupee

toupieren* [tu·'piː·ran] *vt* ■ **sich/jdm die Haare ~** to tease one's/sb's hair

Tour <-, -en> [tuːɐ̯] *f* ① (*Geschäftsfahrt*) trip ② (*Ausflugsfahrt*) tour; **eine ~ machen** to go on a tour ►WENDUNGEN: **jdm auf die dumme ~ kommen** to try to cheat sb; **in einer ~** (*fam*) nonstop; **auf ~en kommen** (*fam*) to get into high gear

Tourismus <-> [tu·'rɪs·mʊs] *m kein pl* tourism

Tourist(in) <-en, -en> [tu·'rɪst] *m(f)* tourist

Tournee <-, -n> [tʊr·'neː] *f* tour; **auf ~ gehen** to go on tour

toxisch ['tɔk·sɪʃ] *adj* toxic

Trab <-[e]s> [traːp] *m kein pl* trot ►WENDUNGEN: **jdn auf ~ bringen** (*fam*) to make sb get a move on

traben ['traː·bn̩] *vi* ① **haben o sein** (*im Trab laufen o reiten*) to trot ② **sein** (*sich irgendwohin bewegen*) to trot

Tracht <-, -en> [traxt] *f* ① (*Volkstracht*) traditional attire ② (*Berufskleidung*) uniform ►WENDUNGEN: **eine ~ Prügel** (*fam*) a walloping

trächtig ['trɛç·tɪç] *adj Tier* pregnant

Tradition <-, -en> [tra·di·'tsi̯oːn] *f* tradition

traditionell [tra·di·tsi̯o·'nɛl] *adj meist attr* traditional

tragbar *adj* ① (*portabel*) portable ② (*akzeptabel*) acceptable

träge ['trɛː·gə] **I.** *adj* ① (*schwerfällig*) lethargic ② PHYS, CHEM inert **II.** *adv* lethargically

tragen <trägt, trug, getragen> ['traː·gn̩] **I.** *vt* ① (*schleppen*) to carry ② (*mit sich führen*) ■ **etw bei sich** *dat* ~ to carry sth on one; **tragen Sie Waffen bei sich?** do you have any weapons on you? ③ MODE to wear; **einen Bart ~** to have a beard; **das Haar kurz/lang ~** to have short/long hair ④ (*stützen*) to support ⑤ AGR, HORT to produce ⑥ (*für etwas aufkommen*) to

bear **II.** *vi* ① AGR, HORT to produce ② (*trächtig sein*) to be pregnant ③ (*das Begehen aushalten*) to withstand weight ④ MODE to wear; **sie trägt lieber kurz** she prefers to wear short clothing ►WENDUNGEN: **zum T~ kommen** to come into effect **III.** *vr* ① (*geh*) **sich** *akk* **mit den Gedanken ~, etw zu tun** *dat* to contemplate the idea of doing sth ② FIN ■ **sich** *akk* ~ to pay for itself

Träger <-s, -> *m* ① *meist pl* MODE strap ② BAU girder

Tragetasche *f* [tote] bag

Tragfläche *f* wing

Trägheit <-, *selten* -en> *f* ① *kein pl* (*Schwerfälligkeit*) sluggishness; (*Faulheit*) laziness ② PHYS inertia

Tragik <-> ['traː·gɪk] *f kein pl* tragedy

tragisch ['traː·gɪʃ] **I.** *adj* tragic; **es ist nicht [so] ~** (*fam*) it's not the end of the world **II.** *adv* tragically; **nimm's nicht so ~!** (*fam*) don't take it to heart!

Tragödie <-, -n> [tra·'gøː·di̯ə] *f* tragedy

Tragweite *f* scale; (*einer Entscheidung, Handlung*) consequence

Trainer(in) <-s, -> ['trɛː·nɐ] *m(f)* coach

Trainer <-s, -> ['trɛː·nɐ] *m* SCHWEIZ tracksuit

trainieren* [trɛ·'niː·rən] **I.** *vt* ① (*üben*) to practice ② (*auf Wettkämpfe vorbereiten*) ■ **jdn ~** to coach sb **II.** *vi* ① (*üben*) to practice ② (*sich auf Wettkämpfe vorbereiten*) to train

Training <-s, -s> ['trɛː·nɪŋ] *nt* practice

Trainingsanzug ['trɛː·nɪŋs-] *m* tracksuit

Trakt <-[e]s, -e> ['trakt] *m* ARCHIT wing

Traktor <-s, -toren> ['trak·toːɐ̯] *m* tractor

Tram <-, -s o -s, -s> ['tram] *f o nt* SCHWEIZ streetcar

trampen [trɛmpn̩] *vi sein* to hitchhike

Trampolin <-s, -e> ['tram·po·liːn] *nt* trampoline

Träne <-, -n> ['trɛː·nə] *f* tear; **in ~n aufgelöst** in tears; **den ~n nahe sein** to be close to tears; **jdm kommen die ~n** sb is starting to cry

T

tränken ['trɛŋ·kn̩] *vt* ❶ (*durchnässen*) to soak ❷ *Tier* to water

Transfer <-s, -s> [trans·'feːɐ̯] *m* transfer

Transformator <-s, -en> [trans·fɔr·'maː·toːɐ̯] *m* transformer

Transistor <-s, -en> [tran·'zɪs·toːɐ̯] *m* transistor

transitiv ['tran·zi·tiːf] *adj* LING transitive

Transitverkehr [tran·'zɪt-] *m* transit traffic

transparent [trans·pa·'rɛnt] *adj* transparent

Transparent <-[e]s, -e> [trans·pa·'rɛnt] *nt* banner

Transport <-[e]s, -e> [trans·'pɔrt] *m* transport

Transporter <-s, -> [trans·'pɔr·tɐ] *m* (*Lieferwagen*) van

transportfähig *adj* transportable

transportieren* [trans·pɔr·'tiː·rən] *vt* ❶ (*befördern*) to transport; (*Person*) to move ❷ FOTO to wind

Transportmittel *nt* means of transportation

Transportunternehmen *nt* trucking company

transsexuell [trans·zɛ·'ksu̯·ɛl] *adj* transsexual

Transvestit <-en, -en> [trans·vɛs·'tiːt] *m* transvestite

Trapez <-es, -e> [tra·'peːts] *nt* ❶ MATH trapezoid ❷ (*Artistenschaukel*) trapeze

tratschen ['traː·tʃn̩] *vi* (*fam*) to gossip (*über* +*akk* about)

Traube <-, -n> ['trau̯·bə] *f* (*Weintraube*) grape *usu pl*

Traubensaft *m* grape juice

Traubenzucker *m* glucose

trauen¹ ['trau̯·ən] *vt* to join in marriage; ▪ **sich** *akk* ~ **lassen** to marry

trauen² ['trau̯·ən] **I.** *vi* (*vertrauen*) to trust **II.** *vr* ▪ **sich** *akk* ~, **etw** *akk* **zu tun** to dare to do sth

Trauer <-> ['trau̯·ɐ] *f kein pl* grief

Trauerfall *m* bereavement

Trauerkleidung *f* mourning attire [*or* dress]

trauern ['trau̯·ɐn] *vi* to mourn (**um** +*akk* for)

Traum <-[e]s, Träume> ['trau̯m] *m* dream; **es war immer mein ~, mal so eine Luxuslimousine zu fahren** I've always dreamed of driving a luxury car like this ▸WENDUNGEN: **aus der ~!** so much for that!; **etw fällt jdm im ~ nicht ein** sb wouldn't dream of sth

Trauma <-s, Traumen> ['trau̯·ma] *nt* trauma

traumatisch [trau̯·'maː·tɪʃ] *adj* traumatic

träumen ['trɔy·mən] *vt, vi* to dream (**von** +*dat* about); **schlecht ~** to have bad dreams

Träumer(in) <-s, -> ['trɔy·mɐ] *m(f)* [day]dreamer

traurig ['trau̯·rɪç] **I.** *adj* sad; ▪ [**es ist**] **~, dass ...** it's unfortunate that ..., unfortunately ... **II.** *adv* sadly ▸WENDUNGEN: **mit etw** *dat* **sieht es ~ aus** sth doesn't look too good

Traurigkeit <-> *f kein pl* sadness

Trauring *m* wedding ring [*or* band]

Trauung <-, -en> ['trau̯·ʊŋ] *f* marriage [*or* wedding] ceremony

Trauzeuge, -zeugin *m, f* best man, witness to a marriage

Treff <-s, -s> [trɛf] *m* (*fam*) ❶ (*Treffen*) get-together ❷ (*Treffpunkt*) meeting point

treffen <trifft, traf, getroffen> ['trɛ·fn̩] **I.** *vt* haben ❶ (*zusammenkommen*) to meet ❷ (*antreffen*) to find; **ich habe ihn zufällig in der Stadt getroffen** I bumped into him in town ❸ (*mit einem Wurf, Schlag etc.*) to hit ❹ *Abmachung, Entscheidung* to make; *Maßnahmen, Vorkehrungen* to take ❺ (*wählen*) **den richtigen Ton ~** to strike the right chord; **auf dem Foto bist du wirklich gut getroffen** that's a really good picture of you; **du hättest es auch schlechter ~ können** it could have been worse ❻ (*kränken*) to hurt **II.** *vi* ❶ *sein* (*antreffen*) ▪ **auf jdn ~** to meet sb ❷ *haben* (*ins Ziel*) to hit ❸ *haben* (*verletzen*) to hurt **III.** *vr* haben ▪ **sich**

akk [**mit jdm**] ~ to meet [sb]; **das trifft sich** [**gut**] that works out [great]
Treffen <-s, -> ['trɛ·fn] *nt* meeting
treffend *adj* appropriate
Treffer <-s, -> *m* ❶ (*aufs Ziel*) hit ❷ (*Tor*) goal ❸ (*Gewinnlos*) winner
Treffpunkt *m* meeting point
treiben <trieb, getrieben> ['trai·bn] I. *vt haben* ❶ (*drängen*) to drive; **jdn in den Wahnsinn** ~ to drive sb mad ❷ (*fortbewegen*) ■**jdn/etw** [**irgend-wohin**] ~ (*durch Wasser*) to wash sb/ sth [somewhere]; (*durch Wind*) to blow sb/sth [somewhere] ❸ *Nagel* to drive (**in** +*akk* into) ❹ BOT to sprout ❺ (*fam: anstellen*) ■**etw** ~ to be up to sth; **dass ihr mir bloß keinen Blödsinn treibt!** don't you [guys] try to pull any nonsense now!; **es zu bunt/wild** ~ to go too far ❻ (*betreiben*) *Gewerbe* to carry out; *Handel* to trade ❼ (*sl: Sex haben*) **es** [**mit jdm**] ~ to do it [with sb] II. *vi* ❶ *sein* (*sich fortbewegen*) to drift; ■**sich** *akk* [**von etw** *dat*] ~ **lassen** to let oneself be carried along [by sth] ❷ *haben* BOT to sprout ❸ *haben* KOCHK to rise ❹ *haben* (*diuretisch wirken*) to have a diuretic effect ▶WENDUNGEN: **sich** *akk* ~ **lassen** to drift
Treiben <-s> ['trai·bn] *nt kein pl* ❶ (*pej: üble Aktivität*) dirty tricks ❷ (*ge-schäftige Aktivität*) hustle and bustle
Treibhaus *nt* greenhouse
Treibhauseffekt *m kein pl* ■**der** ~ the greenhouse effect
Treibstoff *m* fuel
Trend <-s, -s> ['trɛnt] *m* trend; **voll im** ~ **liegen** to be very popular at the moment
trennen ['trɛ·nən] I. *vt* ❶ (*abtrennen*) ■**etw von etw** *dat* ~ to cut sth off sth ❷ (*auseinanderbringen, teilen*) to separate (**von** +*dat* from) ❸ LING *Wort* to divide II. *vr* ■**sich** *akk* ~ LING (*getrennt weitergehen*) to part company ❷ (*die Beziehung lösen*) to split up (**von** +*dat* with) ❸ (*weggehen*) to part (**von** +*dat* with) III. *vi* to differentiate (**zwischen** +*dat* between)

Trennung <-, -en> *f* ❶ (*Scheidung*) separation; **in** ~ **leben** to be separated ❷ (*Unterscheidung*) distinction ❸ LING division
Trennungsstrich *m* hyphen
Trennwand *f* partition [wall]
Treppe <-, -n> ['trɛ·pə] *f* stairs *pl*
Treppengeländer *nt* handrail
Treppenhaus *nt* stairwell
Treppenstufe *f* step
Tresen <-s, -> ['tre:·zn] *m* ❶ (*Theke*) bar ❷ (*Ladentisch*) counter
Tresor <-s, -e> (*Tre·zo:ɐ̯*) *m* ❶ (*Safe*) safe ❷ (*Tresorraum*) strong room
treten <tritt, trat, getreten> ['tre:·tn] I. *vt haben* to kick II. *vi* ❶ *haben* (*mit dem Fuß*) to kick ❷ *sein* (*einen Schritt machen*) to step; ~ **Sie bitte zur Seite** please step aside; **pass auf, wohin du trittst** watch where you step [or your step] ❸ *sein o haben* (*den Fuß setzen*) to tread (**auf** +*akk* on) ❹ *sein o haben* (*betätigen*) to step (**auf** +*akk* on); **auf die Bremse** ~ to put on the brakes
treu ['trɔy] I. *adj* ❶ (*loyal*) loyal; **sich** *dat* **selbst** ~ **bleiben** to remain true to oneself ❷ (*verlässlich*) loyal ❸ (*keinen Seitensprung machend*) faithful II. *adv* ❶ (*loyal*) loyally ❷ (*treuherzig*) trustingly
Treue <-> ['trɔyə] *f kein pl* ❶ (*Loyalität, Verlässlichkeit*) loyalty ❷ (*monogames Verhalten*) fidelity
treulos *adj* unfaithful
Tribüne <-, -n> [tri·ˈbyː·nə] *f* stand
Trichter <-s, -> ['trɪç·tɐ] *m* ❶ (*Einfüll-trichter*) funnel ❷ (*Explosionskrater*) crater
Trick <-s, -s> ['trɪk] *m* trick
Trickbetrüger(in) *m(f)* con artist [*or* man]
Trickfilm *m* cartoon [*or* animated] movie
trieb ['tri:p] *imp von* **treiben**
Trieb[1] <-[e]s, -e> ['tri:p] *m* BOT shoot
Trieb[2] <-[e]s, -e> ['tri:p] *m* PSYCH [sex] drive
Triebwerk *nt* engine
triefen <triefte *o geh* troff, getrieft> ['tri:·fn] *vi* to run; (*Auge*) to water;

■aus etw *dat* ~ to pour from [*or* out of] sth; **vor Nässe** ~ to be dripping wet

triftig ['trɪf·tɪç] I. *adj* good; *Argument, Grund* convincing II. *adv* convincingly

Trikot[1] <-s> [tri·ˈkoː, ˈtri·ko] *m or* kein *pl* (*dehnbares Gewebe*) tricot

Trikot[2] <-s, -s> [tri·ˈkoː, ˈtri·ko] *nt* MODE, SPORT jersey

Trillerpfeife [ˈtrɪ·lɐ·] *f* whistle

trinkbar *adj* drinkable

trinken <trank, getrunken> [ˈtrɪŋ·kn̩] I. *vt* to drink; **möchten Sie lieber Kaffee oder Tee** ~? would you prefer coffee or tea [to drink]?; **etwas zu** ~ something to drink; [**mit jdm**] **einen** ~ **gehen** (*fam*) to go for a drink [with sb] II. *vi* ■**auf jdn/etw** ~ to drink to sb/sth

Trinker(in) <-s, -> *m(f)* drunk[ard]

Trinkgeld *nt* tip; ~ **geben** to give a tip

Trinkspruch *m* toast

Trinkwasser *nt* drinking water

Trinkwasseraufbereitung *f* drinking water purification

tritt [trɪt] *3. pers sing pres von* **treten**

Tritt <-[e]s, -e> [trɪt] *m* ① (*Fußtritt*) kick ② (*Schritt*) step

Triumph <-[e]s, -e> [tri·ˈʊmf] *m* triumph

Triumphbogen *m* triumphal arch

triumphieren* [tri·ʊm·ˈfiː·rən] *vi* ① (*frohlocken*) to rejoice ② (*erfolgreich sein*) to triumph (**über** +*akk* over)

triumphierend I. *adj* triumphant II. *adv* triumphantly

trocken [ˈtrɔ·kn̩] I. *adj* dry; *Buch* dull; **im T~en** out of the rain; ~**er Wein** dry wine ►WENDUNGEN: **auf dem T~en sitzen** (*fam*) to be broke II. *adv* etw ~ **aufbewahren** to keep sth in a dry place; **sich** *akk* ~ **rasieren** to use an electric razor, to dry shave

Trockenheit <-, selten -en> *f* ① (*Dürreperiode*) drought ② (*trockene Beschaffenheit*) a. eines Gebietes dryness

trocken|legen *vt* ① (*windeln*) **ein Baby** ~ to change a baby['s diaper] ② (*entwässern*) to drain

Trockenzeit *f* dry season

trocknen [ˈtrɔk·nən] I. *vi sein* to dry II. *vt haben* to dry

trödeln [ˈtrøː·dl̩n] *vi* ① *haben* (*langsam sein*) to dilly-dally ② *sein* (*langsam schlendern*) to [take a] stroll

Trödler(in) <-s, -> [ˈtrøːd·lɐ] *m(f)* ① (*Altwarenhändler*) second-hand dealer ② (*fam: trödelnder Mensch*) dilly-dallier

Trommel <-, -n> [ˈtrɔ·ml̩] *f* drum

Trommelfell *nt* eardrum

trommeln [ˈtrɔ·ml̩n] *vi* to drum

Trompete <-, -n> [trɔm·ˈpeː·tə] *f* trumpet

Trompeter(in) <-s, -> *m(f)* trumpeter

Tropen [ˈtroː·pn̩] *pl* ■**die** ~ the tropics *pl*

Tropenkrankheit *f* tropical disease

Tropf <-[e]s, -e> [trɔpf] *m* MED drip

tropfen [ˈtrɔp·fn̩] *vi* ① *haben* to drip; (*Nase*) to run ② *sein* ■**aus etw** *dat* [**irgendwohin**] ~ to drip from sth [somewhere]

Tropfen <-s, -> [ˈtrɔp·fn̩] *m* ① (*kleine Menge Flüssigkeit*) drop ② *pl* PHARM, MED drops *pl* ►WENDUNGEN: **ein** ~ **auf den heißen** <u>Stein</u> (*fam*) just a drop in the ocean

Tropfsteinhöhle *f* cave with stalactites and stalagmites

Trophäe <-, -n> [tro·ˈfɛː·ə] *f* trophy

tropisch [ˈtroː·pɪʃ] *adj* tropical

Trost <-[e]s> [ˈtroːst] *m* kein *pl* ① (*Linderung*) consolation; **das ist ein schöner** ~ (*iron*) some comfort that is; **ein schwacher** ~ **sein** to be of little consolation ② (*Zuspruch*) words of comfort; **jdm** ~ **spenden** to comfort sb ►WENDUNGEN: **nicht** [**ganz**] **bei** ~ **sein** (*fam*) to have taken leave of one's senses

trösten [ˈtrøːs·tn̩] I. *vt* to comfort; ■**etw tröstet jdn** sth is of consolation to sb II. *vr* ■**sich** *akk* [**mit jdm**] ~ to find consolation [with sb]; ■**sich** *akk* [**mit etw** *dat*] ~ to console oneself [with sth]

tröstlich *adj* comforting

trostlos *adj* ① (*deprimierend*) miserable ② (*öde und hässlich*) desolate; *Landschaft* bleak

Trostpreis *m* consolation prize

Trott <-s> ['trɔt] *m kein pl* routine

Trottel <-s, -> ['trɔ·tl̩] *m* (*fam*) bone-head *sl*

trotten ['trɔ·tn̩] *vi sein* to trudge [along]

trotz ['trɔts] *präp* +*gen* despite

Trotz <-es> ['trɔts] *m kein pl* defiance; **aus ~** [**gegen jdn/etw**] out of spite [for sb/sth]; **jdm/etw zum ~** in defiance of sb/sth

Trotzalter *nt* difficult age, the terrible twos

trotzdem ['trɔts·de:m] *adv* neverthe-less; (*aber*) still

trotzen ['trɔ·tsn̩] *vi* ■**jdm/etw ~** to defy sb/sth

trotzig ['trɔ·tsɪç] *adj* defiant

trübe ['try:·bə] *adj* ❶ (*unklar*) murky; *Saft, Urin* cloudy; *Glas, Spiegel* dull ❷ (*matt*) dim ❸ *Himmel* dull ❹ (*deprimierend*) bleak; *Stimmung* gloomy ►WENDUNGEN: **mit etw** *dat* **sieht es ~ aus** the prospects [for sth] are [looking] bleak

Trubel <-s> ['tru:·bl̩] *m kein pl* hustle and bustle

trüben ['try:·bn̩] I. *vt* ■**etw ~** ❶ (*unklar machen*) to make sth murky [*or* cloudy] ❷ (*beeinträchtigen*) to cast a cloud over sth; *Beziehungen, ein Verhältnis* to strain II. *vr* ■**sich** *akk* **~** to become murky

trübselig *adj* ❶ (*betrübt*) miserable; *Miene* gloomy ❷ (*trostlos*) bleak

Trübung <-, -en> *f* ❶ *von Wasser etc.* clouding ❷ (*von Beziehungen*) straining

Trüffel <-, -n> ['tryfl̩] *f* (*Pilz, Praline*) truffle

trügen <trog, getrogen> ['try:gn̩] I. *vt* **wenn mich nicht alles trügt** unless I'm very much mistaken II. *vi* to be deceptive

Truhe <-, -n> ['tru:ə] *f* chest

Trümmer ['trʏ·me] *pl* rubble; *eines Flugzeugs* wreckage; **in ~n liegen** to lie in ruins *pl*

Trumpf <-[e]s, Trümpfe> ['trʊmpf] *m* ❶ KARTEN trump [card]; **~ sein** to be trumps ❷ (*fig: entscheidender Vorteil*) trump card; **noch einen ~ in der Hand haben** to have another ace up one's sleeve

Trunkenheit <-> *f kein pl* drunkenness; **~ am Steuer** drunk driving

Truppe <-, -n> ['trʊ·pə] *f* ❶ MIL troop; **Rückzug der ~n** troop withdrawal ❷ THEAT company

Truthahn ['tru:t·ha:n] *m* turkey

Tschad <-s> ['tʃat] *nt* Chad; *s. a.* **Deutschland**

Tscheche, Tschechin <-n, -nen> ['tʃɛ·çə] *m, f* Czech; *s. a.* **Deutsche(r)**

tschechisch ['tʃɛ·çɪʃ] *adj* Czech; *s. a.* **deutsch**

Tschechische Republik *f* Czech Republic; *s. a.* **Deutschland**

T-Shirt <-s, -s> ['tiː·ʃøːɐ̯t] *nt* T-shirt

Tube <-, -n> ['tu:·bə] *f* tube ►WENDUNGEN: **auf die ~ drücken** (*fam*) to step on it

Tuberkulose <-, -n> [tu·bɐr·ku·'lo:·zə] *f* tuberculosis

Tuch <-[e]s, Tücher> ['tu:x] *nt* ❶ (*Kopftuch*) [head]scarf; (*Halstuch*) scarf ❷ (*dünne Decke*) cloth

tüchtig ['tʏç·tɪç] I. *adj* ❶ (*fähig*) capable; (*fleißig*) hard-working ❷ (*fam: groß*) big II. *adv* (*fam*) **~ essen** to eat heartily; **~ regnen/schneien** to rain/snow hard

Tücke <-, -n> ['tʏkə] *f* ❶ *kein pl* (*Heimtücke*) malice ❷ (*Unwägbarkeiten*) ■**~n** *pl* vagaries *pl*; **seine ~n haben** to be temperamental ►WENDUNGEN: **das ist die ~ des Objekts** these things have a will of their own!

tückisch ['tʏ·kɪʃ] *adj* ❶ (*hinterhältig*) malicious ❷ *Krankheit* pernicious ❸ (*gefährlich*) treacherous

tüfteln ['tʏf·tl̩n] *vi* (*fam*) to fiddle around (**an** +*dat* with)

Tugend <-, -en> ['tu:·gnt] *f* virtue

Tulpe <-, -n> ['tʊl·pə] *f* tulip

tummeln ['tʊ·ml̩n] *vr* ■**sich** *akk* **~** to romp [around]

Tumor <-s, -en> ['tu:·mo:ɐ̯] *m* tumor

Tumult <-[e]s, -e> [tu·'mʊlt] *m* ❶ *kein*

T

pl (*lärmendes Durcheinander*) commotion ② *meist pl* (*Aufruhr*) disturbance

tun <tat, getan> ['tuːn] **I.** *vt* ① + *unbestimmtem Objekt* (*machen*) to do; **was sollen wir bloß ~?** what the heck should we do?; **was tut er nur den ganzen Tag?** what does he do all day?; **so etwas tut man nicht!** you just don't do [things like] that!; **noch viel ~ müssen** to still have a lot to do; **etw aus Liebe ~** to do sth out of love; **~ und lassen können, was man will** to do as one pleases; **~, was man nicht lassen kann** to do sth if one has to ② (*unternehmen*) ■**etwas/nichts/einiges für jdn ~** to do something/nothing/a lot for sb; **was tut man nicht alles für seine Kinder!** the things we do for our children!; **was kann ich für Sie ~?** ÖKON can [*or* may] I help you?; ■**etw gegen etw** *akk* **~** *gegen Belästigungen, Pickel, Unrecht etc.* to do sth about sth; **ich will sehen, was sich da ~ lässt** I'll see what I can do [about it] [*or* do what I can] ③ (*fam: legen o stecken*) ■**etw irgendwohin ~** to put sth somewhere ④ (*fam: funktionieren*) **tut es dein altes Tonbandgerät eigentlich noch?** [by the way,] is your old tape recorder still working? ⑤ (*fam: ausmachen*) **das tut nichts** it doesn't matter, no problem ⑥ (*fam: genug sein*) **für heute tut's das** that'll do for today ⑦ (*sl: Sex haben*) ■**es [mit jdm] ~** to do it [with sb] **II.** *vr impers* ■**etwas/nichts/einiges tut sich** something/nothing/a lot is happening **III.** *vi* ① (*sich benehmen*) to act; **er ist doch gar nicht wütend, er tut nur so[, als ob]** he's not angry at all; he's just pretending [to be] ② (*Dinge erledigen*) ■**zu ~ haben** to be busy ▸WENDUNGEN: **es mit jdm zu ~ bekommen** (*fam*) to get into trouble with sb; **es mit jdm zu ~ haben** to be dealing with sb; **etwas/nichts mit jdm/etw zu ~ haben** to have something/nothing to do with sb/sth **IV.** *aux vb modal* ① + *vorgestelltem Infinitiv* (*fam*) **singen tut sie ja gut** she sure is a good singer ② + *nachgestelltem Infinitiv* DIAL **ich tu nur schnell den Braten anbraten** I'll just quickly sear the roast ③ *konjunktivisch, + vorgestelltem Infinitiv* DIAL **er täte zu gerne wissen, warum ...** he would love to know why ...

Tunesien <-s> [tu·'neː·ziən] *nt* Tunisia; *s. a.* **Deutschland**

Tunesier(in) <-s, -> [tu·'neː·ziɐ] *m(f)* Tunisian; *s. a.* **Deutsche(r)**

tunesisch [tu·'neː·zɪʃ] *adj* Tunisian; *s. a.* **deutsch**

Tunfisch[RR] *m s.* **Thunfisch**

Tunnel <-s, -> ['tʊnl̩] *m* tunnel; (*für Fußgänger*) pedestrian underpass

Tür <-, -en> ['tyːɐ̯] *f* door; **an die ~ gehen** to get the door ▸WENDUNGEN: **zwischen ~ und Angel** (*fam*) in passing; **jdm [fast] die ~ einrennen** (*fam*) to pester sb constantly; **mit der ~ ins Haus fallen** (*fam*) to blurt it [right] out; **[bei jdm] [mit etw** *dat*] **offene ~en einrennen** to be preaching to the choir [with sth]; **jdn vor die ~ setzen** (*fam*) to kick sb out; **vor der ~ sein** (*ganz in der Nähe*) to be just around the corner

turbulent [tʊr·bu·'lɛnt] **I.** *adj* turbulent **II.** *adv* turbulently; **~ verlaufen** to be turbulent

Türgriff *m* door handle, doorknob

Türke(in) <-n, -n> ['tʏr·kə] *m(f)* Turk; *s. a.* **Deutsche(r)**

Türkei <-> [tʏr·'kai] *f* ■**die ~** Turkey; *s. a.* **Deutschland**

türkis [tʏr·'kiːs] *adj* turquoise

türkisch ['tʏr·kɪʃ] *adj* Turkish; *s. a.* **deutsch**

Turm <-[e]s, Türme> ['tʊrm] *m* ① ARCHIT tower; (*spitzer Kirchturm*) spire, steeple ② SPORT (*Sprungturm*) diving platform ③ (*Schachfigur*) castle

türmen[1] ['tʏr·mən] *vt, vr* ■**[sich** *akk*] **~** *dat* to pile up *sep*

türmen[2] ['tʏr·mən] *vi sein* (*fam*) **aus dem Knast ~** to break out of jail

Turmspringen *nt kein pl* high diving

turnen ['tʊr·nən] *vi haben* ① SPORT to do

gymnastics ❷ *sein (fam: sich flink bewegen)* to dash

Turnen <-s> ['tʊr·nən] *nt kein pl* ❶ SPORT gymnastics + *sing vb* ❷ SCH physical education, PE

Turner(in) <-s, -> ['tʊr·nɐ] *m(f)* gymnast

Turnhalle *f* gymnasium, gym *fam*

Turnier <-s, -e> [tʊr·'niːɐ̯] *nt* HIST, SPORT *(längerer Wettbewerb)* tournament; *der Springreiter* show jumping competition

Turnschuh *m* tennis shoe

Turnübung *f* gymnastics exercise

Türöffner *m* automatic door opener

Türschild *nt* nameplate

Tusche <-, -n> ['tʊ·ʃə] *f* Indian ink

tuscheln ['tʊ·ʃln] *vi* ■ **[über jdn/etw] ~** to gossip secretly [about sb/sth]

Tüte <-, -n> ['tyː·tə] *f* bag; **eine ~ Popcorn** a bag of popcorn; **Suppe aus der ~** instant soup ▸WENDUNGEN: **[das] kommt nicht in die ~!** *(fam)* no way!

TÜV <-s, -s> [tʏf] *m Akr von* **Technischer Überwachungsverein** Technical Inspection Association *(performs vehicle inspections)*; **jds/der ~ läuft ab** sb's/the annual car inspection needs to be renewed; **durch den ~ kommen** to get [a vehicle] through its inspection

TV <-[s], -s> [teː·'faʊ, *a.* tiː·'viː] *nt Abk von* **Television** TV

twittern ['tvɪ·tɐn] *vt, vi* INET to tweet, to post on Twitter

Typ <-s, -en> ['tyːp] *m* ❶ *(Ausführung)* model ❷ *(Art Mensch)* type [of person] *fam;* **was ist er für ein ~, dein neuer Chef?** what type of person is your new boss?; ■ **der ~ ... sein, der ...** to be the type of ... who ...; **dein ~ ist nicht gefragt** *(fam)* we don't want your type [around] here ❸ *(sl: Kerl, Freund)* guy ❹ *(fam: merkwürdiger Mensch)* character; **was ist denn das für ein ~?** what a weirdo!

typisch ['tyː·pɪʃ] I. *adj* typical **(für** +*akk* of); **[das ist] ~!** *(fam)* [that's] [just] typical! II. *adv* ■ **~ jd** [that's] typical of sb; **~ Frau/Mann!** typical woman/man!; **~ amerikanisch/deutsch** typically American/German

Tyrann(in) <-en, -en> [tʏ·'ran] *m(f)* tyrant

tyrannisch [tʏ·'ra·nɪʃ] I. *adj* tyrannical II. *adv* tyrannically

tyrannisieren* [tʏ·ra·ni·'ziː·rən] *vt* to tyrannize; ■ **sich** *akk* **[von jdm/etw] ~ lassen** to [allow oneself to] be tyrannized [by sb/sth]

T

Uu

U, u <-, -> [u:] nt U, u; **~ wie Ulrich** U as in Uniform

u. konj Abk von **und**

U-Bahn [u:-] f subway

übel ['y:bl] **I.** adj ❶ (schlimm) bad, nasty; Affäre ugly ❷ (unangenehm) nasty ❸ (verkommen) rotten; Stadtviertel bad ❹ (schlecht) ■jdm ist/wird ~ sb feels nauseous **II.** adv ❶ (unangenehm) **was riecht hier so ~?** what's that awful smell [[in] here]? ❷ (schlecht) badly; **nicht ~** not that bad [at all]; **jdn ~ behandeln** to treat sb badly

Übel <-s, -> ['y:bl] nt evil ▶WENDUNGEN: **das <u>kleinere</u> ~** the lesser evil; **ein <u>not-wendiges</u> ~** a necessary evil

Übelkeit <-, -en> f nausea

Übeltäter(in) m(f) wrongdoer

üben ['y:bn] **I.** vt, vi to practice **II.** vr ■**sich** akk **in etw** dat ~ to practice sth

über ['y:bɐ] **I.** präp ❶ +dat (oberhalb von) above ❷ +akk (quer hinüber) over ❸ +akk (höher als) above, over ❹ +akk (etw erfassend) over; **ein Überblick ~ etw** an overview of sth ❺ +akk (quer darüber) over; **er strich ihr ~ das Haar/die Wange** he stroked her hair/cheek ❻ +akk (jdn/etw betreffend) about ❼ +dat (zahlenmäßig größer als) above ❽ (durch jdn/etw) through ❾ (via) via ❿ (während) during; **habt ihr ~ die Feiertage/das Wochenende schon was vor?** do you have anything planned for the holiday/weekend? ▶WENDUNGEN: **~ <u>alles</u>** more than anything **II.** adv ❶ (älter als) over ❷ (mehr als) more than ▶WENDUNGEN: **~ <u>und</u> ~** completely **III.** adj (fam: übrig) ■**~ sein** to be left; Essen to be left [over]

überall [y:bɐ·'?al] adv ❶ (an allen Orten) everywhere; (an jeder Stelle) all over [the place]; **~ <u>wo</u>** wherever ❷ (wer weiß wo) anywhere ❸ (in allen Dingen) everything; **er kennt sich ~ aus**

he knows something about everything ❹ (bei jedermann) everyone; **er ist ~ beliebt** everyone likes him

überanstrengen* [y:bɐ·'?an·ʃtrɛŋ·ən] **I.** vt ■**etw** ~ to put too great a strain on sth **II.** vr ■**sich** akk ~ to overexert oneself

überarbeiten* [y:bɐ·'?ar·bai·tn̩] **I.** vt to revise **II.** vr ■**sich** akk ~ to overwork oneself

überaus ['y:bɐ·'?aus] adv extremely

überbacken* [y:bɐ·'ba·kn̩] vt irreg **etw mit Käse ~** to top sth with cheese and bake it

überbelasten* vt to overload

überbelichten* vt to overexpose

überbewerten* vt **du überbewertest diese Äußerung** you're placing too much importance on this comment

überbieten* [y:bɐ·'bi:·tn̩] vt irreg ❶ SPORT to better (**um** +akk by); Rekord to break ❷ (durch höheres Gebot) to outbid (**um** +akk by)

Überbleibsel <-s, -> ['y:bɐ·blaip·sl̩] nt (fam) ❶ (Relikt) relic ❷ (Rest) remnant

Überblick ['y:bɐ·blɪk] m view (**über** +akk of); **den ~ [über etw** akk**] verlieren** to lose track [of sth]

überblicken* [y:bɐ·'blɪ·kn̩] vt ❶ (Sicht haben) to look out over ❷ (erfassen) Lage, Situation etc. to have an overview of

überbringen* [y:bɐ·'brɪ·ŋən] vt irreg to deliver

überbrücken* [y:bɐ·'brʏ·kn̩] vt to bridge

überdenken* [y:bɐ·'dɛŋ·kn̩] vt irreg to think over

Überdosis f overdose (**an** +dat of)

Überdruck m excess pressure

Überdruss^RR <-es>, **Überdruß**^ALT <-sses> ['y:bɐ·drʊs] m kein pl aversion; **bis zum ~** ad nauseam

überdrüssig ['y:bɐ·drʏ·sɪç] adj ■**jds/**

einer S. *gen* ~ **sein/werden** to be/ grow tired of sb/sth

überdurchschnittlich I. *adj* above-average *attr*; above average *pred* **II.** *adv* above average

übereinander [y:be·ʔai·'nan·də] *adv* ❶ (*eins über dem anderen/das andere*) on top of each other ❷ (*über sich*) about each other

übereinander|schlagen *vt irreg* **die Beine** ~ to cross one's legs

überein|kommen [y:be·'ʔain·kɔ·mən] *vi irreg sein* to agree

überein|stimmen [y:be·'ʔain·ʃti·mən] *vi* ❶ (*der gleichen Meinung sein*) to agree (**in** +*dat* on) ❷ (*sich gleichen*) ■ [**mit etw** *dat*] ~ to match [sth]

Übereinstimmung *f* agreement (**in** +*dat* on)

überempfindlich *adj* oversensitive; MED hypersensitive (**gegen** +*akk* to)

überfahren* [y:be·'fa:·rən] *vt irreg* ❶ (*niederfahren*) to run over *sep* ❷ (*nicht beachten*) **eine rote Ampel** ~ to run a red light ❸ (*fam: übertölpeln*) ■**jdn** ~ to railroad sb

Überfall *m* attack; (*Raubüberfall*) robbery

überfallen* [y:be·'fal·ən] *vt irreg* ❶ (*angreifen*) to mug; **Bank** to rob; **Land** to attack; MIL to raid ❷ (*überraschend besuchen*) ■**jdn** ~ to descend [up]on sb ❸ (*bestürmen*) to bombard (**mit** +*dat* with)

überfliegen* [y:be·'fli:·gn] *vt irreg* ❶ LUFT to fly over ❷ (*flüchtig ansehen*) to take a quick look at; **Text** *a.* to skim through

Überflussᴿᴿ *m kein pl* abundance; **im** ~ **vorhanden sein** to be in plentiful supply; **etw im** ~ **haben** to have plenty of sth ▶WENDUNGEN: **zu allem** ~ to top it all off

überflüssig *adj* superfluous; *Anschaffungen, Bemerkung* unnecessary

überfluten* [y:be·'flu:·tn] *vt* (*a. fig*) to flood

überfordern* [y:be·'fɔr·dən] *vt* to be

too much for; ■**überfordert sein** to be out of one's league

überführen* [y:be·'fy:·rən] *vt* ❶ (*transportieren*) to transfer; *Leiche* to transport ❷ JUR to convict; **jdn des Mordes** ~ to convict sb of murder

überfüllt *adj* overcrowded

Übergabe *f* ❶ (*das Übergeben*) handing over ❷ MIL surrender

Übergangszeit *f* transition; (*zwischen Jahreszeiten*) off-season

übergeben* [y:be·'ge:·bn] *irreg* **I.** *vt* ❶ (*überreichen*) ■**jdm| etw** ~ to hand over *sep* sth [to sb] ❷ (*ausliefern*) ■**jdn jdm** ~ to hand over *sep* sb to sb ❸ MIL (*überlassen*) to surrender **II.** *vr* ■**sich** *akk* ~ to vomit

über|gehen¹ ['y:be·ge·ən] *vi irreg sein* ❶ (*wechseln*) ■**zu etw** *dat* ~ to move on to sth ❷ **in anderen Besitz** ~ to become sb else's property ❸ **in Fäulnis/ Gärung/Verwesung** ~ to begin to rot/ ferment/decay ❹ (*verschwimmen*) ■**ineinander** ~ to merge into one another

über|gehen*² [y:be·'ge:·ən] *vt irreg* ❶ (*nicht berücksichtigen*) to pass over *sep* ❷ (*nicht beachten*) to ignore ❸ (*auslassen*) to skip [over *sep*]

übergeordnet *adj* ❶ (*vorrangig*) superior ❷ (*vorgesetzt*) higher

Übergewicht *nt kein pl* ❶ (*zu hohes Körpergewicht*) excess weight; ~ **haben** to be overweight ❷ (*vorrangige Bedeutung*) predominance

übergewichtig *adj* overweight

überglücklich I. *adj* extremely happy, overjoyed *pred* **II.** *adv* **~ lächeln** to smile blissfully

über|greifen *vi irreg* to spread (**auf** +*akk* to)

Übergröße *f* extra large size

über|hängen ['y:be·hɛ·ŋən] *vt* ■**sich/ jdm etw** ~ *dat* to put sth around one's/ sb's shoulders

überhäufen* [y:be·'hɔy·fn] *vt* ■**jdn mit etw** *dat* ~ (*a. fig*) to heap sth [up]on sb

überhaupt [y:be·'haupt] **I.** *adv* ■**~ kei-**

U

n(e, r) nobody/nothing/none at all;
~ **kein Geld haben** to have no money
at all; ~ **nicht/nichts** not/nothing at
all; ~ **[noch] nie** never [at all] II. *part*
(*eigentlich*) **was soll das ~?** what's
that supposed to mean?; **wissen Sie ~,
wer ich bin?** don't you even know
who I am?

überheblich [yːbɐˈheːplɪç] I. *adj* arrogant II. *adv* arrogantly

Überheblichkeit <-> *f kein pl* arrogance

überhöht *adj* excessive; **mit ~er
Geschwindigkeit fahren** to speed

überholen* [yːbɐˈhoːlən] *vt* ❶(*vorbeifahren*) to pass ❷(*übertreffen*) to surpass ❸ *Motor, Gerät* to overhaul

Überholspur *f* fast lane

überholt *adj* outdated

Überholverbot *nt* restriction on passing; (*Strecke*) no passing zone

überhören* [yːbɐˈhøːrən] *vt* ❶(*nicht
hören*) to not hear ❷(*nicht hören wollen*) to ignore

über|kochen [ˈyːbɐkɔxn̩] *vi sein* to boil over

überladen* [yːbɐˈlaːdn̩] *vt irreg* to overload

überlassen* [yːbɐˈlasn̩] *vt irreg*
❶(*zur Verfügung stellen*) ■**jdm
etw ~** to let sb have sth ❷(*entscheiden lassen*) ■**jdm etw ~** to leave
sth to sb ❸(*preisgeben*) **sich** *dat*
selbst ~ sein to be left to one's own
devices

Überlastung <-, -en> *f* ❶*eines Menschen* excess strain ❷TRANSP *des Verkehrs* congestion

überlaufen*¹ [yːbɐˈlaufn̩] *vt irreg* **es
überlief mich kalt** a cold shiver ran
down my spine

über|laufen² [ˈyːbɐlaufn̩] *vi irreg sein*
❶(*über den Rand*) to overflow; *Tasse
a.* to run over *a. poet* ❷(*überkochen*)
to boil over ❸MIL to desert

überlaufen³ [yːbɐˈlaufn̩] *adj* overrun

überleben* [yːbɐˈleːbn̩] I. *vt* ❶(*lebend überstehen*) to survive ❷(*lebend
überdauern*) ■**etw ~** to live through

sth ❸(*über jds Tod hinaus leben*)
■**jdn ~** to outlive sb II. *vi* to survive

Überlebende(r) *f(m) dekl wie adj* survivor

überlegen*¹ [yːbɐˈleːgn̩] I. *vt, vi* to
think [about it]; **überleg [doch] mal!**
just [stop and] think about it!; **das wäre
zu ~** it is worth considering; **nach kurzem/langem Ü~** after short/long deliberation; **ohne zu ~** without thinking
II. *vr* ■**sich** *dat* **etw ~** to consider sth;
ich will es mir noch einmal ~ I'll
think it over again; **wenn man es sich
recht überlegt** on second thought;
sich *dat* **etw reiflich ~** to give serious
thought to sth; **es sich** *dat* **[anders] ~**
to change one's mind

überlegen² [yːbɐˈleːgn̩] I. *adj* superior; *Sieg* convincing; ■**jdm ~ sein** to be
superior to sb (**auf/in** +*dat* in) II. *adv*
❶(*mit großem Vorsprung*) convincingly ❷(*herablassend*) superciliously *pej*

überlegt [yːbɐˈleːkt] I. *adj* [well-]considered II. *adv* with consideration

Überlegung <-, -en> *f* consideration

über|leiten *vi* to lead (**zu** +*dat* to)

überliefern* [yːbɐˈliːfɐn] *vt* to hand
down *sep*

Überlieferung *f* tradition; **mündliche ~** oral tradition

überlisten* [yːbɐˈlɪstn̩] *vt* to outwit

übermächtig *adj* ❶(*überlegen*) superior ❷(*überwältigend*) overpowering;
Verlangen overwhelming

Übermaß *nt kein pl* excess

übermäßig I. *adj* excessive; *Freude,
Trauer* intense; *Schmerz* violent II. *adv*
excessively; **sich** *akk* **~ anstrengen** to
try too hard

übermorgen [ˈyːbɐmɔrgn̩] *adv* the
day after tomorrow

übermüdet [yːbɐˈmyːdət] *adj* overtired; (*erschöpft a.*) overfatigued *form*

Übermut *m* high spirits *npl*; **aus ~** just
for the hell of it *fam*

übermütig [ˈyːbɐmyːtɪç] I. *adj*
high-spirited; (*zu dreist*) cocky *fam*
II. *adv* boisterously

übernächste(r, s) [ˈyːbɐnɛːçstə, -tə,

-təs] *adj attr* ~**s Jahr**/~ **Woche** the year/week after next, in two years/weeks; **die** ~ **Tür** two doors down

übernachten* [y:bɐ·ˈnax·tn̩] *vi* ■**bei jdm**] ~ to spend the night [at sb's place]

Übernachtung <-, -en> *f* ❶ *kein pl* (*das Übernachten*) spending the night [*or* a]; (*bei Kindern*) sleepover ❷ (*verbrachte Nacht*) overnight stay; **mit zwei** ~**en in Bangkok** with two nights in Bangkok; ~ **mit Frühstück** bed and breakfast

Übernahme <-, -n> [ˈy:bɐ·na:·mə] *f* ❶ (*Inbesitznahme*) taking possession ❷ (*das Übernehmen*) assumption; *von Verantwortung a.* acceptance ❸ ÖKON takeover

übernatürlich *adj* supernatural

übernehmen* [y:bɐ·ˈne:·mən] *irreg* I. *vt* ❶ (*in Besitz nehmen*) to take; (*kaufen*) to buy; *Geschäft* to take over *sep* ❷ (*auf sich nehmen, annehmen*) to accept; *Auftrag, Verantwortung a.* to take on *sep*; *Kosten a.* to pay; *Verpflichtungen* to assume ❸ (*weiterbeschäftigen*) to take over *sep*; **jdn ins Angestelltenverhältnis** ~ to employ sb on a permanent basis II. *vr* ■**sich** *akk* ~ to take on too much

überprüfen* [y:bɐ·ˈpry:·fn̩] *vt* ❶ (*durchchecken*) to vet; *Papiere, Rechnung* to check (**auf** +*akk* for) ❷ (*die Funktion nachprüfen*) to examine ❸ (*erneut bedenken*) to examine

überqueren* [y:bɐ·ˈkve:·rən] *vt* ❶ (*sich über etw hinweg bewegen*) to cross [over] ❷ (*über etw hinwegführen*) to lead over

überragen*¹ [y:bɐ·ˈra:·gn̩] *vt* ❶ (*größer sein*) to tower above (**um** +*akk* by); *Mensch* to be taller than ❷ (*übertreffen*) to outclass

über|ragen² [ˈy:bɐ·ra:·gn̩] *vi* (*überstehen*) to project

überraschen* [y:bɐ·ˈra·ʃn̩] *vt* to surprise (**mit** +*dat* with); **lassen wir uns** ~! (*fam*) let's wait and see [what happens]; ■**jdn dabei** ~, **wie er etw tut** to catch sb doing sth; **vom Regen**

überrascht werden to get caught in the rain

überraschend I. *adj* unexpected II. *adv* unexpectedly

Überraschung <-, -en> *f* surprise

überreden* [y:bɐ·ˈre:·dn̩] *vt* to persuade; ■**jdn zu etw** *dat* ~ to talk sb into [doing] sth

überreichen* [y:bɐ·ˈrai·çn̩] *vt* ■**jdm etw** ~ to hand over *sep* sth to sb; (*feierlich*) to present sth to sb

Überrest *m meist pl* remains *npl*; **jds sterbliche** ~**e** sb's [mortal] remains

überschätzen* [y:bɐ·ˈʃɛ·tsn̩] I. *vt* to overestimate II. *vr* ■**sich** *akk* ~ to think too highly of oneself

überschlagen* [y:bɐ·ˈʃla:·gn̩] *irreg* I. *vt* ❶ *Buchseite* to skip [over] ❷ (*ungefähr berechnen*) to [roughly] estimate II. *vr* ■**sich** *akk* ~ ❶ *Fahrzeug* to overturn; *Mensch* to fall head over heels ❷ *Ereignisse* to follow in quick succession ❸ *Stimme* to crack

überschneiden* [y:bɐ·ˈʃnai·dn̩] *vr irreg* ■**sich** *akk* ~ ❶ (*zeitlich*) to overlap (**um** +*akk* by) ❷ *Linien* to intersect

überschreiten* [y:bɐ·ˈʃrai·tn̩] *vt irreg* ❶ (*geh: zu Fuß*) to cross [over] ❷ (*über etw hinausgehen*) to exceed (**um** +*akk* by)

Überschrift *f* title; *Zeitung* headline

Überschussᴿᴿ *m* ❶ (*Reingewinn*) profit ❷ (*überschüssige Menge*) surplus (**an** +*dat* of)

überschüssig [ˈy:bɐ·ʃy·sɪç] *adj* surplus *attr*

überschwänglichᴿᴿ I. *adj* effusive II. *adv* effusively

überschwemmen* [y:bɐ·ˈʃvɛ·mən] *vt* to flood

Überschwemmung <-, -en> *f* flood[ing]

überschwenglichᴬᴸᵀ [ˈy:bɐ·ʃvɛŋ·lɪç] *adj, adv s.* **überschwänglich**

Übersee [ˈy:bɐ·ze:] *kein art* ■**aus** ~ from overseas; ■**in/nach** ~ overseas

übersehbar [y:bɐ·ˈze:·ba:ɐ̯] *adj* ❶ (*abschätzbar*) *Auswirkungen* containable;

U

Dauer, Kosten, Schäden assessable; *Konsequenzen* clear; ■**etw ist/ist noch nicht ~** sth is in sight/sth is still not known ② (*mit Blicken zu erfassen*) visible

übersehen* [y:bɐˈze:·ən] *vt irreg* ① (*nicht bemerken*) to overlook ② (*abschätzen*) to assess ③ (*mit Blicken erfassen*) to have a view of

übersetzen*¹ [y:bɐˈzɛ·tsn̩] *vt, vi* to translate; [**etw**] **aus dem Deutschen ins Englische ~** to translate [sth] from German into English

überǀsetzen² [ˈy:bɐ·zɛ·tsn̩] **I.** *vt haben* ■**jdn ~** to ferry across *sep* sb **II.** *vi sein* to cross [over]

Übersetzer(in) <-s, -> *m(f)* translator

Übersetzung <-, -en> *f* ① LING translation ② TECH transmission ratio

Übersicht <-, -en> *f* ① *kein pl* (*Überblick*) overall view ② (*knappe Darstellung*) outline

übersichtlich I. *adj* ① (*rasch erfassbar*) clear ② (*gut zu überschauen*) open *attr* **II.** *adv* clearly

übersinnlich *adj* paranormal

überspitzt I. *adj* exaggerated **II.** *adv* in an exaggerated fashion

überspringen*¹ [y:bɐˈʃprɪ·ŋən] *vt irreg* ① (*über etw hinüber*) to jump; *Mauer* to skip ② (*auslassen*) to skip [over] ③ SCH *Klasse* to skip

überǀspringen² [ˈy:bɐ·ʃprɪ·ŋən] *vi irreg sein* to spread (**auf** +*akk* to)

überstehen* [y:bɐˈʃte:·ən] *vt irreg* to get through; *Krankheit, Operation* to get over; **die nächsten Tage ~** to make it through the next few days

übersteigen* [y:bɐˈʃtai·gn̩] *vt irreg* ① (*über etw klettern*) to climb over; *Mauer* to scale ② (*über etw hinausgehen*) to exceed

überstimmen* [y:bɐˈʃtɪ·mən] *vt* ① (*mit Stimmenmehrheit besiegen*) to outvote ② (*mit Stimmenmehrheit ablehnen*) to defeat

Überstunde *f* hour of overtime; ■**~n** overtime

überstürzen* [y:bɐˈʃtʏr·tsn̩] **I.** *vt*

■**etw ~** to rush into sth **II.** *vr* ■**sich** *akk* **~** to follow in quick succession

übertragbar [y:bɐˈtra:k·ba:ɐ̯] *adj* ① *Krankheit* communicable *form* (**auf** +*akk* to); (*durch Berührung*) contagious ② (*anderweitig anwendbar*) to be applicable (**auf** +*akk* to) ③ *Ticket* transferable

übertragen*¹ [y:bɐˈtra:·gn̩] *irreg* **I.** *vt* ① (*senden*) to broadcast ② *Krankheit* to communicate (**auf** +*akk* to) ③ (*übergeben*) *Besitz* to transfer (**auf** +*akk* to); ■**jdm die Verantwortung ~** to entrust sb with the responsibility ④ (*geh: übersetzen*) to translate **II.** *vr* ① MED ■**sich** *akk* [**auf jdn**] **~** to be communicated [to sb] ② (*beeinflussen*) ■**sich** *akk* **auf jdn ~** to spread to sb

übertragen² [y:bɐˈtra:·gn̩] **I.** *adj* figurative **II.** *adv* figuratively

übertreffen* [y:bɐˈtrɛ·fn̩] *vt irreg* ① (*besser/größer sein*) to surpass (**an/in** +*dat* in) ② (*über etw hinausgehen*) to exceed (**um** +*akk* by)

übertreiben* [y:bɐˈtrai·bn̩] *irreg* **I.** *vi* to exaggerate **II.** *vt* to overdo; ■**ohne zu ~** I'm not joking

Übertreibung <-, -en> *f* exaggeration

überǀtreten¹ [ˈy:bɐ·tre:·tn̩] *vi irreg sein* ① (*konvertieren*) to convert (**zu** +*dat* to) ② SPORT to overstep

übertreten*² [y:bɐˈtre:·tn̩] *vt irreg* *Gesetz, Vorschrift* to break

Übertretung <-, -en> [y:bɐˈtre:·tʊŋ] *f* violation

übertrieben I. *adj* exaggerated; *Vorsicht* excessive **II.** *adv* excessively

überwachen* [y:bɐˈva:·xn̩] *vt* ① (*heimlich beobachten*) *Verdächtigen* to keep under surveillance; *Telefon* to bug ② (*kontrollieren*) to supervise; (*durch eine Kamera*) to monitor

Überwachung <-, -en> *f* ① (*heimliches Beobachten*) *eines Verdächtigen* surveillance; *eines Telefons* bugging ② (*Kontrolle*) supervision; (*durch eine Kamera*) monitoring

überwältigen* [y:bɐˈvɛl·tɪ·gn̩] *vt* ① (*bezwingen*) to overpower ② (*über-*

mannen) ■ etw überwältigt jdn sth overwhelms sb

überwältigend _adj_ overwhelming; _Schönheit_ stunning; _Sieg_ crushing

überweisen* [y:bɐ'vai·sn̩] _vt irreg_ ❶ _Geld_ to transfer ❷ _Patienten_ to refer (**an** +_akk_ to)

Überweisung <-, -en> _f_ ❶ _von Geld_ transfer ❷ _eines Patienten_ referral (**an** +_akk_ to); (_Überweisungsformular_) referral form

überwiegend ['y:bɐ·vi:·gn̩t] I. _adj_ predominant; _Mehrheit_ vast II. _adv_ mainly

überwinden* [y:bɐ·'vɪn·dn̩] _irreg_ I. _vt_ to overcome II. _vr_ ■ **sich** _akk_ ~ to overcome one's feelings/inclinations etc.; ■ **sich** _akk_ **zu etw** _dat_ ~ to force oneself to do sth

Überwindung <-> _f kein pl_ ❶ (_das Überwinden_) overcoming ❷ (_Selbstüberwindung_) conscious effort; **jdn** ~ **kosten**|, **etw zu tun**| to take sb a lot of will power [to do sth]

überwintern* [y:bɐ·'vɪn·ten] _vi_ to [spend the] winter; _Pflanzen_ to overwinter

überzeugen* [y:bɐ·'tsɔy·gn̩] I. _vt_ to convince (**von** +_dat_ of); (_umstimmen a._) to persuade II. _vi_ ❶ (_überzeugend sein_) to be convincing ❷ (_sich bewähren_) ■ **bei etw** _dat_ ~ to prove oneself in sth III. _vr_ ■ **sich** _akk_ [**selbst**] ~ to convince oneself; ~ **Sie sich selbst!** [go and] see for yourself!

überzeugend I. _adj_ convincing; (_umstimmend a._) persuasive II. _adv_ convincingly

Überzeugung <-, -en> [y:bɐ·'tsɔy·gn̩] _f_ convictions _npl_; **zu der** ~ **gelangen, dass ...** to become convinced that ...

überziehen*[1] [y:bɐ·'tsi:·ən] _vt irreg_ ❶ (_bedecken_) to cover; (_Kuchen mit Glasur_) to coat ❷ _Konto_ to overdraw (**um** +_akk_ by) ❸ (_zu weit treiben_) ■ **etw** ~ to carry sth too far; ■ **überzogen** exaggerated

über|ziehen[2] [y:bɐ·tsi:·ən] _vt irreg_

(_anziehen_) ■ [**sich** _dat_] **etw** ~ to put on _sep_ sth

Überzug _m_ coat[ing]; (_dünner_) film; (_Zuckerguss_) frosting

üblich ['y:p·lɪç] _adj_ usual; **es ist bei uns hier** [**so**] ~ that's the custom around here

U-Boot ['u:bo:t] _nt_ submarine

übrig ['y:b·rɪç] _adj_ remaining, rest of _attr_; (_andere a._) other _attr_; ■ **die Ü~en** the remaining ones; ■ **das Ü~e** the rest; ■ ~ **sein** to be left [over]; **es wird ihm nichts anderes** ~ **bleiben** he won't have any [other] choice; [**jdm**] **etw** ~ **lassen** to leave sth [for sb]

übrigens ['y:b·rɪ·gn̩s] _adv_ by the way

übrig|haben[RR] _vt irreg_ ■ **für jdn/etw nichts/viel** ~ to be not at all/very interested in sb/sth

Übung <-, -en> ['y:bʊŋ] _f_ ❶ _kein pl_ (_das Üben_) practice; **das ist alles nur** ~ it [all] comes with practice; **zur** ~ for practice ❷ (_Übungsstück_) exercise ❸ SPORT exercise ❹ (_Probe für den Ernstfall_) drill ❺ (_Lehrveranstaltung_) lab (**zu** +_dat_ on) ▸WENDUNGEN: ~ **macht den Meister** (_prov_) practice makes perfect

Ufer <-s, -> ['u:fɐ] _nt_ (_Flussufer_) bank; (_Seeufer_) shore; **ans** ~ **schwimmen** to swim ashore

Ufo, UFO <-[s], -s> ['u:fo] _nt Abk von_ **Unbekanntes Flugobjekt** UFO

Uganda <-> [u'gan·da] _nt_ Uganda; _s. a._ **Deutschland**

Ugander(in) <-s, -> [u'gan·dɐ] _m(f)_ Ugandan; _s. a._ **Deutsche(r)**

ugandisch [u'gan·dɪʃ] _adj_ Ugandan; _s. a._ **deutsch**

Uhr <-, -en> [u:ɐ] _f_ ❶ (_Gerät_) clock; (_Armbanduhr_) watch; **die** ~ [**auf Sommer-/Winterzeit**] **umstellen** to set the clock/one's watch [an hour forward/backward at daylight saving time]; **diese** ~ **geht nach/vor** this watch is slow/fast; **rund um die** ~ round-the-clock, 24 hours a day ❷ (_Zeitangabe_) o'clock; **wie viel** ~ **ist es?** what time is it?; **um wie viel** ~? [at]

U

what time?; **um** 10 ~ at ten [o'clock]; 10 ~ **morgens/abends** ten [o'clock] in the morning/in the evening; **15** ~ 3 o'clock [in the afternoon], 3 p.m.; **7** ~ **30** half past 7, seven thirty; **8** ~ **23** 23 minutes after 8, eight twenty-three

Uhrzeigersinn *m* ■**im** ~ clockwise; ■ **gegen den** ~ counterclockwise

Uhrzeit *f* time [of day]

Uhu <-s, -s> ['uːhu] *m* eagle owl

Ukraine <-> [ukraˈiːnə] *f* ■**die** ~ [the] Ukraine; *s. a.* **Deutschland**

Ukrainer(in) <-s, -> [ukraˈiːnɐ] *m(f)* Ukrainian; *s. a.* **Deutsche(r)**

ukrainisch [ukraˈiːnɪʃ] *adj* Ukrainian; *s. a.* **deutsch**

ulkig ['ʊlkɪç] *adj* ❶ (*lustig*) funny ❷ (*seltsam*) odd

Ultimatum <-s, -s> [ʊlˈtiˈmaːtʊm] *nt* ultimatum; **jdm ein ~ stellen** to give sb an ultimatum

Ultraschall ['ʊltraˈʃal] *m* ultrasound

Ultraschalluntersuchung *f* ultrasound

ultraviolett [ʊltraˈvi̯oˈlɛt] *adj* ultraviolet

um [ʊm] **I.** *präp* +*akk* ❶ (*etw umgebend*) ■~ **etw** [**herum**] around sth; **ganz um etw** [**herum**] all around sth ❷ (*gegen*) ~ **Ostern/den 15./die Mitte des Monats** [**herum**] around Easter/the 15th/the middle of the month ❸ (*über*) ~ **etw streiten** to argue about sth ❹ *Unterschiede im Vergleich ausdrückend* ~ **einiges besser** quite a bit better; ~ **einen Kopf größer/kleiner** taller/shorter by a head; ~ **10 cm länger/kürzer** 4 inches longer/shorter ❺ (*wegen*) ■~ **jds/einer S.** *gen* **willen** for sb's sake/for the sake of sth; ~ **meinetwillen** for my sake ❻ (*für*) **Minute** ~ **Minute** minute by minute ❼ (*nach allen Richtungen*) ~ **sich** *akk* **schlagen/treten** to hit/kick out in all directions ❽ (*vorüber*) ■~ **sein** to be over; *Zeit* to be up; *Frist* to expire **II.** *konj* ■~ **etw zu tun** [in order] to do sth **III.** *adv* ■ **die 80 Meter** about 250 feet

um|ändern *vt* to alter

umarmen* [ʊmˈʔarˈmən] *vt* to embrace; (*fester*) to hug

Umarmung <-, -en> *f* embrace, hug

um|bauen ['ʊmbauˈən] **I.** *vt* to rebuild **II.** *vi* to renovate

um|benennen* *vt irreg* to rename

um|biegen *irreg* **I.** *vt haben* to bend **II.** *vi sein* (*kehrtmachen*) to turn back

um|binden ['ʊmbɪnˈdn̩] *vt irreg* **jdm ein Tuch** ~ to put a scarf around sb's neck; (*mit Knoten a.*) to tie a scarf around sb's neck; ■**sich** *dat* **etw** ~ to put [*or* tie] on sth

um|blättern *vi* to turn over

um|blicken *vr* ❶ (*nach hinten*) ■**sich** *akk* ~ to look back; ■**sich** *akk* **nach jdm/etw** ~ to turn around to look at sb/sth ❷ (*zur Seite*) **sich** *akk* **nach links/rechts/allen Seiten** ~ to look to the left/right/in all directions; (*vor Straßenüberquerung a.*) to look left/right/both ways

um|bringen *irreg* **I.** *vt* to kill; (*vorsätzlich a.*) to murder (**durch** +*akk* with); **jdn mit einem Messer** ~ to stab sb to death **II.** *vr* ■**sich** *akk* ~ to kill oneself ❷ **sich** *akk* **vor Freundlichkeit/ Höflichkeit** [**fast**] ~ to go out of one's way to be friendly/polite

Umbruch ['ʊmbrʊx] *m* radical change

um|buchen *vt* ❶ *Reise* to change one's booking/reservation (**auf** +*akk* to); **den Flug auf einen anderen Tag** ~ to change one's flight reservation to another day ❷ *Geld* to transfer (**auf** +*akk* to)

um|definieren* *vt* to redefine

um|denken *vi irreg* to change one's ideas/views (**in** +*dat* of)

um|drehen **I.** *vt haben* ❶ (*auf die andere Seite*) to turn over *sep* ❷ (*herumdrehen*) to turn **II.** *vr haben* ■**sich** *akk* ~ to turn around **III.** *vi sein o haben* to turn around; *Mensch a.* to turn back

Umdrehungszahl *f* number of revolutions [per minute/second]

umeinander [ʊmʔaiˈnanˈdɐ] *adv* about each other

um|fahren ['ʊmfaːˈrən] *vt irreg* (*fam*)

to run over *sep;* ■**umgefahren werden** to be hit by a vehicle

um|fallen *vi irreg sein* ❶ (*umkippen*) to topple over; *Baum a.* to fall [down] ❷ (*zu Boden fallen*) to fall over; (*schwerfällig*) to slump to the floor/ground; **tot** ~ to drop dead ❸ (*fam: die Aussage widerrufen*) to retract one's statement

Umfang <-[e]s, Umfänge> *m* ❶ (*Perimeter*) circumference; *vom Bauch* girth ❷ (*Ausdehnung*) area ❸ (*Ausmaß*) **in großem** ~ on a large scale; **in vollem** ~ completely

umfangreich *adj* extensive; *Buch* thick

umfassen* [ʊmˈfa·sn̩] *vt* ❶ (*umschließen*) to clasp; (*umarmen*) to embrace ❷ (*aus etw bestehen*) to comprise

umfassend [ʊmˈfa·snt] I. *adj* ❶ (*weitgehend*) extensive ❷ (*alles enthaltend*) full II. *adv* ~ **über etw** *akk* **berichten** to report all the details of sth; **jdn** ~ **informieren** to keep sb informed about everything

Umfeld *nt* sphere

Umfrage *f* survey; POL [opinion] poll; **eine** ~ **machen** to conduct a survey (**zu** +*dat* on/about, **über** +*akk* on/about)

Umgang *m* ❶ (*gesellschaftlicher Verkehr*) dealings *pl;* **kein** ~ **für jdn sein** to not be fit company for sb ❷ (*Beschäftigung*) ■**jds** ~ **mit etw** *dat* sb's dealing[s] with sth

umgänglich [ˈʊm·gɛŋ·lɪç] *adj* friendly; (*entgegenkommend*) obliging

Umgangsformen *pl* [social] manners *pl*

Umgangssprache *f* LING colloquial speech; **die deutsche** ~ colloquial German

Umgangston *m* way of speaking

umgeben* [ʊmˈge·bn̩] *irreg* I. *vt* to surround II. *vr* ■**sich** *akk* **mit jdm/etw** ~ to surround oneself with sb/sth

Umgebung <-, -en> [ʊmˈge·bʊŋ] *f* ❶ (*umgebende Landschaft*) environment, surroundings *pl;* *einer Stadt a.* environs *npl;* (*Nachbarschaft*) vicinity

❷ (*jdn umgebender Kreis*) people around one

um|gehen¹ [ˈʊm·ge·ən] *vi irreg sein* ❶ (*behandeln*) to treat; **mit jdm nicht** ~ **können** to not know how to deal with sb; **mit etw** *dat* **gleichgültig/vorsichtig** ~ to handle sth indifferently/carefully ❷ *Gerücht* to circulate

umgehen*² [ʊmˈge·ən] *vt irreg* (*vermeiden*) to avoid

Umgehungsstraße [ʊmˈge·ʊŋs-] *f* bypass

umgekehrt I. *adj* reverse *attr; Richtung* opposite; **in** ~**er Reihenfolge** in reverse order; [**es ist**] **gerade** ~! [it's] just the opposite! II. *adv* the other way around

um|graben *vt irreg* to dig over *sep*

Umhang *m* cape

um|hängen [ˈʊm·hɛ·ŋən] *vt* ■**sich** *dat* **etw** ~ to put on *sep* sth; ■**jdm etw** ~ to wrap sth around sb

Umhängetasche *f* shoulder bag

umher [ʊmˈheːɐ̯] *adv* around; **überall** ~ everywhere

um|hören *vr* ■**sich** *akk* ~ to ask around

um|kehren I. *vi sein* to turn back II. *vt haben* to reverse

um|kippen I. *vi sein* ❶ (*seitlich umfallen*) to tip over; *Stuhl, Fahrrad* to fall over ❷ (*fam: bewusstlos umfallen*) to pass out ❸ (*fam: die Meinung ändern*) to come around ❹ ÖKOL to become polluted ❺ (*ins Gegenteil umschlagen*) *Laune* to change; ■**in etw** *akk* ~ to turn into sth II. *vt haben* to tip over *sep*

umklammern* [ʊmˈkla·mɐn] *vt* ■**jdn** ~ to cling [on] to sb; ■**etw** ~ to hold sth tight

Umkleideraum *m* changing room

um|kommen *vi irreg sein* ❶ (*sterben*) to be killed (**bei/in** +*dat* in) ❷ (*fam: verderben*) to go bad ❸ (*fam: es nicht mehr aushalten*) **vor Hunger/Durst** ~ to be dying of hunger/thirst; **vor Langeweile** ~ to be bored to death

Umkreis *m* vicinity; **im** ~ **von 100 Metern** within a radius of 100 Meters

U

umkreisen* [ʊmˈkrai̯·zn̩] *vt* ASTRON, RAUM to orbit

um|krempeln *vt* (*grundlegend umgestalten*) ■**jdn/etw ~** to shake up *sep* sb/sth

Umlauf [ˈʊm·lau̯f] *m* ❶ ASTRON rotation ❷ **etw in ~ bringen** to circulate sth; *Gerücht, Lüge* to spread sth; *Geld* to put into circulation

Umlaufbahn *f* orbit

Umlaut *m* umlaut

um|legen [ˈʊm·leː·gn̩] *vt* ❶ *Schalter* to turn ❷ (*um Körperteil legen*) ■**sich/jdm etw ~** *dat* to put sth around oneself/sb ❸ (*sl: umbringen*) ■**jdn ~** to bump off *sep* sb ❹ (*[auf einen anderen Zeitpunkt] verlegen*) to reschedule (**auf** +*akk* for)

um|leiten *vt* to divert

Umleitung *f* detour

um|pflügen [ˈʊm·pflyː·gn̩] *vt* to plow up *sep*

um|räumen I. *vi* to rearrange II. *vt* *Möbel, Zimmer* to rearrange

Umrechnungskurs *m* exchange rate

um|rennen *vt irreg* ■**jdn/etw ~** to [run into and] knock sb/sth over

Umriss[RR] *m meist pl* contour, outline; **in ~en** in outline

um|rühren *vt, vi* to stir

Umsatz *m* turnover

Umsatzsteuer *f* sales tax

um|schalten *vi* ❶ RADIO, TV to switch over; **auf einen anderen Sender ~** to change the channel ❷ *Ampel* to change; **auf Rot/Grün ~** to turn red/green ❸ (*fam: sich einstellen*) to shift gears *fig* (**auf** +*akk* to)

um|schauen *vr s.* **umsehen**

Umschlag *m* ❶ (*Briefumschlag*) envelope ❷ (*Schutzumschlag*) jacket ❸ MED compress ❹ *kein pl* ÖKON transfer

um|schlagen [ˈʊm·ʃlaː·gn̩] *irreg* I. *vt haben* ❶ *Kragen* to turn down *sep*; *Ärmel* to turn up ❷ (*umladen*) to transfer II. *vi sein* METEO to change

umschließen* [ʊmˈʃliː·sn̩] *vt irreg* ❶ (*umgeben, umzingeln*) to enclose

❷ (*umarmen*) **jdn/etw mit den Armen ~** to take sb/sth into one's arms

umschlingen* [ʊmˈʃlɪŋ·ən] *vt irreg* ❶ (*eng umfassen*) to embrace; **jdn mit den Armen ~** to wrap one's arms around sb ❷ BOT to climb

um|schulen *vt* ❶ (*für andere Tätigkeit ausbilden*) to retrain (**zu** +*dat* as) ❷ (*auf andere Schule schicken*) to transfer to another school

Umschwung *m* ❶ (*plötzliche Veränderung*) drastic change ❷ SCHWEIZ (*umgebendes Gelände*) surrounding property

um|sehen *vr irreg* ❶ (*in Augenschein nehmen*) ■**sich** *akk* **irgendwo/bei jdm ~** to have a look around somewhere/in sb's home ❷ (*nach hinten blicken*) ■**sich** *akk* **~** to look back ❸ (*suchen*) ■**sich** *akk* **nach jdm/etw ~** to look around for sb/sth

um|setzen [ˈʊm·ze·tsn̩] *vt* ❶ (*an anderen Platz*) to move ❷ (*umwandeln*) to convert (**in** +*akk* into); **etw in die Praxis ~** to put sth [in]to practice ❸ (*verkaufen*) to turn over

umsonst [ʊmˈzɔnst] *adv* ❶ (*gratis*) for free, free of charge ❷ (*vergebens*) in vain; ■**~ sein** to be pointless; **nicht ~** not without reason

Umstand *m* ❶ (*wichtige Tatsache*) fact; **mildernde Umstände** mitigating circumstances; **den Umständen entsprechend** [**gut**] [as good] as can be expected under the circumstances; **unter diesen Umständen** under these circumstances; **unter Umständen** possibly ❷ *pl* (*Schwierigkeiten*) trouble; **bitte keine Umstände!** please don't go to any trouble! ▸WENDUNGEN: **in anderen Umständen sein** to be expecting

umständlich [ˈʊm·ʃtɛnt·lɪç] I. *adj* ❶ (*mit großem Aufwand verbunden*) laborious; *Anweisung, Beschreibung* elaborate; *Aufgabe, Reise* complicated; *Erklärung, Anleitung* long-winded ❷ (*unpraktisch veranlagt*) ■**~ sein** to be awkward II. *adv* ❶ (*weitschweifig*) long-windedly ② (*mühselig und aufwändig*) laboriously

um|steigen *vi irreg sein* ❶ TRANSP to change ② (*überwechseln*) to switch [over] (**auf** +*akk* to)

um|stellen¹ ['ʊm·ʃtɛ·lən] **I.** *vt* ❶ *Möbel* to move ② *die Uhr* ~ to turn the clock back/forward ③ *die Ernährung* ~ to change one's diet **II.** *vi* ■ **auf etw** *akk* ~ to change over to sth **III.** *vr* (*sich anpassen*) ■ **sich** *akk* ~ to adapt (**auf** +*akk* to)

um|stellen*² ['ʊm·ʃtɛ·lən] *vt* (*umringen*) ■ **jdn/etw** ~ to surround sb/sth

Umstellung *f* change (**auf** +*akk* to)

um|stimmen *vt* ■ **jdn** ~ to change sb's mind; ■ **sich** *akk* [**von jdm**] ~ **lassen** to let oneself be persuaded [by sb]

umstritten [ʊm·'ʃtrɪ·tn̩] *adj* controversial

Umsturz *m* coup [d'état]

um|stürzen I. *vi sein* to fall **II.** *vt haben* to knock over *sep; politisches Regime etc.* to overthrow

Umtausch *m* exchange

um|tauschen *vt* to exchange (**in/gegen** +*akk* for); *Währung* to change (**in** +*akk* into)

um|wandeln ['ʊm·van·dl̩n] *vt* to convert (**in** +*akk* into); *wie umgewandelt sein* to be a changed person

Umweg *m* detour

Umwelt ['ʊm·vɛlt] *f kein pl* environment

Umweltbelastung *f* environmental damage

Umweltbewusstseinᴿᴿ *nt kein pl* environmental consciousness

umweltfeindlich *adj* harmful to the environment

umweltfreundlich *adj* environmentally friendly

Umweltgefährdung *f* environmental threat

Umweltpolitik *f* environmental policy

Umweltschäden *pl* environmental damage

Umweltschutz *m* environmental protection

Umweltschützer(in) *m(f)* environmentalist

Umweltverschmutzung *f* pollution

umweltverträglich *adj* environmentally friendly

Umweltzerstörung *f* destruction of the environment

umwerben* [ʊm·'vɛr·bn̩] *vt irreg* to woo

um|werfen *vt irreg* ❶ (*zum Umfallen bringen*) to knock over *sep* ② (*fam: fassungslos machen*) to bowl over *sep* ③ (*zunichtemachen*) *Ordnung, Plan* to upset

um|ziehen* ['ʊm·tsiː·ən] *irreg* **I.** *vi sein* to move [house] **II.** *vr* ■ **sich** *akk* ~ to get changed

Umzug *m* ❶ (*Wohnungswechsel*) move ② (*Parade*) parade

unabhängig ['ʊn·ʔap·hɛ·ŋɪç] *adj* ❶ (*von niemandem abhängig*) independent (**von** +*dat* of/from) ② (*ungeachtet*) ■ ~ **von etw** *dat* regardless of sth; ~ **davon, ob/wann ...** regardless of whether/when ...; ~ **voneinander** separately

Unabhängigkeit *f kein pl a.* POL independence (**von** +*dat* of/from)

unabsichtlich ['ʊn·ʔap·zɪçt·lɪç] **I.** *adj* unintentional; *Beschädigung* accidental **II.** *adv* accidentally

Unachtsamkeit *f* carelessness

unangebracht ['ʊn·ʔan·gə·braxt] *adj* inappropriate

unangemessen ['ʊn·ʔan·gə·mɛ·sn̩] **I.** *adj* ❶ *Preise* unreasonable ② *Verhalten* inappropriate **II.** *adv* unreasonably

unangenehm ['ʊn·ʔan·gə·neːm] **I.** *adj* ❶ (*nicht angenehm*) unpleasant ② (*peinlich*) ■ **jdm ist etw** ~ sb feels bad about sth ③ (*unsympathisch*) unpleasant; **sie kann ganz schön** ~ **werden** she can get quite nasty **II.** *adv* unpleasantly

Unannehmlichkeit ['ʊn·ʔan·neːm·lɪç·kait] *f meist pl* trouble

unanständig ['ʊn·ʔan·ʃtɛn·dɪç] **I.** *adj* ❶ (*obszön*) dirty ② (*rüpelhaft*) rude **II.** *adv* rudely

U

unappetitlich ['ʊn·ʔape·tiːt·lɪç] *adj* ❶ *(nicht appetitlich)* unappetizing ❷ *(ekelhaft)* disgusting

unartig ['ʊn·ʔaːɐ̯·tɪç] *adj* naughty

unauffällig ['ʊn·ʔauf·fɛ·lɪç] I. *adj* discrete II. *adv* discretely

unaufgefordert ['ʊn·ʔauf·gə·fɔr·dɐt] *adv* without having been asked; **~ eingesandte Manuskripte** unsolicited manuscripts

unaufhörlich ['ʊn·ʔauf·ˈhøːɐ̯·lɪç] I. *adj* constant II. *adv* ❶ *(fortwährend)* constantly ❷ *(ununterbrochen)* incessantly

unaufmerksam ['ʊn·ʔauf·mɛrk·zaːm] *adj* ❶ *(nicht aufmerksam)* inattentive ❷ *(nicht zuvorkommend)* thoughtless

Unaufmerksamkeit *f kein pl* ❶ *(unaufmerksames Verhalten)* inattentiveness ❷ *(unzuvorkommende Art)* thoughtlessness

unausgeglichen ['ʊn·ʔaus·gə·glɪ·çn̩] *adj* unbalanced; *Mensch* moody; *Wesensart* uneven

unausstehlich [ʊn·ʔaus·ˈʃteː·lɪç] *adj* intolerable; *Mensch, Art a.* insufferable

unausweichlich [ʊn·ʔaus·ˈvaiç·lɪç] I. *adj* inevitable II. *adv* inevitably

unbarmherzig ['ʊn·barm·ˈhɛr·tsɪç] I. *adj* merciless II. *adv* mercilessly

unbeabsichtigt I. *adj* ❶ *(versehentlich)* accidental ❷ *(nicht beabsichtigt)* unintentional II. *adv* accidentally

unbedenklich ['ʊn·bə·dɛŋk·lɪç] I. *adj* harmless; *Situation, Vorhaben* acceptable II. *adv* quite safely

unbedeutend ['ʊn·bə·dɔy·tn̩t] I. *adj* ❶ *(nicht bedeutend)* insignificant ❷ *(geringfügig)* minimal; *Änderung* minor II. *adv* insignificantly

unbedingt ['ʊn·bə·dɪŋt] I. *adj attr* absolute II. *adv (auf jeden Fall)* really; **erinnere mich ~ daran, sie anzurufen** [whatever you do,] don't forget to remind me to call her; **nicht ~** not necessarily; **~!** absolutely!

unbefangen ['ʊn·bə·faŋ·ən] I. *adj* ❶ *(unvoreingenommen)* objective; *Ansicht* unbiased ❷ *(nicht gehemmt)*

uninhibited II. *adv* ❶ *(unvoreingenommen)* objectively ❷ *(nicht gehemmt)* uninhibitedly

unbefriedigend ['ʊn·bə·friː·dɪ·gnt] I. *adj* unsatisfactory II. *adv* in an unsatisfactory way

unbefristet ['ʊn·bə·frɪs·tət] I. *adj* lasting for an indefinite period; *Aufenthaltserlaubnis, Visum* permanent; ■ **~ sein** to be [valid] for an indefinite period II. *adv* indefinitely

unbefugt ['ʊn·bə·fuːkt] I. *adj* unauthorized II. *adv* without authorization

unbegrenzt ['ʊn·bə·grɛntst] I. *adj* unlimited; *Vertrauen* boundless II. *adv* indefinitely

unbegründet ['ʊn·bə·grʏn·dət] *adj* ❶ *(grundlos)* unfounded; *Kritik, Maßnahme* unwarranted ❷ JUR unfounded

unbehaglich ['ʊn·bə·haːk·lɪç] I. *adj* uneasy II. *adv* uneasily

unbeholfen ['ʊn·bə·hɔl·fn̩] I. *adj* ❶ *(schwerfällig)* clumsy; ❷ *(wenig gewandt)* awkward II. *adv* clumsily

unbekannt ['ʊn·bə·kant] *adj* unknown; ■ **jdm ~ sein** to be unknown to sb; *Gesicht, Name, Wort* to be unfamiliar to sb; „**~ verzogen**" "moved — address unknown"

Unbekannte(r) *f(m)* stranger

unbekümmert ['ʊn·bə·kʏ·mɐt] I. *adj* carefree II. *adv* in a carefree manner

unbelastet ['ʊn·bəlas·tət] I. *adj* ❶ *(frei)* free (**von** +*dat* of) ❷ FIN unencumbered II. *adv* freely

unbeliebt ['ʊn·bəliːpt] *adj* unpopular

unbenutzt ['ʊn·bə·nʊtst] *adj* unused; *Bett* not slept in *pred; Kleidung* unworn

unbeobachtet ['ʊn·bə·ʔoːbax·tət] *adj* unnoticed; *Gebäude, Platz* unwatched

unbequem ['ʊn·bə·kveːm] I. *adj* ❶ *Stuhl, Sofa* uncomfortable ❷ *Frage* awkward II. *adv* ❶ *(nicht bequem)* uncomfortably ❷ *(lästig)* awkwardly

unberechenbar [ʊn·bə·ˈrɛ·çn̩·baːɐ̯] *adj* ❶ *(nicht einschätzbar)* Gegner, Mensch unpredictable ❷ *(nicht vorhersehbar)* unforeseeable

unberührt ['ʊn·bə·ry·ɐ̯t] *adj* ❶ *(im*

Naturzustand erhalten) unspoiled ❷ (*nicht benutzt*) untouched

unbeschädigt *adj, adv* undamaged

unbeschränkt ['ʊn·bə·ʃrɛŋkt] *adj* unrestricted; *Macht* limitless; *Möglichkeiten* unlimited

unbeschreiblich ['ʊn·bɛ·ʃraip·lɪç] I. *adj* ❶ (*maßlos*) tremendous ❷ (*nicht zu beschreiben*) indescribable II. *adv* **sich** *akk* ~ **ärgern/freuen** to be terribly angry/enormously happy

unbeschwert ['ʊn·bə·ʃveːɐ̯t] *adj* carefree

unbesiegbar [ʊn·bə·ˈziːk·baːɐ̯] *adj* ❶ MIL (*a. fig*) invincible ❷ SPORT unbeatable

unbesorgt [ʊn·bə·zɔrkt] I. *adj* unconcerned; **sei/seinen Sie ~!** don't worry! II. *adv* without worrying; **die Pilze kannst du ~ essen** you needn't worry about eating the mushrooms

unbeständig ['ʊn·bə·ʃtɛn·dɪç] *adj* ❶ METEO unsettled ❷ (*wankelmütig*) fickle

unbestechlich ['ʊn·bɛ·ʃtɛç·lɪç] *adj* ❶ (*nicht bestechlich*) incorruptible ❷ (*nicht zu täuschen*) unerring

unbestimmt ['ʊn·bɛ·ʃtɪmt] *adj* ❶ (*unklar*) vague ❷ (*nicht festlegbar*) indefinite; *Alter* uncertain; *Anzahl, Menge* indeterminate; *Grund, Zeitspanne* unspecified

unbestritten ['ʊn·bɛ·ʃtrɪ·tn̩] I. *adj* ❶ (*nicht bestritten*) undisputed; *Argument* irrefutable ❷ JUR uncontested II. *adv* ❶ (*wie nicht bestritten wird*) unquestionably ❷ (*unstreitig*) unarguably

unbeteiligt ['ʊn·bə·tai·lɪçt] *adj* ❶ (*an etw nicht beteiligt*) uninvolved ❷ (*desinteressiert*) indifferent; (*in einem Gespräch*) uninterested

unbeweglich ['ʊn·bɛ·veːk·lɪç] *adj* ❶ (*starr*) fixed; *Konstruktion, Teil* immovable ❷ (*unveränderlich*) inflexible; *Gesichtsausdruck* rigid; (*fig*) unmoved

unbewohnt *adj* ❶ (*nicht besiedelt*) uninhabited ❷ (*nicht bewohnt*) unoccupied

unbewusstᴿᴿ ['ʊn·bə·vʊst] I. *adj* unconscious II. *adv* unconsciously

unbezahlbar [ʊn·bə·ˈtsaːl·baːɐ̯] *adj* ❶ (*nicht aufzubringen*) unaffordable ❷ (*äußerst nützlich*) invaluable ❸ (*immens wertvoll*) priceless

unblutig ['ʊn·bluː·tɪç] I. *adj* bloodless II. *adv* without bloodshed

unbrauchbar ['ʊn·braux·baːɐ̯] *adj* useless

und [ʊnt] *konj* and; ~ **dann?** then what?; (*nun*) well?; **na ~?** so what?

undankbar ['ʊn·daŋk·baːɐ̯] *adj* ❶ (*nicht dankbar*) ungrateful ❷ (*nicht lohnend*) thankless

undenkbar [ʊn·ˈdɛŋk·baːɐ̯] *adj* unthinkable

undeutlich ['ʊn·dɔyt·lɪç] I. *adj* indistinct; *Schrift* illegible II. *adv* ~ **sprechen** to mumble

undicht ['ʊn·dɪçt] *adj* (*luftdurchlässig*) not airtight; (*wasserdurchlässig*) not watertight

Unding ['ʊn·dɪŋ] *nt kein pl* **ein ~ sein|, etw zu tun|** to be absurd [to do sth]

undurchsichtig ['ʊn·dʊrç·zɪç·tɪç] *adj* ❶ (*nicht transparent*) nontransparent; *Glas* opaque ❷ (*fig*) *Geschäfte* shadowy; *Motive* obscure

uneben ['ʊn·ʔeːbn̩] *adj* uneven; *Straße* bumpy

unecht ['ʊn·ʔɛçt] *adj* ❶ (*imitiert*) fake *usu pej*; *Haar* artificial; *Zähne* false ❷ (*unaufrichtig*) false

unehelich ['ʊn·ʔeːə·lɪç] *adj Kind* illegitimate

uneigennützig ['ʊn·ʔai·ɡn̩·nʏ·tsɪç] *adj* selfless

uneingeschränkt ['ʊn·ʔain·ɡə·ʃrɛŋkt] I. *adj* absolute; *Handel* free; *Lob* unreserved II. *adv* absolutely, unreservedly

unempfindlich ['ʊn·ʔɛmp·fɪnt·lɪç] *adj* insensitive (**gegen** +*akk* to); (*durch Erfahrung*) hardened, seasoned; *Pflanze* hardy; *Material* practical

unendlich [ʊn·ˈʔɛnt·lɪç] *adj* ❶ (*nicht überschaubar*) infinite ❷ (*unbegrenzt*) endless

Unendlichkeit <-> *f kein pl* infinity

U

unentbehrlich ['ʊnˈʔɛntˌbeːɐ̯ˌlɪç] *adj* ❶ (*unbedingt erforderlich*) essential ❷ (*unverzichtbar*) indispensable

unentgeltlich ['ʊnˈʔɛntˌgɛltˌlɪç] **I.** *adj* free of charge; **die ~e Benutzung von etw** *dat* the free use of sth **II.** *adv* for free

unentschieden ['ʊnˈʔɛntˌʃiːdn̩] **I.** *adj* ❶ SPORT tied ❷ (*noch nicht entschieden*) undecided **II.** *adv* SPORT **~ ausgehen** to end in a tie; **~ spielen** to tie

Unentschieden <-s, -> ['ʊnˈʔɛntˌʃiːdn̩] *nt* SPORT tie

Unentschlossenheit *f* indecision

unerbittlich [ʊnˈʔɛɐ̯ˈbɪtˌlɪç] *adj* ❶ (*nicht umzustimmen*) unrelenting ❷ (*gnadenlos*) merciless

unerfahren [ʊnˈʔɛɐ̯ˈfaːˌrən] *adj* inexperienced

unerfreulich [ʊnˈʔɛɐ̯ˈfrɔɪˌlɪç] **I.** *adj* unpleasant; *Neuigkeiten, Nachrichten* bad; *Zwischenfall* unfortunate **II.** *adv* unpleasantly

unergründbar [ʊnˈʔɛɐ̯ˈgrʏntˌbaːɐ̯], **unergründlich** [ʊnˈʔɛɐ̯ˈgrʏntˌlɪç] *adj* puzzling; *Blick, Lächeln* enigmatic

unerhört ['ʊnˈɛɐ̯ˈhøːɐ̯t] *adj attr* ❶ (*pej: skandalös*) outrageous ❷ (*außerordentlich*) incredible

unerklärbar [ʊnˈʔɛɐ̯ˈklɛːɐ̯ˌbaːɐ̯], **unerklärlich** [ʊnˈʔɛɐ̯ˈklɛːɐ̯ˌlɪç] *adj* inexplicable; ▪**jdm ist ~, warum/wie ...** sb cannot understand why/how ...

unerlaubt ['ʊnˈʔɛɐ̯ˌlaupt] **I.** *adj* unauthorized; JUR illegal **II.** *adv* without permission

unermüdlich [ʊnˈʔɛɐ̯ˈmyːtˌlɪç] **I.** *adj* tireless **II.** *adv* tirelessly

unerreichbar [ʊnˈʔɛɐ̯ˈraɪçˌbaːɐ̯] *adj* unattainable; (*telefonisch*) unavailable

unersättlich [ʊnˈʔɛɐ̯ˈzɛtˌlɪç] *adj* insatiable; *Wissensdurst* unquenchable

unerschütterlich [ʊnˈʔɛɐ̯ˈʃʏtɐˌlɪç] **I.** *adj* unshakable **II.** *adv* unshakably

unerschwinglich [ʊnˈʔɛɐ̯ˈʃvɪŋˌlɪç] *adj* exorbitant; ▪**für jdn ~ sein** to be beyond sb's means

unersetzlich [ʊnˈʔɛɐ̯ˈzɛtsˌlɪç] *adj* indispensable; *Wertgegenstand* irreplaceable; *Schaden* irreparable

unerträglich [ʊnˈʔɛɐ̯ˈtrɛːkˌlɪç] **I.** *adj* ❶ (*nicht auszuhalten*) *Lärm, Schmerzen* unbearable ❷ (*pej*) *Mensch* impossible **II.** *adv* (*nicht auszuhalten*) unbearably

unerwartet ['ʊnˈʔɛɐ̯varˌtət] **I.** *adj* unexpected **II.** *adv* unexpectedly

unerwünscht ['ʊnˈʔɛɐ̯vʏnʃt] *adj* ❶ (*nicht willkommen*) unwelcome ❷ (*lästig*) undesirable

unfähig ['ʊnˈfɛːɪç] *adj* ❶ (*inkompetent*) incompetent ❷ (*nicht imstande*) incapable (**zu** +*dat* of)

unfair ['ʊnˈfɛːɐ̯] **I.** *adj* unfair (**gegenüber** +*dat* to) **II.** *adv* unfairly

Unfall ['ʊnˌfal] *m* accident

Unfallflucht *f* leaving the scene of an accident, hit-and-run

Unfallversicherung *f* accident insurance

unfassbar^{RR}, **unfaßbar**^{ALT} [ʊnˈfasˌbaːɐ̯], **unfasslich**^{RR}, **unfaßlich**^{ALT} [ʊnˈfasˌlɪç] *adj* ❶ (*unbegreiflich*) incomprehensible; *Phänomen* incredible ❷ (*unerhört*) outrageous

unfehlbar [ʊnˈfeːlˌbaːɐ̯] **I.** *adj* infallible; *Geschmack* impeccable; *Gespür, Instinkt* unerring **II.** *adv* without fail

unförmig ['ʊnˌfœrˌmɪç] **I.** *adj* shapeless; (*groß*) cumbersome; *Gesicht* misshapen; *Bein* unshapely **II.** *adv* shapelessly

unfreiwillig ['ʊnˌfraɪˌvɪˌlɪç] **I.** *adj* ❶ (*gezwungen*) compulsory ❷ (*unbeabsichtigt*) unintentional **II.** *adv* ▪**etw ~ tun** to be forced to do sth

unfreundlich ['ʊnˌfrɔʏntˌlɪç] **I.** *adj* ❶ (*nicht liebenswürdig*) unfriendly ❷ (*unangenehm*) unpleasant; *Klima* inhospitable; *Jahreszeit, Tag* dreary; *Raum* cheerless **II.** *adv* **jdn ~ behandeln** to be unfriendly to sb

unfruchtbar ['ʊnˌfrʊxtˌbaːɐ̯] *adj* MED infertile; (*agr a.*) barren

Unfruchtbarkeit *f kein pl* ❶ MED infertility ❷ AGR barrenness

Unfug <-s> ['ʊnˌfuːk] *m kein pl* nonsense; **~ machen** to be up to no good

Ungar(in) <-n, -n> ['ʊŋ·gar] *m(f)* Hungarian; *s. a.* **Deutsche(r)**

ungarisch ['ʊŋ·ga·rɪʃ] *adj* Hungarian; *s. a.* **deutsch**

Ungarn <-s> ['ʊŋ·garn] *nt* Hungary; *s. a.* **Deutschland**

ungebeten ['ʊn·gə·be:·tn̩] I. *adj* unwelcome II. *adv* ① (*ohne eingeladen zu sein*) without being invited ② (*ohne aufgefordert zu sein*) without an invitation

ungebildet ['ʊn·gə·bɪl·dət] *adj* uneducated

ungeboren ['ʊn·gəbo:·rən] *adj* unborn

ungebräuchlich ['ʊn·gə·brɔyç·lɪç] *adj* uncommon, not in use *pred*

ungebunden ['ʊn·gə·bʊn·dn̩] *adj* unattached

Ungeduld ['ʊn·gə·dʊlt] *f* impatience

ungeduldig ['ʊn·gə·dʊl·dɪç] I. *adj* impatient II. *adv* impatiently

ungeeignet ['ʊn·gə·ʔaig·nət] *adj* unsuitable (**für** +*akk* for/to)

ungefähr ['ʊn·gə·fɛːɐ̯] I. *adv* ① (*zirka*) approximately, about *fam*; **um ~ … Zeit** at around … ② (*etwa*) **~ da/hier** around there/here; **~ so** something like this/that ③ (*in etwa*) more or less II. *adj attr* approximate

ungefährlich ['ʊn·gəfɛːɐ̯·lɪç] *adj* harmless; ■ **~ sein, etw zu tun** to be safe to do sth

ungeheuer ['ʊn·gə·hɔy·ɐ] I. *adj* ① (*ein gewaltiges Ausmaß besitzend*) enormous ② (*größte Intensität, Bedeutung besitzend*) tremendous II. *adv* ① (*äußerst*) terribly ② (*ganz besonders*) enormously

Ungeheuer <-s, -> ['ʊn·gə·hɔy·ɐ] *nt* monster

ungehindert ['ʊn·gə·hɪn·dɐt] I. *adj* unhindered II. *adv* without hindrance

ungehorsam ['ʊn·gə·ho:ɐ̯·za:m] *adj* disobedient (**gegenüber** +*dat* toward)

Ungehorsam ['ʊn·gə·ho:ɐ̯·za:m] *m* disobedience

ungeklärt ['ʊn·gəklɛːɐ̯t] *adj, adv* ① (*nicht aufgeklärt*) unsolved ② *Abwässer* untreated

ungelegen ['ʊn·gə·le:·gn̩] *adj* inconvenient; [**jdm**] **~ kommen** to be inconvenient [for sb]; (*zeitlich*) to be an inconvenient time [for sb]

ungelernt ['ʊn·gə·lɛrnt] *adj attr* unskilled

ungemütlich ['ʊn·gə·my:t·lɪç] *adj* ① (*nicht gemütlich*) uninviting ② (*unerfreulich*) uncomfortable ▶ WENDUNGEN: **~ werden** (*fam*) to become nasty

ungenau ['ʊn·gə·nau] I. *adj* ① (*nicht exakt*) vague ② (*nicht korrekt*) inaccurate II. *adv* ① (*nicht exakt*) vaguely ② (*nicht korrekt*) incorrectly

Ungenauigkeit <-, -en> *f* inaccuracy

ungenießbar ['ʊn·gə·ni:s·ba:ɐ] *adj* ① (*nicht zum Genuss geeignet*) inedible; *Getränke* undrinkable ② (*schlecht schmeckend*) unpalatable ③ (*fam: unausstehlich*) unbearable

ungenügend ['ʊn·gə·ny:·gn̩t] I. *adj* ① (*nicht ausreichend*) insufficient; *Information* inadequate ② SCH unsatisfactory, ≈ F II. *adv* insufficiently, inadequately

ungenutzt ['ʊn·gə·nʊtst] *adj* unused; *materielle/personelle Ressourcen* unexploited; *Gelegenheit* missed

ungepflegt ['ʊn·gə·pfle:kt] *adj* Haus, Garten neglected; *Person* unkempt

ungerade ['ʊn·gə·ra:·də] *adj* odd

ungerecht ['ʊn·gə·rɛçt] I. *adj* unjust; ■ **~ sein** to be unfair (**gegen** +*akk* to) II. *adv* unjustly, unfairly

Ungerechtigkeit <-, -en> *f* injustice

ungern ['ʊn·gɛrn] *adv* reluctantly

ungeschickt ['ʊn·gə·ʃɪkt] *adj* ① (*unbeholfen*) clumsy; (*unbedacht*) careless ② DIAL, SÜDD (*unhandlich*) unwieldy; (*ungelegen*) awkward

ungeschoren ['ʊn·gə·ʃo:·rən] I. *adj* unshorn II. *adv* unscathed; **~ davonkommen** to get away with it

ungesetzlich ['ʊn·gə·zɛts·lɪç] *adj* unlawful

ungestört ['ʊn·gə·ʃtø:ɐ̯t] I. *adj* undisturbed; **~ sein wollen** to want to be left alone II. *adv* without being disturbed

U

ungestraft ['ʊn·gə·ʃtra:ft] *adv* with impunity; ~ **davonkommen** to get away scot-free

ungestüm ['ʊn·gə·ʃty:m] I. *adj* *Art, Temperament* enthusiastic; *Begrüßung* enthusiastic II. *adv* enthusiastically

ungesund ['ʊn·gə·zʊnt] I. *adj* unhealthy II. *adv* unhealthily

ungeübt ['ʊn·gə·ʔy:pt] *adj* unpracticed; *Lehrlinge* inexperienced; ■ **in etw** *dat* ~ **sein** to lack experience in sth

ungewissRR ['ʊn·gə·vɪs] *adj* uncertain

UngewissheitRR <-, -en> *f* uncertainty

ungewöhnlich ['ʊn·gə·vø:n·lɪç] I. *adj* ① *(vom Üblichen abweichend)* unusual ② *(außergewöhnlich)* remarkable II. *adv* ① *(äußerst)* exceptionally ② *(in nicht üblicher Weise)* unusually

ungewohnt ['ʊn·gə·vo:nt] *adj* unusual

ungewollt ['ʊn·gə·vɔlt] I. *adj* unintentional; *Schwangerschaft* unwanted II. *adv* unintentionally; **ich musste ~ grinsen** I couldn't help grinning

Ungeziefer <-s> ['ʊn·gə·tsi:·fɐ] *nt kein pl* pests *pl*

ungezogen ['ʊn·gə·tso:·gn̩] I. *adj Kind* naughty II. *adv* impertinently; **sich** *akk* ~ **benehmen** to behave badly

ungezwungen ['ʊn·gə·tsvʊŋən] *adj* informal

ungläubig ['ʊn·glɔy·bɪç] *adj* ① *(etw nicht glauben wollend)* disbelieving; **ein ~es Kopfschütteln** an incredulous shake of the head ② REL unbelieving

unglaublich ['ʊn·glaup·lɪç] I. *adj* ① *(nicht glaubhaft)* unbelievable ② *(unerhört)* outrageous II. *adv* *(fam: überaus)* incredibly

unglaubwürdig ['ʊn·glaup·vyr·dɪç] I. *adj* implausible; *Zeuge* unreliable II. *adv* implausibly

ungleich ['ʊn·glaɪç] I. *adj* unequal; *Belastung* uneven; *Paar* odd; *Gegenstände* dissimilar II. *adv* ① *(unterschiedlich)* unequally ② *vor komp (weitaus)* far III. *präp* +*dat (geh)* unlike

ungleichmäßig I. *adj* ① *(unregelmäßig)* irregular ② *(nicht zu gleichen Teilen)* uneven II. *adv* ① *(unregelmäßig)* irregularly ② *(ungleich)* unevenly

Unglück <-glücke> ['ʊn·glʏk] *nt* ① *(Pech)* bad luck; **zu allem ~** to make matters worse ② *(katastrophales Ereignis)* disaster ③ *kein pl (Elend)* unhappiness ▸WENDUNGEN: **ein ~ kommt selten allein** *(prov)* when it rains it pours

unglücklich ['ʊn·glʏk·lɪç] I. *adj* ① *(betrübt)* unhappy ② *(ungünstig, ungeschickt)* unfortunate II. *adv* unfortunately; ~ **verliebt sein** to be lovelorn

unglücklicherweise *adv* unfortunately

Unglücksfall *m* ① *(Unfall)* accident ② *(unglückliche Begebenheit)* mishap

ungültig ['ʊn·gʏl·tɪç] *adj* ① *(nicht mehr gültig)* invalid; *Tor, Treffer* disallowed ② *(nichtig)* [null and] void

ungünstig ['ʊn·gʏns·tɪç] *adj Zeit[punkt]* inconvenient; *Wetter* inclement

ungut ['ʊn·gu:t] *adj* bad; *Verhältnis* strained ▸WENDUNGEN: **nichts für ~!** no offense!

unhandlich ['ʊn·hant·lɪç] *adj* unwieldy

Unheil ['ʊn·haɪl] *nt* disaster; **großes ~ anrichten** to wreak havoc

unheilbar ['ʊn·haɪl·ba:ɐ] I. *adj* incurable II. *adv* incurably

unheimlich ['ʊn·haɪm·lɪç] I. *adj* ① *(Grauen erregend)* eerie ② *(fam: unglaublich, sehr)* incredible ③ *(fam: sehr groß, sehr viel)* terrific *fig* II. *adv* *(fam)* incredibly

unhöflich ['ʊn·hø:f·lɪç] I. *adj* impolite II. *adv* impolitely

unhygienisch ['ʊn·hy·gie:·nɪʃ] *adj* unhygienic

Uniform <-, -en> [uni·'fɔrm, 'uni·fɔrm] *f* uniform

Universität <-, -en> [uni·vɛr·zi·'tɛ:t] *f* university

Universum <-s, Universen> [uni·'vɛr·zʊm] *nt* universe

unkenntlich ['ʊn·kɛnt·lɪç] *adj* unrecognizable; *Eintragung* indecipherable

Unkenntnis ['ʊn·kɛnt·nɪs] *f kein pl* ignorance

unklar ['ʊn·kla:ɐ] I. *adj* ① *(unverständ-*

lich) unclear ②(*ungeklärt*) unclear; [**sich** *dat*] **im U~en sein** to be uncertain (**über** +*akk* about); **jdn im U~en lassen** to leave sb in the dark (**über** +*akk* about) ③(*verschwommen*) indistinct; *Wetter* hazy; *Umrisse* blurred; *Erinnerungen* vague II.*adv* (*unverständlich*) unclearly

Unklarheit <-, -en> *f* ① *kein pl* (*Ungewissheit*) uncertainty ②(*Undeutlichkeit*) lack of clarity

unklug ['ʊn·kluːk] *adj* unwise

unkompliziert ['ʊn·kɔmp·li·tsiːɐ̯t] *adj* straightforward; *Fall* simple; *Mensch* uncomplicated

unkonzentriert ['ʊn·kɔn·tsɛn·triːɐ̯t] *adj* distracted

Unkosten ['ʊn·kɔs·tn̩] *pl* costs *npl*

Unkraut ['ʊn·kraʊt] *nt* weed

unkündbar ['ʊn·kʏnt·baːɐ̯] *adj Stellung* tenured; *Vertrag* not subject to termination

unleserlich ['ʊn·leː·ze·lɪç] I.*adj Schrift* illegible II.*adv* illegibly

unlogisch I.*adj* illogical II.*adv* illogically

unlöslich [ʊn·ˈløːs·lɪç] I.*adj* ①(*nicht zu lösen*) *Problem* unsolvable; *Widerspruch* irreconcilable ② CHEM insoluble II.*adv* (*untrennbar*) indissolubly

Unlust ['ʊn·lʊst] *f kein pl* reluctance

unmäßig ['ʊn·mɛː·sɪç] I.*adj* excessive II.*adv* excessively

unmenschlich ['ʊn·mɛnʃ·lɪç] I.*adj* ① *Bedingungen, Verhältnisse* appalling, inhuman[e]; *Diktator, Grausamkeit* brutal ②*Hitze, Leid* tremendous II.*adv* ①(*grausam*) in an inhuman[e] manner ②(*entsetzlich*) appallingly

unmerklich ['ʊn·mɛrk·lɪç] I.*adj* imperceptible II.*adv* imperceptibly

unmissverständlichRR ['ʊn·mɪs·fɛg·ʃtɛnt·lɪç] I.*adj* unequivocal; *Antwort* blunt II.*adv* unequivocally

unmittelbar ['ʊn·mɪ·t]·baːɐ̯] I.*adj* direct; **in ~er Nähe von etw** in the immediate vicinity of sth II.*adv* ①(*sofort*) immediately ②(*ohne Umweg*) directly

unmöglich ['ʊn·møː·k·lɪç] I.*adj* ①(*nicht machbar*) impossible; *Vorhaben* infeasible ②(*pej fam: nicht tragbar, lächerlich*) impossible II.*adv* (*fam*) not possibly

unmoralisch ['ʊn·mo·raː·lɪʃ] *adj* immoral

unmündig ['ʊn·mʏn·dɪç] *adj* ①(*noch nicht volljährig*) underage ②(*geistig unselbstständig*) dependent

unmusikalisch ['ʊn·mu·zi·kaː·lɪʃ] *adj* unmusical

unnachahmlich ['ʊn·naːx·ʔaːm·lɪç] *adj* inimitable

unnachgiebig ['ʊn·naːx·giː·bɪç] I.*adj* adamant II.*adv* adamantly

unnahbar [ʊn·ˈnaː·baːɐ̯] *adj* unapproachable

unnatürlich ['ʊn·na·tyːɐ̯·lɪç] *adj* ①(*nicht natürlich*) unnatural; (*abnorm*) abnormal ②(*gekünstelt*) artificial

unnötig ['ʊn·nøː·tɪç] *adj* unnecessary

unordentlich ['ʊn·ʔɔr·dnt·lɪç] I.*adj* messy; *Schrift* sloppy II.*adv* messily; *schreiben* sloppily; **~ arbeiten** to work carelessly

Unordnung ['ʊn·ʔɔrd·nʊŋ] *f kein pl* mess

unparteiisch ['ʊn·par·taiˀɪʃ] I.*adj* impartial II.*adv* impartially

unpassend ['ʊn·pa·snt] *adj* ①(*unangebracht*) inappropriate ②(*ungelegen*) inconvenient; *Augenblick* inopportune

unpersönlich ['ʊn·pɛr·zøːn·lɪç] *adj* ①(*distanziert*) *Mensch* distant; *Gespräch, Art* impersonal ② LING impersonal

unpraktisch ['ʊn·prak·tɪʃ] *adj* ①(*nicht handwerklich veranlagt*) unpractical ②(*nicht praxisgerecht*) impractical

unpünktlich ['ʊn·pʏŋkt·lɪç] I.*adj* ①(*generell nicht pünktlich*) unpunctual ②(*verspätet*) late II.*adv* late

Unrecht ['ʊn·rɛçt] *nt kein pl* ①(*unrechte Handlung*) wrong; **jdm ein ~ antun** to do sb an injustice ②(*dem Recht entgegengesetztes Prinzip*) **im ~ sein** to be [in the] wrong; **zu ~** wrongly

U

unrechtmäßig ['ʊn·rɛçt·mɛː·sɪç] I. *adj* illegal II. *adv* illegally

unregelmäßig ['ʊn·reː·gl·mɛː·sɪç] I. *adj* irregular II. *adv* irregularly

unreif ['ʊn·raif] *adj* ① AGR, HORT unripe, green ② *Person* immature

Unruhe ['ʊn·ruːə] *f* ① (*Ruhelosigkeit*) restlessness ② (*ständige Bewegung*) agitation ③ (*erregte Stimmung*) agitation; ~ **stiften** to cause trouble ④ (*Aufstand*) ■ ~**n** *pl* riots *pl*

unruhig ['ʊn·ruː·ɪç] I. *adj* ① (*ständig gestört*) restless; *Zeit* troubled; (*ungleichmäßig*) uneven; *Herzschlag* irregular ② (*laut*) noisy ③ (*ruhelos*) agitated; *Leben* eventful; *Geist* restless; *Schlaf* fitful II. *adv* ① (*ruhelos*) anxiously ② (*unter ständigen Störungen*) restlessly

uns [ʊns] I. *pron pers* ① *dat von* **wir** [to/for] us; ■ **bei** ~ at our house ② *akk von* **wir** us II. *pron refl* ① *akk o dat von* **wir** ourselves ② (*einander*) each other

unsachgemäß ['ʊn·zax·gə·mɛːs] I. *adj* improper II. *adv* improperly

unsanft ['ʊn·zanft] I. *adj* rough; *Erwachen* rude II. *adv* roughly

unsauber ['ʊn·zau·bɐ] I. *adj* ① (*schmutzig*) dirty ② (*unordentlich*, *nachlässig*) careless; (*unpräzise*) unclear II. *adv* carelessly

unschädlich ['ʊn·ʃɛːt·lɪç] *adj* harmless

unscharf ['ʊn·ʃarf] I. *adj* ① (*ohne klare Konturen*) blurred ② (*nicht scharf*) out of focus ③ (*nicht präzise*) imprecise II. *adv* ① (*nicht präzise*) out of focus ② (*nicht exakt*) imprecisely

unscheinbar ['ʊn·ʃain·baːɐ̯] *adj* inconspicuous

unschlagbar [ʊn·'ʃlaːk·baːɐ̯] *adj* unbeatable (**in** + *dat* at)

unschlüssig ['ʊn·ʃlʏ·sɪç] *adj* indecisive

Unschuld ['ʊn·ʃʊlt] *f* ① (*Schuldlosigkeit*) innocence ② (*Reinheit*) purity; (*Naivität*) innocence ③ (*veraltend*: *Jungfräulichkeit*) virginity

unschuldig ['ʊn·ʃʊl·dɪç] I. *adj* innocent II. *adv* ① JUR despite sb's/one's innocence ② (*arglos*) innocently

unselbständig ['ʊn·zɛlp·ʃtɛn·dɪç], **unselbstständig**ᴿᴿ ['ʊn·zɛlp·ʃtʃtɛn·dɪç] *adj* dependent [on others]

unser ['ʊn·zɐ] I. *pron poss, adjektivisch* our II. *pron pers gen von* **wir** (*geh*) of us

unsere(r, s) ['ʊn·zə·rə, -zərə, -zə·rəs] *pron poss, substantivisch* (*geh*) ours

unseresgleichen ['ʊn·zes·'glai·çn̩] *pron* people *npl* like us

unsicher ['ʊn·zɪ·çɐ] I. *adj* ① (*gefährlich*) unsafe; *Gegend* dangerous ② (*gefährdet*) insecure, at risk *pred* ③ (*nicht selbstsicher*) unsure; *Blick* uncertain ④ (*unerfahren, ungeübt*) **sich** *akk* ~ **fühlen** to feel unsure of oneself ⑤ (*schwankend*) unsteady; *Hand* shaky ⑥ (*ungewiss*) uncertain ⑦ (*nicht verlässlich*) unreliable *fam* II. *adv* ① (*schwankend*) unsteadily ② (*nicht selbstsicher*) ~ **fahren** to drive with little confidence

Unsicherheit *f* ① *kein pl* (*mangelnde Selbstsicherheit*) insecurity ② *kein pl* (*mangelnde Verlässlichkeit*) unreliability ③ *kein pl* (*Ungewissheit*) uncertainty ④ (*Gefährlichkeit*) dangers *pl* ⑤ *meist pl* (*Unwägbarkeit*) uncertainty

Unsinn ['ʊn·zɪn] *m kein pl* nonsense; ~ **machen** to mess around

unsinnig ['ʊn·zɪ·nɪç] I. *adj* ridiculous II. *adv* (*fam: unerhört*) terribly

unsittlich ['ʊn·zɪt·lɪç] I. *adj* indecent II. *adv* indecently

unsozial ['ʊn·zo·tsi̯aːl] I. *adj* antisocial II. *adv* antisocially

unsportlich ['ʊn·ʃpɔrt·lɪç] I. *adj* ① *Person* unathletic ② (*nicht fair*) unsportsmanlike II. *adv* (*nicht fair*) **sich** *akk* ~ **verhalten** to behave in an unsportsmanlike way

unsterblich ['ʊn·ʃtɛrp·lɪç] I. *adj* ① (*ewig lebend*) immortal ② (*unvergänglich*) *Liebe* undying II. *adv* (*fam: über alle Maßen*) incredibly

Unsterblichkeit <-> *f kein pl* immortality

unsympathisch ['ʊn·zym·paː·tɪʃ] *adj* unpleasant

untätig ['ʊn·tɛ:·tɪç] I. *adj* idle II. *adv* idly

untauglich ['ʊn·tauk·lɪç] *adj* unsuitable; MIL unfit

unteilbar [ʊn·'tail·baːɐ̯] *adj* indivisible

unten ['ʊn·tn̩] *adv* ❶ (*an einer tieferen Stelle*) down; **dort ~** down there; **weiter ~** farther down; **ich habe die Bücher ~ ins Regal gelegt** I put the books down below on the shelf; **~ links/rechts** on the bottom left/right ❷ (*Unterseite*) bottom ❸ (*in einem tieferen Stockwerk*) downstairs; **der Aufzug fährt nach ~** the elevator is going down ❹ (*in sozial niedriger Position*) bottom ❺ (*hinten im Text*) **siehe ~** see below ❻ (*am hinteren Ende*) at the bottom

unter ['ʊn·tɐ] I. *präp* ❶ +*dat* (*unterhalb von etw*) under, underneath; **~ freiem Himmel** outdoors ❷ +*akk* (*unterhalb von etw*) under; **sich** *akk* **~ einen Baum stellen** to stand under a tree ❸ +*dat* (*weniger, niedriger*) less; **~ dem Durchschnitt liegen** to be below average ❹ +*dat* (*zwischen*) among[st]; (*von*) among; **~ uns gesagt** between you and me; **~ anderem** among other things ❺ +*dat* (*begleitet von, hervorgerufen durch*) under; **~ Zwang** under duress; **~ Lebensgefahr** at risk to one's life; **~ der Bedingung, dass ...** on the condition that ...; **~ Umständen** possibly ❻ +*dat* (*in einem Zustand*) under; **~ Druck stehen** to be under pressure; **~ einer Krankheit leiden** to suffer from an illness ❼ +*dat* SÜDD (*während*) during; **~ der Woche** during the week II. *adv* ❶ (*jünger als*) under ❷ (*weniger als*) less than

Unterarm ['ʊn·tɐ·ʔarm] *m* forearm

Unterbewusstsein[RR] ['ʊn·tɐ·bə·vʊst·zain] *nt* ■**das/jds ~** the/sb's subconscious; **im ~** subconsciously

unterbrechen* [ʊn·tɐ·'brɛ·çn̩] *vt irreg* ❶ (*vorübergehend beenden*) to interrupt ❷ (*räumlich auflockern*) to break up *sep*

unter|bringen *vt irreg* ❶ (*Unterkunft verschaffen*) ■**jdn ~** to put sb up; **die Kinder sind gut untergebracht** the children are being well looked after ❷ (*abstellen*) ■**etw ~** to put sth somewhere ❸ (*fam: eine Anstellung verschaffen*) ■**jdn ~** to get sb a job

unterdrücken* [ʊn·tɐ·'drʏ·kn̩] *vt* ❶ (*niederhalten*) ■**jdn ~** to oppress sb ❷ (*zurückhalten*) ■**etw ~** to suppress sth

Unterdrückung <-, -en> *f* ❶ *kein pl* (*das Unterdrücken*) *der Bürger, Einwohner, des Volks* oppression; *von Aufstand, Unruhen* suppression ❷ (*das Unterdrücktsein*) oppression

untere(r, s) ['ʊn·tə·rə, -tə·rɐ, -tə·rəs] *adj attr* lower

untereinander [ʊn·tɐ·ʔai·'nan·dɐ] *adv* ❶ (*räumlich*) one below the other ❷ (*gegenseitig*) among yourselves/themselves etc.; **sich** *akk* **~ helfen** to help each other

unterernährt *adj* undernourished

Unterführung [ʊn·tɐ·'fyː·rʊŋ] *f* underpass

Untergang *m* ❶ *eines Schiffs* sinking ❷ *der Sonne* setting ❸ (*Zerstörung*) destruction; *einer Zivilisation* decline

Untergebene(r) *f(m) dekl wie adj* subordinate

unter|gehen *vi irreg sein* ❶ (*versinken*) to sink ❷ *Sonne* to set ❸ (*zugrunde gehen*) to be destroyed

untergeordnet *adj* ❶ (*zweitrangig*) secondary ❷ (*subaltern*) subordinate

Untergeschoss[RR] *nt* basement

Untergrund ['ʊn·tɐ·grʊnt] *m* ❶ GEOL subsoil ❷ *kein pl* (*politische Illegalität*) underground; **im ~** underground ❸ KUNST (*unterste Farbschicht*) undercoat

unterhalb ['ʊn·tɐ·halp] I. *präp* +*gen* (*darunter befindlich*) below II. *adv* (*tiefer gelegen*) below; *eines Flusses* downstream; ■**~ von etw** *dat* below sth

Unterhalt <-[e]s> ['ʊn·tɐ·halt] *m kein pl* ❶ (*Lebensunterhalt*) keep; (*Unter-*

U

haltsgeld) alimony ❷ (*Instandhaltung*) upkeep

unterhalten* [ʊn·tɐ·ˈhal·tn̩] *irreg* **I.** *vt* ❶ (*für jds Lebensunterhalt sorgen*) to support ❷ (*instand halten, pflegen*) to maintain ❸ (*betreiben*) to run ❹ (*die Zeit vertreiben*) to entertain **II.** *vr* ❶ (*sich vergnügen*) ▪ **sich** *akk* ~ to keep oneself amused ❷ (*sprechen*) ▪ **sich** *akk* [**mit jdm**] ~ to talk [to sb] (**über** +*akk* about); **wir müssen uns mal** ~ we need to have a talk

unterhaltsam [ʊn·tɐ·ˈhalt·zaːm] *adj* entertaining

Unterhaltspflicht *f kein pl* obligation to pay maintenance

Unterhaltung <-, -en> *f* ❶ *kein pl* (*Instandhaltung*) maintenance ❷ *kein pl* (*Betrieb*) running ❸ (*Gespräch*) conversation ❹ *kein pl* (*Zeitvertreib*) entertainment; **gute** ~! enjoy [yourselves]!

Unterhaus [ˈʊn·tɐ·haus] *nt* lower house, ≈ House of Representatives

Unterhemd [ˈʊn·tɐ·hɛmt] *nt* undershirt

Unterhose [ˈʊn·tɐ·hoː·zə] *f* underwear

unterirdisch [ˈʊn·tɐ·ʔɪr·dɪʃ] **I.** *adj* underground; *Fluss* subterranean **II.** *adv* underground

Unterkunft <-, Unterkünfte> [ˈʊn·tɐ·kʊnft] *f* accommodation; ~ **mit Frühstück** bed and breakfast; ~ **und Verpflegung** room and board

Unterlage [ˈʊn·tɐ·laː·gə] *f* ❶ (*zum Unterlegen*) mat ❷ *pl* (*Dokumente*) ▪ ~ **n** documents

unterlassen* [ʊn·tɐ·ˈla·sn̩] *vt irreg* ❶ (*nicht ausführen*) ▪ **etw** ~ to fail to do sth ❷ (*mit etw aufhören*) ▪ **etw** ~ to refrain from doing sth

unter|legen¹ [ˈʊn·tɐ·leː·gn̩] *vt* (*darunter platzieren*) to put under[neath]

unterlegen*² [ʊn·tɐ·ˈleː·gn̩] *vt* **einen Film mit Musik** ~ to put music to a film

unterlegen³ [ʊn·tɐ·ˈleː·gn̩] *adj* ❶ (*schwächer als andere*) inferior; **zahlenmäßig** ~ **sein** to be outnumbered ❷ *SPORT* ▪ **jdm** ~ **sein** to be defeated by sb

Unterleib *m* [lower] abdomen

unterliegen* [ˈʊn·tɐ·liː·gn̩] *vi irreg* ❶ *sein* (*besiegt werden*) ▪ [**jdm**] ~ to lose [to sb] ❷ *haben* (*unterworfen sein*) **einer Täuschung** ~ to be the victim of deception; **der Schweigepflicht** ~ to be bound to maintain confidentiality

Unterlippe *f* lower lip

Untermiete [ˈʊn·tɐ·miː·tə] *f* subtenancy; **jdn in** ~ **nehmen** to sublet a room/apartment to sb; **zur** ~ **wohnen** to rent [a room/apartment] from an existing tenant

Untermieter(in) *m(f)* subtenant

unternehmen* [ʊn·tɐ·ˈneː·mən] *vt irreg* ❶ (*in die Wege leiten*) **etwas/nichts** ~ to take action/no action (**gegen** +*akk* against) ❷ (*machen*) **wollen wir nicht etwas zusammen** ~? why don't we do something together?; **einen Ausflug** ~ to take a trip; **einen Versuch** ~ to make an attempt

Unternehmen <-s, -> [ʊn·tɐ·ˈneː·mən] *nt* ❶ *ÖKON* company ❷ (*Vorhaben*) venture

Unternehmensberater(in) *m(f)* management consultant

Unternehmer(in) <-s, -> [ʊn·tɐ·ˈneː·mɐ] *m(f)* entrepreneur

unternehmungslustig *adj* enterprising

Unteroffizier [ˈʊn·tɐ·ʔɔfi·tsiːɐ̯] *m* non-commissioned officer

unter|ordnen I. *vt* ❶ (*hintanstellen*) ▪ **etw etw** *dat* ~ to put sth before sth ❷ (*jdm/einer Institution unterstellen*) ▪ **jdm/etw untergeordnet sein** to be subordinate to sb/sth **II.** *vr* ▪ **sich** *akk* [**jdm**] ~ to take on a subordinate role [to sb]

Unterricht <-[e]s, -e> [ˈʊn·tɐ·rɪçt] *m pl selten* lesson, class; **der** ~ **beginnt um zehn vor acht** classes begin at ten to eight; **heute fällt der** ~ **in Mathe aus** there's no math class today; **im** ~ **sein** to be in class; **theoretischer/praktischer** ~ theoretical/practical classes

unterrichten* [ʊn·tɐ·ˈrɪç·tn̩] **I.** *vt* ❶ (*lehren*) to teach ❷ (*informieren*) to inform (**über** +*akk* about) **II.** *vi* to teach

Unterrichtsstunde *f* lesson, class

Unterrock ['ʊn·tɐ·rɔk] *m* petticoat

untersagen* [ʊn·tɐ·'za:·gn̩] *vt (form)*
s. **verbieten**

Untersatz ['ʊn·tɐ·zats] *m* mat

unterschätzen* [ʊn·tɐ·'ʃɛ·tsn̩] *vt* to
underestimate

unterscheiden* [ʊn·tɐ·'ʃai·dn̩] *irreg*
I. *vt* ① *(differenzieren)* to distinguish
(**zwischen** +*dat* between) ② *(auseinanderhalten)* to tell the difference between; **ich kann die beiden nie ~**
I can never tell the difference between
the two; **etw von etw** *dat* ~ to tell sth
from sth II. *vi* [**zwischen Dingen**] ~ to
differentiate [between things] III. *vr*
sich *akk* **von jdm/etw** ~ to differ
from sb/sth

Unterschenkel *m* lower leg; *vom Hähnchen* drumstick

Unterschied <-[e]s, -e> ['ʊn·tɐ·ʃi:t] *m*
difference; **im ~ zu dir bin ich vor-
sichtiger** unlike you, I'm more careful;
ohne ~ indiscriminately; **einen/kei-
nen ~** [**zwischen Dingen**] **machen** to
draw a/no distinction [between things]

unterschiedlich ['ʊn·tɐ·ʃi:t·lɪç] I. *adj*
different; **~er Auffassung sein** to have
different views II. *adv* differently

unterschlagen* [ʊn·tɐ·'ʃla:·gn̩] *vt irreg*
① *(unrechtmäßig für sich behalten)* to
misappropriate; *Geld* to embezzle;
Brief, Beweise to withhold ② *(vorenthalten)* **jdm etw** ~ to withhold sth
from sb

unterschreiben* [ʊn·tɐ·'ʃrai·bn̩] *vt, vi*
irreg to sign

Unterschrift ['ʊn·tɐ·ʃrɪft] *f* ① *(eigene
Signatur)* signature ② *(Bildunterschrift)*
caption

Unterseite *f* underside

untersetzt [ʊn·tɐ·'zɛtst] *adj* stocky

unterste(r, s) ['ʊn·tɐs·tə, -tes·tə, -tes·
tas] *adj superl von* **untere(r, s)** ▶WEN-
DUNGEN: **das U~ zuoberst kehren**
(fam) to turn everything upside down

unterstehen*¹ [ʊn·tɐ·'ʃte:·ən] *irreg*
I. *vi* **jdm/etw** ~ to be subordinate to
sb/sth II. *vr* **sich** *akk* ~ **etw zu tun** to

have the audacity to do sth; **untersteh
dich!** don't you dare!

unter|stehen² ['ʊn·tɐ·ʃte:·ən] *vi irreg*
haben SÜDD, ÖSTERR, SCHWEIZ *(Schutz
suchen)* to take shelter

unterstellen*¹ [ʊn·tɐ·'ʃtɛ·lən] *vt* ① *(un-
terordnen)* **jdm jdn/etw** ~ to put sb
in charge of sb/sth ② *(unterschieben)*
jdm etw ~ to imply that sb has said/
done sth

unter|stellen² ['ʊn·tɐ·ʃtɛ·lən] I. *vt*
① *(abstellen)* **etw irgendwo** ~ to
store sth somewhere; **ein Auto bei
jdm** ~ to leave one's car at sb's house
② *(darunterstellen)* **einen Eimer** ~ to
put a bucket underneath II. *vr* **sich**
akk ~ to take shelter

Unterstellung *f (falsche Behauptung)*
insinuation

unterstreichen* [ʊn·tɐ·'ʃtrai·çn̩] *vt*
irreg ① *(markieren)* to underline ② *(betonen)* to emphasize

unterstützen* [ʊn·tɐ·'ʃty·tsn̩] *vt*
① *(helfen)* to support (**bei/in** +*dat* in)
② *(sich dafür einsetzen)* to back

Unterstützung *f* ① *kein pl (Hilfe)* support ② *(finanzielle Hilfe)* financial aid;
(Arbeitslosenunterstützung) unemployment benefit

untersuchen* [ʊn·tɐ·'zu:·xn̩] *vt* ① *(den
Gesundheitszustand überprüfen)* to examine (**auf** +*akk* for) ② *(überprüfen)* to
investigate; *Fahrzeug* to check ③ *(genau betrachten)* to scrutinize ④ *(durchsuchen)* to search (**auf** +*akk* for) ⑤ *(auf-
zuklären suchen)* to investigate

Untersuchung <-, -en> *f* ① *(Überprüfung des Gesundheitszustandes)* [medi-
cal] examination ② *(Durchsuchung)*
search ③ *(Überprüfung)* investigation
④ *(analysierende Arbeit)* investigation

Untersuchungshaft *f* custody; **in ~
sein** to be in detention pending trial

Untersuchungsrichter(in) *m(f)* magis-
trate judge

Untertasse *f* saucer

unter|tauchen ['ʊn·tɐ·tau·xn̩] I. *vt
haben* **jdn** ~ to dunk sb's head under
the water II. *vi sein* ① *(tauchen)* to

U

dive [under]; *U-Boot* to submerge ❷ (*sich verstecken*) to go underground; ■**irgendwo ~** to disappear somewhere; ■**bei jdm ~** to hide out at sb's place

Untertitel ['ʊn·tɐ·tiː·tl̩] *m* subtitle

untervermieten* *vt, vi* to sublet

unterversorgt *adj* undersupplied

Unterversorgung *f kein pl* shortage

Unterwäsche <-> ['ʊn·tɐ·vɛ·ʃə] *f kein pl* underwear

unterwegs [ʊn·tɐ·'veːks] *adv* on the way; **er hat mich von ~ angerufen** he called me while he was on the road; **für ~** for the trip

Unterwelt ['ʊn·tɐ·vɛlt] *f kein pl* underworld

unterwerfen* [ʊn·tɐ·'vɛr·fn̩] *irreg* I. *vt* to subjugate II. *vr* ■**sich** *akk* **jdm/etw ~** to submit to sb/sth

unterzeichnen* [ʊn·tɐ·'tsaɪç·nən] *vt* to sign

unterziehen*[1] [ʊn·tɐ·'tsiː·ən] *irreg vr* ■**sich** *akk* **etw** *dat* **~** to undergo sth

unter|ziehen[2] [ʊn·tɐ·'tsiː·ən] *vt irreg Kleidung* to put on *sep* underneath

untragbar [ʊn·'traː·k·baːɐ̯] *adj* ❶ (*unerträglich*) unbearable ❷ (*nicht tolerabel*) intolerable

untrennbar [ʊn·'trɛn·baːɐ̯] *adj* inseparable

untreu ['ʊn·trɔy] *adj* unfaithful; ■**jdm ~ sein** to be unfaithful to sb; **sich** *dat* **~ werden** to be untrue to oneself; **etw** *dat* **~ werden** to be disloyal to sth

Untreue *f* ❶ (*untreues Verhalten*) unfaithfulness ❷ JUR embezzlement

untröstlich [ʊn·'trøːst·lɪç] *adj* inconsolable

untypisch *adj* untypical

unübersichtlich ['ʊn·ʔy·bɐ·zɪçt·lɪç] *adj* ❶ (*nicht übersichtlich*) confusing ❷ (*schwer zu überblicken*) unclear

unübertroffen [ʊn·ʔy·bɐ·'trɔ·fn̩] *adj* unsurpassed; *Rekord* unbroken

umumstritten [ʊn·ʔʊm·'ʃtrɪ·tn̩] I. *adj* undisputed II. *adv* undisputedly

ununterbrochen ['ʊn·ʔʊn·tɐ·brɔ·xn̩] I. *adj* ❶ (*unaufhörlich andauernd*) in-

cessant ❷ (*nicht unterbrochen*) uninterrupted II. *adv* incessantly

unveränderlich [ʊn·fɛɐ̯·'ʔɛn·dɐ·lɪç] *adj* unchanging

unverändert ['ʊn·fɛɐ̯·ʔɛn·dɐt] *adj* ❶ (*keine Änderungen aufweisend*) unrevised ❷ (*gleich bleibend*) unchanged; *Einsatz, Fleiß* unchanging

unverantwortlich [ʊn·fɛɐ̯·'ʔant·vɔrt·lɪç] I. *adj* irresponsible II. *adv* irresponsibly

unverbesserlich [ʊn·fɛɐ̯·'bɛ·sɐ·lɪç] *adj* incorrigible; *Optimist* incurable

unverbindlich [ʊn·fɛɐ̯·'bɪnt·lɪç] I. *adj* ❶ (*nicht verpflichtend*) not binding *pred* ❷ (*distanziert*) detached II. *adv* without obligation

unvereinbar [ʊn·fɛɐ̯·'ʔain·baːɐ̯] *adj* incompatible; *Gegensätze* irreconcilable

unvergänglich ['ʊn·fɛɐ̯·gɛŋ·lɪç] *adj* ❶ *Eindruck* lasting ❷ (*nicht vergänglich*) immortal

unvergesslich[RR] [ʊn·fɛɐ̯·'gɛs·lɪç] *adj* unforgettable

unvergleichlich [ʊn·fɛɐ̯·'glaiç·lɪç] I. *adj* incomparable II. *adv* incomparably

unverhältnismäßig ['ʊn·fɛɐ̯·hɛlt·nɪs·mɛː·sɪç] *adv* excessively

unverhofft ['ʊn·fɛɐ̯·hɔft] I. *adj* unexpected II. *adv* unexpectedly

unverkäuflich ['ʊn·fɛɐ̯·kɔyf·lɪç] *adj* not for sale *pred*

unverkennbar [ʊn·fɛɐ̯·'kɛn·baːɐ̯] *adj* unmistakable; ■**~ sein, dass ...** to be clear that ...

unverletzt ['ʊn·fɛɐ̯·lɛtst] *adj* unhurt

unvermeidlich [ʊn·fɛɐ̯·'mait·lɪç] *adj* unavoidable

unvermindert ['ʊn·fɛɐ̯·mɪn·dɐt] I. *adj* undiminished II. *adv* unabated

Unvermögen ['ʊn·fɛɐ̯·møː·gn̩] *nt kein pl* powerlessness; ■**jds ~, etw zu tun** sb's inability to do sth

unvermutet ['ʊn·fɛɐ̯·muː·tət] I. *adj* unexpected II. *adv* unexpectedly

unvernünftig ['ʊn·fɛɐ̯·nynf·tɪç] *adj* unreasonable

unverschämt ['ʊn·fɛɐ̯·ʃɛːmt] I. *adj*

U

Lüge, Preise outrageous II. *adv* outrageously

Unverschämtheit <-, -en> *f* ❶ *kein pl* (*Dreistigkeit*) insolence ❷ (*Bemerkung*) impertinent remark; [**das ist eine**] ~! that's outrageous! ❸ (*Handlung*) impertinence

unverschuldet ['ʊn·fɛɐ̯·ʃʊl·dət] *adj, adv* through no fault of one's own

unversöhnlich ['ʊn·fɛɐ̯·zøːn·lɪç] *adj* irreconcilable

unverständlich ['ʊn·fɛɐ̯·ʃtɛnt·lɪç] *adj* ❶ (*akustisch nicht zu verstehen*) unintelligible ❷ (*unbegreifbar*) incomprehensible

unverträglich ['ʊn·fɛɐ̯·trɛː·lɪç] *adj* indigestible

unverwechselbar [ʊn·fɛɐ̯·'vɛk·sl̩·baːɐ̯] *adj* unmistakable

unverwundbar [ʊn·fɛɐ̯·'vʊnt·baːɐ̯] *adj* invulnerable

unverwüstlich [ʊn·fɛɐ̯·'vyːst·lɪç] *adj* tough; *Gesundheit* robust

unverzeihlich [ʊn·fɛɐ̯·'tsai·lɪç] *adj* inexcusable

unvollständig ['ʊn·fɔl·ʃtɛn·dɪç] I. *adj* incomplete II. *adv* incompletely

unvorbereitet ['ʊn·foːɐ̯·bə·rai·tət] I. *adj* unprepared II. *adv* ❶ (*ohne sich vorbereitet zu haben*) without [any] preparation ❷ (*unerwartet*) unexpectedly

unvoreingenommen ['ʊn·foːɐ̯·ʔain·gə·nɔ·mən] I. *adj* unbiased II. *adv* impartially

unvorhergesehen ['ʊn·foːɐ̯·he:g·gə·ze:·ən] I. *adj* unforeseen; *Besuch* unexpected II. *adv* unexpectedly

unvorsichtig ['ʊn·foːɐ̯·zɪç·tɪç] I. *adj* ❶ (*unbedacht*) rash ❷ (*nicht vorsichtig*) careless II. *adv* ❶ (*unbedacht*) rashly ❷ (*nicht vorsichtig*) carelessly

unvorstellbar [ʊn·foːɐ̯·'ʃtɛl·baːɐ̯] I. *adj* inconceivable II. *adv* inconceivably

unwahr ['ʊn·vaːɐ̯] *adj* untrue, false

unwahrscheinlich ['ʊn·vaːɐ̯·ʃain·lɪç] I. *adj* ❶ (*kaum denkbar*) unlikely; *Zufall* remarkable ❷ (*fam: unerhört*) incredible II. *adv* (*fam*) incredibly

unweigerlich ['ʊn·vai·gə·lɪç] I. *adj attr* inevitable II. *adv* inevitably

unweit ['ʊn·vait] *adv* ■~ **von etw** *dat* not far from sth

Unwetter <-s, -> ['ʊn·vɛ·tɐ] *nt* thunderstorm

unwichtig ['ʊn·vɪç·tɪç] *adj* unimportant

unwiderstehlich [ʊn·vi:·de·'ʃte:·lɪç] *adj* irresistible

unwillig ['ʊn·vɪ·lɪç] I. *adj* ❶ (*verärgert*) angry ❷ (*widerwillig*) reluctant II. *adv* reluctantly

unwillkürlich ['ʊn·vɪl·ky:g·lɪç] I. *adj* involuntary II. *adv* involuntarily

unwirklich ['ʊn·vɪrk·lɪç] *adj* unreal

unwirksam ['ʊn·vɪrk·za:m] *adj* ineffective

Unwissenheit <-> ['ʊn·vɪ·sn̩·hait] *f kein pl* ignorance

unwohl ['ʊn·vo:l] *adj* ■**jdm ist ~** ❶ (*gesundheitlich nicht gut*) sb feels sick ❷ (*unbehaglich*) sb feels uneasy

Unwohlsein <-s> ['ʊn·vo:l·zain] *nt kein pl* [slight] nausea

unwürdig ['ʊn·vyr·dɪç] *adj* ❶ (*nicht würdig*) unworthy ❷ (*schändlich*) disgraceful

unzählig ['ʊn·tsɛː·lɪç] *adj* countless

unzerbrechlich ['ʊn·tsɛɐ̯·brɛç·lɪç] *adj* unbreakable

unzufrieden ['ʊn·tsu·fri:·dn̩] *adj* dissatisfied

Unzufriedenheit *f* dissatisfaction

unzugänglich ['ʊn·tsu:·gɛn·lɪç] *adj* ❶ (*schwer erreichbar*) inaccessible ❷ (*nicht aufgeschlossen*) unapproachable

unzulänglich ['ʊn·tsu:·lɛŋ·lɪç] *adj* inadequate; *Erfahrungen, Kenntnisse* insufficient II. *adv* inadequately

unzulässig ['ʊn·tsu:·lɛ·sɪç] *adj* inadmissible

unzumutbar ['ʊn·tsu:·mu:t·baːɐ̯] *adj* unreasonable

unzurechnungsfähig ['ʊn·tsu:·rɛç·nʊŋs·fɛː·ɪç] *adj* of unsound mind *pred*; **jdn für ~ erklären** to certify [*or* declare] sb mentally incompetent

U

unzusammenhängend ['ʊn·tsu·za·mən·hɛŋ·ənt] *adj* incoherent

unzuverlässig ['ʊn·tsu·fɛɐ̯·lɛ·sɪç] *adj* unreliable

üppig ['ʏpɪç] *adj* ① *Figur* voluptuous ② *Mahlzeit* sumptuous

uralt ['uːɐ̯·ʔalt] *adj* ① (*sehr alt*) very old ② (*schon lange existent*) ancient ③ (*fam: schon lange bekannt*) ancient; *Problem* old, perennial

Uran <-s> [u'raːn] *nt kein pl* uranium

Uraufführung *f* eines *Theaterstücks* first performance; eines *Films* first release

Ureinwohner(in) *m(f)* indigenous person

Urenkel(in) ['uːɐ̯·ʔɛŋ·kl̩] *m(f)* great-grandchild, great-grandson *masc*, great-granddaughter *fem*

Urgeschichte ['uːɐ̯·gə·ʃɪç·tə] *f kein pl* prehistory

Urgroßeltern ['uːɐ̯·groːs·ʔɛl·tɐn] *pl* great-grandparents *pl*

Urgroßmutter ['uːɐ̯·groːs·mʊ·tɐ] *f* great-grandmother

Urgroßvater *m* great-grandfather

Urheberrecht *nt* ① (*Recht des Autors*) copyright (**an** +*dat* on) ② (*urheberrechtliche Bestimmungen*) copyright law

urheberrechtlich I. *adj* copyright *attr* II. *adv* ~ **geschützt** copyright[ed]

Urin <-s, -e> [u'riːn] *m* urine

urinieren* [uɾ·i'niː·ɾən] *vi* (*geh*) to urinate

Urkunde <-, -n> ['uːɐ̯·kʊn·də] *f* (*Auszeichnung*) certificate; (*rechtskräftig*) document

Urkundenfälschung *f* document forgery

Urlaub <-[e]s, -e> ['uːɐ̯·laup] *m* vacation; ~ **machen** to go on vacation; **in** ~ **sein** to be on vacation

Urlauber(in) <-s, -> *m(f)* vacationer

Urlaubsgeld *nt* vacation pay

Urne <-, -n> ['ʊr·nə] *f* ① (*Graburne*) urn ② (*Wahlurne*) ballot box

Ursache *f* cause (**für** +*akk* of) ►WENDUNGEN: **keine** ~! you're welcome!

Ursprung ['uːɐ̯·ʃprʊŋ] *m* origin

ursprünglich ['uːɐ̯·ʃprʏŋ·lɪç] I. *adj* ① *attr* (*anfänglich*) original ② (*im Urzustand befindlich*) unspoiled ③ (*urtümlich*) ancient II. *adv* originally

Urteil <-s, -e> ['ʊr·taɪl] *nt* ① JUR judgment, verdict ② (*Meinung*) opinion (**über** +*akk* on)

urteilen ['ʊr·taɪ·lən] *vi* to pass judgment (**über** +*akk* on)

Urteilsbegründung *f* basis for a judgment

Urwald ['uːɐ̯·valt] *m* primeval [*or* virgin] forest

urwüchsig *adj* ① (*im Urzustand erhalten*) unspoiled ② (*unverbildet*) earthy ③ (*ursprünglich*) original

Urzeit *f* ■**die** ~ primeval times *pl* ►WENDUNGEN: **seit** ~**en** for eons; **vor** ~**en** eons ago

Urzustand *m kein pl* original state

USB-Stick <-s, -s> [uː·ʔɛs·'beː·stɪk, ju·ʔɛs·'biː-] *m* COMPUT flash drive

Utopie <-, -n> [uto·'piː] *f* Utopia

utopisch [u'toː·pɪʃ] *adj* utopian

UV-Strahlen *pl* UV rays *pl*

U

Vv

V, v <-, -> [fau] *nt* V, v; ~ **wie Viktor** V as in Victor

V *Abk von* **Volt** V

Vagabund(in) <-en, -en> [va·ga·'bʊnt] *m(f)* vagabond

vage ['va:·gə] I. *adj* vague II. *adv* vaguely

Vagina <-, Vaginen> ['va:·gi·na] *f* vagina

Vakuum <-s, Vakuen> ['va:·ku·ʊm] *nt* vacuum

vakuumverpackt *adj* vacuum-packed

Vampir <-s, -e> [vam·'pi:ɐ̯] *m* vampire

Vandale, Vandalin <-n, -n> [van·'da:·lə, van·'da:·lɪn] *m, f* vandal

Vandalismus <-> [van·da·'lɪs·mʊs] *m kein pl* vandalism

Vanille <-, -en> [va·'nɪlə] *f* vanilla

variabel [va·'rịa:·bl̩] *adj* variable

Variante <-, -n> [va·'rịan·tə] *f* ❶ (*Abwandlung*) variation ❷ (*veränderte Ausführung*) variant

variieren* [va·ri·'i:rən] *vi* to vary

Vase <-, -n> ['va:·zə] *f* vase

Vater <-s, Väter> ['fa:·tɐ] *m* father

Vaterland *nt* fatherland

väterlich ['fɛ·tɐ·lɪç] I. *adj* ❶ (*dem Vater gehörend*) **das ~ e Geschäft** his/her father's business ❷ (*zum Vater gehörend*) paternal ❸ (*fürsorglich*) fatherly II. *adv* like a father

väterlicherseits *adv* on sb's father's side

Vaterschaftsklage *f* paternity suit

Vaterunser <-s, -> [fa:·te·'ʔʊn·ze] *nt* REL ■**das ~** the Lord's Prayer

Vati <-s, -s> ['fa:·ti] *m* (*fam*) daddy

Vatikan <-s> [va·ti·'ka:n] *m* Vatican

V-Ausschnitt ['fau-] *m* V-neck; **ein Pullover mit ~** a V-neck sweater

Vegetarier(in) <-s, -> [ve·ge·'ta:·ri·ɐ] *m(f)* vegetarian

vegetarisch [ve·ge·'ta:·rɪʃ] I. *adj* vegetarian II. *adv* **sich** *akk* **~ ernähren** to be a vegetarian

Vegetation <-, -en> [ve·ge·ta·'tsị̯o:n] *f* vegetation

Veilchen <-s, -> ['fail·çən] *nt* violet

Velo <-s, -s> ['ve:·lo] *nt* SCHWEIZ (*Fahrrad*) bicycle, bike *fam*

Velours <-, -> [və·'lu:ɐ̯] *nt*, **Veloursleder** *nt* suede

Vene <-, -n> ['ve:·nə] *f* vein

Ventil <-s, -e> [vɛn·'ti:l] *nt* valve

Ventilator <-s, -toren> [vɛn·ti·'la:·to:ɐ̯] *m* fan

verabreden* I. *vr* ■**sich** *akk* [**mit jdm**] **~** to set up a date [*or* make plans] [with sb]; ■[**mit jdm**] **verabredet sein** to have plans [*or* a date] [with sb] II. *vt* **etw** [**mit jdm**] **~** to arrange [*or* set up] sth [with sb]; ■**verabredet** agreed

Verabredung <-, -en> *f* ❶ (*Treffen*) meeting; (*Rendezvous*) date ❷ (*Vereinbarung*) arrangement

verabscheuen* *vt* to detest, to loathe

verabschieden* I. *vr* ■**sich** *akk* **~** to say goodbye (**von** + *dat* to) II. *vt Gesetz* to pass

verachten* *vt* ❶ (*verächtlich finden*) to despise ❷ (*nicht achten*) to scorn; **nicht zu ~ sein** [sth is] not to be sneezed at *fam*

verächtlich [fɛɐ̯·'ʔɛçt·lɪç] I. *adj* ❶ (*Verachtung zeigend*) contemptuous, scornful ❷ (*verabscheuungswürdig*) despicable II. *adv* contemptuously, scornfully

Verachtung *f* contempt, scorn

verallgemeinern* I. *vt* ■**etw ~** to generalize about sth II. *vi* to generalize

veralten* [fɛɐ̯·'ʔal·tn̩] *vi sein* to become obsolete; *Ansichten, Methoden* to become outdated; ■**veraltet** obsolete; *Reiseführer, Stadtplan* old

Veranda <-, Veranden> [ve·'ran·da] *f* veranda

veränderlich *adj* variable

verändern* *vt, vr* to change

V

Veränderung f change; (leicht) alteration, modification

veranlagt [fɛɐ̯ˈʔanˌlaːkt] adj **ein künstlerisch ~er Mensch** a person with an artistic disposition; **er ist praktisch ~** he is practically minded

Veranlagung <-, -en> f disposition (zu + dat to)

veranlassen* vt ❶ (in die Wege leiten) to arrange; **■ ~, dass etw geschieht** to see to it that sth happens ❷ (dazu bringen) **■jdn zu etw** dat **~** to cause sb to do sth

Veranlassung <-, -en> f cause; **auf jds ~** at sb's instigation

veranschaulichen* [fɛɐ̯ˈʔanˌʃau̯lɪçn̩] vt to illustrate

veranstalten* [fɛɐ̯ˈʔanˌʃtaltn̩] vt to organize

Veranstalter(in) <-s, -> m(f) organizer

Veranstaltung <-, -en> f ❶ kein pl (das Durchführen) organizing ❷ (Ereignis) event

Veranstaltungsort m venue

verantworten* I. vt **■etw ~** to take responsibility for sth II. vr **■sich** akk **[vor jdm] ~** to answer [to sb] (für + akk for)

verantwortlich adj responsible

Verantwortung <-, -en> f responsibility; **die ~ [für etw** akk**] tragen/übernehmen** to be responsible/take responsibility [for sth]; **auf eigene ~** on one's own responsibility, at one's own risk

verantwortungsbewusst^RR I. adj responsible II. adv responsibly

verantwortungslos I. adj irresponsible II. adv irresponsibly

verarbeiten* vt ❶ (verwenden) to use; Lebensmittel, Rohstoffe to process; **■etw zu etw** dat **~** to make sth into sth ❷ PSYCH to assimilate, to come to terms with

verärgern* vt to annoy

Verarmung <-, -en> f impoverishment

verarschen* [fɛɐ̯ˈʔarˌʃn̩] vt (derb) **■jdn ~** to mess around with sb

verarzten* [fɛɐ̯ˈʔaːɐ̯tstn̩] vt (fam) to treat

verausgaben* [fɛɐ̯ˈʔau̯sˌɡaːbn̩] vr **■sich** akk **~** (körperlich) to overexert; (finanziell) to overspend

Verb <-s, -en> [vɛrp] nt verb

verbal [vɛrˈbaːl] I. adj verbal II. adv verbally

Verband <-[e]s, Verbände> [fɛɐ̯ˈbant] m ❶ (Bund) association ❷ MED bandage, dressing

Verband(s)kasten m first-aid kit

Verbannung <-, -en> f exile, banishment

verbergen* vt irreg to hide, to conceal (vor + dat from)

verbessern* I. vt ❶ (besser machen) to improve ❷ (korrigieren) to correct II. vr **■sich** akk **~** to improve

Verbesserung <-, -en> f ❶ (qualitative Anhebung) improvement ❷ (Korrektur) correction

verbeugen* vr **■sich** akk **~** to bow

Verbeugung f bow

verbiegen* vt, vr irreg **■[sich** akk**] ~** to bend; **■verbogen** bent

verbieten <verbot, verboten> vt to forbid, to ban; (offiziell) to outlaw; **■jdm ~, etw zu tun** to forbid sb to do sth; **ich habe es dir doch verboten** I told you you weren't allowed to do that

verbinden*¹ vt irreg Wunde to dress; **■jdn ~** to dress sb's wound[s]

verbinden*² vt irreg ❶ (zusammenfügen) to join (mit + dat to) ❷ TELEK **■jdn [mit jdm] ~** to connect sb [to sb]; **falsch verbunden!** wrong number! ❸ TRANSP to connect, to link ❹ (verknüpfen) to combine; **das Nützliche mit dem Angenehmen ~** to combine business with pleasure ❺ (assoziieren) **■etw [mit etw** dat**] ~** to associate sth [with sth]

verbindlich [fɛɐ̯ˈbɪntˌlɪç] I. adj ❶ (bindend) binding ❷ (entgegenkommend) friendly II. adv ❶ (bindend) **~ zusagen** to make a binding commitment ❷ (entgegenkommend) in a friendly manner

Verbindung f ❶ (direkte Beziehung) contact; **in ~ bleiben** to keep in touch; **~en zu jdm/etw haben** to have connections pl with sb/sth; **sich**

akk **mit jdm in ~ setzen** to contact sb ❷ TELEK, TRANSP connection (**nach** +*dat* to) ❸ (*Zusammenhang*) **jdn mit etw** *dat* **in ~ bringen** to connect sb with sth; **in ~ mit** in connection with ❹ CHEM compound ❺ UNIV fraternity

verbissen I. *adj* ❶ (*hartnäckig*) dogged ❷ (*verkrampft*) grim II. *adv* doggedly

verbitten* *vr irreg* ■**sich** *dat* **etw ~** to not tolerate sth

verbittert I. *adj* embittered, bitter II. *adv* bitterly

Verbitterung <-, *selten* -en> *f* bitterness

verblassen* *vi sein* ❶ (*blasser werden*) to pale ❷ (*schwächer werden*) to fade

verbleit *adj* leaded

verblöden* [fɛɐ̯ˈbløːˌdn̩] *vi sein* (*fam*) to turn into a zombie

verblüffen* [fɛɐ̯ˈblʏfn̩] *vt* to astonish

verblühen* *vi sein* to wilt

verbluten* *vi sein* to bleed to death

verbohrt *adj* obstinate

verborgen *adj* hidden

Verbot <-[e]s, -e> [fɛɐ̯ˈboːt] *nt* ban

verboten [fɛɐ̯ˈboːtn̩] *adj* prohibited, forbidden; **Parken ~!** you're not allowed to park here!

Verbotsschild *nt* sign prohibiting sth

Verbrauch *m kein pl* consumption (**an** +*dat* of)

verbrauchen* *vt* ❶ to consume ❷ *Vorräte* to use up *sep*

Verbraucher(in) <-s, -> *m(f)* consumer

verbraucherfreundlich *adj* consumer-friendly

verbraucht *adj* (*aufgebraucht*) exhausted; *Mensch a.* burned-out *fam*

verbrechen <verbrach, verbrochen> *vt* (*fam*) to be up to

Verbrechen <-s, -> *nt* crime

Verbrecher(in) <-s, -> *m(f)* criminal

verbrecherisch *adj* criminal

verbreiten* *vt, vr* to spread

verbreitern* [fɛɐ̯ˈbraɪtɐn] *vt* to widen

verbreitet *adj* popular; ■**[weit] ~ sein** to be [very] widespread

Verbreitung <-, -en> *f* ❶ *kein pl* (*das Verbreiten*) dissemination ❷ MEDIA distribution ❸ MED spread

verbrennen* *irreg* I. *vt haben* to burn II. *vr haben* **sich** *dat* **die Zunge ~** to burn one's tongue; **sich** *dat* **die Finger [an etw** *dat*] **~** to burn one's fingers [on sth] III. *vi sein* to burn; ■**verbrannt** burned

Verbrennung <-, -en> *f* ❶ *kein pl* (*das Verbrennen*) burning ❷ MED burn

verbrühen* *vt* to scald

verbuchen* *vt* to mark up *sep* (**als** +*akk* as)

verbummeln* *vt* (*fam*) ❶ (*vertrödeln*) to waste ❷ (*verlieren*) to misplace

verbünden* [fɛɐ̯ˈbʏndn̩] *vr* ■**sich** *akk* **~** to form an alliance

Verbundenheit <-> *f kein pl* closeness

Verbündete(r) *f(m) dekl wie adj* ally

verbürgen* I. *vt* ■**sich** *akk* **für jdn/etw ~** to vouch for sb/sth II. *vt* to guarantee

verbüßen* *vt* JUR to serve

verchromt *adj* chrome-plated

Verdacht <-[e]s> [fɛɐ̯ˈdaxt] *m kein pl* suspicion; **~ erregen** to arouse suspicion; **jdn im ~ haben** to suspect sb

verdächtig [fɛɐ̯ˈdɛçtɪç] I. *adj* suspicious; **jdm ~ vorkommen** to seem suspicious to sb; **sich** *akk* **~ machen** to arouse suspicion II. *adv* suspiciously

Verdächtige(r) *f(m) dekl wie adj* suspect

verdächtigen* [fɛɐ̯ˈdɛçtɪ·gn̩] *vt* to suspect

verdammen* [fɛɐ̯ˈda·mən] *vt* to condemn

verdammt *adj* (*fam*) ❶ (*Ärger ausdrückend*) damned; **~!** damn! ❷ (*sehr groß*) **wir hatten ~es Glück!** we were damn lucky!

verdampfen* *vi sein* to evaporate

verdanken* *vt* ❶ (*durch etw erhalten*) **diesen Erfolg verdanke ich dir** thanks to you, this has been a success ❷ SCHWEIZ (*Dank aussprechen*) ■**[jdm] etw ~** to express one's thanks [to sb]

verdauen* [fɛɐ̯ˈdaʊ·ən] *vt* ❶ *Nahrung* to digest ❷ *Niederlage etc.* to get over

V

verdaulich *adj* digestible; **gut/ schwer ~** easy/hard to digest

Verdauung <-> *f kein pl* digestion

Verdeck <-[e]s, -e> *nt* convertible top

verdecken* *vt* ① (*die Sicht nehmen*) to cover [up *sep*] ② (*maskieren*) to conceal

verderben <verdarb, verdorben> [fɛɐˈdɛrbn̩] I. *vt haben* ① (*moralisch*) to corrupt ② (*zunichtemachen*) Spaß to spoil ③ (*verscherzen*) **es sich** *dat* **mit niemandem ~ wollen** to try to please everyone II. *vi sein* to spoil; *Lebensmittel* to go bad

verderblich [fɛɐˈdɛrplɪç] *adj Lebensmittel* perishable

verdeutlichen* [fɛɐˈdɔytlɪçn̩] *vt* to explain

verdichten* I. *vt* PHYS to compress II. *vr* ■ **sich** *akk* ~ *Eindruck, Gefühl* to intensify; *Verdacht* to grow

verdienen* I. *vt* ① (*als Verdienst bekommen*) to earn ② (*Gewinn machen*) to make (**an** +*dat* off of) ③ (*zustehen*) to deserve II. *vi* ① (*einen Verdienst bekommen*) to earn [money] ② (*Gewinn machen*) to make a profit (**an** +*dat* off of)

Verdienst¹ <-[e]s, -e> [fɛɐˈdiːnst] *m* FIN income, earnings *npl*

Verdienst² <-[e]s, -e> [fɛɐˈdiːnst] *nt* merit; **es ist sein ~, dass ...** it's thanks to him [*or* to his credit] that ...

Verdienstausfall *m* loss of earnings *pl*

verdoppeln* I. *vt* ① (*erhöhen*) to double ② (*verstärken*) to redouble II. *vr* ■ **sich** *akk* ~ to double

verdorben [fɛɐˈdɔrbn̩] I. *pp von* **verderben** II. *adj* ① (*ungenießbar*) bad ② (*moralisch korrumpiert*) corrupt ③ MED **einen ~en Magen haben** to have an upset stomach

verdorren* [fɛɐˈdɔrən] *vi sein* to wither

verdrängen* *vt* ① (*vertreiben*) to drive out ② (*unterdrücken*) Erinnerung, Gefühl to suppress

verdrehen* *vt* ① (*wenden*) to twist; *Augen* to roll ② *Tatsachen* to distort

▶WENDUNGEN: **jdm den Kopf ~** to turn sb's head

verdreifachen* [fɛɐˈdraifaxn̩] I. *vt* to triple II. *vr* ■ **sich** *akk* ~ to triple

verdrießlich [fɛɐˈdriːslɪç] *adj Gesicht* sullen; *Stimmung* morose

verdrossen [fɛɐˈdrɔsn̩] *adj* sullen, morose

verdrücken* I. *vt* (*fam: verzehren*) to polish off *sep* II. *vr* (*fam: verschwinden*) ■ **sich** *akk* ~ to slip away

VerdrussRR <-sses, -sse> **Verdruß**ALT <-sses, -sse> [fɛɐˈdrʊs] *m meist sing* annoyance; **jdm ~ bereiten** to annoy sb

verdunkeln* I. *vt* ① (*abdunkeln*) to black out ② (*verdüstern*) to darken II. *vr* (*dunkler werden*) ■ **sich** *akk* ~ to darken

verdünnen* [fɛɐˈdʏnən] *vt* to dilute

verdunsten* *vi sein* to evaporate

verdursten* *vi sein* to die of thirst

verdutzt [fɛɐˈdʊtst] I. *adj* (*fam*) ① (*verwirrt*) baffled, confused ② (*überrascht*) taken aback *pred* II. *adv* in a baffled manner

verehren* *vt* ① (*bewundernd*) to admire ② REL to worship

Verehrer(in) <-s, -> *m(f)* admirer

Verehrung *f kein pl* ① (*Bewunderung*) admiration ② REL worship

vereidigen* [fɛɐˈʔaidɪɡn̩] *vt* to swear in *sep*

vereidigt [fɛɐˈʔaidɪçt] *adj* sworn; **gerichtlich ~** certified before the court

Verein <-[e]s, -e> [fɛɐˈʔain] *m* club, association; **eingetragener ~** registered association; **gemeinnütziger ~** charitable organization

vereinbar *adj* compatible (**mit** +*dat* with)

vereinbaren* [fɛɐˈʔainbaːrən] *vt* ① (*absprechen*) ■ **etw** [**mit jdm**] ~ to agree to [*or* arrange] sth [with sb] ② (*in Einklang bringen*) to reconcile; ■ **sich** *akk* ~ **lassen** to be compatible

Vereinbarung <-, -en> *f* ① *kein pl* (*das Vereinbaren*) arranging ② (*Abma-*

chung) agreement; **laut** ~ as agreed; **nach** ~ by arrangement

vereinen* *vt* to unite

vereinfachen* [fɛɐ̯·ˈʔain·fa·xn̩] *vt* to simplify

vereinheitlichen* [fɛɐ̯·ˈʔain·hait·lɪ·çn̩] *vt* to standardize

vereinigen *vr* ∎**sich** *akk* ~ to merge

vereinsamen [fɛɐ̯·ˈʔain·za·mən] *vi sein* to become lonely

vereinsamt *adj* lonely

Vereinsamung <-> *f kein pl* loneliness

vereinzelt [fɛɐ̯·ˈʔain·tsl̩t] *adj* occasional

vereisen* I. *vi sein* to ice up; **eine vereiste Fahrbahn** an icy road II. *vt haben* (*lokal anästhesieren*) to freeze

vereiteln* [fɛɐ̯·ˈʔaitl̩n] *vt* to thwart

vereitern* *vi sein* to go septic

vererben* I. *vt* ∎**jdm** etw ~ ① (*hinterlassen*) to leave [sb] sth ② (*durch Vererbung weitergeben*) to pass on *sep* sth [to sb] ③ (*schenken*) to hand down *sep* sth [to sb] II. *vr* ∎**sich** *akk* ~ to be hereditary

vererblich *adj* hereditary

verewigen* [fɛɐ̯·ˈʔeːvɪ·gn̩] I. *vr* ∎**sich** *akk* ~ to leave one's mark [for posterity] II. *vt* (*unsterblich machen*) to immortalize

verfahren*¹ [fɛɐ̯·ˈʔfaː·rən] *vi irreg sein* ① (*vorgehen*) to proceed ② (*umgehen*) ∎**mit jdm** ~ to deal with sb

verfahren*² [fɛɐ̯·ˈʔfaː·rən] *irreg* I. *vt Benzin* to use up *sep* II. *vr* ∎**sich** *akk* ~ to get lost [while driving]

verfahren*³ [fɛɐ̯·ˈʔfaː·rən] *adj* muddled; **völlig** ~ **sein** to be a total mess

Verfahren <-s, -> [fɛɐ̯·ˈʔfaː·rən] *nt* ① (*Methode*) process ② (*Gerichtsverfahren*) [legal [*or* criminal]] proceedings *npl*

Verfall [fɛɐ̯·ˈfal] *m kein pl* ① (*Verwahrlosung*) dilapidation ② (*moralisch*) decline

verfallen*¹ *vi irreg sein* ① (*zerfallen*) to decay ② (*immer schwächer werden*) to deteriorate ③ (*ungültig werden*) *Ticket, Gutschein* to expire; *Anspruch* to lapse ④ (*erliegen*) ∎**jdm** ~ to be captivated

by sb; ∎**etw** *dat* ~ to become addicted to sth

verfallen² *adj* ① (*völlig baufällig*) dilapidated ② (*abgelaufen*) expired

Verfallsdatum *nt* ÖKON ① (*der Haltbarkeit*) use-by date ② (*der Gültigkeit*) expiration date

verfälschen* *vt* ① (*falsch darstellen*) to distort ② (*in der Qualität mindern*) to adulterate (**durch** +*akk* with)

verfärben* I. *vr* ∎**sich** *akk* ~ to change color; *Wäsche* to discolor II. *vt* to discolor

verfassen* *vt* to write; *Gesetz, Urkunde* to draw up

Verfasser(in) <-s, -> [fɛɐ̯·ˈfa·sɐ] *m(f)* author

Verfassung *f* ① *kein pl* (*Zustand*) condition; (*körperlich*) state [of health]; (*seelisch*) state [of mind] ② POL constitution

Verfassungsschutz *m* domestic intelligence agency

verfassungswidrig *adj* unconstitutional

verfaulen* *vi sein* to rot

Verfechter(in) *m(f)* advocate, champion

verfehlen* *vt* ① (*nicht treffen, verpassen*) to miss; **nicht zu** ~ **sein** to be impossible to miss ② (*nicht erreichen*) to not achieve; **das Thema** ~ to be off the subject; **seinen Beruf** ~ to miss one's calling

verfeinden* [fɛɐ̯·ˈfain·dn̩] *vr* ∎**sich** *akk* ~ to fall out; ∎**verfeindet sein** to be enemies; **verfeindete Staaten** enemy states

verfeinern* [fɛɐ̯·ˈfai·nɐn] *vt* ① KOCHK to improve (**mit** +*dat* with) ② (*raffinierter gestalten*) *Methode, Stil* to refine

Verfilmung <-, -en> *f kein pl* (*das Verfilmen*) filming ② (*Film*) film

verfinstern* [fɛɐ̯·ˈfɪns·tɐn] *vr* ∎**sich** *akk* ~ to darken

verfliegen* *vi irreg sein* ① *Zorn* to pass; *Kummer* to vanish ② *Geruch* to evaporate

verfluchen* *vt* to curse

V

verflüssigen* [fɛɐ̯ˈflʏˑsɪˑɡn̩] *vt, vr* to liquefy

verfolgen* *vt* ① (*nachgehen*) to follow ② (*aus politischen etc. Gründen*) to persecute ③ (*zu erreichen suchen*) to pursue; **eine Absicht ~** to have sth in mind ④ (*belasten*) **vom Pech verfolgt sein** to be dogged by bad luck

Verfolger(in) <-s, -> *m(f)* pursuer

Verfolgte(r) [fɛɐ̯ˈfɔlktə, -tə] *f/m* dekl wie adj victim of persecution

Verfolgung <-, -en> *f* ① (*das Verfolgen*) pursuit ② (*aus politischen Gründen*) persecution ③ JUR prosecution

Verfolgungsjagd *f* pursuit, chase

Verfolgungswahn *m* persecution complex

verformen* I. *vt* to distort II. *vr* ■**sich** *akk* ~ to become distorted [*or* misshapen]

verfressen* *adj* (*pej fam*) [overly] greedy

verfrüht *adj* premature

verfügbar *adj* available

verfügen* I. *vi* ■**über etw** *akk* ~ to have sth at one's disposal II. *vt* (*anordnen*) to order

Verfügung <-, -en> *f* ① (*Anordnung*) order; **einstweilige ~** JUR temporary injunction ② (*Disposition*) **etw zur ~ haben** to have sth at one's disposal; **jdm zur ~ stehen** to be available to sb; **[jdm] etw zur ~ stellen** to make sth available [to sb]

verführen* *vt* ① (*verleiten*) to entice; (*sexuell*) to seduce ② (*hum: verlocken*) to tempt

verführerisch [fɛɐ̯ˈfyːˑrəˑrɪʃ] *adj* ① (*verlockend*) tempting ② (*aufreizend*) seductive

Verführung *f* ① (*Verleitung*) seduction; **~ Minderjähriger** JUR seduction of minors ② (*Verlockung*) temptation

Vergabe [fɛɐ̯ˈɡaːˑbə] *f von Arbeit, Studienplätzen* allocation; *eines Auftrags, Preises* award

vergammelt <-er, -este> *adj* (*fam*) scruffy

vergangen *adj* past, former

Vergangenheit <-, *selten* -en> [fɛɐ̯ˈɡaŋən·haɪt] *f* ① *kein pl* (*Vergangenes*) past ② LING past [tense]

vergänglich [fɛɐ̯ˈɡɛŋ·lɪç] *adj* transient

Vergaser <-s, -> *m* AUTO carburetor

vergeben* *irreg* I. *vi* to forgive II. *vt* ① (*verzeihen*) to forgive ② (*zuteilen*) to allocate sth (**an** +*akk* to); *Preis, Auftrag* to award

vergeblich [fɛɐ̯ˈɡeːp·lɪç] I. *adj* (*erfolglos bleibend*) futile II. *adv* (*umsonst*) in vain

Vergebung <-, -en> *f* forgiveness

vergehen* [fɛɐ̯ˈɡeːˑən] *irreg* I. *vi sein Zeit* to pass II. *vr haben* ■**sich** *akk* **an jdm ~** to sexually assault sb

Vergehen <-s, -> [fɛɐ̯ˈɡeːˑən] *nt* offense

vergelten *vt irreg* ■**[jdm] etw ~** to repay sb for sth

Vergeltung <-, -en> *f* revenge

Vergeltungsschlag *m* retaliatory strike

vergessen <vergisst, vergaß, vergessen> [fɛɐ̯ˈɡɛˑsn̩] I. *vt* ① (*nicht mehr daran denken*) to forget; **nicht zu ~ ...** keep [*or* bear] in mind that ... ② (*liegen lassen*) to leave behind II. *vr* (*die Beherrschung verlieren*) ■**sich** *akk* ~ to lose oneself

vergesslichᴿᴿ, **vergeßlich**ᴬᴸᵀ [fɛɐ̯ˈɡɛsˑlɪç] *adj* forgetful

vergeuden* [fɛɐ̯ˈɡɔy·dn̩] *vt* to waste

vergewaltigen* [fɛɐ̯·ɡə·ˈval·tɪ·ɡn̩] *vt* to rape

Vergewaltigung <-, -en> *f* rape

vergewissern* [fɛɐ̯·ɡə·ˈvɪ·sɐn] *vr* ■**sich** *akk* ~, **dass ...** to make sure that ...

vergießen* *vt irreg Tränen, Blut* to shed

vergiften* *vt* to poison

Vergiftung <-, -en> *f kein pl* poisoning

vergilbt *adj* yellowed

Vergissmeinnichtᴿᴿ, **Vergißmeinnicht**ᴬᴸᵀ <-[e]s, -[e]> [fɛɐ̯·ˈɡɪs·maɪn·nɪçt] *nt* forget-me-not

Vergleich <-[e]s, -e> [fɛɐ̯ˈɡlaɪç] *m* comparison; **im ~ [zu jdm/etw]** in comparison [with sb/sth], compared to [sb/sth] ▸WENDUNGEN: **der ~ hinkt** that's a poor comparison

vergleichbar adj comparable (**mit** +dat to/with)

vergleichen* vt irreg to compare (**mit** +dat to/with)

vergleichsweise adv comparatively; **das ist ~ wenig/viel** that is a little/a lot in comparison

vergnügen* [fɛɐ̯ˈgnyː·gn̩] vr ■**sich** akk ~ to amuse [or enjoy] oneself

Vergnügen <-s, -> [fɛɐ̯ˈgnyː·gn̩] nt (Freude) enjoyment; (Genuss) pleasure ▸WENDUNGEN: **viel ~!** have a good time!

vergnügt [fɛɐ̯ˈgnyːkt] I. adj happy, cheerful II. adv happily, cheerfully

Vergnügungspark m amusement park

vergöttern* [fɛɐ̯ˈgœ·tɐn] vt to idolize

vergraben* irreg I. vt to bury II. vr ■**sich** akk **in Arbeit ~** to bury oneself in work

vergreifen* vr irreg ❶ (stehlen) ■**sich** akk **an etw** dat ~ to steal sth ❷ (Gewalt antun) ■**sich** akk **an jdm ~** to assault sb ❸ (sich unpassend ausdrücken) ■**sich** akk **im Ton ~** to adopt the wrong tone

vergriffen adj Buch out of print pred; Ware unavailable

vergrößern* [fɛɐ̯ˈgrøː·sɐn] I. vt ❶ Fläche, Umfang to extend, to enlarge (**um** +akk by, **auf** +akk to) ❷ Distanz to increase ❸ Firma to expand ❹ (größer erscheinen lassen) to magnify ❺ FOTO to enlarge, to blow up sep II. vr ■**sich** akk ~ (anschwellen) to become enlarged

Vergrößerung <-, -en> f ❶ (das Vergrößern) enlargement, increase; einer Firma expansion; (technisch) magnification ❷ (vergrößertes Foto) enlargement, blowup ❸ (Anschwellung) enlargement

Vergrößerungsglas m magnifying glass

Vergünstigung <-, -en> f ❶ (finanzieller Vorteil) perk ❷ (Ermäßigung) reduction, concession

Vergütung <-, -en> f ❶ (das Ersetzen) refund, reimbursement ❷ (Geld-

summe) payment, remuneration; (Honorar) fee

verhaften* vt to arrest; **Sie sind verhaftet!** you're under arrest!

Verhaftung <-, -en> f arrest

verhalten* [fɛɐ̯ˈhal·tn̩] vr irreg ■**sich** akk ~ to behave

Verhalten <-s> [fɛɐ̯ˈhal·tn̩] nt kein pl behavior

Verhaltensforschung f kein pl behavioral research

verhaltensgestört adj disturbed

Verhaltensweise f behavior

Verhältnis <-ses, -se> [fɛɐ̯ˈhɛlt·nɪs] nt ❶ (Relation) ratio; **im ~** in a ratio (**von** +dat of, **zu** +dat to); **in keinem ~ zu etw** dat **stehen** to bear no relation to sth ❷ (persönliche Beziehung) relationship (**zu** +dat with); (Affäre) affair ❸ pl (Bedingungen) conditions pl; **klare ~se schaffen** to get things straightened out ❹ pl (Lebensumstände) circumstances pl; **über seine ~se** pl **leben** to live beyond one's means pl

verhältnismäßig adv relatively

verhandeln* I. vi to negotiate II. vt ❶ (aushandeln) to negotiate ❷ JUR to hear

Verhandlung f ❶ meist pl (das Verhandeln) negotiations npl ❷ JUR trial, hearing

Verhängnis <-, -se> [fɛɐ̯ˈhɛŋ·nɪs] nt disaster; **jdm zum ~ werden** to be sb's undoing

verhängnisvoll adj disastrous, fatal

verharmlosen* [fɛɐ̯ˈharm·loː·zn̩] vt to play down sep

verharren* vi sein o haben (geh) to pause

verhaspeln* vr ■**sich** akk ~ to get [all] mixed up

verhasstRR, **verhaßt**ALT [fɛɐ̯ˈhast] adj hated

verhätscheln vt to spoil, to pamper

verhauen* <verhaute, verhauen> vt (fam) ❶ (verprügeln) to beat up sep ❷ SCH (fam) **ich habe den Aufsatz**

V

[gründlich] ~! I've made a [complete] mess of the essay!

verheddern* [fɛɡ·ˈhɛ·dən] *vr* ■**sich akk ~** ① (*sich verfangen*) to get tangled up ② (*sich versprechen*) to get [all] mixed up

verheerend I. *adj* devastating **II.** *adv* **sich akk ~ auswirken** to have a devastating effect

verheilen* *vi sein* to heal [up]

verheimlichen* [fɛɡ·ˈhaim·lɪ·çn̩] *vt* ■**[jdm] etw ~** to conceal sth [or keep sth secret] [from sb]; **ich habe nichts zu ~** I have nothing to hide

verheißungsvoll I. *adj* promising; **wenig ~** not very promising **II.** *adv* full of promise

verhelfen* *vi irreg* ■**jdm zu etw** *dat* **~** to help sb [to] achieve sth

verherrlichen* [fɛɡ·ˈhɛr·lɪ·çn̩] *vt* to glorify

verhexen* *vt* to bewitch

verhindern* *vt* to prevent

verhöhnen* *vt* to mock

Verhör <-[e]s, -e> [fɛɡ·ˈhøːɡ] *nt* questioning, interrogation

verhüllen* *vt* to cover

verhungern* *vi sein* to starve [to death]

verhüten* I. *vt* to prevent **II.** *vi* (*Verhütungsmittel anwenden*) to use contraception

Verhütung <-, -en> *f* ① (*das Verhindern*) prevention ② (*Empfängnisverhütung*) contraception

Verhütungsmittel *nt* contraceptive

verirren* *vr* ■**sich** *akk* **~** to get lost

verjagen* *vt* to chase away *sep*

verkabeln* *vt* to connect to the cable network

verkalken* *vi sein* ① (*Kalk einlagern*) to clog up; ■**verkalkt** clogged up ② *Arterien* to harden

Verkalkung <-, -en> *f* ① (*das Verkalken*) clogging ② *von Arterien* hardening

verkatert [fɛɡ·ˈkaː·tet] *adj* (*fam*) hungover *pred*

Verkauf <-s, Verkäufe> [fɛɡ·ˈkauf] *m* ① (*das Verkaufen*) sale, selling; **zum ~ stehen** to be [up] for sale ② *kein pl* (*Ver-*

kaufsabteilung) sales *no art,* + *sing/pl vb*

verkaufen* I. *vt* to sell (**an** +*akk* to); **zu ~ sein** to be for sale **II.** *vr* ■**sich** *akk* **~** to sell; **das Buch verkauft sich gut** the book is selling well

Verkäufer(in) [fɛɡ·ˈkɔy·fe] *m(f)* ① (*in Geschäft*) sales assistant ② (*verkaufender Eigentümer*) seller; JUR vendor

verkäuflich *adj* for sale *pred*

Verkaufspreis *m* retail price

Verkehr <-[e]s> [fɛɡ·ˈkeːɡ] *m kein pl* ① (*Straßenverkehr*) traffic ② (*Umgang*) contact, dealings *pl* ③ (*Handel*) **etw aus dem ~ ziehen** to withdraw sth from circulation ④ (*Geschlechtsverkehr*) intercourse

verkehren* I. *vi* ① *sein o haben* (*fahren*) to run; **der Zug verkehrt nur zweimal am Tag** the train only runs twice a day ② *haben* (*häufiger Gast sein*) to visit regularly ③ *haben* (*Umgang pflegen*) ■**[mit jdm] ~** to associate [with sb] **II.** *vr haben* (*sich umkehren*) ■**sich** *akk* **in etw** *akk* **~** to turn into sth

Verkehrsampel *f* traffic lights *pl*

verkehrsberuhigt *adj* traffic-calmed

Verkehrschaos *nt* traffic mess

Verkehrsfunk *m* traffic report

Verkehrskontrolle *f* police checkpoint

Verkehrsmittel *nt* means + *sing/pl vb* of transportation; **öffentliches/privates ~** public/private transportation

Verkehrsnetz *nt* transportation system

Verkehrsregel *f* traffic regulation

Verkehrsschild *nt* traffic sign

Verkehrssünder(in) *m(f)* (*fam*) traffic offender

Verkehrstote(r) *f(m) dekl wie adj* traffic fatality

Verkehrsverein *m* tourist [information] office

verkehrswidrig *adj* in violation of traffic regulations *pl*

Verkehrszeichen *nt s.* Verkehrsschild

verkehrt I. *adj* wrong; **die ~e Richtung** the wrong direction; ■**der V~e** the wrong person **II.** *adv* wrong; **~ herum** the wrong way around

verklagen* *vt* ■ **jdn ~** to take sb to court; **jdn auf Schadenersatz ~** to sue sb for damages

verkleiden* **I.** *vt* ➊ (*kostümieren*) to dress up *sep* ➋ (*überdecken*) to cover; (*innen*) to line **II.** *vr* ■ **sich** *akk* **~** to dress up

Verkleidung *f* ➊ (*zur Tarnung*) disguise; (*Kostüm*) costume ➋ (*Auskleidung*) lining

verkleinern* [fɛɐˈklaɪ·nɐn] **I.** *vt* ➊ (*verringern*) to reduce ➋ FOTO to reduce; COMPUT to scale down **II.** *vr* ■ **sich** *akk* **~** ➊ (*sich verringern*) to be reduced in size ➋ (*schrumpfen*) to shrink

Verkleinerungsform *f* LING diminutive [form]

verklemmt *adj* uptight [about sex *pred*]

Verknappung *f* shortage

verkneifen* *vr irreg* (*fam*) ■ **sich** *dat* **etw ~** ➊ (*nicht offen zeigen*) to repress sth; **ich konnte mir ein Grinsen nicht ~** I couldn't help grinning ➋ (*sich versagen*) to do without sth

verknittern* *vt* to crumple

verknoten* *vt* ■ **etw miteinander ~** to knot together *sep* sth

verknüpfen* *vt* ➊ (*verknoten*) to tie [together] *sep* ➋ (*verbinden*) to combine ➌ (*in Zusammenhang bringen*) to link (**mit** +*dat* to)

verkommen*[1] *vi irreg sein Gebäude* to decay; *Mensch* to go to the dogs; *Moral* to degenerate

verkommen[2] *adj* ➊ (*verfallen*) *Anwesen, Gebäude* dilapidated ➋ (*verwahrlost*) *Mensch* down-at-heel *attr*; down at heel *pred* ➌ (*moralisch*) degenerate

verkorkst <-er, -este> *adj* screwed-up; *Magen* upset

verkörpern* [fɛɐˈkœr·pɐn] *vt* ➊ FILM, THEAT to play [the part of] ➋ (*personifizieren*) to personify

verkrachen* *vr* (*fam*) ■ **sich** *akk* **~** to fall out

verkraften* [fɛɐˈkraf·tn̩] *vt* ■ **etw ~** to cope with sth

verkrampft **I.** *adj* tense **II.** *adv* tensely

verkriechen* *vr irreg* ■ **sich** *akk* **~** to crawl away

verkrüppelt <-er, -este> *adj* ➊ *Pflanzen* stunted ➋ *Mensch, Körperteil* crippled

verkümmern* *vi sein* ➊ (*eingehen*) to [shrivel up and] die ➋ (*verloren gehen*) to wither away ➌ (*die Lebenslust verlieren*) to waste away

verkürzen* **I.** *vt* ➊ (*kürzer machen*) to shorten (**auf** +*akk* to, **um** +*akk* by) ➋ (*zeitlich vermindern*) to reduce (**auf** +*akk* to, **um** +*akk* by); *Urlaub* to cut short *sep* **II.** *vr* ■ **sich** *akk* **~** to become shorter

Verkürzung *f* ➊ (*das Verkürzen*) shortening, cutting short ➋ (*zeitliche Verminderung*) reduction

verladen* *vt irreg* to load

Verlag <-[e]s, -e> [fɛɐˈlaːk] *m* publisher, publishing house

verlagern* *vt* to move; **den Schwerpunkt ~** to shift the emphasis

verlangen* **I.** *vt* ➊ (*fordern*) to demand (**von** +*dat* of); *Preis* to ask ➋ (*erfordern*) to require ➌ (*erwarten*) to expect; **das ist nicht zu viel verlangt** that is not too much to expect **II.** *vi* ■ **nach etw** *dat* **~** ➊ (*fordern*) to demand sth ➋ (*um etw bitten*) to ask for sth

Verlangen <-s, -> *nt* ➊ (*dringender Wunsch*) desire (**nach** +*dat* for) ➋ (*Forderung*) demand; **auf ~** [up]on demand; **auf ihr ~** [hin] at her request

verlängern* [fɛɐˈlɛŋɐn] **I.** *vt* ➊ (*länger machen*) to lengthen, to extend (**um** +*akk* by) ➋ (*länger dauern lassen*) to extend; *Leben* to prolong; *Vertrag* to renew **II.** *vr* ■ **sich** *akk* **~** to increase (**um** +*akk* by), to become longer (**um** +*akk* by); *Leben, Leid* to be prolonged

Verlängerung <-, -en> *f* ➊ (*räumlich*) lengthening; (*durch ein Zusatzteil*) extension ➋ *kein pl* (*zeitliche*) extension ➌ SPORT overtime

Verlängerungskabel *nt*, **Verlängerungsschnur** *f* extension cord

V

verlangsamen* [fɛɐ̯ˈlaŋ·za·mən] I. vt to slow down sep II. vr ■ sich akk ~ to slow [down]

verlassen*¹ irreg I. vt ❶ (im Stich lassen) to abandon; **der Mut verließ ihn** he lost [his] courage ❷ (fortgehen) to leave II. vr ■ sich akk auf jdn/etw ~ to rely on sb/sth; **worauf du dich ~ kannst!** you bet!, I guarantee it!

verlassen² adj deserted; (verwahrlost) desolate

verlässlichᴿᴿ, **verläßlich**ᴬᴸᵀ [fɛɐ̯ˈlɛs·lɪç] adj reliable

Verlauf [fɛɐ̯ˈlauf] m course; **einen guten ~ nehmen** to go well; **im ~ der nächsten Monate** over the course of the next few months

verlaufen* irreg I. vi sein ❶ (ablaufen) **das Gespräch verlief nicht wie erhofft** the discussion didn't go as hoped ❷ (sich erstrecken) to run II. vr (sich verirren) ■ sich akk ~ to get lost

Verlaufsform f LING continuous form

verlebt adj ruined, haggard

verlegen*¹ [fɛɐ̯ˈleː·gn̩] vt ❶ Schlüssel etc. to misplace ❷ Termin to postpone (auf +akk until) ❸ Gleise, Kabel, Teppich to lay ❹ Buch to publish ❺ Abteilung, Patient to transfer

verlegen² [fɛɐ̯ˈleː·gn̩] I. adj embarrassed; **er ist nie um eine Entschuldigung ~** he's never lost for an excuse II. adv in embarrassment

Verlegenheit <-, -en> f kein pl embarrassment

Verleger(in) <-s, -> m(f) publisher

Verleih <-[e]s, -e> [fɛɐ̯ˈlai] m ❶ (Unternehmen) rental company ❷ kein pl (das Verleihen) renting out

verleihen* vt irreg ❶ (verborgen) to lend (an +akk to); (gegen Geld) to rent out sep ❷ (jdn mit etw auszeichnen) **jdm einen Preis ~** to award sb a prize ❸ (geben) Kraft to give

verleiten* vt ■ jdn [zu etw dat] ~ ❶ (dazu bringen) to persuade sb [to do sth] ❷ (verführen) to entice sb [to do sth]

verlernen* vt to forget; **das Tanzen ~** to forget how to dance

verletzbar adj s. **verletzlich**

verletzen* [fɛɐ̯ˈlɛtsn̩] vt ❶ (verwunden) to injure [or hurt] ❷ (kränken) to offend; Gefühle to hurt ❸ (übertreten) to violate

verletzend adj hurtful

verletzlich adj vulnerable

Verletzte(r) f/m dekl wie adj injured person; (Opfer) casualty; ■ **die ~n** the injured + pl vb

Verletzung <-, -en> f ❶ MED injury ❷ kein pl (Übertretung) violation

verleugnen* vt to deny

verleumden* [fɛɐ̯ˈlɔym·dn̩] vt to slander; (schriftlich) to libel

Verleumdung <-, -en> f slander, libel

verlieben* vr ■ sich akk [in jdn] ~ to fall in love [with sb]; (für jdn schwärmen) to have a crush on sb

verliebt adj infatuated; ■ ~ **sein** to be in love (in +akk with)

verlieren <verlor, verloren> [fɛɐ̯ˈliː·rən] I. vt to lose ▶ WENDUNGEN: **du hast hier nichts verloren** (fam) you have no business being here II. vr ■ sich akk ~ to disappear

Verlierer(in) <-s, -> m(f) loser

Verlies <-es, -e> [fɛɐ̯ˈliːs] nt dungeon

verloben* vr ■ sich akk ~ to get engaged (mit +dat to)

Verlobte(r) f/m dekl wie adj fiancé masc, fiancée fem

Verlobung <-, -en> f engagement

verlockend adj tempting

verlogen [fɛɐ̯ˈloː·gn̩] adj ❶ (lügnerisch) lying attr; ~ **sein** Behauptung to be a lie; Mensch to be a liar ❷ (heuchlerisch) insincere, phony

verloren [fɛɐ̯ˈloː·rən] I. pp von **verlieren** II. adj ~ **gehen** to get lost

verlosen* vt to raffle

Verlosung f raffle, drawing

Verlust <-[e]s, -e> [fɛɐ̯ˈlʊst] m loss; ~ **e machen** to be losing money

vermachen* vt to bequeath

Vermächtnis <-ses, -se> [fɛɐ̯ˈmɛçt·nɪs] nt legacy

vermählen* [fɛɐ̯ˈmɛːlən] *vr* (*geh*) ■ **sich** *akk* [mit jdm] ~ to marry [sb] *attr*

vermarkten* *vt* to market

vermasseln* [fɛɐ̯ˈmasl̩n] *vt* to mess up *sep*

vermehren* *vr* ■ **sich** *akk* ~ ➊ (*sich fortpflanzen*) to reproduce; (*stärker*) to multiply ➋ (*zunehmen*) to increase (**um** +*akk* by)

Vermehrung <-, -en> *f* ➊ (*Fortpflanzung*) reproduction; (*stärker*) multiplying ➋ (*das Anwachsen*) increase

vermeiden* *vt irreg* to avoid; **sich** *akk* **nicht ~ lassen** to be inevitable

Vermerk <-[e]s, -e> [fɛɐ̯ˈmɛrk] *m* note

vermessen* [fɛɐ̯ˈmɛsn̩] *vt irreg* to measure; *Grundstück, Gebäude* to survey

vermessen² [fɛɐ̯ˈmɛsn̩] *adj* presumptuous

vermieten* *vt* to rent out *sep* (**an** +*akk* to); „**zu ~**" "for rent"

Vermieter(in) *m(f)* landlord *masc*, landlady *fem*

vermindern* I. *vt* to reduce II. *vr* ■ **sich** *akk* ~ to decrease, to diminish

vermischen* I. *vt* ➊ to mix; (*um eine bestimmte Qualität zu erreichen*) to blend II. *vr* ■ **sich** *akk* [miteinander] ~ to mix

vermissen* *vt* ➊ (*das Fehlen bemerken*) ■ **etw** ~ to have lost sth ➋ (*jds Abwesenheit bedauern*) ■ **jdn** ~ to miss sb ➌ (*jds Abwesenheit feststellen*) **wir ~ unsere Tochter** our daughter is missing

Vermisste(r)ᴿᴿ, **Vermißte(r)**ᴬᴸᵀ *f(m) dekl wie adj* missing person

vermitteln* I. *vt* ➊ (*beschaffen*) **jdm eine Stellung ~** to find sb a job; **jdn an eine Firma ~** to place sb with a company ➋ (*weitergeben*) to pass on *sep*; **jdm ein schönes Gefühl ~** to give sb a good feeling ➌ (*arrangieren*) to arrange II. *vi* to mediate

Vermittlung <-, -en> *f* ➊ (*Vermitteln*) *einer Stelle, Wohnung* finding ➋ (*Schlichtung*) mediation ➌ (*Telefon-zentrale*) operator ➍ (*das Weitergeben*) imparting

Vermögen <-s, -> [fɛɐ̯ˈmøːɡn̩] *nt* FIN assets *pl*; (*Geld*) capital; (*Eigentum*) property; (*Reichtum*) fortune, wealth

vermögend [fɛɐ̯ˈmøːɡn̩t] *adj* wealthy

Vermögenssteuer *f* property tax

vermummt *adj* masked

vermuten* *vt* to suspect

vermutlich I. *adj attr* probable, likely II. *adv* probably

Vermutung <-, -en> *f* assumption

vernachlässigen* [fɛɐ̯ˈnax.lɛ.sɪ.ɡn̩] *vt* ➊ (*sich nicht genügend kümmern*) to neglect ➋ (*unberücksichtigt lassen*) to ignore

vernarben* *vi sein* to form a scar; ■ **vernarbt** scarred

vernehmen* *vt irreg* JUR to question

Vernehmung <-, -en> *f* JUR questioning

verneigen* *vr* ■ **sich** *akk* ~ to bow

verneinen* [fɛɐ̯ˈnai̯nən] *vt* ➊ (*negieren*) to say no; **eine Frage ~** to answer a question in the negative ➋ (*leugnen*) to deny

Verneinung <-, -en> *f* LING negation

vernetzen* *vt* ➊ COMPUT to network, to link up *sep* ➋ (*fig: verknüpfen*) ■ [mit **etw** *dat*] **vernetzt sein** to be linked [up] [to sth]

vernetzt *adj* COMPUT networked

vernichten* [fɛɐ̯ˈnɪçtn̩] *vt* ➊ (*zerstören*) to destroy ➋ (*ausrotten*) to exterminate

vernichtend I. *adj* devastating; *Niederlage* crushing II. *adv* **jdn ~ schlagen** to inflict a crushing defeat on sb

Vernichtung <-, -en> *f* ➊ (*Zerstörung*) destruction ➋ (*Ausrottung*) extermination

Vernunft <-> [fɛɐ̯ˈnʊnft] *f kein pl* reason, common sense; **jdn zur ~ bringen** to bring sb to his/her senses

vernünftig [fɛɐ̯ˈnʏnftɪç] I. *adj* ➊ (*klug*) reasonable, sensible ➋ (*fam: ordentlich*) (*anständig, gut*) decent; **~e Preise** decent prices II. *adv* (*fam*) properly, decently

V

veröffentlichen* [fɛɐ̯·ˈʔœfn̩t·lɪ·çn̩] *vt* to publish

Veröffentlichung <-, -en> *f* publication

verordnen* *vt* MED to prescribe

verpachten* *vt* to lease (**an** +*akk* to)

verpacken* *vt* to pack [up *sep*]; (*als Geschenk*) to wrap [up *sep*]

Verpackung <-, -en> *f* ❶ *kein pl* (*das Verpacken*) packing ❷ (*Hülle*) packaging

verpassen* *vt* ❶ (*versäumen*) to miss ❷ (*fam: aufzwingen*) ■ **jdm etw** ~ to give sb sth; **jdm einen Denkzettel** ~ to give sb a warning

verpesten* [fɛɐ̯·ˈpɛs·tn̩] *vt* to pollute

verpetzen* *vt* (*fam*) ■ **jdn** ~ to tell on sb

verpfänden* *vt* to pawn; *Grundstück, Haus* to mortgage

verpflanzen* *vt* ❶ (*umpflanzen*) to replant ❷ MED ■ **jdm ein Organ** ~ to give sb an organ transplant

verpflegen* *vt* to cater for

Verpflegung <-, *selten* -en> *f* ❶ *kein pl* (*das Verpflegen*) catering; **mit voller** ~ with full board ❷ (*Nahrung*) food

verpflichten* [fɛɐ̯·ˈpflɪç·tn̩] I. *vt* ❶ (*eine Pflicht auferlegen*) ■ **jdn** [**zu etw** *dat*] ~ to oblige sb to do sth ❷ (*einstellen*) ■ **jdn** [**für etw** *akk*] ~ to hire sb [to do sth] II. *vr* ■ **sich** *akk* **zu etw** *dat* ~ to commit oneself to doing sth

Verpflichtung <-, -en> *f* ❶ *meist pl* (*Pflichten*) duty; **seinen** ~**en nachkommen** to fulfill one's obligations; **finanzielle** ~**en** financial commitments ❷ *kein pl* (*das Engagieren*) engagement

verpfuschen* *vt* ■ **etw** ~ to make a mess of sth

verpixeln *vt* (*fam*) COMPUT ■ **to be** ~**t** to be pixelated [*or* pixelated]

verplappern* *vr* ■ **sich** *akk* ~ to blab

verpönt [fɛɐ̯·ˈpøːnt] *adj* deprecated

verprassen* *vt* to squander

verprügeln* *vt* to beat up *sep*; (*als Strafe*) to give sb a beating

Verputz *m* plaster

verputzen* *vt* ❶ (*mit Putz versehen*) to plaster ❷ (*fam: aufessen*) to polish off *sep*

verqualmt <-er, -este> *adj* smoke-filled *attr*, full of smoke *pred*

verquollen *adj* swollen

Verrat <-[e]s> [fɛɐ̯·ˈraːt] *m* ❶ *kein pl* betrayal (**an** +*dat* of) ❷ JUR treason

verraten <verriet, verraten> I. *vt* ❶ (*ausplaudern*) to give away *sep* ❷ (*Verrat üben, preisgeben*) to betray ❸ (*erkennen lassen*) to show II. *vr* ■ **sich** *akk* ~ to give oneself away

Verräter(in) <-s, -> [fɛɐ̯·ˈrɛː·tɐ] *m(f)* traitor

verrechnen* I. *vr* ■ **sich** *akk* ~ to miscalculate II. *vt* ■ **etw mit etw** *dat* ~ to set off *sep* sth against sth

Verrechnungsscheck *m* a check [endorsed] for deposit only

verregnet <-er, -este> *adj* spoiled by rain; *Tag* rainy

verreisen* *vi sein* to go away; **geschäftlich verreist sein** to be away on business

verrenken* *vt* to twist; **sich** *dat* **ein Gelenk** ~ to dislocate a joint

Verrenkung <-, -en> *f* distortion; *Gelenk* dislocation

verrichten* *vt* to perform

verriegeln* *vt* to bolt

verringern* [fɛɐ̯·ˈrɪŋɐn] I. *vt* to reduce (**um** +*akk* by) II. *vr* ■ **sich** *akk* ~ to decrease

Verringerung <-> *f kein pl* reduction

verrosten* *vi sein* to rust

verrotten* [fɛɐ̯·ˈrɔ·tn̩] *vi sein* ❶ (*faulen*) to rot ❷ (*verwahrlosen*) to decay

verrücken* *vt* to move

verrückt [fɛɐ̯·ˈrʏkt] *adj* ❶ (*wahnsinnig*) nuts, crazy; **bist du** ~? are you out of your mind?; **jdn** ~ **machen** to drive sb crazy ❷ (*in starkem Maße*) **wie** ~ like crazy ❸ (*ausgefallen*) crazy, wild ❹ (*versessen*) ■ ~ **nach jdm/etw sein** to be crazy about sb/sth

Verrückte(r) *f(m) dekl wie adj* lunatic

verrufen* *adj* disreputable

verrühren* *vt* to stir

verrutschen* *vi sein* to slip

Vers <-es, -e> [fɛrs] *m* verse, lines *pl*

versagen* I. *vi* to fail, to choke *sl* II. *vt* ▪**jdm etw ~** to refuse sb sth

Versagen <-s> *nt kein pl* failure; **menschliches ~** human error

Versager(in) <-s, -> *m(f)* failure

versalzen* *vt irreg* to put too much salt in/on

versammeln* I. *vr* ▪**sich** *akk* **~** to gather, to assemble II. *vt* (*zusammenkommen lassen*) to call together; *Truppen* to rally

Versammlung *f* ① (*Zusammenkunft*) meeting ② (*versammelte Menschen*) assembly

Versand <-[e]s> [fɛɐ̯ˈzant] *m kein pl* ① (*das Versenden*) dispatch ② (*Versandabteilung*) dispatch, distribution

Versandhandel *m* mail order *no art*

Versandhaus *nt* mail-order company

versäumen* *vt* to miss

verschaffen* *vt* ▪**sich/jdm etw ~** to get [a hold of] sth for oneself/sb; **jdm eine Stellung ~** to get sb a job; **sich** *dat* **Gewissheit ~** to make certain

verschämt [fɛɐ̯ˈʃɛːmt] *adj* shy, bashful

verschanzen* *vr* ▪**sich** *akk* **~** ① MIL to take up a fortified position ② (*verstecken*) to take refuge

verschärfen* I. *vr* ▪**sich** *akk* **~** to get worse; *Krise* to intensify II. *vt* ① (*rigoroser machen*) to make more rigorous; *Strafe* to make more severe ② (*zuspitzen*) *Situation* to aggravate

verschenken* *vt* ① (*schenken*) to give away *sep* (**an** *+akk* to) ② (*ungenutzt lassen*) to waste

verscherzen* *vr* ▪**sich** *akk* **~** to lose sth; ▪**es sich** *dat* **mit jdm ~** to have a falling out with sb

verscheuchen* *vt* to chase away *sep*

verschicken* *vt* to send

verschieben* *irreg* I. *vt* ① *Gegenstand* to move (**um** *+akk* by) ② *Termin* to postpone (**auf** *+akk* until, **um** *+akk* by) II. *vr* ▪**sich** *akk* **~** ① (*später stattfinden*) to be postponed ② (*verrutschen*) to slip

Verschiebung *f* postponement

verschieden [fɛɐ̯ˈʃiː·dn̩] I. *adj* ① (*unterschiedlich*) different; (*mehrere*) various ② *attr* (*einige*) several *attr*; a few *attr*; ▪**V~es** various things *pl* II. *adv* differently

verschiedenartig *adj* different kinds of *attr*; diverse

Verschiedenheit <-, -en> *f* (*Unterschiedlichkeit*) difference; (*Unähnlichkeit*) dissimilarity

verschimmeln* *vi sein* to get moldy

verschlafen*¹ *irreg* I. *vi* to oversleep II. *vt* ① (*fam*) to miss ② (*schlafend verbringen*) to sleep through

verschlafen² *adj* sleepy

verschlagen*¹ *vt irreg* ① (*nehmen*) **jdm die Sprache ~** to leave sb speechless ② (*geraten*) **es hatte mich nach Argentinien ~** I ended up in Argentina

verschlagen² I. *adj* devious, sly *pej*; **ein ~er Blick** a furtive glance II. *adv* slyly; (*verdächtig*) shiftily

verschlampen* *vt* ▪**etw ~** to manage to lose sth

verschlechtern* [fɛɐ̯ˈʃlɛç·tɐn] I. *vt* to make worse II. *vr* ▪**sich** *akk* **~** to get worse, to worsen

Verschlechterung <-, -en> *f* worsening

verschleiern* [fɛɐ̯ˈʃlai·ɐn] *vt* ① (*mit einem Schleier bedecken*) to cover with a veil ② (*verdecken*) to cover up *sep*

verschleiert *adj Gesicht* veiled

Verschleiß <-es, -e> [fɛɐ̯ˈʃlais] *m* wear [and tear]

verschleißen <verschliss, verschlissen> *vt, vi sein* to wear out

verschleppen* *vt* ① (*deportieren*) to take away *sep* ② (*hinauszögern*) to prolong ③ MED to delay treatment

verschleudern* *vt* to sell off *sep* cheaply

verschließen* *irreg* I. *vt* ① (*zumachen*) to close ② (*zuschließen*) to lock ③ (*wegschließen*) to lock away *sep* ④ (*versagt bleiben*) ▪**jdm verschlos-**

sen bleiben to be closed off to sb II. *vr* ■ **sich** *akk* **etw** *dat* ~ to ignore sth

verschlimmern* I. *vt* to make worse II. *vr* ■ **sich** *akk* ~ to get worse; *Zustand, Lage a.* to deteriorate

Verschlimmerung <-, -en> *f* deterioration

verschlingen* *vt irreg Essen, Buch* to devour

verschlissen I. *pp von* **verschleißen** II. *adj* worn-out

verschlossen [fɛɐ̯ˈʃlɔsn̩] *adj* ① (*zugemacht*) closed ② (*abgeschlossen*) locked ③ (*zurückhaltend*) reserved; (*schweigsam*) taciturn

verschlucken* I. *vt* ① (*hinunterschlucken*) to swallow ② (*undeutlich aussprechen*) to slur; (*nicht aussprechen*) to bite back II. *vr* ■ **sich** *akk* ~ to choke (**an** +*dat* on)

verschlungen I. *pp von* **verschlingen** II. *adj* entwined

Verschluss^RR, **Verschluß**^ALT *m* ① *von Tasche, Brosche* clasp; **etw unter ~ halten** to keep sth under lock and key ② (*Deckel*) lid; *Flasche* top

verschlüsseln* [fɛɐ̯ˈʃlʏsl̩n] *vt* to [en]code

verschmähen* *vt* to reject; (*stärker*) to scorn

verschmelzen* *irreg* I. *vi sein* to melt together II. *vt* (*löten*) to solder; (*verschweißen*) to weld

verschmieren* I. *vt* ① (*verstreichen*) to apply; *Creme etc.* to spread ② (*verwischen*) to smear ③ (*beschmieren*) to make dirty II. *vi* to smear, to get smeared

verschmutzen* I. *vt* to make dirty; ÖKOL to pollute II. *vi sein* to get dirty; ÖKOL to get polluted

verschneit *adj* snow-covered *attr*, covered in snow *pred*

verschnörkelt *adj* adorned with flourishes

verschnupft [fɛɐ̯ˈʃnʊpft] *adj* (*fam*) ■ ~ **sein** ① (*erkältet*) to have a cold ② (*indigniert*) to be in a huff

verschnüren* *vt* to tie up *sep* [with a string]

verschollen [fɛɐ̯ˈʃɔlən] *adj* missing

verschonen* *vt* to spare; **verschone mich mit den Einzelheiten!** spare me the details!; **von etw** *dat* **verschont bleiben** to escape sth

verschönern* [fɛɐ̯ˈʃøːnɐn] *vt* to brighten up *sep*

verschränken* *vt* **die Arme/Beine ~** to fold one's arms/cross one's legs

verschreiben* *irreg* I. *vt* ■ **jdm etw ~** to prescribe sb sth (**gegen** +*akk* for) II. *vr* ① (*falsch schreiben*) ■ **sich** *akk* ~ to make a slip of the pen ② (*sich widmen*) ■ **sich** *akk* **etw** *dat* ~ to devote oneself to sth

verschreibungspflichtig *adj* available by prescription only *pred*

verschrotten* *vt* to scrap

verschüchtert *adj* intimidated

verschulden* I. *vt* ■ **etw ~** to be to blame for sth II. *vi sein* ■ **verschuldet sein** to be in debt III. *vr* ■ **sich** *akk* ~ to get into debt

Verschulden <-s> *nt kein pl* fault

Verschuldung <-, -en> *f* (*Schulden*) debts *pl*

verschütten* [fɛɐ̯ˈʃʏtən] *vt* ① (*danebenschütten*) to spill ② (*unter etw begraben*) to bury

verschwägert [fɛɐ̯ˈʃvɛːɡɐt] *adj* related by marriage *pred*

verschweigen* *vt irreg* to keep secret (**vor** +*dat* from); *Informationen* to withhold; ■ **jdm ~, dass ...** to keep from sb the fact that ...

verschwenden* *vt* to waste

Verschwender(in) <-s, -> *m(f)* wasteful person; *Geld a.* spendthrift

verschwenderisch I. *adj* ① (*sinnlos ausgebend*) wasteful ② (*sehr üppig*) extravagant, sumptuous II. *adv* wastefully

Verschwendung <-, -en> *f* waste

verschwiegen [fɛɐ̯ˈʃviːɡn̩] *adj* discreet

verschwimmen* *vi irreg sein* to become blurred

verschwinden* *vi irreg sein* ① (*nicht*

mehr da sein) to disappear; ■**verschwunden [sein]** [to be] missing; **etw in etw** *dat* ~ **lassen** to slip sth into sth ❷(*sich auflösen*) to vanish ❸(*fam: sich davonmachen*) to disappear; **verschwinde!** beat it!, scram!

Verschwinden <-s> *nt kein pl* disappearance

verschwommen *adj* ❶(*undeutlich*) blurred ❷(*unklar*) hazy, vague

verschwören* *vr irreg* ■**sich** *akk* ~ to conspire [*or* plot] (**gegen** +*akk* against)

Verschwörung <-, -en> *f* conspiracy, plot

Versehen <-s, -> [fɛɐ̯ˈzeːən] *nt* mistake; **aus** ~ inadvertently; (*aufgrund einer Verwechslung a.*) by mistake

versehentlich [fɛɐ̯ˈzeːənt.lɪç] *adv* inadvertently; (*aufgrund einer Verwechslung a.*) by mistake

versenden* *vt irreg o reg* to send

versenken* *vt* to sink

versessen [fɛɐ̯ˈzɛsn̩] *adj* ■**auf etw** *akk* ~ **sein** to be crazy about sth

versetzen I. *vt* ❶(*an eine andere Stelle*) to move; (*aus Berufsgründen*) to transfer ❷sch **einen Schüler** ~ to move up *sep* [*or* promote] a student ❸(*bringen*) **jdn in Begeisterung** ~ to fill sb with enthusiasm; **jdn in Panik/ Wut** ~ to send sb into a panic/a rage ❹(*verpfänden*) to pawn ❺(*warten lassen*) ■**jdn** ~ to stand sb up ❻(*mischen*) **etw mit etw** *dat* ~ to mix sth with sth II. *vr* (*sich hineindenken*) ■**sich** *akk* **in jdn** ~ to put oneself in sb's place

Versetzung <-, -en> *f* ❶(*beruflich*) transfer ❷sch moving up, promotion

verseuchen* [fɛɐ̯ˈzɔy̯çn̩] *vt* to contaminate; *Umwelt* to pollute

versichern*¹ *vt* to insure

versichern*² *vt* ■**jdm** ~, **[dass]** ... to assure sb [that] ...

Versicherte(r) *f(m) dekl wie adj* insured

Versicherung¹ *f* ❶(*Vertrag*) insurance policy ❷(*Gesellschaft*) insurance company

Versicherung² *f* (*Beteuerung*) assurance

Versicherungsschutz *m kein pl* insurance coverage

Versicherungsvertreter(in) *m(f)* insurance agent

versickern* *vi sein* to seep away

versiegeln* *vt* to seal [up *sep*]

versinken *vi irreg sein* to sink

versöhnen* [fɛɐ̯ˈzøː.nən] I. *vr* ■**sich** *akk* **mit jdm** ~ to make up with sb II. *vt* ❶(*aussöhnen*) to reconcile ❷(*besänftigen*) to mollify

Versöhnung <-, -en> *f* reconciliation

versorgen* *vt* ❶(*betreuen*) ■**jdn** ~ to take care of [*or* look after] sb ❷(*versehen*) to supply; ■**sich** *akk* **mit etw** *dat* ~ to provide oneself with sth; **sich** *akk* **selbst** ~ to look after oneself

Versorgung <-> *f kein pl* ❶(*das Versorgen*) care ❷(*das Ausstatten*) supply

verspäten* [fɛɐ̯ˈʃpɛː.tn̩] *vr* ■**sich** *akk* ~ to be [running] late

verspätet I. *adj* ❶(*zu spät eintreffend*) delayed ❷(*zu spät erfolgend*) late II. *adv* late; (*nachträglich*) belatedly

Verspätung <-, -en> *f* delay; **haben** to be late; **mit einer Stunde** ~ **ankommen** to arrive an hour late

versperren* *vt* to block

verspielen* *vt* ❶(*beim Glücksspiel*) to gamble away *sep* ❷ *Chance* to squander

verspotten* *vt* to mock

versprechen* *irreg* I. *vt* to promise II. *vr* ❶(*sich erhoffen*) ■**sich** *dat* **etw von jdm/etw** ~ to hope for sth from sb/sth; **ich verspreche mir nicht viel davon** I don't expect much ❷(*falsch sprechen*) ■**sich** *akk* ~ to misspeak

Versprechen <-s, -> *nt* promise

verspritzen* *vt* to spray

verstaatlichen* [fɛɐ̯ˈʃtaːt.lɪ.çn̩] *vt* to nationalize

verstand [fɛɐ̯ˈʃtant] *imp von* **verstehen**

Verstand <-[e]s> [fɛɐ̯ˈʃtant] *m kein pl* reason; **du bist wohl nicht bei** ~! you're out of your mind!; **bei klarem** ~

V

sein to be lucid; **jdn um den ~ bringen** to drive sb out of his/her mind

verständig [fɛɐ̯·ˈʃtɛn·dɪç] *adj* (*einsichtig*) cooperative

verständigen* [fɛɐ̯·ˈʃtɛn·dɪ·gn̩] I. *vt* to notify (**von** +*dat* of) II. *vr* ■ **sich** *akk* ~ ① (*sich verständlich machen*) to communicate ② (*sich einigen*) to reach an agreement

Verständigung <-, *selten* -en> *f* ① (*Benachrichtigung*) notification ② (*Kommunikation*) communication ③ (*Einigung*) agreement, understanding

verständlich [fɛɐ̯·ˈʃtɛnt·lɪç] I. *adj* ① (*begreiflich*) understandable; **sich** *akk* ~ **machen** to make oneself understood ② (*gut zu hören*) clear, intelligible ③ (*leicht zu verstehen*) clear, comprehensible II. *adv* ① (*vernehmbar*) clearly ② (*verstehbar*) comprehensibly

Verständnis <-ses, *selten* -se> [fɛɐ̯·ˈʃtɛnt·nɪs] *nt* understanding; **für etw** *akk* ~ **haben** to have sympathy for sth

verständnislos I. *adj* uncomprehending; **ein ~er Blick** a blank look II. *adv* uncomprehendingly, blankly

verständnisvoll *adj* understanding, sympathetic

verstärken* *vt* ① (*stärker machen*) to strengthen; (*durch stärkeres Material a.*) to reinforce ② (*intensivieren*) *Gefühle* to intensify ③ (*erhöhen*) to increase

Verstärker <-s, -> *m* TECH amplifier, amp *fam*

Verstärkung *f* ① (*das Verstärken*) strengthening ② (*Vergrößerung*) reinforcement ③ (*Erhöhung*) increase

verstauchen* *vt* ■ **sich** *dat* **das Handgelenk** ~ to sprain one's wrist

verstauen* *vt* to pack [away *sep*]

Versteck <-[e]s, -e> [fɛɐ̯·ˈʃtɛk] *nt* hiding place

verstecken* *vt* to hide (**vor** +*dat* from)

versteckt *adj* ① (*verborgen*) hidden; (*vorsätzlich a.*) concealed ② (*abgelegen*) secluded ③ (*unausgesprochen*) veiled

verstehen <verstand verstanden>

I. *vt* ① (*hören*) to hear; ~ **Sie mich gut?** can you hear me okay? ② (*begreifen*) to understand ③ (*können*) to understand; ■ **es** ~, **etw zu tun** to know how to do sth; **er versteht nichts von Musik** he doesn't know a thing about music ④ (*auslegen*) **was verstehst du unter teuer?** what's "expensive" to you?; **wie darf ich das ~?** how am I supposed to interpret that?; **dieser Brief ist als Drohung zu** ~ this letter has to be taken as a threat II. *vr* ① (*auskommen*) ■ **sich** *akk* **mit jdm** ~ to get along with sb ② (*beherrschen*) ■ **sich** *akk* **auf etw** *akk* ~ to know all about sth ③ (*zu verstehen sein*) **etw versteht sich von selbst** sth goes without saying III. *vi* **verstehst du?** [do you] understand?, you know?

versteifen* *vr* ■ **sich** *akk* ~ ① (*auf etw beharren*) to insist (**auf** +*akk* on) ② MED to stiffen [up]

versteigern* *vt* to auction [off]

Versteigerung *f* auction

Versteinerung <-, -en> *f* fossil

verstellbar *adj* adjustable

verstellen* I. *vt* ① (*anders einstellen*) to adjust ② (*woandershin stellen*) to move ③ (*unzugänglich machen*) to block ④ (*verändern*) to disguise II. *vr* ■ **sich** *akk* ~ to put on an act

versteuern* *vt* ■ **etw** ~ to pay tax on sth

verstimmt *adj* ① MUS out of tune ② (*verärgert*) ■ ~ **sein** to be disgruntled ③ *Magen* upset

verstockt *adj* obstinate

verstohlen [fɛɐ̯·ˈʃtoː·lən] I. *adj* furtive II. *adv* furtively

verstopfen* I. *vt* to block up *sep* II. *vi sein* to become blocked [up]

verstopft *adj* blocked, congested

Verstopfung <-, -en> *f* MED constipation; ~ **haben** to be constipated

verstorben [fɛɐ̯·ˈʃtɔr·bn̩] *adj* deceased, late *attr*

Verstorbene(r) *f(m) dekl wie adj* deceased

verstört [fɛɐ̯ˈʃtøːɐ̯t] I. *adj* distraught II. *adv* in distress

Verstoß [fɛɐ̯ˈʃtoːs] *m* violation (**gegen** +*akk* of); JUR offense

verstoßen* *irreg* I. *vi* ■**gegen etw** *akk* ~ to violate sth II. *vt* ■**jdn** ~ to expel sb

verstreichen* *irreg* I. *vt* Farbe to apply; Butter to spread II. *vi* sein Zeit to pass [by]; Zeitspanne a. to elapse

Verstümmelung <-, -en> *f* mutilation

Versuch <-[e]s, -e> [fɛɐ̯ˈzuːx] *m* ❶ (Bemühen) attempt, try ❷ (Experiment) experiment

versuchen* *vt* ❶ (probieren) to try; ■~, etw zu tun to try doing/to do sth; ■es mit jdm/etw ~ to give sb/sth a try ❷ (in Versuchung sein) ■versucht sein, etw zu tun to be tempted to do sth

Versuchskaninchen *nt* guinea pig

Versuchstier *nt* laboratory animal

Versuchung <-, -en> *f* temptation; jdn in ~ führen to tempt sb; in ~ geraten to be tempted

versunken [fɛɐ̯ˈzʊŋkn̩] *adj* ❶ (untergegangen) sunken ❷ in Gedanken ~ sein to be lost in thought

versüßen* *vt* to sweeten

vertagen* *vt* to adjourn (**auf** +*akk* until); Entscheidung to postpone

vertauschen* *vt* to switch; (unabsichtlich) to mix up *sep*

verteidigen* [fɛɐ̯ˈtai̯dɪɡn̩] *vt, vi* to defend

Verteidiger(in) <-s, -> *m(f)* ❶ JUR defense counsel ❷ SPORT defender

Verteidigung <-, -en> *f* defense

Verteidigungsministerium *nt* Defense Department

verteilen* I. *vt* ❶ (austeilen) to distribute (**an** +*akk* on) ❷ (platzieren) to place ❸ (ausstreuen, verstreichen) to spread (**auf** +*dat* on) II. *vr* (sich verbreiten) ■sich *akk* ~ to spread out

Verteilung *f* distribution

verteuern* [fɛɐ̯ˈtɔy̯ɐn] I. *vt* to increase the price (**um** +*akk* by) II. *vr* ■sich *akk* ~ to become more expensive

vertiefen* [fɛɐ̯ˈtiːfn̩] I. *vt* to deepen II. *vr* ■sich *akk* in etw *akk* ~ to become absorbed in sth; in Gedanken vertieft sein to be deep in thought

Vertiefung <-, -en> *f* ❶ (vertiefte Stelle) depression ❷ kein pl von Beziehung, Freundschaft deepening

vertikal [vɛɐ̯tiˈkaːl] I. *adj* vertical II. *adv* vertically

vertippen* *vr* (fam) ■sich *akk* ~ to make a typo *fam*

Vertrag <-[e]s, Verträge> [fɛɐ̯ˈtraːk] *m* contract; (international) treaty; jdn unter ~ nehmen to contract sb

vertragen* *irreg* I. *vt* ❶ (aushalten) to bear, to stand ❷ (wegstecken können) to tolerate ❸ (fam: zu sich nehmen können) ich vertrage keinen Alkohol alcohol doesn't agree with me ❹ (fam: benötigen) das Haus könnte einen neuen Anstrich ~ the house could use a new coat of paint ❺ SCHWEIZ (austragen) to deliver II. *vr* ❶ (auskommen) ■sich *akk* mit jdm ~ to get along with sb ❷ (zusammenpassen) ■sich *akk* mit etw *dat* ~ to go with sth

vertraglich [fɛɐ̯ˈtraːklɪç] I. *adj* contractual II. *adv* contractually, by contract; ~ festgelegt sein to be laid down in a contract

verträglich [fɛɐ̯ˈtrɛːklɪç] *adj* ❶ (umgänglich) good-natured ❷ (bekömmlich) gut/schwer ~ easily digestible/hard to digest; Medikament well-[·]/not well[·]tolerated

VertragsabschlussRR *m* acceptance of the terms and conditions of a contract

Vertragsbruch *m* breach of contract

vertrauen* *vi* ■jdm ~ to trust sb; ■auf jdn ~ to trust in sb; auf Gott ~ to put one's trust in God; ■darauf ~, dass ... to be confident that ...

Vertrauen <-s> *nt kein pl* trust, confidence (**zu** +*dat* in); ~ erweckend sein to inspire confidence; im ~ [gesagt] [told] in [strict] confidence

Vertrauensbruch *m* breach of confidence

V

vertrauensvoll I. *adj* trusting, based on trust *pred* II. *adv* trustingly

vertrauenswürdig *adj* trustworthy

vertraulich I. *adj* ❶ *(geheim)* [*streng*] ~ [strictly] confidential ❷ *(freundschaftlich)* familiar, chummy *fam* II. *adv* confidentially

verträumt *adj* ❶ *(idyllisch)* sleepy ❷ *(realitätsfern)* dreamy

vertraut *adj* ❶ *(wohlbekannt)* familiar; **sich** *akk* **mit etw** *dat* ~ **machen** to familiarize oneself with sth; **sich** *akk* **mit dem Gedanken ~ machen, dass ...** to get used to the idea that ... ❷ *(eng verbunden)* close, intimate

Vertraute(r) *f(m) dekl wie adj* confidant *masc*, confidante *fem*

vertreiben* *vt irreg (verjagen)* to drive away [*or* out] *sep*

vertretbar *adj* ❶ *(zu vertreten)* tenable ❷ *(akzeptabel)* justifiable

vertreten*¹ *vt irreg* ❶ *(vorübergehend ersetzen)* ■**jdn** ~ to cover for sb; **durch jdn ~ werden** to be replaced by sb ❷ *(repräsentieren)* to represent ❸ *(verfechten)* **Ansicht** to take; **Meinung** to hold

vertreten*² *vr irreg (verstauchen)* **sich** *dat* **den Fuß ~** to twist one's ankle ▶WENDUNGEN: **sich** *dat* **die Beine ~** to stretch one's legs

Vertreter(in) <-s, -> *m(f)* ❶ *(Stellvertreter)* deputy, stand-in ❷ *(Handelsvertreter)* sales representative ❸ *(Repräsentant)* representative

Vertretung <-, -en> *f* ❶ *(Stellvertreter)* deputy ❷ ÖKON agency

Vertrieb <-[e]s, -e> *m* ❶ *kein pl (das Vertreiben)* sale[s *pl*] ❷ *(Vertriebsabteilung)* sales department

Vertriebene(r) *f(m) dekl wie adj* deportee, displaced person

vertrocknen* *vi sein* **Vegetation** to dry out

vertrösten* *vt* to put off *sep* (**auf** +*akk* until)

vertuschen* *vt* to hush up *sep*

verübeln* [fɛɐ̯ˈʔyːbl̩n] *vt* ■**jdm etw ~** to hold sth against sb

verunglücken* [fɛɐ̯ˈʔʊn·ɡlʏ·kn̩] *vi sein* to have an accident; **tödlich ~** to be killed in an accident

verunsichern* [fɛɐ̯ˈʔʊn·zɪ·çɐn] *vt* to unsettle

verunsichert <-er, -este> *adj* insecure

verunstalten* [fɛɐ̯ˈʔʊn·ʃtal·tn̩] *vt* to disfigure

veruntreuen* [fɛɐ̯ˈʔʊn·trɔy·ən] *vt* to embezzle

verursachen* [fɛɐ̯ˈʔuː·ɐ·za·xn̩] *vt* to cause

Verursacher(in) <-s, -> *m(f) (Person)* person responsible

verurteilen* *vt* ❶ *(für schuldig befinden)* to convict; ■**jdn zu etw** *dat* ~ to sentence sb to sth ❷ *(verdammen)* to condemn; **zum Scheitern verurteilt sein** to be bound to fail

Verurteilung <-, -en> *f* conviction

verwählen* *vr* TELEK ■**sich** *akk* ~ to dial the wrong number

verwahrlost <-er, -este> *adj* neglected

verwaist *adj* orphaned; *(fig: verlassen)* deserted, abandoned

verwalten* *vt* ❶ FIN, ADMIN to administer; *Besitz* to manage ❷ COMPUT to manage

Verwalter(in) <-s, -> *m(f)* administrator; *Gut* manager; *Nachlass* trustee

Verwaltung <-, -en> *f* administration

Verwaltungsbezirk *m* administrative district

verwandeln* I. *vt* ❶ *(umwandeln)* ■**jdn in etw** *akk* ~ to turn sb into sth; **er ist wie verwandelt** he is a changed person ❷ TECH to convert ❸ *(anders erscheinen lassen)* to transform II. *vr* ■**sich** *akk* **in etw** *akk* ~ to turn into sth

Verwandlung *f* ❶ *(Umformung)* transformation ❷ TECH conversion

verwandt¹ [fɛɐ̯ˈvant] *adj* related (**mit** +*dat* to); *Methoden* similar

verwandt² [fɛɐ̯ˈvant] *pp von* **verwenden**

Verwandte(r) *f(m) dekl wie adj* relative, relation

Verwandtschaft <-, -en> *f* ❶ *(die Ver-*

wandten) relatives *pl* ❷ (*gemeinsamer Ursprung*) affinity

Verwarnung *f* warning, caution

Verwechslung <-, -en> [-'vɛks·lʊŋ] *f* mix-up, confusion

verwegen [fɛɐ̯·'ve:·gn̩] *adj* daring, bold

verweigern* *vt, vi* to refuse

Verweigerung *f* refusal

verweint *adj* *Augen* red from crying; *Gesicht* tear-stained

Verweis <-es, -e> [fɛɐ̯·'vais] *m* ❶ (*Tadel*) reprimand ❷ (*Hinweis*) reference (**auf** +*akk* to); (*Querverweis*) cross-reference

verweisen* *vt, vi irreg* to refer (**an/auf** +*akk* to)

verwelken* *vi sein* to wilt

verwendbar *adj* usable

verwenden <verwendete *o* verwandte *o* verwandt> *vt* to use (**für** +*akk* for)

Verwendung <-, -en> *f* use

Verwendungszweck *m* purpose

verwerten* *vt* ❶ (*ausnutzen, heranziehen*) to use ❷ (*nutzbringend anwenden*) to exploit

Verwertung <-, -en> *f* use

verwesen* [fɛɐ̯·'ve:·zn̩] *vi sein* to rot, to decompose

Verwesung <-> *f kein pl* decomposition

verwickeln* I. *vt* ▪**jdn in etw** *akk* ~ to involve sb in sth; **jdn in ein Gespräch** ~ to engage sb in conversation II. *vr* ▪**sich** *akk* ~ to get tangled up

verwickelt *adj* complicated, intricate

verwildert *adj* ❶ *Garten* overgrown ❷ *Tier* feral

verwirren* *vt* to confuse

verwirrt <-er, -este> *adj* confused

Verwirrung <-, -en> *f* ❶ (*Verstörtheit*) confusion ❷ (*Chaos*) chaos

verwitwet [fɛɐ̯·'vɪt·vət] *adj* widowed

verwöhnt *adj* (*anspruchsvoll*) discriminating

verworren [fɛɐ̯·'vɔ·rən] *adj* confused

verwunderlich *adj* odd, strange; **das ist nicht** ~ that's not surprising

Verwunderung <-> *f kein pl* amazement

verwundet *adj* (*fig a.*) wounded, hurt

Verwundete(r) *f(m) dekl wie adj* casualty, wounded person

Verwundung <-, -en> *f* wound

verwünschen* *vt* ❶ (*verfluchen*) to curse ❷ (*verzaubern*) to cast a spell on

verwurzelt *adj* rooted

verwüsten* *vt* to devastate; *Wohnung* to wreck; *Land* to ravage

Verwüstung <-, -en> *f meist pl* devastation

verzählen* *vr* ▪**sich** *akk* ~ to miscount

verzaubern* *vt* ❶ (*verhexen*) ▪**jdn** ~ to cast a spell on sb; **jdn in einen Vogel** ~ to turn sb into a bird ❷ (*betören*) to enchant

Verzehr <-[e]s> [fɛɐ̯·'tse:ɐ̯] *m kein pl* consumption

verzehren* I. *vt* ❶ (*essen*) to consume ❷ (*verbrauchen*) to use up II. *vr* ▪**sich** *akk* **nach jdm** ~ to pine for sb

Verzeichnis <-ses, -se> *nt* list; (*Tabelle*) table; (*Computer*) directory

verzeihen <verzieh, verziehen> I. *vt* to forgive II. *vi* to excuse; *Unrecht, Sünde* to forgive; ~ **Sie!** excuse me!, I beg your pardon!

Verzeihung <-> *f kein pl* forgiveness; **jdn] um** ~ **bitten** to apologize [to sb]; ~ **!** sorry!

verzerren* I. *vt* ❶ (*verziehen, entstellen*) to distort ❷ *Muskel* to pull; *Sehne* to strain II. *vr* (*sich verziehen*) ▪**sich** *akk* ~ to become contorted

verzichten* [fɛɐ̯·'tsɪç·tn̩] *vi* to go without; **auf Alkohol/Zigaretten** ~ to abstain from drinking/smoking

verziehen*¹ *vr irreg* ▪**sich** *akk* ~ to disappear; *Gewitter* to pass; **verzieh dich!** beat it!, scram!

verziehen² *irreg* I. *vt* **das Gesicht** ~ to grimace II. *vr* ▪**sich** *akk* ~ *Holz* to warp

verziehen³ *pp von* **verzeihen**

verzieren* *vt* to decorate

Verzierung <-, -en> *f* decoration; (*an Gebäuden*) ornamentation

V

verzinsen* vt etw [mit 3 Prozent] ~ to pay [3 Percent] interest on sth

verzogen [fɛɐ̯'tsoːɡn̩] adj badly brought up; Kinder spoiled

verzögern* I. vt ❶ (später erfolgen lassen) to delay (um +akk by/for) ❷ (verlangsamen) to slow down II. vr (später erfolgen) ■sich akk ~ to be delayed (um +akk by/for)

Verzögerung <-, -en> f delay, holdup fam; (Verlangsamung) slowing down

verzollen* vt ■etw ~ to pay customs on sth; **haben Sie etwas zu ~?** do you have anything to declare?

Verzug <-[e]s> m kein pl delay; [mit etw dat] in ~ geraten to fall behind [with sth]

verzweifeln* vi sein to despair (an +dat of)

verzweifelt I. adj ❶ (völlig verzagt) despairing; **ein ~es Gesicht machen** to look desperate ❷ (hoffnungslos) desperate II. adv (völlig verzagt) despairingly, desperately

Verzweiflung <-> f kein pl (Gemütszustand) despair; (Ratlosigkeit) desperation; **jdn zur ~ bringen** to drive sb to despair

verzwickt [fɛɐ̯'tsvɪkt] adj tricky

Veteran <-en, -en> [ve·te·'raːn] m veteran

Veto <-s, -s> ['veː·to] nt veto

Vetorecht nt right of veto

Vetter <-s, -n> ['fɛ·tɐ] m cousin

Vetternwirtschaft f kein pl nepotism

Viadukt <-[e]s, -e> [via·'dʊkt] m o nt viaduct

Vibration <-, -en> [vi·bra·'tsi̯oːn] f vibration

Videoaufzeichnung f video recording

V **Videokamera** f video camera

Vieh <-[e]s> [fiː] nt kein pl ❶ AGR livestock; (Rinder) cattle ❷ (fam: Tier) animal, beast

Viehzucht f cattle [or livestock] breeding

viel [fiːl] I. adj <mehr, meiste> ❶ sing, adjektivisch a lot of; **er braucht ~ Geld** he needs lots of money;

~ **Erfolg!** good luck!; ~ **Spaß!** have a good time! ❷ sing, + art, poss **das ~e Essen ist mir nicht bekommen** all that food hasn't done me any good ❸ substantivisch a lot, much; **ich habe zu ~ zu tun** I have too much to do; **obwohl er ~ weiß, ...** although he knows a lot, ... ❹ pl, adjektivisch ■~e a lot of, many; **und ~e andere** and many others ❺ + pl, substantivisch (eine große Anzahl) ■~e a lot; (von Menschen a.) many [people] II. adv <mehr, am meisten> ❶ (häufig) a lot; ~ **diskutiert** much-discussed; **eine ~ befahrene Straße** a [very] busy street ❷ (wesentlich) a lot; ~ **zu groß** much too big

vieldeutig adj ambiguous

Vielfalt <-> ['fiːl·falt] f diversity, [great] variety (an +dat of)

vielfältig ['fiːl·fɛl·tɪç] adj diverse, varied

vielleicht [fi·'laɪçt] I. adv ❶ (eventuell) perhaps, maybe ❷ (ungefähr) about II. part ❶ (bitte [mahnend]) please; **würdest du mich ~ einmal ausreden lassen?** would you please let me finish what I'm saying for once? ❷ (etwa) by any chance; **erwarten Sie ~, dass ich Ihnen das Geld gebe?** I don't suppose you expect me to give me the money, do you? ❸ (wirklich) really; **du erzählst ~ einen Quatsch** what are you talking about?

vielmehr ['fiːl·meːɐ̯] adv rather

vielseitig ['fiːl·zai̯·tɪç] I. adj Mensch, Maschine versatile; Angebot, Arbeit varied II. adv ❶ (in vieler Hinsicht) widely ❷ (in verschiedener Weise) **etw ist ~ anwendbar** sth can be used in a variety of ways

Vielzahl f kein pl ■eine ~ von etw dat a large number of sth

vier [fiːɐ̯] adj four; s. a. **acht¹** ▶WENDUNGEN: **ein Gespräch unter ~ Augen führen** to have a private conversation

Vier <-, -en> [fiːɐ̯] f ❶ (Zahl) four ❷ (Zeugnisnote) **er hat in Deutsch eine ~ ≈** he got a D in German ▶WENDUNGEN: **auf allen ~en** on all fours

Viereck ['fiːɐ̯ʔɛk] nt square; MATH quadrilateral

viereckig ['fiːɐ̯ʔɛkɪç] adj rectangular

vierfach, 4fach I. adj fourfold; **die ~e Menge** four times the amount **II.** adv fourfold, four times over

vierhundert ['fiːɐ̯ˈhʊndɐt] adj four hundred

viermal, 4-malRR ['fiːɐ̯maːl] adv four times; *s. a.* **achtmal**

Vierradantrieb m four-wheel drive

vierspurig adj four-lane attr

vierstellig adj **eine ~e Zahl** a four-digit number

vierte(r, s) ['fiːɐ̯tə -tə -təs] adj ❶ (an vierter Stelle) fourth; *s. a.* **achte(r, s) 1** ❷ (Datum) fourth, 4th; *s. a.* **achte(r, s) 2**

viertel ['fɪrtl̩] adj quarter, fourth; **drei ~** three-quarters, three-fourths

Viertel¹ <-s, -> ['fɪrtl̩] nt district, quarter

Viertel² <-s, -> ['fɪrtl̩] nt o SCHWEIZ m ❶ (der vierte Teil) quarter ❷ (15 Minuten) **~ vor/nach drei** [a] quarter to [or of]/after three

Vierteljahr [fɪrtl̩ˈjaːɐ̯] nt three months, quarter spec

vierteljährlich [fɪrtl̩ˈjɛːɐ̯lɪç] adj, adv quarterly

Viertelstunde [fɪrtl̩ˈʃtʊndə] f quarter of an hour, fifteen minutes

vierzehn ['fɪrtseːn] adj fourteen; **~ Tage** two weeks; *s. a.* **acht**¹

vierzehntägig ['fɪrtseːn-] adj o NORDD two-week attr

vierzehnte(r, s) adj ❶ (an vierzehnter Stelle) fourteenth; *s. a.* **achte(r, s) 1** ❷ (Datum) fourteenth, 14th; *s. a.* **achte(r, s) 2**

vierzig ['fɪrtsɪç] adj forty; *s. a.* **achtzig 1, 2**

vierzigste(r, s) adj fortieth; *s. a.* **achte(r, s) 1**

Vietnam <-s> [viɛtˈnam] nt Vietnam; *s. a.* **Deutschland**

Vikar(in) <-s, -e> [viˈkaːɐ̯] m(f) vicar

Villa <-, Villen> ['vɪla] f villa

violett [vi̯oˈlɛt] adj violet, purple

Violine <-, -n> [vi̯oˈliːnə] f violin

virtuell [vɪrˈtuˑɛl] adj virtual

Virus <-, Viren> ['viːrʊs] nt o m virus

Vision <-, -en> [viˈzi̯oːn] f vision

Visite <-, -n> [viˈziːtə] f (Arztbesuch) round

Visitenkarte [viˈziːtən-] f business card

Viskose <-> [vɪsˈkoːzə] f kein pl viscose

Visum <-s, Visa> ['viːzʊm] nt visa

vital [viˈtaːl] adj ❶ (Lebenskraft besitzend) lively, vigorous ❷ (lebenswichtig) vital

Vitalität <-> [vitaliˈtɛt] f kein pl vitality, vigor

Vitamin <-s, -e> [vitaˈmiːn] nt vitamin

Vitaminmangel m vitamin deficiency

Vitrine <-, -n> [viˈtriːnə] f (Schaukasten) display case; (Glasvitrine) glass cabinet

Vizepräsident(in) m(f) vice president

Vogel <-s, Vögel> ['foːgl̩] m ❶ (Tier) bird ❷ (fam: auffallender Mensch) **ein lustiger ~** a real joker; **ein seltsamer ~** a strange bird ▸WENDUNGEN: **einen ~ haben** to have a screw loose

Vogelfutter nt bird food

Vogelscheuche <-, -n> f scarecrow

Vokabel <-, -n> [voˈkaːbl̩] f word; **~n** pl **lernen** to memorize vocabulary words

Vokabular <-s, -e> [vokabuˈlaːɐ̯] nt vocabulary

Vokal <-s, -e> [voˈkaːl] m vowel

Volk <-[e]s, Völker> [fɔlk] nt ❶ (Nation) nation, people ❷ kein pl (Menschen) people npl; **sich** akk **unters ~ mischen** to mingle with the people

Völkergemeinschaft f international community

Völkerkunde <-> f kein pl ethnology

Völkermord m genocide

Völkerrecht nt kein pl international law

Volksabstimmung f referendum

Volksfest nt folk festival

Volksheld(in) m(f) national hero

V

Volkshochschule f adult education center

Volkslied nt folk song

Volksstamm m tribe

Volkstanz m folk dance

volkstümlich ['fɔlks·ty:m·lɪç] adj traditional

Volkswirtschaft f national economy

Volkszählung f [national] census

voll [fɔl] I. adj ❶ (gefüllt) full; **eine Hand ~ Reis** a handful of rice; **~ sein** (fam: satt) to be full ❷ (vollständig) full, whole; **etw in ~en Zügen genießen** to enjoy sth to the fullest; **ein ~er Erfolg** a total success; **jede ~e Stunde** every hour on the hour; **bei ~em Bewusstsein** fully conscious ❸ (kräftig) Stimme rich; Haar thick ❹ (fam: betrunken) ■~ **sein** to be hammered ▶WENDUNGEN: **sie nimmt ihn nicht für ~** she doesn't take him seriously; **aus dem V~en schöpfen** to draw on plentiful resources II. adv ❶ (vollkommen) completely ❷ (uneingeschränkt) fully; **~ und ganz** totally ❸ (mit aller Wucht) right, smack; **der Wagen war ~ gegen den Pfeiler geprallt** the car ran smack into the pillar

vollautomatisch I. adj fully automatic II. adv fully automatically

Vollbart m full beard

Vollblut nt thoroughbred

vollbringen* vt irreg to accomplish; Wunder to perform

Volleyball ['vɔli-] m volleyball

Vollgas nt kein pl full speed; **~ geben** to put one's foot down

völlig ['fœ·lɪç] I. adj complete II. adv completely; **Sie haben ~ recht** you're absolutely right

volljährig ['fɔl·jɛ:·rɪç] adj of age; ■~ **werden** to come of age

Vollkaskoversicherung f comprehensive car insurance [coverage]

vollklimatisiert adj fully air-conditioned

vollkommen [fɔl·'kɔ·mən] I. adj ❶ (perfekt) perfect ❷ (völlig) complete II. adv completely

Vollkornbrot nt whole-grain bread

Vollmacht <-, -en> ['fɔl·maxt] f authorization; (Schriftstück) power of attorney; **jdm [die] ~ für etw** akk **geben** to authorize sb to do sth; **eine ~ haben** to have power of attorney

Vollmilch f whole milk

Vollmond m kein pl full moon; **bei ~** when there's a full moon

Vollpension f kein pl [mit] ~ full board

vollschlank adj plump

vollständig ['fɔl·ʃtɛn·dɪç] I. adj complete II. adv completely

Vollstreckung <-, -en> f execution

Volltreffer m ❶ (direkter Treffer) bull's eye fig fam ❷ (fam: voller Erfolg) complete success

Vollversammlung f general meeting

vollwertig adj ❶ ~**e Kost** whole foods ❷ Ersatz fully adequate

Vollwertkost f kein pl whole foods pl

vollzählig ['fɔl·tsɛ:·lɪç] I. adj (komplett) complete, whole; ■~ **sein** to be all present II. adv at full strength

vollziehen* [fɔl·'tsi:·ən] irreg I. vt to carry out sep; Urteil to execute; Ehe consummate II. vr ■**sich** akk ~ to take place

Vollzugsanstalt f penal institution

Volontär(in) <-s, -e> [vo·lɔn·'tɛ:ɐ̯] m(f) intern, trainee

Volt <-[e]s, -> [vɔlt] nt volt

Volumen <-s, -> [vo·'lu:·mən] nt volume

von [fɔn] präp +dat ❶ räumlich (ab, herkommend) from; **~ woher…?** where … from?, from where…?; **~ rechts** from the right; **~ diesem Fenster kann man alles sehen** you can see everything from this window; **~ unserem eigenen Garten** from our own garden; (aus … herab/heraus) off; **er fiel ~ der Leiter** he fell off [or from] the ladder ❷ räumlich (etw entfernend) from, off; **die Wäsche ~ der Leine nehmen** to take the laundry off the line; **Schweiß ~ der Stirn wischen** to wipe sweat from one's brow ❸ zeitlich (stammend) from; **die Zeitung ~**

gestern yesterday's [news]paper; **ich kenne sie ~ früher** I know her from a long time ago; **~ jetzt an** from now on ④ (*Urheber, Ursache*) **~ jdm gelobt werden** to be praised by sb; **~ wem ist dieses Geschenk?** who is this present from?; **~ wem weißt du das?** who told you that?; **~ wem ist dieser Roman?** who wrote this novel?; **das war nicht nett ~ dir!** that wasn't nice of you! ⑤ *statt gen* (*Zugehörigkeit*) of; **die Musik ~ Beethoven's** Beethoven's music ⑥ (*Gruppenangabe*) of; **einer ~ vielen** one of many; **keiner ~ uns** none of us; **ein Student ~ mir** a student of mine, one of my students ⑦ (*bei Maßangaben*) of; **ein Abstand ~ zwei Metern** a distance of six feet; **eine Pause ~ zehn Minuten** a ten-minute break ▸ WENDUNGEN: **~ wegen!** no way!

voneinander [fɔnˈʔaiˈnanˈdə] *adv* from each other; **die beiden Städte sind 25 Kilometer ~ entfernt** the two cities are 25 kilometers apart

vor [foː̯] **I.** *präp* ① (*räumlich*) in front of; **8 km ~ der Stadt** 8 km outside of town ② (*zeitlich*) before; **es ist zehn ~ zwölf** it is ten to twelve; **ich war ~ dir dran** I was before you; **vor kurzem/hundert Jahren** a short time/a hundred years ago ③ (*bedingt durch*) with; **starr ~ Schreck** scared stiff; **~ Kälte zittern** to shiver [with cold] **II.** *adv* forward; **~ und zurück** forwards and backwards

Vorabend <-s,-e> [ˈfoː̯ɐˈʔaːbn̩t] *m* **am ~** [**einer S.** *gen*] on the evening before [sth], on the eve [of sth]

Vorahnung *f* premonition

voran|gehen *vi irreg sein* ① (*an der Spitze gehen*) ▪ **jdm ~** to go ahead of sb ② *a. impers* (*Fortschritte machen*) to make progress; **die Arbeiten gehen zügig voran** the work is progressing rapidly ③ (*einer Sache vorausgehen*) to precede

voran|kommen *vi irreg sein* ① (*vorwärtskommen*) to make headway ② (*Fortschritte machen*) to make pro-

gress; **wie kommt ihr voran mit der Arbeit?** how's your work coming along[, guys]?

Voranmeldung [ˈfoː̯ʔanˈmɛlˈdʊŋ] *f* appointment, booking

Vorarbeiter(in) *m(f)* foreman *masc,* forewoman *fem*

voraus [foˈʀaʊ̯s] *adv* in front, ahead; **jdm ~ sein** to be ahead of sb; **im V~** in advance

voraus|gehen [foˈʀaʊ̯sˈgeːˈən] *vi irreg sein* to go on ahead; **einem Unwetter geht meistens ein Sturm voraus** bad weather is usually preceded by a storm

vorausgesetzt *adj* ▪ **~,** [**dass**] ... provided [that] ...

Voraussage <-, -en> *f* prediction

voraus|sagen *vt* to predict

voraus|setzen *vt* ① (*als selbstverständlich erachten*) to assume ② (*erfordern*) to require

Voraussetzung <-, -en> *f* ① (*Vorbedingung*) condition; ▪ **~-en** (*für eine Arbeit*) qualifications *npl;* **unter der ~, dass** ... on the condition that ...; **unter bestimmten ~en** under certain conditions ② (*Annahme*) assumption, premise

voraussichtlich [foˈʀaʊ̯sˈzɪçtˈlɪç] **I.** *adj* (*erwartet*) expected **II.** *adv* (*wahrscheinlich*) probably

Vorauszahlung *f* advance payment

Vorbehalt <-[e]s, -e> [ˈfoː̯ɐˈbəˈhalt] *m* reservation (**gegen** +*akk* about); **ohne ~** without reservation; **mit ~en** with reservations *pl*

vorbehaltlos **I.** *adj* unreserved **II.** *adv* unreservedly, without reservation

vorbei [foˈʀaʊ̯ˈbai] *adv* ① (*vorüber*) ▪ **an etw** *dat* ~ past sth; **wir sind schon an München ~** we already passed Munich; **schon wieder ~, ich treffe nie** missed again — I never hit the target ② (*vergangen*) ▪ **~ sein** to be over; **es ist drei Uhr ~** it's [already] past three o'clock; **aus und ~** over and done

vorbei|fahren *vi irreg sein* ① (*vorüberfahren*) to drive past; **im V~** while driving past ② (*kurz aufsuchen*) ▪ **bei etw**

V

dat ~ Apotheke, Supermarkt to stop off at sth

vorbei|gehen [fo:ɐ̯ˈbai̯·ɡe:·ən] *vi irreg sein* **❶** (*vorübergehen*) to go past; (*überholen*) to pass; (*danebengehen*) *Schuss* to miss; **sie ging dicht an uns vorbei** she walked right past us **❷** (*aufsuchen*) to go to; **gehe doch bitte bei der Apotheke vorbei** please stop off at the drugstore **❸** (*vergehen*) **die Ferien gingen schnell ~** vacation went by fast

vorbei|kommen *vi irreg sein* **❶** (*passieren*) to pass **❷** (*besuchen*) to drop in (**bei** +*dat* at) **❸** (*vorbeigehen können*) to get past

vorbei|lassen *vt irreg* to let past; **lassen Sie uns bitte vorbei!** please let us through!

vorbei|reden *vi* **am Thema ~** to miss the point; **aneinander ~** to be talking at cross-purposes *pl*

vorbelastet *adj* at a disadvantage; **erblich ~ sein** to have a genetic predisposition

vor|bereiten* I. *vt* to prepare II. *vr* ∎ **sich** *akk* ~ to prepare oneself

Vorbereitung <-, -en> *f* preparation

Vorbesitzer(in) <-s, -> *m(f)* previous owner

vor|bestellen* *vt* to order in advance; **ich möchte zwei Karten ~** I'd like to reserve two tickets

Vorbestellung *f* advance booking

vorbestraft *adj* previously convicted (**wegen** +*dat* for/of); **nicht ~ sein** to not have a criminal record

vor|beugen I. *vt* (*nach vorne beugen*) to bend forward II. *vi* (*Prophylaxe betreiben*) to take preventive measures; ∎ **etw** *akk* ~ **Gefahr, Krankheit** to prevent sth III. *vr* ∎ **sich** *akk* ~ to lean forward

Vorbeugung <-, -en> *f* prevention; **zur ~** [**gegen etw** *akk*] as a preventive measure [against sth]

Vorbild <-[e]s, -er> ['fo:ɐ̯·bɪlt] *nt* example; [**jdm**] **als ~ dienen** to serve as an example [for sb]

vorbildlich I. *adj* exemplary II. *adv* in an exemplary manner

vor|bringen *vt irreg* **Argument** to put forward; **Bedenken** to express; **Einwand** to raise

vorchristlich *adj attr* **in ~er Zeit** in pre-Christian times

Vorderachse *f* front axle

Vorderasien <-s> *nt* Near East

vordere(r, s) ['fɔr·də·rə, -rɛ, -rəs] *adj* front

Vordergrund *m* foreground

Vordermann *m* ∎ **mein ~** the person in front of me

Vorderrad *nt* front wheel

Vorderradantrieb *m* front-wheel drive

Vorderseite *f* front [side]

vorderste(r, s) ['fɔr·də·stə, -stɛ, -stəs] *adj superl von* **vordere(r, s)** foremost; **die ~n Plätze** the seats at the very front

vor|drängeln, vor|drängen *vr* ∎ **sich** *akk* ~ to push one's way to the front

vor|dringen *vi irreg sein* to reach, to get as far as

vorehelich *adj attr* premarital

voreilig ['fo:ɐ̯·ʔai̯·lɪç] I. *adj* rash, over-hasty II. *adv* rashly, hastily

voreingenommen ['fo:ɐ̯·ʔai̯n·ɡə·nɔ·mən] *adj* prejudiced (**gegenüber** +*dat* against)

Vorentscheidung *f* preliminary decision

vorerst ['fo:ɐ̯·ʔe:ɐ̯st] *adv* for the time being

Vorfahr(in) <-en, -en> ['fo:ɐ̯·fa:ɐ̯] *m(f)* ancestor

Vorfahrt ['fo:ɐ̯·fa:ɐ̯t] *f kein pl* right of way; **jdm die ~ nehmen** to not yield to sb

Vorfahrtsstraße *f* main road

Vorfall *m* incident, occurrence

vor|fallen *vi irreg sein* to happen, to occur

vor|finden *vt irreg* to find

Vorfreude *f* [excited] anticipation (**auf** +*akk* of)

vor|führen *vt* **❶** **Gerät** to demonstrate **❷** (*darbieten*) to perform

Vorführung f FILM screening

Vorgang <-gänge> m ❶ (*Geschehnis*) event ❷ (*Prozess*) process

Vorgänger(in) <-s, -> m(f) predecessor

Vorgarten m front yard

vor|geben vt irreg ❶ (*vorschützen*) to use as an excuse; ■~, **dass** ... to pretend that ... ❷ (*festlegen*) to set in advance

Vorgebirge nt foothills pl

vor|gehen vi irreg sein ❶ (*vorausgehen*) to go on ahead ❷ (*zu schnell gehen*) to be fast; **meine Uhr geht fünf Minuten vor** my watch is five minutes fast ❸ (*Priorität haben*) to have priority, to come first ❹ (*Schritte ergreifen*) to take action ❺ (*sich abspielen*) to be going on; **was ging in ihr vor?** what was going on inside her? ❻ (*verfahren*) to proceed (**bei** +dat in/ with)

Vorgeschmack m kein pl foretaste

Vorgesetzte(r) f(m) dekl wie adj superior

vorgestern ['foːɐ̯ɡɛsˌtɐn] adv the day before yesterday; ~ **Morgen/Nacht** the morning/night before last

vor|haben ['foːɐ̯ˌhaːˌbn̩] vt irreg to have planned; **hast du etwa vor, noch weiterzuarbeiten?** do you intend to keep on working?

Vorhaben <-s, -> ['foːɐ̯ˌhaːˌbn̩] nt plan, project

vor|halten irreg I. vt ■**jdm etw** ~ ❶ (*vorwerfen*) to reproach sb for sth ❷ (*davorhalten*) *Spiegel* to hold sth in front of sb II. vi to last

vorhanden [foːɐ̯ˈhandn̩] adj ❶ (*verfügbar*) available ❷ (*existierend*) existing

Vorhang <-s, Vorhänge> ['foːɐ̯ˌhaŋ] m curtain

Vorhängeschloss^{RR} nt padlock

Vorhaut f ANAT foreskin

vorher [foːɐ̯ˈheːɐ̯] adv beforehand; **kurz** ~ just before; **ich muss** ~ **noch essen** I have to eat first

vorher|bestimmen* vt to predetermine; ■**vorherbestimmt sein** to be predestined

vorherig [foːɐ̯ˈheːˌrɪç] adj attr prior; *Abmachung, Vereinbarung* previous

Vorhersage [foːɐ̯ˈheːɐ̯ˌzaːˌɡə] f ❶ METEO forecast ❷ (*Voraussage*) prediction

vorher|sagen vt to predict

vorhersehbar adj foreseeable

vorher|sehen vt irreg to foresee

vorhin [foːɐ̯ˈhɪn] adv a moment ago, just [now]

vorig ['foːˌrɪç] adj attr last, previous

Vorjahr nt last year

Vorkehrung <-, -en> f precaution; ~**en treffen** to take precautions

vor|kochen vt KOCHK to precook

vor|kommen vi irreg sein ❶ (*passieren*) to happen; ■**es kommt vor, dass** ... it can happen that ...; **das kann [schon mal]** ~ these things [can] happen ❷ (*vorhanden sein*) to be found, to occur ❸ (*erscheinen*) to seem; **jdm bekannt** ~ to sound familiar to sb; **du kommst dir wohl sehr schlau vor?** you think you're real clever, don't you? ❹ (*nach vorn kommen*) to come [up] to the front ❺ (*zum Vorschein kommen*) [**hinter etw** dat] ~ to come out [from behind sth]

Vorkommen <-s, -> nt ❶ kein pl (*Auftreten*) incidence ❷ meist pl GEOL deposit

Vorkriegszeit f prewar period

Vorladung f JUR ❶ (*das Vorladen*) summoning ❷ (*Schreiben*) summons

Vorlage f ❶ kein pl (*das Vorlegen*) presentation ❷ (*Muster*) pattern ❸ SCHWEIZ (*Vorleger*) mat

vor|lassen vt irreg ❶ (*den Vortritt lassen*) to let go first ❷ (*nach vorn durchlassen*) to let past

Vorläufer(in) m(f) precursor

vorläufig ['foːɐ̯ˌlɔy̯fɪç] I. adj temporary; *Ergebnis* provisional; *Regelung* interim II. adv for the time being

vorlaut ['foːɐ̯ˌlau̯t] adj cheeky, impertinent

vor|lesen irreg I. vt ■**[jdm] etw** ~ to read out sep sth [to sb] II. vi to read aloud (**aus** +dat from)

Vorlesung f lecture (**über** +akk on)

V

vorletzte(r, s) ['foːɐ̯·lɛts·tə, -s·tɐ, -s·təs] *adj* before last *pred*

Vorliebe [foːɐ̯·'liː·bə] *f* preference; **eine ~ für jdn/etw haben** to be particularly fond of sb/sth

vorlliegen *vi irreg* ❶ (*eingereicht sein*) ◼ **jdm ~** to have been received by sb; **uns liegen keine Beweise vor** we have no proof ❷ (*bestehen*) to be

vorllügen *vt irreg* ◼ **jdm etw ~** to lie to sb

vorlmachen *vt* ❶ (*täuschen*) ◼ **sich/ jdm etw ~** to fool oneself/sb; **machen wir uns doch nichts vor** let's not kid ourselves ❷ (*demonstrieren*) ◼ **jdm etw ~** to show sb [how to do] sth

vorlmerken *vt* **ich habe mir den Termin vorgemerkt** I've made a note of the appointment

Vormittag ['foːɐ̯·mɪ·taːk] *m* morning; **am [frühen/späten] ~** [early/late] in the morning

vormittags ['foːɐ̯·mɪ·taːks] *adv* in the morning

Vormund <-[e]s, -e> ['foːɐ̯·mʊnt] *m* guardian

Vormundschaft <-, -en> ['foːɐ̯·mʊnt·ʃaft] *f* guardianship

vorn [fɔrn] *adv* at the front; **~ im Bus** at the front of the bus; **nach ~** to the front; **von ~** (*von der Vorderseite her*) from the front; (*von Anfang an*) from the beginning; **jetzt kann ich wieder von ~ anfangen** now I have to start from scratch all over again; **von ~ bis hinten** (*fam*) from beginning to end

Vorname *m* first name

vornehm ['foːɐ̯·neːm] *adj* ❶ (*elegant*) elegant; *Mensch, Benehmen* distinguished ❷ (*luxuriös*) *Gegend, Restaurant* exclusive ▶ WENDUNGEN: **~ tun** (*pej*) to put on airs

vorlnehmen *irreg* **I.** *vt* (*ausführen*) to carry out *sep*; **Änderungen ~** to make changes **II.** *vr* (*planen*) ◼ **sich** *dat* **etw ~** to plan sth

vornherein ['fɔrn·hɛ·rain] *adv* ◼ **von ~** from the start

Vorort ['foːɐ̯·ʔɔrt] *m* suburb

Vorplatz *m* forecourt

vorprogrammiert *adj* pre-programmed; (*vorbestimmt*) predetermined

Vorrang *m kein pl* ❶ (*Priorität*) priority (**vor** +*dat* over) ❷ ÖSTERR (*Vorfahrt*) right of way

vorrangig **I.** *adj* priority *attr*; of prime importance *pred*; ◼ **~ sein** to have priority **II.** *adv* as a matter of priority

Vorrat <-[e]s, Vorräte> ['foːɐ̯·raːt] *m* stock, supply (**an** +*dat* of); **Vorräte anlegen** to stock up on sth; **so lange der ~ reicht** while supplies last

vorrätig ['foːɐ̯·rɛ·tɪç] *adj* in stock *pred*; **etw ~ haben** to have sth in stock

Vorrecht *nt* privilege

Vorrichtung <-, -en> *f* device, gadget

vorlrücken **I.** *vi sein* ❶ MIL to advance (**gegen** +*akk* on) ❷ (*nach vorn rücken*) to move forward **II.** *vt haben* to move forward

Vorruhestand *m* early retirement

Vorrunde *f* SPORT preliminary round

Vorsaison *f* low season

Vorsatz <-[e]s, Vorsätze> ['foːɐ̯·zats] *m* resolution; **den ~ fassen, etw zu tun** to resolve to do sth

vorsätzlich ['foːɐ̯·zɛts·lɪç] **I.** *adj* deliberate, intentional **II.** *adv* deliberately, intentionally

vorlschieben *vt irreg* ❶ (*vorschützen*) to use as an excuse ❷ (*für sich agieren lassen*) ◼ **jdn ~** to use sb as a front man/woman ❸ (*nach vorn schieben*) to push forward ❹ (*vor etw schieben*) *Riegel* to push across

vorlschießen *vt irreg* *Geld* to advance

Vorschlag *m* suggestion; **jdm einen ~ machen** to make a suggestion [to sb]; **auf jds ~ [hin]** on sb's recommendation

vorlschlagen *vt irreg* ❶ (*als Vorschlag unterbreiten*) to suggest ❷ (*empfehlen*) to recommend

vorlschreiben *vt irreg* ◼ **jdm etw ~** to stipulate sth to sb; **schreib mir nicht vor, was ich machen soll!** don't tell me what to do!

Vorschrift *f* ADMIN regulation, rule; (*Anweisung*) instructions *pl*; (*polizei-*

lich) orders *pl;* **~ sein** to be the rule[s];
jdm ~en machen to tell sb what to do
vorschriftsmäßig *adj, adv* according to [the] regulations
Vorschulalter *nt kein pl* preschool age; **im ~ sein** to be of preschool age
Vorschule *f* preschool
Vorschuss^RR <-es, Vorschüsse>, **Vorschuß**^ALT <-sses, Vorschüsse> ['foːɐ̯ʃʊs] *m* advance
vor|schweben *vi* to have in mind
vor|sehen *irreg* I. *vr* **■ sich** *akk* ~ to watch out (**vor** +*dat* for); **sieh dich vor!** watch it! II. *vt* (*planen*) **es ist vorgesehen, dass …** it is planned that …; **das Geld war für den Urlaub vorgesehen** the money was intended for the vacation; **Sie hatte ich für eine andere Aufgabe vorgesehen** I had you in mind for a different job
Vorsehung <-> ['foːɐ̯zeː·ʊŋ] *f kein pl* providence
Vorsicht <-> ['foːɐ̯zɪçt] *f kein pl* caution; **~!** watch out!
vorsichtig I. *adj* ❶ (*umsichtig*) careful ❷ (*zurückhaltend*) cautious II. *adv* ❶ (*umsichtig*) carefully ❷ (*zurückhaltend*) cautiously
vorsichtshalber *adv* as a precaution, just to be on the safe side
Vorsichtsmaßnahme *f* precaution; **~n treffen** to take precautions
Vorsilbe *f* prefix
vor|singen *vt irreg* to sing first
Vorsitzende(r) *f(m) dekl wie adj* chairman/-woman/-person
Vorsorge *f* provisions *pl;* **~ für etw** *akk* **treffen** to make provisions for sth
vor|sorgen *vi* to provide
Vorsorgeuntersuchung *f* medical checkup
Vorspeise *f* starter, appetizer
Vorspiel *nt* ❶ MUS prelude; (*zur Probe*) audition ❷ (*vor dem Liebesakt*) foreplay
vor|spielen I. *vt* ❶ MUS to play ❷ (*vorheucheln*) to put on II. *vi* MUS to play
Vorsprung *m* lead
Vorstadt *f* suburb
Vorstand *m* ❶ (*Geschäftsführung*)

[management] board; (*einer Partei, eines Vereins*) [executive] committee ❷ (*Vorstandsmitglied*) director, board member; (*einer Partei*) executive; (*eines Vereins*) [member of the] executive [committee]
Vorsteher(in) <-s, -> ['foːɐ̯ʃteː·ɐ] *m(f)* head
vor|stellen I. *vt* ❶ (*gedanklich sehen*) **■ sich** *dat* **etw ~** to imagine sth; **das muss man sich mal ~!** just imagine [it]! ❷ (*als angemessen betrachten*) **■ sich** *dat* **etw ~** to have sth in mind ❸ (*bekannt machen*) **■ jdm jdn ~** to introduce sb to sb ❹ (*präsentieren*) **■ jdm etw ~** to present sth to sb ❺ (*vorrücken*) *Uhr* to set forward II. *vr* **■ sich** *akk* ~ ❶ (*bekannt machen*) to introduce oneself ❷ *bei Arbeitgeber* to have an interview
Vorstellung *f* ❶ (*gedankliches Bild*) idea; **falsche ~en haben** to have false hopes ❷ THEAT performance; FILM screening
Vorstellungsgespräch *nt* interview
Vorstellungskraft *f kein pl,* **Vorstellungsvermögen** *nt kein pl* [powers *npl* of] imagination
Vorstrafe *f* previous conviction
Vortag *m* **am ~** the day before; **vom ~** from yesterday
vor|täuschen *vt Unfall* to fake; *Interesse* to feign
Vorteil <-s, -e> ['foːɐ̯taɪl] *m* advantage; **er ist nur auf seinen ~ bedacht** he only ever thinks of his own interests; **im ~ sein** to have an advantage (**gegenüber** +*dat* over); **von ~ sein** to be advantageous (**für** +*akk* for/to)
vorteilhaft *adj* favorable (**für** +*akk* for); *Geschäft* lucrative, profitable
Vortrag <-[e]s, Vorträge> ['foːɐ̯traːk] *m* lecture; **einen ~ halten** to give a lecture (**über** +*akk* about/on)
vor|tragen *vt irreg* ❶ (*berichten*) to present; *Wunsch* to express ❷ (*rezitieren*) to recite; *Lied* to sing
vortrefflich [foːɐ̯trɛf·lɪç] I. *adj* excel-

V

lent; (*Gedanke, Idee a.*) splendid **II.** *adv* excellently

vor|treten *vi irreg sein* ❶ (*nach vorn treten*) to step forward ❷ (*vorstehen*) to jut out

Vortritt[1] *m* precedence, priority; **jdm den ~ lassen** to let sb go first

Vortritt[2] *m kein pl* SCHWEIZ (*Vorfahrt*) right of way

vorüber [fo·'ry:·bə] *adv* ■~ **sein** ❶ *räumlich* to have gone past ❷ *zeitlich* to be over; *Schmerz* to be gone

vorüber|gehen [fo·'ry:·bə·ge:·ən] *vi irreg sein* to pass; *Schmerz* to go

vorübergehend **I.** *adj* temporary **II.** *adv* for a short time; **~ geschlossen** temporarily closed

Vorurteil ['fo:ɐ·ʔʊr·tail] *nt* prejudice; **~e haben** to be prejudiced (**gegenüber** +*dat* against)

Vorverkaufsstelle *f* advance ticket office

vor|verlegen* *vt* to move up (**auf** +*akk* to)

Vorwahl *f* ❶ (*vorherige Auswahl*) pre-selection [process] ❷ POL primary [election] ❸ TELEK area code

Vorwand <-[e]s, Vorwände> ['fo:ɐ·vant] *m* pretext, excuse; **unter einem ~** on a pretext

vorwärts ['fo:ɐ·vɛrts] *adv* forward; **~!** onward!, move it!

vorwärts|bringen *vt irreg* ■**jdn ~** to help sb make progress

Vorwärtsgang <-gänge> *m* forward gear

vorwärts|kommen *vi irreg sein* to make progress

vorweg|nehmen [fo·ɐ·'vɛk·ne:·mən] *vt irreg* to anticipate

vorweihnachtlich *adj* pre-Christmas

vor|werfen *vt irreg* ■**jdm etw ~** to reproach sb for [doing] sth

vorwiegend *adv* predominantly, mainly

vorwitzig *adj* cocky

Vorwort <-worte> *nt* foreword, preface

Vorwurf <-[e]s, Vorwürfe> *m* reproach; **jdm Vorwürfe machen** to reproach sb (**wegen** +*gen* for)

vorwurfsvoll **I.** *adj* reproachful **II.** *adv* reproachfully

Vorzeichen *nt* ❶ (*Omen*) omen ❷ (*Anzeichen*) sign

vor|zeigen *vt* to show

vorzeitig ['fo:ɐ·tsai·tɪç] *adj* early; *Tod* untimely

vor|ziehen *vt irreg* ❶ (*bevorzugen*) to prefer ❷ (*zuerst erfolgen lassen*) *Termin* to move up ❸ (*nach vorn ziehen*) to pull forward

Vorzimmer *nt* ❶ (*Sekretariat*) secretary's office ❷ ÖSTERR (*Diele*) hall

Vorzug <-[e]s, Vorzüge> ['fo:ɐ·tsu:k] *m* ❶ (*gute Eigenschaft*) asset ❷ (*Vorteil*) advantage ❸ (*Bevorzugung*) **etw** *dat* **den ~ geben** to prefer sth

vorzüglich [fo:ɐ·'tsy:g·lɪç] **I.** *adj* excellent **II.** *adv* excellently

Vorzugspreis *m* discount fare

Votum <-s, Voten> ['vo:·tʊm] *nt* ❶ (*Entscheidung*) decision ❷ POL vote

vulgär [vʊl·'gɛ:ɐ] **I.** *adj* vulgar **II.** *adv* **sich** *akk* **~ ausdrücken** to use vulgar language

Vulkan <-[e]s, -e> [vʊl·'ka:n] *m* volcano

Vulkanausbruch [vʊ-] *m* volcanic eruption

vulkanisch [vʊl·'ka:·nɪʃ] *adj* volcanic

Ww

W, w <-, -> [veː] *nt* W, w; **~ wie Wilhelm** W as in Whiskey

Waage <-, -n> ['vaː·gə] *f* ① TECH scale ② *kein pl* ASTROL Libra

waagerecht ['vaː·gə·reçt] I. *adj* horizontal II. *adv* horizontally

wach [vax] *adj* awake; ■~ **werden** to wake up

Wache <-, -n> ['va·xə] *f* ① *kein pl* (*Wachdienst*) guard duty; ~ **stehen** to be on guard duty ② (*Wachposten*) guard ③ (*Polizeiwache*) police station

wachen ['va·xn̩] *vi* ① (*Wache halten*) to keep watch ② ■**über etw** *akk* ~ to ensure that sth is done

wach|rufen *vt irreg Erinnerungen* to evoke

Wachs <-es, -e> [vaks] *nt* wax

wachsam ['vax·zaːm] I. *adj* vigilant, watchful II. *adv* vigilantly, watchfully

wachsen[1] <wächst, wuchs, gewachsen> ['vak·sn̩] *vi sein* to grow (**um** +*akk* by)

wachsen[2] ['vak·sn̩] *vt* (*mit Wachs einreiben*) to wax

Wächter(in) <-s, -> [vɛç·tɐ] *m(f)* ① (*einer Anstalt*) guard; (*Wachmann*) [night] watchman ② ([*moralischer*] *Hüter*) guardian

Wackelkontakt *m* loose connection

wackeln ['va·kl̩n] *vi Konstruktion* to shake

Wade <-, -n> ['vaː·də] *f* calf

Waffe <-, -n> ['va·fə] *f* weapon

Waffel <-, -n> ['va·fl̩] *f* waffle

Waffenhandel *m* arms trade

Waffenruhe *f* ceasefire

Waffenschein *m* gun license

Waffenstillstand *m* armistice

wagemutig *adj* daring

wagen ['vaː·gn̩] I. *vt* ① (*riskieren*) to risk ② (*sich trauen*) ■**es ~, etw zu tun** to dare [to] do sth ▶WENDUNGEN: **wer nicht wagt, der nicht gewinnt** (*prov*) nothing ventured, nothing gained II. *vr* ■**sich** *akk* **irgendwohin ~** to venture out to somewhere

Wagen <-, - SÜDD, ÖSTERR Wägen> ['vaː·gn̩] *m* (*Auto, Zug*) car

Wagenheber <-s, -> *m* jack

Waggon <-s, -s> [va·ɡɔŋ] *m* RAIL car

waghalsig ['vaːk·hal·zɪç] *adj* daring

Wagnis <-ses, -se> ['vaːk·nɪs] *nt* ① (*riskantes Vorhaben*) risky venture ② (*Risiko*) risk

Wagon <-s, -s> [va·ɡɔŋ] *m s.* **Waggon**

Wahl <-, -en> [vaːl] *f* ① POL election ② (*Auswahl*) choice; **jdm keine ~ lassen** to leave sb no choice

wahlberechtigt *adj* entitled to vote *pred*

Wahlbeteiligung *f* [voter] turnout

wählen ['vɛː·lən] *vt, vi* ① (*auswählen*) to choose ② POL to vote; ■**jdn ~** to vote for sb; ■**jdn zu etw** *dat* ~ to elect sb as sth ③ TELEK to dial

Wähler(in) <-s, -> *m(f)* voter

Wahlergebnis *nt* election result

wählerisch ['vɛː·lə·rɪʃ] *adj* particular, choos[e]y *fam*; (*Kunde*) discerning

Wahlkampf *m* election campaign

wahllos ['vaːl·loːs] I. *adj* indiscriminate II. *adv* indiscriminately

Wahlniederlage *f* electoral defeat

Wahlplakat *nt* election poster

Wahlrecht *nt kein pl* [right to] vote

Wahlsieg *m* election victory

Wahlspruch *m* motto, slogan

wahlweise *adv* as desired

Wahn <-[e]s> [vaːn] *m kein pl* ① (*irrige Vorstellung*) delusion ② (*Manie*) mania

Wahnsinn *m kein pl* ① (*Geisteskrankheit*) insanity ② (*fam: Unsinn*) madness; **~!** amazing!

wahnsinnig I. *adj* ① (*geisteskrank*) insane; **jdn ~ machen** (*fam*) to drive sb crazy ② (*fam: unsinnig*) crazy ③ *attr* (*fam: gewaltig*) terrible, dreadful II. *adv*

W

(*fam: sehr*) terribly, dreadfully; ~ **viel** a whole lot

Wahnsinnige(r) *f(m) dekl wie adj* lunatic

wahr [vaːɐ̯] *adj* ❶ (*zutreffend*) true ❷ *attr* (*wirklich*) real; ~ **werden** to become a reality ▶WENDUNGEN: **das darf doch nicht ~ sein!** (*verärgert*) I don't believe this [is happening]!; (*entsetzt*) this can't be true!; **da ist etwas W~es dran** there is some truth in it; (*als Antwort*) you're right about that; **etw ist [auch] nicht das W~e** sth is not the real McCoy *fam*

während [ˈvɛːrənt] **I.** *präp +gen* during **II.** *konj* ❶ (*zur selben Zeit*) while ❷ (*wohingegen*) whereas

wahrhaben *vt* **etw nicht ~ wollen** to not want to admit sth

Wahrheit <-, -en> [ˈvaːɐ̯hait] *f* truth

wahrnehmbar *adj* perceptible; *Geräusch* audible

wahrlnehmen [ˈvaːɐ̯neːmən] *vt irreg* ❶ (*merken*) to perceive; *Geräusch, Geschmack* to detect ❷ (*nutzen*) *Gelegenheit* to take advantage of; *Interessen* to look after; *Termin* to keep

Wahrnehmung <-, -en> *f Geräusch* detection; *Geruch* perception

wahrlsagen [ˈvaːɐ̯zaːɡn̩] *vi* to tell fortunes

Wahrsager(in) <-s, -> [ˈvaːɐ̯zaːɡɐ] *m(f)* fortune teller

wahrscheinlich [vaːɐ̯ˈʃainlɪç] **I.** *adj* probable, likely **II.** *adv* probably

Wahrscheinlichkeit <-, -en> *f* probability; **aller ~ nach** in all probability

Währung <-, -en> [ˈvɛːrʊŋ] *f* currency

Währungsreform *f* currency reform

Währungsunion *f* monetary union; ■**die Europäische ~** the European Monetary Union

Wahrzeichen [ˈvaːɐ̯tsaiçn̩] *nt* landmark

Waise <-, -n> [ˈvaizə] *f* orphan

Waisenhaus *nt* orphanage

Wal <-[e]s, -e> [vaːl] *m* whale

Wald <-[e]s, Wälder> [valt] *m* forest, woods *pl*

Waldbrand *m* forest fire

Waldsterben *nt* [forest] dieback

Waldweg *m* forest path

Wales <-> [weɪlz] *nt* Wales; *s. a.* **Deutschland**

Waliser(in) <-s, -> [vaˈliːzɐ] *m(f)* Welshman *masc*, Welshwoman *fem*; *s. a.* **Deutsche(r)**

walisisch [vaˈliːzɪʃ] *adj* Welsh; *s. a.* **deutsch**

Wall <-[e]s, Wälle> [val] *m* embankment; *Burg* rampart

Wallfahrer(in) *m(f)* pilgrim

Wallfahrt [ˈvalfaːɐ̯t] *f* pilgrimage

Walnuss[RR] [ˈvalnʊs] *f* walnut

Walpurgisnacht *f* eve of May 1st, according to German folklore: the night of the Witches' Sabbat on the Blocksberg

Walross[RR] <-es, -e>, **Walroß**[ALT] <-rosses, -rosse> [ˈvalrɔs] *nt* walrus

Walze <-, -n> [ˈvaltsə] *f* roller

wälzen [ˈvɛltsn̩] **I.** *vt* ❶ (*rollen*) to roll ❷ *Probleme* to turn over in one's mind ❸ *Bücher* to pore over **II.** *vr* ■**sich** *akk* ~ to roll (**in** +*dat* in); **sie wälzte sich im Bett hin und her** she tossed and turned in bed

Walzer <-s, -> [ˈvaltsɐ] *m* waltz

Wampe <-, -n> [ˈvampə] *f* (*fam*) [beer] belly

wand *imp von* **winden**

Wand <-, Wände> [vant] *f* wall

Wandel <-s> [ˈvandl̩] *m kein pl* change

wandeln [ˈvandl̩n] *vt, vr* ■**sich** *akk* ~ to change

Wanderausstellung *f* traveling exhibit

Wanderer, Wanderin <-s, -> [ˈvandərə] *m, f* hiker

Wanderkarte *f* trail map

wandern [ˈvandɐn] *vi* ❶ (*eine Wanderung machen*) to hike ❷ ZOOL to migrate

Wanderung <-, -en> [ˈvandərʊŋ] *f* hike

Wandschrank *m* built-in wall closet

Wange <-, -n> [ˈvaŋə] *f* cheek

wankelmütig ['vaŋ·kl·my:·tɪç] *adj* inconsistent

wanken ['vaŋ·kn̩] *vi* ❶ *haben* (*schwanken*) to sway ❷ *sein* (*wankend gehen*) to stagger

wann [van] *adv* when; **seit ~** since when; **~** |**auch**| **immer** whenever

Wanne <-, -n> ['va·nə] *f* tub

Wanst <-[e]s, Wänste> [vanst] *m* belly

Wanze <-, -n> ['van·tsə] *f* bug

wappnen ['vap·nən] *vr* ■**sich** *akk* |**gegen etw** *akk*| **~** to prepare oneself |for sth|

Ware <-, -n> ['va:·rə] *f* article, product

Warenangebot *nt* range of products

Warenhaus *nt* department store

warm <wärmer, wärmste> [varm] *adj* warm; **etw ~ halten** to keep sth warm; **etw ~ machen** to heat sth up; **den Motor ~ laufen lassen** to let the engine warm up; **mir ist zu ~** I'm hot ▶WENDUNGEN: **etw wärmstens empfehlen** to highly recommend sth; **mit jdm ~ werden** to warm to sb

Wärme <-> ['vɛr·mə] *f kein pl* warmth

wärmen ['vɛr·mən] I. *vt* to warm up II. *vi* to be warm III. *vr* ■**sich** *akk* **gegenseitig ~** to keep each other warm

Wärmeregler *m* thermostat

Wärmflasche *f* hot-water bottle

warmherzig *adj* warm-hearted

Warmstart *m* COMPUT soft reset

Warnblinkanlage *f* AUTO hazard lights *pl*, hazards *pl fam*

Warndreieck *nt* hazard warning triangle

warnen ['var·nən] *vt* to warn (**vor** +*dat* about)

Warnlicht *nt* AUTO hazard lights *pl*

Warnschild *nt* warning sign

Warnschuss^RR *m* warning shot

Warnstreik *m* warning strike

Warnung <-, -en> *f* warning (**vor** +*dat* about)

Warschau <-s> ['var·ʃau] *nt* Warsaw

Wartehalle *f* waiting room

Warteliste *f* waiting list

warten ['var·tn̩] I. *vi* to wait (**auf** +*akk* for); **auf sich** *akk* **~ lassen** to be a long

time [in] coming; **warte mal!** hold on!; **na warte!** just you wait! II. *vt Gerät* to service

Wärter(in) <-s, -> ['vɛr·tɐ] *m(f)* ❶ (*Gefängniswärter*) prison guard ❷ (*Tierpfleger*) keeper

Warteraum *m* waiting room

Warteschlange *f* line

Wartezeit *f* wait

Wartezimmer *nt* waiting room

Wartung <-, -en> *f* service, maintenance

warum [va·ˈrʊm] *adv* why

Warze <-, -n> ['var·tsə] *f* wart

was [vas] I. *pron interrog* what; **~ bedeutet das?** what does that mean?; **~ kostet das?** how much does that cost?; **~ ist?** what's up?; **~ für ein ...** what kind of ...; **~ für ein Glück!** what luck! II. *pron rel* what; **alles, ~ du willst** everything you want; **alles, ~ ich weiß** all [that] I know III. *pron indef* (*fam: etwas*) something; (*in Fragesätzen*) anything; **ist ~?** is anything wrong?; **gibt es ~ Neues?** have you heard anything [new]?

Waschanlage *f* car wash

waschbar *adj* washable

Waschbär *m* raccoon

Waschbecken *nt* sink

Wäsche <-> *f kein pl* ❶ (*das Waschen, Schmutzwäsche*) laundry, wash ❷ (*Unterwäsche*) underwear ❸ (*Haushaltswäsche*) linens *pl*

waschecht *adj* ❶ (*typisch*) genuine, real ❷ (*nicht verbleichend*) colorfast

Wäscheklammer *f* clothespin

Wäschekorb *m* laundry basket

Wäscheleine *f* [clothes]line

waschen <wäscht, wusch, gewaschen> ['va·ʃn̩] *vt* to wash

Wäscherei <-, -en> [vɛ·ʃə·ˈrai] *f* laundry

Wäscheschrank *m* linen cupboard

Wäscheständer *m* clotheshorse, drying rack

Wäschetrockner <-s, -> *m* drier

Waschküche *f* laundry room

W

Waschlappen m ① (*Lappen*) washcloth ② (*fam: Feigling*) wimp

Waschmaschine f washing machine

Waschmittel nt detergent

Waschpulver nt laundry powder

Waschraum m laundry room

Waschsalon m laundromat

Waschstraße f car wash

Wasser <-s, -> ['va·se] nt water; ~ **abweisend** water-repellent ▶WEN·DUNGEN: **ins ~ fallen** to fall through; **das ~ bis zum Hals stehen haben** to be up to one's ears in debt; **sich über ~ halten** to keep oneself above water; **jdm läuft das ~ im Mund zusammen** (*fam*) sb's mouth is watering

Wasseranschlussᴿᴿ m water main connection

Wasseraufbereitungsanlage f water treatment plant

Wasserball m ① kein pl (*Sport*) water polo ② (*Ball*) beach ball

Wasserbett nt waterbed

Wasserdampf m steam

wasserdicht adj watertight, waterproof

Wasserfall m waterfall

Wasserglas nt glass, tumbler

Wasserhahn m [water] faucet

Wasserkraftwerk nt hydroelectric power station

Wasserleitung f water pipe

Wassermann ['va·se·man] m ASTROL Aquarius

Wassermelone f watermelon

wässern ['vɛ·sen] vt to water

Wasserpistole f water pistol

Wasserrohr nt water pipe

wasserscheu adj scared of water

Wasserschutzgebiet nt water protection area

Wasserski m ① kein pl (*Sportart*) waterskiing ② (*Sportgerät*) waterski

Wassersport m water sports pl

Wasserstand m water level

Wasserstrahl m jet of water

Wasserverbrauch m water consumption

Wasserversorgung f water supply

Wasserwaage f level

Wasserwerk nt waterworks + sing/pl vb

wässrigᴿᴿ, **wäßrig**ᴬᴸᵀ ['vɛ·rɪç] adj ① Augen, Suppe watery ② CHEM Lösung aqueous

waten ['va:·tn̩] vi sein to wade

watscheln ['va:·tʃl̩n] vi sein to waddle

Watt¹ <-s, -> [vat] nt PHYS watt

Watt² <-[e]s, -en> [vat] nt mud flats pl

Watte <-, -n> ['va·tə] f cotton wool

Wattestäbchen nt cotton swab, Q-tip®

wattieren* [va·'tiː·rən] vt to pad

WC <-s, -s> [ve:'tse:] nt Abk von **watercloset** bathroom; (*public*) restroom

weben <webte o geh wob, gewebt o geh gewoben> ['ve:·bn̩] vt, vi to weave

Webseite f INET Web page

Website <-, -s> ['wɛb·saɪt] f INET Web site

Wechsel <-s, -> ['vɛk·sl̩] m change

Wechselgeld nt kein pl change

wechselhaft ['vɛk·sl̩·] adj changeable

Wechseljahre pl menopause

Wechselkurs m exchange rate

wechseln ['vɛk·sl̩n] vt, vi to change

wechselseitig adj mutual

Wechselstrom m alternating current

Wechselstube f exchange booth

Wechselwirkung f interaction

wecken ['vɛ·kn̩] vt ① (*aufwecken*) to wake [up] ② (*hervorrufen*) to bring back sep; Assoziationen to create; Interesse, Verdacht to arouse

Wecker <-s, -> ['vɛ·ke] m alarm clock

wedeln ['ve:·dl̩n] vi ■mit etw dat ~ to wave sth; (*mit dem Schwanz*) to wag sth

weder ['ve:·de] konj ~ ... noch ... neither ... nor ...; ~ **du noch er** neither you nor him; ~ **noch** neither

weg [vɛk] adv ① (*fort*) ■~ **sein** to have left, to be gone; ~ **mit dir!** go away!; **nichts wie ~ hier!** let's get out of here!; ~ **da!** [get] out of the way! ② (*fam: hinweggekommen*) ■**über etw** akk ~ **sein** to have gotten over sth

Weg <-[e]s, -e> [ve:k] m ① (*Pfad*) path

② (*unbefestigte Straße*) track **③** (*Strecke*) way; **auf dem ~ sein** to be on one's way; **auf jds ~ liegen** to be on sb's way; **sich** *akk* **auf den ~ machen** to take off **④** (*Methode*) way ▶WENDUNGEN: **auf dem ~e der** <u>Besserung</u> **sein** to be on the road to recovery; **jdm auf** <u>halbem</u> **~e entgegenkommen** to meet sb halfway; **jdm/etw aus dem ~ gehen** to avoid sb/sth; **jdm über den ~** <u>laufen</u> to run into sb; **etw in die ~e** <u>leiten</u> to arrange sth; **etw aus dem ~ räumen** to remove sth; **sich** *akk* **jdm in den ~** <u>stellen</u> to block sb's path; **jdm nicht über den ~** <u>trauen</u> to not trust sb for a second

weg|bleiben *vi irreg sein* to stay away; **bleib nicht so lange weg!** don't stay out too long

weg|bringen *vt irreg* to take away

wegen ['veː·ɡn̩] *präp* +*gen* **①** (*aufgrund von*) because of, due to; **~ ihm** (*fam*) because of him **②** (*bezüglich*) regarding

weg|fahren *irreg* I. *vi sein* **①** (*abfahren*) to drive off, to leave **②** (*verreisen*) to leave on a trip II. *vt haben* (*wegbringen*) to drive [*or* take] away

weg|fallen *vi irreg sein* to cease to apply

weg|fliegen *vi irreg sein* **①** *Vogel* to fly away **②** *Hut, Blätter* to be blown away, to fly off

weg|führen *vt, vi* to lead away

weg|geben *vt irreg* to give away *sep*

weg|gehen *vi irreg sein* **①** (*fortgehen*) to walk away **②** (*ausgehen*) to go out **③** (*fam: sich entfernen lassen*) to go away; **der Fleck geht nicht weg** the stain won't come out

weg|jagen *vt* to drive away *sep*

weg|kommen *vi irreg sein* (*fam*) **①** (*weggehen können*) to get away **②** (*abhandenkommen*) to disappear **③** (*fam: abschneiden*) [**bei etw** *dat*] **gut/schlecht ~** to do/not do well [on sth] ▶WENDUNGEN: <u>mach</u>, **dass du wegkommst!** get out of here!

weg|lassen *vt irreg* **①** (*auslassen*) to leave out *sep* **②** (*weggehen lassen*) to let go

weg|laufen *vi irreg sein* to run away (**vor** +*dat* from)

weg|legen *vt* **①** (*beiseitelegen*) to put down *sep* **②** (*aufbewahren*) to put aside *sep*

weg|müssen *vi irreg* to have to go

weg|nehmen *vt irreg* to take (**von** +*dat* off); **■jdm etw ~** to take away sth *sep* from sb; **■etw [von etw** *dat*] **~** to take sth *sep* [off sth]

weg|räumen *vt* to clear away *sep*

weg|schaffen *vt* to remove *sep*

weg|schicken *vt* **①** *Person* to send away **②** *Brief* to send off *sep*

weg|schmeißen *vt irreg* (*fam*) *s.* **wegwerfen**

weg|schütten *vt* to pour away *sep*

weg|sehen *vi irreg* to look away *sep*

weg|stecken *vt* **①** (*einstecken*) to put away *sep* **②** (*verkraften*) to get over

weg|stellen *vt* to move out of the way *sep*

weg|stoßen *vt irreg* to push away *sep*; (*mit dem Fuß*) to kick away *sep*

weg|tragen *vt irreg* to carry away *sep*

weg|tun *vt irreg* **①** (*wegwerfen*) to throw away *sep* **②** (*weglegen*) to put down *sep*

Wegweiser <-s, -> *m* signpost

weg|werfen *vt irreg* to throw away *sep*

weg|wischen *vt* to wipe away *sep*

weg|ziehen *irreg* I. *vi sein* to move away II. *vt haben* to pull away *sep*

wehen ['veː·ən] *vi* **①** *Wind* to blow **②** *Haare* to blow around; *Fahne* to flutter

wehleidig *adj* oversensitive

wehmütig ['veː·myː·tɪç] *adj* melancholy; *Erinnerung* nostalgic

Wehr [veːɐ̯] *f* **sich** *akk* **zur ~ setzen** to defend oneself

Wehrdienst *m kein pl* military service

Wehrdienstverweigerer *m* conscientious objector

wehren ['veː·rən] *vr* **①** (*sich widersetzen*) **■sich** *akk* **gegen etw** *akk* **~** to fight against sth **②** (*sich sträuben*) **■sich** *akk* **dagegen ~, etw zu tun** to resist doing sth

wehrlos I. *adj* defenseless (**gegen** +*akk*

W

against) **II.** *adv* in a defenseless state;
etw *dat* ~ **gegenüberstehen** to be
defenseless against sth

Wehrpflicht *f kein pl* mandatory military service

wehrpflichtig *adj* obliged to enlist for
military service

Weib <-[e]s, -er> [vaip] *nt* woman

Weibchen <-s, -> ['vaip·çən] *nt* female

Weiberheld *m* (*pej*) lady-killer *sl*

weiblich ['vaip·lıç] *adj* ❶ (*fraulich*)
feminine ❷ ANAT female ❸ LING feminine

Weiblichkeit <-> *f kein pl* femininity

weich [vaiç] **I.** *adj* soft ▶WENDUNGEN:
~ **werden** to weaken **II.** *adv* softly

weichen <wich, gewichen> ['vai·çn] *vi*
sein (*weggehen*) to go; **er wich nicht
von der Stelle** he didn't budge from
the spot; **jdm nicht von der Seite** ~ to
not leave sb's side

weichherzig *adj* soft-hearted

Weichkäse *m* soft cheese

Weichling <-s, -e> ['vaiç·lıŋ] *m* (*pej*)
weakling

Weide <-, -n> ['vai·də] *f* ❶ BOT willow
❷ AGR meadow

weiden ['vai·dn] **I.** *vi* (*grasen*) to graze
II. *vr* ■ **sich** *akk* **an etw** *dat* ~ to feast
one's eyes on sth; (*schadenfroh*) to rev-
el in sth

weigern ['vai·gɐn] *vr* ■ **sich** *akk* ~ to refuse

Weigerung <-, -en> *f* refusal

Weihnachten <-, -> ['vai·nax·tn] *nt*
Christmas, Xmas *fam*; **fröhliche** ~!
Merry Christmas!

weihnachtlich **I.** *adj* Christmassy, festive **II.** *adv* festively

Weihnachtsabend *m* Christmas Eve

Weihnachtsbaum *m* Christmas tree

Weihnachtsfest *nt* Christmas

Weihnachtsgeld *nt* Christmas bonus

Weihnachtsgeschenk *nt* Christmas
present

Weihnachtslied *nt* [Christmas] carol

Weihnachtsmann *m* Santa Claus, Father Christmas

Weihnachtsmarkt *m* Christmas market

weil [vail] *konj* because, since

Weile <-> ['vai·lə] *f kein pl* while; **eine
ganze** ~ quite a while

Wein <-[e]s, -e> [vain] *m* ❶ (*Getränk*)
wine ❷ *kein pl* (*Weinrebe*) [grape]vines
pl ▶WENDUNGEN: **jdm reinen** ~ **einschenken** to tell sb the truth

Weinbeere *f* ❶ (*Traube*) grape ❷ SÜDD,
ÖSTERR, SCHWEIZ (*Rosine*) raisin

Weinberg *m* vineyard

Weinbrand *m* brandy

weinen ['vai·nən] *vi* to cry (**um** +*akk*
for)

weinerlich **I.** *adj* tearful **II.** *adv* tearfully

Weinflasche *f* wine bottle

Weinglas *nt* wine glass

Weingut *nt* winery

Weinkeller *m* wine cellar

Weinlese *f* grape harvest

Weinprobe *f* wine tasting

Weinrebe *f* grape[vine]

weinrot *adj* burgundy[-colored]

Weinstube *f* wine bar

Weintraube *f* grape

weise ['vai·zə] **I.** *adj* wise **II.** *adv* wisely

Weise <-, -n> ['vai·zə] *f* way; **auf
diese/eine bestimmte** ~ in this/a certain way; **in gewisser** ~ in certain
respects

weisen <wies, gewiesen> ['vai·zn] **I.** *vt*
❶ **jdm den Weg** ~ to show sb the way
❷ **etw von sich** *dat* ~ to reject sth **II.** *vi*
■ **irgendwohin** ~ to point somewhere

Weisheit <-, -en> ['vais·hait] *f* ❶ *kein
pl* (*Klugheit*) wisdom ❷ *meist pl* (*wei-
ser Rat*) words *pl* of wisdom ▶WENDUN-
GEN: **mit seiner** ~ **am Ende sein** to be
at one's wits' end

Weisheitszahn *m* wisdom tooth

weis|machen *vt* ■ **jdm etw** ~ to lead sb
to believe sth

weiß¹ [vais] *adj* white

weiß² [vais] *3. pers sing pres von* **wissen**

Weissagung <-, -en> *f* prophecy

Weißbrot *nt* white bread

Weiße(r) *f(m)* (*dekl wie adj*) white, white
man/woman; ■ **die** ~**n** white people

Weißglut *f* ▶WENDUNGEN: **jdn zur** ~
bringen to make sb livid with rage

Weißkohl m, **Weißkraut** nt SÜDD, ÖSTERR white cabbage

Weißwein m white wine

weit [vait] I. adj long; Kleidung baggy; **bis dahin ist es noch ~** we still have a way to go before we get there II. adv ① (räumlich) far; **~ weg** far away; **es noch ~ haben** to have a long way to go; **8 km ~er** 8 km ahead; **etw ~ öffnen** to open sth wide ② (erheblich) s. **weitaus 1** ③ **~ reichend** extensive; **~ verbreitet** widespread ④ (zeitlich) **~ zurückliegen** to be a long time ago ▶WENDUNGEN: **bei/von ~em** by/from far; **bei ~em nicht** not nearly; **~ und breit** for miles around; **~ hergeholt** far-fetched; **mit etw** dat **ist es nicht ~ her** sth is nothing much to write home about

weitab [vait·'ʔap] adv far away; ■ **~ von etw** dat far from sth

weitaus ['vait·ʔaus] adv ① vor komp (erheblich) far, much; **~ schlechter sein** to be far [or much] worse ② vor superl (bei weitem) [by] far

weiten ['vai·tn̩] I. vt MODE to widen II. vr ■ **sich** akk **~** to widen; (Pupille) to dilate

weiter ['vai·tɐ] adv ① (sonst) **wenn es ~ nichts ist, ...** well, if that's all ... ② (weiterhin) **~ bestehen** to continue to exist

weiter|bilden vr ■ **sich** akk **in etw** dat **~** to [further] develop one's knowledge of sth

Weiterbildung f kein pl continuing education

weiter|bringen vt irreg to help along

weiter|empfehlen* vt irreg to recommend

weiter|führen vt (fortsetzen) to continue

weiter|geben vt irreg to pass on sep (**an** +akk to)

weiter|gehen vi irreg sein ① (seinen Weg fortsetzen) to keep going ② (seinen Fortgang nehmen) to go on; **so kann es nicht ~** things can't go on like this

weiter|helfen vi irreg to keep helping; (auf die Sprünge helfen) to help along

weiterhin ['vai·tɐ·'hɪn] adv ① (immer noch) still ② (außerdem) furthermore, in addition

weiter|kommen vi irreg sein to get farther along

weiter|machen vi to continue

weiter|sagen vt to pass on sep; **nicht ~!** don't tell anyone!

weitgehend I. adj (umfassend) extensive II. adv extensively, to a large extent

weitläufig ['vait·lɔy·fɪç] I. adj ① (ausgedehnt) extensive ② (entfernt) distant II. adv extensively, distantly

weitreichend adj extensive

weitsichtig ['vait·zɪç·tɪç] adj (a. med) farsighted

Weizen <-s, -> ['vai·tsn̩] m wheat

welche(r, s) I. pron interrog which II. pron rel (der, die, das: Mensch) who; (Sache) which III. pron indef ① (etwas) some; **wenn du Geld brauchst, kann ich dir ~s leihen** if you need money, I can lend you some ② pl (einige) some; ■ **~, die ...** some [people], who

welk [vɛlk] adj ① (verwelkt) wilted ② (schlaff) worn-out

welken ['vɛl·kn̩] vi sein to wilt

Wellblech nt corrugated iron

Welle <-, -n> ['vɛ·lə] f wave

wellen ['vɛ·lən] vr ■ **sich** akk **~** to be/become wavy; (Papier) to crinkle

Wellenbrecher <-s, -> m breakwater

Wellenlänge f PHYS wavelength

Wellenreiten nt surfing

Wellensittich m parakeet

wellig ['vɛ·lɪç] adj ① (gewellt) wavy ② (wellenförmig) uneven

WellnessRR <-> ['vɛl·nɛs] f kein pl ① (Wohlbefinden) well-being ② (wohltuende Behandlung) spa treatment

WellnesshotelRR nt spa, health resort

Welpe <-n, -n> ['vɛl·pə] m puppy, whelp

Welt <-, -en> [vɛlt] f world; **auf der ~** in the world ▶WENDUNGEN: **alle ~** (fam) the whole world; **in aller ~** all over the

W

world; **die** <u>Dritte</u> **~** the Third World; **auf die** <u>**kommen**</u> to be born; **in einer anderen** <u>**leben**</u> to live on another planet; **um nichts in der ~** not for the world

Weltall *nt* universe

Weltanschauung *f* worldview, philosophy of life

Weltausstellung *f* world's fair

weltberühmt *adj* world-famous

Weltbevölkerung *f kein pl* world population

Weltenbummler(in) <-s, -> *m(f)* globetrotter

weltfremd *adj* unworldly

Weltkarte *f* world map

Weltkrieg *m* world war; **der Erste/ Zweite ~** World War I/II

weltlich ['vɛlt-lɪç] *adj* ❶ *(irdisch)* worldly ❷ *(profan)* mundane

Weltmacht *f* world power

Weltmeer *nt* ocean

Weltmeister(in) *m(f)* world champion **(in** +*dat in)*

Weltmeisterschaft *f* world championship

Weltraum *m kein pl* [outer] space

Weltraumfähre *f* space shuttle

Weltraumtourismus *m* ■ **der ~** space tourism

Weltreise *f* **eine ~ machen** to go on a trip around the world

Weltrekord *m* world record

Weltsicherheitsrat *m* [United Nations] Security Council

Weltstadt *f* international city

Weltuntergang *m* end of the world

weltweit I. *adj* global, worldwide II. *adv* globally

Weltwirtschaft *f* world economy

Weltwirtschaftsgipfel *m* world economic summit

W **Weltwunder** *nt* **die sieben ~** the Seven Wonders of the World

wem [ve:m] I. *pron indef dat von* **wer** *(fam)* who ... to, to whom *form*; **~ gehört dieser Schlüssel?** who does this key belong to?; **mit/von ~** with/from

whom III. *pron rel* ■ **~ ...,** [der] ... the person to whom ..., the person who ... to

wen [ve:n] I. *pron indef akk von* **wer** *(fam)* somebody II. *pron interrog* who, whom; **an/für ~** to/for whom *form,* who ... to/for III. *pron rel* ■ **~ ...,** [der] ... the person who[m] ...; **an/für ~** to/ for whom *form,* who ... to/for

Wende <-, -n> ['vɛn-də] *f* change, turn

Wendekreis *m* AUTO turning circle

Wendeltreppe *f* spiral staircase

wenden ['vɛn-dn̩] I. *vr* <wendete *o geh* wandte, gewendet *o geh* gewandt> ❶ *(sich drehen)* **sich** *akk* **nach links/ rechts ~** to turn left/right ❷ *(kontaktieren)* ■ **sich** *akk* [**in etw** *dat*] **an jdn ~** to turn to sb [regarding sth] ❸ *(zielen)* ■ **sich akk an jdn ~** to be directed at sb ❹ *(entgegentreten)* ■ **sich** *akk* **gegen jdn ~** to turn against sb; ■ **sich** *akk* **gegen etw** *akk* **~** to oppose sth ❺ *(sich verkehren)* **sich** *akk* **zum Besseren/ Schlechteren ~** to take a turn for the better/worse II. *vt* <wendete, gewendet> *(umdrehen)* to turn over *sep* III. *vi* <wendete, gewendet> AUTO to turn

Wendepunkt *m* turning point

wendig ['vɛn-dɪç] *adj* maneuverable

Wendung <-, -en> *f* ❶ *(Veränderung)* turn ❷ *(Redewendung)* expression

wenig ['ve:-nɪç] I. *pron indef* ❶ *sing (nicht viel)* little; **~ Zeit/Geld haben** to have little time/money; **zu ~ Freizeit** not enough free time; ■ **~ sein** to be not [very] much ❷ *pl (nicht viele)* ■ **~e** a few; **~ Stunden später** a few hours later; **das wissen nur ~e** only a few [people] know about it II. *adv* little; **~ interessant** of little interest; **zu ~ schlafen** to not get enough sleep

weniger ['ve:-nɪ-gɐ] I. *adj komp von* **wenig:** ■ **~ als ...** less ... than II. *pron indef* ❶ *(unzählbar)* Zeit, Geld less ❷ *(zählbar)* Menschen, Bücher fewer III. *adv* less; **~ bekannt sein** to be less known

wenigste(r, s) I. *pron* ■ **die ~n** very

few; ■**das ~, was ...** the least that …
II. *adv* least; *pl* fewest; **am ~n** least of
all
wenigstens ['veːnɪçs·tns] *adv* at least
wenn [vɛn] *konj* ① (*falls*) if; **~ das so ist**
if that's true [*or* the way it is] ② (*sobald*)
as soon as
wenngleich [vɛn·ˈglaiç] *konj* although
wer <*gen* wessen, *dat* wem, *akk* wen>
[veːɐ] I. *pron interrog* who; **~ von beiden?** which of the two? II. *pron rel* **~
das sagt, [der] lügt** whoever says that
is lying III. *pron indef* (*fam*) s. **jemand**
▶WENDUNGEN: **~ sein** to be somebody
fam
Werbeagentur *f* advertising agency
Werbefernsehen *nt* commercials *pl*
Werbefilm *m* promotional film
Werbegeschenk *nt* promotional gift
Werbekampagne *f* advertising campaign
werben <wirbt, warb, geworben> ['vɛr-
bn̩] I. *vt* ■**jdn [für etw** *akk*] **~** to recruit sb [for sth] II. *vi* ① (*Reklame
machen*) ■**für etw** *akk* **~** to advertise [*or* promote] sth ② (*zu erhalten
suchen*) **um eine Frau ~** to woo a
woman; **um neue Wähler ~** to try to
attract new voters
Werbeslogan *m* advertising slogan
Werbespot *m* commercial
Werbung <-> *f kein pl* ① (*Reklame*) advertisement; **~ für etw** *akk* **machen** to
advertise sth ② (*Werbespot*) commercial; (*Werbeprospekt*) promotional brochure ③ (*Branche*) advertising
Werdegang *m* career
werden ['veːɐ·dn̩] I. *vi* <wird, wurde,
geworden> *sein* ① (*seinen Zustand
ändern*) to become, to get; **es wird
dunkel** it is getting dark; **es wird besser ~** it is going to get better; **es wird
Sommer** summer is coming [*or* almost
here]; **sie ist gerade 98 geworden** she
[has] just turned 98; **alt/älter ~** to get
old/older; **kalt ~** to get cold; **jdm wird
heiß/übel** sb feels hot/sick; **Wirklichkeit ~** to become reality ② (*eine Ausbildung machen*) to become; **sie will**

Ärztin werden she wants to become a
doctor; **was möchtest du einmal ~?**
what do you want to be [when you
grow up]? ③ (*sich entwickeln*) ■**zu
etw** *dat* **~** to turn into sth; **es wird
schon [wieder] ~** it'll turn out okay in
the end II. *aux vb* ① *zur Bildung des
Futurs* ■**etw tun ~** to be going to do
sth; ■**es wird etw geschehen** sth is
going to happen; ■**jd wird etw getan
haben** sb will have done sth ② *zur Bildung des Konjunktivs* ■**jd würde etw
tun** sb would do sth ③ *mutmaßend* **es
wird gegen 20 Uhr sein** it's probably
[*or* I'm guessing it's] about 8 o'clock
III. *aux vb* <wird, wurde, worden> *sein*
zur Bildung des Passivs **du wirst gerufen** you are being called; **gebissen ~** to
be bitten; **sie wurde entlassen** she
was laid off [*or* fired]; **das wird bei uns
häufig gemacht** we do that a lot here
werfen <wirft, warf, geworfen> ['vɛr-
fn̩] *vt, vi* ① (*schleudern*) to throw
(**nach** +*dat* at) ② (*Junge gebären*) to
throw *spec*, to give birth
Werft <-, -en> [vɛrft] *f* shipyard
Werk <-[e]s, -e> [vɛrk] *nt* ① (*Buch,
Kunstwerk*) work ② (*Gesamtwerk*)
works *pl* ③ (*Fabrik*) factory ▶WENDUN-
GEN: **ein gutes ~ tun** to do a good deed
Werk(s)angehörige(r) *f(m) dekl wie
adj* factory employee
Werksgelände *nt* factory premises *npl*
Werkstatt *f* ① (*Arbeitsraum*) workshop
② AUTO garage
Werktag *m* workday
werktags *adv* on workdays
werktätig ['vɛrk·tɛː·tɪç] *adj* **die ~e
Bevölkerung** the working population
Werkzeug <-[e]s, -e> *nt* tool *usu pl*
Werkzeugkasten *m* toolbox
wert [veːɐt] *adj* ① (*einen Wert besitzen*)
■**[jdm] etw ~ sein** to be worth sth [to
sb] ② (*verdienen*) ■**einer S.** *gen* **~
sein** to be worthy of sth
Wert <-[e]s, -e> [veːɐt] *m* ① (*Preis*)
value; **im ~ steigen** to increase in
value; **an ~ verlieren** to decrease in
value; **im ~e von etw** *dat* worth sth

W

② *pl* (*Daten*) results *pl* **③** (*Wichtigkeit*) ~ **auf etw** *akk* **legen** to think sth is important **④** (*Wertvorstellung*) value ▶WENDUNGEN: **das hat keinen** ~ (*fam*) it's useless

werten *vt* to rate

wertfrei *adj* impartial

wertlos *adj* worthless

Wertschätzung *f* esteem

wertvoll *adj* valuable

Wertvorstellung *f meist pl* moral concept *usu pl*

Wesen <-s, -> ['ve:·zn̩] *nt* **①** (*Geschöpf*) being; (*tierisch*) creature **②** *kein pl* (*Grundzüge*) nature

Wesenszug *m* characteristic

wesentlich ['ve:·zn̩t·lɪç] **I.** *adj* **①** (*erheblich*) considerable **②** (*wichtig*) essential; **■das W~e** the essential part; **im W~en** essentially **II.** *adv* considerably

weshalb [vɛs·'halp] *adv* why

Wespe <-, -n> ['vɛs·pə] *f* yellow jacket

wessen ['vɛ·sn̩] *pron interrog gen von* **wer** whose

Wessi <-, -s> ['vɛ·si] *m o f* (*fam*) West German

Weste <-, -n> ['vɛs·tə] *f* vest

Westen <-s-s> ['vɛs·tn̩] *m kein pl, kein indef art* **①** (*Himmelsrichtung*) west; *s. a.* **Norden 1 ②** (*südliche Gegend*) west; **der Wilde** ~ the Wild West; *s. a.* **Norden 2**

Westentasche *f* vest pocket

Western <-[s], -> ['vɛs·tɐn] *m* western

Westfalen <-s-s> [vɛst·'fa:·lən] *nt* Westphalia

Westküste *f* West Coast

westlich ['vɛst·lɪç] **I.** *adj* **①** (*Himmelsrichtung*) western; *s. a.* **nördlich I 1 ②** (*im Westen liegend*) western; *s. a.* **nördlich I 2 ③** (*von/nach Westen*) westward, westerly; *s. a.* **nördlich I 3** **II.** *adv* ■~ **von** to the west of **III.** *präp* +*gen* [to the] west of

weswegen [vɛs·'ve:·gn̩] *adv* why

Wettbewerb <-[e]s, -e> ['vɛt·bə·vɛrp] *m* competition

Wettbewerber(in) *m(f)* competitor

Wette <-, -n> ['vɛ·tə] *f* bet; **die ~ gilt!**

you're on!; **jede ~ eingehen, dass ...** to bet anything that ...; **um die ~ laufen** to race [each other]

wetteifern *vi* ■**miteinander ~** to contend with each other

wetten ['vɛ·tn̩] *vt, vi* to bet (**auf** +*akk* on); ■**[mit jdm] um etw** *akk* ~ to bet [sb] sth; [**wollen wir**] ~? [do you] want to bet?

Wetter <-s-> ['vɛ·tɐ] *nt kein pl* weather; **bei jedem** ~ rain or shine

Wetterbericht *m* weather report

Wetterdienst *m* weather service

wetterfühlig *adj* sensitive to weather changes *pred*

Wetterhahn *m* rooster weathervane

Wetterkarte *f* weather map

Wetterlage *f* weather situation

wettern ['vɛ·tɐn] *vi* ■**gegen jdn/etw**] ~ to curse [sb/sth]

Wetterumschwung *m* sudden change in the weather

Wettervorhersage *f* weather forecast

Wettkampf *m* competition

Wettlauf *m* race

wett|machen ['vɛt·ma·xn̩] *vt* **①** (*aufholen*) to make up **②** (*gutmachen*) to make up for

Wettrennen *nt* race

Wettrüsten <-s-> *nt kein pl* arms race

Wettstreit ['vɛt·ʃtrait] *m* competition

wetzen ['vɛ·tsn̩] **I.** *vt haben* **①** (*schleifen*) to whet **②** (*reiben*) to rub (**an** +*dat* on) **II.** *vi sein* (*fam: rennen*) to scoot [off]

WG <-, -s> [ve:·'ge:] *f Abk von* **Wohngemeinschaft**

wichsen ['vɪk·sn̩] **I.** *vi* (*vulg*) to jack [*or* jerk] off *vulg sl* **II.** *vt Schuhe* to polish

wichtig ['vɪç·tɪç] *adj* important

Wichtigtuer(in) <-s, -> [-tu:ɐ] *m(f)* stuffed shirt

wickeln ['vɪ·kl̩n] *vt* **①** (*binden*) to wrap (**um** +*akk* around, **in** +*akk* in) **②** *Baby* to change

Widder <-s, -> ['vɪ·dɐ] *m* **①** ZOOL ram **②** *kein pl* ASTROL Aries

widerfahren* [vi:·də·'fa:·rən] *vi irreg sein* to happen, to befall

W

Widerhall <-s, -e> ['viː·dɐ·hal] m echo

widerlegen* [viː·dɐ·'leː·gn̩] vt to refute

widerlich ['viː·dɐ·lɪç] I. adj ① (ekelhaft) disgusting ② (unsympathisch) repulsive II. adv (überaus) süß, kalt awfully

Widerrede ['viː·dɐ·reː·də] f keine ~! don't argue [with me]!

widerrufen* [viː·dɐ·'ruː·fn̩] vt irreg ① (für ungültig erklären) to revoke ② (zurücknehmen) to retract

Widersacher(in) <-s, -> ['viː·dɐ·za·xɐ] m(f) antagonist

widersetzen* [viː·dɐ·'zɛ·tsn̩] vr ■sich akk jdm ~ to resist sb; ■sich akk etw dat ~ to refuse to comply with sth

widerspenstig ['viː·dɐ·ʃpɛns·tɪç] adj unruly; Mensch, Pferd stubborn; Haar unmanageable

wider|spiegeln ['viː·dɐ·ʃpiː·gl̩n] I. vt to mirror, to reflect II. vr sich akk ~ to be reflected

widersprechen* [viː·dɐ·'ʃprɛ·çn̩] irreg I. vi to contradict II. vr ■sich dat ~ Aussage, Angaben to be contradictory

Widerspruch ['viː·dɐ·ʃprʊx] m ① kein pl (das Widersprechen) contradiction; auf ~ stoßen to meet with opposition ② (Unvereinbarkeit) inconsistency; in ~ zu etw dat stehen to conflict with sth

widersprüchlich ['viː·dɐ·ʃprʏç·lɪç] adj inconsistent; ■~ sein to be contradictory

widerspruchslos adv without protest

Widerstand <-[e]s, -stände> ['viː·dɐ·ʃtant] m ① kein pl (Gegenwehr) opposition, resistance ② ELEK (Schaltelement) resistor

widerstandsfähig adj resistant (gegen +akk to)

Widerstandskraft f robustness, resistance (gegen +akk to)

widerstandslos adv without resistance

widerstehen* [viː·dɐ·'ʃteː·ən] vi irreg ① (standhalten) to withstand ② (nicht nachgeben) Person, Versuchung to resist

widerstreben* [viː·dɐ·'ʃtreː·bn̩] vi

■jdm widerstrebt es, etw zu tun sb is reluctant to do sth

Widerstreben <-s> [viː·dɐ·'ʃtreː·bn̩] nt kein pl reluctance

widerwärtig ['viː·dɐ·vɛr·tɪç] I. adj disgusting; (Kerl) nasty II. adv disgustingly

Widerwille ['viː·dɐ·vɪlə] m distaste (gegen +akk for)

widerwillig I. adj reluctant II. adv reluctantly

widmen ['vɪt·mən] I. vt to dedicate to II. vr ① (sich kümmern) ■sich akk jdm ~ to attend to sb ② (sich beschäftigen) ■sich akk etw dat ~ to devote oneself to sth

Widmung <-, -en> ['vɪt·mʊŋ] f dedication

widrig ['viː·drɪç] adj adverse; Umstände, Verhältnisse unfavorable

wie [viː] I. adv how; ~ geht es dir? how are you?; ~ heißt er? what's his name?; ~ war das Wetter? what was the weather like?; ~ viel/viele how much/many; ~ sehr how much; ~ wär's mit ...? how about ...? II. konj ① (vergleichend) so alt/groß ~ ... as big/old as ...; er ist genau ~ du he's just like you ② (beispielsweise) like

wieder ['viː·dɐ] adv again, once more; ~ mal again; Verhandlungen ~ aufnehmen to resume negotiations; Kontakt ~ aufnehmen to reestablish contact; etw ~ einführen to reintroduce sth

Wiederaufbau [viː·dɐ·'ʔaʊf·baʊ] m kein pl reconstruction

wieder|bekommen* vt irreg to get back

wieder|beleben* vt to revive

wieder|bringen ['viː·dɐ·brɪ·ŋən] vt irreg to bring back sep

wieder|erkennen* vt irreg to recognize; **nicht wiederzuerkennen sein** to be unrecognizable **W**

Wiedereröffnung f reopening

wieder|finden irreg I. vt ① (auffinden) to find again ② (Fassung) to regain II. vr ■sich akk ~ to turn up again

Wiedergabe <-, -n> ['viː·də·ga·

bǝ] f ❶ (*Schilderung*) account, report ❷ PHOTO, TYPO reproduction

wieder|geben ['vi:·dǝ·ge:·bn̩] *vt irreg* ❶ (*zurückgeben*) to give back ❷ (*zitieren*) to quote

wieder|gewinnen* ['vi:·dǝ·gǝ·vɪ·nǝn] *vt irreg* ❶ (*zurückgewinnen*) to reclaim ❷ (*wiedererlangen*) to regain

Wiedergutmachung <-, -en> *f* compensation

wieder|her|stellen [vi:·dǝ·ˈheːɐ̯·ʃtɛ·lǝn] *vt* ❶ (*restaurieren*) to restore ❷ *Ordnung, Kontakt, Gesundheit* to reestablish

wiederholen*¹ [vi:·dǝ·ˈhoː·lǝn] I. *vt* ❶ (*erneut machen*) to repeat ❷ *Lernstoff* to revise II. *vr* ■ **sich** *akk* ~ *Ereignis* to happen again; *Person* to repeat oneself

wieder|holen² ['vi:·dǝ·hoː·lǝn] *vt s.* **zurückholen**

wiederholt I. *adj* repeated II. *adv* repeatedly

Wiederholung <-, -en> [vi:·dǝ·ˈhoː·lʊŋ] *f* ❶ (*erneutes Tun*) repetition ❷ (*im Radio/TV*) repeat ❸ *von Lernstoff* review

wieder|kehren ['vi:·dǝ·ke:·rǝn] *vi sein* ❶ *Mensch* to return ❷ *Problem* to reoccur

wieder|kommen ['vi:·dǝ·kɔ·mǝn] *vi irreg sein* ❶ (*zurückkommen*) to come back ❷ (*erneut kommen*) to come again; *Gelegenheit* to reoccur

wieder|sehen ['vi:·dǝ·ze:·ǝn] *irreg* I. *vt* ■ **jdn** ~ to see sb again II. *vr* ■ **sich** *akk* ~ to meet again

Wiedersehen <-s, -> ['vi:·dǝ·ze:·ǝn] *nt* [another] meeting; (*nach längerer Zeit*) reunion; [auf] ~ **sagen** to say goodbye

wiederum ['vi:·dar·ʊm] *adv* ❶ (*abermals*) again ❷ (*andererseits*) on the other hand, though ❸ (*für jds Teil*) in turn

wieder|vereinigen* *vt* POL to reunify

Wiedervereinigung ['vi:·dǝ·fɛɐ̯·ʔai·nɪ·ɡʊŋ] *f* POL reunification

wieder|verwerten* *vt* to recycle

Wiederverwertung *f* recycling

Wiederwahl ['vi:·dǝ·va:l] *f* POL reelection

Wiege <-, -n> ['vi:·gǝ] *f* cradle

wiegen <wog, gewogen> ['vi:·gn̩] *vt, vi* to weigh

Wiegenlied *nt* lullaby

wiehern ['vi:·ɐn] *vi* to neigh

Wien <-s> [vi:n] *nt* Vienna

Wiener ['vi:·nɐ] *adj attr* Viennese

Wiese <-, -n> [vi:·zǝ] *f* meadow

Wiesel <-s, -> ['vi:·zl̩] *nt* weasel

wieso [vi·ˈzo:] *adv* why

wild [vɪlt] I. *adj* ❶ BOT, ZOOL wild ❷ *Kampf* frenzied ❸ (*illegal*) illegal ❹ (*sehr gereizt*) furious; ~ **werden** to go wild ▶WENDUNGEN: **halb so** ~ **sein** (*fam*) to not be important; ~ **auf jdn/ etw sein** (*fam*) to be crazy about sb/ sth; **wie** ~ (*fam*) wildly II. *adv* ❶ (*ungeordnet*) strewn around ❷ (*hemmungslos*) wildly, furiously ❸ (*in freier Natur*) wild *pred*

Wild <-[e]s> [vɪlt] *nt kein pl* ❶ KOCHK game ❷ ZOOL wild animals

Wilderer, Wilderin <-s, -> ['vɪl·dǝ· rǝ] *m, f* poacher

wildern ['vɪl·dɐn] *vi* to poach

wildfremd ['vɪlt·ˈfrɛmt] *adj* completely strange

Wildhüter(in) <-s, -> *m(f)* gamekeeper

Wildnis <-, -se> ['vɪlt·nɪs] *f* wilderness

Wildschwein *nt* wild boar

Wildwestfilm [vɪlt·ˈvɛst-] *m* western

Wille <-ns> ['vɪ·lǝ] *m kein pl* will; **seinen eigenen** ~**n haben** to have a mind of one's own; **seinen** ~**n durchsetzen** to get one's way ▶WENDUNGEN: **jds letzter** ~ sb's last will and testament

willenlos *adj* spineless

Willenskraft *f kein pl* willpower

willensstark *adj* strong-willed

willig ['vɪ·lɪç] *adj* willing

willkommen [vɪl·ˈkɔ·mǝn] *adj* welcome; ■ **jdm** ~ **sein** to be welcomed [by sb]; **jdn** ~ **heißen** to welcome sb

Willkommen <-s, -> [vɪl·ˈkɔ·mǝn] *nt* welcome; **ein herzliches** ~ a warm welcome

Willkür <-> ['vɪl·ky·ɐ̯] *f kein pl* arbitrariness

willkürlich ['vɪl·ky·ɐ̯·lɪç] I. *adj* arbitrary II. *adv* arbitrarily

wimmeln ['vɪ·m|n] *vi impers* ■ **es wimmelt von etw** *dat* it is teeming with sth; *Menschen* it is swarming with

wimmern ['vɪ·mɐn] *vi* to whimper

Wimper <-, -n> ['vɪm·pɐ] *f* [eye]lash ▶WENDUNGEN: **ohne mit der ~ zu zucken** without batting an eyelid

Wimperntusche *f* mascara

Wind <-[e]s, -e> [vɪnt] *m* wind ▶WENDUNGEN: **viel ~ um etw machen** to make a fuss about sth; **bei ~ und Wetter** rain or shine

Winde <-, -n> ['vɪn·də] *f* TECH winch

Windel <-, -n> ['vɪn·d|] *f* diaper

windelweich *adv* **jdn ~ schlagen** to beat sb black and blue

winden <wand, gewunden> ['vɪn·dn̩] I. *vr* ■ **sich** *akk* ~ ❶ *(nach Ausflüchten suchen)* to attempt to wriggle out ❷ *(sich krümmen)* to writhe (**vor** + *dat* in) ❸ BOT to wind [itself] (**um** + *akk* around) II. *vt* ■ **etw um etw** *akk* ~ to wind sth around sth

Windenergie *f* wind energy

windgeschützt I. *adj* sheltered [from the wind] II. *adv* in a sheltered place

windig ['vɪn·dɪç] *adj* windy

Windjacke *f* windbreaker

Windmühle *f* windmill

Windpocken *pl* chickenpox *sing*

Windrad *nt* wind turbine

windschief *adj* crooked

Windschutzscheibe *f* windshield

Windstärke *f* wind force

windstill *adj* windless; ■ **~ sein** to be calm

Windstoß *m* gust of wind

Wink <-[e]s, -e> [vɪŋk] *m* ❶ *(Hinweis)* hint; **einen ~ bekommen** to receive a tip ❷ *(Handbewegung)* signal ▶WENDUNGEN: **ein ~ mit dem Zaunpfahl** a broad hint

Winkel <-s, -> ['vɪŋ·kl̩] *m* ❶ MATH angle; **rechter ~** right angle ❷ *(Ecke)* corner ▶WENDUNGEN: **toter ~** blind spot

winken <gewinkt *o* DIAL gewunken> ['vɪŋ·kn̩] I. *vi* to wave; ■ **mit etw** *dat* ~ to wave sth; **einem Taxi ~** to hail a taxi II. *vt* ■ **jdn zu sich** *dat* ~ to beckon sb over [to one's side]

winseln ['vɪn·z|n] *vi* to whimper; ■ **um etw** *akk* ~ to plead for sth

Winter <-s, -> ['vɪn·tɐ] *m* winter

Wintergarten *m* winter garden

Winterkleidung *f* winter clothes *pl*

winterlich ['vɪn·tɐ·lɪç] I. *adj* wintry; **~e Temperaturen** winter temperatures II. *adv* **~ gekleidet** dressed for winter

Wintermantel *m* winter coat

Winterreifen *m* winter tire

Winterschlaf *m* hibernation; **~ halten** to hibernate

Wintersport *m* winter sport

Winzer(in) <-s, -> ['vɪn·tsɐ] *m(f)* wine grower

winzig ['vɪn·tsɪç] *adj* tiny; **~ klein** minute

Winzling <-s, -e> ['vɪnts·lɪŋ] *m* tiny thing

Wippe <-, -n> ['vɪ·pə] *f* seesaw

wippen ['vɪ·pn̩] *vi* to bob up and down (**auf** + *dat* on); *(auf einer Wippe)* to seesaw

wir <*gen* unser, *dat* uns, *akk* uns> [viːɐ̯] *pron pers* we; **~ nicht** not us

Wirbel <-s, -> ['vɪr·bl̩] *m* ❶ *(Rückenwirbel)* vertebra ❷ *(Haarwirbel)* cowlick ❸ *(fam: Trubel)* turmoil

Wirbelsäule *f* spinal column

Wirbelsturm *m* whirlwind

wirken ['vɪr·kn̩] *vi* ❶ *(Wirkung haben)* to have an effect; *(beabsichtigten Effekt haben)* to work; **dieses Medikament wirkt sofort** this medicine takes effect immediately; **etw auf sich** *akk* ~ **lassen** to take sth in ❷ *(erscheinen)* to seem, to appear

wirklich ['vɪrk·lɪç] I. *adj* real II. *adv* really

Wirklichkeit <-, -en> *f* reality; **~ werden** to come true

wirksam ['vɪrk·zaːm] I. *adj* effective II. *adv* effectively

Wirkstoff *m* active ingredient

Wirkung <-, -en> ['vɪr·kʊŋ] f effect

wirkungslos adj ineffective

wirkungsvoll adj effective

wirr [vɪr] adj ① (unordentlich) tangled ② (verworren) weird ③ (durcheinander) confused

Wirren ['vɪ·rən] pl confusion sing

Wirrwarr <-s> ['vɪr·var] m kein pl ① (Durcheinander) confusion ② (Unordnung) tangle

Wirt(in) <-[e]s, -e> [vɪrt] m(f) innkeeper, ≈ restaurant/tavern manager/owner

Wirtschaft <-, -en> ['vɪrt·ʃaft] f ① ÖKON economy ② (Gastwirtschaft) tavern, pub

wirtschaftlich ['vɪrt·ʃaft·lɪç] I. adj ① ÖKON economic ② (sparsam) economical II. adv economically

Wirtschaftsabkommen nt economic agreement [or treaty]

Wirtschaftsflüchtling m economic refugee

Wirtschaftshilfe f economic aid

Wirtschaftskriminalität f white-collar crime

Wirtschaftslage f economic situation

Wirtschaftsminister(in) m(f) Secretary of Commerce, Commerce Secretary

Wirtschaftsministerium nt Department of Commerce, Commerce Department

Wirtschaftspolitik f economic policy

Wirtschaftswachstum nt economic growth

Wirtschaftswissenschaft f meist pl economics sing

Wirtschaftszweig m branch of industry

Wirtshaus nt tavern, restaurant, inn

wischen ['vɪ·ʃn] vt ① (abwischen) to wipe ② SCHWEIZ (fegen) to sweep

Wischlappen m cloth

wispern ['vɪs·pen] vt, vi to whisper

wissbegierigRR, **wißbegierig**ALT adj eager to learn

wissen <weiß, wusste, gewusst> ['vɪ·sn] vt, vi ① (Kenntnis haben) to know; **man kann nie ~!** you never know!; **woher soll ich das ~?** how

should I know that?; **wenn ich nur wüsste, ...** if only I knew ...; **soviel ich weiß** as far as I know; **jdn etw ~ lassen** to let sb know sth ② (sich erinnern) **weißt du noch?** do you remember? ③ (können) **etw zu schätzen ~** to appreciate sth; **sich** dat **zu helfen ~** to be resourceful ▸WENDUNGEN: **von jdm/etw nichts [mehr] ~ wollen** (fam) to not want to have anything [more] to do with sb/sth

Wissen <-s> ['vɪ·sn] nt kein pl knowledge

Wissenschaft <-, -en> ['vɪ·sn·ʃaft] f science

Wissenschaftler(in) <-s, -> m(f) scientist

wissenschaftlich ['vɪ·sn·ʃaft·lɪç] I. adj scientific; (akademisch) academic II. adv scientifically; (akademisch) academically

Wissensdrang m, **Wissensdurst** m thirst for knowledge

Wissensgebiet nt field of knowledge

wissenswert adj worth knowing

wissentlich ['vɪ·snt·lɪç] I. adj deliberate II. adv deliberately, knowingly

wittern ['vɪ·ten] vt (ahnen) to suspect

Witterung <-, -en> f METEO weather

Witterungsverhältnisse pl weather conditions pl

Witwe <-, -n> ['vɪt·və] f fem form von **Witwer** widow fem; **~ werden** to be widowed

Witwer <-s, -> ['vɪt·və] m widower masc; **~ werden** to be widowed

Witz <-es, -e> [vɪts] m ① (Scherz) joke; **einen ~ machen** to tell a joke ② kein pl (Esprit) wit

Witzbold <-[e]s, -e> m joker

witzeln ['vɪ·tsln] vi to joke (**über** +akk about)

witzig ['vɪ·tsɪç] adj funny

WM <-, -s> f Abk von **Weltmeisterschaft** world championship; (im Fußball) World Cup

wo [voː] I. adv ① (räumlich) where; **pass auf, ~ du hintrittst!** watch your step! [or where you're going!] ② (zeit-

W

lich) when; **zu dem Zeitpunkt, ~ ...** when ... when **II.** *konj* (*zumal*) when, as; **~ er doch wusste, dass ich keine Zeit hatte** when he knew that I had no time

woanders [voˈʔanˌdɛs] *adv* somewhere else, elsewhere

wobei [voˈbai] *adv* ❶ *interrog* how; **~ ist das passiert?** how did that happen? ❷ *rel* in which; **~ mir gerade einfällt ...** which reminds me ...

Woche <-, -n> [ˈvɔxə] *f* week

Wochenblatt *nt* weekly

Wochenende [ˈvɔxn̩ˌʔɛndə] *nt* weekend; **schönes ~!** have a nice weekend!; **am ~** on the weekend

Wochenkarte *f* TRANSP weekly pass

wochenlang [ˈvɔxn̩ˌlaŋ] *adj, adv* for weeks

Wochentag *m* weekday; **was ist heute für ein ~?** what day of the week is it today?

wöchentlich [ˈvœçntˌlɪç] *adj, adv* weekly

wodurch [voˈdʊrç] *adv* ❶ *interrog* how ❷ *rel* which

wofür [voˈfyːɐ̯] *adv* ❶ *interrog* for what, what ... for; **~ hast du denn so viel Geld bezahlt?** what did you pay so much money for? ❷ *rel* for which

Woge <-, -n> [ˈvoːgə] *f* wave ▸WENDUNGEN: **wenn sich die ~n geglättet haben** when things have calmed down

wogegen [voˈgeːgn̩] *adv* ❶ *interrog* against what; **~ hilft dieses Mittel?** what is this medicine for? ❷ *rel* against what/which

woher [voˈheːɐ̯] *adv* ❶ *interrog* where ... from; **~ hast du dieses Buch [from]?** where did you get this book [from]? ❷ *rel* from which, where ... [from]

wohin [voˈhɪn] *adv* ❶ *interrog* where [to]; **~ damit?** where should I put it? ❷ *rel* where

wohl [voːl] *adv* ❶ (*gut, gesund*) well; **sich** *akk* **~ fühlen** to feel well; **sich** *akk* **irgendwo ~ fühlen** to feel at home somewhere ❷ (*gut*) **~ geformt** well-formed; *Körperteil* shapely; **~ überlegt**

well thought out ❸ (*wahrscheinlich*) probably; **~ kaum** hardly ❹ ▪**jdm ist ~ bei etw** *dat* sb is comfortable with sth; ▪**jdm ist nicht ~ bei etw** *dat* sb is uneasy about sth ❺ (*zirka*) about ▸WENDUNGEN: **~ oder übel** whether you like it or not

Wohl <-[e]s> [voːl] *nt kein pl* welfare, well-being; **auf jds ~ trinken** to drink to sb's health; **zum ~!** cheers!

wohlauf [voːlˈʔauf] *adj pred* ▪**~ sein** to be well

Wohlbefinden <-s> *nt kein pl* well-being

Wohlbehagen <-s> *nt kein pl* feeling of well-being

wohlbehalten *adv* safe and sound

Wohlfahrtsstaat *m* welfare state

Wohlgefallen [ˈvoːlgəˌfalən] *nt* ▸WENDUNGEN: **sich** *akk* **in ~ auflösen** (*fam*) to vanish into thin air

wohlgesinnt <wohlgesinnter, wohlgesinnteste> *adj* ▪**jdm ~ sein** to be well-disposed toward sb

wohlhabend <wohlhabender, wohlhabendste> *adj* well-to-do

wohlriechend <wohlriechender, wohlriechendste> *adj* fragrant

wohlschmeckend <wohlschmeckender, wohlschmeckendste> *adj* palatable

Wohlstand *m kein pl* affluence, prosperity

Wohlstandsgesellschaft *f* affluent society

Wohltat *f* ❶ *kein pl* (*Erleichterung*) relief ❷ (*Unterstützung*) good deed

Wohltäter(in) *m(f)* benefactor *masc*, benefactress *fem*

wohltätig *adj* charitable

Wohltätigkeitsveranstaltung *f* charity event

wohltuend <wohltuender, wohltuendste> *adj* agreeable

Wohlwollen <-s> [ˈvoːlˌvɔlən] *nt kein pl* goodwill

wohlwollend <wohlwollender, wohlwollendste> **I.** *adj* benevolent **II.** *adv* benevolently

W

Wohnanlage f housing development

Wohnblock m apartment building

wohnen ['vo:·nən] vi to live; (im Hotel) to stay

Wohnfläche f living space

Wohngebiet nt residential area

Wohngeld nt housing subsidy

Wohngemeinschaft f communal residence, shared house [or apartment]; **in einer ~ leben** to share a house/apartment with sb

Wohnhaus nt residential building

Wohnheim nt (Studentenwohnheim) residence hall, dormitory; (Arbeiterwohnheim) rooming house [for workers]

Wohnküche f eat-in kitchen

wohnlich ['vo:n·lɪç] adj cozy

Wohnmobil <-s, -e> nt camper

Wohnort m place of residence

Wohnsitz m ADMIN domicile; **erster ~** permanent residence; **ohne festen ~** without a fixed residence

Wohnung <-, -en> f apartment

Wohnungsmarkt m housing market

Wohnungsnot f kein pl serious housing shortage

Wohnungssuche f apartment hunting; **auf ~ sein** to be apartment hunting

Wohnviertel nt residential area

Wohnwagen m (zum Campen) RV

Wohnzimmer nt living room

wölben ['vœl·bn̩] vr ❶ (sich biegen) ■**sich** akk ~ to bend ❷ (überspannen) ■**sich** akk **über etw** akk ~ to arch over sth

Wolf <-[e]s, Wölfe> [vɔlf] m wolf

Wolke <-, -n> ['vɔl·kə] f cloud ▶WENDUNGEN: **aus allen ~n fallen** (fam) to be flabbergasted

Wolkenbruch m cloudburst

Wolkendecke f cloud cover

Wolkenkratzer m skyscraper

wolkenlos adj cloudless

wolkig ['vɔl·kɪç] adj cloudy

Wolldecke f [wool] blanket

Wolle <-, -n> ['vɔ·lə] f wool

wollen ['vɔ·lən] I. aux vb <will, wollte, wollen> modal ❶ (zu tun beabsichtigen) ■**etw tun ~** to want to do sth; ■**etw gerade tun ~** to be [just] about to do sth; ■**etw haben ~** to want [to have] sth; **~ wir uns nicht setzen?** why don't we sit down? ❷ (behaupten) ■**etw getan haben ~** to claim to have done sth; **und so jemand will Arzt sein!** and he calls himself a doctor! ❸ passivisch **diese Aktion will gut vorbereitet sein** this operation has to be carefully planned II. vi <will, wollte, gewollt> ❶ (den Willen haben) to want; **ob du willst oder nicht** whether you like it or not; **wenn du willst** if you['d] like; **[ganz] wie du willst** whatever is good for you, as you wish ❷ (gehen wollen) ■**irgendwohin ~** to want to go somewhere; **zu wem ~ Sie?** who[m] do you wish to see? III. vt <will, wollte, gewollt> ❶ (haben wollen) ■**etw [von jdm] ~** to want sth [from sb]; **willst du lieber Tee oder Kaffee?** would you prefer tea or coffee?; **ich will, dass du jetzt sofort gehst!** I want you to go right now [or leave immediately] ❷ (bezwecken) ■**etw mit etw** dat ~ to want sth with [or for] sth; **ohne es zu ~** without wanting to

Wolljacke f wool cardigan

wollüstig ['vɔl·lʏs·tɪç] adj lascivious

womit [vo·'mɪt] adv ❶ interrog with what, what … with; **~ reinigt man Seidenhemden?** what do you use to clean silk shirts [with]?; **~ habe ich das verdient?** what did I do to deserve this? ❷ rel with which

womöglich [vo·'mø:k·lɪç] adv possibly

wonach [vo·'na:x] adv ❶ interrog what … for, what … of; **~ suchst du?** what are you looking for?; **~ riecht das hier?** what's that smell [in here]? ❷ rel which [or what] … for, of which

Wonne <-, -n> ['vɔ·nə] f joy, delight

woran [vo·'ran] adv ❶ interrog (an welchem/welchen Gegenstand) what … on, on what; **~ soll ich das befestigen?** what should I fasten this to? ❷ interrog (an welchem/welchen Umstand) what … of, of what;

~ haben Sie ihn erkannt? how did you recognize him?; **~ denkst du?** what are you thinking of?; **~ ist sie gestorben?** what did she die of? ❸ *rel (an welchem/welchen Gegenstand)* on which; **das Seil, ~ der Kübel befestigt war, riss** the rope [that] the pail was fastened to broke ❹ *rel (an welchem/welchen Umstand)* by which; **das ist das einzige, ~ ich mich noch erinnere** that's the only thing I can remember

worauf [voˈrauf] *adv* ❶ *interrog* on what …, what … on; **~ wartest du noch?** what are you waiting for?; **~ stützen sich deine Behauptungen?** what do you base your claims on? ❷ *rel* on which; **das Bett, ~ wir liegen …** the bed [that] we're lying on …

woraus [voˈraus] *adv* ❶ *interrog* what … out of, out of what; **und ~ schließen Sie das?** and what do you base your conclusion[s] on? ❷ *rel* from which, what … out of, out of which

worin [voˈrɪn] *adv* ❶ *interrog* in what, what … in; **~ besteht der Unterschied?** where is the difference? ❷ *rel* in which; **es gibt etwas, ~ sich Original und Fälschung unterscheiden** there is something that the original and the forgery do not have in common

Wort <-[e]s, Wörter> [vɔrt] *nt* ❶ word; **mit anderen ~en** in other words; **etw in ~e fassen** to put sth into words; **jdm fehlen die ~e** sb is speechless; **ein ernstes ~ mit jdm reden** to have a serious talk with sb ❷ *kein pl (Ehrenwort)* **jdm sein ~ geben** to give sb one's word; **sein ~ brechen/halten** to break/keep one's word; **das glaube ich dir aufs ~** I can believe it, trust me, I believe you ❸ *kein pl (Rede[erlaubnis])* **jdm ins ~ fallen** to interrupt sb; **zu ~ kommen** to get a chance to speak ▶WENDUNGEN: **das ist ein ~!** [it's [or that's] a] deal!; **jdm das ~ im Munde herumdrehen** to twist sb's words

wortbrüchig *adj* treacherous

Wörterbuch *nt* dictionary

wortkarg *adj* taciturn

Wortklauberei <-, -en> [vɔrtˈklau·bə·ˈrai] *f (pej)* hairsplitting

wörtlich [ˈvœrt·lɪç] I. *adj* ❶ *Wiedergabe* word-for-word, verbatim ❷ *Übersetzung* literal II. *adv* ❶ *wiedergeben* word for word ❷ *übersetzen* literally

wortlos I. *adj* silent II. *adv* silently, without saying a word

Wortschatz *m* vocabulary

Wortspiel *nt* play on words

Wortwechsel *m* verbal exchange

wortwörtlich [ˈvɔrt·ˈvœrt·lɪç] I. *adj* word-for-word II. *adv* word for word

worüber [voˈry·bə] *adv* what … about, about what; **~ habt ihr euch unterhalten?** what was it you talked about? [*or fam* did you guys talk about?]

worum [voˈrʊm] *adv* what … about; **~ handelt es sich?** what is it about?

worunter [voˈrʊn·tə] *adv* what … from; **~ leidet Ihre Frau?** what is your wife suffering from?

wovon [voˈfɔn] *adv* what … about; **~ bist du denn so müde?** what has made you so tired?; **~ soll ich leben?** what am I supposed to live on?

wovor [voˈfoːɐ̯] *adv* what … of; **~ fürchtest du dich denn?** what are you afraid of?

wozu [voˈtsuː] *adv* why, how come, what … for; **~ soll das gut sein?** what's the purpose of that?

Wrack <-[e]s, -s> [vrak] *nt* ❶ *(Schiffswrack)* wreck; *(Flugzeug-, Autowrack)* wreckage ❷ *(pej: Mensch)* wreck

Wucher <-s> [ˈvuː·xɐ] *m kein pl* extortion; *(Zinsen)* usury; **das ist ~!** that's highway robbery!

wuchern [ˈvuː·xɐn] *vi sein o haben* ❶ *Pflanze* to grow rampant ❷ *Geschwür* to proliferate

Wucherpreis *m (pej)* extortionate price

wuchs [vuːks] *imp von* **wachsen**[1]

Wucht <-> [vʊxt] *f kein pl* force; *eines Schlags* brunt; **mit voller ~** with full force ▶WENDUNGEN: **eine ~ sein** *(fam)* to be smashing

wuchtig [ˈvʊx·tɪç] *adj* ❶ *(mit großer*

W

Wucht) forceful; *Schlag* powerful ❷(*massig*) massive

wühlen ['vy:·lən] I. *vi* ■**in etw** *dat* [**nach etw** *dat*] ~ (*kramen*) to rummage through sth [for sth] II. *vr* ■**sich akk durch etw** *akk* ~ to burrow one's way through sth

Wühltisch *m* discount table

Wulst [vʊlst] *m* <-[e]s, Wülste>, *f* <-, Wülste> bulge

wulstig ['vʊls·tɪç] *adj* bulging; (*Lippen*) thick

wund [vʊnt] I. *adj* sore II. *adv* **sich** *akk* ~ **liegen** to get bedsores; **sich** *dat* **die Füße** ~ **laufen** to walk until one's feet are sore

Wunde <-, -n> ['vʊn·də] *f* wound

Wunder <-s, -> ['vʊn·dɐ] *nt* miracle; **wie durch ein** ~ miraculously ▶WENDUNGEN: **sein blaues** ~ **erleben** (*fam*) to be in for a nasty surprise; **es ist kein** ~, **dass ...** (*fam*) it is no wonder that ...; ~ **wirken** (*fam*) to work wonders

wunderbar ['vʊn·dɐ·baːɐ̯] I. *adj* ❶(*herrlich*) wonderful, marvelous ❷(*wie ein Wunder*) miraculous II. *adv* (*fam*) wonderfully

Wunderkind *nt* child prodigy

wunderlich ['vʊn·dɐ·lɪç] *adj* odd, strange

wundern ['vʊn·dɐn] I. *vt* ■**jdn** ~ to surprise sb; **das wundert mich** [**nicht**] I'm [not] surprised at that II. *vr* ■**sich** *akk* ~ to be surprised (**über** +*akk* at/about); **du wirst dich** ~! you'll be surprised!

wunderschön ['vʊn·dɐ·ʃøːn] *adj* wonderful

wundervoll *adj, adv s.* **wunderbar**

Wundsalbe *f* ointment

Wundstarrkrampf *m kein pl* tetanus

W **Wunsch** <-[e]s, Wünsche> [vʊnʃ] *m* ❶(*Verlangen*) wish; (*stärker*) desire; (*Bitte*) request; **jdm jeden** ~ **erfüllen** to grant sb's every wish; **auf jds** ~ [**hin**] at/on sb's request ❷ *meist pl* (*Glückwunsch*) wish; **mit besten Wünschen** best wishes

Wunschdenken <-s> *nt kein pl* wishful thinking

wünschen ['vʏn·ʃn] *vt* ❶(*als Geschenk erbitten*) ■**sich** *dat* **etw** [**von jdm**] ~ to ask for sth [from sb]; **was wünschst du dir?** what would you like? [*or* can I get [for] you?]; **nun darfst du dir etwas** ~ now you can say what you'd like for a present ❷(*erhoffen*) to wish; **ich wünschte, der Regen würde aufhören** I wish the rain would stop; ■**jdm etw** ~ to wish sb sth; **jdm zum Geburtstag alles Gute** ~ to wish sb a happy birthday; **ich will dir ja nichts Böses** ~ I don't mean to wish you any harm; ■~, **dass** to hope that ❸(*haben wollen*) ■**sich** *dat* **etw** ~ to want sth; **man hätte sich kein besseres Wetter** ~ **können** one couldn't have wished for better weather ▶WENDUNGEN: **nichts/viel zu** ~ **übrig lassen** to leave nothing/much to be desired

wünschenswert *adj* desirable

Wunschkind *nt* planned child

Wunschtraum *m* dream

Wunschzettel *m* wish list

Würde <-> ['vʏr·də] *f kein pl* dignity

würdig ['vʏr·dɪç] I. *adj* ❶(*ehrbar*) dignified ❷(*wert*) worthy; **einer S.** *gen* [**nicht**] ~ **sein** to [not] be worthy of sth II. *adv* ❶(*mit Würde*) with dignity ❷(*gebührend*) worthy

würdigen ['vʏr·dɪ·gn̩] *vt* ❶(*anerkennend erwähnen*) to acknowledge ❷(*schätzen*) **etw zu** ~ **wissen** to appreciate sth

Wurf <-[e]s, Würfe> [vʊrf] *m* ❶(*das Werfen*) throw ❷(*Tierjunge*) litter

Würfel <-s, -> ['vʏr·fl̩] *m* ❶(*Spielwürfel*) dice *pl,* die ❷(*Kubus*) cube; **etw in** ~ **schneiden** to dice sth ▶WENDUNGEN: **die** ~ **sind gefallen** the die is cast

Würfelbecher *m* shaker

Würfelspiel *nt* dice game

Würfelzucker *m kein pl* sugar cube[s]

würgen ['vʏr·gn̩] I. *vt* to strangle II. *vi* ■**an etw** *dat* ~ to choke on sth

Wurm <-[e]s, Würmer> [vʊrm] *m*

worm ▸WENDUNGEN: **da ist der ~ <u>drin</u>** (*fam*) there's something fishy about it

wurmen ['vʊr·mən] *vt* (*fam*) to bug; **das wurmt mich sehr** that really bugs me

wurmstichig ['vʊrm·ʃtɪ·çɪç] *adj* Apfel maggoty; *Holz* full of woodworms

Wurst <-, Würste> [vʊrst] *f* sausage; (*Brotauflage*) cold cuts *pl* ▸WENDUNGEN: **jetzt <u>geht</u> es um die ~** (*fam*) the moment of truth has come

Würstchen <-s, -> ['vʏrst·çən] *nt dim von* **Wurst** little sausage; **Frankfurter/ Wiener ~** hot dog, frankfurter

Würstchenbude *f*, **Würstchenstand** *m* hot dog stand

Wurzel <-, -n> ['vʊr·tsl̩] *f* (*a. fig*) root; **~n schlagen** (*a. fig*) to put down roots

wurzeln ['vʊr·tsl̩n] *vi* to be rooted (**in** +*dat* in)

würzen ['vʏr·tsn̩] *vt* to season

würzig ['vʏr·tsɪç] I. *adj* tasty II. *adv* tastily

wüst [vyːst] I. *adj* ❶ (*öde*) waste, desolate ❷ (*fig: wild, derb*) vile, rude ❸ (*unordentlich*) hopeless, terrible II. *adv* vilely, terribly; **jdn ~ beschimpfen** to curse at sb

Wüste <-, -n> ['vyːs·tə] *f* desert, wasteland *fig;* **die ~ Gobi** the Gobi Desert

Wüstling <-s, -e> ['vyːst·lɪŋ] *m* (*pej*) lecher

Wut <-> [vuːt] *f kein pl* fury, rage; **eine ~ [auf jdn] haben** to be furious [with sb]; **vor ~ kochen** to seethe with rage

Wutausbruch *m* tantrum

wüten ['vyː·tn̩] *vi* to rage; *Sturm* to cause havoc

wütend I. *adj* furious (**auf** +*akk* with) II. *adv* furiously, in a rage

WWW <-[s]> [veː·veː·ˈveː] *nt* INET *Abk von* **World Wide Web** WWW

X, x <-, -> [ɪks] *nt* ❶ (*Buchstabe*) X, x; **~ wie Xanthippe** X as in X-ray ❷ (*eine unbestimmte Zahl*) x amount of; **~ Bücher** x number of books

X-Beine ['ɪks·bai·nə] *pl* knock-knees *pl*

x-beliebig [ɪks·bə·ˈliː·bɪç] I. *adj* (*fam*) any old; **jeder ~e Ort** any old place II. *adv* (*fam*) as often as one likes

x-mal ['ɪks·maːl] *adv* (*fam*) umpteen times

Xylofon[RR], **Xylophon** <-s, -e> [ksy·lo·ˈfoːn] *nt* xylophone

X

Yy

Y, y <-, -> [ˈʏpsi·lɔn] *nt* Y, y; **~ wie Ypsilon** Y as in Yankee
Yacht <-, -en> [jaxt] *f* yacht

Yoga <-[s]> [ˈjoː·ga] *m o nt* yoga
Ypsilon <-[s], -s> [ˈʏpsi·lɔn] *nt s.* **Y**
Yuppie <-s, -s> [ˈjʊ·pi] *m* yuppie

Zz

Z, z <-, -> [tsɛt] *nt* Z, z; **~ wie Zacharias** Z as in Zulu
zackig [ˈtsa·kɪç] *adj* ① (*gezackt*) jagged; *Stern* pointed ② (*schnell*) *Bewegungen* brisk; *Musik* upbeat
zaghaft [ˈtsaːk·haft] *adj* timid
zäh [tsɛː] **I.** *adj* ① (*eine feste Konsistenz aufweisend*) tough ② (*zähflüssig*) glutinous ③ (*hartnäckig*) tenacious; *Gespräch* long-drawn-out; *Verhandlungen* tough **II.** *adv* tenaciously
zähflüssig *adj* thick; (*fig*) *Verkehr* slow-moving
Zahl <-, -en> [tsaːl] *f* number; **arabische/römische ~en** Arabic/Roman numerals
zahlen [ˈtsaː·lən] *vt, vi* to pay; **~ bitte!** the check please!
zählen [ˈtsɛː·lən] **I.** *vt* ① (*addieren*) count ② (*dazurechnen*) ■ **sich/jdn zu etw** *dat* **~** to regard oneself/sb as belonging to sth **II.** *vi* to count ▶WENDUNGEN: **auf jdn/etw ~** to count on sb/sth; **zu etw** *dat* **~** to belong to sth
zahlenmäßig **I.** *adj* numerical **II.** *adv* (*an Anzahl*) in number
Zahlenschloss^RR *nt* combination lock
Zähler <-s, -> *m* ① TECH meter ② MATH numerator
zahllos *adj* countless
zahlreich **I.** *adj* ① (*sehr viele*) numerous ② (*eine große Anzahl*) large **II.** *adv* (*in großer Anzahl*) **~ erscheinen** to appear in large numbers
Zahlung <-, -en> *f* payment
Zählung <-, -en> *f* count
Zahlungsmittel *nt* means of payment + *sing vb*
Zahlungsverkehr *m* payment transactions *pl*
Zahlwort <-wörter> *nt* numeral
zahm [tsaːm] *adj* tame
zähmen [ˈtsɛː·mən] *vt* to tame
Zahn <-[e]s, Zähne> [tsaːn] *m* ① (*Teil des Gebisses*) tooth; **Zähne bekommen** to be teething; **sich** *dat* **die Zähne putzen** to brush one's teeth; **sich** *dat* **einen ~ ziehen lassen** to have a tooth pulled ② (*fam: Tempo*) **einen ~ draufhaben** to drive at breakneck speed; **einen ~ zulegen** to step on it ▶WENDUNGEN: **sich** *dat* **an jdm/ etw die Zähne ausbeißen** (*fam*) to have a tough time with sb/sth; **jdm auf den ~ fühlen** (*fam*) to grill sb
Zahnarzt, -ärztin *m, f* dentist
Zahnbehandlung *f* dental treatment
Zahnbelag *m kein pl* plaque
Zahnbürste *f* toothbrush
zahnen [ˈtsaː·nən] *vi* *Baby* to teethe
Zahnfäule *f kein pl* tooth decay
Zahnfleisch *nt* gum[s *pl*]
Zahnfüllung *f* filling
Zahnlücke *f* gap between the teeth
Zahnpasta *f* toothpaste

Zahnpflege f kein pl dental hygiene

Zahnprothese f dentures pl

Zahnrad nt AUTO gearwheel; TECH cogwheel

Zahnradbahn f cog railway [or railroad]

Zahnschmelz m [tooth] enamel

Zahnschmerzen pl toothache

Zahnseide f dental floss

Zahnspange f braces pl

Zahnstein m kein pl tartar

Zahnstocher <-s, -> m toothpick

Zange <-, -n> ['tsaŋə] f pliers npl, a pair of pliers; von Hummer, Krebs pincers npl; MED forceps npl; (für Zucker) tongs npl ▶WENDUNGEN: **jdn in die ~ nehmen** (fam) to give sb the third degree

Zank <-[e]s> [tsaŋk] m kein pl fight

zanken ['tsaŋ·kn̩] I. vi to fight II. vr ■ **sich** akk ~ to have a fight (**um** +akk over)

zänkisch ['tsɛŋ·kɪʃ] adj quarrelsome

Zäpfchen <-s, -> ['tsɛpf·çən] nt MED suppository

zapfen ['tsap·fn̩] vt Bier to draw

Zapfen <-s, -> ['tsap·fn̩] m ❶ BOT, ANAT cone ❷ (Eiszapfen) icicle

Zapfhahn m tap

Zapfsäule f gas pump

zappelig ['tsa·pə·lɪç] adj ❶ (sich unruhig bewegend) fidgety ❷ (voller Unruhe) restless

zappeln ['tsa·pl̩n] vi to fidget ▶WENDUNGEN: **jdn ~ lassen** (fam) to keep sb in suspense

Zar(in) <-en, -en> [tsaːɐ̯] m(f) czar masc, czarina fem

zart [tsaːɐ̯t] adj ❶ (mürbe) tender; Gebäck delicate ❷ (weich) delicate; Haut soft ❸ (leicht) mild; Berührung, Andeutung gentle; Farbe, Duft delicate

zärtlich ['tsɛːɐ̯t·lɪç] I. adj tender, affectionate II. adv tenderly, affectionately

Zärtlichkeit <-, -en> f ❶ kein pl (zärtliches Wesen) tenderness ❷ pl (Liebkosung) caresses pl; (zärtliche Worte) tender words pl

Zauber <-s, -> ['tsau·bɐ] m ❶ (magische Handlung) magic; (magische Wirkung) spell ❷ kein pl (Faszination, Reiz) charm

Zauberei <-, -en> [tsau·bə·'rai] f kein pl magic

Zauberer, Zauberin <-s, -> ['tsau·bə·rɐ, 'tsau·bə·rɪn] m, f ❶ (Magier) sorcerer masc, sorceress fem, wizard ❷ (Zauberkünstler) magician

zauberhaft adj enchanting; Kleid gorgeous; Abend, Urlaub splendid

Zauberkünstler(in) m(f) magician

Zauberkunststück nt magic trick

zaubern ['tsau·bɐn] I. vt to conjure (**aus** +dat from); **einen Hasen aus einem Hut ~** to pull a rabbit out of a hat II. vi ❶ (Magie anwenden) to do magic ❷ (Zauberkunststücke vorführen) to do magic tricks

Zauberspruch m magic spell

Zauberstab m magic wand

Zaum <-[e]s, Zäume> [tsaum] m bridle; **sich/jdn/etw in ~ halten** (fig) to keep oneself/sb/sth in check

zäumen ['tsɔy·mən] vt Tier to bridle

Zaun <-[e]s, Zäune> [tsaun] m fence

Zaunkönig m wren

Zebra <-s, -s> ['tseː·bra] nt zebra

Zebrastreifen m pedestrian crossing, crosswalk

Zecke <-, -n> ['tsɛ·kə] f, **Zeck** <-[e]s, -en> [tsɛk] m ÖSTERR (fam) tick

ZeckenbissRR m tick bite

Zeh <-s, -en> [tseː] m, **Zehe** <-, -n> ['tseː·ə] f ANAT toe

Zehennagel m toenail

Zehenspitze f tip of the toe; ■ **auf den ~n** on one's tiptoes

zehn [tseːn] adj ten; s. a. **acht**[1]

Zehn <-, -en> [tseːn] f ten; s. a. **Acht**[1]

Zehnerkarte f TRANSP ten-trip ticket; TOURIST ticket good for ten admissions

Zehnkampf ['tseːn·kampf] m decathlon

zehnmal, 10-malRR ['tseːn·maːl] adv ten times; s. a. **achtmal**

zehntausend ['tseːn·'tau·znt] adj ❶ (Zahl) ten thousand ❷ (sehr viele) ■ **Z~e von ...** tens of thousands of ...

zehntel ['tseːn·tl̩] adj tenth

Z

Zehntel <-s, -> ['tseːn·tl̩] *nt* ■ein ~ a tenth

zehren ['tseː·rən] *vi* ■an jdm/etw ~ to wear sb/sth out; **an jds Gesundheit ~** to ruin sb's health

Zeichen <-s, -> ['tsai·çn̩] *nt* ① (*Symbol*) symbol; (*Schriftzeichen*) character; (*Satzzeichen*) punctuation mark ② (*Markierung*) sign ③ (*Hinweis*) sign ④ (*Symptom*) symptom ⑤ (*Signal*) signal ⑥ ASTROL sign

Zeichenblock <-blöcke> *m* sketch pad

Zeichenbrett *nt* drawing board

Zeichenerklärung *f* key; (*Landkarte*) legend

Zeichensetzung <-> *f kein pl* punctuation

Zeichensprache *f* sign language

Zeichentrickfilm *m* cartoon

zeichnen ['tsaiç·nən] I. *vt* KUNST, ARCHIT to draw II. *vi* KUNST ■an etw *dat* ~ to draw sth

Zeichnung <-, -en> *f* ① KUNST drawing ② BOT, ZOOL markings *pl* ③ FIN subscription

Zeigefinger *m* index finger

zeigen ['tsai·gn̩] I. *vt* ① (*deutlich machen*) to show ② (*vorführen*) to show; **zeig mal, was du kannst!** (*fam*) let's see what you can do!; ■es jdm ~ (*fam*) to show sb II. *vi* ① (*deuten*) to point (**auf** +*akk* at); **nach rechts/hinten ~** to point to the right/back ② (*erkennen lassen*) ■~, **dass ...** to show that ... III. *vr* ■sich *akk* ~ ① (*sich sehen lassen*) to show oneself; **komm, zeig dich mal!** come on, let me see what you look like; **sich** *akk* **von seiner besten Seite ~** to show oneself at one's best ② (*erkennbar werden*) to appear

Zeiger <-s, -> ['tsai·gɐ] *m* (*Uhrzeiger*) hand

Zeile <-, -n> ['tsai·lə] *f* line; **jdm ein paar ~n schrieben** to drop sb a line

zeit [tsait] *präp* +*gen* ~ **meines Lebens** all my life

Zeit <-, -en> [tsait] *f* ① *kein pl* (*verstrichener zeitlicher Ablauf*) time; **mit**

der ~ in time; **~ raubend** time-consuming; **~ sparend** time-saving ② (*Zeitraum*) time; **eine ~ lang** for a while; **die ganze ~** [über] the whole time; **in letzter ~** lately; **in nächster ~** in the near future; **auf unbestimmte ~** for an indefinite period; **~ gewinnen** to gain time; **zwei Tage ~ haben[, etw zu tun]** to have two days [to do sth]; **haben Sie einen Augenblick ~?** do you have a moment to spare?; **das hat noch ~** that can wait; **[sich] time [mit etw *dat*] lassen** to take one's time [with sth]; **jdm die ~ stehlen** to waste sb's time ③ (*Zeitpunkt*) time; **es ist höchste Zeit, dass wir die Tickets kaufen** it's about time we bought the tickets; **seit dieser ~** since then; **von ~ zu ~** from time to time; **zur ~** at the moment; **zu jeder ~** [at] any time ④ (*Epoche, Lebensabschnitt*) time, age ⑤ LING tense ⑥ SPORT time; **eine gute ~ laufen** to run a good time

Zeitalter *nt* age; **in unserem ~** nowadays

Zeitarbeit *f kein pl* temporary work

Zeitbombe *f* time bomb

Zeitdruck *m kein pl* time pressure

Zeiteinteilung *f* time management

zeitgemäß *adj, adv* up-to-date, modern

Zeitgenosse, -genossin ['tsait·gə·nɔ·sə, -gən·sɪn] *m, f* contemporary

zeitgenössisch ['tsait·gə·nœ·sɪʃ] *adj* contemporary

Zeitgeschichte *f kein pl* contemporary history

zeitig ['tsai·tɪç] *adj, adv* early

Zeitkarte *f* TRANSP monthly/weekly/ weekend pass

zeitlebens [tsait·'leː·bn̩s] *adv* all one's life

zeitlich I. *adj* chronological II. *adv* **etw ~ abstimmen** to synchronize sth; **~ begrenzt** for a limited time

zeitlos *adj* timeless; *Kleidung* classic

Zeitlupe *f kein pl* slow motion *no art*

Zeitlupentempo *nt* ■**im ~** in slow motion

Zeitplan *m* schedule

Zeitpunkt *m* time; **zum jetzigen ~** at this moment in time

Zeitraffer <-s> *m kein pl* time-lapse photography

Zeitraum *m* period of time

Zeitrechnung *f* calendar; **vor unserer ~** before Christ, BC; **unserer ~** anno Domini, AD

Zeitschrift ['tsait·ʃrɪft] *f* magazine; (*wissenschaftlich*) journal

Zeitspanne *f* period of time

Zeitung <-, -en> ['tsai·tʊŋ] *f* newspaper

Zeitungsanzeige *f* newspaper advertisement

Zeitungsartikel *m* newspaper article

Zeitungspapier *nt* newspaper

Zeitverschiebung *f* time difference

Zeitverschwendung *f kein pl* waste of time

Zeitvertreib <-[e]s, -e> *m* pastime; **zum ~** to pass the time

zeitweise *adv* ① (*gelegentlich*) occasionally ② (*vorübergehend*) temporarily

zelebrieren* [tse·le·'bri:·rən] *vt* to celebrate

Zelle <-, -n> ['tsɛ·lə] *f* cell

Zellgewebe *nt* cell tissue

Zellkern *m* nucleus [of a cell]

Zellstoff ['tsɛl·ʃtɔf] *m s.* **Zellulose**

Zellteilung *f* cell division

Zellulitis <-, Zellulitiden> [tsɛ·lu·'li:·tɪs] *f meist sing* MED cellulitis

Zellulose <-, -n> [tsɛ·lu·'lo:·zə] *f* cellulose

Zelt <-[e]s, -e> [tsɛlt] *nt* tent; (*Festzelt*) exhibit tent; (*Zirkuszelt*) big top

zelten ['tsɛl·tn̩] *vi* to camp

Zeltlager *nt* camp

Zement <-[e]s, -e> [tse·'mɛnt] *m* cement

zementieren* [tse·mɛn·'ti:·rən] *vt* ① (*a. fig*) to cement

Zenit <-[e]s> [tse·'ni:t] *m kein pl* zenith

zensieren* [tsɛn·'zi:·rən] *vt* ① SCH to grade ② (*der Zensur unterwerfen*) to censor

Zensur <-, -en> [tsɛn·'zu:ɐ̯] *f* ① SCH

grade ② *kein pl* (*prüfende Kontrolle*) censorship

Zentimeter [tsɛn·ti·'me:·tɐ] *m o nt* centimeter

Zentner <-s, -> ['tsɛnt·nɐ] *m* 50 kg (*110 lbs*); ÖSTERR, SCHWEIZ 100 kg (*220 lbs*)

zentral [tsɛn·'tra:l] I. *adj* central II. *adv* centrally

Zentralbank *f* FIN central bank; ■**die Europäische ~** the European Central Bank

Zentrale <-, -n> [tsɛn·'tra:·lə] *f* ① (*Hauptgeschäftsstelle: Bank, Firma*) head office; (*Militär, Polizei, Taxiunternehmen*) headquarters + *sing/pl vb*; (*Busse*) depot ② TELEK operator; *Firma* switchboard

Zentralheizung *f* central heating

zentralisieren* [tsɛn·tra·li·'zi:·rən] *vt* to centralize

Zentralverriegelung <-, -en> *f* power locks *npl*

Zentrifugalkraft *f* centrifugal force

Zentrifuge <-, -n> [tsɛn·tri·'fu:·gə] *f* centrifuge

Zentrum <-s, Zentren> ['tsɛn·trʊm] *nt* center

zerbeißen* [tsɛɐ̯·'bai·sn̩] *vt irreg* ① (*kaputtbeißen*) to chew; *Bonbon* to crunch ② (*überall stechen*) to bite

zerbrechen* *irreg* I. *vt haben* (*in Stücke zerbrechen*) ■**etw ~** to break sth [in]to pieces; *Glas, Teller* to smash; *Kette* to break II. *vi sein* ① (*entzweibrechen*) to break [in]to pieces ② (*in die Brüche gehen*) to be destroyed; *Partnerschaft* to break up ③ (*seelisch zugrunde gehen*) ■**an etw** *dat* **~** to be destroyed by sth

zerbrechlich *adj* ① (*leicht zerbrechend*) fragile ② (*zart*) frail

zerbröckeln* I. *vt haben* to crumble II. *vi sein* to crumble

zerdrücken* *vt* ① (*zu einer Masse pressen*) to crush; *Kartoffeln* to mash ② *Zigarette* to put out *sep* ③ *Stoff* to crease

Zeremonie <-, -n> [tse·re·mo·'ni:] *f* ceremony

Z

zerfallen* *vi irreg sein* ❶ (*sich zersetzen*) *Fassade, Gebäude* to disintegrate; *Körper, Materie* to decompose; *Gesundheit* to decline ❷ (*auseinanderbrechen*) *Reich, Sitte* to decline

zerkleinern* [tsɛɐ̯ˈklai·nɐn] *vt* to cut up *sep*

zerknirscht [tsɛɐ̯ˈknɪrʃt] *adj* remorseful

zerknittern* *vt* to crease

zerknüllen* *vt* to crumple up *sep*

zerkratzen* *vt* to scratch

zerlassen* *vt irreg Butter* to melt

zerlegen* *vt* ❶ KOCHK to cut [up *sep*]; *Braten* to carve ❷ (*auseinandernehmen*) to take apart *sep*; *Maschine* to dismantle; *Getriebe, Motor* to strip down *sep*

zerlumpt *adj* ragged; ~ **sein** to be in tatters

zermürben* [tsɛɐ̯ˈmyr·bn̩] *vt* to wear down *sep*

zerquetschen* *vt* to squash

zerreiben* *vt irreg* to crush

zerreißen* *irreg* **I.** *vt haben* ❶ (*in Stücke*) to tear to pieces ❷ (*durchreißen*) to tear; *Brief, Scheck* to tear up *sep* **II.** *vi sein* to tear; *Seil, Faden* to break

zerren [ˈtsɛ·rən] **I.** *vt* to drag **II.** *vi* to tug (**an** +*dat* at/on); **an den Nerven** ~ to be nerve-racking **III.** *vr* MED **sich** *dat* **einen Muskel** ~ to pull a muscle

Zerrung <-, -en> *f* MED (*Muskelzerrung*) pulled muscle; (*Sehnenzerrung*) pulled tendon

zerrütten* [tsɛɐ̯ˈrʏ·tn̩] *vt* to destroy; *Ehe* to ruin

zerschellen* *vi sein* to be smashed to pieces

zerschlagen*¹ *irreg* **I.** *vt* ❶ *Glas, Teller etc.* to smash to pieces ❷ (*zerstören*) to break up *sep*; *Angriff* to crush; *Plan* to shatter **II.** *vr* ■ **sich** *akk* ~ *Plan* to fall through

zerschlagen² *adj pred* shattered

zerschneiden* *vt irreg* ❶ (*in Stücke*) to cut up *sep* ❷ (*durchschneiden*) to cut in two

zersetzen* *vr* (*sich auflösen*) ■ **sich** *akk* ~ to decompose

zerstäuben* *vt* to spray

Zerstäuber <-s, -> *m* atomizer

zerstochen *adj von Stechmücken* covered in bites, bitten all over

zerstören* *vt* to destroy; *Plan, Gesundheit* to ruin

zerstörerisch **I.** *adj* destructive **II.** *adv* destructively

Zerstörung <-, -en> *f* ❶ *kein pl* destruction ❷ (*Verwüstung*) devastation

zerstreuen* **I.** *vt Ängste, Sorgen* to dispel **II.** *vr* (*entspannen*) ■ **sich** *akk* ~ to amuse oneself

zerstreut *adj* ❶ (*gedankenlos*) absent-minded ❷ (*weit verteilt*) scattered

Zerstreuung <-, -en> *f* (*Unterhaltung*) diversion

zerteilen* *vt* to cut up *sep* (**in** +*akk* into)

zertrümmern* [tsɛɐ̯ˈtrʏ·mɐn] *vt* to smash

zetern [ˈtseː·tɐn] *vi* (*pej*) to nag

Zettel <-s, -> [ˈtsɛ·tl̩] *m* piece of paper

Zeug <-[e]s> [tsɔyk] *nt kein pl* (*fam*) ❶ (*Sachen*) stuff; **altes** ~ junk ❷ (*Quatsch*) crap *fam* ▶WENDUNGEN: **was das** ~ **hält** (*fam*) for all one is worth; **sich** *akk* **ins** ~ **legen** (*fam*) to put one's shoulder to the wheel

Zeuge, Zeugin <-n, -n> [ˈtsɔy·gə, ˈtsɔy·gɪn] *m, f* witness

zeugen¹ [ˈtsɔy·gn̩] *vt Kind* to father

zeugen² [ˈtsɔy·gn̩] *vi* ■ **von etw** *dat* ~ to show sth

Zeugenaussage *f* testimony

Zeugenstand *m* witness stand

Zeugnis <-ses, -se> [ˈtsɔyk·nɪs] *nt* ❶ SCH report card ❷ (*Empfehlung*) certificate of recommendation; (*Arbeitszeugnis*) reference

zeugungsfähig *adj* fertile

zeugungsunfähig *adj* sterile

z. H(d). *Abk von* **zu Händen** attn.

zicken [ˈtsɪ·kən] *vi* (*fam*) to kick up a fuss

Zickzack [ˈtsɪk·tsak] *m* zigzag

Ziege <-, -n> [ˈtsiː·gə] *f* goat

Ziegel <-s, -> [ˈtsiː·gl̩] *m* ❶ (*Ziegelstein*) brick ❷ (*Dachziegel*) tile

Z

Ziegelstein *m* brick
Ziegenbock *m* billy goat
Ziegenkäse *m* goat cheese
Ziegenpeter <-s, -> ['tsiː·gn̩·peː·tɐ] *m* (*fam: Mumps*) mumps + *sing/pl vb*
ziehen <zog, gezogen> ['tsiː·ən] I. *vt haben* ❶ (*hinter sich her schleppen, zerren*) to pull; (*fester*) to drag ❷ *Handbremse* to put on *sep* ❸ (*herausziehen*) *Fäden, Zahn* to take out *sep; Revolver, Spielkarte* to draw ❹ (*züchten*) *Pflanzen* to grow; *Tiere* to breed ❺ *Kreis, Linie* to draw ❻ (*anziehen*) ■ etw auf sich *akk* ~ to attract sth ❼ (*zur Folge haben*) ■ etw nach sich *dat* ~ to have consequences II. *vi* ❶ *haben* (*zerren*) to pull (an *+dat* on) ❷ *sein* (*umziehen*) to move; ■ zu jdm ~ to move in with sb; nach München ~ to move to Munich ❸ *sein* (*irgendwohin gehen*) *Menschenmenge* to march; *Rauch, Wolke* to drift; *Gewitter* to move; durch die Stadt ~ to wander through [the] town/the city; in den Krieg ~ to go to war ❹ *haben* (*saugen*) an einer Zigarette ~ to drag on a cigarette ❺ *haben Tee* to brew III. *vi impers haben* es zieht there is a draft IV. *vt impers haben* es zog ihn in die weite Welt he felt a strong urge to see the world; was zieht dich hierhin? what brings you here? V. *vr haben* ■ sich *akk* ~ *Gespräch, Verhandlungen* to drag on
Ziehharmonika *f* concertina
Ziel <-[e]s, -e> [tsiːl] *nt* ❶ (*angestrebtes Ergebnis*) goal, aim; am ~ sein to be at one's destination ❷ SPORT, MIL target; durchs ~ gehen to cross the finish line ❸ (*Reiseziel*) destination ▶WENDUNGEN: über das ~ __hinausschießen__ (*fam*) to overshoot the mark
zielen ['tsiː·lən] *vi* to aim (auf *+akk* at)
Zielfernrohr *nt* scope
Zielgerade *f* home stretch
Zielgruppe *f* target group
ziellos I. *adj* aimless II. *adv* aimlessly
Zielort *m* destination
Zielscheibe *f* target
Zielsetzung <-, -en> *f* aim

zielsicher *adj* unerring
zielstrebig ['tsiːl·ʃtreː·bɪç] I. *adj* single-minded II. *adv* single-mindedly
ziemlich ['tsiːm·lɪç] I. *adj attr* (*beträchtlich*) considerable II. *adv* ❶ (*weitgehend*) quite ❷ (*beinahe*) almost; so ~ more or less; so ~ alles just about everything; so ~ dasselbe pretty much the same
Zierde <-, -n> ['tsiːɐ̯·də] *f* decoration
zieren ['tsiː·rən] I. *vr* ■ sich *akk* ~ to make a fuss; *Mädchen* to act coyly; ohne sich *akk* zu ~ without having to be pressed II. *vt* to adorn
zierlich ['tsiːɐ̯·lɪç] *adj* dainty
Zierpflanze *f* ornamental plant
Ziffer <-, -n> ['tsɪ·fɐ] *f* ❶ (*Zahlzeichen*) digit ❷ *s.* Zahl
zig [tsɪç] *adj* (*fam*) umpteen; ~mal umpteen times
Zigarette <-, -n> [tsi·ga·ˈrɛ·tə] *f* cigarette
Zigarillo <-s, -s> [tsi·ga·ˈrɪ·lo] *m o nt* cigarillo
Zigarre <-, -n> [tsi·ˈga·rə] *f* cigar
Zigeuner(in) <-s, -> [tsi·ˈgɔy·nɐ] *m(f)* Gypsy
Zimmer <-s, -> ['tsɪ·mɐ] *nt* room; ~ frei haben to have vacancies
Zimmerantenne *f* indoor antenna
Zimmerdecke *f* ceiling
Zimmermädchen *nt* [chamber]maid
Zimmermann <-leute> *m* carpenter
zimmern ['tsɪ·mɐn] *vt* to make from wood
Zimmerpflanze *f* house plant
Zimmervermittlung *f* accommodations service
zimperlich ['tsɪm·pɐ·lɪç] *adj* squeamish
Zimt <-[e]s, -e> [tsɪmt] *m* cinnamon
Zink <-[e]s> [tsɪŋk] *nt kein pl* zinc
Zinn <-[e]s> [tsɪn] *nt kein pl* tin
zinnoberrot *adj* vermilion
Zinsertrag *m* interest yield
Zinseszins *m* compound interest
zinslos *adj* interest-free
Zipfelmütze *f* pointed cap
zirka ['tsɪr·ka] *adv* about

Z

Zirkel <-s, -> ['tsɪr·kl̩] m ❶(*Gerät*) compass ❷(*Gruppe*) group

Zirkus <-, -se> ['tsɪr·kʊs] m circus; **mach nicht so einen ~!** (*fig fam*) don't make such a fuss!

Zirkuszelt nt big top

zischen ['tsɪ·ʃn̩] vi haben to hiss; *Fett* to sizzle

Zischen <-s> ['tsɪ·ʃn̩] nt kein pl hiss

Zitat <-[e]s, -e> [tsi·'ta:t] nt quotation

zitieren* [tsi·'ti:·ran] vt to quote

Zitrone <-, -n> [tsi·'tro:·nə] f lemon

Zitronenschale f lemon peel

Zitrusfrucht ['tsi:·trʊs·] f citrus fruit

zittern ['tsɪ·tɐn] vi to tremble; **vor Angst ~** to tremble with fear

zittrig ['tsɪt·rɪç] adj shaky

Zivil <-s> [tsi·'vi:l] nt kein pl ■**in ~** in civilian clothes

Zivilbevölkerung f civilian population

Zivildienst m kein pl community service as an alternative to military service

Zivilisation <-, -en> [tsi·vi·li·za·'tsi̯o:n] f civilization

zivilisiert I. adj civilized II. adv civilly

Zivilist(in) <-en, -en> [tsi·vi·'lɪst] m(f) civilian

Zivilrecht nt civil law

zocken ['tsɔ·kn̩] vi (sl) to gamble

Zoff <-s> [tsɔf] m kein pl (fam) trouble

zögern ['tsø:·gɐn] vi to hesitate; **ohne zu ~** without hesitation

Zölibat <-[e]s, -e> [tsø·li·'ba:t] nt o m celibacy

Zoll¹ <-[e]s, -> [tsɔl] m (*Maß*) inch

Zoll² <-[e]s, Zölle> [tsɔl] m ❶ÖKON customs npl, duty; **für etw** akk **~ bezahlen** to pay customs on sth ❷kein pl (*Zollverwaltung*) customs npl

Zollbeamte(r), -beamtin m, f customs officer

Zollfahndung f customs investigation department

zollfrei adj, adv duty-free

zollpflichtig adj dutiable

Zollstock m ruler

Zone <-, -n> ['tso:·nə] f zone

Zoo <-s, -s> [tso:] m zoo

Zoologie <-> [tsoo·lo·'gi:] f kein pl zoology

zoomen ['zu:·mən, 'tso:·mən] vt ■jdn/etw ~ to zoom in on sb/sth

Zopf <-[e]s, Zöpfe> [tsɔpf] m braid

Zorn <-[e]s> [tsɔrn] m kein pl anger

zornig ['tsɔr·nɪç] adj angry (**auf** +akk with/at)

zottelig ['tsɔ·tə·lɪç] adj (fam) shaggy

zu [tsu:] I. präp +dat ❶(*wohin*) to; **ich muss ~m Arzt** I have to go see a doctor; **~ Fuß/Pferd** on foot/horseback ❷(*örtlich: Richtung*) **~m Meer/~r Stadtmitte hin** toward the sea/downtown; **das Zimmer liegt ~r Straße hin** the room faces the street ❸(*neben*) ■**~ jdm/etw** next to sb/sth; **setz dich ~ uns** [come and] sit with us ❹*zeitlich* at; **~ Ostern/Weihnachten** at Easter/Christmas; **~m Wochenende fahren wir weg** we're going away on the weekend ❺(*anlässlich*) **etw ~m Geburtstag bekommen** to get sth for one's birthday; **jdn ~m Essen einladen** to invite sb for a meal; **~ dieser Frage möchte ich Folgendes sagen** I would like to say the following regarding this question ❻(*für etw bestimmt*) **das Zeichen ~m Aufbruch** the signal to leave; **~m Frühstück trinkt sie immer Tee** she always has tea with breakfast ❼(*um etw herbeizuführen*) **~r Entschuldigung** in apology; **~ was soll das gut sein?** what is that [supposed to be good] for? ❽+ substantiviertem Infinitiv **nichts ~m Essen** nothing to eat; **etwas ~m Spielen** something to play with; **das ist ja ~m Lachen** that's ridiculous ❾(*Veränderung*) **~ etw werden** to turn into sth; **~m Vorsitzenden gewählt werden** to be elected [to the post of] chairman ❿(*Beziehung*) **Liebe ~ jdm** love for sb; **aus Freundschaft ~ jdm** because of one's friendship with sb; **meine Beziehung ~ ihr** my relationship with her ⓫(*Verhältnis*) **im Verhältnis 1 ~ 4** in a 1:4 [or 1 to 4] ratio; **unsere Chancen stehen 50**

~ **50** we have a fifty-fifty chance; SPORT **sie gewannen mit 5 ~ 1** they won 5-1, 5 to 1 ⑫ *bei Mengenangaben* ~ **drei Prozent** at three percent; **sechs [Stück] fünfzig Cent** six for fifty cents; ~**m halben Preis** at [*or* for] half price; ~**m ersten Mal** for the first time ⑬ (*örtlich: Lage*) in; ~ **Hause** at home; ~ **seiner Rechten/Linken** on his right/left[-hand side] ⑭ (*in Wendungen*) ~**m Beispiel** for example; ~**r Belohnung/Strafe** as a reward/punishment; ~**m Glück** luckily; **jdm ~ Hilfe kommen** to come to sb's aid; ~ **Hilfe!** help!; ~**r Probe** on a trial basis; SCHWEIZ ~**r Hauptsache** mainly II. *adv* ① (*allzu*) too; ~ **sehr** too much; **ich wäre ~ gern mitgefahren** I would have loved to have gone along ② (*geschlossen*) shut, closed; **Tür ~!** shut the door!; **mach die Augen ~** close your eyes ③ (*fam: betrunken sein*) ■~ **sein** to be drunk ④ (*in Wendungen*) **nur ~!** go [right] ahead; **mach ~** hurry up III. *konj* ① + *infin* to; **etw ~ essen** sth to eat; **sie hat ~ gehorchen** she has to obey; **ohne es ~ wissen** without knowing it ② + *part* ~ **bezahlende Rechnungen** outstanding bills; **nicht ~ unterschätzende Probleme** problems [that are] not to be underestimated

zuallererst [tsu·'ʔalɐ·ʔeːɐ̯st] *adv* first of all

zuallerletzt [tsu·'ʔalɐ·lɛtst] *adv* last of all

Zubehör <-[e]s, *selten* -e> ['tsu·bə·høːɐ̯] *nt o m* accessories *pl*

zu|beißen *vi irreg* to bite

zu|bereiten* *vt* to prepare

Zubereitung <-, -en> *f* preparation

zu|billigen *vt* ■jdm etw ~ to grant sb sth

zu|binden *vt irreg* Schuhe to tie

Zucchini <-, -> [tsʊ·'kiː·ni] *f meist pl* zucchini

Zucht <-, -en> [tsʊxt] *f kein pl* (*Pflanzenzucht*) cultivation; (*Tierzucht*) breeding

züchten ['tsʏç·tn̩] *vt Pflanzen* to grow; *Tiere* to breed

Züchter(in) <-s, -> *m(f) Tierzüchter* breeder; *Pflanzenzüchter* grower

Zuchthaus *nt* HIST prison

Zuchthengst *m* stud horse

züchtigen ['tsʏç·tɪ·gn̩] *vt* to beat

zucken ['tsʊ·kn̩] *vi* ① *haben* (*ruckartig bewegen*) *Augenlid* to flutter; *Mundwinkel* to twitch; **mit den Achseln ~** to shrug one's shoulders ② *haben Blitz* to flash

zücken ['tsʏ·kn̩] *vt Messer* to draw

Zucker¹ <-s, -> ['tsʊ·kɐ] *m* sugar

Zucker² <-s> ['tsʊ·kɐ] *m kein pl* MED diabetes

ZuckergussRR *m* icing

Zuckerhut ['tsʊ·kɐ·huːt] *m* GEOL sugar loaf

zuckerkrank *adj* diabetic

Zuckerkranke(r) *f(m)* diabetic

Zuckerrohr *nt* sugar cane

Zuckerrübe *f* sugar beet

zuckersüß ['tsʊ·kɐ·'zyːs] *adj* as sweet as sugar *pred*

Zuckung <-, -en> *f meist pl* twitch

zu|decken *vt* to cover [up *sep*]

zu|drehen *vt* ① (*verschließen*) to screw on *sep* ② (*abstellen*) to turn off *sep* ③ (*festdrehen*) to tighten ④ (*zuwenden*) **jdm den Rücken ~** to turn one's back on sb

zudringlich ['tsuː·drɪŋ·lɪç] *adj* pushy

zu|drücken *vt* to press shut *sep*

zueinander [tsu·ʔaiˈnanˈdɐ] *adv* to each other; ~ **passen** *Menschen* to suit each other; *Farben, Kleider* to go well together

zuerst [tsu·'ʔeːɐ̯st] *adv* ① (*als Erster*) the first; (*als Erstes*) first ② (*anfangs*) at first ③ (*zum ersten Mal*) for the first time

Zufahrt ['tsuː·faːɐ̯t] *f* entrance

Zufall *m* coincidence; (*Schicksal*) chance; **etw dem ~ überlassen** to leave sth to chance

zu|fallen *vi irreg sein* ① *Tür* to close ② (*zuteilwerden*) ■jdm ~ to go to sb

zufällig I. *adj* chance *attr* II. *adv* by **Z**

chance; **rein ~** by pure chance; **jdn ~ treffen** to happen to meet sb; **wissen Sie ~, ob …?** do you happen to know whether …?

Zufallstreffer *m* fluke *fam*

Zuflucht <-, -en> ['tsu:flʊxt] *f* refuge
▶WENDUNGEN: **jds letzte ~ sein** to be sb's last resort

Zufluss^RR, **Zufluß**^ALT *m* ❶ *kein pl* (*das Zufließen*) inflow ❷ (*Nebenfluss*) tributary

zu|flüstern *vt* ■**jdm etw ~** to whisper sth to sb

zufolge [tsu·'fɔl·gə] *präp +dat* according to

zufrieden [tsu·'fri:·dn̩] I. *adj* (*befriedigt*) satisfied (**mit** +*dat* with); (*glücklich*) contented (**mit** +*dat* with) II. *adv* with satisfaction; (*glücklich*) contentedly; ~ **stellend** satisfactory

zufrieden|geben *vr irreg* ■**sich** *akk* [**mit etw** *dat*] ~ to be satisfied [with sth]

Zufriedenheit <-> *f kein pl* satisfaction; (*Glücklichsein*) contentedness

zufrieden|lassen *vt irreg* ■**jdn ~** to leave sb alone

zu|frieren *vi irreg sein* to freeze [over]

zu|fügen *vt* to cause; **jdm Schaden ~** to harm sb; **jdm Unrecht ~** to do sb an injustice

Zufuhr <-, -en> ['tsu:·fu:ɐ] *f* supply

Zug^1 <-[e]s, Züge> [tsu:k] *m* train
▶WENDUNGEN: **der ~ ist abgefahren** (*fam*) you missed the boat

Zug^2 <-[e]s, Züge> [tsu:k] *m* ❶ (*inhalierte Menge*) puff (**an** +*dat* on/at) ❷ *kein pl* (*Luftzug*) draft ❸ (*Spielzug*) move; **am ~ sein** to be sb's move ❹ (*Kolonne*) procession ❺ (*Gesichtszug*) feature ❻ (*Charakterzug*) characteristic ❼ (*Schritt*) ~ **um** step by step; **in einem ~** in one stroke ❽ (*Umriss*) **in groben Zügen** in broad terms

Zugabe ['tsu:·ga:·bə] *f* MUS encore

Zugabteil *nt* train compartment

Zugang <-[e]s, Zugänge> ['tsu:·gaŋ] *m* ❶ (*Eingang*) entrance ❷ *kein pl* (*Zutritt, Zugriff*) access (**zu** +*dat* to)

zugänglich ['tsu:·gɛŋ·lɪç] *adj* ❶ (*erreichbar*) accessible ❷ *Mensch* approachable; ■**für etw** *akk* ~ **sein** to be receptive to sth

Zugbrücke *f* drawbridge

zu|geben *vt irreg* to admit

zugegen [tsu·'ge:·gŋ] *adj* ■**bei etw** *dat* ~ **sein** to be present at sth

zu|gehen *irreg* I. *vi sein* ❶ *Tür* to shut ❷ (*zubewegen*) ■**auf jdn/etw ~** to approach sb/sth ❸ (*sich versöhnen*) ■**aufeinander ~** to become reconciled II. *vi impers sein* (*Party*) **bei ihren Partys geht es immer sehr lustig zu** her parties are always very great fun

zugehörig ['tsu:·gə·hø:·rɪç] *adj attr* accompanying *attr*

Zugehörigkeit <-> *f kein pl* (*Verbundenheit*) affiliation (**zu** +*dat* to); **ein Gefühl der ~** a sense of belonging

zugeknöpft *adj* ❶ *Hemd* buttoned-up ❷ *Mensch* reserved

Zügel <-s, -> ['tsy:·gl̩] *m* reins *npl*

zügellos *adj* unrestrained

zügeln ['tsy:·gln̩] I. *vt* ❶ (*im Zaum halten*) to rein in *sep* ❷ (*beherrschen*) to curb ❸ (*zurückhalten*) ■**sich/jdn ~** to restrain oneself/sb II. *vi sein* SCHWEIZ (*umziehen*) ■**[irgendwohin] ~** to move [somewhere]

Zugeständnis ['tsu:·gə·ʃtɛnt·nɪs] *nt* concession

zu|gestehen* *vt irreg* to concede

zugetan ['tsu:·gə·ta:n] *adj* ■**jdm/etw ~ sein** to be taken with sb/sth

Zugführer(in) *m(f)* BAHN conductor

zugig ['tsu:·gɪç] *adj* drafty

zugleich [tsu·'glaɪç] *adv* ❶ (*ebenso*) both ❷ (*gleichzeitig*) at the same time

Zugluft *f kein pl* draft

Zugmaschine *f* AUTO tractor

Zugpferd *nt* ❶ (*Tier*) draft horse ❷ (*besondere Attraktion*) crowd pleaser

zu|greifen *vi irreg* ❶ (*sich bedienen*) to help oneself ❷ COMPUT ■**auf etw** *akk* ~ to access sth

Zugrestaurant *nt* dining car

Zugriffsberechtigung *f* COMPUT access authorization

Z

zugrunde, zu Grunde[RR] [tsu·'grʊn·də] *adv* [**an etw** *dat*] ~ **gehen** to be destroyed [by sth]; **etw** *dat* ~ **liegen** to form the basis of sth

Zugschaffner(in) *m(f)* train conductor

zugunsten, zu Gunsten[RR] [tsu·'gʊns·tn̩] *präp +gen* in favor of

zugute|halten[RR] [tsu·'gu:·tə-] *vt irreg* ■ **jdm** etw ~ to make allowances for sb's sth

zugute|kommen[RR] *vi irreg sein* ■ **jdm/ etw** ~ to be for the benefit of sb/sth

Zugverbindung *f* train connection

Zugvogel *m* migratory bird

zu|haben *vi irreg (fam)* to be closed

zu|halten *vt irreg* to hold closed; **sich/ jdm den Mund** ~ to hold one's hand over one's/sb's mouth; **sich** *dat* **die Nase** ~ to hold one's nose

Zuhälter(in) <-s, -> ['tsu:·hɛl·tɐ] *m(f)* pimp

Zuhause <-s> [tsu·'hau·zə] *nt kein pl* home

zu|hören *vi* ■ **jdm** ~ to listen to sb

Zuhörer(in) *m(f)* listener; ■ **die** ~ (*Publikum*) the audience + *sing/pl vb*; (*Radiozuhörer a.*) the listeners

zu|jubeln *vi* to cheer

zu|knöpfen *vt* to button up *sep*

zu|kommen *vi irreg sein* ➊ (*sich nähern*) ■ **auf jdn/etw** ~ to come toward sb/sth ➋ (*bevorstehen*) ■ **auf jdn** ~ to be in store for sb; **alles auf sich** ~ **lassen** to take things as they come ➌ (*geben*) **jdm etw** ~ **lassen** to send sb sth

Zukunft <-> ['tsu:·kʊnft] *f kein pl* ➊ (*das Bevorstehende*) future; **in ferner/naher** ~ in the distant/near future ➋ LING future [tense]

zukünftig ['tsu:·kʏnf·tɪç] I. *adj* future *attr* II. *adv* in future

Zukunftsaussichten *pl* future prospects *pl*

Zukunftsmusik *f* ▶WENDUNGEN: ~ **sein** (*fam*) to be a long way off

zu|lächeln *vi* ■ **jdm** ~ to smile at sb

zu|langen *vi (fam)* ➊ (*zugreifen*) to help oneself ➋ (*zuschlagen*) to land a punch

➌ (*hohe Preise fordern*) to ask a fortune

zu|lassen *vt irreg* ➊ (*dulden*) to allow ➋ (*fam*) *Tür* to keep shut *sep* ➌ (*die Genehmigung erteilen*) ■ **jdn** ~ to admit sb (**zu** +*dat* to) ➍ (*anmelden*) to register

zulässig ['tsu:·lɛ·sɪç] *adj* permissible

Zulassung <-, -en> *f* ➊ *kein pl* (*Genehmigung*) authorization; (*Lizenz*) license; **die** ~ **entziehen** to revoke sb's license ➋ (*Anmeldung*) registration ➌ (*Fahrzeugschein*) [motor vehicle] registration

Zulassungsbeschränkung *f* admission restriction

Zulassungsprüfung *f* ADMIN, SCH entrance exam

zu|legen I. *vt (fam: zunehmen)* to put on *sep* ▶WENDUNGEN: **einen Zahn** ~ (*fam*) to step on it II. *vi* ➊ (*fam: zunehmen*) to put on weight ➋ (*fam: das Tempo steigern*) to get a move on; *Läufer* to increase the pace III. *vr* (*fam*) ■ **sich** *dat* **jdn/etw** ~ to get oneself sb/ sth

zuleide, zu Leide[RR] [tsu·'lai·də] *adv* **jdm etwas/nichts** ~ **tun** (*veraltend*) to harm/not harm sb

zuletzt [tsu·'lɛtst] *adv* ➊ (*als Letzte(r)*) ~ **eingetroffen** to be the last to arrive; ~ **durchs Ziel gehen** to finish last ➋ (*zum Schluss*) **bis** ~ until the end; **ganz** ~ right at the end ➌ (*letztmalig*) last; **nicht** ~ not least [of all]

zuliebe [tsu·'li:·bə] *adv* ■ **jdm/etw** ~ for sb['s sake]

zum [tsʊm] = **zu dem** *s.* **zu**

zu|machen *vt, vi* ➊ (*verschließen*) to close; **eine Flasche/ein Glas** ~ to put the top on a bottle/lid on a jar ➋ (*zukleben*) *Brief* to seal ➌ (*zuknöpfen*) to button [up *sep*] ➍ (*den Betrieb einstellen*) to close [down *sep*]

zumal [tsu·'ma:l] I. *konj* particularly as II. *adv* particularly

zumindest [tsu·'mɪn·dəst] *adv* at least

zumute, zu Mute[RR] [tsu·'mu:·tə] *adv* **Z**

mir ist nicht zum Scherzen ~ I'm not in a joking mood

zu|muten ['tsu:·mu:·tn̩] vt ■jdm etw ~ to expect sth of sb; **jdm zu viel** ~ to expect too much of sb; ■**sich** dat **etw** ~ to undertake sth; **sich** dat **zu viel** ~ to overtax oneself

Zumutung f unreasonable demand; **das ist eine** ~! it's just too much!

zunächst [tsu·'nɛçst] adv ❶ (anfangs) initially ❷ (vorerst) for the moment

Zunahme <-, -n> ['tsu:·na:·mə] f increase

Zuname ['tsu:·na:·mə] m (geh) surname

zünden ['tsʏndn̩] vt, vi ❶ TECH to fire spec ❷ (zu brennen anfangen) to catch fire; **Streichholz** to light

zündend adj **Rede** stirring; **Idee** great

Zünder <-s, -> ['tsʏn·dɐ] m detonator

Zündholz <-es, -hölzer> nt DIAL match

Zündholzschachtel f DIAL matchbox

Zündkabel nt ignition cable

Zündkerze f spark plug

Zündschlüssel m ignition key

Zündschnur f fuse

Zündung <-, -en> f ❶ AUTO ignition ❷ TECH firing

zu|nehmen vi irreg ❶ **Gewicht** to gain weight ❷ (sich verstärken) to increase

zu|neigen I. vi ■**etw** dat ~ to be inclined toward sth II. vr **sich** akk **dem Ende** ~ to draw to a close

Zuneigung f affection

Zunft <-, Zünfte> [tsʊnft] f HIST guild

zünftig ['tsʏnf·tɪç] adj (veraltend fam) proper

Zunge <-, -n> ['tsʊŋə] f tongue; **auf der** ~ **zergehen** to melt in one's mouth ▶WENDUNGEN: **etw liegt jdm auf der** ~ sth is on the tip of sb's tongue

Zungenbrecher <-s, -> m (fam) tongue twister

ZungenkussRR m French kiss

Zungenspitze f tip of the tongue

zunichte|machenRR [tsu·'nɪç·tə-] vt to wreck; **Hoffnungen** to ruin

zunutze, zu NutzeRR [tsu·'nu·tsə] adv

sich dat **etw** ~ **machen** to make use of sth

zu|ordnen ['tsu·'ʔɔrd·nən] vt ■**etw etw** dat ~ to assign sth to sth

zu|packen vi ❶ (zufassen) to grip; (schneller) to make a grab ❷ (mithelfen) ■|**mit** ~ to lend a [helping] hand

zupfen ['tsʊp·fn̩] vt ❶ (ziehen) ■**jdn an etw** dat ~ to pluck at sb's sth; (stärker) to tug at sb's sth ❷ (herausziehen) ■**etw aus/von etw** dat ~ to pull sth out of/off [of] sth; **sich** dat **die Augenbrauen** ~ to pluck one's eyebrows

zur [tsu:ɐ̯, tsʊr] = **zu der** s. **zu**

zurechnungsfähig adj JUR responsible for one's [own] actions pred

zurecht|finden [tsu·'rɛçt·fɪn·dn̩] vr irreg ■**sich** akk **irgendwo** ~ to get used to a place; **sich** akk **in einer Großstadt** ~ to find one's way around a city

zurecht|kommen vi irreg sein ❶ (auskommen) to get along (**mit** +dat with) ❷ (klarkommen) to cope (**mit** +dat with)

zurecht|legen vr ■**sich** dat **etw** ~ (sich etw griffbereit hinlegen) to get sth ready; (sich im Voraus überlegen) to work out sep sth

zurecht|machen I. vt ❶ (vorbereiten) to get ready ❷ (zubereiten) to prepare II. vr ■**sich** akk ~ to put on sep one's makeup

zurecht|weisen vt irreg to reprimand (**wegen** +gen for)

zu|reden ['tsu·re:·dn̩] vi ■**jdm** [**gut**] ~ to encourage sb

zu|richten ['tsu·rɪç·tn̩] vt **jdn übel** ~ to beat up sep sb badly; **etw übel** ~ to make a mess of sth

Zurschaustellung f (meist pej) flaunting

zurück [tsu·'rʏk] adv ❶ (wieder da) back (**von** +dat from) ❷ (Rückfahrt, -flug) return; **hin und** ~ **oder einfach?** roundtrip or one-way? ▶WENDUNGEN: ~! back up!

zurück|bekommen* vt irreg to get back sep

zurück|bezahlen* *vt* to repay, to pay back *sep*

zurück|bleiben *vi irreg sein* ❶ (*nicht mitkommen*) to stay behind ❷ (*zurückgelassen werden*) to be left [behind] ❸ (*nicht mithalten können*) to fall behind

zurück|blicken [tsuˈrʏk·blɪ·kn̩] *vi* to look back (**auf** +*akk* on/at)

zurück|bringen *vt irreg* to bring back *sep*

zurück|denken *vi irreg* to think back (**an** +*akk* to)

zurück|drängen *vt* to force back *sep*

zurück|erstatten* *vt* ■ **jdm** **etw** ~ to refund sb's sth

zurück|fahren *irreg* I. *vi sein* (*zum Ausgangspunkt fahren*) to drive back II. *vt* ❶ (*rückwärtsfahren*) to reverse ❷ (*mit dem Auto*) to drive back *sep* ❸ (*reduzieren*) to cut back *sep*

zurück|fallen *vi irreg sein* ❶ SPORT to fall behind ❷ (*in früheren Zustand*) to lapse back (**in** +*akk* in) ❸ (*angelastet werden*) ■ **auf jdn** ~ to reflect on sb

zurück|finden *vi irreg* to find one's way back

zurück|fordern *vt* to demand back (**von** +*dat* from)

zurück|führen *vt* ❶ (*Ursache bestimmen*) ■ **etw auf etw** *akk* ~ to attribute sth to sth ❷ (*zum Ausgangsort zurückbringen*) ■ **jdn irgendwohin** ~ to take sb back somewhere

zurück|geben *vt irreg* to return; **ein Kompliment** ~ to return a compliment

zurückgeblieben *adj* slow

zurück|gehen *vi irreg sein* ❶ (*zurückkehren*) to return, to go back ❷ (*abnehmen*) to go down ❸ MED (*sich zurückbilden*) to go down; *Geschwulst* to be in recession

zurückgezogen *adj, adv* secluded

zurück|greifen *vi irreg* ■ **auf etw** *akk* ~ to fall back [up]on sth

zurück|halten *irreg* I. *vr* ■ **sich** *akk* ~ ❶ (*sich beherrschen*) to restrain oneself ❷ (*reserviert sein*) to be reserved II. *vt* ❶ (*aufhalten*) to hold up *sep* ❷ (*abhal-*

ten) ■ **jdn** [**von etw** *dat*] ~ to keep sb from doing sth

zurückhaltend I. *adj* ❶ (*reserviert*) reserved ❷ (*vorsichtig*) cautious II. *adv* cautiously

Zurückhaltung *f kein pl* reserve

zurück|holen *vt* (*zurückbringen*) to bring back *sep*; (*in seinen Besitz*) to get back *sep*

zurück|kehren *vi sein* to return (**zu** +*dat* to); **nach Hause** ~ to return home

zurück|kommen *vi irreg sein* ❶ (*erneut zum Ausgangsort kommen*) to return; **nach Hause/aus dem Ausland** ~ to return home/from abroad ❷ (*erneut aufgreifen*) ■ **auf etw** *akk* ~ to come back to sth; ■ **auf jdn** ~ to get back to sb

zurück|lassen *vt irreg* to leave behind *sep*

zurück|legen *vt* ❶ (*wieder hinlegen*) to put back *sep* ❷ (*reservieren*) ■ **jdm etw** ~ to set sth aside for sb ❸ (*hinter sich bringen*) **5 km** ~ to go 5 km; (*zu Fuß a.*) to walk 5 km; (*mit dem Auto a.*) to drive 5 km ❹ (*sparen*) to put away *sep*

zurück|liegen *vi irreg* **etw liegt vier Jahre zurück** it's been four years since sth

zurück|nehmen *vt irreg* ❶ (*als Retour annehmen*) to take back *sep* ❷ (*widerrufen*) to take back *sep* ❸ (*rückgängig machen*) to withdraw; **ich nehme alles zurück** I take it all back

zurück|reisen *vi sein* to travel back

zurück|rufen *irreg* I. *vt* ❶ (*zurück telefonieren*) to call back *sep* ❷ (*zurückbeordern*) to recall II. *vi* to call back

zurück|schalten *vi* AUTO to downshift (**in** +*akk* into)

zurück|schauen *vi* to look back (**auf** +*akk* on/at)

zurück|schicken *vt* to send back *sep*

zurück|schlagen *irreg* I. *vt* ❶ SPORT to hit back ❷ (*umschlagen*) to turn back *sep* II. *vi* ■ **auf jdn/etw** ~ to have an effect on sb/sth

zurück|schrecken *vi irreg sein* ❶ (*Be-*

Z

denken vor etw haben) to shrink (**vor** +*dat* from); **vor nichts** ~ (*völlig skrupellos sein*) to stop at nothing; (*keine Angst haben*) to not flinch at anything ② (*erschrecken*) to start back

zurück|sehnen *vr* **sich** *akk* **nach Hause** ~ to long to return home

zurück|stecken I. *vt* to put back *sep* II. *vi* to back down

zurück|stehen *vi irreg* ① (*weiter entfernt stehen*) to stand back ② (*hintangesetzt werden*) ■ **[hinter jdm]** ~ to be behind [sb]

zurück|stellen *vt* ① (*wieder hinstellen*) to put back *sep* ② (*nach hinten stellen*) to move back *sep* ③ *Heizung* to turn down *sep* ④ (*aufschieben*) to put back *sep;* (*verschieben*) to postpone; **die Uhr** ~ to turn back *sep* the clock ⑤ *Wünsche* to put aside ⑥ ÖSTERR (*zurückgeben*) to return

zurück|stufen *vt* to downgrade

zurück|treten *vi irreg sein* ① (*nach hinten treten*) to step back (**von** +*dat* from) ② (*von einem Amt*) to resign

zurück|versetzen* *vr* ■ **sich** *akk* ~ to be transported back

zurück|weichen *vi irreg sein* to draw back (**vor** +*dat* from)

zurück|weisen *vt irreg* ■ **jdn** ~ to turn away *sep* sb; ■ **etw** ~ to reject sth

zurück|werfen *vt irreg* ① (*jdm etw wieder zuwerfen*) to throw back *sep* ② (*Position verschlechtern*) **das wirft uns um Jahre zurück** that will set us back years

zurück|zahlen *vt* ■ **[jdm]** **etw** ~ to repay [sb] sth

zurück|ziehen *irreg* I. *vt* ① (*nach hinten ziehen*) to pull back *sep; Vorhang* to draw back *sep* ② (*widerrufen*) to withdraw II. *vr* ■ **sich** *akk* ~ to withdraw (**aus** +*dat* from) III. *vi sein* **nach Hamburg** ~ to move back to Hamburg

zu|rufen *vt irreg* ■ **jdm etw** ~ to shout sth to sb

zurzeit [tsʊrˈtsait] *adv* at present

Zusage [ˈtsuːˌzaːɡə] *f* acceptance

zu|sagen I. *vt* to promise II. *vi* ■ **jdm** ~

① (*die Teilnahme versichern*) to accept sb ② (*gefallen*) to appeal to sb

zusammen [tsuˈzamən] *adv* ① (*gemeinsam*) together (**mit** +*dat* with); ■ **mit jdm** ~ **sein** to be with sb ② (*ein Paar sein*) ■ ~ **sein** to be going out ③ (*insgesamt*) altogether

Zusammenarbeit *f kein pl* cooperation

zusammen|arbeiten *vi* ■ **mit jdm** ~ to cooperate [*or* work [together]] with sb

zusammen|bauen *vt* to assemble

zusammen|beißen *vt* **die Zähne** ~ to clench one's teeth

zusammen|bleiben *vi irreg sein* to stay together; ■ **mit jdm** ~ to stay with sb

zusammen|brechen *vi irreg sein* to collapse

zusammen|bringen *vt irreg* ① (*in Kontakt bringen*) ■ **jdn [mit jdm]** ~ to introduce [sb to sb] ② (*anhäufen*) to amass

Zusammenbruch *m* collapse

zusammen|drücken *vt* ① (*zerdrücken*) to crush ② (*aneinanderdrücken*) to press together

zusammen|fahren *vi irreg sein* to start; (*vor Schmerzen*) to flinch

zusammen|fallen *vi irreg sein* ① (*einstürzen*) ■ **[in sich]** ~ to collapse; *Gebäude a.* to cave in ② (*gleichzeitig stattfinden*) *Ereignisse* to coincide

zusammen|falten *vt* to fold [up *sep*]

zusammen|fassen I. *vt* ① (*resümieren*) to summarize ② (*vereinigen*) ■ **jdn/etw in etw** *dat* ~ to unite sb/sth into sth; **die Bewerber in Gruppen** ~ to divide the applicants into groups II. *vi* to summarize; **..., wenn ich kurz ~ darf** to sum up, ...

Zusammenfassung *f* summary

zusammen|fügen I. *vt* to assemble; **die Teile eines Puzzles** ~ to piece together a jigsaw puzzle II. *vr* **die Teile fügen sich nahtlos zusammen** the parts fit together seamlessly

zusammen|führen *vt* to bring together *sep; eine Familie* to reunite

zusammen|gehören* *vi* ① (*zueinander gehören*) to belong together ② (*ein*

Ganzes bilden) to go together; *Socken* to form a pair

Zusammengehörigkeit <-> *f kein pl* unity

Zusammengehörigkeitsgefühl *nt kein pl* sense of togetherness

zusammengesetzt *adj* compound *attr*

zusammengestöpselt [tsu·'za·mən-gə·ʃtœp·slt] *adj* (*pej fam*) [hastily] thrown together

zusammengewürfelt *adj* mismatched

Zusammenhalt *m kein pl* solidarity

zusammen|halten *irreg* I. *vi* to stick together II. *vt* ❶ (*beisammenhalten*) **seine Gedanken ~** to keep one's thoughts together; **sein Geld ~ müssen** to have to be careful with one's money ❷ (*verbinden*) to hold together

Zusammenhang <-[e]s, -hänge> *m* connection; (*Verbindung*) link (**zwischen** +*dat* between); (*in ~) (zwischen* +*dat* between); **jdn/etw mit etw** *dat* **in ~ bringen** to connect sb/sth with [*or* to] sth; **etw aus dem ~ reißen** to take sth out of context; **im ~ mit etw** *dat* in connection with [*or* to] sth; **im ~ mit etw** *dat* **stehen** to be connected with [*or* to] sth

zusammen|hängen *vi irreg* ❶ (*in Zusammenhang stehen*) ■**mit etw** *dat* **~** to be connected with [*or* to] sth ❷ (*verbunden sein*) to be joined [together]

zusammenhängend I. *adj* ❶ (*kohärent*) coherent ❷ (*betreffend*) ■**mit etw** *dat* **~** connected with [*or* to] sth II. *adv* coherently

zusammenhang(s)los I. *adj* incoherent II. *adv* incoherently

zusammen|klappen I. *vt haben* to fold up *sep* II. *vi sein* (*a. fig fam*) to collapse

zusammen|kommen *vi irreg sein* ❶ (*sich treffen*) to come together; ■**mit jdm ~** to meet sb; **zu einer Besprechung ~** to get together for a discussion ❷ (*sich akkumulieren*) to combine; **heute kommt wieder alles zusammen!** it's another of those days! ❸ *Schulden* to mount [up]; *Spenden* to be collected

zusammen|krachen *vi sein* (*fam*) ❶ (*einstürzen*) *Brücke* to crash down; *Bett, Stuhl* to collapse with a crash; *Börse, Wirtschaft* to crash ❷ (*zusammenstoßen*) to smash together; *Auto a.* to crash [into each other]

zusammen|laufen *vi irreg sein* to meet (**in** +*dat* at), to converge (**in** +*dat* at); *Flüsse* to flow together; *Menschen* to gather

zusammen|leben *vi* to live together

Zusammenleben *nt kein pl* living together *no art*

zusammen|legen I. *vt* ❶ (*zusammenfalten*) to fold [up *sep*] ❷ (*vereinigen*) to combine (**mit** +*dat* into), to join II. *vi* (*Geld sammeln*) to pitch in

zusammen|nehmen *irreg* I. *vt* to summon [up *sep*]; **den Verstand ~** to get one's thoughts together; ■**alles zusammengenommen** all in all II. *vr* ■**sich** *akk* **~** to control oneself

zusammen|passen *vi Menschen* to suit each other; **gut/schlecht ~** to be well-matched/a poor match; *Farben* to go together; *Kleidungsstücke* to match

Zusammenprall *m* collision

zusammen|prallen *vi sein* to collide

zusammen|pressen *vt* to press together *sep;* **die Faust ~** to clench one's fist; **zusammengepresste Lippen** pinched lips

zusammen|rechnen *vt* to add up *sep;* **alles zusammengerechnet** all in all

zusammen|reimen *vr* ■**sich** *dat* **etw ~** to put two and two together from [doing] sth

zusammen|reißen *vr irreg* (*fam*) ■**sich** *akk* **~** to pull oneself together, to get a grip *fam*

zusammen|rücken I. *vi sein* (*enger aneinanderrücken*) to move up closer; (*enger zusammenhalten*) to join in a common cause II. *vt haben* to move closer together

zusammen|schlagen *vt irreg haben* ❶ (*verprügeln*) to beat up *sep* ❷ (*zertrümmern*) to smash [up *sep*]

zusammen|schließen *irreg* I. *vt* to lock

Z

together *sep* II. *vr* ■ **sich** *akk* ~ ➊ (*sich vereinigen*) to join together ➋ (*sich verbinden*) to join forces

Zusammenschluss^{RR}, **Zusammenschluß**^{ALT} *m* union; *Firmen* merger

zusammen|schreiben *vt irreg* to write as one word

zusammen|schustern *vt* (*pej fam*) to throw together *sep*

Zusammensein <-s> *nt kein pl* meeting; (*zwanglos*) get-together

zusammen|setzen I. *vt* ➊ (*aus Teilen herstellen*) to assemble ➋ (*nebeneinandersetzen*) **Schüler/Tischgäste ~** to seat students/guests beside each other II. *vr* ➊ (*sich zueinandersetzen*) ■ **sich** *akk* ~ to sit together; (*um etw zu besprechen*) to get together ➋ (*bestehen*) ■ **sich** *akk* **aus etw** *dat* ~ to be composed of sth

Zusammensetzung <-, -en> *f* ➊ (*Struktur*) composition; *Mannschaft* lineup ➋ (*Kombination der Bestandteile*) ingredients *pl*; *Rezeptur, Präparat* composition; *Teile* assembly

Zusammenspiel *nt kein pl* ➊ SPORT teamwork ➋ MUS ensemble playing ➌ (*fig*) interplay

zusammen|stellen *vt* ➊ (*auf einen Fleck stellen*) to place side by side ➋ (*aufstellen*) to compile; *Delegation* to assemble

Zusammenstoß *m* ➊ (*Zusammenprall*) collision ➋ (*Auseinandersetzung*) clash

zusammen|stoßen *vi irreg sein* ➊ (*kollidieren*) to collide; ■ **mit jdm** ~ to bump into sb ➋ (*aneinandergrenzen*) to adjoin

zusammen|stürzen *vi sein* to collapse

zusammen|tragen *vt irreg* to collect

zusammen|treffen *vi irreg sein* ➊ (*sich treffen*) to meet; ■ **mit jdm** ~ to meet sb; (*unverhofft*) to encounter sb ➋ *Umstände* to coincide

Zusammentreffen *nt* ➊ (*Treffen*) meeting ➋ *von Umständen* coincidence

zusammen|tun *irreg* I. *vt* (*fam*) to put together II. *vr* (*fam*) ■ **sich** *akk* ~ to get together

zusammen|wirken *vi* ➊ (*gemeinsam tätig sein*) to work together ➋ (*vereint wirken*) to combine

zusammen|zählen *vt* to add up *sep*; **alles zusammengezählt** all in all

zusammen|ziehen *irreg* I. *vi sein* to move in together II. *vr* ■ **sich** *akk* ~ ➊ (*sich verengen*) to contract; *Schlinge* to tighten ➋ *Sturm, Unheil* to be brewing; *Wolken* to gather III. *vt* **die Augenbrauen ~** to frown

Zusatz ['tsu:ˌzats] *m* ➊ (*zugefügter Teil*) appendix ➋ (*Nahrungszusatz*) additive; **ohne ~ von Farbstoffen** no artificial colors added

Zusatzgerät *nt* attachment; COMPUT peripheral [device]

zusätzlich ['tsu:ˌzɛts·lɪç] I. *adj* further *attr*; *Kosten* additional II. *adv* in addition; **jdn ~ belasten** to put extra pressure on sb

zu|schauen *vi s.* **zusehen**

Zuschauer(in) <-s, -> *m(f)* ➊ SPORT spectator; TV viewer ➋ FILM, THEAT ■ **die ~** the audience

Zuschauerraum *m* auditorium

Zuschauertribüne *f* stands *pl*

zu|schicken *vt* to send; **sich** *dat* **etw ~ lassen** to send for sth

Zuschlag <-[e]s, Zuschläge> *m* ➊ (*Preisaufschlag*) surcharge ➋ (*zusätzliches Entgelt*) bonus

zu|schlagen *irreg* I. *vt haben* ➊ (*schließen*) to slam [shut] *sep*; *Buch* to close ➋ (*zuspielen*) **jdm den Ball ~** to kick [*or* hit] the ball to sb II. *vi* ➊ *haben* (*einen Hieb versetzen*) to strike ➋ *sein Tür* to slam shut

zu|schließen *vt irreg* to lock

zu|schneiden *vt irreg* ➊ MODE *Stoff* to cut out *sep* ➋ (*fig*) **auf jdn [genau] zugeschnitten sein** to be cut out for sb

zu|schnüren *vt* ➊ (*durch Schnüren verschließen*) to tie ➋ (*fig*) **die Angst schnürte ihr die Kehle zu** she was choked with fear

zu|schreiben *vt irreg* ➊ (*beimessen*) ■ **jdm etw ~** to attribute sth to sb ➋ (*zur Last legen*) **jdm/etw die**

Schuld an etw *dat* ~ to blame sb/sth for sth

Zuschrift *f* (*geh*) reply

zu|schulden, zu Schulden[RR] [tsuːʃʊldn̩] *adv* **sich** *dat* **etwas/nichts ~ kommen lassen** to do something/nothing wrong

Zuschuss[RR] <-es, Zuschüsse>, **Zuschuß**[ALT] <-sses, Zuschüsse> ['tsuːʃʊs] *m* subsidy

zu|sehen *vi irreg* ❶ (*mit Blicken verfolgen*) to watch ❷ (*etw geschehen lassen*) ■**etw** *dat* to sit back and watch sth; **tatenlos musste er ~, wie ...** he could only stand and watch while ... ❸ (*dafür sorgen*) ■**~, dass ...** to see [to it] that ...

zusehends ['tsuːzeːənts] *adv* noticeably

zu|senden *vt irreg s.* **zuschicken**

zu|setzen I. *vt* ■**[etw** *dat*] **etw ~** to add sth [to sth] II. *vi* (*bedrängen*) ■**jdm ~** to badger sb

zu|sichern *vt* ■**jdm etw ~** to assure sb of sth; **jdm seine Hilfe ~** to promise to help sb

zu|spielen *vt* ❶ SPORT ■**jdm den Ball ~** to pass the ball to sb ❷ (*zukommen lassen*) **etw der Presse ~** to leak sth [to the press]

zu|spitzen I. *vr* ■**sich** *akk* to come to a head II. *vt* to sharpen

Zuspruch *m kein pl* ❶ (*Popularität, Anklang*) **etw erfreut sich großen ~s** sth is very popular ❷ (*Worte*) **ermutigender ~** words of encouragement

Zustand <-[e]s, Zustände> ['tsuːʃtant] *m* ❶ (*Verfassung*) state, condition; **im wachen ~** while awake ❷ *pl* (*Verhältnisse*) conditions; **das ist doch kein ~!** what a disgrace!

zustande, zu Stande[RR] [tsuːʃtandə] *adv* **etw ~ bringen** to manage [to do] sth; **die Arbeit ~ bringen** to get the work done; **eine Einigung ~ bringen** to reach an agreement; **~ kommen** to materialize; (*stattfinden*) to take place

zuständig ['tsuːʃtɛndɪç] *adj* responsible; **der ~e Beamte** the official in

charge; **dafür ist er ~** that's his responsibility

zu|stecken *vt* ■**jdm etw ~** to slip sb sth

zu|stehen *vi irreg* ❶ (*gehören*) ■**etw steht jdm zu** sb is entitled to sth ❷ (*zukommen*) **es steht dir nicht zu, so über ihn zu reden** it's not for you to speak of him like that

zu|stellen *vt* ❶ (*form: überbringen*) ■**jdm] etw ~** to deliver sth [to sb] ❷ (*fam: blockieren*) to block

Zustellung <-, -en> *f* delivery

zu|stimmen *vi* ■**jdm/etw** *dat*] **~** to agree [with sb/to sth]

Zustimmung *f* agreement; (*Einwilligung*) consent

zu|stoßen *irreg* I. *vi sein* ■**jdm ~** to happen to sb II. *vt* **die Tür mit dem Fuß ~** to kick the door shut

zutage, zu Tage[RR] [tsuːˈtaːɡə] *adj* **etw ~ bringen** to bring sth to light; **~ treten** to come to light

zu|teilen *vt* to allocate; **jdm eine Aufgabe/Rolle ~** to assign a task/role to sb

zuteil|werden[RR] [tsuːˈtaɪl-] *vi* ■**jdm wird etw zuteil** sb is given sth; ■**jdm etw ~ lassen** to grant sb sth

zutiefst [tsuːˈtiːfst] *adv* deeply

zu|trauen *vt* **jdm viel Mut ~** to believe sb has great courage; **sich** *dat* **nichts ~** to have no self-confidence; **sich** *dat* **zu viel ~** to take on too much; **das hätte ich dir nie zugetraut!** I never would have expected that from you!

Zutrauen <-s> *nt kein pl* confidence (**zu** + *dat* in)

zutraulich ['tsuːtrau̯lɪç] *adj* trusting; **Hund** friendly

zu|treffen *vi irreg* ❶ (*richtig sein*) to be correct; (*wahr sein*) to be true ❷ (*anwendbar sein*) ■**auf jdn** [**nicht**] **~** to [not] apply to sb; **genau auf jdn ~** *Beschreibung* to fit sb's description] perfectly

zutreffend I. *adj* ❶ (*richtig*) correct; **Z~es bitte ankreuzen** [please] check where applicable ❷ (*anwendbar*) **eine auf jdn ~e Beschreibung** a fitting description sb II. *adv* correctly

Z

Zutritt m kein pl admission (**zu** +dat to); (Zugang) access; [**keinen**] ~ **zu etw** dat **haben** to [not] be admitted to sth; ~ **verboten!** [o **kein** ~ !] no admittance

Zutun nt **ohne jds** ~ (ohne jds Hilfe) without sb's help; (ohne jds Schuld) through no fault of sb's own

zuverlässig ['tsuː·fɛɐ̯·lɛ·sɪç] adj reliable

Zuverlässigkeit <-> f kein pl reliability

Zuversicht <-> ['tsuː·fɛɐ̯·zɪçt] f kein pl confidence

zuversichtlich adj confident

zuvor [tsu·'foːɐ̯] adv before; (zunächst) beforehand; **im Jahr** ~ the year before; **noch nie** ~ never before

zuvor|kommen vi irreg sein ① (schneller handeln) ■**jdm** ~ to beat sb to it ② (verhindern) ■**etw** dat ~ to forestall

zuvorkommend I. adj (gefällig) accommodating; (höflich) courteous II. adv (gefällig) obligingly; (höflich) courteously

Zuvorkommenheit <-> f kein pl courtesy

Zuwachs <-es, Zuwächse> ['tsuː·vaks] m increase

zu|wachsen vi irreg sein ① (überwuchert werden) to become overgrown ② (Wunde) to heal [over [or up]]

Zuwachsrate f growth rate

zuwege, zu Wege^RR [tsu·'veː·gə] adv **gut** ~ **sein** to be in good health; **etw** ~ **bringen** to achieve sth

zu|weisen vt irreg ■**jdm etw** ~ Aufgabe to assign sth to sb

zu|wenden irreg I. vt **jdm das Gesicht/den Rücken** ~ to turn one's face toward/back on sb; **etw** dat **seine Aufmerksamkeit** ~ to turn one's attention to sth II. vr **sich** akk **jdm/ etw** ~ to devote oneself to sth/sb; **wollen wir uns dem nächsten Thema** ~? shall we go on to the next topic?

Zuwendung f ① kein pl (intensive Hinwendung) love and care ② (Geld) [financial] contribution

zuwider^1 [tsu·'viː·dɐ] adv ■**jdm ist jd/**

etw ~ sb finds sb/sth unpleasant; (stärker) sb loathes sb/sth

zuwider^2 [tsu·'viː·dɐ] präp ■**etw** dat ~ contrary to sth; **allen Verboten** ~ in defiance of all bans

zu|ziehen irreg I. vt haben ① Schnur to tighten ② Gardinen to draw; Tür to pull ③ Experten, Gutachter to consult II. vr haben ① (erleiden) **sich** dat **eine Krankheit** ~ to catch a disease; **sich** dat **eine Verletzung** ~ to sustain an injury form ② (einhandeln) **sich** dat **jds Zorn** ~ to incur sb's wrath form ③ (sich eng zusammenziehen) ■**sich** akk ~ to tighten III. vi sein to move into the area

zuzüglich ['tsuː·tsyː·glɪç] präp ■~ **einer S.** gen plus sth

zwang [tsvaŋ] imp von **zwingen**

Zwang <-[e]s, Zwänge> [tsvaŋ] m ① (Gewalt) force; (Druck) pressure; **gesellschaftliche Zwänge** social constraints ② (Notwendigkeit) compulsion; **aus** ~ out of necessity

zwängen ['tsvɛŋ·ən] vt **Sachen in einen Koffer** ~ to cram things into a suitcase; **sich** akk **durch die Menge** ~ to force one's way through the crowd

zwanglos I. adj (ungezwungen) casual; (ohne Förmlichkeit) informal II. adv (ungezwungen) casually; (ohne Förmlichkeit) informally

Zwangsarbeit f kein pl hard labor

Zwangsjacke f straitjacket

Zwangslage f predicament

zwangsläufig I. adj inevitable II. adv inevitably; **dazu musste es ja** ~ **kommen** it had to happen

Zwangsräumung f eviction

Zwangsversteigerung f foreclosure sale

zwangsweise I. adj compulsory II. adv compulsorily

zwanzig ['tsvan·tsɪç] adj twenty; s. a. **achtzig 1, 2**

zwanzigjährig, 20-jährig^RR ['tsvan·tsɪç·jɛː·rɪç] adj twenty-year-old attr; twenty years old pred

zwanzigste(r, s) ['tsvan·tsɪç·stə, -stɐ, -stəs] adj ① (an zwanzigster Stelle)

Z

twentieth; *s. a.* **achte(r, s) 1** ② (*Datum*) twentieth, 20th; *s. a.* **achte(r, s) 2**

zwar [tsvaːɐ̯] *adv* (*einschränkend*) **sie ist ~ 47, sieht aber wie 30 aus** she may be 47, but she looks like 30; **das mag ~ stimmen, aber ...** that may be true, but ...; ■ **und ~** namely

Zweck <-[e]s, -e> [tsvɛk] *m* ① (*Verwendungszweck*) purpose; **ein guter ~** a good cause ② (*Absicht*) aim; **seinen ~ verfehlen** to fail to achieve its/one's object; **zu welchem ~?** for what purpose? ③ (*Sinn*) point; **das hat doch alles keinen ~!** there's no point in any of that ►WENDUNGEN: **der ~ heiligt die Mittel** (*prov*) the end justifies the means

zweckentfremden* *vt* to use for an unintended purpose

zwecklos *adj* futile

zweckmäßig *adj* ① (*geeignet*) suitable ② (*sinnvoll*) appropriate

zwecks [tsvɛks] *präp* ■ **~ einer S.** *gen* for the purpose of sth

zwei [tsvai] *adj* two; *s. a.* **acht¹**

Zweibettzimmer *nt* double room

zweideutig ['tsvai·dɔy·tɪç] I. *adj* ambiguous; (*anrüchig*) suggestive II. *adv* ambiguously; (*anrüchig*) suggestively

zweidimensional I. *adj* two-dimensional II. *adv* in two dimensions

Zweidrittelmehrheit *f* two-thirds majority

zweifach, 2fach ['tsvai·fax] I. *adj* **die ~e Menge** twice as much; **in ~er Ausfertigung** in duplicate II. *adv* **etw ~ ausfertigen** to issue sth in duplicate

Zweifamilienhaus [tsvai·fa·ˈmiː·li̯ən·haus] *nt* two-family house

Zweifel <-s, -> ['tsvai·fl̩] *m* doubt; **da habe ich meine ~!** I'm not sure about that!; **jdm kommen ~** sb begins to doubt; **es steht außer ~, dass ...** it is beyond [all] doubt that ...

zweifelhaft *adj* ① (*anzuzweifeln*) doubtful ② (*pej*) dubious

zweifellos ['tsvai·fl̩·loːs] *adv* undoubtedly

zweifeln ['tsvai·fl̩n] *vi* ■ **an jdm/etw ~**

to doubt sb/sth; ■ **[daran] ~, ob ...** to doubt whether ...

Zweifelsfall *m* ■ **im ~** if [*or* when] in doubt

Zweig <-[e]s, -e> [tsvaik] *m* ① (*Ast*) branch; (*kleiner*) twig ② (*Sparte*) branch ►WENDUNGEN: **auf keinen grünen ~ kommen** (*fam*) to get nowhere

zweigleisig ['tsvai·glai·zɪç] I. *adj* two-track *attr* II. *adv* ① on two tracks ② (*fig*) **~ fahren** to pursue a dual-track policy

Zweigstelle *f* branch office

zweihundert ['tsvai·hʊn·dɐt] *adj* two hundred

zweijährig, 2-jährig^RR *adj* ① (*Alter*) two-year-old *attr*; two years old *pred*; *s. a.* **achtjährig 1** ② (*Zeitspanne*) two-year *attr*; two years *pred*; *s. a.* **achtjährig 2**

Zweikampf *m* duel

Zweiklassengesellschaft *f* SOZIOL, POL divided society

zweimal, 2-mal^RR ['tsvai·maːl] *adv* twice, two times; **sich** *dat* **etw ~ überlegen** to think over *sep* sth carefully; *s. a.* **achtmal**

Zweirad *nt* (*Fahrrad*) bicycle; (*Motorrad*) motorcycle

zweireihig ['tsvai·rai·ɪç] *adj Anzug* double-breasted

zweischneidig ['tsvai·ʃnai·dɪç] *adj* two-edged ►WENDUNGEN: **ein ~es Schwert** a double-edged sword

zweisprachig ['tsvai·ʃpraː·xɪç] I. *adj* bilingual II. *adv* **~ erzogen sein** to be brought up speaking two languages

zweit [tsvait] *adv* **wir sind zu ~** there are two of us

zweite(r, s) ['tsvai·tə, 'tsvai·te, 'tsvai·təs] *adj* ① (*hinsichtlich der Reihenfolge*) second, 2nd; **in der ~n Klasse sein** to be in second grade ② (*bei der Datumsangabe*) 2nd; **am ~n Mai** on May 2nd ③ (*hinsichtlich des Preises, des Prestiges*) second; **ein Fahrschein ~r Klasse** a second-class ticket; *s. a.* **achte(r, s) 2**

zweitens ['tsvai·tns] *adv* secondly; (*bei Aufzählung a.*) second

zweitklassig *adj* (*pej*) second-rate

Zweitstimme *f* second vote

Zweitürer *m* two-door [car]

Zweitwohnung *f* second home

Zwerchfell ['tsvɛrç·çfɛl] *nt* diaphragm

Zwerg(in) <-[e]s, -e> [tsvɛrk] *m(f)* dwarf

Zwergwuchs *m* dwarfism

Zwetschge <-, -n> ['tsvɛtʃ·gə] *f* damson plum

Zwetschgenwasser *nt* plum brandy

zwicken ['tsvi·kn] *vt, vi* to pinch

Zwickmühle *f* ▶WENDUNGEN: **in der ~ sein** (*fam*) to be in a dilemma

Zwieback <-[e]s, -e> ['tsvi·bak] *m* zwieback

Zwiebel <-, -n> ['tsvi·bl] *f* ❶ (*Gemüse*) onion ❷ (*Blumenzwiebel*) bulb

Zwiebelturm *m* cupola

Zwielicht ['tsvi·lɪçt] *nt kein pl* twilight

zwielichtig *adj* (*pej*) dubious

Zwiespalt ['tsvi·ʃpalt] *m kein pl* conflict

zwiespältig ['tsvi·ʃpɛl·tɪç] *adj* conflicting; *Charakter* ambivalent; *Gefühle* mixed

Zwietracht <-> ['tsvi·traxt] *f kein pl* discord

Zwilling <-s, -e> ['tsvi·lɪŋ] *m* ❶ *meist pl* twin ❷ *pl* ASTROL Gemini

Zwillingsbruder *m* twin brother

Zwillingsschwester *f* twin sister

zwingen <zwang, gezwungen> ['tsvi·ŋən] I. *vt* to force; ■**gezwungen sein, etw zu tun** to be forced into doing [*or* to do] sth II. *vr* ■**sich** *akk* **zu etw** *dat* **~** to force oneself to do sth

zwingend I. *adj* urgent; *Gründe* compelling II. *adv* **sich** *akk* **~ ergeben** to follow conclusively

Zwinger <-s, -> ['tsvi·ŋə] *m* cage

zwinkern ['tsvɪŋ·kɐn] *vi* to blink; **mit einem Auge ~** to wink

Zwirn <-s, -e> [tsvɪrn] *m* thread

zwischen ['tsvɪ·ʃn] *präp* ❶ +*dat* (*räumlich: zwischen 2 Personen, Dingen*) be-

tween; (*zwischen mehreren: unter*) among[st] ❷ +*dat* (*zeitlich*) between ❸ +*dat* (*Beziehung*) **~ dir und mir** between you and me

Zwischenaufenthalt *m* stopover

Zwischenbemerkung *f* interruption

Zwischenbilanz *f* FIN interim balance

zwischendurch [tsvɪ·ʃn·'dʊrç] *adv* ❶ *zeitlich* in between times ❷ *örtlich* in between [them]

Zwischenfall *m* ❶ (*unerwartetes Ereignis*) incident ❷ *pl* (*Ausschreitungen*) serious incidents

Zwischengröße *f* in-between size

Zwischenhändler(in) *m(f)* middleman

Zwischenlandung *f* stopover

zwischenmenschlich *adj* interpersonal

Zwischenprüfung *f* ≈ qualifying exams *npl*

Zwischenraum *m* ❶ (*Lücke*) gap ❷ (*zeitlicher Intervall*) interval

Zwischenruf *m* interruption; ■**~e** heckling

Zwischenstation *f* stop; **in einer Stadt ~ machen** to stop [off] in a town

Zwischenstück *nt* connecting [*or* middle] piece

Zwischenzeit *f* ■**in der ~** [in the] meantime

zwischenzeitlich *adv* meanwhile

Zwischenzeugnis *nt* (*vorläufiges Schulzeugnis*) midterm report card

Zwist <-es, -e> [tsvɪst] *m* discord

zwitschern ['tsvɪt·ʃɐn] *vt, vi* to twitter, to chirp

Zwitter <-s, -> ['tsvɪ·tɐ] *m* hermaphrodite

zwo [tsvo:] *adj* (*fam*) two

zwölf [tsvœlf] *adj* twelve; *s. a.* **acht**[1]

Zwölffingerdarm [tsvœlf·'fɪŋɐ·darm] *m* duodenum

Zyankali <-s> [tsÿ·a:n·'ka:·li] *nt kein pl* potassium cyanide

Zyklon <-s, -e> [tsy·'klo:n] *m* cyclone

Zyklus <-, Zyklen> ['tsy:·klʊs] *m* cycle; *von Vorträgen* series

Zylinder <-s, -> [tsi·'lɪn·dɐ] *m* ❶ MATH, TECH cylinder ❷ (*Hut*) top hat

Zylinderkopf *m* cylinder head

Zyniker(in) <-s, -> ['tsyː·ni·kɐ] *m(f)*
cynic

zynisch ['tsyː·nɪʃ] I. *adj* cynical II. *adv*
cynically

Zypern ['tsyː·pɐn] *nt* Cyprus; *s. a.*
Deutschland

Zypresse <-, -n> [tsy·'prɛ·sə] *f* cypress

Zyste <-, -n> ['tsʏs·tə] *f* cyst

Aa

A <*pl* -'s>, **a** <*pl* -'s> [eɪ] *n* ❶ (*letter*) A *nt*, a *nt*; **~ as in Alpha** A wie Anton ❷ MUS A *nt*, a *nt*

a [eɪ, ə], *before vowel* **an** [æn, ən] *art indef* ❶ (*undefined*) ein(e) ❷ *after neg* ■**not ~** kein(e); **there was not ~ person to be seen** es war niemand zu sehen ❸ (*one*) ein(e); **can I have ~ knife and fork, please?** kann ich bitte Messer und Gabel haben?; **one and ~ half** eineinhalb ❹ *before profession, nationality* **she's ~ teacher** sie ist Lehrerin ❺ (*per*) **three times ~ day** dreimal täglich

aback [əˈbæk] *adv* **to be taken ~** erstaunt sein

abacus <*pl* -es> [ˈæb·ə·kəs] *n* MATH Abakus *m*

abandon [əˈbæn·dən] *vt* ❶ (*leave*) verlassen; *baby* aussetzen; **to ~ sb to his/ her fate** jdn seinem Schicksal überlassen ❷ zurücklassen; *car* stehen lassen ❸ aufgeben; *attempt* abbrechen

abandoned [əˈbæn·dənd] *adj* ❶ (*discarded*) verlassen; *baby* ausgesetzt ❷ *building* leer stehend

abashed [əˈbæʃt] *adj* verlegen

abattoir [ˈæb·ə·twar] *n* Schlachthof *m*

abbreviate [əˈbri·vi·eɪt] *vt* abkürzen

abbreviation [ə‧bri‧viˈeɪ‧ʃən] *n* Abkürzung *f*

ABC [ˌeɪ·biˈsi] *n* (*alphabet*) ABC *nt;* **as easy as ~** kinderleicht

abdicate [ˈæb·dɪ·keɪt] *vi monarch* abdanken

abdomen [ˈæb·də·mən] *n* MED Unterleib *m*

abduction [æbˈdʌk·ʃən] *n* Entführung *f*

aberration [ˌæb·əˈreɪ·ʃən] *n* (*deviation*) Abweichung *f*

abeyance [əˈbeɪ·əns] *n* **in ~** [vorübergehend] außer Kraft [gesetzt]

abhorrent [æbˈhɔr·ənt] *adj* abscheulich

abide [əˈbaɪd] *vt* <abode *or* abided, abode *or* abided> *usu neg* (*not like*) ausstehen

◆**abide by** *vt rules* befolgen; **to ~ by the law** sich an das Gesetz halten

ability [əˈbɪl·ɪ·ti] *n* (*capability*) Fähigkeit *f;* **to the best of my ~** so gut ich kann

ablaze [əˈbleɪz] *adj* ❶ (*burning*) ■**to be ~** in Flammen stehen ❷ (*fig: impassioned*) **to be ~ with anger** vor Zorn glühen

able [ˈeɪ·bəl] *adj* <more *or* better ~, most *or* best ~> (*can do*) ■**to [not] be ~ to do sth** etw [nicht] tun können

able-bodied [ˌeɪ·bəlˈbad·ɪd] *adj* gesund

ABM [eɪ·biˈem] *n abbrev of* **antiballistic missile** Antiraketenrakete *f*

abnormal [æbˈnɔr·məl] *adj* anormal; *weather* a. ungewöhnlich

abnormality [ˌæb·nɔrˈmæl·ɪ·ti] *n* ❶ MED Anomalie *f* ❷ (*unusualness*) Abnormität *f*

aboard [əˈbɔrd] *adv, prep* (*on plane, ship*) an Bord; (*on train*) im Zug

abode [əˈboʊd] *n* ❶ (*hum: home*) Wohnung *f* ❷**of no fixed ~** ohne festen Wohnsitz

abolish [əˈbal·ɪʃ] *vt* abschaffen; *law* aufheben

abolition [ˌæb·əˈlɪʃ·ən] *n* Abschaffung *f; of a law* Aufhebung *f*

abominable [əˈbam·ə·nə·bəl] *adj* furchtbar

abomination [əˌbam·əˈneɪ·ʃən] *n* (*loathing*) Abscheu *m*

abort [əˈbɔrt] *vt baby, fetus* abtreiben; *pregnancy* abbrechen

abortion [əˈbɔr·ʃən] *n* Abtreibung *f*

abortive [əˈbɔr·tɪv] *adj attempt* gescheitert; *plan* misslungen

about [əˈbaʊt] **I.** *prep* ❶ (*on the subject of*) über +*akk;* **anxiety ~ the future**

A

Angst *f* vor der Zukunft; **to ask sb ~ sth/sb** jdn nach etw/jdm fragen ❷ (*affecting*) gegen +*akk;* **to do something ~ sth** etw gegen etw machen ❸ *after vb* (*expressing movement*) **to wander ~ the house** im Haus herumlaufen ▶PHRASES: **how** ~ sb/sth? wie wäre es mit jdm/etw?; **what** ~ it? was ist damit? II. *adv* ❶ (*approximately*) ungefähr; ~ **eight** [**o'clock**] [so] gegen acht [Uhr] ❷ (*almost*) fast ❸ (*intending*) **we're just ~ to have supper** wir wollen gerade zu Abend essen ▶PHRASES: **that's ~ all** [*or* **it**] das wär's

about-'face *n* ❶ *esp* MIL. Kehrtwendung *f* ❷ (*fig*) **they've done a complete** ~ sie haben ihre Meinung um 180° geändert

above [ə·'bʌv] I. *prep* ❶ (*over*) über +*dat* ❷ (*greater than*) über +*akk;* **to be barely** ~ **freezing** kaum über dem Gefrierpunkt sein ❸ (*more importantly than*) **they value freedom** ~ **all else** für sie ist die Freiheit wichtiger als alles andere; ~ **all** vor allem II. *adv* ❶ (*on higher level*) oberhalb, darüber; **they live in the apartment** ~ sie wohnen in der Wohnung darüber ❷ (*overhead*) **from** ~ von oben ❸ (*earlier in text*) oben III. *adj* obige(r, s); **the** ~ **address** die oben genannte Adresse

above'board *adj* (*fam*) einwandfrei

above'mentioned *adj* oben genannte(r, s)

abracadabra [ˌæb·rə·kə·'dæb·rə] *interj* (*fam*) Simsalabim!

abrasion [ə·'breɪ·ʒən] *n* (*injury*) Abschürfung *f*

abrasive [ə·'breɪ·sɪv] I. *adj* abreibend; ~ **cleaner** Scheuermittel *nt* II. *n* MECH Schleifmittel *nt*

abreast [ə·'brest] *adv* ❶ (*side by side*) nebeneinander ❷ (*up to date*) **to keep** ~ **of sth** sich über etw *akk* auf dem Laufenden halten

abridge [ə·'brɪdʒ] *vt* kürzen

abroad [ə·'brɔd] *adv* (*in foreign country*) im Ausland; **to go** ~ ins Ausland fahren

abrupt [ə·'brʌpt] *adj* ❶ (*sudden*) abrupt; *departure* plötzlich ❷ (*brusque*) schroff

ABS [ˌeɪ·bi·'es] *n abbrev of* **antilock braking system** ABS *nt*

abscess <*pl* -es> ['æb·ses] *n* Abszess *m*

absence ['æb·səns] *n* ❶ (*nonappearance*) Abwesenheit *f;* (*from school, work*) Fehlen *nt* ❷ (*lack*) Fehlen *nt;* ■**in the** ~ **of sth** in Ermangelung einer S. *gen*

absent I. *adj* ['æb·sənt] ❶ (*not there*) abwesend; **to be** ~ **from work/school** auf der Arbeit/in der Schule fehlen ❷ (*lacking*) ■**to be** ~ fehlen II. *vt* [əb·'sent] ■**to** ~ **oneself** sich zurückziehen

absentee [ˌæb·sən·'ti] *n* Abwesende(r) *f(m)*, Fehlende(r) *f(m)*

absenteeism [ˌæb·sən·'ti·ɪz·əm] *n* häufiges Fernbleiben

absent-'minded *adj* (*momentarily*) geistesabwesend; (*habitually*) zerstreut

absent-mindedness *n* (*momentary*) Geistesabwesenheit *f;* (*habitual*) Zerstreutheit *f*

absolute ['æb·sə·lut] *adj* ❶ absolut ❷ *angel* wahr; *disaster* einzig; *ruler* unumschränkt

absolutely [ˌæb·sə·'lut·li] *adv* absolut; ~ **not!** nein, überhaupt nicht!; ~ **delicious** einfach köstlich; ~ **nothing** überhaupt nichts

absorb [əb·'sɔrb] *vt* ❶ (*soak up*) aufnehmen ❷ *blow* abfangen; *light* absorbieren; *noise* dämpfen ❸ ■**to be** ~**ed in sth** in etw *akk* vertieft sein

absorbent [əb·'sɔr·bənt] *adj* absorptionsfähig; *cotton, paper* saugfähig

absorbing [əb·'sɔr·bɪŋ] *adj* fesselnd; *problem* kniffelig

absorption [əb·'sɔrp·ʃən] *n* Aufnahme *f*

abstain [əb·'steɪn] *vi* ■**to** ~ [**from sth**] sich [einer S. *gen*] enthalten

abstinence ['æb·stə·nəns] *n* Abstinenz *f*

abstract I. *adj* ['æb·strækt] abstrakt; ~ **noun** Abstraktum *nt* II. *n* ❶ (*summary*) Zusammenfassung *f* ❷ (*generalized form*) ■**the** ~ das Abstrakte

A

abstraction [əb·ˈstræk·ʃən] *n* Abstraktion *f*

absurd [əb·ˈsɜrd] *adj* absurd; **to look ~** lächerlich aussehen

abundance [əb·ˈbʌn·dəns] *n* Fülle *f;* **in ~** in Hülle und Fülle

abundant [əb·ˈbʌn·dənt] *adj* reichlich; *harvest* reich

abuse **I.** *n* [ə·ˈbjus] ❶ *(affront)* [**verbal**] ~ Beschimpfung[en] *f(pl);* **a term of ~** ein Schimpfwort ❷ *(mistreatment, misuse)* Missbrauch *m;* **child ~** Kindesmissbrauch *m* **II.** *vt* [ə·ˈbjuz] ❶ *(verbally)* beschimpfen ❷ *(maltreat, exploit)* missbrauchen

abusive [ə·ˈbju·sɪv] *adj* ❶ *(insulting)* beleidigend ❷ *(mistreating)* misshandelnd

abysmal [ə·ˈbɪz·məl] *adj* entsetzlich

abyss [ə·ˈbɪs] *n (a. fig)* Abgrund *m*

AC [ˌeɪ·ˈsi] *n* ❶ *abbrev of* **air conditioning** ❷ *abbrev of* **alternating current** WS

academic [ˌæk·ə·ˈdem·ɪk] *adj* akademisch; **~ year** Studienjahr *nt*

academy [ə·ˈkæd·ə·mi] *n* Akademie *f*

accelerate [ək·ˈsel·ə·reɪt] *vt, vi* beschleunigen

acceleration [ək·sel·ə·ˈreɪ·ʃən] *n* Beschleunigung *f*

accelerator [ək·ˈsel·ə·reɪ·tər] *n (in car)* Gas[pedal] *nt*

accent [ˈæk·sent] *n* ❶ LING Akzent *m* ❷ *(stress)* Betonung *f;* **to put the ~ on sth** etw in den Mittelpunkt stellen

accentuate [ək·ˈsen·tʃu·eɪt] *vt* betonen

accept [ək·ˈsept] *vt* ❶ *(take)* annehmen; *award* entgegennehmen; *bribe* sich bestechen lassen ❷ *(acknowledge)* anerkennen; *blame* auf sich *akk* nehmen; *decision* akzeptieren

acceptable [ək·ˈsep·tə·bəl] *adj (satisfactory)* akzeptabel **(to** für +*akk*)

acceptance [ək·ˈsep·təns] *n* ❶ *(accepting)* Annahme *f; of idea* Zustimmung *f* ❷ *(recognition)* Anerkennung *f*

accepted [ək·ˈsep·tɪd] *adj* anerkannt

access [ˈæk·ses] **I.** *n* Zugang *m;* (*to* *information)* Zugriff *m* **II.** *vt* COMPUT *data* zugreifen auf +*akk*

accessibility [æk·ˌses·ə·ˈbɪl·ɪ·ti] *n* Zugänglichkeit *f*

accessible [ək·ˈses·ə·bəl] *adj* ❶ *(approachable)* [leicht] erreichbar ❷ ■**to be ~ to sb** jdm zugänglich sein

accessory [ək·ˈses·ə·ri] *n* ❶ FASHION Accessoire *nt* ❷ *(equipment)* Zubehör *nt* ❸ *(criminal)* Helfershelfer(in) *m(f)*

accident [ˈæk·sɪ·dənt] *n* ❶ *(with injury)* Unfall *m;* **car ~** Verkehrsunfall *m* ❷ *(chance)* Zufall *m;* **by ~** zufällig

accidental [ˌæk·sɪ·ˈden·təl] *adj* ❶ *(unintentional)* unbeabsichtigt ❷ *(chance)* zufällig

acclimate [ˈə·klaɪ·mɪt] *vt, vi* sich akklimatisieren (**to** an +*akk*); **to new conditions** sich gewöhnen

acclimation [ˌæk·lə·ˈmeɪ·ʃən], **acclimatization** [ə·ˌklaɪ·mə·tɪ·ˈzeɪ·ʃən] *n* Akklimatisation *f*

acclimatize [ə·ˈklaɪ·mə·taɪz] *vt, vi see* **acclimate**

accommodate [ə·ˈkam·ə·deɪt] *vt (have room for)* unterbringen

accommodation [ə·ˌkam·ə·ˈdeɪ·ʃən] *n* *(lodging)* ■ **~s** *pl* Unterkunft *f*

accompaniment [ə·ˈkʌm·pə·nɪ·mənt] *n* Begleitung *f;* **to be the perfect ~ to …** ideal passen zu …

accompanist [ə·ˈkʌm·pə·nɪst] *n* MUS Begleiter(in) *m(f)*

accompany <-ie-> [ə·ˈkʌm·pə·ni] *vt* begleiten

accomplice [ə·ˈkam·plɪs] *n* Komplize *m,* Komplizin *f*

accomplish [ə·ˈkam·plɪʃ] *vt* schaffen; *goal* erreichen

accomplished [ə·ˈkam·plɪʃt] *adj* fähig; *actor* versiert

accomplishment [ə·ˈkam·plɪʃ·mənt] *n* ❶ Vollendung *f* ❷ *usu pl (skill)* Fähigkeit *f*

accord [ə·ˈkɔrd] *n (treaty)* Vereinbarung *f* ▸PHRASES: **of one's/its own ~** *(voluntarily)* von sich *dat* aus; *(without external cause)* von alleine

A

accordance [ə·ˈkɔr·dəns] *prep* **in ~ with** gemäß +*dat*

accordingly [ə·ˈkɔr·dɪŋ·li] *adv* (*appropriately*) [dem]entsprechend

according to [ə·ˈkɔr·dɪŋ·tə] *prep* nach +*dat*

accordion [ə·ˈkɔr·di·ən] *n* Akkordeon *nt*

account [ə·ˈkaʊnt] *n* ① (*description*) Bericht *m;* **by** [*or* **from**] **all ~s** nach allem, was man so hört ② (*at bank*) Konto *nt* ③ (*bill*) Rechnung *f* ④ (*records*) **■ ~s** *pl* [Geschäfts]bücher *pl* ⑤ (*reason*) **■ on ~ of** aufgrund +*gen;* **on my ~** meinetwegen ⑥ (*importance*) **to be of no ~** keinerlei Bedeutung haben ▶PHRASES: **to settle ~s with sb** mit jdm abrechnen

◆ **account for** *vt* (*explain*) erklären

accountability [ə·ˌkaʊn·tə·ˈbɪl·ɪ·ti] *n* Verantwortlichkeit *f*

accountable [ə·ˈkaʊn·tə·bəl] *adj* verantwortlich

accountant [ə·ˈkaʊn·tənt] *n* [Bilanz]buchhalter(in) *m(f)*

accredit [ə·ˈkred·ɪt] *vt* ① (*approve*) **■ to have been ~ed** *degree, school* anerkannt worden sein ② (*authorize*) **■ to be ~ed to sb/sth** *ambassador* bei jdm/etw akkreditiert sein

acct. *n abbrev of* **account** Kto.

accumulate [ə·ˈkjum·jə·leɪt] *vt, vi* [sich] ansammeln

accuracy [ˈæk·jər·ə·si] *n* Genauigkeit *f*

accurate [ˈæk·jər·ɪt] *adj* genau

accusation [ˌæk·ju·ˈzeɪ·ʃən] *n* ① (*charge*) Anschuldigung *f;* LAW Anklage *f* ② (*accusing*) Vorwurf *m*

accusative [ə·ˈkju·zə·tɪv] *n* **~ [case]** Akkusativ *m*

accuse [ə·ˈkjuz] *vt* ① (*charge*) **■ to ~ sb [of sth]** jdn (wegen einer S. *gen*) anklagen ② (*claim*) **■ to ~ sb of sth** jdn einer S. *gen* beschuldigen

accused <*pl* -> [ə·ˈkjuzd] *n* **■ the ~** die/der Angeklagte

accustomed [ə·ˈkʌs·təmd] *adj* **■ to be ~ to sth** etw gewohnt sein

AC/DC [ˌeɪ·si·ˈdi·si] I. *n abbrev of* **alter-**nating current/direct current WS/GS II. *adj* (*sl: bisexual*) bi *fam*

ace [eɪs] I. *n* Ass *nt* II. *adj* (*fam*) klasse III. *vt* (*fam*) **to ~ a test** einen Test mit Leichtigkeit bestehen

acetic 'acid *n* Essigsäure *f*

ache [eɪk] I. *n* (*pain*) Schmerz[en] *m[pl]* II. *vi* (*feel pain*) schmerzen

achieve [ə·ˈtʃiv] *vt* erreichen; *fame* erlangen; *success* erzielen

achievement [ə·ˈtʃiv·mənt] *n* Leistung *f*

acid [ˈæs·ɪd] I. *n* ① CHEM Säure *f* ② (*sl: LSD*) Acid *nt sl* II. *adj* sauer

acid 'rain *n* saurer Regen

'acid test *n* (*fig*) Feuerprobe *f*

acknowledge [ək·ˈnɑl·ɪdʒ] *vt* ① (*admit*) zugeben ② (*respect*) anerkennen ③ *greeting* erwidern; *receipt* bestätigen

acne [ˈæk·ni] *n* Akne *f*

acorn [ˈeɪ·kɔrn] *n* Eichel *f*

acoustic [ə·ˈku·stɪk] *adj* akustisch

acoustic gui'tar *n* Akustikgitarre *f*

acoustics [ə·ˈku·stɪks] *n* Akustik *f*

acquaint [ə·ˈkweɪnt] *vt* vertraut machen

acquaintance [ə·ˈkweɪn·təns] *n* Bekannte(r) *f(m)*

acquiesce [ˌæk·wi·ˈes] *vi* **■ to ~ [to sth]** [in etw *akk*] einwilligen

acquire [ə·ˈkwaɪr] *vt* erwerben; *reputation* bekommen

acquisition [ˌæk·wɪ·ˈzɪʃ·ən] *n* ① (*purchase*) Anschaffung *f* ② (*acquiring*) Erwerb *m; of company* Übernahme *f*

acquit <-tt-> [ə·ˈkwɪt] *vt* freisprechen

acquittal [ə·ˈkwɪt·əl] *n* Freispruch *m*

acre [ˈeɪ·kər] *n* (*unit*) ≈ Morgen *m*

acrid [ˈæk·rɪd] *adj smell* stechend; *smoke* beißend

acrobat [ˈæk·rə·bæt] *n* Akrobat(in) *m(f)*

acrobatic [ˌæk·rə·ˈbæt·ɪk] *adj* akrobatisch

acronym [ˈæk·rə·nɪm] *n* Akronym *nt*

across [ə·ˈkrɔs] I. *prep* ① (*on other side of*) über +*dat;* **~ town** am anderen Ende der Stadt ② (*from one side to other*) über +*akk* ▶PHRASES: **~ the board** allgemein II. *adv* ① (*to other side*) hinüber; (*from other side*) herüber ② (*on other side*) drüben; **~ from sb/sth** jdm/etw gegenüber ❸ *(wide)* breit ▸PHRASES: **to get one's point** ~ sich verständlich machen

act [ækt] **I.** n ❶ *(deed)* Tat f; ~ **of kindness** Akt m der Güte ❷ *(of a play)* Akt m ❸ *(pretence)* Schau f ▸PHRASES: **to get in on the** ~ mitmischen; **to get one's** ~ **together** sich am Riemen reißen **II.** vi ❶ *(take action)* handeln; **to** ~ [**up**]**on sb's advice** jds Rat befolgen ❷ *(represent)* ■**to** ~ **for sb** jdn vertreten ❸ *(behave)* sich benehmen ❹ *(play)* spielen
  ◆ **act out** vt *(realize)* ausleben
  ◆ **act up** vt *(fam)* ❶ *person* Theater machen ❷ *thing* Ärger machen

acting ['æk·tɪŋ] adj stellvertretend

action ['æk·ʃən] n ❶ *(activeness)* Handeln nt; *course of* ~ Vorgehensweise f; **to put into** ~ in die Tat umsetzen ❷ *(act)* Handlung f, Tat f ❸ *(combat)* Einsatz m; **to go into** ~ ins Gefecht ziehen; **to be killed in** ~ fallen ▸PHRASES: **to want a piece of the** ~ eine Scheibe vom Kuchen abhaben wollen

'**action-packed** adj spannungsgeladen

activate ['æk·tə·veɪt] vt aktivieren; *alarm* auslösen

active ['æk·tɪv] adj aktiv; *children* lebhaft

activist ['æk·tə·vɪst] n Aktivist(in) m(f)

activity [æk·'tɪv·ɪ·t̬i] n Aktivität f

actor ['æk·tər] n Schauspieler m

actress <pl -es> ['æk·trɪs] n Schauspielerin f

actual ['æk·tʃʊ·əl] adj *(real)* eigentlich; *facts* konkret; **in** ~ **fact** tatsächlich

actually ['æk·tʃʊ·ə·li] adv ❶ *(in fact)* eigentlich ❷ *(really)* wirklich; **did you** ~ **say that?** hast du das tatsächlich gesagt?

actuate ['æk·tʃʊ·eɪt] vt in Gang setzen

acupuncture ['æk·jʊ·pʌŋk·tʃər] n Akupunktur f

acute [ə·'kjut] adj ❶ *(serious)* akut; *anxiety* ernsthaft ❷ *hearing* fein; *sense of smell* ausgeprägt ❸ *angle* spitz

acutely [ə·'kjut·li] adv äußerst

ad [æd] n *(fam)* short for **advertisement** Anzeige f

AD [ˌeɪ·'di] adj abbrev of **anno Domini** n. Chr.

Adam's 'apple n Adamsapfel m

adapt [ə·'dæpt] **I.** vt ❶ *(modify)* anpassen *(to* an +akk) ❷ *(rewrite)* bearbeiten **II.** vi ■**to** ~ [**to sth**] sich [einer S. dat] anpassen

adaptable [ə·'dæp·tə·bəl] adj anpassungsfähig

adaptation [ˌæd·æp·'teɪ·ʃən] n ❶ *(adapting)* Anpassung f ❷ *(modification)* Umbau m

adapter, **adaptor** [ə·'dæp·tər] n ELEC Adapter m

add [æd] vt ❶ hinzufügen ❷ MATH ■**to** ~ [**together**] addieren; ■**to** ~ **sth to sth** etw zu etw dat [dazu]addieren
  ◆ **add up I.** vi ❶ *(fam: make sense)* **it doesn't** ~ **up** es macht keinen Sinn ❷ *(total)* ■**to** ~ **up to sth** *bill* sich auf etw akk belaufen **II.** vt addieren

adder ['æd·ər] n Otter f

addict ['æd·ɪkt] n Süchtige(r) f(m); **drug** ~ Drogenabhängige(r) f(m)

addicted [ə·'dɪk·tɪd] adj süchtig *(to* nach +dat)

addiction [ə·'dɪk·ʃən] n Sucht f

addictive [ə·'dɪk·tɪv] adj süchtig

addition [ə·'dɪʃ·ən] n ❶ MATH Addition f ❷ *(extra)* Ergänzung f ❸ ■**in** ~ außerdem

additional [ə·'dɪʃ·ən·əl] adj zusätzlich; ~ **charge** Aufpreis m, Zuschlag m

additionally [ə·'dɪʃ·ən·əl·i] adv außerdem

additive ['æd·ɪ·t̬ɪv] n Zusatz m

address ['æd·res] **I.** n <pl -es> Adresse f **II.** vt ❶ *(write address)* adressieren *(to* an +akk) ❷ *(speak to)* anreden

addressee [ˌæd·re·'si] n Empfänger(in) m(f)

adept [ə·'dept] adj geschickt *(at* in +dat)

adequacy ['æd·ɪ·kwə·si] n Angemessenheit f

adequate ['æd·ɪ·kwət] adj ausreichend

adhere [æd·'hɪr] vi kleben *(to* an +akk)

A

adhesive [æd·'hi·sɪv] I. adj haftend II. n Klebstoff m

adjacent [ə·'dʒeɪ·sənt] adj angrenzend

adjectival [ˌædʒ·ɪk·'taɪ·vəl] adj adjektivisch

adjective ['ædʒ·ɪk·tɪv] n Adjektiv nt

adjoining [ə·'dʒɔɪ·nɪŋ] adj angrenzend

adjourn [ə·'dʒɜrn] I. vt (interrupt) unterbrechen; (suspend) verschieben II. vi (stop temporarily) eine Pause einlegen

adjust [ə·'dʒʌst] I. vt (set) [richtig] einstellen II. vi (adapt) ■to ~ to sth sich an etw akk anpassen

adjustable [ə·'dʒʌst·ə·bəl] adj verstellbar

adjustment [ə·'dʒʌst·mənt] n ❶ (mental) Anpassung f ❷ (mechanical) Einstellung f

ad-lib <-bb-> [ˌæd·'lɪb] vt, vi improvisieren

admin ['æd·mɪn] n (fam) ❶ short for **administration** Verwaltung f ❷ COMPUT short for **administrator** Administrator(in) m(f)

administration [æd·ˌmɪn·ɪ·'streɪ·ʃən] n ❶ Verwaltung f ❷ (government) Regierung f

administrative [æd·'mɪn·ɪ·streɪ·tɪv] adj administrativ, Verwaltungs-

administrator [æd·'mɪn·ɪ·streɪ·tər] n Verwaltungsbeamte(r) m/-beamtin f

admirable ['æd·mər·ə·bəl] adj bewundernswert

admiral ['æd·mər·əl] n Admiral(in) m(f)

admiration [ˌæd·mə·'reɪ·ʃən] n Bewunderung f

admire [əd·'maɪr] vt bewundern

admirer [əd·'maɪr·ər] n Anhänger(in) m(f)

admissible [æd·'mɪs·ə·bəl] adj zulässig

admission [æd·'mɪʃ·ən] n ❶ Zutritt m; (into a hospital) Einlieferung f ❷ (entrance fee) Eintritt[spreis] m

admit <-tt-> [əd·'mɪt] vt ❶ (acknowledge) zugeben ❷ (allow entrance) hereinlassen/hineinlassen; ■to ~ sb to the hospital jdn ins Krankenhaus einliefern

admittance [æd·'mɪt·əns] n Zutritt m; "no ~" „Betreten verboten"

admittedly [æd·'mɪt·ɪd·li] adv zugegebenermaßen

adolescence [ˌæd·əl·'es·əns] n Jugend[zeit] f

adolescent [ˌæd·əl·'es·ənt] I. adj heranwachsend, jugendlich II. n Jugendliche(r) f(m)

adopt [ə·'dapt] vt ❶ (raise) adoptieren ❷ (put into practice) annehmen; strategy verfolgen

adoption [ə·'dap·ʃən] n ❶ Adoption f ❷ (taking on) Annahme f; of a technology Übernahme f

adorable [ə·'dɔr·ə·bəl] adj entzückend

adore [ə·'dɔr] vt ❶ (love) über alles lieben ❷ (like very much) to ~ sth etw wunderbar finden

adoring [ə·'dɔr·ɪŋ] adj (devoted) hingebungsvoll

adorn [ə·'dɔrn] vt schmücken

adrenalin(e) [ə·'dren·ə·lɪn] n Adrenalin nt

adrift [ə·'drɪft] adv to cut ~ losmachen

adroit [ə·'drɔɪt] adj geschickt

adult [ə·'dʌlt] I. n Erwachsene(r) f(m) II. adj (grown-up) erwachsen; animal ausgewachsen; behavior reif

adult edu'cation n Erwachsenenbildung f

adultery [ə·'dʌl·tə·ri] n Ehebruch m

advance [əd·'væns] I. vi ❶ (make progress) Fortschritte machen ❷ (move forward) sich vorwärtsbewegen; MIL vorrücken II. vt ❶ career vorantreiben ❷ money vorschießen III. n ❶ (progress) Fortschritt m ❷ (ahead of time) in ~ im Voraus IV. adj vorherig

advanced [əd·'vænst] adj ❶ (in skills) fortgeschritten ❷ (in development) fortschrittlich

advancement [əd·'væns·mənt] n ❶ (furtherance) Förderung f ❷ (in career) Aufstieg m

advance 'notice n Vorankündigung f

advantage [əd·'væn·tɪdʒ] n Vorteil m; to take ~ of sb (pej) jdn ausnutzen

advent ['æd·vənt] n REL ■A~ Advent m

adventure [æd·'ven·tʃər] *n* Abenteuer *nt*

adventurous [əd·'ven·tʃər·əs] *adj* (*daring*) abenteuerlustig

adverb ['æd·vɜrb] *n* Adverb *nt*

adverbial [æd·'vɜr·bi·əl] *adj* adverbial

adverse [æd·'vɜrs] *adj* ungünstig; *criticism, effect* negativ

advertise [æd·vər·taɪz] I. *vt* Werbung machen für +*akk*; (*in a newspaper*) inserieren II. *vi* ❶ (*publicize*) werben ❷ (*in a newspaper*) inserieren

advertisement [ˌæd·vər·'taɪz·mənt] *n* Werbung *f*; (*in a newspaper*) Anzeige *f*; **TV ~** Werbespot *m*; (*fig*) Reklame *f*

advertising ['æd·vər·ˌtaɪ·zɪŋ] *n* Werbung *f*

'advertising agency *n* Werbeagentur *f*

'advertising campaign *n* Werbekampagne *f*

advice [əd·'vaɪs] *n* (*recommendation*) Rat *m*; **some ~** ein Rat[schlag] *m*; **to take sb's ~** jds Rat[schlag] *m* befolgen

advisable [əd·'vaɪ·zə·bəl] *adj* ratsam

advise [əd·'vaɪz] I. *vt* beraten; ■ **to ~ sb to do sth** jdm [dazu] raten, etw zu tun II. *vi* raten

adviser, advisor [əd·'vaɪ·zər] *n* Berater(in) *m(f)*

advisory [æd·'vaɪ·zə·ri] *adj* beratend

aerate ['er·eɪt] *vt* durchlüften; *soil* auflockern

aerial ['er·i·əl] I. *adj* Luft- II. *n* Antenne *f*

aerobatics [ˌer·ə·'bæt̬·ɪks] *n* + *sing vb* Kunstflug *m*

aerobics [ə·'roʊ·bɪks] *n* (*exercise*) Aerobic *nt*

aerodynamic [ˌer·oʊ·daɪ·'næm·ɪk] *adj* aerodynamisch

aerodynamics [ˌer·oʊ·daɪ·'næm·ɪks] *n* Aerodynamik *f*

aeronautics [ˌer·ə·'nɔ·t̬ɪks] *n* + *sing vb* Luftfahrt[technik] *f*

aerosol ['er·ə·sɔl] *n* Spraydose *f*

aesthetic [es·'θet̬·ɪk] *adj* ästhetisch

afar [ə·'far] *adv* **from ~** aus der Ferne

affair [ə·'fer] *n* ❶ (*matter, event*) Angelegenheit *f* ❷ (*situation, relationship*) Affäre *f*

affect [ə·'fekt] *vt* ■ **to ~ sb/sth** sich auf jdn/etw auswirken; (*concern*) jdn/etw betreffen

affected [ə·'fek·tɪd] *adj* ❶ (*insincere*) affektiert ❷ (*influenced*) betroffen

affection [ə·'fek·ʃən] *n* Zuneigung *f*

affectionate [ə·'fek·ʃə·nɪt] *adj* liebevoll

affiliate [ə·'fɪl·i·eɪt] *n* Konzernunternehmen *nt*

affiliation [ə·ˌfɪl·i·'eɪ·ʃən] *n* Angliederung *f*

affirmative [ə·'fɜr·mə·t̬ɪv] I. *adj* zustimmend; *answer* positiv II. *n* Bejahung *f*; **to answer in the ~** mit Ja antworten III. *interj* **~!** jawohl!

affix [ə·'fɪks] *vt* (*attach*) befestigen (**to** an +*dat*); (*stick on*) ankleben (**to** an +*akk*)

afflict [ə·'flɪkt] *vt* plagen

affluence ['æf·lu·əns] *n* Wohlstand *m*

affluent ['æf·lu·ənt] *adj* reich

afford [ə·'fɔrd] *vt* (*have money, time for*) sich *dat* leisten; **you can't ~ to miss this opportunity** diese Gelegenheit darfst du dir nicht entgehen lassen

affordable [ə·'fɔr·də·bəl] *adj* erschwinglich

Afghan ['æf·gæn] I. *n* ❶ (*person*) Afghane *m*, Afghanin *f* ❷ (*dog*) Afghane *m* II. *adj* afghanisch

Afghanistan [æf·'gæn·ɪ·stæn] *n* Afghanistan *nt*

afloat [ə·'floʊt] *adj* (*a. fig*) über Wasser; ■ **to be ~** schwimmen

afraid [ə·'freɪd] *adj* ❶ (*frightened*) verängstigt; **to be ~ [of sb/sth]** Angst haben [vor jdm/etw]; **to be ~ that ...** befürchten, dass ... ❷ (*expressing regret*) **I'm ~ so** leider ja

Africa ['æf·rɪ·kə] *n* Afrika *nt*

African ['æf·rɪ·kən] I. *n* Afrikaner(in) *m(f)* II. *adj* afrikanisch

African American [ˌæf·rɪ·kən·ə·'mer·ɪ·kən], **Afro-American** [ˌæf·roʊ·ə·'mer·ɪ·kən] *n* Afroamerikaner(in) *m(f)*

after ['æf·tər] I. *prep* ❶ (*later time*) nach +*dat*; **~ lunch** nach dem Mittagessen; **[a] quarter ~ six** [um] Viertel nach Sechs ❷ (*following*) nach +*dat* ❸ **~ all**

A

schließlich; (*in spite of*) trotz +*gen*; **he couldn't come ~ all** er konnte doch nicht kommen II. *adv* danach; **shortly ~** kurz darauf

'after·ef·fect *n* Nachwirkung *f*

'after·math [-mæθ] *n* Folgen *pl*

after·noon [ˌæf·tər·'nun] *n* Nachmittag *m;* **good ~!** guten Tag!; **late ~** am späten Nachmittag; **in the ~** am Nachmittag, nachmittags

'after·shave *n* Aftershave *nt*

'after·shock *n usu pl* GEOL Nachbeben *nt*

'after·taste *n* Nachgeschmack *m*

'after·thought *n* **as an ~** im Nachhinein

after·ward, after·wards ['æf·tər·wərdz] *adv* (*later*) später; **shortly ~** kurz danach

again [ə·'gen] *adv* ❶ (*as a repetition*) wieder; (*one more time*) noch einmal; **~ and ~** immer wieder ❷ (*anew*) noch einmal

against [ə·'genst] I. *prep* gegen +*akk;* **~ one's better judgment** wider besseres Wissen II. *adv* gegen; **only 14 voted ~** es gab nur 14 Gegenstimmen

age [eɪdʒ] I. *n* ❶ (*length of existence*) Alter *nt;* **he's about your ~** er ist ungefähr so alt wie du; **to be 45 years of ~** 45 [Jahre alt] sein; **sb looks their ~** man sieht jdm sein Alter an ❷ (*era*) Zeitalter *nt* ❸ (*long time*) **■an ~** eine Ewigkeit; **the meeting took ~s** die Besprechung dauerte ewig [lang] II. *vi* altern III. *vt* (*make look older*) älter machen

'age bracket *n* Altersgruppe *f*

aged¹ [eɪdʒd] *adj* **children ~ 8 to 12** Kinder [im Alter] von 8 bis 12 Jahren

aged² ['eɪ·dʒɪd] *adj* (*old*) alt

'age group *n* Altersgruppe *f*

'age lim·it *n* Altersgrenze *f*

agen·cy ['eɪ·dʒən·si] *n* ❶ (*private business*) Agentur *f* ❷ (*of government*) Behörde *f*

agen·da [ə·'dʒen·də] *n* Tagesordnung *f*

agent ['eɪ·dʒənt] *n* Agent(in) *m(f)*

ag·gra·vate ['æg·rə·veɪt] *vt* ❶ (*worsen*) verschlechtern ❷ (*fam: annoy*) auf die Nerven gehen

ag·gra·vat·ing ['æg·rə·veɪ·t̬ɪŋ] *adj* (*fam: annoying*) ärgerlich

ag·gre·gate ['æg·rɪ·gɪt] *adj* Gesamt·

ag·gres·sion [ə·'greʃ·ən] *n* Aggression *f;* **act of ~** Angriffshandlung *f*

ag·gres·sive [ə·'gres·ɪv] *adj* aggressiv; *salesman* aufdringlich

ag·ile ['æ·dʒəl] *adj* geschickt; *fingers* flink; *mind* rege

agil·i·ty [ə·'dʒɪl·ɪ·t̬i] *n* Flinkheit *f*

ag·ing ['eɪ·dʒɪŋ] *adj person* alternd; *machinery* veraltend

ag·i·tate ['æ·dʒɪ·teɪt] *vt* ❶ (*make nervous*) aufregen ❷ (*shake*) schütteln

ag·i·ta·tion [ˌæ·dʒɪ·'teɪ·ʃən] *n* Aufregung *f*

ag·i·ta·tor ['æ·dʒɪ·teɪ·t̬ər] *n* Agitator(in) *m(f)*

ag·nos·tic [æg·'nɑs·tɪk] *n* Agnostiker(in) *m(f)*

ago [ə·'goʊ] *adv* **a year ~** vor einem Jahr; [**not**] **long ~** vor [nicht] langer Zeit

ago·nize ['æg·ə·naɪz] *vi* **■to ~ about** [*or* **over**] **sth** sich über etw *akk* den Kopf zermartern

ago·niz·ing ['æg·ə·naɪ·zɪŋ] *adj pain* unerträglich

ago·ny ['æg·ə·ni] *n* Todesqualen *pl;* **■to be in ~** große Schmerzen leiden

agree [ə·'gri] I. *vi* ❶ (*have same opinion*) zustimmen; **to ~ to sth** mit etw *dat* einverstanden sein; **■to ~ with sb** mit jdm einer Meinung sein ❷ (*consent to*) zustimmen; **~d!** einverstanden! II. *vt* **■to ~ that …** sich darauf einigen, dass …

agree·able [ə·'gri·ə·bəl] *adj* ❶ (*pleasant*) angenehm; *weather* freundlich ❷ (*acceptable*) **■to be ~ to sb** für jdn akzeptabel sein

agree·ment [ə·'gri·mənt] *n* ❶ (*same opinion*) Übereinstimmung *f;* **■to be in ~ with sb** mit jdm übereinstimmen ❷ (*contract*) Vertrag *m*

ag·ri·cul·tur·al [ˌæg·rɪ·'kʌl·tʃər·əl] *adj* landwirtschaftlich

ag·ri·cul·ture ['æg·rɪ·kʌl·tʃər] *n* Landwirtschaft *f*

aground [ə·'graʊnd] *adv* **to run ~** auf Grund laufen

ah [a] *interj* (*in realization*) ach so; (*in happiness*) ah; (*in sympathy*) oh

ahead [ə·ˈhed] *adv* ① (*in front*) vorn; **full speed ~** volle Kraft voraus; **to go ~** *project* vorangehen ② (*in the future*) **to look ~** nach vorne sehen

AI [ˌeɪˈaɪ] *n* ① COMPUT *abbrev of* **artificial intelligence** künstliche Intelligenz ② SCI *abbrev of* **artificial insemination** künstliche Befruchtung

aid [eɪd] I. *n* ① (*assistance*) Hilfe *f* ② (*helpful tool*) [Hilfs]mittel *nt;* **hearing ~** Hörgerät *nt* II. *vt* helfen +*dat*

aide [eɪd] *n* ① (*advisor*) Berater(in) *m(f)* ② (*assistant*) Hilfskraft *f* (*im Unterricht*)

AIDS [eɪdz] *n abbrev of* **acquired immune deficiency syndrome** Aids *nt*

aim [eɪm] I. *vi* ① (*point*) zielen (**at** auf +*akk*) ② (*try to achieve*) ▪**to ~ at** [*or* **for**] **sth** etw zum Ziel haben; **to ~ to please** gefallen wollen ▶PHRASES: **to ~ high** hoch hinaus wollen II. *vt* ▪**to ~ sth at sb/sth** mit etw *dat* auf jdn/etw zielen III. *n* (*goal*) Ziel *nt*

aimless [ˈeɪm·lɪs] *adj* ziellos

ain't [eɪnt] (*sl*) ① = **am not, is not, are not** *see* **be** ② = **has not, have not** *see* **have**

air [er] I. *n* ① Luft *f;* **by ~** mit dem Flugzeug ② TV, RADIO Äther *m;* **on/off the ~** auf Sendung/nicht mehr auf Sendung sein II. *vt* ① (*ventilate*) lüften; *clothes* auslüften [lassen] ② (*express*) *thoughts* äußern III. *vi* ① TV, RADIO gesendet werden ② (*ventilate*) auslüften

'air bag *n* Airbag *m*

'airbase *n* Luftwaffenstützpunkt *m*

'airborne *adj disease* durch die Luft übertragen; **~ troops** Luftlandetruppen *pl*

'air brake *n* Druckluftbremse *f*

'air bubble *n* Luftblase *f*

'air-conditioned *adj* klimatisiert

'air conditioner *n* Klimaanlage *f*

'air conditioning *n* Klimaanlage *f*

'air-cooled *adj* luftgekühlt

'aircraft <*pl* -> *n* Luftfahrzeug *nt*

'aircraft carrier *n* Flugzeugträger *m*

'aircrew *n* Crew *f,* Flugpersonal *nt*

'airfield *n* Flugplatz *m*

'air force *n* Luftwaffe *f*

'air freight *n* Luftfracht *f*

airless [ˈer·lɪs] *adj* stickig

'airline *n* Fluggesellschaft *f;* **budget** [*or* **no-frills**] **~** Billigfluglinie *f,* Billigflieger *m fam*

'airliner *n* Verkehrsflugzeug *nt*

'airmail I. *n* Luftpost *f* II. *vt* per Luftpost schicken

airman *n* MIL Flieger *m*

'airplane [ˈer·pleɪn] *n* Flugzeug *nt*

'airport *n* Flughafen *m*

'air raid *n* Luftangriff *m*

'airspace *n* Luftraum *m*

'airstrip *n* Start- und Landebahn *f*

'airtight *adj* luftdicht; (*fig*) hieb- und stichfest

'air traffic *n* Flugverkehr *m*

air traffic con'trol *n* Flugleitung *f*

air traffic con'troller *n* Fluglotse *m,* Fluglotsin *f*

'airway *n see* **airline**

airy [ˈer·i] *adj* luftig

aisle [aɪl] *n* Gang *m; of church* Seitenschiff *nt*

AK *abbrev of* **Alaska**

aka [ˌeɪ·keɪ·ˈeɪ] *abbrev of* **also known as** alias

AL, Ala. *abbrev of* **Alabama**

Alabama [ˌæl·ə·ˈbæm·ə] *n* Alabama *nt*

alarm [ə·ˈlɑrm] I. *n* ① (*worry*) Angst *f;* **to give sb cause for ~** jdm einen Grund zur Sorge geben ② (*signal*) Alarm *m* ③ (*device*) Alarmanlage *f* II. *vt* ① erschrecken ② (*warn of danger*) alarmieren

a'larm clock *n* Wecker *m*

alarming [ə·ˈlɑr·mɪŋ] *adj* (*worrying*) beunruhigend; (*frightening*) erschreckend

Alas. *abbrev of* **Alaska**

Alaska [ə·ˈlæs·kə] *n* Alaska *nt*

Albania [æl·ˈbeɪ·ni·ə] *n* Albanien *nt*

albatross <*pl* -es> [ˈæl·bə·trɔs] *n* Albatros *m*

albino [æl·ˈbaɪ·noʊ] *n* Albino *m*

album [ˈæl·bəm] *n* Album *nt*

alcohol [ˈæl·kə·hɔl] *n* Alkohol *m*

A

alcohol-free [ˌæl·kə·hɔlˈfri] *adj* alkoholfrei

alcoholic [ˌæl·kəˈhɔ·lɪk] I. *n* Alkoholiker(in) *m(f)* II. *adj person* alkoholsüchtig; *drink* alkoholisch

alcoholism [ˈæl·kə·hɔ·lɪz·əm] *n* Alkoholismus *m*

alcove [ˈæl·koʊv] *n* Nische *f*

ale [eɪl] *n* Ale *nt*

alert [əˈlɜrt] I. *adj* ❶ (*mentally*) aufgeweckt ❷ (*watchful*) wachsam; (*attentive*) aufmerksam II. *n* Alarmbereitschaft *f;* ■ **to be on the ~** [**for sth**] [vor etw] auf der Hut sein III. *vt* ■ **to ~ sb to** [*or* **of**] **sth** (*warn*) jdn vor etw *dat* warnen

algae <*pl* -e> [ˈæl·gə] *n usu pl* Alge *f*

Algeria [ælˈdʒɪr·i·ə] *n* Algerien *nt*

alias [ˈeɪ·li·əs] I. *n* Deckname *m* II. *adv* alias

alibi [ˈæl·ə·baɪ] *n* Alibi *nt*

alien [ˈeɪ·li·ən] I. *adj* fremd II. *n* ❶ (*foreigner*) Ausländer(in) *m(f)* ❷ (*from space*) Außerirdische(r) *f(m)*

alienate [ˈeɪ·li·ə·neɪt] *vt* befremden

alight [əˈlaɪt] *vi* ❶ (*from train*) aussteigen (**from** aus + *dat*) ❷ *bird* landen (**on** auf + *dat*)

align [əˈlaɪn] *vt* ■ **to ~ sth** [**with sth**] etw [auf etw *akk*] ausrichten

alignment [əˈlaɪn·mənt] *n* Ausrichten *nt*

alike [əˈlaɪk] I. *adj* ❶ (*identical*) gleich ❷ (*similar*) ähnlich II. *adv* gleich; **to look ~** sich *dat* ähnlich sehen

alimony [ˈæl·ɪ·moʊ·ni] *n* Unterhalt *m*

alive [əˈlaɪv] *adj* lebendig, lebend; **to keep sb ~** jdn am Leben erhalten; **to make sth come ~** *story* etw lebendig werden lassen

alkali <*pl* -s> [ˈæl·kə·laɪ] *n* Alkali *nt*

alkaline [ˈæl·kə·laɪn] *adj* alkalisch

all [ɔl] I. *adj* ❶ + *pl n* (*every one of*) alle; **~ her children** alle ihre Kinder; **on ~ fours** auf allen Vieren; **~ the people** alle [Leute]; **why her, of ~ people?** warum ausgerechnet sie? ❷ + *sing n* (*the whole* (*amount*) *of*) der/die/das ganze; **~ her life** ihr ganzes Leben; **~ week**

die ganze Woche ❸ (*the greatest possible*) all; **in ~ honesty** ganz ehrlich II. *pron* ❶ (*every one*) alle; **the best of ~** der Beste von allen ❷ (*everything*) alles; **~ it takes is a little luck** man braucht nur etwas Glück; **for ~ I know, ...** soviel ich weiß ...; **first of ~** zuerst; (*most importantly*) vor allem; **most of ~** am meisten ❸ (*for emphasis*) **at ~** überhaupt; **nothing at ~** überhaupt nichts III. *adv* ❶ (*entirely*) ganz; **she's been ~ over the world** sie war schon überall auf der Welt; **~ along** die ganze Zeit; **to be ~ over** aus und vorbei sein ❷ ■ **the ...** umso ...; **~ the better!** umso besser!; **~ but** fast ❸ (*for emphasis*) **that's ~ very well, but ...** das ist ja schön und gut, aber ...; **~ too ...** nur zu ...; **not ~ there** (*fam*) nicht ganz richtig [im Kopf]

Allah [ˈæl·ə] *n* Allah

all-'around *adj* Allround-

all 'clear *n* Entwarnung *f;* **to give the ~** Entwarnung geben

allegation [ˌæl·ɪˈgeɪ·ʃən] *n* Behauptung *f;* **to make an ~ against sb** jdn beschuldigen

allege [əˈledʒ] *vt* behaupten

alleged [əˈledʒd] *adj* angeblich

allegiance [əˈli·dʒəns] *n* Loyalität *f;* **to pledge ~ to sb** jdm Treue schwören

allergen [ˈæl·ər·dʒən] *n* Allergen *nt*

allergic [əˈlɜr·dʒɪk] *adj* allergisch (**to** gegen + *akk*)

allergy [ˈæl·ər·dʒi] *n* Allergie *f*

alleviate [əˈli·vi·eɪt] *vt fears* abbauen; *pain* lindern

alley [ˈæl·i] *n* (*between buildings*) Gasse *f*

alliance [əˈlaɪ·əns] *n* Allianz *f;* **to form an ~** ein Bündnis schließen

allied [ˈæl·aɪd] *adj* (*united*) verbündet; MIL alliiert

alligator [ˈæl·ɪ·geɪ·tər] *n* Alligator *m*

allocate [ˈæl·ə·keɪt] *vt* zuteilen; *funds* bereitstellen

allocation [ˌæl·əˈkeɪ·ʃən] *n usu sing* (*assignment*) Zuteilung *f;* *of funds* Bereitstellung *f*

all-'out *adj* umfassend; ~ **attack** Großangriff *m*

allow [ə'laʊ] *vt* (*permit*) erlauben
◆ **allow for** *vt* berücksichtigen; *error, delay* einkalkulieren

allowable [ə'laʊ·ə·bəl] *adj* zulässig

allowance [ə'laʊ·əns] *n* ❶ (*permitted amount*) Zuteilung *f* ❷ (*pocket money*) Taschengeld *nt* ❸ (*additional pay*) Zulage *f*

alloy ['æl·ɔɪ] *n* Legierung *f;* ~ **wheels** Alu-Felgen *pl*

all-'purpose *adj* Allzweck-

all 'right I. *adj* ❶ (*OK*) in Ordnung; **that's ~** (*apologetically*) das macht nichts; (*you're welcome*) keine Ursache; ■ **to be ~ with sb** jdm recht sein ❷ (*healthy*) gesund; (*safe*) gut II. *interj* (*in agreement*) o. k., in Ordnung III. *adv* ❶ (*doubtless*) auf jeden Fall ❷ (*quite well*) ganz gut

all-'round *adj see* **all-around**

alluring [ə'lʊr·ɪŋ] *adj* anziehend

allusion [ə'lu·ʒən] *n* Anspielung *f*

'all-weather *adj* Allwetter-

ally I. *n* ['æl·aɪ] Verbündete(r) *f(m)* II. *vt* <-ie-> [ə'laɪ] ■ **to ~ oneself with** sich verbünden mit +*dat*

almond ['a·mənd] *n* Mandel *f*

almost ['ɔl·moʊst] *adv* fast, beinahe; **we're ~ there** wir sind gleich da

aloe vera [ˌæl·oʊ·'ver·ə] *n* Aloe vera *f*

alone [ə'loʊn] *adj, adv* allein; **to leave sb ~** jdn in Ruhe lassen ▸PHRASES: **to go it ~** sich selbständig machen; (*act independently*) etw im Alleingang machen

along [ə'lɑŋ] I. *prep* entlang; *before n* + *dat;* **the trees ~ the river** die Bäume entlang dem Fluss; *after n* + *akk;* ~ **the way** unterwegs II. *adv* **you go ahead — I'll be ~ in a minute** geh du vor — ich komme gleich nach; ■~ **with** [zusammen] mit +*dat;* **to bring ~** mitbringen

alongside [ə'lɑŋ·saɪd] I. *prep* neben + *dat* II. *adv* daneben; **the truck pulled up ~** der Laster fuhr heran

aloof [ə'luf] *adj* zurückhaltend

aloud [ə'laʊd] *adv* laut

alphabet ['æl·fə·bet] *n* Alphabet *nt*

alphabetical [ˌæl·fə·'bet·ɪ·kəl] *adj* alphabetisch

alpine ['æl·paɪn] *n* BOT [Hoch]gebirgspflanze *f*

already [ɔl·'red·i] *adv* schon

alright [ɔl·'raɪt] *adj, adv, interj see* **all right**

also ['ɔl·soʊ] *adv* ❶ (*too*) auch ❷ (*furthermore*) außerdem

altar ['ɔl·tər] *n* Altar *m*

alter ['ɔl·tər] I. *vt* ändern; **that doesn't ~ the fact that ...** das ändert nichts an der Tatsache, dass ... II. *vi* sich ändern

alteration [ˌɔl·tər·'eɪ·ʃən] *n* Änderung *f*

alternate I. *vi* ['ɔl·tər·neɪt] abwechseln II. *vt* **he ~d working in the office with working at home** abwechselnd arbeitete er mal im Büro und mal zu Hause III. *adj* ['ɔl·tɜr·nət] *attr* (*by turns*) abwechselnd

alternating ['ɔl·tər·neɪ·tɪŋ] *adj* alternierend

alternative [ɔl·'tɜr·nə·tɪv] I. *n* Alternative *f* II. *adj* alternativ

alternatively [ɔl·'tɜr·nə·tɪv·li] *adv* stattdessen

although [ɔl·'ðoʊ] *conj* obwohl

altitude ['æl·tə·tud] *n* Höhe *f*

alto ['æl·toʊ] *n* ❶ (*singer*) Altist(in) *m(f)* ❷ (*vocal range*) Altstimme *f*

altogether [ˌɔl·tə·'geð·ər] *adv* ❶ (*completely*) völlig ❷ (*in total*) insgesamt

aluminum [ə·'lu·mə·nəm] *n* Aluminium *nt*

aluminum 'foil *n* Alufolie *f*

always ['ɔl·weɪz] *adv* immer

am [əm, *stressed:* æm] *vi first pers. sing of* **be**

a.m. [ˌeɪ·'em] *abbrev of* **ante meridiem: at 6 ~** um sechs Uhr morgens

amalgamate [ə·'mæl·gə·meɪt] I. *vt companies* fusionieren II. *vi* sich zusammenschließen

amalgamation [əˌmæl·gə·'meɪ·ʃən] *n* Vereinigung *f*

amass [ə·'mæs] *vt* anhäufen

amateur ['æm·ə·tʃər] I. *n* Amateur(in) *m(f)* II. *adj* Hobby-; SPORT Amateur-

A **amateurish** [ˌæm·ə·ˈtʃɜr·ɪʃ] *adj* (*pej*) dilettantisch

amaze [ə·ˈmeɪz] *vt* erstaunen

amazement [ə·ˈmeɪz·mənt] *n* Verwunderung *f*

amazing [ə·ˈmeɪ·zɪŋ] *adj* ❶ (*very surprising*) erstaunlich ❷ (*fam: excellent*) toll

Amazon [ˈæm·ə·zan] *n* ■ the ~ [River] der Amazonas

ambassador [æm·ˈbæs·ə·dər] *n* Botschafter(in) *m(f)*

amber [ˈæm·bər] *n* Bernstein *m*

ambidextrous [ˌæm·bɪ·ˈdek·strəs] *adj* beidhändig

ambiguity [ˌæm·bɪ·ˈgju·ɪ·t̬i] *n* Zweideutigkeit *f*

ambiguous [æm·ˈbɪg·ju·əs] *adj* zweideutig

ambition [æm·ˈbɪʃ·ən] *n* ❶ (*wish to succeed*) Ehrgeiz *m* ❷ (*aim*) Ambition[en] *f(pl)*

ambitious [æm·ˈbɪʃ·əs] *adj* ehrgeizig; *target* hochgesteckt

amble [ˈæm·bəl] *vi* schlendern

ambulance [ˈæm·bju·ləns] *n* Krankenwagen *m*; ~ **service** Rettungsdienst *m*

ambush [ˈæm·bʊʃ] I. *vt* ■ to be ~ed aus dem Hinterhalt überfallen werden II. *n* Überfall *m* aus dem Hinterhalt

ameba <*pl* -s> [ə·ˈmi·bə] *n* see **amoeba**

amen [eɪ·ˈmen] *interj* Amen

amend [ə·ˈmend] *vt* [ab]ändern

amendment [ə·ˈmend·mənt] *n* Änderung *f*; **the Fifth A~** der Fünfte Zusatzartikel [zur Verfassung]

amenities [ə·ˈmen·ə·t̬iz] *n* Freizeiteinrichtungen *pl*

America [ə·ˈmer·ɪ·kə] *n* Amerika *nt*

American [ə·ˈmer·ɪ·kən] I. *adj* amerikanisch II. *n* Amerikaner(in) *m(f)*

American Indian *n* Indianer(in) *m(f)*

Americanize [ə·ˈmer·ɪ·kə·naɪz] *vt* amerikanisieren

American Revolutionary War *n* amerikanischer Unabhängigkeitskrieg

amethyst [ˈæm·ɪ·θɪst] *n* Amethyst *m*

amiable [ˈeɪ·mi·ə·bəl] *adj* freundlich

amicable [ˈæm·ɪ·kə·bəl] *adj* freundlich; *settlement* gütlich

amid [ə·ˈmɪd], **amidst** [ə·ˈmɪdst] *prep* inmitten +*gen*

ammonia [ə·ˈmoʊn·jə] *n* ❶ (*gas*) Ammoniak *nt* ❷ (*liquid*) Salmiakgeist *m*

ammunition [ˌæm·jə·ˈnɪʃ·ən] *n* Munition *f*

amnesia [æm·ˈni·ʒə] *n* Amnesie *f*

amnesty [ˈæm·nɪ·sti] *n* Amnestie *f*

amoeba <*pl* -s> [ə·ˈmi·bə] *n* Amöbe *f*

among [ə·ˈmʌŋ], **amongst** [ə·ˈmʌŋst] *prep* ❶ (*between*) unter +*dat*; ~ **other things** unter anderem ❷ (*in midst of*) inmitten +*gen*

amoral [ˌeɪ·ˈmɔr·əl] *adj* amoralisch

amorous [ˈæm·ər·əs] *adj* amourös; *look* verliebt

amortization [ˌæm·ər·t̬ɪ·ˈzeɪ·ʃən] *n* Amortisation *f*

amortize [ə·ˈmɔr·taɪz] *vt* amortisieren

amount [ə·ˈmaʊnt] *n* (*quantity*) Menge *f*; *of money* Betrag *m*

amp [æmp] ❶ *short for* **ampere** Ampere *nt* ❷ *short for* **amplifier** Verstärker *m*

ampere [ˈæm·pɪr] *n* Ampere *nt*

amphibian [æm·ˈfɪb·i·ən] *n* (*animal*) Amphibie *f*

amphibious [æm·ˈfɪb·i·əs] *adj* amphibisch

ample <-r, -st> [ˈæm·pəl] *adj* reichlich

amplifier [ˈæm·plə·faɪ·ər] *n* Verstärker *m*

amplify <-ie-> [ˈæm·plə·faɪ] *vt* verstärken

amputate [ˈæm·pju·teɪt] *vt, vi* amputieren

amuse [ə·ˈmjuz] *vt* ❶ (*make laugh*) amüsieren ❷ (*entertain*) unterhalten

amusement [ə·ˈmjuz·mənt] *n* Belustigung *f*

a'musement park *n* Freizeitpark *m*

amusing [ə·ˈmju·zɪŋ] *adj* amüsant

an [ən, *stressed:* æn] *art indefin*e(n) (*unbestimmter Artikel vor Vokalen oder stimmlosem* h); *see also* **a**

anabolic steroid [æn·ə·ˈbɑl·ɪk·ˈster·ɔɪd] *n* anaboles Steroid

anachronism [ə·'næk·rə·nız·əm] *n* Anachronismus *m*

anagram ['æn·ə·græm] *n* Anagramm *nt*

analgesic [ˌæn·əl·'dʒɛl·zɪk] *n* Analgetikum *nt*

analogy [ə·'næl·ə·dʒi] *n* (*similarity*) Analogie *f*

analysis <*pl* -ses> [ə·'næl·ə·sɪs] *n* ❶ Analyse *f* ❷ PSYCH [Psycho]analyse *f*

analyst ['æn·ə·lɪst] *n* FIN Analyst(in) *m(f)*; (*psychoanalyst*) Psychoanalytiker(in) *m(f)*

analytical [ˌæn·ə·'lɪt·ɪ·kəl] *adj* analytisch

analyze ['æn·ə·laɪz] *vt* analysieren

anarchist ['æn·ər·kɪst] *n* Anarchist(in) *m(f)*

anarchy ['æn·ər·ki] *n* Anarchie *f*

anatomical [ˌæn·ə·'tam·ɪ·kəl] *adj* anatomisch

anatomy [ə·'næt̬·ə·mi] *n* Anatomie *f*

ancestor ['æn·ses·tər] *n* Vorfahr[e] *m*, Vorfahrin *f*

ancestry ['æn·ses·tri] *n* Abstammung *f*

anchor ['æŋ·kər] I. *n* ❶ Anker *m* ❷ TV Moderator(in) *m(f)* II. *vt* ❶ verankern ❷ *radio/TV program* moderieren

anchorage ['æŋ·kər·ɪdʒ] *n* Ankerplatz *m*

'anchorman *n* TV Moderator *m*

'anchorwoman *n* TV Moderatorin *f*

anchovy ['æn·tʃoʊ·vi] *n* An[s]chovis *f*, Sardelle *f*

ancient ['eɪn·ʃənt] *adj* alt; (*fam*) uralt

and [ænd, ənd] *conj* und; **more ~ more** immer mehr; **~ so on** und so weiter

Andes ['æn·diz] *npl* ■**the ~** die Anden *pl*

android ['æn·drɔɪd] *n* Androide *m*

anemia [ə·'ni·mi·ə] *n* Anämie *f*

anemic [ə·'ni·mɪk] *adj* anämisch; (*fig*) saft- und kraftlos

anesthesia [ˌæn·ɪs·'θi·ʒə] *n* Anästhesie *f*

anesthesiologist [ˌæn·ɪs·ˌθi·zi·'ɑl·ə·dʒɪst] *n* Narkosearzt, -ärztin *m, f*

anesthetic [ˌæn·ɪs·'θet̬·ɪk] *n* Betäubungsmittel *nt*

anesthetize [ə·'nes·θɪ·taɪz] *vt* betäuben

angel ['eɪn·dʒl] *n* Engel *m*

angelic [æn·'dʒɛl·ɪk] *adj* engelhaft

anger ['æŋ·gər] *n* Ärger *m*; (*fury*) Wut *f*

angle ['æŋ·gəl] *n* ❶ Winkel *m* ❷ (*perspective*) Blickwinkel *m*

angler ['æŋ·glər] *n* Angler(in) *m(f)*

angling ['æŋ·glɪŋ] *n* Angeln *nt*

angora [æŋ·'gɔ·rə] *n* Angorawolle *f*

angry ['æŋ·gri] *adj* (*annoyed*) verärgert; (*enraged*) wütend

angst [æŋkst] *n* [neurotische] Angst

anguish ['æŋ·gwɪʃ] *n* Qual *f*

angular ['æŋ·gju·lər] *adj* kantig

animal ['æn·ɪ·məl] *n* Tier *nt*

animal 'rights *npl* das Recht der Tiere auf Leben und artgerechte Haltung

animate ['æn·ɪ·meɪt] *vt* beleben

animated ['æn·ɪ·meɪ·t̬ɪd] *adj* ❶ lebhaft ❷ **~ cartoon** [Zeichen]trickfilm *m*

animator ['æn·ɪ·meɪ·t̬ər] *n* Trickfilmzeichner(in) *m(f)*

anise ['æn·ɪs] *n* Anis *m*

ankle ['æŋ·kəl] *n* [Fuß]knöchel *m*

'ankle bone *n* Sprungbein *nt*

'ankle-deep *adj* knöcheltief

'ankle sock *n* Söckchen *nt*

annex I. *vt* [ə·'neks] annektieren II. *n* <*pl* -es> ['æn·eks] ❶ (*building*) Anbau *m* ❷ *to a letter* Anlage *f*; *to an e-mail* Anhang *m*

annihilate [ə·'naɪ·ə·leɪt] *vt* vernichten

annihilation [ə·ˌnaɪ·ə·'leɪ·ʃən] *n* Vernichtung *f*

anniversary [ˌæn·ə·'vɜr·sə·ri] *n* Jahrestag *m*

announce [ə·'naʊns] *vt* bekannt geben

announcement [ə·'naʊns·mənt] *n* Bekanntmachung *f*; (*at airport*) Durchsage *f*

announcer [ə·'naʊn·sər] *n* [Fernseh]sprecher(in) *m(f)*

annoy [ə·'nɔɪ] *vt* ärgern

annoyance [ə·'nɔɪ·əns] *n* (*anger*) Ärger *m*; (*weaker*) Verärgerung *f*

annoying [ə·'nɔɪ·ɪŋ] *adj* ärgerlich

annual ['æn·ju·əl] *adj* jährlich; **~ income** Jahreseinkommen *nt*

A

annually ['æn·ju·ə·li] *adv* [all]jährlich

annul <-ll-> [ə·'nʌl] *vt* annullieren; *contract* auflösen

anomaly [ə·'nam·ə·li] *n* Anomalie *f*

anonymous [ə·'nan·ə·məs] *adj* anonym

anorak ['æn·ə·ræk] *n* Anorak *m*

anorexia [ˌæn·ə·'rek·si·ə], **anorexia nervosa** [ˌæn·ə·'rek·si·ə nɜr·'vou·sə] *n* Magersucht *f*

anorexic [ˌæn·ə·'rek·sɪk] *adj* magersüchtig

another [ə·'nʌð·ər] I. *adj* ❶ (*one more*) noch eine(r, s) ❷ (*similar to*) ein zweiter/zweites/eine zweite; **the Gulf War could have been ~ Vietnam** der Golfkrieg hätte ein zweites Vietnam sein können ❸ (*not the same*) ein anderer/anderes/eine andere; **that's ~ story** das ist eine andere Geschichte II. *pron* ❶ (*different one*) ein anderer/eine andere/ein anderes; **one way or ~** irgendwie ❷ (*additional one*) noch eine(r, s) ❸ (*each other*) **one ~** einander

answer ['æn·sər] I. *n* ❶ (*reply*) Antwort *f*; (*reaction a.*) Reaktion *f* ❷ MATH Ergebnis *nt* II. *vt* beantworten, antworten auf +*akk*; **to ~ the telephone** ans Telefon gehen; ▪ **to ~ sb** jdm antworten III. *vi* antworten
  ◆ **answer for** *vt* Verantwortung tragen für +*akk*
  ◆ **answer to** *vt* ▪ **to ~ to sb** jdm Rede und Antwort stehen

'answering machine *n* Anrufbeantworter *m*

ant [ænt] *n* Ameise *f*

antagonism [æn·'tæg·ə·nɪz·əm] *n* Feindseligkeit *f*

antagonize [æn·'tæg·ə·naɪz] *vt* sich *dat* zum Feind machen

Antarctica [ænt·'ark·tɪ·kə] *n* die Antarktis

antelope <*pl* -s> ['æn·tɪ·loup] *n* Antilope *f*

antenna [æn·'ten·ə] *n* ❶ <*pl* -nae> *of an insect* Fühler *m* ❷ <*pl* -s> (*aerial*) Antenne *f*

anthem ['æn·θəm] *n* Hymne *f*

anthill ['ænt·hɪl] *n* Ameisenhaufen *m*

anthracite ['æn·θrə·saɪt] *n* Anthrazit *m*

anthropologist [ˌæn·θrə·'pal·ə·dʒɪst] *n* Anthropologe *m*, Anthropologin *f*

anthropology [ˌæn·θrə·'pal·ə·dʒi] *n* Anthropologie *f*

anti ['æn·ti] *prep* gegen +*akk*

anti'aircraft *adj* Flugabwehr-*f*

antibiotic [ˌæn·ti·baɪ·'at·ɪk] *n* Antibiotikum *nt*

'antibody *n* Antikörper *m*

anticipate [æn·'tɪs·ə·peɪt] *vt* (*expect*) erwarten; (*foresee*) vorhersehen

anti'climax *n* Enttäuschung *f*

anti'cyclone *n* Hochdruckgebiet *nt*

antide'pressant *n* Antidepressivum *nt*

antidote ['æn·tɪ·dout] *n* Gegenmittel *nt*

'antifreeze *n* Frostschutzmittel *nt*

anti'histamine *n* Antihistamin *nt*

antilock 'braking system *n* Antiblockiersystem *nt*

anti'oxidant *n* Antioxidationsmittel *nt*

antiperspirant [ˌæn·tɪ·'pɜr·spər·ənt] *n* Antitranspirant *nt*

antiquarian [ˌæn·tɪ·'kwer·i·ən] *n* Antiquitätensammler(in) *m(f)*

antiquated ['æn·tɪ·kwei·tɪd] *adj* antiquiert

antique [æn·'tik] I. *n* (*iron a.*) Antiquität *f* II. *adj* antik

anti'rust *adj* Rostschutz-

anti-'Semitic *adj* antisemitisch

anti'septic I. *n* Antiseptikum *nt* II. *adj* antiseptisch; (*fig*) steril

anti'social *adj* ❶ (*harmful*) unsozial ❷ (*not sociable*) ungesellig

anti'static *adj* antistatisch

antler ['ænt·lər] *n* Geweihstange *f*

antonym ['æn·tə·nɪm] *n* Antonym *nt*

antsy ['ænt·si] *adj* (*fam*) *child* zappelig *fam*

anus ['eɪ·nəs] *n* Anus *m*

anvil ['æn·vɪl] *n* Amboss *m*

anxiety [æŋ·'zaɪ·ɪ·ti] *n* ❶ (*feeling of concern*) Sorge *f* ❷ (*concern*) Angst *f*

anxious ['æŋk·ʃəs] *adj* ❶ (*concerned*) besorgt ❷ (*eager*) bestrebt

any ['en·i] I. *adj* ❶ *in questions, conditional* [irgend]eine(e); *with uncountables* etwas; **do you have ~ brothers**

or sisters? haben Sie Geschwister? ❷ *with neg* **I don't have ~ money** ich habe kein Geld ❸ *(every)* jede(r, s); **in ~ case** *(whatever happens)* auf jeden Fall; *(anyway)* außerdem ❹ *(whichever you like)* jede(r, s) [beliebige]; *(all)* alle; *(not important which)* irgendein(e); *(with pl n)* irgendwelche II. *pron* ❶ *(some of many)* welche; *(one of many)* eine(r, s); **do you have ~ [at all]?** haben Sie [überhaupt] welche? ❷ *(some of a quantity)* welche(r, s); **hardly ~** kaum etwas ❸ *(with negative)* **don't you have ~ at all?** haben Sie denn überhaupt keine? *(not important which)* irgendeine(r, s); **~ will do** egal welche III. *adv* ❶ *(emphasizing)* noch; *(a little)* etwas; *(at all)* überhaupt; **are you feeling ~ better?** fühlst du dich [denn] etwas besser?; **~ more** noch mehr ❷ *(expressing termination)* **not ~ longer/more** nicht mehr

anybody ['en·ɪ·bad·i] *pron* ❶ *(each person)* jede(r, s) ❷ *(someone)* jemand; **does ~ else want coffee?** möchte noch jemand Kaffee?

anyhow ['en·ɪ·haʊ] *adv (in any case)* sowieso

anyone ['en·ɪ·wʌn] *pron see* **anybody**

anyplace ['en·ɪ·pleɪs] *adv (fam)* irgendwo

anything ['en·ɪ·θɪŋ] *pron* ❶ *(each thing)* alles ❷ *(something)* **is there ~ I can do to help?** kann ich irgendwie helfen?; **hardly ~** kaum etwas ❸ *(nothing)* **not ~** nichts; **not ~ like ...** nicht annähernd ... ▶PHRASES: **[as] ... as ~** ausgesprochen ...

anytime ['en·ɪ·taɪm] *adv* jederzeit

anyway ['en·ɪ·weɪ] *adv,* **anyways** ['en·ɪ·weɪz] *adv (fam)* ❶ *(in any case)* sowieso ❷ *(well)* jedenfalls; **~!** na ja!

anywhere ['en·ɪ·wer] *adv* ❶ *(in any place)* überall; **~ else** irgendwo anders ❷ *(some place)* irgendwo; **I'm not getting ~** ich komme einfach nicht weiter; **to go ~** irgendwohin gehen

apart [ə·'part] *adv* ❶ *(not together)* aus-

einander ❷■**~ from** abgesehen von +*dat*

apartment [ə·'part·mənt] *n* Wohnung *f* **a'partment building,** **a'partment house** *n* Wohnhaus *nt;* *(with smaller apartments)* Ap[p]art[e]menthaus *nt*

apathy ['æp·ə·θi] *n* Apathie *f*

ape [eɪp] *n* [Menschen]affe *m*

aperitif [ə·,per·ə·'tif] *n* Aperitif *m*

aperture ['æp·ər·tʃʊr] *n* [kleine] Öffnung; PHOT Blende *f*

apex <*pl* -es> ['eɪ·peks] *n* Spitze *f*

aphid ['eɪ·fɪd] *n* Blattlaus *f*

aphrodisiac [,æf·rə·'dɪ·zi·æk] *n* Aphrodisiakum *nt*

apiece [ə·'pis] *adv* das Stück; *(per person)* jeder

apocalypse [ə·'pak·ə·lɪps] *n* Apokalypse *f*

apologetic [ə·,pal·ə·'dʒet·ɪk] *adj* entschuldigend

apologize [ə·'pal·ə·dʒaɪz] *vi* sich entschuldigen **(to** bei +*dat)*

apology [ə·'pal·ə·dʒi] *n* Entschuldigung *f*

apostrophe [ə·'pas·trə·fi] *n* Apostroph *m*

Appalachian Mountains *npl* ■**the ~** die Appalachen *pl*

appall [ə·'pɔl] *vt* entsetzen

appalling [ə·'pɔ·lɪŋ] *adj* entsetzlich

apparatus [,æp·ə·'ræt·əs] *n* **[piece of]** **~** Gerät *nt*

apparent [ə·'pær·ənt] *adj* ❶ *(obvious)* offensichtlich ❷ *(seeming)* scheinbar

apparently [ə·'pær·ənt·li] *adv* ❶ *(obviously)* offensichtlich ❷ *(seemingly)* anscheinend

appeal [ə·'pil] I. *vi* ❶ *(attract)* ■**to ~ to sb/sth** jdn/etw reizen; *(aim to please)* jdn/etw ansprechen ❷ *(protest formally)* Einspruch einlegen ❸ *(plead)* bitten II. *n* ❶ *(attraction)* Reiz *m* ❷ *(formal protest)* Einspruch *m;* **Court of A~** Berufungsgericht *nt*

appealing [ə·'pi·lɪŋ] *adj* ❶ *(attractive)* attraktiv; **idea** verlockend ❷ *(beseeching)* flehend

A

appealingly [ə·'pi·lɪŋ·li] *adv* (*attractively*) reizvoll

appear [ə·'pɪr] *vi* ① (*become visible*) erscheinen; (*be seen a.*) sich *dat* zeigen; (*arrive a.*) auftauchen ② *film* anlaufen; *newspaper* erscheinen ③ (*seem*) scheinen

appearance [ə·'pɪr·əns] *n* ① (*instance of appearing*) Erscheinen *nt;* (*on TV, theater*) Auftritt *m;* **to make an ~** auftreten ② (*looks*) Aussehen *nt*

appendicitis [ə‚pen·dɪ·'saɪ·tɪs] *n* Blinddarmentzündung *f*

appendix [ə·'pen·dɪks] *n* ① <*pl* -es> (*body part*) Blinddarm *m* ② <*pl* -dices> (*in book*) Anhang *m*

appetite ['æp·ə·taɪt] *n* Appetit *m*

appetizer ['æp·ə·taɪ·zər] *n* Vorspeise *f*

applaud [ə·'plɔd] I. *vi* applaudieren II. *vt* ① (*clap*) **to ~ sb** jdm applaudieren ② *decision* begrüßen

applause [ə·'plɔz] *n* [**a round of**] ~ Applaus *m*

apple ['æp·əl] *n* Apfel *m*

'apple juice *n* Apfelsaft *m*

apple 'pie *n* FOOD gedeckter Apfelkuchen

'applesauce *n* Apfelmus *nt*

'apple tree *n* Apfelbaum *m*

appliance [ə·'plaɪ·əns] *n* Gerät *nt*

applicable [ə·'plɪ·kə·bəl] *adj* anwendbar (**to** auf +*akk*); (*on application form*) **not** ~ nicht zutreffend

applicant ['æp·lɪ·kənt] *n* Bewerber(in) *m(f)*

application [‚æp·lɪ·'keɪ·ʃən] *n* ① *for a job* Bewerbung *f; for a permit* Antrag *m* ② (*implementation*) Anwendung *f* ③ COMPUT Anwendung *f*

appli'cation form *n* (*for job*) Bewerbungsformular *nt;* (*for permit*) Antragsformular *nt*

applied [ə·'plaɪd] *adj* angewandt

apply <-ie-> [ə·'plaɪ] I. *vi* ① **to ~** [**to sb**] [**for sth**] (*for a job*) sich [bei jdm] [um etw *akk*] bewerben; (*for permission, passport*) etw [bei jdm] beantragen ② (*pertain*) gelten; **to ~ to** betreffen II. *vt* ① (*put on*) an-

wenden (**to** auf +*akk*); *makeup* auftragen ② (*use*) gebrauchen; *force* anwenden

appoint [ə·'pɔɪnt] *vt* **to ~ sb** [**as**] **sth** jdn zu etw *dat* ernennen

appointed [ə·'pɔɪn·tɪd] *adj* ① (*selected*) ernannt ② (*designated*) vereinbart

appointment [ə·'pɔɪnt·mənt] *n* ① (*being selected*) Ernennung *f* ② (*official meeting*) Verabredung *f;* **by ~ only** nur nach Absprache

appraisal [ə·'preɪ·zəl] *n* Bewertung *f*

appreciate [ə·'pri·ʃi·eɪt] *vt* ① (*value*) schätzen; (*be grateful for*) zu schätzen wissen ② (*understand*) Verständnis haben für +*akk*

appreciation [ə‚pri·ʃi·'eɪ·ʃən] *n* ① (*gratitude*) Anerkennung *f* ② (*understanding*) Verständnis *nt*

appreciative [ə·'pri·ʃə·tɪv] *adj* ① (*grateful*) dankbar (**of** für +*akk*) ② (*showing appreciation*) anerkennend

apprehensive [‚æp·rɪ·'hen·sɪv] *adj* besorgt; (*scared*) ängstlich

apprentice [ə·'pren·tɪs] *n* Auszubildende(r) *f(m)*

apprenticeship [ə·'pren·tɪs·ʃɪp] *n* ① (*training*) Ausbildung *f* ② (*period of training*) Lehrzeit *f*

approach [ə·'proʊtʃ] I. *vt* ① (*come closer*) **to ~ sb/sth** sich jdm/etw nähern; (*come toward(s)*) auf jdn/etw zukommen ② (*ask*) **to ~ sb** jdn ansprechen (**about** wegen +*gen*) ③ *problem, issue* angehen II. *vi* sich nähern III. *n* ① (*coming*) Nähern *n* ② (*preparation to land*) [Lande]anflug *m* ③ (*method*) Ansatz *m*

approachable [ə·'proʊ·tʃə·bəl] *adj person* umgänglich

appropriate *adj* [ə·'proʊ·pri·ət] angemessen

approval [ə·'pru·vəl] *n* (*consent*) Zustimmung *f* ▶PHRASES: **on ~** ECON zur Ansicht; (*to try*) zur Probe

approve [ə·'pruv] I. *vi* ① (*agree with*) **to ~ of sth** etw *dat* zustimmen ② (*like*) **to ~ of sth** etw gutheißen

A

II. *vt* (*permit*) genehmigen; (*consent to*) billigen

approved [ə·'pruvd] *adj* ❶ (*agreed*) bewährt ❷ (*sanctioned*) [offiziell] anerkannt

approving [ə·'pru·vɪŋ] *adj* zustimmend

approvingly [ə·'pru·vɪŋ·li] *adv* anerkennend

approx. *adv abbrev of* **approximately** ca.

approximately [ə·'prak·sɪ·mət·li] *adv* ungefähr

approximation [ə·ˌprak·sɪ·'meɪ·ʃən] *n* Annäherung *f*

APR [ˌeɪ·piˈar] *n* FIN *abbrev of* **annual percentage rate** Jahreszinssatz *m*

Apr. *n abbrev of* **April** Apr.

apricot ['eɪ·prɪ·kat] *n* Aprikose *f*

April ['eɪ·prəl] *n* April *m; see also* **February**

April 'Fools' Day *n* der erste April

apron ['eɪ·prən] *n* Schürze *f*

apt [æpt] *adj* passend; *remark* treffend

'aptitude test *n* Eignungstest *m*

aquarium <*pl* -s> [ə·'kwer·i·əm] *n* Aquarium *nt*

Aquarius [ə·'kwer·i·əs] *n* ASTROL Wassermann *m*

aquatic [ə·'kwæt·ɪk] *adj* Wasser·

AR *abbrev of* **Arkansas**

Arab ['ær·əb] I. *n* Araber(in) *m(f)* II. *adj* arabisch

Arabic ['ær·ə·bɪk] I. *n* Arabisch *nt* II. *adj* arabisch

arbitrary ['ar·bɪ·trer·i] *adj* willkürlich

arbitrate ['ar·bɪ·treɪt] *vi* vermitteln

arbitrator ['ar·bɪ·treɪ·tər] *n* Schlichter(in) *m(f)*

arbor ['ar·bər] *n* Laube *f*

arc [ark] *n* Bogen *m*

arcade ['ær·keɪd] *n* ❶ (*for playing games*) Spielhalle *f* ❷ ARCHIT Arkade *f*

arch [artʃ] I. *n* Bogen *m* II. *vt back* krümmen

archaic [ar·'keɪ·ɪk] *adj* veraltet

arch'enemy *n* Erzfeind(in) *m(f)*

archeologist [ˌar·ki·'al·ə·dʒɪst] *n* Archäologe *m*, Archäologin *f*

archeology [ˌar·ki·'al·ə·dʒi] *n* Archäologie *f*

archery ['ar·tʃə·ri] *n* Bogenschießen *nt*

archipelago <*pl* -s> [ˌar·kə·'pel·ə·goʊ] *n* Archipel *m*

architect ['ar·kɪ·tekt] *n* Architekt(in) *m(f)*

architecture ['ar·kɪ·tek·tʃər] *n* Architektur *f*

archive ['ar·kaɪv] *n* Archiv *nt*

'archway *n* Torbogen *m*

'arc lamp, 'arc light *n* Bogenlampe *f*

Arctic ['ark·tɪk] I. *n* ■the ~ die Arktis II. *adj* arktisch; *expedition* Arktis·

ardent ['ar·dənt] *adj* leidenschaftlich

arduous ['ar·dʒu·əs] *adj* anstrengend

are [ər, *stressed:* ar] *vt, vi see* **be**

area ['er·i·ə] *n* ❶ Gebiet *nt* ❷ (*surface measure*) Fläche *f*

'area code *n* Vorwahl *f*

arena [ə·'ri·nə] *n* Arena *f*

Argentina [ˌar·dʒən·'ti·nə] *n* Argentinien *nt*

arguably ['ar·gju·ə·bli] *adv* wohl

argue ['ar·gju] *vi* ❶ (*disagree*) [sich] streiten; **don't ~ [with me]**! keine Widerrede! ❷ (*reason*) argumentieren

argument ['ar·gjə·mənt] *n* ❶ (*heated discussion*) Auseinandersetzung *f* ❷ (*case*) Argument *nt*

argumentative [ˌar·gjə·'men·tə·t̬ɪv] *adj* streitsüchtig

aria ['a·ri·ə] *n* Arie *f*

arid ['ær·ɪd] *adj* dürr

Aries ['er·iz] *n* ASTROL Widder *m*

arise <arose, arisen> [ə·'raɪz] *vi* (*come about*) sich ergeben

arisen [ə·'rɪz·ən] *pp of* **arise**

aristocrat [ə·'rɪs·tə·kræt] *n* Aristokrat(in) *m(f)*

aristocratic [e·ˌrɪs·tə·'kræt̬·ɪk] *adj* aristokratisch

arithmetic *n* [ə·'rɪθ·mɪ·tɪk] Arithmetik *f*

Ariz. *abbrev of* **Arizona**

Arizona [ˌær·ɪ·'zoʊ·nə] *n* Arizona *nt*

ark [ark] *n* Arche *f*

Ark. *abbrev of* **Arkansas**

Arkansas ['ar·kən·sɔ] *n* Arkansas *nt*

Arlington National Cemetery *n* Na·

A

tionalfriedhof Arlington, der Gräber von mehr als 60.000 amerikanischen Soldaten sowie die bekannter amerikanischer Persönlichkeiten beherbergt

arm[1] [arm] n ❶ ANAT, GEOG Arm m ❷ (armrest) Armlehne f ▶ PHRASES: **to keep sb at ~'s length** jdn auf Distanz halten

arm[2] [arm] I. vt ❶ (supply with weapons) bewaffnen ❷ bomb scharf machen II. n ■~s pl Waffen pl

'armband n Armbinde f

'armchair n Sessel m

armed [armd] adj bewaffnet

armed 'forces npl Streitkräfte pl

armful ['arm·ful] n Armvoll m

armhole ['arm·houl] n Armloch nt

armor-'plated adj gepanzert

armpit n Achselhöhle f

'armrest n Armlehne f

'arms control n Abrüstung f

'arms race n Wettrüsten nt

army ['ar·mi] n Armee f; **to join the ~** zum Militär gehen

aroma [ə·'rou·mə] n Duft m

aroma'therapy n Aromatherapie f

aromatic [ˌær·ə·'mæt·ɪk] adj aromatisch

arose [ə·'rouz] pt of **arise**

around [ə·'raund] I. adv ❶ (on all sides) rundum; **from miles ~** von weither; **he's the biggest crook ~** er ist der größte Gauner, den es gibt ❷ (with circular motion) umher ❸ (here and there) herum; **to show sb ~** jdn herumführen ▶ PHRASES: **see you ~** bis demnächst mal II. prep ❶ um +akk; **from all ~ the world** aus aller Welt ❷ ungefähr

arouse [ə·'rauz] vt ❶ suspicion erregen ❷ (sexually excite) erregen

arrange [ə·'reɪndʒ] I. vt ❶ (organize) arrangieren; matters regeln ❷ (put in order) ordnen II. vi festlegen; ■**to ~ to do sth** etw vereinbaren

arrangement [ə·'reɪndʒ·mənt] n ❶ ■~s pl (preparations) Vorbereitungen pl ❷ (agreement) Abmachung f; **by [prior] ~** nach [vorheriger] Absprache

arrears [ə·'rɪrz] npl Rückstände pl; **in ~** in Verzug

arrest [ə·'rest] I. vt verhaften II. n Verhaftung f

arrival [ə·'raɪ·vəl] n (at a destination) Ankunft f; of a baby Geburt f

arrive [ə·'raɪv] vi bus ankommen; baby, mail kommen

arrogant ['ær·ə·gənt] adj arrogant

arrow ['ær·ou] n Pfeil m

arson ['ar·sən] n Brandstiftung f

art [art] n Kunst f; ■**the ~s** pl die Kunst

artery ['ar·tə·ri] n Arterie f

arthritis [ar·'θraɪ·tɪs] n Gelenkentzündung f

artichoke ['ar·tɪ·tʃouk] n Artischocke f

article ['ar·tɪ·kəl] n Artikel m; **~ of clothing** Kleidungsstück nt

articulate [ar·'tɪk·jə·lət] adj ❶ person redegewandt ❷ speech verständlich

artificial [ˌar·tə·'fɪʃ·əl] adj ❶ (not natural) künstlich; **~ leg** Beinprothese f ❷ (pej: not genuine) aufgesetzt; smile unecht

artillery [ar·'tɪl·ə·ri] n Artillerie f

artist ['ar·tɪst] n Künstler(in) m(f)

artiste [ar·'tist] n THEAT, TV Artist(in) m(f)

artistic [ar·'tɪs·tɪk] adj künstlerisch; arrangement kunstvoll

'artwork n Illustrationen pl

arty ['ar·ti], **artsy** ['art·si] adj gewollt bohemienhaft

as [æz, əz] I. conj ❶ (while) während ❷ (in the way that, like) wie; ■**it were** sozusagen; **~ if** [or though] als ob ❸ (because) weil ▶ PHRASES: **~ for ...** was ... betrifft; **~ of** ab II. prep als; **~ a child** als Kind; **~ a matter of principle** aus Prinzip III. adv ❶ (in comparisons) wie; ■**[just] ~ ... ~ ...** [genau]so ... wie ... ❷ (indicating an extreme) **~ little ~** nur

asbestos [æs·'bes·təs] n Asbest m

ascend [ə·'send] I. vt hinaufsteigen II. vi aufsteigen; elevator hinauffahren

ascent [ə·'sent] n Aufstieg m

asexual [ˌeɪ·'sek·ʃu·əl] adj asexuell; reproduction ungeschlechtlich

ash[1] [æʃ] n (from burning) Asche f; ■ ~es pl Asche f kein pl

ash[2] [æʃ] n (tree) Esche f

ashamed [ə·'feɪmd] adj ■to be ~ [of sb/sth] sich [für jdn/etw] schämen

ashore [ə·'ʃɔr] adv to swim ~ ans Ufer schwimmen

'ashtray n Aschenbecher m

Ash 'Wednesday n Aschermittwoch m

Asia ['eɪ·ʒə] n Asien nt

Asian ['eɪ·ʒən] I. n Asiat m, Asiatin f II. adj asiatisch

aside [ə·'saɪd] adv zur Seite; **to leave sth ~** etw [weg]lassen

aside from prep abgesehen von + dat

ask [æsk] I. vt ① (request information) fragen; **to ~ a question** [about sth] [zu etw dat] eine Frage stellen ② (request) bitten [um + dat]; **she ~ed me for help** sie bat mich, ihr zu helfen ③ (invite) einladen II. vi (request information) fragen; ■**to ~ about sb/sth** nach jdm/etw fragen

askew [ə·'skju] adj, adv schief

asking ['æs·kɪŋ] n it's yours for the ~ du kannst es gerne haben

asleep [ə·'slip] adj ■**to be ~** schlafen; **to fall ~** einschlafen

asparagus [ə·'spær·ə·gəs] n Spargel m

aspect ['æs·pekt] n Aspekt m

aspen ['æs·pən] n Espe f

asphalt ['æs·fɑlt] n Asphalt m

asphyxiation [əs·fɪk·si·'eɪ·ʃən] n Erstickung f

aspiration [ˌæs·pə·'reɪ·ʃən] n Ambition f

aspire [ə·'spaɪr] vi anstreben

aspirin ['æs·pə·rɪn] n Aspirin nt

aspiring [ə·'spaɪr·ɪŋ] adj aufstrebend

ass[1] <pl -es> [æs] n Esel m

ass[2] <pl -es> [æs] n (vulg: rear end) Arsch m ▶PHRASES: **my ~!** (fam: emphatically not) wahrlich nicht

assassin [ə·'sæs·ɪn] n Mörder(in) m(f); (esp political) Attentäter(in) m(f)

assassination [ə·ˌsæs·ə·'neɪ·ʃən] n Attentat nt

assault [ə·'sɔlt] I. n Angriff m II. vt angreifen

assemble [ə·'sem·bəl] I. vi sich versammeln II. vt zusammenbauen

assembly [ə·'sem·bli] n ① (gathering) Versammlung f; ■**the A~** das Unterhaus ② TECH Montage f; ~ **line** Fließband nt

assert [ə·'sɜrt] vt ① (state firmly) beteuern ② independence behaupten

assertion [ə·'sɜr·ʃən] n ① (claim) Behauptung f ② of authority Geltendmachung f

assertive [ə·'sɜr·tɪv] adj ■**to be ~** Durchsetzungsvermögen zeigen

assertiveness [ə·'sɜr·tɪv·nɪs] n Durchsetzungsvermögen nt

assess [ə·'ses] vt einschätzen; damage schätzen (**at** auf + akk)

assessment [ə·'ses·mənt] n ① of damage Schätzung f ② (evaluation) Beurteilung f

asset ['æs·et] n ① Pluspunkt m ② FIN ■ ~s pl Vermögenswerte pl

assign [ə·'saɪn] vt zuweisen; task zuteilen

assignment [ə·'saɪn·mənt] n Aufgabe f

assimilate [ə·'sɪm·ə·leɪt] vt integrieren; information aufnehmen

assimilation [ə·ˌsɪm·ə·'leɪ·ʃən] n Eingliederung f

assist [ə·'sɪst] vt, vi helfen (**with** bei + dat)

assistance [ə·'sɪs·təns] n Hilfe f

assistant [ə·'sɪs·tənt] n Assistent(in) m(f); (in store) Verkäufer(in) m(f)

associate I. n [ə·'sou·ʃi·ət] Kollege m, Kollegin f; **business ~** Geschäftspartner(in) m(f) II. vt [ə·'sou·ʃi·eɪt] in Verbindung bringen

association [ə·ˌsou·si·'eɪ·ʃən] n ① (organization) Vereinigung f ② (mental connection) Assoziation f

assorted [ə·'sɔr·tɪd] adj gemischt; colors verschieden

assortment [ə·'sɔrt·mənt] n Sortiment nt

assume [ə·'sum] vt ① (regard as true) annehmen ② (adopt) annehmen; role übernehmen

A

assumed [ə·'sumd] *adj* **under an ~ name** unter einem Decknamen

assumption [ə·'sʌmp·ʃən] *n* (*supposition*) Annahme *f;* (*presupposition*) Voraussetzung *f*

assurance [ə·'ʃʊr·əns] *n* ❶ (*promise*) Zusicherung *f* ❷ (*self-confidence*) Selbstsicherheit *f*

assure [ə·'ʃʊr] *vt* ❶ (*confirm certainty*) zusichern ❷ (*promise*) ■ **to ~ sb of sth** jdm etw zusichern

assured [ə·'ʃʊrd] *adj* selbstsicher

asterisk ['æs·tə·rɪsk] *n* Sternchen *nt*

asteroid ['æs·tə·rɔɪd] *n* Asteroid *m*

asthma ['æz·mə] *n* Asthma *nt*

asthmatic [æz·'mæt·ɪk] *adj* asthmatisch

astonish [ə·'stɑn·ɪʃ] *vt* erstaunen

astonishing [ə·'stɑn·ɪʃ·ɪŋ] *adj* erstaunlich

astound [ə·'staʊnd] *vt* verblüffen

astounding [ə·'staʊn·dɪŋ] *adj* erstaunlich; *fact* verblüffend

astray [ə·'streɪ] *adv* verloren

astride [ə·'straɪd] *prep* rittlings auf +*dat*

astrologer [ə·'strɑl·ə·dʒər] *n* Astrologe *m,* Astrologin *f*

astrology [ə·'strɑl·ə·dʒi] *n* Astrologie *f*

astronaut ['æs·trə·nɔt] *n* Astronaut(in) *m(f)*

astronomer [ə·'strɑn·ə·mər] *n* Astronom(in) *m(f)*

astronomical [ˌæs·trə·'nɑm·ɪ·kəl] *adj* (*a. fig*) astronomisch

astronomy [ə·'strɑn·ə·mi] *n* Astronomie *f*

asylum [ə·'saɪ·ləm] *n* (*protection*) Asyl *nt;* **~ seeker** Asylbewerber(in) *m(f)*

asymmetric(al) [ˌeɪ·sɪ·'met·rɪk(əl)] *adj* asymmetrisch

at [ət, æt] *prep* ❶ (*in location of*) an +*dat;* **~ the bakery** beim Bäcker; **~ home** zu Hause; **~ work** bei der Arbeit ❷ (*during time of*) **~ night** in der Nacht, nachts; **~ 10:00 [a.m.]** um 10:00 Uhr; **~ the same time** (*simultaneously*) zur gleichen Zeit; (*on the other hand*) auf der anderen Seite ❸ (*to amount of*) **~ 80 miles per hour** mit

80 Meilen pro Stunde; **~ regular intervals** in regelmäßigen Abständen ❹ (*in state of*) **~ a disadvantage** im Nachteil; **~ fault** im Unrecht ❺ (*in ability to*) bei +*dat;* **good ~** *math* gut in Mathematik ▶PHRASES: **~ all** überhaupt; **not ~ all** (*definitely not*) keineswegs

ate [eɪt] *pt of* **eat**

atheism ['eɪ·θi·ɪz·əm] *n* Atheismus *m*

atheist ['eɪ·θi·ɪst] *n* Atheist(in) *m(f)*

athlete ['æθ·lit] *n* Athlet(in) *m(f)*

athletic [æθ·'let·ɪk] *adj* athletisch, sportlich

athletics [æθ·'let·ɪks] *n* SCH, UNIV [Schul]sport *m kein pl*

Atlantic [ət·'læn·tɪk] *n* ■ **the ~ [Ocean]** der Atlantik

atlas <*pl* -**es**> ['æt·ləs] *n* Atlas *m*

ATM [ˌeɪ·ti·'em] *n abbrev of* **automated teller machine** Geldautomat *m*

atmosphere ['æt·mə·sfɪr] *n* Atmosphäre *f a. fig*

atom ['æt·əm] *n* Atom *nt*

'atom bomb *n* Atombombe *f*

atomic [ə·'tɑm·ɪk] *adj* Atom-

atrocious [ə·'troʊ·ʃəs] *adj* grässlich; *weather* scheußlich

atrocity [ə·'trɑs·ɪ·ʈi] *n* Gräueltat *f*

attach [ə·'tætʃ] *vt* ❶ (*fix*) befestigen (**to** an +*dat*) ❷ (*connect*) verbinden (**to** mit +*dat*) ❸ (*send as enclosure*) ■ **to ~ sth [to sth]** etw [etw *dat*] beilegen

atta'ché case *n* Aktenkoffer *m*

attachment [ə·'tætʃ·mənt] *n* ❶ (*fondness*) Sympathie *f* ❷ (*for appliances*) Zusatzgerät *nt* ❸ COMPUT Anhang *m*

attack [ə·'tæk] I. *n* Angriff *m* II. *vt, vi* angreifen

attacker [ə·'tæ·kər] *n* Angreifer(in) *m(f)*

attainable [ə·'teɪn·ə·bəl] *adj* erreichbar

attempt [ə·'tempt] I. *n* Versuch *m* II. *vt* versuchen

attend [ə·'tend] I. *vt* (*be present at*) besuchen II. *vi* (*be present*) teilnehmen

attendance [ə·'ten·dəns] *n* ❶ (*being present*) Anwesenheit *f* ❷ (*number of people present*) Besucherzahl *f*

attendant [ə·'ten·dənt] *n* Aufseher(in) *m(f)*

attention [əˈten.ʃən] n ❶ (*notice*) Aufmerksamkeit m; ~! Achtung!; **to pay ~ to sth** auf etw *akk* achten ❷ MED Behandlung f

at'tention span n Konzentrationsvermögen f

attentive [əˈten.tɪv] adj aufmerksam

attic [ˈæt̬.ɪk] n Dachboden m

attitude [ˈæt̬.ɪ.tud] n Einstellung f

attorney [əˈtɜr.ni] n Anwalt m, Anwältin f

attorney 'general <pl attornies general> n Justizminister [und Generalstaatsanwalt], Justizministerin [und Generalstaatsanwältin] m, f

attract [əˈtrækt] vt anziehen; *attention* erregen

attraction [əˈtræk.ʃən] n ❶ Anziehung f ❷ (*appeal*) Reiz m

attractive [əˈtræk.tɪv] adj attraktiv

attribute [ˈæt̬.rɪ.bjut] n Eigenschaft f

auburn [ˈɔ.bərn] adj rotbraun

auction [ˈɔk.ʃən] I. n Auktion f, Versteigerung f II. vt ■**to ~ [off]** versteigern

auctioneer [ˌɔk.ʃəˈnɪr] n Auktionator(in) m(f)

audible [ˈɔ.də.bəl] adj hörbar

audience [ˈɔ.di.əns] n (*at performance*) Publikum nt; (*theater a.*) Besucher pl; TV Zuschauer pl

audio [ˈɔ.di.oʊ] adj Audio-

audit [ˈɔ.dɪt] I. n Rechnungsprüfung f II. vt [amtlich] prüfen

audition [ˈɔ.dɪʃ.ən] I. n (*for actor*) Vorsprechen nt; (*for singer*) Vorsingen nt II. vi vorsprechen, vorsingen III. vt vorsprechen/vorsingen lassen

auditor [ˈɔ.də.t̬ər] n Rechnungsprüfer(in) m(f)

auditorium <pl -s> [ˌɔ.dəˈtɔr.i.əm] n THEAT Zuschauerraum m; (*for concerts*) Konzerthalle f

Aug. n abbrev of **August** Aug.

August [ˈɔ.gəst] n August m; *see also* **February**

aunt [ænt] n Tante f

aural [ˈɔr.əl] adj akustisch

austere [ɔˈstɪr] adj karg; *room* schmucklos

austerity [ɔˈster.ɪ.t̬i] n ❶ (*absence of comfort*) Rauheit f ❷ (*sparseness*) Kargheit f

Australia [ɔˈstreɪl.jə] n Australien nt

Austria [ˈɔ.stri.ə] n Österreich nt

Austrian [ˈɔ.stri.ən] I. n (*person*) Österreicher(in) m(f) II. adj österreichisch

authentic [ɔˈθen.tɪk] adj authentisch

authenticate [ɔˈθen.tɪ.keɪt] vt [die Echtheit] bestätigen

authenticity [ˌɔ.θənˈtɪs.ɪ.t̬i] n Echtheit f

author [ˈɔ.θər] n Schriftsteller(in) m(f)

authoritative [əˈθɔr.ə.teɪ.t̬ɪv] adj maßgebend

authority [əˈθɔr.ɪ.t̬i] n ❶ (*right of control*) Autorität f; **in ~** verantwortlich ❷ (*permission*) Befugnis f; (*to act on sb's behalf*) Vollmacht f ❸ (*organization*) Behörde f

authorization [ˌɔ.θər.ɪˈzeɪ.ʃən] n Genehmigung f

authorize [ˈɔ.θə.raɪz] vt genehmigen

auto [ˈɔ.toʊ] I. n Auto nt II. adj ❶ (*concerning cars*) Auto- ❷ (*automatic*) automatisch

autobiography [ˌɔ.t̬ə.baɪˈag.rə.fi] n Autobiografie f

autograph [ˈɔ.t̬ə.græf] I. n Autogramm nt II. vt signieren

automate [ˈɔ.t̬ə.meɪt] vt automatisieren

automated 'teller machine n Geldautomat m

automatic [ˌɔ.t̬əˈmæt̬.ɪk] I. adj automatisch II. n ❶ (*nonmanual machine*) Automat m ❷ (*rifle*) Selbstladegewehr nt

automatic 'pilot n Autopilot m

automatic 'teller machine n see **automated teller machine**

automation [ˌɔ.t̬əˈmeɪ.ʃən] n Automatisierung f

automobile [ˈɔ.t̬ə.moʊ.bil] n Auto nt

autopsy [ˈɔ.tap.si] n Autopsie f

autumn [ˈɔ.t̬əm] n Herbst m

auxiliary [ɔgˈzɪl.jə.ri] I. n ❶ Hilfskraft f ❷ LING Hilfsverb nt II. adj Hilfs-; (*additional*) Zusatz-

A

available [ə·'veɪ·lə·bəl] *adj* ❶ verfügbar; **to make ~** zur Verfügung stellen ❷ ECON erhältlich; (*in stock*) lieferbar

avalanche ['æv·ə·læntʃ] *n* Lawine *f*

avant-garde [ˌa·vant·'gard] *adj* avantgardistisch

Ave. *n abbrev of* **avenue**

avenue ['æv·ə·nu] *n* ❶ (*street*) Avenue *f* ❷ (*fig: possibility*) Weg *m*

average ['æv·ər·ɪdʒ] **I.** *n* Durchschnitt *m;* **on ~** im Durchschnitt **II.** *adj* durchschnittlich; **~ income** Durchschnittseinkommen *nt* **III.** *vt* im Durchschnitt betragen

aversion [ə·'vɜr·ʒən] *n* Abneigung *f*

avert [ə·'vɜrt] *vt* verhindern

avg. *n, adj abbrev of* **average**

aviation [ˌeɪ·vi·'eɪ·ʃən] *n* Luftfahrt *f;* **~ industry** Flugzeugindustrie *f*

avid ['æv·ɪd] *adj* eifrig, begeistert

avocado <*pl* -s> [ˌæv·ə·'ka·doʊ] *n* Avocado *f*

avoid [ə·'vɔɪd] *vt* ❶ (*stay away from*) meiden ❷ (*prevent sth from happening*) vermeiden

avoidable [ə·'vɔɪ·də·bəl] *adj* vermeidbar

avoidance [ə·'vɔɪd·əns] *n* Vermeidung *f; of taxes* Umgehung *f*

await [ə·'weɪt] *vt* erwarten; **long ~ed** lang ersehnt

awake [ə·'weɪk] *adj* wach

awakening [ə·'weɪ·kə·nɪŋ] *n* **rude ~** böses Erwachen

award [ə·'wɔrd] *n* Auszeichnung *f*

aware [ə·'wer] *adj* ❶ (*knowing*) ▪**to be ~ of sth** sich *dat* einer S. *gen* bewusst sein ❷ (*physically sensing*) ▪**to be ~ of sb/sth** jdn/etw [be]merken ❸ (*well informed*) informiert

awareness [ə·'wer·nɪs] *n* Bewusstsein *nt*

awash [ə·'waʃ] *adj* ▪**to be ~** unter Wasser stehen

away [ə·'weɪ] **I.** *adv* ❶ (*distant*) weg; **to be ~ on business** geschäftlich unterwegs sein; **two days ~** in zwei Tagen ❷ SPORT auswärts **II.** *adj* SPORT **~ game** Auswärtsspiel *nt*

awe [ɔ] *n* Ehrfurcht *f*

'awe-inspiring *adj* Ehrfurcht gebietend

awesome ['ɔ·səm] *adj* ❶ (*impressive*) beeindruckend ❷ (*sl: very good*) spitze

awful ['ɔ·fəl] *adj* ❶ (*extremely bad*) furchtbar; **to look ~** schrecklich aussehen ❷ (*great*) außerordentlich; **an ~ lot** eine riesige Menge

awfully ['ɔ·fə·li] *adv* furchtbar; **~ good** besonders gut

awkward ['ɔk·wərd] *adj* ❶ (*difficult*) schwierig ❷ (*embarrassing*) peinlich ❸ (*inconvenient*) ungünstig

awning ['ɔ·nɪŋ] *n* (*on building*) Markise *f;* (*on camper*) Vorzelt *nt*

ax, axe [æks] *n* Axt *f*

axis <*pl* axes> ['æk·sɪs] *n* Achse *f*

axle ['æk·səl] *n* Achse *f*

aye [aɪ] *interj* NAUT **~, ~, sir!** zu Befehl, Herr Kapitän!

AZ *abbrev of* **Arizona**

azalea [ə·'zeɪl·jə] *n* Azalee *f*

azure ['æʒ·ər] *adj* azur[blau]

Bb

B <*pl* -'s>, **b** <*pl* -'s> [bi] *n* ❶ (*letter*) B *nt*, b *nt*; ~ **as in Bravo** B wie Berta ❷ MUS H *nt*, h *nt* ❸ (*school mark*) ≈ Zwei *f*

BA [ˌbiˈeɪ] *n abbrev of* **Bachelor of Arts** B.A.

babble [ˈbæb·əl] I. *n* Geplapper *nt* II. *vt, vi* plappern; (*stammer*) stammeln; *baby* babbeln

babe [beɪb] *n* (*fam*) ❶ (*address*) Schatz *m* ❷ (*person*) Süße(r) *f(m)*

baboon [bæˈbun] *m* Pavian *m*

baby [ˈbeɪ·bi] I. *n* ❶ (*child*) Baby *nt*; **to have a ~** ein Baby bekommen ❷ (*fam: address*) Baby *nt* II. *adj* klein

'baby carriage *n* Kinderwagen *m*

'baby-sit I. *vi* babysitten *fam* II. *vt* ▪ **to ~ sb** auf jdn aufpassen

'babysitter *n* Babysitter(in) *m(f)*

bachelor [ˈbætʃ·ə·lər] *n* ❶ Junggeselle *m* ❷ UNIV **B~ of Arts/Science** Bakkalaureus *m* der philosophischen/naturwissenschaftlichen Fakultät (*unterster akademischer Grad in englischsprachigen Ländern*)

back [bæk] I. *n* ❶ (*of body*) Rücken *m*; *of building, page* Rückseite *f*; *of car* Heck *nt*; *of chair* Lehne *f* II. *adj* Hinter-; ~ **pocket** Gesäßtasche *f*; (*of body*) Rücken- III. *adv* (*to previous place*) [wieder] zurück; **there and ~** hin und zurück; ~ **and forth** hin und her; (*in past*) **that was ~ in 1950** das war [schon] 1950 IV. *vt* (*support*) unterstützen
  ◆ **back away** *vi* zurückweichen
  ◆ **back down** *vi* nachgeben
  ◆ **back off** ~ **off!** lass mich in Ruhe!
  ◆ **back out** *vi* einen Rückzieher machen
  ◆ **back up** I. *vi traffic* sich stauen II. *vt* (*support*) unterstützen ❷ COMPUT sichern ❸ (*reverse*) zurücksetzen

'backbone *n* Rückgrat *nt a. fig*

back 'door *n* Hintertür *f*

'backfire *vi* ❶ AUTO fehlzünden ❷ (*go wrong*) fehlschlagen

background [ˈbæk·graʊnd] *n* Hintergrund *m*

backing [ˈbæk·ɪŋ] *n* Unterstützung *f*

'backlash *n* Gegenreaktion *f*

'backlog *n usu sing* Rückstand *m*

'backpack I. *n* Rucksack *m* II. *vi* mit dem Rucksack reisen

'backpacker *n* Rucksackreisende(r) *f(m)*

'back seat *n* Rücksitz *m*

'backside *n* (*fam*) Hintern *m*

'backstroke *n* Rückenschwimmen *nt*

'back talk *n* (*fam*) Widerrede *f*

'backtrack *vi* ❶ (*go back*) [wieder] zurückgehen ❷ (*change opinion*) einlenken

'backup [ˈbæk·ʌp] *n* ❶ (*support*) Unterstützung *f* ❷ COMPUT Sicherung *f*, Backup *nt*

backward [ˈbæk·wərd] *adj* ❶ (*facing rear*) rückwärtsgewandt; (*reversed*) Rück[wärts]- *m* ❷ (*slow to learn*) zurückgeblieben ❸ (*underdeveloped*) rückständig

backward(s) [ˈbæk·wərd(z)] *adv* ❶ (*toward the back*) nach hinten ❷ (*in reverse*) rückwärts ❸ (*into past*) zurück

back'yard *n* Hinterhof *m*

bacon [ˈbeɪ·kən] *n* [Schinken]speck *m*

bacteria [bækˈtɪr·i·ə] *npl* Bakterien *pl*

bad <worse, worst> [bæd] I. *adj* schlecht; *dream* böse; *smell* übel II. *adv* (*fam*) sehr

badge [bædʒ] *n* Abzeichen *nt*

badger [ˈbædʒ·ər] I. *n* Dachs *m* II. *vt* bedrängen

badly <worse, worst> [ˈbæd·li] *adv* ❶ (*poorly*) schlecht ❷ (*very much*) sehr

badminton [ˈbæd·mɪn·tən] *n* Federball *m*

baffle [ˈbæf·əl] *vt* verwirren

baffling [ˈbæf·əl·ɪŋ] *adj* verwirrend, rätselhaft

B

bag [bæg] n Tasche f; (of plastic etc) Tüte f; (handbag) Handtasche f

bagel ['beɪ·gəl] n Bagel m

baggage ['bæg·ɪdʒ] n Gepäck nt

'baggage allowance n Freigepäck nt

'baggage check n Gepäckkontrolle f

'baggage claim n Gepäckausgabe f

baggy ['bæg·i] adj [weit] geschnitten

'bagpipes npl Dudelsack m

Bahamas [bə·'ha·məz] npl ■the ~ die Bahamas

bail [beɪl] I. n Kaution f II. vt ■to ~ sb jdn gegen Kaution freilassen
 ◆ **bail out** I. vt ■to ~ out ○ sb für jdn [die] Kaution stellen II. vi AVIAT [mit dem Fallschirm] abspringen

bailiff ['beɪ·lɪf] n Justizwachtmeister(in) m(f)

bait [beɪt] n Köder m a. fig

bake [beɪk] vt, vi backen

baker ['beɪ·kər] n Bäcker(in) m(f)

bakery ['beɪ·kə·ri] n Bäckerei f

'baking powder n Backpulver nt

'baking soda n Natron nt

balance ['bæl·əns] I. n ❶ Gleichgewicht nt a. fig ❷ FIN Kontostand m II. vt balancieren; (achieve equilibrium) ein Gleichgewicht herstellen

balcony ['bæl·kə·ni] n Balkon m

bald [bɔld] adj glatzköpfig; **to go** ~ eine Glatze bekommen

bale [beɪl] n Ballen m

balk [bɔk] vi zurückschrecken

ball [bɔl] n ❶ Ball m ❷ (dance) Ball m
 ►PHRASES: **to have a** ~ Spaß haben

ballad ['bæl·əd] n Ballade f

ballast ['bæl·əst] n Ballast m

ball 'bearing n Kugellager nt

ballerina [ˌbæl·ə·'ri·nə] n Ballerina f

ballet [bæ·'leɪ] n Ballett nt

bal'let dancer n Balletttänzer(in) m(f)

'ball game n Baseballspiel nt

ballistic [bə·'lɪs·tɪk] adj ballistisch
 ►PHRASES: **to go** ~ (fam) ausflippen fam

balloon [bə·'lun] n Ballon m

ballot ['bæl·ət] n ❶ Stimmzettel m ❷ (vote) geheime Abstimmung; (election) Geheimwahl f

'ballot box n Wahlurne f

'ballpark n Baseballstadion nt

'ballplayer n Baseballspieler(in) m(f)

'ballpoint, ballpoint 'pen n Kugelschreiber m

'ballroom n Ballsaal m

ballroom 'dancing n Gesellschaftstanz m

balls [bɔlz] n pl (vulg, sl: testicles) Eier pl derb

Baltic ['bɔl·tɪk] n ■the ~ die Ostsee

bamboo [bæm·'bu] n Bambus m

bamboozle [bæm·'bu·zəl] vt (fam) ❶ (confuse) verwirren ❷ (trick) übers Ohr hauen

ban [bæn] I. n Verbot nt II. vt <-nn-> act, event verbieten; person ausschließen

banal [bə·'næl] adj banal

banana [bə·'næn·ə] n Banane f

band[1] [bænd] n ❶ of metal, cloth Band nt ❷ of color Streifen m

band[2] [bænd] n MUS Band f; (traditional) Kapelle f; of criminals Bande f

bandage ['bæn·dɪdʒ] I. n Verband m; (of cloth) Binde f II. vt bandagieren; wound verbinden

'Band-Aid® n Pflaster nt

B & B [ˌbi·ən(d)·'bi] n abbrev of **bed and breakfast**

bandit ['bæn·dɪt] n Bandit(in) m(f)

'bandwagon n ►PHRASES: **to jump on the** ~ auf den fahrenden Zug aufspringen

bang [bæŋ] I. n ❶ (sound) Knall m ❷ (blow) Schlag m ❸ ■~s pl (fringe) [kurzer] Pony II. vi Krach machen; door knallen III. vt door zuschlagen

bangle ['bæŋ·gəl] n Armreif[en] m

banister ['bæn·ə·stər] n usu pl [Treppen]geländer nt

banjo <pl -s> ['bæn·ʒoʊ] n Banjo nt

bank[1] [bæŋk] n Ufer nt; (raised area) Abhang m

bank[2] [bæŋk] I. n FIN Bank f II. vi ■to ~ with sb bei jdm ein Konto haben
 ◆ **bank on** vt ■to ~ on sth (rely on) auf etw dat zählen; (expect) mit etw dat rechnen

'bank account n Bankkonto nt

B

'bank balance n Kontostand m
banker ['bæŋ·kər] n Banker(in) m(f)
banking ['bæŋ·kɪŋ] n Bankwesen nt
'bank robber n Bankräuber(in) m(f)
bankrupt ['bæŋk·rʌpt] I. adj bankrott; **to go ~** in Konkurs gehen II. n Konkursschuldner(in) m(f)
bankruptcy ['bæŋk·rəp·si] n Konkurs m
'bank statement n Kontoauszug m
banner ['bæn·ər] n Banner nt
banquet ['bæŋ·kwət] n Bankett nt
baptism ['bæp·tɪz·əm] n Taufe f
Baptist ['bæp·tɪst] n Baptist(in) m(f)
baptize ['bæp·taɪz] vt taufen
bar [bar] I. n ① (rod) Stange f; of cage Gitterstab m; **to be behind ~s** hinter Schloss und Riegel sein ② of chocolate Riegel m; of soap Stück nt ③ (for drinking) Lokal nt, Bar f; (counter) Theke f ④ LAW **to be admitted to the ~** als Anwalt/Anwältin [vor Gericht] zugelassen werden II. vt <-rr-> ① (fasten) verriegeln ② (obstruct) blockieren ③ (prohibit) something verbieten; somebody ausschließen III. prep außer
barbarian [bar·'ber·i·ən] n Barbar(in) m(f)
barbaric [bar·'ber·ɪk] adj barbarisch
barbecue ['bar·bɪ·kju] I. n Grill m; (event) Grillparty f II. vt grillen
barbed 'wire n Stacheldraht m
barber ['bar·bər] n [Herren]friseur m
'bar code n Strichcode m
bare [ber] adj ① nackt, bloß ② **the ~ essentials** das Allernotwendigste
'bareback I. adj auf ungesatteltem Pferd nach n II. adv ohne Sattel
'barefaced adj unverschämt
'barefoot, bare'footed I. adj barfüßig II. adv barfuß
barely ['ber·li] adv ① (hardly) kaum ② (scantily) karg
bargain ['bar·gɪn] I. n ① Handel m ② (good buy) guter Kauf II. vi [ver]handeln; (haggle) feilschen
◆ **bargain for** vt rechnen mit +dat
barge [bardʒ] I. n Lastkahn m II. vi ■**to ~ into sb** jdn anrempeln
baritone ['ber·ə·toʊn] n Bariton m

bark¹ [bark] n (of tree) [Baum]rinde f
bark² [bark] I. vi dog bellen II. n Bellen nt
barley ['bar·li] n Gerste f
'barmaid n Bardame f
'barman n Barmann m
barn [barn] n Scheune f
barometer [bə·'ram·ə·tər] n Barometer nt
baroque [bə·'roʊk] adj barock
barracks ['ber·əks] npl + sing/pl vb Kaserne f
barrel ['ber·əl] n ① Fass nt ② of gun Lauf m
barren ['ber·ən] adj unfruchtbar; landscape karg
barrette [bə·'ret] n Haarspange f
barricade ['ber·ə·keɪd] I. n Barrikade f II. vt verbarrikadieren
barrier ['ber·i·ər] n Barriere f; (man-made) Absperrung f; RAIL Schranke f
barring ['bar·ɪŋ] prep ausgenommen
barrio [ba·rioʊ] n Barrio m (spanischsprachiges Viertel in amerikanischen Städten)
barrow ['ber·oʊ] n Schubkarren m
bartender ['bar·ten·dər] n Barkeeper m
barter ['bar·tər] I. n Tausch[handel] m II. vi Tauschhandel [be]treiben
base [beɪs] I. n ① (bottom) Fuß m ② (HQ) Hauptsitz m; MIL Basis f ③ SPORT Base f II. vt ① **to be ~d** company seinen Sitz haben; soldier stationiert sein ② (taken from) ■**to be ~d on sth** auf etw dat basieren
'baseball n Baseball m o nt
bash [bæʃ] (fam) I. n <pl -es> ① (blow) [heftiger] Schlag ② (party) Party f II. vi ■**to ~ into** zusammenstoßen mit +dat III. vt verhauen
bashful ['bæʃ·fəl] adj schüchtern
basic ['beɪ·sɪk] I. adj ① (fundamental) grundlegend ② (very simple) [sehr] einfach II. n ■**the ~s** pl die Grundlagen
basically ['beɪ·sɪ·kə·li] adv im Grunde
basil ['ber·zəl] n Basilikum nt
basin ['beɪ·sɪn] n Schüssel f; (washbasin) Waschbecken nt

basis <*pl* **bases**> ['beɪ·sɪs] *n* Basis *f*, Grundlage *f*

B

bask [bæsk] *vi* sich *akk* aalen *a. fig*

basket ['bæs·kɪt] *n* Korb *m*

basketball ['bæs·tərd] *n* Basketball *m*

bass[1] [beɪs] *n* MUS Bass *m*

bass[2] [bæs] *n* (*fish*) Barsch *m*

bassoon [bə·'sun] *n* Fagott *nt*

bastard ['bæs·tərd] *n* Bastard *m*

bat[1] [bæt] *n* ZOOL Fledermaus *f*

bat[2] [bæt] I. *n* SPORT Schläger *m* II. *vt, vi* <-tt-> SPORT schlagen

batch <*pl* -es> [bætʃ] *n* Stapel *m*

bated ['beɪ·tɪd] *adj* **with ~ breath** mit angehaltenem Atem

bath [bæθ] *n* Bad *nt;* **to take** [*or* **have**] **a ~** ein Bad nehmen, baden; (*tub*) [Bade]wanne *f*

bathe [beɪð] I. *vi* ein Bad nehmen; (*swim*) schwimmen II. *vt* baden

bather ['beɪ·ðər] *n* Badende(r) *f(m)*

bathing ['beɪ·ðɪŋ] *n* Baden *nt*

'bathing suit *n* Badeanzug *m;* (*trunks*) Badehose *f*

'bathrobe *n* Bademantel *m*

'bathroom *n* Bad[ezimmer] *nt;* **to go to the ~** auf die Toilette gehen

'bathtub *n* Badewanne *f*

baton [bə·'tan] *n* ❶ (*conductor's*) Taktstock *m* ❷ SPORT Staffelholz *nt* ❸ (*majorette*) [Kommando]stab *m*

battalion [bə·'tæl·jən] *n* Bataillon *nt*

batter[1] ['bæt·ər] *n* FOOD [Back]teig *m*

batter[2] ['bæt·ər] *n* SPORT Schlagmann *m*

batter[3] ['bæt·ər] I. *vt* ■**to ~ sb** jdn verprügeln; ■**to ~ sth** auf etw *akk* einschlagen II. *vi* schlagen; (*with fists*) hämmern

battered ['bæt·ərd] *adj* ❶ (*beaten*) misshandelt ❷ (*damaged*) böse zugerichtet; *car* verbeult ❸ FOOD paniert

battery ['bæt·ə·ri] *n* Batterie *f*

'battery charger *n* [Batterie]ladegerät *nt*

battle ['bæt·əl] I. *n* Kampf *m*, Schlacht *f* II. *vi* kämpfen *a. fig*

'battlefield, 'battleground *n* Schlachtfeld *nt*

'battleship *n* Schlachtschiff *nt*

bawl [bɔl] I. *vi* (*weep*) heulen, plärren; (*bellow*) brüllen II. *vt* schreien

bay [beɪ] *n* Bucht *f*

'bay leaf *n* Lorbeerblatt *nt*

bayonet [ˌbeɪ·ə·'net] *n* Bajonett *nt*

bay 'window *n* Erkerfenster *nt*

bazaar [bə·'zar] *n* Basar *m*

BC [ˌbi·'si] *adv abbrev of* **before Christ** v. Chr.

be <**was, been**> [bi] *vi* + *n/adj* ❶ (*describes*) sein; **she's a doctor** sie ist Ärztin; **what do you want to ~ when you grow up?** was willst du einmal werden, wenn du erwachsen bist? ❷ (*location*) sein; *town, country* liegen; **there is/are ...** es gibt ... ❸ (*in imperatives*) **~ quiet!** sei still!; **please ~ seated!** setzen Sie sich bitte! ❹ (*expressing continuation*) **it's raining** es regnet; **you're always complaining** du beklagst dich dauernd ❺ (*expressing passive*) **to ~ asked** gefragt werden; **what is to ~ done?** was kann getan werden?

beach [bitʃ] *n* <*pl* -es> Strand *m*

'beach ball *n* Wasserball *m*

'beachwear *n* Strandkleidung *f*

bead [bid] *n* Perle *f*

beak [bik] *n* Schnabel *m*

beaker ['bi·kər] *n* Becherglas *nt*

beam [bim] *n* ❶ (*light*) [Licht]strahl *m* ❷ (*rafter*) Balken *m* II. *vi* strahlen

bean [bin] *n* Bohne *f;* **baked ~s** Baked Beans *pl*

'bean sprouts *npl* Sojabohnensprossen *pl*

bear[1] [ber] *n* (*animal*) Bär(in) *m(f)*

bear[2] <**bore, born(e)**> [ber] I. *vt* ❶ (*carry*) tragen ❷ (*endure*) ertragen; *suspense* aushalten ❸ (*harbor*) **to ~ sb a grudge** einen Groll gegen jdn hegen ❹ (*keep*) **I'll ~ that in mind** ich werde das berücksichtigen II. *vi* **to ~ right** sich rechts halten

beard [bɪrd] *n* Bart *m*

bearded ['bɪr·dɪd] *adj* bärtig

bearing ['ber·ɪŋ] *n* Peilung *f;* **to lose one's ~s** die Orientierung verlieren

beast [bist] n Tier nt; **~ of burden** Lasttier nt; (person) Biest nt, Bestie f

beastly ['bist·li] adj scheußlich, ekelhaft

beat [bit] I. n ❶ (throb) Schlag m ❷ (act) Schlagen nt; of heart Klopfen nt ❸ MUS Takt m ❹ usu sing (route) Runde f II. adj (fam) fix und fertig III. vt <beat, beaten or beat> ❶ (hit) schlagen; ■to ~ sth gegen/auf etw akk schlagen; **to ~ sb to death** jdn totschlagen ❷ FOOD schlagen ❸ (defeat) schlagen; **it ~s me how/why ...** (fam) es ist mir ein Rätsel, wie/warum ... ▶PHRASES: **~ it!** (fam) hau ab! IV. vi <beat, beaten or beat> ❶ (throb) schlagen; heart a. klopfen ❷ (strike) ■to ~ **against/on sth** gegen etw akk schlagen

◆**beat down** I. vi rain [her]niederprasseln; sun [her]niederbrennen II. vt herunterhandeln

◆**beat off** vt abwehren; MIL zurückschlagen

◆**beat up** I. vt zusammenschlagen II. ■to ~ **up on** verprügeln

beater ['bi·t̮ər] n Rührbesen m

beautician [bju·'tɪʃ·ən] n Kosmetiker(in) m(f)

beautiful ['bju·t̮ə·fəl] adj ❶ (attractive) schön ❷ (uplifting) herrlich, großartig

beauty ['bju·t̮i] n Schönheit f

beauty contest, 'beauty pageant n Schönheitswettbewerb m

beauty parlor n Schönheitssalon m

beaver ['bi·vər] n Biber m

became [bɪ·'keɪm] pt of **become**

because [bɪ·'kɔz] I. conj weil; (since) da; (for) denn II. prep ■~ **of** wegen +gen

beckon ['bek·ən] vi winken a. fig

become <became, become> [bɪ·'kʌm] vt, vi werden; **what became of ...?** was ist aus ... geworden?

becoming [bɪ·'kʌm·ɪŋ] adj clothes vorteilhaft

bed [bed] n ❶ Bett nt; **to go to ~** ins Bett gehen ❷ (for flowers) Beet nt

bed and 'breakfast n Zimmer nt mit Frühstück

'bedclothes npl Bettzeug nt kein pl

bedding ['bed·ɪŋ] n ❶ Bettzeug nt ❷ AGR [Ein]streu f

'bed linen n Bettwäsche f

'bedridden adj bettlägerig

'bedroom n Schlafzimmer nt

bedside 'table n Nachttisch m

'bedspread n Tagesdecke f

'bedtime n Schlafenszeit f

bee [bi] n Biene f

beech [bitʃ] n Buche f

beef [bif] n Rindfleisch nt

'beefsteak n Beefsteak nt

beefy ['bi·fi] adj (fam) muskulös

'beehive n Bienenstock m; (rounded) Bienenkorb m

'beeline n **to make a ~ for sb/sth** schnurstracks auf jdn/etw zugehen

been [bɪn] pp of **be**

beep [bip] I. vt ❶ (toot) **to ~ one's horn** hupen ❷ (on pager) anpiepen II. vi piepen; (in car) hupen III. n Piep[s]ton m; of car Hupen nt

beeper ['bi·pər] n Piepser m

beer [bɪr] n Bier nt

'beer garden n Biergarten m

beet [bit] n (plant) [Runkel]rübe f; (edible root) Rote Bete

beetle ['bi·t̮əl] n Käfer m

before [bɪ·'fɔr] I. prep ❶ (earlier) vor +dat; **~ long** in Kürze ❷ (in front of) vor +dat; with verbs of motion vor +akk II. conj ❶ (at previous time) bevor ❷ (rather than) bevor, ehe ❸ (until) bis; ■**not ~** erst, wenn III. adv zuvor, vorher; **I have never seen that ~** das habe ich noch nie gesehen IV. adj after n zuvor

beforehand [bɪ·'fɔr·hænd] adv vorher

befriend [bɪ·'frend] vt sich anfreunden mit +dat

beg <-gg-> [beg] I. vt bitten; **to ~ sb's forgiveness** jdn um Verzeihung bitten; **I ~ your pardon** entschuldigen Sie bitte II. vi ❶ (seek charity) betteln ❷ (request) **to ~ for mercy** um Gnade flehen ❸ dog Männchen machen

began [bɪ·'gæn] pt of **begin**

beggar ['beg·ər] n Bettler(in) m(f)

B

begin <-nn-, began, begun> [bɪ-ˈgɪn] *vt, vi* anfangen, beginnen; **she was ~ning to get angry** sie wurde allmählich wütend; **to ~ with** zunächst einmal

beginner [bɪ-ˈgɪn-ər] *n* Anfänger(in) *m(f)*

beginning [bɪ-ˈgɪn-ɪŋ] *n* Anfang *m*; (*in time*) Beginn *m*; **at** [*or* **in**] **the ~** am Anfang

begrudge [bɪ-ˈgrʌdʒ] *vt* ■**to ~ sb sth** jdm etw missgönnen

begun [bɪ-ˈgʌn] *pp of* **begin**

behalf [bɪ-ˈhæf] *n* **on ~ of sb** [*or* **on sb's ~**] (*speaking for*) im Namen einer Person; (*as authorized by*) im Auftrag von jdm

behave [bɪ-ˈheɪv] I. *vi* ❶ *people* sich benehmen; **~!** benimm dich! ❷ *object, substance* sich verhalten II. *vt* ■**to ~ oneself** sich [anständig] benehmen

behavior [bɪ-ˈheɪv-jər] *n* Benehmen *nt*, Verhalten *nt*

behind [bɪ-ˈhaɪnd] I. *prep* ❶ hinter +*dat*; *with verbs of motion* hinter +*akk* ❷ (*fig*) **I'm ~ you all the way** ich stehe voll hinter dir II. *adv* hinten III. *adj* ❶ (*in arrears*) im Rückstand ❷ (*slow*) **to be** [**way**] **~** [weit] zurück sein IV. *n* (*fam*) Hintern *m*

beige [beɪʒ] *adj* beige[farben]

being [ˈbiː-ɪŋ] I. *n* ❶ (*creature*) Wesen *nt* ❷ (*existence*) Dasein *nt* II. *adj* **for the time ~** vorerst

belated [bɪ-ˈleɪ-tɪd] *adj* verspätet

belch [beltʃ] I. *n* <*pl* -es> Rülpser *m* II. *vi* rülpsen

belfry [ˈbel-fri] *n* Glockenturm *m*

Belgian [ˈbel-dʒən] I. *n* Belgier(in) *m(f)* II. *adj* belgisch

Belgium [ˈbel-dʒəm] *n* Belgien *nt*

belief [bɪ-ˈlif] *n* ❶ (*faith*) Glaube *m kein pl* ❷ (*view*) Überzeugung *f*

believable [bɪ-ˈliː-və-bəl] *adj* glaubwürdig

believe [bɪ-ˈliv] I. *vt* ❶ glauben; **would you ~ it?** kannst du dir das vorstellen? ❷ (*pretend*) **to make ~** [**that**] … so tun, als ob … II. *vi* ❶ (*be certain of*)

glauben (**in** an +*akk*) ❷ (*have confidence*) ■**to ~ in sb/sth** auf jdn/etw vertrauen ❸ (*support sincerely*) ■**to ~ in sth** viel von etw *dat* halten ❹ (*think*) glauben; **I ~ so** ich glaube schon

believer [bɪ-ˈliː-vər] *n* Gläubige(r) *f(m)*

bell [bel] *n* Glocke *f*; (*smaller*) Glöckchen *nt*; (*on door*) [Tür]klingel *f*

ˈbellboy *n* [Hotel]page *m*

belligerent [bɪ-ˈlɪdʒ-ər-ənt] *adj* kampflustig

bellow [ˈbel-oʊ] I. *vt, vi* brüllen II. *n* Gebrüll *nt*

bellows [ˈbel-oʊz] *npl* Blasebalg *m*

belly [ˈbel-i] *n* Bauch *m*

ˈbellyache *n* (*fam*) Bauchschmerzen *pl*, Bauchweh *nt kein pl*

ˈbelly button *n* (*fam*) [Bauch]nabel *m*

ˈbelly dancer *n* Bauchtänzerin *f*

belong [bɪ-ˈlaŋ] *vi* ❶ (*be owned*) ■**to ~ to sb** jdm gehören; **where do these spoons ~?** wohin gehören diese Löffel? ❷ (*fit in*) [dazu]gehören

belongings [bɪ-ˈlaŋ-ɪŋz] *npl* Hab und Gut *nt kein pl*

beloved [bɪ-ˈlʌv-ɪd] I. *n* Geliebte(r) *f(m)* II. *adj* geliebt

below [bɪ-ˈloʊ] I. *adv* ❶ (*lower*) unten, darunter ❷ (*on page*) unten II. *prep* unter +*dat*; *with verbs of motion* unter +*akk*

belt [belt] I. *n* Gürtel *m*; (*conveyor*) Band *nt*; (*area*) Gebiet *nt* II. *vt* hauen; *ball* knallen

bemused [bɪ-ˈmjuzd] *adj* verwirrt

bench <*pl* -es> [bentʃ] *n* Bank *f*; LAW ■**the ~** die [Richter]bank

ˈbenchmark *n* Maßstab *m*

ˈbenchwarmer *n* SPORT Ersatzspieler(in) *m(f)* (*der/die kaum eingesetzt wird*)

bend [bend] I. *n* (*in road*) Kurve *f*; (*in river*) Biegung *f* II. *vi* <bent, bent> ❶ (*turn*) *road* biegen; **to ~ forward** sich vorbeugen ❷ (*be flexible*) sich biegen; *tree* sich neigen III. *vt* biegen; (*deform*) verbiegen; **to ~ the rules** (*fig*) sich nicht ganz an die Regeln halten

♦ **bend down** *vi* sich niederbeugen

beneath [bɪ-ˈniθ] I. *prep* unter +*dat*;

with verbs of motion unter +*akk* **II.** *adv* unten, darunter

benefactor ['ben·ə·fæk·tər] *n* Wohltä-ter(in) *m(f)*

beneficiary [ˌben·ə·'fɪʃ·i·ər·i] *n* Nutz-nießer(in) *m(f)*

benefit ['ben·ə·fɪt] **I.** *n* ❶ (*advantage*) Vorteil *m;* (*profit*) Nutzen *m* ❷ (*welfare*) Beihilfe *f* **II.** *vi* <-t-> ■ **to ~ from sth** von etw *dat* profitieren **III.** *vt* <-t-> ■ **to ~ sb/sth** jdm/etw nützen

bent [bent] **I.** *pt, pp of* **bend II.** *n* Nei-gung *f* **III.** *adj* umgebogen; *wire* ver-bogen; *person* gekrümmt

bequest [bɪ·'kwest] *n* Vermächtnis *nt*

bereaved [bɪ·'riːvd] **I.** *adj* trauernd **II.** *n* ■ **the ~** *pl* die Hinterbliebenen

bereavement [bɪ·'riːv·mənt] *n* Trauer-fall *m*

beret [bə·'reɪ] *n* Baskenmütze *f;* MIL Ba-rett *nt*

Bermuda shorts [bər·ˌmjuː·də·'ʃɔrts] *npl* Bermudas *pl*

berry ['ber·i] *n* Beere *f*

berserk [bər·'sɜrk] *adj* außer sich *dat;* **to go ~** [fuchsteufels]wild werden

berth [bɜrθ] *n* (*for ship*) Liegeplatz *m;* (*bed*) [Schlaf]koje *f;* RAIL Schlafwagen-bett *nt*

beside [bɪ·'saɪd] *prep* ❶ (*next to*) neben +*dat; with verbs of motion* neben +*akk* ❷ (*irrelevant to*) **~ the point** nicht der Punkt

besides [bɪ·'saɪdz] **I.** *adv* außerdem **II.** *prep* ❶ (*in addition to*) außer +*dat* ❷ (*except for*) abgesehen von +*dat*

besiege [bɪ·'siːdʒ] *vt* belagern

best [best] **I.** *adj superl of* **good** ❶ (*fin-est*) ■ **the ~ ...** der/die/das beste ...; **~ wishes** herzliche Grüße ❷ (*most fa-vorable*) **what's the ~ way to ...** wie komme ich am besten zum/zur ...; ■ **to be ~** am besten sein **II.** *adv superl of* **well** am besten; **~ of all** am allerbesten **III.** *n* ❶ (*finest person, thing*) ■ **the ~** der/die/das Beste ❷ (*most favorable*) **all the ~!** (*fam*) alles Gute!; **at ~** bes-tenfalls

best 'man *n* Trauzeuge *m* (*des Bräuti-gams*)

best'seller *n* Bestseller *m*

bet [bet] **I.** *n* Wette *f;* **to make a ~ with sb** mit jdm wetten **II.** *vt, vi* <-tt-, bet *or* -ted, bet *or* -ted> wetten; **I ~ you 25 dollars that ...** ich wette mit dir um 25 Dollar, dass ...

betray [bɪ·'treɪ] *vt* ❶ (*be disloyal to*) verraten; (*deceive*) betrügen ❷ (*reveal*) *feelings* zeigen

betrayal [bɪ·'treɪ·əl] *n* Verrat *m*

better ['bet·ər] **I.** *adj comp of* **good** bes-ser; **she is much ~ at tennis than I am** sie spielt viel besser Tennis als ich; **to get ~** sich erholen **II.** *adv comp of* **well** ❶ (*more skillfully*) besser ❷ (*to a greater degree*) mehr; **there's nothing I like ~ than ...** ich tue nichts lieber als ... **III.** *n* **to change for the ~** sich zum Guten wenden; **all** [*or* **so much**] **the ~** umso besser

betting ['bet·ɪŋ] *n* Wetten *nt*

between [bɪ·'twin] **I.** *prep* zwischen +*dat; with verbs of motion* zwischen +*akk;* **~ you and me** unter uns gesagt **II.** *adv* ■ **[in] ~** dazwischen

beverage ['bev·ər·ɪdʒ] *n* Getränk *nt*

beware [bɪ·'wer] *vt, vi* sich in Acht neh-men (**of** vor +*dat*); **"~ of the dog"** „[Vorsicht,] bissiger Hund!"

bewilder [bɪ·'wɪl·dər] *vt* verwirren

bewilderment [bɪ·'wɪl·dər·mənt] *n* Verwirrung *f*

bewitch [bɪ·'wɪtʃ] *vt* ❶ (*by magic*) ver-zaubern ❷ (*delight*) bezaubern

beyond [bɪ·'jɑnd] **I.** *prep* ❶ (*on other side*) über +*akk,* jenseits +*gen* ❷ (*after*) nach +*dat* ❸ (*further than*) über +*akk* ❹ (*surpassing*) **~ help** nicht mehr zu helfen **II.** *adv* (*in space*) jenseits; (*in time*) darüber hinaus

biannual [ˌbaɪ·'æn·ju·əl] *adj* halbjähr-lich

bias ['baɪ·əs] **I.** *n usu sing* ❶ (*prejudice*) Vorurteil *nt* ❷ (*predisposition*) Nei-gung *f* **II.** *vt* <-s-> ■ **to ~ sb against sth** jdn gegen etw *akk* einnehmen

biased ['baɪ·əst] *adj* voreingenommen

B

bib [bɪb] *n* Lätzchen *nt*

Bible ['baɪ·bəl] *n* Bibel *f*

'Bible belt *n* Bibelgürtel *m* (*sehr christliche Gebiete der USA*)

biblical ['bɪb·lɪ·kəl] *adj* biblisch

bibliography [ˌbɪb·liˈɑg·rə·fi] *n* Bibliografie *f*

bicarbonate [baɪˈkar·bə·nɪt], **bicarbonate of 'soda** *n* Natriumbikarbonat *nt*; (*in cooking*) Natron *nt*

bicentennial [baɪ·senˈten·ɪ·əl], **bicentenary** [baɪˈsen·ten·ə·ri] *n* zweihundertjähriges Jubiläum

biceps <*pl* -> ['baɪ·seps] *n* Bizeps *m*

bicker ['bɪk·ər] *vi* sich zanken

bicycle ['baɪ·sɪk·əl] *n* Fahrrad *nt*

bid¹ <-dd-, bid *or* bade, bid *or* bidden> [bɪd] *vt* **to ~ sb farewell** jdm Lebewohl sagen

bid² [bɪd] I. *n* ❶ (*offer*) Angebot *nt*; (*at auction*) Gebot *nt* ❷ (*attempt*) Versuch *m* II. *vt, vi* <-dd-, bid, bid> bieten

biennial [baɪˈen·ɪ·əl] *adj* zweijährlich

big <-gg-> [bɪg] *adj* ❶ groß; *tip* großzügig ❷ (*significant*) bedeutend

bigamist ['bɪg·ə·mɪst] *n* Bigamist(in) *m(f)*

bigamy ['bɪg·ə·mi] *n* Bigamie *f*

Big 'Apple *n* (*fam*) ■**the ~** New York *nt*

big 'cheese *n* (*fam*) hohes Tier *fam*

Big 'Easy *n* ■**the ~** New Orleans *nt*

bigot ['bɪg·ət] *n* Eiferer, Eiferin *m, f*

bigoted ['bɪg·ə·t̬ɪd] *adj* fanatisch

bigotry ['bɪg·ə·tri] *n* Fanatismus *m*

'big shot *n* (*fam*) hohes Tier

'big time *n* (*fam*) **to hit the ~** den großen Durchbruch schaffen

bike [baɪk] *n* (*fam: bicycle*) [Fahr]rad *nt*; (*motorcycle*) Motorrad *nt*

biker ['baɪ·kər] *n* (*fam: bicycle rider*) Fahrradfahrer; (*motorcycle rider*) Motorradfahrer(in) *m(f)*; (*in gang*) Rocker(in) *m(f)*

bikini [bɪˈki·ni] *n* Bikini *m*

bile [baɪl] *n* Galle *f*

bilious ['bɪl·jəs] *adj* MED **~ attack** Gallenkolik *f*

bill¹ [bɪl] *n* ❶ (*invoice*) Rechnung *f*; **could we have the ~, please?** könnten wir bitte zahlen? ❷ (*money*) Geldschein *m*; **[one-]dollar ~** Dollarschein *m* ❸ (*placard*) Plakat *nt*

bill² [bɪl] *n of bird* Schnabel *m*

'billboard *n* Reklamefläche *f*

'billfold *n* Brieftasche *f*

billiards ['bɪl·jərdz] *n* + *sing vb* Billard *nt*

billion ['bɪl·jən] *n* Milliarde *f*

'billy goat *n* Ziegenbock *m*

bimbo <*pl* -es> ['bɪm·bou] *n* (*pej fam*) Puppe *f pej*

bin [bɪn] *n* (*for garbage*) Mülleimer *m*; (*for storage*) Behälter *m*

binary ['baɪ·nə·ri] *adj* binär

bind [baɪnd] I. *n* (*fam*) **to be a ~** lästig sein ❷ **to be in a ~** in der Klemme stecken II. *vt* <bound, bound> ■**to ~ sb** jdn fesseln; ■**to ~ sth** etw festbinden

binder ['baɪn·dər] *n* Einband *m*

binding ['baɪn·dɪŋ] I. *n* ❶ (*covering*) Einband *m* ❷ (*on ski*) Bindung *f* II. *adj* verbindlich

binge [bɪndʒ] *n* (*fam*) Gelage *nt*

bingo ['bɪŋ·gou] I. *n* Bingo *nt* II. *interj* bingo

binoculars [bɪˈnak·jə·lərz] *npl* [**pair of**] **~** Fernglas *nt*

bio'chemistry *n* Biochemie *f*

biode'gradable *adj* biologisch abbaubar

'biofuel *n* Biotreibstoff *m*

'biogas *n* Biogas *nt*

biographer [baɪˈag·rə·fər] *n* Biograf(in) *m(f)*

biographical [ˌbaɪ·ouˈgræf·ɪ·kəl] *adj* biografisch

biography [baɪˈag·rə·fi] *n* Biografie *f*

biological [ˌbaɪ·əˈladʒ·ɪ·kəl] *adj* biologisch

biologist [baɪˈal·ə·dʒɪst] *n* Biologe, -in *m, f*

biology [baɪˈal·ə·dʒi] *n* Biologie *f*

biopsy ['baɪ·ap·si] *n* Biopsie *f*

biped ['baɪ·ped] *n* Zweifüß[l]er(in) *m(f)*

birch <*pl* -es> [bɜrtʃ] *n* Birke *f*

bird [bɜrd] *n* Vogel *m*

'birdcage *n* Vogelkäfig *m*

B

birdie ['bɜr·di] n ❶ (esp childspeak) Piepmatz m ❷ SPORT Federball m

'**birdseed** n Vogelfutter nt

'**bird's-eye 'view** n Vogelperspektive f

'**bird watching** n das Beobachten von Vögeln

birth [bɜrθ] n ❶ (event) Geburt f; **date of ~** Geburtsdatum nt; **to give ~ to a child** ein Kind zur Welt bringen ❷ (family) Abstammung f; **American by ~** gebürtiger Amerikaner/gebürtige Amerikanerin

'**birth certificate** n Geburtsurkunde f

'**birth control** n Geburtenkontrolle f

birthday ['bɜrθ·deɪ] n Geburtstag m; **happy ~ [to you]!** alles Gute zum Geburtstag!

'**birthday cake** n Geburtstagstorte f

'**birthday card** n Geburtstagskarte f

'**birthday party** n Geburtstagsparty f

'**birthday present** n Geburtstagsgeschenk nt

'**birthmark** n Muttermal nt

'**birthplace** n Geburtsort m

biscuit ['bɪs·kɪt] n Brötchen nt

bisect ['baɪ·sekt] vt zweiteilen

bisexual [ˌbaɪ·ˈsek·ʃʊ·əl] I. n Bisexuelle(r) f(m) II. adj bisexuell

bishop ['bɪʃ·əp] n ❶ REL Bischof m ❷ CHESS Läufer m

bison <pl -s> ['baɪ·sən] n Bison m; (European) Wisent m

bit[1] [bɪt] n ❶ (piece) Stück nt ❷ (part) Teil m; of a story Stelle f ❸ (a little) ■**a ~** ein bisschen ❹ (quite a lot) [quite] **a ~ of money** ziemlich viel Geld

bit[2] [bɪt] vt, vi pt of bite

bitch [bɪtʃ] n <pl -es> ❶ (pej fam) Miststück nt ❷ (dog) Hündin f

bite [baɪt] I. n Biss m; of insect Stich m; **to have a ~ to eat** (fam) eine Kleinigkeit essen II. vt <bit, bitten> beißen; insect stechen; **to ~ one's nails** an seinen Nägeln kauen III. vi <bit, bitten> dog, snake beißen; insect stechen

bitten ['bɪt·ən] vt, vi pp of bite

bitter ['bɪt·ər] adj <-er, -est> ❶ taste bitter ❷ (fig) bitter ❸ (resentful) verbittert

bitterly ['bɪt·ər·li] adv bitter; **~ cold** bitterkalt; **~ disappointed** schwer enttäuscht

bitterness ['bɪt·ər·nɪs] n Verbitterung f; FOOD Bitterkeit f

bizarre [bɪ·ˈzɑr] adj bizarr; behavior seltsam

blab <-bb-> [blæb] vi (fam) ausplaudern

black [blæk] I. adj schwarz a. fig; **~ and blue** grün und blau II. n ❶ (person) Schwarze(r) f(m) ❷ (color) Schwarz nt

blackberry ['blæk·ˌber·i] n Brombeere f

'**blackbird** n Amsel f

'**blackboard** n Tafel f

black 'box n AEROSP Flugschreiber m

black 'eye n blaues Auge

'**blackhead** n Mitesser m

black 'hole n schwarzes Loch a. fig

blackjack ['blæk·dʒæk] n CARDS Siebzehnundvier nt

'**blacklist** I. n schwarze Liste II. vt auf die schwarze Liste setzen

'**blackmail** I. n Erpressung f II. vt erpressen

'**blackmailer** n Erpresser(in) m(f)

black 'market n Schwarzmarkt m

blackout ['blæk·aʊt] n ❶ (unconsciousness) Ohnmachtsanfall m ❷ ELEC [Strom]ausfall m

Black 'Sea n ■**the ~** das Schwarze Meer

bladder ['blæd·ər] n [Harn]blase f

blade [bleɪd] n Klinge f; **~ of grass** Grashalm m

blame [bleɪm] I. vt ■**to ~ sb/sth for sth** [or sth on sb/sth] jdm/etw die Schuld an etw dat geben II. n Schuld f; **to take the ~** die Schuld auf sich nehmen

blameless ['bleɪm·lɪs] adj schuldlos; life untadelig

bland [blænd] adj fade; (fig) vage

blank [blæŋk] I. adj ❶ (empty) leer; **my mind went ~** ich hatte ein totales Blackout ❷ (without emotion) aus-

B

drucklos; (*without comprehension*) verständnislos II. *n* Leerstelle *f*, Lücke *f*

blanket ['blæŋ·kɪt] I. *n* Decke *f* II. *vt* bedecken

blare [blerᵊ] I. *n* Geplärr[e] *nt* II. *vi radio* plärren; *music* dröhnen

blast [blæst] I. *n* ❶ (*explosion*) Explosion *f* ❷ ~ **of air** Luftstoß *m*; **at full** ~ *radio* in voller Lautstärke II. *vt* sprengen

blasted ['blæs·tɪd] *adj attr* (*fam*) verdammt

blastoff ['blæst·ɑf] *n* [Raketen]start *m*

blatant ['bleɪ·tənt] *adj* offensichtlich; *lie* unverfroren

blaze [bleɪz] I. *n* ❶ (*fire*) Brand *m* ❷ (*light*) Glanz *m* II. *vi fire* [hell] lodern; *eyes* glänzen; *sun* brennen

blazer ['bleɪ·zər] *n* Blazer *m*

blazing ['bleɪ·zɪŋ] *adj fire* lodernd; *argument* heftig; *sun* grell

bleach [blitʃ] I. *vt* bleichen II. *n* <*pl* -es> Bleichmittel *nt*; (*for hair*) Blondierungsmittel *nt*

bleachers ['bli·tʃərz] *npl* unüberdachte [Zuschauer]tribüne

bleak [blik] *adj* öde; (*fig*) trostlos

bleary ['blɪr·i] *adj* (*sleepy*) verschlafen; *eyes* müde

bleat [blit] *vi sheep* blöken; *person* jammern

bled [bled] *pt, pp of* **bleed**

bleed [blid] *vi* <bled, bled> bluten

bleep [blip] I. *n* Piepton *m* II. *vi* piepsen

blemish ['blem·ɪʃ] *n* <*pl* -es> Makel *m*

blend [blend] I. *n* Mischung *f* II. *vt* [miteinander] vermischen III. *vi* (*not be noticed*) ■**to ~ into sth** mit etw *dat* verschmelzen

blender ['blen·dər] *n* Mixer *m*

bless <-ed *or* blest, -ed *or* blest> [bles] *vt* segnen ▸PHRASES: ~ [**him**/**her**]! der/die Gute!; ~ **you!** (*after a sneeze*) Gesundheit!; (*as thanks*) das ist lieb von dir!

blessing ['bles·ɪŋ] *n* Segen *m*

blew [blu] *pt of* **blow**

blind [blaɪnd] I. *n* ❶ Jalousie *f* ❷ (*people*) ■**the ~** *pl* die Blinden II. *vt*

blind machen; (*temporarily*) blenden III. *adj* blind *a. fig*

blind 'alley *n* Sackgasse *f a. fig*

blinders ['blaɪn·dərz] *n pl* Scheuklappen *pl a. fig*

blindfold ['blaɪnd·foʊld] I. *n* Augenbinde *f* II. *vt* ■**to ~ sb** jdm die Augen verbinden

blinding ['blaɪnd·ɪŋ] *adj* blendend, grell

blindness ['blaɪnd·nɪs] *n* Blindheit *f*

blink [blɪŋk] I. *vi* blinzeln; (*intentionally*) zwinkern; *of light* blinken II. *n* Blinzeln *nt*; (*intentionally*) Zwinkern *nt*

blinker ['blɪŋ·kər] *n* AUTO Blinker *m*

bliss [blɪs] *n* Glück[seligkeit *f*

blissful ['blɪs·fəl] *adj* glückselig; *smile* selig

blister ['blɪs·tər] I. *n* Blase *f* II. *vi paint* Blasen werfen; *skin* Blasen bekommen

blitz [blɪts] I. *n* [plötzlicher] Luftangriff *m* II. *vt* bombardieren

blizzard ['blɪz·ərd] *n* Schneesturm *m*

bloated ['bloʊ·tɪd] *adj* aufgedunsen; (*overindulged*) vollgestopft

blob [blab] *n* ❶ (*spot*) Klecks *m* ❷ (*mass*) Klümpchen *nt*

block [blak] I. *n* ❶ Block *m*; *of wood* Holzklotz *m* ❷ (*neighborhood*) [Häuser]block *m* II. *vt* blockieren; *artery, pipeline* verstopfen; *exit, passage* versperren

◆**block up** *vt* blockieren; (*clog*) verstopfen

blockade [bla·'keɪd] I. *n* Blockade *f* II. *vt* abriegeln

blockage ['blak·ɪdʒ] *n* Verstopfung *f*

block 'capitals, block 'letters *npl* Blockbuchstaben *pl*; **in ~** in Blockschrift

blond(e) [bland] I. *adj* blond II. *n* Blonde(r) *f(m)*; (*woman a.*) Blondine *f*

blood [blʌd] *n* Blut *nt*

'blood bank *n* Blutbank *f*

'bloodbath *n* Blutbad *nt*

'bloodcurdling *adj* markerschütternd

'blood donor *n* Blutspender(in) *m(f)*

'blood group *n* Blutgruppe *f*

'blood poisoning *n* Blutvergiftung *f*

'blood pressure *n* Blutdruck *m*

'bloodshed *n* Blutvergießen *nt*

'bloodshot *adj* blutunterlaufen

'bloodsucker *n* Blutsauger *m a. fig*

'blood test *n* Bluttest *m*

'bloodthirsty *adj* blutrünstig

'blood type *n* Blutgruppe *f*

'blood vessel *n* Blutgefäß *nt*

bloody ['blʌd·i] *adj* blutig

bloom [blum] **I.** *n* Blüte *f* **II.** *vi* blühen

blossom ['blas·əm] **I.** *n* [Baum]blüte *f* **II.** *vi* blühen *a. fig*

blot [blat] *n* Klecks *m*

blotch <*pl* -es> [blatʃ] *n* Fleck *m*

blotchy ['blatʃ·i] *adj* fleckig

blouse [blaʊs] *n* Bluse *f*

blow[1] [bloʊ] **I.** *vi* <blew, blown> *wind* wehen; (*exhale*) blasen; *fuse* durchbrennen; *tire* platzen **II.** *vt* <blew, blown> ① blasen; *wind* wehen; **to ~ one's nose** sich *dat* die Nase putzen ② (*fam*) **you've ~n it!** du hast es vermasselt!

◆ **blow away** **I.** *vt* *wind* wegwehen; (*fam: kill*) wegpusten; (*fig fam: impress*) umhauen *fig fam* **II.** *vi* wegfliegen, verwehen

◆ **blow down** **I.** *vi* umgeweht werden **II.** *vt* umwehen

◆ **blow out** **I.** *vt* ① (*extinguish*) ausblasen ② **to ~ one's brains** sich *dat* eine Kugel durch den Kopf jagen **II.** *vi* ① *candle* verlöschen ② *tire* platzen

◆ **blow up** **I.** *vi* explodieren; (*fig: get angry*) an die Decke gehen **II.** *vt* (*inflate*) aufblasen; (*fig: exaggerate*) hochspielen; (*enlarge*) vergrößern; (*destroy*) [in die Luft] sprengen

blow[2] [bloʊ] *n* ① (*hit*) Schlag *m* ② (*setback*) [Schicksals]schlag *m*

'blow-dry **I.** *vt* <-ie-> fönen **II.** *n* Fönen *nt*

blown [bloʊn] *vt, vi pp* of **blow**

blowout ['bloʊ·aʊt] *n* ① (*of tire*) Platzen *nt* [eines Reifens] ② (*fam: meal*) Schlemmerei *f*

'blowup *n* PHOT Vergrößerung *f*; (*fam: argument*) Krach *m*

blue [blu] **I.** *adj* <-r, -st> ① blau ② (*depressed*) traurig **II.** *n* Blau *nt*

'bluebell *n* [blaue Wiesen]glockenblume

'blueberry *n* Heidelbeere *f*

'blueprint *n* Blaupause *f*; (*fig*) Plan *m*

blues [bluz] *npl* ① (*fam*) **to have the ~** melancholisch drauf sein *fam* ② (*music*) Blues *m*

bluff [blʌf] **I.** *vi* bluffen **II.** *vt* täuschen **III.** *n* Bluff *m*

blunder ['blʌn·dər] **I.** *n* schwer|wiegend|er Fehler **II.** *vi* ① (*make mistake*) einen groben Fehler machen ② ■ **to ~ into sth** in etw *akk* hineinplatzen

blunt [blʌnt] *adj* ① (*not sharp*) stumpf ② (*outspoken*) direkt

bluntly ['blʌnt·li] *adv* direkt

blur [blɜr] **I.** *vi* <-rr-> verschwimmen **II.** *vt* <-rr-> verschwimmen lassen

blurred [blɜrd], **blurry** ['blɜri] *adj* verschwommen; *picture* unscharf

blush [blʌʃ] **I.** *vi* erröten **II.** *n* (Scham-)röte *f*

blusher ['blʌʃ·ər] *n* Rouge *nt*

bluster ['blʌs·tər] **I.** *vi* poltern **II.** *n* Theater *nt fig*

boa ['boʊ·ə] *n* Boa *f*

board [bɔrd] **I.** *n* ① Brett *nt*; (*blackboard*) Tafel *f*; (*bulletin board*) Schwarzes Brett; (*sign*) [Aushänge]schild *nt* ② ADMIN Behörde *f*; **~ of directors** Vorstand *m* ③ **on ~** an Bord *a. fig* **II.** *vt* ① ■ **to ~ up** mit Brettern vernageln ② *plane, ship* besteigen; *bus, train* einsteigen in +*akk* **III.** *vi* ① SCH im Internat wohnen ② AVIAT **Flight 345 is now ready for ~ing** Flug 345 ist nun fertig zum Einsteigen

boarder ['bɔr·dər] *n* ① SCH Internatsschüler(in) *m(f)* ② (*lodger*) Pensionsgast *m*

'board game *n* Brettspiel *nt*

'boarding card *n* Bordkarte *f*

'boarding house *n* Pension *f*

'boarding pass *n* Bordkarte *f*

'boarding school *n* Internat *nt*

'boardwalk *n* Uferpromenade *f* (*aus Holz*)

boast [boʊst] **I.** *vi* angeben **II.** *n* großspurige Behauptung

boat [boʊt] *n* Boot *nt*; (*bigger*) Schiff *nt*

B

'boat trip n Bootsfahrt f
bob[1] [bab] n abbrev of **bobsleigh** Bob m
bob[2] <-bb-> [bab] vi ■to ~ [up and down] sich auf und ab bewegen
'bobsled n Bob[sleigh] m
bode [boʊd] vt, vi to ~ well/ill etwas Gutes/Schlechtes bedeuten
bodice ['bad·ɪs] n Oberteil nt
bodily ['bad·əl·i] I. adj körperlich II. adv gewaltsam
body ['bad·i] n ❶ Körper m ❷ (group) Gruppe f ❸ (central part) Hauptteil m ❹ (corpse) Leiche f; (of animal) Kadaver m ❺ (substance) of hair Fülle f
'body bag n Leichensack m
'bodyguard n Bodyguard m; (group) Leibwache f
'body language n Körpersprache f
'body lotion n Körpermilch f
'body search n Leibesvisitation f
'bodywork n AUTO Karosserie f
bog [bag] n Sumpf m
'bogeyman n Schreckgespenst nt
boggle ['bag·əl] vi sprachlos [o fassungslos] sein
bogus ['boʊ·gəs] adj unecht; documents, name falsch
boil [bɔɪl] I. n ❶ to come to a ~ anfangen zu kochen ❷ MED Furunkel m o nt II. vi ❶ kochen ❷ CHEM den Siedepunkt erreichen III. vt kochen; (bring to boil) zum Kochen bringen
boiler ['bɔɪ·lər] n Boiler m
'boiler room n Kesselraum m
boiling ['bɔɪ·lɪŋ] adj kochend; weather sehr heiß; I'm ~ ich komme um vor Hitze
'boiling point n Siedepunkt m a. fig
boisterous ['bɔɪ·stər·əs] adj ❶ (rough) wild; (noisy) laut ❷ (exuberant) übermütig
bold [boʊld] adj ❶ (brave) mutig ❷ colors kräftig; pattern auffällig ❸ ~ type Fettdruck m
bologna [bə·'loʊ·ni] n ≈ Fleischwurst f
bolster ['boʊl·stər] I. n Nackenrolle f II. vt ❶ (prop up) stützen ❷ (increase) erhöhen

bolt [boʊlt] I. vi (move quickly) rasen; (run away) ausreißen; horse durchgehen II. vt ❶ (gulp down) hinunterschlingen ❷ (lock) verriegeln III. n ❶ of lightning Blitz[schlag] m ❷ (lock) Riegel m ❸ (screw) Schraubenbolzen m
bomb [bam] I. n Bombe f II. vt bombardieren
bombard [bam·'bard] vt bombardieren a. fig
bomber ['bam·ər] n (plane) Bombenflugzeug nt; (person) Bombenleger(in) m(f)
bombing ['bam·ɪŋ] n MIL Bombardierung f; (terrorist attack) Bombenanschlag m
'bombproof adj bombensicher
'bombshell n Bombe f a. fig; to drop a ~ (fig) die Bombe platzen lassen
bona fide [ˌboʊ·nə·'faɪd] adj echt; offer seriös
bonanza [bə·'næn·zə] n Goldgrube f
bond [band] I. n ❶ Bindung f ❷ FIN Schuldschein m II. vi haften
bondage ['ban·dɪdʒ] n ❶ (slavery) Sklaverei f ❷ (sexual act) Fesseln nt
bone [boʊn] n Knochen m; of fish Gräte f
'bone marrow n Knochenmark nt
bonfire ['ban·faɪr] n Freudenfeuer nt
bonnet ['ban·ɪt] n Mütze f; (dated) Haube f
bonus ['boʊ·nəs] n ❶ FIN Prämie f; **Christmas ~** Weihnachtsgratifikation f; **productivity ~** Ertragszulage f ❷ (fig: sth extra) Bonus m
bony ['boʊ·ni] adj ❶ knochig ❷ (full of bones) fish voller Gräten; meat knochig
boo [bu] I. interj ❶ (to surprise) huh ❷ (to show disapproval) buh II. vi buhen III. vt ausbuhen IV. n Buhruf m
boob [bub] n usu pl (sl) big ~s große Titten derb
'booby prize n Trostpreis m
'booby trap n getarnte Bombe
book [bʊk] I. n ❶ Buch nt ❷ FIN ■the ~s die [Geschäfts]bücher pl II. vt buchen; ■to ~ sth for sb etw für jdn

reservieren; **to be fully ~ed** *hotel* ausgebucht sein III. *vi* buchen, reservieren
'**bookcase** *n* Bücherschrank *m*
bookie ['bʊk·i] *n* (*fam*) Buchmacher(in) *m(f)*
'**booking** ['bʊk·ɪŋ] *n* Reservierung *f*
'**bookkeeper** *n* Buchhalter(in) *m(f)*
'**bookkeeping** *n* Buchhaltung *f*
booklet ['bʊk·lɪt] *n* Broschüre *f*
'**bookmark** *n* (*in book, Internet*) Lesezeichen *nt*
'**book review** *n* Buchbesprechung *f*
'**bookseller** *n* Buchhändler(in) *m(f)*
'**bookshelf** *n* Bücherregal *nt*
'**bookstore** *n* Buchgeschäft *nt*
boom[1] [bʊm] ECON I. *vi* florieren II. *n* Aufschwung *m*
boom[2] [bʊm] I. *n* Dröhnen *nt kein pl* II. *vi* dröhnen
boomerang ['bu·mə·ræŋ] *n* Bumerang *m*
boost [bust] I. *n* Auftrieb *m* II. *vt* ansteigen lassen; *morale* heben
'**booster seat** *n* AUTO Kindersitz *m*
boot [but] *n* ❶ Stiefel *m* ❷ (*fam*) **to get the ~** (*fig fam*) hinausfliegen; **to give sb the ~** (*fig fam*) jdn hinauswerfen
◆**boot out** *vt* (*fam*) rausschmeißen
booth [buθ] *n* ❶ (*cubicle*) Kabine *f*; (*in restaurant*) Sitzecke *f* ❷ (*at fair*) Stand *m*
'**bootleg** *adj* ❶ (*sold illegally*) geschmuggelt ❷ (*illegally made*) illegal hergestellt
booty ['bu·ti] *n* Beutegut *nt*
booze [buz] (*fam*) I. *n* Alk *m* II. *vi* saufen
border ['bɔr·dər] *n* Grenze *f*; (*edge*) Begrenzung *f*; *of picture* Umrahmung *f*; FASHION Borte *f*; (*in garden*) Rabatte *f*
◆**border on** *vi* grenzen an +*akk*
borderline ['bɔr·dər·laɪn] I. *n* Grenze *f* II. *adj* Grenz-
bore[1] [bɔr] I. *n* (*thing*) langweilige Sache; (*person*) Langweiler(in) *m(f)* II. *vt* langweilen
bore[2] [bɔr] *pt of* **bear**
bore[3] [bɔr] *vt, vi* bohren
bored [bɔrd] *adj* gelangweilt

boredom ['bɔr·dəm] *n* Langeweile *f*
boring ['bɔr·ɪŋ] *adj* langweilig
born [bɔrn] *adj* geboren
'**born-again** *adj* überzeugt
borne [bɔrn] *vi pt of* **bear**
borough ['bɜr·oʊ] *n* Verwaltungsbezirk *m*
borrow ['bar·oʊ] *vt* leihen; (*from library*) ausleihen
borrower ['bar·oʊ·ər] *n* (*from bank*) Kreditnehmer(in) *m(f)*; (*from library*) Entleiher(in) *m(f)*
Bosnia ['baz·ni·ə] *n* Bosnien *nt*
bosom ['bʊz·əm] *n usu sing* Busen *m*
bosom 'buddy *n* Busenfreund(in) *m(f)*
boss [bas] I. *n* Chef(in) *m(f)* II. *vt* ■**to ~ [around** ⟳**] sb** jdn herumkommandieren
bossy ['ba·si] *adj* (*fam*) herrschsüchtig
botanical [bə·'tæn·ɪ·kəl] *adj* botanisch
botanist ['bat·ən·ɪst] *n* Botaniker(in) *m(f)*
botany ['bat·ən·i] *n* Botanik *f*
botch [batʃ] *vt* (*fam*) verpfuschen
both [boʊθ] I. *adj, pron* beide II. *adv* **~ men and women** sowohl Männer als auch Frauen
bother ['bað·ər] I. *n* ❶ (*effort*) Mühe *f*; (*work*) Aufwand *m*; **not worth the ~** kaum der Mühe wert ❷ (*nuisance*) **to be a ~** lästig sein II. *vi* **no, don't ~** nein, nicht nötig III. *vt* ❶ (*worry*) beunruhigen; **what's ~ing you?** was hast du?; **it doesn't ~ me** das macht mir nichts aus ❷ (*disturb*) stören; **I'm sorry to ~ you, but …** entschuldigen Sie bitte [die Störung], aber … ❸ (*annoy*) belästigen
bottle ['bat·əl] *n* Flasche *f*
'**bottle-feed** *vt* mit der Flasche füttern
'**bottleneck** *n* Engpass *m a. fig*
'**bottle opener** *n* Flaschenöffner *m*
bottom ['bat·əm] I. *n* ❶ Boden *m;* **pajama ~s** Pyjamahose *f;* **from top to ~** von oben bis unten ❷ (*end*) **at the ~ of the street** am Ende der Straße ❸ ANAT Hinterteil *nt* ▶PHRASES: **to get to the ~ of sth** einer Sache *dat* auf den Grund gehen II. *adj* untere(r, s)

B

B

bottom 'line *n usu sing* ❶ FIN Bilanz *f* ❷ (*fig: main point*) Wahrheit *f*

bought [bɔt] *vt pt of* **buy**

boulder ['boʊl·dər] *n* Felsbrocken *m*

boulevard ['bʊl·ə·vard] *n* Boulevard *m*

bounce [baʊns] I. *n of ball* Aufprall; (*spring*) Sprungkraft *f*; hair Elastizität *m* II. *vi* ❶ ball aufspringen; (*bob*) hüpfen ❷ (*fam*) check platzen III. *vt* ❶ aufspringen lassen; *baby* schaukeln ❷ (*fam*) check platzen

bouncer ['baʊn·sər] *n* Rausschmeißer(in) *m(f)*

bound¹ [baʊnd] I. *vi* springen; *kangaroo* hüpfen II. *n* Sprung *m*

bound² [baʊnd] *adj* ▪ **to be ~ for X** unterwegs nach X sein

bound³ [baʊnd] I. *pt, pp of* **bind** II. *adj* **it was ~ to happen** das musste so kommen

boundary ['baʊn·də·ri] *n* Grenze *f*

bounds [baʊndz] *npl* Grenzen *pl*; **to be out of ~s** *ball* im Aus sein; *area* Sperrgebiet sein

bounty ['baʊn·ti] *n* ❶ Kopfgeld *nt* ❷ (*liter: generosity*) Freigebigkeit *f*

bouquet [boʊ·'keɪ] *n* Bukett *nt*

bourbon ['bɜr·bən] *n* Bourbon *m*

bourgeois [bʊr·'ʒwa] *adj* [spieß]bürgerlich

bout [baʊt] *n* ❶ Anfall *m* ❷ (*in boxing*) Boxkampf *m*; (*in wrestling*) Ringkampf *m*

boutique [bu·'tik] *n* Boutique *f*

bow¹ [boʊ] *n* ❶ (*weapon*) Bogen *m* ❷ MUS Bogen *m* ❸ (*knot*) Schleife *f*

bow² [baʊ] I. *vi* sich verbeugen II. *vt* **to ~ one's head** den Kopf senken III. *n* ❶ (*gesture*) Verbeugung *f* ❷ NAUT Bug *m*

bowel ['baʊ·əl] *n usu pl* MED ▪ **~s** Darm *m*

'bowel movement *n* Stuhl[gang] *m*

bowl¹ [boʊl] *n* Schüssel *f*; (*shallower*) Schale *f*; (*for doing dishes*) Spülschüssel *f*

bowl² [boʊl] SPORT I. *vi* bowlen; (*lawn bowling*) Bowls spielen II. *vt* (*bowling*)

werfen; (*lawn bowling*) rollen III. *n* Kugel *f*

bowler ['boʊ·lər] *n* ❶ Bowlingspieler(in) *m(f)*; (*lawn bowling*) Bowlsspieler(in) *m(f)* ❷ (*hat*) Melone *f*

bowling ['boʊ·lɪŋ] *n* Bowling *nt*

'bowling alley *n* Bowlingbahn *f*

bow 'tie *n* Fliege *f*

box¹ [baks] *vi* boxen

box² [baks] *n* ❶ (*container*) Kiste *f*; *carton* Karton *m*; *of candy, matches* Schachtel *f* ❷ (*space*) Kästchen *nt*

boxer ['bak·sər] *n* ❶ (*dog*) Boxer *m* ❷ (*person*) Boxer(in) *m(f)*

boxers ['bak·sərz], **'boxer shorts** *npl* Boxershorts *pl*

boxing ['bak·sɪŋ] *n* Boxen *nt*

'boxing gloves *npl* Boxhandschuhe *pl*

'boxing match *n* Boxkampf *m*

'boxing ring *n* Boxring *m*

'box office *n* Kasse *f* (*im Theater oder Kino*)

boy [bɔɪ] I. *n* ❶ Junge *m* ❷ (*fam: friends*) ▪ **the ~s** *pl* die Kumpels *pl* II. *interj* [oh] ~! Junge, Junge!

boycott ['bɔɪ·kat] I. *vt* boykottieren II. *n* Boykott *m*

'boyfriend *n* Freund *m*

boyhood ['bɔɪ·hʊd] *n* Kindheit *f*

boyish ['bɔɪ·ɪʃ] *adj* jungenhaft

'Boy Scout *n* Pfadfinder *m*

bra [bra] *n* BH *m*

brace [breɪs] I. *n* Stützapparat *m*; (*for teeth*) ▪ **~s** *pl* Zahnspange *f* II. *vt* ❶ (*prepare for*) ▪ **to ~ oneself for sth** sich auf etw *akk* vorbereiten ❷ (*support*) [ab]stützen; (*horizontally*) verstreben

bracelet ['breɪs·lɪt] *n* Armband *nt*

bracken ['bræk·ən] *n* Adlerfarn *m*

bracket ['bræk·ɪt] I. *n* ❶ *usu pl* in [round/square/angle] ~s in [runden/eckigen/spitzen] Klammern ❷ (*class*) Klasse *f*, Gruppe *f* ❸ (*support*) [Winkel]stütze *f* II. *vt* in Klammern setzen

brag <-gg-> [bræg] *vt, vi* ▪ **to ~ [about sth]** [mit etw] prahlen

braid [breɪd] I. *n* ❶ (*on cloth*) Borte *f*; (*on uniform*) Litze *f*; (*with metal* *threads*) Tresse[n] *f(pl)* ❷ (*in hair*) Zopf *m* II. *vt, vi* flechten

Braille [breɪl] *n* Blindenschrift *f*

brain [breɪn] *n* ❶ (*organ*) Gehirn *nt;* ■~s *pl* [Ge]hirn *nt* ❷ (*intelligence*) Verstand *m;* ■~s *pl* Intelligenz *f kein pl*

'**brain dead** *adj* [ge]hirntot

'**brainstorm** *n* (*fam: idea*) Geistesblitz *m*

'**brainstorming** *n* Brainstorming *nt*

'**brainwash** *vt* einer Gehirnwäsche unterziehen

'**brainwashing** *n* Gehirnwäsche *f*

'**brainwave** *n* Geistesblitz *m*

brainy ['breɪ·ni] *adj* (*fam*) gescheit

braise [breɪz] *vt* FOOD schmoren

brake [breɪk] I. *n* Bremse *f* II. *vi* bremsen

'**brake fluid** *n* Bremsflüssigkeit *f*

bran [bræn] *n* Kleie *f*

branch [brɑːntʃ] *n* ❶ Zweig *m; of trunk* Ast *m* ❷ (*office*) Zweigstelle *f,* Filiale *f*

brand [brænd] I. *n* ❶ (*product*) Marke *f* ❷ (*fig: type*) Art *f* ❸ (*mark*) Brandzeichen *nt* II. *vt* brandmarken

brandish ['bræn·dɪʃ] *vt* [drohend] schwingen

'**brand name** *n* Markenname *m*

brand 'new *adj* [funkel]nagelneu

brandy ['bræn·di] *n* Weinbrand *m*

brash [bræʃ] *adj* ❶ (*cocky*) dreist ❷ (*gaudy*) grell

brass [bræs] *n* ❶ (*metal*) Messing *nt* ❷ + *sing/pl vb* MUS ■**the ~** die Blechinstrumente *pl*

brass 'band *n* Blaskapelle *f*

brat [bræt] *n* (*hum o pej*) Balg *m o nt*

brave [breɪv] *adj* ❶ mutig ❷ (*stoical*) tapfer

bravery ['breɪ·və·ri] *n* Tapferkeit *f,* Mut *m*

brawl [brɔl] I. *n* [lautstarke] Schlägerei II. *vi* sich [lautstark] schlagen

brawn [brɔn] *n* Muskelkraft *f*

brawny ['brɔ·ni] *adj* (*fam*) muskulös

bray [breɪ] I. *vi donkey* schreien; *person* kreischen II. *n* [Esels]schrei *m*

brazen ['breɪ·zən] *adj* unverschämt

Brazil [brə·'zɪl] *n* Brasilien *nt*

Brazilian [brə·'zɪl·jən] I. *n* Brasilianer(in) *m(f)* II. *adj* brasilianisch

Bra'zil nut *n* Paranuss *f*

breach [brɪtʃ] I. *n* ❶ (*infringement*) Verletzung *f;* **~ of contract** Vertragsbruch *m* ❷ (*estrangement*) Bruch *m* II. *vt* ❶ (*break*) verletzen; *contract* brechen ❷ *defense* durchbrechen

bread [bred] *n* Brot *nt*

bread and 'butter *n* Butterbrot *nt*

'**breadcrumb** *n* Brotkrume *f;* ■~s *pl* (*for coating food*) Paniermehl *nt kein pl*

breadth [bredθ] *n* Breite *f;* (*fig*) Ausdehnung *f*

'**breadwinner** *n* Ernährer(in) *m(f)*

break [breɪk] I. *n* ❶ (*fracture*) Bruch *m* ❷ (*gap*) Lücke *f* ❸ (*interruption*) Unterbrechung *f;* (*shorter*) Pause *f;* **to take a ~** eine Pause machen ❹ (*opportunity*) Chance *f* II. *vt* <broke, broken> ❶ (*shatter*) zerbrechen; (*damage*) kaputtmachen; *window* einschlagen; **to ~ one's arm** sich *dat* den Arm brechen ❷ (*momentarily interrupt*) unterbrechen ❸ (*put an end to*) brechen; *habit* aufgeben ❹ (*violate*) *agreement* verletzen; *law* übertreten; *promise* brechen ❺ *code* entschlüsseln III. *vi* <broke, broken> ❶ (*stop working*) kaputtgehen, zusammenbrechen, auseinanderbrechen; (*shatter*) zerbrechen ❷ *voice* **the boy's voice is ~ing** der Junge ist [gerade] im Stimmbruch ❸ METEO *dawn, day* anbrechen; *storm* losbrechen ❹ *news* bekannt werden ❺ (*billiards*) anstoßen; (*boxing*) sich trennen

◆**break down** I. *vi* ❶ (*stop working*) stehen bleiben; *engine* versagen ❷ (*dissolve*) sich auflösen; *marriage* scheitern ❸ (*emotionally*) zusammenbrechen II. *vt* ❶ (*force open*) aufbrechen; (*with foot*) eintreten ❷ (*separate into parts*) aufgliedern; CHEM aufspalten

◆**break in** I. *vi* ❶ einbrechen ❷ (*interrupt*) unterbrechen II. *vt* ❶ *shoes* einlaufen ❷ (*tame*) zähmen; (*train*) abrichten; *horse* zureiten

◆**break into** *vt* ❶ einbrechen in + *akk;*

B

car aufbrechen ② **to ~ into a run** [plötzlich] zu rennen anfangen
◆**break off** I. *vt* abbrechen; (*terminate*) beenden; *engagement* lösen II. *vi* abbrechen
◆**break out** *vi* ① (*escape*) ausbrechen ② (*begin*) ausbrechen; *storm* losbrechen
◆**break up** I. *vt* ① (*end*) beenden; *marriage* zerstören ② (*split up*) aufspalten; *family* auseinanderreißen II. *vi* ① (*end relationship*) sich trennen ② (*come to an end*) enden; *marriage* scheitern ③ (*fall apart*) auseinandergehen; *aircraft, ship* zerschellen
breakage ['breɪ·kɪdʒ] *n* Bruch *m*
'**breakdown** *n* ① (*collapse*) Zusammenbruch *m*; (*failure*) Scheitern *nt* ② AUTO Panne *f* ③ (*list*) Aufschlüsselung *f* ④ PSYCH [Nerven]zusammenbruch *m*
'**breakfast** ['brek·fəst] *n* Frühstück *nt*
'**break-in** *n* Einbruch *m*
'**breakthrough** *n* Durchbruch *m*
'**breakup** *n* Auseinanderbrechen *nt; of marriage* Scheitern *nt; of group* Auflösung *f*
'**breakwater** *n* Wellenbrecher *m*
breast [brest] *n* Brust *f*
'**breastbone** *n* Brustbein *nt*
'**breast cancer** *n* Brustkrebs *m*
'**breastfeed** <-fed, -fed> *vt, vi* stillen
'**breaststroke** *n* Brustschwimmen *nt*
breath [breθ] *n* Atem *m*; (*inhalation*) Atemzug *m*; **bad ~** Mundgeruch *m*; **out of ~** außer Atem; **to catch one's ~** [*or* **get one's ~ back**] verschnaufen; **to take a deep ~** tief Luft holen; **to take sb's ~ away** jdm den Atem rauben
Breathalyzer® ['breθ·ə·laɪ·zər] *n* Alcotest® *m*
breathe [brið] I. *vi* atmen II. *vt* (*exhale*) [aus]atmen
'**breathing** ['bri·ðɪŋ] *n* Atmung *f*
'**breathing apparatus** *n* Sauerstoffgerät *nt*
'**breathing room, 'breathing space** *n* (*fig*) Bewegungsfreiheit *f*
breathless ['breθ·lɪs] *adj* atemlos

'**breathtaking** *adj* atemberaubend
'**breath test** *n* Alkoholtest *m*
bred [bred] *pt, pp of* **breed**
breed [brid] I. *vt* <bred, bred> züchten II. *vi* <bred, bred> sich fortpflanzen; *birds* brüten; *rabbits* sich vermehren III. *n* (*of animal*) Rasse *f*; (*of plant*) Sorte *f*
breeder ['bri·dər] *n* Züchter(in) *m(f)*
breeze [briz] *n* ① Brise *f* ② (*fam*) Kinderspiel *nt*
breezy ['bri·zi] *adj* ① windig ② unbeschwert
brevity ['brev·ɪ·ti] *n* Kürze *f*
brew [bru] I. *n* Gebräu *nt*; (*fig*) Mischung *f* II. *vi* (*fig*) *trouble* sich zusammenbrauen III. *vt* brauen
brewer ['bru·ər] *n* [Bier]brauer(in) *m(f)*
brewery ['bru·ə·ri] *n* Brauerei *f*
bribe [braɪb] I. *vt* bestechen II. *n* Bestechung *f*
bribery ['braɪ·bə·ri] *n* Bestechung *f*
bric-a-brac ['brɪk·ə·bræk] *n* Nippes *pl*
brick [brɪk] *n* Backstein *m*
bricklayer *n* Maurer(in) *m(f)*
'**brickwork** *n* Mauerwerk *nt*
bride [braɪd] *n* Braut *f*
bridegroom ['braɪd·ˌgrum] *n* Bräutigam *m*
'**bridesmaid** *n* Brautjungfer *f*
bridge [brɪdʒ] *n* ① Brücke *f* ② (*for teeth*) [Zahn]brücke *f; of nose* Nasenrücken *m; of glasses* Brillensteg *m* ③ (*on ship*) Kommandobrücke *f* ④ (*card game*) Bridge *nt*
bridle ['braɪd·əl] *n* Zaumzeug *nt*
brief [brif] I. *adj* kurz II. *n* ① LAW Unterlagen *pl* zu einer Rechtssache ② ■ **~s** *pl* (*for men*) Herrenunterhose *f; (for women*) Slip *m*, [Damen]schlüpfer *m* III. *vt* informieren
briefcase ['brif·keɪs] *n* Aktentasche *f*
briefing ['bri·fɪŋ] *n* [Einsatz]besprechung *f*
briefly ['brif·li] *adv* kurz
brigade [brɪ·'geɪd] *n* Brigade *f*
bright [braɪt] *adj* ① *light* hell; (*blinding*) grell; *star* leuchtend; *sunshine* strahlend ② (*vivid*) **~ blue** strahlend blau;

B

~ **red** leuchtend rot ③ intelligent; *idea* glänzend *a.* iron

brighten ['braɪt·ən] *vi* ■to ~ [up] ① fröhlicher werden ② METEO sich aufklären

brilliant ['brɪl·jənt] *adj* ① *color, eyes* leuchtend; *smile, sun* strahlend ② *person* hoch begabt; *plan* brillant; *idea* glänzend

brim [brɪm] *n* ① *of hat* Krempe *f* ② (*top*) Rand *m;* **full to the ~** randvoll

brine [braɪn] *n* [Salz]lake *f*

bring <brought, brought> [brɪŋ] *vt* ① (*convey*) mitbringen ② (*cause to come, happen*) bringen; **so what ~s you here to Chicago?** was hat dich hier nach Chicago verschlagen? ③ LAW **to ~ charges against sb** Anklage gegen jdn erheben

♦ **bring about** *vt* verursachen

♦ **bring around** *vt* ① (*persuade*) überreden ② (*bring back to consciousness*) wieder zu Bewusstsein bringen ③ (*bring along*) mitbringen

♦ **bring back** *vt* zurückbringen; *memories* wecken; (*reintroduce*) wieder einführen

♦ **bring off** *vt* zustande bringen

♦ **bring on** *vt* herbeiführen; MED verursachen

♦ **bring out** *vt* ① (*get out*) herausbringen ② COMM (*launch*) herausbringen

♦ **bring up** *vt* ① (*carry up*) heraufbringen ② (*rear*) großziehen ③ (*mention*) zur Sprache bringen

brink [brɪŋk] *n* Rand *m a.* fig

brisk [brɪsk] *adj* ① zügig; *walk* stramm ② (*busy*) lebhaft ③ *wind* frisch

bristle ['brɪs·əl] *n* Borste *f;* (*on face*) [Bart]stoppel *f meist pl*

bristly ['brɪs·li] *adj* borstig; *chin* stoppelig

Brit [brɪt] *n* (*fam*) Brite, -in *m, f*

Britain ['brɪt·ən] *n* Großbritannien *nt*

British ['brɪt·ɪʃ] I. *adj* britisch II. *npl* ■the ~ die Briten *pl*

British 'Isles *npl* **the ~** die Britischen Inseln

Briton ['brɪt·ən] *n* Brite, -in *m, f*

brittle ['brɪt·əl] *adj* zerbrechlich; *bones* brüchig

broach [broʊtʃ] *vt subject* anschneiden

broad [brɔd] *adj* ① (*wide*) breit ② (*general*) allgemein; *generalization* grob ③ (*wide-ranging*) weitreichend; *interests* vielseitig

'**broadband** *n* INET Breitband *nt*

broadcast ['brɔd·kæst] I. *n* Übertragung *f;* (*program*) Sendung *f* II. *vt, vi* <broadcast *or* broadcasted, broadcast *or* broadcasted> senden; *game* übertragen

broaden ['brɔd·ən] I. *vi* breiter werden II. *vt* ① (*make wider*) verbreitern ② (*fig*) vergrößern; *discussion* ausweiten

broadly ['brɔd·li] *adv* ① (*widely*) breit ② (*generally*) *agree* weitgehend

broad-'minded *adj* tolerant

Broadway *n* der Broadway

broccoli ['brak·ə·li] *n* Brokkoli *m*

brochure [broʊ·'ʃʊr] *n* Broschüre *f*

broil [brɔɪl] *vt* grillen

broiler ['brɔɪ·lər] *n* Bratrost *nt*

broke [broʊk] I. *pt of* **break** II. *adj pred* (*fam*) pleite

broken ['broʊ·kən] I. *pp of* **break** II. *adj arm* gebrochen; *bottle* zerbrochen; *watch* kaputt

'**broken-down** *adj* ① (*not working*) kaputt ② (*dilapidated*) verfallen

broken'hearted *adj* untröstlich

broker ['broʊ·kər] *n* ① ECON [Börsen]makler(in) *m(f)* ② (*negotiator*) Vermittler(in) *m(f)*

bronchitis [braŋ·'kaɪ·tɪs] *n* Bronchitis *f*

bronze [branz] I. *n* Bronze *f* II. *adj* **the B~ Age** die Bronzezeit; ~ **medal** Bronzemedaille *f*

brooch <*pl* -es> [broʊtʃ] *n* Brosche *f*

brood [brud] I. *n* Brut *f a.* fig II. *vi* ■to ~ **on sth** über etw *dat* brüten

brook [brʊk] *n* Bach *m*

broom [brum] *n* ① (*brush*) Besen *m* ② BOT Ginster *m*

broomstick ['brum·stɪk] *n* Besenstiel *m*

broth [brɔθ] *n* Brühe *f*

brothel ['braθ·əl] *n* Bordell *nt*

B

brother ['brʌð·ər] n ① Bruder m; ~s and sisters Geschwister pl ②(fam) Kumpel m

brotherhood ['brʌð·ər·hʊd] n ①(group) Bruderschaft f ②(feeling) Brüderlichkeit f

'brother-in-law <pl brothers-in-law> n Schwager m

brotherly ['brʌð·ər·li] adj brüderlich

brought [brɔt] pt, pp of **bring**

brow [braʊ] n Augenbraue f, Stirn f

browbeat <-beat, -beaten> ['braʊ·bit] vt einschüchtern

brown [braʊn] I. n Braun nt II. adj braun

brown 'bread n locker gebackenes Brot aus dunklerem Mehl, etwa wie Mischbrot

brownie ['braʊ·ni] n FOOD kleiner Schokoladenkuchen mit Nüssen

Brownie ['braʊ·ni] n (Girl Scout) junge Pfadfinderin

'brownie point n (hum fam) Pluspunkt m

brown 'rice n ungeschälter Reis

browse [braʊz] I. vi to ~ through a magazine eine Zeitschrift durchblättern; to ~ [around a store] sich [in einem Geschäft] umsehen II. vt COMPUT durchsehen

bruise [bruz] I. n blauer Fleck; (on fruit) Druckstelle f II. vt to ~ one's arm sich am Arm stoßen

brunch <pl -es> [brʌntʃ] n Brunch m

brunette [bru·'net] I. n Brünette f II. adj brünett

brunt [brʌnt] n to bear the ~ of sth etw am stärksten zu spüren bekommen

brush [brʌʃ] I. n <pl -es> ①(for hair, cleaning) Bürste f; (broom) Besen m; (for painting) Pinsel m ②(act) Bürsten nt ③(encounter) Zusammenstoß m II. vt ①abbürsten; to ~ one's hair sich dat die Haare bürsten ②(touch lightly) leicht berühren III. vi ■ to ~ against sb/sth jdn/etw streifen

◆**brush aside** vt ①(push aside) wegschieben ②(dismiss) thing abtun; person ignorieren

◆**brush up** I. vi ■to ~ up on sth etw auffrischen II. vt auffrischen

'brush-off n to get the ~ from sb jdm einen Korb bekommen

brusque [brʌsk] adj schroff

Brussels ['brʌs·əlz] n Brüssel nt

Brussel(s) 'sprout n ■~s pl Rosenkohl m kein pl

brutal ['brut·əl] adj brutal a. fig

brutality [bru·'tæl·ɪ·ti] n Brutalität f

brute [brut] I. n brutaler Kerl II. adj ~ force rohe Gewalt

BS [ˌbi·es] n ①abbrev of **Bachelor of Science** Bakkalaureus m der Naturwissenschaften ②(vulg) abbrev of **bullshit**

bubble ['bʌb·əl] I. n Blase f II. vi kochen a. fig; water, fountain sprudeln; champagne perlen

'bubble bath n Schaumbad nt

'bubblegum n Bubblegum m o nt

bubbly ['bʌb·li] I. n (fam) Schampus m fam II. adj drink sprudelnd; person temperamentvoll

buck¹ [bʌk] n (fam) Dollar m

buck² [bʌk] I. n <pl -> (deer) Bock m; (rabbit) Rammler m II. vi bocken

buck³ [bʌk] n (fam) to pass the ~ [to sb] die Verantwortung [auf jdn] abwälzen

◆**buck up** I. vi [wieder] Mut fassen; ~ up! Kopf hoch! II. vt aufmuntern

bucket ['bʌk·ɪt] n Eimer m

buckle ['bʌk·əl] I. n Schnalle f II. vt ①belt [zu]schnallen ②(bend) verbiegen III. vi sich verbiegen

◆**buckle up** vi AUTO (fam) sich anschnallen

buckskin ['bʌk·skɪn] n Wildleder nt

bud [bʌd] I. n Knospe f II. vi <-dd-> knospen

Buddhism ['bu·dɪz·əm] n Buddhismus m

Buddhist ['bu·dɪst] I. n Buddhist(in) m(f) II. adj buddhistisch

budding ['bʌd·ɪŋ] adj (fig) angehend

buddy ['bʌd·i] n (fam) Kumpel m

budge [bʌdʒ] I. vi ①(move) sich [vom Fleck] rühren ②(change mind) nachgeben II. vt ①(move) [von der Stelle] bewegen ② *(cause to change mind)* umstimmen

budget ['bʌdʒ·ɪt] I. *n* Budget *nt* II. *vi* ■to ~ for sth etw [im Budget] vorsehen III. *adj* preiswert

buff¹ [bʌf] I. *adj* ① *(color)* gelbbraun ② *(sl)* muskulös II. *vt* ■to ~ [up] sth etw polieren

buff² [bʌf] *n (fam)* Fan *m*

buffalo <*pl* -> ['bʌf·ə·lou] *n* Büffel *m*

buffer ['bʌf·ər] *n* Puffer *m*

buffet [bə·'feɪ] *n* Büfett *nt*

buffoon [bə·'fun] *n* Clown *m*

bug [bʌg] I. *n* ① Wanze *f*; ■~s *pl (insects)* Ungeziefer *nt kein pl* ② MED Bazillus *m* ③ COMPUT Bug *m* ④ *(listening device)* Wanze *f* II. *vt* <-gg-> ① *(fam: annoy)* ■to ~ sb jdm auf die Nerven gehen *dat* ② *(install bugs)* verwanzen ③ *(eavesdrop on)* abhören

'**bugbear** *n* Ärgernis *nt*

buggy ['bʌg·i] *n* ① *(horse-drawn)* leichter Einspänner ② *(for baby)* Buggy *m*

bugle ['bju·gəl] *n* Horn *nt*

bugler ['bju·glər] *n* Hornist(in) *m(f)*

build [bɪld] I. *n* Körperbau *m* II. *vt* <built, built> ① *(construct)* bauen ② *(fig)* aufbauen III. *vi* <built, built> ① *(construct)* bauen ② *(increase)* zunehmen; *tension* steigen
◆ **build up** I. *vt* aufbauen; *lead* ausbauen; *speed* erhöhen II. *vi* zunehmen; *traffic* sich verdichten

builder ['bɪl·dər] *n* Bauarbeiter(in) *m(f)*; *(contractor)* Bauherr(in) *m(f)*

building ['bɪl·dɪŋ] *n* Gebäude *nt*

'**building contractor** *n* Bauunternehmer(in) *m(f)*

'**building site** *n* Baustelle *f*

'**buildup** *n* ① *(increase)* Zunahme *f* ② *(hype)* Werbung *f* ③ *(preparations)* Vorbereitung *f*

built [bɪlt] *pt, pp of* **build**

built-in ['bɪlt·ɪn] *adj* eingebaut, Einbau-

built-up ['bɪlt·ʌp] *adj area* verbaut

bulb [bʌlb] *n* ① BOT Zwiebel *f* ② ELEC [Glüh]birne *f*

Bulgaria [bʌl·'gerˑiˑə] *n* Bulgarien *nt*

Bulgarian [bʌl·'gerˑiˑən] I. *adj* bulga-

risch II. *n* ① *(person)* Bulgare, -in *m, f* ② *(language)* Bulgarisch *nt*

bulge [bʌldʒ] I. *n* ① Wölbung *f*; *(in tire)* Wulst *m* II. *vi* sich runden; *eyes* hervortreten

bulimia [buˑ'liˑmiˑə] *n* Bulimie *f*

bulk [bʌlk] *n* ① *(mass)* Masse *f* ② *(size)* Ausmaß *nt* ③ *(quantity)* in ~ in großen Mengen ④ *(largest part)* Großteil *m*

bulky ['bʌl·ki] *adj* ① *luggage* sperrig ② *person* massig

bull [bʊl] *n (steer)* Stier *m; elephant, walrus also* Bulle *m*

'**bulldog** *n* Bulldogge *f*

bulldozer ['bʊl·dou·zər] *n* Bulldozer *m*

bullet ['bʊl·ɪt] *n* Kugel *f*

bulletin ['bʊl·ə·tɪn] *n* Bulletin *nt,* [kurzer] Lagebericht

'**bulletin board** *n* Schwarzes Brett

'**bulletproof** *adj* kugelsicher

'**bullfight** *n* Stierkampf *m*

'**bullfighter** *n* Stierkämpfer(in) *m(f)*

'**bullfrog** *n* Ochsenfrosch *m*

bullion ['bʊl·jən] *n* **gold ~** Goldbarren *pl*

bullock ['bʊl·ək] *n* Ochse *m*

'**bullring** *n* Stierkampfarena *f*

'**bull's eye** *n* Zentrum *nt* der Zielscheibe; **to hit the ~** einen Volltreffer landen *a. fig*

'**bullshit** *(vulg, sl)* I. *n* Schwachsinn *m* II. *vt* <-tt-> verscheißern *derb* III. *vi* <-tt-> Scheiß erzählen *pej derb*

bully ['bʊl·i] I. *n* Tyrann *m* II. *vt* <-ie-> tyrannisieren

bum [bʌm] *(fam)* I. *n* Penner(in) *m(f)* II. *vt* <-mm-> ■to ~ sth off sb etw von jdm schnorren
◆ **bum around** *vi (fam)* ① *(hang out)* herumgammeln *fam* ② *(travel)* herumziehen

bumblebee ['bʌm·bəl·bi] *n* Hummel *f*

bumbling ['bʌm·blɪŋ] *adj* tollpatschig

bump [bʌmp] I. *n* ① *(on head)* Beule *f*; *(in road)* Unebenheit *f* ② *(light blow)* leichter Stoß ③ *(thud)* Bums *m* II. *vt* ① zusammenstoßen mit +*dat*; ■to ~ oneself sich [an]stoßen ② *usu passive* **to get ~ed from a flight** von der Passa-

gierliste gestrichen werden
- **bump into** vi ■**to ~ into sth** gegen etw akk stoßen; ■**to ~ into sb** (knock) mit jdm zusammenstoßen; (meet) jdm [zufällig] in die Arme laufen
- **bump off** vt (fam) umlegen

bumper ['bʌm·pər] n Stoßstange f; RAIL Prellbock m

'**bumper car** n [Auto]skooter m

'**bumper sticker** n Autoaufkleber m

bumpy ['bʌm·pi] adj holp[e]rig; flight, ride unruhig

bun [bʌn] n ❶ Brötchen nt (für Hamburger verwendetes, weiches Brötchen) ❷ [Haar]knoten m ❸ (fam: buttock) ■~s Hintern m kein pl fam

bunch <pl -es> [bʌntʃ] n of bananas Büschel m; of carrots Bund m; of flowers Strauß m; of people Haufen m; ~ of grapes Weintraube f; ~ of keys Schlüsselbund m

bundle ['bʌn·dəl] I. n Bündel nt II. vt to ~ **sb into a car** jdn in ein Auto verfrachten

'**bungee jumping** ['bʌn·dʒi-] n Bungeespringen nt

bungle ['bʌn·gəl] vt verpfuschen

bunk [bʌŋk] n ❶ (in boat) Koje f ❷ (part of bed) **bottom/top ~** unteres/oberes Bett (eines Etagenbetts)

'**bunk bed** n Etagenbett nt

bunker ['bʌŋ·kər] n Bunker m

bunny ['bʌn·i] n Häschen nt

buoy [bɔɪ] n Boje f

buoyant ['bɔɪ·jənt] adj schwimmfähig, tragend

burden ['bɜr·dən] I. n Last f; (fig) Belastung f II. vt beladen; (bother) belasten

burdensome ['bɜr·dən·səm] adj belastend

bureau <pl -x> ['bjʊr·oʊ] n ❶ Amt nt, Behörde f ❷ (office) [Informations]büro nt ❸ (furniture) Kommode f

bureaucracy [bjʊ·'rak·rə·si] n Bürokratie f

bureaucrat ['bjʊr·ə·kræt] n Bürokrat(in) m(f)

bureaucratic [,bjʊr·ə·'kræt̬·ɪk] adj bürokratisch

burger ['bɜr·gər] n short for **hamburger** [Ham]burger m

burglar ['bɜr·glər] n Einbrecher(in) m(f)

'**burglar alarm** n Alarmanlage f

burglarize ['bɜr·glə·raɪz] vt einbrechen in +akk

burglary ['bɜr·glə·ri] n Einbruch[diebstahl] m

burgundy ['bɜr·gən·di] n Burgunder m

burial ['ber·i·əl] n Beerdigung f

burly ['bɜr·li] adj kräftig [gebaut]

burn [bɜrn] I. n ❶ (injury) Verbrennung f, Brandwunde f ❷ (damage) Brandfleck m II. vi <burned or burnt, burned or burnt> ❶ brennen ❷ FOOD anbrennen ❸ (sunburn) einen Sonnenbrand bekommen III. vt <burned or burnt, burned or burnt> ❶ (damage with heat) verbrennen; village niederbrennen ❷ FOOD anbrennen lassen ❸ calories verbrennen; oil verbrauchen
- **burn down** I. vt abbrennen II. vi building niederbrennen; forest abbrennen; candle, fire herunterbrennen
- **burn out** I. vi ❶ fire, candle herunterbrennen ❷ rocket ausbrennen II. vt ■**to ~ [oneself] out** sich völlig verausgaben
- **burn up** I. vi ❶ verbrennen ❷ (fig: be feverish) glühen ❸ rocket verglühen II. vt verbrauchen; calories verbrennen

burner ['bɜr·nər] n Brenner m; (on stove) Kochplatte f

burning ['bɜr·nɪŋ] adj brennend a. fig

burnt [bɜrnt] I. vt, vi pt, pp of **burn** II. adj (completely) verbrannt; (partly) food angebrannt; (from sun) verbrannt

burp [bɜrp] I. n Rülpser m; of baby Bäuerchen nt II. vi rülpsen fam; baby ein Bäuerchen machen

burrow ['bɜr·oʊ] I. n Bau m II. vt graben III. vi einen Bau graben

burst [bɜrst] I. n Ausbruch m II. vi <burst, burst> ❶ (explode) platzen a. fig; bubble zerplatzen; dam bersten ❷ ■**to be ~ing** (be full) suitcase zum Bersten voll sein III. vt <burst, burst> zum Platzen bringen; balloon platzen lassen

◆**burst in** *vi* herein-/hineinstürzen

◆**burst out** *vi* ❶herausstürzen ❷**to ~ out crying/laughing** in Tränen/Gelächter ausbrechen

bury <-ie-> ['ber·i] *vt person* begraben; *thing* vergraben *a. fig*

bus [bʌs] *n* <*pl* -es> |Omni|bus *m*

'**bus driver** *n* Busfahrer(in) *m(f)*

bush <*pl* -es> [buʃ] *n* Busch *m*

bushy ['buʃ·i] *adj* buschig

busily ['bɪz·ɪ·li] *adv* eifrig

business <*pl* -es> ['bɪz·nɪs] *n* ❶(*commerce*) Handel *m;* **to do ~ with sb** mit jdm Geschäfte machen; **on ~** geschäftlich ❷(*profession*) Branche *f* ❸(*company*) Unternehmen *nt* ❹(*matter*) Angelegenheit *f;* **that's none of your ~** das geht dich nichts an

'**business card** *n* Visitenkarte *f*

'**business class** *n* Businessclass *f*

'**business hours** *npl* Geschäftszeiten *pl*

'**businesslike** *adj* geschäftsmäßig

'**businessman** *n* Geschäftsmann *m*

'**business trip** *n* Dienstreise *f,* Geschäftsreise *f*

'**businesswoman** *n* Geschäftsfrau *f*

'**bus station** *n* Busbahnhof *m*

'**bus stop** *n* Bushaltestelle *f*

bust[1] [bʌst] *n* ❶(*statue*) Büste *f* ❷(*breasts*) Büste *f;* (*measurement*) Oberweite *f*

bust[2] [bʌst] (*fam*) I. *n* ❶(*recession*) [wirtschaftlicher] Niedergang ❷(*raid*) Razzia *f* II. *adj* ❶(*broken*) kaputt ❷(*bankrupt*) **to go ~** Pleite machen III. *vt* <bust *or* busted, bust *or* busted> ❶(*break*) kaputtmachen ❷(*arrest*) festnehmen

bustle ['bʌs·əl] *n* Getriebe *nt*

busy ['bɪz·i] *adj* ❶(*occupied*) [viel] beschäftigt ❷*life* bewegt; *street* belebt ❸TELEC besetzt

'**busybody** *n* Wichtigtuer(in) *m(f)*

'**busy signal** *n* TELEC Besetztzeichen *nt*

but [bʌt] I. *conj* ❶(*although, however*) aber ❷(*except*) als ❸(*rather*) sondern; **not only ... ~ also ...** nicht nur[,] ... sondern auch ... II. *prep* außer; **nothing ~ trouble** nichts als Ärger

butch [butʃ] *adj* maskulin

butcher ['butʃ·ər] I. *n* Metzger(in) *m(f)* II. *vt* ❶(*slaughter*) schlachten ❷(*murder*) niedermetzeln

butler ['bʌt·lər] *n* Butler *m*

butt [bʌt] I. *n* ❶*of rifle* Kolben *m; of cigarette* Stummel *m* ❷(*fam*) Hintern *m* II. ◼**to ~ sb** *person* jdm einen Stoß mit dem Kopf versetzen; *goat* jdn mit den Hörnern stoßen

butter ['bʌt·ər] I. *n* Butter *f* II. *vt* mit Butter bestreichen

'**buttercup** *n* Butterblume *f*

'**butterfly** ['bʌt·ər·flaɪ] *n* ❶Schmetterling *m* ❷(*in swimming*) Butterfly *m*

'**buttermilk** *n* Buttermilch *f*

'**buttock** ['bʌt·ək] *n* ❶[Hinter]backe *f;* ◼**~s** *pl* Gesäß *nt*

button ['bʌt·ən] I. *n* ❶Knopf *m* ❷(*badge*) Button *m* II. *vt* zuknöpfen

◆**button up** *vt* zuknöpfen

'**buttonhole** I. *n* Knopfloch *nt* II. *vt* (*fam*) zu fassen kriegen

buy [baɪ] I. *n* Kauf *m* II. *vt* <bought, bought> ❶kaufen ❷(*fam: believe*) abkaufen

buyer ['baɪ·ər] *n* Käufer(in) *m(f);* (*as job*) Einkäufer(in) *m(f)*

'**buyout** *n* Übernahme *f*

buzz [bʌz] I. *vi bee, buzzer* summen; *fly* brummen; *ears* dröhnen II. *vt* (*fam*) anrufen III. *n* <*pl* -es> ❶*of bee, buzzer* Summen *nt; of fly* Brummen *nt* ❷(*fam: call*) **to give sb a ~** jdn anrufen

buzzard ['bʌz·ərd] *n* Truthahngeier *m*

buzzer ['bʌz·ər] *n* Summer *m*

by [baɪ] I. *prep* ❶(*beside*) neben +*akk/dat* ❷(*not later than*) bis +*akk;* **~ February 14**|th] [spätestens] bis zum 14.02.; **~ now** inzwischen ❸(*during*) bei +*dat;* **~ day/night** tagsüber/nachts ❹(*happening progressively*) **little ~ little** nach und nach; **day ~ day** Tag für Tag ❺(*agent*) von +*dat* ❻(*by means of*) durch +*akk,* mit +*dat;* **~ hand** mit der Hand; **~ boat/bus** mit dem Schiff/Bus ❼(*amount*) um +*akk;* **to go up ~ 20%** um 20 % steigen II. *adv* ❶(*past*) vorbei ❷**close ~** ganz in der Nähe

▶PHRASES: ~ **and large** im Großen und Ganzen; ~ **oneself** (alone) allein; (unaided) selbst

bye [baɪ] interj (fam) tschüs

bye-bye [ˌbaɪˈbaɪ] interj (fam) tschüs

'bygone I. adj attr vergangen II. n ▶PHRASES: **to let ~s be ~s** die Vergangenheit ruhen lassen

'bylaw n Gemeindeverordnung f

'bypass I. n ❶ Umgehungsstraße f ❷ MED Bypass m II. vt ❶ (detour) umfahren ❷ (not consult) übergehen

'byproduct n Nebenprodukt nt

'bystander n Zuschauer(in) m(f)

'byway n Nebenstraße f, Seitenweg m

Cc

C <pl -'s>, **c** <pl -'s> [siː] n ❶ (letter) C nt, c nt; ~ **as in Charlie** C wie Cäsar ❷ MUS C nt, c nt ❸ (school grade) ≈ Drei f

C after n abbrev of **Celsius** C

CA abbrev of **California**

cab [kæb] n ❶ (taxi) Taxi nt ❷ (of truck) Führerhaus nt

cabaret [ˌkæb·əˈreɪ] n Varieté nt

cabbage ['kæb·ɪdʒ] n Kohl m kein pl, Kraut nt kein pl bes SÜDD

cabbie, cabby ['kæb·i], **'cabdriver** n Taxifahrer(in) m(f)

cabin ['kæb·ɪn] n ❶ (wooden house) [Block]hütte f; (for vacation) Ferienhütte f ❷ (on ship) Kabine f

cabinet ['kæb·ɪ·nɪt] n ❶ Schrank m ❷ POL Kabinett nt

cable ['keɪ·bəl] n ❶ ELEC [Leitungs]kabel nt, Leitung f ❷ NAUT Tau nt ❸ TV Kabelfernsehen nt

'cable car n Drahtseilbahn f; (on street) Kabelbahn f

cable 'television, cable T'V n Kabelfernsehen nt

cache [kæʃ] n ❶ (hiding place) Versteck nt ❷ COMPUT Cache m

cackle ['kæk·əl] I. vi gackern II. n (chicken noise) Gackern nt kein pl; (laughter) Gegacker nt

cactus <pl -es> ['kæk·təs] n Kaktus m

caddie, caddy ['kæd·i] n Caddie m

cadet [kəˈdet] n MIL Kadett m

Caesarean [sɪˈzeː·ri·ən] n MED Kaiserschnitt m

café, cafe [kæ·ˈfeɪ] n Café nt

cafeteria [ˌkæf·ɪ·ˈtɪr·i·ə] n Cafeteria f; UNIV Mensa f

caffeine [kæf·ˈiːn] n Koffein nt

cage [keɪdʒ] n Käfig m

cagey ['keɪ·dʒi] adj (fam) vorsichtig

cake [keɪk] n ❶ Kuchen m; (layered) Torte f ❷ (patty) Küchlein nt ▶PHRASES: **a piece of ~** (fam) ein Klacks

calcium ['kæl·si·əm] n Kalzium nt

calculate ['kæl·kjə·leɪt] I. vt berechnen; (estimate) veranschlagen II. vi rechnen

calculated ['kæl·kjə·leɪ·t̬ɪd] adj beabsichtigt; risk kalkuliert

calculating ['kæl·kjə·leɪ·t̬ɪŋ] adj berechnend

calculation [ˌkæl·kjə·ˈleɪ·ʃən] n ❶ Berechnung f; (estimate) Schätzung f ❷ (process) Rechnen nt

calculator ['kæl·kjə·leɪ·t̬ər] n Rechner m

calendar ['kæl·ən·dər] n Kalender m

calf <pl calves> [kæf] n ❶ (animal) Kalb nt ❷ ANAT Wade f

caliber ['kæl·ə·bər] n ❶ (diameter) Kaliber nt ❷ (quality) Niveau nt

California [ˌkæl·ə·ˈfɔr·njə] n Kalifornien nt

call [kɔl] I. n ❶ (on phone) [Telefon]anruf m, [Telefon]gespräch nt ❷ (visit) Besuch m ❸ (shout) Ruf m; **to be on ~**

Bereitschaftsdienst haben II. vt ① (on phone) anrufen; ■ to ~ sb back jdn zurückrufen ② (name) nennen; **what's that animal ~ed?** wie heißt dieses Tier? ③ (summon) [auf]rufen; **to ~ a doctor** einen Arzt rufen III. vi ① rufen; animal schreien; **to ~ for sb** jdn rufen; **to ~ for help** um Hilfe rufen ② (telephone) anrufen; **who's ~ing, please?** wer ist am Apparat? ③ (drop by) vorbeischauen

◆**call for** vi ① taxi, food bestellen ② **this ~s for a celebration** das muss gefeiert werden

◆**call in** I. vt specialist, expert hinzuziehen; (ask to come) kommen lassen II. vi sich telefonisch melden; **to ~ in sick** sich [telefonisch] krankmelden

◆**call off** vt ① (cancel) absagen; (stop) abbrechen ② (order back) dog zurückrufen

◆**call on** vt ① (visit) bei jdm vorbeischauen ② (appeal to) ■ to ~ on sb to do sth jdn dazu auffordern, etw zu tun ③ (use) in Anspruch nehmen

◆**call out** vt ① (shout) rufen ② fire department alarmieren

◆**call up** vt ① (telephone) anrufen ② COMPUT aufrufen ③ MIL einberufen

◆**call upon** vi see **call on**

caller ['kɔ·lər] n ① (on telephone) Anrufer(in) m(f) ② (visitor) Besucher(in) m(f)

callous ['kæl·əs] adj hartherzig

calm [kam] I. adj ruhig II. n ① Ruhe f ② METEO Windstille f III. vt beruhigen

◆**calm down** I. vt beruhigen II. vi sich akk beruhigen

calorie ['kæl·ə·ri] n Kalorie f

Cambodia [kæm·'bou·di·ə] n Kambodscha nt

came [keɪm] vi pt of **come**

camel ['kæm·əl] n Kamel nt

cameo <pl -os> ['kæm·i·ou] n Kamee f

camera ['kæm·ər·ə] n Kamera f

'**cameraman** n Kameramann m

'**camerawoman** n Kamerafrau f

camomile ['kæm·ə·mil] n Kamille f

camouflage ['kæm·ə·ˌflaʒ] I. n (a. fig) Tarnung f II. vt (a. fig) tarnen

camp [kæmp] I. n MIL [Feld]lager nt II. vi zelten

campaign [kæm·'peɪn] I. n ① Kampagne f; (for election) Wahlkampf m ② MIL Feldzug m II. vi kämpfen, sich engagieren

camper ['kæm·pər] n ① (person) Camper(in) m(f) ② (vehicle) Wohnmobil nt

'**campfire** n Lagerfeuer nt

'**campground** n Campingplatz m

camping ['kæm·pɪŋ] n Camping nt; **to go ~** zelten gehen

'**campsite** n Campingplatz m

campus ['kæm·pəs] n Campus m; **on ~** auf dem Campus

can[1] <could, could> [kæn] aux vb (be able to) können; (be allowed to) dürfen; (less formal) können; **~ you hear me?** kannst du mich hören?, hörst du mich?; **you ~'t park here** hier dürfen Sie nicht parken

can[2] [kən] n ① Dose f, Büchse f; of paint Farbtopf m ② (sl: bathroom) Klo nt

Canada ['kæn·ə·də] n Kanada nt

Canadian [kə·'neɪ·di·ən] I. n Kanadier(in) m(f) II. adj kanadisch

canal [kə·'næl] n Kanal m

canary [kə·'ner·i] n Kanarienvogel m

cancel <-l-> ['kæn·səl] I. vt ① (call off) absagen ② (remove from schedule) streichen ③ check, reservation stornieren ④ (discontinue) beenden; subscription kündigen; COMPUT abbrechen II. vi absagen

cancellation [ˌkæn·sə·'leɪ·ʃən] n ① Absage f ② (from schedule) Streichung f ③ (revocation) Widerruf m; FIN Stornierung f ④ (discontinuation) Kündigung f; of subscription Abbestellung f

cancer ['kæn·sər] n ① (a. fig: disease) Krebs m ② (growth) Krebsgeschwulst f

Cancer ['kæn·sər] n ASTROL Krebs m

cancerous ['kæn·sər·əs] adj krebsartig

candelabra <pl -> [ˌkæn·dəl·'a·brə] n Leuchter m

candid ['kæn·dɪd] adj offen

C

candidate ['kæn·dɪ·dət] n Kandidat(in) m(f)

candle ['kæn·dəl] n Kerze f

'candlelight n Kerzenlicht nt

'candlestick n Kerzenständer m

candor ['kæn·dər] n Offenheit f

candy ['kæn·di] n Süßigkeiten pl; (piece) Bonbon m o nt

'candy bar n Schokoriegel m

'candy store n Süßwarenladen m

cane [keɪn] n ❶ (of plant) Rohr nt; ~ sugar Rohrzucker m ❷ (stick) [Rohr]stock m

canine ['keɪ·naɪn] adj Hunde-

canister ['kæn·ɪ·stər] n Behälter m; (for oil, gasoline) Kanister m

cannabis ['kæn·ə·bɪs] n Cannabis m

cannibal ['kæn·ɪ·bəl] n Kannibale m, Kannibalin f

cannibalism ['kæn·ɪ·bəl·ɪz·əm] n Kannibalismus m

cannon ['kæn·ən] n Kanone f

'cannonball n Kanonenkugel f

cannot ['kæn·at] aux vb = **can not** see **can**

canoe [kə·'nu] n Kanu nt

canoeist [kə·'nu·ɪst] n Kanufahrer(in) m(f)

'can opener n Dosenöffner m

canopy ['kæn·ə·pi] n Baldachin m

can't [kænt] (fam) = **cannot** see **can**

cantankerous [kæn·'tæŋ·kər·əs] adj streitsüchtig

canteen [kæn·'tin] n Feldflasche f

canter ['kæn·tər] I. n Handgalopp m II. vi leicht galoppieren

canvas <pl -es> ['kæn·vəs] n Segeltuch nt; (for painting) Leinwand f

canvass ['kæn·vəs] vt ❶ (poll) befragen ❷ POL werben

canyon ['kæn·jən] n Schlucht f

cap [kæp] I. n ❶ (hat) Mütze f, Kappe f ❷ (top) Verschlusskappe f II. vt <-pp-> bedecken; teeth überkronen

capability [ˌkeɪ·pə·'bɪl·ɪ·ti] n Fähigkeit f

capable ['keɪ·pə·bəl] adj ❶ (competent) fähig; worker tüchtig ❷ (able) fähig

capacity [kə·'pæs·ɪ·ti] n ❶ Fassungsvermögen nt ❷ Kapazität f ❸ (position) Funktion f; (role) Eigenschaft f

cape[1] [keɪp] n FASHION Umhang m, Cape nt

cape[2] [keɪp] n GEOG Kap nt; **C~ Horn** Kap Hoorn

capital ['kæp·ɪ·təl] n ❶ (city) Hauptstadt f ❷ (letter) Großbuchstabe m ❸ FIN Kapital nt

capitalism ['kæp·ɪ·təl·ɪz·əm] n Kapitalismus m

capitalist ['kæp·ɪ·təl·ɪst] I. n Kapitalist(in) m(f) II. adj kapitalistisch

capitalize ['kæp·ɪ·tə·laɪz] vt ❶ LING großschreiben ❷ FIN kapitalisieren

capital 'letter n Großbuchstabe m

capital 'punishment n Todesstrafe f

Capitol ['kæ·pə·təl] n ■the ~ das Kapitol

Capitol 'Hill n Capitol Hill; **on ~** im amerikanischen Kongress

capitulate [kə·'pɪtʃ·ə·leɪt] vi kapitulieren

cappuccino <pl -s> [ˌkæp·ə·'tʃi·nou] n Cappuccino m

Capricorn ['kæp·rɪ·kɔrn] n ASTROL Steinbock m

capsize ['kæp·saɪz] vi NAUT kentern

capsule ['kæp·səl] n Kapsel f

captain ['kæp·tɪn] n Kapitän(in) m(f); (in army) Hauptmann m

caption ['kæp·ʃən] n ❶ Bildunterschrift f ❷ TV, FILM Untertitel m ❸ (heading) Überschrift f

captivate ['kæp·tə·veɪt] vt faszinieren

captive ['kæp·tɪv] n Gefangene(r) f(m)

captivity [kæp·'tɪv·ɪ·ti] n Gefangenschaft f

capture ['kæp·tʃər] I. vt ❶ gefangen nehmen; police festnehmen ❷ COMPUT erfassen II. n of a person Gefangennahme f; (by police) Festnahme f

car [kar] n ❶ Auto nt, Wagen m ❷ RAIL Waggon m, Wagen m

carafe [kə·'ræf] n Karaffe f

caramel ['kar·məl] n Karamellbonbon nt; (burnt sugar) Karamell m

carat <pl -s> ['ker·ət] n Karat nt

caraway ['kær·ə·weɪ] n Kümmel m

carbohydrate [ˌkar·boʊ·'haɪ·dreɪt] *n* Kohle[n]hydrat *nt*

'car bomb *n* Autobombe *f*

carbon ['kar·bən] *n* CHEM Kohlenstoff *m*

carbonated ['kar·bə·neɪ·tɪd] *adj* sprudelnd

'carbon copy *n* Durchschlag *m*; (*fig*) Ebenbild *nt*

carbon di'oxide *n* Kohlendioxid *nt*

carbon 'footprint *n* CO$_2$-Bilanz *f*, CO$_2$-Fußabdruck *m*

carbon mon'oxide *n* Kohlenmonoxid *nt*

carbs *n pl* (*fam*) *short for* **carbohydrates** Kohle[n]hydrat *nt*

carbuncle ['kar·bʌŋ·kəl] *n* MED Karbunkel *m*

carburetor ['kar·bə·reɪ·tər] *n* Vergaser *m*

carcinogenic [ˌkar·sɪn·ə·'dʒen·ɪk] *adj* Krebs erregend

card [kard] *n* Karte *f*; (*postcard*) [Post]karte *f*; [**game of**] **~s** *pl* Kartenspiel *nt*

'cardboard *n* Pappe *f*

cardiac ['kar·dɪ·æk] *adj* Herz-

cardigan ['kar·dɪ·gən] *n* Strickjacke *f*

cardinal ['kar·dɪn·əl] **I.** *n* REL Kardinal *m* **II.** *adj* **~ number** Kardinalzahl *f*

care [ker] **I.** *n* ❶ (*looking after*) Betreuung *f*; (*of children etc.*) Pflege *f*; (*in a hospital*) Versorgung *f*; **take ~** [**of yourself**]! pass auf dich auf!; ▪**to take ~ of sth** für etw *akk* sorgen; **~ of ...** zu Händen von ... ❷ (*carefulness*) Sorgfalt *f*; **to handle sth with ~** etw vorsichtig behandeln ❸ (*worry*) Sorge *f*; **to not have a ~ in the world** keinerlei Sorgen haben **II.** *vi* ❶ **who ~s?** (*it's not important*) wen interessiert das schon?; (*so what*) was soll's? ❷ (*look after*) ▪**to ~ for sb/sth** sich um jdn/etw kümmern ❸ ▪**to ~ for sth** *drink, dessert* etw mögen **III.** *vt* ▪**sb does not ~ what/who/whether ...** jdm ist es egal, was/wer/ob ...

career [kə·'rɪr] *n* ❶ (*profession*) Beruf *m* ❷ (*working life*) Karriere *f*, Laufbahn *f*

ca'reer woman *n* Karrierefrau *f*

'carefree *adj* sorgenfrei

careful ['ker·fəl] *adj* ❶ (*cautious*) vorsichtig; *driver* umsichtig ❷ (*meticulous*) sorgfältig, gründlich; *consideration* reiflich

careless ['ker·lɪs] *adj* ❶ (*inattentive*) unvorsichtig; *driver* leichtsinnig ❷ (*casual*) *remark* unbedacht; *talk* gedankenlos ❸ (*not painstaking*) nachlässig

carelessness ['ker·lɪs·nɪs] *n* ❶ (*neglecting*) Nachlässigkeit *f* ❷ (*not careful*) Unvorsichtigkeit *f*

caress [kə·'res] **I.** *n* <*pl* -es> Streicheln *nt*; ▪**~es** *pl* Zärtlichkeiten *pl* **II.** *vt* streicheln

'caretaker *n* Hausverwalter(in) *m(f)*

cargo <*pl* -s> ['kar·goʊ] *n* Fracht *f*; (*load*) Ladung *f*

Caribbean [ˌker·ɪ·'bi·ən] **I.** ▪**the ~** die Karibik **II.** *adj* karibisch; **the ~ Islands** die Karibischen Inseln

caricature ['ker·ə·kə·tʃʊr] **I.** *n* Karikatur *f* **II.** *vt* (*draw*) karikieren; (*parody*) parodieren

caring ['ker·ɪŋ] *adj* warmherzig; *person* fürsorglich

'car insurance *n* Kfz-Versicherung *f*

'carjacking *n* Autoentführung *f*

carnage ['kar·nɪdʒ] *n* Gemetzel *nt*

carnation [kar·'neɪ·ʃən] *n* Nelke *f*

carnival ['kar·nə·vəl] *n* ❶ Volksfest *nt*; (*traveling amusement park*) Jahrmarkt *m* ❷ (*pre-Lent*) Karneval *m*, Fasching *m bes* SÜDD, ÖSTERR

carnivore ['kar·nə·vɔr] *n* Fleischfresser *m*

carnivorous [kar·'nɪv·ər·əs] *adj* Fleisch fressend

carol ['ker·əl] *n* [**Christmas**] **~** Weihnachtslied *nt*

carousel [ˌkær·ə·'sel] *n* ❶ Karussell *nt* ❷ AVIAT [Gepäck]ausgabeband *nt*

carp <*pl* -> [karp] *n* Karpfen *m*

carpenter ['kar·pən·tər] *n* Zimmermann *m*

carpet ['kar·pət] **I.** *n* Teppich *m*; (*fitted*) Teppichboden *m* **II.** *vt* [mit einem Teppich] auslegen

'carpet sweeper *n* Teppichkehrer *m*

'carpool *n* Fahrgemeinschaft *f*

'car rental *n* Autovermietung *f*

carriage ['ker·ɪdʒ] *n* Kutsche *f*

carrier ['kæ·ri·ər] *n* ❶ (*person*) Träger(in) *m(f)* ❷ MIL (*vehicle*) Transporter *m*; [**aircraft**] ~ Flugzeugträger *m* ❸ (*transportation company*) *for people* Personenbeförderungsunternehmen *nt*; *for freight* Transportunternehmen *nt*, Spedition *f*; (*by air*) Fluggesellschaft *f* ❹ (*entrepreneur, person*) Frachtunternehmer(in) *m(f)*, Spediteur(in) *m(f)* ❺ MED [Über]träger(in) *m(f)* ❻ TELEC **wireless ~** Mobilfunkanbieter *m*

carrot ['ker·ət] *n* Möhre *f*, Karotte *f*

carry <-ie-> ['ker·i] I. *vt* ❶ (*bear*) tragen *a. fig* ❷ (*transport*) transportieren ❸ (*transmit*) MED übertragen; *electricity, oil* leiten ❹ *usu passive* motion annehmen II. *vi sound* zu hören sein

◆ **carry away** *vt* ❶ (*take away*) wegtragen ❷ *usu passive* ▪ **to get carried away** (*be overcome by*) sich mitreißen lassen; (*be enchanted by*) hingerissen sein

◆ **carry off** *vt* ❶ (*take away*) wegtragen; SPORT vom Spielfeld tragen ❷ (*succeed*) hinbekommen

◆ **carry on** I. *vt* ❶ fortführen; *discussion* fortsetzen ❷ (*conduct*) führen II. *vi* ❶ (*continue*) weitermachen ❷ (*fam: behave stupidly*) sich danebenbenehmen; (*make a fuss*) ein [furchtbares] Theater machen

◆ **carry out** *vt* ❶ hinaus-/heraustragen ❷ (*perform*) durchführen; *order, plan* ausführen; *threat* wahr machen

CARS [kɑːrz] *n no pl acr for* **Car Allowance Rebate System** Verschrottungsprämie *f*, Abwrackprämie *f*

cart [kɑrt] *n* ❶ Wagen *m*, Karren *m*; (*in supermarket*) Einkaufswagen *m* II. *vt* (*fam*) schleppen

cartilage ['kɑr·təl·ɪdʒ] *n* MED Knorpel *m*

carton ['kɑr·tən] *n* Karton *m*; (*small*) Schachtel *f*

cartoon [kɑr·'tun] *n* ❶ (*drawing*) Cartoon *m o nt* ❷ FILM Zeichentrickfilm *m*

car'toonist *n* ❶ Karikaturist(in) *m(f)* ❷ FILM Trickzeichner(in) *m(f)*

cartridge ['kɑr·trɪdʒ] *n* (*for ink, ammunition*) Patrone *f*; (*for film*) Kassette *f*

'cartwheel *n* SPORT Rad *nt*; **to turn a ~** ein Rad schlagen

carve [kɑrv] *vt* ❶ ART schnitzen; (*with a chisel*) meißeln; (*cut a pattern*) [ein]ritzen ❷ FOOD tranchieren

carving ['kɑr·vɪŋ] *n in wood* Schnitzerei *f*; *in stone* Skulptur *f*

'carving knife *n* Tranchiermesser *nt*

'car wash *n* Autowaschanlage *f*

cascade [kæs·'keɪd] I. *n* (*natural*) Wasserfall *m*; (*artificial*) Kaskade *f a. fig* II. *vi* sich ergießen

case¹ [keɪs] *n* ❶ (*instance*) Fall *m*; **in ~ of [an] emergency** im Notfall; **in most ~s** meistens; **in ~ ... falls ...;** **in any ~** (*regardless*) jedenfalls ❷ LAW [Rechts]fall *m*; (*suit*) Verfahren *nt* ❸ LING Fall *m*, Kasus *m*

case² [keɪs] *n* ❶ (*container*) Schatulle *f*; (*for eyeglasses*) Etui *nt*; (*for CD, umbrella*) Hülle *f*; *of beer* Kiste *f*; ❷ (*suitcase*) Koffer *m*

cash [kæʃ] I. *n* Bargeld *nt*; **to pay [in] ~** bar bezahlen II. *vt* ▪ **to ~ [in]** ⟳ sth etw einlösen; *chips* etw eintauschen III. *vi* ▪ **to ~ in on sth** von etw *dat* profitieren

cashew ['kæʃ·u] *n* Cashewnuss *f*

cashier [kæ·'ʃɪr] *n* Kassierer(in) *m(f)*

'cash machine *n* Geldautomat *m*, Bankomat *m* SCHWEIZ, ÖSTERR

cashmere ['kæʒ·mɪr] *n* Kaschmir *m*

'cash register *n* [Registrier]kasse *f*

casino <*pl* -os> [kə·'si·noʊ] *n* [Spiel]kasino *nt*

casket ['kæs·kɪt] *n* ❶ (*coffin*) Sarg *m* ❷ (*box*) Kästchen *nt*

casserole ['kæs·ə·roʊl] *n* Auflaufform *f*, Schmortopf *m*; **tuna/potato ~** Thunfisch-/Kartoffelauflauf *m*

cassette [kə·'set] *n* Kassette *f*

cas'sette player, cas'sette recorder *n* Kassettenrecorder *m*

cast [kæst] I. *n* ❶ THEAT, FILM Besetzung *f* ❷ MED Gips[verband] *m* II. *vt* <cast,

cast> ① (*throw*) werfen *a. fig; fishing line* auswerfen ② *ballots, votes* abgeben ③ THEAT, FILM *part, role* besetzen; *person* eine Rolle geben ④ (*make in a mold*) gießen

◆ **cast off** NAUT I. *vt* losmachen II. *vi* ablegen

castanet [ˌkæs·tə·'net] *n* Kastagnette *f*

caster ['kæs·tər] *n* (*wheel*) Laufrolle *f*

'**casting vote** *n* entscheidende Stimme

cast 'iron *n* Gusseisen *nt*

cast-'iron *adj* ① aus Gusseisen ② (*fig*) *alibi* wasserdicht

castle ['kæs·əl] *n* ① (*fortress*) Burg *f*; (*mansion*) Schloss *nt* ② CHESS (*fam*) Turm *m*

'**castoff** I. *n* ■~s *pl* abgelegte Kleidung II. *adj* (*secondhand*) gebraucht; (*discarded*) abgelegt

castor ['kæs·tər] *n see* **caster**

castrate [ˈkæs·treɪt] *vt* kastrieren

casual ['kæʒ·u·əl] *adj* ① (*informal*) lässig, salopp; *clothing* leger ② (*not planned*) zufällig; *acquaintance, glance* flüchtig

casualty ['kæʒ·u·əl·ti] *n* (*accident victim*) [Unfall]opfer *nt*; (*injured*) Verletzte(r) *f(m)*; (*dead*) Todesfall *m*

cat [kæt] *n* Katze *f*

catalog ['kæt·əl·ag] I. *n* Katalog *m* II. *vt* katalogisieren

catalyst ['kæt·əl·ɪst] *n* Katalysator *m*

catamaran [ˌkæt·ə·mə·'ræn] *n* Katamaran *m*

catapult ['kæt·ə·pʌlt] I. *n* Katapult *nt* II. *vt* katapultieren

cataract ['kæt·ə·rækt] *n* ① MED grauer Star ② GEOG Katarakt *m*

catastrophe [kə·'tæs·trə·fi] *n* Katastrophe *f*

catastrophic [ˌkæt·ə·'straf·ɪk] *adj* katastrophal

catch [kætʃ] I. *n* <*pl* -es> ① (*of ball*) Fang *m* ② (*fish*) Fang *m* kein *pl* ③ (*fastener*) Verschluss *m*; (*bolt*) Riegel *m*; (*hook*) Haken *m* ④ (*disadvantage*) Haken *m* II. *vt* <caught, caught> ① *ball* fangen; *light* einfangen; *person* auffangen ② *person* ergreifen; (*arrest*) fest-

nehmen; *animal* fangen; *escaped animal* einfangen ③ (*surprise*) erwischen; **to be caught in a thunderstorm** von einem Gewitter überrascht werden ④ MED **to ~ [a] cold** sich erkälten ⑤ (*take*) *bus/train* nehmen; (*arrive in time for*) kriegen ⑥ **to ~ sight** [*or* **a glimpse**] **of sb/sth** etw [kurz] sehen; (*by chance*) etw [zufällig] sehen III. *vi* <caught, caught> ■**to ~ on sth** an etw *dat* hängen bleiben

◆ **catch on** *vi* (*fam*) ① (*understand*) kapieren ② (*become popular*) sich durchsetzen

◆ **catch up** *vi* ■**to ~ up with sb** jdn einholen *a. fig*; ■**to ~ up on sth** etw aufarbeiten; ■**to ~ up on sleep** Schlaf nachholen

catcher ['kætʃ·ər] *n* Fänger(in) *m(f)*; (*in baseball*) Catcher *m*

catching ['kætʃ·ɪŋ] *adj* ansteckend

'**catch phrase** *n* Slogan *m*

catchy ['kætʃ·i] *adj* eingängig

categorical [ˌkæt·ə·'gɔr·ɪ·kəl] *adj* kategorisch

category ['kæt·ə·gɔr·i] *n* Kategorie *f*

cater ['keɪ·tər] *vi* ① für Speise und Getränke sorgen; *company* Speisen und Getränke liefern ② sich kümmern (**to** um +*akk*)

caterer ['keɪ·tər·ər] *n* (*company*) Cateringservice *m*; (*for parties*) Partyservice *m*

caterpillar ['kæt·ər·pɪl·ər] *n* Raupe *f*

'**catfish** *n* <*pl* -> Seewolf *m*

cathedral [kə·'θi·drəl] *n* Kathedrale *f*, Dom *m*

Catholic ['kæθ·ə·lɪk] I. *n* Katholik(in) *m(f)* II. *adj* katholisch

Catholicism [kə·'θal·ə·sɪz·əm] *n* Katholizismus *m*

'**catkin** *n* BOT Kätzchen *nt*

'**catnap** (*fam*) I. *n* Nickerchen *nt* II. *vi* <-pp-> kurz schlafen

cattle ['kæt·əl] *npl* Rinder *pl*

catty ['kæt·i] *adj* gehässig; *remark* bissig

'**catwalk** *n* Laufsteg *m*

Caucasian [kɔ·'keɪ·ʒən] I. *n* Weiße(r) *f(m)* II. *adj* weiß

caught [kɔt] *pt, pp of* **catch**

cauliflower ['kɔ·lɪ·ˌflaʊ·ər] *n* Blumenkohl *m*, Karfiol *m* SÜDD, ÖSTERR

cause [kɔz] **I.** *n* ① (*of effect*) Ursache *f*; (*reason*) Grund *m* ② **a good ~** ein guter Zweck **II.** *vt* verursachen; *trouble* stiften

'cause [kəz] *conj* (*fam*) *abbrev of* **because**

causeway ['kɔz·ˌweɪ] *n* Damm *m*

caustic ['kɔ·stɪk] *adj* ätzend *a. fig*; *humor* beißend

caution ['kɔ·ʃən] **I.** *n* (*carefulness*) Vorsicht *f*; (*warning*) Vorwarnung *f* **II.** *vt* (*form*) warnen

cautious ['kɔ·ʃəs] *adj* (*careful*) vorsichtig; (*prudent*) umsichtig

cavalry ['kæv·əl·ri] *n usu + pl vb* ■ **the ~** die Kavallerie

cave [keɪv] *n* Höhle *f*

◆ **cave in** *vi* ① (*collapse*) einstürzen ② (*give in*) kapitulieren

'caveman *n* Höhlenmensch *m*

cavern ['kæv·ərn] *n* Höhle *f*

caviar(e) ['kæv·i·ɑr] *n* Kaviar *m*

cavity ['kæv·ɪ·ti] *n* Loch *nt*; (*hollow space*) Hohlraum *m*; (*in tooth*) Loch *nt*

cayenne [kaɪ·'en], **cayenne 'pepper** [kaɪ·'en-] *n* Cayennepfeffer *m*

CB [ˌsi·'bi] *n* RADIO *abbrev of* **citizens band** CB-Funk *m*

CD [ˌsi·'di] *n abbrev of* **compact disc** CD *f*

C'D player *n* CD-Spieler *m*

CD-ROM [ˌsi·di·'rɑm] *n abbrev of* **compact disc read-only memory** CD-ROM *f*

cease [sis] (*form*) **I.** *vi* aufhören **II.** *vt* beenden; *fire* einstellen

'ceasefire *n* Waffenruhe *f*

cedar ['si·dər] *n* Zeder *f*

ceiling ['si·lɪŋ] *n* [Zimmer]decke *f*; (*fig*) Obergrenze *f*

celebrate ['sel·ɪ·breɪt] *vt, vi* feiern

celebrated ['sel·ɪ·breɪ·tɪd] *adj* berühmt

celebration [ˌsel·ɪ·'breɪ·ʃən] *n* Feier *f*

celebrity [sə·'leb·rɪ·ti] *n* berühmte Persönlichkeit

celeriac [sə·'ler·i·æk] *n* [Knollen]sellerie *m of*

celery ['sel·ə·ri] *n* [Stangen]sellerie *m of*

celibate ['sel·ɪ·bət] *adj* zölibatär

cell [sel] *n* ① BIOL Zelle *f* ② (*in prison*) Zelle *f* ③ (*fam*) *see* **cell phone**

cellar ['sel·ər] *n* Keller *m*

cellist ['tʃel·ɪst] *n* Cellist(in) *m(f)*

cello <*pl* -s> ['tʃel·oʊ] *n* Cello *nt*

cellophane ['sel·ə·feɪn] *n* Cellophan® *nt*

'cell phone *n* Mobiltelefon *nt*, Handy *nt*, Natel *nt* SCHWEIZ

cellulite ['sel·jə·laɪt] *n* Zellulitis *f*

celluloid ['sel·jʊ·lɔɪd] *n* Zelluloid *nt*

cellulose ['sel·jʊ·loʊs] *n* Zellulose *f*

Celsius ['sel·si·əs] *n* Celsius

cement [sɪ·'ment] **I.** *n* Zement *m* **II.** *vt* ① (*with concrete*) betonieren; (*with cement*) zementieren; (*with glue*) kitten ② (*a. fig: bind*) festigen

ce'ment mixer *n* Betonmischmaschine *f*

cemetery ['sem·ə·ter·i] *n* Friedhof *m*

censor ['sen·sər] **I.** *n* Zensor(in) *m(f)* **II.** *vt* zensieren

censorship ['sen·sər·ʃɪp] *n* Zensur *f*

censure ['sen·ʃər] **I.** *n* Tadel *m* **II.** *vt* tadeln

census ['sen·səs] *n* Zählung *f*

cent [sent] *n* Cent *m*

centenarian [ˌsen·tə·'ner·i·ən] *n* Hundertjährige(r) *f/m*

centennial [sen·'teni·əl] *n* Hundertjahrfeier *f*

center ['sen·tər] *n* ① Zentrum *nt*, Mittelpunkt *m*; POL Mitte *f* ② SPORT Center *m*

centigrade ['sen·tə·greɪd] *n* Celsius

centimeter ['sen·tə·ˌmi·tər] *n* Zentimeter *m*

centipede ['sen·tə·pid] *n* Tausendfüßler *m*

central ['sen·trəl] *adj* ① (*middle*) zentral ② (*vital*) wesentlich

centrifugal [sen·'trɪf·jə·gəl] *adj* zentrifugal

century ['sen·tʃə·ri] *n* Jahrhundert *nt*

CEO [ˌsi·i·'oʊ] *n abbrev of* **chief executive officer** Generaldirektor(in) *m(f)*

ceramics [səˈræm·ɪks] *n* + *sing vb* Keramik *f*

cereal [ˈsɪr·i·əl] *n* ❶ *(for breakfast)* Frühstückszerealien *pl* (*Cornflakes, Müsli ...*) ❷ *(crop)* Getreide *nt*

ceremonial [ˌser·əˈmoʊ·ni·əl] *adj* zeremoniell

ceremonious [ˌser·əˈmoʊ·ni·əs] *adj* förmlich

ceremony [ˈser·ə·moʊ·ni] *n* Zeremonie *f*, Feier *f*

certain [ˈsɜr·tən] *adj* ❶ *(sure)* sicher; *(unavoidable)* bestimmt; **to make ~ [that ...]** darauf achten[, dass ...]; **for ~** ganz sicher ❷ *(particular)* gewiss

certainly [ˈsɜr·tən·li] *adv* ❶ *(surely)* sicher[lich]; *(without a doubt)* gewiss ❷ *(gladly)* gern[e]; *(of course)* [aber] selbstverständlich; **~ not** auf [gar] keinen Fall

certainty [ˈsɜr·tən·ti] *n* Gewissheit *f*

certificate [sərˈtɪf·ɪ·kət] *n* *(document)* Urkunde *f*; *(attestation)* Bescheinigung *f*

certified [ˈsɜr·tə·faɪd] *adj* ❶ *copy* beglaubigt ❷ *(trained)* ausgebildet, -meister, -in *m, f*; *(by the state)* staatlich anerkannt

certify <-ie-> [ˈsɜr·tə·faɪ] *vt* bescheinigen, bestätigen; LAW beglaubigen

cervical [ˈsɜr·vɪ·kəl] *adj* ANAT ❶ *(of neck)* zervikal ❷ *(of cervix)* Gebärmutterhals-

cervix <*pl* -es> [ˈsɜr·vɪks] *n* Gebärmutterhals *m*

cesspit [ˈses·pɪt], **cesspool** [ˈses·pul] *n* Jauchegrube *f*; *(fig, pej)* Sumpf *m*

CFC [ˌsi·ef·ˈsi] *n abbrev of* **chlorofluorocarbon** FCKW *nt*

chafe [tʃeɪf] *vt* [wund]scheuern

chain [tʃeɪn] I. *n* ❶ Kette *f* ❷ *(fig: of shops)* [Laden]kette *f* II. *vt* [an]ketten

chain reˈaction *n* Kettenreaktion *f*

ˈ**chain saw** *n* Kettensäge *f*

ˈ**chain smoker** *n* Kettenraucher(in) *m(f)*

ˈ**chain store** *n* Kettenladen *m*

chair [tʃer] I. *n* ❶ Stuhl *m* ❷ UNIV Lehrstuhl *m* ❸ *(chairperson)* Vorsitzende(r) *f(m)* II. *vt* ▪ **to ~ sth** bei etw *dat* den Vorsitz führen

ˈ**chair lift** *n* Sessellift *m*

ˈ**chairman** *n* Vorsitzende(r) *m*

ˈ**chairmanship** *n* Vorsitz *m*

ˈ**chairperson** *n* Vorsitzende(r) *f(m)*

ˈ**chairwoman** *n* Vorsitzende *f*

chalk [tʃɔk] I. *n* ❶ Kreide *f*; *(rock)* Kalkstein *m* II. *vt* mit Kreide schreiben/zeichnen

challenge [ˈtʃæl·ɪndʒ] I. *n* Herausforderung *f* II. *vt* ❶ herausfordern ❷ *findings* in Frage stellen

challenger [ˈtʃæl·ɪn·dʒər] *n* *(for title)* Titelanwärter(in) *m(f)*

challenging [ˈtʃæl·ɪn·dʒɪŋ] *adj* [heraus]fordernd

chamber [ˈtʃeɪm·bər] *n* ❶ *(judge's offices)* ▪ **~s** Amtszimmer *nt* ❷ *(in firearm)* Patronenlager ❸ *(old)* Kammer *f*

ˈ**chambermaid** *n* Zimmermädchen *nt*

ˈ**chamber music** *n* Kammermusik *f*

chameleon [kəˈmi·li·ən] *n* Chamäleon *nt a. fig*

chamois <*pl* -> [ˈʃæm·i] *n* ❶ ZOOL Gämse *f* ❷ *(cloth)* Fensterleder *nt*

champ [tʃæmp] *n short for* **champion** Champion *m*

champagne [ʃæmˈpeɪn] *n* Champagner *m*

champion [ˈtʃæm·pi·ən] *n* ❶ Champion *m* ❷ Verfechter(in) *m(f)*

championship [ˈtʃæm·pi·ən·ʃɪp] *n* Meisterschaft *f*

chance [tʃæns] I. *n* ❶ Zufall *m*; **by ~** zufällig ❷ *(prospect)* Chance *f*; **no ~!** *(fam)* niemals! ❸ *(risk)* Risiko *nt*; **to take ~s** *or* **a ~** etwas riskieren II. *vt* *(fam)* riskieren; **to ~ it** es wagen

chancellor [ˈtʃæn·sə·lər] *n* ❶ Kanzler(in) *m(f)* ❷ UNIV Rektor(in) *m(f)*

chandelier [ˌʃæn·dəˈlɪr] *n* Kronleuchter *m*

change [tʃeɪndʒ] I. *n* ❶ *(alteration)* [Ver]änderung *f* ❷ *(substitution)* Wechsel *m* ❸ *(variety)* Abwechslung *f*; **for a ~** zur Abwechslung ❹ *(coins)* Kleingeld *nt*; *(money returned)* Wechselgeld *nt*, Retourgeld *nt* SCHWEIZ II. *vi* ❶ sich [ver]ändern; *traffic light* umspringen; *weather* umschlagen; *wind* sich

C

drehen ②(*substitute*) ■**to ~ [over] to sth** zu etw *dat* wechseln ③TRANSP umsteigen ④(*dress*) sich umziehen III.*vt* ①(*make different*) [ver]ändern; (*transform*) verwandeln; **to ~ one's mind** seine Meinung ändern ②(*exchange*) wechseln; **to ~ places with sb** mit jdm den Platz tauschen; (*fig*) mit jdm tauschen ③(*make fresh*) *baby* [frisch] wickeln; *bed* neu beziehen; *socks, underwear* wechseln; **to get ~d** sich umziehen ④(*money*) wechseln; **to ~ $100 into euros** $100 in Euros umtauschen ⑤TRANSP *buses, trains* umsteigen

changeable ['tʃeɪn·dʒə·bəl] *adj* unbeständig; *moods* wechselna

'**changeover** *n usu sing* Umstellung *f*

channel ['tʃæn·əl] I.*n* ①Programm *nt* ②[Fluss]bett *nt*; (*artificial*) Kanal *m* II.*vt* <-l-> (*direct*) leiten; *one's energies, money* stecken

chant [tʃænt] I.*n* ①REL [Sprech]gesang *m* ②SPORT Sprechchor *m* II.*vt* ①REL singen ②SPORT im Sprechchor rufen

chaos ['keɪ·as] *n* Chaos *nt*, Durcheinander *nt*

chaotic [keɪ·'at·ɪk] *adj* chaotisch

chap <-pp-> [tʃæp] *vt, vi* aufspringen

chapel ['tʃæp·əl] *n* Kapelle *f*

chaplain ['tʃæp·lɪn] *n* Kaplan *m*

Chap Stick® *n* ≈ Labello® *m*

chapter ['tʃæp·tər] *n* Kapitel *nt*

char <-rr-> [tʃar] *vt, vi* verkohlen

character ['ker·ək·tər] *n* ①Charakter *m* ②LIT [Roman]figur *m* ③TYPO Zeichen *nt*

characteristic [ˌker·ək·tə·'rɪs·tɪk] I.*n* charakteristisches Merkmal II.*adj* charakteristisch, typisch

characterize ['ker·ək·tə·raɪz] *vt* kennzeichnen

charcoal ['tʃar·koʊl] *n* Holzkohle *f*; (*for drawing*) Kohle *f*

charge [tʃardʒ] I.*n* ①(*cost*) Gebühr *f*; **free of ~** kostenlos ②LAW Anklage *f*; ■**~s** *pl* Anklagepunkte *pl*; (*in civil cases*) Ansprüche *pl* ③(*responsibility*) Verantwortung *f*; **to be in ~** die Verant-

wortung tragen; **she's in ~ of the department** sie leitet die Abteilung ④ELEC Ladung *f* ⑤(*attack*) Angriff *m* II.*vi* ①(*attack*) [vorwärts]stürmen ②(*move quickly*) stürmen III.*vt* ①(*demand payment*) berechnen; **how much do you ~ for that?** was kostet das bei Ihnen? ②LAW **to ~ sb with murder** jdn des Mordes anklagen ③*battery* aufladen

'**charging station** *n* Ladestation *f*; (*for electric vehicles*) Stromtankstelle *f*

chariot ['tʃær·i·ət] *n* Streitwagen *m*

charisma [kə·'rɪz·mə] *n* Charisma *nt*

charismatic [ˌkə·rɪz·'mæt·ɪk] *adj* charismatisch

charitable ['tʃer·ɪ·tə·bəl] *adj* ①(*generous*) großzügig; (*uncritical*) gütig ②(*of charity*) karitativ; **~ organization** Wohltätigkeitsorganisation *f*

charity ['tʃer·ɪ·ti] *n* ①(*generosity*) Barmherzigkeit *f* ②Wohltätigkeitsorganisation *f*; **the proceeds go to ~** die Erträge sind für wohltätige Zwecke bestimmt

charm [tʃarm] *n* ①(*quality*) Charme *m* ②(*jewelry*) Anhänger *m*; **lucky ~** Glücksbringer *m*

charming ['tʃar·mɪŋ] *adj* bezaubernd, reizend

chart [tʃart] *n* ①(*visual*) Diagramm *nt* ②MUS ■**the ~s** *pl* die Charts

charter ['tʃar·tər] I.*n* ①(*constitution*) Charta *f*; (*of society*) Satzung *f* ②TRANSP Charter *m* II.*vt* chartern

'**charter flight** *n* Charterflug *m*

chase [tʃeɪs] I.*n* ①Verfolgungsjagd *f* ②HUNT Jagd *f* II.*vi* ■**to ~ after sb** hinter jdm herlaufen III.*vt* ①(*pursue*) verfolgen ②■**to ~ away** vertreiben, verjagen

chasm ['kæz·əm] *n* Kluft *f a. fig*

chassis <*pl* -> ['ʃæs·i] *n* Fahrgestell *nt*

chaste [tʃeɪst] *adj* (*form*) keusch

chastity ['tʃæs·tɪ·ti] *n* Keuschheit *f*

chat [tʃæt] I.*n* (*fam*) Schwatz *m*; **to have a ~ [with sb]** [mit jdm] quatschen II.*vi* <-tt-> ①plaudern ②COMPUT chatten

'chat room *n* Chatroom *m*

chatter ['tʃæt·ər] **I.** *n* Geschwätz *nt* **II.** *vi* ❶ (*converse*) plaudern ❷ *teeth* klappern; *machines* knattern

chatty ['tʃæt·i] *adj* (*fam*) *person* gesprächig; (*pej*) geschwätzig

chauffeur ['ʃoʊ·fər] *n* Chauffeur(in) *m(f)*

cheap [tʃip] *adj* billig *a. fig*; (*reduced*) ermäßigt

'cheapskate *n* (*pej fam*) Geizkragen *m*

cheat [tʃit] **I.** *n* ❶ (*person*) Betrüger(in) *m(f)*; (*in school*) Schummler(in) *m(f)* ❷ (*fraud*) Täuschung *f* **II.** *vi* betrügen; (*in exam*) abschreiben; ▪ **to ~ on sb** jdn betrügen **III.** *vt* täuschen; (*financially*) betrügen

check [tʃek] **I.** *n* ❶ (*inspection*) Kontrolle *f* ❷ (*search*) Suchlauf *m* ❸ (*restraint*) Kontrolle *f* ❹ (*mark*) Haken *m* ❺ CHESS Schach *nt* ❻ FIN Scheck *m*; (*bill*) Rechnung *f* ❼ (*pattern*) Karo[muster] *nt* **II.** *vt* ❶ (*inspect*) überprüfen ❷ *advance* aufhalten ❸ CHESS Schach bieten ❹ *box* abhaken **III.** *vi* ❶ (*examine*) nachsehen ❷ (*consult*) ▪ **to ~ with sb** bei jdm nachfragen

◆ **check in I.** *vi* sich abmelden **II.** *vt* *passengers* abfertigen; *hotel guests* anmelden; *luggage* einchecken

◆ **check out I.** *vi* sich abmelden **II.** *vt* ❶ (*investigate*) untersuchen ❷ (*sl: observe*) ~ **it out!** schau dir bloß das an!

◆ **check up** *vi* ▪ **to ~ up on sb/sth** jdn/etw überprüfen [*o* kontrollieren]

'checkbook *n* Scheckheft *nt*

checked [tʃekt] *adj* kariert

'checkerboard *n* Damebrett *nt*

checkered ['tʃek·ərd] *adj* ❶ (*patterned*) kariert ❷ (*fig*) *past, career* bewegt

'check-in ['tʃek·ɪn] *n* ❶ (*for flight*) Einchecken *nt* ❷ *see* **check-in counter**

'check-in counter, 'check-in desk *n* (*airport*) Abfertigungsschalter *m*; (*hotel*) Rezeption *f*

'checking account *n* Girokonto *nt*

'checklist *n* Checkliste *f*

'checkmate *n* CHESS Schachmatt *nt*

'checkout *n* Kasse *f*

'check room *n* (*for coats*) Garderobe *f*; (*for luggage*) Gepäckaufbewahrung *f*

'checkup *n* [Kontroll]untersuchung *f*

cheek [tʃik] *n* ❶ (*of face*) Backe *f* ❷ (*impertinence*) Frechheit *f*

'cheekbone *n usu pl* Backenknochen *m*

cheeky ['tʃi·ki] *adj* frech

cheep [tʃip] **I.** *n* (*sound*) Piepser *m*; (*action*) Piepen *nt* **II.** *vi* piep[s]en

cheer [tʃɪr] **I.** *n* ❶ Beifallsruf *m*; **three ~s for ...** ein dreifaches Hoch auf +*akk* ... ❷ Aufmunterung *f* **II.** *vi* mit Beifall begrüßen

◆ **cheer up I.** *vi* ~ **up!** Kopf hoch! **II.** *vt* aufmuntern

cheerful ['tʃɪr·fʊl] *adj* ❶ (*happy*) fröhlich, heiter ❷ (*bright*) heiter; *tune* fröhlich

cheering ['tʃɪr·ɪŋ] **I.** *n* Jubel *m* **II.** *adj* jubelnd

'cheerleader *n* Cheerleader *m*

cheers [tʃɪrz] *interj* (*fam*) prost

cheese [tʃiz] *n* Käse *m*

'cheeseburger *n* Cheeseburger *m*

'cheesecake *n* Käsekuchen *m*

cheesy ['tʃi·zi] *adj* ❶ käsig ❷ (*pej fam*) abgedroschen *fam*

cheetah ['tʃi·tə] *n* Gepard *m*

chef [ʃef] *n* Koch *m*, Köchin *f*

chemical ['kem·ɪ·kəl] **I.** *n* (*substance*) Chemikalie *f*; (*additive*) chemischer Zusatz **II.** *adj* chemisch

chemist ['kem·ɪst] *n* Chemiker(in) *m(f)*

chemistry ['kem·ɪ·stri] *n* Chemie *f*

chemotherapy [ˌki·moʊ·ˈθer·ə·pi] *n* Chemotherapie *f*

cherish ['tʃer·ɪʃ] *vt* hegen

cherry ['tʃer·i] *n* Kirsche *f*

cherry to'mato *n* Cocktailtomate *f*

chervil ['tʃɜr·vɪl] *n* Kerbel *m*

chess [tʃes] *n* Schach[spiel] *nt*

'chessboard *n* Schachbrett *nt*

'chessman, 'chesspiece *n* Schachfigur *f*

chest [tʃest] *n* ❶ Brust *f* ❷ (*trunk*) Truhe *f*; (*box*) Kiste *f*

chestnut ['tʃes·nʌt] I. n Kastanie f
II. adj kastanienbraun

chesty ['tʃes·ti] adj (fam) ❶ (arrogant)
eingebildet ❷ (big-bosomed) vollbusig

chew [tʃu] vt, vi kauen

'chewing gum n Kaugummi m o nt

chic [ʃik] I. n Schick m II. adj schick

chick [tʃɪk] n ❶ (chicken) Küken nt
❷ (sl: woman) Puppe f pej

chicken ['tʃɪk·ən] n ❶ (bird) Huhn n
❷ (meat) Hähnchen nt ❸ (pej sl)
Angsthase m

'chickenpox n Windpocken pl

'chick flick n (sl) Frauenfilm f (Film mit
besonders emotionaler Handlung)

chickpea ['tʃɪk·pi] n Kichererbse f

chicory ['tʃɪk·ə·ri] n Chicorée m o f; (in
drink) Zichorie f

chief [tʃif] I. n ❶ (boss) Chef(in) m(f)
❷ (leader) Führer(in) m(f); (head of
clan) Oberhaupt nt; (head of tribe)
Häuptling m II. adj Haupt-, oberste(r, s)

chief ex'ecutive n Präsident(in) m(f);
(of organization) ~ [officer] Generaldirektor(in) m(f)

chief 'justice n Oberrichter(in) m(f)

chiefly ['tʃif·li] adv hauptsächlich

chiffon [ʃɪ·'fan] n Chiffon m

child <pl -dren> [tʃaɪld] n Kind nt

'child abuse n Kindesmisshandlung f

'childbirth n Geburt f

childhood ['tʃaɪld·hʊd] n Kindheit f

childish ['tʃaɪl·dɪʃ] adj (pej) kindisch

'childlike adj kindlich

'childproof adj kindersicher

children ['tʃɪl·drən] n pl of **child**

chili <pl -es> ['tʃɪl·i] n Chili m

chili con carne [,tʃɪl·i·kan·'kar·ni] n Chili con Carne nt

chill [tʃɪl] I. n ❶ Kühle f; (feeling of coldness) Kältegefühl nt II. vi ❶ abkühlen
❷ (fam) ~ [out] chillen sl III. vt [ab]kühlen [lassen]

chilling ['tʃɪl·ɪŋ] adj ❶ (freezing) eisig
❷ (frightening) abschreckend

chilly ['tʃɪl·i] adj kühl a. fig, frostig

chime [tʃaɪm] I. n Glockenspiel nt; (of
single one) Glockenschlag m; (of door-

bell) Läuten nt kein pl II. vi klingen;
church bells läuten

chimney ['tʃɪm·ni] n Schornstein m; (of
factory) Schlot m

'chimney sweep n Schornsteinfeger(in)
m(f)

chimpanzee [tʃɪm·'pæn·zi] n Schimpanse m

chin [tʃɪn] n Kinn nt

china ['tʃaɪ·nə] n Porzellan nt

China ['tʃaɪ·nə] n China nt

Chinese <pl -> [tʃaɪ·'niz] I. n ❶ (person) Chinese, -in m, f; ■the ~ pl die
Chinesen ❷ (language) Chinesisch nt
II. adj chinesisch

chink [tʃɪŋk] n Spalt m

'chin-up n Klimmzug m

chip [tʃɪp] I. n ❶ Splitter m; (of wood)
Span m ❷ this cup has a ~ in it diese
Tasse ist angeschlagen ❸ usu pl FOOD
[potato] ~s Chips pl ❹ COMPUT Chip m
II. vt <-pp-> ❶ (damage) abschlagen;
(break off) abbrechen ❷ SPORT ball, puck
chippen

◆ **chip in** vt, vi etw beisteuern

chipmunk ['tʃɪp·mʌŋk] n Backenhörnchen nt

chiropractor ['kaɪ·roʊ·,præk·tər] n Chiropraktiker(in) m(f)

chirp [tʃɜrp] I. n Zwitschern nt II. vt, vi
zwitschern

chisel ['tʃɪz·əl] I. n Meißel m II. vt <-l->
meißeln

chitchat ['tʃɪt·tʃæt] n (fam) Geplauder nt

chivalrous ['ʃɪv·əl·rəs] adj ritterlich

chives [tʃaɪvz] npl Schnittlauch m
kein pl

chlorine ['klɔr·in] n Chlor nt

chlorofluorocarbon [,klɔr·oʊ·,flʊr·oʊ·
'kar·bən] n Fluorchlorkohlenwasserstoff m

chlorophyll ['klɔr·ə·fɪl] n Chlorophyll nt

chock [tʃak] n Bremsklotz m

chock-'full adj (fam) proppenvoll, vollgestopft

chocolate ['tʃak·lət] n ❶ Schokolade f;
dark ~ Zartbitterschokolade f ❷ (in
box) Praline f

chocolate 'chip n Schokoladenstückchen nt

choice [tʃɔɪs] I. n ➊ (selection) Wahl f; **to make a ~** eine Wahl treffen ➋ (variety) Auswahl f II. adj ausgesucht

choir ['kwaɪr] n Chor m

choke [tʃoʊk] I. n AUTO Choke m II. vt ➊ erwürgen; (suffocate) ersticken ➋ (block) verstopfen III. vi ➊ keine Luft bekommen; **to ~ to death** ersticken ➋ (sl: fail) versagen

cholera ['kɑl·ər·ə] n Cholera f

cholesterol [kə·'les·tə·rɑl] n Cholesterin nt

choose <chose, chosen> [tʃuz] I. vt [aus]wählen II. vi (select) wählen; (decide) sich entscheiden

choosy ['tʃu·zi] adj (fam) wählerisch

chop [tʃɑp] I. vt <-pp-> wood hacken; ■**to ~ sth** ◯ [up] etw klein schneiden II. vi <-pp-> hacken III. n ➊ (meat) Kotelett nt ➋ (blow) Schlag m
♦**chop down** vt fällen
♦**chop off** vt abhacken

chopper ['tʃɑp·ər] n ➊ (sl: helicopter) Hubschrauber m ➋ (sl: motorcycle) Chopper m ➌ (ax, cleaver) Hackbeil nt

'chopping board n Hackbrett nt

choppy ['tʃɑp·i] adj NAUT bewegt

'chopstick n usu pl |Ess|stäbchen nt

choral ['kɔr·əl] adj Chor-

chord [kɔrd] n Akkord m

chore [tʃɔr] n Hausarbeit f

choreographer [ˌkɔr·i·'ag·rə·fər] n Choreograf(in) m(f)

choreography [ˌkɔr·i·'ag·rə·fi] n Choreografie f

chorus ['kɔr·əs] n <pl -es> ➊ Refrain m ➋ Chor m

chose [tʃoʊz] pt of **choose**

chosen ['tʃoʊ·zən] pp of **choose**

chowder ['tʃaʊ·dər] n sämige Suppe mit Fisch, Muscheln etc.

Christ [kraɪst] n Christus m

christen ['krɪs·ən] vt ➊ (baptize, name) taufen ➋ (use for first time) einweihen

christening ['krɪs·ə·nɪŋ] n Taufe f

Christian ['krɪs·tʃən] I. n Christ(in) m(f) II. adj christlich

Christianity [ˌkrɪs·tʃi·'æn·ɪ·t̬i] n Christentum nt

Christmas <pl -es> ['krɪs·məs] n Weihnachten nt; **Merry ~!** Frohe [o Fröhliche] Weihnachten!

'Christmas card n Weihnachtskarte f

'Christmas carol n Weihnachtslied nt

Christmas 'Day n erster Weihnachtsfeiertag

Christmas 'Eve n Heiligabend m

'Christmas tree n Weihnachtsbaum m

chrome [kroʊm], **chromium** ['kroʊ·mi·əm] n Chrom m

chromosome ['kroʊ·mə·soʊm] n Chromosom nt

chronic ['krɑn·ɪk] adj chronisch

chronological [ˌkrɑn·ə·'ladʒ·ɪ·kəl] adj chronologisch

chubby ['tʃʌb·i] adj pummelig; face pausbäckig

chuck [tʃʌk] vt (fam) ➊ (throw) schmeißen ➋ (throw out) wegschmeißen
♦**chuck out** vt (fam) wegschmeißen

chuckle ['tʃʌk·əl] I. n Gekicher nt kein pl II. vi in sich hineinlachen

chug [tʃʌg] vi <-gg-> tuckern

chum [tʃʌm] n (fam) Freund(in) m(f)

chummy ['tʃʌm·i] adj (fam) freundlich

chump [tʃʌmp] n (fam) Trottel m

chump change n (sl) Kleingeld

chunk [tʃʌŋk] n Brocken m; of bread [großes] Stück; (fig fam) großer Batzen

chunky ['tʃʌŋ·ki] adj person stämmig; peanut butter mit ganzen Stücken

church [tʃɜrtʃ] n <pl -es> Kirche f

'churchgoer n Kirchgänger(in) m(f)

churn [tʃɜrn] I. n Butterfass nt II. vt milk quirlen; ground, sea aufwühlen III. vi (fig) sich heftig drehen

chute[1] [ʃut] n Rutsche f

chute[2] [ʃut] n short for **parachute** Fallschirm m

CIA [ˌsi·aɪ·'eɪ] n abbrev of **Central Intelligence Agency** CIA m o f

cider ['saɪ·dər] n Apfelwein m

cigar [sɪ·'gar] n Zigarre f

cigarette [ˌsɪg·ə·'ret] n Zigarette f

cigarette butt n Kippe f

cinch <*pl* -es> [sɪntʃ] *n usu sing* ■ **a ~** ein Kinderspiel *nt*

cinder ['sɪn·dər] *n* Zinder *m*; ■ **~s** *pl* Asche *f kein pl*

Cinderella [ˌsɪn·də·'rel·ə] *n* Aschenputtel *nt*

cinema ['sɪn·ə·mə] *n* Kino *nt*

cinnamon ['sɪn·ə·mən] *n* Zimt *m*

cipher ['saɪ·fər] *n* ❶ [Geheim]code *m*; (*symbol*) Chiffre *f*

circle ['sɜr·kəl] **I.** *n* Kreis *m* **II.** *vt* ❶ (*draw around*) umkringeln ❷ (*walk around*) umkreisen **III.** *vi* kreisen

circuit ['sɜr·kɪt] *n* ❶ ELEC Stromkreis *m*; **short ~** Kurzschluss *m* ❷ (*circular route*) Rundgang *m*

circular ['sɜr·kjə·lər] **I.** *adj* [kreis]rund **II.** *n* Rundschreiben *nt*; (*advertisement*) Wurfsendung *f*

circular 'saw *n* Kreissäge *f*

circulate ['sɜr·kjə·leɪt] **I.** *vt news* in Umlauf bringen; *petition* herumgehen lassen **II.** *vi* zirkulieren; *rumors* kursieren

circulation [ˌsɜr·kjʊ·'leɪ·ʃən] *n* ❶ MED [Blut]kreislauf *m*, Durchblutung *f* ❷ (*copies sold*) Auflage *f*

circumcise ['sɜr·kəm·saɪz] *vt* beschneiden

circumcision [ˌsɜr·kəm·'sɪʒ·ən] *n* Beschneidung *f*

circumference [sər·'kʌm·fər·əns] *n* Umfang *m*

circumstance ['sɜr·kəm·stæns] *n* Umstand *m*; **in** [*or* **under**] **no/these ~s** unter keinen/diesen Umständen

circumstantial [ˌsɜr·kəm·'stæn·ʃəl] *adj* indirekt; **~ evidence** Indizienbeweis *m*

circus ['sɜr·kəs] *n* Zirkus *m*

cistern ['sɪs·tərn] *n* Wasserspeicher *m*

citation [saɪ·'teɪ·ʃən] *n* ❶ Zitat *nt* ❷ JUR Vorladung *f*

cite [saɪt] *vt* ❶ (*mention*) anführen ❷ (*quote*) zitieren ❸ LAW vorladen

citizen ['sɪt·ɪ·zən] *n* [Staats]bürger(in) *m(f)*

citizenship ['sɪt·ɪ·zən·ʃɪp] *n* Staatsbürgerschaft *f*

citrus <*pl* ->ˈ ['sɪt·rəs] *n* Zitrusgewächs *nt*; **~ fruit** Zitrusfrucht *f*

city ['sɪt̬·i] *n* [Groß]stadt *f*

city 'clerk *n* Magistratsbeamte(r), -beamtin *m, f*

city 'council *n* Stadtrat *m*, Stadtverwaltung *f*

city 'hall *n* Rathaus *nt*

City 'Hall *n* Stadtverwaltung *f*

'city slicker *n* (*pej fam*) Großstädter(in) *m(f)*

civic ['sɪv·ɪk] *adj* städtisch; (*of citizenship*) bürgerlich

civics ['sɪv·ɪks] *n* + *sing vb* SCH Gemeinschaftskunde *f*

civil ['sɪv·əl] *adj* ❶ (*nonmilitary*) zivil; (*of ordinary citizens*) bürgerlich ❷ (*courteous*) höflich

civil 'court *n* Zivilgericht *nt*

civil engi'neer *n* Bauingenieur(in) *m(f)*

civilian [sɪ·'vɪl·jən] **I.** *n* Zivilist(in) *m(f)* **II.** *adj* Zivil-

civility [sɪ·'vɪl·ɪ·ti] *n* Höflichkeit *f*

civilization [ˌsɪv·ə·lɪ·'zeɪ·ʃən] *n* Zivilisation *f*

civilize ['sɪv·ə·laɪz] *vt* zivilisieren

civil 'law *n* Zivilrecht *nt*

civil 'rights *npl* Bürgerrechte *pl*

civil 'servant *n* [Staats]beamte(r) *m*, [Staats]beamte [*o* -in] *f*

civil 'service *n* öffentlicher Dienst

civil 'union *n* eingetragene Lebenspartnerschaft *f*

civil 'war *n* Bürgerkrieg *m*

claim [kleɪm] **I.** *n* ❶ (*assertion*) Behauptung *f* ❷ (*demand for money*) Forderung *f* ❸ (*right*) Anspruch *m* ❹ **insurance ~** Versicherungsanspruch *m* **II.** *vt* ❶ (*declare ownership*) auf etw *akk* Anspruch erheben; *luggage* abholen; *throne* beanspruchen ❷ (*demand*) beantragen; *damages, refund* fordern ❸ (*assert*) behaupten; *responsibility* übernehmen; *victory* für sich in Anspruch nehmen ❹ (*take violently*) *lives* fordern

clairvoyant [ˌkler·'vɔɪ·ənt] **I.** *n* Hellseher(in) *m(f)* **II.** *adj* ■ **to be ~** hellsehen können

clam [klæm] *n* Venusmuschel *f*

clamber ['klæm·bər] *vi* klettern

clam 'chowder n [sämige] Muschelsuppe

clammy ['klæm·i] adj feuchtkalt

clamor ['klæm·ər] I. vi schreien (**for** nach +dat) II. n (outcry) Aufschrei m; (demand) lautstarke Forderung; (noise) Lärm m

clamp [klæmp] n Klammer f; (screwable) Klemme f

clan [klæn] n Clan m

clandestine [klæn·'des·tɪn] adj heimlich

clang [klæŋ] I. vi scheppern; bell [laut] läuten II. vt klappern mit +dat, schlagen III. n usu sing Scheppern nt; bell [lautes] Läuten

clank [klæŋk] I. vi klirren; chain rasseln II. vt klirren mit +dat III. n usu sing Klirren nt

clap [klæp] I. n ① (applause) Klatschen nt ② ~ **of thunder** Donner[schlag] m II. vt <-pp-> **to ~ one's hands [together]** in die Hände klatschen III. vi <-pp-> [Beifall] klatschen

clarification [ˌkler·ɪ·fɪ·'keɪ·ʃən] n Klarstellung f

clarify <-ie-> ['kler·ɪ·faɪ] vt klarstellen

clarinet [ˌkler·ə·'net] n Klarinette f

clarity ['kler·ɪ·ti] n Klarheit f

clash [klæʃ] I. vi ① (conflict) zusammenstoßen ② (compete against) aufeinandertreffen ③ (contradict) im Widerspruch stehen ④ colors sich beißen II. n <pl -es> ① (hostile encounter) Zusammenstoß m ② (contest) Aufeinandertreffen nt

clasp [klæsp] I. n ① (fastener) Verschluss m ② (firm grip) Griff m II. vt umklammern

class [klæs] I. n <pl -es> ① (lesson) [Unterrichts]stunde f; sport Kurs[us] m ② (students) [Schul]klasse f ③ (in society) Klasse f, Schicht f ④ (category) Klasse f II. vt einstufen

classic ['klæs·ɪk] I. adj klassisch II. n Klassiker m

classical ['klæs·ɪ·kəl] adj klassisch

classification [ˌklæs·ə·fɪ·'keɪ·ʃən] n Klassifikation f

classified ['klæs·ɪ·faɪd] adj geheim; ~ **advertisement** Kleinanzeige f

classify <-ie-> ['klæs·ɪ·faɪ] vt klassifizieren

'classmate n Klassenkamerad(in) m(f)

'classroom n Klassenzimmer nt

clatter ['klæt̬·ər] I. vt klappern mit +dat II. vi klappern III. n Klappern nt

clause [klɔz] n ① (in sentence) Satzglied nt ② (in contract) Klausel f

claustrophobia [ˌklɔ·strə·'fou·bi·ə] n Klaustrophobie f

claustrophobic [ˌklɔ·strə·'fou·bɪk] adj person klaustrophobisch

claw [klɔ] n Kralle f; of bird of prey, big cat Klaue[n] f(pl); of sea creature Schere[n] f(pl)

clay [kleɪ] n Lehm m; (for pottery) Ton m

clean [klin] I. adj ① sauber; sheets frisch ② (not offensive) sauber; joke anständig II. adv ① sauber ② (fam: completely) total, glatt III. vt (remove dirt) sauber machen, reinigen; car waschen; floor wischen; shoes, teeth putzen IV. vi ① (remove dirt) reinigen ② (become free of dirt) sich reinigen lassen

◆ **clean out** vt ① [gründlich] sauber machen; (with water) auswaschen ② (fam) person [wie eine Weihnachtsgans] ausnehmen

◆ **clean up** I. vt ① (make clean) sauber machen; room, mess aufräumen ② (fig) säubern II. vi ① (make clean) aufräumen; (freshen oneself) sich frisch machen ② (sl: make profit) absahnen

'clean-cut adj anständig

cleaner ['kli·nər] n ① (substance) Reiniger m ② (person) Reinigungskraft f

cleaning ['kli·nɪŋ] n **to do the ~** sauber machen

'cleaning lady, 'cleaning woman n Putzfrau f

cleanliness ['klen·lɪ·nɪs] n Sauberkeit f

cleanly ['klen·li] adv sauber

cleanse [klenz] vt reinigen

cleanser ['klen·zər] n Reiniger m; (for skin) Reinigungscreme f

clean-'shaven adj glatt rasiert

clear [klɪr] **I.** *adj* ❶ klar; (*definite*) eindeutig; *signs* deutlich; **to make one-self ~** sich deutlich ausdrücken ❷ **to be ~ about sth** sich *dat* über etw *akk* im Klaren sein ❸ *glass* durchsichtig; *liquid* klar ❹ (*unobstructed*) *path, view* frei ❺ *conscience* rein ❻ *picture* scharf **II.** *n* **to be in the ~** außer Verdacht sein **III.** *vt* ❶ (*remove clutter from*) [weg]räumen; **to ~ one's throat** sich räuspern ❷ (*empty*) ausräumen; *building* räumen; *table, desks* abräumen ❸ (*clear legally*) freisprechen; *name* reinwaschen ❹ (*give permission*) genehmigen **IV.** *vi* (*weather*) sich [auf]klären; *fog* sich auflösen

◆ **clear out I.** *vt* ausräumen; *attic* entrümpeln **II.** *vi* (*fam*) verschwinden

◆ **clear up I.** *vt* klären; *mystery* aufklären; (*fig: put in order*) *mess* aufräumen **II.** *vi* ❶ METEO aufhören zu regnen; (*brighten up*) sich aufklären ❷ (*become cured*) verschwinden, sich legen

clearance ['klɪr·əns] *n* ❶ (*action*) Beseitigung *f*; (*of slums*) Sanierung *f* ❷ (*space*) Spielraum *m*; (*of a door*) lichte Höhe ❸ (*official permission*) Genehmigung *f*

'clearance sale *n* Räumungsverkauf *m*

'clear-cut *adj* ❶ (*sharply outlined*) klar umrissen ❷ (*not ambiguous*) klar; *case* eindeutig

clearing ['klɪr·ɪŋ] *n* Lichtung *f*

clearly ['klɪr·li] *adv* ❶ (*distinctly*) klar, deutlich ❷ (*obviously*) offensichtlich; (*unambiguously*) eindeutig; (*undoubtedly*) zweifellos

cleavage ['kli·vɪdʒ] *n* Dekolletee *nt*

cleaver ['kli·vər] *n* Hackbeil *nt*

clef [klef] *n* [Noten]schlüssel *m*

cleft [kleft] **I.** *adj* gespalten; **~ palate** Gaumenspalte *f* **II.** *n* Spalt *m*

clematis <*pl* -> ['klem·ə·təs] *n* Klematis *f*

clemency ['klem·ən·si] *n* Milde *f*

clench [klentʃ] *vt fist* ballen; *teeth* fest zusammenbeißen

clergy ['klɜr·dʒi] *n + sing/pl vb* **the ~** die Geistlichkeit

'clergyman *n* Geistliche(r) *m*

'clergywoman *n* Geistliche *f*

clerk [klɜrk] *n* Büroangestellte(r) *f(m)*; (*in hotel*) Empfangschef *m*/Empfangsdame *f*

clever ['klev·ər] *adj* ❶ klug, clever *a. pej; trick* raffiniert ❷ (*dexterous*) geschickt

cleverness ['klev·ər·nɪs] *n* ❶ (*intelligence*) Klugheit ❷ (*dexterity*) Geschicklichkeit *f*

cliché [kli·'ʃeɪ] *n* Klischee *nt*

click [klɪk] **I.** *n* ❶ (*sound*) Klicken *nt;* (*of lock*) Einschnappen *nt* ❷ COMPUT Klick *m* **II.** *vi* ❶ (*make sound*) klicken; *lock* einschnappen ❷ (*fam: become friendly*) sich auf Anhieb verstehen ❸ (*fam: become understandable*) [plötzlich] klar werden ❹ COMPUT **to ~ on sth** etw anklicken **III.** *vt* ❶ *heels* zusammenklappen; **to ~ one's fingers** [mit den Fingern] schnippen ❷ COMPUT anklicken

client ['klaɪ·ənt] *n* Kunde *m*, Kundin *f*; LAW Klient(in) *m(f)*

clientele [ˌklaɪ·ən·'tel] *n* Kundschaft *f*

cliff [klɪf] *n* Klippe *f*

'cliffhanger *n* Thriller *m*

climate ['klaɪ·mɪt] *n* Klima *nt*

'climate change *n* Klimaveränderung *f*

climax ['klaɪ·mæks] *n* ❶ (*culmination*) Höhepunkt *m* ❷ (*orgasm*) Orgasmus *m*

climb [klaɪm] **I.** *n* Aufstieg *m* **II.** *vt* **to ~ [up] a hill** auf einen Hügel [hinauf]steigen; **to ~ [up] a tree** auf einen Baum [hoch]klettern **III.** *vi* ❶ (*ascend*) [auf]steigen; *plant* hochklettern ❷ (*increase rapidly*) [an]steigen

◆ **climb down** *vi* heruntersteigen; (*from summit*) absteigen; (*from tree*) herunterklettern

climber ['klaɪ·mər] *n* ❶ (*mountaineer*) Bergsteiger(in) *m(f)*; (*of rock faces*) Kletterer, Kletterin *m, f* ❷ (*plant*) Kletterpflanze *f*

clinch [klɪntʃ] **I.** *n* <*pl* -es> Umschlingung *f* **II.** *vt* entscheiden; *deal* perfekt machen

cling <clung, clung> [klɪŋ] *vi* ❶ (*hold*

tightly) [sich] klammern (**to** an +_akk_) ② (_stick_) kleben

clinic ['klɪn·ɪk] _n_ MED Klinik _f_, Ärztepraxis _f_

clinical ['klɪn·ɪ·kəl] _adj_ ① MED klinisch ② (_emotionless_) distanziert

clink [klɪŋk] I. _vt, vi_ klirren [mit] +_dat; esp metal_ klimpern [mit] +_dat_ II. _n_ Klirren _nt; (of coins)_ Klimpern _nt_

clip[1] [klɪp] I. _n_ ① (_trim_) Haarschnitt _m_ ② FILM Ausschnitt _m_ II. _vt_ <-pp-> ① _dog_ trimmen; _hedge_ stutzen; _sheep_ scheren; _nails_ schneiden ② (_cut out_) _coupons_ abtrennen, abschneiden

clip[2] [klɪp] I. _n_ ① Klipp _m; (for hair)_ [Haar]spange _f_ ② (_for gun_) Ladestreifen _m_ II. _vt_ <-pp-> anheften, anklammern

clipping ['klɪp·ɪŋ] _n_ (_from newspaper_) Zeitungsausschnitt _m_

clique [klik] _n_ (_pej_) Clique _f_

clitoris ['klɪt·ər·əs] _n_ Klitoris _f_, Kitzler _m_

cloak [kloʊk] I. _n_ ① Umhang _m_ ② (_fig_) Deckmantel _m_ II. _vt_ verhüllen

'cloakroom _n_ Garderobe _f_

clock [klɑk] _n_ Uhr _f_
◆**clock in, clock out** _vi_ stechen

clock 'radio _n_ Radiowecker _m_

clockwise ['klɑk·waɪz] _adj, adv_ im Uhrzeigersinn

'clockwork _n_ Uhrwerk _nt_

clod [klɑd] _n_ Klumpen _m_

clog [klɑg] I. _n_ Holzschuh _m; (modern)_ Clog[s] _m[pl]_ II. _vt, vi_ <-gg-> ■**to ~ [up]** verstopfen

cloister ['klɔɪ·stər] _n usu pl_ Kreuzgang _m_

clone [kloʊn] I. _n_ Klon _m_ II. _vt_ klonen

close[1] [kloʊs] I. _adj_ ① (_near_) nah[e]; ■**to be ~ to sth** in der Nähe einer S. gen liegen ② (_intimate_) eng; _relatives_ nah; ■**to be ~ to sb** jdm [sehr] nahestehen ③ (_almost equal_) knapp ④ (_exact_) genau; **to pay ~ attention to sb** jdm gut zuhören II. _adv_ (_near_) nahe; **she came ~ to getting the job** fast hätte sie die Stelle bekommen; **to hold sb ~** jdn fest an sich drücken; ■**~ together** dicht beieinander

close[2] [kloʊz] I. _vt_ ① schließen; _factory a._ stilllegen; _book, mouth_ zumachen; _curtains_ zuziehen; _road_ sperren ② (_end_) abschließen; _bank account_ auflösen; _meeting_ beenden II. _vi_ ① (_shut_) door zugehen; _shop_ schließen; _eyes_ zufallen ② (_shut down_) schließen; _shop_ zumachen ③ (_end_) zu Ende gehen; _meeting_ schließen III. _n_ Ende _nt,_ Schluss _m_
◆**close down** I. _vi business_ schließen, zumachen; _factory_ stillgelegt werden II. _vt_ schließen; _factory_ stilllegen
◆**close in** _vi_ ■**to ~ on sb/sth** sich jdm/etw nähern; (_surround_) jdn/etw umzingeln
◆**close up** I. _vi_ ① (_lock up_) abschließen ② (_shut_) _flower, wound_ sich schließen ③ (_get nearer_) _people_ zusammenrücken; _troops_ aufschließen II. _vt_ [ab]schließen

closed [kloʊzd] _adj_ geschlossen, zu; **behind ~ doors** (_fig_) hinter verschlossenen Türen

'close-knit _adj family_ eng verbunden

closely ['kloʊs·li] _adv_ ① (_near_) dicht ② (_intimately_) eng ③ (_exactly_) genau ④ (_carefully_) sorgfältig

closeness ['kloʊs·nɪs] _n_ Nähe _f; (intimacy)_ Vertrautheit _f_

closet ['klɑz·ɪt] _n_ Abstellraum _m_ ▸PHRASES: **to come out of the ~** seine Homosexualität bekennen

'close-up _n_ Nahaufnahme _f_

closing ['kloʊ·zɪŋ] _adj_ abschließend

'closing date _n_ Einsendeschluss _m_

'closing time _n_ (_for shop_) Ladenschluss _m; (for staff)_ Feierabend _m; (for bars)_ Sperrstunde _f_

closure ['kloʊ·ʒər] _n_ (_of institution_) Schließung _f; (of street)_ Sperrung _f; (of factory)_ Stilllegung _f_

clot [klɑt] I. _n_ MED [Blut]gerinnsel _nt_ II. _vi_ <-tt-> gerinnen

cloth [klɔθ] _n_ ① (_material_) Tuch _nt,_ Stoff _m_ ② (_for cleaning_) Lappen _m_

clothe [kloʊð] _vt_ <clothed _or_ clad, clothed _or_ clad> [be]kleiden _a. fig_

clothes [kloʊz] _npl_ Kleider _pl; (collectively)_ Kleidung _f kein pl_

'clothes hanger n Kleiderbügel m

'clothesline n Wäscheleine f

'clothespin n Wäscheklammer f

clothing ['kloʊ·ðɪŋ] n Kleidung f

cloud [klaʊd] I. n ① Wolke f; of insects Schwarm m; ~ ash ~ Aschewolke f ▶PHRASES: **every ~ has a silver lining** (prov) jedes Unglück hat auch sein Gutes; **to be under a ~** keinen guten Ruf haben II. vt issue verschleiern
◆**cloud over** vi sich bewölken

'cloudburst n Wolkenbruch m

cloudless ['klaʊd·lɪs] adj wolkenlos

cloudy ['klaʊ·di] adj ① (overcast) bewölkt, bedeckt ② liquid trüb

clout [klaʊt] n (fam) ① (fam: influence) Schlagkraft f ② (hit) Schlag m

clove [kloʊv] n ① Gewürznelke f ② of garlic Knoblauchzehe f

clover ['kloʊ·vər] n Klee m

clown [klaʊn] I. n ① Clown m ② (funny person) Kasper m; (pej) Trottel m II. vi ■**to ~ around** herumalbern

club [klʌb] n ① (group) Klub m, Verein m ② (nightclub) Diskothek f, Klub m ③ (golf) Schläger m ④ (weapon) Knüppel m ⑤ CARDS Kreuz nt

clubbing ['klʌb·ɪŋ] n **to go ~** clubben gehen

'club foot n MED Klumpfuß m

'clubhouse n Klubhaus nt

club 'soda n Sodawasser nt

cluck [klʌk] vi gackern

clue [klu] n ① Hinweis m; (hint) Tipp m; (in police work) Spur f ② (idea) **I don't have a ~!** [ich hab'] keine Ahnung!

clueless ['klu·lɪs] adj (fam) ahnungslos

clump [klʌmp] n ① (group) Gruppe f ② (lump) Klumpen m

clumsiness ['klʌm·zi·nɪs] n Ungeschicktheit f

clumsy ['klʌm·zi] adj ① (bungling) ungeschickt, unbeholfen ② (ungainly) klobig

clung [klʌŋ] pt, pp of **cling**

cluster ['klʌs·tər] I. n Bündel nt; of people Traube f II. vi ■**to ~ around sth** sich um etw akk scharen

clutch [klʌtʃ] I. vi sich klammern (**at** an +akk) II. vt umklammern III. n ① usu sing AUTO Kupplung f ② **to fall into the ~es of sb** jdm in die Klauen fallen

clutter ['klʌt̬·ər] I. n ① (mess) Durcheinander nt ② (unorganized stuff) Kram m II. vt durcheinanderbringen

cm <pl -> n abbrev of **centimeter** cm

c'mon [kə'mɑn] (fam) see **come on**

CO [ˌsiˈoʊ] n ① GEOG abbrev of **Colorado** ② MIL abbrev of **Commanding Officer** Befehlshaber(in) m(f)

Co. [koʊ] n abbrev of **company**

c/o [ˌsiˈoʊ] abbrev of **care of** c/o, bei

coach [koʊtʃ] I. n ① SPORT Trainer(in) m(f); (teacher) Nachhilfelehrer(in) m(f) ② (horse-drawn) Kutsche f; RAIL [Eisenbahn]wagen m II. vt ① SPORT trainieren ② (help to learn) Nachhilfe geben

coaching ['koʊtʃ·ɪŋ] n ① SPORT Training nt ② (teaching) Nachhilfe f

coal [koʊl] n Kohle f

coalition [ˌkoʊ·əˈlɪʃ·ən] n Koalition f

'coal mine n Kohlenbergwerk nt

'coal mining n Kohle[n]bergbau m

coarse [kɔrs] adj ① (rough) grob ② (vulgar) derb

coast [koʊst] I. n Küste f II. vi die Küste entlangfahren; **to ~ [along]** mühelos vorankommen

coastal ['koʊ·stəl] adj Küsten-

coaster ['koʊ·stər] n ① (for glass) Untersetzer m ② (ship) Küstenmotorschiff nt ③ (roller coaster) Achterbahn

'coast guard, 'Coast Guard n Küstenwache f

'coastline n Küste[nlinie] f

coat [koʊt] I. n ① (garment) Mantel m ② (of animal) Fell nt ③ (layer) Schicht f II. vt überziehen

'coat hanger n Kleiderbügel m

coating ['koʊ·t̬ɪŋ] n ① Schicht f, Überzug m; of paint Anstrich m

coax [koʊks] vt ■**to ~ sb into doing sth** jdn dazu bringen, etw zu tun
◆**cobble together** vt zusammenschustern

cobbled ['kab·əld] *adj* street mit Kopfsteinpflaster

cobbler ['kab·lər] *n* [Flick]schuster *m*

'cobblestone *n* Kopfstein *m*

cobra ['koʊ·brə] *n* Kobra *f*

cobweb ['kab·web] *n* Spinnennetz *nt*

cocaine [koʊ·'keɪn] *n* Kokain *nt*

cock [kak] I. *n* ❶ (*chicken*) Hahn *m* ❷ (*vulg, sl: penis*) Schwanz *m* II. *vt* head auf die Seite legen; ears spitzen

cock-a-doodle-doo [ˌkak·ə·ˌduˈdəl·'du] *n* Kikeriki *nt*

cockatoo <*pl* -s> ['kak·ə·'tu] *n* Kakadu *m*

cockeyed ['kak·aɪd] *adj* (*fam*) ❶ (*not straight*) schief ❷ (*ridiculous*) verrückt

cockle ['kak·əl] *n* Herzmuschel *f*

cockpit ['kak·pɪt] *n* Cockpit *nt*

cockroach ['kak·roʊtʃ] *n* Küchenschabe *f*

cocktail ['kak·teɪl] *n* Cocktail *m*

cocky ['kak·i] *adj* (*fam*) großspurig

cocoa ['koʊ·koʊ] *n* Kakao *m*

coconut ['koʊ·kə·nʌt] *n* Kokosnuss *f*

cocoon [kə·'kun] I. *n* Kokon *m* II. *vt* (*fig*) abschirmen

cod <*pl* -> [kad] *n* Kabeljau *m*

coddle ['kad·əl] *vt* ❶ verhätscheln ❷ (*cook gently*) langsam köcheln lassen; eggs pochieren

code [koʊd] I. *n* ❶ (*cipher*) Kode *m* ❷ LAW Kodex *m* II. *vt* chiffrieren

codeine ['koʊ·din] *n* Kodein *nt*

'code name *n* Deckname *m*

code of 'conduct *n* Verhaltensregeln *pl*

'code word *n* Kennwort *nt*

cod-liver 'oil *n* Lebertran *m*

co-ed [ˌkoʊ·'ed] *adj* SCH gemischt

coefficient [ˌkoʊ·ɪ·'fɪʃ·ənt] *n* Koeffizient *m*

coerce [koʊ·'ɜrs] *vt* (*form*) ■ **to ~ sb into doing sth** jdn dazu zwingen, etw zu tun

coercion [koʊ·'ɜr·ʒən] *n* (*form*) Zwang *m*

coexist [ˌkoʊ·ɪg·'zɪst] *vi* nebeneinander bestehen

coexistence [ˌkoʊ·ɪg·'zɪs·təns] *n* Koexistenz *f*

coffee ['kɔ·fi] *n* Kaffee *m*

'coffee bean *n* Kaffeebohne *f*

'coffee break *n* Kaffeepause *f*

'coffee cup *n* Kaffeetasse *f*

'coffee grinder *n* Kaffeemühle *f*

'coffeemaker *n* Kaffeemaschine *f*

'coffeepot *n* Kaffeekanne *f*

'coffee shop *n* Café *nt*

'coffee table *n* Couchtisch *m*

coffin ['kɔ·fɪn] *n* Sarg *m*

cog [kag] *n* ❶ (*part of wheel*) Zahn *m* ❷ (*wheel*) Zahnrad *nt*

cognac ['koʊn·jæk] *n* Cognac *m*

cohabit [koʊ·'hæb·ɪt] *vi* (*form*) zusammenleben; LAW in eheähnlicher Gemeinschaft leben

cohabitation [koʊ·ˌhæb·ɪ·'teɪ·ʃən] *n* Zusammenleben *nt;* LAW eheähnliche Gemeinschaft

coherence [koʊ·'hɪr·əns] *n* Zusammenhang *m*

coherent [koʊ·'hɪr·ənt] *adj* zusammenhängend

coherently [koʊ·'hɪr·ənt·li] *adv* zusammenhängend; speak verständlich

cohesion [koʊ·'hi·ʒən] *n* Zusammenhalt *m*

coil [kɔɪl] I. *n* ❶ (*spiral*) Rolle *f* ❷ ELEC Spule *f* II. *vi* sich winden III. *vt* aufwickeln

coiled [kɔɪld] *adj* gewunden; ~ **spring** Sprungfeder *f*

coin [kɔɪn] *n* Münze *f*

coincide [ˌkoʊ·ɪn·'saɪd] *vi* ❶ (*happen at same time*) zusammenfallen ❷ (*correspond*) übereinstimmen

coincidence [koʊ·'ɪn·sɪ·dəns] *n* ❶ (*chance event*) Zufall *m* ❷ (*simultaneity*) Zusammenfallen *nt*

coincidental [koʊ·ˌɪn·sɪ·'den·təl] *adj* zufällig

coincidentally [koʊ·ˌɪn·sɪ·'dən·təl·i] *adv* zufällig[erweise]

coke [koʊk] *n* (*sl*) Koks *m*

Coke® [koʊk] *n* short for **Coca Cola®** Cola *f*

col. [kal] *n* abbrev of **column** Sp.

Col. *n* abbrev of **colonel**

colander ['kʌl·ən·dər] *n* Sieb *nt*

cold [koʊld] **I.** *adj* kalt; **as ~ as ice** eiskalt; **to feel ~** frieren; **I'm ~** mir ist kalt **II.** *n* ➊ (*low temperature*) Kälte *f* ➋ MED Erkältung *f*, Schnupfen *m*; **to have a ~** erkältet sein

cold-blooded [ˌkoʊld·'blʌd·ɪd] *adj* kaltblütig

'**cold cuts** *npl* Aufschnitt *m kein pl*

cold-'hearted *adj* kaltherzig

coldness ['koʊld·nɪs] *n* Kälte *f*

'**cold sore** *n* Bläschenausschlag *m*

cold 'storage *n* **to put in ~** kühl lagern; (*fig*) auf Eis legen

cold 'turkey *n* (*sl*) kalter Entzug

'**cold war** *n* kalter Krieg

coleslaw ['koʊl·slɔ] *n* Krautsalat *m*

colic ['kal·ɪk] *n* Kolik *f*

collaborate [kə·'læb·ə·reɪt] *vi* ➊ zusammenarbeiten ➋ (*with enemy*) kollaborieren

collaboration [kə·ˌlæb·ə·'reɪ·ʃən] *n* ➊ Zusammenarbeit *f* ➋ (*with enemy*) Kollaboration *f*

collaborative [kə·'læb·ə·rə·tɪv] *adj* effort gemeinsam

collaborator [kə·'læb·ə·reɪ·tər] *n* ➊ (*colleague*) Mitarbeiter(in) *m(f)* ➋ (*pej: traitor*) Kollaborateur(in) *m(f)*

collapse [kə·'læps] **I.** *vi* ➊ *things, buildings* zusammenbrechen, einstürzen; *people* zusammenbrechen ➋ (*fail*) zusammenbrechen; *enterprise* zugrunde gehen; *talks* scheitern **II.** *n* ➊ (*fall*) Einsturz *m*, Zusammenbruch *m* ➋ (*failure*) Zusammenbruch *m* ➌ MED Kollaps *m*

collar ['kal·ər] **I.** *n* Kragen *m*; (*for animals*) Halsband *nt* **II.** *vt* (*fam*) schnappen

'**collarbone** *n* Schlüsselbein *nt*

collateral 'damage *n* Kollateralschaden *m*

colleague ['kal·ig] *n* [Arbeits]kollege, -in *m, f*

collect [kə·'lekt] **I.** *adj* TELEC ~ **call** R-Gespräch *nt* **II.** *adv* TELEC **to call** |**sb**| ~ jdn per R-Gespräch anrufen **III.** *vi* ➊ (*gather*) sich versammeln; (*accumulate*) sich ansammeln **IV.** *vt* ➊ (*gather*) einsammeln; *money, stamps* sammeln ➋ (*pick up*) abholen

collected [kə·'lek·tɪd] *adj* beherrscht

collection [kə·'lek·ʃən] *n* ➊ (*of money, objects*) Sammlung *f*; (*in church*) Kollekte *f*; (*of people*) Ansammlung *f* ➋ FASHION Kollektion *f* ➌ (*act of collecting*) Abholung *f*; (*from mailbox*) [Briefkasten]leerung *f*

collective [kə·'lek·tɪv] *adj* gemeinsam; *leadership* kollektiv

collective 'bargaining *n* Tarifverhandlungen *pl*

collector [kə·'lek·tər] *n* Sammler(in) *m(f)*

college ['kal·ɪdʒ] *n* ➊ (*institution*) Universität *f*, College *nt*, Hochschule *f*; **to go to ~** studieren ➋ (*division of an institution*) Abteilung *f*, Fakultät *f*

collide [kə·'laɪd] *vi* ■ **to ~** |**with sb/sth**| [mit jdm/etw] zusammenstoßen

collie ['kal·i] *n* Collie *m*

collision [kə·'lɪʒ·ən] *n* Zusammenstoß *m*

colloquial [kə·'loʊ·kwi·əl] *adj* umgangssprachlich; ~ **language** Umgangssprache *f*

Colo. *abbrev of* **Colorado**

colon ['koʊ·lən] *n* ➊ ANAT Dickdarm *m* ➋ LING Doppelpunkt *m*

colonel ['kɜr·nəl] *n* Oberst *m*

colonial [kə·'loʊ·ni·əl] **I.** *adj* Kolonial- **II.** *n* Kolonist(in) *m(f)*

colonize ['kal·ə·naɪz] *vt* kolonisieren

colony ['kal·ə·ni] *n* Kolonie *f*

color ['kal·ər] **I.** *n* ➊ Farbe *f*; ~ **photos** Farbfotos *pl* ➋ (*of complexion*) Gesichtsfarbe *f*; *of skin* Hautfarbe *f*; *of hair* Haarfarbe *f* **II.** *vt* ➊ (*change color of*) färben ➋ (*distort*) beeinflussen **III.** *vi* *face* rot werden; *leaves* sich *akk* verfärben

Colorado [ˌkal·ərad·'oʊ] *n* Colorado *nt*

coloration [ˌkʌl·ə·'reɪ·ʃən] *n* Färbung *f*

'**colorblind** *adj* farbenblind

colored ['kʌl·ərd] *adj* farbig; ~ **pencil** Buntstift *m*

'**colorfast** *adj* farbecht

colorful ['kʌl·ər·fəl] *adj* ➊ *paintings* farbenfroh; *clothing* bunt ➋ (*vivid*) lebendig; *description* anschaulich ❸ *past* bewegt

coloring [ˈkʌl·ər·ɪŋ] *n* ❶ (*complexion*) Gesichtsfarbe *f* ❷ (*chemical*) Farbstoff *m*

colorless [ˈkʌl·lɪs] *adj* farblos

colossal [kəˈlɑs·əl] *adj* ungeheuer, riesig

colossus <*pl* -es> [kəˈlɑs·əs] *n* Gigant(in) *m(f)*

colt [koʊlt] *n* [Hengst]fohlen *nt*

Columbus Day *n wird in den USA am zweiten Montag im Oktober zu Ehren der Entdeckung der Neuen Welt durch Christoph Kolumbus gefeiert*

column [ˈkɑl·əm] *n* ❶ (*pillar*) Säule *f* ❷ JOURN Kolumne *f*, Spalte *f* ❸ (*vertical row*) Kolonne *f*, Reihe *f*

coma [ˈkoʊ·mə] *n* Koma *nt*

comb [koʊm] I. *n* Kamm *m* II. *vt* ❶ kämmen ❷ (*search*) durchkämmen

combat [ˈkɑm·bæt] I. *n* Kampf *m* II. *vt* <-tt- *or* -t-> bekämpfen

combatant [kəmˈbæt·ənt] *n* Kämpfer(in) *m(f)*

combination [ˌkɑm·bə·ˈneɪ·ʃən] *n* Kombination *f*

combine[1] [kəmˈbaɪn] I. *vt* verbinden II. *vi* ❶ (*mix together*) verbinden ❷ (*work together*) sich verbünden

combine[2] [ˈkɑm·baɪn] *n* Mähdrescher *m*

combined [kəmˈbaɪnd] *adj* vereint

come [kʌm] *vi* <came, come> ❶ (*move towards*) kommen ❷ (*arrive*) ankommen; **Christmas is coming** bald ist Weihnachten; ■ **to ~ for sb/sth** jdn/ etw abholen ❸ (*accompany someone*) mitkommen ❹ (*originate from*) stammen; **where is that awful smell coming from?** wo kommt dieser schreckliche Gestank her? ❺ (*have priority*) **to ~ before sth** wichtiger als etw sein; **to ~ first** [bei jdm] an erster Stelle stehen ❻ (*happen*) geschehen; **~ what may** komme, was wolle; **you could see it coming** das war ja zu erwarten; **how ~?** wieso? ❼ (*be, become*) **to ~ under pressure** unter Druck geraten; **all my dreams came true** all meine

Träume haben sich erfüllt; **nothing came of it** daraus ist nichts geworden ▶ PHRASES: **~ again?** [wie] bitte?

◆**come about** *vi* passieren

◆**come across** *vi person* [zufällig] begegnen +*dat*; ■ **to ~ across sth** [zufällig] auf etw *akk* stoßen

◆**come along** *vi* ❶ mitgehen, mitkommen; **I'll ~ along later** ich komme später nach ❷ *job, opportunity* sich bieten ❸ **how's your German coming along?** wie geht's mit deinem Deutsch voran?

◆**come apart** *vi* auseinanderfallen

◆**come around** *vi* ❶ [wieder] zu sich kommen ❷ seine Meinung ändern

◆**come back** *vi* zurückkommen; *name* wieder einfallen

◆**come by** *vi* ❶ (*visit*) vorbeikommen ❷ (*obtain*) kriegen

◆**come down** *vi* ❶ fallen; *pants* rutschen; (*collapse*) einstürzen; (*move down*) herunterkommen; (*become less*) sinken ❷ **to ~ down with the flu** die Grippe bekommen

◆**come forward** *vi* sich melden

◆**come in** *vi* ❶ hereinkommen; **~ in!** herein! ❷ ankommen; *results* eintreffen; *train* einfahren; *tide* kommen; *money* reinkommen; *news* hereinkommen ❸ + *adj* (*be*) **to ~ in handy** gelegen kommen; **to ~ in useful** sich als nützlich erweisen ❹ (*play a part*) **where do I ~ in?** welche Rolle spiele ich dabei?

◆**come off** *vi* (*detach itself*) abgehen

◆**come on** *vi* **~ on!** (*impatient*) komm jetzt [endlich]!; (*encouraging*) komm schon!; (*expressing disbelief*) ach, komm!; (*annoyed*) jetzt hör aber auf!

◆**come out** *vi* ❶ herauskommen; (*go out socially*) ausgehen ❷ *book, CD* herauskommen; *movie* anlaufen ❸ (*become known*) bekannt werden ❹ (*end up*) herauskommen, enden ❺ *flowers, buds* herauskommen; *stars* zu sehen sein ❻ (*reveal homosexuality*) sich outen

◆**come over** *vi* vorbeikommen

♦come through vi ❶ (*be noticeable*) durchkommen ❷ (*survive*) überleben

♦come to vi ❶ (*regain consciousness*) [wieder] zu sich kommen ❷ **the total ~s to 25 dollars** das macht 25 Dollar ❸ (*reach*) **to ~ to the point** zum Punkt kommen ❹ **when it ~s to travelling ...** wenn's ums Reisen geht, ...

♦come under vi ❶ (*be listed under*) stehen unter ❷ **to ~ under fire** unter Beschuss geraten

♦come up vi ❶ hochkommen; *sun, moon* aufgehen ❷ (*be mentioned*) aufkommen; *name* erwähnt werden ❸ (*happen unexpectedly*) [unerwartet] passieren ❹ *plants* herauskommen

comeback ['kʌm·bæk] n Comeback nt

comedian [kə·'mi·di·ən] n Komiker(in) m(f)

comedienne [kə·ˌmi·di·'ən] n Komikerin f

comedown ['kʌm·daʊn] n (*fam*) Abstieg m

comedy ['kam·ə·di] n Komödie f

come-on ['kʌm·ɔn] n (*fam*) Anmache f

comet ['kam·ɪt] n Komet m

comfort ['kʌm·fərt] I. n ❶ Bequemlichkeit f ❷ (*consolation*) Trost m ❸ (*pleasurable things*) ■ **~s** pl Komfort m kein pl II. vt trösten

comfortable ['kʌm·fər·tə·bəl] adj bequem; *house, room* komfortabel; *temperature* angenehm; **to feel ~** sich wohl fühlen; **to make oneself ~** es sich dat bequem machen

comforter ['kʌm·fər·tər] n Oberbett nt, Federbett nt

comforting ['kʌm·fər·ţɪŋ] adj *thoughts* beruhigend; *words* tröstend

comfy ['kʌm·fi] adj (*fam*) bequem

comic ['kam·ɪk] I. n Komiker(in) m(f) II. adj komisch

comical ['kam·ɪ·kəl] adj komisch

comics ['kam·ɪks] npl Comic-Heft nt sing

comma ['kam·ə] n Komma nt

command [kə·'mænd] I. vt ❶ (*order*) befehlen ❷ MIL *company* leiten; *ship* befehligen; ■ **to ~ sth** den Oberbefehl

über etw akk haben II. n ❶ (*order*) Befehl m ❷ (*authority*) Kommando nt ❸ (*knowledge*) Beherrschung f

commandant ['kam·ən·dænt] n Kommandant(in) m(f)

commandeer [ˌkam·ən·'dɪr] vt beschlagnahmen

commander [kə·'mæn·dər] n ❶ MIL Kommandant(in) m(f) ❷ NAUT Fregattenkapitän(in) m(f)

commanding [kə·'mæn·dɪŋ] adj ❶ (*authoritative*) gebieterisch ❷ *position, lead* beherrschend

commandment [kə·'mænd·mənt] n REL **the Ten C~s** die Zehn Gebote pl

commemorate [kə·'mem·ə·reɪt] vt gedenken +gen

commemoration [kə·ˌmem·ə·'reɪ·ʃən] n Gedenken nt

commemorative [kə·'mem·ər·ə·tɪv] adj Gedenk-

commence [kə·'mens] vi (*form*) beginnen, anfangen

commencement [kə·'mens·mənt] n (*form*) ❶ Beginn m, Anfang m ❷ SCH, UNIV Abschlussfeier (*mit Verleihung der Diplome*)

commend [kə·'mend] vt ❶ (*praise*) loben ❷ (*recommend*) empfehlen

commendable [kə·'men·də·bəl] adj lobenswert

comment ['kam·ent] I. n Kommentar m II. vi einen Kommentar abgeben, sich äußern über +akk

commentary ['kam·ən·ter·i] n Kommentar m

commentator ['kam·ən·teɪ·ţər] n Kommentator(in) m(f), Reporter(in) m(f)

commerce ['kam·ərs] n Handel m

commercial [kə·'mɜr·ʃəl] I. adj ❶ kaufmännisch, Handels- ❷ (*profit-orientated*) kommerziell II. n Werbespot m

commiserate [kə·'mɪz·ə·reɪt] vi ■ **to ~ with sb** mit jdm mitfühlen

commiserations [kə·ˌmɪz·ə·'reɪ·ʃənz] npl Beileid nt kein pl

commission [kə·'mɪʃ·ən] I. vt *portrait, work* in Auftrag geben II. n ❶ (*order*)

Auftrag m ②(*system of payment*) Provision f ③(*investigative body*) Kommission f ④**in/out of** ~ *machine* in/außer Betrieb

commissioner [kə·ˈmɪʃ·ə·nər] n Beauftragte(r) f(m)

commit <-tt-> [kə·ˈmɪt] I. vt ①*crime* begehen ②*money* bereitstellen; ■**to ~ oneself to doing sth** sich verpflichten, etw zu tun II. vi ■**to ~ to sth** sich auf etw akk festlegen

commitment [kə·ˈmɪt·mənt] n ①(*obligation*) Verpflichtung f ②(*dedication*) Engagement nt

committed [kə·ˈmɪt̬·ɪd] adj ①verpflichtet ②(*dedicated*) engagiert

committee [kə·ˈmɪt̬·i] n + sing/pl vb Ausschuss m, Komitee nt

commodity [kə·ˈmɑd·ɪ·ti] n (*product*) Ware f; (*raw material*) Rohstoff m

common [ˈkɑm·ən] adj <-er, -est or more ~, most ~> ①üblich, gewöhnlich; *disease* weit verbreitet; *name* gängig ②**it is** ~ **knowledge/practice …** es ist allgemein bekannt/üblich … ③gemeinsam; **in** ~ gemeinsam ④<-er, -est> (*pej*) *behavior* vulgär

commonly [ˈkɑm·ən·li] adv häufig, (*usually*) gemeinhin

'commonplace I. adj ①(*normal*) alltäglich ②(*pej: trite*) banal II. n Gemeinplatz m

common 'sense n gesunder Menschenverstand

commotion [kə·ˈmoʊ·ʃən] n (*fuss*) Theater nt; (*noisy confusion*) Spektakel m

communal [kə·ˈmju·nəl] adj gemeinsam

communicate [kə·ˈmju·nɪ·keɪt] I. vt mitteilen; *knowledge* vermitteln II. vi ①(*give information*) kommunizieren ②(*be in touch*) in Verbindung stehen; (*socially*) sich verstehen

communication [kə·ˌmju·nɪ·ˈkeɪ·ʃən] n ①Kommunikation f ②*of ideas* Vermittlung f; *of information* Übermittlung f; *of emotions* Ausdruck m

communicative [kə·ˈmju·nə·keɪ·tɪv] adj gesprächig

Communion [kə·ˈmjun·jən] n ■[**Holy**] ~ (*Protestant*) das [heilige] Abendmahl; (*Catholic*) die [heilige] Kommunion

communism [ˈkɑm·jə·nɪz·əm] n Kommunismus m

communist [ˈkɑm·jə·nɪst] I. n Kommunist(in) m(f) II. adj kommunistisch

community [kə·ˈmju·nɪ·ti] n Gemeinde f; **the business** ~ die Geschäftswelt; ■**the** ~ die Allgemeinheit

commute [kə·ˈmjut] vi pendeln

commuter [kə·ˈmju·tər] n Pendler(in) m(f)

com'muter train n Pendlerzug m

compact [ˈkɑm·pækt] I. adj kompakt; *snow* fest; *style* knapp II. n ①(*cosmetics*) Puderdose f ②AUTO Kompaktwagen m

compact 'disc, compact 'disk n Compactdisc f

companion [kəm·ˈpæn·jən] n Begleiter(in) m(f); (*associate*) Gefährte, -in m, f

companionship [kəm·ˈpæn·jən·ʃɪp] n (*company*) Gesellschaft f; (*friendship*) Kameradschaft f

company [ˈkʌm·pə·ni] n ①Firma f, Unternehmen nt ②(*companionship*) Gesellschaft f ③(*visitors*) Besuch m kein pl ④THEAT Schauspieltruppe f; MIL Kompanie f

comparable [ˈkɑm·pər·ə·bəl] adj vergleichbar (**to/with** mit +dat)

comparative [kəm·ˈper·ə·tɪv] I. n Komparativ m II. adj ①(*involving comparison*) vergleichend ②(*relative*) relativ

comparatively [kəm·ˈper·ə·tɪv·li] adv ①(*relatively*) verhältnismäßig ②(*by comparison*) im Vergleich

compare [kəm·ˈper] I. vt vergleichen (**to/with** mit +dat) II. vi vergleichbar sein

comparison [kəm·ˈper·ɪ·sən] n Vergleich m

compartment [kəm·ˈpɑrt·mənt] n RAIL [Zug]abteil nt, Coupé nt ÖSTERR

compass <pl -es> [ˈkʌm·pəs] n ①(*showing north*) Kompass m ②(*for drawing circles*) Zirkel m

compassion [kəmˈpæʃ·ən] *n* Mitgefühl *nt*

compassionate [kəmˈpæʃ·ə·nɪt] *adj* mitfühlend

compatibility [kəmˌpæt̬·ə·ˈbɪl·ɪ·ti] *n* Vereinbarkeit *f*

compatible [kəmˈpæt̬·ə·bəl] *adj* ❶ ■to be ~ zusammenpassen ❷ COMPUT, MED kompatibel ❸ (*consistent*) vereinbar

compel <-ll-> [kəmˈpel] *vt* ■to ~ sb to do sth jdn [dazu] zwingen, etw zu tun

compelling [kəmˈpel·ɪŋ] *adj reason* zwingend; *performance* fesselnd

compensate [ˈkam·pən·seɪt] I. *vt* (*financiell*) entschädigen II. *vi* kompensieren; ■to ~ for sth etw ausgleichen

compensation [ˌkam·pen·ˈseɪ·ʃən] *n* Entschädigung[sleistung] *f*, Schadenersatz *m*

compete [kəmˈpit] *vi* konkurrieren; ■to ~ [with sb] [gegen jdn] kämpfen (for um +*akk*)

competence [ˈkam·pɪ·təns], **competency** [ˈkam·pɪ·tən·si] *n* ❶ Fähigkeiten *pl*, Kompetenz *f* ❷ LAW Zuständigkeit *f*

competent [ˈkam·pɪ·tənt] *adj* ❶ fähig; (*qualified*) kompetent ❷ LAW zuständig

competition [ˌkam·pə·ˈtɪʃ·ən] *n* ❶ (*contest*) Wettbewerb *m* ❷ COMM Konkurrenz *f*, Wettbewerb *m*

competitive [kəmˈpet̬·ɪ·tɪv] *adj* ❶ kampfbereit; ~ **sports** Leistungssport *m* ❷ COMM konkurrenzfähig, wettbewerbsfähig

competitiveness [kəmˈpet̬·ə·tɪv·nɪs] *n* ❶ (*ambition*) Konkurrenzdenken *nt* ❷ COMM Wettbewerbsfähigkeit *f*

competitor [kəmˈpet̬·ɪ·tər] *n* ❶ (*opponent*) [Wettkampf]gegner(in) *m(f)*; (*participant*) [Wettbewerbs]teilnehmer(in) *m(f)* ❷ COMM Konkurrent(in) *m(f)*

compile [kəmˈpaɪl] *vt* ❶ *list* erstellen ❷ COMPUT kompilieren

complacence [kəmˈpleɪ·səns], **complacency** [kəmˈpleɪ·sən·si] *n* (*pej*) Selbstzufriedenheit *f*

complacent [kəmˈpleɪ·sənt] *adj* (*pej*) selbstzufrieden

complain [kəmˈpleɪn] *vi* klagen, sich beklagen (**about/of** über +*akk*)

complaint [kəmˈpleɪnt] *n* ❶ Beschwerde *f*, Klage *f* ❷ LAW Klageschrift *f*

complement [ˈkam·plɪ·mənt] I. *vt* ergänzen; **to ~ each other** sich [gegenseitig] ergänzen II. *n* Ergänzung *f*

complementary [ˌkam·plə·ˈmen·tə·ri] *adj* [einander] ergänzend

complete [kəmˈplit] I. *vt* ❶ vervollständigen; *form* [vollständig] ausfüllen ❷ (*finish*) fertigstellen; *course* absolvieren; *studies* zu Ende bringen II. *adj* ❶ (*with nothing missing*) vollständig, komplett ❷ (*including*) ~ **with** inklusive ❸ (*total*) absolut; *breakdown* total; *darkness, stranger, surprise* völlig

completely [kəmˈplit·li] *adv* völlig

completeness [kəmˈplit·nɪs] *n* Vollständigkeit *f*

completion [kəmˈpli·ʃən] *n* Fertigstellung *f*

complex [ˈkam·pleks] I. *adj* komplex; (*complicated*) kompliziert; *issue, personality* vielschichtig; *plot* verwickelt II. *n* <*pl* -es> Komplex *m*

complexion [kəmˈplek·ʃən] *n* Teint *m*

complexity [kəmˈplek·sɪ·ti] *n* Komplexität *f*

complicate [ˈkam·plɪ·keɪt] *vt* [noch] komplizierter machen

complicated [ˈkam·plɪ·keɪ·t̬ɪd] *adj* kompliziert

complication [ˌkam·plɪ·ˈkeɪ·ʃən] *n* Komplikation *f*

compliment [ˈkam·plə·mənt] I. *n* Kompliment *nt;* **to pay sb a ~** jdm ein Kompliment machen II. *vt* ■to ~ sb jdm ein Kompliment machen

complimentary [ˌkam·plə·ˈmen·tə·ri] *adj* ❶ schmeichelhaft ❷ (*free*) Frei-

comply [kəmˈplaɪ] *vi* sich fügen

component [kəmˈpou·nənt] *n* [Bestand]teil *m*

compose [kəmˈpouz] I. *vi* komponieren II. *vt* ❶ MUS komponieren ❷ LIT verfassen ❸ (*comprise*) ■**to be ~d of sth** aus etw *dat* bestehen

composer [kəm·ˈpou·zər] *n* Komponist(in) *m(f)*

composition [ˌkam·pə·ˈzɪʃ·ən] *n* ❶ (*piece*) Komposition *f* ❷ (*arrangement*) Gestaltung *f*; (*of painting*) Komposition *f* ❸ (*makeup*) Zusammenstellung *f*; CHEM Zusammensetzung *f*

compost [ˈkam·poust] *n* Kompost *m*

composure [kəm·ˈpou·ʒər] *n* Fassung *f*

compound [ˈkam·paund] I. *adj* zusammengesetzt II. *n* ❶ (*combination*) Mischung *f* ❷ CHEM Verbindung *f*

compound ˈinterest *n* FIN Zinseszins *m meist pl*

comprehend [ˌkam·prɪ·ˈhend] *vt, vi* begreifen, verstehen

comprehensible [ˌkam·prɪ·ˈhen·sə·bəl] *adj* verständlich

comprehension [ˌkam·prɪ·ˈhen·ʃən] *n* Verständnis *nt*

comprehensive [ˌkam·prɪ·ˈhen·sɪv] *adj* umfassend; *list* vollständig

compress¹ [kəm·ˈpres] *vt* ❶ (*squeeze together*) zusammendrücken; *air, gas* komprimieren ❷ (*condense*) zusammenfassen

compress² <*pl* -es> [ˈkam·pres] *n* MED Kompresse *f*

compressed [kəm·ˈprest] *adj* komprimiert; **~ air** Druckluft *f*

comprise [kəm·ˈpraɪz] *vt* (*form*) umfassen

compromise [ˈkam·prə·maɪz] I. *n* Kompromiss *m* II. *vi* Kompromisse eingehen

compromising [ˈkam·prə·maɪ·zɪŋ] *adj* kompromittierend

compulsion [kəm·ˈpʌl·ʃən] *n* Zwang *m*

compulsive [kəm·ˈpʌl·sɪv] *adj* ❶ (*obsessive*) zwanghaft; *liar* notorisch ❷ (*captivating*) fesselnd

compulsory [kəm·ˈpʌl·sə·ri] *adj* obligatorisch; **~ subject** Pflichtfach *nt*

compute [kəm·ˈpjut] *vt* berechnen

computer [kəm·ˈpju·tər] *n* Computer *m*

comˈputer game *n* Computerspiel *nt*

computerize [kəm·ˈpju·tə·raɪz] *vt* ❶ (*store on computer*) [im Computer] speichern ❷ (*equip with computers*) computerisieren

computer ˈprogrammer *n* Programmierer(in) *m(f)*

computing [kəm·ˈpju·tɪŋ] *n* ❶ (*calculating*) Berechnen *nt* ❷ COMPUT EDV *f*

comrade [ˈkam·ræd] *n* ❶ POL Genosse, -in *m, f* ❷ (*friend*) Kamerad(in) *m(f)*

con¹ [kan] (*fam*) I. *vt* <-nn-> reinlegen II. *n* (*trick*) Schwindel *m kein pl*

con² [kan] *n* (*sl: convict*) Knacki *m sl*

concave [ˈkan·keɪv] *adj* konkav

conceal [kən·ˈsil] *vt* verbergen

concealment [kən·ˈsil·mənt] *n* Verheimlichung *f*; (*of feelings*) Verbergen *nt*

concede [kən·ˈsid] I. *vt* ❶ (*acknowledge*) zugeben; **to ~ defeat** sich geschlagen geben ❷ (*grant*) *privileges, rights* einräumen II. *vi* sich geschlagen geben

conceit [kən·ˈsit] *n* Einbildung *f*

conceited [kən·ˈsi·tɪd] *adj* eingebildet

conceivable [kən·ˈsiv·ə·bəl] *adj* vorstellbar

conceive [kən·ˈsiv] I. *vt* sich *dat* vorstellen II. *vi* ❶ (*imagine*) ■**to ~ of sth** sich *dat* etw vorstellen ❷ (*become pregnant*) empfangen

concentrate [ˈkan·sən·treɪt] I. *vi* ■**to ~ [on sth]** sich *akk* [auf etw *akk*] konzentrieren II. *vt* konzentrieren

concentrated [ˈkan·sən·treɪ·tɪd] *adj* konzentriert; *attack* geballt; *effort* gezielt

concentration [ˌkan·sən·ˈtreɪ·ʃən] *n* Konzentration *f*

concenˈtration camp *n* Konzentrationslager *nt*

concept [ˈkan·sept] *n* ❶ (*idea*) Vorstellung *f* ❷ (*plan*) Entwurf *m*, Konzept *nt*

conception [kən·ˈsep·ʃən] *n* ❶ (*basic understanding*) Vorstellung *f* ❷ (*idea*) Idee *f*, Konzept *nt* ❸ BIOL Empfängnis *f*

concern [kən·ˈsɜrn] I. *n* ❶ (*interest*) Anliegen *nt*, Angelegenheit *f* ❷ (*worry*) Sorge *f*, Besorgnis *f* ❸ COMM Handelsun-

C

ternehmen *nt* II. *vt* ① (*be about*) handeln von +*dat* ② (*apply to*) angehen; (*affect*) betreffen; **as far as I'm ~ed** was mich betrifft ③ (*involve*) ■**to ~ oneself with sth** sich mit etw *dat* befassen ④ (*worry*) beunruhigen

concerning [kən·'sɜr·nɪŋ] *prep* bezüglich +*gen*

concert ['kan·sərt] *n* Konzert *nt*

concerted [kən·'sɜr·tɪd] *adj* effort gemeinsam

concerto <*pl* -s> [kən·'tʃer·toʊ] *n* Konzert *nt*

concession [kən·'seʃ·ən] *n* ① Zugeständnis *nt* ② (*admission of defeat*) Eingeständnis *nt* [einer Niederlage] ③ ECON Konzession *f*

conciliatory [kən·'sɪl·i·ə·tɔr·i] *adj* versöhnlich; (*mediating*) beschwichtigend

concise [kən·'saɪs] *adj* präzise; *answer* kurz und bündig; *style* a. knapp

conclude [kən·'klud] I. *vi* enden, schließen II. *vt* ① (*finish*) [ab]schließen ② (*infer*) ■**to ~ [from sth] that ...** [aus etw] schließen, dass ...

concluding [kən·'klu·dɪŋ] *adj* abschließend

conclusion [kən·'klu·ʒən] *n* ① (*end*) Abschluss *m*; (*of a story*) Schluss *m* ② (*decision*) **to come to a ~** einen Beschluss fassen ③ (*inference*) Schluss *m*, Schlussfolgerung *f*

conclusive [kən·'klu·sɪv] *adj* ① (*convincing*) schlüssig ② (*decisive*) eindeutig; *evidence* stichhaltig

concoct [kən·'kakt] *vt* aushecken; *dish* zusammenstellen; *drink* mixen

concoction [kən·'kak·ʃən] *n* Erfindung *f*; (*dish*) Kreation *f*; (*drink*) Gebräu *nt*

concrete ['kan·krit] I. *n* Beton *m* II. *adj* ① *surface* betoniert ② *proof* eindeutig; *suggestion* konkret III. *vt* betonieren

'**concrete mixer** *n* Betonmischmaschine *f*

concur <-rr-> [kən·'kɜr] *vi* übereinstimmen

concurrent [kən·'kʌr·ənt] *adj* gleichzeitig

concussion [kən·'kʌʃ·ən] *n* Gehirnerschütterung *f*

condemn [kən·'dem] *vt* ① verurteilen; (*fig*) verdammen ② (*declare unsafe*) für unbrauchbar erklären; *building* für unbewohnbar erklären

condemnation [ˌkan·dem·'neɪ·ʃən] *n* Verurteilung *f*; (*fig*) Verdammung *f*

condensation [ˌkan·den·'seɪ·ʃən] *n* Kondensation *f*; (*droplets*) Kondenswasser *nt*

condense [kən·'dens] I. *vt* ① *gas* komprimieren; *liquid* eindicken; **~d milk** Kondensmilch *f* ② (*shorten*) zusammenfassen II. *vi* kondensieren

condescending [ˌkan·dɪ·'sen·dɪŋ] *adj* herablassend

condiment ['kan·də·mənt] *n* Würzmittel *nt*; (*sauce*) Soße *f*

condition [kən·'dɪʃ·ən] I. *n* ① (*state*) Zustand *m*; (*of person*) Verfassung *f* ② (*circumstances*) ■**~s** *pl* Bedingungen *pl* ③ (*stipulation*) Bedingung *f* II. *vt* ① (*train*) konditionieren ② (*accustom*) gewöhnen; *hair* eine Pflegespülung machen

conditional [kən·'dɪʃ·ə·nəl] I. *adj* bedingt II. *n* LING ■**the ~** der Konditional

conditionally [kən·'dɪʃ·ə·nə·li] *adv* unter Vorbehalt

conditioner [kən·'dɪʃ·ə·nər] *n* Pflegespülung *f*

condo ['kan·doʊ] *n* (*fam*) *short for* **condominium** Eigentumswohnung *f*

condolences [kən·'doʊ·lənsɪz] *npl* Beileid *nt kein pl*

condom ['kan·dəm] *n* Kondom *nt*

condominium [ˌkan·də·'mɪn·i·əm] *n* Eigentumswohnung *f*; (*building*) Wohnblock *m* [mit Eigentumswohnungen]

condone [kən·'doʊn] *vt* [stillschweigend] dulden

conduct I. *vt* [kən·'dʌkt] ① (*carry out*) durchführen; *negotiations* führen; *service* abhalten ② (*direct*) leiten; *orchestra* dirigieren ③ ELEC leiten ④ (*guide*) führen II. *vi* [kən·'dʌkt] MUS dirigieren

III. n ['kan·dʌkt] Benehmen nt, Verhalten nt

conductor [kən·'dʌk·tər] n ❶ MUS Dirigent(in) m(f) ❷ PHYS Leiter m ❸ RAIL Schaffner(in) m(f)

conduit ['kan·du·ɪt] n (pipe) [Rohr]leitung f; (channel) Kanal m

cone [koʊn] n MATH Kegel m; BOT Zapfen m; **ice cream ~** Eistüte f

confectioner [kən·'fek·ʃə·nər] n Süßwarenhändler(in) m(f)

confectionery [kən·'fek·ʃə·ner·i] n (candy) Süßwaren pl; (chocolate) Konfekt nt

confederacy [kən·'fed·ər·ə·si] n Konföderation f; ■**the C~** HIST die Konföderierten Staaten pl von Amerika

confederate [kən·'fed·ər·ət] **I.** n Komplize, -in m, f **II.** adj HIST ■**C~** Südstaaten-

confederation [kən·ˌfed·ə·'reɪ·ʃən] n POL Bund m; ECON Verband m

confer <-rr-> [kən·'fɜr] **I.** vt ■**to ~ sth [up]on sb** jdm etw verleihen **II.** vi sich beraten

conference ['kan·fər·əns] n Konferenz f, Tagung f

confess [kən·'fes] vt, vi ❶ (admit) zugeben; ■**to ~ [to] sth** etw gestehen ❷ REL beichten

confession [kən·'feʃ·ən] n Geständnis nt; REL Beichte f

confessional [kən·'feʃ·ə·nəl] n Beichtstuhl m

confessor [kən·'fes·ər] n Beichtvater m

confetti [kən·'fet·i] n Konfetti nt

confidant ['kan·fɪ·ˌdant] n Vertraute(r) m

confidante ['kan·fɪ·ˌdant] n Vertraute f

confide [kən·'faɪd] **I.** vt gestehen **II.** vi ■**to ~ in sb** sich jdm anvertrauen

confidence ['kan·fɪ·dəns] n ❶ (trust) Vertrauen nt ❷ no pl (self-assurance) Selbstvertrauen nt

confident ['kan·fɪ·dənt] adj ❶ (certain) zuversichtlich; ■**to be ~ of sth** von etw dat überzeugt sein ❷ (self-assured) selbstbewusst

confidential [ˌkan·fɪ·'den·ʃəl] adj vertraulich

confidentially [ˌkan·fɪ·'den·ʃə·li] adv vertraulich

configure [kən·'fɪg·jər] vt konfigurieren

confine vt [kən·'faɪn] ❶ (restrict) beschränken (**to** auf +akk) ❷ (shut in) einsperren

confinement [kən·'faɪn·mənt] n ❶ Einsperrung f; **solitary ~** Einzelhaft f ❷ MED Geburt f

confirm [kən·'fɜrm] **I.** vt ❶ (verify) bestätigen ❷ REL ■**to be ~ed** (Catholic) gefirmt werden; (Protestant) konfirmiert werden **II.** vi bestätigen

confirmation [ˌkan·fər·'meɪ·ʃən] n ❶ (verification) Bestätigung f ❷ REL (Catholic) Firmung f; (Protestant) Konfirmation f

confiscate ['kan·fɪ·skeɪt] vt beschlagnahmen

conflict **I.** n ['kan·flɪkt] (clash) Konflikt m; (battle) Kampf m **II.** vi [kən·'flɪkt] dates, events sich überschneiden; ■**to ~ with sth** im Widerspruch zu etw dat stehen

conflicting [kən·'flɪk·tɪŋ] adj widersprüchlich; claims entgegengesetzt

conform [kən·'fɔrm] vi sich einfügen; ■**to ~ to [or with] sth** etw dat entsprechen

conformist [kən·'fɔr·mɪst] **I.** n Konformist(in) m(f) **II.** adj konformistisch

confront [kən·'frʌnt] vt ❶ (face) ■**to ~ sth** sich etw dat stellen; danger ins Auge sehen; ■**to ~ sb** jdn zur Rede stellen gen ❷ (compel to deal with) konfrontieren

confrontation [ˌkan·frən·'teɪ·ʃən] n Konfrontation f

confuse [kən·'fjuz] vt verwirren, durcheinanderbringen; (misidentify) verwechseln

confused [kən·'fjuzd] adj person verwirrt, durcheinander; situation verworren

confusing [kən·'fju·zɪŋ] adj verwirrend

confusion [kən·'fju·ʒən] n ❶ (perplexity) Verwirrung f ❷ (mix-up) Verwechslung f ❸ (disorder) Durcheinander nt

congeal [kən·'dʒil] *vi* fest werden

congenial [kən·'dʒin·jəl] *adj* angenehm; *people* sympathisch

congenital [kən·'dʒen·ɪ·təl] *adj* angeboren

congested [kən·'dʒes·tɪd] *adj* ❶ überfüllt; *road* verstopft ❷ MED verstopft

congestion [kən·'dʒes·tʃən] *n* Überfüllung *f;* (*on roads*) Stau *m;* **nasal ~** MED verstopfte Nase

conglomerate [kən·'glam·ə·reɪt] *n* Konglomerat *nt*

congratulate [kən·'grætʃ·ə·leɪt] *vt* **to ~ sb** [**on sth**] jdm [zu etw] gratulieren

congratulation [kən·grætʃ·ə·'leɪ·ʃən] *n* Glückwunsch *m;* **~ s!** herzlichen Glückwunsch!

congregate ['kaŋ·grɪ·geɪt] *vi* sich [ver]sammeln

congregation [ˌkaŋ·grɪ·'geɪ·ʃən] *n* REL [Kirchen]gemeinde *f*

congress ['kaŋ·grəs] *n* Kongress *m;* **C~** POL der Kongress

congressional [kəŋ·'greʃ·ə·nəl] *adj* Kongress-

'congressman *n* [Kongress]abgeordneter *m*

'congresswoman *n* [Kongress]abgeordnete *f*

conifer ['kan·ə·fər] *n* Nadelbaum *m*

conjecture [kən·'dʒek·tʃər] *n* Vermutung *f*

conjunction [kən·'dʒʌŋk·ʃən] *n* ❶ LING Bindewort *nt* ❷ (*combination*) **■in ~ with sth** in Verbindung mit etw *dat;* **■in ~ with sb** zusammen mit jdm

conjunctivitis [kən·ˌdʒʌŋk·tə·'vaɪ·tɪs] *n* Bindehautentzündung *f*

conjure ['kan·dʒər] *vi* zaubern
◆**conjure up** *vt images, pictures* hervorzaubern; *meal* zaubern

conjurer ['kan·dʒər·ər] *n* Zauberkünstler(in) *m(f)*

'con man *n* Schwindler *m*

Conn. *abbrev of* **Connecticut**

connect [kə·'nekt] I. *vi* ❶ (*plug in*) **■to ~ to sth** an etw *akk* angeschlossen werden ❷ (*feel affinity*) **■to ~ with sb** sich auf Anhieb gut mit jdm verstehen II. *vt*

❶ ELEC verbinden (**to/with** mit +*dat*); (*plug in*) anschließen (**to/with** an +*akk*) ❷ (*associate*) in Verbindung bringen *dat* ❸ TELEC verbinden

Connecticut [kə·'net̬·ɪ·kət] *n* Connecticut *nt*

connection [kə·'nek·ʃən] *n* ❶ (*joining, link*) Verbindung *f* (**to/with** mit +*dat*); ELEC Anschluss *m* (**to** an +*akk*) ❷ TRANSP Verbindung *f;* (*connecting train, flight*) Anschluss *m* ❸ (*contacts*) **■~s** *pl* Beziehungen *pl* ❹ **in that/this ~** in diesem Zusammenhang *m*

conniving [kə·'naɪ·vɪŋ] *adj* hinterhältig

conquer ['kaŋ·kər] *vt person, disease* besiegen; *thing* erobern *a. fig*

conqueror ['kaŋ·kər·ər] *n* (*of sth*) Eroberer, Eroberin *m, f;* (*of sb*) Sieger(in) *m(f)*

conquest ['kaŋ·kwest] *n* (*of thing*) Eroberung *f;* (*of person*) Sieg *m*

conscience ['kan·ʃəns] *n* Gewissen *nt*

conscientious [ˌkan·ʃi·en·ʃəs] *adj* gewissenhaft; (*dutiful*) pflichtbewusst; *work* gründlich

conscious ['kan·ʃəs] *adj* ❶ MED bei Bewusstsein ❷ *decision* bewusst ❸ (*aware*) bewusst; **fashion-~** modebewusst

consciousness ['kan·ʃəs·nɪs] *n* Bewusstsein *nt*

conscript I. *n* ['kan·skrɪpt] Wehrpflichtige(r) *m* II. *vt* [kən·'skrɪpt] einziehen, einberufen

conscription [kən·'skrɪp·ʃən] *n* MIL Wehrpflicht *f;* (*act of conscripting*) Einberufung *f*

consecrate ['kan·sə·kreɪt] *vt* weihen

consecration [ˌkan·sə·'kreɪ·ʃən] *n* Weihe *f*

consecutive [kən·'sek·jə·t̬ɪv] *adj days, months* aufeinanderfolgend; *numbers* fortlaufend

consecutively [kən·'sek·jə·t̬ɪv·li] *adv* hintereinander

consensus [kən·'sen·səs] *n* Übereinstimmung *f*

consent [kən·'sent] (*form*) I. *n* Zustimmung *f* II. *vi* **■to ~ to sth** etw *dat* zustimmen; ■**to ~ to do sth** einwilligen, etw zu tun

consequence ['kan·sɪ·kwəns] *n* ❶ (*result*) Folge *f*, Auswirkung *f* ❷ (*significance*) Bedeutung *f*; **of no ~** unwichtig

consequent [ˌkan·sɪ·kwənt], **consequential** [ˌkan·sɪ·'kwən·ʃəl] *adj* daraus folgend

consequently ['kan·sɪ·kwənt·li] *adv* folglich

conservation [ˌkan·sər·'veɪ·ʃən] *n* Schutz *m*; (*preservation*) Erhaltung *f*

conservationist [ˌkan·sər·'veɪ·ʃə·nɪst] *n* Naturschützer(in) *m(f)*

conservative [kən·'sɜr·və·tɪv] **I.** *adj* ❶ (*in dress, opinion*) konservativ ❷ *estimate* vorsichtig **II.** *n* POL Konservative(r) *f(m)*

conservatory [kən·'sɜr·və·tɔr·i] *n* ❶ (*for plants*) Wintergarten *m* ❷ MUS Konservatorium *nt*

conserve **I.** *vt* [kən·'sɜrv] (*save*) sparen; *strength* schonen **II.** *n* ['kan·sɜrv] Eingemachtes *nt kein pl*

consider [kən·'sɪd·ər] *vt* ❶ (*think about*) ■**to ~ sth** sich *dat* etw *akk* überlegen ❷ (*look at*) betrachten; (*think of*) denken an +*akk*; (*take into account*) bedenken ❸ (*regard as*) ■**to ~ sb/sth [as [or to be]] sth** jdn/etw für etw *akk* halten

considerable [kən·'sɪd·ər·ə·bəl] *adj* erheblich, beträchtlich

considerate [kən·'sɪd·ər·ɪt] *adj* rücksichtsvoll

consideration [kən·ˌsɪd·ə·'reɪ·ʃən] *n* ❶ (*thought*) Überlegung *f*; **to take into ~** berücksichtigen ❷ (*factor*) Gesichtspunkt *m* ❸ (*regard*) Rücksicht *f*

considered [kən·'sɪd·ərd] *adj opinion* wohl überlegt

considering [kən·'sɪd·ər·ɪŋ] **I.** *prep* ■**~ how/what ...** wenn man bedenkt, wie/was ... **II.** *conj* ■**~ that ...** dafür, dass ...

consignment [kən·'saɪn·mənt] *n* Warensendung *f*

consist [kən·'sɪst] *vi* ■**to ~ of sth** aus etw *dat* bestehen

consistency [kən·'sɪs·tən·si] *n* ❶ (*firmness*) Konsistenz *f* ❷ (*constancy*) Beständigkeit *f*

consistent [kən·'sɪs·tənt] *adj* ❶ (*compatible*) vereinbar, übereinstimmend ❷ (*steady*) beständig; *improvement* ständig

consolation [ˌkan·sə·'leɪ·ʃən] *n* Trost *m*

console¹ [kən·'soʊl] *vt* trösten

console² ['kan·soʊl] *n* Schaltpult *nt*; COMPUT Konsole *f*

consolidate [kən·'sal·ə·deɪt] *vt*, *vi* ❶ (*unite*) [sich] vereinigen ❷ (*strengthen*) [sich] festigen

consonant ['kan·sə·nənt] *n* Konsonant *m*

consortium <*pl* -s> [kən·'sɔr·ti·əm] *n* Konsortium *nt*

conspicuous [kən·'spɪk·ju·əs] *adj* (*noticeable*) auffallend; (*clearly visible*) unübersehbar

conspiracy [kən·'spɪr·ə·si] *n* Verschwörung *f*

conspirator [kən·'spɪr·ə·ṭər] *n* Verschwörer(in) *m(f)*

conspire [kən·'spaɪr] *vi* (*a. fig*) sich verschwören

constant ['kan·stənt] *adj* ❶ (*continuous*) ständig ❷ (*unchanging*) gleich bleibend; MATH konstant

constantly ['kan·stənt·li] *adv* ständig

constellation [ˌkan·stə·'leɪ·ʃən] *n* Sternbild *nt*

consternation [ˌkan·stər·'neɪ·ʃən] *n* Bestürzung *f*

constipated ['kan·stə·peɪ·ṭɪd] *adj* verstopft; **to be ~** [eine] Verstopfung haben

constipation ['kan·stə·peɪ·ʃən] *n* Verstopfung *f*

constituency [kən·'stɪtʃ·u·ən·si] *n* POL Wahlkreis *m*

constituent [kən·'stɪtʃ·u·ənt] *n* ❶ (*voter*) Wähler(in) *m(f)* ❷ (*part*) Bestandteil *m*

constitute ['kan·stɪ·tut] *vt* ❶ (*make up*) bilden ❷ (*form: be*) sein

constitution [ˌkan·strɪ·'tu·ʃən] *n* ❶ (*structure*) Zusammensetzung *f*

C

C

② POL Verfassung *f* ③ (*health*) Konstitution *f*

constitutional [ˌkan·strɪ·'tuː·ʃə·nəl] I. *adj* konstitutionell II. *n* (*hum*) [regelmäßiger] Spaziergang *m*

constraint [kən·'streɪnt] *n* ① (*compulsion*) Zwang *m* ② (*restriction*) Beschränkung *f*

constrict [kən·'strɪkt] I. *vt* ① verengen; (*squeeze*) einschnüren ② (*hinder*) behindern II. *vi* sich zusammenziehen

constriction [kən·'strɪk·ʃən] *n* ① Verengung *f*; (*squeezing*) Einschnüren *nt* ② (*hindrance*) Behinderung *f*

construct [kən·'strʌkt] *vt* ① (*build*) bauen; *dam* errichten ② *theory* entwickeln

construction [kən·'strʌk·ʃən] *n* ① (*activity*) Bau *m*; **the ~ industry** die Bauindustrie; **under ~** im Bau ② (*how sth is built*) Bauweise *f* ③ (*object*) Konstruktion *f*; (*building*) Gebäude *nt*

constructive [kən·'strʌk·tɪv] *adj* konstruktiv

consul ['kan·səl] *n* Konsul(in) *m(f)*

consulate ['kan·sə·lət] *n* Konsulat *nt*

consult [kən·'sʌlt] I. *vi* sich beraten II. *vt* ① (*ask*) um Rat fragen; *doctor, lawyer* konsultieren, zu Rate ziehen ② (*look at*) *dictionary* nachschlagen in +*dat*

consultancy [kən·'sʌl·tən·si] *n* (*company*) Beratungsdienst *m*

consultant [kən·'sʌl·tənt] *n* Berater(in) *m(f)*

consultation [ˌkan·sʌl·'teɪ·ʃən] *n* ① Beratung *f*; (*with lawyer, accountant*) Rücksprache *f* ② MED Konsultation *f*

consume [kən·'sum] *vt* ① (*eat, drink*) konsumieren ② (*use up*) verbrauchen

consumer [kən·'su·mər] *n* Verbraucher(in) *m(f)*

consumerism [kən·'su·mə·rɪz·əm] *n* Konsumdenken *nt*

consumption [kən·'sʌm(p)·ʃən] *n no pl* ① (*using up*) Verbrauch *m*; (*using*) Konsum *m*; **energy ~** Energieverbrauch *m* ② (*eating, drinking*) Konsum *m*; *of food also* Verzehr *m*; **unfit for human ~** nicht für den menschlichen Verzehr geeignet ③ (*fig: use*) **for inter-**

nal ~ zur internen Nutzung ④ *no pl* MED (*hist*) Schwindsucht *f*

contact ['kan·tækt] I. *n* ① (*communication*) Kontakt *m*, Verbindung *f* ② (*person*) Kontaktperson *f*; **business ~s** Geschäftskontakte *pl* ③ (*touch*) Kontakt *m* II. *vt* ■ **to ~ sb** sich mit jdm in Verbindung setzen; (*by phone*) jdn [telefonisch] erreichen

'**contact lens** *n* Kontaktlinse *f*

contagious [kən·'teɪ·dʒəs] *adj* ansteckend

contain [kən·'teɪn] *vt* ① (*hold*) enthalten ② (*limit*) in Grenzen halten; (*hold back*) aufhalten; **she could barely ~ herself** sie konnte kaum an sich halten

container [kən·'teɪ·nər] *n* ① Behälter *m* ② TRANSP Container *m*

contaminate [kən·'tæm·ə·neɪt] *vt* verunreinigen; (*with radioactivity etc.*) verseuchen

contamination [kən·ˌtæm·ɪ·'neɪ·ʃən] *n* Verunreinigung *f*; (*by radioactivity etc.*) Verseuchung *f*

contemplate ['kan·tem·pleɪt] I. *vi* nachdenken II. *vt* ① (*consider*) in Erwägung ziehen; (*reflect upon*) über etw *akk* nachdenken; *suicide* denken an +*akk* ② (*gaze at*) betrachten

contemplation [ˌkan·tem·'pleɪ·ʃən] *n* ① (*thought*) Nachdenken *nt* ② (*gazing*) Betrachtung *f*

contemplative [kən·'tem·plə·tɪv] *adj* ① *mood* nachdenklich ② REL besinnlich; *life* beschaulich

contemporary [kən·'tem·pə·rer·i] I. *n* ① (*from same period*) Zeitgenosse, -in *m, f* ② (*of same age*) Altersgenosse, -in *m, f* II. *adj* zeitgenössisch

contempt [kən·'tempt] *n* ① (*scorn*) Verachtung *f*; (*disregard*) Geringschätzung *f* ② LAW **~ [of court]** Missachtung *f* [des Gerichts]

contemptuous [kən·'temp·tʃu·əs] *adj* verächtlich

contend [kən·'tend] *vi* ■ **to ~ with sth** mit etw *dat* fertigwerden müssen

contender [kən·'ten·dər] *n* Bewerber(in) *m(f)*, Anwärter(in) *m(f)*

content[1] ['kɑn·tent] n ❶ Inhalt m ❷ Gehalt m; **to have a high/low fat ~** einen hohen/niedrigen Fettgehalt aufweisen

content[2] [kən·'tent] **I.** adj zufrieden **II.** vt ■**to ~ oneself with sth** sich mit etw dat zufriedengeben

contented [kən·'ten·tɪd] adj zufrieden

contention [kən·'ten·ʃən] n SPORT **in ~ for sth** [noch] im Rennen um etw akk

contentious [kən·'ten·ʃəs] adj umstritten

contentment [kən·'tent·mənt] n Zufriedenheit f

contents ['kɑn·tents] npl Inhalt m; **[table of] ~** Inhaltsverzeichnis nt

contest I. n ['kɑn·test] ❶ (event) Wettbewerb m; SPORT Wettkampf m ❷ Wettstreit m **II.** vt [kən·'test] ❶ (compete for) kämpfen um +akk ❷ (dispute) bestreiten

contestant [kən·'tes·tənt] n (in competition) Wettbewerbsteilnehmer(in) m(f); SPORT Wettkampfteilnehmer(in) m(f); (on game show) Kandidat(in) m(f)

context ['kɑn·tekst] n Kontext m, Zusammenhang m

continent ['kɑn·tə·nənt] n GEOG Kontinent m, Erdteil m

continental [ˌkɑn·tə·'nen·təl] adj ❶ kontinental ❷ (of the American colonies) Kontinental-; **C~ Congress** Kontinentalkongress m

contingent [kən·'tɪn·dʒənt] n ❶ Gruppe f ❷ MIL [Truppen]kontingent nt

continual [kən·'tɪn·ju·əl] adj ständig, andauernd

continually [kən·'tɪn·ju·əl·i] adv ständig, [an]dauernd

continuation [kən·ˌtɪn·ju·'eɪ·ʃən] n Fortsetzung f

continue [kən·'tɪn·ju] **I.** vi ❶ (persist) andauern; (go on) weitergehen; (in an activity) weitermachen; ■**to ~ doing/ to do sth** weiter[hin] etw tun ❷ (remain) bleiben ❸ (resume) weitergehen; speaking fortfahren **II.** vt ❶ (carry on) fortführen; an action mit etw dat

weitermachen; education fortsetzen ❷ (resume) fortsetzen

continuity [ˌkɑn·tə·'nu·ɪ·ti] n ❶ (consistency) Kontinuität f ❷ FILM Drehbuch nt

continuous [kən·'tɪn·ju·əs] adj ununterbrochen; (steady) stetig; (unbroken) durchgehend; line a. durchgezogen; pain anhaltend

contort [kən·'tɔrt] vi (in pain) sich verzerren

contortion [kən·'tɔr·ʃən] n Verrenkung f

contortionist [kən·'tɔr·ʃə·nɪst] n Schlangenmensch m

contour ['kɑn·tʊr] n ❶ (outline) Kontur f meist pl ❷ GEOG Höhenlinie f

contraband ['kɑn·trə·bænd] **I.** n Schmuggelware f **II.** adj geschmuggelt

contraception [ˌkɑn·trə·'sep·ʃən] n [Empfängnis]verhütung f

contraceptive [ˌkɑn·trə·'sep·tɪv] **I.** n Verhütungsmittel nt **II.** adj empfängnisverhütend

contract[1] **I.** n ['kɑn·trækt] Vertrag m **II.** vi ■**to ~ to do sth** sich vertraglich verpflichten, etw zu tun
  ◆**contract out** vt vergeben (**to** an +akk)

contract[2] [kən·'trækt] **I.** vt ❶ muscles zusammenziehen; (shrink) zusammenschrumpfen ❷ MED bekommen; pneumonia sich dat zuziehen **II.** vi [kən·'trækt] sich zusammenziehen; pupils sich verengen

contraction [kən·'træk·ʃən] n ❶ (shrinkage) Zusammenziehen nt ❷ (of muscle) Kontraktion f ❸ LING Kontraktion f

contractor [kən·'træk·tər] n (person) Auftragnehmer(in) m(f); (company) beauftragte Firma

contractual [kən·'træk·tʃu·əl] adj vertraglich

contradict [ˌkɑn·trə·'dɪkt] vt widersprechen

contradiction [ˌkɑn·trə·'dɪk·ʃən] n Widerspruch m

contradictory [ˌkɑn·trə·'dɪk·tə·ri] adj widersprüchlich

contralto <pl -s> [kən·ˈtræl·toʊ] n ❶ (singer) Altist(in) m(f) ❷ (voice) Alt m

contrary [ˈkɑn·trer·i] I. n Gegenteil nt; **on the ~** ganz im Gegenteil II. adj ❶ interests, views entgegengesetzt; **~ to** im Gegensatz zu +dat ❷ (argumentative) widerspenstig

contrast I. n [ˈkɑn·træst] Gegensatz m, Kontrast m (**to/with** zu +dat) II. vt [kən·ˈtræst] **■to ~ sth with sth** etw dat gegenüberstellen III. vi [kən·ˈtræst] kontrastieren

contrasting [kən·ˈtræs·tɪŋ] adj gegensätzlich; colors, flavors konträr

contribute [kən·ˈtrɪb·jut] vt, vi money, food, equipment beisteuern; ideas beitragen; (to retirement plan etc.) einen Beitrag leisten

contribution [ˌkɑn·trɪ·ˈbju·ʃən] n Beitrag m; (to charity) Spende f

contributor [kən·ˈtrɪb·jə·tər] n ❶ (donor) Spender(in) m(f) ❷ (writer) Mitarbeiter(in) m(f)

contrive [kən·ˈtraɪv] I. vt ❶ (devise) sich dat ausdenken ❷ (fabricate) entwerfen, einfädeln II. vi **■to ~ to do sth** es schaffen, etw zu tun

control [kən·ˈtroʊl] I. n ❶ Kontrolle f; of a company Leitung f; **out of ~** außer Kontrolle ❷ TECH Schalter m, Regler m II. vt <-ll-> ❶ (direct) kontrollieren; car steuern; company leiten ❷ TECH (limit) valve, volume regulieren; inflation eindämmen ❸ emotions beherrschen; temper zügeln

controller [kən·ˈtroʊ·lər] n (director) Leiter(in) m(f); (of radio station) Intendant(in) m(f); (supervisor) Aufseher(in) m(f)

controversial [ˌkɑn·trə·ˈvɜr·ʃəl] adj umstritten

controversy [ˈkɑn·trə·vɜr·si] n Kontroverse f

convalesce [ˌkɑn·və·ˈles] vi genesen

convalescence [ˌkɑn·və·ˈles·əns] n Genesung f; (time) Genesungszeit f

convalescent [ˌkɑn·və·ˈles·ənt] I. n Genesende(r) f(m) II. adj ❶ (recover-

ing) genesend ❷ (for convalescents) Genesungs-

convene [kən·ˈvin] (form) I. vi sich versammeln; committee zusammentreten II. vt zusammenrufen; committee, meeting einberufen

convenience [kən·ˈvin·jəns] n ❶ (comfort) Annehmlichkeit f ❷ (device) Annehmlichkeit f

con'venience store n Laden m an der Ecke

convenient [kən·ˈvin·jənt] adj ❶ (useful) zweckmäßig; (comfortable) bequem; excuse passend ❷ date, time passend, günstig ❸ (accessible) location günstig gelegen

convent [ˈkɑn·vənt] n [Nonnen]kloster nt

convention [kən·ˈven·ʃən] n ❶ (custom) Brauch m; (social code) Konvention f ❷ (agreement) Abkommen nt; on human rights Konvention f ❸ (assembly) [Mitglieder]versammlung f; (conference) Konferenz f; **~ center** Tagungszentrum nt

conventional [kən·ˈven·ʃə·nəl] adj konventionell; **~ medicine** Schulmedizin f

converge [kən·ˈvɜrdʒ] vi lines zusammenlaufen

conversation [ˌkɑn·vər·ˈser·ʃən] n Gespräch nt, Unterhaltung f

conversational [ˌkɑn·vər·ˈser·ʃə·nəl] adj Gesprächs-, Unterhaltungs-

converse¹ [kən·ˈvɜrs] vi (form) sich akk unterhalten

converse² [ˈkɑn·vɜrs] n (form) **■the ~** das Gegenteil

conversely [kən·ˈvɜrs·li] adv umgekehrt

conversion [kən·ˈvɜr·ʒən] n ❶ (change) Umwandlung f; TECH Umrüstung f ❷ REL Konversion f, Bekehrung f ❸ MATH Umrechnung f ❹ (in football) Conversion f; (in hockey, soccer) Verwandlung f

convert I. n [ˈkɑn·vɜrt] REL Bekehrte(r) f(m); **to become a ~ to Islam** zum Islam übertreten II. vi [kən·ˈvɜrt] ❶ REL übertreten ❷ (change in function) sich verwandeln lassen III. vt [kən·ˈvɜrt]

① REL (*a. fig*) bekehren **②** (*change*) ■to ~ **sth** [**into**] etw umwandeln [in] +*akk*; ARCHIT etw umbauen [zu]; TECH etw umrüsten [zu] **③** (*calculate*) umrechnen; (*exchange*) umtauschen **④** (*in football*) *extra point* erfolgreich abschließen; (*in hockey, soccer*) *penalty* verwandeln

convertible [kən·ˈvɜr·tə·bəl] **I.** *n* Kabrio[lett] *nt*, Kabriole *nt* ÖSTERR **II.** *adj* **①** (*changeable*) verwandelbar **②** FIN konvertierbar

convex [ˈkan·veks] *adj* konvex

convey [kən·ˈveɪ] *vt* **①** (*transport*) befördern **②** (*transmit*) überbringen; (*impart*) vermitteln; (*make clear*) deutlich machen

conveyor [kən·ˈveɪ·ər] *n* ~ [**belt**] Förderband *nt*; (*in factory*) Fließband *nt*

convict I. *n* [ˈkan·vɪkt] Strafgefangene(r) *f(m)* **II.** *vi* [kən·ˈvɪkt] *auf schuldig erkennen* **III.** *vt* [kən·ˈvɪkt] verurteilen

conviction [kən·ˈvɪk·ʃən] *n* **①** (*judgment*) Verurteilung *f* (**for** wegen +*dat*) **②** (*belief*) Überzeugung *f*

convince [kən·ˈvɪns] *vt* überzeugen

convincing [kən·ˈvɪn·sɪŋ] *adj* überzeugend

convoluted [ˌkan·və·ˈluːtɪd] *adj* (*form*) *sentence* verschachtelt; *plot* verschlungen

convoy [ˈkan·vɔɪ] *n* Konvoi *m*

convulsion [kən·ˈvʌl·ʃən] *n usu pl* Krampf *m*

coo [kuː] *vi* gurren

cook [kʊk] **I.** *n* Koch, Köchin *m, f* **II.** *vt, vi* kochen

ˈcookbook *n* Kochbuch *nt*

cooker [ˈkʊ·kər] *n* BRIT **①** (*stove*) Herd *m;* **induction** ~ Induktionsherd *m* **②** (*fam: cooking apple*) Kochapfel *m*

cookie [ˈkʊk·i] *n* **①** (*cake*) Keks *m*, Plätzchen *nt* **②** (*sl: person*) **a tough** ~ eine harte Nuss **③** COMPUT Cookie *nt* ▸PHRASES: **that's the way the ~ crumbles** (*saying*) so ist das nun mal im Leben

cooking [ˈkʊk·ɪŋ] *n* **①** (*act*) Kochen *nt* **②** (*style*) Küche *f*

cool [kuːl] **I.** *adj* **①** (*pleasantly cold*) kühl; (*unpleasantly cold*) kalt; *clothing, material* luftig **②** (*calm*) ruhig, besonnen **③** *reception* kühl **④** (*fam: trendy, great*) cool *sl*, geil *sl* **II.** *n* **①** (*cold*) Kühle *f* **②** (*calm*) Ruhe *f* **III.** *vi* **①** (*lose heat*) abkühlen **②** *tempers* nachlassen **IV.** *vt* **①** (*make cold*) kühlen; (*cool down*) abkühlen **②** (*sl*) **|just| ~ it!** reg dich ab!

cooler [ˈkuː·lər] *n* Kühlbox *f*; *for wine bottles* Kühler *m*

ˈcoolˈheaded *adj* besonnen

coolly [ˈkuː·li] *adv* kühl, distanziert; (*in a relaxed manner*) cool *sl*

coolness [ˈkuːl·nɪs] *n* **①** (*low temperature*) Kühle *f* **②** (*unfriendliness*) Kühle *f*, Distanziertheit *f*

coop [kuːp] **I.** *n* Hühnerstall *m* **II.** *vt* ■to ~ **up** einsperren

co-op [ˈkoʊ·ap] *n abbrev of* **cooperative I**

cooperate [koʊ·ˈap·ə·reɪt] *vi* **①** (*help*) kooperieren; (*comply a.*) mitmachen **②** (*act jointly*) kooperieren, zusammenarbeiten

cooperation [koʊ·ˌap·ə·ˈreɪ·ʃən] *n* **①** (*assistance*) Kooperation *f*, Mitarbeit *f* **②** (*joint work*) Zusammenarbeit *f*, Kooperation *f*

cooperative [koʊ·ˈap·ər·ə·tɪv] **I.** *n* Genossenschaft *f*, Kooperative *f* **II.** *adj* **①** ECON genossenschaftlich, kooperativ **②** (*willing*) kooperativ

coordinate [ˌkoʊ·ˈɔr·dɪn·eɪt] **I.** *n usu pl* MATH Koordinate *f* **II.** *vi* [*gut*] zusammenarbeiten **III.** *vt* koordinieren

coordination [ˌkoʊ·ɔr·də·ˈneɪ·ʃən] *n* **①** (*coordinating*) Koordination *f* **②** (*dexterity*) Sinn *m* für Koordination

coordinator [koʊ·ˈɔr·də·neɪ·tər] *n* Koordinator(in) *m(f)*

cop [kap] *n* **①** (*fam*) Bulle *m* **II.** *vt* <-pp-> **to ~ a plea** LAW *sich schuldig bekennen und dafür eine mildere Strafe aushandeln*

cope [koʊp] *vi* **①** (*mentally*) zurechtkommen; **to ~ with a problem** ein

Problem bewältigen ②(*physically*) gewachsen sein

copier ['kap·i·ər] *n* Kopiergerät *nt*

copilot ['koʊ‚paɪ·lət] *n* Kopilot(in) *m(f)*

copious ['koʊ·pi·əs] *adj* zahlreich

copper ['kap·ər] *n* Kupfer *nt*

copy ['kap·i] I. *n* ① (*duplicate*) Kopie *f*; (*of document*) Abschrift *f*; (*of photo*) Abzug *m* ②(*issue*) Exemplar *nt* II. *vt* <-ie-> ① (*duplicate*) kopieren; (*write down*) *from text* abschreiben; *from speech* niederschreiben; ②*person* nachmachen; *style* nachahmen; *picture* abmalen ③(*plagiarize*) abschreiben

'**copycat** *n* (*pej fam*) Nachmacher(in) *m(f)*

copyright ['kap·i·raɪt] *n* Copyright *nt*, Urheberrecht *nt*

'**copywriter** *n* [Werbe]texter(in) *m(f)*

coral ['kɔr·əl] *n* Koralle *f*

'**coral reef** *n* Korallenriff *nt*

cord [kɔrd] *n* (*for package*) Schnur *f*; ELEC Kabel *nt*

cordial ['kɔr·dʒəl] I. *adj* ①freundlich, herzlich; *relations* freundschaftlich ②(*form: fervent*) heftig; *dislike* tief II. *n* Likör *m*

cordless ['kɔrd·lɪs] *adj* schnurlos

cordon ['kɔr·dən] I. *n* Kordon *m* II. *vt* ■to ~ off ↻ sth etw absperren

corduroy ['kɔr·də·rɔɪ] *n* ① (*material*) Cordsamt *m*; ~ **jacket** Cordjacke *f* ②(*pants*) ■~ **s** *pl* Cordhose *f*

core [kɔr] I. *n* ① (*of apple*) Kerngehäuse *nt*; (*of rock*) Innere[s] *nt*; (*of planet*) Mittelpunkt *m*; (*of reactor*) [Reaktor]kern *m*; (*fig*) Kern *m* II. *adj* zentral

coriander ['kɔr·i·æn·dər] *n* Koriander *m*

cork [kɔrk] I. *n* ① (*material*) Kork *m* ②(*stopper*) Korken *m* II. *vt* zukorken

'**corkscrew** *n* Korkenzieher *m*

corn[1] [kɔrn] *n* FOOD Mais *m*

corn[2] [kɔrn] *n* MED Hühnerauge *nt*

'**corncob** *n* Maiskolben *m*

corner ['kɔr·nər] I. *n* ① Ecke *f*; (*of table*) Kante *f*; **out of the ~ of one's eye** aus dem Augenwinkel ②(*in soccer*) Ecke *f*, Eckball *m* ▶PHRASES: **to cut ~ s** (*financially*) Kosten sparen; (*in*

procedure) das Verfahren abkürzen II. *adj* Eck- III. *vt* in die Enge treiben IV. *vi* *vehicle* eine Kurve/Kurven nehmen

'**cornerstone** *n* (*a. fig*) Eckstein *m*

cornet [kɔr·'net] *n* MUS Kornett *nt*

'**corn flakes** *npl* Cornflakes *pl*

'**cornstarch** *n* Maisstärke *f*

corny ['kɔr·ni] *adj* (*fam: sentimental*) kitschig; (*dopey*) blöd

coronary ['kɔr·ə·ner·i] I. *n* Herzinfarkt *m* II. *adj* koronar, Herzkranz-

coronation [‚kɔr·ə·'neɪ·ʃən] *n* Krönung[szeremonie] *f*

coroner ['kɔr·ə·nər] *n* Coroner *m* (*Beamter, der unter verdächtigen Umständen eingetretene Todesfälle untersucht*)

corp. [kɔrp] *n* ① *short for* **corporation** ② *short for* **corporal**

corporal ['kɔr·pər·əl] *n* Unteroffizier *m*

corporate ['kɔr·pər·ət] *adj* (*of corporation*) körperschaftlich

corporation [‚kɔr·pə·'reɪ·ʃən] *n* COMM [Kapital]gesellschaft *f*

corps <*pl* -> [kɔr] *n* Korps *nt*

corpse [kɔrps] *n* Leiche *f*

corpuscle ['kɔr·pʌs·əl] *n* Blutkörperchen *nt*

corral [kə·'ræl] I. *n* [Fang]gehege *nt* II. *vt* <-ll-> einpferchen

correct [kə·'rekt] I. *vt* korrigieren II. *adj* richtig; (*proper a.*) korrekt

correction [kə·'rek·ʃən] *n* ① (*change*) Korrektur *f* ②(*improvement*) Verbesserung *f*, Berichtigung *f*

correctional [kə·'rek·ʃə·nəl] *adj* ~ **facility** Strafanstalt für junge Straftäter

corrective [kə·'rek·tɪv] I. *adj* ①(*counteractive*) korrigierend; ~ **surgery** Korrekturoperation *f* ②(*improving behavior*) Besserungs- II. *n* Korrektiv *nt*

correctly [kə·'rekt·li] *adv* korrekt, richtig

correctness [kə·'rekt·nɪs] *n* Korrektheit *f*, Richtigkeit *f*

correspond [‚kɔr·ə·'spand] *vi* ①(*be equivalent of*) ■to ~ to sth etw *dat* entsprechen; (*be same as*) übereinstim-

men (**with** mit +*dat*) ❷ (*write*) korrespondieren

correspondence [ˌkɔr·ə·ˈspan·dəns] *n*
Korrespondenz *f*

correspondent [ˌkɔr·ə·ˈspan·dənt] *n*
❶ (*letter writer*) Briefschreiber(in)
m(f) ❷ (*journalist*) Berichterstatter(in)
m(f), Korrespondent(in) *m(f)*

corresponding [ˌkɔr·ə·ˈspan·dɪŋ] *adj*
entsprechend

corridor [ˈkɔr·ɪ·dər] *n* Gang *m*, Korridor *m*

corroborate [kə·ˈrab·ə·reɪt] *vt* bestätigen

corroboration [kə·ˌrab·ə·ˈreɪ·ʃən] *n* Bestätigung *f*

corrode [kə·ˈroʊd] *vt, vi* korrodieren

corrosion [kə·ˈroʊ·ʒən] *n* Korrosion *f*

corrosive [kə·ˈroʊ·sɪv] *adj* korrosiv; *acid*
ätzend

corrugated [ˈkɔr·ə·geɪ·tɪd] *adj* *iron,
cardboard* gewellt

corrupt [kə·ˈrʌpt] I. *adj* ❶ (*dishonest*)
korrupt, bestechlich ❷ *file* unlesbar;
disk kaputt II. *vt* ❶ (*ethically*) korrum-
pieren; (*morally*) [moralisch] verderben;
(*bribe*) bestechen ❷ COMPUT *data, file*
ruinieren

corruption [kə·ˈrʌp·ʃən] *n* ❶ *of moral
standards* Korruption *f*; *of computer file* Zerstörung *f* ❷ (*dishonesty*)
Unehrenhaftigkeit *f*; (*bribery*) Korruption *f*

corset [ˈkɔr·sɪt] *n* Korsett *nt*; MED
Stützkorsett *nt*

cosmetic [kaz·ˈmeṭ·ɪk] I. *n* Kosmetik *f*;
~**s** *pl* Kosmetika *pl* II. *adj* kosmetisch

cosmic [ˈkaz·mɪk] *adj* kosmisch

cosmology [kaz·ˈmal·ə·dʒi] *n* Kosmolo-
gie *f*

cosmonaut [ˈkaz·mə·nɔt] *n* Kosmo-
naut(in) *m(f)*

cosmopolitan [ˌkaz·mə·ˈpal·ɪ·tən] *adj*
kosmopolitisch

cosmos [ˈkaz·məs] *n* Kosmos *m*

cost [kɔst] I. *vt* ❶ <cost, cost> kosten ❷ <-ed, -ed> FIN *job, project*
[durch]kalkulieren II. *n* ❶ Preis *m*, Kosten *pl* (**of** für +*akk*) ❷ (*fig*) Aufwand *m*

kein pl; **at all** ~[**s**] [*or* **at any** ~] um
jeden Preis

costly [ˈkɔst·li] *adj* kostspielig

costume [ˈkas·tum] *n* Kostüm *nt*

cosy [ˈkoʊ·zi] *adj, vi see* **cozy**

cot [kat] *n* (*camping bed*) Feldbett *nt*;
(*foldout bed*) Klappbett *nt*; (*for children*) Kinderbett *nt*

cottage [ˈkat·ɪdʒ] *n* Cottage *nt*

cottage '**cheese** *n* Hüttenkäse *m*

cotton [ˈkat·ən] I. *n* Baumwolle *f*;
(*thread*) Garn *nt* II. *adj* Baumwoll-
III. *vi* (*fam*) ■ **to** ~ [**on**] **to** [**sth**] [etw] kapieren

cotton '**candy** *n* Zuckerwatte *f*

'**cotton mill** *n* Baumwollspinnerei *f*

couch [kaʊtʃ] I. *n* <*pl* -es> Couch *f*
II. *vt* formulieren

'**couch potato** *n* (*fam*) *jd, der den ganzen Tag nur auf der Couch sitzt und
fernsieht*

cougar [ˈku·gər] *n* ZOOL Puma *m*

cough [kɔf] I. *n* Husten *m* II. *vt, vi* husten

◆**cough up** I. *vt* ❶ *blood* husten
❷ (*fam: pay*) herausrücken II. *vi* (*fam*)
herausrücken

'**cough medicine** *n* (*in liquid form*)
Hustensaft *m*

could [kʊd] *pt, subjunctive of* **can**

council [ˈkaʊn·səl] *n* Rat *m*

councilor, councillor [ˈkaʊn·sə·lər] *n*
Ratsmitglied *nt*

counsel [ˈkaʊn·səl] I. *vt* <-l-> empfehlen, raten II. *n* Anwalt, Anwältin *m, f*;
~ **for the defense** Verteidiger(in) *m(f)*

counseling, counselling [ˈkaʊn·sə·lɪŋ]
n psychologische Betreuung

counselor, counsellor [ˈkaʊn·sə·lər] *n*
❶ (*advisor*) Berater(in) *m(f)* ❷ (*lawyer*)
Anwalt *m*, Anwältin *f*

count[1] [kaʊnt] I. *n* ❶ (*action*) Zählung *f*;
POL Auszählung *f* ❷ (*total*) [An]zahl *f*;
Ergebnis *nt* ❸ LAW Anklagepunkt *m*
❹ (*in boxing*) Auszählung *f*; (*in baseball*)
Count *m*, Zählung *f* II. *vt* ❶ (*number*)
zählen; *change* nachzählen ❷ **to** ~ **sb
as a friend** jdn als Freund betrachten;
to ~ **oneself lucky** sich glücklich

schätzen **III.** *vi* zählen; ■**to ~ against sb** gegen jdn sprechen; **that's what ~s** darauf kommt es an

◆**count down** *vi* rückwärts bis null zählen; AEROSP den Countdown durchführen

◆**count on** *vi* zählen auf +*akk*

count² [kaʊnt] *n* Graf *m*

countdown ['kaʊnt·daʊn] *n* Countdown *m*

counter¹ ['kaʊn·tər] **I.** *vt* ausgleichen; *arguments* widersprechen **II.** *adv* entgegen; **to run ~ to sth** etw *dat* zuwiderlaufen

counter² ['kaʊn·tər] *n* ❶ (*in store*) Theke *f*; (*in bank, post office*) Schalter *m*; **over the ~** *medication* rezeptfrei; **under the ~** (*fig*) unterm Ladentisch ❷ (*disc*) Spielmarke *f*

counter'act *vt* entgegenwirken +*dat*; *poison* neutralisieren

'**counterattack I.** *n* Gegenangriff *m* **II.** *vt* im Gegenzug angreifen **III.** *vi* zurückschlagen; SPORT kontern

counterbalance I. *n* ['kaʊn·tər·bæl·əns] Gegengewicht *nt* **II.** *vt* [ˌkaʊn·tər·'bæl·əns] ausgleichen; (*fig*) ein Gegengewicht zu etw *dat* darstellen

counter'clockwise *adv* gegen den Uhrzeigersinn

counter'espionage *n* Spionageabwehr *f*

counterfeit ['kaʊn·tər·fɪt] **I.** *adj* gefälscht **II.** *vt* fälschen **III.** *n* Fälschung *f*

counterin'telligence *n* Spionageabwehr *f*

'**countermeasure** *n* Gegenmaßnahme *f*

'**counterpart** *n* Gegenstück *nt*; POL Amtskollege, -in *m, f*

counterpro'ductive *adj* kontraproduktiv

counter'terrorism *n* Terrorismusbekämpfung *f*

countess <*pl* -es> ['kaʊn·tɪs] *n* Gräfin *f*

countless ['kaʊnt·lɪs] *adj* zahllos

country ['kʌn·tri] **I.** *n* ❶ (*nation*) Land *nt* ❷ (*rural areas*) ■**in the ~** auf dem Land ❸ (*land*) Land *nt*, Gebiet *nt*; **open ~** freies Land ❹ (*music*) Country-

music *f* **II.** *adj* *cottage, road* Land-; *customs* ländlich

'**country club** *n* Country Club *m*

'**countryman** *n* [**fellow**] ~ Landsmann *m*

'**country music** *n* Countrymusic *f*

'**countryside** *n* Land *nt*; (*scenery*) Landschaft *f*

'**countrywide I.** *adj* landesweit **II.** *adv* im ganzen Land

'**countrywoman** *n* [**fellow**] ~ Landsmännin *f*

county ['kaʊn·ti] *n* [Verwaltungs]bezirk *m*

county 'seat *n* Bezirkshauptstadt *f*

coup [ku] *n* ❶ (*achievement*) Coup *m* ❷ POL Staatsstreich *m*

coup de grâce <*pl* coups de grâce> [ˌku·də·'gras] *n* Gnadenstoß *m*

coup d'état <*pl* coups d'état> [ˌku·deɪ·'ta] *n* Staatsstreich *m*

coupé [ku·'peɪ] *n* Coupé *nt*

couple ['kʌp·əl] **I.** *n* ❶ (*a few*) ■**a ~ of ...** einige ..., ein paar ... ❷ (*two people*) Paar *nt* **II.** *vt* ❶ (*join*) koppeln (**to** mit +*dat*) ❷ *usu passive* (*put together*) ■**to be ~d with sth** mit etw *dat* verbunden sein

couplet ['kʌp·lɪt] *n* Verspaar *nt*

coupling ['kʌp·lɪŋ] *n* Kupplung *f*

coupon ['ku·pan] *n* Coupon *m*, Gutschein *m*

courage ['kɜr·ɪdʒ] *n* Mut *m*

courageous [kə·'reɪ·dʒəs] *adj* mutig

courier ['kʊr·i·ər] *n* Kurier(in) *m(f)*

course [kɔrs] *n* ❶ (*series*) SCH, UNIV Kurs *m*; MED *of treatment* Behandlung *f* ❷ (*of aircraft, ship*) Kurs *m*; **off** ~ nicht auf Kurs; (*fig*) aus der Bahn geraten; **on** ~ auf Kurs; (*fig*) auf dem [richtigen] Weg ❸ *of road* Verlauf *m*; *of river, history* Lauf *m* ❹ *of action* Vorgehen *nt* ❺ **in the ~ of sth** im Verlauf einer S. gen ❻ (*part of meal*) Gang *m* ❼ (*for golf*) Golfplatz *m* ▸PHRASES: **of ~** natürlich; **of ~ not** natürlich nicht

court [kɔrt] *n* ❶ LAW Gericht *nt*; **to go to ~** vor Gericht gehen; **out of ~** außergerichtlich; **to take sb to ~** jdn vor Ge-

richt bringen ② (*room*) Gerichtssaal *m*
③ (*playing area*) [Spiel]platz *m* ④ *of
king, queen* Hof *m*
courteous [ˈkɜr·ti·əs] *adj* höflich
courtesy [ˈkɜr·tə·si] *n* (*politeness, polite gesture*) Höflichkeit *f* ▶PHRASES:
~ **of** *sb/sth* (*thanks to*) dank jdm/etw;
(*with the permission of*) mit freund-
licher Genehmigung von jdm/etw
ˈcourthouse *n* Gerichtsgebäude *nt*
courtier [ˈkɔr·ti·ər] *n* Höfling *m*
court-ˈmartial I. *n* <*pl* -s *or form
courts martial*> Kriegsgericht *nt* II. *vt*
<-l-> vor ein Kriegsgericht stellen
ˈcourtroom *n* Gerichtssaal *m*
courtship [ˈkɔrt·ʃɪp] *n* Werben *nt*
ˈcourtyard *n* Hof *m*; (*walled-in*) Innenhof *m*
cousin [ˈkʌz·ɪn] *n* Cousin, Cousine *m, f*
cove [koʊv] *n* kleine Bucht
covenant [ˈkʌv·ə·nənt] *n* ① (*legal agreement*) vertragliches Abkommen ② REL
Bündnis *nt*
cover [ˈkʌv·ər] I. *n* ① (*covering*) Abde-
ckung *f*; (*sheath-like*) Hülle *f*; (*protective top*) Deckel *m*; (*for bed*) [Bett]de-
cke *f*; (*for furniture*) [Schon]bezug *m*;
■ **the ~s** *pl* das Bettzeug ② (*of a book*)
Einband *m*; (*of a magazine*) Titelseite *f*
③ (*shelter*) Schutz *m*; **to take ~** (*from
rain*) sich unterstellen; (*from danger*)
sich verstecken ④ MIL Deckung *f* II. *vt*
① (*put over*) bedecken; (*against dust
a.*) überziehen ② (*protect*) abdecken
③ (*hide*) verdecken ④ (*extend over*)
sich erstrecken über +*akk* ⑤ (*fig*) zuständig sein für +*akk* ⑤ (*travel*) fahren; **to ~
a lot of ground** eine große Strecke zurücklegen; (*make progress*) gut vorankommen; (*be wide-ranging*) sehr umfassend sein ⑥ (*deal with*) sich befassen
mit +*dat* ⑦ (*report on*) berichten über
+*akk* ⑧ (*insure*) versichern (**against/
for** gegen +*akk*) ⑨ MIL decken III. *vi*
(*substitute*) ■ **to ~ for sb** jdn vertreten
◆ **cover up** I. *vt* ① (*hide*) verdecken;
spot abdecken ② (*keep secret*) vertuschen II. *vi* alles vertuschen; ■ **to ~ up
for sb** jdn decken

coverage [ˈkʌv·ər·ɪdʒ] *n* ① (*reporting*)
Berichterstattung *f* ② (*dealing with*) Behandlung *f* ③ (*insurance*) Versicherungsschutz *m*
ˈcoveralls *npl* Overall *m*
ˈcover charge *n* (*in nightclub*) Eintritt *m*; (*in restaurant*) Kosten *pl* für das
Gedeck
covered [ˈkʌv·ərd] *adj* ① (*roofed*) über-
dacht; ~ **wagon** Planwagen *m* ② (*insured*) versichert
ˈcover girl *n* Covergirl *nt*
covering [ˈkʌv·ər·ɪŋ] *n* Bedeckung *f*,
Überzug *m*
ˈcover letter *n* Begleitschreiben *nt*
ˈcover story *n* Titelgeschichte *f*
covert [ˈkoʊ·vɜrt] *adj* verdeckt, geheim;
glance verstohlen
ˈcover-up *n* Vertuschung *f*
cow [kaʊ] *n* Kuh *f*
coward [ˈkaʊ·ərd] *n* Feigling *m*
cowardice [ˈkaʊ·ər·dɪs], **cowardliness**
[ˈkaʊ·ərd·li·nɪs] *n* Feigheit *f*
cowardly [ˈkaʊ·ərd·li] *adj* feige
ˈcowboy *n* Cowboy *m*
cower [ˈkaʊ·ər] *vi* kauern
ˈcowhide *n* Rindsleder *nt*
cowl [kaʊl] *n* Kapuze *f*
coworker [ˈkoʊ·wɜr·kər] *n* Mitarbei-
ter(in) *m(f)*
coxswain [ˈkɑk·sən] *n* Steuermann *m*
(*beim Rudern*)
coy [kɔɪ] *adj* ① (*pretending to be shy*)
geziert ② (*secretive*) geheimnistuerisch
coyote [kaɪˈoʊ·ti] *n* Kojote *m*
coziness [ˈkoʊ·zɪ·nɪs] *n* Gemütlichkeit *f*
cozy, cosy [ˈkoʊ·zi] I. *adj* ① gemütlich, behaglich; *atmosphere* heimelig
② (*pej*) bequem; ~ **deal** Kuhhandel *m*
II. *vi* <-ie-> ■ **to ~ up to sb/sth**
① (*snuggle up*) sich an jdn/etw an-
schmiegen ② (*fam: ingratiate oneself*)
mit jdm/etw einen Kuhhandel machen
CPA [ˌsi·pi·ˈeɪ] *n* ECON, FIN *abbrev of* **certified public accountant** Wirtschafts-
prüfer(in) *m(f)*
Cpl, Cpl., CPL. *n short for* **corporal**
crab¹ [kræb] *n* Krebs *m*
crab² [kræb] *vi* <-bb-> (*fam*) nörgeln

C

crabby ['kræb·i] *adj* (*fam*) mürrisch

crack [kræk] I. *n* ❶ (*fissure*) Riss *m*; (*narrow space*) Ritze *f* ❷ *of a breaking branch* Knacken *nt*; *of breaking ice, thunder* Krachen *nt* ❸ (*sharp blow*) Schlag *m* ❹ (*illegal drug*) Crack *nt o m* ❺ (*attempt*) Versuch *m* II. *vt* ❶ (*break*) **to ~ sth** einen Sprung in etw *akk* machen ❷ (*open*) **■ to ~ sth** ○ [*open*] etw aufbrechen; *bottle* aufmachen; *egg* aufschlagen; *nuts, safe* knacken ❸ (*hit*) **to ~ one's head open** sich den Kopf aufschlagen ❹ (*make noise*) **to ~ one's knuckles** mit den Fingern knacken; **to ~ a whip** mit einer Peitsche knallen ▶PHRASES: **to ~ a joke** einen Witz reißen III. *vi* ❶ (*break*) [zer]brechen, zerspringen; *lips, paint* aufspringen, rissig werden ❷ (*break down*) zusammenbrechen; *voice* versagen ❸ (*make noise*) *ice, thunder* krachen; *shot, whip* knallen

◆ **crack up** I. *vi* (*fam*) ❶ (*laugh*) lachen müssen ❷ (*have nervous breakdown*) zusammenbrechen; (*go crazy*) durchdrehen II. *vt* ❶ **it's not all it's ~ed up to be** es hält nicht alles, was es verspricht ❷ (*fam: amuse*) zum Lachen bringen

'crackdown *n* scharfes Vorgehen

cracked [krækt] *adj* rissig; *cup, glass* gesprungen; *lips* aufgesprungen

cracker ['kræk·ər] *n* ❶ Kräcker *m* ❷ Knallbonbon *nt*

crackle ['kræk·əl] I. *vi* knistern *a. fig*; *telephone line* knacken II. *n* (*on telephone line, radio*) Knacken *nt*; *of paper* Knistern *nt*; *of fire a.* Prasseln *nt*

crackling ['kræk·lɪŋ] *n* ❶ *see* **crackle** ❷ (*pork skin*) **■ ~s** *pl* [Braten]kruste *f*

'crackpot *n* (*fam*) Spinner(in) *m(f)*

cradle ['kreɪ·dəl] I. *n* ❶ Wiege *f* ❷ (*hanging platform*) Hängebühne *f* II. *vt* (*sanft*) halten; *sb's head* betten

craft [kræft] *n* ❶ <*pl* -> (*ship*) Schiff *nt*; (*boat*) Boot *nt* ❷ (*trade*) Handwerk *nt kein pl*; **■ ~s** *pl* Kunsthandwerk *nt kein pl*

'craftsman *n* gelernter Handwerker

crafty ['kræf·ti] *adj* schlau, gerissen

crag [kræg] *n* Felsmassiv *nt*

craggy ['kræg·i] *adj* zerklüftet; *features* markant

cram <-mm-> [kræm] I. *vt* stopfen II. *vi* büffeln, pauken

cramp [kræmp] I. *n* [Muskel]krampf *m* II. *vt* einengen

cramped [kræmpt] *adj* beengt

cranberry ['kræn·ber·i] *n* Kranichbeere *f*

crane [kreɪn] I. *n* ❶ (*device*) Kran *m* ❷ (*bird*) Kranich *m* II. *vt* **to ~ one's neck** den Hals recken

crank [kræŋk] I. *n* ❶ MECH Kurbel *f* ❷ (*fam: eccentric*) Spinner(in) *m(f)* II. *vt* **■ to ~ sth [up]** (*make louder*) *music, volume* aufdrehen

'crankshaft *n* Kurbelwelle *f*

cranky ['kræŋ·ki] *adj* (*fam*) mürrisch

cranny ['kræn·i] *n* Ritze *f*

crap [kræp] I. *vi* <-pp-> (*vulg*) kacken *vulg* II. *n usu sing* (*vulg*) Mist *m*

crash [kræʃ] I. *n* <*pl* -es> ❶ Unfall *m*; (*of plane*) Absturz *m* ❷ (*noise*) Krach *m kein pl* ❸ COMM Zusammenbruch *m* ❹ COMPUT Absturz *m* II. *vi* ❶ *driver, car* verunglücken; *plane* abstürzen ❷ (*collide with*) **■ to ~ into sb/sth** mit etw/jdm zusammenstoßen ❸ (*move noisily*) poltern; *door* knallen ❹ COMM *stock market* zusammenbrechen ❺ COMPUT abstürzen ❻ (*sl: sleep*) pennen *sl* III. *vt* ❶ (*damage in accident*) zu Bruch fahren; **to ~ a plane** eine Bruchlandung machen; (*deliberately*) einen Unfall/Absturz absichtlich verursachen ❷ (*fam*) **to ~ a party** uneingeladen zu einer Party kommen

'crash course *n* Intensivkurs *m*

'crash helmet *n* Sturzhelm *m*

crash 'landing *n* Bruchlandung *f*

crass [kræs] *adj* krass, grob; *behavior* derb

crate [kreɪt] *n* Kiste *f*; (*for bottles*) [Getränke]kasten *m*

crater ['kreɪ·tər] *n* Krater *m*; (*made by bomb*) Trichter *m*

crave [kreɪv] *vt* begehren

craving ['kreɪ·vɪŋ] *n* heftiges Verlangen (**for** nach +*dat*)

crawfish ['krɔ·fɪʃ] *n* Languste *f*

crawl [krɔl] I. *vi* ① (*on all fours*) krabbeln ② (*move slowly*) kriechen II. *n* ① (*slow pace*) **to move at a** ~ im Schneckentempo fahren ② (*swimming style*) Kraulen *nt*

crayfish ['kreɪ·fɪʃ] *n* Flusskrebs *m*

crayon ['kreɪ·ən] *n* Buntstift *m*

craze [kreɪz] *n* Mode[erscheinung] *f*, Fimmel *m pej*, Begeisterung *f* (**for** für +*akk*)

crazed [kreɪzd] *adj* wahnsinnig

crazy ['kreɪ·zi] *adj* verrückt (**about** nach +*dat*); **to drive sb** ~ jdn zum Wahnsinn treiben

creak [krik] *vi furniture* knarren; *door* quietschen

cream [krim] I. *n* ① FOOD Sahne *f*, Obers *nt* ÖSTERR ② (*cosmetic*) Creme *f* ③ (*color*) Creme *nt* ④ (*fig: the best*) Elite *f* II. *adj* cremefarben

cream 'cheese *n* [Doppelrahm]frischkäse *m*

creamy ['kri·mi] *adj* ① (*smooth*) cremig, sahnig ② (*off-white*) cremefarben

crease [kris] I. *n* ① [Bügel]falte *f* II. *vt* zerknittern III. *vi* knittern

create [kri·'eɪt] *vt* ① (*make*) erschaffen ② (*cause*) erzeugen; *confusion* stiften; *impression* erwecken; *sensation* erregen

creation [kri·'eɪ·ʃən] *n* ① (*making*) [Er]schaffung *f*; (*founding*) Gründung *f*; REL Schöpfung *f* ② (*product*) Produkt *nt*; FASHION Kreation *f*

creative [kri·'eɪ·tɪv] *adj* kreativ, schöpferisch

creator [kri·'eɪ·tər] *n* Schöpfer(in) *m(f)*

creature ['kri·tʃər] *n* Kreatur *f*, Wesen *nt*, Geschöpf *nt*

credentials [krɪ·'den·ʃəlz] *npl* ① (*documents*) Zeugnisse *pl* ② (*letter of recommendation*) Empfehlungsschreiben *nt sing*

credibility [ˌkred·ə·'bɪl·ɪ·ti] *n* Glaubwürdigkeit *f*

credible ['kred·ə·bəl] *adj* glaubwürdig

credit ['kred·ɪt] I. *n* ① (*recognition*) Anerkennung *f*; (*respect*) Achtung *f*; (*honor*) Ehre *f* ② COMM Kredit *m* ③ FIN Haben *nt* ④ FILM, TV ■ ~**s** *pl* Abspann *m* ⑤ UNIV Credit [Point] *m*, Leistungspunkt *m* II. *vt* ① (*believe*) glauben ② (*attribute*) zuschreiben ③ FIN gutschreiben

creditable ['kred·ɪ·tə·bəl] *adj* ehrenwert; *result* verdient

'credit card *n* Kreditkarte *f*

creditor ['kred·ɪ·tər] *n* Gläubiger(in) *m(f)*

'credit slip *n* Gutschrift *f*

credulous ['kredʒ·ə·ləs] *adj* (*form*) leichtgläubig

creed [krid] *n* Glaubensbekenntnis *nt*

creek [krik] *n* Bach *m*; (*tributary*) Nebenfluss *m*

creep [krip] I. *n* ① (*fam*) (*person*) Mistkerl *m* ② (*feeling*) ■ **the** ~ **s** *pl* das Gruseln *kein pl* II. *vi* <crept, crept> kriechen

♦ **creep up** *vi* ① (*increase steadily*) [an]steigen ② (*sneak up on*) sich anschleichen *a. fig* (**behind/on** an +*akk*)

creeper ['kri·pər] *n* BOT Kriechgewächs *nt*; (*up a wall*) Kletterpflanze *f*

creepy ['kri·pi] *adj* (*fam*) grus[e]lig, schaurig

creepy-'crawly [-'krɔ·li] *n* (*fam*) Krabbeltier *nt*

cremate ['kri·meɪt] *vt* einäschern

cremation [krɪ·'meɪ·ʃən] *n* Einäscherung *f*

crematorium <*pl* -s> [ˌkri·mə·'tɔr·i·əm], **crematory** ['kri·mə·tɔr·i] *n* Krematorium *nt*

crêpe [kreɪp] *n* ① FOOD Crêpe *f* ② (*fabric*) Krepp *m*

crept [krept] *pt, pp of* **creep**

crescent ['kres·ənt] *n* ① (*moon*) Mondsichel *f* ② halbkreisförmige Straße

crest [krest] *n* ① (*peak*) Kamm *m* ② *of rooster* Kamm *m*; *of bird* Schopf *m* ③ (*insignia*) Emblem *nt*

'crestfallen *adj* niedergeschlagen

Crete [krit] *n* Kreta *nt*

C

cretin ['kri·tən] n (pej fam) Schwachkopf m

crevasse [krə·'væs] n Gletscherspalte f

crevice ['krev·ɪs] n Spalte f

crew [kru] n ❶ AVIAT, NAUT Crew f, Besatzung f ❷ (fam: gang) Bande f

crib [krɪb] n ❶ Kinderbett nt, Gitterbett nt ❷ REL Krippe f

'crib death n see **sudden infant death syndrome**

crib sheet n SCH (fam) Spickzettel m, Schummler m ÖSTERR

cricket¹ ['krɪk·ɪt] n ZOOL Grille f

cricket² ['krɪk·ɪt] n SPORT Kricket nt

crime [kraɪm] n ❶ (illegal act) Verbrechen nt ❷ (criminality) Kriminalität f

criminal ['krɪm·ə·nəl] I. n Verbrecher(in) m(f) II. adj ❶ verbrecherisch; behavior kriminell; offense strafbar ❷ (fig) schändlich

criminality [ˌkrɪm·ə·'næl·ɪ·ti] n Kriminalität f

crimson ['krɪm·zən] I. n Purpur[rot] nt II. adj purpurrot

cringe [krɪndʒ] vi ❶ (cower) sich ducken ❷ (shiver) schaudern

crinkle ['krɪŋ·kəl] I. vt [zer]knittern II. vi dress, paper knittern; face, skin [Lach]fältchen bekommen

crinkly ['krɪŋ·kli] adj ❶ paper zerknittert; skin knittrig ❷ (wavy and curly) gekräuselt

cripple ['krɪp·əl] I. n Krüppel m II. vt person zum Krüppel machen; thing gefechtsunfähig machen; (fig) lahmlegen

crippling ['krɪp·əl·ɪŋ] adj debts erdrückend; pain lähmend

crisis <pl -ses> ['kraɪ·sɪs] n Krise f

crisp [krɪsp] I. adj ❶ (hard and brittle) knusprig; snow knirschend ❷ apple, lettuce knackig ❸ paper, tablecloth steif; banknote druckfrisch ❹ style präzise; reply knapp II. n ❶ burnt to a ~ verkohlt ❷ FOOD Obstdessert nt (mit Streuseln überbacken)

'crispbread n Knäckebrot nt

'crisscross I. vt durchqueren II. vi sich kreuzen

criterion <pl -ria> [kraɪ·'tɪr·i·ən] n Kriterium nt

critic ['krɪt·ɪk] n Kritiker(in) m(f)

critical ['krɪt·ɪ·kəl] adj ❶ (judgmental) kritisch ❷ (crucial) entscheidend ❸ MED condition kritisch

criticism ['krɪt·ɪ·sɪz·əm] n Kritik f

criticize ['krɪt·ɪ·saɪz] vt, vi kritisch beurteilen, kritisieren

critter ['krɪt·ər] n (fam: creature) Lebewesen nt, Kreatur f

croak [kroʊk] vi ❶ frog quaken; person krächzen ❷ (sl: die) abkratzen sl

Croatia [kroʊ·'eɪ·ʃə] n Kroatien nt

crochet [kroʊ·'ʃeɪ] vt, vi häkeln

crockery ['krak·ə·ri] n Geschirr nt

crocodile <pl -> ['krak·ə·daɪl] n Krokodil nt

crocus ['kroʊ·kəs] n Krokus m

croissant [krwa·'saŋ] n Croissant nt

crony ['kroʊ·ni] adj (pej fam) Spießgeselle m, Haberer m ÖSTERR

crook [krʊk] I. n ❶ (fam: rogue) Gauner m ❷ (staff) Hirtenstab m II. vt arm beugen; finger krümmen

crooked ['krʊk·ɪd] adj ❶ (fam: dishonest) unehrlich; (illegal) krumm; politician, cop korrupt ❷ (not straight) krumm; grin, teeth schief

crop [krap] I. n ❶ (plant) Feldfrucht f; (harvest) Ernte f ❷ (hair cut) Kurzhaarschnitt m ❸ (whip) Reitgerte f II. vt <-pp-> ❶ hair kurz schneiden ❷ PHOT zurechtschneiden

♦ crop up vi (fam) auftauchen

croquet [kroʊ·'keɪ] n Krocket[spiel] nt

cross [krɔs] I. n ❶ Kreuz nt ❷ (hybrid) Kreuzung f; (fig) Mittelding nt (**between** zwischen +dat) II. vt ❶ (go over) überqueren; bridge, road also gehen über; (person) Flanke f II. vt ❶ (go over) überqueren; bridge, road also gehen über; border passieren; threshold überschreiten; (traverse) durchqueren ❷ (in soccer) flanken ❸ (place crosswise) [über]kreuzen; arms verschränken; legs übereinanderschlagen ❹ REL ■ to ~ oneself sich bekreuz[ig]en ❺ (breed) kreuzen ▶PHRASES: **to keep one's**

<u>fingers</u> ~ed [for sb] [jdm] die Daumen drücken; to ~ one's <u>mind</u> jdm einfallen III. vi ❶ (intersect) sich kreuzen ❷ (traverse a road) die Straße überqueren; (on foot) über die Straße gehen

◆ **cross off** vt streichen [von]

◆ **cross out** vt ausstreichen, [durch]streichen

◆ **cross over** vi hinübergehen, überqueren; (on boat) übersetzen

'**crossbar** n SPORT Querlatte f; of bicycle [Quer]stange f

'**crossbow** n Armbrust f

'**crossbreed** n ZOOL Kreuzung f; (half-breed) Mischling m

'**crosscheck** vt nachprüfen

cross-'**country** I. adj ~ race Geländerennen nt; ~ skiing Langlauf m II. adv quer durchs Land; (through countryside) querfeldein

cross-exami'**nation** n Kreuzverhör nt

cross-ex'**amine** vt ins Kreuzverhör nehmen a. fig

'**cross-eyed** adj schielend; ■ to be ~ schielen

'**crossfire** n Kreuzfeuer nt; to be caught in the ~ ins Kreuzfeuer geraten a. fig

crossing ['krɔ·sɪŋ] n ❶ (place to cross) Übergang m; (crossroads) [Straßen]kreuzung f ❷ (journey) Überfahrt f

cross-'**legged** [ˌkrɔs·'leg·əd] adv to sit ~ im Schneidersitz [da]sitzen

cross-'**reference** n Querverweis m

'**crossroads** <pl -> n Kreuzung f; (fig) Wendepunkt m

cross-'**section** n Querschnitt m

'**crosswalk** n Fußgängerübergang m

'**crossword**, '**crossword puzzle** n Kreuzworträtsel nt

crotch [krɑtʃ] n Unterleib m; of pants Schritt m

crotchety ['krɑtʃ·ə·ti] adj (fam) quengelig

crouch [kraʊtʃ] I. n usu sing Hocke f II. vi sich kauern

crow[1] [kroʊ] n Krähe f ▶PHRASES: as the ~ **flies** [in der] Luftlinie

crow[2] [kroʊ] vi <crowed, crowed> ❶ (cry) rooster krähen ❷ (express happiness) jauchzen; (gloatingly) triumphieren

'**crowbar** n Brecheisen nt

crowd [kraʊd] I. n ❶ (throng) [Menschen]menge f; SPORT, MUS Zuschauermenge f ❷ (fam: clique) Clique f II. vt ❶ (fill) stadium füllen; streets bevölkern ❷ (fam: pressure) [be]drängen III. vi ■to ~ into sth sich in etw akk hineindrängen

◆ **crowd out** vt herausdrängen

crowded ['kraʊ·dɪd] adj überfüllt; schedule übervoll

crown [kraʊn] I. n ❶ (of monarch) Krone f ❷ (top of head) Scheitel m; (of tooth, tree, hat) Krone f II. vt krönen; teeth überkronen

crown 'jewels npl Kronjuwelen pl

crown 'prince n Kronprinz m

'**crow's feet** npl (wrinkles) Krähenfüße pl

crucial ['kru·ʃəl] adj (decisive) entscheidend (to für +akk); (critical) kritisch; (very important) äußerst wichtig

crucible ['kru·sɪ·bəl] n TECH Schmelztiegel m

crucifix ['kru·sɪ·fɪks] n Kruzifix nt

crucifixion [ˌkru·sɪ·'fɪk·ʃən] n Kreuzigung f

crucify ['kru·sɪ·faɪ] vt kreuzigen; (fig fam) verreißen

crude [krud] I. adj ❶ (rudimentary) primitiv ❷ (vulgar) derb ❸ (unprocessed) roh; ~ **oil** Rohöl nt II. n Rohöl nt

cruel <-l-> ['kru·əl] adj (unkind) grausam; remark gemein ❷ (harsh) hart; disappointment schrecklich

cruelty ['kru·əl·ti] n Grausamkeit f; ~ **to animals** Tierquälerei f; ~ **to children** Kindesmisshandlung f

cruise [kruz] I. n Kreuzfahrt f II. vi ❶ (take a cruise) eine Kreuzfahrt machen; (ship) kreuzen ❷ (go at constant speed) airplane [mit Reisegeschwindigkeit] fliegen; car [konstante Geschwindigkeit] fahren ❸ (fam: drive around aimlessly) herumfahren

'**cruise control** n Temporegler m

cruiser ['kruːzər] n ❶ (*warship*) Kreuzer m ❷ (*pleasure boat*) Motoryacht f ❸ *see* **squad car**

'cruise ship n Kreuzfahrtschiff nt

crumb [krʌm] n ❶ Krümel m, Brösel m ÖSTERR a. nt; *of bread a.* Krume f ❷ (*fig*) **a ~ of comfort** ein kleiner Trost

crumble ['krʌm·bəl] I. vt zerkrümeln, zerbröckeln II. vi ❶ (*disintegrate*) zerbröckeln ❷ (*fig*) *opposition, relationship* [allmählich] zerbrechen; *resistance* schwinden; *support* abbröckeln

crummy ['krʌm·i] adj (*fam*) mies; *house* schäbig

crumple ['krʌm·pəl] I. vt zerknittern; *paper* zerknüllen, zusammenknüllen II. vi ❶ (*become wrinkled*) sich verziehen ❷ (*collapse*) zusammenbrechen

crunch [krʌntʃ] I. n ❶ *usu sing* (*noise*) Knirschen nt kein pl ❷ (*fam: difficult situation*) Krise f II. vt FOOD geräuschvoll verzehren III. vi *gravel, snow* knirschen

'crunch time n **it's ~** (*fam*) jetzt kommt es drauf an!

crunchy ['krʌn·tʃi] adj *apple* knackig; *cereal, toast* knusprig; *snow* verharscht

crusade [kruː·'seɪd] n Kreuzzug m; ■the C~s pl HIST die Kreuzzüge pl

crush [krʌʃ] I. vt ❶ (*compress*) zusammendrücken; (*causing serious damage*) zerquetschen; MED [sich] etw quetschen ❷ FOOD zerdrücken; *grapes* zerstampfen; *ice* zerstoßen ❸ (*defeat*) vernichten; *hopes* zunichtemachen; *rebellion* niederschlagen; *resistance* zerschlagen II. n ❶ (*crowd*) Gedränge nt ❷ (*drink*) Fruchtsaft m mit zerstoßenem Eis ❸ (*infatuation*) Schwarm m; **to have a ~ on sb** in jdn verknallt sein

crushing ['krʌʃ·ɪŋ] adj schrecklich; *blow* hart; *defeat* vernichtend

crust [krʌst] n ❶ Kruste f; (*pastry shell*) Boden m

crustacean [krʌ·'steɪ·ʃən] n Krustentier nt

crusty ['krʌs·ti] adj *bread* knusprig

crutch [krʌtʃ] n ❶ MED Krücke f ❷ (*fig*) Stütze f, Halt m

crux [krʌks] n Kernfrage f

cry <-ie-> [kraɪ] I. n ❶ (*loud utterance*) Schrei m; (*shout a.*) Ruf m; **~ for help** Hilferuf m ❷ ZOOL, ORN Schreien nt kein pl, Geschrei nt kein pl II. vi weinen; *baby* schreien III. vt (*exclaim*) rufen
◆**cry out** I. vi ❶ (*shout*) aufschreien ❷ (*fig: need*) ■**to be ~ing out for sth** nach etw dat schreien II. vt rufen; (*scream*) schreien

crypt [krɪpt] n Krypta f

cryptic ['krɪp·tɪk] adj rätselhaft; *message a.* geheimnisvoll

crystal ['krɪs·təl] n ❶ CHEM Kristall m ❷ (*glass*) Kristallglas nt ❸ (*on a watch, clock*) [Uhr]glas nt

crystal 'ball n Kristallkugel f

crystal 'clear adj ❶ (*transparent*) *water* kristallklar ❷ (*obvious*) glasklar; **she made it ~ that ...** sie stellte unmissverständlich klar, dass ...

crystallize ['krɪs·tə·laɪz] I. vi CHEM kristallisieren; (*fig*) *feelings* fassbar werden II. vt (*fig*) herausbilden

CST [ˌsiː·es·'ti] n *abbrev of* **Central Standard Time** Zentral Standardzeit f

CT *abbrev of* **Connecticut**

cub [kʌb] n ❶ ZOOL Junge[s] nt ❷ (*Cub Scout*) Wölfling m

Cuba ['kjuː·bə] n Kuba nt

cubbyhole ['kʌb·i·hoʊl] n Kämmerchen nt

cube [kjub] I. n ❶ (*shape*) Würfel m ❷ MATH Kubikzahl f II. vt ❶ FOOD in Würfel schneiden ❷ MATH hoch drei nehmen; **2 ~d equals 8** 2 hoch 3 ist 8

cubic ['kjuː·bɪk] adj MATH Kubik-

cubicle ['kjuː·bɪ·kəl] n (*for working*) Arbeitsnische f

cuckoo ['kuː·ku] I. n ORN Kuckuck m II. adj (*fam*) übergeschnappt

'cuckoo clock n Kuckucksuhr f

cucumber ['kjuː·kʌm·bər] n [Salat]gurke f

cuddle ['kʌd·əl] I. n [liebevolle] Umarmung II. vt liebkosen III. vi kuscheln

cuddly ['kʌd·əl·i] adj knudd[el]ig

cue[1] [kju] n (*billiards*) Queue nt ÖSTERR a. m, Billardstock m

cue² [kju] *n* THEAT Stichwort *nt*; *(fig a.)* Zeichen *nt*

cuff¹ [kʌf] *n* ❶ *(of sleeve)* Manschette *f* ❷ *(of pants leg)* [Hosen]aufschlag *m* ❸ *(fam)* ■~s *pl* Handschellen *pl*
▸ PHRASES: **off the** ~ aus dem Stegreif

cuff² [kʌf] *vt* ■**to** ~ **sb** *(strike)* jdm einen Klaps geben

'cuff link *n* Manschettenknopf *m*

cuisine [kwɪˈzin] *n* Küche *f*

cul-de-sac <*pl* -s *or* culs-de-sac> [ˈkʌl·dəˌsæk] *n* Sackgasse *f a. fig*

culinary [ˈkʌl·əˌner·i] *adj* kulinarisch

cull [kʌl] I. *vt* *(kill)* erlegen *(um den Bestand zu reduzieren)* II. *n* Abschlachten *nt kein pl; (fig)* Abschuss *m kein pl*

culminate [ˈkʌl·mɪ·neɪt] *vi* gipfeln *(in in +dat)*

culmination [ˌkʌl·mɪ·ˈneɪ·ʃən] *n* Höhepunkt *m*

culpable [ˈkʌl·pə·bəl] *adj* *(form)* schuldig

culprit [ˈkʌl·prɪt] *n* Schuldige(r) *f(m); (hum)* Missetäter(in) *m(f)*

cult [kʌlt] *n* Kult *m*

cultivate [ˈkʌl·tə·veɪt] *vt* ❶ *crops* anbauen; *land* bestellen ❷ *(fig form)* entwickeln; *accent, contacts* pflegen

cultivated [ˈkʌl·təˈveɪ·tɪd] *adj* ❶ *field* bestellt; *land, soil a.* bebaut ❷ *(fig)* kultiviert

cultivation [ˌkʌl·təˈveɪ·ʃən] *n of crops, vegetables* Anbau *m; of land* Bebauung *m*, Bestellung *m*

cultivator [ˈkʌl·tʃər·əl] *n* Grubber *m*

cultural [ˈkʌl·tʃər·əl] *adj* kulturell

culture [ˈkʌl·tʃər] *n* Kultur *f*

cultured [ˈkʌl·tʃərd] *adj* kultiviert

cumbersome [ˈkʌm·bər·səm] *adj luggage* unhandlich; *clothing* unbequem

cumin [ˈkju·mɪn] *n* Kreuzkümmel *m*

cumulative [ˈkju·mjə·lə·tɪv] *adj* kumulativ

cunning [ˈkʌn·ɪŋ] I. *adj (ingenious) idea* clever, raffiniert; *person a.* schlau, gerissen II. *n* Cleverness *f*, Gerissenheit *f*

cup [kʌp] *n* ❶ *(container)* Tasse *f*; **a ~ of coffee/tea** eine Tasse Kaffee/Tee; *(made of paper, plastic)* Becher *m*

❷ SPORT Pokal *m* ❸ *(part of bra)* Körbchen *nt; (size)* Körbchengröße *f*

cupboard [ˈkʌb·ərd] *n* Schrank *m*, Kasten *m* ÖSTERR

curator [ˈkjʊ·reɪ·tər] *n* Konservator(in) *m(f)*

curb [kɜrb] I. *vt* zügeln; *expenditures* senken; *inflation* bremsen II. *n* ❶ *(beside road)* Randstein *m* ❷ *(restraint)* Beschränkung *f*

curd [kɜrd] *n* Quark *m*

curdle [ˈkɜr·dəl] I. *vi* gerinnen II. *vt* gerinnen lassen

cure [kjʊr] I. *vt* ❶ *(heal)* heilen *a. fig* *(of* von *+dat); cancer* besiegen ❷ FOOD haltbar machen; *(by smoking)* räuchern; *(by salting)* pökeln; *(by drying)* trocknen II. *n (remedy)* [Heil]mittel *nt* *(for* gegen *+akk); (fig: solution)* Lösung *f*

curfew [ˈkɜr·fju] *n* Ausgangssperre *f*

curiosity [ˌkjʊr·ɪ·ˈas·ɪ·ti] *n* ❶ *(feeling)* Neugier[de] *f* ❷ *(object)* Kuriosität *f*

curious [ˈkjʊr·i·əs] *adj* ❶ *(inquisitive)* neugierig *(about* auf *+akk)* ❷ *(peculiar)* seltsam, merkwürdig

curl [kɜrl] I. *n* ❶ *(of hair)* Locke *f* ❷ *(spiral)* Kringel *m* II. *vi hair* sich locken III. *vt* ❶ **to** ~ **one's hair** sich *dat* Locken drehen ❷ *lips, leaves* kräuseln

curler [ˈkɜr·lər] *n* Lockenwickler *m*

curling [ˈkɜr·lɪŋ] *n* SPORT Curling *nt*, Eisstockschießen *nt*

'curling iron *npl* Lockenstab *m*

curly [ˈkɜr·li] *adj leaves* gewellt, gekräuselt; *hair a.* lockig

currency [ˈkɜr·ən·si] *n* ❶ *(money)* Währung *f*; [**foreign**] ~ Devisen *pl* ❷ *(acceptance)* [weite] Verbreitung *f*

current [ˈkɜr·ənt] I. *adj* gegenwärtig; *issue* aktuell II. *n* ❶ *(of air, water)* Strömung *f* ❷ ELEC Strom *m*

current af'fairs, current e'vents *npl* POL Zeitgeschehen *nt kein pl*

currently [ˈkɜr·ənt·li] *adv* zurzeit

curriculum vitae <*pl* -s *or* curricula vitae> [ˈ·viˌtaɪ] *n* Lebenslauf *m*

curry [ˈkɜr·i] *n* FOOD Curry *nt o m*

curse [kɜrs] I. *vi* fluchen II. *vt* ❶ *(swear*

C

at) verfluchen ②(put under spell) verwünschen; ■to be ~d with sth mit etw dat geschlagen sein III. n Fluch m; to put a ~ on sb jdn verwünschen

cursor ['kɜr·sər] n COMPUT Cursor m

cursory ['kɜr·sə·ri] adj (form) glance flüchtig; examination oberflächlich

curt [kɜrt] adj (pej) schroff, barsch

curtail [kɜr·'teɪl] vt ①(reduce) kürzen ②(shorten) verkürzen

curtain ['kɜr·tən] n ①Vorhang m, Gardine f ②(fig) Schleier m, Vorhang m

curtsy, curtsey ['kɜrt·si] I. vi knicksen (to vor +dat) II. n [Hof]knicks m

curvature ['kɜr·və·tʃər] n Krümmung f; ~ of the spine Rückgratverkrümmung f

curve [kɜrv] I. n ①of a figure, vase Rundung f, Wölbung f; of a road Kurve f; of a river Bogen m ②MATH Kurve f II. vi river, road eine Kurve machen; line eine Kurve beschreiben III. vt biegen

cushion ['kʊʃ·ən] I. n ①(pillow) Kissen nt, Polster m ÖSTERR ②(fig: buffer) Polster nt o ÖSTERR a. m II. vt dämpfen a. fig

cushy ['kʊʃ·i] adj (pej fam) bequem; job ruhig

custard ['kʌs·tərd] n (dessert) ≈ Vanillepudding m

custodial [kʌs·'toʊ·di·əl] adj ~ sentence Freiheitsstrafe f

custodian [kʌs·'toʊ·di·ən] n ①(janitor) Hausmeister(in) m(f) ②(keeper) Aufseher(in) m(f); of valuables Hüter(in) m(f)

custody ['kʌs·tə·di] n ①(guardianship) Obhut f; LAW Sorgerecht nt (of für +akk) ②(detention) Haft f; to keep sb in ~ jdn in Gewahrsam halten; to take sb into ~ jdn verhaften

custom ['kʌs·təm] I. n ①(tradition) Brauch m, Sitte f ②(habit) Gewohnheit f II. adj attr maßgeschneidert

customary ['kʌs·tə·mer·i] adj üblich

'custom-built adj spezialangefertigt

customer ['kʌs·tə·mər] n ①(buyer) Kunde, -in m, f ②(fam: person) Typ m

customer 'service n Kundendienst m

customize ['kʌs·tə·maɪz] vt nach Kundenwünschen anfertigen

custom-'made adj auf den Kunden zugeschnitten; shirt maßgeschneidert; shoes maßgefertigt

customs ['kʌs·təmz] npl Zoll m

'customs declaration n Zollerklärung f

'customs duties npl Zollabgaben pl

'customs officer, 'customs official n Zollbeamte(r), -in m, f

cut [kʌt] I. n ①(act) Schnitt m ②of meat Stück nt ③(fit) [Zu]schnitt m; of shirt, pants Schnitt m ④(wound) Schnittwunde f ⑤(decrease) Senkung f; ~ in production Produktionseinschränkung f; ~ in staff Personalabbau m ⑥(less spending) ■~s pl Kürzungen pl II. adj ①(sliced) bread [auf]geschnitten; ~ flowers Schnittblumen pl ②(fitted) glass, gemstones geschliffen III. interj FILM ~! Schnitt! IV. vt <-tt-, cut, cut> ①(slice) schneiden; bread aufschneiden; slice of bread abschneiden; to ~ sth in[to] several pieces etw in mehrere Teile zerschneiden; to ~ open aufschneiden ②(sever) durchschneiden ③(trim) [ab]schneiden; hair, fingernails schneiden; grass mähen; to have [or get] one's hair ~ sich dat die Haare schneiden lassen ④(decrease) costs senken; prices herabsetzen; overtime reduzieren; wages kürzen ⑤film kürzen; scene herausschneiden; to ~ sb short jdn unterbrechen ⑥CARDS abheben V. vi <-tt-, cut, cut> ①(slice) knife schneiden ②(slice easily) material sich schneiden lassen

◆**cut away** vt wegschneiden

◆**cut back** I. vt ①FIN kürzen; production zurückschrauben ②HORT zurückschneiden II. vi ■to ~ back on sth etw kürzen; on spending die Ausgaben reduzieren

◆**cut down** I. vt ①(fell) tree umhauen ②(reduce) einschränken; workforce abbauen; production zurückfahren ③(abridge) kürzen II. vi ■to ~ down on sth smoking, spending etw einschränken

◆cut in I. vi ❶ (interrupt) unterbrechen ❷ AUTO einscheren; ■ to ~ in in front of sb jdn schneiden ❸ (jump line) sich vordräng[l]n; ■ to ~ in on [or in front of] sb sich vor jdn drängeln ❹ (activate) sich einschalten II. vt ❶ (share with) jdn [am Gewinn] beteiligen

◆cut off vt ❶ (remove) abschneiden; ■ to ~ sth off [of] sth etw von etw dat abschneiden ❷ (interrupt) unterbrechen ❸ (disconnect) unterbinden; electricity abstellen; gas supply abdrehen; phone conversation unterbrechen ❹ (isolate) abschneiden; ■ to ~ oneself off sich zurückziehen

◆cut out I. vt ❶ (excise) herausschneiden; (from paper) ausschneiden ❷ (delete) streichen ❸ (fam: desist) aufhören mit; ~ it out! [or that] hör auf damit! ❹ (disinherit) ■ to ~ sb out of one's will jdn aus seinem Testament streichen ▸PHRASES: to have one's <u>work</u> ~ out for one alle Hände voll zu tun haben; to be ~ <u>out</u> for sth für etw akk geeignet sein II. vi ❶ (stop operating) sich ausschalten; plane's engine aussetzen ❷ AUTO ausscheren

◆cut up vt (slice) zerschneiden; food for a child klein schneiden

cut-and-'dried adj ❶ (fixed) abgemacht; decision klar ❷ (routine) eindeutig

cutback ['kʌt·bæk] n Kürzung f

cute <-r, -st> [kjut] adj ❶ (sweet) süß, niedlich ❷ (clever) schlau

cuticle ['kju·tə·kəl] n Nagelhaut f

cutlery ['kʌt·lə·ri] n Besteck nt

cutlet ['kʌt·lɪt] n ❶ (meat) Kotelett nt ❷ (patty) Frikadelle f

cutoff ['kʌt·ɔf] n ❶ (limit) Obergrenze f ❷ (stop) Beendigung f; ~ date Endtermin m

'cutoffs npl abgeschnittene Jeans f

cutout ['kʌt·aʊt] n ❶ (shape) Ausschneidefigur f ❷ (stereotype) cardboard ~ [Reklame]puppe f ❸ (switch) Unterbrecher m

'cut-price adj goods Billig-; clothing herabgesetzt

cutter ['kʌt·ər] n ❶ (tool) Schneider m ❷ (person) [Zu]schneider(in) m(f); FILM Cutter(in) m(f)

'cutthroat adj competition, pricing gnadenlos

cutting ['kʌt·ɪŋ] I. n HORT Ableger m II. adj ❶ (that cuts) tool schneidend ❷ (abrasive) comment scharf; remark bissig

cutting 'edge I. n ❶ (blade) Schneide f ❷ (latest stage) ■ to be at the ~ an vorderster Front stehen II. adj attr supermodern, Hightech-

cyanide ['saɪ·ə·naɪd] n Zyanid nt

cybernetics [ˌsaɪ·bər'neṭ·ɪks] n + sing vb Kybernetik f

cyberspace ['saɪ·bər·speɪs] n Cyberspace m

cycle¹ ['saɪ·kəl] short for bicycle I. n [Fahr]rad nt II. vi Rad fahren

cycle² ['saɪ·kəl] n Zyklus m; of washing machine Arbeitsgang m

cyclist ['saɪ·klɪst] n Radfahrer(in) m(f)

cyclone ['saɪ·kloʊn] n METEO Zyklon m

cygnet ['sɪg·nɪt] n junger Schwan

cylinder ['sɪl·ɪn·dər] n ❶ AUTO, MATH Zylinder m ❷ TECH Walze f

cylindrical [sɪ'lɪn·drɪ·kəl] adj zylindrisch

cymbal ['sɪm·bəl] n ■ ~s Becken nt

cynic ['sɪn·ɪk] n Zyniker(in) m(f)

cynical ['sɪn·ɪ·kəl] adj zynisch

cynicism ['sɪn·ɪ·sɪz·əm] n Zynismus m

cypher n see cipher

cypress ['saɪ·prəs] n Zypresse f

Cyprus ['saɪ·prəs] n Zypern nt

cyst [sɪst] n MED Zyste f

cystitis [sɪ'staɪ·ṭɪs] n Blasenentzündung f

czar [zar] n Zar m

czarina [zɑ·'ri·nə] n Zarin f

Czech [tʃek] I. n ❶ (person) Tscheche, -in m, f ❷ (language) Tschechisch nt II. adj tschechisch

Czech Re'public n ■ the ~ die Tschechische Republik

Dd

D

D <pl -'s>, **d** <pl -'s> [di:] n ① (letter) D nt, d nt; **~ as in Delta** D wie Dora ② MUS D nt, d nt ③ (school grade) ≈ Vier f

DA [ˌdiˈeɪ] n LAW abbrev of **district attorney**

dab [dæb] vt, vi <-bb-> betupfen

dabble ['dæb·əl] vi dilettieren; ■**to ~ in** [or **with**] **sth** sich nebenbei mit etw dat beschäftigen

dad [dæd] n (fam) Papa m

daddy ['dæd·i] n (fam) Vati m, Papi m

daddy 'longlegs <pl -> n (fam) Weberknecht m

daffodil ['dæf·ə·dɪl] n Osterglocke f

daffy ['dæf·i] adj (fam) doof pej sl, blöd fam, bescheuert sl

dagger ['dæg·ər] n Dolch m

daily ['deɪ·li] I. adj, adv täglich II. n Tageszeitung f

dainty ['deɪn·ti] adj fein

dairy ['der·i] n ① (company) Molkerei f; **~ products** Molkereiprodukte pl ② (farm) Milchbetrieb m; **~ farmer** Milchbauer, Milchbäuerin m, f

daisy ['deɪ·zi] n Gänseblümchen nt

dam [dæm] n [Stau]damm m II. vt <-mm-> stauen

damage ['dæm·ɪdʒ] I. vt ■**to ~ sth** ① (wreck) vehicle etw [be]schädigen ② (blemish) reputation etw dat schaden II. n Schaden m

damn [dæm] (fam) I. interj (in anger) ■**~** [it]! verdammt [noch mal]! II. adj ① (cursed) Scheiß- ② (emph: extreme) verdammt; **to be a ~ sight better** entschieden besser sein III. vt ① (curse) verfluchen; **~ you!** hol dich der Teufel! ② (condemn) verurteilen IV. adv (vulg) verdammt V. n **to not give a ~ about sb/sth** sich nicht den Teufel um jdn/ etw scheren fam

damnation [dæmˈneɪ·ʃən] I. n Verdammnis f II. interj verdammt!

damned [dæmd] I. adj (vulg) ① (cursed) Scheiß- ② (emph: extreme) verdammt II. adv (vulg) verdammt

damning ['dæm·ɪŋ] adj evidence erdrückend; report belastend

damp [dæmp] I. adj feucht II. n Feuchtigkeit f

dance [dæns] I. vt, vi tanzen a. fig II. n Tanz m

'dance music n Tanzmusik f

dancer ['dæn·sər] n Tänzer(in) m(f)

dancing ['dæn·sɪŋ] n Tanzen nt

dandelion ['dæn·də·laɪ·ən] n Löwenzahn m

dandruff ['dæn·drəf] n [Kopf]schuppen pl

Dane [deɪn] n Däne, -in m, f

danger ['deɪn·dʒər] n Gefahr f

dangerous ['deɪn·dʒər·əs] adj gefährlich

dangle ['dæŋ·gəl] I. vi herabhängen; earrings baumeln (**from** an +dat) II. vt ① (swing) **to ~ one's feet** mit den Füßen baumeln ② (tempt with) ■**to ~ sth in front of sb** jdm etw [verlockend] in Aussicht stellen

Danish ['deɪ·nɪʃ] I. n <pl -es> ① (language) Dänisch nt ② (cake) see **Danish pastry** II. adj dänisch

Danish 'pastry n Blätterteiggebäck nt

dank [dæŋk] adj nasskalt

Danube ['dæn·jub] n **the ~** die Donau

dappled ['dæp·əld] adj horse scheckig; light gesprenkelt

dare [der] I. vt herausfordern; **I ~ you!** trau dich! II. vi sich trauen; ■**to ~ to** [to] **do sth** es wagen, etw zu tun ►PHRASES: **don't you ~**! untersteh dich!; **I ~ say** (supposing) ich nehme an; (confirming) das glaube ich gern III. n Mutprobe f

'daredevil (fam) I. n Draufgänger(in) m(f) II. adj tollkühn; stunt, tactics halsbrecherisch

daring ['der·ɪŋ] I. *adj person* kühn, wagemutig; *action* waghalsig II. *n* Kühnheit *f*

dark [dɑrk] I. *adj* ❶ (*unlit*) dunkel, finster; (*gloomy*) düster ❷ (*in color*) dunkel ❸ (*fig*) *period* dunkel; *look* finster II. *n* ■ **the** ~ die Dunkelheit; **after** ~ nach Einbruch der Dunkelheit ▶PHRASES: **to keep sb in the** ~ jdn im Dunkeln lassen

'**Dark Ages** *npl* HIST ■ **the** ~ das frühe Mittelalter

darken ['dɑr·kən] I. *vi* ❶ *sky* dunkel werden ❷ *face, mood* sich verdüstern II. *vt* verdunkeln; *room* abdunkeln

darkness ['dɑrk·nɪs] *n* ❶ (*no light*) Dunkelheit *f* ❷ (*night*) Finsternis *f*

'**darkroom** *n* Dunkelkammer *f*

darling ['dɑr·lɪŋ] I. *n* Liebling *m*, Schatz *m*, Schätzchen *nt* II. *adj* entzückend

darn[1] [dɑrn] I. *vt* stopfen II. *n* gestopfte Stelle

darn[2] [dɑrn] *interj* (*euph*) *see* **damn**

dart [dɑrt] I. *n* ❶ (*weapon*) Pfeil *m* ❷ SPORT Wurfpfeil *m*; ~ **s** + *sing vb* (*game*) Darts *nt* II. *vi* flitzen

'**dartboard** *n* Dartscheibe *f*

dash [dæʃ] I. *n* <*pl* -**es**> ❶ (*rush*) Hetze *f*; **to make a** ~ **for the door** zur Tür stürzen ❷ SPORT Kurzstreckenlauf *m* ❸ (*little bit*) ■ **a** ~ [**of**] ein kleiner Zusatz ❹ (*punctuation*) Gedankenstrich *m* II. *vi* (*hurry*) sausen; **I've got to** ~ ich muss fort III. *vt* ❶ (*strike forcefully*) schleudern ❷ (*destroy*) *hopes* zunichtemachen

'**dashboard** *n* Armaturenbrett *nt*

dashing ['dæʃ·ɪŋ] *adj* schneidig

data ['deɪ·tə] *npl* + *sing/pl vb* Daten *pl*

'**database** *n* Datenbank *f*

data 'processing *n* Datenverarbeitung *f*

date[1] [deɪt] I. *n* ❶ (*by calendar*) Datum *nt*; **out of** ~ überholt; **up to** ~ *technology* auf dem neuesten Stand; *style* zeitgemäß ❷ (*on coins*) Jahreszahl *f* ❸ (*engagement*) *business* Termin *m*; *social* Verabredung *f*; *romantic* Date *nt*; **to make a** ~ sich verabreden;

to go out on a ~ ausgehen ❹ (*person*) Date *nt* II. *vt* ❶ (*have relationship*) ■ **to** ~ **sb** mit jdm gehen ❷ (*find age of*) datieren III. *vi* ❶ (*have a relationship*) miteinander gehen ❷ (*go back to*) ■ **to** ~ **from sth** auf etw *akk* zurückgehen; *tradition* aus etw *dat* stammen

date[2] [deɪt] *n* FOOD Dattel *f*

dated ['deɪ·tɪd] *adj* überholt

'**date rape** *n* Vergewaltigung *f* durch eine dem Opfer bekannte Person

dative ['deɪ·tɪv] *n* LING Dativ *m*

daub [dɔb] I. *vt* beschmieren II. *n* Spritzer *m*; *of paint* Farbklecks *m*

daughter ['dɔ·tər] *n* Tochter *f a. fig*

'**daughter-in-law** <*pl* **daughters-**> *n* Schwiegertochter *f*

daunting ['dɔn·tɪŋ] *adj* entmutigend

dawdle ['dɔd·əl] *vi* trödeln

dawn [dɔn] I. *n* ❶ (*daybreak*) [Morgen]dämmerung *f*; **at** ~ bei Tagesanbruch, im Morgengrauen ❷ (*fig*) Anfang *m* II. *vi* ❶ (*start*) anbrechen *a. fig* ❷ (*become apparent*) bewusst werden, dämmern; **it suddenly** ~**ed on me that ...** auf einmal fiel mir siedend heiß ein, dass ...

day [deɪ] *n* Tag *m*; **any** ~ [**now**] jeden Tag; **one** ~ eines Tages; **the other** ~ neulich; **some** ~ irgendwann [einmal]; **the** ~ **after tomorrow** übermorgen; **the** ~ **before yesterday** vorgestern; **these** ~**s** (*recently*) in letzter Zeit; (*nowadays*) heutzutage; (*at the moment*) zurzeit; **one of these** ~**s** eines Tages; (*soon*) demnächst [einmal]; **in those** ~**s** damals ▶PHRASES: **to call it a** ~ Schluss machen [für heute]

'**daybreak** *n* **at** ~ bei Tagesanbruch

'**daycare** *n of preschoolers* Vorschulkinderbetreuung *f*; *of the elderly* Altenbetreuung *f*; ~ **center** (*for preschoolers*) Kindertagesstätte *f*, Kinderkrippe *f*; (*for the elderly*) Altentagesstätte *f*

'**daydream** I. *vi* vor sich *akk* hinträumen II. *n* Tagtraum *m*

'**daylight** *n* Tageslicht *nt*; **in broad** ~ am helllichten Tag[e]

'**daytime** *n* Tag *m*; **in the** ~ tagsüber

day-to-'day *adj* (*daily*) [tag]täglich; (*normal*) alltäglich

'day trip *n* Tagesausflug *m*

daze [deɪz] I. *n* Betäubung *f*; **in a ~** ganz benommen II. *vt* ■**to be ~d** wie betäubt sein

dazzle ['dæz·əl] *vt* ❶ (*blind*) blenden ❷ (*amaze*) verwundern

'dazzled *adj* geblendet *a.fig*, überwältigt *a.fig*

DC [ˌdiˈsi] *n* ❶ ELEC *abbrev of* **direct current** Gleichstrom *m* ❷ *abbrev of* **District of Columbia** D.C.

DE *abbrev of* **Delaware**

dead [ded] I. *adj* ❶ (*not alive*) tot; **~ body** Leiche *f* ❷ *custom* ausgestorben; *fire, match, volcano* erloschen; *language* tot ❸ (*numb*) *limbs* taub ❹ (*deserted*) *city* [wie] ausgestorben; *party* öde ❺ (*fam: exhausted*) tot *fam*, kaputt *fam* ❻ (*not functioning*) *phone* tot; *batteries* leer II. *adv* ❶ (*fam: totally*) absolut; **~ certain** todsicher *fam*; **~ drunk** stockbetrunken; **~ silent** totenstill ❷ (*exactly*) genau; **~ on time** auf die Minute genau III. *n* ❶ (*people*) ■**the ~** *pl* die Toten ❷ (*middle*) **in the ~ of night** mitten in der Nacht

'deadbeat *n* (*sl*) ❶ (*debtor*) Schnorrer(in) *m(f)* ❷ (*lazy person*) Faulpelz *m*; (*feckless person*) Gammler(in) *m(f)*

deaden ['ded·ən] *vt* ❶ (*numb*) *pain* abtöten *a. fig* ❷ (*diminish*) *sound* dämpfen

dead 'end *n* Sackgasse *f a. fig*

dead-'end *adj job* aussichtslos

dead 'heat *n* totes Rennen

'deadline *n* letzter Termin, Deadline *f*

deadlock ['ded·lɑk] *n* toter Punkt

deadly ['ded·li] I. *adj* ❶ (*able to kill*) *weapon* tödlich ❷ (*implacable*) **~ enemies** Todfeinde *pl* ❸ (*pej fam: very boring*) todlangweilig II. *adv* **~ serious** todernst

'deadpan *adj* ausdruckslos; *humor* trocken

Dead 'Sea *n* ■**the ~** das Tote Meer

deaf [def] I. *adj* (*unable to hear*) taub; (*hard of hearing*) schwerhörig II. *n* ■**the ~** *pl* die Tauben

deafen ['def·ən] *vt* taub machen; (*fig*) betäuben

deafening ['def·ə·nɪŋ] *adj* ohrenbetäubend

deaf-'mute *n* Taubstumme(r) *f(m)*

deafness ['def·nɪs] *n* (*complete*) Taubheit *f*; (*partial*) Schwerhörigkeit *f*

deal [dil] I. *n* ❶ **a great** [*or* **good**] **~** eine Menge ❷ (*in business*) Geschäft *nt*, Deal *m sl*; **to do a ~ with sb** mit jdm ein Geschäft abschließen ❸ (*agreement*) Abmachung *f*; **it's a ~!** abgemacht ❹ (*treatment*) **a raw** [*or* **rough**] **~** eine ungerechte Behandlung ❺ CARDS Geben *nt* ▶PHRASES: **big ~!** (*fam*) was soll's? II. *vi* <-t, -t> ❶ CARDS geben ❷ (*sl: sell drugs*) dealen III. *vt* <-t, -t> ❶ (*give*) ■**to ~ [out]** verteilen; **to ~ sb a blow** jdm einen Schlag versetzen *a. fig* ❷ (*sell*) ■**to ~ sth** *drugs* mit etw *dat* dealen

◆**deal with** *vi* ❶ (*handle*) sich befassen mit, sich kümmern um ❷ (*treat*) handeln von ❸ (*do business*) Geschäfte machen mit

dealer ['di·lər] *n* ❶ COMM Händler(in) *m(f)*; *of drugs* Dealer(in) *m(f)* ❷ CARDS [Karten]geber(in) *m(f)*

dealership ['di·lər·ʃɪp] *n* Verkaufsstelle *f*

dealing ['di·lɪŋ] *n* ❶ ■**~s** *pl* (*transactions*) Geschäfte *pl*; (*contact*) Umgang *m kein pl* ❷ (*behavior*) Verhalten *nt*; (*in business*) Geschäftsgebaren *nt*

dealt [delt] *pt, pp of* **deal**

dean [din] *n* Dekan(in) *m(f)*

dear [dɪr] I. *adj* ❶ (*much loved*) lieb; (*lovely*) *baby, kitten* süß ❷ (*in letters*) **D~ Mr. Jones** Sehr geehrter Herr Jones; **D~ Jane** Liebe Jane ❸ (*costly*) teuer II. *interj* **~ me!** du liebe Zeit!; **oh ~!** du meine Güte! III. *n* ❶ (*nice person*) Schatz *m* ❷ (*term of endearment*) **my ~[est]** [mein] Liebling *m*

dearly ['dɪr·li] *adv love* von ganzem Herzen; **to pay ~** (*fig*) teuer bezahlen

dearth [dɜrθ] n (form) Mangel m (of an + dat)

death [deθ] n Tod m; **to be bored to ~** sich zu Tode langweilen

'death certificate n Sterbeurkunde f

deathly ['deθ·li] adj, adv tödlich

'death penalty n Todesstrafe f

death 'row n Todestrakt m

'death sentence n Todesurteil nt

'death trap n Todesfalle f

debacle [dɪˈbɑ·kəl] n Debakel nt

debatable [dɪˈbeɪ·t̬ə·bəl] adj umstritten; ■**it's ~ whether ...** es ist fraglich, ob ...

debate [dɪˈbeɪt] I. n Debatte f II. vt, vi debattieren

debauchery [dɪˈbɔ·tʃə·ri] n Ausschweifungen pl

debilitating [dɪˈbɪl·ɪ·teɪ·t̬ɪŋ] adj schwächend

debit ['deb·ɪt] I. n Debet nt, Soll nt II. vt abbuchen

'debit card n Debitkarte f, Geldautomatenkarte f

debris [də·ˈbri] n Trümmer pl

debt [det] n Schuld f; **to be [heavily] in ~ [to sb]** [jdm] [große] Schulden [bei jdm] haben

'debt collector n Schuldeneintreiber(in) m(f)

debtor ['det̬·ər] n Schuldner(in) m(f)

debug <-gg-> [ˌdiˈbʌg] vt ■**to ~ sth** ❶ COMPUT bei etw dat die Fehler beseitigen ❷ (remove microphones) etw entwanzen

debut [deɪˈbju] I. n of performer Debüt nt II. vi debütieren

Dec. n abbrev of **December** Dez.

decade ['dek·eɪd] n Jahrzehnt nt

decadence ['dek·ə·dəns] n Dekadenz f

decadent ['dek·ə·dənt] adj dekadent; (hum) üppig

decaf ['di·kæf] (fam) I. adj abbrev of **decaffeinated**, koffeinfrei, koffeinfrei II. n entkoffeinierter Kaffee

decaffeinated [ˌdiˈkæf·ɪ·neɪ·t̬ɪd] adj entkoffeiniert, koffeinfrei

decant [dɪˈkænt] vt umfüllen

decanter [dɪˈkæn·t̬ər] n Karaffe f

decapitate [dɪˈkæp·ɪ·teɪt] vt köpfen

decathlon [dɪˈkæθ·lən] n Zehnkampf m

decay [dɪˈkeɪ] I. n ❶ (deterioration) Verfall m ❷ BIOL Verwesung f; BOT Fäulnis f; PHYS Zerfall m II. vi ❶ (deteriorate) verfallen ❷ BIOL verwesen, [ver]faulen; BOT verblühen; PHYS zerfallen

deceased [dɪˈsist] (form) I. n <pl -> ■**the ~** der/die Verstorbene, die Verstorbenen pl II. adj verstorben

deceit [dɪˈsit] n Betrug m

deceitful [dɪˈsit·fəl] adj [be]trügerisch

deceive [dɪˈsiv] vt betrügen; ■**to ~ oneself** sich [selbst] täuschen; ■**to be ~d by sth** von etw dat getäuscht werden

December [dɪˈsem·bər] n Dezember m; see also **February**

decency ['di·sən·si] n (respectability) Anstand m; (goodness) Anständigkeit f

decent ['di·sənt] adj ❶ (socially acceptable) anständig ❷ (good) person nett ❸ (appropriate) angemessen ❹ (good-sized) anständig; helping ordentlich ❺ (acceptable) job, proposal annehmbar ❻ (fam: dressed) angezogen

deception [dɪˈsep·ʃən] n Täuschung f

deceptive [dɪˈsep·tɪv] adj täuschend

decibel ['des·ə·bəl] n Dezibel nt

decide [dɪˈsaɪd] I. vi sich entscheiden (on für +akk); ■**to ~ to do sth** beschließen [o sich entschließen], etw zu tun II. vt entscheiden

decided [dɪˈsaɪ·dɪd] adj (definite) entschieden; dislike ausgesprochen

deciduous [dɪˈsɪdʒ·u·əs] adj ~ **tree** Laubbaum m

decimal ['des·ə·məl] n Dezimalzahl f, Dezimale f; ~ **place** Dezimalstelle f; ~ **point** Komma nt

decipher [dɪˈsaɪ·fər] vt entziffern; code entschlüsseln

decision [dɪˈsɪʒ·ən] n Entscheidung f, Entschluss m; **to come to [or reach] a ~** zu einer Entscheidung gelangen; **to make a ~** eine Entscheidung treffen

decisive [dɪˈsaɪ·sɪv] adj ❶ (determin-

D

D

ing) bestimmend; *battle* entscheidend ➋ (*firm*) *measure* entschlossen

deck [dek] *n* ➊ (*on ship, bus*) Deck *nt*; **on ~** an Deck ➋ (*raised porch*) Veranda *f* ➌ CARDS [Karten]spiel *nt*

declaration [ˌde·klə·ˈreɪ·ʃən] *n* Erklärung *f*

Declaration of Independence *n* Unabhängigkeitserklärung *f* (*der Vereinigten Staaten*)

declare [dɪ·ˈkler] *vt* ➊ (*make known*) verkünden; *intention* kundtun; *support* zusagen ➋ (*state*) erklären; **to ~ war on sb** jdm den Krieg erklären ➌ (*for customs, tax*) deklarieren; **do you have anything to ~?** haben Sie etwas zu verzollen?

decline [dɪ·ˈklaɪn] **I.** *n* ➊ (*decrease*) Rückgang *m* ➋ (*deterioration*) Verschlechterung *f* **II.** *vi* ➊ (*refuse*) ablehnen ➋ (*diminish*) *popularity* sinken, nachlassen; *health* sich verschlechtern; *strength* abnehmen **III.** *vt* ➊ (*refuse*) ablehnen ➋ LING deklinieren, beugen

decode [ˌdiˈkoʊd] *vt* entschlüsseln

decompose [ˌdiˈkəmˈpoʊz] *vi* sich zersetzen

decomposition [ˌdiˈkam·pə·ˈzɪʃ·ən] *n* Zersetzung *f*

decongestant [ˌdiˈkənˈdʒes·tənt] *n* abschwellendes Mittel, Mittel, das die Atemwege frei macht

decontaminate [ˌdiˈkənˈtæm·ɪ·neɪt] *vt* entseuchen

decontamination [ˌdiˈkən·tæm·ɪ·ˈneɪ·ʃən] *n* Entseuchung *f*

decor [ˈdeɪ·kɔr] *n* Ausstattung *f*; THEAT Dekor *m* *o* *nt*

decorate [ˈdek·ə·reɪt] *vt* ➊ (*adorn*) schmücken; *cake, store window* dekorieren ➋ *usu passive* (*honor*) ■ **to be ~ [for sth]** [für etw *akk*] ausgezeichnet werden

decoration [ˌdek·ə·ˈreɪ·ʃən] *n* ➊ (*for party*) Dekoration *f*; (*for Christmas tree*) Schmuck *m* kein *pl* ➋ (*medal*) Auszeichnung *f*

decorative [ˈdek·ər·ə·t̬ɪv] *adj* dekorativ

decorum [dɪ·ˈkɔr·əm] *n* (*form*) Schicklichkeit *f*

decoy [ˈdiˈkɔɪ] *n* Lockvogel *m*

decrease I. *vi* [dɪ·ˈkris] abnehmen, zurückgehen **II.** *vt* [dɪ·ˈkris] reduzieren **III.** *n* [ˈdiˈkris] Abnahme *f*; *numbers* Rückgang *m*

decree [dɪ·ˈkri] *n* (*form*) Erlass *m*

decrepit [dɪ·ˈkrep·ɪt] *adj* klapprig

dedicate [ˈded·ɪ·keɪt] *vt* widmen

dedicated [ˈded·ɪ·ker·t̬ɪd] *adj* engagiert

dedication [ˌded·ɪ·ˈkeɪ·ʃən] *n* ➊ (*hard work*) Engagement *nt* ➋ (*in book*) Widmung *f*

deduce [dɪ·ˈdus] *vt* folgern; ■ **to ~ whether …** feststellen, ob …

deduct [dɪ·ˈdʌkt] *vt* abziehen; FIN ausgleichen

deductible [dɪ·ˈdʌk·tə·bəl] *adj* absetzbar

deduction [dɪ·ˈdʌk·ʃən] *n* ➊ (*inference*) Schlussfolgerung *f* ➋ (*subtraction*) Abzug *m*

deed [did] *n* ➊ (*action*) Tat *f*; **to do a good ~** eine gute Tat vollbringen ➋ LAW Eigentumsurkunde *f*

deep [dip] *adj, adv* tief; *disappointment* schwer; *regret* groß; **the snow was 3 feet ~** der Schnee lag 3 Fuß hoch; **to be in ~ trouble** in großen Schwierigkeiten stecken; **~ blue** tiefblau; **~ space** äußerer Weltraum

deepen [ˈdi·pən] **I.** *vt* ➊ (*make deeper*) tiefer machen ➋ (*intensify*) vertiefen **II.** *vi* ➊ *voice, water* tiefer werden ➋ (*intensify*) sich vertiefen; *crisis* sich verschärfen

'deep freeze *n* Tiefkühlschrank *m*; (*chest*) Tiefkühltruhe *f*

deep-'fry *vt* frittieren

'deep fryer *n* Fritteuse *f*

deeply [ˈdip·li] *adv* tief, äußerst

deep-'seated *adj* tief sitzend

deer <*pl* -> [dɪr] *n* Hirsch *m*; (*roe deer*) Reh *nt*

deface [dɪ·ˈfeɪs] *vt* verunstalten

defamation [ˌdef·ə·ˈmeɪ·ʃən] *n* (*form*) Diffamierung *f*

defamatory [dɪˈfæm·ə·tɔr·i] *adj* (*form*) diffamierend

default [dɪˈfɔlt] I. *vi* FIN in Verzug geraten (**on** mit +*dat*) II. *n* ❶ *of contract* Nichterfüllung *f*; (*failure to pay debt*) Versäumnis *nt* ❷ ▪**by ~** automatisch ❸COMPUT Voreinstellung *f* III. *adj* Standard-

defeat [dɪˈfit] I. *vt* besiegen; (*at games, sports*) schlagen; *proposal, government bill* ablehnen II. *n* Niederlage *f*

defeatism [dɪˈfi·tɪ·zəm] *n* (*pej*) Defätismus *m*, Defaitismus *m* SCHWEIZ

defeatist [dɪˈfi·tɪst] I. *adj* defätistisch, defaitistisch SCHWEIZ II. *n* Defätist(in) *m(f)*, Defaitist(in) *m(f)* SCHWEIZ

defecate [ˈdef·ə·keɪt] *vi* (*form*) den Darm entleeren

defect[1] [ˈdi·fekt] *n* Fehler *m*; TECH Defekt *m*

defect[2] [dɪˈfekt] *vi* POL überlaufen (**to** in +*akk*)

defection [dɪˈfek·ʃən] *n* Flucht *f*; POL Überlaufen *nt*

defective [dɪˈfek·tɪv] *adj* fehlerhaft; TECH defekt

defend [dɪˈfend] *vt*, *vi* verteidigen; ▪**to ~ oneself** sich wehren

defendant [dɪˈfen·dənt] *n* LAW Angeklagte(r) *f(m)*

defense[1] [dɪˈfens] *n* ❶ Verteidigung *f a. fig*; **~ witness** Zeuge, -in *m*, *f* der Verteidigung ❷MED ▪**~s** *pl* Abwehrkräfte *pl*

defense[2] [ˈdiˈfens] *n* *esp* SPORT Abwehr *f*; **to play** [**on**] **~** Abwehrspieler/ Abwehrspielerin sein

defenseless [dɪˈfens·lɪs] *adj* wehrlos

Deˈfense Secretary *n* Verteidigungsminister(in) *m(f)*

defensible [dɪˈfen·sə·bəl] *adj* vertretbar

defensive [dɪˈfen·sɪv] I. *adj* defensiv II. *n* **to be on the ~** in der Defensive sein

defer <-rr-> [dɪˈfɜr] I. *vi* (*form*) ▪**to ~ to sb/sth** sich jdm/etw beugen; *to sb's judgment* sich fügen II. *vt* verschieben; FIN, LAW aufschieben

deference [ˈdef·ər·əns] *n* (*form*) Respekt *m*

deferential [ˌdef·əˈren·tʃəl] *adj* respektvoll

defiance [dɪˈfaɪ·əns] *n* Aufsässigkeit *f*; ▪**in ~ of sb/sth** jdm/etw zum Trotz

defiant [dɪˈfaɪ·ənt] *adj* aufsässig

deficiency [dɪˈfɪʃ·ən·si] *n* Mangel *m*

deficient [dɪˈfɪʃ·ənt] *adj* unzureichend; ▪**to be ~ in sth** an etw *dat* mangeln

deficit [ˈdef·ɪ·sɪt] *n* Defizit *nt*

define [dɪˈfaɪn] *vt* ❶ *word, meaning* definieren ❷ (*specify*) festlegen

definite [ˈdef·ə·nɪt] *adj* sicher; *answer* klar; *improvement, increase* eindeutig; *place, time limit* bestimmt

definite ˈarticle *n* LING bestimmter Artikel

definitely [ˈdef·ɪ·nət·li] *adv* eindeutig; **to decide sth ~** etw endgültig beschließen

definition [ˌdef·ɪˈnɪʃ·ən] *n* ❶ (*meaning*) Definition *f* ❷ (*distinctness*) Schärfe *f*

definitive [dɪˈfɪn·ɪ·tɪv] *adj* ❶ (*conclusive*) endgültig; *proof* eindeutig ❷ (*most authoritative*) ultimativ

deflate [dɪˈfleɪt] I. *vt* ❶ Luft aus etw *dat* ablassen ❷ECON *currency* deflationieren II. *vi* Luft verlieren

deflation [dɪˈfleɪ·ʃən] *n* ECON Deflation *f*

deflect [dɪˈflekt] I. *vt* ablenken; *ball* abfälschen; *blow* abwehren II. *vi* ▪**to ~ off sb/sth** *ball* von jdm/etw *dat* abprallen

deflection [dɪˈflek·ʃən] *n* Ablenkung *f*; SPORT Abpraller *m*

defogger [ˌdiˈfɔ·gər] *n* AUTO Gebläse *nt*

deforestation [di·ˌfɔr·ɪˈsteɪ·ʃən] *n* Abholzung *f*, Entwaldung *f*

deform [dɪˈfɔrm] I. *vt* deformieren II. *vi* sich verformen

deformed [dɪˈfɔrmd] *adj* verformt

deformity [dɪˈfɔr·mɪ·ti] *n* Missbildung *f*

defraud [dɪˈfrɔd] *vt* betrügen

defray [dɪˈfreɪ] *vt* (*form*) *costs* tragen

defrost [ˌdiˈfrɔst] *vt*, *vi* auftauen; *refrig-*

D

erator abtauen; *window, windshield* enteisen

deft [deft] *adj* geschickt

defunct [dɪˈfʌŋkt] *adj* (*form*) gestorben; *institution* ausgedient

defy <-ie-> [dɪˈfaɪ] *vt* ▪ **to** ~ **sb/sth** sich jdm/etw widersetzen; (*fig: resist, withstand*) sich etw *dat* entziehen

deg. *n abbrev of* **degree**

degenerate I. *vi* [dɪˈdʒen·ə·reɪt] degenerieren; ▪ **to** ~ **into sth** zu etw *dat* entarten II. *adj* [dɪˈdʒen·ə·rət] degeneriert III. *n* [dɪˈdʒen·ə·rət] jd, der keine moralischen Werte mehr hat

degrade [dɪˈɡreɪd] *vt* ❶ *person* erniedrigen ❷ CHEM abbauen

degree [dɪˈɡri] *n* ❶ (*amount*) Maß *nt*; (*extent*) Grad *m*; **by** ~**s** nach und nach; **to some** ~ bis zu einem gewissen Grad ❷ MATH, METEO Grad *m* ❸ UNIV Abschluss *m*; (*document*) Abschlusszeugnis *nt*

dehydrate [ˌdi·haɪˈdreɪt] I. *vt* **to become** ~**d** austrocknen II. *vi* MED dehydrieren

dehydration [ˌdi·haɪˈdreɪ·ʃən] *n* MED Dehydration *f*

deice [ˌdiˈaɪs] *vt* enteisen

deity [ˈdi·ə·ti] *n* Gottheit *f*

dejected [dɪˈdʒek·tɪd] *adj* niedergeschlagen

dejection [dɪˈdʒek·ʃən] *n* Niedergeschlagenheit *f*

Del. *abbrev of* **Delaware**

Delaware [ˈdel·ə·wer] *n* Delaware *nt*

delay [dɪˈleɪ] I. *vt* ❶ (*postpone*) verschieben ❷ (*hold up*) **to be** ~**ed** [**by 10 minutes**] [zehn Minuten] Verspätung haben; **I was** ~**ed** ich wurde aufgehalten; ~ **tactics** Verzögerungstaktiken *pl* II. *vi* verschieben III. *n* Verzögerung *f*; TRANSP Verspätung *f*

delectable [dɪˈlek·tə·bəl] *adj food, drink* köstlich; (*esp hum*) *person* bezaubernd

delegate I. *n* [ˈdel·ɪ·ɡət] Delegierte(r) *f(m)* II. *vt* [ˈdel·ɪ·ɡeɪt] ❶ (*appoint*) als Vertreter(in) [aus]wählen; ▪ **to** ~ **sb to do sth** jdn dazu bestimmen, etw zu tun

❷ (*assign*) ▪ **to** ~ **sth to sb** etw auf jdn übertragen III. *vi* [ˈdel·ɪ·ɡeɪt] delegieren

delegation [ˌdel·ɪˈɡeɪ·ʃən] *n* Delegation *f*

delete [dɪˈlit] *vt* ❶ (*in writing*) streichen ❷ COMPUT löschen

deletion [dɪˈli·ʃən] *n* Streichung *f*, Löschung *f*; *of a file* Löschen *nt*

deli [ˈdel·i] *n* (*fam*) *short for* **delicatessen** Feinkostgeschäft *nt*; (*in supermarket*) Frischtheke, an der Wurst- und Käseaufschnitt, frische Salate etc. verkauft werden

deliberate I. *adj* [dɪˈlɪb·ər·ət] ❶ (*intentional*) absichtlich; *decision, lie* bewusst ❷ (*careful*) *pace* vorsichtig II. *vi* [dɪˈlɪb·ə·reɪt] (*form*) [gründlich] nachdenken (**on** über +*akk*)

deliberately [dɪˈlɪb·ər·ət·li] *adv* absichtlich

deliberation [dɪˌlɪb·ə·ˈreɪ·ʃən] *n* ❶ (*carefulness*) Bedächtigkeit *f* ❷ (*form: consideration*) Überlegung *f*

delicacy [ˈdel·ɪ·kə·si] *n* ❶ FOOD Delikatesse *f* ❷ (*discretion*) Feingefühl *nt* ❸ (*fineness*) Feinheit *f*; *of features* Zartheit *f*

delicate [ˈdel·ɪ·kət] *adj* ❶ (*sensitive*) empfindlich; *china* zerbrechlich ❷ (*tricky*) heikel ❸ (*fine*) fein; *aroma, color* zart; ~ **cycle** Feinwaschgang *m*

delicatessen [ˌdel·ɪ·kə·ˈtes·ən] *n* Feinkostgeschäft *nt*

delicious [dɪˈlɪʃ·əs] *adj* köstlich, lecker

delight [dɪˈlaɪt] I. *n* Freude *f* II. *vt* erfreuen

delighted [dɪˈlaɪ·tɪd] *adj* hocherfreut; *smile* vergnügt; ▪ **to be** ~ **to do sth** etw mit [großem] Vergnügen tun

delightful [dɪˈlaɪt·fəl] *adj* wunderbar; *evening, village* reizend; *smile, person* charmant

delinquency [dɪˈlɪŋ·kwən·si] *n* Straffälligkeit *f*

delinquent [dɪˈlɪŋ·kwənt] I. *n* Delinquent(in) *m(f)* II. *adj* straffällig

delirious [dɪˈlɪr·i·əs] *adj* ❶ im Delirium

② (*extremely happy*) außer sich *dat* [vor Freude]

deliver [dɪˈlɪv·ər] **I.** *vt* ① (*bring*) liefern; (*by mail*) zustellen; *newspapers* austragen; *message* überbringen ② (*recite*) *speech* halten; *verdict* verkünden ③ (*direct*) *blow* geben; *rebuke* halten ④ (*give birth*) zur Welt bringen; (*aid in giving birth*) entbinden **II.** *vi* ① (*supply*) liefern ② (*fulfill*) ■**to ~ on sth** *promise* etw einhalten

delivery [dɪˈlɪv·ə·ri] *n* ① (*of goods*) Lieferung *f*; (*of mail*) Zustellung *f* ② (*manner of speaking*) Vortragsweise *f* ③ (*birth*) Entbindung *f*

deˈlivery room *n* Kreißsaal *m*

deˈlivery van *n* Lieferwagen *m*

delta [ˈdel·tə] *n* Delta *nt*

delude [dɪˈlud] *vt* täuschen

deluge [ˈdel·judʒ] **I.** *n* ① (*downpour*) Regenguss *m*; (*flood*) Flut *f* ② (*fig*) Flut *f* **II.** *vt* ■**to be ~d** überflutet werden; (*fig*) überschüttet werden

delusion [dɪˈlu·ʒən] *n* Täuschung *f*

deluxe [dɪˈlʌks] *adj* Luxus-

demand [dɪˈmænd] **I.** *vt* ① (*insist on*) verlangen ② (*need*) *skill, patience* erfordern **II.** *n* ① (*request*) Forderung *f* (**for** nach + *dat*) ② (*requirement*) Bedarf *m*; COMM Nachfrage *f*; **in ~** gefragt ③ (*expectations*) **to make ~s on sb/ sth** Anforderungen *pl* an jdn/etw stellen

demanding [dɪˈmæn·dɪŋ] *adj child, work* anstrengend; *job, person, test* anspruchsvoll

demeanor [dɪˈmi·nər] *n* (*form: behavior*) Verhalten *nt*; (*bearing*) Erscheinungsbild *nt*

demented [dɪˈmen·tɪd] *adj* verrückt

demerit [dɪˈmer·ɪt] *n* ① (*fault*) Schwäche *f* ② (*black mark*) Minuspunkt *m*

demise [dɪˈmaɪz] *n* (*form*) Ableben *nt*

democracy [dɪˈmak·rə·si] *n* Demokratie *f*

democrat [ˈdem·ə·kræt] *n* Demokrat(in) *m(f)*

democratic [ˌdem·əˈkræt·ɪk] *adj* demokratisch

demolish [dɪˈmal·ɪʃ] *vt* ① *building* abreißen; *wall* einreißen ② (*refute*) zunichtemachen; *argument* widerlegen

demolition [ˌdem·əˈlɪʃ·ən] *n* Abriss *m*

demon [ˈdi·mən] *n* (*evil spirit*) Dämon *m*; (*fig: wicked person*) Fiesling *m*

demonic [dɪˈman·ɪk] *adj* ① (*devilish*) dämonisch ② (*evil*) bösartig

demonstrable [dɪˈman·strə·bəl] *adj* nachweislich

demonstrate [ˈdem·ən·streɪt] **I.** *vt* ① (*show*) zeigen; *operation* vorführen; *authority, knowledge* demonstrieren; *loyalty* beweisen ② (*prove*) nachweisen **II.** *vi* demonstrieren

demonstration [ˌdem·ənˈstreɪ·ʃən] *n* ① (*act of showing*) Demonstration *f*, Vorführung *f* ② (*proof*) Beweis *m* ③ (*protest*) Demonstration *f*

demonstrator [ˈdem·ənˈstreɪ·tər] *n* ① (*of product*) Vorführer(in) *m(f)* ② (*protester*) Demonstrant(in) *m(f)*

demoralize [dɪˈmɔr·ə·laɪz] *vt* demoralisieren

demote [dɪˈmoʊt] *vt* zurückstufen; MIL degradieren

demotion [dɪˈmoʊ·ʃən] *n* MIL Degradierung *f*

demure [dɪˈmjʊr] *adj* ① (*shy*) [sehr] schüchtern ② (*composed and reserved*) gesetzt

den [den] *n* ① (*lair*) Bau *m* ② (*study*) Arbeitszimmer *nt*; (*private room*) Bude *f*, Hobbyraum *m* ③ (*children's playhouse*) Verschlag *m*

denial [dɪˈnaɪ·əl] *n* ① (*statement*) Dementi *nt*; (*action*) Leugnen *nt kein pl* ② (*refusal*) Ablehnung *f* ③ PSYCH **to be in ~** sich der Realität verschließen

denim [ˈden·ɪm] *n* ① (*material*) Denim® *m* ② (*fam*) ■**~s** *pl* Jeans *f(pl)*

Denmark [ˈden·mark] *n* Dänemark *nt*

denomination [dɪˌnam·əˈneɪ·ʃən] *n* ① REL Konfessionsgemeinschaft *f* ② (*unit of value*) Währungseinheit *f*

denominator [dɪˈnam·ə·neɪ·tər] *n* MATH Nenner *m*

denote [dɪˈnoʊt] *vt* bedeuten

denounce [dɪˈnaʊns] *vt* ① (*criticize*)

D

anprangern ❷ (*accuse*) entlarven; ▪to ~ sb to sb jdn bei jdm denunzieren

dense <-r, -st> [dens] *adj* ❶ (*thick*) dicht ❷ (*fam: stupid*) dumm

densely ['dens·li] *adv* dicht

density ['den·sə·ti] *n* Dichte *f*

dent [dent] **I.** *n* Beule *f*, Delle *f* **II.** *vt* einbeulen

dental ['den·təl] *adj* Zahn-

dentist ['den·tɪst] *n* Zahnarzt, Zahnärztin *m, f*

dentistry ['den·tɪ·stri] *n* Zahnmedizin *f*

dentures ['den·tʃərz] *npl* [Zahn]prothese *f*

denunciation [dɪˌnʌn·si·'eɪ·ʃən] *n* ❶ (*condemnation*) Anprangerung *f* ❷ LAW (*denouncing*) Denunziation *f*

Denver boot *n* Parkkralle *f*

deny <-ie-> [dɪ·'naɪ] *vt* ❶ (*declare untrue*) abstreiten; *accusation* zurückweisen ❷ (*refuse to grant*) ▪to ~ sth to sb [*or* sb sth] jdm etw verweigern; *request* ablehnen

deodorant [di·'oʊ·dər·ənt] *n* Deo[dorant] *nt*

dep. [dep] *n* ❶ TRANSP *short for* **departure** Abf.; *aircraft* Abfl. ❷ *short for* **department** Abt.

depart [dɪ·'part] *vi* ❶ (*leave*) fortgehen; *plane* abfliegen, starten; *train* abfahren; *ship a.* ablegen ❷ (*differ*) abweichen (**from** von +*dat*)

department [dɪ·'part·mənt] *n* ❶ UNIV Institut *nt*; **the Philosophy D~** die philosophische Fakultät ❷ COMM Abteilung *f* ❸ POL Ministerium *nt* ❹ ADMIN Amt *nt*

departmental [ˌdi·part·'men·təl] *adj* ❶ UNIV Instituts- ❷ COMM Abteilungs- ❸ POL Ministerial- ❹ ADMIN Amts-

Department of De'fense *n* Verteidigungsministerium *nt*

Department of Motor 'Vehicles *n* Kfz-Zulassungsstelle *f*

de'partment store *n* Kaufhaus *nt*

departure [dɪ·'par·tʃər] *n* ❶ (*on trip*) Abreise *f*, Abfahrt *f*; *ship a.* Ablegen *nt*; *plane* Abflug *m* ❷ (*deviation*) Abweichung *f*; *from policy* Abkehr *f*

de'parture lounge *n* Abfahrthalle *f*; AVIAT Abflughalle *f*

de'parture time *n* Abfahrtzeit *f*; AVIAT Abflugzeit *f*

depend [dɪ·'pend] *vi* ❶ (*be dictated by*) ▪to ~ [up]on sth von etw *dat* abhängen; **that ~s** kommt darauf an ❷ (*get help from*) ▪to ~ [up]on sb/sth von jdm/etw abhängig sein; *financially* finanziell auf jdn/etw angewiesen sein ❸ (*rely on*) ▪to ~ [up]on sb/sth sich auf jdn/etw verlassen

dependability [dɪˌpen·də·'bɪl·ɪ·ti] *n* Zuverlässigkeit *f*, Verlässlichkeit *f*

dependable [dɪ·'pen·də·bəl] *adj* zuverlässig, verlässlich

dependence [dɪ·'pen·dəns] *n* Abhängigkeit *f*

dependent [dɪ·'pen·dənt] **I.** *adj* ❶ (*conditional*) ▪to be ~ [up]on sth von etw *dat* abhängen ❷ (*reliant on*) ▪to be ~ [up]on sth von etw *dat* abhängig sein; *help, goodwill* auf etw *akk* angewiesen sein **II.** *n* [finanziell] abhängige(r) Angehörige(r) *f(m)*

depict [dɪ·'pɪkt] *vt* (*form*) darstellen

depiction [dɪ·'pɪk·ʃən] *n* Darstellung *f*

deplete [dɪ·'plit] *vt* vermindern

depleted [dɪ·'pli·tɪd] *adj* verbraucht

depletion [dɪ·'pli·ʃən] *n* Abbau *m*; *of resources, capital* Erschöpfung *f*

deplorable [dɪ·'plɔr·ə·bəl] *adj* beklagenswert; *conditions* erbärmlich

deplore [dɪ·'plɔr] *vt* ❶ (*disapprove*) verurteilen ❷ (*regret*) beklagen

deploy [dɪ·'plɔɪ] *vt* einsetzen

deployment [dɪ·'plɔɪ·mənt] *n* Einsatz *m*

deport [dɪ·'pɔrt] *vt* ausweisen; *prisoner* deportieren

deportation [ˌdi·pɔr·'teɪ·ʃən] *n* Ausweisung *f*, Abschiebung *f*; *of prisoner* Deportation *f*

deportment [dɪ·'pɔrt·mənt] *n* (*form*) Benehmen *nt*

depose [dɪ·'poʊz] *vt* absetzen; *monarch* entthronen

deposit [dɪ·'paz·ɪt] **I.** *vt* ❶ (*leave*) *person* absetzen; *thing* ablegen, abstellen;

luggage deponieren ❷ (*in bank*) einzahlen; (*as first installment*) anzahlen II. *n* ❶ (*sediment*) Bodensatz *m*; (*layer*) Ablagerung *f* ❷ (*in bank*) Einzahlung *f*; (*first installment*) Anzahlung *f*; (*security*) Kaution *f*; (*on bottle*) Pfand *nt*

deposition [ˌdep·ə·ˈzɪʃ·ən] *n* ❶ (*form: removal from power*) Absetzung *f* ❷ LAW (*written statement*) Aussage *f*

depot [ˈdi·poʊ] *n* Depot *nt*

depraved [dɪ·ˈpreɪvd] *adj* verdorben

depravity [dɪ·ˈpræv·ɪ· t̬i] *n* Verdorbenheit *f*

depreciate [dɪ·ˈpri·ʃi·eɪt] I. *vi* an Wert verlieren II. *vt* entwerten

depreciation [dɪ·ˌpri·ʃi·ˈeɪ·ʃən] *n* Wertminderung *f*; *of currencies* Entwertung *f*

depress [dɪ·ˈpres] *vt* ❶ (*deject*) deprimieren ❷ (*reduce*) *prices* drücken ❸ (*push*) *button, lever* niederdrücken

depressed [dɪ·ˈprest] *adj* ❶ (*dejected*) deprimiert (**about/at/by/over** wegen +*gen*) ❷ (*reduced*) *levels* reduziert, verringert ❸ ECON *region, sector* heruntergekommen *fam*

depressing [dɪ·ˈpres·ɪŋ] *adj* deprimierend

depression [dɪ·ˈpreʃ·ən] *n* ❶ (*sadness*) Depression *f* ❷ ECON Wirtschaftskrise *f* ❸ METEO Tiefdruckgebiet *nt*

depressive [dɪ·ˈpres·ɪv] I. *n* Depressive(r) *f(m)* II. *adj* depressiv

deprivation [ˌdep·rɪ·ˈveɪ·ʃən] *n* Entbehrung *f*

deprive [dɪ·ˈpraɪv] *vt* ■**to ~ sb [of] sth** jdm etw entziehen [*o* vorenthalten]

deprived [dɪ·ˈpraɪvd] *adj* sozial benachteiligt

dept. *n abbrev of* **department** Abt.

depth [depθ] *n* Tiefe *f a. fig*; **in the ~s of the forest** mitten im Wald; **in the ~s of despair** zutiefst verzweifelt; **in ~** gründlich

deputation [ˌdep·jə·ˈteɪ·ʃən] *n* Abordnung *f*

deputize [ˈdep·jə·taɪz] *vi* ■**to ~ for sb** für jdn einspringen, jdn vertreten

deputy [ˈdep·jə·t̬i] I. *n* Stellvertreter(in) *m(f)* II. *adj* stellvertretend

derail [dɪ·ˈreɪl] *vt* ❶ *train* entgleisen lassen; ■**to be ~ed** entgleisen ❷ *plan, process* zum Scheitern bringen

deranged [dɪ·ˈreɪndʒd] *adj* geistesgestört

derby [ˈdɜr·bi] *n* ❶ SPORT Derby *nt* ❷ (*hat*) Melone *f*

derelict [ˈder·ə·lɪkt] I. *adj* verlassen II. *n* Obdachlose(r) *f(m)*

dereliction [ˌder·ə·ˈlɪk·ʃən] *n* ❶ (*negligence*) ~ **of duty** Pflichtvernachlässigung *f* ❷ (*dilapidation*) Verwahrlosung *f*

derision [dɪ·ˈrɪʒ·ən] *n* Spott *m*

derisive [dɪ·ˈraɪ·sɪv] *adj* spöttisch

derisory [dɪ·ˈraɪ·sə·ri] *adj* ❶ (*derisive*) spöttisch ❷ (*ridiculously small*) lächerlich

derivation [ˌder·ɪ·ˈveɪ·ʃən] *n* ❶ (*origin*) Ursprung *m* ❷ (*process*) Ableitung *f*

derivative [dɪ·ˈrɪv·ə·t̬ɪv] I. *adj* (*pej*) nachgemacht II. *n* Ableitung *f*, Derivat *nt*

derive [dɪ·ˈraɪv] I. *vt* gewinnen II. *vi* ■**to ~ from sth** sich von etw *dat* ableiten [lassen]

dermatitis [ˌdɜr·mə·ˈtaɪ·t̬əs] *n* Hautreizung *f*, Dermatitis *f*

dermatologist [ˌdɜr·mə·ˈtɑl·ə·dʒɪst] *n* Dermatologe, -in *m, f*, Hautarzt, Hautärztin *m, f*

dermatology [ˌdɜr·mə·ˈtɑl·ə·dʒi] *n* Dermatologie *f*

derogatory [dɪ·ˈrɑg·ə·tɔr·i] *adj* abfällig

derrick [ˈder·ɪk] *n* ❶ (*crane*) Lastkran *m* ❷ (*over oil well*) Bohrturm *m*

desalination [di·ˌsæl·ɪ·ˈneɪ·ʃən] *n* Entsalzung *f*

descend [dɪ·ˈsend] I. *vi* ❶ (*go down*) *path* herunterführen; *person* heruntergehen ❷ (*be related*) ■**to be ~ed from sb/sth** von jdm/etw abstammen ❸ (*fall*) herabsinken II. *vt* hinuntersteigen

descendant [dɪ·ˈsen·dənt] *n* Nachkomme *m*

descent [dɪ·ˈsent] *n* ❶ (*by plane*) [Lan-

de|**anflug** *m* ➋ (*way down*) Abstieg *m* kein pl ➌ (*fig: ancestry*) Abstammung *f*

describe [dɪˈskraɪb] *vt* beschreiben; *experience* schildern

description [dɪˈskrɪp·ʃən] *n* Beschreibung *f*; **of every ~** jeglicher Art

D **descriptive** [dɪˈskrɪp·tɪv] *adj* beschreibend

desecrate [ˈdes·ɪ·kreɪt] *vt* schänden

desecration [ˌdes·ɪˈkreɪ·ʃən] *n* Schändung *f*

desegregate [ˌdiˈseg·rɪ·geɪt] *vt* **to ~ schools/universities** die Rassentrennung in der Schule/an der Universität aufheben

desegregation [dɪˌseg·rɪˈgeɪ·ʃən] *n* Aufhebung *f* der Rassentrennung

desert[1] [ˈdez·ərt] *n* Wüste *f a. fig;* **~ island** verlassene Insel

desert[2] [dɪˈzɜrt] I. *vi* MIL desertieren II. *vt* verlassen

deserted [dɪˈzɜr·tɪd] *adj* verlassen; *of town* ausgestorben

deserter [dɪˈzɜr·tər] *n* Deserteur(in) *m(f)*

desertion [dɪˈzɜr·ʃən] *n* Verlassen *nt;* MIL Desertion *f*

deserts [dɪˈzɜrts] *npl* ■**to get one's |just|** ~ seine Quittung bekommen

deserve [dɪˈzɜrv] *vt* verdienen

deservedly [dɪˈzɜr·vɪd·li] *adv* verdientermaßen

deserving [dɪˈzɜr·vɪn] *adj* verdienstvoll

design [dɪˈzaɪn] I. *vt* ➊ (*plan*) entwerfen; *cars* konstruieren ➋ (*intend*) **to be ~ed for sb** für jdn konzipiert sein; **these measures are ~ed to reduce pollution** diese Maßnahmen sollen die Luftverschmutzung verringern II. *n* ➊ (*plan*) Entwurf *m* ➋ (*art*) Design *nt; of building* Bauart *f; of machine* Konstruktion *f;* (*pattern*) Muster *nt*

designate [ˈdez·ɪg·neɪt] I. *vt* ■**to ~ sb** jdn ernennen (**as** zu +*dat*) II. *adj af-ter n* designiert

designated ˈdriver *n* Person, die sich bereit erklärt, nüchtern zu bleiben und die Freunde sicher nach Hause zu fahren

designer [dɪˈzaɪ·nər] I. *n* Designer(in) *m(f)* II. *adj* Designer-

desirable [dɪˈzaɪr·ə·bəl] *adj* ➊ (*worth having*) erstrebenswert; (*popular*) begehrt; *advantageous* erwünscht ➋ (*sexually attractive*) begehrenswert

desire [dɪˈzaɪr] I. *vt* ➊ (*want*) wünschen ➋ (*sexually*) begehren II. *n* ➊ (*strong wish*) Verlangen *nt;* (*stronger*) Sehnsucht *f;* (*request*) Wunsch *m* ➋ (*sexual need*) Begierde *f*

desist [dɪˈsɪst] *vi* (*form*) einhalten

desk [desk] *n* ➊ (*for writing*) Schreibtisch *m* ➋ (*counter*) Schalter *m*

ˈdesk lamp *n* Schreibtischlampe *f*

ˈdesktop *n* ➊ COMPUT Desktop *m* ➋ (*desk surface*) Tischoberfläche *f*

desolate [ˈdes·ə·lət] *adj* ➊ (*barren*) trostlos ➋ (*unhappy*) niedergeschlagen

desolation [ˌdes·əˈleɪ·ʃən] *n* ➊ (*barrenness*) Trostlosigkeit *f* ➋ (*sadness*) Verzweiflung *f*

despair [dɪˈsper] I. *n* Verzweiflung *f;* **in ~** verzweifelt II. *vi* verzweifeln (**at/ of** an +*dat*); **to ~ of doing sth** die Hoffnung aufgeben, etw zu tun

despairing [dɪˈsper·ɪn] *adj* verzweifelt

despatch [dɪˈspætʃ] *n, vt see* **dispatch**

desperate [ˈdes·pər·ɪt] *adj* **attempt** verzweifelt; (*great*) dringend; ■**to be ~ for sth** etw dringendst brauchen

desperation [ˌdes·pəˈreɪ·ʃən] *n* Verzweiflung *f;* **in ~** aus Verzweiflung

despicable [dɪˈspɪk·ə·bəl] *adj* abscheulich

despise [dɪˈspaɪz] *vt* verachten

despite [dɪˈspaɪt] *prep* trotz +*gen*

despondent [dɪˈspan·dənt] *adj* niedergeschlagen

dessert [dɪˈzɜrt] *n* Nachtisch *m,* Dessert *nt*

destination [ˌdes·təˈneɪ·ʃən] *n* Ziel *nt; of trip* Reiseziel *nt; of letter* Bestimmungsort *m*

destiny [ˈdes·tə·ni] *n* Schicksal *nt*

destitute [ˈdes·tɪ·tut] I. *adj* mittellos II. *n* ■**the ~** *pl* die Bedürftigen

destitution [ˌdes·trˈtu·ʃən] *n* Armut *f*

destroy [dɪˈstrɔɪ] *vt* ➊ (*demolish*)

structure zerstören ② (*do away with*) *possibility* vernichten ③ (*kill*) *herd* abschlachten; *pet* einschläfern ④ (*ruin*) zunichtemachen; *reputation* ruinieren

destroyer [dɪ'strɔɪ-ər] *n* MIL Zerstörer *m*

destruction [dɪ'strʌk-ʃən] *n* Zerstörung *f*; **mass** ~ Massenvernichtung *f*

destructive [dɪ'strʌk-tɪv] *adj* zerstörerisch; *influence, person* destruktiv

desultory ['des-əl-tɔr-i] *adj* (*form*) halbherzig

detach [dɪ'tætʃ] *vt* abnehmen; (*without reattaching*) abtrennen

detachable [dɪ'tætʃ-ə-bəl] *adj* abnehmbar

detached [dɪ'tætʃt] *adj* ① (*separated*) abgelöst ② (*aloof*) distanziert

detachment [dɪ'tætʃ-mənt] *n* ① (*aloofness*) Distanziertheit *f* ② (*of soldiers*) Einsatztruppe *f*

detail [dɪ'teɪl] **I.** *n* ① (*item of information*) Detail *nt*, Einzelheit *f*; **further ~s** nähere Informationen; **to go into ~** ins Detail gehen, auf die Einzelheiten eingehen; **in ~** im Detail ② (*unimportant item*) Kleinigkeit *f* ■ **~s** *pl* (*vital statistics*) Personalien *pl* **II.** *vt* ① (*explain*) ausführlich erläutern ② (*specify*) einzeln aufführen

detailed [dɪ'teɪld] *adj* detailliert; *description, report* ausführlich; *study* eingehend

detain [dɪ'teɪn] *vt* ① LAW in Haft nehmen, inhaftieren ② (*form: delay*) aufhalten

detainee [ˌdi-teɪ'ni] *n* Häftling *m*

detect [dɪ'tekt] *vt* ① (*discover*) entdecken; *disease* feststellen; *smell* bemerken; *sound* wahrnehmen ② (*catch in act*) ertappen

detectable [dɪ'tek-tə-bəl] *adj* feststellbar; *change* wahrnehmbar

detection [dɪ'tek-ʃən] *n* ① Entdeckung *f*; *of disease* Feststellung *f* ② (*by detective*) Ermittlungsarbeit *f*

detective [dɪ'tek-tɪv] *n* ① (*police officer*) Kriminalbeamte(r) *m*, Kriminal-

beamte [*o* -in] *f* ② (*private*) [Privat]detektiv(in) *m(f)*

detention [dɪ'ten-ʃən] *n* ① (*state*) Haft *f* ② (*act*) Festnahme *f* ③ SCH Nachsitzen *nt kein pl*; **to get ~** nachsitzen müssen

de'tention center *n* Untersuchungsgefängnis *nt*

deter <-rr-> [dɪ'tɜr] *vt* verhindern; (*put off*) *person* abschrecken, abhalten (**from** von +*dat*)

detergent [dɪ'tɜr-dʒənt] *n* Reinigungsmittel *nt*; (*for clothes*) Waschmittel *nt*

deteriorate [dɪ'tɪr-i-ə-reɪt] *vi* ① (*become worse*) sich verschlechtern ② (*disintegrate*) verfallen; *leather, wood* sich zersetzen; *rubber, leather* brüchig werden

deterioration [dɪˌtɪr-i-ə-'reɪ-ʃən] *n* ① (*worsening*) Verschlechterung *f* ② ECON, TECH Qualitätsverlust *m* ③ (*disintegration*) Verfall *m*; *of metal, wood* Zersetzung *f*

determination [dɪˌtɜr-mɪ-'neɪ-ʃən] *n* ① (*resolve*) Entschlossenheit *f* ② (*determining*) Bestimmung *f*

determine [dɪ'tɜr-mɪn] *vt* ① (*decide*) entscheiden ② (*find out*) ermitteln, feststellen, herausfinden ③ (*influence*) bestimmen

determined [dɪ'tɜr-mɪnd] *adj* entschlossen

deterrent [dɪ'tɜr-ənt] *n* Abschreckung *f*, Abschreckungsmittel *nt*

detest [dɪ'test] *vt* verabscheuen

detonate ['det-ə-neɪt] *vt, vi* detonieren

detonation [ˌdet-ə-'neɪ-ʃən] *n* Detonation *f*

detonator ['det-ə-neɪ-tər] *n* [Spreng]zünder *m*

detour ['di-tʊr] *n* ① TRANSP Umleitung *f* ② (*deviation*) Umweg *m*

detox ['di-taks] *n short for* **detoxification** Entzug *m*

detract [dɪ'trækt] *vi* ■ **to ~ from sth** etw beeinträchtigen

detriment ['det-rə-mənt] *n* Nachteil *m*

detrimental [ˌdet-rɪ-'men-təl] *adj* schädlich

D

deuce [dus] *n* ① (*cards, dice*) Zwei *f* ② TENNIS Einstand *m*

devaluation [ˌdiˈvæl·ju·ˈeɪ·ʃən] *n* Abwertung *f*

devalue [ˌdiˈvæl·ju] *vt* abwerten

devastate ['dev·ə·steɪt] *vt* vernichten; *region* verwüsten; (*fam*) umhauen

devastated ['dev·ə·steɪ·tɪd] *adj* völlig fertig *fam*, total down *sl*

devastating ['dev·ə·steɪ·tɪŋ] *adj* ① (*destructive*) verheerend, vernichtend *a. fig* ② (*fig fam: positively overwhelming*) umwerfend; (*negatively*) niederschmetternd

devastation [ˌdev·ə·ster·ʃən] *n* ① (*destruction*) Verwüstung *f* ② (*of person*) Verzweiflung *f*

develop [dɪˈvel·əp] **I.** *vi* sich entwickeln (**into** zu +*dat*); *abilities* sich entfalten **II.** *vt* ① entwickeln; *habit* annehmen; *plan* ausarbeiten; *skills* weiterentwickeln ② ARCHIT erschließen [und bebauen] ③ PHOT entwickeln

developed [dɪˈvel·əpt] *adj* ① entwickelt ② ARCHIT erschlossen

developer [dɪˈvel·ə·pər] *n* ① (*person*) Bauunternehmer(in) *m(f)*; (*company*) Baufirma *f*, Bauunternehmen *nt* ② PHOT Entwickler *m*

development [dɪˈvel·əp·mənt] *n* ① (*act, event, process*) Entwicklung *f* ② ARCHIT Bau *m*; (*area*) Baugebiet *nt*; (*buildings*) housing ~ Siedlung *f*

deviant ['di·vi·ənt] SOCIOL **I.** *n* to be a [*sexual*] ~ [im sexuellen Verhalten] von der Norm abweichen **II.** *adj behavior* abweichend

deviate ['di·vi·eɪt] *vi from norm* abweichen; *from route* sich entfernen

deviation [ˌdi·vi·ˈeɪ·ʃən] *n* Abweichung *f*

device [dɪˈvaɪs] *n* ① (*machine*) Gerät *nt*, Vorrichtung *f* ② (*method*) Verfahren *nt* ③ (*bomb*) Sprengsatz *m*

devil ['dev·əl] *n* ① REL Teufel *m* ② (*fig*) Teufel(in) *m(f)* ③ (*fam: affectionately*) little ~ kleiner Schlingel *fam;* lucky ~ Glückspilz *m*

devilish ['dev·ə·lɪʃ] *adj* teuflisch; *situation* verteufelt

devious ['di·vi·əs] *adj* ① (*dishonest*) *person* verschlagen; *plan* krumm ② (*roundabout*) gewunden

devise [dɪˈvaɪz] *vt* erdenken; *plan* aushecken

devoid [dɪˈvɔɪd] *adj* ■to be ~ of sth ohne etw sein

devolve [dɪˈvalv] *vi* (*form*) übergehen ([**up**]**on** auf +*akk*)

devote [dɪˈvoʊt] *vt* widmen; *one's time* opfern

devoted [dɪˈvoʊ·tɪd] *adj admirer* begeistert; *dog* anhänglich; *follower, friend* treu; *husband, mother* hingebungsvoll

devotee [ˌdev·ə·ˈti] *n of an artist* Verehrer(in) *m(f)*; *of a leader* Anhänger(in) *m(f)*; *of a cause* Verfechter(in) *m(f)*; *of music* Liebhaber(in) *m(f)*

devotion [dɪˈvoʊ·ʃən] *n* ① (*loyalty*) Ergebenheit *f* ② (*dedication*) Hingabe *f* (**to** an +*akk*) ③ (*affection*) *of husband, wife* Liebe *f*; *of children* Anhänglichkeit *f*; *of an admirer* Verehrung *f*

devour [dɪˈvaʊ·ər] *vt* verschlingen *a. fig*

devout [dɪˈvaʊt] *adj* REL fromm; (*fig*) [sehr] engagiert; *hope, wish* sehnlich

dew [du] *n* Tau *m*

'dewdrop *n* Tautropfen *m*

dexterity [ˌdek·ˈster·ɪ·ti] *n* Geschicklichkeit *f*

dexterous ['dek·stər·əs] *adj* gewandt; *fingers* geschickt

dextrous ['dek·strəs] *adj see* **dexterous**

diabetes [ˌdaɪ·ə·ˈbi·tɪz] *n* Zuckerkrankheit *f*

diabetic [ˌdaɪ·ə·ˈbet·ɪk] **I.** *n* Diabetiker(in) *m(f)* **II.** *adj* ① (*having diabetes*) zuckerkrank ② (*for diabetics*) Diabetiker-

diabolical [ˌdaɪ·ə·ˈbal·ɪ·kəl] *adj* ① (*of Devil*) Teufels- ② (*evil*) teuflisch

diagnose [ˌdaɪ·əg·ˈnoʊs] *vt* ① MED diagnostizieren ② (*discover*) erkennen; *fault, problem* feststellen

diagnosis <*pl* -ses> [ˌdaɪ·əg·ˈnoʊ·

sis] *n* **①** *of disease* Diagnose *f* **②** *of problem* Beurteilung *f*

diagnostic [ˌdaɪ·əg·ˈnɑs·tɪk] *adj* diagnostisch

diagonal [daɪ·ˈæg·ə·nəl] I. *adj line* diagonal, schräg **②.** *n* Diagonale *f*

diagram [ˈdaɪ·ə·græm] *n* schematische Darstellung; MATH Diagramm *nt*

dial [ˈdaɪ·əl] I. *n* **①** *of clock* Zifferblatt; *of instrument, radio* Skala *f*; *of telephone* Wählscheibe *f* II. *vt, vi* <-l-> wählen; **to ~ the wrong number** sich verwählen

dialect [ˈdaɪ·ə·lekt] *n* Dialekt *m*

dialogue, dialog [ˈdaɪ·ə·lɑg] *n* Dialog *m*

'dial tone *n* Wählton *m*

dialysis [daɪ·ˈæl·ə·sɪs] *n* Dialyse *f*

diameter [daɪ·ˈæm·ə·tər] *n* Durchmesser *m*

diametrically [ˌdaɪ·ə·ˈmet·rɪ·kə·li] *adv* ~ **opposed** völlig entgegengesetzt

diamond [ˈdaɪ·ə·mənd] *n* **①** *(stone)* Diamant *m* **②** MATH Raute *f*, Rhombus *m* **③** CARDS Karo *nt*

diamond anni'versary *n* diamantene Hochzeit

diaper [ˈdaɪ·pər] *n* Windel *f*

diaphragm [ˈdaɪ·ə·fræm] *n* **①** ANAT Zwerchfell *nt* **②** *(contraceptive)* Diaphragma *nt*, Pessar *nt*

diarrhea [ˌdaɪ·ə·ˈri·ə] *n* Durchfall *m*

diary [ˈdaɪ·ə·ri] *n* **①** *(journal)* Tagebuch *nt* **②** *(schedule)* [Termin]kalender *m*

dice [daɪs] I. *n* **①** *pl of* **die** Würfel *m* **②** *(game)* Würfelspiel *nt* ▶PHRASES: **no ~** *(sl)* kommt [überhaupt] nicht in Frage *fam*; *(of no use)* vergiss es *fam* II. *vt* FOOD würfeln

dicey [ˈdaɪ·si] *adj (fam)* riskant

dick [dɪk] *n* **①** *(vulg: penis)* Schwanz *m* **②** *(offensive: jerk)* Idiot *m pej*

Dictaphone® [ˈdɪk·tə·foʊn] *n* Diktaphon® *nt*

dictate [ˈdɪk·teɪt] I. *vt* **①** *(command)* befehlen **②** *letter, memo* diktieren II. *vi* **①** *(issue commands)* ■**to ~ to sb** jdm

Vorschriften machen **②** *(read aloud)* diktieren

dictation [dɪk·ˈteɪ·ʃən] *n* Diktat *nt*

dictator [ˈdɪk·teɪ·tər] *n* Diktator *m*

dictatorial [ˌdɪk·tə·ˈtɔr·i·əl] *adj* diktatorisch

dictatorship [dɪk·ˈteɪ·tər·ʃɪp] *n* Diktatur *f*

diction [ˈdɪk·ʃən] *n* Ausdrucksweise *f*

dictionary [ˈdɪk·ʃə·ner·i] *n* Wörterbuch *nt*

did [dɪd] *pt of* **do**

diddle [ˈdɪd·əl] *vi (fam)* ■**to ~ [around] with sth** an etw *dat* [he]rummachen

didn't [ˈdɪd·ənt] = **did not** *see* **do**

die[1] <-y-> [daɪ] *vi* **①** sterben, umkommen *(of* vor +*dat*); **to ~ of cancer** an Krebs sterben; **to ~ laughing** sich totlachen, sich kaputtlachen; **to ~ of hunger** verhungern; **to ~ of thirst** verdursten **②** *(fig fam: stop functioning)* kaputtgehen; *engine* stehen bleiben; *battery* leer werden; *flame, light* [v]erlöschen ▶PHRASES: **to be dying to do sth** darauf brennen, etw zu tun; **to be dying for sth** großes Verlangen nach etw *dat* haben

◆**die away** *vi* schwinden; *sound* verhallen

◆**die down** *vi noise* leiser werden; *rain, wind* schwächer werden; *storm* sich legen; *excitement* abklingen

◆**die off** *vi* aussterben; BOT absterben

◆**die out** *vi* aussterben

die[2] [daɪ] *n <pl* **dice**> *(for games)* Würfel *m*

'diehard I. *n (pej)* Dickschädel *m* II. *adj* unermüdlich; *liberal* Erz-

diesel [ˈdi·zəl] *n* **①** *(fuel)* Diesel[kraft-stoff] *m* **②** *(vehicle)* Dieselfahrzeug *nt*, Diesel *m*

'diesel engine *n* Dieselmotor *m*

'diesel oil *n* Dieselöl *nt*

diet [ˈdaɪ·ət] I. *n* **①** *(food and drink)* Nahrung *f* **②** MED Diät *f*, Schonkost *f* **③** *(for losing weight)* Diät *f*, Schlankheitskur *f*; **to go on a ~** eine Diät machen II. *vi* Diät halten III. *adj* Diät-

dietary [ˈdaɪ·ɪ·ter·i] *adj* **①** *(of usual*

D

food) Ernährungs-, Ess- ② (*of medical diet*) Diät-

dietary 'fiber *n* Ballaststoffe *pl*

dietician, dietitian [ˌdaɪ·ə·ˈtɪʃ·ən] *n* Diätassistent(in) *m(f)*

differ [ˈdɪf·ər] *vi* ① (*be unlike*) sich unterscheiden ② (*not agree*) verschiedener Meinung sein

difference [ˈdɪf·ər·əns] *n* ① Unterschied *m;* **to make all the ~** die Sache völlig ändern ② FIN Differenz *f;* MATH (*after subtraction*) Rest *m* ③ (*disagreement*) ~ |**of opinion**| Meinungsverschiedenheit *f*

different [ˈdɪf·ər·ənt] *adj* ① anders *pred,* andere(r, s) *attr;* ■ **to be ~ from** |*or* **than**| **sb/sth** sich von jdm/etw unterscheiden ② (*unusual*) ungewöhnlich

differential [ˌdɪf·ə·ˈren·tʃəl] **I.** *n* ① MATH Differenzial *nt* ② MECH Differenzial|getriebe| *nt* ③ (*difference*) Unterschied *m;* ECON Gefälle *nt* **II.** *adj* ① (*different*) unterschiedlich *f* ② MATH, MECH Differenzial-

differentiate [ˌdɪf·ə·ˈren·tʃi·eɪt] *vt, vi* unterscheiden

difficult [ˈdɪf·ɪ·kəlt] *adj* schwierig, schwer; *job, trip* beschwerlich

difficulty [ˈdɪf·ɪ·kəl·ti] *n* ① (*effort*) **with ~** mit Mühe ② (*problematic nature*) Schwierigkeit *f* ③ (*trouble*) Problem *nt,* Schwierigkeit *f;* **to have ~ doing sth** Schwierigkeiten dabei haben, etw zu tun

diffident [ˈdɪf·ɪ·dənt] *adj* (*form*) ① (*shy*) zaghaft ② (*reserved*) zurückhaltend

dig [dɪg] **I.** *n* ① ARCHEOL Ausgrabung *f* ② (*thrust*) Stoß *m* **II.** *vi* <-gg-, dug, dug> graben **III.** *vt* <-gg-, dug, dug> ① (*with shovel*) graben; *ditch* ausheben ② **to ~ sb in the ribs** jdn [mit dem Ellenbogen] anstoßen

◆**dig in I.** *vi* ① MIL sich eingraben ② (*fam: start eating*) reinhauen *fam* **II.** *vt fertilizer* untergraben

◆**dig up** *vt* ① (*turn over*) umgraben ② (*remove*) ausgraben; ARCHEOL freilegen ③ (*fig: find out*) herausfinden

digest *vt* [daɪˈdʒest] ① verdauen *a. fig* ② CHEM auflösen

digestion [daɪˈdʒes·tʃən] *n* Verdauung *f*

digit [ˈdɪdʒ·ɪt] *n* ① MATH Ziffer *f* ② (*finger*) Finger *m;* (*toe*) Zehe *f*

digital [ˈdɪdʒ·ɪ·t̬əl] *adj* digital, Digital-

digital 'radio *n* Digitalradio *nt*

digital 'television *n* Digitalfernsehen *nt*

dignified [ˈdɪg·nɪ·faɪd] *adj* würdig, würdevoll

dignitary [ˈdɪg·nə·ter·i] *n* Würdenträger(in) *m(f)*

dignity [ˈdɪg·nɪ·t̬i] *n* Würde *f*

digress [daɪˈgres] *vi* abschweifen

dike[1] [daɪk] *n* ① (*wall*) Deich *m* ② (*drainage channel*) |Abfluss|graben *m*

dike[2] *n* (*pej sl: lesbian*) *see* **dyke**[2]

dilapidated [dɪˈlæp·ɪ·deɪ·t̬ɪd] *adj house* verfallen; *car* klapprig

dilate [ˈdaɪ·leɪt] **I.** *vi* sich weiten **II.** *vt* erweitern

dilemma [dɪˈlem·ə] *n* Dilemma *nt*

diligence [ˈdɪl·ɪ·dʒəns] *n* ① (*industriousness*) Fleiß *m;* (*enthusiasm*) Eifer *m* ② LAW (*carefulness*) Sorgfalt *f*

diligent [ˈdɪl·ɪ·dʒənt] *adj* ① (*hardworking*) fleißig; (*enthusiastic*) eifrig ② (*painstaking*) sorgfältig

dill [dɪl] *n* Dill *m*

dilly-dally <-ie-> [ˈdɪl·i·dæl·i] *vi* (*pej fam*) schwanken

dilute [daɪˈlut] *vt* verdünnen

dim <-mm-> [dɪm] **I.** *adj* ① (*not bright*) schwach, trüb; (*poorly lit*) schumm[e]rig ② (*indistinct*) undeutlich; *recollection, shape* verschwommen ③ (*fam: slow to understand*) schwer von Begriff **II.** *vt* abdunkeln; *headlights* abblenden

dime [daɪm] *n* Dime *m,* Zehncentstück *nt* ▶PHRASES: **a ~ a dozen** spottbillig

dimension [dɪˈmen·ʃən] *n* Dimension *f*

diminish [dɪˈmɪn·ɪʃ] **I.** *vt* vermindern **II.** *vi* sich vermindern; *pain* nachlassen; *influence, value* abnehmen

diminutive [dɪˈmɪn·jə·t̬ɪv] **I.** *adj*

① (*tiny*) winzig **②** LING diminutiv II. *n* LING Verkleinerungsform *f*

dimmer ['dɪm·ər], **dimmer switch** ['dɪm·ər-] *n* Dimmer *m*, Helligkeitsregler *m*; AUTO Abblendschalter *m*

dimple ['dɪm·pəl] *n* (*in cheeks, chin*) Grübchen *nt*

dimpled ['dɪm·pəld] *adj* mit Grübchen

din [dɪn] *n* (*liter*) Lärm *m*

dine [daɪn] *vi* (*form*) speisen

diner ['daɪ·nər] *n* **①** (*person*) Speisende(r) *f(m)*; (*in restaurant*) Gast *m* **②** (*café*) Restaurant am Straßenrand mit Theke und Tischen **③** RAIL *see* **dining car**

dinghy ['dɪŋ·i] *n* Ding[h]i *nt*

dingy ['dɪn·dʒi] *adj* düster, schmuddelig; *color* trüb

dining car ['daɪ·nɪŋ,-] *n* RAIL Speisewagen *m*

'dining room *n* (*in house*) Esszimmer *nt*; (*in public building*) Speisesaal *m*

dinky ['dɪŋ·ki] *adj* (*pej fam*) klein

dinner ['dɪn·ər] *n* **①** (*evening meal*) Abendessen *nt*; DIAL (*warm lunch*) Mittagessen *nt*; **to go out for ~** essen gehen **②** (*formal meal*) Diner *nt*, Festessen *nt*

'dinner party *n* Abendgesellschaft *f* [mit Essen]

'dinner table *n* (*in house*) Esstisch *m*; (*at formal event*) Tafel *f*

'dinnertime *n* Essenszeit *f*

dinosaur ['daɪ·nə·sɔr] *n* Dinosaurier *m a. fig*

diocese ['daɪ·ə·sɪs] *n* Diözese *f*

dip [dɪp] I. *n* **①** FOOD Dip *m* **②** (*brief swim*) kurzes Bad; **to go for a ~** kurz reinspringen **③** *in road* Vertiefung *f*, Senke *f* II. *vi* <-pp-> **①** (*go down*) [ver]sinken; (*lower*) sich senken **②** (*decline*) fallen; *profits* zurückgehen III. *vt* <-pp-> **①** (*immerse*) [ein]tauchen; FOOD [ein]tunken **②** (*lower*) senken; *flag* dippen

◆ **dip into** *vi* **①** (*study casually*) ■ **to ~ into sth** *book* einen kurzen Blick auf etw *akk* werfen **②** *savings* angreifen

diphtheria [dɪf·'θɪr·i·ə] *n* MED Diphtherie *f*

diphthong ['dɪf·θaŋ] *n* LING Doppellaut *m*

diploma [dɪ·'plou·mə] *n* **①** SCH, UNIV Diplom *nt* **②** (*honorary document*) [Ehren]urkunde *f*

diplomacy [dɪ·'plou·mə·si] *n* Diplomatie *f a. fig*

diplomat ['dɪp·lə·mæt] *n* Diplomat(in) *m(f) a. fig*

diplomatic [,dɪp·lə·'mæt̬·ɪk] *adj* diplomatisch *a. fig*

'dipstick *n* **①** AUTO [Öl]messstab *m* **②** (*sl: idiot*) Idiot(in) *m(f) pej*, Dummkopf *m pej*

dire ['daɪr] *adj* **①** (*dreadful*) entsetzlich, furchtbar; *situation* aussichtslos; **in ~ straits** in einer ernsten Notlage **②** (*ominous*) *warning, forecast* unheilvoll

direct [dɪ·'rekt] I. *adj* direkt; **the ~ opposite** das genaue Gegenteil II. *adv* direkt III. *vt* **①** (*control*) leiten, führen; *traffic* regeln **②** (*aim*) richten (**at/to** an +*akk*); *attention* lenken (**at/to** auf +*akk*) **③** (*give directions*) ■ **to ~ sb to sth** jdm den Weg zu etw *dat* zeigen **④** THEAT, FILM Regie führen bei; MUS dirigieren

direct 'current *n* ELEC Gleichstrom *m*

direct 'hit *n* Volltreffer *m*

direction [dɪ·'rek·ʃən] *n* **①** (*course*) Richtung *f*; **in the ~ of the bedroom** in Richtung Schlafzimmer; **sense of ~** Orientierungssinn *m*; **in opposite ~s** in entgegengesetzter Richtung; **to give sb ~s** jdm den Weg beschreiben **②** (*supervision*) Leitung *f*, Führung *f* **③** (*instructions*) ■ **~s** *pl* Anweisungen *pl*

directive [dɪ·'rek·tɪv] *n* [An]weisung *f*

directly [dɪ·'rekt·li] *adv* direkt

direct 'object *n* direktes Objekt

director [dɪ·'rek·tər] *n* **①** ADMIN *of company* Direktor(in) *m(f)* **②** FILM, THEAT Regisseur(in) *m(f)*; *of orchestra* Dirigent(in) *m(f)*; *of choir* Chorleiter(in) *m(f)*

directory [dɪ·'rek·tə·ri] *n* (*phone book*) Telefonbuch *nt*; (*list*) Verzeichnis *nt*

D

directory as'sistance *n* [Telefon]auskunft *f kein pl*

dirt [dɜrt] *n* ❶ (*filth*) Schmutz *m*, Dreck *m* ❷ (*soil*) Erde *f*

dirt 'cheap *adj* (*fam*) spottbillig

dirt 'road *n* Schotterstraße *f*

dirty ['dɜr· t̬i] I. *adj* ❶ (*unclean*) dreckig, schmutzig; *needle* benutzt ❷ (*fam: nasty*) gemein; *liar* dreckig; *rascal* gerissen ❸ (*fam: lewd*) schmutzig; *language* vulgär ❹ (*unfriendly*) *look* böse II. *adv* ❶ (*dishonestly*) unfair ❷ (*obscenely*) vulgär III. *vt* beschmutzen

disability [ˌdɪs·ə·'bɪl·ɪ·t̬i] *n* Behinderung *f*; ~ **benefit** Erwerbsunfähigkeitsrente *f*

disable [dɪs·'eɪ·bəl] *vt person* arbeitsunfähig machen; *thing* funktionsunfähig machen

disabled [dɪs·'eɪ·bəld] I. *adj* ❶ (*handicapped*) behindert ❷ (*for the handicapped*) Behinderten- II. *n* ■**the ~** *pl* die Behinderten

disadvantage [ˌdɪs·əd·'væn·tɪdʒ] I. *n* Nachteil *m*; (*state*) Benachteiligung *f*; **to put sb at a ~** jdn benachteiligen II. *vt* benachteiligen

disadvantageous [ˌdɪs·ˌæd·væn·'teɪdʒəs] *adj* nachteilig

disaffected [ˌdɪs·ə·'fek·tɪd] *adj* (*form: dissatisfied*) unzufrieden; (*estranged*) entfremdet

disagree [ˌdɪs·ə·'gri] *vi* ❶ (*dissent*) nicht übereinstimmen; (*with plan, decision*) nicht einverstanden sein; (*with sb else*) anderer Meinung sein ❷ (*argue*) eine Auseinandersetzung haben ❸ FOOD **something that ~s with me** etwas, das mir nicht bekommt

disagreeable [ˌdɪs·ə·'gri·ə·bəl] *adj* ❶ (*unpleasant*) unangenehm ❷ (*unfriendly*) unsympathisch

disagreement [ˌdɪs·ə·'gri·mənt] *n* ❶ (*lack of agreement*) Uneinigkeit *f* ❷ (*argument*) Meinungsverschiedenheit *f*

disallow [ˌdɪs·ə·'laʊ] *vt* ❶ nicht erlauben; SPORT nicht anerkennen; *goal* annullieren ❷ LAW abweisen

disappear [ˌdɪs·ə·'pɪr] *vi* verschwinden

disappearance [ˌdɪs·ə·'pɪr·əns] *n* Verschwinden *nt*

disappoint [ˌdɪs·ə·'pɔɪnt] *vt* enttäuschen

disappointed [ˌdɪs·ə·'pɔɪn·t̬ɪd] *adj* enttäuscht (**at/about** über +*akk*, **in/with** mit +*dat*)

disappointing [ˌdɪs·ə·'pɔɪn·t̬ɪŋ] *adj* enttäuschend

disappointment [ˌdɪs·ə·'pɔɪnt·mənt] *n* Enttäuschung *f*

disapproval [ˌdɪs·ə·'pru·vəl] *n* Missbilligung *f*

disapprove [ˌdɪs·ə·'pruv] *vi* dagegen sein; ■**to ~ of sth** etw missbilligen; ■ ~ **of sb** jdn ablehnen

disarm [dɪs·'arm] I. *vt person* entwaffnen *a. fig; bomb* entschärfen II. *vi* abrüsten

disarmament [dɪs·'ar·mə·mənt] *n* Abrüstung *f*

disarming [dɪs·'ar·mɪŋ] *adj* entwaffnend

disarray [ˌdɪs·ə·'reɪ] *n* ❶ (*disorder*) Unordnung *f* ❷ (*confusion*) Verwirrung *f*

disaster [dɪ·'zæs·tər] *n* Katastrophe *f a. fig*

disastrous [dɪ·'zæs·trəs] *adj* katastrophal

disband [dɪs·'bænd] I. *vi* sich auflösen II. *vt meeting, club* auflösen

disbelief [ˌdɪs·bɪ·'lif] *n* Unglaube *m*

disbelieve [ˌdɪs·bɪ·'liv] *vt* (*form*) ■**to ~ sb** jdm nicht glauben; ■**to ~ sth** etw bezweifeln

disc [dɪsk] *n see* **disk**

discard ['dɪs·kard] *vt* ❶ (*throw away*) wegwerfen ❷ CARDS abwerfen

'disc brake *n* Scheibenbremse *f*

discern [dɪ·'sɜrn] *vt* (*form*) wahrnehmen

discernible [dɪ·'sɜr·nə·bəl] *adj* wahrnehmbar, erkennbar

discerning [dɪ·'sɜr·nɪŋ] *adj* urteilsfähig; *palate* fein; *reader* kritisch

discernment [dɪ·'sɜrn·mənt] *n* (*good judgment*) Urteilskraft *f*

discharge I. *vt* [dɪs·'tʃardʒ] ❶ (*re-*

lease) entlassen (**from** aus +*dat*); *soldier* verabschieden ② (*emit*) absondern; *sewage* ablassen ③ (*pay off*) *debt* begleichen II. *vi* [dɪsˈtʃɑrdʒ] (*pour out*) sich ergießen; *wound* eitern III. *n* [ˈdɪsˈtʃɑrdʒ] ① *of person* Entlassung *f* ② (*of liquid*) Ausströmen *nt kein pl* ③ (*liquid emitted*) Ausfluss *m kein pl*; *from wound* Absonderung *f*

disciple [dɪˈsaɪ·pəl] *n* Anhänger(in) *m(f)*; (*of Jesus*) Jünger *m*

disciplinary [ˈdɪs·ə·plə·ner·i] *adj* Disziplinar-

discipline [ˈdɪs·ə·plɪn] I. *n* Disziplin *f* II. *vt* (*punish*) bestrafen

'disc jockey *n* Diskjockey *m*

disclaim [dɪsˈkleɪm] *vt* abstreiten; *responsibility* ablehnen

disclaimer [dɪsˈkleɪ·mər] *n* Verzichtserklärung *f*; INET Disclaimer *m*

disclose [dɪsˈkloʊz] *vt* ① (*reveal*) bekannt geben ② (*uncover*) enthüllen

disclosure [dɪsˈkloʊ·ʒər] *n* (*form*) *of information* Bekanntgabe *f*; *of secret* Enthüllung *f*

disco [ˈdɪs·koʊ] *n short for* **discotheque** Disco *f*, Disko *f*

discolor [dɪsˈkʌl·ər] I. *vi* sich verfärben II. *vt* verfärben

discomfort [dɪsˈkʌm·fərt] *n* ① (*slight pain*) Beschwerden *pl* ② (*inconvenience*) Unannehmlichkeit *f*

disconcert [ˌdɪs·kən·ˈsɜrt] *vt* beunruhigen

disconnect [ˌdɪs·kə·ˈnekt] *vt* trennen; *electricity, gas, phone* abstellen

disconnected [ˌdɪs·kə·ˈnek·tɪd] *adj* ① (*turned off*) [ab]getrennt; (*left without supply*) abgestellt ② (*incoherent*) *speech* zusammenhang[s]los

disconsolate [dɪsˈkan·sə·lət] *adj* (*dejected*) niedergeschlagen; (*inconsolable*) untröstlich

discontent [ˌdɪs·kən·ˈtent] *n* Unzufriedenheit *f*

discontented [ˌdɪs·kən·ˈten·tɪd] *adj* unzufrieden (**with** mit +*dat*)

discontinue [ˌdɪs·kən·ˈtɪn·ju] *vt* abbre-

chen; *product* auslaufen lassen; *service* einstellen; *visits* aufgeben

discord [ˈdɪsˈkɔrd] *n* ① (*form*) Uneinigkeit *f*, Zwietracht *f* ② MUS Disharmonie *f*

discordant [dɪˈskɔr·dənt] *adj* ① entgegengesetzt; *views* gegensätzlich ② MUS disharmonisch

discotheque [ˈdɪs·kə·tek] *n* Diskothek *f*

discount I. *n* [ˈdɪsˈkaʊnt] Rabatt *m*; **~ for cash** Skonto *nt o m* II. *vt* [dɪsˈkaʊnt] ① (*disregard*) unberücksichtigt lassen; *possibility* nicht berücksichtigen; *testimony* nicht einbeziehen ② (*reduce*) *article* herabsetzen; *price* reduzieren

discourage [dɪˈskɜr·ɪdʒ] *vt* ① (*dishearten*) entmutigen ② (*dissuade*) ■ **to ~ sth** von etw *dat* abraten; ■ **to ~ sb from doing sth** jdm davon abraten, etw zu tun

discouragement [dɪˈskɜr·ɪdʒ·mənt] *n* ① (*feeling*) Mutlosigkeit *f* ② (*deterrence*) Abschreckung *f*; (*dissuasion*) Abraten *nt*

discouraging [dɪˈskɜr·ɪdʒ·ɪŋ] *adj* entmutigend

discourteous [dɪsˈkɜr·ti·əs] *adj* (*form*) unhöflich

discover [dɪˈskʌv·ər] *vt* ① (*find out*) herausfinden ② (*find first*) entdecken *a. fig* ③ (*find*) finden

discovery [dɪˈskʌv·ə·ri] *n* Entdeckung *f a. fig*

discredit [dɪsˈkred·ɪt] I. *vt* ① (*disgrace*) in Verruf bringen, diskreditieren ② (*cause to appear false*) unglaubwürdig machen II. *n* Misskredit *m*

discreet [dɪˈskrit] *adj* ① (*unobtrusive*) diskret; *color, pattern* dezent ② (*tactful*) taktvoll

discrepancy [dɪˈskrep·ən·si] *n* (*form*) Diskrepanz *f*

discretion [dɪˈskref·ən] *n* ① (*behavior*) Diskretion *f* ② (*good judgment*) **to use one's ~** nach eigenem Ermessen handeln

discriminate [dɪˈskrɪm·ə·neɪt] *vi* ① (*differentiate*) unterscheiden ② (*be* *prejudiced*) diskriminieren; **to ~ in favor of sb** jdn bevorzugen; ■**to ~ against sb** jdn diskriminieren

discriminating [dɪˈskrɪm·ə·neɪˌtɪŋ] *adj* (*approv*) kritisch; *palate* fein

discrimination [dɪˌskrɪm·ɪˈneɪ·ʃən] *n* ❶(*prejudice*) Diskriminierung *f* ❷(*taste*) [kritisches] Urteilsvermögen *nt*

discriminatory [dɪˈskrɪm·ɪ·nə·tɔr·i] *adj* diskriminierend

discus <*pl* -es> [ˈdɪs·kəs] *n* SPORT Diskus *m*; (*event*) Diskuswerfen *nt*

discuss [dɪˈskʌs] *vt* ❶(*talk about*) besprechen ❷(*debate*) erörtern, diskutieren

discussion [dɪˈskʌʃ·ən] *n* Diskussion *f*

disdain [dɪsˈdeɪn] I. *n* Verachtung *f* II. *vt* (*despise*) verachten; (*reject*) verschmähen

disdainful [dɪsˈdeɪn·fəl] *adj* (*form*) verächtlich

disease [dɪˈziz] *n* Krankheit *f* a. *fig*

diseased [dɪˈzizd] *adj* krank; *plant* befallen

disembark [ˌdɪs·ɪmˈbark] *vi* von Bord gehen

disentangle [ˌdɪs·ɪnˈtæŋ·gəl] *vt* entwirren; (*fig*) herauslösen (**from** aus +*dat*); ■**to ~ oneself** sich befreien

disfavor [ˌdɪsˈfeɪ·vər] *n* Missfallen *nt*

disfigure [dɪsˈfɪg·jər] *vt* entstellen

disfigurement [dɪsˈfɪg·jər·mənt] *n* Entstellung *f*

disgrace [dɪsˈgreɪs] I. *n* Schande *f* II. *vt* Schande bringen über +*akk*

disgraceful [dɪsˈgreɪs·fəl] *adj* schändlich; *behavior* skandalös

disgruntled [dɪsˈgrʌn·təld] *adj* verstimmt

disguise [dɪsˈgaɪz] I. *vt* verbergen; *voice* verstellen; ■**to ~ oneself** sich verkleiden II. *n* (*for body*) Verkleidung *f*; (*for face*) Maske *f*; **in ~** verkleidet

disgust [dɪsˈgʌst] I. *n* ❶(*revulsion*) Ekel *m* ❷(*indignation*) Empörung *f*; **in ~** entrüstet, empört II. *vt* ❶(*sicken*) anwidern, anekeln ❷(*appall*) entrüsten, empören

disgusted [dɪsˈgʌs·tɪd] *adj* ❶(*sickened*) angeekelt, angewidert ❷(*indignant*) empört, entrüstet

disgusting [dɪsˈgʌs·tɪŋ] *adj* ❶(*repulsive*) widerlich ❷(*unacceptable*) empörend

dish <*pl* -es> [dɪʃ] *n* ❶(*for serving*) Schale *f*; (*plate*) Teller *m* ❷(*after meal*) ■**the ~es** *pl* das Geschirr *kein pl*; **to do** [*or* **wash**] **the ~es** [ab]spülen ❸(*meal*) Gericht *nt* ❹TELEC Schüssel *f*

◆**dish out** *vt* ❶(*give freely*) großzügig verteilen (**to an** +*akk*) ❷(*serve*) *food* servieren

◆**dish up** *vt* (*fam*) auftischen

ˈ**dishcloth** *n* Geschirrtuch *nt*

dishearten [dɪsˈhar·tən] *vt* entmutigen

disheveled [dɪˈʃev·əld] *adj* unordentlich; *hair* zerzaust

dishonest [dɪsˈan·ɪst] *adj* unehrlich

dishonesty [dɪsˈan·əs·ti] *n* Unehrlichkeit *f*

dishonor [dɪsˈan·ər] (*form*) I. *n* Schande *f* II. *vt* ❶(*disgrace*) ■**to ~ sb/sth** dem Ansehen einer Person/Sache schaden ❷(*not respect*) *agreement* verletzen; *promise* nicht einlösen

dishonorable [dɪsˈan·ər·ə·bəl] *adj* unehrenhaft

ˈ**dishtowel** *n* Geschirrtuch *nt*

ˈ**dishwasher** *n* ❶(*machine*) Geschirrspülmaschine *f* ❷(*person*) Tellerwäscher(in) *m(f)*

ˈ**dishwater** *n* Spülwasser *nt* a. *fig*

disillusion [ˌdɪs·ɪˈlu·ʒən] I. *vt* desillusionieren II. *n* Ernüchterung *f*

disillusioned [ˌdɪs·ɪˈlu·ʒənd] *adj* desillusioniert

disinclination [ˌdɪs·ɪn·klɪˈneɪ·ʃən] *n* Abneigung *f*

disinclined [ˌdɪs·ɪnˈklaɪnd] *adj* abgeneigt

disinfect [ˌdɪs·ɪnˈfekt] *vt* desinfizieren

disinfectant [ˌdɪs·ɪnˈfek·tənt] *n* Desinfektionsmittel *nt*

disingenuous [ˌdɪs·ɪnˈdʒen·ju·əs] *adj* (*form*) unaufrichtig

disinherit [ˌdɪs·ɪnˈher·ɪt] *vt* enterben

disintegrate [dɪs·ˈɪn·tə·greɪt] *vi* zerfallen

disintegration [dɪs·ˌɪn·tə·ˈgreɪ·ʃən] *n* Zerfall *m*

disinterested [dɪs·ˈɪn·trɪ·stɪd] *adj* (*impartial*) unparteiisch

disjointed [dɪs·ˈdʒɔɪn·tɪd] *adj* zusammenhanglos

disk, disc [dɪsk] *n* ❶ (*object*) Scheibe *f;* MED Bandscheibe *f* ❷ MUS (*CD*) CD *f;* (*record*) [Schall]platte *f* ❸ COMPUT Diskette *f;* ~ **drive** Laufwerk *nt*

'**disk brake** *n see* **disc brake**

'**disk jockey** *n see* **disc jockey**

dislike [dɪs·ˈlaɪk] **I.** *vt* nicht mögen; **to ~ doing sth** etw nicht gern tun **II.** *n* Abneigung *f* (**of/for** gegen +*akk*)

dislocate [dɪs·ˈloʊ·keɪt] *vt* ■**to ~ sth** sich *dat* etw ausrenken

dislodge [dɪs·ˈlɑdʒ] *vt thing* lösen; *person* verdrängen

disloyal [dɪs·ˈlɔɪ·əl] *adj* illoyal (**to** gegenüber +*dat*)

dismal [ˈdɪz·məl] *adj* ❶ (*dreary*) düster, trostlos; *outlook, weather* trüb ❷ (*inadequate*) *performance* kläglich

dismantle [dɪs·ˈmæn·təl] *vt* zerlegen

dismay [dɪs·ˈmeɪ] **I.** *n* Bestürzung *f* **II.** *vt* schockieren

dismayed [dɪs·ˈmeɪd] *adj* bestürzt; *expression* betroffen

dismember [dɪs·ˈmem·bər] *vt* zerstückeln

dismiss [dɪs·ˈmɪs] *vt* ❶ (*ignore*) abtun; **to ~ a thought** [**from one's mind**] sich *dat* einen Gedanken aus dem Kopf schlagen ❷ (*send away*) wegschicken; *class* gehen lassen ❸ (*fire*) entlassen

dismissal [dɪs·ˈmɪs·əl] *n* ❶ (*disregard*) Abtun *nt* ❷ (*firing*) Entlassung *f*

dismissive [dɪs·ˈmɪs·ɪv] *adj* geringschätzig

dismount [dɪs·ˈmaʊnt] *vi* absteigen

disobedience [ˌdɪs·ə·ˈbi·di·əns] *n* Ungehorsam *m*

disobedient [ˌdɪs·ə·ˈbi·di·ənt] *adj* ungehorsam

disobey [ˌdɪs·ə·ˈbeɪ] *vt person* nicht gehorchen; *orders* nicht befolgen; *rules* sich nicht halten an +*akk*

disorder [dɪs·ˈɔr·dər] *n* ❶ (*disarray*) Unordnung *f* ❷ MED [Funktions]störung *f* ❸ (*riot*) Aufruhr *m*

disorderly [dɪs·ˈɔr·dər·li] *adj* ❶ (*untidy*) unordentlich ❷ (*unruly*) aufrührerisch

disorganized [dɪs·ˈɔr·gə·naɪzd] *adj* schlecht organisiert

disorient [dɪs·ˈɔr·i·ent] *vt usu passive* ❶ (*lose bearings*) **to be/get** [**totally**] ~**ed** [völlig] die Orientierung verloren haben/verlieren ❷ (*be confused*) ■**to be ~ed** orientierungslos sein

disown [dɪs·ˈoʊn] *vt* verleugnen; (*hum a.*) nicht mehr kennen

disparaging [dɪ·ˈsper·ɪdʒ·ɪŋ] *adj* geringschätzig

disparity [dɪ·ˈsper·ɪ·t̬i] *n* Ungleichheit *f*

dispassionate [dɪs·ˈpæʃ·ə·nɪt] *adj* objektiv

dispatch [dɪ·ˈspætʃ] **I.** *n* <*pl* -es> (*sending*) Verschicken *nt; of a person* Entsendung *f* **II.** *vt thing* senden; *person* entsenden

dispel <-ll-> [dɪ·ˈspel] *vt mist* auflösen; *rumors* zerstreuen

dispensable [dɪ·ˈspen·sə·bəl] *adj* entbehrlich

dispensary [dɪ·ˈspen·sə·ri] *n* [Krankenhaus]apotheke *f*

dispense [dɪ·ˈspens] **I.** *vt* austeilen; *medicine* ausgeben **II.** *vi* ■**to ~ with sth** auf etw *akk* verzichten

dispenser [dɪ·ˈspen·sər] *n* Automat *m*

dispersal [dɪ·ˈspɜr·səl] *n* ❶ (*scattering*) Zerstreuung *f; of a crowd* Auflösung *f* ❷ (*wide distribution*) Verstreutheit *f*

disperse [dɪ·ˈspɜrs] **I.** *vt* ❶ (*dispel*) auflösen; *crowd* zerstreuen ❷ (*distribute*) verteilen **II.** *vi crowd* auseinandergehen; *mist* sich auflösen

dispirited [dɪ·ˈspɪr·ɪ·t̬ɪd] *adj* entmutigt

displace [dɪs·ˈpleɪs] *vt* ❶ (*force out*) vertreiben ❷ (*replace*) ersetzen

displaced 'person *n* Heimatlose(r) *f(m)*

display [dɪ·ˈspleɪ] **I.** *vt* ❶ (*on board*) aushängen; (*in store window*) auslegen ❷ (*demonstrate*) *strength* zeigen **II.** *n*

① (*in museum, store*) Auslage *f*; **to be on ~** ausgestellt sein ② (*demonstration*) Demonstration *f* ③ COMPUT Display *nt*

dis'play case, dis'play cabinet *n* Vitrine *f*

D **displease** [dɪs-ˈpliz] *vt* ■**to ~ sb** jdm missfallen

displeasure [dɪs-ˈpleʒ-ər] *n* Missfallen *nt*

disposable [dɪ-ˈspoʊ-zə-bəl] *adj* ① *articles* Wegwerf- *m* ② FIN *income* verfügbar

disposal [dɪ-ˈspoʊ-zəl] *n* ① Beseitigung *f*; *of waste* Entsorgung *f* ② (*control*) Verfügung *f*; ■**to be at sb's ~** zu jds Verfügung stehen
◆**dispose of** *vt* (*get rid of*) beseitigen; (*sell*) veräußern

disposed [dɪ-ˈspoʊzd] *adj* **to be well ~ toward sb/sth** jdm/etw wohlgesinnt sein

disposition [ˌdɪs-pə-ˈzɪʃ-ən] *n* ① (*nature*) Art *f* ② (*tendency*) Veranlagung *f*

dispossess [ˌdɪs-pə-ˈzes] *vt* enteignen

disproportionate [ˌdɪs-prə-ˈpɔr-ʃə-nɪt] *adj* unangemessen

disprove [dɪs-ˈpruv] *vt* widerlegen

disputable [dɪ-ˈspju-tə-bəl] *adj* strittig

dispute [dɪ-ˈspjut] I. *vt* ① (*argue*) sich streiten über +*akk* ② (*oppose*) bestreiten II. *vi* streiten III. *n* (*argument*) Streit *m*; **to be beyond ~** außer Frage stehen

disqualification [dɪs-ˌkwal-ə-fɪ-ˈkeɪ-ʃən] *n* Ausschluss *m*; SPORT Disqualifikation *f*

disqualify <-ie-> [dɪs-ˈkwal-ə-faɪ] *vt* ausschließen; SPORT disqualifizieren

disregard [ˌdɪs-rɪ-ˈgard] I. *vt* ignorieren II. *n* Gleichgültigkeit *f*; (*for a rule, the law*) Missachtung *f*

disrepair [ˌdɪs-rɪ-ˈper] *n* Baufälligkeit *f*; **to fall into ~** verfallen

disreputable [dɪs-ˈrep-jə-tə-bəl] *adj* verrufen

disrepute [ˌdɪs-rɪ-ˈpjut] *n* Verruf *m* kein pl

disrespect [ˌdɪs-rɪ-ˈspekt] I. *n* Respektlosigkeit *f* II. *vt* (*fam*) beleidigen

disrespectful [ˌdɪs-rɪ-ˈspekt-fəl] *adj* respektlos

disrupt [dɪs-ˈrʌpt] *vt* stören

disruption [dɪs-ˈrʌp-ʃən] *n* ① (*interruption*) Unterbrechung *f* ② (*disrupting*) Störung *f*

disruptive [dɪs-ˈrʌp-tɪv] *adj* störend

dissatisfaction [dɪs-ˌsæt-ɪs-ˈfæk-ʃən] *n* Unzufriedenheit *f*

dissatisfied [dɪs-ˈsæt-ɪs-faɪd] *adj* unzufrieden

dissect [dɪ-ˈsekt] *vt* ① (*cut open*) sezieren ② (*fig*) analysieren

dissent [dɪ-ˈsent] I. *n* ① (*disagreement*) Meinungsverschiedenheit *f* ② (*protest*) Widerspruch *m* II. *vi* dagegen stimmen; (*disagree*) anderer Meinung sein

dissenter [dɪ-ˈsen-tər] *n* Andersdenkende(r) *f(m)*; POL Dissident(in) *m(f)*

dissertation [ˌdɪs-ər-ˈteɪ-ʃən] *n* Dissertation *f*

disservice [dɪs-ˈsɜr-vɪs] *n* **to do sb a ~** jdm einen schlechten Dienst erweisen

dissident [ˈdɪs-ɪ-dənt] I. *n* Dissident(in) *m(f)* II. *adj* regimekritisch

dissimilar [dɪ-ˈsɪm-ɪ-lər] *adj* unterschiedlich

dissimilarity [ˌdɪ-sɪm-ɪ-ˈler-ɪ-ti] *n* Unterschied *m*

dissipate [ˈdɪs-ɪ-peɪt] I. *vi* allmählich verschwinden; *crowd, mist* sich auflösen II. *vt* ① (*disperse*) auflösen ② (*squander*) verschwenden

dissipated [ˈdɪs-ɪ-peɪ-tɪd] *adj* (*liter*) ausschweifend

dissociate [dɪ-ˈsoʊ-ʃi-eɪt] *vt* getrennt betrachten; ■**to ~ oneself from sb/ sth** sich von jdm/etw distanzieren

dissolute [ˈdɪs-ə-lut] *adj* (*liter*) *life* ausschweifend; *person* zügellos

dissolve [dɪ-ˈzalv] I. *vi* ① (*in liquid*) sich auflösen ② (*subside*) **to ~ in[to] tears** in Tränen ausbrechen II. *vt* ① (*liquefy*) [auf]lösen ② (*annul*) auflösen; *marriage* scheiden

dissuade [dɪ-ˈsweɪd] *vt* abbringen

distance [ˈdɪs-təns] I. *n* (*to a place*)

Strecke *f*; (*between places*) Entfernung *f*; **in the ~** in der Ferne; **from** [*or* **at**] **a distance** von weitem **II.** *vt* **■to ~ oneself** sich distanzieren

'**distance learning** *n* Fernunterricht *m*

distant ['dɪs·tənt] *adj* ❶ (*far away*) fern; (*fig*) *look* abwesend; *relative* entfernt ❷ (*aloof*) unnahbar

distantly ['dɪs·tənt·li] *adv* **~ related** entfernt verwandt

distaste [dɪs·'teɪst] *n* Widerwille *m*

distasteful [dɪs·'teɪst·fəl] *adj* abscheulich

distill [dɪ·'stɪl] *vt* CHEM destillieren; *brandy* brennen

distiller [dɪ·'stɪl·ər] *n* ❶ (*company*) Destillerie *f* ❷ (*person*) Destillateur *m*

distillery [dɪ·'stɪl·ə·ri] *n* Brennerei *f*

distinct [dɪ·'stɪŋkt] *adj* ❶ (*different*) verschieden; **as ~ from sth** im Unterschied zu etw *dat* ❷ (*clear*) deutlich

distinction [dɪ·'stɪŋk·ʃən] *n* ❶ (*difference*) Unterschied *m* ❷ (*eminence*) **of** [**great**] **~** von hohem Rang ❸ (*award*) Auszeichnung *f*; **■with ~** ausgezeichnet

distinctive [dɪ·'stɪŋk·tɪv] *adj* charakteristisch

distinguish [dɪ·'stɪŋ·gwɪʃ] **I.** *vi* unterscheiden **II.** *vt* ❶ (*tell apart*) unterscheiden ❷ (*discern*) ausmachen [können] ❸ (*excel*) **■to ~ oneself in sth** sich in etw *dat* auszeichnen

distinguished [dɪ·'stɪŋ·gwɪʃt] *adj* ❶ (*eminent*) *career* hervorragend; *person* von hohem Rang ❷ (*stylish*) distinguiert

distort [dɪ·'stɔrt] *vt* ❶ (*twist*) verzerren ❷ (*fig*) verdrehen

distortion [dɪ·'stɔr·ʃən] *n* ❶ (*twisting*) Verzerrung *f* ❷ (*fig*) Verdrehung *f*

distract [dɪ·'strækt] *vt* ablenken (**from** von +*dat*)

distracted [dɪ·'stræk·tɪd] *adj* verwirrt; (*worried*) besorgt

distraction [dɪ·'stræk·ʃən] *n* ❶ (*disturbance*) Störung *f* ❷ (*diversion*) Ablenkung *f*

distraught [dɪ·'strɔt] *adj* verzweifelt, außer sich *dat*

distress [dɪ·'stres] **I.** *n* ❶ (*pain*) Leid *nt*; (*anguish*) Kummer *m*, Sorge *f* ❷ (*trouble*) Not *f* **II.** *vt* quälen

distressed [dɪ·'strest] *adj* ❶ (*unhappy*) bekümmert ❷ (*shocked*) erschüttert (**at** über +*dat*) ❸ (*old-looking*) *fabric* verwaschen; *jeans, furniture* Used-Look- **D**

distressing [dɪ·'stres·ɪŋ], **distressful** [dɪ·'stres·fəl] *adj* ❶ (*worrying*) erschreckend ❷ (*painful*) schmerzlich

distribute [dɪ·'strɪb·jut] *vt* verteilen; *goods* vertreiben

distribution [ˌdɪs·trɪ·'bju·ʃən] *n* ❶ (*sharing*) Verteilung *f* ❷ (*scattering*) Verbreitung *f* ❸ ECON Vertrieb *m*

distributor [dɪ·'strɪb·jə·tər] *n* ❶ COMM Vertriebsgesellschaft *f* ❷ AUTO Verteiler *m*

district ['dɪs·trɪkt] *n* (*area*) Gebiet *nt*; (*within a town/country*) Bezirk *m*

district at'torney *n* Staatsanwalt, Staatsanwältin *m*, *f*

district 'court *n* [Bundes]bezirksgericht *nt*

District of Columbia *n* amerikanischer Regierungsbezirk

distrust [dɪs·'trʌst] **I.** *vt* misstrauen +*dat* **II.** *n* Misstrauen *nt* (**of** gegen +*akk*)

distrustful [dɪs·'trʌst·fəl] *adj* misstrauisch

disturb [dɪ·'stɜrb] *vt* ❶ (*interrupt*) stören; "**do not ~**" „bitte nicht stören" ❷ (*worry*) beunruhigen

disturbance [dɪ·'stɜr·bəns] *n* ❶ (*annoyance*) Belästigung *f* ❷ (*riot*) **to cause a ~** Unruhe stiften

disturbed [dɪ·'stɜrbd] *adj* ❶ (*worried*) beunruhigt ❷ PSYCH [geistig] verwirrt; **mentally ~** psychisch gestört

disturbing [dɪ·'stɜr·bɪŋ] *adj* beunruhigend

disuse [dɪs·'jus] *n* Nichtgebrauch *m*; **to fall into ~** nicht mehr benutzt werden

ditch [dɪtʃ] **I.** *n* <*pl* -**es**> Graben *m* **II.** *vt* ❶ (*discard*) wegwerfen; *proposal, job* aufgeben; *car* stehen lassen

D

②(*abandon*) *person* versetzen ③ *plane* im Bach landen III. *vi* AVIAT auf dem Wasser landen

dither ['dɪð·ər] I. *n* **in a ~** ganz aufgeregt II. *vi* schwanken

ditto ['dɪt̬·oʊ] *adv* (*likewise*) dito; (*me too*) ich auch

divan [dɪ·'van] *n* Diwan *m*

dive [daɪv] I. *n* ① (*into water*) [Kopf]sprung *m* ② (*by plane*) Sturzflug *m* ③ (*drop in price*) [Preis]sturz *m* ④ (*fam: dingy place*) Spelunke *f* II. *vi* <dived *or* dove, dived *or* dove> ① (*into water*) einen Kopfsprung ins Wasser machen; (*underwater*) tauchen ② *plane* einen Sturzflug machen ③ (*move quickly*) ■ **to ~ for sth** nach etw *dat* hechten

diver ['daɪ·vər] *n* ① (*underwater*) Taucher(in) *m(f)*; SPORT Turmspringer(in) *m(f)* ② (*bird*) Taucher *m*

diverge [dɪ·'vɜrdʒ] *vi* auseinandergehen

divergence [dɪ·'vɜr·dʒəns] *n* ① (*difference*) Divergenz *f* ② (*deviation*) Abweichung *f*

divergent [dɪ·'vɜr·dʒənt] *adj* (*differing*) abweichend; *opinions* auseinandergehend

diverse [dɪ·'vɜrs] *adj* ① (*varied*) vielfältig ② (*not alike*) unterschiedlich

diversification [dɪ·ˌvɜr·sɪ·fɪ·'keɪ·ʃən] *n* Diversifikation *f*

diversify <-ie-> [dɪ·'vɜr·sɪ·faɪ] I. *vi* vielfältiger werden II. *vt* umfangreicher machen

diversion [dɪ·'vɜr·ʃən] *n* ① (*rerouting*) Verlegung *f*; *of traffic* Umleitung *f* ② (*distraction*) Ablenkung *f*

diversity [dɪ·'vɜr·sɪ·t̬i] *n* Vielfalt *f*

divert [dɪ·'vɜrt] *vt* ① (*reroute*) verlegen; *traffic* umleiten ② (*reallocate*) *funds* anders einsetzen ③ (*distract*) ablenken

diverting [dɪ·'vɜr·t̬ɪŋ] *adj* unterhaltsam

divest [dɪ·'vest] *vt* ① (*deprive*) berauben ② (*sell*) verkaufen

divide [dɪ·'vaɪd] I. *n* ① (*gulf*) Kluft *f* ② GEOG (*watershed*) Wasserscheide *f* II. *vt* ① (*split*) teilen ② (*share*) *profits* aufteilen; **to ~ sth equally** [*or* **evenly**]

etw in gleichen Teilen aufteilen ③ MATH teilen (**by** durch +*akk*) ④ (*separate*) trennen III. *vi* sich teilen

◆**divide off** *vt* [ab]teilen

◆**divide up** I. *vt* aufteilen II. *vi* sich teilen

divided [dɪ·'vaɪ·dɪd] *adj* uneinig

divided 'highway *n* Schnellstraße *f*

dividend ['dɪv·ɪ·dend] *n* FIN Dividende *f*; (*fig*) **to pay ~s** sich bezahlt machen

dividers [dɪ·'vaɪ·dərz] *npl* [**a pair of**] ~ [ein] Zirkel *m*

di'viding line *n* Trennlinie *f*

divine [dɪ·'vaɪn] I. *adj* ① (*of God*) göttlich ② (*splendid*) himmlisch II. *vt* erraten; *future* vorhersehen

diving ['daɪ·vɪŋ] *n* ① (*into water*) Tauchen *nt*; SPORT Turmspringen *nt* ② (*underwater*) Tauchen *nt*

'diving board *n* Sprungbrett *nt*

'diving suit *n* Taucheranzug *m*

di'vining rod *n* Wünschelrute *f*

divisible [dɪ·'vɪz·ə·bəl] *adj* teilbar (**by** durch +*akk*)

division [dɪ·'vɪʒ·ən] *n* ① (*sharing*) Verteilung *f* ② (*breakup*) Teilung *f* ③ MATH Division *f* ④ (*section*) Teil *m* ⑤ (*department*) Abteilung *f* ⑥ (*league*) Liga *f* ⑦ (*disagreement*) Meinungsverschiedenheit *f*

divisive [dɪ·'vaɪ·sɪv] *adj* entzweiend

divorce [dɪ·'vɔrs] I. *n* LAW Scheidung *f* II. *vt* ■ **to ~ sb** [*or* **get ~d from sb**] sich von jdm scheiden lassen III. *vi* sich scheiden lassen

divorcé [dɪ·'vɔr·seɪ] *n* Geschiedener *m*

divorced [dɪ·'vɔrst] *adj* geschieden

divorcée [dɪ·ˌvɔr·'seɪ] *n* Geschiedene *f*

divulge [dɪ·'vʌldʒ] *vt* enthüllen; *information* weitergeben

dizziness ['dɪz·ɪ·nɪs] *n* Schwindel *m*

dizzy ['dɪz·i] *adj* ① (*unsteady*) schwindlig; ~ **spells** Schwindelanfälle *pl* ② (*rapid*) atemberaubend ③ (*fam: scatterbrained*) dumm, einfältig

DJ ['di·dʒeɪ] *n abbrev of* **disc jockey** DJ *m*

DMV [ˌdi·em·'vi] *n abbrev of* **Depart-**

ment of Motor Vehicles Kfz-Zulassungsstelle f

DNA [ˌdiː·en·'eɪ] *n abbrev of* **deoxyribonucleic acid** DNS f

do [du] I. *aux vb* <does, did, done> ❶ *(negating verb)* **Fred ~esn't like olives** Fred mag keine Oliven; **I ~n't want to go yet!** ich will noch nicht gehen! ❷ *(forming question)* **you like children?** magst du Kinder?; **what did you say?** was hast du gesagt? ❸ *(for emphasis)* **can I come? — please ~!** kann ich mitkommen? – aber bitte!; **you ~ look tired** du siehst wirklich müde aus ❹ *(replacing verb)* **she runs much faster than he ~es** sie läuft viel schneller als er; **who ate the cake? — I did!/didn't!** wer hat den Kuchen gegessen? – ich!/ich nicht!; **... so ~ I ...** ich auch II. *vt* <does, did, done> ❶ tun, machen; **that was a stupid thing to ~** das war dumm!; **what did you ~ with my coat?** wo hast du meinen Mantel hingetan?; **what ~es your father ~?** was macht dein Vater beruflich?; **where ~ you get your hair done?** zu welchem Friseur gehst du?; **let me ~ the talking** überlass mir das Reden ❷ *(fam: finish)* **are you done?** bist du jetzt fertig? ❸ *(travel at)* **to ~ 80** 80 fahren ❹ *(suffice)* ▪ **to ~ sb** jdm genügen ❺ *(fam: cheat)* ▪ **to ~ sb out of sth** jdn übers Ohr hauen ❻ *(vulg, sl: have sex with)* **to ~ it with sb** mit jdm schlafen *euph* ▶ PHRASES: **that ~es it!** so, das war's jetzt! III. *vi* <does, did, done> ❶ *(behave)* tun; **~ as you're told** tu, was man dir sagt; **to ~ well to do sth** gut daran tun, etw zu tun ❷ *(fare)* **sb is ~ing fine** jdm geht es gut; **mother and baby are ~ing well** Mutter und Kind sind wohlauf; **our daughter is ~ing well in school** unsere Tochter ist gut in der Schule ❸ *(suffice)* **that'll ~** das ist o. k. so; *(angrily)* jetzt reicht's aber!; **will this room ~?** ist dieses Zimmer o. k. für Sie? ▶ PHRASES: **how ~ you ~?** *(form: as introduction)* angenehm IV. *n* ❶ **the ~s and ~n'ts**

was man tun und was man nicht tun sollte ❷ *(fam: party)* Fete f

◆ **do away with** *vi* ❶ *(discard)* abschaffen ❷ *(fam: kill)* um die Ecke bringen

◆ **do up** *vt* ❶ *(dress)* ▪ **to ~ oneself up** sich zurechtmachen ❷ *(adorn)* herrichten; *house* renovieren ❸ *(close)* zumachen

◆ **do with** *vi* ❶ *(fam: need)* brauchen; **I could ~ with some sleep** ich könnte jetzt etwas Schlaf gebrauchen ❷ *(be related to)* um etw *akk* gehen; **to have nothing to ~ with sth** mit etw *dat* nichts zu tun haben ❸ *(concern)* **sth has nothing to ~ with sb** etw geht jdn nichts an

◆ **do without** *vi* ❶ *(not have)* auskommen ohne ❷ *(prefer not to have)* verzichten auf +*akk*

docile ['das·əl] *adj* sanftmütig

dock[1] [dak] I. *n* ❶ *(wharf)* Dock *nt*; ▪ **the ~s** *pl* die Hafenanlagen *pl*; **dry ~** Trockendock *nt* ❷ *(pier)* Kai *m* II. *vi* ❶ NAUT anlegen ❷ AEROSP andocken *(with* an +*akk)*

dock[2] [dak] *n* LAW Anklagebank f

dock[3] [dak] *vt* ❶ *(reduce)* kürzen; *(deduct)* abziehen ❷ *(cut off)* [den Schwanz] kupieren

docker ['dak·ər] *n* Hafenarbeiter(in) *m(f)*

'dockyard *n* Werft f

doctor ['dak·tər] I. *n* ❶ *(medic)* Arzt, Ärztin *m, f*; **good morning, D~ Smith** guten Morgen, Herr/Frau Doktor Smith ❷ *(academic)* Doktor *m* II. *vt* ❶ *(falsify)* fälschen, frisieren ❷ *(poison)* vergiften

doctorate ['dak·tər·ət] *n* Doktor[titel] *m*

doctrine ['dak·trɪn] *n* ❶ *(set of beliefs)* Doktrin f ❷ *(belief)* Grundsatz *m*

document ['dak·jə·mənt] I. *n* Dokument *nt* II. *vt* dokumentieren

documentary [ˌdak·jə·'men·tə·ri] I. *n* Dokumentation f, Dokumentarfilm *m* II. *adj* dokumentarisch, Dokumentar-

doddering ['dad·ər·ɪŋ] *adj (fam)* tattrig

dodge [dadʒ] I. *vt* ❶ *(avoid)* *blow* ausweichen +*dat* ❷ *(evade)* sich ent-

D

D

ziehen; *military service* sich drücken vor; *question* ausweichend beantworten **II.** *vi* ausweichen **III.** *n* (*fam*) Trick *m*

doe [dou] *n* ❶ (*deer*) Hirschkuh *f*, [Reh]geiß *f* ❷ (*hare or rabbit*) Häsin *f*

does [dʌz] *vt, vi, aux vb 3rd pers. sing of* **do**

doesn't ['dʌz·ənt] = **does not** *see* **do** I, II

dog [dɔg] **I.** *n* ❶ (*canine*) Hund *m* ❷ (*pej sl: ugly woman*) Bratze *f* **II.** *vt* <-gg-> ❶ (*follow*) ständig verfolgen ❷ (*beset*) begleiten

'dog biscuit *n* Hundekuchen *m*

'dog collar *n* ❶ (*for dog*) Hundehalsband *nt* ❷ (*fam: of a minister*) Halskragen *m* [eines Geistlichen]

'dog-eared *adj* mit Eselsohren

dogged ['dɔ·gɪd] *adj* verbissen, zäh

doggerel ['dɔ·gər·əl] *n* Knittelvers *m*

'doghouse *n* Hundehütte *f* ▸ PHRASES: **to be in the ~** in Ungnade gefallen sein

dogma ['dɔg·mə] *n* Dogma *nt*

dogmatic [dɔg·'mæt̬·ɪk] *adj* dogmatisch

dog-'tired *adj* (*fam*) hundemüde

doing ['du·ɪŋ] *n* ❶ (*sb's work*) **to be sb's** ~ jds Werk sein; **to take some** ~ ganz schön anstrengend sein ❷ *pl* (*activities*) ■ ~s Tätigkeiten *pl*

do-it-yourself [ˌdu·ɪt·jər·'self] *n* Heimwerken *nt*

doldrums ['doʊl·drəmz] *npl* (*fig*) **to be in the** ~ (*in low spirits*) deprimiert sein; (*in stagnant state*) in einer Flaute stecken

dole [doʊl] *vt* ■ **to ~ out** sparsam austeilen

doll [dal] **I.** *n* ❶ (*toy*) Puppe *f* ❷ (*fam: attractive woman*) Puppe *f* **II.** *vt* ■ **to ~ oneself up** sich herausputzen

dollar ['dal·ər] *n* Dollar *m*

dollop ['dal·əp] *n* Klacks *m kein pl*

dolly ['dal·i] *n* ❶ TRANSP [Transport]wagen *m* ❷ (*esp childspeak: doll*) Püppchen *nt*

dolphin ['dal·fɪn] *n* Delphin *m*

domain [doʊ·'meɪn] *n* ❶ Reich *nt*, Gebiet *nt* ❷ COMPUT Domäne *f*; TELEC Domain *f*

dome [doʊm] *n* Kuppel *f*

domestic [də·'mes·tɪk] *adj* ❶ (*household*) häuslich; ~ **appliance** [elektrisches] Haushaltsgerät ❷ ECON, POL inländisch, Inland[s]-; ~ **policy** Innenpolitik *f*; ~ **market** Binnenmarkt *m*

domesticate [də·'mes·tɪ·keɪt] *vt* ❶ (*tame*) zähmen ❷ (*accustom to home life*) häuslich machen

domesticity [ˌdoʊ·me·'stɪs·ɪ·t̬i] *n* Häuslichkeit *f*, häusliches Leben

domestic 'violence *n* Gewalt *f* in der Familie, häusliche Gewalt

domicile ['dam·ə·saɪl] (*form*) **I.** *n* Wohnsitz *m* **II.** *vi* **to be ~d in ...** in ... ansässig sein

dominance ['dam·ə·nəns] *n* ❶ (*superior position*) Vormacht[stellung] *f* ❷ (*being dominant*) Dominanz *f*, Vorherrschaft *f*

dominant ['dam·ə·nənt] *adj* ❶ (*controlling*) *color, culture* vorherrschend; *issue, position* beherrschend; *personality* dominierend ❷ BIOL, MUS dominant

dominate ['dam·ə·neɪt] *vt* ❶ beherrschen ❷ PSYCH dominieren

domineering [ˌdam·ə·'nɪr·ɪŋ] *adj* herrschsüchtig, herrisch

domino <*pl* -es> ['dam·ə·noʊ] *n* ❶ (*piece*) Dominostein *m* ❷ (*game*) ■ ~es + *sing vb*, *no art* Domino[spiel] *nt*

don [dan] *n* (*sl*) Mafiaboss *m*

donate ['doʊ·neɪt] *vt, vi* spenden (**to** für + *akk*)

donation [doʊ·'neɪ·ʃən] *n* ❶ (*contribution*) [Geld]spende *f*; (*endowment*) Stiftung *f*; LAW Schenkung *f*; **charitable ~s** Spenden *pl* für wohltätige Zwecke ❷ (*act of donating*) Spenden *nt*

done [dʌn] *pp of* **do**

donkey ['daŋ·ki] *n* Esel *m a. fig*

donor ['doʊ·nər] *n* Spender(in) *m(f)*; (*of large sums*) Stifter(in) *m(f)*; LAW Schenker(in) *m(f)*

don't [doʊnt] *see* **do not** *see* **do** I, II

donut ['doʊ·nʌt] *n see* **doughnut**

doodle ['du·dəl] I. *vi* vor sich *akk* hinkritzeln II. *n* Gekritzel *nt kein pl*

doom [dum] *n* ❶ (*grim destiny*) Verhängnis *nt kein pl*, [schlimmes] Schicksal ❷ (*disaster*) Unheil *nt*

doomed [dumd] *adj* ❶ (*destined to end badly*) verdammt ❷ (*condemned*) verurteilt

door [dɔr] *n* ❶ (*entrance*) Tür *f*; *out of* ~**s** im Freien, draußen ❷ (*house*) *two* ~**s** *away* zwei Häuser weiter; *next* ~ nebenan; ~ *to* ~ von Tür zu Tür

'doorbell *n* Türklingel *f*

'doorframe *n* Türrahmen *m*

'doorknob *n* Türknauf *m*

'doorman *n* Portier *m*

'doormat *n* ❶ (*thing*) Fußmatte *f*, Fußabstreifer *m bes* SÜDD ❷ (*fig, pej: person*) Waschlappen *m*

'doorstep *n* Türstufe *f*; *right on one's* ~ (*fig*) direkt vor der Haustür

door-to-'door *adj* von Haus zu Haus

'doorway *n* [Tür]eingang *m*

doozy ['du·zi] *n* (*sl: difficult job*) *to be a* [**real**] ~ eine Heidenarbeit sein

dope [doʊp] I. *n* ❶ (*fam: illegal drug*) Rauschgift *nt*, Stoff *m sl* ❷ (*sl: stupid person*) Trottel *m* II. *vt* dopen

dopey ['doʊ·pi] *adj* ❶ (*drowsy*) benebelt ❷ (*pej: stupid*) blöd

dorm [dɔrm] *n* Studentenwohnheim *nt*

dormant ['dɔr·mənt] *adj* ❶ (*inactive*) *volcano* untätig ❷ BOT, BIOL ■ *to be* ~ ruhen; *to lie* ~ schlafen; *seeds* ruhen

dormer [dɔr·mər], **dormer window** [dɔr·mər'-] *n* Mansardenfenster *nt*

dormitory ['dɔr·mɪ·tɔ·ri] *n* ❶ (*student housing*) Studentenwohnheim *nt* ❷ (*sleeping quarters*) Schlafsaal *m*

dormouse ['dɔr·maʊs] *n* Haselmaus *f*

dorsal ['dɔr·səl] *adj* Rücken-

dosage ['doʊ·sɪdʒ] *n* (*size of dose*) Dosis *f*

dose [doʊs] I. *n* (*dosage*) Dosis *f a. fig* II. *vt* [medizinisch] behandeln

dossier ['das·i·eɪ] *n* Dossier *nt*

dot [dat] I. *n* Punkt *m*; (*on material*) Tupfen *m* II. *vt* <-tt-> ❶ (*make a dot*) mit einem Punkt versehen ❷ *usu pas-sive* (*scatter*) ■ *to be* ~*ted with sth* mit etw *dat* übersät sein

doting ['doʊ·tɪŋ] *adj* vernarrt

double ['dʌb·əl] I. *adj* ❶ (*twice, two*) doppelt; ~ *the price* doppelt so teuer; *the number is: six,* ~ *three, five* die Nummer ist die sechs, zweimal die drei, fünf ❷ (*with two parts*) Doppel-; *pneumonia* doppelseitig; ~ *life* Doppelleben *nt* II. *adv* ❶ (*twice as much*) doppelt so viel; *to charge sb* ~ jdm das Doppelte berechnen ❷ (*two times*) *to see* ~ doppelt sehen ❸ (*in the middle*) *to be bent* ~ sich niederbeugen; (*with laughter, pain*) sich krümmen III. *n* ❶ (*double quantity*) das Doppelte [*o* Zweifache] ❷ (*whiskey, gin*) Doppelte(r) *m* ❸ (*person*) Doppelgänger(in) *m(f)*; FILM Double *nt* ❹ SPORT ■ ~**s** *pl* Doppel *nt*; *mixed* ~**s** gemischtes Doppel ❺ (*in baseball*) Double *m* IV. *vt* ❶ verdoppeln ❷ (*fold in two*) doppelt nehmen V. *vi* ❶ (*increase twofold*) sich verdoppeln ❷ (*serve a second purpose*) *the kitchen table* ~*s as my desk* der Küchentisch dient auch als mein Schreibtisch ❸ (*in baseball*) einen Double schlagen

◆**double back** *vi* kehrtmachen

◆**double up** *vi* ❶ (*bend over*) sich krümmen (*in/with* vor +*dat*) ❷ (*share a room*) sich *dat* ein Zimmer teilen

double-'barreled *adj gun* doppelläufig

double 'bass *n* Kontrabass *m*

double 'bed *n* Doppelbett *nt*

double-'breasted *adj* zweireihig

double-'check *vt* noch einmal überprüfen

double 'chin *n* Doppelkinn *nt*

double-'click COMPUT I. *vt* doppelt anklicken II. *vi* doppelklicken

double-'cross[1] *vt* ■ *to* ~ *sb* mit jdm ein falsches Spiel treiben

double-'cross[2], **double 'cross** *n* <*pl* -es> Doppelspiel *nt*

double-'dealing (*pej*) I. *n* Betrügerei *f* II. *adj* betrügerisch

double-'decker *n* Doppeldecker *m*

double-'edged *adj* zweischneidig *a. fig*

D

double-'park *vt, vi* in der zweiten Reihe parken

doubly ['dʌb·li] *adv* doppelt

doubt [daʊt] **I.** *n* ① (*lack of certainty*) Zweifel *m* (**about** an +*dat*); **no ~** zweifellos; **to cast ~ on sth** etw in Zweifel ziehen ② (*feeling of uncertainty*) Ungewissheit *f*, Bedenken *pl*; **to have ~s about sth** Zweifel an etw *dat* haben **II.** *vt* ■**to ~ sb** (*mistrust*) jdm misstrauen; (*not believe*) jdm nicht glauben; ■**to ~ sth** Zweifel an etw *dat* haben; ■**to ~ that …** bezweifeln, dass …

doubtful ['daʊt·fəl] *adj* ① (*expressing doubt*) zweifelnd ② (*uncertain*) unsicher, unschlüssig; ■**to be ~ about sth** über etw *akk* im Zweifel sein ③ (*questionable*) fragwürdig, zweifelhaft

doubtless ['daʊt·lɪs] *adv* sicherlich

dough [doʊ] *n* ① (*for baking*) Teig *m* ② (*sl: money*) Knete *f*, Kohle *f*

doughnut ['doʊ·nʌt] *n* Donut *m*

dour [dʊr] *adj person* mürrisch; *expression* finster; *struggle* hart[näckig]

douse [daʊs] *vt* ① (*drench*) übergießen ② (*extinguish*) ausmachen; *fire* löschen

dove¹ [dʌv] *n* Taube *f a. fig*

dove² [doʊv] *vi pt of* **dive**

dovetail I. *vi* übereinstimmen **II.** *vt* TECH *in wood* verschwalben; *in metal* verzinken **III.** *n* (*wood*) Schwalbenschwanz *m*; (*metal*) Zinken *m*

dowdy ['daʊ·di] *adj* (*pej*) ohne jeden Schick

down¹ [daʊn] **I.** *adv* ① (*to lower position*) hinunter; (*toward the speaker*) herunter ② (*downwards*) nach unten ③ (*in a lower position*) unten; **~ there** dort unten ④ (*in the south*) im Süden, unten *fam*; (*toward the south*) in den Süden, runter *fam* ⑤ (*ill*) **to be ~ with sth** an etw *dat* erkrankt sein ⑥ SPORT im Rückstand ⑦ (*including*) **from the mayor ~** angefangen beim Bürgermeister ⑧ (*written*) **to have sth ~ in writing** [*or on paper*] etw schriftlich haben ⑨ (*as initial payment*) als Anzahlung; **to pay 100 dollars ~** 100 Dollar anzahlen ⑩ (*in crosswords*) senkrecht

II. *prep* ① (*downward/downhill*) hinunter; (*toward the speaker*) herunter ② (*along*) entlang; **go ~ the street** gehen Sie die Straße entlang **III.** *adj* ① (*moving downward*) abwärtsführend ② (*fam: unhappy*) niedergeschlagen, down *fam* ③ (*not functioning*) außer Betrieb; *telephone lines* tot **IV.** *vt* ① (*knock down*) *person* zu Fall bringen ② (*shoot down*) *plane* abschießen **V.** *n* (*in football*) Versuch *m* **VI.** *interj* "**~!**" (*to a dog*) „Platz!"; **~ with the dictator!** nieder mit dem Diktator!

down² [daʊn] *n* (*soft feathers*) Daunen *pl*

down-and-'out I. *adj* heruntergekommen **II.** *n* (*pej*) Penner(in) *m(f)*

'downbeat *adj* (*sad*) pessimistisch, düster

'downcast *adj* ① (*sad*) niedergeschlagen ② (*looking down*) gesenkt

'downfall *n* ① (*ruin*) Untergang *m*, Fall *m fig*; *of government* Sturz *m* ② (*cause of ruin*) Ruin *m*

'downgrade I. *vt person* degradieren; *thing* herunterstufen **II.** *n* Gefälle *nt*

down'hearted *adj* niedergeschlagen

'downhill *adv* (*downwards*) bergab, abwärts; **to go ~** *person* heruntergehen; *vehicle* herunterfahren; *road, path* bergab führen; (*fig*) *person* bergab gehen; *situation* sich verschlechtern

'download *vt* COMPUT herunterladen (**to** auf +*akk*)

down'market *adj* weniger anspruchsvoll, für den Massenmarkt

down 'payment *n* Anzahlung *f*

down'play *vt* herunterspielen

'downpour *n* Regenguss *m*, Platzregen *m*

'downright I. *adj* völlig; *lie* glatt; *nonsense* komplett **II.** *adv* (*completely*) ausgesprochen

'downside *n* Kehrseite *f*

'downsize *vi* ECON Personal abbauen

'downstairs I. *adv* (*to lower floor*) treppab, die Treppe hinunter; (*on lower floor*) unten *fam*; *stairs* hinunten; **II.** *adj* ① (*one floor down*) im unteren Stockwerk ➋ (*on the ground floor*) im Erdgeschoss III. *n* Erdgeschoss *nt*

'**downstream** *adv* stromabwärts

'**downtime** *n* MECH Ausfallzeit *f*

down-to-'earth *adj* nüchtern

'**downtown** I. *n* Innenstadt *f*, Zentrum *nt* II. *adj, adv* in der Innenstadt, im Zentrum; *go in* die Innenstadt, ins Zentrum

'**downtrodden** *adj* unterdrückt

'**downturn** *n* ECON Rückgang *m*

downward ['daʊn·wərd] I. *adj* nach unten [gerichtet] II. *adv* ➊ (*in/toward a lower position*) abwärts, nach unten, hinunter ➋ (*to a lower amount*) nach unten

downwards ['daʊn·wərdz] *adv see* **downward**

dowry ['daʊ·ri] *n* Mitgift *f*

dowse [daʊz] *vt see* **douse**

doze [doʊz] I. *n* Nickerchen *nt* II. *vi* ■ **to ~** [**off**] dösen

dozen ['dʌz·ən] *n* Dutzend *nt;* *half a ~* ein halbes Dutzend

Dr. *n abbrev of* **doctor** Dr.

drab <-bb-> [dræb] *adj* trist; *colors* trüb; *surroundings* trostlos

draft [dræft] I. *n* ➊ (*air current*) [Luft]zug *m kein pl* ➋ **on ~** vom Fass ➌ MIL Einberufung *f* ➍ (*preliminary version*) [**first/rough**] ~ [erster/roher] Entwurf *m* II. *adj* ➊ ~ **animal** Zugtier *nt* ➋ ~ **beer** Fassbier *nt* ➌ MIL Einberufungs-; ~ **board** Wehrersatzbehörde *f* ➍ (*preliminary*) Entwurfs-; ~ **contract** Vertragsentwurf *m* III. *vt* ➊ (*prepare*) entwerfen; *bill* verfassen; *contract* aufsetzen; *proposal* ausarbeiten ➋ MIL **to ~ sb into the army** jdn zum Wehrdienst einberufen

'**draft dodger** *n* (*shirker*) Drückeberger(in) *m(f);* (*conscientious objector*) Wehrdienstverweigerer, -in *m, f*

'**draftsman** *n* [technischer] Zeichner

drafty ['dræf·ti] *adj* zugig

drag [dræg] I. *n* ➊ PHYS Widerstand *m;* AVIAT Luftwiderstand *m* ➋ (*fig: impediment*) Hemmschuh *m* ➌ (*fam: bore*) langweilige Sache; *what a ~!* so'n Mist!

sl ➍ (*fam: puff*) Zug *m* ➎ (*fam: road*) **the main** ~ die Hauptstraße ➏ (*fam: clothing of opposite sex*) Fummel *m;* ~ **queen** Künstler, der in Frauenkleidern auftritt II. *vt* <-gg-> ➊ (*pull along*) ziehen; **to ~ one's heels** [*or* **feet**] schlurfen; (*fig*) sich *dat* Zeit lassen; **to ~ oneself along** sich dahinschleppen ➋ (*take despite resistance*) schleifen; **I don't want to ~ you away** ich will dich hier nicht wegreißen ➌ (*force*) ■ **to ~ sth out of sb** etw aus jdm herausbringen III. *vi* <-gg-> ➊ (*trail along*) schleifen ➋ (*pej: proceed tediously*) sich [da]hinziehen

◆ **drag in** *vt person* hineinziehen; *thing* aufs Tapet bringen

◆ **drag on** *vi* (*pej*) sich [da]hinziehen

◆ **drag out** *vt* in die Länge ziehen

dragon ['dræg·ən] *n* ➊ (*mythical creature*) Drache *m* ➋ (*woman*) Drachen *m*

'**dragonfly** *n* Libelle *f*

drain [dreɪn] I. *n* ➊ (*pipe*) Rohr *nt;* (*under sink*) Abflussrohr *nt;* (*in road*) Gully *m;* **to go down the ~** (*fig*) vor die Hunde gehen, den Bach runtergehen *fam* ➋ (*constant outflow*) Belastung *f* (*on* für +*akk*) II. *vt* ➊ (*remove liquid*) entwässern; *liquid* ablaufen lassen; *vegetables* abgießen; *noodles/rice* abtropfen lassen; *abscess* drainieren ➋ (*form: empty*) austrinken ➌ (*exhaust*) [völlig] auslaugen III. *vi* ➊ (*flow away*) ablaufen ➋ (*empty*) leeren

◆ **drain away** *vi liquid* ablaufen; (*fig*) [dahin]schwinden

◆ **drain off** *vt water* abgießen

drainage ['dreɪ·nɪdʒ] *n* ➊ (*water removal*) Entwässerung *f* ➋ (*system*) *for land* Entwässerungssystem *nt; for houses* Kanalisation *f*

'**drain board** *n* Abtropfbrett *nt*

'**drainpipe** *n* (*for rainwater*) Regenrohr *nt;* (*for sewage*) Abflussrohr *nt*

drake [dreɪk] *n* Enterich *m*, Erpel *m*

drama ['drɑ·mə] *n* ➊ (*theater art*) Schauspielkunst *f* ➋ (*play, event*) Drama *nt a. fig* ➌ (*dramatic quality*) Dramatik *f*

D

D

dramatic [drə-'mæt·ɪk] *adj* **①** dramatisch **②** (*pej: theatrical*) theatralisch

dramatist ['dræm·ə·tɪst] *n* Dramatiker(in) *m(f)*

dramatization [ˌdræm·ə·tɪ·'zeɪ·ʃən] *n* **①** (*of a work*) Dramatisierung *f;* THEAT Bühnenbearbeitung *f;* FILM Kinobearbeitung *f;* TV Fernsehbearbeitung *f* **②** (*usu pej: exaggeration*) Dramatisieren *nt*

dramatize ['dræm·ə·taɪz] *vt* **①** (*adapt*) bearbeiten **②** (*usu pej: exaggerate*) dramatisieren

drank [dræŋk] *pt of* **drink**

drape [dreɪp] **I.** *vt* **①** (*cover loosely*) bedecken (**in/with** mit +*dat*) **②** (*place on*) drapieren, legen **II.** *n* ■**~s** *pl* Vorhänge *pl*

drastic ['dræs·tɪk] *adj* drastisch; *change, measures* radikal

draw [drɔ] **I.** *n* **①** (*celebrity*) Publikumsmagnet *m;* (*popular film, etc.*) Kassenschlager *m* **②** (*in chess, soccer*) Unentschieden *nt;* **to end in a ~** unentschieden ausgehen **③** (*drawing lots*) Verlosung *f* **II.** *vt* <drew, -n> **①** (*make a picture*) zeichnen; *line* ziehen **②** (*depict*) darstellen **③** (*pull*) ziehen; (*close*) *curtains* zuziehen; (*open*) aufziehen **④** (*attract*) anlocken; **to ~ [sb's] attention [to sb/sth]** [jds] Aufmerksamkeit *f* [auf jdn/etw] lenken; ■**to feel ~n to sb** sich zu jdm hingezogen fühlen **⑤** (*formulate*) *comparison* anstellen; *conclusion, parallel* ziehen **⑥** (*pull out*) *weapon* ziehen **⑦** (*earn, get from source*) beziehen, erhalten **⑧** (*select by chance*) ziehen, auslosen; **to ~ lots for sth** um etw *akk* losen **⑨** FIN *money* abheben; *check* ausstellen **III.** *vi* <drew, -n> **①** (*make pictures*) zeichnen **②** (*make use of*) ■**to ~ on sth** auf etw *akk* zurückgreifen **③** (*in chess, soccer*) unentschieden spielen

◆**draw out** *vt* in die Länge ziehen; *vowels* dehnen

◆**draw up** *vt* aufsetzen; *agenda, list* aufstellen; *guidelines* festlegen; *plan* entwerfen; *proposal, questionnaire* ausarbeiten; *report* erstellen; *will* errichten

'**drawback** *n* Nachteil *m*

drawer [drɔr] *n* **①** (*storage*) Schublade *f;* **chest of ~s** Kommode *f* **②** (*hum*) ■**~s** *pl* (*underwear*) Unterwäsche *f*

drawing ['drɔ·ɪŋ] *n* **①** (*art*) Zeichnen *nt* **②** (*picture*) Zeichnung *f*

'**drawing board** *n* Zeichenbrett *nt;* **to go back to the ~** (*fig*) noch einmal von vorn anfangen

'**drawing room** *n* (*form*) Wohnzimmer *nt*

drawl [drɔl] **I.** *n* schleppende Sprache **II.** *vi* schleppend sprechen

drawn [drɔn] **I.** *pp of* **draw II.** *adj* abgespannt

dread [dred] **I.** *vt* ■**to ~ sth** sich vor etw *dat* [sehr] fürchten; ■**to ~ doing sth** [große] Angst haben, etw zu tun **II.** *n* Furcht *f*

dreadful ['dred·fəl] *adj* **①** (*awful*) schrecklich, furchtbar **②** (*of very bad quality*) miserabel, erbärmlich

dreadfully ['dred·fə·li] *adv* **①** (*in a terrible manner*) schrecklich, entsetzlich **②** (*extremely*) schrecklich, furchtbar

dream [drim] **I.** *n* Traum *m a. fig;* **in your ~s!** du träumst wohl! **II.** *vt, vi* <dreamed *or* dreamt, dreamed *or* dreamt> träumen *a. fig;* **I wouldn't ~ of asking him for money!** es würde mir nicht im Traum einfallen, ihn um Geld zu bitten

◆**dream up** *vt* sich *dat* ausdenken

dreamt [dremt] *pt, pp of* **dream**

dreamy ['dri·mi] *adj* **①** (*lost in thought*) verträumt **②** (*fam: gorgeous*) zum Träumen

dreary ['drɪr·i] *adj* **①** (*depressing*) trostlos; *day* trüb **②** (*monotonous*) eintönig

dredge [dredʒ] **I.** *n* [Schwimm]bagger *m* **II.** *vt river* ausbaggern

dredger ['dredʒ·ər] *n* [Schwimm]bagger *m*

dregs [dregz] *npl* **①** (*of drink*) [Boden]satz *m kein pl* **②** (*fig*) Abschaum *m kein pl*

drench [drentʃ] *vt* durchnässen

dress [dres] **I.** *n* <*pl* -es> **①** (*woman's garment*) Kleid *nt* **②** (*clothing*) Klei-

dung f II. vi ❶ (put on clothing) ■to ~ [or get ~ed] sich anziehen ❷ (wear clothing) sich kleiden; to ~ casually sich leger anziehen III. vt ❶ (put on clothing) ■to ~ sb/oneself jdn/sich anziehen ❷ FOOD salad anmachen ❸ (treat) wound verbinden
◆dress up I. vi ❶ (wear nice clothes) sich fein anziehen ❷ (disguise oneself) sich verkleiden II. vt ❶ (in a costume) verkleiden ❷ (improve) verschönern
dressing ['dresɪŋ] n ❶ (for salad) Dressing nt ❷ (for injury) Verband m
dressing-'down n (fam) Standpauke f
'dressing room n (in theater) [Künstler]garderobe f; SPORT Umkleidekabine f
'dressing table n Schminktisch m, Frisierkommode f
'dressmaker n [Damen]schneider(in) m(f)
'dressmaking n Schneidern nt
dress re'hearsal n THEAT Generalprobe f
dressy ['dres·i] adj (fam) ❶ (stylish) elegant ❷ (requiring formal clothes) vornehm

drew [dru] pt of draw
dribble ['drɪb·əl] I. vi ❶ (trickle) tropfen ❷ baby sabbern ❸ SPORT dribbeln II. vt SPORT dribbeln mit III. n ❶ (saliva) Sabber m ❷ SPORT Dribbling nt kein pl
dried [draɪd] I. pt, pp of dry II. adj getrocknet
dried up adj pred, dried-up adj attr ausgetrocknet
drift [drɪft] I. vi ❶ treiben; balloon schweben; mist, fog, clouds ziehen; snow angeweht werden; to ~ along (fig) sich treiben lassen; to ~ away people davonschlendern II. n ❶ (slow movement) Strömen nt ❷ (snowdrift) Verwehung f ❸ (general idea) Kernaussage f; to catch sb's ~ verstehen, was jd sagen will
◆drift apart vi einander fremd werden
◆drift off vi einschlummern
drifter ['drɪf·tər] n Gammler(in) m(f)
'drift ice n Treibeis nt
'driftwood n Treibholz nt
drill [drɪl] I. n ❶ (tool) Bohrer m ❷ (ex-

ercise) Übung f; MIL Drill m ❸ (fam: routine procedure) to know the ~ wissen, wie es geht II. vt ❶ holes bohren ❷ MIL, SCH drillen III. vi ❶ (make holes) bohren ❷ MIL exerzieren
'drilling platform n Bohrinsel f
drink [drɪŋk] I. n ❶ Getränk nt; can I get you a ~? kann ich Ihnen etwas zu trinken bringen?; to have a ~ etw trinken ❷ (alcoholic drink) Drink m, Gläschen nt ❸ (alcohol) Alkohol m II. vt, vi <drank, drunk> trinken; to ~ and drive unter Alkoholeinfluss fahren; I'll ~ to that darauf trinke ich; (fig) dem kann ich nur zustimmen
◆drink in vt [begierig] in sich akk aufnehmen
drinker ['drɪŋ·kər] n Trinker(in) m(f)
drinking ['drɪŋ·kɪŋ] I. n Trinken nt II. adj Trink-
'drinking water n Trinkwasser nt
drip [drɪp] I. vi <-pp-> (continually) tropfen; (in individual drops) tröpfeln II. vt <-pp-> [herunter]tropfen lassen III. n ❶ (act of dripping) Tropfen nt; of rain Tröpfeln nt ❷ (drop) Tropfen m ❸ MED Tropf m ❹ (fam: fool) Flasche f pej fam, Null f pej fam
drip-dry I. vt <-ie-> tropfnass aufhängen II. vi clothes, dishes abtropfen III. adj bügelfrei
dripping ['drɪp·ɪŋ] I. adj ❶ (dropping drips) tropfend ❷ (extremely wet) klatschnass (hum, iron: be covered with sth) ■to be ~ with sth über und über mit etw dat behängt sein II. adv ~ wet klatschnass
drive [draɪv] I. n ❶ (trip) Fahrt f; to go for a ~ eine Spazierfahrt machen; it is a 20-minute ~ to the airport zum Flughafen sind es [mit dem Auto] 20 Minuten ❷ (driveway) Einfahrt f; (to larger building) Auffahrt f; (approach road) Zufahrt[sstraße] f ❸ (energy) Tatkraft f; (vigor) Schwung m, Elan m, Drive m; (motivation) Tatendrang m; PSYCH Trieb m ❹ (campaign) Aktion f ❺ COMPUT Laufwerk nt II. vt <drove, -n> ❶ fahren ❷ (force onwards) antreiben;

D

to ~ sb to suicide jdn in den Selbstmord treiben; to ~ sb mad/crazy jdn wahnsinnig/verrückt machen ❸ (power) engine antreiben; COMPUT treiben III. vi <drove, -n> ❶ fahren ❷ rain, snow peitschen; clouds jagen ❸ (fig) what are you driving at? worauf wollen Sie [eigentlich] hinaus?

◆drive away I. vt ❶ (transport) wegfahren ❷ (expel) vertreiben ❸ (fig: dispel) zerstreuen II. vi wegfahren

◆drive back I. vt ❶ (in vehicle) zurückfahren ❷ (force back) zurückdrängen; animals zurücktreiben; enemy zurückschlagen II. vi zurückfahren

◆drive off I. vt ❶ (expel) vertreiben ❷ (repel) zurückschlagen II. vi wegfahren

◆drive out vt hinausjagen; (fig) austreiben

◆drive up I. vt prices hochtreiben II. vi vorfahren

'drive-in I. adj Drive-in- II. n ❶ (restaurant) Drive-in nt ❷ (movie theater) Autokino nt

drivel ['drɪv·əl] n (pej) Gefasel nt

driven ['drɪv·ən] I. pp of drive II. adj ❶ (very ambitious) ehrgeizig ❷ (powered) angetrieben

driver ['draɪ·vər] n ❶ Fahrer(in) m(f); of locomotive Führer(in) m(f) ❷ (golf club) Driver m

'driver's license n Führerschein m

'drive-through I. adj attr Drive-through- II. n Durchfahrt f

'driveway n (to small building) Einfahrt f; (to larger building) Auffahrt f; (longer) Zufahrt[sstraße] f

driving ['draɪ·vɪŋ] I. n (of vehicle) Fahren nt II. adj (on road) Fahr-; ~ conditions Straßenverhältnisse pl ❷ (lashing) rain peitschend ❸ (powerfully motivating) treibend; force, ambition stark

'driving instructor n Fahrlehrer(in) m(f)

'driving lesson n Fahrstunde f

'driving license n see driver's license

'driving school n Fahrschule f

'driving test n Fahrprüfung f

drizzle ['drɪz·əl] I. n METEO Nieselregen m II. vi impers nieseln III. vt FOOD träufeln

droll [droʊl] adj drollig

drone [droʊn] I. n ❶ (male bee) Drohne f ❷ (aircraft) ferngesteuertes Flugzeug; (missile) ferngesteuerte Rakete ❸ of a machine Brummen nt; of insects Summen nt II. vi ❶ (make sound) summen; engine brummen ❷ (speak monotonously) leiern

drool [drul] I. vi ❶ (dribble) sabbern ❷ (fig) ■to ~ over sb/sth von jdm/etw hingerissen sein II. n Sabber m

droop [drup] vi ❶ (hang down) schlaff herunterhängen; flowers die Köpfe hängen lassen; eyelids zufallen ❷ (lack energy) schlapp sein

droopy ['drup·i] adj [schlaff] herabhängend attr

drop [drap] I. n ❶ (vertical distance) Gefälle nt ❷ (decrease) Rückgang m ❸ of liquid Tropfen m; ■~s pl MED Tropfen pl II. vt <-pp-> ❶ (cause to fall) fallen lassen; anchor [aus]werfen; bomb, leaflets abwerfen ❷ (lower) senken ❸ (dismiss) entlassen ❹ (give up) aufgeben; charges fallen lassen; demands abgehen von; to ~ everything alles stehen und liegen lassen ❺ (abandon) ■to ~ sb (fig) jdn fallen lassen; (end a relationship) mit jdm Schluss machen ❻ (fam: tell indirectly) to ~ [sb] a hint [jdm gegenüber] eine Anspielung machen III. vi <-pp-> ❶ (descend) [herunter]fallen; jaw herunterklappen ❷ (become lower) land sinken; prices, temperatures fallen ❸ (fam: become exhausted) umfallen; ~ dead! (fam) scher dich zum Teufel!

◆drop behind vi zurückfallen

◆drop in vi (fam) vorbeischauen (on bei + dat)

◆drop off I. vt (fam) person abliefern; thing absetzen II. vi ❶ (fall off) abfallen ❷ (decrease) zurückgehen; support, interest nachlassen ❸ (fam: fall asleep) einschlafen

◆drop out vi ❶ (give up membership)

ausscheiden; **to ~ out of college** das Studium abbrechen ❷ *of society* aussteigen

drop-down '**menu** *n* COMPUT Pull-down-Menü *nt*

'**dropout** *n* ❶ *(from university)* [Studien]abbrecher(in) *m(f)*; *(from school)* Schulabgänger(in) *m(f)* ❷ *(from conventional lifestyle)* Aussteiger(in) *m(f)*

dropper ['drap·ər] *n* Tropfer *m*

droppings ['drap·ɪŋz] *npl of bird* Vogeldreck *m; (of horse)* Pferdeäpfel *pl; of rodents, sheep* Köttel *pl*

'**drop shot** *n* TENNIS Stopp[ball] *m*

dross [dras] *n* Schrott *m a. fig*

drought [draʊt] *n* Dürre[periode] *f*

drove [droʊv] *pt of* **drive**

drown [draʊn] I. *vt* ❶ *(kill)* ertränken; ▪**to be ~ed** ertrinken ❷ *(make inaudible)* übertönen II. *vi* ertrinken *a. fig* ◆ **drown out** *vt* niederschreien

drowsy ['draʊ·zi] *adj* schläfrig; *(after waking up)* verschlafen

drudge [drʌdʒ] *n (person)* Kuli *m*

drudgery ['drʌdʒ·ə·ri] *n* Schufterei *f*

drug [drʌg] I. *n* ❶ *(medicine)* Medikament *nt* ❷ *(narcotic)* Droge *f*, Rauschgift *nt* II. *vt* <-gg-> ❶ MED Beruhigungsmittel verabreichen ❷ *(secretly)* unter Drogen setzen

'**drug abuse** *n* Drogenmissbrauch *m*

'**drug addict** *n* Drogensüchtige(r) *f(m)*

'**drug addiction** *n* Drogenabhängigkeit *f*

'**drug dealer** *n* Drogenhändler(in) *m(f)*, Dealer(in) *m(f)*

'**drugstore** *n* Drogerie *f* [in der man auch Medikamente erhält]

'**drug trafficker** *n* Drogenhändler(in) *m(f)*

'**drug trafficking** *n* Drogenhandel *m*

drum [drʌm] I. *n* ❶ MUS Trommel *f*; ▪**~s** *pl (drum kit)* Schlagzeug *nt* ❷ *(for storage, machine part)* Trommel *f* II. *vi* <-mm-> ❶ MUS trommeln ❷ *(for a drum kit)* Schlagzeug spielen ❷ *(strike repeatedly)* trommeln (**on** auf +*akk*) III. *vt* <-mm-> *(fam)* ❶ *(make noise)* **to ~ one's fingers** [**on the table**] [mit den Fingern] auf den Tisch trommeln ❷ *(re-*

peat) ▪**to ~ sth into sb** jdm etw einhämmern

'**drumbeat** *n* Trommelschlag *m*

drummer ['drʌm·ər] *n* MUS Trommler(in) *m(f); (playing a drum kit)* Schlagzeuger(in) *m(f)*

'**drumstick** *n* ❶ MUS Trommelstock *m* ❷ FOOD Keule *f*, Schlegel *m* SÜDD, ÖSTERR

drunk [drʌŋk] I. *adj* ❶ *(inebriated)* betrunken; **to get ~** sich betrinken; **~ driving** Trunkenheit *f* am Steuer ❷ *(fig: overcome)* trunken II. *n (pej)* Betrunkene(r) *f(m)* III. *vt, vi pp of* **drink**

drunkard ['drʌŋ·kərd] *n (pej)* Trinker(in) *m(f)*

drunken ['drʌŋ·kən] *adj (pej)* ❶ *person* betrunken ❷ *(involving alcohol)* **~ brawl** Streit *m* zwischen Betrunkenen

drunkenness ['drʌŋ·kən·nɪs] *n* Betrunkenheit *f*

dry [draɪ] I. *adj* <-ier, -iest *or* -er, -est> ❶ trocken ❷ *(without alcohol)* alkoholfrei II. *vt* <-ie-> trocknen; *fruit, meat* dörren; *(dry out)* austrocknen; *(dry up)* abtrocknen; **~ your eyes!** wisch dir die Tränen ab!; **to ~ one's hands** sich *dat* die Hände abtrocknen III. *vi* <-ie-> ❶ *(lose moisture)* trocknen ❷ *(dry up)* abtrocknen

◆ **dry up** I. *vi* ❶ *(become dry)* austrocknen; *spring, well* versiegen ❷ *(dry the dishes)* abtrocknen ❸ *(fig: run out)* *funds* schrumpfen; *source* versiegen; *supply* ausbleiben; *conversation* versiegen II. *vt* ❶ *dishes* abtrocknen ❷ *(dry out)* austrocknen

'**dry-clean** *vt* chemisch reinigen

'**dry cleaner** *n* Reinigung *f*

'**dry cleaning** *n* [chemische] Reinigung *f*

dryer ['draɪ·ər] *n* ❶ *(for laundry)* [Wäsche]trockner *m* ❷ *(for hair)* Fön *m; (overhead)* Trockenhaube *f*

dry 'land *n* Festland *nt*

'**dry rot** *n* ❶ *(in wood)* Hausschwamm *m* ❷ *(in plants)* Trockenfäule *f*

DSL [ˌdiːesˈel] *n* INET, COMPUT, TELEC *acr*

D

for **digital subscriber line** DSL *kein art*

dual ['du·əl] *adj* ❶ (*double*) doppelt; (*two different*) zweierlei; ~ **role** Doppelrolle *f*

dub <-bb-> [dʌb] *vt* ❶ FILM synchronisieren ❷ (*call*) nennen

dubbing ['dʌb·ɪŋ] *n* FILM Synchronisation *f*

dubious ['du·bi·əs] *adj* ❶ (*questionable*) zweifelhaft, fragwürdig ❷ (*unsure*) unsicher; **to feel ~ about sth** an etw *dat* zweifeln

duchess <*pl* -es> ['dʌtʃ·ɪs] *n* Herzogin *f*

duck¹ [dʌk] *n* Ente *f*

duck² [dʌk] I. *vi* sich ducken; (*out of sight*) sich verstecken; **to ~ under water** [unter]tauchen II. *vt* ❶ **to ~ one's head** den Kopf einziehen ❷ (*avoid*) ■**to ~ sth** etw *dat* ausweichen *a. fig*

duckling ['dʌk·lɪŋ] *n* Entenküken *nt*, Entchen *nt*

duct [dʌkt] *n* ❶ (*pipe*) [Rohr]leitung *f* ❷ ANAT Kanal *m*

dud [dʌd] (*fam*) I. *n* ❶ (*bomb*) Blindgänger *m* ❷ (*useless thing*) **this pen is a ~** dieser Füller taugt nichts; (*failure*) Reinfall *m* II. *adj* (*worthless*) mies; *checks* gefälscht

dude [dud] *n* (*fam*) ❶ (*smartly dressed urbanite*) feiner Pinkel ❷ (*fellow*) Typ *m*, Kerl *m*; **what's up, ~?** wie geht's, Alter? *sl*

due [du] I. *adj* ❶ (*payable*) fällig; ~ **date** Fälligkeitstermin *m* ❷ (*appropriate*) gebührend; **with** [**all**] ~ **respect** bei allem [gebotenen] Respekt ❸ (*expected*) **in ~ course** zu gegebener Zeit; ~ **date** (*for work*) Abgabetermin *m*; (*for entries*) Einsendeschluss *m*; **their baby is ~ in January** sie erwarten ihr Baby im Januar ❹ (*because of*) ■~ **to sth** wegen [*o* auf Grund] einer S. *gen*; ■**to be ~ to sb/sth** jdm/etw zuzuschreiben sein II. *n* ❶ (*fair treatment*) **to give sb his/her ~** jdm Gerechtigkeit widerfahren lassen ❷ (*fees*) ■~**s** *pl* Gebühren *pl* III. *adv* ~ **north** genau nach Norden

duel ['du·əl] I. *n* Duell *nt* II. *vi* <-l-> sich duellieren

duet [du·'et] *n* (*for instruments*) Duo *nt*; (*for voices*) Duett *nt*

dug [dʌg] *pt, pp of* **dig**

dugout *n* ❶ MIL Schützengraben *m* ❷ (*in baseball, soccer*) [überdachte] Spielerbank ❸ (*canoe*) Einbaum *m*

duke [duk] *n* Herzog *m*

dull [dʌl] I. *adj* ❶ (*pej: boring*) langweilig, eintönig ❷ (*not bright*) *animal's coat* glanzlos; *weather* trüb; *color* matt II. *vt* (*lessen*) schwächen; *pain* betäuben

dullness ['dʌl·nɪs] *n* Langweiligkeit *f*, Eintönigkeit *f*

duly ['du·li] *adv* ❶ (*appropriately*) gebührend ❷ (*at the expected time*) wie erwartet

dumb [dʌm] *adj* ❶ (*pej fam: stupid*) dumm ❷ (*mute*) stumm

dumbfounded *adj* sprachlos

dumbstruck *adj* sprachlos

dummy ['dʌm·i] I. *n* ❶ (*mannequin*) Schaufensterpuppe *f*; (*for crash tests*) Dummy *m*; (*for ventriloquist*) [Bauchredner]puppe *f* ❷ (*pej: fool*) Dummkopf *m* II. *adj* (*duplicate*) nachgemacht; (*false*) falsch

dump [dʌmp] I. *n* ❶ (*for garbage*) Müll[ablade]platz *m*; (*fig, pej: messy place*) Dreckloch *nt*; (*badly run place*) Sauladen *m* ❷ (*storage place*) Lager *nt* ❸ COMPUT Speicherabzug *m* II. *vt* ❶ (*offload*) abladen ❷ (*put down carelessly*) hinknallen ❸ (*fam: abandon*) *plan* fallen lassen; *sth unwanted* loswerden ❹ (*fam: end a relationship*) ■**to ~ sb** jdm den Laufpass geben, mit jdm Schluss machen III. *vi* ❶ (*throw out garbage*) **"No ~ing"** „Müll abladen verboten" ❷ (*fam: treat unfairly*) ■**to ~ on sb** jdn fertigmachen

dumpling ['dʌmp·lɪŋ] *n* Knödel *m*, Kloß *m*

dump truck *n* Kipper *m*

dumpy ['dʌm·pi] *adj* pummelig

dunce [dʌns] *n* (*pej: poor pupil*)

D

schlechter Schüler, schlechte Schülerin; (*stupid person*) Dummkopf *m*

dune [dun] *n* Düne *f*

dung [dʌŋ] *n* Dung *m*

dungarees [ˌdʌŋ·gə·ˈriz] *npl* Jeans[hose] *f*

dungeon [ˈdʌn·dʒən] *n* Verlies *nt*, Kerker *m*

dunk [dʌŋk] **I.** *vt* ① (*immerse*) [ein]tunken ② SPORT *basketball* dunken **II.** *vi* SPORT dunken **III.** *n* SPORT Dunking *m*

duo [ˈdu·ou] *n* Duo *nt*

duodenum <*pl* -na> [ˌdu·ə·ˈdi·nəm] *n* Zwölffingerdarm *m*

dupe [dup] **I.** *n* Betrogene(r) *f(m)* **II.** *vt* betrügen

duplex [ˈdu·pleks] *n* <*pl* -es> ① (*house*) Doppelhaus *nt* ② (*apartment*) Maisonette[wohnung] *f*

duplicate I. *vt* [ˈdu·plɪ·keɪt] ■ **to ~ sth** eine zweite Anfertigung von etw *dat* machen; (*repeat an activity*) etw noch einmal machen **II.** *adj* [ˈdu·plɪ·kət] Zweit-; ~ **key** Nachschlüssel *m* **III.** *n* [ˈdu·plɪ·kət] Duplikat *nt; of a document* Zweitschrift *f*; **in** ~ in zweifacher Ausfertigung

duplicity [du·ˈplɪs·ɪ·t̬i] *n* (*pej: in speech*) Doppelzüngigkeit *f*; (*in behavior*) Doppelspiel *nt*

durability [ˌdʊr·ə·ˈbɪl·ɪ·t̬i] *n of a product* Haltbarkeit *f*; *of a machine* Lebensdauer *f*

durable [ˈdʊr·ə·bəl] *adj* ① (*long-lasting*) strapazierfähig, dauerhaft ② ECON *goods* langlebig

duration [dʊ·ˈreɪ·ʃən] *n* Dauer *f*

duress [dʊ·ˈres] *n* (*form*) Zwang *m*, Nötigung *f*

during [ˈdʊr·ɪŋ] *prep* während +*gen*

dusk [dʌsk] *n* [Abend]dämmerung *f*

dusky [ˈdʌs·ki] *adj* dunkel

dust [dʌst] **I.** *n* Staub *m*; **covered in** ~ (*outside*) staubbedeckt; (*inside*) völlig verstaubt **II.** *vt* ① (*clean*) *objects* abstauben; *rooms* Staub wischen in ② (*spread over finely*) bestäuben; (*using grated material*) bestreuen **III.** *vi* Staub wischen

'dust cover *n* (*for furniture*) Schonbezug *m*; (*for devices*) Abdeckhaube *f*; (*on a book*) Schutzumschlag *m*; (*for clothes*) Staubschutz *m kein pl*

'duster [ˈdʌs·tər] *n* Staubtuch *nt*

'dust jacket *n* Schutzumschlag *m*

'dust mite *n* Hausmilbe *f*

'dustpan *n* Schaufel *f*

'dust storm *n* Staubsturm *m*

dusty [ˈdʌs·ti] *adj* staubig; *objects* verstaubt

Dutch [dʌtʃ] **I.** *adj* holländisch, niederländisch **II.** *n* ① (*language*) Holländisch *nt*, Niederländisch *nt* ② (*people*) ■ **the** ~ *pl* die Holländer **III.** *adv* **to go** ~ getrennte Kasse machen

'Dutchman *n* Holländer *m*

'Dutchwoman *n* Holländerin *f*

dutiful [ˈdu·t̬ɪ·fəl] *adj* ① *person* pflichtbewusst; (*obedient*) gehorsam ② *act* pflichtschuldig

duty [ˈdu·t̬i] *n* ① (*obligation*) Pflicht *f* ② (*work*) Dienst *m*; **to be off** ~ [dienst]frei haben; **to be on** ~ Dienst haben ③ (*revenue*) Zoll *m*; **customs duties** Zollabgaben *pl*; **to pay** ~ **on sth** etw verzollen **II.** *adj nurse, officer* diensthabend

duty-'free *adj* zollfrei

duvet [du·ˈveɪ] *n* Steppdecke *f*, Daunendecke *f*

DVD [ˌdi·vi·ˈdi] *n abbrev of* **digital video disk** DVD *f*

DVR [ˌdi·vi·ˈar] *n abbrev of* **digital video recorder** digitaler Videorecorder *m*

dwarf [dwɔrf] **I.** *n* <*pl* -s> Zwerg(in) *m(f)* **II.** *adj* Zwerg- **III.** *vt* überragen; (*fig*) in den Schatten stellen

dwell <dwelt *or* dwelled, dwelt *or* dwelled> [dwel] *vi* ① (*reside*) wohnen ② (*think about*) nachdenken (**on** über +*akk*)

dweller [ˈdwel·ər] *n* (*form*) Bewohner(in) *m(f)*

dwelling [ˈdwel·ɪŋ] *n* (*form*) Wohnung *f*

dwelt [dwelt] *pt, pp of* **dwell**

dwindle [ˈdwɪn·dəl] *vi* abnehmen; *numbers* zurückgehen; *money, supplies* schrumpfen

dye [daɪ] I. vt färben II. n Färbemittel nt
dyed-in-the-'wool adj Erz-
dying ['daɪ·ɪŋ] adj sterbend; (fig) aussterbend
dyke[1] [daɪk] n (wall) see **dike**[1]
dyke[2] [daɪk] n (offensive sl: lesbian) Lesbe f
dynamic [daɪ·'næm·ɪk] adj dynamisch
dynamics [daɪ·'næm·ɪks] n Dynamik f

dynamite ['daɪ·nə·maɪt] I. n Dynamit nt a. fig II. vt mit Dynamit sprengen
dynasty ['daɪ·nə·sti] n Dynastie f
dysentery ['dɪs·ən·ter·i] n Ruhr f
dysfunctional [dɪs·'fʌŋk·ʃə·nəl] adj SOCIOL gestört
dyslexia [dɪ·'sleksiə] n Legasthenie f
dyslexic [dɪs·'lek·sɪk] adj legasthenisch

Ee

E <pl -'s> [i], **e** <pl -'s> [i] n E nt, e nt; ~ **as in Echo** E wie Emil
E n ❶ abbrev of **east** O ❷ (in baseball) abbrev of **error** Fehlpass m
each [itʃ] adj, adv, pron jede(r, s); ~ **one** jede einzelne; **one of ~** von jedem eins
each other pron after vb einander; **for ~** füreinander
eager <-er, -est> ['i·gər] adj begierig; (expectant) erwartungsvoll
eagerness ['i·gər·nəs] n Eifer m
eagle ['i·gəl] n Adler m
'eagle-eyed adj scharfsichtig
ear [ɪr] n ❶ Ohr nt ❷ (grain) Ähre f; **from ~ to ~** von einem Ohr zum anderen ▶PHRASES: **to be all ~s** ganz Ohr sein
'earache n Ohrenschmerzen pl
'eardrum n Trommelfell nt
earl [ɜrl] n Graf m
'earlobe n Ohrläppchen nt
early <-ier, -iest> ['ɜr·li] I. adj früh; (ahead) vorzeitig; **from an ~ age** von klein auf II. adv früh; (ahead) vorzeitig; (prematurely) zu früh; (earlier) [früh]zeitig
'earmuffs npl Ohrenschützer pl
earn [ɜrn] vt verdienen; respect gewinnen
earnest ['ɜr·nɪst] I. adj ernst[haft] II. n Ernst m; **in ~** ernst
'earphone n Kopfhörer m

'earplug n usu pl Ohrenstöpsel nt
'earring n Ohrring m
'earshot n [with]in/out of ~ in/außer Hörweite
earth [ɜrθ] n (planet, soil) Erde f; **on ~** in der Welt; **how on ~ ...** wie um alles in der Welt ... ▶PHRASES: **down to ~** natürlich und umgänglich
Earth Day n wird seit 1990 alljährlich am 22. April begangen, um auf die globale Gefährdung unserer Umwelt aufmerksam zu machen
earthly ['ɜrθ·li] adj (fam) **of no ~ use** nicht im Geringsten nützlich
'earthquake n Erdbeben nt
'earthworm n Regenwurm m
'earwax n Ohrenschmalz m
'earwig n Ohrwurm m
ease [iz] I. n. Leichtigkeit f; **to be at ~** sich akk wohl fühlen II. vt pain lindern; strain mindern III. vi nachlassen; tension sich beruhigen
◆**ease off** vi nachlassen; ■**to ~ off on sb** jdn in Ruhe lassen
◆**ease up** vi nachlassen; (relax) sich akk entspannen
easel ['i·zəl] n Staffelei f
easily ['i·zə·li] adv leicht; (effortlessly) mühelos; (probably) [sehr] leicht; ■**to be ~ the ...** + superl bei weitem der/die/das ... sein
east [ist] I. n Osten m; **to the ~** nach

Osten; ■**the E~** der Osten **II.** *adj* östlich; **~ wind** Ostwind *m* **III.** *adv* nach Osten

Easter ['iːstər] *n* Ostern *nt*

'**Easter egg** *n* Osterei *nt*

eastern ['iːstərn] *adj* ❶ östlich; **the ~ seaboard** die Ostküste ❷ ■**E~** orientalisch

easterner ['iːstərnər] *n* Oststaatler(in) *m(f)*

Easter 'Sunday *n* Ostersonntag *m*

East 'Germany *n* HIST Ostdeutschland *nt*

eastwards ['iːstwərdz] *adj, adv* nach Osten

easy <-ier, -iest> ['iːzi] **I.** *adj* einfach; (*effortless*) mühelos; (*trouble-free*) angenehm **II.** *adv* |**take it**| ~ |**now**|! immer mit der Ruhe!; **to take things ~** (*fam*) sich *akk* schonen; (*rest*) sich *dat* keinen Stress machen **III.** *interj* (*fam*) locker

'**easy-care** *adj* pflegeleicht

'**easy chair** *n* Sessel *m*

easy'going *adj* unkompliziert; (*relaxed*) gelassen

eat <ate, eaten> |it| **I.** *vt* essen; *animal* fressen; **to ~ breakfast** frühstücken ▶PHRASES: **what's ~ing you?** was bedrückt dich? **II.** *vi* essen; *animal* fressen

 ◆**eat out** *vi* essen gehen

 ◆**eat up** *vt, vi* aufessen; *animal* auffressen

eaten ['iːtən] *pp of* **eat**

eatery ['iːtəri] *n* (*fam*) Esslokal *nt*

eau de cologne [ˌoʊdəkə'loʊn] *n* Kölnischwasser *nt*

eavesdrop <-pp-> ['iːvzdrap] *vi* |heimlich| lauschen; ■**to ~ on sb/sth** jdn/etw belauschen

ebb |eb| *n* Ebbe *f*; (*fig*) **to be at a low ~** auf einem Tiefstand sein; *funds* knapp bei Kasse sein

ebony ['ebəni] *n* Ebenholz *nt*

EC [ˌiː'siː] *n* HIST *abbrev of* **European Community:** ■**the ~** die EG

eccentric [ɪk'sentrɪk] **I.** *n* Exzentriker(in) *m(f)* **II.** *adj* exzentrisch

ecclesiastic [ɪˌkliːziˈæstɪk] (*form*) **I.** *n*

Geistliche(r) *m* **II.** *adj* kirchlich, geistlich

ECG [ˌiːsiːˈdʒiː] *n abbrev of* **electrocardiogram** EKG *nt*

echo ['ekoʊ] **I.** *n* <*pl* -es> Echo *nt*; (*fig*) Anklang *m* **II.** *vi* |wider|hallen; (*repeat*) wiederholen **III.** *vt* wiedergeben; *parrot* wiederholen

eclipse [ɪ'klɪps] **I.** *n* Finsternis *f*; (*fig*) Niedergang *m* **II.** *vt* verfinstern; (*fig*) in den Schatten stellen

ecological [ˌiːkə'ladʒɪ·kəl] *adj* ökologisch; **~ disaster** Umweltkatastrophe *f*

ecologist [iˈkal·ə·dʒɪst] *n* Ökologe, -in *m, f*

ecology [iˈkal·ə·dʒi] *n* Ökologie *f*

e-commerce ['iːkam·ɜrs] *n short for* **electronic commerce** E-Commerce *m*

economic [ˌiːkə'nam·ɪk] *adj* wirtschaftlich; (*profitable*) rentabel

economical [ˌiːkə'nam·ɪ·kəl] *adj* wirtschaftlich; (*frugal*) sparsam

economics [ˌiːkə'nam·ɪks] *n* + *sing vb* Wirtschaftswissenschaft|en| *f(pl)*; (*aspect*) wirtschaftlicher Aspekt

economist [ɪˈkan·ə·mɪst] *n* Wirtschaftswissenschaftler(in) *m(f)*

economize [ɪˈkan·ə·maɪz] *vi* sparen

economy [ɪˈkan·ə·mi] *n* Wirtschaft *f*; (*thriftiness*) Sparsamkeit *f kein pl*

e'conomy class *n* Touristenklasse *f*

e'conomy pack, e'conomy size *n* Sparpackung *f*

ecosystem ['eˌkoʊ·] *n* Ökosystem *nt*

ecstasy ['ek·stə·si] *n* Ekstase *f*; ■**E~** Ecstasy *f*

ecstatic [ek·'stæt·ɪk] *adj* ekstatisch

eddy ['ed·i] **I.** *vi* <-ie-> wirbeln **II.** *n* Wirbel *m*

edge [edʒ] *n* Rand *m*; (*sharp*) Kante *f*; (*sharpness*) Schärfe *f*

edgewise ['edʒ·waɪz] *adv* **to** |**not**| **get a word in ~** |nicht| zu Wort kommen

edgy <-ier, -iest> ['edʒ·i] *adj* (*fam*) nervös

edible ['ed·ɪ·bəl] *adj* essbar

edifying ['edɪ·faɪ·ɪŋ] *adj* erbaulich

edit ['ed·ɪt] *vt* redigieren; *text* bearbeiten

E

◆**edit out** vt [heraus]streichen; *scene* herausschneiden

edition [ɪ·'dɪ·ʃən] n Ausgabe f

editor ['ed·ɪ·tər] n Herausgeber(in) m(f); (of newspaper) Redakteur(in) m(f)

editorial [,ed·ə·'tɔːr·i·əl] I. n Leitartikel m II. adj ~ **staff** Redaktion f

educate ['edʒ·ə·keɪt] vt unterrichten; (train) ausbilden; (enlighten) aufklären

educated ['edʒ·ə·keɪ·tɪd] adj gebildet; **to be Harvard-~** in Harvard studiert haben

education [,edʒ·ʊ·'keɪ·ʃən] n Bildung f; (system) Erziehungswesen nt

educational [,edʒ·ʊ·'keɪ·ʃə·nəl] adj Bildungs-; (school) schulisch; (enlightening) lehrreich

eel [il] n Aal m

eerie <-r, -st> ['ɪr·i] adj unheimlich

effect [ɪ·'fekt] I. n Auswirkung f; (success) Erfolg m; **in ~** eigentlich; **to come into ~** in Kraft treten II. vt bewirken

effective [ɪ·'fek·tɪv] adj effektiv; (successful) erfolgreich; (real) tatsächlich; **~ January 1** mit Wirkung vom 1. Januar

effectively [ɪ·'fek·tɪv·li] adv effektiv; (successfully) erfolgreich; (basically) eigentlich

effectiveness [ɪ·'fek·tɪv·nəs] n Effektivität f

efficiency [ɪ·'fɪʃ·ən·si] n Leistungsfähigkeit f

efficient [ɪ·'fɪʃ·ənt] adj leistungsfähig

effort ['ef·ərt] n Anstrengung f; **to make an ~** sich anstrengen

effortless ['ef·ərt·lɪs] adj mühelos

EFL [,i·ef·'el] n abbrev of **English as a Foreign Language** Englisch nt als Fremdsprache

e.g. [i·'dʒi] abbrev of **exempli gratia** z. B.

e-generation [i·,dʒen·ə·'reɪ·ʃən] n Internetgeneration f

egg [eg] I. n Ei nt ▶PHRASES: **to put all one's ~s in one basket** alles auf eine Karte setzen II. vt ■to ~ **on** ⟳ **sb** jdn anstacheln

'eggplant n Aubergine f

'egg timer n Eieruhr f

ego ['i·goʊ] n Ego nt

egocentric [,i·goʊ·'sen·trɪk] adj egozentrisch

egoism ['i·goʊ·ɪz·əm] n Egoismus m

egoist ['i·goʊ·ɪst] n Egoist(in) m(f)

egoistic [,i·goʊ·'ɪs·tɪk] adj egoistisch

'ego trip n Egotrip m

Egypt ['i·dʒɪpt] n Ägypten nt

Egyptian [ɪ·'dʒɪp·ʃən] I. n Ägypter(in) m(f) II. adj ägyptisch

eh [eɪ] interj ■~? (pardon?) hä?; (you know?) nicht [wahr]?

eiderdown ['aɪ·dər·daʊn] n [Eider]daunen pl

eight [eɪt] I. adj acht; **there are ~ of us** wir sind [zu] acht; **~ times** achtmal; **one in ~** jeder Achte; **at ~ [o'clock]** um acht [Uhr]; **half past ~** halb neun; **at ~ twenty/forty-five** um zwanzig nach acht/Viertel vor neun II. n Acht f; **~ of clubs** Kreuzacht f

eighteen [,eɪ·'tin] I. adj achtzehn II. n Achtzehn f; see also **eight**

eighteenth [,eɪ·'tinθ] I. adj achtzehnte(r, s) II. n ❶ ■the ~ der/die/das Achtzehnte ❷ (fraction) Achtzehntel nt

eighth [eɪtθ] I. adj achte(r, s); **every ~ person** jeder Achte; **the ~ largest ...** der/die/das achtgrößte ... II. n ❶ ■the ~ der/die/das Achte ❷ ■the ~ [of the month] der 8. [des Monats]; **on February ~** am 8. Februar ❸ (fraction) Achtel nt

eightieth ['eɪ·ti·əθ] I. adj achtzigste(r, s) II. n ❶ ■the ~ der/die/das Achtzigste ❷ (fraction) Achtzigstel nt; see also **eight**

eighty ['eɪ·ti] I. adj achtzig; see also **eight** II. n Achtzig f; **in one's eighties** in den Achtzigern; ■the eighties pl die 80er Jahre

Eire ['erə] n Eire nt

either ['i·ðər] I. conj ~ ... or ... entweder ... oder ... II. adv + neg I don't/haven't ~ ich auch nicht; it's good and

not very expensive ~ es ist gut – und nicht einmal sehr teuer **III.** *adj* ❶ (*each*) **on ~ side** auf beiden Seiten ❷ (*one*) eine(r, s) [von beiden] **IV.** *pron* **~ of you** eine(r) von euch beiden

eject [ɪ·ˈdʒekt] *vt* hinauswerfen

elaborate [ɪ·ˈlæb·ər·ət] *adj* kompliziert; *decorations* kunstvoll [gearbeitet]

elaboration [ɪ·ˌlæb·ə·ˈreɪ·ʃən] *n of plan* Ausarbeitung *f*

elastic [ɪ·ˈlæs·tɪk] **I.** *adj* elastisch **II.** *n* Gummi *m*

elastic 'band *n see* **rubber band**

elbow [ˈel·boʊ] **I.** *n* Ellbogen *m* **II.** *vt* **she ~ed him in the ribs** sie stieß ihm den Ellbogen in die Rippen

'elbow grease *n* Muskelkraft *f*

elder[1] [ˈel·dər] **I.** *n* Ältere(r) *f(m)*; **church ~** Kirchenälteste(r) *f(m)* **II.** *adj* ältere(r, s)

elder[2] [ˈel·dər] *n* (*tree*) Holunder *m*

elderly [ˈel·dər·li] **I.** *adj* ältere(r, s) **II.** *n* ■**the ~** *pl* ältere Menschen

eldest [ˈel·dɪst] **I.** *adj* älteste(r, s) **II.** *n* ■**the ~** der/die Älteste

e-learning [ˈiː·ˌlɜː·nɪŋ] *n no pl* E-Learning *nt*

elect [ɪ·ˈlekt] *vt* wählen

election [ɪ·ˈlek·ʃən] *n* Wahl *f*

e'lection campaign *n* Wahlkampf *m*

E'lection Day *n* Wahltag *m*

electoral 'college *n* Wahlausschuss *m*; (*of US president*) Wahlmännergremium *nt*

electric [ɪ·ˈlek·trɪk] *adj* elektrisch; (*exciting*) elektrisierend

electrical [ɪ·ˈlek·trɪ·kəl] *adj* elektrisch

electrician [ɪ·ˌlek·ˈtrɪʃ·ən] *n* Elektriker(in) *m(f)*

electricity [ɪ·ˌlek·ˈtrɪs·ə·ti] *n* [elektrischer] Strom; **heated by ~** elektrisch beheizt

electrify [ɪ·ˈlek·trɪ·faɪ] *vt* elektrifizieren; (*fig*) elektrisieren

electrocute [ɪ·ˈlek·trə·kjut] *vt* durch einen Stromschlag töten; (*execute*) auf dem elektrischen Stuhl hinrichten

electrocution [ɪ·ˌlek·trə·ˈkju·ʃən] *n* Tötung *f* durch Stromschlag; (*execution*) Hinrichtung *f* durch den elektrischen Stuhl

electron [ɪ·ˈlek·tran] *n* Elektron *nt*

electronic [ɪ·ˌlek·ˈtran·ɪk] *adj* elektronisch

electronics [ɪ·ˌlek·ˈtran·ɪks] *n + sing vb* Elektronik *f kein pl*

elegance [ˈel·ɪ·gəns] *n* Eleganz *f*

elegant [ˈel·ɪ·gənt] *adj* elegant

element [ˈel·ə·mənt] *n* Element *nt*

ele'mentary school *n* Grundschule *f*

elephant [ˈel·ə·fənt] *n* Elefant *m*

elevate [ˈel·ə·veɪt] *vt* [empor]heben

elevated [ˈel·ə·veɪ·t̬ɪd] *adj* erhöht; (*important*) gehoben

elevation [ˌel·ɪ·ˈveɪ·ʃən] *n* [Boden]erhebung *f*; (*promotion*) Beförderung *f*

elevator [ˈel·ə·veɪ·t̬ər] *n* Aufzug *m*

eleven [ɪ·ˈlev·ən] **I.** *adj* elf **II.** *n* Elf *f*; *see also* **eight**

eleventh [ɪ·ˈlev·ənθ] **I.** *adj* elfte(r, s) **II.** *n* ❶ **the ~** der/die/das Elfte ❷ (*fraction*) Elftel *nt*; *see also* **eighth**

elf <*pl* elves> [elf] *n* Elf *m*, Elfe *f*

eligibility [ˌel·ɪ·dʒə·ˈbɪl·ə·ti] *n* Eignung *f*; (*entitlement*) Berechtigung *f*

eligible [ˈel·ɪ·dʒə·bəl] *adj* ❶ ■**to be ~ for sth** für etw *akk* qualifiziert sein; (*entitled*) zu etw *dat* berechtigt sein ❷ (*desirable*) begehrt

eliminate [ɪ·ˈlɪm·ɪ·neɪt] *vt* beseitigen; (*exclude*) ausschließen; ■**to be ~d** SPORT ausscheiden

elimination [ɪ·ˌlɪm·ɪ·ˈneɪ·ʃən] *n* Beseitigung *f*; **process of ~** Ausleseverfahren *nt*

elite [ɪ·ˈliːt] **I.** *n* Elite *f* **II.** *adj* Elite-; **~ university** Eliteuniversität *f*

elitism [ɪ·ˈli·tɪz·əm] *n* Elitedenken *nt*

elitist [ɪ·ˈli·tɪst] *adj* elitär

elk <*pl* -> [elk] *n* Wapitihirsch *m*

ellipse [ɪ·ˈlɪps] *n* Ellipse *f*

elliptic(al) [ɪ·ˈlɪp·tɪ·k(əl)] *adj* elliptisch

elm [elm] *n* Ulme *f*

elope [ɪ·ˈloʊp] *vi* durchbrennen *fam*

elopement [ɪ·ˈloʊp·mənt] *n* Durchbrennen *nt fam*

eloquent [ˈel·ə·kwənt] *adj* sprachgewandt

E

else [els] *adv* ❶ **anybody** ~ jeder andere; **anywhere/nowhere** ~ irgendwo/nirgendwo anders; **everybody** ~ alle anderen; **everything** ~ alles andere; **everywhere** ~ überall sonst; **nobody/nothing** ~ niemand/nichts anders; **someone/something** ~ jemand/etwas anders; **somewhere** ~ woanders; **why** ~ ...? warum sonst ...? ❷ (*additional*) sonst noch; **I don't want anyone ~ to come but you** ich will, dass außer dir [sonst] keiner kommt; **there's nothing ~ to do** es gibt nichts mehr zu tun; **nobody/nothing** ~ sonst niemand/nichts; **somewhere** ~ noch woanders ❸ **or** ~! (*fam*) sonst gibt's was!

elsewhere ['els·wer] *adv* woanders

elusive [ɪˈluˈsɪv] *adj* ausweichend; (*hard to find*) schwer zu fassen

elves [elvz] *n pl of* **elf**

emaciated [ɪˈmeɪˈʃiˈeɪˈtɪd] *adj* [stark] abgemagert

e-mail ['iˈmeɪl] I. *n abbrev of* **electronic mail** E-Mail *f* II. *vt* [e-]mailen

emancipated [ɪˈmænˈsəˈpeɪˌtɪd] *adj* emanzipiert

emancipation [ɪˌmænˈsɪˈpeɪˈʃən] *n* Emanzipation *f*

embalm [emˈbam] *vt* [ein]balsamieren

embankment [emˈbæŋkˈmənt] *n* Damm *m*

embargo [emˈbarˈgoʊ] *n* <*pl* -es> Embargo *nt*

embarrass [emˈbærˈəs] *vt* in Verlegenheit bringen

embarrassed [emˈbærˈəst] *adj* verlegen

embarrassing [emˈbærˈəsɪŋ] *adj* peinlich; *generosity* beschämend

embarrassment [emˈbærˈəsˈmənt] *n* Peinlichkeit *f*; (*feeling*) Verlegenheit *f*

embassy ['emˈbəˈsi] *n* Botschaft *f*

embellish [emˈbelˈɪʃ] *vt* schmücken; *truth* beschönigen

embers ['emˈbərz] *npl* Glut *f*

embezzle [ɪmˈbezˈəl] *vt* unterschlagen

embezzlement [ɪmˈbezˈəlˈmənt] *n* Unterschlagung *f*

emblem ['emˈbləm] *n* Emblem *nt*

embodiment [emˈbadˈɪˈmənt] *n* Verkörperung *f*; **the ~ of virtue** die Tugend selbst

embody [emˈbadˈi] *vt* verkörpern; (*show*) zum Ausdruck bringen

embrace [emˈbreɪs] I. *vt* umarmen; (*fig*) [bereitwillig] übernehmen II. *n* Umarmung *f*

embroider [emˈbrɔɪˈdər] *vt, vi* sticken; *cloth* besticken

embroidery [emˈbrɔɪˈdəˈri] *n* Stickerei *f*

embryo ['emˈbriˈoʊ] *n* Embryo *m o* ÖSTERR *a. nt*

emcee [emˈsi] *n* (*fam*) Conférencier *m*; TV Showmaster *m*

emerald ['emˈərˈəld] *n* Smaragd *m*

emerge [ɪˈmɜrdʒ] *vi* herauskommen; (*surface*) auftauchen; *truth* an den Tag kommen

emergence [ɪˈmɜrˈdʒəns] *n* Auftauchen *nt*; *of country* Entstehung *f*; *of ideas* Aufkommen *nt*

emergency [ɪˈmɜrˈdʒənˈsi] *n* ❶ Notfall *m*; **state of** ~ Ausnahmezustand *m* ❷ (*emergency room*) Notaufnahme *f*

e'mergency room, ER *n* Notaufnahme *f*

'emery board *n* Nagelfeile *f*

emigrant ['emˈɪˈgrənt] *n* Auswanderer, -in *m, f*

emigrate ['emˈɪˈgreɪt] *vi* auswandern

emigration [ˌemˈɪˈgreɪˈʃən] *n* Auswanderung *f*

eminent ['emˈɪˈnənt] *adj* [hoch] angesehen

eminently ['emˈɪˈnəntˈli] *adv* überaus

emission [ɪˈmɪʃˈən] *n* Emission *f*; *of gas, liquid* Ausströmen *nt*; *of heat, light* Ausstrahlen *nt*

emit <-tt-> [ɪˈmɪt] *vt* abgeben; *fumes, cry* ausstoßen; *gas, odor* verströmen; *heat, sound* abgeben; *rays* aussenden

emoticon [ɪˈmoʊˈtɪˈkən] *n* INET Emoticon *nt*

emotion [ɪˈmoʊˈʃən] *n* Gefühl *nt*

emotional [ɪˈmoʊˈʃəˈnəl] *adj* emotio-

nal; *reception* herzlich; *speech* gefühlsbetont

emotionless [ɪ·'moʊ·ʃən·lɪs] *adj* emotionslos; *face* ausdruckslos

emperor ['em·pər·ər] *n* Kaiser *m*

emphasis <*pl* -ses> ['em·fə·sɪs] *n* Betonung *f*

emphasize ['em·fə·saɪz] *vt* betonen

empire ['em·paɪr] *n* Imperium *nt*

employ [em·'plɔɪ] *vt* beschäftigen;
(*staff*) einstellen

employee [em·plɔɪ·'i] *n* Angestellte(r)
f(m); ■~**s** *pl* (*staff*) Belegschaft *f*

employer [em·'plɔɪ·ər] *n* Arbeitge-
ber(in) *m(f)*

employment [em·'plɔɪ·mənt] *n* ❶ Beschäftigung *f*; (*taking on*) Anstellung *f*;
in ~ erwerbstätig ❷ (*profession*) Beruf *m*

em'ployment agency *n* Stellenvermittlung *f*

empress <*pl* -es> ['em·prɪs] *n* Kaise-
rin *f*

emptiness ['emp·tɪ·nɪs] *n* Leere *f*

empty ['emp·ti] **I.** *adj* leer; *house*
leer stehend; *stomach* nüchtern **II.** *vt*
<-ie-> [ent]leeren; (*pour*) schütten
III. *vi* <-ie-> sich leeren **IV.** *n* ■**empties** *pl* Leergut *nt*

 ◆**empty out I.** *vt* ausleeren; (*pour*)
ausschütten **II.** *vi* sich leeren

empty-'handed *adj* mit leeren Händen
nach 'n

empty-'headed *adj* hohlköpfig

emu <*pl* -> ['i·mju] *n* Emu *m*

emulsion [ɪ·'mʌl·ʃən] *n* Emulsion *f*

enable [ɪ·'neɪ·bəl] *vt* ■**to** ~ **sb to
do sth** jdm ermöglichen, etw zu
tun

enact [ɪ·'nækt] *vt role* spielen; *play* aufführen; LAW erlassen

enamel [ɪ·'næm·əl] *n* Email *nt*; (*dental*)
Zahnschmelz *m*

encapsulate [ɪn·'kæp·sə·leɪt] *vt* um-
manteln

encased [en·'keɪs] *adj* ummantelt

enchant [en·'tʃænt] *vt* entzücken

enchanting [en·'tʃæn·tɪŋ] *adj* entzückend

encircle [en·'sɜr·kəl] *vt* umgeben; MIL
umzingeln

encl. *adj, n abbrev of* **enclosed, enclosure** Anl.

enclose [en·'kloʊz] *vt* umgeben; (*shut
in*) einschließen; *mail* beilegen

enclosure [en·'kloʊ·ʒər] *n* eingezäuntes
Grundstück; (*for animals*) Gehege *nt*;
(*in mail*) Anlage *f*

encompass [en·'kʌm·pəs] *vt* umfassen

encore ['an·kɔr] *n* Zugabe *f*

encounter [en·'kaʊn·tər] **I.** *vt* stoßen
auf +*akk*; (*meet*) [unerwartet] treffen
II. *n* Begegnung *f*; MIL Zusammenstoß *m*

encourage [en·'kɜr·ɪdʒ] *vt* ❶ ermuti-
gen; (*give hope*) unterstützen; ■**to** ~
sb to do sth jdn [dazu] ermuntern, etw
zu tun; (*advise*) jdm [dazu] raten, etw
zu tun ❷ (*promote*) fördern

encouragement [en·'kɜr·ɪdʒ·mənt] *n*
Ermutigung *f*; (*urging*) Ermunterung *f*;
(*support*) Unterstützung *f*

encouraging [en·'kɜr·ɪdʒ·ɪŋ] *adj* ermu-
tigend

encyclopedia [en·ˌsaɪ·klə·'pi·di·ə] *n* Lexikon *nt*

encyclopedic [en·ˌsaɪ·klə·'pi·dɪk] *adj*
universal

end [end] **I.** *n* ❶ Ende *nt*; (*completion*)
Schluss *m*; **until the** ~ bis zuletzt; **no** ~
of trouble reichlich Ärger; ~ **to** ~ der
Länge nach; **on** ~ hochkant ❷ *usu pl*
(*aims*) Ziel *nt*; (*purpose*) Zweck *m*
❸ SPORT [Spielfeld]hälfte *f* ▶PHRASES: **at
the** ~ **of the day** [*or* **in the** ~] (*all considered*) letzten Endes; (*finally*) schließlich; **to go off the deep** ~ hochgehen;
to make ~**s meet** mit seinem Geld zurechtkommen **II.** *vt* beenden **III.** *vi* enden; **to** ~ **in a tie** unentschieden ausgehen

 ◆**end up** *vi* enden; **to** ~ **up in prison**
[schließlich] im Gefängnis landen; **to** ~
up teaching schließlich Lehrer/Lehre-
rin werden

endanger [en·'deɪn·dʒər] *vt* gefährden;
an ~**ed species** eine vom Aussterben
bedrohte Art

E

E

endearing [enˈdɪr·ɪŋ] *adj* lieb|ens-
wert|; *smile* gewinnend
endeavor [enˈdev·ər] I. *vi* sich bemühen II. *n* Bemühung *f*
ending [ˈen·dɪŋ] *n* Schluss *m; of story,
book* Ausgang *m;* **happy ~** Happy-
end *nt*
endive [ˈen·daɪv] *n* Endivie *f*
endless [ˈend·lɪs] *adj* endlos; *(countless)* unzählig
endorse [enˈdɔrs] *vt* billigen; *(promote)* unterstützen; *check* auf der
Rückseite unterschreiben
endorsement [enˈdɔrs·mənt] *n* Billi-
gung *f; (signature)* Giro *nt fachspr*
endow [enˈdaʊ] *vt prize* stiften; ■ **to be
~ed with sth** mit etw *dat* ausgestattet
sein
endowment [enˈdaʊ·mənt] *n* Stiftung *f*
endurable [enˈdʊr·ə·bəl] *adj* erträglich
endurance [enˈdʊr·əns] *n* Ausdauer *f*
endure [enˈdʊr] I. *vt* ertragen; *(suffer)*
erleiden II. *vi* fortdauern
enemy [ˈen·ə·mi] I. *n* Feind(in) *m(f)*
II. *adj* feindlich
energetic [ˌen·ərˈdʒet·ɪk] *adj* ener-
giegeladen; *(resolute)* energisch
energy [ˈen·ər·dʒi] *n* Energie *f; (vigor
also)* Kraft *f;* **~ crisis** Energiekrise *f*
enforce [enˈfɔrs] *vt* durchsetzen
enforcement [enˈfɔrs·mənt] *n* Erzwingung *f; of regulation* Durchsetzung *f; of
law* Vollstreckung *f*
engage [enˈgeɪdʒ] *vt (employ)* anstellen; *clutch* einschalten; MIL angreifen
engaged [enˈgeɪdʒd] *adj* verlobt; **to
get ~ [to sb]** sich [mit jdm] verloben
engagement [enˈgeɪdʒ·mənt] *n* Verlobung *f; (appointment)* Verabredung *f*
en'gagement ring *n* Verlobungsring *m*
engaging [enˈgeɪ·dʒɪŋ] *adj* einnehmend; *smile* gewinnend
engine [ˈen·dʒɪn] *n* Motor *m; jet* Trieb-
werk *nt;* RAIL Lok|omotive *f*
engineer [ˌen·dʒɪˈnɪr] I. *n* Ingenieur(in)
m(f); (train driver) Lok|omotiv|füh-
rer(in) *m(f)* II. *vt* konstruieren; *(contrive)* arrangieren

engineering [ˌen·dʒɪˈnɪr·ɪŋ] *n* Technik *f; (studies)* Ingenieurwissenschaft *f*
England [ˈɪŋ·glənd] *n* England *nt*
English [ˈɪŋ·glɪʃ] I. *n* Englisch *nt;*
■ **the ~** *pl* die Engländer II. *adj* englisch; **~ department** Institut *nt* für An-
glistik
'**Englishman** *n* Engländer *m*
'**Englishwoman** *n* Engländerin *f*
engrave [enˈgreɪv] *vt* [ein]gravieren;
(on stone) einmeißeln; *(on wood)* ein-
schnitzen
engraving [enˈgreɪ·vɪŋ] *n* ❶ *(print)*
Stich *m; (from wood)* Holzschnitt *m*
❷ *(design)* Gravur *f*
engulf [enˈgʌlf] *vt* verschlingen
enhance [ɪnˈhæns] *vt* verbessern; *(intensify)* hervorheben
enigma [ɪˈnɪg·mə] *n* Rätsel *nt*
enjoy [enˈdʒɔɪ] *vt* genießen; **did you ~
the movie?** hat dir der Film gefallen?;
■ **to ~ doing sth** etw gern[e] tun; ■ **to ~
oneself** sich amüsieren; **~ yourself!**
viel Spaß!
enjoyable [enˈdʒɔɪ·ə·bəl] *adj* angenehm; *(entertaining)* unterhaltsam
enjoyment [enˈdʒɔɪ·mənt] *n* Vergnügen *nt*
enlarge [enˈlardʒ] *vt* vergrößern; *(expand)* erweitern
enlighten [enˈlaɪ·tən] *vt* aufklären
enlightened [enˈlaɪ·tənd] *adj* aufgeklärt
enlightenment [enˈlaɪ·tən·mənt] *n*
■ **the E~** die Aufklärung
enlist [enˈlɪst] I. *vi* sich melden II. *vt* anwerben; *support* gewinnen
en masse [anˈmæs] *adv* alle zusammen
enormity [ɪˈnɔr·mə·ti] *n* ungeheures
Ausmaß
enormous [ɪˈnɔr·məs] *adj* enorm; *difficulties* ungeheuer
enough [ɪˈnʌf] I. *adj* genug; **that
should be ~** das dürfte reichen; **just
~ room** gerade Platz genug II. *adv*
❶ **are you warm ~?** ist es dir warm
genug? ❷ **he seems nice ~** er
scheint so weit recht nett zu sein;
strangely ~ seltsamerweise III. *pron*

there's ~ **for everybody** es ist für alle genug da; **that's ~!** jetzt reicht es!

enquire [en·ˈkwaɪr] *vi see* **inquire**

enquiry [en·ˈkwaɪr·i] *n see* **inquiry**

enrage [en·ˈreɪdʒ] *vt* wütend machen

enraged [en·ˈreɪdʒd] *adj* wütend

enrich [en·ˈrɪtʃ] *vt* bereichern

enroll, enrol [en·ˈroʊl] *vi* sich einschreiben; *for course* sich anmelden

enrollment, enrolment [en·ˈroʊl·mənt] *n* Einschreibung *f*; (*for course*) Anmeldung *f*

en route [ˌan·ˈrut] *adv* unterwegs

ensemble [an·ˈsam·bəl] *n* Ensemble *nt*

enslave [en·ˈsleɪv] *vt* zum Sklaven machen

ensure [en·ˈʃʊr] *vt* sicherstellen

entangle [en·ˈtæŋ·gəl] *vt* **to get ~d in** sth sich in etw *dat* verfangen; (*fig*) sich in etw *akk* verwickeln

enter [ˈen·tər] **I.** *vt* ❶ hineingehen in +*akk*; *room* betreten; *phase* eintreten in +*akk*; (*penetrate*) eindringen in +*akk* ❷ *data* eingeben; (*in register*) eintragen ❸ (*join*) beitreten +*dat*; **to ~ sb in** sth jdn für etw *akk* anmelden **II.** *vi* ❶ THEAT auftreten ❷ (*register*) **to ~ in** sth sich für etw *akk* [an]melden
◆ **enter into** *vi* **to ~ into an alliance** ein Bündnis schließen; **to ~ into negotiations** in Verhandlungen eintreten

'enter key *n* COMPUT Eingabetaste *f*

enterprise [ˈen·tər·praɪz] *n* Unternehmen *nt*; (*initiative*) Unternehmungsgeist *m*

enterprising [ˈen·tər·praɪ·zɪŋ] *adj* unternehmungslustig; (*ingenious*) einfallsreich

entertain [ˌen·tər·ˈteɪn] **I.** *vt* unterhalten; *guests* zu sich einladen; (*give meal*) bewirten **II.** *vi* Gäste haben

entertainer [ˌen·tər·ˈteɪ·nər] *n* Entertainer(in) *m(f)*

entertaining [ˌen·tər·ˈteɪ·nɪŋ] **I.** *adj* unterhaltsam **II.** *n* **to do a lot of ~** häufig Leute bewirten

entertainment [ˌen·tər·ˈteɪn·mənt] *n* Unterhaltung *f*

enthusiasm [ɪn·ˈθu·zɪ·æz·əm] *n* Begeisterung *f*

enthusiast [ɪn·ˈθu·zɪ·æst] *n* Enthusiast(in) *m(f)*

enthusiastic [ɪn·ˌθu·zɪ·ˈæs·tɪk] *adj* begeistert

entire [en·ˈtaɪr] *adj* ganz; (*complete*) vollständig

entirely [en·ˈtaɪr·li] *adv* ganz; *agree* völlig

entirety [en·ˈtaɪ·rə·t̬i] *n* Gesamtheit *f*

entitle [en·ˈtaɪ·t̬əl] *vt* **to be ~d to do** sth dazu berechtigt sein, etw zu tun

entrails [ˈen·treɪlz] *npl* Eingeweide *pl*

entrance [ˈen·trəns] *n* Eingang *m*; (*for car*) Einfahrt *f*; (*entering*) Eintritt *m*; THEAT Auftritt *m*

'entrance exam(ination) *n* Aufnahmeprüfung *f*

entrepreneur [ˌan·trə·prə·ˈnɜr] *n* Unternehmer(in) *m(f)*

entrust [en·ˈtrʌst] *vt* **to ~ sth to sb** jdm etw anvertrauen

entry [ˈen·tri] *n* ❶ Eintritt *m*; (*by car*) Einfahrt *f*; (*into country*) Einreise *f*; (*into organization*) Aufnahme *f*; **"no ~"** „Zutritt verboten" ❷ (*entrance*) Eingang *m*; (*road*) Einfahrt *f*

'entry form *n* Antragsformular *nt*; (*for competition*) Teilnahmeformular *nt*

envelop [en·ˈvel·əp] *vt* einhüllen

envelope [ˈen·və·loʊp] *n* Briefumschlag *m*

enviable [ˈen·vi·ə·bəl] *adj* beneidenswert

envious [ˈen·vi·əs] *adj* neidisch

environment [en·ˈvaɪ·ərn·mənt] *n* ❶ **the ~** die Umwelt ❷ (*surroundings*) Umgebung *f*; *social* Milieu *nt*

environmental [en·ˌvaɪ·ərn·ˈmen·t̬əl] *adj* Umwelt-

environmentalist [en·ˌvaɪ·ərn·ˈmen·t̬əl·ɪst] *n* Umweltschützer(in) *m(f)*

environmentally [en·ˌvaɪ·ərn·ˈmen·t̬əli] *adv* **~ damaging** umweltschädlich

environment-'friendly *adj* umweltfreundlich

envoy [ˈan·vɔɪ] *n* Gesandte(r) *f(m)*

envy [ˈen·vi] **I.** *n* Neid *m*; **he's the ~ of**

E

the school with his new car die ganze Schule beneidet ihn um sein neues Auto II. *vt* <-ie-> ■to ~ sb sth jdn um etw *akk* beneiden

enzyme ['en·zaɪm] *n* Enzym *nt*

eon ['iː·an] *n* Äon *m*

epic ['ep·ɪk] I. *n* Epos *nt* II. *adj* episch; *(fig)* abenteuerlich; ~ **poet** Epiker(in) *m(f)*; ■ **proportions** unvorstellbare Ausmaße

epicenter ['ep·ɪ·sen·tər] *n* Epizentrum *nt*

epidemic [,ep·ɪ·'dem·ɪk] *n* Epidemie *f*

epilepsy ['ep·ɪ·lep·si] *n* Epilepsie *f*

epileptic [,ep·ɪ·'lep·tɪk] I. *n* Epileptiker(in) *m(f)* II. *adj* epileptisch

epilogue, epilog ['ep·ɪ·lag] *n* Epilog *m*

Epiphany [ɪ·'pɪf·ə·ni] *n* Dreikönigsfest *nt*

episode ['ep·ɪ·soʊd] *n* Episode *f*

epitaph ['ep·ɪ·tæf] *n* Grabinschrift *f*

epitome [ɪ·'pɪt̬·ə·mi] *n* Inbegriff *m*; **the ~ of elegance** die Eleganz selbst

epoch ['ep·ək] *n* Epoche *f*

equal ['iː·kwəl] I. *adj* ❶ *(same)* gleich; **of ~ size** gleich groß ❷ *(able)* **to be ~ to a task** einer Aufgabe gewachsen sein II. *n* Gleichgestellte(r) *f(m)*; **to have no ~** unübertroffen sein III. *vt* <-l- *or* -ll-> ❶ MATH ergeben ❷ *(match)* herankommen an *+akk; record* erreichen

equality [ɪ·'kwal·ə·t̬i] *n no pl* Gleichberechtigung *f*; **racial ~** Rassengleichheit *f*; ■ **the E~ Act** EU das Allgemeine Gleichbehandlungsgesetz, das AGG

equally ['iː·kwə·li] *adv* ebenso; **~ good** gleich gut; **to divide sth ~** etw gleichmäßig aufteilen

equal oppor'tunity *n* Chancengleichheit *f*

'equal sign *n* Gleichheitszeichen *nt*

equation [ɪ·'kweɪ·ʒən] *n* Gleichung *f*

equator [ɪ·'kweɪ·t̬ər] *n* Äquator *m*; **on the ~** am Äquator

equilibrium [,i·kwɪ·'lɪb·ri·əm] *n* Gleichgewicht *nt*

equip <-pp-> [ɪ·'kwɪp] *vt* ausstatten; *(fig)* rüsten

equipment [ɪ·'kwɪp·mənt] *n* Ausstattung *f*

equivalence [ɪ·'kwɪv·ə·ləns] *n* Äquivalenz *f*

equivalent [ɪ·'kwɪv·ə·lənt] I. *adj* äquivalent; ■ **to be ~ to sth** etw *dat* entsprechen II. *n* Äquivalent *nt*

equivocal [ɪ·'kwɪv·ə·kəl] *adj* zweideutig

ER [,i·'ar] *n abbrev of* **emergency room** Notaufnahme *f*

era ['ɪr·ə] *n* Ära *f*

erase [ɪ·'reɪs] *vt* entfernen; *memories* auslöschen; *(rub out)* ausradieren

eraser [ɪ·'reɪ·sər] *n* Radiergummi *m*

erect [ɪ·'rekt] I. *adj* aufrecht; *penis* erigiert II. *vt* errichten; *(upright)* aufstellen

erection [ɪ·'rek·ʃən] *n* Errichtung *f*; *(penis)* Erektion *f*

ergonomic [,ɜr·gə·'nam·ɪk] *adj* ergonomisch

ermine ['ɜr·mɪn] *n* Hermelin *nt*

erode [ɪ·'roʊd] I. *vt* erodieren; *soil* abtragen; *(fig)* untergraben II. *vi* erodiert werden; *soil* abgetragen werden

erosion [ɪ·'roʊ·ʒən] *n* Erosion *f*; *(fig)* [Dahin]schwinden *nt*

erotic [ɪ·'rat̬·ɪk] *adj* erotisch

errand ['er·ənd] *n* Besorgung *f*

erratic [ɪ·'ræt̬·ɪk] *adj* sprunghaft

erroneous [ɪ·'roʊ·ni·əs] *adj* falsch

error ['er·ər] *n* Fehler *m*; *(in baseball)* Fehlpass *m*

'error message *n* COMPUT Fehlermeldung *f*

'error-prone *adj* fehleranfällig

erupt [ɪ·'rʌpt] *vi* ausbrechen; *(fig)* explodieren

eruption [ɪ·'rʌp·ʃən] *n* Ausbruch *m*

escalate ['es·kə·leɪt] I. *vi* eskalieren II. *vt* ausweiten

escalation [,es·kə·'leɪ·ʃən] *n* Eskalation *f; of fighting* Ausweitung *f*

escalator ['es·kə·leɪ·t̬ər] *n* Rolltreppe *f*

escapade [,es·kə·'peɪd] *n* Eskapade *f*

escape [ɪ·'skeɪp] I. *vi* ❶ fliehen; *(successfully)* entkommen; *(from cage, prison)* ausbrechen; *zoo animal* entlaufen; *bird* entfliegen ❷ *(avoid* *harm*) [mit dem Leben] davonkommen; **to ~ unhurt** unverletzt bleiben II. *vt* ❶ fliehen; (*successfully*) entkommen; **to ~ the fire** dem Feuer entkommen ❷ (*avoid*) entgehen +*dat;* **she was lucky to ~ injury** sie hatte Glück, dass sie nicht verletzt wurde ❸ **to ~ sb's attention** jds Aufmerksamkeit entgehen III. *n* Flucht *f; from prison* Ausbruch *m;* (*avoidance*) Entkommen *nt; that was a lucky ~!* da haben wir wirklich noch einmal Glück gehabt!; **to have a narrow ~** gerade noch einmal davongekommen sein

e'scape key *n* COMPUT Esc-Taste *f*

escapism [ɪˈskeɪ·pɪz·əm] *n* Realitätsflucht *f*

escort I. *vt* [ɪsˈkɔrt, esˈkɔrt] eskortieren; MIL Geleitschutz geben +*dat;* **to ~ sb upstairs** jdn hinaufbringen II. *n* [ˈesk·ɔrt] Begleitung *f;* (*guard*) Eskorte *f*

esp. *adv abbrev of* **especially** bes.

especially [ɪˈspeʃ·ə·li] *adv* besonders

espionage [ˈes·pi·ə·nɑʒ] *n* Spionage *f*

espresso [ɪˈspres·oʊ] *n* Espresso *m*

essay [ˈes·eɪ] *n* Essay *m o nt*

essence [ˈes·əns] *n* Wesen *nt;* (*gist*) Wesentliche(s) *nt;* FOOD Essenz *f*

essential [ɪˈsen·ʃəl] I. *adj* unbedingt erforderlich; *vitamins* lebenswichtig; *difference* grundlegend II. *n* ■ the **~s** *pl* das Wesentliche

essentially [ɪˈsen·ʃə·li] *adv* im Grunde [genommen]

EST [ˌi·es·ˈti] *n abbrev of* **Eastern Standard Time** Ostküsten Standardzeit *f*

est. *adj* ❶ *abbrev of* **estimated** ❷ *abbrev of* **established** gegr.

establish [ɪˈstæb·lɪʃ] *vt* ❶ gründen; *relations* aufbauen; *rule* aufstellen; **to ~ order** für Ordnung sorgen ❷ (*prove*) feststellen; *claim* nachweisen

established [ɪˈstæb·lɪʃt] *adj* (*standard*) fest; (*proven*) nachgewiesen; (*founded*) gegründet; **it is ~ practice …** es ist üblich, …

establishment [ɪˈstæb·lɪʃ·mənt] *n* ❶ Gründung *f;* (*institution*) Unternehmen *nt;* **educational ~** Bildungseinrichtung *f* ❷ ■ the **~** das Establishment

estate [ɪˈsteɪt] *n* Gut *nt;* **country ~** Landgut *nt*

esteem [ɪˈstim] *n* **to hold sb in high ~** jdn hoch schätzen

esthetic [esˈθet·ɪk] *adj see* **aesthetic**

estimate I. *vt* [ˈes·tɪ·meɪt] [ein]schätzen II. *n* [ˈes·tɪ·mɪt] Schätzung *f*

estimated [ˈes·tɪ·meɪ·tɪd] *adj* geschätzt; (*expected*) voraussichtlich

estimation [ˌes·tɪ·ˈmeɪ·ʃən] *n* Einschätzung *f; in my ~* meiner Ansicht nach

estranged [ɪˈstreɪndʒd] *adj couple* getrennt

estrogen [ˈes·trə·dʒən] *n* Östrogen *nt*

estuary [ˈes·tʃu·er·i] *n* Flussmündung *f*

ETA [ˌi·ti·ˈeɪ] *n abbrev of* **estimated time of arrival** voraussichtliche Ankunft

etc. *adv abbrev of* **et cetera** usw., etc.

etch [etʃ] *vt* ätzen; (*in copper*) kupferstechen

eternal [ɪˈtɜr·nəl] *adj* ewig; *complaints* endlos

eternity [ɪˈtɜr·nə·ti] *n* Ewigkeit *f*

ethical [ˈeθ·ɪkəl] *adj* ethisch

ethics [ˈeθ·ɪks] *n* Ethik *f*

ethnic [ˈeθ·nɪk] *adj* ethnisch; **~ costumes** Landestrachten *pl*

etiquette [ˈet·ɪ·kɪt] *n* Etikette *f*

eunuch [ˈju·nək] *n* Eunuch *m*

euphemism [ˈju·fə·mɪz·əm] *n* Euphemismus *m*

euphemistic [ˌju·fə·ˈmɪs·tɪk] *adj* euphemistisch

euphoria [juˈfɔr·i·ə] *n* Euphorie *f*

euphoric [juˈfɔr·ɪk] *adj* euphorisch

euro [ˈjʊr·oʊ] *n* Euro *m*

euro 'bailout fund, eurozone 'bailout fund *n* FIN Euro-Rettungsschirm *m*

Europe [ˈjʊr·əp] *n* Europa *nt*

European [ˌjʊr·ə·ˈpi·ən] I. *adj* europäisch II. *n* Europäer(in) *m(f)*

European 'Union *n* Europäische Union

euthanasia [ˌju·θə·ˈneɪ·ʒə] *n* Sterbehilfe *f*

evacuate [ɪˈvæk·ju·eɪt] *vt people* evakuieren; *area* räumen

E

evacuation [ɪˌvæk·juˈeɪ·ʃən] n Evakuierung f; (of building) Räumung f

evade [ɪˈveɪd] vt ausweichen +dat; police entgehen +dat; taxes hinterziehen

evaluate [ɪˈvæl·juˌeɪt] vt bewerten; results auswerten

evaluation [ɪˌvæl·juˈeɪ·ʃən] n Schätzung f

evangelical [ˌi·væn·ˈdʒel·ɪ·kəl] adj evangelisch

evangelist [ɪˈvæn·dʒə·lɪst] n Wanderprediger(in) m(f)

evaporate [ɪˈvæp·əˌreɪt] vi verdunsten; (fig) sich in Luft auflösen

evaporation [ɪˌvæp·əˈreɪ·ʃən] n Verdunstung f

evasion [ɪˈveɪ·ʒən] n Ausweichen nt; (avoidance) Umgehung f; tax ~ Steuerhinterziehung f

evasive [ɪˈveɪ·sɪv] adj to take ~ action ein Ausweichmanöver machen; ■to be ~ ausweichen

eve [iv] n Vorabend m

Eve [iv] n Eva f

even [ˈi·vən] I. adv ❶ (also) selbst; ~ Chris was there selbst Chris war da ❷ (indeed) sogar; not ~ [noch] nicht einmal; did he ~ read it? hat er es überhaupt gelesen? ❸ (despite) ~ if ... selbst wenn ...; ~ so/then trotzdem ❹ + comp ~ colder noch kälter II. adj ❶ (flat) eben; row gerade ❷ (equal) gleich [groß]; distribution gleichmäßig; (in race) gleichauf; (in points) punktegleich ❸ MATH gerade
◆**even out** I. vt ausgleichen II. vi sich ausgleichen

evening [ˈiv·nɪŋ] n Abend m; on Friday ~s freitagabends

evenly [ˈi·vən·li] adv gleichmäßig; (calmly) gelassen

event [ɪˈvent] n ❶ Ereignis nt; sporting ~ Sportveranstaltung f ❷ (case) in the ~ that ... falls ...; in any ~ auf jeden Fall ❸ SPORT Wettkampf m

eventful [ɪˈvent·fəl] adj ereignisreich

eventual [ɪˈven·tʃʊ·əl] adj schließlich; (possible) etwaig

eventuality [ɪˌven·tʃʊˈæl·ə·ti] n Eventualität f

eventually [ɪˈven·tʃʊ·ə·li] adv schließlich; (some day) irgendwann

ever [ˈev·ər] adv ❶ (at any time) je[mals]; nothing ~ happens here hier ist nie was los; have you ~ been there? bist du schon einmal dort gewesen?; hardly ~ kaum; worse than ~ schlimmer als je zuvor ❷ (always) ~ since ... seitdem ... ❸ (of all time) the first performance ~ die allererste Darbietung ❹ (as intensifier) how could anyone ~ ...? wie kann jemand nur ...?; when are we ~ going to get this finished? wann haben wir das endlich fertig?

'everglade n Sumpfgebiet nt; ■the E~s pl die Everglades pl

'evergreen I. n immergrüne Pflanze; (tree) immergrüner Baum II. adj immergrün; (fig) immer aktuell

everlasting [ˌev·ərˈlæs·tɪŋ] adj immerwährend; gratitude ewig; (unceasing) endlos

every [ˈev·ri] adj ❶ (each) jede(r, s) ❷ (as emphasis) ganz und gar; ~ bit as ... as ... genauso ... wie ...

everybody [ˈev·riˌbad·i], **everyone** [ˈev·riˌwʌn] pron indef, + sing vb jede(r); ~ but Jane alle außer Jane

'everyday adj alltäglich; ~ life Alltagsleben nt

everyone [ˈev·riˌwʌn] pron see **everybody**

everything [ˈev·riˌθɪŋ] pron indef alles

everywhere [ˈev·riˌwer] adv überall

evict [ɪˈvɪkt] vt kündigen +dat

eviction [ɪˈvɪk·ʃən] n Zwangsräumung f; ~ order Räumungsbefehl m

evidence [ˈev·ɪ·dəns] n ❶ (proof) Beweis[e] m[pl]; to find no ~ of sth keinen Anhaltspunkt für etw akk haben ❷ LAW Beweisstück m

evil [ˈi·vəl] I. adj böse II. n Übel nt; the lesser of two ~s das kleinere von zwei Übeln

evolution [ˌev·əˈlu·ʃən] n Evolution f; (fig) Entwicklung f

evolve [ɪ·'vɒlv] I. *vi* sich entwickeln II. *vt* entwickeln

ewe [ju] *n* Mutterschaf *nt*

ex <*pl* -es> [eks] *n* (*fam*) Ex-Mann, Ex-Frau *m, f;* (*lover*) Ex-Freund(in) *m(f)*

exact [ɪg·'zækt] *adj* genau; **the ~ opposite** ganz im Gegenteil

exactly [ɪg·'zækt·li] *adv* ❶ genau; ~! ganz genau! ❷ ■ **not** ~ eigentlich nicht

exaggerate [ɪg·'zædʒ·ə·reɪt] *vt, vi* übertreiben

exaggerated [ɪg·'zædʒ·ə·reɪ·t̬ɪd] *adj* übertrieben

exaggeration [ɪg·ˌzædʒ·ə·'reɪ·ʃən] *n* Übertreibung *f*

exam [ɪg·'zæm] *n* Prüfung *f;* UNIV Examen *nt*

examination [ɪg·ˌzæm·ɪ·'neɪ·ʃən] *n* ❶ Prüfung *f;* UNIV Examen *nt* ❷ (*investigation*) Untersuchung *f; of evidence* Überprüfung *f;* **to be under** ~ untersucht werden

examine [ɪg·'zæm·ɪn] *vt* prüfen; (*scrutinize*) untersuchen

examiner [ɪg·'zæm·ɪn·ər] *n* Prüfer(in) *m(f);* **medical** ~ Gerichtsmediziner(in) *m(f)*

example [ɪg·'zæm·pəl] *n* Beispiel *nt;* **for** ~ zum Beispiel; **to make an ~ of sb** an jdm ein Exempel statuieren

exasperate [ɪg·'zæs·pə·reɪt] *vt* zur Verzweiflung bringen

exasperating [ɪg·'zæs·pə·reɪ·t̬ɪŋ] *adj* ärgerlich

exasperation [ɪg·ˌzæs·pə·'reɪ·ʃən] *n* Verzweiflung *f*

excavate ['ek·skə·veɪt] I. *vt site* ausgraben; *hole* ausheben II. *vi* Ausgrabungen machen

excavation [ˌek·skə·'veɪ·ʃən] *n* Ausgrabung *f;* (*of hole*) Ausheben *nt*

excavator ['ek·skə·veɪ·t̬ər] *n* Bagger *m*

exceed [ɪk·'sid] *vt* übersteigen; *limit* überschreiten

exceedingly [ɪk·'si·dɪŋ·li] *adv* äußerst

excel <-ll-> [ɪk·'sel] I. *vi* ■ **to ~ at sth** sich bei etw *dat* hervortun II. *vt* ■ **to ~ oneself** sich *akk* selbst übertreffen

excellence ['ek·sə·ləns] *n* Vorzüglich-keit *f; of performance* hervorragende Qualität

Excellency ['ek·sə·lən·si] *n* **His/Your ~** Seine/Eure Exzellenz

excellent ['ek·sə·lənt] *adj* ausgezeichnet

except [ɪk·'sept] I. *prep* ■ ~ [**for**] außer +*dat* II. *conj* ❶ (*only*) **I want to buy it,** ~ **I don't have any money** (*fam*) ich will es kaufen, ich habe nur kein Geld ❷ (*besides*) außer

excepting [ɪk·'sep·tɪŋ] *prep* außer +*dat;* **not** ~ nicht ausgenommen

exception [ɪk·'sep·ʃən] *n* Ausnahme *f;* **without** ~ ausnahmslos

exceptional [ɪk·'sep·ʃə·nəl] *adj* außer-gewöhnlich

excerpt ['ek·sɜrpt] *n* Auszug *m*

excess [ɪk·'ses] *n* <*pl* -es> Übermaß *nt;* (*surplus*) Überschuss *m*

excessive [ɪk·'ses·ɪv] *adj* übermäßig; *claim* übertrieben

exchange [ɪks·'tʃeɪndʒ] I. *vt* austauschen; *in store* umtauschen; *looks, words* wechseln II. *n* ❶ Tausch *m; in* ~ **dafür** ❷ (*interchange*) Wortwechsel *m;* ~ **of blows** Schlagabtausch *m*

ex'change rate *n* Wechselkurs *m*

ex'change student *n* Austauschschüler(in) *m(f);* UNIV Austauschstudent(in) *m(f)*

excitable [ɪk·'saɪ·t̬ə·bəl] *adj* erregbar

excite [ɪk·'saɪt] *vt* begeistern; *imagination* anregen

excited [ɪk·'saɪ·t̬ɪd] *adj* aufgeregt; (*thrilled*) begeistert; **to be ~ about sth** (*now*) von etw *dat* begeistert sein; (*in near future*) sich auf etw *akk* freuen

excitement [ɪk·'saɪt·mənt] *n* Aufregung *f*

exciting [ɪk·'saɪ·t̬ɪŋ] *adj* aufregend; *story* spannend

excl. *adj, prep abbrev of* **excluding, exclusive** exkl.

exclaim [ɪk·'skleɪm] I. *vi* **to ~ in delight** vor Freude aufschreien II. *vt* ausrufen

exclamation [ˌek·sklə·'meɪ·ʃən] *n* Ausruf *m*

excla'mation point, excla'mation mark n Ausrufezeichen nt

exclude [ɪk·'sklud] vt ausschließen

excluding [ɪk·'sklu·dɪŋ] prep ausgenommen +gen

exclusion [ɪk·'sklu·ʒən] n Ausschluss m

exclusive [ɪk·'sklu·sɪv] I. adj ausschließlich; (select) exklusiv II. n Exklusivbericht m

excommunicate [ˌeks·kə·'mju·nɪ·keɪt] vt exkommunizieren

excommunication [ˌeks·kə·ˌmju·nɪ·'keɪ·ʃən] n Exkommunikation f

excrement ['ek·skrə·mənt] n Exkremente pl

excruciating [ɪk·'skru·ʃi·eɪ·tɪŋ] adj schmerzhaft; suffering entsetzlich

excursion [ɪk·'skɜr·ʒən] n Ausflug m

excuse I. vt [ɪk·'skjuz] entschuldigen; (ignore) hinwegsehen über +akk; ~ **me!** entschuldigen Sie bitte!; ~ **me?** wie bitte?; ■**to ~ sb from sth** jdn von etw dat befreien II. n [ɪk·'skjus] Entschuldigung f; (justification) Ausrede f; **doctor's ~** Krankmeldung f

execute ['ek·sɪ·kjut] vt ausführen; (kill) hinrichten

execution [ˌek·sɪ·'kju·ʃən] n Ausführung f; (killing) Hinrichtung f

executioner [ˌek·sɪ·'kju·ʃə·nər] n Scharfrichter m

executive [ɪg·'zek·jʊ·tɪv] I. n leitender Angestellter/leitende Angestellte; **junior/senior ~** untere/höhere Führungskraft II. adj ~ **editor** Chefredakteur(in) m(f); ~ **producer** leitender Produzent/leitende Produzentin

exemplary [ɪg·'zem·plə·ri] adj vorbildlich

exempt [ɪg·'zempt] I. vt befreien; draftee freistellen II. adj ~ **from tax** gebührenfrei

exercise ['ek·sər·saɪz] I. vt ➊ trainieren; dog spazieren führen; horse bewegen ➋ (use) üben; authority, control ausüben; right geltend machen II. vi trainieren III. n ➊ Bewegung f; (training)

Übung f; **to do ~s** Gymnastik machen ➋ MIL Übung f; SCH, UNIV Aufgabe f

'exercise bike n Heimfahrrad nt

'exercise book n Heft nt

exerciser ['ek·sər·saɪ·zər] n Trainingsgerät nt

exert [ɪg·'zɜrt] vt ausüben; influence geltend machen; ■**to ~ oneself** sich anstrengen

exertion [ɪg·'zɜr·ʃən] n Anstrengung f

exhale [eks·'heɪl] vt, vi ausatmen

exhaust [ɪg·'zɔst] I. vt ermüden; (use up) erschöpfen; ■**to ~ oneself** sich strapazieren II. n ➊ ~ [fumes] Abgase pl ➋ (tailpipe) Auspuff m

exhausted [ɪg·'zɔs·tɪd] adj erschöpft; (used up) aufgebraucht

exhausting [ɪg·'zɔs·tɪŋ] adj anstrengend

exhaustion [ɪg·'zɔs·tʃən] n Erschöpfung f

exhaustive [ɪg·'zɔs·tɪv] adj erschöpfend; inquiry eingehend; list vollständig; research tief greifend

ex'haust pipe n Auspuffrohr nt

exhibit [ɪg·'zɪb·ɪt] I. n ➊ Ausstellungsstück nt ➋ LAW (evidence) Beweisstück nt II. vt, vi ausstellen

exhibition [ˌek·sɪ·'bɪʃ·ən] n Ausstellung f

exhibitor [ɪg·'zɪb·ɪ·tər] n Aussteller(in) m(f)

exhilarating [ɪg·'zɪl·ə·reɪ·tɪŋ] adj aufregend; (energizing) belebend

exhilaration [ɪg·'zɪl·ə·reɪ·ʃən] n Hochgefühl nt

exhumation [ˌeg·zju·'meɪ·ʃən] n Exhumierung f

exhume [ɪg·'zum] vt exhumieren

exile ['ek·saɪl] I. n ➊ Exil nt; **to go into ~** ins Exil gehen ➋ (person) Verbannte(r) f(m); **tax ~** Steuerflüchtling m II. vt verbannen

exist [ɪg·'zɪst] vi existieren; (survive) überleben

existence [ɪg·'zɪs·təns] n Existenz f; **means of ~** Lebensgrundlage f

existent [ɪg·'zɪs·tent] adj vorhanden

existing [ɪg·'zɪs·tɪŋ] adj bestehend; rules gegenwärtig

exit ['eg·sɪt] I. n ❶ Ausgang m; (road) Ausfahrt f ❷ (departure) Weggehen nt kein pl; (from room) Hinausgehen nt kein pl II. vt verlassen III. vi hinausgehen; (in car) eine Ausfahrt nehmen

'**exit visa** n Ausreisevisum nt

exodus <pl -es> ['ek·sə·dəs] n Auszug m; **general ~** allgemeiner Aufbruch

exorbitant [ɪg·'zɔr·bə·tənt] adj überhöht

exorcism ['ek·sɔr·sɪz·əm] n Exorzismus m

exorcist ['ek·sɔr·sɪst] n Exorzist(in) m(f)

exotic [ɪg·'zɑt·ɪk] adj exotisch

expand [ɪk·'spænd] I. vi zunehmen; (physically) sich ausdehnen; economy a. expandieren; horizons sich erweitern II. vt erweitern; (physically) ausdehnen

expanse [ɪk·'spæns] n Weite f; **~ of lawn** ausgedehnte Rasenfläche

expansion [ɪk·'spæn·ʃən] n Erweiterung f; (physically) Ausdehnung f; of territory Expansion f

expansionism [ɪk·'spæn·ʃə·nɪz·əm] n Expansionspolitik f

expansive [ɪk·'spæn·sɪv] adj umgänglich; (effusive) überschwänglich

expatriate n [ek·'speɪ·tri·ət] [ständig] im Ausland Lebende(r) f(m)

expect [ɪk·'spekt] vt ❶ erwarten; **that was to be ~ed** das war zu erwarten; ■**to ~ to do sth** damit rechnen, etw zu tun ❷ (fam) **I ~ so** ich denke schon

expectancy [ɪk·'spek·tən·si] n Erwartung f; **with an air of ~** erwartungsvoll

expectant [ɪk·'spek·tənt] adj erwartungsvoll; mother werdend

expectation [ˌek·spek·'teɪ·ʃən] n Erwartung f

expedition [ˌek·spɪ·'dɪʃ·ən] n Expedition f; MIL Feldzug m

expel <-ll-> [ɪk·'spel] vt ausschließen; SCH verweisen; breath ausstoßen

expenditure [ɪk·'spen·dɪ·tʃər] n Ausgabe f; (sum spent) Aufwendungen pl

expense [ɪk·'spens] n ❶ [Un]kosten pl; ■**~s** pl (offsettable) Spesen pl; **at one's own ~** auf eigene Kosten ❷ (fig)

at sb's ~ auf jds Kosten pl ▶PHRASES: **no ~s spared** [die] Kosten spielen keine Rolle

ex'pense account n Spesenrechnung f

expensive [ɪk·'spen·sɪv] adj teuer; (overly) kostspielig

experience [ɪk·'spɪr·i·əns] I. n ❶ Erfahrung f; (event also) Erlebnis nt; **to learn by ~** durch Erfahrung lernen II. vt erleben; (endure) erfahren; difficulties stoßen auf +akk; (feel) empfinden

experienced [ɪk·'spɪr·i·ənst] adj erfahren; eye geschult; ■**to be ~ at sth** Erfahrung in etw dat haben

experiment I. n [ɪk·'sper·ɪ·mənt] Experiment nt II. vi [ɪk·'sper·ɪ·ment] experimentieren

experimental [ɪk·ˌsper·ɪ·'men·təl] adj Versuchs-

expert ['ek·spɜrt] I. n Experte, ·in m, f II. adj ❶ fachmännisch; (skilled) erfahren ❷ (excellent) ausgezeichnet; liar perfekt

expertise [ˌek·spɜr·'tiz] n Fachkenntnis f; (skill) Können nt

expert o'pinion n Expertenmeinung f; LAW Sachverständigengutachten nt

expire [ɪk·'spaɪr] vi ablaufen; contract auslaufen; (die) verscheiden

expiry [ɪk·'spaɪ·ri] n Ablauf m

explain [ɪk·'spleɪn] vt erklären; **you'd better ~ yourself** du solltest mir das erklären

◆**explain away** vt eine [einleuchtende] Erklärung für etw akk haben

explanation [ˌek·splə·'neɪ·ʃən] n Erklärung f; **by way of ~ [for sth]** als Erklärung [für etw akk]

explanatory [ɪk·'splæn·ə·tɔr·i] adj erklärend

explicit [ɪk·'splɪs·ɪt] adj deutlich; agreement ausdrücklich; (detailed) unverhüllt

explode [ɪk·'sploud] I. vi explodieren; tire platzen; **to ~ with anger** vor Wut platzen II. vt bomb zünden; container sprengen; argument widerlegen

exploit I. n ['ek·splɔɪt] Heldentat f II. vt

[ɪk·'splɔɪt] *worker* ausbeuten; *friend* ausnutzen; (*utilize*) nutzen

exploitation [ˌek·splɔɪ·'teɪ·ʃən] *n* Ausbeutung *f*; *of friend* Ausnutzung *f*; (*use*) Nutzung *f*

exploration [ˌek·splɔ·'reɪ·ʃən] *n* Erforschung *f*; (*examination*) Untersuchung *f*

E **exploratory** [ɪk·'splɔr·ə·tɔr·i] *adj* Forschungs-; *drilling, well* Probe-; ~ **talks** Sondierungsgespräche *pl*

explore [ɪk·'splɔr] I. *vt* erforschen; (*examine*) untersuchen II. *vi* sich umschauen

explorer [ɪk·'splɔr·ər] *n* Forscher(in) *m(f)*

explosion [ɪk·'sploʊ·ʒən] *n* Explosion *f*

explosive [ɪk·'sploʊ·sɪv] I. *adj* explosiv; *issue* [hoch] brisant II. *n* Sprengstoff *m* kein *pl*

export I. *vt, vi* [ɪk·'spɔrt] exportieren II. *n* ['ek·spɔrt] Export *m*; (*product*) Exportartikel *m*

exporter [ɪk·'spɔr·tər] *n* Exporteur *m*; (*country*) Exportland *nt*

expose [ɪk·'spoʊz] *vt* freilegen; *to danger, ridicule* aussetzen; (*reveal*) offenbaren; *scandal* aufdecken; *spy* entlarven

exposed [ɪk·'spoʊzd] *adj* ungeschützt; *position* exponiert; (*bare*) freigelegt

exposure [ɪk·'spoʊ·ʒər] *n* ❶ Aussetzung *f*; (*to weather*) Ausgesetztsein *nt* ❷ (*contact*) Kontakt *m* ❸ *of plot* Aufdeckung *f*; *of affair* Enthüllung *f*; *of person* Entlarvung *f* ❹ (*photo*) Aufnahme *f*

express [ɪk·'spres] I. *vt* ❶ ausdrücken; (*say*) aussprechen; ■**to ~ oneself** sich ausdrücken ❷ (*send*) per Express schicken II. *adj* ❶ **by ~ delivery** per Express ❷ (*explicit*) ausdrücklich; **for the ~ purpose** eigens zu dem Zweck III. *adv* per Express IV. *n* Express[zug] *m*

expression [ɪk·'spreʃ·ən] *n* Ausdruck *m*; (*on face*) [Gesichts]ausdruck *m*; **freedom of ~** Freiheit *f* der Meinungsäußerung

expressionless [ɪk·'spreʃ·ən·lɪs] *adj* ausdruckslos

expressive [ɪk·'spres·ɪv] *adj* ausdrucksvoll; *voice* ausdrucksstark

expressly [ɪk·'spres·li] *adv* ausdrücklich; (*particularly*) extra

ex'pressway *n* Schnellstraße *f*

expulsion [ɪk·'spʌl·ʃən] *n* Ausschluss *m*; *from country* Ausweisung *f*; *from school* Verweisung *f*

exquisite ['ek·skwɪ·zɪt] *adj* exquisit

extend [ɪk·'stend] I. *vt* ausstrecken; (*prolong*) verlängern; (*pull out*) verlängern; *ladder, table* ausziehen; (*expand*) erweitern; *influence* ausdehnen II. *vi* sich erstrecken; *over time* sich hinziehen

extended [ɪk·'sten·dɪd] *adj* verlängert; *bulletin* umfassend

extension [ɪk·'sten·ʃən] *n* ❶ Ausstrecken *nt*; *of muscles* Dehnung *f*; (*lengthening*) Verlängerung *f*; (*expansion*) Erweiterung *f*; *of power* Ausdehnung *f*; (*prolongation*) Verlängerung *f*; ~ **table** Ausziehtisch *m*; **by ~** im weiteren Sinne ❷ (*annex*) Anbau *m* ❸ (*phone line*) Nebenanschluss *m*; (*number*) [Haus]apparat *m*

ex'tension cord *n* Verlängerungskabel *nt*

extensive [ɪk·'sten·sɪv] *adj* ausgedehnt; *grounds* weitläufig; (*far-reaching*) weitreichend; *damage* beträchtlich; *knowledge* breit; *repairs* umfangreich

extent [ɪk·'stent] *n* Ausdehnung *f*; (*range*) Umfang *m*; (*degree*) Maß *nt* kein *pl*; **to a certain/great ~** in gewissem/hohem Maße

exterior [ɪk·'stɪr·i·ər] I. *n* Außenseite *f*; (*look*) Äußere *nt* II. *adj* Außen-

external [ɪk·'stɜr·nəl] *adj* äußerlich; (*from outside*) äußere(r, s); (*on surface*) äußerlich; ~ **affairs** Außenpolitik *f*

extinct [ɪk·'stɪŋkt] *adj* ausgestorben; *language* tot; (*inactive*) erloschen; **to become ~** aussterben; *volcano* erlöschen

extinction [ɪk·'stɪŋk·ʃən] *n* Aussterben *nt*; (*deliberate act*) Ausrottung *f*; (*inactivity*) Erlöschen *nt*

extinguish [ɪkˈstɪŋ·gwɪʃ] *vt* [aus]löschen

extinguisher [ɪkˈstɪŋ·gwɪʃ·ər] *n* Feuerlöscher *m*

extort [ɪkˈstɔrt] *vt* erzwingen; *money* erpressen

extortion [ɪkˈstɔr·ʃən] *n* Erzwingung *f*; *of money* Erpressung *f*; **that's sheer ~!** das ist ja Wucher!

extortionate [ɪkˈstɔr·ʃə·nɪt] *adj* übermäßig; (*using force*) erpresserisch; **~ prices** Wucherpreise *pl*

extra [ˈek·strə] **I.** *adj* zusätzlich; **some ~ money** etwas mehr Geld; **to take ~ care** besonders vorsichtig sein; **~ charge** Aufschlag *m* **II.** *adv* ① mehr; **to charge ~** einen Aufpreis verlangen; **postage and handling ~** zuzüglich Porto und Versand ② (*especially*) besonders **III.** *n* ① (*charge*) Aufschlag *m*; (*perk*) Zusatzleistung *f*; (*option*) Extra *nt* ② (*newspaper*) Sonderausgabe *f*

extract I. *vt* [ɪkˈstrækt] [heraus]ziehen; *bullet* entfernen; *tooth* ziehen; *confession* abringen **II.** *n* [ˈek·strækt] ① (*excerpt*) Auszug *m* ② (*concentrate*) Extrakt *m*

extraction [ɪkˈstræk·ʃən] *n* Herausziehen *nt*; *of bullet* Entfernen *nt*; *of tooth* [Zahn]ziehen *nt*; *of confession* Abringen *nt*

extradite [ˈek·strə·daɪt] *vt* ausliefern

extradition [ˌek·strəˈdɪʃ·ən] *n* Auslieferung *f*

extraneous [ɪkˈstreɪ·ni·əs] *adj* **~ substance** Fremdstoff *m*

extraordinary [ɪkˈstrɔr·də·ner·i] *adj* außerordentlich; *coincidence* merkwürdig

extraterrestrial [ˈek·strə·tə·ˈres·tri·əl] **I.** *adj* außerirdisch **II.** *n* außerirdisches [Lebe]wesen

extravagance [ɪkˈstræv·ə·gəns] *n* Verschwendungssucht *f*; (*luxury*) Luxus *m* *kein pl*

extravagant [ɪkˈstræv·ə·gənt] *adj* extravagant; (*wasteful*) verschwenderisch

extravaganza [ɪkˌstræv·ə·ˈgæn·zə] *n* opulente Veranstaltung

extreme [ɪkˈstrim] **I.** *adj* äußerste(r, s); *difficulties, weather* extrem **II.** *n* Extrem *nt*; **to go from one ~ to the other** von einem Extrem ins andere fallen

extremely [ɪkˈstrim·li] *adv* äußerst

extreme sports *npl* Extremsportarten *pl*

E

extremism [ɪkˈstri·mɪz·əm] *n* Extremismus *m*

extremist [ɪkˈstri·mɪst] **I.** *n* Extremist(in) *m(f)* **II.** *adj* radikal

extrovert [ˈek·strə·vɜrt] *n* extravertierter Mensch

extroverted [ˈek·strə·vɜr·tɪd] *adj* extravertiert

exuberance [ɪgˈzu·bər·əns] *n* Überschwänglichkeit *f*; *of feelings* Überschwang *m*

exuberant [ɪgˈzu·bər·ənt] *adj* überschwänglich; *mood* überschäumend

exultant [ɪgˈzʌl·tənt] *adj* jubelnd; *laugh* triumphierend

eye [aɪ] **I.** *n* ① Auge *nt*; **black ~** blaues Auge; **as far as the ~ can see** so weit das Auge reicht ② (*eyelet*) Öse *f*; (*in needle*) Öhr *nt* ▶PHRASES: **to keep an** [*or* one's] **~ on sb/sth** ein [wachsames] Auge auf jdn/etw haben; **to keep one's ~s open** [*or* **peeled**] die Augen offen halten; **with one's ~s shut** mit geschlossenen Augen; **to turn a blind ~** [**to sth**] [bei etw] beide Augen zudrücken **II.** *vt* <-d, -d, -ing *or* eying> beäugen; ■**to ~ sb up and down** (*carefully*) jdn von oben bis unten mustern; (*with desire*) mit begehrlichen Blicken betrachten

'**eyeball I.** *n* Augapfel *m* **II.** *vt* (*fam*) mit einem durchdringenden Blick ansehen; (*measure*) nach Augenmaß einschätzen

'**eyebrow** *n* Augenbraue *f*

'**eye-catching** *adj* auffallend

'**eye contact** *n* **to make ~** [**with sb**] Blickkontakt [mit jdm] aufnehmen

'**eyedrops** *n pl* Augentropfen *pl*

'**eyeful** *n* **to get an ~ of dust** Staub ins

Auge bekommen ▶PHRASES: **to get an ~ of sth** einen Blick auf etw *akk* werfen

'**eyelash** *n* Wimper *f*

'**eyelid** *n* Augenlid *nt*

'**eyeliner** *n* Eyeliner *m*

'**eye opener** *n* ▪**to be an ~ for sb** (*enlightening*) jdm die Augen öffnen; (*startling*) alarmierend für jdn sein

'**eye shadow** *n* Lidschatten *m*

'**eyesight** *n* Sehvermögen *nt*

'**eyesore** *n* Schandfleck *m*

'**eyetooth** *n* Augenzahn *m*; **I'd give my eyeteeth for that** (*fig*) ich würde alles darum geben

'**eyewash** *n* Augenwasser *nt*; (*fam: nonsense*) Blödsinn *m*

eye'**witness** *n* Augenzeuge, -in *m, f*

F

Ff

F <*pl* -'s>, **f** <*pl* -'s> [ef] *n* (*letter*) F *nt*, f *nt*; **~ as in Foxtrot** F wie Friedrich

fable ['feɪ·bəl] *n* Fabel *f*

fabric ['fæb·rɪk] *n* Stoff *m*

fabulous ['fæb·jə·ləs] *adj* fabelhaft

façade [fə·'sad] *n* Fassade *f a. fig*

face [feɪs] **I.** *n* ❶ Gesicht *nt a. fig*; **with a smile on one's ~** mit einem Lächeln im Gesicht; **~ down/up** mit dem Gesicht nach unten/oben; **to look sb in the ~** jdm in die Augen schauen; **to shut the door in sb's ~** jdm die Tür vor der Nase zuschlagen; **~ to ~** von Angesicht zu Angesicht; **to come ~ to ~ with sth** direkt mit etw *dat* konfrontiert werden ❷ *of a building* Fassade *f*; *of a mountain* Wand *f* ❸ (*reputation*) **to lose/save ~** das Gesicht verlieren/wahren ▶PHRASES: **get out of my face!** (*fam*) lass mich in Ruhe!; **in the ~ of sth** (*despite*) trotz einer S. *gen*; **to show one's ~** sich blicken lassen **II.** *vt* ❶ (*look toward*) *person* ▪**to ~ sb/sth** sich jdm/etw zuwenden; ▪**to ~** [*or sit facing*] **sb** jdm gegenübersitzen ❷ (*look toward*) ▪**to ~ sth** *object* zu etw *dat* hinzeigen; (*be situated across from*) gegenüber etw *dat* liegen ❸ (*confront*) ▪**to ~ sth/sb** etw/jdm ins Auge sehen; **it's time we ~d [the] facts** es wird Zeit, dass wir den Tatsachen ins Auge

sehen ▶PHRASES: **to ~ the music** für die Folgen geradestehen **III.** *vi* ❶ (*point*) **to ~ backward[s]** nach hinten zeigen ❷ (*look onto*) **to ~ south** *garden* nach Süden liegen ❸ (*look*) *person* blicken; **facing forward[s]** mit dem Gesicht nach vorne

◆**face out** *vi* nach außen zeigen

◆**face up** *vi* ▪**to ~ up to sth/sb** etw/jdm ins Auge sehen; **to ~ up to one's problems** sich seinen Problemen stellen

'**face cream** *n* Gesichtscreme *f*

'**facelift** *n* [Face]lifting *nt*

'**face pack** *n* Gesichtsmaske *f*

facet ['fæs·ɪt] *n* Facette *f a. fig*

facetious [fə·'si·ʃəs] *adj* (*usu pej*) [gewollt] witzig

face 'value *n* Nennwert *m*; **to take sth at ~** etw für bare Münze nehmen

facial ['feɪ·ʃəl] *n* [kosmetische] Gesichtsbehandlung

facilitate [fə·'sɪl·ɪ·teɪt] *vt* erleichtern

facilitator [fə·'sɪl·ɪ·teɪ·tər] *n* Vermittler(in) *m(f)*

facility [fə·'sɪl·ə·t̬i] *n* ❶ (*natural ability*) Begabung *f* (**for** für +*akk*) ❷ (*building and equipment*) Einrichtung *f*, Anlage *f*; **sports ~** Sportanlage *f*

facsimile [fæk·'sɪm·ə·li] *n* Faksimile *nt*

fact [fækt] *n* ❶ (*truth*) Wirklichkeit *f* ❷ (*single truth*) Tatsache *f*

'fact-finding *adj* Untersuchungs-

faction ['fæk·ʃən] *n* POL [Splitter]gruppe *f*

factor ['fæk·tər] *n* Faktor *m;* **by a ~ of four** um das Vierfache

factory ['fæk·tə·ri] *n* Fabrik *f*

factory 'farm *n* [voll] automatisierter landwirtschaftlicher Betrieb

factual ['fæk·tʃu·əl] *adj* sachlich

faculty ['fæk·əl·ti] *n* ① SCH, UNIV Lehrkörper *m* ② Fähigkeit *f*

fad [fæd] *n* Modeerscheinung *f*

fade [feɪd] I. *vi* ① (*lose color*) ausbleichen ② (*lose intensity*) nachlassen; **the light is fading** es wird dunkel; *sound* verklingen; *color* verbleichen II. *vt* ausbleichen

◆**fade away** *vi hope* schwinden; *memories* verblassen; *beauty* verblühen

◆**fade in** *vt* FILM, TV einblenden

◆**fade out** *vt* ausblenden

fag [fæg] *n* ① (*pej fam: homosexual*) Schwule(r) *m*

fail [feɪl] I. *vi* ① *person* versagen; *plan* scheitern; **if all else ~s** zur Not ② (*not do*) ■**to ~ to do sth** versäumen, etw zu tun; **I ~ to see what ...** ich verstehe nicht, was ... ③ SCH, UNIV durchfallen ④ *brakes* versagen; *harvest* ausfallen II. *vt* ① (*not pass*) durchfallen; ■**to ~ sb** (*not grant a passing grade*) jdn durchfallen lassen ② (*let down*) im Stich lassen III. *n* ▶ PHRASES: **without ~** auf jeden Fall

failing ['feɪ·lɪŋ] I. *adj* **~ eyesight** Sehschwäche *f* II. *n* Schwäche *f*

'fail-safe *adj* abgesichert

failure ['feɪl·jər] *n* ① (*lack of success*) Scheitern *nt; of business* Bankrott *m; of crop* Missernte *f;* **~ rate** SCH, UNIV Durchfallquote *f* ② Misserfolg *m* ③ MED, TECH Versagen *nt kein pl*

faint [feɪnt] I. *adj* ① *light, smile* matt; *sound, suspicion* leise; *scent, pattern* zart; *chance* gering; **to not have the ~est idea** nicht die geringste Ahnung haben ② *line* undeutlich ③ (*physically weak*) **to feel ~** sich schwach fühlen; **to be ~ with hunger** vor Hunger fast umfallen II. *vi* ohnmächtig werden

faint-'hearted *adj* zaghaft; **to be not for the ~** nichts für schwache Nerven sein

faintly ['feɪnt·li] *adv* ① (*weakly*) leicht ② (*not clearly*) schwach; **~ visible** schwach zu sehen

fair¹ [fer] I. *adj* ① (*reasonable*) fair; *salary* angemessen; (*legitimate*) berechtigt; **you're not being ~** das ist unfair; **it's ~ to say that ...** man kann [wohl] sagen, dass ... ② (*just, impartial*) gerecht, fair; **to get one's ~ share** seinen Anteil bekommen ③ (*large*) ziemlich; **there's still a ~ bit of work to do** es gibt noch einiges zu tun ④ *skin* hell; *hair* blond II. *adv* (*according to rules*) **to play ~** fair sein

fair² [fer] *n* ① (*carnival*) Jahrmarkt *m* ② (*trade*) Messe *f*

'fairground *n* Rummel[platz] *m bes* NORDD

fair-'haired <fairer-, fairest- *or more* ~, most ~> *adj* blond

fairly ['fer·li] *adv* ① (*quite*) ziemlich ② (*justly*) fair

fair-'minded <fairer-, fairest- *or more* ~, most ~> *adj* unvoreingenommen

fairness ['fer·nɪs] *n* ① Fairness *f* ② *of hair* Helligkeit *f*

fair 'play *n* Fairplay *nt*

fairy ['fer·i] *n* Fee *f*

'fairy tale *n* Märchen *nt a. fig*

faith [feɪθ] *n* ① (*trust*) Vertrauen *nt;* **to put one's ~ in sb/sth** auf jdn/etw vertrauen ② REL Glaube *m* ③ (*sincerity*) **to act in good ~** in gutem Glauben handeln

faithful ['feɪθ·fəl] *adj* ① (*loyal*) treu ② (*accurate*) originalgetreu; *account* detailliert

faithfully ['feɪθ·fəl·i] *adv* ① (*loyally*) treu ② (*exactly*) genau; *reproduce* originalgetreu

fake [feɪk] I. *n* ① (*counterfeit object*) Fälschung *f* ② (*impostor*) Hochstapler(in) *m(f)* II. *adj* Kunst-; *jewel* imitiert; *passport* gefälscht III. *vt* ① (*make a copy*) fälschen ② (*pretend*) vortäuschen; *illness* simulieren

falcon ['fæl·kən] *n* Falke *m*
fall [fɔl] **I.** *n* ❶ (*drop*) Fall *m;* (*harder*) Sturz *m;* **she broke her leg in the ~** sie brach sich bei dem Sturz das Bein; **the bushes broke his ~** die Büsche haben seinen Sturz abgefangen ❷ (*decrease*) Rückgang *m; in support* Nachlassen *nt* (in +*gen*); **~ in value** Wertverlust *m* ❸ *of a regime* Sturz *m;* **the ~ of the Roman Empire** der Untergang des Römischen Reiches ❹ (*autumn*) Herbst *m* ▸PHRASES: **to take a** [*or* **the**] **~ for sb/sth** für jdn/etw die Schuld auf sich *akk* nehmen **II.** *adj* Herbst- **III.** *vi* <fell, fallen> ❶ (*tumble*) fallen; (*harder*) stürzen; *person* hinfallen; *tree* umfallen; **to ~ to one's death** in den Tod stürzen; **to ~ flat on one's face** auf die Nase fallen; **to ~ down dead** tot umfallen ❷ (*hang*) fallen; **her hair fell to her waist** ihr Haar reichte ihr bis zur Taille ❸ (*decrease*) sinken, fallen; **church attendance has ~en dramatically** die Anzahl der Kirchenbesucher ist drastisch zurückgegangen ❹ (*become*) **to ~ asleep** einschlafen; **to ~ ill** krank werden ❺ (*enter a particular state*) **to ~ out of favor** [**with sb**] [bei jdm] nicht mehr gefragt sein; **to ~ in love** [**with sb/sth**] sich [in jdn/ etw] verlieben

◆**fall apart** *vi* ❶ (*disintegrate*) auseinanderfallen ❷ (*fig: fail*) auseinanderfallen; *system* zusammenbrechen; *marriage* auseinandergehen

◆**fall away** *vi* ❶ (*detach itself*) abfallen ❷ (*decrease*) sinken, zurückgehen

◆**fall back** *vi* ❶ zurückweichen ❷ (*resort to*) *thing* zurückgreifen ([**up**]**on** +*akk*)

◆**fall behind** *vi* ❶ (*slow*) zurückfallen ❷ (*achieve less*) zurückbleiben; (*at school*) hinterherhinken; ■**to ~ behind with sth** mit etw *dat* in Verzug geraten

◆**fall down** *vi* ❶ (*tumble*) hinunterfallen; (*topple*) *person* hinfallen; *object* umfallen; ■**to ~ down sth** etw hinunterfallen; *hole, well* hineinfallen in +*akk*

❷ (*collapse*) einstürzen; *tent* zusammenfallen

◆**fall for** *vt* ❶ (*love*) sich verlieben in +*akk* ❷ (*be deceived by*) hereinfallen auf +*akk*

◆**fall in** *vi* ❶ (*drop*) hineinfallen ❷ (*collapse*) einstürzen

◆**fall off** *vi* ❶ ■**to ~ off sth** von etw *dat* fallen ❷ (*decrease*) zurückgehen

◆**fall on** *vi* ❶ (*attack*) ■**to ~ on sb** über jdn herfallen ❷ (*be assigned to*) ■**to ~ on sb** jdm zufallen

◆**fall out** *vi* ❶ (*drop*) herausfallen; *hair* ausfallen ❷ (*argue*) ■**to ~ out** [**with sb**] sich [mit jdm] [zer]streiten

◆**fall over** *vi* ❶ (*topple*) *person* hinfallen; *object* umfallen ❷ (*trip*) ■**to ~ over sth** über etw *akk* fallen

◆**fall through** *vi* scheitern

fallacy ['fæl·ə·si] *n* Irrtum *m*

fallen ['fɔ·lən] *adj* ❶ *apple* abgefallen; *tree* umgestürzt ❷ *dictator* gestürzt

'**fall guy** *n* (*sl*) Prügelknabe *m*

fallible ['fæl·ə·bəl] *adj* *person* fehlbar; *thing* fehleranfällig

'**fall-off** *n* Rückgang *m*

'**fallout** *n* ❶ radioaktive Strahlung; **~ shelter** Atombunker *m* ❷ (*fig*) Konsequenzen *pl*

false [fɔls] *adj* falsch; **~ start** Fehlstart *m a. fig*

falsehood ['fɔls·hʊd] *n* Unwahrheit *f*

falseness ['fɔls·nɪs] *n* Falschheit *f*

false 'teeth *n pl* Gebiss *nt*

falsify <-ie-> ['fɔl·sɪ·faɪ] *vt* fälschen

falter ['fɔl·tər] *vi* stocken

fame [feɪm] *n* Ruhm *m*

familiar [fə·'mɪl·jər] *adj* ❶ (*well-known*) vertraut; *faces* bekannt ❷ (*acquainted*) ■**to be ~ with sth/sb** etw/ jdn kennen ❸ (*informal*) vertraulich; **the ~ form** [**of the second person**] LING die Du-Form

familiarity [fə·ˌmɪl·i·'er·ə·t̬i] *n* ❶ (*well-known quality*) Vertrautheit *f* ❷ (*knowledge*) Kenntnis *f*

familiarize [fə·'mɪl·jə·raɪz] *vt* ■**to ~ oneself/sb with sth** sich/jdn mit etw *dat* vertraut machen; **with work** sich/jdn einarbeiten (**with** in +*akk*)

family ['fæm·ə·li] *n* Familie *f*

family 'doctor *n* Hausarzt, Hausärztin *m*,*f*

famine ['fæm·ɪn] *n* Hungersnot *f*

famished ['fæm·ɪʃt] *adj* (*fam*) ausgehungert

famous ['feɪ·məs] *adj* berühmt

fan[1] [fæn] *n* (*enthusiast, admirer*) Bewunderer, Bewunderin *m*, *f*; **a football** ~ ein Footballfan

fan[2] [fæn] **I.** *n* Ventilator *m* **II.** *vt* <-nn-> *flames* anfachen; (*fig*) schüren

fanatic [fə·'næt̬·ɪk] *n* ❶ (*pej: obsessed*) Fanatiker(in) *m(f)* ❷ (*enthusiast*) **fit-ness** ~ ein Fitnessfan *m*

fanatical [fə·'næt̬·ɪ·kəl] *adj* (*obsessed*) besessen (**about** von +*dat*); *support* bedingungslos

'fan belt *n* AUTO Keilriemen *m*

'fan club *n* Fanclub *m*

fancy ['fæn·si] **I.** *adj* ❶ *decorations* aufwändig; *car* schick; (*fig*) *talk* geschwollen; **nothing** ~ nichts Ausgefallenes ❷ (*whimsical*) versponnen **II.** *n* ❶ (*liking*) Vorliebe *f*; **to take a** ~ **to sth/sb** Gefallen an etw/jdm finden ❷ (*whim*) Laune *f* **III.** *vt* <-ie-> ~ **that!** stell dir das [mal] vor!

fanfare ['fæn·fer] *n* Fanfare *f*

fang [fæŋ] *n* Giftzahn *m*

'fan mail *n* Fanpost *f*

fanny ['fæn·i] *n* (*fam*) Hintern *m*

fantasize ['fæn·t̬ə·saɪz] *vi* fantasieren

fantastic [fæn·'tæs·tɪk] *adj* (*fam: wonderful*) fantastisch, toll; **to look** ~ *person* umwerfend aussehen

fantasy ['fæn·t̬ə·si] *n* Fantasie *f*; ■**to have fantasies about** [**doing**] **sth** von etw *dat* träumen; LIT Fantasy *f*

fanzine ['fæn·zin] *n* Fanmagazin *f*

far [far] **I.** *adv* ❶ (*in space*) weit; **how much farther is it?** wie weit ist es denn noch?; ~ **and wide** weit und breit ❷ (*in time*) weit; **some time** ~ **in the future** irgendwann in ferner Zukunft; ~ **into the night** bis spät in die Nacht

hinein; **to plan further ahead** weiter voraus planen ❸ (*in progress*) weit; **to not get very** ~ **with** [**doing**] **sth** mit etw *dat* nicht besonders weit kommen ❹ (*much*) weit, viel; ~ **better** viel besser ▶PHRASES: **as** ~ **as** (*in space*) bis; **as** ~ **as the eye can see** so weit das Auge reicht; (*in degree*) **as** ~ **as I know** soweit ich weiß; ~ **and away** mit Abstand; **I'd** ~ **rather ...** ich würde viel lieber ...; ~ **from it!** weit gefehlt; **sb will go** ~ jd wird es zu etwas bringen; **so** ~, **so good** so weit, so gut; **so** ~, **so** ~ (*until now*) bisher **II.** *adj* ❶ (*further away*) **at the** ~ **end** am anderen Ende ❷ (*distant*) fern ▶PHRASES: **to be a** ~ **cry from sth/sb** mit etw/jdm nicht zu vergleichen sein

faraway ['far·ə·weɪ] *adj* ❶ (*distant*) fern ❷ (*dreamy*) *look* verträumt

fare [fer] *n* Fahrpreis *m*

farewell [ˌfer·'wel] **I.** *interj* (*form*) leb wohl; **to bid** [*or* say] ~ **to sb/sth** sich von jdm/etw verabschieden **II.** *n* Abschied *m*

far-'fetched *adj* weit hergeholt

far-'flung *adj* ❶ (*widespread*) weitläufig ❷ (*remote*) abgelegen

farm [farm] **I.** *n* Bauernhof *m* **II.** *vt* bebauen

♦**farm out** *vt work* abgeben (**to** an +*akk*)

farmer ['far·mər] *n* Bauer, Bäuerin *m*, *f*

'farmhand *n* Landarbeiter(in) *m(f)*

'farmhouse *n* Bauernhaus *nt*

'farmland *n* Ackerland *nt*

'farmstead *n* Farm *f*

'farmyard *n* Hof *m*

'far-off *adj* fern

far-'reaching *adj* weit reichend

'farsighted *adj* *decision* weitsichtig; *person* vorausschauend

fart [fart] **I.** *n* (*vulg*) Furz *m* **II.** *vi* (*vulg*) furzen

farther ['far·ðər] **I.** *adv comp of* **far** weiter; **how much** ~ **is it to the airport?** wie weit ist es noch zum Flughafen? **II.** *adj comp of* **far**: **at the** ~ **end** am anderen Ende; *see also* **further**

F

farthest ['far·ðɪst] I. adv superl of **far** am weitesten II. adj superl of **far** am weitesten

fascinate ['fæs·ə·neɪt] vt faszinieren

fascinating ['fæs·ə·neɪ·t̬ɪŋ] adj faszinierend

fascination [ˌfæs·ə·'neɪ·ʃən] n Faszination f

fascism ['fæʃ·ɪz·əm] n Faschismus m

fascist ['fæʃ·ɪst] n Faschist(in) m(f)

fashion ['fæʃ·ən] n ① (style) Mode f; **to be in** ~ in Mode sein ② ~ [or **the** ~ **industry**] die Modebranche

fashionable ['fæʃ·ə·nə·bəl] adj modisch

'fashion designer n Modedesigner(in) m(f)

'fashion show n Modenschau f

fast¹ [fæst] I. adj ① schnell; **to be a** ~ **runner** schnell laufen ② clock ▪ **to be** ~ vorgehen II. adv schnell

fast² [fæst] I. vi fasten II. n Fastenzeit f

fasten ['fæs·ən] I. vt ① (close) schließen; coat zumachen; **to** ~ **one's seat belt** sich anschnallen ② (secure) festigen (**on/to** an + dat); (with glue) festkleben II. vi (close) sich schließen lassen
  ◆ **fasten down** vt befestigen
  ◆ **fasten up** vt zumachen; buttons zuknöpfen

fastener ['fæs·ə·nər] n Verschluss m

fast 'food n Fast Food nt

fast-'forward vt, vi vorspulen

fastidious [fæ·'stɪd·i·əs] adj wählerisch; **to be very** ~ **about doing sth** sehr sorgsam darauf bedacht sein, etw zu tun

fat [fæt] I. adj <-tt-> ① (fleshy) dick; animal fett ② (thick) dick II. n Fett nt

fatal ['feɪt̬·əl] adj tödlich

fatalist ['feɪt̬·əl·ɪst] n Fatalist(in) m(f)

fatality [feɪ·'tæl·ə·t̬i] n Todesopfer nt

fatally ['feɪt̬·əl·i] adv ① (mortally) tödlich; ~ **ill** sterbenskrank ② (disastrously) hoffnungslos

'fat cat n (pej) Bonze m

fate [feɪt] n Schicksal nt

'fat-free adj fettfrei

'fathead n (fam) Schafskopf m

father ['fa·ðər] n Vater m

'father-in-law <pl fathers-> n Schwiegervater m

fatherless ['fa·ðər·lɪs] adj vaterlos

fatherly ['fa·ðər·li] adj väterlich

fatigue [fə·'tig] n ① Ermüdung f; **donor** ~ Nachlassen nt der Spendenfreudigkeit ② MIL ▪ ~ **s** pl (uniform) Arbeitskleidung f kein pl

fattening ['fæt̬·ən·ɪŋ] adj **to be** ~ dick machen

fatty ['fæt̬·i] adj ① (containing fat) fetthaltig ② (consisting of fat) Fett-

faucet ['fɔ·sɪt] n Wasserhahn m

fault [fɔlt] I. n ① (responsibility) Schuld f; **it's your own** ~ du bist selbst schuld daran; **to find** ~ **with sb/sth** etw an jdm/etw auszusetzen haben; **through no** ~ **of his own** ohne sein eigenes Verschulden ② TENNIS Fehler m II. vt ▪ **to** ~ **sb/sth** [einen] Fehler an jdm/etw finden

faultless ['fɔlt·lɪs] adj fehlerfrei

faulty ['fɔl·t̬i] adj ① (unsound) fehlerhaft ② (defective) defekt

favor ['feɪ·vər] I. n ① (approval) **in** ~ **of** für; ▪ **to be in** ~ dafür sein; **all those in** ~, ... alle, die dafür sind, ...; **to fall out of** ~ in Ungnade fallen ② (advantage) **in** ~ **of** für; **to reject sb/sth in** ~ **of sb/sth** jdm/etw einem jdm/etw den Vorzug geben ③ (kind act) Gefallen m kein pl; **to do sb a** ~ [or **a** ~ **for sb**] jdm einen Gefallen tun II. vt ① (prefer) vorziehen ② (approve) gutheißen; ▪ **to** ~ **doing sth** es gutheißen, etw zu tun

favorable ['feɪ·vər·ə·bəl] adj ① (approving) positiv ② (advantageous) günstig (**to** für + akk)

favored ['feɪ·vərd] adj ① (preferred) bevorzugt ② (privileged) begünstigt

favorite ['feɪ·vər·ɪt] I. adj Lieblings- II. n ① (best-liked) person Liebling m; thing; **which one's your** ~? welches magst du am liebsten? ② (contestant) Favorit(in) m(f)

favoritism ['feɪ·vər·ɪ·tɪz·əm] n (pej) Begünstigung f

fawn [fɔn] I. n Rehkitz nt II. adj rehbraun

fax [fæks] I. n Fax nt II. vt faxen

'fax machine n Fax[gerät] nt

FBI [ˌef·biˈaɪ] n abbrev of **Federal Bureau of Investigation** FBI nt

fear [fɪr] I. n ❶ (dread) Angst f, Furcht f; **to have a ~ of sth** vor etw dat Angst haben ❷ (worry) **~s for sb's safety** Sorge f um jds Sicherheit II. vt fürchten; **nothing to ~** nichts zu befürchten III. vi ■**to ~ for sb/sth** sich dat um etw/jdn Sorgen machen

fearful [ˈfɪr·fəl] adj ❶ (anxious) ängstlich ❷ (terrible) schrecklich

fearless [ˈfɪr·lɪs] adj furchtlos

feasibility [ˌfi·zə·ˈbɪl·ɪ·ti] n Machbarkeit f

feasible [ˈfi·zə·bəl] adj durchführbar; **technically ~** technisch machbar

feast [fist] n Festessen nt

feat [fit] n ❶ (brave deed) Heldentat f ❷ (skillful action) [Meister]leistung f; **no mean ~** keine schlechte Leistung

feather [ˈfeð·ər] n Feder f

'featherweight n Federgewicht nt

feathery [ˈfeð·ə·ri] adj fed[e]rig

feature [ˈfi·tʃər] I. n ❶ (aspect) Merkmal nt, Kennzeichen nt; **special ~** Besonderheit f ❷ (of face) ■**~s** pl Gesichtszüge pl ❸ FILM, TV (report) Sonderbeitrag m; (film) Spielfilm m II. vt ❶ (show) aufweisen ❷ (star) **featuring sb** mit jdm in der Hauptrolle

Feb. n abbrev of **February** Febr.

February [ˈfeb·ru·er·i] n Februar m, Feber m ÖSTERR; **at the beginning of** [or **in early**] **~** Anfang Februar; **in the middle of ~** Mitte Februar; **in the first half of ~** in der ersten Februarhälfte; **for the whole of ~** den ganzen Februar über; **last/next/this ~** vergangenen [o letzten]/kommenden [o nächsten]/ diesen Februar; **in/during ~** im Februar; **on ~ 14th** am 14. Februar

feces [ˈfi·siz] npl (form) Fäkalien pl

Fed [fed] n ❶ (bank) Zentralbankrat m ❷ (police) FBI-Agent(in) m(f)

federal [ˈfed·ər·əl] adj föderativ; **~ law**

Bundesgesetz nt; **~ income tax** nationale Einkommenssteuer

federalism [ˈfed·ər·ə·lɪz·əm] n Föderalismus m

federation [ˌfed·ə·ˈreɪ·ʃən] n Föderation f

'fed up adj (fam) ■**to be ~ up** [**with sb/sth**] die Nase voll haben [von jdm/ etw]

fee [fi] n Gebühr f; **membership ~**[s] Mitgliedsbeitrag m

feeble <-r, -st> [ˈfi·bəl] adj schwach

feed [fid] I. n ❶ (fodder) Futter nt ❷ TECH (supply) Zufuhr f II. vt <fed, fed> ❶ (give food to) ■**to ~ sb** jdm zu essen geben; animal, baby füttern; plant düngen; ■**to ~ sth to an animal** etw an ein Tier verfüttern ❷ (provide food for) ernähren ❸ (thread) führen; rope fädeln III. vi <fed, fed> (eat) animal weiden; baby gefüttert werden

◆**feed off, feed on** vi sich ernähren von

'feedback n Feedback nt

feel [fil] I. vt <felt, felt> ❶ (sense, touch) fühlen; **to ~ one's age** sein Alter spüren; **to ~ nothing for sb** für jdn nichts empfinden, ich musste mich die Wand entlangtasten ❷ (think) halten; ■**to ~ that ...** der Meinung sein, dass ... II. vi <felt, felt> ❶ + adj (have a feeling) sich fühlen; **my mouth ~s dry** mein Mund fühlt sich trocken an; **my eyes ~ sore** meine Augen brennen; **how do you ~ about it?** was sagst du dazu?; **to ~ angry** wütend sein; **to ~ better** sich besser fühlen; **to ~ foolish** sich dat dumm vorkommen; **to ~ free to do sth** etw ruhig tun; **sb ~s hot** jdm ist heiß; ■**to ~ as if one were doing sth** das Gefühl haben, etw zu tun; ■**to ~ like sth** sich akk wie etw fühlen; **to ~ like one's old self** [**again**] [wieder] ganz der/die Alte sein ❷ + adj (seem) scheinen ❸ (search) tasten (**for** nach +dat) ❹ (want) ■**to ~ like sth** zu etw dat Lust haben III. n ❶ (texture) **the ~ of wool** das Gefühl von Wolle ❷ (touch) ■**to ~ sth** Berühren nt ❸ (talent) Ge-

F

F

spür nt; ~ **for language** Sprachgefühl nt

◆**feel up** I. vt (fam) begrapschen II. vi ■**to ~ up to sth** sich etw dat gewachsen fühlen

feeler ['fi·lər] n usu pl Fühler m

'feel-good adj ein Wohlgefühl erzeugend

feeling ['fi·lɪŋ] n ① Gefühl nt; **to cause bad ~s** böses Blut verursachen; **no hard ~s!** nichts für ungut!; **to have a ~ that ...** das Gefühl haben, dass ... ② (opinion) Ansicht f

feet [fit] n pl of **foot**

feign [feɪn] vt vortäuschen

feline ['fi·laɪn] adj katzenartig

fell¹ [fel] pt of **fall**

fell² [fel] vt (cut down) fällen

fellow ['fel·oʊ] I. n ① (fam: man) Kerl m ② (graduate student) Fellow m II. adj ~ **citizen** Mitbürger(in) m(f); ~ **sufferer** Leidensgenosse, -in m, f

felt¹ [felt] pt, pp of **feel**

felt² [felt] n Filz m

'felt tip, felt tip 'pen n Filzstift m

female ['fi·meɪl] I. adj weiblich II. n ① (animal) Weibchen nt ② (woman) Frau f

feminine ['fem·ə·nɪn] adj weiblich

feminism ['fem·ə·nɪz·əm] n Feminismus m

feminist ['fem·ə·nɪst] n Feminist(in) m(f)

fence [fens] I. n ① (barrier) Zaun m ② (sl: criminal) Hehler(in) m(f) II. vi fechten

fencer ['fen·sər] n Fechter(in) m(f)

fencing ['fen·sɪŋ] n SPORT Fechten nt

fend [fend] vi (care) ■**to ~ for oneself** für sich selbst sorgen

◆**fend off** vt ■**to ~ off** ↻ **sb/sth** jdn/etw abwehren; criticism zurückweisen

fender ['fen·dər] n AUTO Kotflügel m

ferment I. vt [fər·'ment] fermentieren II. vi [fər·'ment] gären

fermentation [ˌfɜr·mən·'teɪ·ʃən] n Gärung f

fern [fɜrn] n Farn m

ferocious [fə·'roʊ·ʃəs] adj wild; fighting heftig

ferociousness [fə·'roʊ·ʃəs·nɪs], **ferocity** [fə·'ras·ə·ti] n Wildheit f; of attack, storm Heftigkeit f

Ferris wheel ['fer·ɪs·ˌhwil] n Riesenrad nt

ferry ['fer·i] n Fähre f

fertile ['fɜr·təl] adj fruchtbar; (fig) imagination lebhaft

fertilization [ˌfɜr·təl·ɪ·'zeɪ·ʃən] n Befruchtung f

fertilize ['fɜr·təl·aɪz] vt ① AGR düngen ② BIOL befruchten

fertilizer ['fɜr·təl·aɪ·zər] n Dünger m

fervent ['fɜr·vənt] adj (form) supporter glühend

fester ['fes·tər] vi ① MED eitern ② (fig) gären

festival ['fes·tə·vəl] n Festival nt

festive ['fes·tɪv] adj festlich

festivity [fes·'tɪv·ɪ·ti] n ① (celebrations) ■**festivities** pl Feierlichkeiten pl ② (festiveness) Feststimmung f

fetal ['fiːt·l] adj fetal

fetch [fetʃ] vt ① (get, collect) abholen ② (be sold for) erzielen

fetching ['fetʃ·ɪŋ] adj schick

fetid ['fet·ɪd] adj übel riechend

fetish ['fet·ɪʃ] n Fetisch m

fetus ['fi·təs] n Fetus m

feud [fjud] n Fehde f

fever ['fi·vər] n ① (temperature) Fieber nt kein pl ② (excitement) Aufregung f

feverish ['fi·vər·ɪʃ] adj fiebrig

few [fju] I. adj ① (some) **a ~** ein paar, einige; **quite a ~** ziemlich viele ② (not many) wenige; ~**er people** weniger Menschen; **as ~ as ...** nur ... ▶PHRASES: ~ **and far between** dünn gesät II. pron ① (some) **a ~ of us** einige von uns ② (not many) wenige; **the ~ who came ...** die paar, die kamen, ...; ~ **of the houses** nur wenige Häuser

fiancé [ˌfi·ɑn·'seɪ] n Verlobte(r) m

fiancée [ˌfi·ɑn·'seɪ] n Verlobte f

fib [fɪb] vi <-bb-> (fam) schwindeln

fiber ['faɪ·bər] n ❶ Faser f ❷ FOOD Ballaststoffe pl

'fiberglass n glasfaserverstärkter Kunststoff

fiber optic 'cable n Glasfaserkabel nt

fiber 'optics n + sing vb TELEC, COMPUT Glasfasertechnik f

fickle ['fɪk·l] adj (pej) wankelmütig

fiction ['fɪk·ʃən] n LIT Erzählliteratur f

fictional ['fɪk·ʃə·nəl] adj erfunden

fictitious [fɪk·'tɪʃ·əs] adj ❶ (false) falsch ❷ (imaginary) [frei] erfunden; character fiktiv

fiddle ['fɪd·l] I. n ❶ (fam) MUS Fidel f ▶PHRASES: [as] fit as a ~ kerngesund II. vi geigen

fiddler ['fɪd·lər] n (fam) Geiger(in) m(f)

fidget ['fɪdʒ·ɪt] vi zappeln

field [fild] I. n ❶ Feld nt ❷ SPORT [Spiel]feld nt, Platz m ❸ (area of knowledge) Gebiet nt II. vi SPORT als Fänger m spielen, fielden III. vt ❶ ball fangen ❷ questions parieren; phone calls abweisen

fielder ['fil·dər] n SPORT Fielder(in) m(f), Fänger(in) m(f)

'field glasses npl Feldstecher m

'field trip n Exkursion f

'fieldwork n Feldforschung f

fierce [fɪrs] adj ❶ animal wild ❷ attack, competition scharf; fighting erbittert

fierceness ['fɪrs·nɪs] n Wildheit f

fiery ['faɪr·i] adj (passionate) leidenschaftlich

fifteen [fɪf·'tin] I. adj fünfzehn II. n Fünfzehn f; see also eight

fifteenth [fɪf·'tinθ] I. adj fünfzehnte(r, s) II. n ❶ (order) ■the ~ der/die/das Fünfzehnte ❷ (date) ■the ~ der Fünfzehnte ❸ (fraction) Fünfzehntel nt

fifth [fɪfθ] I. adj fünfte(r, s); every ~ person jeder Fünfte II. n ❶ (order) ■the ~ der/die/das Fünfte ❷ (date) the ~ der Fünfte ❸ (fraction) Fünftel nt; see also eighth

fiftieth ['fɪf·ti·əθ] I. adj fünfzigste(r, s) II. n ❶ (order) ■the ~ der/die/das Fünfzigste ❷ (fraction) Fünfzigstel nt III. adv fünfzigstens; see also eighth

fifty ['fɪf·ti] I. adj fünfzig II. n ❶ (number) Fünfzig f ❷ (paper money) Fünfziger m; see also eight

fig [fɪg] n FOOD Feige f

fig. [fɪg] n abbrev of **figure** Abb. f

fight [faɪt] I. n Kampf m; to put up a ~ sich wehren II. vi <fought, fought> ❶ kämpfen; children sich raufen; ■to ~ with sb (against) gegen jdn kämpfen; (on same side) an jds Seite f kämpfen ❷ (argue) sich streiten (about/over um +akk) III. vt <fought, fought> ❶ kämpfen (against gegen +akk); battle schlagen; fire bekämpfen; disease ankämpfen gegen ❷ (in boxing) boxen gegen +akk

◆**fight back** I. vi zurückschlagen II. vt tears unterdrücken

◆**fight off** vt ■to ~ off ○ sb jdn abwehren

fighter ['faɪ·tər] n ❶ Kämpfer(in) m(f) ❷ (boxer) Boxer(in) m(f)

fighting ['faɪ·t̬ɪŋ] I. n Kämpfe pl II. adj kämpferisch

figure ['fɪg·jər] I. n ❶ (shape) Figur f ❷ (person) Gestalt f ❸ MATH (digit) Ziffer f; (numeral) Zahl f; he is good with ~s er ist ein guter Rechner II. vt (envisage) voraussehen; (estimate) schätzen III. vi ❶ (count on) ■to ~ on sth mit etw dat rechnen ❷ (make sense) that [or it] ~s das hätte ich mir denken können

◆**figure out** vt ❶ (work out) herausfinden; MATH ausrechnen ❷ (understand) begreifen; ■to ~ out ○ sth/sb etw/jdn verstehen

'figure skater n Eiskunstläufer(in) m(f)

filament ['fɪl·ə·mənt] n ❶ (fiber) Faden m ❷ ELEC Glühfaden m

file¹ [faɪl] I. n ❶ (folder) [Akten]hefter m ❷ (database) Akte f ❸ COMPUT Datei f II. vt ❶ (put in folder) ablegen, abheften; (in order) einordnen ❷ (submit) abgeben; JOURN einsenden

file² [faɪl] n (line) Reihe f

file³ [faɪl] I. n Feile f II. vt feilen

filet [fɪ·'leɪ, 'fɪ·leɪ] n, vt see **fillet**

filibuster ['fɪl·ɪ·bʌs·tər] n Obstruktion f

filing ['faɪ·lɪŋ] n ❶ (archiving) Ablage f ❷ (registration) Einreichung f

'**filing cabinet** n Aktenschrank m

fill [fɪl] I. n **to have one's ~ of sth** genug von etw dat haben II. vt ❶ (make full) füllen; gap schließen; vacancy besetzen ❷ (pervade) room erfüllen
♦ **fill in** I. vt ❶ (inform) ▪ **to ~ in ○ sb [on sth]** jdn [über etw akk] informieren ❷ (complete) form ausfüllen II. vi ▪ **to ~ in [for sb]** [für jdn] einspringen
♦ **fill out** I. vt ausfüllen II. vi ▪ fülliger werden
♦ **fill up** I. vt ❶ (make full) vollfüllen ❷ (occupy entire space) ausfüllen ❸ AUTO volltanken II. vi ❶ (become full) sich füllen ❷ AUTO [voll]tanken

filler ['fɪl·ər] n Spachtelmasse f

fillet ['fɪl·ɪt], **filet** [fɪ·'leɪ, 'fɪ·leɪ] I. n FOOD Filet nt II. vt ❶ (remove bones) fish entgräten; meat entbeinen ❷ (cut into pieces) filetieren

filling ['fɪl·ɪŋ] I. n ❶ (for teeth) Füllung f ❷ FOOD Füllung f II. adj sättigend

'**filling station** n Tankstelle f

film [fɪlm] I. n ❶ FILM, PHOT Film m ❷ (layer) Schicht f; **~ of oil** Ölfilm m II. vt filmen III. vi filmen, drehen

filter ['fɪl·tər] I. n Filter m II. vt ❶ (purify) filtern ❷ (fig) selektieren
♦ **filter through** vi light durchscheinen; liquid durchsickern

filth [fɪlθ] n ❶ (dirt) Dreck m ❷ (pej: obscenity) Schmutz m

filthy ['fɪl·θi] adj ❶ (dirty) schmutzig, dreckig fam ❷ temper aufbrausend ❸ (pej fam: obscene) schmutzig

filtration [fɪl·'treɪ·ʃən] n Filterung f

fin [fɪn] n Flosse f

final ['faɪ·nəl] I. adj ❶ (last) letzte(r, s); **in the ~ analysis** letzten Endes; **~ score** Endstand m ❷ (decisive) endgültig; **that's ~!** und damit basta! II. n ❶ (concluding match) Endspiel nt ❷ ▪ **~ s** pl UNIV [Schluss]examen nt

finale [fɪ·'næl·i] n Finale nt

finalist ['faɪ·nə·lɪst] n Finalist(in) m/f

finalize ['faɪ·nə·laɪz] vt zum Abschluss bringen

finally ['faɪ·nə·li] adv ❶ endlich ❷ (in conclusion) zum Schluss

finance ['faɪ·næns] I. n ❶ (money management) Finanzwirtschaft f ❷ (money) ▪ **~ s** pl Geldmittel pl II. vt finanzieren

'**finance company** n Finanzierungsgesellschaft f

financial [faɪ·'næn·ʃəl] adj finanziell, Finanz-

finch < pl -es> [fɪntʃ] n Fink m

find [faɪnd] vt <found, found> finden; money for sth aufbringen; **she was found unconscious** sie wurde bewusstlos aufgefunden; ▪ **to ~ sb/sth [to be sth]** jdn/etw [als etw] empfinden; **to ~ sb guilty** jdn für schuldig erklären; ▪ **to ~ that ...** feststellen, dass ...; (come to realize) sehen, dass ...; **I wish I could ~ more time for reading** ich wünschte, ich hätte mehr Zeit zum Lesen
♦ **find out** vt ❶ (detect) erwischen ❷ (discover) herausfinden

finding ['faɪn·dɪŋ] n ❶ (discovery) Entdeckung f ❷ usu pl (result of investigation) Ergebnis nt

fine¹ [faɪn] I. adj ❶ (acceptable) in Ordnung; **seven's ~ by me** sieben [Uhr] passt mir gut ❷ (excellent) glänzend; wine erlesen ❸ (slender, cut small) fein; slice dünn ❹ METEO schön II. adv ❶ (all right) fein, [sehr] gut ❷ (thinly) fein

fine² [faɪn] I. n (punishment) Geldstrafe f II. vt person zu einer Geldstrafe verurteilen

fineness ['faɪn·nɪs] n Feinheit f

fine 'print n ▪ **the ~** das Kleingedruckte

finesse [fɪ·'nes] n ❶ (delicacy) Feinheit f ❷ (skill) Geschick nt

fine-tooth '**comb**, **fine-toothed** '**comb** n ▸ PHRASES: **to go through [or over] sth with a ~** etw sorgfältig unter die Lupe nehmen

fine-'tune vt ▪ **to ~ sth** etw fein abstimmen

finger ['fɪŋ·gər] I. n Finger m ▸ PHRASES: **to keep one's ~s crossed [for sb]**

[jdm] die Daumen drücken; **to put one's ~ on sth** etw genau ausmachen **II.** *vt* ❶ anfassen ❷ (*fam: inform on*) verpfeifen (**to bei** + *dat*)

'fingernail *n* Fingernagel *m*

'fingerprint I. *n* Fingerabdruck *m* **II.** *vt* ■ **to ~ sb** jdm die Fingerabdrücke abnehmen

'fingertip *n* Fingerspitze *f*

finish ['fɪn·ɪʃ] **I.** *n* ❶ (*final stage*) Ende *nt*; *of race* Finish *nt*; (*finishing line*) Ziel *nt* ❷ (*final treatment*) letzter Schliff **II.** *vi* ❶ enden, aufhören; (*conclude*) schließen; **to ~ second** als Zweiter fertig sein; SPORT Zweiter werden; ■ **to ~ with sth** etw nicht mehr brauchen **III.** *vt* ❶ (*bring to end*) beenden; *book* zu Ende lesen; ■ **to ~ doing sth** mit etw *dat* fertig sein ❷ (*give final treatment*) etw *dat* den letzten Schliff geben ❸ *food* aufessen; *drink* austrinken

◆ **finish off I.** *vt* ❶ (*get done*) fertigstellen ❷ (*make nice*) den letzten Schliff geben ❸ (*sl: murder*) erledigen **II.** *vi* ❶ (*end*) abschließen ❷ (*get work done*) fertig werden

◆ **finish up I.** *vi* fertig werden **II.** *vt* *food* aufessen; *drink* austrinken

finished ['fɪn·ɪʃt] *adj* ❶ fertig; **the ~ product** das Endprodukt ❷ (*ruined*) erledigt; *career* zu Ende

'finish line *n* SPORT Ziellinie *f*

Finland ['fɪn·lənd] *n* Finnland *nt*

fir [fɜr] *n* Tanne *f*

fire ['faɪr] **I.** *n* ❶ Feuer *nt*; **to play with ~** mit dem Feuer spielen *a. fig* ❷ (*destructive burning*) Brand *m*; **destroyed by ~** völlig abgebrannt; **to be on ~** brennen; **to catch ~** Feuer fangen, in Brand geraten; **to set sth on ~** etw in Brand stecken ❸ MIL Feuer *nt*; **to open ~** das Feuer eröffnen **II.** *vt* ❶ (*shoot*) abfeuern; *gun* schießen; (*fig*) **to ~ questions at sb** jdn mit Fragen bombardieren ❷ (*dismiss*) feuern ❸ (*excite*) begeistern **III.** *vi* ❶ (*shoot*) feuern, schießen (**at** auf + *akk*) ❷ (*start up*) zünden

◆ **fire off** *vt* abfeuern

◆ **fire up** *vt person* begeistern (**about** für + *akk*); *engine* zünden

'fire alarm *n* Feuermelder *m*

'firearm *n* Schusswaffe *f*

'firebomb *n* Brandbombe *f*

'firecracker *n* Kracher *m*

'fire department *n* Feuerwehr *f*

'fire drill *n* Feueralarmübung *f*

'fire engine *n* Feuerwehrauto *nt*

'fire escape *n* Feuertreppe *f*

'fire exit *n* Notausgang *m*

'fire extinguisher *n* Feuerlöscher *m*

'firefighter *n* Feuerwehrmann, -frau *m, f*

'firefly *n* Leuchtkäfer *m*

'fire house *n see* **fire station**

'fire hydrant *n* Hydrant *m*

'fire insurance *n* Feuerversicherung *f*

'fireman *n* Feuerwehrmann *m*

'firepower *n* Feuerkraft *f*

'fireproof I. *adj* feuerfest **II.** *vt* feuerfest machen

'fire station *n* Feuerwache *f*

'firewall *n* ❶ ARCHIT Brandmauer *f* ❷ COMPUT Firewall *f*

'firewoman *n* Feuerwehrfrau *f*

'firewood *n* Brennholz *nt*

'firework *n* ■ **~s** *pl* (*display*) Feuerwerk *nt*; (*fig*) [Riesen]krach *m kein pl*

firing ['faɪr·ɪŋ] *n* ❶ (*shooting*) Abfeuern *nt* ❷ (*dismissal*) Rauswurf *m*

'firing line *n* (*fig*) Schusslinie *f*

'firing squad *n* Exekutionskommando *nt*

firm[1] [fɜrm] **I.** *adj* fest; COMM stabil; *offer* verbindlich; ■ **to be ~ with sb** jdm gegenüber bestimmt auftreten **II.** *adv* fest; **to hold** [*or* **stand**] **~** standhaft bleiben

firm[2] [fɜrm] *n* Firma *f*

firmness ['fɜrm·nɪs] *n* ❶ (*solidity*) Festigkeit *f* ❷ (*resoluteness*) Entschlossenheit *f*

first [fɜrst] **I.** *adj* erste(r, s); **~ thing tomorrow** morgen als Allererstes ▶PHRASES: **in the ~ place** (*at beginning*) zunächst [einmal]; (*most importantly*) in erster Linie; **~ things ~** eins nach dem anderen **II.** *adv* ❶ (*before doing some-*

F

thing else) zuerst; **~ of all** zu[al-ler]erst ② (*before other things, people*) als Erste(r, s) ▶PHRASES: **~ and foremost** vor allem III. *n* ① ■**the ~** der/die/das Erste ② (*start*) ■**at ~** anfangs

first 'aid *n* erste Hilfe; **~ kit** Verbandskasten *m*

'firstborn *n* Erstgeborene(r) *f(m)*

'first-class *adj* Erste[r]-Klasse-

first class *adv* erster Klasse

first-degree 'murder *adj* schwerer Mord

first 'floor *n* Erdgeschoss *nt*

'firsthand¹ *adj attr* aus erster Hand; **to experience sth ~** etw am eigenen Leib erfahren

first'hand² *adv* aus erster Hand

first 'lady *n* ■**the ~** die First Lady

firstly ['fɜrst·li] *adv* erstens

'first name *n* Vorname *m*

first-'rate *adj* erstklassig

first 'strike *n* MIL Erstschlag *m*

fiscal ['fɪs·kəl] *adj* fiskalisch

fiscal 'year *n* Geschäftsjahr *nt*

fish [fɪʃ] **I.** *n* <*pl* -es> Fisch *m* **II.** *vi* ① (*catch fish*) fischen; (*with rod*) angeln (**for** auf +*akk*) ② (*look for*) herumsuchen; ■**to ~ for sth** (*fig*) nach etw *dat* suchen; **to ~ for information** auf der Suche nach Informationen sein

'fish bone *n* [Fisch]gräte *f*

'fishbowl *n* [Gold]fischglas *nt*

'fisherman *n* (*professional*) Fischer *m*; (*for hobby*) Angler *m*

'fishhook *n* Angelhaken *m*

fishing ['fɪʃ·ɪŋ] *n* (*catching fish*) Fischen *nt*; (*with rod*) Angeln *nt*

'fishing line *n* Angelleine *f*

'fishing rod *n* Angel[rute] *f*

'fish stick *n* Fischstäbchen *nt*

fishy ['fɪʃ·i] *adj* ① (*tasting of fish*) fischig ② (*pej fam: dubious*) verdächtig

fission ['fɪʃ·ən] *n* PHYS [Kern]spaltung *f*

fist [fɪst] *n* Faust *f*

fit¹ [fɪt] **I.** *adj* <-tt-> ① (*suitable*) geeignet; **that's all he's ~ for** das ist alles, wozu er taugt ② (*appropriate*) angebracht ③ (*healthy*) fit **II.** *n* FASHION Sitz *m* **III.** *vt* <fitted *or* fit, fitted *or*

fit> ① (*be the right size*) ■**to ~ sb** jdm passen ② (*be appropriate*) ■**to ~ sb/ sth** sich für jdn/etw eignen ③ (*correspond with*) ■**to ~ sth** etw *dat* entsprechen; **the key ~s the lock** der Schlüssel passt ins Schloss ④ (*install*) montieren ⑤ (*supply*) ■**to ~ sth with sth** etw mit etw *dat* versehen **IV.** *vi* <fitted *or* fit, fitted> ① (*be correct size*) passen; **~ well** gut sitzen; ■**to ~ into sth** in etw *akk* hineinpassen ② (*agree*) *facts* übereinstimmen

◆**fit in** *vi* ① (*get along well*) sich einfügen ② (*conform*) dazupassen

fit² [fɪt] *n* Anfall *m*; **to be in ~s of laughter** sich kaputtlachen

fitness ['fɪt·nɪs] *n* Fitness *f*

fitted ['fɪt·ɪd] *adj jacket* tailliert

fitter ['fɪt·ər] *n* TECH [Maschinen]schlosser(in) *m(f)*

fitting ['fɪt·ɪŋ] *n* Anprobe *f*

five [faɪv] **I.** *adj* fünf **II.** *n* ① (*number, symbol*) Fünf *f* ② (*five minutes*) **to take ~** (*fam*) sich *dat* eine kurze Pause genehmigen; *see also* **eight**

'fivefold *adj, adv* fünffach

fiver ['faɪ·vər] *n* (*fam*) Fünfdollarschein *m*

fix [fɪks] **I.** *n* ① (*fam: dilemma*) Klemme *f* ② (*sl: drugs*) Schuss *m*, Fix *m* ③ NAUT, AVIAT Position *f* **II.** *vt* ① (*repair*) reparieren, in Ordnung bringen ② (*fasten*) festmachen (**to** an +*akk*) ③ (*decide*) festlegen ④ (*fam: prepare*) **to ~ one's hair** sich frisieren; **shall I ~ you something?** soll ich dir was zu essen machen? ⑤ (*concentrate*) *eyes, thoughts* richten (**on** auf +*akk*) **III.** *vi* (*sl*) *drugs* fixen

◆**fix on** *vt* ■**to ~ on** [*or* **upon**] **sth** sich auf etw *akk* festlegen

◆**fix up** *vt* ① (*supply*) ■**to ~ sb ↻ up** jdn versorgen ② (*arrange*) arrangieren ③ (*fam: repair*) in Ordnung bringen

fixation [fɪk·'seɪ·ʃən] *n* PSYCH Fixierung *f*

fixed [fɪkst] *adj* fest; *gaze* starr; *idea* fix; **how are you ~ for cash?** wie steht's bei dir mit Geld?

F

fixer ['fɪk·sər] n (fam: person) Schieber(in) m(f)

fixture ['fɪks·tʃər] n eingebautes Teil; ■ ~s pl Ausstattung f

fizz [fɪz] I. vi sprudeln II. n Sprudeln nt; **the tonic water has lost its ~** in dem Tonicwater ist keine Kohlensäure mehr

fizzle vi zischen

fjord [fjɔrd] n Fjord m

FL, Fla. abbrev of **Florida**

flabby ['flæb·i] adj schwabbelig

flag [flæg] I. n ❶ (pennant) Fahne f; (national) Flagge f ❷ (marker) Markierung f II. vt <-gg-> markieren III. vi <-gg-> ❶ enthusiasm abflauen; interest nachlassen; strength erlahmen

Flag Day n am 14. Juni zum Gedenken daran, dass an diesem Tag 1777 die jetzige Flagge der Vereinigten Staaten von Amerika zur Nationalfahne ernannt wurde

'flagpole, 'flagstaff n Fahnenmast m, Flaggenmast m

'flagstaff n see **flagpole**

flair [fler] n ❶ (talent) Talent nt ❷ (style) Stil m

flak [flæk] n ❶ Flakfeuer nt ❷ (fig) scharfe Kritik

flake [fleɪk] I. n ❶ of chocolate Raspel f; of pastry Krümel m; of snow Schneeflocke f ❷ (sl: odd person) Spinner(in) m(f) II. vi sich schuppen

flaky ['fleɪ·ki] adj ❶ (with layers) flockig; pastry blättrig; skin schuppig ❷ (sl: unreliable) schusselig

flamboyant [flæm·'bɔɪ·ənt] adj extravagant

flame [fleɪm] I. n Flamme f a. fig II. vi brennen; (fig) glühen

flaming ['fleɪ·mɪŋ] adj color flammend

flamingo <pl -s> [flə·'mɪŋ·goʊ] n Flamingo m

flammable ['flæm·ə·bəl] adj leicht entflammbar

flan [flæn] n Kuchen mit einer Füllung aus Vanillepudding

flannel ['flæn·l] n Flanell m

flap [flæp] I. vt <-pp-> **to ~ one's wings** mit den Flügeln schlagen II. vi <-pp-> (flutter) flattern; wings schlagen III. n ❶ (flutter) Flattern nt ❷ of cloth Futter nt ❸ (fam: commotion) helle Aufregung

flapjack ['flæp·dʒæk] n Pfannkuchen m

flare [fler] I. n ❶ Leuchtkugel f II. vi ❶ (burn up) aufflammen ❷ FASHION aufweiten

♦ **flare up** vi ❶ auflodern a. fig ❷ MED sich bemerkbar machen

flash [flæʃ] I. n <pl -es> ❶ (light) [Licht]blitz m; of jewelry, metal [Auf]blitzen nt kein pl; ~ **of lightning** Blitz m ❷ (fig) ~ **of inspiration** Geistesblitz m ❸ PHOT Blitz m; **to use [a] ~** mit Blitzlicht fotografieren ▶PHRASES: **like a ~** blitzartig; **in a ~** im Nu II. adj ❶ (sudden) Blitz-; ~ **frost** Blitzeis nt; ~ **mob** TELEC, INET Flashmob m ❷ (pej fam: showy) protzig III. vt ❶ light aufleuchten lassen ❷ (pej fam: flaunt) **to ~ sth around** mit etw protzen IV. vi ❶ (shine) blitzen ❷ (fig: appear) kurz auftauchen ❸ (move) **to ~ by** [or past] vorbeirasen

♦ **flash back** vi ■**to ~ back to sth** sich plötzlich [wieder] an etw akk erinnern

'flashback n FILM Rückblende f

'flashbulb n PHOT Blitz[licht]lampe f

'flash card n SCH Zeigekarte f

flasher ['flæʃ·ər] n AUTO ■ ~s pl (hazard lights) Lichthupe f

flash 'flood n flutartige Überschwemmung

'flashlight n Taschenlampe f

'flashpoint n ❶ CHEM Flammpunkt m ❷ (fig: trouble spot) Unruheherd m

flashy ['flæʃ·i] adj protzig

flask [flæsk] n [bauchige] Flasche; for spirits Flachmann m

flat [flæt] I. adj <-tt-> ❶ (horizontal) flach; surface eben; nose platt ❷ drinks schal ❸ tire platt; person niedergeschlagen ❹ COMM, ECON (slack) market flau II. adv <-tt-> ❶ (horizontally) flach; **to fall ~ on one's face** der Länge nach hinfallen ❷ (level) platt; **to knock sth ~** wall, building etw platt walzen ❸ (fam: absolutely) rundheraus, glatt-

F

weg ④ **to fall ~** *attempt* scheitern; *joke* nicht ankommen ④ (*level surface*) flache Seite ② (*tire*) Platte(r) *m*

flat 'feet *npl* Plattfüße *pl*

flat-'footed *adj* plattfüßig

flatly ['flæt·li] *adv* (*absolutely*) glatt[weg]

flatness ['flæt·nɪs] *n* Flachheit *f*; *of ground, track* Ebenheit *f*

'flat rate I. *n* Pauschaltarif *m*, Pauschale *f*; INET, TELEC Flatrate *f* II. *adj* Pauschal-; TELEC, INET Flatrate-

flatten ['flæt·n] *vt* ④ (*level*) flach machen; *ground, path* eben machen; *dent* ausbeulen ② *tree* umlegen; *person* niederstrecken

flatter[1] ['flæt·ər] ■**to ~ sb** jdm schmeicheln; **don't ~ yourself!** bilde dir ja nichts ein!

flatter[2] ['flæt·ər] *adj comp of* **flat**

flatterer ['flæt·ər·ər] *n* Schmeichler(in) *m(f)*

flattering ['flæt·ə·rɪŋ] *adj* (*approv*) schmeichelhaft; (*pej*) schmeichlerisch

flattery ['flæt·ə·ri] *n* Schmeicheleien *pl*

flaunt [flɔnt] *vt* (*esp pej*) zur Schau stellen

flautist ['flɔ·tɪst] *n* Flötist(in) *m(f)*

flavor ['fleɪ·vər] I. *n* (*taste*) [Wohl]geschmack *m*; (*particular taste*) Geschmacksrichtung *f* II. *vt* würzen

flavoring ['fleɪ·vər·ɪŋ] *n* Geschmacksstoff *m*

flaw [flɔ] *n* Fehler *m*; TECH Defekt *m*

flawed [flɔd] *adj* fehlerhaft; *diamond* unrein

flawless ['flɔ·lɪs] *adj* fehlerlos; *diamond* lupenrein; *performance* vollendet

flax [flæks] *n* Flachs *m*

flea [fli] *n* Floh *m*

'flea market *n* Flohmarkt *m*

fleck [flek] *n* Fleck[en] *m*

fled [fled] *vt, vi pt, pp of* **flee**

fledg(e)ling ['fledʒ·lɪŋ] I. *n* Jungvogel *m* II. *adj* neu, Jung-

flee <fled, fled> [fli] I. *vi* (*run away*) fliehen (**from** vor +*dat*) II. *vt* **to ~ the country** aus dem Land fliehen

fleece [flis] I. *n* ④ *of sheep* Schaffell *nt* ② (*fabric*) Flausch *m* ③ (*clothing*)

Vliesjacke *f* II. *vt* (*fig fam: cheat*) schröpfen

fleet [flit] *n* ④ NAUT Flotte *f* ② (*group of vehicles*) Fuhrpark *m*

fleeting ['fli·tɪŋ] *adj* flüchtig; *beauty* vergänglich

flesh [fleʃ] *n* Fleisch *nt*; *of fruit* [Frucht]fleisch *nt* ▶ PHRASES: **to be** [**only**] **~ and blood** auch [nur] ein Mensch sein; **in the ~** in Person

'flesh wound *n* Fleischwunde *f*

flew [flu] *vt, vi pt, pp of* **fly**

flex [fleks] I. *vt, vi* [sich] beugen; *muscles* [sich] [an]spannen II. *n* [Anschluss]kabel *nt*

flexibility [ˌflek·sə·ˈbɪl·ɪ·ti] *n* ④ Biegsamkeit *f* ② (*fig*) Flexibilität *f*

flexible ['flek·sə·bəl] *adj* ④ biegsam ② (*fig*) flexibel; **~ working hours** gleitende Arbeitszeit

flextime ['fleks·taɪm] *n* Gleitzeit *f*

flick [flɪk] I. *n* ④ (*movement*) kurze Bewegung; *of switch* Klicken *nt*; *of wrist* kurze Drehung ② (*fam: movie*) Film *m* II. *vt* ④ (*move*) ■**to ~ sth** etw mit einer schnellen Bewegung ausführen; *whip* schnalzen mit ② (*remove*) wegwedeln

flicker ['flɪk·ər] I. *vi* flackern; *TV* flimmern; *tongue* züngeln II. *n* Flackern *nt kein pl*; *of TV pictures* Flimmern *nt kein pl*

flier ['flaɪ·ər] *n* ④ Flieger(in) *m(f)*; **frequent ~** Vielflieger(in) *m(f)* ② (*leaflet*) Flugblatt *nt*

flight[1] [flaɪt] *n* ④ (*flying*) Flug *m*; **to take ~** auffliegen ② *of stairs* Treppe *f*

flight[2] [flaɪt] *n* (*fleeing*) Flucht *f*

'flight deck *n* ④ (*on plane*) Cockpit *nt* ② (*on ship*) Flugdeck *nt*

'flight number *n* Flugnummer *f*

'flight recorder *n* Flugschreiber *m*

flighty ['flaɪ·ti] *adj* (*usu pej*) flatterhaft

flimsy ['flɪm·zi] *adj* ④ *construction* instabil, unsolide ② *clothing* dünn, leicht ③ (*fig*) *excuse* schwach

flinch [flɪntʃ] *vi* (*wince*) [zusammen]zucken

fling [flɪŋ] I. *n* (*fig: relationship*) **to have a ~ with sb** mit jdm etwas haben

II. vt <flung, flung> werfen; **to ~ open** aufreißen; ■**to ~ oneself into sth** (*fig*) sich in etw *akk* stürzen

◆**fling off** vt *clothing* abwerfen a. *fig; blanket* wegstoßen

flip [flɪp] I. vt <-pp-> ① *switch* drücken ② (*turn over*) umdrehen; *coin* werfen II. vi <-pp-> ① ■**to ~** [over] sich [schnell] [um]drehen; *vehicle* sich überschlagen ② (*fig sl*) ausflippen III. n ① (*throw*) Werfen nt ② (*movement*) Ruck m; **to have a** [quick] ~ **through sth** etw im Schnellverfahren tun

'**flip chart** n Flipchart m o nt

'**flip-flop** n Badelatsche f

flippant ['flɪp·ənt] adj leichtfertig

flipper ['flɪp·ər] n [Schwimm]flosse f

'**flip side** n B-Seite f

flirt [flɜrt] I. vi flirten II. n [gern] flirtende(r) Mann/Frau

flirtatious [flɜr·'teɪ·ʃəs] adj kokett

flit <-tt-> [flɪt] vi huschen a. *fig; (fly)* flattern

float [floʊt] I. n ① (*for fishing*) [Kork]schwimmer m ② (*for swimming*) Schwimmkork m ③ (*in parade*) Festzugswagen m II. vi ① (*be buoyant*) schwimmen ② (*move in liquid or gas*) *objects* treiben; *people* sich treiben lassen III. vt ① ECON *business* gründen; *currency* freigeben ② (*on water*) treiben lassen ③ (*fig*) *idea* zur Diskussion stellen

◆**float around** vi (*fig*) *rumor* in Umlauf sein; *person* sich herumtreiben

floatation [floʊ·'teɪ·ʃən] n see **flotation**

floating ['floʊ·t̬ɪŋ] adj (*in water*) schwimmend, treibend; *crane* Schwimm-

flock [flak] I. n *of animals* Herde f; *of people, birds* Schar f II. vi sich scharen

floe [floʊ] n Eisscholle f

flood [flʌd] I. n ① (*excess water*) Überschwemmung f; ■**the F~** REL die Sintflut ② (*tide*) ~ [tide] Flut f II. vt ① (*overflow*) überschwemmen a. *fig; room* unter Wasser setzen ② AUTO *engine* absaufen lassen III. vi ① *place*

überschwemmt werden; *river* über die Ufer treten ② (*fig*) strömen

'**floodlight** n Flutlicht nt

floor [flɔr] I. n ① (*surface*) [Fußbo]den m ② (*story*) Stock m, Stockwerk nt II. vt ① zu Boden schlagen a. (*fig*) umhauen

'**floorboard** n Diele f

flooring ['flɔr·ɪŋ] n Boden[belag] m

'**floor lamp** n Stehlampe f

'**floor plan** n Grundriss m (*eines Stockwerks*)

flop [flap] I. vi <-pp-> ① (*move*) sich fallen [o plumpsen] lassen ② (*fail*) ein Flop sein II. n ① (*movement*) Plumps m ② (*failure*) *thing* Flop m

floppy ['flap·i] I. adj schlaff; *hair* [immer wieder] herabfallend II. n COMPUT (*fam*) Floppy [Disk] f

floral ['flɔr·əl] adj Blumen-

Florida ['flɔr·ɪ·də] n Florida nt

florist ['flɔr·ɪst] n Florist(in) m(f); ■~ [shop] Blumengeschäft nt

floss [flas] I. n Zahnseide f II. vt *teeth* mit Zahnseide reinigen

flotation [floʊ·'teɪ·ʃən] n ECON Gründung f; **stock-market** ~ Börsengang m

flounder ['flaʊn·dər] vi ① stolpern; *in snow* waten; *in water* [herum]rudern ② (*fig: be in difficulty*) sich abmühen

flour ['flaʊ·ər] n Mehl nt

flourish ['flɜr·ɪʃ] I. vi blühen II. vt herumfuchteln mit *dat*, schwingen III. n (*movement*) schwungvolle Bewegung; (*gesture*) überschwängliche Geste

flourishing ['flɜr·ɪʃ·ɪŋ] adj (a. *fig*) *plants* prächtig; *business* blühend

flow [floʊ] I. vi fließen a. *fig; air, warmth* strömen; **many rivers ~ into the North Sea** viele Flüsse münden in die Nordsee II. n *usu sing* Fluss m a. *fig* ▶PHRASES: **to go against/with the ~** gegen den/mit dem Strom schwimmen

'**flow chart**, '**flow diagram** n Flussdiagramm nt

flower ['flaʊ·ər] I. n (*plant*) Blume f; (*blossom*) Blüte f; **to be in ~** blühen II. vi blühen a. *fig*

'**flower bed** n Blumenbeet nt

'flowerpot n Blumentopf m

flowery ['flaʊ·ə·ri] adj ❶ material geblümt ❷ (fig) language blumig

flowing ['floʊ·ɪŋ] adj flüssig; hair wallend

flown [floʊn] vt, vi pp of **fly**

fl. oz. n abbrev of **fluid ounce** 29,57 ml

flu [flu] n short for **influenza** Grippe f

flub [flʌb] vt (fam) **to ~ one's lines** seinen Text verpatzen

fluctuate ['flʌk·tʃʊ·eɪt] vi schwanken; ECON fluktuieren

flue [flu] n Abzugsrohr nt; (in chimney) Rauchabzug m

fluent ['flu·ənt] adj in a foreign language fließend; style, movements flüssig

fluff [flʌf] I. n ❶ (particle) Fusseln pl ❷ ORN, ZOOL Flaum m II. vt vermasseln; exam verhauen

fluffy ['flʌf·i] adj ❶ (soft) feathers flaumig; animal kuschelig [weich] ❷ (light) clouds aufgelockert; egg whites schaumig

fluid ['flu·ɪd] I. n Flüssigkeit f II. adj ❶ flüssig ❷ (fig: changeable) veränderlich

fluid 'ounce n 29,57 ml

flung [flʌŋ] pt, pp of **fling**

flunk [flʌŋk] vt (fam) durchfallen in +dat

fluorescent [flɔ·'res·ənt] adj fluoreszierend; ~ **light** Neonlicht nt

fluoride ['flɔr·aɪd] n Fluorid nt

flurry ['flɜr·i] n ❶ METEO **snow ~** [Schnee]schauer m ❷ (excitement) Unruhe f

flush¹ [flʌʃ] adj (flat) eben; ~ **with sth** mit etw dat auf gleicher Ebene

flush² [flʌʃ] I. vi ❶ (blush) erröten (with vor +dat) ❷ (empty) spülen; **the toilet won't ~** die Spülung geht nicht II. vt spülen III. n usu sing Röte f kein pl
◆**flush out** vt ❶ (cleanse) ausspülen ❷ (drive out) hinaustreiben

flushed [flʌʃt] adj rot im Gesicht

fluster ['flʌs·tər] vt nervös machen

flute [flut] n Flöte f

flutter ['flʌt·ər] vi flattern

flux [flʌks] n **in a state of ~** im Fluss

fly [flaɪ] I. vi <flew, flown> ❶ (through the air) fliegen ❷ flag wehen ❸ (speed) sausen; **the door flew open** die Tür flog auf II. vt <flew, flown> ❶ (pilot, transport) fliegen ❷ flag wehen lassen; kite steigen lassen III. n ❶ (insect) Fliege f ❷ (zipper) Hosenschlitz m ▶PHRASES: **the ~ in the <u>ointment</u>** das Haar in der Suppe IV. adj <-er, -est> (sl) cool
◆**fly in** vt, vi einfliegen (from aus +dat)

flyer ['flaɪ·ər] n see **flier**

flying ['flaɪ·ɪŋ] I. n Fliegen nt II. adj fliegend

FM [ˌef·'em] n abbrev of **frequency modulation** FM

foal [foʊl] n Fohlen nt

foam [foʊm] n ❶ (bubbles) Schaum m ❷ (plastic) Schaumstoff m

foam 'rubber n Schaumgummi m

fob [fab] I. n Schlüsselanhänger m II. vt <-bb-> ■**to ~ sth off on sb** jdm etw andrehen

focal ['foʊ·kəl] adj ~ **point** Brennpunkt m

focus <pl -es or form foci> ['foʊ·kəs] I. n ❶ (center) Mittelpunkt m ❷ **in/out of ~** scharf/nicht scharf eingestellt II. vi <-s- or -ss-> sich konzentrieren ([up]on auf +akk) III. vt <-s- or -ss-> ❶ attention konzentrieren (on auf +akk) ❷ camera scharf einstellen (on auf +akk); eyes richten (on auf +akk)

fodder ['fad·ər] n Futter nt

fog [fag] n Nebel m

'fogbound adj airport wegen Nebels geschlossen

foggy ['fa·gi] adj neblig

'foghorn n Nebelhorn nt

'fog lamp, 'fog light n Nebelscheinwerfer m

foil¹ [fɔɪl] n Folie f

foil² [fɔɪl] vt thing verhindern; plan durchkreuzen

fold [foʊld] I. n Falte f II. vt ❶ (bend) falten (into zu +dat); letter zusammenfalten; arms verschränken ❷ FOOD (mix) heben (into unter +akk) III. vi ❶ (bend) zusammenklappen ❷ (fail) eingehen

F

◆**fold up** vt, vi zusammenfalten

folder ['foʊl·dər] n ❶ Mappe f ❷ COMPUT Ordner m

folding ['foʊl·dɪŋ] adj ~ **bed** Klappbett nt; ~ **top** Verdeck nt

foliage ['foʊ·lɪ·ɪdʒ] n Laub nt

folk [foʊk] I. n ❶ pl (fam: people) Leute pl ❷ (music) Folk m II. adj ❶ (traditional) Volks- ❷ (connected with folk music) Folk-

'**folk dance** n Volkstanz m

'**folk music** n Folk m

folksy ['foʊk·si] adj (fam) volkstümlich

follow ['fal·oʊ] I. vt ❶ (take same route as) folgen +dat ❷ (pursue) verfolgen ❸ (happen next) folgen auf +akk ❹ (obey) befolgen; guidelines sich halten an +akk II. vi ❶ (take the same route, happen next) folgen; **in the hours that ~ed …** in den darauffolgenden Stunden … ❷ (result) sich ergeben (**from** aus +dat); (be the consequence) die Folge sein

◆**follow through** vt zu Ende verfolgen

◆**follow up** I. vt (investigate) weiterverfolgen; MED nachuntersuchen II. vi ■**to ~ up with sth** etw folgen lassen

follower ['fal·oʊ·ər] n Anhänger(in) m(f)

following ['fal·oʊ·ɪŋ] I. adj folgende(r, s) II. n ❶ + pl vb (listed) ■**the ~ persons** folgende Personen; objects Folgendes ❷ usu sing (fans) Anhänger pl III. prep nach +dat

'**follow-up** I. n Fortsetzung f II. adj visit, interviews Folge-; ~ **treatment** Nachbehandlung f

fond [fand] adj memories teuer; smile liebevoll; ■**to be ~ of sb/sth** jdn/etw gerne mögen

fondle ['fan·dl] vt streicheln

font [fant] n TYPO Schriftart f

food [fud] n ❶ (eatables) Essen nt; **cat ~** Katzenfutter nt ❷ (foodstuff) Nahrungsmittel pl

'**food chain** n Nahrungskette f

'**food poisoning** n Lebensmittelvergiftung f

'**food processor** n Küchenmaschine f

'**foodstuff** n Nahrungsmittel pl

fool [ful] I. n (idiot) Dummkopf m; **to make a ~ of oneself** sich zum Narren machen II. adj (fam) blöd III. vt täuschen

◆**fool around** vi ❶ (carelessly) herumspielen ❷ (amusingly) herumblödeln

foolish ['fu·lɪʃ] adj töricht; **to look ~** sich blamieren

'**foolproof** adj idiotensicher

foot [fʊt] n <pl feet> ❶ (limb) Fuß m; **what size are your feet?** welche Schuhgröße haben Sie?; **to put one's feet up** die Füße hochlegen; **to set ~ in sth** einen Fuß in etw akk setzen; **at sb's feet** zu jds Füßen; **on ~** zu Fuß ❷<pl feet> (length) Fuß m (= 0,3048 Meter) ❸<pl feet> (base) Fuß m; of page Ende nt ▸PHRASES: **to land on one's feet** Glück haben; **to put one's ~ down** (insist) ein Machtwort sprechen; **to put one's ~ in one's mouth** ins Fettnäpfchen treten

footage ['fʊt·ɪdʒ] n Filmmaterial nt

foot-and-'mouth disease n Maul- und Klauenseuche f

football ['fʊt·bɔl] n ❶ (game) [American] Football m ❷ (ball) Football m

'**footbridge** n Fußgängerbrücke f

'**foothold** n Halt m [für die Füße]

'**footing** ['fʊt·ɪŋ] n on [an] **equal ~** auf gleicher Basis

'**footlights** npl Rampenlicht nt kein pl

'**footnote** n Fußnote f

'**footpath** n Fußweg m

'**footprint** n Fußabdruck m

'**footrest** n Fußstütze f

'**footstep** n Schritt m ▸PHRASES: **to follow in sb's ~** in jds Fußstapfen treten

'**footstool** n Fußbank f, Schemel m SÜDD, ÖSTERR

'**footwear** n Schuhe pl

'**footwork** n Beinarbeit f

for [fɔr] I. conj denn II. prep ❶ für; **to be all ~ sth** ganz für etw akk sein; **to make it easy ~ sb** es jdm einfach machen; **luckily ~ me** zu meinem Glück; **what did you do that ~?** wozu hast du

F

das getan?; **to apply ~ a job** sich um eine Stelle bewerben; **I feel sorry ~ her** sie tut mir leid; **to head ~ home** sich auf den Heimweg machen, auf dem Heimweg sein; **to prepare ~ sth** sich auf etw *akk* vorbereiten; **say hi ~ me** grüß ihn/sie von mir; **to trade sth ~ sth** etw gegen etw *akk* [ein]tauschen; **to work ~ sb/sth** bei jdm/etw arbeiten; **a check ~ 100 dollars** eine Scheck über 100 Dollar; **if it hadn't been ~ him, ...** ohne ihn ...; **~ your information** zu Ihrer Information; **to be arrested ~ murder** wegen Mordes verhaftet werden; **~ various reasons** aus verschiedenen Gründen; **~ rent/sale** zu vermieten/verkaufen; **what's the Spanish word ~ "vegetarian"?** was heißt „Vegetarier" auf Spanisch? ② *(with time, distance)* **to practice ~ half an hour** eine halbe Stunde üben; **~ the next two days** in den beiden nächsten Tagen; **~ a while** eine Weile; **~ a long time** seit langem; **~ some time** seit längerem; **~ the time being** für den Augenblick; **~ the first time** zum ersten Mal

forbade [fərˈbæd] *pt of* **forbid**

forbid <-dd-, forbad(e), forbidden> [fərˈbɪd] *vt* ▪ **to ~ sb sth** jdm etw verbieten; ▪ **to ~ sb from doing** [*or* **to do**] **sth** jdm verbieten, etw zu tun

forbidden [fərˈbɪd·ən] I. *adj* verboten II. *pp of* **forbid**

forbidding [fərˈbɪd·ɪŋ] *adj* abschreckend

force [fɔrs] I. *n* ① *(power)* Kraft *f*; *(intensity)* Stärke *f*; **to be come into** [*or* **take**] **~ in** Kraft treten ② *(violence)* Gewalt *f*; **by ~** mit Gewalt ③ *(group)* Truppe *f*; **armed ~s** Streitkräfte *pl* ▶PHRASES: **to join ~s** sich zusammenschließen, um etw zu tun II. *vt (compel)* zwingen; *door* aufbrechen; ▪ **to ~ sth on sb** jdm etw aufzwingen

◆ **force back** *vt* ① *(repel)* zurückdrängen; *(fig) tears* unterdrücken ② *(push back)* zurückdrücken

◆ **force down** *vt* ① *plane* zur Landung zwingen ② *food* hinunterwürgen

◆ **force open** *vt* mit Gewalt öffnen

forced [fɔrst] *adj* ① erzwungen; **~ landing** Notlandung ② *smile* gezwungen

'**force-feed** *vt* zwangsernähren

forceful [ˈfɔrs·fəl] *adj personality* stark

forcible [ˈfɔr·sə·bəl] *adj* gewaltsam

ford [fɔrd] I. *n* Furt *f* II. *vt* durchqueren; *(on foot)* durchwaten

forearm [ˈfɔr·arm] *n* Unterarm *m*

forecast [ˈfɔr·kæst] *n* ① *(prediction)* Prognose *f* ② **weather ~** [Wetter]vorhersage *f*

forecaster [ˈfɔr·kæst·ər] *n* METEO Meteorologe *m*/Meteorologin *f*

'**forefinger** *n see* **index finger**

'**forefront** *n* **at the ~** an der Spitze

forego <-went, -gone> [fɔrˈgoʊ] *vt see* **forgo**

foregone con'clusion *n* ausgemachte Sache

'**foreground** *n* Vordergrund *m*

'**forehand** *n* Vorhand *f*

'**forehead** [ˈfɔr·hed] *n* Stirn *f*

foreign [ˈfɔr·ɪn] *adj* ① *(from another country)* ausländisch ② *(involving other countries)* **~ policy** Außenpolitik *f* ③ *(not belonging)* fremd

foreign af'fairs *npl* Außenpolitik *f kein pl*

foreign corre'spondent *n* Auslandskorrespondent(in) *m(f)*

foreigner [ˈfɔr·ɪ·nər] *n* Ausländer(in) *m(f)*

foreign ex'change *n* Devisen *pl*

'**foreman** *n* ① *(workman)* Vorarbeiter *m* ② LAW Sprecher *m (der Geschworenen)*

foremost [ˈfɔr·moʊst] *adj* führend

forensic [fəˈren·sɪk] *adj* forensisch

'**foreplay** *n* Vorspiel *nt*

foresee <-saw, -seen> [fɔrˈsi] *vt* vorhersehen

foreseeable [fɔrˈsi·ə·bəl] *adj* absehbar; **in the ~ future** in absehbarer Zeit

'**foresight** *n* Weitblick *m*; ▪ **to have the ~ to do sth** so vorausschauend sein, etw zu tun

forest [ˈfɔr·ɪst] *n* Wald *m a. fig*; **the Black F~** der Schwarzwald

forester ['fɔr·ɪ·stər] *n* Förster(in) *m(f)*

'forest fire *n* Waldbrand *m*

'forest ranger *n* Förster(in) *m(f)*

forestry ['fɔr·ɪ·stri] *n* Forstwirtschaft *f*

forever [fɔr·'ev·ər] *adv* **①** (*for all time*) ewig *a. fig* **②** (*continually*) ständig

forewarn [fɔr·'wɔrn] *vt* vorwarnen
▶PHRASES: **~ed is forearmed** (*prov*) bist du gewarnt, bist du gewappnet

'foreword *n* Vorwort *nt*

forfeit ['fɔr·fɪt] *vt* (*surrender*) einbüßen; *right* verwirken

forgave [fər·'geɪv] *n pt of* **forgive**

forge [fɔrdʒ] **I.** *n* **①** (*furnace*) Glühofen *m* **②** (*workshop*) Schmiede *f* **II.** *vt* **①** (*heat and shape*) schmieden **②** (*copy*) fälschen

forger ['fɔr·dʒər] *n* Fälscher(in) *m(f)*

forgery ['fɔr·dʒə·ri] *n* Fälschung *f*

forget <-got, -gotten *or* -got> [fər·'get] *vt, vi* vergessen; **to ~ the past** die Vergangenheit ruhen lassen

forgetful [fər·'get·fəl] *adj* vergesslich

for'get-me-not *n* BOT Vergissmeinnicht *nt*

forgive <-gave, -given> [fər·'gɪv] *vt* ▪ **to ~ sb** [**for**] **sth** jdm etw verzeihen; *sin* vergeben; **to ~ and forget** vergeben und vergessen

forgiven [fər·'gɪv·ən] *pp of* **forgive**

forgiveness [fər·'gɪv·nɪs] *n* Vergebung *f*

forgiving [fər·'gɪv·ɪŋ] *adj* versöhnlich

forgo <-went, -gone> [fər·'goʊ] *vt* verzichten auf *akk*

forgot [fər·'gat] *pt of* **forget**

forgotten [fər·'gat·n] **I.** *pp of* **forget** **II.** *adj* vergessen

fork [fɔrk] **I.** *n* **①** (*tool*) Gabel *f* **②** *in road* Abzweigung *f* **II.** *vt* mit einer Gabel bearbeiten **III.** *vi* sich gabeln
◆ **fork out** *vt* **to ~ out $40** 40 Dollar springen lassen *fam*

forked [fɔrkt] *adj* gegabelt; **~ lightning** Linienblitz *m*

'forklift *n* Gabelstapler *m*

forlorn [fɔr·'lɔrn] *adj place* verlassen; *hope* schwach

form [fɔrm] **I.** *n* **①** (*type*) Form *f*, Art *f*; *of energy* Typ *m*; *art* ~ Kunstform *f*;

~ **of exercise** Sportart *f*; **life** ~ Lebensform *f* **②** (*particular way*) Form *f*, Gestalt *f*; **in some** ~ **or other** auf die eine oder andere Art **③** (*document*) Formular *nt*; *application* ~ Bewerbungsbogen *m* **④** (*shape*) Form *f*; *of a person* Gestalt *f* **⑤** (*physical/mental condition*) Form *f*, Kondition *f* **II.** *vt* **①** (*shape*) formen *a. fig* (**into** zu +*dat*) GEOG **to be ~ed from** entstehen aus **②** (*arrange*) bilden; **they ~ed themselves into three lines** sie stellten sich in drei Reihen auf **③** (*set up*) gründen; *government* bilden; **to ~ an alliance with sb** sich mit jdm verbünden **III.** *vi* sich bilden; *idea* Gestalt annehmen

formal ['fɔr·məl] *adj* **①** (*ceremonious*) formell; **~ wear** Gesellschaftskleidung *f* **②** (*serious*) förmlich

formality [fɔr·'mæl·ɪ·ţi] *n* **①** (*ceremoniousness*) Förmlichkeit *f* **②** (*matter of form*) Formsache *f*

formalize ['fɔr·mə·laɪz] *vt agreement* formell bekräftigen

formally ['fɔr·məl·i] *adv* offiziell

format ['fɔr·mæt] **I.** *n* Format *nt* **II.** *vt* <-tt-> formatieren

formation [fɔr·'meɪ·ʃən] *n* Bildung *f*

former ['fɔr·mər] *adj* **①** (*previous*) ehemalig **②** (*first of two*) erstere(r, s)

formerly ['fɔr·mər·li] *adv* früher

formidable ['fɔr·mɪ·də·bəl] *adj* **①** (*difficult*) schwierig; (*tremendous*) kolossal; *opponent* Furcht erregend **②** (*powerful*) eindrucksvoll

'form letter *n* Briefvorlage *f*

formula <*pl* -s> ['fɔr·mjʊ·lə] *n* **①** Formel *f* **②** FOOD Babymilchpulver *nt*

formulate ['fɔr·mjʊ·leɪt] *vt* ausarbeiten; *law* formulieren; *theory* entwickeln

formulation [ˌfɔr·mjʊ·'leɪ·ʃən] *n* (*drawing up*) Entwicklung *f*; *of law* Fassung *f*

fort [fɔrt] *n* Fort *nt* ▶PHRASES: **to hold the ~** die Stellung halten

forth [fɔrθ] *adv* **back and ~** vor und zurück ▶PHRASES: **[and so on] and so ~** und so weiter [und so fort]

forthcoming [ˌfɔrθ·'kʌm·ɪŋ] *adj* **①** (*planned*) bevorstehend **②** (*coming* *out soon*) in Kürze erscheinend; *film* in Kürze anlaufend

fortieth [ˈfɔr·tɪ·əθ] **I.** *adj* vierzigste(r, s) **II.** *n* ❶ (*order*) ■**the** ~ der/die/das Vierzigste ❷ (*fraction*) Vierzigstel *nt*; *see also* **eighth**

fortification [ˌfɔr·tə·fɪˈkeɪ·ʃən] *n* (*structures*) ■**-s** *pl* Befestigungsanlagen *pl*

fortify <-ie-> [ˈfɔr·tə·faɪ] *vt* MIL befestigen

fortress <*pl* -es> [ˈfɔr·trɪs] *n* Festung *f*

fortunate [ˈfɔr·tʃə·nɪt] *adj* glücklich; ■**to be** ~ Glück haben

fortunately [ˈfɔr·tʃə·nɪt·li] *adv* zum Glück

fortune [ˈfɔr·tʃən] *n* ❶ (*money*) Vermögen *nt* ❷ (*luck*) **to tell sb's** ~ jds Schicksal vorhersagen

'fortune teller *n* Wahrsager(in) *m(f)*

forty [ˈfɔr·ti] **I.** *adj* vierzig **II.** *n* Vierzig *f*; *see also* **eight**

forum [ˈfɔr·əm] *n* Forum *nt*

forward [ˈfɔr·wərd] **I.** *adv* (*toward front*) nach vorn[e]; (*onwards*) vorwärts; **to lean** ~ sich vorlehnen; **from that day** ~ von jenem Tag an **II.** *adj* ❶ (*toward front*) Vorwärts- ❷ (*near front*) vordere(r, s) ❸ (*of future*) Voraus- *f*; ~ **buying** Terminkauf *m* **III.** *n* SPORT Stürmer(in) *m(f)* **IV.** *vt* weiterleiten (**to an** +*akk*)

forwarding ad'dress *n* Nachsendeadresse *f*

'forward-looking *adj* vorausschauend

forwards [ˈfɔr·wərdz] *adv see* **forward**

forwent [fɔrˈwent] *pt of* **forgo**

fossil [ˈfɑs·əl] *n* Fossil *nt*; ~ **fuel** fossiler Brennstoff

foster [ˈfɑ·stər] *vt* ❶ *child* in Pflege nehmen ❷ (*encourage*) fördern

'foster child *n* Pflegekind *nt*

fought [fɔt] *pt, pp of* **fight**

foul [faʊl] **I.** *adj* ❶ (*disgusting*) abscheulich; *smell* faul ❷ (*polluted*) verpestet ❸ *mood* fürchterlich; *language* anstößig **II.** *n* SPORT Foul *nt* **III.** *vt* SPORT foulen

foul-'mouthed *adj* unflätig

foul 'play *n* SPORT Foulspiel *nt*

found [faʊnd] *pt, pp of* **find**

foundation [faʊnˈdeɪ·ʃən] *n* ❶ (*basis*) Fundament *nt a. fig*; **to be without** ~ (*fig*) der Grundlage entbehren ❷ (*make-up*) Grundierung *f*

foun'dation stone *n* Grundstein *m*

founder [ˈfaʊn·dər] *n* Gründer(in) *m(f)*

Founding 'Fathers *npl* Gründerväter *pl*

foundry [ˈfaʊn·dri] *n* Gießerei *f*

fountain [ˈfaʊn·tən] *n* Brunnen *m*

four [fɔr] **I.** *adj* vier **II.** *n* (*number, symbol*) Vier *f*; *see also* **eight**

'four-by-four *n* AUTO allrad-/vierradangetriebenes Auto

'fourfold *adj, adv* vierfach

four-'footed *adj* vierfüßig

four-leaf 'clover *n* vierblättriges Kleeblatt

four-letter 'word *n* Schimpfwort *nt*

'foursome *n* Vierergruppe *f*; (*golf*) Vierer *m*

fourteen [ˌfɔrˈtin] **I.** *adj* vierzehn; ~ **hundred hours** *spoken* vierzehn Uhr; **1400 hours** *written* 14:00 **II.** *n* Vierzehn *f*; *see also* **eight**

fourteenth [ˌfɔrˈtinθ] **I.** *adj* vierzehnte(r, s) **II.** *n* ❶ (*fraction*) Vierzehntel *nt* ❷ (*date*) ■**the** ~ der Vierzehnte

fourth [fɔrθ] **I.** *adj* vierte(r, s) **II.** *n* ❶ (*order*) ■**the** ~ der/die/das Vierte ❷ (*date*) **the** ~ der Vierte ❸ (*fraction*) Viertel *nt*; *see also* **eighth**

Fourth of July *amerikanischer Unabhängigkeitstag am 4. Juli*

four-wheel 'drive *n* Allrad-/Vierradantrieb *m*

fowl <*pl* -> [faʊl] *n* Geflügel *nt kein pl*

fox [fɑks] **I.** *n* ❶ (*animal*) Fuchs *m a. fig*; (*fur*) Fuchspelz *m* ❷ (*sl: attractive woman*) scharfe Braut *pej sl*; (*attractive man*) heißer Typ *pej sl* **II.** *vt* verblüffen

foxy [ˈfɑk·si] *adj* ❶ (*crafty*) gerissen ❷ (*fam: sexy*) sexy

foyer [ˈfɔɪ·ər] *n* Foyer *nt*

fracas <*pl* -es> [ˈfreɪ·kəs] *n* lautstarke Auseinandersetzung

fraction [ˈfræk·ʃən] *n* ❶ (*number*)

Bruchzahl f ②(*proportion*) Bruchteil m; (*fig*) **by a ~** um Haaresbreite
fractional ['fræk·ʃə·nəl] *adj* minimal
fracture ['fræk·tʃər] I. *vt, vi* brechen II. *n* Bruch m
fragile ['frædʒ·əl] *adj* ①(*breakable*) zerbrechlich ②(*unstable*) brüchig; *peace* unsicher
fragment ['fræg·mənt] *n* ①(*broken piece*) Splitter m ②(*incomplete piece*) Brocken m
fragrance ['freɪ·grəns] *n* Duft m
fragrant ['freɪ·grənt] *adj* duftend
frail [freɪl] *adj* gebrechlich
frame [freɪm] I. *n* ①(*of picture*) Bilderrahmen m ②(*of door, window*) Rahmen m ③(*of eyeglasses*) **■ ~s** *pl* Brillengestell nt ④(*body*) Körper m II. *vt* ①(*put in framework*) einrahmen ②(*fam: falsely incriminate*) verleumden
'**frame-up** *n* (*fam*) abgekartetes Spiel
'**framework** *n* ①Gerüst nt ②(*fig*) Rahmen m
France [fræns] *n* Frankreich nt
franchise ['fræn·tʃaɪz] *n* Franchise nt
frank¹ [fræŋk] I. *adj* aufrichtig; **■ to be ~ [with sb] [about sth]** ehrlich [zu jdm] [über etw *akk*] sein II. *vt* envelope frankieren
frank² [fræŋk] *n* (*fam: frankfurter*) Frankfurter f
frankencorn ['fræŋ·kən·kɔːrn] *n* no *pl* (*pej fam*) Genmais m, Horrormais m sl
frankly ['fræŋk·li] *adv* offen
frantic ['fræn·tɪk] *adj* ①(*distracted*) verrückt (**with** vor +*dat*) ②(*hurried*) hektisch
fraternity [frə·'tɜr·nɪ·t̬i] *n* ①(*group*) Vereinigung f ②UNIV Burschenschaft f
fraternize ['fræt̬·ər·naɪz] *vi* sich verbrüdern
fraud [frɔd] *n* ①(*deceit*) Betrug m ②(*deceiver*) Betrüger(in) m(f)
fraudulent ['frɔ·dʒə·lənt] *adj* betrügerisch
fraught [frɔt] *adj* **to be ~ with difficulties** voller Schwierigkeiten stecken
fray [freɪ] *vi* fabric ausfransen

freak [frik] *n* ①(*abnormal thing*) etwas Außergewöhnliches; **a ~ of nature** eine Laune der Natur ②(*abnormal person*) Missgeburt f
◆ **freak out** *vi* (*fam*) ausflippen
freckle ['frek·əl] *n* usu *pl* Sommersprosse f
freckled ['frek·əld] *adj* sommersprossig
free [fri] I. *adj* ①frei; **~ speech** Redefreiheit f; **■ to be ~ [to do sth]** Zeit haben[, etw zu tun]; **you are ~ to come and go as you please** Sie können kommen und gehen, wann Sie wollen; **to break ~ [of [or from] sth]** sich [aus etw] befreien *a. fig*; **to walk ~** straffrei ausgehen ②(*costing nothing*) frei ▶PHRASES: **there's no such thing as a ~ lunch** nichts ist umsonst II. *adv* frei, gratis; **~ of charge** kostenlos III. *vt* freilassen; *hands* frei machen
◆ **free up** *vt* freimachen
freebie ['fri·bi] *n* (*fam*) Werbegeschenk nt
freedom ['fri·dəm] *n* Freiheit f; **~ of information** freier Informationszugang; **~ of speech** Redefreiheit f
'**free-for-all** *n* allgemeines Gerangel
'**freehand** *adj* Freihand-
free 'kick *n* SPORT Freistoß m
freelance ['fri·læns] *n* Freiberufler(in) m(f)
'**freeload** *vi* (*pej*) schnorren (**off** bei +*dat*)
'**freeloader** *vi* (*pej*) Schnorrer(in) m(f)
freely ['fri·li] *adv* ①(*unrestrictedly*) frei ②(*without obstruction*) ungehindert ③(*generously*) großzügig
'**free 'port** *n* Freihafen m
'**free-range** *adj* Freiland
free 'speech *n* Redefreiheit f
free'standing *adj* frei stehend
'**freestyle** *n* Freistil m
free 'trade *n* Freihandel m
'**freeware** *n* COMPUT Freeware f
'**freeway** *n* Fern[verkehrs]straße f
free 'will *n* freier Wille; **■ to do sth of one's own ~** etw aus freien Stücken tun
freeze [friz] I. *n* ①METEO Frost m

F

F

② ECON Einfrieren *nt* II. *vi* <froze, frozen> ① *water* gefrieren; *pipes* einfrieren; **to ~ solid** festfrieren ② (*a. fig: get very cold*) [sehr] frieren; **to ~ to death** erfrieren ③ (*be still*) erstarren III. *vt* <froze, frozen> ① (*turn to ice*) gefrieren lassen ② (*preserve*) einfrieren ③ *image* festhalten

♦ **freeze up** *vi* einfrieren

freezer ['fri·zər] *n* Gefrierschrank *m*
freezer bag *n* Kühltasche *f*
freezing ['fri·zɪŋ] I. *adj* frostig; **it's ~** es ist eiskalt; **I'm ~** mir ist eiskalt II. *n* (*preserving*) Einfrieren *nt*
'**freezing point** *n* Gefrierpunkt *m*
freight [freɪt] *n* ① (*goods*) Frachtgut *nt* ② (*charge*) Frachtgebühr *f*
'**freight car** *n* Güterwagen *m*
freighter ['freɪ·tər] *n* Frachter *m*
'**freight train** *n* Güterzug *m*
French [frentʃ] I. *adj* französisch II. *n* ① (*language*) Französisch *nt* ② (*people*) ■**the ~** *pl* die Franzosen
French 'doors *npl* Verandatür *f*
'**French fries** *npl* Pommes frites *pl*
French 'toast *n* FOOD armer Ritter *m*
frenetic [frə·'neṭ·ɪk] *adj* hektisch
frenzied ['fren·zɪd] *adj* fieberhaft; *attack* wild
frenzy ['fren·zi] *n* Raserei *f*
frequency ['fri·kwən·si] *n* ① Häufigkeit *f* ② RADIO Frequenz *f*
frequent *adj* ['fri·kwənt] (*often*) häufig; (*regular*) regelmäßig
frequently [fri·kwənt·li] *adv* häufig
fresh [freʃ] *adj* ① frisch *a. fig*; **~ start** Neuanfang *m*; **to get a breath of ~ air** frische Luft schnappen ② (*fam: cheeky*) frech
freshen ['freʃ·ən] I. *vt drink* auffüllen; *room* durchlüften II. *vi wind* auffrischen
freshman ['freʃ·mən] *n* ① (*college student*) Studienanfänger *m* ② (*ninth-grade high school student*) Gymnasiast *m* im ersten Jahr
freshness ['freʃ·nɪs] *n* Frische *f*
'**freshwater** *adj* Süßwasser-
fret [fret] *vi* <-tt-> sich *dat* Sorgen machen

friction ['frɪk·ʃən] *n* Reibung *f*
Friday ['fraɪ·di] *n* Freitag *m; see also* **Tuesday**
fridge [frɪdʒ] *n* (*fam*) Kühlschrank *m*
fried [fraɪd] *adj* (*of food*) gebraten; **~ potatoes** Bratkartoffeln *pl*
fried 'egg *n* Spiegelei *nt*
friend [frend] *n* Freund(in) *m(f)*
friendly ['frend·li] *adj* ① (*showing friendship*) freundlich ② *atmosphere* angenehm
friendship ['frend·ʃɪp] *n* Freundschaft *f*
fries [fraɪz] *npl* Pommes frites *pl*
fright [fraɪt] *n* ① (*feeling*) Angst *f* ② *usu sing* (*experience*) Schrecken *m;* **to get a ~** erschrecken
frighten ['fraɪ·ṭən] *vt* ■**to ~ sb** jdm Angst machen

♦ **frighten away** *vt* abschrecken
frightened ['fraɪ·ṭənd] *adj* verängstigt; ■**to be ~ of sth/sb** sich vor etw/jdm fürchten
frightening ['fraɪ·ṭən·ɪŋ] *adj* Furcht erregend
frigid ['frɪdʒ·ɪd] *adj* ① (*of manner*) frostig ② (*sexually*) frigid[e]
frigidity [frɪ·'dʒɪd·ɪ·ti] *n* ① (*of manner*) Kälte *f*
frill [frɪl] *n* Rüsche *f*
frilly ['frɪl·i] *adj* mit Rüschen
fringe [frɪndʒ] I. *n* ① (*edging*) Franse *f* ② (*of area*) Rand *m a. fig* II. *adj* **~ benefits** zusätzliche Leistungen *pl*
frisk [frɪsk] *vt* abtasten (**for** nach +*dat*)
frisky ['frɪs·ki] *adj horse* lebhaft
fritter ['frɪṭ·ər] *n* Fettgebackenes *nt* (*mit Obst-/Gemüsefüllung*)
frivolous ['frɪv·ə·ləs] *adj* ① (*pej*) *person* leichtfertig ② (*pej: unimportant*) belanglos
frizzy ['frɪz·i] *adj* gekräuselt
fro [froʊ] *adv* **to and ~** hin und her
frog [frag] *n* Frosch *m*
from [fram] *prep* ① (*off*) von; (*out of, made of, originating in*) aus ② (*as seen from*) **~ here** von hier [aus]; **~ my point of view** aus meiner Sicht ③ (*as starting location*) von; **~ the north** von Norden ④ (*as starting time*) von, ab;

~ **tomorrow** on[ward] ab morgen; ~ **time to time** ab und zu ⑤ (*as starting condition*) bei; ~ **25 to 200** von 25 auf 200 ⑥ (*considering*) aufgrund, wegen; ~ **the evidence** aufgrund des Beweismaterials ⑦ (*caused by*) an +*dat*; **he died** ~ **his injuries** er starb an seinen Verletzungen; **the risk** ~ **radiation** [**exposure**] das Risiko einer Verstrahlung ⑧ (*indicating protection*) vor; **to protect sb** ~ **sth** jdn vor etw *dat* schützen

front [frʌnt] I. *n* ① *usu sing* (*forward-facing part*) Vorderseite *f*; *of building* Front *f*; **to lie on one's** ~ auf dem Bauch liegen ② (*front area*) ■**the** ~ der vordere Bereich; ■**at the** ~ vorn[e] ③ (*ahead of*) ■**in** ~ vorn[e]; ■**in** ~ **of sth/sb** vor etw/jdm ④ (*in advance*) ■**up** ~ im Voraus ⑤ MIL, METEO, POL **Front** *f* II. *adj* (*at the front*) vorder[st]e(r, s); ~ **wheel** Vorderrad *nt* III. *vt* (*be head of*) vorstehen +*dat*

frontage ['frʌn·tɪdʒ] *n* [Vorder]front *f*
frontal ['frʌn·təl] *adj* Frontal-; ~ **view** Vorderansicht *f*
front 'door *n* Haustür *f*
frontier [frʌn·'tɪr] *n* (*outlying areas*) ■**the** ~ der ehemalige Wilde Westen der USA
front 'line *n* ① MIL Frontlinie *f* ② (*fig*) vorderste Front
front 'page *n* Titelseite *f*
'front-runner *n* Spitzenreiter(in) *m(f)* a. *fig*
front-wheel 'drive *n* Vorderradantrieb *m*
front 'yard *n* Vorgarten *m*
frost [frɑst] *n* Frost *m*
'frostbite *n* Erfrierung *f*
frosted ['frɑ·stɪd] *adj* (*opaque*) ~ **glass** Milchglas *nt*
frosting ['frɑ·stɪŋ] *n* FOOD Glasur *f*
frosty ['frɑ·sti] *adj* frostig
froth [frɑθ] I. *n* Schaum *m* II. *vi* schäumen
frothy ['frɑ·θi] *adj* schaumig
frown [fraʊn] I. *vi* die Stirn runzeln; ■**to**

~ **on** [*or* **upon**] **sth** etw missbilligen II. *n* Stirnrunzeln *nt kein pl*
froze [froʊz] *pt of* **freeze**
frozen ['froʊ·zn] I. *pp of* **freeze** II. *adj* ① (*of water*) gefroren ② FOOD [tief]gefroren; ~ **food** Tiefkühlkost *f*
frugal ['fru·gəl] *adj* ① (*economical*) sparsam ② *meal* karg
fruit [frut] I. *n* Frucht *f* a. *fig*; (*collectively*) Obst *nt* II. *vi* [Früchte] tragen
'fruitcake *n* ① Früchtebrot *nt* ② (*sl: eccentric*) Spinner(in) *m(f)*
fruition [fru·'ɪʃ·ən] *n* **to come to** [*or* **reach**] ~ verwirklicht werden
fruitless ['frut·lɪs] *adj* fruchtlos
fruit 'salad *n* Obstsalat *m*
fruity ['fru·ti] *adj* fruchtig
frustrate ['frʌs·treɪt] *vt* ① (*annoy*) frustrieren ② (*prevent*) hindern
frustrating ['frʌs·treɪ·tɪŋ] *adj* frustrierend
frustration [frʌ·'streɪ·ʃən] *n* Frustration *f*
fry [fraɪ] *vt, vi* <-ie-> braten
frying pan ['fraɪ·ɪŋ-] *n* Bratpfanne *f*
ft. *n abbrev of* **feet** ft
fuck [fʌk] (*vulg*) I. *n* ① (*act*) Fick *m* ② (*used as expletive*) **who gives a** ~**?** wen interessiert es schon? II. *interj* Scheiße! III. *vt* ① (*have sex with*) vögeln ② (*damn*) [**oh**] ~ **it!** verdammte Scheiße! IV. *vi* ficken
◆ **fuck off** *vi* (*vulg*) sich verpissen
fucker ['fʌk·ər] *n* (*vulg*) ① (*person*) Arsch *m* ② (*thing*) Scheiß *m*
fucking ['fʌk·ɪŋ] *adj, adv* (*vulg*) verdammt, Scheiß-; **to be** ~ **useless** zu gar nichts taugen; (*sl*) echt, verflixt
'fuckup *n* (*vulg, sl: mess*) Scheiß *m pej derb*; (*confusion*) Durcheinander *nt*
fudge [fʌdʒ] I. *n* Fondant *m o nt* II. *vt, vi figures* frisieren *fam*
fuel ['fju·əl] I. *n* Brennstoff *m* II. *vt* <-l-> (*fig*) nähren; *resentment* schüren
'fuel consumption *n* Treibstoffverbrauch *m*
'fuel gauge *n* Tankanzeige *f*
fuel-injection 'engine *n* Einspritzmotor *m*

F

F

'**fuel pump** n Kraftstoffpumpe f

fugitive ['fjuːdʒɪtɪv] n Flüchtige(r) f(m)

fulfill [fʊl'fɪl] vt ❶ (satisfy) erfüllen; potential ausschöpfen ❷ contract, promise erfüllen

fulfillment [fʊl'fɪlmənt] n Erfüllung f

full [fʊl] I. adj voll; (after eating) satt; explanation vollständig; theater ausverkauft; ■ to be ~ of sth (enthusiastic) von etw dat ganz begeistert sein; with one's mouth ~ mit vollem Mund; [at] ~ speed mit voller Geschwindigkeit; in ~ swing voll im Gang II. adv voll III. n in ~ zur Gänze

'**fullback** n (in football) Fullback m; (in soccer) Außenverteidiger(in) m(f)

full-'blooded adj ❶ (of descent) reinrassig ❷ (vigorous) kraftvoll

full-'blown adj disease voll ausgebrochen

full-'bodied adj wine vollmundig

full-'frontal adj völlig nackt

full-'grown adj ausgewachsen

full-'length I. adj film abendfüllend; mirror groß II. adv to lie ~ on the floor sich der Länge nach auf den Boden legen [o der Länge nach auf dem Boden liegen]

full 'moon n Vollmond m

fullness ['fʊlnɪs] n Völle f

'**full-page** adj ganzseitig

'**full-scale** adj ❶ (original size) in Originalgröße nach ❷ (all-out) umfassend

full 'time n (in soccer) Spielende nt

'**full-time** I. adj Ganztags- II. adv ganztags

fully ['fʊliː] adv völlig; ~ booked ausgebucht

fumble ['fʌmbəl] I. vi ❶ ■ to ~ [around [or about]] for sth nach etw dat tasten ❷ SPORT den Ball fallen lassen, fumbeln II. vt ball fallen lassen, fumbeln III. n SPORT Fumble m

fume [fjuːm] vi vor Wut schäumen

fumes [fjuːmz] n pl Dämpfe pl; of car Abgase pl

fun [fʌn] I. n Spaß m; it was lots of ~ es hat viel Spaß gemacht; in ~ im Spaß; have ~! viel Spaß!; to make ~ of sb

sich über jdn lustig machen II. adj (fam) lustig

function ['fʌŋkʃən] I. n ❶ (task) of a person Aufgabe f ❷ MATH Funktion f ❸ (social event) Veranstaltung f II. vi funktionieren

functional ['fʌŋkʃənəl] adj funktionstüchtig

'**function key** n COMPUT Funktionstaste f

fund [fʌnd] I. n ❶ (stock) Fonds m; disaster ~ Notfonds m ❷ (money) ■ ~s pl [finanzielle] Mittel II. vt finanzieren

fundamental [ˌfʌndə'mentəl] adj grundlegend (to für +akk); difference wesentlich

fundamentalism [ˌfʌndə'mentəlɪzəm] n Fundamentalismus m

fundamentalist [ˌfʌndə'mentəlɪst] n Fundamentalist(in) m(f)

fundamentally [ˌfʌndə'mentəliː] adv ❶ (basically) im Grunde ❷ (in all important aspects) grundsätzlich

funding ['fʌndɪŋ] n Finanzierung f

'**fundraiser** n (event) Wohltätigkeitsveranstaltung f

'**fundraising** I. adj ~ campaign Spendenaktion f II. n Geldbeschaffung f

funeral ['fjuːnərəl] n Beerdigung f

'**funeral director** n Leichenbestatter(in) m(f)

fungus <pl -es> ['fʌŋgəs] n Pilz m

funicular [fjuː'nɪkjuːlər], **funicular 'railway** n Seilbahn f

funk [fʌŋk] n MUS Funk m

funky ['fʌŋkiː] adj (sl) ❶ (hip) flippig ❷ MUS funkig

'**fun-loving** adj lebenslustig

funnel ['fʌnəl] I. n ❶ (tool) Trichter m ❷ (on ship) Schornstein m II. vt <-l-> [mit einem Trichter] einfüllen

funnies ['fʌniːz] npl ■ the ~ der Witzteil (einer Zeitung)

funny ['fʌniː] I. adj ❶ (amusing) lustig, witzig ❷ (strange) komisch, merkwürdig; to have a ~ feeling that ... so eine Ahnung haben, dass ... ❸ (dishonest) verdächtig ▸ PHRASES: ~ ha-ha or ~ peculiar [or weird]? lustig oder merkwürdig? II. adv (fam) komisch, merkwürdig

fur [fɜr] *n* ❶ (*on animal*) Fell *nt* ❷ FASHION Pelz *m*

furious ['fjʊr·i·əs] *adj* ❶ (*angry*) [sehr] wütend; *argument* heftig; ■**to be ~ with sb/about** [*or* **at**] **sth** wütend auf jdn/über etw *akk* sein ❷ (*intense*) *storm* heftig; **at a ~ pace** in rasender Geschwindigkeit; **fast and ~** rasant

furnace ['fɜr·nɪs] *n* ❶ (*industrial*) Hochofen *m* ❷ (*domestic*) [Haupt]heizung *f*

furnished ['fɜr·nɪʃt] *adj* möbliert

furnishings ['fɜr·nɪ·ʃɪŋz] *npl* Einrichtung *f*

furniture ['fɜr·nɪ·tʃər] *n* Möbel *pl*

furor ['fjʊr·ɔr] *n* Aufruhr *m*

furrow ['fɜr·oʊ] *n* Furche *f*

furry ['fɜr·i] *adj* (*short fur*) pelzig; (*long fur*) wollig

further ['fɜr·ðər] **I.** *adj comp of* **far** ❶ (*additional*) weiter; **until ~ notice** bis auf weiteres ❷ (*more distant*) weiter [entfernt] **II.** *adv comp of* **far** ❶ (*to a greater degree*) weiter; **to take sth ~** mit etw *dat* weitermachen; (*pursue*) *matter* etw weiterverfolgen ❷ (*more*) [noch] weiter; **I have nothing ~ to say** ich habe nichts mehr zu sagen. ❸ (*more distant*) weiter; **~ back** (*in place*) weiter zurück; (*in time*) früher

furthermore ['fɜr·ðər·mɔr] *adv* außerdem

furthest ['fɜr·ðɪst] **I.** *adj superl of* **far** ❶ (*fig*) extremste(r, s) ❷ am weitesten entfernte(r, s) **II.** *adv superl of* **far** am weitesten

furtive ['fɜr·tɪv] *adj glance* verstohlen; *action* heimlich

fury ['fjʊr·i] *n* Wut *f*

fuse¹ [fjuz] *n of a bomb* Zündvorrichtung *f*

fuse² [fjuz] **I.** *n* Sicherung *f* **II.** *vt* verbinden

'**fuse box** *n* Sicherungskasten *m*

fuselage ['fju·sə·laʒ] *n* [Flugzeug]rumpf *m*

fuss [fʌs] **I.** *n* ❶ (*excitement*) [übertriebene] Aufregung ❷ (*attention*) [übertriebener] Aufwand, Getue *nt pej;* **to make** [*or* **kick up**] **a ~** einen Aufstand machen **II.** *vi* (*be nervously active*) [sehr] aufgeregt sein

'**fussbudget** *n* (*fam*) **to be a ~** penibel sein

fussy ['fʌs·i] *adj* ❶ (*pej: about things*) pingelig; (*about food*) mäkelig ❷ (*pej: overly decorated*) [zu] verspielt

futile ['fju·təl] *adj* sinnlos

futon ['fu·tan] *n* Futon *nt*

future ['fju·tʃər] **I.** *n usu sing* ❶ (*in time*) Zukunft *f;* **to have no ~** keine Zukunft[saussichten] haben ❷ LING **~ tense** Futur *nt* **II.** *adj* zukünftig

'**futures market** *n* ECON Terminbörse *f*

fuze [fjuz] *n, vt see* **fuse¹**

fuzz¹ [fʌz] *n* ❶ (*fluff*) Fussel[n] *pl* ❷ (*fluffy hair*) Flaum *m*

fuzz² [fʌz] *n* (*sl: police*) ■**the ~** die Bullen *pl*

fuzzy ['fʌz·i] *adj* ❶ (*fluffy*) flaumig ❷ (*distorted*) verschwommen

FYI *adv* (*fam*) *abbrev of* **for your information** z. K.

Gg

G <pl -'s>, g <pl -'s> [dʒi] n (letter) G nt, g nt; ~ as in Golf G wie Gustav

G adj FILM abbrev of General Audiences: rated ~ jugendfrei

GA, Ga. abbrev of Georgia

gab [gæb] vi <-bb-> (pej fam) quatschen

gabble ['gæb·əl] vi quasseln

gable ['geɪ·bəl] n Giebel m

gadget ['gædʒ·ɪt] n [praktisches] Gerät

gaffer ['gæf·ər] n FILM, TV ≈ Filmtechniker m

gag [gæg] n ➊ (for mouth) Knebel m ➋ (joke) Gag m

gaga ['ga·ga] adj (fam) vertrottelt

gage [geɪdʒ] n, vt see gauge

'gag order n (fam) Nachrichtensperre f

gaily ['geɪ·li] adv fröhlich

gain [geɪn] I. n Zunahme f kein pl II. vt ➊ (obtain) gewinnen; experience sammeln; independence erlangen; to ~ control of sth etw unter [seine] Kontrolle bekommen ➋ (increase) ▪to ~ sth an etw dat gewinnen; self-confidence entwickeln; to ~ speed schneller werden; to ~ weight zunehmen III. vi ➊ (increase) zunehmen ➋ (profit) profitieren

gait [geɪt] n Gang m kein pl; of a horse Gangart f

gala ['geɪ·lə] n (social event) Gala f

galaxy ['gæl·ək·si] n Galaxie f

gale [geɪl] n Sturm m

gall [gɔl] n ANAT ~ bladder Gallenblase f

gallery ['gæl·ə·ri] n Galerie f

galley ['gæl·i] n of a ship Kombüse f; of an airplane Bordküche f

gallon ['gæl·ən] n Gallone f

gallop ['gæl·əp] vi galoppieren

gallows ['gæl·ouz] n + sing vb Galgen m

'gallstone n Gallenstein m

galvanize ['gæl·və·naɪz] vt TECH galvanisieren

gambit ['gæm·bɪt] n ➊ (in chess) Gambit nt ➋ (tactic, remark) Schachzug m

gamble ['gæm·bəl] I. n usu sing Risiko nt II. vi [um Geld] spielen; to ~ on the stock market an der Börse spekulieren

gambler ['gæm·blər] n Spieler(in) m(f)

gambling ['gæm·bəlɪŋ] n Glücksspiel nt

game¹ [geɪm] n Spiel nt; a ~ of tennis eine Partie Tennis; what's your ~? (fig fam) was soll das?; to play ~s with sb (fig) mit jdm spielen ▸PHRASES: to beat sb at their own ~ jdn mit seinen eigenen Waffen schlagen; two can play at that ~ was du kannst, kann ich schon lange; the ~'s up das Spiel ist aus

game² [geɪm] n (animal) Wild nt

'game show n Spielshow f

gaming ['geɪ·mɪŋ] n Spielen nt

gander ['gæn·dər] n Gänserich m

gang [gæŋ] n of criminals Bande f; of youths Gang f

'gangplank n Landungssteg m

gangster ['gæŋ·stər] n Gangster(in) m(f)

gang 'warfare n Bandenkrieg m

'gangway I. n NAUT, AERO Gangway f II. interj (fam) ~! Platz da!

gap [gæp] n Lücke f a. fig

gape [geɪp] vi glotzen

gaping ['geɪ·pɪŋ] adj weit geöffnet

garage [gə·'raʒ] n ➊ Garage f ➋ (repair shop) [Kfz-]Werkstatt f

ga'rage sale n privater Flohmarkt in der Garage

garbage ['gar·bɪdʒ] n Müll m a. fig

'garbage can n Mülleimer m

'garbage truck n Müllauto m

garble ['gar·bəl] vt durcheinanderbringen

garden ['gar·dən] n Garten m; ▪~s pl Gartenanlage f

gardener ['gard·nər] n Gärtner(in) m(f)

gardening ['gard·nɪŋ] *n* Gartenarbeit *f;* ~ **tools** Gartengeräte *pl*

gargle ['gar·gəl] *vi* gurgeln

garish ['ger·ɪʃ] *adj (pej)* knallbunt

garland ['gar·lənd] *n* Kranz *m*

garlic ['gar·lɪk] *n* Knoblauch *m*

garment ['gar·mənt] *n* Kleidungsstück *nt*

garnish ['gar·nɪʃ] *n <pl -es>* Garnierung *f*

garrison ['ger·ə·sən] *n* Garnison *f*

gas [gæs] I. *n <pl -es>* ❶ *(not solid or liquid)* Gas *nt;* **natural ~** Erdgas *nt* ❷ *(fam: gasoline)* Benzin *nt;* **to step on the ~** *(fig)* Gas geben II. *vt <-ss->* vergasen

'gasbag *n (pej sl)* Quasselstrippe *f*

gas chamber *n* Gaskammer *f*

gaseous ['gæs·i·əs] *adj* gasförmig

'gas gauge *n* Benzinuhr *f*

'gas guzzler *n (fam)* Benzinfresser *m fam*

gash [gæʃ] *n <pl -es>* [tiefe] Schnittwunde

'gas heating *n* [zentrale] Gasheizung *f*

'gas mask *n* Gasmaske *f*

'gas meter *n* Gaszähler *m*

gasoline ['gæs·ə·lin] *n* Benzin *nt*

'gas oven *n* Gasherd *m*

gasp [gæsp] I. *vi (pant)* keuchen; *(catch one's breath)* tief einatmen; **to ~ for air** nach Luft schnappen II. *vt* hervorstoßen

'gas pedal *n* Gaspedal *nt*

'gas pipe *n* Gasleitung *f*

'gas pump *n* Zapfsäule *f*

'gas station *n* Tankstelle *f*

'gas stove *n* Gasherd *m*

gastric ['gæs·trɪk] *adj* MED Magen-

gastronomy [gæ·'stran·ə·mi] *n* Gastronomie *f*

gate [geɪt] *n* ❶ *(at an entrance)* Tor *nt;* *(at an airport)* Flugsteig *m,* Gate *nt* ❷ SPORT **starting ~** Startmaschine *f*

'gatecrasher *n (fam)* un[ein]geladener Gast

'gateway *n* ❶ Eingangstor *nt* ❷ *(fig)* Tor *nt*

gather ['gæð·ər] I. *vt* ❶ *(collect)* sammeln; **to ~ intelligence** sich *dat*

[geheime] Informationen beschaffen ❷ FASHION kräuseln ❸ *(understand)* verstehen; ■**to ~ from sb that ...** von jdm erfahren haben, dass ... II. *vi* people sich versammeln

gathering ['gæð·ər·ɪŋ] *n* Versammlung *f*

gauche [gouʃ] *adj* unbeholfen

gaudy ['gɔ·di] *adj* knallig

gauge [geɪdʒ] I. *n* ❶ *(device)* Messgerät *nt;* *(for water level)* Pegel *m* ❷ *(thickness)* of metal Stärke *f;* *(diameter)* of a gun Durchmesser *m* II. *vt* ❶ *(measure)* messen ❷ *(estimate)* [ab]schätzen

gaunt [gɔnt] *adj* hager

gauntlet ['gɔnt·lɪt] *n* [Stulpen]handschuh *m* ▶PHRASES: **to throw down the ~** den Fehdehandschuh hinwerfen geh

gauze [gɔz] *n* Gaze *f*

gave [geɪv] *pt of* **give**

gavel ['gæv·əl] *n* Hammer *m*

gay [geɪ] *adj (homosexual)* schwul, gay; **~ bar** Schwulenlokal *nt*

gaze [geɪz] I. *vi* starren; **to ~ out of the window** aus dem Fenster starren II. *n* Blick *m*

gazette [gə·'zet] *n* Blatt *nt,* Anzeiger *m*

GB [ˌdʒiˑ'bi] *n <pl ->* ❶ *abbrev of* **gigabyte** GByte *nt* ❷ *abbrev of* **Great Britain** GB

GDP [ˌdʒiˑdiˑ'pi] *n abbrev of* **gross domestic product** BIP *nt*

gear [gɪr] I. *n* ❶ TECH Gang *m;* **to shift ~s** schalten ❷ *(equipment)* Ausrüstung *f* II. *vt* ausrichten *(to auf +akk)*

'gearbox *n* Getriebe *nt*

'gearshift *n* Schalthebel *m*

GED [ˌdʒiˑiˑ'di] *n abbrev of* **general equivalency diploma** ≈ SfE *f (Kurs zur Erlangung der US-Hochschulreife auf dem zweiten Bildungsweg)*

gee [dʒi] *interj (fam)* Mannomann

gel [dʒel] *n* Gel *nt*

gelatin, gelatine ['dʒel·ət·ɪn] *n* Gelatine *f*

gem [dʒem] *n* Edelstein *m*

G

Gemini ['dʒem·ɪ·naɪ] *n* ASTROL Zwillinge *pl;* **to be a ~** [ein] Zwilling sein

gen. [dʒen] *n* ❶ *short for* **general** allgem. ❷ *short for* **generation** Gen.

gender ['dʒen·dər] *n* Geschlecht *nt*

gene [dʒin] *n* Gen *nt*

genealogy [ˌdʒi·nɪ·'æl·ə·dʒi] *n* Genealogie *f*

'gene bank *n* Genbank *f*

general ['dʒen·ər·əl] **I.** *adj* allgemein; **~ idea** ungefähre Vorstellung; **~ impression** Gesamteindruck *m;* **~ meeting** Vollversammlung *f;* **it is ~ practice** es ist allgemein üblich; **in ~** [*or* **as a ~ rule**] im Allgemeinen **II.** *n* MIL General(in) *m(f)*

General A'merican *n* die amerikanische Standardsprache

general anes'thetic *n* Vollnarkose *f*

General As'sembly *n* [UNO-]Vollversammlung *f*

general de'livery *n* postlagernd

generality [ˌdʒen·ə·'ræl·ə·ti] *n* (*general statement*) **to talk in generalities** (*generalize*) verallgemeinern; **to talk about/of generalities** sich über Allgemeines unterhalten

generalization [ˌdʒen·ər·ə·lɪ·'zeɪ·ʃən] *n* Verallgemeinerung *f*

generalize ['dʒen·ər·ə·laɪz] *vt, vi* ■**to ~ [about sth]** [etw] verallgemeinern

generally ['dʒen·ər·ə·li] *adv* ❶ (*usually*) normalerweise ❷ (*mostly*) im Großen und Ganzen ❸ (*widely*) **~ speaking** im Allgemeinen

general prac'titioner *n* praktischer Arzt/praktische Ärztin

general 'public *n* **the ~** die Öffentlichkeit

general 'store *n* Gemischtwarenladen *m*

general 'strike *n* Generalstreik *m*

generate ['dʒen·ə·reɪt] *vt controversy* hervorrufen; *electricity* erzeugen

generation [ˌdʒen·ə·'reɪ·ʃən] *n* ❶ (*set*) Generation *f* ❷ (*production*) Erzeugung *f*

generator ['dʒen·ə·reɪ·tər] *n* Generator *m*

generic [dʒɪ·'ner·ɪk] *adj* ❶ (*general*) generisch; **~ term** Oberbegriff *m;* BIOL Gattungsbegriff *m* ❷ (*not name-brand*) *product* markenlos

generosity [ˌdʒen·ə·'ras·ə·ti] *n* Großzügigkeit *f*

generous ['dʒen·ər·əs] *adj person, tip* großzügig; *portion* groß

genesis <*pl* -ses> ['dʒen·ə·sɪs] *n usu sing* REL Genese *f;* **G~** das erste Buch Mose

gene 'therapy *n usu sing* Gentherapie *f*

genetic [dʒɪ·'net·ɪk] *adj* genetisch; **~ disease** Erbkrankheit *f*

genetically 'modified *adj* genmanipuliert

genetics [dʒɪ·'net·ɪks] *n* Genetik *f*

genial ['dʒi·ni·əl] *adj* freundlich

genie <*pl* -nii> ['dʒi·ni] *n* Geist *m*

genitalia [dʒen·ɪ·'teɪ·li·ə] *npl* (*form*), **genitals** ['dʒen·ə·təlz] *npl* Geschlechtsorgane *pl*

genitive ['dʒen·ɪ·tɪv] *n* Genitiv *m*

genius <*pl* -es> ['dʒin·jəs] *n* ❶ (*person*) Genie *nt* ❷ (*intelligence, talent*) Genialität *f*

genocide ['dʒen·ə·saɪd] *n* Völkermord *m*

gent [dʒent] *n* (*hum fam*) *short for* **gentleman** Gentleman *m*

gentian ['dʒen·tiən] *n* Enzian *m*

gentile ['dʒen·taɪl] *n* Nichtjude *m*, Nichtjüdin *f*

gentle ['dʒen·təl] *adj* sanft; *slope* leicht; **~ exercise** leichte sportliche Betätigung

gentleman ['dʒen·təl·mən] *n* Gentleman *m;* **a perfect ~** ein wahrer Gentleman

gentleness ['dʒen·təl·nɪs] *n* Sanftheit *f*

genuine ['dʒen·ju·ɪn] *adj* ❶ (*not fake*) echt ❷ (*sincere*) ehrlich

genus <*pl* -nera> ['dʒi·nəs] *n* BIOL Gattung *f*

geography [dʒi·'ag·rə·fi] *n* Erdkunde *f*

geologist [dʒi·'al·ə·dʒɪst] *n* Geologe, -in *m, f*

geology [dʒi·'al·ə·dʒi] *n* Geologie *f*

geometric(al) [ˌdʒiˑəˈmetˑrɪk(əl)] *adj* geometrisch

geometry [dʒiˈamˑəˑtri] *n* Geometrie *f*

geophysics [ˌdʒiˑouˈfɪzˑɪks] *n* Geophysik *f*

Georgia [ˈdʒɔrˑdʒə] *n* Georgia *nt*

geranium [dʒiˈreɪˑniˑəm] *n* Geranie *f*

geriatric [ˌdʒerˑiˈætˑrɪk] *adj* geriatrisch

geriatrics [ˌdʒerˑiˈætˑrɪks] *n + sing vb* Altersheilkunde *f*

germ [dʒɜrm] *n* MED, BIOL Keim *m*

German [ˈdʒɜrˑmən] **I.** *n* ⓵ (*person*) Deutsche(r) *f(m)* ⓶ (*language*) Deutsch *nt* **II.** *adj* deutsch

German 'measles *n + sing vb* Röteln *pl*

German 'shepherd *n* (*dog*) Schäferhund *m*

Germany [ˈdʒɜrˑməˑni] *n* Deutschland *nt*

'germ-free *adj* keimfrei

germicide [ˈdʒɜrˑməˑsaɪd] *n* keimtötendes Mittel

germinate [ˈdʒɜrˑməˑneɪt] *vi* keimen

germination [ˌdʒɜrˑməˈneɪˑʃən] *n* Keimen *nt*

germ 'warfare *n* Bakterienkrieg *m*

gerrymander [ˈdʒerˑəˌmænˑdər] *vi* POL die Wahlbezirksgrenzen manipulieren

gesticulate [dʒeˈstɪkˑjəˑleɪt] *vi* (*form*) gestikulieren

gesture [ˈdʒesˑtʃər] **I.** *n* Geste *f* **II.** *vt*, *vi* deuten

get <got, got *or* gotten> [get] **I.** *vt* ⓵ (*obtain*) erhalten; **to ~ time off** frei bekommen; **where did you ~ your cell phone?** woher hast du dein Handy? ⓶ (*receive*) bekommen ⓷ (*experience*) erleben; **to ~ a surprise** überrascht sein ⓸ (*deliver*) **to ~ sth to sb** jdm etw bringen ⓹ (*go and obtain*) **to ~ [sb] sth** [*or* **sth for sb**] jdm etw besorgen ⓺ TRANSP (*travel with*) plane, taxi nehmen; (*catch*) erwischen ⓻ + *pp* (*cause to be*) **to ~ sth confused** etw verwechseln ⓼ (*induce*) **to ~ sb/sth to do sth** jdn/etw dazu bringen, etw zu tun ⓽ (*hear, understand*) verstehen; **to ~ the message** [es] kapieren ⓾ (*prepare*) meal zubereiten **II.** *vi* ⓵ (*become*) werden; **I got cold** mir wurde

kalt; **~ well soon!** gute Besserung!; **to ~ used to sth** sich an etw *akk* gewöhnen; **to ~ married** heiraten ⓶ (*reach*) kommen ⓷ (*must*) ▪ **to have got to do sth** etw machen müssen

◆ **get across** *vt* verständlich machen

◆ **get along** *vi* ⓵ (*be friends*) sich verstehen ⓶ (*continue*) ▪ **to ~ along with sth** *job, project* weitermachen

◆ **get around I.** *vi* ⓵ ▪ **to ~ around to** [**doing**] **sth** es schaffen, etw zu tun ⓶ *news* sich verbreiten **II.** *vt* ⓵ (*evade*) umgehen ⓶ (*deal with*) angehen

◆ **get at** *vi* ⓵ (*reach*) rankommen ⓶ (*fam: suggest*) ▪ **to ~ at sth** auf etw *akk* hinauswollen ⓷ (*discover*) ▪ **to ~ at sth** etw aufdecken

◆ **get away** *vi* ⓵ (*leave*) wegkommen ⓶ (*escape*) ▪ **to ~ away** [**from sth/sb**] jdm/etw entkommen ⓷ (*avoid punishment*) ▪ **to ~ away with sth** mit etw *dat* ungestraft davonkommen

◆ **get back I.** *vt* (*actively*) zurückholen; *strength* zurückgewinnen; (*passively*) zurückbekommen **II.** *vi* ⓵ (*return*) zurückkommen ⓶ ▪ **to ~ back to** [**doing**] **sth** zu etw *dat* wieder zurückgehen; **to ~ back to sleep** wieder einschlafen

◆ **get behind** *vi* ⓵ (*support*) unterstützen ⓶ (*be slow*) in Rückstand geraten

◆ **get by** *vi* ▪ **to ~ by** [**on/with sth**] mit etw *dat* auskommen

◆ **get down I.** *vt* (*remove*) runternehmen (**from/off** von + *dat*) **II.** *vi* ⓵ (*descend*) herunterkommen (**from/off** von + *dat*) ⓶ (*bend down*) sich runterbeugen ⓷ (*start*) ▪ **to ~ down to** [**doing**] **sth** sich an etw *akk* machen

◆ **get in I.** *vt* ⓵ (*say*) *word* einwerfen ⓶ (*bring inside*) hereinholen **II.** *vi* ⓵ (*arrive*) ankommen ⓶ (*return*) zurückkehren ⓷ (*become elected*) an die Macht kommen

◆ **get into I.** *vi* ⓵ (*enter*) [ein]steigen in + *akk* ⓶ (*have interest for*) sich interessieren für **II.** *vt* *argument* verwickelt werden in + *akk*

◆ **get off I.** *vi* ⓵ (*exit*) *bus, train* aussteigen ⓶ (*dismount*) absteigen

G

❸ (*evade punishment*) davonkommen
II. *vt* **❶** (*remove*) nehmen von; **to ~ sb off sth** *bus, train, plane* herausbringen aus; *boat, roof* herunterholen von **❷** LAW freibekommen **❸** (*send to sleep*) [los]schicken; **to ~ sb off to sleep** jdn in den Schlaf wiegen

◆get on I. *vt* **❶** (*put on*) anziehen; *lid* drauftun **II.** *vi* **❶** (*be friends*) sich verstehen **❷** (*continue*) weitermachen **❸** (*age*) alt werden; **to be ~ting on [in years]** an Jahren zunehmen

◆get out I. *vi secret* herauskommen; *news* durchsickern **II.** *vt* **❶** (*bring out*) rausbringen (**of** aus +*dat*) **❷** (*remove*) herausbekommen

◆get over I. *vi* **❶** ■**to ~ over sb/sth** über jdn/etw hinwegkommen; *illness* sich erholen von **❷** ■**to ~ sth over [with]** etw hinter sich *akk* bringen **II.** *vt idea* rüberbringen

◆get through I. *vi* **❶** (*make oneself understood*) ■**to ~ through to sb that/how ...** jdm klarmachen, dass/wie ... **❷** (*contact*) ■**to ~ through to sb** *on the phone* zu jdm durchkommen **II.** *vt* **❶** (*use up*) aufbrauchen **❷** (*finish*) *work* erledigen

◆get together *vi* sich treffen

◆get up I. *vt* **❶** (*climb*) hinaufsteigen **❷** (*fam: wake*) wecken **II.** *vi* **❶** (*get out of bed*) aufstehen **❷** (*stand up*) sich erheben

'**getaway** *n* (*fam*) Flucht *f*
'**get-together** *n* (*fam*) Treffen *nt*
'**getup** *n* (*fam: outfit*) Kluft *f*
geyser ['gaɪ·zər] *n* Geysir *m*
gherkin ['gɜr·kɪn] *n* Essiggurke *f*
ghetto <*pl* -s> ['geṭ·oʊ] *n* G[h]etto *nt*
ghost [goʊst] *n* Geist *m*
ghostly ['goʊst·li] *adj* geisterhaft
'**ghost town** *n* Geisterstadt *f*
'**ghostwriter** *n* Ghostwriter *m*
G'I *n* (*fam: soldier*) GI *m*
giant ['dʒaɪ·ənt] **I.** *n* Riese *m* a. *fig* **II.** *adj* riesig
gibber ['dʒɪb·ər] *vi* stammeln
gibe [dʒaɪb] **I.** *n* Stichelei *f* **II.** *vi* ■**to ~ at sb/sth** über jdn/etw spötteln

giddy ['gɪd·i] *adj* schwind(e)lig
gift [gɪft] *n* **❶** (*present*) Geschenk *nt* a. *fig* **❷** (*talent*) Talent *nt*; **to have a ~ for languages** sprachbegabt sein
'**gift certificate** *n* Geschenkgutschein *m*
gifted ['gɪf·tɪd] *adj* begabt
'**gift shop** *n* Geschenkartikelladen *m*
gig [gɪg] *n* Gig *m*
gigabyte ['gɪg·ə·baɪt] *n* COMPUT Gigabyte *nt*
gigantic [dʒaɪ·'gæn·tɪk] *adj* gigantisch
giggle ['gɪg·əl] *vi* kichern (**at** über +*akk*)
gilt [gɪlt] *adj* vergoldet
gimmick ['gɪm·ɪk] *n* (*esp pej*) Trick *m*; **advertising ~** Werbetrick *m*
gin [dʒɪn] *n* (*drink*) Gin *m*
ginger ['dʒɪn·dʒər] **I.** *n* Ingwer *m* **II.** *adj* gelblich braun
'**gingerbread** *n* Lebkuchen *m*
gingerly ['dʒɪn·dʒər·li] *adv* behutsam
Gipsy *n see* **Gypsy**
giraffe <*pl* -s> [dʒə·'ræf] *n* Giraffe *f*
girder ['gɜr·dər] *n* Träger *m*
girdle ['gɜr·dəl] *n* (*corset*) Korsett *nt*
girl [gɜrl] *n* Mädchen *nt*
'**girlfriend** *n* Freundin *f*
'**Girl Scout** *n* Pfadfinderin *f*
girth [gɜrθ] *n* Umfang *m*
gist [dʒɪst] *n* **to get the ~ of sth** den Sinn von etw *dat* verstehen
give [gɪv] **I.** *vt* <gave, given> **❶** ■**to ~ sb sth** jdm etw geben; (*as present*) jdm etw schenken; (*donate*) jdm etw spenden; **to ~ sb a cold** jdn mit seiner Erkältung anstecken; **to ~ sb his/her due** jdm Ehre erweisen; **to ~ a speech** eine Rede halten; **to ~ sb/sth a bad name** jdn/etw in Verruf bringen; **to ~ sb the news** [*or* about] **sth** jdm etw mitteilen; **don't ~ me that!** (*fig*) komm mir doch nicht damit!; **~ her my best wishes** grüß' sie schön von mir! **❷** (*emit*) **to ~ a cry** aufschreien **❸** (*produce*) *result, number* ergeben; *warmth* spenden **II.** *vi* <gave, given> **❶** (*donate*) spenden (**to** für +*akk*); **to ~ and take** [gegenseitige] Kompromisse machen **❷** (*bend, yield*) nachgeben;

rope reißen ▶PHRASES: **to ~ as good as one gets** Gleiches mit Gleichem vergelten III. *n* Nachgiebigkeit *f*; (*elasticity*) Elastizität *f*

◆**give away** *vt* ❶ (*offer for free*) verschenken ❷ (*betray*) *secret* verraten; ■**to ~ oneself away** sich verraten

◆**give back** *vt* zurückgeben (**to** +*dat*)

◆**give in** *vi* ❶ (*to pressure*) nachgeben (**to** +*dat*); **to ~ in to temptation** der Versuchung erliegen ❷ (*surrender*) aufgeben

◆**give off** *vt* abgeben; *smell, smoke* ausströmen

◆**give out** I. *vi* ❶ (*run out*) ausgehen; *energy* zu Ende gehen ❷ (*stop working*) versagen II. *vt* ❶ (*distribute*) verteilen (**to** an +*akk*); *books* austeilen ❷ (*emit*) von sich *dat* geben

◆**give over** *vt* übergeben

◆**give up** I. *vi* aufgeben II. *vt* ❶ (*quit*) aufgeben; *habit* ablegen; ■**to ~ up doing sth** mit etw *dat* aufhören ❷ (*surrender*) *territory* abtreten; **to ~ oneself up** [**to the police**] sich *akk* [der Polizei] stellen

give-and-'take *n* Geben und Nehmen *nt*

'giveaway I. *n* Werbegeschenk *nt* II. *adj* ~ **price** Schleuderpreis *m*

given ['gɪv·ən] I. *n* gegebene Tatsache; **to take sth as a ~** etw als gegeben annehmen II. *adj* ❶ (*certain*) gegeben ❷ (*specified*) festgelegt III. *prep* ~ **sth** angesichts einer S. *gen* IV. *pp of* **give**

'given name *n* Vorname *m*

giver ['gɪv·ər] *n* Spender(in) *m(f)*

glacier ['gleɪ·ʃər] *n* Gletscher *m*

glad <-dd-> [glæd] *adj* froh; **to be ~ about sth** sich über etw *akk* freuen

gladiator ['glæd·i·eɪ·tər] *n* Gladiator *m*

gladly ['glæd·li] *adv* gerne

gladness ['glæd·nɪs] *n* Freude *f*

'glad rags *npl* (*hum*) Festkleidung *f*

glamor ['glæm·ər] *n see* **glamour**

glamorize ['glæm·ə·raɪz] *vt* verherrlichen

glamorous ['glæm·ə·rəs] *adj* glamourös

glamour ['glæm·ər] *n* Glanz *m*

glance [glæns] I. *n* Blick *m*; **at first ~** auf den ersten Blick II. *vi* ■**to ~ at sth** auf etw *akk* schauen

◆**glance off** *vi* abprallen

gland [glænd] *n* Drüse *f*

glare [gler] I. *n* ❶ (*stare*) wütender Blick ❷ (*light*) grelles Licht II. *vi* (*stare*) ■**to ~ [at sb]** [jdn an]starren

glaring ['gler·ɪŋ] *adj* ❶ (*staring*) stechend ❷ (*blinding*) blendend; *light* grell ❸ (*obvious*) *mistake* eklatant

glass [glæs] *n* ❶ Glas *nt* ❷ *pl* (*spectacles*) [**a pair of**] **~es** [eine] Brille *f*

'glassful *n* Glas *nt* voll

'glassware *n* Glaswaren *pl*

glassy ['glæs·i] *adj eyes* glasig

glaze [gleɪz] I. *n* (*on food, pottery*) Glasur *f* II. *vt* ❶ *food, pottery* glasieren ❷ (*fit with glass*) verglasen

gleam [glim] I. *n* Schimmer *m* II. *vi* schimmern

gleaming ['glim·ɪŋ] *adj* glänzend

glee [gli] *n* Entzücken *nt*; (*gloating joy*) Schadenfreude *f*

glen [glen] *n* Schlucht *f*

glib <-bb-> [glɪb] *adj person* zungenfertig; *answer* unbedacht

glide [glaɪd] *vi* ❶ (*move smoothly*) hingleiten ❷ (*fly*) gleiten

glider ['glaɪ·dər] *n* Segelflugzeug *nt*

gliding ['glaɪ·dɪŋ] *n* Segelfliegen *nt*

glimmer ['glɪm·ər] *vi* schimmern

glimpse [glɪmps] I. *vt* flüchtig sehen II. *n* [kurzer/flüchtiger] Blick

glint [glɪnt] *vi* glitzern

glisten ['glɪs·ən] *vi* glitzern

glitch [glɪtʃ] *n* (*fam: fault*) Fehler *m*; **computer ~** Computerstörung *f*

glitter ['glɪt·ər] *vi* glitzern; *eyes* funkeln ▶PHRASES: **all that ~s is not gold** (*prov*) es ist nicht alles Gold, was glänzt

glittering ['glɪt̬·ər·ɪŋ] *adj* ❶ (*sparkling*) glitzernd ❷ (*impressive*) *career* glanzvoll

glitz [glɪts] *n* Glanz *m*

glitzy ['glɪt·si] *adj* glanzvoll

gloat [gloʊt] *vi* sich hämisch freuen

global ['gloʊ·bəl] *adj* ❶ (*worldwide*) global; ~ **warming** globale Erwärmung

G

@ (*complete*) umfassend ▶PHRASES: **to go ~** (*fam*) auf den Weltmarkt vorstoßen

globalization [ˌgloʊ·bə·lɪ·ˈzeɪ·ʃən] *n* Globalisierung *f*

global 'warming *n* Erwärmung *f* der Erdatmosphäre

globe [gloʊb] *n* Globus *m*

'globetrotter *n* Globetrotter(in) *m(f)*, Weltbummler(in) *m(f)*

gloom [glum] *n* ❶ (*depression*) Hoffnungslosigkeit *f* ❷ (*darkness*) Düsterheit *f*; **to emerge from the ~** aus dem Dunkel auftauchen

gloomy [ˈglu·mi] *adj* ❶ (*dismal*) trostlos ❷ (*dark*) düster

glorify <-ie-> [ˈglɔr·ə·faɪ] *vt* verherrlichen

glorious [ˈglɔr·i·əs] *adj* ❶ *victory* glorreich ❷ *weather* herrlich

glory [ˈglɔr·i] *n* ❶ (*honor*) Ruhm *m* ❷ (*splendor*) Herrlichkeit *f*, Pracht *f*

gloss [glas] *n* ❶ (*shine*) Glanz *m*; **in ~ or matte** glänzend oder matt ❷ *see* **gloss paint**
 ◆ **gloss over** *vt* schönfärben

glossary [ˈglas·ə·ri] *n* Glossar *nt*

'gloss paint *n* Glanzlack *m*

glossy [ˈglas·i] **I.** *adj* glänzend; **~ magazine** Hochglanzmagazin *nt* **II.** *n* (*photo*) [Hoch]glanzabzug *m*

glove [glʌv] *n usu sing* Handschuh *m*; **to fit like a ~** wie angegossen passen

'glove box, 'glove compartment *n* AUTO Handschuhfach *nt*

glow [gloʊ] **I.** *n* Leuchten *nt*; *of a lamp* Scheinen *nt*; *of a cigarette* Glühen *nt*; **a healthy ~** eine gesunde Farbe **II.** *vi* ❶ (*shed light*) leuchten; *fire, light* scheinen ❷ (*be red and hot*) glühen ❸ (*fig: look radiant*) strahlen; **to ~ with health** vor Gesundheit strotzen

glower [ˈglaʊ·ər] *vi* verärgert aussehen; **to ~ at sb** jdn zornig anstarren

glowing [ˈgloʊ·ɪŋ] *adj* ❶ *candle* leuchtend; *cigarette* glühend ❷ *review* überschwänglich

'glowworm *n* Glühwürmchen *nt*

glucose [ˈglu·koʊs] *n* Traubenzucker *m*

glue [glu] **I.** *n* Klebstoff *m* **II.** *vt* ❶ kleben; ■**to ~ sth together** etw zusammenkleben ❷ (*fig*) ■**to be ~d to sth** an etw *dat* kleben; **to be ~d to the spot** wie angewurzelt dastehen

'glue sniffing *n* Schnüffeln *nt*

'glue stick *n* Klebestift *m*

glum <-mm-> [glʌm] *adj* niedergeschlagen

glut [glʌt] *n* Überangebot *nt*

gluten [ˈglu·tən] *n* Gluten *nt*

glutton [ˈglʌt·ən] *n* (*pej*) Vielfraß *m*

gnarled [narld] *adj* *branch* knorrig, *finger* knotig

gnash [næʃ] *vt* **to ~ one's teeth** mit den Zähnen knirschen

gnat [næt] *n* [Stech]mücke *f*

gnaw [nɔ] *vi* nagen *a. fig* (**on/at/away at** an +*dat*)

gnawing [ˈnɔ·ɪŋ] *adj* nagend

gnome [noʊm] *n* Gnom *m*; [*garden*] ~ Gartenzwerg *m*

GNP [ˌdʒi·en·ˈpi] *n abbrev of* **Gross National Product** BSP *nt*

go [goʊ] **I.** *vi* <goes, went, gone> ❶ (*proceed*) gehen; *vehicle, train* fahren; *plane* fliegen; **we have a long way to ~** wir haben noch einen weiten Weg vor uns; ■**to ~ toward[s] sb/sth** auf jdn/etw zugehen; **to ~ home** nach Hause gehen; **to ~ to the hospital/a party/prison/the bathroom** ins Krankenhaus/auf eine Party/ins Gefängnis/ auf die Toilette gehen ❷ (*travel*) reisen; **to ~ on vacation** in Urlaub gehen; **to ~ to Italy** nach Italien fahren; **to ~ on a trip** verreisen, eine Reise machen; **to ~ abroad** ins Ausland gehen ❸ (*disappear*) verschwinden; **where did my keys go?** wo sind meine Schlüssel hin?; **my toothache's gone!** meine Zahnschmerzen sind weg!; **half of my salary ~es on rent** die Hälfte meines Gehaltes geht für die Miete drauf; **there ~es another one!** und wieder eine/einer weniger! ❹ (*leave*) gehen; **let's ~!** los jetzt! ❺ (*do*) **to ~ swimming etc.** schwimmen etc. gehen; **to ~ looking for sb/sth** jdn/etw suchen gehen ❻ (*attend*) **to ~ to church** in die Kir-

G

che gehen; **to ~ to school** in die Schule gehen **❼** + *adj* (*become*) werden; **to ~ bankrupt** bankrottgehen; (*out of control*) außer Kontrolle geraten; (*malfunction*) verrücktspielen; **to ~ public** an die Öffentlichkeit treten; STOCKEX an die Börse gehen; **to ~ to sleep** einschlafen **❽** + *adj* (*be*) sein; **to ~ hungry** hungern; **to ~ unnoticed** unbemerkt bleiben **❾** (*turn out*) gehen, und, wie läuft's?; **to ~ according to plan** nach Plan laufen; **to ~ wrong** schieflaufen **❿** (*pass*) vergehen; **only two days to ~ ...** nur noch zwei Tage ... **⓫** (*fail*) kaputtgehen; *hearing, memory* nachlassen; *rope* reißen **⓬** (*die*) sterben **⓭** (*belong*) hingehören; **the silverware ~es in this drawer** das Besteck gehört in diese Schublade **⓮** (*lead*) *path, road* führen **⓯** (*extend*) gehen; **the meadow ~es all the way down to the stream** die Weide erstreckt sich bis hinunter zum Bach **⓰** (*function*) *business* laufen; **to get/keep sth ~ing** etw in Gang bringen/halten; **to keep a conversation ~ing** eine Unterhaltung am Laufen halten **⓱** (*have recourse*) gehen; **to ~ to war** in den Krieg ziehen **⓲** (*match, be compatible*) ■ **to ~ together** [*or* with sth] zu etw passen; **these two colors don't ~ together** [at all] diese beiden Farben beißen sich ▸PHRASES: **there you ~** bitte schön!; **that ~es without saying** das versteht sich von selbst II. *aux vb future tense* ■ **to be ~ing to do sth** etw tun werden; **we are ~ing to have a party tomorrow** wir geben morgen eine Party III. *vt* <goes, went, gone> **❶** (*travel*) *route* nehmen **❷** (*fam: say*) **she ~es to me: I never want to see you again!** sie sagt zu mir: ich will dich nie wiedersehen! IV. *vt* <*pl* -es> **❶** (*turn*) **can I have a ~?** darf ich mal? **❷** (*attempt*) Versuch *m*; **in one ~** auf einen Schlag **❸** (*energy*) Antrieb *m* ▸PHRASES: **from the word ~** von Anfang an; **to make a ~ of sth** mit etw *dat* Erfolg haben

◆**go about** *vt* **to ~ about one's business** seinen Geschäften nachgehen

◆**go after** *vi* **❶** (*in succession*) ■ **to ~ after sb/sth** nach jdm/etw gehen **❷** (*chase*) etw verfolgen

◆**go against** *vi* **❶** (*be negative for*) ■ **to ~ against sb** zu jds Ungunsten *pl* ausgehen **❷** (*contradict*) **that ~es against everything I believe in** das geht gegen all das, woran ich glaube

◆**go ahead** *vi* **❶** (*go before*) vorgehen; (*in vehicle*) vorausfahren **❷** (*proceed*) vorangehen; *event* stattfinden; ■ **to ~ ahead with sth** etw durchführen

◆**go along** *vi* **❶** (*on foot*) entlanggehen; (*in vehicle*) entlangfahren **❷** (*accompany*) mitgehen [*o* mitkommen] **❸** (*agree*) ■ **to ~ along with sth/sb** etw/jdm zustimmen; (*join in*) sich etw/jdm anschließen

◆**go around** *vi* **❶** (*travel around*) **they went around Europe for two months** sie reisten zwei Monate lang durch Europa **❷** (*visit*) ■ **to ~ around and see sb** [*or* to sb's house] bei jdm vorbeischauen **❸** (*be in circulation*) *rumor* [he]rumgehen **❹** (*move in a curve*) herumgehen um +*akk*; **to ~ around the world** eine Weltreise machen ▸PHRASES: **what ~es around, comes around** (*saying*) alles rächt sich früher oder später

◆**go at** *vi* **❶** (*attack*) ■ **to ~ at sb** [with sth] auf jdn [mit etw *dat*] losgehen **❷** (*work hard*) ■ **to ~ at sth** sich an etw *akk* machen; **to ~ at it** loslegen

◆**go away** *vi* **❶** (*travel*) weggehen; (*for vacation*) wegfahren **❷** (*leave*) [weg]gehen **❸** (*disappear*) verschwinden

◆**go back** *vi* **❶** (*return*) zurückgehen; *school* wieder anfangen; ■ **to ~ back to sb** zu jdm zurückkehren; **to ~ back to the beginning** noch mal von vorne anfangen; **to ~ back to normal** sich wieder normalisieren **❷** (*not fulfill*) **to ~ back on one's promise** sein Versprechen nicht halten

◆**go beyond** *vi* ■ **to ~ beyond sth** **❶** (*proceed past*) an etw *dat* vorüber-

G

gehen ② (*exceed*) über etw *akk* hinausgehen

♦ **go by** *vi* ① (*move past*) vorbeigehen;
vehicle vorbeifahren ② (*of time*) vergehen ③ (*be guided by*) ■**to ~ by sth**
nach etw *dat* gehen; **to ~ by the book**
sich an die Vorschriften halten

♦ **go down** *vi* ① (*move downward*) hi-
nuntergehen; *sun* untergehen; *ship a.*
sinken; *plane* abstürzen; **to ~ down on
all fours** sich auf alle viere begeben
② (*decrease*) *attendance, wind* nachlassen; *water level* zurückgehen; *prices*
sinken ③ (*break down*) *computer* ausfallen ④ (*be defeated*) verlieren (**to** gegen +*akk*); (*sport etc.*) unterliegen
⑤ (*on foot*) entlanggehen; (*in vehicle*)
entlangfahren; **she was ~ing down
the road on her bike** sie fuhr auf
ihrem Fahrrad die Straße entlang; **to ~
down a list** eine Liste [von oben nach
unten] durchgehen ⑥ (*extend*) hinunterreichen

♦ **go for** *vi* ① (*fetch*) holen; **to ~ for a
newspaper** eine Zeitung holen gehen
② (*try to achieve*) **~ for it!** nichts wie
ran! ③ (*attack*) **to ~ for the jugular**
(*fig*) an die Gurgel springen *fam*
④ (*fam: like*) ■**to ~ for sth/sb** auf
etw/jdn stehen

♦ **go in** *vi* ① (*enter*) hineingehen
② (*fit*) hineinpassen

♦ **go into** *vi* ① gehen in +*akk;* **to ~ into
action** in Aktion treten; **to ~ into reverse** in den Rückwärtsgang schalten
② (*examine*) ■**to ~ into sth** etw erörtern; **to ~ into detail** ins Detail gehen
③ (*join*) **to ~ into the Army** zur Armee gehen; **to ~ into the hospital** ins
Krankenhaus gehen

♦ **go off** *vi* ① (*stop working*) *lights* ausgehen; *electricity* ausfallen ② (*ring*)
alarm clock klingeln ③ (*detonate*)
bomb hochgehen; *gun* losgehen ④ (*diverge*) abgehen; **to ~ off the subject**
vom Thema abschweifen

♦ **go on** *vi* ① (*go further*) weitergehen;
vehicle weiterfahren; **to ~ on ahead**
vorausgehen; *vehicle* vorausfahren

② (*extend*) sich erstrecken; *time* voranschreiten ③ (*continue*) weitermachen;
fighting anhalten; ■**to ~ on with sth**
mit etw *dat* fortfahren; **I can't ~ on** ich
kann nicht mehr ④ (*continue speaking*)
weiterreden; **sorry, please ~ on** Entschuldigung, bitte fahren Sie fort; **he
went on to say that ...** dann sagte er,
dass ... ⑤ (*happen*) passieren; **what's
~ing on here?** was geht denn hier vor?
⑥ (*move on, proceed*) **he went on to
become a teacher** später wurde er
Lehrer ⑦ *lights* angehen ⑧ (*as encouragement*) **~ on!** los, mach schon!;
~ on, tell me! jetzt sag' schon!
⑨ (*start, embark on*) anfangen; **to ~ on
a diet** auf Diät gehen; **to ~ on welfare**
stempeln gehen ⑩ (*belong on*) gehören
auf +*akk*

♦ **go out** *vi* ① (*leave home*) [hinaus]ge-
hen; **to ~ out to work** arbeiten gehen;
to ~ out jogging joggen gehen
② (*enjoy social life*) ausgehen; **to ~ out
to eat** essen gehen ③ (*date*) **to ~ out
with sb** mit jdm gehen ④ *fire* ausgehen; *light a.* ausfallen ⑤ *tide* zurückgehen ⑥ (*become unfashionable*) aus der
Mode kommen ▶PHRASES: **to ~ all out**
sich ins Zeug legen

♦ **go over** *vi* ① (*cross*) hinübergehen;
(*in vehicle*) hinüberfahren; *river, street*
überqueren ② (*fig: change*) ■**to ~ over
to sth** zu etw *dat* übergehen; POL zu
etw *dat* überwechseln ③ (*examine*)
durchgehen; *apartment* durchsuchen
④ (*exceed*) überschreiten; **to ~ over a
time limit** überziehen ⑤ (*be received*)
to [not] ~ over well [with sb] [nicht]
gut ankommen [bei jdm]

♦ **go through** *vi* ① (*pass in and out of*)
durchgehen; *vehicle* durchfahren ② (*experience*) durchmachen ③ (*use up*)
aufbrauchen ④ *plan* durchgehen; *divorce* durchkommen; *business deal*
[erfolgreich] abgeschlossen werden
⑤ (*carry out*) ■**to ~ through with sth**
durchziehen; **he has to ~ through
with it now** jetzt gibt es kein Zurück
mehr für ihn

◆**go together** *vi* zusammenpassen

◆**go under** *vi* ❶(*sink*) untergehen ❷*person* scheitern; *business* eingehen ❸(*move below*) ■**to ~ under sth** unter etw *akk* druntergehen

◆**go up** *vi* ❶(*move higher*) hinaufgehen; *curtain* hochgehen; *balloon* aufsteigen ❷(*increase*) steigen; **everything is ~ing up!** alles wird teurer! ❸(*approach*) ■**to ~ up to sb/sth** auf jdn/etw zugehen ❹(*move as far as*) ■**to ~ up to sth** [bis] zu etw *dat* hingehen ❺(*ascend*) *mountain, street* ansteigen

◆**go with** *vt* ❶(*accompany*) ■**to ~ with sb** mit jdm mitgehen ❷(*date*) ■**to ~ with sb** mit jdm gehen ❸(*harmonize*) passen zu

◆**go without** *vi* ■**to ~ without sth** ohne etw auskommen

goad [goʊd] *vt* (*provoke*) ■**to ~ sb into [doing] sth** jdn dazu anstacheln, etw zu tun

go-ahead ['goʊ·ə·hed] *n* Erlaubnis *f;* **to give the ~** grünes Licht geben

goal [goʊl] *n* ❶(*aim*) Ziel *nt* ❷SPORT Tor *nt*

goalie ['goʊ·li] *n* (*fam*), **'goalkeeper** ['goʊl·ˌki·pər] *n* Tormann, -frau *m, f*

'**goal line** *n* Torlinie *f*

'**goalpost** *n* Torpfosten *m*

goat [goʊt] *n* Ziege *f*

goatee [goʊ·'ti] *n* Spitzbart *m*

gobble ['gab·əl] *vt* (*fam*) [hinunter]schlingen

gobbledegook ['gab·əl·di·ˌguk], **gobbledygook** *n* (*pej fam*) Kauderwelsch *nt*

go-between ['goʊ·bə·ˌtwin] *n* Vermittler(in) *m(f)*

'**go-cart** *n* Gokart *m*

god [gad] *n* Gott *m*

God [gad] *n* Gott *m;* **to believe in ~** an Gott glauben; **my ~!** mein Gott!; **thank ~!** Gott sei Dank!

god-'awful *adj* (*fam*) beschissen

'**goddamn** (*vulg*) **I.** *adj* (*emphasizing annoyance*) gottverdammt **II.** *interj* verdammt

'**goddaughter** *n* Patentochter *f*

goddess <*pl* -es> ['gad·ɪs] *n* Göttin *f;* **screen ~** [Film]diva *f*

'**godfather** *n* (*male godparent*) Patenonkel *m; a. Mafia leader* Pate *m*

godlike ['gad·laɪk] *adj* göttlich

'**godmother** *n* Patentante *f,* Patin *f*

'**godsend** *n* (*fam*) Gottesgeschenk *nt*

'**godson** *n* Patensohn *m*

goer ['goʊ·ər] *n* (*fam: person or thing that goes*) Geher *m*

goes [goʊz] *3rd pers. sing of* **go**

go-getter [ˌgoʊ·'get·ər] *n* Tatmensch *m*

goggle ['gag·əl] **I.** *vi* (*fam*) glotzen; ■**to ~ at sb/sth** jdn/etw anglotzen **II.** *n* [a **pair of**] **~s** [eine] [Schutz]brille; **ski ~s** Skibrille *f;* **swimming ~s** Schwimmbrille *f*

going ['goʊ·ɪŋ] **I.** *n* ❶(*act of leaving*) Gehen *nt* ❷(*departure*) Weggang *m* ❸(*conditions*) **rough ~** ungünstige Bedingungen; **while the ~ is good** solange es gut läuft **II.** *adj* ❶(*current*) aktuell; **what's the ~ rate for baby-sitters nowadays?** wie viel zahlt man heutzutage üblicherweise für einen Babysitter? ❷(*in action*) am Laufen; **~ concern** gutgehendes Unternehmen

going-'over <*pl* goings-over> *n* **to give sth a [good] ~** (*search thoroughly*) etw gründlich durchsuchen; (*clean thoroughly*) etw gründlich reinigen

gold [goʊld] *n* Gold *nt* ▶PHRASES: [as] **good as ~** mustergültig

'**gold dust** *n* Goldstaub *m*

golden ['goʊl·dən] *adj* golden *a. fig;* **~ brown** goldbraun

'**goldfish** *n* Goldfisch *m*

gold 'leaf *n* Blattgold *nt*

gold 'medal *n* Goldmedaille *f*

'**gold mine** *n* Goldmine *f;* (*fig*) Goldgrube *f*

gold 'plating *n* Vergoldung *f*

'**goldsmith** *n* Goldschmied(in) *m(f)*

golf [galf] *n* Golf *nt*

'**golf ball** *n* Golfball *m*

'golf club n ❶ (*implement*) Golfschläger m ❷ (*association*) Golfclub m

'golf course n Golfplatz m

golfer ['gɑl·fər] n Golfer(in) m(f)

gondola ['gɑn·də·lə] n Gondel f

gone [gɔn] I. *pp* of **go** II. *adj* (*no longer there*) weg; (*used up*) verbraucht

goner ['gɔ·nər] n (*fam*) **to be a** ~ (*be bound to die*) es nicht mehr lange machen; (*be irreparable*) hoffnungslos kaputt sein

gong [gaŋ] n Gong m

gonna ['gɑn·ə] (*sl*) **what you** ~ **do about it?** was willst du dagegen machen?

gonorrhea [ˌgɑn·ə·ˈri·ə] n Tripper m

goo [gu] n (*fam*) Schmiere f

good [gʊd] I. *adj* <better, best> ❶ gut; *weather* schön; (*healthy*) *appetite* gesund; **have a** ~ **day!** schönen Tag noch!; **to have a** ~ **time** [viel] Spaß haben; **it's** ~ **to see you again** schön, dich wiederzusehen; ~ **dog!** braver Hund!; **to do a** ~ **job** gute Arbeit leisten; ~ **luck!** viel Glück!; ~ **sense** Geistesgegenwart f; **in** ~ **time** rechtzeitig; ■**to be** ~ **at sth** gut in etw *dat* sein; **he's a** ~ **runner** er ist ein guter Läufer; **he's not very** ~ **at math** er ist nicht besonders gut in Mathe; **to be** ~ **for nothing** zu nichts taugen; **sb looks** ~ **in sth** etw steht jdm; **too** ~ **to be true** zu schön, um wahr zu sein ❷ (*kind, understanding*) **it was very** ~ **of you to help us** es war sehr lieb von dir, uns zu helfen ❸ (*thorough*) gut; **to have a** ~ **laugh** ordentlich lachen; **to have a** ~ **look at sth** sich *dat* etw genau ansehen ❹ (*substantial*) beträchtlich; **to make** ~ **money** gutes Geld verdienen; **a** ~ **deal of ...** jede Menge ... ❺ (*able to provide*) **he is always** ~ **for a laugh** er ist immer gut für einen Witz ▶PHRASES: **it's as** ~ **as it gets** besser wird's nicht mehr II. *n* ❶ (*moral force*) Gute *nt* ❷ (*benefit*) Wohl *nt;* **this will do you a world of** ~ das wird Ihnen unglaublich guttun; **to do more harm than** ~ mehr schaden als nützen; **for one's own** ~ zu seinem eigenen Besten ❸ (*ability*) ■**to be no** ~ **at sth** etw nicht gut können

goodbye [ɡʊ(d)·ˈbaɪ], **good-by** *interj* auf Wiedersehen; **to say** ~ **to sb/sth** sich von jdm/etw verabschieden; **to kiss sb** ~ jdm einen Abschiedskuss geben; **to kiss sth** ~ (*fig*) etw abschreiben

'good-for-nothing I. n (*pej*) Taugenichts m II. *adj* (*pej*) nichtsnutzig

Good 'Friday n *no art* Karfreitag m

good-humored [ˌɡʊd·ˈhju·mərd] *adj* fröhlich

good-'looking *adj* <more ~, most ~ *or* better-looking, best-looking> gut aussehend

good 'looks *npl* gutes Aussehen

good-'natured *adj* gutmütig

goodness ['ɡʊd·nɪs] n ❶ Güte f ❷ (*for emphasis*) **for ~' sake** du liebe Güte

goods [ɡʊdz] *npl* Waren *pl,* Güter *pl;* **sporting** ~ Sportartikel *pl;* **manufactured** ~ Fertigprodukte *pl*

'good-sized *adj* [recht] groß

'goodwill n ❶ guter Wille (**towards** gegenüber +*dat*); **feeling of** ~ Atmosphäre f des guten Willens ❷ ECON Goodwill m

goody ['ɡʊd·i] n ❶ (*desirable object*) tolle Sache ❷ FOOD Leckerbissen m

gooey ['ɡu·i] *adj* (*fam*) ❶ (*sticky*) klebrig ❷ (*fig, pej*) schmalzig

goof [ɡuf] (*fam*) I. n (*mistake*) Patzer m II. *vi* ■**to** ~ [**up**] Mist bauen
  ◆**goof around** *vt* herumblödeln *fam*

goofy ['ɡu·fi] *adj* (*fam*) doof

goose [ɡus] n <*pl* geese> Gans f ▶PHRASES: **to cook sb's** ~ jdm die Suppe versalzen

'goose bumps *npl,* **goose flesh,** n, **'goose pimples** *npl* Gänsehaut f *kein pl*

gopher ['ɡoʊ·fər] n Ziesel m

gore [ɡɔr] n Blut *nt*

gorge[1] n Schlucht f

gorge[2] [ɡɔrdʒ] *vi* sich vollessen

gorgeous ['ɡɔr·dʒəs] *adj* ❶ (*very beautiful*) herrlich, großartig ❷ (*very pleasurable*) ausgezeichnet

gorilla [gəˈrɪl·ə] n Gorilla m a. fig
gory [ˈgɔ·ri] adj blutig; film blutrünstig
gospel [ˈgas·pəl] n ❶ the G~ according to Saint Mark [or St Mark's Gospel] das Evangelium nach Markus ❷ (music) Gospel nt
gossamer [ˈgas·ə·mər] I. n Spinnfäden pl II. adj hauchdünn
gossip [ˈgas·əp] I. n (usu pej) ❶ (rumors) Klatsch m; idle ~ leeres Geschwätz ❷ (pej: person) Tratschbase f II. vi schwatzen
'gossip column n Klatschspalte f
gossipy [ˈgas·ə·pi] adj schwatzhaft
got [gat] pt, pp of **get**
gotta [ˈgat·ə] (fam) = [have] got to müssen
gotten [ˈgat·ən] pp of **got**
gouge [gaʊdʒ] I. n (indentation) Rille f II. vt ■to ~ out aushöhlen; eye ausstechen
goulash [ˈgu·laʃ] n Gulasch nt
gourd [gɔrd] n Kürbisflasche f
gourmet [ˈgʊrˌmeɪ] n Feinschmecker(in) m(f)
gout [gaʊt] n Gicht f
Gov. n ❶ abbrev of **government** ❷ abbrev of **governor**
govern [ˈgʌv·ərn] vt, vi regieren
governing [ˈgʌv·ərn·ɪŋ] adj regierend; ~ **body** Vorstand m
government [ˈgʌv·ərn·mənt] n Regierung f, Staat m; local ~ Kommunalverwaltung f; ~ **agency** Behörde f; ~ **policy** Regierungspolitik f; ~ **spending** Staatsausgaben pl; ~ **subsidy** Subvention f
governmental [ˌgʌv·ərnˈmen·təl] adj Regierungs-
governor [ˈgʌv·ər·nər] n POL Gouverneur m
gown [gaʊn] n MED Kittel m
GP [ˌdʒiˈpi] n MED abbrev of **general practitioner**
GPS [ˈdʒiˌpiːˈes] acr for **global navigation system** (fam) Navi nt fam, Navigationsgerät nt
grab [græb] I. n (snatch) Griff m ►PHRASES: **to be up for** ~s zu haben

sein II. vt <-bb-> ❶ [sich dat] schnappen; ■to ~ **hold of** sb/sth jdn/etw festhalten ❷ (fig) attention erregen; **to ~ a bite** [to eat] schnell einen Happen essen III. vi <-bb-> (snatch) grapschen
grace [greɪs] n ❶ (of movement) Grazie f ❷ (of behavior) Anstand m kein pl; **social ~s** gesellschaftliche Umgangsformen
graceful [ˈgreɪs·fəl] adj ❶ (in movement) graziös ❷ (in appearance) elegant
graceless [ˈgreɪs·lɪs] adj taktlos
gracious [ˈgreɪ·ʃəs] I. adj (kind) liebenswürdig; (merciful) gnädig II. interj [good [or goodness]] ~ [me] [du] meine Güte
grade [greɪd] I. n ❶ (rank) Rang m ❷ (of salary) Gehaltsstufe f ❸ SCH (score) Note f; (class) Klasse m ❹ (gradient) Neigung f; [steep] ~ (upwards) [starke] Steigung; (downwards) [starkes] Gefälle II. vt SCH, UNIV benoten
grader [ˈgreɪ·dər] n SCH **the second** ~s die Schüler(innen) mpl(fpl) der zweiten Klasse
'grade school n Grundschule f
gradient [ˈgreɪ·di·ənt] n Neigung f
grading system Notensystem der USA mit den Buchstaben A, B, C, D, E und F, wobei A für die beste Note steht und F durchgefallen bedeutet
gradual [ˈgrædʒ·u·əl] adj allmählich
graduate I. n [ˈgrædʒ·u·ət] ❶ UNIV Absolvent(in) m(f); ~ **student** Student(in) m(f) mit Universitätsabschluss (Studenten mit einem „Bachelor's Degree", die eine weitere Stufe zur Erlangung des „Master's Degrees" absolvieren) ❷ SCH Schulabgänger(in) m(f) II. vi [ˈgrædʒ·u·eɪt] ❶ UNIV einen akademischen Grad erwerben ❷ SCH die Abschlussprüfung bestehen ❸ (complete training) die Ausbildung abschließen; UNIV das Studium abschließen
graduated [ˈgrædʒ·u·eɪt·ɪd] adj gestaffelt
graduation [ˌgrædʒ·u·ˈeɪ·ʃən] n ❶ SCH, UNIV (completion of studies) [Studi-

G

en|abschluss *m* ❷(*ceremony*) Abschlussfeier *f*

graffiti [grə·'fi·ti] *n* Graffiti *nt*

graft [græft] **I.** *n* ❶MED Transplantat *nt* ❷(*corruption*) Schiebung *f* **II.** *vt* übertragen (**on|to** auf +*akk*)

grain [greɪn] *n* ❶(*particle*) Korn *nt*, Körnchen *nt* ❷(*crop*) Getreide *nt*

gram [græm] *n* Gramm *nt*

grammar ['græm·ər] *n* Grammatik *f*

grammatical [grə·'mæt·ɪ·kəl] *adj* grammati|kali|sch

grand [grænd] **I.** *adj* ❶(*splendid*) prächtig, großartig; **to make a ~ entrance** einen großen Auftritt haben ❷(*excellent*) großartig ❸(*large, far-reaching*) große Pläne; **on a ~ scale** in großem Rahmen **II.** *n* <*pl* -> (*fam: one thousand dollars*) Mille *f*

grandad ['græn·dæd] *n* (*fam*) *see* **granddad**

'**grandchild** *n* Enkelkind *nt*

'**granddad** *n* (*fam*) ❶(*grandfather*) Opa *m*, Opi *m* ❷(*pej: old man*) Opa *m*, Alter *m*

'**granddaughter** *n* Enkeltochter *f*

grandeur ['græn·dʒər] *n* ❶ Größe *f*; **delusions of ~** Größenwahn *m*

'**grandfather** *n* Großvater *m*

grand 'jury *n* Anklagejury *f*

'**grandma** *n* (*fam*) Oma *f*, Omi *f*

'**grandmother** *n* Großmutter *f*

'**grandpa** *n* (*fam*) Opa *m*, Opi *f*

grand pi'ano *n* [Konzert]flügel *m*

'**grandson** *n* Enkel|sohn *m*

'**grandstand I.** *n* [Haupt]tribüne *f* **II.** *vi* Effekthascherei betreiben

grand 'sum, grand 'total *n* Gesamtsumme *f*

granite ['græn·ɪt] *n* Granit *m*

grannie ['græn·i], **granny** ['græn·i] *n* (*fam*) Oma *f*, Omi *f*

grant [grænt] **I.** *n* ❶UNIV Stipendium *nt* ❷(*subsidy*) Subvention *f* **II.** *vt* ❶(*allow*) ■**to ~ sb sth** jdm etw gewähren; *money* jdm etw bewilligen; *visa* jdm etw erteilen ❷(*admit*) zugeben; **~ed, …** zugegeben, …

granulated ['græn·jə·leɪ·tɪd] *adj* **~ sugar** Kristallzucker *m*

granule ['græn·jul] *n* ■**-s** *pl* Granulat *nt*

grape [greɪp] *n* [Wein]traube *f*

'**grapefruit** <*pl* -> ['greɪp·frut] *n* Grapefruit *f*

'**grapevine** *n* Weinstock *m* ▶PHRASES: **I heard** |**it**| **on the ~ that …** es ist mir zu Ohren gekommen, dass …

graph [græf] *n* Diagramm *nt*; **~ paper** Millimeterpapier *nt*

graphic ['græf·ɪk] *adj* ❶(*diagrammatic*) grafisch ❷(*vividly descriptive*) anschaulich; **in ~ detail** haarklein

graphics ['græf·ɪks] *npl* Grafik *f*; **~ card** Grafikkarte *f*

graphite ['græf·aɪt] *n* Graphit *m*

grasp [græsp] **I.** *n* ❶(*grip*) Griff *m* ❷(*fig*) Reichweite *f*; **to be within sb's ~** zum Greifen nahe sein **II.** *vt* ❶(*take firm hold*) |fest| |er|greifen; **to ~ sb by the arm** jdn am Arm fassen ❷(*fig: understand*) begreifen

grasping ['græs·pɪŋ] *adj* (*fig, pej*) habgierig

grass <*pl* -es> [græs] *n* ❶Gras *nt*; (*lawn*) Rasen *m* ❷(*sl: marijuana*) Gras *nt* *sl*

'**grasshopper** *n* Heuschrecke *f*

'**grassland** *n* Grasland *nt*

grass'roots *npl of a party, organization* Basis *f* *kein pl*; **~ opinion** Volksmeinung *f*

'**grass snake** *n* Grasnatter *f*

'**grassy** ['græs·i] *adj* grasbewachsen

grate [greɪt] **I.** *n* Kamin *m* **II.** *vi* **to ~ on sb|'s nerves|** jdm auf die Nerven gehen **III.** *vt* FOOD reiben; *vegetables* raspeln

grateful ['greɪt·fəl] *adj* dankbar

grater ['greɪ·tər] *n* Reibe *f*

gratifying ['græt·ə·faɪ·ɪŋ] *adj* erfreulich

grating ['greɪ·tɪŋ] *n* Gitter *nt*

gratitude ['græt·ə·tud] *n* Dankbarkeit *f*

gratuitous [grə·'tu·ɪ·təs] *adj* ❶(*free*) kostenlos ❷(*pej: unnecessary*) überflüssig

gratuity [grə·'tu·ɪ·ti] *n* (*tip*) Trinkgeld *nt*

grave [greɪv] I. n Grab nt II. adj ernst; *news* schlimm

gravel ['græv·əl] n Kies m

'gravel pit n Kiesgrube f

gravely ['greɪv·li] adv ernst; ~ **ill** schwer krank

'gravestone n Grabstein m

'graveyard n Friedhof m

gravitate ['græv·ɪ·teɪt] vi ■to ~ to[ward] sth/sb von etw/jdm angezogen werden

gravity ['græv·ɪ·ti] n ❶ PHYS Schwerkraft f ❷ (seriousness) Ernst m

gravy ['greɪ·vi] n ❶ [Braten]soße f ❷ (fig sl: easy money) leicht verdientes Geld

'gravy boat n Sauciere f

'gravy train n (fig) **to get on the** ~ sich dat ein Stück vom Kuchen abschneiden

gray [greɪ] adj grau a. fig

'gray matter n (fam) graue Zellen pl

graze¹ [greɪz] vi grasen, weiden

graze² [greɪz] I. n Schürfwunde f II. vt streifen; **to ~ one's elbow** sich dat den Ellbogen aufschürfen

grease [gris] n Fett nt

'greasepaint n THEAT Fettschminke f

greasy ['gri·si] adj hair, skin fettig; fingers, objects a. schmierig; food fett; (slippery) glitschig

great [greɪt] I. adj ❶ (very big) groß; **to a ~ extent** im Großen und Ganzen ❷ (famous) groß; (important) bedeutend ❸ (fam: wonderful) großartig II. adv (extremely) sehr; ~ **big** riesengroß III. n (person) Größe f; (in titles) **Catherine the G~** Katharina die Große

Great 'Britain n Großbritannien nt

Greater ['greɪt·ər] (in cities) ~ **Los Angeles** Großraum m Los Angeles

great-'grandchild n Urenkel(in) m(f)

Great 'Lakes npl GEOG ■**the ~** die Großen Seen

greatly ['greɪt·li] adv sehr; ~ **impressed** tief beeindruckt

greatness ['greɪt·nɪs] n Bedeutsamkeit f

Great Plains npl Große Ebenen pl (eine der wichtigsten Getreideregionen der Welt)

Greece [gris] n Griechenland nt

greed [grid], **greediness** ['gri·dɪ·nɪs] n Gier f

greedy ['gri·di] adj gierig; (for money, things) habgierig

Greek [grik] I. n ❶ (person) Grieche, -in m, f ❷ (language) Griechisch nt II. adj griechisch ▶PHRASES: **it's all ~ to me** das sind alles böhmische Dörfer für mich

green [grin] I. n ❶ (color) Grün nt ❷ FOOD ■~ **s** pl Blattgemüse nt kein pl II. adj ❶ grün; ~ **with envy** grün vor Neid ❷ (environmental) grün, umweltfreundlich; ~ **issues** pl Umweltschutzfragen

'greenback n (fam) Dollar[schein] m

'green card n Aufenthaltserlaubnis f mit Arbeitsgenehmigung

greenery ['gri·nə·ri] n Grün nt

'greenhouse n Gewächshaus nt; ~ **effect** Treibhauseffekt m

greenish ['gri·nɪʃ] adj grünlich

green 'pepper n grüne Paprikaschote

greet [grit] vt (welcome) [be]grüßen; (receive) empfangen; **to ~ each other [by shaking hands]** sich [mit Handschlag] begrüßen

greeting ['gri·tɪŋ] n Begrüßung f; ■~ **s** pl Grüße pl

gregarious [grɪ·'ger·i·əs] adj gesellig

grenade [grə·'neɪd] n Granate f

grew [gru] pt of **grow**

grey [greɪ] adj see **gray**

'greyhound n Windhund m

grid [grɪd] n ❶ Gitter nt ❷ ELEC Netz nt

griddle ['grɪd·əl] n Heizplatte f

gridiron ['grɪd·aɪ·ərn] n SPORT Footballfeld nt

gridlock ['grɪd·lɑk] n Verkehrskollaps m

grief [grif] n tiefe Trauer, Kummer m

grievance ['gri·vəns] n Beschwerde f

grieve [griv] vi bekümmert sein; ■**to ~ for sb** um jdn trauern; ■**to ~ over sth** über etw akk betrübt sein

grill [grɪl] I. n (over charcoal) [Grill]rost m; (restaurant) Grillrestaurant nt II. vt ❶ grillen ❷ (fig fam: interrogate) ausquetschen

G

grille [grɪl] n Gitter nt

grilling ['grɪl·ɪŋ] n (fig fam) strenges Verhör

grim [grɪm] adj ❶ (forbidding) grimmig ❷ (very unpleasant) picture trostlos; landscape unwirtlich; situation schlimm; **things were looking** ~ die Lage sah langsam düster aus

grimace ['grɪm·əs] n Grimasse f

grime [graɪm] n Schmutz m

grimy ['graɪ·mi] adj schmutzig

grin [grɪn] I. n Grinsen nt kein pl II. vi grinsen

grind [graɪnd] I. n (fam) **the daily** ~ der tägliche Trott II. vt <ground, ground> ❶ (crush); meat fein hacken; **to** ~ **sth** [in]**to a powder** etw fein zermahlen ❷ (sharpen) schleifen III. vi <ground, ground> **to** ~ **to a halt** production stocken; negotiations sich festfahren

♦**grind down** vt ❶ mill zerkleinern ❷ (mentally wear out) zermürben

♦**grind out** vt (produce continuously) ununterbrochen produzieren

grinder ['graɪn·dər] n ❶ (mill) Mühle f ❷ (mincer) Fleischwolf m

grindstone ['graɪnd·stoʊn] n Schleifstein m

grip [grɪp] I. n Griff m kein pl a. fig; **to be in the** ~ **of sth** von etw dat betroffen sein; **to get to** ~**s with sth** etw in den Griff bekommen; **to lose one's** ~ **on reality** den Bezug zur Realität verlieren II. vt <-pp-> packen III. vi <-pp-> greifen

gripe [graɪp] vi (fam) nörgeln

gripping ['grɪp·ɪŋ] adj packend

grisly ['grɪz·li] adj grausig

gristle ['grɪs·əl] n Knorpel m

grit [grɪt] n (small stones) Splitt m; (for icy roads) Streusand m

gritty ['grɪt·i] adj ❶ (like grit) grob[körnig] ❷ (full of grit) sandig

grizzled ['grɪz·əld] adj ergraut

grizzly ['grɪz·li] I. adj gräulich II. n Grizzlybär m

groan [groʊn] I. n Stöhnen nt kein pl II. vi [auf]stöhnen

groceries ['groʊ·sə·riz] npl Lebensmittel pl

groggy ['grag·i] adj angeschlagen

groin [grɔɪn] n ANAT Leiste f

groom [grum] I. n ❶ (bridegroom) Bräutigam m ❷ (for horses) Pferdepfleger(in) m(f) II. vt horse striegeln

groove [gruv] n Rille f

groovy ['gru·vi] adj (sl) klasse fam, cool fam

grope [groʊp] I. vi ■**to** ~ **for sth** nach etw dat tasten II. vt (fam) ■**to** ~ **sb** jdn befummeln

gross [groʊs] I. adj ❶ (disgusting) ekelhaft; (big and ugly) abstoßend ❷ FIN Brutto‑ nt II. vt FIN brutto einnehmen

grossly ['groʊs·li] adv extrem

grotesque [groʊ·'tesk] adj grotesk

grouchy ['graʊ·tʃi] adj griesgrämig

ground¹ [graʊnd] I. n ❶ [Erd]boden m, Erde f; **below** ~ unter der Erde; MIN unter Tage; **to get off the** ~ (fig fam) plan verwirklicht werden; **to get sth off the** ~ (fig fam) etw realisieren ❷ (area of land) [ein Stück] Land nt; **waste** ~ brachliegendes Land; **to gain** ~ MIL Boden gewinnen; (fig) an Boden gewinnen ❸ ELEC (earth) Erdung f ❹ (fig: area of discussion) **to find common** ~ Gemeinsamkeiten entdecken; **to be on safe** ~ sich auf sicherem Boden bewegen ❺ pl ■~**s** (reasons) Grund m; ~ **for divorce** Scheidungsgrund m ▶PHRASES: **to break new** ~ Neuland betreten; **to work oneself into the** ~ sich kaputtmachen II. vt ❶ ■**to be** ~**ed** (fig fam) Hausarrest haben ❷ ELEC erden

ground² [graʊnd] I. n ❶ vt pt of **grind** II. adj gemahlen

'**groundbreaking** adj bahnbrechend

'**ground control** n AVIAT Bodenkontrolle f

'**ground crew** n AVIAT Bodenpersonal nt kein pl

ground 'floor n Erdgeschoss nt ▶PHRASES: **to get in on the** ~ [of sth] von Anfang an [bei etw dat] dabei sein

'**ground frost** n Bodenfrost m

groundhog ['graʊnd·hag] n Waldmurmeltier nt

'**Groundhog Day** n Murmeltiertag m

groundless ['graʊnd·lɪs] adj grundlos

'**ground rules** npl Grundregeln pl

'**ground staff** n AVIAT Bodenpersonal nt

'**groundwater** n Grundwasser nt

'**groundwork** n Vorarbeit f

group [grup] n ❶ Gruppe f ❷ ECON Konzern m

groupie ['gru·pi] n (fam) Groupie nt

group 'practice n Gemeinschaftspraxis f

group 'therapy n Gruppentherapie f

grouse [graʊs] vi (fam) meckern

grove [groʊv] n Wäldchen nt; **olive ~** Olivenhain m

grovel <-l-> ['grav·əl] vi (behave obsequiously) ■**to ~** [before sb] [vor jdm] zu Kreuze kriechen

grow <grew, grown> [groʊ] I. vi wachsen; **to ~ taller** größer werden; sales zunehmen; **to ~ to like sth** langsam beginnen, etw zu mögen II. vt ❶ anbauen; flowers züchten; **to ~ sth from seed** etw aus Samen ziehen ❷ hair wachsen lassen

◆**grow apart** vi **to ~ apart from sb** sich jdm [allmählich] entfremden

◆**grow into** vi hineinwachsen in +akk

◆**grow out of** vi **to ~ out of a habit** eine Angewohnheit ablegen

◆**grow up** vi erwachsen werden

grower ['groʊ·ər] n AGR **coffee ~** Kaffeepflanzer(in) m(f)

growing ['groʊ·ɪŋ] adj ❶ boy, girl im Wachstumsalter; **~ pains** (fig) Anfangsschwierigkeiten pl ❷ (increasing) zunehmend

growl [graʊl] vi knurren; ■**to ~ at sb** jdn anknurren

grown [groʊn] I. adj erwachsen; **fully ~** ausgewachsen II. pp of **grow**

grown-up ['groʊn·ʌp] adj (fam) erwachsen

growth [groʊθ] n Wachstum nt

grub [grʌb] n Larve f

grubby ['grʌb·i] adj (fam) schmudd[e]lig; hands schmutzig

grudge [grʌdʒ] n Groll m kein pl

grudging ['grʌdʒ·ɪŋ] adj widerwillig

grueling ['gru·lɪŋ] adj time aufreibend; journey strapaziös

gruesome ['gru·səm] adj grausig

gruff [grʌf] adj barsch

grumble ['grʌm·bəl] vi murren

grumpy ['grʌm·pi] adj (fam) mürrisch, brummig

grunt [grʌnt] I. n ❶ (sound) Grunzen nt kein pl ❷ MIL gemeiner Soldat/gemeine Soldatin II. vi grunzen

G-string ['dʒi·strɪŋ] n String-Tanga m

guarantee [ˌger·ən·'ti] I. n Garantie f; **money-back ~** Rückerstattungsgarantie f II. vt garantieren; ■**to ~ that ...** gewährleisten, dass ...

guarantor [ˌger·ən·'tɔr] n Garant(in) m(f); LAW Bürge, -in m, f

guard [gɑrd] I. n ❶ (person) Wache f; (sentry) Wach[t]posten m; **security ~** Sicherheitsbeamte(r) f(m), -beamtin f ❷ (group of guards) Garde f ❸ (protective device) Schutz m II. vt (keep watch) bewachen; **heavily ~ed** scharf bewacht; (protect) [be]schützen (**against** vor +dat)

'**guard dog** n Wachhund m

guarded ['gɑr·dɪd] adj (reserve) zurückhaltend; (cautious) vorsichtig

'**guardhouse** n Wache f

guardian ['gɑr·di·ən] n LAW Vormund m

guardian 'angel n Schutzengel m a. fig

'**guard rail** n [Schutz]geländer nt

'**guardroom** n Wachstube f

'**guardsman** n (member of National Guard) Gardesoldat m

gubernatorial [ˌgu·bər·nə·'tɔr·i·əl] adj Gouverneurs-

gue(r)rilla [gə·'rɪl·ə] n Guerillakämpfer(in) m(f); **~ warfare** Guerillakrieg m

guess [ges] I. n <pl -es> Vermutung f; (estimate) Schätzung f; **I'll give you three ~es** dreimal darfst du raten; **lucky ~** Glückstreffer m; **to take a ~** raten ►PHRASES: **it's anyone's ~** weiß der Himmel II. vi ❶ (conjecture) [er]raten; **to keep sb ~ing** jdn auf die Folter spannen ❷ (suppose) denken; (sus-

G

pect) annehmen; **I ~ you're right** du wirst wohl recht haben **III.** vt raten; **~ what?** stell dir vor!

guessing game ['ges·ɪŋ·ˌgeɪm] n Ratespiel nt a. fig

guesstimate ['ges·tɪ·mət] n (fam) grobe Schätzung

guesswork ['ges·wɜrk] n Spekulation f meist pl

guest [gest] **I.** n Gast m **II.** vi als Gaststar auftreten

'guesthouse n Gästehaus nt, Pension f

'guestroom n Gästezimmer nt

guidance ['gaɪ·dəns] n ❶ (advice) Beratung f; (direction) [An]leitung f ❷ (steering system) Steuerung f

guide [gaɪd] **I.** n Führer(in) m(f); TOURIST Fremdenführer(in) m(f); **tour ~** Reiseführer(in) m(f) **II.** vt ❶ (show) ■ **to ~ sb** jdn führen a. fig; (show the way) jdm den Weg zeigen ❷ (steer) führen

'guidebook n Reiseführer m

guided ['gaɪ·dɪd] adj geführt; **~ tour** Führung f

'guide dog n Blindenhund m

'guideline n usu pl Richtlinie f

guiding 'principle n Richtschnur f

guilt [gɪlt] n Schuld f; **feelings of ~** Schuldgefühle pl

guiltless ['gɪlt·lɪs] adj schuldlos

'guilt-ridden adj von Schuldgefühlen geplagt

guilty ['gɪl·ti] adj schuldig; **~ conscience** schlechtes Gewissen; **to feel ~ about sth** ein schlechtes Gewissen wegen einer S. gen haben; **to prove sb ~** jds Schuld f beweisen

'guinea pig n Meerschweinchen nt; (fig) Versuchskaninchen nt

guise [gaɪz] n ❶ (appearance) Gestalt f; **in the ~ of a monk** als Mönch verkleidet ❷ (pretense) Vorwand m

guitar [gɪ·'tɑr] n Gitarre f

guitarist [gɪ·'tɑr·ɪst] n Gitarrist(in) m(f)

gulch [gʌltʃ] n Schlucht f

gulf [gʌlf] n GEOG Golf m; **the G~ of Mexico** der Golf von Mexiko; **the G~ states** die Golfstaaten pl

gull [gʌl] n Möwe f

gullible ['gʌl·ə·bəl] adj leichtgläubig

gulp [gʌlp] **I.** n (großer) Schluck; **to get a ~ of air** Luft holen **II.** vt [hinunter]schlucken **III.** vi **to ~ for air** nach Luft schnappen

gum¹ [gʌm] **I.** n ❶ (sticky substance) Gummi nt; (glue) Klebstoff m ❷ (candy) Kaugummi m o nt **II.** vt <-mm-> kleben

gum² [gʌm] n ANAT ■ ~[s] Zahnfleisch nt kein pl

gumbo ['gʌm·bou] n Okraschote f

gummy ['gʌm·i] adj (sticky) klebrig

gumption ['gʌmp·ʃən] n (fam) Grips m

gun [gʌn] n [Schuss]waffe f; (pistol) Pistole f; (revolver) Revolver m; (rifle) Gewehr nt

◆**gun down** vt niederschießen

'gunfight n Schießerei f

'gunfire n Schießerei f

'gun license n Waffenschein m

'gunman n Bewaffnete(r) m

'gunner ['gʌn·ər] n Artillerist m

'gunpoint n **at ~** mit vorgehaltener Waffe

'gunrunner n Waffenschmuggler(in) m(f)

'gunshot n (shot) Schuss m; **~ wound** Schusswunde f

gurgle ['gɜr·gəl] vi baby glucksen; water gluckern

gush [gʌʃ] vi ❶ (flow out) [hervor]strömen; (at high speed) [hervor]schießen ❷ (praise) [übertrieben] schwärmen

gusher ['gʌʃ·ər] n [natürlich sprudelnde] Ölquelle

gushing ['gʌʃ·ɪŋ] adj schwärmerisch

gust [gʌst] n [Wind]stoß m

gusto ['gʌs·tou] n ■ **with ~** mit Begeisterung

gusty ['gʌs·ti] adj böig

gut [gʌt] **I.** n ❶ (fam: abdomen) Bauch m ❷ (fam: courage) ■ ~s pl Mumm m kein pl ▶ PHRASES: **to bust a ~** sich abrackern **II.** adj (fam) feeling instinktiv; reaction spontan

gutsy ['gʌt·si] adj mutig

gutter ['gʌt·ər] n of road Rinnstein m; (of roof) Dachrinne f

guy [gaɪ] n ❶ (*fam: man*) Kerl m, Typ m ❷ pl (*fam: people*) **are you ~s coming to lunch?** kommt ihr [mit] zum Essen?

guzzle [ˈgʌz·əl] vt (*fam: drink*) in sich akk hineinkippen

gym [dʒɪm] n ❶ *short for* **gymnasium** Turnhalle f ❷ *short for* **PE**

gymnasium <pl -s> [dʒɪmˈneɪ·zi·əm] n Turnhalle f

gymnast [ˈdʒɪm·næst] n Turner(in) m(f)

gymnastic [dʒɪmˈnæs·tɪk] adj turnerisch, Turn-

gymnastics [dʒɪmˈnæs·tɪks] npl Turnen nt kein pl

gynecologist [ˌgaɪ·nəˈkal·ə·dʒɪst] n Gynäkologe, -in m, f

gynecology [ˌgaɪ·nəˈkal·ə·dʒi] n Gynäkologie f

Gypsy [ˈdʒɪp·si] n Zigeuner(in) m(f)

gyrate [ˈdʒaɪ·reɪt] vi sich drehen

gyroscope [ˈdʒaɪ·rə·skoʊp] n NAUT, AVIAT Gyroskop nt

H

Hh

H <pl -'s>, **h** <pl -'s> [eɪtʃ] n H nt, h nt; **~ as in Hotel** H wie Heinrich

habit [ˈhæb·ɪt] n ❶ (*repeated action*) Gewohnheit f; **a bad ~** eine schlechte [An]gewohnheit ❷ (*fam: drug addiction*) **to have a heroin ~** heroinsüchtig sein

habitable [ˈhæb·ɪ·ţə·bəl] adj bewohnbar

habitat [ˈhæb·ɪ·tæt] n Lebensraum m

habitual [həˈbɪtʃ·u·əl] adj gewohnt

hack [hæk] I. vt ❶ (*chop*) hacken ❷ (*sl: cope with*) aushalten; **he can't ~ it** er bringt's einfach nicht II. vi COMPUT ■**to ~ into sth** in etw akk eindringen

hacker [ˈhæk·ər] n COMPUT Hacker(in) m(f)

ˈhacksaw n Bügelsäge f

had [hæd, *unstressed:* həd] vt ❶ pt, pp of **have** ❷ (*fam*) **to have ~ it** (*want to stop*) genug haben; (*to be broken*) kaputt sein

haddock <pl -> [ˈhæd·ək] n Schellfisch m

hadn't [ˈhæd·ənt] = **had not** *see* **have**

haggle [ˈhæg·əl] vi ■**to ~** [**over sth**] [um etw akk] feilschen

Hague [heɪg] n GEOG ■**The ~** Den Haag kein art

hail¹ [heɪl] I. n Hagel m II. vi hageln

hail² [heɪl] vt *taxi* rufen

ˈhailstone n Hagelkorn nt

hair [her] n (*single strand*) Haar nt; (*on head*) Haar nt, Haare pl

ˈhairbrush n Haarbürste f

ˈhair care n Haarpflege f

ˈhair conditioner n Pflegespülung f

ˈhaircut n Frisur f

ˈhairdresser n Friseur m, Friseuse f

ˈhair drier, ˈhair dryer n Föhn m

hairless [ˈher·lɪs] adj unbehaart; *person* glatzköpfig

ˈhairline n Haaransatz m

ˈhairpiece n Haarteil nt

ˈhairpin n Haarnadel f

ˈhair-raising adj (*fam*) haarsträubend

ˈhair remover n Enthaarungsmittel nt

ˈhairspray n Haarspray nt

ˈhairstyle n Frisur f

ˈhairstylist n Friseur m, Friseuse f

hairy [ˈher·i] adj haarig

half [hæf] I. n <pl **halves**> ❶ (*fifty percent*) Hälfte f; **~ an apple** ein halber Apfel; **three and a ~ pounds** eineinhalb Kilo ❷ SPORT (*period*) Spielhälfte f, Halbzeit f ▶ PHRASES: **given ~ a chance** wenn man die Möglichkeit hätte II. adj halbe(r, s); **~ a percent** ein halbes Prozent **III.** *adv* ❶ (*almost*) fast ❷ (*time*) **[at] ~ past nine** [um] halb zehn

'**halfback** *n* SPORT Läufer(in) *m(f)*

'**half brother** *n* Halbbruder *m*

'**half dozen, half a 'dozen** *n* ein halbes Dutzend

half-'empty *adj* halb leer

half-'full *adj* halb voll

half-'hearted *adj* halbherzig

half 'moon *n* Halbmond *m*

half-'price *adj, adv* zum halben Preis

'**half sister** *n* Halbschwester *f*

'**halftime** *n* SPORT Halbzeit *f*; (*break*) Halbzeitpause *f*

half'way **I.** *adj* halb **II.** *adv* in der Mitte; **it's ~ between the two** es liegt genau auf halber Strecke zwischen den beiden; **~ through dinner** mitten beim Abendessen

'**half-wit** *n* (*pej*) Dummkopf *m*

half-'yearly *adj, adv* halbjährlich

hall [hɔl] *n* ❶ (*corridor*) Flur *m* ❷ (*large building*) Halle *f*; (*public room*) Saal *m*; **city ~** Rathaus *nt*

'**hallmark** ['hɔl·mɑrk] *n* Kennzeichen *nt*

Halloween [ˌhæl·ə·'win] *n* Halloween *nt*

hallucinate [hə·'lu·sɪ·neɪt] *vi* halluzinieren

hallucination [hə·ˌlu·sɪ·'neɪ·ʃən] *n* Halluzination *f*

'**hallway** *n* Flur *m*

halo <*pl* -s> ['heɪ·loʊ] *n* Heiligenschein *m*

halogen 'bulb *n* Halogenglühbirne *f*

halt [hɔlt] **I.** *n* ❶ Stillstand *m* ❷ (*break*) Pause *f* **II.** *vt* zum Stillstand bringen; *fight* beenden **III.** *vi* zum Stillstand kommen

halter ['hɔl·tər] *n* ❶ (*for animals*) Halfter *nt* ❷ FASHION *see* **halter-top**

'**halter-top** *n* FASHION rückenfreies Oberteil (*mit Nackenverschluss*)

halting ['hɔl·tɪŋ] *adj speech* stockend

halve [hæv] *vt* ❶ (*cut in two*) halbieren ❷ (*lessen by 50 percent*) um die Hälfte reduzieren

ham [hæm] *n* ❶ FOOD Schinken *m*

❷ THEAT (*pej*) Schmierenkomödiant(in) *m(f)*

hamburger ['hæm·bɜr·gər] *n* FOOD ❶ (*cooked*) Hamburger *m* ❷ (*raw*) Hackfleisch *nt*

ham-'fisted, ham-'handed *adj* (*pej*) ungeschickt

hamlet ['hæm·lət] *n* Weiler *m*

hammer ['hæm·ər] **I.** *n* ❶ (*tool*) Hammer *m* ❷ SPORT [Wurf]hammer *m* **II.** *vt* ❶ *nail* einschlagen; *ball* [kräftig] schlagen; **to ~ sth into sb** (*fig*) jdm etw einhämmern ❷ (*fam: defeat*) **New England ~ed Pittsburgh 35-3** New England war Pittsburgh mit 35:3 haushoch überlegen ▸PHRASES: **to ~ sth home** etw *dat* Nachdruck verleihen **III.** *vi* hämmern *a. fig*

◆**hammer in** *vt* ❶ *nail* einschlagen ❷ (*fig*) ■**to ~ sth into sb** *fact* jdm etw einbläuen

◆**hammer out** *vt* ❶ *dent* ausbeulen ❷ *settlement* aushandeln

hammock ['hæm·ək] *n* Hängematte *f*

hamper[1] ['hæm·pər] *n* [Deckel]korb *m*

hamper[2] ['hæm·pər] *vt* behindern

hamster ['hæm·stər] *n* Hamster *m*

hamstring ['hæm·strɪŋ] *n* Kniesehne *f*

hand [hænd] **I.** *n* ❶ ANAT Hand *f*; **~s up!** Hände hoch!; **to be good with one's ~s** geschickte Hände haben; **by ~** von Hand; **on [one's] ~s and knees** auf allen vieren ❷ (*control*) **to be in good/ safe ~s** in guten/sicheren Händen sein; **to turn one's ~ to sth** sich an etw *akk* machen ❸ (*assistance*) **to give [or lend] sb a ~** jdm helfen ❹ (*on clock*) Zeiger *m* ❺ **to give sb a big ~** jdm einen großen Applaus spenden ▸PHRASES: **to keep a firm ~ on sth** etw fest im Griff behalten; **on the one ~ ... on the other** [~] ... einerseits ... andererseits **II.** *vt* ■**to ~ sb sth** jdm etw [über]geben ▸PHRASES: **you've got to ~ it to sb** man muss es jdm lassen

◆**hand back** *vt* zurückgeben

◆**hand down** *vt* weitergeben; *tradition* überliefern

◆**hand in** vt einreichen; *homework* abgeben

◆**hand out** vt *papers, test* austeilen (**to** an +*akk*); *homework, advice* geben

◆**hand over** vt ❶ *(pass)* herüberreichen; *(away from one)* hinüberreichen; *(present)* übergeben ❷ TV, RADIO weitergeben (**to** an +*akk*)

'**handbag** n Handtasche *f*

'**handball** n Handball *m*

'**handbook** n Handbuch *nt*

'**hand brake** n Notbremse *f*

'**handcuff** n ■ ~ **s** pl Handschellen pl

'**handful** n Handvoll *f*; **a ~ of hair** ein Büschel *nt* Haare; **a ~ of people** wenige Leute

'**hand grenade** n Handgranate *f*

'**handgun** n Handfeuerwaffe *f*

hand-'held adj attr tragbar

handicap ['hæn·dɪ·kæp] I. n Handicap *nt* II. vt <-pp-> benachteiligen

handicapped ['hæn·dɪ·kæpt] adj behindert

handicraft ['hæn·dɪ·kræft] n [Kunst]handwerk *nt kein pl*

handkerchief ['hæŋ·kər·tʃɪf] n Taschentuch *nt*

handle ['hæn·dəl] I. n *of a tool* Griff *m*; *of a door* Klinke *f*; *of a handbag* Bügel *m* ▶PHRASES: **to fly off the ~** hochgehen II. vt ❶ *(grasp)* anfassen ❷ *(work on)* bearbeiten; *luggage* abfertigen; **to ~ sb's affairs** sich um jds Angelegenheiten kümmern ❸ *(deal with)* umgehen mit +*dat*, behandeln

'**handlebars** npl Lenkstange *f sing*

handler ['hænd·lər] n ❶ **baggage ~** Gepäckmann ❷ *(dog trainer)* Hundeführer(in) *m(f)*

handling ['hænd·lɪŋ] n ❶ *(act of touching)* Berühren *nt* ❷ *(treatment)* Handhabung *f*

'**hand luggage** n Handgepäck *nt*

hand'made adj handgearbeitet

'**hand-me-down** n abgelegtes Kleidungsstück

'**handout** n Almosen *nt*

'**handover** n Übergabe *f*

hand-'picked adj handverlesen a. fig

'**handrail** n Geländer *nt*

'**handset** n TELEC Hörer *m*

'**handshake** n Händedruck *m*

handsome ['hæn·səm] adj gut aussehend

'**handstand** n Handstand *m*

'**handwriting** n Handschrift *f*

'**handwritten** adj handgeschrieben

handy ['hæn·di] adj ❶ *(user-friendly)* praktisch, nützlich; *(easy to handle)* handlich ❷ *(convenient)* nützlich ❸ *(conveniently close)* thing griffbereit, greifbar

'**handyman** n Heimwerker(in) *m(f)*

hang [hæŋ] I. n ❶ *of clothes* Sitz *m* ❷ *(fig fam)* **to get the ~ of sth** bei etw *dat* den [richtigen] Dreh herausbekommen II. vt <hung, hung> ❶ *(mount)* aufhängen **(on** an +*dat*) ❷ *(decorate)* behängen ❸<-ed, -ed> *(execute)* [auf]hängen ❹ *head* hängen lassen III. vi <hung, hung> ❶ *(be suspended)* hängen (**from** an +*dat*) ❷<hanged, hanged> *(by execution)* hängen ❸<hung, hung> *mist, smell* hängen ▶PHRASES: **to ~ in there** am Ball bleiben

◆**hang around** vi ❶ *(loiter)* rumhängen fam ❷ *(waste time)* herumtrödeln fam

◆**hang back** vi ❶ *(be slow)* sich zurückhalten; *(hesitate)* zögern

◆**hang on** vi ❶ *(fam: persevere)* durchhalten ❷ *(grasp)* **to ~ on to sth** sich an etw *dat* festhalten; *(stronger)* sich an etw *akk* klammern ❸ *(wait briefly)* warten; *(on the telephone)* dranbleiben; **~ on, ...** Moment mal, ...

◆**hang out** I. vt heraushängen; *laundry* aufhängen II. vi ❶ *(project)* heraushängen ❷ *(sl: loiter)* [he]rumhängen; *(waste time)* herumtrödeln ▶PHRASES: **to let it all ~ out** die Sau rauslassen fam

◆**hang together** vi *argument* schlüssig sein

◆**hang up** I. vi auflegen II. vt ❶ *(suspend)* aufhängen ❷ *phone* auflegen

hangar ['hæŋ·ər] n AVIAT Hangar *m*

hanger ['hæŋ·ər] n *(Kleider)*bügel *m*

'**hang glider** n *(person)* Drachenflieger(in) *m(f)*; *(device)* Drachen *m*

'hang-gliding n Drachenfliegen nt

hanging ['hæŋ·ɪŋ] **I.** n ❶(execution) Hinrichtung f durch den Strang ❷(decorative fabric) Behang m **II.** adj hängend

'hangman n Henker m

'hangover n Kater m

'hang-up n (fam) Komplex m

hankie, hanky ['hæŋ·ki] n (fam) short for **handkerchief** Taschentuch nt

haphazard [hæp·'hæz·ərd] adj willkürlich

happen ['hæp·ən] vi ❶(occur) geschehen, passieren; event stattfinden; **these things** ~ das kann vorkommen ❷(by chance) ▪ **to** ~ **to do sth** zufällig etw tun

happening ['hæp·ə·nɪŋ] n usu pl Ereignis nt; (unplanned) Vorfall m

happily ['hæp·ɪ·li] adv ❶(contentedly) glücklich; (cheerfully) fröhlich ❷(willingly) gern

happiness ['hæp·ɪ·nɪs] n Glück nt; (contentment) Zufriedenheit f

happy ['hæp·i] adj ❶(pleased) glücklich; (contented) zufrieden; (cheerful) fröhlich; ▪ **to be** ~ **about** [or **with**] **sb/ sth** mit jdm/etw zufrieden sein ❷(willing) ▪ **to be** ~ **to do sth** etw gerne tun ❸(in greetings) ~ **birthday** alles Gute zum Geburtstag

happy-go-'lucky adj sorglos, unbekümmert

happy 'medium n goldene Mitte

harass [hə·'ræs] vt (intimidate) schikanieren; (pester) ständig belästigen

harassment [hə·'ræs·mənt] n Schikane f; **sexual** ~ sexuelle Belästigung

harbor ['har·bər] n Hafen m

hard [hard] **I.** adj ❶(solid) hart ❷ person zäh, hart ❸(difficult) schwierig; **to find sth** ~ **to believe** etw kaum glauben können ❹(laborious) anstrengend; **to be** ~ **work** harte Arbeit sein ❺(harmful) ▪ **to be** ~ **on sth** etw stark strapazieren; ▪ **to be** ~ **on sb** hart für jdn sein ❻ water, drug hart; frost, winter streng ▶PHRASES: ~ **and fast** rule verbindlich **II.** adv ❶(solid) hart

❷(vigorously) fest[e], kräftig; fight, work hart; rain stark; **to try** ~ sich akk sehr bemühen ❸(severely) schwer

'hardboard n Hartfaserplatte f

hard-'boiled adj egg hart gekocht

hard 'copy n COMPUT Ausdruck m

'hard-core, hardcore adj ❶(loyal) supporter eingefleischt ❷(explicit) hart

'hardcover adj gebunden

hard 'currency n harte Währung

'hard disk, 'hard drive n COMPUT Festplatte f

harden ['har·dən] **I.** vt ❶(make harder) härten; arteries verhärten ❷(make tougher) attitude verhärten **II.** vi ❶(become hard) hart werden ❷(become tough) sich verhärten; face sich versteinern

hard-'fought adj battle, match hart

'hard hat n [Schutz]helm m

hard-'hearted adj hartherzig

hard 'labor n Zwangsarbeit f

hard'liner n POL Hardliner m

hardly ['hard·li] adv kaum; ~ **ever** so gut wie nie

hardness ['hard·nɪs] n Härte f

hard-'nosed adj nüchtern; person abgebrüht

hard-'pressed adj bedrängt

hard 'sell n aggressive Verkaufsmethoden pl

hardship ['hard·ʃɪp] n Not f

'hardware n ❶Haushaltswaren pl ❷COMPUT Hardware f

'hardwood n Hartholz nt

hard-'working adj fleißig

hardy ['har·di] adj ❶(tough) zäh ❷BOT winterhart

hare <pl -s> [her] n [Feld]hase m

'harebrained adj verrückt

harem ['her·əm] n Harem m

harm [harm] **I.** n Schaden m; **to mean no** ~ es nicht böse meinen **II.** vt ▪ **to** ~ **sth** etw dat Schaden zufügen; ▪ **to** ~ **sb** jdm schaden; (hurt) jdn verletzen

harmful ['harm·fəl] adj schädlich

harmless ['harm·lɪs] adj harmlos

harmonious [har·'moʊ·ni·əs] adj harmonisch a. fig

H

harmonization [ˌhar·mə·nɪˈzeɪ·ʃən] *n* Harmonisierung *f a. fig*

harmony [ˈhar·mə·ni] *n* Harmonie *f*

harness [ˈhar·nɪs] I. *n* <*pl* -es> (*for animal*) Geschirr *nt*; (*for person*) Gurtzeug *nt* II. *vt animal* anschirren; *person* anschnallen

harp [harp] *n* Harfe *f*

harpoon [har·ˈpun] *n* Harpune *f*

harrowing [ˈher·oʊ·ɪŋ] *adj* grauenvoll

harsh [harʃ] *adj* ❶ rau; *winter* streng; *light* grell ❷ (*severe*) hart; (*critical*) scharf

harvest [ˈhar·vɪst] I. *n* Ernte *f*; *of grapes* Lese *f* II. *vt* ernten

has [hæz, həz] *3rd pers. sing of* **have**

hash [hæʃ] *n* ❶ FOOD Haschee *nt* ❷ (*fam: shambles*) **to make a ~ of sth** etw vermasseln

hash browns *npl* Kartoffelpuffer *pl*, ≈ Rösti *pl* SÜDD, SCHWEIZ

hasn't [ˈhæz·ənt] = **has not** *see* **have**

hassle [ˈhæs·əl] I. *n* (*fam*) Mühe *f kein pl* II. *vt* (*fam: pester*) schikanieren; (*harass*) bedrängen

haste [heɪst] *n* Eile *f*; (*rush*) Hast *f*

hasten [ˈheɪ·sən] *vi* sich *akk* beeilen

hasty [ˈheɪ·sti] *adj* ❶ eilig ❷ (*rash*) übereilt

hat [hæt] *n* Hut *m*

hatch[1] <*pl* -es> [hætʃ] *n* ❶ (*opening*) Durchreiche *f* ❷ NAUT Luke *f*

hatch[2] [hætʃ] I. *vi* schlüpfen II. *vt* ausbrüten *a. fig*

hatchback [ˈhætʃ·bæk] *n* ❶ (*door*) Heckklappe *f* ❷ (*vehicle*) Wagen *m mit* Heckklappe

hatchet [ˈhætʃ·ɪt] *n* Beil *nt* ▶PHRASES: **to bury the ~** das Kriegsbeil begraben

hate [heɪt] I. *n* Hass *m* II. *vt* hassen; **I ~ going to the dentist** ich hasse es, zum Zahnarzt zu gehen.

ʹhate crime *n* LAW Verbrechen, das aus [Rassen]hass oder Vorurteilen begangen wird

hatred [ˈheɪ·trɪd] *n* Hass *m*

ʹhat trick *n* Hattrick *m*

haul [hɔl] I. *n* Ausbeute *f* II. *vt* ❶ (*pull*) ziehen; *sth heavy* schleppen ❷ (*trans-*

port) befördern

◆ **haul off** *vt* wegziehen; **to ~ sb off to jail** (*fig*) jdn ins Gefängnis werfen

hauler [ˈhɔ·lər] *n* freight ~ Transportunternehmen *nt*, Spedition[sfirma] *f*

haunt [hɔnt] *vt* ❶ *ghost* spuken in +*dat* ❷ *memories* heimsuchen

haunted [ˈhɔn·tɪd] *adj* ~ **house** Gespensterhaus *nt*

haunting [ˈhɔn·tɪŋ] *adj* ❶ (*disturbing*) quälend ❷ (*stirring*) sehnsuchtsvoll

have [hæv, həv] I. *aux vb* <*has, had, had*> ❶ (*forming past tenses*) **he has never been to New York before** er war noch nie zuvor in New York; **we had been swimming** wir waren schwimmen gewesen ❷ (*render*) ■ **to ~ sth done** etw tun lassen ❸ (*must*) ■ **~ to do sth** etw tun müssen II. *vt* <*has, had, had*> ❶ (*possess*) ■ **to ~ sth** etw haben; **~ a nice day!** viel Spaß!; (*to customers*) einen schönen Tag noch! ❷ *bath* nehmen; *nap, party* machen; **to ~ a talk with sb** mit jdm sprechen ❸ *food* essen; *cigarette* rauchen; **to ~ lunch** zu Mittag essen ❹ (*be obliged*) ■ **to ~ sth to do** etw tun müssen ❺ (*pregnant*) **to ~ a baby** ein Baby bekommen ❻ (*induce*) ■ **to ~ sb do sth** jdn [dazu] veranlassen, etw zu tun ▶PHRASES: **to ~ had it** (*be broken*) hinüber sein; (*be exhausted*) fix und fertig sein; **to ~ had it with sb/sth** von jdm/etw die Nase voll haben

◆ **have around** *vt* zur Hand haben

◆ **have back** *vt* (*object*) zurückhaben; (*person*) wieder nehmen

◆ **have in** *vt* ■ **to ~ sb in** [**to do sth**] jdn kommen lassen[, um etw zu tun] ▶PHRASES: **to ~ it** **in for sb** jdn auf dem Kieker haben

◆ **have on** *vt* ❶ *clothes* tragen ❷ (*know about*) ■ **to ~ sth on sb/sth** evidence, facts etw über jdn/etw [in der Hand] haben

◆ **have out** *vt* ❶ (*remove*) sich *dat* herausnehmen lassen ❷ (*fam: argue*) ■ **to ~ it out** [**with sb**] es [mit jdm] ausdiskutieren

◆**have over** *vt* ■**to ~ sb over** jdn zu sich *dat* einladen

haven ['heɪ·vən] *n* Zufluchtsort *m*

haven't ['hæv·ənt] = **have not** *see* **have**

havoc ['hæv·ək] *n* Verwüstungen *pl;* **to play ~ with sth** *(fig)* etw völlig durcheinanderbringen

Hawaii [hə·'waɪ·i] *n* Hawaii *nt*

hawk [hɔk] I. *n* ① *(bird)* Habicht *m* ② POL Falke *m* II. *vt* ■**to ~ sth** mit etw *dat* hausieren gehen

hawker ['hɔ·kər] *n* Hausierer(in) *m(f)*

'**hawk-eyed** *adj* ■**to be ~** Adleraugen haben

hawthorn ['hɔ·θɔrn] *n* Weißdorn *m*

hay [heɪ] *n* Heu *nt*

'**hay fever** *n* Heuschnupfen *m*

'**haystack** *n* Heuhaufen *m*

hazard ['hæz·ərd] *n* Gefahr *f*

'**hazard lights** *npl* AUTO Warnblinkanlage *f*

hazardous ['hæz·ər·dəs] *adj (dangerous)* gefährlich; *(risky)* riskant

haze [heɪz] I. *n* Dunst[schleier] *m* II. *vt* schikanieren

'**hazelnut** *n* Haselnuss *f*

hazy ['heɪ·zi] *adj* ① *(with haze)* dunstig, diesig ② *(confused)* unklar; *(indistinct)* verschwommen

he [hi] I. *pron pers (male person)* er; *(unspecified person)* er/sie/es II. *n* Er *m*

head [hed] I. *n* ① Kopf *m;* **she's got a good ~ for figures** sie kann gut mit Zahlen umgehen; **to use one's ~** seinen Verstand benutzen ② **a** [*or per*] **~** pro Kopf ③ *of bed, table* Kopfende *nt; of nail, coin* Kopf *m; of line* Anfang *m* ④ *(leader)* Chef(in) *m(f); of a project, department* Leiter(in) *m(f); of church, state* Oberhaupt *nt* ▶PHRASES: **to be ~ over heels in love** bis über beide Ohren verliebt sein; **to not be able to make ~s or tails of sth** aus etw *dat* nicht schlau werden; **to go to sb's ~** jdm zu Kopf steigen II. *vt* leitend III. *vt* ① *(be at the front of)* anführen ② *(be in charge of) organization* leiten IV. *vi* **to**

~ [for] home sich *akk* auf den Heimweg machen

◆**head back** *vi* zurückgehen; *with transport* zurückfahren

◆**head off** I. *vt* abfangen II. *vi* ■**to ~ off to[ward] sth** sich zu etw *dat* begeben

◆**head out** *vi* losziehen

◆**head up** *vt* leiten

'**headache** *n* Kopfschmerzen *pl*

'**headband** *n* Stirnband *nt*

'**headdress** <*pl* -es> *n* Kopfschmuck *m*

header ['hed·ər] *n* ① *(at top of page)* Kopfzeile *f* ② *(in email)* Header *m*

head'first *adv* kopfüber

'**headhunter** *n* Headhunter(in) *m(f)*

heading ['hed·ɪŋ] *n* Überschrift *f*

'**headlamp** *n* Scheinwerfer *m*

'**headlight** *n* Scheinwerfer *m*

'**headline** *n* Schlagzeile *f*

'**headliner** *n* Hauptattraktion *f*

'**headmaster** *n* Schulleiter *m*, Rektor *m*

'**headmistress** *n* Schulleiterin *f*, Rektorin *f*

head 'office *n* Zentrale *f*

head-'on I. *adj* Frontal- II. *adv* frontal; *(fig)* direkt

'**headphones** *npl* Kopfhörer *m*

'**headquarters** *npl* + *sing/pl vb* MIL Hauptquartier *nt; (of company)* Hauptsitz *m*

'**headrest** *n* Kopfstütze *f*

'**headroom** *n* lichte Höhe

'**headscarf** *n* Kopftuch *nt*

'**headset** *n* Kopfhörer *m*

head 'start *n* Vorsprung *m*

'**headstrong** *adj* eigensinnig

head-to-'head *adj contest* Kopf-an-Kopf-

'**headwaters** *n pl* Quellgewässer *pl*

'**headway** *n* **to make ~** [gut] vorankommen (**in** bei +*dat*, **with** mit +*dat*)

'**headwind** *n* Gegenwind *m*

'**headword** *n* LING Stichwort *nt*

heal [hil] *vt, vi* heilen

healing ['hi·lɪŋ] I. *adj attr process* heilsam II. *n* Heilung *f*

health [helθ] *n* Gesundheit *f*

'**health care** *n* Gesundheitsfürsorge *f*

'**health center** n Ärztehaus nt

'**health club** n Fitnessclub m

'**health food** n Reformkost f

'**health food store** n Naturkostladen m

'**health hazard** n Gesundheitsrisiko nt

'**health insurance** n Krankenversicherung f; ~ **company** Krankenkasse f

healthy ['hel·θi] adj gesund a. fig

heap [hip] I. n Haufen m a. fig fig II. vt aufhäufen; (fig) **to ~ praise on sb** jdn überschwänglich loben

hear <heard, heard> [hɪr] I. vt ① (perceive) hören; **Jane ~d him go out** Jane hörte, wie er hinausging ② LAW case verhandeln II. vi hören (**about/of** von +dat)

heard [hɜrd] pt, pp of **hear**

hearing ['hɪr·ɪŋ] n ① (ability to hear) Gehör nt; **to be hard of ~** schwerhörig sein ② (official examination) Anhörung f

'**hearing aid** n Hörgerät nt

'**hearing-impaired** adj schwerhörig

hearsay ['hɪr·seɪ] n Gerüchte pl

hearse [hɜrs] n Leichenwagen m

heart [hart] n ① Herz nt; **from the bottom of one's ~** aus tiefstem Herzen; **the ~ of the matter** der Kern der Sache; **to have one's ~ set on sth** sein [ganzes] Herz an etw akk hängen ② (courage) Mut m ③ CARDS ■~s pl Herz nt kein pl; **queen of ~s** Herzdame f ▶PHRASES: **by ~** auswendig; **to have a change of ~** sich akk anders besinnen

'**heartache** n Kummer m

'**heart attack** n Herzinfarkt m

'**heartbeat** n Herzschlag m

'**heartbreaking** adj herzzerreißend

'**heartbroken** adj todunglücklich

'**heartburn** n Sodbrennen nt

'**heart disease** n Herzkrankheit f

'**heart failure** n Herzversagen nt

heartily ['har·tɪ·li] adv herzlich; applaud begeistert

'**heartland** n of region Herz nt

heartless ['hart·lɪs] adj herzlos

'**heart-rending** adj herzzerreißend

'**heartthrob** n (fam) Schwarm m

'**heart transplant** n Herztransplantation f

'**heartwarming** adj herzerfreuend

hearty ['har·ti] adj ① (warm) herzlich ② breakfast herzhaft; appetite gesund

heat [hit] I. n ① (warmth) Wärme f; (high temperature) Hitze f ② SPORT Vorlauf m ▶PHRASES: **if you can't stand the ~, get out of the kitchen** (prov) wenn es dir zu viel wird, dann lass es lieber sein II. vt erhitzen, heiß machen; food aufwärmen; house heizen; pool beheizen

◆ **heat up** I. vt heiß machen; food aufwärmen; house [auf]heizen II. vi room warm werden; engine warm laufen; (fig) discussion sich erhitzen

heated ['hi·tɪd] adj ① discussion heftig ② (warm) erhitzt; room geheizt; pool beheizt

heater ['hi·tər] n [Heiz]ofen m, Heizgerät nt; (in car) Heizung f

heathen ['hi·ðən] n Heide m, Heidin f

heather ['heð·ər] n Heidekraut nt

heating ['hi·tɪŋ] n ① (action) Heizen nt; of room [Be]heizen nt; of substances Erwärmen nt ② (appliance) Heizung f

'**heat-resistant** adj hitzebeständig; ovenware feuerfest

'**heat shield** n Hitzeschild m

'**heat stroke** n Hitzschlag m

'**heat treatment** n Wärmebehandlung f

'**heat wave** n Hitzewelle f

heave [hiv] I. n Ruck m II. vt [hoch]hieven III. vi ① (pull) hieven ② (move) sich heben und senken; chest, sea wogen

heaven ['hev·ən] n Himmel m a. fig ▶PHRASES: **good ~s!** du lieber Himmel!

heavenly ['hev·ən·li] adj himmlisch

heavily ['hev·ɪ·li] adv ① (to great degree) stark; gamble leidenschaftlich ② (with weight) schwer; move schwerfällig; ~ **built** kräftig gebaut ③ (severely) schwer; **to snow ~** stark schneien

heavy ['hev·i] I. adj ① (weighty) schwer a. fig; fine hoch ② rain, drinker stark

❸ (*fig: oppressive*) drückend; *weather* schwül **❹** (*difficult*) schwierig; *breathing* schwer **❺** *beard* dicht; *coat* dick; *traffic* stark **II.** *n* (*sl: thug*) Schläger[typ] *m*

heavy-'duty *adj* robust; *clothes* strapazierfähig

heavy-'handed *adj* ungeschickt

heavy 'industry *n* Schwerindustrie *f*

heavy 'metal *n* **❶** (*metal*) Schwermetall *nt* **❷** (*music*) Heavymetal *m*

'heavyweight *n* Schwergewicht *nt* a. fig

Hebrew ['hi·bru] *n* **❶** (*person*) Hebräer(in) *m(f)*; (*language*) Hebräisch *nt*

heck [hek] *interj* (*euph sl*) **where the ~ have you been?** wo, zum Teufel, bist du gewesen?

hectic ['hek·tɪk] *adj* hektisch

he'd [hid] = **he had/he would** *see* **have I, II, would**

hedge [hedʒ] *n* BOT Hecke *f*

'hedgehog *n* Igel *m*

heebie-jeebies ['hi·bɪ·'dʒi·biz] *npl* (*sl*) **to get the ~** Zustände kriegen

heed [hid] (*form*) **I.** *vt* beachten **II.** *n* Beachtung *f*; **to pay ~ to** [*or* **take ~ of**] **sth** auf etw *akk* achten

heedless ['hid·lɪs] *adj* (*form*) achtlos

heel [hil] **I.** *n* **❶** ANAT Ferse *f* **❷** *of shoe* Absatz *m* ▶PHRASES: **to dig one's ~s in** sich auf die Hinterbeine stellen **II.** *interj* ■~! bei Fuß!

hefty ['hef·ti] *adj* **❶** (*strong*) kräftig; (*heavy*) schwer **❷** *price, fine* hoch, saftig *fam*

height [haɪt] *n* **❶** (*top to bottom*) Höhe *f*; *of a person* [Körper]größe *f*; **to be 20 feet in ~** 20 Fuß hoch sein **❷** (*high places*) ■~s *pl* Höhen *pl* **❸** (*fig*) Höhepunkt *m*

heighten ['haɪ·tən] *vt* verstärken; *tension* steigern

heir [er] *n* Erbe *m*, Erbin *f*

heiress <*pl* -es> ['er·ɪs] *n* Erbin *f*

heirloom ['er·lum] *n* Erbstück *nt*

heist [haɪst] *n* Raub/überfall] *m*

held [held] *vt, vi pt, pp of* **hold**

helicopter ['hel·ɪ·kap·tər] *n* Hubschrauber *m*

helipad ['hel·ɪ·pæd] *n* Hubschrauberlandeplatz *m*

'heliport *n* Heliport *m*, Hubschrauberlandeplatz *m*

helium ['hi·li·əm] *n* Helium *nt*

hell [hel] *n* **❶** Hölle *f* **❷** (*fig fam*) **to ~ with it!** ich hab's satt!; **to scare the ~ out of sb** jdn zu Tode erschrecken **❸** (*fam: for emphasis*) **he's one ~ of a guy!** er ist echt total in Ordnung!; **a ~ of a lot** verdammt viel ▶PHRASES: **come ~ or high water** komme, was wolle; **go to ~!** scher dich zum Teufel!

he'll [hil] = **he will/he shall** *see* **will, shall**

hellish ['hel·ɪʃ] *adj* höllisch a. fig

hello [hə·'lou] **I.** *n* Hallo *nt* **II.** *interj* hallo!

helm [helm] *n* Ruder *nt* a. fig

helmet ['hel·mɪt] *n* Helm *m*

help [help] **I.** *n* Hilfe *f*; (*financial*) Unterstützung *f*; **to cry for ~** um Hilfe rufen **II.** *interj* ■~! Hilfe! **III.** *vi* helfen (**with** bei +*dat*) **IV.** *vt* **❶** (*assist*) ■**to ~ sb** jdm helfen (**with** bei +*dat*); **can I ~ you?** (*in shop*) kann ich Ihnen behilflich sein? **❷** (*improve*) verbessern; (*alleviate*) lindern **❸** (*prevent*) **I can't ~ it!** ich kann nichts dagegen machen!; ■**sth can't be ~ed** etw ist nicht zu ändern **❹** (*take*) ■**to ~ oneself** sich *akk* bedienen

◆ help along *vt* ■**to ~ sb along** jdm [auf die Sprünge] helfen; ■**to ~ sth along** etw vorantreiben

◆ help out *vt* ■**to ~ out** ⟳ **sb** jdm [aus]helfen **II.** *vi* aushelfen

◆ help up *vt* ■**to ~ sb up** jdm aufhelfen

helper ['hel·pər] *n* Helfer(in) *m(f)*; (*assistant*) Gehilfe *m*, Gehilfin *f*

helpful ['help·fəl] *adj* *person* hilfsbereit; *suggestion* hilfreich

helping ['hel·pɪŋ] **I.** *n* *of food* Portion *f* **II.** *adj* hilfreich; **to give** [*or* **lend**] **sb a ~ hand** jdm helfen

helpless ['help·lɪs] *adj* hilflos; (*powerless*) machtlos

'helpline *n* Notruf *m*

helter-skelter [ˌhel·tər·ˈskel·tər] I. *adj* hektisch II. *adv* Hals über Kopf

hem [hem] *n* Saum *m*
  ◆**hem in** *vt* ❶ (*surround*) umgeben ❷ (*fig*) einengen

hemisphere [ˈhem·ɪ·sfɪr] *n* GEOG, ASTRON [Erd]halbkugel *f*

hemophiliac [ˌhi·moʊ·ˈfɪl·i·æk] *n* MED Bluter(in) *m(f)*

hemorrhage [ˈhem·ər·ɪdʒ] *n* MED [starke] Blutung

hemorrhoids [ˈhem·ər·ɔɪdz] *npl* MED Hämorrhoiden *pl*

hemp [hemp] *n* Hanf *m*

hen [hen] *n* ZOOL Henne *f*, Huhn *nt*

hence [hens] *adv* ❶ *after n* (*from now*) von jetzt an; **four weeks ~** in vier Wochen ❷ (*therefore*) daher

henceforth [ˌhens·ˈfɔrθ], **henceforward** [ˌhens·ˈfɔr·wərd] *adv* (*form*) von nun an

'**henpecked** *adj* **~ husband** Pantoffelheld *m*

hepatitis [ˌhep·ə·ˈtaɪ·t̬ɪs] *n* Leberentzündung *f*

heptathlon [hep·ˈtæθ·lən] *n* Siebenkampf *m*

her [hɜr] I. *pron pers* sie *in akk*, ihr *in dat*; **it was ~** sie war's II. *adj poss* ihr(e, n); (*ship, country*) sein(e, n); **what's ~ name?** wie heißt sie?

herald [ˈher·əld] *n* Bote *m*, Botin *f*

herb [ɜrb] *n* [Gewürz]kraut *nt meist pl*; (*for medicine*) [Heil]kraut *nt meist pl*

herbal [ˈɜr·bəl] *adj* Kräuter·

herbicide [ˈhɜr·bɪ·saɪd] *n* Unkrautvertilgungsmittel *nt*

herd [hɜrd] I. *n* Herde *f* II. *vt* treiben
  ◆**herd together** I. *vt* zusammentreiben II. *vi* sich zusammendrängen

'**herd instinct** *n* Herdentrieb *m*

'**herdsman** *n* Hirt[e] *m*

here [hɪr] I. *adv* hier; (*with movement*) hierher, hierhin; **come ~!** komm [hier]her!; **give it ~!** (*fam*) gib mal her!; **~ I am!** hier bin ich!; **~ comes the train** da kommt der Zug; **~ and now** [jetzt] sofort; **from ~ on in** [*or* out] von jetzt an II. *interj* **~!** hier!

hereabout [ˌhɪr·ə·ˈbaʊt], **hereabouts** [ˌhɪr·ə·ˈbaʊts] *adv* hier [in dieser Gegend]

hereditary [hə·ˈred·ɪ·ter·i] *adj* erblich; *disease* angeboren

heredity [hə·ˈred·ɪ·t̬i] *n* (*transmission of characteristics*) Vererbung *f*; (*genetic makeup*) Erbgut *nt*

heresy [ˈher·ə·si] *n* Ketzerei *f*

heretic [ˈher·ə·t̬ɪk] *n* Ketzer(in) *m(f)*

heritage [ˈher·ɪ·t̬ɪdʒ] *n* Erbe *nt*

hermit [ˈhɜr·mɪt] *n* Eremit(in) *m(f)* a. *fig*, Einsiedler(in) *m(f)* a. *fig*

hernia <*pl* -s> [ˈhɜr·ni·ə] *n* MED Bruch *m*

hero <*pl* -es> [ˈhɪr·oʊ] *n* Held(in) *m(f)*

heroic [hɪ·ˈroʊ·ɪk] *adj* heldenhaft; **~ deed** Heldentat *f*

heroin [ˈher·oʊ·ɪn] *n* Heroin *nt*

heroine [ˈher·oʊ·ɪn] *n* Heldin *f*

heroism [ˈher·oʊ·ɪz·əm] *n* Heldentum *nt*

heron <*pl* -s> [ˈher·ən] *n* Reiher *m*

herpes [ˈhɜr·piz] *n* MED Herpes *m*

herring <*pl* -s> [ˈher·ɪŋ] *n* Hering *m*

hers [hɜrz] *pron pers* (*of person/animal*) ihre(r, s)

herself [hɜr·ˈself] *pron refl* ❶ *after vb, prep* sich *in akk o dat* ❷ (*emph: personally*) selbst; **she told me ~** sie hat es mir selbst erzählt ❸ (*alone*) [**all**] **by ~** ganz alleine

he's [hiz] = **he is/he has** *see* be, have I, II

hesitant [ˈhez·ɪ·tənt] *adj person* unschlüssig; *answer* zögernd; *speech* stockend

hesitantly [ˈhez·ɪ·tənt·li] *adv act* unentschlossen

hesitate [ˈhez·ɪ·teɪt] *vi* zögern

hesitation [ˌhez·ɪ·ˈteɪ·ʃən] *n* (*indecision*) Zögern *nt*; (*reluctance*) Bedenken *pl*

heterogeneous [ˌhet̬·ər·ə·ˈdʒi·ni·əs] *adj* uneinheitlich

heterosexual [ˌhet̬·ə·roʊ·ˈsek·ʃu·əl] I. *adj* heterosexuell II. *n* Heterosexuelle(r) *f(m)*

HEV [ˌeɪtʃ·iː·ˈviː] *n abbrev of* **hybrid**

electric vehicle Hybridauto *nt*, Hybridfahrzeug *nt*

hexagon ['hek·sə·gan] *n* Sechseck *nt*

hexagonal [hek·'sæg·ə·nəl] *adv* sechseckig

hey [heɪ] *interj* (*fam*) he!

HI *abbrev of* **Hawaii**

hi [haɪ] *interj* hallo!

hibernate ['haɪ·bər·neɪt] *vi* Winterschlaf halten

hibernation [haɪ·bər·'neɪ·ʃən] *n* Winterschlaf *m*

hiccup, hiccough ['hɪk·ʌp] I. *n* ❶ Schluckauf *m*; **to have the ~s** einen Schluckauf haben ❷ (*fig: setback*) Schwierigkeit *f meist pl* II. *vi* hicksen DIAL

hick [hɪk] *n* (*pej fam*) Provinzler(in) *m(f) pej fam*

hickory ['hɪk·ə·ri] *n* Hickory[baum] *m*

hid [hɪd] *vt pt of* **hide**

hidden ['hɪd·ən] I. *vt pp of* **hide** II. *adj* versteckt; *agenda* heimlich

hide[1] [haɪd] I. *vt* <hid, hidden> ❶ (*out of sight*) verstecken (**from** vor +*dat*) ❷ *emotions* verbergen; *facts* verheimlichen II. *vi* <hid, hidden> sich *akk* verstecken (**from** vor +*dat*)
◆ **hide away** I. *vt* verstecken II. *vi* sich *akk* verstecken
◆ **hide out, hide up** *vi* sich *akk* versteckt halten

hide[2] [haɪd] *n* (*skin*) Haut *f a. fig*; (*with fur*) Fell *nt*; (*leather*) Leder *nt*

'hide-and-go-seek, **'hide-and-seek** *n* Versteckspiel *nt*

'hideaway *n* (*fam*) Versteck *nt a. fig*

hideous ['hɪd·i·əs] *adj* grässlich, scheußlich

'hideout *n* Versteck *nt*

hiding ['haɪ·dɪŋ] *n* **to be in ~** sich versteckt halten

hierarchy ['haɪ·rar·ki] *n* Hierarchie *f*

hi-fi ['haɪ·faɪ] *n short for* **high fidelity** Hi-Fi-Anlage *f*

high [haɪ] I. *adj* ❶ *building, speed* hoch präd, hohe(r, s) *attr*; *winds* stark; *marks* gut; **~ in calories** kalorienreich; **~ and mighty** (*pej*) herablassend ❷ (*on drugs*) high II. *adv* hoch; (*fig*) **emotions were running ~** die Gemüter erhitzten sich III. *n* ❶ (*high[est] point*) Höchststand *m* ❷ METEO Hoch *nt*

high 'beams *npl* AUTO Fernlicht *nt*

'highbrow *adj* hochgeistig

'highchair *n* Hochstuhl *m*

'high-class *adj* erstklassig; *product* hochwertig

'high court *n see* **Supreme Court**

higher edu'cation *n* Hochschulbildung *f*

high'flier *n* (*fig*) Überflieger(in) *m(f)*

high 'frequency *n* Hochfrequenz *f*

high'handed *adj* selbstherrlich

high 'heels *npl* ❶ (*shoes*) hochhackige Schuhe ❷ (*parts of a shoe*) hohe Absätze

'high jump *n* Hochsprung *m*

highlands ['haɪ·ləndz] *npl* Hochland *nt kein pl*

'high-level *adj* auf höchster Ebene nach *n*

high life *n* exklusives Leben

'highlight I. *n* ❶ (*best part*) Höhepunkt *m* ❷ (*in hair*) **■~s** *pl* Strähnchen *pl* II. *vt* hervorheben; *text* markieren

highly ['haɪ·li] *adv* hoch; **to think ~ of someone** eine hohe Meinung von jdm haben

High 'Mass *n* Hochamt *nt*

Highness ['haɪ·nɪs] *n* **■Your ~** Eure Hoheit

high-'pitched *adj voice* hoch; *roof* steil

'high point *n* Höhepunkt *m*

high-'powered *adj* ❶ *machine* Hochleistungs-; *car* stark ❷ (*influential*) einflussreich; *delegation* hochrangig

high-'pressure I. *adj* ❶ METEO, TECH Hochdruck- ❷ ECON **~ sales techniques** aggressive Verkaufstechniken II. *vt* AM unter Druck setzen

high 'priest *n* REL Hohe(r) Priester *m*

high-'profile *adj* profiliert

high-'protein *adj* eiweißreich

high-'ranking *adj* hochrangig

high-reso'lution *adj* mit hoher Auflösung

'high-rise, high-rise 'building n Hochhaus nt

high-'risk adj hochriskant

'high school n Highschool f, ≈ Gymnasium nt

high 'seas npl hohe See; on the ~ auf hoher See

high 'season n Hochsaison f

high-speed 'train n Hochgeschwindigkeitszug m

high-'spirited adj ausgelassen

high 'spirits npl Hochstimmung f kein pl

'high spot n Höhepunkt m

'hightail vt, vi (fam) to ~ [it] abhauen

high-'tech adj Hightech-

high tech'nology n Hochtechnologie f

high 'tide n Flut f

high 'treason n Hochverrat m

high-'water mark n Hochwassermarke f

'highway n Highway m

hijack ['haɪ·dʒæk] I. vt entführen II. n Entführung f

hijacker ['haɪ·dʒæk·ər] n Entführer(in) m(f)

hijacking ['haɪ·dʒæk·ɪŋ] n Entführung f

hike [haɪk] I. n ⓵ (long walk) Wanderung f ⓶ (fam: increase) Erhöhung f II. vi wandern III. vt (fam) erhöhen

hiker ['haɪ·kər] n Wanderer m, Wanderin f

hiking ['haɪ·kɪŋ] n Wandern nt

hilarious [hɪ·'ler·i·əs] adj urkomisch; mood ausgelassen

hill [hɪl] n Hügel m; (higher) Berg m; (slope) Steigung f

hillbilly ['hɪl·bɪl·i] n Hinterwäldler(in) m(f)

'hillside n Hang m

'hilltop n Hügelkuppe f

hilly ['hɪl·i] adj hügelig

hilt [hɪlt] n (handle) Griff m; of sword Heft nt

him [hɪm] pron object ihn in akk, ihm in dat; who? ~? wer? der?

Himalayas [ˌhɪm·ə·'leɪ·əz] npl GEOG Himalaja m

himself [hɪm·'self] pron refl ⓵ after vb, prep sich in akk o dat ⓶ (emph: personally) selbst; he told me ~ er hat es mir selbst erzählt ⓷ (alone) [all] by ~ ganz alleine

hind [haɪnd] adj hintere(r, s)

hinder ['hɪn·dər] vt behindern

Hindi ['hɪn·di] n Hindi nt

'hindquarters npl Hinterteil nt; of a horse Hinterhand f

hindrance ['hɪn·drəns] n Hindernis nt

'hindsight n in [or with [the benefit of]] ~ im Nachhinein

Hindu ['hɪn·du] n Hindu m o f

hinge [hɪndʒ] n Angel f; of gate Scharnier nt

hint [hɪnt] I. n ⓵ usu sing (trace) Spur f; at the slightest ~ of trouble beim leisesten Anzeichen von Ärger ⓶ (allusion) Andeutung f; OK, I can take a ~ OK, ich verstehe schon ⓷ (advice) Tipp m II. vt, vi andeuten

hip [hɪp] I. n ANAT Hüfte f; of pants Hüftweite f II. adj (fam) hip

'hip flask n Flachmann m

hippie ['hɪp·i] n Hippie m

hippo ['hɪp·oʊ] n (fam) short for hippopotamus

hippopotamus <pl -es> [ˌhɪp·ə·'pɑt·ə·məs] n Nilpferd nt

hippy ['hɪp·i] n see hippie

hire [haɪr] vt einstellen

◆ hire out vt to ~ oneself ⟳ out seine Dienste anbieten

his [hɪz] I. pron pers seine(r, s); some friends of ~ einige seiner Freunde II. adj poss (of person) sein(e)

Hispanic [hɪs·'pæn·ɪk] I. adj hispanisch II. n Hispanoamerikaner(in) m(f)

hiss [hɪs] I. vt, vi zischen; cat fauchen II. n <pl -es> Zischen nt kein pl; of cat Fauchen nt kein pl

historian [hɪ·'stɔr·i·ən] n Historiker(in) m(f)

historic [hɪ·'stɔr·ɪk] adj historisch

historical [hɪ·'stɔr·ɪk·əl] adj geschichtlich, historisch

history ['hɪs·tə·ri] n ⓵ (past events) Geschichte f ⓶ (fig) to be ~ person vergessen sein, passé sein fam ⓷ usu sing

H

(*background*) Vorgeschichte *f;* **her family has a ~ of heart problems** Herzprobleme liegen bei ihr in der Familie

hit [hɪt] I. *n* ❶ (*blow*) Schlag *m* ❷ (*shot*) Treffer *m;* **to suffer a direct ~** direkt getroffen werden ❸ (*success, in baseball*) Hit *m* ❹ (*fam: murder*) Mord *m* ❺ INET Besuch *m* einer Webseite, Hit *m* II. *vt* <-tt-, *hit, hit*> ❶ (*strike*) schlagen ❷ (*come in contact*) treffen *a. fig* ❸ button drücken; **key** drücken *auf +akk* ❹ (*crash into*) **to ~ sth** gegen etw *akk* stoßen ❺ SPORT treffen; **basket** erzielen ❻ (*fam: arrive at*) **to ~ the headlines** in die Schlagzeilen kommen; **to ~ rock bottom** einen historischen Tiefstand erreichen III. *vi* ❶ (*strike*) ■ **to ~ [at sb/sth]** [nach jdm/etw] schlagen; **to ~ hard** kräftig zuschlagen ❷ (*attack*) ■ **to ~ at sb** jdn attackieren *a. fig*
♦**hit back** *vi* zurückschlagen; ■ **to ~ back at sb** jdm Kontra geben
♦**hit off** *vt* ■ **to ~ it off [with sb]** (*fam*) sich prächtig [mit jdm] verstehen
♦**hit on** *vt* ❶ (*think of*) kommen auf *+akk* ❷ (*sl: make sexual advances*) ■ **to ~ on sb** jdn anmachen
♦**hit upon** *vt* **idea** kommen auf *+akk*
hit-and-'miss *adj* zufällig; **a ~ affair** [reine] Glückssache
hit-and-'run *n* AUTO Fahrerflucht *f*
hitch [hɪtʃ] I. *n* <*pl* -es> (*difficulty*) Haken *m;* **to go off without a ~** reibungslos ablaufen II. *vt* ❶ (*fasten*) festmachen (**to** an *+dat*); **trailer** anhängen (**to** an *+akk*) ❷ (*fam: hitchhike*) **to ~ a ride** [*or* **lift**] trampen, per Anhalter fahren III. *vi* (*fam*) trampen
♦**hitch up** *vt* ❶ festmachen (**to** an *+dat*); **trailer** anhängen (**to** an *+akk*); **to ~ a horse up to a cart** ein Pferd vor einen Wagen spannen ❷ **pants** hochziehen
hitcher ['hɪtʃ·ər] *n see* **hitchhiker**
'hitchhike *vi* per Anhalter fahren, trampen
'hitchhiker *n* Anhalter(in) *m(f),* Tramper(in) *m(f)*

hi-'tech *adj see* **high-tech**
'hit man *n* Killer *m*
HIV [ˌeɪtʃ·aɪˈvi] *n abbrev of* **human immunodeficiency virus** HIV *nt*
hive [haɪv] *n* Bienenstock *m*
HMO [ˌeɪtʃ·em·ˈoʊ] *n abbrev of* **health maintenance organization** *eine in der Regel vom Arbeitgeber getragene, preisgünstige Krankenversicherung mit begrenzter Ärzteauswahl*
hoagie ['hoʊ·gi] *n* Riesensandwich *nt*
hoard [hɔrd] I. *n* (*of money, food*) Vorrat *m* (**of** an *+dat*); (*treasure*) Schatz *m* II. *vt* horten; **food** *a.* hamstern
hoarse [hɔrs] *adj* heiser
hoax [hoʊks] I. *n* (*deception*) Täuschung *f;* (*joke*) Streich *m;* (*false alarm*) blinder Alarm II. *adj* vorgetäuscht III. *vt* [he]reinlegen; **to ~ sb into believing** [*or* **thinking**] **sth** jdm etw weismachen
hoaxer ['hoʊks·ər] *n* jd, der falschen Alarm auslöst
hobble ['hab·əl] *vi* hinken, humpeln
hobby ['hab·i] *n* Hobby *nt*
hobo <*pl* -s> ['hoʊ·boʊ] *n* Penner(in) *m(f)*
hock [hak] *n* (*fam*) ❶ (*in debt*) **to be in ~** Schulden haben ❷ (*pawned*) **in ~** verpfändet
hockey ['hak·i] *n* [Eis]hockey *nt*
hodgepodge ['hadʒ·padʒ] *n* Mischmasch *m* (**of** aus *+dat*)
hoe [hoʊ] I. *n* Hacke *f* II. *vt, vi* hacken
hog [hɔg] *n* Schwein *nt*
hoist [hɔɪst] I. *vt* hochheben; **flag, sail** hissen II. *n* Winde *f*
hold [hoʊld] I. *n* ❶ (*grasp*) Halt *m* kein *pl;* **to keep ~ of sth** etw festhalten; **to take ~** (*fig*) **fire, epidemic** übergreifen ❷ SPORT Griff *m* ❸ **to be on ~** auf Eis liegen *fig;* TELEC in der Warteschleife sein; **to put on ~ project, plans** auf Eis legen ❹ NAUT, AVIAT Frachtraum *m* II. *vt* <*held, held*> ❶ (*grasp*) ■ **to ~ sb/sth** [**tight** [*or* **tightly**]] jdn/etw [fest]halten; **to ~ sth in place** etw an seinem Platz halten; **to ~ sb's attention** [*or* **interest**] jdn fesseln; **to ~ its value** seinen

Wert behalten ⑤ (*delay, stop*) zurückhalten; PHOT **OK, ~ it!** gut, bleib so!; TELEC **to ~ the line** am Apparat bleiben ④ (*contain*) fassen; COMPUT speichern

◆ **hold against** vt ■ **to ~ sth against sb** jdm etw vorwerfen

◆ **hold back** I. vt (*stop*) aufhalten; (*impede development*) hindern; *information* geheim halten II. vi (*refrain*) **to ~ back from doing sth** etw unterlassen

◆ **hold down** vt niederhalten; *prices* niedrig halten

◆ **hold forth** vi ■ **to ~ forth [about sth]** sich [über etw *akk*] auslassen

◆ **hold in** vt *emotions* zurückhalten; *stomach* einziehen

◆ **hold off** I. vt ① MIL *enemy* abwehren ② (*postpone*) verschieben II. vi warten

◆ **hold on** vi ① (*affix, attach*) ■ **to be held on by [or with] sth** mit etw *dat* befestigt sein ② (*manage to keep going*) durchhalten ③ (*wait*) **~ on!** Moment bitte!

◆ **hold onto** vt ① (*grasp*) festhalten ② (*keep*) behalten

◆ **hold out** I. vt ausstrecken II. vi (*manage to resist*) durchhalten

◆ **hold over** vt ① (*defer*) aufschieben ② (*extend*) verlängern

◆ **hold to** vt **can I ~ you to that?** bleibst du bei deinem Wort?

◆ **hold together** vt, vi zusammenhalten

◆ **hold up** I. vt ① (*raise*) hochhalten; *hand* heben ② (*support*) stützen ③ (*delay*) aufhalten II. vi ① (*endure*) durchhalten, aushalten ② (*remain convincing*) standhalten

holder ['hoʊl·dər] n ① (*device*) Halter m ② (*person*) Besitzer(in) m(f)

holding ['hoʊl·dɪŋ] n ① (*land*) Pachtbesitz m ② FIN Beteiligung f

'**holdup** n ① (*crime*) Raubüberfall m ② (*delay*) Verzögerung f

hole [hoʊl] I. n ① (*gap*) Loch nt a. fig; of *fox, rabbit* Bau m ② (*fig: fault*) **to pick ~s [in sth]** [etw] kritisieren ③ (*fig fam: difficulty*) **to get sb out of a ~** jdm aus der Patsche helfen II. vt (*in golf*) einlochen

◆ **hole up** vi (*fam*) sich verkriechen

holiday ['hal·ɪ·deɪ] n Feiertag m ▸ PHRASES: **Happy ~s!** Frohe Weihnachten!

Holland ['hal·ənd] n Holland nt

holler ['hal·ər] vt, vi (*fam*) brüllen

hollow ['hal·oʊ] I. adj ① (*empty, sunken*) hohl ② (*fig*) wertlos; *victory* schal II. n ① (*hole*) Senke f ② (*valley*) Tal nt III. vt ■ **to ~ [out]** aushöhlen

holly ['hal·i] n Stechpalme f

holocaust ['hal·ə·kɔst] n ① (*destruction*) Inferno nt ② (*genocide*) Massenvernichtung f; ■ **the H~** der Holocaust

hologram ['hal·ə·græm] n Hologramm nt

holster ['hoʊl·stər] n [Pistolen]halfter nt o f

holy ['hoʊ·li] adj heilig

Holy Com'munion n (*service*) heilige Kommunion

Holy 'Spirit n ■ **the ~** der Heilige Geist

'**holy water** n Weihwasser nt

homage ['ham·ɪdʒ] n Huldigung f

home [hoʊm] I. n ① (*abode*) Zuhause nt; **a ~ away from ~** ein zweites Zuhause; **to make oneself at ~** es sich *dat* gemütlich machen; **at ~** zu Hause, zuhause ÖSTERR, SCHWEIZ ② (*house*) Haus nt; (*apartment*) Wohnung f ③ (*institution*) Heim nt ④ (*place of origin*) Heimat f ▸ PHRASES: **to feel at ~ with sb** sich bei jdm wohl fühlen II. adv ① (*at one's abode*) zu Hause, zuhause ÖSTERR, SCHWEIZ, daheim bes SÜDD, ÖSTERR, SCHWEIZ; (*to one's abode*) nach Hause, nachhause ÖSTERR, SCHWEIZ ② (*to sb's understanding*) **to bring sth ~ [to sb]** [jdm] etw klarmachen III. vi ■ **to ~ in on sth** genau auf etw *akk* zusteuern; (*fig*) [sich *dat*] etw herausgreifen

'**home address** n Heimatadresse f

'**home advantage** n Heimvorteil m

home-'baked adj selbst gebacken

home 'banking n Homebanking nt

'**homecoming** n ① (*return*) Heimkehr f kein pl ② (*reunion*) Ehemaligentreffen nt; **~ queen** Schönheitskönigin beim Ehemaligentreffen

H

home 'cooking n Hausmannskost f
home eco'nomics n + sing vb Hauswirtschaft[slehre] f
'home game n Heimspiel nt
home-'grown adj aus eigenem Anbau
home 'help n Haushaltshilfe f
'homeland n (origin) Heimat f, Heimatland nt; ~ security innere Sicherheit, Heimatschutz m
homeless ['houm·lɪs] I. adj heimatlos; ■to be ~ obdachlos sein II. n the ~ pl die Obdachlosen pl
'home loan n Hypothek f
homely ['houm·li] adj ❶ (pej: ugly) unansehnlich ❷ (plain) schlicht aber gemütlich
home'made adj hausgemacht; cake selbst gebacken
'homemaker n Hausmann, -frau m, f
homeopath ['hou·mi·ou·pæθ] n Homöopath(in) m(f)
homeopathy [,hou·mi·'ap·ə·θi] n Homöopathie f
'homeowner n Hausbesitzer(in) m(f)
'home page n COMPUT Homepage f
home 'plate n (in baseball) Homeplate f, Schlagmal nt
home 'run n (in baseball) Punkt bringender Lauf um alle vier Male beim Baseball
home'schooling n Unterricht m zu Hause
'homesick adj to be [or feel] ~ Heimweh haben
'homesickness n Heimweh nt
homestead ['houm·sted] n Eigenheim nt
home'stretch n Zielgerade f a. fig
'home team n Heimmannschaft f
home'town n Heimatstadt f
homeward ['houm·wərd] adv heimwärts, nach Hause
homewards ['houm·wərdz] adv heimwärts
'homework n Hausaufgaben pl a. fig
homey ['hou·mi] adj (cozy) heimelig
homicidal [,ham·ɪ·'saɪ·dəl] adj gemeingefährlich
homicide ['ham·ɪ·saɪd] n LAW ❶ (murdering) Mord m ❷ (death) Mordfall m; ~ squad Mordkommission f
homogenize [hə·'madʒ·ə·naɪz] vt homogenisieren
homosexual [,hou·mə·'sek·ʃu·əl] (form) I. adj homosexuell II. n Homosexuelle(r) f(m)
homosexuality [,hou·mə·sek·ʃu·'æl·ə·ţi] n Homosexualität f
Honduras [han·'dur·əs] n Honduras nt
honest ['an·ɪst] adj ❶ (truthful) ehrlich ❷ (trusty) redlich
honestly ['an·ɪst·li] I. adv ehrlich II. interj ❶ (promising) [ganz] ehrlich! ❷ (disapproving) also ehrlich!
honesty ['an·ɪ·sti] n Ehrlichkeit f
honey ['hʌn·i] n ❶ (from bees) Honig m ❷ (fam: sweet person) Schatz m
'honeybee n [Honig]biene f
'honeycomb n (wax) Bienenwabe f; (food) Honigwabe f
honeydew 'melon n Honigmelone f
'honeymoon n ❶ (after marriage) Flitterwochen pl ❷ usu sing (fig) Schonfrist f
honk [haŋk] I. n ❶ of goose Schrei m ❷ of horn Hupen nt II. vi ❶ goose schreien ❷ horn hupen III. vt to ~ one's horn auf die Hupe drücken
honor ['an·ər] I. n ❶ Ehre f ❷ (award) Auszeichnung f II. vt ehren
honorable ['an·ər·əb·əl] adj ehrenhaft; person ehrenwert
honorary ['an·ə·rer·i] adj ehrenamtlich
'honor roll n SCH, UNIV Ehrenrolle f
'honors degree n UNIV akademischer Grad mit Prüfung im Spezialfach
hood¹ [hʊd] n ❶ (head covering) Kapuze f ❷ AUTO [Motor]haube f
hood² [hʊd] n (gangster) Kriminelle(r) f(m)
hood³ [hʊd] n (sl) Nachbarschaft f
hoodlum ['hud·ləm] n (gangster) Kriminelle(r) f(m)
hoodwink ['hʊd·wɪŋk] vt hereinlegen
hoof [hʊf] n <pl hooves> Huf m
hook [hʊk] I. n Haken m; to leave the phone off the ~ den Telefonhörer nicht auflegen ►PHRASES: to be off the ~

aus dem Schneider sein; **to let sb off the ~** jdn herauspauken II. vt ① *(fasten)* festhaken **(to** an +*dat)* ② *(grab with hook)* **she ~ed the shoe out of the water** sie angelte den Schuh aus dem Wasser ③ *fish* an die Angel bekommen

◆ **hook up** I. vt ① *(connect)* anschließen **(to** an +*akk)* ② *(fasten)* zumachen ③ *(hang)* aufhängen II. vi ① *(connect)* ■ **to ~ up [to sth]** sich [an etw *akk]* anschließen ② *(sl: get together)* **to ~ up [with sb]** sich [mit jdm] treffen

hooked [hʊkt] adj ① *(curved)* hakenförmig; **~ nose** Hakennase ② *(addicted)* abhängig ③ *(interested)* ■ **to be ~** total begeistert sein

hooker ['hʊk·ər] n *(fam)* Nutte f sl

hooky ['hʊk·i] n *(fam)* **to play ~** die Schule schwänzen

hooligan ['huː·lɪ·gən] n Hooligan m

hoop [huːp] n Reifen m

hooray [həˈreɪ] interj see **hurray**

hoot [huːt] I. n *(owl call)* Schrei m II. vi *owl* schreien

hop¹ [hap] I. vi <-pp-> ① hüpfen ② *sport* springen II. vt <-pp-> ① *(jump)* springen über +*akk* ② *(fam: board)* steigen in +*akk* III. n ① *(jump)* Hüpfer m ② *(fam: flight stage)* Flugabschnitt m

◆ **hop in, hop on** vt, vi *(fam)* einsteigen

◆ **hop off, hop out** vt, vi *(fam)* aussteigen

hop² [hap] n *bot* Hopfen m

hope [hoʊp] I. n Hoffnung f; **to give up ~** die Hoffnung aufgeben; **in the ~ of doing sth** in der Hoffnung, etw zu tun II. vi hoffen **(for** auf +*akk)*

hopeful ['hoʊp·fəl] adj zuversichtlich; ■ **to be ~ of sth** auf etw *akk* hoffen

hopefully ['hoʊp·fəl·i] adv ① *(in hope)* hoffnungsvoll ② *(it is hoped)* hoffentlich

hopeless ['hoʊp·lɪs] adj hoffnungslos; *situation* aussichtslos; ■ **to be ~** *(fam: incompetent)* ein hoffnungsloser Fall sein

hopping ['hap·ɪŋ] adj *(fam)* auf hundertachtzig; **to be ~ mad at sb** stinksauer auf jdn sein

hopscotch ['hap·skatʃ] n Himmel und Hölle nt

horde [hɔrd] n Horde f

horizon [hə·ˈraɪ·zən] n Horizont m

horizontal [ˌhɔr·ɪ·ˈzan·təl] adj horizontal, waag[e]recht

hormone ['hɔr·moʊn] n Hormon nt

horn [hɔrn] n ① *zool* Horn nt ② *mus* Horn nt ③ *auto* Hupe f

hornet ['hɔr·nɪt] n Hornisse f

horny ['hɔr·ni] adj ① *(hard)* hornartig ② *(fam: sexually excited)* geil   **H**

horoscope ['hɔr·ə·skoʊp] n Horoskop nt

horrendous [hə·ˈren·dəs] adj schrecklich; *conditions* entsetzlich; *prices* horrend

horrible ['hɔr·ə·bəl] adj schrecklich; *weather* scheußlich; *(unkind)* gemein

horrific [hə·ˈrɪf·ɪk] adj ① *(shocking)* entsetzlich, grausig ② *(extreme)* *prices* horrend

horrify <-ie-> ['hɔr·ə·faɪ] vt entsetzen

horror ['hɔr·ər] n Entsetzen nt

horse [hɔrs] n Pferd nt; **~ and buggy** Pferdewagen m ▶ PHRASES: **to hear sth [straight] from the ~'s mouth** etw aus erster Hand haben

'**horseback** n **on ~** zu Pferd

'**horse chestnut** n Rosskastanie f

'**horseman** n Reiter m

'**horsepower** <pl -> n Pferdestärke f

'**horse race** n Pferderennen nt

'**horse racing** n Pferderennsport m

'**horseradish** n Meerrettich m

'**horseshoe** n Hufeisen nt

'**horse trailer, 'horse van** n Pferdetransporter m

'**horsewoman** n Reiterin f

hors(e)y ['hɔr·si] adj *(fam)* pferdenärrisch

horticulture ['hɔr·ţɪ·ˌkʌl·tʃər] n Gartenbau m

hose [hoʊz] n Schlauch m

◆ **hose down, hose off** vt ■ **to ~ sth**

○ **down** [*or* **off**] etw [mit einem Schlauch] abspritzen

hospice ['hɑs·pɪs] *n* Hospiz *nt*

hospitable ['hɑs·pɪ·tə·bəl] *adj* gastfreundlich

hospital ['hɑs·pɪ·təl] *n* Krankenhaus *nt*, Spital *nt* SCHWEIZ

hospitality [ˌhɑs·pɪ·'tæl·ɪ·ti] *n* ❶ (*welcome*) Gastfreundschaft *f* ❷ (*food*) Bewirtung *f*

hospitalize ['hɑs·pɪ·tə·laɪz] *vt* ■ **to be ~ d** ins Krankenhaus eingewiesen werden

host [hoʊst] **I.** *n* ❶ (*party giver*) Gastgeber(in) *m(f)* ❷ TV Showmaster(in) *m(f)* **II.** *adj* ~ **country** Gastland *nt* **III.** *vt* ❶ (*stage*) ausrichten ❷ TV präsentieren

hostage ['hɑs·tɪdʒ] *n* Geisel *f*

hostel ['hɑs·təl] *n* Wohnheim *nt;* [**youth**] ~ Jugendherberge *f*

hostess <*pl* -es> ['hoʊ·stɪs] *n* ❶ (*at home, on TV*) Gastgeberin *f* ❷ (*at restaurant*) Wirtin *f* ❸ (*at exhibition*) Hostess *f*

hostile ['hɑs·təl] *adj* ❶ (*unfriendly*) feindselig ❷ (*difficult*) hart, widrig; *climate* rau ❸ ECON, MIL feindlich

hostility [hɑ·'stɪl·ɪ·ti] *n* ❶ Feindseligkeit *f* ❷ MIL ■ **hostilities** *pl* Feindseligkeiten *pl*

hot [hɑt] *adj* <-tt-> ❶ (*temperature*) heiß; **she was ~** ihr war heiß ❷ *food* scharf ❸ (*fam: dangerous*) *situation* brenzlig; *stolen items* heiß ❹ (*sl: sexy*) echt geil ▶PHRASES: **to be all ~ and bothered** ganz aufgeregt sein

hot-'air balloon *n* Heißluftballon *m*

hot-'blooded *adj* (*easy to anger*) hitzköpfig; (*passionate*) heißblütig

'**hot dog** *n* (*sausage*) Wiener Würstchen *nt;* (*in a bun*) Hotdog *m*

hotel [hoʊ·'tel] *n* Hotel *nt*

hotel 'industry *n* Hotelgewerbe *nt*

'**hotfoot** *vt* (*fam*) **to ~ it home** schnell nach Hause rennen

'**hothead** *n* Hitzkopf *m*

'**hothouse** *n* Treibhaus *nt*

'**hotline** *n* Hotline *f;* POL heißer Draht

hotly ['hɑt·li] *adv* heftig; ~ **contested** heiß umkämpft

'**hotplate** *n* (*for cooking*) Kochplatte *f;* (*food warmer*) Warmhalteplatte *f*

hot po'tato *n* POL *fig* heißes Eisen

'**hotshot** *n* (*fam*) Kanone *f*

'**hot spot** *n* ❶ (*popular place*) heißer Schuppen ❷ (*area of conflict*) Krisenherd *m*

hot 'stuff *n* ❶ (*fam: skillful*) ■ **to be ~** ein Ass sein ❷ (*sl: sexy woman*) heiße Braut, Schnecke *f sl;* (*sexy man*) heißer Typ, Schmacko *m sl*

hot-'tempered *adj* heißblütig

'**hot tub** *n* Jacuzzi® *m*

hot-'water bottle *n* Wärmflasche *f*

'**hot-wire** *vt* (*fam*) *car* kurzschließen

hound [haʊnd] **I.** *n* [Jagd]hund *m* **II.** *vt* jagen

hour [aʊr] *n* Stunde *f;* **50 miles an** [*or* **per**] ~ 50 Meilen pro Stunde; ~**s of business** Öffnungszeiten *pl;* **to be paid by the** ~ pro Stunde bezahlt werden; **to work long ~s** lange arbeiten; **for ~s** stundenlang

'**hour hand** *n* Stundenzeiger *m*

hourly ['aʊr·li] *adj, adv* stündlich; ~ **rate** Stundensatz *m*

house I. *n* [haʊs] Haus *nt;* **the White H~** das Weiße Haus; **in ~** im Hause; **on the** ~ auf Kosten des Hauses **II.** *vt* [haʊz] *person* unterbringen; *criminal* Unterschlupf gewähren +*dat; thing* beherbergen

'**house arrest** *n* Hausarrest *m*

'**housebreaker** *n* Einbrecher(in) *m(f)*

'**housebroken** *adj* stubenrein

'**house call** *n* Hausbesuch *m*

'**housefly** *n* Stubenfliege *f*

'**household** *n* Haushalt *m*

'**householder** *n* Hauseigentümer(in) *m(f)*

'**house-hunt** *vi* nach einem Haus suchen

'**househusband** *n* Hausmann *m*

'**housekeeper** *n* Haushälter(in) *m(f)*

'**housekeeping** *n* Haushalten *nt*

House of Repre'sentatives *n* ■ **the** ~ das Repräsentantenhaus

'houseplant n Zimmerpflanze f
house-to-'house adj, adv von Haus zu Haus
'housewarming, **'housewarming party** n Einweihungsparty f
'housewife n Hausfrau f
'housework n Hausarbeit f
housing ['haʊ·zɪŋ] n ❶ (living quarters) Wohnungen pl ❷ (casing) Gehäuse nt
'housing development n Wohnsiedlung f
'housing market n Wohnungsmarkt m
'housing project n Sozialwohnungen pl
HOV [ˌeɪtʃ·oʊ·'vi] n AUTO abbrev of **high occupancy vehicle** Fahrzeug nt mit mindestens zwei Insassen; ~ **lane** Fahrspur f für Fahrzeuge mit mindestens zwei Insassen
hover ['hʌv·ər] vi schweben; hawk a. stehen; (fig) herumlungern
'hovercraft <pl -> n Luftkissenboot nt
how [haʊ] adv wie; ~ **are you?** wie geht es Ihnen?; ~ **do you do?** (meeting sb) Guten Tag/Abend!; ~ **come?** wie das?; ~ **do you know that?** woher weißt du das?; **and ~!** und ob [o wie]!; ~ **far/ many** wie weit/viele; ~ **much** wie viel
howdy ['haʊ·di] interj (fam) Tag fam
however [haʊ·'ev·ər] I. adv ❶ (showing contradiction) jedoch; **I love ice cream — ~, I am trying to lose weight, so ...** ich liebe Eis – aber ich versuche gerade abzunehmen, daher ... ❷ + adj (to whatever degree) egal wie ❸ (by what means) wie um alles ... II. conj ❶ (in any way) wie auch immer; ~ **you do it, ...** wie auch immer du es machst, ... ❷ (nevertheless) jedoch
howl [haʊl] I. n of animal, wind Heulen nt kein pl II. vi ❶ animal, wind heulen; person schreien ❷ (fam: laugh) brüllen
howler ['haʊ·lər] n (mistake) Schnitzer m
hp [ˌeɪtʃ·'pi] n abbrev of **horsepower** PS
HQ [ˌeɪtʃ·'kju] n abbrev of **headquarters**
HR n abbrev of **human resources** Personalabteilung f

hr. n abbrev of **hour** Std.
ht. n abbrev of **height**
hub [hʌb] n ❶ TECH Nabe f ❷ (fig: center) Zentrum nt
hubbub ['hʌb·ʌb] n (noise) Lärm m; (commotion) Tumult m
hubby ['hʌb·i] n (hum fam) [Ehe]mann m
hubcap ['hʌb·kæp] n Radkappe f
huckleberry ['hʌk·əl·ber·i] n amerikanische Heidelbeere
huddle ['hʌd·əl] n ❶ (close group) [wirrer] Haufen; of people Gruppe f ❷ (in football) **to make** [or **form**] **a ~** die Köpfe zusammenstecken
hue [hju] n Farbe f; (shade) Schattierung f ▶PHRASES: ~ **and cry** Geze- ter nt
huff [hʌf] I. vi **to ~ and puff** schnaufen und keuchen II. n (fam) **to be in a ~** eingeschnappt sein
huffy ['hʌf·i] adj ❶ (easily offended) empfindlich ❷ (in a huff) beleidigt
hug [hʌg] I. vt <-gg-> ❶ umarmen ❷ (fig) **the dress ~ged her body** das Kleid lag eng an ihrem Körper an II. vi <-gg-> sich umarmen III. n Umarmung f
huge [hjudʒ] adj riesig
hugely ['hjudʒ·li] adv ungeheuer
hulking ['hʌl·kɪŋ] adj massig
hull [hʌl] n [Schiffs]rumpf m
hum [hʌm] I. vi <-mm-> ❶ brausen; engine brummen; small machine surren; bee summen ❷ (sing) summen II. vt <-mm-> summen III. n Brausen nt; of machinery Brummen nt; of insects Summen nt
human ['hju·mən] I. n Mensch m II. adj menschlich
humane [hju·'meɪn] adj human
humanitarian [hju·ˌmæn·ɪ·'ter·i·ən] adj humanitär
humanities [hju·'mæn·ɪ·tiz] npl ■**the** ~ die Geisteswissenschaften pl
humanity [hju·'mæn·ɪ·t̬i] n ❶ (people) die Menschheit ❷ (quality) Menschlichkeit f
humanly ['hju·mən·li] adv menschlich;

H

to do everything ~ possible alles Menschenmögliche tun

human 'nature *n* die menschliche Natur

human 'race *n* ■**the ~** die menschliche Rasse

human 'resources *npl + sing vb* (*department*) Personalabteilung *f*

human 'rights *npl* Menschenrechte *pl*

humble ['hʌm·bəl] *adj* <-r, -st> ❶(*modest*) bescheiden ❷(*respectful*) demütig

humdrum ['hʌm·drʌm] *adj* langweilig, fad[e]

humid ['hju·mɪd] *adj* feucht

humidifier [hju·'mɪd·ɪ·faɪ·ər] *n* Luftbefeuchter *m*

humidity [hju·'mɪd·ɪ·ți] *n* [Luft]feuchtigkeit *f*

humiliate [hju·'mɪl·i·eɪt] *vt* ❶(*humble*) demütigen ❷(*embarrass*) blamieren

humiliation [hju·mɪl·i·'eɪ·ʃən] *n* Demütigung *f*

humor ['hju·mər] I. *n* Humor *m* II. *vt* ■**to ~ sb** (*indulge*) jdm seinen Willen lassen; (*keep happy*) jdn bei Laune halten *fam*

humorless ['hju·mər·lɪs] *adj* humorlos

humorous ['hju·mər·əs] *adj person* humorvoll; *book, situation* lustig; *idea* witzig

hump [hʌmp] I. *n* ❶(*hill*) kleiner Hügel ❷(*on camel*) Höcker *m*; (*on a person*) Buckel *m* II. *vt* (*vulg, sl: have sex with*) bumsen

'**humpback** *n* ❶(*person*) Buck[e]lige(r) *f(m)* ❷(*back*) Buckel *m* ❸(*whale*) Buckelwal *m*

'**humpbacked** *adj person* bucklig; *bridge* gewölbt

hunch [hʌntʃ] I. *n* <*pl* -es> (*feeling*) Gefühl *nt*; **to have a ~ that ...** das [leise] Gefühl haben, dass ... II. *vi* sich krümmen III. *vt shoulders* hochziehen; **to ~ one's back** einen Buckel machen

'**hunchback** *n* Bucklige(r) *f(m)*

hundred ['hʌn·drəd] I. *n* ❶(*number*) Hundert *f*; **~s of cars** Hunderte von Autos; **eight ~** achthundert ❷**the**

eighteen ~s das neunzehnte Jahrhundert II. *adj* hundert; **a ~ percent** hundertprozentig; **a ~ and five** [ein]hundert[und]fünf

hundredth ['hʌn·drədθ] I. *n* ❶(*in line*) Hundertste(r) *f(m)* ❷(*fraction*) Hundertstel *nt* II. *adj* ❶(*in series*) hundertste(r, s) ❷(*in fraction*) hundertstel

hung [hʌŋ] *pt, pp of* **hang** II, III

Hungarian [hʌŋ·'ger·i·ən] I. *n* ❶(*person*) Ungar(in) *m(f)* ❷(*language*) Ungarisch *nt* II. *adj* ungarisch

Hungary ['hʌŋ·gə·ri] *n* Ungarn *nt*

hunger ['hʌŋ·gər] I. *n* Hunger *m a. fig* II. *vi* ■**to ~ after** [*or* **for**] **sth** nach etw *dat* hungern

hung 'over *adj* (*from drinking*) verkatert

hungry ['hʌŋ·gri] *adj* hungrig *a. fig*; ■**to be ~** Hunger haben

hunk [hʌŋk] *n* ❶(*piece*) Stück *nt* ❷(*fam: man*) **a ~ of a man** ein Bild *nt* von einem Mann

hunt [hʌnt] I. *n* ❶(*chase*) Jagd *f* ❷(*search*) Suche *f* II. *vt* ❶(*chase to kill*) jagen ❷(*search for*) Jagd machen auf *+akk*; **the police are ~ing for the terrorists** die Polizei fahndet nach den Terroristen III. *vi* ❶(*chase to kill*) jagen ❷(*search*) suchen; ■**to ~ through sth** etw durchsuchen

hunter ['hʌn·tər] *n* Jäger(in) *m(f)*

hunting ['hʌn·tɪŋ] *n* Jagen *nt,* Jagd *f*

'**hunting ground** *n* Jagdrevier *nt*

'**hunting license** *n* Jagdschein *m*

'**hunting season** *n* Jagdzeit *f*

'**huntsman** *n* Jäger *m*

hurdle ['hɜr·dəl] I. *n* Hürde *f a. fig;* SPORT ■**~s** *pl* (*for people*) Hürdenlauf *m* II. *vt* überspringen

hurdler ['hɜrd·lər] *n* Hürdenläufer(in) *m(f)*

hurl [hɜrl] *vt* schleudern; **to ~ abuse at sb** jdm Beschimpfungen an den Kopf werfen

hurly-burly ['hɜr·li·bɜr·li] *n* Rummel *m*

hurrah [hə·'ra], **hurray** [hə·'reɪ] *interj* hurra

hurricane ['hɜr·ɪ·keɪn] *n* Orkan *m;* (*tropical*) Hurrikan *m*

hurried ['hɜr·id] *adj* hastig; *departure* überstürzt

hurry ['hɜr·i] I. *n* Eile *f;* **to leave in a ~** hastig aufbrechen; **to need sth in a ~** etw sofort brauchen II. *vi* <-ie-> sich beeilen III. *vt* <-ie-> ■ **to ~ sb** jdn hetzen
♦ **hurry along** I. *vi* sich beeilen II. *vt person* [zur Eile] antreiben; *process* beschleunigen
♦ **hurry away, hurry off** I. *vi* schnell weggehen II. *vt* schnell wegbringen
♦ **hurry out** I. *vi* hinauseilen II. *vt* schnell hinausbringen
♦ **hurry up** I. *vi* sich beeilen; **~ up!** beeil dich! II. *vt* *person* zur Eile antreiben; *process* beschleunigen

hurt [hɜrt] I. *vi* <hurt, hurt> ❶ (*be painful*) wehtun ❷ (*do harm*) schaden *a. fig* II. *vt* <hurt, hurt> ❶ (*a. fig: cause pain*) ■ **to ~ sb** jdm wehtun; (*injure*) jdn verletzen; ■ **to ~ oneself** sich verletzen; **to ~ one's leg** sich *dat* am Bein wehtun ❷ (*harm*) ■ **to ~ sb/sth** jdm/etw schaden III. *adj* ❶ (*in pain*) verletzt ❷ (*fig*) *feelings* verletzt; *look, voice* gekränkt IV. *n* (*pain*) Schmerz *m;* (*injury*) Verletzung *f*

hurtful ['hɜrt·fəl] *adj* verletzend

husband ['hʌz·bənd] *n* Ehemann *m*

hush [hʌʃ] I. *n* Stille *f* II. *interj* ■ **~!** pst! III. *vt* zum Schweigen bringen; (*soothe*) beruhigen
♦ **hush up** *vt* vertuschen

'hush money [*fam*] Schweigegeld *nt*

husk [hʌsk] I. *n* Schale *f* II. *vt* *corn* schälen

husky[1] ['hʌs·ki] *adj* ❶ *voice* rau ❷ *person* kräftig [gebaut]

husky[2] ['hʌs·ki] *n* (*dog*) Husky *m*, Schlittenhund *m*

hustle ['hʌs·əl] I. *vt* ❶ (*hurry*) ■ **to ~ sb somewhere** jdn irgendwohin treiben ❷ (*coerce*) ■ **to ~ sb into doing sth** jdn [be]drängen, etw zu tun II. *vi* ❶ (*work quickly*) schnell erledigen ❷ SPORT (*play aggressively*) stoßen *fam* III. *n* Gedränge *nt;* **~ and bustle** geschäftiges Treiben

hustler ['hʌs·lər] *n* ❶ (*swindler*) Betrüger(in) *m(f)* ❷ (*prostitute*) Strichjunge *m*, Strichmädchen *nt*

hut [hʌt] *n* Hütte *f*

hutch [hʌtʃ] *n* Käfig *m;* (*for rabbits*) Stall *m*

hybrid ['haɪ·brɪd] I. *n* ❶ BOT, ZOOL Kreuzung *f* ❷ AUTO Hybrid *m* II. *adj* ❶ BOT, ZOOL Misch-, hybrid ❷ AUTO hybrid, Hybrid-; **~ powertrain** Hybridantrieb *m;* **~ electric vehicle** Hybridauto *nt*

hydrant ['haɪ·drənt] *n* Hydrant *m*

hydraulic [haɪ·'drɑ·lɪk] *adj* hydraulisch

hydraulics [haɪ·'drɑ·lɪks] *n* + *sing vb* Hydraulik *f*

hydrocarbon [ˌhaɪ·drə·'kar·bən] *n* Kohlenwasserstoff *m*

hydroelectric [ˌhaɪ·drou·ɪ·'lek·trɪk] *adj* hydroelektrisch

hydrogen ['haɪ·drə·dʒən] *n* Wasserstoff *m;* **~ bomb** Wasserstoffbombe *f*

hyena [haɪ·'i·nə] *n* Hyäne *f*

hygiene ['haɪ·dʒin] *n* Hygiene *f;* **personal ~** Körperpflege *f*

hygienic [ˌhaɪ·dʒi·'en·ɪk] *adj* hygienisch

hymn [hɪm] *n* REL Kirchenlied *nt*

hymnal ['hɪm·nəl], **hymnbook** ['hɪm·bʌk] *n* Gesangbuch *nt*

hype [haɪp] I. *n* Reklameaufwand *m;* **media ~** Medienrummel *m* II. *vt* *film* [in den Medien] hochjubeln

hyper ['haɪ·pər] *adj* (*fam*) aufgedreht, hyper *sl*

hyperactive [ˌhaɪ·pər·'æk·tɪv] *adj* hyperaktiv

hyper'sensitive *adj* überempfindlich; ■ **to be ~ to sth** auf etw *akk* überempfindlich reagieren

hyphen ['haɪ·fən] *n* (*between words*) Bindestrich *m;* (*at end of line*) Trennstrich *m*

hyphenate ['haɪ·fə·neɪt] *vt* mit Bindestrich schreiben

hypnosis [hɪp·'nou·sɪs] *n* Hypnose *f*

hypnotic [hɪp·'nɑt·ɪk] *adj* hypnotisierend

hypnotist ['hɪp·nə·tɪst] *n* Hypnotiseur(in) *m(f)*

hypnotize ['hɪp·nə·taɪz] vt hypnotisieren a. fig

hypochondriac [,haɪ·pə·'kan·drɪ·æk] n Hypochonder(in) m(f)

hypocrisy [hɪ·'pak·rə·si] n Heuchelei f

hypocrite ['hɪp·ə·krɪt] n Heuchler(in) m(f)

hypocritical [,hɪp·ə·'krɪt·ɪ·kəl] adj heuchlerisch

hypodermic [,haɪ·pə·'dɜr·mɪk] adj subkutan; ~ **syringe** Injektionsspritze f

hypothermia [,haɪ·pou·'θɜr·mi·ə] n Unterkühlung f

hypothesis <pl -ses> [haɪ·'paθ·ɪ·sɪs] n Hypothese f

hypothetical [,haɪ·pə·'θeṭ·ɪ·kəl] adj hypothetisch

hysteria [hɪ·'ster·i·ə] n Hysterie f

hysterical [hɪ·'ster·ɪk·əl] adj ❶ (emotional) hysterisch ❷ (fam: hilarious) ausgelassen heiter

---

I i

I¹ <pl -'s>, **i** <pl -'s> [aɪ] n (letter) I nt, i nt; ~ **as in India** I wie Ida

I² [aɪ] pron personal ich; ~ **for one ...** ich meinerseits ...

IA, Ia. abbrev of **Iowa**

ibex <pl -es> ['aɪ·beks] n Steinbock m

ice [aɪs] I. n Eis m ▶PHRASES: **to break the** ~ das Eis zum Schmelzen bringen; **to put sth on** ~ etw auf Eis legen II. vt glasieren
  ◆**ice over** vi road vereisen; lake zufrieren

'Ice Age n Eiszeit f

'iceberg n Eisberg m

'icebox n Kühlschrank m

'icebreaker n Eisbrecher m

'ice cap n Eiskappe f (an den Polen)

ice-'cold n eiskalt

'ice cream n Eiscreme f

'ice-cream maker n Eismaschine f

'ice cube n Eiswürfel m

iced [aɪst] adj ❶ (frozen) eisgekühlt ❷ cake glasiert

'ice floe n Eisscholle f

'ice hockey n Eishockey nt

Iceland ['aɪs·lənd] n Island nt

Icelander ['aɪs·lən·dər] n Isländer(in) m(f)

Icelandic [aɪs·'læn·dɪk] I. n Isländisch nt II. adj isländisch

'ice pack n ❶ (for swelling) Eisbeutel m ❷ (sea ice) Packeis nt

'ice pick n Eispickel m

'ice rink n Schlittschuhbahn f

'ice skate n Schlittschuh m

'ice-skate vi Schlittschuh laufen, eislaufen

'ice skating n Schlittschuhlaufen nt

icicle ['aɪ·sɪ·kəl] n Eiszapfen m

icing ['aɪ·sɪŋ] n Zuckerguss m ▶PHRASES: **to be the** ~ **on the cake** (pej: unnecessary) [bloß] schmückendes Beiwerk sein; (approv: extra) das Sahnehäubchen sein fam

icon ['aɪ·kan] n ❶ (painting) Ikone f ❷ COMPUT Symbol nt, Icon nt

icy ['aɪ·si] adj eisig [kalt]; road vereist

ID¹ [,aɪ·'di] n abbrev of **identification** Ausweis m

ID², Id. n abbrev of **Idaho**

I'd [aɪd] = I would, I had see would, have I, II

Idaho ['aɪ·də·hou] n Idaho nt

I'D card n [Personal]ausweis m

idea [aɪ·'di·ə] n ❶ (notion) Vorstellung f, Idee f; **what gave you that** ~? wie kommst du denn auf die Idee?; **don't get any** ~**s!** (fam) komm nicht auf dumme Gedanken!; **don't give him any** ~**s!** (fam) bring ihn nicht auf dumme Gedanken! ❷ (*knowledge*) Begriff *m;* **to have an ~ of sth** eine Vorstellung von etw *dat* haben; **to have no ~** keine Ahnung haben

ideal [aɪˈdiːəl] I. *adj* ideal II. *n* Ideal *nt*

idealism [aɪˈdiːəˌlɪzəm] *n* Idealismus *m*

idealist [aɪˈdiːəlɪst] *n* Idealist(in) *m(f)*

idealistic [ˌaɪdiːəˈlɪstɪk] *adj* idealistisch

idealize [aɪˈdiːəlaɪz] *vt* idealisieren

ideally [aɪˈdiːli] *adv* ideal

identical [aɪˈdentɪkəl] *adj* identisch (**to** mit +*dat*)

identifiable [aɪˌdentəˈfaɪəbəl] *adj* erkennbar; *substance* nachweisbar

identification [aɪˌdentəfɪˈkeɪʃən] *n* ❶ *of person, criminal* Identifizierung *f* ❷ (*sympathy*) Identifikation *f* (**with** mit +*dat*)

identifiˈcation papers *npl* Ausweispapiere *pl*

identify <-ie-> [aɪˈdentəfaɪ] I. *vt* ❶ (*recognize*) identifizieren ❷ (*name*) ■**to ~ sb** jds Identität *f* feststellen II. *vi* ■**to ~ with sb** sich mit jdm identifizieren

identity [aɪˈdentəti] *n* Identität *f*

iˈdentity card *n* [Personal]ausweis *m*

ideological [ˌaɪdiːəˈlɑdʒɪkəl] *adj* ideologisch

ideology [ˌaɪdiːˈalədʒi] *n* Ideologie *f*

idiom [ˈɪdiːəm] *n* LING ❶ (*phrase*) [idiomatische] Redewendung ❷ (*language*) Idiom *nt*

idiomatic [ˌɪdiːəˈmætɪk] *adj* idiomatisch

idiot [ˈɪdiːət] *n* Idiot(in) *m(f)*

idiotic [ˌɪdiːˈatɪk] *adj* idiotisch

idle [ˈaɪdəl] *adj* ❶ (*lazy*) faul ❷ (*inactive*) untätig; *machine* außer Betrieb *präd* ❸ *chatter* hohl; *threats* leer

idol [ˈaɪdəl] *n* ❶ (*model*) Idol *nt* ❷ REL Götzenbild *m*

idolize [ˈaɪdəlaɪz] *vt* vergöttern

idyllic [aɪˈdɪlɪk] *adj* idyllisch

i.e. [ˌaɪˈiː] *n abbrev of* **id est** d.h.

if [ɪf] I. *conj* ❶ (*in case*) wenn, falls; **even ~ ...** selbst [dann,] wenn ...;

■**~ ..., then ...** wenn ..., dann ... ❷ (*whether*) ob ❸ (*although*) wenn auch ▶PHRASES: **barely/hardly/rarely ... ~ at all** kaum ..., wenn überhaupt; **~ ever** wenn [überhaupt] je[mals] II. *n* Wenn *nt* ▶PHRASES: **no ~s, ands, or buts** kein Wenn und Aber *fam*

igloo [ˈɪɡlu] *n* Iglu *m o nt*

ignite [ɪɡˈnaɪt] I. *vi* Feuer fangen; ELEC zünden II. *vt* (*form*) anzünden; (*arouse*) entfachen

ignition [ɪɡˈnɪʃən] *n* Zündung *f*

igˈnition key *n* Zündschlüssel *m*

igˈnition switch <-es> *n* Zündschalter *m*

ignorance [ˈɪɡnərəns] *n* Unwissenheit *f* (**about** über +*akk*)

ignorant [ˈɪɡnərənt] *adj* unwissend; ■**to be ~ about** [*or* **of**] **sth** von etw *dat* keine Ahnung haben

ignore [ɪɡˈnɔr] *vt* ignorieren

iguana [ɪˈɡwanə] *n* Leguan *m*

IL *abbrev of* **Illinois**

ill [ɪl] I. *adj* ❶ (*sick*) krank; **to be critically ~** in Lebensgefahr schweben ❷ (*bad*) schlecht; (*harmful*) schädlich; *effects* negativ; **~ health** angegriffene Gesundheit II. *adv* (*badly*) schlecht; **to speak ~ of sb** schlecht über jdn sprechen

III. *abbrev of* **Illinois**

I'll [aɪl] = **I will** *see* **will**

ill-adˈvised *adj* unklug

illegal [ɪˈliːɡəl] I. *adj* illegal II. *n* Illegale(r) *f(m)*

illegible [ɪˈledʒəbəl] *adj* unleserlich

illegitimate [ˌɪlɪˈdʒɪtɪmət] *adj* ❶ *child* unehelich ❷ (*unauthorized*) unzulässig

ill-eˈquipped *adj* schlecht ausgestattet

ill-ˈfitting *adj* schlecht sitzend *attr*

illicit [ɪˈlɪsɪt] *adj* [gesetzlich] verboten

ill-inˈformed *adj* schlecht informiert

Illinois [ˌɪləˈnɔɪ] *n* Illinois *nt*

illiterate [ɪˈlɪtərɪt] *n* Analphabet(in) *m(f)*

illness [ˈɪlnɪs] *n* Krankheit *f*

illogical [ɪˈladʒɪkəl] *adj* unlogisch

ill-'tempered adj schlecht gelaunt; (by nature) mürrisch

ill-'timed adj ungelegen

ill-'treat vt misshandeln

ill-'treatment n Misshandlung f

illuminate [ɪˈluːməˌneɪt] vt erhellen; (spotlight) beleuchten; (fig) erläutern

illuminating [ɪˈluːməˌneɪtɪŋ] adj aufschlussreich

illumination [ɪˌluːməˈneɪʃən] n Beleuchtung f

illusion [ɪˈluːʒən] n Illusion f

illusive [ɪˈluːsɪv], **illusory** [ɪˈluːsəri] adj ❶ (deceptive) illusorisch ❷ (imaginary) imaginär

illustrate [ˈɪləˌstreɪt] vt ❶ illustrieren ❷ (fig: explain) aufzeigen

illustration [ˌɪləˈstreɪʃən] n ❶ Illustration f ❷ (fig: example) Beispiel nt

I'm [aɪm] = **I am** see **be**

image [ˈɪmɪdʒ] n ❶ (picture) Bild nt ❷ (reputation) Image nt

imaginable [ɪˈmædʒənəbəl] adj erdenklich

imaginary [ɪˈmædʒəˌneri] adj imaginär

imagination [ɪˌmædʒəˈneɪʃən] n Fantasie f

imaginative [ɪˈmædʒənəˌtɪv] adj fantasievoll

imagine [ɪˈmædʒɪn] vt ■ **to ~ sb/ sth** sich dat jdn/etw vorstellen ❷ (suppose) sich dat denken; **I can't ~ what you mean** ich weiß wirklich nicht, was du meinst ▶PHRASES: **~ that!** stell dir das mal vor!

imbalance [ˌɪmˈbæləns] n Ungleichgewicht nt

IMF [ˌaɪemˈef] n abbrev of **International Monetary Fund**: ■ **the ~** der IWF

imitate [ˈɪmɪˌteɪt] vt imitieren

imitation [ˌɪmɪˈteɪʃən] I. n Imitation f II. adj leather, silk Kunst-; pearl, gold, silver unecht

immaculate [ɪˈmækjʊlət] adj makellos

immature [ˌɪməˈtʃʊr] adj unreif

immeasurable [ɪˈmeʒərəbəl] adj unermesslich

immediate [ɪˈmiːdiɪt] adj direkt

immediately [ɪˈmiːdiɪtli] adv ❶ (at once) sofort ❷ (closely) direkt

immense [ɪˈmens] adj riesig, immens

immigrant [ˈɪmɪˌɡrənt] I. n Einwanderer m/Einwanderin f, Immigrant(in) m(f) II. adj attr Immigranten-, Einwanderer-

immigrate [ˈɪmɪˌɡreɪt] vi einwandern, immigrieren

immigration [ˌɪmɪˈɡreɪʃən] n ❶ (action) Einwanderung f, Immigration f ❷ (authority) Grenzkontrolle f, ≈ Grenzschutz m (an Flughäfen)

immobile [ɪˈmoʊbəl] adj unbeweglich

immobility [ˌɪmoʊˈbɪlɪti] n Unbeweglichkeit f

immodest [ɪˈmɑdɪst] adj unbescheiden, eingebildet; behavior, clothing unanständig

immoral [ɪˈmɔrəl] adj unmoralisch

immortal [ɪˈmɔrtəl] I. adj unsterblich II. n Unsterbliche(r) f(m)

immortality [ˌɪmɔrˈtælɪti] n Unsterblichkeit f

immune [ɪˈmjun] adj pred ❶ immun a. fig (**to** gegen/für +akk) ❷ (safe) sicher (**from** vor +dat)

im'mune system n Immunsystem nt

immunity [ɪˈmjunɪti] n ❶ Immunität f ❷ (fig) Unempfindlichkeit f

immunize [ˈɪmjəˌnaɪz] vt immunisieren

immunodeficiency [ˌɪmjənoʊdɪˈfɪʃənsi] n MED Immunschwäche f

impair [ɪmˈper] vt beeinträchtigen

impartial [ɪmˈpɑrʃəl] adj unparteiisch

impasse [ˈɪmˌpæs] n Sackgasse f a. fig; **to reach an ~** sich festfahren

impatience [ɪmˈpeɪʃəns] n Ungeduld f

impatient [ɪmˈpeɪʃənt] adj ungeduldig (**with** gegenüber +dat)

impeach [ɪmˈpitʃ] vt anklagen (**for** wegen +gen)

impeachment [ɪmˈpitʃmənt] n Amtsenthebungsverfahren nt

impede [ɪmˈpid] vt behindern

impel <-ll-> [ɪmˈpel] *vt* [an]treiben; (*force*) nötigen

impending [ɪmˈpend·ɪŋ] *adj attr* bevorstehend

imperative [ɪmˈper·ə·tɪv] I. *adj* unbedingt erforderlich II. *n* LING ■**the ~** der Imperativ

imperfect [ɪmˈpɜr·fɪkt] I. *adj* fehlerhaft, unvollkommen II. *n* LING ■**the ~** der Imperfekt

imperial [ɪmˈpɪr·i·əl] *adj* ❶ (*of empire*) Reichs-; (*of emperor*) kaiserlich; (*imperialistic*) imperialistisch ❷ *measures, weights* britisch

imperialism [ɪmˈpɪr·i·ə·lɪz·əm] *n* Imperialismus *m*

imperialist [ɪmˈpɪr·i·ə·lɪst] I. *n* Imperialist(in) *m(f)* II. *adj* imperialistisch

impermeable [ɪmˈpɜr·mi·ə·bəl] *adj* undurchlässig

impersonal [ˌɪmˈpɜr·sə·nəl] *adj* (*a. ling*) unpersönlich

impersonate [ɪmˈpɜr·sə·neɪt] *vt* imitieren

impertinent [ɪmˈpɜr·tə̬·nənt] *adj* unverschämt

impetuous [ɪmˈpetʃ·u·əs] *adj* impulsiv; *nature* hitzig

implant I. *n* [ˈɪm·plænt] Implantat *nt* II. *vt* [ɪmˈplænt] einpflanzen

implausible [ɪmˈplɔ·zə·bəl] *adj* unglaubwürdig

implement I. *n* [ˈɪm·plɪ·mənt] Gerät *nt;* (*tool*) Werkzeug *nt* II. *vt* [ˈɪm·plɪ·ment] einführen; *plan* in die Tat umsetzen

implicate [ˈɪm·plɪ·keɪt] *vt* ❶ (*involve*) ■**to ~ sb in sth** jdn mit etw *dat* in Verbindung bringen ❷ (*imply*) andeuten

implied [ɪmˈplaɪd] *adj* indirekt

implore [ɪmˈplɔr] *vt* anflehen

imploring [ɪmˈplɔr·ɪŋ] *adj* flehend

imply <-ie-> [ɪmˈplaɪ] *vt* andeuten

impolite [ˌɪm·pə·ˈlaɪt] *adj* unhöflich

impoliteness [ˌɪm·pə·ˈlaɪt·nɪs] *n* Unhöflichkeit *f*

import I. *vt, vi* [ɪmˈpɔrt] importieren (**from** aus +*dat*) II. *n* [ˈɪm·pɔrt] Import *m*

importance [ɪmˈpɔr·təns] *n* Bedeutung *f*

important [ɪmˈpɔr·tənt] *adj* wichtig

importation [ˌɪm·pɔr·ˈteɪ·ʃən] *n* Import *m*

'import duty *n* [Import]zoll *m*

impose [ɪmˈpoʊz] I. *vt* auferlegen; *order* verhängen; *law* verfügen; *taxes* erheben (**on** auf +*akk*) II. *vi* ■**to ~ on sb** sich jdm aufdrängen

imposing [ɪmˈpoʊ·zɪŋ] *adj* beeindruckend; *person* stattlich

impossible [ɪmˈpɑs·ə·bəl] I. *adj* unmöglich II. *n* ■**the ~** das Unmögliche

impossibly [ɪmˈpɑs·ə·bli] *adv* unvorstellbar

impostor, imposter [ɪmˈpɑs·tər] *n* Hochstapler(in) *m(f)*

impotent [ˈɪm·pə·tənt] *adj* ❶ machtlos ❷ (*sexually*) impotent

impoverished [ɪmˈpɑv·ər·ɪʃt] *adj* verarmt

impractical [ɪmˈpræk·tɪ·kəl] *adj* unpraktisch

imprecise [ˌɪm·prɪ·ˈsaɪs] *adj* ungenau

impregnate [ɪmˈpreg·neɪt] *vt usu passive* ❶ *animal, egg* befruchten ❷ (*saturate*) imprägnieren

impress [ɪmˈpres] I. *vt* ❶ beeindrucken ❷ (*convince*) ■**to ~ sth [up]on sb** jdn von etw *dat* überzeugen II. *vi* Eindruck machen, imponieren; **to fail to ~** keinen [guten] Eindruck machen

impression [ɪmˈpreʃ·ən] *n* Eindruck *m*

impressionism [ɪmˈpreʃ·ə·nɪz·əm] *n* Impressionismus *m*

impressive [ɪmˈpres·ɪv] *adj* beeindruckend

imprison [ɪmˈprɪz·ən] *vt usu passive* inhaftieren

imprisonment [ɪmˈprɪz·ən·mənt] *n* Haft *f*

improbability [ˌɪm·prɑb·ə·ˈbɪl·ɪ·t̬i] *n* Unwahrscheinlichkeit *f*

improbable [ɪmˈprɑb·ə·bəl] *adj* unwahrscheinlich

improper [ɪmˈprɑp·ər] *adj* ❶ (*not correct*) falsch ❷ (*inappropriate*) unpassend

improve [ɪmˈpruv] **I.** *vt* verbessern **II.** *vi* sich verbessern; ■ **to ~ on sth** etw [noch] verbessern; **you can't ~ on that!** da ist keine Steigerung mehr möglich!

improvement [ɪmˈpruv·mənt] *n* Verbesserung *f*; *of illness* Besserung *f*; [**home**] **~**[**s**] Renovierungsarbeiten *pl* (*Ausbau- und Modernisierungsarbeiten am eigenen Heim*)

improvisation [ɪmˌprɑv·ɪˈzeɪ·ʃən] *n* Improvisation *f*

improvise [ˈɪm·prə·vaɪz] *vt, vi* improvisieren

imprudent [ɪmˈpru·dənt] *adj* leichtsinnig

impudence [ˈɪm·pjʊ·dəns] *n* Unverschämtheit *f*

impudent [ˈɪm·pjʊ·dənt] *adj* unverschämt

impulse [ˈɪm·pʌls] *n* (*a. elec*) Impuls *m*

impulsive [ɪmˈpʌl·sɪv] *adj* impulsiv

impure [ɪmˈpjʊr] *adj* unrein

in [ɪn] **I.** *prep* ❶ (*describing location*) in + *dat*; **he is deaf ~ his left ear** er hört auf dem linken Ohr nichts; **~ the street** auf der Straße ❷ (*into*) in + *akk*; **to get ~ the car** ins Auto steigen ❸ (*describing state*) **~ pain** vor Schmerzen; **~ secret** heimlich; **to** [**not**] **be ~ doubt** [nicht] zweifeln ❹ **~ French** auf Französisch ❺ (*during*) **she assisted the doctor ~ the operation** sie assistierte dem Arzt bei der Operation; **~ the end** am Ende; **~ March** im März; **~ the morning** morgens ❻ (*describing job*) **she works ~ publishing** sie arbeitet bei einem Verlag ❼ (*wearing*) **the woman ~ the hat** die Frau mit dem Hut ❽ + -*ing* (*while*) **~ attempting to save the child, ...** bei dem Versuch, das Kind zu retten, ...; **~ doing so** dabei, damit ❾ (*state, condition*) **to be equal ~ height/weight** gleich groß sein/ gleich viel wiegen ❿ (*of every*) pro; **one ~ ten people** jeder zehnte ⓫ *after n* **he had no say ~ the decision** er hatte keinen Einfluss auf die Entscheidung; **to have confidence ~ sb** jdm vertrauen ▶PHRASES: **~ all** [*or* **total**] insgesamt; **~ between** dazwischen **II.** *adv* ❶ (*to speaker*) herein; **come ~!** herein! ❷ (*submitted*) **to hand sth ~** etw abgeben ▶PHRASES: **to let sb ~ on sth** jdn in etw *akk* einweihen **III.** *adj* ❶ *pred* (*there*) da; (*at home*) zu Hause ❷ (*in fashion*) in ▶PHRASES: **to be ~ on sth** über etw *akk* Bescheid wissen **IV.** *n* ▶PHRASES: **to know the ~s and outs of sth** sich in einer S. *gen* genau auskennen

IN *abbrev of* **Indiana**

inability [ˌɪn·əˈbɪl·ɪ·ţi] *n* Unfähigkeit *f*

inaccessible [ˌɪn·ækˈses·ə·bəl] *adj* unzugänglich

inaccuracy [ɪnˈæk·jər·ə·si] *n* Ungenauigkeit *f*

inaccurate [ɪnˈæk·jər·ɪt] *adj* ungenau

inactive [ɪnˈæk·tɪv] *adj* untätig, inaktiv

inadequate [ɪnˈæd·ɪ·kwɪt] *adj* unangemessen

inadvisable [ˌɪn·ədˈvaɪ·zə·bəl] *adj* nicht empfehlenswert

inanimate [ɪnˈæn·ɪ·mət] *adj* leblos

inapplicable [ɪnˈæp·lɪ·kə·bəl] *adj* unanwendbar

inappropriate [ˌɪn·əˈprou·pri·ɪt] *adj* unpassend

inattentive [ˌɪn·əˈten·tɪv] *adj* unaufmerksam

inaudible [ɪnˈɔ·də·bəl] *adj* unhörbar

inaugural [ɪnˈɔ·gjʊ·rəl] *adj attr* ❶ Einweihungs- ❷ POL Antritts-

inauguration [ɪnˌɔ·gjʊˈreɪ·ʃən] *n* ❶ (*induction*) Amtseinführung *f* ❷ *of monument, stadium* Einweihung

in-be·tween *adj attr* Zwischen-, Übergangs-

'in box *n* COMPUT Posteingangsordner *m*

inbred [ˈɪn·bred] *adj* ❶ durch Inzucht erzeugt ❷ (*inherent*) angeboren

Inc. *adj after n* ECON *abbrev of* **incorporated** [als Kapitalgesellschaft] eingetragen

incapability [ɪnˌkeɪ·pə·ˈbɪl·ɪ·ţi] *n* Unfähigkeit *f*

incapable [ɪnˈkeɪ·pə·bəl] *adj* unfähig (**of** zu + *dat*)

incapacity [ˌɪn·kə·ˈpæs·ə·t̬i] *n* Unfähigkeit *f*

incense¹ [ˈɪn·sens] *n* (*in church*) Weihrauch *m*

incense² [ɪn·ˈsens] *vt* empören

incentive [ɪn·ˈsen·tɪv] *n* Anreiz *m*

in'centive plan *n* Prämiensystem *nt*

incessant [ɪn·ˈses·ənt] *adj* ununterbrochen

incest [ˈɪn·sest] *n* Inzest *m*

incestuous [ɪn·ˈses·tʃu·əs] *adj* inzestuös

inch [ɪntʃ] **I.** *n* <*pl* -es> Zoll *m* (*2,54 cm*) **II.** *vi* sich [ganz] langsam bewegen

incidence [ˈɪn·sɪ·dəns] *n* Auftreten *nt*

incident [ˈɪn·sɪ·dənt] *n* [Vor]fall *m*, Ereignis *nt*

incidentally [ˌɪn·sɪ·ˈden·təl·i] *adv* ❶ (*by the way*) übrigens ❷ (*in passing*) nebenbei; (*accidentally*) zufällig

incinerate [ɪn·ˈsɪn·ə·reɪt] *vt* verbrennen

incinerator [ɪn·ˈsɪn·ə·reɪ·tər] *n* Verbrennungsanlage *f*

incision [ɪn·ˈsɪʒ·ən] *n* MED [Ein]schnitt *m*

incisor [ɪn·ˈsaɪ·zər] *n* Schneidezahn *m*

incite [ɪn·ˈsaɪt] *vt* aufstacheln; *revolt, riot* anzetteln

inclination [ˌɪn·klɪ·ˈneɪ·ʃən] *n* Neigung *f*

incline I. *vi* [ɪn·ˈklaɪn] ❶ (*tend*) tendieren (**toward[s** zu +*dat*) ❷ (*lean*) sich neigen **II.** *vt* [ɪn·ˈklaɪn] ❶ *usu passive* (*dispose*) ▪to be ~d to do sth dazu neigen, etw zu tun ❷ *head* neigen

inclined [ɪn·ˈklaɪnd] *adj pred* bereit; **to be ~ to agree** eher zustimmen

include [ɪn·ˈklud] *vt* ❶ (*contain*) beinhalten; ▪to be ~d in sth in etw *akk* eingeschlossen sein; **everything is ~d** alles ist inklusive; ▪to ~ sb/sth in sth jdn/etw in etw *akk* einbeziehen ❷ (*add*) beifügen

including [ɪn·ˈklu·dɪŋ] *prep* einschließlich

inclusion [ɪn·ˈklu·ʒən] *n* Einbeziehung *f*

inclusive [ɪn·ˈklu·sɪv] *adj* einschließlich

incognito [ˌɪn·kag·ˈni·toʊ] *adv* inkognito

incoherent [ˌɪn·koʊ·ˈhɪr·ənt] *adj* zusammenhanglos

income [ˈɪn·kʌm] *n* Einkommen *nt*

'income tax *n* Einkommensteuer *f*

incoming [ˈɪn·kʌm·ɪŋ] *adj attr* ❶ ankommend; ~ **call** [eingehender] Anruf; ~ **freshman** *Studienanfänger an einer amerikanischen Hochschule oder High-school* ❷ (*recently elected*) neu [gewählt]

incomparable [ɪn·ˈkam·pər·ə·bəl] *adj* unvergleichbar

incompatibility [ˌɪn·kəm·ˌpæt̬·ə·ˈbɪl·ɪ·t̬i] *n* Unvereinbarkeit *f*

incompatible [ˌɪn·kəm·ˈpæt̬·ə·bəl] *adj* unvereinbar, inkompatibel; ▪persons nicht zusammenpassen

incompetence [ɪn·ˈkam·pə·təns], **incompetency** [ɪn·ˈkam·pə·tən·si] *n* Inkompetenz *f*

incompetent [ɪn·ˈkam·pə·tənt] *adj* ❶ inkompetent, unfähig ❷ LAW unzuständig

incomplete [ˌɪn·kəm·ˈplit] *adj* unvollständig

incomprehensible [ˌɪn·kam·prɪ·ˈhen·sə·bəl] *adj* unverständlich

inconceivable [ˌɪn·kən·ˈsi·və·bəl] *adj* unvorstellbar

inconsequential [ɪn·ˌkan·sɪ·ˈkwen·ʃəl] *adj* ❶ (*illogical*) unlogisch ❷ (*unimportant*) belanglos

inconsiderable [ˌɪn·kən·ˈsɪd·ər·ə·bəl] *adj* unbeträchtlich

inconsiderate [ˌɪn·kən·ˈsɪd·ər·ɪt] *adj* ❶ (*disregarding*) rücksichtslos (**toward[s** gegenüber +*dat*) ❷ (*insensitive*) gedankenlos; *remark* taktlos

inconsistent [ˌɪn·kən·ˈsɪs·tənt] *adj* ❶ (*contradicting*) widersprüchlich ❷ (*erratic*) unbeständig

inconsolable [ˌɪn·kən·ˈsoʊ·lə·bəl] *adj* untröstlich

inconspicuous [ˌɪn·kən·ˈspɪk·ju·əs] *adj* unauffällig

incontestable [ˌɪn·kən·ˈtes·tə·bəl] *adj* unbestreitbar; *evidence* unwiderlegbar

incontinent [ɪn·ˈkan·tə·nənt] *adj* MED inkontinent

inconvenience [ˌɪn·kən·ˈvin·jəns] **I.** *n* Unannehmlichkeit *f* **II.** *vt* ▪to ~ sb jdm Unannehmlichkeiten bereiten

inconvenient [ˌɪn·kənˈviːn·jənt] *adj*
time ungelegen; *place* ungünstig [gelegen]

incorrect [ˌɪn·kəˈrekt] *adj* ❶(*untrue*)
falsch ❷(*improper*) unkorrekt

incorruptible [ˌɪn·kəˈrʌp·tə·bəl] *adj*
unbestechlich

increase I. *vi* [ɪnˈkriːs] *prices, rates*
[an]steigen; *pain, troubles* zunehmen;
population, wealth wachsen II. *vt* [ɪnˈkriːs] erhöhen; (*strengthen*) verstärken; (*enlarge*) vergrößern III. *n* [ˈɪnˌkriːs] Anstieg *m*, Zunahme *f*; *in production* Steigerung *f*; **to be on the ~** ansteigen

increasing [ɪnˈkriːs·ɪŋ] *adj* steigend, zunehmend

increasingly [ɪnˈkriːs·ɪŋ·li] *adv* zunehmend

incredible [ɪnˈkred·ə·bəl] *adj* unglaublich

incredibly [ɪnˈkred·ɪbli] *adv* + *adj*
(*very*) unglaublich

incredulous [ɪnˈkredʒ·ə·ləs] *adj* ungläubig

incubator [ˈɪn·kju·beɪ·tər] *n* Brutapparat *m*; (*for babies*) Brutkasten *m*

incur <-rr-> [ɪnˈkɜr] *vt* ❶ sich zuziehen;
debts machen; *losses* erleiden ❷(*bring on*) hervorrufen; **to ~ the anger of sb** jdn verärgern

incurable [ɪnˈkjʊr·ə·bəl] *adj* unheilbar

Ind. *abbrev of* **Indiana**

indebted [ɪnˈdeʈ·ɪd] *adj pred* ❶FIN
verschuldet ❷■**to be ~ to sb for sth**
jdm für etw *akk* dankbar sein

indecency [ɪnˈdiː·sən·si] *n* ❶(*impropriety*) Ungehörigkeit *f* ❷(*assault*)
sexueller Übergriff (**against** auf +*akk*)

indecent [ɪnˈdiː·sənt] *adj* ❶(*improper*)
ungehörig ❷(*lewd*) unanständig; *proposal* unsittlich

indecision [ˌɪn·dɪˈsɪʒ·ən] *n* Unentschlossenheit *f*

indecisive [ˌɪn·dɪˈsaɪ·sɪv] *adj* unentschlossen

indeed [ɪnˈdiːd] I. *adv* ❶(*for emphasis*)
wirklich; (*actually*) tatsächlich ❷(*affirmation*) allerdings ❸(*for strengthen-*

ing) ja II. *interj* [ja,] wirklich, ach, wirklich

indefinable [ˌɪn·dɪˈfaɪ·nə·bəl] *adj* undefinierbar

indefinite [ɪnˈdef·ə·nɪt] *adj* unbestimmt

indefinite ˈarticle *n* unbestimmter Artikel

indefinitely [ɪnˈdef·ən·ət·li] *adv* auf
unbestimmte Zeit

indemnify <-ie-> [ɪnˈdem·nɪ·faɪ] *vt*
❶(*insure*) versichern ❷(*compensate*)
entschädigen

indemnity [ɪnˈdem·nɪ·ti] *n* ❶(*insurance*) Versicherung *f* ❷(*compensation with liability*) Schaden[s]ersatz *m*;
(*without liability*) Entschädigung *f*

independence [ˌɪn·dɪˈpen·dəns] *n* Unabhängigkeit *f*

Indeˈpendence Day *n* amerikanischer
Unabhängigkeitstag

independent [ˌɪn·dɪˈpen·dənt] I. *adj*
unabhängig (**from** von +*dat*) II. *n* POL
Parteilose(r) *f(m)*

in-depth [ˈɪn·depθ] *adj attr* gründlich;
report detailliert

indescribable [ˌɪn·dɪˈskraɪ·bə·bəl] *adj*
unbeschreiblich

indestructible [ˌɪn·dɪˈstrʌk·tə·bəl] *adj*
unzerstörbar; *toy* unverwüstlich

index <*pl* -es> [ˈɪn·deks] *n* ❶<*pl* -es>
(*in book*) Index *m*; (*of sources*) Quellenverzeichnis *nt* ❷<*pl* -dices> (*indicator*) Index *m*, Anzeichen *nt* (**of** für
+*akk*)

ˈindex card *n* Karteikarte *f*

ˈindex finger *n* Zeigefinger *m*

India [ˈɪn·di·ə] *n* Indien *nt*

India ink *n* Tusche *f*

Indian [ˈɪn·di·ən] I. *adj* ❶(*Asian*) indisch ❷(*native American*) indianisch,
Indianer- II. *n* ❶(*Asian*) Inder(in) *m(f)*
❷(*native American*) Indianer(in) *m(f)*

Indiana [ˌɪn·diˈæn·ə] *n* Indiana *nt*

Indian ˈcorn *n* FOOD Mais *m*

Indian ˈfile *n see* **single file**

Indian ˈOcean *n* ■**the ~** der Indische
Ozean

Indian ˈsummer *n* Altweibersommer *m*

indicate ['ɪn·dɪ·keɪt] *vt* ❶ (*show*) [an]zeigen ❷ (*imply*) auf etw *akk* hindeuten ❸ (*point to*) ■ **to ~ sb/sth** auf jdn/etw hindeuten

indication [ˌɪn·dɪ·'keɪ·ʃən] *n* ❶ (*sign*) [An]zeichen *nt* (**of** für +*akk*), Hinweis *m* (**of** auf +*akk*) ❷ *on gauge, meter* Anzeige *f*

indicator [ˈɪn·dɪ·keɪ·tər] *n* ❶ (*evidence*) Indikator *m* ❷ TECH (*gauge, meter*) [An]zeiger *m*

indices ['ɪn·dɪ·siz] *n pl of* **index 2**

indict [ɪn·'daɪt] *vt* anklagen

indie ['ɪn·di] *adj short for* **independent** *film, music* Indie-

indifference [ɪn·'dɪf·ər·əns] *n* Gleichgültigkeit *f* (**to**[**ward**] gegenüber +*dat*)

indifferent [ɪn·'dɪf·ər·ənt] *adj* ❶ (*uninterested*) gleichgültig (**to** gegenüber +*dat*) ❷ (*mediocre*) [mittel]mäßig

indigenous [ɪn·'dɪdʒ·ə·nəs] *adj* [ein]heimisch

indigestible [ˌɪn·dɪ·'dʒəs·tə·bəl] *adj* (*a. fig*) unverdaulich

indigestion [ˌɪn·dɪ·'dʒəs·tʃən] *n* Magenverstimmung *f*; (*chronic*) Verdauungsstörung[en] *f*[*pl*]

indignant [ɪn·'dɪg·nənt] *adj* empört (**at/about** über +*akk*)

indignation [ˌɪn·dɪg·'neɪ·ʃən] *n* Empörung *f* (**at/about** über +*akk*)

indignity [ɪn·'dɪg·nɪ·ti] *n* Demütigung *f*

indigo ['ɪn·dɪ·goʊ] I. *n* Indigo *m o nt* II. *adj* indigoblau

indirect [ˌɪn·dɪ·'rekt] *adj* indirekt; ~ **remark** Anspielung *f*

indirect 'object *n* LING indirektes Objekt, Dativobjekt *nt*

indirect 'tax *n* FIN indirekte Steuer

indiscernible [ˌɪn·dɪ·'sɜr·nə·bəl] *adj* nicht wahrnehmbar; (*invisible*) nicht erkennbar

indiscreet [ˌɪn·dɪ·'skrit] *adj* indiskret

indiscretion [ˌɪn·dɪ·'skreʃ·ən] *n* Indiskretion *f*

indiscriminate [ˌɪn·dɪ·'skrɪm·ə·nɪt] *adj* ❶ (*unthinking*) unüberlegt ❷ (*uncritical*) unkritisch ❸ (*random*) wahllos

indispensable [ˌɪn·dɪ·'spen·sə·bəl] *adj* unentbehrlich (**for/to** für +*akk*)

indisputable [ˌɪn·dɪ·'spju·tə·bəl] *adj* unbestreitbar; *evidence* unanfechtbar; *skill, talent* unbestritten

indistinct [ˌɪn·dɪ·'stɪŋkt] *adj* undeutlich; *memory* verschwommen

indistinguishable [ˌɪn·dɪ·'stɪŋ·gwɪ·ʃə·bəl] *adj* nicht unterscheidbar; (*imperceptible*) nicht wahrnehmbar

individual [ˌɪn·dɪ·'vɪdʒ·u·əl] I. *n* ❶ Einzelne(r) *f(m)*, Individuum *nt* ❷ (*original person*) [selbstständige] Persönlichkeit II. *adj* ❶ *attr* (*separate*) einzeln ❷ (*particular*) individuell

individualist [ˌɪn·dɪ·'vɪdʒ·u·ə·lɪst] *n* Individualist(in) *m(f)*

individually [ˌɪn·dɪ·'vɪdʒ·u·ə·li] *adv* ❶ einzeln ❷ (*distinctively*) individuell

indivisible [ˌɪn·dɪ·'vɪz·ə·bəl] *adj* unteilbar

indolence ['ɪn·də·ləns] *n* Trägheit *f*

indolent ['ɪn·də·lənt] *adj* träge

Indonesia [ˌɪn·də·'ni·ʒə] *n* Indonesien *nt*

Indonesian [ˌɪn·də·'ni·ʒən] I. *adj* indonesisch II. *n* ❶ Indonesier(in) *m(f)* ❷ (*language*) Indonesisch *nt*

indoor [ˌɪn·'dɔr] *adj attr* ❶ (*inside*) Innen-; ~ **plant** Zimmerpflanze *f*; SPORT Hallen- ❷ (*for use inside*) Haus-; SPORT Hallen-

indoors [ˌɪn·'dɔrz] *adv* (*to inside*) herein/hinein; (*in building*) drinnen

induce [ɪn·'dus] *vt* ❶ (*persuade*) ■ **to ~ sb to do sth** jdn dazu bringen, etw zu tun ❷ (*cause*) hervorrufen ❸ MED *birth, labor* einleiten

inducement [ɪn·'dus·mənt] *n* Anreiz *m*

induct [ɪn·'dʌkt] *vt usu passive* ❶ **to be ~ed into office** in ein Amt eingesetzt werden ❷ MIL **to be ~ed** [**into the Army**] eingezogen werden

induction [ɪn·'dʌk·ʃən] *n* ❶ (*into office*) [Amts]einführung *f*; (*into organization*) Aufnahme *f* (**into** in +*akk*); ~ **into the military** Einberufung *f* [zum Wehrdienst] ❷ MED *of birth* Einleitung *f* ❸ ELEC, PHYS, TECH Induktion *f fachspr*; *of* *engine* Ansaugung *f;* ~ **range** [*or* **stove**] Induktionsherd *m*

indulge [ɪnˈdʌldʒ] I. *vt* ➊ (*allow*) nachgeben +*dat;* **to ~ sb's every wish** jdm jeden Wunsch erfüllen ➋ (*spoil*) verwöhnen II. *vi* ■**to ~ in sth** in etw *dat* schwelgen

indulgence [ɪnˈdʌldʒəns] *n* (*in food, drink, pleasure*) Frönen *nt*

indulgent [ɪnˈdʌldʒənt] *adj* nachgiebig

industrial [ɪnˈdʌstriəl] *adj* industriell; *product, city* Industrie-; *training, development* betrieblich; ~ **area** Industriegebiet *nt;* ~ **output** Industrieproduktion *f*

industrialism [ɪnˈdʌstriəlɪzəm] *n* Industrialismus *m*

industrialist [ɪnˈdʌstriəlɪst] *n* Industrielle(r) *f(m)*

industrialization [ɪnˌdʌstriəlɪˈzeɪʃən] *n* Industrialisierung *f*

industrialize [ɪnˈdʌstriəlaɪz] *vt* industrialisieren

industrial 'park *n* Industriepark *m*

Industrial Revo'lution *n* HIST ■**the ~** die Industrielle Revolution

industrious [ɪnˈdʌstriəs] *adj* fleißig

industry [ˈɪndəstri] *n* Industrie *f;* (*trade*) Branche *f*

inedible [ɪnˈedəbəl] *adj* nicht essbar; (*disgusting*) ungenießbar

ineducable [ɪnˈedʒəkəbəl] *adj* schwer erziehbar; (*handicapped*) lernbehindert

ineffective [ˌɪnɪˈfektɪv] *adj measure* unwirksam; *person* untauglich

ineffectual [ˌɪnɪˈfektʃʊəl] *adj* ineffektiv

inefficiency [ˌɪnɪˈfɪʃənsi] *n* Ineffizienz *f geh; of person* Inkompetenz *f*

inefficient [ˌɪnɪˈfɪʃənt] *adj* ineffizient

inelegant [ɪnˈelɪgənt] *adj* unelegant

ineligible [ɪnˈelɪdʒəbəl] *adj* (*for benefits*) nicht berechtigt (**for** zu +*dat*); (*for office*) nicht wählbar (**for** in +*dat*)

inequality [ˌɪnɪˈkwalɪti] *n* Ungleichheit *f*

inescapable [ˌɪnɪˈskeɪpəbəl] *adj* un-

vermeidlich; *fate* unentrinnbar; *truth* unbestreitbar

inestimable [ɪnˈestɪməbəl] *adj* unschätzbar

inevitable [ɪnˈevɪtəbəl] I. *adj* unvermeidlich; *result* zwangsläufig II. *n* ■**the ~** das Unvermeidbare

inexact [ˌɪnɪgˈzækt] *adj* ungenau

inexcusable [ˌɪnɪkˈskjuːzəbəl] *adj* unverzeihlich

inexhaustible [ˌɪnɪgˈzɔːstəbəl] *adj* unerschöpflich

inexpensive [ˌɪnɪkˈspensɪv] *adj* preisgünstig

inexperience [ˌɪnɪkˈspɪriəns] *n* Unerfahrenheit *f*

inexperienced [ˌɪnɪkˈspɪriənst] *adj* unerfahren; ■**to be ~ in sth** mit etw *dat* nicht vertraut sein; ■**to be ~ with sth** sich mit etw *dat* nicht auskennen

inexplicable [ˌɪnəkˈsplɪkəbəl] *adj* unerklärlich

infallible [ɪnˈfæləbəl] *adj* unfehlbar

infamous [ˈɪnfəməs] *adj* berüchtigt

infancy [ˈɪnfənsi] *n* früh[est]e Kindheit; (*fig*) Anfangsphase *f*

infant [ˈɪnfənt] I. *n* Säugling *m* II. *adj* ~ **daughter** kleines Töchterchen

infanticide [ɪnˈfæntəsaɪd] *n* Kindestötung *f*

infantile [ˈɪnfəntaɪl] *adj* (*pej*) kindisch *meist pej*

infant mor'tality *n* Säuglingssterblichkeit *f*

infantry [ˈɪnfəntri] I. *n* ■**the ~** + *sing/ pl vb* die Infanterie II. *adj* Infanterie-

infantryman *n* Infanterist *m*

infatuated [ɪnˈfætʃueɪtɪd] *adj* vernarrt (**with** in +*akk*); (*in love*) verknallt *fam* (**with** in +*akk*)

infect [ɪnˈfekt] *vt* (*a. fig*) anstecken, infizieren

infection [ɪnˈfekʃən] *n* Infektion *f;* **throat ~** Halsentzündung *f*

infectious [ɪnˈfekʃəs] *adj* (*a. fig*) ansteckend

infer <-rr-> [ɪnˈfɜr] *vt* schließen (**from** aus +*dat*)

inferior [ɪnˈfɪriər] I. *adj* ➊ minderwertig; *mind* unterlegen ❷ (*lower*) *in rank* [*rang*]niedriger; *in status* untergeordnet II. *n* ■-s *pl* Untergebene *pl*

inferi'ority complex *n* Minderwertigkeitskomplex *m*

infernal [ɪn·ˈfɜr·nəl] *adj* (*a. fig*) höllisch, Höllen-

infertile [ɪn·ˈfɜr·təl] *adj* unfruchtbar

infertility [ˌɪn·fər·ˈtɪl·ə·t̬i] *n* Unfruchtbarkeit *f*

infest [ɪn·ˈfest] *vt* befallen (**with** von +*dat*)

infidelity [ˌɪn·fɪ·ˈdel·ɪ·t̬i] *n* ❶ (*disloyalty*) Verrat *m* (**to** gegenüber/an +*dat*) ❷ (*sexual*) Untreue *f*; ■**infidelities** *pl* Seitensprünge *pl*

infiltrate [ɪn·ˈfɪl·treɪt] *vt* ❶ unterwandern; *building, enemy lines* eindringen in +*akk*; *agent, spy* einschleusen (**into** in +*akk*) ❷ *idea, theory* durchdringen

infinite [ˈɪn·fə·nɪt] *adj* ❶ unendlich ❷ (*great*) grenzenlos

infinitely [ˈɪn·fən·ɪt·li] *adv* ❶ unendlich; ~ **small** winzig klein ❷ (*much*) unendlich viel

infinitive [ɪn·ˈfɪn·ɪ·t̬ɪv] *n* Infinitiv *m*

infinity [ɪn·ˈfɪn·ɪ·t̬i] *n* Unendlichkeit *f*

infirm [ɪn·ˈfɜrm] I. *adj* gebrechlich II. *n* ■**the** ~ *pl* die Kranken und Pflegebedürftigen

infirmary [ɪn·ˈfɜr·mə·ri] *n* ❶ Krankenhaus *nt* ❷ (*smaller*) Krankenzimmer *nt*; (*in prison*) Krankenstation *f*

infirmity [ɪn·ˈfɜr·mɪ·t̬i] *n* ❶ (*state*) Gebrechlichkeit *f* ❷ (*illness*) Gebrechen *nt*

inflame [ɪn·ˈfleɪm] *vt* ❶ (*arouse*) entfachen ❷ (*anger*) aufbringen; *with anger* in Wut versetzen; *with desire* mit Verlangen erfüllen

inflammable [ɪn·ˈflæm·ə·bəl] *adj* [leicht] entzündbar; *situation* explosiv

inflammation [ˌɪn·flə·ˈmeɪ·ʃən] *n* Entzündung *f*

inflammatory [ɪn·ˈflæm·ə·tɔr·i] *adj* ❶ entzündlich, Entzündungs- ❷ (*provoking*) aufrührerisch

inflatable [ɪn·ˈfleɪ·t̬ə·bəl] *adj* aufblasbar

inflate [ɪn·ˈfleɪt] I. *vt* ❶ aufblasen; (*with pump*) aufpumpen ❷ (*exaggerate*) aufblähen *pej* ❸ (*raise*) in die Höhe treiben II. *vi* sich mit Luft füllen

inflated [ɪn·ˈfleɪ·t̬ɪd] *adj* aufgeblasen

inflation [ɪn·ˈfleɪ·ʃən] *n* ❶ ECON Inflation *f* ❷ Aufblasen *nt*; (*with pump*) Aufpumpen *nt*

inflationary [ɪn·ˈfleɪ·ʃə·ne·ri] *adj* FIN inflationär, Inflations-

inflect [ɪn·ˈflekt] *vt* LING beugen

inflexible [ɪn·ˈflek·sə·bəl] *adj* ❶ (*fixed*) starr; *person* unflexibel ❷ (*stiff*) steif

influence [ˈɪn·flu·əns] I. *n* Einfluss *m* (**on** auf +*akk*) II. *vt* beeinflussen

influential [ˌɪn·flu·ˈen·ʃəl] *adj* einflussreich

influenza [ˌɪn·flu·ˈen·zə] *n* Grippe *f*

influx [ˈɪn·flʌks] *n* Zustrom *m* (**of** an +*dat*); *of capital* Zufuhr *f* (**of** an +*dat*)

infomercial [ˌɪn·fou·ˈmɜr·ʃəl] *n* TV, MEDIA Infomercial *nt fachspr* (*als Informationssendung getarntes Werbevideo*)

inform [ɪn·ˈfɔrm] *vt* informieren

informal [ɪn·ˈfɔr·məl] *adj* ❶ informell; *atmosphere, party* zwanglos; (*casual*) leger ❷ (*unofficial*) inoffiziell

informant [ɪn·ˈfɔr·mənt] *n* Informant(in) *m(f)*

information [ˌɪn·fər·ˈmeɪ·ʃən] *n* ❶ Information *f*; **a piece of** ~ eine Information; **a lot of** ~ viele Informationen *pl* ❷ (*phone service*) Auskunft *f*

infor'mation science *n usu pl* Informatik *f kein pl*

informative [ɪn·ˈfɔr·mə·t̬ɪv] *adj* informativ

informed [ɪn·ˈfɔrmd] *adj* [gut] informiert

informer [ɪn·ˈfɔr·mər] *n* Informant(in) *m(f)*, Spitzel(in) *m(f)*

infotainment [ˈɪn·fou·teɪn·mənt] *n* Infotainment *nt*

infrared [ˈɪn·frə·ˈred] *adj* infrarot

infrastructure [ˈɪn·frə·ˌstrʌk·tʃər] *n* Infrastruktur *f*

infrequent [ɪn·ˈfri·kwənt] *adj* selten

infringe [ɪn·ˈfrɪndʒ] *vt* verletzen; *law* verstoßen (**against** gegen +*akk*)

infuriate [ɪnˈfjʊrˌiˌeɪt] vt wütend machen

ingratitude [ɪnˈgrætˌəˌtud] n Undankbarkeit f

ingredient [ɪnˈgriˌdiˌənt] n Zutat f

ingrown [ˈɪnˌgroʊn] adj usu attr eingewachsen

inhabit [ɪnˈhæbˌɪt] vt bewohnen

inhabitant [ɪnˈhæbˌəˌtənt] n Einwohner(in) m(f)

inhale [ɪnˈheɪl] vt, vi einatmen; smoker inhalieren

inherent [ɪnˈhɪrˌənt] adj ■ to be ~ in sth etw dat eigen sein

inherit [ɪnˈherˌɪt] vt, vi erben (from von +dat)

inheritance [ɪnˈherˌɪˌtəns] n Erbe nt kein pl

inhibit [ɪnˈhɪbˌɪt] vt ① (restrict) hindern ② (deter) hemmen

inhibition [ˌɪnˌhəˈbɪʃˌən] n Hemmung f

inhospitable [ɪnˈhasˌpɪˌtəˌbəl] adj ungastlich

in-house I. adj attr hauseigen II. adv intern, im Hause

inhuman [ɪnˈhjuˌmən] adj unmenschlich

inhumane [ˌɪnˌhjuˈmeɪn] adj barbarisch

initial [ɪˈnɪʃˌəl] I. adj attr anfänglich, erste(r, s) II. n Initiale f

initialize [ɪˈnɪʃˌəˌlaɪz] vt COMPUT initialisieren

initially [ɪˈnɪʃˌəˌli] adv anfangs

initiate [ɪˈnɪʃˌiˌeɪt] vt ① (start) in die Wege leiten ② (admit) einführen (into in +akk); (officially) [feierlich] aufnehmen (into in +akk)

initiative [ɪˈnɪʃˌəˌtɪv] n Initiative f

inject [ɪnˈdʒekt] vt spritzen (into in +akk)

injection [ɪnˈdʒekˌʃən] n Spritze f; TECH Einspritzung f

in-joke n Insiderwitz m fam

injunction [ɪnˈdʒʌŋkˌʃən] n LAW [gerichtliche] Verfügung

injure [ˈɪnˌdʒər] vt verletzen

injured [ˈɪnˌdʒərd] I. adj verletzt II. n ■ the ~ pl die Verletzten pl

injury [ˈɪnˌdʒəˌri] n Verletzung f

injustice [ɪnˈdʒʌsˌtɪs] n Ungerechtigkeit f

ink [ɪŋk] n Tinte f; ART Tusche f; (for stamp) Farbe

ink-jet 'printer n Tintenstrahldrucker m

'ink pad n Stempelkissen nt

inland adj [ˈɪnˌlənd] usu attr Binnen-

in-laws [ˈɪnˌlɔz] npl Schwiegereltern pl

inlay n [ˈɪnˌleɪ] ① Einlegearbeit[en] f(pl) ② (for tooth) Inlay nt

inlet [ˈɪnˌlet] n ① GEOG [schmale] Bucht; (of sea) Meeresarm m ② TECH Einlass[kanal] m; (pipe) Zuleitung f

inmate [ˈɪnˌmeɪt] n Insasse, -in m, f

inn [ɪn] n Gasthaus nt

innards [ˈɪnˌərdz] npl (fam) Eingeweide pl; FOOD Innereien pl

innate [ɪˈneɪt] adj natürlich, angeboren

inner [ˈɪnˌər] adj usu attr innere(r, s) attr

inner 'city n Innenstadt f, [Stadt]zentrum nt

innermost [ˈɪnˌərˌmoʊst] adj attr ① innerste(r, s) ② (secret) geheimste(r, s), intimste(r, s)

'inner tube n Schlauch m

inning [ˈɪnˌɪŋ] n SPORT (in baseball) Inning nt

innocence [ˈɪnˌəˌsəns] n Unschuld f

innocent [ˈɪnˌəˌsənt] I. adj unschuldig; mistake unbeabsichtigt II. n ■ to be an ~ naiv sein

innovation [ˌɪnˌəˈveɪˌʃən] n ① Neuerung f; (new product) Innovation f ② (creating) [Ver]änderung f

innovative [ˈɪnˌəˌveɪˌtɪv] adj innovativ

innumerable [ɪˈnuˌmərˌəˌbəl] adj unzählig

inoculate [ɪˈnakˌjəˌleɪt] vt impfen (against gegen +akk)

inoculation [ɪˌnakˌjəˈleɪˌʃən] n Impfung f

inoffensive [ˌɪnˌəˈfenˌsɪv] adj harmlos

inoperable [ˌɪnˈapˌərˌəˌbəl] adj ① MED inoperabel ② (not working) nicht funktionsfähig

inopportune [ˌɪnˌapˌərˈtun] adj ① (in-

convenient) ungünstig ② (*unsuitable*)
unpassend

inorganic [ˌɪn·ɔr·ˈgæn·ɪk] *adj* CHEM anorganisch

'inpatient *n* stationärer Patient/stationäre Patientin

input ['ɪn·pʊt] *n* ❶ Beitrag *m*; (*of work*) [Arbeits]aufwand *m* ❷ ELEC Anschluss *m* ❸ COMPUT (*data*) Input *m*; (*entering*) Eingabe *f*

inquest ['ɪn·kwest] *n* LAW gerichtliche Untersuchung [der Todesursache]

inquire [ɪn·ˈkwaɪr] *vt, vi* sich erkundigen (**about/as to** nach + *dat*); ■ **to ~ into sth** etw untersuchen

inquiry [ɪn·ˈkwaɪ·ri] *n* ❶ (*question*) Anfrage *f*, Erkundigung *f* ❷ (*investigation*) Untersuchung *f*; **to make inquiries** Nachforschungen anstellen

inquisition [ˌɪn·kwɪ·ˈzɪʃ·ən] *n* ❶ Verhör *nt* ❷ HIST ■ **the I~** die Inquisition

inquisitive [ɪn·ˈkwɪz·ɪ·tɪv] *adj* wissbegierig; (*curious*) neugierig; *look, face* fragend *attr*; *child* fragelustig

insane [ɪn·ˈseɪn] *adj* ❶ (*mentally ill*) geistesgestört ❷ (*fam: crazy*) verrückt

insanitary [ɪn·ˈsæn·ɪ·ter·i] *adj* unhygienisch

insanity [ɪn·ˈsæn·ɪ·t̬i] *n* Wahnsinn *a. fig*

inscription [ɪn·ˈskrɪp·ʃən] *n* Inschrift *f*; (*in book*) Widmung *f*

insect ['ɪn·sekt] *n* Insekt *nt*

insecticide [ɪn·ˈsek·tɪ·saɪd] *n* Insektenvernichtungsmittel *nt*

insecure [ˌɪn·sɪ·ˈkjʊr] *adj* unsicher

insecurity [ˌɪn·sɪ·ˈkjʊr·ə·t̬i] *n* Unsicherheit *f*

inseminate [ɪn·ˈsem·ɪ·neɪt] *vt woman* [künstlich] befruchten

insemination [ɪn·ˌsem·ɪ·ˈneɪ·ʃən] *n* Befruchtung *f*

insensible [ɪn·ˈsen·sə·bəl] *adj* ❶ (*unconscious*) bewusstlos ❷ (*numb*) gefühllos; (*to pain*) [schmerz]unempfindlich

insensitive [ɪn·ˈsen·sɪ·tɪv] *adj* ❶ (*uncaring*) gefühllos; *remark* taktlos ❷ *usu pred* (*numb*) unempfindlich (**to** gegenüber + *dat*)

inseparable [ɪn·ˈsep·rə·bəl] *adj* ❶ *friends* unzertrennlich ❷ (*connected*) untrennbar [miteinander verbunden]

insert *vt* [ɪn·ˈsɜrt] ❶ [hinein]stecken; *coins* einwerfen ❷ (*write*) einfügen; (*on form*) eintragen

'in-service *adj attr* **~ training** [innerbetriebliche] Fortbildung

inside [ɪn·ˈsaɪd] **I.** *n* ❶ Innere *nt*; **from the ~** von innen ❷ *of hand, door* Innenseite *f*; SPORT Innenbahn *f* **II.** *adv* ❶ innen ❷ (*indoors*) drinnen; (*direction*) hinein/herein ❸ (*fam: jailed*) hinter Gittern *fam* **III.** *adj attr* ❶ Innen-, innere(r, s) ❷ (*indoor*) Innen- **IV.** *prep* ❶ (*direction*) ■ **~ sth** in etw *akk* [hinein] ❷ (*location*) ■ **~ sth** in etw *dat* ❸ (*within*) **~ of two hours** in[nerhalb von] zwei Stunden

insider ['ɪn·saɪ·dər] *n* Insider(in) *m(f)*

insight ['ɪn·saɪt] *n* Einblick *m* (**into** in + *akk*)

insignificant [ˌɪn·sɪg·ˈnɪf·ɪ·kənt] *adj* unbedeutend; *remark* belanglos; *sum, difference* geringfügig

insincere [ˌɪn·sɪn·ˈsɪr] *adj* unaufrichtig; *person* falsch; *smile, praise* unecht; *flattery* heuchlerisch

insinuate [ɪn·ˈsɪn·ju·eɪt] *vt* (*imply*) andeuten

insinuation [ɪn·ˌsɪn·ju·ˈeɪ·ʃən] *n* Anspielung *f*

insist [ɪn·ˈsɪst] **I.** *vi* bestehen ([up]on auf + *dat*); ■ **to ~** [up]on doing sth sich nicht von etw *dat* abbringen lassen **II.** *vt* ■ **to ~ that …** ❶ (*claim*) fest behaupten, dass … ❷ (*demand*) darauf bestehen, dass …

insistence [ɪn·ˈsɪs·təns] *n* Bestehen *nt* (**on** auf + *dat*)

insistent [ɪn·ˈsɪs·tənt] *adj* beharrlich; *demand* nachdrücklich

insofar as [ˌɪn·soʊ·ˈfar·əz] *adv* soweit

insole ['ɪn·soʊl] *n* Einlegesohle *f*

insolence ['ɪn·sə·ləns] *n* Unverschämtheit *f*

insolent ['ɪn·sə·lənt] *adj* unverschämt

insoluble [ɪnˈsal·jə·bəl] *adj* ❶ unlösbar ❷ *minerals* nicht löslich

insolvency [ɪnˈsal·vən·si] *n* Zahlungsunfähigkeit *f*

insolvent [ɪnˈsal·vənt] *adj* zahlungsunfähig

insomnia [ɪnˈsam·ni·ə] *n* Schlaflosigkeit *f*

inspect [ɪnˈspekt] *vt* [über]prüfen, kontrollieren

inspection [ɪnˈspek·ʃən] *n* [Über]prüfung *f*, Kontrolle *f*

inspector [ɪnˈspek·tər] *n* Inspektor(in) *m(f)*; **tax ~** Steuerprüfer(in) *m(f)*

inspiration [ˌɪn·spəˈreɪ·ʃən] *n* Inspiration *f*

inspire [ɪnˈspaɪr] *vt* ❶ inspirieren ❷ *feeling* hervorrufen (**in** bei +*dat*)

inspired [ɪnˈspaɪrd] *adj* ❶ *poet, athlete* inspiriert ❷ *(excellent)* großartig ❸ *(motivated)* motiviert

instability [ˌɪn·stəˈbɪl·ə·t̬i] *n* ❶ Instabilität *f* ❷ PSYCH Labilität *f*

install [ɪnˈstɔl] *vt* *machinery* aufstellen; *computer, heating* installieren; *bathroom, kitchen* einbauen; *wiring, pipes* verlegen; *phone, washing machine* anschließen

installation [ˌɪn·stəˈleɪ·ʃən] *n* ❶ *of machinery* Aufstellen *nt*; *of appliance, heating* Installation *f*; *of kitchen, bathroom* Einbau *m*; *of wiring, pipes* Verlegung *f*; *of phone, washing machine* Anschluss *m* ❷ *(facility)* Anlage *f* ❸ ART Installation *f*

installment [ɪnˈstɔl·mənt] *n* ❶ *(part)* Folge *f* ❷ *(payment)* Rate *f*

in'stallment purchase *n* Ratenkauf *m*

instance [ˈɪn·stəns] *n* ❶ *(case)* Fall *m* ❷ **for ~** zum Beispiel

instant [ˈɪn·stənt] I. *n* ❶ Moment *m*, Augenblick *m*; **this ~** sofort ❷ *(as soon as)* ■ **the ~ ...** sobald ... II. *adj* ❶ sofortige(r, s) *attr*; **to take ~ effect** sofort wirken ❷ *(in bags)* Tüten-; *(in cans)* Dosen-; **~ coffee** Pulverkaffee *m*

instantly [ˈɪn·stənt·li] *adv* sofort

instant 'replay *n* TV Wiederholung *f*

instead [ɪnˈsted] I. *adv* stattdessen

II. *prep* ■ **~ of sb/sth** [an]statt einer Person/einer S. *gen*; ■ **~ of doing sth** [an]statt etw zu tun

instinct [ˈɪn·stɪŋkt] *n* Instinkt *m*

instinctive [ɪnˈstɪŋk·tɪv] *adj* instinktiv

institute [ˈɪn·strɪ·tut] *n* Institut *nt*

institution [ˌɪn·strɪˈtu·ʃən] *n* ❶ *of reforms* Einführung *f* ❷ *(building)* Heim *nt*, Anstalt *f* ❸ *(organization)* Einrichtung *f*, Institution *f*

instruct [ɪnˈstrʌkt] *vt* ❶ *(teach)* unterrichten ❷ *(order)* anweisen

instruction [ɪnˈstrʌk·ʃən] *n* ❶ *usu pl* *(order)* Anweisung *f* ❷ *(teaching)* Unterweisung *f* ❸ *(directions)* **~s for use** Gebrauchsanweisung *f*

in'struction book, in'struction manual *n* Handbuch *nt*; *for device* Gebrauchsanweisung *f*

instructive [ɪnˈstrʌk·tɪv] *adj* lehrreich, aufschlussreich

instructor [ɪnˈstrʌk·tər] *n* ❶ *(teacher)* Lehrer(in) *m(f)* ❷ *(at university)* Dozent(in) *m(f)*

instrument [ˈɪn·strə·mənt] *n* Instrument *nt*

instrumental [ˌɪn·strəˈmen·təl] *adj* ❶ MUS instrumental ❷ *(influential)* förderlich

'instrument panel *n* AUTO Armaturenbrett *nt*; AVIAT, NAUT Instrumententafel *f*

insufficient [ˌɪn·səˈfɪʃ·ənt] *adj* zu wenig *präd*, unzureichend

insular [ˈɪn·sə·lər] *adj* provinziell

insulate [ˈɪn·sə·leɪt] *vt* ❶ ELEC isolieren ❷ *(fig: shield)* [be]schützen (**from** vor +*dat*)

insulating [ˈɪn·sə·leɪ·t̬ɪŋ] *adj* Isolier-

'insulating tape *n* Isolierband *nt*

insulation [ˌɪn·səˈleɪ·ʃən] *n* ❶ Isolierung *f* ❷ *(fig: protection)* Schutz *m*

insulin [ˈɪn·sə·lɪn] *n* Insulin *nt*

insult I. *vt* [ɪnˈsʌlt] beleidigen II. *n* [ˈɪn·sʌlt] Beleidigung *f* ▶ PHRASES: **to add ~ to injury** um dem Ganzen die Krone aufzusetzen

insurance [ɪnˈʃʊr·əns] *n* Versicherung *f*; **to take out ~** [**against sth**] sich [gegen etw *akk*] versichern ❷ *(payout)*

Versicherungssumme *f* ❸(*premium*) [Versicherungs]prämie *f*

in'surance agent *n* Versicherungsmakler(in) *m(f)*

in'surance company *n* Versicherung[sgesellschaft] *f*

in'surance policy *n* Versicherungspolice *f*

in'surance premium *n* [Versicherungs]prämie *f*

insure [ɪn·'ʃʊr] I. *vt* versichern II. *vi* sich versichern (**with** bei +*dat*, **against** gegen +*akk*)

insured [ɪn·'ʃʊrd] I. *adj* versichert II. *n* <*pl* -> ∎**the ~** der/die Versicherte

insurer [ɪn·'ʃʊr·ər] *n* Versicherung[sgesellschaft] *f*

insurgent [ɪn·'sɜr·dʒənt] *n* POL *Parteimitglied, das sich der Parteidisziplin nicht beugt*

intact [ɪn·'tækt] *adj usu pred* intakt, unversehrt

intake ['ɪn·teɪk] I. *n* ❶(*act*) Aufnahme *f*; **~ of breath** Luftholen *nt* ❷(*amount*) aufgenommene Menge; **~ of calories** Kalorienzufuhr *f* II. *adj* TECH Ansaug-, Saug-

intangible [ɪn·'tæn·dʒə·bəl] *adj* nicht greifbar

integrate ['ɪn·tɪ·ɡreɪt] I. *vt* integrieren (**into** in +*akk*) II. *vi* sich integrieren

integrated ['ɪn·tɪ·ɡreɪ·tɪd] *adj* einheitlich; *person* integriert (**in** in +*akk*); **~ school** (*hist*) Schule *f* ohne Rassentrennung

integrated 'circuit, I 'C *n* ELEC integrierter Schaltkreis

intellect ['ɪn·təl·ekt] *n* Verstand *m*, Intellekt *m*

intellectual [ˌɪn·tə·'lek·tʃʊ·əl] I. *n* Intellektuelle(r) *f(m)* II. *adj* intellektuell, geistig

intelligence [ɪn·'tel·ə·dʒəns] I. *n* ❶ Intelligenz *f* ❷(*department*) Geheimdienst *m* ❸(*information*) [nachrichtendienstliche] Informationen; **according to our latest ~** unseren letzten Meldungen zufolge II. *adj* Nachrichten-; **~ report** Geheimdienstbericht *m*

in'telligence agency *n* Geheimdienst *m*

in'telligence test *n* Intelligenztest *m*

intelligent [ɪn·'tel·ə·dʒənt] *adj* klug, intelligent

intend [ɪn·'tend] *vt* beabsichtigen; **I don't think she ~ed me to hear the remark** ich glaube nicht, dass ich die Bemerkung hören sollte; **no disrespect ~ed** [das] war nicht böse gemeint

intended [ɪn·'ten·dɪd] *adj* beabsichtigt; ∎**to be ~ for sth** für etw *akk* gedacht sein

intense [ɪn·'tens] *adj* ❶(*forceful*) intensiv; *odor* stechend; *cold* bitter; *desire, heat* glühend; *excitement* groß; *feeling, friendship* tief; *hatred* rasend; *love* leidenschaftlich; *pain* heftig ❷(*serious*) ernst

intensify <-ie-> [ɪn·'ten·sɪ·faɪ] I. *vt* intensivieren; *conflict* verschärfen; *fears* verstärken; *pressure* erhöhen II. *vi heat* stärker werden; *feeling, competition a.* zunehmen

intensity [ɪn·'ten·sə·ti] *n* Stärke *f*; *of feelings* Intensität *f*; *of explosion, anger* Heftigkeit *f*

intensive [ɪn·'ten·sɪv] *adj* intensiv; *analysis* gründlich; *bombardment* heftig

intensive 'care *n* Intensivpflege *f*; **to be in ~** auf der Intensivstation sein

intent [ɪn·'tent] *n* Absicht *f*; ∎**with ~ to do sth** mit dem Vorsatz, etw zu tun

intention [ɪn·'ten·ʃən] *n* Absicht *f*; **full of good ~s** voller guter Vorsätze

intentional [ɪn·'ten·ʃə·nəl] *adj* absichtlich

interact [ɪn·tər·'ækt] *vi* aufeinander einwirken

interaction [ˌɪn·tər·'æk·ʃən] *n* Wechselwirkung *f*; *of groups, people* Interaktion *f*

interactive [ˌɪn·tər·'æk·tɪv] *adj* interaktiv

interbreed <-bred, -bred> [ˌɪn·tər·'brid] I. *vt* kreuzen II. *vi* sich kreuzen

intercept [ˌɪn·tər·'sept] *vt* abfangen; **~ a call** eine Fangschaltung legen; **to ~ a pass** SPORT einen Pass abfangen

interception [ˌɪn·tər·ˈsep·ʃən] n Abfangen nt; of calls Abhören nt

interceptor [ˌɪn·tər·ˈsep·tər] n MIL Abfangjäger m

interchange [ˈɪn·tər·tʃeɪndʒ] n ① Austausch m ② (road) Autobahnkreuz nt

interchangeable [ˌɪn·tər·ˈtʃeɪn·dʒə·bəl] adj austauschbar; word synonym

intercity [ˌɪn·tər·ˈsɪt·i] adj attr transportation Intercity-

intercom [ˈɪn·tər·kam] n [Gegen]sprechanlage f; (for doors) [Tür]sprechanlage f

intercontinental [ˌɪn·tər·kan·tə·ˈnen·təl] adj interkontinental

intercourse [ˈɪn·tər·kɔrs] n ① (sex) [Geschlechts]verkehr m ② (dealings) Umgang m

interdict [ˌɪn·tər·ˈdɪkt] LAW I. n Verbot nt II. vt verbieten

interest [ˈɪn·trɪst] I. n ① Interesse nt (in an + dat); **in the ~ of safety** aus Sicherheitsgründen ② FIN Zinsen pl; **rate of ~** Zinssatz m II. vt interessieren (**in** für + akk)

interested [ˈɪn·trɪ·stɪd] adj ① (concerned) interessiert; **to be ~ in sb/sth** sich für jdn/etw interessieren ② (involved) beteiligt; witness befangen

interest-'free adj FIN zinslos; credit unverzinslich

interesting [ˈɪn·trɪ·stɪŋ] adj interessant

interface n [ˈɪn·tər·feɪs] Schnittstelle f; COMPUT, TECH Interface nt

interfere [ˌɪn·tər·ˈfɪr] vi ① (meddle) ■to ~ [in sth] sich [in etw akk] einmischen ② (hit) ■to ~ with one another aneinanderstoßen

interference [ˌɪn·tər·ˈfɪr·əns] n ① Einmischung f ② RADIO, TECH Störung f

interim [ˈɪn·tər·ɪm] I. n Zwischenzeit f II. adj attr vorläufig; ~ **government** Übergangsregierung f

interior [ɪn·ˈtɪr·i·ər] I. adj attr ① (inside) Innen- ② (country) Inlands-, Binnen- II. n ① (inside) Innere nt ② POL ■the I~ das Innere; **the Department of the I~** das Innenministerium; **Secretary of the I~** Innenminister(in) m(f)

interior de'signer n Innenarchitekt(in) m(f)

interject [ˌɪn·tər·ˈdʒekt] I. vt einwerfen II. vi dazwischenreden

interjection [ˌɪn·tər·ˈdʒek·ʃən] n ① (interruption) Zwischenbemerkung f ② LING Interjektion f

intermediate [ˌɪn·tər·ˈmi·di·ɪt] adj ① (level) mittel; (between two things) Zwischen- ② (level of skill) Mittel-; ~ **course** Kurs m für fortgeschrittene Anfänger/Anfängerinnen

intermezzo <pl -s> [ˌɪn·tər·ˈmet·soʊ] n Intermezzo nt

interminable [ɪn·ˈtɜr·mɪ·nə·bəl] adj endlos

intermission [ˌɪn·tər·ˈmɪʃ·ən] n Pause f

intermittent [ˌɪn·tər·ˈmɪt·ənt] adj periodisch

intern I. vt [ɪn·ˈtɜrn] internieren II. vi [ɪn·ˈtɜrn] ein Praktikum absolvieren III. n [ˈɪn·tɜrn] Praktikant(in) m(f); [hospital] ~ Assistenzarzt, Assistenzärztin m, f

internal [ɪn·ˈtɜr·nəl] adj innere(r, s); (within company) innerbetrieblich; (within country) Binnen-; investigation, memo intern; ~ **affairs** innere Angelegenheiten pl

internalize [ɪn·ˈtɜr·nə·laɪz] vt verinnerlichen

Internal 'Revenue Service n ■the ~ ≈ das Finanzamt

international [ˌɪn·tər·ˈnæʃ·ə·nəl] adj international

International Court of 'Justice n Internationaler Gerichtshof

International 'Monetary Fund n Internationaler Währungsfonds

International O'lympic Committee n Internationales Olympisches Komitee

Internet [ˈɪn·tər·net] I. n Internet nt; **to surf the ~** im Internet surfen; **on the ~** im Internet II. adj Internet-

Internet 'banking n Internetbanking nt

internist [ɪn·ˈtɜr·nɪst] n Internist(in) m(f)

internment [ɪn·ˈtɜrn·mənt] n Internierung f

in'ternment camp n Internierungslager nt

interpersonal [ˌɪn·tər·ˈpɜr·sə·nəl] adj zwischenmenschlich; ~ **skills** soziale Kompetenz

interplanetary [ˌɪn·tər·ˈplæn·ə·ter·i] adj interplanetarisch

interplay [ˈɪn·tər·pleɪ] n Zusammenspiel nt (**of** von +dat), Wechselwirkung f (**between** zwischen +dat)

Interpol [ˈɪn·tər·pal] n no art Interpol f

interpolate [ɪn·ˈtɜr·pə·leɪt] vt einfügen; opinion einfließen lassen

interpret [ɪn·ˈtɜr·prɪt] I. vt ① (explain) interpretieren; (understand) auslegen ② (perform) wiedergeben; role auslegen II. vi dolmetschen

interpretation [ɪn·ˌtɜr·prɪ·ˈteɪ·ʃən] n Interpretation f; of rules Auslegung f; of dream Deutung f

interpreter [ɪn·ˈtɜr·prɪ·tər] n Dolmetscher(in) m(f)

interpreting [ɪn·ˈtɜr·prɪ·tɪŋ] n Dolmetschen nt

interrogate [ɪn·ˈter·ə·geɪt] vt verhören

interrogation [ɪn·ˌter·ə·ˈgeɪ·ʃən] n Verhör nt

interrogatory [ˌɪn·tə·ˈrag·ə·tɔr·i] adj fragend attr

interrupt [ˌɪn·tə·ˈrʌpt] vt, vi unterbrechen

interruption [ˌɪn·tə·ˈrʌp·ʃən] n Unterbrechung f

intersection [ˌɪn·tər·ˈsek·ʃən] n ① Schnittpunkt m ② (junction) [Straßen]kreuzung f

interstate [ˈɪn·tər·ˈsteɪt] I. adj attr zwischenstaatlich II. n [Bundes]autobahn f

interstate 'highway n [Bundes]autobahn f

interval [ˈɪn·tər·vəl] n ① (gap) Abstand m ② (break) Pause f, Intervall nt

intervene [ˌɪn·tər·ˈvin] vi ① (step in) einschreiten ② (interrupt) sich einmischen

intervening [ˌɪn·tər·ˈvin·ɪŋ] adj attr dazwischenliegend attr

intervention [ˌɪn·tər·ˈven·ʃən] n Eingreifen nt

interview [ˈɪn·tər·vju] I. n ① (with media) Interview nt ② (for job) Vorstellungsgespräch nt ③ (with police) Verhör nt II. vt ■ **to ~ sb** (by reporter) jdn interviewen; (for job) mit jdm ein Vorstellungsgespräch führen; (by police) jdn befragen

interviewee [ˌɪn·tər·vju·ˈi] n Interviewte(r) f(m); (by police) Befragte(r) f(m); **job ~** Kandidat(in) m(f)

interviewer [ˈɪn·tər·vju·ər] n (reporter) Interviewer(in) m(f); (in job interview) Leiter(in) m(f) des Vorstellungsgesprächs

intestine [ɪn·ˈtes·tɪn] n usu pl Darm m, Eingeweide pl

intimacy [ˈɪn·tə·mə·si] n Intimität f; (sexual) Intimitäten pl

intimate [ˈɪn·tə·mɪt] adj ① (close) eng, vertraut; atmosphere gemütlich; friend eng; relationship intim ② (detailed) gründlich; knowledge umfassend ③ (private) ~ **details** intime Einzelheiten

intimidate [ɪn·ˈtɪm·ɪ·deɪt] vt einschüchtern

intimidating [ɪn·ˈtɪm·ɪ·deɪt·ɪŋ] adj beängstigend; manner einschüchternd

intimidation [ɪn·ˌtɪm·ɪ·ˈdeɪ·ʃən] n Einschüchterung f

into [ˈɪn·tə, -tu] prep ① (to inside) in +akk; **to go ~ town** in die Stadt gehen ② (toward) in +akk; **she looked ~ the mirror** sie sah in den Spiegel ③ (through time) **sometimes we work late ~ the evening** manchmal arbeiten wir bis spät in den Abend ④ (fam: interested) **to be ~ sb/sth** an jdm/etw interessiert sein; **what kind of music are you ~?** auf welche Art von Musik stehst du? ⑤ (transition) **to translate ~ French** ins Französische übersetzen

intolerable [ɪn·ˈtal·ər·ə·bəl] adj unerträglich

intolerance [ɪn·ˈtal·ər·əns] n a. MED Intoleranz f (**of** gegenüber +dat)

intolerant [ɪn·ˈtal·ər·ənt] adj ① intolerant ②MED überempfindlich (**of** gegenüber +*dat*)

intoxicating [ɪn·ˈtak·sɪ·keɪ·t̬ɪŋ] *adj* berauschend *a. fig*

Intranet [ˌɪn·trə·ˈnet] *n* Intranet *nt*

intransitive [ɪn·ˈtræn·sɪ·t̬ɪv] *adj* intransitiv

intravenous [ˌɪn·trə·ˈvi·nəs] *adj* intravenös

intricate [ˈɪn·trɪ·kɪt] *adj* kompliziert

intrigue I. *vi* [ɪn·ˈtrig] intrigieren II. *n* [ˈɪn·trig] Intrige *f*

intriguing [ɪn·ˈtri·gɪŋ] *adj* faszinierend

introduce [ˌɪn·trə·ˈdus] *vt* einführen; ■ to ~ **sb** [**to sb**] jdn [jdm] vorstellen

introduction [ˌɪn·trə·ˈdʌk·ʃən] *n* Einführung *f*

intro'ductory course *n* Einführungskurs *m*

introspection [ˌɪn·trə·ˈspek·ʃən] *n* Selbstbeobachtung *f*

introvert [ˈɪn·trə·ˌvɜrt] *n* introvertierter Mensch

introverted [ˈɪn·trə·ˌvɜr·t̬ɪd] *adj* introvertiert

intrude [ɪn·ˈtrud] *vi* stören, sich einmischen (**into in** +*akk*); **am I intruding?** störe ich gerade?; ■ to ~ **on sb's privacy** in jds Privatsphäre eindringen

intruder [ɪn·ˈtru·dər] *n* Eindringling *m;* (*thief*) Einbrecher(in) *m(f)*

intrusion [ɪn·ˈtru·ʒən] *n* Störung *f,* Einmischung *f*

intrusive [ɪn·ˈtru·sɪv] *adj* aufdringlich

intuition [ˌɪn·tu·ˈɪʃ·ən] *n* Intuition *f*

intuitive [ɪn·ˈtu·ɪ·t̬ɪv] *adj* intuitiv

invade [ɪn·ˈveɪd] I. *vt* ①**to ~ a country** in ein Land einmarschieren ②(*fig: breach*) **to ~ sb's privacy** jds Privatsphäre verletzen II. *vi* einfallen

invader [ɪn·ˈveɪ·dər] *n* Angreifer(in) *m(f);* (*encroacher*) Eindringling *m*

invalid[1] [ˈɪn·və·lɪd] I. *n* Invalide(r) *m(f)* II. *adj* invalide, körperbehindert

invalid[2] [ɪn·ˈvæl·ɪd] *adj* (*void*) ungültig; (*unsound*) nicht stichhaltig; *theory* nicht begründet

invalidate [ɪn·ˈvæl·ɪ·deɪt] *vt argument*

widerlegen; *judgment* aufheben; *results* annullieren; *theory* entkräften

invalidity [ˌɪn·və·ˈlɪd·ə·t̬i] *n* ①MED Invalidität *f* ②LAW ~ **of a contract** Nichtigkeit *f* eines Vertrags

invaluable [ɪn·ˈvæl·ju·ə·bəl] *adj* unbezahlbar; *source* unverzichtbar

invariable [ɪn·ˈver·i·ə·bəl] *adj* unveränderlich

invariably [ɪn·ˈver·i·ə·bli] *adv* ausnahmslos

invasion [ɪn·ˈveɪ·ʒən] *n* ①MIL Invasion *f* ②(*interference*) Eindringen *nt kein pl* (**of in** +*akk*)

invent [ɪn·ˈvent] *vt* erfinden

invention [ɪn·ˈven·ʃən] *n* Erfindung *f;* (*creativity*) Einfallsreichtum *m*

inventive [ɪn·ˈven·t̬ɪv] *adj* einfallsreich, fantasievoll

inventiveness [ɪn·ˈven·t̬ɪv·nɪs] *n* Einfallsreichtum *m*

inventor [ɪn·ˈven·tər] *n* Erfinder(in) *m(f)*

inventory [ˈɪn·vən·tɔr·i] I. *n* Inventar *nt,* [Lager]bestand *m;* **to take ~** Inventur machen II. *adj* Bestands-

invert [ɪn·ˈvɜrt] *vt* umkehren

invertebrate [ɪn·ˈvɜr·t̬ə·brɪt] I. *n* wirbelloses Tier II. *adj* wirbellos

invest [ɪn·ˈvest] I. *vt* investieren II. *vi* ■ to ~ **in sth** [sein Geld] in etw *akk* investieren

investigate [ɪn·ˈves·tɪ·geɪt] *vt* untersuchen

investigation [ɪn·ˌves·tɪ·ˈgeɪ·ʃən] *n* Untersuchung *f; of affair* [Über]prüfung *f;* (*by police*) Ermittlung *f;* (*inquiry*) Nachforschung *f*

investigator [ɪn·ˈves·tɪ·geɪ·tər] *n* (*form*) Ermittler(in) *m(f)*

investment [ɪn·ˈvest·mənt] I. *n* ①(*act*) Investierung *f* ②(*instance*) Investition *f* ③(*share*) Einlage *f* II. *adj* Anlage-, Investitions-, Investment-

in'vestment bank *n* FIN Investmentbank *f*

in'vestment fund *n* Investmentfonds *m*

investor [ɪn·ˈves·tər] *n* [Kapital]anleger(in) *m(f)*, Investor(in) *m(f)*

invigorate [ɪn·ˈvɪg·ə·reɪt] *vt* ❶ stärken ❷ (*fig: stimulate*) beleben

invigorating [ɪn·ˈvɪg·ə·reɪ·tɪŋ] *adj* ❶ stärkend ❷ (*fig: stimulating*) belebend

invincible [ɪn·ˈvɪn·sə·bəl] *adj* ❶ (*unbeatable*) unschlagbar ❷ (*insuperable*) unüberwindlich

invisible [ɪn·ˈvɪz·ə·bəl] *adj* unsichtbar

invitation [ˌɪn·vɪ·ˈteɪ·ʃən] *n* ❶ (*request*) Einladung *f* (**to** zu +*dat*) ❷ (*incitement*) Aufforderung *f* (**to** zu +*dat*) ❸ (*chance*) Gelegenheit *f*

invite I. *n* [ˈɪn·vaɪt] (*fam*) Einladung *f* (**to** zu +*dat*) II. *vt* [ɪn·ˈvaɪt] ❶ (*to party*) einladen ❷ (*request*) ▪ **to ~ sb to do sth** jdn auffordern, etw zu tun ❸ (*fig: cause*) herausfordern; **to ~ trouble** Unannehmlichkeiten hervorrufen

inviting [ɪn·ˈvaɪ·tɪŋ] *adj* ❶ *sight, weather* einladend; *appearance, fashion* ansprechend ❷ (*tempting*) verlockend; *gesture, smile* einladend

in vitro [ɪn·ˈviˈtroʊ] I. *adj* künstlich, In-Vitro- II. *adv* künstlich, in vitro *fachspr*

in vitro fertiliˈzation *n* künstliche Befruchtung

invoice [ˈɪn·vɔɪs] I. *vt* ▪ **to ~ sb** jdm eine Rechnung ausstellen II. *n* [Waren]rechnung *f*

involuntary [ɪn·ˈval·ən·ter·i] *adj* ❶ unfreiwillig ❷ (*unintentional*) unbeabsichtigt

involve [ɪn·ˈvalv] *vt* ❶ (*include*) beinhalten; (*encompass*) umfassen; (*entail*) mit sich bringen; (*mean*) bedeuten ❷ (*affect*) betreffen; **that doesn't ~ her** sie hat damit nichts zu tun; **this incident ~s us all** dieser Zwischenfall geht uns alle an ❸ (*bring in*) ▪ **to ~ sb in sth** jdn an etw *dat* beteiligen; (*unwillingly*) jdn in etw *akk* verwickeln; **I don't want to get ~d** ich will damit nichts zu tun haben ❹ *usu passive* ▪ **to be ~d in sth** (*be busy*) mit etw *dat* zu tun haben; (*be engrossed*) von etw *dat* gefesselt sein; ▪ **to be ~d with sb** (*have to do with*) mit jdm zu tun haben;

(*relationship*) mit jdm eine Beziehung haben; (*affair*) mit jdm ein Verhältnis haben

involved [ɪn·ˈvalvd] *adj* kompliziert; *affair* verwickelt; *issue* komplex

involvement [ɪn·ˈvalv·mənt] *n* ❶ (*participation*) Beteiligung *f* (**in** an +*dat*), Verwicklung *f* (**in** in +*dat*) ❷ (*complexity*) Komplexität *f* ❸ (*relationship*) Verhältnis *nt*

invulnerable [ɪn·ˈvʌl·nər·ə·bəl] *adj* ❶ unverwundbar ❷ (*fig*) unantastbar

inward [ˈɪn·wərd] I. *adj* ❶ (*ingoing*) nach innen gehend ❷ (*incoming*) Eingangs-, eingehend ❸ (*usu fig: internal*) innere(r, s), innerlich II. *adv* einwärts, nach innen

inwardly [ˈɪn·wərd·li] *adv* innerlich

inwards [ˈɪn·wərdz] *adv* nach innen

IOC [ˌaɪ·oʊ·ˈsi] *n* + *sing/pl vb abbrev of* **International Olympic Committee:** ▪ **the ~** das IOC

iodine [ˈaɪ·ə·daɪn] *n* Jod *nt*

ion [ˈaɪ·ən] *n* Ion *nt*

IOU [ˌaɪ·oʊ·ˈju] *n* (*fam*) *abbrev of* **I owe you** Schuldschein *m*

Iowa [ˈaɪ·ə·wə] *n* Iowa *nt*

IQ [ˌaɪ·ˈkju] *n abbrev of* **intelligence quotient** IQ *m*

IRA [ˌaɪ·aɾ·ˈeɪ] *n* ❶ FIN *abbrev of* **Individual Retirement Account** [steuerbegünstigte] Altersvorsorge ❷ *abbrev of* **Irish Republican Army:** ▪ **the ~** die IRA

Iran [ɪ·ˈræn] *n* [der] Iran

Iranian [ɪ·ˈreɪ·ni·ən] I. *n* Iraner(in) *m(f)* II. *adj* iranisch

Iraq [ɪ·ˈrak] *n* [der] Irak

Iraqi [ɪ·ˈrak·i] I. *n* Iraker(in) *m(f)* II. *adj* irakisch

Ireland [ˈaɪr·lənd] *n* Irland *nt*

iris <*pl* -es> [ˈaɪ·rɪs] *n* ANAT, BOT Iris *f*

Irish [ˈaɪ·rɪʃ] I. *adj* irisch II. *n pl* ▪ **the ~** die Iren *pl*

ˈIrishman *n* Ire *m*

ˈIrishwoman *n* Irin *f*

iron [ˈaɪ·ərn] I. *n* ❶ Eisen *nt* ❷ (*appliance*) [Bügel]eisen *nt* ❸ (*club*) Golfschläger *m* ▶ PHRASES: **to have many/**

other ~s in the <u>fire</u> viele/andere Eisen im Feuer haben **II.** *adj* Eisen-; (*fig: strict*) eisern **III.** *vt, vi* bügeln

'**Iron Age I.** *n* Eisenzeit *f* **II.** *adj* eisenzeitlich

iron '**curtain** *n* (*hist*) ■the I~ C~ der Eiserne Vorhang

ironic [aɪˈran·ɪk] *adj* ironisch

ironing [ˈaɪ·ər·nɪŋ] *n* Bügeln *nt*; (*laundry*) Bügelwäsche *f*

'**ironing board** *n* Bügelbrett *nt*

iron '**lung** *n* eiserne Lunge

iron '**ore** *n* Eisenerz *nt*

'**ironworks** *n* + *sing/pl vb* Eisenhütte *f*

irony [ˈaɪ·rə·ni] *n* Ironie *f*

irrational [ɪˈræʃ·ə·nəl] *adj* irrational

irreconcilable [ɪˌrek·ənˈsaɪ·lə·bəl] *adj* ideas, views unvereinbar; enemies unversöhnlich

irregular [ɪˈreg·jə·lər] *adj* ❶ (*asymmetrical*) unregelmäßig; surface uneben ❷ (*unorthodox*) conduct regelwidrig; action ungesetzlich; dealings zwielichtig

irrelevant [ɪˈrel·ə·vənt] *adj* belanglos

irreparable [ɪˈrep·ər·ə·bəl] *adj* irreparabel; damage, loss unersetzlich

irreplaceable [ˌɪr·ɪˈpleɪ·sə·bəl] *adj* unersetzlich; resources nicht erneuerbar

irresistible [ˌɪr·ɪˈzɪs·tə·bəl] *adj* unwiderstehlich; argument schlagend

irrespective [ˌɪr·ɪˈspek·tɪv] *adv* ■~ of sth ohne Rücksicht auf etw *akk*, ungeachtet einer S. *gen*; ~ of what … unabhängig davon, was …

irresponsible [ˌɪr·ɪˈspan·sə·bəl] *adj* ❶ (*inconsiderate*) unverantwortlich; person verantwortungslos ❷ LAW unzurechnungsfähig

irretrievable [ˌɪr·ɪˈtri·və·bəl] *adj* losses unersetzlich

irreversible [ˌɪr·ɪˈvɜr·sə·bəl] *adj* nicht umkehrbar, irreversibel

irrevocable [ɪˈrev·ə·kə·bəl] *adj* unwiderruflich, endgültig

irrigate [ˈɪr·ɪ·geɪt] *vt* bewässern

irrigation [ˌɪr·ɪˈgeɪ·ʃən] **I.** *n* Bewässerung *f*; of crops Berieselung *f* **II.** *adj* Bewässerungs-

irritable [ˈɪr·ɪ·tə·bəl] *adj* reizbar, gereizt; organ, tissue [über]empfindlich

irritant [ˈɪr·ɪ·tənt] *n* ❶ (*substance*) Reizstoff *m* ❷ (*annoyance*) Ärgernis *nt*

irritate [ˈɪr·ɪ·teɪt] *vt* ❶ (*anger*) [ver]ärgern ❷ (*inflame*) to ~ skin Hautreizungen hervorrufen

irritating [ˈɪr·ɪ·teɪt·ɪŋ] *adj* ärgerlich, lästig; conduct irritierend

irritation [ˌɪr·ɪˈteɪ·ʃən] *n* ❶ (*annoyance*) Verärgerung *f* ❷ (*nuisance*) Ärgernis *nt* ❸ (*inflammation*) Reizung *f*; to cause ~ eine Reizung hervorrufen

IRS [ˌaɪ·ɑrˈes] *n* FIN abbrev of **Internal Revenue Service** Finanzamt *nt*

is [ɪz] aux vb 3rd pers. sing of be

ISBN [ˌaɪ·es·biˈen] *n* abbrev of **International Standard Book Number** ISBN-Nummer *f*

ISDN [ˌaɪ·es·diˈen] *n* TELEC abbrev of **integrated services digital network** ISDN

Islam [ɪzˈlam] *n* [der] Islam

Islamic [ɪzˈlam·ɪk] *adj* islamisch

island [ˈaɪ·lənd] *n* Insel *f a. fig*

islander [ˈaɪ·lən·dər] *n* Insulaner(in) *m(f)*

isle [aɪl] *n* (*liter*) Eiland *nt*

isn't [ˈɪz·ənt] = is not see be

isolate [ˈaɪ·sə·leɪt] *vt* isolieren (**from** von +*dat*); ■to ~ oneself sich abkapseln; to ~ a problem ein Problem gesondert betrachten

isolated [ˈaɪ·sə·leɪ·tɪd] *adj* ❶ (*outlying*) abgelegen; (*detached*) building, house frei stehend ❷ (*solitary*) einsam [gelegen]; village abgeschieden ❸ (*excluded*) country isoliert

isolation [ˌaɪ·səˈleɪ·ʃən] **I.** *n* Isolation *f*; of building, house Abgelegenheit *f*; ~ **from** noise Isolierung *f* gegen Schall **II.** *adj* block, cell Isolations-; resistor, switch Trenn-

iso'lation ward *n* Isolierstation *f*

ISP [ˌaɪ·es·ˈpi] *n* INET, TELEC abbrev of **Internet service provider** ISP *m*

Israel [ˈɪz·ri·əl] *n* Israel *nt*

Israeli [ɪzˈreɪ·li] **I.** *n* Israeli *m o f* **II.** *adj* israelisch

Israelite ['ɪz·ri·ə·laɪt] n Israelit(in) m/f
issue ['ɪʃ·u] **I.** n ❶ (topic) Thema nt; **to make an ~ of sth** etw aufbauschen ❷ (question) Frage f, Problem nt; **that's not the ~!** darum geht es doch gar nicht!; **to raise an ~** eine Frage aufwerfen; **the point at ~** der strittige Punkt f ❸ (affair) Sache f ❹ (edition) Ausgabe f; **date of ~** Erscheinungsdatum nt ❺ FIN of shares Emission f; of check, document Ausstellung f **II.** vt ❶ (produce) ausstellen; currency in Umlauf bringen; bonds ausgeben; newsletter veröffentlichen; command erteilen; ultimatum stellen; statement abgeben; **to ~ an arrest warrant** einen Haftbefehl erlassen ❷ (supply with) ■ **to ~ sb with sth** jdn mit etw dat ausstatten

it [ɪt] pron ❶ (unknown thing) es; (known thing) er/es/sie; **a room with two beds in ~** ein Raum mit zwei Betten darin ❷ (in time phrases) **what time is ~?** wie spät ist es?; **what day is ~?** welchen Tag haben wir heute? ❸ subject (referring to following) **it's important/a shame that ...** es ist wichtig/schade, dass ...; **~'s true I don't like Stephanie** es stimmt, ich mag Stephanie nicht ❹ (in passive with verbs of opinion) **~ is said that ...** es heißt, dass ... ❺ (emph) **~ was Paul who came here in September, not Bob** Paul kam im September, nicht Bob ❻ (situation) **~ appears that we have lost** mir scheint, wir haben verloren; **~ takes me an hour to ...** ich brauche eine Stunde, um ...; **if ~'s convenient** wenn es Ihnen/dir passt ❼ (right thing) **that's exactly ~ — what a great find!** das ist genau das – ein toller Fund!; **that's ~!** das ist es! ❽ (the end) **that's ~** das war's ▶PHRASES: **go for ~!** mach es!; **go for ~, girl!** du schaffst es, Mädchen!; **this is ~** jetzt geht's los; **that's ~** das ist der Punkt

IT [aɪ'ti] n COMPUT abbrev of **information technology** IT f
Italian [ɪ'tæl·jən] **I.** n ❶ (person) Italiener(in) m/f ❷ (language) Italienisch nt **II.** adj italienisch
italic [ɪ'tæl·ɪk] adj TYPO kursiv
italics [ɪ'tæl·ɪks] npl TYPO Kursivschrift f
Italy ['ɪt·ə·li] n Italien nt
itch [ɪtʃ] **I.** n <pl -es> Juckreiz m; **I've got an ~ on my back** es juckt mich am Rücken **II.** vi ❶ (prickle) jucken ❷ (fig fam: desire) ■ **to be ~ing to do sth** ganz wild darauf sein, etw zu tun
itchy ['ɪtʃ·i] adj juckend; clothes kratzig
item ['aɪ·təm] n ❶ (thing) Gegenstand m; (in catalog) Artikel m; **~ of furniture** Möbelstück nt; **luxury ~** Luxusartikel m ❷ (on agenda) Punkt m; (on list) Posten m; **~ by ~** Punkt für Punkt
itinerary [aɪ'tɪn·ə·rer·i] n Reiseroute f
it'll ['ɪt·əl] = **it will/it shall** see **will¹, shall**
its [ɪts] pron poss sein(e)/ihr(e)
it's [ɪts] = **it is, it has** see **be, have I, II**
itself [ɪt·'self] pron refl ❶ after vb, prep sich [selbst] ❷ (specifically) **the store ~ opened 15 years ago** das Geschäft selbst öffnete vor 15 Jahren ❸ (alone) **[all] by ~** [ganz] allein
IUD [aɪ·ju·'di] n abbrev of **intrauterine device** Intrauterinpessar nt
IV [aɪ·'vi] adj abbrev of **intravenous** intravenös
I've [aɪv] = **I have** see **have I, II**
IVF [aɪ·vi·'ef] n abbrev of **in vitro fertilization** IVF f
ivory ['aɪ·və·ri] **I.** n Elfenbein nt **II.** adj Elfenbein-; **~-colored** elfenbeinfarben
'Ivory Coast n ■ **the ~** die Elfenbeinküste
ivy ['aɪ·vi] n Efeu m
Ivy 'League I. n ■ **the ~** Eliteuniversitäten im Nordosten der USA **II.** n modifier der Ivy League angehörende Eliteuniversitäten

Jj

J <pl -'s>, j <pl -'s> [dʒeɪ] n J nt, j nt;
~ **as in Juliet** J wie Julius

jab [dʒæb] I. n Stoß m; (with knife)
Stich m; (in boxing) Gerade f II. vt
<-bb-> schlagen; (with knife) stechen
III. vi <-bb-> (in boxing) eine [kurze]
Gerade schlagen

jack [dʒæk] n ❶ AUTO Wagenheber m
❷ CARDS Bube m
◆**jack off** vi (vulg) wichsen vulg
◆**jack up** vi ❶ car aufbocken ❷ (fig)
erhöhen; prices, rent in die Höhe treiben II. vi (sl) fixen fam

jackal ['dʒæk·əl] n Schakal m

jackdaw ['dʒæk·dɔ] n Dohle f

jacket ['dʒæk·ɪt] n ❶ FASHION Jacke f
❷ (of a book) Schutzumschlag m

jackhammer ['dʒæk·ˌhæm·ər] n Press-
lufthammer m

'jackknife n Klappmesser nt; SPORT
Hechtsprung m

jack-of-'all-trades n Alleskönner(in)
m(f)

'jack-o'-lantern n Kürbislaterne f

'jackpot n Hauptgewinn m

Jacuzzi® [dʒə·'kuː·zi] n Whirlpool m

jade [dʒeɪd] I. n Jade m o f II. adj jade-
grün

jagged ['dʒæg·ɪd] adj ❶ gezackt; coastline, rocks zerklüftet; cut, tear ausge-
franst ❷ (fig) nerves angeschlagen

jaguar ['dʒæg·wɑr] n Jaguar m

jail [dʒeɪl] I. n Gefängnis nt II. vt einsperren

'jailbird n (fam) Knastbruder m

'jailbreak n Gefängnisausbruch m

'jailer [dʒeɪ·lər] n Gefängnisaufseher(in)
m(f)

jam¹ [dʒæm] n Marmelade f

jam² [dʒæm] I. n ❶ (fam: awkward
situation) Klemme f ❷ (of people Gedränge nt; of traffic Stau m II. vt
<-mm-> ❶ (block) verklemmen; **to ~
sth open** etw aufstemmen ❷ (cram in-

side) [hinein]zwängen (**into** in +akk)
III. vi <-mm-> sich verklemmen;
brakes blockieren

Jamaica [dʒə·'meɪ·kə] n Jamaika nt

Jamaican [dʒə·'meɪ·kən] I. n Jamaika-
ner(in) m(f) II. adj jamaikanisch

'jam-packed adj (fam) bus, store gerammelt voll; bag, box randvoll; suitcase vollgestopft

Jan. n abbrev of **January** Jan.

janitor ['dʒæn·ɪ· t̬ər] n Hausmeister(in)
m(f)

January ['dʒæn·ju·er·i] n Januar m; see
also **February**

Japan [dʒə·'pæn] n Japan nt

Japanese [ˌdʒæp·ə·'niz] I. n <pl ->
❶ (person) Japaner(in) m(f) ❷ (language) Japanisch nt II. adj japanisch

jar [dʒɑr] n (of glass) Glas|gefäß nt; (of
metal or clay) Topf m

jargon ['dʒɑr·gən] n [Fach]jargon m

jasmine ['dʒæs·mɪn] n Jasmin m

jaundice ['dʒɔn·dɪs] n Gelbsucht f

javelin ['dʒæv·lɪn] n Speer m; (event)
Speerwerfen nt

jaw [dʒɔ] n Kiefer m; **lower/upper** ~
Unter-/Oberkiefer m

'jawbone n Kieferknochen m

'jawbreaker n ❶ FOOD großes, rundes,
steinhartes Bonbon ❷ (fam: tongue
twister) Zungenbrecher m

jay [dʒeɪ] n Eichelhäher m

'jaywalker n unachtsamer Fußgänger/
unachtsame Fußgängerin

'jaywalking n unachtsames Überqueren
einer Straße

jazz [dʒæz] n ❶ (music) Jazz m ❷ (pej
fam: nonsense) Quatsch m fam ▶PHRAS-
ES: **and all that** ~ (fam) und all so was
◆**jazz up** vt (fam) ❶ MUS verjazzen
❷ (fig) aufpeppen

jazzy ['dʒæz·i] adj ❶ MUS Jazz-, jazzartig
❷ (fig) colors knallig; piece of clothing
poppig

jealous ['dʒel·əs] *adj* ① (*resentful*) eifersüchtig (**of** auf +*akk*) ② (*envious*) neidisch (**of** auf +*akk*)

jealousy ['dʒel·ə·si] *n* ① (*resentment*) Eifersucht *f* ② (*envy*) Neid *m*

jeans [dʒinz] *npl* Jeans[hose] *f*; **a pair of** ~ eine Jeans[hose]

jeep [dʒip] *n* Jeep *m*, Geländewagen *m*

jeer [dʒɪr] **I.** *vt* ausbuhen **II.** *vi* spotten (**at** über +*akk*) **III.** *n* höhnische Bemerkung

Jehovah [dʒɪ'hoʊ·və] *n* Jehova *m*

jell [dʒel] *vi see* **gel**

jellied ['dʒel·id] *adj* in Aspik eingelegt

Jell-O® ['dʒel·oʊ] *n* Wackelpudding *m*

jelly ['dʒel·i] *n* ① FOOD Gelee *m o nt* ② (*substance*) Gelee *nt*

'jellybean *n* [bohnenförmiges] Geleebonbon

'jellyfish *n* ① (*sea animal*) Qualle *f* ② (*pej fam: cowardly person*) Waschlappen *m*

jeopardize ['dʒep·ər·daɪz] *vt* gefährden; *career, future* aufs Spiel setzen

jeopardy ['dʒep·ər·di] *n* Gefahr *f*

jerk [dʒɜrk] **I.** *n* ① (*movement*) Ruck *m* ② (*pej sl: annoying person*) Trottel *m* *fam* **II.** *vi* zucken; **to** ~ **upwards** hochschnellen; **to** ~ **to a halt** abrupt zum Stillstand kommen **III.** *vt* ■**to** ~ **sb/sth** jdn/etw mit einem Ruck ziehen; ■**to** ~ **sb out of sth** (*fig*) jdn aus etw *dat* reißen

♦ **jerk off** *vi* (*vulg*) wichsen

jerkin ['dʒɜr·kɪn] *n* ärmellose Jacke

jerky ['dʒɜr·ki] **I.** *adj movement* ruckartig; *speech* abgehackt **II.** *n* luftgetrocknetes Fleisch

jersey ['dʒɜr·zi] *n* ① (*garment*) Pullover; SPORT Trikot *nt* ② (*cloth*) Jersey *m*

jest [dʒest] *n* (*form*) Scherz *m*, Spaß *m*

Jesuit ['dʒeʒ·u·ɪt] **I.** *n* Jesuit *m* **II.** *adj* jesuitisch, Jesuiten-

Jesus ['dʒi·zəs], **Jesus Christ** [ˌdʒi·zəs 'kraɪst] **I.** *n* Jesus *m*, Jesus Christus *m* **II.** *interj* (*pej sl*) Mensch! *fam*

jet [dʒet] *n* ① AVIAT [Düsen]jet *m* ② (*thin stream*) Strahl *m* ③ (*nozzle*) Düse *f* **II.** *vi* <-tt-> jetten *fam*

'jet-black *adj* pechschwarz

jet 'engine *n* Düsentriebwerk *nt*

jet 'fighter *n* Düsenjäger *m*

'jetfoil *n* Tragflügelboot *nt*

'jet lag *n* Jetlag *m*

'jet plane *n* Düsenflugzeug *nt*

jet-pro'pelled *adj* mit Düsenantrieb *nach n*

'jet set *n* (*fam*) Jetset *m*

Jew [dʒu] *n* Jude, Jüdin *m, f*

jewel ['dʒu·əl] *n* Edelstein *m*, Juwel *m o nt*

jeweler, jeweller ['dʒu·ə·lər] *n* Juwelier(in) *m(f)*

jewelry ['dʒu·əl·ri] *n* Schmuck *m*

Jewish ['dʒu·ɪʃ] *adj* jüdisch

'jigsaw *n* ① (*hand-operated*) Laubsäge *f*; (*electric*) Stichsäge *f* ② (*puzzle*) Puzzle[spiel] *nt*

jihad [dʒɪ'had] *n* Dschihad *m*

jimmy ['dʒɪm·i] **I.** *n* Brecheisen *nt* **II.** *vt* <-ie-> ■**to** ~ **open** ⊃ **sth** etw aufbrechen

jingle ['dʒɪŋ·gəl] **I.** *vt bells* klingeln lassen; **to** ~ **coins** mit Münzen klimpern **II.** *vi bells* bimmeln; *coins* klimpern

jive [dʒaɪv] **I.** *n* ① (*dance*) Jive *m* ② (*sl: dishonest talk*) Gewäsch *nt fam* **II.** *vi* Jive tanzen

job [dʒab] *n* ① (*employment*) Stelle *f*; **full-time/part-time** ~ Vollzeit-/Teilzeitstelle *f*; **to be out of a** ~ arbeitslos sein; **to give up one's** ~ kündigen ② (*piece of work*) Arbeit *f*; (*task*) Aufgabe *f*; **she's only doing her** ~ sie tut nur ihre Pflicht; **to do a good** ~ **on sth** bei etw *dat* gute Arbeit leisten; **nose** ~ (*fam*) Nasenkorrektur *f* ③ (*sl: crime*) Ding *nt fam*

'job application *n* Bewerbung *f*

jobber ['dʒab·ər] *n* Großhändler(in) *m(f)*

'job creation *n* Arbeitsbeschaffung *f*

'job cuts *npl* Stellenabbau *m kein pl*

'job description *n* Stellenbeschreibung *f*

'job hunt *n* (*fam*) Stellensuche *f*

'job interview *n* Bewerbungsgespräch *nt*

J

jobless ['dʒɑb·lɪs] I. *adj* arbeitslos II. *n*
■ **the ~** *pl* die Arbeitslosen *pl*

'job market *n* Arbeitsmarkt *m*

'job-sharing *n* Arbeitsplatzteilung *f*

'job title *n* Berufsbezeichnung *f*

jockey ['dʒɑk·i] I. *n* Jockey *m* II. *vi* ■ **to
~ for sth** um etw *akk* konkurrieren

jog [dʒɑg] I. *n* (*run*) Dauerlauf *m;* **to go
for a ~** joggen gehen II. *vi* <-gg-> joggen

jogger ['dʒɑg·ər] *n* Jogger(in) *m(f)*

jogging ['dʒɑg·ɪŋ] *n* Joggen *nt*

john [dʒɑn] *n* ❶ (*fam: bathroom*) Klo *nt*
❷ (*sl: prostitute's client*) Freier *m fam*

join [dʒɔɪn] I. *vt* ❶ (*connect*) ■ **to ~ sth
[to sth]** etw [mit etw *dat*] verbinden;
(*add*) etw [an etw *akk*] anfügen ❷ (*offer
company*) ■ **to ~ sb** sich zu jdm gesel-
len; **would you like to ~ us for
dinner?** möchtest du mit uns zu Abend
essen? ❸ (*enroll*) beitreten; *club, party*
Mitglied werden; **to ~ the army** Soldat
werden ❹ (*participate*) ■ **to ~ sb bei**
etw *dat* mitmachen; **let's ~ the dancing** lass uns mittanzen ❺ (*support*) ■ **to
~ sb in [doing] sth** jdm bei etw *dat* zur
Seite stehen II. *vi* ❶ (*connect*) ■ **to ~
[with sth]** sich [mit etw *dat*] verbinden
❷ (*cooperate*) ■ **to ~ with sb in doing
sth** mit jdm *dat* zusammenschließen, um etw zu tun ❸ (*enroll*) beitreten, Mitglied werden III. *n* (*seam*) Verbindung[sstelle] *f*

◆ **join up I.** *vi* ❶ MIL zum Militär gehen
❷ (*meet*) ■ **to ~ up with sb** sich mit
jdm zusammentun II. *vt* ■ **to ~ up** ○
sth etw [miteinander] verbinden; *parts*
etw zusammenfügen

joint [dʒɔɪnt] I. *adj* gemeinsam II. *n*
❶ (*connection*) Verbindungsstelle *f*
❷ ANAT Gelenk *nt;* **to put sth out of ~**
etw ausrenken ❸ (*fam: cheap bar*) Laden *m* ❹ (*cannabis cigarette*) Joint *m sl*
▶ PHRASES: **to be out of ~** aus den Fugen
sein

joint ac'count *n* Gemeinschaftskonto *nt*

jointly ['dʒɔɪnt·li] *adv* gemeinsam

joint 'owner *n* Miteigentümer(in) *m(f);*
of a company Mitinhaber(in) *m(f)*

joint-stock 'company *n* Aktiengesellschaft *f*

joint 'venture *n* Joint Venture *nt*

joist [dʒɔɪst] *n* [Quer]balken *m*

joke [dʒoʊk] I. *n* ❶ Spaß *m;* (*trick*)
Streich *m;* (*amusing thing, person*)
Witz *m;* **to crack/tell ~s** Witze rei-
ßen/erzählen; **to make a ~ of sth** etw
ins Lächerliche ziehen II. *vi* scherzen;
you must be joking! das meinst du
doch nicht im Ernst!; ■ **to ~ about sth**
sich über etw *akk* lustig machen

joker ['dʒoʊ·kər] *n* ❶ (*person*) Spaßvogel *m* ❷ CARDS Joker *m*

joking ['dʒoʊk·ɪŋ] I. *adj* scherzhaft II. *n*
~ **aside** Spaß beiseite

jokingly ['dʒoʊk·ɪŋ·li] *adv* im Scherz

jolly ['dʒɑl·i] *adj* lustig

Jolly 'Roger *n* Totenkopfflagge *f*

jolt [dʒoʊlt] *n* Stoß *m,* Ruck *m*

joss stick ['dʒɑs-] *n* Räucherstäbchen *nt*

jostle ['dʒɑs·əl] I. *vt* [an]rempeln II. *vi*
[sich *akk*] drängeln

journal ['dʒɜr·nəl] *n* ❶ (*periodical*)
Zeitschrift *f;* (*newspaper*) Zeitung *f*
❷ (*diary*) Tagebuch *nt*

journalism ['dʒɜr·nə·lɪz·əm] *n* Journa-
lismus *m*

journalist ['dʒɜr·nə·lɪst] *n* Journalist(in)
m(f)

journalistic [ˌdʒɜr·nə·'lɪs·tɪk] *adj* journa-
listisch

journey ['dʒɜr·ni] *n* Reise *f*

joy [dʒɔɪ] *n* Freude *f,* Vergnügen *nt;* **to
jump for ~** einen Freudensprung ma-
chen

joyful ['dʒɔɪ·fəl] *adj face, person* fröhlich; *event, news* freudig

joyless ['dʒɔɪ·lɪs] *adj* freudlos

'joy ride *n* [waghalsige] Spritztour (*in
einem gestohlenen Auto*)

'joystick *n* ❶ AVIAT Steuerknüppel *m*
❷ COMPUT Joystick *m*

JP *n abbrev of* **Justice of the Peace**

Jr. *adj after n short for* **junior** jun.

jubilant ['dʒu·bɪ·lənt] *adj* glücklich;
crowd jubelnd *attr*

jubilation [ˌdʒu·bɪ·'leɪ·ʃən] *n* Jubel *m*

jubilee ['dʒu·bə·li] *n* Jubiläum *nt*

Judaism [ˈdʒu·dɪ·ɪz·əm] *n* Judaismus *m*, Judentum *nt*

judge [dʒʌdʒ] **I.** *n* ❶ LAW Richter(in) *m(f)* ❷ *(at a competition)* Preisrichter(in) *m(f)*; *(in boxing, gymnastics, wrestling)* Punktrichter(in) *m(f)*; *(in track and field, swimming)* Kampfrichter(in) *m(f)* ❸ *(expert)* of literature, wine Kenner(in) *m(f)* **II.** *vi* ❶ *(decide)* urteilen; ~**ing by his comments**, ... seinen Äußerungen nach zu urteilen, ... ❷ *(estimate)* schätzen **III.** *vt* ❶ *(decide)* beurteilen ❷ *(estimate)* schätzen ❸ SPORT ■**to** ~ **sth** bei etw *dat* Kampfrichter sein

judg(e)ment [ˈdʒʌdʒ·mənt] *n* ❶ LAW Urteil *nt*; **to pass** ~ **[on sb/sth]** *(a. fig)* ein Urteil [über jdn/etw] fällen ❷ *(opinion)* Urteil *nt*; **error of** ~ Fehleinschätzung *f*; **against one's better** ~ wider besseres Wissen

judicial [dʒuˈdɪʃ·əl] *adj* gerichtlich; ~ **authorities** Justizbehörden *pl*; ~ **review** gerichtliche Überprüfung *f* (*der Vorinstanzentscheidung*), Normenkontrolle *f* (*Prüfung der Gesetze auf ihre Verfassungsmäßigkeit*)

judo [ˈdʒu·dou] *n* Judo *nt*

jug [dʒʌg] *n* Krug *m*

juggle [ˈdʒʌg·əl] **I.** *vt* ■**to** ~ **sth** ❶ mit etw *dat* jonglieren ❷ *(fig, pej: manipulate)* etw manipulieren **II.** *vi* ❶ jonglieren ❷ *(fig, pej: manipulate)* ■**to** ~ **with sth** *facts, information* etw manipulieren

juggler [ˈdʒʌg·lər] *n* Jongleur(in) *m(f)*

juice [dʒus] *n* ❶ *(of fruit, vegetables)* Saft *m*; **lemon** ~ Zitronensaft *m* ❷ *pl* *(liquid in meat)* [Braten]saft *m kein pl* ❸ *(fam: electricity)* Saft *m sl*

juicy [ˈdʒu·si] *adj* ❶ *(succulent)* saftig ❷ *(fam: plentiful)* saftig; **profit** fett ❸ *(fam: suggestive)* joke, story schlüpfrig; *details, scandal* pikant

jukebox [ˈdʒuk·baks] *n* Jukebox *f*

Jul. *n abbrev of* **July**

julep [ˈdʒu·ləp] *n* Julep *m o nt* (*alkoholisches Eisgetränk, oft mit Pfefferminze*)

July [dʒuˈlaɪ] *n* Juli *m*; *see also* **February**

jumbo [ˈdʒʌm·bou] **I.** *adj attr* Riesen- **II.** *n* AVIAT *(fam)* Jumbo *m*

jumbo 'jet *n* Jumbojet *m*

jump [dʒʌmp] **I.** *n* *(a. fig)* Sprung *m*; **high/long jump** SPORT Hoch-/Weitsprung *m*; *in prices, temperatures* [sprunghafter] Anstieg; *in profits* [sprunghafte] Steigerung; **to wake up with a** ~ aus dem Schlaf hochfahren **II.** *vi* ❶ *(leap)* springen; **to** ~ **to one's feet** aufspringen; **to** ~ **up and down** herumspringen; ■**to** ~ **in[to] sth** *car, water* in etw *akk* [hinein]springen ❷ *(rise)* sprunghaft ansteigen, in die Höhe schnellen ❸ *(be startled)* einen Satz machen; **to make sb** ~ jdn erschrecken ▸PHRASES: **to** ~ **to conclusions** voreilige Schlüsse ziehen **III.** *vt* überspringen ▸PHRASES: **to** ~ **the gun** *(fam)* überstürzt handeln
◆**jump at** *vt* ■**to** ~ **at sth** *idea, suggestion* sofort auf etw *akk* anspringen *fam*; *offer* sich auf etw *akk* stürzen
◆**jump in** *vi* hineinspringen
◆**jump out** *vi* ❶ *(leave)* **to** ~ **out of bed** aus dem Bett springen ❷ *(fig: stand out)* ■**to** ~ **out at sb** jdm sofort auffallen
◆**jump up** *vi* aufspringen

jumper¹ [ˈdʒʌm·pər] *n* *(person)* Springer(in) *m(f)*; *(horse)* Springpferd *nt*

jumper² [ˈdʒʌm·pər] *n* *(pinafore)* Trägerkleid *nt*

'jumper cables *npl* Starthilfekabel *nt*

'jump rope *n* Springseil *nt*

'jump-start *vt* **to** ~ **sb's car** jdm Starthilfe geben

'jump suit *n* Overall *m*

jumpy [ˈdʒʌm·pi] *adj* *(fam)* ❶ *(nervous)* nervös ❷ *(easily frightened)* schreckhaft ❸ *(unsteady)* market unsicher

Jun. *n abbrev of* **June**

junction [ˈdʒʌŋk·ʃən] *n* *(road)* Kreuzung *f*; *(freeway)* Autobahnkreuz *nt*

June [dʒun] *n* Juni *m*; *see also* **February**

jungle ['dʒʌŋ·gəl] n (a. fig) Dschungel m

junior ['dʒun·jər] I. adj ❶ (younger) junior nach n ❷ attr SPORT Junioren-, Jugend- ❸ attr SCH ~ **college** Juniorencollege nt (die beiden ersten Studienjahre umfassende Einrichtung); ~ **high school** Aufbauschule f (umfasst in der Regel die Klassenstufen 6–9) ❹ (low rank) untergeordnet; ~ **partner** Juniorpartner(in) m(f) II. n ❶ (son) Sohn m ❷ (younger) Jüngere(r) f(m); **he's two years my** ~ er ist zwei Jahre jünger als ich ❸ SCH, UNIV (third-year student) Student (in) m(f) im vorletzten Studienjahr ❹ (low-ranking person) unterer Angestellter/untere Angestellte

juniper ['dʒu·nɪ·pər] n Wacholder m

junk¹ [dʒʌŋk] n ❶ (worthless stuff) Ramsch m fam ❷ (sl: heroin) Stoff m

junk² [dʒʌŋk] n NAUT Dschunke f

'junk food n Schnellgerichte pl; (pej) ungesundes Essen

junkie ['dʒʌŋ·ki] n (sl) Fixer(in) m(f) fam; **fitness** ~ (hum) Fitnessfreak m

'junk mail n Wurfsendungen pl, Reklame f

'junk shop n Trödelladen m

'junkyard n Schrottplatz m

junta ['hʊn·tə] n Junta f

Jupiter ['dʒu·pɪ·tər] n no art Jupiter m

juror ['dʒʊr·ər] n LAW Geschworene(r) f(m)

jury ['dʒʊr·i] n ❶ LAW ■the ~ die Geschworenen pl ❷ (competition) Jury f

just I. adv [dʒʌst] ❶ (in a moment) gleich; **we're** ~ **about to leave** wir wollen gleich los; **I was** ~ **going to call you** ich wollte dich eben anrufen ❷ (directly) direkt, gleich ❸ (recently) gerade [eben], [so]eben ❹ (now) gerade; ■**to be** ~ **doing sth** gerade dabei sein, etw zu tun ❺ (exactly) genau; **that's** ~

what I was going to say genau das wollte ich gerade sagen; **that's** ~ **it!** das ist es ja gerade!; ~ **now** gerade; ~ **then** gerade in diesem Augenblick; ~ **as well** ebenso gut; ~ **as/when** ... gerade in dem Augenblick, als ... ❻ (only) nur, bloß fam; (simply) einfach; **she's** ~ **a baby** sie ist noch ein Baby; ~ **for fun** nur [so] zum Spaß; **[not]** ~ **anybody** [nicht] einfach irgendjemand ❼ (barely) gerade noch/mal; ~ **in time** gerade noch rechtzeitig ❽ with imperatives ~ **imagine!** stell dir das mal vor!; ~ **look at this!** schau dir das mal an! ▶PHRASES: ~ **a minute!** (please wait) einen Augenblick [bitte]!; (as interruption) Moment [mal]!; **it's** ~ **one of those things** (saying) so etwas passiert eben II. adj [dʒʌst] ❶ (fair) gerecht (**to** gegenüber +dat) ❷ (justified) punishment gerecht; **to have** ~ **cause to do sth** einen triftigen Grund haben, etw zu tun ▶PHRASES: **to get one's** ~ **deserts** bekommen, was man verdient hat

justice ['dʒʌs·tɪs] n ❶ (fairness) Gerechtigkeit f ❷ (administration of the law) Justiz f ❸ (judge) Richter(in) m(f)

Justice of the 'Peace n Friedensrichter(in) m(f)

justification [ˌdʒʌs·tə·fɪ·'keɪ·ʃən] n Rechtfertigung f

justified ['dʒʌs·tə·faɪd] adj gerechtfertigt, berechtigt

justify <-ie-> ['dʒʌs·tə·faɪ] vt rechtfertigen; ■**to** ~ **oneself to sb** sich jdm gegenüber rechtfertigen

justly ['dʒʌst·li] adv zu Recht; **to act** ~ gerecht handeln

jute [dʒut] n Jute f

juvenile ['dʒu·və·naɪl] I. adj Jugend-, jugendlich II. n Jugendliche(r) f(m)

juvenile de'linquent n jugendlicher Straftäter/jugendliche Straftäterin

Kk

K <pl -'s>, **k** <pl -'s> [keɪ] n K nt, k nt; ~ **as in Kilo** K wie Kaufmann

K[1] <pl -> n (fam) 1.000 Dollar

K[2] <pl -> n abbrev of **kilobyte** KB

K[3] <pl -> n abbrev of **karat** kt.

kale [keɪl] n [Grün]kohl m

kangaroo <pl -s> [ˌkæn·gə·'ru] n Känguru nt

Kans. abbrev of **Kansas**

Kansas ['kæn·zəs] n Kansas nt

karat ['ker·ət] n Karat nt

karate [kə·'ra·ti] n Karate nt

karma ['kar·mə] n Karma nt

kayak ['kaɪ·æk] n Kajak m o selten a. nt

'kayaking n Kajakfahren nt

KB n abbrev of **kilobyte** KB

kebab [kə·'bab] n Kebab m

keel [kil] n NAUT Kiel m

◆ **keel over** vi 1 NAUT kentern 2 (fam: swoon) umkippen

keen [kin] adj 1 (enthusiastic) leidenschaftlich; ■ **to not be ~ on** [doing] **sth** etw nicht [tun] wollen, etw nicht gerne tun 2 (perceptive) mind, eyesight scharf 3 (extreme) competition scharf; desire heftig; interest lebhaft 4 (piercing) wind schneidend 5 (sharp) blade scharf

keep [kip] I. n [Lebens]unterhalt m II. vt <kept, kept> 1 (hold onto) behalten; bills, receipts aufheben 2 (store) medicine, money aufbewahren 3 (detain) **to ~ sb waiting** jdn warten lassen 4 (prevent) ■ **to ~ sb from doing sth** jdn davon abhalten, etw zu tun 5 (maintain) **to ~ one's balance** das Gleichgewicht halten; **to ~ sb/sth under control** jdn/etw unter Kontrolle halten; **to ~ count of sth** etw mitzählen; **to ~ sb/sth in mind** jdn/etw im Gedächtnis behalten; **to ~ one's mouth shut** den Mund halten; **to ~ time** watch richtig gehen; MUS Takt halten; **to ~ track of sb/sth** jdn/etw im

Auge behalten; **to ~ sb awake** jdn wach halten; **to ~ sb/sth warm** jdn/etw warm halten 6 (not reveal) ■ **to ~ sth from sb** jdm etw akk vorenthalten; secret hüten 7 (stick to) appointment, treaty einhalten; oath, promise halten 8 (make records) **to ~ a record of sth** über etw akk Buch führen III. vi <kept, kept> 1 (stay fresh) food sich halten 2 (wait) Zeit haben; **your questions can ~ until later** deine Fragen können noch warten 3 (stay) bleiben; **to ~ quiet** still sein; **to ~ to the left/right** sich links/rechts halten 4 (continue) **don't ~ asking silly questions** stell nicht immer so dumme Fragen; ■ **to ~ at sth** mit etw dat weitermachen 5 (stop oneself) ■ **to ~ from doing sth** etw unterlassen 6 (adhere to) ■ **to ~ to sth** an etw dat festhalten; (not digress) bei etw dat bleiben; **to ~ to an agreement** sich an eine Vereinbarung halten; **to ~ to a schedule** einen Zeitplan einhalten

◆ **keep away** I. vi sich fernhalten (**from** von +dat) II. vt fernhalten (**from** von +dat)

◆ **keep back** I. vi zurückbleiben; (stay at distance) Abstand halten II. vt 1 (restrain) zurückhalten 2 (prevent advance) ■ **to ~ back** ⟳ **sb** jdn aufhalten; ■ **to ~ sb back from doing sth** jdn daran hindern, etw zu tun 3 (withhold) information verschweigen; payment einbehalten

◆ **keep down** I. vi unten bleiben, sich ducken II. vt 1 (suppress) unterdrücken 2 food bei sich dat behalten ▶ PHRASES: **~ it down!** sei still!

◆ **keep in** vt one's anger, feelings zurückhalten

◆ **keep off** vt 1 (not touch) **to ~ one's hands off sb/sth** die Hände von jdm/etw lassen; **"Keep Off The Grass"**

„Betreten des Rasens verboten" ② (fam: not consume) **to ~ off the booze** das Trinken lassen ③ (not talk about) **to ~ off a subject** ein Thema vermeiden; **to ~ one's mind off sth** sich von etw dat ablenken

◆**keep on I.** vi (continue) ■**to ~ on doing sth** etw weiter[hin] tun **II.** vt **~ your jacket on — it's cold** behalte den Mantel an, es ist kalt

◆**keep out** vi draußen bleiben; **"Keep Out"** „Zutritt verboten"; ■**to ~ out of sth** etw nicht betreten; (fig) sich aus etw dat heraushalten

◆**keep together** vt zusammenhalten ▶PHRASES: **~ it together!** bleib bei der Sache!

◆**keep up I.** vt ① (maintain) fortführen; conversation in Gang halten; **~ it up!** [nur] weiter so! ② (hold up) hochhalten; **these poles ~ the tent up** diese Stangen halten das Zelt aufrecht ③ (not let sleep) wach halten **II.** vi ① (not fall behind) ■**to ~ up with sb/sth** mit jdm/etw mithalten ② (continue) noise, rain andauern, anhalten; courage, strength bestehen bleiben

keeper ['ki·pər] n in a zoo Wärter(in) m(f)

keeping ['ki·pɪŋ] n ① (guarding) Verwahrung f; (care) Obhut f ② (obeying) Einhalten nt, Befolgen nt; **in ~ with an agreement** entsprechend einer Vereinbarung

keepsake ['kip·seɪk] n Andenken nt

keg [keg] n kleines Fass

kelp [kelp] n Seetang m

kennel ['ken·əl] n ① (dog boarding) Hundepension f ② (doghouse) Hundehütte f

Kentucky [kən·'tʌk·i] n Kentucky nt

Kenya ['ken·jə] n Kenia nt

Kenyan ['ken·jən] **I.** n Kenianer(in) m(f) **II.** adj kenianisch

kept [kept] vt, vi pt, pp of **keep**

kernel ['kɜr·nəl] n ① (fruit center) Kern m; (grain center) Getreidekorn nt ② (fig) **a ~ of truth** ein Körnchen nt Wahrheit

kerosene, kerosine ['ker·ə·sin] n Kerosin nt

ketchup ['ketʃ·əp] n Ketschup m o nt

kettle ['ketʃ·əl] n [Wasser]kessel m ▶PHRASES: **to be a [whole] different ~ of fish** etwas ganz anderes sein

key[1] [ki] **I.** n ① (a. fig: for a lock) Schlüssel m ② (button) of a computer, piano Taste f ③ (to symbols) Zeichenerklärung f ④ MUS Tonart f **II.** adj factor, figure, role Schlüssel-; **~ contribution** Hauptbeitrag m

key[2] [ki] n [Korallen]riff nt; **the Florida ~s** die Florida Keys

◆**key in** vt **to ~ in text** Text eingeben

'**keyboard I.** n ① (of a computer) Tastatur f; (of a piano) Klaviatur f ② (musical instrument) Keyboard nt **II.** vt, vi tippen

'**keyhole** n Schlüsselloch nt

'**keynote** n ① Hauptthema nt; of a speech Grundgedanke m ② POL Parteilinie f

'**keynote address, 'keynote speech** n programmatische Rede

'**keypad** n Tastenfeld nt

'**key ring** n Schlüsselring m

'**keyword** n ① (important word) Schlüsselwort nt ② (for identifying) Kennwort nt

kg n abbrev of **kilogram** kg

khaki ['kæk·i] adj Khaki-; (color) khakifarben

kHz n abbrev of **kilohertz** kHz

KIA [ˌkeɪ·aɪ·'eɪ] adj abbrev of **killed in action** gef.

kibbutz [kɪ·'bʊts] n Kibbuz m

kick [kɪk] **I.** n ① (with foot) [Fuß]tritt m, Stoß m; (in sports) Schuss m; of a horse Tritt m ② (fam: exciting feeling) Nervenkitzel m ③ (gun jerk) Rückstoß m **II.** vt ① (hit with foot) [mit dem Fuß] treten; **to ~ a ball** einen Ball schießen ② (get rid of) habit aufgeben fam ▶PHRASES: **to ~ the bucket** ins Gras beißen **III.** vi (with foot) treten (**at** nach +dat); horse ausschlagen ▶PHRASES: **to be alive and ~ing** gesund und munter sein

◆**kick around I.** *vi* (*fam*) [he]rumliegen **II.** *vt* (*with foot*) ■**to ~ sth around** etw [in der Gegend] herumkicken *fam*

◆**kick back I.** *vt* zurücktreten; *ball* zurückschießen **II.** *vi* (*fam: relax*) relaxen *fam*

◆**kick in I.** *vt* ❶ (*with foot*) *door, window* eintreten ❷ (*contribute*) dazugeben, beisteuern **II.** *vi* ❶ (*start*) *drug, measure* wirken; *device, system* anspringen ❷ (*to contribute*) ■**to ~ in for sth** einen Beitrag zu etw *dat* leisten

◆**kick off I.** *vi* beginnen, anfangen; (*in soccer, football*) anstoßen **II.** *vt* (*start, launch*) beginnen

◆**kick out** *vt* hinauswerfen

◆**kick over I.** *vi car* anfahren **II.** *vt* ■**to ~ over ◌ sth** etw umrempeln

◆**kick up** *vi* **to ~ up dust** (*a. fig*) Staub aufwirbeln; **to ~ up a fuss** (*fig*) einen Wirbel machen *fam*

kicker ['kɪkˑər] *n* (*in football*) Fußballspieler(in) *m(f)*; (*in soccer*) Freistoßnehmer(in) *m(f)*

'**kickoff** *n* (*in football, in soccer*) Anstoß *m*

kid [kɪd] **I.** *n* ❶ (*child*) Kind *nt*; (*young person*) Jugendliche(r) *f(m)*; (*male*) Bursche *m*; (*female*) Mädchen *nt*; **~ brother/sister** kleiner Bruder/ kleine Schwester ❷ (*young goat*) Zicklein *nt* **II.** *vi* <-dd-> (*fam*) Spaß machen; **just ~ding!** war nur Spaß!; **no ~ding?** ohne Scherz? **III.** *vt* (*fam*) ■**to ~ sb** jdn verulken

kidnap ['kɪdˑnæp] **I.** *vt* <-pp-> entführen **II.** *n* Entführung *f*

kidnapper ['kɪdˑnæpˑər] *n* Entführer(in) *m(f)*

kidnapping ['kɪdˑnæpˑɪŋ] *n* Entführung *f*

kidney ['kɪdˑni] *n* ANAT, FOOD Niere *f*

'**kidney bean** *n* Kidneybohne *f*

'**kidney donor** *n* Nierenspender(in) *m(f)*

'**kidney failure** *n* Nierenversagen *nt*

kidney-'shaped *adj* nierenförmig

'**kidney stone** *n* Nierenstein *m*

kill [kɪl] **I.** *n* HUNT [Jagd]beute *f* **II.** *vi* (*end life*) *criminal* töten; *disease* tödlich sein **III.** *vt* ❶ (*end life*) umbringen *a. fig;* **to ~ sb by drowning/strangling** jdn ertränken/erwürgen; **to be ~ed in an accident** bei einem Unfall ums Leben kommen ❷ (*destroy*) zerstören; **to ~ the taste of sth** etw *dat* den Geschmack [völlig] nehmen ❸ (*spoil*) *fun, joke* [gründlich] verderben ❹ (*stop*) *engine, lights* ausmachen; *pain* stillen; *plan, project* fallen lassen ❺ (*fam: amuse*) ■**to ~ oneself with laughter** sich totlachen ►PHRASES: **to ~ time** (*spend time*) sich *dat* die Zeit vertreiben; (*waste time*) die Zeit totschlagen; **to ~ two birds with one stone** (*prov*) zwei Fliegen mit einer Klappe schlagen

killer ['kɪlˑər] **I.** *n* ❶ (*person*) Mörder(in) *m(f)*; (*thing*) Todesursache *f* ❷ (*agent*) Vertilgungsmittel *nt*; **weed ~** Unkrautvertilgungsmittel *nt* **II.** *adj attr* (*deadly*) *flu, virus* tödlich; *hurricane, wave* mörderisch

'**killer whale** *n* Schwertwal *m*

killing ['kɪlˑɪŋ] **I.** *n* ❶ (*act*) Tötung *f* ❷ (*case*) Mord[fall] *m* **II.** *adj attr* ❶ (*causing death*) tödlich ❷ (*fig: difficult*) mörderisch *fam*

kilo ['kiˑloʊ] *n* Kilo *nt*

kilobyte ['kɪlˑəˑbaɪt] *n* Kilobyte *nt*

kilogram ['kɪlˑəˑgræm] *n* Kilogramm *nt*

kilometer [kɪˑ'lɑmˑɪˑtər] *n* Kilometer *m*

kilowatt ['kɪlˑəˑwat] *n* Kilowatt *nt*

kilt [kɪlt] *n* Kilt *m*

kimono [kəˑ'moʊˑnə] *n* Kimono *m*

kind¹ [kaɪnd] *adj* ❶ (*generous, helpful*) nett; **with ~ regards** (*in a letter*) mit freundlichen Grüßen ❷ (*gentle*) ■**to be ~ to sb/sth** jdn/etw schonen

kind² [kaɪnd] **I.** *n* ❶ (*group*) Art *f;* **he's not that ~ of person** so einer ist der nicht *fam;* **all ~s of animals** alle möglichen Tiere; **to be one of a ~** einzigartig sein; **his/her ~** (*pej*) so jemand [wie er/sie] ❷ (*limited*) **you could call this success of a ~** man könnte das als so etwas wie einen Erfolg bezeichnen ❸ (*similar*) **nothing of the ~** nichts

K

dergleichen II. *adv* ■ ~ **of** irgendwie; **to be ~ of interesting** irgendwie interessant sein

kindergarten ['kɪn·dər·gar·dən] *n* SCH Vorschule *f*

kind-'hearted *adj* gütig

kindle ['kɪn·dəl] *vt* ❶ *fire* anzünden ❷ *(fig) imagination* wecken

kindly ['kaɪnd·li] I. *adj person* freundlich; *smile, voice* sanft II. *adv (please)* freundlich, freundlicherweise; **you are ~ requested to leave the building** Sie werden freundlich[st] gebeten, das Gebäude zu verlassen

kindness <*pl* -es> ['kaɪnd·nɪs] *n* ❶ *(attitude)* Freundlichkeit *f* ❷ *(act)* Gefälligkeit *f*

kinfolk ['kɪn·foʊk] *n* + *pl vb* Verwandtschaft *f*

king [kɪŋ] *n* König *m*

kingdom ['kɪŋ·dəm] *n* ❶ *(country)* Königreich *nt* ❷ *(domain)* Reich *nt;* **animal ~** Tierreich *nt*

'kingfisher *n* Eisvogel *m*

'king-size(d) *adj* extragroß

kiosk ['ki·ask] *n* Kiosk *m*

kiss [kɪs] I. *n* <*pl* -es> Kuss *m;* **to blow sb a ~** jdm eine Kusshand zuwerfen II. *vi (sich)* küssen; **to ~ and tell** mit intimen Enthüllungen an die Öffentlichkeit gehen III. *vt* küssen; **to ~ sb goodbye** jdm einen Abschiedskuss geben ▶PHRASES: **to ~ sb's ass** *(vulg)* jdm in den Arsch kriechen *derb*

kit [kɪt] *n* ❶ *(set)* Ausrüstung *f;* *(for a model)* Bausatz *m;* **first-aid ~** Verbandskasten *m* ❷ *(outfit)* Ausrüstung *f*

'kit bag *n* Kleidersack *m*

kitchen ['kɪtʃ·ɪn] *n* Küche *f*

kitchenette [ˌkɪtʃ·ɪ·'net] *n* Kochnische *f*

kitchen 'knife *n* Küchenmesser *nt*

kitchen 'sink *n* Spüle *f*

kitchen 'table *n* Küchentisch *m*

kite [kaɪt] *n* Drachen *m* ▶PHRASES: **go fly a ~!** *(fam)* mach die Fliege! *sl;* **to be as high as a ~** *(drunk)* sternhagelvoll sein *fam;* *(high)* völlig zugedröhnt sein *sl*

kitsch [kɪtʃ] I. *n (pej)* Kitsch *m* II. *adj* kitschig

kitten ['kɪt·ən] *n (young cat)* Kätzchen *nt*

kitty ['kɪt·i] *n* ❶ *(childspeak: kitten)* Miezekatze *f;* **here, ~ ~!** komm, miez, miez! ❷ *(money)* gemeinsame Kasse; *(in games)* [Spiel]kasse *f*

'Kitty Litter® *n* Katzenstreu *f*

kiwi ['ki·wi] *n (bird, fruit)* Kiwi *m*

Kleenex® ['kli·neks] *n* Tempo[taschentuch]® *nt*

kleptomaniac [ˌklep·toʊ·'meɪ·ni·æk] *n* Kleptomane *m,* Kleptomanin *f*

km *n abbrev of* **kilometer** km

knack [næk] *n* ❶ *(trick)* Kniff *m;* **to get the ~ of sth** herausfinden, wie etw geht *fam* ❷ *(talent)* Geschick *nt*

knapsack ['næp·sæk] *n* Rucksack *m*

knead [nid] *vt dough* kneten

knee [ni] I. *n* Knie *nt;* **to put sb on one's ~** jdn auf den Schoß nehmen ▶PHRASES: **to bring sb to their ~s** jdn in die Knie zwingen *geh* II. *vt* ■**to ~ sb** jdn mit dem Knie stoßen

'kneecap I. *n* Kniescheibe *f* II. *vt* <-pp-> ■**to ~ sb** jdm die Kniescheibe zerschießen

'knee-high *n* FASHION Kniestrumpf *m*

kneel <knelt *or* kneeled, knelt *or* kneeled> [nil] *vi* knien

knelt [nelt] *pt of* **kneel**

knew [nu] *pt of* **know**

knife [naɪf] I. *n* <*pl* knives> Messer *nt* ❷ **to go under the ~** MED unters Messer kommen *fam* II. *vt* ■**to ~ sb** auf jdn einstechen

knight [naɪt] I. *n* ❶ *(hist: soldier)* Ritter *m* ❷ CHESS Springer *m* II. *vt* ■**to ~ sb** jdn zum Ritter schlagen

knit [nɪt] I. *n (stitch)* Strickart *f* II. *vi* <knitted *or* knit, knitted *or* knit> ❶ *(with yarn)* stricken; *(do basic stitch)* eine rechte Masche stricken ❷ *(heal)* *broken bone* zusammenwachsen III. *vt* <knitted *or* knit, knitted *or* knit> *(with yarn)* stricken ▶PHRASES: **to ~ one's brows** die Augenbrauen zusammenziehen, die Stirn runzeln

◆ **knit together** I. *vi* ❶ *(combine)* sich zusammenfügen ❷ *(heal) broken bone*

zusammenwachsen **II.** *vt* zusammen-
stricken

knitting ['nɪt·ɪŋ] *n* ❶ (*action*) Stricken *nt* ❷ (*product*) Gestrickte(s) *nt*;
(*unfinished*) Strickzeug *nt*

'**knitting needle** *n* Stricknadel *f*

'**knitwear** *n* Stricksachen *pl*

knob [nab] *n* of a door Griff *m*; of a
radio [Dreh]knopf *m*

knobby ['nab·i] *adj* knubbelig; *tree,*
wood astreich

knock [nak] **I.** *n* ❶ (*sound*) Klopfen *nt*;
there was a ~ on the door es hat [an
der Tür] geklopft ❷ (*blow*) Schlag *m*
❸ (*fam: criticism*) **he's taken a few ~ s**
er musste sich einiges anhören **II.** *vi*
❶ (*strike noisily*) klopfen; **to ~ at the**
door an die Tür klopfen ❷ (*collide*
with) stoßen (**into/against** gegen
+*akk*) ❸ TECH *engine, pipes* klopfen
▶PHRASES: **to ~ on wood** dreimal auf
Holz klopfen **III.** *vt* ❶ (*hit*) ∎**to ~ sth**
gegen etw *akk* stoßen ❷ (*blow*) ∎**to ~**
sb jdm einen Schlag versetzen; (*less*
hard) jdm einen Stoß versetzen; **to ~ sb**
unconscious jdn bewusstlos schlagen
❸ (*drive*) ∎**to ~ sth out of sb** jdm etw
austreiben; **to ~ some sense into sb**
jdn zur Vernunft bringen ❹ (*fam: criti-*
cize) ∎**to ~ sb/sth** jdn/etw schlechtmachen

◆**knock around I.** *vi* (*fam: travel aim-*
lessly) [he]rumziehen **II.** *vt* ❶ (*beat*)
∎**to ~ sb around** jdn verprügeln
❷ (*travel through*) **to ~ around**
Europe in Europa herumreisen

◆**knock back** *vt* (*fam: drink quickly*)
hinunterkippen

◆**knock down** *vt* ❶ (*cause to fall*) umstoßen; (*with a car, motorcycle*) umfahren ❷ (*demolish*) niederreißen ❸ (*re-*
duce) *price* herunterhandeln

◆**knock off I.** *vt* ❶ (*cause to fall off*)
hinunterstoßen ❷ (*produce quickly*)
schnell erledigen; (*easily*) etw mit links
machen *fam* ❸ (*fam: stop*) ~ **it off!** hör
auf damit!; **to ~ off work early** früh
Feierabend machen ❹ (*fam: rob*) **to ~**
off a bank eine Bank ausräumen ❺ (*sl:*

copy) klauen *fam* **II.** *vi* (*fam*) Schluss
machen

◆**knock out** *vt* ❶ (*render uncon-*
scious) ∎**to ~ out ◌ sb** jdn bewusstlos
werden lassen; (*in a fight*) jdn k. o.
schlagen ❷ (*forcibly remove*) **to ~ out**
two teeth sich *dat* zwei Zähne ausschlagen ❸ (*eliminate*) ausschalten; **to**
be ~ ed out of a competition
aus einem Wettkampf ausscheiden
❹ (*render useless*) außer Funktion setzen ❺ (*fam: produce quickly*) hastig
entwerfen ❻ (*fam: astonish and im-*
press) umhauen

◆**knock over** *vt* (*cause to fall*) umstoßen; (*with a bike, car*) umfahren

◆**knock up** *vt* (*sl*) schwängern

'**knockdown** *adj attr* ❶ (*very cheap*) su-
pergünstig *sl*; **~ price** Schleuderpreis *m*
fam ❷ (*physically violent*) **a ~ fight** eine handfeste Auseinandersetzung

knocker ['nak·ər] *n* ❶ (*on door*) Tür-
klopfer *m* ❷ *pl* (*sl: breast*) ∎**big ~ s** dicke Titten *derb*

'**knockout I.** *n* K. o. *m* **II.** *adj* **~ blow**
K.-o.-Schlag *m*

knot [nat] **I.** *n* ❶ (*in rope, material*)
Knoten *m* ❷ (*in hair*) [Haar]knoten *m*
❸ (*in wood*) Ast *m* ❹ (*of people*) Knäuel *m o nt* ▶PHRASES: **to tie the ~** heiraten
II. *vt* <-tt-> knoten; *a tie* binden **III.** *vi*
<-tt-> *muscles* sich verspannen; *stom-*
ach sich zusammenkrampfen

know [noʊ] **I.** *vt* <knew, known>
❶ (*have information, knowledge*) wissen; *facts, results* kennen; **do you ~**
where the post office is? können Sie
mir bitte sagen, wo die Post ist?; **I ~**
what I am talking about ich weiß,
wovon ich rede; ∎**to ~ how to do sth**
wissen, wie man etw macht; **to ~ sth**
by heart etw auswendig können; **to let**
sb ~ sth jdn etw wissen lassen (*be*
certain) ∎**to not ~ whether ...** sich
dat nicht sicher sein, ob ...; **to ~ for a**
fact that ... ganz sicher wissen, dass ...
❸ (*be acquainted with*) ∎**to ~ sb** jdn
kennen; **she ~ s Philadelphia well** sie
kennt sich in Philadelphia gut aus;

K

surely you ~ me better than that! du solltest mich eigentlich besser kennen!; **to ~ sb by name** jdn dem Namen nach kennen; **to get to ~ sb/each other** jdn/sich kennen lernen ④ (*have understanding*) verstehen; **do you ~ what I mean?** verstehst du, was ich meine? ⑤ (*experience*) **I've never ~n anything like this** so etwas habe ich noch nie erlebt ⑥ (*be able to differentiate*) **to ~ right from wrong** Gut und Böse unterscheiden können ▶PHRASES: **to ~ no bounds** keine Grenzen kennen; **to ~ the score** wissen, was gespielt wird; **to ~ a thing or two about sth** sich mit etw *dat* auskennen **II.** *vi* <knew, known> ① (*have knowledge*) [Bescheid] wissen; **ask Kate — she's sure to ~** frag Kate, sie weiß es bestimmt; **as far as I ~** so viel ich weiß; **how should I ~?** wie soll ich das wissen? ② (*fam: understand*) begreifen; **I don't ~ why you can't ever be on time** ich begreife einfach nicht warum du nie pünktlich sein kannst ▶PHRASES: **you ought to ~ better** du solltest es eigentlich besser wissen

'know-how *n* Know-how *nt*

knowing ['nɔʊ·ɪŋ] *adj* wissend *attr; look, smile* viel sagend

knowingly ['nɔʊ·ɪŋ·li] *adv* ① (*meaningfully*) viel sagend ② (*with full awareness*) bewusst

know-it-all ['nɔʊ·ɪt̬·ɔl] *n* (*pej fam*) Besserwisser(in) *m(f) pej*

knowledge ['nɑl·ɪdʒ] *n* ① (*body of learning*) Kenntnisse *pl* (**of** in +*dat*); **~ of French** Französischkenntnisse *pl* ② (*acquired information, awareness*) Wissen *nt*; **to be common ~** allgemein bekannt sein

known [nɔʊn] **I.** *vt, vi pp of* **know** **II.** *adj* ① (*publicly recognized*) bekannt; **it is a little-/well-~ fact**

that ... es ist kaum/allgemein bekannt, dass ... ② (*understood*) bekannt; **no ~ reason** kein erkennbarer Grund ③ (*tell publicly*) **to make sth ~** etw bekannt machen

knuckle ['nʌk·əl] *n* ① ANAT [Finger]knöchel *m* ② (*cut of meat*) Hachse *f*, Haxe *f* SÜDD; **~ of pork** Schweinshaxe *f* SÜDD

◆ **knuckle down** *vi* sich dahinterklemmen

KO [ˌkeɪ·'oʊ] **I.** *n abbrev of* **knockout** K. o. *m* **II.** *vt* <KO'd, KO'd> *abbrev of* **knock out**: ■ **to ~ sb** jdn k. o. schlagen

koala *n*, **koala bear** [koʊ·'al·ə-] *n* Koala[bär] *m*

kooky ['ku·ki] *adj* (*sl*) ausgeflippt

Koran [kə·'ræn] *n* ■ **the ~** der Koran

Korea [kə·'ri·ə] *n* Korea *nt*; **North/South ~** Nord-/Südkorea *nt*

Korean [kə·'ri·ən] **I.** *adj* koreanisch **II.** *n* ① (*inhabitant*) Koreaner(in) *m(f)* ② LING Koreanisch *nt*

kosher ['koʊ·ʃər] *adj* (*a. fig*) koscher

Kremlin ['krem·lɪn] *n* ■ **the ~** der Kreml

KS *abbrev of* **Kansas**

Ku Klux Klan ['ku·ˌklʌks·'klæn] *n* + *sing/pl vb* ■ **the ~** der Ku-Klux-Klan

kung fu [ˌkʊŋ·'fu] *n* Kung-Fu *nt*

Kurd [kɜrd] *n* Kurde *m*, Kurdin *f*

Kurdish ['kɜr·dɪʃ] **I.** *adj* kurdisch **II.** *n* LING Kurdisch *nt*

Kurdistan [ˌkɜr·dɪ·'stæn] *n* Kurdistan *nt*

Kuwait [ku·'weɪt] *n* Kuwait *nt*

Kuwaiti [ku·'weɪ·t̬i] **I.** *adj* kuwaitisch **II.** *n* ① (*inhabitant*) Kuwaiter(in) *m(f)* ② LING Kuwaitisch *nt*

kW <*pl* -> *n abbrev of* **kilowatt** kW

Kwanzaa, Kwanza ['kwan·zə] *n* von Amerikanern afrikanischer Herkunft vom 26. Dezember bis 1. Januar gefeiertes, nicht-religiöses Fest

KY, Ky. *abbrev of* **Kentucky**

L <*pl* -'s>, **l** <*pl* -'s> [el] *n* L *nt*, l *nt;* ~ **as in Lima** L wie Ludwig

l [el] I. *n* ❶ *abbrev of* **left** l. ❷ <*pl* -> *abbrev of* **liter** l ❸ <*pl* ll> TYPO *abbrev of* **line** Z. II. *adj abbrev of* **left** l., L III. *adv abbrev of* **left** l.

L. *n abbrev of* **lake**

LA, La. *abbrev of* **Louisiana**

lab [læb] *n short for* **laboratory** Labor *nt*

label ['leɪ·bəl] I. *n* ❶ *(on bottles)* Etikett *nt;* *(in clothes)* Schild[chen] *nt* ❷ *(brand name)* Marke *f* II. *vt* <-l-> *(affix labels)* etikettieren; *(write on)* beschriften

labeling, labelling ['leɪ·bəl·ɪŋ] *n* Etikettierung *f;* *(with a price)* Auszeichnung *f*

labor ['leɪ·bər] I. *n* ❶ *(work)* Arbeit *f;* **manual** ~ körperliche Arbeit ❷ *(workers)* Arbeitskräfte *pl* ❸ *(childbirth)* Wehen *pl;* **to go into** ~ Wehen bekommen II. *vi* hart arbeiten, sich abmühen

laboratory ['læb·rə·ˌtɔri] *n* Labor[atorium] *nt*

'laboratory assistant *n* Laborant(in) *m(f)*

Labor Day *n* amerikanischer Tag der Arbeit, der am ersten Montag im September gefeiert wird

'labor dispute *n* Arbeitskampf *m*

laborer ['leɪb·ər·ər] *n* Hilfsarbeiter(in) *m(f)*

'labor force *n* + *sing/pl vb* *(population)* Arbeiterschaft *f;* *(staff)* Belegschaft *f*

labor-in'tensive *adj* arbeitsintensiv

laborious [lə·'bɔr·i·əs] *adj* mühsam

'labor market *n* Arbeitsmarkt *m*

'labor-saving *adj* arbeitssparend

'labor shortage *n* Arbeitskräftemangel *m*

Labrador ['læb·rə·dɔr], **Labrador re-'triever** *n* Labrador[hund] *m*

labyrinth ['læb·ə·rɪnθ] *n* Labyrinth *nt*

lace [leɪs] I. *n* ❶ *(cloth)* Spitze *f;* *(edg-*

ing) Spitzenborte *f* ❷ *(cord)* Band *nt;* **shoe** ~**s** Schnürsenkel *pl bes* NORDD, MITTELD II. *vt* ❶ *(fasten)* shoes zubinden ❷ *(add drug)* einen Schuss [Rauschmittel] dazugeben

◆**lace up** *vt* zuschnüren

lacerate ['læs·ə·rəɪt] *vt* aufreißen

'lace-ups *npl* Schnürschuhe *pl*

lack [læk] I. *n* Mangel *m;* ~ **of funds** fehlende Geldmittel II. *vt* ■**to** ~ **sth** etw nicht haben

lackadaisical [ˌlæk·ə·'deɪ·zɪ·kəl] *adj* lustlos

lacking ['læk·ɪŋ] *adj pred* ■**to be** ~ **in sth** an etw *dat* mangeln

lacquer ['læk·ər] I. *n* Lack *m* II. *vt* lackieren

lacrosse [lə·'krɑs] *n* SPORT Lacrosse *nt*

ladder ['læd·ər] *n* Leiter *f*

laden ['leɪ·dən] *adj* beladen

'ladies' room *n* Damentoilette *f*

ladle ['leɪ·dəl] I. *n* [Schöpf]kelle *f* II. *vt* austeilen

lady ['leɪ·di] *n* ❶ *(woman)* Frau *f* ❷ *(form: polite address)* **ladies and gentlemen!** meine [sehr verehrten] Damen und Herren!

'ladybug *n* Marienkäfer *m*

'ladylike *adj* damenhaft

lag [læg] I. *n* *(lapse)* Rückstand *m;* *(falling behind)* Zurückbleiben *nt kein pl;* **time** ~ Zeitabstand *m* II. *vi* <-gg-> zurückbleiben (**behind** hinter +*dat*)

lagoon [lə·'gun] *n* Lagune *f*

laid [leɪd] *pt, pp of* **lay**

laid-'back *adj* *(fam: relaxed)* locker; *(calm)* gelassen

lain [leɪn] *pp of* **lie**

lake [leɪk] *n* See *m*

lam [læm] *n* *(fam)* **to be on the** ~ auf der Flucht sein

lamb [læm] *n* ❶ *(sheep)* Lamm *nt fam* ❷ *(meat)* Lamm[fleisch] *nt*

'lambskin *n* Lammfell *nt*

'lambswool *n* Lammwolle *f*

lame [leɪm] *adj* lahm

lameness ['leɪm·nɪs] *n* Lähmung *f*

lament [lə·'ment] I. *n* Klagelied *nt* II. *vt* ■ **to ~ sb** um jdn trauern

laminate I. *n* ['læm·ɪ·nɪt] Laminat *nt* II. *vt* ['læm·ɪ·neɪt] beschichten

laminated ['læm·ɪ·neɪ·t̬ɪd] *adj* geschichtet; *(with plastic)* beschichtet

lamp [læmp] *n* Lampe *f*; **street ~** Straßenlaterne *f*

lampoon [læm·'pun] *vt* verspotten

'lamppost *n* Laternenpfahl *m*

'lampshade *n* Lampenschirm *m*

LAN [læn] *n acr for* **local area network** LAN *nt*; **wireless ~** WLAN *nt*; **~ party** LAN-Party *f*

lance [læns] *vt* MED aufschneiden

land [lænd] I. *n* Land *nt* II. *adj attr* ❶ MIL, AGR Boden- ❷ *(real estate)* Grundstücks III. *vi* ❶ AVIAT, AEROSP landen **(on** auf +*dat)* ❷ NAUT *vessel* anlegen; *people* an Land gehen ❸ *(come down)* landen **(in/on/outside** in/ auf/außerhalb +*dat)*; **to ~ on one's feet** auf den Füßen landen; *(fig)* [wieder] auf die Füße fallen IV. *vt* ❶ *plane* landen; *boat, fish* an Land ziehen ❷ *(unload)* an Land bringen; *cargo* löschen

'landfill *n* Deponiegelände *nt*

'land forces *npl* MIL Landstreitkräfte *pl*

landing ['læn·dɪŋ] *n* ❶ *of stairs* Treppenabsatz *m* ❷ *of ship, plane* Landung *f;* **emergency ~** Notlandung *f*

'landing gear *n* Fahrgestell *nt*

'landing strip *n* Landebahn *f*

'landlady *n (owner)* Hausbesitzerin *f; (leaser) of apartments* Hauswirtin *f*

'landlocked *adj* von Land umgeben; **~ country** Binnenstaat *m*

'landlord *n (owner)* Hausbesitzer *m; (leaser) of apartments* Hauswirt *m*

'landmark *n* ❶ *(point of recognition)* Erkennungszeichen *nt* ❷ *(event)* Meilenstein *m*

'landmine *n* MIL Landmine *f*

'landowner *n* Grundbesitzer(in) *m(f)*

'landscape I. *n* Landschaft *f* II. *adj attr*

TYPO *(format)* **in ~ format** im Querformat

'landscape architect *n* Landschaftsarchitekt(in) *m(f)*

'landslide *n* ❶ *(of earth)* Erdrutsch *m* ❷ *(majority)* Erdrutsch[wahl]sieg *m;* **to win by a ~** mit einer überwältigenden Mehrheit siegen

lane [leɪn] *n* ❶ *(road)* Gasse *f* ❷ *of freeway* [Fahr]spur *f;* SPORT Bahn *f*

language ['læŋ·gwɪdʒ] *n* ❶ Sprache *f;* **native ~** Muttersprache *f* ❷ *(words)* Sprache *f; (style a.)* Ausdrucksweise *f;* **bad ~** Schimpfwörter *pl*

'language laboratory *n* Sprachlabor *nt*

languid ['læŋ·gwɪd] *adj* ❶ *(weak)* schwach ❷ *(listless)* gelangweilt

lank [læŋk] *adj hair* strähnig

lanky ['læŋ·ki] *adj* hoch aufgeschossen

lanolin(e) ['læn·ə·lɪn] *n* Lanolin *nt*

lantern ['læn·tərn] *n* Laterne *f*

lap¹ [læp] *n* Schoß *m*

lap² [læp] I. *n* SPORT Runde *f;* **~ of honor** Ehrenrunde *f* II. *vt* <-pp-> *(overtake)* überrunden

lap³ [læp] I. *vt* lecken II. *vi waves* [sanft] schlagen **(against** gegen +*akk)*
◆ **lap up** *vt* ❶ *(drink)* [auf]lecken ❷ *(fig: accept)* [gierig] aufsaugen *fig*

'lapdog *n* ❶ *(dog)* Schoßhündchen *nt* ❷ *(fig: person)* Spielball *m*

lapel [lə·'pel] *n* Revers *nt*

lapis lazuli [ˌlæp·ɪs·'læz·ə·li] *n* Lapislazuli *m*

lapse [læps] I. *n* ❶ *(error)* Versehen *nt; (moral)* Fehltritt *m;* **~ of memory** Gedächtnislücke *f* ❷ *(time)* Zeitspanne *f;* **after a ~ of a few days** nach Verstreichen einiger Tage II. *vi* ❶ *concentration* abschweifen; *quality* nachlassen ❷ *(end)* ablaufen; *subscription* auslaufen

lapsed [læpst] *adj attr (former) Catholic* vom Glauben abgefallen; *member* ehemalig

'laptop, laptop com'puter *n* Laptop *m*

larceny ['lar·sə·ni] *n* JUR Diebstahl *m*

larch <*pl* -es> [lartʃ] *n* Lärche *f*

lard [lard] *n* Schweineschmalz *nt*

large [lɑrdʒ] **I.** *adj* ❶ *size* groß ❷ *quantity, extent* groß, beträchtlich; **a ~ amount of work** viel Arbeit ▶PHRASES: **by and ~** im Großen und Ganzen **II.** *n* ■**at ~** auf freiem Fuß

largely ['lɑrdʒ·li] *adv* größtenteils

largeness ['lɑrdʒ·nɪs] *n* (*size*) Größe *f*; (*extensiveness*) Umfang *m*

'**large-scale** *adj usu attr* ❶ (*extensive*) umfangreich *m* ❷ (*made large*) in großem Maßstab *nach n*; **a ~ map** eine Karte mit großem Maßstab

lariat ['ler·i·ət] *n* Lasso *nt*

lark [lɑrk] *n* (*bird*) Lerche *f*

larva <*pl* -vae> ['lɑr·və] *n* Larve *f*

laryngitis [ˌler·ɪn·'dʒɑɪ·tɪs] *n* Kehlkopfentzündung *f*

lasagna, lasagne [lə·'zɑn·jə] *n* Lasagne *f*

lascivious [lə·'sɪv·i·əs] *adj* lüstern *geh*

laser ['leɪ·zər] *n* Laser *m*

'**laser beam** *n* Laserstrahl *m*

'**laser printer** *n* Laserdrucker *m*

lash¹ [læʃ] **I.** *n* <*pl* -es> ❶ (*whip*) Peitsche *f* ❷ (*eyelash*) [Augen]wimper *f* **II.** *vt* ❶ (*whip*) auspeitschen ❷ (*strike*) ■**to ~ sth** rain gegen etw prasseln **III.** *vi* (*strike*) schlagen (**at** gegen +*akk*); (*fig*) rain, wave peitschen (**at** gegen +*akk*)

◆**lash out** *vi* ❶ (*attack physically*) ■**to ~ out at sb** [**with sth**] [mit etw *dat*] auf jdn einschlagen ❷ (*attack verbally, in writing*) ■**to ~ out at sb/sth** jdn/etw scharf kritisieren

lash² *vt* (*tie*) [fest]binden (**to** an +*dat*)

lasso ['læs·oʊ] **I.** *n* <*pl* -s> Lasso *nt* **II.** *vt* mit einem Lasso einfangen

last¹ [læst] **I.** *adj* ❶ *attr* (*after all the others*) ■**the ~ ...** der/die/das letzte ...; **to come ~** als Letzte(r) *f(m)* kommen; **next to ~** vorletzte(r, s); **the ~ one** der/die/das Letzte; **she was the ~ one to arrive** sie kam als Letzte an ❷ (*lowest in order, rank*) letzte(r, s); ■**to be ~** Letzte(r) *f(m)* sein ❸ *attr* (*final, remaining*) letzte(r, s); **at the ~ moment** im letzten Moment ❹ *attr* (*most recent, previous*) letzte(r, s);

~ night gestern Abend; **the week before ~** vorletzte Woche ▶PHRASES: **to have the ~ laugh** zuletzt lachen *fig*; (*show everybody*) es allen zeigen; **to be the ~ straw** das Fass [endgültig] zum Überlaufen bringen *fig* **II.** *adv* ❶ (*after the others*) als Letzte(r, s) ❷ (*most recently*) das letzte Mal ❸ (*lastly*) zuletzt, zum Schluss; ■**but not least** nicht zuletzt **III.** *n* <*pl* -> ❶ (*one after all the others*) ■**the ~** der/die/das Letzte; **she was the ~ to arrive** sie kam als Letzte ❷ (*final one, previous one*) **the ~** der/die/das Letzte ❸ (*fam: end*) **to see the ~ of sth** (*fam*) etw nie wiedersehen müssen; **at ~** endlich

last² [læst] **I.** *vi* ❶ *battle, game* [an]dauern ❷ *car, machine* halten; *supplies etc.* ausreichen; **to make sth ~** etw sparsam verwenden **II.** *vt* (*serve*) *car* halten; *supplies etc.* [aus]reichen; **to ~ [sb]** a **lifetime** ein Leben lang halten

lasting ['læs·tɪŋ] *adj* dauerhaft; *impression* nachhaltig

lastly ['læst·li] *adv* schließlich

last-'minute *adj* in letzter Minute *nach n*

'**last name** *n* Nachname *m*

latch [lætʃ] *n* Riegel *m*

◆**latch on to, latch onto** *vi* (*attach oneself to*) ■**to ~ on to sb** sich an jdn hängen

'**latchkey child** *n* Schlüsselkind *nt*

late [leɪt] **I.** *adj* <-r, -st> ❶ (*behind time*) verspätet *attr;* ■**to be ~** bus, flight, train Verspätung haben; *person* zu spät kommen; ■**to be ~ for sth** zu spät zu etw *dat* kommen ❷ (*in the day*) spät; **let's go home - it's getting ~** lass uns nach Hause gehen, es ist schon spät ❸ *attr* (*towards the end*) spät; **in the afternoon** spät am Nachmittag; **to be in one's ~ thirties** Ende dreißig sein ❹ *attr* (*dead*) verstorben **II.** *adv* <-r, -s> ❶ (*after the expected time*) spät; **the train arrived ~** der Zug hatte Verspätung; **to stay up ~** bis spät aufbleiben; **to work ~** Überstunden machen ❷ (*at an advanced time*) **we talked ~**

L

into the night wir haben bis spät in die Nacht geredet; **~ in the afternoon** am späten Nachmittag; **~ in the day** spät [am Tag]; (*fig: at the very last moment*) im [aller]letzten Augenblick

'latecomer n Nachzügler(in) m(f)

lately ['leɪt·li] adv kürzlich, in letzter Zeit

lateness ['leɪt·nɪs] n Verspätung f

'late-night adj attr Spät-

latent ['leɪ·tənt] adj sci latent

later ['leɪ·tər] I. adj comp of **late** ① attr (*at future time*) date, time später ② pred (*less punctual*) später II. adv comp of **late** ① (*at later time*) später, anschließend; **see you** [or fam **ya**] **~!** bis später! ② (*afterwards*) später, danach

lateral ['læt·ər·əl] adj esp attr seitlich; *thinking* unorthodox

latest ['leɪ·tɪst] I. adj superl of **late**: ■**the ~ ...** der/die/das jüngste [o letzte] ...; **her ~ movie** ihr neuester Film II. n **have you heard the ~?** hast du schon das Neueste gehört?

latex ['leɪ·teks] n Latex m

lathe [leɪð] n Drehbank f

lather ['læð·ər] I. n [Seifen]schaum m II. vt einseifen

Latin ['læt·ən] I. n Latein nt II. adj (*of Latin origin*) Latein-

Latina [lə·'ti·nə] n Latina f

Latino [lə·'ti·noʊ] n Latino m

latitude ['læt·ɪ·tud] n Breite f, Breitengrad m

latrine [lə·'trin] n Latrine f

latter ['læt·ər] pron ■**the ~** der/die/das Letztere

lattice ['læt·ɪs] n Gitter[werk] nt

laudable ['lɔ·də·bəl] adj lobenswert

laugh [læf] I. n Lachen nt kein pl II. vi ① (*express amusement*) lachen (**at** über + akk); **to make sb ~** jdn zum Lachen bringen ② (*fig*) ■**to ~ at sb** (*find funny*) über jdn lachen; (*find ridiculous*) jdn auslachen ▶PHRASES: **to ~ in sb's** <u>face</u> jdn auslachen; **no ~ing** <u>matter</u> nicht zum Lachen

◆**laugh off** vt mit einem Lachen abtun

laughable ['læf·ə·bəl] adj lächerlich pej, lachhaft pej

'laughing stock n ■**to be a ~** die Zielscheibe des Spotts sein

laughter ['læf·tər] n Gelächter nt, Lachen nt

launch¹ [lɔntʃ] I. n ① (*of boat*) Stapellauf m; (*of rocket, spacecraft*) Start m ② (*presentation*) Präsentation f II. vt ① (*send out*) boat zu Wasser lassen; *ship* vom Stapel lassen; *spacecraft* starten; *satellite* in den Weltraum schießen ② (*begin*) beginnen; *campaign, show* starten; *inquiry* anstellen; **to ~ an attack** zum Angriff übergehen ③ (*hurl*) ■**to ~ oneself at sb** sich auf jdn stürzen

◆**launch into** vi ■**to ~ into sth** sich [begeistert] in etw akk stürzen

launch² [lɔntʃ] n (*boat*) Barkasse f

'launching pad, 'launch pad n Abschussrampe f

launder ['lɔn·dər] vt ① (*wash*) waschen [und bügeln] ② (*fig*) *money* waschen sl

Laundromat® ['lɔn·drə·mæt] n Waschsalon m

laundry ['lɔn·dri] n ① (*dirty clothes*) Schmutzwäsche f; **to do the ~** Wäsche waschen ② (*washed clothes*) frische Wäsche

'laundry service n ① (*facility*) Wäscheservice m ② (*business*) Wäscherei f

lava ['la·və] n Lava f; (*stone*) Lavagestein nt

lavatory ['læv·ə·tɔr·i] n Toilette f

lavender ['læv·ən·dər] I. n Lavendel m II. adj lavendelfarben

lavish ['læv·ɪʃ] I. adj ① *meal* üppig ② (*generous*) großzügig; *praise* überschwänglich II. vt ■**to ~ sth on sb** jdn mit etw dat überhäufen; **to ~ great effort on sth** viel Mühe in etw akk stecken

law [lɔ] n ① (*rule*) Gesetz nt ② (*system*) ■**the ~** das Gesetz; **against the ~** illegal ③ (*subject*) Jura kein art

'lawbreaker n Gesetzesbrecher(in) m(f)

'law court n Gericht nt

'law enforcement n Gesetzesvollzug *m;* **in most countries, ~ is in the hands of the police** in den meisten Ländern ist es Aufgabe der Polizei, für die Einhaltung der Gesetze zu sorgen

law firm, law office *n* Anwaltsbüro *nt,* Kanzlei *f*

lawful ['lɔ·fəl] *adj* gesetzlich; *heir* gesetzmäßig

lawless ['lɔ·lɪs] *adj* ❶ (*without laws*) gesetzlos ❷ (*illegal*) gesetzwidrig

'lawmaker *n* Gesetzgeber(in) *m(f)*

lawn [lɔn] *n* Rasen *m*

'lawn bowling *n* Bowls *pl*

'lawnmower *n* Rasenmäher *m*

'law school *n* juristische Fakultät

'law student *n* Jurastudent(in) *m(f)*

'lawsuit *n* Klage *f,* Prozess *m*

lawyer ['lɔ·jər] *n* Rechtsanwalt, -anwältin *m, f*

lax [læks] *adj* (*careless*) lax *oft pej; security* mangelnd

laxative ['læk·sə·tɪv] *n* Abführmittel *nt*

laxity ['læk·sɪ·ti] *n* Laxheit *f*

lay¹ [leɪ] I. *vt* <laid, laid> ❶ (*spread*) legen (**on** auf +*akk*), breiten (**over** über +*akk*) ❷ *egg* legen ❸ (*put down*) verlegen; **to ~ the blame on sb** (*fig*) jdn für etw *akk* verantwortlich machen ❹ (*render*) **to ~ sb/sth open to criticism** jdn/etw der Kritik aussetzen ❺ (*present*) ∎**to ~ sth before sb** jdm etw vorlegen ❻ (*vulg, sl: have sex*) **to get laid** flachgelegt werden *sl* ►PHRASES: **to ~ eyes on** [erstmals] zu sehen bekommen; **to ~ sth to rest** etw beschwichtigen II. *vi* ❶ (*shape*) **the ~ of the land** (*fig*) die Lage ❷ (*vulg, sl: sex partner*) **to be a good ~** gut im Bett sein *fam*

◆**lay aside** *vt* ❶ (*put away, save*) beiseitelegen ❷ (*fig: forget*) *one's differences* beilegen

◆**lay down** *vt* ❶ (*deposit*) hinlegen (**on** auf +*akk*) ❷ *weapons* niederlegen ❸ *rules* festlegen ►PHRASES: **to ~ down the law** [about sth] [über etw *akk*] Vorschriften machen

◆**lay into** *vi* (*fam*) ∎**to ~ into sb** (*physically*) jdn angreifen; (*verbally*) jdn

zur Schnecke machen *fam*

◆**lay off** I. *vt* kündigen; ∎**to ~ off ↻ sb** jdn entlassen II. *vi* aufhören

◆**lay on** *vt* auftragen

◆**lay out** *vt* ❶ (*arrange*) planen; *schedule* organisieren ❷ *usu passive* (*design*) ∎**to be laid out** angeordnet sein; *garden* angelegt sein

lay² [leɪ] *adj attr* laienhaft

lay³ [leɪ] *pt of* **lie**

layer ['leɪ·ər] I. *n* ❶ Schicht *f;* ∎**~s** *pl* (*in hair*) Stufen *pl* ❷ (*fig: level*) Stufe *f* II. *vt* ∎**to ~ sth** [with sth] etw [abwechselnd mit etw *dat*] in Schichten anordnen

layette [leɪ·'et] *n* Babyausstattung *f*

'layman *n* Laie *m*

'layoff *n* Entlassung *f*

'layout *n* ❶ (*plan*) *of building* Raumaufteilung *f; of town* Plan *m* ❷ (*of text*) Layout *nt*

'layover *n* Aufenthalt *m;* (*of plane*) Zwischenlandung *f*

laze [leɪz] *vi* faulenzen

laziness ['leɪ·zɪ·nɪs] *n* Faulheit *f*

lazy ['leɪ·zi] *adj* faul

'lazybones *n + sing vb* (*pej*) Faulenzer(in) *m(f)*

lb. <*pl* -> *n abbrev of* **pound** Pfd.

LCD [,el·si·'di] *n abbrev of* **liquid crystal display** LCD *nt*

lead¹ [lid] I. *vt* <led, led> ❶ (*command*) führen; *delegation* leiten ❷ (*guide*) führen (**into/over/through** in/über/durch +*akk,* **to** zu +*dat*) ❸ (*go in advance*) **to ~ the way** vorangehen; (*in car*) voranfahren ►PHRASES: **to ~ sb down the garden path** (*fam*) jdn an der Nase herumführen II. *vi* <led, led> ❶ (*command*) die Leitung innehaben ❷ (*be guide*) vorangehen ❸ (*cause to happen*) ∎**to ~ to sth** zu etw *dat* führen ❹ (*be in the lead*) führen; SPORT in Führung liegen III. *n* ❶ THEAT, FILM Hauptrolle *f* ❷ (*front position*) Führung *f;* ∎**to be in the ~** führend sein; **to take over the ~** sich an die Spitze setzen ❸ (*advance position*) Vorsprung *m* ❹ (*leash*) Leine *f*

◆**lead off I.** vt ❶ (initiate) ■**to ~ off ○ sth [with sth]** etw [mit etw dat] eröffnen **II.** vi ❶ (begin) beginnen ❷ road wegführen; **to ~ off to the left** nach links abgehen

◆**lead on** vt (pej) ■**to ~ on ○ sb** (deceive) jdm etw vormachen

◆**lead up to** vi ■**to ~ up to sth** ❶ (precede) etw dat vorangehen ❷ (approach) subject zu etw dat hinführen

lead² [led] n ❶ (metal) Blei nt ❷ (of pencil) Mine f

leaded ['led·əd] adj gasoline verbleit

leader ['li·dər] n ❶ (head) Leiter(in) m(f), Führer(in) m(f) ❷ (competitor) Erste(r) f(m) ❸ MUS (conductor) Dirigent(in) m(f)

leadership ['li·dər·ʃɪp] n ❶ (action) Führung f ❷ (position) Leitung f, Führung f

lead-free ['led·fri] adj bleifrei

leading ['li·dɪŋ] adj attr führend

leading 'edge n ❶ of wing Flügelvorderkante f ❷ of development ■**to be at the ~ [of sth]** auf dem neuestem Stand [einer S. gen] sein

leading 'question n Suggestivfrage f

lead pencil [led'-] n Bleistift m

lead poisoning ['led-] n Bleivergiftung f

lead singer [led'-] n Leadsänger(in) m(f)

lead 'story [lid'-] n Leitartikel m

lead time [lid'-] n Vorlaufzeit f

leaf [lif] **I.** n < pl leaves> Blatt nt ►PHRASES: **to shake like a ~** wie Espenlaub zittern **II.** vi <-s, -ed> ■**to ~ through sth** etw durchblättern

leaflet ['lif·lɪt] n (for advertising) Prospekt m ÖSTERR a. nt; (for instructions) Merkblatt nt; (brochure) Broschüre f

leafy ['li·fi] adj ❶ (of place) belaubt ❷ HORT Blatt-, blattartig

league [lig] n ❶ (group) Bund m ❷ SPORT Liga f

leak [lik] **I.** n ❶ Leck nt; gas ~ undichte Stelle in der Gasleitung **II.** vi ❶ container undicht sein; ship lecken; faucet tropfen; tire Luft verlieren **III.** vt ❶ gas, liq-

uid austreten lassen ❷ (fig) information durchsickern lassen

leaky ['li·ki] adj leck

lean¹ [lin] **I.** vi ❶ (incline) sich beugen; (prop) sich lehnen; ■**to ~ forward** sich nach vorne lehnen **II.** vt <leaned, leaned> lehnen (against/on an/auf +akk)

◆**lean on** vi ❶ (rely on) sich verlassen auf +akk ❷ (fam: put under pressure) unter Druck setzen

lean² [lin] adj ❶ (not fat) mager; person a. schlank ❷ budget schmal

leap [lip] **I.** n (a. fig) Sprung m **II.** vi <leaped or leapt, leaped or leapt> ❶ (jump) springen (across/over über +akk, from von +dat); ■**to ~ on sth** sich auf etw stürzen ❷ (rush) **to ~ to sb's defense** (fig) zu jds Verteidigung eilen ❸ (fig: increase) prices in die Höhe schießen **III.** vt <leaped or leapt, leaped or leapt> springen über +akk, überspringen

◆**leap out** vi ❶ (jump out) herausspringen (of aus +dat) ❷ (fig: grab attention) ■**to ~ out at sb** jdm ins Auge springen

'leapfrog n Bockspringen nt

leapt [lept] vt, vi pt, pp of **leap**

'leap year n Schaltjahr nt

learn [lɜrn] **I.** vt <learned or learnt, learned or learnt> lernen; ■**to ~ how to do sth** lernen, wie man etw tut ►PHRASES: **to ~ sth by heart** etw auswendig lernen **II.** vi <learned or learnt, learned or learnt> ❶ (master) lernen ❷ (become aware) (about über +akk) ■**to ~ about sth** von etw dat erfahren

learner ['lɜr·nər] n Lernende(r) f(m); **to be a quick ~** schnell lernen

learnt [lɜrnt] vt, vi pt, pp of **learn**

lease [lis] **I.** vt ❶ (grant use) vermieten (to an +akk) ❷ (rent) mieten; property pachten; equipment leasen **II.** n of apartment, house Mietvertrag m; of equipment Leasingvertrag m

leash [liʃ] **I.** n ❶ Leine f; (for children) Laufgurt m **II.** vt dog anleinen

leasing ['li·sɪŋ] n ❶ (granting of use) of

land Verpachten nt; (of equipment) Leasing nt ② (renting) of land Pachten nt; of equipment Leasen nt

least [liːst] I. adv am wenigsten; **the ~ little thing** die kleinste Kleinigkeit; **~ of all** am allerwenigsten II. adj det (tiniest amount) geringste(r, s); **at ~** (minimum) mindestens; (if nothing else) zumindest

leather ['leð·ər] n Leder nt

leathery ['leð·ə·ri] adj led[e]rig; hands, skin ledern

leave [liːv] I. n ① (farewell) Abschied m ② (permission) Erlaubnis f ③ (off work) Urlaub m II. vt <left, left> ① (depart) verlassen; (train) abfahren ② (permanently) husband, wife verlassen; job aufgeben; **to ~ school** die Schule beenden ③ (not take) [zurück]lassen (**with** bei +dat); message, note hinterlassen ④ (forget) vergessen ⑤ (cause to remain) **to ~ sth open** etw offen lassen ⑥ (not change) lassen ⑦ (not eat) übrig lassen ⑧ (bequeath) hinterlassen ▶PHRASES: **to ~ nothing to <u>chance</u>** nichts dem Zufall überlassen; **to ~ sb <u>alone</u>** jdn in Ruhe lassen III. vi <left, left> [weg]gehen; vehicle abfahren; plane abfliegen

◆**leave behind** vt ① (not take) zurücklassen ② traces hinterlassen ③ (fig: forget on purpose) ■ **to ~ behind** ⟳ **sth** hinter sich dat lassen

◆**leave off** vt ① (omit) auslassen; **to ~ sb's name off a list** jds Namen nicht in eine Liste aufnehmen ② (not put on) **to ~ a lid on sth** keinen Deckel auf etw akk geben

◆**leave out** vt ① (omit) auslassen; facts weglassen; (accidentally) vergessen ② (exclude) ausschließen

◆**leave over** vt usu passive ■ **to be left over** [**from sth**] [von etw dat] übrig geblieben sein

leaves [liːvz] n pl of **leaf**

leaving ['liː·vɪŋ] n Abreise f

lecherous ['letʃ·ər·əs] adj geil oft pej

lectern ['lek·tərn] n [Redner]pult nt

lecture ['lek·tʃər] I. n ① (speech) Vortrag m; UNIV Vorlesung f ② (criticism) Standpauke f fam II. vi UNIV eine Vorlesung halten III. vt ■ **to ~ sb on** [or about] **sth** ① (give speech) jdm über etw akk einen Vortrag halten; UNIV vor jdm über etw akk eine Vorlesung halten ② (criticize) jdm wegen einer S. eine Standpauke halten fam

'**lecture hall** n Hörsaal m

lecturer ['lek·tʃər·ər] n ① (speaker) Redner(in) m(f) ② (university) Dozent(in) m(f)

'**lecture tour** n Vortragsreise f

led [led] pt, pp of **lead**

ledge [ledʒ] n Sims m o nt; (of rock) Felsvorsprung m

lee [liː] n Windschatten m; GEOG, NAUT Lee f o nt fachspr

leek [liːk] n Lauch m

leer [lɪr] I. vi ■ **to ~ at sb** jdm anzügliche Blicke zuwerfen II. n anzügliches Grinsen

leeway ['liː·weɪ] n Spielraum m

left[1] [left] I. n ① (direction) **from ~ to right** von links nach rechts ② (turn) **to make a ~** [nach] links abbiegen ③ (side) ■ **the ~** die linke Seite; POL die Linke; ■ **on** [or to] **sb's ~** zu jds Linken, links von jdm II. adj linke(r, s) III. adv (direction) nach links; (side) links; **to keep ~** sich links halten ▶PHRASES: **~, right and <u>center</u>** überall

left[2] [left] pt, pp of **leave**

'**left-hand** adj attr (on left side) linke(r, s)

left-'handed I. adj person linkshändig II. adv SPORT **to throw ~** mit links werfen

left-'hander n (person) Linkshänder(in) m(f)

'**leftovers** npl (food) Reste pl

left 'wing n ■ **the ~** ① POL die Linke ② MIL, SPORT der linke Flügel

left-'wing adj linksgerichtet, links präd

leg [leg] n ① (limb, support) Bein nt ② (meat) Keule f ③ (stage) Etappe f ▶PHRASES: **to be on one's <u>last</u> ~** auf dem letzten Loch pfeifen sl; **to <u>pull</u> sb's ~** (fam) jdn auf den Arm nehmen

L

legacy ['leg·ə·si] n LAW Vermächtnis nt, Erbe nt a. fig

legal ['li·gəl] adj ① (permitted by law) legal ② (statutory) gesetzlich [vorgeschrieben] ③ (under law) rechtmäßig ④ (of paper) nordamerikanische Standardgröße für Papierformat: 21,6 cm x 35,6 cm

legalese [ˌli·gəl·'iz] n (pej fam) Juristenjargon m oft pej

legalize ['li·gə·laɪz] vt legalisieren geh

legally ['li·gə·li] adv ① (permissible) legal ② (required) ~ obliged gesetzlich verpflichtet ③ (according to the law) rechtmäßig

'legal pad n Schreibblock m

legend ['ledʒ·ənd] n ① (saga) Sage f ② (person) Legende f

legendary ['ledʒ·ən·der·i] adj ① (mythical) sagenhaft ② (famous) legendär

leggings ['leg·ɪŋz] npl Leggings pl

legible ['ledʒ·ə·bəl] adj lesbar

legion ['li·dʒən] n HIST Legion f; the [Foreign] L~ die Fremdenlegion

Legion'naires' disease n die Legionärskrankheit

legislate ['ledʒ·ɪ·sleɪt] vi ein Gesetz erlassen (against gegen +akk)

legislation [ˌledʒ·ɪ·'sleɪ·ʃən] n ① (laws) Gesetze pl ② (lawmaking) Gesetzgebung f

legislative ['ledʒ·ɪ·sleɪ·tɪv] adj esp attr gesetzgebend

legislator ['ledʒ·ɪ·sleɪ·tər] n Gesetzgeber(in) m(f)

legislature ['ledʒ·ɪ·sleɪ·tʃər] n Legislative f; member of the ~ Parlamentsmitglied nt

legitimate adj [lə·'dʒɪt·ə·mɪt] ① (legal) rechtmäßig ② (reasonable) gerechtfertigt; complaint begründet ③ child ehelich

legitim(at)ize [lə·'dʒɪt·ə·m(ə·t)aɪz] vt (make legal) für rechtsgültig erklären

'legroom n Beinfreiheit f

legume [lə·'gjum] n BOT Hülsenfrucht f

leisure ['li·ʒər] n Freizeit f ▶PHRASES: at [one's] ~ in aller Ruhe

leisurely ['li·ʒər·li] I. adj ruhig, geruh-

sam; picnic, breakfast gemütlich II. adv gemächlich

'leisurewear n Freizeit[be]kleidung f

lemon ['lem·ən] n ① (fruit) Zitrone f ② (color) Zitronengelb nt

lemonade [ˌlem·ə·'neɪd] n Zitronenlimonade f

'lemon peel, 'lemon rind n Zitronenschale f

lend <lent, lent> [lend] vt ① (loan) leihen ② (be suitable) ■to ~ itself to sth sich für etw akk eignen

lender ['len·dər] n Verleiher(in) m(f); (of money) Kreditgeber(in) m(f)

lending ['len·dɪŋ] n Leihen nt

'lending library n Leihbibliothek f

length [leŋkθ] n ① (measurement) Länge f; 6 feet in ~ 6 Fuß lang ② (piece) Stück nt; of cloth Bahn f ③ (duration) Dauer f; at ~ (in detail) ausführlich ▶PHRASES: to go to great ~s sich dat alle Mühe geben

lengthen ['leŋk·θən] I. vt verlängern; clothes länger machen II. vi [immer] länger werden

lengthwise ['leŋk·waɪz], **lengthways** ['leŋk·weɪz] adv der Länge nach

lengthy ['leŋk·θi] adj ① (long time) [ziemlich] lange; delay beträchtlich ② (tedious) langwierig

lenience ['li·ni·əns], **leniency** ['li·ni·ən·si] n Nachsicht f, Milde f

lenient ['li·ni·ənt] adj nachsichtig, milde

lens <pl -es> [lenz] n Linse f; of camera Objektiv nt; of glasses Glas nt; [contact] ~ Kontaktlinse f

lent [lent] vt, vi pt, pp of **lend**

lentil ['len·təl] n Linse f

Leo ['li·ou] n ASTRON, ASTROL ① no art der Löwe ② (person) Löwe m; she is a ~ sie ist Löwe

leopard ['lep·ərd] n Leopard(in) m(f)

leotard ['li·ə·tard] n Trikot nt; (for gymnastics a.) Turnanzug m

leprosy ['lep·rə·si] n Lepra f

lesbian ['lez·bi·ən] I. n Lesbierin f, Lesbe f II. adj lesbisch

less [les] I. adv comp of **little** weniger; the ~ ... the better je weniger ..., umso besser; **~ and ~** immer weniger II. *adj comp of* little weniger III. *pron indef* weniger; **a lot ~** viel weniger; **I've been seeing ~ of her lately** ich sehe sie in letzter Zeit weniger; **~ of a problem** ein geringeres Problem

lessen ['les·ən] *vi* schwächer werden; *pain* nachlassen

lesser ['les·ər] *adj attr* ❶ (*smaller*) geringer; **the ~ of two evils** das kleinere Übel ❷ (*minor*) unbedeutend

lesson ['les·ən] *n* ❶ (*at school*) Stunde *f*; ■ **~s** *pl* Unterricht *m kein pl* (in *+dat*) ❷ (*experience*) Lehre *f*; **to teach sb a ~** jdm eine Lektion erteilen

let[1] [let] *vt* <-tt-, let, let> ❶ (*allow*) ■ **to ~ sth/sb do sth** etw/jdn tun lassen; **to ~ sb go** (*allow to depart*) jdn gehen lassen; (*release from grip*) jdn loslassen; **I'll ~ you go** (*on the phone*) ich will Sie nicht länger aufhalten; **to ~ sth go** (*neglect*) etw vernachlässigen; (*let pass*) etw durchgehen lassen ❷ (*give permission*) ■ **to ~ sb do sth** jdm etw tun lassen ❸ (*in suggestions*) **~'s go out to dinner!** lass uns Essen gehen! ▶ PHRASES: **~ alone …** geschweige denn …; **~ it rip** (*fam*) es [mal so richtig] krachen lassen *fam*

◆**let down** *vt* ❶ ■ **to ~ down** ⟳ **sb** (*disappoint*) jdn enttäuschen; (*fail to support*) jdn im Stich lassen ❷ (*lower*) ■ **to ~ down** ⟳ **sth** etw herunterlassen

◆**let in** *vt* hereinlassen; ■ **to ~ oneself in** aufschließen

◆**let into** *vt* ■ **to ~ sb into sth** jdn in etw *akk* lassen

◆**let off** *vt* ❶ (*not punish*) **to ~ sb off with a warning** jdn mit einer Verwarnung davonkommen lassen ❷ (*emit*) ausstoßen; *bad smell* verbreiten; **to ~ off steam** (*a. fig*) Dampf ablassen

◆**let on** *vi* (*fam*) ■ **to ~ on about sth** [to sb] [jdm] etwas von etw *dat* verraten

◆**let out** I. *vt* ❶ (*release*) herauslassen; **I'll ~ myself out** ich finde selbst hinaus ❷ (*emit*) ausstoßen; **to ~ out** ⟳ **a shriek** aufschreien ❸ *seam* auslassen II. *vi* enden; **when does school ~ out**

for the summer? wann beginnen die Sommerferien?

◆**let through** *vt* durchlassen

◆**let up** *vi* (*fam: decrease*) aufhören; *rain a.* nachlassen; *fog, weather* aufklaren

let[2] [let] *n* SPORT Netzball *m*

lethal ['li·θəl] *adj* tödlich

lethargic [lɪ·ˈθɑr·dʒɪk] *adj* ❶ (*not energetic*) lethargisch ❷ (*apathetic*) lustlos

letter ['let·ər] I. *n* ❶ (*message*) Brief *m*; **to inform sb by ~** jdn schriftlich verständigen ❷ (*of alphabet*) Buchstabe *m* II. *adj* (*of paper*) nordamerikanische Standardgröße für Papierformat: 21,6 cm x 27,9 cm

'letter bomb *n* Briefbombe *f*

lettuce ['let·ɪs] *n* (*plant*) Blattsalat *m*; (*with firm head*) Kopfsalat *m*

leukemia [lu·ˈki·mi·ə] *n* Leukämie *f*

level ['lev·əl] I. *adj* ❶ (*plane*) horizontal, waag[e]recht ❷ (*flat*) eben ❸ *pred* (*at equal height*) auf gleicher Höhe (**with** mit *+dat*) ❹ (*calm*) *voice* ruhig II. *n* ❶ (*quantity, standard*) Niveau *nt*; (*height*) Höhe *f*; **above sea ~** über dem Meeresspiegel ❷ (*extent*) Ausmaß *nt* ❸ (*story*) Stockwerk *nt*; **on ~ four** im vierten Stock ❹ (*rank*) Ebene *f* III. *vt* <-l-> ❶ (*flatten*) *ground* [ein]ebnen; (*raze*) *building* dem Erdboden gleichmachen ❷ (*direct*) *pistol* richten (**at** auf *+akk*)

◆**level off, level out** I. *vi* ❶ (*after dropping*) *plane* sich fangen; *pilot* das Flugzeug abfangen; (*after rising*) horizontal fliegen ❷ *road* flach werden II. *vt* [ein]ebnen

◆**level with** *vi* (*fam*) ■ **to ~ with sb** ehrlich zu jdm sein

level-'headed *adj* vernünftig

lever ['lev·ər] I. *n* ❶ Hebel *m* ❷ (*fig: threat*) Druckmittel *nt* II. *vt* ■ **to ~ sth up** etw aufstemmen

leverage ['lev·ər·ɪdʒ] *n* ❶ TECH Hebelkraft *f* ❷ (*fig: pressure*) Einfluss *m*

levitate ['lev·ɪ·teɪt] I. *vi* schweben II. *vt* schweben lassen

levy ['lev·i] I. *n* Steuer *f*, Abgaben *pl*

L

II. vt <-ie-> erheben; *tax* auferlegen (**on** +*dat*)

lewd [lud] *adj* (*indecent*) unanständig; *gesture* obszön

lexical ['lek·sɪ·kəl] *adj* lexikalisch

lexicography [ˌlek·sɪ·'kag·rə·fi] *n* Lexikographie *f*

lexicon ['lek·sɪ·kan] *n* Wörterbuch *nt*

liability [ˌlaɪ·ə·'bɪl·ɪ·ti] *n* ❶ (*responsibility*) Haftung *f* ❷ FIN ■**liabilities** *pl* Verbindlichkeiten *pl* ❸ (*handicap*) Belastung *f*

liable ['laɪ·ə·bəl] *adj* ❶ JUR haftbar ❷ (*likely*) ■**to be ~ to do sth** Gefahr laufen, etw zu tun

liaise [lɪ·'eɪz] *vi* ■**to ~ with sb/sth** (*establish contact*) eine Verbindung zu jdm/etw herstellen; (*be go-between*) als Verbindungsstelle zu jdm/etw fungieren

liaison ['li·eɪ·zan] *n* (*contact*) Verbindung *f*; **to work in close ~ with sb** mit jdm eng zusammenarbeiten

liar ['laɪ·ər] *n* Lügner(in) *m(f)*

libel ['laɪ·bəl] JUR **I.** *n* Verleumdung *f* **II.** *vt* <-l-> verleumden

libelous, libellous ['laɪ·bə·ləs] *adj* verleumderisch

liberal ['lɪb·ər·əl] **I.** *adj* liberal; *attitude* tolerant **II.** *n* Liberale(r) *f(m)*

liberal 'arts I. *n pl* ■**the ~** die Geisteswissenschaften *pl* **II.** *adj* geisteswissenschaftlich

liberalism ['lɪb·ər·ə·lɪz·əm] *n* Liberalismus *m*

liberalization [ˌlɪb·ər·ə·lɪ·'zeɪ·ʃən] *n* Liberalisierung *f*

liberalize ['lɪb·ər·ə·laɪz] *vt* liberalisieren

liberate ['lɪb·ə·reɪt] *vt* befreien (**from** von +*dat*)

liberation [ˌlɪb·ə·'reɪ·ʃən] *n* Befreiung *f* (**from** von +*dat*)

liberty ['lɪb·ər·ti] *n* ❶ (*freedom*) Freiheit *f*; **to be at ~** frei sein ❷ (*incorrect behavior*) **to take liberties with sb** sich *dat* bei jdm Freiheiten herausnehmen

libido [lɪ·'bi·doʊ] *n* Libido *f*

Libra ['li·brə] *n* ASTRON, ASTROL ❶ die

Waage ❷ (*person*) Waage *f*; **she is a ~** sie ist Waage

librarian [laɪ·'brer·i·ən] *n* Bibliothekar(in) *m(f)*

library ['laɪ·brer·i] *n* Bibliothek *f*; (*public a.*) Bücherei *f*; **public ~** Leihbücherei *f*

lice [laɪs] *n pl of* **louse**

license ['laɪ·səns] **I.** *n* (*permit*) Genehmigung *f*, Erlaubnis *f*; **driver's ~** Führerschein *m* **II.** *vt* ■**to ~ sb to do sth** jdm die Lizenz erteilen, etw zu tun

licensed ['laɪ·sənst] *adj* zugelassen

'license plate *n* Nummernschild *nt*

'license plate number *n* Kfz-Kennzeichen *nt*

licensing ['laɪ·sən·sɪŋ] *n* Lizenzvergabe *f*

lichen ['laɪ·kən] *n* Flechte *f*

lick [lɪk] **I.** *n* ❶ Lecken *nt kein pl*, Schlecken *nt kein pl* **II.** *vt* ❶ lecken; *lollipop* schlecken an +*dat* ❷ (*fam: beat*) ■**to ~ sb** jdn [doch glatt] in die Tasche stecken

licking ['lɪk·ɪŋ] *n* (*fam*) **to give sb a** [**good**] **~** (*beating*) jdm eine Tracht Prügel verpassen *fam*; (*defeat*) jdn haushoch schlagen

licorice ['lɪk·ər·ɪʃ] *n* Lakritze *f*

lid [lɪd] *n* ❶ (*cover*) Deckel *m* ❷ (*eyelid*) Lid *nt*

lie[1] [laɪ] **I.** *n* Lage *f* **II.** *vi* <-y-, lay, lain> ❶ (*repose*) liegen; **to ~ awake** wach [da]liegen ❷ (*become horizontal*) sich hinlegen ❸ (*be in particular state*) **to ~ in wait** auf der Lauer liegen ❹ (*be situated*) liegen; **to ~ to the east of sth** im Osten einer S. *gen* liegen ▶PHRASES: **to ~ low** (*escape search*) untergetaucht sein; (*avoid notice*) sich unauffällig verhalten

◆**lie around** *vi* [he]rumliegen *fam*

◆**lie ahead** *vi* ❶ (*in space, position*) ■**to ~ ahead** [**of sb**] vor jdm liegen ❷ (*in time*) bevorstehen

◆**lie back** *vi* sich zurücklegen

◆**lie behind** *vi* (*be cause of*) ■**to ~ behind sth** etw zugrunde liegen

◆**lie down** *vi* sich hinlegen

lie[2] [laɪ] **I.** *vi* <-y-> lügen; ■**to ~ about**

sb über jdn die Unwahrheit erzählen;
■ to ~ to sb jdn belügen II. n Lüge f
'lie detector n Lügendetektor m
lieu [lu] n in ~ of sth an Stelle einer S.
gen
Lieut. n attr abbrev of Lieutenant Lt.
lieutenant [luˈtɛn·ənt] n ❶ MIL Leut-
nant m ❷ LAW ≈ Polizeihauptwacht-
meister(in) m(f)
lieutenant 'governor n POL Vizegouver-
neur m
life <pl lives> [laɪf] n ❶ [das] Leben; to
save sb's ~ jdm das Leben retten ❷ (living things collectively) das Leben;
plant ~ die Pflanzenwelt ❸ (energy)
Lebendigkeit f; to bring sth to ~ etw
lebendiger machen ❹ (time until death)
das/sein Leben; ■ for ~ friendship le-
benslang ❺ (duration) of battery Lebensdauer f; of a contract Laufzeit f
▶PHRASES: to frighten the ~ out of sb
jdn zu Tode erschrecken; that's ~! so
ist das Leben [eben]!
'lifeboat n Rettungsboot nt
'life cycle n Lebenszyklus m
'life expectancy n Lebenserwartung f
'life form n Lebewesen f
'lifeguard n (at swimming pool) Bade-
meister(in) m(f); (on beach) Rettungs-
schwimmer(in) m(f)
life im'prisonment n lebenslängliche
Freiheitsstrafe
'life insurance n Lebensversicherung f
'life jacket n Schwimmweste f
lifeless ['laɪf·lɪs] adj ❶ (inanimate) leblos ❷ (dull) game langweilig; hair
stumpf
'lifelike adj lebensecht; imitation a. naturgetreu
'lifeline n ❶ (rope) Rettungsleine f
❷ (fig: vital link) [lebenswichtige] Verbindung
'life preserver n Schwimmweste f
lifer ['laɪ·fər] n (fam: prisoner) Lebens-
längliche(r) f(m) fam
'life raft n Rettungsfloß nt; (dinghy)
Schlauchboot nt
'lifesaver n (fam: thing) die Rettung fig;
(person) [Lebens]retter(in) m(f) fig

life 'sentence n lebenslängliche Freiheitsstrafe
'life-size(d) adj in Lebensgröße nach n,
lebensgroß
'lifestyle n Lebensstil m
'life support system n MED lebenserhal-
tender Apparat
'life-threatening adj illness lebensbe-
drohend; situation lebensgefährlich
'lifetime n usu sing ❶ (time one is alive)
Lebenszeit f; to last a ~ memories das
ganze Leben [lang] andauern ❷ (time
sth exists) Lebensdauer f kein pl
▶PHRASES: the chance of a ~ eine ein-
malige Chance
'life vest n see life jacket
lift [lɪft] I. n ❶ (for skiers) Skilift m
❷ (act of lifting) [Hoch]heben nt kein pl
❸ (ride) Mitfahrgelegenheit f; to give
sb a ~ jdn [im Auto] mitnehmen II. vt
❶ (raise) [hoch]heben ❷ (direct upward) eyes aufschlagen; head heben
❸ (airlift) fliegen; supplies auf dem
Luftweg transportieren ❹ usu passive
(in surgery) face straffen lassen, liften
❺ (end) restrictions aufheben III. vi
❶ (be raised) sich heben ❷ fog sich auflösen
◆ lift off vi ❶ (leave earth) abheben
❷ (come off) sich hochheben lassen
◆ lift up vt hochheben; lid hochklappen
'liftoff n AEROSP Start m
ligament ['lɪg·ə·mənt] n ANAT Band nt;
to tear a ~ sich dat einen Bänderriss
zuziehen
light¹ [laɪt] I. n ❶ Licht nt ❷ (source of
brightness) Licht nt; (lamp) Lampe f;
to turn the ~ off das Licht ausschalten
❸ (fire) Feuer nt ❹ usu pl (traffic light)
Ampel f ❺ (fig: perspective) to show
sth in a good ~ etw in einem guten
Licht erscheinen lassen ▶PHRASES: to
come to ~ ans Licht kommen II. adj
hell III. vt <lit or lighted, lit or light-
ed> ❶ erhellen; room beleuchten
❷ match, fire anzünden
◆ light up I. vt ❶ (illuminate) erhellen
❷ cigar anzünden II. vi ❶ (smoke) sich
dat eine [Zigarette] anstecken fam

L

❷ (*become animated*) *eyes* aufleuchten *fig*

light² [laɪt] I. *adj* ❶ leicht ❷ (*for small loads*) Klein-; **~ airplane** Kleinflugzeug *nt* ❸ (*low-fat*) fettarm ❹ (*low in intensity*) **~ rain** Nieselregen *m* ❺ *kiss* zart; *touch* sanft ▶PHRASES: **to make ~ of sth** etw bagatellisieren II. *adv* **to travel ~** mit leichtem Gepäck reisen

'light bulb *n* Glühbirne *f*

lighten ['laɪ·tən] *vt* ❶ (*make less heavy*) leichter machen ❷ (*fig: make less serious*) aufheitern; *mood* heben

◆**lighten up** *vi* **~ up, would you?** mach bitte nicht so ein ernstes Gesicht

lighter ['laɪ·tər] *n* Feuerzeug *nt*

light'headed *adj* (*faint*) benommen; (*dizzy*) schwind[e]lig

light'hearted *adj* unbeschwert

'lighthouse *n* Leuchtturm *m*

lighting ['laɪ·tɪŋ] *n* Beleuchtung *f*; (*equipment*) Beleuchtungsanlage *f*

lightly ['laɪt·li] *adv* ❶ (*not seriously*) leichtfertig; **to not take sth ~** etw nicht leichtnehmen ❷ (*gently*) leicht; (*not much*) wenig; **I tapped ~ on the door** ich klopfte leise an [die Tür] ❸ (*slightly*) leicht

lightness¹ ['laɪt·nɪs] *n* (*brightness*) Helligkeit *f*

lightness² ['laɪt·nɪs] *n* (*not heaviness*) Leichtheit *f*

lightning ['laɪt·nɪŋ] *n* Blitz *m*; **thunder and ~** Blitz und Donner; **to be struck by ~** vom Blitz getroffen werden

'lightning rod *n* Blitzableiter *m a. fig*

'light pen *n* COMPUT Lichtstift *m*

'lightweight I. *n* (*boxer*) Leichtgewichtler(in) *m(f)* II. *adj* ❶ SPORT Leichtgewichts- ❷ (*weighing little*) leicht

'light year *n* ASTRON Lichtjahr *nt*

likable ['laɪ·kə·bəl] *adj* liebenswert

like¹ [laɪk] I. *vt* ❶ (*enjoy*) mögen; ▪to **~ doing sth** etw gern[e *fam*] tun ❷ (*want*) wollen; **whether you ~ it or not** ob es dir passt oder nicht; **would you ~ a drink?** möchten Sie etwas trinken? ❸ (*prefer*) **I ~ to get up early** ich

stehe gern[e *fam*] früh auf II. *vi* **as you ~** wie Sie wollen

like² [laɪk] I. *prep* ❶ (*similar to*) wie; **~ most people** wie die meisten Leute; **~ father, ~ son** wie der Vater, so der Sohn; **what does it taste ~?** wie schmeckt es?; **he looks ~ his brother** er sieht seinem Bruder ähnlich; **there's nothing ~ a good cup of coffee** es geht doch nichts über eine gute Tasse Kaffee ❷ *after n* (*such as*) wie ▶PHRASES: **it looks ~ rain** es sieht nach Regen aus II. *conj* (*fam*) ❶ (*the same as*) wie; **let's go swimming in the lake ~ we used to** lass uns im See schwimmen gehen wie früher ❷ (*as if*) als ob; **she acts ~ she's the boss** sie tut so, als sei sie die Chefin

likeable ['laɪ·kə·bəl] *adj see* likable

likelihood ['laɪk·li·hʊd] *n* Wahrscheinlichkeit *f*

likely ['laɪk·li] I. *adj* <-ier, -iest *or* more ~, most ~> wahrscheinlich; **please remind me, because I'm ~ to forget** erinnere mich bitte unbedingt daran, sonst vergesse ich es wahrscheinlich II. *adv* <more ~, most ~> **very ~** sehr wahrscheinlich

like-'minded *adj* gleich gesinnt

likewise ['laɪk·waɪz] *adv* ebenfalls, gleichfalls; **to do ~** es genauso machen

liking ['laɪ·kɪŋ] *n* Vorliebe *f*; **to develop a ~ for sth** eine Vorliebe für etw *akk* entwickeln

lilac ['laɪ·læk] I. *n* ❶ (*bush*) Flieder *m* ❷ (*color*) Lila *nt* II. *adj* lila

lilt [lɪlt] *n of voice* singender Tonfall

lily ['lɪl·i] *n* Lilie *f*

limb [lɪm] *n* ANAT Glied *nt* ▶PHRASES: **to risk life and ~** [to do sth] Kopf und Kragen riskieren[, um etw zu tun] *fam*

limber ['lɪm·bər] I. *adj* <-er, -est *or* more ~, most ~> (*supple*) geschmeidig ❷ (*flexible*) gelenkig II. *vi* ▪to **~ up** sich warm machen

limbo¹ ['lɪm·boʊ] *n* **to be in ~** *plan* in der Schwebe sein; *person* in der Luft hängen *fam*

limbo² ['lɪm·boʊ] *n* (*dance*) Limbo

lime[1] [laɪm] n (fruit) Limette f

lime[2] [laɪm] n Kalk m

'limelight n Rampenlicht nt; **to be in the ~** im Rampenlicht stehen

'limestone n Kalkstein m

limit ['lɪm·ɪt] **I.** n ❶ (utmost) [Höchst]grenze f; (boundary) Grenze f ❷ of person Grenze[n] f(pl); **to reach one's ~** an seine Grenze[n] kommen ❸ (restriction) Beschränkung f; of blood alcohol Promillegrenze f; **speed ~** [zulässige] Höchstgeschwindigkeit f ▶PHRASES: **to be off ~s** [to sb] [für jdn] gesperrt sein **II.** vt einschränken

limitation [ˌlɪm·ɪ·'teɪ·ʃən] n Begrenzung f

limited ['lɪm·ɪ·t̬ɪd] adj begrenzt (**to** auf +akk)

limited lia'bility company n ≈ Gesellschaft f mit beschränkter Haftung

limitless ['lɪm·ɪt̬·lɪs] adj grenzenlos

limousine ['lɪm·ə·zin] n [Luxus]limousine f

limp [lɪmp] **I.** vi hinken; (fig) mit Müh und Not vorankommen **II.** n Hinken nt **III.** adj ❶ (not stiff) schlaff; cloth weich ❷ (weak) schlapp; handshake lasch

limpid ['lɪm·pɪd] adj eyes, water klar

linchpin ['lɪntʃ·pɪn] n (essential element) Stütze f

linden ['lɪn·dən] n Linde f

line[1] [laɪn] **I.** n ❶ (mark, contour) Linie f; **dividing ~** Trennungslinie f ❷ (wrinkle) Falte f ❸ (boundary) Grenze f ❹ TELEC [Telefon]leitung f; (connection) Anschluss m; **please hold the ~!** bitte bleiben Sie am Apparat! ❺ (of words, poem) Zeile f ❻ (row) Reihe f ❼ (people waiting) Schlange f; **to be first in ~** an erster Stelle stehen; (fig) ganz vorne dabei sein ▶PHRASES: **right down the ~** voll und ganz; **to be out of ~** behavior aus dem Rahmen fallen; person sich danebenbenehmen **II.** vt (make rows) **to ~ the streets** die Straßen säumen geh

◆ **line up I.** vt ❶ (put in row) ■**to ~ up ○ sth** etw in einer Reihe aufstellen ❷ (organize) **do you have anyone ~d up to do the catering?** haben Sie jemanden für das Catering engagiert? **II.** vi sich [in einer Reihe] aufstellen; MIL, SPORT antreten

line[2] [laɪn] vt clothing füttern; drawers von innen auslegen

linear ['lɪn·i·ər] adj ❶ (of line) Linien- ❷ (of length) Längen-

linen ['lɪn·ɪn] n Leinen nt; **bed ~** Bettwäsche f

liner[1] ['laɪ·nər] n NAUT Liniendampfer m

liner[2] ['laɪ·nər] n (lining) Einsatz m

'linesman n SPORT Linienrichter m

'lineup n SPORT [Mannschafts]aufstellung f; (in baseball) Lineup f fachspr

linger ['lɪŋ·gər] vi anhalten; **the smell ~ed in the kitchen for days** der Geruch hing tagelang in der Küche

lingerie [ˌlɑn·ʒə·'reɪ] n [Damen]unterwäsche f

lingering ['lɪŋ·gər·ɪŋ] adj attr ❶ (lasting) verbleibend; fears [fort]bestehend; regrets nachhaltig ❷ ausgedehnt; death schleichend; illness langwierig **L**

lingo <pl -s> ['lɪŋ·goʊ] n (esp hum fam) ❶ (language) Sprache f ❷ (jargon) Jargon m

linguist ['lɪŋ·gwɪst] n Linguist(in) m(f)

linguistics [lɪŋ·'gwɪs·tɪks] n + sing vb die Sprachwissenschaft

lining ['laɪ·nɪŋ] n ❶ (fabric) Futter nt ❷ of stomach Magenschleimhaut f; of brake Bremsbelag m

link [lɪŋk] **I.** n ❶ (connection) Verbindung f ❷ INET, COMPUT Link m fachspr ❸ of chain [Ketten]glied nt **II.** vt verbinden

'linkup n Verbindung f

linoleum [lɪ·'noʊ·li·əm] n Linoleum nt

linseed ['lɪn·sid] n Leinsamen m

'linseed oil n Leinöl nt

lint [lɪnt] n MED Mull m

lion ['laɪ·ən] n ❶ Löwe m ❷ ASTROL Löwe m

lioness <pl -es> ['laɪ·ə·nes] n Löwin f

lip [lɪp] n ❶ Lippe f ❷ of pitcher Schnabel m

'lip balm n Lippenpflege f

'lip-gloss n Lipgloss m

liposuction ['lɪp·oʊ·ˌsʌk·ʃən] n Fettabsaugen nt

'lip-read <-read, -read> vi von den Lippen ablesen

'lip service n (pej) Lippenbekenntnis nt; **to pay ~ to sth** ein Lippenbekenntnis zu etw ablegen

'lipstick n Lippenstift m

liquefy <-ie-> ['lɪk·wə·faɪ] vt, vi [sich] verflüssigen

liqueur [lɪˈkɜr] n Likör m

liquid ['lɪk·wɪd] I. adj ❶ (watery) flüssig; **~ soap** Seifenlotion f ❷ FIN [frei] verfügbar II. n Flüssigkeit f

liquidate ['lɪk·wɪ·deɪt] vt ❶ ECON, FIN company auflösen; assets verfügbar machen ❷ (kill) liquidieren geh

liquidation [ˌlɪk·wɪ·ˈdeɪ·ʃən] n ❶ FIN of company Auflösung f; **to go into ~** in Liquidation gehen ❷ (killing) Liquidierung f geh

liquidize ['lɪk·wɪ·daɪz] vt food pürieren

liquify ['lɪk·wə·faɪ] vt, vi see **liquefy**

liquor ['lɪk·ər] n Alkohol m; **hard ~** Schnaps m

'liquor store n Wein- und Spirituosengeschäft nt

lisp [lɪsp] vt, vi lispeln

list [lɪst] I. n Liste f; **~ of names** Namensliste f; (in books) Namensverzeichnis nt; **shopping ~** Einkaufszettel m II. vt auflisten

listen ['lɪs·ən] vi ❶ (hear) zuhören; ■ **to ~ to sb** jdm zuhören; **~ to this!** hör dir das an! fam; **to ~ to the radio** Radio hören ❷ (heed) hören; **don't ~ to them** hör nicht auf sie

◆ **listen in** vi (secretly) mithören; (without participating) mitanhören

listener ['lɪs·nər] n Zuhörer(in) m(f)

listing ['lɪs·tɪŋ] n ❶ (list) Auflistung f ❷ (entry in list) Eintrag m ❸ (program) **television ~s** Fernsehprogramm nt

listless ['lɪst·lɪs] adj ❶ (unenergetic) person teilnahmslos ❷ (unenthusiastic) lustlos

lit [lɪt] vt, vi pt, pp of **light**

liter ['li·tər] n Liter m o nt; **two ~s** [of milk] zwei Liter [Milch]

literacy ['lɪt·ər·ə·si] n Lese- und Schreibfähigkeit f

literal ['lɪt·ər·əl] adj ❶ (word-for-word) wörtlich; **~ meaning** eigentliche Bedeutung ❷ (unexaggerated) buchstäblich

literally ['lɪt·ər·ə·li] adv ❶ (word-for-word) [wort]wörtlich ❷ (actually) buchstäblich

literary ['lɪt·ə·rer·i] adj attr criticism Literatur-; language literarisch; **~ career** Schriftstellerkarriere f

literate ['lɪt·ər·ɪt] adj ❶ (able to read and write) ■ **to be ~** lesen und schreiben können ❷ **to be computer·~** sich mit Computern auskennen

literature ['lɪt·ər·ə·tʃər] n ❶ (works) Literatur f ❷ (printed matter) Informationsmaterial nt

lithe [laɪð] adj geschmeidig

lithium ['lɪθ·i·əm] n Lithium nt

lithography [lɪ·ˈθɑg·rə·fi] n Lithographie f

litigant ['lɪt·ɪ·gənt] n LAW prozessführende Partei

litigation [ˌlɪt·ɪ·ˈgeɪ·ʃən] n LAW Prozess m

litigious [lɪ·ˈtɪdʒ·əs] adj LAW prozessfreudig iron

litmus ['lɪt·məs] n Lackmus m o nt

'litmus paper n Lackmuspapier nt

'litmus test n (fig: indication) entscheidendes [An]zeichen

litter ['lɪt·ər] I. n ❶ (trash) Müll m ❷ ZOOL Wurf m II. vt ❶ (make untidy) **dirty clothes ~ed the floor** dreckige Wäsche lag über den Boden verstreut ❷ usu passive (fig: fill) ■ **to be ~ed with sth** mit etw dat übersät sein

'litter box n Katzenklo nt

'litterbug n (fam) Umweltverschmutzer(in) m(f)

little ['lɪt·əl] I. adj ❶ (small, young) klein; (for emphasis) richtige(r, s), kleine(r, s) ❷ attr distance kurz II. adv ❶ (somewhat) ■ **a ~** ein wenig ❷ (hardly) wenig; **[a] ~ more than an**

hour ago vor kaum einer Stunde III. *pron sing* ❶ (*small quantity*) ∎ **a ~** ein wenig (**of** von +*dat*) ❷ (*not much*) wenig; **as ~ as possible** möglichst wenig ❸ (*short time*) **it's a ~ after six** es ist kurz nach sechs ▶ PHRASES: **precious ~** herzlich wenig

live¹ [laɪv] I. *vi* ❶ (*be alive, spend life*) leben; **will she ~?** wird sie überleben? ❷ (*reside*) wohnen; **where do you ~?** wo wohnst du? ▶ PHRASES: **you'll ~ to regret that!** das wirst du noch bereuen! II. *vt* to ~ one's own life sein eigenes Leben leben ▶ PHRASES: **to ~ a lie** mit einer Lebenslüge leben

◆**live down** *vt* ∎ **to ~ down ○ sth** über etw *akk* hinwegkommen

◆**live for** *vi* ∎ **to ~ for sth** für etw *akk* leben ▶ PHRASES: **to ~ for the moment** ein sorgloses Leben führen

◆**live off, live off of** *vi* (*depend on*) ∎ **to ~ off sb** auf jds Kosten leben

◆**live on** *vi* ❶ (*continue*) weiterleben; *tradition* fortbestehen; **~ in memory** in Erinnerung bleiben ❷ (*support oneself*) ∎ **to ~ on sth** von etw *dat* leben

◆**live out** *vt* to ~ out ○ one's **dreams** seine [Wunsch]träume verwirklichen

◆**live through** *vi* überstehen

◆**live together** *vi* zusammenleben

◆**live up** *vt* to ~ **it up** (*fam*) die Puppen tanzen lassen *fam*

◆**live up to** *vi* to ~ up to sb's expectations jds Erwartungen gerecht werden

◆**live with** *vi* ❶ (*cohabit*) zusammenleben ❷ (*tolerate*) sich abfinden mit +*dat*

live² [laɪv] I. *adj* ❶ *attr* (*living*) lebend ❷ MUS, RADIO, TV live ❸ ELEC geladen; **~ wire** Hochspannungskabel *nt* II. *adv* MUS, RADIO, TV live

livelihood ['laɪv·li·hʊd] *n* Lebensunterhalt *m;* **to lose one's ~** seine Existenzgrundlage verlieren

liveliness ['laɪv·li·nɪs] *n of story* Lebendigkeit *f; of person* Lebhaftigkeit *f*

lively ['laɪv·li] *adj* ❶ (*energetic*) lebhaft; *child, eyes* munter; *nature* aufgeweckt ❷ (*bright*) *colors* hell ❸ (*brisk*) rege; *pace* flott

liven ['laɪ·vən] I. *vt* ∎ **to ~ up ○ sth** Leben in etw *akk* bringen; ∎ **to ~ up ○ sb** jdn aufmuntern II. *vi* ∎ **to ~ up** *person* aufleben; *party* in Schwung kommen

liver ['lɪv·ər] *n* Leber *f*

'**liver damage** *n* Leberschaden *m*

'**liverwurst** *n* Leberwurst *f*

'**livestock** *n* Vieh *nt,* Viehbestand *m*

live wire *n* ❶ ELEC unter Strom stehende Leitung ❷ (*fig fam*) Feger *m*

livid ['lɪv·ɪd] *adj* (*fam*) wütend

living ['lɪv·ɪŋ] I. *n* ❶ *usu sing* (*livelihood*) Lebensunterhalt *m* ❷ (*lifestyle*) Lebensstil *m;* **standard of ~** Lebensstandard *m* ❸ *pl* ∎ **the ~** die Lebenden *pl* II. *adj* ❶ (*alive*) lebend *attr;* **~ creatures** Lebewesen *pl* ❷ (*in use*) lebendig; *language* lebend ▶ PHRASES: **to scare the ~ daylights out of sb** jdn zu Tode erschrecken

'**living conditions** *n* Lebensbedingungen *pl*

'**living room** *n* Wohnzimmer *nt*

living 'will *n* LAW Willenserklärung eines Patienten, die seine medizinische Behandlung festlegt

lizard ['lɪz·ərd] *n* Eidechse *f*

load [loʊd] I. *n* ❶ (*amount carried*) Ladung *f* ❷ (*burden*) Last *f* ❸ (*fam: lots*) **a ~ of work** ein Riesenberg *m* an Arbeit ▶ PHRASES: **get a ~ of this!** (*fam*) hör dir das an! II. *adv* ∎ **~s** *pl* (*fam*) tausendmal *fam* III. *vt* ❶ (*fill*) laden; *container* beladen; *washing machine* füllen ❷ (*fig: burden*) aufladen; **to ~ sb with responsibility** jdm sehr viel Verantwortung aufladen ❸ (*insert*) DVD einlegen

◆**load down** *vt thing* schwer beladen

◆**load up** I. *vt* aufladen; **to ~ up ○ a container** einen Container beladen II. *vi* beladen

loaded ['loʊ·dɪd] *adj* ❶ (*carrying load*) beladen ❷ *gun* geladen ❸ (*excessive*) überladen (**with** mit +*dat*) ❹ *pred*

L

(*fam: rich*) steinreich ⑤ *pred* (*fam: drunk*) besoffen *fam*

'loading dock *n* Laderampe *f*

loaf¹ [loʊf] *n* <*pl* loaves> [loʊf] *n* (*bread*) Brot *nt;* (*unsliced a.*) Brotlaib *m*

loaf² [loʊf] *vi* faulenzen; **to ~ around** herumgammeln *fam*

loafer ['loʊ·fər] *n* Faulenzer(in) *m(f) pej*

Loafer® ['loʊ·fər] *n* FASHION [leichter] Halbschuh

loan [loʊn] I. *n* ①(*money*) Kredit *m* ②**to be on ~** verliehen sein II. *vt* leihen

'loanword *n* Lehnwort *nt*

loath [loʊθ] *adj pred* ■**to be ~ to do sth** etw ungern tun

loathe [loʊð] *vt thing* nicht ausstehen können; *person* verabscheuen

loathing ['loʊ·ðɪŋ] *n* (*hate*) Abscheu *m*

loathsome ['loʊð·səm] *adj* abscheulich

loaves [loʊvz] *n pl of* **loaf**

lob [lɑb] I. *vt* <-bb-> lobben II. *n* ①(*stroke*) Lobspiel *nt kein pl* ②(*ball*) Lob *m*

lobby ['lɑb·i] I. *n* ①ARCHIT Eingangshalle *f;* *hotel* ~ Hotelfoyer *nt* ②POL Lobby *f* II. *vi* <-ie-> ■**to ~ for sth** [mittels eines Interessenverbandes] für etw geltend machen

lobe [loʊb] *n* Lappen *m; of ear* Ohrläppchen *nt*

lobster ['lɑb·stər] *n* Hummer *m*

local ['loʊ·kəl] I. *adj* ①(*neighborhood*) hiesig, örtlich; ~ **radio station** Lokalsender *m;* ~ **bar** Stammkneipe *f* ②MED lokal II. *n* ①*usu pl* (*inhabitant*) Ortsansässige(r) *f(m)* ②(*trade union*) örtliches Gewerkschaftsbüro

local anes'thetic *n* örtliche Betäubung

'local call *n* Ortsgespräch *nt*

local 'government *n* *of city* Stadtverwaltung *f; of community* Kommunalverwaltung *f*

locality [loʊ·kæl·ɪ·ti] *n* Gegend *f*

localize ['loʊ·kə·laɪz] *vt* ①*government* dezentralisieren ②(*pinpoint*) lokalisieren *geh*

local 'newspaper *n* Lokalblatt *nt*

'local time *n* Ortszeit *f*

locate [loʊ·keɪt] I. *vt* ①(*find*) ausfindig machen; *sunken ship* orten ②(*situate*) bauen; **to be centrally ~d** zentral liegen II. *vi* sich niederlassen

location [loʊ·keɪ·ʃən] *n* ①(*place*) Lage *f* ②FILM Drehort *m* ③(*act*) Positionsbestimmung *f*

lock [lɑk] I. *n* ①(*fastener*) Schloss *nt* ②NAUT Schleuse *f* ▶PHRASES: **to be under ~ and key** hinter Schloss und Riegel sitzen *fam* II. *vt* abschließen; *suitcase* verschließen III. *vi* ①(*become secured*) schließen ②(*become fixed*) binden

◆**lock away** *vt* ①(*secure*) wegschließen ②(*imprison*) einsperren *fam*

◆**lock on** *vi* MIL **to ~ on to a target** ein genaues Ziel ausmachen

◆**lock up** I. *vt* ①(*shut, secure*) abschließen; *money* wegschließen ②(*put in custody*) ■**to ~ up** ○ **sb** LAW jdn einsperren *fam,* jdn einlochen *sl* II. *vi* abschließen

locker ['lɑk·ər] *n* Schließfach *nt;* MIL, SCH, SPORT Spind *m*

'locker room *n* Umkleideraum [mit Schließfächern] *m*

locket ['lɑk·ɪt] *n* Medaillon *nt*

'lockout *n* Aussperrung *f*

'locksmith *n* Schlosser(in) *m(f)*

'lockup *n* Gefängnis *nt;* (*for drunks*) Ausnüchterungszelle *f*

locomotive [ˌloʊ·kə·ˈmoʊ·tɪv] *n* Lokomotive *f*

lode [loʊd] *n* MIN Ader *f a. fig*

lodge [lɑdʒ] I. *n* ①(*house*) Hütte *f* ②(*in resort*) Lodge *f* II. *vt* ①(*submit*) *complaint* einlegen; *protest* erheben ②(*fix*) hineintun III. *vi* stecken bleiben

lodger ['lɑdʒ·ər] *n* Untermieter(in) *m(f)*

lodging ['lɑdʒ·ɪŋ] *n* Unterkunft *f*

loft [lɑft] *n* (*attic*) Speicher *m;* (*for living*) Dachwohnung *f,* Loft *m*

lofty ['lɑf·ti] *adj* ①(*high*) hoch [aufragend] ②(*noble*) erhaben; *ambitions* hochfliegend; *ideals* hohe(r, s)

log [lɒg] I. *n* ①(*branch*) [gefällter]

Baumstamm; (*firewood*) [Holz]scheit *nt* ❷ (*systematic record*) Aufzeichnungen *pl* II. *vt* <-gg-> ❶ (*enter into record*) aufzeichnen; *phone calls* registrieren ❷ *trees* fällen III. *vi* <-gg-> Bäume fällen

◆ **log in** *vi* sich einloggen
◆ **log off** *vi* sich ausloggen
◆ **log on** *vi* sich einloggen (**to** in +*akk*)
◆ **log out** *vi* sich ausloggen (**of** aus +*dat*)

loganberry ['loʊ·gən·berˌi] *n* Logan-beere *f*

'**logbook** *n* NAUT Logbuch *nt*; AVIAT Bord-buch *nt*

log '**cabin** *n* Blockhaus *nt*

logger ['lɔ·gər] *n* Holzfäller(in) *m(f)*

logic ['lɑdʒ·ɪk] *n* Logik *f*

logical ['lɑdʒ·ɪ·kəl] *adj* ❶ logisch ❷ (*sensible*) vernünftig

logistics [loʊ·'dʒɪs·tɪks] *n* + *sing/pl vb* Logistik *f*

'**logjam** *n* ❶ (*logs*) Anstauung *f* von Floßholz ❷ (*deadlock*) toter Punkt; **to break a ~** wieder aus einer Sackgasse herauskommen

logo ['loʊ·goʊ] *n* Logo *m o nt*

'**logrolling** *n* POL (*fam*) Kuhhandel *m*

loiter ['lɔɪ·tər] *vi* ❶ (*idle*) **to ~** [around] herumhängen *fam* ❷ (*dawdle*) [he-rum]trödeln

loll [lɑl] *vi* (*idle*) lümmeln; (*sit*) faul da-sitzen

lollipop ['lɑl·iˌpɑp] *n* Lutscher *m*

lone [loʊn] *adj attr* einsam

loneliness ['loʊn·lɪ·nɪs] *n* Einsamkeit *f*

lonely <-ier, -iest *or* more ~, most ~> ['loʊn·li] *adj* ❶ (*alone*) einsam ❷ (*un-frequented*) abgeschieden; *street* still

loner ['loʊ·nər] *n* Einzelgänger(in) *m(f)*

lonesome ['loʊn·səm] *adj* ❶ (*alone*) einsam ❷ (*unfrequented*) abgelegen

long¹ [lɔŋ] I. *adj* ❶ (*in space*) lang; *dis-tance* weit; (*fig*) **to have come a ~ way** von weit her gekommen sein ❷ (*in time*) lang; (*tedious*) lang[wierig]; **a ~ day** ein langer [und anstrengender] Tag; *friendship* langjährig; *memory* gut; **to work ~ hours** einen langen Ar-

beitstag haben ▸PHRASES: **in the ~ run** auf lange Sicht [gesehen] II. *adv* ❶ (*for a long time*) lang[e]; **I won't be ~** (*be-fore finishing*) ich bin gleich fertig; (*be-fore appearing*) ich bin gleich da ❷ (*at a distant time*) lange; **~ ago** vor langer Zeit ❸ (*after implied time*) lange; **how much ~er will it take?** wie lange wird es noch dauern? ▸PHRASES: **as ~ as ...** (*during*) solange ...; (*provided that*) vorausgesetzt, dass ... III. *n* ▸PHRASES: **before** [**very**] **~** schon [sehr] bald

long² [lɔŋ] *vi* sich sehnen (**for** nach +*dat*); ■ **to ~ to do sth** sich danach sehnen, etw zu tun

long³ *n* GEOG *abbrev of* **longitude** Län-ge *f*

long-'distance I. *adj attr* (*between places*) Fern-, Weit-; **~ flight** Langstre-ckenflug *m* II. *adv* **to call ~** ein Fernge-spräch führen

'**long-haired** <longer-, longest-> *adj* langhaarig; *animals* Langhaar-

'**longhand** *n* Langschrift *f*; **to write sth in ~** etw mit der Hand schreiben

long 'haul *n* ❶ (*long distance*) Lang-streckentransport *m* ❷ (*long time*) **over the ~** auf lange Sicht

long-'haul *adj* **~ flight** Langstrecken-flug *m*

'**longhorn** *n* (*breed of cattle*) Long-horn *nt*

longing ['lɔŋ·ɪŋ] *n* Sehnsucht *f*

longish ['lɔŋ·ɪʃ] *adj* (*fam*) ziemlich lang

longitude ['lɑn·dʒɪ·tud] *n* GEOG Länge *f*

'**long johns** *npl* (*fam*) lange Unterhose *f*

'**long jump** *n* SPORT Weitsprung *m*

'**long-lasting** *adj* strapazierfähig

'**long-life** *adj batteries* langlebig

'**long-lost** *adj attr* lang verloren ge-glaubt; *person* lang vermisst geglaubt

long-range *adj* Langstrecken-

'**long shot** *n usu sing* ■ **to be a ~** ziem-lich aussichtslos sein

long-'standing *adj* seit langem beste-hend; *friendship, relationship* langjäh-rig

long-'suffering *adj* langmütig

'**long-term** *adj attr* langfristig; ~ **strat-egy** Langzeitstrategie *f*

long-'winded *adj* langatmig

loofa, loofah ['luˈfə] *n* Luffa-schwamm *m*

look [lʊk] I. *n* ❶ (*glance*) Blick *m;* **to get a good ~ at sb/sth** jdn/etw genau sehen können; **to have** [*or* **take**] **a ~ around** [**for sth**] sich [nach etw *dat*] umsehen ❷ (*on face*) [Gesichts]aus-druck *m* ❸ (*examination*) Betrach-tung *f;* (*search*) **to have** [*or* **take**] **a ~ around for sth** nach jdm/etw su-chen ❹ (*appearance*) Aussehen *nt* ►PHRASES: **if ~s could kill** wenn Blicke töten könnten II. *interj* (*explanatory*) pass mal auf *fam;* (*protesting*) hör mal *fam* III. *vi* ❶ (*glance*) schauen; **to ~ away** wegsehen ❷ (*search*) suchen; (*in an encyclopedia*) nachschlagen ❸ (*ap-pear*) **she doesn't ~ her age** man sieht ihr ihr Alter nicht an; **to ~ tired** müde aussehen; ■**to ~ like sb** jdm ähnlich sehen ❹ (*face*) blicken (**onto** auf +*akk*); *window* [hinaus]gehen (**onto** auf +*akk*)

◆**look after** *vi* (*care for*) ■**to ~ after sb** sich um jdn kümmern; (*keep eye on*) ■**to ~ after sb/sth** auf jdn/etw aufpassen

◆**look ahead** *vi* (*fig: plan*) voraus-schauen

◆**look around** *vi* ❶ (*glance*) sich um-sehen ❷ (*search*) ■**to ~ around for sth** sich nach etw umsehen

◆**look at** *vi* ❶ (*glance*) ansehen ❷ (*ex-amine*) ■**to ~ at sth/sb** sich *dat* etw/ jdn ansehen ❸ (*regard*) ■**to ~ at sth** etw betrachten

◆**look back** *vi* ❶ (*glance*) zurück-schauen ❷ (*remember*) zurückblicken (**on/over/at** auf +*akk*) ►PHRASES: **sb never ~ed back** für jdn ging es bergauf

◆**look down** *vi* ❶ (*glance*) nach unten sehen; ■**to ~ down at/on sb/sth** zu jdm/etw hinuntersehen ❷ (*examine*) **to ~ down a list** eine Liste von oben bis unten durchgehen

◆**look for** *vi* (*seek*) ■**to ~ for sb** nach jdm suchen; **to ~ for a job** Arbeit su-chen

◆**look forward** *vi* ❶ (*glance*) nach vorne sehen ❷ (*anticipate*) sich freuen (**to** auf +*akk*)

◆**look in** *vi* ❶ (*glance*) hineinsehen ❷ (*visit*) ■**to ~ in** [**on sb**] [bei jdm] vor-beischauen *fam*

◆**look into** *vi* ■**to ~ into sth** ❶ (*glance*) in etw *akk* [hinein]sehen ❷ (*examine*) etw untersuchen; **to ~ into a complaint** eine Beschwerde prü-fen

◆**look on** *vi* zusehen

◆**look out** *vi* ❶ (*take care*) aufpassen ❷ (*watch*) Ausschau halten (**for** nach +*dat*) ❸ (*face*) blicken (**onto/over** auf +*akk*); *window* hinausgehen (**onto/ over** auf +*akk*)

◆**look over** I. *vi* ❶ (*glance*) blicken über +*akk*; ■**to ~ over to sb** zu jdm hi-nübersehen ❷ (*offer view*) blicken über +*akk*; *room* [hinaus]gehen auf +*akk* II. *vt* ❶ (*view*) besichtigen ❷ (*examine*) *letter* überfliegen

◆**look through** *vi* ❶ (*glance*) ■**to ~ through sth** durch etw *akk* [hin-durch]sehen ❷ (*peruse*) durchsehen; *magazine* durchblättern

◆**look to** *vi* (*anticipate*) **to ~ to the fu-ture** in die Zukunft blicken

◆**look toward(s)** *vi* ❶ (*glance*) ■**to ~ toward sth/sb** zu etw/jdm sehen ❷ (*face*) ■**to ~ toward sth** auf etw *akk* blicken; *window* auf etw *akk* [hi-naus]gehen

◆**look up** I. *vi* ❶ (*glance*) ■**to ~ up at sb/sth** zu jdm/etw hinaufsehen ❷ (*im-prove*) besser werden II. *vt* ❶ (*fam: visit*) ■**to ~ up** ᴑ **sb** bei jdm vorbei-schauen ❷ (*search for*) nachschlagen

◆**look upon** *vi see* **look on**

◆**look up to** *vi* ■**to ~ up to sb** zu jdm aufsehen

'**lookalike** *n* Doppelgänger(in) *m(f)*

'**lookout** *n* ❶ (*person*) Wache *f* ❷ (*watch*) **to keep a ~** [**for sb**] [nach jdm] Ausschau halten

loom[1] [lum] *vi* ❶ (*come into view*) [drohend] auftauchen ②(be ominously near) sich drohend abzeichnen; storm sich zusammenbrauen a. fig

loom² [lum] n Webstuhl m

loony ['lu·ni] n (fam) Irre(r) f(m)

loop [lup] I. n ①(shape) Schleife f; of string Schlinge f; of belt Schlaufen pl ②COMPUT [Programm]schleife f ③(contraceptive) Spirale f II. vi eine Schleife machen; road sich schlängeln

'**loophole** n LAW Gesetzeslücke f

loose [lus] adj ①(relaxed, not tight) locker; papers los; skin schlaff; ~ cash/coins Kleingeld nt; to come ~ sich lösen ②hair offen ③(not confined) frei ④(not exact) ungefähr attr; (not strict) lose; translation frei ⑤clothing weit, locker ▶PHRASES: to **hang** ~ (fam) cool bleiben

'**loose-leaf** adj attr ~ **binder** Ringbuch nt

loosely ['lus·li] adv ①(not tightly) lose; to **hang** ~ schlaff herunterhängen ②(not exactly) ungefähr; ~ **speaking** grob gesagt

loosen ['lu·sən] I. vt ①collar aufmachen; tie lockern ②(relax) muscles lockern ▶PHRASES: to ~ **sb's tongue** jdm die Zunge lösen II. vi sich lockern

loot [lut] I. n ①(plunder) [Diebes]beute f ②(fam: money) Zaster m II. vt ①(plunder) [aus]plündern ②(steal) stehlen III. vi plündern

looting ['lu·t̬ɪŋ] n Plünderei f

lop [lap] vt <-pp-> streichen; budget kürzen

◆**lop off** vt ①branches abhacken ②(reduce) expenses [ver]kürzen

lope [loʊp] vi in großen Sätzen springen; hare hoppeln

'**lopsided** adj schief

lord [lɔrd] n ①(nobleman) Lord m ②(fam: powerful man) Herr m

Lord [lɔrd] n REL ■**the ~** der Herr

lose <lost, lost> [luz] I. vt ①(forfeit) verlieren; ■**to ~ sth to sb** etw an jdn verlieren; **to ~ one's breath** außer Atem kommen ②(through death) **she lost her son in the fire** ihr Sohn ist

beim Brand umgekommen ③usu passive ■**to be lost** things verschwunden sein; victims umgekommen sein; plane, ship verloren sein ④(waste) opportunity versäumen; time verlieren ▶watch to ~ **time** nachgehen ⑥(not find) verlieren; (mislay) verlegen; **to ~ one's way** sich verirren ⑥(not win) verlieren ▶PHRASES: to ~ **heart** den Mut verlieren; to ~ **it** (fam) durchdrehen; **to ~ touch [with sb]** den Kontakt [zu jdm] verlieren II. vi (be beaten) verlieren (to gegen +akk) ▶PHRASES: **you can't** ~ du kannst nur gewinnen

◆**lose out** vi ①(be deprived) schlecht wegkommen fam ②(be beaten) ■**to ~ out to sb/sth** jdm/etw unterliegen

loser ['lu·zər] n ①(defeated person) Verlierer(in) m(f) ②(fam: habitually) Verlierer[typ] m

loss <pl -es> [lɔs] n Verlust m ▶PHRASES: to **be at a ~** nicht mehr weiterwissen

lost [lɔst] I. pt, pp of lose II. adj ①(unable to find way) **to get ~** sich verirren; (on foot) sich verlaufen haben; (using vehicle) sich verfahren haben ②(misplaced) **to get ~ [in the mail]** [in der Post] verschwinden ③pred (helpless) **to feel ~** sich verloren fühlen; ■**to be ~** (not understand) nichts verstehen ④soldiers gefallen; planes, ships zerstört ⑤(not won) battle, contest verloren ▶PHRASES: **get ~!** (fam) hau ab!, zieh Leine! sl

lost and 'found n Fundbüro nt

lot [lat] I. pron ①(much, many) ■**a ~** viel/viele; **a ~ of people** viele [o eine Menge] Leute ②(many things) ■**~s [of sth]** + sing/pl vb viel [o fam jede Menge] [etw]; **there's ~s to do here** es gibt hier jede Menge zu tun fam ③(everything) ■**the [whole] ~** alles II. adv (fam) ■**a ~** viel; **thanks a ~!** vielen Dank! III. n ①(land) Stück nt Land; **parking ~** Parkplatz m ②(movie studio) Filmgelände

loth [loʊθ] adj see loath

lotion ['loʊ·ʃən] n Lotion f

lottery ['lɑt̬·ə·ri] n Lotterie f

'lotus position n Lotossitz m

loud [laʊd] **I.** adj ❶ (audible) laut ❷ (garish) auffällig; colors grell, schreiend **II.** adv laut; **to laugh out ~** lauthals loslachen

'loudmouth n (fam) Großmaul nt

loudness ['laʊd·nɪs] n Lautstärke f

'loudspeaker n Lautsprecher m

Louisiana [lu·ˌi·zi·'æn·ə] n Louisiana nt

lounge [laʊndʒ] **I.** n Lounge f; **departure ~** Abflughalle f **II.** vi (lie) [faul] herumliegen; (sit) [faul] herumsitzen
◆**lounge around** vi (lie) [faul] herumliegen; (sit) [faul] herumsitzen

'lounge chair n Klubsessel m

louse I. n [laʊs] ❶ <pl lice> (parasite) Laus f ❷ <pl -s> (fam: person) miese Type pej **II.** vt [laʊz] (fam) ■**to ~ up** ⟳ **sth** etw vermasseln

lousy ['laʊ·zi] adj ❶ (fam: bad) lausig; **I'm ~ at math** in Mathe bin ich eine absolute Null ❷ pred (fam: ill) **to feel ~** sich hundeelend [o mies] fühlen ❸ (inadequate) armselig; **a ~ 20 dollars** lumpige 20 Dollar

louver ['lu·vər] n Jalousie f; (slat) Lamelle f [einer Jalousie]

lovable ['lʌv·ə·bəl] adj liebenswert

love [lʌv] **I.** n ❶ (affection) Liebe f; **to be in ~** verliebt sein; **to fall in ~ with sb** sich in jdn verlieben ❷ (interest) Leidenschaft f; (with activities) Liebe f; **she has a great ~ of music** sie liebt die Musik sehr ❸ TENNIS null **II.** vt (be in love with) lieben; (greatly like) sehr mögen **III.** vi lieben; **I would ~ for you to come to dinner tonight** ich würde mich freuen, wenn du heute zum Abendessen kämst

'love affair n [Liebes]affäre f

love-'hate relationship n Hassliebe f

loveless ['lʌv·lɪs] adj childhood, marriage ohne Liebe nach n

'love letter n Liebesbrief m

'love life n Liebesleben nt kein pl

loveliness ['lʌv·lɪ·nɪs] n Schönheit f

lovely ['lʌv·li] adj ❶ (beautiful) schön; house wunderschön; **to look ~** reizend

aussehen ❷ (fam: pleasant) wunderbar, herrlich

lover ['lʌv·ər] n ❶ (partner) Liebhaber(in) m(f) ❷ (fan) Liebhaber(in) m(f) (**of** von +dat); **sports ~** Sportfan m

'love song n Liebeslied nt

'love story n Liebesgeschichte f

loving ['lʌv·ɪŋ] adj liebevoll

low [loʊ] **I.** adj ❶ (not high) niedrig; neckline, voice tief ❷ (in number) gering, wenig; blood pressure niedrig; **~ in calories** kalorienarm ❸ (depleted) knapp; stocks gering ❹ morale schlecht; quality minderwertig; self-esteem gering; **to have a ~ opinion of sb** von jdm nicht viel halten **II.** adv ❶ (in height) niedrig; **to be cut ~** dress tief ausgeschnitten sein ❷ (to low level, not high-pitched) tief; **turn the oven on ~** stell den Ofen auf kleine Hitze **III.** n ❶ (low level) Tiefpunkt m ❷ METEO Tief nt

low-'alcohol adj alkoholarm

'lowbrow adj (pej) book, film geistig anspruchslos, seicht

low-'cal ['loʊ·kæl] adj (fam), **low-'calorie** adj kalorienarm

'low-cost adj billig

'low-cut adj dress tief ausgeschnitten

'lowdown n (fam) ■**the ~** ausführliche Informationen

lower ['loʊ·ər] **I.** adj ❶ (less high) niedriger; (below) untere(r, s), Unter- ❷ status niedere(r, s), untere(r, s) **II.** vt ❶ (move down) herunterlassen; hem herauslassen; lifeboat zu Wasser lassen; **to ~ one's eyes** die Augen niederschlagen ❷ (decrease) verringern; voice senken; quality mindern; **to ~ one's sights** seine Ansprüche zurückschrauben **III.** vi sinken

lower 'house n Unterhaus nt

low-'fat adj fettarm

low-'key adj unauffällig; color gedämpft

lowland ['loʊ·lənd] n Flachland nt

'low-level adj ❶ (not high) tief ❷ (of low status) niedrig; official klein meist pej ❸ COMPUT niedere(r, s)

lowly ['loʊ·li] adj einfach; status niedrig

lowness ['lou·nɪs] n ① (in height) Niedrigkeit f; of neckline Tiefe f ② of note Tiefe f; of voice Gedämpftheit f

low-'pitched adj tief

low 'pressure n PHYS Niederdruck m; METEO Tiefdruck m

low 'profile n Zurückhaltung f; **to keep a ~** sich zurückhalten; (fig) im Hintergrund bleiben

low-'spirited adj niedergeschlagen

low-'tech adj [technisch] einfach, Lowtech-

low 'tide n Niedrigwasser nt; of sea Ebbe f

loyal ['lɔɪ·əl] adj treu (**to** + dat)

loyalty ['lɔɪ·əl·ti] n (faithfulness) Treue f

'loyalty card n Kundenkarte f

LSD [ˌel·es·'di] n abbrev of **lysergic acid diethylamide** LSD nt

lube [lub] (fam) I. n see **lubricant** II. vt see **lubricate**

lubricant ['lu·brɪ·kənt] n MED Gleitmittel nt; TECH Schmiermittel nt

lubricate ['lu·brɪ·keɪt] vt schmieren

lubrication [ˌlu·brɪ·'keɪ·ʃən] n Schmieren nt

lucid ['lu·sɪd] adj klar

luck [lʌk] I. n ① (fortune) Glück nt; **as ~ would have it** wie es der Zufall wollte; **just my ~!** Pech gehabt!; **to be out of ~** kein Glück haben ② (success) Erfolg m II. vi (fam) ▪ **to ~ into sth** etw durch Zufall ergattern

luckily ['lʌ·kɪ·li] adv glücklicherweise

lucky ['lʌk·i] adj ① (fortunate) glücklich ② (bringing fortune) glückbringend

lucrative ['lu·krə·tɪv] adj einträglich

ludicrous ['lu·dɪ·krəs] adj (ridiculous) lächerlich; (absurd) absurd

lug [lʌg] vt <-gg-> (carry) schleppen; (pull) zerren; ▪ **to ~ sth along** etw herumschleppen

luggage ['lʌg·ɪdʒ] n [Reise]gepäck nt; **piece of ~** Gepäckstück nt

'luggage rack n Gepäckablage f

lukewarm [ˌluk·'wɔrm] adj lau[warm]

lull [lʌl] vt ① (soothe) fears zerstreuen; **to ~ sb to sleep** jdn in den Schlaf lullen ② (trick) einlullen; **to ~ sb into a false**

sense of security jdn in trügerischer Sicherheit wiegen

lullaby ['lʌl·ə·baɪ] n Schlaflied nt

lumber[1] ['lʌm·bər] n (timber) Bauholz nt

lumber[2] ['lʌm·bər] vi person schwerfällig gehen; animal trotten; bear [behäbig] tapsen

lumberjack ['lʌm·bər·dʒæk] n Holzfäller(in) m(f)

'lumberyard n Holzlager nt

luminous ['lu·mə·nəs] adj ① (bright) leuchtend a. fig ② (phosphorescent) phosphoreszierend

lump [lʌmp] I. n ① (chunk) Klumpen m ② (swelling) Schwellung f; (in breast) Knoten m II. vt (combine) ▪ **to ~ sth with sth** etw mit etw dat zusammentun fam

lump 'sum n Einmalzahlung f

lumpy ['lʌm·pi] adj liquid klumpig; figure plump

lunacy ['lu·nə·si] n Wahnsinn m fam

lunar ['lu·nər] adj attr Mond-

lunatic ['lu·nə·tɪk] I. n ① Geistesgestörte(r) f(m) ② (fool) Verrückte(r) f(m) fam II. adj verrückt fam

lunch [lʌntʃ] n <pl -es> ① (noon meal) Mittagessen nt; **to have ~** zu Mittag essen ② (noon break) Mittagspause f ▶PHRASES: **to be out to ~** (hum fam) nicht ganz richtig im Kopf sein fam

'lunch break n Mittagspause f

'lunch hour n Mittagspause f

'lunchtime n (noon) Mittagszeit f; (break) Mittagspause f; **at ~** mittags

lung [lʌŋ] n Lungenflügel m; ▪ **the ~s** pl die Lunge[n pl]

'lung cancer n Lungenkrebs m

lunge [lʌndʒ] I. n Satz m nach vorn; (in fencing) Ausfall m II. vi ▪ **to ~ forward** einen Satz nach vorne machen

lupin(e) ['lu·pɪn] n Lupine f

lurch [lɜrtʃ] I. n <pl -es> Ruck m a. fig II. vi person torkeln; ship schlingern

lure [lʊr] I. vt [an]locken; ▪ **to ~ sb away from sth** jdn von etw dat weglocken II. n (attraction) Reiz m

lurid ['lʊr·ɪd] adj ① (glaring) grell

L

[leuchtend]; *colors* schreiend ❷ (*sensational*) reißerisch *pej; article* reißerisch aufgemacht *pej*

lurk [lɜrk] *vi* lauern *a. fig; (fig)* stecken (**behind** hinter +*dat*)

luscious ['lʌʃ·əs] *adj* ❶ (*sweet*) *taste, smell* [herrlich] süß; *fruit* saftig [süß] ❷ (*voluptuous*) *curves* üppig; *lips* voll

lush¹ [lʌʃ] *adj* ❶ *grass* saftig [grün]; *vegetation* üppig ❷ *décor* luxuriös

lush² [lʌʃ] *n* <*pl* -es> (*fam*) Säufer(in) *m(f) pej sl*

lust [lʌst] I. *n* ❶ (*sexual drive*) Lust *f* ❷ (*desire*) Begierde *f;* (*greed*) Gier *f* II. *vi* ■**to ~ after sth** gierig nach etw *dat* sein

luster ['lʌs·tər] *n* Glanz *m*

lusty ['lʌs·ti] *adj* (*strong and healthy*) *person* gesund [und munter]; *cry* laut

lute [lut] *n* Laute *f*

Lutheran ['lu·θər·ən] *n* REL Lutheraner(in) *m(f)*

luxuriant [lʌg·'ʒʊr·i·ənt] *adj* (*abundant*) üppig; *hair* voll

luxuriate [lʌg·'ʒʊr·i·eɪt] *vi* sich aalen

luxurious [lʌg·'ʒʊr·i·əs] *adj* luxuriös, Luxus-

luxury ['lʌk·ʃər·i] *n* ❶ (*self-indulgence*) Luxus *m* ❷ (*luxurious item*) Luxus[artikel] *m*

Lycra® ['laɪ·krə] *n* Lycra® *nt*

lye [laɪ] *n* Lauge *f*

lying¹ ['laɪ·ɪŋ] *vi* present participle of **lie**

lying² ['laɪ·ɪŋ] I. *adj attr* verlogen, lügnerisch II. *n* Lügen *nt*

'lymph gland, 'lymph node *n* Lymphknoten *m*

lynch [lɪntʃ] *vt* lynchen

lynchpin ['lɪntʃ·pɪn] *n see* **linchpin**

lynx <*pl* -es> [lɪŋks] *n* Luchs *m*

lyric ['lɪr·ɪk] *n* ■**~s** *pl* [Lied]text *m*

lyrical ['lɪr·ɪ·kəl] *adj* gefühlvoll, schwärmerisch

lyricist ['lɪr·ɪ·sɪst] *n* Texter(in) *m(f)*

M

Mm

M <*pl* -'s>, **m** <*pl* -'s> [em] *n* (*letter*) M *nt,* m *nt; ~* **as in Mike** M wie Martha

M [em] *n* <*pl* -> *abbrev of* **million** Mill., Mio.

m I. *n* <*pl* -> ❶ *abbrev of* **mile** ❷ *abbrev of* **meter** m ❸ *abbrev of* **minute** Min. II. *adj* ❶ *abbrev of* **male** männl. ❷ *abbrev of* **masculine** m ❸ *abbrev of* **married** verh.

MA [ˌem·'eɪ] *n* ❶ *abbrev of* **Master of Arts** ❷ *abbrev of* **Massachusetts**

ma [ma] *n* (*fam: mother*) Mama *f*

Mac [mæk] *n* (*fam*) *short for* **Macintosh®** Mac *m*

macabre [məˈkab·rə] *adj* makaber

macaroni [ˌmæk·ə·'roʊ·ni] *n* Makkaroni *pl*

mace [meɪs] *n* BOT, FOOD Mazis *m*

Mace® [meɪs] I. *n* ≈ Tränengas *nt* II. *vt* mit Tränengas besprühen

Mach [mak] *n* AEROSP, PHYS Mach *nt*

machete [məˈʃet·i] *n* Machete *f*

machine [məˈʃin] I. *n* Maschine *f* II. *vt* (*produce*) maschinell herstellen

ma'chine gun *n* Maschinengewehr *nt*

machine-'readable *adj* COMPUT (*by device*) maschinenlesbar; (*by computer*) computerlesbar

machinery [məˈʃi·nə·ri] *n* ❶ (*machines*) Maschinen *pl* ❷ (*mechanism*) Mechanismus *m*

ma'chine tool *n* Werkzeugmaschine *f*

machinist [məˈʃi·nɪst] *n* Maschinist(in) *m(f)*

macho ['matʃ·oʊ] *adj* (*pej fam*) machohaft, Macho-

mackerel <*pl* -s> ['mæk·rəl] *n* Makrele *f*

macro ['mæk·roʊ] *n* COMPUT Makro *nt*

macrobiotic [ˌmæk·roʊ·baɪ·'aṭ·ɪk] *adj* makrobiotisch

mad <-dd-> [mæd] *adj* ❶ (*fam: angry*) sauer; **to make sb ~** jdn rasend machen ❷ (*fam: insane*) wahnsinnig, verrückt; **to go ~** den Verstand verlieren ❸ (*frantic*) **like ~** wie verrückt ❹ (*fam: enthusiastic*) verrückt (**about** nach +*dat*)

madam ['mæd·əm] *n* (*form of address*) gnädige Frau; (*in titles*) **M~ President** Frau Präsidentin

mad 'cow disease *n* Rinderwahnsinn *m*

maddening ['mæd·n̩·ɪŋ] *adj* äußerst ärgerlich; (*situation*) nervend

made [meɪd] I. *pt, pp of* **make** II. *adj* **to have [got] it ~** es geschafft haben *fam*

made-to-'measure *adj* maßgeschneidert

made-'up *adj* ❶ (*imaginary*) ausgedacht ❷ (*wearing makeup*) geschminkt

madly ['mæd·li] *adv* ❶ (*insanely*) wie verrückt ❷ (*fam: very much*) wahnsinnig

'madman *n* (*fig fam*) Verrückter *m*

madness ['mæd·nɪs] *n* Wahnsinn *m*

'madwoman *n* (*fig fam*) Verrückte *f* *fam*

mafia ['ma·fiə] *n* + *sing/pl vb* Mafia *f*

mag [mæg] *n* (*fam*) *short for* **magazine** Blatt *nt*

magazine ['mæg·ə·zin] *n* ❶ (*publication*) Zeitschrift *f* ❷ (*gun part*) Magazin *nt*

maggot ['mæg·ət] *n* Made *f*

magic ['mædʒ·ɪk] I. *n* ❶ (*sorcery*) Magie *f*, Zauber *m* ❷ (*tricks*) Zaubertrick[s] *m[pl]*; **to do ~** zaubern II. *adj* ❶ (*supernatural*) magisch, Zauber-; **they had no ~ solution** sie konnten keine Lösung aus dem Ärmel zaubern ❷ (*extraordinary*) *moment* zauberhaft, wundervoll; *powers* magisch

magical ['mædʒ·ɪk·əl] *adj* ❶ (*magic*) magisch ❷ (*extraordinary*) *moment* zauberhaft; *powers* magisch

magically ['mæ·dʒɪk·li] *adv* ❶ (*by magic*) wie von Zauberhand ❷ (*extraordinarily*) zauberhaft

magic 'carpet *n* fliegender Teppich

magician [mə·'dʒɪʃ·ən] *n* Zauberer *m*/Zauberin *f*; (*on stage*) Zauberkünstler(in) *m(f)*

magnate ['mæg·neɪt] *n* Magnat *m*

magnet ['mæg·nɪt] *n* Magnet *m*

magnetic [mæg·'neṭ·ɪk] *adj* ❶ *steel* magnetisch; **~ strip** Magnetstreifen *m* ❷ (*fig*) *attraction* unwiderstehlich; *charm* anziehend

mag'netic field *n* Magnetfeld *nt*

magnetism ['mæg·nə·tɪz·əm] *n* ❶ Magnetismus *m* ❷ *of person* Ausstrahlung *f*

magnetize ['mæg·nə·taɪz] *vt* PHYS magnetisieren

magnification [ˌmæg·nɪ·fɪ·'keɪ·ʃən] *n* Vergrößerung *f*

magnificent [mæg·'nɪf·ɪ·sənt] *adj* *house, concert* wunderbar, großartig

magnify <-ie-> ['mæg·nɪ·faɪ] *vt* (*make bigger*) vergrößern; (*make worse*) verschlimmern

'magnifying glass *n* Lupe *f*   **M**

magnitude ['mæg·nɪ·tud] *n* (*size*) Größe *f*; *of project* Ausmaß *nt*; *of earthquake* Stärke *f*

magnolia [mæg·'noʊl·jə] *n* Magnolie *f*

mahogany [mə·'hag·ə·ni] *n* Mahagoni[holz] *nt*

maid [meɪd] *n* (*servant*) Dienstmädchen *nt*; (*in hotel*) Zimmermädchen *nt*

maiden ['meɪ·dən] I. *n* (*old*) Jungfer *f* II. *adj attr* (*first*) Jungfern-

'maiden name *n* Mädchenname *m*

mail¹ [meɪl] I. *n* Post *f*; **to send sth through** [*or* **in**] **the ~** etw mit der Post [ver]schicken II. *vt* (*at post office*) *letter, package* aufgeben; (*in mailbox*) einwerfen

mail² [meɪl] *n* **chain ~** Kettenpanzer *m*

'mailbag *n* Postsack *m*

'mailbox *n* Briefkasten *m*

'mailing list *n* Adressenliste *f*, Mailingliste *f*

'mailman *n* Briefträger *m*, Postbote *m*

'mail order *n* [Direkt]versand *m*; (*by catalog*) Katalogbestellung *f*

maim [meɪm] *vt* verstümmeln

main [meɪn] **I.** *adj attr* Haupt- **II.** *n* TECH
water ~ Wasserhauptleitung *f*

main 'drag *n* (*fam*) Haupt|einkaufs|stra-
ße *f*

Maine [meɪn] *n* Maine *nt*

'mainframe *n* Hauptrechner *m*

mainly ['meɪn·li] *adv* hauptsächlich, in
erster Linie

'mainstream I. *n* ■the ~ (*fig*) der
Mainstream; **to enter the ~ of poli-**
tics am alltäglichen politischen All-
tag|sgeschäft| teilnehmen **II.** *adj book,*
music kommerziell

'main street *n* Haupt|einkaufs|straße *f*

maintain [meɪn·'teɪn] *vt* ❶ (*keep*)
[bei]behalten; *status quo* aufrechterhalten; *dignity* bewahren; **to ~ the lead** in
Führung bleiben ❷ (*in good condition*)
instand halten ❸ (*provide for*) *family*
unterhalten

maintenance ['meɪn·tə·nəns] *n* ❶ *of*
relations Beibehaltung *f* ❷ *of car* Pflege *f*; *of building* Instandhaltung *f*; *of*
machine Wartung *f* ❸ (*maintenance*
costs) Unterhaltung *f*

majestic [mə·'dʒes·tɪk] *adj* majestätisch; *proportions* stattlich

majesty ['mædʒ·ɪ·sti] *n* ❶ (*royal title*)
[Her/His/Your] M~ [Ihre/Seine/Eure]
Majestät ❷ (*beauty*) *of sunset* Herrlich-
keit *f; of person* Würde *f*

major ['meɪ·dʒər] **I.** *adj* ❶ *attr* (*im-*
portant) bedeutend, wichtig; (*main*)
Haupt-; (*large*) groß ❷ *attr crime*
schwer; *illness* schwerwiegend **II.** *n*
❶ MIL (*officer rank*) Major(in) *m(f)*
❷ UNIV (*primary subject*) Hauptfach *nt*;
(*person studying*) **she was a philoso-**
phy ~ sie hat Philosophie im Hauptfach
studiert **III.** *vi* UNIV **to ~ in physics** Physik als Hauptfach studieren

major 'general *n* Generalmajor(in) *m(f)*

majority [mə·'dʒɔr·ɪ·ti] *n* ❶ + *sing/pl*
vb Mehrheit *f*; **in the ~ of cases** in der
Mehrzahl der Fälle ❷ POL (*winning mar-*
gin) |Stimmen|mehrheit *f*

make [meɪk] **I.** *n* ❶ ECON (*brand*) Marke *f* ❷ (*pej*) **to be on the ~** geldgierig
sein **II.** *vt* <made, made> ❶ (*produce*)

machen; (*manufacture*) herstellen;
movie drehen; **this sweater is made**
of wool dieser Pullover ist aus Wolle
❷ *dinner* machen; **to ~ coffee** Kaffee
kochen ❸ (*become*) **I don't think he**
will ever ~ a good lawyer ich glaube,
aus ihm wird nie ein guter Rechtsanwalt
[werden]; **to ~** [for] **fascinating read-**
ing faszinierend zu lesen sein ❹ (*cause*)
machen; **to ~ sb laugh** jdn zum Lachen
bringen ❺ (*force*) ■**to ~ sb do sth** jdn
zwingen, etw zu tun ❻ + *adj* (*cause to*
be) machen; **to ~ sth public** etw veröffentlichen ❼ *mistake, suggestion* machen; *appointment* vereinbaren; *deal*
schließen; **to ~ a call** anrufen; **to ~ an**
effort sich anstrengen; **to ~ way** den
Weg frei machen ❽ (*earn, get*) **he ~s**
50,000 dollars a year er verdient
50.000 Dollar im Jahr; **to ~ friends**
Freundschaften schließen; **to ~ a**
killing einen Riesengewinn machen
❾ (*fam: reach*) **could you ~ a meeting**
at 8 a.m.? schaffst du ein Treffen um 8
Uhr morgens?; **to ~ the finals** sich für
das Finale qualifizieren; **to ~ it** es schaffen **III.** *vi* <made, made> (*pretend*) **he**
made as if to leave the room er
machte Anstalten, das Zimmer zu verlassen; ■**to ~ like ...** so tun, als ob ...
▶PHRASES: **to ~ do without sth** ohne
etw auskommen

♦**make for** *vi* ❶ (*head for*) zugehen
auf +*akk*; (*by car or bus*) zufahren auf
+*akk* ❷ (*promote*) **constant arguing**
doesn't ~ for a good relationship
ständiges Streiten ist einer guten Beziehung nicht gerade förderlich

♦**make of** *vt* ❶ (*understand*) **I don't**
know what to ~ of it ich weiß nicht,
wie ich das deuten soll ❷ (*think*) **what**
do you ~ of his speech? was hältst du
von seiner Rede?

♦**make off** *vi* (*fam*) ❶ (*leave*) abhauen
❷ (*steal*) ■**to ~ off with sth** etw mitgehen lassen *fam*

♦**make out I.** *vi* (*fam*) ❶ (*manage*)
person zurechtkommen ❷ (*sl: kiss*
passionately) [he]rummachen, [he]rum-

fummeln (**with** mit +*dat*) II. *vt* ❶ ausschreiben; *check* ausstellen ❷ (*see*) *writing* entziffern; *distant object* ausmachen

◆ **make over** *vt* (*change appearance*) *house* umändern; *person* verändern

◆ **make up** I. *vt* ❶ (*invent*) ■ **to ~ up** ↻ **sth: she made the whole thing up** sie hat das alles nur erfunden ❷ (*prepare*) fertig machen ❸ (*put on makeup*) ■ **to ~ oneself up** sich schminken ❹ (*compensate*) *deficit* ausgleichen; **to ~ up time** Zeit wieder gutmachen; *train* Zeit wieder herausfahren; (*repay favor*) ■ **to ~ it up to sb** jdm gegenüber etw wiedergutmachen II. *vi* sich versöhnen (**with** mit +*dat*); **kiss and ~ up** küsst euch und vertragt euch wieder

◆ **make up for** *vt* entschädigen für +*akk*; *mistake* wiedergutmachen; **to ~ up for lost time** verlorene Zeit wieder aufholen

'**make-believe** I. *n* Fantasie *f* II. *vi* <made-, made-> ■ **to ~ [that]** ... sich *dat* vorstellen, dass ...

maker ['meɪ·kər] *n* (*manufacturer*) ■ **the ~** Hersteller(in) *m(f)*

'**makeshift** *adj* Not-, behelfsmäßig

'**makeup** *n* ❶ (*cosmetics*) Make-up *nt*; **to put on ~** sich schminken ❷ *of group* Zusammensetzung *f*

'**makeup artist** *n* Visagist(in) *m(f)*

making ['meɪ·kɪŋ] *n* ❶ (*production*) Herstellung *f*; **her problems with that child are of her own ~** ihre Probleme mit diesem Kind hat sie selbst verschuldet ❷ (*qualities, ingredients*) ■ **~s** *pl* Anlagen *pl*; **she has the ~s of a great violinist** sie hat das Zeug zu einer großartigen Geigerin

maladjusted [ˌmæl·ə·'dʒʌs·tɪd] *adj* verhaltensgestört

malaise [mæ·'leɪz] *n* Unbehagen *nt*

malaria [mə·'ler·i·ə] *n* Malaria *f*

male [meɪl] I. *adj* männlich; **~-dominated** von Männern dominiert II. *n* (*person*) Mann *m;* (*animal*) Männchen *nt*

malformation [ˌmæl·fɔr·'meɪ·ʃən] *n* Missbildung *f*

malfunction [ˌmæl·'fʌŋk·ʃən] I. *vi* (*not work properly*) nicht funktionieren; (*stop working*) ausfallen II. *n* Ausfall *m;* *of liver, kidney* Funktionsstörung *f*

malice ['mæl·ɪs] *n* Boshaftigkeit *f*

malicious [mə·'lɪʃ·əs] *adj* boshaft

malignant [mə·'lɪg·nənt] *adj* MED bösartig

mall [mɔl] *n* [überdachtes] Einkaufszentrum

mallard <*pl* -s> ['mæl·ərd] *n* Stockente *f*

malleable ['mæl·i·ə·bəl] *adj* *metal* formbar; (*fig*) *person* gefügig

mallet ['mæl·ɪt] *n* (*hammer*) [Holz]hammer *m;* (*in croquet*) Krockethammer *m*

malnutrition [ˌmæl·nu·'trɪʃ·ən] *n* Unterernährung *f*

malpractice [ˌmæl·'præk·tɪs] *n* (*faulty work*) Berufsvergehen *nt;* (*criminal misconduct*) [berufliches] Vergehen; **medical ~** ärztlicher Kunstfehler

malt [mɔlt] *n* ❶ (*grain*) Malz *nt* ❷ (*malted milk*) Malzmilch *f;* **chocolate ~** Schokoladenshake mit Zusatz von Malzextrakt

mammal ['mæm·əl] *n* Säugetier *nt*, Säuger *m*

mammography [mə·'mag·rə·fi] *n* Mammographie *f*

mammoth ['mæm·əθ] I. *n* Mammut *nt* II. *adj* (*fig*) Mammut-, riesig

man [mæn] *n* <*pl* men> ❶ (*male adult*) Mann *m;* **the men's [room]** die Herrentoilette ❷ (*person*) Mensch *m;* **to be sb's right-hand ~** jds rechte Hand sein ❸ (*mankind*) der Mensch ❹ (*particular type*) **to be a family ~** ein Familienmensch *m* sein ❺ *pl* (*soldiers, workers*) Männer *pl*, Leute *pl* II. *interj* (*fam*) Mensch, Mann III. *vt* <-nn-> *fortress* besetzen; *ship* bemannen

manage ['mæn·ɪdʒ] I. *vt* ❶ (*run*) leiten ❷ (*control*) steuern; (*administer*) verwalten; (*organize*) organisieren ❸ (*accomplish*) schaffen; *task* bewältigen; **to**

~ **a smile** ein Lächeln zustande bringen II. vi ❶ (*succeed*) es schaffen; (*cope, survive*) zurechtkommen; **we'll ~!** wir schaffen das schon! ❷ (*get by*) ■**to ~ without sth** ohne etw auskommen

manageable ['mæn·ɪ·dʒə·bəl] *adj* ❶ (*doable*) job leicht zu bewältigen; task überschaubar ❷ (*feasible*) erreichbar; deadline realistisch

management ['mæn·ɪdʒ·mənt] *n* ❶ of business Management *nt*, [Geschäfts]führung *f* ❷ (*managers*) Management *nt*; of hospital, theater Direktion *f* ❸ (*handling*) Umgang *m*

management 'buyout *n* Management-Buy-out *nt* (*Übernahme einer Firma durch die leitenden Direktoren*)

management con'sultant *n* Unternehmensberater(in) *m(f)*

management 'skills *npl* Führungsqualitäten *pl*

'management studies *n + sing/pl vb* Betriebswirtschaft[slehre] *f*

manager ['mæn·ɪ·dʒər] *n* ❶ Geschäftsführer(in) *m(f)*; (of performer) Manager(in) *m(f)*; (of department) Abteilungsleiter(in) *m(f)* ❷ (chief adviser) **campaign** ~ Wahlkampfleiter *m* ❸ SPORT (coach) [Chef]trainer(in) *m(f)*

managerial [ˌmæn·ə·'dʒɪr·i·əl] *adj* Manager; **at ~ level** auf Führungsebene

managing di'rector *n* [Haupt]geschäftsführer(in) *m(f)*

mandarin ['mæn·də·rɪn] *n* Mandarine *f*

Mandarin ['mæn·də·rɪn] *n* LING Mandarin *nt*

mandate ['mæn·deɪt] I. *n usu sing* (authority) Mandat *nt*; (command) Verfügung *f* II. *vt* (order) anordnen; (authorize) ein Mandat erteilen für +akk

mandatory ['mæn·də·tɔr·i] *adj* gesetzlich vorgeschrieben

mandolin ['mæn·də·lɪn] *n* MUS Mandoline *f*

mane [meɪn] *n* Mähne *f*

'man-eater *n* ❶ (animal) Tier, das Menschen tötet ❷ (hum fam: woman) männermordender Vamp

maneuver [mə·'nu·vər] I. *n* ❶ usu pl (military exercise) Manöver *nt* ❷ (planned move) Manöver *nt*; (fig) Schachzug *m* ❸ **to have room for ~** Spielraum haben II. *vt* (move) manövrieren; vehicle lenken III. *vi* manövrieren

maneuverability [mə·ˌnu·vər·ə·'bɪl·ɪ·ti] *n* Beweglichkeit *f*, Manövrierfähigkeit *f*

maneuverable [mə·'nu·vər·ə·bəl] *adj* beweglich; ship manövrierfähig

mangle ['mæŋ·gəl] *vt usu passive* (crush) zerstören; limbs verstümmeln; car zerdrücken

mango <*pl* -s> ['mæŋ·gou] *n* Mango *f*

mangrove ['mæn·grouv] *n* Mangrovenbaum *m*

manhandle ['mæn·hæn·dəl] *vt* (handle roughly) grob behandeln

'manhole cover *n* Einstiegsverschluss *m*

manhood ['mæn·hʊd] *n* (adulthood) Erwachsenenalter *nt* (eines Mannes); **to reach ~** zum Manne werden

'man-hour *n* Arbeitsstunde *f*

'manhunt *n* Verbrecherjagd *f*

mania ['meɪ·ni·ə] *n* Manie *f*

maniac ['meɪ·ni·æk] *n* (fam) Verrückte(r) *f(m)*

maniacal [mə·'naɪ·ə·kəl] *adj* (crazy) verrückt, irrsinnig

manic ['mæn·ɪk] *adj* manisch; (highly energetic) wild

manic de'pression *n* manische Depression

manic de'pressive *n* Manisch-Depressive(r) *f(m)*

manicure ['mæn·ɪ·kjʊr] *n* Maniküre *f*

manicurist ['mæn·ɪ·kjʊr·ɪst] *n* Handpflegerin *f*

manifest ['mæn·ɪ·fest] I. *adj* offenkundig II. *n* TRANSP (list of passengers) Passagierliste *f*; (cargo list) [Ladungs]manifest *nt*

manifesto <*pl* -s> [ˌmæn·ɪ·'fes·tou] *n* Manifest *nt*

manifold ['mæn·ɪ·foʊld] *n* TECH Verteilerrohr *nt*

Manil(l)a 'envelope [mə·'nɪl·ə·] *n* Briefumschlag *m* aus Manilapapier

manipulate [mə·ˈnɪp·jə·leɪt] vt ❶ (*esp pej: manage cleverly*) ■**to ~ sb** geschickt mit jdm umgehen ❷ (*with hands*) handhaben; *machine* bedienen; COMPUT *text* bearbeiten

manipulation [mə·ˌnɪp·jə·ˈleɪ·ʃən] n ❶ (*esp pej: clever management*) Manipulation f ❷ (*handling*) Handgriff m

manipulative [mə·ˌnɪp·jə·ˈlə·tɪv] adj (*esp pej*) manipulativ

mankind [ˌmæn·ˈkaɪnd] n Menschheit f

manly [ˈmæn·li] adj männlich

man-ˈmade adj künstlich

manna [ˈmæn·ə] n Manna nt; **~ from heaven** ein wahrer Segen

manned [mænd] adj AEROSP bemannt

manner [ˈmæn·ər] n ❶ (*way*) Weise f, Art f; **in a ~ of speaking** sozusagen ❷ (*behavior to others*) Betragen nt ❸ (*polite behavior*) ■**~s** pl Manieren pl

mannerism [ˈmæn·ə·rɪz·əm] n Eigenart f

mannish [ˈmæn·ɪʃ] adj (*esp pej: of woman*) männlich

ˈmanpower n Arbeitskräfte pl

mansion [ˈmæn·ʃən] n Villa f

manslaughter [ˈmæn·slɔ·tər] n Totschlag m

mantel [ˈmæn·təl] n Kaminsims m o nt

ˈman-to-man adj von Mann zu Mann

manual [ˈmæn·ju·əl] I. adj manuell, Hand-; **~ transmission** AUTO Schaltgetriebe nt II. n Handbuch nt

manually [ˈmæn·ju·ə·li] adv manuell

manufacture [ˌmæn·ju·ˈfæk·tʃər] vt herstellen

manufacturer [ˌmæn·ju·ˈfæk·tʃər·ər] n Hersteller m

manufacturing [ˌmæn·jə·ˈfæk·tʃər·ɪŋ] n Fertigung f

manure [mə·ˈnʊr] n Dung m

manuscript [ˈmæn·ju·skrɪpt] n Manuskript nt

many [ˈmen·i] pron (*a great number*) viele; **too ~** zu viele; **as ~ as …** so viele wie …

many-ˈsided adj vielseitig; (*complex*) vielschichtig

map [mæp] n GEOG [Land]karte f; *of town* Stadtplan m; **road ~** Straßenkarte f

◆**map out** vt genau festlegen; *route* planen

maple [ˈmeɪ·pəl] n Ahorn m

ˈmaple leaf n Ahornblatt nt

maple ˈsyrup n Ahornsirup m

mar <-rr-> [mar] vt stören

Mar. n abbrev of **March**

marathon [ˈmær·ə·θən] n Marathon[lauf] m; **~ runner** Marathonläufer(in) m(f)

marauder [mə·ˈrɔ·dər] n (*raider*) Plünderer(in) m(f)

marble [ˈmar·bəl] n ❶ (*stone*) Marmor m ❷ (*for games*) Murmel f

ˈmarble cake n Marmorkuchen m

march [martʃ] I. n <pl -es> Marsch m II. vi marschieren III. vt ■**to ~ sb off** jdn wegführen; *police* jdn abführen

March <pl -es> [martʃ] n März m; see also **February**   **M**

Mardi Gras [ˈmar·di·ˌgra] n (*carnival on Shrove Tuesday*) ≈ Fastnachtsdienstag m, Karneval m

mare [mer] n Stute f

margarine [ˈmar·dʒər·ɪn] n Margarine f

margin [ˈmar·dʒɪn] n ❶ (*outer edge*) Rand m; TYPO [Seiten]rand m ❷ (*amount*) Abstand m ❸ (*provision*) Spielraum m; **a ~ of error** eine Fehlerspanne

marginal [ˈmar·dʒə·nəl] adj ❶ (*slight*) geringfügig ❷ (*insignificant*) nebensächlich

marginalize [ˈmar·dʒɪ·nə·laɪz] vt an den Rand drängen

marigold [ˈmær·ɪ·goʊld] n Studentenblume f

marijuana, marihuana [ˌmær·ɪ·ˈwa·nə] n Marihuana nt

marina [mə·ˈri·nə] n Jachthafen m

marinade [ˌmær·ɪ·ˈneɪd] n Marinade f

marinate [ˈmær·ɪ·neɪt] vt marinieren

marine [mə·ˈrin] I. adj attr ❶ (*of sea*) Meeres-, See- ❷ (*of shipping*) Schiffs- II. n Marineinfanterist m

marine bi'ologist n Meeresbiologe m/ -biologin f

Ma'rine Corps n Marineinfanterie-korps nt

marital ['mær·ɪ·təl] adj ehelich, Ehe-; **~ status** Familienstand m

maritime 'law n Seerecht nt

marjoram ['mar·dʒər·əm] n Majoran m

mark [mark] **I.** n ❶(spot, stain) Fleck m; (trace) Spur f; (fingerprint) Abdruck m ❷(identifying feature) [Kenn]zeichen nt, Merkmal nt ❸(indication) Zeichen nt ▸PHRASES: **to leave its/one's ~ on sb** seine Spuren bei jdm hinterlassen **II.** vt ❶(stain) schmutzig machen ❷(indicate) markieren ❸(commemorate) **▪to ~ sth** an etw akk erinnern **III.** vi (get dirty) schmutzig werden; (scratch) Kratzer bekommen

◆ **mark down** vt ❶(reduce the price of) heruntersetzen ❷(give a lower grade) **▪to ~ down ↻ sb** jdm eine schlechtere Note geben

◆ **mark off** vt (separate off) abgrenzen

◆ **mark out** vt abstecken, markieren

◆ **mark up** vt (increase the price of) heraufsetzen

marked [markt] adj ❶(clear) deutlich; (striking) auffallend, markant; **in ~ contrast to sth** im krassen Gegensatz zu etw dat ❷(with distinguishing marks) markiert

markedly ['mar·kəd·li] adv deutlich

marker ['mar·kər] n ❶(sign, symbol) [Kenn]zeichen nt ❷(felt tip pen) Filzstift m

market ['mar·kɪt] **I.** n Markt m; **to put sth on the ~** etw auf den Markt bringen **II.** vt (sell) vermarkten

market 'forces npl Marktkräfte pl

marketing ['mar·kɪ·tɪŋ] n Marketing nt

market 'leader n Marktführer m

'marketplace n ❶(place) Marktplatz m ❷(commercial environment) Markt m

market 'research n Marktforschung f

marking ['mar·kɪŋ] n ▪**~s** pl Markie-

rungen pl; on animals Zeichnung f kein pl

marksman ['marks·mən] n Schütze m

marksmanship ['marks·mən·ʃɪp] n Treffsicherheit f

markswoman ['marks·wʊm·ən] n Schützin f

markup ['mark·ʌp] n [Kalkulations]aufschlag m

marmalade ['mar·mə·leɪd] n Orangenmarmelade f

maroon[1] [mə·'run] vt (abandon) aussetzen

maroon[2] [mə·'run] adj kastanienbraun, rötlichbraun

marquee [mar·'ki] n beleuchtete Werbetafel über Kino-/Theatereingängen

marriage ['mær·ɪdʒ] n ❶(wedding) Heirat f ❷(relationship) Ehe f

'marriage certificate n Heiratsurkunde f

marriage counselor n Eheberater(in) m(f)

'marriage license n Heiratserlaubnis f

'marriage vow n usu pl Ehegelübde nt geh

married ['mer·id] adj verheiratet; **to get ~ [to sb]** [jdn] heiraten

marrow ['mær·oʊ] n (of bone) [Knochen]mark nt

marry ['mær·i] **I.** vt ❶(wed) heiraten ❷(officiate at ceremony) trauen, verheiraten ❸(combine) verbinden (**to/with** mit +dat) **II.** vi heiraten

Mars [marz] n Mars m

marsh <pl -es> [marʃ] n Sumpf m

marshal ['mar·ʃəl] n ❶(federal agent) Gerichtsdiener(in) m(f); **fire ~** Branddirektor(in) m(f) ❷MIL (army officer) Marschall m

'marshland n Sumpfland nt

marshmallow ['marʃ·mel·oʊ] n Marshmallow nt

marshy ['mar·ʃi] adj sumpfig

martial 'arts npl SPORT Kampfsport m kein pl, Kampfsportarten pl

martial 'law n Kriegsrecht nt

martyr ['mar·tər] n Märtyrer(in) m(f)

martyrdom ['mar·tər·dəm] n (being a

martyr) Märtyrertum *nt*; (*death*) Märtyrertod *m*

marvel ['mar·vəl] I. *n* (*wonderful thing*) Wunder *nt* II. *vi* <-I-> (*wonder*) sich wundern (**at** über +*akk*)

marvelous ['mar·və·ləs] *adj* wunderbar, großartig

Marxist ['mark·sɪst] I. *n* Marxist(in) *m(f)* II. *adj* marxistisch

Maryland ['mer·ə·lənd] *n* Maryland *nt*

marzipan ['mar·zɪ·pæn] *n* Marzipan *nt o m*

masc. *adj abbrev of* **masculine**

mascara [mæ·'skær·ə] *n* Wimperntusche *f*

mascot ['mæs·kat] *n* Maskottchen *nt*

masculine ['mæs·kjə·lɪn] *adj* männlich, maskulin

mash [mæʃ] I. *n* Brei *m* II. *vt* zerdrücken, [zer]stampfen
 ◆ **mash up** *vt food* zerdrücken

mashed po'tatoes *n pl* Kartoffelbrei *m*, [Kartoffel]püree *nt*

mask [mæsk] I. *n* Maske *f* II. *vt* verbergen

masked [mæskt] *adj* maskiert

masking tape ['mæs·kɪŋ-] *n* Tesakrepp® *nt*

masochist ['mæs·ə·kɪst] *n* Masochist(in) *m(f)*

mason ['meɪ·sən] *n* Steinmetz(in) *m(f)*

masonry ['meɪ·sən·ri] *n* Mauerwerk *nt*

masquerade [ˌmæs·kə·'reɪd] I. *n* Maskerade *f* II. *vi* ■ **to ~ as sb** sich als jdn ausgeben

mass [mæs] I. *n* ① *usu sing* Masse *f* ② *usu sing* (*large quantity*) Menge *f*; **a ~ of contradictions** eine Reihe von Widersprüchen ③ (*common people*) ■ **the ~es** *pl* **music for the ~** Musik für die breite Masse II. *vi crowd* sich ansammeln

Mass [mæs] *n* REL, MUS Messe *f*

Mass. *abbrev of* **Massachusetts**

Massachusetts [ˌmæs·ə·'tʃu·sɪts] *n* Massachusetts *nt*

massacre ['mæs·ə·kər] I. *n* Massaker *nt* II. *vt* ① (*kill*) massakrieren ② (*defeat*) vernichtend schlagen

massage [mə·'sadʒ] I. *n* Massage *f*; **to give sb a ~** jdn massieren II. *vt* (*rub*) massieren; **to ~ cream into the skin** Creme einmassieren

mas'sage parlor *n* (*for sex*) Massagesalon *m euph*

masseur [mæ·'sɜr] *n* Masseur *m*

masseuse [mæ·'sɜz] *n* Masseurin *f*

massive ['mæs·ɪv] *adj* riesig, enorm; *heart attack* schwer

mass 'market *n* Massenmarkt *m*

mass 'media *n* + *sing/pl vb* ■ **the ~** die Massenmedien *pl*

mass 'murderer *n* Massenmörder(in) *m(f)*

mass-pro'duce *vt* serienmäßig herstellen

mass pro'duction *n* Massenproduktion *f*

mass 'transit *n* öffentliche Verkehrsmittel

mast [mæst] *n* ① NAUT [Schiffs]mast *m* ② RADIO, TV Sendeturm *m*

master ['mæs·tər] I. *n* ① (*of slave*) Herr *m*; (*of dog*) Herrchen *nt* ② (*expert*) Meister(in) *m(f)* II. *vt* ① (*cope with*) meistern ② (*become proficient*) beherrschen

master 'bedroom *n* großes Schlafzimmer

'master class *n* Meisterklasse *f*

master 'craftsman *n* Handwerksmeister(in) *m(f)*

masterful ['mæs·tər·fəl] *adj* ① (*authoritative*) bestimmend ② (*skillful*) meisterhaft

'master key *n* Generalschlüssel *m*

'mastermind I. *n* führender Kopf II. *vt* federführend leiten

Master of 'Arts *n* ≈ Magister Artium *m*

Master of 'Ceremonies *n* Zeremonienmeister *m*

Master of 'Science ■ **to have a ~** ≈ ein Diplom *nt* in einer Naturwissenschaft haben

'masterpiece *n* Meisterwerk *nt*

'master plan *n* Grundplan *m*

Master's, Master's degree ['mæs-

M

tərz-] *n* ≈ Magister *m*; **to study for one's ~** ≈ seinen Magister machen

'**master switch** *n* Hauptschalter *m*

'**masterwork** *n see* **masterpiece**

mastiff ['mæs·tɪf] *n* englische Dogge

masturbate ['mæs·tər·beɪt] *vi* masturbieren

masturbation [ˌmæs·tər·'beɪ·ʃən] *n* Masturbation *f*

mat [mæt] *n* ❶ (*for floor*) Matte *f*; (*decorative mat*) Deckchen *nt* ❷ (*thick layer*) **a ~ of hair** dichtes Haar; (*on the head*) eine Mähne *fam*

match¹ [mætʃ] **I.** *n* <*pl* -**es**> ❶ *usu sing* (*complement*) **to be a good ~** gut zusammenpassen ❷ (*one of pair*) Gegenstück *nt* ❸ *usu sing* (*equal*) ebenbürtiger Gegner/ebenbürtige Gegnerin; **to have met one's ~** seine bessere Hälfte gefunden haben *hum fam* ❹ SPORT Spiel *nt*; **tennis ~** Tennisspiel *nt*; CHESS Partie *f* ❺ COMPUT (*hit*) Treffer *m* **II.** *vi* (*harmonize*) zusammenpassen **III.** *vt* ❶ (*complement*) passen *zu* +*dat* ❷ (*find complement*) ■**to ~ sth** [**with sth**] etw [auf etw *akk*] abstimmen ❸ (*correspond to*) ■**to ~ sth** etw *dat* entsprechen, zu etw *dat* passen
◆ **match up I.** *vi* (*be aligned*) aufeinander abgestimmt sein **II.** *vt* (*find complement*) ■**to ~ up ◌ socks** die zusammengehörigen Socken finden

match² <*pl* -**es**> [mætʃ] *n* (*for lighting*) Streichholz *nt*

'**matchbox** *n* Streichholzschachtel *f*

matching ['mætʃ·ɪŋ] *adj attr* [zusammen]passend

match 'point *n* TENNIS Matchball *m*

'**matchstick** *n* Streichholz *nt*

mate¹ [meɪt] **I.** *n* ❶ (*sexual partner*) Partner(in) *m(f)* ❷ (*ship's officer*) Schiffsoffizier *m* **II.** *vi* BIOL *animals* sich paaren (**with** mit +*dat*)

mate² [meɪt] CHESS **I.** *n* [Schach]matt *nt* **II.** *vt* [schach]matt setzen

material [mə·'tɪr·i·əl] **I.** *n* ❶ (*substance*) Material *nt* a. *fig*; **raw ~** Rohmaterial *nt* ❷ (*type of cloth*) Stoff *m* ❸ (*information*) [Informations]materi-

al *nt* **II.** *adj* ❶ (*physical*) materiell; **~ damage** Sachschaden *m* ❷ (*important*) wesentlich; ■**to be ~ to sth** für etw *akk* relevant sein

materialism [mə·'tɪr·i·ə·lɪz·əm] *n* Materialismus *m*

materialistic [mə·ˌtɪr·i·ə·'lɪs·tɪk] *adj* materialistisch

materialize [mə·'tɪr·i·ə·laɪz] *vi dream* sich verwirklichen, in Erfüllung gehen; *plan* in die Tat umgesetzt werden

maternal [mə·'tɜr·nəl] *adj* mütterlich

maternity [mə·'tɜr·nɪ·ti] *n* Mutterschaft *f*

ma'ternity dress *n* Umstandskleid *nt*

ma'ternity leave *n* Mutterschaftsurlaub *m*

math [mæθ] *n* (*fam*) *short for* **mathematics** Mathe *f*

mathematical [ˌmæθ·ə·'mæt·ɪ·kəl] *adj* mathematisch

mathematics [ˌmæθ·ə·'mæt·ɪks] *n* + *sing vb* Mathematik *f*

matinee [mæt·ə·'neɪ] *n* Matinee *f*; (*afternoon performance*) Frühvorstellung *f*

mating ['meɪ·tɪŋ] *n* Paarung *f*

matrices ['meɪ·trɪ·siz] *n pl of* **matrix**

matriculate [mə·'trɪk·jə·leɪt] *vi* UNIV sich immatrikulieren

matrimonial [ˌmæt·rə·'moʊ·ni·əl] *adj* (*form*) Ehe-, ehelich

matrimony ['mæt·rə·moʊ·ni] *n* Ehe *f*; **to be joined in holy ~** in den heiligen Stand der Ehe treten

matrix <*pl* -**es**> ['meɪ·trɪks] *n* (*rectangular arrangement*) Matrix *f*

matronly ['meɪ·trən·li] *adj* (*esp hum*) matronenhaft *meist pej*

matte [mæt] *adj* matt

matted ['mæt·ɪd] *adj* verflochten; *hair* verfilzt

matter ['mæt·ər] **I.** *n* ❶ (*material*) Materie *f*; **reading ~** Lesestoff *m* ❷ (*affair*) Angelegenheit *f*, Sache *f*; **this is a ~ for the police** das sollte man der Polizei übergeben; **a ~ of urgency** etwas Dringendes ❸ (*question*) Frage *f*; **as a ~ of fact** (*by the way*) übrigens; (*expressing* *agreement or disagreement*) in der Tat; **a ~ of taste** eine Geschmacksfrage ❹ (*topic*) Thema *nt;* **it's no laughing ~** das ist nicht zum Lachen ❺ (*problem*) **is anything the ~?** stimmt etwas nicht?; **what's the ~ with you?** was ist los mit dir? II. *vi* (*be of importance*) von Bedeutung sein; **that's the only thing that ~s** das ist das Einzige, was zählt; **it doesn't ~** das ist egal, das macht nichts

matter-of-'fact *adj* ❶ (*emotionless*) sachlich ❷ (*straightforward*) geradeheraus *präd,* direkt

mattress <*pl* -es> ['mæt·rɪs] *n* Matratze *f*

mature [mə·'tʃʊr] I. *adj* ❶ (*adult*) erwachsen ❷ (*ripe*) reif; *wine* ausgereift II. *vi* (*physically*) erwachsen werden, heranreifen; (*mentally and emotionally*) reifer werden III. *vt* FOOD reifen lassen

maturity [mə·'tʃʊr·ɪ·ti] *n* ❶ (*adulthood*) Erwachsensein *nt;* **to reach ~** (*of person*) erwachsen werden; (*of animal*) ausgewachsen sein ❷ (*developed form*) Reife *f*

maudlin ['mɔd·lɪn] *adj* [weinerlich] sentimental

maul [mɔl] *vt* ❶ (*wound*) verletzen; (*attack*) anfallen ❷ (*criticize*) heruntermachen

mausoleum [ˌmɔ·sə·'li·əm] *n* Mausoleum *nt*

mauve [moʊv] *adj* mauve

maverick ['mæv·ər·ɪk] *n* Einzelgänger(in) *m(f)*

max [mæks] (*fam*) I. *n short for* **maximum** max. II. *adv* **it'll cost you 40 dollars ~** das wird dich maximal 40 Dollar kosten

♦ **max out** *vt* (*fam*) ■**to ~ out** ⟳ **sth** *credit card* etw ausschöpfen

maxim ['mæk·sɪm] *n* Maxime *f*

maximize ['mæk·sɪ·maɪz] *vt* maximieren

maximum ['mæk·sɪ·məm] I. *adj attr* maximal, Höchst- II. *n* <*pl* -ima> Maximum *nt*

maximum-security 'prison *n* Hochsicherheitsgefängnis *nt*

may <*3rd pers. sing* may, might, might> [meɪ] *aux vb* ❶ (*indicating possibility*) können; **there ~ be side effects from the drug** diese Arznei kann Nebenwirkungen haben ❷ (*be allowed*) dürfen, können; **~ I ask you a question?** darf ich Ihnen [mal] eine Frage stellen? ❸ (*expressing wish*) mögen; **~ she rest in peace** möge sie in Frieden ruhen *form*

May [meɪ] *n* Mai *m; see also* **February**

maybe ['meɪ·bi] *adv* ❶ (*perhaps*) vielleicht ❷ (*approximately*) circa, ungefähr

'mayday *n* Mayday *kein art* (*internationaler Notruf*)

mayhem ['meɪ·hem] *n* Chaos *nt*

mayo ['meɪ·oʊ] *n* (*fam*) *short for* **mayonnaise** Mayo *f*

mayonnaise [ˌmeɪ·ə·'neɪz] *n* Mayonnaise *f*

mayor ['meɪ·ər] *n* Bürgermeister(in) **M** *m(f)*

maze [meɪz] *n* Labyrinth *nt*

MBA [ˌem·bi·'eɪ] *n abbrev of* **Master of Business Administration** MBA *m*

MC [ˌem·'si] *n abbrev of* **Master of Ceremonies**

MD [ˌem·'di] *n* ❶ *abbrev of* **Maryland** ❷ *abbrev of* **Doctor of Medicine** Dr. med.

me [mi] *pron object* (*1st person singular*) mir *in dat,* mich *in akk;* **why are you looking at ~?** warum siehst du mich an?; **hi, it's ~** hallo, ich bin's; **between you and ~** unter uns [gesagt] ▶PHRASES: **dear ~!** du liebe Güte!

ME, Me. *abbrev of* **Maine**

meadow ['med·oʊ] *n* Wiese *f*

meager ['mi·gər] *adj* mager

meal¹ [mil] *n* Mahlzeit *f,* Essen *nt; to* ***go out for a ~*** essen gehen

meal² [mil] *n* AGR [grobes] Mehl

'mealtime *n* Essenszeit *f*

'mealy-mouthed *adj* (*pej*) ausweichend; *expressions* schönfärberisch

mean[1] [min] *adj* ❶ (*unkind*) gemein, fies *fam* ❷ (*vicious*) aggressiv

mean[2] <meant, meant> [min] *vt* ❶ (*signify*) *word, symbol* bedeuten; **no ~s no** nein heißt nein ❷ (*intend to convey*) meinen; **what do you ~ by that?** was willst du damit sagen? ❸ (*intend*) wollen; **it was ~t to be a surprise** das sollte eine Überraschung sein; **to ~ business** es ernst meinen; **to be ~t for each other** füreinander bestimmt sein

mean[3] [min] *adj* durchschnittlich

meander [mɪˈæn·dər] I. *n* Windung *f* II. *vi* sich schlängeln [*o* winden]

meaning [ˈmi·nɪŋ] *n* Bedeutung *f*

meaningful [ˈmi·nɪŋ·fəl] *adj* ❶ (*important*) bedeutsam, wichtig ❷ (*implying something*) bedeutungsvoll

meaningless [ˈmi·nɪŋ·lɪs] *n* (*nonsensical*) sinnlos; (*empty*) nichts sagend

meanness [ˈmin·nɪs] *n* Gemeinheit *f*, Gehässigkeit *f*

means <pl -> [minz] *n* ❶ (*method*) Weg *m;* (*possibility*) Möglichkeit *f;* (*device*) Mittel *nt; ~* **of transport** Transportmittel *nt* ❷ (*income*) ▪ ~ *pl* Geldmittel *pl;* **to live beyond one's ~** über seine Verhältnisse leben ▸PHRASES: **by all ~** (*form*) unbedingt; (*of course*) selbstverständlich; **by no ~** auf keinen Fall

meant [ment] *pt, pp of* **mean**

'meantime *n* **in the ~** inzwischen, in der Zwischenzeit

meanwhile [ˈmin·hwaɪl] *adv* inzwischen

measles [ˈmi·zəlz] *n* + *sing vb* Masern *pl*

measly [ˈmi·zli] *adj* (*pej fam*) mickrig, schäbig

measurable [ˈmeʒ·ər·ə·bəl] *adj* messbar; *perceptible* nachweisbar

measure [ˈmeʒ·ər] I. *n* ❶ (*unit*) Maß *nt*, Maßeinheit *f;* **a ~ of length** ein Längenmaß *nt* ❷ (*measuring instrument*) Messgerät *nt;* (*ruler, indicator*) Messstab *m* ❸ *usu pl* (*action*) Maßnahme *f* II. *vt* [ab]messen III. *vi* messen

♦**measure out** *vt* abmessen

♦**measure up** I. *vt* ▪ **to ~ up** ⟳ **sb** jdn einschätzen II. *vi* den Ansprüchen genügen

measured [ˈmeʒ·ərd] *adj* gemäßigt; *voice* bedächtig

measurement [ˈmeʒ·ər·mənt] *n* ❶ (*size*) ▪**sb's ~s** *pl* jds Maße *pl*, jds Größe *f* ❷ (*measuring*) Messung *f*

measuring cup [ˈmeʒ·ər·ɪŋ-] *n* Messbecher *m*

meat [mit] *n* Fleisch *nt*

'meatball *n* Fleischklößchen *nt*

'meat grinder *n* Fleischwolf *m*

'meat loaf *n* Hackbraten *m*

Mecca [ˈmek·ə] *n* Mekka *nt a. fig*

mechanic [mɪˈkæn·ɪk] *n* Mechaniker(in) *m(f)*

mechanical [mɪˈkæn·ɪk·əl] *adj* ❶ *machines* mechanisch; (*by machine*) maschinell ❷ (*machine-like*) mechanisch

mechanical engi'neering *n* Maschinenbau *m*

mechanical 'pencil *n* Drehbleistift *m*

mechanics [mɪˈkæn·ɪks] *n* ❶ + *sing vb* AUTO, TECH Mechanik *f* ❷ + *pl vb* (*fam: practicalities*) Mechanismus *m*

mechanism [ˈmek·ə·nɪz·əm] *n* Mechanismus *m*

mechanize [ˈmek·ə·naɪz] *vt* mechanisieren

med I. *adj* (*fam*) *see* **medical** II. *n* (*fam*) ▪~**s** *pl* Medizin *f*

med. I. *n* *abbrev of* **medicine** II. *adj* ❶ *abbrev of* **medieval** ma. ❷ *abbrev of* **medium**

medal [ˈmed·əl] *n* Orden *m;* SPORT Medaille *f*

medalist [ˈmed·əl·ɪst] *n* Medaillengewinner(in) *m(f)*

medallion [məˈdæl·jən] *n* Medaillon *nt*

meddle [ˈmed·əl] *vi* sich einmischen (**in** in +*akk*)

media [ˈmi·di·ə] *n* ❶ *pl of* **medium** ❷ + *sing/pl vb* (*the press*) ▪**the ~** die Medien *pl*

mediaeval [ˌmi·di·ˈi·vəl] *adj* *see* **medieval**

'median (strip) *n* Mittelstreifen *m*

'media studies *npl* ≈ Kommunikationswissenschaft *f*

mediate ['mi·di·eɪt] *vi* vermitteln

mediator ['mi·di·eɪ·ʈər] *n* Vermittler(in) *m(f)*

medic ['med·ɪk] *n* (*fam*) ❶ MIL, NAUT Sanitäter(in) *m(f)* ❷ (*doctor*) Doktor *m fam*

Medicaid ['med·ɪ·keɪd] *n* Gesundheitsfürsorgeprogramm in den USA für einkommensschwache Gruppen

medical ['med·ɪ·kəl] **I.** *adj* facilities, research medizinisch; advice, treatment ärztlich **II.** *n* (*fam*) ärztliche Untersuchung; **to have a ~** sich ärztlich untersuchen lassen

'medical certificate *n* ärztliches Attest

medical exami'nation *n* ärztliche Untersuchung

Medicare ['med·ɪ·ker] *n* staatliche Gesundheitsfürsorge [für Senioren]

medicate ['med·ɪ·keɪt] *vt usu passive* (*treat with drug*) **to be ~d** medikamentös behandelt werden

medication [ˌmed·ɪ·'keɪ·ʃən] *n* MED Medikamente *pl*

medicinal [mə·'dɪs·ə·nəl] *adj* medizinisch

medicine ['med·ɪ·sɪn] *n* ❶ (*for illness*) Medizin *f* ❷ (*substance*) Medikament *nt* ❸ (*medical science*) Medizin *f*; **to practice ~** den Arztberuf ausüben

'medicine cabinet, 'medicine chest *n* Hausapotheke *f*

medieval [ˌmi·di·'i·vəl] *adj* mittelalterlich

mediocre [ˌmi·di·'oʊ·kər] *adj* mittelmäßig

meditate ['med·ɪ·teɪt] *vi* ❶ (*think deeply*) nachdenken (**on/about** über +*akk*) ❷ (*as spiritual exercise*) meditieren

meditation [ˌmed·ɪ·'teɪ·ʃən] *n* ❶ (*spiritual exercise*) Meditation *f* ❷ (*serious thought*) Nachdenken *nt*

Mediterranean [ˌmed·ɪ·tə·'reɪ·ni·ən] *n* Mittelmeer *nt*

medium ['mi·di·əm] **I.** *adj* ❶ (*average*) durchschnittlich; **of ~ height** von mittlerer Größe ❷ FOOD steak halb durch **II.** *n* <*pl* -s> ❶ (*means*) Medium *nt*, Mittel *nt*; **advertising ~** Werbeträger *m* ❷ (*art material*) Medium *nt*

medium-'rare *adj* FOOD englisch

'medium-size(d) *adj* mittelgroß

medley ['med·li] *n* ❶ (*mixture*) Gemisch *nt* ❷ (*of tunes*) Medley *nt*

meek [mik] *adj* ❶ (*gentle*) sanftmütig ❷ (*pej: submissive*) unterwürfig

meet [mit] **I.** *n* (*sporting event*) Sportveranstaltung *f* **II.** *vt* <met, met> ❶ (*by chance*) treffen ❷ (*by arrangement*) ■**to ~ sb** sich mit jdm treffen ❸ (*make acquaintance of*) kennen lernen ❹ (*fulfill*) erfüllen; *deadline* einhalten ▶PHRASES: **to make ends ~** über die Runden kommen **III.** *vi* <met, met> ❶ (*by chance*) sich begegnen ❷ (*by arrangement*) sich treffen; **to ~ for a drink** sich auf einen Drink treffen ❸ (*get acquainted*) sich kennen lernen; **no, we haven't met** nein, wir kennen uns noch nicht ❹ (*join*) zusammentreffen; *roads* zusammenlaufen

◆ **meet with** *vi* ❶ (*have meeting*) treffen ❷ (*experience*) problems stoßen auf +*akk*; **to ~ with success** Erfolg haben

meeting ['mi·tɪŋ] *n* (*organized gathering*) Versammlung *f*, Sitzung *f*, Besprechung *f*; **to hold a ~** eine Besprechung abhalten

'meeting point *n* ❶ (*place to gather*) Treffpunkt *m* ❷ (*point of contact*) Schnittpunkt *m*

mega ['megə] *adj* (*fam*) Riesen-, Mega-

mega- ['megə] *in compounds* + *adj* (*fam*) mega- *fam*; **~-cool** megacool *sl*, geil *sl*

'megabucks *npl* (*fam*) Schweinegeld *nt kein pl sl*

'megabyte *n* Megabyte *nt*

'megahertz *n* Megahertz *nt*

megalomania [ˌmeg·ə·loʊ·'meɪ·ni·ə] *n* (*lust for power*) Größenwahn *m pej*

'megaphone *n* Megaphon *nt*

'megawatt *n* Megawatt *nt*

M

melancholy ['mel·ən·kal·i] I. *n* Melancholie *f* II. *adj* melancholisch, schwermütig

melee ['meɪ·leɪ] *n usu sing* Handgemenge *nt*

mellow ['mel·ou] I. *adj* <-er, -est *or* more ~, most ~> ❶ (*relaxed*) *person* abgeklärt, locker *fam* ❷ (*not harsh*) sanft; *flavor* mild; *wine* lieblich II. *vi colors* weicher werden; *flavor* milder werden

melodic [mə·'lad·ɪk] *adj* melodisch

melodramatic [,mel·ou·drə·'mæt·ɪk] *adj* melodramatisch

melody ['mel·ə·di] *n* Melodie *f*

melon ['mel·ən] *n* Melone *f*

melt [melt] I. *n* ❶ (*thaw*) Schneeschmelze *f* ❷ FOOD *patty* ~ Sandwich *mit geschmolzenem Käse* II. *vt, vi* schmelzen

'meltdown *n* ❶ TECH [Ein]schmelzen *nt* ❷ (*fam: collapse*) Zusammenbruch *m*

'melting point *n* Schmelzpunkt *m*

'melting pot *n* (*fig*) Schmelztiegel *m*

member ['mem·bər] *n* (*of group*) Angehörige(r) *f(m); of club, party* Mitglied *nt*

membership ['mem·bər·ʃɪp] *n* ❶ (*people*) ■**the** ~ die Mitglieder *pl;* (*number of people*) Mitgliederzahl *f* ❷ (*being member*) Mitgliedschaft *f*

'membership card *n* Mitgliedsausweis *m*

membrane ['mem·breɪn] *n* Membran *f*, Häutchen *nt*

memento <*pl* -s> [mə·'men·tou] *n* Andenken *nt*

memoir ['mem·war] *n* ❶ (*personal account*) Erinnerungen *pl* ❷ (*autobiography*) ■~**s** *pl* Memoiren *pl*

'memo pad *n* Notizblock *m*

memorabilia [,mem·ər·ə·'bɪl·i·ə] *npl* Souvenirs *pl*

memorable ['mem·ər·ə·bəl] *adj* unvergesslich

memorial [mə·'mɔr·i·əl] *n* Denkmal *nt*

Me'morial Day *n* Volkstrauertag *m* (*wird in den Vereinigten Staaten am letzten Montag im Mai gefeiert*)

memorize ['mem·ə·raɪz] *vt facts* sich

dat einprägen; *poem, song* auswendig lernen

memory ['mem·ə·ri] *n* ❶ (*ability to remember*) Gedächtnis *nt* (**for** für +*akk*) ❷ (*remembered event*) Erinnerung *f* ❸ COMPUT Speicher *m*

'memory bank *n* COMPUT Speicherbank *f*

men [men] *n pl of* **man**

menace ['men·əs] I. *n* Drohung *f* II. *vt* bedrohen

menacing ['men·ɪs·ɪŋ] *adj attr* drohend

mend [mend] I. *vt* reparieren ▶PHRASES: **to** ~ **one's ways** sich bessern II. *vi* gesund werden *a. fig; bone* heilen

menial ['mi·ni·əl] *adj* niedrig; ~ **labor** Hilfsarbeit *f*

meningitis [,men·ɪn·'dʒaɪ·ṭɪs] *n* Gehirnhautentzündung *f*

menopause ['men·ə·pɔz] *n* Wechseljahre *pl*

men's room *n* Herrentoilette *f*

menstruation [,men·stru·'eɪ·ʃən] *n* Menstruation *f geh*, Periode *f*

mental ['men·təl] *adj* ❶ (*of the mind*) geistig, mental; ~ **process** Denkprozess *m* ❷ (*psychological*) psychisch, seelisch; ~ **illness** Geisteskrankheit *f*; (*fam: crazy*) verrückt

'mental hospital *n* psychiatrische Klinik

mentally ['men·təl·i] *adv* ❶ (*psychologically*) psychisch ❷ (*intellectually*) geistig

menthol ['men·θɔl] *n* Menthol *nt*

mention ['men·ʃən] I. *n* (*reference*) Erwähnung *f* II. *vt* erwähnen

menu ['men·ju] *n* ❶ (*in restaurant*) Speisekarte *f* ❷ COMPUT Menü *nt*

'menu bar *n* COMPUT Menüleiste *f*

meow [mi·'aʊ] *vi* miauen

mercenary ['mɜr·sə·ner·i] *n* Söldner *m*

merchandise ['mɜr·tʃən·daɪz] *n* ECON Handelsware *f*

merchant ma'rine *n* Handelsmarine *f*

'merchant ship *n* Handelsschiff *nt*

merciful ['mɜr·sɪ·fəl] *adj* gnädig

merciless ['mɜr·sɪ·lɪs] *adj* ❶ (*showing no mercy*) gnadenlos ❷ (*relentless*) unnachgiebig

mercury ['mɜr·kjə·ri] *n* Quecksilber *nt*

mercy ['mɜr·si] *n* (*compassion*) Mitleid *nt*, Erbarmen *nt*; (*forgiveness*) Gnade *f* ▶PHRASES: **to be at the ~ of sb** jdm auf Gnade oder Ungnade ausgeliefert sein

mere [mɪr] *adj* nur, nichts als

merely ['mɪr·li] *adv* nur, bloß *fam*

merge [mɜrdʒ] **I.** *vi* ❶ (*join*) zusammenkommen; *roads* zusammenlaufen ❷ ECON *companies* fusionieren ❸ (*fuse*) verschmelzen (**with**/**into** mit +*dat*) ❹ AUTO **to ~ left** sich rechts einordnen **II.** *vt companies* zusammenschließen

merger ['mɜr·dʒər] *n* ECON Fusion *f*

meridian [mə·'rɪd·i·ən] *n* GEOG Meridian *m*

meringue [mə·'ræŋ] *n* Baiser *nt*, Meringe *f*

merit ['mer·ɪt] **I.** *n* ❶ (*worthiness*) Verdienst *nt* ❷ (*good quality*) gute Eigenschaft, Vorzug *m* **II.** *vt* verdienen

mermaid ['mɜr·meɪd] *n* Seejungfrau *f*

merry ['mer·i] *adj* fröhlich; **M~ Christmas** Frohe [*o* Fröhliche] Weihnachten

'merry-go-round *n* (*fairground ride*) Karussell *nt*

mesh [meʃ] **I.** *n* Geflecht *nt* **II.** *vi gears* ineinandergreifen

mesmerize ['mez·mə·raɪz] *vt* faszinieren

mess <*pl* -es> [mes] *n* ❶ *usu sing* (*messy state*) Unordnung *f*, Durcheinander *nt* ❷ *usu sing* (*disorganized state*) Chaos *nt;* **to be in a ~** sich in einem schlimmen Zustand befinden

♦ **mess around** *vi* ❶ (*behave foolishly*) herumblödeln *fam*, Unfug treiben ❷ (*waste time*) herumspielen ❸ (*tinker*) herumspielen, herumfummeln (**with** an +*dat*)

♦ **mess up** *vt* (*fam*) ❶ (*botch up*) verpfuschen; *plan* vermasseln ❷ (*make messy*) in Unordnung bringen

♦ **mess with** *vi* ❶ (*get involved with*) ■**to ~ with sb** sich mit jdm einlassen; (*cause trouble to*) jdn schlecht behandeln; **don't ~ with me!** verarsch mich

bloß nicht! *derb* ❷ ■**to ~ with sth** (*tamper*) an etw *dat* herumspielen

message ['mes·ɪdʒ] *n* (*communication*) Nachricht *f*; **to leave a ~** eine Nachricht hinterlassen ▶PHRASES: **to get the ~** (*fam*) kapieren

messenger ['mes·ɪn·dʒər] *n* Bote *m*, Botin *f*

'mess hall *n* Kasino *nt*

messy ['mes·i] *adj* ❶ (*untidy*) unordentlich; *person* schlampig ❷ (*dirty*) schmutzig

met [met] *vt, vi pt of* **meet**

metabolism [mɪ·'tæb·ə·lɪz·əm] *n* Stoffwechsel *m*

metal ['met·əl] **I.** *n* Metall *nt;* **precious ~** Edelmetall *nt* **II.** *adj* aus Metall nach *n*

metallic [mə·'tæl·ɪk] *adj* metallisch; **~ paint** Metalleffektlack *m*

metallurgy ['mət·əl·ɜr·dʒi] *n* Metallurgie *f*

'metalwork *n* Metallarbeit *f*

metaphor ['met·ə·fɔr] *n* Metapher *f*

metaphoric(al) [,met·ə·'fɔr·ɪk(əl)] *adj* metaphorisch

mete [mit] *vt* ■**to ~ out ○ sth** [**to sb**] [jdm] etw auferlegen

meteor ['mi·ti·ər] *n* Meteor *m*

meteoric [,mi·ti·'ɔr·ɪk] *adj* ❶ ASTRON meteorisch ❷ (*rapid*) kometenhaft

meteorological [,mi·ti·ə·rə·'ladʒ·ɪ·kəl] *adj* meteorologisch

meteorologist [,mi·ti·ə·'ral·ə·dʒɪst] *n* Meteorologe *m*, Meteorologin *f*

meter[1] ['mi·tər] *n* Messuhr *f*, Zähler *m;* [**parking**] ~ Parkuhr *f*

meter[2] ['mi·tər] *n* (*unit of measurement*) Meter *m*

methane ['meθ·eɪn] *n* Methan *nt*

methanol ['meθ·ə·nɔl] *n* Methanol *nt*

method ['meθ·əd] *n* (*way of doing sth*) Methode *f*; TECH Verfahren *nt*

methodical [mə·'θad·ɪ·kəl] *adj* methodisch, systematisch

Methodist ['meθ·ə·dɪst] *n* Methodist(in) *m(f)*

methyl alcohol [,meθ·əl·'æl·kə·hɔl] *n see* **methanol**

M

meticulous [mɪˈtɪk·jʊ·ləs] *adj* peinlich genau; **~ detail** kleinstes Detail

metric [ˈmet·rɪk] *adj* metrisch

metro [ˈmet·roʊ] *adj attr short for* **metropolitan** Stadt-

metropolitan [ˌmet·rəˈpɑl·ə·tən] *adj* (*of large city*) weltstädtisch; **~ area** Metropolregion *f*

mew [mju] *vi* miauen

Mexican [ˈmek·sɪ·kən] **I.** *n* Mexikaner(in) *m(f)* **II.** *adj* mexikanisch

Mexico [ˈmek·sɪ·koʊ] *n* Mexiko *nt*

mg *n* <*pl* -> *abbrev of* **milligram** mg

MHz *n* <*pl* -> *abbrev of* **megahertz** MHz

MI *abbrev of* **Michigan**

mica [ˈmaɪ·kə] *n* Glimmererde *f*

mice [maɪs] *n pl of* **mouse**

Mich. *abbrev of* **Michigan**

Michigan [ˈmɪʃ·ɪ·gən] *n* Michigan *nt*

'Mickey Mouse *adj attr* (*pej fam*) Scherz- *fam*; **~ computer** Spielzeugcomputer *m*

microbe [ˈmaɪ·kroʊb] *n* Mikrobe *f*

microbi'ology [ˌmaɪ·kroʊ-] *n* Mikrobiologie *f*

'microchip *n* Mikrochip *m*

'microclimate *n* Mikroklima *nt*

microelec'tronics *n* + *sing vb* Mikroelektronik *f*

'microfilm *n* Mikrofilm *m*

micro'organism *n* Mikroorganismus *m*

'microphone *n* Mikrofon *nt*

'microprocessor *n* Mikroprozessor *m*

microscope [ˈmaɪ·krə·skoʊp] *n* Mikroskop *nt*

microscopic [ˌmaɪ·krəˈskɑp·ɪk] *adj* ❶ (*fam: tiny*) winzig; **to look at sth in ~ detail** etw haargenau prüfen ❷ *analysis, examination* mikroskopisch

'microwave **I.** *n* Mikrowellenherd *m*, Mikrowelle *f* **II.** *vt* in der Mikrowelle kochen/erwärmen

mid'day *n* Mittag *m*; **at ~** mittags

middle [ˈmɪd·əl] **I.** *n* ❶ (*center; between things*) Mitte *f*; *of fruit, nuts* Innere[s] *nt*; (*center part*) *of book, movie* Mittelteil *m* ❷ (*in time, space*) mitten; **in the ~ of the road** mitten auf der

Straße; **in the ~ of the night** mitten in der Nacht; **in the ~ of nowhere** (*fig*) am Ende der Welt; **to be in the ~ of eating** (*busy with*) mitten dabei sein zu essen ❸ (*fam: waist*) Taille *f* **II.** *adj attr* mittlere(r, s)

middle 'age *n* mittleres Alter

middle-'aged *adj* mittleren Alters nach n

middle 'class *n* ▪ **the ~** der Mittelstand

'middle-class *adj* Mittelstands-, mittelständisch

Middle 'East *n* ▪ **the ~** der Nahe Osten

'middleman *n* ❶ ECON (*person*) Zwischenhändler(in) *m(f)* ❷ (*go-between*) Mittelsmann *m*

middle 'name *n* zweiter Vorname

middle-of-the-'road *adj film, music* mittelmäßig

'middleweight *n* SPORT Mittelgewichtler(in) *m(f)*

Mid'east *n* ▪ **the ~** der Nahe [*o* Mittlere] Osten

midge [mɪdʒ] *n* [kleine] Mücke

midget [ˈmɪdʒ·ɪt] **I.** *n* (*dwarf*) Liliputaner(in) *m(f)* **II.** *adj* (*small*) winzig

'midnight *n* Mitternacht *f*

'midpoint *n usu sing* Mittelpunkt *m*

midriff [ˈmɪd·rɪf] *n*, **midsection** [ˈmɪd·sek·ʃən] *n* Taille *f*

mid'summer *n* Hochsommer *m*

mid'term *n* (*midpoint*) *of political office* Halbzeit *f* der Amtsperiode; *of school year* Schulhalbjahr *nt*

midway [ˈmɪd·weɪ] **I.** *adv* auf halbem Weg; **the projector broke ~ through the film** mitten im Film ging der Projektor kaputt **II.** *n* Mittelweg einer Ausstellung oder eines Jahrmarktes, an dem sich die Hauptattraktionen befinden

mid'week *n* Wochenmitte *f*

midwife [ˈmɪd·waɪf] *n* Hebamme *f*

mid'winter *n* Mitte *f* des Winters

might[1] [maɪt] *n* ❶ (*authority*) Macht *f* ❷ (*strength*) Kraft *f*; MIL Stärke *f*

might[2] [maɪt] **I.** *pt of* **may** **II.** *aux vb* ❶ (*expressing possibility*) **I ~ go to the movies tonight** vielleicht gehe ich heute Abend ins Kino; (*could*) **someone**

called at six; **it ~ have been him** um
sechs rief jemand an, das könnte er gewesen sein; (*expressing probability*)
könnte(n) ② (*form: polite form of may*)
~ I ...? dürfte ich [vielleicht] ...?; **~ I
make a suggestion?** dürfte ich vielleicht einen Vorschlag machen?
mighty ['maɪ·ti] **I.** *adj river* gewaltig;
country mächtig; *warrior* stark **II.** *adv*
(*fam*) sehr; **that was ~ nice of you** das
war wirklich nett von dir
migraine ['maɪ·greɪn] *n* Migräne *f*
migrant ['maɪ·grənt] *n* ① (*person*) Zu-
wanderer *m*, Zuwanderin *f* ② (*bird*)
Zugvogel *m*
migrate ['maɪ·greɪt] *vi* (*change habitat*)
wandern, umherziehen; **to ~ south**
birds nach Süden ziehen
migration [maɪ·'greɪ·ʃən] *n* Wanderung *f*; *of birds* Zug *m*
migratory ['maɪ·grə·tɔr·i] *adj animals*
Wander-; **~ bird** Zugvogel *m*
mike [maɪk] *n* (*fam*) *short for* **microphone** Mikro *nt*
mild [maɪld] *adj* ① (*gentle*) *person*
sanft; *soap* schonend; (*not severe*)
shock leicht; *climate* mild ② MED *infection* leicht ③ (*not strong in flavor*)
cheese mild; *cigarette* leicht
mildew ['mɪl·du] *n* Schimmel *m*; (*on
plants*) Mehltau *m*
mildly ['maɪld·li] *adv* ① (*gently*) leicht;
clean schonend; (*not severely*) milde
② (*as an understatement*) **to put it ~**
um es [mal] milde auszudrücken
mildness ['maɪld·nɪs] *n* ① *of person*
Sanftmut *f* ② *of weather* Milde *f*
mile [maɪl] *n* ① (*distance*) Meile *f*; **we
could see for ~s and ~s** wir konnten
meilenweit sehen ② (*fam: far from*) **to
be ~s from the truth** weit von der
Wahrheit entfernt sein
mileage, milage ['maɪ·lɪdʒ] *n* ① (*gasoline efficiency*) Kraftstoffverbrauch *m*
② (*distance traveled*) Meilenstand *m*
'**milestone** *n* (*a. fig*) Meilenstein *m*
militant ['mɪl·ɪ·tənt] *adj* militant
militaristic [ˌmɪl·ɪ·tə·'rɪs·tɪk] *adj* milita-
ristisch

military ['mɪl·ɪ·ter·i] *n pl* ■**the ~** das
Militär
military po'lice *npl* ■**the ~** die Militär-
polizei
military 'service *n* Wehrdienst *m*
militia [mɪ·'lɪʃ·ə] *n* Miliz *f*
milk [mɪlk] **I.** *n* Milch *f*; (*breast milk*)
Muttermilch *f*; (*in coconuts*) Kokos-
milch *f*; **whole ~** Vollmilch *f* **II.** *vt cow*
melken
milk 'chocolate *n* Milchschokolade *f*
'**milkman** *n* Milchmann *m*
'**milk shake** *n* Milchshake *m*
milky ['mɪl·ki] *adj* ① (*with milk*) mit
Milch *nach n* ② (*not clear*) *glass, water*
milchig; *skin* sanft
Milky 'Way *n* ■**the ~** die Milchstraße
mill [mɪl] **I.** *n* ① (*building, machine*)
Mühle *f* ② (*factory*) Fabrik *f*; **steel ~**
Stahlwerk *nt* **II.** *vt grain* mahlen; *metal*
walzen
millennium <*pl* -s> [mɪ·'len·i·əm] *n*
Jahrtausend *nt*
miller ['mɪl·ər] *n* Müller(in) *m(f)*
millet ['mɪl·ət] *n* Hirse *f*
milligram ['mɪl·ɪ·græm] *n* Milli-
gramm *nt*
milliliter ['mɪl·ɪ·ˌli·tər] *n* Milliliter *m*
millimeter ['mɪl·ɪ·ˌmi·tər] *n* Millimeter *m*
million ['mɪl·jən] *n* ① (*1,000,000*) Million *f*; **a ~ dollars** eine Million Dollar
② (*fam: countless number*) **I've already heard that story a ~ times** diese Geschichte habe ich schon tausendmal gehört
millionaire [ˌmɪl·jə·'ner] *n* Millionär *m*
'**millstone** *n* Mühlstein *m*
mime [maɪm] **I.** *n* THEAT Pantomime *m*,
Pantomimin *f* **II.** *vt* THEAT pantomimisch
darstellen; (*mimic*) mimen
mimic ['mɪm·ɪk] *vt* <-ck-> nachahmen;
(*when teasing*) nachäffen *peJ*
min. I. *n* ① *abbrev of* **minimum** Min.
② *abbrev of* **minute** Min. **II.** *adj abbrev
of* **minimum** min.
minaret [ˌmɪn·ə·'ret] *n* Minarett *nt*
mince [mɪns] *vt* FOOD hacken; (*in
grinder*) durch den Fleischwolf drehen;

M

onions klein schneiden ▶PHRASES: **to not ~ [one's] words** kein Blatt vor den Mund nehmen

'**mincemeat** *n süße Gebäckfüllung aus Dörrobst und Gewürze*

mincer ['mɪnsər] *n* Fleischwolf *m*

mind [maɪnd] **I.** *n* ❶(*brain, intellect*) Geist *m*; (*sanity a.*) Verstand *m*; **to have a logical ~** logisch denken können; **to use one's ~** seinen Verstand gebrauchen ❷(*thoughts*) Gedanken *pl*; **what's on your ~?** woran denkst du?; **to bear sth in ~** etw nicht vergessen; **to have sb/sth in ~** an jdn/etw denken ❸(*intention*) **to make up one's ~** sich entscheiden; **to set one's ~ to sth** sich *dat* etw in den Kopf setzen ❹*usu sing* (*opinion*) Meinung *f*; **to change one's ~** es sich *dat* anders überlegen ▶PHRASES: **to be out of one's ~** (*crazy*) übergeschnappt sein **II.** *vt* ❶(*be careful of, look after*) aufpassen auf +*akk* ❷(*care about*) **don't ~ me** kümmere dich nicht um mich; **I don't ~ the heat** die Hitze macht mir nichts aus ❸(*fam: object*) **do you ~ if I smoke?** stört es Sie, wenn ich rauche?; **I wouldn't ~ a cup of coffee** gegen eine Tasse Kaffee hätte ich nichts einzuwenden ▶PHRASES: **~ you** allerdings **III.** *vi* ❶(*care*) sich *dat* etwas daraus machen; **I don't ~** das ist mir egal; **never ~!** [ist doch] egal! ❷(*object*) etwas dagegen haben

'**mind-bending** *adj* (*fam*) *puzzle* knifflig

'**mind-blowing** *adj* (*sl*) irre *fam*

'**mind-boggling** *adj* (*fam*) irrsinnig *fam*, verrückt

minded ['maɪn·dɪd] *adj pred* **to be mathematically ~** eine mathematische Neigung haben

mindful ['maɪnd·fəl] *adj pred* **to be ~ of sb's feelings** jds Gefühle berücksichtigen

mindless ['maɪnd·lɪs] *adj* ❶(*pointless*) sinnlos; *violence, jealousy* blind ❷(*not intellectual*) *work* geistlos; *entertainment* anspruchslos

'**mind reader** *n* Gedankenleser(in) *m(f)*

'**mindset** *n* Denkart *f*

mine¹ [maɪn] **I.** *n* ❶Bergwerk *nt*; (*fig: valuable source*) Fundgrube *f* ❷MIL (*explosive*) Mine *f* **II.** *vt* *coal, iron* abbauen, fördern; *gold* schürfen **III.** *vi* **to ~ for gold** nach Gold graben

mine² [maɪn] *pron poss* (*belonging to me*) meine(r, s); **she's an old friend of ~** sie ist eine alte Freundin von mir

'**minefield** *n* Minenfeld *nt*; (*fig*) gefährliches Terrain

miner ['maɪ·nər] *n* Bergarbeiter(in) *m(f)*

mineral ['mɪn·ər·əl] *n* Mineral *nt*

'**mineral deposits** *npl* Erzlagerstätten *pl*

mineralogist [,mɪn·ə·'ral·ə·dʒɪst] *n* Mineraloge *m*, Mineralogin *f*

'**mineral water** *n* Mineralwasser *nt*; (*carbonated*) Sprudel *m*

'**minesweeper** *n* NAUT Minenräumer *m*

mingle ['mɪŋ·gəl] **I.** *vt usu passive* mischen **II.** *vi* ❶(*socialize*) sich untereinander vermischen ❷(*mix*) sich vermischen

mini- ['mɪni] *in compounds* Mini-

miniature ['mɪn·i·ə·t∫ər] **I.** *adj attr* Miniatur- *f* **II.** *n* Miniatur *f*

'**minibus** *n* Kleinbus *m*

minimal ['mɪn·ɪ·məl] *adj* minimal, Mindest-

minimize ['mɪn·ɪ·maɪz] *vt* (*reduce*) auf ein Minimum beschränken, minimieren

minimum ['mɪn·ɪ·məm] **I.** *n* <*pl* -s> Minimum *nt* **II.** *adj* ❶(*lowest possible*) Mindest-; **~ requirements** Mindestanforderungen *pl* ❷(*very low*) Minimal-

minimum-security 'prison *n* offenes Gefängnis

minimum 'wage *n* Mindestlohn *m*

mining ['maɪ·nɪŋ] *n* Bergbau *m*

'**mining engineer** *n* Bergbauingenieur(in) *m(f)*

'**miniskirt** *n* Minirock *m*

minister ['mɪn·ɪ·stər] *n* ❶(*protestant priest*) Pfarrer(in) *m(f)* ❷(*in government*) Minister(in) *m(f)*

ministerial [,mɪn·ɪ·'stɪr·i·əl] *adj* Minister-, ministeriell

ministry ['mɪn·ɪ·stri] *n* Ministerium *nt*

mink [mɪŋk] *n* <*pl* -> Nerz *m*

Minn. *abbrev of* **Minnesota**

Minnesota [ˌmɪn·ɪ·'sou·tə] *n* Minnesota *nt*

minor ['maɪ·nər] **I.** *adj* ❶ (*small, not serious*) *detail* nebensächlich; *crime* geringfügig; *repair* unwichtig; *illness* leicht ❷ (*low-ranking*) untergeordnet **II.** *n* (*underage person*) Minderjährige(r) *f(m)*

minority [maɪ·'nɔr·ɪ·ti] *n* Minderheit *f*; **in a ~ of cases** in wenigen Fällen

mint¹ [mɪnt] **I.** *n* ❶ (*coin factory*) Münzanstalt *f*, Prägeanstalt *f* ❷ (*fam: lots of money*) **to make a ~** einen Haufen Geld machen *fam* **II.** *vt money* prägen; *gold, silver* münzen

mint² [mɪnt] *n* ❶ (*herb*) Minze *f* ❷ (*candy*) Pfefferminz[bonbon] *nt*

minus ['maɪ·nəs] **I.** *prep* MATH minus; **what is 57 ~ 39?** was ist 57 minus 39? **II.** *n* <*pl* -es> Minus[zeichen] *nt* **III.** *adj attr* (*number*) minus; **~ ten [degrees] Fahrenheit** minus zehn Grad Fahrenheit

minuscule ['mɪn·ə·skjul] *adj* winzig

minute¹ ['mɪn·ɪt] **I.** *n* ❶ Minute *f* ❷ (*short time*) Moment *m*; [**wait**] **just a ~!** (*for delay*) einen Moment noch!; (*in disbelief*) Moment mal! **II.** *adj attr* **~ hand** Minutenzeiger *m*

minute² [maɪ·'nut] *adj* winzig; **in ~ detail** bis ins kleinste Detail

minutely [maɪ·'nut·li] *adv* bis ins kleinste Detail

miracle ['mɪr·ə·kəl] *n* Wunder *nt a. fig*

miraculous [mɪ·'ræk·jə·ləs] *adj* wunderbar; **to make a ~ recovery** wie durch ein Wunder genesen

mirage [mə·'rɑʒ] *n* (*fig*) Trugbild *nt*, Illusion *f*

mirror ['mɪr·ər] **I.** *n* Spiegel *m* **II.** *vt* widerspiegeln

mirror 'image *n* Spiegelbild *nt*

misapprehension [ˌmɪs·æprɪ·'hen·ʃən] *n* Missverständnis *nt*

misappropriate [ˌmɪs·ə·'prou·pri·eɪt] *vt funds* veruntreuen

misbehave [ˌmɪs·bɪ·'heɪv] *vi* (*behave badly*) *adult* sich schlecht benehmen; *child* ungezogen sein

misbehavior [ˌmɪs·bɪ·'heɪv·jər] *n by adult* schlechtes Benehmen; *by child* Ungezogenheit *f*

misc. *adj short for* **miscellaneous** verschiedene(r, s)

miscalculate [ˌmɪs·'kæl·kjə·leɪt] *vt* ❶ MATH falsch berechnen ❷ (*misjudge*) falsch einschätzen

miscarriage ['mɪs·ˌkær·ɪdʒ] *n* ❶ MED Fehlgeburt *f* ❷ LAW **~ of justice** Justizirrtum *m*

miscellaneous [ˌmɪs·ə·'leɪ·ni·əs] *adj* verschiedene(r, s), diverse(r, s)

mischief ['mɪs·tʃɪf] *n* Unfug *m*; **to keep sb out of ~** jdn davon abhalten, Dummheiten zu machen; **to mean ~** Unfrieden stiften wollen

mischievous ['mɪs·tʃə·vəs] *adj* immer zu Streichen aufgelegt; **~ child** Schlingel *m*

misconception [ˌmɪs·kən·'sep·ʃən] *n* falsche Vorstellung

M

misconduct [ˌmɪs·'kɑn·dʌkt] *n* (*bad behavior*) schlechtes Benehmen; MIL schlechte Führung; **professional ~** standeswidriges Verhalten

misconstrue [ˌmɪs·kən·'stru] *vt* missdeuten, missverstehen, falsch auslegen

misdemeanor [ˌmɪs·dɪ·'mi·nər] *n* ❶ (*minor bad action*) [leichtes] Vergehen, [leichter] Verstoß ❷ LAW geringfügiges Vergehen

misdirect [ˌmɪs·dɪ·'rekt] *vt* ❶ (*send in wrong direction*) in die falsche Richtung schicken; *letter* falsch adressieren ❷ (*aim wrongly*) *hockey puck* in die falsche Richtung lenken

miser ['maɪ·zər] *n* Geizhals *m*

miserable ['mɪz·ə·bəl] *adj* ❶ (*unhappy*) unglücklich, elend; **to make life ~ [for sb]** [jdm] das Leben unerträglich machen ❷ *attr* (*bad-tempered*) griesgrämig; (*fam: as insult*) mies, Mist-

miserably ['mɪz·ər·ə·bli] *adv* ❶ (*unhappily*) traurig ❷ (*extremely*) schrecklich, furchtbar ❸ (*utterly*) jämmerlich

miserliness ['maɪ·zər·li·nɪs] *n* Geiz *m*

miserly ['maɪ·zər·li] *adj* geizig

misery ['mɪz·ə·ri] *n* ❶ (*suffering*) Elend *nt*, Not *f* ❷ (*unhappiness*) Jammer *m* ▶PHRASES: **to make sb's life a ~** jdm das Leben zur Qual [*o* Hölle] machen

misfire *vi* [mɪs·'faɪr] *engine* eine Fehlzündung haben; *gun* versagen

misfit ['mɪs·fɪt] *n* Außenseiter(in) *m(f)*

misfortune [,mɪs·'fɔr·tʃən] *n* (*bad luck*) Pech *nt*, Unglück *nt*

misguided [mɪs·'gaɪ·dɪd] *adj attempt, measures* unsinnig; *effort, policy* verfehlt; *enthusiasm* falsch, unangebracht; **to be ~ in sth** mit etw *dat* falschliegen

mishandle [,mɪs·'hæn·dəl] *vt* (*mismanage*) falsch behandeln; *business* schlecht führen; *investigation* [grobe] Fehler machen bei +*dat*

mishap ['mɪs·hæp] *n* Unfall *m*, Panne *f*

mishear [,mɪs·'hɪr] I. *vt* <-heard, -heard> falsch hören II. *vi* <-heard, -heard> sich verhören

mishmash ['mɪʃ·mæʃ] *n* Mischmasch *m fam*

misinform [,mɪs·ɪn·'fɔrm] *vt* falsch informieren

misinterpret [,mɪs·ɪn·'tɜr·prɪt] *vt* missverstehen; *text* falsch interpretieren

misinterpretation [,mɪs·ɪn·tɜr·prɪ·'teɪ·ʃən] *n* Missverständnis *nt*, Fehlinterpretation *f*

misjudge [,mɪs·'dʒʌdʒ] *vt situation* falsch einschätzen [*o* beurteilen]; *amount, distance* falsch schätzen

mislay <-laid, -laid> [,mɪs·'leɪ] *vt* verlegen

mislead <-led, -led> [mɪs·'lid] *vt* (*deceive*) täuschen

misleading [mɪs·'li·dɪŋ] *adj* irreführend

mismanage [,mɪs·'mæn·ɪdʒ] *vt* falsch umgehen mit +*dat*; *business* schlecht führen

mismanagement [,mɪs·'mæn·ɪdʒ·mənt] *n* schlechte Verwaltung [*o* Führung]

misnomer [,mɪs·'noʊ·mər] *n* (*inappro-* *priate name*) unzutreffende Bezeichnung

misogynist [mɪ·'sadʒ·ə·nɪst] *n* Frauenfeind *m*

misplace [,mɪs·'pleɪs] *vt* verlegen

misprint ['mɪs·,prɪnt] *n* Druckfehler *m*

mispronounce [,mɪs·prə·'naʊns] *vt* falsch aussprechen

misread <-read, -read> [,mɪs·'rid] *vt* ❶ (*read incorrectly*) falsch lesen ❷ (*misinterpret*) falsch verstehen

misrepresent [,mɪs·,rep·rɪ·'zent] *vt* falsch darstellen

misrepresentation [,mɪs·,rep·rɪ·zen·'teɪ·ʃən] *n* falsche Darstellung; LAW falsche Angabe

miss¹ [mɪs] I. *n* <*pl* -es> (*failure*) Fehlschlag *m;* SPORT (*in basketball*) Fehlwurf *m* II. *vi* nicht treffen; *projectile a.* danebengehen; *person, weapon a.* danebenschießen III. *vt* ❶ (*not hit*) nicht treffen ❷ *train* verpassen; *deadline* nicht [ein]halten ❸ (*be absent*) versäumen; **to ~ school** in der Schule fehlen ❹ *opportunity* verpassen ❺ (*not notice*) nicht bemerken; (*deliberately*) übersehen ❻ (*notice loss, long for*) vermissen

♦ **miss out** *vi* zu kurz kommen; ■ **to ~ out on sth** *chance, opportunity* sich *dat* etw entgehen lassen

miss² [mɪs] *n* ■ **M~** Fräulein *nt*

Miss. *abbrev of* **Mississippi**

misshapen [,mɪs·'ʃeɪ·pən] *adj* (*out of shape*) unförmig

missile ['mɪs·əl] *n* MIL Flugkörper *m*, Rakete *f*

'missile base *n* Raketenstützpunkt *m*

'missile launcher *n* [Raketen]abschussrampe *f*

missing ['mɪs·ɪŋ] *adj* ❶ (*disappeared*) *thing* verschwunden; *person* vermisst; (*not there*) fehlend; **to report sb ~** jdn als vermisst melden ❷ MIL **~ in action** [nach Kampfeinsatz] vermisst

missing 'link *n* ❶ (*in evolution*) unbekannte Zwischenstufe ❷ (*connector*) Bindeglied *nt*

missing 'person *n* Vermisste(r) *f(m)*

mission ['mɪʃ·ən] n ① (*task*) Einsatz m, Mission f ② (*goal*) Ziel nt

mission con'trol n Bodenkontrolle f

Mississippi [mɪs·ɪ·'sɪ·pi] n Mississippi nt

Missouri [mɪ·'zʊr·i] n Missouri nt

misspell <-spelled or -spelt, -spelled> [ˌmɪs·'spel] vt (*spell wrongly*) falsch buchstabieren

mist [mɪst] n ① (*light fog*) [leichter] Nebel, Dunst m ② (*condensation*) Beschlag m

mistake [mɪ·'steɪk] I. n Fehler m, Irrtum m; **spelling ~** Rechtschreibfehler m; **by ~** aus Versehen, versehentlich II. vt <-took, -taken> falsch verstehen; **there's no mistaking a painting by Picasso** ein Gemälde von Picasso ist unverwechselbar

mistaken [mɪ·'steɪ·kən] I. pp of **mistake** II. adj *announcement* irrtümlich; *idea* falsch; **~ identity** Personenverwechslung f; **to be ~** sich irren (*about* in +dat)

Mister ['mɪs·tər] n ① (*Mr.*) Herr m ② (*a. iron fam: form of address*) Chef m; **hey, ~!** he, Sie da! fam

mistletoe ['mɪs·əl·toʊ] n Mistel f

mistook [mɪ·'stʊk] pt of **mistake**

mistreat [ˌmɪs·'trit] vt misshandeln

mistress <pl -es> ['mɪs·trɪs] n (*sexual partner*) Geliebte f

mistrial ['mɪs·ˌtraɪ·əl] n (*misconducted trial*) fehlerhaftes Gerichtsverfahren

mistrust [ˌmɪs·'trʌst] I. n Misstrauen nt II. vt misstrauen

mistrustful [ˌmɪs·'trʌst·fəl] adj misstrauisch (*of* gegenüber +dat)

misty ['mɪs·ti] adj ① (*slightly foggy*) [leicht] neblig ② (*blurred*) undeutlich

misunderstand <-stood, -stood> [ˌmɪs·ˌʌn·dər·'stænd] I. vt missverstehen II. vi sich irren

misunderstanding [ˌmɪs·ʌn·dər·'stæn·dɪŋ] n ① (*misinterpretation*) Missverständnis nt ② (*quarrel*) Meinungsverschiedenheit f

misuse I. n [ˌmɪs·'jus] (*wrong use*) of *funds, position* Missbrauch m, falscher Gebrauch [o Umgang] II. vt [ˌmɪs·'juz] *funds, position* missbrauchen, falsch gebrauchen

mitten ['mɪt·ən] n Fäustling m

mix [mɪks] I. n ① (*combination*) Mischung f ② (*premixed ingredients*) Fertigmischung f; **sauce ~** Fertigsauce f II. vi ① (*combine*) sich mischen [lassen]; (*go together*) zusammenpassen ② (*make contact with people*) unter Leute gehen; *host* sich unter die Gäste mischen III. vt ① (*blend*) [miteinander] [ver]mischen; *drinks* mixen; *paint* mischen ② *sound tracks* mischen

◆ **mix in** I. vi sich einfügen II. vt untermischen

◆ **mix up** vt ① (*mistake for another*) verwechseln ② (*combine ingredients*) vermischen ③ usu passive (*be involved with*) **to be/get ~ed up in sth** in etw akk verwickelt sein/werden

mixed [mɪkst] adj (*positive and negative*) gemischt; **~ blessing** kein reiner Segen

mixed 'doubles npl SPORT gemischtes Doppel

mixed e'conomy n gemischte Wirtschaftsform

mixer ['mɪk·sər] n ① (*machine*) Mixgerät nt ② (*drink*) **~ [drink]** Mixgetränk nt

mixture ['mɪks·tʃər] n ① (*combination*) Mischung f; *of ingredients* Gemisch nt ② (*mixed fluid substance*) Mischung f; AUTO Gemisch nt

'mix-up n (*confused state*) Durcheinander nt, Verwirrung f

ml <pl -> n abbrev of **milliliter** ml

MLB [ˌem·el·'bi] n SPORT abbrev of **Major League Baseball** MLB f

mm n abbrev of **millimeter** mm

MN abbrev of **Minnesota**

MO [ˌem·'oʊ] n ① abbrev of **Missouri** ② abbrev of **modus operandi** Arbeitsweise f ③ abbrev of **Medical Officer** Stabsarzt m, Stabsärztin f

mo. [moʊ] n abbrev of **month**

moan [moʊn] I. n ① (*groan*) Stöhnen nt; *of the wind* Heulen nt II. vi ① (*groan*)

M

stöhnen; *wind* heulen ❷ (*complain*) klagen, sich beschweren (**at** bei +*dat*)

mob [mab] **I.** *n* ❶ (*usu pej: crowd*) Mob *m;* **angry** ~ aufgebrachte Menge ❷ (*criminal gang*) Verbrecherbande *f,* Gang *f;* ■**the M**~ die Mafia **II.** *vt* <-bb-> (*surround*) umringen

mobile ['moʊ·bəl] **I.** *adj* ❶ (*able to move, flexible*) beweglich ❷ (*in a vehicle*) mobil, fahrbar; ■**to be** ~ motorisiert sein **II.** *n* (*ceiling decoration*) Mobile *nt*

mobile 'home *n* [großer] Wohnwagen *m,* Trailer *m*

mobility [moʊ·'bɪl·ɪ·ţi] *n* Mobilität *f*

mobilize ['moʊ·bə·laɪz] *vt* ❶ (*prepare for war*) *army* mobilisieren ❷ (*organize*) *supporters* aktivieren, mobilisieren ❸ (*put to use*) einsetzen; *snowplows* zum Einsatz bringen

mobster ['mab·stər] *n* (*fam*) Gangster *m*

moccasin ['mak·ə·sɪn] *n* Mokassin *m*

mock [mak] **I.** *adj* ❶ nachgemacht, Schein-; *sympathy* gespielt **II.** *vt* (*ridicule*) lächerlich machen, verspotten

mockery ['mak·ə·ri] *n* (*ridicule*) Spott *m,* Hohn *m*

'mockingbird *n* ORN Spottdrossel *f*

mode [moʊd] *n* ❶ (*way*) Weise *f,* Methode *f;* ~ **of operation** Betriebsart *f* ❷ COMPUT, TECH (*operation*) Betriebsart *f,* Modus *m*

model ['mad·əl] **I.** *n* ❶ Modell *nt;* COMPUT [schematical] Darstellung, Simulation *f* ❷ (*example*) Vorbild *nt* ❸ (*perfect example*) Muster *nt* ❹ *fashion* Model *nt* **II.** *vt* <-ll-> ❶ (*make figure*) modellieren ❷ (*on computer*) [schematisch] darstellen, simulieren ❸ (*show clothes*) vorführen

modem ['moʊ·dəm] *n* Modem *nt*

moderate I. *adj* ['mad·ər·ət] ❶ (*neither large nor small*) *amount, quantity, size* mittlere(r, s); *prices* angemessen ❷ (*not excessive*) mäßig, gemäßigt; LAW *sentence* mild **II.** *n* POL Gemäßigte(r) *f(m)* **III.** *vt* ['mad·ər·eɪt] (*make less extreme*) mäßigen

moderation [ˌmad·ə·'reɪ·ʃən] *n* Mäßigung *f;* **in** ~ in Maßen

moderator ['mad·ə·reɪ·ţər] *n* ❶ (*mediator*) Vermittler(in) *m(f)* ❷ (*of discussion*) Moderator(in) *m(f)*

modern ['mad·ərn] *adj* modern

modernize ['mad·ər·naɪz] **I.** *vt* modernisieren **II.** *vi* modern werden

modest ['mad·ɪst] *adj* ❶ (*not boastful*) bescheiden ❷ (*fairly small*) *income* bescheiden, mäßig

modesty ['mad·ɪ·sti] *n* ❶ (*without boastfulness*) Bescheidenheit *f* ❷ (*chasteness*) Anstand *m*

modification [ˌmad·ɪ·fɪ·'keɪ·ʃən] *n* Modifikation *f*

modifier ['mad·ɪ·faɪ·ər] *n* LING näher bestimmendes Wort; (*as an adjective*) Beiwort *nt;* (*as an adverb*) Umstandswort *nt*

modify <-ie-> ['mad·ɪ·faɪ] *vt* ❶ (*change*) [ver]ändern ❷ (*alter*) *engine* modifizieren

modular ['madʒ·ə·lər] *adj* modular, Baukasten-

module ['madʒ·ul] *n* Modul *nt*

mohair ['moʊ·her] *n* Mohair *m*

moist [mɔɪst] *adj* feucht; *cake* saftig

moisten ['mɔɪ·sən] *vt* anfeuchten

moisture ['mɔɪs·tʃər] *n* Feuchtigkeit *f*

moisturize ['mɔɪs·tʃə·raɪz] *vt* befeuchten

moisturizer ['mɔɪs·tʃə·raɪ·zər] *n* Feuchtigkeitscreme *f*

molasses [moʊ·'læs·ɪz] *n* Melasse *f*

mold[1] [moʊld] **I.** *n* ❶ (*shape*) Form *f* ❷ (*fig*) Typ *m;* **to break the** ~ [of sth] neue Wege in etw *dat* gehen **II.** *vt* formen

mold[2] [moʊld] *n* BOT Schimmel *m*

molding ['moʊl·dɪŋ] *n* ARCHIT Fries *m;* ART [Zier]leiste *f*

moldy ['moʊl·di] *adj* *food* schimmelig

mole[1] [moʊl] *n* ANAT [kleines] Muttermal

mole[2] [moʊl] *n* ZOOL Maulwurf *m*

molecular [mə·'lek·jə·lər] *adj* molekular, Molekular-

molecule ['mal·ɪ·kjul] *n* Molekül *nt*

molehill ['moʊl·hɪl] n Maulwurfshügel m

molest [mə·'lest] vt ❶ (annoy) belästigen ❷ (attack sexually) [sexuell] belästigen

mollusk, mollusc ['mal·əsk] n Molluske f, Weichtier nt

molt [moʊlt] vi birds [sich] mausern; cats, dogs haaren; snakes, insects sich häuten

molten ['moʊl·tən] adj geschmolzen

mom [mam] n Mama f, Mutti f bes NORDD

mom-and-pop store n Tante-Emma-Laden m fam

moment ['moʊ·mənt] n ❶ (very short time) Moment m, Augenblick m; at any ~ jeden Augenblick; in a ~ gleich, sofort ❷ (specific time) Zeitpunkt m; ■ at the ~ im Augenblick, momentan

momentarily [,moʊ·mən·'ter·ɪ·li] adv ❶ (briefly) kurz, eine Weile ❷ (very soon) gleich

momentary ['moʊ·mən·ter·i] adj kurz

momentous [moʊ·'men·təs] adj bedeutsam, folgenschwer; day bedeutend

momentum [moʊ·'men·təm] n (force) Schwung m, Wucht f; to gain ~ in Schwung kommen

momma ['ma·mə] n (childspeak) Mama f

mommy ['mam·i] n (childspeak) Mama f, Mami f

monarchy ['man·ər·ki] n Monarchie f

monastery ['man·ə·ster·i] n [Mönchs]kloster nt

monastic [mə·'næs·tɪk] adj REL mönchisch

Monday ['mʌn·di] n Montag m; see also **Tuesday**

monetary ['man·ə·ter·i] adj ECON Geld-, Währungs-

money ['mʌn·i] n ❶ (cash) Geld nt; to be short on ~ knapp bei Kasse sein fam; to put ~ into sth Geld in etw akk stecken fam ❷ (fam: pay) Bezahlung f, Verdienst m ▶ PHRASES: **easy** ~ leicht verdientes Geld

moneyed ['mʌn·id] adj (form) vermögend

'moneymaker n ❶ (person) erfolgreicher Geschäftsmann/erfolgreiche Geschäftsfrau ❷ (profitable business) gewinnbringendes Geschäft fam ❸ (profitable product) Verkaufsschlager m fam

'money market n Geldmarkt m

mongrel ['maŋ·grəl] n ❶ BOT, ZOOL (result of crossing) Kreuzung f ❷ (esp pej: dog breed) Promenadenmischung f hum o pej

monitor ['man·ɪ·tər] I. n ❶ Bildschirm m, Monitor m ❷ POL (observer) Beobachter(in) m(f) II. vt ❶ (check) beobachten, kontrollieren ❷ RADIO, TELEC, TV (view, listen in on) abhören ❸ (maintain quality, keep under surveillance) überwachen

monk [mʌŋk] n Mönch m

monkey ['mʌŋ·ki] n Affe m

♦ **monkey around** vi (fam) ❶ (waste time) seine Zeit verschwenden ❷ (pej: play) ■ to ~ around with sth mit etw dat herumspielen

'monkey business n ❶ (silliness) Blödsinn m ❷ (trickery) faule Tricks pl

'monkey wrench n Universal[schrauben]schlüssel m

monochrome ['man·oʊ·kroʊm] adj PHOT Schwarzweiß-

monogamy [mə·'nag·ə·mi] n Monogamie f

monogram ['man·ə·græm] n Monogramm nt

monolingual [,man·oʊ·'lɪŋ·gwəl] adj einsprachig

monologue, monolog ['man·ə·lag] n Monolog m

monopolize [mə·'nap·ə·laɪz] vt ❶ ECON (control) monopolisieren ❷ (keep for oneself) ganz für sich akk beanspruchen; conversation an sich akk reißen

monopoly [mə·'nap·ə·li] n Monopol nt

monorail ['man·oʊ·reɪl] n Einschienenbahn f

monosodium glutamate [,man·oʊ·

M

sou·di·əm·'glu·tə·meıt] n CHEM [Mo-no]natriumglutamat nt, Glutamat nt

monosyllabic [,man·ə·sı·'læb·ık] adj (pej: taciturn) wortkarg

monotonous [mə·'nat·ən·əs] adj eintönig, monoton

monsoon [man·'sun] n ▪the ~[s] der Monsun kein pl

monster ['man·stər] I. n ❶ (imaginary creature) Monster nt, Ungeheuer nt ❷ (unpleasant person) Scheusal nt; (inhuman person) Unmensch m ❸ (fam: huge thing) Ungetüm nt, Monstrum nt II. adj attr (fam: huge) ungeheuer

monstrous ['man·strəs] adj ❶ (huge) ungeheuer, monströs ❷ (awful) scheußlich; cruelty abscheulich

Mont. abbrev of **Montana**

montage [man·'taʒ] n Montage f

Montana [man·'tæn·ə] n Montana nt

month [mʌnθ] n Monat m; to take a two-~ vacation zwei Monate Urlaub nehmen

monthly ['mʌnθ·li] I. adj, adv monatlich II. n Monatsschrift f

monument ['man·jə·mənt] n ❶ (fig: memorial) Mahnmal nt ❷ (historical structure) Denkmal nt

monumental [,man·jə·'men·təl] adj ❶ (tremendous) gewaltig, kolossal ❷ ART (large-scale) monumental

moo [mu] vi muhen

mood [mud] n Laune f, Stimmung f; in a good ~ gut gelaunt; to not be in the ~ to do sth zu etw dat keine Lust haben

moodiness ['mu·dı·nıs] n (sullenness) Missmut m, Verdrossenheit f; (grumpiness) Übellaunigkeit f

moody ['mu·di] adj ❶ (temperamental) launisch ❷ (sullen) missmutig

moon [mun] n ASTRON Mond m; full ~ Vollmond m ▶PHRASES: to be over the ~ about sth über etw akk überglücklich sein

'**moonbeam** n Mondstrahl m

'**moonlight** I. n (moonshine) Mondlicht nt II. vi <-lighted> (fam: work at a second job) schwarzarbeiten

'**moonshine** n (fam: liquor) schwarzgebrannter Alkohol

moor[1] [mʊr] vt, vi NAUT festmachen

moor[2] [mʊr] n Heideland nt, [Hoch]moor nt

mooring ['mʊr·ıŋ] n NAUT (berth) Liegeplatz m

moose <pl -> [mus] n Elch m

mop [map] I. n ❶ (for cleaning) Mopp m ❷ (wiping) to give sth a ~ etw moppen II. vt <-pp-> feucht wischen

mope [moʊp] vi Trübsal blasen

♦**mope around** vi (fam) trübsinnig herumschleichen

moral ['mɔr·əl] I. adj ❶ (ethical) moralisch, ethisch ❷ (virtuous) person moralisch, anständig II. n ❶ (of story) Moral f ❷ (standards of behavior) ▪~s pl Moralvorstellungen pl

morale [mə·'ræl] n Moral f

morality [mə·'ræl·ı·ti] n ❶ (moral principles) moralische Grundsätze ❷ (moral system) Ethik f

moralize ['mɔr·ə·laız] vi moralisieren

moratorium <pl -s> [,mɔr·ə·'tɔr·i·əm] n ❶ (period of waiting) Warfrist f ❷ COMM Moratorium nt

morbid ['mɔr·bıd] adj (unhealthy) morbid, krankhaft

more [mɔr] I. adj comp of many, much noch mehr; two ~ days until Christmas noch zwei Tage bis Weihnachten; we can't take any ~ calls wir können keine weiteren Anrufe entgegennehmen; some ~ coffee? noch etwas Kaffee? II. pron ❶ (greater amount) mehr; ~ and ~ came es kamen immer mehr; is there any ~? ist noch etwas da?; no ~ nichts weiter; (countable) keine mehr ❷ all the ~ ... umso mehr ...; the ~ the better je mehr, desto besser III. adv ❶ (forming comparatives) let's find a ~ sensible way of doing it wir sollten eine vernünftigere Lösung finden; ~ importantly wichtiger noch ❷ (to a greater extent) you should listen ~ and talk less du solltest besser zuhören und weniger reden

▶PHRASES: **~ or less** (all in all) mehr oder weniger; (approximately) ungefähr

morgue [mɔrg] n Leichen[schau]haus nt

Mormon ['mɔr·mən] n Mormone m, Mormonin f

morning ['mɔr·nɪŋ] I. n Morgen m, Vormittag m; **tomorrow ~** morgen Vormittag; **yesterday ~** gestern Morgen II. interj (fam) Morgen!; **good ~!** guten Morgen!

'morning sickness n morgendliche Übelkeit

moron ['mɔr·ɑn] n (pej fam) Trottel m

moronic [mɔˈrɑn·ɪk] adj (pej fam) blöde

morose [məˈroʊs] adj mürrisch

morphine ['mɔr·fin] n Morphium nt

Morse [mɔrs], **Morse 'code** n Morsealphabet nt

morsel ['mɔr·səl] n (of food) Bissen m, Happen m

mortal ['mɔr·təl] adj ① sterblich ② (fatal) tödlich

mortality [mɔrˈtæl·ɪ·t̬i] n Sterblichkeit f

mortar ['mɔr·tər] n ① ARCHIT, TECH (mixture) Mörtel m ② CHEM Mörser m; **~ and pestle** Mörser m und Stößel m

'mortar shell n Mörsergranate f

mortgage ['mɔr·gɪdʒ] n Hypothek f

mortician [mɔrˈtɪʃ·ən] n Leichenbestatter(in) m(f)

mortify <-ie-> ['mɔr·t̬ə·faɪ] vt usu passive ■ **to be mortified** (be humiliated) gedemütigt sein; (be embarrassed) sich ärgern

mortuary ['mɔr·tʃu·er·i] n Leichen[schau]haus nt

mosaic [moʊˈzeɪ·ɪk] n Mosaik nt

Moscow ['mɑs·kaʊ] n Moskau nt

Moslem ['mɑz·ləm] adj, n see **Muslim**

mosque [mɑsk] n Moschee f

mosquito <pl -es> [məˈski·t̬oʊ] n Moskito m; **~ net** Moskitonetz nt

moss <pl -es> [mɑs] n (plant) Moos m

mossy ['mɑs·i] adj ① (overgrown with moss) moosbedeckt ② (resembling moss) moosartig

most [moʊst] I. pron ① (largest quantity) ■ **the ~** am meisten; **at the |very| ~** [aller]höchstens ② pl (the majority) die Mehrheit ③ (best) ■ **the ~** höchstens; **to make the ~ of sth** das Beste aus etw dat machen II. adj ① (greatest in amount, degree) am meisten ② (majority of, nearly all) die meisten ▶PHRASES: **for the ~ part** im Allgemeinen III. adv ① (forming superlative) im Deutschen durch Superlativ ausgedrückt; **~ easily** am leichtesten ② (form: extremely) höchst, äußerst; **~ certainly** ganz bestimmt ③ (to the greatest extent) am meisten; **at ~** höchstens

mostly ['moʊst·li] adv ① (usually) meistens ② (mainly) größtenteils ③ (chiefly) hauptsächlich

motel [moʊˈtel] n Motel nt

moth [mɑθ] n Motte f, Nachtfalter m

'mothball I. n Mottenkugel f II. vt usu passive (put away for a while) einmotten

mother ['mʌð·ər] n Mutter f

'mother-in-law <pl mothers-> n Schwiegermutter f

motherly ['mʌð·ər·li] adj mütterlich; **~ love** Mutterliebe f

mother-of-'pearl n Perlmutt nt

'Mother's Day n Muttertag m

mother 'tongue n Muttersprache f

motif [moʊˈtif] n Motiv nt

motion ['moʊ·ʃən] I. n ① (movement) Bewegung f; **in slow ~** in Zeitlupe ② POL (proposal) Antrag m II. vi ■ **to ~ to sb to do sth** jdn durch einen Wink auffordern, etw zu tun

motionless ['moʊ·ʃən·lɪs] adj bewegungslos

motion 'picture n [Spiel]film m

motivate ['moʊ·t̬ə·veɪt] vt ① (provide with motive) **they are ~d by a desire to help people** ihre Handlungsweise wird von dem Wunsch bestimmt, anderen zu helfen ② (arouse interest) motivieren

motivation [ˌmoʊ·t̬əˈveɪ·ʃən] n ① (reason) Begründung f, Veranlassung f ② (drive) Motivation f

M

motive ['mou·tɪv] n Beweggrund m; **ulterior** ~ tieferer Beweggrund

motor ['mou·tər] n Antriebsmaschine f, [Verbrennungs]motor m

'**motorbike** n (fam) Motorrad nt

'**motorboat** n Motorboot nt

'**motorcycle** n Motorrad nt

motoring ['mou·tər·ɪŋ] n Fahren nt

motorist ['mou·tər·ɪst] n Kraftfahrer(in) m(f)

motorized ['mou·tə·raɪzd] adj motorisiert; ~ **wheelchair** elektrisch betriebener Rollstuhl

'**motor racing** n Autorennsport m

'**motor scooter** n Motorroller m

'**motor vehicle** n Kraftfahrzeug nt

motto <pl -s> ['mat·ou] n Motto nt

mound [maund] n Haufen m; (small hill) Hügel m; (in baseball) **pitcher's** ~ Mound m

mount [maunt] **I.** n ❶ (horse) Pferd nt ❷ (setting) of picture Halterung f; of jewel Fassung f ❸ (mountain) Berg m; **M~ Everest** Mount Everest m; **M~ Etna** der Ätna **II.** vt ❶ (get on to ride) [auf]steigen auf +akk ❷ (fix securely) aufhängen; **to ~ a camera on a tripod** eine Kamera auf ein Stativ montieren ❸ stairs hochgehen ❹ (organize) organisieren; campaign starten **III.** vi ❶ (increase) wachsen, [an]steigen, größer werden ❷ (get on a horse) aufsteigen

mountain ['maun·tən] n Berg m; pl a. Gebirge nt

mountaineer [,maun·tə·'nɪr] n Bergsteiger(in) m(f)

mountainous ['maun·tə·nəs] adj gebirgig

'**mountain range** n Gebirgszug m

mounted ['maun·tɪd] adj beritten geh

mounting ['maun·tɪŋ] **I.** n ❶ (on a horse) Besteigen nt ❷ (display surface) picture Halterung f; of machine Sockel m **II.** adj attr (increasing) steigend

Mount Rushmore n Mount Rushmore m (Granitfelsen, in dem die Büsten von George Washington, Thomas Jefferson, Theodore Roosevelt und Abraham Lincoln eingehauen sind)

mourn [mɔrn] vt, vi trauern (**for** um +akk)

mourner ['mɔr·nər] n Trauernde(r) f(m)

mournful ['mɔrn·fəl] adj (sad) traurig; (gloomy) trübsinnig

mouse <pl mice> [maus] n ZOOL, COMPUT Maus f

'**mouse pad** n COMPUT Mauspad nt

'**mousetrap** n Mausefalle f

mousse [mus] n ❶ FOOD Mousse f ❷ (cosmetics) Schaum m

moustache ['mʌs·tæʃ] n see **mustache**

mousy ['mau·si] adj farblos; hair mausgrau

mouth [mauθ] n ❶ (of human) Mund m; of animal Maul nt; **to have a big ~** (fig) ein großes Mundwerk haben fam ❷ (opening) Öffnung f; of river Mündung f

mouthful ['mauθ·fʊl] n of food Bissen m; of drink Schluck m

'**mouthpiece** n of musical instrument Mundstück nt; of telephone Sprechmuschel f

mouth-to-'mouth, mouth-to-mouth resusci'tation n Mund-zu-Mund-Beatmung f

'**mouthwash** n Mundwasser nt

'**mouth-watering** adj [sehr] appetitlich, köstlich

movable ['mu·və·bəl] adj beweglich

move [muv] **I.** n ❶ (movement) Bewegung f; **to be on the ~** unterwegs sein; **to make a ~** (fam: leave) sich auf den Weg machen; (start) loslegen fam ❷ (step) Schritt m; (measure) Maßnahme f ❸ (in games) Zug m; **it's your ~** du bist dran ❹ (change of residence) Umzug m; (change of job) Stellenwechsel m ▶PHRASES: **to get a ~ on** (fam) sich beeilen **II.** vi ❶ (change position) sich bewegen; **no one ~d** keiner rührte sich; **to ~ [out of the way]** aus dem Weg gehen ❷ (change) **that's my final decision, and I am not going to ~ [on it]** das ist mein letztes Wort und dabei bleibt es ❸ (progress) vorankommen; **to ~ forward** Fortschritte machen ❹ (change address) umziehen

III. *vt* **➊** (*change position of*) bewegen; (*place somewhere else*) woanders hinstellen; (*clear*) wegräumen; (*transport*) befördern **➋** (*transfer*) verlegen; (*to another job, class*) versetzen **➌** (*cause emotions*) bewegen; **to ~ sb to tears** jdn zu Tränen rühren

move around I. *vi* **➊** (*go around*) herumgehen **➋** (*travel*) umherreisen **➌** (*change jobs*) oft wechseln; (*change house*) oft umziehen II. *vt* (*change position of*) [hin und her] bewegen; *furniture* umstellen

◆ **move along** I. *vt* ▪**to ~ sb ◯ along** jdn zum Weitergehen bewegen II. *vi* **➊** (*walk farther on*) weitergehen; (*drive farther on*) weiterfahren **➋** (*make room*) aufrücken

◆ **move away** I. *vi* **➊** (*leave*) weggehen; *vehicle* wegfahren **➋** (*move to new house*) wegziehen II. *vt* wegräumen; (*push away*) wegrücken

◆ **move down** I. *vi* **➊** (*change position*) sich nach unten bewegen; (*slip down*) runterrutschen *fam* **➋** (*change value*) *prices* fallen II. *vt* (*change position of*) nach unten bewegen; (*place lower down*) nach unten stellen

◆ **move in** I. *vi* **➊** (*enter a new home*) einziehen; ▪**to ~ in with sb** zu jdm ziehen **➋** (*advance to attack*) anrücken; **to ~ in for the kill** zum tödlichen Schlag ausholen II. *vt* (*change position of*) nach innen bewegen **➋** (*send*) einsetzen; *troops, police* einrücken lassen

◆ **move off** I. *vi* sich in Bewegung setzen II. *vt* wegräumen

◆ **move on** I. *vi* **➊** (*continue a trip*) sich wieder auf den Weg machen **➋** (*progress in career*) beruflich weiterkommen **➌** (*change subject*) ▪**to ~ on to sth** zu etw *dat* übergehen II. *vt* (*force to leave*) vertreiben

◆ **move out** I. *vi* **➊** (*stop inhabiting*) ausziehen **➋** (*leave*) *troops* abziehen II. *vt* **➊** (*clear*) wegräumen; (*take outside*) hinausbringen **➋** (*make leave*) *tenant* kündigen

◆ **move over** I. *vi* **➊** (*make room*) Platz machen **➋** (*switch*) ▪**to ~ over to sth** zu etw *dat* übergehen II. *vt* herüberschieben; (*put aside*) zur Seite räumen

◆ **move up** I. *vi* **➊** (*advance*) aufrücken; (*professionally, socially*) aufsteigen **➋** (*make room*) aufrücken **➌** (*increase*) *prices* steigen II. *vt* (*change position of*) nach oben bewegen

movement ['muːv·mənt] *n* **➊** Bewegung *f* **➋** FIN, STOCKEX Schwankung[en] *f(pl)* **➌** MUS Satz *m* **➍** (*tendency*) Trend *m* **➎** (*mechanism*) *of clock* Uhrwerk *nt*

movie ['muː·vi] *n* [Kino]film *m*; ▪**the ~ s** *pl* das Kino

'movie camera *n* Filmkamera *f*

'moviegoer *n* Kinogänger(in) *m(f)*

'movie star *n* Filmstar *m*

'movie theater *n* Kino *nt*

moving ['muː·vɪŋ] *adj* **➊** *attr* MECH beweglich **➋** (*causing emotion*) bewegend, ergreifend

mow <mowed, mowed *or* mown> [moʊ] *vt lawn* mähen; *field* abmähen

M

mower ['moʊ·ər] *n* Rasenmäher *m*

mown [moʊn] *pp of* **mow**

mpg [ˌem·piˈdʒi] *abbrev of* **miles per gallon** Meilen pro Gallone

mph [ˌem·piˈeɪtʃ] *abbrev of* **miles per hour** Meilen pro Stunde

Mr. ['mɪs·tər] *n* (*title for man*) Herr *m*

Mrs. ['mɪs·ɪz] *n* (*title for married woman*) Frau, Fr.

MS [ˌem·es] *n* **➊** *abbrev of* **Master of Science** **➋** *abbrev of* **Mississippi** Mississippi *m* **➌** *abbrev of* **multiple sclerosis** MS *f*

Ms. [mɪz] *n* (*title for woman, married or unmarried*) Fr., Frau (*Alternativbezeichnung zu Mrs und Miss, die sowohl für verheiratete als auch für unverheiratete Frauen zutrifft*)

ms [ˌem·es] *n* **➊** *abbrev of* **manuscript** Mskr. **➋** *abbrev of* **millisecond** ms

MSG [ˌem·es·ˈdʒi] *n* CHEM *abbrev of* **monosodium glutamate**

MST [ˌem·es·ˈti] *n abbrev of* **Mountain**

Standard Time Mountain Standardzeit f

MT abbrev of **Montana**

Mt. n abbrev of **mount I 3**

much [mʌtʃ] **I.** adj <more, most> + sing viel; **how ~ ...?** wie viel ...?; **twice as ~** doppelt so viel **II.** pron **①** (relative amount) viel; **however ~ you dislike her ...** wie unsympathisch sie dir auch sein mag, ... **②** (great deal) viel; **~ of what you say is right** vieles von dem, was Sie sagen, ist richtig **③** with neg (pej: poor example) **he's not ~ to look at** er sieht nicht gerade umwerfend aus **III.** adv <more, most> **①** (greatly) sehr; **~ to our surprise** zu unserer großen Überraschung; **to not be ~ good at sth** in etw dat nicht sehr gut sein **②** (nearly) fast; **~ the same** fast so **③** (specifying degree) **I like him as ~ as you do** ich mag ihn genauso sehr wie du; **thank you very ~** herzlichen Dank **IV.** conj (although) auch wenn; **~ as I like you, ...** so gern ich dich auch mag, ...

muck [mʌk] n **①** (dirt) Dreck m fam **②** (euph: excrement) Haufen m fam

mucus ['mju·kəs] n Schleim m

mud [mʌd] n Schlamm m

muddle ['mʌd·əl] n Durcheinander nt

muddy ['mʌd·i] **I.** vt verschmutzen **II.** adj schlammig; ground matschig

'mud flap n of car Kotflügel m; of bicycle Schutzblech nt

'mudpack n Gesichtsmaske f

'mudslide n Schlammlawine f

muff [mʌf] vt (fam) vermasseln

muffin ['mʌf·ɪn] n Muffin nt (kleiner, hoher, runder, meist süßer Kuchen aus Rührteig)

muffle ['mʌf·əl] vt dämpfen; (fig) [ab]schwächen

muffler ['mʌf·lər] n of car Auspufftopf m

mug¹ [mʌg] n (cup) Becher m (mit Henkel)

mug² [mʌg] **I.** n (pej: face) Visage f **II.** vt <-gg-> (rob) überfallen und ausrauben

mugger ['mʌg·ər] n [Straßen]räuber(in) m(f)

mugging ['mʌg·ɪŋ] n [Straßen]raub m, Überfall m (auf offener Straße)

muggy ['mʌg·i] adv weather schwül

mulberry ['mʌl·ber·i] n Maulbeere f

mule¹ [mjul] n (animal) Maultier nt

mule² [mjul] n (shoe) halboffener Schuh

mull [mʌl] vt **①** (spice) **~ed wine** Glühwein m **②** (ponder) ■**to ~ sth** [over] sich dat etw durch den Kopf gehen lassen

mullet ['mʌl·ɪt] n Meeräsche f

multi'colored adj mehrfarbig

multi'cultural adj multikulturell

multi'lateral adj POL multilateral geh

multi'lingual adj mehrsprachig

multi'media **I.** n Multimedia f **II.** adj multimedial

multimillion'aire n Multimillionär(in) m(f)

multi'national **I.** n multinationaler Konzern, Multi m **II.** adj multinational

multiplayer ['mʌl·ti·pler·ər] adj attr computer game Multiplayer-

multiple ['mʌl·tə·pəl] **I.** adj attr vielfach, vielfältig **II.** n Vielfache[s]

multiplex ['mʌl·tə·pleks] n Multiplex-Kino nt

multiplier ['mʌl·tə·plaɪ·ər] n Multiplikator m

multiply <-ie-> ['mʌl·tə·plaɪ] vt multiplizieren (**by** mit + dat)

multi'purpose adj multifunktional, Mehrzweck-

multi'racial adj gemischtrassig; **~ society** Gesellschaft, die aus den Angehörigen verschiedener Rassengruppen besteht

multi'tasking n COMPUT Ausführen nt mehrerer Programme, Multitasking nt

mum [mʌm] adj (fam: silent) still; **to keep ~** den Mund halten

mumble ['mʌm·bəl] vi (speak unclearly) nuscheln

mumbo jumbo [,mʌm·boʊ·'dʒʌm·boʊ] n (fam) Quatsch m

mummy ['mʌm·i] n Mumie f

mumps [mʌmps] *n + sing vb* Mumps *m*

munch [mʌntʃ] *vt, vi* mampfen

mundane [mʌn·'deɪn] *adj* (*unexciting*) *question* banal; (*routine*) *activity, task* alltäglich

municipal [mju·'nɪs·ə·pəl] *adj* Stadt-, kommunal

munitions [mju·'nɪʃ·ənz] *npl* (*weapons*) Waffen *pl*; (*weapons and ammunition*) Kriegsmaterial *nt kein pl*; (*ammunition*) Munition *f kein pl*

mural ['mjʊr·əl] *n* Wandgemälde *nt*

murder ['mɜr·dər] I. *n* Mord *m*, Ermordung *f* II. *vt* ermorden, umbringen *a. fig*

murderer ['mɜr·dər·ər] *n* Mörder(in) *m(f)*

murky ['mɜr·ki] *adj* düster; *night* finster; *water* trübe

murmur ['mɜr·mər] *vt, vi* murmeln

muscle ['mʌs·əl] *n* ❶ (*contracting tissue*) Muskel *m* ❷ (*fig: influence*) Stärke *f*
 ◆**muscle in** *vi* sich [rücksichtslos] einmischen; ■**to ~ in on sth** sich irgendwo [mit aller Gewalt] hineindrängen

'muscleman *n* Muskelprotz *m*

muscular ['mʌs·kjə·lər] *adj* ❶ (*relating to muscles*) muskulär ❷ (*with well-developed muscles*) muskulös

museum [mju·'zi·əm] *n* Museum *nt*

mush [mʌʃ] *n* (*fam*) Brei *m*, Mus *nt*

mushroom ['mʌʃ·rum] *n* Pilz *m*

mushy ['mʌʃ·i] *adj* ❶ (*pulpy*) breiig ❷ (*soppily romantic*) schnulzig

music ['mju·zɪk] *n* Musik *f*

musical ['mju·zɪ·kəl] I. *adj* musikalisch II. *n* Musical *nt*

'music box *n* Spieluhr *f*

musician [mju·'zɪʃ·ən] *n* Musiker(in) *m(f)*

musk [mʌsk] *n* Moschus *m*

muskrat ['mʌs·kræt] *n* Moschusratte *f*

Muslim ['mʌz·ləm] I. *n* Moslem(in) *m(f)*, Muslim(in) *m(f)* II. *adj* moslemisch, muslimisch

muss [mʌs] *vt* durcheinanderbringen

mussel ['mʌs·əl] *n* [Mies]muschel *f*

must [mʌst] I. *aux vb* ❶ (*be obliged, be required*) müssen; **for security reasons, all bags ~ be left at the cloakroom** lassen Sie bitte aus Sicherheitsgründen alle Handtaschen in der Garderobe; ■**~ not** [*or* **~n't**] nicht dürfen; **you ~n't say anything to anyone about this matter** darüber darfst du mit niemandem sprechen ❷ (*should*) **you really ~ read this book** dieses Buch sollten Sie wirklich einmal lesen ❸ (*be certain to*) müssen; **she ~ be wondering where I am** sie wird sich bestimmt fragen, wo ich abgeblieben bin II. *n* Muss *nt kein pl*

mustache ['mʌs·tæʃ] *n* Schnurrbart *m*

mustang ['mʌs·tæŋ] *n* Mustang *m*

mustard ['mʌs·tərd] *n* Senf *m*

muster ['mʌs·tər] *vt soldiers* [zum Appell] antreten lassen

'must-have *adj attr* (*fam*) unentbehrlich

mustn't ['mʌs·ənt] *short for* **must not** *see* **must**

'must-see *n* **this film is a ~** diesen Film muss man gesehen haben

musty ['mʌs·ti] *adj book* mod[e]rig; *room, smell* muffig

mutation [mju·'teɪ·ʃən] *n* Mutation *f fachspr*

mute [mjut] I. *n* ❶ (*person*) Stumme(r) *f(m)* ❷ MUS (*quieting device*) Dämpfer *m* II. *vt sound* dämpfen III. *adj* stumm

muted ['mju·tɪd] *adj* (*not loud*) gedämpft; (*fig*) schweigend; *colors* gedeckt

mutilate ['mju·tə·leɪt] *vt* verstümmeln; (*fig*) verschandeln

mutilation [ˌmju·tə·'leɪ·ʃən] *n* Verstümmelung *f*; (*fig*) Verschandelung *f*

mutinous ['mju·tə·nəs] *adj* meuterisch; *shareholders* rebellisch

mutiny ['mju·tɪ·ni] I. *n* Meuterei *f* II. *vi* <-ie-> meutern

mutter ['mʌt·ər] *vi* (*mumble*) ■**to ~** [**to oneself**] irgendetwas [vor sich *akk* hin]murmeln

mutton ['mʌt·ən] *n* Hammelfleisch *nt*

mutual ['mju·tʃu·əl] *adj* gegenseitig;

M

friends gemeinsam; *agreement* wechselseitig

'**mutual fund** *n* FIN offener Investmentfond

mutually ['mjuː·tʃʊ·ə·li] *adv* gegenseitig

Muzak® ['mjuː·zæk] *n* Musikberieselung *f*

muzzle ['mʌz·əl] I. *n* ❶ (*animal mouth*) Maul *nt* ❷ (*mouth covering*) Maulkorb *m* ❸ (*gun end*) Mündung *f* II. *vt* *animal* einen Maulkorb anlegen; (*fig*) *person, press* mundtot machen

MW *n* PHYS *abbrev of* **megawatt** MW *nt*

my [maɪ] *adj poss* mein(e); ~ **brother and sister** mein Bruder und meine Schwester; **I hurt ~ foot** ich habe mir den Fuß verletzt; **I need a car of ~ own** ich brauche ein eigenes Auto

myopic [maɪ·'ɒp·ɪk] *adj* (*form or fig*) kurzsichtig

myself [maɪ·'self] *pron refl* ❶ (*direct object of verb*) mir +*dat*, mich +*akk*; **I caught sight of ~ in the mirror** ich

sah mich im Spiegel ❷ (*emph form: I, me*) ich; **people like ~** Menschen wie ich ❸ (*emph: me personally*) ich persönlich; **I wrote it ~** ich schrieb es selbst ❹ (*me alone*) **I never get an hour to ~** ich habe nie eine Stunde für mich; [**all**] **by ~** (ganz) alleine

mysterious [mɪ·'stɪr·i·əs] *adj* geheimnisvoll, mysteriös

mystery ['mɪs·tə·ri] *n* (*secret*) Geheimnis *nt*; (*puzzle*) Rätsel *nt*

mystical ['mɪs·tɪ·kəl] *adj* mystisch

mystification [ˌmɪs·tɪ·fɪ·'keɪ·ʃən] *n* Verwunderung *f*

mystify <-ie-> ['mɪs·tə·faɪ] *vt* ■ **to ~ sb** jdn vor ein Rätsel stellen

myth [mɪθ] *n* ❶ (*ancient story*) Mythos *m* ❷ (*pej: false idea*) Ammenmärchen *nt*

mythical ['mɪθ·ɪ·kəl] *adj* ❶ (*fictional*) sagenhaft ❷ (*supposed*) imaginär

mythological [ˌmɪθ·ə·'lɑdʒ·ɪ·kəl] *adj* mythologisch

Nn

N <*pl* -'s>, **n** <*pl* -'s> [en] *n* N *nt*, n *nt*; ~ **as in November** N wie Nordpol

N I. *n abbrev of* **North** N *m* II. *adj abbrev of* **North, Northern** nördl.

n *n* ❶ *abbrev of* **noun** Subst. ❷ *abbrev of* **neuter** nt

nab <-bb-> [næb] *vt* (*fam*) stibitzen

nag [næg] I. *vi* <-gg-> [herum]nörgeln (**at** an +*dat*) II. *vt* <-gg-> ■ **to ~ sb** (*annoy*) jdn nicht in Ruhe lassen

nagging ['næg·ɪŋ] I. *n* Nörgelei *f* II. *adj* (*persistent*) quälend

nail [neɪl] I. *n* ❶ Nagel *m*; **to cut one's ~s** sich *dat* die Nägel schneiden II. *vt* ❶ (*fasten*) nageln (**to** an +*akk*) ❷ (*sl: catch*) *police* schnappen *fam*

'**nail-biting** *adj* nervenzerreißend; *film* spannend

'**nail clippers** *npl* Nagelknipser *m*

'**nail file** *n* Nagelfeile *f*

'**nail polish** *n* Nagellack *m*

'**nail scissors** *npl* Nagelschere *f*

naïve, naive [na·'iv] *adj* (*esp pej*) naiv *pej*

naked ['neɪ·kɪd] *adj* (*a. fig*) nackt; *flame* offen; **to the ~ eye** für das bloße Auge

nakedness ['neɪ·kɪd·nɪs] *n* Nacktheit *f*

namby-pamby [ˌnæm·bi·'pæm·bi] *adj attr* (*pej fam: weak*) *person* verweichlicht

name [neɪm] I. *n* ❶ (*title*) Name *m*; **my ~'s Peter** ich heiße Peter; **first/last ~** Vor-/Nachname *m* ❷ (*reputation*) Name *m*, Ruf *m*; **to make a ~ for oneself** sich *dat* einen Namen machen II. *vt* nennen

nameless ['neɪm·lɪs] *adj* namenlos

namely ['neɪm·li] *adv* nämlich

'**nameplate** *n* (*on door*) Türschild *nt*; *of company* Firmenschild *nt*

'**namesake** *n* Namensvetter *m*

nana ['naen·ə] *n* (*fam*) Omi *f*

nanny ['næn·i] *n* Kindermädchen *nt*

nanosecond ['nan·ə·ˌsek·ənd] *n* Nanosekunde *f*

nap [næp] **I.** *n* Nickerchen *nt* **II.** *vi* <-pp-> (*fam*) ein Nickerchen machen

napkin ['næp·kɪn] *n* Serviette *f*

narc, nark [nɑrk] *n* (*sl: narcotics agent*) Rauschgiftfahnder(in) *m(f)*

narcissus <*pl* -es> [nɑr·'sɪs·əs] *n* Narzisse *f*

narcotic [nɑr·'kɑt·ɪk] **I.** *n* Rauschgift *nt* **II.** *adj* MED narkotisch; (*sleep-inducing*) einschläfernd

narrate ['nær·eɪt] *vt* ① (*provide commentary*) erzählen ② (*give account of*) schildern

narrator ['nær·eɪ·tər] *n* Erzähler(in) *m(f)*

narrow ['nær·ou] **I.** *adj* ① (*thin*) eng, schmal ② *margin, victory* knapp **II.** *vi* enger werden; *gap* sich schließen

narrowly ['nær·ou·li] *adv* (*barely*) knapp

narrow-'minded *adj* engstirnig

NASA ['næs·ə] *n abbrev of* **National Aeronautics and Space Administration** NASA *f*

nasal ['neɪ·zəl] *adj* Nasen-

nastiness ['næs·ti·nɪs] *n* Gemeinheit *f*

nasturtium [nə·'stɜr·ʃəm] *n* [Kapuziner]kresse *f*

nasty ['næs·ti] *adj* ① (*mean*) *person* gemein; *surprise* böse ② (*bad*) *smell* scheußlich; *shock* furchtbar ③ (*serious*) schlimm, böse; **to turn ~** *situation, animal* unangenehm werden

nation ['neɪ·ʃən] *n* ① (*country, state*) Nation *f*, Land *nt* ② (*people*) Volk *nt*; **the Apache N~** der Stamm der Apachen

national ['næʃ·ə·nəl] **I.** *adj* ① (*of a nation, nationwide*) *matter, organization* national; *flag, team* National-

② (*particular to a nation*) Landes-, Volks- **II.** *n* Staatsangehörige(r) *f(m)*

national 'anthem *n* Nationalhymne *f*

national 'debt *n* Staatsverschuldung *f*

National 'Guard *n* Nationalgarde *f*

nationalist ['næʃ·ə·nə·lɪst] **I.** *adj* nationalistisch **II.** *n* Nationalist(in) *m(f)*

nationality [ˌnæʃ·ə·'næl·ə·ti] *n* ① (*esp cultural*) Nationalität *f* ② (*legal*) Staatsangehörigkeit *f*

nationalize ['næʃ·ə·nə·laɪz] *vt* *company, steel industry* verstaatlichen

national 'park, National 'Park *n* Nationalpark *m*

nation-'state *n* Nationalstaat *m*

'**nationwide** **I.** *adv* landesweit, im ganzen Land **II.** *adj* *campaign* landesweit

native ['neɪ·tɪv] **I.** *adj* ① (*of one's birth*) beheimatet; **~ country** Heimatland *nt* ② *traditions* einheimisch; *population* eingeboren ③ BOT, ZOOL *animal, plant* beheimatet, einheimisch **II.** *n* (*local inhabitant*) Einheimische(r) *m(f)*; (*indigenous*) Eingeborene(r) *f(m)*

Native A'merican *n* amerikanischer Ureinwohner/amerikanische Ureinwohnerin

native-'born *adj* gebürtig

native 'speaker *n* Muttersprachler(in) *m(f)*

na'tivity play *n* Krippenspiel *nt*

NATO ['neɪ·tou] *n acr for* **North Atlantic Treaty Organization** NATO *f*

natural ['nætʃ·ər·əl] **I.** *adj* ① (*not artificial*) *flavor, ingredients* natürlich; *color* Natur- ② (*as in nature*) *harbor, reservoir* natürlich; *fabric, wood* naturbelassen; **~ state** Naturzustand *m* ③ (*caused by nature*) natürlich; **~ disaster** Naturkatastrophe ④ (*normal*) natürlich, normal **II.** *n* (*approv fam*) Naturtalent *nt*

natural 'gas *n* Erdgas *nt*

natural 'history *n* Naturgeschichte *f*; (*as topic of study*) Naturkunde *f*

naturalistic [ˌnætʃ·ər·ə·'lɪs·tɪk] *adj* ART, LIT, PHILOS naturalistisch

naturalization [ˌnætʃ·ər·ə·lɪ·'zeɪ·ʃən] *n* Einbürgerung *f*

N

naturalize ['nætʃ·ər·ə·laɪz] *vt* einbür-
gern
naturally ['nætʃ·ər·ə·li] *adv* ❶ natürlich; (*as expected*) verständlicherweise
❷ (*without special training*) natürlich;
dancing comes ~ to him Tanzen fällt
ihm leicht
natural re'sources *npl* Bodenschätze *pl*
natural se'lection *n* natürliche Auslese
nature ['neɪ·tʃər] *n* ❶ *no art* (*natural environment*) Natur *f* ❷ (*innate qualities*)
Art *f*; **by** ~ von Natur aus
nature conser'vation *n* Naturschutz *m*
'nature preserve *n* Naturschutzgebiet *nt*
'nature study *n* Naturkunde *f*
'nature trail *n* Naturlehrpfad *m*
naughty ['nɔ·ti] *adj* ❶ *children* ungezogen; (*iron*) *adults* ungehörig ❷ (*hum
fam: sinful*) unanständig
nausea ['nɔ·zi·ə] *n* Übelkeit *f*; (*fig*)
Ekel *m*
nauseate ['nɔ·zi·eɪt] *vt usu passive*
(*form*) ■ **to be ~d by sth** (*fig, pej*) von
etw *dat* angeekelt sein

N **nauseating** ['nɔ·zi·eɪ·tɪŋ] *adj* Übelkeit
erregend *attr*
nauseous ['nɔ·ʃəs] *adj* ❶ (*having nausea*) **she is** ~ ihr ist übel ❷ (*fig: causing
nausea*) widerlich
nautical ['nɔ·tɪ·kəl] *adj* nautisch;
~ **mile** Seemeile *f*
naval ['neɪ·vəl] *adj* (*of a navy*) Marine-;
(*of ships*) See-; ~ **base** Flottenstütz-
punkt *m*
navel ['neɪ·vəl] *n* ANAT Nabel *m*
navigable ['næv·ɪ·gə·bəl] *adj* (*passable*) schiffbar
navigate ['næv·ɪ·geɪt] *vt* ❶ (*steer*) navi-
gieren ❷ (*pilot*) steuern; AUTO lenken
navigation [,næ·vɪ·'geɪ·ʃən] *n no pl*
❶ (*navigating*) Navigation *f*; ~ **system** Navigationssystem *nt* ❷ (*assisting
operator*) Lotsen *nt*
navigator ['næv·ɪ·geɪ·tər] *n* Naviga-
tor(in) *m(f)*; AUTO Beifahrer(in) *m(f)*
navy ['neɪ·vi] **I.** *n* ■ **the N~** die Marine
II. *adj* marineblau
Nazi ['nɑt·si] *n* Nazi *m*

Nazism ['nɑt·sɪz·əm], **Naziism** ['nɑt·si·
ɪz·əm] *n* (*hist*) Nazismus *m*
NB [,en·'bi] *adv abbrev of* **nota bene** NB
NC, N.C. *abbrev of* **North Carolina**
NCO [,en·si·'oʊ] *n abbrev of* **noncommissioned officer** Uffz. *m*
ND, N.D. *abbrev of* **North Dakota**
NE *abbrev of* **Nebraska**
near [nɪr] **I.** *adj* ❶ (*close in space*) nahe,
in der Nähe; **where's the ~est phone
booth?** wo ist die nächste Telefonzelle?
❷ (*close in time*) nahe ▸ PHRASES: **to be
a ~ miss** knapp danebengehen **II.** *adv*
❶ (*close in space*) nahe; **do you live
somewhere ~?** wohnst du hier irgendwo in der Nähe? ❷ (*close in time*) nahe; **the time is drawing ~** die Zeit
rückt näher ❸ (*almost*) beinahe, fast
III. *prep* ❶ (*in proximity to*) nahe [bei]
+*dat;* **do you live ~ here?** wohnen Sie
hier in der Nähe? ❷ (*close to a state*)
we came ~ to being killed wir wären
beinahe getötet worden
nearby [,nɪr·'baɪ] **I.** *adj* nahe gelegen
II. *adv* in der Nähe
Near 'East *n* Naher Osten
nearly ['nɪr·li] *adv* fast, beinahe
near'sighted *adj* kurzsichtig
near'sightedness *n* Kurzsichtigkeit *f*
neat [nit] *adj* ❶ (*well-maintained*) ordentlich; *appearance* gepflegt ❷ (*approv fam: very good*) toll ❸ (*undiluted*)
pur
neaten ['ni·tən] *vt* in Ordnung bringen
neatly ['nit·li] *adv* ❶ (*tidily*) sauber
❷ (*skillfully*) geschickt
neatness ['nit·nɪs] *n* Ordentlichkeit *f*
Nebr. *abbrev of* **Nebraska**
Nebraska [nə·'bræs·kə] *n* Nebraska *nt*
nebulous ['neb·jə·ləs] *adj* nebelhaft;
fear, promise vage
necessarily [,nes·ɪ·'ser·ə·li] *adv* (*consequently*) notwendigerweise; (*inevitably*) unbedingt; (*of necessity*)
zwangsläufig
necessary ['nes·ɪ·ser·i] *adj* notwendig
necessitate [nə·'ses·ɪ·teɪt] *vt* erfordern
necessity [nə·'ses·ə·ti] *n* ❶ (*being necessary*) Notwendigkeit *f* ❷ (*necessary*

thing) **the necessities of life** das Lebensnotwendige

neck [nek] n ❶ ANAT Hals; (nape) Nacken m ❷ (narrow part) Hals m ▶ PHRASES: **to be breathing down sb's ~** jdm im Nacken sitzen

necklace ['nek·lɪs] n [Hals]kette f

'neckline n Ausschnitt m

'necktie n Krawatte f

nectar ['nek·tər] n Nektar m

nectarine [ˌnek·təˈrin] n Nektarine f

née [neɪ] adj pred geborene

need [nid] I. n ❶ (requirement) Bedarf m ❷ (yearning) Bedürfnis nt; **I'm in ~ of some fresh air** ich brauche etwas frische Luft ❸ (poverty) Not f II. vt ❶ (require) brauchen ❷ (must) ■ **to ~ to do sth** etw tun müssen III. aux vb ~ I **say more?** (iron) muss ich noch mehr sagen?

needed ['nid·ɪd] adj notwendig; **much·~** dringend nötig

needle ['ni·dəl] I. n Nadel f II. vt ärgern

needless ['nid·lɪs] adj unnötig; **~ to say ...** selbstverständlich ...

needn't ['ni·dənt] = **need not** see **need III**

needy ['ni·di] adj (poor) bedürftig, Not leidend attr

negate [nɪˈgeɪt] vt (nullify) zunichtemachen

negative ['neg·ə·tɪv] I. adj negativ; **~ answer** ablehnende Antwort; **to be ~ about sth** etw gegenüber negativ eingestellt sein II. n ❶ (negation) Verneinung f ❷ PHOT Negativ nt

negatively ['neg·ə·tɪv·li] adv negativ; (saying no) ablehnend

neglect [nɪˈglekt] I. vt vernachlässigen; ■ **to ~ to do sth** [es] versäumen, etw zu tun II. n (lack of care) Vernachlässigung f; (disrepair) Verwahrlosung f

neglected [nɪˈglekt·ɪd] adj (uncared for) verwahrlost; (overlooked) vernachlässigt

neglectful [nɪˈglekt·fəl] adj nachlässig (of gegenüber +dat)

negligence ['neg·lɪ·dʒəns] n (lack of

care) Nachlässigkeit f; (neglect) Vernachlässigung f

negligible ['neg·lɪ·dʒə·bəl] adj unbedeutend

negotiable [nɪˈgoʊ·ʃi·ə·bəl] adj ❶ (discussable) verhandelbar ❷ (traversable) passierbar; road befahrbar

negotiate [nɪˈgoʊ·ʃi·eɪt] I. vt (discuss) aushandeln; treaty abschließen II. vi verhandeln (for/on über +akk)

negotiation [nɪˌgoʊ·ʃiˈeɪ·ʃən] n Verhandlung f

negotiator [nɪˈgoʊ·ʃi·eɪ·tər] n Unterhändler(in) m(f)

neigh [neɪ] vi wiehern

neighbor ['neɪ·bər] I. n (person) Nachbar(in) m(f); (fig: country) Nachbarland nt II. vi [an]grenzen (on an +akk)

neighborhood ['neɪ·bər·hʊd] n ❶ (district) Viertel nt; (people) Nachbarschaft f ❷ (vicinity) Nähe f kein pl

neighborhood 'watch n Nachbarschaftswachdienst m

neighboring ['neɪ·bər·ɪŋ] adj attr (nearby) benachbart; (bordering) angrenzend

neighborly ['neɪ·bər·li] adj (community-friendly) gutnachbarlich; (kindly) freundlich

neither ['ni·ðər] I. adv ❶ (not either) weder; **~ ... nor ... [nor ...]** weder ... noch ... [oder ...] ❷ (a. not) auch nicht ▶ PHRASES: **to be ~ here nor there** völlig nebensächlich sein II. adj attr keine(r, s) von beiden III. pron (not either of two) keine(r, s) von beiden IV. conj ❶ (not either) ■ **~ ... nor ...** weder ... noch ❷ after neg (also not) weder; **I can't be at the meeting, and ~ can Andrew** ich kann nicht zum Treffen kommen und Andrew auch nicht

neon ['ni·an] n Neon nt; **~ sign** Leuchtreklame f

neo-Nazi [ˌni·oʊˈnat·si] n Neonazi m

nephew ['nef·ju] n Neffe m

nerd [nɜrd] n (sl: geek) Streber(in) m(f) pej; **computer ~** Computerfreak m sl

nerdy ['nɜr·di] adj (fam) doof

N

nerve [nɜrv] n ❶ ANAT Nerv m ❷ (*courage*) Mut m; **to lose one's ~** die Nerven verlieren ❸ (*impudence*) Frechheit f ▶ PHRASES: **to get on sb's ~s** (*fam*) jdm auf die Nerven [*o* den Wecker] gehen

'**nerve center** n Nervenzentrum nt a. fig

'**nerve gas** n Nervengas nt

'**nerve-racking**, '**nerve-wracking** adj nervenaufreibend

nervous ['nɜr·vəs] adj (*high-strung*) nervös; (*tense*) aufgeregt

nervous 'breakdown n Nervenzusammenbruch m

nervously ['nɜr·vəs·li] adv nervös; (*overexcitedly*) aufgeregt; (*timidly*) ängstlich

nervousness ['nɜr·vəs·nɪs] n (*nervous state*) Nervosität f

'**nervous system** n Nervensystem nt

nervy ['nɜr·vi] adj (*pej*) unverschämt

nest [nest] I. n Nest nt II. vi ORN nisten

'**nest egg** n (*fig*) Notgroschen m

nesting ['nest·ɪŋ] adj attr ❶ (*of sets*) ineinanderstapelbar ❷ (*of nests*) Nist-

nestle ['nes·əl] I. vt **she ~d the baby lovingly in her arms** sie hielt das Baby liebevoll in ihren Armen II. vi object **■to ~ in sth** in etw akk eingebettet sein

nestling ['nest·lɪŋ] n ORN Nestling m

Net [net] n INET, COMPUT **■the ~** das Netz

net¹ [net] I. n Netz nt a. fig II. vt <-tt-> fish mit einem Netz fangen; (*fig*) criminals fangen

net² [net] I. adj netto, rein, Netto-, Rein-; **~ profit** Reingewinn m ❷ attr (*fig: final*) End-; **~ result** Endergebnis nt II. vt (*after tax*) netto verdienen

Netherlands ['neð·ər·ləndz] n **■the ~** die Niederlande pl

netiquette ['net·ɪ·ˌket] n COMPUT Netiquette f

netting ['net·ɪŋ] n Netzgewebe nt

nettle ['net·əl] n Nessel f; stinging **~s** Brennnesseln pl

network ['net·ˌwɜrk] I. n ❶ (*structure*) Netz[werk] nt ❷ (*fig: people*) Netz nt ❸ TELEC [Kommunikations]netzwerk nt; **cable ~** Kabelnetz nt; **telephone ~** Telefonnetz nt; **television** [*or* **TV**] **~** Sendernetz nt ❹ ECON Netz nt ❺ TRANSP **rail|road|**~ [Eisen]bahnnetz nt ❻ INET Netzwerk nt; **social ~** soziales Netzwerk, Social Network nt II. vt (*link*) also COMPUT vernetzen (**to** mit) III. vi Kontakte knüpfen und nutzen, netzwerken; **■to ~ with sb** mit jdm Kontakt knüpfen

'**networker** n Networker(in) m(f)

networking ['net·ˌwɜrk·ɪŋ] n ❶ (*making contacts*) Kontaktknüpfen nt ❷ COMPUT Vernetzen nt

neural ['nʊr·əl] adj attr COMPUT **~ network** Neuronennetz nt

neurologist [nʊ·ˈral·ə·dʒɪst] n Neurologe m, Neurologin f

neurology [nʊ·ˈral·ə·dʒi] n Neurologie f

neuroscience [ˌnʊr·oʊ·ˈsaɪ·əns] n Neurobiologie f

neurosis <pl -ses> [nʊ·ˈroʊ·sɪs] n Neurose f

neurosurgery [ˌnʊr·oʊ·ˈsɜr·dʒə·ri] n Neurochirurgie f

neurotic [nʊ·ˈrat·ɪk] adj neurotisch

neuter ['nu·tər] I. adj sächlich; **~ noun** Neutrum nt II. vt male animal kastrieren

neutral ['nu·trəl] I. adj neutral II. n AUTO Leerlauf m; **in ~** im Leerlauf

neutrality [nu·ˈtræl·ə·ti] n Neutralität f

neutralize ['nu·trə·laɪz] vt (*nullify*) neutralisieren; bomb entschärfen

neutron ['nu·tran] n Neutron nt

Nev. abbrev of **Nevada**

Nevada [nə·ˈvad·ə] n Nevada nt

never ['nev·ər] adv nie, niemals; **~ again!** nie wieder!; **~ before** noch nie [zuvor]

never-'ending adj endlos

never-'never land n (*fam*) Fantasiewelt f

nevertheless [ˌnev·ər·ðə·ˈles] adv dennoch

new [nu] adj neu; **~ boy/girl/kid** (a. fig: in school) Neue(r) f(m); **I'm ~ around here** ich bin neu hier

newbie ['nu·bi] n Anfänger(in) m(f)

'newborn adj attr neugeboren

'newcomer n (new arrival) Neuankömmling m; (stranger) Fremde(r) f(m)

new'fangled adj (fam) neumodisch

'newfound adj neu[entdeckt]

New Hampshire [,nu·'hæmp·ʃər] n New Hampshire nt

newish ['nu·ɪʃ] adj (fam) relativ neu

New Jersey [,nu·'dʒɜr·zi] n New Jersey nt

newly ['nu·li] adv kürzlich, neulich; ~ painted frisch gestrichen

'newlywed n Jungverheiratete(r) f(m)

New Mexico [,nu·'mek·sɪ·koʊ] n New Mexico nt

new 'moon n Neumond m

new po'tatoes npl neue Kartoffeln pl

news [nuz] n ① (new information) Neuigkeit f; to break the ~ to sb jdm die schlechte Nachricht überbringen ② (media) Nachrichten pl; to be in the ~ in den Schlagzeilen sein

'newscast n Nachrichtensendung f

'news conference n Pressekonferenz f

'newsflash n Kurzmeldung f

'newsgroup n INET Newsgroup f

'news item n Nachricht f

'newsletter n Rundschreiben nt

'newspaper n Zeitung f

'newsprint n Zeitungspapier nt

'news report n Meldung f

'newsroom n Nachrichtenredaktion f

'newsstand n Zeitungsstand m

'newsworthy adj berichtenswert

New 'Testament n the ~ das Neue Testament

New 'Year n Neujahr nt kein pl; Happy ~ gutes neues Jahr

New 'Year's n (fam: January 1) Neujahrstag m; (December 31) Silvester nt

New Year's 'Day n Neujahr nt, Neujahrstag m

New Year's 'Eve n Silvester nt

New York [,nu·'jɔrk] n New York nt

New Zealand [,nu·'zi·lənd] n Neuseeland nt

next [nekst] I. adj ① (coming immediately after) nächste(r, s); ~ month

nächsten Monat ② (next in order, space) nächste(r, s), folgende(r, s); who's ~? wer ist der/die Nächste? II. adv ① (subsequently) dann, gleich darauf; so what happened ~? was geschah als Nächstes? ② (second) zweit-; the ~ best thing die zweitbeste Sache ③ (to one side) ■~ to prep neben etw/jdm ④ (almost) ~ to nothing fast gar nichts ▶PHRASES: what ~? und was kommt dann? III. n (following one) der/die/das Nächste

next 'door adj pred buildings nebenan nach n; people benachbart

next-'gen adj (fam) short for next-generation futuristisch

next of 'kin n + sing/pl vb nächste(r) Angehörige(r)

NH, N.H. abbrev of New Hampshire

nibble ['nɪb·əl] vt, vi knabbern

Nicaragua [,nɪk·ə·'rag·wə] n Nicaragua nt

Nicaraguan [,nɪk·ə·'rag·wən] n Nicaraguaner(in) m(f)

nice [naɪs] adj (approv) ① nett; (pleasant) schön, angenehm; neighborhood freundlich; ~ to meet you! es freut mich, Sie/dich kennen zu lernen! ② (amiable) nett, freundlich

nice-'looking adj gut aussehend, hübsch

nicely ['naɪs·li] adv ① (pleasantly) nett, hübsch ② (well) gut, nett; that'll do ~ das reicht völlig

niche [nɪtʃ] n Nische f

nick [nɪk] n (chip) Kerbe f

nickel ['nɪk·əl] n ① (metal) Nickel nt ② (coin) Fünfcentstück nt

nickel-'plated adj vernickelt

nickname ['nɪk·neɪm] n Spitzname m; (affectionate) Kosename m

nicotine ['nɪk·ə·tin] n Nikotin nt

niece [nis] n Nichte f

nifty ['nɪf·ti] adj (approv fam: stylish) elegant; (skillful) geschickt

niggle ['nɪg·əl] vi ① (criticize) nörgeln ② (worry) beunruhigen

niggling ['nɪg·lɪŋ] adj attr (troubling) nagend fig

N

night [naɪt] *n* ❶ (*darkness*) Nacht *f;* **at ~** nachts ❷ (*evening*) Abend *m;* **to have a ~ out** [abends] ausgehen

'nightcap *n* (*drink*) Schlaftrunk *m*

'nightclothes *npl* Nachtwäsche *f kein pl;* (*pajamas*) Schlafanzug *m*

'nightclub *n* Nachtklub *m*

'night cream *n* Nachtcreme *f*

'nightdress, 'nightgown, *fam* **nightie** ['naɪ·ti] *n* Nachthemd *nt*

nightingale ['naɪ·tɪŋ·geɪl] *n* Nachtigall *f*

'nightlife *n* Nachtleben *nt*

'nightlight *n* Nachtlicht *nt*

'nightmare ['naɪt·mer] *n* Alptraum *m*

nightmarish ['naɪt·mer·ɪʃ] *adj* alptraumhaft

'night owl *n* (*fam*) Nachteule *f hum*

nights [naɪts] *adv* nachts; **to work ~** nachts arbeiten

'night school *n* Abendschule *f*

'night shift *n* Nachtschicht *f*

'nightspot *n* (*fam*) Nachtklub *m*

'nightstand *n* Nachttisch *m*

'nighttime *n* Nacht[zeit] *f*

night 'watchman *n* Nachtwächter *m*

'nightwear *n* Nachtwäsche *f*

nihilistic [ˌnaɪ·əˈlɪs·tɪk] *adj* nihilistisch

Nikkei Index [nɪ·ˈkeɪ-] *n* Nikkei Index *m*

nil [nɪl] *n* Nichts *nt,* Null *f*

nimble ['nɪm·bəl] *adj* (*usu approv: agile*) gelenkig; (*quick*) flink

NIMBY <*pl* -s> ['nɪm·bi] *n* (*pej*) *acr for* **not in my back yard** *Person, die sich gegen umstrittene Bauvorhaben in der eigenen Nachbarschaft stellt, aber nichts dagegen hat, wenn diese woanders realisiert werden*

nine [naɪn] *adj* neun ▶PHRASES: **the whole ~ yards** (*fam*) ganz und gar

9-11, 9/11 [naɪn·ɪ·ˈlev·ən] *n* der 11. September (*Terrorangriffe am 11.9.2001 auf das World Trade Center in New York und das Pentagon in Washington*)

nineteen [ˌnaɪnˈtin] I. *n* Neunzehn *f* II. *adj* neunzehn

nineteenth [ˌnaɪnˈtinθ] *adj* neunzehnte(r, s)

nineties ['naɪn·tiz] *npl* (*decade*) ◼the **~** die Neunziger *pl*

ninetieth ['naɪn·ti·əθ] *adj* neunzigste(r, s)

'nine-to-five *adv* **to work ~** von neun bis fünf [Uhr] arbeiten

ninety ['naɪn·ti] I. *n* Neunzig *f* II. *adj* neunzig

ninth [naɪnθ] *adj* neunte(r, s)

nip[1] [nɪp] I. *vt* <-pp-> (*bite*) beißen; (*pinch*) zwicken II. *vi* <-pp-> beißen *dat* III. *n* ❶ (*pinch*) Kniff *m;* (*bite*) Biss *m* ❷ (*chill*) Kälte *f;* **there's a ~ in the air** es ist frisch

nip[2] [nɪp] *n* (*fam: sip*) Schluck *m*

nipple ['nɪp·əl] *n* ❶ ANAT Brustwarze *f* ❷ (*of baby bottle*) Sauger *m*

nippy ['nɪp·i] *adj* (*fam*) kühl

nit [nɪt] *n* Nisse *f*

nitpicking ['nɪt·pɪk·ɪŋ] I. *adj* (*pej fam*) pingelig II. *n* (*pej fam*) Krittelei *f*

nitric ['naɪ·trɪk] *adj* Stickstoff-; **~ acid** Salpetersäure *f*

nitrogen ['naɪ·trə·dʒən] *n* Stickstoff *m*

nitroglycerin(e) [ˌnaɪ·troʊ·ˈglɪs·ər·ɪn] *n* Nitroglyzerin *nt*

nitty-gritty [ˌnɪt·i·ˈgrɪt·i] *n* (*fam*) **to get down to the ~** zur Sache kommen

nitwit ['nɪt·wɪt] *n* (*pej fam: stupid person*) Schwachkopf *m*

nix [nɪks] *vt* (*fam*) ablehnen

NJ, N.J. *abbrev of* **New Jersey**

NM, N.M. *abbrev of* **New Mexico**

no [noʊ] I. *adj* ❶ (*not any*) kein(e); **~ one** keiner ❷ (*on signs*) "~ **parking**" „Parken verboten" II. *adv* ❶ (*not at all*) nicht; **~ less than sth** nicht weniger als etw ❷ (*negation*) nein III. *interj* ❶ (*refusal*) nein ❷ (*distress*) **oh, ~!** oh nein!

Noah's ark [ˌnoʊ·əzˈark] *n* die Arche Noah

Nobel Prize [ˌnoʊ·belˈ-] *n* Nobelpreis *m*

nobility [noʊ·ˈbɪl·ə·ti] *n* (*aristocracy*) ◼the **~** der Adel

noble ['noʊ·bəl] I. *adj* ❶ (*aristocratic*) ad[e]lig ❷ (*approv: estimable*) *person* edel *geh* II. *n* Ad[e]lige(r) *f(m)*

nobody ['noʊ·bad·i] *pron indef sing* (*no people*) niemand, keiner; ~ **else** niemand anders

no-brainer ['noʊ·breɪ·nər] *n* (*fam*) ■ **to be a ~** ein Kinderspiel sein

nocturnal [nak·'tɜr·nəl] *adj* (*of the night*) nächtlich *attr*; Nacht-; ZOOL (*active at night*) nachtaktiv

nod [nad] I. *n usu sing* Nicken *nt kein pl*; **to get the ~** (*fig*) grünes Licht bekommen II. *vt* <-dd-> **to ~ one's head** mit dem Kopf nicken III. *vi* <-dd-> (*as signal*) nicken
♦ **nod off** *vi* (*involuntarily*) einnicken; (*voluntarily*) ein Nickerchen machen

node [noʊd] *n* (*intersection*) Schnittpunkt *m*; COMPUT Schnittstelle *f*

no-'fault *adj attr* Vollkasko-

no-'fly zone *n* Flugverbotszone *f*

no-'frills *adj attr* shop [schlicht und] einfach; ~ **service** Service *m* ohne Extras

no-go 'area, **no-go 'zone** *n* ❶ (*prohibited*) verbotene Zone ❷ MIL Sperrgebiet *nt*

nohow ['noʊ·haʊ] *adv* (*fam*) auf gar keinen Fall

no-'iron *adj clothes* bügelfrei

noise [nɔɪz] *n* ❶ (*loudness*) Lärm *m* ❷ (*sound*) Geräusch *nt*

noiseless ['nɔɪz·lɪs] *adj* geräuschlos

'noise pollution *n* Lärmbelästigung *f*

noise prevention *n* Lärmvermeidung *f*

noisy ['nɔɪ·zi] *adj* laut

nomadic [noʊ·'mæd·ɪk] *adj* nomadisch, Nomaden-

nominal ['nam·ə·nəl] *adj* ❶ (*titular*) nominell ❷ (*small*) *sum of money* gering

nominate ['nam·ə·neɪt] *vt* ❶ (*propose*) nominieren ❷ (*appoint*) ernennen

nomination [ˌnam·ə·'neɪ·ʃən] *n* ❶ (*proposal*) Nominierung *f* ❷ (*appointment*) Ernennung *f*

nominative ['nam·ə·nə·tɪv] *n* ■ **the ~** der Nominativ

nominee [ˌnam·ə·'ni] *n* Kandidat(in) *m(f)*

nonag'gression *n* Gewaltverzicht *m*; ~ **treaty** Nichtangriffspakt *m*

nonalco'holic *adj drink* alkoholfrei

nonat'tendance *n* (*at school, a hearing*) Abwesenheit *f*

nonchalant [ˌnan·ʃə·'lant] *adj* gleichgültig

noncommissioned 'officer *n* MIL Unteroffizier(in) *m(f)*

noncommittal [ˌnan·kə·'mɪt·əl] *adj tone* unverbindlich

noncom'pliance *n with an order* Nichtbeachtung *f*

noncon'formist *adj* nonkonformistisch

noncon'tributory *adj* beitragsfrei

noncoope'ration *n* Kooperationsverweigerung *f*

nondeposit 'bottle *n* Einwegflasche *f*

nondescript [ˌnan·dɪ·'skrɪpt] *adj person, building* unscheinbar; *color, taste* undefinierbar

none [nʌn] I. *pron* ❶ (*not any*) keine(r, s); ~ **of it matters anymore** das spielt jetzt keine Rolle mehr; ~ **at all** gar keine(r, s) ❷ (*no person, no one*) ~ **other than ...** kein Geringerer/keine Geringere als ... ▶ PHRASES: **to be ~ of sb's business** jdn nichts angehen II. *adv* kein bisschen; ~ **too pleased** (*form*) nicht sonderlich erfreut

nonentity [nan·'en·tə·t̬i] *n* (*pej: nobody*) ■ **a ~** ein Niemand *m*

nones'sential *adj* überflüssig

nonex'istent *adj* nicht vorhanden

non'fat *adj food* fettfrei

non'fiction I. *n* Sachliteratur *f* II. *adj* ~ **books** Sachbücher *pl*

non'flammable *adj material* nicht entflammbar

nonne'gotiable *adj* ❶ LAW *terms* nicht verhandelbar ❷ FIN *document* nicht übertragbar

'no-no <*pl* -es> *n* (*fam*) Unding *nt*; **that's a ~!** das macht man nicht!

nonpol'luting *adj byproduct* ungiftig

nonpro'ductive *adj* unproduktiv; FIN *investment* nicht Gewinn bringend *attr*

non'profit I. *adj* nicht gewinnorientiert II. *n* gemeinnützige Organisation

nonre'fundable *adj payment* nicht zurückzahlbar

nonrenewable 'resources *npl* nicht erneuerbare Energien *pl*
non'resident *adj* ① *(not local)* auswärtig ② COMPUT nicht resident
nonre'turnable *adj* nicht zurücknehmbar
nonsense ['nan·sens] **I.** *n* Unsinn *m* **II.** *adj attr* unsinnig, sinnlos **III.** *interj* ■~! Quatsch!, Unsinn!
nonsensical [,nan·'sen·sɪ·kəl] *adj plan* unsinnig
non'shrink *adj clothing* einlaufsicher
non'slip *adj surface* rutschfest
non'smoking *adj section* Nichtraucher-
non'starter *n (idea)* Reinfall *m*
non'stick *adj* antihaftbeschichtet
non'stop **I.** *adj* Nonstop- **II.** *adv rain* ununterbrochen
non'toxic *adj substance* ungiftig
non'verbal *adj communication* nonverbal
non'violent *adj protest* gewaltfrei
noob [nu:b] *n* COMPUT, INET Newbie *m* *fam*
noodle ['nu·dəl] *n* Nudel *f*
nook [nʊk] *n* Nische *f*, Ecke *f* ►PHRASES: [in] every ~ **and cranny** in allen Ecken und Winkeln
noon [nun] *n* Mittag *m*
no one ['noʊ·wʌn] *pron see* **nobody**
noose [nus] *n* Schlinge *f a. fig*
nope [noʊp] *adv (sl)* nö *fam*
nor [nɔr] *conj* noch; **neither … ~ …** weder … noch …
norm [nɔrm] *n* Norm *f*
normal ['nɔr·məl] **I.** *adj* ① *(ordinary) person, day* normal ② *(usual) behavior* normal **(for** für *+akk)*; **as [is]** ~ wie üblich **II.** *n* Normalzustand *m;* **to return to** ~ sich normalisieren
normalize ['nɔr·mə·laɪz] *vt, vi* [sich] normalisieren
normally ['nɔr·mə·li] *adv* normalerweise
north [nɔrθ] **I.** *n* ① *(direction)* Norden *m;* ■**to the** ~ nach Norden [hin] ② *(region)* ■**the N~** der Norden **II.** *adj* nördlich, Nord- **III.** *adv* nordwärts
North A'merica *n* Nordamerika *nt*

North A'merican *adj* nordamerikanisch
North Carolina [,nɔrθ·,kær·ə·'laɪ·nə] *n* North Carolina *nt*
North Dakota [,nɔrθ·də·'koʊ·də] *n* Norddakota *nt*
north'east **I.** *n (direction)* Nordosten *m* **II.** *adj* nordöstlich; ~ **wind** Wind *m* von Nordost **III.** *adv* nordostwärts **(of** von *+dat)*
north'eastern *adj attr* nordöstlich, Nordost-
northerly ['nɔr·ðər·li] *adj* nördlich, Nord-
northern ['nɔr·ðərn] *adj attr* nördlich
northerner ['nɔr·ðər·nər] *n* Nordstaatler(in) *m(f)*
Northern 'Ireland *n* Nordirland *nt*
North 'Pole *n* ■**the** ~ der Nordpol
northward ['nɔrθ·wərd] **I.** *adj migration* nach Norden *nach n,* Nord- **II.** *adv* nach Norden
north'west **I.** *n* Nordwesten *m;* ■**to the** ~ **[of sth]** nordwestlich [von etw *dat]* **II.** *adj* nordwestlich, Nordwest-
nose [noʊz] **I.** *n* ① *(organ)* Nase *f;* **to blow one's** ~ sich *dat* die Nase putzen ② *(front)* Schnauze *f fam; of aircraft* Flugzeugnase *f* **II.** *vi* **to** ~ **forward** sich vorsichtig vorwärtsbewegen
 ♦ **nose around** *vi (fam)* herumstöbern *fam*
 ♦ **nose out** *vt secrets* herausfinden
'nosebleed *n* Nasenbluten *nt*
'nosedive **I.** *n* ① AVIAT Sturzflug *m* ② *(fig)* Einbruch *m* **II.** *vi* FIN *economy* einbrechen
'nose job *n (fam)* Nasenkorrektur *f*
nosey ['noʊ·zi] *adj (pej) see* **nosy**
no-'smoking *adj area* Nichtraucher-
nostalgic [na·'stæl·dʒɪk] *adj* nostalgisch
no-'strike agreement *n* Streikverbotsabkommen *nt*
nostril ['nas·trəl] *n of a person* Nasenloch *nt*
nosy ['noʊ·zi] *adj (pej)* neugierig
not [nat] *adv* ① *after aux vb* nicht; **it's** ~ **unusual** das ist nicht ungewöhnlich ② *in tag question* **it's cold, isn't it?** es ist kalt, nicht [wahr]? ③ *before n* kein,

nicht; **it's a girl, ~ a boy** es ist ein Mädchen, kein Junge ④ *before adj, adv* (*meaning opposite*) nicht; **~ much** nicht viel ▸PHRASES: **~ at all!** (*polite answer*) überhaupt nicht!; (*denying vehemently*) überhaupt nicht!
notable ['nou·tə·bəl] *adj* ① (*eminent*) bedeutend ② (*remarkable*) beachtlich
notably ['nou·tə·bli] *adv* ① (*particularly*) insbesondere ② (*perceptibly*) merklich
notary 'public <*pl* -ies public> [ˌnou·tə·ri-] *n* Notar(in) *m(f)*
notch <*pl* -es> [natʃ] *n* Einkerbung *f*
note [nout] I. *n* ① Notiz *f*; **to leave a ~** eine Nachricht hinterlassen ② MUS Note *f* II. *vt* (*notice*) wahrnehmen; ▪**to ~ that ...** zur Kenntnis nehmen, dass ...
'notebook *n* ① (*book*) Notizbuch *nt* ② COMPUT Notebook *nt*
noted ['nou·tɪd] *adj attr* bekannt
'notepad *n* Notizblock *m*
noteworthy ['nout·ˌwɜr·ði] *adj results* beachtenswert; **nothing ~** nichts Besonderes
not-for-'profit *adj organization* nicht auf Gewinn ausgerichtet *attr*
nothing ['nʌθ·ɪŋ] I. *pron indef* ① (*not anything*) nichts, nix *fam*; **all or ~** alles oder nichts; **~ else** nichts weiter, sonst nichts ② (*of no importance*) nichts; **to mean ~ to sb** jdm nichts bedeuten ③ (*zero*) Null *f* ▸PHRASES: **[all] for ~** [vollkommen] umsonst; **there's ~ to it** (*easy*) dazu gehört nicht viel; (*not true*) da ist nichts dran *fam* II. *adv* überhaupt nicht; **to look ~ like sb** jdm nicht ähnlich sehen
notice ['nou·tɪs] I. *vt* ① (*see*) bemerken; (*perceive*) wahrnehmen ② (*pay attention to*) beachten; ▪**to ~ sb** (*become aware of*) auf jdn aufmerksam werden II. *n* ① (*attention*) Beachtung *f*; **to take no ~ of the fact that ...** die Tatsache ignorieren, dass ... ② (*information in advance*) **until further ~** bis auf weiteres ③ (*to end an arrangement*) **to give [one's] ~** kündigen

noticeable ['nou·tɪs·ə·bəl] *adj* merklich
notification [ˌnou·tə·fɪ·'keɪ·ʃən] *n* Mitteilung *f*
notify <-ie-> ['nou·tə·faɪ] *vt* ▪**to ~ sb [of sth]** jdn [über etw *akk*] unterrichten
notorious [nou·'tɔːr·i·əs] *adj temper* notorisch; *criminal* berüchtigt
noun [naun] *n* Hauptwort *nt*, Substantiv *nt*
nourishing ['nɜr·ɪʃ·ɪŋ] *adj* (*healthy*) nahrhaft
nourishment ['nɜr·ɪʃ·mənt] *n* ① (*food*) Nahrung *f* ② (*vital substances*) Nährstoffe *pl*
Nov. *n abbrev of* **November** Nov.
novel¹ ['nav·əl] *n* (*book*) Roman *m*; **detective ~** Kriminalroman *m*
novel² ['nav·əl] *adj* (*new*) neuartig
novelist ['nav·ə·lɪst] *n* Romanautor(in) *m(f)*
novelty ['nav·əl·ti] *n* ① (*new thing*) Neuheit *f* ② (*newness*) Neuartigkeit *f*
November [nou·'vem·bər] *n* November *m*; *see also* **February**
novice ['nav·ɪs] *n* Anfänger(in) *m(f)*
now [nau] I. *adv* ① (*at present*) jetzt; **until ~** bis jetzt ② (*at once*) **[right] ~** jetzt, sofort, gleich ③ (*up to present*) jetzt, nun; **for two years ~** seit zwei Jahren ④ (*short time ago*) **just ~** gerade eben ▸PHRASES: **[it's/it was] ~ or never** (*saying*) jetzt oder nie II. *conj* **~ that ...** jetzt, wo ...
nowadays ['nau·ə·deɪz] *adv* heutzutage
nowhere ['nou·hwer] *adv* nirgends, nirgendwo; **~ to be seen** nirgends zu sehen
nozzle ['naz·əl] *n* Düse *f*; *of gasoline pump* [Zapf]hahn *m*
nuclear ['nu·kli·ər] *adj* Kern-, Atom-
nuclear 'family *n* Kernfamilie *f*
nuclear 'medicine *n* Nuklearmedizin *f*
nuclear 'power plant *n* Kernkraftwerk *nt*
nucleus <*pl* -clei> ['nu·kli·əs] *n* Kern *m*
nude [nud] I. *adj* nackt II. *n* ART Akt *m*
nudge [nʌdʒ] I. *vt* stoßen II. *n* ① (*push*)

N

Schubs m ❷ (*encouragement*) Anstoß m

nudist ['nu·dɪst] n Nudist(in) m(f)

nudity ['nu·də·t̬i] n Nacktheit f

nugget ['nʌg·ɪt] n (*lump*) Klumpen m; **gold ~** Goldnugget nt

nuisance ['nu·səns] n ❶ (*pesterer*) Belästigung f ❷ (*annoyance*) Ärger m; **what a ~!** wie ärgerlich!

nuke [nuk] vt MIL (*sl*) atomar angreifen

null, null and 'void [nʌl-] adj pred LAW null und nichtig

numb [nʌm] I. adj ❶ *limbs* taub; **to go ~** *limbs* einschlafen ❷ (*torpid*) benommen II. vt ❶ (*deprive of feeling*) taub machen ❷ (*lessen*) **to ~ the pain** den Schmerz betäuben

number¹ ['nʌm·bər] I. n ❶ Zahl f; (*identifying number*) Nummer f ❷ + *sing/pl vb* (*amount*) [An]zahl f II. vt nummerieren

number² ['nʌm·ər] adj comp of **numb**

numbering ['nʌm·bər·ɪŋ] n Nummerierung f

numbness ['nʌm·nɪs] n ❶ *of limbs* Taubheit f ❷ (*torpor*) Benommenheit f

N **numbskull** n see **numskull**

numeral ['nu·mər·əl] n Ziffer f

numerical [nuˈmer·ɪ·kəl] adj **in ~ order** in numerischer Reihenfolge

numeric 'keypad n COMPUT Ziffernblock m

numerous ['nu·mər·əs] adj zahlreich

numskull ['nʌm·skʌl] n Hohlkopf m pej fam

nun [nʌn] n Nonne f

nurse [nɜrs] I. n ❶ (*in a hospital*) [Kranken]schwester f; (*male*) Krankenpfleger m ❷ (*nanny*) Kindermädchen nt

II. vt ❶ (*care for*) pflegen ❷ (*breastfeed*) stillen

nursery ['nɜr·sə·ri] n ❶ (*daycare*) Kindergarten m; (*preschool*) Vorschule f ❷ HORT Gärtnerei f

'nursery rhyme n Kinderreim m

'nursery school n Vorschule f

nursing ['nɜr·sɪŋ] n ❶ (*taking care*) [Kranken]pflege f ❷ (*feeding*) Stillen nt

nut [nʌt] n ❶ (*fruit*) Nuss f ❷ TECH Mutter f ❸ (*fam: crazy person*) Bekloppte(r) f(m) sl ▶PHRASES: **to go ~s** durchdrehen

'nutcracker n Nussknacker m

nutmeg ['nʌt·meg] n Muskat m

nutrient ['nu·tri·ənt] n Nährstoff m

nutrition [nu·ˈtrɪʃ·ən] n Ernährungswissenschaft f

nutritional [nu·ˈtrɪʃ·ən·əl] adj Ernährungs-; **~ supplement** Nahrungsergänzung f

nutritionist [nu·ˈtrɪʃ·ə·nɪst] n Ernährungswissenschaftler(in) m(f)

nutritious [nu·ˈtrɪʃ·əs] adj nahrhaft

nuts [nʌts] adj pred ❶ (*crazy*) ■ **to be ~** verrückt sein ❷ (*angry*) ■ **to go ~** ausrasten ❸ (*enthusiastic*) ■ **to be ~ about sb** verrückt nach jdm sein

'nutshell n Nussschale f

nutty ['nʌt̬·i] adj ❶ (*full of nuts*) mit vielen Nüssen ❷ (*tasting like nuts*) taste, aroma nussig

nuzzle ['nʌz·əl] vt [sanft] berühren

NV abbrev of **Nevada**

NY, N.Y. abbrev of **New York**

nylon ['naɪ·lɑn] n Nylon nt

nymphomaniac [ˌnɪm·fə·ˈmeɪ·ni·æk] n (*pej*) Nymphomanin f

NZ n abbrev of **New Zealand**

Oo

O <pl -'s>, **o** <pl -'s> [ou] n ❶ (*letter*) O nt, o nt; ~ **as in Oscar** O wie Otto ❷ (*zero*) Null f

O. abbrev of **Ohio**

oaf [ouf] n (*pej fam*) Tölpel m fam

oafish ['ou·fɪʃ] adj (*pej fam*) ❶ (*rude*) rüpelhaft ❷ (*clumsy*) tölpelig fam

oak [ouk] n Eiche f

oar [ɔr] n Ruder nt

oasis <pl -ses> [ou·'eɪ·sɪs] n (a. fig) Oase f

oat [out] n Hafer m

oath [ouθ] n (*promise*) Eid m; **to be under** ~ unter Eid stehen

'oatmeal n Haferbrei m

obedient [ou·'bi·di·ənt] adj gehorsam

obese [ou·'bis] adj fett pej; esp MED fettleibig

obesity [ou·'bi·sə·ti] n Fettheit f pej; esp MED Fettleibigkeit f

obey [ou·'beɪ] vt, vi gehorchen

obituary [ou·'bɪtʃ·u·er·i] n Nachruf m

object¹ ['ab·dʒɪkt] n ❶ (*thing, ling*) Objekt nt ❷ (*subject*) Gegenstand m

object² [əb·'dʒekt] vi (*oppose*) dagegen sein; (*dislike*) etwas dagegen haben; ■**to** ~ **to sth** (*oppose*) gegen etw akk sein; (*dislike*) etwas gegen etw akk haben

objection [əb·'dʒek·ʃən] n Einwand m

objectionable [əb·'dʒek·ʃə·nə·bəl] adj (*offensive*) anstößig; smell übel

objective [əb·'dʒek·tɪv] I. n (*aim*) Ziel nt II. adj objektiv

objectively [əb·'dʒek·tɪv·li] adv (*without bias*) objektiv

'object lesson n (*approv*) Paradebeispiel nt

objector [əb·'dʒek·tər] n Gegner(in) m(f)

obligation [ˌab·lə·'geɪ·ʃən] n Verpflichtung f

obligatory [ə·'blɪg·ə·tɔr·i] adj obligatorisch a. hum

oblige [ə·'blaɪdʒ] I. vt ❶ (*force*) ■**to be** ~**d to do sth** verpflichtet sein, etw zu tun ❷ (*please*) ■**to** ~ **sb** [**by doing sth**] jdm [durch etw akk] einen Gefallen erweisen II. vi helfen; **I'll be happy to** ~ ich werde bereitwillig helfen

obliging [ə·'blai·dʒɪŋ] adj (*approv*) behavior entgegenkommend; person zuvorkommend

oblique [ou·'blik] adj ❶ (*indirect*) indirekt ❷ (*slanting*) schief

obliterate [ə·'blɪt·ə·reɪt] vt ❶ (*destroy*) vernichten ❷ (*efface*) verwischen

oblivion [ə·'blɪv·i·ən] n ❶ (*obscurity*) Vergessenheit f ❷ (*unconsciousness*) Besinnungslosigkeit f

oblivious [ə·'blɪv·i·əs] adj ■**to be** ~ **of** [or **to**] **sth** sich dat einer S. gen nicht bewusst sein; (*not notice*) etw gar nicht bemerken

oblong ['ab·lɑŋ] I. n Rechteck nt II. adj rechteckig

oboe ['ou·bou] n Oboe f

obscene [əb·'sin] adj (*offensive*) obszön; joke zotig

obscenity [əb·'sen·ə·ti] n Obszönität f

obscure [əb·'skjʊr] adj ❶ author, place unbekannt ❷ (*unclear*) unbestimmt; text schwer verständlich; **for some** ~ **reason** aus irgendeinem unerfindlichen Grund

obscurity [əb·'skjʊr·ə·ti] n (*anonymity*) Unbekanntheit f; (*of no importance*) Unbedeutendheit f; **to sink into** ~ in Vergessenheit geraten

observable [əb·'zɜr·və·bəl] adj wahrnehmbar

observant [əb·'zɜr·vənt] adj (*approv: sharp-eyed*) aufmerksam

observation [ˌab·zər·'veɪ·ʃən] n Beobachtung f; LAW (*surveillance*) Überwachung f

obser'vation tower n Aussichtsturm m

observatory [əb·ˈzɜr·və·tɔr·i] *n* Observatorium *nt*

observe [əb·ˈzɜrv] *vt* ❶ (*watch closely*) beobachten; *by police* überwachen ❷ (*study by watching*) *stars* beobachten ❸ (*form: obey*) *ceasefire* einhalten; *law* befolgen; **to ~ the speed limit** sich an die Geschwindigkeitsbegrenzung halten

observer [əb·ˈzɜr·vər] *n* (*watcher*) Beobachter(in) *m(f)*; (*spectator*) Zuschauer(in) *m(f)*

obsess [əb·ˈses] *vt* verfolgen; **to be ~ed by sb** von jdm besessen sein

obsession [əb·ˈsef·ən] *n* (*preoccupation*) Manie *f*; **to have an ~ with sth** von etw *dat* besessen sein

obsessive [əb·ˈses·ɪv] *adj* zwanghaft

obsolete [ˌab·sə·ˈlit] *adj* veraltet; *design* altmodisch; *method* überholt

obstacle [ˈab·stə·kəl] *n* Hindernis *nt*

'obstacle course *n* Hindernisstrecke *f*

obstetrician [ˌab·stə·ˈtrɪʃ·ən] *n* Geburtshelfer(in) *m(f)*

obstinate [ˈab·stə·nɪt] *adj* hartnäckig; *person* eigensinnig

obstruct [əb·ˈstrʌkt] *vt* ❶ (*block*) blockieren; *path* versperren; *pipe* verstopfen; *progress* behindern ❷ SPORT sperren

obstruction [əb·ˈstrʌk·ʃən] *n* ❶ (*blockage*) Blockierung *f*; (*med, of pipes*) Verstopfung *f*; **to cause an ~** *for traffic* den Verkehr behindern ❷ (*Baseball, law*) Behinderung *f*; SPORT Sperre *f*

obstructive [əb·ˈstrʌk·tɪv] *adj* (*pej*) hinderlich

obtain [əb·ˈteɪn] *vt* ■ **to ~ sth [from sb]** (*to be given*) etw [von jdm] bekommen; (*to go and get*) sich *dat* etw [von jdm] verschaffen; *permission* erhalten

obtainable [əb·ˈteɪ·nə·bəl] *adj* erhältlich

obtuse [ab·ˈtus] *adj* MATH (*angle*) stumpf

obvious [ˈab·vi·əs] *adj* offensichtlich; *comparison, solution* naheliegend; *displeasure* deutlich; ■ **to be ~ [that]** ... offenkundig sein, dass ...

obviously [ˈab·vi·əs·li] *adv* offensichtlich; **he was ~ very upset** er war sichtlich sehr aufgebracht

occasion [ə·ˈkeɪ·ʒən] *n* (*particular time*) Gelegenheit *f*; (*event*) Ereignis *nt*; **on another ~** ein anderes Mal; **on several ~s** mehrmals

occasional [ə·ˈkeɪ·ʒə·nəl] *adj* gelegentlich

occasionally [ə·ˈkeɪ·ʒə·nə·li] *adv* gelegentlich; **to see sb ~** jdn ab und zu treffen

occult [ə·ˈkʌlt] *n* ■ **the ~** das Okkulte

occupation [ˌak·jə·ˈpeɪ·ʃən] *n* ❶ (*form: profession*) Beruf *m* ❷ MIL Besetzung *f*

occupational [ˌak·jə·ˈpeɪ·ʃə·nəl] *adj* Berufs-, beruflich

occupational 'therapy *n* Beschäftigungstherapie *f*

occupier [ˈak·jə·paɪ·ər] *n* ❶ (*tenant*) Bewohner(in) *m(f)* ❷ (*conqueror*) Besatzer(in) *m(f)*

occupy <-ie-> [ˈak·ju·paɪ] *vt* ❶ (*fill*) ausfüllen; (*live in*) bewohnen ❷ (*take control of*) besetzen; **~ing forces** Besatzungstruppen *pl*

occur <-rr-> [ə·ˈkɜr] *vi* ❶ (*take place*) geschehen; *accident* sich ereignen; *change* stattfinden ❷ (*come to mind*) ■ **to ~ to sb** jdm einfallen

occurrence [ə·ˈkɜr·əns] *n* ❶ (*event*) Vorfall *m* ❷ (*incidence*) Vorkommen *nt*

ocean [ˈoʊ·ʃən] *n* Ozean *m*

oceanography [ˌoʊ·ʃə·ˈnag·rə·fi] *n* Ozeanographie *f*

ocelot [ˈas·ə·lat] *n* Ozelot *m*

ocher, ochre [ˈoʊ·kər] *n* Ocker *m* o nt

o'clock [ə·ˈklak] *adv* **two ~** zwei Uhr

Oct. *n abbrev of* **October** Okt.

octagonal [ak·ˈtæg·ə·nəl] *adj* achteckig

octane [ˈak·teɪn] *n* Oktanzahl *f*

octave [ˈak·tɪv] *n* Oktave *f*

October [ak·ˈtoʊ·bər] *n* Oktober *m; see also* **February**

octopus <*pl* -es> [ˈak·tə·pəs] *n* Tintenfisch *m*

OD [ˌoʊ·ˈdi] (*sl*) *abbrev of* **overdose** I. *vi* ■ **to ~ on sth** eine Überdosis einer S. *gen* nehmen *fig* II. *n* Überdosis *f*

odd [ad] I. *adj* ❶ (*strange*) merkwürdig; *person* eigenartig ❷ MATH ungerade ❸ *attr shoe, sock* einzeln II. *n* ■ **~s** *pl* (*probability*) **the ~s are 3 to 1** die Chancen stehen 3 zu 1; ■**the ~s are ...** es ist sehr wahrscheinlich, dass ...; **the ~s on/against sb doing sth** die Chancen, dass jd etw tut/nicht tut ►PHRASES: **against all the ~s** entgegen allen Erwartungen; **~s and ends** Krimskrams *m kein pl*

oddball ['ad·bɔl] (*fam*) **I.** *n* Verrückte(r) *f(m)* **II.** *adj attr* verrückt

oddity ['ad·ə·t̬i] *n* Kuriosität *f*

oddly ['ad·li] *adv* seltsam; **~ enough** merkwürdigerweise

odometer [oʊ·'dam·ə·t̬ər] *n* Kilometerzähler *m*

odor ['oʊ·dər] *n* Geruch *m*

odorless ['oʊ·dər·ləs] *adj* (*form*) geruchlos

odyssey ['ad·ɪ·si] *n usu sing* (*liter. or a. fig*) Odyssee *f*

of [ʌv, əv] *prep* ❶ *after n* (*expressing relationship*) von; **the employees ~ the company** die Angestellten des Unternehmens; **the destruction ~ the rain forest** die Zerstörung des Regenwalds; **the works ~ Shakespeare** die Werke Shakespeares; **a friend ~ mine** ein Freund von mir ❷ *after n* (*relating a part to the whole*) von; **both ~ us** wir beide; **all ~ us** wir alle; **most ~ them** die meisten von ihnen; **a third ~ the people** ein Drittel der Leute; **one ~ the smartest** eine(r) der Schlauesten ❸ *after n* (*expressing quantities*) **a cup ~ coffee** eine Tasse Kaffee; **two pounds ~ apples** ein Kilo Äpfel *nt;* **a piece ~ cake** ein Stück Kuchen ❹ *after vb, n* (*consisting of*) aus; **a sweater made ~ the finest lambswool** ein Pullover aus feinster Schafswolle ❺ *after vb* (*concerning*) **he was accused ~ fraud** er wurde wegen Betrugs angeklagt; *after adj;* **to be unsure ~ oneself** sich seiner selbst nicht sicher sein; **to be afraid ~ sb** vor jdm Angst haben; **to be fond ~ swimming** gerne schwimmen; **to be sick ~ sth** etw satthaben; *after n;* **memories ~ sb/sth** Erinnerungen an jdn/etw ❻ *after n* (*expressing position*)

von; **north ~** nördlich von; **on the corner ~ the street** an der Straßenecke ❼ *after n* (*in time phrases*) **the eleventh ~ March** der elfte März; (*to*) vor; **it's a quarter ~ five** es ist viertel vor fünf

off [ɔf] **I.** *prep* ❶ (*indicating removal*) von; **he wiped the dust ~ the table** er wischte den Staub von dem Tisch; **he cut a piece ~ the cheese** er schnitt ein Stück Käse ab; **to be ~ the air** RADIO, TV nicht mehr senden; **~ the record** nicht für die Öffentlichkeit bestimmt ❷ *after vb* (*moving down*) hinunter [von]; (*towards sb*) herunter [von]; **they jumped ~ the cliff** sie sprangen von der Klippe; **the boy fell ~ his bike** der Junge fiel von seinem Fahrrad herunter ❸ (*away from*) [weg] von; (*at sea*) von +*dat;* **six miles ~ the coast of Florida** sechs Meilen vor der Küste Floridas; **to lead ~ sth** von etw *dat* wegführen; **far/a long way ~ sth** weit entfernt von etw *dat* ❹ (*absent from*) **to be ~ work** am Arbeitsplatz fehlen **II.** *adv* ❶ (*not on*) aus; **to switch/turn sth ~** etw ausschalten ❷ (*away*) weg; **to go/drive ~** weggehen/-fahren; **I'm ~ now — see you tomorrow** ich gehe jetzt – wir sehen uns morgen; **to see sb ~** jdn verabschieden ❸ (*removed*) ab-; **I'll take my jacket ~** ich ziehe meine Jacke aus; **to come ~** button abgehen ❹ (*discounted*) reduziert; **to get money ~** Rabatt bekommen **III.** *adj* ❶ (*not working*) außer Betrieb; (*switched ~*) aus[geschaltet]; *faucet* zugedreht ❷ (*not at work*) ■**to be ~** freihaben; **to take some time ~** einige Zeit freinehmen

'offbeat *adj* unkonventionell; *sense of humor* ausgefallen

off-'center *adj* nicht in der Mitte *präd*

'off day *n* schlechter Tag

off-'duty *adj* ■**to be ~** dienstfrei haben

offend [ə·'fend] **I.** *vi* (*commit a criminal act*) eine Straftat begehen **II.** *vt* (*insult*) beleidigen; (*hurt*) kränken

offender [ə·'fen·dər] *n* [Straf]täter(in) *m(f)*

offense [ə·ˈfens] *n* ❶ LAW Straftat *f* ❷ (*upset feelings*) Beleidigung *f*; **to cause ~** Anstoß erregen; **to take ~** [at sth] (*wegen einer S. gen*) gekränkt/beleidigt sein ❸ SPORT (*attack*) Angriff *m*

offensive [ə·ˈfen·sɪv] I. *adj* ❶ (*causing offense*) anstößig; *joke* anzüglich II. *n* MIL Angriff *m*; **to go on the ~** in die Offensive gehen

offer [ˈɔ·fər] I. *n* Angebot *nt* II. *vt* ❶ (*present for acceptance*) anbieten ❷ (*put forward*) vorbringen; *explanation* abgeben; *information* geben

offering [ˈɔ·fər·ɪŋ] *n usu pl* Spende *f*

off'hand *adj* ❶ (*uninterested*) gleichgültig ❷ (*informal*) lässig; **~ remark** nebenbei fallen gelassene Bemerkung

office [ˈɔ·fɪs] *n* ❶ (*room*) Büro *nt*; (*of company*) Geschäftsstelle *f* ❷ POL (*authoritative position*) Amt *nt*; **to come into ~** sein Amt antreten

'office building *n* Bürohaus *nt*

'office hours *npl* Geschäftszeit[en] *f(pl)*

officer [ˈɔ·fɪ·sər] *n* ❶ MIL Offizier(in) *m(f)* ❷ (*office holder*) Beamte(r) *m*, Beamte [*o* -in] *f*; (*police*) **~** Polizeibeamte(r) *f(m)*, Polizist(in) *m(f)*

O **'office supplies** *npl* Bürobedarf *m* *kein pl*

'office worker *n* Büroangestellte(r) *f(m)*

official [ə·ˈfɪʃ·əl] I. *n* ❶ (*holding public office*) Amtsperson *f*, Beamte(r) *m*, Beamte [*o* -in] *f* ❷ SPORT Schiedsrichter, -in *m, f* II. *adj* ❶ (*relating to an office*) offiziell, amtlich; **~ residence** Amtssitz *m* ❷ (*authorized*) offiziell; *inquiry* amtlich

officially [ə·ˈfɪʃ·ə·li] *adv* offiziell

officious [ə·ˈfɪʃ·əs] *adj* (*pej*) ❶ (*bossy*) schikanierend ❷ (*interfering*) aufdringlich

off-'key *adj* verstimmt

off-'limits *adj pred* ■ **to be ~ to sb** für jdn tabu sein

off'line *adj* offline

'offload *vt* ❶ (*unload*) ausladen ❷ (*get rid of*) loswerden *fam*; **to ~ the responsibility** [onto sb] die Verantwortung [auf jdn] abladen

off-'peak *adj telephone call* außerhalb der Hauptsprechzeiten *nach n*

off-'piste *adv* abseits der Skipiste

'off-season *n* ■ **the ~** die Nebensaison

offset [ˈɔf·set] *vt* <-set, -set> *usu passive* (*compensate for*) ■ **to be ~ by** [doing] **sth** durch etw *akk* ausgeglichen werden

off-'site *adj* Außen-

offspring <*pl ->* [ˈɔf·sprɪŋ] *n* (*a. hum: person's child*) Nachkomme *m*

off'stage *adv* ❶ (*away from the stage*) hinter der Bühne ❷ (*privately*) privat

off-street 'parking *n* Parken auf Parkplätzen außerhalb des Stadtzentrums

off-the-'rack *adj* Konfektions-

often [ˈɔ·fən] *adv* oft; **every so ~** gelegentlich

oftentimes *adv* (*fam*) häufig

ogle [ˈoʊ·gəl] *vt* angaffen *pej*

ogre [ˈoʊ·gər] *n* Menschenfresser *m*; (*fig fam*) Scheusal *nt pej*

OH *abbrev of* Ohio

oh[1] [oʊ] *interj* ❶ (*to show surprise, disappointment, pleasure*) oh; **~ well** na ja ❷ (*by the way*) ach, übrigens

oh[2] [oʊ] *n* (*in phone numbers*) Null *f*

Ohio [oʊ·ˈhaɪ·oʊ] *n* Ohio *nt*

oil [ɔɪl] I. *n* ❶ (*lubricant*) Öl *nt* ❷ (*petroleum*) [Erd]öl *nt* ❸ FOOD [Speise]öl *nt* II. *vt* (*lubricate*) ölen

'oilcan *n* Ölkännchen *nt*

'oil change *n* Ölwechsel *m*

'oil company *n* Ölfirma *f*

'oil field *n* Ölfeld *nt*

'oil painting *n* Ölbild *nt*

'oil pipeline *n* Ölpipeline *f*

'oil rig *n* Bohrinsel *f*

'oilskin *n* ■ **~s** *pl* Ölzeug *nt kein pl*

'oil tanker *n* Öltanker *m*

'oil well *n* Ölquelle *f*

oily [ˈɔɪ·li] *adj* ❶ *food* ölig ❷ *hair* fettig

ointment [ˈɔɪnt·mənt] *n* Salbe *f*

OK, okay [oʊ·ˈkeɪ] (*fam*) I. *adj* ❶ *pred* (*acceptable*) okay ❷ *pred* (*healthy*) *person* in Ordnung ❸ *pred* (*not outstanding*) nicht schlecht ❹ *pred* (*have no problems*) **to be ~ for money** genug Geld haben II. *interj* okay; **~ then**

also gut **III.** *vt* ■**to ~ sth** zu etw *dat* sein Okay geben **IV.** *adv* gut; **did you get there ~?** bist du dort gut angekommen?

OK *abbrev of* **Oklahoma**

Okla. *abbrev of* **Oklahoma**

Oklahoma [ˌoʊ·klə·ˈhoʊ·mə] *n* Oklahoma *nt*

okra [ˈoʊk·rə] *n* Okra *f*

old [oʊld] **I.** *adj* ① alt ② *after n (denoting an age)* alt; **three years ~** drei Jahre alt ③ *attr (former)* ehemalig; *job* alt ▶PHRASES: **you can't teach an ~ dog new tricks** (*prov*) der Mensch ist ein Gewohnheitstier **II.** *n* **young and ~** Jung und Alt

old 'age *n* Alter *nt*

old-'fashioned *adj (esp pej)* altmodisch

old 'lady *n* ① *(elderly female)* alte Dame ② *(fam: wife, mother)* ■**the ~** die Alte

old 'man *n* ① *(elderly male)* alter Mann ② *(fam: husband, father)* ■**the ~** der Alte *fam*

old 'master *n* alter Meister

Old 'Testament *n* ■**the ~** das Alte Testament

old-'timer *n (fam)* ① *(old man)* Oldie *m* hum *fam* ② *(long-time worker)* alter Hase *fam*

old 'wives' tale *n* Ammenmärchen *nt*

oleander [ˌoʊ·li·ˈæn·dər] *n* Oleander *m*

olive [ˈal·ɪv] *n* Olive *f*

'olive branch *n (fig)* Ölzweig *m*

'olive grove *n* Olivenhain *m*

'olive oil *n* Olivenöl *nt*

Olympic 'Games, Olympics [oʊ·ˈlɪm·pɪks] *n pl* ■**the ~** die Olympischen Spiele

omelet, omelette [ˈam·lət] *n* Omelett *nt*

omen [ˈoʊ·mən] *n* Omen *nt*

ominous [ˈam·ə·nəs] *adj* unheilvoll

omission [oʊ·ˈmɪʃ·ən] *n* Auslassung *f*

omit <-tt-> [oʊ·ˈmɪt] *vt* auslassen

omnivorous [am·ˈnɪv·ər·əs] *adj* alles fressend

on [an] **I.** *prep* ① *(on top of)* auf +*dat;* **the book's ~ the table** das Buch liegt auf dem Tisch ② *with verbs of motion (onto)* auf +*akk;* **to go out ~ the balcony** auf die Terrasse hinausgehen ③ *(indicating position)* an +*dat,* auf +*dat;* **to lie ~ the beach** am Strand liegen; **he had a scratch ~ his arm** er hatte einen Kratzer am Arm; **~ the right** auf der rechten Seite ④ *(indicating contact)* an +*dat;* **I hit my head ~ the shelf** ich stieß mir den Kopf am Regal an; **to stumble ~ sth** über etw *akk* stolpern ⑤ *(about)* über +*akk;* **a debate ~ the crisis** eine Debatte über die Krise; **he needs some advice ~ how to dress** er braucht ein paar Tipps, wie er sich anziehen soll ⑥ *(based on)* auf … hin; ~ **account of** wegen; **to rely ~ sb/sth** sich auf jdn/etw verlassen ⑦ *(against)* auf +*akk;* **to place a limit ~ sth** etw begrenzen ⑧ *(indicating a medium)* auf +*dat;* **what's ~ TV tonight?** was kommt heute Abend im Fernsehen?; **to come out ~ video** als Video herauskommen ⑨ *(traveling by)* in +*dat,* mit +*dat;* ~ **foot** zu Fuß ⑩ *(indicating date)* an +*dat;* ~ **Friday** am Freitag **II.** *adv* ① *(in contact with)* auf; **to screw sth ~** etw anschrauben ② *(on body)* an; **to try sth ~** etw anprobieren ③ *(indicating continuance)* weiter; **if the line's busy, keep ~ trying!** wenn besetzt ist, probier es weiter! ④ *(in forward direction)* vorwärts; **from that day ~** von diesem Tag an ⑤ *(functioning)* an; **to leave the light ~** das Licht anlassen; **to switch/turn sth ~** etw einschalten ⑥ *(aboard)* **to get ~ bus, train** einsteigen; *horse* aufsitzen ▶PHRASES: ~ **and off** ab und zu *fam;* **you're ~!** abgemacht! *fam*

once [wʌns] **I.** *adv* ① *(one time)* einmal; **just this ~** nur dieses eine Mal ② *(in the past)* früher; ~ **upon a time …** *(liter)* es war einmal … ▶PHRASES: **at ~** *(simultaneously)* auf einmal; *(immediately)* sofort; ~ **more** *(one more time)* noch einmal; *(again, as before)* wieder; ~ **or twice** ein paar Mal **II.** *conj (as soon as)* sobald

'once-over *n (fam: cursory examina-*

tion) **to give sth the ~** etw flüchtig ansehen

oncoming ['ɑn·kʌm·ɪŋ] *adj attr vehicle* entgegenkommend; **~ traffic** Gegenverkehr *m*

one [wʌn] **I.** *n* ❶ (*unit*) eins; **a hundred and ~** einhundert[und]eins ❷ (*numeral*) Eins *f* **II.** *adj* ❶ *attr* (*not two*) ein(e); **~ hundred** einhundert; **~ million** eine Million ❷ *attr* (*one of a number*) ein(e); **he can't tell ~ wine from another** er schmeckt bei Weinen keinen Unterschied ❸ *attr* (*single, only*) einzige(r, s); **we should paint the bedroom all ~ color** wir sollten das Schlafzimmer nur in einer Farbe streichen ❹ *attr* (*some future*) irgendein(e); **~ day** irgendwann ❺ *attr* (*some in the past*) ein(e); **~ evening** eines Abends ▶PHRASES: **~ way or another** (*somehow*) irgendwie **III.** *pron* ❶ (*single item*) eine(r, s); **not a single ~** kein Einziger/keine Einzige/kein Einziges; **~ after another** eine(r, s) nach dem/der anderen; **this/that ~** diese(r, s)/jene(r, s) ❷ (*single person*) eine(r); **she thought of her loved ~s** sie dachte an ihre Lieben; **~ by ~** nacheinander; **she's ~ of my favorite writers** sie ist eine meiner Lieblingsautoren ❸ (*expressing alternatives*) **~ or the other** der/die/das eine oder der/die/das andere ❹ (*form: any person, most people*) man; (*I*) ich; **~ gets the impression that ...** man hat den Eindruck, dass ... ▶PHRASES: **to be ~ of the family** zur Familie gehören *fig*; **in ~s and twos** (*in small numbers*) immer nur ein paar; (*alone or in a pair*) allein oder paarweise

'one-armed *adj* einarmig

'one-eyed *adj attr* einäugig

one-'handed I. *adv* mit einer Hand **II.** *adj attr* einhändig

one-'liner *n* Einzeiler *m*

one-night 'stand *n* ❶ (*sexual relationship*) Abenteuer *nt* für eine Nacht ❷ (*performance*) einmaliges Gastspiel

'one-piece, one-piece 'swimsuit *n* Einteiler *m*

oneself [wʌn'self] *pron refl* ❶ *after vb, prep* (*direct object*) sich ❷ (*personally*) selbst; **to see sth for ~** etw selbst sehen ❸ (*alone*) [**all**] **by ~** [ganz] alleine

one-'sided *adj* einseitig

'one-time *adj attr* ❶ (*former*) ehemalig ❷ (*happening only once*) einmalig

one-track 'mind *n* **to have a ~** immer nur eins im Kopf haben

one-way 'street *n* Einbahnstraße *f*

one-way 'ticket *n* einfache Fahrkarte, Einzelfahrschein *m*

ongoing ['ɑn·gou·ɪŋ] *adj* laufend *attr*

onion ['ʌn·jən] *n* Zwiebel *f*

online [ɑn·'laɪn] COMPUT **I.** *adj* Online- **II.** *adv* online

onlooker ['ɑn·lʊk·ər] *n* (*a. fig*) Zuschauer(in) *m(f)*

only ['oʊn·li] **I.** *adj attr* einzige(r, s); **the ~ one** der/die/das Einzige; **the ~ way** die einzige Möglichkeit **II.** *adv* ❶ (*exclusively*) nur; **for members ~** nur für Mitglieder ❷ (*just*) erst ❸ (*merely*) nur, bloß; **not ~ ..., but also ...** nicht nur ..., sondern auch ... ❹ (*unavoidably*) nur, unweigerlich; **the situation can ~ get better** die Situation kann sich nur verbessern **III.** *conj* (*however*) aber, jedoch; **he's a good athlete, ~ he smokes too much** er ist ein guter Sportler, bloß raucht er zu viel

onset ['ɑn·set] *n* Beginn *m*

onshore ['ɑn·ʃɔr] *adv* an Land

on-'site I. *adj* Vor-Ort- **II.** *adv* vor Ort

onstage [ɑn·'steɪdʒ, ɑn-] *adv* auf die Bühne

on-the-job 'training *n* Ausbildung *f* am Arbeitsplatz

onto, on to ['ɑn·tu] *prep after vb* auf +*akk*; **to get ~ a bus/train** in einen Bus/einen Zug einsteigen; **to load sth ~ sth** etw auf etw *akk* laden ▶PHRASES: **to be ~ sb/sth** jdm/etw auf der Spur sein

onward ['ɑn·wərd] **I.** *adj attr* (*of trip*) Weiter- **II.** *adv* ❶ (*into the future*) **from that day ~** von diesem Tag an ❷ (*of direction*) weiter

onyx ['ɑn·ɪks] *n* Onyx *m*

oops [ʊps] *interj* (*fam*) hoppla

ooze [uz] **I.** *vi* (*seep out*) tropfen (**from** aus +*dat*); *water* sickern; **to ~ with oil** vor Öl triefen **II.** *vt* (*fig: overflow with*) *charm* ausstrahlen; *sex appeal* versprühen

opal ['oʊ·pəl] *n* Opal *m*

opalescent [ˌoʊ·pə·'les·ənt] *adj* schillernd

opaque [oʊ·'peɪk] *adj* (*not transparent*) undurchsichtig; *window* trüb

OPEC ['oʊ·pek] *n acr for* **Organization of Petroleum Exporting Countries** OPEC *f*

open ['oʊ·pən] **I.** *adj* ❶ (*not closed*) offen, geöffnet, auf *präd*; *book* aufgeschlagen; *flower* aufgeblüht; **wide ~** [sperr-angel]weit geöffnet; **to burst ~** *case* aufgehen ❷ *pred* (*for customers*) *shop* geöffnet, offen ❸ (*not yet decided*) *question* offen; **to keep an ~ mind** unvoreingenommen bleiben ❹ (*not enclosed*) offen; **to be in the ~ air** an der frischen Luft sein ❺ *pred* (*frank*) *person* offen ❻ *pred* (*exposed*) offen, ungeschützt; **to be ~ to criticism** kritisierbar sein **II.** *vi* ❶ (*from closed*) sich öffnen, aufgehen ❷ (*for business*) shop öffnen; (*for the first time*) eröffnen ❸ *story* beginnen, anfangen ❹ *play* Premiere haben **III.** *vt* ❶ *book* aufschlagen; *window, bottle* aufmachen; *eyes, letter* öffnen; (*a. fig*) *mouth* aufmachen ❷ *bank account* eröffnen ▶PHRASES: **to ~ sb's eyes to sb** jdm die Augen über jdn öffnen **IV.** *n* ❶ (*out of doors*) ■[out] **in the ~** draußen; (*in the open air*) **[out]** im Freien ❷ (*not secret*) **to come out into the ~** ans Licht kommen

◆open out I. *vi* ❶ (*move apart*) sich ausbreiten ❷ *map* sich auffalten lassen; *flower* aufblühen ❸ (*grow wider*) sich erweitern; *river* breiter werden **II.** *vt* (*unfold*) **to ~** ⟳ **a map** eine [Land]karte auseinanderfalten

◆open up I. *vi* ❶ *store, etc.* eröffnen ❷ (*start shooting*) das Feuer eröffnen, losfeuern **II.** *vt* ❶ *pipe* passierbar machen; *house* aufschließen; *door* aufma-

chen ❷ (*make available*) ■**to ~ up** ⟳ **sth** [**to** sb/sth] [jdm/etw] etw zugänglich machen

'open-air *adj* im Freien *nach n*

opener ['oʊ·pə·nər] *n* (*opening device*) Öffner *m*

open-'faced *adj sandwich* belegt

open-heart 'surgery *n* Operation *f* am offenen Herzen

opening ['oʊ·pə·nɪŋ] *n* ❶ (*action*) Öffnen *nt* ❷ (*hole*) Öffnung *f*; (*in traffic*) Lücke *f* ❸ (*job*) freie Stelle ❹ (*introduction*) *of a film* Anfang *m*

'opening hours *npl* Öffnungszeiten *pl*

'opening time *n* Öffnungszeit *f*

openly ['oʊ·pən·li] *adv* ❶ (*frankly*) offen ❷ (*publicly*) öffentlich

open 'market *n* offener Markt

open-'minded *adj* (*to new ideas*) aufgeschlossen; (*not prejudiced*) unvoreingenommen

openness ['oʊ·pən·nəs] *n* Offenheit *f*

opera ['ap·rə] *n* Oper *f*

'opera house *n* Opernhaus *nt*

operate ['ap·ə·reɪt] **I.** *vi* ❶ (*work*) funktionieren ❷ (*perform surgery*) ■**to ~ on sb** jdn operieren ❸ (*do business*) operieren *geh* **II.** *vt* (*work*) bedienen

'operating room *n* MED Operationssaal *m*

'operating system, OS [ˌoʊ·'es] *n* COMPUT Betriebssystem *nt*

operation [ˌap·ə·'reɪ·ʃən] *n* ❶ (*way of functioning*) Funktionsweise *f*; **day-to-day ~** gewöhnlicher Betriebsablauf ❷ (*functioning state*) Betrieb *m*; **to come into ~** *law* in Kraft treten ❸ (*process*) Vorgang *m* ❹ (*activity*) Unternehmung *f*; MIL Operation *f*; **rescue ~** Rettungsaktion *f* ❺ (*surgery*) Operation *f*

operational [ˌap·ə·'reɪ·ʃə·nəl] *adj* (*functioning*) betriebsbereit

operative ['ap·ər·ə·tɪv] **I.** *n* (*in a factory*) [Fach]arbeiter(in) *m(f)* **II.** *adj* (*functioning*) in Betrieb *präd*

operator ['ap·ə·reɪ·tər] *n* ❶ (*worker*) Bediener(in) *m(f)* ❷ (*switchboard worker*) Telefonist(in) *m(f)*

O

operetta [ˌap·ə·ˈreṭ·ə] n Operette f

ophthalmologist [ˌaf·θəl·ˈmɑl·ə·dʒɪst] n Augenarzt, -ärztin m, f

opiate [ˈoʊ·pi·ɪt] n Opiat nt

opinion [ə·ˈpɪn·jən] n ❶ (belief) Meinung f ❷ (view on topic) Einstellung f, Standpunkt m; **difference of** ~ Meinungsverschiedenheit f; **to have a high ~ of sb** von jdm eine hohe Meinung haben

opinionated [ə·ˈpɪn·jə·neɪ·ṭɪd] adj (pej) rechthaberisch

o'pinion poll n Meinungsumfrage f

opium [ˈoʊ·pi·əm] n Opium nt

opossum <pl -s> [ə·ˈpɑs·əm] n Opossum nt

opponent [ə·ˈpoʊ·nənt] n POL Widersacher(in) m(f); SPORT Gegner(in) m(f)

opportune [ˌap·ər·ˈtun] adj angebracht

opportunism [ˌap·ər·ˈtu·nɪz·əm] n Opportunismus m

opportunist [ˌap·ər·ˈtu·nɪst] n Opportunist(in) m(f)

opportunity [ˌap·ər·ˈtu·nə·ṭi] n ❶ (occasion) Gelegenheit f; **a window of** ~ eine Chance ❷ (for advancement) Möglichkeit f

oppose [ə·ˈpoʊz] vt ❶ (disapprove) ablehnen ❷ (resist) ■**to** ~ **sb/sth** gegen jdn/etw vorgehen ❸ SPORT ■**to** ~ **sb** gegen jdn antreten

opposed [ə·ˈpoʊzd] adj pred ■**to be** ~ **to sth** gegen etw akk sein

opposing [ə·ˈpoʊz·ɪŋ] adj attr entgegengesetzt; opinion gegensätzlich; team gegnerisch

opposite [ˈap·ə·zɪt] I. n Gegenteil nt II. adj ❶ (contrary) gegensätzlich ❷ (facing) gegenüberliegend; directions entgegengesetzt III. adv gegenüber IV. prep (across from) gegenüber

opposition [ˌap·ə·ˈzɪʃ·ən] n ❶ (resistance) Widerstand m ❷ (party not in power) Opposition[spartei] f; (opposing team) gegnerische Mannschaft

oppression [ə·ˈpreʃ·ən] n Unterdrückung f

oppressive [ə·ˈpres·ɪv] adj ❶ regime unterdrückerisch ❷ heat, weather drückend

opt [apt] vi ■**to** ~ **for sth** sich für etw akk entscheiden

◆ **opt in** vi sich beteiligen

◆ **opt out** vi nicht mitmachen; (withdraw) aussteigen fam

optical [ˈap·tɪ·kəl] adj optisch

optician [ap·ˈtɪʃ·ən] n Optiker(in) m(f)

optimism [ˈap·tə·mɪz·əm] n Optimismus m

optimist [ˈap·tə·mɪst] n Optimist(in) m(f)

optimize [ˈap·tə·maɪz] vt optimieren

optimum [ˈap·tə·məm] adj optimal

option [ˈap·ʃən] n Wahl f; (possibility) Möglichkeit f; **to not be an** ~ nicht in Frage kommen

optional [ˈap·ʃə·nəl] adj wahlfrei

opulence [ˈap·jə·ləns] n (luxury) Luxus m

opulent [ˈap·jə·lənt] adj ❶ (affluent) wohlhabend ❷ (luxurious) luxuriös

OR n abbrev of **Oregon**

or [ɔr] conj ❶ (as a choice) oder ❷ (otherwise) sonst; ■**either ... ~ ...** entweder...[,] oder ❸ (and a. not) ■**not ... ~ ...** weder ... noch ...

oral [ˈɔr·əl] I. adj mündlich II. n ■~**s** pl mündliches Examen

orange [ˈɔr·ɪndʒ] I. n (fruit) Orange f II. adj orange[farben]

'orange juice n Orangensaft m

'orange peel n Orangenschale f

orangutan [ɔ·ˈræŋ·ə·tæn], **orangoutang** [ɔ·ˈræŋ·ə·tæŋ] n Orang-Utan m

orator [ˈɔr·ə·ṭər] n Redner(in) m(f)

orbit [ˈɔr·bɪt] I. n ❶ (constant course) Umlaufbahn f; **in** ~ **around the earth** in einer Erdumlaufbahn ❷ (fig: influence) [Einfluss]bereich m II. vt (circle around) umkreisen

orchard [ˈɔr·tʃərd] n Obstgarten m

orchestra [ˈɔr·kɪ·strə] n Orchester nt

orchestral [ɔr·ˈkes·trəl] adj orchestral

'orchestra pit n Orchestergraben m

'orchestra seats npl Parkett nt

orchestrate [ˈɔr·kɪ·streɪt] vt ❶ (arrange

for orchestra) orchestrieren ② (*fig*) *event* organisieren

orchid ['ɔr·kɪd] *n* Orchidee *f*

ordeal [ɔr·'dil] *n* (*fig: painful experience*) Zerreißprobe *f*

order ['ɔr·dər] I. *n* ① (*neatness*) Ordnung *f* ② (*sequence*) Reihenfolge *f*; **word ~** Wortstellung *f*; **in alphabetical ~** in alphabetischer Reihenfolge ③ (*command*) Befehl *m*; **doctor's ~s** ärztliche Anweisung ④ Bestellung *f*; (*request to make sth a.*) Auftrag *m* ⑤ (*correct behavior*) Ordnung *f*; **to restore ~** die Ordnung wiederherstellen ⑥ (*condition*) Zustand *f*; **to be in working ~** (*ready for use*) funktionsbereit sein; (*functioning*) funktionsbereit sein; **"out of ~"** „außer Betrieb" ⑦ (*intention*) **■in ~ to do sth** um etw zu tun II. *vi* bestellen III. *vt* ① (*command*) befehlen ② COMM (*request from company or in restaurant*) bestellen

◆ **order around** *vt* herumkommandieren *fam*

'order form *n* Bestellformular *nt*

orderly ['ɔr·dər·li] I. *n* (*hospital attendant*) ~ [Kranken]pfleger(in) *m(f)* II. *adj* ① (*methodical*) geordnet; (*neat*) ordentlich ② *demonstration* friedlich

ordinal, ordinal number ['ɔr·də·nəl·] *n* Ordinalzahl *f*

ordinary ['ɔr·də·ner·i] I. *adj* gewöhnlich, normal II. *n* (*normal state*) **nothing out of the ~** nichts Ungewöhnliches

ore [ɔr] *n* Erz *nt*

Ore. *n abbrev of* **Oregon**

oregano [ə·'reg·ə·noʊ] *n* Oregano *nt*

Oregon ['ɔr·ɪ·gən] *n* Oregon *nt*

organ ['ɔr·gən] *n* ① MUS Orgel *f* ② ANAT Organ *nt*

'organ donor *n* Organspender(in) *m(f)*

organic [ɔːr·'gæn·ɪk] *adj* ① (*of bodily organs*) organisch ② (*living*) organisch ③ AGR, ECOL biologisch, Bio-; **~ fruit** Obst *nt* aus biologischem Anbau; **~ farming methods** biologische Anbaumethoden; **~ label** Bio-Siegel *nt*; **~ supermarket** Biosupermarkt *m*

organism ['ɔr·gə·nɪz·əm] *n* Organismus *m*

organist ['ɔr·gə·nɪst] *n* Organist(in) *m(f)*

organization [,ɔr·gə·nɪ·'zeɪ·ʃən] *n* Organisation *f*

Organization of Petroleum Exporting 'Countries *n* die Organisation Erdöl exportierender Länder

organize ['ɔr·gə·naɪz] *vt* ① *activities* organisieren; *books, files* ordnen; *space* aufteilen ② vorbereiten; *committee, team* zusammenstellen

organized ['ɔr·gə·naɪzd] *adj* organisiert

organized 'crime *n* organisiertes Verbrechen

organizer ['ɔr·gə·naɪ·zər] *n* ① (*book*) Terminplaner *m* ② (*person*) Organisator(in) *m(f)*

orgasm ['ɔr·gæz·əm] *n* Orgasmus *m*

orgy ['ɔr·dʒi] *n* Orgie *f*

orient ['ɔr·i·ənt] I. *n* GEOG **■the O~** der Orient II. *vt* (*determine position*) **■to ~ oneself** [**by sth**] sich [nach etw *dat*] orientieren

oriental [,ɔr·i·'en·təl] *adj* orientalisch

orientation [,ɔr·i·en·'teɪ·ʃən] *n* Orientierung *f*; **sexual ~** sexuelle Neigung

orienteering [,ɔr·i·en·'tɪr·ɪŋ] *n* Orientierungslauf *m*

origin ['ɔr·ə·dʒɪn] *n* ① (*beginning, source*) Ursprung *m* ② (*place sth/sb comes from*) Herkunft *f kein pl*

original [ə·'rɪdʒ·ɪ·nəl] I. *n* ① Original *nt* II. *adj* ① (*first*) ursprünglich; **the ~ version** die Originalversion; *of a book* die Originalausgabe ② (*unique*) originell; (*innovative*) bahnbrechend ③ (*from creator*) original; **~ painting** Original *nt*

originality [ə·,rɪdʒ·ɪ·'næl·ə·t̬i] *n* Originalität *f*

originally [ə·'rɪdʒ·ɪ·nə·li] *adv* ursprünglich

originate [ə·'rɪdʒ·ɪ·neɪt] I. *vi* entstehen; **■to ~ from sth** aus etw *dat* stammen II. *vt* erfinden

ornament ['ɔr·nə·mənt] *n* ① Ziergegenstand *m*; (*figurine*) Figürchen *nt* ② (*adornment*) Schmuck *m*

ornamental [ˌɔr·nə·ˈmen·təl] *adj* Zierteiliges

ornate [ɔrˈneɪt] *adj object* prunkvoll; *music* ornamentreich; *language, style* kunstvoll

ornithology [ˌɔr·nə·ˈθɑl·ə·dʒi] *n* Ornithologie *f fachspr*

orphan [ˈɔr·fən] *n* Waise *f*

orphanage [ˈɔr·fə·nɪdʒ] *n* Waisenhaus *nt*

orthodontist [ˌɔr·θə·ˈdɑn·tɪst] *n* Kieferorthopäde, -in *m, f*

orthodox [ˈɔr·θə·dɑks] *adj* ❶ (*generally accepted*) herkömmlich ❷ (*strictly religious*) strenggläubig ❸ REL **Greek ~** griechisch orthodox; **the O~ Church** die christlich orthodoxe Kirche

orthopedic [ˌɔr·θə·ˈpi·dɪk] *adj* orthopädisch

orthopedist [ˌɔr·θə·ˈpi·dɪst] *n* Orthopäde, -in *m, f*

OS [ˌoʊ·ˈes] *n* COMPUT *abbrev of* **operating system**

oscillate [ˈɑs·ə·leɪt] *vi* (*swing*) schwingen

oscillation [ˌɑs·ə·ˈleɪ·ʃən] *n* (*movement*) Schwingung *f*

osmosis [ɑz·ˈmoʊ·sɪs] *n* BIOL, CHEM Osmose *f fachspr*

ostensible [ɑ·ˈsten·sə·bəl] *adj* angeblich

ostensibly [ɑ·ˈsten·səb·li] *adv* angeblich

ostentatious [ˌɑs·tən·ˈteɪ·ʃəs] *adj* prahlerisch; *lifestyle* protzig

osteoporosis [ˌɑs·ti·oʊ·pə·ˈroʊ·sɪs] *n* MED Osteoporose *f fachspr*

ostracize [ˈɑs·trə·saɪz] *vt* ächten

ostrich [ˈɑs·trɪtʃ] *n* ORN Strauß *m*

other [ˈʌð·ər] **I.** *adj det* ❶ (*different*) andere(r, s); **in ~ words** mit anderen Worten; **~ people** andere [Leute] ❷ (*additional*) andere(r, s), weitere(r, s) ❸ (*alternative*) andere(r, s); **on the ~ hand** andererseits; **every ~** jede(r, s) zweite **II.** *pron* (*the remaining one*) ■**the ~** der/die/das andere; **one or the ~** eines davon; **the ~s** die anderen

otherwise [ˈʌð·ər·waɪz] **I.** *adv* ❶ (*differently*) anders; **unless you let me know ~,** ... sofern ich nichts Gegen-

teiliges von dir höre, ... ❷ (*except for this*) sonst **II.** *conj* andernfalls

otter [ˈɑt·ər] *n* Otter *m*

ouch [aʊtʃ] *interj* aua, autsch

ought [ɔt] *aux vb* ❶ (*indicating duty*) ■**sb ~ to do sth** jd sollte etw tun; **we ~ not to have agreed** wir hätten nicht zustimmen sollen ❷ (*indicating probability*) **we ~ to be home by 7 o'clock** um sieben müssten wir eigentlich zu Hause sein; **ten minutes ~ to be enough time** zehn Minuten müssten eigentlich genügen

ounce [aʊns] *n* Unze *f*

our [aʊr] *adj poss* unser(e)

ours [aʊrz] *pron poss* (*belonging to us*) unsere(r, s); **he's a cousin of ~** er ist ein Cousin von uns

ourselves [aʊr·ˈselvz] *pron refl* ❶ *after vb, prep* (*direct object*) uns; **we enjoyed ~ at the party very much** wir hatten großen Spaß bei der Party ❷ (*emph: personally*) wir persönlich; **to see sth for ~** etw selbst sehen

oust [aʊst] *vt* (*expel*) vertreiben; (*by taking their position*) verdrängen

out [aʊt] **I.** *adj pred* ❶ (*not at a place*) ■**to be ~** nicht da sein; (*not at home*) nicht zu Hause sein; **to be ~ and about** unterwegs sein; (*after an illness*) wieder auf den Beinen sein ❷ (*outside*) ■**to be ~** draußen sein; *prisoner* [wieder] draußen sein *fam* ❸ (*visible*) ■**to be ~** sun, moon, stars am Himmel stehen; (*in blossom*) blühen; (*available*) erhältlich sein; (*on the market*) auf dem Markt sein ❹ (*known*) ■**to be ~** heraus sein; *secret* gelüftet sein; *news* bekannt sein ❺ (*finished*) aus; **before the month is ~** vor Ende des Monats ❻ SPORT ■**to be ~** (*not playing*) nicht [mehr] im Spiel sein; (*in cricket, baseball*) aus sein; (*outside a boundary*) im Aus sein ❼ *light, TV* aus; *fire a.* erloschen **II.** *adv* ❶ (*not in sth*) außen; (*not in a room, apartment*) draußen; (*outdoors*) draußen, im Freien; **to keep sb ~** jdn nicht hereinlassen ❷ (*outwards*) heraus;

(*seen from inside*) hinaus; (*facing the outside*) nach außen; (*out of a room, building a.*) nach draußen; **get ~!** raus hier! *fam* ❸ (*away from home, for a social activity*) **to eat ~** im Restaurant essen; **to go ~** ausgehen ❹ (*removed*) [he]raus; (*extinguished*) aus; **to put a fire ~** ein Feuer löschen; **to cross sth ~** etw ausstreichen ❺ (*fully*) **burned ~** (*a. fig*) ausgebrannt; *fuse* durchgebrannt ❻ (*aloud*) **to call ~ to sb** jdm zurufen; **to cry ~ in pain** vor Schmerzen aufschreien ❼ (*unconscious*) **to knock sb ~** jdn bewusstlos schlagen ❽ (*open*) **to open sth ~** (*unfold*) etw auseinanderfalten; (*spread out*) etw ausbreiten **III.** *vt* ■ **to ~ sb** *homosexual* jdn outen *fam* **IV.** *prep* (*fam*) aus + *dat;* **to run ~ the door** zur Tür hinausrennen

'out-and-out *adj attr* ausgemacht

'outback *n* Hinterland *nt* [Australiens]

out'bid <-bid, -bid> *vt* überbieten

'outboard, outboard 'motor *n* Außenbordmotor *m*

'outbreak *n of a disease, a war* Ausbruch *m*

'outburst *n* Ausbruch *m*

'outcast *n* Ausgestoßene(r) *f(m)*; **social ~** gesellschaftlicher Außenseiter/ gesellschaftliche Außenseiterin

out'class *vt* in den Schatten stellen

'outcome *n* Ergebnis *nt*

'outcry *n* lautstarker Protest

out'dated *adj* veraltet; *ideas, views* überholt

out'do <-did, -done> *vt* übertreffen

'outdoor *adj clothes* für draußen *nach n;* **~ swimming pool** Freibad *nt*

outdoors [ˌaʊtˈdɔːz] *adv* im Freien

outdoorsy [ˌaʊtˈdɔːɹzi] *adj* (*fam*) ■ **to be ~** gern in der freien Natur [*o* an der frischen Luft] sein

outer [ˈaʊtər] *adj* ❶ (*external*) äußerlich ❷ (*far from center*) äußere(r, s)

outermost [ˈaʊtər·moʊst] *n attr* äußerste(r, s)

'outfield *n* Outfield *nt*

'outfit *n* ❶ (*clothes*) Kleidung *f*; **cow-**

boy ~ Cowboykostüm *nt* ❷ (*fam: group*) Verein *m*; (*musicians*) Truppe *f*

'outflow *n* Ausfluss *m*

out'going *adj* (*approv: extrovert*) kontaktfreudig

out'grow <-grew, -grown> *vt* (*become too big for*) ■ **to ~ sth** aus etw *dat* herauswachsen

'outgrowth *n* Auswuchs *m a. fig;* (*development*) Weiterentwicklung *f*

outing [ˈaʊ·tɪŋ] *n* ❶ (*trip*) Ausflug *m;* **to go on an ~** einen Ausflug machen ❷ (*revealing homosexuality*) Outing *f*

out'last *vt* überdauern; ■ **to ~ sb** jdn überleben

outlaw [ˈaʊt·lɔ] *n* (*criminal*) Bandit(in) *m(f)*; (*fugitive from law*) Geächtete(r) *f(m)*

'outlay *n* Aufwendungen *pl*

'outlet *n* ❶ ELEC Steckdose *f* ❷ (*exit*) Ausgang *m; for water* Abfluss *m* ❸ (*means of expression*) Ventil *nt fig* ❹ (*store*) Verkaufsstelle *f;* **factory ~** Fabrikverkauf *m*

'outline I. *n* ❶ (*brief description*) Übersicht *f* ❷ (*contour*) Umriss *m* **II.** *vt* ■ **to ~ sth** ❶ (*draw*) die Umrisse von etw *dat* zeichnen ❷ (*summarize*) etw [kurz] umreißen

out'live *vt* (*live longer than*) ■ **to ~ sb** jdn überleben; ■ **to ~ sth** etw überdauern

'outlook *n* ❶ (*view*) Aussicht *f* ❷ (*future prospect*) Aussicht[en] *f(pl)* ❸ (*attitude*) Einstellung *f*

'outlying *adj attr region, town* abgelegen

outma'neuver *vt* ausmanövrieren

outmoded [ˌaʊtˈmoʊ·dɪd] *adj* (*pej*) altmodisch; *ideas* überholt

out'number *vt* zahlenmäßig überlegen sein

'out of *prep* ❶ *after vb* (*towards outside*) aus ❷ *after vb* (*situated away from*) außerhalb; **she's ~ the office at the moment** sie ist zurzeit nicht an ihrem [Arbeits]platz; *after vb* außerhalb ❸ *after vb* (*from*) von; **she had to pay for it ~ her own pocket** sie musste es aus der

O

eigenen Tasche bezahlen ④(*excluded from*) aus; **I'm glad to be ~ it** ich bin froh, dass ich das hinter mir habe; **to be ~ the question** nicht in Frage kommen ⑤*after n* (*ratio of*) von; **nine times ~ ten** neun von zehn Malen ⑥(*without*) **they were ~ luck** sie hatten kein Glück [mehr]; **to run ~ cash** kein Bargeld mehr haben ⑦(*beyond*) außer; **~ reach** außer Reichweite; **~ focus** *photo* unscharf; **get ~ the way!** aus dem Weg! ▸PHRASES: **~ sight, ~ mind** aus den Augen, aus dem Sinn; **~ place** fehl am Platz

out-of-court 'settlement *n* LAW außergerichtliche Einigung

out of 'date *adj pred*, **'out-of-date** *adj attr* veraltet; *clothing* altmodisch; *ideas* überholt

out of the 'way *adj pred*, **'out-of-the-way** *adj attr* place abgelegen

'outpatient *n* ambulanter Patient/ambulante Patientin

out'play *vt* ■**to ~ sb** besser spielen als jd

'outpost *n* ①MIL (*base*) Stützpunkt *m* ②(*remote branch*) Außenposten *m*

'outpouring *n* (*of emotion*) Ausbruch *m*

'output I. *n* ECON Ausstoß *m*; COMPUT Ausgabe *f* **II.** *vt* data ausgeben

'outrage I. *n* Empörung *f*; (*deed*) Schandtat *f*; (*disgrace*) Schande *f kein pl* **II.** *vt* (*arouse indignation*) ■**to be ~d by sth** entrüstet über etw *akk* [sein]

outrageous [aʊtˈreɪ·dʒəs] *adj* ①(*terrible*) empörend; (*unacceptable*) unerhört ②(*unusual and shocking*) außergewöhnlich; *outfit a.* gewagt ③(*exaggerated*) ungeheuerlich; *story* unwahrscheinlich; *lie* schamlos

'outreach *adj* **~ work** soziales Engagement; **~ program** Programm *nt* zur sozialen Unterstützung

'outright I. *adj attr* ①(*total*) total; *disaster* absolut ②(*undisputed*) offensichtlich; *winner* eindeutig **II.** *adv* ①(*totally*) total ②(*clearly*) eindeutig ③(*immediately*) sofort; **to be killed ~** auf der Stelle tot sein

out'run <-ran, -run, -nn-> *vt* ■**to ~ sb** jdm davonlaufen

'outset *n* Anfang *m*; ■**from the ~** von Anfang an

out'side I. *n* ①(*exterior*) Außenseite *f*; *of a fruit* Schale *f*; ■**from the ~** (*fig*) von außen ②(*external appearance*) ■**on the ~** äußerlich **II.** *adj attr* ①(*outer*) *door* äußere(r, s); **~ wall** Außenmauer *f* ②(*external*) außenstehend; **the world ~** die Welt draußen **III.** *adv* ①(*not in building*) außen ②(*in open air*) im Freien **IV.** *prep* außerhalb (*of* von +*dat*)

outsider [aʊtˈsaɪ·dər] *n* Außenseiter(in) *m(f)*

'outsize *adj attr* (*very large*) übergroß

'outskirts [ˈaʊt·skɜrts] *npl* Stadtrand *m*

outsourcing [ˈaʊt·ˌsɔr·sɪŋ] *n* Outsourcing *nt fachspr*; *of production* Produktionsauslagerung *f*

outspoken [ˌaʊtˈspoʊ·kən] *adj* offen; *criticism* unverblümt; *opponent* entschieden

out'standing *adj* ①(*excellent*) außergewöhnlich; *effort, contribution* bemerkenswert; *performance* brillant; *achievement* überragend ②(*not dealt with*) unerledigt; *problems* ungelöst

out'stay *vt stay too long* **to ~ one's welcome** länger bleiben, als man erwünscht ist

outstretched [ˌaʊt·ˈstretʃt] *adj* ausgestreckt

out'strip <-pp-> *vt* ①(*surpass*) übertreffen ②(*be greater*) übersteigen

out'vote *vt* überstimmen

outward [ˈaʊt·wərd] **I.** *adj attr* ①(*exterior*) äußere(r, s), Außen-; (*superficial*) äußerlich ②(*going out*) ausgehend; **~ flight** Hinflug *m* **II.** *adv* nach außen

outwardly [ˈaʊt·wərd·li] *adv* äußerlich, nach außen hin

outwards [ˈaʊt·wərdz] *adv* nach außen

out'weigh *vt* (*in importance*) ■**to ~ sth** etw wettmachen; **the advantages ~ the disadvantages** die Vorteile überwiegen die Nachteile

out'wit <-tt-> *vt* austricksen

oval ['əʊ·vəl] *adj* oval

Oval 'Office *n* POL ■**the ~** das Oval Office (*Büro des US-Präsidenten*)

ovary ['əʊ·və·ri] *n* Eierstock *m*

ovation [əʊ·'veɪ·ʃən] *n* Applaus *m*

oven ['ʌv·ən] *n* [Back]ofen *m*

'ovenproof *adj* hitzebeständig

'oven-ready *adj* bratfertig, backfertig

over ['əʊ·vər] I. *adv pred* ❶ (*across*) hinüber; **~ here** hier herüber; (*on the other side*) drüben; **~ there** dort drüben ❷ (*another way up*) to **turn ~** umdrehen ❸ (*downwards*) **to fall ~** hinfallen; **to knock sth ~** etw umstoßen ❹ (*finished*) ■**to be ~** vorbei sein ❺ (*remaining*) übrig ❻ (*again*) noch einmal; **~ and ~** immer wieder II. *prep* ❶ (*across*) über ❷ (*on the other side of*) über ❸ (*above*) über; (*moving above*) über; **a flock of geese passed ~** eine Schar von Gänsen flog über uns hinweg ❹ (*everywhere*) [überall] in; **all ~ the world** in der ganzen Welt ❺ (*during*) in, während; **~ the years, he became more and more depressed** mit den Jahren wurde er immer deprimierter ❻ (*through*) **he told me ~ the phone** er sagte es mir am Telefon ❼ (*more than*) über; **this shirt cost me ~ $50!** dieses Hemd hat mich über 50 Dollar gekostet! ❽ (*past*) **to get ~ sb/sth** über jdn/etw hinweg kommen

overa'bundant *adj* übermäßig

over'act *vi* THEAT übertreiben

overall I. *n* ['əʊ·vər·ɔl] ■**~s** *pl* Latzhose *f* II. *adj* ['əʊ·vər·ɔl] *attr* Gesamt- III. *adv* [ˌəʊ·vər·'ɔl] insgesamt

over'bearing *adj* (*pej: arrogant*) anmaßend

'overboard *adv* NAUT über Bord ►PHRASES: **to go ~** zu weit gehen, es übertreiben

over'book I. *vt usu passive* ■**to be ~ed** überbucht sein II. *vi* zu viele Buchungen vornehmen

over'cast *adj* sky bedeckt

over'charge *vi* zu viel berechnen

'overcoat *n* Mantel *m*

over'come <-came, -come> I. *vt* ❶ *fear* überwinden; *temptation* widerstehen; *enemy forces* besiegen ❷ *usu passive* (*render powerless*) ■**to be ~ by sth** *sleep* von etw *dat* überwältigt werden; *fumes* von etw *dat* ohnmächtig werden II. *vi* siegen

over'compensate *vi* ■**to ~ for sth** etw *akk* überkompensieren

over'confident *adj* (*extremely self-assured*) übertrieben selbstbewusst; (*too optimistic*) übertrieben zuversichtlich

over'crowded *adj* überfüllt; *town* übervölkert

over'do <-did, -done> *vt* **to ~ it** sich überanstrengen; (*go too far*) zu weit gehen

over'done *adj* (*overcooked*) *in water* verkocht; *in oven* verbraten

overdose I. *n* ['əʊ·vər·dəʊs] Überdosis *f* II. *vi* [ˌəʊ·vər·'dəʊs] eine Überdosis nehmen

'overdraft *n* Kontoüberziehung *f*

over'draw <-drew, -drawn> *vt account* überziehen

over'dress *vi* sich zu fein anziehen

'overdrive *n* ❶ AUTO Schongang *m* ❷ (*fig: effort*) ■**to be in ~** auf Hochtouren laufen

over'due *adj usu pred* überfällig

over 'easy *adj, adv usu pred* **~ egg** auf beiden Seiten gebratenes Spiegelei

over'eat <-ate, -eaten> *vi* zu viel essen

over'emphasize *vt* überbetonen

overes'timate [ˌəʊ·vər·'es·tə·meɪt] *vt* überschätzen

overex'cited *adj usu pred* ■**to be ~** ganz aufgeregt sein

overex'pose *vt* ■**to be ~d** ❶ PHOT überbelichtet sein ❷ *usu passive* **to be ~d to risks** zu starken Risiken ausgesetzt sein

overex'tend *vt* ■**to ~ oneself** [on sth] sich [bei etw *dat*] [finanziell] übernehmen

overflow I. *n* ['əʊ·vər·fləʊ] ❶ (*act of spilling*) Überlaufen *nt* ❷ (*overflowing liquid*) überlaufende Flüssigkeit ❸ (*out-*

let) Überlauf m **II.** vi [ˌoʊ·vər·'floʊ] *river, tank* überlaufen

overhang [ˌoʊ·vər·'hæŋ] vt <-hung, -hung> (*project over*) ■ **to ~ sth** über etw *akk* hinausragen

overhaul vt [ˌoʊ·vər·'hɔl] (*repair*) überholen

overhead I. n ['oʊ·vər·hed] (*running costs of business*) laufende Geschäftskosten **II.** adj ['oʊ·vər·hed] attr (*above head level*) Hoch-; ELEC oberirdisch **III.** adv [ˌoʊ·vər·'hed] in der Luft; **a plane circled ~** ein Flugzeug kreiste über uns

over'hear <-heard, -heard> vt ■ **to ~ sth** etw zufällig mithören; ■ **to ~ sb** jdn unabsichtlich belauschen

over'heat vi sich überhitzen a. *fig*

overin'dulge vi (*eat too much*) sich *dat* den Bauch vollschlagen *fam*; (*drink too much*) sich volllaufen lassen *fam*

overjoyed [ˌoʊ·vər·'dʒɔɪd] adj *pred* überglücklich

'overkill n (*pej: excessiveness*) Übermaß nt

overland I. adj ['oʊ·vər·lænd] attr Überland- **II.** adv [ˌoʊ·vər·'lænd] auf dem Landweg

overlap I. n ['oʊ·vər·læp] ❶ (*overlapping part*) Überlappung f ❷ (*similarity*) Überschneidung f **II.** vi <-pp-> [ˌoʊ·vər·'læp] ❶ (*lie edge over edge*) sich überlappen ❷ (*be partly similar*) sich überschneiden

overload I. n ['oʊ·vər·loʊd] ❶ ELEC Überlast[ung] f; TRANSP Übergewicht nt ❷ (*excess*) Überbelastung f **II.** vt [ˌoʊ·vər·'loʊd] (*overburden*) *vehicle* überladen; *system, person* überlasten

overlook vt [ˌoʊ·vər·'lʊk] ❶ (*look out onto*) überblicken ❷ (*not notice*) übersehen

overly ['oʊ·vər·li] adv allzu

over'night I. adj ❶ attr (*for a night*) Nacht-; **~ stay** Übernachtung f ❷ (*for next day*) *delivery* über Nacht ❸ (*sudden*) ganz plötzlich; **~ success** Blitzerfolg m **II.** adv ❶ (*until next day*) in der Nacht, über Nacht ❷ (*fig: suddenly*) in kurzer Zeit

'overpass n Überführung f

over'pay <-paid, -paid> vt für etw *akk* zu viel bezahlen

over'populated adj überbevölkert

over'powering adj überwältigend; *smell* durchdringend

overpro'duce vt ■ **to ~ sth** von etw *dat* zu viel produzieren

over'rated adj (*pej*) überbewertet

over'rule vt ■ **to ~ oneself** sich übernehmen

overre'act vi überreagieren

over'ride I. n Übersteuerung f; **manual ~** Automatikabschaltung f **II.** vt <-rid, -ridden> ❶ (*outweigh*) überwiegen ❷ (*control*) abschalten

over'riding adj attr vorrangig

over'rule vt überstimmen; *objection* zurückweisen

over'run I. vt <-ran, -run> ❶ MIL (*occupy*) überrollen ❷ (*spread over*) sich in etw *dat* ausbreiten ❸ *budget* überschreiten **II.** vi <-ran, -run> (*exceed time*) überziehen

overseas I. adj ['oʊ·vər·siz] attr (*abroad*) Übersee-; **in Übersee** nach n **II.** adv [ˌoʊ·vər·'siz] (*in foreign country*) im Ausland; (*to foreign country*) ins Ausland

over'see <-saw, -seen> vt beaufsichtigen

overseer ['oʊ·vər·ˌsi·ər] n Aufseher, -in m, f

over'shadow vt ❶ (*make insignificant*) in den Schatten stellen ❷ (*cast gloom over*) überschatten

'overshoe n Überschuh m

over'shoot <-shot, -shot> vt ■ **to ~ sth** über etw *akk* hinausschießen; **the plane overshot the runway** das Flugzeug schoss über die Rennbahn hinaus

'oversight n (*mistake*) Versehen nt; ■ **by an ~** aus Versehen

over'simplify <-ie-> vt grob vereinfachen

'oversize, 'oversized adj überdimensional

over'sleep <-slept, -slept> *vi* verschlafen

over'spend <-spent, -spent> I. *vi* zu viel [Geld] ausgeben II. *vt* budget überschreiten

over'staffed *adj* überbesetzt

over'state *vt* übertreiben; **to ~ a case** einen Fall übertrieben darstellen

over'stay *vt* **to ~ a visa** ein Visum überschreiten

over'supply *n* (supply) Überangebot *nt*

overt ['oʊ·vɜrt] *adj* offenkundig; racism unverhohlen

over'take <-took, -taken> *vt* überholen a. fig

over-the-'counter *adj attr* drugs, remedies rezeptfrei

over-the-'top *adj* (fam) übertrieben

overthrow I. *n* ['oʊ·vər·θroʊ] (removal from power) Sturz *m* II. *vt* <-threw, -thrown> [,oʊ·vər·'θroʊ] (topple) stürzen; regime zu Fall bringen

'overtime I. *n* ❶ (extra work) Überstunden *pl* ❷ SPORT (extra time) Verlängerung *f* II. *adv* **to work ~** Überstunden machen

over'tired *adj* übermüdet

overture ['oʊ·vər·tʃər] *n* Ouvertüre *f*

over'turn I. *vi* umstürzen; boat kentern II. *vt* ❶ (turn upside down) umstoßen ❷ (reverse) revidieren; government stürzen

over'value *vt* (give excessively high value to) überbewerten

'overview *n* Überblick *m*

overweight [,oʊ·vər·'weɪt] *adj* zu schwer; person a. übergewichtig

overwhelm [,oʊ·vər·'welm] *vt* ❶ (affect powerfully) überwältigen ❷ enemy besiegen

overwhelming [,oʊ·vər·'wel·mɪŋ] *adj* (very powerful) überwältigend; need unwiderstehlich; grief unermesslich

overwork I. *vi* [,oʊ·vər·'wɜrk] sich überarbeiten II. *vt* [,oʊ·vər·'wɜrk] ■**to ~ sb** jdn [mit Arbeit] überlasten

ovulation [,av·ju·'leɪ·ʃən] *n* Eisprung *m*

ow [aʊ] *interj* au

owe [oʊ] *vt* ❶ (be in debt) schulden; **to ~ sb an explanation** jdm eine Erklärung schuldig sein; **to ~ sb thanks** jdm zu Dank verpflichtet sein ❷ (be indebted) ■**to ~ sth to sb** jdm etw verdanken

owing ['oʊ·ɪŋ] *adj pred* ausstehend

'owing to *prep* (form) ■**~ sth** wegen einer S. gen

owl [aʊl] *n* Eule *f*; barn ~ Schleiereule *f*

own [oʊn] I. *pron* (belonging, relating to) his time is his ~ er kann über seine Zeit frei verfügen; **to make sth [all] one's ~** sich dat etw [ganz] zu eigen machen; **to have ideas of one's ~** eigene Ideen haben ▶PHRASES: **[all] on one's/its ~** [ganz] allein[e] II. *adj attr* ❶ (belonging to, individual) eigene(r, s) ❷ (for oneself) ■**on one's ~ mind** sich akk entscheiden ▶PHRASES: **in one's ~ right** (not due to others) aus eigenem Recht; (through one's talents) aufgrund der eigenen Begabung III. *vt* (possess) besitzen

◆**own up** *vi* es zugeben

owner ['oʊ·nər] *n* Besitzer(in) *m(f)*

owner-'occupied *adj* vom Eigentümer/ von der Eigentümerin selbst bewohnt

ox <*pl* -en> [aks] *n* Ochse *m*

oxidize ['ak·sɪ·daɪz] *vt, vi* oxidieren

oxtail 'soup *n* Ochsenschwanzsuppe *f*

oxyacetylene [,ak·sɪ·ə·'set̬·ə·lin] *n* Azetylensauerstoff *m*

oxygen ['ak·sɪ·dʒən] *n* Sauerstoff *m*

'oxygen mask *n* Sauerstoffmaske *f*

oyster ['ɔɪ·stər] *n* Auster[nmuschel] *f*

oz, oz. <*pl* -> *n abbrev of* **ounce**

ozone ['oʊ·zoʊn] *n* Ozon *nt*

'ozone layer *n* Ozonschicht *f*

Pp

P <pl -'s>, **p** <pl -'s> [piː] n p nt, P nt; ~ **as in Papa** P wie Paula

p. [piː] n <pl pp> abbrev of **page** S.

p [piː] adv MUS abbrev of **piano** p

PA, Pa. n abbrev of **Pennsylvania**

pace [peɪs] I. n ❶ (speed) Tempo nt ❷ (step) Schritt m; **to keep ~ with sb** mit jdm Schritt halten II. vi gehen

'pacemaker n ❶ (for heart) [Herz]schrittmacher m ❷ SPORT (speed setter) Schrittmacher(in) m(f)

Pacific [pəˈsɪf·ɪk] n ■**the ~** der Pazifik

pacifier [ˈpæs·ə·faɪ·ər] n (for baby) Schnuller m

pacifist [ˈpæs·ə·fɪst] n Pazifist(in) m(f)

pacify <-ie-> [ˈpæs·ə·faɪ] vt beruhigen

pack [pæk] I. n ❶ (packet) Packung f ❷ (backpack) Rucksack m ❸ of cards [Karten]spiel nt ❹ (group) Gruppe f II. vi packen III. vt ❶ (put into a container) articles, goods [ein]packen ❷ (a. fig: cram) vollpacken (**with** mit + dat); ■**to be ~ed** [**with people**] gerammelt voll [mit Leuten] sein fam

♦ **pack away** vt wegpacken

♦ **pack in** vt (cram in) hineinstopfen; people, animals hineinpferchen ❷ einpacken

♦ **pack into** vt ❶ (put) [ein]packen ❷ (cram) [hinein]stopfen ❸ (fig: fit) [hinein]packen

♦ **pack off** vt (fam) wegschicken

♦ **pack up** I. vt zusammenpacken II. vi (fam) **to ~ up and leave** seine Sachen packen und gehen

package [ˈpæk·ɪdʒ] I. n ❶ (parcel) Paket nt ❷ (pack) of cookies etc. Packung f II. vt ❶ (pack) verpacken ❷ (fig) präsentieren

packaged [ˈpæk·ɪdʒd] adj food verpackt

'package deal n Pauschalangebot nt

packaging [ˈpæk·ɪ·dʒɪŋ] n Verpackung f

packer [ˈpæk·ər] n [Ver]packer(in) m(f)

packet [ˈpæk·ɪt] n Packung f, Schachtel f

pact [pækt] n Pakt m

pad¹ [pæd] I. n ❶ (wad) Pad m o nt ❷ (protector) Polster nt ❸ (of paper) Block m ❹ AEROSP, AVIAT **launch ~** Abschussrampe f II. vt <-dd-> [aus]polstern

pad² [pæd] vi trotten; (walk softly) tappen

padded [ˈpæd·ɪd] adj [aus]gepolstert

padding [ˈpæd·ɪŋ] n Polsterung f

paddle¹ [ˈpæd·əl] I. n Paddel nt II. vi paddeln

paddle² [ˈpæd·əl] vi planschen

paddy [ˈpæd·i] n Reisfeld nt

padlock [ˈpæd·lɑk] n Vorhängeschloss nt

page¹ [peɪdʒ] I. n (single sheet) Blatt nt; COMPUT (single side) Seite f II. vi COMPUT ■**to ~ up/down** auf der Seite nach oben/unten gehen

page² [peɪdʒ] vt (over loudspeaker) ausrufen; (by pager) anpiepsen

pageant [ˈpædʒ·ənt] n ❶ (show) **beauty ~** Schönheitswettbewerb m ❷ (play) Historienspiel nt

pager [ˈpeɪ·dʒər] n Pager m, Piepser m

pagination [ˌpædʒ·əˈneɪ·ʃən] n Seitennummerierung f

paid [peɪd] I. pt, pp of **pay** II. adj attr bezahlt

pail [peɪl] n Eimer m

pain [peɪn] n ❶ (feeling) Schmerz m; **a ~ in one's leg** Schmerzen pl im Bein ❷ (physical suffering) Schmerz[en] m[pl] ❸ (effort) ■**~s** pl Mühe f; **to go to great ~s to do sth** keine Mühe scheuen, etw zu tun

painful [ˈpeɪn·fəl] adj schmerzhaft; death qualvoll

painfully [ˈpeɪn·fəl·i] adv unter Schmerzen

'painkiller n Schmerzmittel nt

painless ['peɪn·lɪs] *adj* ❶ (*without pain*) schmerzlos ❷ (*fig: without trouble*) schmerzlos

painstaking ['peɪnz·teɪ·kɪŋ] *adj* [sehr] sorgfältig

paint [peɪnt] I. *n* ❶ (*substance*) Farbe *f*; (*on car*) Lack *m* ❷ (*art color*) ■~**s** *pl* Farben *pl* II. *vi* ❶ ART malen ❷ (*decorate rooms*) streichen III. *vt* ❶ (*make picture*) malen ❷ *house* anstreichen; *wall* streichen

'**paintbrush** *n* [Farb]pinsel *m*

painter ['peɪn·tər] *n* ❶ (*artist*) [Kunst]maler(in) *m(f)* ❷ (*sb who paints buildings*) Maler(in) *m(f)*

painting ['peɪn·tɪŋ] *n* ❶ (*picture*) Bild *nt* ❷ (*house decorating*) Streichen *nt*

'**paintwork** *n of a house* Anstrich *m*

pair [per] *n* Paar *nt*; **a ~ of gloves** ein Paar *nt* Handschuhe; **a ~ of pants** eine Hose

◆**pair off** I. *vi* einen Partner/eine Partnerin finden II. *vt* ■**to ~ sb off** [**with sb**] jdn [mit jdm] verkuppeln *fam*

pajamas [pə·'dʒɑ·məz] *npl* Pyjama *m*

pal [pæl] *n* (*fam*) Kumpel *m*

palace ['pæl·əs] *n* Palast *m*

palatial [pə·'leɪ·ʃəl] *adj* prachtvoll

pale [peɪl] I. *adj* blass II. *vi* (*go white*) bleich werden

Palestinian [ˌpæl·ə·'stɪn·i·ən] I. *n* Palästinenser(in) *m(f)* II. *adj* palästinensisch

palette ['pæl·ɪt] *n* ART Palette *f*

pall [pɔl] *vi* an Reiz verlieren

pallet ['pæl·ɪt] *n* Palette *f*

palliative ['pæl·i·ə·t̬ɪv] *adj* schmerzstillend *attr*

pallid ['pæl·ɪd] *adj* (*very pale*) fahl

pallor ['pæl·ər] *n* Blässe *f*

palm[1] [pɑm] *n* Handfläche *f*

palm[2] [pɑm] *n* (*tree*) Palme *f*

Palm 'Sunday *n* Palmsonntag *m*

palpable ['pæl·pə·bəl] *adj* ❶ (*obvious*) offenkundig ❷ (*tangible*) spürbar

palpitations [ˌpæl·pə·'teɪ·ʃənz] *npl* Herzklopfen *nt kein pl*

paltry ['pɔl·tri] *adj* (*small*) armselig; *sum* lächerlich

Pampas ['pæm·pəz] *n + sing/pl vb* Pampa *f*

pamper ['pæm·pər] *vt* verwöhnen

pamphlet ['pæm·flɪt] *n* [kleine] Broschüre *f*

pan[1] [pæn] I. *n* Pfanne *f* II. *vt* <-nn-> (*fam: criticize*) verreißen

pan[2] [pæn] *vi* **to ~ to the left** nach links schwenken

◆**pan out** *vi* sich entwickeln

panacea [ˌpæn·ə·'si·ə] *n* Allheilmittel *nt*

panache [pə·'næʃ] *n* Elan *m*

Panama Ca'nal *n* ■**the ~** der Panama-kanal

'**pancake** *n* Pfannkuchen *m*

pancreas <*pl* -es> ['pæŋ·kri·əs] *n* Bauchspeicheldrüse *f*

panda ['pæn·də] *n* Panda *m*

pandemonium [ˌpæn·də·'moʊ·ni·əm] *n* ❶ Chaos *nt* ❷ (*fig: uproar*) Tumult *m*

pane [peɪn] *n* [Fenster]scheibe *f*

panel ['pæn·əl] I. *n* ❶ (*wooden*) [Holz]paneel *nt*; (*metal*) Blech *nt* ❷ **instrument** – AVIAT Instrumentenbrett *nt*; AUTO Armaturenbrett *nt* II. *vt* <-l-> täfeln (**with** mit + *dat*)

paneling ['pæn·ə·lɪŋ] *n* [Holz]täfelung *f*

panelist ['pæn·ə·lɪst] *n* (*on expert team*) Mitglied *nt* [einer Expertengruppe]

'**panhandle** *vi* schnorren

'**panhandler** *n* (*fam*) Schnorrer(in) *m(f)*

panic ['pæn·ɪk] I. *n* Panik *f* II. *vi* <-ck-> in Panik geraten

panicky ['pæn·ɪ·ki] *adj* panisch

'**panic-stricken** *adj* von Panik ergriffen

panorama [ˌpæn·ə·'ræm·ə] *n* Panorama *nt*

panoramic [ˌpæn·ə·'ræm·ɪk] *adj* Panorama-

pansy ['pæn·zi] *n* (*flower*) Stiefmütterchen *nt*

pant[1] [pænt] *vi* (*breathe rapidly*) keuchen

pant[2] [pænt] *n* FASHION ■~**s** *pl* **a pair of ~s** eine [lange] Hose ▶PHRASES: **to be caught with one's ~s down** (*fam*) auf frischer Tat ertappt werden

P

panther <pl -> ['pæn·θər] n Puma m

panties ['pæn·tiz] npl (fam) [Damen]slip m

pantomime ['pæn·tə·maɪm] n Pantomime f

'pantsuit, 'pants suit n Hosenanzug m

'pantyhose npl Strumpfhose f

papa ['pa·pə] n (childspeak fam) Papa m

papacy ['peɪ·pə·si] n Pontifikat nt

papal ['peɪ·pəl] adj päpstlich

paparazzi [ˌpa·pa·ˈra·tsi] npl Paparazzi pl

papaya [pə·ˈpaɪ·ə] n Papaya f

paper ['peɪ·pər] n ❶ Papier nt; **recycled ~** Altpapier nt ❷ (newspaper) Zeitung f ❸ usu pl (document) Dokument nt; (credentials) [Ausweis]papiere pl

'paperback n Taschenbuch nt

paper 'bag n Papiertüte f

'paper chase n Schnitzeljagd f

paper clip n Büroklammer f

paper 'cup n Pappbecher m

'paper mill n Papierfabrik f

'paper money n Papiergeld nt

paper-'thin adj, adv hauchdünn

paper 'towel n Papierhandtuch nt

'paperweight n Briefbeschwerer m

papery ['peɪ·pə·ri] adj skin pergamenten

papier-mâché [ˌpeɪ·pər·mə·ˈʃeɪ] n Pappmaschee nt

papyrus <pl -es> [pə·ˈpaɪ·rəs] n Papyrus m

par [par] n ❶ (standard) **below ~** unter dem Durchschnitt ❷ (equality) ■**to be on** [a] **~ with each other** einander ebenbürtig sein

par. ['perə] n short for **paragraph** Absatz m

parable ['pær·ə·bəl] n Parabel f

parachute ['pær·ə·ʃut] I. n Fallschirm m II. vi mit dem Fallschirm abspringen

'parachute jump n Fallschirmabsprung m

parachutist ['pær·ə·ʃu·tɪst] n Fallschirmspringer(in) m(f)

parade [pə·ˈreɪd] I. n (procession) Parade f II. vi ❶ (walk in procession) einen Umzug machen ❷ (show off) ■**to ~ around** auf und ab stolzieren III. vt ❶ MIL troops aufmarschieren lassen ❷ (fig) knowledge, wealth zur Schau tragen

paradise ['pær·ə·daɪs] n Paradies nt

paradoxical [ˌpær·ə·ˈdak·sɪ·kəl] adj paradox

paraffin ['pær·ə·fɪn] n, **paraffin wax** n Paraffin nt

paragraph ['pær·ə·græf] n ❶ (text) Absatz m ❷ (newspaper article) [kurze] Zeitungsnotiz

parakeet ['pær·ə·kit] n Sittich m

paralegal [ˌpe·rə·ˈli·gəl] n juristische Hilfskraft

parallel ['pær·ə·lel] I. adj ❶ lines parallel ❷ (corresponding) **~ example** Parallelbeispiel nt II. n (similarity) Parallele f III. adv parallel; **to run ~ to sth** zu etw dat parallel verlaufen

parallel 'bars npl Barren m

parallel 'line n Parallele f

paralysis <pl -ses> [pə·ˈræl·ə·sɪs] n Lähmung f a. fig

paralyze ['pær·ə·laɪz] vt ❶ MED (a. fig) lähmen ❷ (bring to halt) lahmlegen

paramedic [ˌpær·ə·ˈmed·ɪk] n Sanitäter(in) m(f)

parameter [pə·ˈræm·ə·tər] n usu pl (set of limits) **~s** pl Leitlinien pl

paranoia [ˌpær·ə·ˈnɔɪ·ə] n PSYCH Paranoia f geh

paranoid ['pær·ə·nɔɪd] adj paranoid

paranormal [ˌpær·ə·ˈnɔr·məl] n ■**the ~** übernatürliche Erscheinungen

paraplegic [ˌpær·ə·ˈpli·dʒɪk] n doppelseitig Gelähmte(r) f(m)

parasite ['pær·ə·saɪt] n Parasit m a. fig

parasol ['pær·ə·sɔl] n Sonnenschirm m

paratrooper ['pær·ə·tru·pər] n Fallschirmjäger(in) m(f)

paratroops ['pær·ə·trups] npl Fallschirmtruppen pl

parboil ['par·bɔɪl] vt **to ~ food** Lebensmittel kurz vorkochen (um sie dann weiterzuverarbeiten)

P

parcel ['par·səl] I. *n* Paket *nt* II. *vt* <-l-> einpacken

parcel 'post *n* Paketpost *f*

parched [partʃt] *adj* (*dried out*) vertrocknet; *throat* ausgedörrt

Parcheesi® [par·'tʃi·zi] *n* Mensch-ärgere-dich-nicht[-Spiel] *nt*

parchment ['partʃ·mənt] *n* Pergament *nt*

pardon ['par·dən] I. *n* LAW Begnadigung *f* II. *vt* ❶ (*forgive*) verzeihen, entschuldigen ❷ LAW begnadigen III. *interj* (*apology*) **I beg your ~!** [*or* **~ me!**] Entschuldigung!, tut mir Leid!; (*request for repetition*) wie bitte?; (*reply to offensiveness*) na, hören Sie mal!

parent ['per·ənt] *n of a child* Elternteil *m*; **■ ~s** Eltern *pl*

parental [pə·'ren·təl] *adj* elterlich

parent 'company *n* Muttergesellschaft *f*

parenthesis <*pl* -ses> [pə·'ren·θə·sɪs] *n usu pl* [runde] Klammern *pl*

parenthood ['per·ənt·hʊd] *n* Elternschaft *f*

parent 'teacher association *n* Eltern-Lehrer-Organisation *f*

parishioner [pə·'rɪʃ·ə·nər] *n* Gemeindemitglied *nt*

parity ['pær·ɪ·t̬i] *n* Gleichheit *f*

park [park] I. *n* Park *m* II. *vt* AUTO [ein]parken III. *vi* parken

parka ['par·kə] *n* Parka *m*

parking ['par·kɪŋ] *n* Parkplatz *m*

'parking garage *n* Parkhaus *nt*

'parking lot *n* Parkplatz *m*

'parking meter *n* Parkuhr *f*

'parking place, 'parking space *n* Parkplatz *m*

'parking ticket *n* Strafzettel *m* für unerlaubtes Parken

'park ranger *n* Parkaufseher(in) *m(f)*

'parkway *n* Schnellstraße *f*

parliament ['par·lə·mənt] *n* (*institution*) **■P~** Parlament *nt*

parliamentary [,par·lə·'men·t̬ə·ri] *adj* parlamentarisch

parlor ['par·lər] *n* Salon *m;* **funeral ~** Bestattungsinstitut *nt*

'parlor game *n* Gesellschaftsspiel *nt*

Parmesan, Parmesan cheese ['par·mə·zan-] *n* Parmesan[käse] *m*

parochial [pə·'roʊ·ki·əl] *adj* ❶ REL Gemeinde- ❷ (*pej: provincial*) provinziell

parochial 'school *n* Konfessionsschule *f*

parody ['pær·ə·di] I. *n* (*a. pej: imitation*) Parodie *f* II. *vt* <-ie-> parodieren

parole [pə·'roʊl] *n* bedingte Haftentlassung

parrot ['pær·ət] *n* Papagei *m*

parse [pars] *vt* COMPUT **to ~ a text** einen Text parsen *fachspr*

parsley ['pars·li] *n* Petersilie *f*

parsnip ['pars·nɪp] *n* Pastinak *m*

parson ['par·sən] *n* Pastor(in) *m(f)*

part [part] I. *n* ❶ Teil *m*; **for the most ~** zum größten Teil; **body ~** Körperteil *m*; **|spare| ~s** Ersatzteile *pl* ❷ (*unit*) [An]teil *m* ❸ FILM, TV Folge *f* ❹ *usu pl* GEOG Gegend *f;* **around these ~s** (*fam*) in dieser Gegend ❺ THEAT (*a. fig*) Rolle *f* II. *adv* teils, teilweise III. *vi* ❶ (*separate*) sich trennen ❷ (*become separated*) *curtains* aufgehen; *lips* sich öffnen IV. *vt* ❶ trennen ❷ *hair* scheiteln ▶PHRASES: **to ~ company** sich trennen ♦ **part with** *vi* **■to ~ with sth** sich von etw *dat* trennen

parted ['par·t̬ɪd] *adj* ❶ (*separated*) getrennt (**from** von +*dat*) ❷ *hair* **her hair is ~ on the side** sie trägt einen Seitenscheitel

P

partial ['par·ʃəl] *adj* ❶ (*incomplete*) Teil-; *paralysis* partiell ❷ (*biased*) parteiisch

partiality [,par·ʃi·'æl·ɪ·t̬i] *n* (*bias*) Parteilichkeit *f*

partially ['par·ʃəl·i] *adv* teilweise

participant [par·'tɪs·ə·pənt] *n* Teilnehmer(in) *m(f)*

participate [par·'tɪs·ə·peɪt] *vi* teilnehmen

participation [par·,tɪs·ə·'peɪ·ʃən] *n* Teilnahme *f*

participle ['par·tɪ·sɪ·pəl] *n* Partizip *nt*

particle ['par·tɪ·kəl] *n* Teilchen *nt*

particular [pər·'tɪk·jə·lər] I. *adj* ❶ *attr* (*individual*) bestimmt ❷ *attr* (*special*) besondere(r, s) ❸ *pred* (*demanding*) anspruchsvoll (**about** hinsichtlich +*gen*) II. *n* (*information*) ■ ~**s** *pl* Einzelheiten *pl* ▶PHRASES: **in** ~ insbesondere

particularly [pər·ˈtɪk·jə·lər·li] *adv* besonders, vor allem

par'ticulate filter *n* Partikelfilter *m* o *nt*; **diesel** ~ Rußpartikelfilter *m* o *nt*

parting 'shot *n* letztes [sarkastisches] Wort

partisan [ˈpɑr·tɪ·zən] *n* MIL Partisan(in) *m(f)*

partition [pɑr·ˈtɪʃ·ən] I. *n* ❶ POL Teilung *f* ❷ (*structure*) Trennwand *f* II. *vt* (*divide*) [unter]teilen

partly [ˈpɑrt·li] *adv* zum Teil, teilweise

partner [ˈpɑːrt·nər] *n* ❶ (*owner*) Teilhaber(in) *m(f)* ❷ (*in sports*) Partner(in) *m(f)* ❸ (*spouse*) Ehepartner(in) *m(f)*; (*unmarried*) [Lebens]partner(in) *m(f)*

partnership [ˈpɑːrt·nər·ʃɪp] *n* ❶ *no pl* (*condition*) Partnerschaft *f* ❷ (*relationship*) **domestic** ~ Lebenspartnerschaft *f*

'partnership agreement *n* Gesellschaftsvertrag *m*

part of 'speech <*pl* parts-> *n* LING Wortart *f*

part-'time I. *adj* Teilzeit- II. *adv* **to work** ~ halbtags arbeiten

part-time 'job *n* Teilzeitarbeit *f*

part-'timer *n* Halbtagskraft *f*

party [ˈpɑr·ti] I. *n* ❶ (*celebration*) Party *f* ❷ POL Partei *f* ❸ (*group*) [Reise]gruppe *f* II. *vi* <-ie-> (*fam*) feiern

party 'line POL Parteilinie *f*

party 'politics *n* + *sing/pl vb* Parteipolitik *f*

pass [pæs] I. *n* <*pl* -es> ❶ (*road, sports*) Pass *m* ❷ SCH, UNIV (*grade*) „Bestanden" ❸ (*permit*) Passierschein *m* II. *vt* ❶ (*go past*) ■**to** ~ **sb/sth** an jdm/etw vorbeigehen; (*in car*) an jdm/etw vorbeifahren ❷ (*overtake*) überholen ❸ (*hand to*) ■**to** ~ **sb sth** [*or* **to** ~ **sth to sb**] jdm etw geben ❹ SPORT **to** ~ **the ball to sb** jdm den Ball zuspielen ❺ (*succeed*) exam, test bestehen, ablegen ▶PHRASES: **to** ~ **the buck to sb** (*fam*) die Verantwortung auf jdn abwäl-

zen III. *vi* ❶ (*move by*) vorbeigehen; *car* vorbeifahren; **to** ~ **unnoticed** unbemerkt bleiben ❷ (*overtake*) überholen ❸ (*go away*) vorübergehen ❹ SPORT (*of a ball*) zuspielen ❺ SCH (*succeed*) bestehen ❻ *time* vergehen ❼ (*be accepted as*) **I don't think you'll** ~ **for 18** keiner wird dir abnehmen, dass du 18 bist

◆**pass along** *vt* ■**to** ~ **along** ⟳ **sth** etw weitergeben

◆**pass around** *vt* herumreichen

◆**pass away** *vi* (*euph: die*) entschlafen

◆**pass by** I. *vi* ❶ *time* vergehen ❷ (*go past*) [an jdm/etw] vorbeigehen II. *vt* (*miss sb*) ■**sth** ~**es sb by** etw geht an jdm vorbei

◆**pass down** *vt* ❶ *usu passive* (*bequeath*) ■**to be** ~**ed down** *tradition* weitergegeben werden ❷ (*hand down*) hinunterreichen

◆**pass off** *vt* ■**to** ~ **sth off as sth** etw *akk* als etw ausgeben

◆**pass on** *vt* ❶ *information* weitergeben ❷ *disease* übertragen ❸ *usu passive* ■**to be** ~**ed on** *clothes* weitergegeben werden; *fortune* [weiter]vererbt werden

◆**pass out** *vi* in Ohnmacht fallen

◆**pass over** *vt* ❶ *usu passive* (*not promote*) ■**to be** ~**ed over** [**for promotion**] [bei der Beförderung] übergangen werden ❷ (*disregard*) übergehen

◆**pass through** *vi* durchreisen

◆**pass up** *vt* ■**to** ~ **up** ⟳ **sth** sich *dat* etw entgehen lassen

passable [ˈpæs·ə·bəl] *adj* ❶ (*traversable*) passierbar ❷ (*satisfactory*) [ganz] passabel

passage [ˈpæs·ɪdʒ] *n* ❶ (*narrow corridor*) Gang *m* ❷ LIT (*excerpt*) [Text]passage *f*; MUS Stück *nt* ❸ (*progression*) *of time* Voranschreiten *nt*

'passageway *n* Korridor *m*, [Durch]gang *m*

passenger [ˈpæs·ən·dʒər] *n* (*on a bus*) Fahrgast *m*; (*on an airline*) Passagier(in) *m(f)*; (*in a car*) Mitfahrer(in) *m(f)*

P

'**passenger seat** *n* (*in car*) Beifahrersitz *m*

passer-by <*pl* passers-> [ˌpæs·ər·'baɪ] *n* Passant(in) *m(f)*

passing ['pæs·ɪŋ] I. *adj attr* ❶ *vehicle* vorbeifahrend; *pedestrian* vorbeigehend; **with each ~ day** mit jedem weiteren Tag[, der vergeht] ❷ *remark* beiläufig ❸ *resemblance* gering II. *n* SPORT Passen *nt*

passion ['pæʃ·ən] *n* ❶ [große] Leidenschaft ❷ (*fancy*) Vorliebe *f*; **to have a ~ for doing sth** etw leidenschaftlich gerne tun

passionate ['pæʃ·ə·nɪt] *adj* leidenschaftlich

'**passion fruit** *n* Passionsfrucht *f*

passive ['pæs·ɪv] *adj* ❶ *role* passiv ❷ (*submissive*) unterwürfig; **to be too ~** sich *dat* zu viel gefallen lassen

'**passkey** *n* ❶ *see* **master key** ❷ *see* **skeleton key**

Passover ['pæs·ˌoʊ·vər] *n* Passah[fest] *nt*

passport ['pæs·pɔrt] *n* [Reise]pass *m*

'**passport control** *n* Passkontrolle *f*

'**password** *n* Parole *f*; COMPUT Passwort *nt*

past [pæst] I. *n* Vergangenheit *f*; (*past life*) Vorleben *nt* II. *adj* ❶ *attr* (*preceding*) vergangen; (*former*) frühere(r, s) ❷ (*over*) vorüber, vorbei III. *adv* **to go ~ sb** an jdm vorbeigehen; *vehicle* an jdm vorbeifahren IV. *prep* ❶ (*to other side*) an ... vorbei; **to drive ~** vorbeifahren; (*at other side*) hinter, nach ❷ (*after the hour of*) nach; **it's a quarter ~ five** es ist Viertel nach Fünf

pasta ['pas·tə] *n* Nudeln *pl*

paste [peɪst] I. *n* ❶ (*soft substance*) Paste *f* ❷ (*sticky substance*) Kleister *m* II. *vt* ❶ (*affix*) kleben (**on**[**to**] auf +*akk*) ❷ COMPUT einfügen

pastel [pæ·'stel] *adj* pastellfarben

pasteurize ['pæs·tʃə·raɪz] *vt usu passive* pasteurisieren

pastor ['pæs·tər] *n* Pfarrer *m*, Pastor *m*

past 'participle *n* Partizip Perfekt *nt*

past 'perfect, **past 'perfect tense** *n* Plusquamperfekt *nt*

pastry ['peɪ·stri] *n* ❶ (*dough*) [Kuchen]teig *m* ❷ (*cake*) Gebäckstück *nt*

'**pastry chef**, '**pastry cook** *n* Konditor(in) *m(f)*

past 'tense *n* Vergangenheit *f*

pasture ['pæs·tʃər] *n* Weide *f*

pasty ['pæs·ti] *adj* (*pej*) *complexion* bleich, käsig *fam*

pat [pæt] I. *vt* <-tt-> tätscheln II. *n* ❶ (*tap*) [freundlicher] Klaps ❷ **a ~ of butter** ein Stückchen *nt* Butter

patch [pætʃ] I. *n* <*pl* -es> ❶ (*piece of fabric*) Flicken *m*; (*for an eye*) Augenklappe *f* ❷ (*spot*) Fleck[en] *m*; ▪**in ~es** stellenweise II. *vt* (*cover*) flicken

◆ **patch up** *vt* ❶ (*repair*) zusammenflicken *fam* ❷ (*fig: conciliate*) **to ~ up an argument** einen Streit beilegen

'**patchwork** *n* Patchwork *n*

patchy ['pætʃ·i] *adj* ❶ METEO ~ **fog** stellenweise Nebel ❷ (*fig: inconsistent*) von sehr unterschiedlicher Qualität *nach n, präd; knowledge* lückenhaft

pâté [pa·'teɪ] *n* Pastete *f*

patent ['pæt·ənt] *n* LAW Patent *nt*; **to take out a ~ on sth** [sich *dat*] etw patentieren lassen

patented ['pæt·ən·tɪd] *adj* (*copyrighted*) patentiert

patent 'leather *n* Lackleder *nt*

'**patent office** *n* Patentamt *nt*

paternal [pə·'tɜr·nəl] *adj* väterlich

pa'ternity leave *n* Vaterschaftsurlaub *m*

pa'ternity suit *n* Vaterschaftsprozess *m*

path [pæθ] *n* ❶ (*way*) Weg *m*, Pfad *m*; **to cross sb's ~** jdm über den Weg laufen ❷ (*direction*) Weg *m*; *of a bullet* Bahn *f*

pathetic [pə·'θet̬·ɪk] *adj* ❶ (*heart-rending*) Mitleid erregend ❷ (*pej: pitiful*) jämmerlich; *excuse* schwach

pathologist [pə·'θal·ə·dʒɪst] *n* Pathologe, -in *m, f*

pathos ['peɪ·θas] *n* Pathos *nt geh*

'**pathway** *n* Weg *m* a. *fig*

patience ['peɪ·ʃəns] *n* Geduld *f*

patient ['peɪ·ʃənt] I. *adj* geduldig; ▪**to be ~ with sb** mit jdm Geduld haben II. *n* MED Patient(in) *m(f)*

P

patina ['pæt·ən·ə] n CHEM, SCI, TECH Film m; (on copper, brass) Patina f

patio ['pæt·i·oʊ] n Terrasse f

patriarchal [,peɪ·tri·'ar·kəl] adj patriarchalisch

patricide ['pæt·rə·saɪd] n Vatermord m

patriotic [,peɪ·tri·'aṭ·ɪk] adj patriotisch

patrol [pə·'troʊl] I. vi <-ll-> patrouillieren II. n Patrouille f; **highway ~** Polizei, die die Highways überwacht

pa'trol car n Streifenwagen m

pa'trolman n Streifenpolizist(in) m(f), Polizeiwachtmeister(in) m(f)

patron ['peɪ·trən] n (benefactor) Schirmherr m; **~ of the arts** Mäzen(in) m(f) der [schönen] Künste

patronize ['peɪ·trə·naɪz] vt (pej) **to ~ sb** jdn herablassend behandeln

patronizing ['peɪ·trə·naɪ·zɪŋ] adj (pej) attitude herablassend; look gönnerhaft

patron 'saint n Schutzpatron(in) m(f)

patter ['pæt·ər] vi feet trippeln; rain prasseln

pattern ['pæt·ərn] n Muster nt

patterned ['pæt·ərnd] adj gemustert

patty ['pæt·i] n Pastetchen nt; **burger ~** Fleischbratling m

paunch <pl -es> [pɔntʃ] n Bauch m

paunchy ['pɔn·tʃi] adj dickbäuchig

pauper ['pɔ·pər] n Arme(r) f(m)

pause [pɔz] I. n Pause f II. vi eine [kurze] Pause machen; speaker innehalten III. vt anhalten

pavement ['peɪv·mənt] n Asphalt m

paving ['peɪ·vɪŋ] n das Pflastern

'paving stone n Pflasterstein m

paw [pɔ] I. n Pfote f; of a big cat, bear Pranke f sl II. vt (fam: touch) begrabschen

pawn[1] [pɔn] vt verpfänden

pawn[2] [pɔn] n CHESS Bauer m

'pawnbroker n Pfandleiher(in) m(f)

pay [peɪ] I. n (wages) Lohn m; (salary) Gehalt nt II. vt <paid, paid> ❶ (give) [be]zahlen; **~ out** etw [aus]zahlen; **to ~ [in] cash** [in] bar [be]zahlen ❷ (settle) bezahlen; **to ~ one's dues** (debts) seine Schulden bezahlen; (fig: obligations) seine Schuldigkeit tun III. vi <paid,

paid> ❶ (give money) [be]zahlen ❷ (be profitable) rentabel sein; **it ~s to do sth** es lohnt sich, etw zu tun ❸ (fig: suffer) **to ~ [for sth]** [für etw akk] bezahlen

◆ **pay back** vt ❶ (give back) zurückzahlen; debts bezahlen ❷ (fig: for revenge) **to ~ sb back for sth** jdm etw heimzahlen

◆ **pay off** I. vt ❶ (repay) abbezahlen; (settle) debt [vollständig] begleichen ❷ **to ~ off ⟲ sb** jdn kaufen II. vi (fig fam) sich auszahlen

◆ **pay out** I. vt ausgeben II. vi FIN **to ~ out [on a policy]** [be]zahlen

◆ **pay up** vi [be]zahlen

'paycheck n Lohnscheck m

'payday n Zahltag m

payer ['peɪ·ər] n Zahler(in) m(f)

paying ['peɪ·ɪŋ] adj attr zahlend

'payload n TRANSP, AEROSP Nutzlast f

payment ['peɪ·mənt] n (sum) Zahlung f

'payoff n ❶ (fam: reward) Lohn m ❷ (fam: bribe) Bestechung f

'payout n FIN Ausschüttung f

pay-per-'view n Pay-per-View nt (System, bei dem der Zuschauer nur für die Sendungen zahlt, die er auch tatsächlich gesehen hat)

'pay phone n Münzfernsprecher m

'pay raise n (for white-collar worker) Gehaltserhöhung f; (for blue-collar worker) Lohnerhöhung f

pay T'V n (fam) Pay-TV nt

PBS [,pi·bi·'es] n abbrev of **Public Broadcasting Service** amerikanischer Fernsehsender

PC [,pi·'si] I. n ❶ abbrev of **personal computer** PC m ❷ abbrev of **political correctness** II. adj abbrev of **politically correct** pc

p.c. [,pi·'si] n abbrev of **percent** p.c.

PDA [,pi·,di·'eɪ] n abbrev of **personal digital assistant** PDA m

PE [,pi·'i] n abbrev of **physical education**

pea [pi] n Erbse f

peace [pis] n ❶ Frieden m ❷ (social order) Ruhe f

'peace conference n Friedenskonferenz f

peaceful ['pis·fəl] adj friedlich; (calm) ruhig

'peace'keeping I. n Friedenssicherung f II. adj ~ force Friedenstruppe f

'peace-loving adj friedliebend

'peacemaking n Befriedung f geh

'peace movement n Friedensbewegung f

'peace settlement n Friedensabkommen nt

'peacetime n Friedenszeiten pl

'peace treaty n Friedensvertrag m

peach [pitʃ] n <pl -es> Pfirsich m

peachy ['pitʃ·i] adj (fam) wunderbar, toll

peacock ['pi·kak] n Pfau m

peak [pik] I. n Gipfel m II. vi athletes [seine] Höchstleistung erbringen; production den Höchststand erreichen

peal [pil] I. n (sound) Dröhnen nt kein pl II. vi bells läuten

peanut ['pi·nʌt] n ❶ (nut) Erdnuss f ❷ (fam: very little) ▪ ~s pl Klacks m

'peanut butter n Erdnussbutter f

pear [per] n Birne f

pearl [pɜrl] n Perle f

peasant ['pez·ənt] n [Klein]bauer, [Klein]bäuerin m, f

peat [pit] n Torf m

'peat bog n Torfmoor nt

pebble ['peb·əl] n Kieselstein m

pecan [pɪ'kan] n Pekannuss f

peck [pek] I. n ❶ (bite) Picken nt kein pl ❷ (fam: quick kiss) Küsschen nt II. vt ❶ (bite) hacken nach +dat ❷ (fam: kiss quickly) to ~ sb on the cheek jdn flüchtig auf die Wange küssen III. vi (with the beak) picken

'pecking order n Hackordnung f

pectoral ['pek·tər·əl] adj Brust-, pektoral fachspr

peculiar [pɪ'kjul·jər] adj ❶ (strange) seltsam, merkwürdig ❷ (belonging to, special) to sb typisch

peculiarity [pɪ·kju·li·'ær·ɪ·ti] n ❶ (strangeness) Eigenartigkeit f ❷ (idiosyncrasy) Eigenart f

peculiarly [pɪ'kjul·jər·li] adv eigenartig

pedal ['ped·əl] I. n Pedal nt II. vi <-l-> Rad fahren

pedantic [pə'dæn·tɪk] adj pedantisch

peddle ['ped·əl] vt ▪ to ~ sth (esp pej: sell) etw verscherbeln pej

peddler ['ped·lər] n Drogenhändler(in) m(f)

pedestal ['ped·ɪ·stəl] n Sockel m

pedestrian [pə'des·tri·ən] n Fußgänger(in) m(f)

pedestrian crossing n Zebrastreifen m

pedestrianize [pə'des·tri·ə·naɪz] vt in eine Fußgängerzone umwandeln

pedestrianized [pɪ'des·tri·ə·naɪzd] adj ~ area Fußgängerzone f

pedestrian 'mall n Fußgängerzone f

pediatrician [ˌpi·di·ə·'trɪʃ·ən] n Kinderarzt, -ärztin m, f

pedicure ['ped·ɪ·kjʊr] n Pediküre f

pedigree ['ped·ɪ·gri] n Stammbaum m

pedometer [pɪ'dam·ə·tər] n Pedometer nt

pedophile ['ped·ə·faɪl] n Pädophile(r) m

pee [pi] (fam) I. n ❶ (urine) Pipi nt Kindersprache ❷ (act) Pinkeln nt; to go ~ (esp childspeak) Pipi machen II. vi pinkeln fam; to ~ in one's pants in die Hose[n] machen

peek [pik] I. n flüchtiger Blick II. vi blinzeln; ▪ to ~ over sth über etw akk gucken

◆ peek out vi hervorgucken

peel [pil] I. n Schale f II. vt fruit schälen; to ~ the paper off sth etw auswickeln III. vi paint, wallpaper sich lösen; skin sich schälen

◆ peel off I. vt schälen; adhesive strip abziehen II. vi (come off) sich lösen

peeler ['pi·lər] n (utensil) Schäler m

peelings ['pi·lɪŋz] npl Schalen pl

peep[1] [pip] I. n usu sing ❶ (bird sound) Piep[ser] m ❷ (answer, statement) Laut m; to not hear [so much as] a ~ out of [or from] sb keinen Mucks von jdm hören II. vi piepsen

peep[2] [pip] I. n (look) [verstohlener] Blick II. vi ❶ verstohlen blicken, spähen

P

② (*appear*) hervorkommen (**through** durch +*akk*)
♦ **peep out** *vi toe, finger* herausgucken

'peephole *n* Guckloch *nt*, Spion *m*

peeping 'Tom *n* Spanner *m fam*

peer [pɪr] *vi* (*look closely*) spähen; **to ~ over sb's shoulder** jdm über die Schulter gucken

peeved [pivd] *adj* (*fam*) sauer

peevish ['piː·vɪʃ] *adj* mürrisch

peg [peg] **I.** *n* (*hook*) Haken *m*; (*stake*) Pflock *m* **II.** *vt* <-gg-> **to ~ prices** Preise stützen

pejorative [pɪ·'dʒɔːr·ə·tɪv] (*form*) abwertend

Pekinese <*pl* -> [ˌpiː·kə·'niːz] *n* (*dog*) Pekinese *m*

pelican ['pel·ɪ·kən] *n* Pelikan *m*

pellet ['pel·ɪt] *n* **①** (*ball*) Kugel *f* **②** (*gunshot*) Schrot *nt o m kein pl*

pelt [pelt] *vt* ■**to ~ sb with sth** jdn mit etw *dat* bewerfen

pelvis <*pl* -es> ['pel·vɪs] *n* Becken *nt*

pen¹ [pen] *n* (*writing utensil*) Feder *f*; **ballpoint ~** Kugelschreiber *m*

pen² [pen] *n* (*enclosed area*) Pferch *m*
♦ **pen in** *vt animal* einsperren; ■**to be ~ned in** *people* eingeschlossen sein

pen³ [pen] *n* (*fam*) *short for* **penitentiary** Knast *m fam*

penal ['piː·nəl] *adj attr* **~ code** Strafgesetz *nt*

penalize ['piː·nə·laɪz] *vt* ■**to ~ sb** [**for sth**] jdn [für etw *akk*] bestrafen

penalty ['pen·əl·ti] *n* LAW (*a. fig*) Strafe *f*

'penalty area *n* Strafraum *m*

'penalty box *n* **①** (*in soccer*) Strafraum *m* **②** (*in hockey*) Strafbank *f*

'penalty clause *n* [restriktive] Vertragsklausel

'penalty shot *n* **to award a ~** (*in hockey*) einen Strafschuss verhängen; (*in soccer*) einen Elfmeter geben

penance ['pen·əns] *n* Buße *f*

pencil ['pen·səl] **I.** *n* (*writing utensil*) Bleistift *m*; FASHION **eyeliner ~** Eyelinerstift *m* **II.** *vt* <-l-> mit Bleistift schreiben
♦ **pencil in** *vt* vormerken

'pencil case *n* Federmäppchen *nt*

'pencil sharpener *n* [Bleistift]spitzer *m*

pendant ['pen·dənt] *n* Anhänger *m*

pending ['pen·dɪŋ] *adj* LAW anhängig; *deal* bevorstehend

pendulum ['pen·dʒə·ləm] *n* Pendel *nt*

penetrate ['pen·ɪ·treɪt] *vt* ■**to ~ sth** **①** (*move into*) in etw *akk* eindringen **②** (*spread through*) *smell* etw durchdringen

penetrating ['pen·ɪ·treɪ·tɪŋ] *adj* durchdringend *attr*; *analysis* eingehend

penguin ['peŋ·gwɪn] *n* Pinguin *m*

penicillin [ˌpen·ɪ·'sɪl·ɪn] *n* Penicillin *nt*

peninsula [pə·'nɪn·sə·lə] *n* Halbinsel *f*

penis <*pl* -es> ['piː·nɪs] *n* Penis *m*

penitent ['pen·ɪ·tənt] *n* REL reuiger Sünder/reuige Sünderin

penitentiary [ˌpen·ɪ·'ten·tʃə·ri] *n* Gefängnis *nt*

'penknife *n* Taschenmesser *nt*

'pen name *n* Pseudonym *nt*

pennant ['pen·ənt] *n* (*flag*) Wimpel *m*; SPORT Siegeswimpel *m*

penniless ['pen·ɪ·lɪs] *adj* mittellos

Pennsylvania [ˌpen·sɪl·'veɪ·ni·ə] *n* Pennsylvania *nt*

penny <*pl* -nies> ['pen·i] *n* Penny *m*
▶PHRASES: **to be worth every ~** sein Geld wert sein

'penny-pinching *adj* geizig

'pen pal *n* Brieffreund(in) *m(f)*

pension ['pen·ʃən] *n* Rente *f*

'pension fund *n* Pensionskasse *f*

'pension plan *n* Altersversorgungsplan *m*

pensive ['pen·sɪv] *adj* nachdenklich

pentagon ['pen·tə·gɑn] *n* Fünfeck *nt*

Pentagon ['pen·tə·gɑn] *n* ■**the ~** das Pentagon

pentathlon [pen·'tæθ·lɑn] *n* Fünfkampf *m*

penthouse ['pent·haʊs] *n* Penthaus *nt*

'pent-up *adj emotions* aufgestaut

peony ['piː·ə·ni] *n* Pfingstrose *f*

people ['piː·pəl] **I.** *n* **①** *pl* (*persons*) Leute *pl*, Menschen *pl*; **rich ~** die Reichen *pl* **②** *pl* (*nation*) Volk *nt* **II.** *adj* **~ skills** Menschenkenntnis *f kein pl*

pep [pep] **I.** *n* (*fam*) Elan *m*,

Schwung *m* II. *vt* <-pp-> ■**to ~ sb** ↺ **up** jdn in Schwung bringen; ■**to ~ sth** ↺ **up** aufpeppen (**with** mit +*dat*)

pepper ['pep·ər] I. *n* ❶(*spice*) Pfeffer *m*; **black ~** schwarzer Pfeffer ❷(*vegetable*) Paprika *f* II. *vt* (*add pepper*) pfeffern

'**peppercorn** *n* Pfefferkorn *nt*

'**pepper mill** *n* Pfeffermühle *f*

'**peppermint** *n* Pfefferminz[bonbon] *nt*

pepperoni [pep·ə·'rou·ni] *n* Salami *f*

'**pepper shaker** *n* Pfefferstreuer *m*

peppery ['pep·ə·ri] *adj* pfeffrig; *dish* scharf

'**pep pill** *n* Aufputschmittel *nt*

'**pep talk** *n* Motivationsgespräch *nt*

per [pɜr] *prep* ❶(*for every, in every*) pro ❷(*according to*) **as ~ usual** wie gewöhnlich

per annum [pər·'æn·əm] *adv* (*form*) per annum

per capita [pər·'kæp·ɪ·ţə] *adj attr* (*form*) Pro-Kopf-

perceive [pər·'siv] *vt* wahrnehmen

percent [pər·'sent] I. *n* Prozent *nt*; **what ~ ...?** wie viel Prozent ...? II. *adv* ·prozentig

percentage [pər·'sen·tɪdʒ] *n* Prozentsatz *m*; **what ~ ...?** wie viel Prozent ...?

per'centage point *n* Prozentpunkt *m*

perceptible [pər·'sep·tə·bəl] *adj* wahrnehmbar

perception [pər·'sep·ʃən] *n usu sing* Wahrnehmung *f kein pl*

perceptive [pər·'sep·tɪv] *adj* einfühlsam; *observer* aufmerksam; *remark* scharfsinnig

perch [pɜrtʃ] I. *n* <*pl* -es> (*for birds*) Sitzstange *f* II. *vi bird* sitzen (**on** auf +*dat*); *person* thronen (**on** auf +*dat*)

percolate ['pɜr·kə·leɪt] I. *vt* filtrieren; **to ~ coffee** Filterkaffee zubereiten II. *vi water* durchsickern

percolator ['pɜr·kə·leɪ·ţər] *n* Kaffeemaschine *f*

percussion [pər·'kʌʃ·ən] *n* Percussion *f*, Schlagzeug *nt*

peregrine 'falcon *n* Wanderfalke *m*

peremptory [pə·'remp·tə·ri] *adj* gebieterisch

perennial [pə·'ren·i·əl] I. *n* mehrjährige Pflanze II. *adj attr* (*lasting through many years*) mehrjährig

perfect I. *adj* ['pɜr·fɪkt] vollkommen, perfekt II. *vt* [pər·'fekt] perfektionieren

perfection [pər·'fek·ʃən] *n* Perfektion *f*

perfectionist [pər·'fek·ʃə·nɪst] *n* Perfektionist(in) *m(f)*

perfectly ['pɜr·fɪkt·li] *adv* vollkommen, perfekt; **~ clear** absolut klar *fam*

perforate ['pɜr·fə·reɪt] *vt* perforieren; (*once*) durchstechen

perforation [ˌpɜr·fə·'reɪ·ʃən] *n* Loch *nt*

perform [pər·'fɔrm] I. *vt* ❶(*entertain*) vorführen; *play, symphony* aufführen; (*on an instrument*) spielen ❷*function* erfüllen ❸ *surgical procedure* durchführen II. *vi* ❶(*on stage*) auftreten; (*play*) spielen ❷(*function*) funktionieren; *car* laufen ❸(*do, act*) **to ~ well** gut sein

performance [pər·'fɔr·məns] *n* ❶(*entertaining, showing*) Vorführung *f*; *of a play, ballet* Aufführung *f*; *of a part* Darstellung *f*; **to give a ~** eine Vorstellung geben ❷(*effectiveness, level of achievement*) Leistung *f*

performer [pər·'fɔr·mər] *n* Künstler(in) *m(f)*

perfume I. *n* ['pɜr·fjum] ❶(*scented liquid*) Parfüm *nt* ❷*of a flower* Duft *m* II. *vt* [pər·'fjum] parfümieren

perfunctory [pər·'fʌŋk·tə·ri] *adj* flüchtig

perhaps [pər·'hæps] *adv* ❶(*maybe*) vielleicht ❷(*approximately*) ungefähr

peril ['per·əl] *n* (*form: danger*) Gefahr *f*; (*risk*) Risiko *nt*

perimeter [pə·'rɪm·ə·ţər] *n* Grenze *f*

period ['pɪr·i·əd] I. *n* ❶(*length of time*) Zeitspanne *f*, Periode *f*; **for a ~ of three months** für die Dauer von drei Monaten ❷(*time in history, development*) Zeit *f*; (*distinct time*) Zeitabschnitt *m*; (*phase*) Phase *f*; **~ of office** Amtszeit *f* ❸(*fam: menstruation*) Periode *f* ❹LING (*a. fig*) Punkt *m* II. *adj clothing, novel* historisch

P

periodical [ˌpɪrˈiˈadˈɪˈkəl] n Zeitschrift f; (specialist journal a.) Periodikum nt fachspr

peripheral [pəˈrɪfˈərˈəl] I. adj ❶ (minor) unbedeutend ❷ (at the edge) Rand- II. n COMPUT Peripherie f fachspr

periscope [ˈperˈɪˈskoʊp] n Periskop nt

perishable [ˈperˈɪʃˈəˈbəl] adj food [leicht] verderblich

perjury [ˈpɜrˈdʒəˈri] n Meineid nt; to commit ~ einen Meineid schwören

perk [pɜrk] n Vergünstigung f
♦ perk up I. vi ❶ (cheer up) aufleben; (become more awake) munter werden ❷ (recover) sich erholen II. vt ❶ (cheer up) aufheitern ❷ (energize) aufmuntern

perky [ˈpɜrˈki] adj (lively) munter

perm¹ [pɜrm] n short for permanent Dauerwelle f

perm² [pɜrm] vt to ~ hair Dauerwellen machen

permafrost [ˈpɜrˈməˈfrɔst] n Dauerfrost[boden] m

permanence [ˈpɜrˈməˈnəns], permanency [ˈpɜrˈməˈnənˈsi] n Beständigkeit f

permanent [ˈpɜrˈməˈnənt] adj permanent, ständig; relationship dauerhaft; ink wasserfest; ~ address fester Wohnsitz; ~ damage bleibender Schaden

permeable [ˈpɜrˈmiˈəˈbəl] adj (a. fig form) durchlässig a. fig

permissible [pərˈmɪsˈəˈbəl] adj gestattet

permission [pərˈmɪʃˈən] n Erlaubnis f; (from an official body) Genehmigung f

permissive [pərˈmɪsˈɪv] adj (pej) nachgiebig; (sexually) freizügig

permit I. n [ˈpɜrˈmɪt] Genehmigung f II. vt <-tt-> [pərˈmɪt] ❶ (give permission) andauern, erlauben ❷ (make possible) ■ to ~ sb to do sth jdm ermöglichen, etw zu tun III. vi [pərˈmɪt] weather ~ting vorausgesetzt, das Wetter spielt mit

permitted [pərˈmɪtˈɪd] adj zulässig

peroxide [pəˈrakˈsaɪd] n Peroxyd nt

perpendicular [ˌpɜrˈpənˈdɪkˈjuˈlər] I. adj senkrecht II. n Senkrechte f; MATH, ARCHIT ■ the ~ das Lot

perpetrate [ˈpɜrˈpəˈtreɪt] vt (form) begehen

perpetrator [ˈpɜrˈpəˈtreɪˈtər] n (form) Täter(in) m(f)

perpetual [pərˈpetʃˈuˈəl] adj attr ständig

perpetuate [pərˈpetʃˈuˈeɪt] vt aufrechterhalten

perplex [pərˈpleks] vt (puzzle) verblüffen

perplexed [pərˈplekst] adj perplex; (puzzled a.) verblüfft

perplexity [pərˈplekˈsɪˈti] n Verblüffung f

persecute [ˈpɜrˈsɪˈkjut] vt usu passive verfolgen

persecution [ˌpɜrˈsɪˈkjuˈʃən] n usu sing Verfolgung f

perseverance [ˌpɜrˈsəˈvɪrˈəns] n Beharrlichkeit f, Ausdauer f

persevere [ˌpɜrˈsəˈvɪr] vi nicht aufgeben; ■ to ~ with sth an etw dat festhalten; (continue) mit etw dat weitermachen

persevering [ˌpɜrˈsəˈvɪrˈɪŋ] adj beharrlich

Persian [ˈpɜrˈʒən] n (cat) Perserkatze f

persist [pərˈsɪst] vi ❶ (continue to exist) andauern; cold, rain anhalten ❷ (to not give up) beharrlich bleiben ❸ (continue) ■ to ~ in doing sth nicht aufhören, etw zu tun

persistence [pərˈsɪsˈtəns] n ❶ (continuation) Anhalten nt ❷ (perseverance) Hartnäckigkeit f

persistent [pərˈsɪsˈtənt] adj ❶ difficulties anhaltend; cough hartnäckig ❷ demand ständig

person <pl people or form -s> [ˈpɜrˈsən] n (human) Person f, Mensch m; not a single ~ came kein Mensch kam; cat ~ Katzenliebhaber(in) m(f); night ~ Nachtmensch m

persona <pl -nae> [pərˈsoʊˈnə] n Fassade f meist pej

personal [ˈpɜrˈsəˈnəl] adj persönlich;

private a. privat; **~ data** Personalien *pl;* **~ quality** Charaktereigenschaft *f*

'personal ad *n* Kontaktanzeige *f*

personal com'puter *n* Personal Computer *m*

personal digital as'sistant *n* PDA *m,* [handflächengroßer] Taschencomputer

personality [ˌpɜr·sə·'næl·ɪ·t̬i] *n* (*character, a celebrity*) Persönlichkeit *f*

personally ['pɜr·sə·nə·li] *adv* persönlich

personal 'pronoun *n* Personalpronomen *nt*

personnel [ˌpɜr·sə·'nel] *n* ❶ *pl* (*employees*) Personal *nt kein pl* ❷ (*department*) Personalabteilung *f*

person'nel department *n* Personalabteilung *f*

personnel 'manager *n* Personalchef(in) *m(f)*

perspective [pər·'spek·tɪv] *n* (*viewpoint*) Perspektive *f;* **from a historical ~** aus geschichtlicher Sicht; **in ~** perspektivisch; **to get sth in ~** etw nüchtern betrachten

perspiration [ˌpɜr·spə·'reɪ·ʃən] *n* Schweiß *m*

perspire [pər·'spaɪr] *vi* schwitzen

persuade [pər·'sweɪd] *vt* überreden; (*convince*) überzeugen

persuasion [pər·'sweɪ·ʒən] *n usu sing* (*talking into*) Überredung *f;* (*convincing*) Überzeugung *f*

persuasive [pər·'sweɪ·sɪv] *adj* überzeugend

pert [pɜrt] *adj* ❶ (*attractively small*) wohl geformt ❷ (*impudent*) frech

pertinent ['pɜr·tən·ənt] *adj* (*form*) relevant; *question* sachdienlich; *remark* treffend

perturb [pər·'tɜrb] *vt* (*form*) beunruhigen

pervasive [pər·'veɪ·sɪv] *adj* (*widespread*) weit verbreitet

perversion [pər·'vɜr·ʒən] *n* (*pej*) ❶ (*unnatural behavior*) Perversion *f* ❷ **~ of justice** Rechtsbeugung *f*

pervert I. *n* ['pɜr·vɜrt] (*pej: sexual deviant*) Perverse(r) *f(m)* II. *vt* [pər·'vɜrt] (*pej*) *truth* verdrehen

perverted [pər·'vɜr·t̬ɪd] *adj* (*sexually deviant*) pervers

pesky ['pes·ki] *adj* (*fam*) verdammt *fam*

pessimist ['pes·ə·mɪst] *n* Pessimist(in) *m(f)*

pessimistic [ˌpes·ə·'mɪs·tɪk] *adj* pessimistisch

pest [pest] *n* ❶ (*destructive animal*) Schädling *m* ❷ (*fig fam: annoying person*) Nervensäge *f fam*

'pest control *n* Schädlingsbekämpfung *f*

pester ['pes·tər] *vt* belästigen; **■ to ~ sb to do sth** jdn drängen, etw zu tun

pesticide ['pes·tə·saɪd] *n* Schädlingsbekämpfungsmittel *nt*

pestle ['pes·əl] *n* Stößel *m*

pet [pet] I. *n* Haustier *nt* II. *adj* ❶ (*concerning animals*) **~ cat** Hauskatze *f* ❷ *project, theory, charity* Lieblings- III. *vt* <-tt-> streicheln

petal ['pet̬·əl] *n* Blütenblatt *nt*

petite [pə·'tit] *adj* (*approv*) *person* zierlich

petition [pə·'tɪʃ·ən] I. *n* ❶ (*signed document*) Petition *f* ❷ LAW (*written request*) Gesuch *nt* II. *vi* LAW (*request formally*) einen Antrag stellen

petitioner [pə·'tɪʃ·ən·ər] *n* LAW Kläger(in) *m(f)*

pet 'name *n* Kosename *m*

petrified ['pet·rə·faɪd] *adj* ❶ (*fossilized*) versteinert ❷ (*terrified*) gelähmt *fig;* **■ to be ~ of sth** vor etw *dat* panische Angst haben

petrochemical [ˌpet·rou·'kem·ɪ·kəl] *adj attr* petrochemisch

petroleum [pə·'trou·li·əm] *n* Erdöl *nt*

petting ['pet̬·ɪŋ] *n* Petting *nt*

petty ['pet̬·i] *adj* (*pej*) ❶ (*insignificant*) unbedeutend ❷ (*small-minded*) kleinkariert

petty 'cash *n* Portokasse *f*

'petty officer *n* NAUT ≈ Marineunteroffizier *m*

pew [pju] *n* Kirchenbank *f*

pewter ['pju·tər] *n* Zinn *nt*

PG [ˌpi·'dʒi] *adj abbrev of* **parental guidance: to be rated ~** bedingt jugendfrei sein

pH [ˌpiːˈeɪtʃ] n usu sing pH-Wert m

phallic [ˈfæl·ɪk] adj phallisch

phantom [ˈfæn·təm] I. n Geist m II. adj attr (caused by mental illusion) Phantom-

pharaoh [ˈfer·oʊ] n Pharao m

pharmaceutical [ˌfar·mə·ˈsuː·tɪ·kəl] adj attr pharmazeutisch

pharma'ceutical industry n Pharmaindustrie f

pharmacist [ˈfar·mə·sɪst] n Apotheker(in) m(f)

pharmacy [ˈfar·mə·si] n ❶ (drugstore) Apotheke f ❷ (profession) Pharmazie f

phase [feɪz] n Phase f
◆**phase in** vt stufenweise einführen
◆**phase out** vt auslaufen lassen

phat [fæt] adj (sl) toll, krass sl

PhD [ˌpiː·eɪtʃˈdiː] n abbrev of **Doctor of Philosophy** Dr., Doktor m

pheasant <pl -s> [ˈfez·ənt] n Fasan m

phenomena [fəˈnɒm·ə·nə] n pl of **phenomenon**

phenomenal [fəˈnɒm·ə·nəl] adj (great) phänomenal

phenomenon <pl -mena> [fəˈnɒm·ə·nən] n Phänomen nt geh

phew [fjuː] interj (fam) puh

philately [fɪˈlæt·ə·li] n Philatelie f

Philippines [ˈfɪl·ə·pinz] npl ■ the ~ die Philippinen pl

philistine [ˈfɪl·ɪ·stin] n (pej) Banause m

philosopher [fɪˈlɒs·ə·fər] n Philosoph(in) m(f)

philosophic(al) [ˌfɪl·ə·ˈsɒf·ɪk(əl)] adj (calm) gelassen

philosophy [fɪˈlɒs·ə·fi] n Philosophie f

phish [fɪʃ] vi INET phischen (im Internet persönliche Daten und Passwörter auskundschaften, um die Betroffenen zu bestehlen)

phlegm [flem] n Schleim m

phobia [ˈfoʊ·bi·ə] n Phobie f

phone [foʊn] I. n Telefon nt; **to answer the** ~ ans Telefon gehen; **on the** ~ am Telefon II. vt anrufen III. vi telefonieren
◆**phone back** vt, vi zurückrufen

◆**phone in** vi anrufen, sich telefonisch melden
◆**phone up** vt anrufen

'**phone book** n Telefonbuch nt

'**phone booth** n Telefonzelle f

'**phone card** n Telefon[kredit]karte f

phonetic [fəˈnet·ɪk] adj LING phonetisch fachspr

phony, **phoney** [ˈfoʊ·ni] (pej) I. adj (fam) accent, smile aufgesetzt, künstlich; documents gefälscht II. n (impostor) Hochstapler(in) m(f); (fake) Fälschung f

phooey [ˈfuː·i] interj (hum fam) pfui

phosphate [ˈfɒs·feɪt] n Phosphat nt

phosphorescent [ˌfɒs·fəˈres·ənt] adj phosphoreszierend

photo [ˈfoʊ·toʊ] n short for **photograph** Foto nt

'**photo album** n Fotoalbum nt

'**photocopier** n [Foto]kopierer m

'**photocopy** I. n [Foto]kopie f II. vt [foto]kopieren

photo 'finish n SPORT Fotofinish nt fachspr

photogenic [ˌfoʊ·toʊ·ˈdʒen·ɪk] adj fotogen

photograph [ˈfoʊ·tə·græf] I. n Fotografie f, Foto nt; **aerial** ~ Luftaufnahme II. vt fotografieren

photographer [fəˈtɒg·rə·fər] n Fotograf(in) m(f)

photography [fəˈtɒg·rə·fi] n Fotografie f

photo'journalism n Fotojournalismus m

photo oppor'tunity n Fototermin m

photo'sensitive adj lichtempfindlich

photo'synthesis n BIOL, CHEM Photosynthese f

phrasal 'verb n LING Phrasal Verb nt (Grundverb mit präpositionaler oder adverbialer Ergänzung)

phrase [freɪz] n (words) Satz m; (idiomatic expression) Ausdruck m

'**phrase book** n Sprachführer m

pH value [ˈpiː·eɪtʃ·ˌ-] n pH-Wert m

physical [ˈfɪz·ɪ·kəl] I. adj condition, love körperlich; **to have a** ~ **disability** körperbehindert sein; **~ contact** Körperkontakt *m* II. *n* MED Untersuchung *f*

physical edu'cation *n* Sport[unterricht] *m*

physically ['fɪz·ɪ·kəl·i] *adv* körperlich

physical 'therapist *n* Physiotherapeut(in) *m(f) fachspr*

physical 'therapy *n* Physiotherapie *f fachspr*

physician [fɪ·'zɪʃ·ən] *n* Arzt, Ärztin *m, f*

physicist ['fɪz·ɪ·sɪst] *n* Physiker(in) *m(f)*

physics ['fɪz·ɪks] *n* + *sing vb* Physik *f*

physiologist [ˌfɪz·i·'al·ə·dʒɪst] *n* Physiologe, -in *m f*

physique [fɪ·'zik] *n* Körperbau *m*

pianist ['pi·æn·ɪst] *n* Klavierspieler(in) *m(f);* (*professional*) Pianist(in) *m(f)*

piano [pi·'æn·oʊ] *n* Klavier *nt,* Piano *nt*

piazza [pɪ·'at·sə] *n* Marktplatz *m*

pick¹ [pɪk] I. *n* (*choice*) Auswahl *f* II. *vt* ❶ (*select*) aussuchen; **to ~ sth at random** etw [völlig] willkürlich aussuchen ❷ (*harvest*) pflücken ❸ (*scratch*) ■ **to ~ sth** an etw *dat* kratzen; **to ~ one's nose** in der Nase bohren ❹ (*take*) ■ **to ~ sth from/off [of] sth** etw aus/von etw *dat* nehmen ❺ *lock* knacken III. *vi* ❶ (*be choosy*) aussuchen ❷ (*toy with*) ■ **to ~ at one's food** in seinem Essen herumstochern

◆**pick off** *vt* (*shoot*) ■ **to ~ off** ⟳ **sb** jdn einzeln abschießen

◆**pick on** *vi* herumhacken auf +*dat*

◆**pick out** *vt* ❶ (*select*) aussuchen ❷ (*recognize*) erkennen

◆**pick over, pick through** *vt* ■ **to ~ sth** ⟳ **over** etw gut durchsehen

◆**pick up** I. *vt* ❶ (*lift*) aufheben; **to ~ up the phone** [den Hörer] abnehmen ❷ (*acquire*) erwerben; **to ~ up an illness** sich mit einer Krankheit anstecken ❸ (*collect*) abholen ❹ (*sl: for sexual purposes*) ■ **to ~ up** ⟳ **sb** jdn abschleppen ❺ *signal* empfangen ❻ (*fam: pay for*) **to ~ up the tab** die Rechnung bezahlen II. *vi* ❶ (*improve*) sich bessern; *numbers* steigen ❷ (*resume*) **to ~ up where one left off** da weitermachen, wo man aufgehört hat

pick² [pɪk] *n* (*pickax*) Spitzhacke *f*

'pickax, 'pickaxe *n* Spitzhacke *f*

picker ['pɪk·ər] *n* (*of crops*) Erntehelfer(in) *m(f)*

picket ['pɪk·ɪt] *n* ❶ (*stake*) Palisade *f* ❷ (*striker*) Streikposten *m*

picket 'fence *n* Palisadenzaun *m*

'picket line *n* Streikpostenkette *f*

pickings ['pɪk·ɪŋz] *npl* **slim ~** magere Ausbeute

pickle ['pɪk·əl] I. *n* FOOD saure Gurke II. *vt* FOOD einlegen

pickled ['pɪk·əld] *adj* eingelegt

'pick-me-up *n* (*fam*) Muntermacher *m*

'pickpocket *n* Taschendieb(in) *m(f)*

'pickup *n* ❶ (*pickup truck*) (offener) Kleintransporter ❷ (*fam: casual sexual acquaintance*) Eroberung *f hum*

'pickup truck *n* (offener) Kleintransporter

picky ['pɪk·i] *adj* (*pej fam*) pingelig; *eater* wählerisch

picnic ['pɪk·nɪk] *n* Picknick *nt*

picture ['pɪk·tʃər] I. *n* ❶ (*painting, drawing*) Bild *nt; photograph* a. Foto *nt* ❷ (*on TV screen*) [Fernseh]bild *nt* ❸ FILM **motion ~** Film *m* II. *vt* (*imagine*) sich *dat* vorstellen

'picture book *n* (*for children*) Bilderbuch *nt*

'picture frame *n* Bilderrahmen *m*

'picture library *n* Bildarchiv *nt*

picturesque [ˌpɪk·tʃə·'resk] *adj scenery* malerisch; *language* bildhaft

'picture window *n* Panoramafenster *n*

piddle ['pɪd·əl] *vi* (*vulg*) pinkeln

pidgin ['pɪdʒ·ɪn] *n* LING Pidgin *f fachspr*

pie [paɪ] *n* [Obst]torte *f;* **spinach ~** Spinatpastete *f*

piece [pis] I. *n* ❶ (*bit*) Stück *nt;* (*part*) Teil *nt o m; of bread* Scheibe *f; of cake* Stück *nt;* [**all**] **in one ~** heil; **to break sth in[to]** [*or* **to**] **~s** etw in Stücke brechen; ■ **~ by ~** Stück für Stück ❷ (*item, coin*) Stück *nt; ~* **of baggage** Gepäckstück *nt;* **a ~ of evidence** ein Beweis *m* ❸ (*in chess*) Figur *f* ❹ MUS, THEAT Stück *nt* ▶PHRASES: **a ~ of the ac-**

P

tion ein Stück nt des Kuchens; **to be a ~ of cake** (fam) kinderleicht sein II. vt ■ **to ~ together** ⊃ sth etw zusammensetzen; (reconstruct) etw rekonstruieren

'**piecemeal** I. adv (bit by bit) Stück für Stück II. adj (bit by bit) stück[chen]weise

'**piece rate** n Akkordlohn m

'**piecework** n Akkordarbeit f

pier [pɪr] n NAUT Pier m o fachspr f; (dock) Landungsbrücke f

pierce [pɪrs] vt (make hole in) durchstechen; (break through) durchbrechen; **to have ~d ears** Ohrlöcher haben

piercing ['pɪr·sɪŋ] I. adj ① durchdringend; (pej) voice schrill ② (cold) eisig ③ question, reply, wit scharf II. n (hole in body) Piercing nt

pig [pɪg] n ① Schwein nt a. fig ② (fam: greedy person) Vielfraß m
◆ **pig out** vi (fam) ■ **to ~ out** [on sth] sich [mit etw dat] vollstopfen

pigeon ['pɪdʒ·ən] n Taube f

'**pigeonhole** I. n (Post)fach nt, Ablage f II. vt (categorize) in eine Schublade stecken

'**pigeon-toed** adj mit einwärtsgerichteten Füßen nach n

P **piggish** ['pɪg·ɪʃ] adj (pej) behavior schweinisch

piggy ['pɪg·i] n (childspeak fam) Schweinchen nt

'**piggyback** n **to give sb a ~** [ride] jdn huckepack nehmen

'**piggy bank** n Sparschwein nt

pig'headed adj (pej) stur

pigment ['pɪg·mənt] n Pigment nt

Pigmy ['pɪg·mi] n, adj see **Pygmy**

'**pigskin** n ① (leather) Schweinsleder nt ② SPORT (fam) Leder nt (Ball beim American Football)

'**pigsty** n (pej, a. fig) Schweinestall m

'**pigtail** n Zopf m

pike¹ [paɪk] n ZOOL Hecht m

pike² [paɪk] n short for **turnpike** Mautstraße f ▸ PHRASES: **sth comes down the ~** etw kommt auf uns zu

pile¹ [paɪl] I. n ① (stack) Stapel m; (fam:

heap) Haufen m ② (sl: fortune) Vermögen nt II. vt stapeln (on|to) auf +dat)
◆ **pile in** vi in etw akk [hinein]strömen
◆ **pile on** vt anhäufen; **you're really piling on the compliments tonight** du bist ja heute Abend so großzügig mit Komplimenten hum
◆ **pile up** vt, vi (sich) anhäufen

pile² [paɪl] n (fabric surface) Flor m

piles [paɪlz] npl (fam) see **hemorrhoids**

'**pile-up** n (fam) Massenkarambolage f

pilfer ['pɪl·fər] vt, vi klauen

pilgrim ['pɪl·grɪm] n Pilger(in) m(f)

pill [pɪl] n ① (tablet) Tablette f ② (contraceptive) ■ **the ~** die Pille

pillar ['pɪl·ər] n Pfeiler m

pillow ['pɪl·oʊ] n ① (for bed) (Kopf)kissen nt ② (decorative cushion) Kissen nt

'**pillowcase** n [Kopf]kissenbezug m

pilot ['paɪ·lət] I. n ① AVIAT Pilot(in) m(f); NAUT Lotse, -in m, f ② TV Pilotfilm m II. vt AVIAT, NAUT aircraft fliegen; ship lotsen

'**pilot light** n Zündflamme f

'**pilot's license** n Pilotenschein m

pimento [pɪ·'men·toʊ], **pimiento** [pɪ·'mjen·toʊ] n ① (sweet red pepper) [rote] Paprika ② (spice) Piment m o nt

pimp [pɪmp] n Zuhälter m

pimple ['pɪm·pəl] n Pickel m

pimply ['pɪm·pli] adj pickelig

pin [pɪn] I. n ① (sharp object) Nadel f ② (brooch) Brosche f II. vt <-nn-> ① (attach with pin) befestigen ([up]on/ [on]to an +dat) ② (hold firmly) ■ **to ~ sb to the floor** jdn auf den Boden drücken
◆ **pin down** vt ① (define exactly) genau definieren ② (make decide) ■ **to ~ down** ⊃ sb [to sth] jdn [auf etw akk] festnageln
◆ **pin up** vt anstecken; hair hochstecken

PIN [pɪn] n abbrev of **personal identification number** PIN

pinafore ['pɪn·ə·fɔr] n [große] Schürze f

'**pinball** n Flipper m

pincer ['pɪn·sər] n ■ **~ s** pl [Kneif]zange f

pinch [pɪntʃ] I. vt ① (nip) kneifen ② (sl: steal) klauen II. vi kneifen; boots, *shoes* drücken III. *n* <*pl* -es> ① (*nip*) Kneifen *nt* ② (*small quantity*) Prise *f* ▶**PHRASES: to take sth with a ~ of** <u>salt</u> etw mit Vorsicht genießen

pinch-'hit *vi* SPORT einspringen

pinch 'hitter *n* SPORT Ersatzspieler(in) *m(f)*

'pincushion *n* Nadelkissen *nt*

pine[1] [paɪn] *n* Kiefer *f*

pine[2] [paɪn] *vi* sich sehnen (**for** nach +*dat*)

pineapple ['paɪn·æp·əl] *n* Ananas *f*

'pinecone *n* Kiefernzapfen *m*

ping [pɪŋ] I. *n* (*sound*) [kurzes] Klingeln II. *vi* [kurz] klingeln

Ping-Pong ['pɪŋ·pɑŋ] *n* (*fam*) Tischtennis *nt*, Pingpong *nt*

'pinhead *n* Stecknadelkopf *m*

pinion ['pɪn·jən] *n* TECH Ritzel *nt*

pink [pɪŋk] *adj* (*pale red*) rosa, pink; *cheeks* rosig

pinkie ['pɪŋ·ki] *n* (*fam*) kleiner Finger

pink slip *n* (*fam*) ① (*notice*) Kündigung *f* ② AUTO (*ownership document*) Kraftfahrzeugbrief *m*

'pinpoint I. *vt* (*genau*) feststellen II. *adj attr* sehr genau; ~ **accuracy** hohe Genauigkeit

'pinprick *n* Nadelstich *m*

pint [paɪnt] *n* Pint *nt* (*0,473 l*)

'pintsize(d) *adj* (*fam*) winzig; (*fig*) unbedeutend

'pinup *n* [Star]poster *nt o m*

pioneer [ˌpaɪ·ə·'nɪr] *n* Pionier(in) *m(f)*

pioneering [ˌpaɪ·ə·'nɪr·ɪŋ] *adj* bahnbrechend; (*innovative*) innovativ

pious ['paɪ·əs] *adj* fromm

pip [pɪp] *n* ① (*on playing card*) Farbe *f* ② HORT Kern *m*

pipe [paɪp] I. *n* ① TECH (*tube*) Rohr *nt*; (*small tube*) Röhre *f*; for gas, water Leitung *f* ② (*for smoking*) Pfeife *f* II. *vt* gas, water leiten

◆**pipe down** *vi* (*fam: be quiet*) den Mund halten; (*be quieter*) leiser sein

◆**pipe up** *vi* den Mund aufmachen

'pipe cleaner *n* Pfeifenreiniger *m*

'pipeline *n* Pipeline *f*; **in the ~** (*fig*) in Planung

piping ['paɪ·pɪŋ] *adv* ~ **hot** kochend heiß

piquant ['pi·kənt] *adj* pikant; (*fig: stimulating*) interessant

pique [pik] *n* Ärger *m*

piracy ['paɪ·rə·si] *n* ① (*at sea*) Piraterie *f*, Seeräuberei *f* ② (*of copyrights*) Raubkopieren *nt*

pirate ['paɪ·rət] I. *n* ① (*buccaneer*) Pirat(in) *m(f)* ② (*plagiarizer*) Raubkopierer(in) *m(f)* II. *adj attr* video, CD raubkopiert

Pisces <*pl* -> ['paɪ·siz] *n* ASTROL Fische *pl, kein art*

piss [pɪs] (*vulg*) I. *n* ① (*urine*) Pisse *f* derb ② *usu sing* (*action*) **to take a ~** schiffen *derb* II. *vi* pinkeln *fam*

pissed [pɪst] *adj* (*vulg*) [stink]sauer

pissed off [pɪst·ɔf] *adj* ■**to be ~ at sb** auf jdn sauer sein

pistachio [pɪ·'stæʃ·i·oʊ] *n* Pistazie *f*

pistol ['pɪs·təl] *n* Pistole *f*

piston ['pɪs·tən] *n* Kolben *m*

pit[1] [pɪt] I. *n* ① (*hole in ground*) Grube *f* ② (*mine*) Bergwerk *nt* ③ (*scar*) Narbe *f* ④ (*sl: the worst*) ■**the ~** *sl* das Allerletzte II. *vt* <-tt-> (*place in competition*) ■**to ~ oneself against sb/sth** sich mit jdm/etw messen

pit[2] [pɪt] FOOD I. *n* Kern *m* II. *vt* <-tt-> entkernen

P

pitch[1] [pɪtʃ] I. *n* <*pl* -es> ① (*delivery from pitcher*) Pitch *m*, Wurf *m* ② (*tone*) Tonhöhe *f*; (*of a voice*) Stimmlage *f* ③ (*persuasion*) [sales] ~ [Verkaufs]sprüche *pl a. pej fam* II. *vt* ① (*throw*) pitchen, werfen ② (*set up*) aufstellen; tent aufschlagen ③ MUS *instrument* stimmen ④ (*target*) ■**to be ~ed at sb** book, film sich an jdn richten III. *vi* SPORT (*in baseball*) pitchen, werfen

◆**pitch in** *vi* (*fam: contribute*) mit anpacken

pitch[2] [pɪtʃ] *n* Pech *nt*

'pitch-black *adj* pechschwarz

pitcher[1] ['pɪtʃ·ər] *n* SPORT (*in baseball*) Pitcher(in) *m(f)* fachspr

pitcher² ['pɪtʃ·ər] n (jug) [Henkel]krug m

pith [pɪθ] n ① (of orange etc.) weiße Innenhaut ② (in plants) Mark nt

pithy ['pɪθ·i] adj ① (succinct) prägnant ② (of citrus fruits) dickschalig

pitiful ['pɪt·ɪ·fəl] adj ① (arousing pity) bemitleidenswert; sight traurig ② (unsatisfactory) jämmerlich

pitiless ['pɪt·ɪ·lɪs] adj erbarmungslos

'pit stop n ① AUTO Boxenstopp m ② usu sing (hum: journey break) Reiseunterbrechung f

pittance ['pɪt·əns] n usu sing (pej) Hungerslohn m

pity ['pɪt·i] I. n ① (compassion) Mitleid nt; **to feel ~ for sb** mit jdm Mitleid haben ② (shame) ■ **to be a ~** schade sein II. vt <-ie-> Mitleid haben mit +dat

pivot ['pɪv·ət] I. n ① MECH, TECH (shaft) [Dreh]zapfen m II. vi ■ **to ~ around sth** (a. fig) um etw akk kreisen

pixel ['pɪk·səl] n Pixel nt fachspr

pixelate, pixellate ['pɪk·sə·leɪt] vt COMPUT verpixeln

pizza ['pit·sə] n Pizza nt

placate ['pleɪ·keɪt] vt beschwichtigen

P

place [pleɪs] I. n ① (location) Ort m; **~ of birth** Geburtsort m; **~ of work** Arbeitsplatz m; **in ~s** stellenweise ② (home) **I'm looking for a ~ to live** ich bin auf Wohnungssuche ③ (fig: position, rank) Stellung f; **if I were in your ~ ...** ich an deiner Stelle ..., wenn ich du wäre ... ④ (proper position) ■ **to be in ~** an seinem Platz sein; (fig: completed) fertig sein; **arrangements** abgeschlossen; **to be out of ~** nicht an der richtigen Stelle sein; **person** fehl am Platz[e] sein ⑤ (job, position) Stelle f; (seat, on team) Platz m ⑥ (ranking) Platz m ▶PHRASES: **in the first/second ~** (firstly, secondly) erstens/zweitens; **to go ~s** (fam) weit kommen, es zu etw dat bringen; **to take ~** stattfinden II. vt ① (position) **to ~ an ad in the paper** eine Anzeige in die Zeitung setzen; **to ~ a bet on sth** auf etw akk

wetten ② (impose) embargo verhängen (on über +akk); **to ~ a limit on sth** etw begrenzen ③ (ascribe) **to ~ the blame on sb** jdm die Schuld geben; **to ~ importance on sth** auf etw akk Wert legen ④ (put in certain condition) **to ~ sb under surveillance** jdn unter Beobachtung stellen ⑤ (appoint to a position) **to ~ sb in charge [of sth]** jdm die Leitung [von etw dat] übertragen III. vi SPORT sich platzieren; (finish first or second) **to bet [a horse] to ~** eine Platzwette abschließen

placebo [plə·'si·boʊ] n MED Placebo nt

'place kick n SPORT Place-Kick m, Platzkick m

'place mat n Set nt o m, Platzdeckchen nt

placement ['pleɪs·mənt] n ① (being placed) Platzierung f ② (by job service) Vermittlung f; (job itself) Stelle f

'place name n Ortsname m

placid ['plæs·ɪd] adj ruhig, friedlich; person a. gelassen

plague [pleɪg] I. n ① (disease) Seuche f; ■ **the ~** die Pest ② (of insects) Plage f II. vt bedrängen; (irritate) ärgern

plaice <pl -> [pleɪs] n Scholle f

plaid [plæd] n FASHION Schottenmuster nt

plain [pleɪn] I. adj ① (simple, uncomplicated) einfach; **~ and simple** ganz einfach ② (clear) klar, offensichtlich; **to make sth ~** etw klarstellen ③ (unattractive) unscheinbar II. adv (fam: downright) einfach III. n GEOG Ebene f

'plainclothes adj attr Zivil-

plainly ['pleɪn·li] adv ① (simply) einfach ② (clearly) deutlich; (obviously) offensichtlich

plainness ['pleɪn·nɪs] n ① (simplicity) Einfachheit f ② (unattractiveness) Unscheinbarkeit f

plain'spoken adj direkt

plaintiff ['pleɪn·tɪf] n Kläger(in) m(f)

plan [plæn] I. n ① **to go according to ~** wie geplant verlaufen ② (intention) Plan m, Absicht f; **what are your ~s for this weekend?** was hast du dieses

Wochenende vor? **II.** *vt* <-nn-> planen **III.** *vi* ❶ (*prepare*) planen ❷ ▪**to ~ on sth** (*expect*) mit etw *dat* rechnen; (*intend*) etw vorhaben

plane[1] [pleɪn] *n* ❶ (*aircraft*) Flugzeug *nt;* **by ~** mit dem Flugzeug ❷ (*level*) Ebene *f*

plane[2] [pleɪn] *n* Hobel *m*

plane[3] [pleɪn] *n* (*tree*) Platane *f*

'**plane crash** *n* Flugzeugunglück *nt*

planet ['plæn·ɪt] *n* Planet *m;* **to be from a different ~** (*fig*) aus einer anderen Welt sein

plank [plæŋk] *n* (*timber*) Brett *nt;* (*in house*) Diele *f*

planner ['plæ·nər] *n* Planer(in) *m(f)*

planning ['plæ·nɪŋ] *n* Planung *f*

plant [plænt] **I.** *n* ❶ (*organism*) Pflanze *f* ❷ (*factory*) Werk *nt,* Betrieb *m* ❸ (*machinery*) Maschinen *pl* **II.** *vt* ❶ pflanzen ❷ (*fam: frame*) [heimlich] platzieren; ▪**to ~ sth on sb** jdm etw unterschieben

plantain ['plæn·tɪn] *n* FOOD, BOT Kochbanane *f*

plantation [plæn·'teɪ·ʃən] *n* Plantage *f*

planter ['plæn·tər] *n* ❶ (*plantation owner*) Pflanzer(in) *m(f)* ❷ (*container*) Blumentopf *m*

plaque [plæk] *n* ❶ (*plate*) Tafel *f;* **brass ~** Messingschild *nt* ❷ MED [Zahn]belag *m*

plasma ['plæz·mə] *n no pl* MED, PHYS, ASTRON Plasma *nt;* **~ screen** Plasmabildschirm *m*

plaster ['plæs·tər] **I.** *n* ARCHIT [Ver]putz *m* **II.** *vt* (*mortar*) verputzen

plastered ['plæs·tərd] *adj pred* (*fam*) stockbesoffen

plastic ['plæs·tɪk] **I.** *n* Plastik *nt kein pl* **II.** *adj* ❶ (*of plastic*) Plastik- ❷ (*pej: artificial*) künstlich

plastic '**bag** *n* Plastiktüte *f*

plastic '**bullet** *n* Gummigeschoss *nt*

plastic ex'**plosive** *n* Plastiksprengstoff *m*

plastic '**surgery** *n* Schönheitschirurgie *f*

'**plastic wrap** *n* Frischhaltefolie *f*

plate [pleɪt] *n* ❶ (*dish*) Teller *m*

❷ (*metal layer*) **gold ~** Vergoldung *f* ❸ AUTO **license ~** Nummernschild *nt*

plateau <*pl* -s> [plæ·'toʊ] *n* ❶ GEOG (*upland*) [Hoch]plateau *nt* ❷ ECON (*flat period*) **to reach a ~** stagnieren

plated ['pleɪ·tɪd] *adj* überzogen

plateful ['pleɪt·fʊl] *n* Teller *m;* **a ~ of lasagna** ein Teller *m* [voll] Lasagne

plate '**glass** *n* Flachglas *nt fachspr*

platform ['plæt·fɔrm] *n* ❶ (*elevated area*) Plattform *f* ❷ RAIL Bahnsteig *m* ❸ (*stage*) Podium *nt*

platform '**shoes** *npl* Plateauschuhe *pl*

plating ['pleɪ·tɪŋ] *n* Überzug *m*

platinum ['plæt·nəm] *n* Platin *nt*

platonic [plə·'tɑn·ɪk] *adj* platonisch

platoon [plə·'tun] *n* MIL Zug *m*

platter ['plæt·ər] *n* Platte *f*

plausibility [ˌplɔ·zə·'bɪl·ɪ·ti] *n* Plausibilität *f*

plausible ['plɔ·zə·bəl] *adj* plausibel

play [pleɪ] **I.** *n* ❶ (*recreation*) Spiel *m* ❷ THEAT [Theater]stück *nt* ❸ (*space for movement*) Spielraum *m* **II.** *vi* spielen; **to ~ for money** um Geld spielen ▶PHRASES: **to ~ for time** versuchen, Zeit zu gewinnen **III.** *vt* ❶ (*take part in*) spielen; **to ~ cards** Karten spielen ❷ (*compete against*) ▪**to ~ sb** gegen jdn spielen ❸ MUS spielen ❹ MUS, THEAT **to ~ the lead** die Hauptrolle spielen ❺ (*gamble*) **to ~ the stock market** an der Börse spekulieren ❻ (*perpetrate*) **~ a trick on sb** jdn hochnehmen *fig fam;* (*practical joke*) [jdm] einen Streich spielen ❼ (*execute*) **to ~ a shot** schießen; (*in pool*) stoßen ▶PHRASES: **to ~ ball** (*sl*) mitspielen *fam;* **to ~ one's cards right** geschickt taktieren; **to ~ it safe** auf Nummer sicher gehen

◆**play along** *vi* ▪**to ~ along with sth** etw [zum Schein] mitmachen

◆**play around** *vi* ❶ (*mess around*) *children* spielen; **stop ~ing around!** hör mir den Blödsinn auf! **play** ❷ (*experiment*) ▪**to ~ around with sth** mit etw *dat* [herum]spielen; (*try out*) etw ausprobieren

P

◆**play back** vt noch einmal abspielen

◆**play down** vt herunterspielen

◆**play off** vt ■**to ~ off** ⟳ **sb against sb** jdn gegen jdn ausspielen

◆**play on** vi ① (*exploit*) ■**to ~ on sth** etw ausnutzen ② (*keep playing*) weiterspielen

◆**play out** I. vt ① *usu passive* (*take place*) ■**to be ~ed out** *scene* sich abspielen ② (*play to end*) **to ~ out the last few seconds** SPORT die letzten Sekunden spielen II. vi zu Ende spielen

◆**play through** vt MUS [von Anfang bis Ende] [durch]spielen

◆**play up** I. vt hochspielen II. vi (*fam*) ■**to ~ up to sb** sich bei jdm einschmeicheln

◆**play with** I. vi ① (*entertain oneself with*) ■**to ~ with sth** mit etw *dat* spielen ② (*play together*) ■**to ~ with sb** mit jdm spielen ③ (*manipulate nervously*) ■**to ~ with sth** mit etw *dat* herumspielen *fam* II. vt (*vulg, fam*) ■**to ~ with oneself** an sich *dat* herumspielen

'**playback** n Playback nt

'**playboy** n (*usu pej*) Playboy m

player ['pleɪ·ər] n ① Spieler(in) m(f); **baseball ~** Baseballspieler(in) m(f) ② (*playback machine*) **CD ~** CD-Player m ③ POL (*participant*) **a key ~** Schlüsselfigur f

playful ['pleɪ·fəl] adj spielerisch

'**playground** n Spielplatz m

'**playhouse** n Spielhaus nt (*für Kinder*)

'**playing card** ['pleɪ·ɪŋ-] n Spielkarte f

'**playing field** ['pleɪ·ɪŋ-] n Sportplatz m

'**playoff** I. n Play-off nt II. adj **~ game** Entscheidungsspiel nt

'**playpen** n Laufstall m

'**playroom** n Spielzimmer nt

'**plaything** n Spielzeug nt

'**playtime** n (*in school*) Pause f

'**playwright** n Dramatiker(in) m(f)

plaza ['plɑ·zə] n [**shopping**] **~** Einkaufszentrum m

plea [pli] n ① (*appeal*) Appell m ② LAW **to enter a ~** eine Einrede erheben

'**plea bargaining** n LAW *Vereinbarung zwischen Staatsanwalt und Angeklag-* *tem, der sich zu einem geringeren Straftatbestand bekennen soll*

plead <pleaded *or* pled, pleaded *or* pled> I. vi ① (*implore*) [flehentlich] bitten, flehen; ■**to ~ with sb** [**to do sth**] jdn anflehen[, etw zu tun] ② LAW (*as advocate*) plädieren; (*speak for*) ■**to ~ for sb** jdn verteidigen ③ + adj LAW (*answer charge*) **to ~ guilty** sich schuldig bekennen II. vt ① (*claim*) behaupten ② (*argue for*) **to ~ a case** LAW eine Sache vor Gericht vertreten

pleading ['pli·dɪŋ] adj flehend

pleasant ['plez·ənt] adj ① *experience* angenehm ② (*friendly*) freundlich

please [pliz] I. *interj* ① (*in requests*) bitte ② (*when accepting sth*) ja, bitte; **more potatoes? — ~** noch Kartoffeln? – gern II. vt (*make happy*) ■**to ~ sb** jdm gefallen; **to be hard to ~** schwer zufrieden zu stellen sein III. vi **eager to ~** [unbedingt] gefallen wollen

pleased [plizd] adj (*happy*) froh, erfreut; (*content*) zufrieden; ■**to be ~ that ...** froh sein, dass ...

pleasing ['pli·zɪŋ] adj angenehm; **to be ~ to the ear** hübsch klingen

pleasurable ['pleʒ·ər·ə·bəl] adj angenehm

pleasure ['pleʒ·ər] n Freude f; **to give sb ~** jdm Freude bereiten; **to take ~ in doing sth** Vergnügen daran finden, etw *akk* zu tun

pleat [plit] n Falte f

pled [pled] vt, vi pt, pp of **plead**

pledge [pledʒ] I. n (*promise*) Versprechen nt; **to make a ~ that ...** geloben, dass ... II. vt versprechen

plentiful ['plen·tɪ·fəl] adj reichlich *präd*

plenty ['plen·ti] I. n (*form: abundance*) Reichtum m II. adv (*fam*) **~ more** noch viel mehr III. pron ① (*more than enough*) mehr als genug; **~ of money/ time** viel Geld/Zeit ② (*a lot*) genug; **~ to see** viel zu sehen

pliable ['plaɪ·ə·bəl] adj biegsam

pliers ['plaɪ·ərz] npl Zange f

plight [plaɪt] n Not[lage] f

plod [plɑd] vi <-dd-> ① (*walk slowly*)

stapfen ② (*work slowly*) ∎ **to ~ through sth** sich durch etw *akk* hindurcharbeiten

◆**plod away** *vi* vor sich *akk* hin arbeiten

plop [plɒp] *vi* <-pp-> ① (*fall into liquid*) platschen *fam* ② (*drop heavily*) plumpsen *fam*

plot [plɒt] I. *n* ① (*conspiracy*) Verschwörung *f* ② LIT (*story line*) Handlung *f* ③ (*of land*) Parzelle *f*; **vegetable ~** Gemüsebeet *nt* II. *vt* <-tt-> (*conspire*) [im Geheimen] planen *a. hum* III. *vi* <-tt-> ∎ **to ~ against sb** sich gegen jdn verschwören

◆**plot out** *vt* ① *route* [grob] planen ② *scene, story* umreißen

plotter ['plɒt·ər] *n* ① (*conspirator*) Verschwörer(in) *m(f)* ② COMPUT Plotter *m*

plow [plaʊ] I. *n* Pflug *m* II. *vt, vi* AGR pflügen

◆**plow into** I. *vi* ∎ **to ~ into sth** in etw *akk* hineinrasen II. *vt* ∎ **to ~ sth into sth** etw in etw *akk* investieren

◆**plow up** *vt land* umpflügen; *lawn* umgraben

ploy [plɔɪ] *n* Plan *m*

pluck [plʌk] I. *n* Mut *m* II. *vt* ① (*pick*) ∎ **to ~ sth [from sth]** *flower* etw [von etw *dat*] abpflücken ② *feathers* ausrupfen; *hair* entfernen

◆**pluck up** *vt* **to ~ up the courage [to do sth]** allen Mut zusammennehmen[, um etw zu tun]

plug [plʌg] I. *n* ① (*connector*) Stecker *m*; **to pull the ~ [on sth]** den Stecker [aus etw *dat*] herausziehen ② (*socket*) Steckdose *f* ③ (*for sink*) Stöpsel *m* II. *vt* <-gg-> ① *leak* stopfen, [zu]stopfen (**with** mit +*dat*) ② (*publicize*) anpreisen

◆**plug away** *vi* verbissen arbeiten (**at** an +*dat*)

◆**plug in** I. *vt* einstöpseln II. *vi* (*electrical device*) sich anschließen lassen

◆**plug up** *vt* zustopfen

'**plug-in** *n* Zusatz *m*

plum [plʌm] I. *n* Pflaume *f* II. *adj* ① (*color*) pflaumenfarben ② *attr* (*desirable*) **~ job** Traumberuf *m*

plumb[1] [plʌm] I. *vt* (*determine depth*) [aus]loten II. *adj pred* gerade III. *adv* ① (*fam: squarely*) genau ② (*fam: completely*) **~ crazy** total verrückt

plumb[2] [plʌm] *vt* ∎ **to ~ sth into sth** etw an etw *akk* anschließen

'**plumb bob** *n* Lot *nt*

plumber ['plʌm·ər] *n* Klempner(in) *m(f)*

plumbing ['plʌm·ɪŋ] *n* Wasserleitungen *pl*

plume [plum] *n* ① (*large feather*) Feder *f* ② (*cloud*) **~ of smoke** Rauchwolke *f*

plummet ['plʌm·ɪt] I. *vi* ① (*plunge*) fallen ② *prices* in den Keller purzeln *fam* II. *n see* **plumb bob**

plump [plʌmp] *adj* (*rounded*) rund; (*euph*) *person* füllig

◆**plump down** (*fam*) I. *vt* ∎ **to ~ down** ↻ **sth** etw hinplumpsen lassen *fam* II. *vi* ∎ **to ~ down in a chair** sich auf einen Stuhl fallen lassen

◆**plump up** *vt cushion* aufschütteln

plumpness ['plʌmp·nɪs] *n* Fülligkeit *f*

plunder ['plʌn·dər] I. *vt, vi* plündern II. *vi* plündern III. *n* (*booty*) Beute *f*

plunge [plʌndʒ] I. *n* (*drop*) Sprung *m*; (*fall*) Sturz *m*; (*dive*) **to make a ~** tauchen II. *vi* ① (*fall*) stürzen (**into** +*akk*) ② (*decrease dramatically*) dramatisch sinken III. *vt* (*immerse*) ∎ **to ~ sth into sth** etw in etw *akk* eintauchen; (*in cooking*) etw in etw *akk* geben

◆**plunge in** *vi* ① (*dive in*) eintauchen ② (*fig: get involved*) sich einmischen

plunger ['plʌn·dʒər] *n* Saugpumpe *f*

plunk [plʌŋk] I. *n* (*fam: sound*) Ploppen *nt* II. *vt* (*fam*) ① (*set down heavily*) ∎ **to ~ sth somewhere** etw irgendwo hinknallen ② (*sit heavily*) **to ~ oneself down on a chair** sich auf einen Stuhl plumpsen lassen

◆**plunk down** *vt* (*fam*) ∎ **to ~ oneself down** sich hinplumpsen lassen

P

pluperfect ['plu·ˌpɜr·fɪkt] *n* LING ■**the ~** das Plusquamperfekt

plural ['plʊr·əl] *n* ■**the ~** der Plural

plus [plʌs] I. *prep* plus II. *n* <*pl* -es> Plus *nt kein pl fam* III. *adj* ❶ *attr* (*above zero*) ~ **two degrees** zwei Grad plus ❷ *pred* (*or more*) mindestens; **20 ~** mindestens 20

plush [plʌʃ] I. *adj* (*luxurious*) exklusiv II. *n* Plüsch *m*

'plus sign *n* Pluszeichen *nt*

plutonium [plu·'tou·ni·əm] *n* Plutonium *nt*

ply[1] [plaɪ] *n* ❶ (*thickness*) Stärke *f* ❷ (*layer*) Schicht *f*

ply[2] <-ie-> [plaɪ] *vt* ❶ (*sell*) drugs handeln ❷ (*supply continuously*) **to ~ sb with wine** jdn mit Wein abfüllen *fam*

'plywood *n* Sperrholz *nt*

pm, p.m. [ˌpiː·'em] *adv abbrev of* **post meridian: eight ~** acht Uhr abends, zwanzig Uhr

PMS [ˌpiː·em·'es] *n* MED *abbrev of* **premenstrual syndrome** PMS *nt*

pneumonia [nu·'moʊn·jə] *n* Lungenentzündung *f*

PO [ˌpiː·'oʊ] *n abbrev of* **Post Office**

poach[1] [poʊtʃ] *vt* pochieren

poach[2] [poʊtʃ] *vt* ❶ (*catch illegally*) wildern ❷ *ideas* stehlen ❸ *employee* abwerben (**from** +*dat*)

poacher ['poʊ·tʃər] *n* Wilderer *m*

P'O box *n abbrev of* **Post Office Box** Postfach

pocket ['pɑk·ɪt] I. *n* ❶ (*in clothing*) Tasche *f* ❷ (*on bag*) Fach *nt* ❸ (*fig: financial resources*) **out of one's own ~** aus eigener Tasche II. *vt* ❶ (*put in one's pocket*) in die Tasche stecken ❷ (*keep sth for oneself*) behalten

'pocketbook *n* Handtasche *f*

'pocketknife *n* Taschenmesser *nt*

'pocket money *n* Taschengeld *nt*

'pocket-size(d) *adj* im Taschenformat *nach n*

pod [pɑd] *n* ❶ (*seed container*) Hülse *f*; *pea* Schote *f* ❷ (*K-cup*) **coffee ~** Kaffeepad *nt*

podiatrist [pə·'daɪ·ə·trɪst] *n* Fußpfleger(in) *m(f)*

podium <*pl* -dia> ['poʊ·di·əm] *n* Podium *nt*

poem ['poʊ·əm] *n* (*a. fig*) Gedicht *nt*

poet ['poʊ·ət] *n* Dichter(in) *m(f)*

poetic(al) [poʊ·'et·ɪk(əl)] *adj* (*relating to poetry*) dichterisch; ~ **language** Dichtersprache *f*

poetry ['poʊ·ɪ·tri] *n* Dichtung *f*

poignant ['pɔɪn·jənt] *adj* bewegend

poinsettia [pɔɪnt·'set·i·ə] *n* Weihnachtsstern *m*

point [pɔɪnt] I. *n* ❶ (*sharp end*) Spitze *f* ❷ (*decimal point*) Komma ❸ (*position*) Punkt *m;* ~ **of contact** Berührungspunkt *m* ❹ (*particular time*) Zeitpunkt *m;* **at that ~** zu diesem Zeitpunkt; (*then*) in diesem Augenblick ❺ (*argument, issue*) Punkt *m;* **she made the ~ that ...** sie wies darauf hin, dass ...; (*stress*) sie betonte, dass ...; **ok, ~ taken** o. k., ich hab schon begriffen *fam* ❻ (*most important idea*) **to come to the ~** auf den Punkt kommen ❼ (*purpose*) Sinn *m*, Zweck *m* ❽ (*stage in process*) Punkt *m;* **from that ~ on ...** von diesem Moment an ...; **up to a ~** bis zu einem gewissen Grad ❾ SPORT Punkt *m* ❿ (*important characteristic*) Merkmal *nt;* **good ~s** gute Seiten II. *vi* ❶ (*with finger*) zeigen (**at/to** auf +*akk*) ❷ (*be directed*) weisen; **to ~ west** nach Westen zeigen ❸ (*indicate*) hinweisen (**to** auf +*akk*) III. *vt* ❶ (*aim*) ■**to ~ sth at sb** *weapon* etw [auf jdn] richten ❷ (*direct*) **to ~ sb in the direction of sth** jdm den Weg zu etw *dat* beschreiben

◆**point out** *vt* ❶ (*show*) ■**to ~ out** ○ **sth** [**to sb**] [jdn] auf etw hinweisen; (*with finger*) [jdn] etw zeigen ❷ (*inform*) ■**to ~ out that ...** darauf aufmerksam machen, dass ...

point-'blank *adv* ❶ (*at very close range*) aus nächster Nähe ❷ (*bluntly*) geradewegs

pointed ['pɔɪn·tɪd] *adj* ❶ (*with sharp*

point) spitz ❷ (*emphatic*) pointiert *geh; criticism* scharf

pointer ['pɔɪn·tər] *n* ❶ (*on dial*) Zeiger *m* ❷ *usu pl* (*fam: tip*) Tipp *m*

pointless ['pɔɪnt·lɪs] *adj* sinnlos, zwecklos

point of 'view <*pl* points of view> *n* Ansicht *f*

poise [pɔɪz] I. *n* Haltung *f* II. *vt usu passive* ❶ (*balance*) balancieren; (*hover*) ■ **to be ~d** schweben ❷ (*fig*) ■ **to be ~d to do sth** (*about to*) nahe daran sein, etw zu tun

poised [pɔɪzd] *adj* beherrscht

poison ['pɔɪ·zən] I. *n* Gift *nt* II. *vt* vergiften

poison 'gas *n* Giftgas *nt*

poisoning ['pɔɪ·zə·nɪŋ] *n* ❶ (*act*) Vergiften *nt* ❷ (*condition*) Vergiftung *f*; **blood ~** Blutvergiftung *f*

poison 'ivy *n* Giftsumach *m*

poisonous ['pɔɪ·zə·nəs] *adj* giftig

poke¹ [poʊk] I. *n* (*jab*) Stoß *m* II. *vt* ❶ (*prod*) anstoßen; (*with umbrella, stick*) stechen; **to ~ a hole in sth** ein Loch in etw *akk* bohren ❷ ■ **to ~ sth into/through sth** (*prod with*) etw in/durch etw *akk* stecken ❸ *fire* schüren ▶PHRASES: **to ~ one's nose into sb's business** (*fam*) seine Nase in jds Angelegenheiten stecken III. *vi* ❶ (*jab repeatedly*) herumfummeln *fam* (**at** an + *dat*) ❷ (*break through*) ■ **to ~ through** durchscheinen

◆ **poke around** *vi* (*fam*) herumstöbern

◆ **poke out** I. *vi* ■ **to ~ out** [**of sth**] [aus etw *dat*] hervorgucken II. *vt* *tongue* herausstrecken

◆ **poke up** *vi* hervorragen

poke² [poʊk] *n* ▶PHRASES: **to buy a pig in a ~** (*pej*) die Katze im Sack kaufen *fig*

poker¹ ['poʊ·kər] *n* (*card game*) Poker *m* o *nt*

poker² ['poʊ·kər] *n* (*fireplace tool*) Schürhaken *m*

pokey, poky ['poʊ·ki] *adj* (*pej: slow*) lahm

Poland ['poʊ·lənd] *n* Polen *nt*

'polar bear *n* Eisbär *m*

polarize ['poʊ·lə·raɪz] *vt, vi* [sich] polarisieren

pole¹ [poʊl] *n* ❶ GEOG, ELEC Pol *m* ❷ (*extreme*) **to be ~s apart** Welten voneinander entfernt sein

pole² [poʊl] *n* Stange *f*; **flag~** Fahnenmast *m*

'pole vault *n* Stabhochsprung *m kein pl*

'pole-vaulter *n* Stabhochspringer(in) *m(f)*

police [pə·'lis] I. *n* + *pl vb* ❶ (*force*) ■ **the ~** die Polizei; **to call the ~** die Polizei rufen ❷ (*police officers*) Polizisten, -innen *mpl, fpl* II. *vt* ❶ (*maintain law and order*) überwachen ❷ (*regulate*) ■ **to ~ sth** etw kontrollieren

po'lice car *n* Polizeiauto *nt*

po'lice department *n* Polizeidienststelle *f*

po'lice dog *n* Polizeihund *m*

po'lice force *n* ❶ (*the police*) ■ **the ~** die Polizei ❷ (*unit of police*) Polizeieinheit *f*

po'liceman *n* Polizist *m*

po'lice officer *n* Polizeibeamte(r) *m*, Polizeibeamte [o -in] *f*

po'lice station *n* Polizeiwache *f*

po'licewoman *n* Polizistin *f*

policy¹ ['pal·ə·si] *n* ❶ (*plan*) Programm *nt* ❷ Politik *f*

policy² ['pal·ə·si] *n* (*for insurance*) Police *f*

'policyholder *n* Versicherungsnehmer(in) *m(f)*

'policymaker *n* Parteiideologe, -ideologin *m, f*

polio [ˌpoʊ·li·oʊ], **poliomyelitis** [ˌpoʊ·li·oʊˌmaɪ·ə·'laɪ·təs] *n* (*spec*) Kinderlähmung *f*

polish ['pal·ɪʃ] I. *n* ❶ (*substance*) Politur *f*; **shoe ~** Schuhcreme *f* ❷ (*fig: refinement*) [gesellschaftlicher] Schliff II. *vt* polieren; *shoes* putzen

◆ **polish off** *vt* ❶ *food* verdrücken *fam* ❷ (*fam: beat*) abfertigen, abservieren

Polish ['poʊ·lɪʃ] I. *n* Polnisch *nt* II. *adj* polnisch

P

polished ['pal·ɪʃt] *adj* ❶ (*gleaming*) glänzend *attr* ❷ *performance* großartig

polite [pə·'laɪt] *adj* höflich

politeness [pə·'laɪt·nɪs] *n* Höflichkeit *f*

political [pə·'lɪt̬·ɪ·kəl] *adj* politisch; **~ leaders** politische Größen *pl*

political cor'rectness *n* politische Korrektheit

politically cor'rect *adj* politisch korrekt

politician [ˌpal·ə·'tɪʃ·ən] *n* Politiker(in) *m(f)*

politics ['pal·ə·tɪks] *npl* ❶ + *sing vb* Politik *f kein pl;* **to go into ~** in die Politik gehen ❷ + *sing/pl vb* (*within group*) **office ~** Büroklüngelei *f pej*

polka ['poʊl·kə] *n* Polka *f*

'polka dot *n usu pl* Tupfen *m*

poll [poʊl] **I.** *n* ❶ (*public survey*) Erhebung *f;* **an opinion ~** eine Meinungsumfrage ❷ (*number of votes cast*) Wahlbeteiligung *f* **II.** *vt* ❶ (*canvass in poll*) befragen ❷ (*receive*) **the party ~ed 67% of the vote** die Partei hat 67 % der Stimmen erhalten

pollen ['pal·ən] *n* Blütenstaub *m*

'pollen count *n* Pollenflug *m kein pl*

polling ['poʊl·ɪŋ] *n* Wahl *f*

'polling booth *n* Wahlkabine *f*

pollutant [pə·'lu·tənt] *n* Schadstoff *m*

pollute [pə·'lut] *vt* verschmutzen

polluter [pə·'lu·tər] *n* Umweltverschmutzer(in) *m(f)*

pollution [pə·'lu·ʃən] *n* Verschmutzung *f;* **environmental ~** Umweltverschmutzung *f*

polo ['poʊ·loʊ] *n* Polo *nt*

'polo shirt *n* Polohemd *nt*

polyester [ˌpal·i·'es·tər] *n* Polyester *m*

polyethylene [ˌpal·ɪ·'eθ·ə·lin] *n* Polyäthylen *nt*

polygamous [pə·'lɪg·ə·məs] *adj* polygam *geh*

polygon ['pal·i·gan] *n* Vieleck *nt*, Polygon *nt fachspr*

polygraph ['pal·i·græf] *n* Lügendetektor *m*

polyp ['pal·ɪp] *n* MED, ZOOL Polyp *m*

polystyrene [ˌpal·i·'staɪ·rin] *n* Styropor® *nt*

polytechnic [ˌpal·i·'tek·nɪk] **I.** *adj* *institute* Technische Hochschule *f* **II.** *n* Fachhochschule *f*

polyunsaturated fats [ˌpal·i·ʌn·'sæt̬·ə·reɪ·tɪd-], **polyunsaturates** [ˌpal·i·ʌn·'sæt̬·ə·reɪts] *npl* (*fatty acids*) mehrfach ungesättigte Fettsäuren; (*fats*) Fette mit einem hohen Anteil an mehrfach ungesättigten Fettsäuren

polyurethane [ˌpal·i·'jʊr·ə·θeɪn] *n* Polyurethan *nt*

pomegranate ['pam·græn·ɪt] *n* Granatapfel *m*

pompon ['pam·pan], **pompom** ['pam·pam] *n* ❶ (*of cheerleader*) Pompon *m* ❷ (*yarn ball*) Quaste *f*

pompous ['pam·pəs] *adj* ❶ *person* selbstgefällig ❷ *language* geschraubt *pej*

poncho ['pan·tʃoʊ] *n* Poncho *m*

pond [pand] *n* ❶ (*body of water*) Teich *m* ❷ (*hum: Atlantic Ocean*) ∎**the ~** der große Teich

ponder ['pan·dər] **I.** *vt* durchdenken **II.** *vi* nachdenken

pone [poʊn] *n* **[corn] ~** Maisbrot *nt*

pontificate [pan·'tɪf·ɪ·kɪt] *vi* (*pej*) ∎**to ~ about sth** sich über etw *akk* auslassen

pontoon [pan·'tun] *n* Ponton *m*

pontoon 'bridge *n* Pontonbrücke *f*

pony ['poʊ·ni] *n* (*small horse*) Pony *nt*

'ponytail *n* Pferdeschwanz *m*

poo [pu] *n* (*childspeak sl*) Aa *nt kein pl*

poodle ['pu·dəl] *n* Pudel *m*

poof [puf] *interj* (*fam*) hui!

pooh [pu] *interj* (*fam: in disgust*) pfui!, igitt!

pooh-pooh [ˌpu·'pu] *vt* (*fam*) abtun

pool¹ [pul] **I.** *n* Becken *nt;* [**swimming**] **~** Schwimmbecken *nt;* (*private*) Swimmingpool *m;* (*public*) Schwimmbad *nt* **II.** *vi liquid* sich stauen

pool² [pul] **I.** *n* SPORT Poolbillard *nt* **II.** *vt* zusammenlegen

'pool hall *n* Billardzimmer *nt*

'pool table *n* Poolbillardtisch *m*

poop¹ [pup] *n* (*of ship*) Heck *nt*

poop² [pup] **I.** *n* (*euph: excrement*) Aa *nt;* **dog ~** Hundedreck *m fam* **II.** *vi* *(fam: defecate)* Aa machen *Kindersprache*

◆**poop** '**out** *vi* ❶ *(become tired)* schlappmachen ❷ *(not persevere)* sich geschlagen geben

pooped [pupt] *adj (fam)* erschöpft, [fix und] fertig

pooper scooper ['pu·pər‚sku·pər] *n (fam)* Kotschaufel *f (Schaufel zum Entfernen von Hundekot)*

poor [pʊr] *adj* ❶ *(lacking money)* arm ❷ *(inadequate)* unzureichend, schlecht; **to be in ~ health** in schlechtem gesundheitlichen Zustand sein ❸ *attr (deserving of pity)* arm

poorly ['pʊr·li] *adv* ~ **dressed** ärmlich gekleidet

poor re'lation *n* arme(r) Verwandte(r) *f(m)*

pop¹ [pap] **I.** *n* ❶ *(noise)* Knall *m* ❷ *usu sing (sl)* **a ~** pro Stück **II.** *adv* **to go ~** *(make noise)* einen Knall machen **III.** *vi* <-pp-> ❶ *(make noise)* knallen ❷ *(burst)* platzen **IV.** *vt* <-pp-> ❶ *(burst)* platzen lassen ❷ *(put quickly)* ~ **the pizza in the oven** schieb' die Pizza in den Ofen ▶PHRASES: **to ~ pills** Pillen schlucken

◆**pop in** *vi* vorbeischauen
◆**pop out** *vi* herausspringen
◆**pop up** *vi* ❶ *(appear unexpectedly)* auftauchen ❷ *(in baseball: hit a short, high fly ball)* einen Popup schlagen

pop² [pap] *n (fam)* Papa *m*
pop³ [pap] *n (music)* Pop *m*
'**pop art** *n* Pop-Art *f*
'**popcorn** *n* Popcorn *nt*
pope [poʊp] *n* Papst *m*
poplar ['pap·lər] *n* Pappel *f*
poplin ['pap·lɪn] *n* Popelin *f*
'**pop music** *n* Popmusik *f*
poppy ['pap·i] *n* Mohnblume *f*
Popsicle® ['pap·sɪ·kəl] *n* Eis *nt* am Stiel
'**pop singer** *n* Popsänger(in) *m(f)*
popular ['pap·jə·lər] *adj* ❶ *(widely liked)* beliebt ❷ *attr (not highbrow)* populär ❸ *attr (widespread)* weit verbreitet; **it is a ~ belief that ...** viele glauben, dass ...

popularity [‚pap·jə·'lær·ɪ·t̬i] *n* Beliebtheit *f*

popularize ['pap·jə·lə·raɪz] *vt (make accessible)* breiteren Kreisen zugänglich machen

popularly ['pap·jə·lər·li] *adv (commonly)* allgemein; **as is ~ believed** wie man allgemein annimmt

populate ['pap·jə·leɪt] *vt usu passive (inhabit)* ■**to be ~d** bevölkert sein; *island* bewohnt sein

population [‚pap·jə·'leɪ·ʃən] *n* ❶ *usu sing (inhabitants)* Bevölkerung *f kein pl* ❷ *(number of people)* Einwohnerzahl *f*

population 'density *n* Bevölkerungsdichte *f*

population ex'plosion *n* Bevölkerungsexplosion *f*

porcelain ['pɔr·sə·lɪn] *n* Porzellan *nt*

porch <*pl* -es> ['pɔrtʃ] *n* ❶ Vordach *nt* ❷ *(veranda)* Veranda *f*

porcupine ['pɔr·kju·paɪn] *n* Stachelschwein *nt*

pore¹ [pɔr] *vi (examine)* brüten (**over** über + *dat*)

pore² [pɔr] *n* Pore *f*

pork [pɔrk] *n* Schweinefleisch *nt*

'**pork chop** *n* Schweinekotelett *nt*

porky ['pɔr·ki] *adj (pej fam)* fett

porn [pɔrn] *n short for* **pornography** *(fam)* Porno *m*

pornographic [‚pɔr·nə·'græf·ɪk] *adj (containing pornography)* pornografisch, Porno-

pornography [pɔr·'nag·rə·fi] *n* Pornografie *f*

porous ['pɔr·əs] *adj* porös

porpoise ['pɔr·pəs] *n* Tümmler *m*

porridge ['pɔr·ɪdʒ] *n* Porridge *m o nt*

port¹ [pɔrt] *n* ❶ *(harbor)* Hafen *m* ❷ *(town)* Hafenstadt *f*

port² [pɔrt] *n* AVIAT, NAUT Backbord *nt*

port³ [pɔrt] *n* COMPUT Anschluss *m*, Port *m fachspr*

port⁴ [pɔrt] *n (wine)* Portwein *m*

portable ['pɔr·t̬ə·bəl] *adj* tragbar

portal ['pɔr·t̬ᵊl] *n* ❶ *(form)* Portal *nt* ❷ INET Portal *nt;* **web** *[or* **Internet***]* ~ Onlineportal *nt,* Internetportal *nt*

P

porter ['pɔr·tər] *n* Gepäckträger *m*

portfolio [pɔrt·'fou·li·ou] *n* ❶ (*of drawings*) Mappe *f* ❷ FIN Portefeuille *nt fachspr*

'porthole *n* NAUT Bullauge *nt;* AVIAT Kabinenfenster *nt*

portion ['pɔr·ʃən] I. *n* ❶ (*part*) Teil *m* ❷ (*serving*) Portion *f;* (*piece*) Stück *nt* II. *vt* ▪ **to ~ out** ⟳ **sth** etw aufteilen

portrait ['pɔr·trɪt] I. *n* Porträt *nt* II. *adj* TYPO **in ~ format** im Hochformat

portray [pɔr·'treɪ] *vt* ❶ (*paint*) porträtieren ❷ (*describe*) darstellen

Portugal ['pɔr·tʃə·gəl] *n* Portugal *nt*

pose [pouz] I. *n* ❶ (*bodily position*) Haltung *f* ❷ *usu sing* (*pretence*) Getue *nt* II. *vi* ❶ (*adopt position*) posieren ❷ (*pretend*) ▪ **to ~ as** sich ausgeben als III. *vt* ❶ (*cause*) aufwerfen; **to ~ a threat to sb** eine Bedrohung für jdn darstellen ❷ (*question*) stellen

poser ['pou·zər] *n* (*pej fam: person*) Angeber(in) *m(f)*

posh [pɑʃ] *adj* (*fam*) vornehm

position [pə·'zɪʃ·ən] I. *n* ❶ (*place*) Platz *m;* (*building*) Lage *f* ❷ (*in navigation*) Position *f* ❸ (*posture*) Stellung *f;* **to change one's ~** eine andere Stellung einnehmen ❹ SPORT (*in team*) [Spieler]position *f* ❺ (*rank*) Position *f;* (*in race, competition*) Platz *m* II. *vt* platzieren

positive ['paz·ɪ·tɪv] *adj* ❶ (*certain*) bestimmt; ▪ **to be ~ about sth** sich *dat* einer S. *gen* sicher sein ❷ (*optimistic, med, math, elec*) positiv

positively ['paz·ɪ·tɪv·li] *adv* ❶ (*definitely*) bestimmt; **promise** fest ❷ **think** positiv

posse ['pɑs·i] *n* (*hist: summoned by sheriff*) [Hilfs]trupp *m*

possess [pə·'zes] *vt* ❶ besitzen ❷ *usu passive* (*control*) **to be ~ed by the Devil** vom Teufel besessen sein

possession [pə·'zeʃ·ən] *n* ❶ (*having*) Besitz *m;* ▪ **to be in sb's ~** sich in jds Besitz befinden ❷ *usu pl* (*something owned*) Besitz *m kein pl*

possessive [pə·'zes·ɪv] *adj* ❶ (*not sharing*) eigen ❷ (*jealous*) besitzergreifend

possibility [ˌpɑs·ə·'bɪl·ɪ·ti] *n* ❶ Möglichkeit *f;* **there's a ~ that ...** es kann sein, dass ... ❷ (*potential*) ▪ **possibilities** *pl* Möglichkeiten *pl*

possible ['pɑs·ə·bəl] *adj* möglich; **it's just not ~** das ist einfach nicht machbar; **as much as ~** so viel wie möglich

possibly ['pɑs·ə·bli] *adv* ❶ (*feasibly*) **he couldn't ~ have known that** das kann er doch unmöglich gewusst haben! ❷ (*perhaps*) möglicherweise; **very ~** durchaus möglich

possum <*pl* -> ['pɑs·əm] *n* Opossum *nt*

post¹ [poust] *n* ❶ (*pole*) Pfosten *m* ❷ (*fam*) **goal ~** [Tor]pfosten *m* II. *vt* COMPUT **to ~ sth on the [Inter]net** etw über das Internet bekannt geben

post² [poust] *n* MIL Stützpunkt *m*

postage ['pou·stɪdʒ] *n* Porto *nt*

'postage meter *n* Frankiermaschine *f*

postal ['pou·stəl] *adj attr* Post- ▸ PHRASES: **to go ~** (*sl*) Amok laufen

'postcard *n* Postkarte *f*

post'date *vt* (*give later date*) vordatieren

poster ['pou·stər] *n* [Werbe]plakat *nt*

post'graduate *n* Postgraduierte(r) *f(m) fachspr*

posthumous ['pɑs·tʃə·məs] *adj* (*form*) post[h]um

posting ['pou·stɪŋ] *n* COMPUT (*message*) Posting *nt*

'postmark I. *n* Poststempel *m* II. *vt usu passive* ▪ **to be ~ed** abgestempelt sein

'postmaster *n* Leiter *m* einer Postdienststelle

post'modern *adj* post-modern

postmortem [ˌpoust·'mɔr·təm] I. *n* ❶ MED *see* **autopsy** ❷ (*fam: discussion*) Manöverkritik *f hum* II. *adj attr* (*done after death*) nach dem Tod *nach n*

'post office *n* ▪ **the ~** die Post *kein pl*

postpone [poust·'poun] *vt* verschieben

'postscript *n* Postskript[um] *nt*

posture ['pɑs·tʃər] *n* [Körper]haltung *f*

posy ['pou·zi] *n* Sträußchen *nt*

pot¹ [pɑt] I. *n* ❶ Topf *m;* **coffee ~** Kaffeekanne f ❷ (*for plants*) Blumentopf m II. vt <-tt-> *plants* eintopfen

pot² [pat] n (*sl*) Pot nt

potassium [pə'tæs·i·əm] n Kalium nt

potato [pə'teɪ·toʊ] n Kartoffel f; **baked ~** Ofenkartoffel f

po'tato chip n usu pl Kartoffelchip m

po'tato peeler n Kartoffelschäler m

potbellied [pat·belid] adj dickbäuchig

potency ['poʊ·tən·si] n ❶ (*strength*) Stärke f; *of temptation, a spell* Macht f; *of a drug* Wirksamkeit f ❷ (*sexual*) Potenz f

potent ['poʊ·tənt] adj ❶ (*strong*) mächtig; *drink* stark; *argument* schlagkräftig ❷ (*sexual*) potent

potential [pə'ten·ʃəl] I. adj potenziell geh, möglich II. n Potenzial nt geh

potentially [pə'ten·ʃə·li] adv potenziell geh; **~ disastrous** möglicherweise verheerend; **sth is ~ fatal** etw kann tödlich sein

'potholder n Topflappen m

'pothole n (*in road*) Schlagloch nt

pot'luck n attr FOOD (*communal meal*) **~ dinner** Abendessen, zu dem jeder eine Speise mitbringt

potpourri [poʊ·pʊ·'ri] n Potpourri nt

'pot roast n Schmorbraten m

'potshot n ❶ (*with gun*) blinder Schuss ❷ (*fig: verbal attack*) Seitenhieb m

potter ['pat·ər] n Töpfer(in) m(f)

pottery ['pat·ə·ri] n ❶ Keramik f *kein pl* ❷ (*factory*) Töpferei f

potty ['pat·i] n Töpfchen nt

pouch <pl -es> [paʊtʃ] n ❶ (*small bag*) Beutel m ❷ ZOOL (*of kangaroo*) Beutel m

poultry ['poʊl·tri] n pl Geflügel nt *kein pl*

pounce [paʊns] vi ❶ (*jump*) losspringen; *animal* einen Satz machen ❷ (*fig: seize opportunity*) zuschlagen

pound¹ [paʊnd] n (*unit of weight*) ≈ Pfund nt (*454 g*)

pound² [paʊnd] I. vt ❶ (*hit repeatedly*) ■**to ~ sth** auf etw akk hämmern ❷ MIL (*bombard*) **to ~ enemy positions** die feindlichen Stellungen bombardieren

II. vi (*beat*) *pulse* schlagen; *heart a.* pochen

pounding ['paʊn·dɪŋ] I. n ❶ (*noise*) *of guns* Knattern nt; (*in head*) Pochen nt; *of waves* Brechen nt ❷ (*attack*) Beschuss m *kein pl*; **to take a ~** unter schweren Beschuss geraten ❸ (*defeat*) Niederlage f; (*in election, match*) Schlappe f II. adj *drum* dröhnend; *head* pochend

pour [pɔr] I. vt ❶ (*cause to flow*) gießen (**into/onto** in/auf +akk); ■**to ~ sb sth** jdm etw einschenken ❷ (*fig: give in large amounts*) *resources* fließen lassen (**into** in +akk); *energy* stecken (**into** in +akk) II. vi ❶ (*flow*) fließen (**into/out of** in/aus +akk) ❷ impers (*rain*) **it's ~ing** [*rain*] es schüttet wie aus Kübeln *fam*

♦**pour in** vi hereinströmen, hineinströmen; *letters, donations* massenweise eintreffen

♦**pour out** I. vt ❶ *liquids* ausgießen, herauskippen; *solids* ausschütten ❷ (*produce quickly*) ausstoßen II. vi (*come out*) ausströmen; *smoke* herausquellen

pout [paʊt] I. vi einen Schmollmund machen II. n Schmollmund m

poverty ['pav·ər·ti] n Armut f

'poverty line n ■**the ~** die Armutsgrenze

'poverty-stricken adj bitterarm

POW [ˌpi·oʊ·'dʌb·əl·ju] n abbrev of **prisoner of war** KG

powder ['paʊ·dər] I. n Pulver nt II. vt pudern

powdered ['paʊ·dərd] adj ❶ (*in powder form*) Pulver-; **~ sugar** Puderzucker m ❷ (*covered with powder*) gepudert

powdery ['paʊ·də·ri] adj pulv[e]rig; (*finer*) pud[e]rig

power ['paʊ·ər] I. n ❶ POL (*control*) Macht f; (*influence*) Einfluss m; **to seize ~** die Macht ergreifen ❷ (*nation*) [Führungs]macht f ❸ (*person, group*) Macht f ❹ (*ability*) Vermögen nt; **to do everything in one's ~** alles in seiner

P

Macht Stehende tun ❺ (*strength*) Kraft *f;* (*output a.*) Leistung *f;* (*of sea, wind, explosion*) Gewalt *f;* (*of nation*) Stärke *f* ❻ (*electricity*) Strom *m;* **nuclear ~** Atomenergie *f* II. *vt* antreiben
◆**power down** I. *vt* ELEC, TECH abschalten; *computer* herunterfahren II. *vi* COMPUT herunterfahren; TECH zum Stillstand kommen
◆**power up** I. *vt* ELEC, TECH einschalten; *computer* hochfahren II. *vi* TECH, COMPUT hochfahren

power-as'sisted *adj attr* Servo-
'powerboat *n see* **motorboat**
power 'brakes *npl* Servobremsen *pl*
'power cable *n* Stromkabel *nt*
powerful ['paʊ·ər·fəl] *adj* ❶ (*mighty*) mächtig; (*influential*) einflussreich ❷ (*physically strong*) stark, kräftig ❸ *effect, influence* stark; *argument* schlagkräftig
powerfully ['paʊ·ər·fə·li] *adv* ❶ (*strongly*) stark; (*very much*) sehr ❷ (*using great force*) kraftvoll
powerless ['paʊ·ər·lɪs] *adj* machtlos
'power line *n* Stromkabel *nt*
'power outage *n* Stromausfall *m*
'power plant *n* Kraftwerk *nt*
power 'steering *n* Servolenkung *f*
'power tool *n* Motorwerkzeug *nt;* (*electric*) Elektrowerkzeug *nt*
PR [piˈar] *n abbrev of* **public relations** PR
practical ['præk·tɪ·kəl] *adj* ❶ (*not theoretical*) praktisch ❷ (*approv: good at doing things*) praktisch [veranlagt] ❸ (*possible*) realisierbar
practicality [ˌpræk·tɪ·ˈkæl·ɪ·ti] *n* ❶ (*feasibility*) Durchführbarkeit *f* ❷ (*practical aspect*) ■**the practicalities** *pl* die praktische Seite
practically ['præk·tɪk·li] *adv* (*almost*) praktisch
practice ['præk·tɪs] I. *n* ❶ (*preparation*) Übung *f;* ■**to be out of ~** aus der Übung sein ❷ (*training session*) [Übungs]stunde *f;* SPORT Training *nt* ❸ (*actual performance, usual procedure*) Praxis *f;* ■**in ~** in der Praxis

❹ (*custom*) Sitte *f* II. *vt* (*rehearse*) ■**to ~ [doing] sth** etw üben; (*improve particular skill*) an etw *dat* arbeiten III. *vi* ❶ (*improve skill*) üben ❷ (*work in a profession*) praktizieren
practiced ['præk·tɪst] *adj* (*experienced*) erfahren; **~ eye** geübtes Auge
practicing ['præk·tɪs·ɪŋ] *adj attr* praktizierend
practitioner [præk·ˈtɪʃ·ə·nər] *n* (*form*) **medical ~** praktischer Arzt/praktische Ärztin
pragmatic [præg·ˈmæt̬·ɪk] *adj attitude* pragmatisch; *idea* vernünftig
prairie ['prer·i] *n* [Gras]steppe *f;* (*in North America*) Prärie *f*
'prairie dog *n* ZOOL Präriehund *m*
praise [preɪz] I. *vt* loben II. *n* (*approval*) Lob *nt;* **to win ~ for sth** für etw *akk* [großes] Lob ernten
praiseworthy ['preɪz·ˌwɜr·ði] *adj* lobenswert
prank [præŋk] *n* Streich *m*
pray [preɪ] *vi* beten
prayer [prer] *n* ❶ Gebet *nt;* **to say a ~ for sb** für jdn beten ❷ (*fig: hope*) Hoffnung *f;* **to not have a ~** (*fam*) kaum Chancen haben
'prayer book *n* Gebetbuch *nt*
'prayer meeting *n* Gebetsstunde *f*
'prayer rug *n* Gebetsteppich *m*
preach [pritʃ] I. *vi* ❶ (*give a sermon*) predigen (**to** vor +*dat*) ❷ (*pej: lecture*) ■**to ~ to sb [about sth]** jdm eine Predigt [über etw *akk*] halten *fig* II. *vt* **to ~ a sermon** eine Predigt halten
preacher ['pri·tʃər] *n* ❶ (*priest*) Geistliche(r) *f(m)* ❷ Prediger(in) *m(f)*
prearrange [ˌpri·ə·ˈreɪndʒ] *vt usu passive* vorplanen
precarious [prɪ·ˈker·i·əs] *adj balance* unsicher
precaution [prɪ·ˈkɔ·ʃən] *n* Vorkehrung *f*
precede [prɪ·ˈsid] *vt* ❶ (*in rank*) rangieren vor *dat;* (*in importance*) wichtiger sein als ❷ (*in time*) vorausgehen *dat*
precedence ['pres·ə·dəns] *n* Vorrang *m*
precedent ['pres·ə·dənt] *n* vergleichbarer Fall, Präzedenzfall *m geh*

preceding [prɪ'siːdɪŋ] *adj attr* vorhergehend; **the ~ page** die vorige Seite

precinct ['priːsɪŋkt] *n* ❶ (*electoral district*) Wahlbezirk *m* ❷ (*police station*) Revier *nt*

precious ['preʃəs] **I.** *adj* (*of great value*) wertvoll; ■**to be ~ to sb** jdm viel bedeuten **II.** *adv* (*fam*) ~ **little** herzlich wenig

precipice ['presəpɪs] *n* (*steep drop*) Abgrund *m*; (*cliff face*) Steilhang *m*

precipitate [prɪ'sɪpɪteɪt] **I.** *vi* ❶ METEO einen Niederschlag bilden ❷ CHEM ■**to ~ [out]** ausfallen *fachspr* **II.** *n* Satz *m*

precipitation [prɪˌsɪpɪ'teɪʃən] *n* ❶ METEO Niederschlag *m* ❷ (*forming into a solid*) Setzen *nt*

precise [prɪ'saɪs] *adj* genau

precisely [prɪ'saɪsli] *adv* ❶ (*exactly*) genau, präzise ❷ (*approv: carefully*) sorgfältig

precision [prɪ'sɪʒən] *n* Genauigkeit *f*

precocious [prɪ'koʊʃəs] *adj* ❶ (*developing early*) frühreif; ~ **talent** frühe Begabung ❷ (*pej: maturing too early*) altklug

preconceived [ˌpriːkən'siːvd] *adj* (*esp pej*) vorgefasst

preconception [ˌpriːkən'sepʃən] *n* (*esp pej*) vorgefasste Meinung *f*

precondition [ˌpriːkən'dɪʃən] *n* Voraussetzung *f*

precooked [ˌpriː'kʊkt] *adj* vorgekocht

predator ['predətər] *n* ❶ (*animal*) Raubtier *nt*; (*bird*) Raubvogel *m* ❷ (*pej: person*) Profiteur(in) *m(f)*

predatory ['predətɔːri] *adj* ❶ (*preying*) Raub-, räuberisch ❷ (*esp pej: exploitative*) raubtierhaft

predecessor ['predəsesər] *n* Vorgänger(in) *m(f)*

predetermine [ˌpriːdɪ'tɜːmən] *vt usu passive* (*form*) vor[her]bestimmen; **at a ~d signal** auf ein verabredetes Zeichen hin

predicament [prɪ'dɪkəmənt] *n* Notlage *f*

predict [prɪ'dɪkt] *vt* vorhersagen; *sb's future etc.* prophezeien

predictable [prɪ'dɪktəbəl] *adj* ❶ (*foreseeable*) vorhersehbar ❷ (*pej: not very original*) berechenbar

prediction [prɪ'dɪkʃən] *n* (*forecast*) Vorhersage *f*; ECON, POL Prognose *f*

predominance [prɪ'dɑːmənəns] *n* ❶ (*greater number*) zahlenmäßige Überlegenheit ❷ (*predominant position*) Vorherrschaft

predominant [prɪ'dɑːmənənt] *adj* vorherrschend; ■**to be ~** führend sein

preempt [ˌpriː'empt] *vt* (*form: act in advance*) ■**to ~ sth** etw zuvorkommen

preemptive [priː'emptɪv] *adj* ❶ (*preventive*) vorbeugend ❷ MIL (*forestalling the enemy*) präventiv

preen [priːn] *vi* ❶ *bird* sich putzen ❷ (*pej*) *person* sich auftakeln

pre-exist [ˌpriːɪg'zɪst] *vi* (*form*) vorher existieren

prefabricated [ˌpriː'fæbrɪkeɪtɪd] *adj* vorgefertigt

preface ['prefɪs] *n* (*introduction*) Einleitung *f*; *to a novel etc.* Vorwort *nt*

prefect ['priːfekt] *n* (*official*) Präfekt(in) *m(f)*

prefer <-rr-> [prɪ'fɜːr] *vt* ■**to ~ doing sth [to doing sth]** etw lieber [als etw] tun

preferable ['prefərəbəl] *adj* besser

preferably ['prefərəbli] *adv* vorzugsweise

preference ['prefərəns] *n* ❶ (*priority*) Priorität *f*; **to be given ~** Vorrang haben ❷ (*greater liking*) Vorliebe *f*

preferential [ˌprefə'renʃəl] *adj attr* Vorzugs-; **to get ~ treatment** bevorzugt behandelt werden

preferred [prɪ'fɜːrd] *adj attr* bevorzugt, Lieblings-

prefix ['priːfɪks] *n* <*pl* -es> LING Präfix *nt fachspr*

pregnancy ['pregnənsi] *n* Schwangerschaft *f*

pregnant ['pregnənt] *adj woman* schwanger; *animal* trächtig

prehistoric [ˌpriːhɪ'stɔːrɪk] *adj* ❶ prähistorisch ❷ (*pej fam: outdated*) steinzeitlich *fig*

P

prejudge [ˌpriːˈdʒʌdʒ] *vt* vorschnell ein Urteil fällen über +*akk*

prejudice [ˈpredʒ·ə·dɪs] **I.** *n* (*preconceived opinion, bias*) Vorurteil *nt;* **racial** ~ Rassenvorurteil *nt* **II.** *vt* ❶ (*harm*) **to** ~ **sb's chances** jds Chancen beeinträchtigen ❷ (*bias*) ■ **to** ~ **sb** [**against/in favor of sb/sth**] jdn [gegen/für jdn/etw] einnehmen

prejudiced [ˈpredʒ·ə·dɪst] *adj* voreingenommen; ■ **to be** ~ **against sb** Vorurteile gegen jdn haben

prelim [ˈpriː·lɪm] *n* SPORT (*fam*) *short for* **preliminary** Vorrunde *f*

preliminary [prɪˈlɪm·ə·ner·i] **I.** *adj attr* einleitend; ~ **arrangements** Vorbereitungen *pl* **II.** *n* ❶ (*introduction*) Einleitung *f* ❷ SPORT Vorrunde *f*

prelude [ˈprel·juːd] *n usu sing* (*preliminary*) Vorspiel *nt*

premarital [ˌpriːˈmær·ɪ·təl] *adj* vorehelich *attr*

premature [ˌpriː·məˈtʃʊr] *adj* ❶ voreilig ❷ MED ~ **baby** Frühgeburt *f*

premeditated [ˌpriːˈmed·ɪ·ter·tɪd] *adj* geplant

premeditation [ˌpriː·med·ɪˈteɪ·ʃən] *n* (*form*) **with** ~ **of a crime** mit Vorsatz

premenstrual [ˌpriːˈmen·stru·əl] *adj attr* prämenstruell

premier [prɪˈmɪr] **I.** *n* Premierminister(in) *m(f)* **II.** *adj attr* **the** ~ **sporting event** der bedeutendste Wettkampf

premiere, première [prɪˈmɪr] **I.** *n* Premiere *f* **II.** *vt* uraufführen

premise [ˈprem·ɪs] *n* Prämisse *f geh;* **to start from the** ~ **that ...** von der Voraussetzung ausgehen, dass ...

premium [ˈpriː·mi·əm] **I.** *n* ❶ (*insurance payment*) [Versicherungs]prämie *f* ❷ (*extra charge*) Zuschlag *m* ❸ (*gasoline*) Super[benzin] *nt* **II.** *adj attr* (*top quality*) Spitzen-; **the** ~ **brand** die führende Marke

premonition [ˌpriː·məˈnɪʃ·ən] *n* [böse] Vorahnung

prenatal [ˌpriːˈneɪ·təl] *adj attr* vorgeburtlich

preoccupation [ˌpriː·ak·jə·ˈper·ʃən] *n* ❶ (*dominant concern*) Sorge *f* ❷ (*state of mind*) ■ [**a**] ~ **with sth** ständige [gedankliche] Beschäftigung mit etw *dat*

preoccupied [priːˈak·ju·paɪd] *adj* ❶ (*distracted*) gedankenverloren; (*absorbed*) nachdenklich ❷ (*worried*) besorgt

preordain [ˌpriː·ɔrˈdeɪn] *vt usu passive* (*form*) ■ **to be** ~**ed** vorherbestimmt sein; *path* vorgezeichnet; **sb is** ~**ed to succeed** der Erfolg ist jdm sicher

prep [prep] *n* (*fam*) Vorbereitung *f*

preparation [ˌprep·əˈreɪ·ʃən] *n* ❶ (*getting ready*) Vorbereitung *f; of food* Zubereitung *f;* **to do a lot of** ~ [**for sth**] sich sehr gut [auf etw *akk*] vorbereiten ❷ (*measures*) ■ ~**s** *pl* Vorbereitungen *pl*

preparatory [prɪˈpær·ə·tɔr·i] *adj* vorbereitend *attr,* Vorbereitungs-

prepare [prɪˈper] **I.** *vt* ❶ (*get ready*) vorbereiten (**for** auf +*akk*); **to** ~ **the way** [**for sb/sth**] den Weg [für jdn/etw] bereiten ❷ (*make*) zubereiten; *meal* machen **II.** *vi* ■ **to** ~ **for sth** sich auf etw *akk* vorbereiten

prepared [prɪˈperd] *adj* ❶ *pred* (*ready*) bereit, fertig *fam;* ■ **to be** ~ **for sth** auf etw vorbereitet sein ❷ *pred* (*willing*) ■ **to be** ~ **to do sth** bereit sein, etw zu tun

prepay <-paid>, -paid> [ˌpriːˈpeɪ] *vt* im Voraus bezahlen

prepayment [ˌpriːˈpeɪ·mənt] *n* Vorauszahlung *f*

preposition [ˌprep·əˈzɪʃ·ən] *n* Verhältniswort *nt,* Präposition *f*

preposterous [prɪˈpas·tər·əs] *adj* absurd, unsinnig

preppy, preppie [ˈprep·i] **I.** *n* Schüler(in) einer privaten „prep school", der/die großen Wert auf gute Kleidung und das äußere Erscheinungsbild legt **II.** *adj appearance* adrett; *clothes, look* popperhaft *meist pej fam*

prerogative [prɪˈrag·ə·tɪv] *n usu sing* (*form: right*) Recht *nt;* (*privilege*) Vorrecht *nt*

preschool [ˈpriː·skuːl] *n* Kindergarten *m*

prescribe [prɪ'skraɪb] *vt* (*medical*) ■to ~ **sth** [**for sb**] [jdm] etw verschreiben

prescription [prɪ'skrɪp·ʃən] *n* (*medical*) Rezept *nt*; **to be available by ~ only** verschreibungspflichtig sein

presence ['prez·əns] *n* ❶ (*attendance*) Anwesenheit *f*; **in my ~** in meiner Gegenwart *f* ❷ (*approv: dignified bearing*) Haltung *f*

present¹ ['prez·ənt] I. *n* (*now*) ■**the ~** die Gegenwart; **at ~** zurzeit, gegenwärtig II. *adj* ❶ *attr* (*current*) derzeitig, gegenwärtig; *month* laufend; **at the ~ moment** im Moment ❷ *attr case* vorliegend ❸ *usu pred* (*in attendance*) anwesend

present² I. *n* ['prez·ənt] Geschenk *nt*; **to get sth as a ~** etw geschenkt bekommen II. *vt* [prɪ'zent] ❶ (*give formally*) ■**to ~ sth** [**to sb/sth**] *gift* [jdm] etw schenken; *award* [jdm] etw überreichen ❷ (*hand over, show*) ■**to ~ sth** [**to sb/sth**] [jdm/etw] etw vorlegen ❸ (*put forward*) ■**to ~ sth** [**to sb/sth**] [jdm/etw] etw präsentieren; *proposal* unterbreiten ❹ (*confront*) **to ~ sb with the facts** jdm die Fakten vor Augen führen ❺ (*arise*) ■**to ~ itself** *opportunity, solution* sich bieten

presentable [prɪ'zen·tə·bəl] *adj person* vorzeigbar; *thing* ansehnlich

presentation [ˌpre·zən'teɪ·ʃən] *n* ❶ (*giving*) Präsentation *f*; *of a thesis* Vorlage *f*; *of awards* [Preis]verleihung *f* ❷ (*lecture*) Präsentation *f* ❸ *of photographs, works* Ausstellung *f*

present-'day *adj usu attr* heutig *attr*

presenter [prɪ'zen·tər] *n* Moderator(in) *m(f)*

presently ['prez·ənt·li] *adv* ❶ (*now*) gegenwärtig ❷ (*soon*) bald, gleich

present 'tense *n* LING Präsens *nt*

preservation [ˌprez·ər·'veɪ·ʃən] *n* ❶ (*upkeep*) Erhaltung *f* ❷ (*conservation*) Bewahrung *f*; *of order* Aufrechterhaltung *f*; *of food* Konservierung *f*

preservative [prɪ'zɜr·və·tɪv] *n* Konservierungsstoff *m*

preserve [prɪ'zɜrv] I. *vt* ❶ (*maintain*) erhalten; *customs* bewahren ❷ (*conserve*) konservieren; *wood* [mit Holzschutzmittel] behandeln; *fruit* einmachen II. *n* ❶ *usu pl* (*jam or jelly*) Marmelade *f*; (*cooked whole*) Eingemachte(s) *nt kein pl* ❷ (*reserve*) **nature ~** Naturschutzgebiet *nt*

preserved [prɪ'zɜrvd] *adj* ❶ (*maintained*) konserviert; *building* erhalten ❷ **~ food** konservierte Lebensmittel

preside [prɪ'zaɪd] *vi* ■**to ~ over sth** etw leiten

presidency ['prez·ɪ·dən·si] *n* Präsidentschaft *f*

president ['prez·ɪ·dənt] *n of country* Präsident(in) *m(f)*; *of company, corporation* [Vorstands-]vorsitzende(r)

presidential [ˌprez·ɪ·'den·tʃəl] *adj usu attr* POL (*of president*) Präsidenten-; (*of office*) Präsidentschafts-

Presidents' Day *n* Präsidententag *m* (*nationaler Feiertag am dritten Montag im Februar*)

press [pres] I. *n* <*pl* -es> ❶ (*push*) Druck *m*; **at the ~ of a button** auf Knopfdruck ❷ (*news media*) ■**the ~** die Presse; (*publicity*) **to get good ~** eine gute Presse bekommen II. *vt* ❶ (*push*) ■**to ~ sth** [auf] etw *akk* drücken; ■**to ~ sth into sth** etw in etw *akk* hineindrücken ❷ (*flatten*) zusammendrücken; *flowers* pressen ❸ (*iron*) bügeln III. *vi* ❶ (*push*) drücken ❷ (*be urgent*) drängen

◆ **press ahead** *vi* ■**to ~ ahead** [**with sth**] etw vorantreiben

◆ **press on** I. *vi* ■**to ~ on** [**with sth**] [mit etw *dat*] [zügig] weitermachen II. *vt* ■**to ~ sth on sb** jdm etw aufdrängen

press agency *n* Nachrichtenagentur *f*

'press clipping *n* Zeitungsausschnitt *m*

'press conference *n* Pressekonferenz *f*

pressing ['pres·ɪŋ] *adj issue* dringend; *requests* nachdrücklich

'press office *n* Pressestelle *f*

'press release *n* Pressemitteilung *f*

pressure ['preʃ·ər] I. *n* ❶ Druck *m*; **to apply ~** Druck ausüben; **~ wash-**

P

er Hochdruckreiniger *m* ❷ (*stress*) Druck *m;* (*stronger*) Überlastung *f;* **to be under ~ to do sth** unter Druck stehen, etw zu tun ❸ (*insistence*) **to put ~ on sb** [**to do sth**] jdn unter Druck setzen[, damit er/sie etw tut] II. *vt* ■ **to ~ sb to do sth** jdn [massiv] dazu drängen, etw zu tun

'**pressure cooker** *n* Schnellkochtopf *m*
'**pressure gauge** *n* Druckmesser *m*

pressurize ['preʃ·ə·raɪz] *vt* druckfest halten

prestige [pre·'stiʒ] *n* Prestige *nt,* Ansehen *nt*

presumably [prɪ·'zu·mə·bli] *adv* vermutlich

presume [prɪ·'zum] *vt* (*suppose, believe*) annehmen; **to be ~d innocent** als unschuldig gelten

presumption [prɪ·'zʌmp·ʃən] *n* (*assumption*) Annahme *f*

presumptuous [prɪ·'zʌmp·tʃu·əs] *adj* *attitude* überheblich; (*forward*) unverschämt

pretax [ˌpri·'tæks] *adj* vor Abzug der Steuern *nach n,* Brutto-

pretend [prɪ·'tend] I. *vt* ❶ (*behave falsely*) vorgeben, vortäuschen; **to ~ that one is asleep** sich schlafend stellen ❷ (*imagine*) ■ **to ~ to be sth** so tun, als sei man etw; **I'll just ~ that I didn't hear that** ich tue einfach so, als hätte ich das nicht gehört II. *vi* (*feign*) ■ **to ~ to sb that …** jdm vormachen, dass …

pretender [prɪ·'ten·dər] *n* *title* Anwärter, Anwärterin *m, f*

pretense ['pri·tens] *n* (*false behavior*) Vortäuschung *f;* **under false ~s** unter Vorspiegelung falscher Tatsachen

pretension [prɪ·'ten·ʃən] *n* ❶ *usu pl* (*claim*) Anspruch *m* ❷ (*pej*) *see* **pretentiousness**

pretentious [prɪ·'ten·ʃəs] *adj* (*pej*) *person* großspurig; *manner, speech, style* hochgestochen

pretentiousness [prɪ·'ten·ʃəs·nɪs] *n* (*arrogance*) Überheblichkeit *f,* Anmaßung *f*

P

pretext ['pri·tekst] *n* Vorwand *m*

pretty ['prɪt·i] I. *adj* *person* hübsch; *thing* nett II. *adv* (*fam*) ❶ (*fairly*) **~ good** (*fam*) ganz gut; **~ damn quick** (*fam*) verdammt schnell ❷ (*almost*) **~ much everything** beinah alles

pretzel ['pret·səl] *n* Brezel *f*

prevail [prɪ·'veɪl] *vi* ❶ (*triumph*) siegen; *person* sich durchsetzen ❷ (*induce*) ■ **to ~ [up]on sb to do sth** jdn dazu bewegen, etw zu tun

prevailing [prɪ·'veɪ·lɪŋ] *adj* *attr wind* vorherrschend; *law* geltend

prevalent ['prev·ə·lənt] *adj* (*common*) vorherrschend *attr; disease* weit verbreitet

prevent [prɪ·'vent] *vt* verhindern; *crime* verhüten; ■ **to ~ sb from doing sth** jdn daran hindern, etw zu tun

preventative [prɪ·'ven·tə·tɪv] *adj* *see* **preventive**

prevention [prɪ·'ven·ʃən] *n of disaster* Verhinderung *f; of accident* Vermeidung *f*

preventive [prɪ·'ven·tɪv] *adj* vorbeugend

preview ['pri·vju] *n of a film sneak ~* Vorpremiere *f;* (*trailer*) Vorschau *f*

previous ['pri·vi·əs] *adj* *attr* ❶ (*former*) vorig; (*prior*) vorherig; **~ conviction** Vorstrafe *f* ❷ (*preceding*) vorhergehend; **on the ~ day** am Tag davor

previously ['pri·vi·əs·li] *adv* (*beforehand*) zuvor; (*formerly*) früher; **~ unreleased** bisher unveröffentlicht

prey [preɪ] I. *n* (*victim*) Beute *f* II. *vi* (*exploit*) ■ **to ~ on sb** jdn ausnutzen; (*abuse*) jdn ausnehmen

price [praɪs] I. *n* Preis *m;* **to pay full ~ for sth** den vollen Preis bezahlen; **not at any ~** um keinen Preis II. *vt* **to be reasonably ~d** einen angemessenen Preis haben

'**price cut** *n* Preissenkung *f*
'**price fixing** *n* Preisabsprache *f*
priceless ['praɪs·lɪs] *adj* unbezahlbar
'**price range** *n* Preislage *f*
'**price tag,** '**price ticket** *n* Preisschild *nt*
'**price war** *n* Preiskrieg *m*

pricey ['praɪ·si] *adj* (*fam*) teuer

pricing ['praɪ·sɪŋ] *n* Preisgestaltung *f*

prick [prɪk] I. *n* ❶ (*act of piercing*) Stechen *nt*; (*fig*) *sharp pain* Stich *m* ❷ (*vulg: penis*) Schwanz *m* II. *vt* stechen; **to ~** one's **finger** sich *dat o akk* in den Finger stechen

◆**prick up** *vt* **to ~ up** one's **ears** die Ohren spitzen

prickle ['prɪk·əl] *n* ❶ (*thorn*) Dorn *m* ❷ (*sensation*) Kratzen *nt*

prickly ['prɪk·li] *adj* ❶ (*thorny*) stachelig ❷ (*fam: easily offended*) [leicht] reizbar

prickly 'pear *n* Kaktusfeige *f*

pride [praɪd] I. *n* ❶ (*satisfaction*) Stolz *m*; **to take ~ in sth** stolz auf etw sein ❷ (*arrogance*) Hochmut *m* ❸ (*animal group*) **a ~ of lions** ein Rudel *nt* Löwen II. *vt* ■**to ~ oneself on sth** auf etw *akk* stolz sein

priest [prist] *n* Priester *m*

prim <-mm-> [prɪm] *adj* (*pej*) steif

primarily [praɪ·'mer·ə·li] *adv* vorwiegend, in erster Linie

primary ['praɪ·mer·i] I. *adj* (*principal*) primär *geh*, Haupt-; **~ concern** Hauptanliegen *nt* II. *n* POL (*election*) Vorwahl *f*

primary 'color *n* Grundfarbe *f*

'primary school *n* Grundschule *f*

primate ['praɪ·meɪt] *n* ZOOL (*mammal*) Primat *m*

prime [praɪm] I. *adj attr* ❶ (*main*) wesentlich, Haupt-; **~ suspect** Hauptverdächtige(r) *f(m)* ❷ (*best*) erstklassig II. *n* Blütezeit *f fig*; **to be in** one's **~** im besten Alter sein III. *vt* ❶ (*prepare*) vorbereiten ❷ *canvas, wood* grundieren

prime 'number *n* Primzahl *f*

primer ['praɪ·mər] *n* Grundierfarbe *f*

'prime time *n* Hauptsendezeit *f*

primitive ['prɪm·ɪ·tɪv] *adj* primitiv

prince [prɪns] *n* (*royal*) Prinz *m*

princess <*pl* -es> ['prɪn·sɪs] *n* Prinzessin *f*

principal ['prɪn·sə·pəl] I. *adj attr* Haupt-, hauptsächlich II. *n* ❶ *in a school* Direktor(in) *m(f)*, Schulleiter(in) *m(f)*; *in a play* Hauptdarsteller(in) *m(f)*

❷ *usu sing* (*of investment*) Kapitalsumme *f*

principally ['prɪn·sə·pli] *adv* hauptsächlich, in erster Linie

principle ['prɪn·sə·pəl] *n* ❶ Prinzip *nt*; **basic ~** Grundprinzip *nt* ❷ (*basis*) Grundlage *f* ▶PHRASES: **on ~** aus Prinzip

print [prɪnt] I. *n* ❶ (*lettering*) Gedruckte(s) *nt*; **to read the fine ~** das Kleingedruckte lesen ❷ (*printed form*) Druck *m*; **out of ~** vergriffen ❸ (*photo*) Abzug *m*; (*copy of artwork*) Druck *m* II. *vt* ❶ TYPO drucken ❷ PUBL veröffentlichen; (*in magazine, newspaper*) abdrucken ❸ COMPUT ausdrucken III. *vi* (*write in unjoined letters*) in Druckschrift schreiben

printable ['prɪn·tə·bəl] *adj* druckfähig; *manuscript* druckfertig

printed 'circuit board *n* Leiterplatte *f*

printer ['prɪn·tər] *n* ❶ (*machine*) Drucker *m* ❷ (*person*) Drucker(in) *m(f)*

printing ['prɪn·tɪŋ] *n* ❶ (*act*) Drucken *nt* ❷ (*handwriting*) Druckschrift *f*

'printout *n* Ausdruck *m*

'print run *n* Auflage *f*

'print shop *n* Grafikhandlung *f*

prior ['praɪ·ər] *adj attr* (*earlier*) frühere(r, s)

prioritize [praɪ·'ɔr·ɪ·taɪz] *vt* ❶ (*order*) der Priorität nach ordnen ❷ (*give preference to*) vorrangig behandeln

priority [praɪ·'ɔr·ɪ·ti] *n* ❶ (*deserving greatest attention*) vorrangige Angelegenheit; **top ~** Angelegenheit *f* von höchster Priorität; **to get** one's **priorities straight** seine Prioritäten richtig setzen ❷ (*precedence*) Vorrang *m* ❸ (*right of way*) Vorfahrt *f*

prior to *prep* ■**~ to sth** vor etw *dat*

prism ['prɪz·əm] *n* Prisma *nt*

prison ['prɪz·ən] *n* (*a. fig: jail*) Gefängnis *nt a. fig*; **to be in ~** im Gefängnis sitzen

'prison camp *n* (*for POWs*) [Kriegs]gefangenenlager *nt*; (*for political prisoners*) Straflager *nt*

prisoner ['prɪz·ə·nər] *n* (*a. fig*) Gefangene(r) *f(m) a. fig*, Häftling *m*

prisoner of 'war <pl prisoners-> n Kriegsgefangene(r) f(m)

'prison sentence n Freiheitsstrafe f

privacy ['praɪ·və·si] n ① (personal realm) Privatsphäre f; **in the ~ of one's [own] home** in den eigenen vier Wänden fam ② (time alone) Zurückgezogenheit f

private ['praɪ·vət] I. adj ① (personal, not open to public) privat ② (confidential) vertraulich; **to keep sth ~** etw für sich akk behalten ③ (secluded) abgelegen II. n ① (not in public) **to speak to sb in ~** jdn [o mit jdm] unter vier Augen sprechen ② (soldier) Gefreiter m

private 'eye n (fam) Privatdetektiv(in) m(f)

privately ['praɪ·vət·li] adv ① (not in public) privat ② (secretly) heimlich

privatization [ˌpraɪ·və·tɪ·'zeɪ·ʃən] n Privatisierung f

privatize ['praɪ·və·taɪz] vt privatisieren

privilege ['prɪv·ə·lɪdʒ] I. n ① (special right) Privileg nt ② (honor) Ehre f II. vt usu passive (give privileges to) privilegieren

privileged ['prɪv·ə·lɪdʒd] adj ① (with privileges) privilegiert ② LAW information vertraulich

prize¹ [praɪz] I. n (sth won) Preis m; (in lottery) Gewinn m II. adj attr (prize-winning) preisgekrönt III. vt usu passive **to ~ sth highly** etw hoch schätzen

prize² [praɪz] vt **to ~ sth open** etw [mit einem Hebel] aufbrechen

'prize-winning adj attr preisgekrönt

pro¹ [proʊ] I. n Pro nt; **the ~s and cons of sth** das Pro und Kontra einer S. gen II. prep (in favor of) für

pro² [proʊ] n (fam) Profi m

proactive [ˌproʊ·'æk·tɪv] adj initiativ geh

probability [ˌprab·ə·'bɪl·ɪ·ti] n Wahrscheinlichkeit f

probable ['prab·ə·bəl] adj wahrscheinlich

probably ['prab·ə·bli] adv wahrscheinlich

probation [proʊ·'beɪ·ʃən] n ① (trial period) Probezeit f; **to be on ~** Probezeit haben; (employee) auf Probe eingestellt sein ② LAW Bewährung f

pro'bation officer n Bewährungshelfer(in) m(f)

probe [proʊb] I. vi ① (investigate) forschen (**for** nach +dat); **to ~ into sb's private life** in jds Privatleben herumschnüffeln pej fam ② (physically search) Untersuchungen durchführen II. vt untersuchen III. n ① (investigation) Untersuchung f ② MED, ELEC, ASTRON Sonde f

problem ['prab·ləm] n ① (difficulty) Schwierigkeit f; **no ~** (sure) kein Problem; (don't mention it) keine Ursache; **what's the ~?** (fam) was ist denn los? ② (task) Aufgabe f; **that's her ~!** das ist ihre Sache!

procedure [prə·'si·dʒər] n ① (particular course of action) Verfahren nt; **standard ~** übliche Vorgehensweise ② (operation) Vorgang m ③ LAW **court ~** Gerichtsverfahren nt

proceed [proʊ·'sid] vi ① (make progress) fortschreiten, vorangehen ② (continue) fortfahren ③ (go on) ∎**to ~ to do sth** sich anschicken, etw zu tun

proceeding [proʊ·'si·dɪŋ] n ① (action) Vorgehen nt kein pl ② usu pl (legal action) Verfahren nt

proceeds ['proʊ·sidz] npl Einnahmen pl

process ['pras·es] I. n <pl -es> ① (series of actions) Prozess m ② (method) Verfahren nt ③ (passage) Verlauf m; **in the ~** dabei II. vt ① (deal with) bearbeiten ② COMPUT verarbeiten ③ (treat) bearbeiten, behandeln

processing ['pras·es·ɪŋ] n ① of application Bearbeitung f ② TECH Weiterverarbeitung f; FOOD Konservierung f ③ COMPUT Verarbeitung f

procession [prə·'seʃ·ən] n Umzug m

processor [pra·'ses·ər] n ① food ~ Küchenmaschine f ② COMPUT Prozessor m

pro-'choice adj für das Recht auf Abtreibung

procreate ['prou·kri·eɪt] *vi* sich fortpflanzen

proctor ['prak·tər] SCH, UNIV I. *n (for exam)* [Prüfungs]aufsicht *f* II. *vi* Aufsicht führen

procure [prou·'kjʊr] *vt (form)* beschaffen

procurement [prou·'kjʊr·mənt] *n (form)* Beschaffung *f*

prod [prad] I. *n* ❶ *(tool)* Ahle *f* ❷ *(poke)* Schubs *m fam,* [leichter] Stoß ❸ *(fig: incitation)* Anstoß *m fig; (reminder)* Gedächtnisanstoß *m* II. *vt* <-dd-> stoßen

prodigal ['prad·ɪ·gəl] *adj* verschwenderisch

prodigy ['prad·ə·dʒi] *n* **child ~** Wunderkind *nt*

produce I. *vt* [prə·'dus] ❶ *(make)* herstellen; *coal, oil* fördern; *electricity* erzeugen ❷ *(bring about)* bewirken; *effect, profits* erzielen ❸ FILM produzieren; THEAT *play* inszenieren II. *vi* [prə·'dus] ❶ *(bring results)* Ergebnisse erzielen ❷ *(give output)* produzieren; *mine* fördern III. *n* ['pra·dus] *(fruits and vegetables)* Obst und Gemüse *nt*

producer [prə·'du·sər] *n* ❶ *(manufacturer)* Hersteller *m;* AGR Erzeuger *m* ❷ FILM, TV Produzent(in) *m(f);* THEAT Regisseur(in) *m(f)*

product ['prad·əkt] *n* ❶ *(sth produced)* Erzeugnis *nt,* Produkt *nt* ❷ *(result)* Ergebnis *nt*

production [prə·'dʌk·ʃən] *n* ❶ Produktion *f,* Herstellung *f; of energy* Erzeugung *f* ❷ FILM, TV, RADIO, MUS Produktion *f;* THEAT Inszenierung *f*

pro'duction line *n* Fließband *nt*

production 'manager *n* Produktionsleiter(in) *m(f)*

productive [prə·'dʌk·tɪv] *adj* ❶ *(with large output)* produktiv; *land, soil* fruchtbar, ertragreich; *(fig) conversation* fruchtbar ❷ *(profitable)* rentabel

productivity [ˌprou·dək·'tɪv·ɪ·ti] *n* Produktivität *f*

prof [praf] *n (fam) short for* **professor** Prof *m*

profanity [prou·'fæn·ɪ·ti] *n* ❶ *(blasphemy)* Gotteslästerung *f* ❷ *(swearing)* Fluchen *nt*

professed [prə·'fest] *adj attr (openly declared) communist* erklärt

profession [prə·'feʃ·ən] *n* ❶ *(field of work)* Beruf *m* ❷ *(body of workers)* **the legal ~** der Anwaltsberuf

professional [prə·'feʃ·ə·nəl] I. *adj* ❶ *(of a profession)* beruflich, Berufs- ❷ *(not tradesman)* freiberuflich, akademisch ❸ *(expert)* fachmännisch ❹ *(approv: businesslike)* professionell; **to do a ~ job** etw fachmännisch erledigen ❺ *(not amateur)* Berufs-; SPORT Profi- II. *n* ❶ *(not an amateur)* Fachmann, Fachfrau *m, f;* SPORT Profi *m* ❷ *(not a tradesman)* Angehörige(r) *f(m)* der freien [*o* akademischen] Berufe

professionalism [prə·'feʃ·ə·nə·lɪz·əm] *n (skill and experience)* Professionalität *f; (attitude)* professionelle Einstellung

professionally [prə·'feʃ·ə·nə·li] *adv* ❶ *(by a professional)* von einem Fachmann/einer Fachfrau ❷ *(not as an amateur)* berufsmäßig

professor [prə·'fes·ər] *n* Professor(in) *m(f)*

proficient [prə·'fɪʃ·ənt] *adj* **to be ~ in a language** eine Sprache beherrschen

profile ['prou·faɪl] *n* ❶ *(side view)* Profil *nt* ❷ *(description)* Porträt *nt fig* ❸ *(public image)* **to raise sb's ~** jdn hervorheben ▶PHRASES: **to keep a low ~** sich zurückhalten

profit ['praf·ɪt] I. *n* Gewinn *m;* **net ~** Reingewinn *m* II. *vi* profitieren

profitability [ˌpraf·ɪ·tə·'bɪl·ɪ·ti] *n* Rentabilität *f*

profitable ['praf·ɪ·tə·bəl] *adj* ❶ *(in earnings)* Gewinn bringend, rentabel ❷ *(advantageous)* nützlich

profiteer [ˌpraf·ɪ·'tɪr] I. *n (pej)* Profitjäger(in) *m(f)* II. *vi (make excessive profit)* riesige Gewinne erzielen

profiteering [ˌpraf·ɪ·'tɪr·ɪŋ] *n* Wucher *m pej*

'profit margin *n* Gewinnspanne *f*

P

'profit sharing n Gewinnbeteiligung f

profound [prə·'faʊnd] adj ❶ (extreme) tief gehend; change tief greifend; impression tief ❷ (strongly felt) tief, heftig; compassion tief empfunden ❸ (intellectual) tiefsinnig a. iron, tiefgründig

profuse [prə·'fjus] adj überreichlich; bleeding stark

prognosis <pl -ses> [prag·'noʊ·sɪs] n Prognose f; to make a ~ eine Prognose stellen

program ['proʊ·græm] I. n ❶ RADIO, TV, COMPUT Programm nt; (single broadcast) Sendung f ❷ (list of events) Programm nt; THEAT Programmheft nt II. vt <-mm-> TECH, COMPUT (instruct) programmieren

programmer ['proʊ·græm·ər] n COMPUT Programmierer(in) m(f)

'programming language n COMPUT Programmiersprache f

progress I. n ['prag·res] ❶ (onward movement) Vorwärtskommen nt; to make good ~ gut vorwärtskommen ❷ Fortschritt m II. vi [prə·'gres] (develop) Fortschritte machen; how's the work ~ing? wie geht's mit der Arbeit voran?

progression [prə·'greʃ·ən] n ❶ (development) Entwicklung f ❷ MATH (series) Reihe f

progressive [prə·'gres·ɪv] adj ❶ (gradual) fortschreitend; (gradually increasing) zunehmend ❷ (forward-looking) progressiv

prohibit [proʊ·'hɪb·ɪt] vt verbieten

prohibition [proʊ·ə·'bɪʃ·ən] n ❶ (ban) Verbot nt ❷ (hist: US alcohol ban) ■P~ no art die Prohibition

prohibitive [proʊ·'hɪb·ɪ·tɪv] adj ❶ price unerschwinglich ❷ (prohibiting) ~ measures Verbotsmaßnahmen pl

project I. n ['pra·dʒekt] ❶ (undertaking) Projekt nt ❷ (plan) Plan m II. vt [prə·'dʒekt] ❶ (forecast) vorhersagen; profit, number veranschlagen ❷ film projizieren III. vi [prə·'dʒekt] (pro-

trude) hervorragen, [hinaus]ragen (over über +akk)

projectile [prə·'dʒek·təl] n (thrown object) Wurfgeschoss nt

projection [prə·'dʒek·ʃən] n ❶ (forecast) Prognose f; of expenses Voranschlag m ❷ (protrusion) Vorsprung m

projectionist [prə·'dʒek·ʃə·nɪst] n Filmvorführer(in) m(f)

project 'manager n Projektmanager(in) m(f)

projector [prə·'dʒek·tər] n Projektor m

proletarian [proʊ·lə·'ter·i·ən] I. n Proletarier(in) m(f) II. adj proletarisch

pro-'life adj gegen das Recht auf Abtreibung

proliferate [proʊ·'lɪf·ə·reɪt] vi stark zunehmen; (animals) sich stark vermehren

prolific [proʊ·'lɪf·ɪk] adj ❶ (productive) produktiv ❷ pred (abundant) ■to be ~ in großer Zahl vorhanden sein

prologue, prolog ['proʊ·lag] n Vorwort nt

prolong [proʊ·'laŋ] vt verlängern

prom n Ball am Ende des Schuljahres der High School

promenade [pram·ə·'neɪd] n (walkway) [Strand]promenade f

prominence ['pram·ə·nəns] n ❶ (conspicuousness) Unübersehbarkeit f; to give sth ~ etw in den Vordergrund stellen ❷ (importance) Bedeutung f

prominent ['pram·ə·nənt] adj ❶ (projecting) vorstehend attr ❷ (distinguished) prominent

promiscuity [pram·ɪ·'skju·ɪ·ţi] n Promiskuität f geh

promiscuous [prə·'mɪs·kju·əs] adj (pej) promisk

promise ['pram·ɪs] I. vt, vi versprechen; I ~! ich verspreche es! II. n ❶ (pledge) Versprechen nt ❷ (potential) to show ~ (person) viel versprechend sein

promising ['pram·ɪ·sɪŋ] adj viel versprechend

promontory ['pram·ən·tɔr·i] n GEOG Vorgebirge nt

promote [prə'moʊt] *vt* ① (*raise in rank*) befördern (**to** zu +*dat*) ② (*encourage*) fördern; **to ~ awareness of sth** etw ins Bewusstsein rufen ③ (*advertise*) für etw *akk* werben

promoter [prə'moʊ·tər] *n* (*organizer*) Veranstalter(in) *m(f)*

promotion [prə'moʊ·ʃən] *n* ① (*in rank*) Beförderung *f* ② (*advertising campaign*) Werbekampagne *f*

prompt [prɑmpt] **I.** *vt* ① THEAT (*remind of lines*) soufflieren ② COMPUT auffordern **II.** *adj* ① (*swift*) prompt; **action** sofortig ② (*punctual*) pünktlich **III.** *n* ① COMPUT Prompt *m fachspr* ② THEAT Stichwort *nt*

promptly ['prɑmpt·li] *adv* ① (*quickly*) prompt ② (*fam: immediately afterward*) gleich danach, unverzüglich

prong [prɑŋ] *n* Zacke *f*

pronoun ['proʊ·naʊn] *n* Pronomen *nt*

pronounce [prə'naʊns] *vt* ① (*speak*) aussprechen ② *verdict* verkünden ③ (*declare*) **to ~ sb dead** jdn für tot erklären

pronounced [prə'naʊnst] *adj* deutlich; *accent* ausgeprägt

pronouncement [prə'naʊns·mənt] *n* Erklärung *f*

pronto ['prɑn·toʊ] *adv* (*fam*) fix

pronunciation [prə·nʌn·sɪ·'eɪ·ʃən] *n* Aussprache *f*

proof [pruf] **I.** *n* ① (*confirmation*) Beweis *m* ② TYPO (*trial impression*) Korrekturfahne *f* ③ *of alcohol* Alkoholgehalt *m* **II.** *vt* (*make waterproof*) wasserdicht machen

'proofread <-read, -read> *vt, vi* Korrektur lesen

'proofreader *n* Korrektor(in) *m(f)*

prop¹ [prɑp] **I.** *n* Stütze *f* **II.** *vt* stützen

prop² [prɑp] *n usu pl* THEAT Requisite *f*

propaganda [ˌprɑp·ə·'gæn·də] *n* (*usu pej*) Propaganda *f*

propagate ['prɑp·ə·geɪt] **I.** *vt* ① *plants* vermehren ② (*form: disseminate*) verbreiten **II.** *vi plants* sich vermehren

propane ['proʊ·peɪn] *n* Propan *nt*

propel <-ll-> [prə·'pel] *vt* antreiben

propellant [prə·'pel·ənt] *n* ① (*fuel*) Treibstoff *m* ② (*gas*) Treibgas *nt*

propeller [prə·'pel·ər] *n* Propeller *m*

proper ['prɑp·ər] *adj* ① (*real, correct*) echt ② (*socially respectable*) anständig

properly ['prɑp·ər·li] *adv* ① (*correctly*) richtig ② (*socially respectably*) anständig

proper 'noun, proper 'name *n* Eigenname *m*

property ['prɑp·ər·ti] *n* ① (*things owned*) Eigentum *nt*; (*owned buildings*) Immobilienbesitz *m*; **private ~** Privatbesitz *m* ② (*attribute*) Eigenschaft *f*

prophecy ['prɑf·ə·si] *n* Prophezeiung *f*

prophesy <-ie-> ['prɑf·ə·saɪ] *vt* prophezeien

prophet ['prɑf·ɪt] *n* (*a. fig*) Prophet *m*

prophetic [prə·'fet·ɪk] *adj* prophetisch

proponent [prə·'poʊ·nənt] *n* Befürworter(in) *m(f)*

proportion [prə·'pɔr·ʃən] *n* ① (*part*) Anteil *m* ② (*relation*) Verhältnis *nt*; **to be out of ~** (**to sth**) in keinem Verhältnis zu etw *dat* stehen

proportional [prə·'pɔr·ʃə·nəl] *adj* proportional (**to** zu +*dat*); **inversely ~** umgekehrt proportional

proportioned [prə·'pɔr·ʃənd] *adj* **beautifully ~** ebenmäßig proportioniert

proposal [prə·'poʊ·zəl] *n* ① (*suggestion*) Vorschlag *m* ② (*offer of marriage*) Antrag *m*

propose [prə·'poʊz] **I.** *vt* ① (*suggest*) vorschlagen ② (*intend*) ▪**to ~ doing sth** beabsichtigen, etw zu tun **II.** *vi* ▪**to ~** (**to sb**) (jdm) einen [Heirats]antrag machen

proposition [ˌprɑp·ə·'zɪʃ·ən] *n* ① (*assertion*) Aussage *f* ② (*proposal*) Vorschlag *m*; **business ~** geschäftliches Angebot

proprietary [prə·'praɪ·ə·ter·i] *adj* ECON, LAW urheberrechtlich geschützt

proprietor [prə·'praɪ·ə·tər] *n* Inhaber(in) *m(f)*

propulsion [prə·'pʌl·ʃən] *n* Antrieb *m*

prorate [ˌproʊˈreɪt] *vt* anteilmäßig aufteilen

prose [proʊz] *n* Prosa *f*

prosecute [ˈpras·ɪ·kjut] I. *vt* LAW ■**to ~ sb** [**for sth**] jdn [wegen einer S. *gen*] strafrechtlich verfolgen II. *vi* (*in court*) für die Anklage zuständig sein

prosecuting [ˈpras·ɪ·kju·tɪŋ] *adj attr* **~ attorney** Staatsanwalt, Staatsanwältin *m, f*

prosecution [ˌpras·ɪ·ˈkju·ʃən] *n* ❶ (*legal action*) strafrechtliche Verfolgung ❷ (*legal team*) ■**the ~** die Anklagevertretung ❸ (*case*) Anklage[erhebung] *f*

prosecutor [ˈpras·ɪ·kju·tər] *n* Ankläger(in) *m(f)*

prospect [ˈpras·pekt] I. *n* ❶ Aussicht *f* ❷ (*opportunities*) ■**~s** *pl* Aussichten *pl*, Chancen *pl* II. *vi* nach Bodenschätzen suchen

prospective [prə·ˈspek·tɪv] *adj* voraussichtlich; *customer* potenziell

prospector [ˈpras·pek·tər] *n* MIN Prospektor(in) *m(f) fachspr*

prospectus [prə·ˈspek·təs] *n* Prospekt *m*

prosperity [pra·ˈsper·ɪ·ti̬] *n* Wohlstand *m*

prosperous [ˈpras·pər·əs] *adj* (*well-off*) wohlhabend

prostitute [ˈpras·tə·tut] *n* Prostituierte *f*; **male ~** Stricher *m pej*

prostitution [ˌpras·tɪ·ˈtu·ʃən] *n* Prostitution *f*

prostrate [ˈpras·treɪt] *adj* ❶ (*face downward*) ausgestreckt ❷ (*overcome*) überwältigt

protect [prə·ˈtekt] *vt* schützen (**against** gegen +*akk*, **from** vor +*dat*)

protection [prə·ˈtek·ʃən] *n* ❶ (*defense*) Schutz *m; of interests* Wahrung *f* ❷ (*paid to criminals*) Schutzgeld *nt*

protective [prə·ˈtek·tɪv] *adj* ❶ (*affording protection*) Schutz- ❷ (*wishing to protect*) fürsorglich (**of/toward** gegenüber +*dat*)

protector [prə·ˈtek·tər] *n* Beschützer(in) *m(f)*

protégé, protégée [ˈproʊ·tə·ʒeɪ] *n* Protegé *m geh*

protein [ˈproʊ·tin] *n* Eiweiß *nt*

protest I. *n* [ˈproʊ·test] ❶ (*strong complaint*) Protest *m* ❷ (*demonstration*) Protestkundgebung *f* II. *vi* [proʊ·ˈtest] protestieren

Protestant [ˈprat·ɪ·stənt] *n* Protestant(in) *m(f)*

protester [prə·ˈtes·tər] *n* (*objector*) Protestierende(r) *f(m)*; (*demonstrator*) Demonstrant(in) *m(f)*

'protest march *n* Protestmarsch *m*

protocol [ˈproʊ·tə·kɔl] *n* Protokoll *nt*

proton [ˈproʊ·tan] *n* PHYS Proton *nt*

prototype [ˈproʊ·tə·taɪp] *n* Prototyp *m*

protractor [proʊ·ˈtræk·tər] *n* MATH Winkelmesser *m*

protrude [proʊ·ˈtrud] *vi* hervorragen (**from** aus +*dat*)

protruding [proʊ·ˈtru·dɪŋ] *adj attr ears* abstehend; *eyes* vortretend

protrusion [proʊ·ˈtru·ʒən] *n* Vorsprung *m*

proud [praʊd] *adj* ❶ stolz (**of** auf +*akk*) ❷ (*pej: arrogant*) eingebildet

proudly [ˈpraʊd·li] *adv* ❶ (*with pride*) stolz ❷ (*pej: haughtily*) hochnäsig *fam*

prove <-d, -d **or** proven> [pruv] I. *vt* (*establish*) beweisen II. *vi + n/adj* sich erweisen; **to ~ successful** sich als erfolgreich erweisen

proven [ˈpru·vən] I. *vt, vi pp of* **prove** II. *adj* nachgewiesen; *remedy* erprobt

proverb [ˈprav·ɜrb] *n* Sprichwort *nt*

proverbial [prə·ˈvɜr·bi·əl] *adj* (*fig: well-known*) sprichwörtlich

provide [prə·ˈvaɪd] I. *vt* zur Verfügung stellen; *explanation* liefern; ■**to ~ sb with sth** jdn mit etw *dat* versorgen II. *vi* ■**to ~ for oneself** für sich selbst sorgen

provided [prə·ˈvaɪ·dɪd] I. *adj* beigefügt II. *conj see* **providing** [**that**]

provider [prə·ˈvaɪ·dər] *n* ❶ (*supplier*) Lieferant(in) *m(f)* ❷ TELEC, INET Anbieter *m;* **Internet** [**service**] **~** Internet Service Provider *m*, Internetdienstan-

bieter m ❸ (*breadwinner*) Ernährer(in) m(f)

providing (**that**) [prə·ˈvaɪ·dɪŋ-] *conj* (*as long as*) sofern

province [ˈprɑv·ɪns] n ❶ (*territory*) Provinz f ❷ (*area of knowledge*) [Fach]gebiet nt

provincial [prə·ˈvɪn·ʃəl] *adj* ❶ (*of a province*) Provinz- ❷ (*pej: unsophisticated*) provinziell

provision [prə·ˈvɪʒ·ən] n ❶ (*providing*) Versorgung f; (*financial precaution*) Vorkehrung f ❷ (*something supplied*) Vorrat m ❸ (*stipulation*) **with the ~ that** ... unter der Bedingung, dass ...

provisional [prə·ˈvɪʒ·ə·nəl] *adj* vorläufig

proviso [prə·ˈvaɪ·zoʊ] n Vorbehalt m

provocation [ˌprɑv·ə·ˈkeɪ·ʃən] n Provokation f

provoke [prə·ˈvoʊk] vt ❶ (*vex*) ■ **to ~ sb** [**into doing sth**] jdn [zu etw *dat*] provozieren ❷ *outrage* hervorrufen

prow [praʊ] n Bug m

prowl [praʊl] I. n (*search*) Streifzug m, Suche f II. vt durchstreifen III. vi ■ **to ~** [**around**] umherstreifen

prowler [ˈpraʊ·lər] n Herumtreiber(in) m(f) fam

proximity [prɑk·ˈsɪm·ɪ·ti] n Nähe f

proxy [ˈprɑk·si] n Bevollmächtigte(r) f(m)

prudent [ˈpru·dənt] *adj* vorsichtig; *action* klug

prudish [ˈpru·dɪʃ] *adj* prüde

prune[1] [prun] n (*plum*) Dörrpflaume f

prune[2] [prun] vt HORT [be]schneiden; (*fig*) reduzieren; *costs* kürzen

pry[1] <-ie-> [praɪ] vi ■ **to ~ into sth** seine Nase in etw *akk* stecken fam

pry[2] <-ie-> [praɪ] vt ■ **to ~ sth open** etw [mit einem Hebel] aufbrechen

prying [ˈpraɪ·ɪŋ] *adj* (*pej*) neugierig

PS [ˌpi·ˈes] n abbrev of **postscript** PS nt

psalm [sam] n REL Psalm m

pseudo [ˈsu·doʊ] *adj* Pseudo-

pseudonym [ˈsu·də·nɪm] n Pseudonym nt

PST [ˌpi·es·ˈti] n abbrev of **Pacific Standard Time** pazifische Zeit

psych [saɪk] vt (*fam: prepare*) ■ **to ~ oneself up** sich *akk* [psychisch] aufbauen

psyched [saɪkt] *adj pred* (*sl: excited*) aufgedreht fam, aufgeputscht

psychedelic [ˌsaɪ·kə·ˈdel·ɪk] *adj* psychedelisch

psychiatric [ˌsaɪ·ki·ˈæt·rɪk] *adj* psychiatrisch

psychiatrist [saɪ·ˈkaɪ·ə·trɪst] n Psychiater(in) m(f)

psychiatry [saɪ·ˈkaɪ·ə·tri] n Psychiatrie f

psychic [ˈsaɪ·kɪk] I. n Medium nt II. *adj* übernatürlich

psychoanalysis [ˌsaɪ·koʊ·ə·ˈnæl·ə·sɪs] n Psychoanalyse f

psychological [ˌsaɪ·kə·ˈlɑdʒ·ɪ·kəl] *adj* (*of the mind, not physical*) psychisch

psychologist [saɪ·ˈkɑl·ə·dʒɪst] n Psychologe, -in m, f

psychology [saɪ·ˈkɑl·ə·dʒi] n Psychologie f

psychopath [ˈsaɪ·kə·pæθ] n Psychopath(in) m(f)

psychotherapist [ˌsaɪ·koʊ·ˈθer·ə·pɪst] n Psychotherapeut(in) m(f)

psychotic [saɪ·ˈkɑt·ɪk] *adj* psychotisch

pt.[1] abbrev of **part** I 2, 3

pt.[2] abbrev of **point** I

pt.[3] abbrev of **pint** Pint nt (*0,568 l*)

PTA [ˌpi·ti·ˈeɪ] abbrev of **Parent-Teacher Association** Eltern-Lehrer-Organisation f

PTO [ˌpi·ti·ˈoʊ] abbrev of **Parent-Teacher Organization** ≈ Elternbeirat m

pub [pʌb] n Kneipe f

puberty [ˈpju·bər·ti] n Pubertät f

public [ˈpʌb·lɪk] I. *adj* öffentlich II. n + *sing/pl vb* ❶ (*the people*) ■ **the ~** die Öffentlichkeit f ❷ (*patrons*) Anhängerschaft f; **the viewing ~** Zuschauer pl

public-ad'dress system n Lautsprecheranlage f

publication [ˌpʌb·lɪ·ˈkeɪ·ʃən] n ❶ (*publishing*) Veröffentlichung f ❷ (*published work*) Publikation f

P

public 'holiday n gesetzlicher Feiertag
public 'interest n öffentliches Interesse
publicist ['pʌb·lɪ·sɪst] n Publizist(in) m(f)
publicity [pʌb·'lɪs·ɪ· t̬i] n ❶ (promotion) Publicity f ❷ (attention) Aufsehen nt
publicize ['pʌb·lɪ·saɪz] vt bekannt machen
public 'library n öffentliche Bibliothek
publicly ['pʌb·lɪk·li] adv öffentlich
public o'pinion n öffentliche Meinung
public re'lations npl MEDIA, POL Public Relations pl
public 'school n öffentliche [o staatliche] Schule
public 'sector n öffentlicher Sektor
public 'television n öffentlich-rechtliches Fernsehen
public transpor'tation n öffentliche Verkehrsmittel
public u'tility n (company) öffentlicher Versorgungsbetrieb
publish ['pʌb·lɪʃ] vt article, result veröffentlichen; book, newspaper herausgeben
publisher ['pʌb·lɪ·ʃər] n MEDIA ❶ (company) Verlag m ❷ (newspaper owner) Herausgeber(in) m(f)
publishing ['pʌb·lɪ·ʃɪŋ] n Verlagswesen nt
'publishing house n Verlag m
puck [pʌk] n SPORT Puck m
pucker ['pʌk·ər] I. vt in Falten legen; lips spitzen II. vi ■to ~ [up] cloth sich kräuseln; lips sich spitzen
pudding ['pʊd·ɪŋ] n Pudding m
puddle ['pʌd·əl] n Pfütze f
pudgy ['pʊdʒ·i] adj rundlich; face schwammig; person pummelig
Puerto Rican [ˌpwer·tə·'ri·kən] I. n Puerto-Ricaner(in) m(f) II. adj puerto-ricanisch
Puerto Rico [ˌpwer·tə·'ri·koʊ] n Puerto Rico nt
puff [pʌf] I. n ❶ (fam: short blast) of breath Atemstoß m; of wind Windstoß m ❷ (pastry) Blätterteig m II. vi ❶ (breathe heavily) schnaufen

❷ (smoke) ■to ~ on a cigar eine Zigarre qualmen III. vt (fam: praise) aufbauschen
◆**puff out** vt aufblähen; feathers aufplustern
◆**puff up** I. vt (fig) ■to ~ oneself up person sich aufblasen II. vi [an]schwellen
puffy ['pʌf·i] adj geschwollen, verquollen
'pug nose n Stupsnase f
puke [pjuk] I. vt (vulg) ■to ~ sth ↻ [up] etw [aus]kotzen sl II. vi (sl) kotzen sl
pull [pʊl] I. n ❶ (tug) Zug m ❷ (force) Zugkraft f; of the earth Anziehungskraft f ❸ (on a cigarette) Zug m; (on a bottle) Schluck m ❹ (attraction) Anziehung f II. vt ❶ (draw) ziehen; trigger abdrücken ❷ MED muscle zerren ❸ (fam) gun ziehen ▶ PHRASES: **to ~ sb's leg** (fam) jdn auf den Arm nehmen; **to ~ strings** Beziehungen spielen lassen III. vi (draw) ■to ~ [at sth] [an etw dat] ziehen
◆**pull ahead** vi ❶ (overtake) **to ~ ahead of sb** jdn überholen ❷ SPORT in Führung gehen
◆**pull apart** vt auseinanderziehen
◆**pull aside** vt ■to ~ sb aside jdn zur Seite nehmen
◆**pull away** I. vi ■to ~ away from sb/sth ❶ (leave) sich von jdm/etw wegbewegen ❷ SPORT runner sich vom Feld absetzen ❸ (recoil) vor jdm zurückweichen II. vt wegreißen
◆**pull back** vi ❶ (recoil) zurückschrecken ❷ MIL (withdraw) sich zurückziehen
◆**pull down** vt ❶ (move down) herunterziehen ❷ building abreißen ❸ (sl: earn) kassieren
◆**pull in** I. vi TRANSP train einfahren; bus anhalten II. vt ❶ (attract) anziehen ❷ (fam: earn) [ab]kassieren
◆**pull off** vt ❶ (take off) [schnell] ausziehen ❷ (fam: succeed) durchziehen; deal zustande bringen
◆**pull on** vt [schnell] überziehen

◆**pull out** I. *vi* ❶ (*move out*) *vehicle* ausscheren ❷ (*depart*) *train* ausfahren; *car* herausfahren ❸ (*withdraw*) aussteigen *fam* II. *vt* ❶ MIL **to ~ out troops** Truppen abziehen ❷ (*take out*) herausziehen

◆**pull over** I. *vt vehicle* anhalten II. *vi vehicle* zur Seite fahren

◆**pull through** *vi* (*survive*) durchkommen

◆**pull together** *vt* (*regain composure*) ■ **to ~ oneself together** sich zusammennehmen

◆**pull up** I. *vt* ❶ (*pull toward one*) heranziehen ❷ (*raise*) hochziehen ❸ *floorboards* herausreißen II. *vi* [heranfahren und] anhalten

pull-down '**menu** *n* Pulldown-Menü *nt*

pulley ['pʊl·i] *n* Flaschenzug *m*

'**pullout** *n* ❶ MIL Rückzug *m* ❷ PUBL [Sonder]beilage *f*

pulp [pʌlp] I. *n* ❶ (*mush*) Brei *m* ❷ FOOD Fruchtfleisch *nt kein pl* II. *vt* zu Brei verarbeiten

pulpit ['pʊl·pɪt] *n* Kanzel *f*

pulsate ['pʌl·seɪt] *vi* pulsieren; (*with noise*) vibrieren

pulse [pʌls] *n* ❶ (*heartbeat*) Puls *m*; **to take sb's ~** jds Puls fühlen ❷ (*fig: mood*) **to have one's finger on the ~** am Ball sein

pulverize ['pʌl·və·raɪz] *vt* pulverisieren

puma ['pu·mə] *n* Puma *m*

pumice ['pʌm·ɪs], **pumice stone** ['pʌm·ɪs·] *n* Bimsstein *m*

pump[1] [pʌmp] I. *n* (*device*) Pumpe *f* II. *vt* pumpen

pump[2] [pʌmp] *n* (*shoe*) Pumps *m*

pumpernickel ['pʌm·pər·nɪk·əl] *n* Pumpernickel *nt*

pumpkin ['pʌmp·kɪn] *n* [Garten]kürbis *m*

pumpkin pie *n* eine Art Kürbiskuchen, der vor allem an Thanksgiving und Weihnachten serviert wird

pun [pʌn] *n* Wortspiel *nt*

punch[1] [pʌntʃ] I. *n* (*piercing tool*) Stanzwerkzeug *nt*; [*hole*] ~ (*for paper*) Lo-

cher *m* II. *vt metal* [aus]stanzen; *paper* lochen

punch[2] [pʌntʃ] I. *n* <*pl* -es> ❶ (*hit*) [Faust]schlag *m*; (*in boxing*) Punch *m kein pl fachspr* ❷ (*strong effect*) Durchschlagskraft *f kein pl*; *of arguments* Überzeugungskraft *f kein pl* II. *vt* (*hit*) ■ **to ~ sb** jdn [mit der Faust] schlagen

punch[3] [pʌntʃ] *n hot or cold* Punsch *m*; *cold* Bowle *f*

'**punch bowl** *n* Punschschüssel *f*, Bowlengefäß *nt*

'**punch line** *n* Pointe *f*

punctual ['pʌŋk·tʃu·əl] *adj* pünktlich

punctuation [ˌpʌŋk·tʃu·'eɪ·ʃən] *n* Zeichensetzung *f*

punctu'ation mark *n* Satzzeichen *nt*

puncture ['pʌŋk·tʃər] I. *vt* ❶ (*pierce*) durchstechen ❷ (*fig*) *hope* zerstören; *mood* verderben II. *vi* (*burst*) *tire* ein Loch bekommen III. *n* Reifenpanne *f*

pungent ['pʌn·dʒənt] *adj* ❶ (*a. pej: strong*) *taste, smell* scharf ❷ (*fig*) *wit, words* scharf *a. pej*; *comment* bissig *pej*

punish ['pʌn·ɪʃ] *vt* ❶ (*penalize*) bestrafen ❷ (*treat roughly*) strapazieren; (*treat badly*) maltrâtieren

punishable ['pʌn·ɪʃ·ə·bəl] *adj* LAW *offense* strafbar; **a ~ infraction of the rules** ein Regelverstoß, der zu ahnden ist

punishing ['pʌn·ɪ·ʃɪŋ] I. *adj attr* (*fig*) ❶ (*heavy*) mörderisch *fig fam* ❷ (*tough*) hart, schwer, anstrengend II. *n* (*severe handling*) Strapazierung *f*; (*rough treatment*) Maltrâtierung *f*; **to take a ~** *equipment* stark beansprucht werden; *boxer* Prügel beziehen

punishment ['pʌn·ɪʃ·mənt] *n* ❶ (*penalty*) Bestrafung *f*, Strafe *f*; **capital ~** Todesstrafe *f* ❷ (*severe handling*) Strapazierung *f*; (*rough treatment*) grobe Behandlung; (*strain*) Strapaze *f*

punk [pʌŋk] *n* ❶ (*pej fam: worthless person*) Dreckskerl *m* ❷ (*music*) Punk[rock] *m*; (*fan*) Punker(in) *m(f)*

punt [pʌnt] SPORT I. *vt*, *vi* punten II. *n* Punt *m*

puny ['pju·ni] *adj* (*pej*) ❶ *person*

P

schwächlich ② (*fig: lacking in power*) schwach; *attempt* schüchtern

pupil¹ ['pju·pəl] *n* Schüler(in) *m(f)*

pupil² ['pju·pəl] *n* ANAT Pupille *f*

puppet ['pʌp·ɪt] *n* (*theater doll*) [Hand]puppe *f*; (*on strings*) Marionette *f a. pej, fig*

'**puppet show** *n* Puppenspiel *nt*, Marionettentheater *nt*

puppy ['pʌp·i] *n* (*baby dog*) junger Hund, Welpe *m*

purchase ['pɜr·tʃəs] I. *vt* (*form: buy*) kaufen II. *n* (*something bought, act of buying*) Kauf *m*

purchaser ['pɜr·tʃə·sər] *n* Käufer(in) *m(f)*

'**purchasing power** *n* Kaufkraft *f kein pl*

pure [pjʊr] *adj* ① (*unmixed*) rein, pur ② *air, water* sauber ③ (*fig: utter*) rein, pur

'**purebred** *adj* reinrassig

purée [pjʊ·'reɪ] I. *vt* <puréed, puréeing> pürieren II. *n* Püree *nt*

purely ['pjʊr·li] *adv* ① (*completely*) rein, ausschließlich ② (*merely*) bloß

purge [pɜrdʒ] I. *vt* (*a. fig: cleanse*) reinigen (**of** von +*dat*); ■**to ~ oneself of sth** *guilt* sich von etw *dat* reinwaschen II. *n* POL Säuberung[saktion] *f*

purification [,pjʊr·ə·fɪ·'keɪ·ʃən] *n* Reinigung *f*

purify ['pjʊr·ə·faɪ] *vt* reinigen (**of/from** von +*dat*)

purist ['pjʊr·ɪst] *n* Purist(in) *m(f)*

puritanical [,pjʊr·ɪ·'tæn·ɪ·kəl] *adj* (*usu pej*) puritanisch

purity ['pjʊr·ɪ·ṭi] *n* ① (*cleanness*) Sauberkeit *f* ② (*freedom from admixture*) Reinheit *f*

purl [pɜrl] *n* linke Masche

purple ['pɜr·pəl] *adj* (*red/blue mix*) violett; (*more red*) lila[farben]; (*crimson*) purpurrot

Purple 'Heart *n* Verwundetenabzeichen *nt*

purpose ['pɜr·pəs] *n* ① (*reason*) Grund *m* ② (*goal*) Absicht *f*, Ziel *nt* ③ (*resoluteness*) **lack of ~** Unentschlossenheit *f*

purposeful ['pɜr·pəs·fəl] *adj* ① (*single-minded*) zielstrebig ② (*resolute*) entschlossen

purposely ['pɜr·pəs·li] *adv* absichtlich, bewusst

purr [pɜr] *vi* (*cat*) schnurren

purse [pɜrs] *n* ① (*handbag*) Handtasche *f* ② SPORT (*prize money*) Preisgeld *nt*

purser ['pɜr·sər] *n* AVIAT Purser *m*; NAUT Zahlmeister(in) *m(f)* fachspr

pursue [pər·'su] *vt* ① (*a. fig*) verfolgen ② (*investigate*) weiterverfolgen ③ (*engage in*) betreiben; *studies* nachgehen

pursuer [pər·'su·ər] *n* Verfolger(in) *m(f)*

pursuit [pər·'sut] *n* ① (*chase*) Verfolgung[sjagd] *f*; *of knowledge, fulfillment* Streben *nt* ② (*activity*) Beschäftigung *f*

pus [pʌs] *n* Eiter *m*

push [pʊʃ] I. *n* <*pl* -es> ① (*shove*) Stoß *m*; (*slight push*) Schubs *m fam*; **to give sb/sth a ~** jdm/etw einen Stoß versetzen ② (*press*) Druck *m*; **at the ~ of a button** auf Knopfdruck *a. fig* ③ (*concerted effort*) Anstrengung[en] *f[pl]*, Kampagne *f* II. *vt* ① (*shove*) schieben; (*in a crowd*) drängeln; (*violently*) stoßen, schubsen; **to ~ sth to the back of one's mind** (*fig*) etw verdrängen ② (*move forcefully*) schieben; (*give a push*) stoßen ③ (*pressure*) ■**to ~ sb into doing sth** jdn [dazu] drängen, etw zu tun; (*force*) jdn zwingen, etw zu tun ④ (*press*) ■**to ~ sth** auf etw *akk* drücken ⑤ (*demand a lot*) ■**to ~ oneself** sich *dat* alles abverlangen ⑥ (*sl: promote*) propagieren; (*sell illegal drugs*) pushen *sl* III. *vi* ① (*exert force*) dränge[l]n; (*move*) schieben; **to ~ and pull** hin- und herschieben ② ■**to ~ past sb** sich an jdm vorbeidrängen

◆**push around** *vt* ① (*violently*) herumstoßen ② (*fig, pej: bully*) herumkommandieren

◆**push back** *vt* ① (*move backwards*) zurückschieben, zurückdrängen ② (*fig: delay*) *date* verschieben

◆**push down** *vt* ① *lever* hinunterdrücken ② *prices* [nach unten] drücken

◆**push forward I.** vt ❶ *(approv, fig)* development [ein großes Stück] voranbringen ❷ *(present forcefully)* in den Vordergrund stellen **II.** vi *(continue)* weitermachen

◆**push in** vt *(press against)* eindrücken

◆**push off I.** vi *(fig, a. fam: leave)* sich verziehen **II.** vt NAUT abstoßen

◆**push out** vt ❶ *(force out)* hinausjagen ❷ *(dismiss)* hinauswerfen

◆**push over** vt umwerfen, umstoßen

◆**push through** **I.** vi *(maneuver through)* ■**to ~ through sth** sich durch etw akk drängen **II.** vt POL *motion* durchdrücken *fam*

◆**push up** vt ❶ *(move higher)* ■**to ~ sb ◯ up** jdn hochheben ❷ ECON *demands* steigern; *prices* hochtreiben

'**pushbutton I.** adj *(automated)* Druckknopf-, [voll]automatisch **II.** n Druckknopf m

pusher ['pʊʃ•ər] n *(pej)* Dealer(in) m(f)

'**pushover** n ❶ *(fig, pej fam: easily defeated opponent)* leichter Gegner/ leichte Gegnerin ❷ *(approv, fig fam: easy success)* Kinderspiel nt kein pl

'**pushpin** n Reißzwecke f

'**pushup** n Liegestütz m

pushy ['pʊʃ•i] adj *(fig fam)* ❶ *(pej)* aufdringlich ❷ *(ambitious)* tatkräftig

pussy ['pʊs•i] n ❶ *(cat)* Mieze[katze] f fam ❷ *(fig, pej vulg: woman's genitals)* Muschi f

'**pussyfoot** vi *(pej fam: move cautiously)* ■**to ~ around** herumreden *fam*

'**pussy willow** n Salweide f

put <-tt-, put, put> [pʊt] vt ❶ *(place)* ■**to ~ sth somewhere** etw irgendwohin stellen; *(lay down)* etw irgendwohin legen; **she ~ some milk in her coffee** sie gab etwas Milch in ihren Kaffee; **to ~ oneself in sb's place** sich in jds Situation versetzen; **I ~ clean sheets on the bed** ich habe das Bett frisch bezogen; **she ~ her arm round him** sie legte ihren Arm um ihn; **to ~ sb to bed** jdn ins Bett bringen ❷ *(invest)* **to ~ effort into sth** Mühe in etw akk

stecken ❸ *(impose)* **to ~ the blame on sb** jdm die Schuld geben; **to ~ pressure on sb** jdn unter Druck setzen; **to ~ sb to the test** jdn auf die Probe stellen ❹ *(include)* **to ~ sth on the agenda** etw auf die Tagesordnung setzen ❺ *(indicating change of condition)* **to ~ sb at risk** jdn in Gefahr bringen; **to ~ one's affairs in order** seine Angelegenheiten in Ordnung bringen; **to ~ a stop to sth** etw beenden ❻ *(express)* **how should I ~ it?** wie soll ich mich ausdrücken?

◆**put across** vt *(make understood)* **to ~ one's point across** etw verständlich machen

◆**put aside** vt ❶ *(save)* zurücklegen; *money a.* sparen; **to ~ sth aside for sb** etw akk für jdn auf die Seite legen ❷ *(postpone)* ■**to ~ aside ◯ sth** *book etc.* etw beiseitelegen

◆**put away** vt ❶ *(tidy up)* wegräumen; *(in storage place)* einräumen ❷ *(save)* auf die hohe Kante legen ❸ *(fam: eat a lot)* ■**to ~ away ◯ sth** etw in sich akk hineinstopfen

◆**put back** vt ❶ *(replace)* zurückstellen ❷ *(reassemble)* ■**to ~ sth back together** etw wieder zusammensetzen

◆**put down** vt ❶ *(set down)* ablegen ❷ *(lower)* *arm, feet* herunternehmen; ■**to ~ sb ◯ down** jdn runterlassen ❸ *(spread)* **to ~ down roots** *(a. fig)* Wurzeln schlagen ❹ *(write)* aufschreiben; ■**to ~ sb down for sth** jdn für etw akk eintragen ❺ ECON *(leave as deposit)* anzahlen ❻ *(deride)* ■**to ~ down ◯ sb/oneself** jdn/sich schlechtmachen

◆**put forward** vt *idea* vorbringen; *candidate* vorschlagen

◆**put in I.** vt ❶ *(place in)* hineinsetzen/-legen/-stellen ❷ *food, ingredients* hinzufügen ❸ *(install)* installieren ❹ *(enter, submit)* **to ~ in an order for sth** etw bestellen **II.** vi ■**to ~ in for sth** *job* sich um etw akk bewerben; *pay raise, transfer* etw beantragen

◆**put off** vt ❶ *(delay)* verschieben

P

❷ (*persuade to not act*) vertrösten ❸ (*discourage*) ■ **to ~ sb off from doing sth** jdm etw *akk* verleiden [*o* madigmachen]

◆ **put on** *vt* ❶ *clothes, shoes* anziehen; *makeup* auflegen; (*fig*) *smile* aufsetzen ❷ (*turn on*) einschalten ❸ (*provide*) bereitstellen; *exhibition* veranstalten ❹ (*increase*) **to ~ on weight** zunehmen

◆ **put out** *vt* ❶ (*place outside*) **to ~ the laundry out** [**to dry**] die Wäsche draußen aufhängen ❷ *hand, foot* ausstrecken ❸ MEDIA (*publish*) veröffentlichen ❹ (*place ready*) ■ **to ~ sth out** [**for sb**] *chairs, clothes* [jdm] etw hinstellen ❺ *fire* löschen; *cigarette* ausmachen; *lights* ausschalten

◆ **put over** *vt* (*fam: fool*) **to ~ one over on sb** sich mit jdm einen Scherz erlauben

◆ **put through** *vt* ❶ (*insert through*) ■ **to ~ sth through sth** etw durch etw *akk* schieben; (*pierce*) etw durch etw *akk* stechen ❷ TELEC (*connect*) ■ **to ~ sb through to sb** jdn mit jdm verbinden ❸ (*carry through*) *plan, proposal* durchbringen

◆ **put together** *vt* ❶ (*assemble*) zusammensetzen; *machine, model, radio* zusammenbauen ❷ (*make*) zusammenstellen; *list* aufstellen ❸ MATH (*add*) **to ~ 10 and 15 together** 10 und 15 zusammenzählen; **she earns more than all the rest of us ~ together** (*fig*) sie verdient mehr als wir alle zusammengenommen

◆ **put up** *vt* ❶ (*hang up*) aufhängen; *flag, sail* hissen ❷ (*raise*) hochheben; *feet* hochlegen; *hair* aufstecken ❸ (*build*) bauen ❹ (*offer*) **to ~ sth up for sale** etw zum Verkauf anbieten ❺ (*give shelter*) unterbringen

◆ **put up with** *vi* **I'm not ~ing up with this any longer** ich werde das nicht länger dulden

'**putdown** *n* verächtliche Bemerkung

putrid ['pju·trɪd] *adj* (*form*) ❶ *smell* faulig ❷ BIOL *organic matter* verfault

putt [pʌt] SPORT **I.** *vt, vi* putten **II.** *n* Putt *m*

putter[1] ['pʌt̬·ər] *n* SPORT *golf club* Putter *m*

putter[2] ['pʌt̬·ər] *vi* (*do nothing in particular*) vor sich *akk* hin werkeln *fam*

putty ['pʌt̬·i] **I.** *n* [Dichtungs]kitt *m* **II.** *vt* <-ie-> [ver]kitten, [ver]spachteln

puzzle ['pʌz·əl] *n* ❶ (*question, test of ingenuity*) Rätsel *nt*; **jigsaw ~** Puzzle *nt* ❷ (*test of patience*) Geduldsspiel *nt*

puzzled ['pʌz·əld] *adj* ratlos

puzzling ['pʌz·əl·ɪŋ] *adj* rätselhaft

PVC [ˌpi·vi·'si] *n abbrev of* **polyvinyl chloride** PVC *nt*

Pygmy ['pɪg·mi] *n* (*pej, a. fig*) Zwerg(in) *m(f)*

pylon ['paɪ·lan] *n* AUTO (*traffic cone*) Pylon *m*

pyramid ['pɪr·ə·mɪd] *n* Pyramide *f*

Pyrex® ['paɪ·reks] *n* Pyrex-Glas®

python <*pl* -s> ['paɪ·θan] *n* Python *m*

Qq

Q <pl -'s>, **q** <pl -'s> [kju] n Q nt, q nt;
~ as in Quebec Q wie Quelle

Q. [kju] n ECON abbrev of **quarter** Quartal nt

q. [kju] n ❶ FOOD abbrev of **quart** Quart nt (0,95 l) ❷ abbrev of **question** Frage f

QR code [kjuː·'ɑː·ʳ-] n abbrev of **Quick Response** INET QR-Code m

qt., qt n FOOD abbrev of **quart** Quart nt (0,95 l)

Q-tip® ['kju·tɪp] n Wattestäbchen nt

quack¹ [kwæk] I. n Quaken nt II. vi quaken

quack² [kwæk] n (pej: fake doctor) Quacksalber(in) m(f) pej

quad¹ [kwad] n short for **quadrangle** Geviert nt; (on campus) Hof

quad² [kwad] n (fam) short for **quadruplet** Vierling m

quadrangle ['kwad·ræŋ·gəl] n (square) Geviert nt

quadrant ['kwad·rənt] n MATH Viertelkreis m

quadraphonic [ˌkwad·rə·'fan·ɪk] adj quadrophon[isch]

quadrilateral [ˌkwad·rɪ·'læt̬·ər·əl] n Viereck nt

quadruped ['kwad·rə·ped] n Vierfüßer m

quadruple [kwa·'dru·pəl] I. vt vervierfachen II. adj vierfach attr

quadruplet [kwa·'dru·plɪt] n Vierling m

quagmire ['kwæg·maɪr] n Morast[boden] m

quail <pl -s> [kweɪl] n ZOOL Wachtel f

quaint [kweɪnt] adj ❶ (charming) reizend; village malerisch; cottage urig ❷ (old-fashioned) altertümlich

quake [kweɪk] I. n (fam) [Erd]beben nt II. vi earth beben

Quaker ['kweɪ·kər] n Quäker(in) m(f)

qualification [ˌkwal·ə·fɪ·'keɪ·ʃən] n ❶ (skill) Qualifikation f ❷ (condition)

[notwendige] Voraussetzung f ❸ (restriction) Einschränkung f

qualified ['kwal·ɪ·faɪd] adj ❶ (competent) qualifiziert ❷ (restricted) bedingt; **to make a ~ statement** eine Erklärung unter Einschränkungen abgeben

qualifier ['kwal·ɪ·faɪ·ər] n Qualifikant(in) m(f)

qualify <-ie-> ['kwal·ɪ·faɪ] I. vt ❶ (make competent) qualifizieren ❷ (make eligible) ■ to ~ sb to do sth jdn berechtigen, etw zu tun ❸ (restrict) einschränken; **to ~ a remark** eine Bemerkung unter Vorbehalt äußern II. vi ❶ (prove competence) sich qualifizieren (for für +akk) ❷ (meet requirements) die [nötigen] Voraussetzungen erfüllen

qualifying ['kwal·ɪ·faɪ·ɪŋ] adj attr ❶ (restrictive) einschränkend ❷ SPORT round Qualifikations-

qualitative ['kwal·ɪ·teɪ·t̬ɪv] adj qualitativ

quality ['kwal·ɪ·t̬i] I. n ❶ (standard) Qualität f; **~ of life** Lebensqualität f ❷ (feature) Merkmal nt; **managerial qualities** Führungsqualitäten pl II. adj [qualitativ] hochwertig

'quality control n usu sing Qualitätskontrolle f

'quality time n die Zeit, die man dafür aufbringt, familiäre Beziehungen zu entwickeln und zu pflegen

qualm [kwam] n ❶ (doubt) ■ ~s pl Bedenken pl ❷ (uneasiness) ungutes Gefühl

quandary ['kwan·də·ri] n usu sing Unentschiedenheit f; **to be in a ~** sich nicht entscheiden können

quantify <-ie-> ['kwan·tə·faɪ] vt mengenmäßig messen

quantitative ['kwan·tə·teɪ·t̬ɪv] adj quantitativ geh

quantity ['kwan·t̬ɪ·t̬i] n ❶ (amount)

Menge f; *of individual items* Stückzahl f ② (*large amount*) große Menge f

quarantine ['kwɔr·ən·ˌtin] n Quarantäne f

quarrel ['kwɔr·əl] I. n (*argument*) Streit m; **to have a ~** sich streiten II. vi <-l-> ① (*argue*) sich streiten (**about** über +akk) ② (*disagree with*) ■**to ~ with sth** etwas an etw dat aussetzen

quarrelsome ['kwɔr·əl·səm] adj streitsüchtig

quarry[1] ['kwɔr·i] I. n Steinbruch m II. vt <-ie-> brechen

quarry[2] ['kwɔr·i] n (*animal*) Jagdbeute f

quart [kwɔrt] n Quart nt (*0,95 l*); **a ~ of milk** ein Quart nt Milch

quarter ['kwɔr·tər] I. n ① (*fourth*) Viertel nt; **the bottle was a ~ full** es war noch ein Viertel in der Flasche; **to divide sth into ~s** etw in vier Teile teilen ② (*coin*) Vierteldollar m ③ (*time*) Viertel nt; *of year* Quartal nt; **a ~ to/after three** Viertel vor/nach drei ④ SPORT (*period*) Viertel nt ⑤ (*area*) Gegend f; **the French Q~** das französische Viertel ⑥ (*lodgings*) ■**~s** pl Wohnung f; MIL Quartier nt ▶PHRASES: **at close ~s with sb** in jds Nähe II. vt vierteln

'**quarterback** n ① SPORT Quarterback m *fachspr* ② (*leader*) Gruppenleiter(in) m(f)

quarter'final n Viertelfinale nt

quarterly ['kwɔr·tər·li] adv, adj vierteljährlich

quartermaster ['kwɔr·tər·ˌmæs·tər] n MIL Quartiermeister m

'**quarter note** n MUS Viertelnote f

quartet, quartette [kwɔr·'tet] n Quartett nt

quartz [kwɔrts] n Quarz m; **rose ~** Rosenquarz m

quash [kwɑʃ] vt ① (*destroy*) zermalmen; (*fig*) *hopes* zunichtemachen ② (*suppress*) *rebellion* niederschlagen; *rumors* zum Verstummen bringen

quasi- ['kwɑ·zi] *in compounds* (*resembling*) Quasi-, quasi-

quaver ['kweɪ·vər] vi ① (*tremble*) *person* zittern; *voice a.* beben ② (*speak*) mit zitternder Stimme sprechen

quay [ki] n Kai m

queasy ['kwi·zi] adj ① *stomach* [über]-empfindlich ② (*upset*) übel *nach* n

queen [kwin] n ① Königin f ② (*chess*) Dame f ③ (*fam: gay*) Tunte f *pej fam*; **drag ~** Transvestit m

queer [kwɪr] I. adj ① (*strange*) seltsam; **to have ~ ideas** schräge Ideen haben ② (*offensive fam: homosexual*) schwul *fam* II. n (*offensive fam*) Schwule(r) m *fam*; *female* Lesbe f *fam*

quell [kwel] vt ① (*suppress*) *revolt* niederschlagen ② (*fig*) *doubts, fears* zerstreuen

quench [kwentʃ] vt löschen; (*fig*) dämpfen

query ['kwɪr·i] I. n Rückfrage f II. vt <-ie-> (*form*) ① (*doubt*) in Frage stellen ② (*ask*) befragen

quest [kwest] n Suche f

question ['kwes·tʃən] I. n ① (*query*) Frage f; **to pop the ~** jdm einen [Heirats]antrag machen ② (*doubt*) Zweifel m; **there's no ~ about it** keine Frage; **without ~** zweifellos ③ (*matter*) Frage f; **to be out of the ~** nicht in Frage kommen II. vt ① (*ask*) befragen (**about** über +akk) ② (*interrogate*) verhören (**about** zu +dat)

questionable ['kwes·tʃə·nə·bəl] adj ① (*uncertain*) zweifelhaft; *future* ungewiss ② (*shady*) fragwürdig

questioning ['kwes·tʃə·nɪŋ] I. n by police Verhör nt II. adj look fragend

'**question mark** n Fragezeichen nt a. fig

questionnaire [ˌkwes·tʃə·'ner] n Fragebogen m

queue [kju] COMPUT I. n Schlange f II. vi anstehen, Schlange stehen

quibble ['kwɪb·əl] I. n (*criticism*) Kritteleï f II. vi sich streiten (**about** über +akk); **no one would ~ with that** das würde niemand bestreiten

quiche <pl -> [kiʃ] n Quiche f

quick [kwɪk] I. adj ① (*fast*) schnell; **in ~ succession** in schneller [Ab]folge; **to have a ~ temper** ein rasch aufbrausendes Temperament haben ② (*short*) kurz; **to have a ~ look at sth** sich dat etw kurz ansehen ③ (*alert*) [geistig] gewandt; ~ **wit** Aufgewecktheit *f; in replying* Schlagfertigkeit *f* II. *adv* schnell, rasch III. *interj* schnell

'**quick-acting** *adj* schnell wirksam

quickie ['kwɪk·i] I. *n* ① (*fast thing*) kurze Sache ② (*sex*) Quickie *m* II. *adj* ~ **divorce** schnelle und unkomplizierte Scheidung

quickly ['kwɪk·li] *adv* schnell, rasch

quickness ['kwɪk·nɪs] *n* ① (*speed*) Schnelligkeit *f* ② (*alertness*) ~ **of mind** scharfer Verstand

'**quicksand** *n* Treibsand *m*

'**quickstep** *n* ■ **the** ~ der Quickstep

quick-'tempered *adj* hitzköpfig

quick-'witted *adj* (*alert*) aufgeweckt; *reply* schlagfertig

quid pro quo ['kwɪd·prou·'kwou] *n* Gegenleistung *f*

quiet ['kwaɪ·ət] I. *adj* <-er, -est *or* more ~, most ~> ① (*not loud*) leise ② (*silent*) ruhig; **please be** ~ Ruhe bitte! ③ (*not talking*) still; *child* ruhig; (*taciturn*) schweigsam ④ (*secret*) heimlich; **to keep sth** ~ etw für sich *akk* behalten ⑤ *street* ruhig ▶ PHRASES: **as** ~ **as a mouse** mucksmäuschenstill *fam* II. *n* ① (*silence*) Stille *f* ② (*lack of excitement*) Ruhe *f*; **peace and** ~ Ruhe und Frieden

◆ **quiet down** I. *vi* ① (*become quiet*) leiser werden ② (*become calm*) sich beruhigen II. *vt* ① (*make less noisy*) zur Ruhe bringen ② (*calm*) beruhigen

quietly ['kwaɪət·li] *adv* ① (*not loudly*) leise ② (*silently*) still; **to wait** ~ ruhig warten ③ (*unobtrusively*) unauffällig; **to be** ~ **confident** insgeheim überzeugt sein

quietness ['kwaɪ·ət·nɪs] *n* Ruhe *f*; (*silence*) Stille *f*

quill [kwɪl] *n* ① (*feather*) Feder *f* ② (*of porcupine*) Stachel *m*

quilt [kwɪlt] I. *n* Steppdecke *f*; **patch-work** ~ Quilt *m* II. *vt* [ab]steppen

quinine ['kwaɪ·naɪn] *n* Chinin *nt*

quintessential [ˌkwɪn·tə·'sen·ʃəl] *adj* essentiell

quintet, quintette [kwɪn·'tet] *n* Quintett *nt*

quintuplet [kwɪn·'tʌp·lɪt] *n* Fünfling *m*

quip [kwɪp] *n* witzige Bemerkung

quirk [kwɜrk] *n* ① (*habit*) Marotte *f* ② (*oddity*) Merkwürdigkeit *f kein pl*

quirky ['kwɜr·ki] *adj* schrullig *fam*

quit <quit *or* quitted, quit *or* quitted> [kwɪt] I. *vi* ① *worker* kündigen; *official* zurücktreten ② COMPUT aussteigen ③ (*give up*) aufgeben II. *vt* ① (*stop*) ~ **wasting my time** hör auf, meine Zeit zu verschwenden; **to** ~ **smoking** das Rauchen aufgeben ② (*give up*) aufgeben; *job* kündigen ③ COMPUT (*end*) aussteigen aus +*dat*

quite [kwaɪt] *adv* ① (*fairly*) ziemlich; **I had to wait** ~ **a long time** ich musste ganz schön lange warten *fam* ② (*completely*) ganz, völlig; ~ **honestly, ...** ehrlich gesagt ...

quits [kwɪts] *adj pred* quitt (**with** mit +*dat*); **to call it** ~ (*fam*) es gut sein lassen

quiver ['kwɪv·ər] *vi* zittern

quixotic [kwɪk·'sɑt·ɪk] *adj idea, vision* unrealistisch; *attempt* naiv

quiz [kwɪz] I. *n* <*pl* -zes> SCH, UNIV [kurze] Prüfung II. *vt* (*question*) befragen (**about** zu +*dat*)

'**quiz show** *n* Quizsendung *f*

quorum ['kwɔr·əm] *n* Quorum *nt geh*

quota ['kwou·tə] *n* Quote *f*

quotation [kwou·'teɪ·ʃən] *n* ① (*citation*) Zitat *nt* ② STOCKEX [Kurs]notierung *f*

quo'tation marks *npl* Anführungszeichen *pl*

quote [kwout] I. *n* ① (*citation*) Zitat *nt* ② (*quotation mark*) ■ ~**s** *pl* Gänsefüßchen *pl fam* ③ (*estimate*) Kostenvoranschlag *m* II. *vt* ① (*cite*) zitieren; ■ **to** ~ **sb on sth** jdn zu etw *dat* zitieren ② (*give*) *price* nennen ③ STOCKEX notieren III. *vi* zitieren; ■ **to** ~ **from sb** jdn zitieren

quotient ['kwou·ʃənt] *n* Quotient *m*

QWERTY keyboard [ˌkwɜr·ti·'ki·bɔrd] *n englische Standardtastatur*

Q

Rr

R <pl -'s>, r <pl -'s> [ar] n R nt, r nt;
~ **as in Romeo** R wie Richard

r adv abbrev of **right** r.

R[1] [ar] adj abbrev of **right** r.

R[2] [ar] adv FILM abbrev of **Restricted**:
rated ~ nicht für Jugendliche unter 17
Jahren

rabbi ['ræb·aɪ] n Rabbiner m

rabbit ['ræb·ɪt] n Kaninchen nt

'**rabble-rousing** adj [auf]hetzerisch

rabid ['ræb·ɪd] adj dog tollwütig; (fig) fanatisch

rabies ['reɪ·biz] n + sing vb Tollwut f

raccoon [ræ·'kun] n Waschbär(in) m(f)

race[1] [reɪs] n (run) Rennen nt; (species) Spezies f

race[2] [reɪs] I. n (run) Rennen nt; (competition) Wettkampf m II. vi Rennen
laufen; vehicles Rennen fahren; (rush)
rennen; ■ **to** ~ **by** time schnell vergehen III. vt ■ **to** ~ **sb** gegen jdn antreten

'**racecar** n Rennwagen m

'**racecourse** n Rennbahn f

'**racehorse** n Rennpferd nt

racer ['reɪ·sər] n [Renn]läufer(in) m(f);
(horse) Rennpferd nt; (bicycle) Renn-
rad nt; (car) Rennwagen m

'**racetrack** n Rennbahn f

racial ['reɪ·ʃəl] adj Rassen-; (racist) rassistisch

racism ['reɪ·sɪz·əm] n Rassismus m

racist ['reɪ·sɪst] I. n Rassist(in) m(f)
II. adj rassistisch

rack [ræk] I. n Regal nt; **clothes** ~ Klei-
derständer m; **magazine** ~ Zeitschrif-
tenständer m II. vt ▸PHRASES: **to** ~ **one's
brains** sich dat den Kopf zerbrechen

racket[1] ['ræk·ɪt] n SPORT Schläger m

racket[2] ['ræk·ɪt] n (fam) ❶ Krach m
❷ **extortion** ~ Schutzgelderpressung f

racketeering [ˌræk·ə·'tɪr] n dunkle Machenschaften pl

racoon [ræ·'kun] n see **raccoon**

racy ['reɪ·si] adj ❶ anzüglich; clothing
gewagt ❷ person draufgängerisch

radar ['reɪ·dar] n Radar m o nt

radiant ['reɪ·di·ənt] adj smile strahlend

radiate ['reɪ·di·eɪt] I. vi ausstrahlen
II. vt ausstrahlen; heat abgeben

radiation [ˌreɪ·di·'eɪ·ʃən] n Strahlung f;
(process) Abstrahlen nt

radiator ['reɪ·di·eɪ·tər] n Heizkörper m;
(on car) Kühler m

radical ['ræd·ɪ·kəl] I. adj radikal; (fundamental) fundamental II. n ❶ (person)
Radikale(r) f(m) ❷ CHEM Radikal nt; **free**
~ **s** freie Radikale

radio ['reɪ·di·oʊ] I. n ❶ Radio nt SÜDD,
ÖSTERR, SCHWEIZ a. m; (communicator)
Funkgerät nt; **on/over the** ~ über
Funk ❷ (broadcasting) Radio nt; **to
listen to the** ~ Radio hören II. vi **to**
~ **for help** über Funk Hilfe anfordern

radioactive [ˌreɪ·di·oʊ·'æk·tɪv] adj radioaktiv

radioactivity [ˌreɪ·di·oʊ·æk·'tɪv·ɪ·ti] n
Radioaktivität f

radiologist [ˌreɪ·di·'al·ə·dʒɪst] n Radio-
loge(in) m(f)

radiology [ˌreɪ·di·'al·ə·dʒi] n Radiolo-
gie f

'**radio station** n Radiosender m

radish <pl -es> ['ræd·ɪʃ] n Rettich m

radium ['reɪ·di·əm] n Radium nt

radius <pl -dii> ['reɪ·di·əs] n Radius m

raffle ['ræf·əl] I. n Tombola f II. vt verlo-
sen

raft [ræft] n Floß nt

rafting ['ræf·tɪŋ] n Rafting nt

rag [ræg] n Lumpen m; (for cleaning)
Lappen m; (for dust) Staubtuch nt
◆ **rag on** vt <gg-> (fam) ■ **to** ~ **on sb**
jdn nerven sl; (scold) auf jdm herumhacken fam

rage [reɪdʒ] I. n ❶ Wut f; **to get in a** ~
sich aufregen ❷ **to be** [all] **the** ~ der
letzte Schrei sein fam II. vi toben; **at sb**
anschreien; fire wüten

R

ragged ['ræg·ɪd] *adj* zerlumpt; *group* unorganisiert

raging ['reɪ·dʒɪŋ] *adj river* reißend; *fire* lodernd; *inferno* flammend; *thirst* schrecklich

'ragtime *n* Ragtime *m*

raid [reɪd] I. *n* ❶ (*attacker*) Angriff *m*; (*by police*) Razzia *f*; (*by bandits*) Überfall *m* II. *vt* ❶ überfallen; (*bomb*) bombardieren; *town* plündern ❷ (*rob*) ausplündern; *bank* überfallen

raider [reɪ·dər] *n* ❶ (*attacker*) Angreifer(in) *m(f)* ❷ (*robber*) Einbrecher(in) *m(f)* ❸ (*pej: investor*) **corporate ~** Heuschrecke *f pej*

rail [reɪl] *n* ❶ Bahn *f*; **by ~** mit der Bahn ❷ (*track*) Schiene *f* ❸ (*on stairs*) Geländer *nt*; (*pole*) Stange *f*

railing ['reɪ·lɪŋ] *n* Geländer *nt*

'railroad *n* ❶ (*Eisen*)bahn *f kein pl* ❷ (*track*) Schienen *pl*; (*stretch*) Strecke *f*

'railroad crossing *n* Bahnübergang *m*

'railroad station *n* Bahnhof *m*

rain [reɪn] I. *n* Regen *m*; **in the ~** im Regen II. *vi impers* **it's ~ing** es regnet

rainbow ['reɪn·boʊ] *n* Regenbogen *m*

'rain cloud *n* Regenwolke *f*

'raincoat *n* Regenmantel *m*

'raindrop *n* Regentropfen *m*

'rainfall *n* Niederschlag *m*; (*quantity*) Niederschlagsmenge *f*

'rain forest *n* Regenwald *m*

'rainproof *adj* wasserdicht

'rainstorm *n* starke Regenfälle *pl*

rainy ['reɪ·ni] *adj* regnerisch

raise [reɪz] I. *n* Gehaltserhöhung *f* II. *vt* ❶ heben; *anchor* lichten; *eyebrow, blinds* hochziehen; *flag, sail* hissen ❷ (*increase*) erhöhen; *quality* verbessern ❸ (*mention*) vorbringen; *issue* aufwerfen ❹ *capital* aufbringen ❺ *children* aufziehen ❻ (*breed*) züchten

raisin ['reɪ·zən] *n* Rosine *f*

rake [reɪk] I. *n* Harke *f* II. *vt* [zusammen]rechen; *soil* harken III. *vi* ■ **to ~ through sth** etw durchsuchen

♦ **rake in** *vt* rechen; (*fam*) *money* kassieren

rally ['ræl·i] I. *n* ❶ [Massen]versammlung *f*; *of troops* Versammlung *f* ❷ SPORT Ballwechsel *m* ❸ (*race*) Rallye *f* II. *vt* <-ie-> *troops* sammeln; *support* gewinnen; *supporters* mobilisieren III. *vi* <-ie-> *prices* sich erholen

♦ **rally 'around** *vi* unterstützen

ram [ræm] I. *n* ❶ Widder *m* ❷ (*weapon*) Rammbock *m* II. *vt* <-mm-> rammen

Ramadan [ˌræm·ə·'dan] *n* Ramadan *m*

ramble ['ræm·bəl] I. *n* Wanderung *f* II. *vi* ❶ wandern ❷ (*pej fam*) faseln *fam*

rambling ['ræm·blɪŋ] I. *n* ■ **~s** *pl* Gefasel *nt kein pl pej* II. *adj* ❶ (*incoherent*) unzusammenhängend ❷ **~ rose** Kletterrose *f*

ramification [ˌræm·ɪ·fɪ·'keɪ·ʃən] *n usu pl* Auswirkung *f*

ramp [ræmp] *n* Rampe *f*

rampage ['ræm·peɪdʒ] I. *n* Randale *f*; **on the ~** am angriffslustig II. *vi* randalieren

rampant ['ræm·pənt] *adj* ungezügelt, wuchernd; *inflation* galoppierend

ramshackle ['ræm·ʃæk·əl] *adj* klapp[e]rig; *building* baufällig

ran [ræn] *pt of* **run**

ranch [ræntʃ] *n* <*pl* -es> Ranch *f*

rancher ['ræn·tʃər] *n* Viehzüchter(in) *m(f)*; (*worker*) Farmarbeiter(in) *m(f)*

rancid ['ræn·sɪd] *adj* ranzig

rancor ['ræn·kər] *n* Verbitterung *f*, Groll *m*

R & B [ˌar·ənd·'bi] *n abbrev of* **rhythm and blues** R & B *m*

random ['ræn·dəm] I. *n* **at ~** willkürlich; (*by chance*) zufällig II. *adj* zufällig; **~ sample** Stichprobe *f*

rang [ræn] *pt of* **ring**

range [reɪndʒ] I. *n* ❶ Auswahl *f*; (*selection*) Angebot *nt* ❷ (*limits*) Bereich *m* ❸ (*distance*) Entfernung *f*; **in/out of ~** in/außer Reichweite ❹ (*mountains*) Bergkette *f* ❺ (*stove*) [Koch]herd *m* II. *vi* schwanken; ■ **to ~ from sth to sth** von etw *dat* bis [zu etw *dat*] reichen

ranger ['reɪn·dʒər] *n* Aufseher(in) *m(f)*;

R

(*soldier*) Ranger(in) *m(f)*; **park ~** Park-
ranger *m*

rank¹ [ræŋk] I. *n* ❶ Position *f*; MIL
Dienstgrad *m* ❷ (*row*) Reihe *f*; **to close
~s** die Reihen schließen; (*fig*) sich zusammenschließen II. *vi* **to ~ second in
the world** auf Platz zwei der Weltrang-
liste stehen; ■ **to ~ above sb** einen hö-
heren Rang als jd einnehmen III. *vt* einstufen

rank² [ræŋk] *adj* ❶ (*smelly*) stinkend
❷ *attr* absolut; *outsider* total

ransack ['ræn·sæk] *vt* durchwühlen;
(*hum*) plündern; (*rob*) ausrauben

ransom ['ræn·səm] I. *n* Lösegeld *nt*
II. *vt* auslösen

rant [rænt] I. *n* Geschimpfe *nt* II. *vi* [vor
sich *akk* hin] schimpfen

rap¹ [ræp] I. *n* ❶ Klopfen *nt kein pl*;
(*fam: rebuke*) Anpfiff *m fam* ❷ (*sl*) **to
take the ~** [**for sth**] die Schuld [für etw
akk] zugeschoben kriegen II. *vt* <-pp->
klopfen; (*fig: criticize*) scharf kritisieren

rap² [ræp] I. *n* MUS Rap *m* II. *vi* MUS rap-
pen

rape [reip] I. *n* Vergewaltigung *f*; (*fig*)
Zerstörung *f* II. *vt* vergewaltigen

rapid ['ræp·ɪd] *adj* schnell; *change,
growth* rasch; *rise* steil; (*sudden*) plötzlich

rapids ['ræp·ɪdz] *npl* Stromschnellen *pl*

rapist ['reɪ·pɪst] *n* Vergewaltiger(in)
m(f)

rapport [ræ·'pɔr] *n* Harmonie *f*

rapture ['ræp·tʃər] *n* Verzückung *f*

rare [rer] *adj* ❶ selten ❷ *meat* blutig

rarely ['rer·li] *adv* selten

rarity ['rer·ɪ·ţi] *n* Seltenheit *f*

rascal ['ræs·kəl] *n* Schlingel *m*; (*child*)
Frechdachs *m*

rash [ræʃ] I. *n* <*pl* -es> Ausschlag *m*
II. *adj* übereilt

raspberry ['ræz·ˌber·i] *n* Himbeere *f*

Rastafarian [ˌras·tə·'far·i·ən] *n* Rasta-
fari *m*

rat [ræt] *n* Ratte *f*

rate [reit] I. *n* ❶ Geschwindigkeit *f*;
(*measure*) Maß *nt*; (*payment, tax*)
Satz *m*; **unemployment ~** Arbeitslo-

senrate *f* ❷ **at any ~** (*whatever
happens*) auf jeden Fall; (*at least*) zu-
mindest II. *vt* [ein|schätzen, halten (**as**
für + *akk*)

rather ['ræð·ər] *adv* ❶ lieber, vielmehr;
I'd ~ rather stay ich würde lieber bleiben ❷ (*very*) ziemlich ❸ **or ~ ...** oder
besser gesagt ... ❹ (*on the contrary*)
eher

ratification [ˌræt·ə·fɪ·'keɪ·ʃən] *n* Ratifi-
zierung *f*

ratify <-ie-> ['ræt·ə·faɪ] *vt* ratifizieren

rating ['reɪ·ţɪŋ] *n* Einschätzung *f*, Ein-
stufung *f*; TV ■ **~s** *pl* [Einschalt]quo-
ten *pl*

ratio ['reɪ·ʃi·oʊ] *n* Verhältnis *nt*

ration ['ræʃ·ən] I. *n* Ration *f* II. *vt* ratio-
nieren

rational ['ræʃ·ə·nəl] *adj* rational

rationalize ['ræʃ·ə·nə·laɪz] *vt, vi* rationa-
lisieren

rationing ['ræʃ·ə·nɪŋ] *n* Rationierung *f*

'rat race *n* ewiger Konkurrenzkampf

rattle ['ræţ·əl] I. *n* ❶ Klappern *nt*; (*of
chains*) Rasseln *nt* ❷ (*toy*) Rassel *f* II. *vi*
❶ klappern; *keys* rasseln ❷ (*move*) rattern ❸ ■ **to ~ on** [drauflos]quasseln *fam*
III. *vt keys* rasseln; *person* durcheinanderbringen

'rattlesnake *n* Klapperschlange *f*

raucous ['rɔ·kəs] *adj* rau, heiser

raunchy ['rɔn·tʃi] *adj* schlüpfrig *fam*;
video, film heiß *fam*

ravage ['ræv·ɪdʒ] *vt* verwüsten

rave [reiv] I. *n* Rave *m* o *nt* II. *adj attr* re-
views glänzend III. *vi* ❶ **to** [**rant and**] ~
toben ❷ (*fam: praise*) schwärmen

raven ['reɪ·vən] *n* Rabe *m*

ravenous ['ræv·ə·nəs] *adj* ausgehungert; *appetite* unbändig

ravine [rə·'vin] *n* Schlucht *f*

raving ['reɪ·vɪŋ] I. *n* ■ **~s** *pl* Hirngespins-
te *pl* II. *adj attr* total *fam* III. *adv* **to be
[stark] ~ mad** (*fam*) völlig verrückt sein

ravioli [ræv·i·'oʊ·li] *n* Ravioli *pl*

ravishing ['ræv·ɪ·ʃɪŋ] *adj* hinreißend

raw [rɔ] *adj* ❶ roh ❷ (*inexperienced*)
unerfahren ❸ (*sore*) wund; (*fig*) *nerves*
empfindlich

R

raw ma'terial n Rohstoff m
ray¹ [reɪ] n Strahl m
ray² [reɪ] n (fish) Rochen m
rayon ['reɪ·ən] n Viskose f
razor ['reɪ·zər] I. n Rasierapparat m II. vt [ab]rasieren
'razor blade n Rasierklinge f
'razor sharp adj pred, **'razor-sharp** adj attr ▪ **to be** ~ scharf wie ein Rasiermesser sein; (fig) [äußerst] scharfsinnig
Rd. n abbrev of **road** Str.
reach [ritʃ] I. n <pl -es> ❶ (arm length, power) Reichweite f; TV, RADIO [Sende]bereich m ❷ (distance to travel) **to be within** [easy] ~ [ganz] in der Nähe sein II. vi ❶ (stretch) greifen ❷ (touch) herankommen ❸ (extend) reichen III. vt ❶ (arrive at) erreichen; destination ankommen ❷ audience erreichen; agreement erzielen ❸ road ▪ **to** ~ **sth** bis zu etw dat führen; hair, clothing bis zu etw dat reichen ❹ (touch) **to be able to** ~ **sth** an etw akk herankommen ❺ (contact) erreichen; (on the phone) [telefonisch] erreichen ❻ (fam: give) hinüberreichen
  ◆ **reach down** vi hinabreichen, herunterreichen
  ◆ **reach out** I. vt **to** ~ **out** ⟳ **one's hand** die Hand ausstrecken II. vi greifen nach + dat
  ◆ **reach out to** vi ▪ **to** ~ **out to sb** (stretch) die Hand nach jdm ausstrecken; (help) für jdn da sein
  ◆ **reach over** vi hinübergreifen
  ◆ **reach up** vi nach oben greifen
react [rɪ·'ækt] vi reagieren
reaction [rɪ·'æk·ʃən] n Reaktion f
reactionary [rɪ·'æk·ʃə·ner·i] I. adj (pej) reaktionär II. n (pej) Reaktionär(in) m(f)
reactor [ri·'æk·tər] n Reaktor m; **nuclear** ~ Kernreaktor m; **fusion** ~ Fusionsreaktor m; **fission** ~ Spaltreaktor m
read¹ [rid] I. n usu sing ❶ (fam) **to be a good** ~ sich gut lesen [lassen] ❷ (act) Lesen nt II. vt <read, read> lesen; (aloud) vorlesen; emotion erraten; ▪ **to** ~ **sb** jdn verstehen; **to** ~ **sth in sb's**

face jdm etw vom Gesicht ablesen III. vi <read, read> lesen; **to** ~ **aloud** laut vorlesen; **to** ~ **well** book sich gut lesen
  ◆ **read off** vt herunterlesen; dial ablesen
  ◆ **read out** vt laut vorlesen; COMPUT auslesen
  ◆ **read over, read through** vt [schnell] durchlesen
  ◆ **read up** vi nachlesen; ▪ **to** ~ **up on sth** sich akk über etw akk informieren
read² [red] I. vt, vi pt, pp of **read** II. adj **well** ~ belesen
reader ['ri·dər] n Leser(in) m(f); (aloud) Vorleser(in) m(f); (proofreader) Lektor(in) m(f)
readily ['red·ə·li] adv bereitwillig; (easily) ohne weiteres
readiness ['red·i·nɪs] n ❶ Bereitwilligkeit f; preparedness a. Bereitschaft f ❷ (quickness) Schnelligkeit f
reading ['ri·dɪŋ] n ❶ Lesen nt ❷ (material) Lesestoff m ❸ (recital) Lesung f
'reading glasses npl Lesebrille f
readjust [ˌri·ə·'dʒʌst] I. vt [wieder] neu anpassen; tie zurechtzücken; machine neu einstellen II. vi ❶ machine sich neu einstellen; clock sich neu stellen ❷ (re-adapt) sich wieder gewöhnen
ready ['red·i] adj ❶ pred fertig; **to get** ~ sich akk fertig machen; **to be** ~ **to go** bereit zum Gehen sein ❷ (available) verfügbar ❸ attr (esp approv: quick) prompt ▶PHRASES: ~, **set, go!** auf die Plätze, fertig, los!
ready-'made adj ❶ (ready for use) gebrauchsfertig; FOOD fertig ❷ FASHION Konfektions- ❸ (available) vorgefertigt
'ready-to-wear adj Konfektions-
reaffirm [ˌri·ə·'fɜrm] vt bestätigen
real [ril] I. adj ❶ wirklich; (genuine) echt; beauty wahr; **a** ~ **bargain** ein echt günstiges Angebot ❷ (fam) disaster echt ▶PHRASES: **the** ~ **thing** (not fake) das Wahre; (true love) die wahre Liebe; **get** ~! (fam) mach dir doch nichts vor! II. adv (fam) wirklich fam
'real estate n Immobilien pl

R

'real estate agent n Immobilienmakler(in) m(f)

realism ['riːlɪzəm] n Realismus m

realist ['riːlɪst] n Realist(in) m(f)

realistic [ˌriːə'lɪstɪk] adj realistisch

reality [riː'ælɪti] n ❶ Realität f; **in** ~ in Wirklichkeit ❷ (fact) Tatsache f; **to become a** ~ wahr werden

realization [ˌriːəlɪ'zeɪʃən] n ❶ (awareness) Erkenntnis f ❷ (fulfillment) Realisierung f

realize ['riːəlaɪz] vt ❶ ■to ~ sth sich dat einer S. gen bewusst sein; (become aware of) etw erkennen ❷ dream verwirklichen

really ['riːəli] I. adv wirklich; (seriously) ernsthaft II. interj (in surprise) wirklich; (in annoyance) also wirklich

realm [relm] n ❶ Reich ❷ **within the ~ s of possibility** im Bereich des Möglichen

reap [riːp] vt ernten a. fig; field abernten; profits realisieren

reappear [ˌriːə'pɪr] vi wieder auftauchen [o erscheinen]

reapply <-ie-> [ˌriːə'plaɪ] vi ■to ~ **for sth** sich nochmals um etw akk bewerben

reappraisal [ˌriːə'preɪzəl] n Neubewertung f

rear¹ [rɪr] I. n ❶ (back) ■**the ~** der hintere Teil ❷ (fam: buttocks) Hintern m II. adj attr Hinter-; auto Heck-; ~ **wheel** Hinterrad nt

rear² [rɪr] I. vt usu passive großziehen; animal aufziehen; (breed) züchten II. vi ❶ horse sich aufbäumen ❷ ■to ~ **above sth** etw überragen

rearm [ˌriː'ɑːm] vi sich akk wieder bewaffnen

rearview 'mirror n Rückspiegel m

rear-wheel 'drive n Hinterradantrieb m

reason ['riːzən] I. n ❶ Grund m; **there is every ~ to ...** es spricht alles dafür, ...; **for some ~** aus irgendeinem Grund ❷ (sense) Vernunft f; (sanity) Verstand m II. vi (judge) ausgehen ❷ ■to ~ **with sb** vernünftig mit jdm re-

den III. vt ■to ~ **that ...** schlussfolgern, dass ...

reasonable ['riːzənəbəl] adj ❶ (sensible) vernünftig ❷ (understanding) einsichtig; **be ~!** sei [doch] vernünftig! ❸ (justified) angebracht ❹ price akzeptable

reasonably ['riːzənəbli] adv ❶ (sensibly) vernünftig ❷ (fairly) ziemlich ❸ ~ **priced** preiswert

reasoning ['riːzənɪŋ] n logisches Denken

reassure [ˌriːə'ʃʊr] vt [wieder] beruhigen

reassuring [ˌriːə'ʃʊrɪŋ] adj beruhigend

rebate ['riːbeɪt] n Rückzahlung f; (discount) [Preis]nachlass m

rebel I. n ['rebəl] Rebell(in) m(f) II. adj ['rebəl] aufständisch III. vi <-ll-> [rɪ'bel] (a. fig) rebellieren

rebellion [rɪ'beljən] n Rebellion f

rebellious [rɪ'beljəs] adj rebellisch; child aufsässig

rebirth [ˌriː'bɜːθ] n Wiedergeburt f

rebound [rɪ'baʊnd] I. vi abprallen; (in basketball) rebounden II. vt (in basketball) rebounden III. n ['riːbaʊnd] Abprallen nt; (in basketball) Rebound

rebuff [rɪ'bʌf] I. vt [schroff] zurückweisen II. n Zurückweisung f

rebuild <rebuilt, rebuilt> [ˌriː'bɪld] vt wieder aufbauen

recall I. vt [rɪ'kɔl] ❶ sich akk erinnern ❷ product zurückrufen II. n ['riːkɔl] Rückruf f

recede [rɪ'siːd] vi ❶ sea, tide zurückgehen ❷ (fig: diminish) weniger werden ❸ hair zurückgehen

receipt [rɪ'siːt] n ❶ Erhalt m ❷ (payment slip) Quittung f

receive [rɪ'siːv] I. vt ❶ erhalten; salary beziehen; degree erhalten; prize [verliehen] bekommen ❷ radio, tv empfangen II. vi sport den Ball bekommen

receiver [rɪ'siːvər] n of telephone Hörer m; of radio Empfänger m

recent ['riːsənt] adj kürzlich; **in ~ times** in der letzten Zeit

recently ['riː·sənt·li] *adv* kürzlich; **until ~** bis vor kurzem

reception [rɪ·'sep·ʃən] *n* Empfang *m*; (*guest area*) Rezeption *f*; **~ desk** Rezeption *f*

receptionist [rɪ·'sep·ʃə·nɪst] *n* Empfangschef *m*; (*female*) Empfangsdame *f*; (*in office*) Empfangssekretärin *f*

recess [rɪ·'ses] I. *n* <*pl* -es> ❶ (*niche*) Nische *f* ❷ [Sitzungs]pause *f*; SCH Pause *f* II. *vt* ❶ (*cut out*) aussparen ❷ (*suspend*) vertagen

recession [rɪ·'seʃ·ən] *n* Rezession *f*

recharge [ˌriː·'tʃɑːrdʒ] *vt* [neu] aufladen; **to ~ one's batteries** (*fig*) neue Kräfte tanken

rechargeable [ˌriː·'tʃɑr·dʒə·bəl] *adj* [wieder]aufladbar

recipe ['res·ə·pi] *n* Rezept *nt*

recipient [rɪ·'sɪp·i·ənt] *n* Empfänger(in) *m(f)*

reciprocal [rɪ·'sɪp·rə·kəl] *adj* (*mutual*) beidseitig; *favor* gegenseitig; (*reverse*) umgekehrt

recital [rɪ·'saɪ·təl] *n* Aufzählung *f*; *of poetry* Vortrag *m*; *of dance* Aufführung *f*

recite [rɪ·'saɪt] *vt* aufzählen; *poem* vortragen; (*at school*) [auswendig] aufsagen

reckless ['rek·lɪs] *adj* rücksichtslos; (*not cautious*) leichtsinnig

recklessness ['rek·lɪs·nɪs] *n* Leichtsinn *m*; *of driving* Rücksichtslosigkeit *f*

reckon ['rek·ən] *vt* ❶ (*calculate*) berechnen ❷ I **~ you won't be seeing her again** ich denke nicht, dass du sie je wiedersehen wirst
 ♦ **reckon with** *vt* ■**to ~ with sth/sb** mit etw/jdm rechnen

reckoning ['rek·ə·nɪŋ] *n* Berechnung *f*

reclaim [rɪ·'kleɪm] *vt* zurückverlangen; *luggage* abholen; **to ~ land from the sea** dem Meer Land abgewinnen

recline [rɪ·'klaɪn] I. *vi* sich *akk* zurücklehnen II. *vt* **to ~ one's seat** die Rückenlehne seines Sitzes nach hinten stellen

recluse ['rek·lus] *n* Einsiedler(in) *m(f)*

recognition [ˌrek·əg·'nɪʃ·ən] *n* ❶ [Wie-

der]erkennen *nt* ❷ (*appreciation*) Anerkennung *f*

recognizable ['rek·əg·naɪ·zə·bəl] *adj* erkennbar

recognize ['rek·əg·naɪz] *vt* (*identify*) erkennen; (*know again*) wiedererkennen; (*acknowledge*) anerkennen

recoil [rɪ·'kɔɪl] I. *vi* zurückspringen; (*draw back*) zurückweichen; *rubber band, spring* zurückschnellen II. *n* Rückstoß *m*

recollect [ˌrek·ə·'lekt] *vt* sich *akk* erinnern an +*akk*

recollection [ˌrek·ə·'lek·ʃən] *n* Erinnerung *f*

recommend [ˌrek·ə·'mend] *vt* empfehlen; *doctor a.* raten

recommendation [ˌrek·ə·mən·'deɪ·ʃən] *n* Empfehlung *f*; (*advice a.*) Rat *m*

recompense ['rek·əm·pens] *n* Belohnung *f*; (*retribution*) Entschädigung *f*

reconcile ['rek·ən·saɪl] *vt* versöhnen; *conflict* schlichten; *differences* beilegen

reconciliation [ˌrek·ən·ˌsɪl·i·'eɪ·ʃən] *n* Versöhnung *f*; (*of differences*) Beilegung *f*

recondition [ˌriː·kən·'dɪʃ·ən] *vt engine* [general]überholen

reconnaissance [rɪ·'kɑn·ə·səns] *n* MIL Aufklärung *f*

reconnoiter [ˌriː·kə·'nɔɪ·tər] *vt* MIL auskundschaften

reconsider [ˌriː·kən·'sɪd·ər] *vt* [noch einmal] überdenken

reconstruct [ˌriː·kən·'strʌkt] *vt* wieder aufbauen; (*restore*) wiederherstellen; *crime* rekonstruieren

reconstruction [ˌriː·kən·'strʌk·ʃən] *n* Rekonstruktion *f*; (*restoration*) Wiederaufbau *m*

record I. *n* ['rek·ərd] ❶ Aufzeichnungen *pl*; (*document*) Akte *f*; *of attendance* Liste *f*; (*minutes*) Protokoll *nt* ❷ **criminal ~** Vorstrafenregister *nt*; **medical ~** Krankenblatt *nt* ❸ (*music*) [Schall]platte *f* ❹ SPORT Rekord *m* ▸PHRASES: **to say sth on/off the ~** etw offiziell/inoffiziell sagen II. *adj* ['rek·ərd] Rekord- III. *vt* [rɪ·'kɔrd] ❶ (*store*) aufzeichnen, regis-

R

trieren; *feelings, ideas* niederschreiben ❷ *(measure)* messen ❸ FILM, MUS aufnehmen

'**record-breaking** *adj attr* Rekord-

recorder [rɪ·ˈkɔr·dər] *n* ❶ **video** ~ Videorekorder *m;* **tape** ~ Kassettenrekorder ❷ MUS Blockflöte *f*

'**record holder** *n* Rekordhalter(in) *m(f)*

recording [rɪ·ˈkɔr·dɪŋ] *n* Aufnahme *f;* *(of program)* Aufzeichnung *f*

'**record player** *n* [Schall]plattenspieler *m*

recount[1] [rɪ·ˈkaʊnt] *vt* [ausführlich] erzählen

recount[2] **I.** *vt* [ˌri·ˈkaʊnt] nachzählen **II.** *n* [ˈri·kaʊnt] erneute Stimmenauszählung

recourse [ˈri·kɔrs] *n* Zuflucht *f*

recover [rɪ·ˈkʌv·ər] **I.** *vt* wiederbekommen; *stolen goods* sicherstellen; *composure* wiederfinden; *data* wiederherstellen; **to be fully ~ed** völlig genesen sein **II.** *vi* sich *akk* erholen

recovery [rɪ·ˈkʌv·ə·ri] *n* Erholung *f;* *(getting back)* Wiedererlangen *nt;* *of survivor* Bergung *f*

recreation [ˌrek·ri·ˈeɪ·ʃən] *n* Freizeitbeschäftigung *f;* *(fun)* Erholung *f*

recreational [ˌrek·ri·ˈeɪ·ʃə·nəl] *adj* Freizeit-

recreational 'vehicle *n* Wohnwagen *m*

rec room [ˈrek·ˌrum] *n* Aufenthaltsraum *m*

R

recruit [rɪ·ˈkrut] **I.** *vt* einstellen; *members* werben; *soldiers* rekrutieren; *volunteers* finden **II.** *vi army* Rekruten anwerben; *company* Neueinstellungen vornehmen; *club* neue Mitglieder werben **III.** *n* MIL Rekrut(in) *m(f);* *party, club* neues Mitglied; *staff* neu eingestellte Arbeitskraft

rectangle [ˈrek·tæŋ·gəl] *n* Rechteck *nt*

rectangular [rek·ˈtæŋ·gjə·lər] *adj* rechteckig

rectify <-ie-> [ˈrek·tə·faɪ] *vt* *(set right)* korrigieren; *omission* nachholen

rector [ˈrek·tər] *n* Pfarrer *m;* UNIV Rektor(in) *m(f)*

rectory [ˈrek·tə·ri] *n* Pfarrhaus *nt*

rectum <*pl* -ta> [ˈrek·təm] *n* MED Mastdarm *m*

recuperate [rɪ·ˈku·pə·reɪt] *vi* sich *akk* erholen

recur <-rr-> [rɪ·ˈkər] *vi* sich wiederholen, wiederkehren

recycle [ˌri·ˈsaɪ·kəl] *vt* recyceln; *(fig)* wiederverwenden

recycling [rɪ·ˈsaɪ·kəl·ɪŋ] *n* Recycling *nt*

red [red] **I.** *adj* <-dd-> rot; *eyes* gerötet **II.** *n* Rot *nt;* **to be in the ~** in den roten Zahlen sein

Red 'Cross *n* ▪ **the ~** das Rote Kreuz

redden [ˈred·ən] **I.** *vi* sich röten; *person* rot werden; *sky* sich rot färben **II.** *vt* rot färben

reddish [ˈred·ɪʃ] *adj* rötlich

redecorate [ˌri·ˈdek·ə·reɪt] **I.** *vt* neu streichen; *(wallpaper)* neu tapezieren **II.** *vi* renovieren

redeem [rɪ·ˈdim] *vt* wiederherstellen; *mistake* wettmachen; *(pay off)* ab[be]zahlen; *mortgage* tilgen; *pledge* einlösen

redevelop [ˌri·dɪ·ˈvel·əp] *vt* sanieren

'**red-eye** *n (fam)* Nachtflug *m*

red-'handed *adj* **to catch sb ~** jdn auf frischer Tat ertappen

'**redhead** *n* Rothaarige(r) *f(m)*

red-'headed *adj* rothaarig

red 'herring *n* Ablenkungsmanöver *nt*

red-'hot *adj* ❶ **to be ~** [rot] glühen; *(fig)* glühend heiß sein ❷ *news* brandaktuell

red-'light district *n* Rotlichtviertel *nt*

red 'meat *n* dunkles Fleisch *(wie Rind, Lamm und Reh)*

'**redneck** *n (pej fam)* weißer Arbeiter aus den Südstaaten, oft mit reaktionären Ansichten

redness [ˈred·nɪs] *n* Röte *f*

redouble [rɪ·ˈdʌb·əl] *vt* verdoppeln

red 'pepper *n* rote(r) Paprika

redress [rɪ·ˈdres] *vt* wiedergutmachen

Red 'Sea *n* ▪ **the ~** das Rote Meer

'**redskin** *n (pej fam)* Rothaut *f pej*

red 'tape *n* Bürokratie *f*

reduce [rɪ·ˈdus] *vt* verringern; *prices* heruntersetzen; *taxes* senken; *photo* verkleinern; *fraction* kürzen; **he was**

~d to begging for help er war gezwungen, seine Eltern um Hilfe zu bitten

reduced [rɪ'dust] *adj attr price* heruntergesetzt; **to be in ~ circumstances** in verarmten Verhältnissen leben

reduction [rɪ'dʌk·ʃən] *n* Reduzierung *f; of photo* Verkleinerung *f; in taxes* Senkung *f; in salary* Kürzung *f*

redundant [rɪ'dʌn·dənt] *adj* überflüssig

red 'wine *n* Rotwein *m*

reed [rid] *n* Schilf[gras] *nt; (in instrument)* Rohrblatt *nt*

reef [rif] *n* Riff *nt*

reek [rik] *vi* übel riechen, stinken

reel [ril] *n* Rolle *f; (for film, tape)* Spule *f; (for fishing line)* Angelrolle *f*

re-elect [,ri·ɪ·'lekt] *vt* wiederwählen

re-enter [,ri·'en·tər] *vt bus, car* wieder einsteigen in +*akk; country* wieder einreisen in +*akk; house, store* wieder hineingehen in +*akk; room* wieder betreten; *earth's atmosphere* wieder eintreten in +*akk*

ref [ref] *n abbrev of* **referee** *(fam)* Schiri *m fam*

ref. [ref] *n abbrev of* **reference** AZ

refectory [rɪ'fek·tə·ri] *n* UNIV Mensa *f*

refer <-rr-> [rɪ'fɜr] I. *vt* verweisen; **he was ~red to a specialist** er wurde an einen Facharzt überwiesen II. *vi* ❶ ■**to ~ to sb/sth** sich *akk* auf jdn/etw beziehen; **~ring to your letter, ...** Bezug nehmend auf Ihren Brief ... ❷ *(consult)* ■**to ~ to sth** *dictionary* in etw *dat* nachschlagen

referee [,ref·ə·'ri] *n* Schiedsrichter(in) *m(f); (arbitrator)* Schlichter(in) *m(f)*

reference ['ref·ər·əns] *n* ❶ Verweis *m* ❷ *(allusion) indirect* Anspielung *f; direct* Bemerkung *f; (direct mention)* Bezugnahme *f;* ■**to ~ to sb/sth** mit Bezug auf jdn/etw ❸ *(in correspondence)* Aktenzeichen *nt* ❹ *(recommendation)* Empfehlungsschreiben *nt*

'reference book *n* Nachschlagewerk *nt*

'reference number *n* Aktenzeichen *nt; (on goods)* Artikelnummer *f*

referendum <*pl* -s> [,ref·ə·'ren·dəm] *n* POL Referendum *nt*

refill I. *n* ['ri·fɪl] ❶ ■**to give sb a ~** *(fam)* jdm nachschenken ❷ *(replacement)* Nachfüll-, Ersatz- II. *vt* [,ri·'fɪl] **to ~ a cup** eine Tasse wieder füllen

refine [rɪ'faɪn] *vt* raffinieren; *(improve)* verfeinern

refined [rɪ'faɪnd] *adj* raffiniert; *food* aufbereitet; *metal* veredelt; *(fig)* kultiviert

refinement [rɪ'faɪn·mənt] *n* Raffinieren *nt; of metal* Veredelung *f; (fig)* Verfeinerung *f*

refinery [rɪ'faɪ·nə·ri] *n* Raffinerie *f*

reflect [rɪ'flekt] I. *vt* ❶ widerspiegeln; *light, sound* reflektieren ❷ *(show)* zeigen II. *vi* ❶ reflektieren ❷ *(ponder)* nachdenken ❸ **to ~ badly on sth** ein schlechtes Licht auf etw *akk* werfen

reflection [rɪ'flek·ʃən] *n* ❶ *(reflecting)* Reflexion *f* ❷ *(image)* Spiegelbild *nt; (fig: sign)* Ausdruck *m*, Zeichen *nt* ❸ *(consideration)* Betrachtung *f*

reflective [rɪ'flek·tɪv] *adj* reflektierend; *person* nachdenklich

reflex <*pl* -es> [ri·fleks] *n* Reflex *m*

reform [rɪ'fɔrm] I. *vt* reformieren; *criminal* bessern II. *vi* sich *akk* bessern III. *n* Reform *f; of criminal* Besserung *f*

reformation [,ref·ər·'meɪ·ʃən] *n (hist)* ■**the R~** die Reformation

reformer [rɪ'fɔr·mər] *n* Reformer(in) *m(f)*

re'form school *n* Erziehungsheim *nt*

refrain [rɪ'freɪn] *vi* sich *akk* zurückhalten; **to ~ from smoking** das Rauchen unterlassen

refresh [rɪ'freʃ] *vt* erfrischen; *(fig) skills* auffrischen; **to ~ one's memory** seinem Gedächtnis auf die Sprünge helfen; **to ~ sb's drink** jds Glas nachfüllen

refresher course [rɪ'freʃ·ər-] *n* Auffrischungskurs *m*

refreshing [rɪ'freʃ·ɪŋ] *adj* erfrischend; *(pleasing)* [herz]erfrischend

refreshment [rɪ'freʃ·mənt] *n* Erfrischung *f;* ■**~s** *pl (drinks)* Erfrischungen *pl; (food)* Snacks *pl*

R

refrigerator [rɪ·ˈfrɪdʒ·ə·reɪ·tər] *n* Kühlschrank *m*

refuel <-l-> [ˌriˈfjuˑəl] *vt, vi* auftanken

refuge [ˈref·judʒ] *n* Zufluchtsort *m;* **women's** ~ Frauenhaus *nt*

refugee [ˌref·juˑˈdʒi] *n* Flüchtling *m*

'**refugee camp** *n* Aufnahmelager *nt*

refund I. *vt* [rɪˈfʌnd] zurückerstatten II. *n* [ˈriˑfʌnd] Rückzahlung *f*

refurbish [ˌriˈfɜr·bɪʃ] *vt* aufpolieren; *house* renovieren

refusal [rɪˈfjuˑzəl] *n* Ablehnung *f; of offer* Zurückweisung *f; of invitation* Absage *f; of food, visa* Verweigerung *f*

refuse[1] [rɪˈfjuz] I. *vi* ablehnen; *horse* verweigern II. *vt* ablehnen; *offer* ausschlagen

refuse[2] [ˈref·jus] *n (form)* Abfall *m*

reg. *adj abbrev of* **regular**

regain [rɪˈgeɪn] *vt* wiederbekommen; *lost ground* zurückgewinnen; *consciousness* wiedererlangen

regal [ˈriˑgəl] *adj* majestätisch

regard [rɪˈgɑrd] I. *vt* ❶ betrachten; ■**to ~ sb/sth as sth** jdn/etw als etw betrachten, jdn/etw für etw *akk* halten ❷ *(concerning)* ■**as ~s ...** was ... angeht, II. *n* ❶ Rücksicht *f;* **without ~ for sb/sth** ohne Rücksicht auf jdn/etw ❷ *(respect)* Achtung *f* ❸ *(aspect)* **in this ~** in dieser Hinsicht ❹ *(concerning)* ■**with ~ to ...** in Bezug auf ... +*akk*

regarding [rɪˈgɑr·dɪŋ] *prep* bezüglich +*gen*

regardless [rɪˈgɑrd·lɪs] *adv* trotzdem; ~ **of the expense** ungeachtet der Kosten; **to press on** ~ trotzdem weitermachen

regards [rɪˈgɑrdz] *n pl* [**best**] ~ [**viele**] Grüße; **Jim sends his** ~ Jim lässt grüßen

regenerate [rɪˈdʒen·ə·reɪt] I. *vt* erneuern; *tissue* neu bilden II. *vi* sich regenerieren; *tissue* sich neu bilden

regent [ˈriˑdʒənt] *n* Regent(in) *m(f)*

reggae [ˈreg·eɪ] *n* Reggae *m*

regime [rəˈʒim] *n* Regime *nt*

regiment [ˈredʒ·ə·mənt] I. *n* Regiment *nt* II. *vt* in Gruppen einordnen

region [ˈriˑdʒən] *n* Region *f; (administrative)* [Verwaltungs]bezirk *m*

regional [ˈriˑdʒəˑnəl] *adj* regional

register [ˈredʒ·ɪ·stər] I. *n* ❶ Register *nt* ❷ *(till)* **cash** ~ Kasse *f* II. *vt* ❶ registrieren; *birth, death* anmelden; *copyright* eintragen ❷ *(measure)* anzeigen ❸ *letter, package* per Einschreiben schicken ❹ **to** ~ **surprise** sich überrascht zeigen III. *vi* ❶ sich melden; *(to vote)* sich eintragen; *(to take classes)* sich einschreiben; **to** ~ **with the authorities** sich behördlich anmelden ❷ *dial* anzeigen ❸ *(show)* sich zeigen

registrar [ˈredʒ·ɪ·strɑr] *n* Standesbeamte(r) *m*, Standesbeamte [o -in] *f;* UNIV höchster Verwaltungsbeamter/höchste Verwaltungsbeamte [o -in]

registration [ˌredʒ·ɪ·ˈstreɪ·ʃən] *n* ❶ Anmeldung *f*, Registrierung *f; (at school)* Einschreibung *f;* UNIV Immatrikulation *f* ❷ *(document)* [**motor vehicle**] ~ Kraftfahrzeugschein *m*

regret [rɪˈgret] I. *vt, vi* <-tt-> bedauern; **I ~** [**to have**] **to inform you that ...** leider muss ich Ihnen mitteilen, dass ... II. *n* Bedauern *nt kein pl;* **to have no ~s about sth** etw nicht bereuen; **to send one's ~s** sich entschuldigen [lassen]

regretful [rɪˈgret·fəl] *adj* bedauernd; *smile* wehmütig

regrettable [rɪˈgret·əˑbəl] *adj* bedauerlich

regular [ˈreg·jəˑlər] I. *adj* ❶ regelmäßig; *price* regulär; *procedure* üblich; *surface* gleichmäßig; **to keep ~ hours** sich an feste Zeiten halten; ~ **gasoline** Normalbenzin *nt* ❷ *attr* ~ **fries** normale Portion Pommes Frites II. *n* Stammgast *m*

regularity [ˌreg·juˑˈler·ɪˑt̬i] *n (in time)* Regelmäßigkeit *f; of shape* Ebenmäßigkeit *f*

regularly [ˈreg·jəˑlɚ·li] *adv* regelmäßig; *(equally)* gleichmäßig

regulate [ˈreg·juˑleɪt] *vt* regeln; *(adjust)* regulieren

R

regulation [ˌreg·ju·'lei·ʃən] *n* Vorschrift *f*; **in accordance with the ~s** vorschriftsmäßig; **fire ~s** Brandschutzbestimmungen *pl*

rehearsal [rɪ·'hɜr·səl] *n* Probe *f*

rehearse [rɪ·'hɜrs] *vt, vi* proben

reign [rein] I. *vi* ① regieren; **to ~ over a country** ein Land regieren ② (*be dominant*) dominieren; **confusion ~s** es herrscht Verwirrung II. *n* Herrschaft *f*

rein [rein] *n usu pl* Zügel *m* ▶PHRASES: **to give free ~ to sb** jdm freie Hand lassen

reincarnation [ˌri·ɪn·kar·'nei·ʃən] *n* Wiedergeburt *f*

reindeer <*pl* -> ['rein·dɪr] *n* Rentier *nt*

reinforce [ˌri·ɪn·'fɔrs] *vt* (*strengthen*) *troops* verstärken; *concrete* armieren; *findings* bestätigen

reinforcement [ˌri·ɪn·'fɔrs·mənt] *n* ① Verstärkung *f*; **steel ~** Stahlträger *m meist pl* ② ■**~s** *pl* Verstärkungstruppen *pl*; (*equipment*) Verstärkung *f*

reinstate [ˌri·ɪn·'steit] *vt* wieder einstellen; *tax* wieder einführen; *law and order* wiederherstellen

reject I. *vt* [rɪ·'dʒekt] ablehnen; *excuse* nicht annehmen; (*snub*) abweisen; *drug* nicht vertragen; *transplant* abstoßen; **to feel ~ed** sich als Außenseiter(in) fühlen II. *n* ['ri·dʒekt] Ausschussware *f*; (*person*) Außenseiter(in) *m(f)*

rejection [rɪ·'dʒek·ʃən] *n* Ablehnung *f*; MED Abstoßung *f*

rejoice [rɪ·'dʒɔɪs] *vi* sich freuen

rejoicing [rɪ·'dʒɔɪ·sɪŋ] *n* Freude *f*

rejoin [ˌri·'dʒɔɪn] *vt* sich wieder vereinigen

relapse I. *n* ['ri·læps] MED Rückfall *m*; (*in economy*) Rückschlag *m* II. *vi* [rɪ·'læps] MED einen Rückfall haben; *economy* einen Rückschlag erleiden

relate [rɪ·'leit] I. *vt* ① in Verbindung bringen ② (*narrate*) erzählen; ■**to ~ sth to sb** jdm etw berichten II. *vi* ① (*fam: get along*) ■**to ~ to sb/sth** eine Beziehung zu jdm/etw finden ② (*be about*) ■**to ~ to sb/sth** von jdm/etw handeln; **chapter nine ~s to inflation** in Kapitel neun geht es um die Inflation

related [rɪ·'lei·tɪd] *adj* ① verbunden; **to be directly ~ to sth** in direktem Zusammenhang mit etw *dat* stehen ② *species* verwandt; **to be ~ by blood** blutsverwandt sein; **distantly ~** entfernt verwandt

relating to [rɪ·'lei·tɪŋ·] *prep* in Zusammenhang mit +*dat*

relation [rɪ·'lei·ʃən] *n* ① Bezug *m*; **in ~ to** in Bezug auf +*akk* ② (*relative*) Verwandte(r) *f(m)*; **is Julia any ~ to you?** ist Julia irgendwie mit dir verwandt? ③ (*between countries*) ■**~s** *pl* Beziehungen *pl*

relationship [rɪ·'lei·ʃən·ʃɪp] *n* ① (*connection*) Beziehung *f* ② (*in family*) Verwandtschaftsverhältnis *nt* ③ (*association*) Verhältnis *nt*; ■**to be in a ~ with sb** mit jdm eine feste Beziehung haben

relative ['rel·ə·tɪv] I. *adj* relevant; (*corresponding*) jeweilige(r, s); (*comparative*) relativ; ■**to be ~ to sth** von etw *dat* abhängen II. *n* Verwandte(r) *f(m)*

relaunch [ˌri·'bɔntʃ] I. *vt* *rocket* erneut starten; *product* erneut auf den Markt bringen II. *n of rocket* Zweitstart *m*; *of ship* zweiter Stapellauf; *of brand* Wiedereinführung *f*

relax [rɪ·'læks] I. *vi* sich entspannen; **~!** entspann dich!; (*don't worry*) beruhige dich! II. *vt* lockern; *muscles a.* entspannen; *security* einschränken

relaxation [ˌri·læk·'sei·ʃən] *n* Entspannung *f*; *of discipline* Nachlassen *nt*; *of laws* Liberalisierung *f*; *of rules* Lockerung *f*

relaxed [rɪ·'lækst] *adj* entspannt; (*easygoing*) locker; *manner* lässig

relay ['ri·lei] I. *vt* mitteilen; *message* weiterleiten; *TV* übertragen II. *n* Staffellauf *m*

release [rɪ·'lis] I. *vt* ① freilassen; *prisoner* [aus der Haft] entlassen; *brake* lösen; *shutter* betätigen; *steam* freisetzen; *grip* lockern ② (*circulate*) verbreiten; (*issue*) veröffentlichen; *CD* herausbringen II. *n* ① Entlassung *f*; *of hostage* Freilassung *f*; *of funds* Freigabe *f*; (*of gases*) Entweichen *nt* ② (*mechanism*)

R

Auslöser *m* ③ (*publication*) Veröffentlichung *f*; **press ~** Pressemitteilung *f* ④ (*new CD*) Neuerscheinung *f*

relegate ['rel·ə·geɪt] *vt usu passive* **the story was ~d to the middle pages of the newspaper** die Story wurde in den Mittelteil der Zeitung verschoben

relent [rɪ·'lent] *vi* nachgeben; *wind, rain* nachlassen

relentless [rɪ·'lent·lɪs] *adj* unnachgiebig; (*rain*) unablässig; *persecution* gnadenlos; *pressure* unaufhörlich

relevance ['rel·ə·vəns], **relevancy** ['rel·ə·vən·si] *n* Bedeutsamkeit *f*; (*significance*) Bedeutung *f*

relevant ['rel·ə·vənt] *adj* relevant; (*important*) bedeutend

reliability [rɪ·ˌlaɪ·ə·'bɪl·ɪ·ţi] *n* Zuverlässigkeit *f*; (*trustworthiness*) Vertrauenswürdigkeit *f*

reliable [rɪ·'laɪ·ə·bəl] *adj* zuverlässig; (*credible*) glaubwürdig; *criterion* sicher; (*trustworthy*) vertrauenswürdig

reliance [rɪ·'laɪ·əns] *n* Verlass *m*; (*trust*) Vertrauen *nt*

reliant [rɪ·'laɪ·ənt] *adj* abhängig

relic ['rel·ɪk] *n* (*a. fig, hum*) Relikt *nt*

relief [rɪ·'lif] *n* ① Entlastung *f*; *of suffering* Linderung *f*; *of tension* Erleichterung *f*; **tax ~** Steuerermäßigung *f*; **to breathe a sigh of ~** erleichtert aufatmen ② (*welfare*) Hilfsgüter *pl* ③ (*next shift*) Ablösung *f* ④ (*sharpness*) Kontrast *m*; **to stand out in sharp ~** sich deutlich von etw *dat* abheben

re'lief worker *n* Mitarbeiter(in) *m(f)* einer Hilfsorganisation; (*in third-world countries*) Entwicklungshelfer(in) *m(f)*

relieve [rɪ·'liv] *vt* ① erträglicher machen; *pressure* verringern; *tension* abbauen; *pain* lindern ② (*unburden*) ■ **to ~ sb of sth** jdm etw abnehmen; (*hum: steal*) jdn um etw *akk* erleichtern; ■ **to ~ one-self** (*hum*) sich *akk* erleichtern *euph* ③ (*take over*) ablösen

relieved [rɪ·'livd] *adj* erleichtert; **to be ~ to hear sth** etw mit Erleichterung hören

religion [rɪ·'lɪdʒ·ən] *n* Religion *f*; (*beliefs*) Glaube *m*; (*system*) Kult *m*

religious [rɪ·'lɪdʒ·əs] *adj* religiös; (*pious a.*) fromm; ■ **organization** Glaubensgemeinschaft *f*

relish ['rel·ɪʃ] I. *n* ① Genuss *m*; ■ **with ~** genüsslich ② (*sauce*) Relish *nt* II. *vt* genießen; **to ~ the thought that …** sich darauf freuen, dass …

reload [ˌri·'loʊd] I. *vt* nachladen; *camera* neu laden; *ship* wieder beladen II. *vi* nachladen

reluctance [rɪ·'lʌk·təns] *n* Widerwillen *m*

reluctant [rɪ·'lʌk·tənt] *adj* widerwillig; ■ **to be ~ to do sth** sich dagegen sträuben, etw zu tun

rely [rɪ·'laɪ] *vi* ① ■ **to ~ on sb/sth** sich auf jdn/etw verlassen; ■ **to ~ on sb/ sth to do sth** sich darauf verlassen, dass jd/etw etw tut ② (*depend on*) ■ **to ~ on sb/sth** von jdm/etw abhängen; ■ **to ~ on sb/sth for** [*or* to do] **sth** darauf angewiesen sein, dass jd/etw etw tut

remain [rɪ·'meɪn] *vi* ① bleiben; **to ~ be-hind** zurückbleiben ② + *n or adj* bleiben; **to ~ untreated** nicht behandelt werden ③ (*survive*) übrig bleiben; *person* überleben; **much ~s to be done** es muss noch vieles getan werden; **the fact ~s that …** das ändert nichts an der Tatsache, dass …

remainder [rɪ·'meɪn·dər] *n* Rest *m*

remaining [rɪ·'meɪ·nɪŋ] *adj attr* übrig

remains [rɪ·'meɪnz] *npl* Überbleibsel *pl*; (*form: corpse*) sterbliche Überreste

remake I. *vt* <-made, -made> [ˌri·'meɪk] *film* neu drehen II. *n* ['ri·meɪk] Neuverfilmung *f*

remark [rɪ·'mark] I. *vt* bemerken II. *vi* eine Bemerkung machen; ■ **to ~ on sth** sich über etw äußern III. *n* Bemerkung *f*

remarkable [rɪ·'mar·kə·bəl] *adj* bemerkenswert; *ability* beachtlich; (*surprising*) merkwürdig

remarkably [rɪ·'mar·kə·bli] *adv* bemerkenswert; (*surprisingly*) überraschenderweise

remarry <-ie-> [ˌri·'mær·i] *vi* wieder heiraten

rematch ['ri·mætʃ] *n* Rückspiel *nt*

remedy ['rem·ə·di] *n* Heilmittel *nt;* (*solution*) Mittel *nt*

remember [rɪ·'mem·bər] **I.** *vt* sich erinnern; (*memorize*) sich *dat* merken; (*commemorate*) gedenken +*gen;* **I never ~ her birthday** ich denke nie an ihren Geburtstag; ■ **to ~ doing sth** sich daran erinnern, etw getan zu haben **II.** *vi* sich erinnern; ■ **to ~ [that]** ... sich daran erinnern, [dass] ...

remind [rɪ·'maɪnd] *vt* erinnern; **that ~s me!** das erinnert mich an etwas!; ■ **to ~ sb about sth** jdn an etw *akk* erinnern

reminder [rɪ·'maɪn·dər] *n* Erinnerung *f;* (*for bill*) Mahnung *f;* **as a ~ to oneself that ...** um sich *akk* daran zu erinnern, dass ...

remnant ['rem·nənt] *n* Rest *m;* **~ sale** Resteverkauf *m*

remorse [rɪ·'mɔrs] *n* Reue *f;* ■ **without ~** erbarmungslos

remorseless [rɪ·'mɔrs·lɪs] *adj* gnadenlos; *attack* brutal; (*relentless*) unerbittlich

remote <-r, -st> [rɪ·'moʊt] *adj* ❶ fern; (*isolated*) abgelegen; (*in time*) lang vergangen; *past, future* fern ❷ (*standoffish*) distanziert

remote con'trol *n* (*device*) Fernbedienung *f;* (*action*) Fernsteuerung *f*

remote-con'trolled *adj* ferngesteuert

removal [rɪ·'mu·vəl] *n* Beseitigung *f;* (*taking off*) Abnahme *f;* (*of stain a.*) Entfernung *f*

remove [rɪ·'muv] *vt* ❶ entfernen; *obstacle* beseitigen; *car* abschleppen; *mine* räumen; *makeup* entfernen ❷ (*form*) **to ~ sb [from office]** jdn [aus dem Amt] entlassen

remover [rɪ·'mu·vər] *n* Reinigungsmittel *nt;* **nail polish ~** Nagellackentferner *m*

Renaissance [ˌren·ə·'sɑns] *n* ■ **the ~** die Renaissance

render ['ren·dər] *vt* (*form*) ❶ **she was ~ed unconscious** sie wurde ohnmächtig; **to ~ sb speechless** jdn sprachlos machen ❷ (*interpret*) wiedergeben; *song* vortragen ❸ (*offer*) leisten

rendering ['ren·dər·ɪŋ] *n* ❶ (*performance*) Interpretation *f;* *of song* Vortrag *m;* *of role* Darstellung *f* ❷ (*account*) Schilderung *f*

rendezvous ['rɑn·deɪ·ˌvu] **I.** *n* <*pl* -> ❶ Rendezvous *nt* ❷ (*place*) Treffpunkt *m* **II.** *vi* sich heimlich treffen

renegade ['ren·ə·ɡeɪd] **I.** *n* Abtrünnige(r) *f(m) pej* **II.** *adj attr* abtrünnig

renew [rɪ·'nu] *vt* erneuern; *passport* verlängern; (*repair*) reparieren; (*patch*) ausbessern; **to ~ a relationship** eine Beziehung wieder aufnehmen

renewal [rɪ·'nu·əl] *n* Erneuerung *f;* (*regeneration*) Entwicklung *f;* *of passport* Verlängerung *f*

renewed [rɪ·'nud] *adj* erneuert *attr; interest* wieder erwacht

renovate ['ren·ə·veɪt] *vt* renovieren

renovation [ˌren·ə·'veɪ·ʃən] *n* Renovierung *f;* (*large-scale*) Sanierung *f;* **to be under ~** gerade renoviert werden

renowned [rɪ·'naʊnd] *adj* (*form, liter*) berühmt

rent [rent] **I.** *n* Miete *f;* (*for land*) Pacht *f;* **"for ~"** „zu vermieten" **II.** *vt* mieten; *land* pachten; *dress* ausleihen; (*rent out*) vermieten **III.** *vi* vermietet werden; ■ **to ~ for sth** gegen etw *akk* zu mieten sein

rental ['ren·təl] *n* Miete *f;* **~ agency** Verleih *m;* **car ~ agency** Autoverleih *m*

rent-'free *adj* mietfrei

reopen [ri·'oʊ·pən] **I.** *vt* wieder aufmachen; *shop* wieder eröffnen; *negotiations* wieder aufnehmen **II.** *vi* wieder eröffnen

reorganize [ri·'ɔr·ɡə·naɪz] *vt, vi* reorganisieren

rep [rep] *n* (*fam: salesperson*) *short for* **representative** Vertreter(in) *m(f)*

repaint [ri·'peɪnt] *vt* neu streichen

repair [rɪ·'per] **I.** *vt* reparieren; *defect* beheben; *road* ausbessern; (*put right*) [wieder] in Ordnung bringen; *damage* wiedergutmachen **II.** *n* Reparatur *f;* (*repaired place*) ausgebesserte Stelle; **beyond ~** irreparabel; **to be in good ~** in gutem Zustand sein; ■ **~s** *pl* Repara-

R

turarbeiten *pl;* **to do ~s** Reparaturen
durchführen

reparable ['rep·ər·ə·bəl] *adj* reparabel

repatriate [ri·'peɪ·tri·eɪt] *vt* [in das Heimatland] zurückschicken

repatriation [ri·ˌpeɪ·tri·'eɪ·ʃən] *n* Repatriierung *f*

repay <-paid, -paid> [ri·'peɪ] *vt* ❶ zurückzahlen; *loan* tilgen; ■**to ~ sb** jdm Geld zurückzahlen ❷ **to ~ a favor** sich für eine Gefälligkeit erkenntlich zeigen; ■**to ~ sb by doing sth** etw mit etw *dat* vergelten

repeal [ri·'pil] I. *vt* aufheben II. *n* Aufhebung *f*

repeat [ri·'pit] I. *vt* wiederholen; **~ after me** bitte mir nachsprechen; **don't ~ this but ...** sag es nicht weiter, [aber] ... II. *vi* sich wiederholen III. *n* Wiederholung *f*

repeatedly [ri·'pi·tɪd·li] *adv* wiederholt; (*several times*) mehrfach

repel <-ll-> [ri·'pel] *vt* ❶ zurückweisen; (*form: repulse*) abwehren ❷ ■**she was ~led by the sight** sie war abgestoßen von dem Anblick

repellent [ri·'pel·ənt] I. *n* Insektenspray *nt* II. *adj* abstoßend

repetition [ˌrep·ə·'tɪʃ·ən] *n* Wiederholung *f*

repetitious [ˌrep·ə·'tɪʃ·əs], **repetitive** [ri·'pet·ə·tɪv] *adj* sich wiederholend *attr*

replace [ri·'pleɪs] *vt* ersetzen; (*return*) [an seinen Platz] zurücklegen; *receiver* wieder auflegen; *bandage* wechseln

replacement [ri·'pleɪs·mənt] I. *n* Ersatz *m;* (*person*) Vertretung *f;* (*substituting*) Ersetzung *f* II. *adj attr* Ersatz-; **~ hip joint** künstliches Hüftgelenk

replay I. *vt* [ˌri·'pleɪ] *game* wiederholen; *video* nochmals abspielen II. *n* ['ri·pleɪ] (*recording*) Wiederholung *f;* (*game*) Wiederholungsspiel *nt*

replica ['rep·lɪ·kə] *n* Kopie *f*

reply [ri·'plaɪ] I. *vi* <-ie-> antworten; **to ~ to letters/a question** Briefe/eine Frage beantworten II. *n* Antwort *f*

report [ri·'pɔrt] I. *n* Meldung *f;* (*statement*) Bericht *m* II. *vt* ❶ ■**to ~ sth** etw berichten; **he was ~ed missing in action** er wurde als vermisst gemeldet; **to ~ a crime** ein Verbrechen anzeigen ❷ (*denounce*) melden; *to the police* anzeigen ❸ **the new management is ~ed to be more popular among the staff** es heißt, dass die neue Geschäftsleitung bei der Belegschaft beliebter sei III. *vi* ❶ Bericht erstatten; ■**to ~ on sth to sb** (*once*) jdm über etw *akk* Bericht erstatten; (*ongoing*) jdn über etw *akk* auf dem Laufenden halten; ■**to ~ [that] ...** mitteilen, [dass] ... ❷ (*be accountable to*) unterstehen ❸ (*arrive*) sich zur Arbeit melden; *to the police* sich bei der Polizei melden

◆ **report back** I. *vt* ■**to ~ back sth [to sb]** [jdm] über etw *akk* berichten II. *vi* Bericht erstatten; ■**to ~ back on sth [to sb]** [jdm] über etw *akk* Bericht erstatten

reporter [ri·'pɔr·tər] *n* Reporter(in) *m(f)*

repossess [ˌri·pə·'zes] *vt* wieder in Besitz nehmen

represent [ˌrep·ri·'zent] *vt* repräsentieren; (*depict*) darstellen; (*symbolize*) symbolisieren; (*be typical of*) widerspiegeln

representation [ˌrep·ri·zen·'teɪ·ʃən] *n* [Stell]vertretung *f;* (*that depicts*) Darstellung *f*

representative [ˌrep·ri·'zen·tə·tɪv] I. *adj* repräsentativ; (*typical*) typisch II. *n* [Stell]vertreter(in) *m(f);* POL Abgeordnete(r) *f(m)*

repressive [ri·'pres·ɪv] *adj* repressiv *geh; regime* unterdrückerisch

reprimand ['rep·rə·mænd] I. *vt* tadeln II. *n* Rüge *f*

reprint I. *vt* [ˌri·'prɪnt] nachdrucken II. *n* ['ri·prɪnt] Nachdruck *m*

reprisal [ri·'praɪ·zəl] *n* Vergeltungsmaßnahme *f*

reproach [ri·'proʊtʃ] I. *vt* ■**to ~ sb [for doing sth]** jdm [wegen einer S. *gen*]

R

Vorwürfe machen II. *n* <*pl* -es> Vorwurf *m*

reproachful [rɪˈprəʊtʃ·fəl] *adj* vorwurfsvoll

reproduce [ˌri·prə·ˈdus] I. *vi* sich fortpflanzen; (*multiply*) sich vermehren II. *vt* reproduzieren; (*in large numbers*) vervielfältigen

reproduction [ˌri·prə·ˈdʌk·ʃən] I. *n* Fortpflanzung *f;* (*multiplying*) Vermehrung *f;* (*copy*) Reproduktion *f;* **sound ~** Wiedergabe *f* II. *adj* **~ furniture** Stilmöbel *pl*

reproductive [ˌri·prə·ˈdʌk·tɪv] *adj* Fortpflanzungs-

reptile [ˈrep·taɪl] *n* Reptil *nt*

republic [rɪˈpʌb·lɪk] *n* Republik *f*

Republican [rɪˈpʌb·lɪ·kən] POL I. *n* Republikaner(in) *m(f)* II. *adj* republikanisch

repulsion [rɪˈpʌl·ʃən] *n* Abscheu *m*

repulsive [rɪˈpʌl·sɪv] *adj* abstoßend

reputable [ˈrep·jə·tə·bəl] *adj* angesehen

reputation [ˌrep·jʊ·ˈteɪ·ʃən] *n* Ruf *m;* (*high regard*) Ansehen *nt;* **to have a ~ for sth** für etw *akk* bekannt sein; **to have a ~ as sth** einen Ruf als etw haben

repute [rɪˈpjut] *n* Ansehen *nt;* **of good ~** von gutem Ruf

reputed [rɪˈpju·tɪd] *adj* vermutet; (*supposed*) mutmaßlich

request [rɪˈkwest] I. *n* ❶ Bitte *f;* **on ~** auf Anfrage ❷ (*formal*) Antrag *m;* **to submit a ~ that …** beantragen, dass … ❸ (*in radio*) [Musik]wunsch *m* II. *vt* ❶ ▪**to ~ sth** (*form*) um etw *akk* bitten; **as ~ed** wie gewünscht ❷ (*in radio*) ▪**to ~ sth** [sich *dat*] etw wünschen

require [rɪˈkwaɪr] *vt* ❶ brauchen; ▪**to be ~d for sth** für etw *akk* erforderlich sein; **~d reading** Pflichtlektüre *f* ❷ (*demand*) ▪**to ~ sth** [of sb] etw [von jdm] verlangen ❸ (*order*) **the rules ~ that …** die Vorschriften besagen, dass …

requirement [rɪˈkwaɪr·mənt] *n* Voraussetzung *f;* **it is a legal ~ that …** es

ist gesetzlich vorgeschrieben, dass …; **to meet the ~s** die Voraussetzungen erfüllen

requisite [ˈrek·wɪ·zɪt] I. *adj attr* (*form*) erforderlich II. *n usu pl* Notwendigkeit *f*

rescue [ˈres·kju:] I. *vt* retten; (*free*) befreien; **to ~ sb from danger** jdn aus einer Gefahr retten II. *n* Rettung *f;* **to come to sb's ~** jdm zu Hilfe kommen III. *adj* **attempt, helicopter** Rettungs-

'rescue company *n* ECON Auffanggesellschaft *f*

'rescue package *n* FIN, POL [Euro]rettungsschirm *m*

research I. *n* [ˈri·sɜrtʃ] ❶ Forschung *f;* (*specific*) Erforschung *f;* **to conduct ~ [into sth]** [etw er]forschen ❷ (*studies*) Untersuchungen *pl* II. *vi* [rɪˈsɜrtʃ] forschen; ▪**to ~ in[to] sth** etw erforschen III. *vt* [rɪˈsɜrtʃ] erforschen; *reporter* recherchieren

researcher [rɪˈsɜrtʃ·ər] *n* Forscher(in) *m(f)*

resemblance [rɪˈzem·bləns] *n* Ähnlichkeit *f;* **to bear a ~ to sb/sth** jdm/etw ähnlich sehen

resemble [rɪˈzem·bəl] *vt* ähneln

resent [rɪˈzent] *vt* sich [sehr] ärgern; ▪**to ~ doing sth** etw [äußerst] ungern tun

resentment [rɪˈzent·mənt] *n* Verbitterung *f*

reservation [ˌrez·ər·ˈveɪ·ʃən] *n* ❶ Reservierung *f;* **to make a ~** reservieren ❷ *usu pl* (*doubt*) Bedenken *pl* ❸ (*land*) Reservat *nt*

reserve [rɪˈzɜrv] I. *n* ❶ Reserve *f;* **to put sth on ~ [for sb]** etw [für jdn] reservieren ❷ (*area*) Reservat *nt;* **wildlife ~** Naturschutzgebiet *nt* ❸ SPORT Ersatzspieler(in) *m(f)* ❹ (*restraint*) Reserviertheit *f* II. *vt* aufheben; (*save*) reservieren; *room, tickets a.* vorbestellen; **to ~ the right to do sth** sich *dat* das Recht vorbehalten, etw zu tun

reserved [rɪˈzɜrvd] *adj* reserviert; (*restrained*) reserviert; *smile* verhalten

reservoir [ˈrez·ər·vwar] *n* Wasserreservoir *nt;* (*fig*) Reservoir *nt*

R

reset <-tt-, -set, -set> [ˌriːˈset] vt clock neu stellen; bone [ein]richten; COMPUT neu starten

residence [ˈrez·ɪ·dəns] n ❶ (form: domicile) Wohnsitz m; **to take up ~ in a country** sich in einem Land niederlassen ❷ (building) Wohngebäude nt; of monarch Residenz f ❸ (for research) Forschungsaufenthalt m; (for teaching) Lehraufenthalt m

resident [ˈrez·ɪ·dənt] I. n Bewohner(in) m(f); local ~ Anwohner(in) m(f); **"~s only"** "Anlieger frei" II. adj ❶ ansässig; (in-house) hauseigen ❷ fears tief sitzend

residential [ˌrez·ɪˈden·ʃəl] adj Wohn-; ~ **district** Wohngebiet nt

residue [ˈrez·ə·du] n usu sing Rückstand m

resign [rɪˈzaɪn] I. vi kündigen; **to ~ from office** von einem Amt zurücktreten II. vt ❶ aufgeben; post niederlegen ❷ (accept) ■to ~ oneself to sth sich mit etw abfinden

resignation [ˌrez·ɪgˈneɪ·ʃən] n (letter, act) Kündigung f; from post Rücktritt m; (acceptance) Resignation f

resigned [rɪˈzaɪnd] adj resigniert; ■to be ~ to sth sich mit etw dat abgefunden haben

resilience [rɪˈzɪl·jəns], **resiliency** [rɪˈzɪl·jən·si] n Widerstandskraft f

resilient [rɪˈzɪl·jənt] adj zäh; health unverwüstlich

resin [ˈrez·ɪn] n Harz nt

resist [rɪˈzɪst] I. vt ❶ (oppose) ■to ~ sth etw dat Widerstand leisten; **to ~ arrest** LAW sich der Verhaftung widersetzen ❷ (refuse) ■to ~ sth gegen etw akk wehren ❸ temptation widerstehen +dat II. vi sich wehren; (refuse) widerstehen

resistance [rɪˈzɪs·təns] n Widerstand m; to illness Widerstandskraft f; ~ **to a disease** Resistenz f gegen eine Krankheit

resistant [rɪˈzɪs·tənt] adj resistent

resolute [ˈrez·ə·lut] adj (form) entschlossen; belief fest

resolution [ˌrez·əˈlu·ʃən] n ❶ Entschlossenheit f; (decision) Entscheidung f; (intention) Vorsatz m; **New Year's ~** gute Vorsätze fürs Neue Jahr ❷ of image Auflösung f

resolve [rɪˈzalv] I. vt ❶ differences beilegen; **the crisis ~d itself** die Krise legte sich von selbst ❷ (form: decide) ■to ~ that ... beschließen, dass ... II. vi beschließen; ■to ~ to do sth beschließen, etw zu tun III. n Entschlossenheit f

resolved [rɪˈzalvd] adj pred entschlossen

resonance [ˈrez·ə·nəns] n [Nach]hall m

resonant [ˈrez·ə·nənt] adj [wider]hallend; ■to be ~ with sth von etw dat widerhallen

resort [rɪˈzɔrt] I. n ❶ Urlaubsort m; (recourse) Einsatz m; **as a last ~** als letzten Ausweg; **you're my last ~!** du bist meine letzte Hoffnung! II. vi ■to ~ to sth auf etw akk zurückgreifen

resound [rɪˈzaʊnd] vi Furore machen; **the rumor ~ed throughout the world** das Gerücht ging um die ganze Welt

resounding [rɪˈzaʊn·dɪŋ] adj attr schallend; (emphatic) unglaublich; success durchschlagend

resource [ˈriː·sɔrs] n pl Ressourcen pl; (wealth) [finanzielle] Mittel; **natural ~s** Bodenschätze pl

resourceful [rɪˈsɔrs·fəl] adj einfallsreich

respect [rɪˈspekt] I. n ❶ Respekt m; (consideration) Rücksicht f; **to have ~ for sb** Rücksicht auf jdn nehmen; **to have no ~ for sth** etw nicht respektieren; **to pay one's ~s** [to sb] jdm einen Besuch abstatten; **to pay one's last ~s to sb** jdm die letzte Ehre erweisen ▸PHRASES: **in many ~s** in vielen Punkten; **in every ~** in jeglicher Hinsicht II. vt respektieren

respectable [rɪˈspek·tə·bəl] adj (decent) anständig; salary ansehnlich; (deserving respect) respektabel; person angesehen

respected [rɪ·ˈspek·təd] *adj* angesehen

respectful [rɪ·ˈspekt·fəl] *adj* respektvoll; **to be ~ of sth** etw respektieren

respective [rɪ·ˈspek·tɪv] *adj attr* jeweilig

respectively [rɪ·ˈspek·tɪv·li] *adv* beziehungsweise

respirator [ˈres·pə·rei·tər] *n* Beatmungsgerät *nt;* (*mask*) Atem[schutz]gerät *nt*

respond [rɪ·ˈspand] I. *vt* ■**to ~ that …** erwidern, dass … II. *vi* antworten; (*react*) reagieren

response [rɪ·ˈspans] *n* Antwort *f;* (*reaction*) Reaktion *f;* **to meet with a good ~** eine gute Resonanz finden; **in ~ to sth** in Erwiderung etw *akk*

responsibility [rɪ·ˌspan·sə·ˈbɪl·ɪ·ti] *n* Verantwortung *f;* (*duty*) Verantwortlichkeit *f;* **to claim ~ for sth** sich für etw *akk* verantwortlich erklären; **to carry a lot of ~** eine große Verantwortung tragen

responsible [rɪ·ˈspan·sə·bəl] *adj* verantwortlich; (*in charge a.*) zuständig; (*sensible*) verantwortungsbewusst; *job* verantwortungsvoll; **to hold sb ~** jdn verantwortlich machen

responsive [rɪ·ˈspan·sɪv] *adj* gut reagierend; **to be ~ to treatment** auf eine Behandlungsmethode ansprechen

rest¹ [rest] I. *n* ➊ Erholung *f;* (*period*) [Ruhe]pause *f;* **to have a [little] ~** eine [kurze] Pause machen; **for a ~** zur Erholung ➋ (*support*) Stütze *f* II. *vt* ➊ **to ~ one's eyes** seine Augen ausruhen ➋ (*support*) lehnen III. *vi* ➊ [aus]ruhen; **to not ~ until …** [so lange] nicht ruhen, bis … ➋ (*be supported*) ruhen ➌ (*depend*) ruhen; (*be based*) beruhen ▶ PHRASES: **[you can] ~ assured [that …]** seien Sie versichert, dass …

rest² [rest] *n + sing/pl vb* ■**the ~** der Rest

restaurant [ˈres·tər·ənt] *n* Restaurant *nt*

restful [ˈrest·fəl] *adj* beruhigend; *atmosphere* entspannt; *place* friedlich

'rest home *n* Altersheim *nt*

restless [ˈrest·lɪs] *adj* unruhig; (*uneasy*) rastlos; (*wakeful*) ruhelos; *night* schlaflos; **to get ~** anfangen, sich unwohl zu fühlen

restoration [ˌres·tə·ˈrei·ʃən] *n* (*act*) Restaurieren *nt;* (*instance*) Restaurierung *f*

restore [rɪ·ˈstɔr] *vt* restaurieren; (*re-establish*) wiederherstellen; **to ~ sb's faith in sth** jdm sein Vertrauen in etw *akk* zurückgeben; **to ~ sb to life** jdn ins Leben zurückbringen; **to ~ sb to power** jdn wieder an die Macht bringen

restrain [rɪ·ˈstrein] *vt* zurückhalten; (*forcefully*) bändigen; ■**to ~ sb from [doing] sth** jdn davon abhalten, etw zu tun; ■**to ~ oneself** sich beherrschen

restrained [rɪ·ˈstreind] *adj* beherrscht; *criticism* verhalten; *manners* gepflegt

restraint [rɪ·ˈstreint] *n* Beherrschung *f;* (*restriction*) Einschränkung *f;* **to exercise ~** Zurückhaltung üben

restrict [rɪ·ˈstrɪkt] *vt* beschränken; *number* begrenzen; ■**to ~ sb from [doing] sth** jdm etw untersagen

restricted [rɪ·ˈstrɪk·tɪd] *adj* begrenzt; *space* eng; (*subject to limitation*) eingeschränkt

restriction [rɪ·ˈstrɪk·ʃən] *n* Begrenzung *f;* (*act*) Einschränken *nt;* **to lift ~s** Restriktionen aufheben

restrictive [rɪ·ˈstrɪk·tɪv] *adj* einschränkend; *measures* restriktiv

'restroom *n* Toilette *f*

restructure [ˌri·ˈstrʌk·tʃər] *vt* umstrukturieren

result [rɪ·ˈzʌlt] I. *n* Folge *f;* (*outcome*) Ergebnis *nt;* (*math a.*) Resultat *nt;* (*satisfactory*) Erfolg *m;* **to have good ~s with sth** gute Ergebnisse mit etw *dat* erzielen II. *vi* resultieren; ■**to ~ in sth** etw zur Folge haben

resume [rɪ·ˈzum] I. *vt* wieder aufnehmen; *journey* fortsetzen; ■**to ~ doing sth** fortfahren, etw zu tun II. *vi* wieder beginnen; (*after short interruption*) weitergehen

résumé [ˈrez·u·mei] *n* Lebenslauf *m*

resumption [rɪ·ˈzʌmp·ʃən] *n* (*act*) Wie-

R

deraufnahme *f*; (*instance*) Wiederbeginn *m kein pl*

retail [ˈriˑteɪl] **I.** *n* Einzelhandel *m* **II.** *vi* **this model of computer ~s for 650 dollars** im Einzelhandel kostet dieses Computermodell 650 Dollar

retailer [ˈriˑteɪˑlər] *n* Einzelhändler(in) *m(f)*

retain [rɪˈteɪn] *vt* behalten; *attention* halten; *dignity* bewahren; (*hold in place*) zurückhalten; (*not lose*) speichern; *thought* behalten; **to ~ control of sth** etw weiterhin in der Gewalt haben; **to ~ the right to do sth** LAW sich das Recht vorbehalten, etw zu tun

retainer [rɪˈteɪˑnər] *n* Vorschuss *m*

retake I. *vt* <-took, -taken> [ˌriˑˈteɪk] (*regain*) wiedergewinnen; *exam* wiederholen; *scene* nochmals drehen **II.** *n* [ˈriˑteɪk] Neuaufnahme

retaliate [rɪˈtælˑiˑeɪt] *vi* Vergeltung üben; *for insults* sich revanchieren

retaliation [rɪˌtælˑiˑˈeɪˑʃən] *n* Vergeltung *f*; (*act*) Vergeltungsschlag *m*

retaliatory [rɪˈtælˑiˑəˌtɔrˑi] *adj attr* Vergeltungs-

retard [ˈriˑtard] *n* (*pej sl*) Idiot *m pej*

retarded [rɪˈtarˑdɪd] *adj* (*pej fam*) zurückgeblieben

retch [retʃ] *vi* würgen; **to make sb ~** jdn zum Würgen bringen

rethink I. *vt* <-thought, -thought> [ˌriˑˈθɪŋk] überdenken **II.** *n* [ˈriˑθɪŋk] Überdenken *nt*; **to have a ~** etw noch einmal überdenken

retina <*pl* -s> [ˈretˑənˑə] *n* Netzhaut *f*

retinue [ˈretˑənˑu] *n* Gefolge *nt kein pl*

retire [rɪˈtaɪr] *vi* ❶ in den Ruhestand treten; *worker* in Rente gehen; *civil servant* in Pension gehen; *self-employed* sich zur Ruhe setzen; *soldier* aus der Armee ausscheiden; *athlete* seine Karriere beenden ❷ (*form: withdraw*) sich zurückziehen

retired [rɪˈtaɪˑərd] *adj* im Ruhestand *präd*; *worker* in Rente *präd*; *civil servant* pensioniert

retirement [rɪˈtaɪrˑmənt] *n* Ruhestand *m*; (*act*) Ausscheiden *nt* aus dem

Arbeitsleben; *of civil servant* Pensionierung *f*; *of soldier* Verabschiedung *f*; *of athlete* Zurücktreten *nt*

re'tirement plan *n* Vorsorgeplan *m*

retiring [rɪˈtaɪˑərˑɪŋ] *adj* zurückhaltend

retort [rɪˈtɔrt] **I.** *vt* ■**to ~ that ...** scharf erwidern, dass ... **II.** *vi* scharf antworten **III.** *n* scharfe Antwort

retouch [ˌriˑˈtʌtʃ] *vt* retuschieren

retrace [riˑˈtreɪs] *vt* zurückverfolgen; *in mind* [geistig] nachvollziehen; **to ~ one's steps** denselben Weg zurückgehen

retract [rɪˈtrækt] **I.** *vt* ❶ zurückziehen; *offer* zurücknehmen ❷ (*draw back*) zurückziehen; (*into body*) einziehen **II.** *vi* eingezogen werden

retrain [riˑˈtreɪn] **I.** *vt* umschulen **II.** *vi* umgeschult werden

retreat [rɪˈtrit] **I.** *vi* zurückweichen; *floodwaters* zurückgehen; (*withdraw*) sich zurückziehen; (*hide*) sich verstecken; ■**to ~ into oneself** sich in sich selbst zurückziehen **II.** *n* Abwendung *f*; MIL Rückzug *m*; (*place*) Zufluchtsort *m*

retrial [ˈriˑtraɪl] *n* LAW Wiederaufnahmeverfahren *nt*

retribution [ˌretˑrəˑˈbjuˑʃən] *n* (*form*) Vergeltung *f*

retrieval [rɪˈtriˑvəl] *n* Wiedererlangen *nt*; (*rescuing*) Rettung *f*; (*of wreckage*) Bergung *f*; **data ~** Datenabruf *m*; (*when lost*) Datenrückgewinnung *f*

retrieve [rɪˈtriv] *vt* wiederfinden; (*fetch*) zurückholen; (*rescue*) retten; (*from wreckage*) bergen; *data* abrufen

retriever [rɪˈtriˑvər] *n* Retriever *m*

retro [ˈretˑrou] *adj* (*fam*) *fashion* Retro-

retroactive [ˌretˑrouˑˈækˑtɪv] *adj* rückwirkend

retrospect [ˈretˑrəˑspekt] *n* **in ~** im Rückblick

retrospective [ˌretˑrəˑˈspekˑtɪv] **I.** *adj* rückblickend; *mood* nachdenklich **II.** *n* Retrospektive *f*

return [rɪˈtɜrn] **I.** *n* ❶ Rückkehr *f*; *of illness* Wiederauftreten *nt*; **~ home** Heimkehr *f* ❷ (*giving back*) Rückgabe *f*; (*stroke*) Rückschlag *m*; (*proceeds*) Gewinn *m;* **~ on capital** Rendite *f* ③ *(key)* Returntaste *f* **II.** *adj after trip* Rück- **III.** *vi* ① zurückkommen; *illness* wiederkommen; **to ~ home** nach Hause gehen/kommen; *(after long absence)* heimkehren; **~ to sender** zurück an Absender ② *(revert)* ■**to ~ to sth** etw wieder aufnehmen; **to ~ to normal** *things* sich wieder normalisieren; *person* wieder zu seinem alten Ich zurückfinden **IV.** *vt* ① zurückgeben; **to ~ sth to its place** etw an seinen Platz zurückstellen ② *(reciprocate)* erwidern; **to ~ a wave** zurückwinken; **to ~ sb's call** jdn zurückrufen ③ *volley* annehmen

re'turn key *n* Eingabetaste *f*

reunification [ˌriː·juː·nə·fɪˈkeɪ·ʃən] *n* Wiedervereinigung *f*

reunion [ˌriːˈjuːn·jən] *n* ① Treffen *nt* ② *(form: bringing together)* Wiedervereinigung *f;* *(coming together)* Wiedersehen *nt*

reunite [ˌriː·juːˈnaɪt] **I.** *vt* wieder zusammenführen; ■**to ~ sb with sb** jdn mit jdm [wieder] zusammenbringen **II.** *vi* sich wiedervereinigen; *people* wieder zusammenkommen

reusable [ˌriːˈjuː·zə·bəl] *adj* wiederverwendbar

reuse [ˌriːˈjuːz] *vt* wiederverwenden

rev¹ [rev] *n (fam) short for* **revolution** Drehzahl *f;* ■**~s** *pl* Umdrehungen *pl* [pro Minute]

rev² <-vv-> [rev] *vt* auf Touren bringen; *(noisily)* aufheulen lassen

◆**rev up I.** *vi* auf Touren kommen; *(noisily)* aufheulen **II.** *vt* auf Touren bringen

Rev. *n abbrev of* **Reverend**

revamp [ˌriːˈvæmp] *vt (fam)* aufpeppen; *room* aufmöbeln; *image* aufpolieren

reveal [rɪˈviːl] *vt* ① zeigen; *(disclose)* enthüllen; *secret* verraten; *identity* zu erkennen geben; ■**to ~ that ...** enthüllen, dass ...; *(admit)* zugeben, dass ...

revealing [rɪˈviː·lɪŋ] *adj* freizügig; *dress* gewagt; *interview* aufschlussreich

revel <-l-> [ˈrev·əl] *vi* feiern

◆**revel in** *vi* ■**to ~ in sth** seine wahre Freude an etw *dat* haben

revelation [ˌrev·əˈleɪ·ʃən] *n* Enthüllung *f* ▶PHRASES: **to be [quite] a ~ to sb** jdm die Augen öffnen

revelry [ˈrev·əl·ri] *n* [ausgelassenes] Feiern; *usu pl (festivity)* [ausgelassene] Feier

revenge [rɪˈvendʒ] **I.** *n* Rache *f;* *(desire)* Rachedurst *m;* **to get one's ~** sich rächen; **~ killing** Vergeltungsmord *m* **II.** *vt* rächen

revenue [ˈrev·ə·nu] *n* Einkünfte *pl;* *(of state)* Staatseinkünfte *pl;* *sales* **~s** Verkaufseinnahmen *pl;* *tax* **~s** Steueraufkommen *nt*

revere [rɪˈvɪr] *vt (form)* verehren; *work* hoch schätzen

reverence [ˈrev·ər·əns] *n* Verehrung *f;* **to treat sth/sb with ~** etw/jdn ehrfürchtig behandeln

reverend [ˈrev·ər·ənd] *n ≈* Pfarrer *m*

reverent [ˈrev·ər·ənt] *adj* ehrfürchtig; *behavior* ehrerbietig

reverential [ˌrev·əˈren·ʃəl] *adj (form)* ehrfürchtig

reversal [rɪˈvɜr·səl] *n (effect)* Wende *f;* *(situation)* Umkehrung *f;* *(misfortune)* Rückschlag *m;* **~ of a trend** Trendwende *f;* **role ~** Rollentausch *m*

reverse [rɪˈvɜrs] **I.** *vt* umkehren; *(turn over)* umdrehen; *coat* wenden; *car* zurücksetzen **II.** *vi car* rückwärtsfahren; *(briefly)* zurücksetzen **III.** *n* ① ■**the ~** das Gegenteil; **to do sth in ~** etw umgekehrt tun ② *(gear)* Rückwärtsgang *m;* **to go into ~** in den Rückwärtsgang schalten ③ *(back)* Rückseite *f;* *of coin a.* Kehrseite *f* **IV.** *adj* umgekehrt; *direction* entgegengesetzt

reversible [rɪˈvɜr·sə·bəl] *adj* zum Wenden *nach n;* *(alterable)* umkehrbar; **~ coat** Wendejacke *f*

revert [rɪˈvɜrt] *vi* ■**to ~ to sth** zu etw *dat* zurückkehren; *bad state* in etw *akk* zurückfallen; **to ~ to a method** auf eine Methode zurückgreifen

review [rɪˈvju] **I.** *vt* ① [erneut] [über]prüfen; *(reconsider)* überdenken; *salaries*

R

revidieren ❷ (*look back over*) zurückblicken auf +*akk*; *lesson* wiederholen; **let's ~ what has happened so far** führen wir uns vor Augen, was bis jetzt passiert ist ❸ (*criticize*) besprechen; *book, play* rezensieren ❹ **to ~ the troops** eine Parade abnehmen II. *vi* lernen III. *n* ❶ Überprüfung *f*; **to come under ~** überprüft werden; *case* wieder aufgenommen werden ❷ (*summary*) Überblick *m*; *of lesson* Wiederholung *f*; **month under ~** ᴇᴄᴏɴ Berichtsmonat *m*; **wage** [*or* **salary**] ~ Gehaltsrevision *f*; ~ **for an exam** Prüfungsvorbereitung *f* ❸ *of book, play* Rezension *f*; *movie* ~ Filmbesprechung *f*

reviewer [rɪˈvjuːər] *n* Kritiker(in) *m(f)*; *of plays a.* Rezensent(in) *m(f)*

revise [rɪˈvaɪz] *vt* umändern; *manuscript* überarbeiten; *book* redigieren; (*reconsider*) überdenken; ■ **to ~ sth upwards/downwards** etw nach oben/unten korrigieren

revision [rɪˈvɪʒən] *n* (*act*) Überarbeitung *f*; (*version*) Neufassung *f*; *of book* überarbeitete Ausgabe; (*alteration*) Änderung *f*

revitalize [riːˈvaɪtəlaɪz] *vt* wieder beleben

revival [rɪˈvaɪvəl] *n* ❶ Wiederbelebung *f*; *of idea* Wiederaufleben *f*; *of custom a.* Renaissance *f*; **economic ~** wirtschaftlicher Aufschwung ❷ (*new production*) Neuauflage *f*; *of film* Neuverfilmung *f*; *of play* Neuaufführung *f*

revive [rɪˈvaɪv] I. *vt* wiederbeleben; (*give new energy*) beleben; (*resurrect*) wieder aufleben lassen; *economy* ankurbeln; *idea* wieder aufgreifen; *interest* wieder erwecken; *spirits* wieder heben; **to ~ sb's hopes** jdm neue Hoffnungen machen II. *vi* (*to consciousness*) wieder zu sich *dat* kommen; (*to health*) sich erholen; (*be resurrected*) sich erholen; *economy a.* wieder aufblühen; *custom* wieder aufleben; *confidence* zurückkehren; *suspicions* wieder aufkeimen

revolt [rɪˈvoʊlt] I. *vi* rebellieren II. *vt*

■ **to ~ sb** jdn abstoßen; ■ **to be ~ed by sth** von etw *dat* angeekelt sein III. *n* Revolte *f*; ~ **against the government** Regierungsputsch *m*

revolting [rɪˈvoʊltɪŋ] *adj* abstoßend; *person* widerlich; *smell* ekelhaft

revolution [ˌrevəˈluːʃən] *n* Revolution *f*; ᴛᴇᴄʜ Umdrehung *f*; ~**s per minute** Drehzahl *f*

revolutionary [ˌrevəˈluːʃənˌneri] I. *n* Revolutionär(in) *m(f)* II. *adj* revolutionär; (*fig*) bahnbrechend

revolutionize [ˌrevəˈluːʃənˌnaɪz] *vt* revolutionieren

revolve [rɪˈvalv] *vi* sich drehen; **to ~ on an axis** sich um eine Achse drehen

♦ **revolve around** *vi* ■ **to ~ around sth** sich um etw *akk* drehen

revolver [rɪˈvalvər] *n* Revolver *m*

revolving [rɪˈvalvɪŋ] *adj attr* rotierend; ~ **door** Drehtür *f*

revue [rɪˈvjuː] *n* Revue *f*

reward [rɪˈwɔːrd] I. *n* Belohnung *f*; *for service* Anerkennung *f*; (*finder's fee*) Finderlohn *m* II. *vt* belohnen

rewarding [rɪˈwɔːrdɪŋ] *adj* befriedigend; *experience* lohnend; *task* dankbar

rewind I. *vt* <-wound, -wound> [ˌriːˈwaɪnd] aufwickeln; *cassette* zurückspulen; *watch* aufziehen II. *vi* <-wound, -wound> [ˌriːˈwaɪnd] zurückspulen III. *adj* [ˈriːwaɪnd] Rückspul-

rewrite <-wrote, -written> I. *vt* [ˌriːˈraɪt] neu schreiben; (*revise*) überarbeiten; (*recast*) umschreiben; **to ~ history** (*fig*) die Geschichte neu schreiben II. *n* [ˈriːraɪt] Überarbeitung *f*

rhapsody [ˈræpsədi] *n* Rhapsodie *f*

rhetoric [ˈretərɪk] *n* (*persuasive*) Redegewandtheit *f*; (*bombastic*) Phrasendrescherei *f pej*; **empty ~** leere Worte

rhetorical [rɪˈtɔːrɪkəl] *adj* rhetorisch; (*overdramatic*) übertrieben dramatisch

rheumatic [ruːˈmætɪk] *adj* rheumatisch; *joint a.* rheumakrank

rheumatism [ˈruːmətɪzəm] *n* Rheuma *nt*

Rhine [raɪn] n GEOG ■**the ~** der Rhein

rhino [ˈraɪnoʊ] n (fam) short for **rhinoceros** Nashorn nt

rhinoceros <pl -es> [raɪˈnɑsˑərˑəs] n Nashorn nt

Rhode Island [ˌroʊdˈaɪˑləd] n Rhode Island nt

Rhodes [roʊdz] n Rhodos nt

rhubarb [ˈruˑbɑrb] n Rhabarber m

rhyme [raɪm] I. n Reim m; (poem) Reim[vers] m; (word) Reimwort nt; ■**in ~** gereimt II. vi ■**to ~ [with sth]** sich [auf etw akk] reimen III. vt reimen

rhythm [ˈrɪðˑəm] n Rhythmus m

rhythmic(al) [ˈrɪðˑmɪk(əl)] adj rhythmisch

RI, R.I. abbrev of **Rhode Island**

rib [rɪb] I. n Rippe f; ■**~s** (food) Rippchen pl; **to break a ~** sich dat eine Rippe brechen II. vt <-bb-> (fam) ■**to ~ sb** jdn aufziehen

ribbon [ˈrɪbˑən] n Band nt; (fig) Streifen m; ■**in ~s** in Fetzen; **to cut sb/sth to ~s** jdn/etw zerfetzen; (fig) jdn/etw in der Luft zerreißen

'**rib cage** n Brustkorb m

rice [raɪs] n Reis m; **brown ~** Naturreis m

rich [rɪtʃ] I. adj reich; land fruchtbar; soil a. fett; vegetation üppig; reward großzügig; (food) gehaltvoll; (hard to digest) schwer; (intense) satt; flavor reich; smell schwer; taste voll; (interesting) reich; life a. erfüllt; history bedeutend; **to get ~ quick** schnell zu Reichtum kommen; ■**in detail** sehr detailliert II. n ■**the ~** pl die Reichen pl

richness [ˈrɪtʃˑnɪs] n Reichtum m; (fattiness) Reichhaltigkeit f; (intensity) Stärke f; of color Sattheit f; **~ of detail** Detailgenauigkeit f

ricksha(w) [ˈrɪkˑʃa, -ʃɔ] n Rikscha f

ricochet [ˈrɪkˑəˑʃeɪ] I. n (act) Abprallen nt; (ball) Abpraller m; (bullet) Querschläger m II. vi abprallen

rid <-dd-, rid, rid> [rɪd] vt ■**to ~ sth/ sb of sth** etw/jdn von etw dat befreien; ■**to be ~ of sb/sth** jdn/etw los

sein; **to get ~ of sb/sth** jdn/etw loswerden

riddance [ˈrɪdˑəns] n ▶PHRASES: **good ~ [to him]**! Gott sei Dank[, dass wir den los sind]!

ridden [ˈrɪdˑən] pp of **ride**

riddle [ˈrɪdˑəl] n Rätsel nt

ride [raɪd] I. n ❶ Fahrt f; (on horse) Ritt m; carousel ~ Karussellfahrt f; **to go for a ~** eine Fahrt machen; (with horse) ausreiten ❷ (lift) Mitfahrgelegenheit f; **to give sb a ~** jdn [im Auto] mitnehmen ▶PHRASES: **to take sb for a ~** (fam) jdn übers Ohr hauen II. vt <rode, ridden> fahren; horse reiten; **I ~ my bicycle to work** ich fahre mit dem Fahrrad zur Arbeit; **to ~ the bus/train** Bus/Zug fahren III. vi <rode, ridden> reiten

rider [ˈraɪˑdər] n Reiter(in) m(f); of vehicle Fahrer(in) m(f)

ridge [rɪdʒ] n Grat m; of roof Dachfirst m; **~ of high/low pressure** Hoch-/Tiefdruckkeil m

ridicule [ˈrɪdˑɪˑkjul] I. n Spott m; **to hold sth up to ~** sich über etw lustig machen II. vt verspotten

ridiculous [rɪˈdɪkˑjuˑləs] adj lächerlich; (inane) absurd

rife [raɪf] adj pred weit verbreitet; **~ with** voller +gen

riffraff [ˈrɪfˑræf] n + sing/pl vb (pej) Gesindel nt kein pl   R

rifle[1] [ˈraɪˑfəl] n Gewehr nt

rifle[2] [ˈraɪˑfəl] I. vi durchwühlen II. vt plündern

'**rifle range** n Schießstand m

rift [rɪft] n Spalt m; GEOL [Erd]spalt m; (fig: disagreement) Spaltung f; (in friendship) Bruch m

rig [rɪg] I. n Vorrichtung f; **drilling ~** Bohrinsel f; **gas/oil ~** Gas-/Ölbohrinsel f; **big ~** [mehrachsiger] Sattelschlepper II. vt <-gg-> boat takeln; sails anschlagen fachspr; (shelter) [behelfsmäßig] zusammenbauen; (manipulate) manipulieren

rigging [ˈrɪgˑɪŋ] n (on ship) Takelung f;

(*manipulation*) Manipulation *f;* **ballot-~** Wahlmanipulation *f*

right [raɪt] I. *adj* ❶ (*good*) richtig; (*fair*) gerecht; **to do the ~ thing** das Richtige tun; **you're ~ to be annoyed** du bist zu Recht verärgert ❷ *exact* genau; **to get sth ~** etw richtig machen; **you were ~ about him** was ihn angeht, haben Sie Recht gehabt; **to be just ~** (*fam*) genau das Richtige sein ❸ ■**~?** oder? ❹ (*best*) richtig; **he's the ~ person for the job** er ist der Richtige für den Job; **to be in the ~ place at the ~ time** zur rechten Zeit am rechten Ort sein ❺ *pred* (*functioning*) in Ordnung; **is your watch ~?** geht deine Uhr richtig? ❻ (*not left*) rechte(r, s); **to make a ~ turn** rechts abbiegen II. *adv* ❶ (*completely*) völlig; **she walked ~ past me** sie lief direkt an mir vorbei; **to be ~ behind sb** voll [und ganz] hinter jdm stehen ❷ (*all the way*) ganz; (*directly*) direkt ❸ (*well*) gut; **things have been going ~ for me** es läuft gut für mich ❹ (*not left*) rechts; **to turn ~** [nach] rechts abbiegen III. *n* ❶ (*goodness*) Recht *nt* ❷ (*morally correct*) das Richtige; **the ~s and wrongs of sth** das Für und Wider einer S. *gen* (*claim*) Recht *nt;* **~ of** [*or* to] **free speech** Recht *nt* auf freie Meinungsäußerung; **women's ~s** die Rechte *pl* der Frau[en] ❹ (*right side*) rechte Seite; **on the ~** rechts; **on my/her ~** rechts [von mir/ ihr] ❺ POL ■**the R~** die Rechte; **the far ~** die Rechtsextremen *pl* IV. *vt* ❶ (*correct position*) aufrichten; (*correct condition*) in Ordnung bringen ❷ (*rectify*) wiedergutmachen V. *interj* (*fam*) ❶ (*okay*) in Ordnung; ~ **you are!** in Ordnung! ❷ (*as introduction*) ~ , **let's go** also, nichts wie los *fam*

'right a·way *adv* sofort; **we have to leave** ~ **away** wir müssen unverzüglich aufbrechen

right·ful ['raɪt·fəl] *adj attr* rechtmäßig

'right-hand *adj attr* rechte(r, s); (*with right hand*) mit der Rechten *nach n;* ~ **punch** rechter Haken

right-hand 'man *n* ■**sb's** ~ jds rechte Hand

right·ly ['raɪt·li] *adv* richtig; (*justifiably*) zu Recht

right-'mind·ed *adj* vernünftig

right of 'way <*pl* rights of way> *n* Durchgangsrecht *nt;* (*on road*) Vorfahrt *f*

'right·wing *adj* rechts *präd,* rechte(r, s)

rigid ['rɪdʒ·ɪd] *adj* steif; (*unalterable*) starr; (*stringent*) streng

rigidity [rɪ·'dʒɪd·ɪ·t̬i] *n* Steifheit *f;* (*pej: intransigence*) Starrheit *f*

rigmarole ['rɪg·mə·roʊl] *n usu sing* (*pej*) Gelabere *nt pej;* (*procedures*) Prozedur *f*

rigor ['rɪg·ər] *n* Genauigkeit *f;* (*strictness*) Strenge *f*

rigor mortis [ˌrɪg·ər·'mɔr·t̬ɪs] *n* Leichenstarre *f*

rigorous ['rɪg·ər·əs] *adj* (*peinlich*) genau; (*disciplined*) strikt; (*demanding*) hart

rile [raɪl] *vt* (*fam*) ärgern; **to get sb ~d** jdn verärgern

rim [rɪm] I. *n* ❶ Rand *m; of wheel* Felge *f;* **on the Pacific R~** am Rande des Pazifiks ❷ *usu pl* (*of spectacles*) Fassung *f* II. *vt* <-mm-> umgeben; (*frame*) umrahmen

rind [raɪnd] *n* Schale *f;* [**grated**] **lemon** ~ [geriebene] Zitronenschale

ring¹ [rɪŋ] I. *n* ❶ Ring *m; of people, things* Kreis *m;* (*clique*) Kartell *nt;* **spy** ~ Spionagering *m* II. *vt usu passive* umringen

ring² [rɪŋ] I. *n* ❶ Klingeln *nt;* (*sound*) Klirren *nt;* **your name has a familiar** ~ Ihr Name kommt mir bekannt vor ❷ *usu sing* (*phone call*) **to give sb a** ~ jdn anrufen II. *vi* <rang, rung> *phone* klingeln; *ears* klingen; **the room rang with laughter** der Raum war von Lachen erfüllt III. *vt* <rang, rung> läuten
◆**ring out** *vi* ertönen

'ring bind·er *n* Ringbuch *nt*

ringer ['rɪŋ·ər] *n* PHRASES: **to be a** dead ~ **for sb** jdm aufs Haar gleichen

'ring fin·ger *n* Ringfinger *m*

R

ringing ['rɪŋ·ɪŋ] I. *adj attr* schallend; **~ cheer** lauter Jubel II. *n* Klingeln *nt*

'ringleader *n* Anführer(in) *m(f)*

ringlet ['rɪŋ·lɪt] *n usu pl* Locke *f*

'ring tone *n* Klingelton *m*

rink [rɪŋk] *n* Bahn *f;* **ice ~** Eisbahn *f*

rinse [rɪns] I. *n* Spülung *f; (for mouth)* Mundspülung *f; (conditioner)* [Haar]spülung *f; (for tinting hair)* Tönung *f* II. *vt* spülen; *hands* abspülen; *mouth* ausspülen III. *vi* spülen

riot ['raɪ·ət] I. *n* Krawall *m;* (*uproar*) Aufstand *m;* **a ~ of color[s]** eine Farbenpracht ② **to run ~** *people* Amok laufen; *emotions* verrückt spielen; **my imagination ran ~** die Fantasie ist mit mir durchgegangen II. *vi* randalieren; *(fig)* wild feiern

rioter ['raɪ·ə·tər] *n* Aufständische(r) *f|m*

rioting ['raɪ·ə·tɪŋ] *n* Randalieren *nt*

rip [rɪp] I. *n* ① *(tear)* Riss *m* ② *usu sing (act)* Zerreißen *nt;* (*with knife*) Zerschlitzen *nt* II. *vt* <-pp-> zerreißen; **to ~ sth to shreds** etw zerfetzen; **to ~ sth open** etw aufreißen; *(with knife)* etw aufschlitzen III. *vi* <-pp-> reißen; *seams* platzen

◆**rip off** *vt (fam: steal)* mitgehen lassen; *ideas* klauen; ■**to ~ off ⟳ sb** (*overcharge*) jdn übers Ohr hauen

◆**rip out** *vt* herausreißen

◆**rip up** *vt* zerreißen; *carpet* herausreißen

RIP [ˌɑːr·aɪ·ˈpiː] *abbrev of* **rest in peace** R.I.P.

ripe [raɪp] *adj* reif; *(matured)* ausgereift; *(intense)* beißend; ■**to be ~ for sth** reif für etw *akk* sein; **to live to a ~ old age** ein hohes Alter erreichen

ripen ['raɪ·pən] *vi* [heran]reifen

ripeness ['raɪp·nɪs] *n* Reife *f*

'rip-off *n (fam)* Wucher *m;* (*fraud*) Schwindel *m;* **that's just a ~ of my idea!** da hat doch bloß einer meine Idee geklaut! *fam*

ripple ['rɪp·əl] I. *n* leichte Welle; *(feeling)* Schauer *m;* (*sound*) Raunen *nt;* (*reaction*) Wirkung *f;* **a ~ of laughter**

ein leises Lachen II. *vi* *water* sich kräuseln; *stream* plätschern; *grain* wogen; **his muscles ~d under his skin** man sah das Spiel seiner Muskeln [unter der Haut] III. *vt* *water* kräuseln; *muscles* spielen lassen

rip-'roaring *adj attr (fam)* sagenhaft

rise [raɪz] I. *n* ① Hochgehen *nt; of sun* Aufgehen *nt;* (*in society*) Aufstieg *m;* **~ to power** Aufstieg *m* an die Macht ② *(height)* Höhe *f;* (*hill*) Anhöhe *f* ③ *(increase)* Anstieg *m* II. *vi* <rose, risen> ① steigen; *curtain* aufgehen; *sun* aufgehen; *(from chair)* sich erheben; *voice* höher werden; *(become louder)* lauter werden; *wind* aufkommen; *ground* ansteigen; *(improve status)* aufsteigen; **to ~ to fame** berühmt werden; ■**to ~ against sb/sth** sich gegen jdn/ etw auflehnen ② *(increase)* [an]steigen; *river, prices* steigen; *dough* aufgehen; *temper* sich erhitzen ▶PHRASES: **to ~ to the bait** anbeißen; **~ and shine!** los, raus aus den Federn!

◆**rise above** *vi* ■**to ~ above sth** *tower* sich über etw *dat* erheben; *person* über etw *dat* stehen; **to ~ above difficulties** Schwierigkeiten überwinden

◆**rise up** *vi (mutiny)* sich auflehnen; *(be visible)* aufragen

risen ['rɪz·ən] *pp of* **rise**

rising ['raɪ·zɪŋ] *adj attr* *politician* aufstrebend; *floodwaters* steigend; *sun* aufgehend; *costs* steigend; *wind* aufkommend; *fury* wachsend; *ground* [auf]steigend

risk [rɪsk] I. *n* Risiko *nt;* **health ~** Gesundheitsrisiko *nt;* **to take a ~** ein Risiko eingehen II. *vt* riskieren; **to ~ life and limb** Leib und Leben riskieren

risky ['rɪs·ki] *adj* riskant

rite [raɪt] *n usu pl* Ritus *m;* **last ~s** Sterbesakramente *pl*

ritual ['rɪtʃ·u·əl] I. *n* Ritual *nt* II. *adj attr* rituell

rival ['raɪ·vəl] I. *n* Rivale(in) *m(f);* ECON Konkurrent *m;* **arch ~** Erzrivale(in) *m(f);* **bitter ~s** scharfe Rivalen;

R

~ **team** gegnerische Mannschaft II. *vt*
<-l-> konkurrieren

rivalry ['raɪ·vəl·ri] *n* Rivalität *f*; ECON
Konkurrenz *f*; **friendly** ~ freundschaft-
licher Wettstreit

river ['rɪv·ər] *n* Fluss *m*; **down/up** ~
stromab-/aufwärts

'**river bed** *n* Flussbett *nt*

'**riverside** *n* [Fluss]ufer *nt*

rivet ['rɪv·ɪt] I. *n* Niete *f* II. *vt* ■**to** ~ **sth**
[**together**] etw [zusammen]nieten; **to**
be ~**ed to the spot** (*fig*) wie angewurzelt stehen bleiben

riveting ['rɪv·ɪ·tɪŋ] *adj* (*fam*) fesselnd

RN [ˌɑr·'en] *n abbrev of* **registered**
nurse examinierte Krankenschwester;
(*male*) examinierter Krankenpfleger

roach <*pl* -es> [roʊtʃ] *n* (*fam*) Küchenschabe *f*; (*sl: butt*) eingedrehter
Pappfilter

road [roʊd] *n* Straße *f*; (*fig*) Weg *m*;
busy ~ stark befahrene Straße; **side** ~
Nebenstraße *f*; **on the** ~ **to recovery**
auf dem Wege der Besserung

'**roadblock** *n* Straßensperre *f*

'**road hog** *n* (*pej fam*) Verkehrsrowdy *m*

'**roadhouse** *n* Raststätte *f*

roadie ['roʊ·di] *n* (*fam*) Roadie *m*

'**roadkill** *n* totgefahrenes Tier; (*action*)
Überfahren *nt* eines Tiers

'**road map** *n* Straßenkarte *f*

'**road rage** *n* aggressives Verhalten im
Straßenverkehr

'**roadside** I. *n* Straßenrand *m* II. *adj*
Straßen-; *café* am Straßenrand gelegen

'**road sign** *n* Verkehrsschild *nt*

'**road-test** *vt* Probe fahren

'**roadway** *n* Fahrbahn *f*

'**roadwork** *n* Straßenbauarbeiten *pl*

roam [roʊm] I. *vi* ❶ **to** ~
around/over/through umherstreifen
❷ *thoughts* abschweifen II. *vt* **to** ~ **the**
streets durch die Straßen ziehen (*fam*);
dog herumstreunen

'**roaming** *n* Roaming *nt* (*per Handy Aus-*
landsgespräche führen)

roar [rɔr] I. *n* Brüllen *nt*; *of cannon* Donnern *nt*; *of engine* [Auf]heulen *nt*; *of fire*
Prasseln *nt*; *of thunder* Grollen *nt*; *of*
waves Tosen *nt*; (*laughter*) schallendes
Gelächter II. *vi* brüllen; *cannon* donnern; *engine* [auf]heulen; *fire* prasseln;
thunder grollen; *waves* tosen; *wind*
heulen; **to** ~ **with laughter** in schallendes Gelächter ausbrechen; ■**to** ~ **at**
sb jdn anbrüllen

roast [roʊst] I. *vt* rösten; *meat* braten;
■**to** ~ **sb** mit jdm hart ins Gericht gehen II. *vi* braten; (*fig*) [vor Hitze] fast
umkommen *fam* III. *adj attr* Brat-;
~ **beef** Rinderbraten *m*; ~ **chicken**
Brathähnchen *nt* IV. *n* Braten *m*;
(*process*) Rösten *nt*; (*of coffee*) Rös-
tung *f*

roasting ['roʊs·tɪŋ] *adj* (*fam*) knallheiß

rob <-bb-> [rɑb] *vt* ❶ *person* bestehlen;
(*violently*) rauben +*dat*; *bank* ausrauben ❷ *usu passive* (*fam: overcharge*)
ausnehmen ❸ (*deprive*) ■**to** ~ **sb of**
sth jdn um etw *akk* bringen

robber ['rɑb·ər] *n* Räuber(in) *m(f)*

robbery ['rɑb·ə·ri] *n* Raubüberfall *m*;
(*theft a.*) Raub *m*; *bank* ~ Bankraub *m*

robe [roʊb] *n usu pl* (*formal*) Talar *m*;
(*bathrobe*) Morgenmantel *m*

robot ['roʊ·bɑt] *n* Roboter *m*

robotics [roʊ·'bɑt·ɪks] *n* + *sing vb* Ro-
botik *f kein pl*

robust [roʊ·'bʌst] *adj* kräftig; *appetite*
gesund; (*sturdy*) widerstandsfähig; *view*
bodenständig; *food* deftig; *wine* kernig

robustness [roʊ·'bʌst·nɪs] *n* Widerstandsfähigkeit *f*; (*determination*) Entschlossenheit *f*

rock[1] [rɑk] *n* Stein *m*; GEOL Gestein *nt*;
(*fam: diamond*) Klunker *m*;
(*boulder*) Felsbrocken *m*; (*embedded*)
Fels[en] *m*; (*in sea*) Riff *nt*; (*fig*) Fels *m*
in der Brandung ▶PHRASES: **on the** ~**s**
(*fam*) am Ende; *marriage* kaputt *fam*;
(*drink*) mit Eis

rock[2] [rɑk] I. *n* Rockmusik *f*; (*sway*)
Schaukeln *nt* II. *vt* schaukeln; (*gently*)
wiegen; *quake* erschüttern III. *vi* schaukeln; (*dance*) rocken *fam*; (*play music*)
Rock[musik] spielen; **he really** ~**s!**
(*fam*) er ist ein Supertyp!

rock-and-'roll *n see* **rock 'n' roll**

rock 'bottom n Tiefpunkt m; **to be at ~** am Tiefpunkt [angelangt] sein; person a. am Boden zerstört sein

rocker ['rak·ər] n (chair) Schaukelstuhl m; of cradle [Wiegen]kufe; (musician) Rockmusiker(in) m(f); (fan) Rockfan m ▶PHRASES: **to be off one's ~** übergeschnappt sein

rocket ['rak·ɪt] I. n [Marsch]flugkörper m; (for space travel) Rakete f; (firework) [Feuerwerks]rakete f II. vi ■ **to ~ [up]** hochschnellen; **to ~ to fame** über Nacht berühmt werden

Rockies ['rak·iz] n ■ **the ~** die Rocky Mountains pl

'rocking chair n Schaukelstuhl m

'rocking horse n Schaukelpferd nt

'rock music n Rockmusik f

rock 'n' 'roll n Rock and Roll m

'rock salt n Steinsalz nt

'rock star n Rockstar m

rocky ['rak·i] adj felsig; soil steinig; (difficult) schwierig; future unsicher

Rocky 'Mountains n ■ **the ~** die Rocky Mountains pl

rod [rad] n Stange f; (for punishing) Rute f; (cane) Rohrstock m; (for fishing) [Angel]rute f ▶PHRASES: **to rule sb/sth with a ~ of iron** jdn/etw mit eiserner Hand regieren

rode [roʊd] pt of ride

rodent ['roʊ·dənt] n Nagetier nt

rodeo ['roʊ·di·oʊ] n Rodeo nt

roger ['radʒ·ər] interj ~! verstanden!

rogue [roʊg] I. n Gauner(in) m(f); (rascal) Spitzbube m II. adj skrupellos; ~ **state** Schurkenstaat m

role [roʊl] n Rolle f; (function a.) Funktion f; **supporting ~** Nebenrolle f

'role model n Rollenbild n

'role play, 'role playing n Rollenspiel nt

roll [roʊl] I. n ①Rolle f; of cloth Ballen m ②(list) [Namens]liste f; (register) Verzeichnis nt ③(bread) Brötchen nt ④(movement) Rollen nt; (overturn) Herumrollen nt; (wallowing) Herumwälzen nt; of ship Schlingern nt ⑤usu sing of thunder [G]rollen nt kein pl;

drum ~ Trommelwirbel m ▶PHRASES: **to be on a ~** (fam) eine Glückssträhne haben II. vt ①rollen; eyes verdrehen; (turn over) drehen; **to ~ one's car** sich mit dem Auto überschlagen ②■ **to ~ sth into sth** etw zu etw dat rollen; **he ~ed the clay into a ball** er formte den Ton zu einer Kugel ③(wind) aufrollen; cigarette drehen; (wrap) ■ **to ~ sth in sth** etw in etw akk einwickeln ④(flatten) walzen; pastry ausrollen III. vi rollen; (overturn) sich herumrollen; (wallow) sich [herum]wälzen; (flow) rollen; tears kullern; ship schlingern; (person) schwanken; (undulate) wallen; thunder [g]rollen; (operate) laufen; **to keep sth ~ing** etw in Gang halten; **to ~ by** (elapse) vorbeiziehen

◆**roll back** vt zurückrollen; (push back) zurückschieben; (fold back) zurückschlagen; (lower) senken; (fig) advances umkehren; **to ~ back the years** die Uhr zurückdrehen fig

◆**roll down** I. vt hinunterrollen; (bring down); window herunterkurbeln II. vi hinunterrollen; (come down) herunterrollen; tears a. herunterlaufen

◆**roll in** I. vi hineinrollen; (come in) hereinrollen; (fam) offers [massenhaft] eingehen; money reinkommen fam; (fam: arrive) hereinplatzen am ▶PHRASES: **to be ~ing in money** (fam) im Geld schwimmen II. vt herein-/hineinrollen

◆**roll on** vi weitergehen; time verfliegen

◆**roll out** I. vt hinaus-/herausrollen; dough ausrollen; metal auswalzen; product herausbringen II. vi product herauskommen

◆**roll over** I. vi herumrollen; dog, bather sich umdrehen; car umkippen; boat kentern; **to ~ over onto one's side** sich auf die Seite rollen II. vt umdrehen

◆**roll up** I. vt hochrollen; sleeves hochkrempeln; window hochkurbeln; (coil) aufrollen; string aufwickeln II. vi hochrollen; (fam: arrive) aufkreuzen

'roll call n Namensaufruf m kein pl

R

roller ['roʊ·lər] n Rolle f; (for hair) Lockenwickler m; TECH Walze f

'Rollerblade® I. n Rollerblade® m II. vi inlineskaten

'roller coaster n Achterbahn f

'roller skate n Rollschuh m

'roller-skate vi Rollschuh laufen

'roller skater n Rollschuhläufer(in) m(f)

rolling ['roʊ·lɪŋ] adj attr hills sanft ansteigend; gait [sch]wankend

'rolling pin n Nudelholz nt

'roll-on n Deoroller m

roly-poly [ˌroʊ·li·'poʊ·li] adj (hum fam) rundlich; baby moppelig fam; child pummelig

ROM [ram] n abbrev of **Read Only Memory** ROM m o nt

Roman ['roʊ·mən] I. adj römisch II. n Römer(in) m(f)

Roman 'Catholic I. adj römisch-katholisch II. n Katholik(in) m(f)

romance [roʊ·'mæns] n Romantik f; (love) romantische Liebe; (affair) Romanze f; (movie) Liebesfilm m; (book) Liebesroman m

Romania [roʊ·'meɪ·ni·ə] n Rumänien nt

Romanian [roʊ·'meɪ·ni·ən] I. adj rumänisch II. n Rumäne(in) m(f); (language) Rumänisch nt

romantic [roʊ·'mæn·tɪk] I. adj romantisch II. n Romantiker(in) m(f)

Rome [roʊm] n Rom nt

romp [ramp] I. vi tollen II. n Tollerei f; (book) Klamauk m

roof [ruf] n Dach nt; (attic) Dachboden m; (ceiling) Decke f; of mouth Gaumen m

'roof rack n Dachgepäckträger m

'rooftop n Dach nt

rook [rʊk] n CHESS Turm m

rookie ['rʊk·i] n (fam) Neuling m; MIL Rekrut(in) m(f)

room [rum] I. n Zimmer nt; (space) Platz m; (scope a.) Raum m; **the whole ~ laughed** alle, die im Zimmer waren, lachten; **double ~** Doppelzimmer nt; **~ for maneuver** Bewegungsspielraum m II. vi wohnen; ■**to ~ with sb** mit jdm zusammen wohnen

'rooming house n Pension f

'roommate n (in room) Zimmergenosse(in) m(f); (in apartment) Mitbewohner(in) m(f)

'room service n Zimmerservice m

room 'temperature n Zimmertemperatur f

roomy ['ru·mi] adj geräumig

roost [rust] I. n Rastplatz m; (for sleep) Schlafplatz m II. vi rasten

rooster ['ru·stər] n Hahn m

root[1] [rut] n Wurzel f; (of potato) Knolle f; (of tulip) Zwiebel f; (fig: origin) Wurzel f; (essential) Kern m; MATH Wurzel f; **to take ~** Wurzeln schlagen; **square ~** Quadratwurzel f

root[2] [rut] vi (fam) **to ~ for a team** eine Mannschaft anfeuern

root around vi (fam) herumwühlen

◆**root out** vt weeds ausgraben; evil ausrotten; (find) aufstöbern

root beer n eine Art Limonade aus verschiedenen Pflanzenextrakten

'root vegetable n Wurzelgemüse nt; (potato) Knolle f

rope [roʊp] I. n Seil nt; NAUT Tau nt; (lasso) Lasso nt II. vt anseilen; **to ~ calves** Kälber mit dem Lasso [ein]fangen

◆**rope in** vt (fam) einspannen

◆**rope off** vt **to ~ off ⊃ an area** ein Gebiet [mit Seilen/einem Seil] absperren

'rope ladder n Strickleiter f

rosary ['roʊ·zə·ri] n Rosenkranz m

rose[1] [roʊz] I. n Rose f; (bush) Rosenbusch m; (tree) Rosenbäumchen nt; (color) Rosa nt II. adj rosa

rose[2] [roʊz] pt of **rise**

'rosebud n Rosenknospe f

'rosebush n Rosenstrauch m

'rose hip n Hagebutte f

rosemary ['roʊz·mer·i] n Rosmarin m

roster ['ras·tər] n Liste f; (plan) Plan m; **duty ~** Dienstplan m

rostrum <pl -s> ['ras·trəm] n Tribüne f

rosy ['roʊ·zi] adj rosig

rot [rɒt] I. n (process) Fäulnis f; (matter) Verfaultes nt; BOT Fäule f II. vi <-tt-> verrotten; teeth, meat verfaulen; woodwork vermodern; (deteriorate) verkommen
◆ **rot away** vi verfaulen

rotary ['rəʊ·tə·ri] n see **traffic circle**

rotate ['rəʊ·teɪt] I. vi rotieren; (alternate) wechseln II. vt drehen; troops auswechseln; crops im Fruchtwechsel anbauen; **to ~ duties** Aufgaben turnusmäßig [abwechselnd] verteilen

rotation [rəʊ·'teɪ·ʃən] n Umdrehung f; **crop ~** Fruchtwechsel m; **in ~** im Wechsel

rote [rəʊt] n **by ~** auswendig

rotor ['rəʊ·tər] n Rotor m

rotten ['rɑt·ən] I. adj verfault; fruit verdorben; tooth faul; wood modrig; (corrupt) korrupt; (fam: bad) mies; joke gemein; cook hundsmiserabel II. adv (fam) total fam; **spoiled ~** child völlig verzogen

rouble ['ru·bəl] n see **ruble**

rouge [ruːʒ] n Rouge nt

rough [rʌf] I. adj rau; ground uneben; landscape unwirtlich; fur struppig; (hard) hart; wine sauer; (fam: difficult) schwer; (makeshift) primitiv; (unrefined) ungehobelt; (imprecise) grob; **to give sb a ~ time** jdm das Leben ganz schön schwer machen; **a ~ idea** eine ungefähre Vorstellung II. n (in golf) ■ **the ~** das Rough fachspr III. vt (fam) **to ~ it** [ganz] primitiv leben

roughage ['rʌf·ɪdʒ] n Ballaststoffe pl; (fodder) Raufutter nt

'rough-and-tumble adj attr ~ **atmosphere** raue Atmosphäre

rough 'draft n Rohfassung f; (sketch) Entwurf m

roughen ['rʌf·ən] I. vt aufrauen II. vi rau werden; society verrohen; weather stürmisch werden

'roughhouse vi Radau machen fam; (fight) sich prügeln; (playfully) sich raufen

roughly ['rʌf·li] adv grob; ~ **sketched** skizzenhaft; ~ **speaking** ganz allgemein gesagt; ~ **the same** ungefähr gleich

'roughneck n (fam) Rohling m; (rig worker) Bohrarbeiter(in) m(f)

roughness ['rʌf·nɪs] n Rauheit f; of ground Unebenheit f; of game Härte f

'roughshod adv **to ride ~ over sb** (fig) jdn unterdrücken

roulette [ru·'let] n Roulette nt

round [raʊnd] I. adj <-er, -est> rund; face rundlich; vowel gerundet II. n (of drinks) Runde f; (series) Folge f; SPORT Runde f; (routine) Trott m; ~ **of talks** Gesprächsrunde f; ~ **of applause** Beifall m; ~ **of ammunition** Ladung f III. vt **to ~ the corner** um die Ecke biegen
◆ **round down** vt abrunden
◆ **round off** vt abrunden
◆ **round up** vt sum aufrunden; people zusammentrommeln fam; things zusammentragen; cattle zusammentreiben; support holen

roundabout ['raʊnd·ə·baʊt] adj umständlich; **to take a ~ route** einen Umweg machen; **to ask sb in a ~ way** jdn durch die Blumen fragen

rounded ['raʊn·dɪd] adj rund; edges abgerundet

roundly ['raʊnd·li] adv (form) gründlich; criticize heftig; defeat haushoch

round 'robin n Wettkampf, in dem jeder gegen jeden antritt

round'table adj attr ~ **discussion** Gespräch nt am runden Tisch

'round-the-clock adj rund um die Uhr nach n

round 'trip I. n Rundreise f II. adv **to fly** ~ ein Rückflugticket haben

round-trip 'ticket n Hin- und Rückfahrkarte f; AVIAT Hin- und Rückflugticket nt

'roundup n Versammlung f; of suspects Festnahme f; of cattle Zusammentreiben nt; (summary) Zusammenfassung f

rouse [raʊz] vt wecken; **to ~ sb to action** jdn zum Handeln bewegen

rousing ['raʊ·zɪŋ] adj mitreißend; cheer stürmisch

route [raʊt] n Strecke f; of parade Ver-

R

lauf m; (delivery path) Runde f; (bus number) Linie f; **the ~ to success** der Weg zum Erfolg; **to have a paper ~** Zeitungen austragen

Route 66 n berühmte Straße von Chicago nach Los Angeles

routine [ruˈtin] I. n Routine f; (dancing) Figur f; (gymnastics) Übung f; COMPUT Programm nt II. adj routinemäßig; performance a. durchschnittlich; **~ inspection** Routineuntersuchung f; **to become ~** zur Gewohnheit werden

row[1] [roʊ] n Reihe f; **in ~s** reihenweise; **in a ~** (in succession) hintereinander

row[2] [roʊ] vt, vi rudern

row[3] [raʊ] I. n Streit m II. vi (fam) sich streiten

rowboat ['roʊˌboʊt] n Ruderboot nt

rowdy ['raʊˌdi] adj rüpelhaft; party wild

'row house n Reihenhaus nt

rowing ['roʊ·ɪŋ] n Rudern nt

royal ['rɔɪ·əl] I. adj <-er, -est> königlich; (fig) fürstlich II. n (fam) Angehörige(r) f(m) der königlichen Familie

royalty ['rɔɪ·əl·ti] n ❶ + sing/pl vb Königshaus nt; **to treat sb like ~** jdn fürstlich behandeln ❷ PUBL ∎**royalties** pl Tantiemen pl

rpm <pl -> [ˌar·piˈem] n abbrev of **revolutions per minute** U/min

RR [ˌar·ˈar] n abbrev of **railroad**

RSVP [ˌar·es·vi·ˈpi] abbrev of **répondez s'il vous plaît** u. A. w. g.

R

rub [rʌb] I. n Reiben nt; **to give sth a ~** hair etw trocken rubbeln; material etw polieren II. vt <-bb-> einreiben; (polish) polieren; **to ~ one's hands together** sich dat die Hände reiben III. vi <-bb-> reiben; shoes scheuern

◆**rub down** vt abreiben; child abfrottieren

◆**rub in** vt einreiben; ∎**to ~ it in** (fam) auf etw dat herumreiten ▶PHRASES: **don't keep on ~bing my nose in it!** hör auf, es mir unter die Nase zu reiben! fam

◆**rub off** I. vi wegreiben; stains rausgehen; ∎**sth ~s off on sb** (fam) etw färbt auf jdn ab II. vt wegwischen

◆**rub out** I. vt ausradieren; ∎**to ~ out sb** (sl) jdn abmurksen sl II. vi herausgehen; (erase) sich ausradieren lassen

rubber ['rʌb·ər] n Gummi m o nt; (sl: condom) Gummi m; ∎**~s** pl (shoes) Überschuhe pl (aus Gummi)

rubber 'band n Gummiband nt

rubber 'boot n Gummistiefel m

rubber 'check n (sl) ungedeckter Scheck

rubberneck ['rʌb·ər·nek] (sl) I. n see **rubbernecker** II. vi gaffen fam

rubbernecker ['rʌb·ər·nek·ər] (sl) n Gaffer(in) m(f) pej fam

'rubber plant n Gummibaum m

'rubber stamp n Stempel m; (fig) Genehmigung f

rubber-'stamp vt genehmigen; decision bestätigen

'rubber tree n Kautschukbaum m

rubbery ['rʌb·ə·ri] adj gummiartig; meat zäh; (fam) legs wackelig

rubbish ['rʌb·ɪʃ] n Müll m; (fam: nonsense) Quatsch m; (fam: junk) Gerümpel nt

rubble ['rʌb·əl] n Trümmer pl; (for building) Bauschutt m; **to reduce sth to ~** etw in Schutt und Asche legen

rubella [ru·ˈbel·ə] n Röteln pl

ruble, rouble ['ru·bəl] n Rubel m

ruby ['ru·bi] I. n Rubin m II. adj Rubin-; (color) rubinrot

rucksack ['rʌk·sæk] n Rucksack m

ruckus ['rʌk·əs] n (fam) Krawall m

rudder ['rʌd·ər] n [Steuer]ruder m

rude [rud] adj unhöflich; behavior unverschämt; gesture ordinär; joke unanständig; surprise böse

rudimentary [ˌru·də·ˈmen·tə·ri] adj elementar; (primitive) primitiv; method einfach

rudiments ['ru·də·mənts] npl ∎**the ~** die Grundlagen pl

ruffian ['rʌf·i·ən] n Schlingel m

ruffle ['rʌf·əl] vt durcheinanderbringen; hair zerzausen; (upset) aus der Ruhe bringen ▶PHRASES: **to ~ sb's feathers** jdn auf die Palme bringen fam

rug [rʌg] n Teppich m; (sl: wig) Haarteil nt

rugby ['rʌg·bi] n Rugby nt

rugged ['rʌg·ɪd] adj uneben; cliff zerklüftet; coast wild; (robust) kräftig; looks markant; vehicle robust; (solid) fest; honesty unerschütterlich

ruin ['ru·ɪn] I. vt zerstören; dress, name ruinieren; hopes zunichtemachen; **to ~ sb's day** jdm den Tag vermiesen; **to ~ sb's chances** jdm die Suppe versalzen II. n Ruine f; (bankruptcy) Ruin m; **■ ~ s** pl of building Ruinen pl; of reputation Reste pl; of hopes Trümmer pl; **to be in ~ s** eine Ruine sein; (after fire) in Schutt und Asche liegen; (fig) zerstört sein

ruinous ['ru·ə·nəs] adj ruinös

rule [rul] I. n ① (instruction) Regel f; **~ s and regulations** Regeln und Bestimmungen; **to be against the ~ s** gegen die Regeln verstoßen ② (control) Herrschaft f; **the ~ of law** die Rechtsstaatlichkeit ▶PHRASES: **as a [general] ~** in der Regel II. vt ① (govern) regieren ② (control) beherrschen ③ (draw) ziehen III. vi herrschen; sovereign a. regieren

♦ **rule out** vt ausschließen

'rule book n Vorschriftenbuch nt

ruler ['ru·lər] n Herrscher(in) m(f); (device) Lineal nt

ruling ['ru·lɪŋ] I. adj attr (governing) herrschend; (primary) hauptsächlich; passion größte(r, s) II. n Entscheidung f

rum [rʌm] n Rum m

Rumania [roʊ·'meɪ·ni·ə] see **Romania**

rumble ['rʌm·bəl] I. n Grollen nt; of stomach Knurren nt; (fam) Schlägerei f II. vi rumpeln; stomach knurren; thunder grollen

rumbling ['rʌm·bəl·ɪŋ] I. n Grollen nt; of distant guns Donnern nt; **■ ~ s** pl (indications) [erste] Anzeichen pl II. adj grollend attr

rummage ['rʌm·ɪdʒ] vi **■ to ~ through sth** etw durchstöbern

'rummage sale n Flohmarkt m

rummy ['rʌm·i] n CARDS Rommé nt

rumor ['ru·mər] I. n Gerücht nt II. vt passive **the president is ~ ed to be seriously ill** der Präsident soll angeblich ernsthaft krank sein; **it is ~ ed that …** es wird gemunkelt, dass …

rump [rʌmp] n ① of animal Hinterbacken pl ② (beef) Rumpsteak nt ③ (hum: buttocks) Hinterteil nt fam

rumpus ['rʌm·pəs] n (fam) Krawall m

run [rʌn] I. n ① Lauf m; **to go for a ~** laufen gehen ② (course) Strecke f ③ (period) Dauer f; **~ of good luck** Glückssträhne f ④ (enclosure) Gehege nt ⑤ SPORT (in baseball) Run m ⑥ (in stocking) Laufmasche f ⑦ (fam) **■ the ~ s** pl (diarrhea) Dünnpfiff m fam ▶PHRASES: **in the long ~** auf lange Sicht gesehen; **in the short ~** kurzfristig II. vi <ran, run> ① laufen; **to ~ for cover** schnell in Deckung gehen; **to ~ for one's life** um sein Leben rennen ② (operate) fahren; engine laufen; machine in Betrieb sein; **work is ~ ning smoothly at the moment** die Arbeit geht im Moment glatt von der Hand ③ (travel) laufen; (lead) verlaufen; ski gleiten; **the route ~ s through the mountains** die Strecke führt durch die Berge ④ (last) [an]dauern; **the film ~ s for two hours** der Film dauert zwei Stunden ⑤ (flow) fließen; **my nose is ~ ning** meine Nase läuft; **the river ~ s [down] to the sea** der Fluss mündet in das Meer ⑥ (candidate) kandidieren; **to ~ for President** für das Präsidentenamt kandidieren ⑦ (fray) eine Laufmasche bekommen ▶PHRASES: **to ~ in the family** in der Familie liegen; **to ~ low** [langsam] ausgehen III. vt <ran, run> ① (pass) **he ran a vacuum cleaner over the carpet** er saugte den Teppich ab; **to ~ one's fingers through one's hair** sich dat mit den Fingern durchs Haar fahren ② machine bedienen; program, engine laufen lassen ③ (manage) leiten; farm betreiben; government, household führen; **don't tell me how to ~ my life!** erklär mir nicht, wie ich mein Leben leben soll! ④ (conduct) an-

R

bieten; *test* durchführen ⑤ *water* laufen
lassen; *bath* einlaufen lassen ⑥ **to ~ a
red light** (*fam*) eine rote Ampel überfahren ▶PHRASES: **to ~ the show** verantwortlich sein

◆**run across** *vi* zufällig treffen; **to ~
across a problem** auf ein Problem stoßen

◆**run after** *vi* hinterherlaufen

◆**run along** *vi* (*fam*) ■~! troll dich!

◆**run around** *vi* herumlaufen; (*bustle*)
herumrennen *fam;* ■**to ~ around with
sb** sich mit jdm herumtreiben *fam*

◆**run away** *vi* weglaufen; *liquid* abfließen; ■**to ~ away from sb** *wife* jdn verlassen

◆**run down** I. *vt* überfahren; *boat* rammen; (*reduce*) reduzieren; *production*
drosseln; *supplies* einschränken; (*fam:
belittle*) runtermachen II. *vi battery* leer
werden; (*become reduced*) reduziert
werden

◆**run into** *vi* hineinrennen; **he ran
into a tree on his motorcycle** er fuhr
mit seinem Motorrad gegen einen
Baum; ■**to ~ into sb** (*bump into*) jdm
über den Weg laufen; **to ~ into difficulties** auf Schwierigkeiten stoßen

◆**run off** I. *vi* abhauen; (*drain*) ablaufen II. *vt* **he quickly ran off some
copies** er machte schnell ein paar Ko-
pien

◆**run on** *vi* ① **the game ran on for
too long** das Spiel zog sich zu lange hin
② ■**to ~ on sth** mit etw *dat* betrieben
werden

◆**run out** *vi* ausgehen; (*expire*) auslaufen; **the milk has ~ out** die Milch ist alle

◆**run over** I. *vt* überfahren II. *vi bath*
überlaufen; (*review*) durchgehen

◆**run through** *vi* (*examine*) durchgehen; (*practice*) durchspielen

◆**run up** I. *vt debt* machen; *costume*
nähen II. *vi* **to ~ up against problems**
auf Probleme stoßen

'**runaround** *n* (*fig*) **to give sb the ~** jdm
keine klare Auskunft geben

'**runaway** I. *adj attr* (*out of control*) au-

ßer Kontrolle geraten; *prices* galoppierend; *prisoner* entlaufen; *horse* durchgegangen II. *n* Ausreißer(in) *m(f) fam*

'**rundown** I. *n* zusammenfassender Bericht II. *adj* verwahrlost; *building* baufällig; (*worn out*) abgespannt

rung[1] [rʌŋ] *n* Sprosse *f;* (*fig*) Stufe *f*

rung[2] [rʌŋ] *pp of* **ring**

'**run-in** *n* (*fam*) Krach *m*

runner ['rʌn·ər] *n* Läufer(in) *m(f);*
(*horse*) Rennpferd *nt;* (*messenger*) Bo-
te(in) *m(f)*

runner-'up *n* Zweite(r); **to be the ~** den
zweiten Platz belegen

running ['rʌn·ɪŋ] I. *n* ① Laufen *nt*
② (*management*) Leitung *f; of machine*
Bedienung *f* ▶PHRASES: **to be out of
the ~** nicht mehr mit im Rennen sein
II. *adj* ① *after n* (*in a row*) nacheinander *nach n* ② (*ongoing*) [fort]laufend
③ (*operating*) betriebsbereit

runny ['rʌn·i] *adj nose* laufend *attr; jam*
dünnflüssig

run-of-the-'mill *adj* durchschnittlich

runt [rʌnt] *n* zurückgebliebenes Jung-
tier; (*pej sl: person*) Wicht *m;* **little ~**
Würmchen *nt*, kleines Ding

'**run-through** *n* THEAT Durchlaufprobe *f;*
(*examination*) Durchgehen *nt*

'**run-up** *n* Anlauf *m* [zum Absprung];
(*fig: prelude*) Vorlauf *m*

'**runway** *n* Start- und Landebahn *f;* (*catwalk*) Laufsteg *m*

rupture ['rʌp·tʃər] I. *vi* zerreißen; *appendix* durchbrechen; *artery* platzen
II. *vt* zerreißen; **to ~ a blood vessel**
ein Blutgefäß zum Platzen bringen III. *n*
Zerreißen *nt; of artery* Platzen *nt;* (*hernia*) Bruch *m;* (*torn muscle*) [Musk-
kel]riss *m*

rural ['rʊr·əl] *adj* ländlich

ruse [ruz] *n* List *f*

rush[1] [rʌʃ] I. *n* ① Eile *f;* **to be in a ~** in Eile sein ② (*rapid movement*) Ansturm *m;*
(*press*) Gedränge *nt* ③ (*surge*)
Schwall *m; of emotions* Anfall *m* II. *vi*
① eilen; **stop ~ing!** hör auf zu hetzen!;
■**to ~ in** hineinstürmen; *water* hinein-
schießen; ■**to ~ out** hinausstürzen;

water herausschießen; ■**to ~ toward sb** auf jdn zueilen ❷ ■**to ~ into sth** *decision* etw überstürzen III. *vt* ❶ **she was ~ed to the hospital** sie wurde auf schnellstem Weg ins Krankenhaus gebracht ❷ (*pressure*) ■**to ~ sb [into sth]** jdn [zu etw *dat*] treiben; **don't ~ me!** dräng mich nicht! ❸ **let's not ~ things** lass uns nichts überstürzen

rush² [rʌʃ] *n* BOT Binse *f*

'rush hour *n* Hauptverkehrszeit *f*

'rush order *n* Eilauftrag *m*

Russia ['rʌʃ·ə] *n* Russland *nt*

Russian ['rʌʃ·ən] I. *adj* russisch II. *n* Russe(in) *m(f)*; (*language*) Russisch *nt*

rust [rʌst] I. *n* Rost *m*; (*color*) Rostbraun *nt* II. *vi* rosten; ■**to ~ away/through** ver-/durchrosten

rustic ['rʌs·tɪk] *adj* rustikal; (*simple*) grob [zusammen]gezimmert; (*fig*) schlicht

rustle ['rʌs·əl] I. *vi* rascheln; *silk* rauschen II. *vt* ❶ **to ~ paper** mit Papier rascheln ❷ *cattle* stehlen III. *n* Rascheln *nt*; *of silk* Knistern *nt*

rustler ['rʌs·lər] *n* Viehdieb(in) *m(f)*

'rustproof *adj* rostbeständig; **~ paint** Rostschutzfarbe *f*

rusty ['rʌs·ti] *adj* rostig; (*fig*) eingerostet; **my Russian is a little ~** ich bin mit meinem Russisch etwas aus der Übung

rut [rʌt] *n* Furche *f*; (*fig*) Trott *m*

ruthless ['ruθ·lɪs] *adj* skrupellos; *measure* hart; *dictatorship* erbarmungslos

ruthlessness ['ruθ·lɪs·nɪs] *n* Unbarmherzigkeit *f*; *of behavior* Rücksichtslosigkeit *f*; *of action* Skrupellosigkeit *f*

RV [ˌɑr·'vi] *n abbrev of* **recreational vehicle**

rye [raɪ] *n* Roggen *m*; **~ [whiskey]** Roggenwhiskey *m*

Ss

S <*pl* -'s>, **s** <*pl* -'s> [es] *n* S *nt*, s *nt*; **~ as in Sierra** S wie Siegfried

S [es] *n, adj* ❶ *abbrev of* **south, southern** S ❷ *abbrev of* **small** S

s <*pl* -> *abbrev of* **second** Sek.

Sabbath ['sæb·əθ] *n* Sabbat *m*

saber ['seɪ·bər] *n* Säbel *m*

sable ['seɪ·bəl] *n* Zobel *m*; (*fur*) Zobelpelz *m*

sabotage ['sæb·ə·tɑʒ] I. *vt* sabotieren; *plans* zunichtemachen II. *n* Sabotage *f*

saccharin ['sæk·ər·ɪn] *n* Süßstoff *m*

sachet [sæ·'ʃeɪ] *n* Päckchen *nt*

sack¹ [sæk] I. *n* Sack *m*; **~ of potatoes** Sack *m* Kartoffeln II. *vt* rausschmeißen *fam*

sack² [sæk] *vt* plündern

'sackful *n* Sack *m kein pl*

sacrament ['sæk·rə·mənt] *n* Sakrament *nt*

sacred ['seɪ·krɪd] *adj* heilig; *tradition* geheiligt

sacrifice ['sæk·rə·faɪs] I. *vt* opfern; (*give up a.*) aufgeben II. *vi* **to ~ to the gods** den Göttern Opfer bringen III. *n* Opfer *nt*; **at great personal ~** unter großem persönlichen Verzicht; **to make ~s** Opfer bringen

sacrilege ['sæk·rə·lɪdʒ] *n* Sakrileg *nt geh*; (*fig*) Verbrechen *nt*

sad <-dd-> [sæd] *adj* traurig; (*regrettable a.*) bedauerlich; *incident* betrüblich; (*pathetic*) bedauernswert; **to look ~** betrübt aussehen; **to make sb ~** jdn traurig machen; **~ to say** bedauerlicherweise

sadden ['sæd·ən] *vt* traurig machen; (*distress*) schwer treffen

saddle ['sæd·əl] I. *n* Sattel *m*; **to be in the ~** im Sattel sein; (*fig: in charge*) im

S

Amt sein **II.** *vt* satteln; **to be ~d with sth** *(fam)* etw *akk* am Hals haben; **to ~ sb with sth** *(fam)* jdm etw *akk* anhalsen

sadism ['seɪ·dɪz·əm] *n* Sadismus *m*

sadist ['seɪ·dɪst] *n* Sadist(in) *m(f)*

sadistic [sə·'dɪs·tɪk] *adj* sadistisch

sadly ['sæd·li] *adv* traurig; *(regrettably)* leider; *(fully)* völlig

sadness ['sæd·nɪs] *n* Traurigkeit *f*

safari [sə·'far·i] *n* Safari *f*

safe [seɪf] **I.** *adj* sicher; *(certain)* [relativ] sicher; *driver* vorsichtig; **[have a] ~ trip!** gute Reise!; **to keep sth in a ~ place** etw sicher aufbewahren ▶ PHRASES: **to be in ~ hands** in guten Händen sein; **to play it ~** auf Nummer Sicher gehen *fam* **II.** *n* Tresor *m*

safe-de'posit box *n* Tresorfach *nt*

safe'keeping *n* **to be in sb's ~** in jds Gewahrsam sein; **to give sth to sb for ~** jdm etw in Verwahrung geben

safely ['seɪf·li] *adv* sicher; *(avoiding risk)* vorsichtig; *(without harm) person* wohlbehalten; *object* heil

safe 'sex *n* Safer Sex *m*

safety ['seɪf·ti] *n* Sicherheit *f; of medicine* Unbedenklichkeit *f*

'safety belt *n* Sicherheitsgurt *m*

'safety catch *n* Sicherung *f*

'safety measures *npl* Sicherheitsmaßnahmen *pl*

'safety pin *n* Sicherheitsnadel *f*

'safety regulations *npl* Sicherheitsvorschriften *pl*

saffron ['sæf·rən] **I.** *n* Safran *m* **II.** *adj* safrangelb

sag [sæg] **I.** *vi* <-gg-> [herab]hängen; *bed, rope* durchhängen; *courage* sinken **II.** *n* Durchhängen *nt*

saga ['sa·gə] *n* Saga *f; (novel)* Familienroman *m; (pej)* [lange] Geschichte

sage [seɪdʒ] *n* Salbei *m*

Sagittarius [ˌsædʒ·ə·'ter·i·əs] *n* ASTROL Schütze *m*

said [sed] *pt, pp of* **say**

sail [seɪl] **I.** *n* Segel *nt; (of windmill)* Flügel *m; (journey)* [Segel]törn *m* ▶ PHRASES: **to set ~** in See stechen **II.** *vi (by ship)*

reisen; *(by yacht)* segeln; **the ball ~ed over the fence** der Ball segelte über den Zaun; **she ~ed into the room** sie kam ins Zimmer gerauscht ▶ PHRASES: **to ~ close to the wind** sich hart an der Grenze des Erlaubten bewegen **III.** *vt ship* steuern; *yacht* segeln; **to ~ the Pacific** den Pazifik befahren

'sailboard *n* Surfbrett *nt*

'sailboat *n* Segelboot *nt*

sailing ['seɪ·lɪŋ] *n* Segeln *nt; (sport)* Segelsport *m*

sailor ['seɪ·lər] *n* Matrose *m; (on sailing boat)* Segler(in) *m(f)*

saint [seɪnt, sənt] *n* Heilige(r) *f(m);* **to make sb a ~** jdn heiligsprechen; **S~ Peter** der heilige Petrus; **to be no ~** *(hum)* nicht gerade ein Heiliger/eine Heilige sein

saintly ['seɪnt·li] *adj* heilig

Saint Patrick's Day *n* der 17. März, an dem die irische Gemeinschaft in den USA ihren heiligen Schutzpatron feiert

'saint's day *n* Heiligenfest *nt*

sake [seɪk] *n* **for the ~ of sth** um einer S. *gen* willen; **for sb's ~** jdm zuliebe ▶ PHRASES: **for goodness' [or heaven's] ~** um Gottes [*o* Himmels] willen

salad ['sæl·əd] *n* Salat *m*

salami [sə·'la·mi] *n* Salami *f*

salary ['sæl·ə·ri] *n* Gehalt *nt; (wage packet)* Lohntüte *f*

sale [seɪl] *n* ① Verkauf *m; (amount sold)* Absatz *m;* **for ~** zu verkaufen; **to be on ~** – erhältlich sein ② *(at cut prices)* Ausverkauf *m; (auction)* Auktion *f;* **to be on ~** im Angebot sein

'sales clerk *n* Verkäufer(in) *m(f)*

'salesman *n* Verkäufer *m;* **door-to-door ~** Hausierer *m*

'salesperson *n* Verkäufer(in) *m(f)*

'sales tax *n* Umsatzsteuer *f*

'saleswoman *n* Verkäuferin *f*

saliva [sə·'laɪ·və] *n* Speichel *m*

salmon ['sæm·ən] *n* <*pl* -> Lachs *m*

salmonella [ˌsæl·mə·'nel·ə] *n* Salmonelle[n] *f(pl)*

saloon [sə·'lun] *n (dated)* Saloon *m*

salt [sɔlt] **I.** *n* Salz *nt;* **a pinch of ~** eine

Prise Salz ▶PHRASES: **to take sth with a pinch of** ~ etw mit Vorsicht genießen *fam* II. *vt* salzen

'salt flats *npl* Salzwüste *f*

salt 'lake *n* Salzsee *m*

'salt shaker *n* Salzstreuer *m*

salt 'water *n* Salzwasser *nt*

salty ['sɔl·ti] *adj* salzig

salutation [,sæl·jə·'teɪ·ʃən] *n* Anrede *f*; (*liter: greeting*) Gruß *m*

salute [sə·'lut] I. *vt* ❶ (*form*) grüßen; (*welcome*) begrüßen ❷ MIL ■**to** ~ **sb** vor jdm salutieren ❷ *vi* MIL salutieren III. *n* Gruß *m*; MIL Salut *m*; (*of guns*) Salut[schuss] *m*; **to give a** ~ salutieren

salvage ['sæl·vɪdʒ] *vt* *cargo* bergen; *reputation* wahren

salvation [sæl·'veɪ·ʃən] *n* Rettung *f*; REL Erlösung *f*

Salvation 'Army *n* Heilsarmee *f*

Samaritan [sə·'mer·ɪ·tən] *n* REL **the good** ~ der barmherzige Samariter

same [seɪm] I. *adj attr* ❶ (*similar*) ■**the** ~ ... der/die/das gleiche ...; (*identical*) der/die/das-selbe; **she's the** ~ **age as me** sie ist genauso alt wie ich ❷ (*not another*) ■**the** ~ ... der/die/das gleiche ...; ■**at the** ~ **time** gleichzeitig; (*nevertheless*) trotzdem ▶PHRASES: **to be in the** ~ **boat** [**as sb**] im gleichen Boot wie jd sitzen II. *pron* ■**the** ~ der/die/dasselbe; **things will never be the** ~ **again** nichts wird mehr so sein wie früher; **to be one and the** ~ ein und der/die/dasselbe sein ▶PHRASES: **all the** ~ trotzdem III. *adv* **I feel just the** ~ [**as you do**] mir geht es genauso [wie dir]

sample ['sæm·pəl] I. *n* Probe *f*; (*of fabric*) Muster *nt*; (*for test*) Stichprobe *f*; **blood** ~ Blutprobe *f* II. *vt* [aus]probieren; *food* kosten

sampler ['sæm·plər] *n* Probeset *nt*

sanction ['sæŋk·ʃən] I. *n* Strafmaßnahme *f*; POL Sanktion *f* II. *vt* unter Strafe stellen

sanctuary ['sæŋk·tʃu·er·i] *n* Heiligtum *nt*; (*refuge*) Zuflucht *f*; (*for animals*) Schutzgebiet *nt*

sand [sænd] I. *n* Sand *m*; ■~**s** *pl* (*beach*) Sandstrand *m*; *of desert* Sand *m kein pl* II. *vt* [ab]schmirgeln

sandal ['sæn·dəl] *n* Sandale *f*

'sandalwood *n* Sandelholz *nt*

'sandbag I. *n* Sandsack *m* II. *vt* <-gg-> mit Sandsäcken schützen; (*fig*) niederschlagen

'sandbox *n* Sandkasten *m*

'sandcastle *n* Sandburg *f*

'sand dune *n* Sanddüne *f*

'sandpaper I. *n* Schmirgelpapier *nt* II. *vt* abschmirgeln

'sandstone *n* Sandstein *m*

'sandstorm *n* Sandsturm *m*

sandwich ['sænd·wɪtʃ] I. *n* <*pl* -es> Sandwich *m o nt* ▶PHRASES: **to be one** ~ **short of a picnic** (*hum fam*) völlig übergeschnappt sein II. *vt* einklemmen; ■**to** ~ **sth** [**in**] **between sth** (*fig*) etw zwischen etw *dat* dazwischenschieben

'sandwich board *n* Reklametafel *f* (*mittels verbindendem Schulterriemen von einer Person auf Brust und Rücken als doppelseitiges Werbeplakat getragen*)

sandy ['sæn·di] *adj* sandig; *color* sandfarben

sane [seɪn] *adj* geistig gesund; LAW zurechnungsfähig; *action* vernünftig

sang [sæŋ] *pt of* sing

sanitary ['sæn·ɪ·ter·i] *adj* hygienisch; *installations* sanitär

'sanitary napkin *n* Damenbinde *f*

sanitation [,sæn·ɪ·'teɪ·ʃən] *n* Hygiene *f*; (*toilets*) sanitäre Anlagen; (*water disposal*) Abwasserkanalisation *f*

sanity ['sæn·ɪ·ti] *n* gesunder Verstand; LAW Zurechnungsfähigkeit *f*; (*sensibleness*) Vernünftigkeit *f*; (*hum*) Verstand *m fam*

sank [sæŋk] *pt of* sink

Santa, Santa Claus [,sæn·tə·'klɔz] *n* der Weihnachtsmann

sap¹ [sæp] *n* ❶ (*of tree*) Saft *m* ❷ (*sl: dope*) Trottel *m fam*

sap² [sæp] *vt* <-pp-> **to** ~ **sb's energy** an jds Energie zehren *geh*

sapling ['sæp·lɪŋ] *n* junger Baum

sapphire ['sæf·aɪr] *n* Saphir *m*

S

Saran® Wrap, Saran® wrap [sə-'ræn-] n Frischhaltefolie f

sarcasm ['sar·kæz·əm] n Sarkasmus m

sarcastic [sar·'kæs·tɪk] adj sarkastisch; *tongue* scharf

sardine [sar·'din] n Sardine f; **packed like ~s** wie die Ölsardinen zusammengepfercht

Sardinia [sar·'dɪn·i·ə] n Sardinien nt

sari ['sa·ri] n Sari m

SARS, Sars [sarz] n MED *acr* for **severe acute respiratory syndrome** SARS *kein art*

SASE [ˌes·eɪ·es·'i] n *abbrev of* **self-addressed stamped envelope** adressierter und frankierter Rückumschlag

sash[1] <pl -es> [sæʃ] n Schärpe f

sash[2] <pl -es> [sæʃ] n (*in windows*) Fensterrahmen m; (*in doors*) Türrahmen m

sat [sæt] pt, pp of **sit**

Satan ['seɪ·tən] n Satan m

satchel ['sætʃ·əl] n [Schul]ranzen m

satellite ['sæt·ə·laɪt] n Satellit m; (*astron a.*) Trabant m

'satellite dish n Satellitenschüssel f *fam*

satin ['sæt·ən] n Satin m

satire ['sæt·aɪr] n Satire f

satirical [sə·'tɪr·ɪ·kəl] adj satirisch; (*mocking*) ironisch

satirist ['sæt·ər·ɪst] n Satiriker(in) m(f)

satirize ['sæt·ə·raɪz] vt satirisch darstellen

satisfaction [ˌsæt·ɪs·'fæk·ʃən] n Zufriedenheit f; (*sth producing satisfaction*) Genugtuung f *geh*; ■**to sb's ~** zu jds Zufriedenheit; **to my great ~** zu meiner großen Genugtuung

satisfactory [ˌsæt·ɪs·'fæk·tə·ri] I. adj befriedigend II. n Ausreichend nt *kein pl* (*Mindestnote für das Bestehen einer Prüfung*)

satisfy <-ie-> ['sæt·ɪs·faɪ] vt zufrieden stellen; *need* befriedigen; *condition* erfüllen; ■**to ~ sb that ...** jdn überzeugen, dass ...

satisfying ['sæt·ɪs·faɪ·ɪŋ] adj zufrieden stellend

saturate ['sætʃ·ə·reɪt] vt durchnässen; (*fill*) [völlig] auslasten; CHEM sättigen

saturated ['sætʃ·ə·reɪ·tɪd] adj durchnässt; *soil* aufgeweicht; CHEM gesättigt

saturation [ˌsætʃ·ə·'reɪ·ʃən] n CHEM Sättigung f; **~ point** Sättigungspunkt m

Saturday ['sæt·ər·deɪ] n Samstag m; *see also* **Tuesday**

Saturn ['sæt·ərn] n Saturn m

sauce [sɔs] I. n ❶ Soße f; **tomato ~** Tomatensoße f; **apple ~** Apfelmus nt ❷ (*pej sl: alcohol*) Alkohol m II. vt (*fam*) ■**to ~ sth up** etw würzen

'saucepan n Kochtopf m

saucer ['sɔ·sər] n Untertasse f

Saudi ['saʊ·di] I. n (*male*) Saudi[-Araber] m; (*female*) Saudi-Araberin f II. adj saudisch

Saudi A'rabia n Saudi-Arabien nt

Saudi A'rabian I. n Saudi-Araber(in) m(f) II. adj saudi-arabisch

sauerkraut ['saʊ·ər·kraʊt] n Sauerkraut nt

sauna ['sɔ·nə] n Sauna f

saunter ['sɔn·tər] vi bummeln *fam*; (*amble*) schlendern; **to ~ along** herumschlendern

sausage ['sɔ·sɪdʒ] n Wurst f; (*small*) Würstchen nt; (*type*) Wurstsorte f

sauté [sɔ·'teɪ] vt <sautéed *or* sautéd> [kurz] [an]braten

savage ['sæv·ɪdʒ] I. adj wild; (*fierce*) brutal II. n (*usu pej*) Wilde(r) f(m) *pej*; (*barbarian*) Barbar(in) m(f) III. vt anfallen; (*fig*) attackieren

savagery ['sæv·ɪdʒ·ri] n Brutalität f

savanna(h) [sə·'væn·ə] n Savanne f

save [seɪv] I. vt ❶ retten; **to ~ sb's life** jds Leben retten ❷ (*retain*) aufheben; *money* sparen ❸ (*collect*) sammeln ❹ *time, energy* sparen ❺ COMPUT speichern ❻ *goal* verhindern; *penalty* abwehren ▶PHRASES: **a stitch in time ~s nine** (*prov*) was du heute kannst besorgen, das verschiebe nicht auf morgen *prov* II. vi ❶ *money* sparen; **to ~ with a bank** im Sparkonto bei einer Bank haben ❷ ■**to ~ on sth** bei etw *dat* sparen III. n Abwehr f

saving ['seɪ·vɪŋ] n ❶ ▪ ~s pl Ersparnisse pl ❷ (act) Einsparung f; (result) Ersparnis f

savings account ['seɪ·vɪŋz·ə·ˌkaʊnt] n Sparkonto nt

'savings bank n Sparkasse, die nicht auf Profitbasis arbeitet und auch für kleine Einlagen Zinsen bietet

savior ['seɪv·jər] n Retter(in) m(f); ▪ the S~ REL der Erlöser

savor ['seɪ·vər] I. n Geschmack m II. vt auskosten

savory ['seɪ·və·ri] adj pikant; (salty) salzig; (appetizing) appetitanregend

savvy ['sæv·i] (fam) I. adj ausgebufft sl II. n Köpfchen nt; (practical) Können nt

saw[1] [sɔ] I. n Säge f II. vt <-ed, -ed or sawn> [zer]sägen; **to ~ a tree down** einen Baum fällen III. vi sägen

saw[2] [sɔ] pt of **see**

'sawdust n Sägemehl nt

'sawmill n Sägemühle f

sawn [sɔn] pp of **saw**

Saxony ['sæk·sə·ni] n Sachsen nt

saxophone ['sæk·sə·foʊn] n Saxophon nt

saxophonist ['sæk·sə·foʊ·nɪst] n Saxophonist(in) m(f)

say [seɪ] I. vt <said, said> ❶ sagen; ▪ **to ~ sth to sb** jdm etw sagen (about über +akk); **to ~ goodbye to sb** sich von jdm verabschieden; **to have nothing to ~** nichts zu sagen haben; **to ~ nothing of the cost** ganz zu schweigen von den Kosten; **it goes without ~ing that ...** es versteht sich von selbst, dass ... ❷ (recite) aufsagen; prayer sprechen ❸ (show) sagen; **the sign ~s ...** auf dem Schild steht ...; **it ~s on the bottle ...** auf der Flasche heißt es ...; **my watch ~s 3 o'clock** auf meiner Uhr ist es 3 [Uhr]; **the way she drives ~s a lot about his character** sein Fahrstil sagt eine Menge über seinen Charakter aus ❹ (instruct) **she said to call her back** sie sagte, du sollst sie zurückrufen; ▪ **to ~ whether/where etc.** sagen, ob/wo usw.; **~ when!** sag stopp! ▶PHRASES: **~ no more!** (fam) alles klar!; **you don't ~!** was du nicht sagst!; **you said it!** (fam) du sagst es! II. vi <said, said> sagen; **where was he going? — he didn't ~** wo wollte er hin? – das hat er nicht gesagt; **hard to ~** schwer zu sagen; **that's not for me to ~** es steht mir nicht zu, das zu entscheiden III. n Meinung f; **to have a/no ~ in sth** bei etw dat ein/kein Mitspracherecht haben IV. interj ❶ (fam: doubting) ~s who? wer sagt das? ❷ (approving) ~, **that's a great idea!** Mensch, das ist ja eine tolle Idee! fam

saying ['seɪ·ɪŋ] n Sprichwort nt

'say-so n (fam) Erlaubnis f

SC, S.C. abbrev of **South Carolina**

scab [skæb] n ❶ Kruste f ❷ (pej fam: strikebreaker) Streikbrecher(in) m(f)

scabby ['skæb·i] adj schorfig; (pej fam) schäbig

scabies ['skeɪ·biz] n Krätze f

scaffold ['skæf·əld] n ❶ [Bau]gerüst nt; (hist: for executions) Schafott nt

scaffolding ['skæf·əl·dɪŋ] n [Bau]gerüst nt

scald [skɔld] I. vt verbrühen; (cook) erhitzen; fruit dünsten; milk abkochen II. n Verbrühung f

scalding ['skɔl·dɪŋ] adj kochend; ~ **hot** kochend heiß

scale[1] [skeɪl] I. n Schuppe f II. vt fish [ab]schuppen

scale[2] [skeɪl] I. n ❶ Skala f; of map Maßstab m; **to ~** maßstab[s]getreu ❷ (extent) Umfang m; **on a national ~** auf nationaler Ebene; **on a large/small ~** im großen/kleinen Rahmen ❸ MUS Tonleiter f II. vt besteigen; **to ~ a wall** auf eine Mauer klettern

◆ **scale down** I. vt reduzieren; production einschränken II. vi verkleinern

◆ **scale up** vt erweitern; production erhöhen

scale[3] [skeɪl] n usu pl Waage f; **to tip the ~s** (fig) den [entscheidenden] Ausschlag geben

scallop ['skal·əp] n Kammmuschel f;

S

(*served*) Jakobsmuschel *f*; **veal ~** Schnitzel *nt*

scalp [skælp] I. *n* Kopfhaut *f* II. *vt* skalpieren; (*pej*) *tickets* unter der Hand verkaufen

scalpel ['skæl·pəl] *n* Skalpell *nt*

scalper ['skæl·pər] *n* (*pej*) Schwarzhändler(in) *m(f)* (*für Eintrittskarten*)

scaly ['skeɪ·li] *adj* schuppig; *kettle* verkalkt

scam [skæm] *n* (*fam*) Betrug *m*

scamper ['skæm·pər] *vi* flitzen *fam*

scan [skæn] I. *vt* <-nn-> absuchen; (*glance*) überfliegen; COMPUT einscannen II. *n* Abtastung *f*; (*med a.*) Scan *m*; (*glance*) [flüchtige] Durchsicht

scandal ['skæn·dəl] *n* Skandal *m*; (*disgrace a.*) Schande *f*; (*gossip*) Skandalgeschichten *pl*

scandalize ['skæn·də·laɪz] *vt* schockieren; (*offend*) empören

scandalous ['skæn·də·ləs] *adv* skandalös; (*shocking*) schockierend

Scandinavia [ˌskæn·dɪ·'neɪ·vi·ə] *n* Skandinavien *nt*

Scandinavian [ˌskæn·dɪ·'neɪ·vi·ən] I. *adj* skandinavisch II. *n* Skandinavier(in) *m(f)*

scanner ['skæn·ər] *n* Scanner *m*

scant [skænt] *adj attr* gering, dürftig

scanty ['skæn·ti] *adj* knapp; (*inadequate*) unzureichend; *evidence* unzulänglich

scapegoat ['skeɪp·goʊt] *n* Sündenbock *m*

S

scar [skar] I. *n* Narbe *f* II. *vt* <-rr-> ■ **to be ~red** [**by sth**] [von etw *dat*] gezeichnet sein; **to be ~red for life** fürs [ganze] Leben gezeichnet sein

scarce [skers] *adj* knapp; (*rare*) rar; **to make oneself ~** sich *akk* aus dem Staub machen *fam*

scarcely ['skers·li] *adv* kaum

scarcity ['sker·sɪ·ti] *n* Knappheit *f*

scare [sker] I. *n* Schreck[en] *m*; (*public panic*) Hysterie *f*; **bomb ~** Bombendrohung *f*; **to give sb a ~** jdm einen Schrecken einjagen II. *vt* ■ **to ~ sb** jdm Angst machen ► PHRASES: **to ~ the** <u>living</u> **day-**

lights out of sb jdn zu Tode erschrecken

♦ **scare away**, **scare off** *vt* verscheuchen; (*discourage*) abschrecken

scarecrow ['sker·kroʊ] *n* Vogelscheuche *f*

scaremonger ['sker·ˌmaŋ·gər] *n* Panikmacher(in) *m(f)*

scarf <*pl* -s *or* scarves> [skarf] *n* Schal *m*

scarlet ['skar·lət] I. *n* Scharlachrot *nt* II. *adj* scharlachrot

scarlet 'fever *n* Scharlach *m*

scary ['sker·i] *adj* Furcht erregend; (*uncanny*) unheimlich

scat [skæt] *interj* (*fam*) ■ **~!** hau ab!

scathing ['skeɪ·ðɪŋ] *adj* versengend; *criticism* scharf; *remark* bissig

scatter ['skæt·ər] I. *vt* verstreuen II. *vi* sich zerstreuen III. *n* (*liter*) [vereinzeltes] Häufchen

'scatterbrain *n* zerstreute Person

'scatterbrained *adj* zerstreut

scattered ['skæt·ərd] *adj* verstreut; (*far apart*) weit verstreut; (*sporadic*) vereinzelt

scavenge ['skæv·ɪndʒ] I. *vi* stöbern; (*feed*) Aas fressen II. *vt* (*find*) aufstöbern; (*get*) ergattern *fam*

scavenger ['skæv·ɪn·dʒər] *n* Aasfresser *m*; (*pej: person*) Aasgeier *m pej fam*

scenario [sə·'ner·i·oʊ] *n* Szenario *nt*; **worst-case ~** schlimmster Fall

scene [sin] *n* ① (*setting*) Schauplatz *m*; (*scenery*) Kulisse *f*; **behind the ~s** (*a. fig*) hinter den Kulissen; **crime ~** Tatort *m* ② (*real-life event*) Szene *f*; (*milieu*) **drug ~** Drogenszene *f*

scenery ['si·nə·ri] *n* Landschaft *f*; THEAT Bühnenbild *nt*

scenic ['si·nɪk] *adj* landschaftlich schön

scent [sent] I. *n* Duft *m*; (*perfume*) Parfüm *nt*; (*of animal*) Fährte *f*; ■ **to be on sb's/sth's ~** (*a. fig*) jdm/etw auf der Fährte sein *a. fig* II. *vt* wittern; (*detect*) ahnen

scepter ['sep·tər] *n* Zepter *nt*

schedule ['skedʒ·ʊl] I. *n* Zeitplan *m*; (*of events*) Programm *nt*; TRANSP Fahrplan *m;* SPORT Spielplan *m;* SCH, UNIV Stundenplan *m;* **ahead of** ~ früher als geplant; **behind** ~ im Verzug; **on** ~ termingerecht; **work** ~ Dienstplan *m* II. *vt usu passive* planen; *meeting* ansetzen; **they've** ~**d him to speak at three o'clock** sie haben seine Rede für drei Uhr geplant

scheduled ['skedʒ·uld] *adj attr* geplant; TRANSP planmäßig

schematic [ski·'mæt̬·ɪk] *adj* schematisch

scheme [skim] I. *n* ❶ [finsterer] Plan; POL Verschwörung *f* ❷ (*pattern*) Gesamtbild *nt;* **it fits into his** ~ **of things** das passt in sein Bild; **color** ~ Farb[en]zusammenstellung *f* II. *vi* planen

scheming ['ski·mɪŋ] I. *adj attr* (*pej*) intrigant *geh;* (*cleverly*) raffiniert II. *n* Intrigieren *nt*

schizophrenia [ˌskɪt·sə·'fri·ni·ə] *n* Schizophrenie *f;* (*fam: behavior*) schizophrenes Verhalten *geh*

schizophrenic [ˌskɪt·sə·'fren·ɪk] I. *adj* schizophren II. *n* Schizophrene(r) *f(m)*

scholar ['skal·ər] *n* Gelehrte(r) *f(m);* (*good learner*) fleißiger Student/fleißige Studentin

scholarly ['skal·ər·li] *adj* wissenschaftlich; (*erudite*) gelehrt

scholarship ['skal·ər·ʃɪp] *n* ❶ **her book is a work of great** ~ ihr Buch ist eine großartige wissenschaftliche Arbeit ❷ (*award*) Stipendium *nt*

school[1] [skul] I. *n* Schule *f;* (*faculty*) Fakultät *f;* (*smaller*) Institut *nt;* **elementary** ~ Grundschule *f;* **public** ~ staatliche Schule *f;* **to attend** ~ zur Schule gehen; **driving** ~ Fahrschule *f;* **graduate** ~ hohe Stufe innerhalb des Hochschulsystems, die das Studium bis zum Master's degree und dem PhD umfasst II. *vt* erziehen; (*train*) schulen; *dog* dressieren

school[2] [skul] *n* ZOOL Schule *f;* (*shoal*) Schwarm *m*

'**school age** *n* schulpflichtiges Alter

'**school bag** *n* Schultasche *f*

'**school board** *n* Schulbehörde *f*

'**schoolbook** *n* Schulbuch *nt*

'**schoolboy** *n* Schuljunge *m,* Schüler *m*

'**schoolchild** *n* Schulkind *nt*

'**schoolgirl** *n* Schulmädchen *nt,* Schülerin *f*

schooling ['sku·lɪŋ] *n* Schulbildung *f;* (*training*) Ausbildung *f*

'**schoolroom** *n* Klassenzimmer *nt*

'**schoolteacher** *n* Lehrer(in) *m(f)*

'**schoolwork** *n* Schularbeiten *pl*

'**schoolyard** *n* Schulhof *m*

schooner ['sku·nər] *n* Schoner *m*

science ['saɪ·əns] *n* [Natur]wissenschaft *f;* (*discipline*) Wissenschaft *f;* **applied** ~ angewandte Wissenschaft

science 'fiction *n* Sciencefiction *f*

scientific [ˌsaɪ·ən·'tɪf·ɪk] *adj* naturwissenschaftlich; *method* wissenschaftlich

scientist ['saɪ·ən·tɪst] *n* Wissenschaftler(in) *m(f)*

sci-fi ['saɪ·faɪ] *n short for* **science fiction** Sciencefiction *f*

scissors ['sɪz·ərz] *npl* Schere *f;* **a pair of** ~ eine Schere

sclerosis [sklɪ·'rou·sɪs] *n* Sklerose *f*

scoff [skaf] *vi* spotten; (*laugh*) lachen; ▪**to** ~ **at sb/sth** sich über jdn/etw lustig machen

scold [skould] *vt* ausschimpfen

scolding ['skoul·dɪŋ] *n* Schimpfen *nt;* **to get a [good]** ~ [furchtbar] ausgeschimpft werden

scone [skoun] *n* weiches, krustenloses Gebäck, das entweder nur mit Butter oder mit Butter und Marmelade gegessen wird

scoop [skup] I. *n* ❶ Schaufel *f;* (*ladle*) Schöpflöffel *m;* **measuring** ~ Messlöffel *m* ❷ (*amount*) Löffel *m; of ice cream* Kugel *f* ❸ JOURN (*fam*) Knüller *m fam* ❹ (*fam*) [Insider]informationen *pl* II. *vt* ❶ schaufeln; *ice cream* löffeln ❷ JOURN **we were** ~**ed by a rival paper** eine konkurrierende Zeitung kam uns zuvor

♦**scoop up** *vt* hochheben

scoot [skut] *vi* (*fam*) rennen

S

scooter ['sku·tər] n [Tret]roller m; **motor ~** Motorroller m

scope [skoʊp] n Rahmen m; (possibility) Möglichkeit f; (freedom) Spielraum m

scorch [skɔrtʃ] I. vt versengen II. vi versengt werden III. n <pl -es> versengte Stelle; **~ mark** Brandfleck m

scorcher ['skɔr·tʃər] n (fam) sehr heißer Tag

scorching ['skɔr·tʃɪŋ] adj sengend; heat glühend

score [skɔr] I. n ❶ Punktestand m; (of game) Spielstand m; **final ~** Endstand m ❷ (dispute) Streit[punkt] m; **to settle a ~** eine Rechnung begleichen ❸ MUS Partitur f ❹ (notch) Kerbe f ❺ (twenty) zwanzig; (three ~ years and ten) siebzig Jahre; **~s of** Dutzende von ▶PHRASES: **to know the ~** wissen, wie der Hase läuft fam; **what's the ~?** (fam) wie sieht's aus? II. vt ❶ SPORT treffen; goal schießen; run scoren ❷ (achieve) erreichen; **to ~ points** (fig) sich dat einen Vorteil verschaffen ❸ (cut) einkerben ❹ (fam) drugs beschaffen III. vi ❶ scoren; (in basketball) einen Punkt machen; (in soccer) ein Tor schießen ❷ (achieve) abschneiden ❸ (sl) [sich dat] Stoff beschaffen ❹ (sl: have sex) jdn ins Bett kriegen

'scoreboard n Anzeigetafel f

scorer ['skɔr·ər] n Torschütze, -schützin m, f; (scorekeeper) Scorer m; **the leading ~** Torschützenkönig m; (in basketball, football) Spieler, der die meisten Punkte erzielt hat

scorn [skɔrn] I. n Verachtung f II. vt verachten; (refuse) ablehnen ▶PHRASES: **hell hath no fury like a woman ~ed** (saying) die Hölle kennt keinen schlimmeren Zorn als den einer verlachten Frau

scornful ['skɔrn·fəl] adj verächtlich

Scorpio ['skɔr·pi·oʊ] n ASTROL Skorpion m

scorpion ['skɔr·pi·ən] n Skorpion m

Scot [skat] n Schotte, Schottin m, f

Scotch <pl -es> [skatʃ] n Scotch m

Scotch 'tape® n Tesa[film]® m

scot-'free adv straffrei; (unchallenged) unbehelligt; (unharmed) ungeschoren

Scotland ['skat·lənd] n Schottland nt

Scots [skats] I. adj schottisch II. n Schottisch nt

'Scotsman n Schotte m

'Scotswoman n Schottin f

Scottish ['skat·ɪʃ] I. adj schottisch II. n ■**the ~** pl die Schotten pl

scoundrel ['skaʊn·drəl] n Schuft m

scour¹ ['skaʊ·ər] I. n Scheuern nt II. vt scheuern; torrent auswaschen; wind abtragen

scour² ['skaʊ·ər] vt ■**to ~ sth** [for sb/sth] etw [nach jdm/etw] absuchen; newspaper etw [nach jdm/etw] durchforsten

scourer ['skaʊ·ər·ər] n Topfreiniger m

scourge [skɜrdʒ] n Geißel f geh; (critic) Kritiker(in) m(f)

scout [skaʊt] I. n Pfadfinder(in) m(f); (talent seeker) Talentsucher(in) m(f) II. vi kundschaften; **to ~ for new talent** nach neuen Talenten suchen III. vt auskundschaften

'scoutmaster n Pfadfinderführer(in) m(f)

scowl [skaʊl] I. n mürrischer [Gesichts]ausdruck II. vi mürrisch [drein]blicken

scrabble ['skræb·əl] vi [herum]wühlen; ■**to ~ for sth** nach etw dat greifen

scram <-mm-> [skræm] vi (fam) abhauen

scramble ['skræm·bəl] I. n Kletterpartie f; (rush) Gedrängel nt fam II. vi klettern; (rush) hasten; **to ~ to one's feet** sich hochrappeln fam III. vt eggs verrühren; (encode) verschlüsseln

scrambled 'eggs npl Rührei nt

scrap [skræp] I. n ❶ Stück[chen] nt; of paper Fetzen m; (metal) Schrott m; ■**~s** pl (leftovers) Speisereste pl II. vt <-pp-> wegwerfen; (metal) verschrotten; (abolish) abschaffen; (fam: abandon) aufgeben

'scrapbook n [Sammel]album nt

scrape [skreɪp] I. n [Ab]kratzen nt; (on

skin) Abschürfung *f*; (*scratch*) Kratzer *m*; (*fam: situation*) Klemme *f* II. *vt* ① [ab]schaben; *dirt* [ab]kratzen ② to ~ sth (*graze*) sich *dat* etw aufschürfen III. *vi* (*rub*) reiben; (*brush*) bürsten; (*scratch*) kratzen; (*economize*) sparen

◆ **scrape by** *vi* mit Ach und Krach durchkommen *fam*

◆ **scrape through** *vi* gerade [mal] so durchkommen *fam*

◆ **scrape together, scrape up** *vt* zusammenbekommen; *money* zusammenkratzen *fam*

scraper ['skreɪ·pər] *n* Spachtel *m o f*; (*for windshields*) Kratzer *m*; (*for shoes*) Abkratzer *m*

'**scrap heap** *n* Schrotthaufen *m*; **to be on the ~** (*fig*) zum alten Eisen gehören *fam*; *plan* verworfen worden sein

'**scrap iron** *n* Alteisen *nt*

scrappy ['skræp·i] *adj* rauflustig

scratch [skrætʃ] I. *n* <*pl* -es> ① (*cut*) Kratzer *m* ② (*itch*) **to give oneself a ~** sich *akk* kratzen ③ **to start** [sth] **from ~** [mit etw *dat*] bei null anfangen II. *vt* zerkratzen; *person* kratzen; (*mark*) verkratzen; *itch* kratzen; **to ~ one's head** sich am Kopf kratzen III. *vi* kratzen; (*itch*) sich kratzen

◆ **scratch out** *vt* auskratzen; *word* durchstreichen

'**scratch card** *n* Rubbellos *nt*

'**scratch paper** *n* Schmierpapier *nt*; (*for draft*) Konzeptpapier *nt*

scratchy ['skrætʃ·i] *adj* kratzig

scrawl [skrɔl] I. *vt* [hin]kritzeln *fam* II. *n* Gekritzel *nt*; (*note*) hingekritzelte Notiz *fam*

scrawny ['skrɔ·ni] *adj* dürr; *vegetation* mager

scream [skrim] I. *n* Schrei *m*; *of animal* Gekreisch[e] *nt kein pl*; *of engine* Heulen *nt*; *of plane* Dröhnen *nt*; ~ **for help** Hilfeschrei *m* II. *vi* schreien; (*with joy*) kreischen; *engine* heulen; *plane* dröhnen; ■ **to ~ at sb** jdn anschreien III. *vt* schreien; (*shout*) lauthals schreien

screech [skritʃ] I. *n* <*pl* -es> Schrei *m*;

of animal Kreischen *nt kein pl*; *of tires* Quietschen *nt kein pl* II. *vi* schreien; *animal* kreischen; *tires* quietschen

screen [skrin] I. *n* ① Leinwand *f*; (*of television*) Bildschirm *m*; (*for radar*) Schirm *m* ② (*panel*) Trennwand *f*; (*for protection*) Schutzschirm *m*; (*against insects*) Fliegengitter *nt* ③ (*that conceals*) Tarnung *f* II. *vt* (*conceal*) abschirmen; (*shield*) schützen; (*examine*) überprüfen; (*show*) vorführen; TV senden; ■ **to ~ sb for sth** MED jdn auf etw *akk* hin untersuchen

screening ['skri·nɪŋ] *n* Vorführen *nt*; *of TV program* Ausstrahlung *f*; (*testing*) Überprüfung *f*; MED Untersuchung *f*; **health** ~ Vorsorgeuntersuchung *f*; (*X-ray*) Röntgenuntersuchung *f*

'**screen saver** *n* Bildschirmschoner *m*

screw [skru] I. *n* Schraube *f*; (*turn*) Drehung *f* ▶ PHRASES: **to have a ~ loose** (*hum fam*) nicht ganz dicht sein *pej* II. *vt* ① ■ **to ~ sth to sth** etw an etw *akk* schrauben ② (*twist*) **to ~ sth tight** etw fest zudrehen; ■ **to ~ sth into/on sth** etw in/auf etw *akk* schrauben ③ (*vulg, sl: have sex with*) vögeln *derb*

◆ **screw around** (*fam*) I. *vi* herumblödeln; (*waste time*) herumtrödeln II. *vt* ■ **to ~ sb around** (*mess about*) jdm auf die Nerven gehen; (*waste time*) jds Zeit *f* verschwenden

◆ **screw on** *vi cap* sich zuschrauben lassen; *nut* sich anziehen lassen

◆ **screw up** I. *vt* ① (*sl: spoil*) vermasseln *fam* ② *twist* verziehen; **to ~ it up** Mist bauen *fam* ② *twist* verziehen; **to ~ up one's eyes** blinzeln II. *vi* (*sl*) ■ **to ~ up** [**on sth**] [bei etw *dat*] Mist bauen *fam*

'**screwball** *n* ① (*in baseball*) Screwball *m* ② (*fam*) Spinner(in) *m(f) pej*

'**screwdriver** *n* Schraubenzieher *m*

screwed [skrud] *adj pred* (*sl*) festgefahren; (*in hopeless situation*) geliefert

'**screw top** *n* Schraubverschluss *m*

'**screwup**, '**screw-up** *n* (*sl*) Schnitzer *m* *fam*

screwy ['skru·i] *adj* (*fam*) verrückt

S

scribble ['skrɪb·əl] I. *vt* [hin]kritzeln II. *vi* kritzeln; (*hum: write*) schriftstellern *fam* III. *n* Gekritzel *nt kein pl pej*; (*handwriting*) Klaue *f pej sl*

scrimp [skrɪmp] *vi* **to ~ and save** knausern *pej fam*

script [skrɪpt] *n* ❶ Drehbuch *nt; of play* Regiebuch *nt; of broadcast* Skript *nt* ❷ (*writing style*) Schrift *f,* Schriftart *f*

'**scriptwriter** *n* Drehbuchautor(in) *m(f)*; RADIO Rundfunkautor(in) *m(f)*

scroll [skroʊl] I. *n* [Schrift]rolle *f* II. *vi* COMPUT scrollen

Scrooge [skruːdʒ] *n* (*pej*) Geizhals *m*

scrounge [skraʊndʒ] (*fam*) I. *vt* (*pej*) ■to ~ sth [off sb] etw [von jdm] schnorren II. *vi* ❶ ■to ~ [around] for sth nach etw *dat* herumsuchen ❷ (*pej*) schnorren

scrounger ['skraʊn·dʒər] *n* (*pej fam*) Schnorrer(in) *m(f)*

scrub[1] [skrʌb] I. *n* to give sth a [good] ~ etw [gründlich] [ab]schrubben *fam* II. *vt* <-bb-> [ab]schrubben *fam*; (*fam: cancel*) fallen lassen; *project* abblasen III. *vi* <-bb-> schrubben *fam*

scrub[2] [skrʌb] *n* (*bushes*) Gestrüpp *nt;* (*area*) Busch *m*

scrubber ['skrʌb·ər], '**scrub brush** *n* Schrubber *m;* (*smaller*) Scheuerbürste *f*

scruffy ['skrʌf·i] *adj* schmuddelig *pej fam; person* vergammelt *pej fam; place* heruntergekommen *fam*

scruple ['skruː·pəl] *n* ■~s *pl* Skrupel *pl*

scrupulous ['skruːp·jʊ·ləs] *adj* gewissenhaft; (*careful*) [peinlich] genau

scrutinize ['skruː·tə·naɪz] *vt* [genau] untersuchen; *text* studieren

scrutiny ['skruː·tə·ni] *n* [genaue] [Über]prüfung

'**scuba diving** *n* Sporttauchen *nt*

scuff [skʌf] *vt* verschrammen; (*wear away*) abwetzen; **to ~ one's feet** schlurfen

scuffle ['skʌf·əl] I. *n* Handgemenge *nt* II. *vi* sich balgen

sculpt [skʌlpt] I. *vt* (*heraus*)meißeln; (*in clay*) modellieren; (*shape*) formen II. *vi* bildhauern *fam*

sculptor ['skʌlp·tər] *n* Bildhauer(in) *m(f)*

sculpture ['skʌlp·tʃər] I. *n* (*art*) Bildhauerei *f;* (*object*) Skulptur *f* II. *vt* [heraus]meißeln; (*in clay*) modellieren; (*shape*) formen; (*model*) modellieren III. *vi* bildhauern *fam*

scum [skʌm] *n* Schaum *m;* (*residue*) Rand *m;* (*layer*) Schmutzschicht *f;* (*pej: evil people*) Abschaum *m*

'**scumbag** *n* (*pej sl: man*) Mistkerl *m fam;* (*woman*) Miststück *nt fam*

scurry ['skɜr·i] *vi* <-ie-> eilen; (*mouse*) huschen

scuttle ['skʌt̬·əl] *vi* hasten; *mouse* huschen

scythe [saɪð] I. *n* Sense *f* II. *vt* [mit der Sense] [ab]mähen; ■to ~ sb/sth [down] (*fig*) jdn/etw niedermähen *fam* III. *vi* preschen

SD, S.D. *abbrev of* **South Dakota**

sea [si] *n* ❶ ■the ~ das Meer; **at the bottom of the ~** auf dem Meeresboden; **by the ~** am Meer; **the high ~s** die hohe See; **the Dead ~** das Tote Meer ❷ (*sea state*) Seegang *m kein pl* ▶PHRASES: **to be [all] at ~** [ganz] ratlos sein

'**seabed** *n* Meeresgrund *m*

'**seaboard** *n* Küste *f*

'**sea dog** *n* Seebär *m fam*

'**seafood** *n* Meeresfrüchte *pl*

'**seafront** *n* Strandpromenade *f;* (*beach*) Strand *m*

'**seagull** *n* Möwe *f*

'**sea horse** *n* Seepferdchen *nt*

seal[1] [sil] I. *n* ❶ (*stamp*) Siegel *nt* ❷ (*join*) Verschluss *m* II. *vt* ❶ (*stamp*) siegeln ❷ (*close*) [fest] verschließen; (*airtight*) luftdicht verschließen; (*watertight*) wasserdicht verschließen; *gaps* abdichten; (*with seal*) versiegeln; (*for customs*) plombieren; (*with adhesive*) zukleben; *border* schließen

◆**seal up** *vt* [fest] verschließen; (*with seal*) versiegeln; (*with adhesive*) zukleben; *gaps* abdichten

seal[2] [sil] *n* ZOOL Seehund *m*

'**sea level** *n* Meeresspiegel *m;* **above ~** über dem Meeresspiegel

'sealing wax n Siegelwachs nt

'sea lion n Seelöwe m

seam [siːm] n Naht f; of coal Schicht f; **to be bursting at the ~s** (fig) aus allen Nähten platzen fam

'seaman ['siːmən] n Seemann m; (rank) Matrose m

seamless ['siːmlɪs] adj nahtlos; (a. fig) robe ohne Nähte nach n

seamlessly ['siːmlɪsli] adv nahtlos

seamy ['siːmi] adj heruntergekommen; (dubious) zwielichtig; **the ~ side of life** die Schattenseite des Lebens

'seaplane n Wasserflugzeug nt

'seaport n Seehafen m

search [sɜːtʃ] I. n Suche f; (for drugs) Durchsuchung f; of person Leibesvisitation f; COMPUT Suchlauf m; **to go off in ~ of sth** sich auf die Suche nach etw dat machen II. vi suchen; ■ **to ~ for sb/sth** nach jdm/etw suchen; ■ **to ~ through sth** etw durchsuchen III. vt durchsuchen; place absuchen; conscience prüfen; memory durchforschen
  ◆ **search out** vt ausfindig machen

'search engine n COMPUT Suchmaschine f

searching ['sɜːtʃɪŋ] adj look forschend; inquiry eingehend; question tief gehend

'searchlight n Suchscheinwerfer m

'search party n Suchtrupp m

'search warrant n Durchsuchungsbefehl m

'seashell n Muschel f

'seashore n Strand m; (coast) [Meeres]küste f

'seasick adj seekrank

'seasickness n Seekrankheit f

'seaside I. n ■ **the ~** die [Meeres]küste; ■ **at the ~** am Meer II. adj attr See-

season ['siːzən] I. n ① Jahreszeit f; **the Christmas ~** die Weihnachtszeit; **the rainy ~** die Regenzeit f; (period) Saison f; (business a.) Hauptzeit f; **oysters are out of ~ at the moment** zurzeit gibt es keine Austern; **at the height of the ~** in der Hochsaison; **high ~** Hochsaison f II. vt würzen; wood ablagern lassen

seasonal ['siːzənəl] adj **~ adjustment** Saisonbereinigung f; **~ work** Saisonarbeit f

seasoned ['siːzənd] adj timber abgelagert; (spiced) gewürzt

seasoning ['siːzənɪŋ] n Gewürz nt; (salt and pepper) Würze f

'season ticket n Dauerkarte f; SPORT Saisonkarte f

seat [siːt] I. n ① [Sitz]platz m; (in car) Sitz m; (in bus, train) Sitzplatz m; (in theater) Platz m; **to take a ~** sich [hin]setzen ② usu sing of chair Sitz m; of pants Hosenboden m ③ (base) Sitz m II. vt **to ~ 2500** 2500 Menschen fassen; **his car ~s five** in seinem Auto haben fünf Leute Platz

'seat belt n Sicherheitsgurt m; **to fasten one's ~** sich anschnallen

seating ['siːtɪŋ] n Sitzgelegenheiten pl; (arrangement) Sitzordnung f; **~ for 6** Sitzplätze pl für 6 Personen

'seating arrangements npl, **'seating plan** n Sitzordnung f

'seawater n Meerwasser nt

'seaweed n [See]tang m

sec. [sek] n short for **second**: **wait a ~!** Moment mal!; **hold on [just] a ~!** warte einen Moment!

secluded [sɪˈkluːdɪd] adj abgelegen; area abgeschieden; life zurückgezogen

seclusion [sɪˈkluːʒən] n Zurückgezogenheit f; of place Abgelegenheit f

second¹ ['sekənd] n Sekunde f; (short time a.) Augenblick m; **I'll only be a ~** ich bin gleich da

second² ['sekənd] I. adj ① usu attr zweite(r, s); **the ~ time** das zweite Mal; **to finish ~** Zweite(r) werden; **to be in ~ place** auf Platz zwei sein ② **~-largest** zweitgrößte(r, s); **Germany's ~ city** Deutschlands zweitwichtigste Stadt; **to be ~ to none** unübertroffen sein ③ attr (another) zweite(r, s); **to give sb a ~ chance** jdm eine zweite Chance geben; **to have ~ thoughts** ▶ es sich dat noch einmal überlegen ▶PHRASES: **to play ~ fiddle to sb** in jds Schatten stehen III. n AUTO zweiter Gang III. adv **to finish ~**

S

den zweiten Platz belegen **IV.** vt motion
unterstützen

secondary ['sek·ən·der·i] adj ① zweitrangig; **to play a ~ role** eine unterge-
ordnete Rolle spielen ② ~ **education**
höhere Schulbildung

'**secondary school** n SCH Highschool f

second 'best n to settle for ~ sich mit
weniger zufriedengeben

second-'best adj zweitbeste(r, s)

second 'class I. n zweite Klasse **II.** adv
to travel ~ zweiter Klasse reisen

second-'guess I. vt ■to ~ sb jdn/etw
im Nachhinein kritisieren **II.** vi vorhersagen, was jd tun wird

'**secondhand I.** adj ① ~ **car** Gebrauchtwagen m; ~ **clothes** Secondhandklei-
dung f ② information aus zweiter Hand
nach n **II.** adv gebraucht; (from inter-
mediary) aus zweiter Hand

second 'hand n Sekundenzeiger m

secondly ['sek·ənd·li] adv zweitens

second-'rate adj (pej) zweitklassig

secrecy ['si·krə·si] n ① Geheimhaltung f;
(ability) Verschwiegenheit f; (secretiveness) Heimlichtuerei f pej; **in ~** im Ge-
heimen

secret ['si·krit] **I.** n Geheimnis nt; **to
keep a ~** ein Geheimnis für sich akk
behalten; ■**in ~** insgeheim; **to do sth
in ~** etw heimlich tun **II.** adj geheim;
(hidden) verborgen; (done in secret)
heimlich

secret 'agent n Geheimagent(in) m(f)

secretary ['sek·rə·ter·i] n Sekretär(in)
m(f)

Secretary ['sek·rə·ter·i] n Minister,
·in m, f; ~ **of Defense** Verteidigungsmi-
nister(in) m(f)

Secretary 'General <pl **Secretaries
General**> n Generalsekretär(in) m(f)

Secretary of 'State n Außenminis-
ter(in) m(f)

secretive ['si·krı·tɪv] adj geheimnisvoll;
character verschlossen

'**Secret Service** n ■the ~ der Geheimdienst

sect [sekt] n Sekte f

section ['sek·ʃən] n ① Teil nt; of road

Teilstrecke f; TECH [Bau]teil nt; of statute
Paragraph m; of book Abschnitt m; of
document Absatz m ② (area) Bereich m; **nonsmoking ~** (in restaurant) Nichtraucherbereich m; (on
train) Nichtraucherabteil nt; **woodwind ~** Holzbläser pl ③ (division) Abteilung f ④ (cut) Schnitt m; **cesar-
ean ~** Kaiserschnitt m
♦ **section off** vt abteilen

sector ['sek·tər] n Sektor m; (of land a.)
Zone f

secure [sɪ·'kjʊr] **I.** adj <-r, -st> sicher;
(guarded) bewacht; phone abhörsicher;
rope fest; door fest verschlossen; **financially** ~ finanziell abgesichert **II.** vt
① rights sich dat sichern ② (make safe)
[ab]sichern; **to ~ sb/sth against
sth** jdn/etw vor etw dat schützen
③ (fasten) befestigen; door fest schließen

security [sɪ·'kjʊr·ɪ·ţi] n ① Sicherheit f;
(guards) Sicherheitsdienst m; **tight ~**
strenge Sicherheitsvorkehrungen; **to
tighten ~** die Sicherheitsmaßnahmen
verschärfen ② usu sing (safeguard) Sicherheit f ③ FIN ■**securities** pl (invest-
ments) Wertpapiere pl; (government
securities) Staatspapiere pl

Se'curity Council n Sicherheitsrat m

se'curity forces npl Sicherheitskräfte pl

se'curity guard n Sicherheitsbeamte(r),
·beamtin m, f

sedan [sɪ·'dæn] n Limousine f

sedate [sɪ·'deɪt] vt MED ruhigstellen

sedation [sɪ·'deɪ·ʃən] n MED Ruhigstel-
lung f

sedative ['sed·ə·ţɪv] n Beruhigungsmittel nt

sediment ['sed·ə·mənt] n Sediment nt;
(in wine) [Boden]satz m

seduce [sɪ·'dus] vt verführen; ■**to ~ sb
into doing sth** jdn dazu verleiten, etw
zu tun

seduction [sɪ·'dʌk·ʃən] n Verführung f;
(quality) Verlockung f

seductive [sɪ·'dʌk·tɪv] adj verführerisch; offer verlockend

see <saw, seen> [si] **I.** vt ① sehen;

movie [sich *dat*] [an]sehen ❷ (*understand*) verstehen; (*discern*) erkennen; I ~ what you mean ich weiß, was du meinst; ~ what I mean? siehst du? ❸ (*consider*) this is how I ~ it so sehe ich die Sache; to ~ sth in a new light etw mit anderen Augen sehen ❹ (*learn*) I'll ~ who it is ich schaue mal nach, wer es ist; that remains to be ~n das wird sich zeigen; to ~ into the future in die Zukunft schauen ❺ (*meet*) sehen; (*by chance*) [zufällig] treffen; we're ~ing friends this weekend wir treffen uns am Wochenende mit Freunden; ~ you later! (*fam: until later*) bis später!; (*goodbye*) tschüs! *fam;* ■to be ~ing sb (*dating*) mit jdm zusammen sein *fam;* I'm not ~ing anyone at the moment ich habe im Moment keine Freundin/keinen Freund ⑥ (*talk to*) sprechen; (*receive*) empfangen; Ms. Miller can't ~ you now Frau Miller ist im Moment nicht zu sprechen; to ~ a doctor zum Arzt gehen ❼ (*accompany*) to ~ sb home/to the door jdn nach Hause/zur Tür bringen ▶PHRASES: to ~ the last of sb [endlich] jdn los sein *fam;* to not ~ the forest for the trees den Wald vor [lauter] Bäumen nicht sehen *hum* II. *vi* ❶ sehen; let me ~! lass mich mal sehen!; can you ~? (*in theater etc.*) können Sie noch sehen? ❷ (*understand*) oh, I ~! aha!; I ~ ich verstehe; I ~ from your report ... Ihrem Bericht entnehme ich, ...; we'll ~ about that das wird sich zeigen ▶PHRASES: to not ~ eye to eye [with sb] nicht derselben Ansicht sein [wie jd]

◆ see in *vt* hineinbringen; to ~ the New Year in das neue Jahr begrüßen
◆ see off *vt* verabschieden; to ~ sb off at the airport jdn zum Flughafen bringen
◆ see out *vt* ❶ (*escort*) hinausbegleiten ❷ (*continue to end of*) durchstehen; (*last until end of*) überstehen; *project* bis zum Ende mitmachen
◆ see through *vt* ❶ ■to ~ through sth durch etw *akk* hindurchsehen

❷ *plan* durchschauen ❸ (*sustain*) ■to ~ sb through jdm über die Runden helfen *fam;* (*comfort*) jdm beistehen; will 30 dollars be enough to ~ you through? reichen dir 30 Dollar? ❹ *project* zu Ende bringen
◆ see to *vt* ■to ~ to sb/sth sich um jdn/etw kümmern; ■to ~ to it that ... dafür sorgen, dass ...

seed [sid] I. *n* ❶ ❶ Samen *m; of grain* Korn *nt;* ■~s *pl* AGR Saat *f kein pl* ❷ (*seeds*) Samen *pl;* to go to ~ Samen bilden; *plants* schießen; (*fig*) *person* herunterkommen *fam* II. *vt* ❶ (*sow*) besäen; ■to ~ itself sich aussäen ❷ *fruit* entkernen ❸ *usu passive* SPORT ■to be ~ed platziert sein

'seedbed *n* Samenbeet *nt;* (*fig*) Grundlage *f*
seedless ['sid·lɪs] *adj* kernlos
seedy ['si·di] *adj* zwielichtig; *character* zweifelhaft; *clothes* schäbig
seeing ['si·ɪŋ] *conj* ~ that ... da ...
seek <sought, sought> [sik] *vt* ❶ (*form*) suchen; (*try to obtain a.*) erstreben; *justice* streben ❷ (*ask for*) erbitten *geh;* *approval* einholen; to ~ advice from sb jdn um Rat bitten
◆ seek out *vt* ausfindig machen; *information* herausfinden

seem [sim] *vi* ❶ he's sixteen, but he ~s younger er ist sechzehn, wirkt aber jünger; he ~s like a very nice man er scheint ein sehr netter Mann zu sein; (*it ~s all right to me*) das scheint mir ganz in Ordnung zu sein; it ~ed like a good idea at the time damals hielt ich das für eine gute Idee ❷ there ~s to have been some mistake da liegt anscheinend ein Irrtum vor; ■it ~s [that] ... anscheinend ...; ■it ~s as if ... es scheint, als ob ...; it ~s to me that he isn't the right person ich finde, er ist nicht der Richtige

seemingly ['si·mɪŋ·li] *adv* scheinbar
seen [sin] *pp of* see
seep [sip] *vi* sickern; (*fig*) *truth* durchsickern
◆ seep away *vi* versickern

S

seesaw ['siːsɔː] I. n Wippe f; (fig) Auf und Ab nt II. vi wippen; (fig) sich auf und ab bewegen; prices steigen und fallen; mood schwanken

seethe [siːð] vi ❶ (be very angry) kochen fam ❷ (be crowded) wimmeln

'see-through adj durchsichtig

segment ['segmənt] n Teil m; of population Gruppe f; (of worm) Segment nt

segregation [ˌsegrəˈgeɪʃən] n Trennung f; **racial ~** Rassentrennung f

seize [siːz] vt ❶ (grab) ergreifen ❷ usu passive (fig) ■to be ~d with sth von etw dat ergriffen werden ❸ (capture) einnehmen; criminal festnehmen; hostage nehmen; power ergreifen; (more aggressively) an sich akk reißen ❹ (confiscate) beschlagnahmen
♦**seize on** vt idea aufgreifen; excuse greifen
♦**seize up** vi engine stehen bleiben; brain aussetzen

seizure ['siːʒər] n MED Anfall m

seldom ['seldəm] adv selten; **~ if ever** fast nie

select [səˈlekt] I. adj (high-class) exklusiv; (chosen) ausgewählt; team auserwählt; fruit ausgesucht II. vt aussuchen; person auswählen; team aufstellen III. vi ■to ~ from sth aus etw dat [aus]wählen

selection [səˈlekʃən] n Auswahl f; BIOL Selektion f geh; **to make one's ~** seine Wahl treffen

selective [səˈlektɪv] adj wählerisch; buyer kritisch; (choosing the best) ausgewählt; process gezielt

self <pl selves> [self] n ■one's ~ das Selbst; **to be [like [or back to]] one's former ~** wieder ganz der/die Alte sein

self-addressed stamped 'envelope n adressierter frankierter Rückumschlag

self-ad'hesive adj selbstklebend

self-ap'pointed adj selbst ernannt

self-as'surance n Selbstvertrauen nt

self-as'sured adj selbstbewusst

self-'centered adj egozentrisch

self-com'posed adj beherrscht; **to remain ~** gelassen bleiben

self-con'fessed adj attr **she's a ~ thief** sie bezeichnet sich selbst als Diebin

self-'confidence n Selbstvertrauen nt

self-'conscious adj gehemmt; smile verlegen

self-con'tained adj selbstgenügsam; community autark; apartment separat

self-con'trol n Selbstbeherrschung f

self-de'ceit, self-de'ception n Selbstbetrug m

self-de'fense n Selbstverteidigung f; **to kill sb in ~** jdn in Notwehr töten

self-de'struct vi sich selbst zerstören; materials zerfallen

self-'discipline n Selbstdisziplin f

self-ef'facing adj bescheiden

self-em'ployed I. adj selbständig II. n ■**the ~** pl die Selbständigen pl

self-es'teem n Selbstwertgefühl nt

self-'evident adj offensichtlich; ■**it is ~ that …** es liegt auf der Hand, dass …

self-ex'planatory adj ■**to be ~** keiner weiteren Erklärung bedürfen

self-ex'pression n Selbstdarstellung f

self-'help n Selbsthilfe f

selfie ['selfiː] n TELEC, INET Selfie nt

self-im'portance n Selbstgefälligkeit f

self-im'portant adj selbstgefällig

self-im'posed adj selbst verordnet

self-in'dulgence n Luxus m; (act) Hemmungslosigkeit f

self-in'dulgent adj genießerisch

self-in'flicted adj selbst zugefügt

self-'interest n Eigeninteresse f

selfish ['selfɪʃ] adj selbstsüchtig; motive eigennützig

selfishness ['selfɪʃnɪs] n Selbstsucht f

selfless ['selfləs] adj selbstlos

self-'made adj selbst gemacht; **~ man** Selfmademan m

self-'portrait n Selbstbildnis nt; **to draw a ~** sich selbst porträtieren

self-pos'sessed adj selbstbeherrscht

self-preser'vation n Selbsterhaltung f

self-re'spect n Selbstachtung f

self-re'specting adj **no ~ person** niemand, der was auf sich hält

self-'righteous adj selbstgerecht

self-rising 'flour n Mehl, dem Backpulver beigemischt ist

self-'sacrifice n Selbstaufopferung f

self-'service n Selbstbedienung f

self-suf'ficiency n Selbstversorgung f

self-suf'ficient adj selbständig

self-'taught adj selbst erlernt; (acquired) autodidaktisch

sell [sel] I. vt <sold, sold> ❶ verkaufen; ■ to ~ sb sth [or sth to sb] jdm etw verkaufen (for für +akk) ❷ (persuade) ■ to ~ sth [to sb] jdn für etw akk gewinnen; ■ to ~ an idea to sb jdm eine Idee schmackhaft machen II. vi <sold, sold> verkaufen; (attract customers) sich verkaufen ▶ PHRASES: to ~ like hotcakes wie warme Semmeln weggehen III. n Ware f; to be a hard/soft ~ schwer/leicht verkäuflich sein

◆ sell off vt verkaufen

◆ sell out I. vi ■ to be/have sold out product, shop, play ausverkauft sein; ■ to ~ out to sb business [seine Firma] an jdn verkaufen; (give in to) sich akk an jdn verkaufen II. vt ❶ ■ to be sold out ausverkauft sein ❷ (fam: betray) verraten

seller ['sel·ər] n Verkäufer(in) m(f); (product) Verkaufsschlager m

'selling price n Kaufpreis m

'sellout n Ausverkauf m; (betrayal) Auslieferung f; the concert was a ~ das Konzert war ausverkauft

selves [selvz] n pl of self

semen ['si·mən] n Sperma nt

semester [sə·'mes·tər] n Semester nt

semi <pl -s> ['sem·i] n (fam) ❶ (truck) Sattelschlepper m ❷ SPORT ■ ~s pl Halbfinale nt

semiauto'matic adj MIL halbautomatisch

'semicircle n Halbkreis m

semi'circular adj halbkreisförmig

'semicolon n Semikolon nt

semicon'ductor n Halbleiter m

semi'conscious adj halb bewusstlos

semi'final n Halbfinale nt

semi'finalist n Halbfinalist(in) m(f)

seminar ['sem·ə·nar] n Seminar nt

semi'precious adj ~ stone Halbedelstein m

semi'skilled adj angelernt

semi'trailer n Sattelschlepper m; (trailer) Anhänger m

semi-vege'tarian n Flexitarier(in) m(f), Halbvegetarier(in) m(f)

semo'lina [,sem·ə·'li·nə] n Gries m

Sen. n POL abbrev of senator

senate ['sen·ɪt] n Senat m

senator ['sen·ə·tər] n Senator(in) m(f)

send <sent, sent> [send] vt ❶ ■ to ~ [sb] sth [or sth [to sb]] jdm etw [zu]schicken; to ~ sth in the mail etw mit der Post schicken; to ~ a signal to sb jdm etw signalisieren ❷ (dispatch) schicken; ■ to ~ sb for sth jdn nach etw dat [los]schicken; to ~ sb to prison jdn ins Gefängnis stecken ❸ (transmit) senden; signal aussenden; (pass on) ■ to ~ sb sth jdm etw übermitteln [lassen]; Maggie ~s [you] her love Maggie lässt [dich] grüßen ❹ (cause) the news sent him running back to the house die Nachricht ließ ihn wieder ins Haus laufen; to ~ sb into a panic jdn in Panik versetzen ▶ PHRASES: to ~ sb flying jdn zu Boden schicken

◆ send away I. vi ■ to ~ away for sth sich dat etw zuschicken lassen II. vt wegschicken

◆ send back vt zurückschicken

◆ send for vi (summon) rufen; brochure anfordern; help holen

◆ send in I. vt bill einreichen; report einschicken; order aufgeben; troops einsetzen II. vi ■ to ~ in for sth sich dat etw zuschicken lassen; for information etw anfordern

◆ send off I. vt abschicken; package aufgeben; (dispatch) fortschicken; to be sent off for fighting (player) einen Platzverweis wegen Rauferei bekommen II. vi ■ to ~ off for sth etw anfordern

◆ send out I. vi ■ to ~ out for sth etw telefonisch bestellen II. vt aussenden; letter verschicken; email versenden

◆ send up vt prices ansteigen lassen;

S

(*pass on*) zuschicken; (*fam: imprison*) hinter Gitter bringen

sender ['sen·dər] *n* Absender(in) *m(f)*

'sendoff *n* Verabschiedung *f*; **to give sb a ~** jdn verabschieden

Senegal [ˌsen·ɪ·ˈɡɔl] *n* Senegal *m*

senile ['si·naɪl] *adj* senil

senility [sə·ˈnɪl·ɪ·ti] *n* Senilität *f*

senior ['sin·jər] **I.** *adj* ❶ (*form*) älter ❷ *employee* vorgesetzt ❸ *attr* SCH, UNIV Senior- **II.** *n* ❶ Senior(in) *m(f)*; (*employee*) Vorgesetzte(r) *f(m)*; **she's my ~ by three years** sie ist drei Jahre älter als ich ❷ SCH, UNIV *Bezeichnung für Schüler einer Highschool- oder einer Collegeabgangsklasse*

senior 'citizen *n* ■**~s** *pl* ältere Menschen

senior 'high school *n* (*Schulform nach der Junior High School, welche die Stufen 9, 10, 11 und 12 enthält*)

seniority [sin·ˈjɔr·ɪ·ti] *n* Alter *nt*; (*rank*) Dienstalter *nt*

senior 'partner *n* Seniorpartner(in) *m(f)*

sensation [sen·ˈseɪ·ʃən] *n* ❶ Gefühl *nt*; **~ of cold** Kälteempfindung *f*; **burning ~** Brennen *nt* ❷ (*stir*) Sensation *f*; **to cause a ~** Aufsehen erregen

sensational [sen·ˈseɪ·ʃə·nəl] *adj* sensationell; (*very good a.*) fantastisch; (*shocking a.*) spektakulär

sensationalism [sen·ˈseɪ·ʃən·əl·ɪ·zəm] *n* Sensationsmache *m pej*

sense [sens] **I.** *n* ❶ Verstand *m*; ■**sb's ~s** *pl* jds gesunder Menschenverstand; **it's time you came to your ~s** es wird Zeit, dass du zur Vernunft kommst ❷ **to make [good] ~** sinnvoll sein; **to see the ~ in sth** den Sinn in etw *dat* sehen; **there's no ~ in doing sth** es hat keinen Sinn, etw zu tun ❸ (*faculty*) Sinn *m*; **~ of hearing** Gehör *nt*; **~ of sight** Sehvermögen *nt*; **~ of smell** Geruchssinn *m*; **sixth ~** sechster Sinn ❹ (*feeling*) Gefühl *nt*; **~ of duty** Pflichtgefühl *nt*; **~ of justice** Gerechtigkeitssinn *m* ❺ (*meaning*) Bedeutung *f*; **to make ~** einen Sinn ergeben; **in**

every ~ in jeder Hinsicht **II.** *vt* wahrnehmen; *danger* wittern; ■**to ~ that ...** spüren, dass ...

senseless ['sens·lɪs] *adj waste* sinnlos; (*foolish*) töricht; (*unconscious*) bewusstlos

sensible ['sen·sə·bəl] *adj* vernünftig; *decision* weis; *person* klug; (*suitable*) angemessen

sensibly ['sen·sə·bli] *adv* vernünftig; (*suitably*) angemessen; *dressed* passend

sensitive ['sen·sɪ·tɪv] *adj* ❶ verständnisvoll; ■**to be ~ to sth** für etw *akk* Verständnis haben ❷ (*secret*) vertraulich ❸ (*responsive*) empfindlich; **to be ~ to cold** kälteempfindlich sein; **~ feelings** verletzliche Gefühle

sensitivity [ˌsen·sə·ˈtɪv·ɪ·ti] *n* Verständnis *nt*; (*confidentiality*) Vertraulichkeit *f*; (*reaction*) Überempfindlichkeit *f*; **~ to light** Licht[über]empfindlichkeit *f*

sensor ['sen·sər] *n* Sensor *m*

sensual ['sen·ʃu·əl] *adj* sinnlich

sensuality [ˌsen·ʃu·ˈæl·ɪ·ti] *n* Sinnlichkeit *f*

sent [sent] *pt, pp of* **send**

sentence ['sen·təns] **I.** *n* ❶ Urteil *nt*; (*punishment*) Strafe *f*; **life ~** lebenslängliche Haftstrafe; **to serve a ~** eine Strafe verbüßen ❷ (*words*) Satz *m* **II.** *vt* verurteilen

sentiment ['sen·tə·mənt] *n* ❶ *usu pl* Ansicht *f*; **my ~s exactly!** ganz meine Meinung!; **popular ~** allgemeine Meinung ❷ (*emotion*) Rührseligkeit *f*

sentimental [ˌsen·tə·ˈmen·təl] *adj* ❶ gefühlvoll; **~ value** ideeller Wert ❷ (*emotional*) sentimental; *music* kitschig; *story* rührselig

sentimentality [ˌsen·tə·men·ˈtæl·ɪ·ti] *n* Sentimentalität *f*

sentry ['sen·tri] *n* Wache *f*

separate **I.** *adj* ['sep·ər·ɪt] getrennt; (*independent*) einzeln *attr*; **a ~ piece of paper** ein extra Blatt *nt* Papier; **to keep sth ~** etw getrennt halten **II.** *vt* ['sep·ə·reɪt] trennen **III.** *vi* ['sep·ə·reɪt] sich trennen; CHEM sich scheiden; *couple* sich trennen; (*divorce*) sich scheiden lassen; **she is ~d from her hus-band** sie lebt von ihrem Mann ge-trennt

separation [ˌsep·ə·ˈreɪ·ʃən] *n* Tren-nung *f;* (*living apart*) (eheliche) Tren-nung

separatist [ˈsep·ər·ə·tɪst] *n* Separa-tist(in) *m(f)*

Sept. *n abbrev of* **September** Sept.

September [sep·ˈtem·bər] *n* Septem-ber *m; see also* **February**

sequel [ˈsiː·kwəl] *n* Fortsetzung *f;* (*fol-low-up*) Nachspiel *nt*

sequence [ˈsiː·kwəns] *n* ❶ Reihenfolge *f; of programs* Sendefolge *f;* (*connected series*) Abfolge *f* ❷ (*part of film*) Se-quenz *f; closing ~* Schlussszene *f*

sequin [ˈsiː·kwɪn] *n* Paillette *f*

Serb [sɜrb] *n* Serbe, Serbin *m, f*

Serbia [ˈsɜr·bi·ə] *n* Serbien *nt*

Serbian [ˈsɜr·bi·ən] **I.** *adj* serbisch **II.** *n* Serbe, Serbin *m, f;* (*language*) Ser-bisch *nt*

Serbo-Croatian [ˌsɜr·boʊ·kroʊ·ˈeɪ-ʃən] *n* Serbokroatisch *nt*

serenade [ˌser·ə·ˈneɪd] **I.** *n* Serenade *f;* (*by lover*) Ständchen *nt* **II.** *vt* ein Ständ-chen bringen

sergeant [ˈsɑr·dʒənt] *n* Unteroffizier *m;* (*police*) ≈ Polizeimeister(in) *m(f)*

sergeant | **major** *n* Oberfeldwebel *m*

serial [ˈsɪr·i·əl] **I.** *n* Fortsetzungsge-schichte *f* **II.** *adj* Serien-

'serial killer *n* Serienmörder(in) *m(f)*

'serial number *n* Seriennummer *f*

series <*pl ->* [ˈsɪr·iz] *n* ❶ Reihe *f;* (*succes-sion*) Folge *f;* (*products*) Serie *f*

serious [ˈsɪr·i·əs] *adj* ❶ ernst; *threat, ar-gument* ernsthaft; *accident* schwer; (*dangerous*) gefährlich; *allegation* schwerwiegend ❷ *attr* (*careful*) ernsthaft ❸ (*significant*) bedeutend; (*thought-provoking*) tiefgründig; *writer* anspruchsvoll

seriously [ˈsɪr·i·əs·li] *adv* ❶ ernst; (*badly*) schwer; (*dangerously*) ernstlich ❷ (*fam: very*) äußerst; **~ funny** urko-misch

seriousness [ˈsɪr·i·əs·nɪs] *n* Ernst *m;*

(*sincerity*) Ernsthaftigkeit *f;* **in all ~** ganz im Ernst

sermon [ˈsɜr·mən] *n* Predigt *f;* (*pej: lec-ture*) [Moral]predigt *f*

serrated [sə·ˈreɪ·tɪd] *adj* gezackt

serum <*pl -s>* [ˈsɪr·əm] *n* Serum *nt*

servant [ˈsɜr·vənt] *n* Bedienstete(r) *f(m);* (*for public*) Angestellte(r) *f(m)* (*im öf-fentlichen Dienst*)

serve [sɜrv] **I.** *n* Aufschlag *m;* (*in volley-ball*) Angabe *f* **II.** *vt* ❶ *customer* bedie-nen; *food* servieren; **this ~s 4 to 5** das ergibt 4 bis 5 Portionen ❷ (*complete*) ableisten; *prison sentence* absitzen *fam* ❸ **to ~ a purpose** einen Zweck erfül-len; **if my memory ~s me right** wenn ich mich recht erinnere ❹ **to ~ the ball** Aufschlag haben; (*in volleyball*) Angabe haben ▶ PHRASES: **~ him right!** (*fam*) das geschieht ihm recht! **III.** *vi* servieren; (*work for*) dienen; (*function a.*) fungie-ren; (*in tennis*) aufschlagen; (*in volley-ball*) angeben

◆ **serve up** *vt* servieren

server [ˈsɜr·vər] *n* Server *m*

service [ˈsɜr·vɪs] *n* ❶ Service *m;* (*paid*) Dienstleistung *f;* (*at shop*) Bedienung *f; customer ~* Kundendienst *m* ❷ (*form*) ■ **to be of ~** [to sb] [jdm] von Nutzen sein; **to need the ~s of an expert** ei-nen Gutachter/eine Gutachterin brau-chen ❸ *ambulance ~* Rettungs-dienst *m; civil ~* öffentlicher Dienst ❹ **to be out of/in ~** außer/in Betrieb sein; *postal ~* Postwesen *nt* ❺ Auf-schlag *m;* (*in volleyball*) Angabe *f* ❻ ■ **the ~s** das Militär *nt kein pl* ❼ Gottesdienst *m;* **morning/eve-ning ~** Frühmesse/Abendandacht *f* ❽ (*maintenance*) Wartung *f;* AUTO In-spektion *f*

'service area *n* Raststätte *f*

'service center *n* Reparaturwerkstatt *f;* (*garage*) Werkstatt *f*

'service charge *n* Bedienungsgeld *nt*

'serviceman *n* Militärangehöriger *m*

'service station *n* Tankstelle *f*

'servicewoman *n* MIL Militärangehöri-ge *f*

S

servile ['sɜr·vəl] adj (pej) unterwürfig; obedience sklavisch

serving ['sɜr·vɪŋ] I. n (a ~ of rice) eine Portion Reis II. adj attr **the longest-~ mayor** der dienstälteste Bürgermeister/ die dienstälteste Bürgermeisterin

servo ['sɜː·voʊ] n AUTO, TECH ❶ short for **servomechanism** Servomechanismus m ❷ short for **servomotor** Servomotor m ❸ AUS (fam: service station) Tanke f fam

sesame ['ses·ə·mi] n Sesam m

session ['seʃ·ən] n Sitzung f; (period) Sitzungsperiode f; (for specific activity) Stunde f; recording ~ Aufnahme f

set¹ [set] I. adj ❶ pred (ready) bereit, fertig; **ready, [get] ~, go!** auf die Plätze, fertig, los!; ■**to be [all] ~ [for sth]** [für etw akk] bereit sein ❷ pattern, time fest[gesetzt]; ~ **phrase** feststehender Ausdruck ❸ look starr ❹ attr (assigned) vorgegebene(r, s); subject a. bestimmte(r, s) II. vt <set, set> ❶ (place) stellen; (on its side) legen; **to ~ foot in/on sth** etw betreten ❷ usu passive **"West Side Story" is ~ in New York** „West Side Story" spielt in New York ❸ **his remarks ~ me thinking** seine Bemerkungen gaben mir zu denken; **to ~ one's/sb's mind at ease** sich/jdn beruhigen; **to ~ sth in motion** etw in Bewegung setzen [o fig a. ins Rollen bringen] ❹ (prepare) vorbereiten; table decken; **to ~ the scene for sth** (create conditions) die Bedingungen für etw akk schaffen; (facilitate) den Weg für etw akk frei machen ❺ (adjust) einstellen; clock stellen ❻ (fix) festsetzen; budget festlegen; date, time ausmachen; deadline setzen ❼ record aufstellen; pace vorgeben; **to ~ a good example for sb** jdm ein Vorbild sein ❽ dislocation einrenken; bone einrichten ❾ hair legen ❿ TYPO setzen ⓫ **to ~ sail for ...** nach ... losfahren III. vi <set, set> ❶ concrete fest werden; sun untergehen

set² [set] n ❶ Satz m; (pair) Paar nt; coffee ~ Kaffeeservice nt ❷ THEAT Büh-

nenbild nt; FILM Szenenaufbau m; **on the ~** bei den Dreharbeiten; (on location) am Set ❸ (appliance) Gerät nt; (television) Fernseher m; (radio) Radio[gerät] nt ❹ (in tennis) Satz m

◆ **set about** vi **to ~ about doing sth** sich daran machen, etw zu tun

◆ **set apart** vt beiseitelegen; **clothes/sth ~ sb/sth ○ apart from sb/sth** etw unterscheidet jdn/etw von jdm/etw; ■**to be ~ apart for sth** für etw akk reserviert sein

◆ **set aside** vt ❶ beiseitelegen; clothes sich dat zurücklegen lassen; money sparen; time einplanen; (differences) begraben

◆ **set back** vt ❶ (delay) zurückwerfen; deadline verschieben ❷ (position) zurücksetzen; **their garden is ~ back from the road** ihr Garten liegt nicht direkt an der Straße

◆ **set down** vt absetzen; plane landen; **to ~ sth down in writing** aufschreiben

◆ **set in** vi weather einsetzen; complications sich einstellen

◆ **set off** I. vi sich auf den Weg machen; (in car) losfahren II. vt (trigger) auslösen; bomb zünden; ■**to ~ sb off** jdn verärgern

◆ **set on** vt (fam) ■**to ~ an animal on sb** ein Tier auf jdn hetzen

◆ **set out** I. vt (arrange) auslegen; chairs aufstellen; idea darlegen II. vi aufbrechen; ■**to ~ out to do sth** beabsichtigen, etw zu tun

◆ **set up** vt camp aufschlagen; business einrichten; program installieren; system konfigurieren; (fam: deceive) übers Ohr hauen fam

'setback n Rückschlag m

setting ['set·ɪŋ] n usu sing Lage f; (surroundings) Umgebung f; (in film) Schauplatz m; (for jewel) Fassung f

settle ['set·əl] I. vi sich niederlassen; (in chair) es sich dat bequem machen; (build up) sich anhäufen; (end dispute) sich einigen; weather beständig werden II. vt ❶ (decide) entscheiden; (deal with) regeln; (end) erledigen; argument beilegen; **that ~s that** damit hat

sich das erledigt ②(*colonize*) besiedeln
▶PHRASES: **to ~ a score [with sb]** [mit jdm] abrechnen

◆ **settle down** I. *vi* sich [häuslich] niederlassen; (*in chair*) es sich *dat* bequem machen; (*calm down*) sich beruhigen II. *vt* ❶ **to ~ oneself down** es sich *dat* bequem machen ②(*calm down*) beruhigen

◆ **settle for** *vi* ■ **to ~ for sth** mit etw *dat* zufrieden sein

◆ **settle in** *vi* sich einleben

◆ **settle on** *vi* ■ **to ~ on sth** sich für etw *akk* entscheiden; (*agree on*) sich auf etw *akk* einigen; *on name* sich für etw *akk* entscheiden

settled ['set·əld] *adj* ❶ *pred* ■ **to be ~** sich eingelebt haben; **to feel ~** sich heimisch fühlen ②(*calm*) ruhig; *lifestyle* geregelt

settlement ['set·əl·mənt] *n* ❶(*resolution*) Übereinkunft *f*; (*agreement*) Vereinbarung *f*; LAW Vergleich *m*; *of conflict* Lösung *f*; *of matter* Regelung *f*; *of strike* Schlichtung *f*; **they reached an out-of-court ~** sie einigten sich außergerichtlich ②(*colony*) Siedlung *f*; (*colonization*) Besiedlung *f*; (*people*) Ansiedlung *f*

settler ['set·lər] *n* Siedler(in) *m(f)*

'**setup** *n* Aufbau *m*; (*arrangement*) Einrichtung *f*; (*fam: deception*) abgekartetes Spiel

seven ['sev·ən] I. *adj* sieben; *see also* **eight** II. *n* Sieben *f*; *see also* **eight**

'**sevenfold** *adj* siebenfach

seventeen [,sev·ən·'tin] I. *adj* siebzehn; *see also* **eight** II. *n* Siebzehn *f*; *see also* **eight**

seventeenth [,sev·ən·'tinθ] I. *adj* siebzehnte(r, s) II. *n* ❶(*date, ordinal*) ■ **the ~** der Siebzehnte ②(*fraction*) Siebzehntel *nt*

seventh ['sev·ənθ] I. *adj* siebte(r, s) II. *n* ❶(*date, ordinal*) ■ **the ~** der Siebte ②(*fraction*) Siebtel *nt*

seventieth ['sev·ən·ti·əθ] I. *adj* siebzigste(r, s) II. *n* Siebzigste(r, s); (*fraction*) Siebzigstel *nt*

seventy ['sev·ən·ti] I. *adj* siebzig II. *n* Siebzig *f*

several ['sev·ər·əl] I. *adj* einige; (*various*) verschiedene II. *pron* einige

'**severance pay** *n* Abfindung *f*

severe [sə·'vɪr] *adj* schwer; *pain* heftig; *cutbacks* drastisch; *criticism* hart; (*strict*) streng; *storm* heftig; *cold* eisig; *frost* streng; (*violent*) gewaltig; *reprimand* scharf

severity [sə·'ver·ɪ·ti] *n* Schwere *f*; (*of situation*) Ernst *m*; (*harshness*) Härte *f*; (*strictness*) Strenge *f*; *of criticism* Schärfe *f*; (*extreme nature*) Rauheit *f*

Seville [sə·'vɪl] *n* Sevilla *nt*

sew <sewed, sewn *or* sewed> [soʊ] I. *vt* [an]nähen II. *vi* nähen

◆ **sew up** *vt* ❶ zunähen; *wound* nähen ②(*fam: end*) zum Abschluss bringen; **to be ~n up** unter Dach und Fach sein

sewage ['su·ɪdʒ] *n* Abwasser *nt*

sewer ['su·ər] *n* Abwasserkanal *m*

sewerage ['su·ər·ɪdʒ] *n* Kanalisation *f*

sewing ['soʊ·ɪŋ] *n* Nähen *nt*; (*things*) Näharbeit *f*

'**sewing basket** *n* Nähkorb *m*

'**sewing machine** *n* Nähmaschine *f*

sewn [soʊn] *pp of* **sew**

sex <*pl* -es> [seks] *n* ❶ Geschlecht *nt*; **the opposite ~** das andere Geschlecht ②(*intercourse*) Sex *m*; **to have ~** Sex haben; **to have ~ with sb** mit jdm schlafen

'**sex appeal** *n* Sexappeal *m*

'**sex education** *n* Sexualerziehung *f*

sexism ['sek·sɪz·əm] *n* Sexismus *m*

sexist ['sek·sɪst] I. *adj* sexistisch II. *n* Sexist(in) *m(f)*

'**sex life** *n* Sexualleben *nt*

'**sex symbol** *n* Sexsymbol *nt*

sextet [sek·'stet] *n* Sextett *nt*

sexual ['sek·ʃu·əl] *adj* geschlechtlich; (*erotic*) sexuell; **~ equality** Gleichheit *f* der Geschlechter

sexual discrimi'nation *n* Diskriminierung *f* aufgrund des Geschlechts

sexual 'harassment *n* sexuelle Belästigung

S

sexual 'intercourse n Geschlechtsverkehr m

sexuality [ˌsek·ʃu·ˈæl·ɪ·t̬i] n Sexualität f

sexy ['sek·si] adj (fam) sexy; (arousing) erregend; (exciting) heiß

Seychelles [seɪ·ˈʃelz] n ▪ the ~ die Seychellen pl

Sgt. n abbrev of **sergeant** Uffz.

shabby ['ʃæb·i] adj schäbig; clothing gammelig; (poorly dressed) ärmlich gekleidet; (unfair) schäbig; (mediocre) mittelmäßig; excuse fadenscheinig

shack [ʃæk] n Hütte f
◆ **shack up** vi (fam) ▪ to ~ up with sb mit jdm zusammenziehen; ▪ to be ~ed up with sb mit jdm zusammenleben

shackle ['ʃæk·əl] I. n ~s pl Fesseln f pl; (fig) Zwänge m pl II. vt [mit Ketten] fesseln; (fig) behindern

shade [ʃeɪd] I. n ❶ Schatten m; **patch of ~** schattiges Plätzchen; **in the ~** im Schatten ❷ (lampshade) [Lampen]schirm m ❸ (color) [Farb]ton m ❹ (fam: sunglasses) ▪ ~s pl Sonnenbrille f II. vt [vor der Sonne] schützen; eyes beschirmen ❷ (draw) schattieren

shading ['ʃeɪ·dɪŋ] n Schattierung f

shadow ['ʃæd·oʊ] I. n Schatten m; (under eye) Augenring m; (trace) Hauch m; **not a ~ of doubt** nicht der leiseste Zweifel II. vt verdunkeln; (follow) beschatten; player decken

'shadowboxing n Schattenboxen nt

shadowy ['ʃæ·doʊ·i] adj schattig; (dark) düster; (dubious) zweifelhaft; ~ **figure** schemenhafte Figur; (fig) rätselhaftes Wesen

shady ['ʃeɪ·di] adj schattig; (fam) fragwürdig; (dishonest) unehrlich

shaft [ʃæft] I. n (hole) Schacht m; (handle) Schaft m; (in engine) Welle f; ~ **of sunlight** Sonnenstrahl m II. vt (fam) betrügen

shaggy ['ʃæg·i] adj struppig; (unkempt) zottelig

Shah [ʃa] n (hist) Schah m

shake [ʃeɪk] I. n ❶ Schütteln nt; **she gave the box a ~** sie schüttelte die

Schachtel ❷ (fam: milkshake) Shake m
▶ PHRASES: **to be no great ~s at sth** bei etw dat nicht besonders gut sein II. vt <shook, shaken> schütteln; (fig) erschüttern; ▪ **well before using** vor Gebrauch gut schütteln; **the news has ~n the whole country** die Nachricht hat das ganze Land schwer getroffen; ▪ **to ~ oneself** sich schütteln; ▪ **to ~ sth over sth** etw über etw akk streuen III. vi <shook, shaken> beben; (with fear a.) zittern (**with** +dat)
▶ PHRASES: **to ~ like a leaf** wie Espenlaub zittern
◆ **shake off** vt abschütteln; (get rid of) überwinden; habit ablegen; illness besiegen; person loswerden; pursuer abschütteln
◆ **shake out** vt ausschütteln
◆ **shake up** vt (mix) mischen; (shock) aufwühlen; (alter) umkrempeln; (reorganize) umstellen

shaken ['ʃeɪ·kən] I. vt, vi pp of **shake** II. adj erschüttert

shaker ['ʃeɪ·kər] n Mixbecher m; **salt/pepper ~** Salz-/Pfefferstreuer m

shakily ['ʃeɪ·kɪ·li] adv wack[e]lig; speak zitt[e]rig; (uncertainly) unsicher

shaky ['ʃeɪ·ki] adj zittrig; ladder wack[e]lig; basis unsicher; economy instabil; **to feel a bit ~** (physically) noch etwas wack[e]lig auf den Beinen sein; (emotionally) beunruhigt sein; **to get off to a ~ start** mühsam in Gang kommen

shall [ʃæl] aux vb (liter) ❶ (future) ▪ **I ~ ...** ich werde ... ❷ (ought to) ▪ **I/ he ~ ...** ich/er soll ...

shallow ['ʃæl·oʊ] adj seicht; (fig a.) oberflächlich

sham [ʃæm] I. n ❶ usu sing Betrug m; **kein ~** (pretense) Verstellung f II. adj gefälscht; ~ **marriage** Scheinehe f III. vt <-mm-> vortäuschen IV. vi <-mm-> sich verstellen

shambles ['ʃæm·bəlz] n + sing vb (fam) **to be [in] a ~** sich in einem chaotischen Zustand befinden

shame [ʃeɪm] I. n Scham f; (disgrace)

Schande f; (a pity) Jammer m; **what a ~!** wie schade!; **~ on you!** (a. hum) schäm dich!; **to bring ~ on sb** Schande über jdn bringen; **it's a |great| ~ that ...** es ist |jammer|schade, dass ... II. vt ❶ beschämen ❷ (bring shame on) ■ **to ~ sb/sth** jdm/etw Schande machen

shamefaced ['ʃeɪm·'feɪst] adj verschämt

shameful ['ʃeɪm·fəl] adj schimpflich; defeat schmachvoll; (disgraceful) empörend; ■ **it's ~ that ...** es ist eine Schande, dass ...

shameless ['ʃeɪm·lɪs] adj schamlos

shampoo [ʃæm·'pu] I. n Shampoo nt II. vt shampoonieren

shamrock ['ʃæm·rak] n weißer Feldklee

shape [ʃeɪp] I. n ❶ Form f; BIOL Gestalt f; MATH Figur f; **in any ~ or form** (fig) in jeder Form; **all ~s and sizes** alle Formen und Größen; **to take ~** Form annehmen ❷ **to be in bad ~** things in schlechtem Zustand sein; people in schlechter Verfassung sein; SPORT nicht in Form sein; **to be in great ~** in Hochform sein ▶ PHRASES: **to whip sb/sth into →** jdn/etw auf Vordermann bringen fam II. vt [aus]formen; (influence) prägen; character formen; destiny gestalten

shapeless ['ʃeɪp·lɪs] adj formlos; ideas vage; (not shapely) unförmig

shapely ['ʃeɪp·li] adj wohlgeformt; figure schön; woman gut gebaut

shard [ʃard] n Scherbe f; of metal Splitter m

share [ʃer] I. n ❶ Anteil m; (in company a.) Aktie f; **one's ~ of the blame** seine Mitschuld; **the lion's ~ of sth** der Löwenanteil von etw dat; **to have had one's fair ~ of sth** (iron) etw reichlich abbekommen haben; **to have a ~ in sth** an etw dat teilhaben II. vi teilen; ■ **to ~ in sth** an etw dat teilhaben; (participate) in etw dat beteiligt sein III. vt ❶ teilen; **to ~ responsibility** Verantwortung gemeinsam tragen ❷ (have in common) gemeinsam haben; opinion

teilen; **to ~ an interest** ein gemeinsames Interesse haben ❸ (communicate) ■ **to ~ sth with sb** etw an jdn weitergeben; **to ~ one's thoughts with sb** jdm seine Gedanken anvertrauen

'**shareholder** n Aktionär(in) m(f)

shark <pl -s> [ʃark] n Hai[fisch] m; (pej fam) Hai m; **loan ~** Kredithai m

sharp [ʃarp] I. adj scharf; (pointed) spitz; features kantig; (stabbing) stechend; (sudden) plötzlich; (marked) drastisch; rise stark; (clear-cut) scharf, deutlich, klar; (perceptive) scharfsinnig; eyes scharf; (penetrating) schrill; **to bring sth into ~ focus** etw klar und deutlich herausstellen II. adv **at 7:30 ~** um Punkt 7.30 Uhr; **to turn ~ left/right** scharf links/rechts abbiegen

sharpen ['ʃar·pən] vt (a. fig) schärfen; pencil spitzen; knife schleifen; (intensify) verschärfen

sharpener ['ʃar·pən·ər] n pencil ~ Bleistiftspitzer m

sharp-'eyed adj scharfsichtig

'**sharpshooter** n Scharfschütze m

sharp-'tempered adj leicht erregbar

sharp-'tongued adj scharfzüngig

sharp-'witted adj scharfsinnig

shat [ʃæt] vi pt, pp of **shit**

shatter ['ʃæt̬·ər] I. vi zerspringen II. vt zertrümmern; health zerrütten; (fig) vernichten; calm zerstören; dreams zunichtemachen

shattered ['ʃæt̬·ərd] adj (fam) am Boden zerstört

shattering ['ʃæt̬·ər·ɪŋ] adj (fam: upsetting) erschütternd; (destructive) vernichtend

shatterproof ['ʃæt̬·ər·pruf] adj bruchsicher; windshield splitterfrei

shave [ʃeɪv] I. n Rasur f; **I need a ~** ich muss mich rasieren; **close ~** Glattrasur f; (fig) knappes Entkommen; **to have a close ~** gerade noch davonkommen II. vi <-d, -d or shaven> sich rasieren III. vt <-d, -d or shaven> rasieren

S

shaven ['ʃeɪ·vən] *adj* rasiert; *head* kahl geschoren

shaver ['ʃeɪ·vər] *n* Rasierapparat *m*

'shaving brush *n* Rasierpinsel *m*

'shaving cream *n* Rasiercreme *f*

'shaving foam *n* Rasierschaum *m*

shawl [ʃɔl] *n* Schultertuch *nt*

she [ʃi] I. *pron sie* I. *pron (country)* es; *(ship)* sie II. *n usu sing* ■a ~ eine Sie; *(animal)* ein Weibchen *nt*

shear <-ed, -ed *or* shorn> [ʃɪr] *vt* scheren

shears [ʃɪrz] *npl* [große] Schere

shed¹ <-dd-, shed, shed> [ʃed] I. *vt* ablegen; *leaves* abwerfen; *hair* verlieren; *blood, tears* vergießen; *light* verbreiten; **to ~ a few pounds** ein paar Kilo abnehmen; **to ~ one's skin** sich häuten II. *vi* sich häuten; *cats* haaren

shed² [ʃed] *n* Schuppen *m;* **garden ~** Gartenhäuschen *nt*

sheep <*pl* -> [ʃip] *n* Schaf *nt;* **flock of ~** Schafherde *f*

'sheepdog *n* Schäferhund *m*

sheepish ['ʃi·pɪʃ] *adj* unbeholfen; *smile* verlegen

'sheepskin *n* Schaffell *nt*

sheer [ʃɪr] *adj* ❶ ~ **bliss** eine wahre Wonne; ~ **nonsense** blanker Unsinn ❷ *cliff* steil

sheet [ʃit] *n Laken nt; of paper* Blatt *nt; of metal* Platte *f*

'sheet metal *n* Blech *nt*

'sheet music *n* Noten *pl*

sheik(h) [ʃik] *n* Scheich *m*

shelf <*pl* shelves> [ʃelf] *n* [Regal]brett *nt; (set of shelves)* Regal *nt*

'shelf life *n* Haltbarkeit *f*

shell [ʃel] I. *n* ❶ Schale *f; of tortoise* Panzer *m; of pea* Hülse *f; (on beach)* Muschel *f* ❷ *(artillery)* Granate *f; (cartridge)* Patrone *f* ►PHRASES: **to come out of one's ~** aus sich *dat* herausgehen II. *vt* schälen; *nut* knacken; *pea* enthülsen; *(bombard)* [mit Granaten] bombardieren

◆**shell out** *(fam)* I. *vt* blechen II. *vi* ■**to ~ out for sb/sth** für jdn/etw bezahlen

'shellfish <*pl* -> *n* Schalentier *nt*

shelling ['ʃəl·ɪŋ] *n* Bombardierung *f*

'shell-shocked *adj (fam)* völlig geschockt

shelter ['ʃel·tər] I. *n* ❶ Schutz *m; (structure)* Unterstand *m; (to sit in)* Häuschen *nt; (for the needy)* Heim *nt* II. *vi* Schutz suchen III. *vt* schützen

sheltered ['ʃel·tərd] *adj* geschützt; *childhood* [über]behütet

shepherd ['ʃep·ərd] I. *n* Schäfer(in) *m(f)* II. *vt* hüten; **to ~ sb toward the door** jdn zur Tür führen

sherbet ['ʃɜr·bət], **sherbert** ['ʃɜr·bɜrt] *n* Fruchteis *nt*

sheriff ['ʃer·ɪf] *n* Sheriff *m*

sherry ['ʃer·i] *n* Sherry *m*

shield [ʃild] I. *n* [Schutz]schild *m; (with coat of arms)* [Wappen]schild *m o nt* II. *vt* beschützen; *eyes* schützen

shift [ʃɪft] I. *vt* [weg]bewegen; *furniture* verschieben; *blame* abwälzen; *emphasis* verlagern; **to ~ gears** schalten II. *vi* sich bewegen; *(change position)* sich bewegen; *[o seine]* Position verändern; **it won't ~** es lässt sich nicht bewegen; **to ~ into reverse** den Rückwärtsgang einlegen III. *n* ❶ Wechsel *m;* **a ~ in the balance of power** eine Verlagerung im Gleichgewicht der Kräfte ❷ *(work, people)* Schicht *f*

◆**shift down** *vi* herunterschalten

◆**shift up** *vi* hochschalten

'shift key *n* COMPUT Shifttaste *f*

'shift work *n* Schichtarbeit *f*

'shift worker *n* Schichtarbeiter(in) *m(f)*

shifty ['ʃɪf·ti] *adj* hinterhältig; **to look ~** verdächtig aussehen

Shiite ['ʃi·aɪt] I. *n* Schiit(in) *m(f)* II. *adj* schiitisch

shimmer ['ʃɪm·ər] I. *vi* schimmern II. *n usu sing* Schimmer *m*

shin [ʃɪn] *n* Schienbein *nt*

shindig ['ʃɪn·dɪg] *n (fam)* [wilde] Fete *f*

shine [ʃaɪn] I. *n* Glanz *m* ►PHRASES: **[come] rain or ~** komme, was da wolle II. *vi* <shone *or* shined, shone *or* shined> scheinen; *stars* leuchten; *metal* glänzen; *eyes* strahlen; *(excel)*

glänzen **III.** *vt* <shone *or* shined, shone *or* shined> **❶** to ~ a light at sb/ sth jdn/etw anstrahlen **❷** (*polish*) polieren
◆**shine out** *vi* [auf]leuchten; (*excel*) herausragen

shiner ['ʃaɪ·nər] *n* (*fam*) Veilchen *nt*

shining ['ʃaɪ·nɪŋ] *adj* glänzend; *eyes* strahlend; (*outstanding*) hervorragend; *example* leuchtend

shiny ['ʃaɪ·ni] *adj* glänzend; *metal* [spiegel]blank

ship [ʃɪp] **I.** *n* Schiff *nt*; ■by ~ mit dem Schiff; (*goods*) per Schiff **II.** *vt* <-pp-> verschiffen; (*transport*) transportieren
◆**ship off** *vt* verschiffen; *goods* per Schiff verschicken; (*fam: send away*) wegschicken
◆**ship out I.** *vt* per Schiff senden **II.** *vi* (*fam*) sich verziehen

'**shipbuilder** *n* Werft *f*

'**shipbuilding** *n* Schiffbau *m*

'**shipload** *n* Schiffsladung *f*

shipment ['ʃɪp·mənt] *n* Sendung *f*; (*dispatching*) Transport *m*

'**shipowner** *n* (*inland*) Schiffseigner(in) *m(f)*; (*ocean*) Reeder(in) *m(f)*

shipper ['ʃɪp·ər] *n* Spediteur(in) *m(f)*; (*business a.*) Spedition *f*

shipping ['ʃɪp·ɪŋ] *n* **❶** Transport *m*; (*by mail*) Versand *m*; (*by ship*) Verschiffung *f* **❷** (*costs*) Transportkosten *pl*; (*by mail*) Postversand *m*; (*by sea*) Versand *m* auf dem Seeweg **❸** (*ships*) Schiffe *pl* [eines Landes]

'**shipping lane** *n* Schifffahrtsweg *m*

'**shipshape** *adj pred* (*fam*) aufgeräumt; **to make sth ~** etw aufräumen

'**shipwreck I.** *n* Schiffbruch *m*; (*remains*) [Schiffs]wrack *nt* **II.** *vt usu passive* ■to be ~ed Schiffbruch erleiden; (*fail*) scheitern

'**shipyard** *n* [Schiffs]werft *f*

shirk [ʃɜrk] *vt* meiden; **to ~ one's responsibilities** sich seiner Verantwortung entziehen

shirt [ʃɜrt] *n* Hemd *nt* ▶PHRASES: **keep your ~ on!** (*fam*) reg dich ab!

'**shirtsleeve** *n usu pl* Hemdsärmel *m*; **in ~s** in Hemdsärmeln

shit [ʃɪt] (*vulg*) **I.** *n* Scheiße *f* derb; **Jackie doesn't take any ~ from anyone** Jackie lässt sich von niemandem was gefallen *fam* ▶PHRASES: **to beat the ~ out of sb** aus jdm Hackfleisch machen *fam*; **the ~ hits the fan** es gibt Ärger; **to not know ~ about sb/sth** keinen blassen Schimmer von jdm/etw haben **II.** *interj* ~! Scheiße! *derb* **III.** *vi* <-tt-, shit *or* shitted *or* shat, shit *or* shitted *or* shat> scheißen *derb* **IV.** *vt* <-tt-, shit *or* shitted *or* shat, shit *or* shitted *or* shat> **to ~ one's pants** sich *dat* [vor Angst] in die Hosen machen *fam*

shitty ['ʃɪt·i] *adj* (*vulg*) beschissen *derb*

shiver ['ʃɪv·ər] **I.** *n* Schauder *m*; **to give sb the ~s** (*fam*) jdn das Fürchten lehren **II.** *vi* zittern; **to ~ with cold** frösteln

shoal [ʃoʊl] *n* Schwarm *m*

shock [ʃak] **I.** *n* Schock *m*; (*electric*) [elektrischer] Schlag; (*health condition*) Schock[zustand] *m*; **prepare yourself for a ~** mach dich auf etwas Schlimmes gefasst; **a ~ to the system** eine schwierige Umstellung; **to be in [a state of] ~** unter Schock stehen **II.** *vt* schockieren; (*deeply*) erschüttern

'**shock absorber** *n* Stoßdämpfer *m*

shocker ['ʃak·ər] *n* (*fam*) Schocker *m*; **the headline was a deliberate ~** die Schlagzeile sollte schockieren

shocking ['ʃak·ɪŋ] *adj* schockierend; *crime* abscheulich; (*surprising*) völlig überraschend

'**shockproof** *adj* bruchsicher

'**shock therapy, 'shock treatment** *n* Schocktherapie *f*

'**shock wave** *n* Druckwelle *f*; **the news sent ~s through the financial world** die Nachricht erschütterte die Finanzwelt

shoddy ['ʃad·i] *adj* schlampig [gearbeitet] *fam*; (*run down*) schäbig; *goods* minderwertig; (*reprehensible*) schäbig

shoe [ʃu] **I.** *n* Schuh *m*; (*horseshoe*)

S

Hufeisen *nt;* **a pair of** ~s ein Paar *nt* Schuhe ▶PHRASES: **to put oneself in sb's** ~**s** sich in jds Lage versetzen; **if I were in your** ~**s** (*fam*) an deiner Stelle II. *vt* <shod *or* shoed, shod *or* shodden *or* shoed> *horse* beschlagen

'**shoehorn** *n* Schuhlöffel *m*

'**shoelace** *n usu pl* Schnürsenkel *m*

'**shoemaker** *n* Schuster(in) *m(f)*

'**shoe polish** *n* Schuhcreme *f*

'**shoe size** *n* Schuhgröße *f*

'**shoestring** *n usu pl* Schnürsenkel *m* ▶PHRASES: **to do sth on a** ~ (*fam*) etw mit wenig Geld tun

shone [ʃoʊn] *pt, pp of* **shine**

shoo [ʃu] (*fam*) I. *interj* husch [husch]! II. *vt* wegscheuchen

shook [ʃʊk] *n pt of* **shake**

shoot [ʃut] I. *n* (*on plant*) Trieb *m;* (*hunt*) Jagd *f;* PHOT Aufnahmen *pl* II. *vi* <shot, shot> ❶ schießen; **to** ~ **to kill** mit Tötungsabsicht schießen ❷ + *adv/ prep* ■**to** ~ **past** vorbeischießen ❸ (*film*) filmen; (*take photos*) fotografieren ❹ (*target*) ■**to** ~ **for sth** etw anstreben III. *vt* <shot, shot> ❶ ■**to** ~ **sth** *gun* mit etw *dat* schießen; *arrow* etw abschießen; *bullet* etw abfeuern ❷ (*hit*) anschießen; (*dead*) erschießen; **to be shot in the leg** ins Bein getroffen werden ❸ *movie* drehen; *photo* machen ❹ **to** ~ **questions at sb** jdn mit Fragen bombardieren ❺ *goal* schießen

◆ **shoot down** *vt* abschießen; (*kill*) erschießen; (*fam*) *accusation* niedermachen

◆ **shoot off** I. *vi* schnell losfahren; *people* eilig aufbrechen II. *vt* abschießen ▶PHRASES: **to** ~ **one's mouth off** (*sl*) sich *dat* das Maul zerreißen

◆ **shoot out** I. *vi* plötzlich hervorschießen; *water* herausschießen; *flames* hervorbrechen II. *vt* ❶ **he shot out a hand** er streckte blitzschnell die Hand aus ❷ ■**to** ~ **it out** etw [mit Schusswaffen] austragen

◆ **shoot up** I. *vi* ❶ *price* schnell ansteigen; *skyscraper* in die Höhe schießen ❷ (*fam*) *child* schnell wachsen ❸ (*sl*)

sich *dat* einen Schuss verpassen *sl* II. *vt* sich *dat* spritzen

shooting [ˈʃu·tɪŋ] *n* ❶ Schießerei *f;* (*killing*) Erschießung *f;* (*sport*) Jagen *nt* ❷ FILM Drehen *nt*

'**shooting range** *n* Schießstand *m*

shooting '**star** *n* Sternschnuppe *f;* (*person*) Shootingstar *m*

'**shootout** *n* Schießerei *f*

shop [ʃap] I. *n* Laden *m;* (*garage*) Werkstatt *f;* **to set up** ~ ein Geschäft eröffnen; (*start out in business*) ein Unternehmen eröffnen II. *vi* <-pp-> einkaufen

'**shopkeeper** *n* Ladeninhaber(in) *m(f)*

'**shoplifter** *n* Ladendieb(in) *m(f)*

'**shoplifting** *n* Ladendiebstahl *m*

shopper [ˈʃap·ər] *n* Käufer(in) *m(f)*

shopping [ˈʃap·ɪŋ] *n* Einkaufen *nt;* **to go** ~ einkaufen gehen

'**shopping bag** *n* Einkaufstasche *f*

'**shopping basket** *n* Einkaufskorb *m*

'**shopping cart** *n* Einkaufswagen *m*

'**shopping center** *n* Einkaufszentrum *nt*

'**shopping list** *n* Einkaufsliste *f*

'**shopping mall** *n* überdachtes Einkaufszentrum

shore [ʃɔr] *n* Küste *f;* (*bank*) Ufer *nt;* (*beach*) Strand *m;* **on** ~ an Land

'**shoreline** *n* Küstenlinie *f*

shorn [ʃɔrn] *pp of* **shear**

short [ʃɔrt] I. *adj* ❶ kurz; *person* klein; **at** ~ **range** aus kurzer Entfernung; **in the** ~ **term** kurzfristig; **Bob's** ~ **for Robert** Bob ist die Kurzform von Robert ❷ **we're still one person** ~ uns fehlt noch eine Person; **to be in** ~ **supply** schwer zu beschaffen sein; ■**sb is** ~ **of sth** jdm mangelt es an etw *dat;* **we're a bit** ~ **of coffee** wir haben nur noch wenig Kaffee; **to be** ~ [**of cash**] knapp bei Kasse sein; **to be** ~ **of breath** außer Atem sein ▶PHRASES: **to have a** ~ **fuse** schnell wütend werden; **to draw the** ~ **straw** den Kürzeren ziehen II. *adv* **to cut sth** ~ etw abkürzen; **to fall** ~ **of expectations** den Erwartungen nicht entsprechen ▶PHRASES: **in** ~ kurz gesagt

shortage [ˈʃɔr·tɪdʒ] *n* Mangel *m kein pl*

'**shortbread** *n* Shortbread *nt* (*Butterge-bäck*)

short'change *vt* ■**to ~ sb** jdm zu wenig Wechselgeld herausgeben

short 'circuit *n* Kurzschluss *m*

short-'circuit **I.** *vt* kurzschließen; (*avoid*) abkürzen **II.** *vi* einen Kurzschluss haben

'**shortcoming** *n usu pl* Mangel *m;* *of person* Fehler *m;* *of system* Unzulänglichkeit *f*

'**shortcut** *n* Abkürzung *f*

shorten ['ʃɔr·tən] **I.** *vt* kürzen; *name* abkürzen **II.** *vi* kürzer werden

'**shortfall** *n* Mangel *m kein pl;* (*deficit*) Defizit *nt*

'**shorthand** *n* Kurzschrift *f*

short-'handed *adj* unterbesetzt; ■**to be ~** zu wenig Personal haben

'**short list** *n* **to be on the ~** in der engeren Wahl sein

'**short-list** *vt* in die engere Wahl ziehen

short-lived [-'lɪvd] *adj* kurzlebig

shortly ['ʃɔrt·li] *adv* in Kürze; **~ afterwards** kurz danach

'**short-range** *adj* Kurzstrecken-; *forecast* kurzfristig

shorts [ʃɔrts] *n pl* kurze Hose; (*underpants*) Unterhose *f*

short'sighted *adj* kurzsichtig *a. fig*

'**short-term** *adj* kurzfristig

shot[1] [ʃat] *n* ❶ Schuss *m* ❷ (*in basketball*) Wurf *m;* (*in tennis, golf*) Schlag *m;* (*in soccer, hockey*) Schuss *m* ❸ (*photograph*) Aufnahme *f;* FILM Einstellung *f* ❹ (*fam: injection*) Spritze *f;* (*fig*) Schuss *m* ❺ (*fam: attempt*) Gelegenheit *f;* **to give it a ~** es mal versuchen *fam* ❻ (*of alcohol*) Schuss *m* ❼ (*remark*) **to take a ~ at sb** jdn runtermachen; (*attack verbally*) über jdn herfallen ▶PHRASES: **like a ~** (*fam*) wie der Blitz

shot[2] [ʃat] **I.** *vt, vi pt, pp of* **shoot II.** *adj* (*fam*) ausgeleiert *fam;* **my nerves are ~** ich bin mit meinen Nerven am Ende

'**shotgun** *n* Schrotflinte *f* ▶PHRASES: **to ride ~** (*fam*) auf dem Beifahrersitz mitfahren (*im Auto/auf dem Motorrad*)

'**shot put** *n* SPORT ■**the ~** Kugelstoßen *nt kein pl*

'**shot putter** *n* SPORT Kugelstoßer(in) *m(f)*

should [ʃʊd] *aux vb* **you ~ be ashamed of yourselves** ihr solltet euch [was] schämen; **~ I apologize to him?** soll[te] ich mich bei ihm entschuldigen?; **there ~n't be any problems** es dürfte eigentlich keine Probleme geben; **I ~ have known that ...** ich hätte es eigentlich wissen müssen, dass ...; **why ~ I?** warum sollte ich?; **where's Stuart? — how ~ I know?** wo ist Stuart? – woher soll[te] ich das wissen?

shoulder ['ʃoʊl·dər] **I.** *n* Schulter *f;* *of road* Bankett *nt;* **to shrug one's ~s** mit den Achseln zucken **II.** *vt* ❶ (*accept*) auf sich *akk* nehmen; *blame* übernehmen ❷ (*push*) **to ~ one's way somewhere** sich irgendwohin drängen

'**shoulder bag** *n* Umhängetasche *f*

'**shoulder blade** *n* Schulterblatt *nt*

'**shoulder pad** *n* Schulterpolster *nt*

shout [ʃaʊt] **I.** *n* Ruf *m;* **a ~ of laughter** lautes Gelächter *nt* **II.** *vi* schreien; ■**to ~ at sb** jdn anschreien; ■**to ~ to sb** jdm zurufen **III.** *vt* rufen; ■**to ~ sth at sb** jdm etw zurufen; **to ~ abuse at sb** jdn lautstark beschimpfen
    ◆ **shout down** *vt* niederschreien *fam*
    ◆ **shout out** *vt* [aus]rufen

shouting ['ʃaʊ·tɪŋ] **I.** *n* Schreien *nt* **II.** *adj* ▶PHRASES: **within ~ distance** in Rufweite; (*fig*) nahe [an] + *dat*

shove [ʃʌv] **I.** *n* Ruck *m;* **to give sth a ~** etw [weg]rücken **II.** *vt* schieben; ■**to ~ sb around** jdn herumstoßen *fam;* **to ~ sth into a bag** etw in eine Tasche stecken **III.** *vi* drängen
    ◆ **shove off** *vi* (*fam*) abhauen *sl*

shovel ['ʃʌv·əl] **I.** *n* Schaufel *f;* *of bulldozer* Baggerschaufel *f;* **a ~ of snow** eine Schaufel [voll] Schnee **II.** *vt, vi* <-l-> schaufeln *a. fig*

show [ʃoʊ] **I.** *n* ❶ Demonstration *f;* **~ of solidarity** Solidaritätsbekundung *f geh*

S

➋ (*display*) Schau *f;* **just for ~** nur der Schau wegen **➌** (*event*) Ausstellung *f;* **slide ~** Diavortrag *m;* ■ **to be on ~** ausgestellt sein **➍** (*entertainment*) Show *f;* (*on TV a.*) Unterhaltungssendung *f;* (*at theater*) Vorstellung *f* ▸PHRASES: **let's get this ~ on the road** (*fam*) lasst uns die Sache [endlich] in Angriff nehmen; **the ~ must go on** (*saying*) die Show muss weitergehen **II.** *vt* <showed, shown *or* showed> **➊** *film* zeigen; (*exhibit*) ausstellen; (*perform*) vorführen; *passport* vorzeigen; **to ~ sb respect** jdm Respekt erweisen **➋** (*reveal*) zeigen; **he started to ~ his age** man konnte ihm langsam sein Alter ansehen; **to ~ common sense** gesunden Menschenverstand beweisen **➌** (*explain*) zeigen; **to ~ sb the way** jdm den Weg zeigen **➍** (*record*) anzeigen; *statistics* [auf]zeigen; *profit* aufweisen **➎** (*prove*) beweisen; ■ **to ~** [*sb*] **how ...** [jdm] zeigen, wie ...; ■ **to ~ oneself** [to be] sth sich als etw erweisen ▸PHRASES: **to ~ one's <u>true</u> colors** Farbe bekennen; **that <u>will</u> ~ you!** (*fam*) das wird dir eine Lehre sein **III.** *vi* <showed, shown *or* showed> **➊** (*be visible*) zu sehen sein; **to let sth ~** sich *dat* etw anmerken lassen **➋** *film* laufen *fam;* **now ~ing at a theater near you!** jetzt in Ihrem Kino!

◆ **show around** *vt* her-/hineinführen
◆ **show in** *vt* her-/hineinführen
◆ **show off I.** *vt* ■ **to ~ off** ⟲ **sb/sth** mit jdm/etw angeben **II.** *vi* angeben
◆ **show through** *vi* durchschimmern
◆ **show up I.** *vi* **➊** (*appear*) sich zeigen; **the drug does not ~ up in blood tests** das Medikament ist in Blutproben nicht nachweisbar **➋** (*fam: arrive*) auftauchen **II.** *vt* **➊** (*expose*) zeigen **➋** (*embarrass*) bloßstellen

show biz ['ʃoʊ·bɪz] *n* (*fam*) *short for* **show business** Showbiz *nt*
'show business *n* Showbusiness *nt*
'showcase *n* Schaukasten *m;* (*opportunity*) Schaufenster *nt*

shower ['ʃaʊ·ər] **I.** *n* Schauer *m;* (*for bathing*) Dusche *f;* **to take a ~** duschen **II.** *vt* bespritzen; **to ~ sb with compliments** jdn mit Komplimenten überhäufen **III.** *vi* duschen
'shower cap *n* Duschhaube *f*
showing ['ʃoʊ·ɪŋ] *n usu sing* Ausstellung *f;* (*broadcasting*) Übertragung *f;* (*performance*) Vorstellung *f*
'show jumping *n* Springreiten *nt*
'showman *n* Showman *m*
shown [ʃoʊn] *vt, vi pp of* **show**
'showoff *n* Angeber(in) *m(f)*
'showroom *n* Ausstellungsraum *m*
'showtime *n* Aufführung[szeit] *f* ▸PHRASES: **it's ~!** es geht los!
showy ['ʃoʊ·i] *adj* auffällig
shrank [ʃræŋk] *vt, vi pt of* **shrink**
shrapnel ['ʃræp·nəl] *n* Granatsplitter *pl*
shred [ʃred] **I.** *n* Streifen *m;* of hope Funke *m;* **there isn't a ~ of evidence** es gibt nicht den geringsten Beweis; **to be in ~s** zerfetzt sein; **to rip sth to ~s** etw in Fetzen reißen **II.** *vt* <-dd-> zerkleinern; *vegetables* hacken
shredder ['ʃred·ər] *n* Reißwolf *m;* (*paper*) Shredder *m*
shrew [ʃru] *n* Spitzmaus *f*
shrewd [ʃrud] *adj* schlau; *eye* scharf; *move* geschickt
shriek [ʃrik] **I.** *n* [schriller, kurzer] Schrei *m* **II.** *vi* kreischen; (*with laughter*) brüllen; (*with pain*) [auf]schreien **III.** *vt* [auf]schreien
shrill [ʃrɪl] *adj* schrill
shrimp <*pl* -s> [ʃrɪmp] *n* Garnele *f;* (*pej fam: person*) Zwerg *m* hum
shrine [ʃraɪn] *n* Heiligtum *nt;* (*for relics*) Schrein *m a. fig;* (*tomb*) Grabmal *nt;* (*for worship*) Pilgerstätte *f*
shrink [ʃrɪŋk] **I.** *vi* <shrank *or* shrunk, shrunk *or* shrunken> **➊** schrumpfen; *sweater* eingehen **➋** ■ **to ~ away** zurückweichen **➌** ■ **to ~ from** [doing] sth sich vor etw *dat* drücken *fam* **II.** *vt* <shrank *or* shrunk, shrunk *or* shrunken> schrumpfen lassen **III.** *n* (*fam*) Psychiater(in) *m(f)*
'shrink-wrap I. *n* Plastikfolie *f* **II.** *vt* in

Frischhaltefolie einpacken; *book* einschweißen

shrivel <-l-> ['ʃrɪv·əl] *vi* [zusammen]schrumpfen; *fruit* schrumpeln; *plants* welken; *skin* faltig werden; *profits* schwinden

◆ **shrivel up** *vi* zusammenschrumpfen; *fruit* schrumpeln

Shrove Tuesday [,ʃroʊv·'tuz·deɪ] *n no art* Fastnachtsdienstag *m*

shrub [ʃrʌb] *n* Strauch *m*

shrubbery ['ʃrʌb·ə·ri] *n* Sträucher *pl*; *(area)* Gebüsch *nt*

shrug [ʃrʌg] I. *n* Achselzucken *nt* II. *vi* <-gg-> die Achseln zucken III. *vt* <-gg-> **to ~ one's shoulders** die Achseln zucken

shrunk [ʃrʌŋk] *vt, vi pt, pp of* **shrink**

shrunken ['ʃrʌŋ·kən] I. *adj* geschrumpft II. *vt, vi pp of* **shrink**

shudder ['ʃʌd·ər] I. *vi* zittern; *ground* beben; **I ~ to think what …** mir graut vor dem Gedanken, was …; **to ~ to a halt** mit einem Rucken zum Stehen kommen II. *n* Schaudern *nt*; **to send a ~ through sb** jdn erschaudern lassen *geh*

shuffle ['ʃʌf·əl] I. *n* Mischen *nt* (*von Karten*); *(rearrangement)* Neuordnung *f*; *of feet* Schlurfen *nt*; **to give the cards a ~** die Karten mischen II. *vt* mischen; *feet* schlurfen; ▪ **to ~ sth around** etw hin- und herschieben III. *vi* Karten mischen; *(with feet)* schlurfen

shun <-nn-> [ʃʌn] *vt* meiden; ▪ **to ~ sb** jdm aus dem Weg gehen

shush [ʃʊʃ] I. *interj* pst! II. *vt* (*fam*) ▪ **to ~ sb** jdm sagen, dass er/sie still sein soll

shut [ʃʌt] I. *adj* geschlossen; *curtains* zugezogen; **to slam a door ~** eine Tür zuschlagen II. *vt* <-tt-, shut, shut> (*close*) schließen; *book* zuklappen; *shop* schließen ▪ PHRASES: ~ **your mouth!** Klappe! *sl* III. *vi* <-tt-, shut, shut> schließen

◆ **shut away** *vt* einsperren

◆ **shut down** I. *vt* abstellen; *factory* stilllegen; *computer* herunterfahren II. *vi* zumachen

◆ **shut in** *vt* einsperren

◆ **shut off** I. *vt* abstellen; *computer* herunterfahren; **to ~ oneself off** sich zurückziehen II. *vi* sich [automatisch] ausschalten

◆ **shut out** *vt* ausschließen; *thoughts* verdrängen; *light* abschirmen

◆ **shut up** I. *vt* ❶ schließen; **to ~ up shop** das Geschäft schließen; (*stop business*) seine Tätigkeit einstellen ❷ (*fam: silence*) zum Schweigen bringen II. *vi* (*fam*) den Mund halten

'**shutdown** *n* Schließung *f*

'**shuteye** *n* (*fam*) Nickerchen *nt*

shutter ['ʃʌt·ər] *n* Fensterladen *m*; PHOT [Kamera]verschluss *m*

shuttle ['ʃʌt·əl] *n* (*train*) Pendelzug *m*; (*plane*) Pendelmaschine *f*; **space ~** Raumfähre *f*

shuttle bus *n* [kostenloser] Zubringer[bus]

shuttlecock ['ʃʌt·əl·kak] *n* Federball *m*

shy [ʃaɪ] *adj* schüchtern; *smile* scheu

◆ **shy away from** *vt* ▪ **to ~ away from [doing] sth** vor etw *dat* zurückschrecken

shyness ['ʃaɪ·nɪs] *n* Schüchternheit *f*

Siamese [,saɪ·ə·'miz] I. *n* <*pl* -> Siamese, Siamesin *m, f*; (*cat*) Siamkatze *f*; (*language*) Siamesisch *nt* II. *adj* siamesisch

Siamese 'twins *npl* siamesische Zwillinge

Sicilian [sɪ·'sɪl·jən] I. *n* Sizilianer(in) *m(f)* II. *adj* sizilianisch

Sicily ['sɪs·ɪ·li] *n* Sizilien *nt*

sick [sɪk] I. *adj* ❶ krank; (*mentally*) geisteskrank; *machine, engine* angeschlagen; **to call in ~** sich krankmelden ❷ *pred* **to be ~** (*vomit*) sich erbrechen; **to feel ~** sich schlecht fühlen ❸ *pred* (*fam*) **to be ~ and tired of sth** etw [gründlich] satthaben; **to be ~ of sb/ sth** von jdm/etw die Nase voll haben ❹ (*fam: cruel*) geschmacklos; *person* pervers; *mind* abartig ▪ PHRASES: **to be worried ~** (*fam*) krank vor Sorge sein II. *n* ▪ **the ~** *pl* die Kranken *pl*

sicken ['sɪk·ən] I. *vi* erkranken II. *vt*

S

(*upset*) krank machen *fam;* (*disgust*) anekeln

sickening ['sɪk·ən·ɪŋ] *adj* entsetzlich; *smell* widerlich; (*annoying*) [äußerst] ärgerlich

sickle ['sɪk·əl] *n* Sichel *f*

'sick leave *n* MED **to be on ~** krankgeschrieben sein

sickly ['sɪk·li] *adj* kränklich; *complexion* blass

sickness <*pl* -es> ['sɪk·nɪs] *n* Krankheit *f;* (*nausea*) Übelkeit *f*

'sick pay *n* Krankengeld *nt*

side [saɪd] I. *n* ❶ Seite *f; of hill* Hang *m; of house* [Seiten]wand *f; of plate, field* Rand *m; of river* [Fluss]ufer *nt; of road* [Straßen]rand *m;* **this ~ up!** oben!; **on all ~s** auf allen Seiten; **to stay at sb's ~** jdm zur Seite stehen; ■ **at the ~ of sth** neben etw *dat* ❷ (*half*) *of bed* Hälfte *f; of town, road* Seite *f* ❸ **to take sb to one ~** jdn auf die Seite nehmen ❹ (*party*) Partei *f;* (*team a.*) Mannschaft *f;* **to change ~s** sich auf die andere Seite schlagen; **to take ~s** Partei ergreifen ❺ **I've listened to your ~ of the story** ich habe jetzt deine Version der Geschichte gehört ▶PHRASES: **the other ~ of the coin** die Kehrseite der Medaille; **to be on the large/small ~** zu groß/klein sein II. *adj* ~ **job** Nebenbeschäftigung *f* III. *vi* ■ **to ~ against sb** sich gegen jdn stellen; ■ **to ~ with sb** zu jdm halten

'sideburns *npl* Koteletten *pl*

'sidecar *n* AUTO Seitenwagen *m*

'side dish *n* FOOD Beilage *f*

'side effect *n* Nebenwirkung *f*

'sideshow *n* Nebenaufführung *f;* (*exhibition*) Sonderausstellung *f*

'sidestep I. *vt* <-pp-> ■ **to ~ sb/sth** jdm/etw ausweichen II. *vi* <-pp-> ausweichen III. *n* Schritt *m* zur Seite; (*fig*) Ausweichmanöver *nt*

'side street *n* Seitenstraße *f*

'sidetrack *vt* ablenken

'sidewalk *n* Bürgersteig *m*

sideways ['saɪd·weɪz] I. *adv* seitwärts;

(*awry*) schief II. *adj* seitlich; *look* von der Seite

siding ['saɪ·dɪŋ] *n* Rangiergleis *nt*

siege [siːdʒ] *n* MIL Belagerung *f;* **to lay ~ to sth** etw belagern

sieve [sɪv] I. *n* Sieb *nt* ▶PHRASES: **to have a mind like a ~** (*fam*) ein Gedächtnis wie ein Sieb haben II. *vt* sieben

sift [sɪft] *vt* ❶ sieben; ~ **some sugar over the cake** bestäuben Sie den Kuchen mit Zucker ❷ (*examine*) durchsieben; *evidence* [gründlich] durchgehen

sigh [saɪ] I. *n* Seufzer *m;* **to give a ~** einen Seufzer ausstoßen II. *vi* seufzen; *wind* säuseln; **to ~ with relief** vor Erleichterung [auf]seufzen

sight [saɪt] *n* ❶ [**sense of**] ~ Sehvermögen *nt* ❷ (*access*) Sicht *f;* (*range a.*) Sichtweite *f;* **get out of my ~!** (*fam*) geh mir aus den Augen!; **to be in/out of ~** in/außer Sichtweite sein; **to keep out of ~** sich nicht sehen lassen ❸ (*act*) Anblick *m; love at first ~* Liebe auf den ersten Blick; **to know sb by ~** jdn vom Sehen [her] kennen ❹ (*attractions*) ■ **~s** *pl* Sehenswürdigkeiten *pl* ❺ (*on gun*) Visier *nt* ▶PHRASES: **out of ~, out of mind** (*prov*) aus den Augen, aus dem Sinn *prov;* **to set one's ~s on sth** sich *dat* etw zum Ziel machen

'sightseeing *n* Besichtigungen *pl;* **to go ~** Sehenswürdigkeiten besichtigen

sightseer ['saɪt·siː·ər] *n* Tourist(in) *m(f)*

sign [saɪn] I. *n* ❶ Zeichen *nt;* **to make the ~ of the cross** sich bekreuzigen ❷ (*notice*) [Straßen]schild *nt;* (*signboard*) Schild *nt;* **traffic ~** Verkehrsschild *nt* ❸ (*symbol*) Zeichen *nt;* (*of zodiac*) Sternzeichen *nt* ❹ (*indication*) [An]zeichen *nt;* (*trace*) Spur *f;* ~ **of life** Lebenszeichen *nt* II. *vt letter* unterschreiben; *contract* unterzeichnen; *book* signieren III. *vi* unterschreiben; **to ~ for a delivery** eine Lieferung gegenzeichnen

◆ **sign in** I. *vi* sich eintragen II. *vt* eintragen

◆ **sign off** *vi* (*end letter*) zum Schluss kommen; (*end work*) Schluss machen

◆**sign on** I. *vi* sich verpflichten; (*for class*) sich einschreiben II. *vt* verpflichten

◆**sign out** *vt books* ausleihen

◆**sign over** *vt* übertragen

◆**sign up** *vi* sich verpflichten; (*for class*) sich einschreiben

signal ['sɪg·nəl] I. *n* Signal *nt;* (*reception*) Empfang *m;* (*gesture*) Zeichen *nt;* (*traffic light*) Ampel *f;* (*for trains*) Signal *nt;* (*on car*) Blinker *m* II. *vi* <-l-> signalisieren; **she ~ed to them to be quiet** sie gab ihnen ein Zeichen, ruhig zu sein

signature ['sɪg·nə·tʃər] *n* ❶ Unterschrift *f;* of artist Signatur *f* ❷ (*characteristic*) Erkennungszeichen *nt*

significance [sɪg·'nɪf·ɪ·kəns] *n* Wichtigkeit *f;* (*meaning*) Bedeutung *f;* **to be of no ~** bedeutungslos sein

significant [sɪg·'nɪf·ɪ·kənt] *adj* bedeutend; (*important*) bedeutsam; *date, event* wichtig; *difference* deutlich; *increase* beträchtlich; *look* viel sagend; **do you think it's ~ that ...** glaubst du, es hat etwas zu bedeuten, dass ...

signify <-ie-> ['sɪg·nə·faɪ] I. *vt* andeuten II. *vi* **it doesn't ~** es macht nichts

'**signpost** I. *n* Wegweiser *m* II. *vt* ausschildern

Sikh [sik] *n* Sikh *m*

silence ['saɪ·ləns] I. *n* Stille *f;* (*of person*) Schweigen *nt;* (*discretion*) Stillschweigen *nt;* (*calmness*) Ruhe *f;* **to work in ~** still arbeiten ▶PHRASES: **~ is golden** (*prov*) Schweigen ist Gold II. *vt* zum Schweigen bringen; *doubts* verstummen lassen

silencer ['saɪ·lən·sər] *n* Schalldämpfer *m*

silent ['saɪ·lənt] *adj* still; (*not talking a.*) schweigsam; ■**to be ~** schweigen; **to keep ~** still sein; **to go ~** verstummen

silhouette [ˌsɪl·u·'et] I. *n* Silhouette *f* II. *vt* ■**to be ~d against sth** sich von etw *dat* abheben

silicon ['sɪl·ɪ·kən] *n* Silizium *nt*

silicon 'chip *n* COMPUT, ELEC Siliziumchip *m*

silicone ['sɪl·ɪ·koʊn] *n* Silikon *nt*

Silicon 'Valley *n* Silicon Valley *nt*

silk [sɪlk] *n* Seide *f*

'**silkworm** *n* Seidenraupe *f*

silky ['sɪl·ki] *adj* seidig; *voice* samtig

sill [sɪl] *n* Fensterbank *f*

silly ['sɪl·i] *adj* albern; **don't be ~!** (*make silly suggestions*) red keinen Unsinn!; (*do silly things*) mach keinen Quatsch! *fam;* **to be bored ~** zu Tode gelangweilt sein

silo ['saɪ·loʊ] *n* Silo *m o nt*

silver ['sɪl·vər] I. *n* Silber *nt;* (*coins*) Münzgeld *nt;* (*cutlery*) [Tafel]silber *nt* II. *adj* Silber- ▶PHRASES: **every cloud has a ~ lining** (*saying*) jedes Unglück hat auch sein Gutes

'**silverfish** <*pl ->* *n* Silberfischchen *nt*

similar ['sɪm·ə·lər] *adj* ähnlich (**to** +*dat*)

similarity [ˌsɪm·ə·'ler·ɪ·ti] *n* Ähnlichkeit *f*

simple <-r, -st> ['sɪm·pəl] *adj* einfach; (*straightforward*) schlicht; (*ignorant*) naiv; **the ~ things in life** die einfachen Dinge des Lebens; **for the ~ reason that ...** aus dem schlichten Grund, dass ...

simple-'minded *adj* einfach; (*naive*) einfältig

simplicity [sɪm·'plɪs·ɪ·ti] *n* Einfachheit *f;* **~ itself** die Einfachheit selbst

simplification [ˌsɪm·plə·fɪ·'keɪ·ʃən] *n* Vereinfachung *f*

simplify <-ie-> ['sɪm·plə·faɪ] *vt* vereinfachen

simply ['sɪm·pli] *adv* einfach; (*just*) nur; (*humbly*) bescheiden

simulate ['sɪm·ju·leɪt] *vt* simulieren; (*resemble*) nachahmen; (*feign*) vortäuschen

simulation [ˌsɪm·ju·'leɪ·ʃən] *n* Simulation *f;* (*feigning*) Vortäuschung *f*

simulator ['sɪm·ju·leɪ·tər] *n* Simulator *m*

simultaneous [ˌsaɪ·məl·'teɪ·ni·əs] *adj* gleichzeitig

sin [sɪn] I. *n* Sünde *f;* **[as] ugly as ~** unglaublich hässlich II. *vi* <-nn-> sündigen

since [sɪns] I. *adv* seitdem; **we haven't seen her** ~ seitdem haben wir sie nicht mehr gesehen; **long** ~ seit langem; **not long** ~ vor kurzem [erst] II. *prep* seit III. *conj* da; [**ever**] ~ seit

sincere [sɪn·'sɪr] *adj* ehrlich; *gratitude* aufrichtig

sincerely [sɪn·'sɪr·li] *adv* ehrlich; (*in letter*) mit freundlichen Grüßen

sinew ['sɪn·ju] *n* Sehne *f*

sing <sang *or* sung, sung> [sɪŋ] *vt, vi* singen; *kettle* pfeifen; *locusts* zirpen; *wind* pfeifen; (*ring*) dröhnen
♦ **sing out** I. *vi* laut singen; (*fam: call out*) schreien II. *vt* (*fam*) ausrufen

sing. I. *n abbrev of* **singular** Sg. II. *adj abbrev of* **singular** im Sing. nach n

Singapore ['sɪŋ·ə·pɔr] *n* Singapur *nt*

Singaporean ['sɪŋ·ə·pɔr·i·ən] I. *adj* aus Singapur *nach n* II. *n* Singapurer(in) *m(f)*

singe [sɪndʒ] I. *vt* ansengen; (*slightly*) versengen II. *vi* angesengt werden; (*slightly*) versengt werden

singer ['sɪŋ·ər] *n* Sänger(in) *m(f)*

singing ['sɪŋ·ɪŋ] *n* Singen *nt*

single ['sɪŋ·gəl] I. *adj* einzige(r, s); (*having one part*) einzelne(r, s); (*unmarried*) ledig; ~ **mother** allein erziehende Mutter; **not a** ~ **soul** keine Menschenseele; **every** ~ **time** jedes Mal II. *n* (*record*) Single *f*; (*room*) Einzelzimmer *nt*; (*in baseball*) Single *m*
♦ **single out** *vt* auswählen; *rejects* herausgreifen

single 'file *n* **in** ~ im Gänsemarsch

single-'handed I. *adv* [ganz] allein II. *adj* allein

single-'minded *adj* zielstrebig

'singles bar *n* Singlekneipe *f*

single-'sex *adj* nach Geschlechtern getrennt

singly ['sɪŋ·gli] *adv* einzeln

singular ['sɪŋ·gjə·lər] I. *adj* Singular-; **to be** ~ im Singular stehen; ~ **form** Singularform *f* II. *n* Singular *m*

Sinhalese [ˌsɪn·hə·'liz] I. *adj* singhale-

sisch II. *n* Singhalese, Singhalesin *m, f*; (*language*) Singhalesisch *nt*

sinister ['sɪn·ɪ·stər] *adj* unheimlich; (*fam: ominous*) unheilvoll; *forces* dunkel

sink [sɪŋk] I. *n* Spülbecken *nt*; (*washbasin*) Waschbecken *nt* II. *vi* <sank *or* sunk, sunk>, *vi* <sank> versinken; (*in mud*) einsinken; *sun* untergehen; (*subside*) sich senken; *head* herabsinken; *sales* zurückgehen; *standards* nachlassen; **to** ~ **to the ground** *person* zu Boden sinken; **to** ~ **to the bottom** auf den Boden sinken ▸PHRASES: **sb's heart** ~**s** (*sad*) jdm wird das Herz schwer; (*discouraged*) jd verliert den Mut III. *vt* <sank *or* sunk, sunk> versenken; *well* bohren; (*ruin*) zunichtemachen
♦ **sink in** *vi* einsinken; *liquid* einziehen; (*be understood*) ins Bewusstsein dringen
♦ **sink into** *vi* ▪**to** ~ **into sth** in etw *dat* einsinken; *lotion* in etw *akk* einziehen; (*lie back*) in etw *akk* [hinein]sinken; **to** ~ **into bed** sich ins Bett fallen lassen; **to** ~ **into a coma** ins Koma fallen

sinking ['sɪŋ·kɪŋ] *adj attr* sinkend; **a** ~ **feeling** ein flaues Gefühl [in der Magengegend]; **with a** ~ **heart** resigniert ▸PHRASES: **to leave the** ~ **ship** das sinkende Schiff verlassen

sinner ['sɪn·ər] *n* Sünder(in) *m(f)*

Sioux [su] I. *adj* Sioux- II. *n* <*pl* -> Sioux *m o f*; (*language*) Sioux *nt*

sip [sɪp] I. *vt* <-pp-> nippen; (*carefully*) etw in kleinen Schlucken trinken II. *n* Schlückchen *nt*

siphon ['saɪ·fən] I. *n* Saugheber *m* II. *vt* [mit einem Saugheber] absaugen

sir [sɜr] *n* Herr *m*; **excuse me,** ~ entschuldigen Sie bitte; **no,** ~**!** (*fam*) auf keinen Fall!; **Dear S~** [**or Madam**] Sehr geehrte Damen und Herren

siren ['saɪ·rən] *n* Sirene *f*

sister ['sɪs·tər] *n* Schwester *f*; (*nun*) [Ordens]schwester *f*

sister city *n* Partnerstadt *f*

'**sister-in-law** <*pl* sisters-> *n* Schwägerin *f*

sisterly ['sɪs·tər·li] *adj* schwesterlich

sit <-tt-, sat, sat> [sɪt] **I.** *vi* sitzen; (*perch a.*) hocken; (*sit down*) sich hinsetzen; (*be located*) liegen; (*in session*) tagen; *court* zusammenkommen; (*fit*) passen; *clothes* sitzen; (*fam: baby-sit*) babysitten; ~! (*to dog*) Platz! ▶PHRASES: **to be ~ting pretty** fein heraus sein; **to ~ tight** sich nicht rühren **II.** *vt* **to ~ oneself** sich *akk* setzen

◆**sit around** *vi* herumsitzen

◆**sit back** *vi* sich zurücklehnen; (*do nothing*) die Hände in den Schoß legen

◆**sit down I.** *vi* sich [hin]setzen; (*be sitting*) sitzen; **to ~ down to dinner** sich zum Essen an den Tisch begeben **II.** *vt* setzen; ■**to ~ oneself down** sich hinsetzen

◆**sit in** *vi* ❶ dabeisitzen; **to ~ in on a meeting** einem Treffen beisitzen ❷ (*hold sit-in*) ein Sit-in halten

◆**sit on** *vi* ❶ **to ~ on a committee** Mitglied eines Komitees sein ❷ (*fam: not act*) ■**to ~ on sth** auf etw *dat* sitzen

◆**sit out** *vt* auslassen; (*until end*) bis zum Ende ausharren

◆**sit through** *vt* über sich *akk* ergehen lassen

◆**sit up** *vi* aufrecht sitzen; **to ~ up straight** sich gerade hinsetzen; **to ~ up and take notice** (*fam*) aufhorchen

sitcom ['sɪt·kam] *n* (*fam*) *short for* **situation comedy** Sitcom *f*

site [saɪt] **I.** *n* Stelle *f*; (*plot*) Grundstück *nt*; *of crime* Tatort *m*; **building ~** Baustelle *f*; **camping ~** Campingplatz *m*; **on ~** vor Ort; **Web ~** Website *f* **II.** *vt* einen Standort bestimmen; **to be ~d out of town** außerhalb der Stadt liegen

'**sit-in** *n* Sit-in *nt*

sitter ['sɪt·ər] *n* Babysitter(in) *m(f)*

situated ['sɪtʃ·u·eɪ·t̬ɪd] *adj pred* ❶ gelegen; ~ **near the church** in der Nähe der Kirche ❷ **to be well ~** [finanziell] gutgestellt sein

situation [ˌsɪtʃ·u·'eɪ·ʃən] *n* Lage *f*; (*location a.*) Standort *m*

six [sɪks] **I.** *adj* sechs; *see also* **eight II.** *pron* sechs; *see also* **eight** ▶PHRASES: ~ **of one and half a dozen of the other** gehupft wie gesprungen *fam* **III.** *n* Sechs *f*; *see also* **eight**

'**six-pack** *n* Sechserpack *m*; *of beer* Sixpack *m*

sixteen [sɪk·'stin] **I.** *adj* sechzehn; *see also* **eight II.** *n* Sechzehn *f*; *see also* **eight**

sixteenth [ˌsɪk·'stinθ] **I.** *adj* sechzehnte(r, s) **II.** *pron* ■**the ~** der/die/das sechzehnte **III.** *adv* als sechzehnte(r, s) **IV.** *n* Sechzehntel *nt*

sixth [sɪksθ] **I.** *adj* sechste(r, s) **II.** *pron* ■**the ~** der/die/das sechste **III.** *adv* als sechste(r, s) **IV.** *n* Sechstel *nt*

sixtieth ['sɪk·sti·əθ] **I.** *adj* sechzigste(r, s) **II.** *pron* ■**the ~** der/die/das sechzigste **III.** *adv* als sechzigste(r, s) **IV.** *n* Sechzigstel *nt*

sixty ['sɪk·sti] **I.** *adj* sechzig **II.** *pron* sechzig **III.** *n* Sechzig *f*

size [saɪz] *n* Größe *f*; *of debt* Höhe *f*; **to double in** ~ seine Größe verdoppeln; **to increase in** ~ größer werden; **shirt/ shoe** ~ Hemd-/Schuhgröße *f*

sizzle ['sɪz·əl] *vi* brutzeln; (*fam*) aufregend sein

skate [skeɪt] **I.** *n* (*for ice*) Schlittschuh *m*; (*roller skate*) Rollschuh *m* **II.** *vi* (*on ice*) Schlittschuh laufen; (*on roller skates*) Rollschuh fahren ▶PHRASES: **to be skating on thin ice** sich auf dünnem Eis bewegen

skateboard ['skeɪt·bɔrd] **I.** *n* Skateboard *nt* **II.** *vi* skaten

skater ['skeɪ·t̬ər] *n* (*on ice*) Schlittschuhläufer(in) *m(f)*; (*on roller skates*) Rollschuhfahrer(in) *m(f)*; **figure** ~ Eiskunstläufer(in) *m(f)*; **speed** ~ Eisschnellläufer(in) *m(f)*

skating ['skeɪ·t̬ɪŋ] *n* (*on ice*) Eislaufen *nt*; (*roller skating*) Rollschuhlaufen *nt*; **figure** ~ Eiskunstlauf *m*; **speed** ~ Eisschnelllauf *m*

S

'skating rink n (of ice) Eisbahn f; (for roller skating) Rollschuhbahn f

skeleton ['skel·ɪ·tən] n Skelett nt; of boat Gerippe nt; of building Skelett nt; of report Entwurf m ▶PHRASES: **to have ~s in the** <u>closet</u> eine Leiche im Keller haben fam

skeptic ['skep·tɪk] n Skeptiker(in) m(f)

skeptical adj skeptisch

sketch [sketʃ] I. n <pl -es> Skizze f; (outline) Überblick m; (comedy) Sketch m II. vt skizzieren; (outline) umreißen III. vi Skizzen machen

'sketchbook n Skizzenbuch nt

sketchy ['sketʃ·i] adj flüchtig; (incomplete) lückenhaft

skewer ['skju·ər] I. n Spieß m II. vt anstechen; (criticize) sticheln

ski [ski] I. n Ski m II. vi Ski fahren; **to ~ down the slope** die Piste hinunterfahren

skid [skɪd] vi <-dd-> rutschen; (in vehicle) schleudern; **to ~ to a halt** schlitternd zum Stehen kommen

'skid mark n Reifenspur f; (from braking) Bremsspur f

skier ['ski·ər] n Skifahrer(in) m(f)

skiing ['ski·ɪŋ] n Skifahren nt

'ski jump n Sprungschanze f; (jump) Skisprung m; (event) Skispringen nt

skill [skɪl] n Geschick nt; (ability) Fähigkeit f; (technique) Fertigkeit f; **language ~s** Sprachkompetenz f

skilled [skɪld] adj ausgebildet; (skillful) geschickt; **highly ~ job** hoch qualifizierte Tätigkeit

skillful ['skɪl·fəl] adj geschickt; (showing skill) gekonnt

skim <-mm-> [skɪm] vt streifen; (read) überfliegen; (froth) abschöpfen

'ski mask n Skimaske f

skin [skɪn] n Haut f; (hide) Fell nt; of fruit Schale f; **to be soaked to the ~** nass bis auf die Haut sein ▶PHRASES: **it's no ~ off my** <u>nose</u> das ist nicht mein Problem; **by the ~ of one's** <u>teeth</u> nur mit knapper Not II. vt <-nn-> häuten; fruit schälen; **to ~ one's knees** sich dat

'skinhead n Skinhead m

skinny ['skɪn·i] adj mager

'skin-tight adj hauteng

skip [skɪp] I. vi <-pp-> ❶ hüpfen; (with rope) seilspringen; **to ~ with joy** einen Freudensprung machen ❷ (omit) ■**to ~ over sth** etw überspringen; **let's ~ to the next one** lasst uns direkt zum Nächsten übergehen II. vt <-pp-> ❶ **to ~ rope** seilspringen ❷ (omit) überspringen ❸ (not participate) nicht teilnehmen; dance auslassen; class schwänzen fam; work blau machen fam; meeting etw sausen lassen III. n Hüpfer m

skirmish <pl -es> ['skɜr·mɪʃ] n Gefecht nt; (argument) Wortgefecht nt

skirt [skɜrt] I. n Rock m II. vt umgeben; (move around) umfahren; (avoid) [bewusst] umgehen

'ski slope n Skipiste f

skulk [skʌlk] vi herumlungern fam; (move) schleichen

skull [skʌl] n Schädel m

skunk [skʌŋk] n Stinktier nt

sky [skaɪ] n Himmel m; **in the ~** am Himmel ▶PHRASES: **the ~'s the** <u>limit</u> alles ist möglich

'sky-blue adj attr himmelblau

'skydiving n Fallschirmspringen nt

'skylight n Oberlicht nt; (in roof) Dachfenster nt

'skyline n of city Skyline f; (horizon) Horizont m

skype [skaɪp] vi, vt TELEC, INET skypen (**with** mit)

'skyscraper n Wolkenkratzer m

slab [slæb] n Platte f; of wood Tafel f; of food [dicke] Scheibe

slack [slæk] I. adj schlaff; (not busy) ruhig; market flau; (lazy) träge; **discipline has become very ~ lately** die Disziplin hat in letzter Zeit sehr nachgelassen II. n **the men pulled on the rope to take up the ~** die Männer zogen am Seil, um es zu spannen; **to cut sb some ~** (fam) jdm Spielraum einräumen m

◆**slack off** *vi* es langsamer angehen lassen

slacken ['slæk·ən] I. *vt* locker lassen; *grip* lockern; *pace* verlangsamen II. *vi* sich lockern; (*diminish*) langsamer werden; *demand* nachlassen

slacks [slæks] *npl* Hose *f;* **a pair of ~** eine Hose

slain [sleɪn] *vt, vi pp of* **slay**

slalom ['slal·əm] *n* Slalom *m*

slam [slæm] I. *n* Knall *m; of door* Zuschlagen *nt;* (*punch*) Schlag *m;* (*push*) harter Stoß II. *vt* <-mm-> *door* zuschlagen; (*hit*) schlagen; (*fam: criticize*) heruntermachen III. *vi* <-mm-> zuschlagen; **to ~ on the brakes** voll auf die Bremse treten

slander ['slæn·dər] I. *n* üble Nachrede; (*statement*) Verleumdung *f* II. *vt* verleumden

slang [slæŋ] *n* Slang *m;* **army ~** Militärjargon *m*

slant [slænt] I. *vi* sich neigen II. *n* Neigung *f;* (*perspective*) Tendenz *f;* **to have a right-wing ~** rechtsgerichtet sein

slanting ['slæn·tɪŋ] *adj* schräg

slap [slæp] I. *n* Klaps *m* fam; (*noise*) Klatschen *nt; ~* **in the face** Ohrfeige *f;* (*fig*) Schlag *m* ins Gesicht II. *vt* <-pp-> ❶ schlagen; **to ~ sb on the back** jdn auf den Rücken schlagen; (*in congratulations*) jdm [anerkennend] auf die Schulter klopfen ❷ (*fam*) **to ~ a fine on sth** eine Geldstrafe auf etw *akk* draufschlagen

'**slapstick** *n* Slapstick *m*

slash [slæʃ] I. *vt* ❶ **to ~ sb's tires** jds Reifen aufschlitzen *fam;* **to ~ one's wrists** sich *dat* die Pulsadern aufschneiden ❷ *budget* kürzen; *prices* senken; *staff* abbauen; *workforce* verringern II. *n* <*pl* -es> Schnittwunde *f;* (*in object*) Schnitt *m;* (*punctuation*) Schrägstrich *m*

slate [sleɪt] I. *n* Schiefer *m;* (*on roof*) [Dach]schindel *f* ▸PHRASES: **to wipe the ~ clean** reinen Tisch machen II. *adj*

Schiefer- III. *vt* ■**to be ~d for sth** für etw *akk* vorgesehen sein

slaughter ['slɔ·tər] I. *vt* abschlachten; *animal* schlachten; (*fam: defeat*) vom Platz fegen II. *n* Abschlachten *nt; of animals* Schlachten *nt;* (*fam: defeat*) Schlappe *f*

Slav [slav] I. *n* Slawe, Slawin *m, f* II. *adj* slawisch

slave [sleɪv] I. *n* Sklave, Sklavin *m, f* II. *vi* schuften; **to ~** [**away**] **at sth** sich mit etw *dat* herumschlagen

slavery ['sleɪ·və·ri] *n* Sklaverei *f*

Slavic ['sla·vɪk] *adj* slawisch

slavish ['sleɪ·vɪʃ] *adj* sklavisch

Slavonic [slə·'van·ɪk] *adj* slawisch

slay <slew, slain> [sleɪ] *vt* ■**to be slain** ermordet werden

sled [sled] I. *n* Schlitten *m* II. *vi* <-dd-> **to go ~ding** Schlittenfahren gehen

sledge [sledʒ] *n* Schlitten *m*

'**sledgehammer** *n* Vorschlaghammer *m*

sleek [slik] *adj* geschmeidig; (*streamlined*) elegant; *car* schnittig; (*fig: in manner*) [aal]glatt *pej;* (*well-groomed*) gepflegt

sleep [slip] I. *n* Schlaf *m;* **to go to ~** einschlafen; **to put sb to ~** jdn einschlafen lassen ▸PHRASES: **he can do it in his ~** er beherrscht es im Schlaf II. *vi* <slept, slept> schlafen; **~ tight!** schlaf schön!; **to ~ late** lange schlafen; **to ~ soundly** [tief und] fest schlafen; ■**to ~ with sb** mit jdm schlafen ▸PHRASES: **to ~ on it** eine Nacht darüber schlafen

◆**sleep in** *vi* ausschlafen

◆**sleep off** *vt hangover* ausschlafen; *headache* sich gesund schlafen

sleeper ['sli·pər] *n* ❶ **to be a light ~** einen leichten Schlaf haben ❷ (*train*) Zug *m* mit Schlafwagenabteil; (*sleeping car*) Schlafwagen *m* ❸ (*pajamas*) ■**~s** *pl* Schlafanzug *m* ❹ (*spy*) Schläfer *m*

sleepiness ['sli·pɪ·nɪs] *n* Schläfrigkeit *f*

sleeping ['sli·pɪŋ] *adj attr* **let ~ dogs lie** (*prov*) schlafende Hunde soll man nicht wecken *prov*

'**sleeping bag** *n* Schlafsack *m*

S

'sleeping pill n Schlaftablette f
sleepless ['slip·lıs] adj schlaflos
'sleepwalk vi schlafwandeln
'sleepwalker n Schlafwandler(in) m(f)
sleepy ['sli·pi] adj schläfrig; town verschlafen fam
sleet [slit] I. n Eisregen m II. vi impers it's ~ing es fällt Eisregen
sleeve [sliv] n Ärmel m; (for record) [Schallplatten]hülle f; **to roll up one's ~s** die Ärmel hochkrempeln ▶ PHRASES: **to have sth up one's ~** etw im Ärmel haben
sleigh [sleı] n Pferdeschlitten m
slender ['slen·dər] adj schlank; object schmal; means knapp
slept [slept] pt, pp of **sleep**
slew [slu] pt of **slay**
slice [slaıs] I. n Scheibe f; of cake Stück nt; (portion) Anteil m II. vt in Scheiben schneiden; cake in Stücke schneiden III. vi ■**to ~ through sth** etw durchschneiden
◆slice off vt abschneiden
◆slice up vt in Scheiben schneiden; bread aufschneiden; cake in Stücke schneiden; profits aufteilen
slick [slık] I. adj gekonnt; (great) geil sl; performance tadellos; answer glatt; (clever) gewieft; hair geschniegelt fam; road glatt II. n Ölteppich m III. vt **to ~ back one's hair** sich dat die Haare nach hinten klatschen fam
slide [slaıd] I. vi <slid, slid or slidden> rutschen; (smoothly) gleiten; currency sinken II. vt <slid, slid or slidden> **she slid the hatch open** sie schob die Luke auf III. n (at playground) Rutsche f; (in photography) Dia nt; **rock ~** Felslawine f
slight [slaıt] adj gering; mistake klein; injury leicht; (slim) zierlich; **there's been a ~ improvement** es hat sich geringfügig gebessert; **he has a ~ tendency to exaggerate** er neigt etwas zu Übertreibungen; **not in the ~est** nicht im Geringsten
slightly ['slaıt·li] adv ein wenig; **to know sb ~** jdn flüchtig kennen

slim [slım] adj <-mm-> schlank; waist schmal; object dünn; chance gering; **~ pickings** magere Ausbeute
◆slim down I. vi abnehmen II. vt reduzieren
slime [slaım] n Schleim m
slimy ['slaı·mi] adj schleimig a. fig
sling [slıŋ] I. n Schlinge f; (for baby) Tragetuch nt; (weapon) Schleuder f II. vt <slung, slung> ❶ schleudern ❷ (hang) ■**to be slung from sth** von etw dat herunterhängen
slip [slıp] I. n ❶ Fall m ❷ (form) Formular nt; (sales slip) Kassenzettel m; **a ~ of paper** ein Stück nt Papier ❸ (mistake) Flüchtigkeitsfehler m; **~ of the tongue** Versprecher m ▶ PHRASES: **to give sb the ~** jdn abhängen II. vi <-pp-> ❶ ausrutschen; hand abrutschen; tires wegrutschen; clutch schleifen ❷ **to ~ into the house** ins Haus schleichen; **to ~ through a gap** durch ein Loch schlüpfen ❸ **to ~ into sth more comfortable** [sich] etwas Bequemeres anziehen ❹ price sinken ❺ (make mistake) sich versprechen; **to let sth ~** etw ausplaudern ❻ **to ~ into bad habits** sich dat schlechte Gewohnheiten aneignen ▶ PHRASES: **to ~ through sb's fingers** jdm entkommen III. vt <-pp-> ❶ **she ~ped the key under the mat** sie schob den Schlüssel unter die Matte; **he ~ped the letter into his pocket** er steckte den Brief in seine Tasche ❷ **to ~ sb's attention** jds Aufmerksamkeit entgehen; **sth ~s sb's mind** jd vergisst etw
◆slip away vi sich wegstehlen; (time) verstreichen geh; control entgleiten
◆slip by vi vorbeihuschen; years verfliegen; mistake durchgehen
◆slip down vi herunterrutschen
◆slip in I. vt einbringen II. vi sich hereinschleichen
◆slip off I. vi sich davonstehlen; (fall off) herunterrutschen II. vt abstreifen
◆slip on vt anziehen; ring sich dat anstecken
◆slip out vi ❶ **to ~ out for a second**

kurz weggehen ② *secret* herausrutschen

◆ **slip up** *vi* einen Fehler begehen

'slip-on I. *adj attr* ~ **shoes** Slipper *pl* II. *n* ■ ~**s** *pl* Slipper *pl*

slipper ['slɪp·ər] *n* Hausschuh *m*

slippery ['slɪp·ə·ri] *adj* rutschig; *situation* unsicher; *road* glatt; (*untrustworthy*) windig *fam* ▶PHRASES: **to be as ~ as an eel** aalglatt sein

slit [slɪt] I. *vt* <-tt-, slit, slit> aufschlitzen; **to ~ one's wrists** sich *dat* die Pulsadern aufschneiden II. *n* Schlitz *m*; *of door* Spalt *m*

slob [slab] *n* (*pej fam*) Gammler(in) *m(f)*

slog [slag] (*fam*) I. *n* Schufterei *f*; (*hike*) [Gewalt]marsch *m* II. *vi* <-gg-> ① **to ~ up the hill** sich auf den Hügel schleppen ② (*work*) sich durcharbeiten

slogan ['slou·gən] *n* Slogan *m*; **campaign ~** Wahlspruch *m*

slop [slap] (*fam*) I. *n* ① (*pej: food*) Schlabber *m* ② (*waste*) ■ ~**s** *pl* Abfälle *pl*; (*food waste*) Essensreste *pl* II. *vt* <-pp-> verschütten III. *vi* <-pp-> überschwappen

slope [sloup] I. *n* Hang *m*; (*angle*) Neigung *f*; *of roof* Schräge *f* II. *vi* *ground* abfallen; *roof* geneigt sein; ■**to ~ down/up** abfallen/ansteigen

sloping ['slou·pɪŋ] *adj attr* schräg; (*upwards*) ansteigend; (*downwards*) abfallend

sloppy ['slap·i] *adj* schlampig; (*romantic*) kitschig

slot [slat] *n* Schlitz *m*; (*for money*) Geldeinwurf *m*; (*for mail*) Briefschlitz *m*; (*on TV*) Sendezeit *f*

sloth [slaθ] *n* Faultier *nt*

'slot machine *n* Spielautomat *m*

slouch [slautʃ] I. *n* <*pl* -es> krumme Haltung ▶PHRASES: **to be no ~** [at [doing] sth] (*fam*) etw gut können II. *vi* gebeugt stehen; **to ~ along the street** die Straße entlangschlendern

Slovak ['slou·vak] I. *n* Slowake, Slowakin *m, f*; (*language*) Slowakisch *nt* II. *adj* slowakisch

Slovakia [slou·'va·ki·ə] *n* die Slowakei

Slovakian [slou·'va·ki·ən] I. *n* Slowake, Slowakin *m, f*; (*language*) Slowakisch *nt* II. *adj* slowakisch

Slovene ['slou·vin] I. *n* Slowene, Slowenin *m, f*; (*language*) Slowenisch *nt* II. *adj* slowenisch

Slovenia [slou·'vi·ni·ə] *n* Slowenien *nt*

Slovenian [slou·'vi·ni·ən] I. *n* Slowene, Slowenin *m, f*; (*language*) Slowenisch *nt* II. *adj* slowenisch

slow [slou] I. *adj* ① langsam; *business* flau ② (*dumb*) begriffsstutzig; **to be [a little] ~ on the uptake** [ein wenig] schwer von Begriff sein ③ *clock* **to be [10 minutes] ~** [10 Minuten] nachgehen II. *vi* langsamer werden; **to ~ to a crawl** fast zum Stillstand kommen

◆ **slow down** I. *vt* verlangsamen; *speed* drosseln II. *vi* langsamer werden; *car* langsamer fahren; (*speak*) langsamer sprechen; (*walk*) langsamer laufen; (*relax*) kürzertreten *fam*

'slowdown *n* economic ~ Konjunkturabschwächung *f*

slowly ['slou·li] *adv* langsam; **~ but surely** langsam, aber sicher

slowness ['slou·nɪs] *n* Langsamkeit *f*

sludge [slʌdʒ] *n* Schlamm *m*

slug[1] [slʌg] *n* Nacktschnecke *f*

slug[2] [slʌg] I. *vt* <-gg-> ■**to ~ sb** jdm eine verpassen *sl*; **to ~ it out** es untereinander ausfechten II. *n* gehöriger Schlag

sluggish ['slʌg·ɪʃ] *adj* träge; *market* flau; *engine* lahm

slum [slʌm] *n* Slum *m*

slump [slʌmp] I. *n* [plötzliche] Abnahme; (*recession*) Rezession *f*; **~ in prices** Preissturz *m*; **economic ~** Wirtschaftskrise *f* II. *vi* ① *prices* stürzen; *sales* zurückgehen ② (*fall heavily*) fallen

slung [slʌŋ] *pt, pp of* sling

slur [slɜr] I. *vt* <-rr-> undeutlich artikulieren; *drunkard* lallen; (*damage*) verleumden II. *n* Verleumdung *f*; **to cast a ~ on sb/sth** jdn/etw in einem schlechten Licht erscheinen lassen

slurp [slɜrp] (*fam*) I. *vi* schlürfen II. *vt* schlürfen III. *n* Schlürfen *nt*

S

slush [slʌʃ] n [Schnee]matsch m; (pej: kitsch) Gefühlsduselei f

slut [slʌt] n (pej) Schlampe f derb

sly [slaɪ] adj verstohlen; smile verschmitzt; (cunning) gerissen; **on the ~** heimlich

smack [smæk] I. n [klatschender] Schlag; (noise) Knall m; (kiss) Schmatz m II. adv ~ **in the middle** genau in der Mitte; **I walked ~ into it** ich lief voll dagegen III. vt ■**to ~ sb** jdm eine knallen fam; **to ~ sb's butt** jdm den Hintern versohlen

small [smɔl] adj klein; amount a. gering; (insignificant) unbedeutend; **in ~ quantities** in kleinen Mengen; ~ **child** Kleinkind nt; ~ **consolation** ein schwacher Trost; **to make sb feel ~** jdn niedermachen fam ► PHRASES: **it's a ~ world!** (prov) die Welt ist klein!

small 'change n Kleingeld nt

'small fry n + sing/pl vb (fam) kleine Fische; (child) junges Gemüse hum

small-'minded adj engstirnig

small 'print n ■**the ~** das Kleingedruckte

'small talk n Smalltalk m o nt

'small-time adj unbedeutend; ~ **crook** kleiner Gauner

'small-town adj attr Kleinstadt-

smart [smart] I. adj schlau; (stylish) schick; (quick) [blitz]schnell; **to make a ~ move** klug handeln II. n ① (sl) ■**the ~s** pl die [nötige] Intelligenz ② (pain) Schmerz m III. vi brennen

smart aleck [ˌsmart·ˈæl·ek] n (pej fam) Schlauberger(in) m(f) fam

'smart-ass n (pej vulg) Klugscheißer(in) m(f) sl

smarten ['smar·tən] I. vt ■**to ~ sth ↻ up** etw herrichten; house etw verschönern; ■**to ~ oneself ↻ up** sich in Schale werfen fam II. vi ■**to ~ up** mehr Wert auf sein Äußeres legen

smartphone, smart phone ['smart·foʊn] n Smartphone nt

smash [smæʃ] I. n <pl -es> ① Krachen nt; SPORT Schlag m; **forehand/backhand ~** Vorhand-/Rückhand-

schmetterball m ② (fam: song) Superhit m; **box-office ~** Kassenschlager m II. vt zerschlagen; window einschlagen; (strike) schmettern; record brechen; ball schmettern III. vi zerbrechen; (strike) prallen

◆**smash in** vt einschlagen

◆**smash up** vt zertrümmern; (crush) zerdrücken; car zu Schrott fahren

smashing ['smæʃ·ɪŋ] adj vernichtend; **to be a ~ success** (fam) ein durchschlagender Erfolg sein

'smashup n schwerer Unfall; (pile-up) Karambolage f

smear [smɪr] I. vt ① ■**to ~ sth on sth** etw mit etw dat beschmieren ② (slur) verunglimpfen II. n Fleck m; (slur) Verleumdung f

smell [smel] I. n Geruch m; of perfume Duft m; (bad) Gestank m; **sense of ~** Geruchssinn m II. vi <smelled or smelt, smelled or smelt> ① riechen ② + adj (give off odor) riechen; (pleasantly) duften; (stink) stinken III. vt <smelled or smelt, smelled or smelt> riechen ► PHRASES: **to ~ a rat** den Braten riechen fam

◆**smell out** vt aufspüren

smelly ['smel·i] adj stinkend attr

smelt [smelt] vt, vi pt, pp of **smell**

smile [smaɪl] I. n Lächeln nt; **to give sb a ~** jdm zulächeln II. vi lächeln; ■**to ~ at sb** jdn anlächeln

smiley ['smaɪ·li], **'smiley face** n INET Smiley m

smirk [smɜrk] I. vi grinsen; ■**to ~ at sb** jdn süffisant anlächeln II. n Grinsen nt

smith [smɪθ] n Schmied m

smock [smak] n [Arbeits]kittel m

smog [smag] n Smog m

smoke [smoʊk] n ① Rauch m ② **to have a ~** eine rauchen fam ③ (fam: cigarettes) ■~**s** pl Glimmstängel pl ► PHRASES: **to go up in ~** in Rauch [und Flammen] aufgehen II. vt rauchen; FOOD räuchern ► PHRASES: **put that in your pipe and ~ it!** schreib dir das hinter die Ohren! III. vi rauchen

◆**smoke out** *vt* ausräuchern; (*fig*) entlarven

smoked [smoʊkt] *adj* geräuchert; ~ **fish** Räucherfisch *m*

smoker ['smoʊ·kər] *n* Raucher(in) *m(f)*; (*compartment*) Raucherabteil *nt*; ~'**s cough** Raucherhusten *m*

'**smokescreen** *n* Vorwand *m*

smoking ['smoʊ·kɪŋ] *n* Rauchen *nt*; ~ **ban** Rauchverbot *nt*

smoky ['smoʊ·ki] *adj* verraucht; (*emitting*) rauchend *attr;* (*tasting*) rauchig

smolder ['smoʊl·dər] *vi* schwelen; *cigarette* glimmen; *dispute* schwelen; **to ~ with rage** vor Zorn glühen

smooth [smuð] **I.** *adj* glatt; *sea* ruhig; (*without difficulty*) problemlos; *flight* ruhig; *landing* sanft; (*mild*) mild; (*suave*) [aal]glatt; ~ **operator** gewiefte Person **II.** *vt* ❶ **to ~ the path** [**to sth**] den Weg [zu etw *dat*] ebnen ❷ (*rub in*) einmassieren

◆**smooth down** *vt* glatt streichen

◆**smooth over** *vt* in Ordnung bringen

smoothly ['smuð·li] *adv* reibungslos; (*suavely*) aalglatt *pej;* **to go ~** glattlaufen *fam*

smother ['smʌð·ər] *vt* ersticken; (*suppress*) unterdrücken; ■**to be ~ed in sth** von etw *dat* völlig bedeckt sein

SMS [ˌes·em·'es] TELEC, INET **I.** *n abbrev of* **short message service** ❶ *no pl* (*service*) [der] SMS ❷ (*message*) SMS *f* **II.** *vt* (*fam*) ■**to ~ sb** jdm simsen *fam*

smudge [smʌdʒ] **I.** *vt* verwischen; (*dirty*) beschmutzen **II.** *vi* verlaufen; *ink* klecksen; *mascara* verschmiert **III.** *n* Fleck *m*

smug <-gg-> [smʌg] *adj* selbstgefällig

smuggle ['smʌg·əl] *vt* schmuggeln

smuggler ['smʌg·lər] *n* Schmuggler(in) *m(f)*

smuggling ['smʌg·lɪŋ] *n* Schmuggel *m*

snack [snæk] *n* Snack *m*

'**snack bar** *n* Imbissstube *f*

snag [snæg] **I.** *n* Haken *m fam;* (*rip*) gezogener Faden; **to hit a ~** auf Schwierigkeiten stoßen **II.** *vt* <-gg-> **don't ~ your coat on the barbed wire** pass

auf, dass du mit deiner Jacke nicht am Stacheldraht hängen bleibst

snail [sneɪl] *n* Schnecke *f*

'**snail mail** *n* (*hum fam*) Schneckenpost *f*

snake [sneɪk] *n* Schlange *f*

'**snake bite** *n* Schlangenbiss *m*

'**snakeskin** *n* Schlangenhaut *f;* FASHION Schlangenleder *nt*

snap [snæp] **I.** *n* Knacken *nt;* (*sound*) Knacks *m;* (*fastener*) Druckknopf *m;* **it was a ~!** (*fam*) es war ein Kinderspiel! **II.** *vi* <-pp-> auseinanderbrechen; (*whip*) peitschen; (*bite*) schnappen; **her patience finally ~ped** (*fig*) ihr riss schließlich der Geduldsfaden; ■**to ~ at sb** (*speak sharply*) jdn anfahren **III.** *vt* <-pp-> entzweibrechen; ■**to ~ sth** ↻ **off** etw abbrechen; **to ~ sth shut** etw zuknallen; *book* etw zuklappen; **to ~ one's fingers** mit den Fingern schnippen; **to ~ sb's head off** jdm den Kopf abreißen *fam*

◆**snap out** *vi* ~ **out of it!** krieg dich wieder ein!

snappy ['ʃnæp·i] *adj* ❶ (*fam: smart*) schick ❷ (*quick*) zackig; **make it ~!** mach fix! *fam*

'**snapshot** *n* Schnappschuss *m*

snare [sner] **I.** *n* Falle *f;* (*noose*) Schlinge *f* **II.** *vt* [mit einer Falle] fangen

snarl [snarl] **I.** *vi* knurren; ■**to ~ at sb** jdn anknurren **II.** *n* Knurren *nt*

snatch [snætʃ] **I.** *n* <*pl* -es> ❶ **to make a ~ at sth** nach etw *dat* greifen ❷ (*fragment*) Fetzen *m* ❸ **to do sth in ~es** etw mit Unterbrechungen tun *nt* **II.** *vt* schnappen; (*steal*) sich *dat* greifen **III.** *vi* greifen

sneak [snik] **I.** *vi* <-ed *or* snuck, -ed *or* snuck> schleichen; **to ~ up on sb/sth** sich an jdn/etw heranschleichen **II.** *vt* <-ed *or* snuck, -ed *or* snuck> **to ~ a look at sb/sth** einen verstohlenen Blick auf jdn/etw werfen; ■**to ~ sb/ sth in** jdn/etw hineinschmuggeln **III.** *n* (*pej*) Schleicher, -in *m, f*

sneaker ['sni·kər] *n usu pl* Turnschuh *m*

sneaky ['sni·ki] *adj* raffiniert

sneer [snɪr] **I.** *vi* spöttisch grinsen; (*utter*) spotten **II.** *n* spöttisches Lächeln

sneeze [sniz] **I.** *vi* niesen ▸PHRASES: **not to be ~d at** nicht zu verachten **II.** *n* Niesen *nt*

sniff [snɪf] **I.** *vi* ❶ die Luft einziehen; *animal* wittern; ■**to ~ at sth** an etw *dat* schnuppern; *animal* die Witterung von etw *dat* aufnehmen ❷ (*show disdain*) ■**to ~ at sth** über etw *akk* die Nase rümpfen **II.** *vt* ■**to ~ sth** an etw *dat* riechen

◆**sniff out** *vt* aufspüren; (*fig*) entdecken

snip [snɪp] **I.** *n* Schnitt *m* **II.** *vt* schneiden

snipe [snaɪp] *vi* aus dem Hinterhalt schießen; (*criticize*) attackieren

sniper [ˈsnaɪpər] *n* Heckenschütze *m*

snitch [snɪtʃ] **I.** *vt* (*fam*) klauen **II.** *vi* (*pej sl*) ■**to ~ on sb** jdn verpetzen **III.** *n* <*pl* -es> (*pej sl*) Petze(r) *f(m)*

snivel [ˈsnɪv·əl] **I.** *vi* <-l-> schniefen *fam*; (*cry*) flennen *pej fam* **II.** *n* Geplärre *nt pej fam*; (*sad*) Schniefen *nt*

sniveling [ˈsnɪv·əl·ɪŋ] **I.** *n* Geheul *nt pej fam* **II.** *adj attr* weinerlich

snob [snab] *n* Snob *m*

snobbery [ˈsnab·ə·ri] *n* Snobismus *m*

snoop [snup] *vi* (*fam*) [herum]schnüffeln; (*pry*) [herum]spionieren; ■**to ~ on sb** jdn ausspionieren

snooze [snuz] (*fam*) **I.** *vi* ein Nickerchen machen **II.** *n* Nickerchen *nt*

snore [snɔr] **I.** *vi* schnarchen **II.** *n* Schnarchen *nt kein pl*

snorkel [ˈsnɔr·kəl] **I.** *n* Schnorchel *m* **II.** *vi* <-l-> schnorcheln

snort [snɔrt] **I.** *vi* schnauben **II.** *vt* [verächtlich] schnauben; **to ~ cocaine** (*sl*) Kokain schnupfen **III.** *n* Schnauben *nt kein pl*

snot [snat] *n* (*fam*) Rotz *m*

snotty [ˈsnat·i] *adj* (*fam*) Rotz-; *handkerchief* vollgerotzt; (*pej: rude*) rotzfrech *sl*; *answer* pampig; *look* unverschämt

snout [snaʊt] *n* Schnauze *f*; *of pig* Rüssel *m*; (*nose*) Rüssel *m sl*

snow [snoʊ] **I.** *n* Schnee *m*; (*snowfall*) Schneefall *m* **II.** *vi impers* **it's ~ing** es schneit

◆**snow in** *vt* **to be ~ed in** eingeschneit sein

'snowball *n* Schneeball *m*

'snowboard **I.** *n* Snowboard *nt* **II.** *vi* Snowboard fahren

'snowbound *adj* eingeschneit; *road* wegen Schnees gesperrt

'snow chains *npl* Schneeketten *pl*

'snowdrift *n* Schneewehe *f*

'snowfall *n* Schneefall *m*; (*amount*) Schneemenge *f*

'snowflake *n* Schneeflocke *f*

'snowman *n* Schneemann *m*

'snowplow *n* Schneepflug *m*

'snowshoe *n usu pl* Schneeschuh *m*

'snowstorm *n* Schneesturm *m*

snow-'white *adj* schneeweiß; *sheets a.* blütenweiß; *face* kalkweiß

Snow 'White *n* Schneewittchen *nt*

snowy [ˈsnoʊ·i] *adj* schneereich; (*snow-covered*) verschneit; *mountain* schneebedeckt; (*color*) schneeweiß

'snub-nosed *adj attr* stupsnasig; *gun* mit kurzem Lauf *nach n*

snuff [snʌf] **I.** *n* Schnupftabak *m* **II.** *vt* **to ~ it** (*fam*) abkratzen *sl*

◆**snuff out** *vt* auslöschen; *cigarette* ausdrücken; *with one's foot* austreten; *hopes* zunichtemachen

snug [snʌg] *adj* kuschelig, gemütlich, mollig warm; (*tight*) eng

so [soʊ] **I.** *adv* **he's pretty nice; more ~ than I was led to believe** er ist ganz nett, viel netter als ich angenommen hatte; **what are you looking ~ unhappy about?** warum bist du so traurig?; **what's ~ wrong about that?** was ist denn daran so falsch?; **I have an enormous amount of work to do — ~ do I** ich habe jede Menge Arbeit – ich auch; **can I watch television? — I suppose ~** darf ich fernsehen? – na gut, meinetwegen; **I'm afraid ~** ich fürchte ja; **~ they say** so sagt man; **I told you ~** ich habe es dir ja gesagt; **is that ~?** stimmt das?; **if ~ ...** wenn das so ist ...; **and ~ it was** und so kam es dann auch; **and ~ forth** und so weiter; **~ to speak** sozusagen ▶PHRASES: **~ long** bis dann; **~ what?** na und? *fam* II. *conj* **I couldn't find you ~ I left** ich konnte dich nicht finden, also bin ich gegangen; **~ what's the problem?** wo liegt denn das Problem?; **be quiet ~ she can concentrate** sei still, damit sie sich konzentrieren kann ▶PHRASES: **~ long as ...** (*if*) sofern; (*for the time*) solange III. *adj* (*sl*) **that's ~ 70's** das ist typisch 70er

soak [souk] I. *n* Einweichen *nt kein pl* II. *vt* einweichen; (*in alcohol*) einlegen; (*wet*) durchnässen III. *vi* eingeweicht werden

◆**soak in** I. *vi* einziehen; (*be understood*) in den Schädel gehen *fam;* **will it ever ~ in?** ob er/sie das wohl jemals kapiert? *fam* II. *vt* einsaugen; (*fig*) in sich *akk* aufnehmen

◆**soak up** *vt* aufsaugen; (*fig*) [gierig] in sich *akk* aufnehmen; *atmosphere* in sich *akk* aufnehmen; *sun[shine]* sich aalen

soaked [soukt] *adj* (*wet*) ■**to be ~** pitschnass sein *fam;* **~ in sweat** schweißgebadet; *shirt* völlig durchgeschwitzt

soaking ['sou·kɪŋ] I. *n* Einweichen *nt kein pl;* (*becoming wet*) Nasswerden *nt kein pl;* **to get a ~** patschnass werden *fam* II. *adj* **~ [wet]** klatschnass *fam*

so-and-so ['sou·ən·sou] *n* (*fam*) Herr/ Frau Soundso; (*thing*) das und das; **what a mean old ~!** das ist ein alter Fiesling! *sl*

soap [soup] I. *n* Seife *f;* (*soap opera*) Seifenoper *f* II. *vt* einseifen

'**soap opera** *n* Seifenoper *f*

soapy ['sou·pi] *adj* seifig; **~ water** Seifenwasser *nt*

soar [sɔr] *vi* aufsteigen; *peaks* sich erheben; *prices* in die Höhe schnellen; *bird* [in großer Höhe] segeln; *glider* gleiten

sob [sab] I. *n* Schluchzen *nt kein pl* II. *vi* <-bb-> schluchzen III. *vt* <-bb-> schluchzen

sober ['sou·bər] I. *adj* nüchtern;

thought a. sachlich; *color* gedeckt; *truth* einfach II. *vt* ernüchtern

◆**sober up** I. *vi* nüchtern werden II. *vt* nüchtern machen

sobering ['sou·bər·ɪŋ] *adj* ernüchternd

so-called [,sou·'kɔld] *adj attr* so genannt

soccer ['sak·ər] *n* Fußball *m*

'**soccer mom** *n* (*pej fam*) *Bezeichnung für Mütter aus den Vorortsiedlungen, die viel Zeit damit verbringen, ihre Kinder von einer Sportveranstaltung zur nächsten zu fahren*

sociable ['sou·ʃə·bəl] *adj* gesellig; (*friendly*) umgänglich

social ['sou·ʃəl] I. *adj* gesellschaftlich; (*of human behavior*) sozial; **I'm a ~ drinker** ich trinke nur, wenn ich in Gesellschaft bin II. *n* Treffen *nt;* **church ~** Gemeindefest *nt*

socialism ['sou·ʃə·lɪz·əm] *n* Sozialismus *m*

socialist ['sou·ʃə·lɪst] I. *n* Sozialist(in) *m(f)* II. *adj* sozialistisch

socialize ['sou·ʃə·laɪz] I. *vi* ■**to ~ with sb** mit jdm gesellschaftlich verkehren II. *vt* sozialisieren; *offender* [re]sozialisieren

socially ['sou·ʃə·li] *adv* gesellschaftlich; **to meet sb ~** jdn privat treffen

social se'curity *n* Sozialhilfe *f;* (*pension*) Sozial[versicherungs]rente *f*

social 'service *n* Sozialarbeit *f;* ■**~s** *pl* (*welfare*) staatliche Sozialleistungen

'**social work** *n* Sozialarbeit *f*

'**social worker** *n* Sozialarbeiter(in) *m(f)*

society [sə·'saɪ·ɪ·t̬i] *n* Gesellschaft *f;* (*elite*) die [feine] Gesellschaft; (*organization*) Verein *m*

sociologist [,sou·si·'al·ə·dʒɪst] *n* Soziologe, Soziologin *m, f*

sociology [,sou·si·'al·ə·dʒi] *n* Soziologie *f*

sock[1] [sak] *n* Socke *f*

sock[2] [sak] *vt* schlagen; (*in soccer*) schießen

socket ['sak·ɪt] *n* Steckdose *f;* (*for lamps*) Fassung *f;* **eye ~** Augenhöhle *f*

soda ['sou·də] *n* ➊ *see* **soft drink** ➋ *see* **soda water**

S

'**soda water** *n* Sodawasser *nt*

sodden ['sad·ən] *adj* durchnässt; *grass* durchweicht

sodium ['sou·di·əm] *n* Natrium *nt*

sodium bi·carbonate *n see* **baking soda**

sodium 'chloride *n* Natriumchlorid *nt*

sofa ['sou·fə] *n* Sofa *nt*

'**sofa bed** *n* Schlafcouch *f*

soft [sɔft] *adj* weich; *skin* zart; *leather* geschmeidig; *hair* seidig; *(weak)* schlaff; *colors* zart; *music* gedämpft; *voice* leise

'**softball** *n* Softball *m*

soft-'boiled *adj* weich [gekocht]

'**soft drink** *n* Limo[nade] *f*

soften ['sɔ·fən] I. *vi* weich werden; *ice cream* schmelzen; *(moderate)* nachgiebiger werden II. *vt* weich werden lassen; *(moderate)* mildern; *color* dämpfen

◆ **soften up** I. *vt* weicher machen; *(win over)* erweichen; *(persuade)* rumkriegen *fam* II. *vi* weich werden

softener ['sɔ·fə·nər] *n* Weichmacher *m*; *(for kettle)* Enthärter *m*; **fabric ~** Weichspüler *m*

soft'hearted *adj* weichherzig; *(gullible)* leichtgläubig

softie ['sɔf·ti] *n (fam) see* **softy**

softly ['sɔft·li] *adv* sanft; *(quietly)* leise; *(dimly)* schwach

softness ['sɔft·nɪs] *n* Weichheit *f*; *(smoothness)* Weichheit *f*; *of skin* Glätte *f*; *of hair* Seidigkeit *f*; *of lighting* Gedämpftheit *f*; *of colors* Zartheit *f*

software ['sɔft·wer] *n* COMPUT Software *f*

softy ['sɔf·ti] *n (fam)* Softie *m sl*

soggy ['sag·i] *adj* durchnässt; *(boggy)* glitschig *fam*; *soil* aufgeweicht; FOOD matschig

soil [sɔɪl] *n* Erde *f*; *(territory)* Boden *m*

solace ['sal·ɪs] *n* Trost *m*

solar ['sou·lər] *adj* Solar-

solar 'cell *n* Solarzelle *f*

solar e'clipse *n* Sonnenfinsternis *f*

solar 'energy *n* Solarenergie *f*

solarium <*pl* -**aria**> [sou·'ler·i·əm] *n* Solarium *nt*; *(porch)* Glasveranda *f*

'**solar system** *n* Sonnensystem *nt*

sold [sould] *pt, pp of* **sell**

solder ['sad·ər] I. *vt* löten II. *n* Lötmetall *nt*

soldier ['soul·dʒər] *n* Soldat(in) *m(f)*

sold 'out *adj* ausverkauft

sole¹ [soul] *n* [Fuß]sohle *f*; *of shoe* [Schuh]sohle *f*

sole² [soul] *adj attr* einzig; *(exclusive)* Allein-

solely ['soul·li] *adv* einzig und allein

solemn ['sal·əm] *adj* feierlich; *oath* heilig; *(grave)* ernst; *voice* getragen

solicitor [sə·'lɪs·ɪ·tər] *n* POL Rechtsreferent(in) *m(f)* *(einer Stadt)*

solid ['sal·ɪd] I. *adj* fest; *wall* solide; *foundation* stabil; *punch* kräftig; *rock* massiv; *(not hollow)* massiv; *(substantial)* verlässlich; *evidence* handfest; *(uninterrupted)* durchgehend; *(dependable)* zuverlässig; *marriage* stabil; *investment* sicher; **~ silver** massives Silber II. *n* **■~s** *pl* feste Nahrung *kein pl* III. *adv* frozen **~** hart gefroren; *plants* steif gefroren

solidarity [ˌsal·ə·'der·ɪ·ti] *n* Solidarität *f*; **S~** *(movement)* Solidarität *f*

solidify <-ie-> [sə·'lɪd·ə·faɪ] *vi* fest werden; *lava* erstarren; *cement* hart werden; *water* gefrieren; *(fig) plans* sich konkretisieren; *idea* konkret[er] werden

solidity [sə·'lɪd·ɪ·ti] *n* fester Zustand; *of wood* Härte *f*; *of foundation* Stabilität *f*; *of facts* Zuverlässigkeit *f*; *of argument* Stichhaltigkeit *f*; *of judgment* Fundiertheit *f*; *of commitment* Verlässlichkeit *f*; *of investment* Solidität *f*; *of company* finanzielle Stärke; *(strength)* Stabilität *f*

solitaire ['sal·ə·ter] *n* Patience *f*

solitary ['sal·ə·ter·i] *adj* einzelne(r, s) *attr*; *(lonely)* einsam; *(remote)* abgeschieden

solitude ['sal·ə·tud] *n* Alleinsein *nt*; *(loneliness)* Einsamkeit *f*; **in ~** alleine

solo ['sou·lou] I. *adj attr* Solo- II. *adv* allein; MUS solo III. *n* MUS Solo *nt*

soloist ['sou·lou·ɪst] *n* Solist(in) *m(f)*

solution [sə·'lu·ʃən] *n* Lösung *f*; (*to puzzle*) [Auf]lösung *f*; (*act*) Lösen *nt*; **software** ~**s** Softwareanwendungen *pl*

solve [salv] *vt* lösen; *crime* aufklären; *mystery* aufdecken

Somali [soʊ·'ma·li] **I.** *n* <*pl* -> Somalier(in) *m(f)*; (*language*) Somali *nt* **II.** *adj* somalisch

Somalia [soʊ·'mal·i·ə] *n* Somalia *nt*

somber ['sam·bər] *adj* düster; *setting* ernst; (*dark*) dunkel; *day* trüb

some [sʌm] **I.** *adj attr* ❶ (*unknown amount*: + *pl*) einige; (+ *sing n*) etwas; **there's ~ cake in the kitchen** es ist noch Kuchen in der Küche; **~ more** noch etwas ❷ (*certain*: + *pl*) gewisse ❸ (*unknown*) irgendein(e); **he's in ~ kind of trouble** er steckt in irgendwelchen Schwierigkeiten; **~ day or another** irgendwann ❹ (*noticeable*) **to ~ extent** bis zu einem gewissen Grad ❺ (*slight*) **there is ~ hope that ...** es besteht noch etwas Hoffnung, dass ... **II.** *pron* ❶ (*unspecified number of persons or things*) welche ❷ (*unspecified amount of sth*) **if you need money, I can lend you ~** wenn du Geld brauchst, kann ich dir gerne welches leihen ❸ (*at least a small number*) einige ❹ + *pl vb* (*among larger number*) **~ of you have already met Betsey** einige von euch kennen Betsey bereits **III.** *adv* **~ sixty or sixty-five feet deep** ungefähr zwanzig Meter tief

somebody ['sʌm·ˌbad·i] *pron indef* ❶ jemand; **~ or other** irgendwer; **~ else** jemand anders; **there's ~ at the door** jemand ist an der Tür ❷ (*one person*) irgendwer ❸ **to be ~** jemand [*o* etwas] sein

somehow ['sʌm·haʊ] *adv* irgendwie

someone ['sʌm·wʌn] *pron see* **somebody**

someplace ['sʌm·pleɪs] *adv* irgendwo; **~ else** woanders/woandershin

somersault ['sʌm·ər·sɔlt] **I.** *n* (*on ground*) Purzelbaum *m*; (*in air*) Salto *m* **II.** *vi* einen Purzelbaum schlagen; (*in air*) einen Salto machen; *car* sich überschlagen

something ['sʌm·θɪŋ] *pron indef* etwas; **~ else** etwas anderes; **~ special/sharp/stronger** etwas Besonderes/Scharfes/Stärkeres; **to do ~** [about sb/sth] etwas [gegen jdn/etw] unternehmen; **I need ~ to write with** ich brauche etwas zum Schreiben; **is there ~ you'd like to say?** möchtest du mir etwas sagen?; **it was ~ of a surprise** es war eine kleine Überraschung; **she works for a bank or ~** sie arbeitet für eine Bank oder so was; **~ like ...** ungefähr wie ...; (*approximately*) um die ... ▶PHRASES: **that's [really] ~** das ist schon was; **there's ~ in it** es ist etwas dran

sometime ['sʌm·taɪm] *adv* irgendwann; **come up and see me ~** komm mich mal besuchen; **~ soon** demnächst irgendwann

sometimes ['sʌm·taɪmz] *adv* manchmal

somewhere ['sʌm·hwer] *adv* irgendwo/irgendwohin; **~ else** woanders/woandershin; **~ between 30 and 40** so zwischen 30 und 40

son [sʌn] *n* Sohn *m*

sonar ['soʊ·nar] *n* Sonar[gerät] *nt*

sonata [sə·'na·tə] *n* Sonate *f*

song [sɔŋ] *n* Lied *nt*; (*singing*) Gesang *m*; *of cricket* Zirpen *nt*

'son-in-law <*pl* sons-> *n* Schwiegersohn *m*

sonnet ['san·ɪt] *n* Sonett *nt*

soon [sun] *adv* bald; (*early*) früh; **~ after sth** kurz nach etw *dat*; **how ~** wie bald; **~er rather than later** lieber früher als später; **as ~ as possible** so bald wie möglich; **the ~er the better** je eher, desto besser; **not a moment too ~** gerade noch rechtzeitig; **I'd ~er not speak to him** ich würde lieber nicht mit ihm sprechen

soot [sʊt] *n* Ruß *m*

soothe [suð] *vt* beruhigen; (*relieve*) lindern

sooty ['sʊt̬·i] *adj* verrußt

S

sop [sap] *vt* ■**to ~ up** ⟳ **sth** etw aufsaugen

sophisticated [sə·ˈfɪs·tə·keɪ·tɪd] *adj* [geistig] verfeinert; (*cultured*) kultiviert; *audience* anspruchsvoll; *restaurant* gepflegt; (*highly developed*) hoch entwickelt; *method* raffiniert; *approach* differenziert

sophomore [ˈsaf·ə·mɔr] *n* (*in college*) Student(in) *m(f)* im zweiten Studienjahr; (*in high school*) Schüler(in) *m(f)* einer Highschool im zweiten Jahr

sopping [ˈsap·ɪŋ] (*fam*) I. *adj* klatschnass II. *adv* ~ **wet** klatschnass

soppy [ˈsap·i] *adj* (*fam*) gefühlsdus[e]lig; *film* schmalzig

soprano [sə·ˈpræn·oʊ] *n* Sopranistin *f*; (*range*) Sopran *m*

sorcerer [ˈsɔr·sər·ər] *n* Zauberer *m*

sorcery [ˈsɔr·sə·ri] *n* Zauberei *f*

sordid [ˈsɔr·dɪd] *adj* schmutzig; (*squalid*) schäbig; *apartment* verkommen

sore [sɔr] I. *adj* schlimm; (*overused*) wund [gescheuert]; ~ **muscles** Muskelkater *m*; ~ **point** (*fig*) wunder Punkt II. *n* wunde Stelle; **to open an old ~** (*fig*) alte Wunden aufreißen

sorely [ˈsɔr·li] *adv* arg; **to be ~ tempted to do sth** stark versucht sein, etw zu tun

sorrow [ˈsar·oʊ] *n* Kummer *m*; (*experience*) Leid *nt*

sorry [ˈsar·i] I. *adj* ❶ *pred* **I'm/she's ~** es tut mir/ihr leid; ■**to be ~ about sth** etw bedauern; **to say ~** [to sb] sich [bei jdm] entschuldigen; **we were ~ to hear** [that] ... es tat uns leid zu hören, dass ...; **sb feels ~ for sb/sth** jd/etw tut jdm leid ❷ *attr* (*wretched*) armselig II. *interj* ■**~!** Verzeihung!

sort [sɔrt] I. *n* ❶ (*type*) Sorte *f* ❷ (*fam*) **I had a ~ of feeling that** ... ich hatte so ein Gefühl, dass ... ❸ **I know your ~!** Typen wie euch kenne ich [zur Genüge]! *fam* II. *adv* (*fam*) ■**~ of** ❶ **that's ~ of difficult to explain** das ist nicht so einfach zu erklären ❷ (*not exactly*) mehr oder weniger III. *vt* sortieren IV. *vi* ■**to ~ through sth** etw sortieren

◆ **sort out** *vt* ordnen; *mess* in Ordnung bringen; (*resolve*) klären; *problem* lösen; (*choose*) aussuchen; (*for throwing out or giving away*) aussortieren

SOS [ˌes·oʊ·ˈes] *n* SOS *nt*; (*fig*) Hilferuf *m*

so-so [ˈsoʊ·soʊ] (*fam*) I. *adj* so lala *präd* II. *adv* so lala

sought [sɔt] *pt, pp of* **seek**

'sought-after *adj* begehrt

soul [soʊl] *n* ❶ Seele *f*; (*feeling a.*) Gefühl *nt*; **not a ~** keine Menschenseele ❷ MUS Soul *m*

'soul-destroying *adj* nervtötend; (*discouraging*) zermürbend

'soul mate *n* Seelenverwandte(r) *f(m)*

'soul-searching *n* Prüfung *f* des Gewissens

sound¹ [saʊnd] I. *n* Geräusch *nt*; *of bell* Klang *m*; (*TV*) Ton *m*; LING Laut *m*; PHYS Schall *m*; **don't make a ~!** sei still! II. *vi* ❶ erklingen; *alarm* ertönen; *alarm clock* klingeln; *bell* läuten ❷ (*fam: complain*) ■**to ~ off** herumtönen ❸ + *adj* (*seem*) klingen III. *vt* *alarm* auslösen; *car horn* hupen

sound² [saʊnd] I. *adj* (*healthy*) gesund; (*in good condition*) in gutem Zustand; (*trustworthy*) solide; (*reasonable*) vernünftig; *advice* gut; *argument* schlagend; *sleep* tief; **to be of ~ mind** bei klarem Verstand sein II. *adv* **to be ~ asleep** tief [und fest] schlafen

'sound bite *n* prägnanter Ausspruch (*eines Politikers*)

soundly [ˈsaʊnd·li] *adv* gründlich; (*clearly*) eindeutig; (*severely*) schwer *fam*; (*reliably*) fundiert *geh*; *sleep* tief

'soundproof I. *adj* schalldicht II. *vt* schalldicht machen

soup [sup] *n* Suppe *f*

'soup kitchen *n* Armenküche *f*

sour [ˈsaʊ·ər] I. *adj* sauer; (*ill-tempered*) griesgrämig; (*embittered*) verbittert II. *vt* sauer machen; (*make unpleasant*) trüben III. *vi* sauer werden; (*fig*) getrübt werden

source [sɔrs] *n* Quelle *f*; (*reason*) Grund *m*; ■**~s** *pl* (*references*) Quellen[angaben] *pl;* **according to government ~s** wie in Regierungskreisen verlautete

south [saʊθ] I. *n* Süden *m;* **to the ~ of sth** südlich von etw; ■**the S~** die Südstaaten *pl* II. *adj* südlich III. *adv* **my room faces ~** mein Zimmer ist nach Süden ausgerichtet; **to drive ~** Richtung Süden fahren

South 'Africa *n* Südafrika *nt*

South 'African I. *adj* südafrikanisch II. *n* Südafrikaner(in) *m(f)*

South A'merica *n* Südamerika *nt*

South A'merican I. *adj* südamerikanisch II. *n* Südamerikaner(in) *m(f)*

South Carolina [ˌsaʊθˌkær·ə·'laɪ·nə] *n* Südkarolina *nt*

South Dakota [ˌsaʊθˌdə·'koʊ·ṭə] *n* Süddakota *nt*

south'east I. *n* Südosten *m* II. *adj* südöstlich III. *adv* südostwärts

southerly ['sʌð·ər·li] I. *adj* südlich II. *adv* südlich; (*going south*) südwärts; (*coming from south*) von Süden III. *n* Südwind *m*

southern ['sʌð·ərn] *adj* südlich

southerner ['sʌð·ər·nər] *n* Südstaatler(in) *m(f)*

southernmost ['sʌð·ərn·moʊst] *adj* ■**the ~ ...** der/die/das südlichste ...

South Ko'rea *n* Südkorea *nt*

South Ko'rean I. *adj* südkoreanisch II. *n* Südkoreaner(in) *m(f)*

South 'Pole *n* Südpol *m*

southward ['saʊθ·wərd] I. *adj* südlich II. *adv* südwärts

southwards ['saʊθ·wərdz] *adv see* **southward** II

south'west I. *n* Südwesten *m* II. *adj* südwestlich III. *adv* südwestwärts

south'western *adj* südwestlich

souvenir [ˌsu·və·'nɪr] *n* Andenken *nt*

sovereign ['sav·rɪn] I. *n* Herrscher(in) *m(f)* II. *adj attr* oberste(r, s); *state* souverän; **~ power** Hoheitsgewalt *f*

sow[1] <sowed, sown *or* sowed> [soʊ] I. *vt* säen; (*a. fig*) *mines* legen; *doubts* wecken II. *vi* säen

sow[2] [saʊ] *n* (*pig*) Sau *f*

sown [soʊn] *vt, vi pp of* **sow**[1]

'soybean *n* Sojabohne *f*

'soy sauce *n* Sojasoße *f*

spa [spa] *n* [Bade]kurort *m;* (*spring*) Heilquelle *f;* **health ~** Heilbad *nt*

space [speɪs] *n* Raum *m;* (*gap, vacancy*) Platz *m;* (*between two things*) Zwischenraum *m;* (*for photo*) freie Stelle; (*between words*) Zwischenraum *m;* (*premises*) Fläche *f;* (*for living*) Wohnraum *m;* (*seat*) [Sitz]platz *m;* (*cosmos*) Weltraum *m;* **blank ~** Lücke *f;* **parking ~** Parklücke *f*

'space bar *n* COMPUT Leertaste *f*

'spacecraft <*pl* -> *n* Raumfahrzeug *nt*

spaced-'out *adj* (*sl*) ■**to be ~** geistig weggetreten sein *fam;* (*scatterbrained*) schusselig sein *fam*

'spaceman *n* [Welt]raumfahrer *m*

'space-saving *adj* Platz sparend

'spaceship *n* Raumschiff *nt*

'space station *n* [Welt]raumstation *f*

space tourism *n* Weltraumtourismus *m*

'spacewoman *n* Raumfahrerin *f*

spacious ['speɪ·ʃəs] *adj* geräumig; *area* weitläufig

spade [speɪd] *n* Spaten *m;* CARDS Pik *nt*

spaghetti [spə·'geṭ·i] *n* Spaghetti *pl*

spaghetti 'western *n* (*fam*) Italowestern *m*

Spain [speɪn] *n* Spanien *nt*

spam [spæm] *n no pl* INET (*sl*) Spam *m o f o nt,* Spammail *f;* **~ filter** Spamfilter *m*

span [spæn] I. *n usu sing* Spanne *f;* (*distance*) Breite *f;* (*scope*) Umfang *m;* **life ~** Lebensspanne *f* II. *vt* <-nn-> überspannen; (*cross*) führen

spangle ['spæŋ·gəl] *n* Paillette *f*

spangled ['spæŋ·gəld] *adj* mit Pailletten besetzt; (*shiny*) glitzernd

Spaniard ['spæn·jərd] *n* Spanier(in) *m(f)*

spaniel ['spæn·jəl] *n* Spaniel *m*

Spanish ['spæn·ɪʃ] I. *n* ❶ (*language*) Spanisch *nt* ❷ + *pl vb* ■**the ~** die Spanier *pl* II. *adj* spanisch

S

spank [spæŋk] *vt* ■to ~ **sb** jdm den Hintern versohlen; (*sexually*) jdm einen Klaps auf den Hintern geben

spanking ['spæŋ·kɪŋ] I. *n* Tracht *f* Prügel II. *adv* ~ **new** funkelnagelneu

spare [sper] I. *vt* verschonen; (*go easy on*) schonen; (*avoid*) ersparen; (*not use*) sparen; **could you** ~ **me** 10 **dollars?** kannst du mir 10 Dollar leihen?; **to** ~ **no cost** keine Kosten scheuen II. *adj* Ersatz-; ~ [**bed**]**room** Gästezimmer *nt* III. *n* AUTO Ersatzreifen *m*

spare 'parts *n pl* Ersatzteile *pl*

'spareribs *npl* [Schäl]rippchen *pl*

spare 'time *n* Freizeit *f*

spare 'tire *n* Ersatzreifen *m*; (*fam: fat*) Rettungsring *m*

sparing ['sper·ɪŋ] *adj* sparsam

spark [spark] I. *n* Funke[n] *m*; ~ **of hope** Fünkchen *nt* Hoffnung; **a bright** ~ ein Intelligenzbolzen *m fam* II. *vt* entfachen *a. fig; interest* wecken; *problems* verursachen III. *vi* Funken sprühen

sparkle ['spar·kəl] I. *vi* funkeln; (*fig: be witty*) sprühen (**with** vor +*dat*) II. *n* Funkeln *nt*; **sth lacks** ~ einer S. *dat* fehlt es an Schwung

sparkling ['spark·lɪŋ] *adj* glänzend; *eyes* funkelnd; (*lively*) vor Leben sprühend; *drink* mit Kohlensäure *nach n*; *wine* schäumend

'spark plug *n* Zündkerze *f*

sparrow ['sper·oʊ] *n* Spatz *m*

sparse [spars] *adj* spärlich; (*meager*) dürftig

Spartan ['spar·tən] I. *adj* spartanisch II. *n* Spartaner(in) *m(f)*

spasm ['spæz·əm] *n* Krampf *m*; (*surge*) Anfall *m*

spastic ['spæs·tɪk] *adj* spastisch; (*fig, offensive sl*) schwach

spat [spæt] *vt, vi pt, pp of* **spit**

spate [speɪt] *n* ■**a** ~ **of sth** eine Flut von etw *dat*

spatter ['spæt·ər] I. *vt* bespritzen; **to** ~ **sb with water** jdn nass spritzen II. *vi* prasseln

spatula ['spætʃ·ə·lə] *n* Spachtel *m o f*

spawn [spɔn] I. *vt frog* ablegen; (*fig*) hervorbringen II. *vi frog* laichen III. *n* (*eggs*) Laich *m*

speak <spoke, spoken> [spik] I. *vi* sprechen; (*make speech a.*) reden; (*converse*) sich unterhalten; **scientifically** ~**ing** wissenschaftlich gesehen; **strictly** ~**ing** genau genommen; **to** ~ **to** [*or* **with**] **sb** [**about sth**] mit jdm [über etw *akk*] reden II. *vt* sagen; **to not** ~ **a word** kein Wort herausbringen; **to** ~ **one's mind** sagen, was man denkt; **to** ~ **English fluently** fließend Englisch sprechen

♦ **speak against** *vi* ■**to** ~ **against sth** sich gegen etw *akk* aussprechen

♦ **speak for** *vi* ■**to** ~ **for sb** in jds Namen sprechen; ■**to** ~ **for oneself** für sich selbst sprechen ▶ PHRASES: ~ **for yourself!** (*fam*) du vielleicht!

♦ **speak out** *vi* seine Meinung deutlich vertreten; ■**to** ~ **out against sth** sich gegen etw *akk* aussprechen

♦ **speak up** *vi* lauter sprechen; (*support*) seine Meinung sagen; **to** ~ **up for sb/sth** für jdn/etw eintreten

speaker ['spi·kər] *n* Redner(in) *m(f)*; (*loudspeaker*) Lautsprecher *m*; **native** ~ Muttersprachler(in) *m(f)*; **the S~ of the House** der/die Vorsitzende des Repräsentantenhauses

speaking ['spi·kɪŋ] I. *n* Sprechen *nt*; (*holding speech*) Reden *nt* II. *adj* ▶ PHRASES: **to be on** ~ **terms** miteinander bekannt sein; **they are no longer on** ~ **terms with each other** sie reden nicht mehr miteinander

spear [spɪr] I. *n* Speer *m* II. *vt* durchbohren

'spearhead I. *n* Speerspitze *f*; (*fig*) Spitze *f* II. *vt* (*a. fig*) anführen

'spearmint *n* grüne Minze

special ['speʃ·əl] I. *adj* besondere(r, s); *circumstances* außergewöhnlich; (*for particular purpose*) speziell; (*for particular use*) Spezial-; **on** ~ **occasions** zu besonderen Gelegenheiten; ■**to be** ~ **to sb** jdm sehr viel bedeuten II. *n*

❶ (*meal*) Tagesgericht *nt* **❷** *pl* (*bargains*) **■ ~ s** Sonderangebote *pl*

special e'dition *n* Sonderausgabe *f*

special ef'fect *n usu pl* Spezialeffekt *m*

specialist ['spef·ə·lɪst] *n* Spezialist(in) *m(f)*

specialization [ˌspef·ə·lɪ·'zeɪ·ʃən] *n* Spezialisierung *f*; (*skill*) Spezialgebiet *nt*

specialize ['spef·ə·laɪz] *vi* sich spezialisieren

specialized ['spef·ə·laɪzd] *adj* spezialisiert; (*particular*) spezial; **~ knowledge** Fachwissen *f*; **~ magazine** Fachzeitschrift *f*

specially ['spef·əl·i] *adv* speziell; (*particularly*) insbesondere; (*very*) besonders

special 'offer *n* Sonderangebot *nt*

specialty ['spef·əl·ti] *n* Spezialität *f*; (*skill*) Fachgebiet *nt*

species <*pl* -> ['spi·ʃiz] *n* Art *f*

specific [spə·'sɪf·ɪk] *adj* genau; (*particular*) speziell; **could you be a little more ~?** könntest du dich etwas klarer ausdrücken?; **~ details** besondere Einzelheiten

specifically [spə·'sɪf·ɪk·li] *adv* speziell; (*clearly*) ausdrücklich

specification [ˌspes·ə·fɪ·'keɪ·ʃən] *n* **❶** (*specifying*) Angabe *f* **❷** (*plan*) **■ ~ s** *pl* detaillierter Entwurf; (*for building*) Bauplan *m* **❸** (*description*) genaue Angabe; (*for patent*) Patentschrift *f*; (*for machines*) Konstruktionsplan *m*

specify <-ie-> ['spes·ə·faɪ] *vt* angeben; (*list*) spezifizieren; (*expressly*) ausdrücklich angeben

specimen ['spes·ə·mən] *n* Exemplar *nt*; MED Probe *f*

speck [spek] *n* Fleck *m*; *of blood* Spritzer *m*; (*particle*) Körnchen *nt*

speckle ['spek·əl] *n* Tupfen *m*

speckled ['spek·əld] *adj* gesprenkelt

specs [speks] *npl* (*fam*) *short for* **spectacles** Brille *f*

spectacle ['spek·tə·kəl] *n* Spektakel *nt*; (*event*) Schauspiel *nt*; (*sight*) Anblick *m*

spectacles ['spek·tə·kəlz] *npl* (*old*) Brille *f*

spectacular [spek·'tæk·ju·lər] *adj* atemberaubend; (*striking*) spektakulär

spectator [spek·'teɪ·tər] *n* Zuschauer(in) *m(f)*

spectrum <*pl* -tra> ['spek·trəm] *n* Spektrum *nt*; (*range*) Palette *f*

speculate ['spek·ju·leɪt] *vi* spekulieren

speculation [ˌspek·ju·'leɪ·ʃən] *n* Spekulation *f*

speculative ['spek·jə·lə·t̬ɪv] *adj* spekulativ

speculator ['spek·ju·leɪ·tər] *n* Spekulant(in) *m(f)*

sped [sped] *pt, pp of* **speed**

speech <*pl* -es> [spitʃ] *n* Sprache *f*; (*style a.*) Redestil *m*; (*oration*) Rede *f*; (*shorter*) Ansprache *f*; (*act*) Sprechen *nt*; **in everyday ~** in der Alltagssprache; **freedom of ~** Redefreiheit *f*

speechless ['spitʃ·lɪs] *adj* sprachlos

speed [spid] I. *n* Geschwindigkeit *f*; (*quickness*) Schnelligkeit *f*; *of engine* Drehzahl *f*; (*sl: drug*) Speed *nt*; **full ~ ahead!** volle Kraft voraus! II. *vi* <sped, sped> sausen; *car* rasen

◆ **speed up** I. *vt* beschleunigen; **■ to ~ up ○ sb/sth** jdn/etw antreiben II. *vi* beschleunigen; *person* sich beeilen

'speedboat *n* Rennboot *nt*

'speed bump *n* Bodenschwelle *f*

'speed dating *n organisierte Partnersuche, wobei man mit jedem Kandidaten nur wenige Minuten spricht*

speeding ['spi·dɪŋ] *n* Geschwindigkeitsüberschreitung *f*

'speed limit *n* Geschwindigkeitsbegrenzung *f*

speedometer [spɪ·'dam·ɪ·tər] *n* Tachometer *m o nt*

'speed skating *n* Eisschnelllauf *m*

'speed trap *n* Radarfalle *f*

speedy ['spi·di] *adj* schnell; *decision, recovery a.* rasch; *delivery* prompt

spell[1] <spelled *or* spelt, spelled *or* spelt> [spel] I. *vt* buchstabieren; (*signify*) bedeuten II. *vi* [richtig] schreiben; (*aloud*) buchstabieren

◆ **spell out** *vt* buchstabieren; (*explain*) klarmachen

S

spell² [spel] n Zauber m; (words) Zauberspruch m; **to cast a ~ on sb** jdn verzaubern; **to be under sb's ~** von jdm verzaubert sein

spell³ [spel] n **to go through a bad ~** eine schwierige Zeit durchmachen; **~ of sunny weather** Schönwetterperiode f; **to suffer from dizzy ~s** unter Schwindelanfällen leiden

spellbinding ['spel·baɪn·dɪŋ] adj fesselnd

spellbound ['spel·baʊnd] adj gebannt; **to hold sb ~** jdn fesseln

'spellchecker n COMPUT Rechtschreibhilfe f

spelling ['spel·ɪŋ] n Rechtschreibung f; (activity) Buchstabieren nt kein pl

'spelling bee n Buchstabierwettbewerb m

spelt¹ [spelt] pt, pp of **spell**

spelt² [spelt] n Dinkel m

spend [spend] I. vt <spent, spent> ausgeben; time verbringen II. vi <spent, spent> Geld ausgeben

spending ['spen·dɪŋ] n Ausgaben pl

spent [spent] I. pt, pp of **spend** II. adj verbraucht; (tired) erschöpft

sperm <pl -> ['spɜrm] n Samenzelle f; (fam: semen) Sperma nt

'sperm whale n Pottwal m

spew [spju] I. vt ausspeien; lava auswerfen; exhaust ausstoßen; (vomit) erbrechen; blood spucken II. vi austreten; ash herausgeschleudert werden; flames hervorschlagen; water hervorsprudeln; (vomit) erbrechen

sphere [sfɪr] n Kugel f; (earth) Erdkugel f; (area) Bereich m

spherical ['sfɪr·ɪ·kəl] adj kugelförmig

spice [spaɪs] I. n Gewürz nt; (fig) Pep m II. vt würzen; (fig) aufpeppen fam

spicy ['spaɪ·si] adj würzig; (hot) scharf; story pikant

spider ['spaɪ·dər] n Spinne f

spike [spaɪk] I. n Nagel m; of fence Spitze f; of animal Stachel m; (on shoes) Spike m pl II. vt ❶ (fam) **to ~ sb's drink** einen Schuss Alkohol in jds

Getränk geben ❷ (injure) verletzen ❸ (fam) story ablehnen; plan einstellen

spill [spɪl] I. n Verschüttete(s) nt; (pool) Lache f; (stain) Fleck m; oil ~ Ölteppich m II. vt <spilled or spilt, spilled or spilt> verschütten; (fam: reveal) ausplaudern ▶PHRASES: **to ~ the beans** das Geheimnis lüften III. vi überlaufen; flour verschüttet werden; crowd strömen; conflict sich ausbreiten IV. adj ▶PHRASES: **don't cry over ~ed milk** (saying) was passiert ist, ist passiert

spilt [spɪlt] pt, pp of **spill**

spin [spɪn] I. n ❶ Drehung f; (in washing machine) Schleudern nt ❷ (drive) Spritztour f fam; **to send a car into a ~** ein Auto zum Schleudern bringen II. vi <-nn-, spun, spun> rotieren; washing machine schleudern; (make thread) spinnen; **to ~ out of control** außer Kontrolle geraten; **my head is ~ning** mir dreht sich alles fam III. vt <-nn-, spun, spun> drehen; clothes schleudern; yarn spinnen

◆ **spin out** I. vi **to ~ out of control** car außer Kontrolle geraten II. vt ■ **to ~ out** ↻ **sth** etw ausdehnen

spinach ['spɪn·ɪtʃ] n Spinat m

'spinal column n Wirbelsäule f

spindle ['spɪn·dəl] n Spindel f

spindly ['spɪnd·li] adj spindeldürr

'spin doctor n ≈ Pressesprecher(in) m(f); POL Spindoktor m

'spin-dry vt schleudern

'spin-dryer n Wäscheschleuder f

spine [spaɪn] n Wirbelsäule f; of book [Buch]rücken m; (spike) Stachel m

spine-chilling ['spaɪn·tʃɪl·ɪŋ] adj gruselig

spineless ['spaɪn·lɪs] adj (pej) rückgratlos

spinning ['spɪn·ɪŋ] n Spinnen nt

'spinning wheel n Spinnrad nt

'spinoff, 'spin-off I. n Nebenprodukt nt II. adj attr ~ **effect** Folgewirkung f

spiny ['spaɪ·ni] adj stach[e]lig; plant a. dornig

spiral ['spaɪ·rəl] I. n Spirale f II. adj attr

spiralförmig **III.** vi <-l-> sich hoch-/hinunterwinden; *smoke, hawk* spiralförmig auf-/absteigen; *prices* ansteigen

spirit ['spɪr·ɪt] n ❶ Geist m; *(ghost a.)* Gespenst nt; *(mood)* Stimmung f; *(vitality)* Temperament nt; ■**the Holy S~** der Heilige Geist; **team ~** Teamgeist m ❷ *(alcohol)* ■**~s** pl Spirituosen pl

spirited ['spɪr·ɪ·t̬ɪd] adj temperamentvoll; *discussion* lebhaft; *person* beherzt; *reply* mutig

spiritual ['spɪr·ɪ·tʃu·əl] **I.** adj geistig; *leader* religiös **II.** n Spiritual nt

spit [spɪt] **I.** n Spucke f **II.** vi <-tt-, spat *or* spit, spat *or* spit> spucken; ■**to ~ at sb** jdn anspucken **III.** vt <-tt-, spat *or* spit, spat *or* spit> ausspucken; *flames* ausstoßen

◆ **spit out** vt ausspucken; *(fam: say angrily)* fauchen; **~ it out!** spuck's schon aus!

spite [spaɪt] **I.** n Bosheit f; ■**in ~ of sth** trotz einer S. *gen* **II.** vt ärgern

spiteful ['spaɪt·fəl] adj gehässig

spitting 'image n Ebenbild nt

splash [splæʃ] **I.** n <pl -es> Platschen nt; *of sauce* Klecks m fam; *(in drink)* Spritzer m **II.** vt verspritzen; *(spray)* bespritzen; **her picture was ~ed all over the newspapers** ihr Bild erschien groß in allen Zeitungen **III.** vi klatschen; *(spill out)* spritzen

splatter ['splæt̬·ər] **I.** vt bespritzen **II.** vi spritzen

spleen [splin] n Milz f

splendid ['splen·dɪd] adj großartig

splendor ['splen·dər] n Pracht f; ■**~s** pl Herrlichkeiten pl

splint [splɪnt] n Schiene f

splinter ['splɪn·tər] n Splitter m

'splinter group n POL Splittergruppe f

split [splɪt] **I.** n Riss m; *(in wood)* Spalt m; *(in opinion)* Kluft f; *(in party)* Spaltung f; *of couple* Trennung f; *(sharing)* Aufteilung f **II.** vt <-tt-, split, split> teilen; *in half* halbieren; *party* spalten; *seam* aufplatzen lassen; **to ~ the difference** *(fig)* sich *akk* auf halbem Weg einigen; **to ~ one's head**

open sich *dat* den Kopf aufschlagen **III.** vi <-tt-, split, split> [entzwei]brechen; *seam* aufplatzen; *hair* splissen; *couple* sich trennen; **to ~ into groups** sich aufteilen; ■**to ~ from sth** *group* sich von etw *dat* abspalten

◆ **split off I.** vt abbrechen; *(with axe)* abschlagen; *(separate)* abtrennen **II.** vi sich lösen; ■**to ~ off from sth** *group* sich von etw *dat* abspalten

◆ **split up I.** vt aufteilen; *group* teilen **II.** vi ❶ **to ~ up into groups** sich in Gruppen aufteilen ❷ *couple* sich trennen

'split-up n Trennung f

splutter ['splʌt̬·ər] **I.** vi stottern; *fire* zischen **II.** vt **to ~ an excuse** eine Entschuldigung hervorstoßen **III.** n Prusten nt; *of car* Stottern nt; *of fire* Zischen nt

spoil [spɔɪl] **I.** n ■**~s** pl Beute f **II.** vt <spoiled *or* spoilt, spoiled *or* spoilt> verderben; *(pamper)* verwöhnen; *child* verziehen; **to ~ sb's chances** jds Chancen ruinieren; **to be spoiled for choice** eine große Auswahl haben **III.** vi <spoiled *or* spoilt, spoiled *or* spoilt> schlecht werden

spoiled [spɔɪld] adj verdorben; *child* verzogen

spoilsport ['spɔɪl·spɔrt] n *(fam)* Spielverderber(in) m/f

spoilt [spɔɪlt] vt, vi pt, pp of **spoil**

spoke[1] [spoʊk] n Speiche f

spoke[2] [spoʊk] pt of **speak**

spoken ['spoʊ·kən] **I.** pp of **speak** **II.** adj attr gesprochen

spokesman ['spoʊks·mən] n Sprecher m

spokesperson <pl -people> n Sprecher(in) m/f

'spokeswoman n Sprecherin f

sponge [spʌndʒ] n Schwamm m

◆ **sponge off I.** vt ■**to ~ off ⟳ sb/sth** jdn/etw schnell [mit einem Schwamm] [ab]waschen **II.** vi *(pej fam)* ausnutzen

'sponge cake n Rührkuchen m; *(without fat)* Biskuit[kuchen] m

S

sponger ['spʌn·dʒər] *n* (*pej*) Schmarotzer(in) *m(f)*

sponsor ['spɑn·sər] I. *vt* sponsern; *candidate* unterstützen II. *n* Sponsor(in) *m(f)*; *of charity* Förderer, Förderin *m, f*

spontaneous [spɑn·'teɪ·ni·əs] *adj* spontan; *laughter* impulsiv

spook [spuk] *n* (*fam*) Gespenst *nt*

spooky ['spu·ki] *adj* (*fam*) schaurig; *uncanny* unheimlich; *film* gespenstisch

spool [spul] *n* Rolle *f*

spoon [spun] *n* Löffel *m*

spoon-feed <-fed, -fed> ['spun·fid] *vt* ■**to** ~ **sb** jdn mit einem Löffel füttern; (*supply*) jdm alles vorgeben

spoonful <*pl* -s *or* spoonsful> ['spun·ful] *n* Löffel *m*

sporadic [spə·'ræd·ɪk] *adj* sporadisch

sport [spɔrt] *n* Sport *m*; (*type*) Sportart *f*; **to be a** [good]/**bad** ~ (*fam*) ein/ kein Spielverderber/eine/keine Spielverderberin sein; ■~**s** *pl* Sport *m*; **to be good at** ~**s** sportlich sein

'sports car *n* Sportwagen *m*

'sportsman *n* Sportler *m*

'sportsmanship *n* Fairness *f*

'sportswoman *n* Sportlerin *f*

sporty ['spɔr·ti] *adj* (*athletic*) sportlich; *car* schnell

spot [spat] I. *n* Fleck *m*; (*dot*) Punkt *m*; (*pattern*) Tupfen *m*; (*place*) Stelle *f*; (*on TV*) Beitrag *m*; **on the** ~ an Ort und Stelle II. *vt* <-tt-> entdecken; (*notice*) bemerken

spot 'check *n* Stichprobe *f*

spotless ['spat·lɪs] *adj* makellos; (*unblemished a.*) tadellos

'spotlight I. *n* Scheinwerfer *m*; **to be in the** ~ (*fig*) im Rampenlicht stehen II. *vt* <-lighted *or* -lit, -lighted *or* -lit> ■**to** ~ **sth** etw beleuchten; (*fig*) auf etw *akk* aufmerksam machen

spotted ['spat·ɪd] *adj* getupft; (*covered*) gesprenkelt

spout [spaʊt] I. *n* Ausguss *m* II. *vt* speien; (*pej: rant*) faseln *fam* III. *vi* hervorschießen; (*pej: rant*) Reden schwingen *fam*

sprain [spreɪn] I. *vt* **to** ~ **one's ankle** sich *dat* den Knöchel verstauchen II. *n* Verstauchung *f*

sprang [spræŋ] *vt, vi pt of* **spring**

sprawl [sprɔl] I. *n* Ausdehnung *f* II. *vi* sich ausbreiten; (*slouch*) herumlümmeln *pej fam*

sprawling ['sprɔ·lɪŋ] *adj* (*pej*) ausgedehnt; (*irregular*) unregelmäßig

spray [spreɪ] I. *n* Spray *m o nt*; (*cloud*) Sprühnebel *m*; *of perfume* Wolke *f*; *of water* Gischt *m o f* II. *vt* besprühen; *plants* spritzen; *paint* sprühen III. *vi* spritzen

spread [spred] I. *n* Verbreitung *f*; (*range*) Vielfalt *f*; (*fam: meal*) Festessen *nt*; (*on bread*) Aufstrich *m*; (*news*) Doppelseite *f* II. *vi* <spread, spread> sich verbreiten; *panic* sich verbreiten; (*stretch*) sich erstrecken III. *vt* <spread, spread> ausbreiten; *net* auslegen; *bread* bestreichen; *sand* verteilen; *fertilizer* streuen; *disease* übertragen; *panic* verbreiten; *rumors* verbreiten

spread-eagled ['spred·'i·gəld] *adj* ausgestreckt

'spreadsheet *n* Tabellenkalkulation *f*

spree [spri] *n* **shopping** ~ Einkaufstour *f*

sprightly ['spraɪt·li] *adj* munter; *old person* rüstig

spring [sprɪŋ] I. *n* (*season*) Frühling *m*; TECH Feder *f*; (*water*) Quelle *f* II. *vi* <sprang *or* sprung, sprung> springen; (*appear*) auftauchen; **to** ~ **to mind** in den Kopf schießen

'springboard *n* Sprungbrett *nt*

spring-'clean I. *vi* Frühjahrsputz machen II. *vt* **to** ~ **a house** in einem Haus Frühjahrsputz machen

'spring roll *n* Frühlingsrolle *f*

'springtime *n* Frühling *m*

sprinkle ['sprɪŋ·kəl] I. *vt* streuen; (*cover*) bestreuen; (*with liquid*) besprengen II. *n* **a** ~ **of snow** leichter Schneefall; **chocolate** ~**s** Schokosplitter *pl*

sprinkler ['sprɪŋ·klər] *n* Bewässerungsanlage *f*; (*for lawn*) Sprinkler *m*; (*for fires*) Sprinkler *m*

sprinkling ['sprɪŋ·klɪŋ] *n* ■ **a ~ of ...** ein paar ...; **a ~ of salt** eine Prise Salz

sprint [sprɪnt] **I.** *vi* sprinten **II.** *n* Sprint *m*

sprinter ['sprɪn·tər] *n* Sprinter(in) *m(f)*

sprout [spraʊt] **I.** *n* Spross *m*; ■ **Brussels ~s** *pl* Rosenkohl *m* **II.** *vi* sprießen; *buds* austreiben *geh*; (*germinate*) keimen **III.** *vt* treiben

 ◆ **sprout up** *vi* aus dem Boden schießen

spruce [sprus] *n* Fichte *f*

sprung [sprʌŋ] *pt, pp of* **spring**

spud [spʌd] *n* (*sl*) Kartoffel *f*

spun [spʌn] *pt, pp of* **spin**

spur [spɜr] **I.** *n* Sporn *m*; (*fig*) Ansporn *m* ▸ PHRASES: **on the ~ of the moment** spontan **II.** *vt* <-rr-> anspornen; (*persuade*) bewegen; (*incite*) anstacheln

spurt [spɜrt] **I.** *n* Strahl *m*; (*surge*) Schub *m*; **to do sth in ~s** etw schubweise machen; **to put on a ~** einen Spurt hinlegen **II.** *vt* [ver]spritzen **III.** *vi* spritzen

sputter ['spʌt·ər] **I.** *n* Knattern *nt* **II.** *vi* zischen; (*car*) stottern **III.** *vt* heraussprudeln; (*stutter*) stottern

spy [spaɪ] **I.** *n* Spion(in) *m(f)* **II.** *vi* spionieren; ■ **to ~ on sb** jdm nachspionieren **III.** *vt* sehen; (*spot*) entdecken

squabble ['skwab·əl] **I.** *n* Zankerei *f* **II.** *vi* sich zanken

squad [skwad] *n* Mannschaft *f*; MIL Trupp *m*

'**squad car** *n* Streifenwagen *m*

squadron ['skwad·rən] *n* Schwadron *f*; (*air force*) Staffel *f*; (*navy*) Geschwader *nt*

squalid ['skwal·ɪd] *adj* schmutzig; (*neglected*) verwahrlost; (*immoral*) verkommen

squalor ['skwal·ər] *n* Schmutz *m*; (*immorality*) Verkommenheit *f*

squander ['skwan·dər] *vt* verschwenden; *opportunity* vertun

square [skwer] **I.** *n* Quadrat *nt*; (*in town*) Platz *m*; (*tool*) Winkelmaß *nt*; MATH Quadratzahl *f* **II.** *adj* quadratisch; *face* kantig; (*on each side*) im Quadrat; (*when squared*) zum Quadrat; *foot, mile* Quadrat-; **to be [all] ~** (*fam*) auf gleich sein **III.** *vt* ❶ ■ **to ~ sth with sth** etw mit etw *dat* in Übereinstimmung bringen ❷ (*settle*) in Ordnung bringen

 ◆ **square up** *vi* (*fam*) abrechnen

'**square dance** *n* Squaredance *m*

squarely ['skwer·li] *adv* aufrecht; (*directly*) direkt

square 'root *n* MATH Quadratwurzel *f*

squash[1] [skwaʃ] *n* (*pumpkin*) Kürbis *m*

squash[2] [skwaʃ] **I.** *n* Squash *nt* **II.** *vt* zerdrücken; *rumors* aus der Welt schaffen; **to ~ sth flat** etw platt drücken

squat [skwat] **I.** *vi* <-tt-> ❶ hocken; ■ **to ~ [down]** sich hinhocken ❷ *on land* sich illegal ansiedeln; **to ~ [in a house]** ein Haus besetzen **II.** *n* Hocke *f*; (*exercise*) Kniebeuge *f*; (*building*) besetztes Haus **III.** *adj* <-tt-> gedrungen

squatter ['skwat·ər] *n* Hausbesetzer(in) *m(f)*

squaw [skwɔ] *n* (*offensive*) Squaw *f*

squawk [skwɔk] **I.** *vi* kreischen **II.** *n* Kreischen *nt*

squeak [skwik] **I.** *n* Quietschen *nt*; *of animal* Quieken *nt*; *of mouse* Pieps[er] *m fam*; *of person* Quiekser *m fam* **II.** *vi* quietschen; *animal, person* quieken; *mouse* piepsen

'**squeaky-clean** *adj* blitzsauber *fam*

squeal [skwil] **I.** *n* [schriller] Schrei; *of tires* Quietschen *nt*; *of brakes* Kreischen *nt*; *of pig* Quieken *nt* **II.** *vi* kreischen; *pig* quieken; *tires* quietschen; *brakes* kreischen

squeamish ['skwi·mɪʃ] **I.** *adj* zimperlich; **he is ~ about seeing blood** er ekelt sich vor Blut **II.** *npl* **to be not for the ~** nichts für schwache Nerven sein

squeeze [skwiz] **I.** *n* ❶ Drücken *nt*; **to give sth a ~** etw drücken ❷ (*limit*) Beschränkung *f* ❸ (*fit*) Gedränge *nt*; **it'll be a tight ~** es wird eng werden **II.** *vt* drücken; *orange* auspressen; *sponge* ausdrücken; (*push in*) [hinein]zwängen;

S

(*push through*) [durch]zwängen; (*constrict*) einschränken III. *vi* ■**to → in/ past/through** sich hinein-/vorbei-/ durchzwängen

squid <*pl* -> [skwɪd] *n* Tintenfisch *m*

squiggle ['skwɪg·əl] *n* Schnörkel *m*

squint [skwɪnt] *vi* blinzeln; ■**to → at sb/sth** einen Blick auf jdn/etw werfen

squirm [skwɜrm] I. *vi* sich winden; **to → in pain** sich vor Schmerzen krümmen II. *n* **to give a → of embarrassment** sich vor Verlegenheit winden

squirrel ['skwɜr·əl] *n* Eichhörnchen *nt*

squirt [skwɜrt] I. *vt* spritzen; ■**to → sb with sth** jdn mit etw *dat* bespritzen II. *vi* ■**to → out** herausspritzen III. *n* Spritzer *m*

Sri Lanka [ˌsri·'lɑŋ·kə] *n* Sri Lanka *nt*

Sri Lankan [ˌsri·'lɑŋ·kən] I. *adj* sri-lankisch; **to be →** aus Sri Lanka sein II. *n* Sri-Lanker(in) *m(f)*

SSW [ˌes·es·'dʌb·əl·ju] *abbrev of* **southsouthwest** SSW

St. *n* ❶ *abbrev of* **street** Str. ❷ *abbrev of* **saint** St.

stab [stæb] I. *vt* <-bb-> ■**to → sb/sth** auf jdn/etw einstechen; **to → sth with a fork** mit einer Gabel in etw *dat* herumstochern; **to → the air** [**with sth**] [mit etw *dat*] in der Luft herumfuchteln II. *vi* <-bb-> ■**to → at sb/sth** auf jdn/ etw einstechen III. *n* Stich *m;* (*wound*) Stichwunde *f;* (*pain*) Stich *m* ▶PHRASES: **to take a → at** [**doing**] **sth** etw [einmal] probieren

stabbing ['stæ·bɪŋ] I. *n* Messerstecherei *f* II. *adj* stechend; *fear* durchdringend

stability [stə·'bɪl·ɪ·t̬i] *n* Stabilität *f*

stabilization [ˌstei·bə·lɪ·'zei·ʃən] *n* Stabilisierung *f*

stabilize ['stei·bə·laɪz] I. *vt* stabilisieren; *prices a.* festigen II. *vi* sich stabilisieren; **his condition has now →d** sein Zustand ist jetzt stabil

stable¹ <-r, -st *or* more ~, most ~> ['stei·bəl] *adj* stabil; *relationship* fest; PSYCH ausgeglichen

stable² ['stei·bəl] *n* Stall *m*

stack [stæk] I. *n* Stapel *m; of papers* Stoß *m;* (*fam: amount*) Haufen *m; hi-fi* Stereoturm *m* II. *vt* [auf]stapeln; *dishwasher* einräumen; *shelves* auffüllen

stadium <*pl* -s> ['stei·di·əm] *n* Stadion *nt*

staff [stæf] I. *n* ❶ + *sing/pl vb* Belegschaft *f;* **nursing ~** Pflegepersonal *nt* ❷ (*stick*) [Spazier]stock *m* II. *vt usu passive* **many charities are ~ed by volunteers** viele Wohltätigkeitsvereine beschäftigen ehrenamtliche Mitarbeiter

stag [stæg] *n* Hirsch *m*

stage [steidʒ] I. *n* ❶ Etappe *f; of race a.* Abschnitt *m;* (*level*) Stufe *f;* **crucial ~** entscheidende Phase ❷ THEAT Bühne *f;* **to take center ~** im Mittelpunkt [des Interesses] stehen II. *vt* aufführen; *concert* geben; *meeting* veranstalten; *strike* organisieren; *game* austragen

'**stage fright** *n* Lampenfieber *nt*

'**stage-manage** *vt* inszenieren

'**stage manager** *n* Bühnenmeister(in) *m(f)*

'**stage name** *n* Künstlername *m*

stagger ['stæg·ər] I. *vi* wanken; (*waver a.*) schwanken; **to → one's feet** sich aufrappeln II. *vt* erstaunen III. *n* Wanken *nt*

staggering ['stæg·ər·ɪŋ] *adj* erstaunlich; *news* unglaublich; (*shocking*) erschütternd

stagnant ['stæg·nənt] *adj* stagnierend; *pool* still; *water* stehend

stagnate ['stæg·neit] *vi* stagnieren; *stream* sich stauen

stagnation [stæg·'nei·ʃən] *n* Stagnation *f*

stain [stein] I. *vt* verfärben; *wood* [ein]färben; (*spot*) Flecken machen auf + *dat; reputation* schaden II. *vi* abfärben; (*discolor*) sich verfärben; (*take dye*) sich färben III. *n* Verfärbung *f;* (*blemish*) Makel *m*

stained [steind] *adj* verfärbt; (*with spots*) fleckig; (*dyed*) gefärbt

'**stained-glass window** *n* Buntglasfenster *nt*

stainless 'steel *n* rostfreier Stahl

'**stain remover** n Fleckenentferner m
'**stair** [ster] n Treppenstufe f; ■~s pl
Treppe f; **flight of ~s** Treppe f
'**staircase** n Treppenhaus nt; **spiral ~**
Wendeltreppe f
'**stairway** n Treppe f
stake [steɪk] I. n ❶ Pfahl m ❷ usu pl
(bet) Einsatz m ❸ (interest) Anteil m
▶PHRASES: **to be at ~** (in question) zur
Debatte stehen; (at risk) auf dem Spiel
stehen II. vt ❶ animal anbinden; plant
hochbinden ❷ (bet) setzen; **to ~ one's
future on sth** seine Zukunft auf etw
akk aufbauen
◆ **stake out** vt ❶ (watch) überwachen
❷ (mark) markieren; border abstecken
'**stakeholder** n Teilhaber(in) m(f)
stalactite [stə'læk·taɪt] n Tropfstein m
stalagmite [stə'læg·maɪt] n Tropfstein m
stale [steɪl] adj schal; beer abgestanden;
air muffig; bread alt; (unoriginal) fanta-
sielos; joke abgedroschen; (without
zest) abgestumpft
stalemate ['steɪl·meɪt] I. n Patt nt;
(deadlock) Stillstand m II. vt patt setzen; (deadlock) zum Stillstand bringen
stalk¹ [stɔk] n Stiel m
stalk² [stɔk] I. vt jagen; ■**to ~ sb** jdm
nachstellen II. vi stolzieren; (angrily)
marschieren
stalker ['stɔː·kər] n ❶ (hunter) Jäger(in)
m(f) ❷ of people Stalker(in) m(f) (Person, die jemanden verfolgt, belästigt
und terrorisiert)
stall¹ [stɔl] I. n Stall m; (booth) [Ver-
kaufs]stand m; (for parking) [markier-
ter] Parkplatz; (toilet) Toilette f II. vi
stehen bleiben; aircraft abrutschen; negotiations zum Stillstand kommen
III. vt abwürgen
stall² [stɔl] I. vi zögern; **to ~ for time**
Zeit gewinnen II. vt verzögern; ■**to ~
sb** (fam) jdn hinhalten
stallion ['stæl·jən] n Hengst m
stamina ['stæm·ə·nə] n Durchhalteverme-
mögen nt
stammer ['stæm·ər] I. n Stottern nt
II. vi stottern

stamp [stæmp] I. n ❶ Stempel m; **~ of
approval** Genehmigungsstempel m;
postage ~ Briefmarke f ❷ (step)
Stampfer m fam; (sound) Stampfen nt
II. vt ❶ |ab|stempeln; **to ~ a letter** ei-
nen Brief frankieren ❷ zertreten; **to ~
one's foot** mit dem Fuß aufstampfen
III. vi stampfen; (walk a.) stapfen; ■**to
~ on sth** auf etw akk treten
◆ **stamp out** vt ausmerzen; crime bekämpfen; disease ausrotten; fire austreten
'**stamp collector** n Briefmarkensamm-
ler(in) m(f)
stampede [stæm·'piːd] I. n wilde
Flucht; of people [Menschen]auflauf m
II. vi durchgehen; people stürzen
stance [stæns] n Haltung f; (attitude)
Standpunkt m
stand [stænd] I. n ❶ Stellung f; (view)
Einstellung f; **to take a ~ on sth** sich
für etw akk einsetzen ❷ (seating) ■**~s**
pl [Zuschauer]tribüne f ❸ (support)
Ständer m ❹ LAW ■**the ~** der Zeugenstand; **to take the ~** vor Gericht aussagen ❺ **to make a ~** klar Stellung beziehen ❻ **taxi ~** Taxistand m II. vi <stood,
stood> ❶ stehen; **~ against the wall**
stell dich an die Wand; **to ~ clear** aus
dem Weg gehen; **to ~ still** stillstehen
❷ (be located) stehen/liegen; **to ~ in
sb's way** jdm im Weg stehen ❸ + adj
to ~ open/empty/in second place
offen/leer/an zweiter Stelle stehen;
**with the situation as it ~s right
now ...** so wie die Sache im Moment
aussieht, ... ❹ (remain valid) gelten;
does that offer still ~? ist das Angebot
noch gültig? ▶PHRASES: **to ~ on one's
own two feet** auf eigenen Füßen stehen III. vt <stood, stood> ❶ ■**to ~ sth
somewhere** etw irgendwohin stellen;
to ~ sth on its head etw auf den Kopf
stellen ❷ (bear) ertragen; **she can't ~
anyone touching her** sie kann es nicht
leiden, wenn man sie anfasst; **to ~ the
test of time** die Zeit überdauern ❸ **to ~
trial** sich vor Gericht verantworten
müssen ▶PHRASES: **to ~ sb in good**

S

stead jdm von Nutzen sein

◆ **stand around** vi herumstehen

◆ **stand back** vi (*take detached view*) etw aus der Distanz betrachten; (*not get involved*) tatenlos zusehen; (*be set back from*) abseitsliegen

◆ **stand by** vi bereitstehen; (*observe*) dabeistehen; *promise* halten; ■**to ~ by sb/one's word** zu jdm/zu seinem Wort stehen

◆ **stand for** vi ❶ (*tolerate*) ■**to not ~ for sth** sich *dat* etw nicht gefallen lassen ❷ (*represent*) ■**to ~ for sth** für etw *akk* stehen

◆ **stand in** vi ■**to ~ in for sb** für jdn einspringen

◆ **stand out** vi hervorragen; (*be distinguishable*) zu unterscheiden sein; (*be identifiable*) gekennzeichnet sein; **to ~ out in a crowd** sich von der Menge abheben

◆ **stand up** vi aufstehen; (*stand*) stehen

standard ['stæn·dərd] I. n ❶ Standard m; (*criterion*) Gradmesser m; **to raise ~s** das Niveau heben ❷ (*principles*) ■**~s** pl Wertvorstellungen pl II. adj Standard-; (*average*) durchschnittlich

standardization [ˌstæn·dər·dɪ·'zeɪ·ʃən] n Standardisierung f

standardize ['stæn·dər·daɪz] vt standardisieren; (*compare*) vereinheitlichen

standby <pl -s> ['stæn(d)·baɪ] I. n ❶ no pl (*readiness*) **on ~** in Bereitschaft; ELEC betriebsbereit; **~ mode** Stand-by-Modus m, Stand-by-Betrieb m ❷ (*backup*) Reserve f ❸ (*plane ticket*) Stand-by-Ticket nt ❹ (*traveler*) Fluggast m mit Stand-by-Ticket II. adj attr Ersatz- III. adv AVIAT, TOURIST **to fly ~** mit einem Stand-by-Ticket fliegen

'**stand-in** n Vertretung f; (*actor*) Ersatz m

standing ['stæn·dɪŋ] I. n ❶ (*status*) Ansehen nt ❷ **to be of long ~** von langer Dauer sein II. adj attr (*upright*) [auf-recht] stehend; (*permanent*) ständig; (*stationary*) stehend

standing o'vation n stehende Ovationen pl

'**standpoint** n Standpunkt m

'**standstill** n Stillstand m; **to be at a ~** zum Erliegen kommen

'**standup** adj attr **~ comedy** Stand-up-Comedy f; **~ comedian** Stand-up-Comedian m

stank [stæŋk] pt of **stink**

staple ['steɪ·pəl] I. n Heftklammer f II. vt heften; ■**to ~ sth together** etw zusammenheften

'**staple gun** n Heftmaschine f

stapler ['steɪp·lər] n Hefter m

star [star] I. n Stern m; (*asterisk*) Sternchen nt; (*performer*) Star m II. vt <-rr-> "**King Lear**" **~ring John Smith as Lear** „King Lear" mit John Smith als Lear III. vi <-rr-> **to ~ in a film** in einem Film die Hauptrolle spielen IV. adj attr Star-; **~ witness** Hauptzeuge, -zeugin m, f

starboard ['star·bərd] n Steuerbord nt kein pl

starch [startʃ] n Stärke f

stare [ster] I. n Starren nt; (*directed*) fester Blick II. vi starren; (*gawk*) große Augen machen; ■**to ~ at sb/sth** jdn/etw anstarren III. vt **to ~ sb in the eye** jdn anstarren; **to ~ sb up and down** jdn anstieren *fam* ▶PHRASES: **to be staring sb in the face** auf der Hand liegen

'**starfish** n Seestern m

staring ['ster·ɪŋ] adj starrend

stark [stark] I. adj krass; **to be a ~ reminder** drastisch an etw *akk* erinnern II. adv **~ naked** splitternfasernackt *fam*; **~ raving mad** (*hum, iron*) völlig übergeschnappt *fam*

starling ['star·lɪŋ] n Star m

'**starry-eyed** adj blauäugig

Stars and Stripes [ˌstarz·ənd·'straɪps] npl + sing vb ■**the ~** die Stars and Stripes pl (*Nationalflagge der USA*)

'**star sign** n Sternzeichen nt

Star-Spangled 'Banner n ■**the ~** das Sternenbanner (*die Nationalflagge der USA*); (*anthem*) der Star Spangled Banner (*die Nationalhymne der USA*)

start [start] I. *n* ❶ Anfang *m;* SPORT Start *m;* **it was an exciting ~** es fing spannend an; **to make a fresh ~** einen neuen Anfang machen; **to have a good ~ in life** einen guten Start ins Leben haben ❷ **to give a ~** zusammenzucken II. *vi* ❶ anfangen; *(on trip)* losfahren; *car* anspringen; *(happen)* beginnen; **~ ing tomorrow** ab morgen; **to ~ with** *(at first)* anfangs; *(firstly)* zunächst einmal ❷ *(jump)* zusammenfahren III. *vt* anfangen; *(switch on)* einschalten; *machine* anstellen; *motor* anlassen; *car* starten; *family* gründen; *(initiate)* ins Leben rufen; **when do you ~ your new job?** wann fängst du mit deiner neuen Stelle an?; **to ~ a fire** Feuer machen; ■**to ~ doing sth** anfangen, etw zu tun
◆**start back** *vi* sich auf den Rückweg machen
◆**start off** I. *vi* **they ~ed off by reading through the script** zuerst lasen sie das Skript durch; ■**to ~ off as sth** seine Laufbahn als etw beginnen; ■**to ~ off with sb/sth** bei jdm/etw anfangen II. *vt* ■**to ~ sth** ↻ **off** etw beginnen; ■**to ~ sb off doing sth** jdn zu etw *dat* veranlassen; ■**to ~ sb off with sth** jdm den Start bei etw *dat* erleichtern
◆**start out** *vi* aufbrechen; *(begin)* anfangen
◆**start up** I. *vt* gründen; *motor* anlassen II. *vi* beginnen; *engine* anspringen
'**starting point** *n* Ausgangspunkt *m*
startle ['star·təl] *vt* erschrecken
startling ['star·təl·ɪŋ] *adj* überraschend; *(alarming)* erschreckend
'**start-up** *n* [Neu]gründung *f; of machine* Inbetriebnahme *f;* COMPUT Hochfahren *nt;* **~ disk** Startdiskette *f*
starvation [star·'veɪ·ʃən] *n* Unterernährung *f; (fatal)* Hungertod *m;* **to die of ~** verhungern
starve [starv] I. *vi* hungern; *(die)* verhungern; *(be malnourished)* unterernährt sein; *(fam)* am Verhungern sein *fam; (crave)* hungern **(for** nach *+dat)* II. *vt* aushungern; ■**to ~ oneself to**

death sich zu Tode hungern; ■**to be ~ d of sth** um etw *akk* gebracht werden
starving ['star·vɪŋ] *adj* ausgehungert; **I'm ~ !** ich bin am Verhungern!
stash [stæʃ] I. *n* <*pl* -**es**> [geheimes] Lager, Vorrat *m* II. *vt (fam)* verstecken; *money* bunkern
state [steɪt] I. *n* ❶ Zustand *m; (bodily)* körperliche Verfassung; **~ of war** Kriegszustand *m;* **a good ~ of health** ein guter Gesundheitszustand; **~ of mind** Gemütszustand *m* ❷ *(nation)* Staat *m; (government a.)* Regierung *f; (in USA)* [Bundes]staat *m; (in Germany)* Land *nt;* ■**the S~s** *pl (fam: the USA)* die Staaten *pl* II. *vt* aussprechen; *objections* vorbringen; *source* angeben; *(fix)* nennen; *demands* stellen; ■**to ~ why …** darlegen, warum …
'**State Department** *n* ■**the ~** das US-Außenministerium
stately ['steɪt·li] *adj* würdevoll; *(splendid)* prächtig
statement ['steɪt·mənt] *n* Erklärung *f; (formal)* Stellungnahme *f;* **to make a ~ to the press** eine Presseerklärung abgeben; *bank* ~ [Konto]auszug *m*
state of the 'art *adj pred,* **state-of-the-'art** *adj attr* auf dem neuesten Stand der Technik *nach n*
'**stateside** I. *adj* in den Staaten *präd* II. *adv* in die Staaten
'**statesman** *n* Staatsmann *m*
'**stateswoman** *n* Staatsfrau *f*
state 'visit *n* Staatsbesuch *m*
static ['stæt̬·ɪk] I. *adj* statisch; *(not changing)* konstant II. *n* statische Elektrizität
static elec'tricity *n* statische Elektrizität
station ['steɪ·ʃən] *n* ❶ *train* ~ Bahnhof *m;* **subway ~** U-Bahn-Haltestelle *f;* **police ~** Polizeiwache *f;* **power ~** Kraftwerk *nt* ❷ TV Sender *m*
stationary ['steɪ·ʃə·ner·i] *adj* ruhend; *(not changing)* unverändert
stationery ['steɪ·ʃə·ner·i] *n* Schreibwaren *pl; (writing paper)* Schreibpapier *nt*
'**station house** *n* Polizeiwache *f*
'**station wagon** *n* Kombi[wagen] *m*

S

statistics [stə·'tɪs·tɪks] *npl* Statistik *f*
statue ['stætʃ·u] *n* Statue *f*
Statue of 'Liberty *n* ■**the ~** die Freiheitsstatue
stature ['stætʃ·ər] *n* Statur *f; (reputation)* Prestige *nt; short ~* kleiner Wuchs
status ['stæ·təs] *n* Status *m; (prestige a.)* Prestige *nt; legal ~* Rechtsposition *f*
'**status symbol** *n* Statussymbol *nt*
statute ['stætʃ·ut] *n* Satzung *f; (law)* Gesetz *nt;* ■**by ~** satzungsgemäß
'**statute book** *n* Gesetzbuch *nt*
statute of limi'tations *n* Verjährungsgesetz *nt*
staunch [stɔntʃ] *adj* standhaft; *Catholic* überzeugt; *opponent* erbittert
stave off *vt* hinauszögern; *(prevent)* abwenden; *hunger* stillen; ■**to ~ off** ⊃ **sb** jdn hinhalten *fam*
stay [steɪ] **I.** *n* Aufenthalt *m; overnight ~* Übernachtung *f* **II.** *vi* ❶ bleiben; **to ~ put** *(fam: keep standing)* stehen bleiben; *(not stand up)* sitzen bleiben; *(not move)* sich nicht vom Fleck rühren ❷ *(reside temporarily)* untergebracht sein; **to ~ overnight** übernachten ❸ *+ n or adj* bleiben; **the stores ~ open until 8 p.m.** die Läden haben bis 20 Uhr geöffnet; **to ~ in touch** in Verbindung bleiben **III.** *vt* ▶PHRASES: **to ~ the course** durchhalten
◆**stay away** *vi* fernbleiben; *(avoid)* meiden
◆**stay behind** *vi* [noch] [da]bleiben; **to ~ behind after school** nachsitzen
◆**stay in** *vi* zu Hause bleiben
◆**stay on** *vi* [noch] bleiben; *lid* draufbleiben; *sticker* haften; *light* an bleiben; *device* eingeschaltet bleiben
◆**stay out** *vi* wegbleiben; **~ out of the kitchen!** bleib aus der Küche!; **to ~ out of trouble** sich *dat* Ärger vom Hals halten *fam*
◆**stay together** *vi* immer zusammen sein; *(always)* unzertrennlich sein; *group* zusammenhalten; *(loyally)* zusammenhalten
◆**stay up** *vi* aufbleiben

steady ['sted·i] **I.** *adj* fest; *(regular)* kontinuierlich; *pulse* regelmäßig; *increase* stetig; *rain* anhaltend; *speed* konstant; *voice* fest; *pain* permanent; *hand* ruhig; *(calm)* verlässlich; *nerves* stark **II.** *vt* <-ie-> stabilisieren; *ladder* festhalten; *nerves* beruhigen; **to ~ oneself** ins Gleichgewicht kommen, Halt finden **III.** *adv* **to ~ hold ~** *prices* stabil bleiben; **to hold sth ~** etw festhalten
steak [steɪk] *n* Rindfleisch *nt; (slice)* [Beef]steak *nt*
steal [stil] **I.** *vt* <stole, stolen> stehlen; *heart* erobern; **she stole a glance at her watch** sie lugte heimlich auf ihre Armbanduhr; **to ~** *[sb's]* **ideas** *[jds]* Ideen klauen *fam* **II.** *vi* <stole, stolen> stehlen; **he stole out of the room** er stahl sich aus dem Zimmer
stealth [stelθ] *n* Heimlichkeit *f;* **by ~** heimlich
stealthy ['stel·θi] *adj* heimlich
steam [stim] **I.** *n* Dampf *m;* **to let off ~** Dampf ablassen **II.** *vi* dampfen
◆**steam up I.** *vi* [sich] beschlagen **II.** *vt* **the windows are ~ed up** die Fenster sind beschlagen; **to get all ~ed up** *[about sth]* *(fam)* sich [über etw *akk*] unheimlich aufregen
'**steamboat** *n* Dampfschiff *nt,* Dampfer *m*
steamer ['sti·mər] *n* Dampfer *m; (pot)* Dampfkochtopf *m*
'**steamroller I.** *n* Dampfwalze *f* **II.** *vt* niederwalzen; ■**to ~ sb into doing sth** jdn unter Druck setzen, etw zu tun
'**steamship** *n* Dampfschiff *nt*
steamy ['sti·mi] *adj* feuchtheiß; *(fam: sexy)* heiß; *novel a.* prickelnd
steel [stil] **I.** *n* Stahl *m;* **nerves of ~** Nerven *pl* wie Drahtseile **II.** *vt* ■**to ~ oneself against/for sth** sich gegen/für etw *akk* wappnen; ■**to ~ oneself** *[to do sth]* all seinen Mut zusammennehmen[, um etw zu tun]
'**steelworker** *n* Stahlarbeiter(in) *m(f)*
'**steelworks** *npl + sing vb* Stahlwerk *nt*
steep [stip] *adj* steil; *slope* abschüssig;

steps hoch; (*dramatic*) drastisch; *decline* deutlich; (*expensive*) überteuert

steepen ['sti·pən] *vi* steiler werden; *slope* ansteigen

steeple ['sti·pəl] *n* Turmspitze *f*; *of church* Kirchturm *m*

'steeplechase *n* Hindernislauf *m*; (*for horses*) Hindernisrennen *nt*

steer¹ [stɪr] *vt, vi* steuern

steer² [stɪr] *n* junger Ochse

steering ['stɪr·ɪŋ] *n* Lenkung *f*; NAUT Steuerung *f*

'steering wheel *n* Steuer[rad] *nt*; *of car a.* Lenkrad *nt*

stem [stem] **I.** *n* Stamm *m*; *of leaf* Stiel *m*; *of grain* Halm *m*; *of glass* [Glas]stiel *m* **II.** *vi* <-mm-> ■**to ~ back to sth** auf etw *akk* zurückgehen; ■**to ~ from sb/sth** auf jdn/etw zurückzuführen sein

stench [stentʃ] *n* Gestank *m*

stencil ['sten·səl] *n* Schablone *f*; (*picture*) Schablonenzeichnung *f*

step [step] **I.** *n* Schritt *m*; (*measure a.*) Vorgehen *nt*; (*of dance*) [Tanz]schritt *m*; (*stair*) Stufe *f*; *of ladder* Sprosse *f*; **"watch your ~"** „Vorsicht, Stufe!"; **to be one ~ ahead** [of sb] [jdm] einen Schritt voraus sein; **~ by ~** Schritt für Schritt; **to take drastic ~s** zu drastischen Mitteln greifen; ■**in ~** im Takt; (*fig*) im Einklang; **to walk in ~** im Gleichschritt laufen **II.** *vi* <-pp-> ❶ **to ~ on sb's foot** jdm auf den Fuß treten; ■**to ~ over sth** über etw *akk* steigen ❷ (*walk*) ■**to ~ somewhere** irgendwohin gehen; **would you care to ~ this way please, sir?** würden Sie bitte hier entlanggehen, Sir?; **to ~ aside** zur Seite gehen; **to ~ out of line** (*fig*) sich danebenbenehmen **III.** *vi* treten (**on** auf +*akk*); **~ on it!** gib Gas! *fam*

◆**step back** *vi* zurücktreten; (*reconsider*) Abstand nehmen

◆**step down** *vi* zurücktreten; *witness* den Zeugenstand verlassen

◆**step in** *vi* eintreten; *car* einsteigen; (*intervene*) eingreifen

◆**step up** *vt* verstärken; *pace* beschleunigen; *volunteer* vortreten

'stepbrother *n* Stiefbruder *m*

'stepdaughter *n* Stieftochter *f*

'stepfamily *n* + *sing/pl vb* Stieffamilie *f*, Patchworkfamilie *f*

'stepfather *n* Stiefvater *m*

'stepladder *n* Stehleiter *f*

'stepmother *n* Stiefmutter *f*

'stepping stone *n* [Tritt]stein *m*; (*fig*) Sprungbrett *nt*

'stepsister *n* Stiefschwester *f*

'stepson *n* Stiefsohn *m*

stereo ['ster·i·oʊ] **I.** *n* <*pl* -os> Stereo *nt*; (*fam: unit*) Stereoanlage *f* **II.** *adj* Stereo-

stereotype ['ster·i·ə·taɪp] **I.** *n* Stereotyp *nt*; (*character*) stereotype Figur **II.** *vt* **to ~ sb/sth** jdn/etw in ein Klischee zwängen

sterile ['ster·əl] *adj* steril

sterilization [ˌster·ə·lɪ·'zeɪ·ʃən] *n* Sterilisierung *f*

sterilize ['ster·ə·laɪz] *vt* sterilisieren; (*disinfect*) desinfizieren; *water* abkochen

stern¹ [stɜrn] *adj* ernst; (*strict*) streng; (*difficult*) hart

stern² [stɜrn] *n* NAUT Heck *nt*

steroid ['ster·ɔɪd] *n* Steroide *pl*

stethoscope ['steθ·ə·skoʊp] *n* Stethoskop *nt*

steward ['stu·ərd] *n* Flugbegleiter *m*; (*on cruise*) Schiffsbegleiter *m*; (*at event*) Ordner(in) *m(f)*

stewardess <*pl* -es> ['stu·ər·dɪs] *n* Flugbegleiterin *f*; (*on cruise*) Schiffsbegleiterin *f*

stick [stɪk] **I.** *n* ❶ Zweig *m*; (*implement*) Stock *m*; **walking ~** Spazierstock *m*; **hockey ~** Hockeyschläger *m*; **celery ~s** Selleriestangen *pl*; **a ~ of chewing gum** ein Stück *nt* Kaugummi ❷ **a ~ in the ribs** ein Stoß *m* in die Rippen **II.** *vi* <stuck, stuck> ❶ kleben; **this glue won't ~** dieser Klebstoff hält nicht ❷ (*not move*) feststecken; *car* stecken

S

bleiben; (be *unmovable*) festsitzen; *door* klemmen; **to ~ in sb's mind** jdm in Erinnerung bleiben ❸ (*persevere*) ■**to ~ with sth** an etw *dat* dranbleiben ❹**to ~ to one's budget** sich an sein Budget halten; **to ~ to a diet** eine Diät einhalten ❺ ■**to ~ by sb/sth** zu jdm/ etw halten ▶PHRASES: **to ~ to one's guns** nicht lockerlassen III. *vt* <stuck, stuck> ❶ kleben (**to an** +*akk*); **~ your things wherever you like** (*fam*) stellen Sie Ihre Sachen irgendwo ab; **to ~ one's head around the door** seinen Kopf durch die Tür stecken ❷ (*fam: burden*) ■**to be stuck with sb** jdn am Hals haben ▶PHRASES: **to ~ one's nose into sb's business** seine Nase in jds Angelegenheiten stecken

◆**stick around** *vi* (*fam*) da bleiben

◆**stick in** I. *vi* stecken bleiben II. *vt* (*fam*) ■**~ sth in sth** etw in etw *akk* einkleben; ■**to ~ sth in**[**to**] **sth** etw in etw *akk* hineinstecken

◆**stick out** I. *vt* ausstrecken; *tongue* herausstrecken; ■**to ~ it out** (*endure*) es [bis zum Ende] durchhalten II. *vi* [her]vorstehen; *ears* abstehen; (*be obvious*) offensichtlich sein; **to ~ out like a sore thumb** wie ein bunter Pudel auffallen *fam*

◆**stick together** I. *vt* zusammenkleben II. *vi* zusammenkleben; (*fig*) immer zusammen sein; (*always*) unzertrennlich sein; *group* zusammenbleiben; (*loyally*) zusammenhalten

◆**stick up** I. *vt* (*fam*) überfallen II. *vi* emporragen; (*on end*) abstehen; ■**to ~ up for sb/sth** sich für jdn/etw einsetzen

sticker ['stɪk·ər] *n* Aufkleber *m*; (*for collecting*) Sticker *m*; **price ~** Preisschild[chen] *nt*

'**stick insect** *n* Gespenstheuschrecke *f*

'**stick-in-the-mud** I. *n* (*fam*) Muffel *m* II. *adj attr* rückständig

stickler ['stɪk·lər] *n* Pedant(in) *m(f) pej*; **to be a ~ for accuracy** pingelig auf Genauigkeit achten

'**stick-on** *adj attr* Klebe-

'**stick-up** *n* (*sl*) Überfall *m*

sticky ['stɪk·i] *adj* klebrig; *weather* schwül; *air* stickig; ■**to be ~ with sth** mit etw *dat* verklebt sein

stiff [stɪf] I. *adj* steif; *paper, dough* fest; *paste* dick; *opposition* stark; *breeze* steif; *criticism* herb II. *adv* **to be scared ~** zu Tode erschrocken sein

stiffen ['stɪf·ən] I. *vi* sich versteifen; *muscles* sich verspannen; (*with nervousness*) sich verkrampfen; (*with fear*) erstarren II. *vt* versteifen; *collar* stärken

stiff-necked ['stɪf·nekt] *adj* halsstarrig; (*arrogant*) arrogant

stifle ['staɪ·fəl] I. *vi* ersticken II. *vt* ersticken; (*suppress*) unterdrücken; **to ~ the urge to laugh** sich *dat* das Lachen verbeißen

stifling ['staɪ·flɪŋ] *adj* erstickend; *air* zum Ersticken *nach n, präd; heat* drückend; *room* stickig; (*repressive*) erdrückend

stiletto <*pl* -os> [stɪ·ˈlɛt·oʊ] *n* Pfennigabsatz *m*; ■**~s** *pl* Schuhe *pl* mit Pfennigabsätzen

stiletto 'heel *n* Pfennigabsatz *m*

still [stɪl] I. *n* Stille *f*; (*photo*) Standfoto *nt* II. *adj* ruhig; (*motionless*) reglos; *water* ohne Kohlensäure *nach n;* **to keep ~** still halten, sich nicht bewegen III. *adv* ❶ [immer] noch, noch immer; (*in future as in past*) nach wie vor; **there's ~ time for us to …** wir können es noch schaffen, … zu … ❷ (*nevertheless*) trotzdem; **…, but he's ~ your brother …**, [aber] er ist immer noch dein Bruder ❸**to want ~ more** immer noch mehr wollen

'**stillbirth** *n* Totgeburt *f*

'**stillborn** *adj* tot geboren

still 'life <*pl* -s> *n* Stillleben *nt*; (*style*) Stilllebenmalerei *f*

stilt [stɪlt] *n usu pl* Stelze *f*

stimulant ['stɪm·jə·lənt] *n* Anreiz *m*; (*drug*) Stimulans *nt*; SPORT Aufputschmittel *nt*

stimulate ['stɪm·jə·leɪt] I. *vt* ankurbeln; (*excite*) stimulieren II. *vi* mitreißen

stimulating ['stɪm·jə·leɪ·t̬ɪŋ] *adj* stimulierend; (*sexually a.*) erregend; *conversation* anregend; *atmosphere* animierend; *exercise* belebend

stimulation [ˌstɪm·jə·ˈleɪ·ʃən] *n* Anregung *f*; (*physical*) belebende Wirkung; (*sexual*) Stimulieren *nt*; (*motivation*) Ankurbelung *m*; (*of interest*) Erregung *f*

stimulus <*pl* -li> [ˈstɪm·jə·ləs] *n* Anreiz *m*; (*motivation*) Ansporn *m*; BIOL Reiz *m*

sting [stɪŋ] **I.** *n* ❶ Stich *m*; (*from ointment, jellyfish*) Brennen *nt*; (*from needle*) Stechen *nt* ❷ (*sl: raid*) Coup *m* **II.** *vi* <stung, stung> stechen; *sunburn* brennen; *cut* schmerzen; *words* schmerzen **III.** *vt* <stung, stung> stechen; **to ~ sb's eyes** jdm in den Augen brennen; **he was stung by her criticism** ihre Kritik hat ihn tief getroffen

stinger [ˈstɪŋ·ər] *n* Stachel *m*

stingray [ˈstɪŋ·reɪ] *n* Stachelrochen *m*

stingy [ˈstɪn·dʒi] *adj* (*fam*) geizig

stink [stɪŋk] **I.** *n usu sing* Gestank *m*; (*fam: trouble*) Stunk *m* **II.** *vi* <stank or stunk, stunk> stinken (**of** nach +*dat*); (*fam: suck*) stinken; (*fam: be wrong*) zum Himmel stinken *sl*; **his acting ~s** (*fam*) er ist ein miserabler Schauspieler

'stink bomb *n* Stinkbombe *f*

stipulate [ˈstɪp·jə·leɪt] *vt* verlangen; (*contract*) festlegen; (*law*) vorschreiben

stipulation [ˌstɪp·jə·ˈleɪ·ʃən] *n* Bedingung *f*; (*clause*) Klausel *f*

stir [stɜr] **I.** *n usu sing* (*with spoon*) [Um]rühren *nt* ❷ (*movement*) Bewegung *f*; *of emotion* Erregung *f*; (*excitement*) Aufruhr *f*; **to cause a ~** Aufsehen erregen **II.** *vt* <-rr-> ❶ rühren; ■ **to ~ sth into sth** etw in etw *akk* [hin]einrühren ❷ (*move*) rühren ❸ (*arouse*) bewegen; *anger* erregen; *emotions* aufwühlen ❹ ■ **to ~ sb into action** jdn zum Handeln bewegen **III.** *vi* <-rr-> rühren; (*move*) sich regen; *water* sich bewegen; (*awaken*) wach werden; ■ **to ~ within sb** sich in jdm regen

'stir-fry I. *n* Wok *m* **II.** *vt* <-ie-> kurz anbraten

stirring [ˈstɜr·ɪŋ] **I.** *n* Regung *f* **II.** *adj* aufwühlend

stirrup [ˈstɜr·əp] *n* Steigbügel *m*

stitch [stɪtʃ] **I.** *n* <*pl* -es> Stich *m*; (*in knitting*) Masche *f*; (*method*) Stichart *f*; (*pain*) Seitenstechen *nt*; **to not have a ~ on** splitterfasernackt sein ▶ PHRASES: **to be in ~es** (*fam*) sich schieflachen **II.** *vt* sticken; (*sew*) nähen **III.** *vt* nähen

stock [stak] **I.** *n* ❶ Vorrat *m*; (*inventory*) Bestand *m*; (*livestock*) Viehbestand *m*; **to be in ~** vorrätig sein ❷ ■ **~s** *pl* (*in company*) Aktien *pl* ❸ FOOD Brühe *f*; **fish ~** Fischfond *m* **II.** *adj attr* Vorrats-; (*standard*) Standard- **III.** *vt* vorrätig haben; (*fill*) füllen; *shelves* auffüllen; (*supply*) beliefern

'stockbroker *n* Börsenmakler(in) *m(f)*

'stock dividend *n* Stockdividende *f*; **~ share** Gratisaktie *f*

'stock exchange *n* Börse *f*

'stockholder *n* Aktionär(in) *m(f)*

stocking [ˈstak·ɪŋ] *n* ■ **~s** *pl* Strümpfe *pl*

'stock market *n* [Wertpapier]börse *f*

'stockpile I. *n* Vorrat *m* **II.** *vt* ■ **to ~ sth** Vorräte an etw *dat* anlegen; **to ~ weapons** ein Waffenarsenal anlegen

stock-'still *adj pred* stocksteif

stocky [ˈstak·i] *adj* stämmig

stoic [ˈstoʊ·ɪk] **I.** *n* stoischer Mensch **II.** *adj* stoisch

stoicism [ˈstoʊ·ɪ·sɪz·əm] *n* stoische Ruhe; (*about sth specific*) Gleichmut *m*

stoke [stoʊk] *vt* schüren; *furnace* beschicken

stole [stoʊl] *pt of* **steal**

stomach [ˈstʌm·ək] **I.** *n* ❶ Magen *m*; (*abdomen*) Bauch *m*; **upset ~** Magenverstimmung *f*; **to have no ~ for sth** keinen Appetit auf etw *akk* haben; (*desire*) keine Lust haben, etw zu tun **II.** *vt* (*fam*) **to not be able to ~ sth** etw nicht ertragen können

'stomachache *n usu sing* Magenschmerzen *pl*

stomp [stamp] **I.** *n* Stampfen *nt* **II.** *vi* stapfen; (*intentionally*) trampeln; ■ **to ~ on sb/sth** auf jdn/etw treten; (*sup-*

S

press) jdn/etw niedertrampeln III. *vt
rebellion* niederschlagen; **to ~ one's
feet** mit den Füßen [auf]stampfen

stone [stəʊn] I. *n* Stein *m;* (*in fruit a.*)
Kern *m;* (*jewel*) [Edel]stein *m;* **to be
[just] a ~'s throw away** [nur] einen
Katzensprung [weit] entfernt sein II. *adj
attr* Stein-; **~ statue** Statue *f* aus Stein
III. *vt* steinigen

'**Stone Age** *n* ■ **the ~** die Steinzeit

stone-'cold I. *adj* eiskalt II. *adv* ~ **sober**
stocknüchtern *fam*

stoned [stəʊnd] *adj* entsteint; (*sl:
drugged*) high; (*drunk*) betrunken; **to
be ~ out of one's mind** total zu[ge-
dröhnt] sein

stone-'deaf *adj* stocktaub *fam*

'**stonemason** *n* Steinmetz(in) *m(f)*

stony ['stəʊ·ni] *adj* steinig; (*unfeeling*)
steinern; *silence* eisig

stood [stʊd] *pt, pp of* **stand**

stool [stuːl] *n* Hocker *m;* (*feces*) Stuhl *m*

stoop[1] [stuːp] I. *n usu sing* Buckel *m*
II. *vi* sich beugen; **we had to ~ to go
through the doorway** wir mussten
den Kopf einziehen, um durch die Tür
zu gehen; ■ **to ~ down** sich bücken; **to
~ so low as to do sth** so weit sinken,
dass man etw tut

stoop[2] [stuːp] *n* offene Veranda

stop [stɑp] I. *vt* <-pp-> anhalten; *traffic*
aufhalten; (*make cease*) beenden; (*temporarily*) unterbrechen; *bleeding* stillen; *clock* anhalten; *machine* abstellen;
(*cease*) aufhören mit +*dat;* ~ **that
man!** haltet den Mann!; **this will ~ the
pain** davon gehen die Schmerzen weg
fam; ~ **it!** hör auf [damit]!; ■ **to ~ sb
[from] doing sth** jdn davon abhalten,
etw zu tun II. *vi* <-pp-> stehen bleiben;
car [an]halten; *bus* halten; *machine*
nicht mehr laufen; *rain* aufhören; *pain*
abklingen; *payments* eingestellt werden; ~! halt!; **to ~ dead** abrupt innehalten; ■ **to ~ [doing sth]** aufhören[, etw
zu tun], [mit etw *dat*] aufhören; **she
~ped drinking** sie trinkt nicht mehr
▶PHRASES: **to ~ at nothing** vor nichts zurückschrecken III. *n* Halt *m;* (*break*)

Pause *f;* (*for bus*) Haltestelle *f;* **to come
to a ~** stehen bleiben; *car a.* anhalten;
rain aufhören; *project* eingestellt werden; **to put a ~ to sth** etw *dat* ein Ende
setzen

◆ **stop by** *vi* vorbeischauen; **to ~ by
sb's house** bei jdm vorbeischauen

◆ **stop off** *vi* kurz bleiben; (*while traveling*) eine Zwischenstation machen

◆ **stop over** *vi* eine Zwischenstation
machen

◆ **stop up** *vt* verstopfen; *hole* [zu]stop-
fen

'**stopgap** *n* Notlösung *f*

'**stoplight** *n* [Verkehrs]ampel *f;* (*brake
light*) Bremslicht *nt*

'**stopover** *n* Zwischenlandung *f;* (*duration*) Zwischenaufenthalt *m*

stoppage ['stɑp·ɪdʒ] *n* Arbeitseinstel-
lung *f;* (*unintentional*) Unterbrechung *f*

stopper ['stɑp·ər] *n* Stöpsel *m*

'**stop sign** *n* Stoppschild *nt*

'**stopwatch** *n* Stoppuhr *f*

storage ['stɔr·ɪdʒ] *n* Lagerung *f;* *of
books* Aufbewahrung *f;* *of data, power*
Speicherung *f;* **to put sth into ~** etw
[ein]lagern

store [stɔr] I. *n* ❶ Vorrat *m;* (*fig*)
Schatz *m;* ■ **~s** *pl* Vorräte *pl;* ■ **to be in
~ [for sb]** (*fig*) [jdm] bevorstehen; **we
have a surprise in ~ for your father**
wir haben für deinen Vater eine Überraschung auf Lager ❷ (*business*) Laden *m;* (*larger*) Geschäft *nt;* (*department store*) Kaufhaus *nt;* (*warehouse*)
Lager *nt* II. *vt* [auf]speichern; *supplies*
lagern; *data* [ab]speichern

'**store card** *n* Kundenkarte *f*

'**storeroom** *n* Lagerraum *m;* (*for food*)
Vorratskammer *f*

stork [stɔrk] *n* Storch *m*

storm [stɔrm] I. *n* Sturm *m;* (*with
thunder*) Gewitter *nt;* (*with rain*) Unwetter *nt;* ~ **of applause** Beifalls-
sturm *m;* **to raise a ~ of protest** einen
[Protest]sturm hervorrufen ▶PHRASES: **to
take sth/sb by ~** etw/jdn im Sturm erobern II. *vi* ❶ *impers* ■ **it's ~ing** es

S

stürmt ❷(*race*) stürmen; ■**to ~ out** hinausstürmen III. *vt* stürmen

'**storm cloud** *n* Gewitterwolke *f*

stormy ['stɔr·mi] *adj* stürmisch; (*fierce*) stürmisch; *life* bewegt; *debate* hitzig

story[1] ['stɔr·i] *n* Geschichte *f;* (*lie a.*) [Lügen]märchen *nt fam;* (*narrative*) Erzählung *f;* (*plot*) Handlung *f;* (*rumor*) Gerücht *nt;* (*report*) Beitrag *m;* (*in newspaper*) Artikel *m;* **the ~ goes that …** man erzählt sich, dass … ▶PHRASES: **to make a long ~ short** um es kurz zu machen

story[2] ['stɔr·i] *n* Stockwerk *nt;* **a three-~ house** ein dreistöckiges Haus

'**storyteller** *n* Geschichtenerzähler(in) *m(f);* (*fam: liar*) Lügner(in) *m(f)*

stout [staʊt] *adj* beleibt; *woman* füllig *euph;* (*strong*) kräftig; *shoes* fest

stoutly ['staʊt·li] *adv* stämmig; (*strongly*) stabil; (*firmly*) entschieden; **to ~ believe in sth** fest an etw *akk* glauben

stove [stoʊv] *n* ❶(*for cooking*) Herd *m;* **induction ~** Induktionsherd *m* ❷(*heater*) Ofen *m*

'**stovepipe** *n* Ofenrohr *nt*

stow [stoʊ] *vt* verstauen; (*hide*) verstecken; (*fill*) vollmachen; *goods* verladen
◆**stow away** I. *vt* verstauen; (*hide*) verstecken II. *vi* als blinder Passagier reisen

stowaway ['stoʊ·ə·weɪ] *n* blinder Passagier/blinde Passagierin

straddle ['stræd·əl] I. *vt* ❶■**to ~ sth** (*standing*) mit gespreizten Beinen über etw *dat* stehen; (*sitting*) rittlings auf etw *dat* sitzen; (*jumping*) [mit gestreckten Beinen] über etw *akk* springen ❷*legs* spreizen ❸**to ~ an issue** bei einer Frage nicht klar Stellung beziehen II. *vi* breitbeinig [da]stehen; (*sit*) mit gespreizten Beinen [da]sitzen

straggler ['stræg·lər] *n* Nachzügler(in) *m(f)*

straight [streɪt] I. *adj* ❶gerade; *hair* glatt; *skirt* gerade geschnitten; *road, row* [schnur]gerade; **the picture isn't ~** das Bild hängt schief ❷(*frank*) offen; (*honest*) ehrlich; *answer* klar ❸(*heterosexual*) heterosexuell ❹(*factual*) tatsachengetreu ❺(*plain*) einfach; (*undiluted*) pur ❻*pred* (*in order*) in Ordnung; (*clarified*) geklärt; **to set things ~** (*tidy*) Ordnung schaffen; (*organize*) etwas auf die Reihe kriegen *fam;* **to set sb ~ about sth** jdm Klarheit über etw *akk* verschaffen II. *adv* ❶(*in a line*) gerade[aus]; **go ~ down this road** folgen Sie immer dieser Straße; **to look ~ ahead** geradeaus schauen ❷**to get ~ to the point** sofort zur Sache kommen ❸**I can't think ~ anymore** ich kann nicht mehr klar denken

straighten ['streɪ·tən] I. *vt* gerade machen; *hair* glätten; *river* begradigen; *tie* zurechtrücken II. *vi* sich aufrichten; *river* gerade werden; *hair* sich glätten
◆**straighten out** I. *vt* gerade machen; *clothes* glatt streichen; (*tidy up*) in Ordnung bringen; (*clarify*) klarstellen; *misunderstanding* aus der Welt schaffen II. *vi* gerade werden
◆**straighten up** I. *vi* sich aufrichten; *ship* [wieder] geradeaus fahren; *aircraft* [wieder] geradeaus fliegen II. *vt* gerade machen; (*tidy*) aufräumen; (*put in order*) regeln

straightforward [ˌstreɪt·ˈfɔr·wərd] *adj* direkt; *explanation* unumwunden; *look* gerade; (*honest*) aufrichtig; (*easy*) einfach

strain[1] [streɪn] I. *n usu sing* Druck *m;* (*overexertion*) [Über]beanspruchung *f;* (*muscle*) Zerrung *f;* **to be under a lot of ~** unter hohem Druck stehen II. *vi* **to ~ at the leash** an der Leine zerren III. *vt* ziehen an +*dat; muscle* zerren; (*overexert*) [stark] beanspruchen; *eyes* überanstrengen; *coffee* filtrieren; *vegetables* abgießen

strain[2] [streɪn] *n* Rasse *f; of plants* Sorte *f; of virus* Art *f*

strained [streɪnd] *adj* bemüht; (*artificial*) gekünstelt; *relations* angespannt; (*stressed*) abgespannt

strainer ['streɪ·nər] *n* Sieb *nt*

'**straitjacket** *n* Zwangsjacke *f*

S

strait-laced ['streɪt·leɪst] *adj* purita-nisch

strand [strænd] *n* Faden *m; of rope* Strang *m; of tissue* Faser *f; of hair* Sträh-ne *f;* **~ of the plot** Handlungsstrang *m*

stranded ['stræn·dɪd] *adj* gestrandet; ■**to be ~** *(fig)* festsitzen; **to leave sb ~** jdn sich *dat* selbst überlassen

strange [streɪndʒ] *adj* sonderbar; *(unusual)* ungewöhnlich; *(weird)* seltsam; *(exceptional)* erstaunlich; *(uneasy)* ko-misch; *(unwell)* unwohl; *(not known)* fremd; *(unfamiliar)* nicht vertraut

strangely ['streɪndʒ·li] *adv* merkwür-dig; **she was ~ calm** sie war auffällig still; **~ enough** seltsamerweise

stranger ['streɪn·dʒər] *n* Fremde(r) *f(m); (new to a place)* Neuling *m;* **are you a ~ here, too?** sind Sie auch fremd hier?

strangle ['stræŋ·gəl] *vt* erdrosseln; ■**to ~ sth** *(fig)* etw unterdrücken

'**stranglehold** *n* Würgegriff *m; (fig)* Vor-macht[stellung] *f*

strangulation [ˌstræŋ·gjʊ·'leɪ·ʃən] *n* Erdrosselung *f*

strap [stræp] I. *n* Riemen *m; (for safety)* Gurt *m; (for clothes)* Träger *m; (hold in vehicle)* Halteschlaufe *f;* **watch ~** Uhrarmband *nt* II. *vt* <-pp-> ■**to ~ sth [to sth]** etw [an etw *dat*] befestigen

strategic [strə·'ti·dʒɪk] *adj* strategisch

strategist ['stræt·ə·dʒɪst] *n* Stratege, -in *m, f*

strategy ['stræt·ə·dʒi] *n* ❶ Strategie *f; (fig a.)* Taktik *f* ❷ *(art of planning)* Tak-tieren *nt; (of war)* Kriegsstrategie *f*

stratum <*pl* -ta> ['streɪ·ṭəm] *n* Schicht *f*

straw [strɔ] *n* Stroh *nt; (stem, tube)* Strohhalm *m;* **to draw ~s** losen ▶PHRAS-ES: **to be the final ~** das Fass zum Über-laufen bringen

strawberry ['strɔ·ˌber·i] *n* Erdbeere *f*

stray [streɪ] I. *vi* streunen; *(go astray)* sich verirren; *(move casually)* umher-streifen; *(digress)* abweichen; *thoughts* abschweifen; **her eyes kept ~ing to the clock** ihre Blicke wanderten immer wieder zur Uhr II. *adj attr* streunend; *(lost)* umherirrend; *(isolated)* verein-zelt; *(occasional)* gelegentlich; **to be hit by a ~ bullet** von einem Blindgän-ger getroffen werden

streak [strik] I. *n* Streifen *m; (on win-dow)* Schliere *f; (run)* Strähne *f;* **lucky ~** Glückssträhne *f;* ■**~s** *pl (in hair)* Strähnen *pl* II. *vt usu passive* ■**to be ~ed** gestreift sein; **~ed with gray hair** von grauen Strähnen durchzogen III. *vi* flitzen *fam*

streaker ['stri·kər] *n (fam)* Flitzer(in) *m(f)*

stream [strim] I. *n* Bach *m; (flow)* Strahl *m; of people* Strom *m; (series)* Schwall *m; (current)* Strömung *f* II. *vi* strömen; *water* fließen; *nose* laufen; *eyes* tränen

streamer ['stri·mər] *n* Wimpel *m; (decoration)* Luftschlange *f*

streaming ['stri:·mɪŋ] *n* INET Stream-ing *nt,* Livestream *m*

streamlined ['strim·laɪnd] *adj* stromli-nienförmig; *car a.* windschnittig; *(effi-cient)* rationalisiert; *(simplified)* verein-facht

street [strit] *n* Straße *f;* ■**in the ~** auf der Straße; **I live on Main S~** ich wohne in der Main Street; **side ~** Sei-tenstraße *f* ▶PHRASES: **the average man/woman/person on the ~** der Mann/die Frau von der Straße

'**streetcar** *n* Straßenbahn *f*

'**street lamp** *n* Straßenlaterne *f*

'**streetlight** *n* Straßenlicht *nt*

strength [streŋkθ] *n* Kraft *f; (of struc-ture)* Belastbarkeit *f; (potency)* Stärke *f; of alcoholic drink a.* Alkoholgehalt *m; of drug* Konzentration *f; of medicine* Wirksamkeit *f; (effectiveness)* Wir-kungsgrad *m; (of argument)* Überzeu-gungskraft *f; (intensity)* Intensität *f; of color* Leuchtkraft *f; of belief* Stärke *f;* **physical ~** körperliche Kraft; **to gain ~** wieder zu Kräften kommen; **to gather ~** an Stabilität gewinnen; **to show great ~ of character** große Cha-rakterstärke zeigen; **to draw ~ from**

S

sth aus etw *dat* Kraft ziehen; **sb's ~s and weaknesses** jds Stärken und Schwächen; **to turn out in ~** in Massen anrücken ▶PHRASES: **on the ~ of sth** aufgrund einer S. *gen*

strengthen ['streŋk·θən] I. *vt* kräftigen; *(fortify)* befestigen; *(increase)* [ver]stärken; *(intensify)* intensivieren; *(improve)* verbessern; *currency* stabilisieren II. *vi* stärker werden; *muscles* kräftiger werden; *wind* auffrischen; *market* an Wert gewinnen; *currency* zulegen

strenuous ['stren·ju·əs] *adj* anstrengend; *(energetic)* energisch; **despite ~ efforts** trotz angestrengter Bemühungen

stress [stres] I. *n* <*pl* -es> Stress *m*; *(emphasis)* Bedeutung *f*; *(force)* Belastung *f*; *(tension)* Spannung *f*; *(pressure)* Druck *m*; **to be under ~** starken Belastungen ausgesetzt sein; *(at work)* unter Stress stehen II. *vt* ❶ betonen; **I'd just like to ~ that ...** ich möchte lediglich darauf hinweisen, dass ... ❷ *(strain)* belasten; **to ~ sb [out]** jdn stressen

stressed [strest] *adj* gestresst; *(pronounced)* betont

stressful ['stres·fʊl] *adj* aufreibend; **~ situation** Stresssituation *f*

'**stress test** *n* Stresstest *m*; MED Belastungstest *m*, Stresstest *m*

stretch [stretʃ] I. *n* <*pl* -es> ❶ *(exercise)* Dehnungsübungen *pl* ❷ *(section)* Stück *nt*; *(of road)* Streckenabschnitt *m*; *(of time)* Zeitspanne *f*; **~ of train tracks** Bahnstrecke *f*; **~ of water** Wasserfläche *f* II. *vi* sich dehnen; *clothes* weiter werden; *body* sich [recken und] strecken; *(exercise)* Dehnungsübungen machen III. *vt* [aus]dehnen; *(tighten)* straff ziehen; *sauce* verlängern; **we're already fully ~ed** wir sind schon voll ausgelastet; **to ~ one's legs** sich *dat* die Beine vertreten; **to ~ the limit** über das Limit hinausgehen; **to ~ sb's patience** jds Geduld auf eine harte Probe stellen

stretcher ['stretʃ·ər] *n* Tragbahre *f*

strew <strewed, strewn *or* strewed> [stru] *vt* [ver]streuen; *(cover)* bestreuen

strict [strɪkt] *adj* streng; *boss* strikt; *penalty* hart; *vegetarian* überzeugt; *limit* festgesetzt; *neutrality* strikt; *(absolute)* streng; **in the ~est confidence** streng vertraulich

strictly ['strɪkt·li] *adv* streng; **~ defined** genau definiert; **~ speaking** genau genommen

stride [straɪd] I. *vi* <strode, stridden> schreiten; **to ~ forward** *(fig)* vorankommen II. *n* Schritt *m*; **to hit one's ~** in Schwung kommen; **to take sth in one's ~** mit etw *dat* gut fertigwerden; **to make ~s forward** Fortschritte machen

strike [straɪk] I. *n* ❶ Angriff *m*; **preemptive ~** Präventivschlag *m*; *(fig)* vorbeugende Maßnahme ❷ *(of labor)* Streik *m*; **to be [out] on ~** streiken; **to call for a ~** einen Streik ausrufen ❸ *(discovery)* Fund *m* ❹ *(in baseball)* Strike *m* II. *vt* <struck, struck *or* stricken> ❶ schlagen; *soccer ball* schießen; **to ~ sth** *(bang against)* gegen etw *akk* schlagen; *(bump into)* gegen etw *akk* stoßen; *(drive against)* gegen etw *akk* fahren; *(collide with)* mit etw *dat* zusammenstoßen; **to ~ one's fist on the table** mit der Faust auf den Tisch schlagen ❷ *usu passive* **to be struck by lightning** vom Blitz getroffen werden ❸ **to ~ a blow** zuschlagen; **to ~ a blow against sb/sth** *(fig)* jdm/etw einen Schlag versetzen ❹ *(devastate)* heimsuchen; **the flood struck New Orleans** die Flut brach über New Orleans herein ❺ **she doesn't ~ me as [being] very motivated** sie scheint mir nicht besonders motiviert [zu sein] ❻ *(impress)* **to be struck by sth** von etw *dat* beeindruckt sein ❼ *(achieve)* erreichen; **to ~ a deal with sb** mit jdm eine Vereinbarung treffen ❽ **to ~ the hour** die [volle] Stunde schlagen ❾ **has it ever struck you that ...?** ist dir je der Gedanke gekommen dass ...? ❿ *match* anzünden

S

⓫ to ~ **oil** auf Öl stoßen; **to ~ it rich** das große Geld machen **III.** *vi* <struck, struck> ❶ treffen; *lightning* einschlagen; **to ~ at the heart of sth** etw vernichtend treffen; ❷ (*act*) zuschlagen; (*attack*) angreifen; *illness* ausbrechen; *fate* zuschlagen ❸ *clock* schlagen ❹ (*not work*) streiken
◆ **strike back** *vi* zurückschlagen
◆ **strike down** *vt* ■to ~ ~ **down** ⟳ sb jdn niederschlagen; (*kill*) jdn töten; (*epidemic*) jdn dahinraffen
◆ **strike out I.** *vt* ❶ (*delete*) ■to ~ **out** ⟳ **sth** etw [aus]streichen ❷ (*in baseball*) ■to ~ **out** ⟳ **sb** jdn ausstriken **II.** *vi* ❶ zuschlagen; ■to ~ **out at sb** nach jdm schlagen; (*fig*) jdn scharf angreifen ❷ **to ~ out on one's own** eigene Wege gehen
◆ **strike up** *vt* anfangen; **to ~ up a friendship with sb** sich mit jdm anfreunden
'strikebreaker *n* Streikbrecher(in) *m(f)*
striker ['straɪ·kər] *n* Streikende(r) *f(m)*; (*in soccer*) Stürmer(in) *m(f)*
striking ['straɪ·kɪŋ] *adj* ❶ bemerkenswert; *differences* erheblich; *feature* herausragend; *parallel* erstaunlich; *personality* beeindruckend; (*good-looking*) umwerfend; **the most ~ aspect of sth** das Bemerkenswerteste an etw *dat* ❷ **within ~ distance [of sth]** in unmittelbarer Nähe [einer S. *gen*]; (*short distance*) einen Katzensprung [von etw *dat*] entfernt
string [strɪŋ] **I.** *n* Schnur *f*; MUS, SPORT Saite *f*; (*chain*) Kette *f*; (*series a.*) Reihe *f*; **ball of ~** Knäuel *m o nt*; **to pull [some] ~s** seine Beziehungen spielen lassen; **[with] no ~s attached** ohne Bedingungen; **~ of pearls** Perlenkette *f*; ■the ~s *pl* (*instruments*) die Streichinstrumente *pl*; (*players*) die Streicher *pl* **II.** *vt* <strung, strung> (*fit*) besaiten; *racket* bespannen; (*attach*) auffädeln
◆ **string up** *vt* (*fam*) jdn [auf]hängen
string 'bean *n* grüne Bohne

string(ed) instrument [ˌstrɪŋd'-] *n* Saiteninstrument *nt*
'string quartet *n* Streichquartett *nt*
stringy ['strɪŋ·i] *adj* faserig; *hair* strähnig
strip [strɪp] **I.** *n* Streifen *m* **II.** *vt* <-pp-> ❶ *house* leer räumen; **to ~ sth bare** etw kahl fressen ❷ (*undress*) ■to ~ **sb** jdn ausziehen ❸ *usu passive* ■to ~ **sb of sth** jdn einer S. *gen* berauben; **to ~ sb of his/her title** jdm seinen Titel aberkennen **III.** *vi* <-pp-> sich ausziehen; **~ped to the waist** mit nacktem Oberkörper
stripe [straɪp] *n* Streifen *m*; MIL [Ärmel]streifen *m*
'strip light *n* Neonröhre *f*
stripper ['strɪp·ər] *n* Stripper(in) *m(f)*; (*solvent*) Farbentferner *m*
'strip search *n* Leibesvisitation, bei der sich der/die Durchsuchte ausziehen muss
'striptease *n* Striptease *m*
strive <strove *or* -d, striven> [straɪv] *vi* sich bemühen; ■to ~ **after sth** nach etw *dat* streben; ■to ~ **for sth** um etw *akk* ringen
strode [stroʊd] *pt of* **stride**
stroke [stroʊk] **I.** *vt* streicheln; **to ~ sth** über etw *akk* streichen; **to ~ sb's hair** jdm übers Haar streichen **II.** *n* Streicheln *nt*; (*mark*) Strich *m*; (*hit*) Schlag *m*; **at the ~ of midnight** um Punkt Mitternacht; **to suffer a ~** einen Schlaganfall bekommen; **breast ~** Brustschwimmen *nt*; **by a ~ of fate** durch eine Fügung des Schicksals; **~ of luck** Glücksfall *m*; **~ of genius** genialer Einfall
stroll [stroʊl] **I.** *n* Spaziergang *m*; (*around town*) Stadtbummel *m*; **to go for a ~** einen Spaziergang machen **II.** *vi* schlendern
stroller ['stroʊ·lər] *n* [Kinder]sportwagen *m*
strong [strɔŋ] **I.** *adj* stark; *desire* brennend; *economy* gesund; *currency* hart; *incentive* groß; *reaction* heftig; *resistance* erbittert; *rivalry* ausgeprägt; (*effective*) gut; (*robust*) stabil; (*tough*) stark;

S

(*deep-seated*) überzeugt; *conviction* fest; *objections* stark; *tendency* deutlich; (*bright*) hell; *light* grell; (*pungent*) streng; *flavor* kräftig; *smell* beißend; **tact is not her ~ point** Takt ist nicht gerade ihre Stärke; ~ **language** derbe Ausdrucksweise; **to be as ~ as an ox** bärenstark sein II. *adv* (*fam*) **to come on ~** (*sexually*) rangehen *fam*; (*aggressively*) in Fahrt kommen *fam*; **still going ~** noch gut in Form

'**strong-arm** I. *adj attr* (*pej*) brutal II. *vt* ■ **to ~ sb** jdn einschüchtern

'**strongbox** *n* [Geld]kassette *f*

'**stronghold** *n* Stützpunkt *m*; (*fig*) Hochburg *f*; (*sanctuary*) Zufluchtsort *m*

strongly ['strɒŋ·li] *adv* stark; *advise* nachdrücklich; *criticize* heftig; *deny* energisch; *recommend* dringend; *smell* stark; ~ **built** kräftig gebaut

strong-'minded *adj* willensstark

strong-'willed *adj* willensstark

strove [strəʊv] *pt of* **strive**

struck [strʌk] *pt, pp of* **strike**

structural ['strʌk·tʃər·əl] *adj* strukturell; (*of building*) baulich

structure ['strʌk·tʃər] I. *n* Aufbau *m*; (*system*) Struktur *f*; (*construction*) Bau[werk] *nt*; (*makeup*) Konstruktion *f* II. *vt* strukturieren; (*construct*) konstruieren; *life* regeln

struggle ['strʌg·əl] I. *n* Kampf *m*; **uphill** ~ harter Kampf II. *vi* kämpfen; (*toil*) sich abmühen; ■ **to ~ with sth** sich mit etw *dat* herumschlagen; **to ~ to one's feet** sich mühsam aufrappeln; **to ~ for survival** ums Überleben kämpfen

strum [strʌm] I. *vt* <-mm-> herumzupfen auf +*dat*; *guitar* herumklimpern auf +*dat* II. *vi* <-mm-> [herum]klimpern III. *n usu sing* (*sound of strumming*) Klimpern *nt*

strung [strʌŋ] *pt, pp of* **string**

strut [strʌt] I. *vi* <-tt-> ■ **to ~ around/ past** herum/vorbeistolzieren II. *vt* <-tt-> **to ~ one's stuff** (*esp hum fam: dance*) zeigen, was man hat; (*show-*

case) zeigen, was man kann III. *n* Strebe *f*

strychnine ['strɪk·naɪn] *n* Strychnin *nt*

stub [stʌb] I. *n of check* Abriss *m*; *of pencil* Stummel *m* II. *vt* <-bb-> **to ~ one's toes** sich die Zehen anstoßen

stubble ['stʌb·əl] *n* Stoppeln *pl*

stubbly ['stʌb·li] *adj* Stoppel-

stubborn ['stʌb·ərn] *adj* starrköpfig; (*persistent*) hartnäckig; *problem* vertrackt

stuck [stʌk] I. *pt, pp of* **stick** II. *adj* ❶ fest; **the door is ~** die Tür klemmt ❷ *pred* **I hate being ~ behind a desk** ich hasse Schreibtischarbeit; ■ **to be ~ in sth** in etw *dat* feststecken; ■ **to be ~ with sb** jdn am Hals haben ❸ *pred* (*at a loss*) ■ **to be ~** nicht klarkommen *fam*; **I'm really ~** ich komme einfach nicht weiter

stuck-'up *adj* (*pej fam*) hochnäsig *fam*

stud¹ [stʌd] *n* Stecker *m*; (*for collar*) Kragenknopf *m*; (*for shirt*) Hemdknopf *m*; (*for cuff*) Manschettenknopf *m*; (*in snow tire*) Spike *m*

stud² [stʌd] *n* Deckhengst *m*; (*farm*) Gestüt *nt*; (*sl: man*) geiler Typ

student ['stu·dənt] *n* Student(in) *m(f)*; (*pupil*) Schüler(in) *m(f)*

student 'teacher *n* Referendar(in) *m(f)*

studied ['stʌd·id] *adj* wohl überlegt

studio ['stu·di·oʊ] *n* Atelier *nt*; (*for photography*) Studio *nt*; (*company*) Filmgesellschaft *f*; (*apartment*) Appartement *nt*

study ['stʌd·i] I. *vt* <-ie-> studieren; (*at school*) lernen; (*look at*) eingehend betrachten; **to ~ for an exam** auf eine Prüfung lernen; ■ **to ~ how/ whether ...** erforschen, wie/ob ... II. *vi* <-ie-> studieren; (*at school*) lernen III. *n* ❶ Untersuchung *f*; (*academic*) Studie *f* ❷ (*studying*) Lernen *nt*; (*at university*) Studieren *nt* ❸ (*room*) Arbeitszimmer *nt* ❹ (*drawing*) Studie *f*

stuff [stʌf] I. *n* ❶ (*fam: indeterminate*) Zeug *nt oft pej fam*; **to know one's ~** sich auskennen ❷ (*possessions*) Sachen *pl* ❸ (*material*) Stoff *m* II. *vt* stopfen;

(*fill*) ausstopfen; *turkey* füllen; ■**to ~ oneself** (*fam*) sich vollstopfen

stuffed animal *n* Kuscheltier *nt*

stuffing ['stʌf·ɪŋ] *n* Füllung *f*

stumble ['stʌm·bəl] *vi* stolpern; (*while speaking*) stocken; ■**to ~ on sth** über etw *akk* stolpern; ■**to ~ around** herumtappen; ■**to ~ across sb/sth** [zufällig] auf jdn/etw stoßen

'**stumbling block** *n* Stolperstein *m*

stump [stʌmp] **I.** *n* Stumpf *m*; *of arm* Armstumpf *m*; *of leg* Beinstumpf *m*; *of tooth* Zahnstummel *m*; **out on the ~** POL im Wahlkampf **II.** *vt* verwirren; **we're all completely ~ed** wir sind mit unserem Latein am Ende

stun <-nn-> [stʌn] *vt* betäuben; (*amaze*) verblüffen; **~ned silence** fassungsloses Schweigen

stung [stʌŋ] *pt, pp of* **sting**

stunk [stʌŋk] *pt, pp of* **stink**

stunning ['stʌn·ɪŋ] *adj* fantastisch; (*amazing*) unfassbar; *blow* betäubend

stunt[1] [stʌnt] *vt growth* hemmen

stunt[2] [stʌnt] *n* Stunt *m*; (*for publicity*) Gag *m*; **to pull a ~** (*fig fam*) etwas Verrücktes tun

stunted ['stʌn·t̬ɪd] *adj* verkümmert; (*underdeveloped*) unterentwickelt

'**stuntman** *n* Stuntman *m*

stupid ['stu·pɪd] **I.** *adj* <-er, -est> dumm; (*silly*) blöd *fam* **II.** *n* (*fam*) Blödmann *m*

stupidity [stu·'pɪd·ɪ·t̬i] *n* Dummheit *f*

stupor ['stu·pər] *n* Benommenheit *f*; **in a drunken ~** im Vollrausch

sturdy ['stɜr·di] *adj* (*robust*) *chair, wall* stabil; *material* robust; *shoes* fest; *arms* kräftig; *body* stämmig

stutter ['stʌt̬·ər] **I.** *vt, vi* stottern **II.** *n* Stottern *nt kein pl*

sty [staɪ] *n* Schweinestall *m*

style [staɪl] **I.** *n* Stil *m*; (*stylishness a.*) Schick *m*; **in the ~ of sb/sth** im Stil einer Person/einer S. *gen*; **that's not my ~** (*fam*) das ist nicht mein Stil; **to have real ~** Klasse haben; **to do things in ~** alles im großen Stil tun; **the lat-**

est ~ die neueste Mode **II.** *vt* gestalten; *hair* frisieren

styling ['staɪ·lɪŋ] *n* Styling *nt; of hair* Frisur *f*

stylish ['staɪ·lɪʃ] *adj* (*approv*) ❶ (*chic*) elegant; (*smart*) flott *fam*; (*fashionable*) modisch, stylisch, stylish ❷ (*polished*) stilvoll, mit Stil *nach n*

stylishly ['staɪ·lɪʃ·li] *adv* (*approv: chic*) elegant; (*smartly*) flott *fam*; (*fashionably*) modisch, stylisch, stylish

stylistic [staɪ·'lɪs·tɪk] *adj* stilistisch

sub [sʌb] **I.** *n* ❶ (*fam*) *short for* **substitute** Vertretung *f* ❷ (*fam*) *short for* **submarine** U-Boot *nt* **II.** *vi* <-bb-> *short for* **substitute**: ■**to ~ for sb** für jdn einspringen

subconscious [ˌsʌb·'kɑn·ʃəs] **I.** *n* Unterbewusstsein *nt* **II.** *adj attr* unterbewusst

subcontractor [ˌsʌb·'kɑn·træk·tər] *n* Subunternehmer(in) *m(f)*

subculture ['sʌb·ˌkʌl·tʃər] *n* Subkultur *f*

subdue [səb·'du] *vt* unter Kontrolle bringen; (*into subjection*) unterwerfen; (*suppress*) unterdrücken; *emotion* bändigen

subdued [səb·'dud] *adj* beherrscht; (*reticent*) zurückhaltend; *voice, lighting* gedämpft; (*quiet*) leise; *mood* gedrückt

subject I. *n* ['sʌb·dʒɪkt] Thema *nt*; (*person*) Versuchsperson *f*; (*field*) Fach *nt*; (*specific*) Spezialgebiet *nt*; (*at school*) [Schul]fach *nt* **II.** *adj* ['sʌb·dʒɪkt] ■**to be ~ to sth** etw *dat* ausgesetzt sein; (*contingent on*) von etw *dat* abhängig sein; **to be ~ to a high rate of tax** einer hohen Steuer unterliegen; **~ to payment** vorbehaltlich einer Zahlung **III.** *vt* [səb·'dʒekt] ■**to ~ sb/sth to sth** jdn/etw etw *dat* aussetzen; **to ~ sb to torture** jdn foltern

subjective [səb·'dʒek·tɪv] *adj* subjektiv

submachine gun [ˌsʌb·mə·'ʃin·ˌgʌn] *n* Maschinenpistole *f*

submarine ['sʌb·mə·rin] **I.** *n* U-Boot *nt* **II.** *adj* Unterwasser-

submerge [səb·'mɜrdʒ] **I.** *vt* tauchen;

(*inundate*) überschwemmen II. *vi* untertauchen

submission [səb·ˈmɪʃ·ən] *n* Unterwerfung *f*; (*to orders*) Gehorsam *m*

submit <-tt-> [səb·ˈmɪt] I. *vt* ❶ **to ~ oneself to sb/sth** sich jdm/etw unterwerfen; **to ~ oneself to treatment** sich einer Behandlung unterziehen ❷ (*hand in*) einreichen; ▪**to ~ sth to sb** jdm etw vorlegen II. *vi* aufgeben; (*yield*) nachgeben; (*unconditionally*) sich unterwerfen

subordinate I. *n* [sə·ˈbɔr·dən·ɪt] Untergebene(r) *f(m)* II. *adj* [sə·ˈbɔr·dən·ɪt] zweitrangig; (*lower in rank*) rangniedriger

subpoena [sə·ˈpi·nə] LAW I. *vt* <-ed, -ed or -'d, -'d> vorladen II. *n* Ladung *f*; **to serve a ~ on sb** jdn vorladen

subscribe [səb·ˈskraɪb] I. *vi* ❶ **to ~ to sth** *magazine* etw abonnieren ❷ (*donate*) spenden II. *vt* spenden

subscriber [səb·ˈskraɪ·bər] *n* Abonnent(in) *m(f)*; *service* Kunde, Kundin *m, f*

subscription [səb·ˈskrɪp·ʃən] *n* Abonnement *nt*, Abonnementgebühr *f*

subsequent [ˈsʌb·sɪ·kwənt] *adj* [nach]folgend; (*later*) später

subsequently [ˈsʌb·sɪ·kwənt·li] *adv* anschließend

subservient [səb·ˈsɜr·vi·ənt] *adj* unterwürfig

subside [səb·ˈsaɪd] *vi* nachlassen; *anger* sich legen

subsidence [səb·ˈsaɪ·dəns] *n* Absenken *nt*

subsidiary [səb·ˈsɪd·i·er·i] *adj* ~ [**company**] Tochtergesellschaft *f*

subsidize [ˈsʌb·sə·daɪz] *vt* subventionieren

subsidy [ˈsʌb·sə·di] *n* Subvention *f*

substance [ˈsʌb·stəns] *n* ❶ Substanz *f*; (*material*) Materie *f*; **chemical ~** Chemikalie *f* ❷ (*significance*) Substanz *f*; (*decisive*) Gewicht *nt*; **the book lacks ~** das Buch hat inhaltlich wenig zu bieten ❸ (*main point*) Wesentliche(s) *nt*

substandard [ˌsʌb·ˈstæn·dərd] *adj* unterdurchschnittlich

substantial [səb·ˈstæn·ʃəl] *adj attr* solide; (*facts*) bedeutend; *contribution* wesentlich; *difference* erheblich; *improvement* deutlich; (*weighty*) überzeugend; **~ evidence** hinreichender Beweis

substantially [səb·ˈstæn·ʃə·li] *adv* erheblich; (*mainly*) im Wesentlichen

substantiate [səb·ˈstæn·ʃi·eɪt] *vt* bekräftigen; *report* bestätigen; *claim* begründen

substitute [ˈsʌb·stə·tut] I. *vt* austauschen; *players* auswechseln II. *vi* einspringen; (*deputize*) als Stellvertreter fungieren III. *n* Ersatz *m*; (*player*) Ersatzspieler(in) *m(f)*; **there's no ~ for him!** es geht doch nichts über ihn!

substitution [ˌsʌb·stə·ˈtu·ʃən] *n* Ersetzung *f*; (*act*) Austausch *m*; *of player* [Spieler]wechsel *m*

subterfuge [ˈsʌb·tər·fjudʒ] *n* List *f*

subterranean [ˌsʌb·tə·ˈreɪ·ni·ən] *adj* unterirdisch; (*fig*) Untergrund-

subtitle [ˈsʌb·taɪ·təl] I. *vt* untertiteln II. *n* Untertitel *m*

subtle <-r, -st> [ˈsʌt·əl] *adj* subtil; *flavor* fein; *charm* unaufdringlich; (*astute*) scharfsinnig; *strategy* geschickt; **~ tact** ausgeprägtes Taktgefühl

subtlety [ˈsʌt·əl·ti] *n* Subtilität *f*; (*astuteness*) Scharfsinnigkeit *f*

subtotal [ˈsʌb·toʊ·təl] *n* Zwischensumme *f*

subtract [səb·ˈtrækt] *vt* abziehen (**from** von +*dat*)

subtraction [səb·ˈtræk·ʃən] *n* Subtraktion *f*

subtropical [ˌsʌb·ˈtrɑp·ɪ·kəl] *adj* subtropisch

suburb [ˈsʌb·ɜrb] *n* Vorort *m*; ▪**the ~s** *pl* der Stadtrand

suburban [sə·ˈbɜr·bən] *adj* Vorstadt-; (*pej: provincial*) spießig *fam*

suburbia [sə·ˈbɜr·bi·ə] *n* Vororte *pl*; (*people*) Vorstadtbewohner *pl*

subversive [səb·ˈvɜr·sɪv] I. *adj* umstürzlerisch II. *n* Umstürzler(in) *m(f)*

subway [ˈsʌb·weɪ] *n* U-Bahn *f*; ▪**by ~**

S

mit der U-Bahn; ~ **station** U-Bahn-Station f

subzero [sʌb·'ziˑroʊ] *adj* unter null [Grad] *nach n;* ~ **temperatures** Minusgrade *pl*

succeed [sək·'siːd] I. *vi* ❶ Erfolg haben; *plan* gelingen; **she ~ed in doing it** es gelang ihr, es zu tun ❷ *(follow)* die Nachfolge antreten; **to ~ to the throne** die Thronfolge antreten II. *vt* **to ~ sb in office** jds Amt übernehmen

succeeding [sək·'siˑdɪŋ] *adj attr* aufeinanderfolgend; **in the ~ weeks** in den darauf folgenden Wochen

success <*pl* -es> [sək·'ses] *n* Erfolg *m;* **to be a big ~ with sb** bei jdm einschlagen *fam;* **to achieve ~** erfolgreich sein; **box-office ~** *(film)* Kassenschlager *m fam*

successful [sək·'ses·fəl] *adj* erfolgreich; *(lucrative a.)* lukrativ; *(effective)* gelungen

succession [sək·'seʃ·ən] *n* ❶ Folge *f; of events a.* Serie *f;* **in** [close] **~** [dicht] hintereinander ❷ *(line of inheritance)* Nachfolge *f;* **~ to the throne** Thronfolge *f*

successive [sək·'ses·ɪv] *adj attr* aufeinanderfolgend; **six ~ weeks** sechs Wochen hintereinander

successor [sək·'ses·ər] *n* Nachfolger(in) *m(f)*

succinct [sək·'sɪŋkt] *adj* kurz [und bündig]

such [sʌtʃ] I. *adj* ❶ *attr* solcher(r, s); **I had never met ~ a person before** so ein Mensch war mir noch nie begegnet; **~ a thing** so etwas; **there's no ~ thing as ghosts** so etwas wie Geister gibt es nicht ❷ **he's ~ an idiot!** er ist so ein Idiot!; **why are you in ~ a hurry?** warum bist du derart in Eile? II. *pron* solche(r, s); *(suchlike)* dergleichen; **~ is life** so ist das Leben; **~ as** wie; **■as ~** an [und für] sich III. *adv* so; **she's ~ an arrogant person** sie ist dermaßen arrogant; **I've never had ~ good coffee** ich habe noch nie [einen] so guten Kaffee getrunken; **~ … that …** so …, dass …

suchlike ['sʌtʃ·laɪk] *pron* dergleichen

suck [sʌk] I. *n* Saugen *nt; on popsicle* Lutschen *nt* II. *vt* **■to ~ sth** an etw *dat* saugen; *sweets* etw lutschen; **■to be ~ed into sth** *(fig)* in etw *akk* hineingezogen werden III. *vi* saugen; *on candy* lutschen; *(sl)* ätzend sein

◆**suck up** I. *vt* aufsaugen II. *vi* *(pej fam)* **■to ~ up to sb** sich bei jdm einschmeicheln

sucker ['sʌk·ər] I. *n* *(fam)* Einfaltspinsel *m;* **to be a ~ for sth** nach etw *dat* verrückt sein II. *vt* **■to ~ sb into sth** jdn zu etw *dat* verleiten

suction ['sʌk·ʃən] *n* [Ab]saugen *nt; (force)* Saugwirkung *f*

suction cup *n* Saugfuß *m*

Sudan [suˑ·'dæn] *n* Sudan *m*

Sudanese [ˌsuˑdə·'niːz] I. *n* Sudanese, Sudanesin *m, f* II. *adj* sudan[es]isch

sudden ['sʌd·ən] *adj* plötzlich; *departure* überhastet; *movement* abrupt; **all of a ~** *(fam)* [ganz] plötzlich

sudden infant death syndrome *n* plötzlicher Kindstod

suddenly ['sʌd·ən·li] *adv* plötzlich

suds [sʌdz] *npl* Seifenwasser *nt; (foam)* Schaum *m; (sl: beer)* Bier *nt*

sue [su] I. *vt* verklagen; **to ~ sb for damages/libel** jdn auf Schadenersatz/wegen Beleidigung verklagen; **to ~ sb for divorce** gegen jdn die Scheidung einreichen II. *vi* prozessieren; **■to ~ for sth** etw einklagen

suede [sweɪd] *n* Wildleder *nt*

suffer ['sʌf·ər] I. *vi* leiden; *(deteriorate a.)* Schaden erleiden; **■to ~ from sth** unter etw *dat* zu leiden haben II. *vt* erleiden; *(put up with)* ertragen; **to ~ neglect** vernachlässigt werden; **to not ~ fools gladly** mit dummen Leuten keine Geduld haben

sufferer ['sʌf·ər·ər] *n* *(chronic)* Leidende(r) *f(m); (acute)* Erkrankte(r) *f(m);* **AIDS ~** AIDS-Kranke(r) *f(m);* **asthma ~** Asthmatiker(in) *m(f)*

suffering ['sʌf·ər·ɪŋ] *n* Leiden *nt; (distress)* Leid *nt*

sufficiency [sə·'fɪʃ·ən·si] *n* Hinlänglichkeit *f*; (*quantity*) ausreichende Menge

sufficient [sə·'fɪʃ·ənt] *adj* ausreichend, genügend; ■**to be ~ for sth/sb** für etw/jdn ausreichen

suffocate ['sʌf·ə·keɪt] *vt, vi* ersticken

suffocating ['sʌf·ə·keɪ·tɪŋ] *adj* erstickend; (*fig*) erdrückend; *air* stickig

suffrage ['sʌf·rɪdʒ] *n* Wahlrecht *nt*

sugar ['ʃʊɡ·ər] *n* Zucker *m*; (*endearment*) Schätzchen *nt fam*

'**sugar beet** *n* Zuckerrübe *f*

'**sugar cane** *n* Zuckerrohr *nt*

'**sugar cube** *n* Stück *nt* Zucker

'**sugar daddy** *n* wohlhabender älterer Mann, der ein junges Mädchen aushält

sugary ['ʃʊɡ·ə·ri] *adj* zuckerhaltig; (*sugar-like*) zuckerig; (*fig*) zuckersüß; *smile* süßlich

suggest [səɡ·'dʒest] *vt* ❶ ■**to ~ sth** [to **sb**] [jdm] etw vorschlagen ❷ (*indicate*) hinweisen; **the footprints ~ that ...** die Fußspuren lassen darauf schließen, dass ... ❸ (*insinuate*) ■**to ~ sth** etw andeuten; ■**to ~ that ...** darauf hindeuten, dass ...; **are you ~ing that ...?** willst du damit sagen, dass ...?

suggestion [səɡ·'dʒes·tʃən] *n* Vorschlag *m*; (*hint*) Andeutung *f*; (*indication*) Hinweis *m*; (*trace*) Spur *f*; **to be always open to ~s** immer ein offenes Ohr haben

suggestive [səɡ·'dʒes·tɪv] *adj* andeutend; (*risqué*) anzüglich

suicidal [su·ɪ·'saɪ·dəl] *adj* selbstmörderisch; *person* selbstmordgefährdet; (*disastrous*) [selbst]zerstörerisch; **that would be ~** das wäre glatter Selbstmord

suicide ['su·ɪ·saɪd] *n* Selbstmord *m*; **to commit ~** Selbstmord begehen

suit [sut] I. *n* Anzug *m*; (*jacket and skirt*) Kostüm *nt*; CARDS Farbe *f*; **ski ~** Skianzug *m* ▶PHRASES: **to follow ~** (*form*) dasselbe tun II. *vt* ■**to ~ sb** jdm passen; *clothes* jdm stehen; ■**to ~ oneself** tun, was man will; **~ yourself!** [ganz,] wie du willst!

suitable ['su·tə·bəl] *adj* geeignet; *clothing* angemessen

'**suitcase** *n* Koffer *m*

suite [swit] *n* Suite *f*; (*furniture*) Garnitur *f*; **~ of offices** Reihe *f* von Büroräumen; **bedroom ~** Schlafzimmereinrichtung *f*

sulfur ['sʌl·fər] *n* Schwefel *m*

sulfuric 'acid *n* Schwefelsäure *f*

sulk [sʌlk] I. *vi* schmollen II. *n* **to be in a ~** schmollen

sulky ['sʌl·ki] *adj* beleidigt; *face* mürrisch

sultan ['sʌl·tən] *n* Sultan *m*

sultry ['sʌl·tri] *adj* schwül; (*sexy*) sinnlich

sum [sʌm] *n* Summe *f*

◆**sum up** I. *vi* zusammenfassen; *judge* resümieren II. *vt* zusammenfassen; (*evaluate*) einschätzen; **to ~ up a situation at a glance** eine Situation auf einen Blick erfassen

summarize ['sʌm·ə·raɪz] *vt, vi* [kurz] zusammenfassen; **to ~, ...** kurz gesagt, ...

summary ['sʌm·ə·ri] I. *n* Zusammenfassung *f*; *of contents* [kurze] Inhaltsangabe II. *adj* knapp; *dismissal* fristlos

summer ['sʌm·ər] I. *n* Sommer *m*; **a ~ 's day** ein Sommertag *m*; **in** [**the**] **~** im Sommer II. *vi* den Sommer verbringen

summer house *n* Ferienhaus *nt*

'**summertime** *n* Sommerzeit *f*; **in the ~** im Sommer

summer 'vacation *n* Sommerurlaub *m*; SCH Sommerferien *pl*

summit ['sʌm·ɪt] *n* Gipfel *m*; (*fig a.*) Höhepunkt *m*

summon ['sʌm·ən] *vt* zu sich *dat* bestellen; LAW vorladen; *help* holen; **to ~ a meeting** eine Versammlung einberufen; **to ~ up the courage to do sth** den Mut aufbringen, etw zu tun

summons ['sʌm·ənz] I. *n* <*pl* -es> LAW [Vor]ladung *f*; (*call*) Aufforderung *f*; **to issue a ~** [vor]laden II. *vt* LAW ■**to ~ sb** jdn vorladen lassen

sumptuous ['sʌmp·tʃu·əs] *adj* luxuriös; *dinner* üppig

S

sun [sʌn] I. *n* Sonne *f;* **to sit in the ~** in der Sonne sitzen; **everything under the ~** alles Mögliche II. *vt* <-nn-> ■**to ~ oneself** sich sonnen

'**sunbathe** *vi* sonnenbaden

'**sunbeam** *n* Sonnenstrahl *m*

'**sunblock** *n* Sunblocker *m*

'**sunburn** I. *n* Sonnenbrand *m* II. *vi* <-ed *or* -burnt, -ed *or* -burnt> sich verbrennen

'**sunburned**, '**sunburnt** *adj* sonnengebräunt; (*red*) sonnenverbrannt

sundae ['sʌn·di] *n* Eisbecher *m*

Sunday ['sʌn·deɪ] *n* Sonntag *m; see also* **Tuesday**

'**Sunday school** *n* Sonntagsschule *f*

'**sundial** *n* Sonnenuhr *f*

'**sundown** *n* Sonnenuntergang *m*

'**sundries** ['sʌn·driz] *n pl* Verschiedenes *nt kein pl*

sundry ['sʌn·dri] *adj attr* verschiedene(r, s) ▶PHRASES: **all and ~** (*fam*) Hinz und Kunz *pej*

'**sunflower** *n* Sonnenblume *f*

sung [sʌŋ] *pp of* **sing**

'**sunglasses** *npl* Sonnenbrille *f*

sunk [sʌŋk] *pp of* **sink**

sunken ['sʌŋ·kən] *adj attr* tief[er] liegend *attr; bathtub* eingelassen; *cheeks* eingefallen

'**sunlight** *n* Sonnenlicht *nt*

'**sunlit** *adj* sonnenbeschienen; *room* sonnig

sunny ['sʌn·i] *adj* sonnig; (*cheery*) heiter; **~ intervals** Aufheiterungen *pl*

'**sunrise** *n* Sonnenaufgang *m*

'**sunroof** *n* Schiebedach *nt*

'**sunscreen** *n* Sonnenschutzmittel *nt*

'**sunset** *n* Sonnenuntergang *m*

'**sunshade** *n* Sonnenblende *f;* (*umbrella*) Sonnenschirm *m*

'**sunshine** *n* sonniges Wetter; (*sunlight*) Sonnenschein *m*

'**sunstroke** *n* Sonnenstich *m*

'**suntan** *n* Sonnenbräune *f;* **to get a ~** braun werden

'**suntan lotion** *n* Sonnencreme *f*

'**suntanned** *adj* sonnengebräunt

'**sunup** *n* Sonnenaufgang *m*

super ['su·pər] (*fam*) I. *adj* klasse II. *interj* super!, spitze! III. *adv* besonders

superb [sə·'pɜrb] *adj* ausgezeichnet; (*impressive*) erstklassig; *view* großartig

Super Bowl *n* Finale *des professionellen amerikanischen Fußballs*

superficial [ˌsu·pər·'fɪʃ·əl] *adj* oberflächlich; *damage* geringfügig; (*apparent*) äußerlich; *treatment* flüchtig

superfluous [su·'pɜr·flu·əs] *adj* überflüssig

super'human *adj* übermenschlich

superimpose [ˌsu·pər·ɪm·'pouz] *vt* überlagern

superintendent [ˌsu·pər·ɪn·'ten·dənt] *n* Aufsicht *f;* *of schools* Oberschulrat, -rätin *m, f;* (*police officer*) Polizeichef(in) *m(f)*

superior [sə·'pɪr·i·ər] I. *adj* vorgesetzt; (*excellent*) übergeordnet; (*better*) überlegen; (*pej: arrogant*) überheblich; **to be ~ in numbers** in der Überzahl sein II. *n* Vorgesetzte(r) *f(m)*

superiority [sə·ˌpɪr·i·'ɔr·ɪ·ti] *n* Überlegenheit *f;* (*pej: arrogance*) Überheblichkeit *f*

'**superman** *n* Superman *m*

supermarket ['su·pər·ˌmar·kɪt] *n* Supermarkt *m*

supernatural [ˌsu·pər·'næʧ·ər·əl] I. *adj* übernatürlich; (*extraordinary*) außergewöhnlich II. *n* ■**the ~** das Übernatürliche

supersonic [ˌsu·pər·'san·ɪk] *adj* Überschall-

'**superstar** ['su·pər·star] *n* Superstar *m*

superstition [ˌsu·pər·'stɪʃ·ən] *n* Aberglaube[n] *m*

superstitious [ˌsu·pər·'stɪʃ·əs] *adj* abergläubisch

'**superstore** ['su·pər·stɔr] *n* Großmarkt *m*

supervise ['su·pər·vaɪz] *vt* beaufsichtigen

supervision [ˌsu·pər·'vɪʒ·ən] *n* Beaufsichtigung *f;* *of prisoners* Überwachung *f*

supervisor ['su·pər·vaɪ·zər] *n* Aufsichtsbeamte(r), -beamtin *m, f;* (*in* *shop*) Abteilungsleiter(in) *m(f)*; (*in factory*) Vorarbeiter(in) *m(f)*; SCH Betreuungslehrer(in) *m(f)*; UNIV Betreuer(in) *m(f)*

supervisory [ˌsuˑpərˈvaɪˑzəˑri] *adj* Aufsichts-

supper [ˈsʌpˑər] *n* Abendessen *nt*

supple [ˈsʌpˑəl] *adj* geschmeidig; *mind* flexibel; *skin* weich

supplement [ˈsʌpˑləˑmənt] **I.** *n* Ergänzung *f*; (*book*) Supplement *nt*; (*section*) Beilage *f*; (*information*) Nachtrag *m* **II.** *vt* ergänzen; **to ~ one's income** sein Einkommen aufbessern

supplementary [ˌsʌpˑləˈmenˑtəˑri], **supplemental** [ˌsʌpˑləˈmenˑtəl] *adj* zusätzlich

supplier [səˈplaɪˑər] *n* Lieferant(in) *m(f)*; (*company a.*) Lieferfirma *f*; *of services* Dienstleister(in) *m(f)*

supply [səˈplaɪ] **I.** *vt* <-ie-> bereitstellen; (*provide sb with sth*) versorgen; *drugs* beschaffen; (*act as source*) liefern **II.** *n* ❶ Vorrat *m*; (*action*) Versorgung *f*; **oil/gas[oline]** ~ Öl-/Benzinzufuhr *f*; **energy** ~ Energieversorgung *f* ❷ ECON Angebot *nt*; **to be in short** ~ Mangelware sein ❸ **supplies** *pl* Versorgung *f*; (*amount needed*) Bedarf *m*; **to cut off supplies** die Lieferungen einstellen

support [səˈpɔrt] **I.** *vt* ❶ **to ~ oneself on sth** sich auf etw *akk* stützen; **the ice is thick enough to ~ our weight** das Eis ist so dick, dass es uns trägt ❷ (*fund*) [finanziell] unterstützen; *lifestyle* finanzieren; *family* unterhalten; ■ **to ~ sb** für jds Lebensunterhalt aufkommen ❸ (*back*) unterstützen; *plan* befürworten; **to ~ a team** für ein Team sein **II.** *n* ❶ Stütze *f*; **to give sth** ~ etw *dat* Halt geben ❷ (*funds*) Unterstützung *f*; LAW Unterhalt *m* ❸ (*backing*) Stütze *f*; (*services*) Support *m*; **to give sb moral ~** jdn moralisch unterstützen

supporter [səˈpɔrˑtər] *n* Anhänger(in) *m(f)*; *of campaign* Befürworter(in) *m(f)*; *of theory* Verfechter(in) *m(f)*

supportive [səˈpɔrˑtɪv] *adj* ■ **to be ~**

of sb jdm eine Stütze sein; ■ **to be ~ of sth** etw unterstützen

suppose [səˈpouz] *vt* ❶ **to ~ [that]** … annehmen, dass …; **I ~ you think that's funny** du hältst das wohl auch noch für komisch; **I don't ~ you could …** Sie könnten mir nicht zufällig …; **you're ~d to be asleep** du solltest eigentlich schon schlafen ❷ (*believe*) glauben; **her new book is ~d to be very good** ihr neues Buch soll sehr gut sein ▶PHRASES: **I ~ so** wenn du meinst

supposed [səˈpouzd] *adj attr* angenommen; *killer* mutmaßlich

supposedly [səˈpouˑzɪdˑli] *adv* angeblich; (*apparently*) anscheinend

supposing [səˈpouˑzɪŋ] *conj* **~ he doesn't show up?** was, wenn er nicht erscheint?

supposition [ˌsʌpˑəˈzɪʃˑən] *n* Spekulation *f*; (*belief*) Vermutung *f*; **on the ~ that …** vorausgesetzt, dass …

suppository [səˈpɑzˑəˑtɔrˑi] *n* Zäpfchen *nt*

suppress [səˈpres] *vt* unterdrücken; *revolution* niederschlagen; *terrorism* bekämpfen; *information* zurückhalten; (*inhibit*) hemmen; (*weaken*) schwächen; *reaction* abschwächen; *memories* verdrängen

suppression [səˈpreʃˑən] *n* Unterdrückung *f*; *of revolt* Niederschlagung *f*; *of terrorism* Bekämpfung *f*; *of information* Zurückhaltung *f*; (*weakening*) Hemmung *f*

supremacy [səˈpremˑəˑsi] *n* Vormachtstellung *f*; SPORT Überlegenheit *f*

supreme [səˈprim] *adj* höchste(r, s); (*extreme*) äußerste(r, s); (*wonderful*) überragend; *moment* einzigartig

Supreme 'Court *n* oberstes Gericht

surcharge [ˈsɜrˑtʃardʒ] *n* Zuschlag *m*; (*penalty*) Strafgebühr *f*

sure [ʃʊr] **I.** *adj pred* sicher; **I'm not really ~** ich weiß nicht so genau; **to feel ~ [that]** … überzeugt [davon] sein, dass …; ■ **to be ~ [that]** … [sich *dat*] sicher sein, dass …; ■ **to be ~ to … ** da-

S

ran denken, dass ...; **be ~ to close the door** vergiss nicht, die Tür zuzumachen ▶PHRASES: **~ thing** (*fam*) sicher!; (*of course*) [na] klar! *fam*; **to be ~** of oneself sehr von sich *dat* überzeugt sein; **to make ~** [that] ... darauf achten, dass ... II. *adv* (*fam*) echt; **I ~ am hungry!** hab ich vielleicht einen Hunger! III. *interj* (*fam*) **~ I will!** aber klar doch!

surely ['ʃʊr·li] *adv* sicher[lich]; **~ you don't expect me to believe that!** du erwartest doch wohl nicht, dass ich dir das abnehme! *fam*; **slowly but ~** langsam, aber sicher

surf [sɜrf] I. *n* Brandung *f* II. *vi* surfen; (*windsurf*) windsurfen III. *vt* **to ~ the Internet** im Internet surfen

surface ['sɜr·fɪs] I. *n* Oberfläche *f*; *of lake* Spiegel *m*; **road ~** Straßenbelag *m* ▶PHRASES: **to scratch the ~** [of sth] [etw] streifen II. *vi* auftauchen

'surface mail *n* Postsendung, die auf dem Land- bzw. Seeweg befördert wird

surfboard ['sɜrf·bɔrd] *n* Surfbrett *nt*

surfer ['sɜr·fər] *n* Surfer(in) *m(f)*; (*windsurfer*) Windsurfer(in) *m(f)*

surfing ['sɜr·fɪŋ] *n* Surfen *nt*; (*windsurfing*) Windsurfen *nt*

surge [sɜrdʒ] I. *vi* wogen; *sea* branden; *profits* [stark] ansteigen; ■**to ~** [up] *emotion* aufwallen; *cheer* aufbrausen II. *n* [plötzlicher] Anstieg; (*wave*) Woge *f*; (*fig*) Ansturm *m*; *of emotion* Woge *f*

surgeon ['sɜr·dʒən] *n* Chirurg(in) *m(f)*

surgery ['sɜr·dʒə·ri] *n* chirurgischer Eingriff

surgical ['sɜr·dʒɪ·kəl] *adj* chirurgisch; (*orthopedic*) medizinisch

surmount [sər·'maʊnt] *vt* meistern; *obstacle* überwinden

surname ['sɜr·neɪm] *n* Familienname *m*

surpass [sər·'pæs] *vt* ■**to ~ oneself** sich selbst übertreffen

surplus ['sɜr·pləs] I. *n* <*pl* -es> Überschuss *m* II. *adj* zusätzlich; (*dispensable*) überschüssig

surprise [sər·'praɪz] I. *n* Überraschung *f*; **~!** (*fam*) Überraschung!; **to take sb by ~** jdn überraschen; **to one's [great] ~** zu seinem [großen] Erstaunen II. *vt* überraschen; ■**to ~ sb doing sth** jdn bei etw *dat* überraschen III. *adj attr* überraschend

surprised [sər·'praɪzd] *adj* überrascht; (*amazed*) erstaunt; *pred* (*disappointed*) enttäuscht; **I wouldn't be ~ if ...** es würde mich nicht wundern, wenn ...; **pleasantly ~** angenehm überrascht

surprising [sər·'praɪ·zɪŋ] *adj* überraschend

surprisingly [sər·'praɪ·zɪŋ·li] *adv* erstaunlich; (*unexpectedly*) überraschenderweise

surrender [sə·'ren·dər] I. *vi* aufgeben; MIL kapitulieren; (*give in a.*) nachgeben; ■**to ~ to sb** sich jdm ergeben; **to ~ to temptation** der Versuchung erliegen II. *n* Kapitulation *f*

surrogate 'mother *n* Leihmutter *f*

surround [sə·'raʊnd] *vt* umgeben; (*encircle*) einkreisen; MIL umstellen

surrounding [sə·'raʊn·dɪŋ] *adj attr* **~ area** Umgebung *f*

sur'roundings *npl* Umgebung *f*; (*living conditions a.*) [Lebens]verhältnisse *pl*

surveillance [sər·'veɪ·ləns] *n* Überwachung *f*

survey I. *vt* [sər·'veɪ] *passers-by* befragen; (*look at*) betrachten; (*carefully*) begutachten; (*overview*) umreißen II. *n* ['sɜr·veɪ] Untersuchung *f*; (*research*) Studie *f*; (*overview*) Übersicht *f*; *of topic* Überblick *m*; *of land* Vermessung *f*; **nationwide ~** landesweite Umfrage

surveyor [sər·'veɪ·ər] *n* [Land]vermesser(in) *m(f)*

survival [sər·'vaɪ·vəl] *n* Überleben *nt*

survive [sər·'vaɪv] I. *vi* überleben; (*fig a.*) erhalten bleiben; *monument* überdauern; *tradition* fortbestehen; ■**to ~ on sth** sich mit etw *dat* am Leben halten II. *vt* überleben; (*fig*) hinwegkommen; *fire* überstehen

surviving [sər·'vaɪ·vɪŋ] *adj* noch lebend; *relative* hinterblieben; (*fig*) [noch] vorhanden

survivor [sər·'vaɪ·vər] *n* Überlebende(r) *f(m)*; (*tough person*) Überlebenskünstler(in) *m(f)*; **she's a cancer ~** sie hat den Krebs besiegt

susceptible [sə·'sep·tə·bəl] *adj* ■**to be ~ to sth** für etw *akk* empfänglich sein

suspect I. *vt* [sə·'spekt] vermuten; (*consider guilty*) verdächtigen; (*doubt*) anzweifeln; *motives* misstrauen; ■**to be ~ed of sth** einer S. *gen* verdächtigt werden II. *n* ['sʌs·pekt] Verdächtige(r) *f(m)* III. *adj* ['sʌs·pekt] verdächtig; (*possibly defective*) zweifelhaft

suspend [sə·'spend] *vt* ❶ [vorübergehend] aussetzen; *worker* suspendieren; *student* [zeitweilig] [vom Unterricht] ausschließen; *player* sperren; **to ~ judgment** mit seiner Meinung zurückhalten ❷ (*hang*) herabhängen

suspender [sə·'spen·dər] *n* ■**~s** *pl* Hosenträger *pl*

suspense [sə·'spens] *n* Spannung *f*; **to keep sb in ~** jdn im Ungewissen lassen

suspension [sə·'spen·ʃən] *n* ❶ [zeitweilige] Einstellung; *of worker, student* Suspendierung *f*; *of player* Sperrung *f* ❷ AUTO Radaufhängung *f*

sus'pension bridge *n* Hängebrücke *f*

suspicion [sə·'spɪʃ·ən] *n* Verdacht *m*; (*mistrust*) Misstrauen *nt*; **to be above ~** über jeglichen Verdacht erhaben sein

suspicious [sə·'spɪʃ·əs] *adj* verdächtig; (*distrustful*) misstrauisch; ■**to be ~ of sth** einer S. *dat* gegenüber skeptisch sein

sustain [sə·'steɪn] *vt* aufrechterhalten; (*keep alive*) [am Leben] erhalten; *family* unterhalten; (*emotionally*) unterstützen

sustainable [sə·'steɪ·nə·bəl] *adj* ❶ (*maintainable*) haltbar; *argument* stichhaltig; ■**sth is ~** etw kann aufrechterhalten werden ❷ ECOL *resources* erneuerbar; *development* nachhaltig

sustained [sə·'steɪnd] *adj* anhaltend; (*determined*) nachdrücklich

swab [swab] I. *n* Tupfer *m*; (*sample*) Abstrich *m* II. *vt* <-bb-> abtupfen

swagger ['swæg·ər] I. *vi* stolzieren; (*behave*) prahlen II. *n* Prahlerei *f*

swallow[1] ['swal·oʊ] I. *n* Schlucken *nt*; (*quantity*) Schluck *m* II. *vt* [hinunter]schlucken; (*greedily*) verschlingen; (*fam: believe*) schlucken; ■**to be ~ed [up] by sth** von etw *dat* geschluckt werden *fam*; **to ~ sth whole** etw *akk* unzerkaut [hinunter]schlucken III. *vi* schlucken

swallow[2] ['swal·oʊ] *n* (*bird*) Schwalbe *f*

swam [swæm] *vt, vi pt of* **swim**

swamp [swamp] I. *vt* überschwemmen; **I'm ~ed with work at the moment** im Moment ersticke ich in Arbeit II. *n* Sumpf *m*

'swampland, 'swamplands *npl* Sumpfland *nt*

swan [swan] *n* Schwan *m*

swap [swap] I. *n* Tausch *m*; (*interchange*) Austausch *m*; (*deal*) Tauschhandel *m* II. *vt* <-pp-> tauschen; *stories* austauschen III. *vi* <-pp-> tauschen; ■**to ~ with sb** mit jdm tauschen

swarm [swɔrm] I. *n* Schwarm *m*; (*people*) Schar *f* II. *vi* schwärmen; ■**to be ~ing with sth** von etw *dat* [nur so] wimmeln

swat [swat] I. *vt* <-tt-> totschlagen; *ball* schmettern II. *n* [heftiger] Schlag; (*swatter*) Fliegenklatsche *f*

sway [sweɪ] I. *vi* schwanken; *trees* sich wiegen II. *vt* schwenken; *wind* wiegen; (*alter*) ändern; ■**to be ~ed by sb/sth** sich von jdm/etw beeinflussen lassen; (*change mind*) von jdm/etw umgestimmt werden

swear <swore, sworn> [swer] I. *vi* fluchen; (*take oath*) schwören II. *vt* schwören; *oath* leisten

◆ **swear in** *vt* vereidigen

'swearing *n* Fluchen *nt*

'swear word *n* Fluch *m*

sweat [swet] I. *n* Schweiß *m*; **to work oneself into a ~ [about sth]** sich [wegen einer S. *dat*] verrückt machen *fam* II. *vi* <sweat *or* sweated, sweat *or* sweated> schwitzen III. *vt* <sweat *or* sweated, sweat *or* sweated> ▶PHRASES:

S

to ~ **blood** Blut [und Wasser] schwitzen *fam*

◆**sweat out** *vt* to ~ it out zittern *fam*

sweater ['swet·ər] *n* Pullover *m*

'**sweatpants** *n pl* Jogginghose *f*

'**sweatshirt** *n* Sweatshirt *nt*

'**sweatshop** *n* Ausbeuterbetrieb *m pej*

sweaty ['swet·i] *adj* verschwitzt; *work* schweißtreibend

Swede [swid] *n* Schwede *m*, Schwedin *f*

Sweden ['swi·dən] *n* Schweden *nt*

Swedish ['swi·dɪʃ] I. *n* Schwedisch *nt* II. *adj* schwedisch

sweep [swip] I. *n* ⟨ Kehren *nt*; (*with saber*) ausholender Hieb; (*range*) Reichweite *f* II. *vt* ⟨swept, swept⟩ ❶ kehren; **she swept the pile of papers into her bag** sie schaufelte den Stapel Papiere in ihre Tasche ❷ ■**to ~ sth** *epidemic* über etw *akk* kommen III. *vi* ⟨swept, swept⟩ kehren; (*move*) gleiten

◆**sweep aside** *vt* [hin]wegfegen; (*dismiss*) beiseiteschieben

◆**sweep away** *vt* [hin]wegfegen; (*fig*) beiseiteschieben; (*carry away*) mitreißen

◆**sweep out** I. *vt* auskehren II. *vi* hinausstürmen

◆**sweep up** I. *vt* zusammenkehren II. *vi* aufkehren

sweeper ['swi·pər] *n* Kehrmaschine *f*; (*person*) [Straßen]kehrer(in) *m(f)*; (*in soccer*) Libero *m*

sweeping ['swi·pɪŋ] *adj* weitreichend; *changes* einschneidend; *cuts* drastisch; (*general*) pauschal; *generalization* grob; *curves* weit

sweepstakes ['swip·steɪks] *npl + sing/ pl vb* Art Lotterie, wobei mit kleinen Einsätzen u. A. auf Pferde gesetzt wird und diese Einsätze auf den Gewinner gehen

sweet [swit] I. *adj* süß; (*pleasant a.*) angenehm; (*endearing*) niedlich; *wine, voice* lieblich; *temper* sanft; (*kind*) lieb II. *n* ■**~s** *pl* Süßigkeiten *pl*

'**sweet-and-sour** *adj* süßsauer

'**sweet corn** *n* [Zucker]mais *m*

sweeten ['swi·tən] *vt* süßen; ■**to ~** [**up** ⟩] *sb* jdn günstig stimmen

sweetener ['swi·tən·ər] *n* Süßstoff *m*; (*pill*) Süßstofftablette *f*; (*inducement*) Versuchung *f*

'**sweetheart** *n* Liebling *m*

sweetness ['swit·nɪs] *n* Süße *f*; (*pleasantness*) Freundlichkeit *f*; *of victory* süßes [*o* wohliges] Gefühl

swell ⟨swelled, swelled *or* swollen⟩ [swel] I. *n* [an]steigen lassen; *sales* steigern II. *vi* ❶ ■**to ~** [**up**] anschwellen ❷ (*increase*) zunehmen; *population* ansteigen; (*get louder*) lauter werden III. *n* *of sound* zunehmende Lautstärke; *of music* Anschwellen *nt*; *of sea* Seegang *m*

swelling ['swel·ɪŋ] *n* Schwellung *f*; (*sudden*) Beule *f*; (*activity*) Anschwellen *nt*

sweltering ['swel·tər·ɪŋ] *adj* drückend heiß; *heat* schwül

swept [swept] *vt, vi pt of* **sweep**

swerve [swɜrv] I. *vi* [plötzlich] ausweichen; *car* ausscheren; (*deviate*) eine Schwenkung vollziehen *geh*; **to ~ from one's principles** von seinen Grundsätzen abweichen II. *n* Schlenker *m*; (*evasion*) Ausweichbewegung *f*; (*fig*) Abweichung *f*; **a ~ to the left/ right** ein Ausscheren *nt* nach links/ rechts

swift [swɪft] I. *adj* schnell II. *n* Mauersegler *m*

swiftly ['swɪft·li] *adv* schnell

swiftness ['swɪft·nɪs] *n* Schnelligkeit *f*

swill [swɪl] I. *n* Schweinefutter *nt*; (*fig, pej: drink*) Gesöff *nt fam*; (*food*) Fraß *m fam* II. *vt* (*usu pej fam*) hinunterstürzen; *beer* hinunterkippen

swim [swɪm] I. *vi* ⟨swam, swum, -mm-⟩ schwimmen; (*whirl*) verschwimmen II. *vt* ⟨swam, swum, -mm-⟩ durchschwimmen; **to ~ a few strokes** ein paar Züge schwimmen III. *n* **to go for a ~** schwimmen gehen

swimming ['swɪm·ɪŋ] *n* Schwimmen *nt*

'**swimming cap** *n* Badekappe *f*

'**swimming pool** n Schwimmbecken nt; (*private*) Swimmingpool m; (*public*) Schwimmbad nt; **indoor/outdoor ~** Hallen-/Freibad nt

'**swimsuit** n Badeanzug m; (*trunks*) Badehose f

'**swim trunks**, '**swimming trunks** npl Badehose f

swindle ['swɪn·dəl] I. vt betrügen; ■**to ~ sb out of sth** jdn um etw akk betrügen II. n Betrug m

swindler ['swɪnd·lər] n Betrüger(in) m(f)

swine <pl -> [swaɪn] n Schwein nt; (*pej fam: person*) Schwein nt

'**swine flu** no pl, '**swine influenza** n no pl Schweinegrippe f

swing [swɪŋ] I. n Schwingen nt; (*punch*) Schlag m; (*in baseball*) Schwung m; (*seat*) Schaukel f; (*change*) Schwankung f; POL Umschwung m ▶PHRASES: **to be in full ~** voll im Gang sein II. vi <swung, swung> ❶ [hin und her] schwingen; (*in circles*) sich drehen; *baseball bat* schwingen; *mood* schwanken; **the door swung open in the wind** die Tür ging durch den Wind auf ❷ (*try to hit*) zum Schlag ausholen; ■**to ~ at sb** nach jdm schlagen ❸ *party* swingen ▶PHRASES: **to ~ into action** loslegen fam III. vt <swung, swung> [hin- und her]schwingen; **do you think you could ~ the job for me?** (fam) glaubst du, du könntest die Sache für mich schaukeln?; **to ~ it** es deichseln

swing around I. vi sich schnell umdrehen; (*in fear*) herumfahren; **she swung around the corner at full speed** sie kam mit vollem Tempo um die Ecke geschossen II. vt ■**to ~ sth around** etw [her]umdrehen; (*in circles*) etw herumschwingen; **to ~ a conversation around to sth** ein Gespräch auf etw akk bringen

swipe [swaɪp] I. vi schlagen II. vt (*fam: steal*) klauen III. n Schlag m; **to take a ~ at sb/sth** auf jdn/etw losschlagen

swirl [swɜrl] I. vi wirbeln II. n of water

Strudel m; of snow, wind Wirbel m; of dust Wolke f

Swiss [swɪs] I. adj Schweizer· II. n <pl -> Schweizer(in) m(f)

switch [swɪtʃ] I. n <pl -es> ❶ Schalter m; **to flick a ~** (*on*) einen Schalter anknipsen; (*off*) einen Schalter ausknipsen ❷ (*substitution*) Wechsel m; (*alteration*) Änderung f; (*change*) Wechsel m II. vi wechseln III. vt ❶ (*adjust settings*) umschalten ❷ *direction* wechseln; (*substitute*) auswechseln

◆ **switch off** I. vt ausschalten II. vi ausschalten; (*lose attention*) abschalten fam

◆ **switch on** I. vt einschalten; *TV a.* anmachen II. vi einschalten

◆ **switch over** vi wechseln

'**switchblade** n Klappmesser nt

'**switchboard** n Vermittlung f

Switzerland ['swɪt·sər·lənd] n Schweiz f

swivel ['swɪv·əl] I. vt <-l-> drehen II. vi <-l-> sich drehen

swollen ['swoʊ·lən] I. pp of **swell** II. adj geschwollen; *face* aufgequollen; (*larger*) angeschwollen

swoop [swup] I. n Sturzflug m; (*fam: attack*) Überraschungsangriff m II. vi herabstoßen; ■**to ~ in on sb/sth** (fam) jdn/etw angreifen; *police* bei jdm/etw eine Razzia machen

sword [sɔrd] n Schwert nt

'**swordfish** n Schwertfisch m

swore [swɔr] pt of **swear**

sworn [swɔrn] I. pp of **swear** II. adj attr ~ **statement** eidliche Aussage; ~ **enemy** Todesfeind(in) m(f)

swum [swʌm] pp of **swim**

swung [swʌŋ] pt, pp of **swing**

sycamore ['sɪk·ə·mɔr] n Platane f

syllable ['sɪl·ə·bəl] n Silbe f

syllabus <pl -es> ['sɪl·ə·bəs] n Lehrplan m; (*list*) Leseliste f

symbiosis [ˌsɪm·bɪ·'oʊ·sɪs] n Symbiose f

symbiotic [ˌsɪm·bɪ·'aʧ·ɪk] adj symbiotisch

symbol ['sɪm·bəl] n Symbol nt

symbolic [sɪm·'bal·ɪk] adj symbolisch

S

symbolize ['sɪm·bə·laɪz] *vt* symbolisieren

symmetrical [sɪ'met·rɪ·kəl] *adj* symmetrisch; *face* ebenmäßig

symmetry ['sɪm·ə·tri] *n* Symmetrie *f*; (*evenness*) Ebenmäßigkeit *f*; (*correspondence*) Übereinstimmung *f*

sympathetic [ˌsɪm·pə·'θet·ɪk] *adj* verständnisvoll; (*sympathizing*) mitfühlend; (*likeable*) sympathisch; ▪ **to be ~ about sth** für etw *akk* Verständnis haben; ▪ **to be ~ to[ward] sb/sth** mit jdm/etw sympathisieren

sympathize ['sɪm·pə·θaɪz] *vi* Verständnis haben; (*show compassion*) Mitleid haben; (*agree with*) sympathisieren

sympathizer ['sɪm·pə·θaɪ·zər] *n* Sympathisant(in) *m(f)*

sympathy ['sɪm·pə·θi] *n* Mitleid *nt*; (*commiseration*) Mitgefühl *nt*; (*understanding*) Verständnis *nt*; (*agreement*) Übereinstimmung *f*; (*affection*) Sympathie *f*; ▪ **sympathies** *pl* (*condolences*) Beileid *nt*

symphony ['sɪm·fə·ni] *n* Symphonie *f*

symptom ['sɪmp·təm] *n* Symptom *nt*; (*fig a.*) [An]zeichen *nt*

symptomatic [ˌsɪmp·tə·'mæt·ɪk] *adj* symptomatisch

synagogue ['sɪn·ə·gag] *n* Synagoge *f*

synchronize ['sɪŋ·krə·naɪz] I. *vt* aufeinander abstimmen; **to ~ watches**

Uhren gleichstellen II. *vi* zeitlich zusammenfallen

synchronous ['sɪŋ·krə·nəs] *adj* synchron

syndicate ['sɪn·də·kɪt] *n* Syndikat *nt*; JOURN Pressesyndikat *nt*

syndrome ['sɪn·droʊm] *n* Syndrom *nt*

synergy ['sɪn·ər·dʒi] *n* Synergismus *m*; (*energy*) Synergie *f*

synonym ['sɪn·ə·nɪm] *n* Synonym *nt*

synonymous [sɪ'nan·ɪ·məs] *adj* synonym

synopsis <*pl* -ses> [sɪ'næp·sɪs] *n* Zusammenfassung *f*

synthesis <*pl* -theses> ['sɪn·θə·sɪs] *n* Synthese *f*

synthesize ['sɪn·θə·saɪz] *vt* künstlich herstellen

synthesizer ['sɪn·θə·saɪ·zər] *n* Synthesizer *m*

synthetic [sɪn'θet·ɪk] I. *adj* synthetisch; (*fig, pej: fake*) künstlich; **~ fiber** Kunstfaser *f* II. *n* synthetischer Stoff

syphilis ['sɪf·ə·lɪs] *n* Syphilis *f*

Syria ['sɪr·i·ə] *n* Syrien *nt*

Syrian ['sɪr·i·ən] I. *adj* syrisch II. *n* Syr[i]er(in) *m(f)*

syringe [sə'rɪndʒ] *n* Spritze *f*

syrup ['sɪr·əp] *n* Sirup *m*; **maple ~** Ahornsirup

system ['sɪs·təm] *n* System *nt*

systematic [ˌsɪs·tə·'mæt·ɪk] *adj* systematisch

S

Tt

T <pl -'s>, **t** <pl -'s> [ti] n T nt, t nt; ~ **as in Tango** T wie Theodor

t. n abbrev of **ton** t

tab [tæb] n Lasche f; (on file) [Kartei]reiter m; (fam: bill) Rechnung f; **to pick up the** ~ die Rechnung übernehmen ▶PHRASES: **to keep** ~**s on sth/sb** (fam) etw/jdn [genau] im Auge behalten

tabby ['tæb·i] adj, n ~ [**cat**] Tigerkatze f

'tab key n COMPUT Tabulatortaste f

table ['teɪ·bəl] n Tisch m; (list) Tabelle f; **to set the** ~ den Tisch decken ▶PHRASES: **to turn the** ~**s on sb** jdm gegenüber den Spieß umdrehen

'tablecloth n Tischtuch nt

'table manners npl Tischmanieren pl

'tablespoon n Esslöffel m

tablet ['tæb·lɪt] n ❶ (pill) Tablette f ❷ (commemorative) [Gedenk]tafel f ❸ (writing pad) Notizblock m ❹ (computer) Tablet nt

'table tennis n Tischtennis nt

tabloid ['tæb·lɔɪd] n Boulevardzeitung f

taboo [tə·'bu] I. n Tabu nt II. adj tabu, Tabu-

tack [tæk] I. n kurzer Nagel; (pin) Reißzwecke f; (stitch) Heftstich m; **to try a different** ~ (fig) eine andere Richtung einschlagen II. vt festnageln; (sew) anheften; hem heften

tackle ['tæk·əl] I. n Ausrüstung f; (hoist) Winde f; (in football) Tackle m; (in soccer) Angriff m; **block and** ~ Flaschenzug m II. vt in Angriff nehmen; (problem) angehen; (manage) fertigwerden; (in football) tackeln; (in soccer) angreifen

tacky ['tæk·i] adj klebrig; (pej fam: in bad taste) billig; (pej fam: shoddy) schäbig

tact [tækt] n Taktgefühl nt; (sensitiveness) Feingefühl nt

tactful ['tækt·fəl] adj taktvoll

tactic ['tæk·tɪk] n Taktik f

tactical ['tæk·tɪ·kəl] adj taktisch; (skillful) geschickt

tactless ['tækt·lɪs] adj taktlos

tadpole ['tæd·poʊl] n Kaulquappe f

taffeta ['tæf·ɪ·tə] n Taft m

tag [tæg] I. n Schild[chen] nt; (on clothes) Etikett nt; (on car) Steuerplakette f; (on suitcase) [Koffer]anhänger m; (security tag) Sicherungsetikett nt; for person elektronische Fessel II. vt <-gg-> mit einem Schild versehen; suitcase mit einem Anhänger versehen; (electronically) ein Sicherungsetikett anbringen; person eine elektronische Fessel anlegen

♦ **tag along** vi (fam) hinterherlaufen; (join) mitkommen

tail [teɪl] I. n Schwanz m; of car Heck nt; (fam: follower) Beschatter(in) m(f); **heads or** ~**s?** Kopf oder Zahl?; **to have sb on one's** ~ jdn auf den Fersen haben; **to put a** ~ **on sb** jdn beschatten lassen ▶PHRASES: **I can't make heads or** ~**s of it** ich werde daraus einfach nicht schlau II. vt (fam) beschatten

♦ **tail off** vi nachlassen; voice schwächer werden

'tailgate I. n Heckklappe f; of truck Ladeklappe f; of van Laderampe f II. vt, vi (fam) [zu] dicht auffahren

'taillight n Rücklicht nt

tailor ['teɪ·lər] I. n Schneider(in) m(f) II. vt [nach Maß] schneidern

tailor-'made adj maßgeschneidert; ■**to be** ~ **for sb/sth** für jdn/etw maßgeschneidert sein

'tailpipe n Auspuffrohr nt

taint [teɪnt] vt verderben; reputation beflecken

Taiwan [ˌtaɪ·'wan] n Taiwan nt

Taiwanese [ˌtaɪ·wə·'niz] I. adj taiwanisch II. n Taiwaner(in) m(f)

Tajikistan [ta·'dʒi·kɪˌstan] n Tadschikistan nt

T

take [teɪk] I. *n* Einnahmen *pl;* (*scene*) Take *m o nt fachspr* ▸ PHRASES: **to be on the ~** (*fam*) Bestechungsgelder nehmen II. *vt* <took, taken> ❶ (*accept*) annehmen; *criticism* akzeptieren; **to ~ sth badly** etw schlecht aufnehmen ❷ (*transport*) bringen; **to ~ sb to the train station** jdn zum Bahnhof fahren ❸ (*seize*) nehmen; *power* ergreifen; *city* einnehmen; (*win*) gewinnen; **to ~ sb by the hand/throat** jdn bei der Hand nehmen/am Kragen packen ❹ (*tolerate*) ertragen; *abuse* hinnehmen ❺ (*hold*) aufnehmen; **my car ~s five people** mein Auto hat Platz für fünf Leute ❻ (*require*) erfordern; **I ~ [a] size five** [*or* **a size five shoe**] ich habe Schuhgröße fünf; ■**it ~s …** man braucht …; **hold on, it won't ~ long** warten Sie, es dauert nicht lange ❼ (*receive*) erhalten ❽ (*remove*) [weg]nehmen; (*steal a.*) stehlen; *chess piece* schlagen ❾ (*travel by*) nehmen; **to ~ the bus** mit dem Bus fahren ❿ (*consume*) zu sich *dat* nehmen; *medicine* einnehmen ⓫ (*engage in*) machen; *bath* nehmen; *exam* schreiben; *notes* sich *dat* machen; *pictures* machen ⓬ (*feel*) **to ~ notice of sb/sth** jdn/etw beachten; **to ~ offense** beleidigt sein ⓭ **I ~ it [that]** … ich nehme an, [dass] … ⓮ (*order*) nehmen ▸ PHRASES: **to ~ sb by surprise** jdn überraschen; **what do you ~ me for?** wofür hältst du mich?

◆**take aback** *vt* verblüffen; (*shock*) schockieren

◆**take along** *vt* mitnehmen

◆**take apart** *vt* auseinandernehmen

◆**take away** *vt* [weg]nehmen; **to ~ away sb's fear** jdm die Angst nehmen; ■**to ~ away ◯ sb** jdn mitnehmen; *police* abführen ▸ PHRASES: **to ~ sb's breath away** jdm den Atem verschlagen

◆**take back** *vt* zurückbringen; (*return*) [wieder] zurückbringen; (*repossess*) [sich *dat*] zurückholen; *territory* zurückerobern; **to ~ sb back [home]** jdn nach Hause bringen

◆**take down** *vt* [sich *dat*] notieren; *particulars* aufnehmen; (*remove*) abnehmen; (*from higher position*) herunternehmen; *picture* abhängen; *tent* abschlagen; *scaffolding* abbauen

◆**take in** *vt* ❶ hineinbringen; *person a.* hineinführen; (*to police station*) festnehmen; (*accommodate*) aufnehmen; *child* zu sich *dat* nehmen; (*admit*) aufnehmen; *university* zulassen; (*deceive*) hereinlegen; (*understand*) aufnehmen; ■**to be ~n in [by sb/sth]** sich [von jdm/etw] täuschen lassen; **to ~ in a situation** eine Situation erfassen ❷ (*tuck*) enger machen

◆**take off** I. *vt* abnehmen; *clothes* ausziehen; *coat a.* ablegen; *hat* absetzen; ■**to ~ sth off sb** (*fam*) jdm etw wegnehmen; **he was ~n off to the hospital** er wurde ins Krankenhaus gebracht II. *vi* abheben; (*fam: leave*) verschwinden; (*flee*) abhauen; *idea* ankommen; *product a.* einschlagen

◆**take on** *vt* auf sich *akk* nehmen; *job* annehmen; (*employ*) einstellen; (*load*) laden; *passengers* aufnehmen

◆**take out** *vt* herausnehmen; *trash* hinausbringen; (*invite*) ausführen; *insurance* abschließen; *loan* aufnehmen; *money* abheben; (*sl: kill*) beseitigen; (*destroy*) vernichten; **to ~ sb out to dinner** jdn zum Abendessen einladen

◆**take over** I. *vt* übernehmen; (*fig*) in Beschlag nehmen; *power* ergreifen II. *vi* ■**to ~ over [from sb]** jdn ablösen; **the night shift ~s over at 10 p.m.** die Nachtschicht übernimmt um 22.00 Uhr

◆**take to** *vi* ❶ (*like*) ■**to ~ to sb/sth** an jdm/etw Gefallen finden ❷ **to ~ to drink** anfangen, zu trinken; ■**to ~ to doing sth** anfangen, etw zu tun ▸ PHRASES: **to ~ to sth like a duck to water** bei etw *dat* gleich in seinem Element sein

◆**take up** I. *vt* hinaufbringen; *carpet* herausreißen; *skirt* kürzen; (*start doing*) anfangen; *job* antreten; (*accept*) annehmen; *opportunity* wahrnehmen;

my job ~s up all my time mein Beruf frisst meine ganze Zeit auf; ■**to ~ sth up with sb** etw mit jdm erörtern; **to ~ up a point** einen Punkt aufgreifen; **to ~ up space** Raum einnehmen II. *vi* ■**to ~ up with sb** sich mit jdm einlassen

taken ['teɪ·kən] I. *vt, vi pp of* **take** II. *adj* ■**to be ~ with sb/sth** von jdm/ etw angetan sein

'**takeoff** *n* Start *m*; SPORT Absprungstelle *f*; **to be ready for ~** startklar sein

'**take-out** *n* Imbissbude *f*; *(food)* Essen *nt* zum Mitnehmen

'**takeover** *n* Übernahme *f*

taker ['teɪ·kər] *n* Wettende(r) *f(m)*; *(at sale)* Interessent(in) *m(f)*; *(buyer)* Käufer(in) *m(f)*; **any ~s?** wer nimmt die Wette an?

taking ['teɪ·kɪŋ] *n* ■**~s** *pl* Einnahmen *pl* ▶PHRASES: **to be there for the ~** zum Mitnehmen sein; *(not settled)* [noch] offen sein

talc [tælk], **talcum** (**powder**) ['tæl·kəm. ˌpaʊ·dər)] *n* Talkpuder *m*; *(perfumed)* Körperpuder *m*

tale [teɪl] *n* Geschichte *f*; LIT Erzählung *f*; *(true story)* Bericht *m*; **fairy ~** Märchen *nt*; **tall ~** [Lügen]märchen *nt* ▶PHRASES: **to** <u>live</u> **to tell the ~** *(fam)* überleben

talent ['tæl·ənt] *n* Talent *nt*

talented ['tæl·ən·t̬ɪd] *adj* begabt

Taliban ['tɑ·lɪ·bæn] *n* Taliban *f*

talisman <*pl* -s> ['tæl·ɪs·mən] *n* Talisman *m*

talk [tɔk] I. *n* Gespräch *nt*; *(conversation)* Unterhaltung *f*; *(private)* Unterredung *f*; *(lecture)* Vortrag *m*; *(things said)* Worte *pl*; **to have a ~ with sb** mit jdm reden; *(conversation)* sich mit jdm unterhalten; **idle ~** leeres Gerede II. *vi* reden; *(converse)* sich unterhalten; **to ~ to sb on the phone** mit jdm telefonieren ▶PHRASES: <u>look</u> **who's ~ing** *(fam)* du hast es gerade nötig, etwas zu sagen III. *vt (fam)* **to ~ politics** über Politik sprechen ▶PHRASES: **~ <u>about</u> ...** so was von ... *fam*

◆**talk around** I. *vt* ■**to ~ sb around**

jdn überreden II. *vi* ■**to ~ around sth** um etw *akk* herumreden

◆**talk back** *vi* eine freche Antwort geben; **don't ~ back!** keine Widerrede!

◆**talk down** *vi* ■**to ~ down to sb** mit jdm herablassend reden

◆**talk out** *vt* **to ~ one's way out of sth** sich aus etw *dat* herausreden; ■**to ~ sb out of [doing] sth** jdm ausreden, etw zu tun

◆**talk over** *vt* durchsprechen

◆**talk through** *vt* durchsprechen; ■**to ~ sb through sth** jdm bei etw *dat* gut zureden

talkative ['tɔk·ə·t̬ɪv] *adj* gesprächig

talking ['tɔk·ɪŋ] I. *adj* sprechend II. *n* Sprechen *nt*; "**no ~, please!**" „Ruhe bitte!"

'**talk show** *n* Talkshow *f*

tall [tɔl] *adj* hoch; *person* groß; *price* ziemlich hoch; **to grow ~** groß werden

tally <-ie-> ['tæl·i] I. *vi* übereinstimmen II. *vt* ❶ ■**to ~ sth** ↻ [up] etw zusammenzählen ❷ *(check off)* nachzählen; *score* notieren III. *n usu sing* Stückliste *f*; **to keep a ~** eine [Strich]liste führen

talon ['tæl·ən] *n* Klaue *f*

tambourine [ˌtæm·bə·'rin] *n* Tamburin *nt*

tame [teɪm] I. *adj* zahm; *(harmless)* friedlich; *book, joke* lahm II. *vt* zähmen; *anger* bezähmen; *impatience* zügeln

tamper ['tæm·pər] *vi* ■**to ~ with sth** etw [in betrügerischer Absicht] verändern

tampon ['tæm·pɑn] *n* Tampon *m*

tan [tæn] I. *vi* <-nn-> braun werden II. *vt* <-nn-> bräunen; *leather* gerben; **to be ~ned** braun gebrannt sein III. *n* [Sonnen]bräune *f*; *(color)* Gelbbraun *nt* IV. *adj* gelbbraun

tandem ['tæn·dəm] *n* Tandem *nt*

tang [tæŋ] *n* [scharfer] Geruch; *(taste)* [scharfer] Geschmack

tangent ['tæn·dʒənt] *n* ▶PHRASES: **to <u>fly</u> off on a ~** [plötzlich] das Thema wechseln

◆**talk around** I. *vt* ■**to ~ sb around**

tangerine [ˌtæn·dʒə·'rin] *n* Mandarine *f*

T

tangible ['tæn·dʒə·bəl] *adj* fassbar; (*real*) real; *advantage* echt; *evidence* handfest

tangle ['tæŋ·gəl] I. *n* [wirres] Knäuel; *of wires* Gewirr *nt;* (*confusion*) Durcheinander *nt;* **to get into a ~** sich verfangen II. *vt* durcheinanderbringen; *threads* verwickeln III. *vi* verfilzen; *wires* sich verwickeln

◆**tangle up** I. *vt* durcheinanderbringen II. *vi* verfilzen; *wires* sich *akk* verwickeln

tango ['tæŋ·goʊ] I. *n* Tango *m* II. *vi* Tango tanzen

tangy ['tæŋ·i] *adj* scharf; *smell* durchdringend

tank [tæŋk] *n* Tank *m;* MIL Panzer *m;* **fish ~** Aquarium *nt*

tanker ['tæŋ·kər] *n* Tanker *m;* (*truck*) Tankwagen *m*

tanned [tænd] *adj* braun [gebrannt]; *leather* gegerbt

'**tanning bed** *n* Sonnenbank *f*

tantalize ['tæn·tə·laɪz] I. *vt* reizen; (*fascinate*) in den Bann ziehen; (*keep in suspense*) auf die Folter spannen II. *vi* reizen

tantalizing ['tæn·tə·laɪ·zɪŋ] *adj* verlockend; *smile* verführerisch

tantamount ['tæn·tə·maʊnt] *adj* ■**to be ~ to sth** mit etw *dat* gleichbedeutend sein

tantrum ['tæn·trəm] *n* Wutanfall *m;* **to throw a ~** einen Wutanfall bekommen

Tanzania [ˌtæn·zə·'ni·ə] *n* Tansania *nt*

tap[1] [tæp] I. *n* ❶ [leichter] Schlag ❷ (*dancing*) Stepp[tanz] *m* II. *vt* <-pp-> [leicht] klopfen; **to ~ sb on the shoulder** jdm auf die Schulter tippen III. *vi* <-pp-> [leicht] klopfen

tap[2] [tæp] I. *n* ❶ Hahn *m;* **to be on ~** (*fig*) [sofort] verfügbar sein ❷ TELEC Abhörgerät *nt* II. *vt* <-pp-> ❶ (*intercept*) abhören ❷ *energy* erschließen ❸ (*drain*) [ab]zapfen; *barrel* anstechen; *beer* zapfen III. *vi* (*fam*) **to ~ into new markets** neue Märkte erschließen

'**tap dance** I. *n* Stepptanz *m* II. *vi* steppen

tape [teɪp] I. *n* Band *nt;* SPORT (*at finish*) Zielband *nt;* (*for measuring*) Maßband *nt;* (*adhesive*) Klebeband *nt;* (*for recording*) [Ton-/Magnet]band *nt;* **audio ~** Audiokassette *f;* **Scotch ~**® Tesafilm® *m* II. *vt* ❶ **she ~d a note to the door** sie heftete eine Nachricht an die Tür ❷ (*record*) aufnehmen

'**tape deck** *n* Tapedeck *nt*

'**tape measure** *n* Maßband *nt*

taper ['teɪ·pər] *vi* sich verjüngen

◆**taper off** *vi* sich verjüngen; (*decrease*) [allmählich] abnehmen; *interest* nachlassen

'**tape recorder** *n* Tonbandgerät *nt*

tapestry ['tæp·əs·tri] *n* Gobelin *m*

'**tapeworm** *n* Bandwurm *m*

'**tap water** *n* Leitungswasser *nt*

tar [tar] I. *n* Teer *m* II. *vt* <-rr-> teeren

▶PHRASES: **to be ~red with the same brush** um kein Haar besser sein

tarantula [tə·'ræn·tʃə·lə] *n* Tarantel *f*

tardy ['tar·di] *adj* unpünktlich; (*overdue*) verspätet; (*sluggish*) langsam; *progress* schleppend

target ['tar·gɪt] I. *n* ❶ Ziel *nt;* **to hit the ~** ins Schwarze treffen; ■**to be on ~** auf [Ziel]kurs liegen; *analysis* zutreffen ❷ (*goal*) Zielsetzung *f;* ■**to be on ~** im Zeitplan liegen II. *vt* <-t-> [ab]zielen III. *adj* Ziel-; *profit* angestrebt

'**target practice** *n* Übungsschießen *nt*

tarnish ['tar·nɪʃ] I. *vi* stumpf werden; (*discolor*) anlaufen; (*fig: lose shine*) an Glanz verlieren; *honor* beschmutzt werden II. *vt* trüben; (*discolor*) anlaufen lassen; (*fig*) den Glanz nehmen; *reputation* beflecken III. *n* Belag *m;* (*fig*) Makel *m*

tarpaulin [tar·'pɔ·lɪn] *n* [Abdeck]plane *f*

tarragon ['tær·ə·gən] *n* Estragon *m*

tart[1] [tart] *adj* scharf; (*sour*) sauer; *irony* beißend; *remark* bissig

tart[2] [tart] *n* [Obst]törtchen *nt;* (*usu pej: whore*) Schlampe *f;* **jam ~** Marmeladentörtchen *nt*

Tartar ['tar·tər] *n* Tatar(in) *m(f);* (*language*) Tatarisch *nt*

task [tæsk] n Aufgabe f ▶PHRASES: **to take sb to ~** jdn zur Rede stellen

'**task force** n Arbeitsgruppe f; MIL Eingreiftruppe f; police Spezialeinheit f

Tasmania [tæz·ˈmeɪ·ni·ə] n Tasmanien nt

Tasmanian [tæz·ˈmeɪ·ni·ən] I. n Tasmanier(in) m(f) II. adj tasmanisch

tassel [ˈtæs·əl] n Quaste f

taste [teɪst] I. n Geschmack m; (liking) Vorliebe f; (encounter) Kostprobe f; **sense of ~** Geschmackssinn m; **to acquire a ~ for sth** an etw dat Geschmack finden; **to have a ~ of sth** einen Vorgeschmack von etw dat bekommen II. vt schmecken; (test) probieren; success [einmal] erleben III. vi schmecken; **to ~ sweet** süß schmecken

tasteful [ˈteɪst·fəl] adj geschmackvoll

tasteless [ˈteɪst·lɪs] adj geschmacksneutral; (unappetizing) fad[e]; beer schal; (offensive) geschmacklos

tasty [ˈteɪ·sti] adj schmackhaft

tatter [ˈtæ·tər] n usu pl Fetzen m; ■**to be in ~s** zerfetzt sein; (fig) reputation ruiniert sein

tattered [ˈtæt·ərd] adj zerlumpt; flag zerrissen; reputation ramponiert

tattoo [tæ·ˈtu] I. n Tattoo m o nt II. vt tätowieren

taught [tɒt] pt, pp of **teach**

taunt [tɒnt] I. vt verspotten; (provoke) sticheln II. n spöttische Bemerkung; (tease) Hänselei f; (provocation) Stichelei f

Taurus [ˈtɔr·əs] n ASTROL Stier m

taut [tɒt] adj straff [gespannt]; muscle gespannt; rubber band stramm; face angespannt

tax [tæks] I. n <pl -es> Steuer f; (burden) Belastung f; (on resources) Beanspruchung f; **income ~** Einkommenssteuer f; **to impose a ~ on sth** etw besteuern II. vt besteuern; (burden) belasten; (make demands) beanspruchen; (confront) beschuldigen; **to be ~ed [heavily]** [hoch] besteuert werden

taxable [ˈtæk·sə·bəl] adj steuerpflichtig

taxation [tæk·ˈseɪ·ʃən] n Besteuerung f; (money) Steuereinnahmen pl

'**tax collector** n Steuerbeamte(r), -beamtin m, f

tax-de'ductible adj steuerlich absetzbar

'**tax dodger** n (fam), '**tax evader** n Steuerhinterzieher(in) m(f)

'**tax evasion** n Steuerhinterziehung f

'**tax-exempt** adj von der Mehrwertsteuer befreit

tax-'free adj steuerfrei

taxi [ˈtæk·si] n Taxi nt

taxidermist [ˈtæk·sɪ·ˌdɜr·mɪst] n [Tier]präparator(in) m(f)

taxidermy [ˈtæk·sɪ·ˌdɜr·mi] n Taxidermie f

'**taxi driver** n Taxifahrer(in) m(f)

taxing [ˈtæk·sɪŋ] adj anstrengend; (hard) schwierig

'**taxi stand** n Taxistand m

'**taxman** n Finanzbeamte(r), -beamtin m, f; ■**the ~** das Finanzamt

'**taxpayer** n Steuerzahler(in) m(f)

'**tax return** n Steuererklärung f

TB [ˌtiˈbi] n abbrev of **tuberculosis** TB

tbsp. <pl -> n abbrev of **tablespoon** EL

tea [ti] n Tee m

'**tea bag** n Teebeutel m

teach <taught, taught> [titʃ] I. vt ❶ unterrichten; ■**to ~ sb sth** [or **sth to sb**] jdm etw beibringen; **to ~ school** Lehrer(in) m(f) sein ❷ **this has taught him a lot** daraus hat er viel gelernt; **to ~ sb a lesson** jdm eine Lehre erteilen II. vi unterrichten

teacher [ˈti·tʃər] n Lehrer(in) m(f)

teaching [ˈti·tʃɪŋ] I. n Unterrichten nt; (profession) Lehrberuf m II. adj Lehr-

'**teacup** n Teetasse f

teak [tik] n Teak[holz] nt; (tree) Teakbaum m

team [tim] I. n Mannschaft f; **research ~** Forschungsgruppe f II. vi ❶ (fam: gather) ein Team bilden ❷ (join) sich [in eine Gruppe] einfügen ◆**team up** vi ❶ ein Team bilden ❷ (join) sich [in eine Gruppe] einfügen

team 'spirit n Teamgeist m

T

'teamwork n Teamarbeit f

'teapot n Teekanne f

tear[1] [ter] I. n Riss m II. vt <tore, torn> zerreißen; **to ~ a muscle** sich dat einen Muskelriss zuziehen III. vi <tore, torn> **①** [zer]reißen; *lining* ausreißen **②** (*fam: rush*) ■**to ~ away** losrasen

◆**tear apart** vt zerreißen; *play* verreißen

◆**tear away** vt ■**to ~ sb ⟲ away** jdn wegreißen; ■**to ~ oneself away** sich losreißen; ■**to ~ sth ⟲ away** etw abreißen

◆**tear down** vt abreißen

◆**tear off** vt abreißen; **to ~ off one's clothes** sich dat die Kleider vom Leib reißen

◆**tear out** vt ausreißen; *page* herausreißen

◆**tear up** vt zerreißen; (*destroy*) kaputtmachen *fam*; *road* aufreißen

tear[2] [tɪr] n Träne f

teardrop ['tɪr·drap] n Träne f

'tear gas n Tränengas nt

'tearjerker n (*fam*) Schnulze f

tease [tiz] I. n Quälgeist m *fam*; (*playfully*) neckische Person; (*erotic*) Aufreißer(in) m(f) II. vt aufziehen; (*playfully*) necken; (*provoke*) provozieren

teaser ['ti·zər] n neckische Person; (*riddle*) harte Nuss *fam*

'teaspoon n Teelöffel m

teat [tit] n Zitze f

technical ['tek·nɪ·kəl] adj technisch; (*detailed*) Fach-; **~ term** Fachausdruck m

technicality [ˌtek·nə·'kæl·ɪ·t̬i] n Formsache f; (*triviality*) unnötiges Detail

technician [tek·'nɪʃ·ən] n Techniker(in) m(f)

technique [tek·'nik] n Technik f; (*method*) Methode f

technology [tek·'nɑl·ə·dʒi] n Technologie f

teddy ['ted·i] n Teddybär m; (*undergarment*) Body m

'teddy bear n Teddybär m

tedious ['ti·di·əs] adj langweilig; *job a.* öde; *conversation* zäh

tedium ['ti·di·əm] n Langeweile f

tee [ti] n Tee nt

◆**tee off** I. vi abschlagen II. vt (*fam*) **to get ~d off** sauer werden *fam*

teeming ['tim·ɪŋ] adj überfüllt

teen [tin] n Teenager m

teenage(d) ['tin·eɪdʒ(d)] adj attr jugendlich; *person* im Teenageralter *nach* n

teenager ['tin·eɪ·dʒər] n Teenager m

teens [tinz] npl Jugendjahre pl

tee shirt ['ti·ʃɜrt] n T-Shirt nt

teeter ['ti·t̬ər] vi + *adv/prep* taumeln; **to ~ on the brink of a disaster** (*fig*) sich am Rande einer Katastrophe bewegen

teeth [tiθ] npl pl of **tooth** ▶ PHRASES: **in the ~ of sth** (*against*) angesichts einer S. *gen*; (*despite*) trotz einer S. *gen*

teethe [tið] vi zahnen

teetotaler [ˌti·'tou·t̬əl·ər] n Abstinenzler(in) m(f)

tel. n abbrev of **telephone number** Tel.

telecommunications ['tel·ɪ·kə·mju·nɪ·'keɪ·ʃənz] npl + *sing vb* Fernmeldewesen nt

telecommuting ['tel·ɪ·kə·mju·t̬ɪŋ] n Telearbeit f

telegenic [ˌtel·ə·'dʒen·ɪk] adj telegen

telegram ['tel·ɪ·græm] n Telegramm nt

telegraph ['tel·ɪ·græf] I. n Telegraf m II. vt telegrafieren; (*inform*) telegrafisch benachrichtigen

telepathic [ˌtel·ə·'pæθ·ɪk] adj telepathisch

telepathy [tə·'lep·ə·θi] n Telepathie f

telephone ['tel·ə·foun] I. n Telefon nt; **cell|ular| ~** Handy nt; ■**by ~** telefonisch II. vt anrufen III. vi telefonieren

'telephone book n Telefonbuch nt

'telephone booth n Telefonzelle f

'telephone call n Telefonanruf m

'telephone directory n Telefonverzeichnis nt

'telephone number n Telefonnummer f

'telephone operator n Vermittlung f

telescope ['tel·ə·skoup] I. n Teleskop nt II. vt ineinanderschieben III. vi sich ineinanderschieben

telescopic [ˌtelˈəˈskapˈɪk] adj Teleskop-; (powered) ausfahrbar; ladder ausziehbar; ~ **lens** Teleobjektiv nt

televise ['telˈəˈvaɪz] vt [im Fernsehen] übertragen

television ['telˈəˈvɪʒˈən] n Fernsehgerät nt; (broadcasting) Fernsehen nt; ■ **on** ~ im Fernsehen

'**television set** n Fernsehapparat m

telex ['telˈeks] n <pl -es> Telex nt

tell [tel] I. vt <told, told> sagen; joke, story erzählen; (discern) erkennen; (notice) [be]merken; (know) wissen; (determine) feststellen; **can you ~ me the way to the train station?** können Sie mir sagen, wie ich zum Bahnhof komme?; **to ~ a lie** lügen; **to ~ [the] time** die Uhr lesen II. vi <told, told> ■ **to ~ [on sb]** jdn verraten

◆ **tell apart** vt auseinanderhalten

◆ **tell off** vt ausschimpfen

teller ['telˈər] n Kassierer(in) m(f)

telling ['telˈɪŋ] adj aufschlussreich

telltale ['telˈteɪl] adj verräterisch

temp [temp] (fam) I. n Gelegenheitsarbeiter(in) m(f) II. vi jobben fam

temp. [temp] n abbrev of **temperature** Temp.

temper ['temˈpər] n usu sing Laune f; **she has a very sweet** ~ sie hat ein sehr sanftes Wesen; **to be in a bad temper** wütend sein; **to lose one's** ~ die Geduld verlieren

temperament ['temˈprəˈmənt] n Temperament nt; **fit of** ~ Temperamentsausbruch m; (angrier) Wutanfall m

temperamental [ˌtemˈprəˈmenˈtəl] adj launisch

temperate ['temˈpərˈɪt] adj gemäßigt

temperature ['temˈpərˈəˈtʃər] n Temperatur f; **to have a** ~ Fieber haben

tempest ['temˈpɪst] n Sturm m

temple ['temˈpəl] n Tempel m; (on head) Schläfe f

tempo <pl -s> ['temˈpou] n Tempo nt

temporary ['temˈpəˈrerˈi] adj vorüber-

gehend; (with specific limit) befristet; ~ **staff** Aushilfspersonal nt

tempt [tempt] vt in Versuchung führen; (attract) reizen; ■ **to be** ~ **ed** schwach werden; ■ **to** ~ **sb into doing sth** jdn dazu verleiten, etw zu tun ▶ PHRASES: **to** ~ **fate** das Schicksal herausfordern

temptation [tempˈteɪˈʃən] n Versuchung f; (thing) Verlockung f

tempting ['tempˈtɪŋ] adj verführerisch

ten [ten] I. adj zehn; see also **eight** II. n Zehn f; ~ **s of thousands** zehntausende; see also **eight**

tenant ['tenˈənt] n Mieter(in) m(f); of leasehold Pächter(in) m(f)

tend[1] [tend] vi ❶ ■ **to** ~ **to[ward]** sth zu etw dat neigen; **he** ~ **s to come early** er kommt meistens früh ❷ (be directed toward) tendieren; **to** ~ **upwards** eine Tendenz nach oben aufweisen

tend[2] [tend] vt sich kümmern

◆ **tend to** vi sich kümmern um +akk

tendency ['tenˈdənˈsi] n Tendenz f; (inclination) Neigung f; (trend) Trend m

tender[1] ['tenˈdər] adj zart; (affectionate) zärtlich; heart weich

tender[2] ['tenˈdər] I. n Angebot nt II. vt **to** ~ **one's resignation** die Kündigung einreichen; (from office) seinen Rücktritt anbieten

tender'hearted adj weichherzig

tenderloin ['tenˈdərˈlɔɪn] n Lendenstück nt

tenderly ['tenˈdərˈli] adv zärtlich; (lovingly) liebevoll

tenderness ['tenˈdərˈnɪs] n Zärtlichkeit f

tendon ['tenˈdən] n Sehne f

tendril ['tenˈdrəl] n Ranke f

tenement ['tenˈəˈmənt] n heruntergekommene Mietwohnung f

Tenn. abbrev of **Tennessee**

Tennessee [ˌtenˈɪˈsi] n Tennessee nt

tennis ['tenˈɪs] n Tennis nt

'**tennis court** n Tennisplatz m

'**tennis racket** n Tennisschläger m

'**tennis shoe** n Turnschuh m

tenor ['tenˈər] n Tenor m; (voice a.) Tenorstimme f

T

tense [tens] **I.** *adj* angespannt; *moment* spannungsgeladen **II.** *vt* anspannen
◆ **tense up** *vi* sich [an]spannen

tension ['ten·ʃən] *n* Spannung *f*; *of muscle* Verspannung *f*; (*uneasiness*) [An]spannung *f*; (*strain*) Spannung[en] *f[pl]*; **to ease the ~** die Spannungen reduzieren

tent [tent] *n* Zelt *nt*; **to pitch a ~** ein Zelt aufschlagen

tentacle ['ten·tə·kəl] *n* Tentakel *m*; (*sensor*) Fühler *m*

tenterhooks ['ten·tər·hʊks] *npl* ▶PHRAS-ES: **to be [kept] on ~** wie auf glühenden Kohlen sitzen

tenth [tenθ] **I.** *n* ■**the ~** der Zehnte; ■**a ~** ein Zehntel *nt* **II.** *adj attr* zehnte(r, s) ■**to be ~** Zehnte(r, s) sein **III.** *adv* als Zehnte(r, s)

tepee ['ti·pi] *n* Indianerzelt *nt*

tepid ['tep·ɪd] *adj* lau[warm]; *applause* schwach

term [tɜrm] **I.** *n* ❶ Semester *nt*; (*trimester*) Trimester *nt*; *of office* Amtszeit *f*; (*range*) Dauer *f*; *prison* ~ Gefängnisstrafe *f*; **in the short** ~ kurzfristig ❷ (*phrase*) Ausdruck *m*; **to be on friendly ~s with sb** mit jdm auf freundschaftlichem Fuß stehen; **in no uncertain ~s** unmissverständlich **II.** *vt* bezeichnen

terminal ['tɜr·mɪ·nəl] **I.** *adj* (*fatal*) End-; ~ **disease** tödlich verlaufende Krankheit **II.** *n* ❶ Terminal *m o nt*; **airport** ~ Flughafengebäude *nt*; **bus** ~ Busbahnhof *m* ❷ (*in circuit*) Anschluss *m*

terminate ['tɜr·mɪ·neɪt] **I.** *vt* beenden; *contract* aufheben; *pregnancy* abbrechen **II.** *vi* enden

termination [ˌtɜr·mɪ·'neɪ·ʃən] *n* Beendigung *f*; *of contract* Aufhebung *f*

terminology [ˌtɜr·mɪ·'nal·ə·dʒi] *n* Terminologie *f*

termite ['tɜr·maɪt] *n* Termite *f*

'term paper *n* UNIV Seminararbeit *f*

terrace ['ter·əs] **I.** *n* Terrasse *f* **II.** *vt* terrassenförmig anlegen

terrain [te·'reɪn] *n* Gelände *nt*

terrestrial [tə·'res·tri·əl] *adj* (*form*) terrestrisch *geh*, Erd-; *animal, plant* Land-

terrible ['ter·ə·bəl] *adj* schrecklich; **to look** ~ schlimm aussehen; **to be a ~ nuisance** schrecklich lästig sein

terribly ['ter·ə·bli] *adv* schrecklich; (*fam: extremely*) außerordentlich

terrier ['ter·i·ər] *n* Terrier *m*

terrific [tə·'rɪf·ɪk] *adj* (*fam*) toll *fam*; (*great*) gewaltig

terrified ['ter·ə·faɪd] *adj* erschrocken; (*scared*) verängstigt; **to be ~ of sth** [große] Angst vor etw *dat* haben

terrify <-ie-> ['ter·ə·faɪ] *vt* fürchterlich erschrecken

terrifying ['ter·ə·faɪ·ɪŋ] *adj* entsetzlich; *speed* Angst erregend; *experience* schrecklich

territorial [ˌter·ə·'tɔr·i·əl] *adj* territorial; *plant* regional begrenzt

territory ['ter·ə·tɔr·i] *n* Gebiet *nt*; POL Hoheitsgebiet *nt*; BIOL Revier *nt*; **forbidden** ~ (*fig*) verbotenes Terrain; **familiar** ~ (*fig*) vertrautes Gebiet ▶PHRASES: **it comes with the ~** es gehört dazu

terror ['ter·ər] *n* schreckliche Angst; (*political violence*) Terror *m*; **reign of** ~ Schreckensherrschaft *f*; **war on** ~ Bekämpfung *f* des Terrorismus

'terror cell *n* Terrorzelle *f*

terrorism ['ter·ə·rɪz·əm] *n* Terrorismus *m*; **act of** ~ Terroranschlag *m*

terrorist ['ter·ə·rɪst] **I.** *n* Terrorist(in) *m(f)* **II.** *adj attr* terroristisch; ~ **attack** Terroranschlag *m*

terrorize ['ter·ə·raɪz] *vt* in Angst und Schrecken versetzen; (*bully*) terrorisieren

'terror-stricken, 'terror-struck *adj* starr vor Schreck *nach n*

terse [tɜrs] *adj* kurz und bündig; *reply* kurz

test [test] **I.** *n* Test *m*; SCH Klassenarbeit *f*; UNIV Klausur *f*; (*challenge*) Herausforderung *f*; **blood** ~ Blutuntersuchung *f*; **driving** ~ Fahrprüfung *f*; **to pass/fail a** ~ eine Prüfung bestehen/nicht bestehen; **to put sb/sth to the** ~ etw/jdn auf die Probe stellen ▶PHRASES:

to stand the ~ of time die Zeit überdauern **II.** *vt* testen; *(by touching)* prüfen; *(by tasting)* probieren; *(examine)* untersuchen; *performance* überprüfen **III.** *vi* einen Test machen

testament ['tes·tə·mənt] *n* Testament *nt;* **the New/Old T~** das Neue/ Alte Testament

'test drive *n* Probefahrt *f*

tester ['tes·tər] *n* Prüfer(in) *m(f);* (*machine*) Prüfgerät *nt*

testicle ['tes·tɪ·kəl] *n* Hoden *m*

testify <-ie-> ['tes·tɪ·faɪ] *vi* [als Zeuge/ Zeugin] aussagen; ■ **to ~ to sth** etw bezeugen; *(fig)* von etw *dat* zeugen *geh*

testimonial [ˌtes·tɪ·'moʊ·ni·əl] *n* Bestätigung *f;* (*tribute*) Ehrengabe *f*

testimony ['tes·tɪ·moʊ·ni] *n* [Zeugen]aussage *f;* (*proof*) Beweis *m*

testing ['tes·tɪŋ] *n* Testen *nt*

'test tube *n* Reagenzglas *nt*

testy ['tes·ti] *adj* leicht reizbar; *answer* gereizt

tetanus ['tet·ə·nəs] *n* Tetanus *m*

tether ['teð·ər] **I.** *n* [Halte]seil *nt* ▶PHRASES: **to be at the end of one's ~** am Ende seiner Kräfte sein **II.** *vt* anbinden

Tex. *abbrev of* **Texas**

Texan ['tek·sən] **I.** *n* Texaner(in) *m(f)* **II.** *adj* texanisch

Texas ['tek·səs] *n* Texas *nt*

text [tekst] **I.** *n* Text *m;* *of document* Inhalt *m;* (*writings*) Schrift *f;* (*textbook*) Lehrbuch *nt;* ~ **message** SMS *f* **II.** *vt* ■ **to ~ [sb] sth** [jdm] eine SMS[-Nachricht] senden

'textbook **I.** *n* Lehrbuch *nt* **II.** *adj attr* Parade-; ~ **landing** Bilderbuchlandung *f*

textile ['teks·taɪl] *n* Stoff *m;* ■ ~**s** *pl* Textilien *pl*

'text message *n* SMS *f*

texture ['teks·tʃər] *n* Struktur *f;* *of surface* [Oberflächen]beschaffenheit *f;* (*consistency*) Konsistenz *f*

Thai [taɪ] **I.** *n* Thai *m o f,* Thailänder(in) *m(f);* (*language*) Thai *nt* **II.** *adj* thailändisch

Thailand ['taɪ·lənd] *n* Thailand *nt*

Thames [temz] *n* Themse *f*

than [ðən] **I.** *prep* **bigger ~** größer als; **rather ~** anstatt +*gen;* **other ~** außer +*dat;* **other ~ that,** ... abgesehen davon, ... **II.** *conj* als

thank [θæŋk] *vt* ■ **to ~ sb** jdm danken; ~ **you [very much]**! danke [sehr]!; **no/ yes, ~ you,** nein, danke/ja, bitte ▶PHRASES: **thank goodness!** Gott sei Dank!

thankful ['θæŋk·fəl] *adj* dankbar; (*pleased*) froh

thankfully ['θæŋk·fəl·i] *adv* glücklicherweise; (*gratefully*) dankbar

thankless ['θæŋk·lɪs] *adj* undankbar

thanks [θæŋks] *npl* Dank *m;* (*thank you*) danke; **many ~**! vielen Dank!; **to express one's ~** seinen Dank zum Ausdruck bringen *geh*

thanksgiving [ˌθæŋks·'gɪv·ɪŋ] *n* Dankbarkeit *f;* **prayer of ~** Dankgebet *nt;* ■ **T~** Thanksgiving *nt* (*amerikanisches Erntedankfest*)

'thank you *n* Danke[schön] *nt*

that [ðæt] **I.** *adj* **dem** der/die/das; **who is ~ girl?** wer ist das Mädchen? **II.** *pron* **➊ dem ~'s a good idea** das ist eine gute Idee; ~**'s why** deshalb **➋ dem,** *after prep* **after/before** ~ danach/davor; **like** ~ (*in such a way*) so; (*of such a kind*) derartig; (*fam: effortlessly*) einfach so **➌ dem ~'s it!** jetzt reicht's!; **I won't agree to it and ~'s** ~ ich stimme dem nicht zu, und damit Schluss **➍ rel** der/die/das; (*when*) als; **the year** ~ **Anna was born** das Jahr, in dem Anna geboren wurde **III.** *conj* dass; **so ~** damit **IV.** *adv* so; **it wasn't [all]** ~ **good** so gut war es [nun] auch wieder nicht

thatched [θætʃt] *adj* reetgedeckt

thaw [θɔ] **I.** *n* Tauwetter *nt* a.*fig* **II.** *vi* auftauen; *ice* schmelzen **III.** *vt* ■ **to ~ sth** ⊙ **out** etw auftauen

the [ðə, ði] **I.** *art definite* **➊** der/die/das; **it's on ~ table** es ist auf dem Tisch; ~ **Smiths** die Schmidts; ~ **inevitable** das Unvermeidliche; ~ **highest/longest** ... der/die/das höchste/längste ... **➋** ■ ~ ... *der/die/das* ...; **Harry's Bar**

is ~ place to go Harry's Bar ist in der Szene total in *fam* ❸ (*with measurements*) pro; **sold by ~ liter** literweise verkauft II. *adv* + *comp* **all ~ better/ worse** umso besser/schlechter; **~ colder it got, ~ more she shivered** je kälter es wurde, desto mehr zitterte sie

theater ['θiː·ə·ţər] *n* Theater *nt;* **movie ~** Kino *nt;* MIL Schauplatz *m;* **to go to the ~** ins Kino/Theater gehen

'theatergoer *n* Theaterbesucher(in) *m(f)*

theatrical [θiː·'æt·rɪ·kəl] *adj* Theater-; (*exaggerated*) theatralisch; **~ agent** Theateragent(in) *m(f)*

theft [θeft] *n* Diebstahl *m*

their [ðer] *adj poss* ihr(e); **the children brushed ~ teeth** die Kinder putzten sich die Zähne; **has everybody got ~ passport?** hat jeder seinen Pass dabei?

theirs [ðerz] *pron* ihr(e, es); **they think everything is ~** sie glauben, dass ihnen alles gehört; **a favorite game of ~** eins ihrer Lieblingsspiele

them [ðem] *pron pers* sie *in akk,* ihnen *in dat;* (*him/her*) ihm/ihr *in dat,* sie *in akk;* **we want to show every customer that we appreciate ~** wir wollen jedem Kunden zeigen, wie sehr wir ihn schätzen

theme [θiːm] *n* Thema *nt;* (*music*) Melodie *f*

'theme music *n* Titelmusik *f*

themselves [ðəm·'selvz] *pron refl* **the children behaved ~ [very well]** die Kinder benahmen sich [sehr gut]; **they tried it for ~** sie versuchten es selbst; **everyone who considers ~ a race car driver** jeder, der sich selbst für einen Rennfahrer hält

then [ðen] *adv* damals; (*after that*) dann; **before ~** davor; **by/until ~** bis dahin; **but ~** aber schließlich

theological [θiː·ə·'lɑdʒ·ɪ·kəl] *adj* Theologie-

theology [θiː·'ɑl·ə·dʒi] *n* Glaubenslehre *f;* (*study*) Theologie *f*

theorem ['θiː·ər·əm] *n* Lehrsatz *m*

theoretical [θiː·ə·'ret·ɪ·kəl] *adj* theoretisch

theorize ['θiː·ə·raɪz] *vi* Theorien aufstellen

theory ['θiː·ə·ri] *n* Theorie *f;* **in ~** theoretisch

therapeutic [θer·ə·'pju·ţɪk] *adj* therapeutisch; (*beneficial*) gesundheitsfördernd

therapist ['θer·ə·pɪst] *n* Therapeut(in) *m(f)*

therapy ['θer·ə·pi] *n* Therapie *f*

there [ðer] I. *adv* ❶ dort; (*to place*) dorthin; **~'s that book you were looking for** hier ist das Buch, das du gesucht hast; **the museum is closed today — we'll go ~ tomorrow** das Museum ist heute zu – wir gehen morgen hin; **here and ~** hier und da; **in/up ~** da drin[nen]/oben; **to get ~** hinkommen; (*fig: succeed*) es schaffen; (*understand*) es verstehen ❷ **~ are lives at stake** es stehen Leben auf dem Spiel; **~ goes my raise** das war's dann wohl mit meiner Gehaltserhöhung; **~'s a good dog** braver Hund; **~ comes a point where …** es kommt der Punkt, an dem … ▸ PHRASES: **been ~, done that** (*fam*) kalter Kaffee; **~ you have it** na siehst du II. *interj* schau!; (*expressing satisfaction*) na bitte!; **~, ~!** schon gut!

'thereby *adv* dadurch

therefore ['ðer·fɔr] *adv* deshalb

thermal ['θɜr·məl] I. *n* ■ **~s** *pl* Thermounterwäsche *f* II. *adj attr* Thermal-

thermal 'underwear *n* Thermounterwäsche *f*

thermometer [θər·'mɑm·ə·ţər] *n* Thermometer *nt*

Thermos®, Thermos® bottle ['θɜr·məs-] *n* Thermosflasche *f*

thermostat ['θɜr·mə·stæt] *n* Thermostat *m*

thesaurus <*pl* -es> [θɪ·'sɔr·əs] *n* Synonymwörterbuch *nt*

these [ðiz] I. *adj* pl of **this** II. *pron dem pl of* **this** diese; **are ~ your bags?** sind das hier deine Taschen?; **~ are my kids** das sind meine Kinder; **~ here** die da

thesis <*pl* -ses> ['θiː·sɪs] *n* wissenschaftliche Arbeit; (*for diploma*) Diplomarbeit *f*; (*for master's degree*) Magisterarbeit *f*

they [ðeɪ] *pron pers* sie; (*he/she*) er/sie; **where are my glasses? ~'re gone!** wo ist meine Brille? sie ist weg!; **ask a friend if ~ can help** frag einen Freund, ob er helfen kann; **~ say ...** es heißt, ...

they'll [ðeɪl] **= they will** *see* will[1]

they're [ðer] **= they are** *see* be

they've [ðeɪv] **= they have** *see* have I, II

thick [θɪk] I. *adj* dick; (*viscous a.*) zähflüssig; (*dense*) dicht; *hair a.* voll ▶PHRASES: **to have ~ skin** ein dickes Fell haben II. *n* (*fam*) ■ **in the ~ of sth** mitten[drin] in etw *dat* III. *adv* **the snow lay ~ on the path** auf dem Weg lag eine dicke Schneedecke ▶PHRASES: **the complaints were coming ~ and fast** es hagelte Beschwerden; **to lay it on ~** dick auftragen

thicken ['θɪk·ən] I. *vt* eindicken II. *vi* dick[er] werden; (*denser*) dicht[er] werden

thicket ['θɪk·ɪt] *n* Dickicht *nt*

thickness ['θɪk·nɪs] *n* Dicke *f*; (*denseness*) Dichte *f*

thick-'skinned *adj* dickhäutig

thief <*pl* thieves> [θiːf] *n* Dieb(in) *m(f)*

thigh [θaɪ] *n* [Ober]schenkel *m*

thimble ['θɪm·bəl] *n* Fingerhut *m*

thin <-nn-> [θɪn] I. *adj* dünn; *line* fein; (*too slim*) hager; *fog* leicht; *crowd* klein; (*fluid*) dünn[flüssig]; (*feeble*) schwach; *disguise* dürftig; *excuse* fadenscheinig ▶PHRASES: **to disappear into ~ air** sich in Luft auflösen; **to be on ~ ice** sich auf dünnem Eis bewegen II. *vt* verdünnen; (*less dense*) ausdünnen

thing [θɪn] *n* Ding *nt*; (*unspecified*) Sache *f*; (*matter a.*) Thema *nt*; **one ~ leads to another** das eine führt zum anderen; **sure ~!** na klar!; **you lucky ~!** du Glückliche(r)!; **[the] poor ~** der/die Ärmste; (*child*) das

arme Ding; **to know a ~ or two** eine ganze Menge wissen; **to be not sb's ~** nicht jds Ding *nt* sein *fam*; **the whole ~** das Ganze; **to do one's own ~** (*fam*) seinen [eigenen] Weg gehen; **just the ~** (*fam*) genau das Richtige; ■ **~s** *pl* (*possessions*) Besitz *m*; (*specific*) Sachen *pl*; **swimming ~s** Schwimmzeug *nt* ▶PHRASES: **to be just one of those ~s** (*unavoidable*) einfach unvermeidlich sein; (*typical*) typisch sein; **to be onto a good ~** (*fam*) etwas Gutes auftun

think [θɪnk] I. *vi* <thought, thought> ❶ denken; (*reflect*) überlegen; **to ~ better of sth** sich *dat* etw anders überlegen; **yes, I ~ so** ich glaube schon; **not everybody ~s like you** nicht jeder denkt wie du; **I thought as much!** das habe ich mir schon gedacht!; **to ~ highly of sb/sth** viel von jdm/etw halten; ■ **to ~ of doing sth** erwägen, etw zu tun ❷ (*come up with*) **to ~ of sth** sich *dat* etw ausdenken; **to ~ of a solution** auf eine Lösung kommen ▶PHRASES: **I can't hear myself ~!** ich kann mein eigenes Wort nicht mehr verstehen! II. *vt* <thought, thought> **to ~ the world of sb/sth** große Stücke auf jdn/etw halten; **who do you ~ you are?** für wen hältst du dich eigentlich?; ■ **to ~ to do sth** daran denken, etw zu tun III. *n* (*fam*) **to give sth a ~** sich *dat* etw überlegen

◆ **think about** *vi* ■ **to ~ about sth** über etw *akk* denken; (*reflect*) über etw *akk* nachdenken; (*consider*) sich *dat* etw überlegen

◆ **think ahead** *vi* vorausdenken; (*be foresighted*) sehr vorausschauend sein

◆ **think back** *vi* zurückdenken

◆ **think over** *vt* überdenken; **I'll ~ it over** ich überleg's mir noch mal

◆ **think through** *vt* [gründlich] durchdenken

◆ **think up** *vt* (*fam*) sich *dat* ausdenken

thinker ['θɪn·kər] *n* Denker(in) *m(f)*

thinking ['θɪn·kɪn] I. *n* Denken *nt*; (*reasoning*) Überlegung *f*; **good ~!** gut ge-

T

dacht!; **to do some ~ about sth** sich *dat* über etw *akk* Gedanken machen II. *adj attr* denkend

'**think tank** *n* Expertenkommission *f*

thinner ['θɪn·ər] I. *n* Verdünnungsmittel *nt;* **paint ~** Farbverdünner *m* II. *adj comp of* **thin**

thin-'skinned *adj* sensibel

third [θɜrd] I. *n* Dritte(r, s); *(fraction)* Drittel *nt;* *(gear)* dritter Gang; **the ~ of September** der dritte September II. *adj* dritte(r, s); **~ best** drittbeste(r, s)

third de'gree *n* Polizeimaßnahme *f (zur Erzwingung eines Geständnisses);* **to give sb the ~** *(fam)* jdn in die Mangel nehmen

third 'party *n* Dritte(r) *f(m)*

Third 'World *n* ■**the ~** die Dritte Welt; **~ country** Drittweltland *nt*

thirst [θɜrst] *n* Durst *m;* *(desire)* Verlangen *nt;* **to die of ~** verdursten; **~ for knowledge** Wissensdurst *m*

thirsty ['θɜr·sti] *adj* durstig; ■**to be ~** Durst haben; ■**to be ~ for sth** nach etw *dat* hungern

thirteen [θɜr·'tin] I. *n* Dreizehn *f; see also* **eight** II. *adj* dreizehn; *see also* **eight**

thirteenth [θɜr·'tinθ] I. *n* ❶ ■**the ~** der/die/das Dreizehnte; *(date)* der Dreizehnte; *see also* **eight** ❷ *(fraction)* Dreizehntel *nt; see also* **eighth** II. *adj* dreizehnte(r, s); *see also* **eighth** III. *adv* als Dreizehnte(r, s); *see also* **eighth**

thirtieth ['θɜrt·i·əθ] I. *n* Dreißigste(r, s); *(fraction)* Dreißigstel *nt;* **the ~** *(date)* der Dreißigste; *see also* **eighth** II. *adj* dreißigste(r, s); *see also* **eighth** III. *adv* als Dreißigste(r, s); *see also* **eighth**

thirty ['θɜr·ti] I. *n* Dreißig *f;* ■**the thirties** *pl* die dreißiger Jahre; **to be in one's thirties** in den Dreißigern sein; *see also* **eight** II. *adj* dreißig; *see also* **eight**

this [ðɪs] I. *adj attr* diese(r, s); **~ minute** sofort; **by ~ time** dann II. *pron* **is ~ your bag?** ist das deine Tasche?; **~ is my husband Steve** das ist mein Ehe-

mann Steve; **what's ~?** was soll das?; **~ is what I was talking about** davon spreche ich ja; **every time I do ~, it hurts** jedes Mal, wenn ich das mache, tut es weh; **like ~** so ▶PHRASES: **~ and that** *(fam)* dies und das III. *adv* so; **~ far and no further** bis hierher und nicht weiter

thistle ['θɪs·əl] *n* Distel *f*

thong [θɑŋ] *n* Lederband *nt;* *(G-string)* Tanga *m;* ■**~s** *pl (flip-flop)* Flip-Flops *pl*

thorn [θɔrn] *n* Dorn *m*

thorny ['θɔr·ni] *adj* dornig; *(difficult)* schwierig; *issue* heikel

thorough ['θɜr·oʊ] *adj* genau; *(careful)* sorgfältig; *reform* durchgreifend

'**thoroughbred** I. *n* Vollblut[pferd] *nt* II. *adj* reinrassig

thoroughly ['θɜr·oʊ·li] *adv* genau; *(completely)* völlig; *enjoy* ausgiebig

thoroughness ['θɜr·oʊ·nɪs] *n* Sorgfältigkeit *f*

those [ðoʊz] I. *adj* pl *of* **that: how much are ~ brushes?** wie viel kosten die Bürsten da?; **I like ~ cookies with the almonds** ich mag die Kekse mit den Mandeln II. *pron* pl *of* **that: these peaches aren't ripe — try ~ on the table** diese Pfirsiche sind noch nicht reif, versuch die auf dem Tisch; **~ are my kids over there** das sind meine Kinder da drüben; ■**~ who ...** diejenigen, die ...; ■**one of ~** eine(r) davon

though [ðoʊ] I. *conj* obwohl; *(however)* [je]doch; ■**as ~** als ob II. *adv* trotzdem

thought [θɔt] I. *n* Nachdenken *nt;* *(idea)* Gedanke *m;* **to be deep in ~** tief in Gedanken versunken sein; **to give sth some ~** sich *dat* Gedanken über etw *akk* machen ▶PHRASES: **it's the ~ that counts** *(fam)* der gute Wille zählt II. *vt, vi pt, pp of* **think**

thoughtful ['θɔt·fəl] *adj* aufmerksam; *(contemplative)* nachdenklich; *(careful)* sorgfältig

thoughtless ['θɔt·lɪs] *adj* rücksichtslos; *(without thinking)* unüberlegt

'thought-provoking *adj* nachdenklich stimmend

thousand ['θaʊ·zənd] **I.** *n* Tausend *f;* **two ~** zweitausend; *(year)* [das Jahr] zweitausend; **a ~ dollars** [ein]tausend Dollar; **■ ~ s** Tausende *pl* **II.** *adj det, attr* tausend; **I've said it a ~ times** ich habe es jetzt unzählige Male gesagt

thousandth ['θaʊ·zəntθ] **I.** *n* Tausendste(r, s); *(fraction)* Tausendstel *nt* **II.** *adj* tausendste(r, s); **■ the ~ ...** der/die/das tausendste ...; **a ~ part** ein Tausendstel *nt*

thrash [θræʃ] *vt* verprügeln; *(fam: defeat)* haushoch schlagen

thrashing ['θræʃ·ɪŋ] *n* Prügel *pl;* **to give sb a [good] ~** jdm eine [anständige] Tracht Prügel verpassen

thread [θred] **I.** *n* Garn *nt;* *(fiber)* Faden *m;* *(groove)* Gewinde *nt;* INET Thread *m* **II.** *vt* ❶ *(put through)* einfädeln; **she ~ed her way through the crowd** sie schlängelte sich durch die Menge ❷ *(put onto a string)* auffädeln

threat [θret] *n* Drohung *f;* *(risk)* Gefahr *f;* **to pose a ~ to sb/sth** eine Gefahr für jdn/etw darstellen; **■ to be under ~ of sth** von etw *dat* bedroht sein

threaten ['θret·ən] **I.** *vt* bedrohen; *(be danger)* gefährden; **■ to ~ sb with sth** jdm mit etw *dat* drohen; *(with weapon)* jdn mit etw *dat* bedrohen **II.** *vi* drohen; **■ to ~ to do sth** damit drohen, etw zu tun

threatening ['θret·ə·nɪŋ] *adj* drohend; *(menacing)* bedrohlich; *clouds* dunkel; **~ letter** Drohbrief *m*

three [θri] **I.** *n* Drei *f;* *(quantity)* drei; *(time)* drei [Uhr]; **in ~ s** in Dreiergruppen; **the ~ of diamonds** die Karodrei; **at ~ p.m.** um drei Uhr [nachmittags]; *see also* **eight** ▶PHRASES: **two's company, ~'s a crowd** drei sind einer zu viel **II.** *adj* drei; **I'll give you ~ guesses** dreimal darfst du raten; *see also* **eight** ▶PHRASES: **~ cheers [for sb/ sth]**! ein dreifaches Hoch [auf jdn/etw]!

three-'D *adj* *(fam)*, **three-di'men-**

sional *adj* dreidimensional; **~ printer** 3-D-Drucker *m*

three-'quarter *adj attr* dreiviertel

three-'wheeler *n* dreirädriges Auto; *(tricycle)* Dreirad *nt*

thresh [θreʃ] *vt* dreschen

'threshing machine *n* Dreschmaschine *f*

threshold ['θreʃ·hoʊld] *n* [Tür]schwelle *f;* *(fig)* Anfang *m;* *(limit)* Grenze *f;* **pain ~** Schmerzgrenze *f*

threw [θru] *pt of* **throw**

thrift [θrɪft] *n* Sparsamkeit *f*

'thrift shop, 'thrift store *n* Laden, in dem gespendete, meist gebrauchte Waren verkauft werden, um Geld für wohltätige Zwecke zu sammeln

thrifty ['θrɪf·ti] *adj* sparsam

thrill [θrɪl] **I.** *n* Erregung *f;* *(titillation)* Nervenkitzel *m* **II.** *vt* erregen; *(fascinate)* faszinieren; *(frighten)* Angst machen; *(delight)* entzücken

thriller ['θrɪl·ər] *n* Thriller *m*

thrilling ['θrɪl·ɪŋ] *adj* aufregend; *story* spannend

thriving ['θraɪ·vɪŋ] *adj* *community* gut funktionierend

throat [θroʊt] *n* Kehle *f;* *(inside neck)* Rachen *m;* **a sore ~** Halsschmerzen *pl;* **to cut sb's ~** jdm die Kehle durchschneiden ▶PHRASES: **to have a lump in one's ~** einen Kloß im Hals haben; **to jump down sb's ~** jdn anschnauzen

throb [θrab] **I.** *n* Klopfen *nt;* *of heart* Pochen *nt;* *of bass* Dröhnen *nt* **II.** *vi* <-bb-> klopfen; *heart* pochen; *bass* dröhnen; **his head was ~bing** er hatte rasende Kopfschmerzen

throne [θroʊn] *n* Thron *m;* REL Stuhl *m*

throng [θraŋ] **I.** *n* [Menschen]menge *f* **II.** *vt* *visitors* **~ed the narrow streets** die engen Straßen wimmelten nur so von Besuchern

throttle ['θraṭ·əl] **I.** *n* Drosselklappe *f;* **at full ~** mit voller Geschwindigkeit; *(fig)* mit Volldampf **II.** *vt* würgen; *(strangle)* erdrosseln; *(fig: hinder)* drosseln

through [θru] **I.** *prep* durch +*akk;* *(be-*

T

cause of a.) wegen +*gen;* (*during*) während +*gen;* (*by means of*) über +*akk;* **she looked ~ her mail** sie sah ihre Post durch; **we're open Monday ~ Friday** wir haben Montag bis Freitag geöffnet; **I can't hear you ~ all this noise** ich kann dich bei diesem ganzen Lärm nicht verstehen; **we were cut off halfway ~ the conversation** unser Gespräch wurde mittendrin unterbrochen; **~ chance** durch Zufall; **to get ~ sth** (*endure*) etw durchstehen **II.** *adj* ❶ *pred* (*finished*) fertig; **we're ~** (*relationship*) mit uns ist es aus; (*job*) es ist alles erledigt ❷ *pred* (*successful*) durch; **Henry is ~ to the final** Henry hat sich für das Finale qualifiziert ❸ *attr bus* durchgehend **III.** *adv* ❶ **the train goes ~ to Hamburg** der Zug fährt bis nach Hamburg durch ❷ (*from beginning to end*) [ganz] durch; **to be halfway ~ sth** etw halb durch haben ❸ **~ and ~** durch und durch; **cooked ~** durchgegart

through'out [θru·'aʊt] **I.** *prep* ❶ **people ~ the country** Menschen im ganzen Land ❷ (*at times during*) während +*gen;* **~ the performance** die ganze Vorstellung über **II.** *adv* vollständig; (*the whole time*) die ganze Zeit [über]

throw [θroʊ] **I.** *n* Wurf *m;* **a stone's ~ [away]** (*fig*) nur einen Steinwurf von hier **II.** *vi* <threw, thrown> werfen **III.** *vt* <threw, thrown> ❶ werfen; (*hurl*) schleudern; *wrestler* zu Fall bringen; *rider* abwerfen; (*direct*) zuwerfen; **to ~ a fit/tantrum** (*fam*) einen Anfall/Wutanfall bekommen; **to ~ a party** eine Party geben; **to ~ a punch at sb** jdm einen Schlag versetzen; ■**to ~ sb sth** [*or* **sth to sb**] jdm etw zuwerfen; ■**to ~ oneself onto sb/sth** sich auf jdn stürzen/auf etw *akk* werfen; ■**to ~ oneself at sb** (*embrace*) sich jdm an den Hals werfen; (*attack*) sich auf jdn stürzen; ■**to ~ sth against sth** etw gegen etw *akk* schleudern ❷ (*fam: confuse*) ■**to ~ sb [off]** jdn durcheinanderbringen ▶PHRASES: **to ~ caution to the**

wind eine Warnung in den Wind schlagen

◆**throw away** *vt* wegwerfen; **to ~ money away on sth** Geld für etw *akk* zum Fenster hinauswerfen

◆**throw back** *vt* nach hinten werfen; *curtains* aufreißen ▶PHRASES: **to ~ sth back in sb's** <u>face</u> jdm etw wieder auftischen

◆**throw off** *vt* herunterreißen; *clothes* schnell ausziehen; ■**to ~ oneself off sth** sich über etw *akk* hinunterstürzen; ■**to ~ sb** ↻ **off** (*escape*) jdn abschütteln; *fluster* jdn aus dem Konzept bringen

◆**throw on** *vt* ❶ **~ a log on the fire, will you?** legst du bitte noch einen Scheit aufs Feuer?; ■**to ~ oneself on sb** sich auf jdn stürzen ❷ *clothes* eilig anziehen ❸ **to ~ suspicion on sb** den Verdacht auf jdn lenken

◆**throw out** *vt* hinauswerfen; (*discard*) wegwerfen; (*dismiss*) entlassen; *player* vom Platz stellen; *lawsuit* abweisen

◆**throw up I.** *vt* hochwerfen; *hands* hochreißen; (*fam: vomit*) erbrechen **II.** *vi* (*fam*) sich übergeben

throwaway ['θroʊ·ə·weɪ] *adj attr* wegwerfbar; (*unimportant*) achtlos dahingeworfen *attr;* **~ razor** Einwegrasierer *m*

thrown [θroʊn] *pp of* **throw**

thru [θru] *prep, adv* (*fam*) *see* **through**

thrush <*pl* -es> [θrʌʃ] *n* Drossel *f*

thrust [θrʌst] **I.** *n* Stoß *m;* (*impetus*) Stoßrichtung *f;* **the main ~ of an argument** die Hauptaussage eines Arguments **II.** *vi* <thrust, thrust> **to ~ at sb with a knife** nach jdm mit einem Messer stoßen **III.** *vt* <thrust, thrust> **to ~ money into sb's hand** jdm Geld in die Hand stecken; ■**to ~ sth on sb** jdm etw auferlegen; ■**to ~ oneself on sb** sich jdm aufdrängen

thud [θʌd] **I.** *vi* <-dd-> dumpf aufschlagen **II.** *n* dumpfer Schlag

thug [θʌg] *n* Schlägertyp *m*

thumb [θʌm] **I.** *n* Daumen *m* ▶PHRASES:

to stand out like a <u>sore</u> ~ unangenehm auffallen II. *vt* ❶ *(fam)* **to** ~ **a ride** per Anhalter fahren ❷ *book* durchblättern III. *vi* **to** ~ **through a newspaper** durch die Zeitung blättern

thumb 'index *n* Daumenregister *nt*

'thumbnail *n* Daumennagel *m*

'thumbtack *n* Reißzwecke *f*

thump [θʌmp] I. *n* dumpfer Knall II. *vt* schlagen III. *vi* schlagen; *heart* klopfen

thunder ['θʌn·dər] I. *n* Donner *m;* *(loud sound)* Getöse *nt;* **rumble of** ~ Donnergrollen *nt* ▶PHRASES: **to** <u>steal</u> **sb's** ~ jdm die Schau stehlen II. *vi* donnern; *(declaim)* schreien; ■ **to** ~ **by** vorbeidonnern; ■ **to** ~ **about sth** sich lautstark über etw *akk* äußern III. *vt* brüllen

'thunderbolt *n* Blitzschlag *m*

'thundercloud *n usu pl* Gewitterwolke *f*

thundering ['θʌn·dər·ɪŋ] I. *n* Donnern *nt* II. *adj* tosend; *voice* dröhnend; *(enormous)* immens; *success a.* riesig

thunderous ['θʌn·dər·əs] *adj attr* donnernd; ~ **applause** Beifallsstürme *pl*

'thunderstorm *n* Gewitter *nt*

'thunderstruck *adj pred* wie vom Donner gerührt

Thursday ['θɜrz·deɪ] *n* Donnerstag *m; see also* Tuesday

thus [ðʌs] *adv* folglich; *(in this way)* so

thwart [θwɔrt] *vt* vereiteln; *escape* verhindern; *plan* durchkreuzen

thyme [taɪm] *n* Thymian *m*

thyroid ['θaɪ·rɔɪd] *n* Schilddrüse *f*

tiara [tɪ·'ær·ə] *n* Tiara *f*

tibia <*pl* -biae> ['tɪb·i·ə] *n* Schienbein *nt*

tic [tɪk] *n* nervöses] Zucken

tick¹ [tɪk] I. *n* Ticken *nt* II. *vi* ticken ▶PHRASES: **what** <u>makes</u> **sb** ~ was jdn bewegt

◆ **tick off** *vt* *(fam)* auf die Palme bringen

tick² [tɪk] *n* ZOOL Zecke *f*

ticker-tape pa'rade *n* Konfettiparade *f*

ticket ['tɪk·ɪt] *n* Karte *f;* *(tag)* Etikett *nt;* **concert** ~ Konzertkarte *f;* **lottery** ~ Lottoschein *m;* **plane** ~ Flugticket *nt;*

price ~ Preisschild *nt;* *(for fine)* Strafzettel *m*

'ticket collector *n* Schaffner(in) *m(f)*

ticking ['tɪk·ɪŋ] *n* Ticken *nt*

tickle ['tɪk·əl] I. *vi* kitzeln II. *vt* kitzeln; **to** ~ **sb's fancy** *(fam)* jdn reizen III. *n* Jucken *nt;* ~ **in one's throat** Kratzen *nt* im Hals

ticklish ['tɪk·lɪʃ] *adj* kitzlig; *(delicate)* heikel

tick-tack-toe, tic-tac-toe [ˌtɪk·tæk·'toʊ] *n* Tic Tac Toe *nt*

'tidal wave *n* Flutwelle *f;* *(fig)* Flut *f*

tidbit ['tɪd·bɪt] *n* Leckerbissen *m;* *juicy* ~**s** *(fig)* pikante Einzelheiten

tiddlywinks ['tɪd·li·wɪŋks] *n pl* Flohhüpfen *nt*

tide [taɪd] *n* Gezeiten *pl;* *(opinion)* öffentliche Meinung; *(trend)* Welle *f;* **the** ~ **has turned** die Meinung ist umgeschlagen; **high** ~ Flut *f;* **low** ~ Ebbe *f;* **to swim against the** ~ gegen den Strom schwimmen

◆ **tide over** *vt* ■ **to** ~ **sb over** jdm über die Runden helfen *fam*

tidiness ['taɪ·dɪ·nɪs] *n* Ordnung *f*

tidy ['taɪ·di] I. *adj* ordentlich; *(fam)* sum beträchtlich II. *vt* aufräumen

tie [taɪ] I. *n* ❶ *(necktie)* Krawatte *f;* **bow** ~ Fliege *f* ❷ *pl* **diplomatic** ~**s** diplomatische Beziehungen; **family** ~**s** Familienbande *pl* ❸ **to end in a** ~ mit einem Unentschieden enden II. *vi* <-y-> ❶ schließen; **to** ~ **in the front/back** vorne/hinten zugebunden werden ❷ ■ **to** ~ **with sb/sth** denselben Platz wie jd/etw belegen III. *vt* <-y-> ❶ fesseln; *knot* machen; *necktie* binden ❷ *(restrict)* ■ **to be** ~**d to sth/somewhere** an etw *akk*/einen Ort gebunden sein ▶PHRASES: **sb's** <u>hands</u> **are** ~**d** jds Hände sind gebunden

◆ **tie back** *vt* zurückbinden

◆ **tie down** *vt* festbinden; ■ **to be** ~**d down** *(restricted)* gebunden sein; ■ **to** ~ **sb down to sth** *(fam)* jdn auf etw *akk* festlegen

◆ **tie in** *vi* ■ **to** ~ **in with sth** mit etw *dat* übereinstimmen

T

tie up *vt* festbinden; *hair* hochbinden; (*delay*) aufhalten; *capital* binden; *game* den Ausgleich erzielen; ■**to be ~d up** (*busy*) beschäftigt sein ▶PHRASES: **to ~ up some loose** <u>ends</u> etwas erledigen

'tiebreaker, 'tiebreak *n* Tie-Break *m o nt*

tier [tɪr] *n* Reihe *f*; (*level*) Lage *f*; **~ of management** Managementebene *f*

'tie-up *n* Stillstand *m*

tiff [tɪf] *n* (*fam*) Plänkelei *f*; **to have a ~** eine Meinungsverschiedenheit haben

tiger ['taɪ·gər] *n* Tiger *m*

tight [taɪt] **I.** *adj* ❶ fest; *clothes* eng; (*close*) dicht; (*taut*) gespannt; *muscles* verspannt; *face* angespannt; (*severe*) streng; *bend* eng; *budget* knapp; **~ spot** (*fig*) Zwickmühle *f* ❷ (*pej fam: miserly*) knauserig ▶PHRASES: **to run a ~** <u>ship</u> ein strenges Regime führen **II.** *adv pred* straff; *seal* fest; **to hang on ~ to sb/sth** sich an jdm/etw festklammern

tighten ['taɪ·tən] **I.** *vt* festziehen; *rope* festbinden; *screw* anziehen; (*boost*) verstärken ▶PHRASES: **to ~ one's** <u>belt</u> den Gürtel enger schnallen **II.** *vi* straff werden

tight'fisted *adj* (*pej fam*) geizig

tight-'fitting *adj* eng anliegend

'tightrope *n* Drahtseil *nt*; **~ walker** Seiltänzer(in) *m(f)*

tights [taɪts] *npl* [**pair of**] **~** Strumpfhose *f*; (*for dancing*) Leggings *pl*

tile [taɪl] **I.** *n* Fliese *f* **II.** *vt* fliesen

till[1] [tɪl] *prep, conj see* **until**

till[2] [tɪl] *n* Kasse *f* ▶PHRASES: **to be caught with one's** <u>hand</u> **in the ~** auf frischer Tat ertappt werden

tilt [tɪlt] **I.** *n* Neigung *f* ▶PHRASES: [**at**] <u>full</u> **~** mit voller Kraft **II.** *vt* neigen; **to ~ the balance** einen Meinungsumschwung herbeiführen **III.** *vi* sich neigen; (*opinion*) sich ab-/zuwenden

timber ['tɪm·bər] *n* Bauholz *nt*; (*beam*) Holzplanke *f*

time [taɪm] **I.** *n* ❶ Zeit *f*; (*occasion*) Mal *nt*; MUS Takt *m*; **~ stood still** die Zeit stand still; **~'s up** (*fam*) die Zeit ist

um; **it will take some ~** es wird eine Weile dauern; **~s are changing** die Zeiten ändern sich; **to keep ~** den Takt halten; **as ~ goes by** im Lauf[e] der Zeit; **for all ~** für immer; **to go through a difficult ~** eine schwere Zeit durchmachen; **free ~** Freizeit *f*; **period of ~** Zeitraum *m*; **a long ~ ago** vor langer Zeit; **to be pressed for ~** in Zeitnot sein; **to take one's ~** sich *dat* Zeit lassen; **for the ~ being** vorläufig; **to tell the ~** die Uhr lesen; **on ~** pünktlich; **for the first ~** zum ersten Mal; **from ~ to ~** ab und zu; **three ~s a week** drei Mal in der Woche; **for the hundredth ~** zum hundertsten Mal; **to be behind the ~s** seiner Zeit hinterherhinken; **to not have much ~ for sb** jdn nicht mögen; **to do ~** (*fam*) [im Knast] sitzen ❷ **two ~s five is ten** zwei mal fünf ist zehn ▶PHRASES: **~ is of the** <u>essence</u> die Zeit drängt; [**only**] **~ will** <u>tell</u> (*saying*) erst die Zukunft wird es zeigen **II.** *vt* ■**to ~ sb in the 100 meters** jds Zeit beim 100-Meter-Lauf nehmen; ■**to ~ sth** [**right**] den richtigen Zeitpunkt wählen

'time bomb *n* Zeitbombe *f*

'time-consuming *adj* zeitintensiv

timeless ['taɪm·lɪs] *adj* zeitlos; *beauty* immer während *attr*

'time limit *n* Frist *f*

timely ['taɪm·li] *adj* rechtzeitig; *remark* passend; *manner* rasch

'timeout **I.** *n* <*pl* **times->** SPORT Auszeit *f*; **to call a ~** ein Time-out nehmen **II.** *interj* Auszeit!

timer ['taɪ·mər] *n* Timer *m*; (*for eggs*) Eieruhr *f*

'time-saving *adj* Zeit sparend

'timetable *n* Fahrplan *m*; (*for events*) Programm *nt*; (*for appointments*) Zeitplan *m*

'time zone *n* Zeitzone *f*

timid <-er, -est> ['tɪm·ɪd] *adj* ängstlich; (*shy*) schüchtern; (*lacking courage*) zaghaft

timing ['taɪ·mɪŋ] *n* Timing *nt*; (*measuring*) Zeitabnahme *f*; *of race* Stoppen *nt*

tin [tɪn] *n* Hauch *m;* (*for baking*) Backform *f;* **cake ~** Kuchenform *f*

tin 'can *n* Blechdose *f*

'tinfoil ['tɪn·fɔɪl] *n* Alufolie *f*

tinge [tɪndʒ] I. *n* Hauch *m;* (*of emotion*) Anflug *m;* **~ of red** [leichter] Rotstich II. *vt usu passive* **to be ~d with orange** mit Orange [leicht] getönt sein; **~d with regret** mit einer Spur von Bedauern

tingle ['tɪŋ·gəl] I. *vi* kribbeln; **to ~ with excitement** vor Aufregung zittern II. *n* Kribbeln *nt*

tinker ['tɪŋ·kər] *vi* ■**to ~** [**around**] [**with sth**] [an etw *dat*] herumbasteln

tinkle ['tɪŋ·kəl] I. *vi* klimpern; *bell* klingen; *fountain* plätschern; (*fam: urinate*) Pipi machen II. *vt* **to ~ a bell** mit einer Glocke klingeln III. *n* Klingen *nt;* (*of water*) Plätschern *nt;* (*fam: urine*) Pipi *nt*

tinny ['tɪn·i] *adj* blechern

tinsel ['tɪn·səl] *n* Lametta *nt*

tint [tɪnt] I. *n* Farbton *m;* (*dye*) Tönung *f* II. *vt* tönen

tiny ['taɪ·ni] *adj* winzig

tip¹ [tɪp] *n* Spitze *f* ▶PHRASES: **it's on the ~ of my tongue** es liegt mir auf der Zunge

tip² [tɪp] I. *vt* <-pp-> umkippen; (*tilt*) neigen; **to ~ the balance** den Ausschlag geben II. *vi* <-pp-> kippen

tip³ [tɪp] I. *n* Trinkgeld *nt;* (*suggestion*) Tipp *m;* **to leave a 15% ~** 15 % Trinkgeld geben II. *vt* <-pp-> Trinkgeld geben; (*inform*) einen Tipp geben III. *vi* <-pp-> Trinkgeld geben

♦ **tip off** *vt* einen Tipp geben

♦ **tip over** *vt, vi* umkippen

'tip-off *n* (*fam*) Tipp *m*

tiptoe ['tɪp·toʊ] I. *n* **on ~**[**s**] auf Zehenspitzen II. *vi* auf Zehenspitzen gehen

tire¹ [taɪr] I. *vt* ermüden; **to ~ oneself doing sth** von etw *dat* müde werden II. *vi* müde werden; ■**to ~ of sth/sb** etw/jdn satthaben; **to ~ never ~ of doing sth** nie müde werden, etw zu tun

tire² [taɪr] *n* Reifen *m;* **spare ~** Ersatzreifen *m;* (*fig fam*) Rettungsring *m*

tired <-er, -est> ['taɪrd] *adj* müde; *excuse* lahm; *phrase* abgedroschen; **to be sick and ~ of sth/sb** von etw/jdm die Nase gestrichen voll haben *fam*

tireless ['taɪr·lɪs] *adj* unermüdlich

tiresome ['taɪr·səm] *adj* mühsam; *habit* unangenehm

tiring ['taɪ·rɪŋ] *adj* ermüdend

tissue ['tɪʃ·u] *n* Seidenpapier *nt;* (*for nose*) Tempo® *nt;* BIOL Gewebe *nt*

tit¹ [tɪt] *n* (*bird*) Meise *f* ▶PHRASES: **~ for tat** wie du mir, so ich dir

tit² [tɪt] *n* (*vulg, sl: breast*) Titte *f*

title ['taɪt·əl] I. *n* Titel *m;* **job ~** Berufsbezeichnung *f* II. *vt* betiteln

'title deed *n* LAW Eigentumsurkunde *f*

'title page *n* Titelblatt *nt*

titter ['tɪt̬·ər] I. *vi* kichern II. *n* Gekicher *nt*

TN *abbrev of* **Tennessee**

to [tu] I. *prep* **they go ~ work on the bus** sie fahren mit dem Bus zur Arbeit; **we moved ~ Germany last year** wir sind letztes Jahr nach Deutschland gezogen; **she goes ~ college** sie geht auf die Universität; **I've asked them ~ dinner** ich habe sie zum Essen eingeladen; **tie the leash ~ the fence** mach die Leine am Zaun fest; **I prefer beef ~ seafood** ich ziehe Rindfleisch Meeresfrüchten vor; **and ~ this day …** und bis auf den heutigen Tag …; **he converted ~ Islam** er ist zum Islam übergetreten; **it's twenty ~ six** es ist zwanzig vor sechs; **here's ~ you!** auf Ihr Wohl!; **the record is dedicated ~ her mother** die Schallplatte ist ihrer Mutter gewidmet; **give that gun ~ me** gib mir das Gewehr; **to be married ~ sb** mit jdm verheiratet sein; **to tell sth ~ sb** jdm etw erzählen; **ten ~ the third power** zehn hoch drei; **~ the north** nördlich; **from place ~ place** von Ort zu Ort; **to point ~ sth** auf etw *akk* zeigen; **cheek ~ cheek** Wange an Wange II. *to form infin* I'll have **~ tell him** ich werde es ihm sagen müssen; **he told me ~ wait**

T

er sagte mir, ich solle warten; **I asked her ~ give me a call** ich bat sie, mich anzurufen; **would you like to go? — yes, I'd love ~** möchtest du hingehen? – ja, sehr gern; **I'm sorry ~ hear that** es tut mir leid, das zu hören; **I don't know what ~ do** ich weiß nicht, was ich tun soll; **to be about ~ do sth** gerade etw tun wollen; **easy ~ use** leicht zu bedienen; **~ be honest** um ehrlich zu sein **III.** adv zu; **to come ~** zu sich dat kommen

toad [toʊd] n Kröte f

'**toadstool** n Giftpilz m

toady ['toʊ·di] (pej) **I.** n Speichellecker m **II.** vi <-ie-> kriechen

to and 'fro I. adv hin und her; (back and forth) vor und zurück **II.** vi (fam) ▪ **to be toing and froing** vor- und zurückgehen; (be indecisive) hin und her schwanken

toast¹ [toʊst] **I.** n Toast m; **slice of ~** Scheibe f Toast ▶PHRASES: **to be ~** (hum fam) erledigt sein fam **II.** vt toasten; nuts rösten

toast² [toʊst] **I.** n Toast m; **to drink a ~ to sb** auf jdn trinken **II.** vt trinken

toaster ['toʊ·stər] n Toaster m

tobacco [tə·'bæk·oʊ] n Tabak m

-to-be [tə·'bi] in compounds zukünftige(r, s) attr; **mother-~** werdende Mutter

toboggan [tə·'bag·ən] **I.** n Schlitten m **II.** vi Schlitten fahren

today [tə·'deɪ] **I.** adv heute; (nowadays) heutzutage **II.** n heutiger Tag; **what's the date ~?** welches Datum haben wir heute?; **cars of ~** Autos pl von heute

toddler ['tad·lər] n Kleinkind nt

to-do [tə·'du] n usu sing (fam) Getue nt pej; (confrontation) Wirbel m; **to make a big ~ about sth** ein großes Theater um etw akk machen

to-'do list n Besorgungsliste f

toe [toʊ] **I.** n Zehe f; (of sock) Spitze f ▶PHRASES: **to keep sb on their ~s** jdn auf Zack halten **II.** vt **to ~ the party line** der Parteilinie folgen

'**toehold** n Vorteil m

'**toenail** n Zehennagel m

toffee ['tɔ·fi] n Toffee nt

together [tə·'geð·ər] **I.** adv zusammen; (collectively a.) gemeinsam; (simultaneously) gleichzeitig; **close ~** nah beisammen; **all ~ now** jetzt alle miteinander **II.** adj (fam) ausgeglichen

togetherness [tə·'geð·ər·nɪs] n Zusammengehörigkeit f

Togo ['toʊ·goʊ] n Togo nt

Togolese [ˌtoʊ·goʊ·'liz] **I.** adj togoisch **II.** n Togoer(in) m(f)

toilet ['tɔɪ·lɪt] n Toilette f

'**toilet bowl** n Toilettenschüssel f

'**toilet paper** n Toilettenpapier nt

toiletries ['tɔɪ·lɪ·triz] npl Toilettenartikel pl

'**toilet seat** n Toilettensitz m

toing and froing [ˌtu·ɪŋ·ənd·'froʊ·ɪŋ] n Hin und Her nt; (back and forth) Vor und Zurück nt

token ['toʊ·kən] **I.** n Zeichen nt; (chip) Chip m ▶PHRASES: **by the same ~** aus demselben Grund fam **II.** adj attr nominell; fine symbolisch; **the ~ woman** die Alibifrau

told [toʊld] pt, pp of **tell**

tolerance ['tal·ər·əns] n Toleranz f; (capacity a.) Widerstandsfähigkeit f; **~ to alcohol** Alkoholverträglichkeit f

tolerant ['tal·ər·ənt] adj tolerant; (resistant) widerstandsfähig; plant resistent

tolerate ['tal·ə·reɪt] vt tolerieren; person ertragen; heat, pain aushalten; drug vertragen

toleration [ˌtal·ə·'reɪ·ʃən] n Toleranz f

toll [toʊl] n Maut f; **truck ~** Lkw-Maut f; (for phone call) [Fernsprech]gebühr f; **death ~** Opferzahl f

'**toll bridge** n Mautbrücke f

'**toll-free** adj gebührenfrei; **~ number** gebührenfreie Telefonnummer

tomahawk ['ta·mə·hak] n Tomahawk m

tomato <pl -es> [tə·'meɪ·toʊ] n Tomate f

tomb [tum] n Grab nt; (mausoleum) Gruft f; (below ground) Grabkammer f

tombstone ['tʊm·stoʊn] n Grabstein m
tomcat ['tam·kæt] n Kater m
tomorrow [tə·'mar·oʊ] I. adv morgen
II. n der morgige Tag; **~'s problems**
Probleme pl von morgen; **a better** – eine bessere Zukunft ▶PHRASES: **~ is another day** (saying) morgen ist auch noch ein Tag
ton <pl -> [tʌn] n Tonne f; **how much money does he have? — ~s** (fam) wie viel Geld besitzt er? – jede Menge; **a ~ of money** (fam) ein Haufen m Geld; **to weigh a ~** (fam) Unmengen wiegen ▶PHRASES: **to come down on sb like a ~ of** <u>bricks</u> jdn völlig fertigmachen
tone [toʊn] n Klang m; of speaking Ton m; (of color) Farbton m; **dial ~** Wählton m; **disrespectful ~** respektloser Ton
◆**tone down** vt abmildern; color abschwächen
'**tone-deaf** adj ▪to be ~ unmusikalisch sein
toner ['toʊ·nər] n Toner m; **~ cartridge** Tonerpatrone f
Tonga ['taŋ·gə] n Tonga nt
Tongan ['taŋ·gən] I. adj tongaisch II. n Tongaer(in) m(f); (language) Tongasprache f
tongs [taŋz] npl Zange f
tongue [tʌŋ] n Zunge f; **cat got your ~?** hat es dir die Sprache verschlagen?; **to bite one's ~** sich dat in die Zunge beißen; **~ of land** Landzunge f ▶PHRASES: **to say sth ~ in** <u>cheek</u> etw als Scherz meinen
'**tongue-tied** adj sprachlos
'**tongue twister** n Zungenbrecher m
tonic[1] ['tan·ɪk] n Tonikum nt; (sth that rejuvenates) Erfrischung f
tonic[2] ['tan·ɪk], **tonic water** ['tanɪk-] n Tonic[water] nt
tonight [tə·'naɪt] I. adv heute Abend; (until after midnight) heute Nacht II. n der heutige Abend
tonsillitis [ˌtan·sə·'laɪ·t̬ɪs] n Mandelentzündung f
tonsils ['tan·səlz] npl Mandeln pl

too [tu] adv ❶ zu; **to be ~ bad** wirklich schade sein; **far ~ difficult** viel zu schwierig; **to be not ~ sure if …** sich dat nicht ganz sicher sein, ob … ❷ (also) auch; **me ~!** ich auch! ❸ (moreover) überdies
took [tʊk] vt, vi pt of **take**
tool [tul] n Werkzeug nt; (aid) Mittel nt; **to be a ~ of the trade** zum Handwerkszeug gehören
'**toolbox** n Werkzeugkiste f
'**tool chest**, '**toolkit** n Werkzeugkasten m
toot [tut] I. n Hupen nt II. vt anhupen; **to ~ a horn** auf die Hupe drücken
tooth <pl teeth> [tuθ] n Zahn m; of comb Zinke f; of saw [Säge]zahn m; of cog Zahn m; **to brush one's teeth** die Zähne putzen; **to grit one's teeth** die Zähne zusammenbeißen ▶PHRASES: **to** <u>sink</u> **one's teeth into sth** sich in etw akk hineinstürzen
'**toothache** n Zahnschmerzen pl
'**toothbrush** n Zahnbürste f
'**toothpaste** n Zahnpasta f
'**toothpick** n Zahnstocher m
top[1] [tap] I. n ❶ oberes Ende; of mountain [Berg]gipfel m; of tree [Baum]krone f; (highest rank) Spitze f; **there was a pile of books on ~ of the table** auf dem Tisch lag ein Stoß Bücher; **from ~ to bottom** von oben bis unten; **to be at the ~ of one's class** Klassenbeste(r) f(m) sein; **to get on ~ of sth** (fig) etw in den Griff bekommen ❷ FASHION Top nt ❸ (lid) Deckel m ▶PHRASES: **off the ~ of one's** <u>head</u> (fam) aus dem Stegreif; **to go** <u>over</u> **the ~** überreagieren II. adj attr oberste(r, s); (best) beste(r, s); (maximum) höchste(r, s); **~ floor** oberstes Stockwerk; **sb's ~ choice** jds erste Wahl; **~ athlete** Spitzensportler(in) m(f); **~ speed** Höchstgeschwindigkeit f III. vt <-pp-> anführen; (surpass) übertreffen; **to ~ a list** oben auf einer Liste stehen
◆**top off** vt garnieren; tank auffüllen; (conclude) abrunden; (crown) krönen
top[2] [tap] n (toy) Kreisel m

topaz ['toʊˌpæz] *n* Topas *m*

'top hat *n* Zylinder *m*

top-'heavy *adj* kopflastig

topic ['tap·ɪk] *n* Thema *nt*

topical ['tap·ɪ·kəl] *adj* aktuell; (*by topics*) thematisch

topicality [ˌtap·ɪ·'kæl·ɪ·t̬i] *n* Aktualität *f*

topless ['tap·lɪs] *adj* oben ohne *präd*

'topmost *adj attr* oberste(r, s)

topography [tə·'pag·rə·fi] *n* Topographie *f*

topping ['tap·ɪŋ] *n* Garnierung *f*

topple ['tap·əl] I. *vt* umwerfen; (*overthrow*) stürzen II. *vi* stürzen; *prices* fallen

◆ **topple over** I. *vt* umwerfen II. *vi* umfallen

top 'quality *n* Spitzenqualität *f*

top 'secret *adj* streng geheim

top 'speed *n* Höchstgeschwindigkeit *f*

topsy-turvy [ˌtap·sɪ·'tɜr·vi] (*fam*) I. *adj* chaotisch II. *adv* **to turn sth ~** etw auf den Kopf stellen

torch [tɔrtʃ] I. *n* <*pl* -es> Fackel *f*; (*blowtorch*) Lötlampe *f*; **Olympic ~** olympisches Feuer II. *vt* (*fam*) in Brand setzen

'torchlight *n* Fackelschein *m*

tore [tɔr] *vt, vi pt of* **tear**

torment I. *n* ['tɔr·ment] Qual *f*; (*physical*) starke Schmerzen *pl*; (*torture*) Tortur *f* II. *vt* [tɔr·'ment] quälen; **to be ~ed by grief** großen Kummer haben

torn [tɔrn] I. *vt, vi pp of* **tear** II. *adj pred* [innerlich] zerrissen

tornado <*pl* -s> [tɔr·'neɪ·doʊ] *n* Tornado *m*

torpedo [tɔr·'pi·doʊ] I. *n* <*pl* -es> Torpedo *m* II. *vt* torpedieren

torrent ['tɔr·ənt] *n* Sturzbach *m*; (*large amount*) Strom *m*

torrential [tɔ·'ren·ʃəl] *adj* sintflutartig

torso ['tɔr·soʊ] *n* Rumpf *m*; (*statue*) Torso *m*

tortoise ['tɔr·təs] *n* [Land]schildkröte *f*

'tortoiseshell *n* Schildpatt *nt*

tortuous ['tɔr·tʃu·əs] *adj* gewunden; (*complicated*) umständlich; *process* langwierig

torture ['tɔr·tʃər] I. *n* Folter *f*; (*suffering*) Qual *f* II. *vt* foltern; (*disturb*) quälen

toss <*pl* -es> [tɔs] I. *n* Wurf *m* II. *vt* werfen; (*fling*) schleudern; *horse* abwerfen; *one's head* zurückwerfen; *salad* schwenken III. *vi* ▶PHRASES: **to ~ and turn** sich hin und her wälzen

◆ **toss out** *vt* hinauswerfen

tot [tat] *n* (*fam*) Knirps *m*

total ['toʊ·t̬əl] I. *n* Gesamtsumme *f*; **in ~** insgesamt II. *adj* gesamt; (*absolute*) völlig; *disaster* rein; **to be a ~ stranger** vollkommen fremd sein III. *vt* <-l-> zusammenrechnen; (*fam*) *car* zu Schrott fahren; **their debts ~ 8,000 dollars** ihre Schulden belaufen sich auf 8.000 Dollar

◆ **total up** *vt* zusammenrechnen

totalitarian [toʊ·ˌtæl·ə·'ter·i·ən] *adj* totalitär

totalitarianism [toʊ·ˌtæl·ə·'ter·i·ə·nɪz·əm] *n* Totalitarismus *m*

totally ['toʊ·t̬ə·li] *adv* völlig

'tote bag *n* Einkaufstasche *f*

totem ['toʊ·t̬əm] *n* Totem *nt*

totter ['tat·ər] *vi* wanken

tottery ['tat̬·ə·ri] *adj* wackelig; *person* zittrig

toucan ['tu·kæn] *n* Tukan *m*

touch [tʌtʃ] I. *n* <*pl* -es> ➊ Tasten *nt*; (*instance*) Berührung *f*; **the material was soft to the ~** das Material fühlte sich weich an; **at the ~ of a button** auf Knopfdruck; **to be/keep in ~ with sb/sth** mit jdm/etw in Kontakt stehen/bleiben ➋ *of salt* Spur *f*; **a ~ of the flu** (*fam*) eine leichte Grippe ▶PHRASES: **to be a soft ~** (*fam*) leichtgläubig sein II. *vt* berühren; (*contact*) in Berührung kommen; (*border*) grenzen; (*emotions*) bewegen ▶PHRASES: **to ~ a [raw] nerve** einen wunden Punkt berühren III. *vi* sich berühren

◆ **touch down** *vi* landen

◆ **touch on, touch upon** *vi* ansprechen

◆ **touch up** *vt* auffrischen; *photograph* retuschieren

touch-and-'go *adj* unentschieden; ■**to**

be ~ **whether** ... auf Messers Schneide stehen, ob ...

'**touchdown** n Landung f; SPORT Touchdown m

touched [tʌtʃt] adj pred gerührt

touchiness ['tʌtʃ·ɪ·nɪs] n (fam) Überempfindlichkeit f; (delicacy) Empfindlichkeit f

touching ['tʌtʃ·ɪŋ] adj rührend

touchy ['tʌtʃ·i] adj (fam) empfindlich; (delicate) heikel

tough [tʌf] adj robust; (hardy, fibrous) zäh; (difficult, harsh) schwierig; climate rau; competition hart; winter, laws streng; (violent) rau; **to be as ~ as nails** nicht unterzukriegen sein ◆**tough out** vt (fam) aussitzen; ■**to ~ it out** es durchhalten

toughen ['tʌf·ən] I. vt verstärken; glass härten II. vi stärker werden

toupee [tu·'peɪ] n Toupet nt

tour [tʊr] I. n Reise f; (period of duty) Tournee f; **guided ~** Führung f II. vt bereisen; (professionally) besuchen; **to ~ Germany** eine Deutschlandtournee machen III. vi ■**to ~ [with sb]** [mit jdm] auf Tournee gehen

'**tour guide** n Reiseführer m; (person a.) Fremdenführer(in) m(f)

touring ['tʊr·ɪŋ] n Reisen nt; **to do some ~** herumreisen

tourism ['tʊr·ɪz·əm] n Tourismus m

tourist ['tʊr·ɪst] n Tourist(in) m(f)

tourist office n Fremdenverkehrsamt nt

'**tourist season** n Hauptsaison f

tournament ['tɜr·nə·mənt] n Turnier nt

tousled ['taʊ·zəlt] adj zerzaust

tow [toʊ] I. n Schleppen nt; **to have sb in ~** jdn im Schlepptau haben II. vt ziehen; car abschleppen

toward(s) [tɔrd(z)] prep in Richtung; **she walked ~ him** sie ging auf ihn zu; **we're up ~ the front of the line** wir sind nahe dem Anfang der Schlange; **~ midnight** gegen Mitternacht; **to count ~ sth** auf etw akk angerechnet werden

towel ['taʊ·əl] I. n Handtuch nt; **paper ~** Papiertuch nt ▶PHRASES: **to throw in the ~** das Handtuch werfen II. vt <-ll-> **to ~ sth dry** etw trockenreiben

'**towel rack** n Handtuchhalter m

tower ['taʊ·ər] n Turm m ▶PHRASES: **a ~ of strength** ein Fels m in der Brandung ◆**tower above**, **tower over** vi aufragen; ■**to ~ above** sb/sth jdn/etw überragen

towering ['taʊ·ər·ɪŋ] adj hoch aufragend; (great) überragend

town [taʊn] n Stadt f; **home ~** Heimatstadt f; **the whole ~** die ganze Stadt; ■**to be in ~** in der Stadt sein ▶PHRASES: **to go to ~ [on sth]** sich [bei etw dat] ins Zeug legen

town 'clerk n Magistratsbeamte(r), -beamtin m, f

town 'hall n Rathaus nt

'**tow truck** n Abschleppwagen m

toxic ['tak·sɪk] adj giftig; **~ waste** Giftmüll m

toxicology [ˌtak·sɪ·'kal·ə·dʒi] n Toxikologie f

toxin ['tak·sɪn] n Toxin nt

toy [tɔɪ] n Spielzeug nt; **stuffed ~** Kuscheltier nt ◆**toy with** vi spielen mit +dat

'**toy store** n Spielwarengeschäft nt

trace [treɪs] I. n Spur f; **without a ~** spurlos; **to put a ~ on a phone call** einen Anruf zurückverfolgen II. vt ① auffinden; phone call zurückverfolgen; ■**to ~ sb** jds Spur verfolgen ② (through paper) durchpausen; (with finger) nachmalen

'**trace element** n Spurenelement nt

'**tracing paper** n Pauspapier nt

track [træk] I. n ① Weg m; RAIL Bahnsteig m; ■**~s** pl Gleise pl; **to get one's life back on ~** sein Leben wieder in die Reihe bringen ② usu pl (prints) Spur f; of deer Fährte f ③ SPORT Laufbahn f; for racecars Rennstrecke f; for bikes Radrennbahn f ④ (athletics) Leichtathletik f ⑤ (in film) Soundtrack m ▶PHRASES: **to be off the beaten ~** abgelegen sein; **to keep ~ of sb/sth** jdn/etw im Auge behalten; **to stop in one's ~s** vor

T

Schreck erstarren II. vt verfolgen; (find) aufspüren; ■to ~ sb jds Spur verfolgen ◆ **track down** vt aufspüren; *information* ausfindig machen

track and 'field n Leichtathletik f

'trackball n Rollkugel f

'track record n Streckenrekord m; of company Erfolgsbilanz f

'track shoe n Laufschuh m

'tracksuit n Trainingsanzug m

tract [trækt] n Gebiet nt; (property) Grundstück nt; **respiratory** ~ Atemwege pl

traction ['træk·ʃən] n to be in ~ im Streckverband liegen

tractor ['træk·tər] n Traktor m

'tractor-trailer n Sattelschlepper m

trade [treɪd] I. n Handel m; (business type) Branche f; (handicraft) Handwerk nt; **building** ~ Baugewerbe nt; to **learn a** ~ ein Handwerk erlernen II. vi tauschen; (do business) Geschäfte machen III. vt austauschen; to ~ **places [with sb]** [mit jdm] den Platz tauschen ◆ **trade in** vt in Zahlung geben

'trade agreement n Handelsabkommen nt

'trade fair n Messe f

'trade-in n Tauschware f; ~ **value** Gebrauchtwert m

'trademark n Warenzeichen nt; (of person) charakteristisches Merkmal

'trade name n Markenname m

'trader ['treɪ·dər] n Händler(in) m(f); (broker) Wertpapierhändler(in) m(f)

'trade route n Handelsweg m

trade 'secret n Betriebsgeheimnis nt

tradesman ['treɪdz·mən] n Handwerker m

'trade union n Gewerkschaft f

'trade wind n Passat m

trading ['treɪ·dɪŋ] n Handel m

tradition [trə·'dɪʃ·ən] n Tradition f; (custom a.) Brauch m; (style a.) Stil m

traditional [trə·'dɪʃ·ə·nəl] adj traditionell; person konservativ

traditionalist [trə·'dɪʃ·ə·nə·lɪst] n Traditionalist(in) m(f)

traffic ['træf·ɪk] I. n Verkehr m; (trade) illegaler Handel; **to get stuck in** ~ im Verkehr stecken bleiben; **data** ~ Datenverkehr m II. vi <-ck-> handeln; to ~ **in arms** Waffenhandel betreiben

'traffic accident n Verkehrsunfall m

'traffic circle n Kreisverkehr m

'traffic cop n (fam) Verkehrspolizist(in) m(f)

'traffic island n Verkehrsinsel f; (median) Mittelstreifen m

'traffic jam n [Rück]stau m

trafficker ['træf·ɪk·ər] n Händler(in) m(f)

'traffic light n Ampel f

tragedy ['trædʒ·ə·di] n Tragödie f; **it's a** ~ **that** ... es ist tragisch, dass ...

tragic ['trædʒ·ɪk] adj tragisch

trail [treɪl] I. n Weg m; (track) Spur f; ■**to be on the** ~ **of sth/sb** etw/jdm auf der Spur sein II. vt **to** ~ **sb** jdm auf der Spur sein; (competitor) hinter jdm liegen III. vi schleifen; vines sich ranken; (be losing) zurückliegen; ■**to** ~ **after sb** hinter jdm her trotten ◆ **trail away** vi verstummen ◆ **trail behind** I. vi zurückbleiben II. vt hinterherlaufen ◆ **trail off** vi verstummen

trailblazer ['treɪl·bleɪ·zər] n Wegbereiter(in) m(f)

trail-blazing ['treɪl·bleɪ·zɪŋ] adj attr bahnbrechend

trailer ['treɪ·lər] n Anhänger m; (home) Wohnwagen m; (advertisement) Trailer m

'trailer park n Wohnwagenabstellplatz m

'trailer trash n (pej sl) weißer Abschaum pej

train [treɪn] I. n Zug m; (retinue) Gefolge nt; (procession) Zug m; (part of dress) Schleppe f; **to lose one's** ~ **of thought** den roten Faden verlieren II. vi trainieren III. vt ausbilden; dog abrichten; vines ziehen; gun richten

trained [treɪnd] adj ausgebildet; dog abgerichtet; eye geschult

trainee [treɪ·'ni] n Auszubildende(r) f(m)

trainer ['treɪ·nər] *n* Trainer(in) *m(f)*; (*of animals*) Dresseur(in) *m(f)*; (*in circus*) Dompteur *m*, Dompteuse *f*

training ['treɪ·nɪŋ] *n* Ausbildung *f*; *of new employee* Schulung *f*; *of dog* Abrichten *nt*; (*practice*) Training *nt*

'**training camp** *n* Trainingscamp *nt*

'**train station** *n* Bahnhof *m*

trait [treɪt] *n* Eigenschaft *f*; **genetic ~** genetisches Merkmal

traitor ['treɪ·tər] *n* Verräter(in) *m(f)*

trajectory [trə·'dʒek·tə·ri] *n* Flugbahn *f*

tramp [træmp] **I.** *vi* marschieren; (*heavily*) trampeln **II.** *n* Vagabund(in) *m(f)*; (*pej: woman*) Flittchen *nt*

trample ['træm·pəl] **I.** *vt* niedertrampeln; *crops* zertrampeln; **to be ~d to death** zu Tode getrampelt werden **II.** *vi* herumtrampeln

trampoline ['træm·pə·lin] *n* Trampolin *nt*

trance [træns] *n* Trance *f*; (*music*) Trance-Musik *f*

tranquil ['træŋ·kwɪl] *adj* ruhig; *expression* gelassen

tranquility [træŋ·'kwɪl·ɪ·ti] *n* Ruhe *f*

tranquilize ['træŋ·kwɪ·laɪz] *vt* ruhigstellen

tranquilizer ['træŋ·kwɪ·laɪ·zər] *n* Beruhigungsmittel *nt*

tranquillity [træŋ·'kwɪl·ɪ·ti] *n see* **tranquility**

tranquillize ['træŋ·kwɪ·laɪz] *vt see* **tranquilize**

tranquillizer ['træŋ·kwɪ·laɪ·zər] *n see* **tranquilizer**

transact [træn·'zækt] *vt* abschließen; *negotiations* durchführen

transaction [træn·'zæk·ʃən] *n* Transaktion *f*; **business ~** Geschäft *nt*

transatlantic [ˌtræns·ət·'læn·tɪk] *adj* transatlantisch; *voyage* über den Atlantik

transcendental [ˌtræn·sen·'den·təl] *adj* transzendent[al]

transcript ['træn·skrɪpt] *n* Abschrift *f*; **~s** *pl* SCH, UNIV Zeugnisse *pl*

transfer ['træns·'fɜr] **I.** *vt* <-rr-> [træns·'fɜr] *money* überweisen; (*reassign*) ver-

setzen; *power* abgeben; *responsibility* übertragen; *call* weiterleiten **II.** *vi* <-rr-> [træns·'fɜr] *employee* überwechseln; (*passenger*) umsteigen **III.** *n* ['træns·fɜr] ❶ Verlegung *f*; *of money* Überweisung *f*; *of ownership* Übertragung *f*; (*at work*) Versetzung *f*; (*player*) Transferspieler(in) *m(f)* ❷ (*pattern*) Abziehbild *nt*; **heat ~** Wärmeübertragung *f*

transfigure [træns·'fɪg·jər] *vt* verwandeln

transfix [træns·'fɪks] *vt usu passive* ■ **to be ~ed by sth/sb** von etw/jdm fasziniert sein; **to be ~ed with horror** starr vor Entsetzen sein

transform [træns·'fɔrm] *vt* verwandeln

transformation [ˌtræns·fər·'meɪ·ʃən] *n* Verwandlung *f*

transformer [træns·'fɔr·mər] *n* Transformator *m*

transfusion [træns·'fju·ʒən] *n* Transfusion *f*

transient ['træn·zi·ənt] *n* Durchreisende(r) *f(m)*

transistor [træn·'zɪs·tər] *n* Transistor *m*

transit ['træn·zɪt] *n* ❶ Transit *m*; **passengers in ~** Transitreisende *pl* ❷ (*public transport*) öffentliches Verkehrswesen; **mass ~** öffentlicher Nahverkehr

'**transit desk** *n* Transitschalter *m*

transition [træn·'zɪʃ·ən] *n* Übergang *m*; ■ **to be in ~** in einer Übergangsphase sein

transitional [træn·'zɪʃ·ə·nəl] *adj* Übergangs-

'**transit visa** *n* Transitvisum *nt*

translate ['træns·leɪt] **I.** *vt* übersetzen; (*simplify*) einfacher ausdrücken; *ideas* umsetzen; **to ~ sth from Greek to Spanish** etw aus dem Griechischen ins Spanische übersetzen **II.** *vi* übersetzen; (*transfer*) sich umsetzen lassen; **to ~ from Hungarian to Russian** aus dem Ungarischen ins Russische übersetzen

translation [træns·'leɪ·ʃən] *n* Übersetzung *f*; (*act*) Übersetzen *nt*; (*conversion*) Umsetzung *f*

T

translator ['træns·leɪ·tər] n Übersetzer(in) m(f)

transmission [træns·'mɪʃ·ən] n Übertragen nt; (broadcast) Sendung f; (gears) Getriebe nt

transmit <-tt-> [træns·'mɪt] I. vt übertragen; (impart) übermitteln; knowledge vermitteln II. vi senden

transmitter [træns·'mɪt·ər] n Sender m

transparency [træns·'per·ən·si] n Lichtdurchlässigkeit f; (slide) Dia nt

transparent [træns·'per·ənt] adj durchsichtig; (fig) transparent

transpire [træn·'spaɪ·ər] vi sich ereignen; (become known) sich herausstellen

transplant I. vt [træns·'plænt] transplantieren; (relocate) umsiedeln II. n ['træns·plænt] Transplantation f; (organ) Transplantat nt

transplantation [ˌtræns·plæn·'teɪ·ʃən] n Transplantation f

transport I. vt [træns·'pɔrt] befördern; to ~ sb to a time jdn in eine Zeit versetzen II. n ['træns·pɔrt] Beförderung f; (traffic) Verkehrsmittel nt; (vehicle) [Transport]fahrzeug nt; means of ~ Transportmittel nt

transportation [ˌtræns·pər·'teɪ·ʃən] n Beförderung f; (means) Transportmittel nt; through ~ Transitverkehr nt; to provide ~ ein Beförderungsmittel zur Verfügung stellen

transporter [træns·'pɔr·tər] n Transporter m

transvestite [træns·'ves·taɪt] n Transvestit m

trap [træp] I. n Falle f; (ambush) Hinterhalt m; to set a ~ eine Falle aufstellen; to fall into a ~ in die Falle gehen; shut your ~! (sl) Klappe! II. vt <-pp-> ❶ [in einer Falle] fangen ❷ usu passive (confine) ■to be ~ped eingeschlossen sein; to feel ~ped sich gefangen fühlen ❸ (trick) in die Falle locken; ■to ~ into sth/doing sth jdn dazu bringen, etw zu tun ❹ finger sich dat einklemmen

'trapdoor n Falltür f; THEAT Versenkung f

trapeze [træ·'piz] n Trapez nt

trappings ['træp·ɪŋz] npl Drumherum nt fam; the ~ of power die Insignien pl der Macht

trash [træʃ] I. n Abfall m; (pej fam) Plunder m; (literature) Schund m; (people) Gesindel nt; (nonsense) Mist m II. vt (fam) kaputt machen; place verwüsten; (criticize) auseinandernehmen; ■to ~ sb über jdn herziehen

'trash can n Mülltonne f

trashy ['træʃ·i] adj (pej fam) wertlos; ~ novels Kitschromane pl

trauma <pl -s> ['trɔ·mə] n Trauma nt

traumatic [trɔ·'mæt·ɪk] adj traumatisch; (upsetting) furchtbar

traumatize ['trɔ·mə·taɪz] vt usu passive ■to be ~d by sth durch etw akk traumatisiert sein

travel ['træv·əl] I. vi <-l-> reisen; (by air) fliegen; (by train) fahren; (move) sich [fort]bewegen; to ~ badly lange Reisen nicht vertragen; freight lange Transporte nicht vertragen II. vt <-l-> to ~ the world die Welt bereisen III. n Reisen nt; ■~s pl (journeys) Reisen pl

'travel agency n Reisebüro nt

'travel agent n Reisebürokaufmann m, Reisebürokauffrau f

traveler ['træv·ə·lər] n Reisende(r) f(m)

'traveler's check n Reisescheck m

'travel expenses npl Reisekosten pl

'travel guide n Reiseführer m

traveling ['træv·ə·lɪŋ] n Reisen nt

traveller n see **traveler**

travelling n see **traveling**

travelog ['træv·ə·lag] n Reisebericht m; (film) Reisebeschreibung f

travesty ['træv·ɪ·sti] n Karikatur f; (burlesque) Travestie f; ~ of justice Hohn m auf die Gerechtigkeit

trawl [trɔl] I. vt mit dem Schleppnetz fangen; (search) durchkämmen II. vi ❶ ■to ~ [for sth] mit dem Schleppnetz [nach etw dat] fischen ❷ (search) ■to ~ through sth etw durchsuchen

trawler ['trɔ·lər] n Trawler m

tray [treɪ] *n* Tablett *nt*; (*for papers*) Ablage *f*

treacherous ['tretʃ·ər·əs] *adj* verräterisch; (*disloyal*) treulos; (*dangerous*) tückisch; *sea* trügerisch

treachery ['tretʃ·ə·ri] *n* (*esp hist*) Verrat *m*

tread [tred] **I.** *vi* <trod *or* treaded, trodden *or* trod> ❶ (*step*) treten; ▪ **to ~ in/on sth** in/auf etw *akk* treten ❷ (*maltreat*) ▪ **to ~ on sb** jdn treten ▶ PHRASES: **to ~ carefully** vorsichtig vorgehen **II.** *vt* <trod *or* treaded, trodden *or* trod> ▪ **to ~ sth down** etw niedertreten; **to ~ water** Wasser treten **III.** *n* Tritt *m*; (*step*) Stufe *f*; *of tire* [Reifen]profil *nt*; *of shoe* [Schuh]profil *nt*

treadmill ['tred·mɪl] *n* Heimtrainer *m*; (*routine*) Tretmühle *f fam*

treason ['tri·zən] *n* [Landes]verrat *m*; **high ~** Hochverrat *m*

treasure ['treʒ·ər] **I.** *n* Schatz *m*; ▪ **~s** *pl* Schätze *pl* **II.** *vt* [hoch]schätzen; *memories* bewahren

'treasure hunt *n* Schatzsuche *f*

treasurer ['treʒ·ər·ər] *n* Schatzmeister(in) *m(f)*; *of club* Kassenwart(in) *m(f)*

'treasure trove *n* Fundgrube *f*

treasury ['treʒ·ə·ri] *n* Schatzkammer *f*; ▪ **the T~** das Finanzministerium

'Treasury Secretary *n* Finanzminister(in) *m(f)*

treat [trit] **I.** *vt* behandeln; (*regard*) betrachten; *sewage* klären; **to ~ sb/sth badly** jdn/etw schlecht behandeln; **to ~ sth with contempt** etw mit Verachtung begegnen; ▪ **to ~ sb [to sth]** jdn [zu etw *dat*] einladen; ▪ **to ~ oneself [to sth]** sich *dat* etw gönnen **II.** *vi* (*fam*) **Jack's ~ing!** Jack gibt einen aus! **III.** *n* [it's] **my ~** das geht auf meine Rechnung; **it is a special ~ to do that** es ist ein besonderes Vergnügen, das zu tun; **to give oneself a ~** sich *dat* etw gönnen

treatise ['tri·tɪs] *n* Abhandlung *f*

treatment ['trit·mənt] *n* Behandlung *f*;

of waste Verarbeitung *f*; **to respond to ~** auf eine Behandlung ansprechen

treaty ['tri·ti] *n* Vertrag *m*

treble ['treb·əl] **I.** *adj attr* Diskant-; **~ voice** Sopranstimme *f* **II.** *n* Sopran *m*

tree [tri] *n* Baum *m*

'tree house *n* Baumhaus *nt*

'tree-lined *adj* von Bäumen gesäumt

'tree surgeon *n* Baumchirurg(in) *m(f)*

'treetops *npl* ▪ **the ~** die [Baum]wipfel *pl*

trek [trek] **I.** *vi* <-kk-> wandern **II.** *n* Wanderung *f*; (*hike*) Marsch *m*

tremble ['trem·bəl] **I.** *vi* zittern; *voice* beben; **to ~ like a leaf** zittern wie Espenlaub **II.** *n* Zittern *nt*

tremendous [trɪ·'men·dəs] *adj* enorm; *scope* riesig; *help* riesengroß *fam*; (*good*) klasse *fam*

tremor ['trem·ər] *n* Zittern *nt*; MED Tremor *m*; (*earthquake*) Beben *nt*; (*fluctuation*) Schwanken *nt*

tremulous ['trem·jʊ·ləs] *adj* zitternd; *voice* zittrig

trench <*pl* -es> [trentʃ] *n* Graben *m*; MIL Schützengraben *m*

'trench coat *n* Trenchcoat *m*

trend [trend] *n* Trend *m*; (*style a.*) Mode *f*; **the latest ~** der letzte Schrei *fam*

trendsetter ['trend·ˌset·ər] *n* Trendsetter(in) *m(f)*

trendy ['tren·di] *adj* modisch

trespass ['tres·pəs] *vi* unbefugt eindringen; **to ~ on sb's land** jds Land unerlaubt betreten

trespasser ['tres·pæs·ər] *n* Eindringling *m*; "**~s will be prosecuted!**" „unbefugtes Betreten wird strafrechtlich verfolgt!"

trial ['traɪ·əl] *n* Prozess *m*; (*test*) Probe *f*; **clinical ~s** klinische Tests *pl*; **~ by jury** Schwurgerichtsverhandlung *f*; **to stand ~** vor Gericht stehen

triangle ['traɪ·æŋ·gəl] *n* Dreieck *nt*; (*object*) dreieckiges Objekt; (*percussion*) Triangel *f*; (*drawing aid*) Zeichendreieck *nt*

triangular [traɪ·'æŋ·gjʊ·lər] *adj* dreieckig

T

tribal ['traɪ·bəl] adj (ethnic) Stammes-; (fam: group) Gruppen-

tribe [traɪb] n Stamm m; (fam: group) Sippe f

tribunal [traɪ·'bju·nəl] n Gericht nt; (investigative body) Untersuchungsausschuss m

tribune ['trɪb·jun] n Tribüne f

tributary ['trɪb·jə·ter·i] n Nebenfluss m

tribute ['trɪb·jut] n Tribut m; **to pay ~ to sb/sth** jdm/etw Tribut zollen geh; ■**to be a ~ to sb/sth** (beneficial) jdm/ etw Ehre machen

trick [trɪk] I. n Trick m; (knack) Kunstgriff m; **he knows all the ~s of the trade** er ist ein alter Hase; **to play a ~ on sb** jdm einen Streich spielen; **dirty ~** gemeiner Trick; **~ of the light** optische Täuschung ►PHRASES: **to not miss a ~** keine Gelegenheit auslassen; **to do the ~** (fam) klappen fam II. adj attr question Fang-; (acrobatic) Kunst- III. vt hintergehen; (fool) reinlegen fam; ■**to ~ sb into doing sth** jdn dazu bringen, etw zu tun

trickery ['trɪk·ə·ri] n Betrug m; (repeated) Betrügerei f

trickle ['trɪk·əl] I. vi sickern; (in drops) tröpfeln; sand rieseln; tear kullern; details durchsickern; **people ~d back into the theatre** die Leute kamen in kleinen Gruppen in den Theatersaal zurück II. vt tröpfeln III. n Rinnsal nt geh; (in drops) Tropfen pl; ■**a ~ of people** wenige Leute

'trick question n Fangfrage f

tricky ['trɪk·i] adj betrügerisch; (sly) raffiniert; (awkward) schwierig; (difficult) kniff[e]lig

tricycle ['traɪ·sɪ·kəl] n Dreirad nt

trident ['traɪ·dənt] n Dreizack m

tried [traɪd] vt, vi pt, pp of **try**

trifle ['traɪ·fəl] n Kleinigkeit f; **a ~ surprised** etwas erstaunt

trifling ['traɪ·flɪŋ] adj unbedeutend; sum geringfügig

trigger ['trɪg·ər] I. n Abzug m; (cause) Auslöser m; **to pull the ~** abdrücken II. vt auslösen

trill [trɪl] I. n Trillern nt; MUS Triller m II. vt, vi trillern

trillion ['trɪl·jən] n ❶ <pl -> Billion f ❷ pl (fam) ■**~s** pl Tausende pl

trilogy ['trɪl·ə·dʒi] n Trilogie f

trim [trɪm] I. n Nachschneiden nt; (edging) Applikation f II. adj <-mer, -mest> ordentlich; lawn gepflegt; (slim) schlank III. vt <-mm-> [nach]schneiden; beard stutzen; (reduce) kürzen; costs a. verringern; (decorate) schmücken

trimming ['trɪm·ɪŋ] n ■**the ~s** pl das Zubehör; **turkey with all the ~s** Truthahn m mit allem Drum und Dran

Trinidad ['trɪn·ɪ·dæd] n Trinidad nt

Trinidadian ['trɪn·ɪ·dæd·i·ən] I. adj trinidadisch II. n Trinidader(in) m(f)

trinity ['trɪn·ɪ·ti] n ■**the [Holy] T~** die [Heilige] Dreifaltigkeit

trinket ['trɪŋ·kɪt] n wertloser Schmuckgegenstand; ■**~s** pl Plunder m

trio <pl -s> ['tri·oʊ] n Trio nt

trip [trɪp] I. n ❶ Reise f; (outing) Ausflug m; **round ~** Rundreise f; **ego ~** Egotrip m ❷ (stumble) Stolpern nt II. vi <-pp-> stolpern; (fam: be on drugs) auf einem Trip sein sl; **to ~ off one's tongue** leicht von der Zunge gehen III. vt <-pp-> ■**to ~ sb** jdm ein Bein stellen

♦ **trip over** vi stolpern; **to ~ over one's words** über seine Worte stolpern

♦ **trip up** I. vt ❶ (unbalance) ■**to ~ up ◯ sb** jdm ein Bein stellen ❷ (foil) zu Fall bringen II. vi einen Fehler machen

tripe [traɪp] n Kutteln pl; (fam: nonsense) Quatsch m

triple ['trɪp·əl] I. adj attr dreifach; (of three parts) Dreier- II. adv dreimal so viel III. vt verdreifachen IV. vi sich verdreifachen; (in baseball) einen Triple schlagen V. n Triple m

triplet ['trɪp·lɪt] n usu pl Drilling m

tripod ['traɪ·pad] n Stativ nt

trite [traɪt] adj abgedroschen

triumph ['traɪ·ʌmf] I. n Triumph m; (joy) Siegesfreude f II. vi triumphieren

triumphant [traɪ·'ʌm·fənt] adj siegreich; (*successful*) erfolgreich; (*exulting*) triumphierend

trivia ['trɪv·i·ə] *npl* Lappalien *pl*

trivial ['trɪv·i·əl] *adj* trivial; *issue* belanglos; *details* bedeutungslos; (*petty*) kleinlich

triviality [ˌtrɪv·i·'æl·ɪ·ti] *n* Belanglosigkeit *f*; (*unimportant thing*) Trivialität *f*

trivialize ['trɪv·i·ə·laɪz] *vt* trivialisieren

trod [trad] *pt, pp of* **tread** I, II

trodden ['trad·ən] *pp of* **tread** I, II

Trojan ['troʊ·dʒən] **I.** *n* Trojaner(in) *m(f)* **II.** *adj* trojanisch

trolley ['tral·i] *n* Straßenbahn *f*

'**trolley bus** *n* Oberleitungsbus *m*

trombone [tram·'boʊn] *n* Posaune *f*

troop [trup] **I.** *n* Truppe *f*; *of animals* Schar *f*; *of soldiers* Trupp *m* **II.** *vi* ■**to ~ off** abziehen *fam*

trooper ['tru·pər] *n* [einfacher] Soldat; *state ~* Polizist(in) *m(f)*

trophy ['troʊ·fi] *n* Preis *m*; (*memento*) Trophäe *f*; *war ~* Kriegsbeute *f*

tropic ['trap·ɪk] *n* **the T~ of Cancer/ Capricorn** der Wendekreis des Krebses/Steinbocks; ■**the ~s** *pl* die Tropen *pl*

tropical ['trap·ɪ·kəl] *adj* Tropen-; *weather* tropisch

trot [trat] **I.** *n* Trab *m*; *of horse* Trott *m* **II.** *vi* <-tt-> trotten; *horse* traben; (*ride*) im Trab reiten; (*run*) laufen

◆ **trot along** *vi* traben

◆ **trot off** *vi* (*fam*) losziehen

trotter ['trat·ər] *n* ■[**pig**] ~**s** *pl* Schweinshaxen *pl*

trouble ['trʌb·əl] **I.** *n* Schwierigkeiten *pl*; (*annoyance*) Ärger *m*; (*problem*) Problem[e] *nt*[*pl*]; (*cause of worry*) Sorge *f*; (*inconvenience*) Umstände *pl*; (*malfunction*) Störung *f*; (*strife*) Unruhe *f*; **the only ~ is that ...** der einzige Haken [dabei] ist, dass ...; **it's no ~ at all** das macht gar keine Umstände; **to spell ~** (*fam*) nichts Gutes bedeuten; **to stay out of ~** sauber bleiben *hum fam*; **to get oneself into a bit of ~** sich in Schwierigkeiten bringen; **engine ~** Motorschaden *m* **II.** *vt* beunruhigen;

(*grieve*) bekümmern; (*cause pain*) plagen; ■**to ~ sb for sth** (*form*) jdn um etw *akk* bemühen *geh*

troubled ['trʌb·əld] *adj* bedrängt; *times* unruhig; (*worried*) besorgt

'**trouble-free** *adj* problemlos

'**troublemaker** *n* Unruhestifter(in) *m(f)*

'**troubleshooting** *n* Fehler-/Störungsbeseitigung *f*; (*searching*) Fehlersuche *f*; (*mediation*) Vermittlung *f*

troublesome ['trʌb·əl·səm] *adj* schwierig

'**trouble spot** *n* Unruheherd *m*

trough [trɔf] *n* Trog *m*; (*low*) Tiefpunkt *m*

troupe [trup] *n* Truppe *f*

trouser ['traʊ·zər] *n* ■[**pair of**] ~**s** Hose *f*

trout <*pl* -s> [traʊt] *n* Forelle *f*

trowel ['traʊ·əl] *n* Maurerkelle *f*; *for gardening* kleiner Spaten

Troy [trɔɪ] *n* (*hist*) Troja *nt*

truancy ['tru·ən·si] *n* [Schule]schwänzen *nt fam*

truant ['tru·ənt] *n* Schulschwänzer(in) *m(f) fam*

truce [trus] *n* Waffenstillstand *m*

truck [trʌk] *n* Last[kraft]wagen *m*; **pickup ~** Lieferwagen *m* ▶PHRASES: **to have no ~ with sb/sth** (*fam*) mit jdm/etw nichts zu tun haben

truck driver, trucker ['trʌk·ər] *n* Lastwagenfahrer(in) *m(f)*; (*over long distances*) Fernfahrer(in) *m(f)*

trucking ['trʌk·ɪŋ] *n* Lkw-Transport *m*; **~ company** Spedition[sfirma] *f*

'**truck stop** *n* Fernfahrerraststätte *f*

trudge [trʌdʒ] **I.** *vi* wandern, trotten **II.** *n* [anstrengender] Fußmarsch

true [tru] **I.** *adj* <-r, -st> wahr; (*accurate*) richtig; *aim* genau; (*actual*) echt; (*loyal*) treu; **it is ~** [**to say**] **that ...** es stimmt, dass ...; **~ love** wahre Liebe; **to be ~ to one's word** zu seinem Wort stehen ▶PHRASES: **sb's ~ colors** jds wahres Gesicht; **~ to form** wie zu erwarten **II.** *adv* ❶ **to ring ~** glaubhaft klingen ❷ (*accurately*) genau

T

'true-'blue adj attr treu; (genuine) waschecht fam

true 'love n ■sb's ~ jds Geliebte(r) f(m)

truffle ['trʌf·əl] n Trüffel f o m

truly ['tru·li] adv wahrhaftig; (very) wirklich; (genuinely a.) echt ▶PHRASES: yours ~ (fam) meine Wenigkeit hum; Yours ~ (at end of letter) mit freundlichen Grüßen

trump [trʌmp] I. n Trumpf m; ■~s pl Trumpffarbe f II. vt übertrumpfen; (better) ausstechen

◆trump up vt erfinden

trumpet ['trʌm·pət] I. n Trompete f II. vi trompeten III. vt ausposaunen fam

trumpeter ['trʌm·pə·tər] n Trompeter(in) m(f)

truncheon ['trʌn·tʃən] n Schlagstock m

trundle ['trʌn·dəl] vi to ~ along zuckeln

trunk [trʌŋk] n Stamm m; (body) Rumpf m; (of elephant) Rüssel m; (of car) Kofferraum m; ■|swim|ming| ~ s pl Badehose f

trust [trʌst] I. n Vertrauen nt; position of ~ Vertrauensposten m; ■in sb's ~ in jds Obhut f II. vt vertrauen; ■to ~ sb to do sth jdm zutrauen, dass er/sie etw tut III. vi ■to ~ in sb/sth auf jdn/etw vertrauen; ■to ~ |that| ... hoffen, |dass| ...

trusted ['trʌs·tɪd] adj attr getreu geh; (proved) bewährt

trustful ['trʌst·fəl] adj vertrauensvoll; (gullible) leichtgläubig

trusting ['trʌs·tɪŋ] adj see trustful

trusty ['trʌs·ti] adj attr zuverlässig; (loyal) treu

truth <pl -s> [truθ] n Wahrheit f; (principle) Grundprinzip nt; there is no ~ in what she says es ist nichts Wahres an dem, was sie sagt

truthful ['truθ·fəl] adj wahr; (sincere) ehrlich; (accurate) wahrheitsgetreu

try [traɪ] I. n Versuch m; to give sth a ~ etw ausprobieren II. vi <-ie-> versuchen; (make an effort) sich bemühen III. vt <-ie-> versuchen; (experiment a.) probieren; (sample) |aus|probieren;

(put on trial) vor Gericht stellen; ■to ~ sb for sth jdn wegen einer S. gen anklagen

◆try for vi sich bemühen

◆try on vt anprobieren

◆try out vt ausprobieren; ■to ~ out ◯ sb/sth jdn/etw testen

trying ['traɪ·ɪŋ] adj anstrengend; (difficult) hart; time schwierig

T-shirt ['ti·ʃɜrt] n T-Shirt nt

tsp. <pl -> n abbrev of teaspoon|ful| TL

T-square ['ti·skwɛr] n Reißschiene f

tsunami [tsu·'na·mi] n Tsunami m

tub [tʌb] n Kübel m; (fam: bath) [Bade]wanne f; (carton) Becher m

tuba ['tu·bə] n Tuba f

tubby ['tʌb·i] adj pummelig

tube [tub] n Röhre f; (bigger) Rohr nt; (container) Tube f; inner ~ Schlauch m; test ~ Reagenzglas nt; ■the ~ (fam: TV) die Glotze pej sl ▶PHRASES: to go down the ~|s| den Bach runter gehen fam

tuberculosis [tu·ˌbɜr·kjə·'loʊ·sɪs] n Tuberkulose f

tuck [tʌk] I. n Abnäher m; tummy ~ Operation, bei der am Bauch Fett abgesaugt wird II. vt to ~ sb into bed jdn ins Bett [ein]packen fam; to ~ one's legs under oneself seine Beine unterschlagen

◆tuck away vt verstauen; (hide) verstecken

◆tuck in vt shirt in die Hose stecken; (put to bed) zudecken

Tuesday ['tuz·deɪ] n Dienstag m; |on| ~ afternoon/evening |am| Dienstagnachmittag/-abend; on ~ afternoons/evenings dienstagnachmittags/-abends; a week/two weeks from ~ Dienstag in einer Woche/zwei Wochen; a week/two weeks ago ~ Dienstag vor einer Woche/zwei Wochen; every ~ jeden Dienstag; last/next/this ~ |am| letzten/nächsten/diesen Dienstag; ~ before last/after next vorletzten/übernächsten Dienstag; |on| ~ |am| Dienstag; on ~ March

4th am Dienstag, den 4. März; [on] ~ s
dienstags

tuft [tʌft] n Büschel nt

tug [tʌg] I. n Ruck m; (boat) Schlepper m; **to give sth a ~** an etw dat zerren II. vt <-gg-> ziehen III. vi <-gg-> zerren

tug of 'war n Tauziehen nt; (struggle a.) Hin und Her nt

tuition [tuˈɪʃ·ən] n Studiengebühr f; at school Schulgeld nt; (teaching) Unterricht m; **private ~** Einzelunterricht m

tulip [ˈtuˈlɪp] n Tulpe f

tumble [ˈtʌm·bəl] I. vi fallen; (faster) stürzen; prices [stark] fallen II. n Sturz m; **to take a ~** stürzen

◆ **tumble over** vi hinfallen; (collapse) umfallen

'tumbledown adj attr baufällig

'tumble dryer n Wäschetrockner m

tumbler [ˈtʌm·blər] n [Trink]glas nt; (acrobat) Bodenakrobat(in) m(f)

tumbleweed [ˈtʌm·bəl·wid] n Steppenhexe f

tummy [ˈtʌm·i] n (fam) Bauch m

tumor [ˈtu·mər] n Geschwulst f

tumult [ˈtu·mʌlt] n Krach m; (disorder) Tumult m; (agitation) Verwirrung f

tumultuous [tuˈmʌl·tʃu·əs] adj lärmend; applause stürmisch; (confused) turbulent; (excited) aufgeregt

tuna [ˈtu·nə] n <pl -s> Thunfisch m

tune [tun] I. n Melodie f; ■ **to the ~ of 2 million dollars** in Höhe von 2 Millionen Dollar; ■ **to be out of ~** falsch spielen ▶PHRASES: **to change one's ~** einen anderen Ton anschlagen II. vt piano stimmen; radio einstellen; car tunen

◆ **tune in** vi ❶ einschalten; **to ~ in to a station** einen Sender einstellen ❷ (fam: be sensitive) ■ **to be ~ d in to sth** eine Antenne für etw akk haben

tuner [ˈtu·nər] n Empfänger m; (person) Stimmer(in) m(f)

'tune-up n **to give a car a ~** einen Wagen [neu] einstellen

tunic [ˈtu·nɪk] n Kittel m

'tuning fork n Stimmgabel f

Tunisia [tuˈni·ʒə] n Tunesien nt

Tunisian [tuˈni·ʒən] I. n Tunesier(in) m(f) II. adj tunesisch

tunnel [ˈtʌn·əl] I. n Tunnel m ▶PHRASES: **to see [the] light at the end of the ~** das Licht am Ende des Tunnels sehen II. vi <-l-> einen Tunnel graben; **to ~ under a river** einen Fluss untertunneln III. vt <-l-> **to ~ one's way out** sich herausgraben

'tunnel vision n Tunnelblick m; (fig) Scheuklappendenken nt

turban [ˈtɜr·bən] n Turban m

turbine [ˈtɜr·bɪn] n Turbine f

'turbocharged adj mit Turboaufladung nach n; (sl: energetic) Turbo-

'turbocharger n Turbolader m

turbulence [ˈtɜr·bju·ləns] n Turbulenz f; air ~ Turbulenzen pl

turbulent [ˈtɜr·bju·lənt] adj turbulent; sea a. unruhig

turd [tɜrd] n (vulg) Scheißhaufen m derb

turf <pl -s or turves> [tɜrf] n Rasen m; (fam: territory) Revier nt; (fam: expertise) Spezialgebiet f; **artificial ~** Kunstrasen m

Turk [tɜrk] n Türke m, Türkin f

turkey [ˈtɜr·ki] n Pute(r) f(m); (meat) Putenfleisch nt

Turkey [ˈtɜr·ki] n Türkei f

Turkish [ˈtɜr·kɪʃ] I. adj türkisch II. n Türkisch nt

turmoil [ˈtɜr·mɔɪl] n Tumult m; **her mind was in ~** sie war völlig durcheinander

turn [tɜrn] I. n Drehung f; (change in direction) Kurve f; **"no left ~"** „Links abbiegen verboten"; **things took an ugly ~** (fig) die Sache nahm eine üble Wendung; **it's my ~ now!** jetzt bin ich dran!; **the ~ of the century** die Jahrhundertwende; **to take ~ s doing sth** etw abwechselnd tun; **to do sb a good ~** jdm einen guten Dienst erweisen ▶PHRASES: **one good ~ deserves another** (saying) eine Hand wäscht die andere II. vt drehen; (switch direction a.) wenden; (aim) richten; **the shock ~ ed her hair gray overnight** durch den Schock wurde sie über Nacht grau;

to ~ the corner um die Ecke biegen; to ~ one's attention to sth seine Aufmerksamkeit etw *dat* zuwenden; ■to ~ sth/sb into sth etw/jdn in etw *akk* umwandeln; ■to ~ sth [over] umdrehen; *page* umblättern ▶PHRASES: to ~ one's back on sb/sth sich von jdm/etw abwenden; to ~ a blind eye to sth die Augen vor etw *dat* verschließen III. *vi* ❶ sich drehen; to ~ around [and around] sich umdrehen ❷ *wind* drehen; (*fig*) sich wenden; to ~ around *person* sich umdrehen; *car* wenden; to ~ left/right [nach] links/rechts abbiegen; to ~ on one's heels auf dem Absatz kehrtmachen ❸ to ~ to sb for help jdn um Hilfe bitten ❹ (*change*) werden; *milk* sauer werden; *leaves* sich verfärben; *luck* sich wenden; his face ~ed green er wurde ganz grün im Gesicht; ■to ~ into sth zu etw *dat* werden ❺ ■to ~ to sth *subject* sich etw *dat* zuwenden ❻ to ~ 20 20 werden ▶PHRASES: to ~ [over] in one's grave sich im Grabe umdrehen

◆turn against I. *vi* sich auflehnen II. *vt* ■to ~ sb against sb/sth jdn gegen jdn/etw aufwiegeln

◆turn away I. *vi* sich abwenden II. *vt* wegrücken; (*repulse*) abweisen

◆turn back I. *vi* [wieder] zurückgehen; there's no ~ing back now! (*fig*) jetzt gibt es kein Zurück [mehr]! II. *vt* zurückschicken; (*at border*) zurückweisen; *sheet* zurückschlagen

◆turn down *vt* abweisen; *offer* ablehnen; *heat* niedriger stellen; *music* leiser stellen; *sheet* zurückschlagen; *collar* herunterschlagen

◆turn in I. *vt* ❶ (*to police*) thing abgeben; *person* verpfeifen; to ~ oneself in to the police sich der Polizei stellen ❷ (*submit*) einreichen ❸ (*inwards*) nach innen drehen II. *vi* ❶ (*fam: go to bed*) sich in die Falle hauen ❷ (*drive in*) einbiegen

◆turn off I. *vt* abschalten; *engine* abstellen; *gas* abdrehen; *lights* ausmachen; *TV* ausschalten; ■to ~ sb off jdm

die Lust nehmen; (*be sexually unappealing*) jdn abtörnen *sl* II. *vi* abbiegen

◆turn on I. *vt* einschalten; *heat* aufdrehen; *lights* anmachen; (*fam: excite*) anmachen; (*sexually a.*) antörnen *sl* II. *vi* einschalten; ■to ~ on sb auf jdn losgehen

◆turn out I. *vi* sich entwickeln; (*be revealed to be*) sich herausstellen; (*arrive*) erscheinen; how did it ~ out? wie ist es gelaufen? *fam* II. *vt* ausmachen; (*kick out*) [hinaus]werfen *fam*; (*empty*) [aus]leeren; *pockets* umdrehen; *products* produzieren

◆turn over I. *vi* sich umdrehen; *boat* kentern; *car* sich überschlagen; *pages* umblättern; (*sell*) laufen; *engine* laufen; (*start*) anspringen II. *vt* umdrehen; *mattress* wenden; *page* umblättern; *soil* umgraben; (*ponder*) sorgfältig überdenken; ■to ~ over ⟳ sth to sb (*delegate responsibility*) jdm etw übertragen; (*give*) jdm etw [über]geben; to ~ sth over in one's head sich *dat* etw durch den Kopf gehen lassen ▶PHRASES: to ~ over a new leaf einen [ganz] neuen Anfang machen

◆turn up I. *vi* erscheinen; (*become available*) sich ergeben; *solution* sich finden; (*happen*) passieren II. *vt* aufdrehen; *music* lauter machen; *heat* höher stellen; *collar* hochschlagen; (*find*) finden

'turnabout *n* Umschwung *m*

'turnaround *n* Wende *f*; *of health* Besserung *f*; *of company* Aufschwung *m*; (*sudden reversal*) Kehrtwendung *f*

'turning point *n* Wendepunkt *m*

turnip ['tɜr·nɪp] *n* [Steck]rübe *f*

'turnoff ['tɜrn·ˌɔf] *n* Abzweigung *f*; (*sth unappealing*) Gräuel *nt*; to be a real ~ (*sexually*) abtörnen *sl*

turnout ['tɜrn·ˌaʊt] *n* Teilnahme *f*; POL Wahlbeteiligung *f*

turnover ['tɜrn·ˌoʊ·vər] *n* ❶ apple ~ Apfeltasche *f* ❷ *of staff* Fluktuation *f* *geh*; *of business* Umsatz *m*

'turnstile *n* Drehkreuz *nt*

'turntable n Drehscheibe f; (for records) Plattenteller m

turpentine ['tɜr·pən·taɪn] n Terpentin nt

turquoise ['tɜr·kwɔɪz] I. n Türkis m II. adj türkis|farben|

turtle <pl -> ['tɜr·təl] n Schildkröte f

'turtledove n Turteltaube f

'turtleneck n Rollkragen m; (sweater) Rollkragenpullover m

tush [tʊʃ] n (sl) Hintern m fam

tusk [tʌsk] n Stoßzahn m

tussle ['tʌs·əl] I. vi sich balgen; ■ to ~ [with sb] over sth [mit jdm] über etw akk streiten II. n Rauferei f; (argument) Streiterei f

tut [tʌt] interj ~ ~ na, na!

tutor ['tu·tər] I. n Nachhilfelehrer(in) m(f); (private teacher) Privatlehrer(in) m(f) II. vt (in addition to school lessons) Nachhilfestunden geben; (private tuition) Privatunterricht erteilen

tuxedo [tʌk·'si·doʊ] n Smoking m

TV [ˌtiˑ·ˈvi] n abbrev of **television** Fernseher m; (programming) Fernsehen nt; ■ on ~ im Fernsehen

twang [twæŋ] I. n Doing nt II. vt zupfen III. vi einen sirrenden Ton von sich geben

tweak [twik] I. vt zupfen; (adjust) gerade ziehen; **this proposal still needs some ~ing** an diesem Vorschlag muss noch etwas gefeilt werden II. n Zupfen nt

tweed [twid] n Tweed m

tweet [twit] I. vi piepsen II. n Piepsen nt

tweeter ['twi·tər] n Hochtonlautsprecher m

tweezers ['twi·zərz] npl ■ |pair of| Pinzette f

twelfth [twelfθ] I. adj zwölfte(r, s) II. adv als zwölfte(r, s) III. n ■ the ~ der/die/das Zwölfte; (date) der Zwölfte

twelve [twelv] I. adj zwölf; see also **eight** II. n Zwölf f; see also **eight**

twentieth ['twen·tiˑ·əθ] I. adj zwanzigste(r, s) II. adv an zwanzigster Stelle III. n ■ the ~ der/die/das Zwanzigste; (date) der Zwanzigste

twenty ['twen·ti] I. adj zwanzig; see also **eight** II. n Zwanzig f; see also **eight**

twice [twaɪs] adv zweimal; (doubly) doppelt; ~ a day zweimal täglich; **she is ~ his age** sie ist doppelt so alt wie er

twiddle ['twɪd·əl] vt [herum]drehen; **to ~ one's thumbs** Däumchen drehen

twig [twɪg] n [kleiner] Zweig

twilight ['twaɪ·laɪt] n Zwielicht nt

twin [twɪn] I. n Zwilling m; (thing) Pendant nt geh; **identical/fraternal ~s** eineiige/zweieiige Zwillinge II. adj Zwillings-; **rooms** miteinander verbunden; **cities** Partner- III. <-nn-> ■ to ~ **sth** [with sth] etw [mit etw dat] [partnerschaftlich] verbinden

twine [twaɪn] I. n Schnur f II. vi sich schlingen III. vt ■ to ~ **sth together** etw ineinanderschlingen

twinge [twɪndʒ] n Stechen nt; ~ of **pain** stechender Schmerz; ~ of **guilt** Anflug m eines schlechten Gewissens

twinkle ['twɪŋ·kəl] I. vi funkeln II. n Funkeln nt; **to do sth with a ~ in one's eye** etw mit einem [verschmitzten] Augenzwinkern tun

twinkling ['twɪŋ·klɪŋ] I. adj funkelnd II. n kurzer Augenblick; **in the ~ of an eye** im Handumdrehen

twin 'room n Zweibettzimmer nt

'twinset, 'twin set n Twinset nt

twirl [twɜrl] I. vi wirbeln II. vt rotieren lassen; (in dancing) [herum]wirbeln III. n Wirbel m; (in dancing) Drehung f

twist [twɪst] I. vt [ver]drehen; (coil) herumwickeln; (sprain) sich verrenken; ■ to ~ **sth off** etw abdrehen; **to ~ sb's arm** (fig) auf jdn Druck ausüben II. vi sich winden; **to ~ and turn road** sich schlängeln III. n Drehung f; (bend) Kurve f; (change) Wendung f; **to give sth a ~** etw [herum]drehen; **cruel ~ of fate** grausame Wendung des Schicksals

twisted ['twɪs·tɪd] adj verdreht; **ankle** gezerrt; (winding) verschlungen; **path** gewunden

twister ['twɪs·tər] n (fam) Tornado m

twitch [twɪtʃ] I. vi zucken II. vt zucken

T

mit +*dat;* (*tug*) zupfen; **to ~ one's nose** *rabbit* schnuppern **III.** *n* <*pl* -es> ❶ **to have a [nervous] ~** nervöse Zuckungen *pl* haben ❷ (*tug*) Ruck *m*

twitter ['twɪ·tər] *vi* ❶ (*chirp*) zwitschern ❷ (*talk rapidly*) ■**to ~ away** vor sich hin plappern ❸ TELEC, INET twittern

two [tu] **I.** *adj* zwei; **~** [**o'clock**] zwei [Uhr]; **to break sth in ~** etw entzwei brechen; **the ~ of you** ihr beide; *see also* **eight** ▸ PHRASES: **to throw in one's ~** cents [worth] seinen Senf dazugeben; **to be ~ of a** kind aus dem gleichen Holz geschnitzt sein; **to be of ~** minds hin- und hergerissen sein; **there are no ~** ways **about it** es gibt keine andere Möglichkeit **II.** *n* Zwei *f; see also* **eight**

'**two-bit** *adj attr* (*pej fam*) billig *pej*

two-di'mensional *adj* zweidimensional; (*pej*) *plot* flach

'**two-faced** *adj* (*pej*) falsch

twofold I. *adj* zweifach; (*with two parts*) zweiteilig **II.** *adv* zweifach; **to increase sth ~** etw verdoppeln

'**two-piece** *n* Bikini *m;* (*suit*) Zweiteiler *m*

twosome ['tu·səm] *n* Duo *nt;* (*couple*) Paar *nt;* **as a ~** zu zweit

'**two-time** *vt* (*fam*) ■**to ~ sb** [**with sb**] jdn [mit jdm] betrügen

TX *abbrev of* **Texas**

TXT *vt short for* **text**: ■**to ~ sth** etw texten

tycoon [taɪ·ˈkun] *n* [Industrie]magnat(in) *m(f)*

tyke [taɪk] *n* (*fam*) Gör *nt*

type [taɪp] **I.** *n* ❶ Art *f; of skin* Typ *m; of food* Sorte *f* ❷ (*character*) Typ *m;* ■**to be one's ~** jds Typ sein *fam* ❸ (*lettering*) Schriftart *f;* **italic ~** Kursivschrift *f* **II.** *vt* tippen; (*classify*) typisieren *geh* **III.** *vi* Maschine schreiben

◆**type out** *vt* tippen

◆**type up** *vt* erfassen

'**typecast** *vt irreg, usu passive* ■**to be ~** auf eine Rolle festgelegt sein/werden

'**typeface** *n* Schrift[art] *f*

'**typescript** *n* maschinengeschriebenes Manuskript

'**typesetter** *n* Setzmaschine *f;* (*printer*) [Schrift]setzer(in) *m(f)*

'**typesetting** *n* Setzen *nt*

'**typewrite** *vt irreg* tippen

'**typewriter** *n* Schreibmaschine *f*

'**typewritten** *adj* maschinengeschrieben

typhoid ['taɪ·fɔɪd], **typhoid 'fever** *n* Typhus *m*

typhoon [taɪ·ˈfun] *n* Taifun *m*

typhus ['taɪ·fəs] *n* Typhus *m*

typical ['tɪp·ɪ·kəl] *adj* typisch; *symptom a.* charakteristisch

typically ['tɪp·ɪ·kəl·i] *adv* typisch; **~, ...** normalerweise ...

'**typing** ['taɪ·pɪŋ] *n* Tippen *nt*

typist ['taɪ·pɪst] *n* Schreibkraft *f*

typo ['taɪ·poʊ] *n* (*fam*) Druckfehler *m*

tyrannical [tɪ·ˈræn·ɪ·kəl] *adj* tyrannisch

tyrannize ['tɪr·ə·naɪz] *vt* tyrannisieren

tyranny ['tɪr·ə·ni] *n* Tyrannei *f*

tyrant ['taɪ·rənt] *n* Tyrann(in) *m(f);* (*bossy man*) [Haus]tyrann *m pej;* (*bossy woman*) [Haus]drachen *m pej fam*

Tyrol [tɪ·ˈroʊl] *n* ■**the ~** Tirol *nt*

tzar [zar] *n see* **czar**

Uu

U <pl -'s>, **u** <pl -'s> [ju] n (letter)
U nt, u nt; ~ **as in Uniform** U wie Ulrich

U¹ [ju] n CHEM see **uranium** U nt

U² [ju] (fam) abbrev of **university** Uni f

UAE [ˌjuˑeɪ'i] n pl abbrev of **United
Arab Emirates:** ■ **the ~** die VAE

U-boat ['juˑboʊt] n U-Boot nt

UFO <pl -s> [ˌjuˑef'oʊ] n abbrev of **unidentified flying object** UFO nt

ugh [ʌg] interj (fam) igitt!

ugliness ['ʌgˑlɪˑnɪs] n Hässlichkeit f; (fig
a.) Scheußlichkeit f

ugly ['ʌgˑli] adj ❶ (not beautiful) hässlich ❷ (unpleasant) rumors übel; mood
unerfreulich; **to turn ~** eine üble Wendung nehmen

UHF [ˌjuˑeɪtʃˈef] n abbrev of **ultrahigh
frequency** UHF

UK [ˌjuˑ'keɪ] n abbrev of **United Kingdom:** ■ **the ~** das Vereinigte Königreich

Ukraine [juˑ'kreɪn] n die Ukraine

ulcer ['ʌlˑsər] n Geschwür nt

ulterior [ʌlˈtɪrˑiˑər] adj ~ **motive** Hintergedanke m

ultimate ['ʌlˑtəˑmɪt] adj attr ❶ (unbeatable) beste(r, s) ❷ (highest) höchs-
te(r, s); deterrent wirksamste(r, s)
❸ (final) endgültig; ~ **destination** End-
ziel nt

ultimately ['ʌlˑtəˑmɪtˑli] adv (in the
end) letztes Endes; (eventually) letztlich

ultimatum <pl -ta> [ˌʌlˑtəˈmeɪˑtəm] n
Ultimatum nt

ultrahigh 'frequency n Ultrahoch-
frequenz f

ultramaˈrine adj ultramarin[blau]

ultraˈsonic adj Ultraschall-

ultraˈviolet adj ultraviolett

um [əm] interj (fam) hm, äh

umˈbilical cord n Nabelschnur f

umbrella [ʌmˈbrelˑə] n Regenschirm m; **folding ~** Knirps® m

umpire ['ʌmˑpaɪr] n SPORT (esp baseball)
Schiedsrichter(in) m(f)

umpteen ['ʌmpˑtin] adj (fam) zig;
~ **times** zigmal

UN [ˌjuˑ'en] n pl abbrev of **United Nations:** ■ **the ~** die UN [o UNO]

unable [ʌnˈeɪˑbəl] adj **to be ~ to do
sth** etw nicht tun können

unabridged [ˌʌnˑəˈbrɪdʒd] adj ungekürzt

unacceptable [ˌʌnˑəkˈsepˑtəˑbəl] adj
inakzeptabel; offer unannehmbar

unaccompanied [ˌʌnˑəˈkʌmˑpəˑnid]
adj ohne Begleitung nach n, präd; baggage herrenlos

unaccounted-for [ˌʌnˑəˈkaʊnˑtɪdˌfɔr]
adj pred ❶ (unexplained) ungeklärt
❷ (not included in count) nicht erfasst;
person vermisst

unaccustomed [ˌʌnˑəˈkʌsˑtəmd] adj **to
be ~ to doing sth** es nicht gewohnt
sein, etw zu tun

unaddressed [ˌʌnˑəˈdrest] adj envelope nicht adressiert

unadorned [ˌʌnˑəˈdɔrnd] adj schlicht

unadulterated [ˌʌnˑəˈdʌlˑtəˑreɪˌtɪd]
adj unverfälscht; alcohol rein

unadventurous [ˌʌnˑədˈvenˑtʃərˑəs]
adj person wenig unternehmungslustig

unaffected [ˌʌnˑəˈfekˑtɪd] adj ❶ (unchanged) unberührt; (unmoved) un-
beeindruckt ❷ (natural) natürlich;
manner ungekünstelt

unaided [ʌnˈeɪˑdɪd] adj ohne fremde
Hilfe nach n

unaltered [ʌnˈɔlˑtərd] adj unverändert

unambiguous [ˌʌnˑæmˈbɪgˑjuˑəs] adj
unzweideutig; statement eindeutig

un-American [ˌʌnˑəˈmerˑɪˑkən] adj un-
amerikanisch; ~ **activities** ≈ Landesverrat m (gegen den amerikanischen Staat
gerichtete Umtriebe)

unanimous [juˈnænˑəˑməs] adj einstimmig

U

unanswerable [ˌʌnˈænsərəbəl] *adj*
❶ ∎**to be ~** nicht zu beantworten sein
❷ (*irrefutable*) unwiderlegbar

unanswered [ˌʌnˈænsərd] *adj* unbeantwortet

unapproachable [ˌʌnəˈproʊtʃəbəl] *adj* unzugänglich; *person a.* unnahbar

unarmed [ˌʌnˈɑrmd] *adj* unbewaffnet

unasked [ˌʌnˈæskt] *adj* ❶ ungefragt; **an ~ question** eine Frage, die keiner zu stellen wagt ❷ (*not requested*) ∎**~-for** ungebeten

unassuming [ˌʌnəˈsuːmɪŋ] *adj* bescheiden

unattached [ˌʌnəˈtætʃt] *adj* ❶ (*not connected*) einzeln ❷ *bachelor* ungebunden

unattended [ˌʌnəˈtendɪd] *adj*
❶ (*alone*) unbegleitet; *baggage* unbeaufsichtigt ❷ (*unmanned*) nicht besetzt

unattractive [ˌʌnəˈtræktɪv] *adj* unattraktiv; *personality* wenig anziehend

unauthorized [ˌʌnˈɔːθəraɪzd] *adj* nicht autorisiert; *person, access* unbefugt *attr*

unavailable [ˌʌnəˈveɪləbəl] *adj* (*not in*) nicht verfügbar; *person* nicht erreichbar

unavoidable [ˌʌnəˈvɔɪdəbəl] *adj* unvermeidlich

unaware [ˌʌnəˈwer] *adj* ∎**to be ~ of sth** sich *dat* einer S. *gen* nicht bewusst sein

unawares [ˌʌnəˈwerz] *adv* **to catch sb ~** jdn überraschen

unbalanced [ˌʌnˈbælənst] *adj* ❶ (*uneven*) schief; *account* nicht ausgeglichen; *diet* unausgewogen ❷ (*unstable*) labil

unbearable [ʌnˈberəbəl] *adj* unerträglich

unbeatable [ʌnˈbiːtəbəl] *adj* ❶ unschlagbar; *army* unbesiegbar ❷ (*perfect*) unübertrefflich

unbeaten [ʌnˈbiːtən] *adj* ungeschlagen

unbeknown [ʌnbɪˈnoʊn], **unbeknownst** [ʌnbɪˈnoʊnst] *adv* ∎**~ to sb** ohne jds Wissen

unbelievable [ˌʌnbɪˈliːvəbəl] *adj*

❶ (*surprising*) unglaublich ❷ (*fam: extraordinary*) sagenhaft

unbelieving [ˌʌnbɪˈliːvɪŋ] *adj* ungläubig

unbend [ʌnˈbend] **I.** *vt* <-bent, -bent> strecken **II.** *vi* <-bent, -bent> (*straighten out*) [wieder] gerade werden; *person* sich aufrichten

unbiased [ʌnˈbaɪəst] *adj* unparteiisch; *report* objektiv

unbleached [ʌnˈbliːtʃt] *adj* ungebleicht

unborn [ʌnˈbɔrn] *adj* ungeboren

unbreakable [ʌnˈbreɪkəbəl] *adj* unzerbrechlich; *habit* fest verankert; *promise* bindend; *rule* unumstößlich

unbroken [ʌnˈbroʊkən] *adj* ❶ unbeschädigt; *record* ungebrochen ❷ *sleep* ungestört

unbuckle [ʌnˈbʌkəl] *vt* aufschnallen; *seatbelt* öffnen

unburden [ʌnˈbɜrdən] *vt* ∎**to ~ oneself [to sb]** [jdm] sein Herz ausschütten

unbutton [ʌnˈbʌtən] *vt, vi* aufknöpfen

uncalled for *adj pred,* **uncalled-for** [ʌnˈkɔːldfɔr] *adj attr* unnötig; *remark* unpassend

uncanny [ʌnˈkæni] *adj* unheimlich

uncared for *adj pred,* **uncared-for** [ʌnˈkerdfɔr] *adj attr* ungepflegt

unceasing [ʌnˈsiːsɪŋ] *adj* unaufhörlich; *efforts* unablässig

uncertain [ʌnˈsɜrtən] *adj* ❶ (*unsure*) unsicher; **in no ~ terms** klar und deutlich ❷ (*unpredictable*) ungewiss; *temper* launenhaft

uncertainty [ʌnˈsɜrtənti] *n* ❶ (*doubtfulness*) Ungewissheit *f* ❷ (*hesitancy*) Unsicherheit *f*

unchallenged [ʌnˈtʃælɪndʒd] *adj* unwidersprochen; **to go ~** unangefochten bleiben

unchanged [ʌnˈtʃeɪndʒd] *adj* unverändert

uncharted [ʌnˈtʃɑrtɪd] *adj* (*fig*) **~ territory** Neuland *nt*

unchecked [ʌnˈtʃekt] *adj* ❶ (*unrestrained*) unkontrolliert; **to continue ~** ungehindert weitergehen ❷ (*not examined*) ungeprüft

U

unclaimed [ˌʌn·ˈkleɪmd] *adj* nicht beansprucht; *baggage* nicht abgeholt

unclassified [ˌʌn·ˈklæs·ɪ·faɪd] *adj* nicht geheim

uncle [ˈʌŋ·kəl] *n* Onkel *m* ▶PHRASES: **to cry** [*or* **say**] ~ (*fam*) klein beigeben

unclean [ˌʌn·ˈklin] *adj* ① (*unhygienic*) verunreinigt ② (*impure*) schmutzig

unclear [ˌʌn·ˈklɪr] *adj* ① (*not certain*) unklar ② (*vague*) vage

Uncle 'Sam *n* Uncle Sam *m* (*Bezeichnung für die USA*)

uncluttered [ˌʌn·ˈklʌt̬·ərd] *adj* ① (*tidy*) aufgeräumt ② (*fig*) *mind* frei

uncomfortable [ˌʌn·ˈkʌm·fər·t̬ə·bəl] *adj* ① (*causing discomfort*) unbequem ② (*uneasy*) unbehaglich; *silence* gespannt

uncommitted [ˌʌn·kə·ˈmɪt̬·ɪd] *adj* unentschieden

uncommon [ʌn·ˈkɑm·ən] *adj* selten

uncommunicative [ˌʌn·kə·ˈmju·nɪ·kə·t̬ɪv] *adj* ■**to be ~ about sth** wenig über etw sprechen

uncompromising [ʌn·ˈkɑm·prə·maɪ·zɪŋ] *adj* kompromisslos

unconcerned [ˌʌn·kən·ˈsɜrnd] *adj* ① (*not worried*) unbekümmert ② (*indifferent*) desinteressiert

unconditional [ˌʌn·kən·ˈdɪʃ·ə·nəl] *adj* bedingungslos; *love a.* rückhaltlos

unconfirmed [ˌʌn·kən·ˈfɜrmd] *adj* unbestätigt

unconscious [ʌn·ˈkɑn·ʃəs] *adj* bewusstlos; ■**to be ~ of sth** sich *dat* einer S. *gen* nicht bewusst sein

unconsciously [ʌn·ˈkɑn·ʃəs·li] *adv* unbewusst

unconsciousness [ʌn·ˈkɑn·ʃəs·nɪs] *n* Bewusstlosigkeit *f*

unconstitutional [ˌʌn·kɑn·stɪ·ˈtu·ʃə·nəl] *adj* verfassungswidrig

uncontested [ˌʌn·kən·ˈtes·tɪd] *adj* ① (*unchallenged*) unbestritten; *claim* unstreitig ② LAW ~ **divorce** einvernehmliche Scheidung

uncontrollable [ˌʌn·kən·ˈtrou·lə·bəl] *adj* unkontrollierbar; *bleeding* unstillbar

uncontrolled [ˌʌn·kən·ˈtrould] *adj* unkontrolliert; *aggression* unbeherrscht

unconventional [ˌʌn·kən·ˈven·ʃə·nəl] *adj* unkonventionell

unconvincing [ˌʌn·kən·ˈvɪn·sɪŋ] *adj* ① (*not persuasive*) nicht überzeugend ② (*not credible*) unglaubwürdig

uncooked [ˌʌn·ˈkʊkt] *adj* roh

uncooperative [ˌʌn·koʊ·ˈɑp·ər·ə·tɪv] *adj* unkooperativ

uncountable [ʌn·ˈkaʊn·tə·bəl] *adj* unzählbar; (*countless*) zahllos

uncouple [ʌn·ˈkʌp·əl] *vt* MECH abkuppeln

uncover [ʌn·ˈkʌv·ər] *vt* ① (*bare*) freilegen ② (*disclose*) entdecken; *secret* aufdecken

uncritical [ʌn·ˈkrɪt̬·ɪ·kəl] *adj* unkritisch

uncrowned [ʌn·ˈkraʊnd] *adj* ungekrönt *a. fig*

uncut [ʌn·ˈkʌt] *adj* ① ungeschnitten ② (*not shortened*) *version* ungekürzt

undated [ʌn·ˈdeɪ·t̬ɪd] *adj* undatiert

undecided [ˌʌn·dɪ·ˈsaɪ·dɪd] *adj* ① (*hesitant*) unentschlossen; ■**to be ~ about sth** sich *dat* über etw *akk* [noch] unklar sein ② *vote* unentschieden

undeclared [ˌʌn·dɪ·ˈklerd] *adj* ① FIN nicht deklariert ② (*unofficial*) ~ **war** Krieg *m* ohne Kriegserklärung

undefined [ˌʌn·dɪ·ˈfaɪnd] *adj* ① unbestimmt ② (*lacking clarity*) vage

undelivered [ˌʌn·dɪ·ˈlɪv·ərd] *adj* nicht zugestellt

undemocratic [ˌʌn·dem·ə·ˈkræt̬·ɪk] *adj* undemokratisch

undemonstrative [ˌʌn·dɪ·ˈmɑn·strə·t̬ɪv] *adj* zurückhaltend

undeniable [ˌʌn·dɪ·ˈnaɪ·ə·bəl] *adj* ~ **evidence** eindeutiger Beweis

U

undeniably [ˌʌn·dɪ·ˈnaɪ·ə·bli] *adv* unbestreitbar

under [ˈʌn·dər] **I.** *prep* ① (*below*) unter +*dat;* *with verbs of motion* unter +*akk* ② (*less than*) unter +*dat;* **to cost** ~ **5 dollars** weniger als fünf Dollar kosten ③ (*governed by*) unter +*dat;* ~ **the supervision of sb** unter jds Aufsicht ④ (*in state of*) unter

+ *dat;* ~ **arrest** unter Arrest; ~ [**no**] **circumstances** unter [keinen] Umständen II. *adv* ❶ (*down*) **to go** ~ untergehen; *company* Pleite machen ❷ (*less*) **suitable for kids aged five and** ~ geeignet für Kinder von fünf Jahren und darunter

under·a'**chieve** *vi* weniger leisten als erwartet

under'**age** *adj* minderjährig

'**underarm** *n* Achselhöhle *f*

under'**charge** *vt, vi* zu wenig berechnen

'**underclothes** *npl see* **underwear**

'**undercoat** I. *n* ❶ (*paint*) Grundierung *f* ❷ (*fur*) Wollhaarkleid *nt* II. *vt* grundieren

'**undercover** I. *adj attr* geheim; ~ **police officer** Geheimpolizist(in) *m(f)* II. *adv* geheim

'**undercurrent** *n* ❶ (*of sea*) Unterströmung *f* ❷ (*fig*) Unterton *m*

under·de'**veloped** *adj* unterentwickelt

'**underdog** *n* Außenseiter(in) *m(f)*

under'**done** *adj* (*undercooked*) nicht gar; *meat* blutig

under'**dressed** *adj* (*too casual*) zu einfach gekleidet

under·e'**quipped** *adj* unzureichend ausgerüstet

under'**estimate** *vt* unterschätzen

under·ex'**pose** *vt photo* unterbelichten

under'**fed** *adj* unterernährt

under'**funding** *n* Unterfinanzierung *f*

under'**go** <-went, -gone> *vt* **to** ~ **surgery** sich einer Operation unterziehen

under'**graduate** *n* Student(in) *m(f)*

'**underground** I. *adj* ❶ unterirdisch; ~ **cable** Erdkabel *nt* ❷ POL Untergrund- II. *adv* ❶ GEOG unter der Erde ❷ POL **to go** ~ in den Untergrund gehen

'**undergrowth** *n* Dickicht *nt*

under'**hand** I. *adj* (*devious*) hinterhältig; ~ **dealings** betrügerische Machenschaften II. *adv* SPORT mit der Hand von unten

under·in'**sured** *adj* unterversichert

under'**lay** *vt pt of* **underlie**

under'**lie** <-y-, -lay, -lain> *vt* zugrunde liegen

under'**line** *vt* ❶ (*draw line*) unterstreichen ❷ (*emphasize*) betonen

under'**lying** *adj attr* zugrunde liegend

under'**manned** *adj* unterbesetzt

under'**mine** *vt* (*weaken*) untergraben; *confidence* schwächen

underneath [ʌn·dər·'niːθ] I. *prep* unter + *dat; with vbs of motion* unter + *akk* II. *adv* darunter

under'**nourished** *adj* unterernährt

under'**paid** *adj* unterbezahlt

'**underpants** *npl* Unterhose *f*

under'**pay** <-paid, -paid> *vt usu passive* unterbezahlen

under'**play** *vt* herunterspielen

under'**populated** *adj* unterbevölkert

under'**privileged** *adj* unterprivilegiert

under'**rated** *adj* unterschätzt

under'**sell** <-sold, -sold> *vt* ❶ (*offer cheaper*) *competitor* unterbieten ❷ (*undervalue*) unterbewerten

'**undershirt** *n* Unterhemd *nt*

'**underside** *n usu sing* Unterseite *f*

'**undersigned** <*pl* -> *n* (*form*) ■**the** ~ der/die Unterzeichnete

'**underskirt** *n* Unterrock *m*

under'**staffed** *adj* unterbesetzt

understand <-stood, -stood> [ʌn·dər·'stænd] I. *vt* ❶ (*perceive meaning*) verstehen; **to not** ~ **a single word** kein einziges Wort verstehen; **to** ~ **one another** sich verstehen ❷ (*comprehend significance*) begreifen ❸ (*sympathize with*) ■**to** ~ **sb** für jdn Verständnis haben ❹ (*be informed*) ■**to** ~ [**that**] ... hören, dass ... II. *vi* ❶ (*comprehend*) verstehen, kapieren *fam* ❷ (*infer*) **to** ~ **from sth that** ... aus etw *dat* schließen, dass ...

understandable [ʌn·dər·'stæn·də·bəl] *adj* verständlich

understanding [ʌn·dər·'stæn·dɪŋ] I. *n* ❶ (*comprehension*) Verständnis *nt* ❷ (*agreement*) Übereinkunft *f*; **tacit** ~ stillschweigendes Abkommen ❸ (*condition*) Bedingung *f*; **to be sth on the** ~ **that** ... etw unter der Bedingung machen, dass ... II. *adj* verständnisvoll

understatement [ʌn·dər·'steɪt·

mənt] n Untertreibung f, Understatement nt

understood [ˌʌn·dərˈstʊd] pt, pp of **understand**

understudy [ˈʌn·dərˌstʌd·i] n THEAT Zweitbesetzung f

undertake <-took, -taken> [ˌʌn·dərˈteɪk] vt ❶ (take on) durchführen ❷ (guarantee) ▪to ~ to do sth sich verpflichten, etw zu tun

undertaker [ˈʌn·dərˌteɪ·kər] n see **funeral director**

undertaking [ˌʌn·dərˈteɪ·kɪŋ] n ❶ (project) Unternehmung f ❷ (pledge) Verpflichtung f

'**undertone** n gedämpfte Stimme

under'used, **under'utilized** adj nicht [voll] ausgelastet

under'value vt unterbewerten; person unterschätzen

'**underwater** I. adj Unterwasser· II. adv unter Wasser

'**underwear** n Unterwäsche f

'**underweight** adj untergewichtig

'**underworld** n Unterwelt f

under'write <-wrote, -written> vt ▪to ~ **a loan** für einen Kredit bürgen

'**underwriter** n Versicherer, Versicherin m, f

undesirable [ˌʌn·dɪˈzaɪ·rə·bəl] adj unerwünscht

undeveloped [ˌʌn·dɪˈvel·əpt] adj ❶ land unerschlossen ❷ ECON unterentwickelt

undid [ʌnˈdɪd] pt of undo

undies [ˈʌn·diz] npl (fam) Unterwäsche f kein pl

undiscovered [ˌʌn·dɪˈskʌv·ərd] adj unentdeckt

undisputed [ˌʌn·dɪˈspju·t̬ɪd] adj unumstritten

undisturbed [ˌʌn·dɪˈstɜrbd] adj ❶ (untouched) unberührt ❷ (uninterrupted) ungestört

undivided [ˌʌn·dɪˈvaɪ·dɪd] adj ungeteilt

undo <-did, -done> [ʌnˈdu] I. vt ❶ (unfasten) öffnen; button, zipper aufmachen ❷ (cancel) damage beheben; **to ~** **the good work** die gute Arbeit zunichtemachen II. vi button aufgehen

undone [ʌnˈdʌn] I. vt pp of **undo** II. adj offen; **to come ~** aufgehen

undoubted [ʌnˈdaʊ·t̬ɪd] adj unbestritten

undoubtedly [ʌnˈdaʊ·t̬ɪd·li] adv zweifellos

undreamed of adj pred, **undreamed-of** [ʌnˈdrimd·ˌʌv] adj attr; **undreamt of** adj pred, **undreamt-of** [ʌnˈdremt·ˌʌv] adj attr unvorstellbar; **success** ungeahnt

undress [ʌnˈdres] vt, vi [sich] ausziehen

undressed [ʌnˈdrest] adj pred unbekleidet

undue [ʌnˈdu] adj ungebührlich; **~ pressure** übermäßiger Druck

unduly [ʌnˈdu·li] adv unangemessen; concerned übermäßig

undying [ˌʌnˈdaɪ·ɪŋ] adj attr unvergänglich; love ewig

unearned [ˌʌnˈɜrnd] adj ❶ (undeserved) unverdient ❷ (not worked for) nicht erarbeitet

unearth [ʌnˈɜrθ] vt (discover) entdecken; truth ans Licht bringen

unearthly [ʌnˈɜrθ·li] adj ❶ (eerie) gespenstisch; noise grässlich ❷ (fam: inconvenient) **at some ~ hour** zu einer unchristlichen Zeit

unease [ʌnˈiz], **uneasiness** [ʌnˈiz·ɪ·nɪs] n Unbehagen nt

uneasy [ʌnˈi·zi] adj ❶ (anxious) besorgt; smile gequält ❷ (causing anxiety) unangenehm; relationship gespannt

uneconomic [ʌnˌek·əˈnam·ɪk] adj unwirtschaftlich

uneducated [ʌnˈedʒ·ə·keɪ·t̬ɪd] adj ungebildet

U

unemotional [ʌn·ɪˈmoʊ·ʃə·nəl] adj ❶ (not feeling emotions) kühl ❷ (not revealing emotions) emotionslos

unemployable [ʌn·ɪmˈplɔɪ·ə·bəl] adj unvermittelbar

unemployed [ʌn·ɪmˈplɔɪd] I. n ▪**the ~** pl die Arbeitslosen II. adj arbeitslos

unemployment [ˌʌn·ɪm·ˈplɔɪ·mənt] *n* Arbeitslosigkeit *f*

unemployment compen'sation, unemployment in'surance *n* Arbeitslosenunterstützung *f*, Arbeitslosengeld *nt*

unemployment office *n* Arbeitsamt *nt*

unenviable [ʌn·ˈen·vi·ə·bəl] *adj* wenig beneidenswert

unequal [ʌn·ˈiː·kwəl] *adj* ❶ (*different*) unterschiedlich; ~ **triangle** ungleichseitiges Dreieck ❷ (*unjust*) ungerecht; *contest* ungleich

unequaled, unequalled *adj* [ʌn·ˈiː·kwəld] unübertroffen

UNESCO [juːˈnes·koʊ] *n acr for* **United Nations Educational, Scientific and Cultural Organization**: ■[the] ~ die UNESCO

unethical [ʌn·ˈeθ·ɪ·kəl] *adj* unmoralisch

uneven [ʌn·ˈiː·vən] *adj* ❶ (*not level*) uneben ❷ (*not parallel*) ungleich; ~ **bars** (*gymnastics*) Stufenbarren *m* ❸ (*unfair*) unterschiedlich; *contest* ungleich ❹ (*odd*) ungerade

uneventful [ʌn·ɪ·ˈvent·fəl] *adj* ereignislos

unexceptional [ʌn·ɪk·ˈsep·ʃə·nəl] *adj* nicht außergewöhnlich

unexciting [ʌn·ɪk·ˈsaɪ·tɪŋ] *adj* (*uneventful*) ereignislos

unexpected [ʌn·ɪk·ˈspek·tɪd] I. *adj* unerwartet; *opportunity* unvorhergesehen II. *n* ■the ~ das Unerwartete

unexplained [ʌn·ɪk·ˈspleɪnd] *adj* unerklärt

unexpressed [ʌn·ɪk·ˈsprest] *adj* unausgesprochen

unfailing [ʌn·ˈfeɪ·lɪŋ] *adj* beständig; *loyalty* unerschütterlich

U

unfair [ʌn·ˈfer] *adj* ungerecht

unfaithful [ʌn·ˈfeɪθ·fʊl] *adj* untreu

unfamiliar [ʌn·fə·ˈmɪl·jər] *adj* unvertraut; *experience* ungewohnt; *place* unbekannt

unfashionable [ʌn·ˈfæʃ·ə·nə·bəl] *adj* unmodisch

unfasten [ʌn·ˈfæs·ən] I. *vt button, belt* öffnen II. *vi* aufgehen

unfavorable [ʌn·ˈfeɪ·vər·ə·bəl] *adj*

❶ (*adverse*) ungünstig; *decision* negativ ❷ (*disadvantageous*) nachteilig

unfeeling [ʌn·ˈfiː·lɪŋ] *adj* gefühllos

unfilled [ʌn·ˈfɪld] *adj* leer; *job* offen

unfinished [ʌn·ˈfɪn·ɪʃt] *adj* ❶ (*incomplete*) unvollendet; ~ **business** offene Fragen *pl* ❷ (*rough*) halbfertig

unfit [ʌn·ˈfɪt] *adj* ❶ (*unhealthy*) nicht fit; **to be ~ for work** arbeitsuntauglich sein ❷ (*incompetent*) ungeeignet

unflappable [ʌn·ˈflæp·ə·bəl] *adj* (*fam*) unerschütterlich

unflinching [ʌn·ˈflɪn·tʃɪŋ] *adj* unerschrocken; *determination* unbeirrbar

unfold [ʌn·ˈfoʊld] I. *vt* (*open*) entfalten; *furniture* aufklappen II. *vi* (*develop*) sich entwickeln ❷ (*open*) aufgehen

unforeseeable [ʌn·fɔr·ˈsiː·ə·bəl] *adj* unvorhersehbar

unforeseen [ʌn·fɔr·ˈsin] *adj* unvorhergesehen

unforgettable [ʌn·fər·ˈget·ə·bəl] *adj* unvergesslich

unforgivable [ʌn·fər·ˈgɪv·ə·bəl] *adj* unverzeihlich

unfortunate [ʌn·ˈfɔr·tʃə·nɪt] *adj* ❶ (*unlucky*) unglücklich ❷ (*regrettable*) bedauerlich; *manner* ungeschickt

unfortunately [ʌn·ˈfɔr·tʃə·nɪt·li] *adv* unglücklicherweise

unfriendly [ʌn·ˈfrend·li] *adj* unfreundlich; (*hostile*) feindlich; **environmentally ~** umweltschädlich

unfulfilled [ʌn·fʊl·ˈfɪld] *adj* *promise, life* unerfüllt

unfurnished [ʌn·ˈfɜr·nɪʃt] *adj* unmöbliert

ungainly [ʌn·ˈgeɪn·li] *adj* unbeholfen

UN General 'Assembly *n* UN-Vollversammlung *f*

ungentlemanly [ʌn·ˈdʒen·təl·mən·li] *adj* ungalant *geh*

ungrateful [ʌn·ˈgreɪt·fəl] *adj* undankbar

unhappy [ʌn·ˈhæp·i] *adj* unglücklich

unharmed [ʌn·ˈhɑrmd] *adj* unversehrt

unhealthy [ʌn·ˈhel·θi] *adj* ❶ (*unwell*) kränklich ❷ (*harmful*) ungesund

unheard [ʌn·ˈhɜrd] *adj* ungehört

un'heard-of *adj* ❶ (*unknown*) unbekannt ❷ (*unthinkable*) undenkbar

unhelpful [ʌn·'help·fʊl] *adj person* nicht hilfsbereit

unhoped-for [ʌn·'hoʊpt·ˌfɔr] *adj* unverhofft

unhurt [ʌn·'hɜrt] *adj* unverletzt

UNICEF ['ju·nɪ·sef] *n acr for* United Nations (International) Children's (Emergency) Fund UNICEF *f*

unidentified [ˌʌn·aɪ·'den·tə·faɪd] *adj* (*unknown*) nicht identifiziert

unification [ˌju·nɪ·fɪ·'keɪ·ʃən] *n* Vereinigung *f*

uniform ['ju·nə·fɔrm] I. *n* ❶ (*outfit*) Uniform *f* ❷ (*fam: police officer*) Polizist(in) *m(f)* II. *adj* ❶ (*same*) einheitlich ❷ (*consistent*) gleich bleibend; *color* einförmig

uniformity [ju·nə·'fɔr·mə·ti] *n* ❶ (*sameness*) Einheitlichkeit *f* ❷ (*consistency*) Gleichmäßigkeit *f*

unilateral [ju·nə·'læt·ər·əl] *adj* einseitig

unimaginable [ˌʌn·ɪ·'mædʒ·ə·nə·bəl] *adj* unvorstellbar

unimportant [ˌʌn·ɪm·'pɔr·tənt] *adj* unwichtig

uninhabited [ˌʌn·ɪn·'hæb·ɪtɪd] *adj building* unbewohnt; *land a.* unbesiedelt

uninhibited [ˌʌn·ɪn·'hɪb·ɪ·tɪd] *adj* ungehemmt

uninjured [ˌʌn·'ɪn·dʒərd] *adj* unverletzt

unintelligent [ˌʌn·ɪn·'tel·ɪ·dʒənt] *adj* unintelligent

unintelligible [ˌʌn·ɪn·'tel·ɪ·dʒə·bəl] *adj* unverständlich

unintentional [ˌʌn·ɪn·'ten·ʃə·nəl] *adj* unabsichtlich

uninterested [ˌʌn·'ɪn·tr·stɪd] *adj* uninteressiert; ■ **to be ~ in sth/sb** kein Interesse an etw/jdm haben

uninteresting [ˌʌn·'ɪn·tr·stɪŋ] *adj* uninteressant

uninterrupted [ˌʌn·ˌɪn·tər·'ʌp·tɪd] *adj* ununterbrochen; *rest* ungestört

union ['jun·jən] *n* ❶ (*state*) Union *f*

❷ (*organization*) Verband *m*; (*labor union*) Gewerkschaft *f*

unique [ju·'nik] *adj* ❶ (*only*) einzigartig ❷ (*exceptional*) einzigartig; *opportunity* einmalig

unisex ['ju·nɪ·seks] *adj* unisex

unison ['ju·nɪ·sən] *n* **to sing in ~** einstimmig singen; **to act in ~** in Übereinstimmung handeln

unit ['ju·nɪt] *n* ❶ (*standard*) Einheit *f* ❷ (*group*) Abteilung *f* ❸ (*furniture*) Element *nt* ❹ MATH Einer *m*

'unit cost *n* COMM Kosten *pl* pro Einheit

unite [ju·'naɪt] *vt, vi* [sich] vereinigen

united [ju·'naɪ·tɪd] *adj* (*joined*) vereinigt ▸ PHRASES: ~ **we stand, divided we fall** (*saying*) nur gemeinsam sind wir stark

United 'Kingdom *n* ■the ~ das Vereinigte Königreich

United 'Nations *n* ■the ~ die Vereinten Nationen *pl*

United 'States *n* + *sing vb* ■the ~ [of America] die Vereinigten Staaten *pl* [von Amerika]

universal [ju·nə·'vɜr·səl] *adj* universell; *agreement* allgemein; **~ truth** allgemein gültige Wahrheit

universe ['ju·nə·vɜrs] *n* ■the ~ das Universum

university [ju·nə·'vɜr·sɪ·ti] *n* Universität *f*

unjust [ʌn·'dʒʌst] *adj* ungerecht

unjustifiable [ʌn·ˌdʒʌs·tɪ·'faɪ·ə·bəl] *adj* nicht zu rechtfertigen *präd*

unjustified [ʌn·'dʒʌs·tɪ·faɪd] *adj* ungerechtfertigt; *complaint* unberechtigt

unkind [ʌn·'kaɪnd] *adj* (*mean*) unfreundlich, gemein

unknowing [ʌn·'noʊ·ɪŋ] *adj* ahnungslos

unknown [ʌn·'noʊn] I. *adj* unbekannt II. *n* ■the ~ das Unbekannte

unlawful [ʌn·'lɔ·fəl] *adj* rechtswidrig

unleaded [ʌn·'led·ɪd] *adj gasoline* bleifrei

unleavened [ʌn·'lev·ənd] *adj* ~ **bread** ungesäuertes Brot

unless [ən·'les] *conj* he won't come ~

U

he has time er wird nicht kommen, außer wenn er Zeit hat

unlicensed [ʌn·ˈlaɪ·sənst] *adj* ohne Lizenz *nach n*

unlike [ʌn·ˈlaɪk] *prep* ❶ (*different*) **to be ~ sb/sth** jdm/etw nicht ähnlich sein ❷ (*not normal for*) **to be ~ sb** für jdn nicht typisch sein

unlikely [ʌn·ˈlaɪk·li] *adj* ❶ (*improbable*) unwahrscheinlich ❷ (*unconvincing*) nicht überzeugend

unlimited [ʌn·ˈlɪm·ɪ·t̬ɪd] *adj* unbegrenzt

unlisted [ʌn·ˈlɪs·t̬ɪd] *adj* ❶ STOCKEX nicht notiert; *securities* unnotiert ❷ TELEC nicht verzeichnet

unload [ʌn·ˈloʊd] **I.** *vt* ❶ *vehicle* entladen; *container* ausladen; *dishwasher* ausräumen ❷ (*get rid*) abstoßen; *garbage* abladen **II.** *vi* ❶ (*empty*) abladen ❷ ECON entladen; *ship* löschen

unlock [ʌn·ˈlak] *vt* aufschließen

unlocked [ʌn·ˈlakt] *adj* unverschlossen

unlucky [ʌn·ˈlʌk·i] *adj* ❶ (*unfortunate*) glücklos ❷ (*causing bad luck*) ▪ **to be ~** Unglück bringen

unmanageable [ʌn·ˈmæn·ɪ·dʒə·bəl] *adj* unkontrollierbar; *child* außer Rand und Band *pred*

unmanned [ʌn·ˈmænd] *adj* unbemannt

unmarked [ʌn·ˈmarkt] *adj* ❶ (*without mark*) unbeschädigt ❷ *grave* namenlos; **~ [police] car** Zivilfahrzeug *nt* der Polizei

unmarried [ʌn·ˈmær·ɪd] *adj* unverheiratet

unmatched [ʌn·ˈmætʃt] *adj* unübertroffen

unmentionable [ʌn·ˈmen·ʃə·nə·bəl] *adj* unaussprechlich; ▪ **to be ~** tabu sein

unmistakable [ˌʌn·mɪ·ˈsteɪ·kə·bəl] *adj* unverkennbar; *symptom* eindeutig

unmitigated [ʌn·ˈmɪt̬·ɪ·geɪ·t̬ɪd] *adj* absolut; *disaster* total

unmoved [ʌn·ˈmuvd] *adj usu pred* unbewegt; (*emotionless*) ungerührt

unnamed [ʌn·ˈneɪmd] *adj* ungenannt

unnatural [ʌn·ˈnætʃ·ər·əl] *adj* unnatürlich; PSYCH abnorm

unnecessarily [ˌʌn·nes·ə·ˈser·ə·li] *adv* unnötigerweise

unnecessary [ʌn·ˈnes·ə·ser·i] *adj* unnötig

unnerve [ʌn·ˈnɜrv] *vt* nervös machen

unnoticed [ˌʌn·ˈnoʊ·t̬ɪst] *adj pred* unbemerkt

UN ob'server *n* UNO-Beobachter(in) *m(f)*

unobtainable [ˌʌn·əb·ˈteɪ·nə·bəl] *adj* unerreichbar

unobtrusive [ˌʌn·əb·ˈtru·sɪv] *adj* unaufdringlich

unoccupied [ˌʌn·ˈak·jə·paɪd] *adj seat* frei

unofficial [ˌʌn·ə·ˈfɪʃ·əl] *adj* inoffiziell

unorganized [ˌʌn·ˈɔr·gə·naɪzd] *adj* unorganisiert

unorthodox [ʌn·ˈɔr·θə·daks] *adj* unkonventionell; *method* ungewöhnlich

unpack [ʌn·ˈpæk] *vt, vi* auspacken; *car* ausladen

unpaid [ʌn·ˈpeɪd] *adj* unbezahlt; *invoice a.* ausstehend

unpalatable [ʌn·ˈpæl·ə·t̬ə·bəl] *adj* (*distasteful*) unangenehm

unperturbed [ˌʌn·pər·ˈtɜrbd] *adj* nicht beunruhigt

unpick [ʌn·ˈpɪk] *vt a seam* auftrennen

unplaced [ʌn·ˈpleɪst] *adj* SPORT unplatziert

unpleasant [ʌn·ˈplez·ənt] *adj* ❶ (*not pleasing*) unangenehm ❷ (*unfriendly*) unfreundlich

unplug <-gg-> [ʌn·ˈplʌg] *vt* ausstecken

unpolluted [ˌʌn·pə·ˈlu·t̬ɪd] *adj* unverschmutzt

unpopular [ʌn·ˈpap·jə·lər] *adj* ❶ (*not liked*) unbeliebt ❷ (*not accepted*) unpopulär

unpopularity [ˌʌn·ˌpap·jə·ˈler·ə·t̬i] *n of person* Unbeliebtheit *f*

unprecedented [ʌn·ˈpres·ə·den·t̬ɪd] *adj* noch nie da gewesen; *action* beispiellos

unpredictable [ˌʌn·prɪ·ˈdɪk·tə·bəl] *adj*

unvorhersehbar; *weather* unberechenbar

unprejudiced [ʌn·'predʒ·ə·dɪst] *adj* unvoreingenommen; *opinion* objektiv

unpretentious [ʌn·prɪ·'ten·ʃəs] *adj* bescheiden; *tastes* einfach

unproductive [ʌn·prə·'dʌk·tɪv] *adj* unproduktiv; *land* unfruchtbar

unprofessional [ʌn·prə·'feʃ·ə·nəl] *adj* ❶ (*amateurish*) unprofessionell ❷ (*unethical*) gegen die Berufsehre *präd*; ~ **conduct** berufswidriges Verhalten

unprofitable [ʌn·'praf·ɪ·tə·bəl] *adj* unrentabel

unprompted [ʌn·'pramp·tɪd] *adj* unaufgefordert

unprovoked [ʌn·prə·'voʊkt] *adj* grundlos

unpublished [ʌn·'pʌb·lɪʃt] *adj* unveröffentlicht

unqualified [ʌn·'kwal·ə·faɪd] *adj* ❶ unqualifiziert ❷ (*unreserved*) bedingungslos; *success* voll

unquestionable [ʌn·'kwes·tʃə·nə·bəl] *adj* fraglos; *honesty* unzweifelhaft

unquestioning [ʌn·'kwes·tʃə·nɪŋ] *adj* bedingungslos; *obedience* absolut

unquote ['ʌn·kwoʊt] *vi* quote ... ~ Zitatanfang ... Zitatende

unravel <-l-> [ʌn·'ræv·əl] I. *vt* ❶ (*undo*) auftrennen ❷ *knot* aufmachen ❸ *mystery* lösen II. *vi* sich auftrennen

unreadable [ʌn·'ri·də·bəl] *adj* ❶ (*illegible*) unleserlich ❷ (*dull*) schwer zu lesen *präd*

unreal [ʌn·'ril] *adj* unwirklich

unrealistic [ʌn·ri·ə·'lɪs·tɪk] *adj* unrealistisch

unreasonable [ʌn·'ri·zə·nə·bəl] *adj* ❶ unvernünftig ❷ *demand* überzogen

unrefined [ʌn·rɪ·'faɪnd] *adj* ❶ CHEM nicht raffiniert ❷ (*coarse*) unkultiviert

unregistered [ʌn·'redʒ·ɪ·stərd] *adj* nicht registriert; *birth* nicht eingetragen

unrelated [ʌn·rɪ·'leɪ·tɪd] *adj* ❶ (*not of family*) nicht [miteinander] verwandt ❷ (*unconnected*) ■ **to be** ~ nicht zusammenhängen (**to** mit +*dat*)

unreliable [ʌn·rɪ·'laɪ·ə·bəl] *adj* unzuverlässig

unrelieved [ʌn·rɪ·'livd] *adj* ununterbrochen; *boredom* dauernd

unremarkable [ʌn·rɪ·'mar·kə·bəl] *adj* nicht bemerkenswert

unrepeatable [ʌn·rɪ·'pi·tə·bəl] *adj* nicht wiederholbar

unrepentant [ʌn·rɪ·'pen·tənt] *adj* reu[e]los

unreserved [ʌn·rɪ·'zɜrvd] *adj* ❶ (*without reservations*) uneingeschränkt; *support* voll ❷ (*not booked*) nicht reserviert

unreservedly [ʌn·rɪ·'zɜrv·ɪd·li] *adv* vorbehaltlos

unrest [ʌn·'rest] *n* Unruhen *pl*; **social** ~ soziale Spannungen

unrestrained [ʌn·rɪ·'streɪnd] *adj* uneingeschränkt; *laughter* ungehemmt

unrestricted [ʌn·rɪ·'strɪk·tɪd] *adj* uneingeschränkt; *access* ungehindert

unripe [ʌn·'raɪp] *adj* unreif

unroll [ʌn·'roʊl] I. *vt* aufrollen II. *vi* sich abrollen [lassen]

unruly <-ier, -iest *or* more ~, most ~> [ʌn·'ru·li] *adj* ❶ (*disorderly*) ungebärdig; *crowd* aufrührerisch ❷ *hair* nicht zu bändigen *präd*

unsafe [ʌn·'seɪf] *adj* (*dangerous*) unsicher; *sex* ungeschützt

unsaid [ʌn·'sed] *adj* ungesagt ▶PHRASES: **what's** <u>said</u> **cannot be** ~ (*prov*) gesagt ist gesagt

UN 'sanction *n* UN-Sanktion *f*

unsatisfactory [ʌn·sæt·ɪs·'fæk·tə·ri] *adj* ❶ unzureichend; *answer* unbefriedigend ❷ SCH (*grade*) ungenügend

unsatisfied [ʌn·'sæt·ɪs·faɪd] *adj* unzufrieden

unsaturated [ʌn·'sætʃ·ə·reɪ·tɪd] *adj* CHEM, FOOD ungesättigt *attr*

unsavory [ʌn·'seɪ·və·ri] *adj* ❶ (*unpalatable*) unappetitlich ❷ (*asocial*) fragwürdig; *character* zwielichtig

unscathed [ʌn·'skeɪðd] *adj* **to emerge** ~ **from sth** (*fig*) etw unbeschadet überstehen

unscheduled [ʌn·'skedʒ·ʊld] *adj* außer-

U

planmäßig; *stop, landing* außerfahrplanmäßig

unscrew [ʌnˈskruː] **I.** *vt* ❶ (*detach*) abschrauben ❷ (*open*) aufschrauben **II.** *vi* (*detach*) sich abschrauben lassen

unscripted [ʌnˈskrɪptɪd] *adj* improvisiert

unscrupulous [ʌnˈskruːpjələs] *adj* skrupellos

unseal [ʌnˈsiːl] *vt* entsiegeln

unsecured [ˌʌnsɪˈkjʊrd] *adj* ❶ FIN **an ~ loan** Blankokredit *m* ❷ (*unfastened*) unbefestigt

UN Se'curity Council *n* UN-Sicherheitsrat *m*

unseen [ʌnˈsiːn] *adj* ungesehen

unselfish [ʌnˈselfɪʃ] *adj* selbstlos

unsettle [ʌnˈseṭəl] *vt* verunsichern

unsettled [ˌʌnˈseṭəld] *adj* ❶ *political climate* unruhig; *weather* unbeständig ❷ (*unresolved*) noch anstehend

unsettling [ˌʌnˈseṭəlɪŋ] *adj* beunruhigend

unshakable, unshakeable [ʌnˈʃeɪkəbəl] *adj belief* unerschütterlich; *alibi* felsenfest

unsightly <-ier, -iest *or* more ~, most ~> [ʌnˈsaɪtli] *adj* unansehnlich

unsigned [ʌnˈsaɪnd] *adj* nicht unterschrieben; *painting* unsigniert

unskilled [ʌnˈskɪld] *adj* ❶ (*inept*) ungeschickt ❷ *laborer* ungelernt

unsociable [ʌnˈsoʊʃəbəl] *adj person* ungesellig

unsocial [ʌnˈsoʊʃəl] *adj* unsozial

unsold [ʌnˈsoʊld] *adj* unverkauft

unsolved [ʌnˈsɑːlvd] *adj mystery, problem* ungelöst

U unsophisticated [ˌʌnsəˈfɪstəkeɪṭɪd] *adj* (*naive*) naiv; *taste* einfach

unsound [ʌnˈsaʊnd] *adj* ❶ (*unstable*) instabil ❷ *argument* nicht stichhaltig; *judgment* anfechtbar

unspecified [ʌnˈspesɪfaɪd] *adj* unspezifiziert

unspoiled [ʌnˈspɔɪld] *adj person* natürlich; *landscape* unberührt

unspoken [ʌnˈspoʊkən] *adj* unausgesprochen; *agreement* stillschweigend

unsportsmanlike [ʌnˈspɔːrtsmenˌlaɪk] *adj* unsportlich; *behavior* unfair

unstable [ʌnˈsteɪbəl] *adj* ❶ (*not firm*) nicht stabil; *furniture* wackelig ❷ (*fig*) instabil

unsteady [ʌnˈstedi] *adj* ❶ (*unstable*) nicht stabil ❷ (*wavering*) zittrig

unstuck [ʌnˈstʌk] *adj* **to come ~** sich [ab]lösen; (*fam: fail*) scheitern

unsubstantial [ˌʌnsəbˈstænʃəl] *adj* unwesentlich

unsuccessful [ˌʌnsəkˈsesfəl] *adj* erfolglos; *candidate* unterlegen; ■ **to be ~ in sth** bei etw *dat* keinen Erfolg haben

unsuitable [ʌnˈsuːṭəbəl] *adj* nicht geeignet

unsung [ʌnˈsʌŋ] *adj* unbesungen; *hero* unbeachtet

unsure [ʌnˈʃʊr] *adj* unsicher; ■ **to be ~ why ...** nicht genau wissen, warum ...

unsuspecting [ˌʌnsəˈspektɪŋ] *adj* ahnungslos

unsustainable [ˌʌnsəˈsteɪnəbəl] *adj* (*not maintainable*) nicht aufrechtzuerhalten *präd*

unsympathetic [ˌʌnsɪmpəˈθeṭɪk] *adj* ❶ ohne Mitgefühl *nach n* ❷ (*disapproving*) verständnislos; ■ **to be ~ toward sb** für jdn kein Verständnis haben

untangle [ʌnˈtæŋgəl] *vt* entwirren *a. fig; mystery* lösen

untapped [ʌnˈtæpt] *adj resources* ungenutzt

untaxed [ʌnˈtækst] *adj* (*tax-free*) steuerfrei

unthinkable [ʌnˈθɪŋkəbəl] *adj* undenkbar

unthinking [ʌnˈθɪŋkɪŋ] *adj* unbedacht; (*unintentional*) unabsichtlich

untidy [ʌnˈtaɪdi] *adj* (*disordered*) unordentlich; *appearance* ungepflegt

untie <-y-> [ʌnˈtaɪ] *vt* ❶ (*undo*) lösen ❷ *boat* losbinden

until [ənˈtɪl] **I.** *prep* ❶ (*up to*) bis +*akk;* **two more days ~ Easter** noch zwei Tage bis Ostern *+akk;* **we didn't eat ~ midnight** wir aßen erst um Mitternacht **II.** *conj* ❶ (*up to time when*) bis; **I laughed ~ tears**

rolled down my face ich lachte, bis mir die Tränen kamen ② (*not before*) ■ **to not do sth ~ ...** etw erst [dann] tun, wenn ...

untimely [ʌnˈtaɪm·li] *adj* (*inopportune*) ungelegen

untold [ʌnˈtoʊld] *adj attr* unsagbar; *damage* immens; *wealth* unermesslich

untouched [ʌnˈtʌtʃt] *adj* ① (*not touched*) unberührt ② (*unaffected*) ■ **to be ~ by sth** von etw *dat* nicht betroffen sein

untoward [ʌnˈtɔrd] *adj* ① (*unfortunate*) ungünstig ② *remark* unpassend

untrained [ʌnˈtreɪnd] *adj* ungeübt; *eye* ungeschult

untranslatable [ʌn·træns·ˈleɪ·t̬ə·bəl] *adj* unübersetzbar

untreated [ʌnˈtriˌt̬ɪd] *adj* unbehandelt; ~ **sewage** ungeklärte Abwässer *pl*

untried [ʌnˈtraɪd] *adj* (*inexperienced*) unerfahren

untrue [ʌnˈtru] *adj* unwahr

untrustworthy [ʌnˈtrʌst·ˌwɜr·ði] *adj* unzuverlässig

untruthful [ʌnˈtruθ·fəl] *adj* unwahr; *person* unaufrichtig

unused[1] [ʌnˈjuzd] *adj* unbenutzt; **to go ~** nicht genutzt werden

unused[2] [ʌnˈjuzd] *adj pred* ■ **to be ~ to sth** an etw *akk* nicht gewöhnt sein

unusual [ʌnˈju·ʒu·əl] *adj* ungewöhnlich

unusually [ʌnˈju·ʒu·ə·li] *adv* ungewöhnlich

unveil [ʌnˈveɪl] *vt* enthüllen

unwanted [ʌnˈwan·tɪd] *adj* unerwünscht; *clothes* abgelegt

unwelcome [ʌnˈwel·kəm] *adj* unwillkommen; **to make sb feel ~** jdm das Gefühl geben, nicht willkommen zu sein

unwell [ʌnˈwel] *adj pred* ■ **sb is ~** jdm geht es nicht gut; **to feel ~** sich unwohl fühlen

unwilling [ʌnˈwɪl·ɪŋ] *adj* ■ **to be ~ to do sth** nicht gewillt sein, etw zu tun

unwillingly [ʌnˈwɪl·ɪŋ·li] *adv* ungern

unwind <unwound, unwound> [ʌnˈwaɪnd] I. *vi* ① (*unroll*) sich abwickeln

② (*relax*) sich entspannen II. *vt* abwickeln

unwise [ʌnˈwaɪz] *adj* unklug

unwittingly [ʌnˈwɪt̬·ɪŋ·li] *adv* ① (*without realizing*) unwissentlich ② (*unintentionally*) unbeabsichtigterweise

unworkable [ʌnˈwɜr·kə·bəl] *adj* undurchführbar

unworldly [ʌnˈwɜrld·li] *adj* (*naive*) weltfremd

unworthy [ʌnˈwɜr·ði] *adj* unwürdig; ~ **of interest** nicht von Interesse

unwrap <-pp-> [ʌnˈræp] *vt contents* auspacken

unwritten [ʌnˈrɪt̬·ən] *adj* nicht schriftlich fixiert; *agreement* stillschweigend

unzip <-pp-> [ʌnˈzɪp] *vt* ① (*open*) ■ **to ~ sth** den Reißverschluss einer S. *gen* aufmachen ② COMPUT auspacken

up [ʌp] I. *adv* ① (*to higher*) nach oben; **halfway ~** auf halber Höhe ② (*erect*) aufrecht; **lean it ~ against the wall** lehnen Sie es gegen die Wand ③ (*out of bed*) auf; ~ **and about** auf den Beinen ④ (*at higher*) oben; ~ **there** da oben ⑤ (*toward*) ■ ~ **to sb/sth** auf jdn/etw zu; **to walk ~ to sb** auf jdn zugehen ⑥ (*to point of*) ~ **until** [*or* **to**] bis +*akk*; ~ **to 300 dollars** bis zu 300 Dollar II. *prep* ① (*to higher*) hinauf/herauf; ~ **the ladder** die Leiter hinauf/herauf ② (*along*) [**just**] ~ **the road** ein Stück die Straße hinauf/herauf; ~ **and down** auf und ab ③ (*against*) ~ **the river** flussauf[wärts] ④ (*at top of*) **he's ~ that ladder** er steht dort oben auf der Leiter ▶ PHRASES: ~ **yours!** (*vulg, sl*) ihr könnt/ du kannst mich mal! III. *adj* ① *attr* (*rising*) nach oben ② *pred* (*finished*) vorbei, um; **your time is ~!** Ihre Zeit ist um! ③ *pred* (*fam: happening*) **what's ~?** was ist los? IV. *n* (*fam*) Hoch *nt*; ~**s and downs** Höhen und Tiefen *pl* V. *vt* <-pp-> erhöhen; *price, tax* anheben; **to ~ the stakes** den Einsatz erhöhen

up-and-ˈcoming *adj attr* aufstrebend

upbeat [ˈʌp·bit] *adj* (*fam*) optimistisch; *mood* fröhlich

U

upbringing ['ʌp·brɪŋ·ɪŋ] n usu sing Erziehung f

upcoming ['ʌp·ˌkʌm·ɪŋ] adj bevorstehend

update I. vt [ʌp·'deɪt] ❶ (modernize) aktualisieren; hardware nachrüsten ❷ (inform) auf den neuesten Stand bringen II. n ['ʌp·deɪt] Update nt fachspr

upend [ʌp·'end] vt hochkant stellen

upfront [ʌp·'frʌnt] adj ❶ pred (frank) offen; **to be ~ about sth** etw offen sagen ❷ attr (advance) Voraus-; **~ payment** Anzahlung f

upgrade ['ʌp·greɪd] I. vt ❶ COMPUT erweitern; hardware nachrüsten ❷ (promote) befördern II. n ❶ COMPUT Aufrüsten nt ❷ (version) verbesserte Version

upheaval [ʌp·'hi·vəl] n Aufruhr m; **political ~** politische Umwälzung[en] f[pl]

uphill [ʌp·'hɪl] adv, adj bergauf

uphold <-held, -held> [ʌp·'hould] vt aufrechterhalten; verdict bestätigen

upholstery [ʌp·'houl·stə·ri] n (padding) Polsterung f; (covering) Bezug m

upkeep ['ʌp·kip] n ❶ (maintenance) Instandhaltung f ❷ of person Unterhalt m; of animals Haltungskosten f

uplift [ʌp·'lɪft] vt ❶ (raise) anheben ❷ (inspire) [moralisch] aufrichten

uplifting [ʌp·'lɪf·tɪŋ] adj erbaulich

upload ['ʌp·loud] INET I. vt, vi hochladen, uploaden II. n Upload m

upon [ə·'pan] prep (form) ❶ (on top of) auf +dat; with verbs of motion auf +akk ❷ (hanging on) an +dat ❸ (at time of) **once ~ a time** [es war einmal] vor langer Zeit

upper ['ʌp·ər] adj attr ❶ (higher) obere(r, s); arm, lip Ober- ❷ rank höhere(r, s) ❸ location höher gelegen

'upper case n TYPO ■**in ~** in Großbuchstaben

upper 'class n Oberschicht f

upper 'deck n Oberdeck nt

uppermost ['ʌp·ər·moust] adj oberste(r, s)

uppity ['ʌp·ə·ti] adj (pej fam) hochnäsig

upright ['ʌp·raɪt] I. adj ❶ (vertical)

senkrecht; (erect) aufrecht ❷ (honest) anständig II. adv (vertical) senkrecht; (erect) aufrecht; **bolt ~** kerzengerade III. n SPORT Pfosten m

uprising ['ʌp·raɪ·zɪŋ] n Aufstand m

uproar ['ʌp·rɔr] n ❶ (noise) Lärm m ❷ (protest) Aufruhr m

uproot [ʌp·'rut] vt ❶ (extract) herausreißen; tree entwurzeln ❷ ■**to ~ oneself** seine Heimat verlassen

upscale [ʌp·'skeɪl] adj goods hochwertig

upset I. vt [ʌp·'set] ❶ (push over) umwerfen; a glass umstoßen ❷ (unsettle) aus der Fassung bringen; (distress) mitnehmen II. adj [ʌp·'set] ❶ pred (nervous) aufgeregt; (angry) aufgebracht; (distressed) bestürzt ❷ **to have an ~ stomach** sich dat den Magen verdorben haben III. n ['ʌp·set] (trouble) Ärger m; (argument) Verstimmung f

upsetting [ʌp·'set·ɪŋ] adj erschütternd; (saddening) traurig

upshot ['ʌp·ʃat] n [End]ergebnis nt

upside 'down I. adj (inverted) auf dem Kopf stehend attr; **that picture is ~** das Bild hängt verkehrt herum II. adv verkehrt herum; **to turn sth ~** etw auf den Kopf stellen a. fig

upstage ['ʌp·steɪdʒ] vt ■**to ~ sb** jdm die Schau stehlen

upstairs [ˌʌp·'sterz] I. adj oben präd, obere(r, s) attr II. adv (to higher) nach oben; (at higher) oben

upstart ['ʌp·start] n (pej) Emporkömmling m

upstate ['ʌp·steɪt] adj im ländlichen Norden [des Bundesstaates] nach n; **in ~ New York** im ländlichen Teil New Yorks

upstream [ʌp·'strim] adv flussaufwärts

upswing ['ʌp·swɪŋ] n ECON Aufschwung m

uptake ['ʌp·teɪk] n ▸PHRASES: **to be slow on the ~** (fam) schwer von Begriff sein

uptight [ʌp·'taɪt] adj (fam) ❶ (nervous) nervös; (anxious) ängstlich ❷ (inhibited) verklemmt 'up-to-'date *adj attr information* aktuell

up-to-the-'minute *adj* hochaktuell

uptown [ˈʌpˌtaʊn] *adj* to live in ~ Manhattan im nördlichen Teil Manhattans leben

upturn [ˈʌpˌtɜrn] *n* Aufschwung *m*

upturned [ʌpˈtɜrnd] *adj* nach oben gewendet; *boat* gekentert

upward [ˈʌpwərd] I. *adj* Aufwärts-II. *adv* nach oben; from childhood ~ von Kindheit an

upwardly [ˈʌpwərdli] *adv* nach oben, aufwärts; ~ mobile aufstrebend und erfolgreich

upwards [ˈʌpwərdz] *adv* nach oben, aufwärts

uranium [juˈreɪniəm] *n* Uran *nt*

urban [ˈɜrbən] *adj attr* städtisch; ~ area Stadtgebiet *nt*

urbane [ɜrˈbeɪn] *adj* weltmännisch; *manner* kultiviert

urbanization [ˌɜrbənɪˈzeɪʃən] *n* Verstädterung *f*

urchin [ˈɜrtʃɪn] *n* ❶ ZOOL Seeigel *m* ❷ (*child*) [street] ~ Straßenkind *nt*

urge [ɜrdʒ] I. *n* Verlangen *nt*; (*compulsion*) Drang *m* II. *vt* ❶ (*persuade*) **to ~ sb** [to do sth] jdn drängen[, etw zu tun] ❷ (*advocate*) ■ **to ~ sth** auf etw *akk* dringen, zu etw *dat* drängen; **to ~ caution** zur Vorsicht mahnen

urgency [ˈɜrdʒənsi] *n* Dringlichkeit *f*; **to be a matter of ~** äußerst dringend sein

urgent [ˈɜrdʒənt] *adj* (*imperative*) dringend; (*on letter*) „eilt"

urgently [ˈɜrdʒəntli] *adv* dringend

urinate [ˈjʊrəˌneɪt] *vi* urinieren

urine [ˈjʊrɪn] *n* Urin *m*

URL [ˌjuˌɑrˈel] *n abbrev of* **uniform resource locator** URL *m*

urn [ɜrn] *n* (*vase*) Krug *m*; (*for remains*) [Grab]urne *f*

us [əs, *stressed:* ʌs] *pron* (*object of we*) uns *dat o akk*; **let ~ know** lassen Sie es uns wissen; **both of ~** wir beide; **it's ~** wir sind's

U.S., US [ˌjuˈes] *n abbrev of* **United States**: ■ **the ~** die USA *pl*

USA, U.S.A. [ˌjuˌesˈeɪ] *n abbrev of* **United States of America**: ■ **the ~** die USA *pl*

USAF [ˌjuˌesˌeɪˈef] *n abbrev of* **United States Air Force**: ■ **the ~** die US-Luftwaffe

usage [ˈjuːsɪdʒ] *n* ❶ (*practice*) Usus *m* geh ❷ (*of word*) Verwendung *f*

USB [ˌjuˌesˈbiː] *n acr for* **Universal Serial Bus** COMPUT USB *m*; ~ **[flash] drive** USB-Stick *m*

use I. *vt* [juz] ❶ (*utilize*) benutzen; *skills, talent* nutzen; *method* anwenden; *dictionary, idea* verwenden; **I could ~ some help** ich könnte etwas Hilfe gebrauchen; **to ~ drugs** Drogen nehmen ❷ (*employ*) einsetzen; **to ~ common sense** seinen gesunden Menschenverstand benutzen ❸ (*consume*) verbrauchen; **this radio ~s four AAA batteries** für dieses Radio braucht man vier AAA Batterien ❹ (*exploit*) ausnutzen II. *n* [jus] ❶ (*utilization*) Verwendung *f*; *of dictionary* a. Benutzung *f*; *of talent, experience* Nutzung *m*; *of method* Anwendung *f*; **directions for ~** Gebrauchsanweisung *f*; **for external ~ only** nur zur äußerlichen Anwendung; **to find a ~ for sth** für etw *akk* Verwendung finden; **to make ~ of sth** etw benutzen; *experience, talent* etw nutzen ❷ (*consumption*) Verwendung *f* ❸ (*usefulness*) Nutzen *m*; **can I be of any ~?** kann ich vielleicht irgendwie behilflich sein?; **it's no ~** [doing sth] es hat keinen Zweck[, etw zu tun]

♦ **use up** *vt* verbrauchen; (*completely*) [völlig] aufbrauchen

used[1] [juzd] *vt only in past* **my father ~ to say ...** mein Vater sagte [früher] immer, ...

used[2] [juzd] *adj* (*old*) gebraucht

used[3] [juzd] *adj* (*accustomed*) ■ **to be ~ to sth** etw gewohnt sein

useful [ˈjusfəl] *adj* ❶ (*practical*) nützlich (**for** für +*akk*) ❷ (*advantageous*) wertvoll; **to come in ~** gut zu gebrauchen sein

U

usefulness ['jus·fəl·nɪs] *n* Nützlichkeit *f*; (*applicability*) Verwendbarkeit *f*

useless ['jus·lɪs] *adj* ❶ (*pointless*) sinnlos ❷ (*fam: inept*) zu nichts zu gebrauchen *präd*; **he's a ~ goalkeeper** er taugt nichts als Torwart ❸ (*unusable*) unbrauchbar

user ['ju·zər] *n* Benutzer(in) *m(f)*; *of software, system a.* Anwender(in) *m(f)*; *of electricity, gas* Verbraucher(in) *m(f)*

'user-friendly *adj* COMPUT benutzerfreundlich

user 'interface *n* COMPUT Benutzeroberfläche *f*

USP [ju·es·'pi] *n* ECON *abbrev of* **unique selling proposition** USP *m*

USPS [ju·es·pi·'es] *n abbrev of* **United States Postal Service** US-amerikanische staatliche Postgesellschaft

USS [ju·es·'es] *n abbrev of* **United States Ship** Schiff aus den Vereinigten Staaten

usual ['ju·ʒu·əl] *adj* üblich, normal; **to find sth in its ~ place** etw an seinem gewohnten Platz vorfinden

usually ['ju·ʒu·ə·li] *adv* normalerweise; **more … than ~** mehr … als sonst

usurp [ju·'sɜrp] *vt* ❶ *power* an sich *akk* reißen ❷ (*oust*) verdrängen

UT, Ut. *abbrev of* **Utah**

Utah ['ju·tɔ] *n* Utah *nt*

utensil [ju·'ten·səl] *n* Utensil *nt*; **kitchen ~s** Küchengeräte *pl*

utility [ju·'tɪl·ɪ·ti] **I.** *n* ❶ (*usefulness*) Nützlichkeit *f* ❷ (*provider*) **public ~** öffentlicher Versorgungsbetrieb **II.** *adj* **~ vehicle** Mehrzweckfahrzeug *nt*

u'tility room *n* Raum, in dem Haushaltsgeräte, wie z. B. Waschmaschine und Trockner stehen, und der ebenfalls als Vorratskeller dient

utilization [ju·tɪ·lɪ·'zer·ʃən] *n* Verwendung *f*

utilize ['ju·tɪ·laɪz] *vt* nutzen

utmost ['ʌt·moust] *adj attr* größte(r, s); **of the ~ importance** von äußerster Wichtigkeit

utter[1] ['ʌt·ər] *adj attr* vollkommen; **~ nonsense** absoluter Blödsinn

utter[2] ['ʌt·ər] *vt* ❶ (*give voice to*) von sich *dat* geben; **without ~ing a word** ohne ein Wort zu sagen ❷ (*speak out*) sagen; *curse* ausstoßen

utterly ['ʌt·ər·li] *adv* vollkommen; **to be ~ convinced that …** vollkommen [davon] überzeugt sein, dass …

U-turn ['ju·tɜrn] *n* ❶ (*of car*) Wende *f* ❷ (*change*) Kehrtwendung *f*

U

Vv

V <pl -'s> n, **v** <pl -'s> [vi] n (letter) V nt, v nt; **~ as in Victor** V wie Viktor
v [vi] **I.** n LING abbrev of **verb** v **II.** prep abbrev of **verse, verso, versus** vs. **III.** adv abbrev of **very**

VA, Va. abbrev of **Virginia**

vac [væk] **I.** n (fam) short for **vacuum cleaner** Staubsauger m **II.** vt, vi <-cc-> (fam) short for **vacuum clean** [staub]saugen

vacancy ['veɪ·kən·si] n ❶ (room) freies Zimmer; **"no vacancies"** „belegt" ❷ (job) freie Stelle; **to fill a ~** eine [freie] Stelle besetzen

vacant ['veɪ·kənt] adj ❶ (empty) bed, seat frei; land unbebaut ❷ job unbesetzt

vacate ['veɪ·keɪt] vt räumen; place, seat frei machen

vacation [veɪ·'keɪ·ʃən] **I.** n ❶ (holiday) Ferien pl, Urlaub m; **to take a ~** Urlaub machen; ■**on ~** im Urlaub ❷ UNIV Semesterferien pl; LAW Gerichtsferien pl **II.** vi Urlaub machen

vacationer [veɪ·'keɪ·ʃə·nər] n Urlauber(in) m(f)

vaccinate ['væk·sə·neɪt] vt impfen

vaccination [ˌvæk·sə·'neɪ·ʃən] n [Schutz]impfung f

vaccine [væk·'sin] n Impfstoff m

vacuum <pl -s> ['væk·jum] **I.** n ❶ Vakuum nt ❷ (fig: gap) Vakuum nt, Lücke f ❸ (vacuum cleaner) Staubsauger m **II.** vt [staub]saugen

'vacuum cleaner n Staubsauger m

'vacuum-packed adj vakuumverpackt

vagina <pl -s> [və·'dʒaɪ·nə] n ANAT Vagina f, Scheide f

vagrant ['veɪ·grənt] n Obdachlose(r) f(m)

vague [veɪg] adj ❶ ungenau, vage; blurred verschwommen ❷ person zerstreut

vagueness ['veɪg·nəs] n Unbestimmtheit f

vain [veɪn] adj ❶ (conceited) eingebildet; (about one's looks) eitel ❷ (futile) sinnlos; hope töricht ❸ (unsuccessful) **in ~** vergeblich

valance ['væl·əns] n ❶ (on bed) Volant m ❷ (on curtain rail) Querbehang m

valedictorian [ˌvæl·ə·dɪk·'tɔr·i·ən] n Abschiedsredner(in) m(f) (Jahrgangsbeste(r), die/der bei Schul- oder Universitätsentlassungsfeiern eine Abschiedsrede hält)

valedictory [ˌvæl·ə·'dɪk·tə·ri] adj (school-leaving) **~ address** Abschiedsrede f

valentine ['væl·ən·taɪn] n Valentinskarte f

'Valentine's Day n Valentinstag m

'valet parking n Parkservice m

valid ['væl·ɪd] adj ❶ (well-founded) begründet; argument stichhaltig; criticism gerechtfertigt ❷ (in force) gültig

validate ['væl·ə·deɪt] vt bestätigen

validity [və·'lɪd·ə·ti] n Gültigkeit f; (value) Wert m

valley ['væl·i] n Tal nt

valuable ['væl·ju·ə·bəl] **I.** adj wertvoll **II.** n usu pl Wertsachen pl

valuation [ˌvæl·ju·'eɪ·ʃən] n ❶ (appraisal) **to make a ~** of sth etw schätzen ❷ (price) Schätzwert m

value ['væl·ju] **I.** n ❶ Wert m; **to be of little ~** wenig Wert haben ❷ (ethics) ■**~s** pl Werte pl **II.** vt schätzen

valued ['væl·jud] adj geschätzt

valueless ['væl·ju·lɪs] adj wertlos

valve [vælv] n Ventil nt

vampire ['væm·paɪr] n Vampir(in) m(f)

van [væn] n (truck) Transporter m; **delivery ~** Lieferwagen m

vandal ['væn·dəl] n Vandale(in) m(f) pej

vandalism ['væn·də·lɪz·əm] n Vandalismus m

vanguard ['væn·gard] n (fig: leader) **to**

V

be in the ~ of sth zu den Vorreitern einer S. gen gehören

vanilla [və·'nɪl·ə] I. *n* Vanille *f* II. *adj* (*fig: ordinary*) **plain ~** nullachtfuffzehn *fam*

vanish ['væn·ɪʃ] *vi* verschwinden; **to ~ into thin air** sich in Luft auflösen

'**vanishing point** *n* Fluchtpunkt *m*

vanity ['væn·ə·ţi] *n* Eitelkeit *f*

vantage ['væn·tɪdʒ] *n* Aussichtspunkt *m*

'**vantage point** *n* ① (*outlook*) Aussichtspunkt *m* ② (*fig: perspective*) Blickpunkt *m*

vapor ['veɪ·pər] *n* Dampf *m*

vaporization [ˌveɪ·pər·ɪ·'zeɪ·ʃən] *n* Verdampfung *f*

vaporize ['veɪ·pə·raɪz] *vt*, *vi* verdampfen

vaporizer ['veɪ·pə·raɪ·zər] *n* Inhalator *m*

'**vapor trail** *n* Kondensstreifen *m*

variable ['vær·i·ə·bəl] I. *n* Variable *f* II. *adj* variabel, veränderlich; *weather* unbeständig

variance ['vær·i·əns] *n* ① ■**to be at ~ with sth** mit etw *dat* nicht übereinstimmen ② (*variation*) Abweichung *f*

variant ['vær·i·ənt] *n* Variante *f*

variation [ˌvær·i·'eɪ·ʃən] *n* ① (*variability*) Abweichung *f* ② (*difference*) Schwankung[en] *f/pl*

varied ['vær·id] *adj* unterschiedlich; *career* bewegt; *group* bunt gemischt

variegated ['vær·i·ə·geɪ·tɪd] *adj* (*multicolored*) mischfarbig; *leaves* bunt

variety [və·'raɪ·ə·ţi] *n* ① (*diversity*) Verschiedenartigkeit *f*; (*in job a.*) Abwechslungsreichtum *m* ② (*assortment*) Vielfalt *f* ③ (*category*) Art *f*; BIOL Spezies *f*

va'riety show *n* Varieteeshow *f*

various ['vær·i·əs] *adj* verschieden

varnish ['var·nɪʃ] I. *n* <*pl* -es> Lack *m* II. *vt* lackieren

vary <-ie-> ['vær·i] I. *vi* ① (*differ*) variieren, verschieden sein; **to ~ greatly** stark voneinander abweichen ② (*change*) sich verändern II. *vt* variieren

varying ['veri·ɪŋ] *adj* unterschiedlich

vase [veɪs] *n* Vase *f*

vast [væst] *adj* gewaltig; *country* weit; *majority* überwältigend

vat [væt] *n* Fass *nt*

Vatican ['væţ·ɪ·kən] *n* ■**the ~** der Vatikan

vault [vɔlt] I. *n* ① (*arch*) Gewölbebogen *m* ② (*strong room*) Tresorraum *m*; (*safe*) Magazin *nt* ③ (*jump*) Sprung *m* II. *vt* ■**to ~ sth** über etw *akk* springen

vaulted ['vɔl·tɪd] *adj* gewölbt

VCR [ˌvi·si·'ar] *n* *abbrev of* **videocassette recorder** Videorekorder *m*

veal [vil] *n* Kalbfleisch *nt*

veg <-gg-> [vedʒ] *vi* (*fam*) ■**to ~ out** herumhängen

vegan ['vi·gən] *n* Veganer(in) *m(f)*

vegetable ['vedʒ·tə·bəl] *n* ① (*edible plant*) Gemüse *nt* ② (*not animal or mineral*) Pflanze *f*

'**vegetable fat** *n* pflanzliches Fett

'**vegetable garden** *n* Gemüsegarten *m*

'**vegetable oil** *n* pflanzliches Öl

vegetarian [ˌvedʒ·ə·'ter·i·ən] *n* Vegetarier(in) *m(f)*

vegetate ['vedʒ·ə·teɪt] *vi* vegetieren

vegetation [ˌvedʒ·ə·'teɪ·ʃən] *n* Pflanzen *pl*

veggie ['vedʒ·i] *n* (*fam*) *short for* **vegetable**

vehement ['vi·ə·mənt] *adj* vehement, heftig; *critic* scharf

vehicle ['vi·ə·kəl] *n* Fahrzeug *nt*

veil [veɪl] *n* Schleier *m* *a. fig*

veiled [veɪld] *adj* (*fig: hidden*) verschleiert; *threat* versteckt

vein [veɪn] *n* ① (*vessel*) Vene *f* ② BOT, ZOOL, MIN Ader *f*

veined [veɪnd] *adj* geädert

Velcro® ['vel·kroʊ] *n* Klettverschluss *m*

velocity [və·'las·ə·ţi] *n* Geschwindigkeit *f*

velvet ['vel·vɪt] *n* Samt *m*

velvety ['vel·və·ţi] *adj* samtig

vend [vend] *vt* verkaufen

vendetta [ven·'deţ·ə] *n* Vendetta *f*

'**vending machine** *n* Automat *m*

vendor ['ven·dər] *n* Straßenverkäufer(in) *m(f)*

veneer [və·'nɪr] *n* ❶ (*layer*) Furnier *nt* ❷ (*fig: front*) Fassade *f*

venerable ['ven·ə·rə·bəl] *adj* ehrwürdig; *tradition* alt

venereal [və·'nɪr·i·əl] *adj* ~ **disease** Geschlechtskrankheit *f*

venetian 'blind *n* Jalousie *f*

Venezuela [ˌven·ə·'zwei·lə] *n* Venezuela *nt*

vengeance ['ven·dʒəns] *n* Rache *f*

venison ['ven·ɪ·sən] *n* Rehfleisch *nt*

venom ['ven·əm] *n* Gift *nt*

venomous ['ven·ə·məs] *adj* giftig *a. fig*

vent [vent] **I.** *n* ❶ (*outlet*) Abzug *m*; **air ~** Luftschacht *m* ❷ (*fig: release*) Ventil *nt*; **to give ~ to one's anger** seinem Ärger Luft machen **II.** *vt* **to ~ one's anger on sb** seine Wut an jdm auslassen

ventilate ['ven·tə·leit] *vt* lüften

ventilation [ˌven·tə·'lei·ʃən] *n* Belüftung *f*

ventilator ['ven·tə·lei·tər] *n* Ventilator *m*

ventriloquist [ven·'trɪl·ə·kwɪst] *n* Bauchredner(in) *m(f)*

venture ['ven·tʃər] **I.** *n* Projekt *nt* **II.** *vt* *opinion* vorsichtig äußern

'venture capital *n* Risikokapital *nt*

venue ['ven·ju] *n* (*site*) Veranstaltungsort *m*; (*for competition*) Austragungsort *m*

veranda(h) [və·'ræn·də] *n* Veranda *f*

verb [vɜrb] *n* Verb *nt*

verbal ['vɜr·bəl] *adj* mündlich

verbalize ['vɜr·bə·laɪz] *vt* ausdrücken

verbally ['vɜr·bə·li] *adv* mündlich

verbatim [vər·'bei·tɪm] *adv* wortwörtlich

verbose [vər·'bous] *adj* wortreich; *speech* weitschweifig

verdict ['vɜr·dɪkt] *n* Urteil *nt*; ~ **of not guilty** Freispruch *m*; **unanimous ~** einstimmiges Urteil; **to return a ~** ein Urteil verkünden

verdigris ['vɜr·dɪ·grɪs] *n* Grünspan *m*

verge [vɜrdʒ] *n* ❶ (*edge*) Rand *m* ❷ (*fig: brink*) **to be on the ~ of collapse** kurz vor dem Zusammenbruch stehen

verifiable [ˌver·ə·'faɪə·bəl] *adj fact* überprüfbar; *theory* nachweisbar

verification [ˌver·ə·fɪ·'kei·ʃən] *n* Verifizierung *f* geh; (*checking*) Überprüfung *f*

verify <-ie-> ['ver·ə·faɪ] *vt* (*check*) überprüfen; (*confirm*) belegen

vermicelli [ˌvɜr·mə·'tʃel·i] *npl* Fadennudeln *pl*

vermin ['vɜr·mɪn] *npl* (*animals*) Schädlinge *pl*; **to control ~** Ungeziefer bekämpfen

Vermont [vər·'mant] *n* Vermont *nt*

vermouth [vər·'muθ] *n* Wermut *m*

vernacular [vər·'næk·jə·lər] *n* Umgangssprache *f*; (*dialect*) Dialekt *m*

versatile ['vɜr·sə·təl] *adj* vielseitig

versatility [ˌvɜr·sə·'tɪl·ə·ti] *n* Vielseitigkeit *f*

verse [vɜrs] *n* ❶ (*poetry*) Dichtung *f*; **in ~** in Versen *m* ❷ (*poem, song*) Strophe *f*

versed [vɜrst] *adj* **to be [well] ~ in sth** (*knowledgeable about*) in etw *dat* [sehr] versiert sein *geh*

version ['vɜr·ʒən] *n* (*variant*) Version *f*; *of book, text* Fassung *f*; **abridged ~** Kurzfassung *f*

versus ['vɜr·səs] *prep* gegen

vertebra <*pl* -brae> ['vɜr·tə·brə] *n* Wirbel *m*

vertebrate ['vɜr·tə·brɪt] *n* Wirbeltier *nt*

vertical ['vɜr·tə·kəl] *adj* senkrecht

vertigo ['vɜr·tə·gou] *n* Schwindel *m*

verve [vɜrv] *n* Begeisterung *f*

very ['ver·i] **I.** *adv* ❶ (*extremely*) sehr, außerordentlich ❷ (*to great degree*) sehr; ~ **much** sehr ❸ + *superl* (*to add force*) aller-; **to do the ~ best one can** sein Allerbestes geben; **at the ~ most** allerhöchstens; **the ~ next day** schon am nächsten Tag **II.** *adj attr* **at the ~ bottom** zuunterst; **the ~ fact that ...** allein schon die Tatsache, dass ...; **they're the ~ opposite of one another** sie sind völlig unterschiedlich

vessel ['ves·əl] *n* ❶ (*ship*) Schiff *nt* ❷ (*container*) Gefäß *nt*

V

vest [vest] n [Anzug]weste f

vestibule ['ves·tə·bjul] n (foyer) Vorraum m; (in theater) Foyer nt

vestige ['ves·tɪdʒ] n (trace) Spur f

vestry ['ves·tri] n Sakristei f

vet[1] [vet] n Tierarzt, Tierärztin m, f

vet[2] [vet] n (fam) short for **veteran** Veteran(in) m(f)

veteran ['veṭ·ər·ən] n (expert, ex-military) Veteran(in) m(f) hum, alter Hase hum

Veteran's Day n Veteranentag m (der 11. November als Andenken an den Waffenstillstand zwischen Deutschland und den Alliierten 1918)

veterinarian [ˌvet·ər·ə·'ner·i·ən] n Tierarzt, Tierärztin m, f

veterinary ['vet·ər·ə·ner·i] adj attr tierärztlich; ~ **medicine** Tiermedizin f

veto ['vi·tou] I. n <pl -es> ❶ (nullification) Veto nt ❷ (right of refusal) Vetorecht nt II. vt ❶ (refuse) ein Veto einlegen gegen +akk ❷ (forbid) untersagen

vex [veks] vt verärgern

VHF [ˌvi·eɪtʃ·'ef] n abbrev of **very high frequency** UKW f

via ['vaɪ·ə] prep ❶ (through) über ❷ (using) per, via

viable ['vaɪ·ə·bəl] adj ❶ (successful) existenzfähig ❷ (feasible) machbar

viaduct ['vaɪ·ə·dəkt] n Viadukt m o nt

vibe [vaɪb] n usu pl (sl: atmosphere) Schwingungen pl; (general feeling) Klima nt

vibrant ['vaɪ·brənt] adj ❶ person lebhaft ❷ atmosphere, place lebendig ❸ color leuchtend

vibrate ['vaɪ·breɪt] vi vibrieren

vibration [vaɪ·'breɪ·ʃən] n Vibration f; of earthquake Erschütterung f

vicarious [vɪ·'ker·i·əs] adj nachempfunden; pleasure indirekt; ~ **satisfaction** Ersatzbefriedigung f

vice[1] [vaɪs] n Laster nt

vice[2] [vaɪs] n see **vise**

vice 'chairman n stellvertretende(r) Vorsitzende(r)

Vice 'President, vice 'president n Vizepräsident(in) m(f)

'vice squad n Sittendezernat nt

vice versa [ˌvaɪ·sə·'vɜr·sə] adv umgekehrt

vicinity [və·'sɪn·ə·ṭi] n Nähe f; ▪ **in the ~ [of sth]** in der Nähe [einer S. gen]

vicious ['vɪʃ·əs] adj (malicious) boshaft, gemein; crime grauenhaft; dog bissig

vicious 'circle, vicious 'cycle n Teufelskreis m

victim ['vɪk·tɪm] n ❶ (harmed) Opfer nt ❷ (sufferer) **cancer ~** Krebskranke(r) f(m)

victimize ['vɪk·tə·maɪz] vt ungerecht behandeln

victor ['vɪk·tər] n Sieger(in) m(f)

Victorian [vɪk·'tɔr·i·ən] adj era viktorianisch

victory ['vɪk·tə·ri] n Sieg m

video ['vɪd·i·ou] n Video nt

'video camera n Videokamera f

videocas'sette recorder, VCR n Videorekorder m

'videoconference n Videokonferenz f

'video game n Videospiel nt

'videophone n Bildtelefon nt

'videotape n ❶ (cassette) Videokassette f ❷ (tape) Videoband nt

Vienna [vi·'en·ə] n Wien nt

Viennese [ˌvi·ə·'niz] I. n <pl -> Wiener(in) m(f) II. adj Wiener-, wienerisch

Vietnam [ˌvi·et·'nam] n Vietnam nt

Vietnamese [vi·et·nə·'miz] I. adj vietnamesisch II. n Vietnamese, -mesin m, f

view [vju] I. n ❶ (sight) Sicht f; **in full ~ of all the spectators** vor den Augen aller Zuschauer; **to come into ~** sichtbar werden ❷ (panorama) [Aus]blick m; **he paints rural ~s** er malt ländliche Motive ❸ (opinion) Ansicht f, Meinung f; **it's my ~ that the price is much too high** meiner Meinung nach ist der Preis viel zu hoch; **point of ~** Standpunkt m; **from my point of ~ ...** meiner Meinung nach ... ❹ (perspective) Ansicht f; ▪ **in ~ of sth** angesichts einer S. gen II. vt ❶ (watch) ▪ **to ~ sb/sth [from sth]** etw [von jdm/etw aus] betrachten; spectator etw dat [von etw dat aus]

zusehen ② (*consider*) ■**to ~ sb/sth**
[**as sb/sth**] jdn/etw [als jdn/etw] betrachten; **we ~ the situation with
concern** wir betrachten die Lage mit
Besorgnis

viewer ['vju·ər] *n* ① (*person*) [Fern-
seh]zuschauer(in) *m(f)* ② (*for film*)
Filmbetrachter *m*

'**viewfinder** *n* PHOT [Bild]sucher *m*

viewing ['vju·ɪŋ] *n* FILM Anschauen *nt*;
TV Fernsehen *nt*

'**viewpoint** *n* ① (*opinion*) Standpunkt *m*
② (*place*) Aussichtspunkt *m*

vigilant ['vɪdʒ·ɪ·lənt] *adj* wachsam

vigor ['vɪg·ər] *n* ① (*liveliness*) Energie *f*;
with ~ mit vollem Eifer ② (*forceful-
ness*) Ausdruckskraft *f*

vigorous ['vɪg·ər·əs] *adj* ① (*strong*)
kräftig, kraftvoll ② *walk* stramm ③ (*passionate*) leidenschaftlich; *criticism* heftig; *denial* energisch

vile [vaɪl] *adj* abscheulich

village ['vɪl·ɪdʒ] *n* Dorf *nt*

villager ['vɪl·ə·dʒər] *n* Dorfbewoh-
ner(in) *m(f)*

villain ['vɪl·ən] *n* (*in novel, film*) Bösewicht *m*

VIN ['viˈaɪˈen] *n* AUTO *acr for* **vehicle
identification number** Kfz-Kennzeichen *nt*

vinaigrette [ˌvɪn·əˈgret] *n* Vinaigrette *f*

vindicate ['vɪn·də·keɪt] *vt* (*justify*) *thing*
rechtfertigen; *person* verteidigen

vindictive [vɪnˈdɪk·tɪv] *adj* nachtragend; (*vengeful*) rachsüchtig

vine [vaɪn] *n* ① (*of grape*) Weinrebe *f*
② (*creeper*) Rankengewächs *nt*

vinegar ['vɪn·ə·gər] *n* Essig *m*

vineyard ['vɪn·jərd] *n* Weinberg *m*

vintage ['vɪn·tɪdʒ] I. *n* ① (*wine*) Jahr-
gangswein *m* ② (*year*) Jahrgang *m*
II. *adj* ① (*classic*) erlesen; **this film is ~
Disney** dieser Film ist ein Disneyklas-
siker ② AUTO **~ car** Oldtimer *m*

vinyl *n* ['vaɪ·nəl] Vinyl *nt*

viola [viˈou·lə] *n* MUS Viola *f*, Bratsche *f*

violate ['vaɪ·ə·leɪt] *vt* (*breach*) brechen;
regulation verletzen; **to ~ a law** gegen
ein Gesetz verstoßen

violation [ˌvaɪ·əˈleɪ·ʃən] *n* Verletzung *f*,
Verstoß *m*

violence ['vaɪ·ə·ləns] *n* ① (*behavior*)
Gewalt *f* ② (*force*) Heftigkeit *f*

violent ['vaɪ·ə·lənt] *adj* ① (*brutal*) gewalttätig; *person a.* brutal; *death* gewaltsam ② (*strong*) heftig; *argument*
heftig

violet ['vaɪ·ə·lɪt] I. *n* Veilchen *nt* II. *adj*
violett

violin [ˌvaɪ·əˈlɪn] *n* Violine *f*, Geige *f*

violinist [ˌvaɪ·əˈlɪn·ɪst] *n* Violinist(in)
m(f), Geiger(in) *m(f)*

V.I.P., VIP [ˌvi·aɪˈpi] *n abbrev of* **very
important person** Promi *m fam*

virgin ['vɜr·dʒɪn] I. *n* ① Jungfrau *f*
② (*novice*) unbeschriebenes Blatt *fam*
II. *adj attr* jungfräulich

Virginia [vərˈdʒɪn·jə] *n* Virginia *nt*

Virgin 'Islands *npl* ■**the ~** die Jung-
ferninseln *pl*

virginity [vərˈdʒɪn·ə·ţi] *n* Jungfräulichkeit *f*

Virgo ['vɜr·gou] *n no art* ASTROL Jungfrau *f*

virile ['vɪr·əl] *adj* potent; (*masculine*)
männlich

virtual ['vɜr·tʃu·əl] *adj* ① (*almost*) so gut
wie, quasi; **to be a ~ unknown** praktisch unbekannt sein ② COMPUT, PHYS virtuell

virtually ['vɜr·tʃu·ə·li] *adv* praktisch, eigentlich

virtual re'ality *n* virtuelle Realität

virtue ['vɜr·tʃu] *n* ① (*quality*) Tugend *f*
② (*advantage*) Vorteil *m* ③ (*benefit*)
Nutzen *m*

virtuoso [ˌvɜr·tʃuˈou·sou] *n* <*pl* -s> Vir-
tuose, -in *m, f*

virus ['vaɪ·rəs] *n* <*pl* -es> ① MED
Virus *nt o fam m* ② COMPUT Virus *m*

visa ['vi·zə] *n* Visum *nt*

vis-à-vis [ˌvi·zəˈvi] *prep* (*concerning*)
bezüglich +*gen*

viscose ['vɪs·kous] *n* Viskose *f*

viscous ['vɪs·kəs] *adj* zähflüssig

vise [vaɪs] *n* Schraubstock *m*

visibility [ˌvɪz·əˈbɪl·ə·ţi] *n* ① (*view*)

V

Sichtweite f ❷ (*being seen*) Sichtbarkeit f

visible ['vɪz·ə·bəl] *adj* sichtbar; **to be barely ~** kaum zu sehen sein

vision ['vɪʒ·ən] *n* ❶ (*sight*) Sehvermögen *nt;* **to have blurred ~** verschwommen sehen ❷ (*mental image*) Vorstellung f ❸ (*forethought*) Weitblick *m*

visionary ['vɪʒ·ə·ner·i] *n* Visionär(in) *m(f) geh*

visit ['vɪz·ɪt] I. *n* ❶ Besuch *m;* **to have a ~ from sb** von jdm besucht werden ❷ (*fam: chat*) Plauderei f II. *vt* besuchen III. *vi* einen Besuch machen; ■**to ~ with sb** sich mit jdm treffen

'**visiting hours** *npl* Besuchszeiten *pl*

visitor ['vɪz·ɪ·tər] *n* Besucher(in) *m(f);* (*at hotel*) Gast *m*

visor ['vaɪ·zər] *n* ❶ (*of cap*) Schild *nt* ❷ AUTO Sonnenblende f

vista ['vɪs·tə] *n* Aussicht f

visual ['vɪʒ·u·əl] I. *adj* visuell; **~ imagery** Bildersymbolik f II. *n* ■**~s** *pl* Bildmaterial *nt*

visual 'aid *n* Anschauungsmaterial *nt*

visualize ['vɪʒ·u·ə·laɪz] *vt* ■**to ~ sth** (*imagine*) sich *dat* etw vorstellen

vital ['vaɪ·təl] *adj* (*essential*) unerlässlich; (*stronger*) lebensnotwendig; **to be of ~ importance** von entscheidender Bedeutung sein

vitality [vaɪ·'tæl·ə·t̬i] *n* Vitalität f

vital 'signs *n pl* MED Lebenszeichen *pl*

vitamin ['vaɪ·t̬ə·mɪn] *n* Vitamin *nt*

'**vitamin deficiency** *n* Vitaminmangel *m*

vittles ['vɪt̬·əls] *n pl* (*hum*) Lebensmittel *pl*

vivacious [vɪ·'veɪ·ʃəs] *adj* (*lively*) lebhaft; (*cheerful*) munter

vivid ['vɪv·ɪd] *adj* ❶ (*graphic*) anschaulich; *memories* lebhaft ❷ *colors* kräftig

vixen ['vɪk·sən] *n* Füchsin f

vocabulary [voʊ·'kæb·jə·ler·i] *n* Wortschatz *m*

vocal ['voʊ·kəl] I. *adj* ❶ stimmlich ❷ (*outspoken*) laut; *minority* lautstark II. *n* MUS Vokalpartie f *fachspr*

'**vocal cords** *n pl* Stimmbänder *pl*

vocalist ['voʊ·kə·lɪst] *n* Sänger(in) *m(f)*

vocalize ['voʊ·kə·laɪz] *vt* LING (*express*) aussprechen; *thoughts* in Worte fassen

vocation [voʊ·'keɪ·ʃən] *n* Berufung f

vocational [voʊ·'keɪ·ʃə·nəl] *adj* beruflich; **~ training** Berufsausbildung f

vodka ['vad·kə] *n* Wodka *m*

vogue [voʊg] *n* Mode f

voice [vɔɪs] I. *n* ❶ Stimme f; **at the top of one's ~** in voller Lautstärke; **inner ~** innere Stimme; **to keep one's ~ down** leise sprechen ❷ (*expression*) **to give ~ to sth** etw zum Ausdruck bringen II. *vt* zum Ausdruck bringen; *complaint* vorbringen

voiceless ['vɔɪs·lɪs] *adj* stumm *a. fig*

'**voice mail** *n* Voicemail f

'**voice-over** *n* TV, FILM Offkommentar *m* *fachspr*

void [vɔɪd] I. *n* (*empty space*) Leere f *kein pl a. fig;* (*in building*) Hohlraum *m* ▶PHRASES: **to fill a** [*or* **the**] **~** die innere Leere ausfüllen II. *adj* (*invalid*) nichtig III. *vt* (*annul*) aufheben

voip [vɔɪp] *vt, vi abbrev of* **Voice over Internet Protocol** INET voipen

vol. *n abbrev of* **volume** (*book*) Bd.; (*measure*) vol.

volatile ['val·ə·təl] *adj* ❶ (*changeable*) unbeständig; (*unstable*) instabil ❷ (*explosive*) explosiv

volcanic [val·'kæn·ɪk] *adj* vulkanisch

volcano <*pl* -**es**> [val·'keɪ·noʊ] *n* Vulkan *m a. fig*

volition [voʊ·'lɪʃ·ən] *n* **of one's own ~** aus freien Stücken

volley ['val·i] I. *n* ❶ (*salvo*) Salve f ❷ SPORT (*in tennis*) Volley *m fachspr* II. *vi* SPORT (*in tennis*) einen Volley schlagen *fachspr*

volleyball ['val·i·bɔl] *n* Volleyball *m*

volt [voʊlt] *n* Volt *nt*

voltage ['voʊl·tɪdʒ] *n* Spannung f

voluble ['val·jə·bəl] *adj* redselig

volume ['val·jum] *n* ❶ (*space*) Volumen *nt* ❷ (*sound*) Lautstärke f ❸ (*book*) Band *m*

'**volume control** *n* Lautstärkeregler *m*

voluntary ['val·ən·ter·i] *adj* freiwillig; **~ work** ehrenamtliche Tätigkeit

voluntary organi'zation *n* Freiwilligenorganisation *f*

volunteer [,val·ən·'tɪr] **I.** *n* ❶ (*worker*) ehrenamtlicher Mitarbeiter/ehrenamtliche Mitarbeiterin ❷ (*helper*) Freiwillige(r) *f(m)* **II.** *vt information* bereitwillig geben; *one's services* anbieten **III.** *vi* ▪ **to ~ to do sth** sich [freiwillig] anbieten, etw zu tun

voluptuous [və·'lʌp·tʃu·əs] *adj* üppig; *woman a.* kurvenreich; (*sumptuous*) verschwenderisch

vomit ['vam·ɪt] *vi* (sich) erbrechen

voodoo ['vu·du] *n* Voodoo *m*

vortex <*pl* -es> ['vɔr·teks] *n* Wirbel *m*

vote [voʊt] **I.** *n* ❶ (*choice*) Stimme *f* ❷ (*election*) Abstimmung *f* ❸ (*right*) ▪ **the ~** das Wahlrecht **II.** *vi* ❶ (*elect*) wählen; ▪ **to ~ against sb** für jdn stimmen ❷ (*decide*) abstimmen (**on** über +*akk*) **III.** *vt* ❶ (*elect*) ▪ **to ~ sb into office** jdn ins Amt wählen ❷ (*declare*) **she was ~d the winner** sie wurde zur Siegerin erklärt

◆ **vote down** *vt* niederstimmen

voter ['voʊ·tər] *n* Wähler(in) *m(f)*

voter regis'tration *n* Eintragung *f* ins Wählerverzeichnis

'voter turnout *n* Wahlbeteiligung *f*

voting ['voʊ·tɪŋ] *n* Wählen *nt*

'voting booth *n* Wahlkabine *f*

'voting machine *n* Wahlmaschine *f*

vouch [vaʊtʃ] *vi* ▪ **to ~ for sb** sich für jdn verbürgen

voucher ['vaʊ·tʃər] *n* Gutschein *m*; **school ~** *öffentliche Mittel, die in Amerika bereitgestellt werden, damit Eltern ihre Kinder in Privatschulen schicken können*

vow [vaʊ] **I.** *vt* geloben *geh* **II.** *n* Versprechen *nt*; ▪ **~s** *pl* (*of marriage*) Eheversprechen *nt*

vowel ['vaʊ·əl] *n* Vokal *m*

voyage ['vɔɪ·ɪdʒ] *n* Reise *f*; (*by sea*) Seereise *f*

voyeur [vɔɪ·'jɜr] *n* Voyeur(in) *m(f)*

VP [,vi·'pi] *n abbrev of* **vice president** Vizepräsident(in) *m(f)*

vs. *prep abbrev of* **versus** vs.

VT, Vt. *abbrev of* **Vermont**

vulcanize ['vʌl·kə·naɪz] *vt* vulkanisieren

vulgar ['vʌl·gər] *adj* ordinär, vulgär; (*bad taste*) abgeschmackt

vulnerable ['vʌl·nər·ə·bəl] *adj* verletzlich; ▪ **to be ~ to sth** anfällig für etw *akk* sein; **to be ~ to criticism** Kritik ausgesetzt sein; **to feel ~** sich verwundbar fühlen

vulture ['vʌl·tʃər] *n* Geier *m a. fig*

V

Ww

W <pl -'s>, **w** <pl -'s> ['dʌb·əl·ju] n W nt, w nt; ~ **as in Whiskey** W wie Wilhelm

W[1] I. adj ❶ abbrev of **West** W- ❷ abbrev of **western** I II. n abbrev of **West** W

W[2] <pl -> n abbrev of **Watt** W

WA abbrev of **Washington**

wacko ['wæk·ou] n (pej sl: person) Querkopf m

wacky ['wæk·i] adj (fam) person, idea verrückt

wad [wad] n ❶ (mass) Knäuel nt; of cotton Wattebausch m ❷ (fam: bundle) ~[s pl] **of money** schöne Stange Geld fam

waddle ['wad·əl] vi watscheln

wade [weid] vi waten

wader ['wei·dər] n Watvogel m

wafer ['wei·fər] n (cookie, cracker) Waffel f

wafer-'thin adj, adv hauchdünn

waffle[1] ['waf·əl] n (food) Waffel f

waffle[2] ['waf·əl] vi (pej fam) herumdrucksen fam

'waffle iron n Waffeleisen nt

wag [wæg] I. vt <-gg-> **to ~ one's finger** mit dem Finger drohen II. vi <-gg-> wedeln

wage [weidʒ] I. n Lohn m; **minimum ~** Mindestlohn m II. vt **to ~ war on sth** (fig) gegen etw akk vorgehen

'wage dumping n Lohndumping nt

'wage earner n Lohnempfänger(in) m(f)

'wage freeze n Lohnstopp m

wagon ['wæg·ən] n Wagen m

waif [weif] n (child) verwahrlostes Kind

wail [weil] vi jammern; siren heulen

wailing ['wei·lɪŋ] adj jammernd; sirens heulend

waist [weist] n Taille f

'waistband n Bund m

waist-'deep adv bis zur Taille

'waistline n Taille f

wait [weit] I. n Warten nt ▶PHRASES: **to lie in ~** [for sb] [jdm] auflauern II. vi warten (**for** auf +akk); **~ a minute!** Moment mal! III. vt (serve) **to ~ tables** als Kellner/Kellnerin arbeiten

♦ **wait around** vi warten

♦ **wait behind** vi zurückbleiben

♦ **wait on** vt (serve) ■ **to ~ on sb** jdn bedienen

♦ **wait up** vi ■ **~ up!** warte mal!

waiter ['wei·tər] n Bedienung f, Kellner m; **~!** Herr Ober!

'waiting list n Warteliste f

'waiting room n Wartezimmer nt

waitress <pl -es> ['wei·trɪs] n Kellnerin f, Bedienung f

waive [weiv] vt verzichten auf +akk

waiver ['wei·vər] n Verzichterklärung f

wake[1] [weik] n NAUT Kielwasser nt; ■ **in the ~ of sth** (fig) infolge einer S. gen

wake[2] <woke or waked, woken or waked> [weik] I. vi aufwachen II. vt aufwecken

♦ **wake up** I. vi aufwachen a. fig II. vt aufwecken

wakeful ['weik·fəl] adj **~ night** schlaflose Nacht

waken ['wei·kən] I. vi aufwachen II. vt [auf]wecken

walk [wɔk] I. n ❶ (going) Gehen nt; (as recreation) Spaziergang m; **to go for a ~** einen Spaziergang machen ❷ (path) Wanderweg m II. vt ❶ **to ~ the streets** (wander) durch die Straßen gehen; prostitute auf den Strich gehen sl ❷ dog ausführen III. vi ❶ (go) zu Fuß gehen ❷ (for recreation) spazieren gehen

♦ **walk away** vi (withdraw) sich zurückziehen (**from** von +dat) ❷ (fam: steal) ■ **to ~ away with sth** etw mitgehen lassen fam

♦ **walk in** vi hereinkommen

♦ **walk in on** vt ■ **to ~ in on sb** bei jdm hereinplatzen fam

W

◆**walk off** vi ❶ (*leave*) weggehen ❷ (*fam: steal*) ■**to ~ off with sth** etw mitgehen lassen *fam*

◆**walk out** vi ❶ (*leave*) ■**to ~ out on sb** jdn im Stich lassen ❷ (*strike*) streiken

◆**walk over** vt (*fam*) ■**to ~ [all] over sb** jdn ausnutzen

◆**walk through** vt ■**to ~ sb through sth** etw mit jdm durchgehen

walker ['wɔ·kər] n Fußgänger(in) m(f); (*for recreation*) Spaziergänger(in) m(f)

walkie-talkie [ˌwɔ·ki·'tɔ·ki] n Walkie-Talkie nt

'**walk-in** adj closet begehbar; clinic Klinik, für die keine Voranmeldung nötig ist

walking ['wɔ·kɪŋ] I. n Gehen nt; (*as recreation*) Spaziergengehen nt II. adj attr **within ~ distance** zu Fuß erreichbar

'**walking shoes** npl Wanderschuhe pl

'**walking stick** n Spazierstock m

Walkman® <pl -men> ['wɔk·mən] n Walkman® m

'**walk-on** adj attr THEAT, FILM ~ **part** [or **role**] Statistenrolle f

'**walkout** n Arbeitsniederlegung f

'**walkover** n leichter Sieg

'**walkway** n [Fuß]weg m

wall [wɔl] n Mauer f; (*in room*) Wand f; **the Great W~ of China** die Chinesische Mauer

◆**wall in** vt usu passive ummauern

◆**wall off** vt usu passive durch eine Mauer abtrennen

'**wall chart** n Schautafel f

'**wall clock** n Wanduhr f

wallet ['wal·ɪt] n (*for money*) Brieftasche f; (*for documents*) Dokumentenmappe f

'**wall hanging** n Wandteppich m

'**wall map** n Wandkarte f

wallop ['wal·əp] (*fam*) I. vt schlagen II. n Schlag m

wallow ['wal·oʊ] vi **to ~ in self-pity** in Selbstmitleid zerfließen

'**wallpaper** I. n Tapete f II. vt tapezieren

'**Wall Street** n Wall Street f

wall-to-'wall adj ❶ ~ **carpeting** Tep-

pichboden m ❷ (*fig: constant*) ständig; ~ **coverage** Berichterstattung f rund um die Uhr

walnut ['wɔl·nʌt] n Walnuss f

walrus <pl -> ['wɔl·rəs] n Walross nt

waltz [wɔlts] I. n <pl -es> Walzer m II. vi Walzer tanzen

◆**waltz in** vi hereintanzen *fam*

wand [wand] n Zauberstab m

wander ['wan·dər] I. vt **to ~ the streets** (*stroll*) durch die Straßen schlendern; (*be lost*) durch die Straßen irren II. vi (*lose concentration*) **my attention is ~ing** ich bin nicht bei der Sache

wandering ['wan·dər·ɪŋ] adj attr wandernd; *tribe* nomadisierend

wane [weɪn] vi abnehmen; **to wax and ~** zu- und abnehmen

wangle ['wæŋ·gəl] vt (*fam*) deichseln; **to ~ one's way out of sth** sich aus etw dat herauswinden

wanna ['wa·nə] (*fam*) = **want to** see want II

wannabe ['wa·nə·bi] adj (*pej fam*) Möchtegern- *iron fam*

want [want] I. n ❶ (*need*) Bedürfnis nt; **to be in ~ of sth** etw benötigen ❷ (*lack*) Mangel m II. vt ❶ (*desire*) wünschen, wollen; (*politely*) mögen; **to be ~ed by the police** polizeilich gesucht werden ❷ (*need*) brauchen ▶PHRASES: **waste** not, ~ not (*prov*) spare in der Zeit, dann hast du in der Not *prov*

◆**want in** vi (*fam*) ■**to ~ in [on sth]** [bei etw dat] dabei sein wollen

◆**want out** vi (*fam*) ■**to ~ out [of sth]** [aus etw dat] aussteigen wollen

wanting ['wan·tɪŋ] adj pred unzulänglich

wanton ['wan·tən] adj leichtfertig; ~ **destruction** mutwillige Zerstörung

WAP [wap] n INET acr for **Wireless Application Protocol** WAP nt

war [wɔr] n Krieg m; **at ~** im Kriegszustand a. fig; **to go to ~** in den Krieg ziehen

'**war baby** n Kriegskind nt

warbler ['wɔr·blər] n Grasmücke f

'war correspondent n Kriegsberichterstatter(in) m(f)

'war crime n Kriegsverbrechen nt

'war criminal n Kriegsverbrecher(in) m(f)

ward [wɔrd] n Station f
  ◆ **ward off** vt abwehren

warden ['wɔr·dən] n ① (in prison) Gefängnisdirektor(in) m(f) ② (official) **game ~** Jagdaufseher(in) m(f)

wardrobe ['wɔrd·roub] n ① (armoire) [Kleider]schrank m ② (clothing) Garderobe f

warehouse ['wer·haʊs] n Lagerhaus nt

warfare ['wɔr·fer] n Krieg[s]führung f

warhead ['wɔr·hed] n Sprengkopf m

warily ['wer·ɪ·li] adv vorsichtig; (suspiciously) misstrauisch

warlike ['wɔr·laɪk] adj ① (military) kriegerisch ② (hostile) militant

'warlord n Kriegsherr m

warm [wɔrm] I. adj ① (not cool) warm ② (hearty) warm; person warmherzig; welcome herzlich II. vt wärmen; food aufwärmen
  ◆ **warm up** I. vi ① engine warm laufen ② (limber up) aufwärmen II. vt engine warm laufen lassen; food aufwärmen

warm-'blooded adj warmblütig

'warm front n METEO Warmfront f

warm-'hearted adj warmherzig

warmly ['wɔrm·li] adv ① to dress ~ sich warm anziehen ② (heartily) herzlich

warmth [wɔrmθ] n ① (heat) Wärme f ② (affection) Herzlichkeit f

'warm-up n [Sich]aufwärmen nt kein pl

warn [wɔrn] I. vi warnen (of vor +dat) II. vt warnen (about vor +dat); ■ to ~ **sb not to do sth** jdn davor warnen, etw zu tun

warning ['wɔr·nɪŋ] n ① (notice) Warnung f ② (threat) Drohung f

'warning sign n ① (signboard) Warnschild nt ② usu pl (symptom) Anzeichen nt

warp [wɔrp] I. vt, vi verziehen II. n ~ **and weft** Kette und Schuss

'warpath n **to be on the ~** auf dem Kriegspfad sein hum

warped [wɔrpt] adj ① (bent) verzogen ② (perverted) verschroben pej

warrant ['wɔr·ənt] **search ~** Durchsuchungsbefehl m

'warrant officer n ranghöchster Unteroffizier

warranty ['wɔr·ən·ti] n Garantie f

warren ['wɔr·ən] n ① (burrows) Kaninchenbau m ② (maze) Labyrinth nt

warship ['wɔr·ʃɪp] n Kriegsschiff nt

wart [wɔrt] n Warze f ▶PHRASES: **~s and all** (fam) mit all seinen/ihren Fehlern und Schwächen

'wartime n Kriegszeit[en] f[pl]

wary ['wer·i] adj vorsichtig

'war zone n Kriegsgebiet nt

was [waz] pt of **be**

wash [waʃ] I. n <pl -es> usu sing (cleaning) Waschen nt kein pl; **to give sth a [good] ~** etw [gründlich] waschen II. vt (clean) waschen; dishes spülen ▶PHRASES: **to ~ one's hands of sth** mit etw nichts zu tun haben wollen III. vi sich waschen
  ◆ **wash away** vt ① sea wegspülen ② (clean) auswaschen
  ◆ **wash down** vt ① (swallow) hinunterspülen ② (clean) waschen
  ◆ **wash off** I. vi sich abwaschen lassen II. vt abwaschen
  ◆ **wash out** I. vi sich herauswaschen lassen II. vt ① (clean) auswaschen ② (remove) herauswaschen
  ◆ **wash over** vi (flow over) ■ **to ~ over sb** über jdn [hinweg]spülen
  ◆ **wash up** vi ① (wash oneself) sich waschen ② usu passive (burn out) ■ **to be ~ed up** [völlig] ausgebrannt sein

Wash. abbrev of **Washington**

washable ['waʃ·ə·bəl] adj garment waschbar; surface abwaschbar; **machine-~** waschmaschinenfest

wash-and-'wear adj bügelfrei

'washbasin n Waschbecken nt

'washcloth n Waschlappen m

washed-out [ˌwaʃt·'aʊt] adj ① clothes verwaschen ② (tired) fertig fam

washer ['waʃ·ər] n ① (*machine*) Waschmaschine f ② (*ring*) Unterlegscheibe f; (*seal*) Dichtung f

'**washing machine** n Waschmaschine f

Washington ['waʃ·ɪŋ·tən] n Washington nt

'**washout** n usu sing (*fam*) Reinfall m fam

'**washroom** n Toilette f

wasn't ['wʌz·ənt] = was not see be

wasp [wasp] n Wespe f

'**wasps' nest** n Wespennest nt

waste [weɪst] I. n ① (*misuse*) Verschwendung f; ~ **of time** Zeitverschwendung f ② (*matter*) Abfall m; **household/industrial** ~ Haushalts-/Industriemüll m; **electronic** ~ Elektroschrott m ③ (*excrement*) Exkremente pl II. vt ① (*misuse*) verschwenden; **don't** ~ **my time!** stiehl mir nicht meine wertvolle Zeit! ② (*fam*) ■**to** ~ **sb** jdn umlegen

◆**waste away** vi immer dünner werden

'**wastebasket** n Papierkorb m

wasted ['weɪs·tɪd] adj (*sl*) ① (*high on drugs*) mit Drogen vollgepumpt ② (*drunk*) betrunken

'**waste disposal** n Abfallbeseitigung f

wasteful ['weɪst·fəl] adj verschwenderisch (**of** mit + dat)

waste 'management n Abfallwirtschaft f

'**waste pipe** n Abflussrohr nt

waste 'product n Abfallprodukt nt

waster ['weɪ·stər] n Verschwender(in) m(f)

watch [watʃ] I. n ① (*timepiece*) Armbanduhr f ② (*duty*) Wache f; **on** ~ auf Wache II. vt ① (*look at*) beobachten; **to** ~ **TV** fernsehen ② (*keep vigil*) aufpassen auf + akk ③ (*be careful*) ~ **it!** pass auf!; **to** ~ **one's weight** auf sein Gewicht achten ▶PHRASES: **to** ~ **one's step** aufpassen III. vi ① (*look*) zusehen ② (*be attentive*) aufpassen

◆**watch out** vi ~ **out!** Achtung!

'**watchband** n Uhr[arm]band nt

'**watchdog** n ① (*dog*) Wachhund m ② (*organization*) Überwachungsgremium nt

watcher ['watʃ·ər] n Zuschauer(in) m(f)

watchful ['watʃ·fəl] adj wachsam

watchmaker ['watʃ·ˌmeɪ·kər] n Uhrmacher(in) m(f)

'**watchman** n **night** ~ Nachtwächter m

'**watchtower** n Wachturm m

water ['wɔ·tər] I. n ① Wasser nt ② (*urine*) **to pass** ~ Wasser lassen ▶PHRASES: **to be** ~ **under the bridge** Schnee von gestern sein fam; **like a fish out of** ~ wie ein Fisch auf dem Trockenen II. vt bewässern; **plants** gießen III. vi ① **eyes** tränen ② (*salivate*) **my mouth is** ~**ing** mir läuft das Wasser im Munde zusammen

◆**water down** vt (*dilute*) verdünnen

'**waterborne** adj ~ **disease** durch das Wasser übertragene Krankheit

'**water bottle** n Wasserflasche f

'**water buffalo** n ZOOL Wasserbüffel m

'**water cannon** n Wasserwerfer m

'**watercolor** n ① (*paint*) Aquarellfarbe f ② (*picture*) Aquarell nt

'**water-cooled** adj wassergekühlt

'**water cooler** n [Trink]wasserspender m

'**watercress** n Brunnenkresse f

'**waterfall** n Wasserfall m

'**waterfowl** n pl Wasservögel pl

'**waterfront** n (*shore*) Ufer nt; (*area*) Hafengebiet nt

watering ['wɔ·tər·ɪŋ] n of land Bewässerung f; of plants Gießen nt

'**watering can** n Gießkanne f

'**watering hole** n ① (*pond*) Wasserloch nt ② (*hum fam: bar*) Kneipe f fam

'**water level** n (*of surface water*) Wasserstand m; of river Pegel[stand] m

'**water lily** n Seerose f

'**waterline** n Wasserlinie f

'**waterlogged** adj ground feucht

'**water main** n Haupt[wasser]leitung f

'**watermark** n (*on paper*) Wasserzeichen nt

'**watermelon** n Wassermelone f

'**water meter** n Wasserzähler m

'**water pipe** n Wasserleitung f

'**water pistol** n Wasserpistole f

'water pollution n Wasserverschmutzung f

'water polo n Wasserball m kein pl

'water power n Wasserkraft f

'water pressure n Wasserdruck m

'waterproof I. adj wasserdicht II. vt wasserundurchlässig machen

water-re'pellent adj Wasser abweisend

'watershed n (fig: change) Wendepunkt m

'water shortage n Wassermangel m kein pl

'water-ski vi Wasserski fahren

water-'soluble adj wasserlöslich

'water supply n (for area) Wasservorrat m; (for households) Wasserversorgung f

'water table n Grundwasserspiegel m

'water tank n Wassertank m

watertight ['wɔ·tər·taɪt] adj wasserdicht

'water vapor n Wasserdampf m

'waterway n Wasserstraße f

'waterworks npl (facility) Wasserwerk nt ▶PHRASES: to turn on the ~ (fam) losheulen fam

watery <more, most or -ier, -iest> ['wɔ·tə·ri] adj ❶ drink dünn; soup wässrig ❷ light, sunshine fahl

watt [wat] n Watt nt

wattage ['waṯ·ɪdʒ] n Wattzahl f

wave [weɪv] I. n ❶ of water, hair Welle f ❷ (fig: feeling) ~ of panic Welle der Panik ❸ of hand Wink m; to give sb a ~ jdm [zu]winken II. vi ❶ (greet) winken; I ~d at him across the room ich winkte ihm durch den Raum zu ❷ flag wehen III. vt (with hand) to ~ goodbye to sb jdm zum Abschied [nach]winken

◆wave aside vt to ~ aside ⟲ an objection einen Einwand abtun

◆wave down vt anhalten

◆wave through vt durchwinken

'waveband n Wellenbereich m

'wavelength n Wellenlänge f

waver ['weɪ·vər] vi ❶ wanken; concentration nachlassen ❷ (be indecisive) schwanken

wavy ['weɪ·vi] adj wellig; hair gewellt

wax [wæks] I. n Wachs nt II. vt ❶ (polish) wachsen; floor bohnern ❷ (remove hair) enthaaren

wax 'paper n Butterbrotpapier nt

waxy ['wæk·si] adj Wachs-, aus Wachs nach n

way [weɪ] I. n ❶ (road) Weg m; one-~-street Einbahnstraße f ❷ (route) we have to go by ~ of Chicago wir müssen über Chicago fahren; to ask the ~ nach dem Weg fragen; to be on the ~ letter, baby unterwegs sein; to get under ~ in Gang kommen; to go the wrong ~ sich verlaufen; (in car) sich verfahren; to lead the ~ vorausgehen; to lose one's ~ sich verirren ❸ (distance) Weg m; to be a long ~ off (in space) weit entfernt sein; (in time) fern sein ❹ (direction) this ~ around so herum; which ~ are you going? in welche Richtung gehst du? ❺ (manner) Art f, Weise f; that is definitely not the ~ to do it so macht man das auf gar keinen Fall!; ~s and means Mittel und Wege; one ~ or another so oder so; no ~! auf gar keinen Fall; no ~! (sl) ausgeschlossen!, kommt nicht in die Tüte! fam II. adv (fam) weit; to be ~ past sb's bedtime für jdn allerhöchste Zeit zum Schlafengehen sein

wayward ['weɪ·wərd] adj eigenwillig

we [wi] pron pers wir; in this section ~ discuss … in diesem Abschnitt besprechen wir ..

weak [wik] adj ❶ schwach; coffee, tea dünn ❷ (ineffective) leader unfähig; argument, attempt schwach

weaken ['wi·kən] I. vi schwächer werden II. vt schwächen

weakling ['wik·lɪŋ] n Schwächling m

weakness <pl -es> ['wik·nɪs] n Schwäche f

wealth [welθ] n Reichtum m; (fortune) Vermögen nt

'wealth tax n Vermögenssteuer f

wealthy ['wel·θi] adj reich

wean [win] vt baby abstillen

weapon ['wep·ən] n Waffe f a. fig; ~s

of mass destruction Massenvernichtungswaffen pl

weaponry ['wep·ən·ri] n Waffen pl

wear [wer] I. n ① (clothing) Kleidung f ② (damage) ~ **and tear** Verschleiß m II. vt <wore, worn> tragen ▸PHRASES: **to ~ one's heart on one's sleeve** das Herz auf der Zunge tragen III. vi <wore, worn> clothes abtragen

◆**wear away** vi sich abnutzen

◆**wear down** vt (tire) fertigmachen fam; (weaken) zermürben

◆**wear off** vi nachlassen

◆**wear out** I. vi abnutzen II. vt erschöpfen

wearable ['wer·ə·bəl] adj tragbar

weary ['wɪr·i] adj müde

weasel ['wi·zəl] n Wiesel nt

weather ['weð·ər] I. n ① Wetter nt; (climate) Witterung f ▸PHRASES: **to be under the ~** (fam) angeschlagen sein fam II. vi verwittern

'**weather-beaten** adj verwittert

'**weather chart** n Wetterkarte f

'**weather conditions** npl Witterungsverhältnisse pl

'**weather forecast** n Wettervorhersage f

'**weatherman** n Wettermann m fam

'**weatherproof** adj wetterfest

weave [wiv] vt, vi <wove or weaved, woven or weaved> weben

weaver ['wi·vər] n Weber(in) m(f)

web [web] n ① of spider Netz nt ② (fig) **a ~ of intrigue** ein Netz nt von Intrigen

'**web browser** n INET [Web-]Browser m fachspr

web-footed ['web·fʊt·ɪd] adj mit Schwimmfüßen nach n

webmaster ['web·mæs·tər] n INET Web-Administrator(in) m(f)

'**web page** n INET Webseite f

'**web portal** n INET Internetportal nt

'**website** n INET Website f

webzine ['web·zin] n INET Webzine nt (Onlinemagazin)

we'd [wid] ① = **we had** see have I, II ② = **we would** see would

wedding ['wed·ɪŋ] n Hochzeit f

'**wedding anniversary** n Hochzeitstag m

'**wedding cake** n Hochzeitstorte f

'**wedding day** n Hochzeitstag m

'**wedding dress** n Brautkleid nt

'**wedding night** n Hochzeitsnacht f

'**wedding present** n Hochzeitsgeschenk nt

'**wedding ring** n Ehering m, Trauring m

wedge [wedʒ] I. n Keil m II. vt einkeilen

Wednesday ['wenz·deɪ] n Mittwoch m; see also **Tuesday**

wee [wi] adj winzig; **in the ~ hours** zwischen 1 und 2 Uhr

weed [wid] I. n Unkraut nt kein pl II. vt garden jäten

weedy ['wi·di] adj (fam) [spindel]dürr

week [wik] n ① (seven days) Woche f; **twice a ~** zweimal die Woche ② (work period) **five-day ~** 5-Tage-Woche

'**weekday** n Wochentag m

'**weekend** n Wochenende nt; ▪**on the ~|s|/on ~s** am Wochenende/an Wochenenden

weekly ['wik·li] I. adj, adv wöchentlich II. n (magazine) Wochenzeitschrift f; (newspaper) Wochenzeitung f

weep [wip] vi <wept, wept> weinen

weeping willow n Trauerweide f

weigh [weɪ] I. vi ① (in measurement) wiegen ② (fig) **to ~ heavily** eine große Bedeutung haben II. vt [ab]wiegen

◆**weigh down** vt niederdrücken; ▪**to be ~ed down with sth** schwer mit etw dat beladen sein

◆**weigh in** vi ① **to ~ in at 132 pounds** 132 Pfund auf die Waage bringen ② (fam: intervene) ▪**to ~ in with sth** opinion etw einbringen

'**weigh-in** n SPORT Wiegen nt

weight [weɪt] I. n ① Gewicht; **to put on** [or gain] ~ zunehmen ▸PHRASES: **to throw one's ~ around** (fam) seinen Einfluss geltend machen II. vt ▪**to ~ sth down** etw beschweren

weightless ['weɪt·lɪs] adj schwerelos

'**weightlifter** n Gewichtheber(in) m(f)

W

weighty ['weɪ·ti] *adj* ❶ (*heavy*) schwer ❷ (*fig: important*) [ge]wichtig

weird [wɪrd] *adj* (*fam*) seltsam, komisch

weirdo <*pl* -os> ['wɪr·doʊ] *n* (*pej fam*) seltsame Person, Freak *m*

welcome ['wel·kəm] I. *vt* ❶ (*greet*) willkommen heißen ❷ (*be glad of*) begrüßen II. *n* ❶ (*reception*) **to give sb a warm ~** jdm einen herzlichen Empfang bereiten ❷ (*approval*) Zustimmung *f* ▶PHRASES: **to overstay one's ~** länger bleiben, als man erwünscht ist III. *adj* ❶ willkommen ❷ **thank you very much — you're ~** vielen Dank – nichts zu danken

welcoming ['wel·kəm·ɪŋ] *adj* **~ smile** freundliches Lächeln

weld [weld] I. *vt* schweißen II. *n* Schweißnaht *f*

welder ['wel·dər] *n* Schweißer(in) *m(f)*

welfare ['wel·fer] *n* Sozialhilfe *f*; ■**to be on ~** von [der] Sozialhilfe leben

'welfare payments *npl* Sozialabgaben *pl*

'welfare services *npl* + *sing vb* (*office*) Sozialamt *nt*

we'll [wil] = **we will** *see* **will**[1]

well[1] [wel] I. *adj* <better, best> *usu pred* ❶ (*healthy*) gesund; **to feel ~** sich gut fühlen; **to get ~** gesund werden ❷ (*okay*) **all's ~ here** hier ist alles in Ordnung; **all ~ and good** gut und schön II. *adv* <better, best> ❶ (*in a good way*) gut; **~ done!** gut gemacht!, super! *fam;* **to be money ~ spent** gut angelegtes Geld sein; **to mean ~** es gut meinen ❷ (*thoroughly*) gut; **to know sb ~** jdn gut kennen ❸ (*used for emphasis*) [sehr] wohl; **to be ~ aware of sth** sich *dat* einer S. *gen* durchaus bewusst sein; **~ and truly** ganz einfach ❹ (*also*) **as ~** auch; (*and*) **... as ~ as ...** ... sowie ... III. *interj* (*introducing, continuing*) nun [ja], also; (*hesitating, resignedly*) tja *fam;* (*surprised*) **~ [, ~]!** sieh mal einer an!

well[2] [wel] *n* ❶ (*for water*) Brunnen *m* ❷ **oil ~** Ölquelle *f*

well-ad'vised *adj pred* ■**to be ~ to do sth** gut beraten sein, etw zu tun

well ap'pointed *adj pred,* **well-ap-'pointed** *adj attr* gut ausgestattet

well 'balanced *adj pred,* **well-'balanced** *adj attr* ❶ *report* objektiv; *team* harmonisch ❷ *diet* ausgewogen

well be'haved *adj pred,* **well-be-'haved** *adj attr child* artig; *dog* brav

well-'being *n* **feeling of ~** wohliges Gefühl

well 'bred *adj pred,* **well-'bred** *adj attr* (*with good manners*) wohlerzogen *geh;* (*refined*) gebildet

well 'chosen *adj pred,* **well-'chosen** *adj attr* gut gewählt; [**to say**] **a few ~ words** ein paar passende Worte [sagen]

well con'nected *adj pred,* **well-con-'nected** *adj attr* ■**to be ~** gute Beziehungen haben

well de'served *adj pred,* **well-de-'served** *adj attr* wohlverdient

well de'veloped *adj pred,* **well-de'veloped** *adj attr* gut entwickelt

well 'done *adj pred,* **well-'done** *adj attr* ❶ (*of meat*) gut durch[gebraten] ❷ (*of work*) gut gemacht

well 'dressed *adj pred,* **well-'dressed** *adj attr* gut gekleidet

well 'educated *adj pred,* **well-'educated** *adj attr* gebildet

well 'founded *adj pred,* **well-'founded** *adj attr* [wohl]begründet

well 'groomed *adj pred,* **well-'groomed** *adj attr* gepflegt

well 'heeled *adj pred,* **well-'heeled** *adj attr* (*fam*) [gut] betucht

well in'formed *adj pred,* **well-in-'formed** *adj attr* **to be ~ on a subject** über ein Thema gut Bescheid wissen

well in'tentioned *adj pred,* **well-in-'tentioned** *adj attr* gut gemeint

well 'kept *adj pred,* **well-'kept** *adj attr* ❶ (*tended*) gepflegt ❷ (*hidden*) **a ~ secret** ein gut gehütetes Geheimnis

well 'known *adj pred,* **well-'known** *adj attr* [allgemein] bekannt; (*famous*) berühmt

well 'meaning *adj pred,* **well-'mean-**

W

ing *adj attr* ~ **advice** gut gemeinte Ratschläge

'wellness *n* Wohlbefinden *nt*

well 'off <better-, best-> *adj pred*, **well-'off** *adj attr* wohlhabend

well pro'portioned *adj pred*, **well-pro'portioned** *adj attr* wohlproportioniert

well 'read *adj pred*, **well-'read** *adj attr* [sehr] belesen

well 'spoken *adj pred*, **well-'spoken** *adj attr* (*polite*) höflich; (*refined*) beredt

well 'timed *adj pred*, **well-'timed** *adj attr* **his remark was ~** seine Bemerkung kam zur rechten Zeit

well-to-'do *adj* (*fam*) [gut] betucht

'well-wisher *n* wohlwollender Freund/ wohlwollende Freundin; (*supporter*) Sympathisant(in) *m(f)*

well 'worn *adj pred*, **well-'worn** *adj attr* *clothes* abgetragen; *object* abgenützt

went [went] *pt of* **go**

wept *pt, pp of* **weep**

were [wɜr] *pt of* **be**

we're [wɪr] = **we are** *see* **be**

weren't [wɜrnt] = **were not** *see* **be**

west [west] **I.** *n* ①(*direction*) Westen *m;* **to be to the ~ of sth** westlich von etw *dat* liegen ■POL **the W~** die westliche Welt **II.** *adj* westlich, West-; **the ~ coast of Florida** die Westküste Floridas **III.** *adv* westwärts; **to travel ~** nach Westen reisen

'westbound *adj* in Richtung Westen

westerly ['wes·tər·li] *adj* westlich

western ['wes·tərn] **I.** *adj attr* West-, westlich; **~ Europe** Westeuropa *nt* **II.** *n* (*film*) Western *m*

westerner ['wes·tər·nər] *n* Abendländer(in) *m(f)*

West Vir'ginia *n* West Virginia *nt*

westward(s) ['west·wərd(z)] *adj* westlich; *road* nach Westen *nach n*

wet [wet] **I.** *adj* <-tt-> ①(*soaked*) nass; ■**soaking** ~ [völlig] durchnässt ②(*covered with moisture*) feucht ③(*not dried*) **"~ paint!"** „frisch gestrichen!" **II.** *vt* <-tt-, wet *or* wetted, wet *or*

wetted> ①(*moisten*) anfeuchten; (*soak*) nass machen ②(*urinate*) **to ~ the bed** das Bett nass machen

'wetback *n* (*pej sl*) illegaler Einwanderer/illegale Einwanderin aus Mexiko

wet 'dream *n* (*fam*) feuchter Traum

'wetness *n* Nässe *f*

'wetsuit *n* Taucheranzug *m*

we've [wiv] = **we have** *see* **have I, II**

whack [hwæk] **I.** *vt* (*sl: murder*) ■**to ~ sb/sth?** jdn umlegen *fam* **II.** *n* (*blow*) Schlag *m*

whacko ['wæ·koʊ] *adj* (*sl*) *see* **wacko**

whale [hweɪl] *n* Wal *m*

whaling ['hweɪ·lɪŋ] *n* der Walfang

wharf <*pl* wharves> [hwɔrf] *n* Kai *m*

what [hwʌt] **I.** *pron* ① *interrog* was; **~ is your name?** wie heißt du?; **~ about sb/sth?** (*fam*) was ist mit jdm/etw?; **~ for?** (*for what purpose?*) wofür?; (*fam: why?*) warum?; **~ if ...?** was ist, wenn ...?; **so ~?** (*fam*) na und? ② *rel* was; **I can't decide ~ to do next** ich kann mich nicht entschließen, was ich als nächstes tun soll ③ *rel* (*whatever*) was; **do ~ you can** tu, was du kannst **II.** *adj* ①(*which*) welche(r, s); **~ time is it?** wie spät ist es? ②(*emphasizing*) was für; **~ a shame!** wie schade! **III.** *interj* ①(*pardon?*) **~?** **I can't hear you** was? ich höre dich nicht ②(*showing surprise, disbelief*) **~!? you left him there alone!?** was?! du hast ihn da allein gelassen?

whatchamacallit ['hwʌtʃ·ə·mə·kɔl·ɪt] *n* (*fam*) Dingsda *m o f o nt fam;* (*object a.*) Dings *nt fam*

whatever [hwʌt·'ev·ər] **I.** *pron* ① was [auch immer]; **I eat ~ I want** ich esse, was ich will ② (*fam*) **or ~** wie du willst **II.** *adj* ①(*any*) was auch immer; **take ~ action is needed** was auch immer nötig ist ②(*regardless*) gleichgültig welche(r, s) **III.** *adv with neg* überhaupt

whatnot ['hwʌt·nɑt] *n* (*fam*) ■**and ~** und was weiß ich noch alles

whatsoever [ˌhwʌt·soʊ·'ev·ər] *adv* überhaupt

wheat [hwit] *n* Weizen *m*

W

'wheat germ *n* Weizenkeim *m*
wheel [hwil] *n* ❶ Rad *nt;* **rear ~** Hinterrad *nt* ❷ *(for steering)* Steuer *nt;* AUTO Lenkrad *nt;* ■ **to be at the ~** am Steuer sitzen ❸ *(fam: vehicle)* ■**~s** *pl* fahrbarer Untersatz *hum*
◆ **wheel around** *vi* sich schnell umdrehen; *(esp shocked)* herumfahren
'wheelbarrow *n* Schubkarre *f*
'wheelchair *n* Rollstuhl *m*
wheeler-dealer [ˌhwiˈlərˈdiˈlər] *n* Schlitzohr *nt*
wheeling [ˈhwiˈlɪŋ] *n* **~ and dealing** Abzockerei *f sl; (shady)* Gemauschel *nt*
wheeze [hwiz] I. *vi* keuchen II. *n* Keuchen *nt kein pl*
when [hwen] I. *adv* ❶ *interrog* wann; **~ do you want to go?** wann möchtest du gehen? ❷ *rel (during)* wenn, wo; **there are times ~ ...** es gibt Momente, wo ... II. *conj* ❶ *(once in past)* als; *(several times in past)* wenn; **I loved that film ~ I was a child** als Kind liebte ich diesen Film ❷ *(after, whenever)* wenn
whenever [hwenˈevˈər] *conj* ❶ wann auch immer ❷ *(every time)* jedes Mal, wenn ...
where [hwer] *adv* ❶ *interrog* wo; *(to where)* wohin; *(from where)* woher; **~ are you going?** wohin gehst du? ❷ *rel* wo; *(to where)* wohin; *(from where)* woher; **Boston, ~ Phil comes from ...** Boston, wo Phil herkommt ...
▶PHRASES: **to see ~ sb's coming from** verstehen, was jd meint
whereabouts I. *n* [ˈhwerˈəˈbaʊts] + *sing/pl vb* Aufenthaltsort *m* II. *adv* [ˌhwerˈəˈbaʊts] wo [genau]; **~ in Manhattan do you live?** wo genau in Manhattan wohnst du?
whereas [hwerˈæz] *conj (in contrast to)* während
wherever [ˌhwerˈevˈər] I. *conj* ❶ *(to whatever place)* wohin auch immer ❷ *(in all places)* wo auch immer II. *adv (in every case)* wann immer; **~ possible** wenn möglich
whether [ˈhweðˈər] *conj* ❶ *(if)* ob; **to**

ask ~ ... fragen, ob ...; **she can't decide ~ to tell him** sie kann sich nicht entscheiden, ob sie es ihm sagen soll ❷ *(no matter)* **~ you like it or not** ob es dir [nun] gefällt oder nicht
whew [hwu] *interj* puh
which [hwɪtʃ] I. *pron* ❶ *interrog (one)* welche(r, s); **~ [one] is mine?** welches gehört mir? ❷ *rel (with defining clause)* der/die/das; **the conference, ~ ended on Friday** die Konferenz, die am Freitag geendet hat ❸ *rel (with non-defining clause)* was; **she says it's Anna's fault, ~ is ridiculous** sie sagt, das ist Annas Schuld, was aber Blödsinn ist II. *adj interrog (one)* welche(r, s); **~ doctor did you see?** bei welchem Arzt warst du?
whichever [hwɪtʃˈevˈər] I. *pron* wer/ was auch immer II. *adj attr* ❶ *(any one)* ■**~ ...** der/die-/dasjenige, der/die/ das ...; **choose ~ brand you prefer** wähle die Marke, die du lieber hast ❷ *(regardless)* egal welche(r, s), welche(r, s) ... auch immer
whiff [hwɪf] *n usu sing* Hauch *m kein pl*
while [hwaɪl] I. *n* Weile *f;* **in a ~** in Kürze II. *conj* ❶ *(during)* während ❷ *(although)* obwohl; **~ I completely understand your point of view, ...** wenn ich Ihren Standpunkt auch vollkommen verstehe, ...
whim [hwɪm] *n* Laune *f*
whimper [ˈhwɪmˈpər] *vi person* wimmern; *dog* winseln
whimsical [ˈhwɪmˈzɪˈkəl] *adj* ❶ *(playful)* skurril *geh* ❷ *(capricious)* launenhaft
whimsy, whimsey [ˈhwɪmˈzi] *n* ❶ *(whim)* Laune *f* ❷ *(playfulness)* Spleenigkeit *f*
whine [hwaɪn] *vi* ❶ *(utter sound)* jammern; *animal* jaulen ❷ *(complain)* meckern
whip [hwɪp] I. *n* Peitsche *f* II. *vt* <-pp-> ❶ *(hit)* [mit der Peitsche] schlagen; *horse* die Peitsche geben ❷ *(fam: defeat)* [vernichtend] schlagen
◆ **whip out** *vt* zücken

♦whip up *vt* ❶ (*excite*) **to ~ up support** Unterstützung finden ❷ (*cook*) zaubern *fig, hum*

'**whiplash** *n* ~ [**injury**] Schleudertrauma *nt*

whipped [hwɪpt] *adj* ~ **cream** Schlagsahne *f*

whippet ['hwɪp-ɪt] *n* Whippet *m*

whipping ['hwɪp-ɪŋ] *n* ❶ (*punishment*) **to get a ~** Prügel beziehen ❷ (*fam: defeat*) Schlappe *f fam*

'**whipping cream** *n* Schlagsahne *f*

whir [hwɜr] *vi* <-rr-> surren

whirl [hwɜrl] **I.** *vt, vi* wirbeln **II.** *n* ❶ (*action*) Wirbeln *nt* ❷ (*activity*) Trubel *m*

whirligig ['hwɜr-lɪ-gɪg] *n* (*top*) Kreisel *m*

whirlpool ['hwɜrl-pul] *n* Whirlpool *m*

whirlwind ['hwɜrl-wɪnd] *n* Wirbelwind *m*

whisk [hwɪsk] **I.** *n* Schneebesen *m* **II.** *vt cream* schlagen

whisker ['hwɪs-kər] *n* ❶ (*of animal*) Schnurrhaar[e] *nt*[*pl*] ❷ (*beard*) **~s** Bartstoppeln *pl* ▶PHRASES: **by a ~** um Haaresbreite

whiskey, **whisky** ['hwɪs-ki] *n* Whisk[e]y *m*

whisper ['hwɪs-pər] **I.** *vi* flüstern **II.** *n* Flüstern *nt kein pl*; **to speak in a ~** etw im Flüsterton sagen

whispering ['hwɪs-pər-ɪŋ] **I.** *n* Flüstern *nt* **II.** *adj attr* flüsternd

whist [hwɪst] *n* Whist *nt*; **game of ~** Partie *f* Whist

whistle ['hwɪs-əl] **I.** *vi* ❶ pfeifen ❷ *bird* zwitschern **II.** *vt* pfeifen **III.** *n* ❶ (*sound*) Pfeifen *nt* ❷ (*device*) Pfeife *f*; **as clean as a ~** blitzsauber

white [hwaɪt] **I.** *n* ❶ Weiß *nt* ❷ *of eye* Weiße *nt* ❸ (*person*) Weiße(r) *f(m)* **II.** *adj* ❶ weiß; **black and ~** schwarzweiß ❷ *coffee* mit Milch *nach vn* ❸ **~ bread** Weißbrot *nt* ❹ (*Caucasian*) weiß ▶PHRASES: **as ~ as a sheet** weiß wie die Wand, kreidebleich

'**white-collar** *adj* ~ **worker** Angestellte(r) *f(m)*

white 'flag *n* weiße Fahne

'**White House** *n* ■**the ~** das Weiße Haus

white 'lie *n* Notlüge *f*

'**white meat** *n* helles Fleisch

whiten ['hwaɪ-tən] **I.** *vt* weiß machen; *teeth* bleichen **II.** *vi* weiß werden

whitener ['hwaɪ-tnər] *n* (*for coffee*) Kaffeeweißer *m*

'**whiteout** *n* ❶ METEO [starker] Schneesturm ❷ TYPO Korrekturflüssigkeit *f*

'**white sale** *n* Weißwäscheausverkauf *m*

'**whitewash I.** *n* ❶ (*solution*) Tünche *f* ❷ (*cover-up*) Schönfärberei *f* **II.** *vt* ❶ (*paint*) weiß anstreichen ❷ (*conceal*) schönfärben

white 'wine *n* Weißwein *m*

whiting <*pl* -> ['hwaɪ-tɪŋ] *n* (*fish*) Weißfisch *m*

Whitsun ['hwɪt-sən] *n* Pfingsten *nt*

whittle ['hwɪt-əl] *vt* schnitzen

♦whittle down *vt* reduzieren

whiz, whizz [hwɪz] **I.** *vi* ❶ **to ~ by** vorbeijagen ❷ *time* rasen **II.** *vt* [mit dem Mixer] verrühren **III.** *n* (*fam*) **computer ~** Computerass *nt fam*

whiz kid *n* Wunderkind *nt*, Genie *nt oft hum*

who [hu] *pron* ❶ *interrog* (*which person*) wer; **~ did this?** wer war das? ❷ *interrog* (*whom*) wem *dat*, wen *akk*; **~ do you want to talk to?** mit wem möchten Sie sprechen? ❸ *rel* der/die/das; **I think it was your dad ~ called** ich glaube, das war dein Vater, der angerufen hat

whoa [hwoʊ] *interj* ❶ (*fam: slow down!*) langsam! ❷ (*fam: wow!*) wow *sl*, toll! *fam*

whodunit, whodunnit [,hu-'dʌn-ɪt] *n* (*fam*) Krimi *m fam*

whoever [hu-'ev-ər] *pron rel* **come out, ~ you are** kommen Sie heraus, wer auch immer Sie sind

whole [hoʊl] **I.** *adj* ❶ (*entire*) ganz; **the ~ [wide] world** die ganze [weite] Welt ❷ (*in one piece*) ganz; (*intact*) intakt **II.** *n* ❶ (*entire thing*) ■**a ~** ein Ganzes *nt* ❷ (*entirety*) ■**the ~** das Ganze ❸ (*in total*) **on the ~** im Großen und

W

Ganzen III. *adv* ganz; **a ~ new approach** ein ganz neuer Ansatz

'whole food *n* Vollwertkost *f*

wholehearted [ˌhoʊlˈhɑr·tɪd] *adj* ❶ (*sincere*) aufrichtig ❷ (*committed*) engagiert

whole 'milk *n* Vollmilch *f*

'whole note *n* MUS ganze Note

'whole rest *n* MUS ganze Pause

wholesale ['hoʊl·seɪl] I. *adj* ❶ *attr* ~ **business** Großhandel *m* ❷ (*extensive*) ~ **reform** umfassende Reform II. *adv* (*in bulk*) in Großmengen

wholesaler ['hoʊl·seɪ·lər] *n* Großhändler(in) *m(f)*

wholesome ['hoʊl·səm] *adj* wohltuend; (*healthy*) gesund

'whole-wheat *adj attr* ~ **bread** Vollkornbrot *nt*

who'll [hul] = **who will** *see* **who**

wholly ['hoʊ·li] *adv* ganz, völlig

whom [hum] *pron* (*form*) ❶ *interrog* wem *dat*, wen *akk*; ~ **did he marry?** wen hat er geheiratet? ❷ *rel* das/der/die; **none of ~ ...** keiner, der ...

'whooping cough *n* Keuchhusten *m*

whoops [hwʊps] *interj* (*fam*) hoppla; **~-a-daisy** hopsala

whop [hwɑp] *vt* <-pp-> (*fam*) schlagen

whopper ['hwɑp·ər] *n* (*fam*) ❶ (*huge thing*) Apparat *m sl;* **that's a ~ of a fish** das ist ja ein Riesenfisch ❷ (*lie*) faustdicke Lüge *fam*

whore [hɔr] *n* (*pej*) Nutte *f sl*

who's [huz] = **who is, who has** *see* **who**

whose [huz] I. *adj* ❶ (*in questions*) wessen; ~ **round is it?** wer ist dran? ❷ (*indicating possession*) dessen; **she's the woman ~ car I rode in** sie ist die Frau, in deren Auto ich gefahren bin II. *pron poss, interrog* wessen

why [hwaɪ] *adv* ❶ (*for what reason*) warum; ~ **did he say that?** warum hat er das gesagt? ❷ (*for that reason*) **the reason ~ I ...** der Grund, warum ich ...

WI *abbrev of* **Wisconsin**

wick [wɪk] *n* Docht *m*

wicked ['wɪk·ɪd] I. *adj* ❶ (*evil*) böse

❷ (*cunning*) raffiniert ❸ (*fam: good*) saugut *sl* II. *interj* (*fam*) super *fam*

wicker ['wɪk·ər] *n* Korbgeflecht *nt*

wicker 'furniture *n* Korbmöbel *pl*

wicket ['wɪk·ɪt] *n* (*croquet hoop*) Tor *nt*

wide [waɪd] I. *adj* ❶ (*broad*) breit ❷ (*considerable*) enorm, beträchtlich ❸ (*open*) breit; *eyes* groß ❹ (*varied*) breit gefächert; ~ **range of goods** großes Sortiment an Waren II. *adv* weit; ~ **apart** weit auseinander

wide-angle 'lens *n* PHOT Weitwinkelobjektiv *nt fachspr*

wide a'wake *adj pred,* wide-a'wake *adj attr* hellwach

widely ['waɪd·li] *adv* ❶ (*broadly*) breit ❷ (*extensively*) weit; ~ **admired** weithin bewundert ❸ (*considerably*) beträchtlich

'widespread *adj* weit verbreitet

widow ['wɪd·oʊ] *n* Witwe *f*

widower ['wɪd·oʊ·ər] *n* Witwer *m*

width [wɪdθ] *n* Breite *f*

wiener ['wi·nər] *n* ❶ (*hot dog*) Wiener Würstchen *nt* ❷ (*childspeak fam: penis*) Pimmel *m fam*

wife <*pl* wives> [waɪf] *n* [Ehe]frau *f*

Wi-Fi® ['waɪ·faɪ] *n no pl abbrev of* **Wireless Fidelity** INET WLAN *nt*

wig [wɪg] *n* Perücke *f*

wiggle ['wɪg·əl] *vt, vi* wackeln

wigwam ['wɪg·wɑm] *n* Wigwam *m*

wild [waɪld] I. *adj* ❶ (*undomesticated*) wild ❷ (*uncultivated*) *landscape* rau, wild; ~ **flowers** wild wachsende Blumen ❸ (*uncontrolled*) unbändig; *behavior* undiszipliniert ❹ (*stormy*) rau, stürmisch ❺ (*fam: angry*) wütend ❻ (*fam: enthusiastic*) ■ **to be ~ about sb** auf jdn ganz wild sein II. *adv* wild; **to run ~** *child* sich *dat* selbst überlassen sein; *animals* frei herumlaufen III. *n* ❶ (*natural environment*) ■ **the ~** die Wildnis ❷ (*fig: remote places*) ■ **the ~s** *pl* die Pampa *f kein pl oft hum fam*

wild 'boar *n* Wildschwein *nt*

'wildcard *n* ❶ CARDS Joker *m* ❷ COMPUT Wildcard *f*

'wildcat *n* Wildkatze *f*

wilderness <*pl* -es> ['wɪl·dər·nɪs] *n* Wildnis *f*; (*desert*) Wüste *f*

'wildfire *n* **to spread like ~** (*fig*) sich wie ein Lauffeuer verbreiten

'wildfowl *n* Federwild *nt kein pl*; FOOD Wildgeflügel *nt kein pl*

wild-'goose chase *n* (*venture*) fruchtloses Unterfangen

'wildlife I. *n* [natürliche] Tier- und Pflanzenwelt **II.** *adj* **~ sanctuary** Wildschutzgebiet *nt*

wildly ['waɪld·li] *adv* ① (*in uncontrolled way*) wild; **to talk ~** wirres Zeug reden *fam* ② (*haphazardly*) ungezielt; **to guess ~** [wild] drauflosraten *fam*

wild 'rice *n* Wildreis *m*

Wild West *n* **the ~** der Wilde Westen

wiles [waɪlz] *npl* Trick *m*; **to use all one's ~** mit allen Tricks arbeiten

wilful ['wɪl·fəl] *adj see* **willful**

will¹ <would, would> [wɪl] *aux vb* ① (*in future tense*) **do you think he ~ come?** glaubst du, dass er kommt [*o* kommen wird]? ② (*repeating question*) **you won't forget to tell him, ~ you?** du vergisst aber nicht, es ihm zu sagen, oder? ③ (*expressing intention*) werden; **I ~ always love you** ich werde dich immer lieben ④ (*expressing facts*) **fruit ~ keep longer in the fridge** Obst hält sich im Kühlschrank länger

will² [wɪl] **I.** *n* ① Wille *m* ② LAW Testament *nt* **II.** *vt* ■**to ~ sb to do sth** jdn [durch Willenskraft] dazu bringen, etw zu tun

willful, wilful ['wɪl·fəl] *adj* ① (*deliberate*) bewusst; *damage* mutwillig ② (*self-willed*) eigensinnig; (*obstinate*) starrsinnig

willies ['wɪl·iz] *npl* (*fam*) **sb has the ~** jd kriegt Zustände

willing ['wɪl·ɪŋ] *adj* ① (*unopposed*) bereit ② (*enthusiastic*) willig

willingness ['wɪl·ɪŋ·nɪs] *n* (*readiness*) Bereitschaft *f*; (*enthusiasm*) Bereitwilligkeit *f*

willow ['wɪl·ou] *n* Weide *f*

'willpower *n* Willenskraft *f*

wily ['waɪ·li] *adj* listig

wimp [wɪmp] *n* (*fam*) Waschlappen *m*

win [wɪn] **I.** *vt* <won, won> ① (*be victorious*) gewinnen ② (*get*) gewinnen, bekommen; *recognition* finden ▶PHRASES: **you can't ~ them** [*or* 'em] **all** (*saying*) man kann nicht immer Glück haben **II.** *vi* <won, won> gewinnen; **to ~ hands down** spielend gewinnen ▶PHRASES: **may the best man ~** dem Besten der Sieg **III.** *n* Sieg *m*

◆**win back** *vt* ① SPORT **to ~ back** ↻ **the trophy** den Pokal zurückholen ② *customers* zurückgewinnen

◆**win over** *vt* (*persuade*) überzeugen

◆**win around** *vt* überzeugen

winch [wɪntʃ] *n* <*pl* -es> Winde *f*

wind¹ [wɪnd] *n* ① (*air*) Wind *m*; **to see which way the ~ is blowing** sehen, woher der Wind weht *a. fig* ② (*breath*) Atem *m* ③ (*flatulence*) Blähungen *pl*

wind² [waɪnd] **I.** *vt* <wound, wound> ① (*wrap*) wickeln; *yarn* aufwickeln; *film* spulen ② *watch* aufziehen ③ (*turn*) winden **II.** *vi* <wound, wound> ① (*meander*) sich schlängeln ② (*coil*) sich wickeln

◆**wind down I.** *vt business* auflösen; *production* drosseln **II.** *vi* (*relax*) [sich] entspannen

◆**wind up I.** *vt* ① (*end*) abschließen; *meeting, speech* beenden ② (*annoy*) ■**to ~ up** ↻ **sb** jdn auf die Palme bringen ③ *clock* aufziehen **II.** *vi* (*fam*) ① (*end*) schließen *fam*; *speech* abschließend bemerken ② (*land*) enden; **to ~ up in prison** im Gefängnis landen *fam*

'windbreak *n* Windschutz *m*

'wind energy *n* Windenergie *f*

winder ['waɪn·dər] *n* Aufziehschraube *f*; (*on watch*) Krone *f*

'windfall *n* ① (*money*) warmer [Geld]regen *fam* ② (*fruit*) ■**~s** *pl* Fallobst *nt kein pl*

'wind farm *n* Windpark *m*

'wind generator *n* Windgenerator *m*

winding ['waɪn·dɪŋ] **I.** *adj* gewunden; *road* kurvenreich **II.** *n* ELEC Wicklung *f*

W

'**wind instrument** n Blasinstrument nt

'**windmill** n ① (for grinding) Windmühle f ② (turbine) Windrad nt

'**window** ['wɪn·doʊ] n ① (a. comput) Fenster nt; of shop Schaufenster nt; **rear** ~ Heckscheibe f ② (opportunity) Gelegenheit f

'**window box** n Blumenkasten m

'**window cleaner** n ① (person) Fensterputzer(in) m(f) ② (detergent) Glasreiniger m

'**window display** n Schaufensterauslage f

'**window frame** n Fensterrahmen m

'**window-shopping** n Schaufensterbummel m

'**windowsill** n (inside) Fensterbank f; (outside) Fenstersims m o nt

'**windpipe** n Luftröhre f

'**wind power** n (energy) Windenergie f

'**windshield** n Windschutzscheibe f

'**windshield wiper** n Scheibenwischer m

windsurfer ['wɪnd·ˌsɜr·fər] n Windsurfer(in) m(f)

'**windswept** adj ① beach windgepeitscht ② appearance [vom Wind] zerzaust

'**wind tunnel** n Windkanal m

'**wind turbine** n Windturbine f

'**windward** ['wɪnd·wərd] adj, adv windwärts

windy[1] ['wɪn·di] adj METEO windig

windy[2] ['waɪn·di] adj road kurvenreich

wine [waɪn] I. n ① Wein m II. vi **to ~ and dine** fürstlich essen

'**wine bottle** n Weinflasche f

'**wine cellar** n Weinkeller m

'**wineglass** n Weinglas nt

winegrower ['waɪn·ˌɡroʊ·ər] n Winzer(in) m(f)

winegrowing ['waɪn·ˌɡroʊ·ɪŋ] n Wein[an]bau m

'**wine list** n Weinkarte f

winery ['waɪ·nə·ri] n Weinkellerei f

'**winetasting** n Weinprobe f

wing [wɪŋ] n ① Flügel m ② THEAT **to be waiting in the ~s** in den Kulissen warten

'**wing chair** n Ohrensessel m

winger ['wɪŋ·ər] n SPORT (left) Linksaußen m; (right) Rechtsaußen m

'**wing nut** n Flügelmutter f

'**wingspan** n Flügelspannweite f

wink [wɪŋk] I. vi (one eye) zwinkern; ▪**to ~ at sb** jdm zuzwinkern II. n [Augen]zwinkern nt ▶PHRASES: **to not sleep a ~** kein Auge zutun

winner ['wɪn·ər] n (victor) Gewinner(in) m(f); (in competition) Sieger(in) m(f)

winning ['wɪn·ɪŋ] I. adj attr (in competition) Sieger-; (victorious) siegreich; **to be on a ~ streak** eine Glückssträhne haben II. n ▪**~s** pl Gewinn m

winter ['wɪn·tər] n Winter m

winter 'sports npl Wintersport m kein pl

'**wintertime** n Winterzeit f

wintry ['wɪn·tri], **wintery** ['wɪn·tə·ri] adj winterlich

wipe [waɪp] I. vt ① (clean) abwischen; feet abtreten; nose putzen ② dishes abtrocknen II. n Reinigungstuch nt

◆ **wipe down** vt abwischen; (with water) abwaschen

◆ **wipe off** vt (clean) wegwischen; (from surface) abwischen

◆ **wipe out** vt ① (destroy) auslöschen; disease ausrotten ② (kill) beseitigen

◆ **wipe up** vt aufwischen

wire ['waɪr] I. n ① (thread) Draht m ② ELEC (cable) Leitung f II. vt ① (fasten) mit Draht binden ② ELEC (connect) mit elektrischen Leitungen versehen

'**wire cutters** npl [pair of] ~ Drahtschere f

'**wireless** adj drahtlos; ~ **network** Funknetz nt

wireless communi'cation n Mobilfunk m

wiretapping ['waɪr·ˌtæp·ɪŋ] n Abhören nt von Telefonleitungen

wiring ['waɪr·ɪŋ] n ① (wires) elektrische Leitungen pl ② (installation) Stromverlegen nt

'**wiring diagram** n Schaltplan m

W

wiry [ˈwaɪ·ri] *adj* ❶ *hair* borstig ❷ (*fig: lean*) drahtig

Wis. *abbrev of* **Wisconsin**

Wisconsin [wɪsˈkɑn·sɪn] *n* Wisconsin *nt*

wisdom [ˈwɪz·dəm] *n* Weisheit *f*

'wisdom tooth *n* Weisheitszahn *m*

wise [waɪz] *adj* ❶ (*sage*) klug; **to be older and ~r** durch Schaden klug geworden sein ❷ (*sensible*) vernünftig; **a ~ choice** eine gute Wahl ❸ *pred* (*fam: aware*) **to get ~ to sb** jdn durchschauen

◆ **wise up** *vi* (*fam*) aufwachen

wisecrack [ˈwaɪz·kræk] **I.** *n* Witzelei[en] *f[pl]* **II.** *vi* witzeln

'wise guy *n* (*fam*) Klugschwätzer *m pej fam*

wish [wɪʃ] **I.** *n* <*pl* -es> ❶ (*desire*) Wunsch *m*, Verlangen *nt* ❷ (*thing desired*) Wunsch *m*; **to grant sb a ~** jdm einen Wunsch erfüllen ❸ (*regards*) ■**~es** *pl* Grüße *pl* **II.** *vt* ❶ (*be desirous*) wünschen; **whatever you ~** was immer du möchtest ❷ (*make a magic wish*) ■**to ~** [**that**] … sich *dat* wünschen, dass … ❸ (*express wishes*) **to ~ sb happy birthday** jdm zum Geburtstag gratulieren **III.** *vi* ❶ (*want*) wollen ❷ (*make a wish*) wünschen

wishbone [ˈwɪʃ·boʊn] *n* Gabelbein *nt*

wishful 'thinking *n* Wunschdenken *nt*

wishy-washy [ˈwɪʃ·i·ˌwɑʃ·i] *adj colors* wässrig

wisp [wɪsp] *n* Büschel *nt*; **~ s of smoke** [kleine] Rauchfahnen

wispy [ˈwɪs·pi] *adj* dünn; *hair* strähnig

wisteria [wɪˈstɪr·i·ə] *n* BOT Glyzin[i]e *f*

wistful [ˈwɪst·fəl] *adj smile* wehmütig; *look* sehnsüchtig

wit [wɪt] *n* ❶ (*humor*) Witz *m*; **dry ~** trockener Humor ❷ (*intelligence*) ■**~s** *pl* geistige Fähigkeiten; **to keep one's ~s** seine fünf Sinne zusammenhalten *fam*

witch <*pl* -es> [wɪtʃ] *n* Hexe *f*

'witchcraft [ˈwɪtʃ·kræft] *n* Hexerei *f*

'witch doctor *n* Medizinmann *m*

'witch-hunt *n* Hexenjagd *f*

with [wɪð, wɪθ] *prep* ❶ (*having*) mit +*dat;* **~ a little luck** mit ein wenig Glück ❷ (*accompanied*) **~ friends** mit Freunden ❸ (*concerning*) **to have something to do ~ sb/sth** etwas mit jdm/etw zu tun haben ❹ (*using*) **she paints ~ watercolors** sie malt mit Wasserfarben ❺ (*while*) **~ things the way they are** so wie die Dinge sind ❻ (*in state of*) vor +*dat;* **she was shaking ~ rage** sie zitterte vor Wut ❼ (*in company of*) bei +*dat;* **to stay ~ relatives** bei Verwandten übernachten

withdraw <-drew, -drawn> [wɪðˈdrɔ] **I.** *vt* ❶ (*remove*) herausziehen; **to ~ one's hand** seine Hand zurückziehen ❷ *money* abheben ❸ (*take back*) *coins* aus dem Verkehr ziehen **II.** *vi* sich zurückziehen

withdrawal [wɪðˈdrɔ·əl] *n* ❶ FIN [Geld]abhebung *f* ❷ MIL Rückzug *m* ❸ (*taking back*) Zurücknehmen *nt;* (*cancel*) Zurückziehen *nt; of funds* Entzug *m; of allegation* Widerruf *m; from contract* Rücktritt *m*

with'drawal symptoms *npl* Entzugserscheinungen *pl*

wither [ˈwɪð·ər] *vi* verdorren

withhold <-held, -held> [wɪðˈhoʊld] *vt* ❶ (*not give*) zurückhalten; **to ~ information** Informationen verschweigen ❷ (*not pay*) etw nicht zahlen; **to ~ benefit payments** Leistungen nicht auszahlen

within [wɪðˈɪn] **I.** *prep* ❶ innerhalb +*gen* ❷ (*in limit of*) **~ reach** in Reichweite **II.** *adv* innen; ■**from ~** von innen [heraus]

'with-it *adj* (*fam*) ❶ (*trendy*) modisch; **to be ~** auf dem neuesten Stand sein ❷ (*alert*) aufmerksam

without [wɪðˈaʊt] *prep* ohne +*akk*

withstand <-stood, -stood> [wɪðˈstænd] *vt* ■**to ~ sth** etw standhalten; **to ~ rough treatment** eine unsanfte Behandlung aushalten

witness [ˈwɪt·nɪs] **I.** *n* <*pl* -es> Zeuge, -in *m, f;* **expert ~** Gutachter(in) *m(f)*

W

II. *vt* beobachten; ■ to ~ sb doing sth sehen, wie jd etw tut

'witness stand *n* Zeugenstand *m kein pl*

witty ['wɪt·i] *adj* (*clever*) geistreich; (*funny*) witzig

wizard ['wɪz·ərd] *n* Zauberer *m*

wobble ['wab·əl] I. *vi* ❶ (*move*) wackeln; *wheel* eiern *fam; knees* zittern ❷ (*tremble*) *voice* zittern II. *vt* rütteln III. *n* Wackeln *nt kein pl*

wobbly ['wab·li] *adj* wack[e]lig

wok [wak] *n* Wok *m*

woke [woʊk] *vt, vi pt of* wake

woken ['woʊ·kən] *vt, vi pp of* wake

wolf [wʊlf] I. *n* <*pl* wolves> Wolf *m* ▶PHRASES: to cry ~ blinden Alarm schlagen II. *vt* ■ to ~ down etw verschlingen

'wolf cub *n* Wolfsjunge(s) *nt*

'wolfhound *n* Wolfshund *m*

'wolf whistle *n* bewundernder Pfiff

woman ['wʊm·ən] *n* <*pl* women> Frau *f*

womanizer ['wʊm·ə·naɪ·zər] *n* Weiberheld *m oft pej*

womanly ['wʊm·ən·li] *adj* weiblich

womb [wʊm] *n* Gebärmutter *f*

womenfolk ['wɪm·ɪn·foʊk] *npl* Frauen *pl*

women's lib [ˌwɪm·ɪnz·'lɪb] *n* (*fam*) *short for* women's liberation die Frauen[rechts]bewegung

won [wʌn] *vt, vi pt, pp of* win

wonder ['wʌn·dər] I. *vi* ❶ (*ask*) sich fragen; why do you ask? — I was just ~ing warum fragst du? — ach, nur so; ■ to ~ about sth sich Gedanken über etw machen ❷ (*surprised*) ■ to ~ at sth sich über etw wundern II. *n* ❶ (*surprise*) Staunen *nt*, Verwunderung *f* ❷ (*marvel*) Wunder *nt*; no ~ ... kein Wunder, dass ...; to work ~s [wahre] Wunder wirken

'wonder boy *n* (*iron, hum fam*) Wunderknabe *m*

'wonder drug *n* Wundermittel *nt*

wonderful ['wʌn·dər·fəl] *adj* wunderbar

'wonderland *n* Wunderland *nt*;

winter ~ winterliche Märchenlandschaft

won't [woʊnt] = will not *see* will[1]

woo [wu] *vt* to ~ voters Wähler umwerben

wood [wʊd] *n* ❶ Holz *nt*; plank of ~ [Holz]brett *nt* ❷ (*forest*) ■~s *pl* Wald *m* ▶PHRASES: to not be out of the ~[s] (*still critical*) noch nicht über den Berg sein *fam*; (*still difficult*) noch nicht aus dem Schneider sein *fam*; knock on ~! unberufen!

'woodcarving *n* ART ❶ (*art genre*) Holzschnitzerei *f* ❷ (*object*) [Holz]schnitzerei *f*

'woodchuck *n* ZOOL Waldmurmeltier *nt*

'woodcut *n* ART Holzschnitt *m*

wooded ['wʊd·ɪd] *adj* ~ area Waldgebiet *nt*

wooden ['wʊd·ən] *adj* ❶ Holz-, aus Holz *nach n* ❷ (*stiff*) *movements* hölzern

'woodland *n* ■~[s] *pl*] Wald *m*

'woodpecker *n* Specht *m*

'woodpile *n* Holzstoß *m*

'wood pulp *n* Zellstoff *m*

'woodwind *n pl* ■the ~s die Holzbläser *pl*

'woodwork *n of building* Holzwerk *nt* ▶PHRASES: to come out of the ~ ans Licht kommen

'woodworking *n* (*carpentry*) Tischlern *nt*; (*business*) Tischlerei *f*

'woodworm <*pl* -> *n* Holzwurm *m*

woof [wʊf] *vi dog* bellen; ~, ~! wau, wau

woofer ['wʊf·ər] *n* Tieftonlautsprecher *m*

wool [wʊl] *n* Wolle *f*

woolen, woollen ['wʊl·ən] *adj* wollen, aus Wolle *nach n*

wooly, woolly ['wʊl·i] *adj* ❶ Woll-, wollen ❷ (*vague*) verschwommen; *thoughts* kraus

woozy ['wu·zi] *adj* (*fam: dizzy*) benommen; (*drunk*) beschwipst *fam*

word [wɜrd] I. *n* ❶ Wort *nt*; in other ~s mit anderen Worten; in a ~ um es kurz zu sagen ❷ (*talk*) [kurzes] Ge-

W

spräch; **to have a ~ with sb** [about sth] mit jdm [über etw *akk*] sprechen ❸ (*promise*) Wort *nt*; **to go back on one's ~** sein Wort brechen ❹ (*lyrics*) ■**~s** *pl* Text *m* ▸PHRASES: **by ~ of** <u>mouth</u> mündlich II. *vt* formulieren

wording ['wɜr·dɪŋ] *n* Formulierung *f*

wordless ['wɜrd·lɪs] *adj* wortlos, ohne Worte

'**word order** *n* Wortstellung *f*

word-'perfect *adj* textsicher

'**wordplay** *n* Wortspiel *nt*

'**word processor** *n* COMPUT ❶ (*computer*) Textverarbeitungssystem *nt* ❷ (*program*) Textverarbeitungsprogramm *nt*

'**word wrap** *n* COMPUT [automatischer] Zeilenumbruch

wore [wɔr] *vt, vi* pt of **wear**

work [wɜrk] I. *n* ❶ (*activity*) Arbeit *f*; **to be hard ~** (*strenuous*) anstrengend sein; (*difficult*) schwierig sein ❷ (*employment*) Arbeit *f*; **to look for ~** auf Arbeitssuche sein; **to be at ~** bei der Arbeit sein ❸ (*opus*) Werk *nt*; **~s of art** Kunstwerke *pl* ❹ (*factory*) ■**~s** + *sing vb* Werk *nt*, Fabrik *f* ❺ (*fam: all*) ■**the ~s** *pl* das ganze Drum und Dran *kein pl* II. *vi* ❶ (*do job*) arbeiten; **to ~ hard** hart arbeiten; **to ~ together** zusammenarbeiten ❷ (*be busy*) arbeiten; ■**to ~ at/on sth** an etw *dat* arbeiten ❸ (*function*) funktionieren; **my cell phone doesn't ~** mein Handy geht nicht ❹ (*succeed*) funktionieren, klappen *fam; medicine* wirken III. *vt* ❶ (*operate*) *machine* bedienen; *equipment* etw betätigen ❷ (*move*) **to ~ sth free** etw losbekommen ❸ (*pay by working*) **to ~ one's way through college** sich *dat* sein Studium finanzieren ▸PHRASES: **to ~ one's <u>fingers</u> to the bone** [for sb/sth] (*fam*) sich *dat* [für jdn/etw] den Rücken krummarbeiten

◆**work away** *vi* vor sich hinarbeiten

◆**work for** *vt* ❶ (*be employed by*) arbeiten für +*akk* ❷ (*appeal to*) ■**to** [**not**] **~ for sb** jdm [nicht] zusagen

◆**work in** *vt* (*mix in*) einarbeiten; (*on skin*) einreiben

◆**work off** *vt* (*counteract*) abarbeiten; *energy* loswerden

◆**work out** I. *vt* ❶ (*calculate*) errechnen ❷ (*develop*) ausarbeiten ❸ (*figure out*) ■**to ~ out** ○ sth hinter etw *akk* kommen ❹ (*solve itself*) **things usually ~ themselves out** die Dinge erledigen sich meist von selbst II. *vi* ❶ (*amount to*) **to ~ out cheaper** billiger kommen ❷ (*develop*) sich entwickeln; **to ~ out well** gut laufen *fam* ❸ (*do exercise*) trainieren

◆**work through** *vt* durcharbeiten; *problems* aufarbeiten

◆**work toward** *vt* **to ~ toward a deadline** auf einen Termin hinarbeiten

◆**work up** I. *vt* ❶ (*generate*) **to ~ up an appetite** Appetit bekommen ❷ (*upset*) ■**to ~ oneself up** sich aufregen ❸ (*develop*) **to ~ up a sweat** ins Schwitzen kommen II. *vi* (*progress to*) ■**to ~ up to sth** sich zu etw *dat* hocharbeiten

workable ['wɜr·ə·bəl] *adj* ❶ (*feasible*) durchführbar ❷ (*able to be manipulated*) bearbeitbar; **~ land** bebaubares Land

workaholic ['wɜr·kə·hɔ·lɪk] *n* (*fam*) Arbeitssüchtige(r) *f(m)*

'**workbench** *n* Werkbank *f*

'**workbook** *n* Arbeitsbuch *nt*

'**work camp** *n* Lager, in dem Freiwillige gemeinnützige Arbeiten verrichten

'**workday** *n* ❶ (*work time*) Arbeitstag *m* ❷ (*not holiday*) Werktag *m*

worker ['wɜr·kər] *n* (*employee*) Arbeiter(in) *m(f)*; **blue-collar ~** [Fabrik]arbeiter(in) *m(f)*

'**work ethic** *n* Arbeitsethos *nt*

'**workforce** *n* Belegschaft *f*

working ['wɜr·kɪŋ] *adj attr* ❶ (*employed*) berufstätig ❷ (*for work*) **~ conditions** Arbeitsbedingungen *pl* ❸ (*functioning*) funktionierend *attr;* **in ~ order** betriebsfähig

working 'class *n* ■**the ~** die Arbeiterklasse *kein pl*

'**workload** *n* Arbeitspensum *nt kein pl;* TECH Leistungsumfang *m*

W

'workman n ❶ (worker) Arbeiter m ❷ (craftsman) Handwerker m
'workmanlike adj fachmännisch
workmanship ['wɜrk·mən·ʃɪp] n Verarbeitung[sgüte] f
work of 'art n Kunstwerk nt
'workout n Fitnesstraining nt
work permit n Arbeitserlaubnis f
'workplace n Arbeitsplatz m
'workshop n ❶ (room) Werkstatt f ❷ (meeting) Workshop m
'workstation n ❶ COMPUT Workstation f fachspr ❷ (work area) Arbeitsplatz m
'work surface n Arbeitsfläche f
world [wɜrld] n ❶ (earth) ▪ the ~ die Welt [o Erde] (planet) Welt f; beings from other ~ s Außerirdische pl ❸ (society) the ancient ~ die antike Welt ▶ PHRASES: to be out of this ~ (fam) himmlisch sein; not for [all] the ~ nie im Leben
World 'Bank n ▪ the ~ die Weltbank
'world-class adj von Weltklasse nach n
world-'famous adj weltberühmt
world popu'lation n Weltbevölkerung f
world 'power n Weltmacht f
world 'record n Weltrekord m
World Series npl Finale der US-amerikanischen Baseball-Profiliga
World's 'Fair n Weltausstellung f
'world view n Weltanschauung f
world 'war n Weltkrieg m; W~ W~ II der 2. Weltkrieg
worldwide ['wɜrld·ˌwaɪd] adj, adv weltweit
World Wide 'Web n INET ▪ the ~ das World Wide Web, das Internet
worm [wɜrm] I. n (comput) Wurm m II. vt (treat for worms) an animal entwurmen
'worm-eaten adj wurmzerfressen
W **worn** [wɔrn] I. vt, vi pp of **wear** II. adj (damaged) abgenutzt; carpet abgetreten
worn 'out adj pred, 'worn-out adj attr ❶ (tired) erschöpft ❷ shoes durchgelaufen
worried ['wɜr·ɪd] adj beunruhigt, be-

sorgt; ▪ to be ~ about sb/sth sich dat um jdn/etw Sorgen machen
worry ['wɜr·i] I. vi <-ie-> sich dat Sorgen machen (about um + akk); I'm sorry — don't ~ about it tut mir leid — das macht doch nichts II. vt <-ie-> beunruhigen III. n Sorge f
worrying ['wɜ·ri·ɪŋ] adj Besorgnis erregend
worse [wɜrs] I. adj comp of **bad** schlechter; (harder, uglier) schlimmer II. adv comp of **badly** (less well) schlechter; (more seriously) schlimmer III. n to change for the ~ schlechter werden
worsen ['wɜr·sən] vt, vi [sich] verschlechtern
worship ['wɜr·ʃɪp] I. n ❶ Verehrung f ❷ (service) Gottesdienst m II. vt <-p-> ❶ (revere) to ~ a deity einer Gottheit huldigen geh ❷ (adore) vergöttern ▶ PHRASES: to ~ the ground sb walks on jdn abgöttisch verehren fam III. vi <-p-> beten
worshiper, worshipper ['wɜr·ʃɪp·ər] n Kirchgänger(in) m(f); devil ~ Teufelsanbeter(in) m(f)
worst [wɜrst] I. adj superl of **bad** ❶ (poorest, least) ▪ the ~ ... der/die/das schlechteste ... ❷ (most dangerous) schlimmste(r, s) ❸ (least advantageous) ungünstigste(r, s) II. adv superl of **badly** ❶ (most severely) am schlimmsten ❷ (least well) am schlechtesten III. n ▪ at ~ schlimmstenfalls ▶ PHRASES: to be at one's ~ sich von seiner schlechtesten Seite zeigen
worsted ['wʊs·tɪd] n Kammgarn nt
worth [wɜrθ] I. adj pred (valued, meriting) wert; to be ~ one's weight in gold Gold wert sein ▶ PHRASES: if a thing is ~ doing, it's ~ doing well (saying) wenn schon, denn schon fam; for what it's ~ (fam) übrigens fam II. n Wert m; of little ~ von geringem Wert
worthless ['wɜrθ·lɪs] adj wertlos a. fig
worthwhile [ˌwɜrθ·'hwaɪl] adj ▪ to be ~ sich lohnen
worthy ['wɜr·ði] adj ❶ (estimable) wür-

dig ❷(*meriting*) ~ **of praise** lobenswert

would [wʊd] *aux vb* ❶(*in indirect speech*) **they promised that they ~ help** sie versprachen zu helfen ❷(*expressing condition*) **what ~ you do if …?** was würdest du tun, wenn …? ❸(*expressing inclination*) **sb ~ rather do sth** jd würde lieber etw tun

'**would-be** *adj attr* Möchtegern- *pej fam*

wouldn't ['wʊd·ənt] = **would not** *see* **would**

wound¹ [wund] I. *n* Wunde *f*; **gunshot ~** Schussverletzung *f* II. *vt* verwunden

wound² [waʊnd] *vt, vi pt, pp of* **wind**

wounded ['wun·dɪd] I. *adj* verletzt II. *n* ■**the ~** *pl* MIL die Verwundeten *pl*

wove [woʊv] *vt, vi pt of* **weave**

woven ['woʊ·vən] I. *vt, vi pp of* **weave** II. *adj* (*on loom*) gewebt; **~ fabric** Gewebe *nt*

wow [waʊ] *interj* (*fam*) wow *sl*, toll! *fam*

wrangle ['ræŋ·gəl] I. *vi* streiten II. *n* Gerangel *nt*

wrap [ræp] I. *n* ❶(*robe*) Umhang *m* ❷(*packaging*) Verpackung *f*; **plastic ~** Frischhaltefolie *f* ❸ FOOD Tortillawrap *m* II. *vt* <-pp-> ❶(*cover*) einpacken; *in paper* einwickeln ❷(*draw around*) ■**to ~ sth around sb** etw um jdn wickeln ▶ PHRASES: **to ~ sb around one's little finger** jdn um den kleinen Finger wickeln

wraparound ['ræp·ə‚raʊnd] I. *adj* herumgezogen II. *n* ❶ FASHION Wickelrock *m* ❷ COMPUT Zeilenumbruch *m*

◆**wrap up** I. *vt* ❶(*cover*) einwickeln ❷ *deal* unter Dach und Fach bringen II. *vi usu passive* ■**to be ~ped up in sb** mit jdm ganz beschäftigt sein

wrapper ['ræp·ər] *n* (*packaging*) Verpackung *f*; *candy ~* Bonbonpapier *nt*

'**wrapping paper** *n* (*for package*) Packpapier *nt*; (*for present*) Geschenkpapier *nt*

wreak [rik] *vt* **to ~ damage** [**on sth**] Schaden [an etw *dat*] anrichten

wreath [riθ] *n* Kranz *m*

wreck [rek] I. *n* ❶ *of ship* Schiffbruch *m* ❷(*remains*) Trümmerhaufen *m* ❸(*accident*) Unfall *m* II. *vt* ❶(*sink*) ■**to be ~ed** *ship* Schiffbruch erleiden ❷(*destroy*) zerstören ❸(*spoil*) ruinieren; *hopes* zunichtemachen

wreckage ['rek·ɪdʒ] *n* Wrackteile *pl*

wrecker ['rek·ər] *n* ❶(*destroyer*) Zerstörer(in) *m(f)* ❷(*truck*) Abschleppwagen *m*

wren [ren] *n* Zaunkönig *m*

wrench [rentʃ] I. *n* <*pl* -es> ❶(*tool*) Schraubenschlüssel *m*; **screw ~** Franzose *m* ❷ *usu sing* (*twisting*) Ruck *m* II. *vt* *muscle* zerren; *joint* verrenken

wrestle ['res·əl] *vi* SPORT ringen

wrestler ['res·lər] *n* Ringer(in) *m(f)*; **Sumo ~** Sumoringer(in) *m(f)*

wrestling ['res·lɪŋ] *n* Ringen *nt*

'**wrestling bout**, '**wrestling match** *n* Ringkampf *m*

wretched ['retʃ·ɪd] *adj* ❶(*unhappy*) unglücklich ❷ *state* jämmerlich

wriggle ['rɪg·əl] *vi* ❶(*twist*) sich winden; **to ~ free** [**of sth**] sich [aus etw *dat*] herauswinden ❷(*move*) schlängeln

wring <wrung, wrung> [rɪŋ] *vt* ❶(*twist*) auswringen ❷(*break*) **to ~ sb's neck** jdm den Hals umdrehen *a. fig*

wrinkle ['rɪŋ·kəl] I. *n* (*crease*) Knitterfalte *f*; (*in face*) Falte *f* II. *vt, vi* zerknittern

wrinkled ['rɪŋ·kli] *adj* zerknittert; *face, skin* faltig

wrist [rɪst] *n* Handgelenk *nt*

'**wristband** *n* ❶(*strap*) Armband *nt* ❷(*absorbent*) Schweißband *nt*

'**wristwatch** *n* Armbanduhr *f*

writ [rɪt] *n* (*gerichtliche*) Verfügung; **to issue a ~ against sb** jdn vorladen

write <wrote, written *or old* writ> [raɪt] I. *vt* ❶(*pen*) schreiben; **to ~ a letter to sb** jdm einen Brief schreiben ❷(*fill out*) ausstellen II. *vi* (*pen letters*) schreiben; **to know how to read and ~** Lesen und Schreiben können

◆**write away** *vi* ■**to ~ away for sth** etw [schriftlich] anfordern

◆ **write back** *vt, vi* zurückschreiben

◆ **write down** *vt* aufschreiben

◆ **write in** I. *vt* ■ **to ~ in ◯ sth** (*in text*) etw einfügen; (*in form*) etw eintragen II. *vi* schreiben; **he wrote in expressing his dissatisfaction** er schickte einen Brief, um seine Unzufriedenheit auszudrücken

◆ **write off** I. *vi* ■ **to ~ off for sth** etw [schriftlich] anfordern II. *vt* abschreiben

◆ **write out** *vt* ❶ (*put in writing*) aufschreiben ❷ (*in full*) ausschreiben

◆ **write up** *vt notes* ausarbeiten; *report* aufschreiben *fam*

'**write-in** *adj* POL **a ~ candidate** ein nachträglich auf der Liste hinzugefügter Kandidat

'**write-off** *n* FIN Abschreibung *f*

'**write-protected** *adj* COMPUT schreibgeschützt

writer ['raɪ·tər] *n* ❶ (*person*) Verfasser(in) *m(f)* ❷ (*author*) Autor(in) *m(f)*

'**write-up** *n of film* Kritik *f*; *of book* a. Rezension *f*

writing ['raɪ·tɪŋ] *n* ❶ (*skill*) Schreiben *nt*; ■ **in ~** schriftlich ❷ (*literature*) Literatur *f* ❸ (*handwriting*) [Hand]schrift *f*

'**writing desk** *n* Schreibtisch *m*

'**writing pad** *n* Schreibblock *m*

'**writing paper** *n* Schreibpapier *nt*

written ['rɪt·ən] I. *vt, vi pp of* **write** II. *adj* **the ~ word** das geschriebene Wort ▶PHRASES: **to have sth ~ all over one's face** jdm steht etw ins Gesicht geschrieben

wrong [rɔŋ] I. *adj* ❶ (*incorrect*) falsch; **it's all ~** das ist völlig verkehrt; **to be proven ~** widerlegt werden; ■ **to be ~ about sth** sich bei etw *dat* irren ❷ *pred* (*amiss*) **what's ~ with you today?** was ist denn heute mit dir los? ▶PHRASES: **to get hold of the ~ end of the stick** etw in den falschen Hals bekommen *fam* II. *adv* ❶ (*incorrectly*) falsch ❷ **to go ~** *things* schiefgehen *fam* III. *n* **to know right from ~** Richtig und Falsch unterscheiden können ▶PHRASES: **to be in the ~** (*mistaken*) sich irren

wrongdoer ['rɔŋ·du·ər] *n* Übeltäter(in) *m(f)*

wrongful ['rɔŋ·fəl] *adj* unrechtmäßig

wrong-'headed *adj* querköpfig *pej*; *idea* hirnverbrannt *fam*

wrongly ['rɔŋ·li] *adv* ❶ (*mistakenly*) fälschlicherweise ❷ (*incorrectly*) falsch

wrote [roʊt] *vt, vi pt of* **write**

wrought [rɔt] *adj attr silver; gold* gehämmert

wrought 'iron *n* Schmiedeeisen *nt*

wrung [rʌŋ] *vt pt, pp of* **wring**

wry <-ier, -iest *or* -er, -est> [raɪ] *adj usu attr humor* trocken; *smile* bitter

wt. *n abbrev of* **weight** Gew.

wuss [wʊs] *n* (*pej fam*) Schlappschwanz *m pej sl*

WV, W.V. *abbrev of* **West Virginia**

WY *abbrev of* **Wyoming**

Wyo. *abbrev of* **Wyoming**

Wyoming [waɪ·'oʊ·mɪŋ] *n* Wyoming *nt*

W

Xx

X <*pl* -'s>, **x** <*pl* -'s> [eks] *n* X *nt*, x *nt*; **~ as in X-ray** X wie Xanthippe

x [eks] I. *vt* ■ **to ~ [out ○] sth** [aus]streichen II. *n* MATH x *nt*; **~-axis** x-Achse *f*

xenophobia [ˌzen·ə·ˈfoʊ·bi·ə] *n* Fremdenhass *m*

xerox [ˈzɪr·aks] *vt* kopieren

Xerox® [ˈzɪr·aks] *n* Kopie *f*

Xmas <*pl* -es> [ˈkrɪs·məs] *n* (*fam*) *short for* **Christmas** Weihnachten *nt*

X-ray [ˈeks·reɪ] I. *n* ❶ (*picture*) Röntgenbild *nt* ❷ (*examination*) Röntgenuntersuchung *f*; **to have an ~** sich röntgen lassen II. *vt* röntgen

xylophone [ˈzaɪ·lə·foʊn] *n* Xylophon *nt*

Yy

Y <*pl* -'s>, **y** <*pl* -'s> [waɪ] *n* Y *nt*, y *nt*; **~ as in Yankee** Y wie Ypsilon

y [waɪ] *n* MATH y *nt*; **~-axis** y-Achse *f*

yacht [jat] *n* Jacht *f*

ˈyachtsman *n* **around-the-world ~** Weltumsegler *m*

yak [jæk] *vi* <-kk-> (*fam*) quasseln

yam [jæm] *n* Jamswurzel *f*

yank [jæŋk] (*fam*) I. *n* Ruck *m* II. *vt* [ruckartig] ziehen an + *dat*
  ♦ **yank out** *vt* herausreißen

Yank [jæŋk] *n* (*usu pej fam*) Ami *m*

Yankee [ˈjæŋ·ki] *n* (*usu pej fam*) ❶ (*person from northern US*) Nordstaatler(in) *m(f)* ❷ (*American*) Ami *m*

yap [jæp] *vi* <-pp-> ❶ *dog* kläffen ❷ (*fam: talk*) quasseln

yard¹ [jard] *n* Yard *nt*; **to sell sth by the ~** etw in Yards verkaufen

yard² [jard] *n* ❶ (*lawn*) Garten *m* ❷ (*worksite*) Werksgelände *nt*; (*for storage*) Lagerplatz *m*

ˈyardstick *n* Maßstab *m*

yarn [jarn] *n* Garn *nt*

yawn [jɔn] I. *vi* gähnen *a. fig* II. *n* Gähnen *nt kein pl*

yawning [ˈjɔ·nɪŋ] *adj* gähnend *a. fig*

yd. *n abbrev of* **yard**¹

yeah [jeə] *adv* (*fam: yes*) ja[wohl]; **oh ~!** [*or* ~, ~!] (*iron*) ja klar!

year [jɪr] *n* ❶ Jahr *nt*; **five times a ~** fünfmal im [*o* pro] Jahr; **two ~s' work** zwei Jahre Arbeit; **last ~** letztes Jahr ❷ (*age*) [Lebens]jahr *nt*; **a two-~-old child** ein zweijähriges Kind ❸ SCH Schuljahr *nt*; UNIV Studienjahr *nt*; (*group*) Klasse *f*

ˈyearbook *n* SCH, UNIV Jahrbuch *nt*

yearly [ˈjɪr·li] *adj*, *adv* jährlich; **twice-~** zweimal pro Jahr

yearn [jɜrn] *vi* sich sehnen (**for** nach + *dat*)

yeast [jist] *n* Hefe *f*

yell [jel] I. *n* ❶ (*shout*) [Auf]schrei *m* ❷ (*cheer*) Schlachtruf *m* II. *vi* **to ~ for help** um Hilfe rufen; ■ **to ~ at sb** jdn anschreien

yellow [ˈjel·oʊ] I. *adj* ❶ (*color*) gelb; (*yellowed*) Werksgilbt ❷ (*fam: cowardly*) feige II. *vi* vergilben

yellow ˈfever *n* Gelbfieber *nt*

yellowish [ˈjel·oʊ·ɪʃ] *adj* gelblich

ˈYellow Pages® *npl* ■ **the ~** die Gelben Seiten

yelp [jelp] *vi* *dog* kläffen; *person* aufschreien

X
Y

yen[1] *<pl ->* [jen] *n* Yen *m*

yen[2] [jen] *n* (*fam*) Faible *nt;* **to have a ~ to do sth** den Drang haben, etw zu tun

yep [jep] *adv* (*fam*) ja

yes [jes] **I.** *adv* ① ja; **~, please** ja bitte; **to say ~** [**to sth**] ja [zu etw *dat*] sagen, etw bejahen ② (*contradicting*) aber ja [doch] **II.** *n <pl -[s]es>* Ja *nt*

'yes-man *n* (*fam*) Jasager *m*

yesterday ['jes·tər·deɪ] **I.** *adv* gestern **II.** *n* Gestern *nt*

yet [jet] **I.** *adv* ① (*until now*) bis jetzt; *+ superl;* **the best ~** der/die/das Beste bisher ② (*already*) schon; **is it time to go ~? — no, not ~** ist es schon Zeit zu gehen? – nein, noch nicht ③ (*despite that*) trotzdem; (*but*) aber [auch]; (*in spite of everything*) schon **II.** *conj* doch

yew [ju] *n* Eibe *f*

Yiddish ['jɪd·ɪʃ] *n* Jiddisch *nt*

yield [jild] **I.** *n* ① Ertrag *m* ② MIN Ausbeute *f* **II.** *vt* ① (*produce*) hervorbringen; **grain** erzeugen; **results** liefern ② FIN abwerfen; **the bonds are currently ~ing 6-7%** die Pfandbriefe bringen derzeit 6-7 % **III.** *vi* (*give right of way*) ■**to ~ to sb** jdm den Vortritt lassen

YMCA [ˌwaɪ·em·siˈeɪ] *n + sing/pl vb abbrev of* **Young Men's Christian Association** CVJM *m*

yoga ['joʊ·gə] *n* Yoga *nt*

yogurt, yoghurt ['joʊ·gərt] *n* Joghurt *m o nt*

yoke [joʊk] **I.** *n* (*for pulling*) Joch *nt a. fig* **II.** *vt* (*fig*) ■**to ~ sth together** etw [miteinander ver]koppeln

yolk [joʊk] *n* Eigelb *nt*

you [ju] *pron* ① (*singular*) du *in nomin*, dich *in akk*, dir *in dat;* (*polite form*) Sie *in nomin, akk,* Ihnen *in dat;* **if I were ~** wenn ich du/Sie wäre, an deiner/Ihrer Stelle ② (*plural*) ihr *in nomin, akk, dat;* (*polite form*) Sie *in nomin, akk,* Ihnen *in dat;* **how many of ~ are there?** wie viele seid ihr? ③ (*one*) man; **~ learn from experience** aus Erfahrung wird man klug; **it's not good for ~** das ist nicht gesund

you'll [jul] *=* **you will** *see* **will**[1]

young [jʌŋ] *adj* jung; **she's ~ for sixteen** für sechzehn ist sie noch recht kindlich; **to be ~ at heart** im Herzen jung [geblieben] sein

youngster ['jʌŋ·stər] *n* Jugendliche(r) *f(m)*

your [jʊr] *adj poss* ① (*singular*) dein(e); (*plural*) euer/eure; (*polite form*) Ihr(e) ② (*one's*) sein(e); **it's enough to break ~ heart** es bricht einem förmlich das Herz

you're [jʊr] *=* **you are** *see* **be**

yours [jʊrz] *pron poss* ① deine/deiner/dein[e]s, Ihre/Ihrer/Ihr[e]s; **is this pen ~?** ist das dein Stift?; **the choice is ~** Sie haben die Wahl ② (*in letter*) **Y~ truly** mit freundlichen Grüßen

yourself *<pl* **yourselves>** [jʊrˈself] *pron* ① (*singular*) dich *akk,* dir *dat;* (*plural*) euch; (*polite form, sing/pl*) sich; **how would you describe ~?** wie würden Sie sich beschreiben?; **help yourselves, boys** bedient euch, Jungs ② (*oneself*) sich; **to have sth [all] to ~** etw für dich [*o* sich] allein haben ③ (*personally*) selbst; **you can do that ~** du kannst das selbst machen; **to be ~** du selbst sein; **to try sth for ~** etw selbst versuchen

youth [juθ] *n* ① (*period*) Jugend *f* ② (*young man*) Jugendliche(r) *m* ③ *pl* (*young people*) **the ~ of today** die Jugend von heute

'youth center, 'youth club *n* Jugendzentrum *nt*

youthful ['juθ·fəl] *adj* jugendlich

'youth hostel *n* Jugendherberge *f*

you've [juv] *=* **you have** *see* **have I, II**

yo-yo *<pl -s>* ['joʊ·joʊ] **I.** *n* Jo-Jo *nt* **II.** *vi* (*fam: vacillate*) schwanken

yucky ['jʌk·i] *adj* (*fam*) ek[e]lig

Yukon Territory ['ju·kən-] *n* Yukon Territory *nt*

'yule log *n* großes Holzscheit, das zur Weihnachtszeit im offenen Feuer brennt

yum [jʌm] *interj* (*fam*) lecker!

yuppie ['jʌp·i] *n* Yuppie *m*

Y

Zz

Z <pl -'s>, **z** <pl -'s> [zi] n Z nt, z nt; **~ as in Zulu** Z wie Zacharias

z [zi] n MATH z nt; **~-axis** z-Achse f

zany ['zeɪ·ni] adj ulkig

zap [zæp] (fam) I. vt <-pp-> ❶ person erledigen; thing kaputtmachen ❷ COMPUT (delete) löschen II. vi <-pp-> TV zappen III. interj schwups!

zeal [zil] n Eifer m

zealous ['zel·əs] adj [über]eifrig

zebra <pl -s> ['zi·brə] n Zebra nt

zero ['zɪr·oʊ] I. n <pl -s> ❶ MATH Null f ❷ (point on scale) Nullpunkt m; **10 degrees below ~** zehn Grad unter null II. adj **~ hour** die Stunde null III. vt auf null einstellen

♦ **zero in** vi (aim) **to ~ in** on a target ein Ziel anvisieren

zero-'energy adj äußerst energiesparend, mit extrem geringem Energieverbrauch nach n; **~ building** Null-Energie-Haus nt

zero 'tolerance n LAW Nulltoleranz f

zest [zest] n ❶ (enthusiasm) Eifer m ❷ lemon ~ Zitronenschale f

zigzag ['zɪg·zæg] I. n Zickzack m II. vi <-gg-> sich im Zickzack bewege

zinc [zɪŋk] n Zink nt

zip [zɪp] I. n ❶ (fam: vigor) Schwung m ❷ (Zip Code) ≈ Postleitzahl f II. pron (fam) null; **I know ~ about computers** ich habe null Ahnung von Compu-

tern III. vt <-pp-> (close) **could you help me ~ [up] my dress?** könntest du mir vielleicht helfen, den Reißverschluss an meinem Kleid zuzumachen?; **to ~ sth together** etw mit einem Reißverschluss zusammenziehen IV. vi <-pp-> ❶ (fasten) **it ~s [up] at the back** es hat hinten einen Reißverschluss ❷ (speed) rasen; **to ~ through** job im Eiltempo erledigen

'Zip Code n ≈ Postleitzahl f

zipper ['zɪp·ər] n Reißverschluss m

zodiac ['zoʊ·di·æk] n **sign of the ~** Tierkreiszeichen nt

zombie ['zam·bi] n Zombie m

zone [zoʊn] n Zone f; **danger ~** Gefahrenzone f; **no-fly ~** Flugverbotszone f

zoning ['zoʊn·ɪŋ] I. n Bodenordnung f II. adj **~ restriction** Planungsbeschränkung f

zoo [zu] n Zoo m

zoologist [zoʊ·'al·ə·dʒɪst] n Zoologe, Zoologin m, f

zoology [zoʊ·'al·ə·dʒi] n Zoologie f

zoom [zum] I. n ❶ [lens] Zoom[objektiv] nt II. vi ❶ (speed) rasen; ■**to ~ ahead** [or off] davonsausen; (in race) vorpreschen ❷ PHOT zoomen

♦ **zoom in** vi [nahe] heranfahren, heranzoomen

♦ **zoom out** vi wegzoomen

zucchini <pl -s> [zu·'ki·ni] n Zucchini f

Anhang
Appendix

Liste der unregelmäßigen deutschen Verben

List of the irregular German verbs

Die einfachen Zeiten unregelmäßiger Verben sind in den Spitzklammern (< >) nach dem Stichwort angegeben. Zusammengesetzte oder präfigierte Verben, deren Formen denen des Grundverbs entsprechen, sind auf der Deutsch-Englischen Seite mit *irreg* markiert. Außerdem gibt das Wörterbuch die unregelmäßigen Formen zusammengesetzter Verben an, die sich anders verhalten als ihre Grundverben. Die Verben, die mit *sein* oder alternativ mit *sein* oder *haben* konjugiert werden, sind entsprechend im Wörterbucheintrag gekennzeichnet. Wenn das Hilfsverb nicht eigens angegeben ist, wird die Perfektform mit *haben* gebildet.

Inflections of irregular verbs are given in angle brackets (< >) after the headword in the main part of the dictionary. Compound verbs and prefixed verbs whose conjugated forms correspond to those of the base verb are marked *irreg* on the German-English side of the dictionary. Conjugated forms of compound verbs are provided, however, when they differ from the conjugated forms of the base verb. Verbs that take *sein* and those that take *sein* or *haben* in the compound past tenses are marked accordingly in the dictionary entry. Whenever the auxiliary verb is not specifically given, one may assume that the compound past tenses are formed with *haben*.

Infinitiv Infinitive	Präteritum Simple past	Partizip Perfekt Past participle
backen	backte o *alt* buk	gebacken
befehlen	befahl	befohlen
beginnen	begann	begonnen
beißen	biss	gebissen
bergen	barg	geborgen
bersten	barst	geborsten
bewegen	bewog	bewogen
biegen	bog	gebogen
bieten	bot	geboten
binden	band	gebunden

Infinitiv Infinitive	Präteritum Simple past	Partizip Perfekt Past participle
bitten	bat	gebeten
blasen	blies	geblasen
bleiben	blieb	geblieben
bleichen	bleichte o *alt* blich	gebleicht o *alt* geblichen
braten	briet	gebraten
brechen	brach	gebrochen
brennen	brannte	gebrannt
bringen	brachte	gebracht
denken	dachte	gedacht

Infinitiv Infinitive	Präteritum Simple past	Partizip Perfekt Past participle	Infinitiv Infinitive	Präteritum Simple past	Partizip Perfekt Past participle
dreschen	drosch	gedro-schen	genesen	genas	genesen
dringen	drang	gedrun-gen	genießen	genoss	genossen
dürfen	durfte	dürfen, gedurft	geraten	geriet	geraten
			geschehen	geschah	geschehen
empfangen	empfing	empfangen	gestehen	gestand	gestanden
empfehlen	empfahl	empfohlen	gewinnen	gewann	gewonnen
empfinden	empfand	empfunden	gießen	goss	gegossen
			gleichen	glich	geglichen
essen	aß	gegessen	gleiten	glitt	geglitten
fahren	fuhr	gefahren	glimmen	glimmte o selten glomm	geglimmt o selten geglommen
fallen	fiel	gefallen			
fangen	fing	gefangen	graben	grub	gegraben
fechten	focht	gefochten	greifen	griff	gegriffen
finden	fand	gefunden	haben	hatte	gehabt
flechten	flocht	geflochten	halten	hielt	gehalten
fliegen	flog	geflogen	hängen	hing (hängte)	gehangen, (gehängt)
fliehen	floh	geflohen			
fließen	floss	geflossen	heben	hob	gehoben
fressen	fraß	gefressen	heißen	hieß	geheißen
frieren	fror	gefroren	helfen	half	geholfen
gären	gärte o gor	gegärt o gegoren	kennen	kannte	gekannt
			klimmen	klimmte o klomm	geklommen o geklimmt
gebären	gebar	geboren			
geben	gab	gegeben	klingen	klang	geklungen
gedeihen	gedieh	gediehen	kneifen	kniff	gekniffen
gefallen	gefiel	gefallen	kommen	kam	gekommen
gehen	ging	gegangen			
gelingen	gelang	gelungen	können	konnte	können, gekonnt
gelten	galt	gegolten	kriechen	kroch	gekrochen

Infinitiv Infinitive	Präteritum Simple past	Partizip Perfekt Past participle
laden	lud	geladen
lassen	ließ	gelassen *nach Infinitiv* lassen
laufen	lief	gelaufen
leiden	litt	gelitten
leihen	lieh	geliehen
lesen	las	gelesen
liegen	lag	gelegen
lügen	log	gelogen
mahlen	mahlte	gemahlen
meiden	mied	gemieden
melken	melkte *o veraltend* molk	gemolken
messen	maß	gemessen
misslingen	misslang	misslungen
mögen	mochte	mögen, gemocht
nehmen	nahm	genommen
nennen	nannte	genannt
pfeifen	pfiff	gepfiffen
preisen	pries	gepriesen
quellen	quoll	gequollen
raten	riet	geraten
reiben	rieb	gerieben
reißen	riss	gerissen
reiten	ritt	geritten
rennen	rannte	gerannt
reichen	roch	gerochen
ringen	rang	gerungen

Infinitiv Infinitive	Präteritum Simple past	Partizip Perfekt Past participle
rinnen	rann	geronnen
rufen	rief	gerufen
salzen	salzte	gesalzen *o selten* gesalzt
saufen	soff	gesoffen
saugen	sog *o* saugte	gesogen *o* gesaugt
schaffen	schuf	geschaffen
schallen	schallte *o* scholl	geschallt
scheiden	schied	geschieden
scheinen	schien	geschienen
scheißen	schiss	geschissen
schelten	schalt	gescholten
scheren	schor	geschoren
schieben	schob	geschoben
schießen	schoss	geschossen
schinden	schindete	geschunden
schlafen	schlief	geschlafen
schlagen	schlug	geschlagen
schleichen	schlich	geschlichen
schleifen	schliff	geschliffen
schließen	schloss	geschlossen

Infinitiv Infinitive	Präteritum Simple past	Partizip Perfekt Past participle
schlingen	schlang	geschlungen
schmeißen	schmiss	geschmissen
schmelzen	schmolz	geschmolzen
schnauben	schnaubte o *veraltet* schnob	geschnaubt o *veraltet* geschnoben
schneiden	schnitt	geschnitten
schrecken *vt* *vi*	schreckte schrak	geschreckt geschrocken
schreiben	schrieb	geschrieben
schreien	schrie	geschrie[e]n
schreiten	schritt	geschritten
schweigen	schwieg	geschwiegen
schwellen	schwoll	geschwollen
schwimmen	schwamm	geschwommen
schwinden	schwand	geschwunden
schwingen	schwang	geschwungen

Infinitiv Infinitive	Präteritum Simple past	Partizip Perfekt Past participle
schwören	schwor	geschworen
sehen	sah	gesehen
senden	sandte o sendete	gesandt o gesendet
sieden	siedete o sott	gesiedet o gesotten
singen	sang	gesungen
sinken	sank	gesunken
sinnen	sann	gesonnen
sitzen	saß	gesessen
sollen	sollte	sollen, gesollt
spalten	spaltete	gespalten o gespaltet
speien	spie	gespie[e]n
spinnen	spann	gesponnen
sprechen	sprach	gesprochen
sprießen	spross o spießte	gesprossen
springen	sprang	gesprungen
stechen	stach	gestochen
stecken	steckte o *geh* stak	gesteckt
stehen	stand	gestanden
stehlen	stahl	gestohlen
steigen	stieg	gestiegen
sterben	starb	gestorben
stieben	stob o stiebte	gestoben o gestiebt
stinken	stank	gestunken

Infinitiv Infinitive	Präteritum Simple past	Partizip Perfekt Past participle
stoßen	stieß	gestoßen
streichen	strich	gestrichen
streiten	stritt	gestritten
tragen	trug	getragen
treffen	traf	getroffen
treiben	trieb	getrieben
treten	trat	getreten
triefen	triefte o geh troff	getrieft o geh getroffen
trinken	trank	getrunken
trügen	trog	getrogen
tun	tat	getan
verbieten	verbot	verboten
verbrechen	verbrach	verbrochen
verderben	verdarb	verdorben
vergessen	vergaß	vergessen
verlieren	verlor	verloren
verraten	verriet	verraten
verstehen	verstand	verstanden
verwenden	verwendete o verwandte	verwendet o verwandt
verzeihen	verzieh	verziehen
wachsen	wuchs	gewachsen

Infinitiv Infinitive	Präteritum Simple past	Partizip Perfekt Past participle
waschen	wusch	gewaschen
weben	webte o geh wob	gewebt o geh gewoben
weichen	wich	gewichen
weisen	wies	gewiesen
wenden	wendete o geh gewandt	gewendet o geh gewandt
werben	warb	geworben
werden	wurde	worden, geworden
werfen	warf	geworfen
wiegen	wog	gewogen
winden	wand	gewunden
winken	winkte	gewinkt o dial gewunken
wissen	wusste	gewusst
wollen	wollte	wollen, gewollt
wringen	wrang	gewrungen
ziehen	zog	gezogen
zwingen	zwang	gezwungen

Die Hilfsverben *sein, haben* und *werden*

The auxiliary verbs *sein, haben,* and *werden*

sein

Präsens Present	Präteritum Simple Past	Perfekt Present Perfect	Plusquamperfekt Past Perfect
bin	war	bin gewesen	war gewesen
bist	warst	bist gewesen	warst gewesen
ist	war	ist gewesen	war gewesen
sind	waren	sind gewesen	waren gewesen
seid	wart	seid gewesen	wart gewesen
sind	waren	sind gewesen	waren gewesen

Futur Future	Konjunktiv I Subjunctive I	Konjunktiv II Subjunctive II	Imperativ Imperative
werde sein	sei	wäre	
wirst sein	seist	wär[e]st	sei
wird sein	sei	wäre	
werden sein	seien	wären	seien wir
werdet sein	seiet	wär[e]t	seid
werden sein	seien	wären	seien Sie

haben

Präsens Present	Präteritum Simple Past	Perfekt Present Perfect	Plusquamperfekt Past Perfect
habe	hatte	habe gehabt	hatte gehabt
hast	hattest	hast gehabt	hattest gehabt
hat	hatte	hat gehabt	hatte gehabt
haben	hatten	haben gehabt	hatten gehabt
habt	hattet	habt gehabt	hattet gehabt
haben	hatten	haben gehabt	hatten gehabt

Futur Future	Konjunktiv I Subjunctive I	Konjunktiv II Subjunctive II	Imperativ Imperative
werde haben	habe	hätte	
wirst haben	habest	hättest	hab[e]
wird haben	habe	hätte	
werden haben	haben	hätten	haben wir
werdet haben	habet	hättet	habt
werden haben	haben	hätten	haben Sie

werden

Präsens Present	Präteritum Simple Past	Perfekt Present Perfect	Plusquamperfekt Past Perfect
werde	wurde	bin geworden	war geworden
wirst	wurdest	bist geworden	warst geworden
wird	wurde	ist geworden	war geworden
werden	wurden	sind geworden	waren geworden
werdet	wurdet	seid geworden	wart geworden
werden	wurden	sind geworden	waren geworden

Futur Future	Konjunktiv I Subjunctive I	Konjunktiv II Subjunctive II	Imperativ Imperative
werde werden	werde	würde	
wirst werden	werdest	würdest	werd[e]
wird werden	werde	würde	
werden werden	werden	würden	werden wir
werdet werden	werdet	würdet	werdet
werden werden	werden	würden	werden Sie

Die Modalverben
The modal verbs

können

Präsens Present	Präteritum Simple Past	Perfekt Present Perfect	Plusquamperfekt Past Perfect
kann	konnte	habe gekonnt	hatte gekonnt
kannst	konntest	hast gekonnt	hattest gekonnt
kann	konnte	hat gekonnt	hatte gekonnt
können	konnten	haben gekonnt	hatten gekonnt
könnt	konntet	habt gekonnt	hattet gekonnt
können	konnten	haben gekonnt	hatten gekonnt

Futur Future	Konjunktiv I Subjunctive I	Konjunktiv II Subjunctive II
werde können	könne	könnte
wirst können	könntest	könntest
wird können	könne	könnte
werden können	können	könnten
werdet können	könn[e]t	könntet
werden können	können	könnten

dürfen

Präsens Present	Präteritum Simple Past	Perfekt Present Perfect	Plusquamperfekt Past Perfect
darf	durfte	habe gedurft	hatte gedurft
darfst	durftest	hast gedurft	hattest gedurft
darf	durfte	hat gedurft	hatte gedurft
dürfen	durften	haben gedurft	hatten gedurft
dürft	durftet	habt gedurft	hattet gedurft
dürfen	durften	haben gedurft	hatten gedurft

Futur Future	Konjunktiv I Subjunctive I	Konjunktiv II Subjunctive II
werde dürfen	dürfe	dürfte
wirst dürfen	dürftest	dürftest
wird dürfen	dürfe	dürfte
werden dürfen	dürfen	dürften
werdet dürfen	dürf[e]t	dürftet
werden dürfen	dürfen	dürften

mögen

Präsens Present	Präteritum Simple Past	Perfekt Present Perfect	Plusquamperfekt Past Perfect
mag	mochte	habe gemocht	hatte gemocht
magst	mochtest	hast gemocht	hattest gemocht
mag	mochte	hat gemocht	hatte gemocht
mögen	mochten	haben gemocht	hatten gemocht
mögt	mochtet	habt gemocht	hattet gemocht
mögen	mochten	haben gemocht	hatten gemocht

Futur Future	Konjunktiv I Subjunctive I	Konjunktiv II Subjunctive II
werde mögen	möge	möchte
wirst mögen	mögest	möchtest
wird mögen	möge	möchte
werden mögen	mögen	möchten
werdet mögen	mög[e]t	möchtet
werden mögen	mögen	möchten

müssen

Präsens Present	Präteritum Simple Past	Perfekt Present Perfect	Plusquamperfekt Past Perfect
muss	musste	habe gemusst	hatte gemusst
musst	musstest	hast gemusst	hattest gemusst
muss	musste	hat gemusst	hatte gemusst
müssen	mussten	haben gemusst	hatten gemusst
müsst	musstet	habt gemusst	hattet gemusst
müssen	mussten	haben gemusst	hatten gemusst

Futur Future	Konjunktiv I Subjunctive I	Konjunktiv II Subjunctive II
werde müssen	müsse	müsste
wirst müssen	müssest	müsstest
wird müssen	müsse	müsste
werden müssen	müssen	müssten
werdet müssen	müss[e]t	müsstest
werden müssen	müssen	müssten

sollen

Präsens Present	Präteritum Simple Past	Perfekt Present Perfect	Plusquamperfekt Past Perfect
soll	sollte	habe gesollt	hatte gesollt
sollst	solltest	hast gesollt	hattest gesollt
soll	sollte	hat gesollt	hatte gesollt
sollen	sollten	haben gesollt	hatten gesollt
sollt	solltet	habt gesollt	hattet gesollt
sollen	sollten	haben gesollt	hatten gesollt

Futur Future	Konjunktiv I Subjunctive I	Konjunktiv II Subjunctive II
werde sollen	solle	sollte
wirst sollen	solltest	solltest
wird sollen	solle	sollte
werden sollen	sollen	sollten
werdet sollen	soll[e]t	solltet
werden sollen	sollen	sollten

wollen

Präsens Present	Präteritum Simple Past	Perfekt Present Perfect	Plusquamperfekt Past Perfect
will	wollte	habe gewollt	hatten gewollt
willst	wolltest	hast gewollt	hattest gewollt
will	wollte	hat gewollt	hatte gewollt
wollen	wollten	haben gewollt	hatten gewollt
wollt	wolltet	habt gewollt	hattet gewollt
wollen	wollten	haben gewollt	hatten gewollt

Futur Future	Konjunktiv I Subjunctive I	Konjunktiv II Subjunctive II
werde wollen	wolle	wollte
wirst wollen	wollest	wolltest
wird wollen	wolle	wollte
werden wollen	wollen	wollten
werdet wollen	woll[e]t	wolltet
werden wollen	wollen	wollten

Übersicht über die wichtigsten unregelmäßigen englischen Verben

List of the most important irregular English verbs

Infinitiv Infinitive	Präteritum Simple past	Partizip Perfekt Past participle	Infinitiv Infinitive	Präteritum Simple past	Partizip Perfekt Past participle
abide	abode, abided	abode, abided	breed	bred	bred
			bring	brought	brought
arise	arose	arisen	broadcast	broadcast, broad-casted	broad-cast, broad-casted
awake	awoke, awaked	awoken, awaked			
be	was *sing*, were *pl*	been	build	built	built
bear	bore	born(e)	burn	burned, burnt	burned, burnt
beat	beat	beaten, beat	burst	burst	burst
become	became	become	bust	bust, busted	bust, busted
begin	began	begun	buy	bought	bought
behold	beheld	beheld	can	could	–
bend	bent	bent	cast	cast	cast
beset	beset	beset	catch	caught	caught
bet	bet, betted	bet, betted	choose	chose	chosen
bid	bid, bade	bid, bidden	cling	clung	clung
			clothe	clothed, clad	clothed, clad
bind	bound	bound			
bite	bit	bitten	come	came	come
bleed	bled	bled	cost	cost	cost
bless	blessed, blest	blessed, blest	creep	crept	crept
			cut	cut	cut
blow	blew	blown	deal	dealt	dealt
break	broke	broken	dig	dug	dug

Infinitiv Infinitive	Präteritum Simple past	Partizip Perfekt Past participle
dive	dived, dove	dived, dove
do	did	done
draw	drew	drawn
dream	dreamed, dreamt	dreamed, dreamt
drink	drank	drunk
drive	drove	driven
dwell	dwelt, dwelled	dwelt, dwelled
eat	ate	eaten
fall	fell	fallen
feed	fed	fed
feel	felt	felt
fight	fought	fought
find	found	found
fit	fitted, fit	fitted, fit
flee	fled	fled
fling	flung	flung
fly	flew	flown
forbid	forbad(e)	forbidden
forecast	forecast, forecasted	forecast, forecasted
forget	forgot	forgotten
forgive	forgave	forgiven
freeze	froze	frozen
get	got	gotten, got
give	gave	given
go	went	gone
grind	ground	ground
grow	grew	grown

Infinitiv Infinitive	Präteritum Simple past	Partizip Perfekt Past participle
hang	hung, LAW hanged	hung, LAW hanged
have	had	had
hear	heard	heard
hide	hid	hidden, hid
hit	hit	hit
hold	held	held
hurt	hurt	hurt
keep	kept	kept
kneel	knelt, kneeled	knelt, kneeled
knit	knitted, knit	knitted, knit
know	knew	known
lay	laid	laid
lead	led	led
lean	leaned	leaned
leap	leaped, leapt	leaped, leapt
learn	learned, learnt	learned, learnt
leave	left	left
lend	lent	lent
let	let	let
lie	lay	lain
light	lit, lighted	lit, lighted
lose	lost	lost
make	made	made
may	might	–
mean	meant	meant
meet	met	met

Infinitiv Infinitive	Präteritum Simple past	Partizip Perfekt Past participle
mistake	mistook	mistaken
mow	mowed	mowed, mown
pay	paid	paid
prove	proved	proved, proven
put	put	put
quit	quit, quitted	quit, quitted
read	read	read
rid	rid, ridded	rid, ridded
ride	rode	ridden
ring	rang	rung
rise	rose	risen
run	ran	run
saw	sawed	sawed, sawn
say	said	said
see	saw	seen
seek	sought	sought
sell	sold	sold
send	sent	sent
set	set	set
sew	sewed	sewn, sewed
shake	shook	shaken
shave	shaved	shaved, shaven
shear	sheared	sheared, shorn
shed	shed	shed
shine	shone	shone

Infinitiv Infinitive	Präteritum Simple past	Partizip Perfekt Past participle
shit	shit, shitted, shat	shit, shitted, shat
shoe	shod, shoed	shod, shodden, shoed
shoot	shot	shot
show	showed	shown, showed
shrink	shrank, shrunk	shrunk, shrunken
shut	shut	shut
sing	sang	sung
sink	sank	sunk
sit	sat	sat
slay	slew	slain
sleep	slept	slept
slide	slid	slid, slidden
sling	slung	slung
slink	slunk	slunk
slit	slit	slit
smell	smelled, smelt	smelled, smelt
sow	sowed	sown, sowed
speak	spoke	spoken
speed	speeded, sped	speeded, sped
spell	spelled, spelt	spelled, spelt
spend	spent	spent
spill	spilled, spilt	spilled, spilt
spin	spun	spun

Infinitiv Infinitive	Präteritum Simple past	Partizip Perfekt Past participle
spit	spat, spit	spat, spit
split	split	split
spoil	spoiled, spoilt	spoiled, spoilt
spread	spread	spread
spring	sprang, sprung	sprung
stand	stood	stood
stave	staved, stove	staved, stove
steal	stole	stolen
stick	stuck	stuck
sting	stung	stung
stink	stank, stunk	stunk
strew	strewed	strewn, strewed
stride	strode	stridden
strike	struck	struck
string	strung	strung
strive	strove, strived	striven
swear	swore	sworn
sweat	sweat, sweated	sweat, sweated
sweep	swept	swept
swell	swelled	swelled, swollen
swim	swam	swum

Infinitiv Infinitive	Präteritum Simple past	Partizip Perfekt Past participle
swing	swung	swung
take	took	taken
teach	taught	taught
tear	tore	torn
tell	told	told
think	thought	thought
thrive	thrived, throve	thrived, thriven
throw	threw	thrown
thrust	thrust	thrust
tread	trod	trodden
understand	understood	understood
wake	woke, waked	woken, waked
wear	wore	worn
weave	wove	woven
wed	wed, wedded	wed, wedded
weep	wept	wept
wet	wet, wetted	wet, wetted
win	won	won
wind	wound	wound
withhold	withheld	withheld
wring	wrung	wrung
write	wrote	written

Die Zahlwörter
Numerals

Die Kardinalzahlen
Cardinal numbers

null	0	nought, zero
eins	1	one
zwei	2	two
drei	3	three
vier	4	four
fünf	5	five
sechs	6	six
sieben	7	seven
acht	8	eight
neun	9	nine
zehn	10	ten
elf	11	eleven
zwölf	12	twelve
dreizehn	13	thirteen
vierzehn	14	fourteen
fünfzehn	15	fifteen
sechzehn	16	sixteen
siebzehn	17	seventeen
achtzehn	18	eighteen
neunzehn	19	nineteen
zwanzig	20	twenty
einundzwanzig	21	twenty-one
zweiundzwanzig	22	twenty-two
dreiundzwanzig	23	twenty-three
dreißig	30	thirty
einunddreißig	31	thirty-one
zweiunddreißig	32	thirty-two
vierzig	40	forty

einundvierzig	41	forty-one
fünfzig	50	fifty
einundfünfzig	51	fifty-one
sechzig	60	sixty
einundsechzig	61	sixty-one
siebzig	70	seventy
einundsiebzig	71	seventy-one
achtzig	80	eighty
einundachtzig	81	eighty-one
neunzig	90	ninety
einundneunzig	91	ninety-one
hundert	100	a [o one] hundred
hundert(und)eins	101	hundred and one
hundert(und)zwei	102	hundred and two
hundert(und)zehn	110	hundred and ten
zweihundert	200	two hundred
dreihundert	300	three hundred
vierhundert(und)einundfünfzig	451	four hundred and fifty-one
tausend	1000	a [o one] thousand
zweitausend	2000	two thousand
zehntausend	10 000	ten thousand
eine Million	1 000 000	a [o one] million
zwei Millionen	2 000 000	two million
eine Milliarde	1 000 000 000	a [o one] billion
eine Billion	1 000 000 000 000	a [o one] trillion

Die Ordnungszahlen
Ordinal numbers

erste	1.	1st	first
zweite	2.	2nd	second
dritte	3.	3rd	third
vierte	4.	4th	fourth
fünfte	5.	5th	fifth
sechste	6.	6th	sixth
siebente	7.	7th	seventh
achte	8.	8th	eighth
neunte	9.	9th	ninth
zehnte	10.	10th	tenth
elfte	11.	11th	eleventh
zwölfte	12.	12th	twelfth
dreizehnte	13.	13th	thirteenth
vierzehnte	14.	14th	fourteenth
fünfzehnte	15.	15th	fifteenth
sechzehnte	16.	16th	sixteenth
siebzehnte	17.	17th	seventeenth
achtzehnte	18.	18th	eighteenth
neunzehnte	19.	19th	nineteenth
zwanzigste	20.	20th	twentieth
einundzwanzigste	21.	21st	twenty-first
zweiundzwanzigste	22.	22nd	twenty-second
dreiundzwanzigste	23.	23rd	twenty-third
dreißigste	30.	30th	thirtieth
einunddreißigste	31.	31st	thirty-first
vierzigste	40.	40th	fortieth
einundvierzigste	41.	41st	forty-first
fünfzigste	50.	50th	fiftieth
einundfünfzigste	51.	51st	fifty-first
sechzigste	60.	60th	sixtieth
einundsechzigste	61.	61st	sixty-first
siebzigste	70.	70th	seventieth

einundsiebzigste	71.	71st	seventy-first
achtzigste	80.	80th	eightieth
einundachtzigste	81.	81st	eighty-first
neunzigste	90.	90th	ninetieth
hundertste	100.	100th	(one) hundredth
hundertunderste	101.	101st	hundred and first
zweihundertste	200.	200th	two hundredth
dreihundertste	300.	300th	three hundredth
vierhundert(und)ein-undfünfzigste	451.	451st	four hundred and fifty-first
tausendste	1000.	1000th	(one) thousandth
tausend(und)einhun-dertste	1100.	1100th	thousand and (one) hundredth
zweitausendste	2000.	200th	two thousandth
einhunderttausendste	100 000.	100 000th	(one) hundred thou-sandth
millionste	1000 000.	1000 000th	millionth
zehnmillionste	10 000 000.	10 000 000th	ten millionth

Die Bruchzahlen

Fractions

ein halb	$\frac{1}{2}$	one [o a] half
ein Drittel	$\frac{1}{3}$	one [o a] third
ein Viertel	$\frac{1}{4}$	one [o a] quarter
ein Fünftel	$\frac{1}{5}$	one [o a] fifth
ein Zehntel	$\frac{1}{10}$	one [o a] tenth
ein Hundertstel	$\frac{1}{100}$	one hundredth
ein Tausendstel	$\frac{1}{1000}$	one thousandth
ein Millionstel	$\frac{1}{1000000}$	one millionth
zwei Drittel	$\frac{2}{3}$	two thirds
drei Viertel	$\frac{3}{4}$	three quarters
zwei Fünftel	$\frac{2}{5}$	two fifths
drei Zehntel	$\frac{3}{10}$	three tenths

anderthalb	$1^1/_2$	one and a half
zwei(und)einhalb	$2^1/_2$	two and a half
fünf drei achtel	$5^3/_8$	five and three eighths
eins Komma eins	1,1 1.1	one point one
zwei Komma drei	2,3 2.3	two point three

Vervielfältigungszahlen

Multiples

einfach	single
zweifach	double
dreifach	threefold, treble, triple

vierfach	fourfold, quadruple
fünffach	fivefold
hundertfach	(one) hundredfold

Gewichte und Maße
Weights and measures

Das Dezimalsystem
Decimal system

Giga	1 000 000 000	G	giga
Mega	1 000 000	M	mega
Hektokilo	100 000	hk	hectokilo
Myria	10 000	ma	myria
Kilo	1 000	k	kilo
Hekto	100	h	hecto
Deka	10	da	deca
Dezi	0,1	d	deci
Centi	0,01	c	centi
Milli	0,001	m	milli
Dezimilli	0,0001	dm	decimilli
Centimilli	0,00001	cm	centimilli
Mikro	0,000001	µ	micro

Umrechnungstabellen
Conversion tables

In den USA ist immer noch das anglo-amerikanische Maßsystem in Gebrauch. In Großbritannien ist man offiziell auf das Dezimalsystem umgestiegen, jedoch bevorzugen viele immer noch das alte System. Für Temperaturen wird die Fahrenheit-Skala verwendet. Nur diejenigen anglo-amerikanischen Maße, die immer noch in Umlauf sind, werden in den Tabellen aufgeführt. Man erhält ein angloamerikanisches Maß, indem man das entprechende metrische mit dem **fett** gedruckten Umrechnungsfaktor multipliziert. Umgekehrt gilt: Ein imperiales Maß, das durch den gleichen Faktor dividiert wird, ergibt das metrische.

Only U. S. Customary units still in common use are given here. To convert a metric measurement to U. S. Customary measures, multiply by the conversion factor in **bold**. Likewise dividing a U. S. Customary measurement by the same factor will give the metric equivalent. Note that the decimal comma is used throughout rather than the decimal point.

Das metrische System
Metric measurement

Anglo-amerikanisches Maßsystem
U.S. Customary System

Längenmaße
Length measures

Seemeile	1852 m	–	nautical mile			
Kilometer	1000 m	km	kilometer	0,62	mile (= 1760 yards)	m, mi
Hektometer	100 m	hm	hectometer			
Dekameter	10 m	dam	decameter			
Meter	1 m	m	meter	1,09 3,28	yard (= 3 feet) foot (= 12 inches)	yd ft
Dezimeter	0,1 m	dm	decimeter			
Zentimeter	0,01 m	cm	centimeter	0,39	inch	in
Millimeter	0,001 m	mm	millimeter			
Mikron	0,000 001 m	µ	micron			
Millimikron	0,000 000 001 m	mµ	millimicron			
Angström	0,000 000 000 1 m	Å	angstrom			

Flächenmaße
Surface measures

Quadrat-kilometer	1 000 000 m²	km²	square kilometer	0,386	square mile (= 640 acres)	sq. m., sq. mi.
Quadrat-hektometer Hektar	10 000 m²	hm² ha	square hectometer hectare	2,47	acre (= 4840 square yards)	a.
Quadrat-dekameter Ar (SCHWEIZ: Are)	100 m²	dam² a	square decameter are			

Quadrat-meter	1 m²	m²	square meter	1.196	square yard (9 square feet)	sq. yd
				10,76	square feet (= 144 square inches)	sq. ft
Quadrat-dezimeter	0,01 m²	dm²	square decimeter			
Quadrat-zentimeter	0,0001 m²	cm²	square centimeter	0,155	square inch	sq. in.
Quadrat-millimeter	0,000 001 m²	mm²	square millimeter			

Kubik- und Hohlmaße

Volume and capacity

Kubikkilo-meter	1 000 000 000 m³	km³	cubic kilo-meter			
Kubikmeter	1 m³	m³	cubic meter	1,308	cubic yard (= 27 cubic feet)	cu. yd
Ster		st	stere	35,32	cubic foot (=1728 cubic inches)	cu. ft
Hektoliter	0,1 m³	hl	hectoliter			
Dekaliter	0,01 m³	dal	decaliter			
Kubik-dezimeter	0,001 m³	dm³	cubic deci-meter	0,26	gallon	gal.
Liter		l	liter	2,1	pint	Pt
Deziliter	0,0001 m³	dl	deciliter			
Zentiliter	0,00001 m³	cl	centiliter	0,352	fluid ounce	fl. oz
				0,338		
Kubik-zentimeter	0,000 001 m³	cm³	cubic centi-meter	0,061	cubic inch	cu. in.
Milliliter	0,000 001 m³	ml	milliliter			
Kubik-millimeter	0,000 000 001 m³	mm³	cubic milli-meter			

Gewichte
Weight

Tonne	1000 kg	t	ton	1,1	[short] ton (= 2000 pounds)	t.
Quintal	100 kg	q	quintal			
Kilogramm	1000 g	kg	kilogram	2,2	pound (= 16 ounces)	lb
Hekto-gramm	100 g	hg	hectogram			
Deka-gramm	10 g	dag	decagram			
Gramm	1 g	g	gram	0,035	ounce	oz
Karat	0,2 g	–	carat			
Dezigramm	0,1 g	dg	decigram			
Zenti-gramm	0,01 g	cg	centigram			
Milligramm	0,001 g	mg	milligram			
Mikro-gramm	0,000 001 g	µg	microgram			

Temperaturumrechnung
Temperature conversion

Fahrenheit – Celsius		Celsius – Fahrenheit	
°F	°C	°C	°F
0	–17,8	–10	14
32	0	0	32
50	10	10	50
70	21,1	20	68
90	32,2	30	86
98,4	37	37	98,4
212	100	100	212
zur Umrechnung 32 abziehen und mit $^5/_9$ multiplizieren		zur Umrechnung mit $^9/_5$ multiplizieren und 32 addieren	
To convert subtract 32 and multiply by $^5/_9$		To convert multiply by $^9/_5$ and add 32	

Notizen

Notizen

Zeichen und Abkürzungen

►	phraseologischer Block	phrase block
|	trennbares Verb	separable verb
=	Kontraktion	contraction
*	Partizip ohne *ge-*	German past participle formed without *ge-*
≈	entspricht etwa	comparable to
ALT	alte Schreibung	unreformed German spelling
RR	reformierte Schreibung	reformed German spelling
○	zeigt variable Stellung des Objektes und der Ergänzung bei Phrasal Verbs auf	indicates the variable position of the object in phrasal verb sentences
®	Warenzeichen	trade mark
a.	auch	also
Abk abbr	Abkürzung	abbreviation
acr	Akronym	acronym
adj	Adjektiv	adjective
ADMIN	Verwaltung	administration
adv	Adverb	adverb
AEROSP	Raum- und Luftfahrt	aerospace
AGR	Landwirtschaft	agriculture
akk	Akkusativ	accusative
Akr	Akronym	acronym
ANAT	Anatomie	anatomy
approv	aufwertend	approving
ARCHÄOL ARCHEOL	Archäologie	archaeology
ARCHIT	Architektur	architecture
art	Artikel	article
ART	Kunst	art
ASTROL	Astrologie	astrology
ASTRON	Astronomie	astronomy
attr	attributiv	attributive
aux	Hilfsverb	auxiliary verb
AVIAT	Luftfahrt	aviation
BAU	Bauwesen	construction
BERGB	Bergbau	mining
BIOL	Biologie	biology
BOT	Botanik	botany
BRD	Binnendeutsch	German of Germany
CHEM	Chemie	chemistry
COMM	Handel	commerce
comp	komparativ in Komposita	comparative in compounds

Symbols and Abbreviations

COMPUT	Informatik	computing
conj	Konjunktion	conjunction
dat	Dativ	dative
def	bestimmt	definite
dekl	dekliniert	declined
dem	demonstrativ	demonstrative
derb	derb	vulgar language
det	Bestimmungswort	determiner
DIAL	dialektal	dialect
dim	Diminutiv	diminutive
ECOL	Ökologie	ecology
ECON	Wirtschaft	economy
ELEK ELEC	Elektrizität	electricity
emph	emphatisch	emphatic
EU	Europäische Union	European Union
euph	euphemistisch	euphemistic
f	Femininum	feminine
fachspr	fachsprachlich	specialist term
fam	umgangssprachlich	informal
FBALL	Fußball	football
fem	feminine Form	feminine form
fig	bildlich	figurative
FIN	Finanzen	finance
FOOD	Kochkunst	food and cooking
form	förmlicher Sprachgebrauch	formal
geh	gehobener Sprachgebrauch	formal
gen	Genitiv	genitive
GEOG	Geographie	geography
GEOL	Geologie	geology
hist	historisch	historical
HIST	Geschichte	history
HORT	Gartenbau	gardening
hum	scherzhaft	humorous
HUNT	Jagd	hunting
imp	Imperfekt	imperfect
imper	Imperativ	imperative
impers	unpersönliches Verb	impersonal use
indef	unbestimmt	indefinite
INET	Internet	internet
infin	Infinitiv	infinitive
interj	Interjektion	interjection
inter-rog	fragend	interrogative
inv	unveränderlich	invariable
iron	ironisch	ironic
irreg	unregelmäßig	irregular

JOURN	Journalismus	journalism
JUR	Jura	law
KARTEN	Karten	cards
KOCHK	Kochkunst	food and cooking
konj	Konjunktion	conjunction
KUNST	Kunst	art
LAW	Jura	law
LING	Linguistik	linguistics
LIT	Literatur	literature
liter	literarisch	literary
LUFT	Luftfahrt	aviation
m	Maskulinum	masculine
masc	maskuline Form	masculine form
MATH	Mathematik	mathematics
MECH	Mechanik	mechanics
MED	Medizin	medicine
MEDIA	Medien	media
METEO	Meteorologie	meteorology
MIL	Militär	military
MIN	Bergbau	mining
MODE	Mode	fashion
MUS	Musik	music
n	Substantiv	noun
NAUT	Seefahrt	navigation
neg	verneinend, Verneinung	negative, negation
nomin	Nominativ	nominative
NORDD	Norddeutsch	language of Northern Germany
nt	Neutrum	neuter
ÖKOL	Ökologie	ecology
ÖKON	Wirtschaft	economics
old	veraltet	old
ORN	Vogelkunde	ornithology
ÖSTERR	österreichisches Deutsch	Austrian German
part	Partizip	participle
pej	abwertend	pejorative
pers	Personal(pronomen)	personal pronoun
pers.	Person	person
PHARM	Pharmazie	pharmacy
PHILOS	Philosophie	philosophy
PHOT	Fotografie	photography
PHYS	Physik	physics
pl	plural	plural
poet	poetisch	poetic
POL	Politik	politics
poss	possessiv	possessive
pp	Partizip Perfekt	past participle
präp	Präposition	preposition
pred	Prädikativ	predicative
prep	Präposition	preposition
pres	Präsens	present
pron	Pronomen	pronoun
prov	Sprichwort	proverb
pt	erste Vergangenheit	past tense
PUBL	Verlagswesen	publishing
RADIO	Rundfunk	radio broadcasting
RAIL	Eisenbahnwesen	railway
rare	selten	rare
RAUM	Raumfahrt	aerospace
refl	reflexiv	reflexive
rel	Religion	religion
S.	Sache	thing
SCH	Schule	school
SCHWEIZ	schweizerisches Deutsch	Swiss German
SCI	Naturwissenschaften	science
sep	trennbar	separable
sing	Einzahl	singular
sl	salopp	slang
SOZIOL SOCIOL	Soziologie	sociology
spec	fachsprachlich	specialist term
SPORT	Sport	sports
STOCKEX	Börse	stock exchange
SÜDD	Süddeutsch	language of Southern Germany
superl	Superlativ	superlative
TECH	Technik	technology
TELEK TELEC	Nachrichtentechnik	telecommunications
TENNIS	Tennis	tennis
THEAT	Theater	theatre
TOURIST	Tourismus	tourism
TRANSP	Transport und Verkehr	transportation
TV	Fernsehen	television
TYPO	Buchdruck	typography
UNIV	Universität	university
usu	gewöhnlich	usually
veraltend	veraltend	dated
veraltet	veraltet	old
VERLAG	Verlagswesen	publishing
vi	intransitives Verb	intransitive verb
vr	reflexives Verb	reflexive verb
vt	transitives Verb	transitive verb
vulg	vulgär	vulgar language
ZOOL	Zoologie	zoology

FREE E-DICTIONARY
DOWNLOADING INSTRUCTIONS

1. To download your FREE e-dictionary visit:
   www.barronsbooks.com/pocket424/

2. Please have the printed book in front of you. You will be asked two security questions. For example, „what is the first headword on page 361?"

3. Follow the prompts.

This e-dictionary can be read on any desktop or laptop with Windows or Mac operating systems. It is not compatible with Tablets or Smartphones.

SYSTEM REQUIREMENTS

Windows:	Mac:
Windows 8.1	Mac OS 10.7 and above
Max 50 MB hard drive space*	Max 70 MB hard drive space*

* with all 4 dictionaries